2007
Gun Digest®

Edited by
Ken Ramage

Published by

Gun Digest Books

An imprint of F+W Publications
700 East State Street • Iola, WI 54990-0001
715-445-2214 • 888-457-2873
www.gunlistonline.com

Our toll-free number to place an order or obtain
a free catalog is (800) 258-0929.

Manuscripts, contributions and inquiries, including first class return postage, should be sent to the GUN DIGEST Editorial Offices, Gun Digest Books, 700 E. State Street, Iola, WI 54990-0001. All materials recieved will receive reasonable care, but we will not be responsible for their safe return. Material accepted is subject to our requirements for editing and revisions. Author payment covers all rights and title to the accepted material, including photos, drawings and other illustrations. Payment is at our current rates.

CAUTION: Technical data presented here, particularly technical data on handloading and on firearms adjustment and alteration, inevitably reflects individual experience with particular equipment and components under specific circumstances the reader cannot duplicate exactly. Such data presentations therefore should be used for guidance only and with caution. Gun Digest Books accepts no responsibility for results obtained using these data.

Library of Congress Catalog Number: 0072-9043

ISBN 13: 978-0-89689-316-0
ISBN 10: 0-89689-316-2

Designed by Kara Grundman, Patsy Howell & Tom Nelsen

Edited by Ken Ramage

Printed in the United States of America

TWENTY-FIFTH ANNUAL
JOHN T. AMBER LITERARY AWARD
John Taffin

John Taffin

Growing up in the wonderful pre-PC days of the late 1940s and early 1950s I was blessed with school librarians who stocked the shelves with the outdoor books and magazines of the time and teachers who encouraged my interests by allowing me to do most of my papers on outdoor subjects. They probably had something to do with me becoming a teacher and spending 31 years teaching thousands of junior high kids the mysteries of algebra and, hopefully, about the wonder of life.

In my early years I eagerly awaited every issue of *Outdoor Life* to see where Jack O'Connor was hunting, and each August was extremely important–– that is when the annual GUN DIGEST arrived. Little did I know that someday my writing would not only appear in the book but that I would also know many of those grand old *pistoleros*: Col. Rex Applegate, Elmer Keith, Bill Jordan and Skeeter Skelton.

My first six-gun was a Ruger Single-Six 22. I still have fond memories of the first smells of powder smoke, followed by Hoppe's #9! That first Ruger was soon joined by a growing collection of handguns. My life has been wrapped around six-guns ever since and I've had a running gun bill for 50 years.

My first article appeared in the long-defunct *GunSport* magazine in 1967. I freelanced for many publications and then joined the staff of *American Handgunner* and sister publication *GUNS* more than 20 years ago. I have had over 1200 articles published, many of these about load development. I have also done four books for GUN DIGEST's publisher, Krause Publications: *Big-Bore Sixguns, Action Shooting Cowboy Style, Big-Bore Handguns* and *Single Action Sixguns*.

I am blessed to have a wife, Diamond Dot, who shares much of my passion for firearms and has a collection of her own, specializing in top-break revolvers. The most important things in life to me are faith, family, friends and firearms. It has been a great half-century of shooting. All the foregoing are possible because of freedom, may we always be truly free.

The only juried literary award in the firearms field, the John T. Amber Award replaced the Townsend Whelen Award originated by the late John T. Amber and later re-named in his honor. Now, a $1000 prize goes to the winner of this annual award.

Nominations for the competition are made by GUN DIGEST editor Ken Ramage and are judged by a distinguished panel of editors experienced in the firearms field. Entries are evaluated for felicity of expression and illustration, originality and scholarship, and subject importance to the firearms field.

This year's Amber Award nominees, in addition to Taffin, were:

Holt Bodinson, *"Ammunition, Ballistics & Components: A 60-Year Overview"*
Norm Flayderman, *"Unsheathing An American Legend: The Bowie Knife"*
Jim Foral, *"The Automatic Question"*
Harvey L. Pennington, *"For Targets and Game: Modify A Ruger No. 1 to 32-40"*
John Taffin, *"The Good Old Days: 60 Years of Six-Guns"*
Tom Turpin, *"Bullets for the Smaller Stuff"*
Terry Wieland, *"Bullets for the Big Stuff"*

Serving as judges for this year's competition were John D. Acquilino, editor of *Inside Gun News*; Bob Bell, former editor-in-chief of *Pennsylvania Game News*; James W. Bequette, editorial director of Primedia's outdoor group; David Brennan, editor of *Precision Shooting*; Sharon Cunningham, director of Pioneer Press; Pete Dickey, former technical editor of *American Rifleman*; Jack Lewis, former editor and publisher of *Gun World*; Bill Parkerson, former editor of *American Rifleman*, now director of research and information for the National Rifle Association, and Dave Petzal, deputy editor of *Field & Stream*.

INTRODUCTION

The past 12 months have been eventful. We welcome the return of several seemingly defunct companies and mourn the demise of an American firearms icon, Winchester/U.S. Repeating Arms Co.

Production of the Model 94 and Model 70 rifles, and the Model 1300 shotgun has ended with the closing of the New Haven, Conn., manufacturing facility. The Winchester brand will continue on the guns from overseas sources, at least for the duration of the current licensing agreement with Olin Corporation.

Are the Model 94 and Model 70 rifles gone for good? There are good arguments on both sides of that question. I think the two rifles will be back. Perhaps they will no longer carry the licensed Winchester name or the familiar New Haven address, but at some point American riflemen will again be able to buy a factory-new specimen of both models––they are too good to fade into obscurity.

The firearms industry news is not all bad, however. Back with us are AMT, Charter Arms and Ithaca Guns USA. These companies are operating a bit differently, and all have new business addresses.

AMT was acquired by High Standard Mfg. Co. and now calls Texas home. I'm told deliveries of AMT pistols have begun.

Charter Arms has returned, and will be marketed exclusively by MKS Supply in Dayton, Ohio. MKS is also the exclusive marketer of the Hi-Point Firearms line. While visiting with Charter president Nick Ecker during the Milwaukee NRA Show, he introduced me to another business endeavor, Chaparral Arms. This new company sends over Italian-made parts and assembles them in the U.S. Presently the cowboy-oriented line is rather short: three lever actions and an 1873 single-action revolver. The show samples I saw looked good. Their address is not in our directory, so query www.chaparralfirearms.com or call 866-769-4867.

Prior to the annual SHOT Show, arms companies host shooting events for writers and editors. Winchester's new Wildcat 22 rimfire caught my eye, and I sent a few rounds downrange.

About This Edition.......

Leading off we have John Malloy's excellent "Sixty Years of Auto Pistols." This should have run in last year's book, but we ran out of room.

Jim Foral's "The Genesis of the Lyman #48 Sight" tracks the history and development of what is arguably the most successful and widely used micrometer receiver sight in the world. Foral is the latest recipient of the John T. Amber Award and a frequent contributor to this book.

There are more articles, too many to mention here. For a complete report on the year's new products, see the contributing editors' reports within. The catalog and directories have been fully updated. Enjoy.

Ithaca rises from the ashes yet again. The business is now located in Upper Sandusky, Ohio. I don't know full details, but I understand the new ownership's initial emphasis will be to service parts needs of existing 37s, and then begin production of finished guns.

I continue to be impressed with Smith & Wesson's resurgence. Not only has the current ownership recovered the ground lost by the preceding offshore ownership, but the company has just entered the law enforcement and military arena in a nicely organized big way. I refer to the M&P line, initially an autoloading pistol with a reinforced polymer frame offered in three chamberings. More recently, the pistols have been joined by several variations of an AR-style rifle, the M&P15.

Last December S&W invited me to a seminar held at the Springfield, Mass., factory to acquaint writers and editors with the new M&P pistol, and the company as well. The new pistol comes in 9mm, 357 SIG and 40 S&W at present; our seminar guns were 40s. Features of the pistol include a three-piece grip insert set that allows the shooter to customize the grip size to fit his hand, an accessory rail forward of the trigger guard and ambidextrous controls. My pistol shot to point of aim, and was exceptional for the consistency of the DA trigger pull, an aspect appreciated by all.

I had another chance to use the new S&W models several months later, during the 2006 SHOT Show in Las Vegas. A number of us were invited to S&W's shooting event held at an indoor range. A competitive program was planned, and we shot different S&W firearms, including the M&P pistol and the M&P15 tactical rifle, for score. I'd like to report I didn't drop a point, but that was not the case. I did have fun, though.

While attending the 2006 Safari Club International Show in Reno, I ran across a very interesting cartridge, the 408 CheyTac. Based on the 505 Gibbs case, and intended for the anti-materiel/military arms market, the cartridge and overall shooting system are designed around a new concept called "Balanced Flight." The bullet is literally needle-sharp...I almost punctured myself fiddling with the dummy round on display. Later, at the SHOT Show, I enjoyed a dinner with Robin Sharpless and Steve Schultz of CheyTac Associates and Tammy Even, sales manager of Jamison International, a sister company and source of the cartridge brass. I heard reports of incredible accuracy at phenomenal distances. This cartridge, and similar anti-materiel rounds, are reported on in the new (July'06) CARTRIDGES OF THE WORLD, 11TH EDITION.

Ken Ramage, Editor
GUN DIGEST

The GUN DIGEST 60th Anniversary Edition
Ruger Rifle

The GUN DIGEST 60th Anniversary Edition Ruger Rifle sweepstakes generated thousands of entries. When the entry deadline passed and the drawing held, Ralph Kloha of Dover, Ohio, won the one-of-a-kind cased Ruger rifle.

This one-of-a-kind Ruger No. 1 now has a new home in Ohio and I seized this last opportunity to enjoy the rifle. Ruger's engraver Paul Lantuch and gunsmith Mitch Schultz did an exceptional job.

Gun Digest Staff

EDITOR
Ken Ramage

CONTRIBUTING EDITORS

Holt Bodinson – Ammunition, Ballistics
   & Components; Web Directory
Raymond Caranta – The Guns of Europe
J. W. "Doc" Carlson – Blackpowder Review
John Campbell – Single-Shot Rifles
John Haviland – Shotgun Review

John Malloy – Handguns Today: Autoloaders
Layne Simpson – Rifle Review
John Taffin – Handguns Today: Six-guns & Others
Tom Turpin – Engraved & Custom Guns
Wayne van Zwoll – Scopes & Mounts

About The Covers

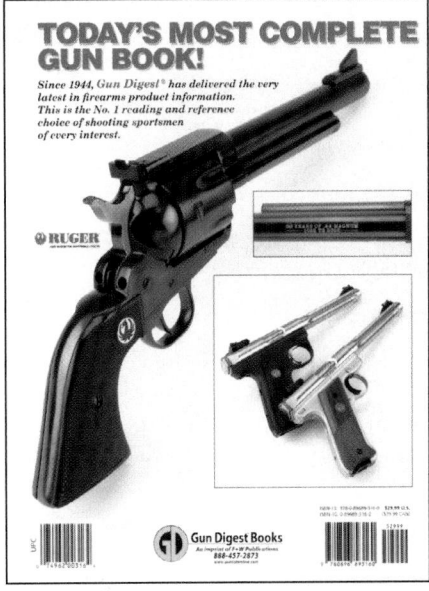

FRONT COVER

Ruger's 10/22 Rifle was introduced in 2004 and features a slim rifle-style stock, adjustable fiber-optic sights and a new 20-inch tapered barrel. It is chambered for the 22LR rimfire cartridge and incorporates the proven Ruger 10/22 action and rotary 10-round magazine. This model, the 10/22RR, proved such a success that the company introduced a compact version for 2006, the 10/22CRR.

The 10/22CRR Compact is essentially a reduced-size version of the 10/22 Rifle introduced in 2004, and seems particularly appealing to shooters of smaller stature or those who want an appreciably smaller, lighter rimfire rifle package. The barrel is 16-1/8 inches, 3-7/8 inches shorter than the full-size Rifle. The stock is shortened proportionally fore and aft, with a 12 3/4-inch length of pull and shortened forend. The Compact weighs four pounds, a full pound less than the Rifle. Both 10/22s have adjustable fiber-optic sights and are fitted with satin-finish hardwood stocks.

The new 22-caliber Ruger Mark III Hunter pistol was named the 2006 Hunting Handgun of the Year by the NRA's American Hunter magazine. The Hunter model shown here is all stainless steel, with a 6 7/8-inch fluted barrel and half-checkered Cocobolo grips. Other features include an adjustable rear sight and fiber-optic front sight, Weaver-style scope adapter, loaded chamber indicator, magazine disconnect and internal lock.

BACK COVER

For 2006, Ruger introduces its new 50th Anniversary 44 Magnum New Model Blackhawk to commemorate the 50th anniversary of the original 44 Magnum "Flattop."

The special edition Flattop 44 50th anniversary pistol will be made only in 2006, and in a limited quantity. The original flattop was the direct predecessor of the Super Blackhawk 44 Magnum, which continues in production to this day.

Notable features include the original, smaller grip frame with checkered "hard rubber" grips that feature original-style black Ruger medallions. The frame is the original flattop style and the barrel measures 6-1/2 inches. The adjustable rear sight is the original micro-style paired with Ruger's traditional ramped blade front sight.

The Flattop 44 comes in a red anniversary hard case, along with a booklet relating the history of the Ruger Blackhawk revolver. A special commemorative rollmark appears on top of the barrel.

INSET: The new Mk III Hunter is available in the two versions shown here. One is all stainless steel with the traditional Ruger slanted grip. The second, designated the 22/45 Mark III Hunter, has a black polymer grip frame that replicates the feel of the GI 1911 autoloading pistol. Otherwise, the two pistols are similar in specifications, to include the latest safety features.

CONTENTS

SIX DECADES OF
AUTOMATIC PISTOLS
by John Malloy

PAGE 8

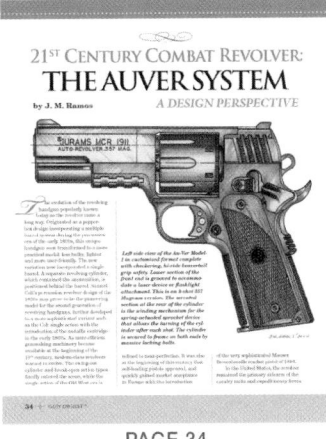

21ST CENTURY COMBAT REVOLVER:
THE AUVER SYSTEM
A DESIGN PERSPECTIVE
by J. M. Ramos

PAGE 34

THE GENESIS OF THE
LYMAN #48 SIGHT
by Jim Foral

PAGE 66

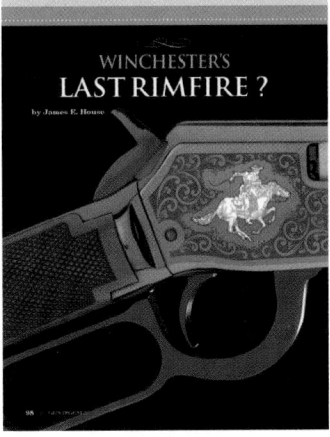

WINCHESTER'S
LAST RIMFIRE ?
by James E. House

PAGE 98

SIX DECADES OF
AUTOMATIC PISTOLS

by John Malloy

Inset: The 2005 Gun Digest cover showed Ruger's new Mark III 22 and the company's trim new 45, the model 345. After only appearing four times in almost four decades of the early covers, autoloading pistols were featured on eight of the last 23 covers.

• THE WORLD'S GREATEST GUN BOOK •

Gun Digest 2005

59th
Annual Edition
Edited by
Ken Ramage

RUGER

Essential
Information
For Shooters,
Collectors and
Students of
the Gun

New Product
Reports:
Firearms Optics
Ammunition
Accessories
...and more!

Complete Illustrated
Catalog of Current
Firearms and
Accessories

Art of the Engraver & Custom Guns in Color

*I*n the final years of the
Great Depression, just before
the start of World War II, only two
U. S. manufacturers produced what
were then known as "automatic" pistols.
Foreign autoloaders were made, but
relatively few were used in America.
The revolver, designed and brought
into common use in America, remained
the most popular type of handgun.

During the World War II, the
American public understood the value
of proficiency and knowledge related to
firearms. After that devastating war
was over, there was a great interest in
firearms of all types, but in particular
in semi-automatic pistols. Servicemen
during the war had been exposed not
only to the U.S. service semi-automatic
pistol, but to those of other countries.
After the war, new developments took
place in America, and foreign makers
were eager to sell to U. S. markets.

The first edition of GUN DIGEST
came out in 1944, during the course
of World War II. The first edition
was well-received, and the second
edition of GUN DIGEST was published
in 1946, immediately after the war. It
soon became an annual reference. It
provided historical information, tips
and advice on how to shoot various
types of firearms, and let post-war
America know what guns were
available. As time went by, students
of firearms realized the publication
was a valuable reference to the history
and evolution of the types of guns
available to the American shooter.

Now, that first thin book has
grown to the present 61st edition.
With sixty-one editions of GUN DIGEST,
we can look back and see the gradual
changes in what has been available in
various types of rifles, shotguns and
handguns. We can also see the pattern
of background events that led to the
offerings of certain types of guns.

However, nowhere has this evolution
been more striking, or the changes
more numerous or more dramatic,
than the field of what were originally
called "automatic" pistols. Starting
with just a handful of possibilities in
the first edition, this category grew

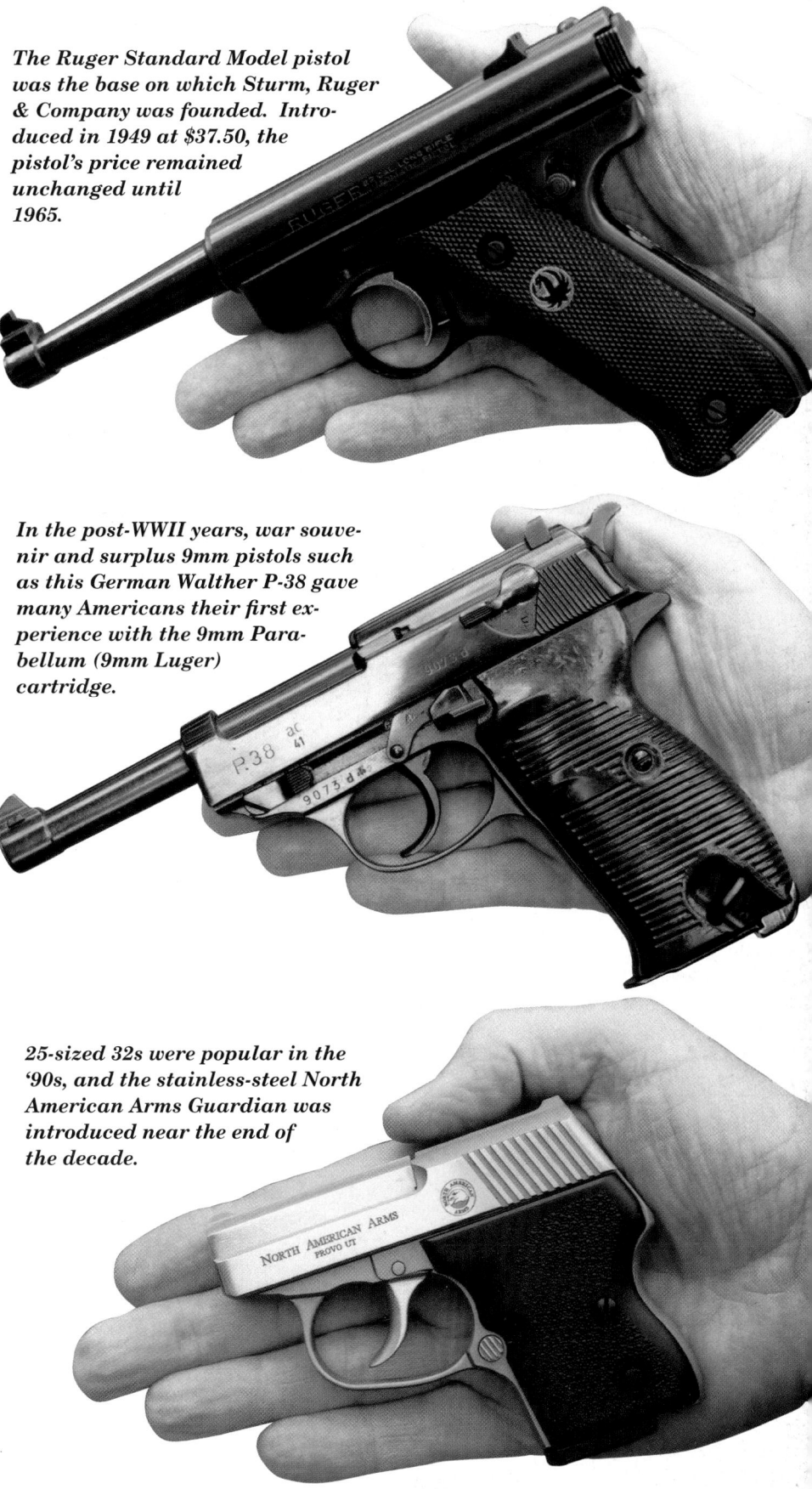

*The Ruger Standard Model pistol
was the base on which Sturm, Ruger
& Company was founded. Introduced in 1949 at $37.50, the
pistol's price remained
unchanged until
1965.*

*In the post-WWII years, war souve-
nir and surplus 9mm pistols such
as this German Walther P-38 gave
many Americans their first experience with the 9mm Parabellum (9mm Luger)
cartridge.*

*25-sized 32s were popular in the
'90s, and the stainless-steel North
American Arms Guardian was
introduced near the end of
the decade.*

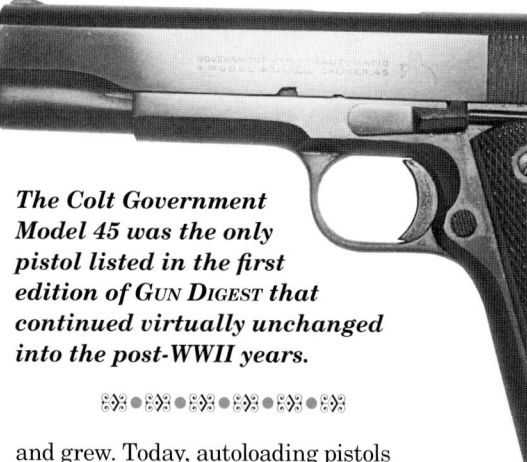

The Colt Government Model 45 was the only pistol listed in the first edition of GUN DIGEST that continued virtually unchanged into the post-WWII years.

❧❧ ● ❧❧ ● ❧❧ ● ❧❧ ● ❧❧ ● ❧❧

and grew. Today, autoloading pistols form a dominant portion of the volume, far outnumbering revolvers or any specific action type of rifle or shotgun.

So, GUN DIGEST is a useful reference to chronicle the history and development of semi-automatic handguns in the six decades since the first slim volume appeared.

Of course, the "automatic" pistol had been introduced to America long before 1944. In 1900, Colt had introduced the 38-caliber autoloader designed by firearms genius John M. Browning. The cartridge, the 38 Automatic Colt Pistol cartridge (38 ACP) is still produced––more than a century later––as the 38 Super. One of Browning's great achievements came in 1911, when the Browning-designed Colt automatic in 45 ACP was adopted by the United States military. If there was any valid criticism of the Colt 1911, it is that the pistol was so good that it discouraged competition by other makers. Savage

and Remington shelved their designs for 45-caliber service pistols.

Those two makers, and others such as Smith & Wesson, Harrington & Richardson and Warner, did challenge Colt in the field of American pocket pistols, but by the late1930s, only the Colt pocket pistols were left.

The 22-caliber automatic pistol arrived in 1915, actually prior to our entry into the First World War, and was another Colt/Browning design. Today, with a wide variety of dependable 22 pistols from which to choose, it is easy to lose sight of the difficulties Browning faced. The rimfire 22 Long Rifle (22 LR) cartridge had been developed only 28 years before, in 1887. 1915 ammunition was loaded with varieties of black, semi-smokeless, and smokeless powders, all with corrosive priming. The greased lead bullets were only lightly held in very thin copper or brass cases. It amazed experts of the time that the new Colt 22, later to be called the Woodsman, worked so well.

Several variants of the Woodsman were made, and became very popular. Non-corrosive priming arrived in 1926 and high-velocity 22 LR cartridges arrived in 1930. By 1932, competition for the Woodsman had also arrived, in the form of the

Hi-Standard 22 automatic. High Standard Manufacturing Co. had acquired a Hartford Arms design for a 22 pistol, and produced it as the Hi-Standard Model B. Similar in shape to the Colt, it was of different construction. Several variations were made in succeeding years.

Colt had brought out several variants of its basic Government Model. In 1929, the 38 Super was introduced. Soon, target versions—the National Match 45 and the Super Match 38—were added. The big frame was adapted to the 22 LR cartridge in the Ace and Service Ace variants.

That was it.

In the period leading up to our involvement in World War II, we had variants of two big-bore automatic pistols, two models of pocket pistols, and a smattering of 22 automatics— all from two manufacturers, Colt and High Standard.

This was the autoloading pistol situation prior to the publication of the first GUN DIGEST in 1944. In addition to the paucity of pre-war self-loading models, wartime production needs meant that few automatic pistols were actually available to civilians.

During the war, the country switched over to wartime production. Firearms that could be used for some military function were kept in production. Others were dropped "for the duration," some to be resumed after the end of hostilities, others to never again be made. The automotive industry also switched to war production, and no cars were made between 1942 and 1945. Ford switched one of its properties to aircraft production, building a mile-long factory that ran 24 hours a day. Parts and materials entered one end, and every hour a four-engine B-24 heavy bomber rolled out the other.

People at home were deeply impressed with the need for guns and shooting. Training programs grew throughout the country to train young men in marksmanship. America was still largely rural then, and hunting was a way to supplement a family's food supply during a period of rationing and "Meatless Tuesdays." Hunting and target shooting continued in the

The Colt Commander of 1950 was the smallest, lightest 45 that had been produced to that time. It was also made for the 9mm Parabellum cartridge, the first 9mm pistol made in America.

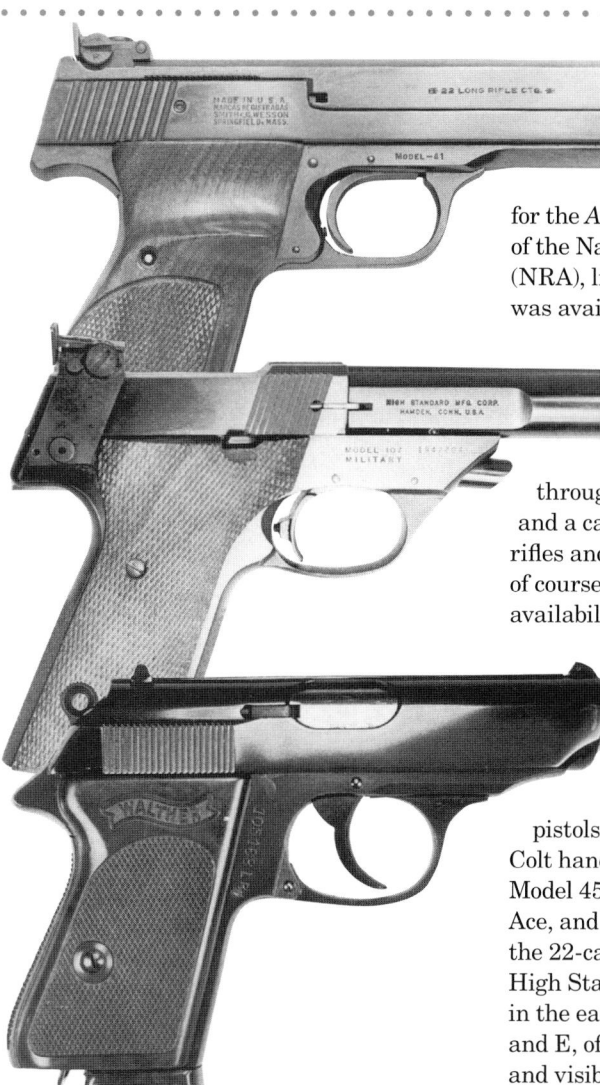

tremendous interest in guns and shooting, but except for the *American Rifleman* magazine of the National Rifle Association (NRA), little published information was available. The 1944 GUN DIGEST introduced the basic format that was to continue through the years—feature articles, and a catalog section of handguns, rifles and shotguns. The catalog section, of course, could not be accurate, as availability changed markedly during the war. Essentially, the catalog section of the first edition listed the guns made prior to the war. The automatic pistol listings consisted only of the pistols by Colt and High Standard. Colt handguns were the Government Model 45, Super 38, and 22-caliber Ace, and their target models, and the 22-caliber Woodsman series. High Standard listings were all 22s, in the early "letter" series A, B, D and E, offered both as hammerless and visible-hammer models.

After the end of fighting in 1945, servicemen began returning home. A joke of the time was that returning servicemen were only interested in two things—and the second one was hunting. The first interest created the baby boom. The second created a demand for inexpensive firearms that could be used for hunting and recreational shooting.

The Second Annual Edition came out in 1946, again published by Klein's Sporting Goods. The addition of "Annual" to the name indicated the intention to revise and publish a new edition each year. A note mentioned that the publication had been "revised since the end of World War II." However, the automatic pistol listings were exactly the same

as they had been in the first edition. Considering the turbulent state of firearms manufacturing at that time, this was certainly understandable.

The U.S. firearms industry had problems switching from expanded wartime production to more restricted peacetime production. A number of companies never put some of their pre-war offerings back into production, and a new section was added to the second GUN DIGEST. "Discontinued Metallic Cartridge Arms" gave shooters an idea as to what was no longer available.

The Third Edition came out in 1947. Colt listings had been changed to include only the Government Model 45, the Super 38, and the Woodsman Target, Sport and Match Target 22s. The Pocket Model 25 was also included, but it was not actually available.

High Standard pistol listings were reduced to only one model. Only the Model H-D Military (which had been made for the military during the war) was then in production, with 4 1/2- or 6 3/4-inch barrels. A note was included that the Model B hammerless "may be produced in 1947."

"Discontinued Models" was continued as a section, and a new section, "Foreign Sporting Arms," was added. Consisting mostly of rifles and shotguns, there were passing references to automatic pistols, primarily as war souvenirs.

❧ ● ❧ ● ❧ ● ❧ ● ❧ ● ❧

In 1970, Colt revised its standby Government Model with a collet-type barrel bushing, and it became the Mk. IV / Series '70.

Top: *In 1957, Smith & Wesson introduced a 22-caliber target pistol, later named the Model 41. The company thus joined Colt, High Standard and Ruger in producing 22 semi-automatic target pistols.*
Middle: *In the mid-1960s, High Standard began using a "military" grip on its line of 22 target pistols, a grip of the same angle as the service Colt 45 pistol.*
Bottom: *After the Gun Control Act of 1968 went into effect, importation of small pistols such as the Walther PPK was no longer allowed.*

❧ ● ❧ ● ❧ ● ❧ ● ❧ ● ❧

face of a dwindling supply of factory ammunition for civilian use.

The first GUN DIGEST came out in 1944, during this period. There was a

The fourth GUN DIGEST began a tradition that was to serve the publication well in some ways. Brought out in 1948, it was listed as the "4th Annual (1949) Edition." This got it into the hands of hunters before the beginning of the 1948-1949 hunting season, and was the most current listing of available firearms. This tradition has been followed ever since, and explains why the book for each year has been copyrighted the year before.

Toward the end of the 1960s, a new 22-caliber pistol was offered by Stoeger. The clever blowback pistol looked like a Luger, and because Stoeger had acquired the rights to that trade name, was the only new pistol that could be called a Luger.

Automatic pistol listings had changed, but only a little. Colt's big news was the redesign of the Woodsman models. The Woodsman now had a longer grip frame, a slide hold-open, a pushbutton magazine latch, and Coltwood plastic grips. The Government Model 45 and 38 Super were still the flagships of the automatic line.

High Standard still offered the H-D Military, and added a new Model G, a 380 pistol with a barrel lock on the frame to permit easy field-stripping. This was to be the beginning of the

The aluminum-frame Star PD was a small 45 of modified 1911 design that was imported from Spain.

Colt had introduced its Gold Cup National Match 45 in 1957, and in 1970, it was modified with Series '70 improvements

interchangeable-barrel system that is still in use in the present day.

More people were interested in handguns, and a new section, "Handgun Facts," was written by Charles Askins, Jr. This section was the predecessor of the "Handguns, Today" sections in the current GUN DIGEST. Askins was the earliest writer of the handguns section, joined in later years by such knowledgeable writers as Julian S. Hatcher, Kent Bellah, Pete Kuhlhoff, Gil Hebard, Dean Grennell, George Nonte, J. B. Wood and others.

Some notable changes were made in the 5th Edition, 1951. Copyrighted and published in 1950, it was still copyrighted by Klein's Sporting Goods, but published by a new entity, The Gun Digest Company. The editor was now John T. Amber, who was to remain in that position for twenty-eight years, through the 33rd Edition, 1979. Charles Askins' report was in the new section, "Handguns Today." A "Foreign Firearms" section made an appearance, with illustrated coverage. In the automatic pistol section were offerings of Astra, Beretta, Bernardelli, Star and Unique, mostly pocket pistols in 25, 32 and 380 calibers, with some 22 target pistols.

This introduction to the 1950s tied in to the changes going on in America.

The 1950s were generally a time of optimism and enthusiasm for America. New cars had once more become available in 1946, but most new designs arrived only in 1949. Styling was to grow more flamboyant and engines more powerful as the '50s went on.

Not even the Korean Conflict of 1950-1953, important as it was, dampened America's enthusiasm. The fighting, however, reinforced the ideas of many that all young men needed firearms training. Shooting clubs, veterans' organizations, police departments and other groups operated youth shooting programs.

Dwight D. Eisenhower was elected President in 1952. The Korean War ended in 1953. "Ike" was reelected in 1956.

Serious motion-picture Westerns—*High Noon, Shane* and *Hondo*—were screened in the early '50s. Also, a new medium—television—began a number of popular Western series. Such entertainment increased interest in single-action revolvers and lever-action revolvers, but did little to spur interest in semi-automatic pistols. However, some new developments were taking place in semi-automatic pistols.

Reporting of new guns was improving, and one of the most important pistols of the time, the Ruger 22-caliber Standard pistol, introduced in 1949, was reported by GUN DIGEST in 1950. This pistol was the one on which Sturm, Ruger & Company was built. 1950 was the year of introduction for the lightweight Colt Commander. With a 4 1/4-inch barrel and weight of 26-1/2 ounces, it was the smallest, lightest 45 automatic made, and was also offered in 38 Super and 9mm Parabellum (9mm Luger). It was the first U. S.-made 9mm pistol. Colt also introduced the Challenger, a low-price version of the Woodsman. High Standard improved new models for competitive target shooting and introduced its Supermatic in 22 LR and the Olympic in 22 Short.

By 1951, Ruger had brought out its Mark I target pistol. That year, High Standard dropped the "letter" designations completely, and had new names for all pistol models.

By 1954, High Standard introduced the simplified Dura-Matic pistol, priced at $37.50 to directly compete with the Ruger Standard. In that year, Smith & Wesson brought out a double-action 9mm pistol. Not numbered for several years, it became the S&W Model 39. In 1954, Belgian-made Browning pistols—the 9mm High Power (HP),

the 380 and the little 25—were imported into the postwar American market for the first time.

1956 saw some modifications of previous designs. The Colt Huntsman was another modified Woodsman, and Sears, Roebuck's J. C. Higgins Model 80 was a High Standard Dura-Matic with some cosmetic changes. (Yes, Sears sold pistols without government paperwork in those carefree days.)

Two new designs also appeared. The Whitney Wolverine was a completely new 22 pistol by firearms designer Robert L. Hillberg. With an aluminum frame and futuristic styling, the light new 22 was unlike anything made before. Praised for its natural pointing features, the Whitney fell victim to company financial problems and disappeared by the early 1960s.

One of the most ambitious new projects of 1956 was the Kimball pistol. It was chambered for the 30 Carbine cartridges that were available as surplus. The Kimball was a delayed blowback design that proved to be not satisfactory for the pressure of the cartridge. The few made are collector items, but the Kimball foreshadowed later attempts to produce handguns for this cartridge.

In 1957, S&W introduced their 22-caliber target pistol. Introduced without a model number, it soon became the S&W Model 41. Target shooters now had a choice of Colt, High Standard, Ruger or S&W pistols for 22-caliber competition.

Colt also introduced its new 45-caliber National Match pistol, the Gold Cup. The new match pistol was

Double-action autoloaders were the coming thing, but Browning did not yet make one. In 1977, the SIG/Sauer P220 was imported with the Browning name on it as the Browning BDA.

Top: *The Rudd stainless-steel pistol was a locked-breech design with a fixed barrel and double-action trigger. Only one specimen was made, this prototype chambered in 45 ACP.*
Middle: *The Walther P5 pistol was the first Walther to offer a frame-mounted decocking lever.*
Bottom: *The delayed-blowback Thomas 45 was an innovative double-action compact pistol.*

considerably more refined than the pre-war National Match, which had not been produced again following the war. Bullseye target shooting was a popular sport in the '50s, and a number of custom gunsmiths were building "accurized" 45s. The appearance of the Gold Cup National Match provided a readily-available pistol that was satisfactory for competition. It soon became the standard target

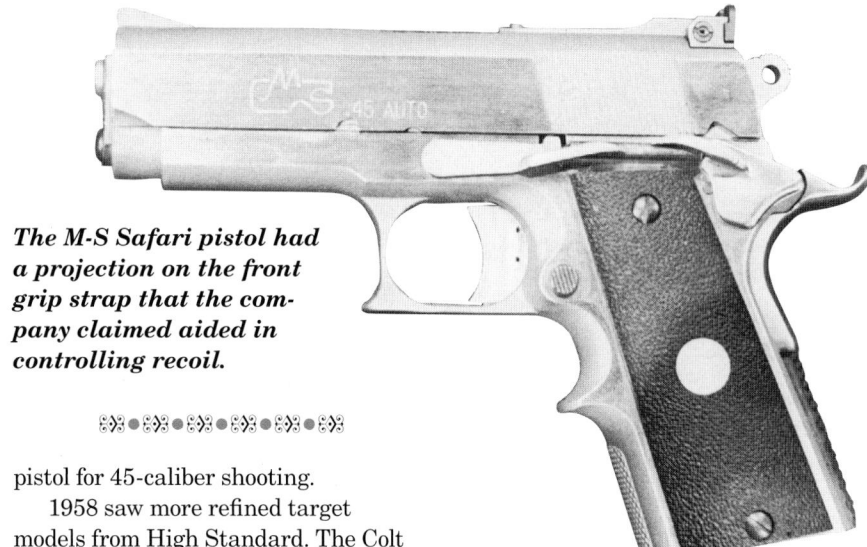

The M-S Safari pistol had a projection on the front grip strap that the company claimed aided in controlling recoil.

※ ● ※ ● ※ ● ※ ● ※ ● ※

pistol for 45-caliber shooting.

1958 saw more refined target models from High Standard. The Colt 25 had not been produced after WWII, but there was a market for a small 25. In 1958, Colt introduced the Colt "Junior" 25, made in Spain by Astra.

Entry-level shooters in the bullseye target sport were price-conscious, and in 1959, S&W offered its 22-caliber Model 46. Mechanically the same as the Model 41, the new Model 46 had plastic grips and a dull finish, and sold at a substantially lower price.

By the latter part of the 1950s, military modernization was taking place. Governments all over the world were clearing their armories of obsolete military equipment, including firearms and ammunition. Most of these items were sold to private citizens in the country with the greatest degree of personal freedom—the United States. Many previously little-known automatic pistols were among the items imported during the late '50s and into the '60s. American shooters

had their first chance to try out Lugers, Walthers, Mausers, Astras, Radoms and other foreign pistols. The pistols were fed with inexpensive surplus ammunition, predominantly 9mm. It was the first time the average shooter had a chance to gain experience with the 9mm round, and set the stage for its later acceptance.

As the guns changed in the 1950s, so did the GUN DIGEST. The "Handgun Review" section, which still combined automatics and revolvers, was a standard feature in every issue. The catalog section relating to American-made autoloaders had grown from a few models made by two companies to a full four pages which featured the pistols of five different companies. In the order of the listings, handguns still came in third behind rifles and shotguns, but this would change with time. Foreign guns were still considered

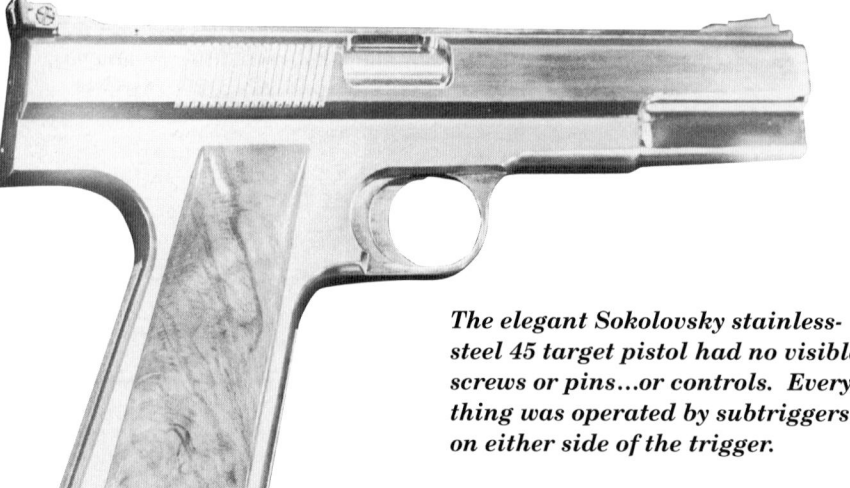

The elegant Sokolovsky stainless-steel 45 target pistol had no visible screws or pins...or controls. Everything was operated by subtriggers on either side of the trigger.

separately, but more and more were being imported, and the foreign handguns were mostly automatics. By the end of the decade, foreign-made autoloaders filled five pages.

With the 1955 edition, a semi-automatic pistol appeared for the first time on the cover of GUN DIGEST. A 9mm Smith & Wesson pistol appeared on both the front and back covers. A single-action version of the S&W Model 39, the pictured Model 44 was never produced.

Most shooters of the '50s were not aware that there was a growing anti-gun sentiment among some public officials. To make people aware, GUN DIGEST dedicated its 1953 edition to the National Rifle Association and encouraged NRA membership. Annual membership was $4, and Junior membership was 50 cents.

The 1960s began as an extension of the 1950s, but changed drastically before the end of the decade.

In 1960, John F. Kennedy was elected President of the United States. When he took office, he was a Life Member of the NRA, as had been Eisenhower and previous presidents. Kennedy was no stranger to firearms, and while a Senator, had acquired an M1 Garand from the Director of Civilian Marksmanship (DCM). Kennedy did not serve his full term. On November 22, 1963, he was assassinated under circumstances that arouse speculation to this day. Officially, a lone killer with unknown motives had committed the murder with a surplus military rifle.

As a result, gun-control advocates stepped up their demands for further restrictions on firearms. Senator Thomas Dodd added surplus military rifles to a restrictive bill he was preparing.

The Civil War Centennial period, 1961-1965, created some new interest in firearms, but primarily the percussion revolvers and rifles used during the Civil War.

By the mid-1960s, the United States was involved in Viet Nam. Protests began against American involvement. Somehow, in the minds of some, firearms became involved with the Asian war. A political viewpoint was formed that was both anti-war and anti-gun.

The 1966 killings at the University of Texas, and the 1968 assassinations of Robert F. Kennedy and Martin Luther King added momentum to the anti-gun bandwagon. In 1968, the year of the Tet Offensive in Vietnam, the Gun Control Act of 1968 (GCA 68) was passed by Congress and signed into law by President Lyndon B. Johnson. The GCA 68, among other things, stopped importation of many firearms, including surplus firearms, placed restrictions on all firearms made after 1898, and initiated federal restrictions for purchasers of firearms.

It was the passing of an era. In that same year, traditional family TV entertainment such as "The Andy Griffith Show" went off the air.

In other forms of entertainment, a change was also obvious. The Beatles, who had achieved popularity in the United States in 1964 with their harmonic versions of rock-and-roll songs, gradually evolved during the '60s into a group performing songs that involved protest and drug use.

The '60s were to involve some changes in the handguns America preferred. In 1960, America was still a revolver country. The 1961 15th Edition GUN DIGEST, which came out in late 1960, showed this in its catalog section. Under "U. S. Handguns," nine pages were devoted to revolvers, and only four to pistols (which included single-shots as well as autoloaders). The foreign handguns, however, were represented by 27 automatics and only three revolvers. During the decade, American interest in autoloading handguns would increase.

In 1961, Colt celebrated its 125th anniversary, and in that year introduced the new 38 Special Gold Cup National Match. High Standard was the largest maker of 22-caliber handguns in the world, but other companies were making 22s. Browning introduced a new 22 LR automatic that year. Walther was importing its Model PP Sport in 22 LR.

By 1962, the Browning 22 line had grown to the Nomad, the Challenger and the Medalist, with increasing features and prices. Smith & Wesson, not to be outdone by Colt's 38 Special

auto, brought out the S&W Model 52 target pistol in 38 Special.

Bullseye target shooting remained very popular and High Standard, S&W and Ruger all introduced bull-barrel 22-caliber target pistols in the mid-60s. By that time, Browning was considered an American, rather than a foreign, company. Also in the mid-60s, an unusual pistol, the Universal Enforcer, was introduced. The Enforcer was a 30-caliber 30-shot pistol with a 12-inch barrel, based on the M1 Carbine. It was the first of a type that would later be demonized as "assault pistols."

In 1965, High Standard introduced its "military-grip" autoloaders, with a grip angle the same as that of the military 19llA1 pistol. The Ruger Standard, which had been introduced in 1949 at a price of $37.50, had its first price increase, to $41.50. Sixteen years of production before a price hike is a record that still stands. The Heckler & Koch HK4 was imported, a novel pistol with interchangeable barrels for 22 LR, 25, 32 and 380.

At the end of the decade, after the passage of GCA 68, little new came from the major manufacturers. Colt put out a series of four World War I commemorative 45 autos. Browning dropped the 25- and 380-caliber pistols due to the new import restrictions.

However, in 1969, two companies introduced new 22-caliber autoloaders. The Sterling pistols were full-size pistols with external hammers and fixed barrels. They looked quite a bit like the early Hi-Standard autos. The other offering was the Stoeger 22-caliber Luger pistol. Stoeger held the trademark on the "Luger" name, and used it for the new pistol, a clever blowback design that had a striking resemblance to the original German pistol.

There were changes in GUN DIGEST during the 1960s. There were a number of editorials relating to the

Top: *In 1986, Smith & Wesson offered its first 45-caliber semi-automatic pistol, the Model 645.* **Bottom:** *ODI introduced the 45-caliber Viking, a 1911 design with the Seecamp double-action mechanism.*

assassinations, proposed legislation and the passage of the Gun Control Act. GUN DIGEST's tradition of putting out each year's edition during the previous year fell afoul of the timing of these events. The Kennedy murder took place in November 1963, after the 1964 edition had been published. Thus, the 1965 edition was the first that had an editorial touching on the tragedy and its effect on the right to bear arms. In similar fashion, the 1970 edition contained the first editorial response to the Gun Control Act of 1968. During the decade, more feature articles dealing with semi-automatic pistols were included, by writers such as Gil Hebard, Larry Sterrett, Kent Bellah, James B. Stewart and Raymond Caranta.

In the 1965/19th Edition, the Townsend Whelen Award was announced, to honor Whelen, who had died in 1961. It offered a $500 prize "for significant contributions to

The 9mm MAB PA-15 was a 15-shot pistol imported from France.

the literature of guns and shooting." The third Townsend Whelen Award presented (23rd-1969 Edition) was won by Raymond Caranta for his feature, "History of French Handguns."

The country moved into the 1970s. In the aftermath of the GCA 68, the restrictions contained in that law kept many ordinary people from acquiring firearms. Because the restrictions applied to those who obeyed laws, criminals ignored them. In the framework of rebellion against authority and drug use by increasing numbers of the younger population, the crime rate skyrocketed.

In the face of increasing crime, many people thought more seriously about guns for protection. Many of the small foreign pistols previously favored were prohibited by GCA 68. Soon, American manufacturers began providing pistols to fill the niche.

Politically and economically, the '70s were a turbulent time. Richard Nixon was reelected President in 1972, but the Watergate scandal forced his resignation, and Gerald Ford assumed the office. A messy retreat from Vietnam did not sit well with America. In 1976, the year of the nation's Bicentennial, Jimmy Carter was elected President.

One of Carter's campaign points had been the increasing rate of inflation, caused initially by the Organization of Petroleum Exporting Countries (OPEC)'s severe cutback on oil production in 1973. Before Carter's term was over, the Arabs turned off the tap

again in 1979, and inflation soared to record levels. The uncertainty caused many businesses to founder or fail.

These conditions also affected the firearms industry. However, interest in autoloading pistols was still strong, and the Gun Control Act actually stimulated the development of new models in the United States. Redesigned foreign pistols began coming back in. George Nonte called this "rebellion by compliance," a situation in which prohibited guns were revised and dressed up to qualify for importation.

An indication of the rapid development of the autoloading handgun during the 1970s is the situation involving the 45 automatic. Surplus 45s were popular, and both custom and home gunsmiths were building target pistols from them. However, in 1970, only one American company—Colt—was making new 45 automatics. In that year, Colt had introduced its Mark IV Series '70 variation, which used a finger-type collet barrel bushing.

Toward the end of the decade, other new designs of 45 ACP pistols, both American and foreign, had begun to arrive on the scene. The Thomas 45 of 1977 was a compact American-made 45 with a unique retarded blowback system. The Spanish Star PD was a compact aluminum-frame locked-breech pistol. Sterling, a company that had started making pistols after GCA 68, developed and displayed (but never commercially produced) their model 450, a double-action 45. Hawes, an American company, by 1977, imported under its name the SIG/Sauer P220 in 45 ACP chambering. Soon, Browning imported the same P220 pistol as the Browning BDA 45.

The Detonics 45, an innovative scaled-down 45 based on a highly-modified 1911 design, appeared on the market. Crown City, a company that had made parts, decided to make complete pistols, essentially slightly-modified 1911s. The Essex company

made 1911-type frames and slides, and surplus parts were available to build complete pistols. Later in the decade, AMT brought out its line of all-stainless-steel 1911-type 45s. These included the Combat Government, the Hardballer (adjustable-sight target version) and the Long Slide Hardballer (with a 7-inch barrel). Llama 45s, modified from the 1911 design, were imported from Spain.

The Heckler & Koch P9S arrived in 1977, first in 9mm and then in 45. The Rudd pistol, an innovative double-action 45, was displayed in prototype but never produced. The Vega, another 1911 look-alike, did go into production. Mossberg advertised, but did not produce, its AIG "Combat Model" pistol, based on a Clerke design.

Other new pistols, primarily small ones, but some large, were designed and manufactured by both old and new companies during the 1970s. The Walther PPK was made in a slightly larger version, the PPK/S, to meet the absurd point system of GCA 68. American-made small pocket pistols also appeared from old companies. S&W brought out its 22 LR Model 61 Escort, and Colt introduced an American-made Colt Junior 25, a new copy of the Astra Cub pistol.

A new company, American Firearms Manufacturing Company, brought out a new stainless-steel 25 auto. The company would later become American Derringer, and would continue the little 25 in with its line of double derringers. From across the seas came the Astra Constable and the Beretta Model 90, modern double-action pocket pistols. The Heckler & Koch HK4 four-caliber pistol qualified for importation by Harrington & Richardson.

With all the interest in pocket pistols, there was a new niche developing. Interest in long-range pistol silhouette shooting and handgun hunting had opened opportunities for more powerful pistols. The '70s saw the introduction of the AutoMag (44 AutoMag) and the Wildey (45 Winchester Magnum), semi-automatic pistols of much greater power than had previously been produced in a practical autoloader.

As the 1970s wound down, the

trends had already begun to develop that would reach a peak in the next decade. These trends were double-action (DA) trigger mechanisms, large-capacity magazines, and stainless-steel construction. Not every new design had all of them, but the trends seemed clear. The DA Smith & Wesson 59, with its 14-round magazine, was introduced about 1973. A few years later, the 18-shot Steyr P-18, and its American counterpart, the stainless-steel LES Rojak P-18, were offered. The HK VP70Z, an 18-shot DAO pistol originally designed as a combination pistol/submachinegun, was approved for importation as a pistol.

Gun Digest itself changed during the decade of the '70s. Foreign guns became such a part of the American handgun scene that U. S. and foreign pistols were grouped together for the first time, and were just listed alphabetically in the catalog section. More feature articles had autoloading handguns as their subjects. Articles about autoloading pistols by Jeff Cooper, Raymond Caranta, George C. Nonte, Mason Williams, Larry Sterrett, James B. Stewart, J. B. Wood, Kenneth L. Waters and others appeared.

The Townsend Whelen awards, which in the early years seemed to favor rifle topics, were presented in 1978 to Donald M. Simmons for "The Remington Model 51," and in 1979 to Dennis Riordan for "The Model of 1911 Colt."

Toward the end of the decade, runaway inflation made it difficult to keep prices current, and some guns were listed in the catalog section without prices.

The company identification had changed from "Gun Digest Publishing Co." in the 25th-1971 Edition to "Digest Books, Inc." the following year. By the 30th-1976 Edition, it was DBI Books. In the last edition published during the 1970s, John T. Amber had stepped down after 28 years as editor. A new editor, Ken Warner, was at the helm.

The decade of the '80s began with the election of Ronald Reagan as President in November 1980. In March 1981, only a few weeks after taking office, President Reagan was shot, and three others were also injured.

Anti-gun forces prepared to use the incident to further their program of further restrictions. However, Reagan stated publicly that he saw no need for additional gun controls.

Economic problems still remained, but whereas President Carter had blamed Americans for a "malaise," President Reagan voiced his optimism and enthusiasm for America. Conditions slowly improved, and he was reelected in 1984.

In 1986, the Firearms Owners Protection Act was passed which modified a number of the provisions of Gun Control Act of 1968. One of the most visible was the resumption, after almost two decades, of importation of surplus firearms.

In 1988, George H. W. Bush was elected President. Bush was not particularly supportive of firearms rights. After the killing of five schoolchildren in Stockton, California in 1989, the useless "Gun Free School Zone" legislation was passed in 1990.

The Berlin Wall came down in 1989. Then, from the standpoint of automatic pistols, the breakup of the Soviet Union opened the door to the importation of new and surplus handguns from the area behind the Iron Curtain.

The first Shooting, Hunting, Outdoor Trade Show (SHOT Show) had been held in January 1979, as a trade show specifically aimed at the shooting and hunting aspects of outdoor sports. Organized by the National Sport Shooting Foundation (NSSF), the new annual show grew steadily through the next decade. The show was to be a factor in providing accurate information on the types of autoloading handguns available each year.

Automatic pistols at the beginning of the 1980s continued the trends of the late 1970s. However, there was a veritable explosion of creativity, and autoloaders gained prominence. There were more double actions, more stainless-steel pistols. The 9mm seemed to be the most popular round, but the 45 got plenty of attention. American police, wedded to the revolver in the previous decades, were adopting automatics in the 1980s.

The category some called the "wondernine" pistols had expanded. With large-capacity magazines and DA triggers, often stainless, the new 9mms were offered by many makers. Development was encouraged by the fact that the U. S. military was conducting testing for a new 9mm pistol to replace the 45. The tests rejuvenated the 9mm/45 controversy, but on January 14, 1985, the United States adopted the Beretta 9mm pistol as the M9. Commercially, it was sold as the Model 92 SB.

Many companies got into the "wondernine" business during the 1980s. At least

Top: *This rare LES P-18 Rojak pistol was the stainless-steel American counterpart of the Austrian Steyr GB pistol.*
Bottom: *Another CZ 75 clone was the TA-90, made by Tanfoglio of Italy.*

four copies of the CZ 75 were offered before the original pistol became available. The Swiss-made AT-84 was handled by Action Arms. FIE offered the Italian TZ 9, and Excam the Italian TA-90. Springfield introduced their P9.

Other foreign designs, such as the South African Mamba pistol, the Spanish pistols Llama Omni and Astra A-80 and Star Models 28 and 30, the French MAB P-15, and the Italian Bernardelli PO 18 were offered. The Browning HP was made in a DA version. The Ruger P85 took a long time getting into production, but eventually joined the group. The 15-shot Walther P88 was a German entry.

One of the most influential new 9mms was the Austrian Glock 17. With a frame of polymer plastic, the 17-shot Glock was immediately denounced by anti-gun politicians as able to pass undetected through airport security devices. It would not, of course, but even long after DC police adopted the Glock, Capital Hill anti-gunners continued to rail against "plastic pistols" that were useful only to criminals and terrorists. The Glock's unique action caused the reevaluation of other mechanisms.

Even amidst a flood of new larger-capacity nines, the 45 auto received plenty of attention. Most, but not all, of the new 45s were copies or modifications of the basic 1911 design. Colt offered its Series '80 pistols, which had a new firing-pin block. A stainless version was offered, and (since the Detonics had already demonstrated the feasibility of a very small 45) the scaled-down Colt Officers ACP was introduced. ODI brought out a commercial 1911-type pistol with a Seecamp double-action trigger system.

During the decade, new copies of the basic 1911 design were offered by Springfield Armory and Auto-Ordnance (Thompson). The Randall company made stainless-steel versions, and then brought out a dramatic true left-hand variant, in which every part was reversed. Randall went out of business during the decade, but a new left-hand pistol, the Falcon Portsider, appeared. Unfortunately for southpaws, Falcon also disappeared.

M-S Safari offered 1911-style pistols, distinguished by a projection on the front strap of the frame that provided a hollow place for the shooter's middle finger. Many felt the configuration helped control recoil. The company closed down, but the Safari-style pistols were acquired and continued in production by Olympic Arms.

Large-frame Spanish Llama 45s were built on the 1911 design, but not all parts would interchange with the Colt. The original Detonics company had gone out of business, but a new company, called New Detonics, took over. The Arminex Tri-Fire pistol was generally based on the 1911, with a number of modifications. The "Tri-Fire" name came from its ability to switch barrels and parts and use 45 ACP, 38 Super or 9mm ammunition.

Not all the new 45s of the '80s were based on the 1911 design. The Sokolovsky was a gorgeous (and expensive) stainless-steel pistol with no external screws, pins or controls. All operations were controlled by two "subtriggers" on either side of the actual trigger. The German Korth and Korriphila pistols were also of unique design and were also in the expensive category. The British Victory pistol was introduced in 45 ACP and other chamberings. Magnum Research planned to

The small Beretta 22 Short pistol of the 1950s evolved into the double-action Model 21 in 22 Long Rifle.

market it in the United States, but the pistol never reached full production status. The SIG/Sauer P220 was imported into America, this time under its own name.

Smith & Wesson, a company that had made large numbers of 45 ACP revolvers, finally introduced a 45 automatic. The double-action Model 645, introduced in 1985, was followed in 1986 by the limited-production single-action Model 745.

Small pistols were in demand. The Budischowsky TP-70 design was made in small quantities by a succession of companies. Other small 22- and 25-caliber pistols were offered by companies such as Wilkinson, Iver Johnson, Raven, RG, Jennings, Seecamp (the Seecamp 25 was modified later into a 32), Sterling and Bauer. CB Arms introduced the 22-caliber Double Deuce. The company changed to Steel City Arms, then Desert Arms, with few pistols produced.

New 32- and 380-caliber pistols were offered by Davis, Sterling and TDE (later AMT). A new polymer-frame 380, the Grendel P-10, was introduced in 1987. Small 9mm pistols were represented by the Detonics Pocket Nine and the Sirkis (later Sardius) DAO 9mm. Both of these early attempts at a very small 9mm were blowbacks, and shooters complained of heavy felt recoil.

More powerful pistols also found a market. The Coonan 357 was a modified 1911 design that handled the 357 Magnum revolver cartridge. The

A 45-caliber BackUp pistol was introduced by AMT in the middle 1990s. Double-action-only, it was made of stainless steel.

Eagle pistol, an Israeli design handled by Magnum Research, was also offered as a 357 Magnum. Before the decade ended, the pistol was called the Desert Eagle, and was also available as a 44 Magnum. The LAR Grizzly, looking like a 1911 on steroids, was offered in 45 Winchester Magnum. The AMT AutoMag III was offered in 30 Carbine in 1989, filling a niche the old Kimball of the '50s could not. Dornaus & Dixon introduced the Bren Ten, chambered for a new 10mm cartridge that got a nod from pistol guru Jeff Cooper.

During the 1980s, a new class of semi-automatic pistol became popular. The new pistols were large and vaguely resembled submachine guns. In the early years of the decade, writer J. B. Wood called them an "as yet unnamed category." It did not take long for the anti-gunners to hate them, and "assault pistol" was the name applied. Used frequently by the major media, the term, unfortunately, has stuck.

The Universal Enforcer in 30 Carbine was still made. However, the category was now also represented by the Bushmaster 223, the Ingram M-10 (45) and M-11 (9mm), the 9mm Interdynamic KG-9 (later KG-99), the UZI pistol, the Holmes MP83, the Goncz and Claridge high-tech pistols, the Intratec TEC-9, the 45-caliber Encom, and the Calico 9mm, with its 100-round helical magazine.

Not all developments were so spectacular. 22-caliber pistols quietly remained popular for hunting, plinking and target shooting. The Ruger Standard pistol had passed the One Million mark by 1988, and had been modified into the Ruger Mark II. However, the High Standard Manufacturing Company, which had made 22 automatics since 1932, and had been the largest manufacturer of 22-caliber handguns, went out of business in late 1984.

Gun Digest noted the tremendous expansion of the autoloading handgun field. Autoloading handguns now came first in the catalog section. More and more articles about semiauto pistols appeared. In the 36th-1982 Edition, the cover showed a Heckler & Koch P9S Target pistol. That same issue instituted the John T. Amber

Literary Award, to honor Amber, the editor emeritus. The new award, which doubled the previous monetary prize, replaced the original Townsend Whelen Award. Amber himself died later in the decade, in 1986. By the end of the decade, in 1989, the John T. Amber Award was awarded to John Malloy for "Early Rivals of the Model 1911 45 Automatic," a history of early autoloaders that had challenged the Colt design.

Much happened during the 1990s, and some events influenced the world of autoloading pistols.

The Gulf War of early 1991 was over quickly, and Americans were impressed with the power of the military. However, the Los Angeles riots of April 1992, in which over 50 people were killed, and the August 1992 tragedy at Ruby Ridge, where government agents killed people at their home, made many uncomfortable with the idea that the government could provide protection for them.

Bill Clinton was elected in November 1992, and the Clinton Justice Department was involved in the killing of at least 74 people near Waco, Texas on April 19, 1993.

Politicians wanted more gun control, and in 1994, the "Brady Bill" and the "Assault Weapons Ban" took effect. In 1996, Clinton was reelected, but Congress reflected gains in pro-gun members. At the state level, "Shall Issue" concealed-carry laws were passed in a number of states.

The tragic murders at Columbine High School, near Littleton, Colorado, occurred on April 19, 1999. The tragedy was played up by the major media, and more calls for restrictive gun control were prompted.

Not content with the way the legislative process was working, a number of municipal politicians began to sue the firearms industry. The excuse was that crimes committed by people with guns cost the cities money. The real intent seemed to be to force companies out of business through legal costs.

All this had an effect on the firearms industry, but did not stop the creativity and the development that had characterized the previous decade. More use of injection-moulded polymers (we no longer said "plastic") created new opportunities for makers of autoloading pistols.

The 1990 introduction of the 40 Smith & Wesson cartridge took some of the fun out of discussions as to whether the 9mm or the 45 ACP was the better cartridge. AMT actually beat Smith & Wesson into production with a 40 S&W, but soon the S&W 4006 appeared. The FBI had adopted the 10mm, but few agents could handle the full-power load well, and a reduced load (some called it "10mm Lite") was used. S&W shrewdly realized that a smaller cartridge could duplicate the reduced load, and the smaller round could be used in smaller pistols. The 40 S&W caught on rapidly, and within a short time, SIG, Taurus, Glock, Browning, Star, Heckler & Koch, Auto-Ordnance, Springfield and others were offering pistols for it.

The Assault Weapons Ban (AWB) of September 1994 had a greater impact on automatic pistols than on the rifles it purported to restrict. With magazine capacity restricted to 10 rounds, interest waned in the large-capacity full-size wondernine. A large-capacity pistol without a large-capacity magazine lost some of its appeal. 9mm pistols became smaller, with magazines that would just hold the "legal limit" of 10 rounds. So, smaller guns, with shorter grips, became popular. Polymer plastic as a frame material allowed

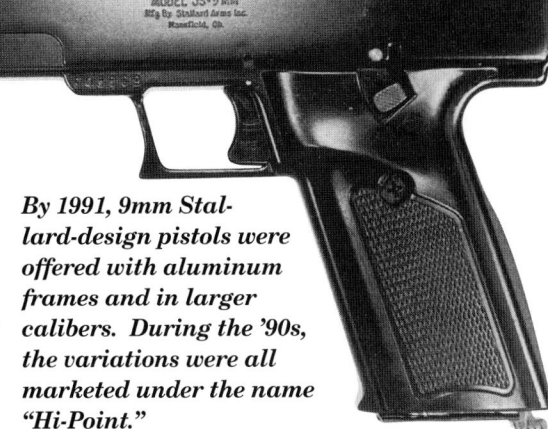

By 1991, 9mm Stallard-design pistols were offered with aluminum frames and in larger calibers. During the '90s, the variations were all marketed under the name "Hi-Point."

Top: *The Taurus PT 145, introduced after the turn of the century, is a compact polymer 45.*
Bottom: *Following the success of their 32-caliber Guardian, North American brought out an enlarged version in 380.*

lighter pistols, faster production and lower-priced offerings. This situation fit well with the nationwide interest in "license-to-carry" legislation that was growing from state to state.

The 45 ACP was seen with even greater favor. Seven or eight rounds of 45 didn't look so bad when compared with ten rounds of 9mm.

Still, large-capacity pistols did not fade away. Many companies had, before the AWB went into effect, cranked out as many big magazines as they could, and offered these as an incentive with their larger pistols.

New cartridges arrived during the '90s. Colt introduced the 9x23, sort of a rimless 38 Super with a reinforced case to take high pressure. In 1993, S&W brought out the 356 TSW (Team Smith & Wesson), a somewhat similar round. AMT brought out the 400 Cor-Bon (a 45 ACP necked to 40) and the 440 Cor-Bon (a 50 AE necked to 44). The 41, 44

and 45 Wildey Magnums were the company's 475 Magnum case necked down appropriately.

Companies came and went. FIE and Excam went, but two companies, Quality Firearms, Inc. (QFI) and European American Armory (EAA) picked up most of the lines of imported pistols.

The Bren Ten had disappeared, but a slightly-modified version was marketed in 1991 as the Peregrine Falcon. It too disappeared after a short while.

Mossberg got back into the pistol business in 1996, planning to market Israeli IMI pistols under the name UZI Eagle. The arrangement ended three years later, with few pistols actually sold.

The LAR Grizzly, a giant 1911-style pistol, started out as a 45 Winchester Magnum and added new chamberings throughout the '90s, including 50 AE. By the end of the decade, however, the Grizzly was no longer made.

The major companies were active. Colt brought out the Double Eagle 45 in 1990. In 1991, the company introduced its lower-price line of 45s, the 1991A1 series. Colt's 9mm All-American 2000, the polymer DAO pistol, didn't work out, and was dropped in 1994. Colt had not made a 22 since the Woodsman, but in 1994 brought out the Colt Cadet, with a Woodsman slant to the grip, and the Colt Target 22 the next year.

Smith & Wesson expanded its line of 9mm, 40 and 45-caliber autos, with conventional double-action and DAO versions. In 1994, the polymer-frame Sigma series made its debut. In 1995, the 45-caliber Model 645 was replaced by the 4506. By 1997, a new line of redesigned 22 pistols appeared.

Ruger also expanded its pistol line, bringing out the 22-caliber Model 22/45 in 1992. The polymer frame had the same grip angle as a 1911. The centerfire line grew, with polymer frames included.

Beretta introduced the Cougar, a compact pistol with a rotating barrel lock, in 1994. Soon, a Mini-Cougar appeared.

Springfield, in early 1994, introduced a wide-frame 45 with a 13-round magazine. The AWB of later

that year refocused the emphasis on the company's line of standard 1911 pistols and 10-shot compacts.

Heckler & Koch introduced the new USP (Universal Self-Loading Pistol) line in 1993, in 9mm and 40 S&W. By 1996, the USP and a new Mark 23 were available in 45 ACP.

Glock had introduced subcompact versions of its original pistols by 1996. A year later, subcompacts in 10mm and 45 were added.

AMT introduced its On Duty, an aluminum-frame departure from its stainless-steel tradition, about 1994. The AutoMag line expanded to 45 Winchester Magnum and 10mm, and later to 50 AE. In 1992, the DAO BackUp 380 arrived. A larger DAO BackUp was offered a few years later. By the end of the decade, in 1998, the rights to manufacture most AMT pistols had been acquired by Galena Industries.

SIGarms brought out a P220 "American" version with side magazine release button, and in 1996, the P239, the first SIG made in the USA, was offered.

Some companies came into prominence during the '90s. Kahr introduced its stainless-steel K9 pistol in 1994. The company expanded, and by the end of the decade, had acquired Auto-Ordnance.

Para-Ordnance, having got its start by making large-capacity replacement frames for 1911 pistols, began marketing complete guns in 1990.

Kel-Tec, with the experience of the polymer-frame Grendel pistols on which to draw, introduced its 14-ounce 11-shot DAO 9mm, the P-11, in 1995. The P-11 introduced a whole new category of popular pistols for concealed carry. It was light, simple to use, shot a relatively powerful cartridge, and didn't cost a whole lot. It was soon made in 40-caliber in 1997. By then, Heritage had introduced its Stealth polymer-frame pistol in 9mm, soon also in 40. In 1997, Republic Arms entered the category with a polymer-frame DAO 45.

Some pistols came with a story. The Raven was a reliable, inexpensive 25 auto, but the factory had burned down in 1984. The design was acquired by another company, and figuratively "rising from the

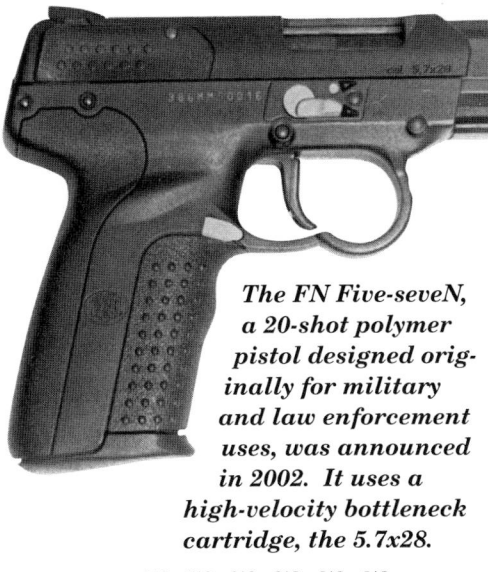

The FN Five-seveN, a 20-shot polymer pistol designed originally for military and law enforcement uses, was announced in 2002. It uses a high-velocity bottleneck cartridge, the 5.7x28.

⊰⊱ ● ⊰⊱ ● ⊰⊱ ● ⊰⊱ ● ⊰⊱ ● ⊰⊱

ashes," the new company became Phoenix Arms. By 1993, Phoenix had added a nice little 22-caliber pistol to its line. Other small companies were active. Lorcin introduced 32 and 380 pistols in 1992. The Wyoming Arms Parker pistol was modified into the Laseraim pistol in 1993.

The 9mm blowback Maverick pistol became the Stallard in 1990. Then, 40- and 45-caliber versions were added in 1991, as the Iberia and Haskell pistols. To avoid confusion, they were all marketed under the name Hi-Point a few years later. Hi-Point grew, and became a leading producer of low-priced but dependable handguns.

Kimber, a rifle company, got into the making of 1911-style pistols in the mid-1990s. The company went into it in a big way, and became one of the leading makers of 1911-type pistols.

Several custom pistol makers realized that many of their customers wanted pistols that were basically similar. They offered such variations as production items. Thus, the appearance of "production custom" pistols, mostly 1911s, took place in the '90s.

GUN DIGEST covered all this, of course. Autoloading handguns were becoming a greater part of the shooting world. They were always listed first now in the catalog section, and filled 38 pages by the end of the decade. Numerous articles, by writers such as Gene Gangarosa, Lee Arten, C. Rodney James, J. B. Wood, C. E. Harris, Holt Bodinson and Raymond

Caranta discussed semi-automatic pistols. One automatic pistol piece, "Blowback Nines" by John Malloy, won the John T. Amber Award for 1993.

The covers featured autoloaders three times. On the 1991-45th Edition, two SIG/Sauer pistols were featured. Two years later, the new Ruger 22/45 appeared. Then, the next edition featured the Heckler & Koch USP pistol.

Following the publication of the 1996-50th Edition, J. B. Wood stepped down, after having written the "Handguns Today, Autoloaders" section for 15 years. John Malloy filled in at that position, and Wood continued to have articles about semi-automatic pistols included.

After the 1990s ended, January 1, 2000 arrived on schedule without much trouble. There had been substantial concern about "Y2K," the possibility of widespread computer failure, as the new year clicked into place. Prudent people had made preparations just in case, and part of the preparations of many involved the protection afforded by firearms.

George W. Bush was elected President of the United States—not in November 2000, but over a month after Election Day—after lengthy court proceedings over vote counts.

On September 11, 2001, America was attacked. Terrorists in highjacked jetliners killed thousands of people. The U. S. economy, already in a slump, went into a nosedive. For a while, the only things selling well were American flags, gas masks, Bibles and… firearms. A lot of people wanted a dependable handgun. The U. S. military responded to the threat of further terrorist action with strikes in Afghanistan, and in March 2003 went into Iraq.

2004 was a significant year for gunowners. On September 13, 2004, the "Assault Weapons Ban" did actually sunset. It was the only time in the memory of many that an onerous gun law had gone away. On November 4 of that year, George W. Bush was reelected.

The period following the 1990s has thus been a time of change for

the firearms world. By 2000, lawsuits had driven Lorcin out of business, and other companies were hard-pressed. Colt discontinued almost all its handgun line, including guns introduced only the year before. Only a few 1911 models, in 45 ACP only, and single-action revolvers were retained. Colt recovered, and the product line gradually increased again. Galena took the AMT operation from hostile California to Sturgis, SD, but things did not work out. By late 2001, AMT was gone. The Davis, Talon and Republic companies were out of business by 2002.

However, useful designs are sometimes just not allowed to fade away. In 2002, Cobra Enterprises had been formed, and was offering improved Davis, Talon and Republic pistol designs again. In 2003, Lorcin-style guns had been added to the Cobra line. In 2004, the newly-formed Crusader Group, which included High Standard, had acquired AMT designs. AMT BackUp and AutoMag pistols were put back into production by 2005.

The 1911 design, with its 100th birthday just down the road, has never been more popular. Besides the traditional Colt offerings, companies such as Springfield, Olympic, Kimber and others had already gone heavily into 1911 production before 2000. Dan Wesson, a name related to revolvers since 1968, introduced its own 1911 line in the year 2000. That same year, High Standard also added a line of 1911 45s. In 2001, Century International Arms brought out an offering of 1911 pistols.

Smith & Wesson introduced their SW1911 in 1903, and Sigarms

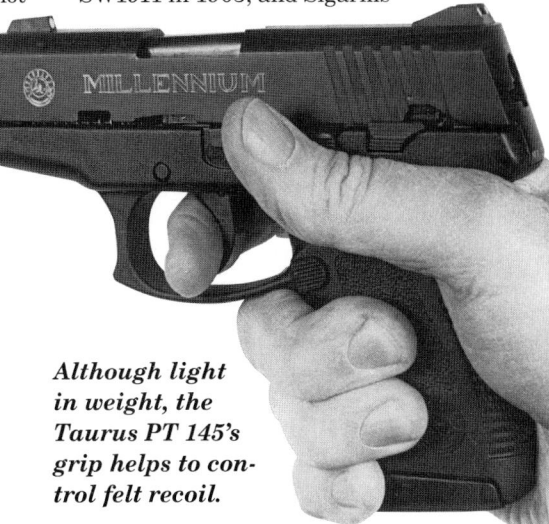

Although light in weight, the Taurus PT 145's grip helps to control felt recoil.

followed the next year with their 1911-type GSR pistol. In 2005, new 1911 pistols from Taurus, U. S. Fire Arms and Iver Johnson also entered the market. Colt has "reissued" older models such as the original World War I-type 1911, the military-style 1911A1 pistol of World War II, the Series '70 and the pre-'70 Government Model.

Polymer frames have become more widespread. Browning brought out its PRO-9 and PRO-40 pistols in 2003. Beretta, between 2000 and 2005, introduced its 9000S polymer compact pistol, its 22-caliber U22 NEOS and the new modular Storm Px4 pistol. Glock, a leader in polymer usage, added its Model 36, a compact single-column 45 ACP, and its later offerings for the new 45 G.A.P. (45 Glock Automatic Pistol) cartridge—the models 37, 38 and 39.

Hi-Point had used polymer for some time, with smaller-caliber 380 and 9mm models. In 2002, the company began phasing in polymer-frame 40- and 45-caliber pistols. HS America had introduced its HS2000 pistol, a polymer-frame design from Croatia with a "Glock-type" trigger, in 2000. By 2002, the design was modified and offered by Springfield Armory as their new XD (Extreme Duty) pistol.

Kel-Tec, whose head was an early pioneer in the use of polymers, had its popular P-32 in use by 2000. The company added a 380 version, slyly called the P-3AT, in 2003. Kahr, beginning with stainless-steel pistols in the '90s, introduced polymer-frame variants in 2000. Kahr's first 45-caliber pistol, the P45, was a polymer-frame design introduced in 2005. Ruger added a new

polymer 45 auto, the P345, in 2004. The company's new Mark III 22/45 pistols also have polymer frames.

Full-size pistols are still here, as are compacts and also very small pistols. Today's small pistols may be of greater power than those of years past. The new little Rohrbaugh 9mm pistol, in production during 2004, weighs less than 13 ounces. North American Arms has introduced powerful new bottleneck cartridges for its little Guardian pocket pistols. The 32 NAA was in production by 2003, the 25 NAA a year later. From their short barrels, the bullets exit at about 1200 feet per second.

GUN DIGEST recorded these developments, and there were some changes to GUN DIGEST itself after the end of the 1990s. In 2000, Ken Warner stepped down as editor-in-chief, after serving in that capacity for twenty years. Ken Ramage, the present editor, took over at that time. He had held the position of senior staff editor prior to then. DBI had already been bought by Krause Publications before 2000, and in 2003, F&W Publications took over Krause. Autoloading pistols remained the largest individual portion of the catalog section, and a number of excellent feature articles added to the store of knowledge about semi-automatics. Writers such as Jerry Burke, Jim Foral, Raymond Caranta and Lee Arten wrote on different aspects of autoloading handguns. In the 2004-58th Edition, the John T. Amber Award was reported won by John L. Marshall for his coverage of "Service 45s of the Twentieth Century." In the following 2005-59th Edition, the front and back covers were graced by new Ruger semi-automatic pistols. The

"Handguns Today, Autoloaders" section in that edition covered 15 pages, the largest single section in the volume. Thirty pages of the catalog section were devoted to current autoloading pistols.

So, after six decades, creativity continues in the field of automatic pistols. Yet, a few things are not much different than they were. In 1944, there were only two American manufacturers of automatic pistols. Both Colt and High Standard, the original two, have had problems, but both are still here. Of the models listed in the first GUN DIGEST, only the Colt 1911 design still survives, only little changed. Many companies have made their own modifications, but the popularity of the original 1911 design lives on.

Foreign automatics were given little coverage in the early years of GUN DIGEST. As the years went by, the foreign autoloaders were given greater coverage, then combined with the American pistols. Because foreign designs are now manufactured in the United States, there would no longer be any way to separate the guns by countries, as was done in the past. Some of the European pistol designs of the pre-WWII era are also still with us, such as the Walther PP and PPK pistols, and the 1935 Browning Hi-Power.

Most of today's companies that make autoloading pistols did not exist in 1944, yet some, such as Ruger, and later Glock, have grown to great importance. Some designs have stayed with us, such as the CZ 75 and the Beretta 92, and their importance has gone beyond their production by the original maker.

The world of autoloading handguns has grown with the years. It is an exciting world. There are always new materials and new manufacturing processes to be tried. New cartridges are introduced that might fill a new niche. There are always new ways to accomplish the functions of feeding cartridges from a magazine into a chamber, firing the cartridge, controlling the pressure, ejecting the empty cartridge case, and then doing it all over again. Some designs arrive, and then fade away. Some designs arrive and thrive. Through it all, for just over six decades, GUN DIGEST has recorded these efforts.

Anti-gun forces seem to hate all autoloading pistols, but they love to hate some more than others. Some, such as this 45-caliber MAC-10, were labeled "assault pistols" and banned by the Assault Weapons Ban of 1994, which finally sunset in 2004.

MILITARY ROLLING BLOCK RIFLES
OF THE RAREST KIND

by George J. Layman

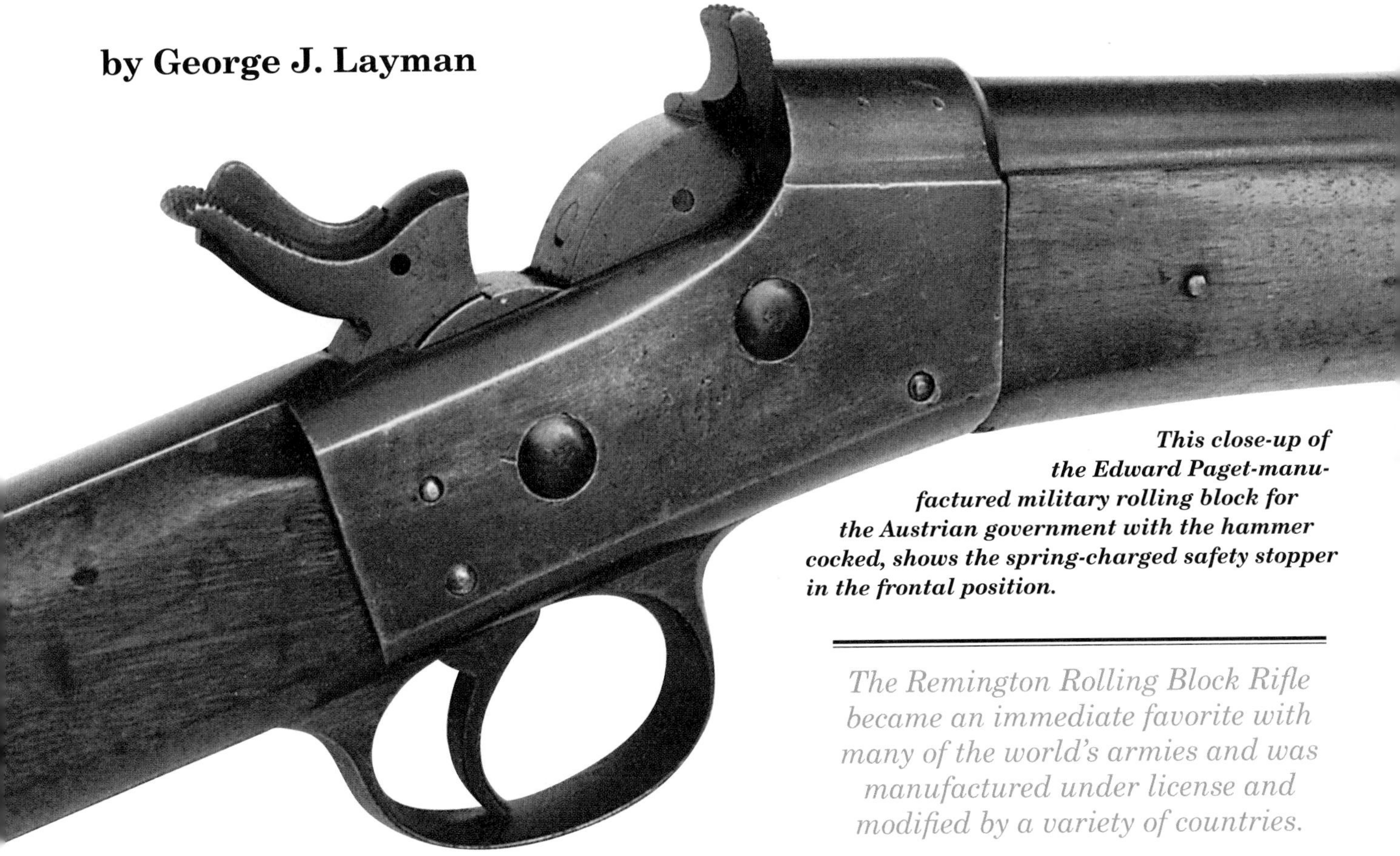

This close-up of the Edward Paget-manufactured military rolling block for the Austrian government with the hammer cocked, shows the spring-charged safety stopper in the frontal position.

The Remington Rolling Block Rifle became an immediate favorite with many of the world's armies and was manufactured under license and modified by a variety of countries.

The story of the Remington rolling block is well known to arms students throughout the world. However, several variations produced in limited numbers are relatively unknown. Herewith, a short overview on the development of the world's greatest single-shot military rifle.

In 1864-65 chief engineer Joseph Rider of the E. Remington and Sons Arms Co. was tasked to redesign and improve the Leonard Geiger breech-loading design. Geiger, a native of Hudson, NY, received his first patent (#37,501) on January 27, 1863; it was reissued in April 17, 1866, whereupon Rider refined the action even further. The complete redesign strengthened the earlier Remington "split breech" action purchased by the government at the end of the Civil War. The split-breech action was based upon the earlier 1864 patent, having its hammer fit between a weaker, slotted, breechblock that was compatible only with low pressure copper-cased cartridges such as the 46 or 56 Spencer rimfire. The new 1866 patent allowed Rider to improve the breechblock by forming it from a solid billet of steel

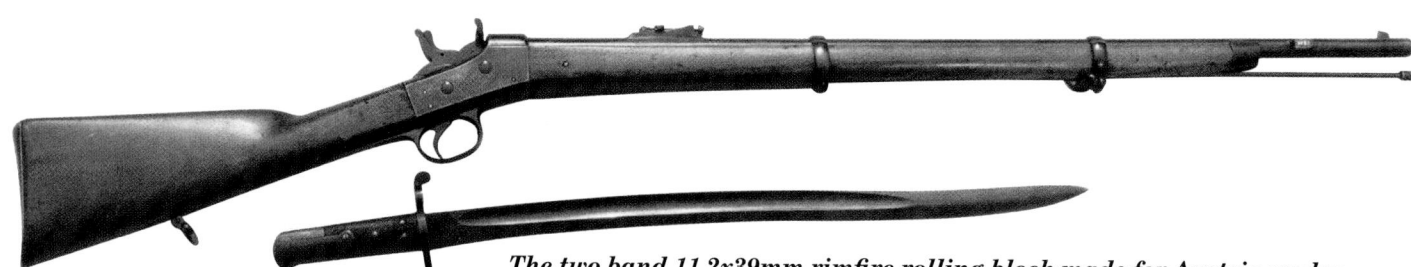

The two band 11.2x39mm rimfire rolling block made for Austria under license by Remington took the standard Werndl bayonet and is considered the rarest of any pre-production foreign-made military rolling block. The majority of these surplus rifles went to China.

drilled for a firing pin channel. The breechblock's solid crescent contour rolled beneath the hammer's crescent cut for loading and extracting a spent case. It was the strongest system known that could handle the largest blackpowder cartridges to arrive in the coming decades. The term "rolling block" became the action's sobriquet for eternity. Because the government's budget was strained by the war, and because there was a surplus of ordnance of all categories, many previously active arms suppliers to the War Department went out of business.

Remington saw this coming and was certain that, unless they quickly found some new business, they would be bankrupt like so many of the other wartime arms manufacturers. Seeking a market for the new rolling block rifle, in the summer of 1866 brother Samuel departed for Europe to demonstrate the qualities of the improved Remington rolling block rifle. It proved a worthwhile journey; ordnance inspectors from Europe and the Middle East were present for Sam Remington's many hands-on demonstrations of the strength, reliability and rapidity of fire of the new Remington breechloader. Spain, Denmark, Sweden, Egypt, Austria––and a host of other countries––were

immediately sold on the remarkable design of the new American breechloader. Once it was awarded a gold medal at the Paris Exposition of 1867, success was at hand.

The Austro-Hungarian Model Of 1866

The Austro-Hungarian delegation became the first nation to obtain licensing rights to produce the rolling block in Vienna. The reason behind such a hasty arrangement was that Austria knew it would soon be at war with Prussia. Upon the particulars being worked out, the Austrian Emperor called on an English firearms engineer, Edward Paget, to come to Vienna to oversee production. After Archduke Wilhelm's special commission concurred the rolling block would be an ideal breechloading arm for his military and police forces, Austria paid Remington the license fees to produce the rifle, and Paget began work immediately. According to an article in a British publication, *The Engineer*, dated 27 July 1866, the Emperor of Austria was said to contract with Paget to produce 6,000 rolling-block breechloaders; a later published source stated the number was 15,000.

In any event, Paget cleverly incorporated a number of changes

⬩⬥⬩⬥⬩⬥⬩⬥⬩⬥⬩

All the Austrian rolling blocks were marked ED.A PAGET WIEN 3. Serial numbers were located on the bayonet lug. Note the breech block and hammer pins are screw-retained, something the Swedes later copied.

on the Austrian 11.2 x 39.7Rmm rimfire rolling-block rifle not found on the American-made versions. First, hammer and breechblock pins were retained by individual screws in lieu of the standard Remington "button" plate. Second, a spring-charged, hammer-shaped, "safety stopper" mechanism was cut into the center of the hammer. Unless both the stopper and hammer were simultaneously thumbed to the rear, the hammer could not be cocked. This modification prevented the hammer from automatically opening if a faulty cartridge exploded––which could *possibly* cock the hammer, slamming the breech block open and sending gases into the shooter's face. The chance of this occurring was very remote when using solid-head centerfire cases but, using the earlier thin copper rimfire cartridge it was a possibility. Single-shot author James J. Grant once credited the Swedes and Norwegians with the safety stopper device; later disproved when I finally obtained one of these rare military rolling-block rifles.

The Austrian Model of 1866, produced in Europe, should be acknowledged as the first (albeit small) foreign contract obtained by Sam Remington before he departed from the continent. My specimen (s/n #1952) displays other unusual features such as a non-Remington oval-shaped trigger guard, a unique stock comb contour and a three-screw buttplate. Overall quality is quite acceptable, and the rifle is marked on the left frame ED. A. PAGET, WIEN J. Only 2000 pieces are said

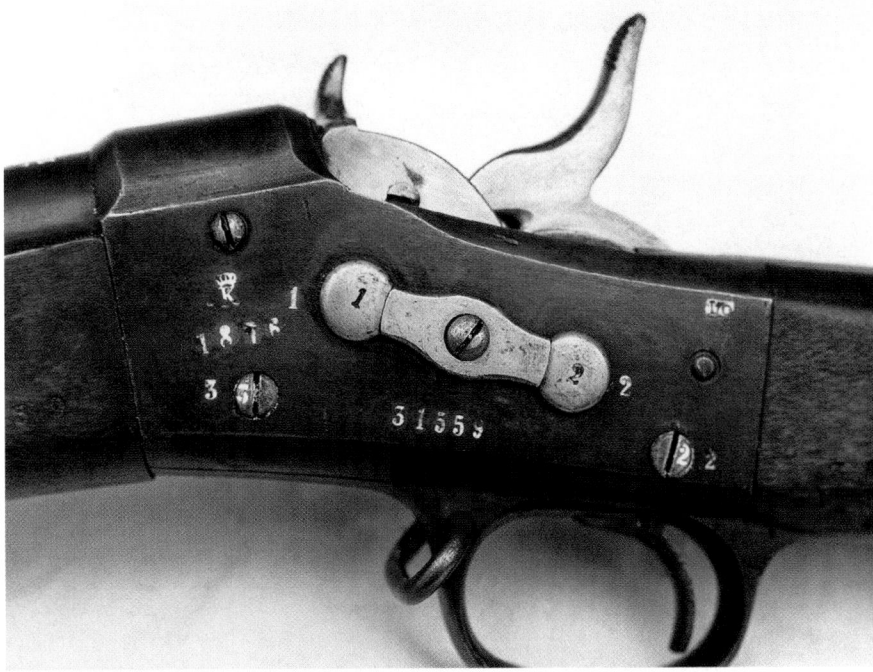

▶ *The left frame of the 1868/74 Norwegian rolling-block rifle made at Konigsberg is one of the most well-inspected Scandinavian military rolling blocks to be found. The markings include the manufacture date, serial number and inspectors' markings—even the screws are numbered. The production precision clearly shows it was made for a special purpose, perhaps for rifle competition.*

⋇⋇●⋇⋇●⋇⋇●⋇⋇●⋇⋇●⋇⋇

to have been completed by Paget when production was halted following the 1866-67 Austrian debacle with the Prussians at Koniggratz.

The Austrian 4th Battalion and the 21st Jager Battalion were selected to conduct the field trials of the new rolling block. The snag that derailed this rolling block design was the issue of nationalism, as the Austrian press hammered the government for considering a foreign design. Between this and the Prussian troubles, the rolling block lost out to Joseph Werndl's system, which Austria finally chose as the national military arm.

Today, the Austrian Edward Paget-made rolling block is indeed *the* rarest of any Remington-sanctioned foreign prototype/limited production in existence. For years, many rolling-block students were left wondering about the disposition of the remaining 2000 arms. I discovered the majority of remaining surplus Paget-made Austrian rolling blocks ended up in Korea and China; surviving examples have been uncovered with Chinese/Korean character cartouches on the buttstock. It is believed they were disposed of through a European version of an American Hartley and Graham military-surplus operation.

▶ *The rear sight, calibrated in "Alens," is itself serial-numbered to the rifle.*

⋇⋇●⋇⋇●⋇⋇●⋇⋇●⋇⋇●⋇⋇

Evidence indicates they could have been used by Korean hostiles and their Chinese allies, who repelled the U.S. landing expeditions from the *USS Colorado* in 1871 during the battles at Kanghwa Island, Korea.

The Danish Model 1867/ 96/ 05 Carbine

In 1867, Denmark became the first quantity purchaser of the Remington rolling-block action, making it their official service arm. Contracting with Remington for 42,000 rifles and 1800 carbines, the Danes received permission to begin domestic production in 1869. When, decades later,

Denmark began to upgrade their older equipment, one of the most radically modified rolling blocks is unquestionably the Danish Model 1867/96/05 *Rytterkarabin* (cavalry carbine). This ultra-rare carbine is chambered for the 11.35x45Rmm Danish Remington carbine centerfire cartridge, which replaced the 11.7x42R

⋇⋇●⋇⋇●⋇⋇●⋇⋇●⋇⋇●⋇⋇

Having the entire comb of the stock stripped flat and drilled to hold ten cartridges beneath a spring-charged aluminum cover is indeed a radical addition.

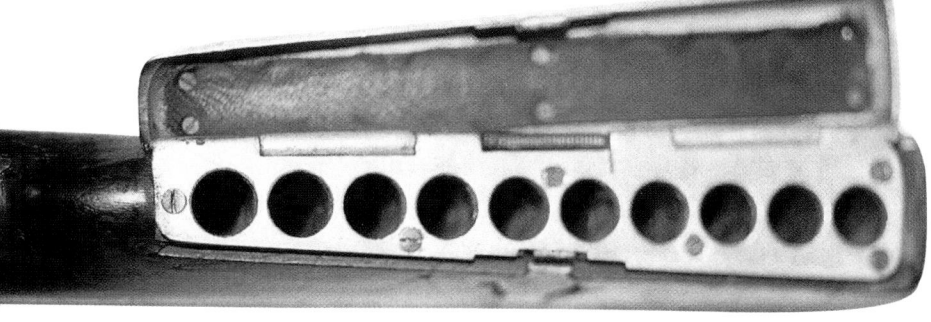

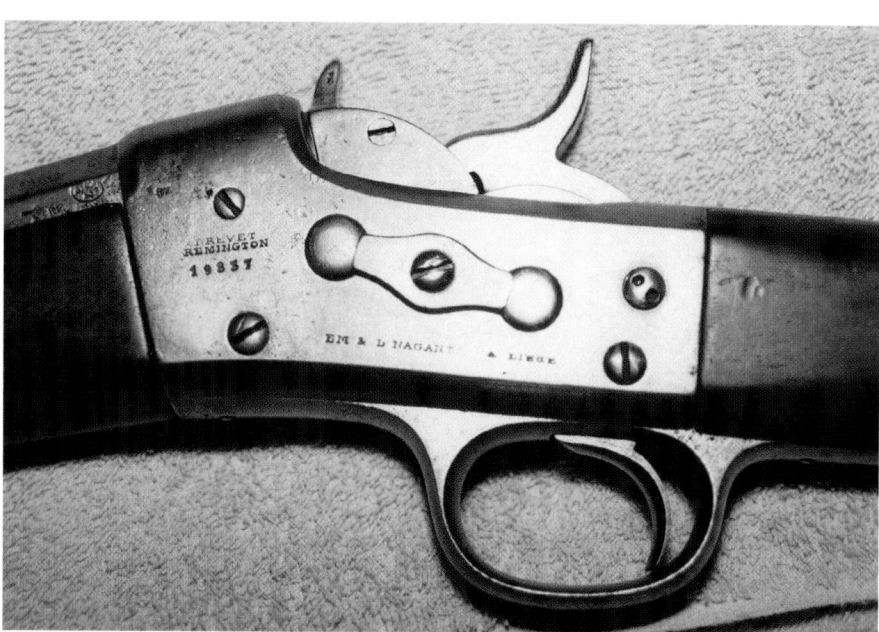

rimfire version (for carbines) some years earlier. Beyond seeing one of these in the Copenhagen Arsenal display in 1968, I hadn't seen one in the United States until 1996. A Danish-American acquaintance brought one to this country in the 1950s and eventually sold it to me after several years of pestering. It is the first—and only—one I have seen in the Lower 48.

For years the Danes had experimented with manufacturing special-purpose rifles and carbines based on the rolling-block action. The 67/96/05 carbines were shortened to an overall length of 35.5 inches and were simply modified from the older 1867 Danish *Bagladeriffels* (infantry rifles) with worn barrels and other defects.

My Model 1867/96/05 was discovered with tang markings of E. Remington and Son indicating its action was from one the original rifles purchased back in 1867. The 67/96/05's designation is derived from the official nomenclature being the Model 1867; '1896' indicated its sling swivels were repositioned, and the regraduation of the rear sight changed from the earlier Danish "Alen" to meters.

The modification of 1905, however, gave the carbine its most radical physical modification. The comb of the buttstock was laterally cut from the thumb rest on back and drilled to hold ten cartridges, thus increasing the soldier's basic ammunition load. Further, a hinged spring-tensioned aluminum cover and base plate kept the cartridges in place. A leather liner pinned inside the cover kept the cartridges silent when they hit against the cover.

Another interesting feature was the rounded, protruding knob installed on the left side of the frame, which served in place of a saddle ring. With its "mushroom"-style head that fit into a clip spring on the saddle, it somewhat resembled the swiveling concept of the "Bridgeport Device" experimented with on Colt single-action revolvers for the U.S. Army.

The 67/96/05 cavalry carbine was fitted with conventional sling swivels

▲ *The hands-down rarest of all Belgian-made military rolling blocks is the Nagant-made Dutch contract carbine of 1873. So few of these have been seen worldwide that it is likely the scarcest foreign-made production rolling block.*

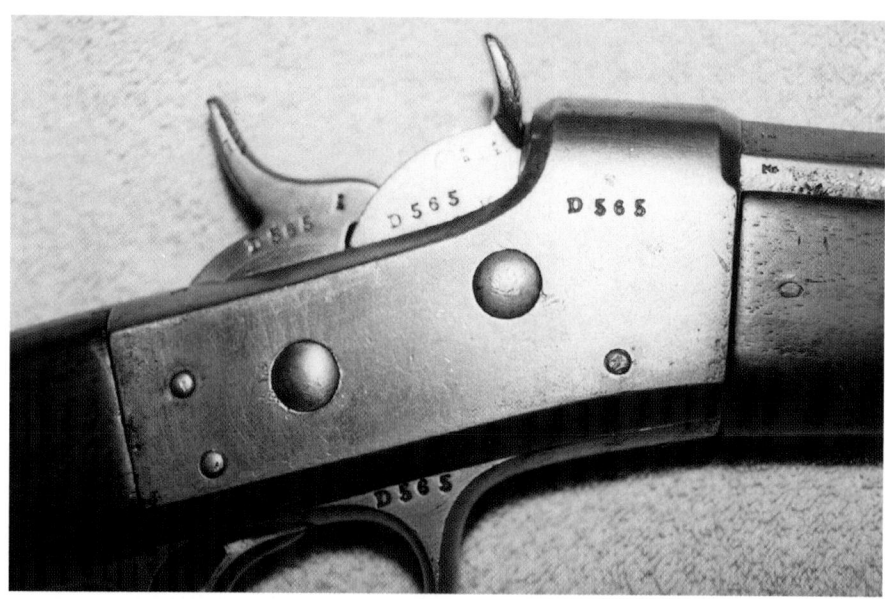

These right and left close-ups of the Nagant Dutch carbine show well-defined markings that identify it. The left frame side (top) *has BREVETTE REMINGTON (Remington copy) over the company's master rolling block serial number. The pentagonal barrel flat shows still more inspectors' stampings.*

A full-length view of my Chinese rimfire carbine has nowhere near the graceful lines of the Nagant-made Dutch contract carbine and seems to have been produced in the shortest amount of time possible.

with the rear swivel being angled on the right wrist, and had lightly-rounded finger grooves on the forend. All in all, it made for a very slick-looking carbine that appears about as far as one could go in modernizing the rolling block. The one feature it lacked was a buttplate.

The total number of 1867/96/05 modified carbines is estimated at 3000. Regarding Danish carbine production as a whole, 2500 Engineer carbines of the Model 1867 were delivered to the army, of which 1950 were altered to centerfire.

With substantial quantities of earlier rimfire ammunition in reserve stocks, a fair number of rimfire rolling-block carbines were left. Thus, breechblocks on some carbines were drilled with two firing pin channels––rim- or centerfire––allowing the firing pin to be moved to either position, depending on the ammunition issued.

Between 1872 and 1883, some 3078 carbines identical to the Engineer Model (with sling swivels on forend and lower buttstock) were received by the Danish navy (Marinen). The only distinguishing feature of service affiliation was the army or navy brass regimental or service disc in the buttstock. One of the reasons for the Danish military carbine upgrade of 1905 was to cover the shortage of 8mm Danish Model 1889 Krag bolt-action rifles. Interestingly, the Model 67/96/05 11.7mm centerfire carbines remained in active service with the regular army until 1914.

The Norwegian 1868/74 Konigsberg Rolling Block Rifle

Another very rare Scandinavian copy of the rolling block made under license was the 1868/74 infantry rifle manufactured at Konigsberg, Norway in 12.11mm Norway/Sweden rimfire. This particular example differs from the typical Swedish-made versions as it has a 38 1/2-inch barrel. This rifle shows the highest quality of workmanship and attention to detail in every single part: the frame, barrel, rear sight, the three barrel bands and all other components were serial-numbered. My specimen is s/n 31559 and is marked 1876 indicating continuous serial numbers on all Konigsberg-made rolling blocks regardless of special or standard issue; otherwise, many more of these unique M1868/74 rifles would be in circulation. I believe it was specially-made as a military match rifle due to the overabundance of inspectors' cartouches and overall precise fit. The Konigsberg arsenal produced thousands of rolling blocks for the Swedish crown, but this high quality example does not compare to the usual Konigsberg-produced rolling-block infantry rifles with dates from 1875 to 1878 that I have observed. Whatever the case, this configuration is truly one to watch for.

❧ ● ❧ ● ❧ ● ❧ ● ❧ ● ❧

With the action open one can see the early grooved channeled breech block was utilized. The million dollar question which evades explanation up to now is who was the Belgian company involved in setting up this operation in China to build these carbines? Also, did the Chinese build these independently upon their departure?

The Belgian Nagant Model 1873 Dutch Carbine

Two of Europe's most prolific arms manufacturers from Belgium were Emil & L. Nagant and August Francotte, both of whom had amicable relations with the Remington company in Ilion, New York. By the early 1870s, Remington found it had to work 24-hour shifts to keep up with orders from Spain, Latin America, Egypt and beyond. To meet production deadlines, the system of granting manufacturing rights to reliable, high-quality foreign arms manufacturing companies proved a profitable venture. Remington, though not receiving a full price for each rifle, would receive a healthy royalty for each unit manufactured under license.

Francotte produced rolling-block rifles and carbines to help fill the large Egyptian order, and independently took orders for Uruguay and El Salvador for a two-band musketoon in 43 Spanish. Nagant also produced an order of two-band musketoons for Tunisia that had a crescent moon inlaid into the stock, with fleur-de-lis designs in the body of the crescent.

The aforementioned Francotte and Nagant rolling blocks are genuine scarcities, but the real prize among Belgian-made rolling blocks are those of the 1873 Dutch carbine contract made by Nagant. These are so difficult to uncover that ten years ago they could bring $1000 in Europe alone. Holland, though adopting the Beaumont rifle in 1870, issued its Snider conversions to the home guard and some colonial troops, then in 1873 decided to also adopt a Remington rolling-block carbine to be made under license by Nagant. It would be chambered for the 11.3x45R or 11mm Dutch Remington centerfire cartridge. The Nagant-made rolling-block carbines served three purposes: to arm the cavalry, engineers, and *gendarmerie* (national police or gendarmes).

The variation shown is part of the collection of Tom Jackson of Kingman, Arizona. I have never owned a Nagant Dutch rolling-block carbine and have heard rumors from Europe that, during the Nazi occupation of Holland, even antiquated Dutch firearms were destroyed or dumped at sea by the Germans to keep them from the resistance groups. If true, this could explain the worldwide rarity of these carbines. The thoroughness of the inspectors' markings on Jackson's Dutch carbine are indicative of the quality Nagant demanded on production that directly represented the Remington company. The left frame is marked Brevette Remington, or "Remington copy," with the number 19337 beneath. This is a "tracking serial number," indicating the total of rolling-block rifle actions the Nagant firm produced for royalty accounting purposes for Remington. Em. & L. Nagant markings are also present with the Liege ELG definitive proof on the barrel. The 1873 on the rear of barrel is the model year number and the 1877 on the buttplate is the year of manufacture. The D 565 appears to be the Nagant in-house serial number of how many carbines were produced on the contract so far. The circular Nagant cartouche on the right butt is very clear and it is obvious this carbine is in near excellent condition and obviously did not live a hard life. It can only be estimated that possibly 2000 to 4000 carbines were produced, conjecture based on military and police population size of the day. I have viewed rare photographs of the capitulation of the Dutch East Indies to the Japanese in World War II that show Dutch colonial police throwing what appeared to be rolling block-type carbines into an arms cache of all varieties of captured weapons. Thus it may be that numerous obsolete Dutch weapons, including Nagant-made carbines, were lost as a result of hostilities with Japan.

A Mysterious Chinese Rolling Block Carbine

Rolling block usage in Asia has traditionally been confined to China and Korea. Partial records indicate that, in 1874, Remington received a rather dubious order for 144,000 rolling-block rifles. I have examined Chinese copies of the rolling block, none of which had any Remington or U.S. markings. Some of these were the surplus Austrian rolling blocks made by Edward Paget as discussed previously, and were strictly a surplus purchase without any connection to Remington.

The second copies I examined were a rifle and a carbine, the latter of which I now own. The carbine is a mysterious piece, without markings aside from the number 21 and two Chinese characters––all other major components have the Chinese character of the number ten "+" which is shaped like a cross. Chambered for an unknown 11mm rimfire cartridge, the carbine appears to be of Belgian design with a Springfield-style muzzleloading rear sight (possibly U.S. surplus or replicated production). Other features include a brass buttplate and a circular channel drilled horizontally through the center of the stock evidently intended for some sort of sling attachment device. The barrel has an octagonal chamber

and an offset witness mark to line up with the frame. I purchased this carbine from a WWII veteran who brought it back from Manchuria after his assignment involving releasing U.S. soldiers from Japanese captivity. He mentioned he saw many carbines and rifles of this design at the Mukden, Manchuria arsenal.

Who assisted the Chinese in manufacturing these? If the tooling came from Belgium, it is odd that no Nagant or Francotte markings are present. Both these firms were known for their strict quality control, and the absence of even a token showing of inspector markings is very odd. Another peculiar note: of all of the surplus military arms coming out of China in the last 20 years or more, not one Remington-marked rolling block has ever been imported. What became of the so-called order of 144,000 rolling blocks? I feel there was a secret (at least at present) arrangement wherein China made an agreement with Remington to produce the arms either in China proper, or in Belgium for subsequent export to the Chinese mainland––or perhaps vice-versa. From a professional

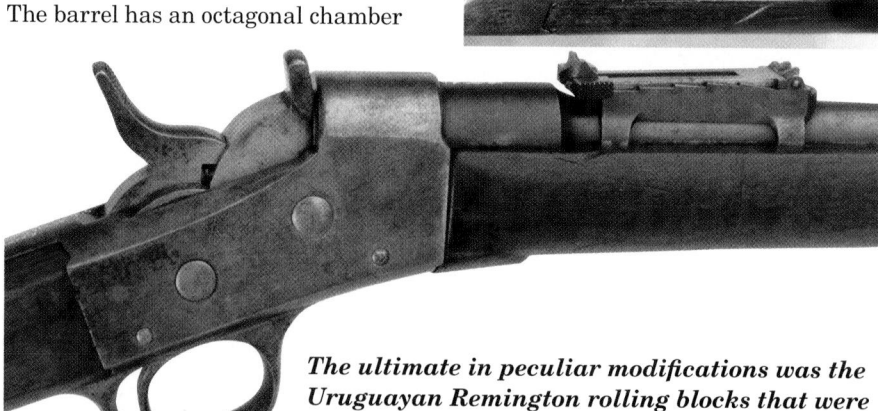

The ultimate in peculiar modifications was the Uruguayan Remington rolling blocks that were replaced with French Model 1895 6.5mm Daudeteau barrels. With only one known so far, what was going on in the mind the Uruguayan engineer, one Mr. Doviitis who initially supervised the rebarreling of obsolete M1871 Mauser rifles in France with upgraded smokeless powder 6.5mm Daudeteau barrels. As shown here (bottom) with a No.1 Remington blackpowder action and a smokeless 6.5 mm Daudeteau barrel and sight, it can be seen by the patent address on the tang (top) that this action was of pre-1888 manufacture.

viewpoint, after having examined over a thousand foreign- and domestic-made Remington military rolling blocks, the theory of tooling and machinery being shipped to China and the arms subsequently manufactured there, under Belgian supervision, seems the most feasible scenario. Given the warlord system of the day, foreign inspector or manufacturers markings may have been purposely omitted since countless warring factions may have had their arms produced on the identical Belgian equipment overseen by the same inspectors!

There have been at least two known sales of Chinese-made rolling-block rifles having this carbine's characteristics (excepting the drilled stock channel). They were sold by Kristopher Gasior, a dealer of rare and unusual military rolling blocks (www. Collectiblefirearms.com). The Chinese-made rolling-block rifles were definitely produced under trained Belgian supervision and––so far––have been two-band military rifles with a cleaning rod and a unique elevated rear sight almost eight inches from the receiver ring! Indeed a peculiar arrangement. Caliber of these rifles appears very similar to that of a 50-70 rimfire cartridge. Regarding the carbine, I know of only one other example––it is in a Massachusetts collection and an exact clone of my carbine. Parts are completely interchangeable, but are marked with the Chinese character number of 216. Perhaps in the future, a long-forgotten arsenal––akin to the recent

find of thousands of arms in Nepal's Lagan Silekhana palace––will be revealed on the Chinese mainland. For now, the so-called Chinese contract of Remington's mysterious "144,000" is a rolling-block version of lost treasure.

The Uruguayan 6.5 Daudeteau/Doviitis Rolling Block Rifle

One nation that earnestly favored the rolling block system was the South American Republic of Uruguay. Whether made by Remington, Francotte or Nagant, they were probably the most prolific customers for this single-shot rifle of any country south of the border. The Uruguayan military first purchased several thousand Remington rolling-block rifles and carbines in 1880 in 43 Spanish, which was the standard chambering of nearly all Latin American countries that were rolling block-equipped. About that same year, Uruguay contracted with August Francotte of Belgium for approximately 2500-3000 two-band artillery musketoons, which are usually found marked "Republica Oriental," the early name for Uruguay.

Since Uruguay was populated by many German, Italian and other European immigrants, there was an ample population of educated machinists on hand, to include former European arms craftsmen. There is a great deal of evidence that they were conducting experiments on rolling block and other existing weapon systems.

Several years ago I obtained a particularly unusual and so far

⚜ ● ⚜ ● ⚜ ● ⚜ ● ⚜ ● ⚜

Unknown until the 1960s, the Canadian purchase of 60 Whitney carbines to arm the Montreal police department was exposed in a 1965 article in a Canadian arms journal. For years American collectors believed it was merely a rumor.

one-of-a-kind specimen, once owned by the late author Jerry Janzen, was obtained by the author several years ago. This Remington rolling-block action was fitted with what is known as the 6.5mm Mauser-Doviitis barrel, one of the great enigmas of foreign converted rolling-block actions. In the 1890s, a mysterious Uruguayan engineer named Dovitiis was tasked by his government to take an unknown number of surplus German Mauser Infanterie Gewehr Model 1871 bolt-action rifles and have them reworked by the French Societe Francaise des Armes Portatives of St. Denis in Paris (abbreviated S.F.A.P / St. Denis). Dovitiis is said to have supervised the installation of new French-made barrels chambered for the 6.5 x 53mm Daudeteau No.12 caliber to replace the old German 11mm (43 Mauser) tubes on the 71 Mauser actions (these barrels came from the now very rare Model 1895 Daudeteau rifle sold to Uruguay, El Salvador and Portugal). No one ever seemed to find a record for this order, though many felt it was an interim purchase by the Uruguayan government to supplement its army's M1893 or M1895 Mauser rifles. Another rumor is they were intended to arm rebel factions in one of the Uruguayan states in the outback.

In any case, the arms were shipped from Antwerp, Belgium to Montevideo, Uruguay. A later rumor circulated that quantities of rolling-block actions were soon after being rebarreled in Montevideo arsenal, also with Doviitis in charge of the operation. Whether intended to serve as government training arms or to supply the army (or rebels?) is unknown.

Up to this point, only a single specimen of the 6.5mm Daudeteau-chambered military rolling block is known to me. The late Mr. Janzen may have obtained this rifle on a trip to Uruguay, but no such record exists. If quantities were reworked and clandestinely issued to rebels, or other factions, perhaps none ever returned to be imported through legal means and could likely have been discarded by insurgents in the jungle outback after the ammunition became obsolete. My specimen is in superb condition.

Shown *(top)* is a full-length view of the Whitney Montreal Police Carbine, complete with its surplus 1861 Springfield angular bayonet. The marking of MONTREAL POLICE *(left)* was accomplished by a subcontractor to Hartley Graham and Company from whom the carbines were ordered. Montreal arms dealer R.H. Kilby of Montreal made the purchase of 60 carbines for the city. It is estimated that less than 18 of this ultra rare carbine have survived. This specimen's condition is excellent.

The barrel is clearly marked with the SFAP ST. DENIS scroll behind the original banded ramp rear sight for the 6.5 mm Daudeteau rifle cartridge. The two-band forend has the French 1895 bayonet lug beneath the front sight band, along with the peculiar cleaning rod mounted offset to the right side. I have requested information regarding this rifle and the Dovitiis connection but to this day however, the Uruguayan government is still secretive of disclosing even 19th century military information because of their past troubles with the 1970s Tupamaro rebels, off-shoots of another era. It would indeed be nice to see another specimen offered not only for sale but to simply compare and examine.

The U.S. Model 1870 Uruguayan-Honduran Carbine Conversion

The Uruguayan-Honduran carbine conversion is a true 19th century multi-national rolling-block carbine that started life as the U.S. Navy Model 1870 rifle, purchased by the Navy and made under contract at the Springfield Armory. Almost 10,000 of these two-band rifles with Remington-marked actions, several thousand had the rear sight installed closer to the receiver ring than specified, and were subsequently rejected by government inspectors. Though another 10,000 were assembled properly for the Navy, many believe this first batch was purposely assembled incorrectly and was nothing more than a ploy to allow American surplus arms dealers to buy them and re-sell them to the French, who were clamoring for military rifles during the Franco-Prussian War.

This clandestine act of "back-door" diplomacy actually succeeded, but the French ultimately lost the war in 1870.

The Hartley and Graham Company is believed to have bought them from the U.S. government at a bargain price, subsequently reselling them to France. Then, after buying the rifles back from France, advertised them as "Franco-Prussian War Surplus," selling them for a profit yet again! Prime markets for such sales were Central and South America, where a ready market existed for rolling-block rifles. Many times, a country's numerous rival political groups would buy their ordnance from the same dealer––such as Hartley & Graham––who could care less which side was right. It was all about money. Uruguay, in 1873-75, again ordered some 2500 rolling blocks from Hartley & Graham, advertised as surplus 1870 Navy rolling blocks in 50-70 Govt. that had been repurchased from the French. The Uruguayans requested the rifles to be rebarreled to 43 Spanish and shortened to carbine length, and fitted with a saddle ring and staple and carbine forend. These modifications would slightly raise the cost per cost of gun, but the contract with Hartley & Graham was nevertheless completed, and Uruguay received the delivery without a hitch. Upon receipt, all were inspected and stamped with the standard Uruguayan circular military cartouche on the left side of the stock with the date and EJERCITO URUGUAYO (Uruguayan Army). Interestingly, the button plate which held the breechblock and hammer pin in place was reversed to the right side of the frame. The reversal button

plate partially obscured the "giveaway origin" of the markings on the carbine actions––the U.S. Springfield 1870 marking and the American eagle motif.

Sometime in the mid-1880s, Uruguay sold a thousand or more of these carbines to Honduras as that rather poor nation could not afford to purchase new rifles from the United States. Over time, some of these carbines were captured by both Honduran rebel factions as well as El Salvadoran troops, and few have survived after years of hard service. My carbine was not terribly abused and its original Uruguayan cartouche is still noticeable. There is also a serial or rack number of "33" on the lower tang, which may be a Honduran addition since I once examined an identical specimen, imported from Uruguay, which lacked any numeration in this area. A "43 Span." stamping over the chamber is also present. Also, an E.H. is found stamped on the comb of the stock which appears to translate to Ejercito Honduras (Honduran Army). Very few of these have surfaced on the U.S. antique firearms market. But one thing is certain; they truly made money for their original American owners at least five times in their heyday!

Right up to the early 1910s, the M. Hartley Company of New York City (formerly Hartley and Graham) remained an agent for the Remington Arms Company, being redesignated as such after the Remington company was reorganized in 1888. As late as the 1900s, the Hartley Co. maintained an extensive inventory of out-of-production blackpowder-era rolling blocks and fulfilled countless orders for the poorer nations of Latin America who could not afford to arm all their soldiers with expensive Mauser bolt-action repeaters. Hartley and Co. produced hundreds of different unique military rolling blocks for numerous countries, which have often been mistaken as genuine factory-correct Remington-made arms. This specimen of the Hartley & Graham-modified Model 1870 Navy rolling block sold to Uruguay, and then to Honduras, is a good example of how specially reworked rolling blocks confuse rolling block students as to being some sort of special-order contract made at the Remington factory. There are literally dozens of Hartley-converted rolling blocks: carbines with bayonet lugs or two-band full-stock carbines with a shortened cleaning rod, all going to Central or South American countries to arm both governments and rebel factions.

The 1870 Navy conversion sold to Uruguay should be considered among the most difficult to uncover, including those indigenously manufactured in a foreign arsenal under Remington license. Rest assured, many variations never before seen are waiting somewhere in the dark jungles of Latin America.

Whitney Rolling Block Rarities

Along with E. Remington & Sons, the firm of the Whitney Arms Co. of New Haven, Conn. competed in manufacturing a rolling block-action rifle which resulted in two different types of actions offered at different periods of time. The earliest was the Whitney-Laidley patent breech-loading system; peculiar in that the breechblock and hammer components consisted of a five-piece assembly comprised of hammer, locking cam, thumb piece plate and breechblock. Its last patent was registered on July 16 1872. In production from 1871 to 1881, the first model action was eventually redesigned and "Remingtonized" to a less complicated system once the Remington patent expired. This allowed Whitney to closely copy its simpler competitor, resulting in an action more

economical to manufacture.

The second model action was produced from 1881 until 1888 when the Whitney Firearms Company closed its doors, and was acquired by the Winchester Repeating Arms Co. Not having come close to the quantities of rolling-block rifles Remington had churned out, Whitney military rolling-block rifles and carbines nevertheless had their following and, in their entirety, were exported outside the United States to countries primarily in Latin America. In nearly every case, those that returned to the U.S. surplus arms market in scanty numbers have been in conditions ranging from good to poor, indicating hard usage. To find any standard or special order Whitney military rolling-block rifle or carbine in excellent condition is truly sensational. Special production Whitney military rolling blocks for foreign customers have been almost non-existent in the past, but it is accurate to say that arms exporters Hartley and Graham made up at least some specially-modified Whitney rolling blocks for overseas buyers.

There is, however, at least one that was revealed by author Gordon Howard in a Canadian arms journal dated 1965. No one in the United States, including antique firearms expert Norm Flayderman, had ever seen the special Whitney Montreal Police Carbine until it was featured in the third edition of my book, *The Military Remington Rolling Block Rifle* (1998 Pioneer Press, Union City TN). Years ago, I heard from several Canadians that this arm existed, but had never owned an example until I purchased a single specimen from a Maine dealer/collector who began going on buying trips to Canada in the 1990s when our northern neighbor's government imposed draconian gun legislation. Many rarities were coming out of the woodwork as average Canadian citizens were frantically selling off their firearms, many of which were highly collectible.

The Whitney Montreal Police Carbine was a standard, first model Whitney military saddle ring carbine chambered in 433 Spanish Remington Carbine, a lighter-recoiling number

than the full-blown 78-grain load of FFg of the standard 43 Spanish cartridge. The carbine was procured specifically for the city of Montreal in December of 1875 after the city police committee decided to pick out 50 men in the department and arm them with carbines in lieu of revolvers.

At the meeting on September 1, the police council stated…."the men shall be armed with carbines, as they are more useful than revolvers and that the number so armed be limited to sixty…" After $1330 was appropriated for the purchase, a Montreal arms agent named R.H. Kilby residing at Saint Catherine St. was to be the contact man for the procurement. Little is known whether Kilby or the Montreal city council specified details of the carbine regarding caliber, including the angular socket-type bayonets that accompanied all sixty pieces, which appear to have been surplus U.S. Springfield-style bayonets. It is generally felt that Kilby ordered the arms and had them stamped "Montreal Police" by Hartley and Graham Co. in New York City. In Gordon Johnson's article, he notes a former police lieutenant he interviewed believes the carbines were never fired except for brief training practice and were used as reserve weapons. In addition, the lieutenant stated that they were mostly used for escorting prisoners from the courthouse to Bordeaux Jail in the north end of Montreal city. All carbines had rack markings on the buttplate, with mine being #7. As with all Whitney rolling blocks, serial numbers are on the lower tang and, from all indications, they were not consecutively numbered.

In the early 1960s, a very small number of these carbines began to appear in Canada and were in from good to very good condition. The highest rack number known is #59, reported by Gordon Johnson. He also noted (in 1965) that no more than 18 to 20 carbines were said to exist. When they were withdrawn from service during World War I, they were stored in wooden cases in the basement of the Montreal Police School. Around 1923, a substantial number were destroyed or disassembled, and ammunition for the carbines was disposed of as late as 1961. The arms were supplied with a two-position carbine open and peep sight for 200 and 500 yards, and were finished in the white, aside from a blued barrel. Fortunately my specimen appears to have had little to no use––which explains its excellent condition. Only slight wear adjacent to the muzzle stems from bayonet installation and removal. For many years rumors circulated that rolling block firearms were being used in official military or police capacities in Canada, but no proof of this surfaced until the 1960s. The importance of the discovery of the Whitney Montreal Carbine caused it to be included as a special category of its own in the latest edition of FLAYDERMAN'S GUIDE TO ANTIQUE AMERICAN FIREARMS...AND THEIR VALUES.

Another extremely rare Whitney rolling block is a second model garden-variety three-band military rifle. What makes it special is that *(a)* it is one of the rare Mexican contract models and *(b)*, its condition is almost at 90 percent, aside from a bullet hole in its stock indicating its violent past. Though the bullet took out a sizeable piece of walnut, especially at the exit, clear cartouches still remain on the wrist and other places. Whitney rifles in 43 Spanish were ordered twice by Mexico, both orders being of the first and second models.

The rifle's fifth-generation owner, whose ancestors lived in California near the Mexican border, told me the rifle was a participant––in the hands of Mexican bandits––in the

second famous raid (the first being in 1875) on the "Old Stone" Trading Post in Campo, California in 1881. The trading-post workers won the shoot-outs and captured the Mexicans guns, a dozen or more Whitney rolling blocks recently stolen from a *Federale* arsenal in Mexico. This attests to the like-new condition with brilliant case colors, and the Mexican Sunburst and R.M. (Republic of Mexico) translating to *Republica Mexicana*.

Whitney rifles in 43 Spanish were ordered twice by Mexico; both orders being of the first and second models.

Remington-Made Rarities of both Black and Smokeless Powder Eras

Genuine Remington factory-made rolling-block military rifles have their share of scarce models. One of the most elusive rolling blocks catalogued in 1870s and 1880s Remington factory literature is the Spanish Civil Guard Model, simply a two-band military rifle with a shorter 30-inch barrel. I've owned a meager total of four different Civil Guard models in the past 35 years: three from the Philippines and one from Costa Rica.

A most peculiar example I uncovered was found in Belize (the former British Honduras). I speculate it was part of a small lot ordered for Her Majesty's colonial militia in the late 1880s. The profusely British proof-marked Civil Guard Model is in 43 Spanish and has a tinned rear sight, a very peculiar addition. It is the second one from Belize that I have seen in "Del Norte" in about 20 years.

Well identified with numerous British proofmarks, the rifle has scattered pitting typical of the humid region; the bore however is surprisingly clean.

Why England ordered these in lieu of issuing the standard British service arm, the Martini-Henry, is unknown. The only practical reason is that all British Honduras' neighboring countries used the 43 Spanish Remington rolling block. Thus perhaps the British reasoned from a logistical standpoint that if ammunition ran low during a skirmish with rebel or other forces from nearby Mexico or Guatemala, the interchangeable captured stocks of 43 Spanish cartridges could be utilized if required. Remember, no countries in that region used British Martini-Henry rifles chambered for the 577/450 cartridge. Definitely a rare interesting rifle!

Another seldom-encountered military rolling-block rifle from that area of Central America, is from the post-1888 order from Guatemala. This period can be verified since the tangs on all these rifles were marked REMINGTON ARMS COMPANY, indicating their manufacture followed the reorganization of E. Remington and Sons after that year. Fragmented records show that fewer than 2500 were exported to Guatemala between 1890 and 1894. Physical proof they were used to the extreme in that humid and politically violent country is obvious in that their condition ranged from fair to (barely) good. Their primary identifier was behind the rear sight, having the stamped metal displaying "EJERCITO

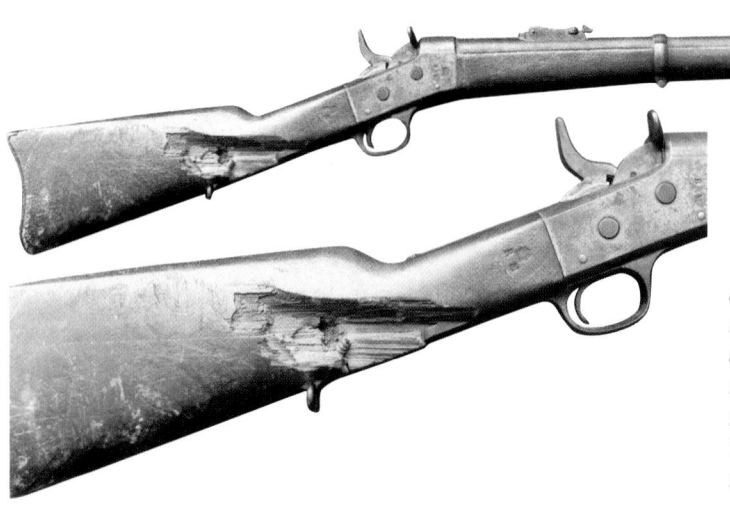

Whitney military rolling-block rifles are indeed scarce and are normally found in pretty rough shape. Aside from a bullet hole in the stock, this Mexican contract model (left), was spared the ravages of time as its fifth generation owner related that one of his ancestors captured the gun from a band of Mexican outlaws. The fine condition of this rifle makes it valuable; the Mexican contract models are almost never found in any condition! The full-length view (bottom) shows the three-band musket is complete.

GUATEMALA" (Guatemalan Army) which was often barely visible. The Guatemalan 43s usually ended up in the rebarreling vise to be converted, reblued, etc. into sporters at a time when military rolling blocks in less than new condition regardless of unusual markings, were looked upon as one step above scrap iron. I have found one intact, with markings, and in very good condition to boot. The Guatemalan army issue model is definitely one to watch for, but look closely for the markings as they are normally very faint.

On the opposite end of the beauty scale, Remington rolling blocks that were made as presentation pieces are in a one-of-a-kind category. One of the most beautiful blackpowder-era examples I had the chance to inspect was a fully engraved three-band rifle in 43 Spanish with a fancy silver inlay on the left side of the buttstock that was presented to a Spanish army general for the capture of Cuban insurrectionist D. Pedro Figueredo on August 10, 1870. The rifle was sold at auction in 2000 by J.C. Devine Auctioneers for well over $7500.

After 1896, the Remington rolling block entered the smokeless era. Examples considered antique scarcities, manufactured during this time frame (1896-1917), are primarily categorized

by caliber and the presence of national crests. Since 7mm Mauser was the most widespread smokeless powder chambering in the Remington Model 1902, to discover one in 236 (6mm) Navy, 30-40 Krag and 7.65mm Mauser is so rare that they currently bring as much as $2500 to $3000 in good to excellent condition. The Remington Model 1897 rifles and carbines of the 1899-1900 Mexican contract, with the national crest stamped on the receiver ring, totaled 14,010 rifles and carbines. Those that returned to the U.S. arms market in the 1960s were, for the most, in very sad shape. The majority of these hardened smokeless steel guns were rebarreled to modern calibers and given complete makeovers. A Mexican-marked Model 1897 rifle or, especially, a carbine in very decent condition today is quite desirable and, price-wise, is a well above the 1962 price of $8.28! The condition of the crest is often the primary factor in determining desirability and price.

Aside from the Mexican contract model, the other crested military rolling block of the smokeless era are those of the El Salvador contract of 1902. These are even more difficult to discover because fewer were manufactured. Those that have been found are, on average, in rough and pitted condition. I've seen only one in very good condition in a private collection. The Salvadoran Model differs from the Mexican contract model not because it is a Model 1902, but because of an oversize upper handguard with a pronounced groove. Find one of these 7mm rifles that worked the humid, wet jungles of El Salvador in excellent condition with a clean national crest, and you have one of the great prizes of the post-1900 era Remington

⧉ ● ⧉ ● ⧉ ● ⧉ ● ⧉ ● ⧉

The final Remington rolling block to finish out its fifty years of production was the French 1915-16 contract model ordered by France in World War I.

military rolling block rifles.

The very last Remington military rolling block of substantial number that closed out a 50-year era of steady production were those of the French contract of 1915-1916. It was basically a supplementary order to provide France with a single-shot rifle in their national caliber of 8mm Lebel. This interim order gave Remington time to tool up for the standard Mannlicher-Berthier repeating bolt-action rifle. The French purchased 100,291 rolling blocks in World War I, with most going to arm colonial forces from Morocco, Algeria and other colonies. The majority of these rifles saw very hard usage and, after the war, many went to far-flung areas such as French Indo-China and French Guyana's infamous Devil's Island. Finding one in excellent condition is difficult, but they are a key piece in a rolling-block collection.

The only other World War I military rolling block that I've seen (once, in Vietnam in 1971), is the elusive 1917 Russian contract model in 7.62mm. Remington records do not report the number produced. This can be probably be attributed to the confusion during the Bolshevik revolution because Remington was also producing the Model 1891 Mosin-Nagant bolt action for Czarist Russia at the same time.

More than any other military single-shot rifle in the world, the rolling block variations––Remington, Whitney, or a foreign-made version; the modified, special purpose or experimental models––are seemingly endless. Only through patience and the passage of time, future generations *might* be able to say each version has been accounted for. Then again, the mists of the past may prolong the hunt indefinitely............ ⊛

BIBLIOGRAPHY

Layman, George J. *The Military Remington Rolling Block Rifle*, 1992, 4th Edition 1998, Pioneer Press, Union City, TN

Sharpe, Philip B., *The Rifle in America* 1938, 2nd printing 1958, Funk & Wagnalls, New York City, NY

M. Hartley & Co. Ledgers and Catalogs., 1890-1903, New York, NY

Notas de Defencia, de Uruguay, 1900-1926, (Ministry of Defense) Montivideo, Uruguay

21ST CENTURY COMBAT REVOLVER:
THE AUVER SYSTEM

by J. M. Ramos

A DESIGN PERSPECTIVE

The evolution of the revolving handgun popularly known today as the revolver came a long way. Originated as a pepperbox design incorporating a multiple barrel system during the percussion era of the early 1800s, this unique handgun soon transformed to a more practical model: less bulky, lighter and more user-friendly. The new variation now incorporated a single barrel. A separate revolving cylinder, which contained the ammunition, is positioned behind the barrel. Samuel Colt's percussion revolver design of the 1830s may prove to be the pioneering model for the second generation of revolving handguns, further developed to a more sophisticated variant such as the Colt single action with the introduction of the metallic cartridge in the early 1860s. As more efficient gunmaking machinery became available at the beginning of the 19th century, modern-class revolvers started to evolve. The swing-out cylinder and break-open action types finally entered the scene, while the single action of the Old West era is

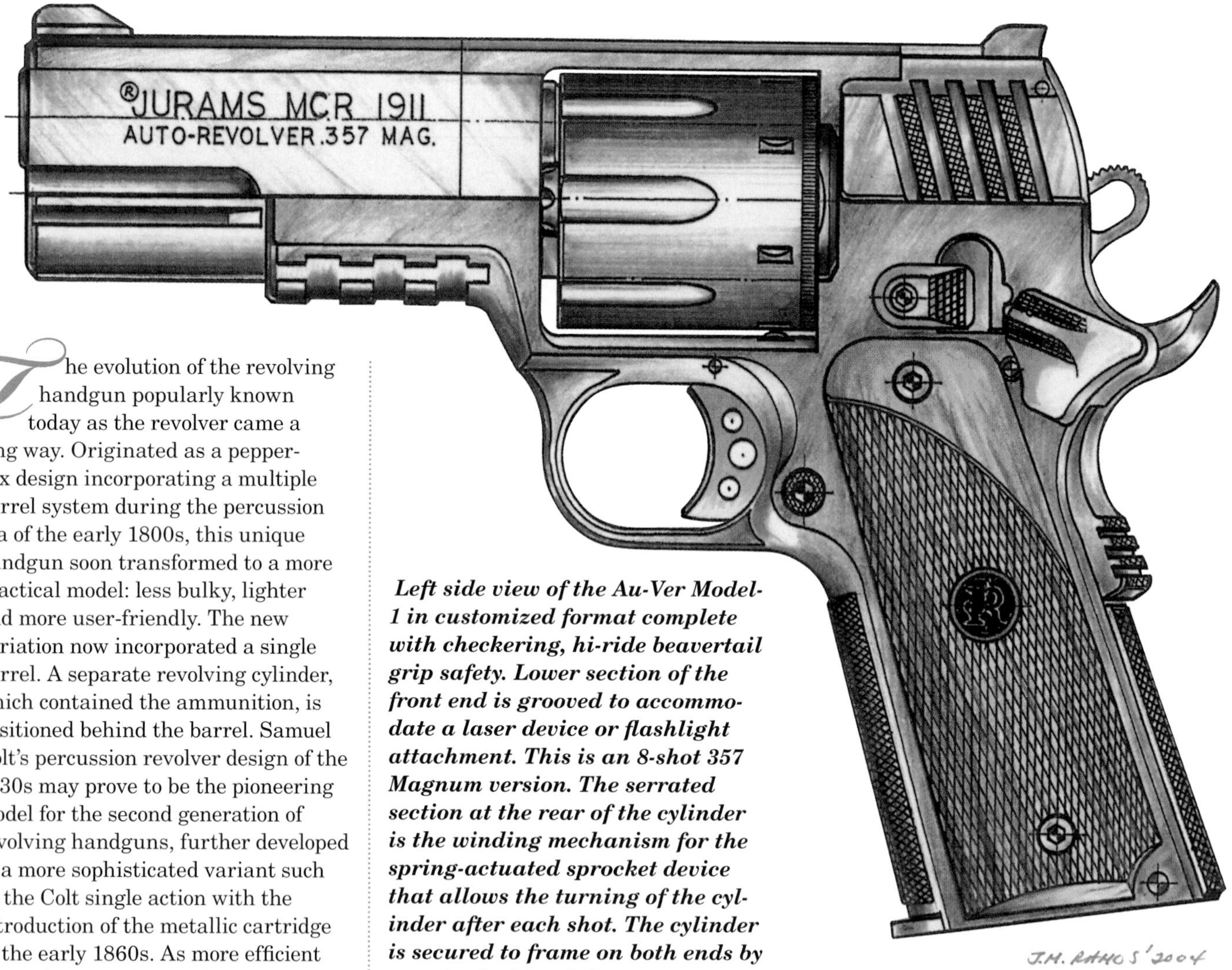

Left side view of the Au-Ver Model-1 in customized format complete with checkering, hi-ride beavertail grip safety. Lower section of the front end is grooved to accommodate a laser device or flashlight attachment. This is an 8-shot 357 Magnum version. The serrated section at the rear of the cylinder is the winding mechanism for the spring-actuated sprocket device that allows the turning of the cylinder after each shot. The cylinder is secured to frame on both ends by massive locking bolts.

refined to near-perfection. It was also at the beginning of this century that self-loading pistols appeared, and quickly gained market acceptance in Europe with the introduction

of the very sophisticated Mauser Broomhandle combat pistol of 1896.

In the United States, the revolver remained the primary sidearm of the cavalry units and expeditionary forces until it was replaced by the venerable Colt 45 automatic in 1911. Despite the switch by the military to John Browning's legendary workhorse, the modern swing-out revolver, of both Colt and Smith & Wesson manufacture, remained with various units of the military up until the Vietnam conflict of the 1960s. By the early 1980s, many U.S. police departments began evaluating the merits of the automatic pistol as a possible replacement for their aging issue revolvers. With many recorded engagements involving officers killed by felons equipped with automatic pistols, the advantage of the self-loader seemed obvious. Soon America's lawmen embraced the self-loader and recognized its fighting capability over the century-old revolver design. Undoubtedly, it was the firepower and speed of reloading time that provided the auto-pistol the edge in a firefight over the wheel-gun, wherein seconds can mean life or death.

From its many transitional stages of evolution, there is one particular revolver design that can be set apart from its siblings. The British Webley-Fosbery is a unique revolver that deserves a close look. This gun was quite advanced for its day. Introduced in 1902, primarily as a combat revolver, the Fosbery incorporated many new features. Externally looking like a normal break-open Webley & Scott revolver, the Fosbery can be best described as an auto-pistol/revolver hybrid. Loading and extraction of cartridges is the same as the regular Webley model, but mechanical functioning––cocking the hammer and turning the cylinder––is accomplished mechanically with the aid of the gun's recoil while on battery. The exterior of the cylinder has special cam-track grooves that glide into a stationary lug mounted on top of the lower frame, where the usual cylinder stop is found.

To make the system work, the Fosbery design utilized two-piece frame construction. The upper half contained the basic barrel and cylinder assembly, while the lower frame has the trigger lockwork. During firing, the recoil will

Schematic diagram showing the internal clockwork of the Au-Ver Model-1 gas-operated semi-auto revolver. The cylinder incorporated an internal sprocket, powered by wire spring, to turn the cylinder after each shot. The return spring for the mini-slide is an extension-type, seen below the firing pin. Note the new-style hammer strut and additional pin mounted below the pivot pin to allow the hammer to rebound automatically, allowing the sear to engage the safety notch while in the 'rest' position.

JM RAMOS 04

AU-VER MODEL 1
AUTOMATIC-REVOLVER .357 MAG.

J.H. RAMOS '2004

cause the top half to move rearward via an internally-machined groove on the lower frame. As the upper half glides rearward, the cylinder will be forced to rotate by the lower frame-mounted lug via the cylinder cam tracks. As the recoil reaches its end stroke, a pivoting pawl, activated by the upper frame, forces the lower *(extended)* section of the hammer to rotate until its cocking

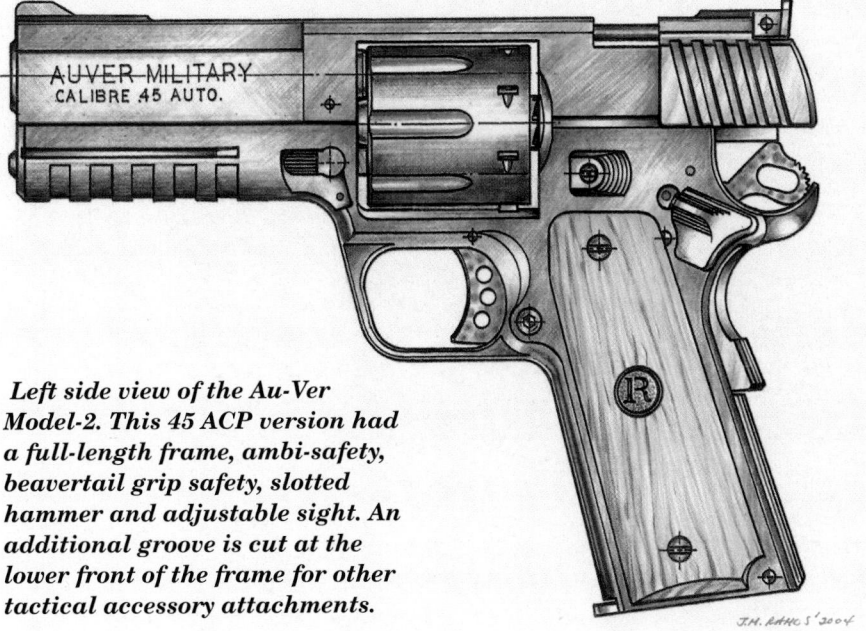

AUVER MILITARY
CALIBRE .45 AUTO.

Left side view of the Au-Ver Model-2. This 45 ACP version had a full-length frame, ambi-safety, beavertail grip safety, slotted hammer and adjustable sight. An additional groove is cut at the lower front of the frame for other tactical accessory attachments.

J.H. RAMOS '2004

notch engages the sear, holding the hammer at the full-cock position, ready for the next shot as soon as the top end returns to normal battery position.

The gun will not fire until both frames are properly lined up, since the trigger connector will only engage the sear while the frame's upper half is in its full forward position. The recoiling action of the upper frame is countered by a powerful spring-loaded pawl mounted on the left side of the grip. A manual safety is positioned on the left side of the frame, between the trigger and top front of the grip. The safety prevents the trigger from being pulled when the safety is applied. The Fosbery revolver saw limited use during WWII in the hands of the British troops in Africa, alongside the regular Webleys. It was reported that the automatic revolver was more susceptible to malfunction than the Webleys when their mechanism was exposed to desert sand, and resulted in its final demise as a promising combat weapon.

The new millennium is now upon us. Ironically, to date––except for few improvements in trigger lockwork and method of disassembly––current revolver designs remain virtually unchanged since the introduction of the swing-out cylinder models by Colt and Smith & Wesson in the latter part of the 18th century. From their original format, the only notable changes are minor improvements in trigger lockwork, method of field-stripping, cylinder latches and wider varieties of cartridge choices.

Let's analyze what is really missing here. In my opinion, a true radical revolver design for the 21st century is long overdue; one that can truly match the automatic pistol in terms of combat effectiveness. This revolver must work and feel like an automatic and be quickly reloaded as fast as––if not faster than––its self-loading rival. For some, this may be viewed as wishful thinking––a dream that will never come true, impossible to achieve and––last but not least––a pure fantasy. Many of the most remarkable and successful weapons in history started as dreams.

We have seen the accomplishments of Sam Colt, Daniel Wesson, John Browning and Bill Ruger just to name a few. Needless to say, great inventors and successful designers are my heroes. Like them, I dream that my concept––a truly radical automatic revolver design, capable of competing with the most formidable automatic pistol (*like a customized 1911*)––will eventually became a reality.

The AUtomatic-revolVER (AU-VER) Design Concept

The first gun my father put in my hand was his issue 1911 Remington Rand 45 ACP automatic pistol. Installed on it was a Colt Service-Ace 22 conversion kit. It was my 7th birthday. We drove to the river bank that Saturday afternoon with a hatful of 22 rimfire ammo. This was a great birthday present from my dad, the day of my indoctrination to firing a gun. In the 1980s, my interest in the 1911 quickly returned as IPSC competition became popular. I became very active in this discipline, and even wrote two books and many articles on stock and custom pistols alike.

Having solely focused my attention to shooting the 1911 the past 25 years, suddenly the nostalgic spell of the wheel-gun struck me once again. The last time I used revolvers was the mid-70s. These were both Smith & Wesson––a 6-inch 357 model and a Chiefs 38 Special snubby. These wheelguns were soon replaced by custom 1911s, in both stock and compensated formats. At the range, I tried several new revolvers from both S&W and Colt and felt very awkward grasping the pistols with my usual two-hand hold that I use on the 1911.

I like the 1911's hi-ride beavertail grip safety resting comfortably over the web of my hand, the natural pointing characteristic of the well-executed pistol grip, the re-assuring feel of the hand-cut checkering and the manual safety that I normally used as a thumb rest and––most importantly––the short, crisp trigger pull of a single action. That's what I want in my revolver. Firing the 357 Magnum or (*worse*) the 44 Magnum is not what I can call comfortable, since

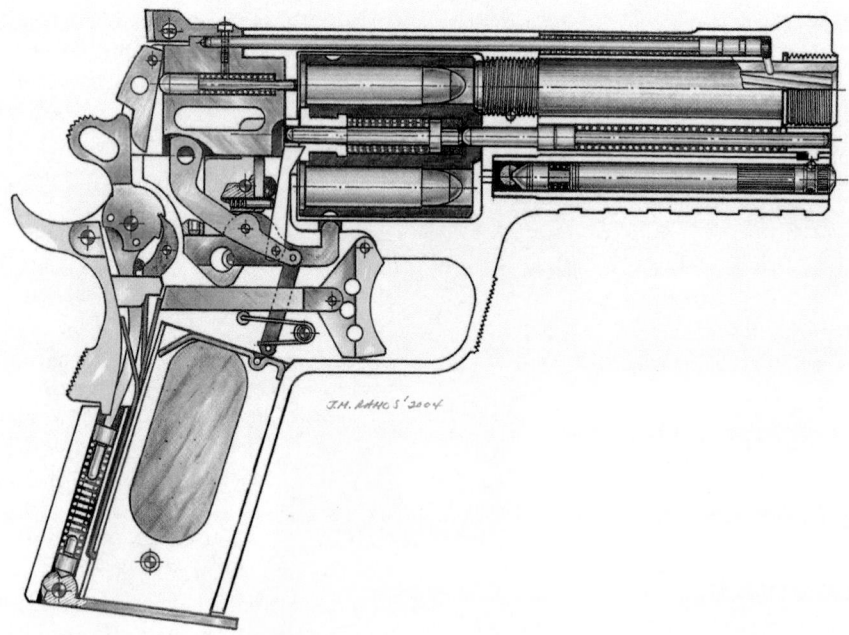

Schematic diagram showing the radical trigger clockwork of the Au-Ver Model-2, the way a 21st century revolver should be made. Take the best features from the legendary 1911, combine them with a gas-operated mechanism and you have one magnificent semi-auto wheel-gun that can easily match—or out-perform—the best service-class autoloader available. Note the mini-laser concealed below the spring-loaded cylinder locking bolt. The automatic cylinder ejector is not included in this view.

your wrist takes most of the pounding, not to mention the muzzle flip each time the wheelgun barks. The feel and comfort of my customized Colt 45 is simply not there. I love the feel of the hi-ride 1911 in my hand. A wheelgun with a grip and operating system designed like this legendary 1911 pistol is definitely the revolver for me.

The Dream is on Me

So there I was in front of my drafting board day dreaming. A 1911 revolver? Why not? Impossible? Maybe not. So we have learned about the Webley-Fosbery; its advantages and its drawbacks. This is the new millennium. The revolver needs serious revamping. We don't need another single action, break-open or a swing-out revolver. What we need is a truly revolutionary design: a gun appreciated by both auto- and wheel-gun shooters alike.

The AU-VER System

The Au-Ver is only a concept gun and is in no way a prototype or gun-in-the-making. I am presenting an idea–– perhaps to stir interest in a new service handgun design concept for those in the military or law enforcement who still prefer the revolver, but want the firepower and quick reloading advantage of the auto-pistol. The auto-revolver has the added advantage of not being affected by limp-wrist shooting, often blamed for loading malfunctions by less experienced big-bore autoloader shooters.

The popularity of the 1911 pistol is unequalled by any service pistol ever made considering it is almost a century-old design. The excitement of action-shooting competition, and the never-ending demand for the new generation 1911 loaded with custom features, soon attracted many big names in the gun manufacturing: Smith & Wesson, Dan Wesson, SIG, CZ and others, onto the 1911 bandwagon. Considering the popularity of the 1911, with its superlative ergonomics and handling characteristics, it seems fitting the Au-Ver design perspective is derived from this legendary pistol. Anyone who is proficient with the 1911 will have no problem mastering and

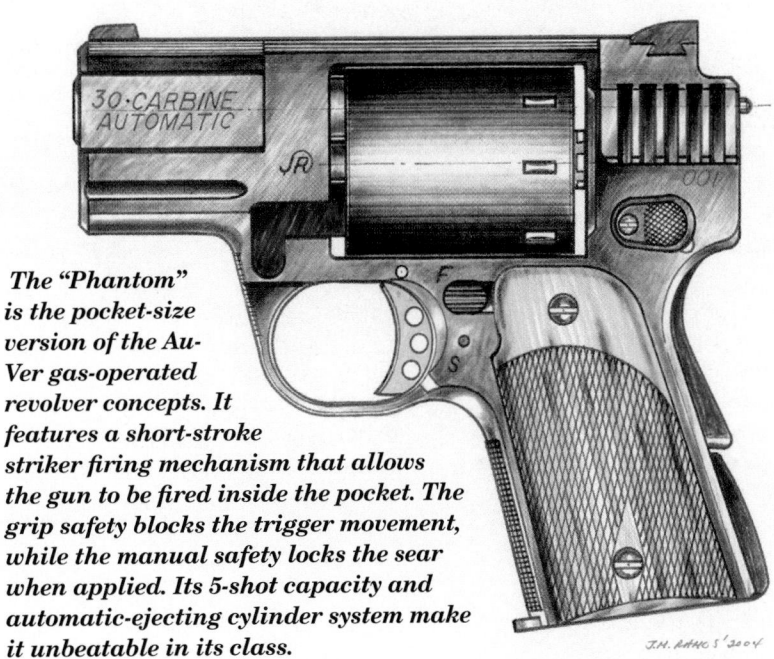

The "Phantom" is the pocket-size version of the Au-Ver gas-operated revolver concepts. It features a short-stroke striker firing mechanism that allows the gun to be fired inside the pocket. The grip safety blocks the trigger movement, while the manual safety locks the sear when applied. Its 5-shot capacity and automatic-ejecting cylinder system make it unbeatable in its class.

appreciating a revolver that shoots and handles like their favorite automatic.

In order to really appreciate the Au-Ver system, let's take a closer look at the many unique features of this futuristic wheel-gun design concept.

Configuration - staying with a winning format is the basic principle in the gun's overall design concept. The gun is so designed that it will feel, operate and fire like a typical 1911 pistol––but with the added element of a mechanically-rotated cylinder and gas-operated mechanism.

Gas-operated system - unlike the Webley-Fosbery design, the Au-Ver does not operate in recoil principle to cock the hammer and rotate the cylinder, rather it works as a gas-operated semi-auto revolver. Assuming the system works, this set-up will result in much milder recoil with magnum calibers or high-intensity small-caliber military rounds like the new Belgian FN 5.7mm and HK's 4.6x30mm––the ideal ammunition for this gun, which may require a large volume of gas energy to reliably power the piston that activates the slide. In the Heckler & Koch P7 and Steyr GB auto-pistols, the gas pressure is harnessed to prevent the rapid opening of the slide while in battery. In the Au-Ver system, the arrangement is reversed. The gas is used to power the piston to

provide the short-recoil action of the ultra-light miniature slide to accomplish mechanical cocking of the hammer and rotation of the cylinder.

The mini-slide format- mechanical functioning of hammer and cylinder in semi-auto fashion is accomplished by incorporating a miniature slide of lightweight material, like titanium or aluminum alloy. The slide is connected to the gas piston which is actuated by gas pressure being bled off a drilled port at the top of the barrel near the muzzle. In Model-2, after a shot is fired, a volume of gas will be diverted towards the piston, forcing it to move rearward, allowing the slide to cock the hammer and activate the lever that controls the hand to rotate the cylinder, aligning the next round with the barrel for the next shot. In Model-1, the rotation of the cylinder is controlled by an internal wire spring powering a built-in sprocket. A separate piece at the rear of the cylinder *(with serrations)* acts as a winder and is turned clockwise until it stops. A round is inserted in the chamber to lock the setting of the sprocket. When the pre-loaded cylinder is snapped into the frame, the spring-loaded bolt positioned underneath the barrel will automatically lock with the front center hole of the cylinder, pushing the cylinder rod rearward to connect with the corresponding hole in the center of the frame shield. The rearward action of the cylinder internal rod will automatically activate the sprocket release mechanism, allowing the cylinder to rotate counter-clockwise under spring tension each time a shot is fired. The principal arrangement is somewhat similar to the Striker revolving shotgun.

Trigger mechanism – as clearly seen on the accompanying diagram, the Au-Ver not only closely resembled the 1911 *(sans rotating cylinder)* but also utilized some of the pistol's trigger components such as the hammer, sear, beavertail grip safety, manual safety, main spring housing assembly and the three-pronged flat spring that powers the trigger bar, the sear and the grip safety. Added to the bottom of the usual mainspring housing is a pivoting grip cover that secures the compartment that originally functioned as a magazine well for the 1911 pistol. The grip compartment will come in handy as storage for extra ammo, laser batteries and other useful survival accessories.

Speed reloading advantage – the Au-Ver revolver design utilized a "drop-in" cylinder reloading system. The operator simply activates the cylinder release latch and the fired cylinder will be automatically ejected by a built-in spring-loaded ejector mounted at the right side of the frame, in front of the cylinder. A fresh pre-loaded cylinder is then snapped in at the opening of the frame, with the extended bottom end of the ejector serving as an automatic guide for quick alignment.

The spring-loaded bolt under the barrel will automatically engage the corresponding pivot hole in the cylinder, pushing the internally-mounted cylinder rod rearward to lock with the connecting hole in the middle of the frame shield. Note that when the fired cylinder is ejected, the front wall of the ejector will automatically depress the protruding end of the spring-loaded locking bolt as the expended cylinder is ejected from its seat, allowing unimpeded insertion of a fresh cylinder into the frame during reloading.

The ejector also acts as a stopper for the cylinder when the latter is snapped into its seat in the frame, so the pivot hole of the cylinder will always precisely align with the locking bolt each time a freshly-loaded cylinder

is brought into action. With the Au-Ver system, the gun can be kept pointed at the target while the fired cylinder is ejected and a pre-loaded cylinder is substituted: without switching the position of the shooting hand during the process. Instead of fumbling with speed-loaders, a pre-loaded cylinder is all it takes to match––or beat––the automatic's reloading time. In the standard model, the cylinder holds 10 rounds of 30 M1 Carbine, 8 rounds in 38 caliber, 7 rounds in 40 and 6 rounds in 44 and 45 calibers.

Disposable Cylinder System

The Au-Ver revolver is designed to meet military or law enforcement applications by incorporating a disposable cylinder system. The cylinder is polymer, with steel inserts to act as chambers. In actual firefights, the combatants rarely go back to retrieve their ejected empty magazines. They just keep going until the battle is over. The same principle is applied in the Au-Ver; you simply snap in a fully-loaded cylinder as fast as the fired one is ejected from the gun. If the Au-Ver design concept becomes reality and is produced, it will give IPSC shooters a run for their money.

Safety features - all of the basic safety system of the 1911 pistol is utilized except the Series-80 auto-firing pin safety. The grip safety blocks the trigger bar. The manual safety locks the sear plus the usual hammer safety notch. The Au-Ver utilized a rebounding hammer, controlled by an additional pin strategically positioned below the pivot pin and working in conjunction with the new-style hammer strut. After the hammer hits the firing pin, the hammer will slightly rebound and its safety notch will automatically engage the sear; it will remain in this position until the slide once again forces it to cock after a shot has been fired. In the event that the next round in the cylinder did not line up properly with the barrel at the end of the index rotation, the slide-mounted lock will rest over the cylinder face between the chambers, or on top of a cartridge rim *(away*

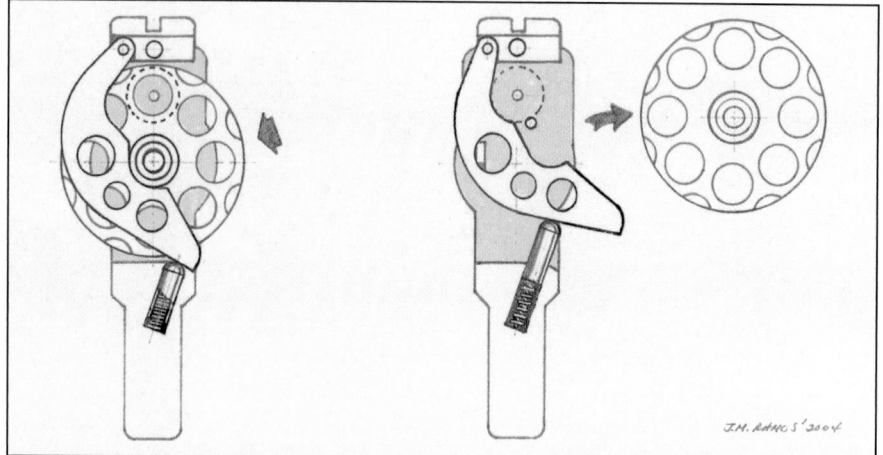

View showing the Au-Ver cylinder ejector system. Left view has the cylinder in its normal position with the gun. The ejector is positioned forward of the cylinder and mounted on the right side of the frame's top strap. A powerful spring-loaded plunger is positioned below the lever, resting against the boss of the cylinder. Right view shows the ejector in action, ejecting the cylinder automatically as soon as the cylinder release latch is activated. To reload, simply snap a fresh pre-loaded cylinder into the frame and resume firing. The Au-Ver is faster to reload than an auto-pistol since it can be reloaded without altering the firing position. Snapping a cylinder on the side of the gun is more natural than canting the grip of an auto-pistol to feed a fresh magazine into the magazine well.

from the primer), thereby creating a large gap between the back of the frame shield and front of the slide. This gap will prevent the firing pin *(mounted in the slide)* from reaching the cartridge in the chamber when the trigger is pulled and the hammer is tripped, thus preventing accidental discharge. The gun will only fire when the slide is fully closed and the cylinder lock is positively engaged.

Sturdy construction – every component of the Au-Ver is designed solid to match the legendary versatility of the 1911 pistol. The auto-revolver concept is based on ergonomics and strength aimed as a first-rate service handgun. It is primarily designed to easily handle high pressure loads for maximum power surpassing that of an average service pistol. The design also has great potential as a powerful, but mild-shooting platform for wildcat and big-bore magnum calibers, much dreaded for their wrist-twisting tendencies.

Accessories - designed to look, feel and function like a 1911 and more. The Au-Ver can be created so that a miniature laser device can be built into the hollowed chamber below the spring loaded cylinder locking bolt. A small rotating switch can be operated to activate or turn off the concealed sighting system. In addition to its concealed laser capability, the additional exterior groove below the barrel will accommodate a small flashlight or other tactical devices for combat applications.

So there it is. I hope you have enjoyed the preview of this fantasy gun; a dream waiting to be turned into reality. Despite the effort of many wheel-gun manufacturers to dress up their latest wares aesthetically, mechanically, it's still the same old boring clunker. Now that you understand my Au-Ver's many outstanding merits as the ideal candidate for the ultimate 21st century wheelgun, capable of taking on the finest big-bore autoloader in the market today, it's your turn to make the next move. We now have the means and technology to bring this revolutionary design to life. ✳

Functioning

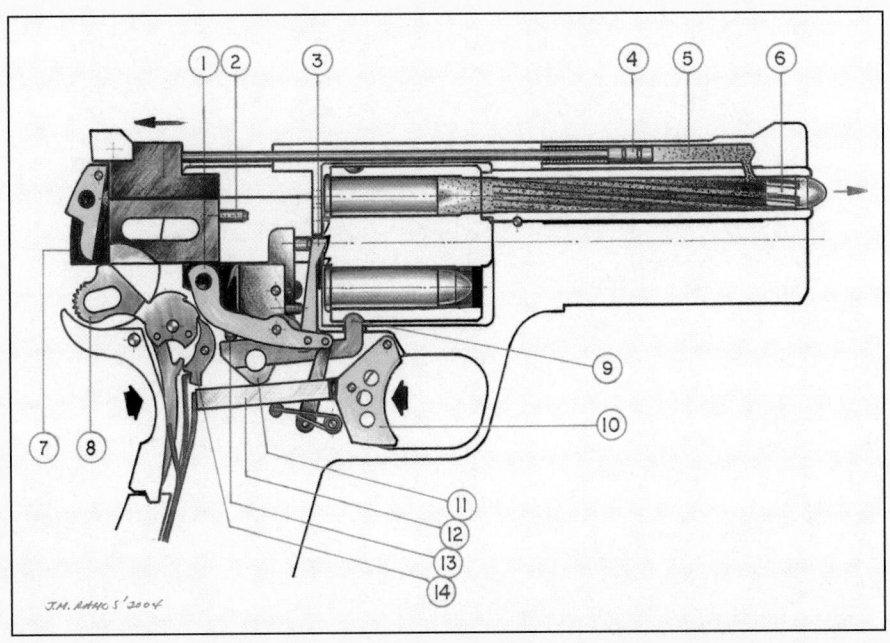

The Au-Ver Model-2 in battery. The bullet (6) is just about to leave the muzzle. The gas pressure (5) being bled off the gas port had operated the piston (4) rearward. The slide (7) connected at the rear of the piston has recoiled forcing the hammer (8) to cock. Simultaneously, the connector (13) and the top hump of the pawl lever (1) was forced downward by the recoiling slide. In this sequence, the top of the disconnector (11) was depressed by the connector, forcing the trigger bar (12) to move downward, disengaging itself from the sear (14) to allow the latter to engage the hammer at the fully cocked position as the slide returns to battery. The hump of the lever being forced down by the recoiling slide raises its front end in a "see-saw" motion, raising the cylinder pawl (3) to rotate the cylinder, aligning the next round to the barrel. The upward movement of the pawl starts as soon as the cylinder lock (2), mounted at the face of the slide, retracts from its connection with the cylinder as the slide starts its rearward cycle. As the slide recoils, the front end (11) of the disconnector raises upward to engage the cylinder stop notch at the bottom of the cylinder, after the hand has rotated the cylinder to its normal indexing for the next shot. The cylinder stop (9) will temporarily restrain the cylinder for the next shot until the slide has fully returned to battery. As the slide comes to a full forward stop, the cylinder lock (2) will once again engage the corresponding hole on the face of the cylinder between chambers. When the pull on the trigger (10) is released, the trigger bar (12), under spring tension, will move forward to re-engage the sear, lifting the disconnector which will, in turn, transfer the motion to the vertically-mounted connector and return it to its normal position. As the disconnector moves upward, its front end (9) will disengage from the cylinder notch, leaving the cylinder lock (2) in complete control of the cylinder during battery. The impact of the hammer at the rear of the slide, when the firing pin is hit during firing, further assists the slide-actuated cylinder lock with its solid lock-up with the cylinder during operation, assuring maximum safety by completely eliminating cylinder-to-barrel misalignment, or play. The gun will not fire unless the slide is fully closed and the cylinder lock is fully engaged in its mating hole with the cylinder.

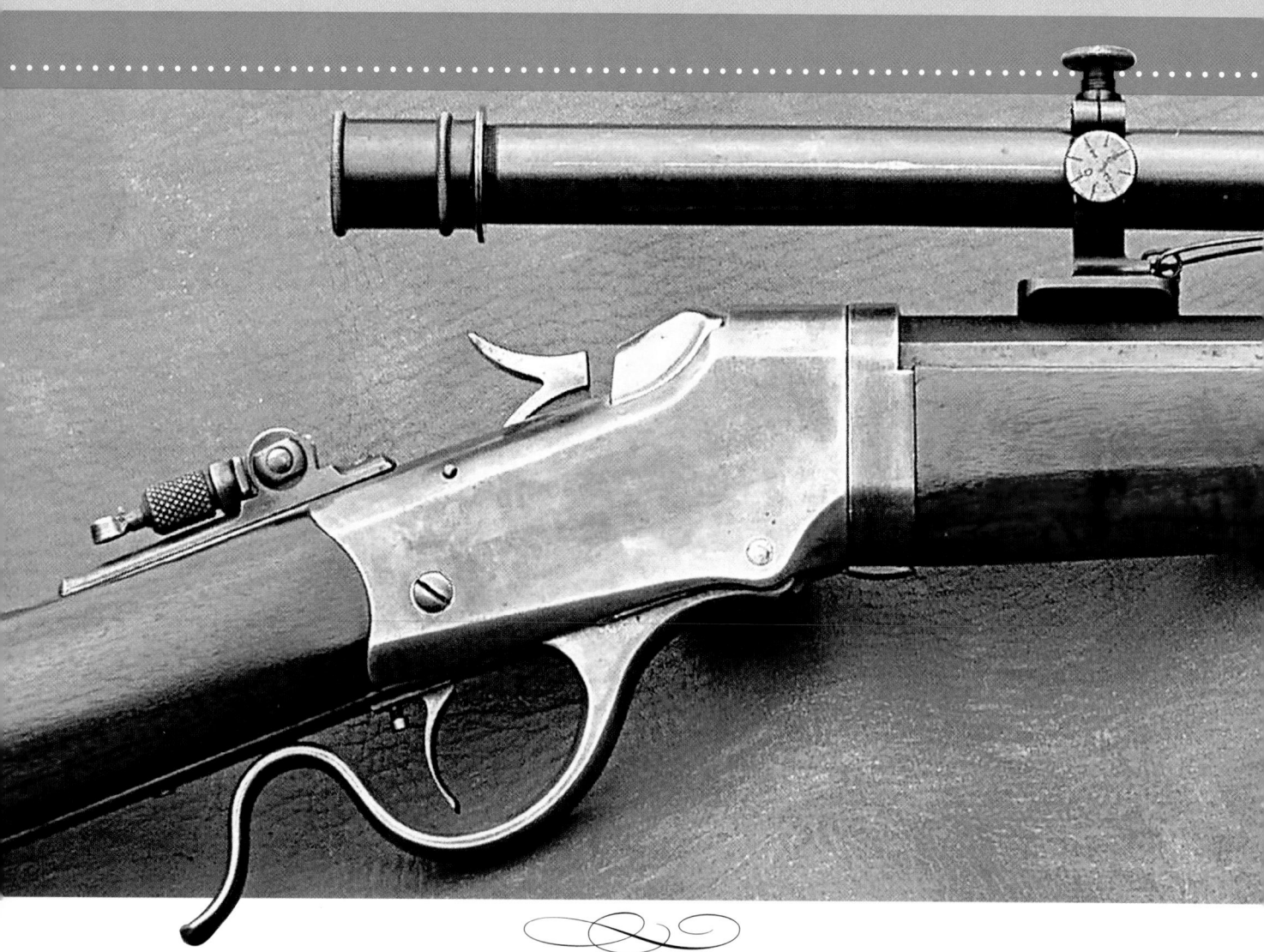

THE WINCHESTER
TELESCOPIC SIGHTS
OF 1909

by Clarence M. Anderson

The dominance in the American arms industry of the colossus that Oliver Winchester founded has manifested itself in far-reaching ways, one of the most unexpected being the extraordinary success of the firm's only venture into the optics trade––the Winchester telescopic sights of 1909. (1) Moreover, owing in part to their long production history, original Winchester scopes have survived to the present in numbers significantly greater than any of their competitors, making what was a relative late-comer to an expanding market the quintessential "antique" scope to many riflemen today.

When the new models (or "styles") A and B telescopes were introduced in Winchester Repeating Arm's general catalog of June, 1910, those American riflemen sophisticated enough to appreciate telescopic

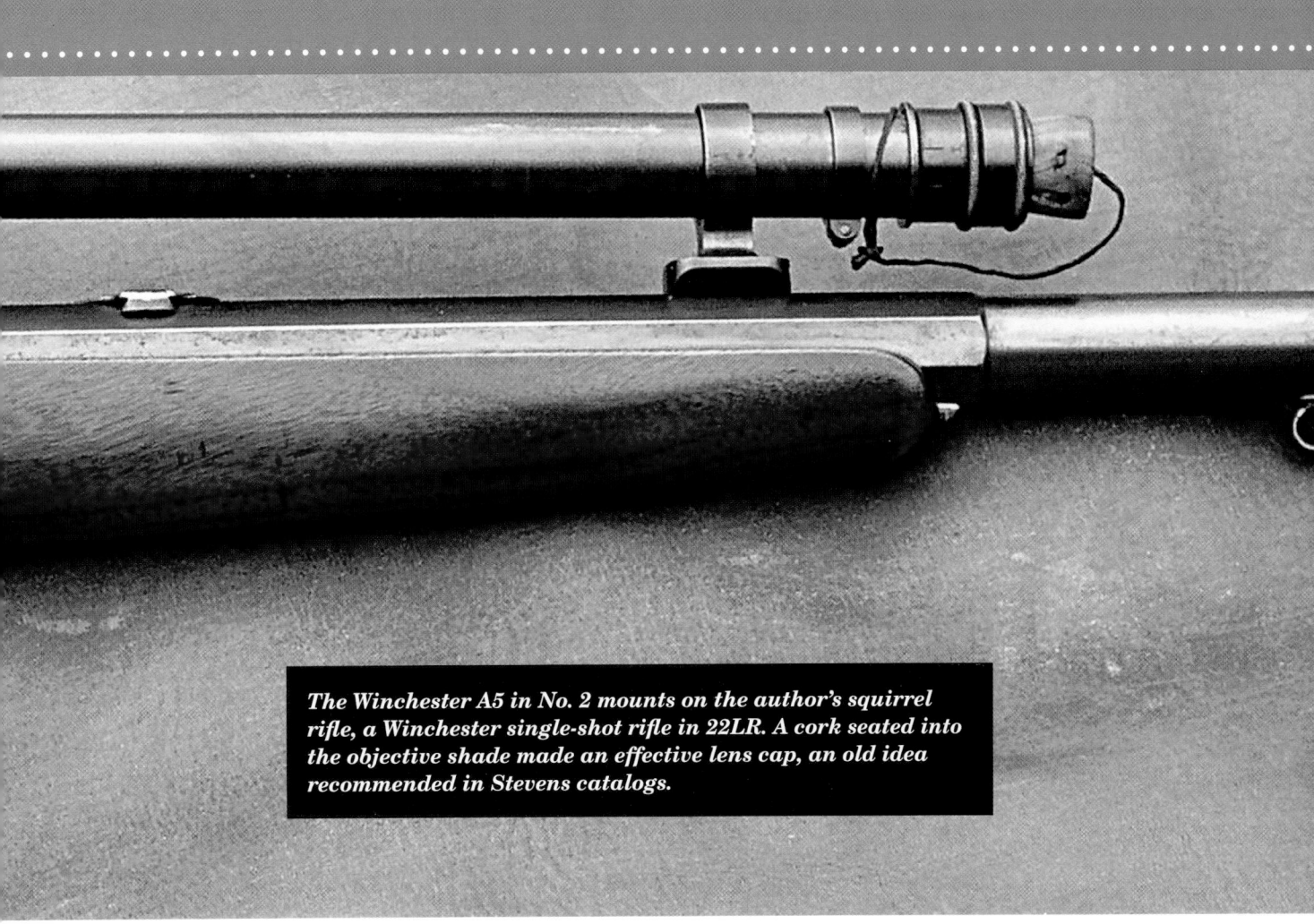

The Winchester A5 in No. 2 mounts on the author's squirrel rifle, a Winchester single-shot rifle in 22LR. A cork seated into the objective shade made an effective lens cap, an old idea recommended in Stevens catalogs.

sighting could already choose from among a generous selection of makes and designs: the legendary Malcolm Co., founded in 1855, but by 1910 in decline; its look-alike rival Mogg; the highly-praised line of John Sidel; the internally-adjustable Cummins; and the part-time work of such legendary gunmakers as Peterson and Niedner. Others could be named, but the most diverse, innovative, and technologically advanced scopes available before June of 1910 were those offered by the J. Stevens Arms Co., which had burst upon the optics market in spectacular fashion in 1902, following purchase of the Cataract Optical Co., briefly celebrated for supplying scopes to the U.S. Army during the era of the Krag.

Rivalry with Stevens, which between 1902 and the onset of World War 1 was boasting itself "the largest manufacturer of sporting arms in the world," quite possibly swayed Winchester management to stake a claim in this booming market. Stevens had displayed remarkable verve and acumen in promoting its new optics, accomplishing the placement of scope-mounted Stevens rifles on the covers of six issues of *Shooting and Fishing* (predecessor of the *American Rifleman*) between late 1903 and early 1904. In one of the most important Schuetzen matches of 1903 (Glendale Park, N. J.), which attracted the most famous marksmen in America, a large majority of competitors were reported by *Shooting and Fishing* to have used Stevens scopes. And between 1903 and 1910, the preferred choice of instrument for factory-mounting on Winchester rifles seems to have been Stevens. Would it be surprising if Stevens' swift success with their new optical products aroused a bit of envy in New Haven?

Carrying the idea of envy to its ultimate conclusion, one highly regarded Winchester study sowed the seeds for much confusion by asserting that Winchester launched its own scope program by purchase of the Stevens optical business! Surely it is enough to note that, although the entire Stevens line was drastically attenuated following the firm's reorganization in 1916 (after a disruptive foray into arms production for the government of Czarist Russia), Stevens scopes continued to be manufactured until the optics line was finally purchased by the Lyman Gun Sight Corp. in 1929. (And where *are* the many thousands of Stevens scopes produced during their 27-year manufacturing history–one would expect them to be encountered more commonly than Winchesters, yet the reverse is true.)

The "orthodox," quasi-official, account of the genesis of Winchester's interest in telescopic sights hangs the tale on a serendipitous personal relationship between W.R.A. Pres. T. G. Bennett and eminent optical engineer Prof. Charles S. Hastings. In the Winchester archives of the Buffalo Bill Historical Center is a letter written in 1969 by former General Director Edwin Pugsley, which asserts that Bennett became acquainted with Hastings through mutual membership in the Colby Club, a small New Haven group of technically-minded intellectuals which gathered in members' homes for scientific and social discourse. Prof. Hastings lectured at Yale's Sheffield Scientific School, from which Bennett had himself graduated in 1870. Seemingly on his own initiative, according to Pugsley, Hastings presented Bennett with a design for an advanced optical system that no would-be competitor could duplicate because the objective lens was configured to produce an "undetectable" optical error that was corrected by a "compensating" error in the ocular lenses.

(It is critical to note that Pugsley's statements of 1969, written in his 85th year, though articulated clearly and cogently, betray in many particulars the consequences of truly egregious memory lapses, as in his recollection that in 1909, "I do not think there were any American-made telescopes available at this time."

Curiously, advertising for these instruments never attempted to exploit the scientific stature of their reputed designer, Prof. Hastings, a consultant in the design of some of the world's most famous astronomical telescopes, nor was the slightest hint ever given of his "compensating errors." The earliest public disclosure of Hasting's involvement was made in 1938 by Phil Sharpe in his influential history of firearms development, *The Rifle in America*. Since industry-insider Sharpe identifies Pugsley as one of his principal informants, the source of his Hastings story may be deduced.

The enduring popularity of Sharpe's magnum opus, reprinted many times, has insured wide dissemination of the Hastings anecdote, and every commentator since Sharpe has recounted the tale with unconcealed relish. Prior to 1938, however, although Winchester scopes were discussed repeatedly and exhaustively by the arms authorities of the era (foremost among whom were E. C. Crossman, and Townsend Whelen), no mention seems to have been made of Hastings or his "errors." Whelen, in particular, was such an ardent student of optical design that, according to a March 15, 1923, *Arms and the Man* column, he revealed, "Before the War, I spent over $1000 of my own money in experimenting with telescopic sights." This testing included "a Winchester A5, one of the first scopes ever put out by that company," and in 1918 he declared in *The Rifle in America* that this model was "the most modern and satisfactory scope manufactured in the U. S.––the best that can be obtained at the present time."

Crossman, likewise, had written extensively (but rather less enthusiastically) about the A5. He had been one of the select few entrusted with testing prototypes of the Army's M1918 sniper scope, a joint Ordnance Dept.-Winchester project that had also, according to Pugsley, involved the direct participation of Prof. Hastings. A figure of even greater prominence than Whelen at the time, and the conduit of virtually all arms industry gossip worth reporting, he never noted the A5's optical design as being in any way unorthodox.

Well known for his cantankerous streak, and merciless in exposing bogus advertising claims, this kind of "oddball story" would surely have aroused his interest, had any hint of it reached his ears.

Theoretically, it is not impossible to grind an objective lens with a distortion, or error, that is corrected by another lens, such as the inverter lens, placed between it and the focal plane or reticle. The ocular lens could *not* be used for this purpose, as it must be rotated to focus on the reticle, and thus would not remain in the same position relative to the objective. Such a deliberately introduced error would be likely to degrade image quality, unless special care was exercised in grinding and mounting both lenses, which would of course add to the cost of producing them. Finally, it is patently untrue, and a violation of basic optical principles to imply, that it would be impossible, or even particularly difficult, to "reverse engineer" such a system by optical tests and measurements of the individual lenses–this, after all, is what optical engineers are *trained* to do. An "undetectable" optical error really is a contradiction in terms. There exists, therefore, a *prima facie* case for rejecting outright this legend of "compensating errors." (This would not be the only questionable claim associated with the Winchester scope, as will be shown presently.)

Winchester A5 scope.

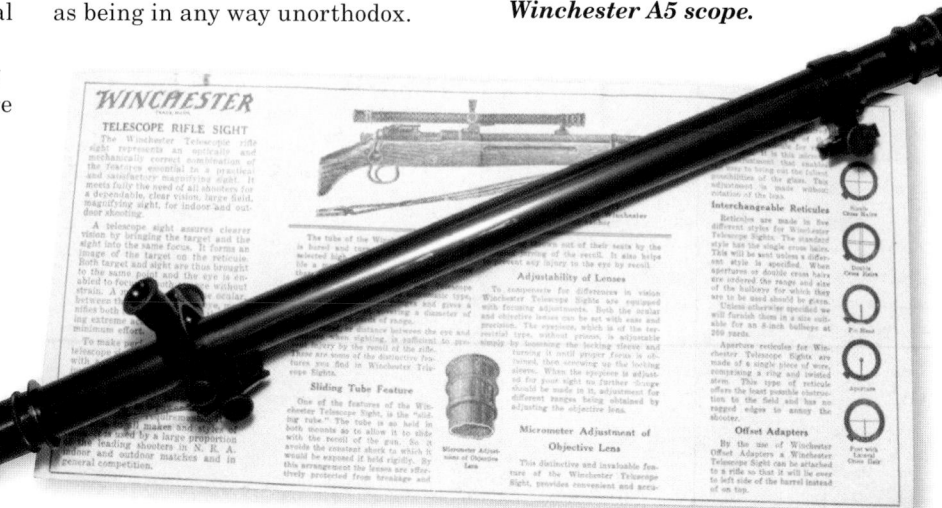

The Telescope

Somewhat like the dog in the famous Sherlock Holmes story that became a significant clue when it did *not* bark, Prof. Hasting's name is, in the several patents pertaining to the Winchester scope, most notable by its absence. The individual actually accorded the honor of being named "inventor" in the patent application of March 8, 1908, (which pertained only to the telescope) is George F. Matteson. Eight points of originality were asserted therein, the first and most enduring being Matteson's "internal rib," a groove in the underside of the objective cell which mated with a corresponding groove in the tube to prevent rotation as the lens was traversed in focusing. (This simple arrangement was still being used when the last Super Targetspot was manufactured.) Illustrating the cooperative nature of the design work, Matteson took pains to distinguish his short groove from the long one in the underside of the tube, which was protected by another Winchester-owned patent.

Another of his claims of novelty was an aperture reticle constructed of twisted wire, strongly promoted for target work in early advertising, but which for all its ingenuity is rarely encountered in surviving instruments. (Stevens, too, offered an aperture.) That reticle, along with the four others offered, was affixed to a stamped brass ring that could be easily and cheaply replaced by the user–Matteson's cleverest idea, since replacement of damaged reticles is the single most frequent scope repair.

The remaining five patent specifications "protected" from imitation what most contemporary users of Winchester scopes regarded as the instrument's very worst flaw–the complicated and unreliable arrangement of tiny screws and internal "movable arms," which expanded to retain the lens cells by friction *alone* against the tube wall. It was a mechanism as needlessly and foolishly complex as the internal rib was sound and simple.

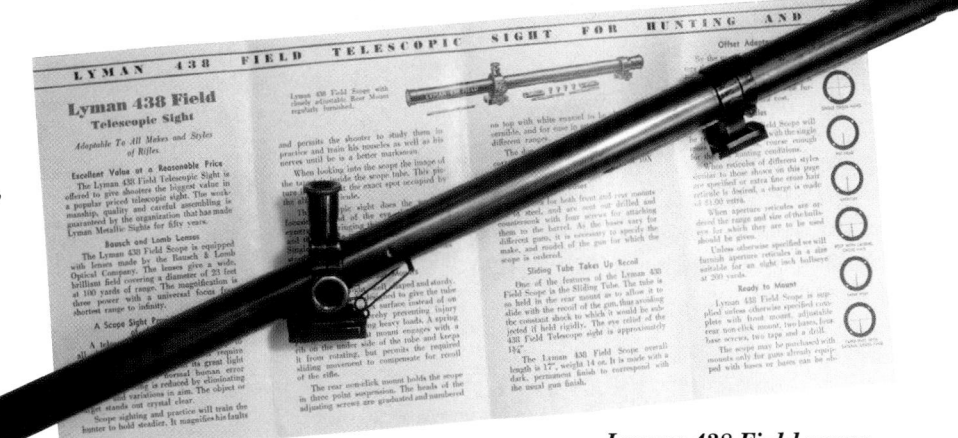

Lyman 438 Field scope.

According to Crossman, C. S. Landis, and most other authorities of the day, the repeated shock of a hard-kicking rifle would eventually cause displacement of the lens cells, despite the buffering action provided by the sliding-tube mounting system (developed c.1890 by H. L. Willard of Walnut Hill fame to protect the internal components, as well as the shooter). In *Small Bore Rifle Shooting* (1927), Crossman declared, with his customary no-nonsense assertiveness, "the ordinary A5 is not fit to use for a long siege on a high-power rifle–it is entirely too delicate in its construction." He also described how the scope might be rebuilt to overcome this deficiency, the same kind of improvement later effected by the Lyman Co. when it transformed the A5 into the 5A.

Yet A5 loyalist Whelen, to the contrary, insisted that the instrument would stand up to any level of recoil not exceeding that of an 8 lb. 30-06 "indefinitely." (He conceded grudgingly that the lens retention system was less than ideal.) This confident assessment appeared, significantly, not in the work of 1918 previously quoted, but in a May, 1928, *American Rifleman* review of the subject–almost 20 years after acquiring his first A5, "the week after the Winchester announcement of its manufacture." That two equally acute and discerning authorities could arrive at such antithetical opinions on this important question is baffling,

but it might be noted that Whelen's personal experience seems to have been confined to what he called "about the oldest A5 in existence, [which] I think has probably had more use than any other in existence." Crossman, on the other hand, who spent much time as a shooting coach and range officer, had observed hundreds of A5s in use by competitors on the high-power firing line.

Whether the lenses do or do not shift under recoil is possibly less important than the susceptibility of their tiny retaining screws to being stripped by users who don't know that they have to be turned not out, but IN, clockwise, to release the cells. Yes, they have left-hand threads, and thus might almost seem to have been *designed* to be abused, which, in any event, they often have been. (What appears to be the slotted head of an ordinary screw is in fact the visible end of a cone-shaped member that wedges the "movable arms" apart as it is rotated.) Many surviving specimens are found to have had their original screw holes re-drilled and tapped for larger, conventional screws, the same modification suggested by Crossman, but probably done out of necessity after being damaged, rather than to "improve" the scope.

The most remarkable aspect of Matteson's patent description is what is NOT claimed to be original–the micrometer adjustable focusing mechanism of the objective lens. Remarkable, because, even if not sufficiently original to warrant patent protection (presumably, some similar system was in use on other optical instruments), it truly *was* a revolutionary innovation in riflescope design, creating a norm for American scope designers that has seldom been challenged. (In any major way, only by J. W. Fecker.) Of course, all previous instruments of good design allowed some means of moving either the objective or inverter lenses (or, rarely, the reticle) to focus for distance and correct for parallax error. The usual solution was a length-wise slot in the tube, which allowed the lens retaining screw to be slid back and forth as needed to achieve proper focus. Fool-proof, but each significant change of range necessitated a bit of trial and error lens manipulation; a given adjustment, in other words, was not quickly and precisely repeatable, nor "scientific and exact," to quote Winchester advertising copy. And reliable repeatability of focus became, after experience with the Winchester micrometer objective, a feature most target shooters, especially those in the new small-bore events, believed to be quite indispensable. Hunters wise enough to focus a glass for the average range, then leave it strictly alone, probably found this feature to be of small utility.

Relevant to observe here is that our modern dichotomy between externally-adjustable "target" and internally-adjustable "hunting" scopes did not exist before the introduction of improved, internally-adjustable hunting models in the mid-1920's. Circa 1910, a purely target scope was considered to be one of higher power, at least 5X, and often up to 20X, and a hunting scope, one of around 5X, or less. Thus, the 5X A and B models would have been viewed, when introduced, as "general purpose" instruments, equally adaptable to field or range. (An important consideration, since the high cost of quality optics obliged most owners to make do with one scope for all their shooting needs. Even scope-connoisseur Whelen speaks of switching his single A5 back and forth among his large battery of rifles.)

Winchester's micrometer focusing adjustment would have been an even greater achievement if, as Winchester literature implied, the published table of range settings actually could have been used to focus perfectly for the range desired. However, those settings were merely approximations, which had to be refined for each individual instrument by trial and error, after which the "true" settings would have to be recorded by the owner. One might wonder why this should be necessary when the machine-made lenses supplied by Bausch & Lomb were, theoretically, ground to identical specifications? The answer is that neither those lenses, nor any others of comparable quality, truly *were* identical, but differed to small degrees in the various parameters of optical correction. J. W. Fecker, whose lenses were ground in his own plant to higher standards of accuracy than those supplied to Winchester, simplified focusing for his customers by going to the trouble of test-focusing each individual instrument, and recording the exact micrometer range settings and serial number on a card that accompanied each scope. (A wasted consideration, as virtually all those cards have been lost.)

The difficulty of manufacturing truly identical lenses (at a production cost that would be acceptable to consumers) also explains why two instruments assembled the same day could differ noticeably in brightness and definition — sometimes the individual lens irregularities combined to act in a way that enhanced their optical performance, sometimes the reverse occurred. This phenomenon prompted C. S. Landis to remark in *.22 Caliber Rifle Shooting* (1932) that "some of the glasses [A5s] vary a good bit in the excellence of their lenses. When you got a good Winchester, you have a first class glass. If you got one with mediocre lenses, you have a very ordinary rifle scope." I would wager that Whelen's much-praised A5 was one of Landis' "first class" examples, if not one hand-selected by a Winchester optician. During the glory days of Camp Perry, an unspoken practice by target scope manufacturers was the sequestering

of instruments found to exhibit exceptional optical performance for purchase by the leading competitors of the time. Unfair, perhaps, but why allow such superior instruments to fall into the hands of untalented shooters?

Today, "Winchester scope" has come to mean "A5," but that outcome is by no means the one that had been originally planned. In the beginning, there was that almost forgotten sibling, the "Style B," in 3, 4, and 5 powers, which merits notice, if only because it was possibly the most ill-designed scope ever placed on the American market. This opprobrium is earned not because it was Winchester's "economy model," selling for about one-third less than the A5 (which equaled in price a Model 1895, the most expensive rifle Winchester then offered), but rather because its designers saw fit to give it excessive eye relief (3.5 in.) at the expense of field of view.

So narrow a field (in 5X, less than half that of the 5A) is bad enough when the user's eye is close to the ocular lens, but when forced as far behind the ocular as it must be with a B model, the visual effect is that of trying to peer through a key hole, with the scope's mediocre luminosity and contrast further diminished by the side-light flooding the user's visual field. Maintaining visual alignment with a small exit pupil becomes much more taxing with the user's eye so far behind the ocular lens–the slightest degree of misalignment with the optical axis causes the narrow field to "black out" completely. (And remember that the low-combed stocks typical of the period provided poor head support for scope usage.) Optical design is always an exercise in compromise, and in "trade-offs," but since any scope in sliding mounts can be placed within eyelash distance of the shooter's face without risk of injury, the "Style B" sacrificed field and brightness to gain nothing of value.

Sharpe reported that only 500 each of the three B variants had been produced by 1917, and they do not appear in the general catalog of 1918. Although this statistic is substantiated by a production record compiled by T. C. Johnson (now in the Winchester archives), and thus must be accepted as accurate, the numbers of B models remaining in circulation seem almost to defy those low production figures. Over only the last 3 years, at least one dozen have been offered for sale on eBay alone, which, relative to the production numbers, strikes me as a remarkable survival rate.

Only one favorable reference to use of any B model has come to my attention, and that, inexplicably, was written by a rifleman of undoubted skill, C. S. Landis himself: in a 1914 *Outers'* piece on squirrel hunting, he called it "very good" except for a "small field." A close reading of this article, however, conveys the impression that this scope was possibly the first one he had owned, and even a mediocre scope, needless to say, will seem quite wonderful compared to metallic sights. Far more characteristic of the majority view was Whelen's remark in his "Dope Bag" column for the Nov. 1, 1922, issue of *Arms and the Man*: "I do not like the Winchester B telescope at all."

One last point pertaining to Winchester's optical design bears brief mention—brief, because the notion is almost too bizarre to merit serious examination. I refer to the groundless belief that some evolutionary relationship exists between the optical system of L. C. Cummins' internally-adjustable "Duplex" scope of 1892, and the "compensating-errors" idea. Copies of Cummins' patents (along with many others) have indeed been found among the W. R. A. records now at the Buffalo Bill Museum. This innocuous circumstance has been construed by some researchers as a "smoking gun" with respect to influence on Winchester's later design, primarily because a light-ray tracing included by Cummins among his patent drawings was misinterpreted by viewers unaware that the strange, asymmetric appearance of the inventor's diagram is merely a technical *convention* in optics science, drawn that way solely for purposes of clarity and convenience. In such diagrams, only rays on *one* side of the optical axis are shown; omission of the opposite side creates a false appearance of asymmetry. To those already convinced of the "compensating errors" dogma, however, this queer-looking illustration seemed to confirm a relationship where none whatsoever exists.

The Front Mount

Interest in the optical properties of a scope seems naturally to take precedence over considerations of the mounting system, but with any externally-adjustable instrument, it must always be remembered that the quality and design of the mounts is *at least* as important as that of the lens system. Without a doubt, better shooting can be done with a second-rate telescope in first-rate mounts, than contrariwise.

Prior to 1910, the best-designed mounts on the market had been the "Stevens Special" No. 4, a double-micrometer, three bearing-point system, introduced in 1904. They were not conclusively bettered until J. W. Fecker introduced mounts of his own design in 1925, but, inexplicably, the No.4s were discontinued soon after 1916 as part of Stevens' "downsizing" program.

Stevens was, in addition, also first (1904) to offer the dovetail mounting blocks later adopted by all

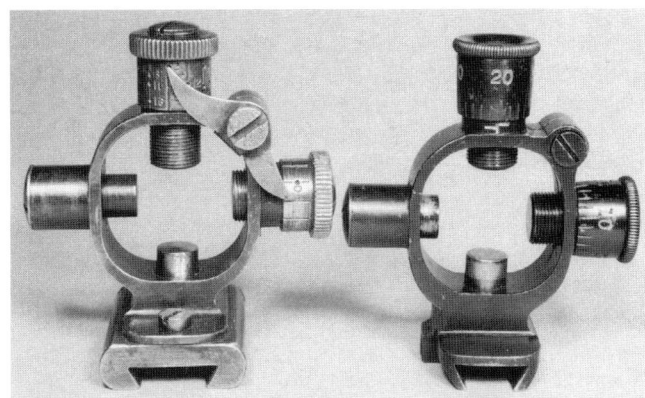

The 5A mount (right), improved by replacement of the "grasshopper" spring with a plunger, compared to an A5 mount (left) modified for U.S. military issue c. WWI; the latter's original base replaced with one that accepts a Mann-Neidner tapered block.

❊ ● ❊ ● ❊ ● ❊

Non-rotating disks on Stevens #8 rear mount (left) prevent changes in one adjustment from influencing the other, a principle eventually adopted by other makers. WRA's #1 mount (right).

❊ ● ❊ ● ❊ ● ❊

Beside Stevens' modern-looking #4 micrometer rear mount of 1904 (left), WRA's #2 micrometer seems a bit archaic.

later makers, although their size and shape differed slightly from those of Winchester. Patent protection for this pivotal innovation was apparently impossible for Stevens to obtain due, presumably, to some prior application of the basic principle, possibly in machine-tool construction, as was the case with Adolf Niedner's tapered blocks. But even if similar mounting blocks had been used previously to attach removable machine parts, Stevens' application of the idea was so novel that one might question the competence of the firm's patent attorneys.

The Nov. 5, 1907, patent date stamped on the base of Winchester mounts pertains to the design work of another staff engineer, Frank Burton, who devised the arrangement of a spring-loaded plunger in the front mount shaped to mate with the longitudinal groove in the underside of the tube, so as to prevent rotation of the tube within its mounts. Curiously, this patent was a revision of an earlier Burton patent application that employed a so-called "Pope" alignment rib to accomplish the same function. Such a rib had also been employed by Stevens on its

❦ ● ❦ ● ❦ ● ❦ ● ❦ ● ❦

WRA's inaugural magazine ad for its new line of scopes, from the June 1910* Outer's Book. *(Courtesy of Jim Foral)

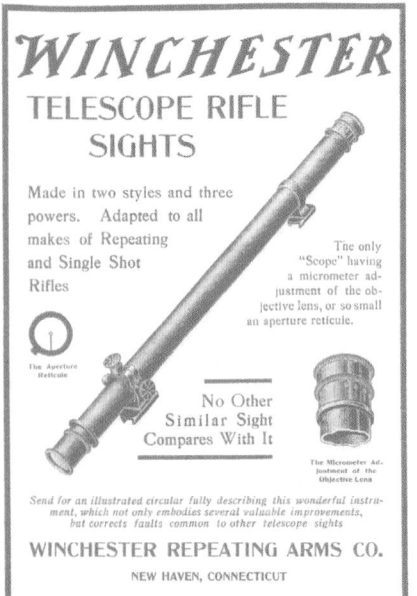

WINCHESTER
TELESCOPE RIFLE
SIGHTS

Made in two styles and three powers. Adapted to all makes of Repeating and Single Shot Rifles

The only "Scope" having a micrometer adjustment of the objective lens, or so small an aperture reticule.

The Aperture Reticule

No Other Similar Sight Compares With It

The Micrometer Ad-justment of the Objective Lens

Send for an illustrated circular fully describing this wonderful instrument, which not only embodies several valuable improvements, but corrects faults common to other telescope sights

WINCHESTER REPEATING ARMS CO.

NEW HAVEN, CONNECTICUT

higher grade models (a V-notch and alignment pin served this purpose on the others), but this, too, was a feature that apparently could not gain patent protection. Since Burton's groove was certainly *not* an improvement over the rib, and later became the object of criticism, the substitution can most reasonably be explained on economic grounds–impressing a groove was a much cheaper manufacturing operation than machining a rib, milling a mortise to receive it, and finally pinning or soldering it in place.

The seamless steel tubing used by Winchester, Stevens, and every other maker, would probably be indistinguishable before machining to receive the internal components–all measure about .030" in wall thickness. But whereas other makers acknowledged purchasing, for this purpose, the kind of high-quality drawn tubing that had been available since the 1880s, Winchester catalogs claimed "the tube is not drawn, but turned and bored from a solid piece of steel." Such a time-consuming procedure obviously makes no economic sense, especially in light of the apparent decision to cut costs by scrapping the rib, nor does it make optical sense. William Brophy reported in *The Springfield 1903 Rifles* that, during developmental work in 1907, 12 prototype tubes actually were "turned and bored" from barrel blanks, but adds that later tubing was purchased. Brophy did not state his source for this information, but it does ring true, and is decidedly more credible than the irrational claim that Winchester advertising continued to assert right through the end of production. (2)

One more item of evidence suggesting that Winchester's tubing was not significantly different from that of other makers concerns the problem of dented tubes experienced with scopes used on rifles of heavy recoil. In such cases, the repeated impact of the tube against the two convex bearing points inside the front mount ring eventually caused the formation of shallow dents in spite of the shock-absorbing action of the sliding tube. The solution was simple–hardening the forward part

of the tube–but the problem serves to demonstrate that this tubing possessed no special advantage in strength.

The Rear Mounts

Matteson and Burton are names not well known even among most Winchester collectors, but the third member of the design team was the inventor of "America's favorite shotgun," the Model 12, along with a parade of other great Winchesters, Thomas C. Johnson. After Winchester's schism with John Browning, Johnson had become the firm's "resident genius," so not surprisingly his ideas for a rear mount were imaginative in every respect. Their novelty, in fact, seems to have provoked a failure of nerve on the part of management, because Johnson's advanced design, though patented on the same date as Burton's mount, never progressed further than the model shop!

Johnson's mount was truly *sui generis,* like nothing else before or since. Windage adjustment is achieved by moving not the tube, but the entire upper half of the mount, as with the Lyman No. 103 tang sight. Elevation adjustment is rather more conventional, but in place of a screw tip bearing against the tube at one point, Johnson employed a "yoke-like shoe" riding like a saddle atop the tube, and thereby denying it lateral movement. A semi-circular "cradle spring," supporting the tube, and thrusting it firmly against the "shoe," betrays itself as the antecedent of that most recognizable feature of the Winchester mount, the so-called "grasshopper" elevation spring.

Given the obvious care invested by Johnson in this design, Winchester's failure to make use of it invites speculation: was there some shortcoming that only became apparent in later testing? Or, as I suspect, did projected production costs alarm the accounting department? (What lover of fine rifles can forget or forgive the cost-cutting zeal that afflicted the great Model 52 with a BB-gun trigger guard?) Whatever the explanation, the mounts that went into production were thoroughly conventional. Paradoxically, the only detail of Johnson's patent to survive (slightly altered) was the element that would generate most criticism among contemporary users, the bent-wire elevation spring.

Crossman derided this spring as "old and weak," and Landis cited it as one of two "principal defects" of Winchester scopes (the other was its susceptibility to rain damage). Neither seem to have swallowed the advertising claim that "the use of two instead of one spring overcomes a defect common to most mounts." The oblique reference here, unmistakably, was to the single spring employed on Stevens' mounts, which subsequent history would prove beyond question was the mechanically superior solution.

Winchester's No. 1 rear mount closely resembled Stevens' No. 2 and No. 8–the only graduations on either are index marks on the heads of the two adjustment screws, without any kind of scale to register complete revolutions. It is generally assumed by collectors that Winchester originally intended to match the lower-priced No. 1 with the B models, and the micrometer-adjustable No. 2 with the "top of the line" A5, but merely reading the catalog price list refutes this misconception: "No. 1 rear mount is standard for both Style A and Style B Telescopes, and will be sent with all orders unless specified otherwise."

Nevertheless, the No. 1 was so harshly criticized by early critics like Landis, who devoted two paragraphs in his 1914 article to disparaging it, and promoting the No. 2, that even the price-conscious buyers of B models appear, usually, to have ordered them fitted with the micrometer model. At least, surviving Bs fitted with No. 2 mounts seem to outnumber those with No. 1s; the latter is in fact scarce on either model. These Bs could have been retrofitted by their owners with No. 2 mounts, but that seems an unlikely explanation, given the Bs disappointing optical properties–it would have been throwing good money after bad. (A dissenting opinion–due to its smaller diameter ring, and uncluttered, low-profile design, I *like* the No. 1, although the coarse pitch of its adjustment screws can make small changes in bullet impact a

trying procedure; its lack of the same adjustment latitude as the No. 2 is not restrictive except at extreme ranges.)

The No. 2 was not without a shortcoming of its own, which eventually became the source of considerable consternation among target shooters, who found that the "zero" mark on the thimble often failed to register exactly on the index line of the main scale. Landis complained that it was " not easy to tell how many complete revolutions you have made," which could spell disaster during competition, when frequent readjustments were necessary. Target shooters comprised a major segment of the market, and after 1925, they could opt for Fecker's new mounts, which, among many other advanced features, featured more easily read graduations. (The paint used to mark these graduations provides one of the few clues available for dating Winchester scopes: red was the original color used, but after May, 1923, it was changed to white.)

Allusion has been made to the precipitous decline of Stevens Arms after 1916, when the higher grade rifles and scopes were discontinued, and Stevens' corporate stature shrank to a shadow of its former eminence in the industry. By this time, as well, John Sidel had been forced into retirement by the combined competition from Stevens and Winchester, and he died in 1919. Thus by default the A5 became America's premium scope. That status it would retain until the introduction of Fecker's early models in 1922 (sold in either Stevens or Winchester mounts), but not until 1925, when Fecker's advanced new mounts became available, did the A5 finally face a "life-threatening" challenge.

Whelen's long admiration for the A5 did not blind him to the superiority of Fecker's advanced engineering, for in the 1928 *Rifleman* article previously quoted he declared that the Fecker "was the most perfect target telescope I had ever seen, superior, both scope and mountings, to the Winchester." This assessment, however, did not imply Winchester scopes should be considered hopelessly antiquated, as Whelen went out of his way in this article to

emphasize that "the Winchester glass is so good that, personally, I do not believe a rifleman would gain very much in turning from a Winchester to a Fecker." Exactly this view was reiterated by Crossman: "the difference [between the two] is not enough to worry the man using the good old A5." For target shooting, he meant, and for field use the older instrument still possessed one advantage, in that the longer and heavier Fecker detracted considerably from the handiness of a light rifle. Then there was the matter of cost: in 1926, the A5 was listed at $40, the 3/4-inch Fecker at $42.50, and the 1 1/8-inch Fecker at $62.50. (In 1926, gun prices ranged from $7 for a Stevens Favorite, to $36 for a Mod. 52, one of Winchester's most expensive.)

Notwithstanding the only slightly diminished prestige of the A5, as reflected in the previous comments, and the continuing allegiance of many other riflemen, corporate planners at Winchester could not have failed to regard without foreboding the innovations of Fecker, and the enthusiasm with which they had been greeted. Not even the magic of the "Winchester" name was advantage enough to forestall indefinitely some concession to changing times and advancing technology. Confronted with a pressing need to modernize this aging design, an opportunity to divest the firm of a faltering old war-horse while it yet enjoyed so much esteem and good will was not to be ignored. "Who approached whom" to initiate sales negotiations is not known, but throughout the latter half of the generally prosperous 1920s, Winchester is known to have suffered chronic financial difficulties, culminating in 1931 in bankruptcy.

Including the 1500 B models, a total of 8000 Winchester scopes had been manufactured by the end of 1924, according to the accounting of T. C. Johnson. Although declining sales in these later years were obviously the root cause of the divestiture, it seems not unreasonable to assume (based on Lyman's subsequent production) annual sales of about 300 for 1925 through 1928, bringing total production up to roughly 9000.

The Successor

To the enterprise and imagination of the Lyman Gun Sight Co., therefore, devolves the distinction of elevating the A5 to its ultimate point of refinement, as the Lyman 5A. The change of ownership, transacted in 1928, provoked relatively little response in the shooting press when the acquisition was announced in Lyman Catalog No. 17, of 1929. (Thus coinciding nicely with the onset of the Great Depression.) The continuity between the Lyman product and its predecessor was emphasized by the notice that Lyman, not Winchester, would thereafter be responsible for service work on A5s. (No corresponding responsibility for Stevens' service was assumed by Lyman, and perhaps this has something to do with the enhanced survival rate of Winchester scopes over their rivals.)

The earliest *Rifleman* advertisement for what was described as "formerly the Winchester A5" appeared in the issue of May, 1929. The June issue provided the first distinct clue that some change had been made in the "good old A5" by announcing it had been "improved optically and internally." However, neither that ad, nor those which followed, made great efforts to emphasize differences between the "original" and the instrument as manufactured by Lyman, despite the fact that important improvements had indeed been achieved. This circumstance, an odd reversal of the usual "new and improved" marketing bluster, suggests that Lyman's management wished, above all, to reassure potential buyers that Winchester quality had in no way been compromised by

❧ ● ❧ ● ❧ ● ❧ ● ❧ ● ❧

***Lyman's initial A5 ad, in the May, 1929* Rifleman.**

LYMAN 5-A
TELESCOPIC SIGHTS

The Lyman 5A Telescopic Sight, formerly the Winchester A5 Scope, now manufactured by Lyman, is ready for delivery. We will mail you a 5A folder on request.

the transition from New Haven to Middlefield. In truth, it had been enhanced, as reason exists to suspect that Winchester's financial stresses of the late '20's had probably impinged on standards of quality-control.

Perhaps it was this strategy of deliberate understatement that persuaded Whelen to report, in the Jan., 1931, *Rifleman,* that the 5A was "exactly the same, except optical qualities of the Lyman are very slightly better." Landis likewise thought it "had been changed very little since its introduction." F. C. Ness, having recently inherited the "Dope Bag" column from Whelen, considered it sufficient to note in the Sept., 1934, *Rifleman,* that "this popular model (formerly the A5 Winchester) is well known to all [target shooting] club members." (The superficial character of these assessments suggests the authors were merely reviewing promotional material, rather than actually testing the new scope.)

Crossman, to the contrary, was much impressed by the rejuvenated instrument, and said so emphatically in one of the great classics of the period, *The Book of the Springfield* (1932): "The Lyman Co. has greatly improved the old Winchester glass. The mountings of the lenses have been greatly improved and strengthened, and the system of watchmakers screws has been abandoned in favor of rear screws with hair on their chests… capable of holding the works under continued use on a high power rifle."

Of the same opinion was Sharpe, who "was not greatly impressed with the performance" of the Winchester, which was "by no means as satisfactory as the 5A." Sharpe went on (*The Rifle in America*) to attribute this improvement to removal of the "compensating errors," but he was the only reviewer to make this connection, and no corroboration of such a change in basic optical design was ever made public by Lyman.

The replacement of the "watchmakers screws" of the A5 with those boasting "hair on their chests" was a crucial improvement, erasing at a single stroke the most serious and persistent criticism of the Winchester scope. By eliminating

the "expanding arms," this change also simplified manufacture of the cells, and possibly reduced production costs. Burton's alignment groove was replaced with his original intention, a Pope-type rib, which also required changing the shape of the front-mount plunger to make it straddle the rib.

Another cause for complaint disappeared in 1932 when Johnson's much maligned elevation spring was replaced by a spring-loaded plunger, a modification that had first been devised, it appears, by Marine Corps armorers for sniper usage during World War I. (USMC modification usually included replacement of the bases of both mounts with bases that accepted Niedner-style taper-blocks.) However, even this new four bearing-point mount was, compared to Fecker's three-point design, somewhat behind the times, and Lyman's own three-point version did not "join the club" until 1937, when it arrived with the Super Targetspot.

Replacing the "grasshopper" spring simplified mounting the 5A to its barrel blocks, as it eliminated the aggravating tendency of that spring to skew the bottom of the mount out of alignment with the barrel block when attempting to engage the two. However, the new mount introduced a peculiar annoyance of its own–any accidental displacement of the tube from its centered position may result, owing to the equal and opposite spring pressure of the four-point design, in the tube "sticking" in its misaligned position. This would not occur if the tube, as recommended, was kept freshly oiled, but its usual condition was more likely to be either dry, or gummy from old oil. The lightest touch will suffice to return the tube to its correct position, but if the misalignment is not noticed, a ""wild" shot is the result. Such a condition is not possible with the three-point design, precisely because of its "unbalanced" thrust against the tube.

Lyman's acquisition of the "good old A5" brought another improvement: serial numbering, and the maintenance of records on each individual instrument (records presently owned by Parsons Optical Co.). Seemingly "trivial," this change implies something of greater significance––a long-range commitment to high standards of service and quality. Even if it could be assumed that Winchesters were assembled with equal care, A5s are "anonymous," but each 5A possesses its own unique "identity." (Occasionally, 5As lacking serial numbers will be found; the conjecture is that these are "off the books" specimens, possibly "lunch-box specials.")

Lyman's use of serial numbering allows identification of what might otherwise appear to be "rebuilt" Winchester scopes. Along with the jigs, fixtures, and other machine tool parts, transferred by Winchester to Lyman in 1928, came an unknown quantity of unassembled component parts, including, it may be deduced, "Winchester"-marked tubes. Such tubes Lyman fitted with its much improved lens cells, retained by conventional screws through the tube walls rather than Matteson's trouble-prone "moveable arms." These components were machined from brass, rather than steel as used by Winchester– some insurance against the formation of rust, the least bit of which renders disassembly difficult or impossible.

It is the appearance of serial numbers on such "Winchester" scopes that excludes the possibility they might be damaged Winchesters repaired with Lyman components. The highest such number known to me is #216. Most reasonable to assume is that Lyman used up all the "inherited" Winchester tubes before assembling scopes with newly manufactured ones. I have also seen one 5A with the Winchester markings blotted out with matting of the type sometimes applied to barrels and ribs, and Lyman markings stamped above the matting, so this may have been an alternate (but highly disfiguring) means of using up these Winchester-marked tubes.

By the early 1930s, telescopic sighting on better quality small-game and varmint rifles had become the rule, not the exception, as it had been in 1910. As a result of that acceptance, the 5A, despite its improvements, faced growing competition from newer rivals such as Fecker's compact Small Game model, similarly priced, and John Unertl's Small Game model,

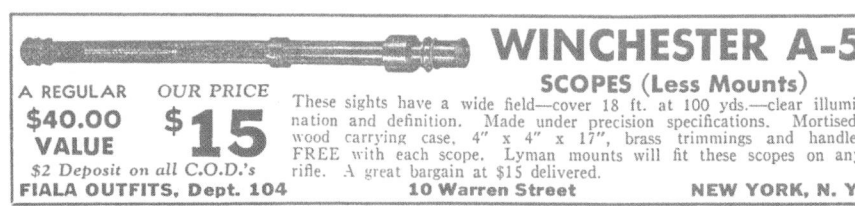
costing even less. For the most serious target work, the 5A had been totally eclipsed by Lyman's first original design, the Targetspot model of 1934 (the brainchild, possibly, of master optician Wray Hageman, hired away from Fecker at about that time).

And if all this competition was not enough to undermine sales of the 5A, the U.S. Army and Navy began about this time to dispose of large numbers of surplus Winchester telescopes, purchased without mounts for use in artillery aiming devices ("bore scopes"). The wooden boxes made up to hold these special appliances are now often sold as "original" Winchester scope cases, despite the glaring incongruity of there being an illustration of the device pasted inside the box. (The only cases ever sold by Winchester were form-fitted leather ones, now worth more than the scope itself.) The dealers who purchased these surplus Winchesters (mostly As, but a few Bs) marketed them in a variety of ways: with the large bronze bushings used in the bore scope still attached, or, more commonly, in new Lyman mounts–either the cheap, "pot metal," mounts of the Stevens-derived Model 438 , or 5A mounts. Even in the latter, these refurbished units were typically sold for only about half Lyman's price for the 5A––a wonderful bargain in those Depression years, but another nail in the 5A's coffin.

Lyman's designers, it soon became apparent, had not rested on their laurels after introducing the Targetspot, but must immediately have begun the planning which culminated in the sensational Super Targetspot, of 1937. This instrument had grown so large that it was paired in the same year with the beautifully proportioned Junior Targetspot. In this expanded product line (the Targetspot also continued to be offered for several more years), there must have seemed little rationale for continued production of the

Examples of the cut-rate competition faced by Lyman from military surplus dealers.

❊ ● ❊ ● ❊ ● ❊ ● ❊ ● ❊

senior member of the family. The last advertised appearance in the *Rifleman* of the 5A occurred in the August 1937 issue, and by December of that year, Lyman was promoting the Junior Targetspot. Although the latter was never explicitly touted as a replacement for the 5A, the circumstantial evidence suggests that such was Lyman's intent.

There remained at least one die-hard 5A loyalist, however, as the last recorded specimen, ser. no. 2824, was manufactured on April 1, 1938, according to Parsons' records. Whoever took possession of that last 5A, on the eve of World War II, brought to an end a manufacturing history that had commenced when lever-actions still reigned supreme among American hunters, black powder-loaded cartridges remained in widespread use, and telescopic sighting was viewed by most riflemen as an impractical luxury.

Endnotes

(1) To sell boxed with special Models 67 and 69 bolt-action 22s, introduced in 1935, Winchester commissioned the manufacture of 3, 5, and 8X brass-tube scopes fitted in primitive stamped steel mounts, and designated merely "No. 3," etc. (The 3 and 5x are listed in catalogs, but seem now to be very scarce; the 8x is not uncommon—far more common than B models, for example.) The tubes are unmarked–only the mounts bear the Winchester name, but many of these are also unmarked. These instruments were first manufactured by the Carolyn Scope Co., which produced under its own name a well-reviewed variable-power that was discontinued by or before 1940, following a production run of only 2 or 3 years. From then until World War 11 disrupted civilian commerce, production was continued by the Saymon Brown Co., a New York City manufacturer of optical accessories for cameras. Production was not resumed after the war.

(2) Mr. Brophy chose to repeat an anecdote that logic suggests is, at best, incomplete. He not only reiterated the apocryphal legend of Prof. Hastings, but added to it the equally questionable tale that all scopes were assembled by a single Winchester employee who "kept his work room locked so that only he knew anything about assembling the telescopes." Would Winchester have approved an arrangement that allowed its investment in the scope business to be totally dependent on one such individual? This strikes me as one of Pugsley's confused recollections, or that of another aging employee straining to remember events of many decades past.

Mannlicher rifles in my family include (L-R): 6.5x55 Swede, 03A3 257 Roberts, Winchester M70 225, Savage M99 22 High Power, Remington Mohawk 222, Falling Block Works Model K 218 Bee, Ruger No. 3 in 22 Hornet and Ruger M77/22 Long Rifle.

MAKE MINE
MANNLICHER

by Ron Terrell

It isn't for everyone. But, then, there isn't much in life that is for everyone—be it cars, art, music or hairstyles. This is especially true in subject matter as personal as sporting goods equipment.

What we're talking about is a rifle stock style known as "Mannlicher"—a standard stock with a forearm that extends the full length of the barrel. This style is credited to Ritter Ferdinand von Mannlicher, a German firearms designer. One of his most notable designs resulted in a bolt-action rifle known as the Mannlicher-Schoenauer. These rifles were chambered for several European big-game cartridges, but the 6.5x54mm Mannlicher-Schoenauer became one of the better known. Partly because they originated in Europe and were chambered mostly for European cartridges, Mannlicher-style rifles never became as popular in the United States as they were abroad.

Like a number of other subjects, full-length gunstocks are in the *personal taste* category. There are those who don't like the looks of the wood going all the way to the muzzle, and there are those weight-conscious riflemen who don't want to add those extra ounces to be carried afield.

And, too, there is the concern on the part of other riflemen that all that extra wood might warp and cause a shift in point of impact from season to season. This latter concern might be the most valid, but since each rifle should be double-checked for zero

Below: *Three of the Mannlichers in author's line-up include* **(L-R): 6.5x55 Swedish Mauser, author's wife's 03A3 .257 Roberts** (the first Mannlicher in the Terrell family) *and the diminutive 218 Bee on a Falling Block Works Model K action.*

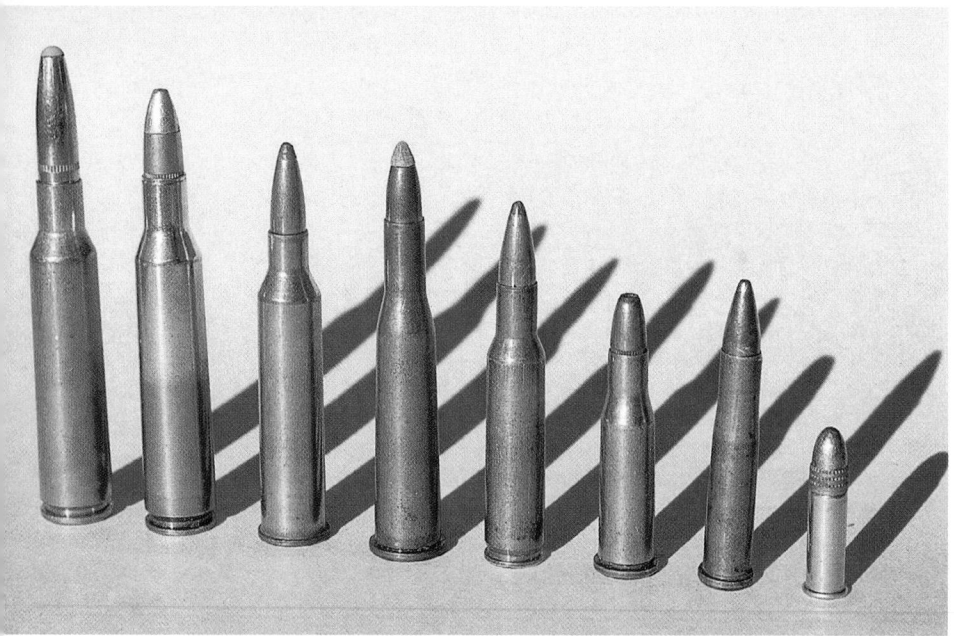

The line-up of cartridges chambered in author's Mannlichers includes (L-R): 6.5x55, 257 Roberts, 225 Winchester, 22 High Power, 222 Remington, 218 Bee, 22 Hornet and 22 Long Rifle.

The one made by Griffin and Howe happens to have a 24-inch barrel! Mr. Ruger acquired these rifles in the '50s, and his later International stock design seems to rely quite heavily on the look of these two Mannlichers.

Normally, in my opinion, the best lengths for Mannlicher stocks are in the 18-20 inch range. Shorter barrels in the 16-17 inch range will work … but sometimes too short is almost as bad as too long. Even 22-inch barrels may be a shade too long for best appearances.

And appearance is what the Mannlicher offers. That extra wood may help balance a muzzle-light rifle but, frankly, it's hard for even me to come up with other advantages of the Mannlicher stock: its looks that count.

The first rifle to wear a Mannlicher stock in our family was a custom 257 Roberts built for my wife. Long-time friend and gunsmith Claude Simmons *(now deceased)* of LaPorte, Colorado, had built a 257 for me on an '03-A3 action, but its 24-inch medium weight barrel and Monte Carlo stock were too much for Bobbie's 5'2" frame. Claude installed a lightweight Douglas barrel on another '03-A3 *(remember back 30-40 years ago when M-98 Mauser and '03 Springfield rifles were readily available at discount prices?)* and shortened it to 18 1/2 inches. I ordered a semi-finished Mannlicher stock from Fajen to finish myself. After the stock work was done, we mounted a Bausch & Lomb 2.5-8x scope in Conetrol base and rings to complete the outfit.

Once it was fitted to her, Bobbie used that rifle with deadly accuracy on everything from prairie dogs and jackrabbits to deer and antelope. Even after Claude built a 7x57mm on another '03-A3 for her, that Mannlicher-stocked 257 remained Bobbie's favorite.

Since that time, a succession of custom rifles has come into our family's possession. A move from

before heading out after game anyway, that shouldn't be a major problem.

Even with these aspects to consider, there are numerous others of us who like the clean lines of a full stock on a compact rifle. And the operative word here is *Compact*. For a Mannlicher stock to really look right, it needs to be on a short-barreled rifle.

One of my old Winchester Model 70s in the 225 Winchester chambering has a 22-inch barrel. Putting a Mannlicher stock on it turned it into a real attention-getter. In addition to the full-length stock with its ebony

forend tip, it has a curved pistol grip and modernistic sculptured cheekpiece. I worked for Reinhart Fajen Gunstocks as a specialty machine carver at the time the M70 was to be restocked and decided to create a triple hybrid pattern. About all I can say is that it looks nice and is a unique style—but maybe that rifle should not have had a Mannlicher stock on it. At least that was my thinking until I read R.L. Wilson's excellent book, *Ruger and His Guns*. On page 103 of that book is a photo of two of Mr. Ruger's rifles, both with Mannlicher stocks.

Rev. Wayne Isrig is so fond of his H&R 17 Remington that he says it has found a permanent home with him. I had the rifle stocked by Fajen Gunstocks shortly after moving to Missouri over 30 years ago.

Colorado to Warsaw, Missouri—home of Fajen Gunstock Company—many years ago provided the opportunity of fitting a variety of quality woods to our long guns. Fajen's was always a top source for gunstocks and custom services and it was a major loss to the shooting sports world when it went out of business. The good news is that Fred Wenig, Fajen's plant manager and custom wood specialist, opened his own shop in nearby Lincoln. Missouri, and hired a number of the original Fajen employees.

Included on the list of Mannlicher-stocked rifles that either are or have been in our gun vaults are some ranging from the 17 Remington to the 30-40 Krag. While working on a story about the 17 Remington 30 some years ago—before Remington introduced that cartridge in their Model 700 rifle—I restocked a sweet little Harrington & Richardson M317 rifle chambered for the 17. Experimentation with the 17-caliber had been going on for over 25 years at that time. Dave Wolfe, founder of *Handloader* and *Rifle* magazines, had developed a 17-223 and it was speculated that the final commercialization of the 17 would take that form. Remington changed the shape of the case slightly when they introduced it so Wolfe's creation remained in the crowd of the other 17 wildcats that had appeared before the Remington version.

The little H&R was based on the small Sako L461 action and sported a slim 20-inch barrel—a perfect choice for a Mannlicher stock. An extra fancy walnut classic stock was fitted to this little beauty and it became one of my favorite field-trip guns. Rural areas of Missouri are more densely populated than the prairies of eastern Colorado and the milder report of the 17 was more acceptable to the local farmers and ranchers. That 17 accounted for numerous crows, a fair number of groundhogs and a few coyotes during the years it stayed with us.

When a decision had to be made about which rifle had to go to make

My grandson, Matt Newsom, carried this FBW Model K in 218 Bee on his first deer hunt with his grandpa. Plans were to use it on coyotes, or other varmint targets of opportunity.

room for another project, Fred bought the H&R for himself. Years later, he was persuaded by his minister to let it transfer to the minister's hands. That minister says this H&R 17 has found a permanent home.

While most rifles suitable for stocking with Mannlicher-style

Delbert Smith, vice president of Wenig Gunstocks, sights in author's Ruger M77/22 that he helped stock as a full-length Mannlicher of fancy walnut.

Author's 6.5x55 Swedish Mauser is propped up by the rack of a Missouri whitetail taken with the rifle in the '03 season.

wood are bolt actions, there are others that will work, too. Sturm, Ruger & Company proves that point. They have had their own version of Mannlicher stocks for years. Theirs is called the International and is currently offered on their 10/22 International, a semi-auto rimfire that has become something of a cult classic in recent years, and M77 RSI bolt action—both of which are one-piece stocks. According to the records-keeping department at Ruger's New Hampshire plant, the 10/22 International was first offered from 1964-1970 and then periodically after that. It is listed as being available in the current catalog in several versions, one of which is the International.

Then there is the Ruger No. 1 single shot, known as the No. 1 RSI International, which has a two-piece stock. Incidentally, according to Wilson's book on Ruger and the company records department, the No. 1 International was brought out with a 20-inch barrel in 1983 and has been offered in that version ever since. Wilson says that Mr. Ruger always had a fondness for the Mannlicher style and our earlier reference to his two custom Mannlichers show that his liking of this style predates his first efforts to add rifles to his production lineup.

The 10/22 International has a slightly slimmer profile than the other Ruger Mannlicher style stocks but, even there, I like an even slimmer appearance. Consequently, I will be taking my early production

10/22 to Wenig's Custom shop for one of their Classic Mannlichers.

Having a rifle with a fuller, heavier forearm was probably one of the reasons a Krag 30-40 did not find a permanent home with me. The surplus Krag had been sporterized by a previous owner and he had done a pretty good job on it. The barrel had been cut to 20 inches, good sights installed, bolt jeweled, barrel and action polished and blued and a medium fancy walnut Mannlicher stock fitted. For my tastes, though, he left the forearm too full and it had more of a "clubby" look than I liked. I did shoot it enough to know that it produced satisfactory accuracy: 3 1/2-inch five-shot groups at 100 yards with open sights. Obviously, a better iron sight shooter and accurate handloads would improve on that. This happened to be one of those rifles that just didn't *grab* me, however, so—Mannlicher or not—it found another home.

But, back to the Ruger rifles: When the No. 1 was introduced, I ordered a barreled action in 22-250 and had a super fancy piece of Fajen walnut fitted to it. I liked that rifle so well that when Ruger introduced another single shot, the No. 3, in 22 Hornet, I ordered one of those, too. I restocked it with a plain piece of walnut in classic style with a Neidner buttplate and, since it had a 20-inch barrel, talked to Wenig about putting a Mannlicher forearm on it. He had to develop a new pattern to accomplish that but, when he did, we had a Ruger Mannlicher

(International?). It looks great and, I think, improves the balance.

Single shots are not the only non-bolt actions that can be used as the basis for Mannlicher-style stocked rifles. Savage's Model 99s have set the standards for quality lever actions for over 100 years. The 99's smooth action and rotary magazine—before modernization changed the feed system to a detachable clip—was first choice for thousands of hunters who liked the fast, strong action. My first Colorado mule deer was taken with an M-99 in 250 Savage.

Years later, two other M-99s were acquired. One is an older 22 Hi-Power takedown and the other an even older M99 in 25-35 chambering, also a takedown model. The wood on both was in poor condition, so new stocks were in order. Since both rifles sported 20-inch barrels, I considered them good prospects for restocking with full-length forearms.

In addition to the necessary woodwork, some minor metal work was required. The original forearms were relatively small and thin and the metal barrel studs were too short for the new wood—so new studs had to be machined, not a difficult task. Other than that, creating Mannlicher-style forearms for these M-99s was relatively simple.

Another lightweight varmint rifle in our family's assortment is Bobbie's custom 222. Years ago, when Remington introduced the Model 600 and then the 660, we had 660s in 243 for our daughter Susan's deer

Ruger's M77/22 with its fancy walnut Mannlicher stock is one of author's favorite plinking and small game rifles.
Bottom Left: This nice Missouri whitetail buck fell to author's 6.5x55 Swede.

and antelope rifle, and a 222 for son Jim's varmint gun. More years later, Remington reintroduced a similar version of that rifle called the Mohawk and, again, in 2003, re-reintroduced that rifle as the 613.

The Mohawk 600 was basically a cheaper 660. By the time it arrived on the scene, Bobbie was thinking about a varmint gun that was lighter and quieter than her 257. So, we picked up a Mohawk, had Claude turn the barrel to a smaller contour, polish and blue the barrel and action and do a few other cosmetics to it. I ordered a fancy Claro walnut Mannlicher semi-finished stock from Roberts Wood Products out of California *(we were still in Colorado at that time)* and set about putting the pieces together. It turned out to be a neat, trim little rifle for those shorter-range jackrabbit jaunts and varmint-calling trips.

One especially unique feature about this rifle is that Claude replaced the original dog leg-shaped bolt handle with a slightly curved handle with a knurled, hollowed-out knob. Our home was just a short distance from Estes Park where knifemaker T.J. Yancey lived and, since we had several of his hunting knives and knew the quality of his custom knife work, we asked for his help with this project. Actually, it was T.J.'s wife, Ann, on whom we called. Ann is quite an artist and, among other medium, does scrimshaw work on T.J.'s knife handles. We didn't have any ivory but Ann did a beautiful job of schrimshanding a red rose on simulated ivory which T.J. then mounted in the hollowed-out portion

of the bolt handle. After 30-odd years, it still holds its color and beauty.

Perhaps the second most popular Mannlicher-stocked rifle in our family is a 6.5x55mm Swedish Mauser. Claude had done all the metalwork on the rifle for me before we left Colorado, but nothing had been done about a stock. The barreled action had been relegated to a back corner of the vault. Hunting opportunities *(and time to use what opportunities there were)* weren't as numerous for me in Missouri, and my 257 met all my needs when opportunities did arise. About the time grandson Matt started getting ready for a deer rifle, the Swede was chosen for customizing.

A relatively plain walnut Fajen Mannlicher stock was fitted to the 18 1/2-inch barreled action—by Fred Wenig, of course—and it was cut to fit Matt's teenage frame. He practiced with that rifle until he was comfortable with it and could consistently place his shots inside a two-inch circle at 100 yards.

Matt's first deer was a nice 5-point buck at a distance of about 65 yards *(which I was able to video - a lifetime treasure)*. The next year, he took a heavy-beamed 10-pointer at about 85 yards, and the next it was a spike at about 60 yards. Now, at 19, Matt considers himself an accomplished deer hunter. He credits the handling characteristics of the Swede for his success and claims it as part of his grandpa-to-grandson inheritance.

One of the most recent additions to our long rifle/long wood battery is a Ruger M77/22. Ruger introduced this full-sized bolt-action 22 in two versions: a bare-barrel model and

an open-sighted model. I ordered barreled actions of each but it was the bare-barrel model that ended up with a Mannlicher stock; it just looks better without those iron sights. Besides, almost all of our family's rifles wear scopes since we don't often use rifles with open sights.

A nicely figured walnut stock was fitted to the 22, a Neidner steel buttplate and grip cap were added and a metal forend cap surrounds the muzzle of the 20-inch barrel. Wenig Gunstocks' craftsmen did the fitting and finishing and Darrel Smith, a genuine artist in creating unique checkering and carving patterns *(Wenig's checkering expert)*, cut a neat 22 lpi *(lines per inch)* pattern on the grip and forearm. A Leupold & Stevens 4x RF Compact scope was clamped in the Ruger rings to finalize the project. This full-sized 22 stands up well against all the other custom-stocked rifles in our family. It is a classy, man-sized 22.

As mentioned earlier, one of the main considerations in deciding about putting a Mannlicher stock on a rifle is barrel length. Almost any bolt- or single-shot action—and even some modern lever actions—will look good wearing a full-length stock, providing barrel length is in the 17 to 22-inch range. Most of today's manufacturers have several choices in their current catalogs and there are thousands of used guns available that would fill the bill.

Some prime candidates for Mannlicher stocks would be Ruger's M77 Ultra Light with its slim 20-inch barrel and USRAC's Model 70 Classic Compact, also with a slim 20-inch barrel. Remington's neat Model 7 with its 18 1/2-inch barrel would really look sharp wearing a Mannlicher-styled stock, too. In fact, Remington's custom department just happens to offer the Model 7 Custom MS rifle with a 20-inch barrel. It is a special order deal but comes with a full-length stock adorned with cut checkering and other extras. With over a dozen cartridges chambered in it, this is a first-class, ready-to-go Mannlicher.

Anschutz is another manufacturer that offers an out-of-the-box

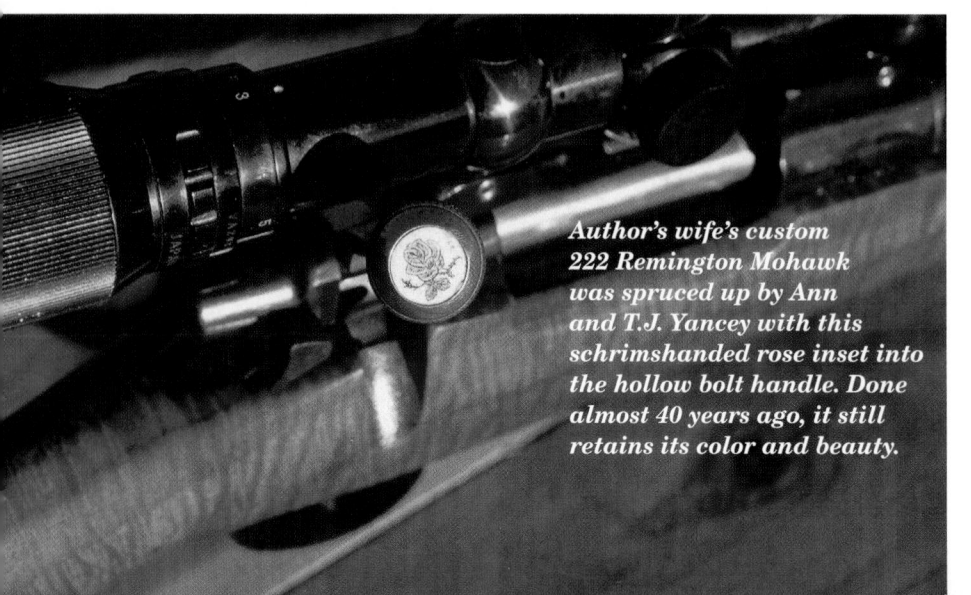

Author's wife's custom 222 Remington Mohawk was spruced up by Ann and T.J. Yancey with this schrimshanded rose inset into the hollow bolt handle. Done almost 40 years ago, it still retains its color and beauty.

Mannlicher-stocked rifle. Barrel length is a shy 20 inches and it wears open sights … but Anschutz' reputation for quality makes this a rifle to consider.

Browning's A Bolt II Short Action, even with its 22-inch barrel, would make another excellent choice. So would the A Bolt II Micro Hunter with its 20-inch barrel.

As mentioned earlier, Ruger offers its M77 RSI in their International carbine with 18 1/2–inch barrel. They also have other M77s: 77/22 Hornet, standard MKII, 77/44 and my favorite, the 77 Ultra Light, with barrel lengths from 18-1/2 to 20 inches. In addition, Ruger's 96/44 lever action would make an interesting Mannlicher project.

Another new model recently introduced by Ruger is made to order for a Mannlicher stock. Cataloged as the M77CR MKII, it sports a 16 1/2-inch barrel and is offered in five chamberings ranging from 223 to 308. During a recent visit to Wenig's plant, I saw my first sample of the Compact. An avid hunter with physical limitations had brought his 223 to Fred for, you guessed it, a Mannlicher stock. Looked like a toy, but is intended for serious hunting!

A high-dollar, factory-issued Mannlicher with a true European flavor, Steyr offers their Mannlicher SBS in a wide variety of chamberings. Pricey at the three grand mark, but Steyr's reputation for jeweler-like precision is well known.

A recent announcement by CZ USA stated that this firm was adding a Mannlicher stock to their full-sized 22 bolt action. They also offer two centerfire models with Mannlicher stocks, one of which is styled like the American classic while the other two follow the European trend.

Perhaps one of the highest compliments to the Mannlicher idea in recent years is that the Firearms Engravers and Gunmakers Guild created a masterpiece rifle for their #19 raffle project in 2003. It was a much-modified M98 Mauser that ended up as a 22 rimfire—with a Mannlicher stock!

Okay, so you agree with this idea and decide to add a Mannlicher-stocked rifle to your gun rack. The question is, if you don't choose one of the above-mentioned company's offerings, what do you do about the factory stock?

If you start with a new rifle for this project, you get the whole thing —lock, barrel and, of course, the stock. Some factory stocks are too nice to just discard. Several years ago, I had a standard Browning A-Bolt 257 Roberts with a stock that would rival many super fancy custom stocks. It would be a shame to replace a stock like that.

Ideally, for your Mannlicher project, you could find a barreled action somewhere and not have to deal with the problem of what to do with the factory stock. In years past, some manufacturers made barreled actions available—and that might still be a possibility. To my knowledge, Ruger is the only company that advertises their rifles as being available as barreled actions only. Ask your dealer to check it out for you.

Left: *Jim, author's then-12-year-old son, especially liked this Mann-licher-stocked G.I. 30 Carbine for plinking and jackrabbit jaunts.*
Middle: *Bobbie with her 257 and daughter Susan with her 243 at the end of a successful antelope hunt on eastern Colorado prairies. Susan bagged this nice buck, but mom and daughter posed together for this photo.*
Right: *A young* (much younger) *author in his pre-mustache days with a nice Colorado bobcat taken with his wife's 257 Roberts, the first Mannlicher in the family.*

<hr/>

If that option isn't possible–and if you're like me–you'll get the rifle you want, remove the factory stock *(putting in on a shelf to gather dust, probably)* and start from there. Nonsense? Maybe. Then, again, maybe not.

In a recent "Cooper's Corner" column in *GUNS & AMMO* magazine, the inimitable Col. Jeff Cooper expressed his opinion as to the best use of a Mannlicher-stocked rifle. According to the Colonel, anyone who has a Mannlicher-stocked rifle and is walking over rough ground should just grab the rifle by that slim muzzle end and use it as a walking stick. Well, Colonel, with all due respect for your experience and opinion *(most of which I agree with)*, when it comes to a custom stock, make mine Mannlicher.

A TALE OF
THREE
OUTDOORSMEN

by Tom Osborne

Below: A trio of classic Outdoorsman revolvers and contemporary ammunition repose on a reprint of a 1936 topo map, along with a World War I- vintage military compass. (Top to bottom: post-war 38/44, prewar 38/44, prewar K-22)

America's two oldest handgun makers have a rich tradition of assigning colorful names to many of their products. Over the years, the folks at Colt's Patent Firearms have brought us the "Lightning," "Thunderer" and "Woodsman" to cite a few examples. Smith & Wesson also applied descriptive sobriquets to a number of their handguns. Names like "Lady Smith," "Regulation Police" and "Combat Masterpiece" all suggest the purpose for which these firearms were intended, or the segment of the gun-buying public towards which they were being marketed. But of all the titles Smith & Wesson ascribed to their revolvers, the one that most captures my imagination is the "Outdoorsman." For me, the name evokes images of an independent, self-reliant individual––a man who is at home in the natural elements.

The term "Outdoorsman" was given to two separate Smith & Wesson handguns. One was a 22-caliber revolver with a 6-inch barrel, utilizing the medium size "Military & Police" or 'K' frame. The other was chambered in 38 Special and was built on the large "New Century" or 'N' frame, which was originally designed for the 44 Special cartridge. Standard barrel length for this gun was 6-1/2 inches. A more powerful 38 Special loading was developed for use in the 44 ('N' frame) guns and was termed the "38/44 S&W Special" cartridge, to distinguish it from the standard 38 Special round.

Both Outdoorsman revolvers were solid-frame "Hand Ejectors" with swing-out cylinders. Both were also equipped with adjustable target sights. Another trait they shared was that they were over-engineered for their chamberings. They were much more massive and rugged than any handgun Smith & Wesson had previously manufactured in either of these calibers.

Actually, the proper name for these guns has been a source of some confusion. The boxes in which both models were packaged were labeled "THE OUTDOORSMAN'S REVOLVER." Yet sales literature such as the 1938 Smith & Wesson catalog listed the larger-framed handgun as "the 38/44 Outdoorsman." Making matters even more confusing, in the first sentence of the catalog narrative the gun is referred to as the "OUTDOORSMAN'S Revolver." Regardless of which term was most correct, both firearms earned well-deserved reputations for accuracy, sturdiness and dependability.

Both models were introduced to the American public while the Nation was in the grip of the Great Depression. The first K-22 Outdoorsman revolvers were completed in late January of 1931. The first of the 38/44 Outdoorsman revolvers followed in November of the same year. The modest wages paid to factory workers of that era allowed an amount of hand labor which would be cost-prohibitive today. The guns exhibited fine polishing and high luster bluing as well as extensive hand fitting of parts. Selecting from an assortment of sideplates, fitters matched them to frames so closely that the seams were nearly invisible. Company promotional material

Unconventional perhaps, but an old tree stump can make a very satisfactory platform for a Ransom Rest. Here the author prepares to touch off a round with his prewar 38/44 Outdoorsman.

A gorgeous mountain meadow—and not a bad- looking 25-yard group from the prewar 38/44 Outdoorsman.

proclaimed there was no stoning of internal components which might compromise their case-hardened surfaces. Triggers, hammers and other moving parts were mated to each other by trial and error until the desired fit was achieved. As a result, the guns were noted for their smooth double-action cycling and crisp single-action trigger pull.

The 38/44 Outdoorsman

Pre-World War II Smith & Wesson Hand Ejectors employed what later came to be referred to as a "long" action. When the trigger was pulled double action, the take-up had a distinctive smoothness that was praised by such noted handgunning authorities as Montana trick shot artist Ed McGivern and Idaho cowpuncher Elmer Keith. In the early 1930s both McGivern and Keith experimented extensively with the 38/44 Outdoorsman as a long-range handgun. They both found that this finely-made revolver, paired with the heavily fortified but inherently accurate 38/44 Special round, was well-suited for perforating distant targets.

The 1932 edition of *Burning Powder*, a booklet edited by Major Douglas B. Wesson, contained an article by Ed McGivern in which he discussed the new 38/44 Outdoorsman.

McGivern wrote: "The new 38/44 S & W Outdoorsman revolver, with the new high speed and high velocity cartridges, opens up the field of long range revolver work with possible results that are very surprising. This particular gun, with 6 1/2-inch barrel, was the greatest and most pleasant surprise I have had since the beginning of my revolver shooting experience. The possibilities at 300 yards are surprising; at 500 yards they are more than intensely interesting, and quite successful. This new gun is, in my opinion, the finest gun ever turned out by anybody at any time."

Ed McGivern tested an Outdoorsman that had been fitted with a telescopic rifle sight by the Lyman Gunsight Company. This had to be one of the earliest 'scoped handguns ever. On page 413 of McGivern's book *Fast and Fancy Revolver Shooting* is a photo of a man-size silhouette target that he hit six out of six times at a distance of 300 yards, using his scope-sighted Outdoorsman and factory metal case 38/44 ammunition. However, McGivern eventually abandoned the Outdoorsman for long-range shooting in favor of the 357 Magnum revolver, which Smith & Wesson introduced in 1935.

In contrast, Elmer Keith found the 38/44 Outdoorsman superior

to the 357 for long-range work, at least when factory ammunition was used. In his classic treatise *Sixguns*, Keith wrote about field-testing the then-new 357 on jackrabbits. Although he achieved hits on rabbits as far away as 180 yards with the magnum, he found that: "the factory 357 load was not as accurate beyond 125 yards as our older Smith & Wesson Outdoorsman with a 6 1/2-inch barrel and either the Remington factory 38/44 load or our handload in the same cases." The handload Keith favored in the big 38 consisted of 13-1/2 grains of 2400 behind a 160-grain hollowpoint semi-wadcutter of his own design. Elmer also considered the 38/44 to be fully the equal of his 44 Special loads for long-range accuracy, but he allowed the 44 did kick up more dirt, making bullet strikes easier to see.

In the April, 1932 issue of *American Rifleman* magazine, W. D. Frazer reviewed the new 38/44 Outdoorsman. Characterizing the Outdoorsman as "a target revolver in every sense of the word," Frazer described a long-range test of the handgun and factory 38/44 Special ammunition. After sighting in, 20 rounds were fired at a police silhouette target some 200 yards away. Bracing his back against a car and holding the revolver in both hands, with forearms supported between his knees, the shooter achieved 17 hits on the distant target.

Development of the 38/44 S&W Special

Details surrounding the origin of the 38/44 S&W Special round have become blurred with the passage of time. The popular version holds that law enforcement agencies during the Prohibition era found that no commercial revolver round was effective against the "bullet-proof" vests worn by some criminals of the day. Nor could the available revolver ammunition be depended upon to penetrate the heavier body metal of newer automobiles. The only handgun round possessing those capabilities was the 38 Super cartridge, which propelled a 130-

grain jacketed bullet at a published velocity of 1300 feet per second. The only handgun chambered for the 38 Super was Colt's semi-auto Government Model. As the story goes, Smith & Wesson realized they did not have a product to compete with their rival and set out to correct the situation.

The 38 S&W Special cartridge was developed in 1899 as a blackpowder round. However, by the early 1900s, the ammunition factories had largely transitioned from blackpowder to smokeless powders. This left the 38 Special case with a much greater internal capacity than was needed for the more efficient smokeless propellant. With all this extra space, the 38 Special had the potential for greater power than it originally possessed.

Walter Roper's book *Experiments of a Handgunner* contains a letter from Major D. B. Wesson in which he recounted the development of the 38/44 S&W Special round. Major Wesson wrote: "From the time I was a kid, my one big wish was that someday I might see S&W build the finest, most powerful revolver ever made. Finally things broke so that I was really able to really think of making my dream revolver. To provide a big 38 caliber revolver, we (I was then one of the firm) had fitted a cylinder and barrel to our Military model, chambered for the 38 Special cartridge. One day Phil Sharpe brought me some high-speed handloads he had found satisfactory. After much experimenting and testing, a new cartridge, the S&W 38/44 was produced and a medium-caliber revolver, more powerful than anything made before, was a fact." Phil Sharpe was a widely recognized authority on firearms and ammunition, with an extensive knowledge of ballistics. He was an inveterate experimenter and author of *The Complete Guide to Handloading*, the definitive text

of that time on the subject of making your own ammunition.

The experimenting and testing referred to by Major Wesson was a collaborative effort between Smith & Wesson and Remington-U.M.C. In the late 1920s, the two companies worked together at developing a more potent 38 Special ammunition to satisfy the needs of law enforcement. The result was the 38/44 S&W Special cartridge, which propelled a 158-grain lead, or "metalpoint" bullet of the same weight, at an advertised velocity of 1125 fps. Compared to the standard 38 Special, which fired a 158-grain slug at a listed speed of 847 fps, the new round delivered about half-again the energy of the regular loading. Although dimensionally identical to the original 38 Special, the 38/44 Special cartridge was meant for use in big-frame revolvers such as the Outdoorsman, and a fixed-sight counterpart of the Outdoorsman called the 38/44 "Heavy Duty." With a standard barrel length of 5 inches, the rugged Heavy Duty was ideally suited for the demands of uniformed police work.

The K-22 Outdoorsman

Until the K-22 Outdoorsman was introduced, Smith & Wesson's only 22-caliber revolver having adjustable sights as a standard feature was their 22/32 target model, which was built on the small "I" frame. The 22/32 was accurate and had certainly won its share of competitions. However, the factory saw a potential market for a heavier, 6-inch-barreled 22 target revolver built on the M&P, or 'K' frame. They reasoned such a gun would be the perfect companion

piece to their 38 M&P target revolver, duplicating the feel and handling qualities of that gun. Additionally, in 1930 Remington introduced their "Hi-Speed" 22 rimfire ammunition. Along with higher velocity, the new 22 round also generated increased pressure. The chambers of the 22/32 revolver were not recessed and did not support the rim of the cartridge. With standard velocity ammunition this was of little concern, but with the "Hi-Speed" 22 ammunition, shooters faced the risk that the unsupported rim might rupture. The K-22 Outdoorsman featured recessed chambers which surrounded and supported the rim of the ammunition, greatly reducing the hazard of a rupture.

Praised as a specimen of precision engineering, the K-22 Outdoorsman was well-received by such firearms experts as Walter Roper. In his book *Pistol and Revolver Shooting*, Roper offered this assessment of the gun: "Like all S & W guns, the K-22 is a beautiful example of fine gunmaking, the action being watch-like in workmanship and a delight to anyone who appreciates quality."

The K-22 Outdoorsman proved to be extremely accurate with both standard and high velocity ammunition. The Novice Pistol Match of the 1931 U.S. Revolver Association National indoor competition was won by a shooter using a K-22 Outdoorsman. The winner was shooting against competitors armed with single-shot target pistols, which dominated the rimfire events of the day. This was the first time in the history of the organization that a revolver won a national competition against the highly specialized single-shot pistols.

The prewar 38/44 shot well with factory wadcutters at 25 yards.

Extreme durability was another characteristic of the K-22 Outdoorsman. Ed McGivern fired over 200,000 rounds through a K-22 Outdoorsman he owned. At that point McGivern sent the gun back to the factory for adjustments. There the revolver was clamped into a machine rest and test-fired with several cylinders-full of ammunition before any work was done on it. Even with all the use the gun had seen, it still produced ragged one-hole groups at 20 yards. After the adjustments were made, the Outdoorsman was again clamped into the machine rest and several more groups were fired. The results of this "before & after" test, as shown on page 166 of *Fast and Fancy Revolver Shooting*, are striking. I was unable to see any appreciable difference between the two sets of groups; both are remarkably small. This is especially impressive in view of the fact that McGivern did the majority of his shooting double-action, which causes greater stress and wear on moving parts than does single-action fire.

Personal Observations

Handguns have been a part of my life longer than I sometimes care to think about. I have owned and used a multitude of them since getting my first revolver at the age of 16. Throughout my 31 years in law enforcement, a sidearm of some type has been a regular part of my working attire. For the past 28 years I have also served as a firearms instructor for the major Southwestern department where I work. My years of handgunning have fostered a real admiration for the quality, durability and accuracy of Smith & Wesson's hand ejectors. The basic design has been around for over 100 years. There have been changes to internal parts and improvements in metallurgy, but their swing-out cylinder revolvers are still being manufactured in a variety of calibers and configurations and they still work as well as they ever did.

It is no coincidence that the majority of the handguns I have owned over the past 40 years have been Smith & Wessons, as I believe they produce a superior product. For the first 18 years of my law enforcement career I carried a 357 Magnum S&W Model 66 revolver. Even after the department for which I worked authorized the optional carry of high-capacity semi-autos, I stubbornly continued to wear that Model 66. It shot well, usually scoring "expert" at range qualification and I didn't feel particularly handicapped by its ammunition capacity. I rationalized that if I couldn't resolve matters with the first six rounds, I might as well pack up and go home. Bravado perhaps, but that gun inspired confidence and, in an armed confrontation, confidence is critical. That Model 66 served me well, but it was finally retired from duty when my department mandated the switch from revolvers to semi-autos. I never did have to test my theory about the first six rounds.

Eventually my interest in S&W hand ejectors focused on those made prior to World War II. This period has sometimes been termed the "golden age" of production, because labor was cheap, and quality was high. Also from a personal standpoint, those guns have a historical "romance" about them that I find intriguing. In pursuit of that interest, I set out to assemble a collection of prewar hand ejectors, with the ultimate goal of having a representative example of each model and caliber made by Smith & Wesson prior to the end of World War II. Over time I have been fortunate enough to acquire some nice prewar specimens. Among them are an early 38/44 Outdoorsman and a K-22 Outdoorsman, both in nearly new condition.

Part of the appeal of collecting old guns is in considering the role a firearm, or its contemporaries, might have played in history. As I examine a vintage piece, I wonder: When was it made, who might have owned it and what kind of use might it have seen? In the case of Smith & Wesson revolvers, the first question (and sometimes the second) can be answered by sending an inquiry to the factory. For a fee (presently $30.00), S&W Historian Roy Jinks will research the chronology of a piece. The requested information is documented under the old Smith & Wesson letterhead and includes a detailed outline of the model's history, the total number of that model manufactured, as well as the shipping date and destination of the particular gun in question.

Research on my 38/44 Outdoorsman revealed that it was shipped from the factory on December 31, 1931 and sent to one of their distributors in Chicago. According to S&W Factory records, the order to produce the first 500 38/44 Outdoorsman revolvers was issued by Harold Wesson on September 18, 1931 and the revolver was introduced to the public on November 21st of that year. Although the letter from Jinks didn't specifically address the subject, I strongly suspect that my 38/44 was part of that first lot of 500 revolvers. Recently I posed that very question to him at the annual Smith & Wesson Collector's Association meeting. He also was of the opinion that my 38/44 Outdoorsman probably was among the first 500 manufactured. A total of 4,761 38/44 Outdoorsman revolvers were produced over the next ten years, before Smith & Wesson discontinued commercial manufacture to concentrate on wartime production.

The K-22 Outdoorsman in my collection was shipped on June 28, 1934 to a distributor in Philadelphia. As a point of interest, Smith & Wesson regards the date of shipment from the factory as the "birthday" of their firearms. A particular gun might languish in a box at the factory for an extended period, but "life" doesn't officially begin for it until the day it is shipped. According to Roy Jinks' book *History of Smith & Wesson*, a total of 17,117 K-22 Outdoorsman revolvers were produced between 1931 and 1940.

Although my two prewar Outdoorsman revolvers are over 70 years old and have obviously seen use, they are both still in excellent condition, with 98 percent of their original bluing. They show no significant wear, other than a light "turning ring" around the cylinders. Fit and finish of both revolvers is impressive. They are sterling examples of an era when mass production methods and precise hand-fitting were combined to create high-quality firearms.

The Post-War Outdoorsman

Since the title of this article is "A Tale of Three Outdoorsmen," this seems an appropriate time to introduce the third character of this cast. This one is not a prewar hand ejector. When Smith & Wesson resumed commercial production after World War II, the first 38/44 Outdoorsman revolvers they made combined the prewar "long" action with a ribbed barrel, topped by their new micrometer sights. One deficiency of prewar target model 'Smiths was the design of the rear sight. Windage adjustments were made by turning two tiny opposing screws. This rather delicate arrangement lacked precision and was prone to loosen, which did nothing to help accuracy. With the development of the new micrometer sight, Smith & Wesson corrected this problem. It could be argued that the post-war, transitional 38/44 Outdoorsman incorporated all of the most desirable features (long action, micrometer sights and the recently introduced "magna" grips) into one package. A total of 2,326 post-war, transitional models were manufactured before the existing supply of parts was used up. Once the supply of prewar parts was exhausted, the factory began producing the 38/44 Outdoorsman with the modern "short" action.

I first saw this transitional model at a gun show some 23 years ago. At the time, I was supporting my family on a patrolman's income and the $315.00 the seller was asking was beyond my immediate means. I took his business card and told him that when I saved up the money, I would give him a call. In addition to being a homemaker, my wife also contributed to the household income with part-time work, so it was only fair that a purchase of that magnitude be a mutual decision. Among my blessings I am fortunate to count an understanding, supportive spouse. Upon hearing about this latest object of my desire, she agreed that we could save the money without undue hardship on the family budget.

A few weeks later, I phoned the seller to tell him I could meet his price. He expressed his regrets as

The transitional, post-war 38/44 Outdoorsman (bottom) combined the desirable prewar "long" action with the new micrometer sights, ribbed barrel and more comfortable "magna" stocks.

he informed me I was too late, he had recently sold the Outdoorsman. Although disappointed, I tried to act philosophical when I told my better half about this turn of events. My disappointment was short-lived, however, as she presented me with the revolver, which she had secretly purchased because she was worried someone else might buy it first.

Upon writing to the factory for historical information on that Outdoorsman, I learned that it started life in 1947, the same year I did. At one time or another, many of us have probably thought: "If I could keep just one of my guns, which one would it be?" In my case, there is no doubt, this one is the keeper. I have other guns that are worth more money, but none of them have the personal value that this fine Smith & Wesson holds for me.

For a number of years I used that post-war Outdoorsman recreationally. It shot well, the weight of the gun contributing to its steadiness in the hand. While I didn't try to wring "magnum" performance out of it, I did shoot heavier handloads in it than I used in my K-frame 38s. Eventually, because guns like this became more sought after by collectors and their values rose, I retired that 38/44. The revolver still looks great, locks up tight and the bore is spotless. That Outdoorsman and I may be the same age, but I

have to admit it has withstood the ravages of time better than I have.

There you have my trio of Outdoorsmen, a prewar 38/44, a prewar K-22 and an early post-war 38/44. The two older guns have been around for over 70 years and the newer one is rapidly approaching 60, but all three are in excellent condition.

The Testing Process

Some time ago, I acquired a full box of 1930s-vintage Remington 38/44 Special, metalpoint ammunition. The box and the ammo were both in nice shape and would likely fetch a tidy sum from a collector. But I was curious. Several questions came to mind, including: How well does factory ammunition retain its potency over 70-plus years? Was factory ammo as accurate in the prewar Outdoorsman as claimed? And finally, did the metalpoint ammunition have the penetration power proclaimed by the manufacturer? Since I had both the gun and the ammo, some empirical testing seemed in order. A purist collector would undoubtedly cringe at the thought of shooting up rare ammunition in a pristine gun just to satisfy an idle curiosity, but I prefer to think of it as 'research to expand the sum of human knowledge.'

Having a Ransom Rest for accuracy testing and a chronograph to measure velocity, I was set. About this time it occurred to me that as long as I was going to violate the virtue of the 38/44, I might just as well include the K-22 in my "research" project. I was also curious to know how accurate the rimfire Outdoorsman might prove to be. In addition to the vintage 38/44 ammunition, I decided to purchase some modern 38 Special target ammo, along with some target-quality 22 Long Rifle ammunition, to measure the accuracy of both prewar revolvers.

Now I have to admit it had been a while since I last bought commercial centerfire handgun ammunition, as I normally use my own handloads for recreational shooting. But I wasn't prepared for what I encountered. Checking for factory-loaded 38 Special wadcutters with five local gun shops, only one had any in stock. That store had a single box of Winchester-Western Super Match, which had been ordered by mistake. Apparently no one shoots 38 wadcutters anymore, at least not in this part of the country. My search for target-quality 22 ammunition proved a little more successful and I bought a box each of CCI Pistol Match, Federal Gold Medal Target and Remington Club Extra.

A camping trip to the Coconino National Forest afforded a perfect opportunity for the accuracy trials. The stately Ponderosa pines of the northern Arizona mountains create a most appropriate setting for testing "Outdoorsman" revolvers. Fortuitously, the remote meadow we favor for our campsite is dotted with large tree stumps, remnants of a bygone logging era. Despite their age, some of these stumps are still quite sound. Experience has taught me that a tough old stump can make an entirely suitable platform upon which to mount a Ransom Rest. Unconventional as it may seem, this "stump shooting" method works very well. With the Ransom Rest secured to a sturdy plywood base, a half-dozen 5-inch lag bolts will anchor the device solidly against the recoil of any handgun.

After clamping the prewar 38/44 into the Ransom Rest, a couple of cylinders full of ammunition were run through it, to settle it into the grip inserts. The target stand was then placed a measured 25 yards out and the testing commenced. Admittedly, firing only one brand of 38 target ammunition hardly constitutes a thorough trial, but the big Outdoorsman acquitted itself well. Six test groups were fired, using all chambers. The best of them clustered under an inch center-to-center, with the overall average for all groups fired calculated at 1.289 inches.

Upon completion of the wadcutter testing, the bore of the big 38 was cleaned with several passes of a dry wire brush. The gun was then loaded with a cylinder-full of the vintage 38/44 metalpoint ammunition. With considerable anticipation, I depressed the trigger on the first round. However, when the hammer fell the only sound heard was the "thunk" of the firing pin striking a dead primer. The second round was a repeat of the first. Then, at the third round, came the report of the stoutly-loaded 38. The process was continued, with only about half of the rounds igniting. Finally after running thirteen rounds through the Outdoorsman, I had six holes in the target. This "group" measured 2-3/4 inches center-to-center. Obviously, the past 70-plus years had not been kind to the old ammunition. In view of the ammo's erratic performance, I scrapped my plan to chronograph the 38/44 rounds.

I do not believe that the single group I shot truly represents the accuracy this 38/44 S&W Special ammunition was originally capable of delivering. If Elmer Keith said he was able to obtain minute-of-jackrabbit precision beyond 125 yards using the big Outdoorsman and factory loads, I am not about to dispute his claim based on the half-dozen rounds I fired.

Accuracy testing was not conducted with the circa-1947 38/44 Outdoorsman, as I already had a good working knowledge of its capabilities and my supply of factory wadcutters was exhausted. That post-war Outdoorsman will consistently put six rounds of its favorite handload inside an inch and a half at 25 yards. I believe that is all one could reasonably ask.

Changing out the grip inserts in the Ransom Rest, the K-22 Outdoorsman was next clamped in for accuracy testing. This revolver demonstrated some definite preferences in brands of 22 target ammo. The best results were obtained using CCI's Pistol Match, which yielded 3/4-inch groups at 25 yards.

The Ransom Rest tests of both prewar Outdoorsman revolvers proved to my satisfaction that the accuracy claims made by Smith & Wesson and contemporary gun writers were not all hyperbole. The guns did not possess any mystical abilities, but they did deliver very respectable results. To be sure, I have some more modern handguns which will equal, or exceed the accuracy of these fine old firearms, but none that exude the sense of adventure these Outdoorsman revolvers hold for me.

While probably not very scientific by today's standards, for many years the test employed by manufacturers to measure the penetrating power of handgun ammunition was the number of 7/8-inch thick, soft pine boards a bullet would pass through. Page 50 of the 1938 Smith & Wesson catalog contains a ballistic table of the factory rounds for which S&W handguns were chambered. This table lists muzzle velocity of the 38/44 S&W Special as 1125 fps and muzzle energy as 444 fpe. According to the ballistic table, penetration of the round was 12 pine boards, 7/8-inch thick.

An obvious variable in using pine boards as a test medium is finding boards of consistent density for valid comparative testing. Also today's dimensional pine boards measure a nominal 3/4-inch thick, as opposed to the 7/8-inch thickness used by the ammunition makers. Despite these minor technicalities, I elected to conduct my own penetration test of the 38/44 metalpoint round. The ballistic table in the 1938 S&W catalog indicates the pine boards in their tests were spaced 7/8 of an inch apart. Since I would be using 3/4-inch boards, it seemed reasonable to use 3/4-inch spacing.

Accordingly, I built a wooden baffle box that allowed the boards to be replaced after each shot. The post-war Outdoorsman was drafted for the penetration test. Firing from less than one foot distance, the metalpoint bullet cleanly punched through 8 boards, breaking them in the process. The bullet dented the 9th board and was recovered un-deformed at the bottom of the box. With all the scientific fervor of a modern-day Isaac Newton, I replaced the damaged boards and the test was repeated. The results were the same. Maximum penetration was 8 boards and other than rifling marks, the bullet was undamaged.

In addition to the recovered bullets, I also pulled the bullets from some of the faulty 38/44 rounds. Unlike modern jacketed handgun bullets which typically have gilding material to the base of the projectile, the "metalpoint" of the 38/44 covers only the exposed portion of the bullet. The bullet's shank is either pure lead or a very soft alloy, with a single, narrow lube groove. Bullet diameter measured exactly .357-inch, using a micrometer. Weighing several of the slugs, they averaged 156.6 grains, with a deviation of +/- .3 grain. The powder charges were also weighed, averaging 7 grains of a disc-type propellant. Visually comparing the powder to two that were available in the 1930s and are still around today, the flakes were smaller than Unique and larger than 2400. A fired case was cross-sectioned to examine its construction. The cases are of solid head design, and other than lacking the shallow rebate found just above the rim on cases of current manufacture, the 38/44 cases appear very similar to modern 38 Specials.

At the conclusion of the tests, the revolvers were given a thorough cleaning. They suffered no harm from the shooting sessions and looked as good as before. A collector's reluctance to fire––or even cycle a rare, mint condition gun is certainly understandable. However, with guns that are in less than perfect condition, being able to use them as was intended only adds to the pleasure of ownership. This doesn't mean that I routinely shoot with my collectibles, but there is a certain satisfaction in knowing that I can. The informal tests I conducted with the Outdoorsman revolvers were both enjoyable and enlightening. The experience left me with an even greater appreciation for the quality

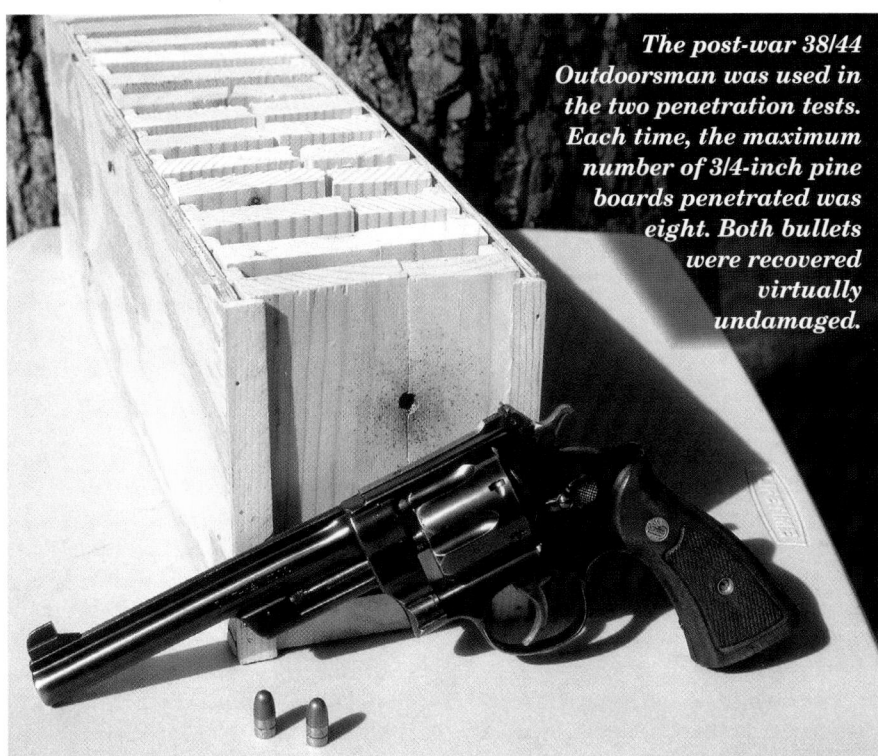

The post-war 38/44 Outdoorsman was used in the two penetration tests. Each time, the maximum number of 3/4-inch pine boards penetrated was eight. Both bullets were recovered virtually undamaged.

and craftsmanship of these handsome pieces of American handgun history.

Conclusion

Gun writers today usually regard the 38/44 Special and the companion Outdoorsman revolver as an evolutionary step in the creation of the 357 Magnum, which was introduced in 1935. It is generally accepted that the 357 Magnum was developed not only to give shooters the most powerful handgun of the time, but also out of concern that the high performance 38/44 Special cartridge might be used in old or small-frame 38 Special revolvers that were not designed to handle the pressure of the round. Despite this, I consider the 38/44 Outdoorsman an end in itself in terms of handgun development. The revolver was a magnificent example of American gunmaking and the 38/44 round achieved substantially more power than the standard 38 Special, while retaining all of its accuracy.

In addition to being a beautifully-crafted firearm, the K-22 Outdoorsman was significant because it legitimized the full-size 22 revolver as a sporting handgun. Use of the 22 revolver for target competition was diminishing, as semi-automatic 22 pistols gained

increasing acceptance among competitors. The semi-auto's advantage wasn't necessarily greater intrinsic accuracy, but they did allow the shooter to maintain a consistent grip on the gun from shot to shot. Firing a revolver in the single-action mode required the shooter to alter his grip each time the gun was cocked, creating a distinct handicap in timed and rapid fire. However, for casual shooting or small-game hunting, the K-frame 22 revolver proved to be an ideal sidearm.

Although Smith & Wesson continued to offer the 38-44 Outdoorsman when commercial production resumed following World War II, demand for the big 38 was fading. The gun-buying public now wanted the 357 Magnum. Revolvers like my post-war Outdoorsman found their niche with knowledgeable shooters who had no need for the roar and thunder of the 357, but who desired a supremely well-made, rugged and accurate 38 Special.

The Outdoorsman revolvers were state of the art firearms in their day and the craftsmanship that went into their manufacture was unexcelled by any other production handgun. This venerable trio of Outdoorsmen has definitely earned a permanent, prominent place in my gun collection. 🔘

THE GENESIS OF THE
LYMAN #48 SIGHT

by Jim Foral

The Lyman #48 on a Lee Enfield. (Lyman Archives)

Bob Kane, as editor of the popular monthly *OUTERS BOOK*, was given to making observations on sporting trends and topics and wordily advancing his analysis via his regular column. The "eye of the rifle" is how Kane, in 1908, appropriately considered the rifle sight. Our rifle—the inanimate but trusted, relied upon, befriended instrument by which we extend ourselves and our vision, has but one sense and no other. By proxy, the faculty of sight has been imparted to our rifle, but they can see no better than the aiming devices furnished them. It was during the Creedmoor era of the mid-1870s that the Remington Arms and Sharps Rifle companies, together with the usually victorious American competitor, proved the practicability of a tiny near-the-eye peephole at the thousand-yard target. On this famous and important range, the aperture rear sight became developed and refined into a condition of perfection previously unknown. To a lesser extent, the set-up was validated concurrently on the great buffalo killing plains. These precise Vernier sights were too delicate to withstand the rough usage incident to military service, or the harsh usage required of them on the Western frontier or Northwoods.

It was in 1878 that William Lyman came to the rescue with a strong, stiff and sturdy working gun sight employing the same proven optical principle that had made the target sight so favorable in certain limited circles. The sighting principle was promoted as if it were his private revelation from Above. This accomplished, the sight seemed to sell itself.

Circumstances forced a repositioning of the back sight from the rifle's tang to the rear end of its frame. When the rearward travel of the Model 1895 Winchester's bolt precluded safe and prudent use of a tang sight, Lyman obliged with the development of the #21, the firm's original receiver-mounted sight and the pattern for the Lyman line for far too long. In 1899, the Lyman people were ready with the goods. Owners of most Winchesters and Marlin models were thus given the option of the familiar Lyman tang or the new-fangled receiver sight. Going eyeball-to-eyepiece with either, they viewed their target through a hole.

In the *weest* years of the century just past, Lyman provided novel receiver sights for the earliest of bolt-action rifles. For the Mannlicher-Schoenauer, there was the ingenious swing-arm #22 of 1909. The hinged-top #25 was cleverly designed for the Winchester-Lee repeater. The #35 was for captured, surplus and commercial Mausers. Owners of Krags, Remington-Lees, and later Springfields, had to settle for the Lyman #33, an essentially compacted #21, modified to better fit bolt actions. The common denominator of the sub-species of the #21 was elevations arrived at by the WAG formula, and the trademark friction thumb lever lock.

The nineteenth century rifleman of the cap-and-ball era settled a low front bead in a shallow U-notch, pulled his trigger and hoped for the best. In the main, this person was quite contented to hit the barn door.

The more complex turn-of-the-century military marksman, in contrast, was possessed of loftier ambitions. With the fullest

The #48C receiver sight fit the '03 Springfield, and the M1922 M-1 and M-2 as well. (Lyman Archives)

expectation of hitting it, he centered the screw-head fastening the hinge to the barn door. His 1903 Springfield and the arsenal cartridges were certainly up to the task; the rear sight, less so. And it was for this sharpshooter that the receiver sight couldn't evolve quickly enough. The rudimentary Krag and Springfield #33 receiver sights Lyman handed the shooters were the basis from which to improve upon. Most shooters agreed that the #33 had a laundry list of faults. The criticisms lodged against the #33 did not represent the peevish rantings of the occasional crackpot here and there. The repeated venting was rather the direction of attention to a general and valid dissatisfaction with a purportedly state-of-the-art, but seriously flawed, article. Secondarily, it was a plea for improvement.

To begin with, the coarse and few graduated marks gashed onto the elevation scale were inexact guidelines only; if they agreed for a particular factory cartridge, they did so either accidentally or providentially. One citizen, complaining for the masses, lamented there was but a one and a half factory notch variation between the 140- and 300-yard range. Early Lyman catalogs intimated that supplemental, more meaningful lines scratched onto the frame of the sight might be necessary. A precise and thorough adjustment of the #33

required patience and diligence—plus an investment that was range time and ammunition-intensive. Windage was friction-adjustable via trial and error. The aperture slide was driven to and fro in its base to center or align the peephole. About 1902, the #34 sight, a #33 with screw-adjustable windage, was introduced.

Another weakness of the #33 was its pointer, which clicked into the generous depressions impersonating as graduations. The pointer often (E.C. Crossman wrote "about half the time") failed to mate with the depression and hold firmly, allowing movement in the slide. Unavoidably, a certain amount of play developed with use. This slackness was not estimated, or expressed in thousandths of an

The Krag Sight Micrometer; the device that inspired the micrometer-adjustable receiver sight in the mind's eye of Townsend Whelen. (Catalog of Stevens-Pope Specialties ca 1902-03, courtesy Rudi Prusok & AS-SRA Library)

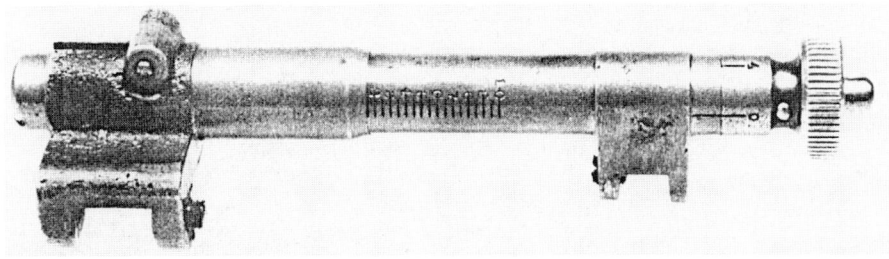

Lyman sights for ever.
Yours faithfully,
S. Stuart White
Dunedin, New Zealand

Send for   Catalogue.
The Lyman Gun Sight Corp., Middlefield, Conn.

Stewart Edward White did not pick up the Lyman banner suddenly in 1910 to lend support to friend E. C. Crossman's cause. Here he is in June 1907, loyally proclaiming "Lyman Sights Forever". (National Sportsman, June 1907)

inch, but in sixty-fourths. The "no good" pointer was either replaced periodically or a sturdier expedient was filed out of sturdier material. One hunter recorded that he's ruled lines on a paper scale to match his Springfield's particular elevations, pasted it over the factory marks, and weatherproofed the improvement with shellac.

Stuart Edward White, the well-traveled novelist and distinguished magazine contributor, was a long-time user and vocal promoter of Lyman sights. Close personal friend and fellow Los Angeles Rifle and Revolver Club member/officer E.C. Crossman described his colleague as an "authority on all things pertaining to life outdoors." Early in 1910, White succinctly nut-shelled the failings of the #33/#34, and advanced his

recommendation for improvement when he wrote: "the Lyman rear is at the right direction from the eye, but it is mighty hard to set and keep set. A micrometer arrangement with a milled head would help a heap and I should think the Lyman people would see that it is to their advantage to put it out in that shape."

Edward C. Crossman was one of the best-informed gun writers of the twentieth century. An enormously knowledgeable and prolific writer, his byline was far-flung and seemingly unavoidable. To be unnecessarily caustic was his nature, and this distanced him from the affections of many, but the opinions and evaluations of this foremost authority commanded the respect of his countless readers. Inside the sporting hardware community, Crossman savored his reputation as the person to please. The up or down of Crossman's thumb was as fateful to the fortunes of manufacturers as the same digital gesture which indicated the prospects of gladiators and Christian lion fodder at the Roman coliseums.

When, in about 1904, Lyman decided to market a satisfactory receiver sight for the 1903 Springfield rifle, there was evidently no studied or painstaking aim taken at the betterment of status quo. What the consumer—the increasingly sophisticated shooter, hunter, and military marksman—was given was the basic #33, about-faced to mount on the right side of the Model 1903. Crossman reacted with a typically disparaging assessment, recorded in a period *Arms and the Man* where he opined "...it resembles something you designed and I made with a sledge hammer and a cold chisel."

Throughout his career, Lt. Townsend Whelen was a wellspring of ideas concerning the refinement of sporting implements, which were unselfishly shared with his vast readership as they sprang to his mind and ripened. Generally, Whelen's conception blossomed into reality, whether through a reader following and fashioning his example or an enterprising commercial establishment appropriating the

inspiration. His occasional inkling, sketch, or diagram of a proposed improvement wasn't a wave of his magic wand, but it often turned out that way. His betterment of canvas articles associated with camping ran the gamut from haversacks to tentage. More satisfactory than the government-issue rifle sling was Whelen's sling incorporating a quickly-fashioned arm loop for steadier prone and offhand holding. Leather lacings—the Lieutenant's idea—substituted for the stock-marring brass rivets. When E.C. Crossman introduced his readers to the Whelen sling, it became the adopted standard almost at once.

Whelen embraced the general modernization of sporting rifle stock architecture as a pet project. The ill-fitting, mass-produced factory stocks followed a century-old pattern with their excessive drop at comb and heel, together with an overly narrow fore-stock and butt. After World War I, he wrote endlessly of the problem and offered his dimensional remedy. The cause made instant headway; major arms makers saw the light and

New LYMAN REAR
SIGHT for MAUSER Rifle
(PATENTED)

No. 35   Price $7.00

Very accurate, and easily adjusted. A specially constructed base, renders it easily attached to bolt stop. When on rifle, there is nothing to interfere with loading from clips. Slightly elevating slide, it is easily turned to one side, allowing removal of bolt.
Send for our 96-page Catalogue

The Lyman Gun Sight Corporation
Middlefield, Conn.

This is how the slide graduations on the #35 looked after Crossman told Lyman how it should be done, and then showed them. (Lyman 1935 catalog)

stepped into the twentieth century. A number of factory model stocks were modified to the officer's prescription, the revamped Remington Model 30S being the most notable example.

An Army-wide, nationally recognized authority on ballistic matters, Whelen dabbled continuously with powder, bullet and theory. A pioneer handloader, he individually was considered the infallible source of loading data. His once-famous low velocity, cast-bulleted 30-caliber small game load has a small following yet. Interspersed with his material contributions were tips on the attainment of comfort in the woods, general camp management, and advice on open fire cookery.

Significantly, Whelen refused to badger or belittle. Courteously explaining his recommendation while pinpointing existing shortcomings was much more his style.

In 1903, Whelen obtained a Pope micrometer sight adjuster and used it to minutely move the sight bar on his competition Krag rifle. During the process, he wondered to himself why a sight could not be manufactured with the micrometer adjustment incorporated into the device. That same year he publicized this mental rambling.

In a round-about way, a 1910 pursuit of Crossman's figured foundationally in a new Lyman sight. During the fall of 1909, Bob Kane planted a mental seed in the head of Mr. Crossman, where it germinated, took root, developed and, about a year later, bore fruit. Kane suggested that the Springfield army rifle had within it the makings of a crackerjack sporting rifle, and that a stock along the lines of the imported sporting Mauser, together with some easily-seen cosmetic refinements, would allow a functional beauty to emerge. A plan was hatched in Los Angeles to fabricate five sporting Springfields, the first of which Stuart Edward White carried on a much-celebrated safari in 1911. Crossman spearheaded the project as a personal mission and devoted himself to the task of design. Execution was the duty of all-around local gunsmith Ludwig Wundhammer,

TWO VIEWS OF THE NEW LYMAN COMBINATION REAR SIGHT (MICROMETER ADJUSTMENT)*

who artfully stocked and finished each of the rifles. "The Metamorphosis of the New Springfield," Crossman's didactic three-part epistle published in *Outers Book* in the winter of 1910-11, made clear the route taken and kept the public abreast of progress. Just as importantly, the series promoted a yearning for a like gun and sparked emulation. The undertaking remains historically significant from the standpoint that it provided, directly or indirectly, the inspiration and impetus for each of the many thousands of converted Springfields during the next forty years.

The rawest ingredients—the necessary component Springfield parts—had to be procured from the Adjutant General of California. Adequately long stock blanks of a befitting grade were to be located and obtained. The stocks would follow a general pattern, but five different physiques requiring individual painstaking must be successfully dealt with. Buttplates, sling swivel fasteners and other oddments of fittings needed to be selected and gathered. Incidental but important details were pored over as they were encountered. In due course, it came time to decide upon sights. Selection was limited almost entirely to the Lyman #34, though it abounded in defects. For want of anything better, it was selected unanimously and by default, was mounted on each of the rifles. At the time, it was lamented that these special rifles

It was only Whelen's fingers in this Lyman pie. Here we have the Lyman tang-mounted #103 for lever-action and single-shot rifles. We can thank Whelen alone for this one. (Outers Book, June 1915)

Pre-production #48 mounted on a sporting Springfield once owned by one of the agitators of the sight, and now in the collection of an anonymous someone.

⚜ ● ⚜ ● ⚜ ● ⚜ ● ⚜ ● ⚜

deserved a better sight than the current Lyman for the Springfield. In Connecticut, meanwhile, such an item was already in the works.

During mid-1910, a receiver sight improvement matured in the mind's

The #33/34 system worked nicely unless the operator needed more than imprecision. Springfield owners were forced to make do for a few years with the right-side-mounted #34 until the perfect receiver sight came down the pike in 1911. (National Sportsman, October 1909)

❊❊❊❊❊❊

The first magazine advertisement introducing the new Lyman #48. (Hunter-Trader-Trapper, November 1911)

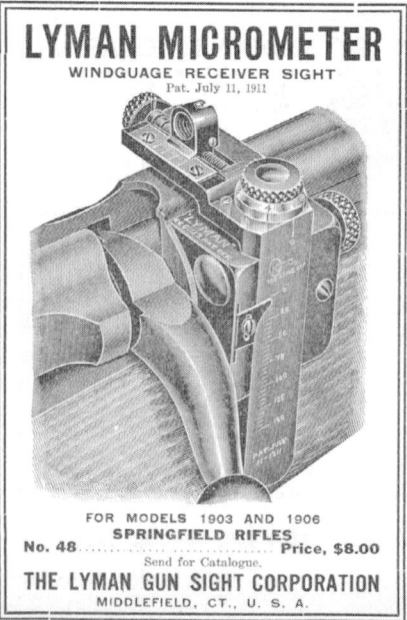

eye of the rifle project's guiding force. Crossman took action and applied to Lyman for a #34 slide, *sans* the offending notches. In their place were lines neatly graduated into 1/50-inch parts. The shallow lines were not prominent and did not contrast with the white steel of the slide, and were thus hard to read, making even careful pointer placement difficult. While not successful, Crossman's mongrel sight was developmentally a step in the right direction. As what was needed and wanted became more and more distinct, Crossman maneuvered towards faultlessness. While he was at it, Mr. Crossman asked to be favored with another slide similarly graduated. His intention was to improve upon the Lyman #35 Mauser sight, which was elevated by a slick rack and pinion arrangement, but hobbled by the identical graduation scratching inflicted upon the #33/34. The custom, and presumably complimentary, slide replaced the original of Crossman's #35, mounted on the left side of his high-grade Sauer Mauser. Enough merit existed in the plan to convince the folks at Lyman to standardize the new Crossman-agitated elevation markings for the Mauser receiver sight.

He then engaged an unnamed "arms accessory company," which evolved for him a receiver sight along the general pattern of the Lyman, though somewhat more substantial. A screw having a knurled head on its top ran through the elevation slide. Turning the head moved the slide up or down for fine elevation adjustments. Each degree of the graduated screw head was equal to one inch for each hundred yards. Crossman calculated the screw pitch and slide graduation specifications of this experimental sight, and it is believed that the novel slide release was also his brainchild. By pressing a button located on the side of the sight, the slide was released from the adjusting screw and moved freely in the fingers for speedy adjustment. It is unclear from Crossman's description whether this custom contrivance was a modification of the standard Lyman #34, or a from-scratch-unit built from the ground up.

There was but one of these sights in all the world, and it went to Africa with S.E. White's partner, R.J. Cuninghame, fixed to the receiver of his Wundhammer sporting Springfield. That this sight-building exercise was for the intended benefit of an established, but seemingly inattentive commercial sightmaker was unintimated; a departure from the usual directness of the Los Angeles writer. Effectively, though, Crossman had skillfully erected in the sporting press a signpost, one that read ALTERNATE ROUTE. Still, this impression was infused into the minds of wide-awake readers, who would be overcome with a queer *deja vu* sensation accompanying a major announcement from a certain sight manufacturer just a few short weeks later.

Radiating from every quarter of the U.S., but seemingly epicentered in Los Angeles, the collective grumblings of the aggravated American shooter funneled eastwardly and converged upon Middlefield, Connecticut. Here the Lyman decision-makers secretly had a solution already in the works.

To the extent that a company like the Lyman Gunsight Corp. could be said to include fixtures, James Windridge, the firm's in-house inventor, exemplified the definition. The maintenance of Lyman's mostly progressive and up-to-date product line was attributed to Windridge's inventive flair, and a portion of the company's success was due to this behind-the-scenes prolifically creative person. A sampling from his patent history suggests a long term and beneficial association with his employer.

With his patented Special Thumb Locking Feature, Windridge eliminated the objectionable wobble from the early #1, Lyman's foundational tang sight. For owners of the Mannlicher-Schoenauer and other contemporary split-receiver bolt actions, he devised a patentable modification of Wm. Lyman's own 1896 swinging sight arm system. This entered the catalogs in 1909 as Lyman Receiver Sight #36. In 1907, Windridge, together with George S. Wilcox, gave the American rifleman

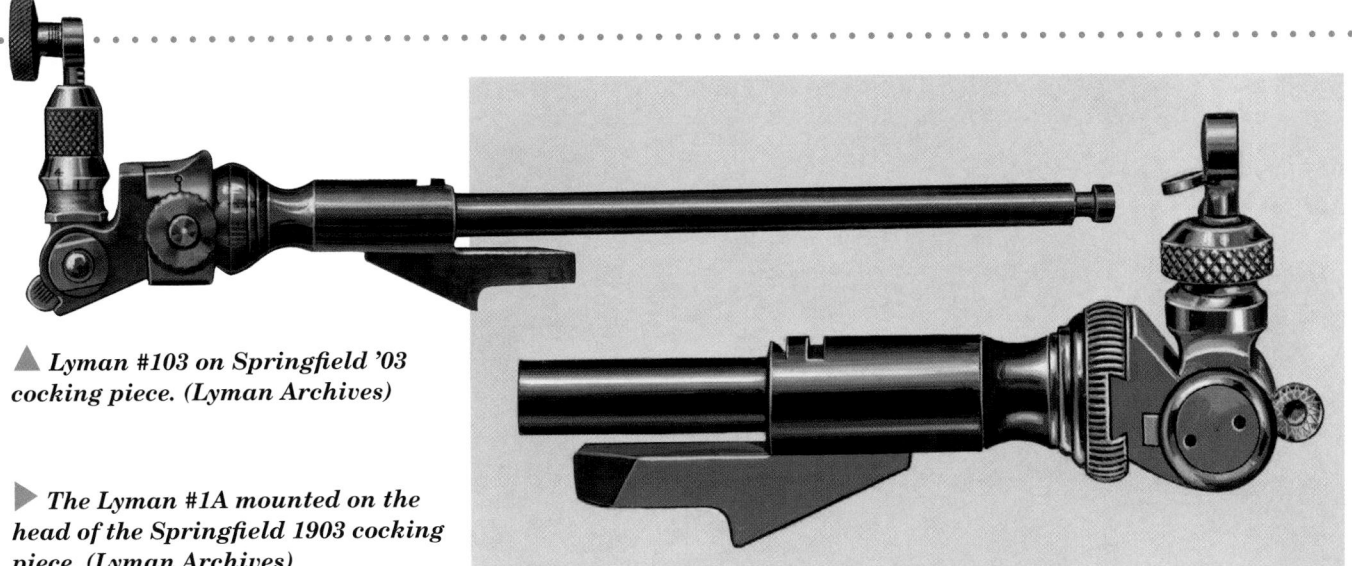

▲ **Lyman #103 on Springfield '03 cocking piece. (Lyman Archives)**

▶ **The Lyman #1A mounted on the head of the Springfield 1903 cocking piece. (Lyman Archives)**

❧●❧●❧●❧●❧

adjustable leaf sights. The winter previously, our man Windridge dreamed up a novel method which allowed the ready removal of the vertical slide of a receiver sight from its base, answering a complaint from the era's more demanding shooters. Also in 1907, he and Wilcox again co-patented a rack-and-pinion elevation system they'd had in the works for more than a year. The patent rights for each of Windridge's brainchildren were assigned to Lyman Gunsight.

In the first months of 1910, Windridge gathered his dividers and his straight-edged rule, and sharpened a pencil. He spread out a clean sheet of paper and proceeded to cover it with straight gray lines of varying lengths. An occasional angle was added, a radius here and there, and only as many circles as was necessary. Presently, the outline of a receiver sight began to take on a recognizable shape. Noticeably absent, however, was the channeled mid-section characteristic of the Lyman line. A stretched-out slide carrying enough compacted lines to give pause to the most optimistic long-distance shooter suggested exciting range possibilities. The crosshatched dials indicated purchase provision for thumb and forefinger and translated only one way—up, down, and sideways adjustability. Overall, there was a sense of substantialness about the sketched sight. Even in two dimensions, the instrument's representation smacked of uncommon soundness and precision.

James Windridge, well versed in Patent office procedure, applied for his "sight for firearms" patent on February 8, 1910. Substantially, the sight was Windridge's design, with some fine-tuning from its primary agitators. There is enough evidence to believe that both Crossman and Lt. Whelen were sent prototypical examples for their evaluation and critique. Crossman suggested making the elevation screw heads with five divisions, and distinguishing by line every five minutes on the slides. Proving that great minds do think alike, Whelen independently proposed the same thing at the same time. The responsible personnel at Lyman Gunsight considered the pair's sage advice and incorporated the recommended changes into the finished product.

Before the patent was granted on July 11, 1911, whisperings were circulating wildly on military ranges, but lacked official confirmation. A flyer introducing the new Lyman #48 was inserted into Lyman's 1911 catalog and first advertisements appeared in the commercial sections of the various outdoor magazines by late summer; by August 1911 it was ready for the market.

Lyman's formal announcement through the popular sporting press was printed in the November, 1911 issue of *Outers Book*. "You only need this sight to make your sporting or military Springfield a perfect arm, for any line of game or target work" was editor Bob Kane's private judgment. A more authoritative validation was published with as little hesitation as magazine lead time allowed. *Outers* published Townsend Whelen's enthusiastically favorable evaluation of the new sight, triumphantly titled "The Perfect Rear Sight at Last" in its February 1912 number. The military "sharks"—the bulk of *Arms and the Man* subscribers—had already been enlightened. Whelen comforted those who naturally peeked first at the illustration and thus were already daunted by the cluster of knurled dials and compressed stack of hash-marks and numerals. Most had struggled with the gadgetry of the government sight. Complexity was the impression here and bewilderment the expectation. In essentials, the sight was a housing containing two screws, each arranged as a micrometer, the Lieutenant explained. The right screw governed elevation and the left one windage. Before elaborating with examples, Whelen whispered the nut-shelled, ultra-simple secret to mastery of the Lyman Micrometer Sight: "A change of one minute in elevation or windage moves the point of impact on the target one inch for every hundred yards of range." Put another way, turning the knurled sight head one graduation resulted in the point of impact at one hundred yards being moved one inch, or two inches at 200 yards, three inches at 300 yards, etc. A spring on the head locked the adjustment and produced an inaudible, but plainly felt "click" each time the sight was raised or lowered one inch. This hard-to-forget formula was dead simple to estimate on the target, and readily combined with published trajectory tables to get required elevations without even firing. "Mighty simple, is it not?" Whelen asked his devoted *Outers Book* readers. Lt. Whelen's assessment centered on the Lyman's absurdly simple operation, but its ruggedness was not overlooked. "It is several times stronger than the ordinary receiver sight, which has had the approval of hunters for the past twenty years." he wrote. His narrative concluded with windage correction tables calculated for the universally-used standard government load (150-grain bullet, 2700 fps) for the 30-1906 cartridge—extremely valuable dope for the military and civilian marksman.

This was not the usual impassively-delivered Whelen report. He was not one to toss about superlatives offhandedly, but the Lieutenant was atypically enthusiastic about the new Lyman sight, and his unbridled delight gushed out across the page. Straightaway, Whelen's obvious zeal transferred to the mind of the knowing reader, alerted to the #48's significance and the ramifications of its use. Suddenly, the mental prospects of shooting a 600-yard match peeping through an abruptly sub-standard #34 was now akin to ciphering long division by counting one's toes. Splitting the difference between the factory-stamped furrows was now—conceivably—a thing of the past. Gone were the days of awkwardly scribed elevation marks, and no more guessing, which was which. Gone too was the wedging of a lever with the hopes it would hold. The understanding was that all that needed to be done to unfailingly direct bullets to the X-ring was to dial in the Whelen-provided windage and elevation dope. As a practical matter, the perception and reality (discounting skillful hard holding and correct wind judgment) meshed pretty closely.

Those flush with a discretionary eight dollars could purchase their liberation from the #34. This investment bought the modern 20th century 20/20-visioned eye of the

rifle, the sight touted as the "most perfect and accurately adjusted rear sight ever developed." With the same speed as the #48 was embraced, the "by guess and by gosh" adjustable #34 Springfield sight was relegated to back-number status. Those riflemen resisting the modernization were hopelessly handicapped against those who conformed, and if they aspired to be competitive, they had themselves to blame for their failure to do so.

After eight years, the sight Whelen had mentally formulated and proposed in print was now a reality. He hadn't lost his touch.

For a number of years after 1911, the #48 was made to fit only the Springfield rifle. Lt. Whelen didn't allow this paltry limitation to deter him from fitting the micrometer sight to his beloved Krag. This was accomplished by mounting the sight on the Krag's port side and reversing the eyepiece. Those who considered emulating his example were advised that the elimination of the magazine cut-off was usually necessary. By recontouring the inside of the sight base, the #48 became adaptable to the 1895 Winchester lever action, and this became a fairly common Whelen-endorsed practice. Indeed, the Lieutenant advised his readers that the top-of-the-line Lyman could be contrived to fit, by a patient man with a file, "all Winchester models." The Lyman's fine adjustability and great strength offset the somewhat bulky protuberance, which resulted. About 1920, Lyman Gun Sight began to offer #48 versions specifically adapted to a growing number of popular rifle models.

After Crossman's broadcasting of the five-rifle Springfield remodeling project, imitation was the sudden craze, and it caught fire with a frenzy. Instantly, Lyman's latest and best micrometer sight became the rear sight of choice to grace the high-grade rifles of those flush enough to afford a restocked army rifle. Fittingly, each complimented the quality of the other. Lt. Whelen, who must have had a dozen custom 1903s at one time or another, may have had the earliest sporter equipped with the new #48.

A cut of his deluxe Fred Adolph remodeled Springfield appeared in *Outers Book* for September of 1911, less than a month after the sight was released for public sale. For two more decades, the Golden and peak years of these conversions, the Lyman #48 remained the only receiver sight worthy of the consideration.

The Lyman Company was particularly accommodating to Whelen. In 1912, he approached the outfit with the matter of a sight to attach to the cocking piece of a pet Springfield. In short order, they developed for him a sight base, a heavy bulbous appendage that was welded to the cocking knob. Secured to this windage-adjustable contrivance was the familiar aperture, sleeve and stem arrangement. This unique sight later was much refined and streamlined and the #1A Combination Rear Sight for the Springfield and Krag, which dovetailed into the cocking head, evolved directly from it. Anxious to see a micrometer sight incorporating the #48's level of perfection applied to other rifles, Whelen leaned on Lyman politely, persistently and firmly. He'd been successful in creating a demand, and instrumental in convincing Lyman that such an article would be a paying proposition. Lyman responded in the summer of 1915 with the #103, the Cadillac of tang sights. The new sight was adaptable to all rifles, which took the old #1 tang sight, benefiting owners of most Winchester, Marlin, and Savage lever-action models. The 1/2-minute adjustable #103, fixed to the tangs of Winchester, Ballard, and Stevens single-shot rifles, saw a lot of use on indoor gallery ranges. Whelen introduced this yet "another perfect sight" to the readers of *Outers Book* in January 1915.

The Lyman #48 didn't just chance upon the sporting scene in 1911. It was brought into being because two hugely influential men knew how to effect its happening. The sight maker, after applying its corporate fingers to the public pulse, ultimately became receptive to a new idea and delivered the goods. The less-noticeable figure in this Lyman #48 history lesson was the sainted Lt. Whelen, who respectfully placed himself subordinate to Mr. Crossman. His exact contribution, apart from consultant and agitator, was never perfectly clear. Alluding to the #48 in 1916, Whelen wrote, as an aside, that he was "almost totally responsible" for the existence of that Lyman sight. Eagerly sharing the credit with Crossman, who was "directly responsible" for bringing the micrometer adjustment method to the attention of Lyman, Whelen allowed in 1912 "Mr. Crossman and I have both had our fingers in the pie..."

Crossman's concocted receiver sight, his "Model of Later 1910," incidentally or co-incidentally, embodied every desirable particular found on Lyman's micrometer sight unleashed some few months later. Questioning which came first is as pointless as the old chicken-or-the-egg debate. Fuzzy things such as arbitrary magazine lead times—as short as two months in those days—further bother the accuracy of timelines. The written historical record appears to be devoid of solid evidence. What exists seems to suggest developments from all points occurring concurrently and independently.

The late, great Lyman #48 had a long and illustrious run. After being moribund for some time, it finally died a natural death in the marketplace. After 63 years of continuous production, and having been adapted to most bolt-action rifles from the 1903 Springfield to the modern Remington Model 700, it was discontinued in 1974. Sounding the death knell of the #48 was the development of the telescopic rifle sight and its mountings into utterly reliable instruments, coupled with the public's readiness for the transition. In the '30s and '40s, the smart hunter mounted to their big-game rifle a #48 as an auxiliary or back-up sight for the early, liable-to-fail telescope sights. Almost overnight, the American hunter abandoned en masse the iron sight in favor of the glass, and for at least the past forty years, we have been, as a culture, dependent optically for our rifles' magnified vision. Now virtually unbreakable and foolproof, the scope sight—until superseded—is here to stay.

Two Lyman #48-equipped rifles (top: 1910 Ross; bottom: Remington M30S) still in use by the author, and still capable of directing five shots into one MOA at a hundred yards.

To the past three generations, the merits of the adjustable aperture sight have been almost wholly lost, to the point there is no longer much reason for metallic barrel sights to be placed on common hunting rifles. Irreversibly spoiled to the scope sight as we are, I dare say that most U.S. hunters have never fired a shot through a receiver-sighted rifle.

For the current crop of budding riflemen, the most likely exposure to a Lyman #48 would be a chanced-upon relic bolt action on a gun show table, where it would be shot a cursory, indifferent glance. Though I've not seen one at a range or in the field in the past thirty years, I understand that some of the cognizant throwbacks use them yet. Lamentably, the Lyman #48, the classic eye of the rifle and institution in Rifleman's progress, has been relegated to a curious and nostalgic artifact of times gone by.

There is certainly no problem acquiring cases for the 45-120 3 1/4-inch cartridge these days. The interest in long-range buffalo-rifle matches has seen to that. The author had different brands of 3 1/4-inch cases on hand that bore the headstamps of "Old Reliable," "C.S.A," as well as these cases by "Bell."

AN AMERICANIZED 450 3¼-INCH
BLACKPOWDER EXPRESS

by Harvey T. Pennington

*I*t wasn't in Africa or India. My quarry wasn't a lion or a tiger. But, I was hunting, armed with a double rifle, loaded with cartridges that were nearly four inches long, and, ballistically identical to the old British 450 3 1/4-inch Blackpowder Express cartridge. So, there was an added degree of excitement on this hunt when I silently cocked the right hammer on my double and prepared to fire....

Without a doubt, the side-by-side exposed-hammer breech-loading double rifle has always been—to me —one of the most intriguing types of firearms. Part of the mystique, obviously, lies in the historic connection of this type of rifle with the incredible hunting found in the African continent and India during the late 19th and early 20th centuries. The double rifle is a reminder to many of us of those times, and of the now-legendary hunters of that period.

One of those hunters was a man by the name of John Taylor, who, arguably, penned one of the most authoritative books ever written regarding rifles and cartridges for hunting big game. Taylor was born in Dublin, Ireland but, for several decades—beginning just prior to the start of World War I, and continuing until his death—he lived the life of

a professional hunter in Africa. His book, of course, was *African Rifles and Cartridges*, (copyright 1948, Reprint Edition 1977, by The Gun Room Press), and in that work, Taylor wrote at length of his (at that point) thirty years' experience of hunting on that great continent. He described—in exquisite detail—the different types of rifles (single-shots, bolt-actions and doubles) that he used in the field, and chronicled the efficiency (or lack thereof) of the many rifles and cartridges which were in use during that period of time. In addition to

his own African experiences, Taylor met—and regularly corresponded with—those who hunted big game in other parts of the world, especially in India and the United States.

❖ ● ❖ ● ❖ ● ❖ ● ❖ ● ❖

Author's Kodiak Mark IV was manufactured in Italy by the Davide Pedersoli Co. It was imported through Trail Guns Armory, of League City, Texas, and came with this fitted, canvas-covered wood trunk.

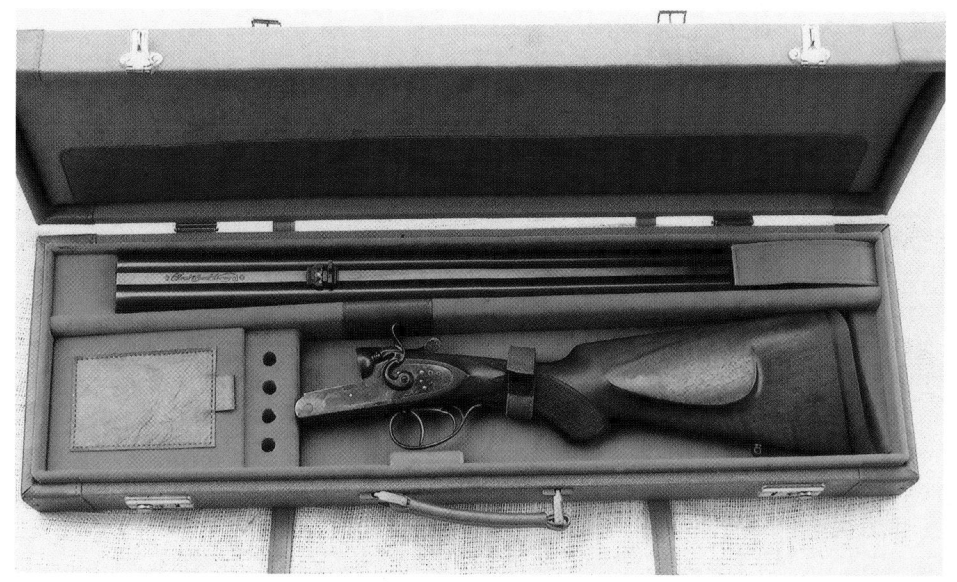

The information contained in John Taylor's well-known work, African Rifles and Cartridges, *helped influence the author's idea of rechambering his rifle. It would be quite difficult to read Taylor's book and not come away with a great appreciation of the double rifle.*

Mr. Taylor left no doubt that the type of rifle he preferred for dangerous game was the double. Although it was the more familiar hammerless doubles (with the sliding tang safeties) that he used primarily, he did have a particular affinity for the older-style doubles and their two visible hammers. On that subject, he wrote:

"I am very fond of the double hammer action because of the absolute silence in which it can be loaded and cocked. I know of more than one man, sitting up at night for man-eating tiger, who scared off his beast by the click of his safety as he prepared to shoot with a hammerless rifle. If you draw back the trigger at the same time as you draw back the hammer on a hammer rifle and then let the trigger go, you will have cocked without a sound of any

sort. Then there is the delightful ease with which the breech opens; powerful double rifles are fitted with extra powerful main springs to obviate any possibility of a misfire; those springs have to be compressed as the breech of a hammerless action is opened and the locks cocked. There is nothing of that with the hammer rifle—you cock with your thumb, one lock at a time. I would happily finish the remainder of my career with nothing but best-grade double hammer rifles. Incidentally, such weapons can occasionally be picked up secondhand at very low prices—not because the hammer action is no good, but simply because fashion favors the hammerless. If you get such a chance, provided the weapon is in good condition, you need not hesitate—it will satisfactorily answer any questions you are ever likely to ask it."

My own interest in double rifles reached a peak in the mid-1980s. I had been reading books not only by Taylor, but also by other noted hunters such as Jim Corbett (*Man-Eaters of Kumaon*); Lt. Col. J.H. Patterson (*The Man-Eaters of Tsavo*); Peter Hathaway Capstick (*Death in the Long Grass*) and Robert Ruark (*Use Enough Gun*), just to name a few.

After a literary diet like that one, I was more than caught up in the allure of the breech-loading double rifle. However, after checking the prices on some of the new and used ones, and finding that their prices ran into the many thousands of dollars, I began to believe that I would never be able to afford one of my own.

But, one day in 1987, while perusing a firearms publication, I read that Trail Guns Armory (a

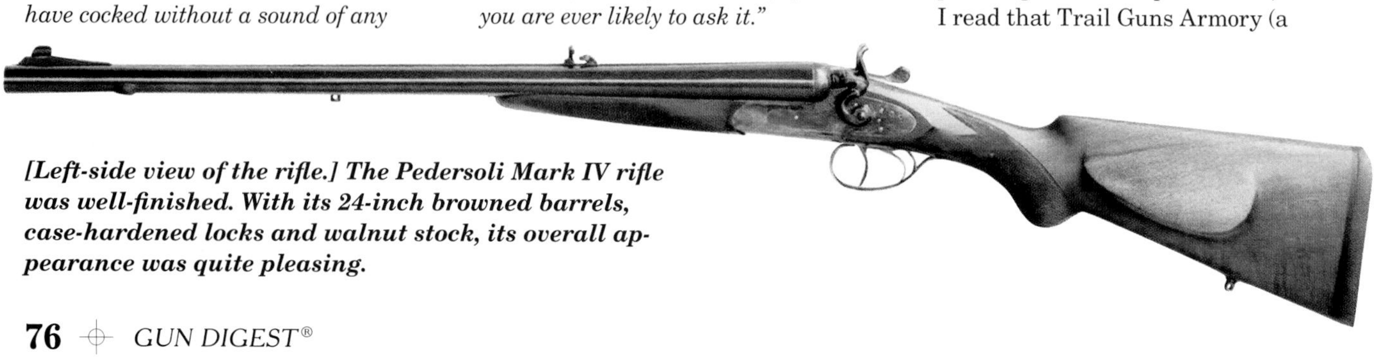

[Left-side view of the rifle.] The Pedersoli Mark IV rifle was well-finished. With its 24-inch browned barrels, case-hardened locks and walnut stock, its overall appearance was quite pleasing.

firearms importing business located in League City, Texas) had plans to begin importing a new breech-loading double rifle manufactured in Italy by Pedersoli. The rifle had exposed hammers, 24-inch browned barrels and was chambered for the 45-70 cartridge. The advertisement also stated that the rifle had case-hardened locks, an adjustable two-leaf rear sight, and came in a fitted case.

After a short while to think it over, I placed an order for the new rifle that had been named the Kodiak Mark IV. I believe the price was then $1,495.

In less time than I expected, a call came in from my local dealer that my order had been received. After picking it up, I anxiously cut open the shipping box, pulled out the heavy canvas-covered wooden case, unbuckled the leather straps, unsnapped the brass locks, and opened it up. When I saw

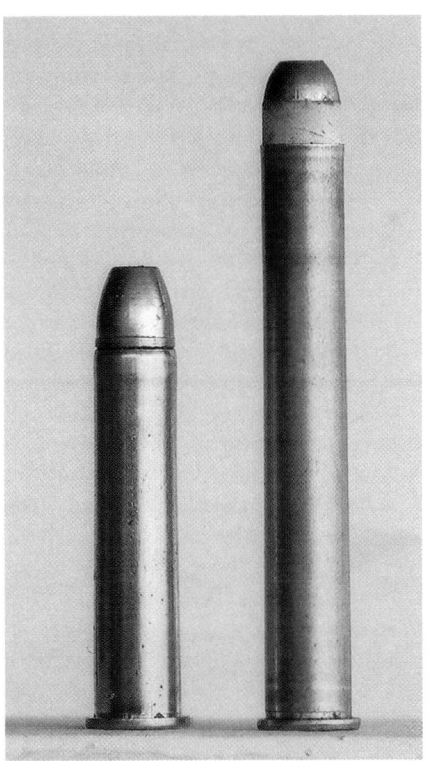

Both the 45-70 (left) and the 45-120 3 1/4-inch (right) can be made to work well with smokeless powders. But the longer case has a big advantage over the 45-70 when using black-powder hunting loads because of its ability to hold charges of up to 120 grains of blackpowder. Obviously, those kinds of charges result in more velocity—and more power.

my new double hammer rifle nestled in its fitted, green felt-lined case, I felt reassured that the purchase had been a good one. A few minutes later, after I had carefully removed the barrels, stock/action and forend from the case, and had completed assembling the rifle, I was further impressed with the close fitting of the parts and the rifle's overall appearance.

By the way, the hunting load recommended by Trail Guns Armory for their new 45/70 double rifle was basically the jacketed 350-grain "Bear Claw" bullets (manufactured by Trophy Bonded Bullets, Houston, TX) loaded to a velocity of 1850 feet per second. I didn't order any of those loads, however, since I planned to do my own reloading. Besides, I knew there was the strong possibility that my rifle might not remain chambered for the 45-70; more on that later.

My initial handloads for the Kodiak Mark IV used bullets commonly available in my area, such as the 350-grain Hornady and the 400-grain Speer. Another bullet that I used in my testing was the Barnes Original 400-grain bullet. All of these gave very satisfactory performance in the 45-70, as did several of my different cast bullets. Based upon the power of the load recommended by TGA, it would seem that the level of handloads usually published for use in the 1886 Winchester should be perfectly acceptable in this rifle.

Obviously, what sets the double rifle apart from the more common rifles is its twin barrels. In order for those two barrels to shoot their individual bullets to the same point of impact, using the same sight, the barrels must be properly "regulated" (i.e., aligned and fitted together). The traditional process of regulating the barrels during manufacture of the rifle is a labor-intensive, time-consuming one, and one of the reasons that double rifles are so expensive. In order to hold down the price of the Kodiak Mark IV rifle, it is not regulated in that same manner. Be that as it may, whatever method is used by Pedersoli to regulate the barrels of their doubles, it certainly seems to work.

Once the re-chambering of the rifle was complete, author re-stamped the bottom flats of the barrels to reflect the new caliber designation— "45-120 BPE." The old chambering (45-70) was crossed out.

✦✦ ● ✦✦ ● ✦✦ ● ✦✦ ● ✦✦ ● ✦✦

From the outset, I was gratified to find the barrels of my new rifle were almost perfectly regulated. That is, at 50-75 yards, proper loads from the left and right barrels grouped together when using the same sight, and would continue to group acceptably close up to at least 100 yards.

I was certainly not alone in my opinion regarding the regulation of the barrels on this new double rifle. In an article in the December, 1989, issue of *Guns & Ammo* magazine about the Kodiak Mark IV, Phil Spangenberger (the well-known feature editor of that magazine) reported that, in addition to the above TGA hand-tailored loads, he also used Remington 405-grain factory loads (at a velocity of about 1330 fps). He stated, "During all of my shooting with the Mark IV, I found that the rear sight worked well for me with either barrel out to about 100 or so yards—with a variety of ammo."

With the intended use for my rifle being close-range big-game hunting, up to 100 yards or so (the traditional duty of a double rifle), my rifle's barrels seemed satisfactorily regulated for that chore. The primary sight on my rifle stays sighted for the shorter ranges, and the second sight may then be sighted for longer range, if desired.

Almost from the time I received this rifle I wasn't sure it would remain chambered for the 45-70. In part, the reason was that the famous old 45-70 U.S. Government cartridge just didn't seem *African* enough for use in this rifle. I wanted something closer to one of the old British cartridges for which the old double hammer rifles used in Africa and India in the late 1800s were chambered. In other words, I wanted something bigger. And, I had a perfect candidate in mind....

Again, I must acknowledge the influence of John Taylor, and his book *African Rifles and Cartridges*. In the chapter entitled "The Large Bores," Taylor introduces the reader to the British 450 3 1/4-inch Blackpowder Express (B.P.E.) cartridge. Essentially, this cartridge was composed of a cartridge case 3-1/4 inches in length, holding 120 grains of blackpowder, and was loaded with either lead copper-tubed bullets or with solid lead-alloy bullets. The copper-tubed bullets could be had in either 270-grain or 325-grain weights, but Taylor complained that they tended to break up prematurely on all but the lightest animals.

However, it was a different story with the 450 B.P.E.'s solid lead-alloy bullets. Those came in weights of either

❦●❦●❦●❦●❦●❦

(A) Whenever grooved cast bullets were used, the author "pan-lubed" them; this method involves placing the bullets base-down in a flat-bottomed pan and pouring melted lube around the bullets until the top lube groove is covered. (B) Once the lube has cooled, the "cake" of lube—along with the bullets—can then be removed. (C) The bullets are then pushed out of the lube, base first. (D) The result is a cast bullet with perfectly filled lube grooves.

310 grains or 365 grains, could be purchased either as "soft" lead bullets or "hardened" and, at least in the latter weight, proved to be quite effective against the heavier game. It was the heavier 365-grain lead-alloy bullet that proved to be Taylor's favorite when using this cartridge. Its velocity was reported to be 1700 fps [From the illustrations that I have seen of the loaded 450 3 1/4-inch cartridges, its lead-alloy bullets were paper-patched.]

Taylor stated that for lighter animals the plain *soft* lead bullet was much better than the copper-tubed slugs. Then he went on to describe the effectiveness of the 450 B.P.E. cartridge, stating: *"I had a falling-block single-loader handling this cartridge and also a double hammerless by Holland. I killed elephant, rhino and buffalo with the 365-gr. hardened lead bullet, and lion with the soft solid bullet of the same weight from both these rifles. In the dry season the smoke with modern blackpowder does not worry you unduly; but it is a decided liability during the rains. My Holland was sighted for 150 yards, with a folding leaf for 250 which I never used. For my work I found the 150-yard sight entirely satisfactory. I was very fond of this little rifle, and only sold it because the stock was much too straight for me having apparently been built for a man who did practically all his shooting from the prone position. If a quick shot was called for, I almost invariably went high. But the rifle did great work for me, and was a real killer."*

Taylor also pointed out that the 450 B.P.E. was Frederick Selous' favorite cartridge, and that Selous used a

Farquarson-actioned single-loader (built by Gibbs) in that chambering for close to 30 years on all types of African game. Like Taylor, Selous preferred the 365-grain solid lead-alloy bullet.

[I cannot leave this point about Taylor and Selous without making one further observation. While researching for this article, I referred (as I often do) to Frank C. Barnes' book, *Cartridges of the World (10th Edition, Revised and Expanded)*, published by Krause Publications. This is a wonderful reference source that I would never be without. But, in his comments on the 450 3 1/4-inch B.P.E. cartridge (at page 382) Mr. Barnes stated, *"...It was a deer cartridge, or for medium-size game at best. Selous and Taylor both used this cartridge to take elephant, but they both knew this was something of a stunt."* Certainly, the 450 Blackpowder Express was not intended as an elephant rifle. There were much more powerful rifles made for that purpose that were available to both of those hunters at the time. But, it seems to me that the statement that the 450 B.P.E was a "deer cartridge, or for medium game at best," sells the cartridge a little short. Perhaps that is all it would be if we only considered its loads using "copper-tubed" bullets; on that subject we need only refer to John Taylor's observation that the 450 B.P.E.'s "copper-tubed" bullets were of inadequate construction for any but the "lightest" game. But, those were not the 450 3 1/4-inch B.P. Express loads that he and Selous used on dangerous game. As noted above, Taylor was quite clear that he considered the cartridge (with the correct loads, using

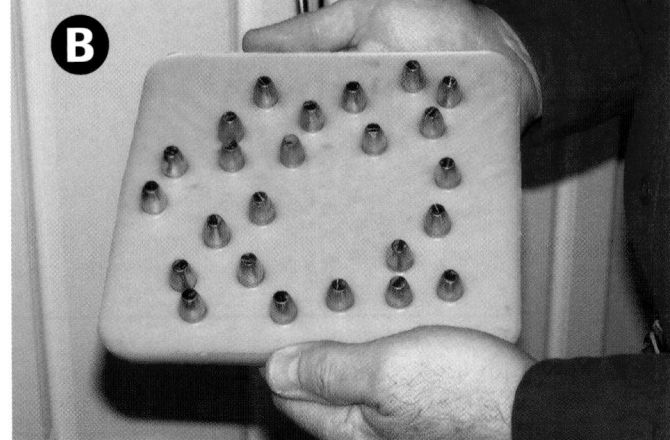

solid lead-alloy bullets) to be "...a real killer" on African game. Such game included the lion, for which he found the 450 3 1/4-inch B.P.E. to be quite satisfactory—and certainly the lion is well above the "deer" or even the ordinary "medium" class of big game.

Finally, in studying John Taylor's writings, it is obvious that when he gave the reader information on particular cartridges, he pulled no punches—he told the bad as well as the good about them. So, when he says that the 450 3 1/4-inch B.P.E. was "a real killer" on African game (with the solid lead-alloy bullets), I think we can take his word for it.]

Of course, the greatest practical advantage of the 450 B.P. Express over the 45-70 (for the person who enjoys shooting blackpowder in these old cartridges) is its ability to hold more blackpowder, thus enabling the shooter to obtain substantially higher velocities than possible with the smaller case. Further, blackpowder loads (or smokeless-powder loads loaded to blackpowder levels) operate at very moderate breech-pressure levels compared to full-power smokeless loads, so there is an extra margin of safety—for both the rifle and the shooter—when using blackpowder loads. Moreover, blackpowder loads (and blackpowder-level smokeless loads) are nicely compatible with cast bullets—and one of my great pleasures in life is using cast bullets for most of my hunting.

So, for the reasons just stated, I suppose it was inevitable that I would re-chamber my new double for a different, larger cartridge. Of course,

the case rim thickness of the 45-70 case is .065-inch—quite a bit greater than the rim of the British 450 B.P. Express case, which measures only .040-inch thick. Therefore, I could not simply re-chamber my rifle for the British cartridge and use original 450 3 1/4-inch B.P.E. cases (assuming I could have found a reliable source for them). To have done so would have created a problem of excessive headspace that could have been solved only with the aid of some very expensive gunsmithing, or an even more costly replacement of my barrels.

The answer, of course, was simply to re-chamber my rifle for the good old 45-120-3 1/4-inch Sharps cartridge, which (with the exception of its greater rim thickness) is a near dead-ringer for the British 450 B.P.E. So, I placed my rifle in the capable hands of Bob Riggs, a gunsmith who lives and works in northeastern Kentucky. In short order, I had my rifle back, this time chambered for the 45-120-3 1/4-inch cartridge—the closest cousin to the British 450/3 1/4-inch Blackpowder Express that I could find.

As soon as the rifle was returned, and to note its new chambering, I stamped "CAL 45-120 BPE" on the bottom flats of the barrels, and X'd out the original 45-70 designation.

Although I did quite a bit of load-testing with the rifle shortly after its return from the gunsmith, I admit I did not get around to hunting with it until recently. Many of you will know what I mean when I say that an interest in other rifles just seemed to get in the way. I even had vague plans to use it on an African hunt,

which I have never yet been able to take. Oh, it wasn't that I totally neglected it. I would occasionally take it out and shoot it, but the big double simply wasn't suited for many of the big-game hunts that I was able to take (such as the antelope hunts or the muzzleloading-season elk hunts). And, even on those certain hunts when the double rifle would have been a good choice, another suitable rifle just simply "got the nod."

However, when my hunting partner, Steve Geurin, and I began to make plans for an expected 2005 Colorado elk hunt, my interest in the big double was, once again, on the top of my agenda. We had plans to backpack in and hunt during the modern-weapons season in an area where close contact with elk did occur with some frequency—close enough that I could feel comfortable using the open sights on the double. I knew the Kodiak should be perfect for such situations, and I was more than anxious to give it a try.

So, out came my reloading dies, bullet moulds, chronograph and targets, and my load testing began again in earnest, with a specific goal in mind—elk.

Loading blackpowder cast-bullet cartridges is an interesting task. The method of doing so is greatly different from loading smokeless-powder cartridges. For those who may not be familiar with loading the blackpowder cartridge, I will outline my usual loading procedure for the larger-capacity rifle cases. Of course, the procedure that I will set out is my own method, but it has evolved from

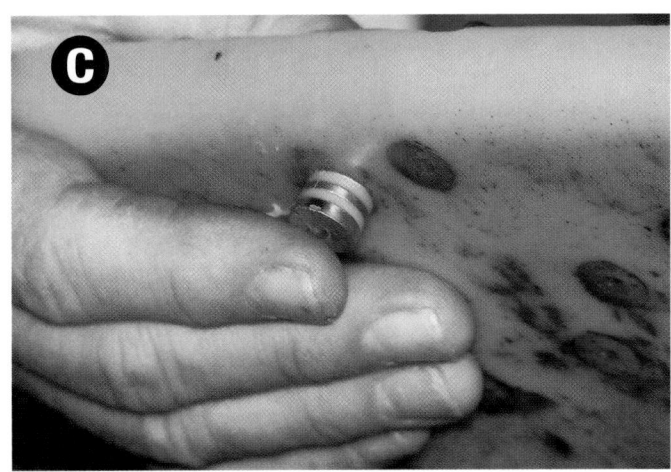

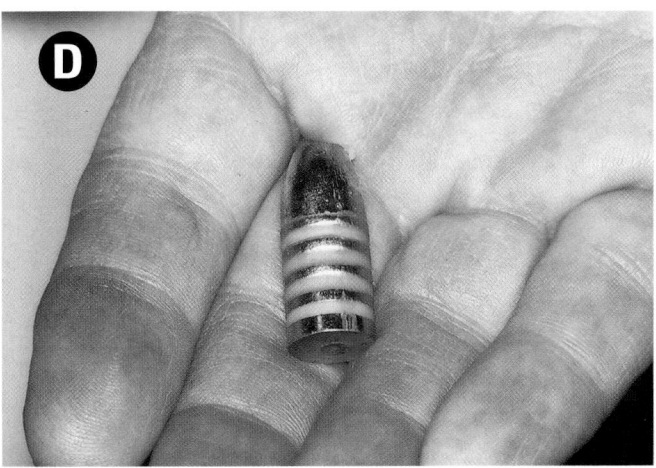

what I have learned from others, yet includes certain modifications and additions that I have incorporated on my own through the years. At any rate, it may prove helpful:

1. The case is sized in the usual manner. I prefer to full-length size, especially in loads that are intended for hunting, so that the round can be chambered with as little resistance as possible.

2. The case mouth is then flared slightly in the neck-expander die—just enough to accept the base of the cast bullet and to help prevent the shaving of lead from the sides of the bullet during the bullet-seating operation.

3. The primer is seated; for the larger cases, I usually find that magnum Large Rifle primers give the best accuracy, especially with the coarser granulations (e.g., Fg); however, this is not always the case, as will be noted below. The shooter must experiment to find the best choice

❧✺●✺●✺●✺●✺●✺

(A) Lube wads are a necessity in paper-patched blackpowder loads intended for hunting, and, at times, they may improve accuracy in blackpowder loads using grooved cast bullets. To produce his lube wads, author uses this lube mould which he made from a steel plate 3/16-inch thick. The melted lube is first poured into the holes of the plate. (B) After the lube has hardened, the excess on top of the mould is scraped off with a dull kitchen knife. (C) The individual lube discs are then punched out of the mould.

for his or her rifle/load combination.

4. The proper amount of blackpowder is trickled through a brass loading-tube 24-30 inches in length, and dropped into the cartridge case. This somewhat compacts the powder and gives a more uniform height to the powder column inside the case. It also promotes cleaner combustion of the charge. The amount of powder is correct when the height of the powder column (including a card wad and, possibly, a lubricating disc *(see steps 5 and 6, below)*, is about 1/4-inch higher than the point in the case where the base of the bullet will be when it is fully seated.

5. A card wad (punched from a waxed orange-juice carton, and of a size that is a tight fit on the inside of the cartridge case) is pressed down with a short dowel rod to the top of the powder. This card wad should be viewed as a necessity in larger cases. It helps to insulate the bullet base, minimizing damage to the base of the bullet at the time the powder is ignited, and, when a lubricating disc [see 6, below] is used, the card wad also keeps the lubricant from mixing with the powder.

6. When appropriate, a lubricating disc (also called "wax disc" or "lube wad") is pressed down into the case with the dowel rod until it is positioned atop the card wad. The lubricating disc is usually about 3/16ths of an inch thick and is ordinarily made of the same lubricant as that which is selected for use in the grooves of the cast bullet. The primary purpose of this disc is to help soften the blackpowder fouling that is left in the

barrel when the shot is fired. Softening such fouling is absolutely imperative in order to maintain accuracy in a breech-loading cartridge rifle. In the larger-capacity cases, (such as the 45-110 2 7/8-inch and 45-120 3 1/4-inch) this disc may be necessary because the grooves of the bullet, alone, simply may not be able to carry an adequate amount of lube. Of course, when paper-patched bullets (which carry no lube at all) are used, a lube disc inside the case is absolutely essential—unless the barrel is to be cleaned after every shot. Several different commercial blackpowder lubes suitable for this task are available, or suitable lubes can be made at home with different formulas using commonly-available ingredients.

7. The bullet is seated in the case. If the powder column is of the correct height, the bullet should compress the column about 1/4-inch when it is seated. Accuracy with cast bullets is generally better when the bullet is seated out far enough in the cartridge case to make contact with the lands of the barrel. However, for hunting loads, the bullet should be seated to its normal depth, so as not to make the chambering of successive cartridges more difficult; this deeper seating of the grooved bullet will also keep all grease grooves inside the case, so dirt and other abrasives will not find its way to the surface of the bullet and then into the barrel.

8. Further, it is best to crimp the bullet in the case when assembling hunting loads—except when using paper-patched bullets. Often, in a fouled chamber, when another unfired cartridge is seated in the chamber and

then later extracted, the fouling can cause the bullet from that cartridge to stick in the chamber, and be pulled from the cartridge case when the case is extracted. A good crimp—and a tight-fitting case neck—will almost always prevent that kind of mishap.

By the way, the bore diameter of the barrels of my double is .444-inch, and the groove diameter measures .458-inch, making the grooves especially deep—.014-inch as compared to the usual .008-inch. Taylor, in his comments about the British 450 B.P.E. stated "…The rifling in a blackpowder Express was deeper than in a nitro-firing [smokeless-powder] weapon…." Based upon that statement, I hoped that the conversion of my rifle to a larger blackpowder cartridge might be even more appropriate than I originally thought.

It certainly is no problem to find 45-120 3 1/4-inch cartridge cases these days. The surge in popularity of long-range buffalo rifle matches has seen to that. As a matter of fact, I already had a variety of such cases ("Old Reliable," "C.S.A" and "Bell") on hand to use as basic cases from which to form the 45-110 2 7/8-inch cases for my Shiloh Sharps. But, now I had a rifle chambered for the full-length case, and I was anxious to start putting together some loads for the re-chambered double.

A 1:25 bullet alloy (one part tin to 25 parts lead) was selected for my cast-bullet loads for this rifle. I expected this alloy would permit reasonable expansion of my cast bullets on game such as elk, deer and/or black bear—for which the rifle would most likely be

put to use—yet not expand so easily that penetration would unduly suffer.

Since my grooved cast bullets were so close to the correct diameter for my barrels, they were used as-cast (unsized), and the lubricant was applied by pan-lubing. That is, the bullets were placed base down in a flat-bottomed pan, and the melted lube was poured in the pan until the top lube grooves of the bullets were covered. Once the lube had cooled and hardened, the "cake" of lube (containing the bullets) was removed from the pan and the bullets were pushed out base first. When done properly, the grooves of the bullets will be perfectly filled with the lubricant.

As mentioned earlier, in the larger cartridges I sometimes use both a card wad and a 3/16-inch lube wad (made from the same lube used on the bullet) between the blackpowder and the base of the bullet. Lube wads are always used in my paper-patched-bullet loads. Those wads can be made in a couple of different ways. The simplest method is to make a mould from a piece of 3/16-inch steel. Holes are drilled in the steel the width of the desired wads needed for the cartridge. The lube can then be melted, poured into the holes of the mould and allowed to cool; a dull kitchen knife can be used to remove the excess lube on top of the mould, and the individual lube wads can then be punched out with a finger or a short dowel rod.

If no lube mould is available, another method for making lube wads is to pour the melted lube 3/16-inch deep onto a flat griddle that has been placed on a level surface. Preferably,

the griddle should be Teflon-coated. Once the melted lube has cooled and hardened, it is carefully separated from the griddle by slowly working a dull kitchen knife underneath the sheet of lube. A piece of the sheet of hardened lube, small enough to be held in one hand, is then broken off and the wads are punched out of the sheet—one at a time—using a cartridge case (with the case head cut off) as the wad cutter. The wad is then pushed out of the cutter with a dowel rod.

The bullet lube that I use most often is a homemade mixture of 60-percent beeswax and 40-percent Wesson (soybean) Oil. In colder

⬧〉◦⬧〉◦⬧〉◦⬧〉◦⬧〉◦⬧〉

Cork wads can sometimes be helpful (in straight-sided cases) as over-the-powder wads. In a 1979 GUN DIGEST article, Jack Lott told of his (and others') use of such wads in the larger British cordite cases when smaller-volume charges of American powders were used. The author used cork wads in some of the smokeless loads for this article. Since composition cork is blown apart immediately upon ignition of the charge, it apparently does not pose the same danger of "ringing" the chamber as does a solid wad. All that is necessary is some 1/8-inch sheet cork, a hollow punch, dowel rod, mallet, and a thick rubber mat. The cork wad is pushed all the way down to the top of the powder, preventing the powder from shifting around inside the case.

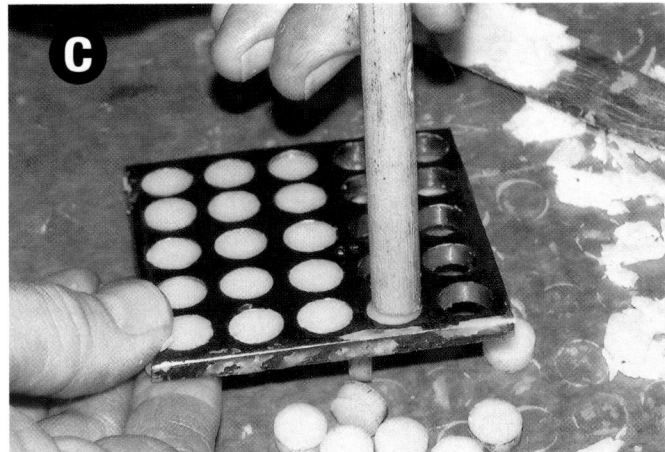

weather, it might be better to soften it some by using a 50-percent beeswax and 50-percent Wesson Oil mix. This lube also works well with smokeless loads. Recently, I have been experimenting with a variation of the above mix, consisting of 5 parts beeswax, 4 parts Crisco and one part Wesson (soybean) Oil. It seems to show great promise with blackpowder loads. As a matter of fact, it performed extremely well with loads using paper-patched bullets. Another mixture that I sometimes use for blackpowder loads consists of half Vaseline, half paraffin and one teaspoon of RCBS case lube per pound. This load is fine in cooler weather, but be advised that it will melt in the hot sun.

Some old-timers simply used the tallow rendered from the fat of buffalo, elk, bear, etc., as the lubricant on the bullet and/or in the case. (Elmer Keith stated he used elk tallow inside the cases of his 45-110 2 7/8-inch Sharps when using paper-patched bullets.) I have used both beef and mutton tallow, and have found them to give satisfactory results in cooler temperatures. In hot weather, mixing in 1 part beeswax to 3 or 4 parts tallow seems to work rather well.

For those shooters who do not wish to manufacture their own blackpowder bullet lubes, there are many commercial lubes available. For instance, the latest Buffalo Arms Co. catalog lists about ten different lubes, the best-known of which would probably be SPG; Lyman Blackpowder Gold; Thompson/Center Bore Butter, and Rooster BP-7. Of course, C. Sharps Arms offers another lube for blackpowder cartridge shooters that is marketed under the name BPC.

When it came time to cast bullets for use in the loads for my 45-120 3 1/4-inch double rifle, I already had several moulds from which to choose. The mould in my collection which would cast a bullet closely matching Taylor's favorite 365-grain load for the 450 B.P. Express was the Lyman # 457122. That bullet, when cast of the 1:25 alloy, weighed 355 grains. The # 457122 is a 3-groove bullet, with a nice, wide flat-nose—very appropriate for hunting. The as-cast diameter of the bullet was

.461-inch, which should, I thought, produce nice accuracy from my barrels with their .458-inch groove diameters.

This was the first cast bullet to be tested, and it did not disappoint. With a load of 112 grains of Cartridge-grade GOEX blackpowder and CCI 250 primer, velocity of the 355-grain bullet was 1570 fps. Accuracy of that load was quite good. For my testing, I fired 4-shot groups—two from each barrel. At 50 yards, it would group its shots from both barrels into a 2 1/2- to 3-inch group. Of course, these groups were shot using the same sight—an open sight—the toughest of all sights for me to use nowadays.

The velocity of that load compared very favorably to Taylor's 450 B.P. Express load, with its 365-grain bullet at a velocity of 1700 fps. It must be kept in mind that the barrels of my rifle are 24 inches in length, and Taylor made a point that "…all British standard ballistics are taken from 28" barrels…." Well, those four extra inches easily explain the missing 130 fps. But what does it really matter, anyway? That small difference in velocity would never be noticed in the field, on elk, bear, deer, or (I think) even on lion.

Besides, some other brands of blackpowder, or other granulations of the same brand, may give faster velocities. For instance, I had a small quantity of Swiss Fg blackpowder on hand and decided to give it a try. I was amazed to find that the Swiss Fg powder actually gave higher velocities than did the GOEX Cartridge powder. Average velocity of the 355-grain bullets, when using 120 grains of that powder, was 1604 fps. No lube wad was used with this load, but I did use a blow tube, giving each

barrel about four long puffs after the first two shots. Groups with this load at 50 yards were about 3-4 inches, somewhat larger than with GOEX Cartridge.

One other blackpowder was tried with the 355-grain bullet—GOEX Fg. (This is the powder that I use for target loads in my 45-110 Sharps.) In the 24-inch barrels of my double, 112 grains of GOEX Fg gave a velocity of 1413 fps. Accuracy was fine—just over 2 inches—on a par of that with GOEX Cartridge powder.

While shooting blackpowder loads is a lot of fun—and certainly authentic for the older cartridges—it does require some extra effort in loading the shells and cleaning up the powder residue left in the barrels and cases after the shooting session. Therefore, I thought it would be useful to develop smokeless loads that would be the ballistic equivalent of the blackpowder ones—what the British would call "nitro-for-black loads."

For that purpose, I chose to work up loads using Accurate Arms' 5744 powder, which has a good reputation for use in some of the blackpowder cases. In the smaller cases, such as the .38-55 and 40-65, it is known as a powder that is not "position sensitive," so no "filler" is necessary inside the case to help confine the powder to the rear of the cartridge near the primer. (My wife, Linda, has used AA 5744

This adjustable bullet mould made by Ballard Bullet Moulds, Clancy, Mt., was used to cast the 377-grain patched bullet (center) and was loaded in author's 45-120. This bullet is almost identical to Taylor's favorite bullet for the British 450 3 1/4-inch Blackpowder Express. This Ballard mould also casts bullets as heavy as 560 grains (right).

loads in both 40-65 and 38-55 rifles in the annual Matthew Quigley Buffalo Rifle match in Forsyth, Montana, and has done just fine on their range with targets up to 800 yards from the firing line.) However, I was not so sure that AA 5744 would perform as well in the big 45-120 3 1/4-inch case, but I was determined to find out.

My smokeless load consisted of 39 grains of AA 5744, giving the 355-grain Lyman bullet a velocity of 1577 fps—almost identical to the blackpowder loads. This load shot very well, giving groups of a little over 2 inches at 50 yards, and they were centered at virtually the same place on the target as the blackpowder loads using the same bullet. As with the GOEX Cartridge blackpowder loads, I used the homemade beeswax/ Wesson Oil lube on the bullet, and a CCI 250 primer. Of course, with this smokeless powder load no lube wad or card wad was needed.

A second mould that I had which would cast a proven hunting bullet was the Lyman # 457193. It has been a favorite cast bullet for hunting for many years in the 45-70 and larger 45-caliber cartridges. This bullet has the same style of wide flat point as the #457122 just mentioned, but the #457193 is longer and heavier, weighing 418 grains when cast with the 1:25 alloy. The as-cast diameter of this bullet from my mould was perfect for my rifle at .460-inch—.002-inch wider than the groove diameter of my barrels.

My blackpowder load for the 418-grain #457193 bullet was 109 grains of GOEX Cartridge powder. All else (bullet lube, lube wad and primer) were the same as the load mentioned for the #457122 bullet. My PACT chronograph registered an average velocity for this load of 1452 fps. Accuracy with the first two shots was on a par with that of the 355-grain bullet, but I did notice that there was a tendency for the third and fourth shots to be wider. But, this is a very powerful load and, given the right opportunity, could be expected to easily bring home some elk meat.

This would probably be a good time to mention that I did not fire "fouling

shots" or "warming shots" while testing my blackpowder loads. It is common to fire such shots when using blackpowder loads in long-range target rifles, because the first shot or two from a clean, cold barrel will usually not land where the rest of the group will be centered. But the double is first and foremost a hunting rifle, and the hunter does not have the option of firing a fouling shot just before taking his shot at the quarry. Therefore, the hunter must know where the first shot from his clean, cold barrel will land, even though the size of his groups on paper will suffer. My rifle would usually place its first two shots close together, and, because of the blackpowder fouling and the warming of the barrels, the next two shots would sometimes land a little farther away. I did some of my testing when the outside temperatures were quite cold, and, on those days, it was common for the first shot from the right barrel to be well-centered, and for the next shot from the left barrel to land higher and a little to the left. On warmer days, that tendency was not as noticeable.

I also tried the Swiss Fg powder with the #457193. I decided to use only a card wad in the case—no lube wad. With a load using 115 grains of Swiss Fg, this bullet had a velocity of 1497 fps, although it did not seem to group as well as with Cartridge-grade GOEX.

The smokeless load that I worked up with the #457193 bullet to match the blackpowder load used 36 grains of AA 5744. Average velocity of this load was 1453 fps, and it seemed accurate, giving about two-inch

Patches for the bullets cast from the Ballard PP mould were cut from bond paper having a thickness of .0025-inch. Besides the paper, necessary items include a template, sharp knife, and a pad (for use when the patches are being cut).

groups. Again, this load printed almost to the same point on the 50-yard target as the blackpowder load.

The third cast bullet that I tested in my re-chambered Kodiak Mark IV was a Lyman #457121, another flat-nosed bullet, and also the heaviest of the three, weighing in at 460 grains. Although the circumference of this bullet was slightly out-of-round, causing the diameter to vary from .455- to .460-inch, there certainly was no need for concern. This heavy bullet shot very accurately when loaded with 97-100 grains of GOEX Cartridge blackpowder. Group sizes at 50 yards were a little over 2 inches. With the 100-grain powder charge, the velocity averaged 1280 fps from my 24-inch barrels. That certainly is impressive velocity, considering the weight of the bullet and the comparatively short barrels from which it was fired. For those hunters who desire certain, deep penetration on heavy game animals, this load and bullet should be perfect. For most hunting needs, however, loads at this lower velocity level would probably improve with the use of a 1:40 (tin-lead) alloy rather than the 1:25 alloy, since the softer alloy would

	LOADS TESTED RIFLE: Trail Guns Armory Kodiak Mark IV CALIBER: .45-120-3 1/2" (custom chambered) BARREL LENGTH: 24 inches BRASS: Bell PRIMER: CCI 250 (unless otherwise noted) LOADS FOR 355-grain Lyman #457122 Cast Bullet (1:25 alloy; .461" diameter, unsized)				
	Powder				
	Bullet	Powder	Charge	Velocity	Additional Load Data/Comments
Load 1	355-gr., cast	Goex CTG	112 grs.	1570 f.p.s.	Bullet Lube: HPG * One .030" card wad One 3/16" HPG * lube wad
Load 2	355-gr., cast	Swiss Fg	120 grs.	1604 f.p.s.	Bullet Lube: HPG* One .030" card wad No lube wad
Load 3	355-gr., cast	Goex Fg	112 grs.	1413 f.p.s.	Bullet Lube: HPG* One .030" card wad No lube wad
Load 4	355-gr., cast	Goex Fg	109 grs.	1389 f.p.s.	Bullet Lube: Tech* One .030" card wad One 3/16" Tech* lube wad
Load 5	355-gr., cast	AA 5744	39.0 grs.	1577 f.p.s.	Bullet Lube: Tech* This is a good black-powder- equivalent load
Load 6	355-gr., cast	AA 5744	39.0 grs.	1648 f.p.s.	Bullet Lube: Tech* 1/8" composition cork wad was placed over powder. Note higher velocity than load 5. The cork wad contributed to better accuracy, and caused the AA 5744 powder to burn cleaner.
Load 7	355-gr., cast	IMR 3031	50.0 grs.	1607 f.p.s.	Bullet lube: Tech* 1/8" composition cork wad seated on powder. Primer: CCI 200

	LOADS FOR 418-grain Lyman #457193 (1:25 alloy; .460" diameter, unsized)				
	Powder				
	Bullet	Powder	Charge	Velocity	Additional Load Data/Comments
Load 8	418 gr., cast	Goex CTG	109 grs.	1452 f.p.s.	Bullet lube: HPG* One .030" card wad One 3/16" HPG* lube wad
Load 9	418 gr., cast	Swiss Fg	115 grs.	1497 f.p.s.	Bullet lube: Tech* One .030" card wad No lube wad
Load 10	418 gr., cast	Swiss Fg	110 grs.	1473 f.p.s.	Bullet lube: Tech* One .030" card wad One 3/16" Tech* lube wad
Load 11	418 gr., cast	AA 5744	36.0 grs.	1453 f.p.s.	Bullet lube: HPG* Good smokeless-for-black load
Load 12	418 gr., cast	AA 5744	35.0 grs.	1480 f.p.s.	Bullet lube: Tech* Composition cork wad seated on top of powder. Very accurate: 3- 1/8" group at 100 yards.
	Composition cork wad seated on top of powder. Very accurate: 3-1/8" group at 100 yards.				

LOADS FOR
460-grain Lyman #457121
(1:25 alloy; .455"-.460" diameter; unsized)

	Bullet	Powder	Charge	Velocity	Additional Load Data/Comments
				Powder	
Load 13	460-gr., cast	Goex CTG	100 grs.	1280 f.p.s.	Bullet lube: HPG* One .030" card wad One 3/16" HPG* lube wad
Load 14	460-gr., cast	Goex CTG	97 grs.	1265 f.p.s.	Bullet lube: HPG* One .030" card wad One 3/16" HPG* lube wad. A very accurate load.
Load 15	460-gr., cast	Swiss Fg	115 grs.	1441 f.p.s.	Bullet lube: HPG* One .030" card wad No lube wad. Very powerful heavy- bullet load.
Load 16	460-gr., cast	AA 5744	33.0 grs.	1273 f.p.s.	Bullet lube: HPG*

LOADS FOR
377-grain paper-patched Ballard bullet
(1:25 alloy; .456" diameter)

	Bullet	Powder	Charge	Velocity	Additional Load Data/Comments
				Powder	
Load 17	377-gr., PP	Goex CTG	110 grs.	1425 (E)	One 3/16" Tech* lube wad sandwiched between two .030" card wads. Very accurate. WLR primer.
Load 18	377-gr., PP	Swiss Fg	110 grs.	1495 f.p.s.	Same as Load 17, except for powder type. Not as accurate as Goex CTG load. WLR primer.

*Formulas For
Homemade Bullet Lubes Used In Tests

The lubricants used in my tests of the above loads were made at home. I have found that it does help to give names to these different lubes for easier reference. The formula for the lube I refer to as "HPG" was given to me by a man whose last name began with the letter H, and he said that he thought it was similar to the commercial SPG lube; hence, the name "HPG." The formula of the second lube that I refer to in my chart was passed on to me by a Brownell's technician during a telephone conversation a few years ago; thus, the name "Tech" seemed appropriate for it.

"HPG" lube is a mixture composed of 60 percent beeswax and 40 percent Wesson (soybean) Oil, by weight. This has proven a most satisfactory lube for me in black-powder loads as well as for use in low- to moderate-velocity smokeless powder loads.

"Tech" lube is composed of 5 parts beeswax, 4 parts Crisco and one part Wesson (soybean) Oil, by weight. I began using this lube only recently, but I think it's going to be very worthwhile. It worked extremely well with the black-powder .45-120 loads using paper-patched bullets. With those loads, the 3/16-inch Tech wads (positioned between two card wads and then placed in the case between the top of the powder and the base of the bullet) did a great job of softening the fouling left by those heavy loads.

Remember that these components are flammable, and should not be melted and mixed over direct heat. A double-boiler should be purchased and used for this purpose.

allow easier expansion on game.

As with the other bullets, velocity increased when the Swiss Fg blackpowder was used. One hundred fifteen grains of that powder gave a velocity of 1441 fps. In my test load, the beeswax/Wesson Oil lube was used on the bullet, but no lube wad was used. This load gave also gave nice accuracy.

A good smokeless-for-black load for this 460-grain bullet was 33 grains of AA 5744, which gave a velocity of 1273 fps, essentially matching the velocity of the GOEX Cartridge load.

I must make a couple of observations about the performance of AA 5744 in the long 45-120-3 1/4-inch case. Especially when using this powder with the lighter bullets, I noticed there were many granules of unburned powder left in the barrel after a shooting session. When that happened, velocities varied a great deal and accuracy suffered—especially in groups fired at 100 yards. Such loose unburned granules could, obviously, jam the action of a double or cause difficulty in chambering new

rounds. In an attempt to correct these deficiencies in my AA 5744 loads, I used a method that first came to my attention in the 1979 GUN DIGEST, in an article written by Jack Lott entitled "The Double Rifle—Its Care and Feeding." That article described the use of American smokeless powders in the large-capacity British double cartridges—both the blackpowder cartridges as well as those originally designed for cordite. Among those credited for the loads which had been printed (in addition to Lott) were Elmer Keith, Ross ("R.") Seyfried and Capt. Wadman.

Besides providing a source to loads developed by those well-known gentlemen, the article gave specific information about the use of cork wads on top of the powder charges in cartridges having straight (i.e., not "bottle-necked") cases. The purpose of the cork wads was to keep the smaller charges of American (usually IMR) powders situated in the rear of those cavernous cartridge cases. Without such a method of controlling the location of the powder, the loads were quite erratic as to the velocities and accuracy they gave, and there could even be dangerous pressure excursions. Mr. Lott reported that he used cork wads in *"...hundreds of rounds for doubles using DuPont powders for over 20 years,"* and that he had *"never had pressure problems unless I loaded them too heavily...."*

Lott also stated that he preferred *"...cork composition gasket material about 1/8" thick... These are easily cut with a hollow punch, they do not turn sideways in the barrel or remain intact, for they're quickly broken up and blown out...."* This last statement explained why such wads did not cause concern about "ringing" the chamber of a rifle, which can be a problem when a solid over-the-powder-wad is used. Apparently, when the charge is ignited, the composition cork wad breaks up and is no longer a "solid" wad.

Based upon the information in that article, I began using cork wads in straight-sided cases many years ago, and, like Jack Lott, have never had a problem. Of course, no near-maximum loads developed without over-powder wads should be used as a starting point for working up loads with the cork wad;

the addition of the wad would cause pressures of such loads to increase.

So, after noticing the abovementioned problems with some of my AA 5744 loads, I worked up some loads using cork wads on top of the AA 5744 powder to find out whether that addition might improve things. It did. Accuracy was immediately improved, and the problem with unburned granules was noticeably lessened. In one of my tests using cork wads over the powder, I fired a 4-shot group at 100-yards using a load of 35 grains of AA 5744 and a #457193 (418-grain) bullet; that group measured slightly over 3-1/8 inches!

Well, unintentionally, I saved the best (or at least the most authentic) load for last. You see, in my attempts to copy the original 365-grain blackpowder load of the British 450 3 1/4-inch Blackpowder Express, I had forgotten that I had a mould that would cast an almost-exact copy of the original bullet. The mould was one that was manufactured for me back in the early 1980s by Tom Ballard (Ballard Bullet moulds, Box 298, Clancy, MT 59634.) It was an adjustable paper-patch bullet mould, which would cast bullets from about 560 grains (on the heavy side) down to a bullet weighing (as I was to discover) only 377 grains. The reason I had overlooked it was that I had only used it for its heavyweight bullet in the past. Once I remembered that it was an adjustable mould, which would cast a lighter bullet close to the original, I was more than enthusiastic to give it a try.

Using a paper-patch template that I had gotten from C. Sharps Arms of Big Timber, MT, many years before, I cut some patches for the 45-caliber bullet from bond paper .0025-inch

thick. After casting some 377-grain bullets from the Ballard mould, I moistened some patches and rolled them on. Two wraps with this paper gave a finished bullet diameter of .456-inch. I allowed the patched bullets to dry. The paper was not lubed.

I chose to try this bullet first with a charge of 110 grains of GOEX Cartridge blackpowder. Between the bullet and the powder I placed a lube wad, which in turn was "sandwiched" between two card wads. [This matched the lube-wad arrangement that I had seen in line drawings of the British Blackpowder Express cartridges.] My lube wad was made from the beeswax/Crisco/Wesson Oil formula that I mentioned earlier. Once the patched bullet was seated, the overall length of the cartridge was 3.72 inches. By the way, I should mention here that I decided to try a change of primer, and, remembering the success reported to me by my Wyoming (and fellow Sharps-shooting) friend, Ken Swick, I decided to try the Winchester Large Rifle primers along with the GOEX Cartridge blackpowder.

This load shot very well from the outset. The first group at 50 yards placed its four shots into a little over 2 inches. The second group—a six-shot group—was 2-7/8 inches overall, but 5 of the six shots were in less than 1-3/4 inches! All indications were that the beeswax/Crisco/Wesson Oil lube-wad had done a great job. While cleaning the rifle's bores, the softness of the fouling was quite noticeable, as was the ease with which it wiped from the barrels. I expect to be using this lube a great deal in the future.

Again, I tried a load with the Swiss Fg powder—110 grains behind the patched 377-grain

The two expanded bullets pictured here were recovered from the hard, packed dirt of author's 50-yard backstop. They both started out as #457122 bullets (center), of 1-25 alloy, weighing 355 grains; the remaining weight of the bullet on the left was 298 grains, and the one on the far right still weighed 332 grains when it was recovered.

bullet. Velocity was impressive at 1495 fps, but, again, it was not as accurate a load in my rifle as the load using GOEX Cartridge powder.

So, with the load-testing out of the way, you may be wondering what happened on the elk hunt I mentioned earlier. Well, the fact is, it sort of turned into a deer hunt. As it happened, my wife had to undergo knee surgery in the fall of 2005. But, the timing of the surgery—and the recuperative period that followed—came right in the heart of the Colorado elk season. So, instead of taking the big double into the high, black-timbered elk country of northern Colorado, I had to settle for a whitetail deer hunt in the hills and hardwood forests near our home in eastern Kentucky.

As I mentioned at the beginning of this piece, using the big Kodiak Mark IV double rifle and 45-120 3 1/4-inch cartridge added a lot of spice to this hunt for me. Even its open sights were different from those I usually hunt with. Although I ordinarily use iron sights for most of my hunting, they are nearly always in the form of aperture ("peep") sights, since those are much easier to use than open sights —especially when the shooter's eyes get some age on them. But, with the use of some eyeglasses that I "prescribed" for myself—and ordered through a local optometrist—I thought I should be able to see the double's open sights without any real problem.

On the opening day of deer season, I was using loads made up of the 355-grain Lyman bullet (with the 1:25 alloy and the beeswax/Wesson Oil bullet lube), powered by 39 grains of AA 5744 powder—my smokeless-for-black load, having a velocity of 1577 fps.

Of course, even the right eyeglasses, rifle, cartridge and sights can't do a deer hunter any good unless he gets some cooperation from the deer. I was musing about that very thing when I saw a flash of antlers through the brush about 60 yards away. A quick peek through my binoculars confirmed the deer was about a six-point buck, and that he was slowly moving my way. The wind was in my favor, and I silently cocked the right hammer on the big double

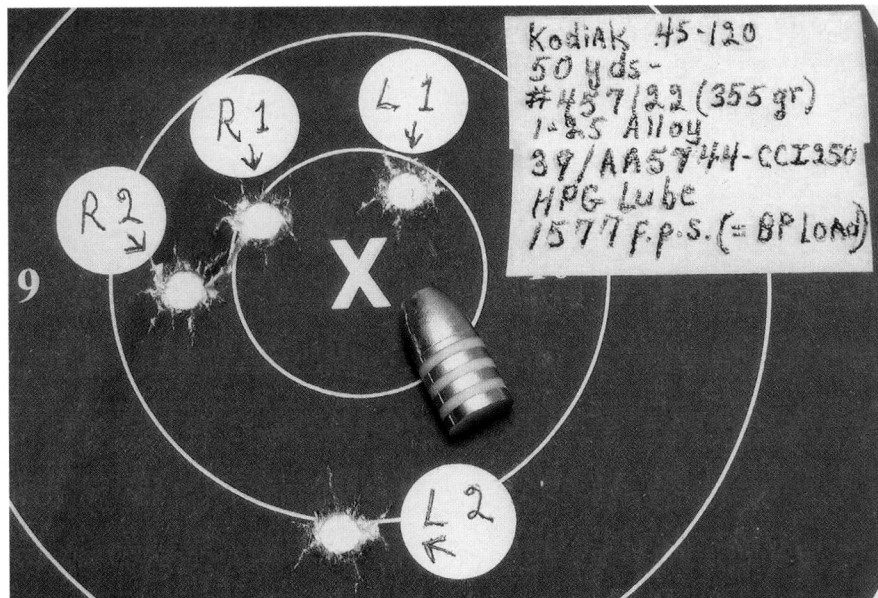

and lined up the sights, waiting for the buck to clear some brush.

As he walked into a small open spot about 30 yards from me, the gold color of my front sight could clearly be seen just behind his near shoulder, and the rifle boomed. The deer immediately went into high gear, making a fast, desperate run that took him only about 25 yards. As he was collapsing, he veered slightly to his left and his forward motion was stopped abruptly when he ran into the trunk of a large black-oak tree. He was stone dead when he hit the ground.

During the brief time of his run, I had been able to cock the left hammer of the double and realign the sights. I had not really practiced this maneuver more than a few times, and was pleased at how naturally and quickly it could be accomplished with the Kodiak double-hammer rifle. But, there was no need to fire a second time, since it had been obvious the buck was about to go down.

After field-dressing the deer, I went back to the place where the buck had been standing when the shot was fired. Evidence of the hit was obvious there, as was the blood trail that led to the black-oak tree where he fell. An easy-to-follow blood trail can be important at times, and a well-designed cast bullet—such as this one—comes as close to guaranteeing that as any bullet I know of. It was obvious that the 45-caliber, flat-pointed 355-grain bullet had

This is a 50-yard group made with the 355-grain Lyman bullet and a charge of 39 grains of AA 5744 powder. This is author's "smoke-less-for-black" load for the #457122 bullet, and it was this load that he used to take the six-point whitetail mentioned in the article. Velocity averaged 1577 fps

§}{ ● §}{ ● §}{ ● §}{ ● §}{ ● §}{

performed its job efficiently. The bullet could not be recovered, of course, having passed completely through the buck.

Well, perhaps next year the double can finally make its elk trip. If so, I will be using blackpowder loads in the rifle and, more than likely, the Ballard 377-grain paper-patched bullet. (I did miss hearing the bigger boom that a blackpowder load would have made on my deer hunt; and I missed seeing the cloud of smoke that would have lingered in the woods for a minute or so before disappearing.)

Working with this rifle, and learning to load for it, has been a great pleasure. And, for someone like me, who has often imagined what it must have been like to hunt in Africa or India in the late 19th century, re-chambering it for an Americanized version of the British 450 3 1/4-inch Blackpowder Express was a project well worth-while.

Who knows? Even John Taylor might have appreciated the effort.

THE ART OF
ENGRAVED & CUSTOM GUNS

by Tom Turpin

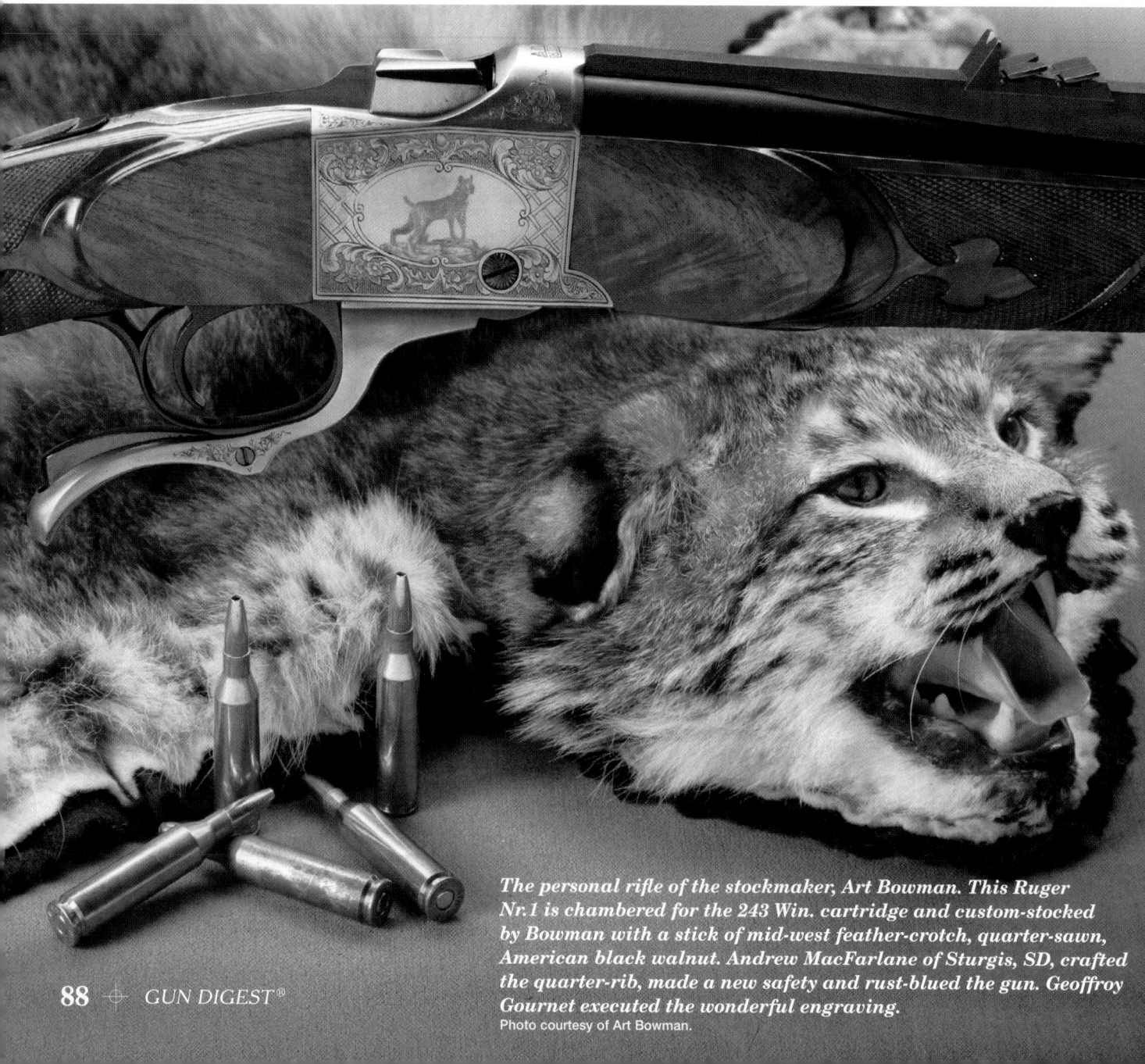

The personal rifle of the stockmaker, Art Bowman. This Ruger Nr.1 is chambered for the 243 Win. cartridge and custom-stocked by Bowman with a stick of mid-west feather-crotch, quarter-sawn, American black walnut. Andrew MacFarlane of Sturgis, SD, crafted the quarter-rib, made a new safety and rust-blued the gun. Geoffroy Gournet executed the wonderful engraving.
Photo courtesy of Art Bowman.

Above: View of a splendid David Miller Co. custom rifle from his Tucson, Arizona shop. Dave and his associate, Curt Crum, craft some of the finest—if not the finest—bolt-action rifles ever made. David and Curt begin with a new classic Model 70 action, which they helped design, and then modify it substantially. The Miller Co. makes two models of rifles, the Marksmen and the Classic. Shown here is a walnut-stocked Marksmen model on a backdrop of several thousand dollars worth of walnut stock blanks.
Tom Turpin photo

Above and Top: Three views of a superb engraving job executed on a Browning Citori O/U shotgun by C. J. Cai, an up-and-coming engraving talent as can be seen in these images. Mr. Cai lives and works in the great state of Hawaii.
Tom Alexander photo

Two views of an unusual custom rifle, a Sharps from C. Sharps Arms Co. Inc., Big Timber, Montana. Engraver Heidi Marsh executed the equally unusual engraving pattern, featuring gold inlaid trains on one side and wolves on the other. Unusual and lovely best describes this rifle. Tom Alexander photo

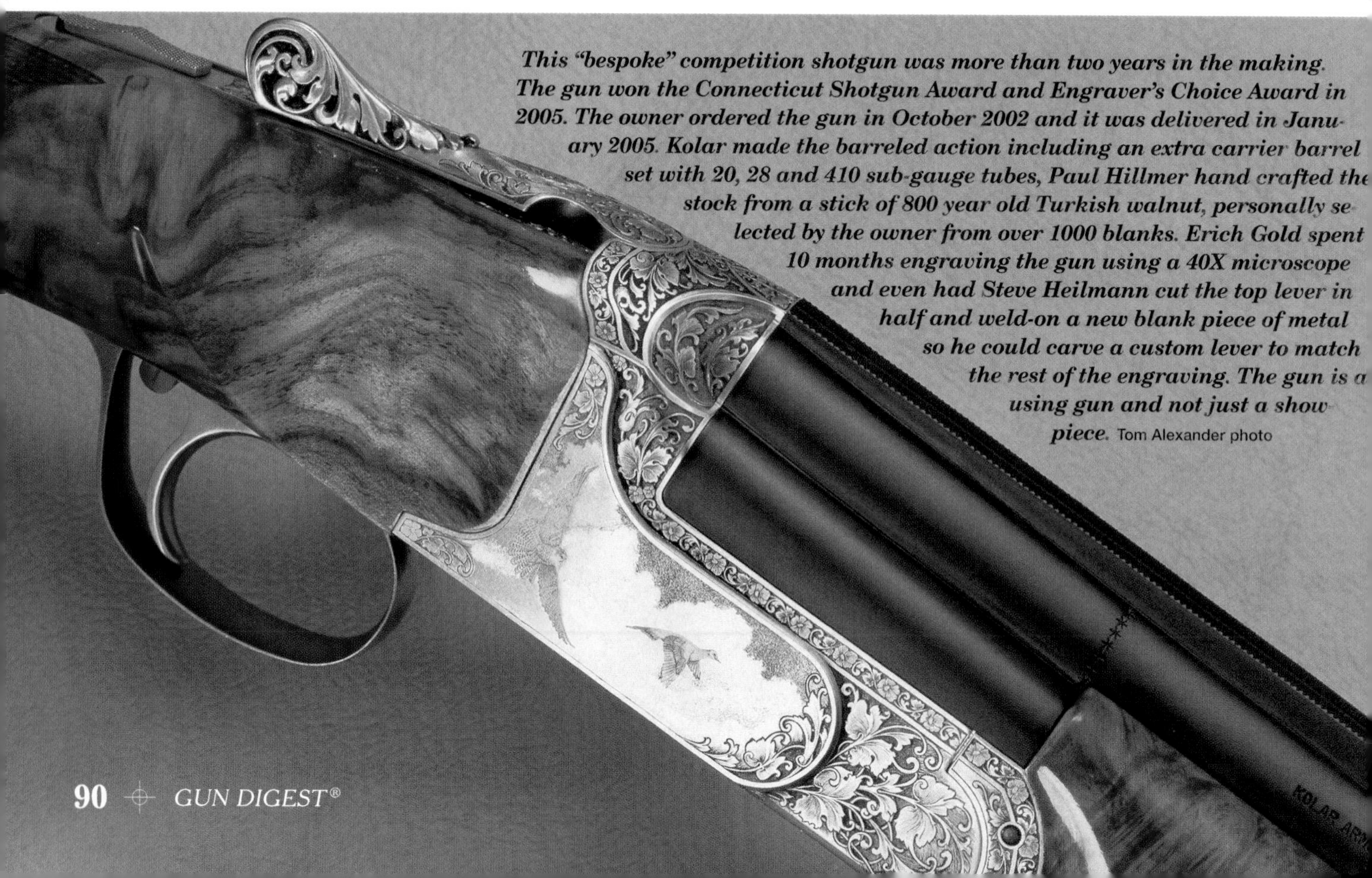

This "bespoke" competition shotgun was more than two years in the making. The gun won the Connecticut Shotgun Award and Engraver's Choice Award in 2005. The owner ordered the gun in October 2002 and it was delivered in January 2005. Kolar made the barreled action including an extra carrier barrel set with 20, 28 and 410 sub-gauge tubes, Paul Hillmer hand crafted the stock from a stick of 800 year old Turkish walnut, personally selected by the owner from over 1000 blanks. Erich Gold spent 10 months engraving the gun using a 40X microscope and even had Steve Heilmann cut the top lever in half and weld-on a new blank piece of metal so he could carve a custom lever to match the rest of the engraving. The gun is a using gun and not just a show-piece. Tom Alexander photo

A wonderful Perazzi shotgun that has been engraved by Lee Griffith. The gun was originally a stock two-barrel set Perazzi MX-11. The owner, avid competition shooter Dave Blomeyer, decided to spiff the gun up considerably. He had it custom stocked in a piece of breath-taking walnut by Larry Garroutte of Tulsa, Okla. He then turned it over to Lee for his exquisite engraving. This gun is no closet queen and is used in competition just about every weekend.
Tom Alexander photo

Our finest engravings begin with a plan by the engraver. Here is engraver Kurt Horvath's plan for a floorplate for a David Miller Co. Classic rifle.
Horvath photo

Below: This is a very interesting and historical shotgun. It was made by James Donn & Bro. of Canton, Illinois. It was made in the late 19th or very early 20th century — Mr. Donn died in 1911 so the gun was crafted well before that date. The gun's owner, Mr. Jack Herrin of Dawson, Ill., arranged for Art Bowman to restore wood on the gun to its previous glory. It was pretty sad at the time with the checkering mostly worn away and the wood was very dirty and gummy with the old linseed oil finish. Bowman also had to reshape the receiver pads to create the tear drops as the originals were completely worn away. Now back in wonderful condition, it is a prime example of little-known but best-quality guns turned out by a handful of makers at the turn-of-the-century.
Photo courtesy of Art Bowman

Right Opposite Page: A pair of bottom metal components for John Bolliger rifles, after having the engraving talents of Mike Dubber lavished upon them. The gold-inlaid Elephant and Lion clearly show these components go on Dangerous Game Rifles.
Mike Duber photo

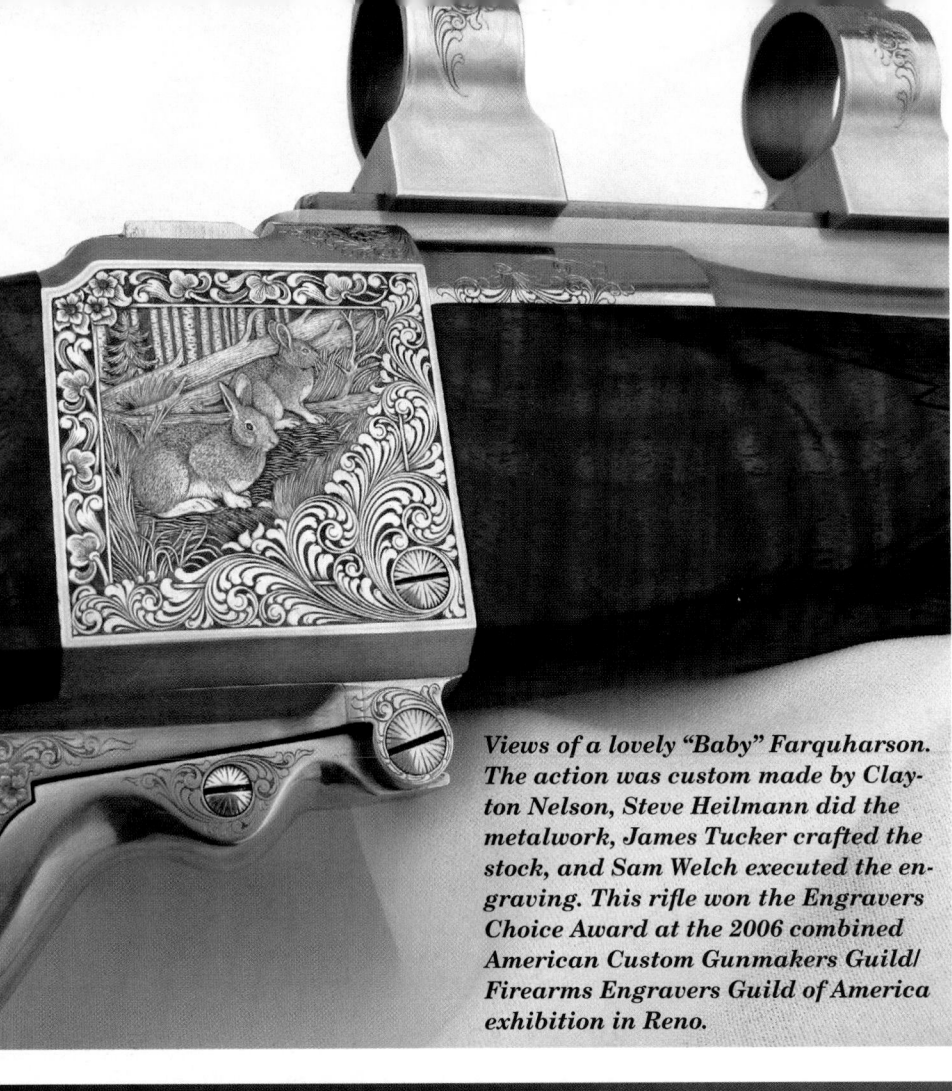

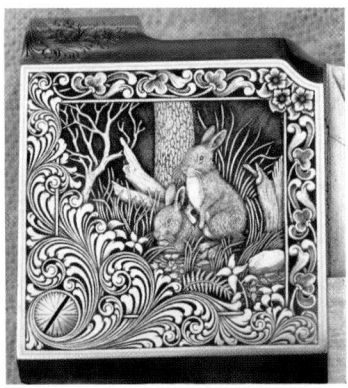

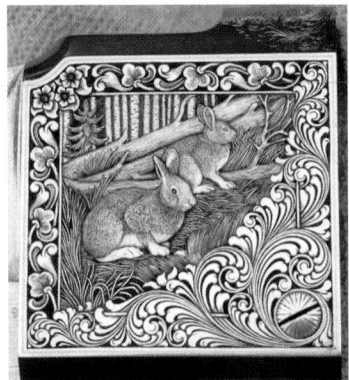

Views of a lovely "Baby" Farquharson. The action was custom made by Clayton Nelson, Steve Heilmann did the metalwork, James Tucker crafted the stock, and Sam Welch executed the engraving. This rifle won the Engravers Choice Award at the 2006 combined American Custom Gunmakers Guild/ Firearms Engravers Guild of America exhibition in Reno.

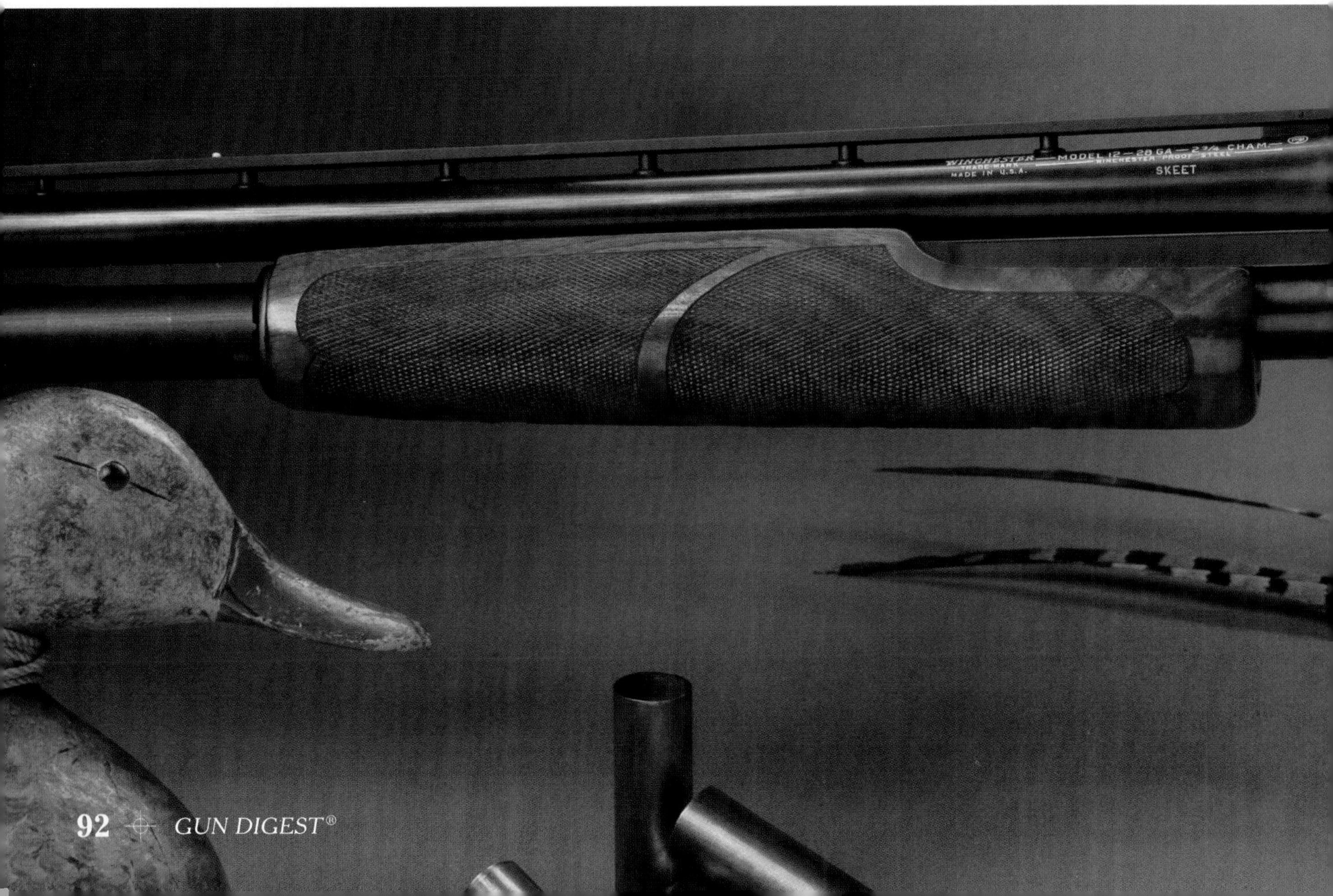

Engraving views of the Savage Model 99 found on the following page.

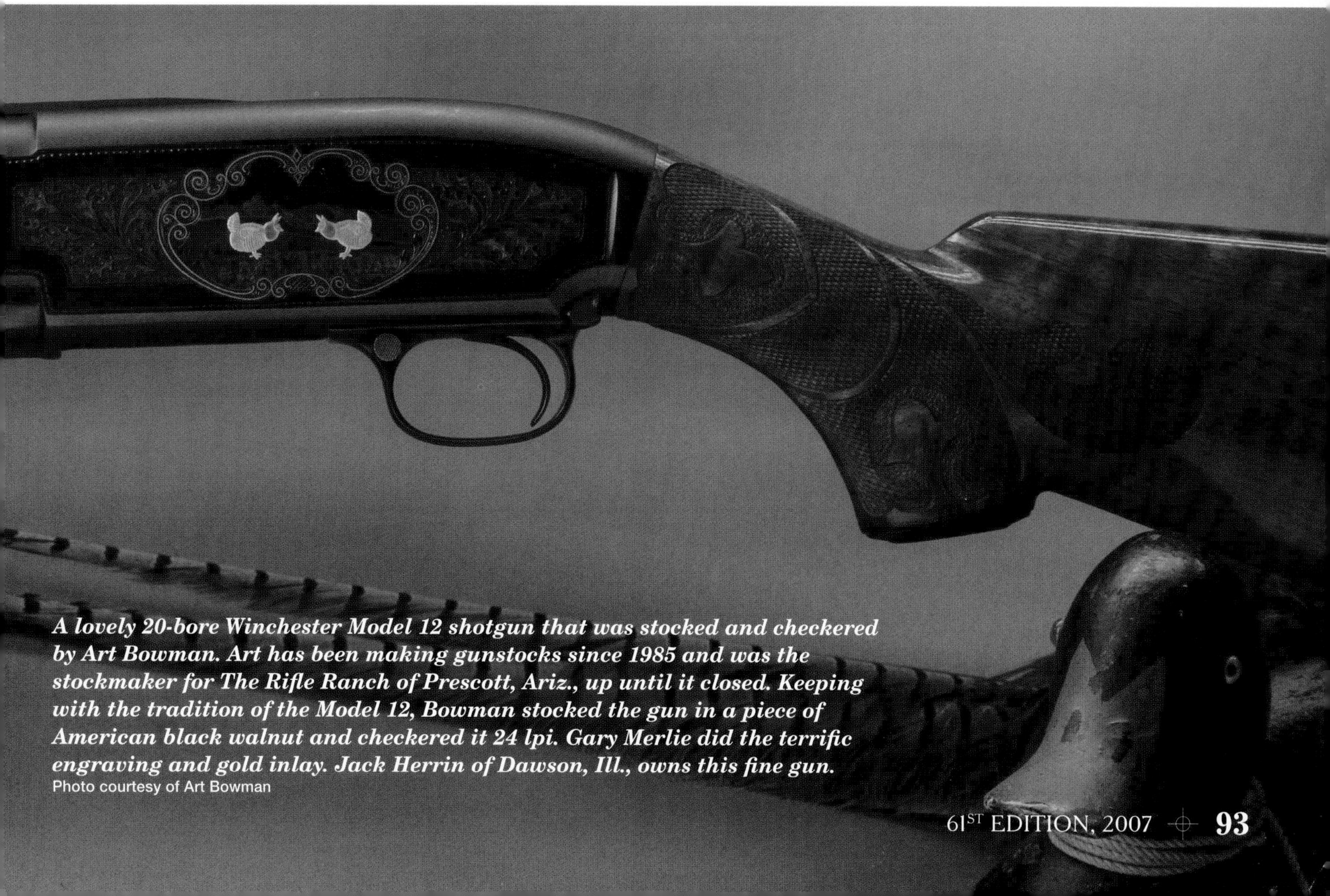

A lovely 20-bore Winchester Model 12 shotgun that was stocked and checkered by Art Bowman. Art has been making gunstocks since 1985 and was the stockmaker for The Rifle Ranch of Prescott, Ariz., up until it closed. Keeping with the tradition of the Model 12, Bowman stocked the gun in a piece of American black walnut and checkered it 24 lpi. Gary Merlie did the terrific engraving and gold inlay. Jack Herrin of Dawson, Ill., owns this fine gun.
Photo courtesy of Art Bowman

Perhaps the most discriminating Savage Model 99 in existence. Clyde Moore of D&D Gunsmiths Ltd. in Troy, Mich. crafted the fine custom stock out of a lovely stick of walnut. Joe Rundell did some modest reshaping of the stock to accommodate the carving and checkering that he executed, in addition to the superb engraving. The rifle is chambered from the 7/08 cartridge and should be a deer-killing machine for its owner, Mr. William Kennedy.
PointSeven Studios photos

A Kimber rimfire rifle after a custom stock job by Art Bowman. Art crafted the new stock from a nice stick of Bastogne walnut. The stock includes a skeleton grip cap, inlet sling swivel studs and a rosewood forend tip. Bowman checkered the stock 24 lpi. He also jeweled and checkered the bolt.
Photo courtesy of Art Bowman

This absolutely lovely lightweight 250-3000 rifle is a joy to shoot and use. Shane Thompson started the crafting process with a ground and detailed Mexican Mauser action. He recontoured the bottom metal and the customer-supplied barrel to a more pleasing shape and whittled out the lovely classic-styled custom stock and checkered it 24 lpi in a no-frills point pattern. The resulting rifle is clean, purely classic, and elegant – exactly what a fine custom rifle should be.
Gene Wright photos

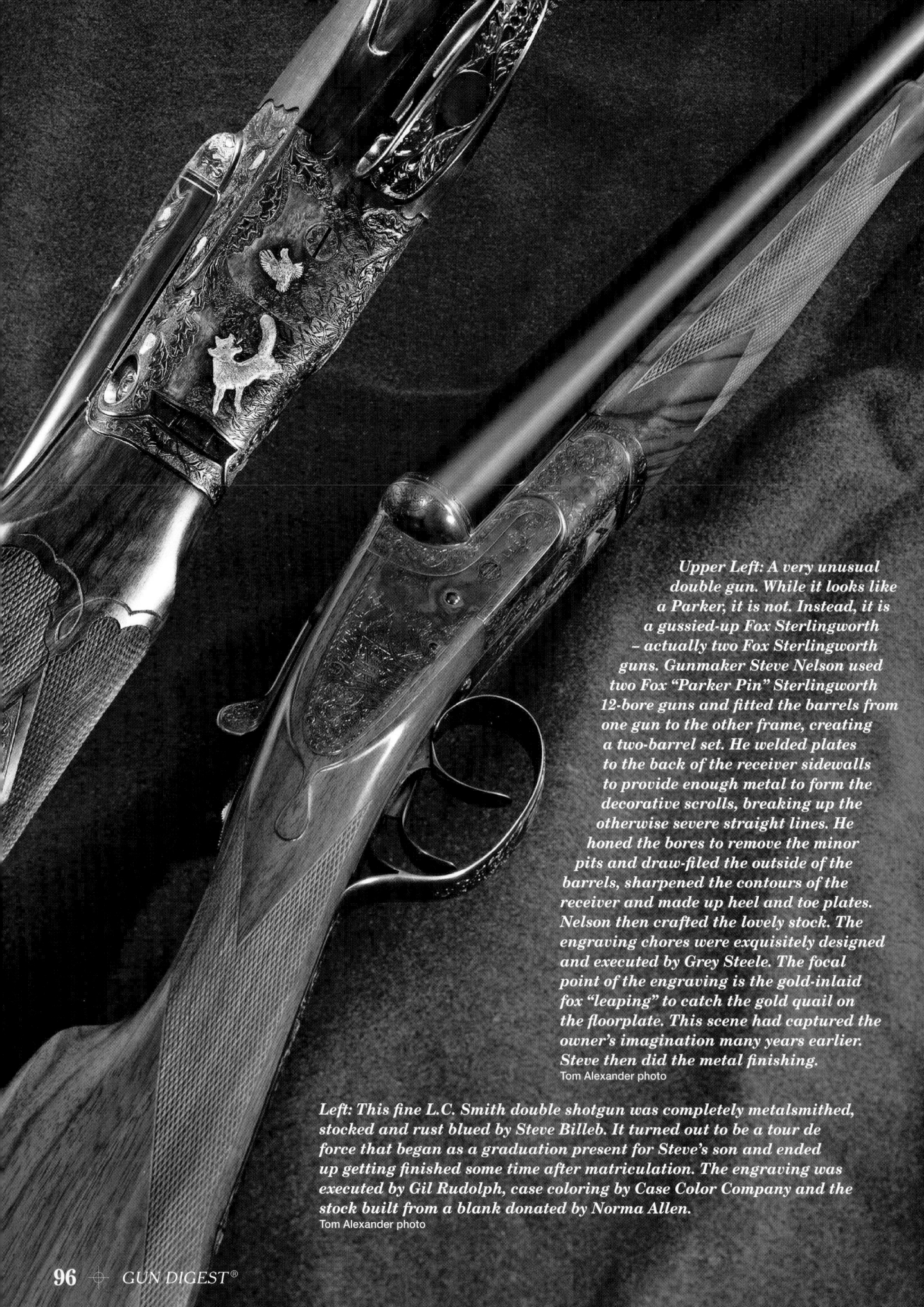

Upper Left: A very unusual double gun. While it looks like a Parker, it is not. Instead, it is a gussied-up Fox Sterlingworth – actually two Fox Sterlingworth guns. Gunmaker Steve Nelson used two Fox "Parker Pin" Sterlingworth 12-bore guns and fitted the barrels from one gun to the other frame, creating a two-barrel set. He welded plates to the back of the receiver sidewalls to provide enough metal to form the decorative scrolls, breaking up the otherwise severe straight lines. He honed the bores to remove the minor pits and draw-filed the outside of the barrels, sharpened the contours of the receiver and made up heel and toe plates. Nelson then crafted the lovely stock. The engraving chores were exquisitely designed and executed by Grey Steele. The focal point of the engraving is the gold-inlaid fox "leaping" to catch the gold quail on the floorplate. This scene had captured the owner's imagination many years earlier. Steve then did the metal finishing.
Tom Alexander photo

Left: This fine L.C. Smith double shotgun was completely metalsmithed, stocked and rust blued by Steve Billeb. It turned out to be a tour de force that began as a graduation present for Steve's son and ended up getting finished some time after matriculation. The engraving was executed by Gil Rudolph, case coloring by Case Color Company and the stock built from a blank donated by Norma Allen.
Tom Alexander photo

Below: A beautiful Hagn and Martini single-shot rifle. Martin Hagn and Ralf Martini did much of the metalwork. Steve Heilmann also did some of the metalwork on the rifle. Richard Boucher started the engraving and completed a good portion of it before falling ill. Unable to complete the engraving, it was turned over to Dennis Reese who finished it. Doug Turnbull did the case coloring and Pete Mazur the other finishing work. The stock was crafted from a lovely stick of California English walnut by Keith Heppler.
Tom Alexander photo

Middle: About as neat a Remington Model 700 as one is ever apt to see. This beautiful rifle was metalsmithed by Pete Grisel and custom stocked by Gary Goudy. It is chambered for the 17 Remington cartridge.
Gary Bolster photo

Bottom: This iron-sighted Mauser is chambered for the 358 Norma Magnum cartridge, an excellent medium bore that is seldom encountered these days. Steve Heilmann did all the wonderful metalsmithing on this rifle. Gary Goudy stocked it in a stick of exquisite Bastogne walnut.
Gary Bolster photo

WINCHESTER'S
LAST RIMFIRE ?

by James E. House

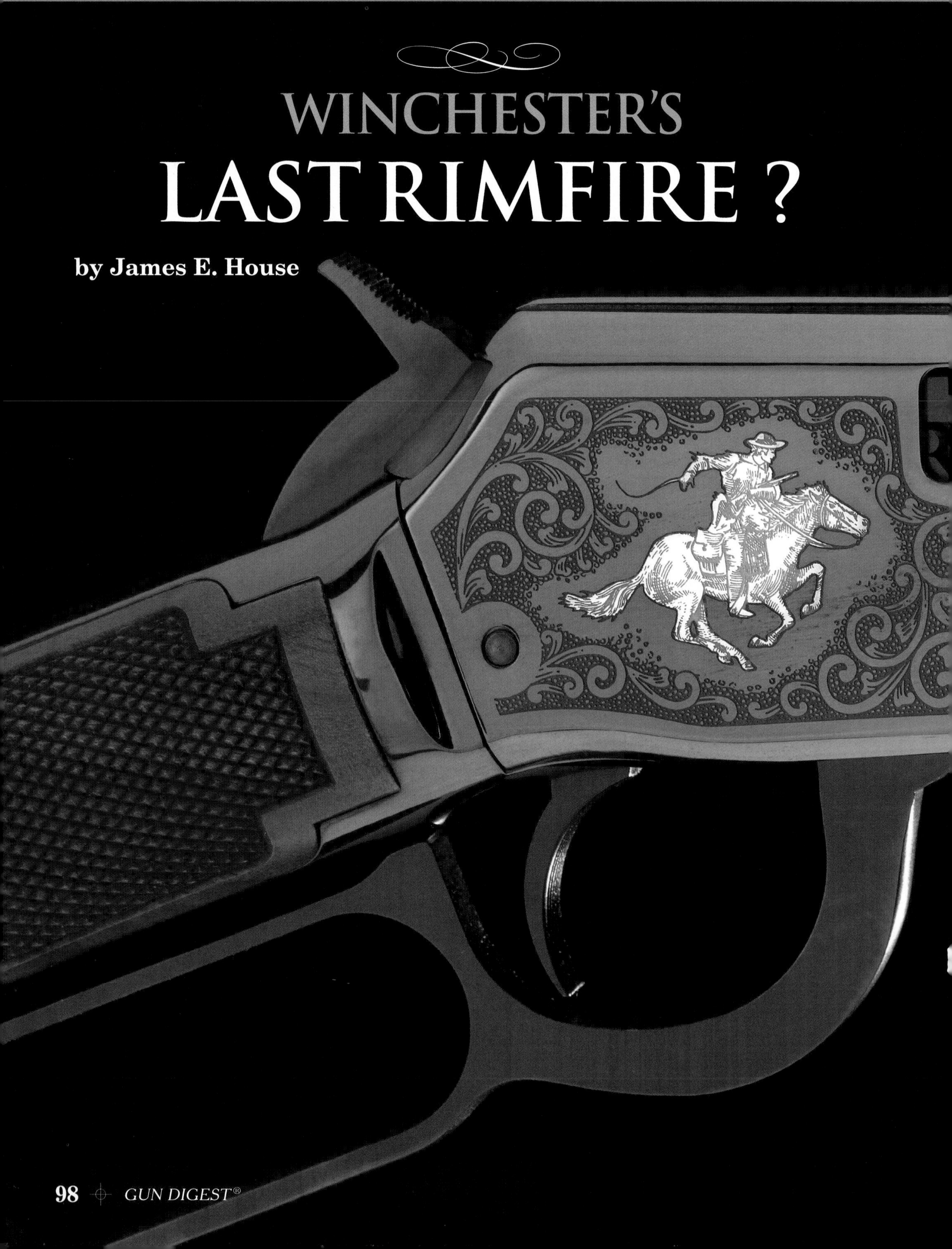

Among the last Winchester Model 9422s produced is the embellished High Grade Tribute version.

here is an old saying that all good things must come to an end. It seems that in the shooting sports we may truly be witnessing the end of an era. About three-score years ago, my introduction to rimfire shooting began with an old Winchester Model 1890 pump chambered for the 22 Short. As a youngster growing up in a rural area, Dad's old rifle was my companion on innumerable walks in the woods and fields. When Dad died, the rifle became mine. But well before 1921 when my old pump was made, Winchester was producing rimfire rifles. At this point, I want to briefly review the history of a few of the

famous Winchester 22s, and relate my association with some of these rifles.

The era of Winchester rimfire rifles began with the Model 1885 single shot and the Model 1873 lever action which was produced in 22-caliber from 1888-1904. Sales of the Model 73 in that caliber were less than stellar, and fewer than 20,000 of the rifles were produced. Winchester introduced the Model 1890 pump with a visible hammer that was essentially the rifle patented by John M. Browning in 1888. The Model 1890 was produced until 1932, and it was followed by the Model 62 slide action (1932-1958). The classic Model 61 hammerless pump was produced from

1932-1963. Many other Winchester rimfire rifles were produced over the years including several single-shot models, as well as autoloaders like the Models 1903, 63, 74, and 77.

In the 1950s, I bought a bolt-action Winchester Model 69A, which by that time was being produced with a grooved receiver. After mounting one of those dinky scopes on it (I could not afford a good scope at that time), I found I had a real shooter. Groups at 50 yards that measured under an inch were obtained when I could find a steady rest. Also during the 1950s, I competed as member of an ROTC rifle team using a Winchester 52D that I found to be unbelievably accurate

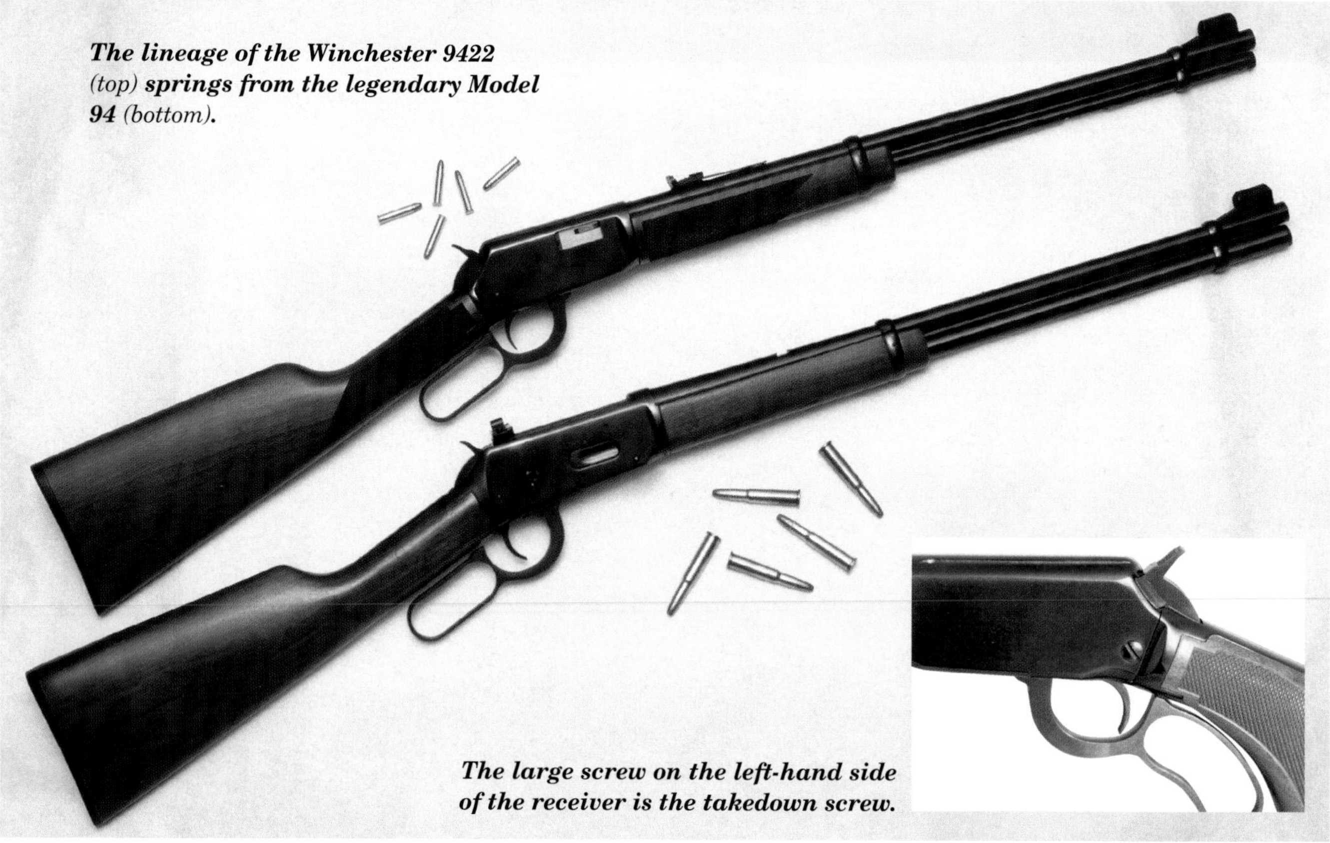

The lineage of the Winchester 9422 (top) springs from the legendary Model 94 (bottom).

The large screw on the left-hand side of the receiver is the takedown screw.

even with its superb metallic sights.

A series of modern-looking rimfires was produced by Winchester in the years from 1963 to 1977. The series included the Model 250 lever action, Model 270 pump, and the Model 290 autoloader. In 22 WMR chambering, the lever action was designated as the Model 255 and the pump as Model 275. With their rounded receivers and sleek appearance, these were appealing rifles. The elegant Model 490 autoloader (1975-1980) which had a steel receiver and a one-piece checkered walnut stock, was even more attractive. As I got into the most pressing and productive years of an academic career, the shooting sports occupied a place of lower priority than teaching, research, meetings, and work in scientific organizations. However, I still admired several rimfire rifles––with Winchesters heading the list. But with priorities being what they were, none of these rifles came my way.

In 1973, another Winchester rimfire did come my way. It was a Model 320 bolt-action clip-fed repeater that was a catalog item for only two or three years. For a time, the Model

320, which had a list price of $57.50, was a bargain among 22s. There was also a Model 310 single shot. Both rifles had a nicely-shaped walnut stock with pressed checkering and an excellent finish on the metal parts. In terms of performance, the Model 320 was on a par with almost any 22 bolt action, but this rifle deserves to be described in an article devoted to it alone. As interesting as these models are, they are not part of this discussion of the Model 9422, but they serve to place the rifle under discussion in the context of other Winchester rimfires.

In 1972, Winchester introduced a lever-action 22 styled after the legendary Model 94. Within a few years, it was the only 22 produced by Winchester as the rifles in the 200 series and the Model 190 autoloader were discontinued. For many years, Winchester's only rimfire rifle has been the Model 9422. It was announced early in 2005 that the Model 9422 was being discontinued as a regular production item. A run of 9,422 rifles will be produced in the Special Edition and High Grade Tribute Series. The Special Edition has the Winchester

Horse and Rider image engraved on the right sideplate of the receiver and a banner reading "Model 9422 Tribute" on the left side. The High Grade models have these images as silver inlays on engraved receivers. Also, 222 high-grade rifles having engraved silver-plated receivers with gold inlays and fancy walnut stocks with special checkering are being produced as a Custom Tribute Series. These special rifles will be the last of the Model 9422s. To those of us who have used Winchester 22s of various types over a period of three-score years, probably the most disturbing aspect of this state of affairs is that the grand old Winchester/USRAC company will have no rimfire rifles in the catalog.

It is not the purpose here to describe and catalog all of the variants of a rifle that was produced for a period of 33 years, but a brief summary is in order. Initially, the Model 9422 was available in 22 LR (which will feed and shoot 22 Short and Long, but the current instruction manuals indicate that Shorts are not recommended) and 22 WMR versions. Early 9422s had a straight-grip walnut stock without checkering. Eventually, the rifles having a straight grip became known as the Traditional while those having a curved grip were called the Legacy. Several special versions were also available over the years. One of these was the Annie Oakley Commemorative Model 9422 which was produced in 1982. Production of this special edition was 6000 rifles.

In 1985, Winchester offered the Model 9422 in two commemorative versions to honor the 75th anniversary of the Boy Scouts of America. One thousand of the Eagle Scout Limited Edition were produced with serial numbers EAGLE 1 through EAGLE 1000. They had receivers, levers, and hammers plated in antique gold, and they were deeply etched on the sides of the receiver and on the lever and hammer. Boy Scout mottos and figures were etched on the receiver, and a gold plated medallion was inlaid in the stock. The Boy Scout Commemorative had a receiver that was plated in antique pewter with etchings on the receiver and lever. A pewter medallion was inlaid in the stock of the Boy Scout Commemorative version which was limited to 15,000 rifles.

In 1986, a high grade Model 9422 was offered through the Winchester Custom Shop. It featured a select-grade walnut stock and a gold inlay of the Statue of Liberty. The same year also marked the introduction of a 9422 chambered only for the 22 WMR that had a green-tone laminated stock that was called WinCam. The 1990 and 1991 Winchester catalogs listed the 9422 with a brown laminated stock that was called the WinTuff stock. Also appearing in the 1985-1987 catalogs was a version known as the Model 9422 XTR Classic Rifle that had a curved grip like the current Legacy but without checkering.

As of 2004, the Model 9422 was offered in the straight grip and curved grip versions in 22 LR, 22 WMR, and 17 HMR (designated as the Model 9417) calibers. If there is one characteristic of the 9422 that attracts attention it is the outstanding construction of these fine rifles. Receivers that are highly polished and blued are made from steel forgings, and barrels and

levers are made of blued steel. The stocks are walnut and although the early rifles had smooth stocks, those produced in the last several years are nicely checkered. Examining a 9422 it is easy to see that these rifles can not be inexpensive. Quality at that level never is. The Model 9422 is an elegant rimfire rifle.

Certainly the elegance of the Model 9422 is one reason for it being discontinued. The latest list prices were $479-515 for the straight-gripped Traditional and $512-551 for the curved-gripped Legacy (depending on chambering), so the Winchester lever-action 9422 and 9417 are rather expensive. The Model 9422 is not a rifle for the shooter who demands highest accuracy, and it costs over twice as much as many of the 22 plinking rifles. But for roaming the woods looking for small game, few rimfire rifles are more appropriate or better suited than the 9422. In the first two decades of production, approximately 600,000 rifles were produced and the total production is approximately 750,000.

The Winchester 9422 had escaped me for many years. I had looked, handled, and wished, but other rimfires were in the cabinet so a Winchester lever action just did not join them. Finally, the opportunity to buy a beautiful Legacy just could not be ignored any longer. At the time, I was involved in a project that required my testing a large number of 22 rifles with no other current Winchester model among them. I spent a great deal of time just getting familiar with the 22 LR Legacy, and the more time I spent with it, the more impressive the rifle became. Later, I added a 22 WMR Traditional 9422 to my rimfire battery. For rimfires, these rifles exude quality. Many rimfire rifles simply are not crafted to the same standards as are centerfires, but the 9422 is.

The 9422 is a takedown rifle that can be

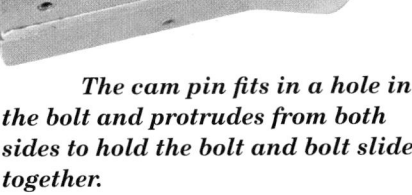

The cam pin fits in a hole in the bolt and protrudes from both sides to hold the bolt and bolt slide together.

❊●❊●❊●❊●❊●❊

disassembled for cleaning and transporting. Loosening and removing the takedown screw at the rear of the left-hand side of the receiver allows separation of the barrel/frame/forearm assembly from the buttstock/lever/trigger assembly. With the major sections apart, the breech bolt and bolt slide can now be removed from off the rear of the receiver while using care to prevent the cam pin (which inserts in a hole through the breech

Special versions of the 9422, like this National Wild Turkey Federation edition, have been produced for specific groups.

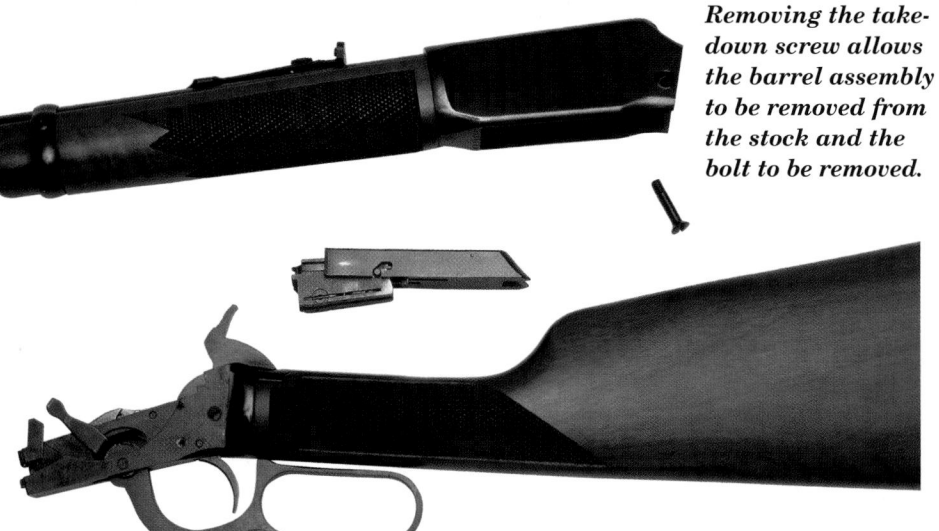

Removing the take-down screw allows the barrel assembly to be removed from the stock and the bolt to be removed.

bolt) from sliding out of the bolt. The bolt and slide can then be separated. Putting the rifle back together begins with attaching bolt, slide, and cam pin, then inserting that assembly into the rear of the receiver. Push the assembly forward until it locks in place, then cock the hammer with the lever closed. Slide the rear section of the frame into the receiver, then insert and tighten the takedown screw.

Working the lever on a 9422 requires very little effort. The action is crisp, smooth, and positive. Being a rifle with an exposed hammer, there is a half cock notch that is intended to hold the hammer away from the firing pin so that if the hammer is

❈●❈●❈●❈●❈●❈

Recently produced Legacy rifles had nice touches like a recessed crown. The front sight is a hooded bead on a ramp.

struck the rifle will not fire. However, a heavy blow on the hammer could cause the hammer to move out of engagement and cause the rifle to fire. Care must be exercised when carrying a lever action rifle of this type with a loaded round in the chamber. The safest practice is to carry the rifle with an empty chamber, then operate the lever to move a cartridge into battery at the time of firing. Although the Traditional and Legacy models have barrel lengths of 20.5 and 22.5 inches, respectively, the magazine capacities are identical. The 22 LR rifles hold 15 cartridges while the 22 WMR rifles hold only 11.

The magazine tube is held in place by a small pin protruding from the brass magazine tube that engages a notch in the front end of the tube housing. When there are no cartridges in the magazine, there is no spring tension pushing it forward to keep the retaining pin in the notch. As a result, the magazine can rotate slightly so that the pin is no longer engaged in the notch, allowing the magazine to fall out if the rifle is pointed downward. Of course this condition does not exist when there are cartridges in the magazine because of the forward pressure generated by the spring

inside the tube. The magazine tube in my Legacy fits tightly enough that it does not rotate as a result of incidental contact. On my 22 WMR Traditional, the magazine tube often fell out when removing the rifle from a case or in other instances in which the knurled piece on the end of the magazine tube was moved. I solved that problem by slipping a 3/8 x 1/2-inch #12 rubber O-ring over the magazine tube between the retaining pin and the knurled end cap. This ring keeps the tube pushed forward so that the retaining pin is held in the notch even when the magazine is empty.

The open sights on the Winchester 9422 are very good examples of that type of sight. The front sight consists of a hooded bead on a ramp, and the rear sight is adjustable. Elevation can be adjusted in steps by means of a notched elevator ramp under the rear sight blade. Two small screws hold the sight blade to the base. Loosening these screws allows the blade to be raised or lowered continuously by any small amount to adjust elevation more precisely than can be done with the notched ramp alone. Adjusting windage requires the entire rear sight to be moved laterally by drifting it in the dove-tailed notch where it is attached to the barrel. The front sight is mounted to the ramp in a dove-tailed notch so it can also be drifted laterally if desired. Because of the quality of the sights and the weight distribution of a lever action rifle, I find it easier to shoot the 9422 than some other rifles in the standing position.

Mounting a scope on the grooved receiver of a 9422 is a simple process, but it can present a minor problem because the receiver is so short. Most scopes have the turret located so that it may be difficult to place one ring in front of the turret and the other behind it without having the eyepiece extend too far back. One solution with some scopes is to place both of the rings behind the turret which then permits the eyepiece to be in a normal position. I have an older Weaver K4 scope that I mount on my 9422M in that way. Also, if the scope is long and a low mount is used, the front of the scope can make contact with the rear sight. The rear sight can easily be removed, but I always leave iron sights on my 22s if possible. Each 9422 is furnished with a hammer extension to facilitate operating the hammer when a scope is mounted on the rifle.

Over the years, I had read several published evaluations of Model 9422 with some authors saying that accuracy was excellent while others said that the rifles were candidates for only plinking. I had always thought that my Model 9422 Legacy performed quite well, so I mounted an old 2-7X Leupold Vari-X II scope on it to do more serious testing. The Leupold scope has the turret in a position that allows one ring to be placed on either side during mounting and still have the eyepiece in about the correct position. Scheels All Sports stores carry a line of optics bearing the Scheels label that includes two rimfire scopes, a 4-12X AO and a 4X AO Compact Elite. The 4-12X model has the turret in a position which allows the scope to be mounted normally on the Model 9422. As indicated in the accompanying table, the Scheels 4-12X scope was used in some of the later tests.

Several types of ammunition were selected for testing, and five 5-shot groups were fired at 50 yards using each type of ammunition. The results obtained are shown in the table above.

ⁿ⋄ⁿ●ⁿ⋄ⁿ●ⁿ⋄ⁿ●ⁿ⋄ⁿ●ⁿ⋄ⁿ●ⁿ⋄ⁿ

Each Model 9422 rifle is furnished with a hammer extension.

Accuracy Results for the 22 LR Winchester 9422 Legacy

Ammunition	Group Size (inches)		
	Smallest	Largest	Average
CCI Standard Velocity	0.52	0.79	0.69
CCI SGB	0.85	1.46	1.22
Federal High Velocity H.P	0.53	1.42	1.03
Lapua Super Club	0.59	1.33	0.94
PMC Scoremaster	0.69	0.94	0.84*
Remington Game Load	0.89	1.52	1.17
SK Jagd Standard Plus	0.37	1.08	0.72*
Winchester Power Point	0.68	1.54	1.12
Wolf Match Target	0.47	0.83	0.60*
		Overall Av.	0.93

*Obtained with the Scheels 4-12X AO rimfire scope attached.

Looking at the results of the accuracy testing shows several interesting facts. First, the Winchester 9422 is capable of giving fine accuracy when appropriate ammunition is selected. The types of ammunition tested represent a broad range, and an overall group size of less than one inch is more than satisfactory. I suspect that most shooters of lever-action rimfires do not test accuracy with Lapua Super Club, CCI Standard Velocity, or Wolf Match Target, but several types of ammunition should always be tested if you are looking for best accuracy. Generally, high velocity, bulk pack, price leader ammo probably will not deliver the highest accuracy in most rifles. Second, I have never subscribed to the old dictum that only bolt-action rifles are accurate. In my experience, it is certainly not true that all rifles with two-piece stocks give groups about the size of a starling at 25 yards, and the data shown confirm this conclusion.

With Wolf Match Target, the groups ranged from 0.47-inch to 0.83-inch with the average group size being only 0.60-inch. With CCI Standard Velocity, the groups ranged from 0.52-inch to 0.79-inch with an average of 0.69-inch. Accuracy at this level rivals that of many 22s that

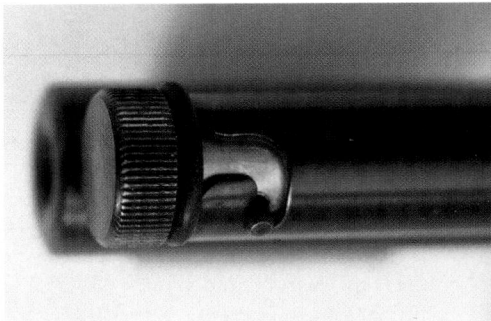

When the magazine is empty, the magazine retaining pin can easily slide out of the notch. A small O-ring between the pin and the knurled cap solved the problem.

ⁿ⋄ⁿ●ⁿ⋄ⁿ●ⁿ⋄ⁿ●ⁿ⋄ⁿ●ⁿ⋄ⁿ●ⁿ⋄ⁿ

The rear sight can be adjusted for elevation by means of a stepped ramp, or by moving the sight blade after loosening two locking screws.

are getting a lot of press coverage, and it is a far cry from the two-inch group size reported in an article I saw some years ago describing the 9422. Lapua Super Club gave an average group size of 0.94-inch but that included one group that measured 1.33 inches, which was much larger than the others. Without that group being included, the other four groups averaged 0.84-inch. The bulk-pack Federal High Velocity hollowpoints averaged 1.03 inches. The four best groups with Winchester Power Points averaged 1.01 inches. Several other types of ammunition gave average group sizes of about 1.1-1.2 inches. Not only is the Legacy a handsome rifle, it shoots very well.

After testing the 22 LR Legacy, I mounted the Scheels 4-12X AO rimfire scope on the 22 WMR 9422M Traditional. Several types of 22 WMR ammunition were tested by firing five 5-shot groups at 50 yards. The results obtained are shown in the table below.

The data obtained show that the 9422M is about as accurate as most 22 WMR rifles I have tested, regardless of the type of action. The overall average group size was only 0.80-inch. Although not capable of benchrest accuracy, the 9422M

delivers accuracy that is similar to several bolt-action sporters I have shot in the same caliber. The Winchester Dynapoint is a lower-powered cartridge that uses a plated bullet and is not really comparable to the other full-power loads. It did not shoot as accurately, and the data for that load was not included in computing the overall average group size. In general, groups were very consistent with most types of ammunition, and with three types the average group size was only about three-quarters of an inch. This level of accuracy is certainly adequate for hunting small game and pests, and with a good scope attached the 9422M is easily a 100-yard varmint rifle on species for which the 22 WMR is a suitable load.

At one point in the testing, I noted that several groups fired in succession seemed to be getting larger. After checking everything, I found that the takedown screw had worked loose. Tightening the screw resulted in an immediate return to more consistent groups.

The results obtained with the 22 LR Legacy and the 22 WMR Traditional show clearly that these rifles give excellent accuracy in spite of the fact that they are takedown

models. Although performance of a rifle is always a primary concern, the more subjective issues of handling and style are also considered when choosing a rifle. In these areas, the Winchester 9422 leaves nothing to be desired. Personally, I do not believe that there is a more beautiful rifle than the lever action. It has a symmetry that is not present when there is a large handle protruding from one side of the action. Lever action rifles are also thin and sleek. Having a magazine tube below the barrel, there is additional weight forward which makes offhand shooting with a lever action rifle somewhat easier than it is with a rifle that has more of the weight between the shooter's hands. Over 6 million Winchester Model 94 centerfire rifles have been produced, at least partially for these reasons. They are equally valid for the Winchester 9422 because it bears a striking resemblance to the legendary Model 94.

I have some extremely accurate bolt-action and autoloader rimfire rifles, but the handy and handsome Winchester 9422 Legacy and Traditional satisfy the vast majority of my rimfire needs. In most sporting situations, they never leave me feeling seriously undergunned regardless of what type of rimfire my shooting companions may be using. Sometimes, I just want to use something other than a bolt action or an autoloader that has had a trigger job, after-market barrel and stock, and other accoutrements. There are times when my mood is better suited to an old-fashioned lever-action than to a bolt-action rimfire sporter. For those times, the Winchester 9422 or 9422M is the perfect companion. I don't know about you but as I approach my 70th birthday my mental state is the most important aspect of being out there with a rifle.

It is hard for me to accept the fact that the time is rapidly approaching when no new rimfire rifles will be produced by Winchester. I am just thankful for the long association I have had with several models. A Winchester rimfire rifle has been and will always be an integral part of many of my pleasant memories.

Results of Accuracy Testing With the Winchester 9422M

Ammunition	Group Size (inches)		
	Smallest	Largest	Average
CCI Maxi Mag H.P. (40 gr.)	0.50	1.08	0.85
Federal H.P. (50 gr.)	0.62	0.98	0.84
Remington Premier (33 gr.)	0.59	0.88	0.76
Remington PSP (40 gr.)	0.55	0.97	0.72
Winchester H.P. (40 gr.)	0.46	0.87	0.76
Winchester Supreme (34 gr.)	0.52	1.03	0.85
Winchester Dynapoint (45 gr.)	0.90	1.14	1.02*
		Overall Av.	0.80

*Not included in calculating the overall average group size.

ACCESSORIES FOR YOUR
AR-15

by Patrick Sweeney

The GG&G A2 is compact, solid, windage-adjustable and works just like an A2. Hard to beat.

The AR-15 is not like other rifles. In the old days, if you wanted a new stock for a rifle you could pick up the process anywhere between sawing the plank off the timber, to applying a finish to a pre-shaped, pre-bedded stock. Not so the AR. Unless you happen to have a milling machine and the experience, you aren't going to be carving a new stock/sight/whatever for your AR out of a block of aluminum, steel or plastic.

That's the bad news.

The good news is that there are a lot of companies who have already done that for you. In the course of writing this article I did a quick web

❁ ● ❁ ● ❁ ● ❁ ● ❁ ● ❁

The Duostock looks odd, but provides a solid and comfortable surface for those who use the high-hold shooting style.

Accessories For Your AR-15

Here we have the GG&G MAD, an EOTech Holosight, and the Redi-Mag—all on one rifle. Not much extra weight, and worth every ounce.

search for "AR-15 accessories" and came up with 712,000 hits. That's a lot of accessories. And someone out there has made it their mission to bolt every single one to an AR that is humanly possible. Me, I like the AR as it is: light, handy, convenient. But there are a few places where prudent selection

of accessories can make it handier and more convenient, even if we do make it a tad bit heavier. Let's take a look at a few, working from back to front.

If you have a solid buttstock and want more magazine carrying capacity, you can lash on a Blackhawk mag pouch. I used to think these

were pretty "mall-ninja" but I've seen lots of them in photos in Iraq and Afghanistan. The troops love them. Just be aware that once it is on you aren't going to be shooting from the other side of the AR. The mag gets in the way. To avoid that, install a Rase stock. The Rase stock uses the hollow interior as a place to store a spare magazine. You give up the trapdoor storage, but gaining a loaded magazine is worth it. Unlike the stock pouch, you can get the spare out without even taking the stock from your shoulder. Those with a tele-stock might want to consider the new Command Arms slider. It has an improved cheekrest, and a compartment that holds spare batteries. Given the number of add-ons we now have that are battery-powered, having spare cells close at hand is a good idea. The CAA stock also has a Picatinny rail and mag holder to put an extra mag on the off-side of the stock. If you already have a tele-stock and slider that works, and you just want battery storage, then CAA also has a sidesaddle. It clips over your slider and holds batteries in a pair of tubes.

Many shooters have been taught to keep their head erect when aiming. The problem with that approach is that the toe of the stock then digs into your chest just above your collar bone. The Duostock has an extension shaped like your chest that gives you a solid stock surface instead of a point. For those used to the "high hold" method, it works great. For those using the old method, the Duostock won't be in your way. One thing to keep in mind when getting a replacement stock for your carbine: there are two tube diameters. There is the mil-spec diameter, and the other, larger, tube. If you have a Colt, a Vltor or an LMT, you have a mil-spec tube. All others are larger. It does matter when you go to fit your new stock on.

Getting a sling on an AR is easy, right? Just lash a strap to the supplied loops. But what if you want something more useful than the traditional sling? Or you want to use a side sling. One approach is to call GG&G and

The Leupold CQ/T offers features from both worlds: a lighted dot, but with magnification and a reticle that still works when your battery goes dead.

get their side-sling adapters. You must have a telestock for the rear, but with the side rings you can have a sling on the left side of your AR. If you get the Sling 'n Light Combo up front you can mount a sling and have a place to put a light. It bolts right into the front sight housing, and stays out of the way. For those who want a single-point sling, GG&G is one of many who make replacement plates. You remove the stock (standard) or unscrew the castle nut and buffer tube (telestock) and then use the adapter plate. You have a choice of ring or loops, depending on what kind of attachment you need for your sling. Some departments don't allow any gunsmithing on an issue weapon that requires tools. If you need to take so much as a screwdriver to the rifle, you can't install the new and improved part. You can install a single-point sling adapter in such cases. Both GG&G and Midwest Industries make slip-on adapters. Remove the slider of your telestock. Slide the adapter over the buffer tube and tighten down. Replace slider. You're done, except for attaching the sling itself. And if the department wants the weapon back, you can simply remove the adapter before you turn in the weapon. (It's your money, right?)

If we all had the same-sized hands, there would only be one size that gloves were made in. If we have different-size gloves, why not pistol grips? The standard works fine for a lot of shooters, but for those who find them lacking, you can go with the Ergo Grip. In shape it is much like the H-K

The Command Arms telestock, with battery storage compartment.

MP5. It also has a riser that comes up the rear of the AR lower, to fill the gap and change the angle of your wrist. If you want more flexibility in selection and adjustment, Magpul makes a modular pistol grip which you can bolt together to the size and contour you prefer. Buffer Technologies makes a pistol grip that is better-contoured than the mil-spec grip, and can be used to store spare batteries or spare parts.

The buttstock isn't the only place you can use to keep extra ammo. The simplest are the mag Cinch from Buffer Technologies, and the mag coupler from Command Arms. Each of them clamps two magazines together. To reload after emptying the first magazine, just grab the mags, press the mag button, pull down, shift over and shove up. You now have more ammo. You need to keep one thing in mind: stagger your mags. The right-hand magazine should be slightly lower in the clamps

than the left. Otherwise, it may interfere with ejection of the empty brass when you're firing from the left-hand magazine. The heavier, but better-protected spare magazine option comes from

The A.R.M.S. 40L is a low-profile BUIS that is spring-loaded and very cool.

Aimpoint's own mount uses a ratcheted locking knob. You can't over-tighten it and you can always check to see if it is tight enough.

Redi-Mag. The Redi-mag (available from The Wilderness) is a sheet-steel housing that acts as a secondary magazine well. Once you have two loaded magazines in your AR, switching is simple. Reach up and grab the spare. Press the mag button. The empty magazine will drop free. Pull the spare out, shift and shove. Be careful. Between the buttstock storage and the Mag Cinch or Redi-mag, you can have so much ammo ready you can't carry your AR.

The big advantage rifles have over other firearms is accuracy at range. To make best use of that accuracy you need more than just irons. (You still need iron sights, but if possible use optics first.) The traditional optics are magnifying optics. Leupold has blended the magnifying optic with a red-dot sight in their CQ/T. You have a regular black reticle (ring and dot) that you can light up with a battery. If the battery dies, you still have a sight. And you can zoom from 1X to 3X for more precision. If you want more than just the 1-3X range then Leupold makes no end of regular scopes that you simply mount as if the AR were any other rifle. Any other rifle with a flat-top, so you can use a hell-for-tough LaRue ring and mount. The sturdiness of LaRue mounts exceeds that of the optics they hold, and sometimes even the rifle itself.

If you do not need magnification (and a lot of AR shooting doesn't) then a red-dot scope is the hot ticket. At the top end you have Aimpoint and EOTech duking it out. Both make extremely tough scopes. Both work hard at improving their scopes. And both deliver superb aiming devices. However, and this is no slam, you can spend almost as much on optics and a mount, as you spent on your rifle. For some of us that isn't a problem. For guys (and gals) who want to learn how to shoot, it can be an obstacle.

Adco to the rescue. Their tactical red-dot looks enough like the Aimpoint that even the most status-conscious mall ninja would be happy. You can buy the Adco, with mount, for about what you'd pay for a mount alone for the Aimpoint. For the beginning shooter, the math is easy: Aimpoint and mount, or EOTech, versus Adco and several thousand rounds of practice ammo. Once you've gotten practice, and know you need more scope, then get the better optics. Although for most shooters, the extra margin of durability is never going to be needed. Sorry, Aimpoint and EOTech, but true. Most of us will not collect paychecks for jumping out of perfectly good aircraft or SWAT vans.

Flat-top rifles are all the rage. But a flat-top rifle removes one of the essential parts of a rifle, the rear sight. Even the most durable optics

Midwest Industries makes a very good A2 BUIS that folds.

Aimpoint scopes can be mounted in other mounts, too, like this A.R.M.S. #68.

break. Even the most energy-packed battery dies. You'll need iron sights, in our case the Back Up Iron Sight, or BUIS. The GG&G MAD (Multiple Aperture Device) is a very compact sight that has two sizes of aperture in it. For those using an A.R.M.S. forearm, they make two BUIS: the 40 and the 40L. The difference is that the 40L is the lower of the two, and fits right behind the top rail of their Selective Integrated Rail. For those not worried about fitting in with accessory rails, and just want a durable and useful sight, Midwest Industries makes their A2 ERS. It has windage adjustments just like the A2 sight, and folds to be out of the way when using your optics.

The hottest new item for the AR is a tactical forearm, or tactical handguards. With lots of rails, there is plenty of room to bolt on more gear. Even if you do not need to bolt a PEQ-2 laser targeting designator, or an M-203 grenade launcher, the railed handguard does a good thing for you: it free-floats your barrel. Free-floating almost always improves accuracy. A.R.M.S. makes the S.I.R. which is cool, rugged, gets high marks in the CDI scale (chicks dig it) and works like a champ. It is also just a bit large in diameter. If you have medium-sized hands it may be large for you. Small-handed shooters may find it too big. Midwest Industries makes railed handguards in all lengths, and even a pair that simply replace your regular handguards. Yes, you lose the free-float option, but you get rails and don't have to use any tools. Samson makes railed handguards that are perhaps the toughest around. (I haven't whacked all brands against a windowsill yet.) If you do have small hands, GG&G makes the best option for you––and for us large-handed shooters, too. Their railed handguard has removable rails. If you want, you can strip the rails off except the one actually holding your light. That leaves a very compact free-float tube that is great for grasping.

And speaking of lights, you can now get as much or as little light on your subject as you like. There is no end of flashlight holders that clamp

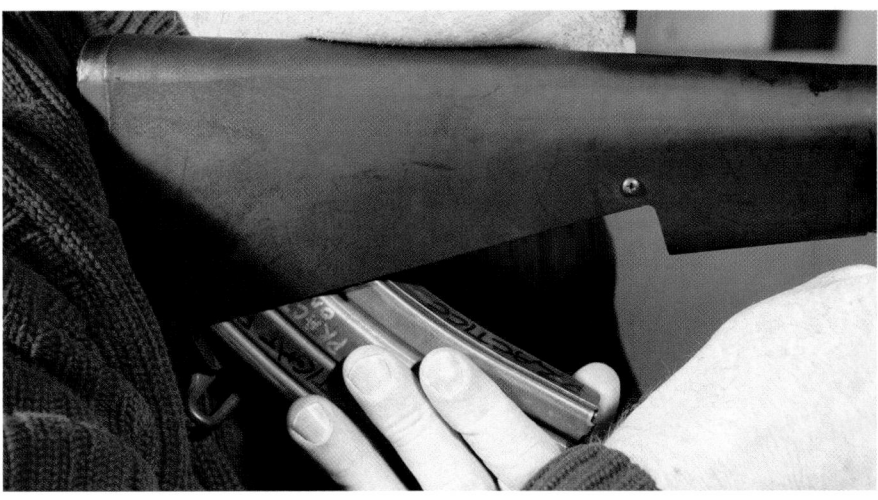

The Rase stock holds a spare loaded magazine in the stock. When you need it, you can get it quickly.

right to your railed handguard. You can install a low-power light for just walking around in the dark, or you can use a Surefire 900-series light pumped up to 500 lumens. That will almost give heat blisters to what you're lighting up. If you want something not removable, the 500 series replace your handguards and also give you the option of up to 500 lumens. For smaller lights, the Surefire X200, the Streamlight M3 or M6, and almost any other handgun-designated tactical light will attach right to your railed handguard. They are all simple to install, and will fit in your pocket.

In all this discussion, you have to keep one word in mind: restraint.

If you went and attached all the possible extra gear to your AR, you can more or less double its weight. It is easy to take a carbine of just under seven pounds and bolt more than seven pounds of stuff to it. An H-Bar would take more work, but you could come close to doubling its nine pounds. You can also break the bank on accessories. If you buy a good AR for a grand, you could easily double your cost with accessories. Remember, you have to actually pick up and carry your AR in order for it to do you any good. And you have to be able to afford practice ammo, if you expect to have any skills to show. ✺

The Adco is a good, inexpensive red-dot for those who want to get shooting, get practice and move up in scopes later. (Or not.)

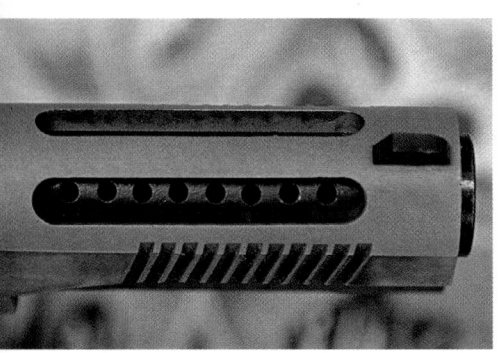

The 45 Super delivers as much downrange punch as a revolver in 41 Magnum, but the out-front weight and 16 gas ports of the Springfield V16 Long Slide make it more comfortable to shoot.

thinning its wall from the inside with a special reamer. He later switched to 451 Detonics brass which still had to be shortened but did not require as much reaming. Due to considerably greater web thickness of a case formed from either of those cases, the area left unsupported by the barrel of the 1911 chamber was able to contain higher pressures than was possible with the 45 ACP case. The fact that the case wall just forward of the web was also thicker didn't hurt anything either. This beefed-up version of the 45 ACP would come to be called the 45 Super.

When Grennell wrote his first article on the 45 Super many years ago, there were several reasons why the cartridge seemed to be destined for great success. For one, it was capable of generating over 700 foot-pounds of energy at the muzzle, a level of power that matched some 41 Magnum and 44 Magnum loads. *(The 45 Winchester Magnum is more powerful but it requires an oversized autoloader and is too long for the 1911 pistol.)* Secondly, and just as important, the hunting of big game with handguns had become quite popular among Americans, so an autoloading pistol of conventional size chambered for a magnum-performance cartridge fell right in step with the parade. Thirdly, transforming a mild-mannered old pistol into a romping, stomping powerhouse was

relatively inexpensive and last, but possibly most important of all, the new cartridge could be safely fired in handguns already owned by millions of shooters around the world. The 45 Super had a lot going for it and why it did not take off like a scalded dog remains something of a mystery.

The 45 Super received a really big boost during the mid-1990s when Starline began to make the brass and a small New York ammunition manufacturer by the name of Triton started loading the ammo. All told, Triton offered five different full-power loads: 165-grain bonded-core hollowpoint (BCHP) at 1400 fps, 185-grain jacketed hollowpoint (JHP) at 1300 fps, 200-grain BCHP at 1200 fps, 230-grain BCHP at 1100 fps, and 230-grain FMJ at the same velocity. I was happy to discover, when first shooting those four loads, their advertised performance was no brag, as each and every one equaled or exceeded those velocity ratings in a five-inch barrel. More recently, I checked out their velocity in the six-inch barrel of a Springfield 1911A1 Long Slide and all were slightly faster than they were supposed to be. In addition to those five, Triton also offered three reduced-velocity loads with 185- 200- and 230-grain bullets loaded about 200 fps slower than the full-throttle loads.

While writing this report I decided to contact Triton to see if any new loads had been added to the list and was surprised to learn the company is no longer loading the 45 Super. As a company spokesman

❦●❦●❦●❦●❦●❦

Since the external dimensions of the 45 Super (left) and 45 ACP (right) are the same, both can be fired in a pistol chambered for either cartridge.

explained to me, 40 is the hot number in handgun cartridges today and a newer cartridge called the 40 Super is selling far better than Grennell's old 45 Super. The 40 Super started out as the 45 Winchester Magnum shortened to the same length as the 10mm Auto and necked down, but such case forming is no longer necessary since Starline offers the brass. The greater popularity of the 40 Super indicates to me that most who are interested in high-performance cartridges in the 1911 pistol are not hunters because as hunting cartridges go the 45 Super should be the better of the two. Something else the 45 Super has in its favor is it can be fired in a standard 45 ACP barrel whereas the 40 Super requires the installation of a barrel chambered specifically for it.

With Triton no longer offering 45 Super ammo, Grennell's fine old cartridge is once again strictly a handloading proposition. Starline still offers excellent unprimed brass quite capable of handling 45 Super chamber pressures. The word I get is the company has no plans to drop it anytime in the near future but, just the same, anyone who has, or will have, a 1911 pistol converted for this cartridge would be wise to stock up on cases now rather than wish they had later. One of the nice things about owning a pistol in 45 Super is that 45 ACP cases can be used for reduced-velocity practice loads and the 45 Super brass reserved for full-power hunting loads.

Something else the 45 Super has going for it is that no special reloading dies are required. Since the external dimensions of its case are the same as those of the 45 ACP, dies reamed for that cartridge work perfectly. The two cartridges also use the same shell holder. The 45 ACP dies I use were made by Redding and consist of a full-length resizer with titanium carbide insert, micrometer-adjustable bullet seater die, and taper crimp die. Bullets of various weights are seated to the same overall length as for the 45 ACP.

For plinking and target shooting, any jacketed bullet works fine, but since most of those available were designed for the slower impact velocities of the 45 ACP, over-expansion and its attendant lack of penetration could be a problem when some bullets are pushed to the higher speeds possible with the 45 Super. This especially holds true if the bullet strikes heavy bone. Based on the very limited amount of expansion testing I have done, I'd say the Triton folks are correct when they recommend the 230-grain Speer Gold Dot hollowpoint and the Hornady jacketed hollowpoint of the same weight as the bullets to use on game up to whitetail deer in size. I also believe the Sierra 240-grain JHP would perform about as well as those two. Expanding bullets of lighter weights are best reserved for lighter targets.

As for choosing the perfect powder, I'll have to say it's a tossup between those I have included in my data chart. Vihtavuori N350 and Alliant Power Pistol burn a bit cleaner than HS7 and AA7 but accuracy was about the same regardless of which of the four propellants was used behind various bullets. The two most accurate loads tried in the Springfield pistol, both averaging 4-1/2 to 5 inches at 50 yards from a sandbag rest, were the Nosler 185-grain JHP pushed along at just over 1300 fps by 11.2 grains of Power Pistol and the Speer 230-grain Gold Dot exiting the muzzle at 1125 fps, compliments of 12.2 grains of Hodgdon's HS7. Interestingly enough, when the 185-grain Nosler was zeroed

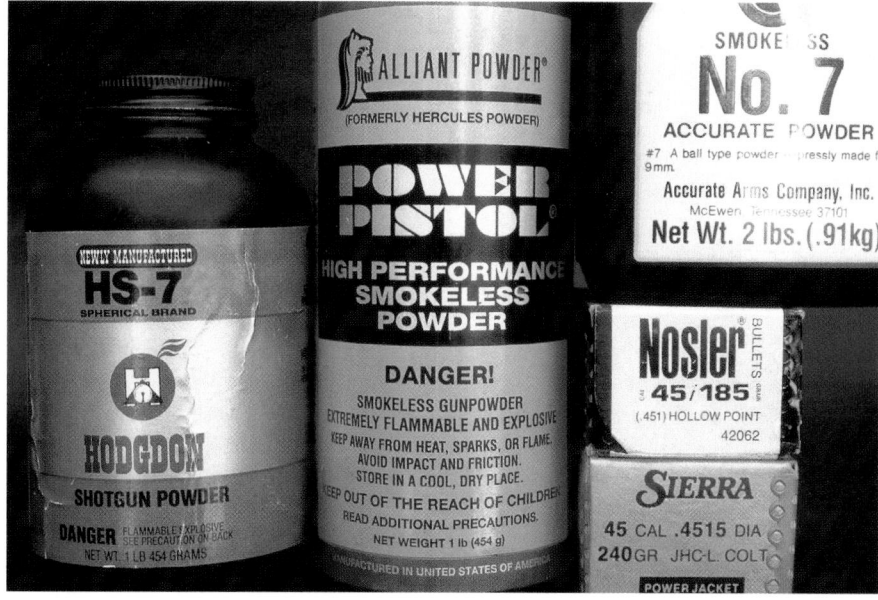

These three powders are top performers in the 45 Super.

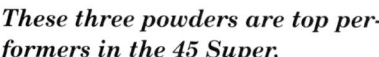

two inches high at 50 yards, it was almost dead on the money at 100 yards where average group size increased to about eight inches. Zeroed the same, the 230-grain Speer landed three inches low at 100 yards with several five-shot groups fired at that range measuring as small as six inches.

Autoloaders in 45 Super are available from Springfield, Inc. and STI International. Actually, with the exception of a heavier recoil spring, they are the same guns those companies offer in 45 ACP. I have not shot the STI gun, but I am quite impressed by how comfortable the Springfield V16 Long Slide pistol is to shoot with full-power loads. When

I first started shooting the gun, a sharp corner on the rear edge of its thumb safety kept digging into the second joint of my thumb, but a sharp file quickly solved that little problem. The 45 Super churns up about the same level of recoil as the 41 Magnum but when fired in the Springfield autoloader I find it to be much easier on the hand than full-power 41 Magnum loads fired in any revolver I have tried. No doubt about it, the extra up-front weight of the autoloader's six-inch barrel and the extra-long slide, along with 16 gas ports in the barrel, do a great job of reducing muzzle jump. Anyone who can handle full-power 45 ACP ammo in a five-inch 1911 pistol will have no problem with full-power 45 Super ammo in the Springfield V-16 Long Slide. In fact, I find the combination easier on the hand than Colt's Lightweight Commander and Officer's ACP with heavy 45 ACP loads.

I tried several 45 ACP loads in the Springfield gun and accuracy was about the same as with 45 Super loads,

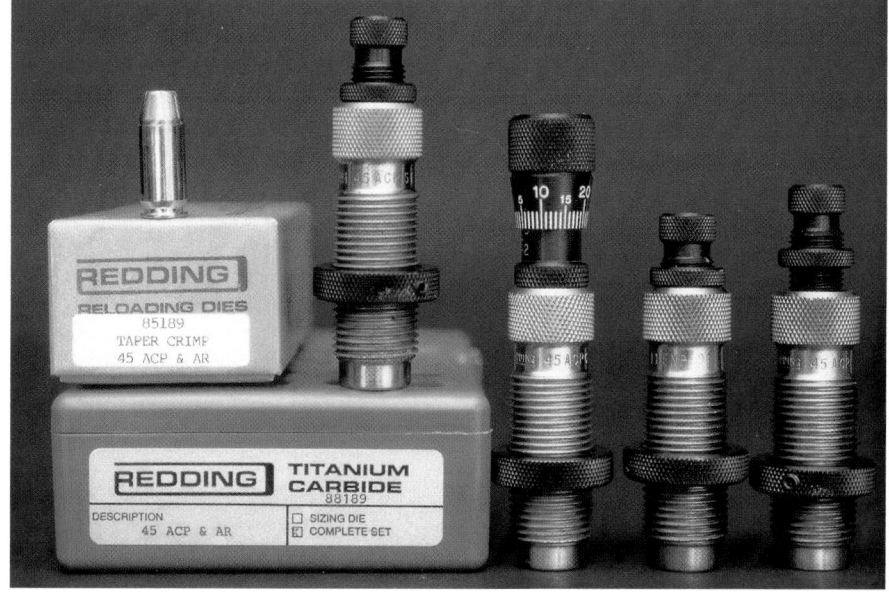

Reloading dies reamed for the 45 ACP and 45 Auto Rim work equally well with the 45 Super.

with a couple of positive exceptions. Federal Premium ammo loaded with the 230-grain Hydra-Shok bullet, and Black Hills ammo loaded with a jacketed hollowpoint of the same weight consistently averaged no worse than 3-1/4 inches at 50 yards. I consider this to be outstanding performance for anything less than a 1911 built for shooting light loads in bullseye competition. Prior to shooting the gun, I had assumed that 45 ACP ammo would not generate enough recoil to cycle its slide reliably unless the 32-pound recoil spring was replaced with a lighter spring. This did not prove to be the case, so long as full-power 45 ACP ammo was used.

When loaded with a bullet capable of expanding and yet holding together for deep penetration at its impact velocities, I consider a 1911 pistol chambered for the 45 Super to be plenty of medicine for certain hunting applications. Hunting wild hogs with hounds where shots usually come fast, close and furious springs immediately to mind. Through the years I've killed lots of hogs with cartridges of less power (including the 40 S&W), so I'm sure the 45 Super is up to that particular job. Neither would I hesitate to use the cartridge out to 50 yards or so on smallish whitetail deer, and might even give it another 50 long paces for those who enjoy seeing how close they can get to a pronghorn antelope rather than shooting from afar. For that job I might switch to the Nosler 185-grain JHP. A treed mountain

Triton no longer offers 45 Super ammo, but unprimed cases are available from Starline.

lion wouldn't stay that way very long if shot in the right place with the 45 Super, and anyone who knows how to use a predator call should find the cartridge fun to use on critters such as coyote and bobcat.

Something I'd like to see become available is a .451-inch hunting bullet designed specifically for the 45 Super and other high-speed cartridges of its caliber. Either a Partition bullet from Nosler or an X-Bullet from Barnes is what I have in mind and, if I had my druthers, it would weigh somewhere in the neighborhood of 220 to 240 grains. In addition to being an excellent option for the 45 Super, such a bullet would also prove useful to those who handload the 45 Winchester Magnum, as well as a more recent introduction called the 460 Rowland.

Something important to remember about the 45 Super is it operates at considerably higher chamber pressures than the 45 ACP. I have not been able to pin down the exact level to which Triton ammo was loaded, but my guess is it is right up there with the 40 S&W, and possibly as high as the 10mm Auto—and those cartridges operate at 30,000 to 37,000 psi, compared to 21,000 psi for the 45 ACP. As Colt proved with the 10mm Auto chambering, the 1911 pistol is capable of handling higher pressures than generated by the 45 ACP, but this does not prove all 1911s capable of handling either the 10mm Auto or the 45 Super.

Editor's note; Layne is field editor for Shooting Times magazine.

45 Super Load Data

Bullet	Powder		MV
	(Type)	(Gr.)	(fps)
185 Nosler	JHP V-N350	10.9	1298
185 Nosler	JHP V-N350	11.1	1322
185 Nosler	JHP Alliant PP	11.2	1318
185 Nosler	JHP HS7	14.6	1322
200 Hornady	JHP V-N350	10.0	1192
200 Hornady	JHP Alliant PP	10.2	1215
200 Speer	JHP HS7	13.6	1244
200 Speer	JHP AA-7	14.5	1236
225 Speer	JHP HS7	2.3	1149
225 Speer	JHP AA-7	13.5	1142
230 Hornady	JHP V-N350	8.5	1043
230 Hornady	JHP V-N350	8.8	1087
230 Hornady	JHP Alliant PP	9.3	1116
230 Speer	GDHP HS7	12.2	1122
230 Speer	GDHP AA-7	13.4	1118
240 Sierra	JHP HS7	12.0	1110
240 Sierra	JHP AA-7	13.2	1125

Triton Factory Loads*

165 BCHP	—	1407
185 JHP	—	1332
200 JHP	—	1224
230 JHP	—	1118

*No longer available

NOTES: WARNING! These loads are maximum and intended only for 1911-style pistols in good serviceable condition, and either professionally modified or originally built to handle 45 Super loads. Reduce all powder charges by 20 percent for starting loads. Starline 45 Super cases and Federal 150 primers were used in all loads. Velocities shown are averages of five or more rounds clocked 12 feet from the muzzle of a six-inch Springfield V-16 Long Slide pistol. Guns with five-inch barrels will average only about 25 feet per second slower.

THE HOWE-WHELEN
Bolt-Sleeve Peep Sight

by Scott Key Shelton, Jr.

Jenkins-Howe-Whelen sight #1 on the author's '03 Springfield.

ol. Townsend Whelen's seminal role in firearms development, and his influence generally, is legend. Just one of his collaborations, with James Virgil Howe, produced what is arguably the most sophisticated, well-thought-out, totally useful,

◆◇◆ ● ◆◇◆ ● ◆◇◆ ● ◆◇◆ ● ◆◇◆

▶ *Right-top view of the Red Jenkins/Howe-Whelen bolt-shroud peep sight. Engraving and gold-inlay by Jim White of Anchorage, Alaska. Rifle is remodeled '03 Springfield.*

and utterly pleasing rifle sight ever conceived or designed or manufactured and used in the history of long arms. This would be the Howe-Whelen bolt-sleeve peep sight.

Much less is known about Howe, as compared to Whelen, but this is the same James V. Howe of the famed Griffin & Howe, formed with Seymour Griffin in 1923. The company was absorbed by Abercrombie & Fitch in 1930. Griffin & Howe rifles remain highly collectible, and relatively rare. The *Blue Book of Gun Values, 21st Edition* (Fjestad) states that fewer than 3000 guns have been produced since 1923, that an average example without special engraving will start at $3150 plus, while elaborate specimens "will command over $10,000." This gives us some rough idea of the quality and rarity arising out of the life and times of James Virgil Howe.

But in addition to this rough idea of value, let us add the fact that Griffin & Howe rifles set a standard which is yet to be surpassed: most truly fine custom rifles to this day exhibit qualities of design and execution first realized in those few superb examples of the gunmaker's craft which bore the name Griffin & Howe. This is to say without

Left view of sight, showing elevation slide.

Top rear view of Jenkins/Howe-Whelen peep sight. Note safety position on right side of assembly.

Right side view of sight in cocked/safe position.

equivocation that Griffin & Howe rifles remain THE BEST examples of American rifle craftmanship... copied by many, matched or surpassed by very few...hence their continuing historical and material value.

If you have a copy of Howe's *The Modern Gunsmith*, you might have stumbled upon the Howe-Whelen peep. But I doubt very much that one out of a thousand of us riflemen have ever even seen one, not in real life, not at a gun collector's show—or even on the rare Griffin & Howe rifle. I certainly would have missed it myself, were it not for Robert "Red" Jenkins, gunsmith extraordinaire, who has actually made not just one, but three of these little marvels, including the engraved and gold-inlaid #3, shown here. For James V. Howe, thoughtful and considerate man that he must have been, includes the technical drawings required for said sight, in the above-mentioned book, on pages 282-5. If he had not published these

drawings, this extraordinary piece of firearms history might have been all but entirely lost to it, and to us.

Howe himself has little to say of an nontechnical nature about the sight itself, except that it was designed with Col. Whelen, places the "peep" two or so inches closer to the shooter's eye than receiver-mounted peep sights (Lyman, Redfield, Weaver, etc.), replaces the standard bolt-shroud on a Springfield or Mauser, and uses the same type of windage/elevation adjustments used by receiver-type sights. And that he likes the safety *(a sight with a built-in safety?!)* on the right side of the sight, because it is easily accessible to the right-handed shooter's thumb. Most of the remaining two pages of copy in *The Modern Gunsmith* are given to technical details, with the comment that further development of such sights must be determined by interested persons. Of note is the front sight which he describes and

shows (drawings) in the preceding paragraphs, which lends itself very nicely to use with the Howe-Whelen bolt-sleeve peep, for target or field use.

Clearly, peep sights, to a very large extent, have seen their day, except for relatively specialized use; specifically target rifles and some dangerous-game guns, and those odd rifles here and there that for one reason or another won't take a scope. What Howe could not have known,

at the time of the development of this sight, is that it would represent in many ways the very pinnacle of peep sight development. For a bolt-action rifle, there exists simply nothing, nor is there likely to be anything, that so effectively addresses the question: What is the best peep sight? There's only one problem; they're not available, for love or money, except to those very few collectors who might just happen to be in possession of one. God knows if Howe kept a record of how few or many he himself made.

I suspect they were made to order, meaning *only* made when ordered. He does note that some good and mediocre examples were produced here and there by others, and we have heard of some versions having been made by Hoffman, and some by Marble-Goss, which may or may not be the ones Howe makes reference to. Seen any? Neither have I.

The problem is this, which Red discovered when he decided to make his first one: they take FIFTY hours of machine shop time and labor, for a master gunsmith. At fifty dollars an hour for a skilled machinist, we're talking about a $2500 item... that, fellow firearms enthusiasts, is why we don't see them, and why they are almost completely unavailable. Even Red won't make any more. It just takes too much time. When you think about it, the H-W peep is and always has been a pretty rarified item: the only guys willing to go the distance for a Howe-Whelen *(when they were available)* on their favorite sporterized Springfield '03 or Mauser '98 were those for whom only the best was good enough, who would shed blood for that additional two inches of sight radius, and sell their mother's dentures to avoid drilling and tapping that pristine action and mangling that gorgeous custom Circassian walnut stock to accommodate a receiver-type sight. Not on what was to be the perfect rifle. So only those guys bought them. You know the type...the few and very far-between. Nowadays they buy Swarovskis for their Dakotas, or take out a second mortgage for a David Miller, or a D'Arcy Echols.

Anyway, in a few short decades after the "golden age" of the peep sight, good, affordable *(and internally adjustable)* rifle scopes began to become available, which soon became more-or-less standard equipment on bolt-action rifles. Peep sights took a back seat to the new Lyman Alaskan, or early Redfield or Leupold scopes. Nevermind the persisting fact that few shooters, then or now, can hit better from practical hunting positions with a scope than with

Top rear view in fired/ safety off position.

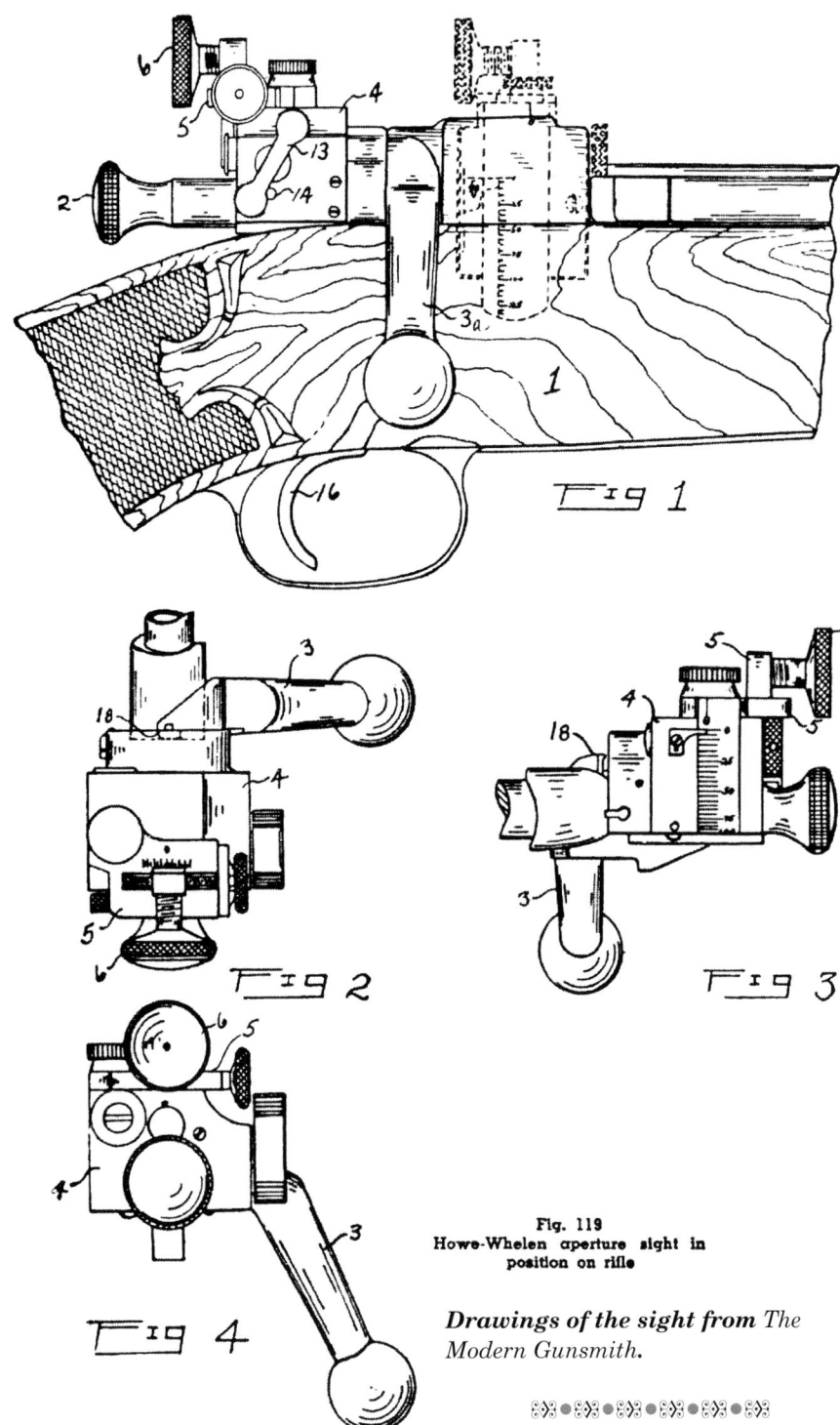

Fig 1

Fig 2

Fig 3

Fig. 119
Howe-Whelen aperture sight in
position on rifle

Drawings of the sight from The
Modern Gunsmith.

Fig 4

a receiver-mounted peep on a Model 54 Winchester 30-06, many, many years ago, fired from the bench. Testing other rifles/loads at the time, I decided to see what the old girl would do to a 300-yard target. Ten shots would have all killed a regulation baseball. Few scope-sighted rifles have I owned that would do as well at that range... and the front bead completely covered the entire paper target! So go figure. Since then I've given peeps all the credit they deserve, using on them on rifles from a 250 Savage Model 99 to a 444 Marlin, from 22s to 45-70s, Lymans, Redfields, and so on... and so does the U.S. military, to this day: in spite of all the fancy optics available for the M16/AR15, basic marksmanship qualification is still done exclusively with a peep sight.

But I wonder, in this CNC-controlled age and investment-cast world of ours, is there—or could there develop—sufficient interest in the finest practical peep sight ever designed, to cause some enterprising manufacturer to reintroduce the Howe-Whelen bolt-sleeve peep sight? Until then you'll just have to do it yourself, now that you have the drawings...or find your own Red Jenkins, and try to talk him out of one...lotsa luck, pardner!

Afterword: That would have been the end of this article, if something rather strange hadn't happened to me. I didn't think I needed to own a Howe-Whelen bolt-shroud peep sight...until all of a sudden I did. So I emailed Red, and asked a silly question: what would you think about letting go of one of them rascals? Not the pretty engraved and gold-inlaid one, of course, but where are number one and number two? Mr. Jenkins had to think about it for a while, giving me time to cajole and come up with extravagant offers. Finally I came up with the right one, and Jenkins-Howe-Whelen bolt-shroud peep sight #1 was soon on its way to Texas, via Red Label shipping. So that's the end of the story, and the beginning of a beautiful friendship... mine, with one of the finest bolt-action rifles ever made, coupled with *the finest peep sight ever made.* Thanks, Red. And thank you, James V. Howe and Col. Townsend Whelen!

a good peep sight, mounted on the same rifle. Add the additional bulk and weight of scopes, and the fact they are all but useless in the really wet and rainy...well, one begins to wonder what all the fuss was about. Nonetheless, scopes now rule as rifle

sights, and the golden age of the peep is behind us. As they say at NASA, "Better is the enemy of good."

I don't know if it's happened to you, but good use of a good peep sight can be a revelation. I remember the first time I ever really gave one a chance;

BROWNING
A-BOLT MOUNTAIN TI & WINCHESTER XP3 BULLET

by Layne Simpson

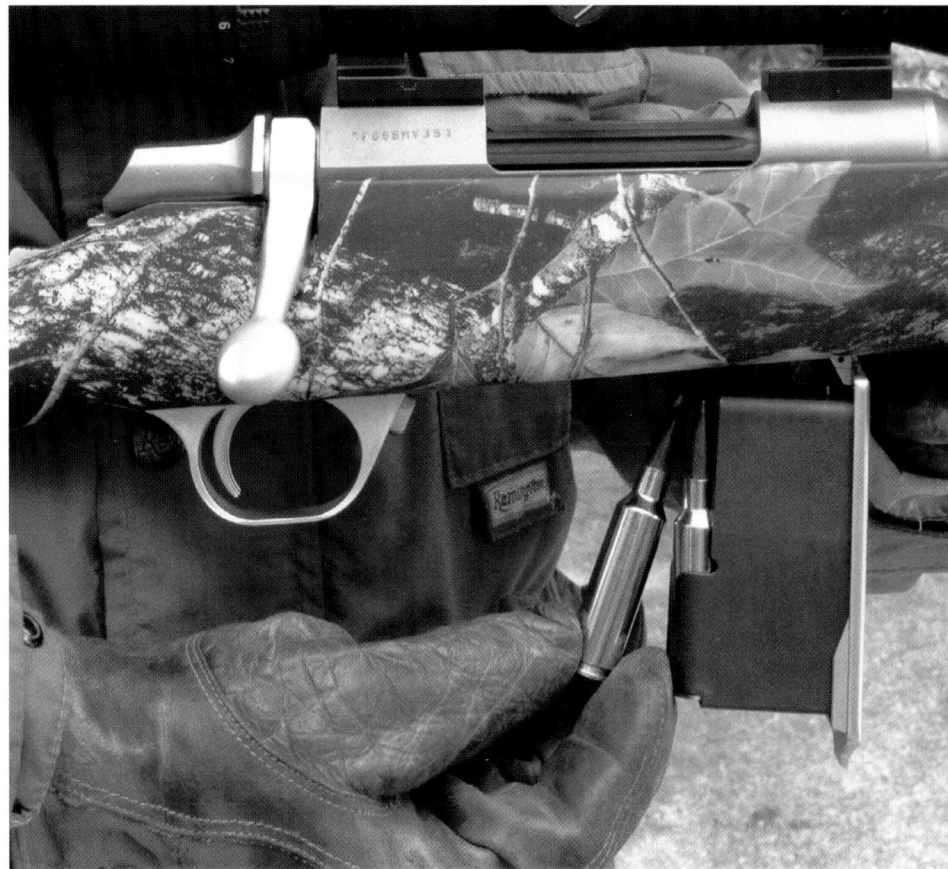

Browning A-Bolt Mountain Ti

In 1984 Browning management made the decision to lighten up and scale down the BBR action and reintroduce it as the A-Bolt. The new rifle weighed about a pound less and among other changes, its bolt had three large locking lugs rather than nine smaller ones and it would also be eventually offered with a left-

hand action. One of the rifle's strong points of both rifles is a swing-down magazine box. It can be loaded with cartridges in four ways: through the ejection port as Paul Mauser would have us do, with the magazine box

swung down but still attached to the hinged floorplate, or with it completely detached from the floorplate. Another option is to remove the empty

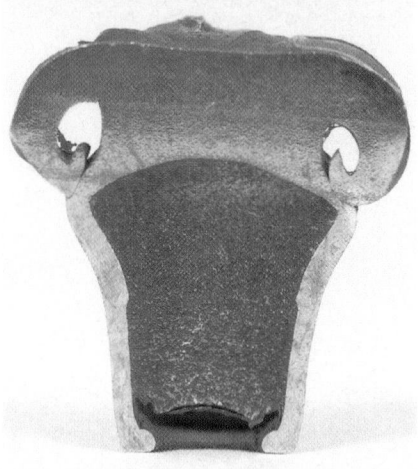

New Winchester XP3 bullet retains about 90 percent of its weight and is an excellent choice for use on game ranging in size from deer and pronghorn antelope to deer and elk.

A drop-down magazine is one of the best features of the A-Bolt rifle.

magazine box from the floorplate and quickly snap-in a loaded one. The latter two methods allow the magazine of the rifle to be recharged while the bolt is closed and locked on a cartridge in the chamber, not a bad option to have on a rifle to be used for hunting potentially dangerous game.

Another nifty idea the A-Bolt borrows from the BBR is scissors-style follower struts in lieu of the more common leaf spring-powered follower. This design discourages the nose of a cartridge from tipping downward in the magazine box as the bolt pushes it toward the chamber. This is why the A-Bolt feeds Winchester's fat and stubby WSM family of cartridges like grease on glass while some other rifles choke. The magazine is also quick and easy to unload—remove the cartridge from its chamber, drop the hinged floorplate, remove the magazine and the rifle is safe to go. The magazine assembly is easily taken apart for cleaning—slide off its bottom retention plate, remove the follower and its spring and the job is done. Magazine capacities depend on the case diameters of various cartridges, five for the 223 Remington, four for the 30-06 and three for the various magnums.

The A-Bolt action is made in three lengths. Latest variant is the Mountain Ti, my favorite for hunting big game where the mountains are tall and steep and the weather often turns nasty. Its titanium receiver trims away four ounces when compared to the steel A-Bolt receiver and the utilization of a synthethic bolt body sleeve sheds another three ounces. Browning ways the synthetic stock is 10 ounces lighter than the synthetic stocks of other A-Bolt rifles. The Mountain Ti in 300 WSM I used to take a very nice New Mexico elk during the 2005 season weighed 7-1/2 pounds complete with a Zeiss 3-9X Diavari MC scope in a Browning two-piece lightweight mount, a Weatherby nylon sling and three cartridges resting in its magazine. The same rifle with its shorter action in 223, 243 and 25 family of WSSM cartridges is

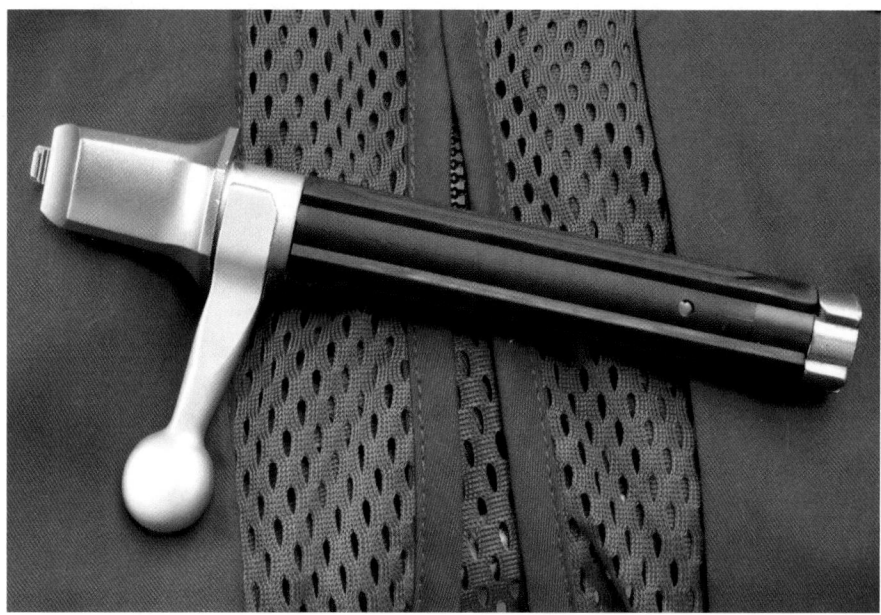
Carbon-fiber sleeve on the Mountain Ti bolt body sheds a few ounces.

rated four ounces lighter. In addition to those three and the 300 WSM I've already mentioned, other chambering options are 243 Winchester, 7mm-08 Remington, 308 Winchester, 270 WSM, 7mm WSM and 325 WSM.

The 23-inch stainless steel barrel of the Mountain Ti screws directly into a hardened steel sleeve inside the titanium receiver and a recoil lug is sandwiched between the two. The barrel measures 1.170 inches in diameter at the receiver and rapidly tapers to a rather slim 0.555 inch at the muzzle. A deep crown protects the rifling at the muzzle from dings in the field. Pulling an average of 32 ounces with a pull-to-pull variation of only two ounces, the trigger is of the ideal weight for a hunting rifle, especially one to be used with fingers made insensitive by extremely cold weather. Lack of detectable creep and a crisp break more than make up for a bit of overtravel in the trigger.

The Dura Touch Armor Coating on the stock of the Mountain Ti is the best I have tried on a synthetic stock. It is warm and friendly to the touch, its velvety texture offers a no-slip gripping surface for cold, wet hands, its dull finish won't spook game like a shiny finish will and it is kind to the cheek. The rifle I hunted

with shot all five of Winchester's 180-grain 300 WSM loads inside two inches at 100 yards and it averaged 1-1/2 inches or less with the Ballistic Silvertip, XP3 and Fail Safe loads. Even from the benchrest the rifle is comfortable to shoot, no doubt due to the excellent shape of the stock and the recoil-absorbing Pachmayr Decelerator recoil pad.

Winchester's New XP3 Big-Game Bullet

Winchester plans to utilize its new line of Supreme Elite ammunition to introduce the very latest in cutting-edge technology as it is developed. First examples to come off the line are eight cartridges loaded with a new big-game bullet called XP3 (short for Extreme Precision, Power and Performance). Described as an improvement over the Fail Safe which it will eventually replace, the XP3 offers the high weight retention and deep, bone-smashing penetration of that bullet but due to a polymer tip positioned at the front of its nose cavity, it will expand at lower impact velocities. The Fail Safe is a great bullet but it is best suited for use on elk, moose and other heavy game while the XP3 should work equally well in that role

Winchester's new line of Supreme Elite ammunition will usher in the latest in technology, with the new XP3 bullet the first offering.

and do a better job of expanding at long range on smaller game such as deer and pronghorn antelope.

Up front, the XP3 is a solid copper alloy with a deep cavity capped off with a polymer tip; a lead core in its rear section is bonded in place. During expansion the midsection of the bullet swells out to about twice its original diameter and it retains that frontal diameter retention even if the front petals are shed. Weight retention should run 90 percent and higher. A Lubalox coating worn by the bullet cuts down on bore fouling. Ballistic coefficients are quite high; the 30-caliber 180-grain XP3 is rated

at .527 compared to .391 for the Fail Safe of the same weight. The 30-caliber 150-grain bullet has a ballistic coefficient of .437 while the 270 and 280 caliber bullets are rated at .496 and .500, respectively. XP3 options slated for availability in 2006 are 150-grain only in 308 Winchester, 150- and 180-grain in 30-06, 300 WSM and 300 Winchester Magnum, 160-grain only in 7mm Remington Magnum and 7mm WSM and 150-grain in 270 Winchester and .270 WSM.

On a hunt in New Mexico with Elite Outfitters (505-937-7767) I used a Browning A-Bolt Mountain Ti in 300 WSM and the 180-grain XP3 load and

got complete penetration through the shoulders of a very nice bull elk at about 95 yards. It was a rather demanding bullet test since impact velocity had to be somewhere in the neighborhood of 2800 fps and heavy bone was struck. Back home, I had found both accuracy and velocity uniformity of Winchester's various 300 WSM loads to be quite good. My chronograph indicated a maximum velocity difference of only 60 fps between the five 180-grain loads with a mere 15 fps difference between four of them. Winchester obviously takes the precision, power and performance of its ammunition quite seriously.

CZ Model 527 American 204 Ruger
BLOND IS BEAUTIFUL

By Steve Gash

*V*armint hunting these days takes a variety of forms, but two styles predominate. One group of riflemen tramps over hill and prairie in search of targets. The other camp finds an area populated with varmints, sets up a portable rest of some sort, and lets fly at critters as far away as they can hit them. This, inevitably, has led to the development of slim-barreled light rifles for toting around, and bull-barreled arms for the "stand" hunters. These distinctions are not new, incidentally. They were detailed decades ago.

The late Warren Page, long-time shooting editor for *Field & Stream* magazine, once penned an article entitled "A Pair of Aces." Page, who graduated *cum laude* in English from Harvard, described two typical varmint rifles of the day, both custom bolt actions. One was a "sitting rifle," with a heavy-barrel for the stationary hunter, and the other a "walking" rifle, a light-weight sporter for roaming the Eastern woodchuck fields. The two riflaes he described were chambered for

the premier varmint cartridges of the day, the 6mm Remington and the 222 Remington, respectively.

The Model 527 American from CZ-USA is a prime example of the "walking" rifle. Slim, trim, highly accurate and chambered for cutting-edge cartridges, it makes a great rig for stalking the prairie. CZ's line of M-527 varmint rifles actually covers both bases, however, ranging from short carbines to more typical heavy-barreled models. All M-527s feature what CZ calls a "true micro

length Mauser-style action" that has the traditional controlled-round feed, hammer-forged barrel, detachable magazine and a single set trigger. Rotating the safety forward blocks the sear and locks the bolt.

I have been a fan of CZ bolt guns since I wrung out a M-550 American in 9.3x62 Mauser awhile back. All of the "American" models (452, 527, and 550) have features specifically designed for the U.S. market. Their

The CZ Model 527 American is styled to American tastes, and features a mini-Mauser action chambered for several popular varmint cartridges, a single set trigger, and detachable box magazine.

main attribute is a stock styled after the classic American sporter, with a straight and high comb suitable for scope use, trim proportions and well executed checkering. One-inch scope rings are included with all American models. Nice bluing and calibers popular stateside don't hurt, either.

At the 2005 SHOT Show in Las Vegas, I stopped by the CZ booth to visit with Mike Eagleshield, CZ's gunsmith who was manning the exhibit. While I was looking at a passel of nice iron, Mike dragged me over to a display of petite rifles, and thrust one into my hands. It was an M-527 American with a lightly-colored, highly-figured maple stock. Trying to be polite, I observed that I have never liked pale stocks, and that I preferred gun handles with dark streaks and figure in the right places. Mike was undeterred, extolled its virtues and noted that the little beauty came in the chambering *du jour*, the 204 Ruger.

But the little rifle was so unique and striking that I was soon hooked, and I ordered one (in 204 Ruger, of course) as soon as I returned home. The gun I received has a beautiful stock of curly blond maple with enough contrast and figure to make a brunette jealous. The 18 lines-per-inch checkering is well done, and the bluing is uniformly dark and lustrous. Guns come and go frequently at our household, so my wife often gives them nicknames to keep things straight; the M-527 almost instantly became the "blond rifle." It seems to fit.

The supplied 1-inch scope rings clamp to cut-outs in the receiver, and line up *perfectly*. I had just finished testing a superb Sightron SIISS 3.5-10x44 scopes on a 300 Winchester Magnum, and found it to be optically and mechanically superb, so I mounted it on the 204. So equipped, the M-527 weighs 7 pounds, 10 ounces, empty.

CZ's bolt guns have a very nice single set trigger, which is adjustable. Unset, the trigger breaks at about 3 pounds, 8 ounces, and set, it is a breathtaking 1 pound, 13 ounces. Use of the set trigger is easy, once you get the hang of it. First, push the trigger forward about 1/2-inch;

this takes considerable effort. The trigger is now set. Pulling the trigger in the set mode requires very little pressure, just a perceivable amount of movement—much more than a light single-stage trigger. The side safety locks the trigger—either set or

unset. To "unset" the trigger, point the rifle in a safe direction, make sure the safety is "on," and just pull the trigger. The trigger is now unset, but the gun is still cocked. This is easier to do than describe, of course.

About the only hiccup I can report

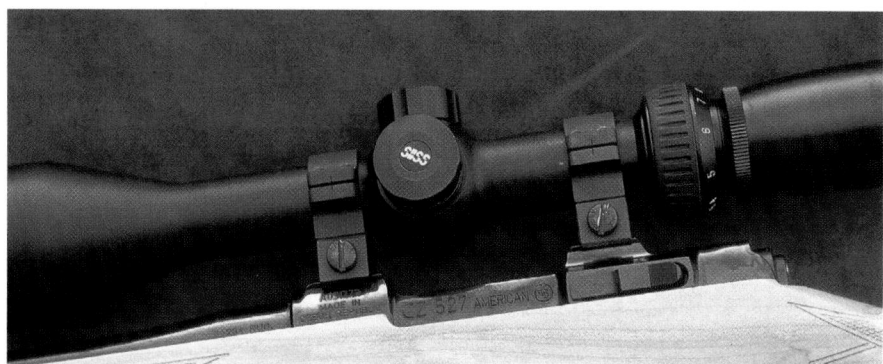

All CZ American model rifles come with 1-inch scope rings that clamp top cut-outs in the receiver, and provide solid and precise alignment for a scope.

The single set trigger is adjustable, but came from the factory at 1 lb., 13 oz., and was a delight to use.

SELECTED HANDLOADS
CZ-USA MODEL 527 AMERICAN 204 RUGER

BRAND	BULLET	VELOCITY (FPS)	STANDARD DEVIATION	GROUP
Remington	32-gr. AccuTip-V	3866	27	1.46
Hornady	32-gr. V-MAX	3999	41	1.24
Winchester	34-gr. hollowpoint	3759	76	1.58
Winchester	34-gr. hollowpoint	3836	36	1.95
HORNADY	40-GR. V-MAX	3615	69	1.38

NOTES:
M-504 has a 21-inch barrel. Chronograph was a Oehler M-35P.

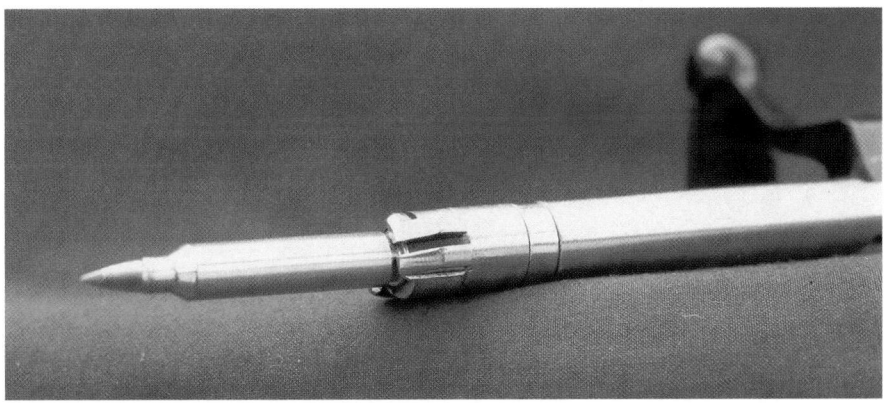

After the bolt grabs a cartridge from the magazine, it controls it into the chamber.

Rotating the M-527's safety forward – covering the red dot – blocks the sear and locks the bolt.

⟨⟩●⟨⟩●⟨⟩●⟨⟩●⟨⟩●⟨⟩

chambered for the Hornet, 222 and 223. Interestingly, the American is the only M-527 offered in one of the best light varmint cartridges ever—the 221 Fireball. After shooting hundreds of rounds through the little rifle, I am delighted to report that the M-527 was impressively accurate, and its barrel accumulated very little jacket fouling, even at these high velocities. Best of all, groups fired after 25-30 rounds were every bit as good as those from a squeaky-clean barrel.

For cleaning chores, I used

The detachable box magazine holds five rounds, and the follower is marked with the caliber.

SELECTED HANDLOADS CZ-USA MODEL 527 AMERICAN 204 RUGER

BULLET	POWDER	CHARGE (GR.)	VELOCITY (FPS)	STANDARD DEVIATION	GROUP (IN.)
BERGER 30-GR. HP	H-322	26.5	3817	37	.75
	BALL C(2)	29.5	3628	63	.71
Hornady 32-gr. V-MAX|	2015BR	25.5	3685	34	.90
	Varget	28.0	3481	41	.59
Sierra 32-gr. Blitzking	2015BR	26.5	3819	36	.92
	Reloder 10	25.5	3771	13	.65
Berger 35-gr. HP	TAC	26.2	3431	34	.53
	X-Terminator	25.7	3428	50	.37
Sierra 39-gr. Blitzking	2015BR	25.0	3522	23	.74
	Benchmark	25.1	3365	19	.71
Berger 40-gr. HP	2015BR	24.0	3406	41	1.02
	Ball C(2)	28.8	3545	13	.37
HORNADY 40-GR. V-MAX	BENCHMARK	25.5	3394	28	.91
	RELODER 15	26.5	3245	48	.91

NOTES:
CZ M-527 has a 21-inch barrel. Winchester cases and Remington No. 7-1/2 primers were used for all handloads. Velocities measured with an Oehler M-35P chronograph.

The 204 Ruger (right) compares favorably with the famous 220 Swift.

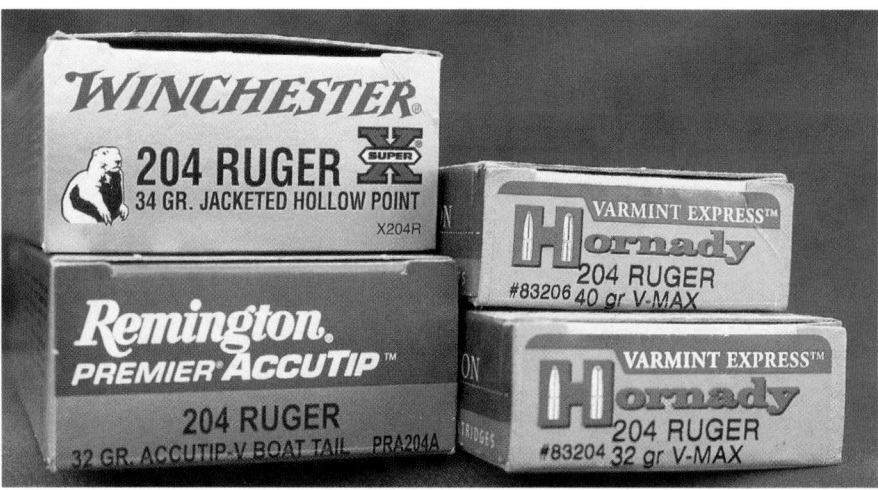

A good selection of 204 Ruger factory loads is available.

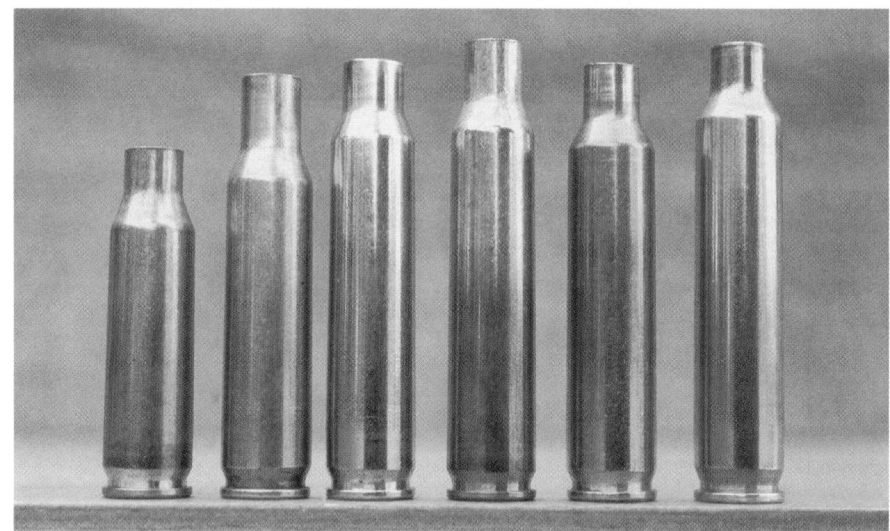

A line-up of great varmint-busters, all based on the 222-headsize (from left): 221 Fireball, 222 and 223 Remington, 222 Remington Magnum, 20 Tactical, and 204 Ruger.

the new and excellent Montana X-TREME and 50 BMG bore solvents from Western Outdoor Products (the Ramshot Powder folks). If you haven't tried this stuff, you're missing out. It whisked out all traces of powder and copper fouling in a jiffy.

Factory 204 Ruger ammo offers great terminal performance and a modest selection of bullet weights, all at warp speeds. For the 32-grain bullets, Hornady's V-MAX and Remington's AccuTip-V Boat Tail are listed at 4225 fps. Winchester's 34-grain hollow point is rated at 4025 fps, and the 40-grain V-MAX from Hornady and the AccuTip-V Boat Tail of the same weight from Remington

are each cataloged at 3900 fps. These speeds are for 24-inch barrels.

In the M-527, Hornady's 32-grain V-MAX came pretty darn close to specs at 3999 fps – a loss of only about 5 percent. (Several individual rounds chronographed over 4000 fps.) Two batches of Winchester's 34-grain HPs averaged 3759 and 3836 fps, while the 40-grain V-MAX averaged 3615 fps. Remington's 32-grain offering hit 3866 fps. These velocity losses are in the 5-8 percent range, and are to be expected from a barrel 3 inches shorter. No prairie dog will ever notice. Promise.

Testing started with Winchester's 34-grain hollowpoint loads, and the

average for three, 5-shot groups was a 1.58 inches. I rustled up a different lot number of this fodder, and it averaged 1.95 inches. This was most puzzling, since at a recent industry Montana prairie dog shoot, this ammo (in other rifles) shot great. Subsequently, three more factory loads were tried. Best of the bunch was Hornady's 32-grain V-MAX. It averaged 1.24 inches, followed closely by that firm's 40-grain V-MAX with a 1.38-inch group average. Rounding out the factory loads was Remington's 32-grain AccuTip-V boattail, which grouped into 1.46 inches. The average accuracy of all factory loads was 1.52 inches.

Okay, so this M-527 doesn't like

Twenty-caliber bullets look tiny because, well, they are. Shown here are (from left): 32- and 39-gr. Sierra BlitzKings, 32- and 40-gr. Hornady V-MAXs, 30-, 35- and 40-gr. Bergers, and a 180-gr. Sierra 30-caliber SP.

A typical M-527/.204 group, shot with the 32-gr. Sierra BlitzKing over 27.3-gr. of Benchmark powder.

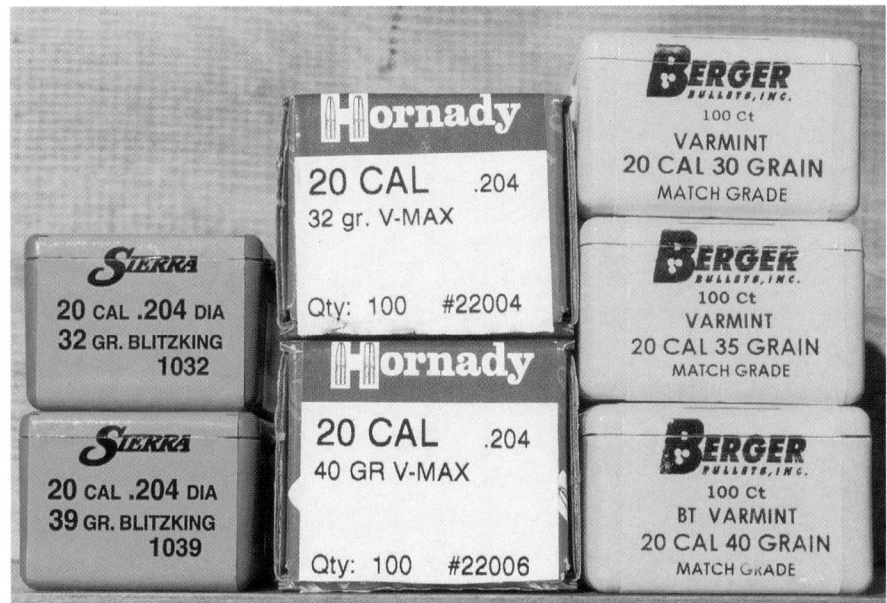

Highly accurate 20-caliber bullets are available from Sierra, Hornady and Berger. All shot well in the M-527 with several loads.

factory loads, but handloads did much better. Loading data for the 204 is available from virtually all component manufacturers, so representative loads with most of the currently available 20-caliber bullets were easy to assemble. I used Hornady New Dimension dies in a Redding T-7 turret press to load test ammo. Toward the end of the project, I started using a new Hornady neck size die just introduced for the 204 Ruger. I could tell no difference between the accuracy of loads put up in full-length and neck-sized cases, but the neck die was a bit easier to use.

Before discussing the handload results, I should point out a problem that affected the group averages and prolonged load testing for almost a year. Wind seriously affected accuracy when testing several loads, producing groups that the benchresters call "weather reports." But I have it on good authority that wind occasionally blows in prairie dog towns, so I reported exactly what happened. Groups were markedly better on the calmer days, however. Just so you know.

After shooting the factory loads, I was somewhat apprehensive before testing the handloads. I shouldn't have worried. In short order, I had numerous groups well under an inch, and some under .5-inch, at velocities that approximated factory loads.

A total of 38 handloads were tested in the M-527 with most suitable powders. Due to low velocities, wide velocity swings, or poor accuracy, many powders were dropped in a hurry. The 14 loads presented are the best two loads for each bullet tested, and represent the ballistic potential of the little Mauser. Group sizes listed in the load tables are the averages of (at least) three, 5-shot groups at 100 yards.

The dainty little 30-grain Berger HPs over 29.5 grains of Ball C(2), averaged 0.71-inch. H-322 also did well, and 26.5 grains of this old favorite of benchrest shooters produced a velocity of 3817 fps and 3/4-inch groups. As might be expected, the wind seemed to drift the lighter bullets a little off course, but for calm days these little Bergers would be a good choice.

Several loads with 30-grain Bergers had to be re-tested because of some

Hornady 45-Grain 204 Ruger Ammo

Hornady's new 45-grain Spire Point load adds a new dimension to the 204 Ruger cartridge, and delivers a heavy-weight punch with top-notch accuracy.

Hide hunters, listen up: Just as this edition of GD was going to press, Hornady announced a new heavy bullet load for the 204 Ruger that expands the capability of the cartridge considerably. The new round is loaded with Hornady's 45-grain Spire Point bullet that's designed for controlled expansion and deeper penetration on larger game.

The new load is cataloged at a velocity of 3625 fps, but in the 21-inch barreled CZ, it clocked 3299 fps, which produces 1088 ft-lb. of muzzle energy. Sighted in for 200 yards, the bullet drops 5.5 and 16.9 inches at 300 and 400 yards, respectively, and drift in a 10 mph crosswind at those same ranges is 4.1 inches and 9.8 inches, according to Hornady data.

I was at first concerned that the heavier bullet would be too long for the CZ's 12-inch twist but, when I dissected a round, I found the Spire Point bullet was actually a trifle shorter than the 40-grain V-MAX, and only slightly longer that the 32-grain V-MAX.

At the range, the average of three 5-shot and one 4-shot group was 0.87-inch, with the smallest measuring 0.67-inch. While not as tiny as some of the handloads tested, it is a huge improvement in factory load performance for this rifle, and is well within MOC (minute-of-coyote). A couple of these groups are shown nearby.

This new load from Hornady should be a welcome addition to the ammo selection for this established varmint-buster, and I'm looking forward to wringing it out in the field this summer. **SG**

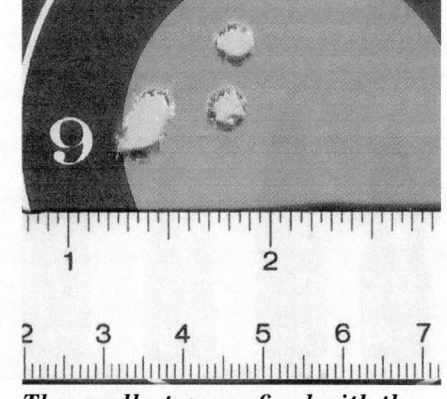

The smallest group fired with the Hornady 45-grain Spire Point ammo measured 0.67-inch.

This group measures 0.87-inch across.

missed velocity readings. Occasionally, these itty-bitty bullets slithered over the Oehler Skyscreen IIIs undetected. Also, on some range sessions, the sun was fairly low in the horizon, and this affects chronograph operation. Chronograph screens can be finicky little devils, and sometimes you have to trick them into compliance. Oehler offers diffusers with 40-watt incandescent bulbs for such situations. Since I have line power to my range, I used them with the M-35P, and experienced no more missed shots. (Oehler recommends unplugging the middle "proof" screen when using the lighted diffusers.)

Sierra's 32-grain BlitzKing was slightly more accurate than Hornady's V-MAX of the same weight, but only by a hair. With 25.5 grains of Reloder 10, velocity was 3771 fps, and groups averaged 0.65-inch. Next best was 26.5 grains of 2015BR, at 3819 fps and a 0.92-inch group average. The Hornady 32-grain V-MAX bullet clearly liked Varget powder. While velocity was a bit slower than with some other propellants, it produced the smallest groups. With 28.0 grains of Varget at 3481 fps, it averaged 0.59-inch. A charge of 25.5-grain of 2015BR was runner-up, at 3685 and groups under an inch.

The Berger 35-grain hollowpoints are a good intermediate weight bullet for the 204. With 25.7 grains of X-Terminator, velocity was 3428 fps, and groups were so small that I was sure it was a fluke. After I re-shot the load, the group average was a measly 0.37-inch. A charge of 26.2 grains of Ramshot's TAC averaged 0.53-inch at 3431 fps.

Top honors for the 39-grain Sierra BlitzKing was a dead heat between 25.1 grains of Benchmark (3365 fps) and 25.0 grains of 2015BR (3522 fps). Both shot these little green-tipped missiles into 0.74-inch or less. Two loads tied with the Hornady 40-grain V-MAX bullet. With either 25.5 grains of Benchmark or 26.5 grains of Reloder 15, groups averaged 0.91-inch. Velocities were 3394 and 3245 fps, respectively. The Berger 40-grain HPs were a little finicky, but the highest velocity and best accuracy was with 28.8 grains of Ball C(2), averaging a measly 0.37-inch at 3545 fps. With 24.0 grains of 2015BR at 3406 fps, this bullet averaged groups a hair over an inch. (Berger also makes a 20-caliber 50-grain BTHP, but they are not recommended for the 12-inch twist of the 204 Ruger.)

After several months of testing, the shooting results indicated that the 204 is more versatile than I at first thought. By careful bullet selection, one can tailor the load somewhat, not only for accuracy, but also for trajectory and down-range energy. The 30- and 32-grain bullets naturally turn in the fastest speeds and (slightly) flatter trajectories. But the 39- and 40-grainers offer a bit more punch down-range. At 400 yards, the 32-grain bullets have about 327 fpe left, compared to 456 fpe for the 40-grain—a 39 percent increase. This is probably not important to the prairie-dogger, but might be to hunters pursuing larger quarry like coyotes.

The 204 is sure to be compared to the most popular varmint round going, the 223 Remington, and the cartridge that got the 4000+ fps ball rolling, the 220 Swift.

Nobody has to sell me on the 220 Swift's attributes; I have owned one since 1972. As can be seen on the Oehler ballistic graphs, the 204 mirrors the 220 in trajectory, and is darn close to it in velocity out to 500 yards. Bullet energy is another matter, where the 204 and 223 are similar, and the Swift cleans the clock of both. So, as the 204 bandwagon rolls on, more and more components make the little cartridge uniquely useful in its own right, not beholding to other contenders—or pretenders.

The concept of two basic styles of varmint rifles is pretty sound, when you think about it, and the trim CZ Model 527 effectively embodies one of them. If Warren Page were alive today, I am sure he'd be smitten by the ballistics and accuracy of the 204 Ruger cartridge, and that he would consider the CZ M-527 American a perfect candidate for the walking varmint hunter—and one of his pair of aces.

CZ MODEL 527 AMERICAN SPECIFICATIONS

Chamberings: 204 Ruger (tested); 22 Hornet, 221 Fireball, 222 and 223 Remington also available

Action type: mini Mauser-type controlled-feed bolt action

Magazine capacity: 5 rounds, detachable box

Trigger: single set, pull weights 1 lb., 2 oz. (set), 3 lb., 4 oz. (unset)

Sights: none

Barrel length: 21.9-in. (555mm)

Twist: 1:12 inches

Finish: bright blue, bolt white

Stock: maple, checkered 18 lpi, sling swivels and rubber buttpad;
American and French walnut, and laminate stocks
also available; no cheekpiece or Monte Carlo

Length of pull: 13-1/2 inches

Overall length: 40-1/4 inches

Weight: 6 lb., 6 oz.; 7 lb., 10 oz., as tested with scope

Accessories: supplied with CZ clamp-on scope rings

MSRP: $633

Manufacturer: Ceska Zbrojovka, Uhersky Brod, Czech Republic

Importer: CZ-USA, PO Box 171073, Kansas City, KS 66117 (800) 955-4486

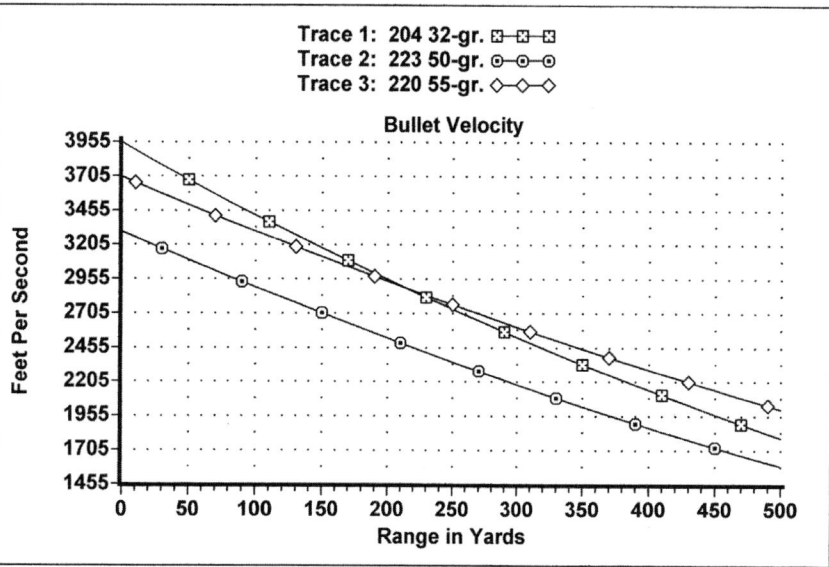

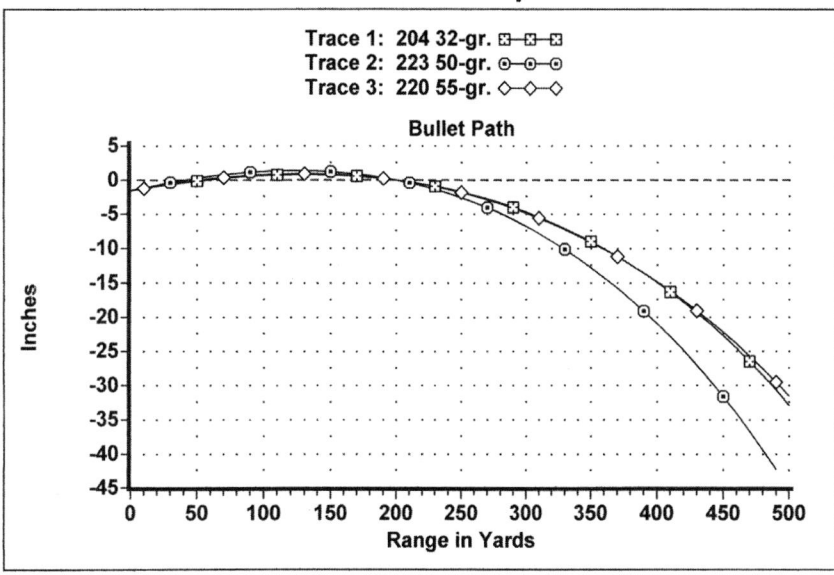

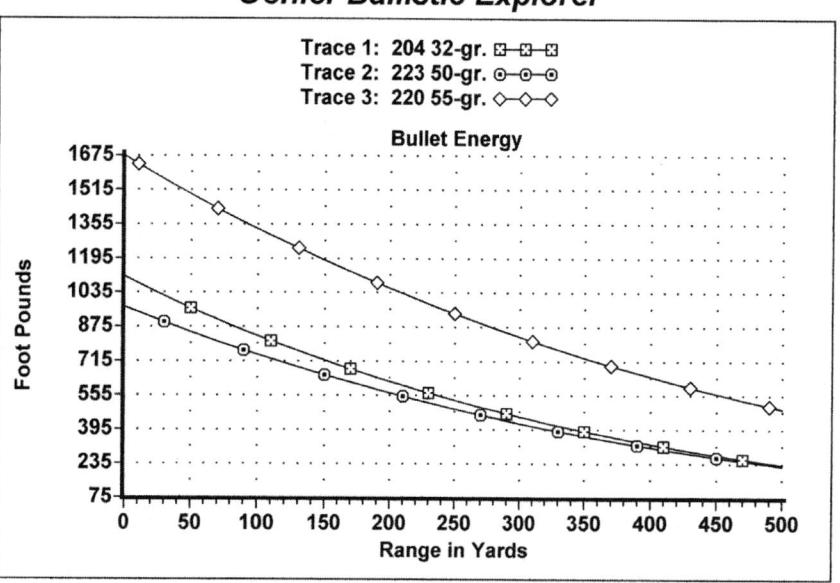

REMINGTON
MODEL 105 CTI

by Layne Simpson

Titanium is about 44 percent lighter than steel and since the receiver of Remington's new Model 105 CTi autoloading shotgun is made of it, overall weight is only about seven pounds. Titanium has other desirable qualities—its yield strength is three times greater than that of the steel alloys used in making shotgun receivers, its fatigue strength is twice that of steel and it is highly resistant to corrosion and rusting. Coat various steel parts such as the bolt and shell carrier with electroless nickel and it all adds up to a weather-resistant shotgun. A TriNyte coating on the inside of the receiver prevents galling and looks a lot like bluing on the outside. Lightening cuts machined through non-stress areas of the receiver walls are hidden from view by a thin carbon fiber shell. A TriNyte coating on the stainless steel magazine tube increases rust resistance and prevents carbon fouling from adhering to its surface; a quick wipe with a paper towel cleans it nicely. The gun is quite comfortable to carry with (receiver depth and width are about the same as for the Remington Model 1100).

Some autoloaders have a rotating bolt head containing locking lugs but the bolt head of the Model 105 remains stationary while a steel ring located just behind it rotates 75 degrees to engage the barrel extension for breech lockup. The fixed boltface eliminates rotational extractor drag on the rim of a shotshell during locking and unlocking and this adds to reliable functioning.

Propellant gas used to operate the action is also handled differently. The most common designs seen in autoloading shotguns utilize some type of relief valve located near the gas port of the barrel to control the amount of gas allowed to impinge on the action bar of the bolt. When a light load is fired the valve remains closed but it opens up to vent excessive gas generated by a heavy load—the heavier the load, the more gas vented and this keeps bolt velocity close to the same regardless of the load fired. Remington design engineers chose to forego a conventional forward-located gas relief valve in the Model 105 and in doing so they eliminated several small parts that are prone to breakage and becoming lost when the gun is field-stripped for cleaning. An oil-filled hydraulic cylinder located in the buttstock is connected to the bolt

The Model 105 is Remington's first bottom-feed eject autoloading shotgun.

The Model 105 weighs a pound less than the Model 1100, but several of its design features make it more comfortable to shoot with heavy loads.

by a steel link. During the firing cycle, propellant gas flows through a vent in the barrel, impinges on the action bar and begins to push the bolt rearward. This forces the piston through the cylinder, causing oil to flow through energy-dissipating ports in the cylinder wall; the higher the velocity of the force applied to the piston, the higher its resistance to movement becomes. So regardless of whether the shell being fired is a 3-inch waterfowl load or a 2-3/4 inch skeet load, bolt velocity remains the same. Once the bolt reaches the limit of its rearward travel, a large spring wound around the magazine tube returns it back into battery so long as another shell is in the magazine (the bolt remains locked back after the last shell is fired). The hydraulic rate reducer also serves to dampen the secondary recoil impulse

caused by the bolt and this, along with a few other things, lessens perceived recoil by a noticeable degree.

An opening in the bottom of the receiver is used to load the magazine and for the ejection of fired cases. A tuning fork-shaped carrier elevates a shell from magazine to chamber level during the feeding cycle and it then reverses direction to propel the fired case downward through the bottom port during the ejection cycle. The gun is easily loaded by pushing a shell into the magazine with the bolt locked open; this automatically releases the bolt and causes that shell to be fed into the chamber (Remington calls it TurboFeed). The magazine is then manually topped off with additional shells. Another way is to load a shell into the magazine with the bolt forward; retracting and

releasing the bolt moves a shell from magazine to chamber. You don't have to cycle shells through the chamber when unloading the magazine; just reach inside the port with a finger, rotate the pivoting shell feed latch downward and shells will slide into your hand, one-by-one. The chamber is then cleared by retracting the bolt.

In the bottom-feed/bottom-eject design of the Model 105, the ejector is not fighting gravity as it flips a spent hull from the gun and since fired shells are ejected downward, they won't ricochet off your partner's head in a duck blind. The bottom ejection of hulls also makes the gun left-hand-shooter friendly and the safety button in the rear of the trigger guard can be reversed. Lack of an ejection port in the side of its receiver means the Model 105 will shed rain

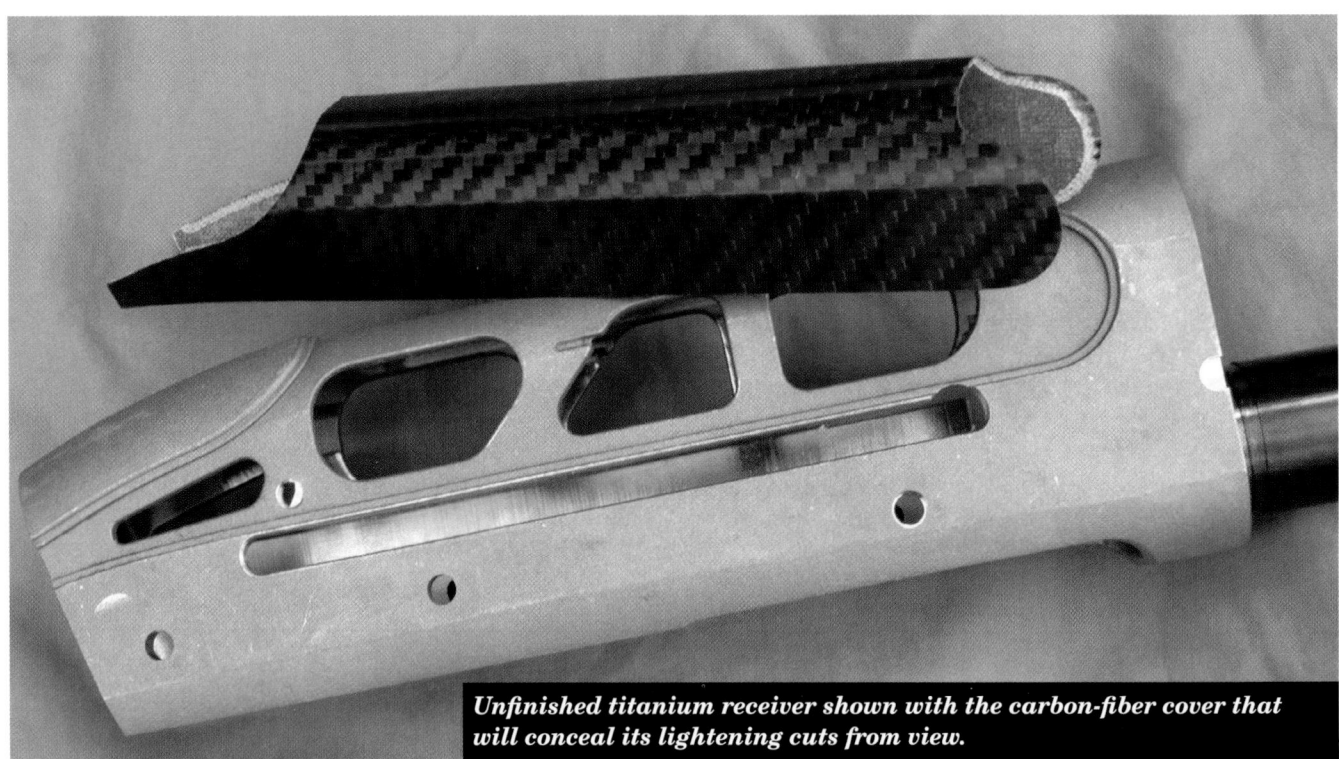

Unfinished titanium receiver shown with the carbon-fiber cover that will conceal its lightening cuts from view.

and snow better than a side-ejecting gun although its carrier does not close off as much of the bottom port as the wide carriers of Remington's Model 1100 and Model 1187 so it may accumulate more field debris; pushing out two pins in the receiver and removing the trigger group allows its innards to be cleaned.

The patented roller-type sear of the Model 105 trigger eliminates creep and overtravel—the one I shot broke crisply at about five pounds. It did have just a bit of initial freetravel (not a bad thing on a hunting gun), but once it moved beyond that point it was like squeezing the trigger of an over-under shotgun. The trigger is absolutely the best I have ever tried on a repeating shotgun.

The walnut stock and forearm have laser-cut checkering spaced 18 lines-per-inch and a special grip cap worn by the first 5000 guns built will commemorate 100 years of Remington autoloading shotguns. The Sims recoil pad has an unusual shape but it does a better job of soaking up recoil than any other pad I have tried. Stock and forearm dimensions are quite close to those of the Remington Model 1100 so it is no surprise that the two guns handle

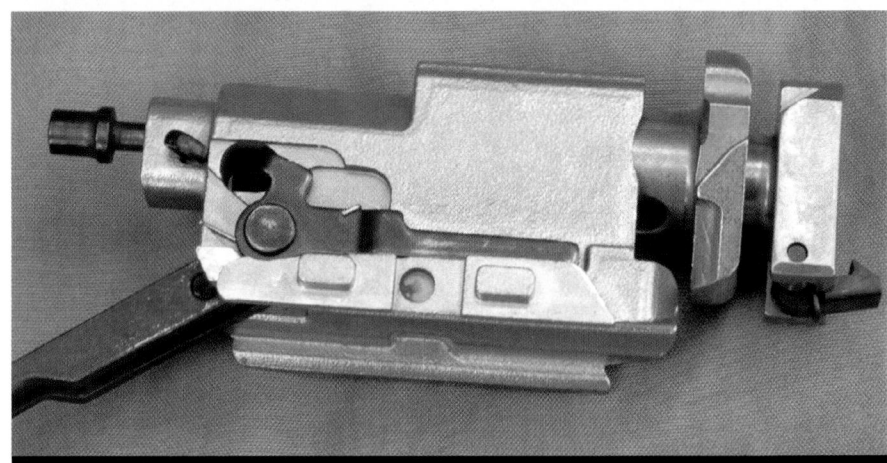

Breech lockup to the barrel extension is accomplished by a rotating steel ring located between the fixed bolt head (right) and the body of the bolt.

and feel much alike. This, by the way, was no accident; those who designed the Model 105 knew that many hunters and target shooters have long considered the Model 1100 to be the best-handling autoloader ever built.

The Model 105 will be available only in 12 gauge with three-inch chamber in 26- and 28-inch barrel lengths. The barrel has a lengthened forcing cone and it is overbored to .735-inch (compared to a nominal .727-inch for the barrels of other Remington field guns). A larger bore diameter calls for a different series of

screw-in chokes; called ProBore, they differ from the standard RemChokes by their front-located threads. Improved Cylinder, Modified and Full come with the gun. I compared perceived recoil of the Model 105 CTi with the Model 1100 by shooting heavy waterfowl loads and even though the new gun is about a pound lighter, it most definitely kicked less. Remington says recoil is 48 percent less than for a recoil-operated shotgun and 26 percent less than for other gas guns, and shooting the gun convinced me that statement is no brag. ✺

THE WELL-TRAVELED ITHACA

by Dave Cournoyer

I've lived in Rhode Island, Arizona, Alaska and Idaho. My Ithaca has taken a variety of game for me in all of these states. The climate, terrain and hunting methods might be very different, but the one constant is that the 12-gauge Ithaca Model 37 seems to jump to my shoulder effortlessly and point exactly where I am looking––every time.

Over 30 years of hunting with the Ithaca started in August of 1973. I was in a gun shop in Rhode Island making the final decision on which 12-gauge pump-action shotgun to buy. Being 18 years old, this would be the first shotgun I purchased. The "Shotguns - Slide

Action" section of the 1973 GUN DIGEST helped narrow the field to a Mossberg, Remington or Ithaca.

I could say that it was a difficult decision, but it really wasn't. I was sold on the bottom ejection, flapless loading port, all-steel construction and lighter weight of the Ithaca Model 37 Featherlight. The action was very smooth, and it handled better than any of the other 12-gauge pump guns. The pistol grip seemed to fit my hand perfectly.

My new Model 37 had a 28-inch plain barrel with Modified choke––the perfect duck gun. It was chambered for 2 3/4-inch shells. At this time, 3-inch magnum loads of steel shot were many years away from widespread use. For most waterfowl hunting, 12-gauge 2 3/4-inch shells were more than adequate.

The genius of John Browning's original 1913 design had resulted in a classic shotgun. Ithaca obtained the rights to this design and began producing the Model 37 in 1937. Not only was it sturdy and reliable, the Featherlight weighed 1/2- to 3/4-pound less than its competitors,

The fast-handling attributes of the author's classic 6 1/2-pound Ithaca Featherlight allowed this jackrabbit to be taken before it got into high gear and out of range.

despite its all-steel construction. With only minor changes, the Model 37 has been in continuous production for more than 68 years.

The first and primary use of my new Ithaca was jump-shooting ducks, and hunting squirrels by canoe on small rivers in Rhode Island and Connecticut. Many of the numerous clear-running rivers, typical of New England, are winding and slow-moving, allowing a carefully maneuvered canoe to silently approach ducks that are just around the next bend. Oaks and other hardwood trees grow tallest along riverbanks and provide excellent squirrel hunting.

Ideally, one person paddles and guides the canoe from the back seat and the shooter sits in the front seat, gun in hand. The shooter can then give his complete attention to watching the shallow water along the riverbanks for mallards or black ducks. If on a combination squirrel and duck hunt, the shooter also has to be watching the trees and riverbanks for bushytails. About half of the time I was float-hunting by myself, which meant I had to paddle and keep the Featherlight ready on a cushion in front of me.

The fast-handling attributes of the Model 37 came in handy when one or more mallards jumped off the water from behind a screen of grass and I had to drop my paddle, pick up the Ithaca, point and shoot in just a few

Ithaca with the 20-inch Deerslayer barrel is compact. The finish on the stock is worn and the bluing is gone around the trigger guard from years of carrying at the ready, finger on the cross-bolt safety.

seconds. The Ithaca didn't let me down.

The next task the Featherlight excelled at was shooting ducks over decoys on ponds, lakes and rivers. The flapless loading port made it easy to reload while keeping my eyes on the skies overhead, watching for the next flight of mallards. In addition to ducks and squirrels, my Ithaca also bagged one Canada goose and two red foxes.

When I moved to Arizona it looked like the Ithaca might be out of a job. The miles and miles of open desert country did not provide opportunities for duck or squirrel hunting. After getting acquainted with the vast desert, land of the towering saguaro cactus, I discovered the Gambels quail.

This colorful game bird with a feather plume on top of his head is often found in flocks of one to four dozen. They are very vocal, always calling to one another and they like to run, it seems, to just outside shotgun range before they take flight. Taking Gambels quail with my Ithaca was almost too easy. I got to shoot standing up, instead of from a moving canoe or cramped duck blind. And the weather was usually sunny and warm! Fortunately, the Featherlight was only called on to dispatch one rattlesnake.

Hours away from the desert, the high mountains of northern and eastern Arizona above 6000 feet are home to the pointy-eared Alberts squirrel. These squirrels are similar in size and coloration to the eastern gray squirrel except for their distinctive pointed ears. Many weekend camping trips in the fall were spent with my Ithaca in those high mountain pine forests between 6000 to 9000 feet elevation pursuing Alberts squirrels. As usual, the Ithaca did its job, averaging not much more than one shot per squirrel.

I moved to south-central Alaska in the early '80s, packing the car and heading north via the Alaska Highway through Canada. The Model 37 was one of the two firearms that accompanied me on the 3800-mile drive. In late May the campgrounds were open, but deserted. Warning signs about bears were posted everywhere and it was comforting to have the Ithaca close at hand when I was alone in my tent at night.

After arriving in Alaska, the Ithaca went along on canoe camping trips primarily as bear protection. One note of interest: I learned that in Alaska any type of short-barreled 12-gauge pump gun was called a "bear gun," available on sale at most sporting good stores in early summer.

The Ithaca and I were once again shooting ducks over decoys. One thing different about Alaska is that there are very few roads and highways. Getting to a hunting area usually means using a floatplane, boat, ATV or a good pair of hiking boots. My favorite duck area was very close to home by Alaskan standards. The trip required boating down a turbulent and murky glacier-fed river at high tide, towing a canoe. The boat was beached; the canoe was carried a few hundred yards to a freshwater marsh and paddled to a tent campsite on high ground. I also used the Model 37 for hunting snowshoe hares in an area of birch trees and small lakes on the Kenai Peninsula.

Two years after moving to Alaska, I became active in shooting practical pistol at my local gun club. For 3-gun competition, I used a Smith & Wesson Model 57 41 Magnum, an M-1 Garand and the Model 37. The addition of a 20-inch Cylinder-bore Deerslayer barrel with rifle sights made the Ithaca competitive with buckshot and slugs. Shooting in these matches once or twice a month provided an opportunity to get out during the long cold winter months, despite temperatures often below zero and daylight hours limited to about 9 A.M. to 3 P.M.

In the mid-'90s, I moved to northern Idaho. My Ithaca is now used to hunt ruffed grouse in dense pine forests. This game bird's explosive take-off and unpredictable dodge-through-the-trees flight make for a difficult target. The 28-inch barrel and Modified choke were not well suited for this task. The grouse were rocketing off and disappearing behind trees and brush long before reaching the effective range of a Modified shot pattern.

A shorter barrel and more open choke would be better suited to the close-range conditions. I decided to try the Deerslayer barrel. This turned the Ithaca into an excellent ruffed grouse gun. The 20-inch barrel swings into action quickly and the Cylinder bore produces an effective pattern at close range. Most shots are less than 20 yards, none are over 25 yards. The rifle sights? I don't notice they are there. And the light weight of the Featherlight with the shorter barrel is welcome when walking the miles of old logging roads open to non-motorized travel in the nearby national forests.

My Ithaca has spent more time afield with me than any other firearm. I'm sure new hunting situations and locations are in the future and I know this shotgun will perform as expected. My Model 37 pump no longer looks factory new, but it still handles and shoots as well as the day I bought it. For me, it has always been one good gun. ✸

AUTOLOADLERS✛

HANDGUNS TODAY

by John Malloy

*T*he world of autoloading handguns is an exciting world, one in which traditional ideas and new concepts share the spotlight together.

What could be more traditional than the Colt/Browning 1911 design, which is now nudging its way toward a century of service? Just within the last few years, companies such as Smith & Wesson, SIG-Sauer and Taurus introduced new 1911-type pistols, and have become new players in the 1911 market. Established companies such as Colt, and somewhat more recent entries such as Auto-Ordnance, Kimber, Para-Ordnance, High Standard and others have kept the 1911 design in continuous production since, well … 1911. Other, generally smaller, companies offer 1911s, often made by other overseas manufacturers. A number of American companies make what have been called "production custom" pistols, and the design used is almost exclusively the 1911. There seems to be no concern the 1911 may not make it to its 100th birthday a few years from now.

At the same time, the semiautomatic pistol market is changing to more modern designs. Several decades ago, a category of full-size large-capacity 9mm autoloading pistols gained popularity

for service and self-protection use. They were commonly dubbed the "wondernines." Although polymer-frame pistols were being made, most of the new big nines had steel frames, sometimes stainless steel. Then came the "Assault Weapons Ban" of 1994, which limited pistol magazines to a capacity of 10 rounds. Ten rounds of 9mm didn't have as much appeal in a large heavy pistol, one that was designed to hold many more than that. So a decade ago, in the aftermath of the magazine ban, we saw the beginning of a new category of pistol. Small polymer-frame 10-shot pistols for personal defense became popular. Concealed-carry legislation had been growing across the country and there was a demand for affordable pistols of small size. Then, in 2004, the ban sunset, and large-capacity magazines came back.

Now, we have seen a new category arise. The magazine ban is gone, but there is no move back to the big heavy full-size pistols of the wondernine days. Instead, large-capacity pistols are being introduced with light polymer frames. The Glock design showed that such pistols could find a large market. So, within the last few years—with some introductions just this year, on these pages—new full-size light polymer-frame pistols have come on the market. This

year's Smith & Wesson M&P and Kimber KPD join a list of recent pistols that include the new Beretta Px4 Storm, the Springfield XD, The Taurus 24/7 and the Walther P99.

It is obvious that what happens in the political arena influences what happens in the world of autoloading handguns. More so perhaps than any other type of firearm in wide use, semiautomatic pistols are related to the world of politics.

So, perhaps it is worthwhile to take a brief look at the political highpoints of the past year or so, just to keep our frame of reference current.

In March 2005, John Bolton became ambassador to the United Nations. Bolton has strongly stated that we will not accept any UN firearms regulations that go against United States citizens' right to keep and bear arms.

In April, Governor Jeb Bush of Florida signed into law an extension of the "Castle Doctrine" that allows citizens to legally defend themselves in places they have a right to be, without retreating. Other states are considering similar legislation.

Starting on July 10, 2005, a series of four devastating hurricanes hit the Gulf Coast. On August 29, Hurricane Katrina hit the upper coast and subsequently flooded the city of New Orleans. Looting began, and many people armed themselves for protection. Local officials announced that only police would be allowed to have guns, and began illegally confiscating firearms from law-abiding residents. People protested, and gun rights organizations filed a lawsuit. By September 23, a court in Louisiana had banned further confiscation and ordered the return of guns taken.

On October 26, President George Bush signed the "Lawful Commerce in Firearms Act," which gives protection to firearms makers when their legal products are used illegally by criminals.

However, on November 9, 2005, a proposition passed in San Francisco that made it illegal to buy, sell or transfer firearms or ammunition in the city. In some ways, this has been interpreted as showing how desperate the antigunners are. For, a similar law was passed before, in 1982, and was struck down in the courts. Another court challenge is sure, but at the time of this writing, no resolution has been made in this situation.

The antigun forces, realizing that "gun control" is not a winning issue in most areas, have tried to cloud the issue by changing the name. The very same objectives of restricting firearms are now presented as "gun safety." We must guard against their getting away with it.

On January 31, 2006, Samuel Alito joined the Supreme Court of the United States. Alito has gone on record in favor of the right to keep and bear arms. He was sworn in by the new Chief Justice, John Roberts, who took his position late in 2005. Roberts is also believed to be a strict constitutionalist.

Antigun forces never rest. In early 2006, a move began to apply New York City restrictions in other cities throughout the country. Antigunners know that if they can win just one battle, they can deprive us of some of our rights, whereas we must win every battle to retain our rights.

However, concealed carry legislation continues to grow across the country. By early 2006, 38 states reportedly had in effect "shall issue"

laws. This type of law requires officials to issue licenses to people who met the qualifications. A number of other states have concealed carry licenses, but they may be issued at the whim of issuing officials.

For the time being, things look positive. Nationally, the Bush administration is generally pro-gun rights. The Supreme Court may now be more inclined to interpret the Constitution as it was written. Local governments in many places have supported concealed carry, and other efforts have been made to allow legal armed access to businesses…and their parking lots.

The sunset of the so-called "Assault Weapons Ban" in 2004 has caused manufacturers to supply larger-capacity pistols to meet increased demand. Along with autoloading pistols, the shooting public seems to like pistol-caliber carbines, often with extended-capacity magazines. Because such carbines are generally not covered in the reports of common hunting and target rifles, they will again be covered here.

With all this in mind, let's take a look at what the companies are doing.

AMT

Since AMT came back into existence, pistols reportedly began shipping in February 2006. The double-action-only AMT Back-Up pistols are now available in 380 and 45 ACP calibers. Other calibers will follow later.

The AutoMag II, in the 6-inch barrel version, is in production. Chamberings are 22 Winchester Magnum Rimfire (22WMR) which was the original caliber, and a new variant, the 17 Hornady Magnum Rimfire (HMR).

ArmaLite

ArmaLite, essentially a rifle manufacturer since the start of the company in the mid-1950s, makes AR-15- and AR-10-type rifles in 223 and 308, and other rifles in larger calibers. Although the company has never offered a pistol before, the ArmaLite name has been associated with pistols in the past. In the

1980s, when Charter Arms was making the ArmaLite-designed AR-7 Explorer 22-caliber survival rifle, that company brought out a pistol version, the Explorer II. Serious readers of these pages may also remember that in the 1998 edition, it was reported that ArmaLite was considering marketing a 45-caliber 1911-style pistol. However, the ArmaLite 45 never materialized.

But now, the company will definitely be in the pistol business. ArmaLite and the Turkish firm of Sarsilmaz announced an agreement on February 11, 2006. Sarsilmaz will produce ArmaLite rifles under license for the Turkish armed forces, and ArmaLite will be their link to the United States handgun market.

The ArmaLite pistols will be based on the Sarsilmaz 9mm "Kilinc" (sword) pistol, which is the standard sidearm of the Turkish military. It is essentially a modified CZ75 design, with a cam-operated tilting-barrel locking system and conventional double-action trigger mechanism. ArmaLite is making modifications, so that the pistols will reflect the tradition of the company.

Three pistol variants will be offered by ArmaLite.

The AR-24 will be all-steel, with forged and machined parts. The large-capacity double-action pistols will be offered in full-size and compact models, and in 9mm and 40 S&W.

The AR-25 will have similar variants, but with lightweight polymer frames replacing the steel frames.

Introduction of the new AR-24 and AR-25 pistols was scheduled for the 3rd quarter of 2006.

In addition, the AR-26, a full-size steel-frame 45 ACP pistol, is in the works.

Beretta

Beretta has three new pistol developments, and some modifications to its Storm pistol-caliber carbine.

The Storm Px4 pistol, introduced on these pages last year, is now in production. Recall that the new polymer-frame sidearm was designed in what Beretta calls a "modular concept." Three interchangeable grip backstraps, reversible controls and a convertible trigger mechanism can customize a gun to meet the specifications of just about any shooter or any organization. It is available in 9mm and 40 S&W. As to the question posed last year about a 45-caliber version? Beretta is "exploring the options."

The M9A1 is a variation of the military M9 pistol with modifications for the U. S. Marine Corps. The new A1 variant has a frame accessory rail and other features. There is checkering on the front and rear frame straps, a chromed-lined bore, and a new sand-resistant magazine.

A new variant, called the 90-TWO (interesting play on words, as it is a modified "92" pistol) has a lightweight aluminum frame with a choice of sizes of a composite one-piece wraparound grip. The 90-TWO uses the same internal parts as the 92/96 series pistols, but the dimensions of the slides and frames are slightly different, and they will not interchange. The new pistol has an integral accessory rail on the frame, but a detachable cover is also provided to smooth out the profile if the rail is not used. Many manufacturers are putting frame rails on their pistols, figuring that users will want to hang things on the guns. However, some shooters hold that the purpose of a rail seems to be to keep one from ever being able to put the pistol in his waistband. Beretta's rail cover should pacify them somewhat.

The Cx4 Storm carbine is now offered with the options of using Px4 or 92/96 series pistol magazines. A kit is also available to adopt the carbine to use Beretta Cougar magazines. The ability to use the same magazines in a pistol and carbine carried together is an obvious advantage.

Browning

Several new variants of Browning's 22-caliber Buck Mark pistol line have been introduced.

The Buck Mark Lite Splash is light in weight, and has gold "splash" anodizing over matte blue. The lightness comes from a sleeved alloy barrel. Barrel lengths are 5.5

and 7.25 inches. This variant has the Ultragrip (a soft nitrile grip with ambidextrous finger grooves) and a fiber-optic front sight.

The Buck Mark Contour has a specially contoured barrel, with a scope base and target sights. It also has the Ultragrip and offers a choice of 5 1/2- or 7 1/4-inch barrels.

The Buck Mark Bullseye Target Stainless has a fluted 7 1/4-inch barrel and adjustable sights. Grips are laminated rosewood.

In addition, a limited number of special John M. Browning presentation pistols will be made, with a portion of the price paid for each pistol to go to the John M. Browning Endowment, to benefit the National Rifle Association (NRA) Shooting Sports Camp Program. The Grade I pistol will be stainless, with Black DymondWood grips and special engraving. Two thousand, five hundred will be made. The High Grade pistol will be engraved, with gold and copper accents. Two barrels and checkered walnut grips come with each High Grade pistol, of which only 1001 will be produced.

All new Buck Mark pistols have gripping flanges (ears, to some) at the rear of the slide now. Earlier versions were criticized for a lack of a positive gripping surface, and retracting the slide when the pistol was uncocked could be difficult.

Bushmaster

Recall that two years ago, Bushmaster acquired Professional Ordnance, and continued the lightweight 223-caliber Carbon 15 pistols and carbines. Carbon 15 variants have receivers made of carbon fiber composite.

In February 2006, Bushmaster added to the Carbon 15 offerings a new 9mm pistol and a 9mm carbine. The new pistol and carbine have the same "AR-15" appearance and controls of the other Bushmaster products. However, in place of the rotating bolt and direct-gas-impingement opening system, the 9mm firearms use the simpler blowback system of operation.

The pistol has a 7 1/2-inch barrel, and an overall length of about 22 inches. Weight is 4.6 pounds. The 9mm carbine has a 16-inch barrel, which gives it an overall length of 34-1/2

Top: Browning's Bullseye Target Stainless pistol has a fluted barrel and rosewood grips.
Below Top: The Buck Mark Lite Splash is also made with a 7 1/4-inch barrel.
Above Bottom: The Browning Buck Mark Lite Splash is a lightweight pistol with gold "splash" decoration. This is the 5 1/2-inch version.
Bottom: The Browning Buck Mark Contour has a specially contoured barrel, with a scope base and target sights.

inches, and a weight of 5.7 pounds. Both the pistol and the carbine come with 30-round magazines.

Century

The Philippine-made S.A.M. (Shooters Arms Manufacturing) 45-caliber pistols that were discontinued last year by Century International Arms have been partially reinstated.

Two variants of the 1911-style pistols have returned to Century's handgun lineup. The Military pistol is essentially a modernized recreation of the WWII-era service pistol. The Elite model has a number of the embellishments many shooters favor, such as beavertail grip safety, skeletonized trigger and hammer, and slam pad on the magazine. Both have 5-inch barrels, and, of course, are in 45 ACP. These are nice pistols, and it is good to see them back.

Another new offering is the Romanian Carpati Model 95, a double-action compact in 380 ACP. For those who like a bonus, the 380 Carpati comes with a cleaning rod, spare magazine and a shoulder holster.

Charles Daly

With the sunset of the "Assault Weapons Ban" in 2004, larger capacity pistols now have advantages for some competition and personal-protection situations. Charles Daly has introduced a new steel frame high-capacity 45 based on the Colt/Browning 1911 design. Most higher-capacity 45 frames are now made of polymer material, but many shooters still prefer a steel frame.

CZ

Since 1998, when CZ-USA was established to import Czech firearms to the United States, the offerings to American shooters have grown. New in the CZ lineup as of February 2006 were a number of autoloading pistols, most modifications of the basic 9mm CZ75.

The CZ75B Stainless is the first stainless-steel firearm to carry the CZ name. Except for rubber grips and an ambidextrous manual safety, the stainless-steel version is functionally the same as the blue-steel CZ75B.

Two new SP-01 models have been introduced. The SP-01 Tactical pistol is a full-size version with a 4.7-inch barrel, a larger version of the standard SP-01 Service Pistol introduced recently. It has a beavertail tang, rubber grips and a full-length frame with an accessory rail.

The SP-01 Shadow is a competition version with adjustable rear sight, fiber-optic front sight and walnut grips. It has a lighter recoil spring and mainspring to handle "minor" power factor 9mm loads. The magazine capacity, as with the other SP-01 pistols, is 19 rounds.

The CZ75 Tactical Sport pistol was built for IPSC competition. It features high sights, a single-action trigger of special configuration, and a full-length frame with beveled magazine well. Available in 9mm (20+1) and 40 S&W (16+1) variants, the Tactical Sport has a nickeled frame with blued slide.

The compact CZ2075 RAMI pistol, introduced recently, is an aluminum-frame subcompact based on the SZ75 mechanism. The little pistol has found a following, and this year, a polymer-frame version with a lightened slide is available. It is offered in 40 S&W (8+1) or 9mm (10+1). An extended 14-round 9mm magazine is also available.

On January 25, 2005, CZ USA purchased the assets and trademark of Dan Wesson. Within the CZ framework, the Dan Wesson group continues a separate product line of revolvers and 1911-type semiautomatic pistol and are now included in the CZ catalog. (See Dan Wesson)

Dan Wesson

The alphabet being arranged as it is, this is certainly a convenient place to report on the Dan Wesson handguns being offered, following the acquisition of the company by CZ-USA.

Some revolvers and three automatic pistols appeared in the 2006 CZ catalog. The autoloaders

are of interest to us here.

The Pointman 7 (PM7) is a 1911-style match-grade pistol with a 5-inch barrel. Enhancements such as adjustable sights, beavertail grip safety, extended thumb safety and extended magazine release are standard.

The Commander Classic Bobtail has many of the same features, but has a 4.25-inch barrel and fixed night sights. The lower rear edge of the grip frame and mainspring housing area has

Top: *The CZ75B Stainless 9mm is the company's first stainless-steel pistol.*
Bottom: *The CZ75 SP-01 Tactical pistol is a larger version of the SP-01 service pistol.*

been beveled off ("bobbed") to make the gun easier to conceal as a carry pistol.

The Razorback is a new 1911-style pistol chambered only for the 10mm Auto cartridge. A 5-inch barrel and fixed sights are standard. While the other Dan Wesson pistols are basically 45s, they may be ordered in 10mm chambering. The Razorback is made as a 10mm only.

Detonics

Detonics USA reports that the short-frame CombatMaster with 3 1/2-inch barrel and the short frame StreetMaster with 5-inch barrel are now in good production, and other models are coming on line. A Detonics Combat Master pistol was used in the motion picture *Mr. and Mrs. Smith,* allowing some recognition outside normal shooting circles.

A new variant, listed as a medium-sized CombatMaster, is now in the catalog. In heritage, it is related to the original 4 1/4-inch ServiceMaster, and in appearance is the ServiceMaster with a short grip, giving a 6+1 capacity.

How do the new Detonics pistols hold up? Pretty well, if a recent 3-day endurance test is any indication. In those three days, 31,000 rounds were fired through a single full-size 5-inch Model 9-11-01 pistol. Students of firearms history will recall that the original Colt 1911 was subjected in that year to a 6000-round test—the longest recorded shooting test of any pistol to that time. Now, Detonics has put over five times that many rounds through one of their pistols. Oh, yes, for good measure, they also shot the pistol out of a mortar before running accuracy tests. The gun functioned well and gave good accuracy.

Because Jerry Ahern, president of Detonics, and pistolmaker L. W. Seecamp have had a long relationship, 100 cased sets of two pistols—a Detonics 45 and a Seecamp 32—are being made up. Both pistols in each set have identical serial numbers, with the prefix DETLWS.

DSA

At the February 2006 SHOT Show, DSA displayed a prototype long-range 308-caliber pistol with an 11-inch barrel. The pistol is a modification of the company's 11-inch "entry rifle" made without a stock. The thinking is that other chamberings—243 Winchester, 260 Remington—may come into the line after production begins.

EAA

European American Armory has introduced the Witness "Elite Match" pistol. Decked out for competition, the new Witness is available in 9mm, 10mm, 40S&W and 45 ACP. Witness pistols are a modified CZ75 design.

EAA is also offering high-end carry guns from their custom shop. Designated "Match Special," the pistols are available in compact and subcompact sizes.

Ed Brown

Ed Brown Products offers a line of high-grade 1911-style pistols. New for 2006 was the Executive Target model, an enhanced 5-inch-barrel pistol. It has many of the features favored by a lot of shooters today, such as adjustable sights, beavertail grip safety, checkered front and back grip straps, and ambidextrous manual safety. It is offered in blue, stainless steel or a blue/stainless two-tone combination.

New also is the Special Forces 5-inch "Government" style pistol. The fixed sights are 3-dot Novak. Front and rear grip straps have a chainlink pattern to provide a gripping surface. The finish is a hard dark coating over forged carbon steel.

Firestorm

Not all that long ago, it seemed as if the 32 ACP cartridge was a dead duck. Because of the perceived superiority of the 380 ACP, no company that made pistols suitable for either cartridge made a 32. Then things changed. Perhaps because of the appearance of 25-sized 32s, or perhaps because of the ballistically-improved ammunition available, the 32 ACP chambering experienced a resurrection. Now, a number of manufacturers make 32s again.

The latest purveyor of 32 ACP pistols is FireStorm. For some years offering compact pocket pistols in 380 ACP, the line now includes a 32 ACP chambering in its MiniFireStorm series. Magazine capacity of the new 32 is 10 rounds, three more than the similar 380. With a 3 1/2-inch barrel, the pistol weighs 23 ounces.

Made in Argentina, the new 32 and other FireStorm pistols are imported by SGS Importers in New Jersey.

The large-frame FireStorm 45-caliber pistols were previously manufactured by Llama in Spain. With the demise of Llama, these pistols are no longer available. (See Llama)

FNH USA

FNH USA is the American company that handles Belgian Fabrique Nationale (FN)-designed firearms. The firm continues to modify their pistol line, and has introduced a carbine that is sure to generate interest.

The FNP 9 and FNP 40 pistols are available in black finish or black with a silver (stainless-steel) slide. New double-action-only variants are also available, and a double decocker version has been introduced.

The Five-seveN pistol, chambered for the interesting 5.7x28mm cartridge has a new variant. Although most makers are putting magazine disconnectors in all their pistols in an attempt to make their products universally salable and ward off lawsuits, most

The new Ed Brown Special Forces Pistol has Novak sights and a chain-link pattern on the grip straps.

law-enforcement officers and others who carry a pistol regularly seem not to prefer them. The pistol has been available in an Individual Officers Model without the disconnect.

Recall that the Five-seveN is a light, mostly-polymer pistol with what is called a delayed-blowback mechanism. Although not locked together, the barrel recoils a short distance with the slide before the slide continues rearward.

The most attention-getting new FNH offering is the new P90 semiautomatic carbine based on the firm's M90 submachine gun. Chambered for the 5.7x28mm cartridge, the new carbine has a 16-inch barrel and can fire single shots only, in autoloading fashion. The magazine, like that of the submachine gun, lies on the top of the gun, and the cartridges in the magazine lie crosswise to the long axis of the gun until they are fed into the feed mechanism. The innovative design allows magazines of different capacities without increasing the size of the firearm. 10-, 30- and 50-round magazines are reported to be available. The appearance is unconventional (to say the least), and the P90 is sure to attract attention.

Heckler & Koch

As of January 2006, Heckler & Koch (HK) has experienced some changes in organization structure. Merkel (shotguns and rifles) is now part of HK, and Anschutz guns are now imported by Merkel. HK itself has been split into two entities—sporting arms will be handled from Trussville, AL, and military and defense items will be handled from Sterling, VA.

High Standard

High Standard has introduced its "Mil-Spec" series of pistols—and carbines. The pistols are 1911-type 45s, and are of, in High Standard's words, "original design, with a few improvements." The Parkerized 45 shares the spotlight with the company's new line of 223-caliber AR-15-style rifles and carbines, dubbed HSA-15. The pistol carries the model number TX1911.

Other 45-caliber 1911-type pistols are new in the line. The "Camp Perry" National Match pistol is tuned for competition, but avoids some of the exotic accessories some like to add on. As were the original military National Match pistols, they will be offered with either fixed or adjustable sights. A "Supermatic" 45 will be offered with a 6-inch barrel. A "Crusader Compact" with a 3 1/2-inch barrel is in the offing. It will be all-steel, with Novak-style sights.

In the world of 22 pistols, High Standard will offer the "Bob Shea" series of specially-constructed pistols. Shea began working for High Standard in 1942, and is still active in repairing and accurizing various models of the 22 pistols. When asked about retirement, Shea replied that he seems to be spending "less time fishing and more time making guns." High Standard has returned to production a limited edition of the old Supermatic Tournament—the early target pistol with the sight on the slide instead of on a bridge. The company will also return the fixed-sight Sport King to production.

Although it is not pertinent to this report, the High Standard team seems to enjoy bringing back old names. The group is forming a company to manufacture ammunition. The name they have acquired may be familiar to many old-timers—U. S. Cartridge Company.

Hi-Point

Hi-Point Firearms now has an association with Charter Arms, and both brands will be distributed by MKS Supply. This relationship should work well. Both brands are American-made, and Hi-Point autoloading pistols and Charter revolvers will complement each other, offering more handgun choices. As a sign the Hi-Point niche is really expanding, note that a line of reproductions of historic lever-action rifles has also been added.

Hi-Point carbines are probably the most popular single brand of pistol-caliber carbine being used today. The popular 9mm and 40-caliber carbines were scheduled to be

joined by a long-awaited 45-caliber version in the Spring of 2006.

With the sunset of the "Assault Weapons Ban," Hi-Point has been working on extended magazines for its carbines, but at the time of this writing, has not marketed any. Charles Brown, president, said that they have not yet been satisfied with the reliability of the prototype extended magazines. Hi-Point products have a reputation for working right, and the company wants the new magazines to continue that reputation.

Iver Johnson

The Iver Johnson 45-caliber 1911-type pistol, introduced on these pages in the last edition, is not yet in production, but was getting close in early 2006. The 45 pistols have steel frames, but an aluminum-frame 22-caliber version is also planned. Twenty-two-caliber kits are under development, and the company is also testing pistols and kits for the 17 Mach 2 cartridge.

Kahr

Kahr has a number of new products in both its traditional Kahr line and in its Auto-Ordnance/Thompson line. In the Kahr line, the new CW series (think "concealed weapon") are designed, not for the armed professional, but for the average citizen who carries a concealed pistol for his or her own personal protection. The CW pistols use some simpler manufacturing processes, and sell at a lower price. The CW pistols have conventional rifling rather than polygonal. The front sight is fixed on the slide instead of fitting in a dovetail. The slide stop, instead of being machined, is an MIM (metal injection molded) part. Such changes allow offering the same basic pistol at a substantially lower price. CW pistols are double-action-only, have polymer frames and matte stainless-steel slides. They are available in 9mm and 40, and have 3 1/2-inch barrels.

The P45 is a new 45 ACP polymer variant, with a blackened stainless-steel slide. The barrel is

3.54 inches long and has polygonal rifling. With a capacity of 6+1, the new 45 weighs just a bit over 20 ounces with its magazine. Like all Kahr pistols, the P45 does not have a magazine disconnector. Many consider this an advantage.

The Auto-Ordnance/Thompson Custom line of 1911-style 45 automatics has two new 4 1/4-inch variants. One is all stainless steel, and the other has a stainless-steel slide and an aluminum frame. The pistols have a number of the enhancements favored by today's shooters.

Thompson long guns may be considered the modern offspring of the original pistol-caliber carbine—the Thompson submachine gun. The several variants of the modern Thompson semiautomatic carbine have been upgraded with more authentic features. Fifty- and 100-round drums are now available (and, interestingly, 10-round drums for those who want the Thompson look, but live in capacity-limited states or localities).

Now, I have walked into a trap by including pistol-caliber carbines in this report. Auto-Ordnance also offers a reproduction of the U. S. M-1 30-caliber carbine. Is the 30 Carbine cartridge really a pistol cartridge? Certainly pistols have been made for it. At any rate, the company is making M-1 carbines.

Kel-Tec

Kel-Tec has introduced a number of new pistols and modifications to its existing pistol models.

The most eye-catching is the PLR-16, a long-range pistol in 223. The big new pistol is a modification of the company's SU-16 rifle design. It has a 9.2-inch barrel and weighs 3.2 pounds. The PLR-16 uses the turning-bolt locking system of the military M-16. The muzzle is threaded for standard attachments.

The company's fortunes were built on the excellent 14-ounce P-11 pistol of 1995, a 10+1 polymer-frame 9mm. For 2006, the basic mechanism was put into an even more compact package—the new PF-9. A single-column magazine offers 7+1 capacity and allows a slimmer, lighter 12.7-ounce pistol. A new simpler extractor has been introduced with the PF-9.

The new extractor design is now also being used by the company's P-32 (32 ACP) and P-3AT (380 ACP) guns. Those two little pocket pistols also have new sights—very low sights with a broad square notch and a broad blade front. The sights are made as part of the slide and are not adjustable.

Kimber

Kimber, one of the largest manufacturers of 1911-type pistols, announced a departure for 2006. The new Kimber Pro Defense (KPD) is a polymer-frame 40-caliber designed for both service and personal defense use. At 25 ounces, the double-action-only pistol has a 4-inch barrel and has 12+1 capacity. Three interchangeable backstraps allow fitting the gun to a specific hand. The stainless-steel slide is covered with a black "Kim Pro II" finish. As most new introductions seem to have, the KPD has an accessory rail on the front of the frame. Introduced in 40 S&W chambering, a 9mm is planned for the near future.

Introduced back in May 2005 (and not yet included on these pages), the Kimber Desert Warrior is an interesting 1911 pistol with an accessory rail––and of all things––a lanyard loop at the butt. Earth tones (sand tones) for the metal finish and grips reflect the desert theme and give the pistol distinctive appearance.

From the Kimber Custom Shop, the Grand Raptor II features scaled serrations, polished flats of the stainless-steel frame, and a matte slide. A full-size 45, the two-tone pistol is loaded with Custom Shop features.

Les Baer

Les Baer Custom builds 1911-style pistols for service, defense and competition use. The company celebrated its 25th anniversary last year. This year, a book, *Les Baer, Sr.– A Legend in His Own Time,* by Charles K. Stroud, Jr., was published. Baer is one of a number of gunmakers who began making guns on a custom basis, then realized many customers wanted similar guns. The result is what many call "production custom" pistols.

Llama

The grand old name of Llama is gone. It was introduced by the Spanish firm of Gabilondo over a century ago, in 1904. A variety of pistols and revolvers have been made under the Llama name. In 1931, the company began making centerfire pistols based on (but not exact copies of) the Colt/Browning 1911 design, and such guns were used during the Spanish Civil War. Stoeger was the long-term importer of Llama pistols into the United States after World War II. In the 1990s, the firm had financial problems, but in 2000, manufacture was continued by a cooperative of Gabilondo employees. Import Sports became the importer.

Now it looks as if Llama is gone for good. The cooperative went out of business in early April 2005. For those who want to keep their Llamas shooting, Eagle Imports of New Jersey has acquired the last supply of Llama parts and magazines. A listing of Llama parts can be seen at www.yourgunparts.com.

Magnum Research

Magnum Research has introduced a line of lightweight rimfire semiautomatic rifles. In limited production (only one production run was planned for 2006) is a pistol version, called the "PiCuda."

The unusual name seems to stem from the fact that it is the "pistol" version, with what the company calls the "barracuda" stock. Based on the Ruger rimfire rifle action, the receiver and sight rail are machined as one piece, and the barrel is a steel tube in a graphite carbon fiber sleeve. The barracuda stock is a design of unusual-shape that does not contact the barrel. It is laminated in a pattern of browns and greens that the company calls "forest camo." The PiCuda has a 10-shot magazine, and is available in 22 Long Rifle or 17 Mach 2.

Majestic Arms

We have not considered Majestic Arms in this report previously, but now that we are covering pistol-caliber carbines, it is worth paying some attention to this company's products. Their autoloading model MA 4 is based on what they call the Majestic Arms Rimfire Rifle System (MARRS). Using a new action patterned after the AR-7 survival rifle action, the company makes interchangeable-barrel carbines that can use 22 Long Rifle (22LR), 17 Mach 2, 22 Winchester Magnum Rimfire (22WMR) and 17 Hornady Magnum Rimfire (17HMR).

Mitchell

Mitchell Manufacturing has brought out a new rimfire semi-auto pistol and carbine duo.

Regular readers of these pages may have noted that similar guns were introduced in the 2005 edition. At that time, they had just been introduced by Excel Arms. In the interim, Mitchell acquired the rights to these interesting guns, and is offering them under the Mitchell name. The pistol is named the White Lightning, and the carbine is marketed as the Black Lightning. Either version is available as one of four rimfire calibers—22LR, 17 Mach 2, 22WMR or 17 HMR. A nine-round magazine works with either the pistol or carbine. A bolt handle on the right of the slide (even on the pistol) aids in operation.

The pistol has an 8 1/2-inch barrel, is equipped with adjustable open sights and has a top rail for mounting optical or electronic sights. The carbine has an 18-inch barrel and a full-length top rail that can mount a variety of scopes and other sights. Scope rings come standard with the carbine.

Nighthawk

A new name has entered the arena of high-end "production custom" semiautomatic pistols based on the 1911 Colt/Browning design. Nighthawk Custom was formed in 2004, but the first large-scale public display of the pistols

was made at the February 2006 SHOT Show, in Las Vegas, NV.

One of their offerings had been called the Global Response Pistol (GRP), a 5-inch 45 suited to extreme conditions. Their newest pistol was a similar gun, but with a 4 1/4-inch barrel. The new arrival has been dubbed the GRP II.

Olympic

Olympic Arms has introduced a series of pistol-caliber carbines based on the AR-15. The code is not hard to break, for the model numbers are K9, K10, K40 and K45. With 16-inch barrels, they are offered in 9mm, 10mm, 40 S&W and 45 ACP. The 9mm uses a 32-round converted Sten magazine. The other calibers use 10-round converted UZI magazines. There are two additional models—models K9-GL and K40-GL. These carbines, in 9mm and 40 calibers, use standard factory Glock magazines of varying capacities. Although the controls are the same, the locked-breech mechanism of the AR-15 is not needed with the pistol calibers, so the new guns are blowback-operated. Pistol-caliber kits (uppers) are also available to convert an existing AR-type rifle to a pistol-caliber 16-inch carbine.

The Whitney Wolverine reincarnation has been in production long enough now that Olympic has a line of accessories available. Adjustable sights are planned as an option. Checkered wood grips, a suitable nylon holster and extra magazines may be had now. The magazines offered will also fit the original Whitneys of the 1950s—a good situation for those who need a magazine for an old Whitney.

Para-Ordnance

Para-Ordnance has brought out a number of new pistols, all variants of the 1911 Colt/Browning design. Most of them can be found in the 2006 Para catalog, but at least one was too new to make it in. Let's look at them:

The "Hog" series has some new members. The Stainless Warthog is the 3.5-inch 10+1 Warthog,

The Para Tac-Five is a 9mm with the LDA trigger system.

made in stainless steel. The Slim Hawg, introduced last year, is now a production item. It is a single-column version of the Warthog, with 6+1 capacity. The Lite Hawg 9 is a modification of the 9mm-chambered Hawg 9 of last year. The "lite" in the new model's name doesn't mean that it is lighter than the original, but that it has a rail on the frame to hold a light. The 12+1 9mm is also joined by a 10+1 Lite Hawg 45.

The Tac-Five has Para's LDA (light double action) trigger mechanism, and is available as an 18+1 9mm. New calibers of Nite-Tac full-size LDA pistols have light rails. They are offered as a 9mm (18+1) or as a 40 S&W (16+1).

The 1911 SSP model is a single-column full-size pistol made in 45 ACP (8+1) and—in 38 Super, with a 9+1 capacity.

Todd Jarrett uses Para pistols in

This Para 1911 SSP is an 8+1 pistol in 45 ACP.

competition, and the company has brought out special pistols to attest to that fact. Todd Jarrett USPSA Limited Edition pistols are available in two versions. A 45 version is a single-column pistol with an 8+1 capacity, and a 40-caliber version has a double-column magazine and holds 16+1 rounds. For every one of these pistols purchased, a portion of the price will go to the United States Practical Shooting Association (USPSA).

A new caliber for Para is 45 G.A.P. A compact single-column Carry model is offered in the 45 G.A.P. chambering, although the new addition did not make it into the catalog.

Rock Island

"Rock Island Arsenal" is the name used on the 1911-style semiautomatic pistols produced for American sales by the Philippine manufacturer Armscor. Along with the standard service model, a new target model with adjustable sights is now available.

Rock River

Rock River Arms makes high-grade 1911-style pistols and AR-15 type rifles and carbines.

New for 2006 were LAR-15 pistols, large AR-type pistols in 223 and 9mm calibers. Either version comes with barrel choices of 7 or 10-1/2 inches. Other choices are AR-15 style sights, or no sights, but with front and rear rails for sight mounting. 223 pistols are locked breech, and 9mm pistols are blow-back operated.

Tooled up for the 9mm AR-style pistol, it is logical to reason that Rock River would also offer 9mm carbines based on the AR design. The company does indeed offer two 9mm blow-back carbines. The CAR A2 has a 16-inch Wilson barrel, and has AR-style front and rear sights. The CAR A4 is similar, but has a front sight and receiver rail that allows different types of rear sight mounting.

Both 9mm carbines and the 9mm pistols use modified 25-round UZI magazines. For those in areas where magazine freedom has not reached, 10-shot magazines are also available.

In their 1911 line, Rock River Arms offers new variants. The Basic Carry is a "dehorned" full-size 45, with edges smoothed out for easier carry. The Tactical Pistol adds a light rail on the forward part of the frame. Two new 9mm Police Competition pistols are offered now, for use in Limited and Unlimited events. The Limited version has a 5-inch barrel, while the Unlimited pistol has a 6-inch barrel.

Rohrbaugh

The lightweight all-metal 9mm Rohrbaugh pistols are now available in three cosmetic variants—black, silver, or black-and-silver (the original version). New variations in grips, and choices of sights (Model R9S) or no sights (Model R9) are offered.

New for 2006 were presentation models. Production has gone well past 1000 pistols, and the landmark serial number R1000 is up for auction. Rohrbaugh pistols have been used in *Mr. and Mrs. Smith* and the *Miami Vice* movie, so they are acquiring recognition outside the shooting world.

RTI

Recoilless Technologies, Inc. is developing recoilless and multi-caliber pistols. Avid readers of these pages may recognize that the company was first reported in the 1997 edition as Ultima Technologies. By the 1998 edition, it had become Recoilless Technologies, to better reflect the operating characteristics of the pistol under development.

The design is of some interest. A collar around the rear portion of the barrel can be removed from the front of the frame. With the collar off, the frame can be opened as if it were a clamshell, hinged at the rear. With the frame open, the barrel can be simply lifted out, allowing easy interchange of barrels. The geometry of the internal parts minimizes recoil. The rearward moving breechblock is linked to an internal mechanism that moves down against spring pressure as the action operates. Inertia of this motion acts against the upward rise from recoil, and diminished felt recoil comes back at near a straight line.

The late 1990s pistol was a 9mm, and it was claimed that loadings to produce very high velocities could be handled safely. At the February 2006 SHOT Show, three different variants were shown, handling 9mm (9x19, 9x21, 9x23), 9mm Winchester Magnum (with reported velocities of 1980 fps) and a special 50 caliber, made by shortening a 300 Winchester Short Magnum (300WSM) case.

Ruger

All right, the big news from Sturm, Ruger & Co. was the 50th Anniversary model of their 44 Magnum revolver. That said, the company did bring out some new variants of autoloading pistols.

Last year, Ruger brought out the stainless-steel Mark III Hunter 22-caliber pistol, with a 6 7/8-inch fluted barrel. This year, the firm is giving the same treatment to the 22/45 pistol line. The new 22/45 Mark III Hunter has the polymer frame, introduced in 1992, which has the same grip angle as the 1911 45-caliber pistol. The polymer frame was slimmed down recently, and the new pistol has this thinner grip frame. The new Hunter version has the long fluted stainless barrel, and an adjustable rear sight with a HiViz front sight. The stainless-steel receiver is drilled and tapped for a scope base adapter, which is included with the gun. Also included are a gun lock and a storage case in, of course, Hunter Green color.

Also new in February 2006 was Model P95 9mm pistol with an integral frame light/accessory rail. The polymer frame has new textured grip areas to provide a better hold, and the trigger guard has been modified to a smoother, more rounded shape. Offered with a manual safety or as a decock-only version, the new P95 pistols have 3.9-inch barrels, weigh 27 ounces and have 15+1 capacity.

Sarsilmaz

The Turkish firm of Sarsilmaz has become a big player in the international handgun field. A few years ago, the reappearance of the Italian Bernardelli pistol line was due largely to association with Sarsilmaz. This year, an agreement with ArmaLite will provide a new line of Sarsilmaz-produced pistols under the ArmaLite name. (see ARMALITE.)

Under the Sarsilmaz name, the Turkish firm offers a line of shotguns and 9mm pistols that are based on the CZ 75 operating mechanism. The pistols they produce run the gamut from full size to compact, from steel-frame to alloy-frame to polymer-frame variants, and from service pistols to competition guns. A version of their steel-frame full-size pistol is the official pistol of Turkish armed forces.

Other companies that base their pistol line on the CZ 75 design often offer variants in 40 S&W as well as the original 9mm. Sarsilmaz, for whatever reason, has chosen not to do this. The firm seemed satisfied with the 9mm chambering. Thus, it was a surprise to see a 45 ACP pistol displayed at the Sarsilmaz booth at the February 2006 SHOT Show. Little could be learned about the company's plans for the Sarsilmaz 45, and it is not mentioned in their catalog.

SIGARMS

After the successful introduction of the SIG-Sauer 1911 a couple years back, it seems safe to say that SIGARMS has embraced the 1911 design. The 2006 catalog lists no fewer than 15 different versions! Called the Granite Series Revolution (GSR) upon its introduction, "Revolution" seems to have won out as the identifier, and all the SIG 1911s are now various Revolution models.

SIGARMS has a number of new entries in its traditional pistols lines. Model P220, P226 and P229 pistols in various calibers now can be had with factory-installed Crimson Trace Lasergrips. Rails and night sights (and the extra set of original factory grips, in case you want to change back) come standard with these pistols.

From the SIGARMS custom shop, a series of "SAS" variants is available for Models P220, P226, P229 and P239. These are good-looking carry pistols that feature

a bright slide, dark frame and strikingly attractive laminated wood grips. The metal has been "dehorned" to give smooth edges. All models wear a Siglite front sight.

Smith & Wesson

Smith & Wesson must have held its corporate breath when it introduced the Chiefs Special automatic pistols a few years ago. The Chiefs Special 38 revolver had been a mainstay in the S&W line for half a century. Would the shooting world accept an autoloader also named Chiefs Special? Apparently it did. Now, S&W has reapplied the Military & Police (M&P) name—a designation applied to a revolver in production since 1899—to a modern semiautomatic pistol. And, not just to a pistol, but to the company's new AR-style 223 rifle!

The rifle is interesting, too, but the pistol is what we will consider here. The new M&P pistol is a full-size gun with a light Zytel polymer frame with a hardened, Melonite-coated stainless-steel slide. It is a locked-breech mechanism with a 6.5-pound trigger that operates a striker-fire ignition system. The M&P has three interchangeable backstrap grip inserts to fit a particular pistol to a particular hand. Slide stop is ambidextrous, and the magazine release is reversible. Barrel length is 4-1/4 inches, and weight is about 24 ounces. The frame has an accessory rail. The M&P pistol was introduced in early 2006 in 40 S&W caliber. 9mm and 347 SIG also were scheduled for introduction shortly thereafter. Compact versions are also in the works.

The M&P was the star of the show for S&W's auto pistols, but the 1911 line has received plenty of attention. No less than 14 different variants appear in the 2006 catalog. Newly introduced in 2006 are the SW1911 Tactical Rail pistols, which have an accessory rail at the front of the frame. Two versions are offered—a stainless steel pistol, and one with a black scandium frame and stainless slide with black Melonite finish.

The Model 1911PD "Gunsite" pistol has a 4 1/4-inch barrel.

The frame is scandium, with a carbon steel slide; both finishes in matte black. Sights are Novak, with a brass bead front sight.

From the performance shop, a new Model 952 Long Slide is available. The pistol is a 9mm version of the old Model 52 target pistol, now with a 6-inch barrel and long slide to match. The single-action pistol is fitted with a Wilson Micro adjustable rear sight.

Springfield

Springfield continues to make lots of 1911-type pistols, but their big news is the new 45-caliber version of their polymer-frame XD pistol. Introduced at the February 2006 SHOT Show, the new XD is chambered for 45 ACP, and has 13+1 capacity.

The company had brought out a 45 G.A.P. version of the XD last year, but the longer 45 ACP cartridge required some redesign. Now the pistols are here, in two variants. The 4-inch barrel XD 45 weighs

Top: *1911 Gunsite L The scandium-frame "Gunsite" pistol from S&W has special grips and a 4 1/4-inch barrel.*
Bottom: *S&W Tactical Rail pistol in stainless steel, left view.*

Top: *Springfield XD 45 ACP pistol, angled*
Bottom: *Spring-field's XD pistol is now available in 45 ACP chambering. This is the 4-inch barrel version.*

30 ounces, and is 7 inches long. The variant with the 5-inch barrel weighs 32 ounces, and has an overall length of 8 inches. Dovetailed 3-dot sights are standard, with Tritium sights as an option.

Steyr

The uncertainty expressed here last year is over. Import arrangements for Steyr firearms have been established, and Steyr pistols (and rifles too) have a new importer, Steyr Arms of Cummins, GA.

Steyr and Mannlicher-branded rifles are being imported, but the Steyr M-A1 pistol is the gun that fits this report. The ergonomic polymer-frame pistol has a 4-inch barrel and is available in 9mm, 40 S&W and 357 SIG. An accessory rail is located at the front of the frame.

Because we are including pistol-caliber carbines here, it is of interest to note that the Steyr AUG—a gun of unusual appearance, and one that antigun forces love to hate—is now available as a 9mm carbine with a 16-inch barrel.

Taurus

In January 2005, Taurus introduced their version of the 45-caliber 1911 Colt/Browning design, the PT-1911. At that time, there were only two specimens in the United States. As of February 2006, the new guns were still not in full production, but Taurus had already brought out four new models.

A full-size 5-inch model in 38 Super is now offered, available in blue or stainless. A second full-size pistol is offered in 40 S&W caliber, also with a choice of blue or stainless, and also with or without a frame accessory rail. The third full-size offering is a 9mm, also blue or stainless. The fourth is a compact 45, with a 4 1/4-inch barrel. Actually, there could be any number of variations, adding up to a very large number of 1911 choices. It seems safe to say that Taurus is definitely in the 1911 business.

Taurus seems to have wanted to provide something for everyone with their new 2006 offerings. How about a full-size PT59 in 380 ACP, with 15+1 capacity? Or the 9mm PT917, with a 20-round magazine, giving a full 21 shots? The PT 745 polymer compact 45 has two new variants, one a long-slide version with a longer 4 1/4-inch barrel.

The other is a version in 45 G.A.P.

The compact Millennium pistol is available in a titanium variant that provides 13+1 rounds of 9mm capacity. The polymer-frame 24/7 service pistol is now available with a titanium slide, as a long-slide version with a 5-inch barrel, or as a short-slide/short grip model with a 3.3-inch barrel. Or, as the short slide/long grip model. You probably get the idea—Taurus offers a lot of variations in its line of autoloading pistols.

Uselton

Uselton's pistol line of "totally customized out of the box" 1911-type pistols had a new addition for 2006. The Officers Damascus variant has a damascus slide, a titanium frame—and grips made from genuine ray skin. The ray skin grips feel as if they would provide a non-slip hold under almost any circumstances.

U. S. Firearms

United States Firearms Manufacturing Co., a company that made its reputation by manufacturing replicas of historic Colt revolvers, surprised a lot of people last year by bring out their first autoloading pistols. The guns were Colt 1911-type pistols, but looked even earlier, as they were fitted with grips that recalled the wide flat grips of the Colt 1905 pistol.

USFA liked the look, and this year they have brought out two new 1911-style handguns with those grips. One is in the 38 Super chambering, with the slide marked "USFA Super 38 Automatic." The second is a recreation of the old Colt Ace 22 pistol, and is marked "USFA ACE .22 Long Rifle." Two appropriate magazines are furnished with each pistol.

Volquartsen

New from Volquartsen is the Predator pistol, a long-range rimfire handgun. Introduced in stainless steel, the company also plans to offer a version with an aluminum receiver and a lightweight sleeved barrel. The Predator comes with a fiberglass stock, and calibers are 22 Winchester Magnum Rimfire (22WMR) and 17 Hornady Magnum Rimfire (17HMR).

Walther

According to Walther records, the Walther PPK pistol was introduced in 1931. Thus, 2006 marked the little pistol's 75th anniversary. Such a milestone obviously called for a special commemorative pistol.

The commemorative pistol will be of carbon steel, with a highly-polished blue finish, accented with engraving on the slide and frame, and the Walther logo in gold. "75th Anniversary" will be engraved on the slide. Serial numbers will be in a separate group, starting with 0000PPK.

The 75th year PPK is close to the original, which was one of the first commercially-made pistols to introduce the double-action trigger mechanism to autoloading handguns. The current version is in 380 ACP and has a 3.3-inch barrel, is six inches long and weighs 20.8 ounces. The original had a very short tang, which could result in "hammer bite" to the web of the shooter's hand; the current production pistol has a longer tang to prevent this. The Anniversary PPK will wear wood grips for the occasion, instead of the plastic grips of the original.

Wildey

Recall that back in the 2004 edition, it was reported that Wildey had reintroduced the 44 AutoMag cartridge as a current chambering in a production pistol. In February 2006, Wildey brought out the 357 AutoMag as a regular

chambering. Wildey plans to provide ammunition, reloading dies and brass for the 357, as they do for all their calibers. Owners of original Automag pistols in the 357 and 44 calibers can also benefit from having a reliable source for these items.

The JAWS Viper pistol, which was developed as a joint venture between Wildey and the country of Jordan, is ready to go into production. Readers may remember that the pistol can be converted to several different calibers by quick replacement of just a few parts. A Wildey representative said that it was hoped that the pistol would be in full production by the end of 2006.

Wilson

Wilson, long known for the company's line of "production custom" pistols based on the 45-caliber 1911 Colt/Browning system, has introduced a new pistol that is a departure for the company. The new gun, called the ADP (Advanced Design Pistol) is a 9mm compact pistol with a polymer frame and a gas-retarded operating mechanism.

Readers of these pages will recall that the Heritage Stealth pistol was introduced about a decade ago. The design went out of production a few years later, but the mechanism, based of the concepts of South African designer Alex Du Plessis, was of interest. The pistol had a unique gas-retarded system, in which a port in front of the chamber allowed gas from a fired round to operate against a piston underneath the barrel that

was attached to the slide. As the slide and piston recoiled rearward, the gas pressure tried to push the assembly forward, thus effectively retarding the initial opening of the mechanism, and softening the felt recoil.

This is the system used on the new Wilson pistol. Alex Du Plessis has worked with Wilson and an improved version of the original pistol has been introduced as the Wilson 9mm ADP. In Wilson literature, the ADP notation signifies Advanced Design Pistol. Note that this designation just happens to also be the initials of the designer.

The Wilson ADP has a number of improvements over the original. A squared-off slide with good grasping serrations allow purchase for retracting the slide. The polymer frame has an ergonomically-shaped rear grip strap and finger-groove front strap that provide a good grip, and the gun offers good control during shooting. The 10+1 pistol weighs just 19 ounces.

Wilson has not ignored developments in its 1911 line. A polymer-frame 9mm, the new KZ is offered in two styles—a full-size 17-round pistol weighing 32 ounces, and a compact 15-rounder that weighs 30 ounces.

The Carry Comp is a compact carry pistol with a 4 1/2-inch barrel, fitted with the company's ACCU-COMP. Wilson states the compensator reduces recoil and muzzle rise, while adding only minimal bulk.

The Sentinel is a 45-caliber compact carry pistol with 3 5/8-inch cone barrel. With a shortened grip frame that allows 6+1 capacity, Wilson feels this pistol reaches the maximum degree of compactness for complete reliability.

Postscript

Those of us who enjoy autoloading handguns should remember that some people just do not like our guns, and will do everything they can to deprive us of them. We have to win *every* political and legislative battle to retain our rights. The antigun forces need only to win once in a while to cause us to gradually lose our rights. Enjoy shooting, but stay informed and stay active.

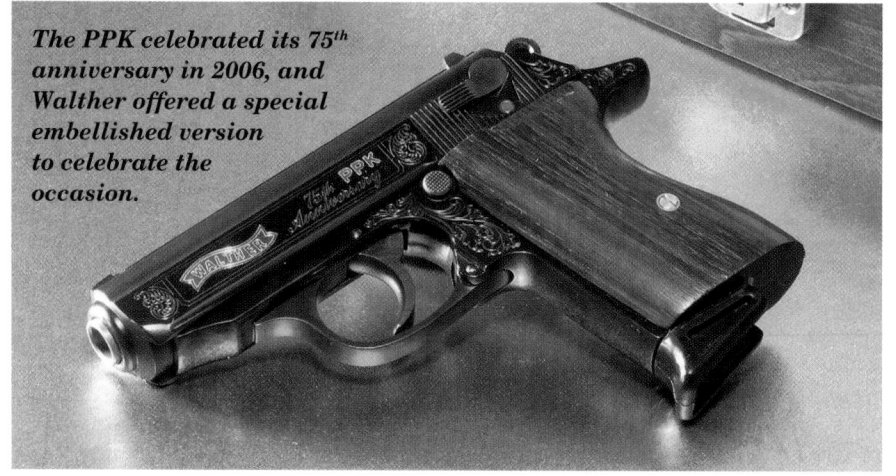

The PPK celebrated its 75th anniversary in 2006, and Walther offered a special embellished version to celebrate the occasion.

SIXGUNS & OTHERS:
HANDGUNS TODAY

by John Taffin

It was 50 years ago I fired a 44 Magnum for the first time. Fifty years is a long time even in light of the old cliché, "I wonder where all the time went?" However, it is something I'll never forget. We were teenagers, we shot together and we thought we had a lot of experience as we all had 1911s, 45 Colts and 357 Magnums—none of which prepared us for the 44 Magnum. Shell's Gun & Archery Farm had one of the earliest 4-inch Smith & Wesson 44s and, instead of selling it, Shell rented it out to all those who were brave enough to try it. We all did and we all lied about how bad it wasn't.

It took a while for the first 44 Magnums to show up on dealer shelves; the first one I saw for sale was not a Smith & Wesson but a Ruger Blackhawk. With its grip frame identical to the size and shape of the Colt Single Action Army (noted for rolling up in recoil), I figured the Blackhawk would kick less than the Smith & Wesson. I was wrong! I touched off that first round of those original 1450 fps+ factory loads and that Blackhawk rotated all right; it rolled backwards and didn't stop it until the hammer dug into my hand between thumb and forefinger, cutting out a good-sized hole. Obviously it would take some

time to learn to handle the recoil; it not only took time but experience and custom grips as well, but I eventually conquered both the Ruger and Smith & Wesson 44 Magnums.

Now both Ruger and Smith & Wesson are celebrating the 50th year of their original 44 Magnums by offering anniversary models. The original 44 Magnum Blackhawk, now known to collectors as the Flat-Top, disappeared from Ruger's catalog in 1963 and

Smith & Wesson's 44 Magnum, which became the Model 29 in 1957 and then went through a long list of 'dash' models (29-1, 29-2, etc.), was pulled from production in 1999; in the latter case the Model 29 had varied considerably from the original by being round-butted and heavy underlug barreled before it was finally dropped.

Both Anniversary Models follow the same general configuration as their original 44 Magnum parents but

From the custom shop of American Western Arms comes this beautifully engraved and stocked 4 3/4-inch 44 by Jerry Harper.

are built to 21ˢᵗ century standards. In addition to these two Anniversary Models, we have a new cartridge from Freedom Arms; several new offerings from both Smith & Wesson and Taurus; Hi-Point and CZ-USA are now part of the six-gun scene; more 19ᵗʰ-century replicas have been added to the lines of several companies; six-guns announced last year are now starting to show up in quantity, and we have two examples of Mare's Legs built on rifle actions. So with that, let's begin our yearly trip —traveling alphabetically —through a long list of manufacturers and importers.

American Western Arms (AWA)

As with most inventions and discoveries the Internet can be used for good or ill. In the case of American Western Arms, the Internet was used in the worst possible way with someone posting erroneous information two years ago stating American Western Arms was going out of business. They definitely were not, however the damage was done and the posting almost became a self-fulfilling prophecy by causing many to cancel orders. The truth then and now is AWA is alive and well and producing first-class six-guns —plus a new surprise.

AWA's standard offering is The Ultimate, a beautifully blued single-action six-gun with a case-colored frame and hammer, one-piece walnut stocks and a coil mainspring. The Ultimate is offered in all the standard single-action chamberings such as, but not limited to, 45 Colt, 44-40, 44 Special and 38-40, with all the standard barrel lengths of 4-3/4, 5-1/2, and 7-1/2 inches. In addition the custom shop takes The Ultimate even further by offering custom stocks, engraving, octagon barrels, and dual cylinder versions. Octagon-barreled versions pictured have cylinders for both the 44 Special and 44-40 as well as custom mesquite stocks by Jim Martin. Martin has specially designed his version of single-action stocks to be a trifle longer to facilitate both point shooting and hip shooting by making the single action point even more naturally. AWA has a

Consecutively numbered to the AWA 10 1/2-inch Ultimate is this 7 1/2-inch version, also with an octagon barrel and two cylinders in 44 Special and 44-40.

AWA's version of the Mare's Leg is the Lightning Bolt slide-action 44-40 handgun. Leather is by Bill Kelly and the knife by Bob Huddleston.

reputation for smooth actions and beautiful finishes; both are evident in standard production models as well as custom models. The finish on both of these custom 44s cannot be captured in a picture; brilliant case colors and deep blue.

The surprise this year from AWA is the Lightning Bolt, which is the handgun version of their Lightning slide- or pump-action rifle. The idea of the Lightning Bolt comes from

the old TV series *Wanted Dead or Alive* in which Steve McQueen used a cut-down lever-action rifle. AWA has applied the idea to their pump rifle, and a slick little "handgun" it is. Yes, it is classified as a handgun by ATF, holds six rounds, has a blued finish with walnut buttstock and forearm, and a saddle ring on the right side that mates with a hook on a special holster. The saddle ring goes over the hook while the barrel snaps

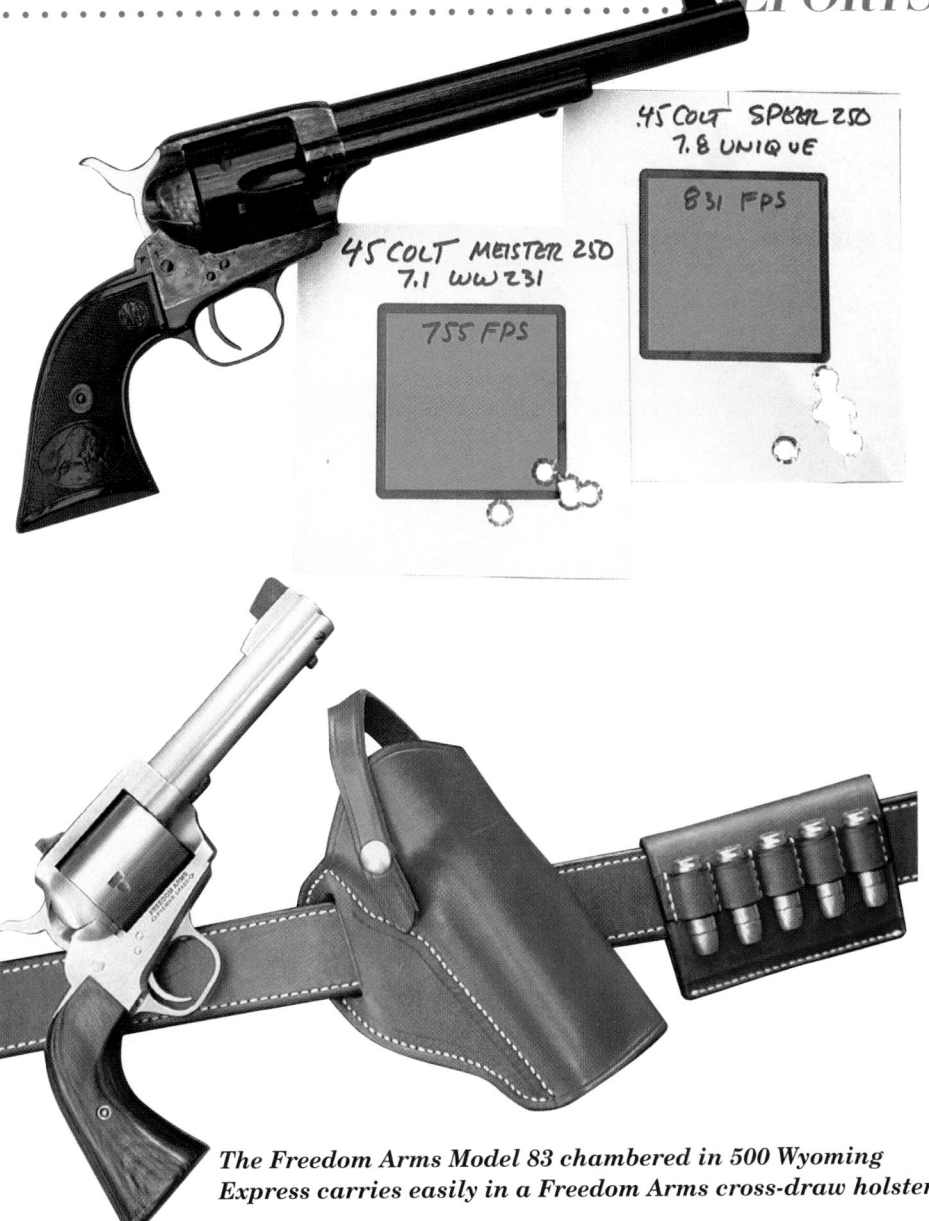

45 COLT MEISTER 250
7.1 WW231

755 FPS

.45 COLT SPEER 250
7.8 UNIQUE

831 FPS

The Freedom Arms Model 83 chambered in 500 Wyoming Express carries easily in a Freedom Arms cross-draw holster.

Beretta's 45 Colt Stampede not only looks and feels good, it also shoots very well.

grips also have a very good shape and feel to them. Although the Stampede has a transfer bar safety allowing it to be carried safely with six rounds, it also operates traditionally in that the loading gate is opened and the hammer placed on half-cock for loading and unloading. In fact, everything works so smoothly it feels like a traditional single-action six-gun. In addition to the Single Action Army version of the Stampede, Beretta is also offering the Bisley Model, complete with wide trigger and hammer and Bisley target-style grip frame.

The newest Beretta/Uberti six-gun is the Smith & Wesson Model #3-styled 45 Colt Laramie, a beautifully blued top-break, automatic-ejecting single-action revolver with a 6 1/2-inch barrel. The six-gun itself is blued, however the hammer, trigger guard and operating latch are all case-colored, and a nickel version is also available. To load or unload, the hammer is placed in the first notch, the combination rear sight/top latch is lifted, allowing the barrel, top strap and cylinder to rotate 90 degrees downwards to automatically eject the cartridge cases. The cylinder is then reloaded, the barrel grasped and rotated upwards 90 degrees and the latch is carefully locked in place.

The Beretta/Uberti Laramie has a rebounding hammer and is safely carried with six rounds. The stocks found on the Laramie are highly functional and feel good, though a trifle thick for my hand; they are near duplicates of the original New Model #3 stocks. When the Schofield Model, the first replica of Smith & Wesson single-action six-guns, arrived nearly 15 years ago, I hoped for a New Model #3; with the arrival of the Model #3 Russian, my hopes went even higher. Now finally we have a version of the New Model #3 —if they would only chamber it in 44 Russian.

CZ/Dan Wesson

In the early days of long-range silhouetting, Dan Wesson revolvers

into a spring clip at the bottom of the holster —a fun gun to be sure.

Beretta/Uberti

I predicted we would see some new offerings from Uberti when they were purchased by Beretta. The first of the new Ubertis to arrive a couple years ago under the Beretta banner was the Single Action Army-styled Stampede, complete with a very smooth action mated with a transfer bar safety, and a beautiful blue/case-colored finish. The very first guns had some problems with broken transfer bars, however that has been solved and the Stampede has proven to be both rugged and reliable. Our test version of the Beretta Stampede is a 45 Colt

with a 7 1/2-inch barrel, blued with a case-colored frame. The deep bluing is carried out on a nicely polished barrel, cylinder, grip frame and ejector rod housing, while the mainframe is finished with brilliant case colors.

Sights are the traditional single-action style with a rear square notch mated with a nicely shaped front sight, again of the traditional style. The smooth trigger is wider than the traditional single-action style; although the action has a trigger-actuated transfer bar the trigger does not set as far forward in the trigger guard as one might expect. Metal-to-metal fit is excellent and the checkered black plastic grips are also well fitted to the grip frame. The were extremely popular for several reasons. They were offered with long barrels, interchangeable front sights, were incredibly accurate, and the manufacturer listened to the needs of shooters. First came the 357 Magnum DW revolver with a 10-inch heavy barrel version; it was followed by the 44 Magnum and the 357 SuperMag. Dan Wesson himself started the company, and then his family lost it, got it back, and finally closed the doors. Dan Wesson Firearms was then purchased by Bob Serva, moved to New York, and, using all new machinery, Wesson Firearms began producing probably the best Dan Wesson revolvers ever.

Now Wesson Firearms is part of CZ-USA and, after concentrating on 1911s the past few years, Wesson is once again building revolvers, beginning with the 445 SuperMag. The 445 is basically a 44 Magnum case stretched to 1.6 inches. Muzzle velocities are substantially higher than the 44 Magnum and the 445 is at its best with 300-grain bullets. In addition to the long-barrel versions of the 445, CZ/Dan Wesson is also offering the Alaskan Guide Special with a barrel length of 4 inches, plus an integral muzzle brake.

Freedom Arms

In this report two years ago I showed three "mystery" cartridges. One of those was a belted 50-caliber six-gun round. The shroud of mystery has now been lifted and the 500 Wyoming Express can be announced. This latest six-gun cartridge was designed by Bob Baker and crew at Freedom Arms and is chambered in their Model 83 five-shot stainless-steel revolver. The Freedom Arms revolver arrived in 1983 chambered in the now legendary 454 Casull, then came the 44 Magnum, 357 Magnum, 41 Magnum, 50 AE and even the 22 Long Rifle. Several years ago the 475 Linebaugh was chambered in a Freedom Arms revolver, and once this project was off and running well, Baker began taking a serious look at the 500 Linebaugh. To chamber such a cartridge in the Freedom Arms cylinder would necessitate cutting into

This 7 1/2-inch Model 83 50AE from Freedom Arms has been fitted with a second cylinder chambered in 500 Wyoming Express. Scope is a LER Leupold on an SSK T'SOB base.

Hard to beat for close encounters with big tough critters is the Freedom Arms Model 83 chambered in 500 Wyoming Express.

the ratchet at the back of the cylinder as well as significantly reducing the rim diameter to fit the cylinder. To make a 500 work in the Model 83, Freedom Arms' cartridge headspaces on a belt rather than the cartridge rim.

Factory-chambered 500 WE revolvers are now available in three barrel lengths: 4 3/4-, 6- and 7 1/2-inch versions. For testing purposes, two revolvers were obtained from Freedom Arms (actually one new revolver and one retrofitted with a 500 WE cylinder). The brand-new Model 83 is my favorite 4 3/4-inch Perfect Packin' Pistol version. I returned my older 7 1/2-inch Model

83 chambered in 50 Action Express to have a new 500 Wyoming Express cylinder fitted. Both the 500 Wyoming Express and the 50 Action Express use the same 0.500-inch diameter bullets, not the 0.511-inch diameter of the original 500 Linebaugh.

The 500 Wyoming Express revolver is capable of major horsepower: 370-grain bullets at 1600 fps; 400-grain bullets at 1550 fps and 440-grain bullets at 1450 fps —through relatively light-weight revolvers. The 4 3/4-inch Model 83 chambered in 500 WE weighs less than three pounds, while the 7 1/2-inch version —even with scope, base and rings —comes

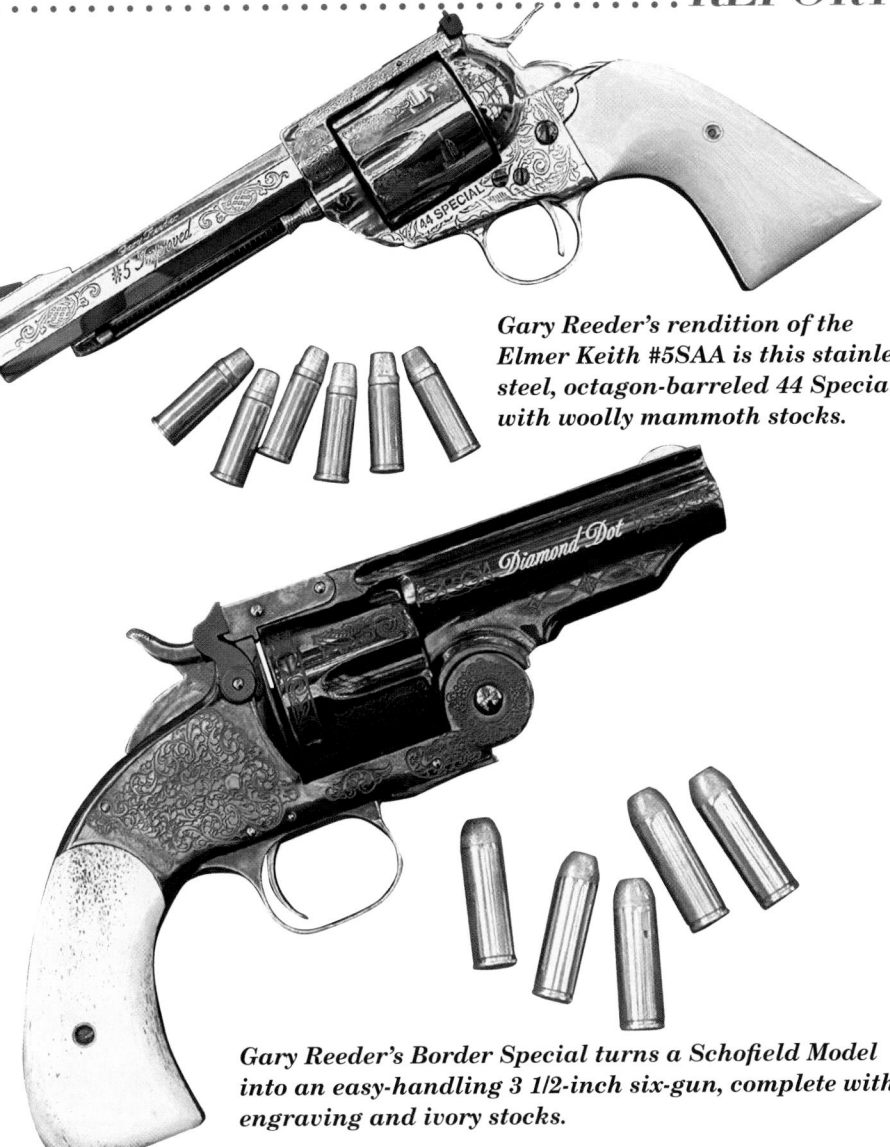

Gary Reeder's rendition of the Elmer Keith #5SAA is this stainless-steel, octagon-barreled 44 Special with woolly mammoth stocks.

Gary Reeder's Border Special turns a Schofield Model into an easy-handling 3 1/2-inch six-gun, complete with engraving and ivory stocks.

in around four pounds. I soon found my upper limit of comfort to be 1200 fps with a 440-grain bullet in the 7 1/2-inch version. With the lighter 4 3/4-inch Model 83 I find 370-grain bullets at the same muzzle velocity about all I want to handle. If you can use it, the horsepower is definitely there; for everyday use, I prefer loads that are more enjoyable. A 440-grain bullet even at 900-1000 fps will handle most six-gunning chores quite well, reserving the really heavy loads for hunting big tough game.

Freedom Arms has a reputation for producing the finest factory made single-action revolvers ever offered to six-gunners. They continue to offer the Model 83, in either Premier Grade or Field Grade, in all calibers mentioned except the 50 Action

Express; they also offer the mid-sized Model 97 (Premier Grade only) in 22 LR/22 Magnum, 32 Magnum/32-20, 357 Magnum, 41 Magnum, 44 Special, and 45 Colt/45 ACP. They have the precision and strength of the proverbial Swiss bank vault.

Gary Reeder Custom Guns

Gary Reeder has long been known for performing custom conversions on single-action and double-action revolvers, as well as Thompson/Center Contenders, thus creating some of the most powerful handguns available. In addition, Reeder also belongs to that select group of connoisseurs who really appreciate the century-old 44 Special. Until the arrival of the 44 Magnum, the handloaded 44 Special

was the most powerful revolver round to be had. The 44 Magnum almost pushed the 44 Special into oblivion —almost, but not quite. It took awhile, but shooters discovered the extra weight and power of a 44 Magnum was not always needed and that the 44 Special really was special, after all.

Reeder is offering three single-action packages made for the 44 Special. The Arizona Classic is built on Reeder's own frame, which he characterizes as "sort of a half breed between the 1st Generation Colt and the early 1st Generation Ruger Three-Screw. Its a small frame, not meant for the big magnums. Internal parts are early Three-Screw Ruger for strength, with coil springs and such." The Arizona Classic has a transfer bar safety and Reeder has made the necessary arrangements with Ruger to use the safety conversion Ruger retrofits in their early Three Screw Blackhawks. The Arizona Classic operates with the standard half-cock position to rotate the cylinder combined with this transfer bar safety. In addition to 44 Special, it is also available in 45 Colt and 357 Magnum.

A second offering from Reeder is the El Diablo, which is built on an Old Model Ruger Blackhawk. Instead of Reeder rechambering the original cylinder, a new 44 Special cylinder is installed and fitted to a 3 1/2-inch premium barrel with a deep dish muzzle crown and special throating. The steel grip frame is the Reeder Gunfighter design, the barrel/cylinder gap is set tightly, an interchangeable gold bead front sight on a ramp is matched with a V-notch rear sight, and the entire package is finished in Black Chromex. Reeder also offers gold or silver bands on the barrel and cylinder, scroll engraving on mainframe and cylinder, with the barrel marked "El Diablo" and the frame "44 Special"—both in script. Grips are Corian ivory and the owner's name is added at no extra charge, resulting in a very attractive and easy-packing 44 Special. The same basic six-gun with a standard barrel length is known as the Wichita Classic and is also available in 41 Special.

It was my good fortune two years ago to test the prototype #5 Improved, one of the most beautiful six-guns ever offered by Gary Reeder, based upon Elmer Keith's #5SAA from the 1920s. This Deluxe Grade all-steel six-gun is of high-polish stainless steel highlighted by bright blue screws, engraved, a deep-crowned octagonal barrel, chambered in 44 Special and stocked with elephant ivory. There is one major change of the Reeder #5 compared to the Keith #5. When Bill Grover built his Texas Longhorn Arms #5 he duplicated Keith's #5 grip frame; however, Keith had very small hands, which is evident in his grip frame. Reeder maintained the same basic grip frame and made it more useable by adding 3/8-inch to the length.

The prototype #5 Improved had to be sent back, and I fully intended to order a #5 44 Special later. Before I could act, my wife, Diamond Dot, got together with Gary Reeder and ordered a very special #5 Improved and I now have one of the first production #5 Improved 44 Specials. Barrel length is 5-1/2 inches, stocks are certificated 20,000-year old wooly mammoth ivory out of Russia with a heart-stopping creamy smooth texture; the high-polish stainless is set off with scroll engraving and blue screws, and the serial number —MPM66 —was specially ordered as it has special significance to me; a very special Special to be passed on in my family for many generations.

Hi-Point/Charter Arms

Four decades ago Charter Arms had a better idea; an idea based on the old British Bulldog 44, but carried out in a much better fashion. The result was the 5-shot, double-action 44 Special Bulldog revolver. The Bulldog was available in both blue and stainless steel versions, and they have a very special part in my heart. Three times in my life I have had to rely on a six-gun in a serious situation. Fortunately the presence of the big-bore revolver was all that was needed and two of those times the six-gun I had with me was the Charter Arms 44 Bulldog.

J.B. Custom is now offering the Mare's Leg built by Rossi on their Model 92 action. Yep, it is a handgun.

Charter Arms is now owned by Hi-Point Firearms, which means we'll be seeing more production and added models. The original 44 Special Bulldog was replaced by the Bulldog Pug several years ago and is available in blue or stainless with a 2 1/2-inch barrel and rubber finger-groove grips. It has now been joined by the Mag Pug, a 2 inch-barreled 357 Magnum also in blue or stainless. Two 38 Specials are offered: the Undercover which was the first Charter Arms revolver ever offered, in a 2-inch blued version and available either with or without a hammer; and the Off Duty, the ultralight version of the Undercover.

Those who shoot 22s are not forgotten. Hi-Point/Charter Arms offers the Pathfinder, a 2-inch stainless steel six-shot revolver available in 22 or 22 Magnum; and the newest revolver from the purchase of Charter Arms by Hi-Point is the Dixie Derringer, a five-shot stainless steel mini-gun also offered in 22 or 22 Magnum. Once all the necessary arrangements are made when one company purchases another, we can expect Charter Arms revolvers to be much easier to locate.

Even with the Boot Grip, the NAA 22 Mini-Gun is still concealable.

JB Custom

The Mare's Leg is back. Two years ago JB Custom offered a limited number of Mare's Legs on Winchester Model 94 actions; they all sold out immediately. The Model 92 action is slightly smaller, much stronger and naturally much smoother in operation than the Model 94. It was the Model 92 that was used by Steve McQueen (Josh Randall) in the TV series *Wanted Dead or Alive*. The natural choice to produce the Mare's Legs was Rossi, a longtime producer of 1892 lever-action replicas dating back to the days when they were known as The Puma. Rossi is definitely a quality producer of lever-action rifles and has now become the only manufacturer of lever-action pistols featuring brand-new actions from their South American plant.

The Mare's Leg, as expected from Rossi, is a quality "handgun" beautifully finished and fitted with a nicely grained walnut forearm and abbreviated buttstock with the wood-

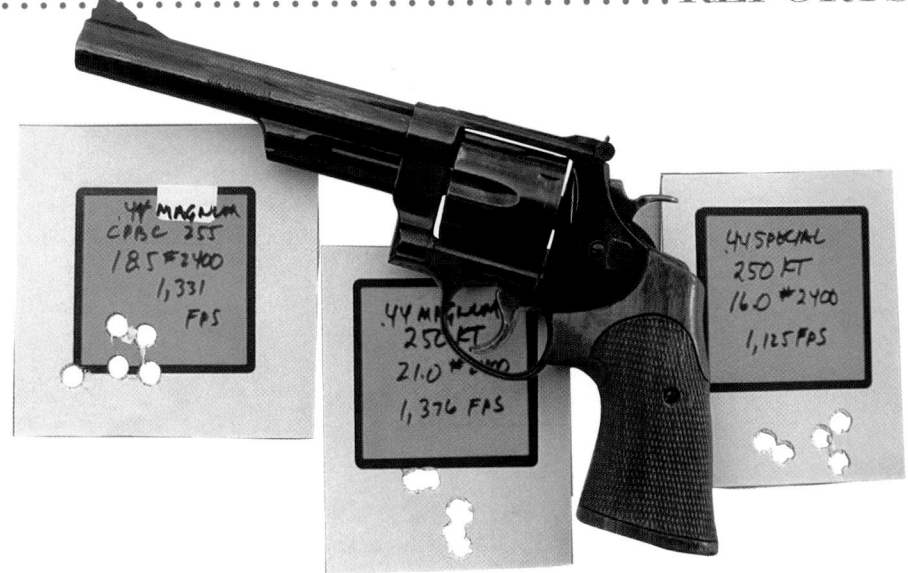

The Model 29 Smith & Wesson is back as the 50th Anniversary Model 44 Magnum.

Smith & Wesson's 50th Anniversary Model 29, here equipped with Herrett's Trooper Stocks from the 1950s, shoots well.

to-metal fit in the 'excellent' category. Sights are the traditional elevation-adjustable buckhorn mated with a brass bead front sight in a dovetail, allowing for windage adjustment. It is currently offered in 45 Colt, 44-40, 44 Magnum and 357 Magnum; a replica of Josh Randall's belt and holster is also available in black or brown. The Mare's Leg holds six rounds of 45 Colt and can be safely carried with one in the chamber as it does have the top-mounted Rossi safety.

North American Arms (NAA)

NAA offers the world's smallest single-action revolvers, five-shooters, with the tiniest being chambered for 22 Short, and the same basic revolver with correspondingly longer cylinders in 22 Long Rifle, 22 Magnum, and also a 22 Magnum with an auxiliary cylinder chambered in 22 Long Rifle. When the 17 HMR was introduced

several years ago, North American Arms added this tiny little cartridge as well as an even smaller version, the 17 Mach 2. In addition to cartridge-firing Mini-Revolvers, NAA also offers 22-caliber blackpowder versions requiring powder, round ball and percussion cap.

NAA has just recently introduced two new versions of their Mini-Revolvers, much easier to hold onto and shoot them quite accurately. The new guns are known as Boot Guns and are simply the basic Mini-Revolvers fitted with a longer grip —a boot grip. As the name implies, they fit nicely into the top of the boot. NAA also offers ankle holsters, clip-on belt holsters, and even a flap holster for their Boot Guns.

Three versions of Boot Gun are offered: the standard 22 Long Rifle, 22 Magnum, and the 22 Magnum/22LR dual-cylinder model —all can be had with 1 1/8- or 1 5/8-inch barrels. The longer boot grip makes the NAA Mini-Revolver slightly harder to conceal but

decidedly easier to shoot well, and the boot grip can also be fitted to the other Mini-Revolvers from NAA. Although they are five-shot revolvers and most single actions are only safe when carried with the hammer down on an empty, these little Mini-Revolvers have a slot between chambers so they can be safely carried with five rounds when the hammer is resting in one of these little slots.

To load or unload the Mini-Revolver it is necessary to remove the cylinder. This is easy because the cylinder base pin is spring-loaded and, when pushed in at the front, the base pin is unlocked and can be removed, and the cylinder with it. Use the base pin to poke out the empty cases, reload the cylinder and replace. With CCI's MiniMax HP+V, the 22 Magnum version clocked out at 1094 fps while with the 22 LR Mini-Revolver, CCI's Mini-Mag +Vs registered 932 fps.

Smith & Wesson

To celebrate fifty years of the 44 Magnum S&W originally introduced, we now have the 50th Anniversary Model of the Smith & Wesson 44 Magnum. The Bright Blue finish almost rivals that of 50 years ago. The sights are a white outline rear and a red ramp front as on the original, and the barrel length is the original 6-1/2 inches —not the 6-inch length found on 29s and 629s since 1979. The hammer and trigger are the original checkered and serrated style; however, the hammer has a decidedly different look and has the best-looking profile I've ever seen on a Smith & Wesson six-gun.

The stocks are the same color, though a lighter shade, as the originals and also have the diamond around the grip screw holes; they also feel much better to me than the originals, being slightly thinner and tapered to the top of the grip frame. The 50th Anniversary Model 44 Magnum also has something we had not seen for quite a while: a square-butt grip frame identical in size and shape to that found on the original 44 Magnum, and original grips will fit. I replaced the factory stocks with a pair of Herrett's

Taffin shooting the Smith & Wesson 50th Anniversary Model 29.

꧁●꧁●꧁●꧁●꧁●꧁

Troopers that are almost as old as the original S&W 44 Magnum.

The Anniversary Model comes in a lockable, padded plastic case. The sides of the barrel are marked as the original were, though in reverse. The left side of the barrel is marked "44 MAGNUM", while the right side carries "SMITH & WESSON". Since this is a 50th Anniversary Model, there is a gold seal on the right side of the frame announcing "50th ANNIVERSARY, SMITH & WESSON" above the S&W logo with "1956-2006, 44 MAGNUM" found below the gold logo.

Last year Smith & Wesson brought back a revolver that had not been seen for nearly 40 years, a 4-inch, fixed-sight, six-shot, blue steel, big-bore six-gun. That was the Model 21-4 Thunder Ranch Special chambered in 44 Special, complete with an enclosed ejector rod. Except for the round butt and 21st century manufacturing requirements it is a dead-ringer for the 44 Special Model 1926 and the 38/44 Heavy Duty of 1930. Now new for this year we have the next version following along the same lines, the Model 22-4 chambered in 45 ACP/45 Auto Rim and as an even further improvement: it has a square butt just like the great guns of the first three-quarters of the 20th century.

The fixed sights on both of these new big-bore six-guns consist of a square notch rear sight cut into the top of the frame in front of the hammer, matched with a half-moon pinned-in front sight. The 44 Special and 45 ACP/Auto Rim also have

From Smith & Wesson's Performance Center comes the 12-inch Magnum Hunter chambered in 460 S&W Magnum.

Smith & Wesson now offers the 460 Magnum as the short-barreled Model 460V "survival gun."

S&W's Model 327 TTR8 Rail Gun features an 8-shot 357 Magnum cylinder.

Remember the old song, "She not very much good for pretty, but she pretty much good for strong"? That pretty well describes the Smith & Wesson Model 357 Rail Gun: both an electric-dot sight and a tactical flashlight are mounted.

Smith & Wesson's scandium/titanium lightweight big-bore revolver this year is the Model 325PD chambered in 45 ACP.

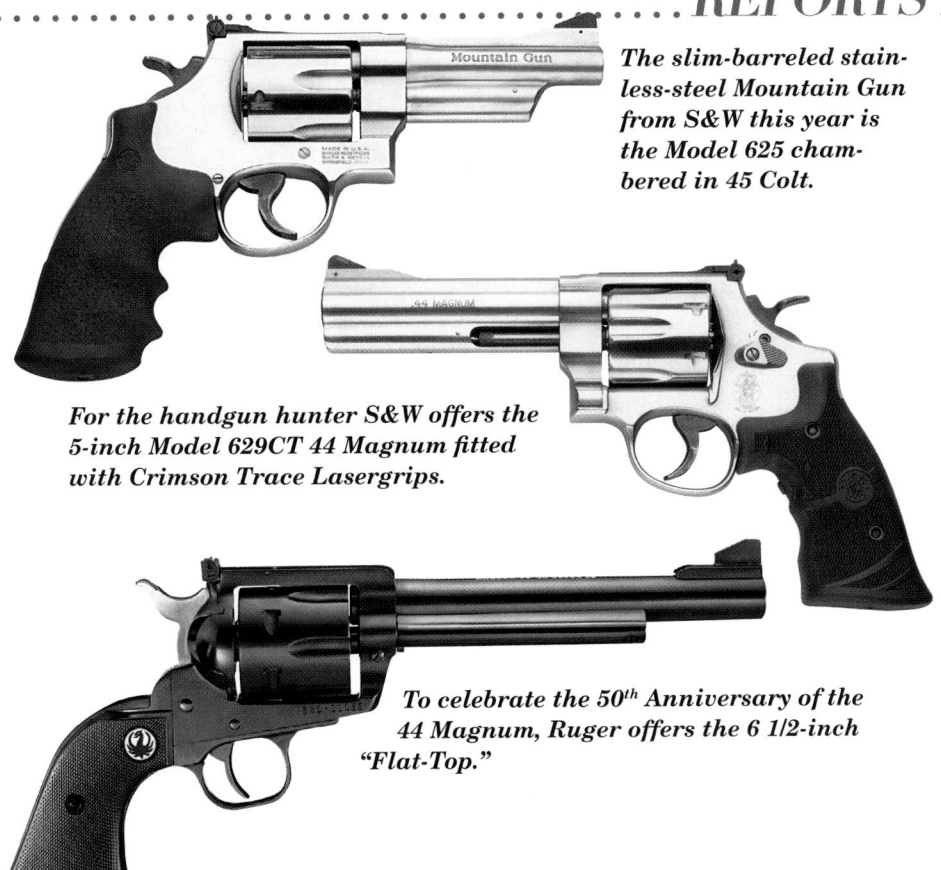

The slim-barreled stainless-steel Mountain Gun from S&W this year is the Model 625 chambered in 45 Colt.

For the handgun hunter S&W offers the 5-inch Model 629CT 44 Magnum fitted with Crimson Trace Lasergrips.

To celebrate the 50th Anniversary of the 44 Magnum, Ruger offers the 6 1/2-inch "Flat-Top."

the Model 325PD, and as anyone with working knowledge of Smith & Wesson revolvers will know, the model number says 45-caliber; in this case 45 ACP, which means it also accepts 45 Auto Rim loads. This gives the six-gunner a very easy-to-carry, lightweight, big-bore revolver without excess recoil. With so many excellent 45 ACP offerings available for defensive use, this revolver would be an excellent choice for the hiker, outdoorsman or fisherman —and an excellent choice for either open carry or CCW use.

Smith & Wesson also offers a second 45 revolver this year: the stainless steel Model 625 Mountain Gun now chambered in 45 Colt. The Mountain Gun concept consists of a 4-inch tapered barrel as found on such old favorites as the original 357 Magnum, the Highway Patrolman and the 1950 Target. Both the 325PD and 625 Mountain Guns are built on the Smith & Wesson N-frame, with adjustable sights and a round-butt grip frame.

Smith & Wesson has offered several models with Crimson Trace Lasergrips for defensive use, and has now expanded this concept to the hunting field with the Model 629CT. The stainless steel 6-shot N-frame 44 Magnum has a heavy-underlug 5-inch barrel with the standard sights consisting of an adjustable rear sight and a red-ramp front sight. Sometimes hunting requires very fast target acquisition, so the Model 629CT comes complete with a Crimson Trace Lasergrip. Anyone who has ever hunted dangerous game up close —such as wild pigs —knows how fast the action can be and a red dot projected on the shoulder of a big mean hog can be very comforting.

SSK Industries: J.D.

Jones as SSK has been offering custom-barreled T/C Contenders for three decades. Two of his very early designs are still the number-one sellers as custom barrels for the Contender. One is the 6.5 JDJ on the 225 Winchester case, and the other the 375 JDJ on a necked-down 444 Marlin. The 375 JDJ uses a 220-grain bullet for deer-sized game and a 270/300-grain

frame-mounted firing pins, instead of the hammer-mounted firing pin Smith & Wesson used in their double-action revolvers for about 100 years.

Last year Smith & Wesson introduced the Model 460XVR (Xtreme Velocity Revolver) chambered in 460 S&W Magnum, and just as they did with their 500 S&W Magnum chambered Model 500, they now offer a shorter-barreled version the Model 460V with a 5-inch barrel. This version has an interchangeable muzzle compensator, and as on the original Model 460, Sorbothane finger-groove rubber grips, and a five-shot cylinder capable of handling the 460 S&W, the 454 Casull and the 45 Colt. All Model 460s feature gain-twist rifling, which means the rate of twist becomes faster towards the muzzle end of the barrel.

Two other versions of the 460XVR are offered by the Smith & Wesson Performance Center. The 10 1/2-inch Compensated Hunter has a 360-degree muzzle brake, an integral Weaver scope base and sling swivels, while the 12-inch Magnum Hunter has integral Picatinny-style bases

on both the top and bottom of the fluted barrel, sling swivels and a bipod adapter at the end of the barrel. These two special Model 460s weigh 82-1/2 and 80 ounces, respectively.

Also from the Performance Center comes the Model 327 TRR8 Rail Gun. This 8-shot 357 Magnum features a scandium frame, steel cylinder, rubber finger groove grips and a 5-inch shrouded steel barrel. It is set up for full-moon clips and has removable Picatinny-style rails both on the top and bottom of the barrel for the installation of a full range of optical or laser sights, and tactical flashlights. With both a red-dot scope mounted on the top of the barrel and a tactical flashlight below, the Model 327 TRR8 is not the prettiest revolver I've ever seen —but it would look awfully good in a serious situation.

Three years ago Smith & Wesson introduced the 4-inch Model 329PD, a scandium-framed, titanium-cylindered, 26-ounce, 6-shot 44 Magnum. Recoil with full-house loads is brutal, but it packs oh, so easy. Now the same basic revolver is offered as

SSK offers custom chamberings in the T/C Encore, such as the 460 and 500 S&W Magnums.

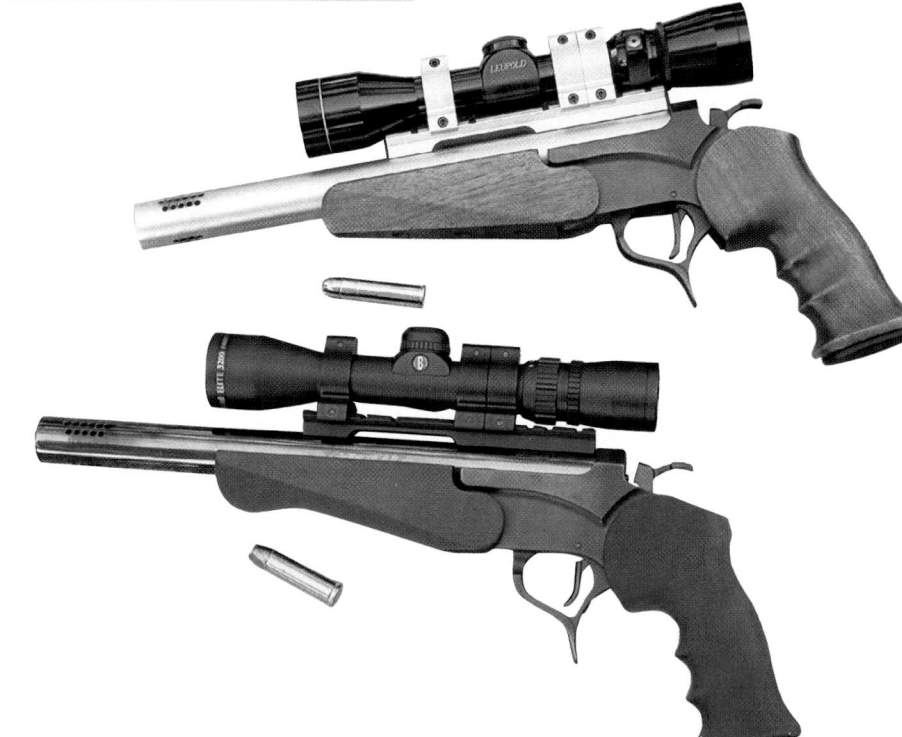

bullet for the big stuff; while the 6.5 JDJ will take care of everything and anything in-between. The 375 is now a standard chambering by Thompson/Center, and factory ammunition is also available. In addition to the 6.5 JDJ, there are others: the 226, 270 and 7mm JDJs, as well as the 309, 8mm, 338 #2 and 416 —JDJs all, plus the 375 JDJ on the 444 Marlin. Currently SSK chambers over 200 cartridges in Contender barrels.

By going to the Thompson/Center Encore, SSK is able to offer more powerful cartridges such the 454 Casull, 500 S&W, 460 S&W, 300 Winchester Magnum, 338 Winchester Magnum, and 375 H&H as well as the 280, 30, 338, 35, 375 and 416 JDJs on the 30-06 case. Currently SSK has more than 300 reamers in stock for custom Encore barrels.

SSK also offers the best available muzzlebrake, the Arrestor Muzzle Brake, and for any heavy-recoiling handgun there is simply no better scope mount base than his T'SOB. This is the only scope mount base I will recommend for really hard-kicking handguns. When installed properly and used with three or four scope rings, the scope will stay in place.

Sturm, Ruger

Ruger's first centerfire single action, the 357 Magnum Blackhawk, now known to collectors as the Flat-Top, arrived in 1955 and only lasted until it was "improved" into what is now known as the Old Model Blackhawk. Last year Ruger offered the 50th Anniversary Model of the original, and per the original —and unlike current Ruger Blackhawks —the Anniversary Model had a true Flat-Top frame the same size as the original with no protective ears around the rear sight, plus the original grip frame size, shape, and black rubber grips complete with the black eagle medallion. The grips are shaped perfectly for my hand and

Ruger's big-bore survival gun is the Super Redhawk Alaskan chambered in 480 Ruger and, as shown, 454 Casull.

feel exceptionally good. As on the original, the barrel length is 4-5/8 inches and the rear sight is Micro-style. Unlike the original, the grip frame is steel and the action is the standard Ruger New Model style, complete with transfer bar safety.

The Anniversary Model feels very good in the hand, has the balance of the original, and shoots as well as —in

many cases better than —the 1950s 357 Flat-Top. It is a beautiful well-made six-gun and I have asked Ruger to not only keep it in the line as a standard offering, but also to chamber it in the 44 Special and 357 Magnum.

This year is the 50th anniversary of Ruger's first 44 Magnum and that original Ruger 44 Magnum, the Flat-Top Blackhawk, is now

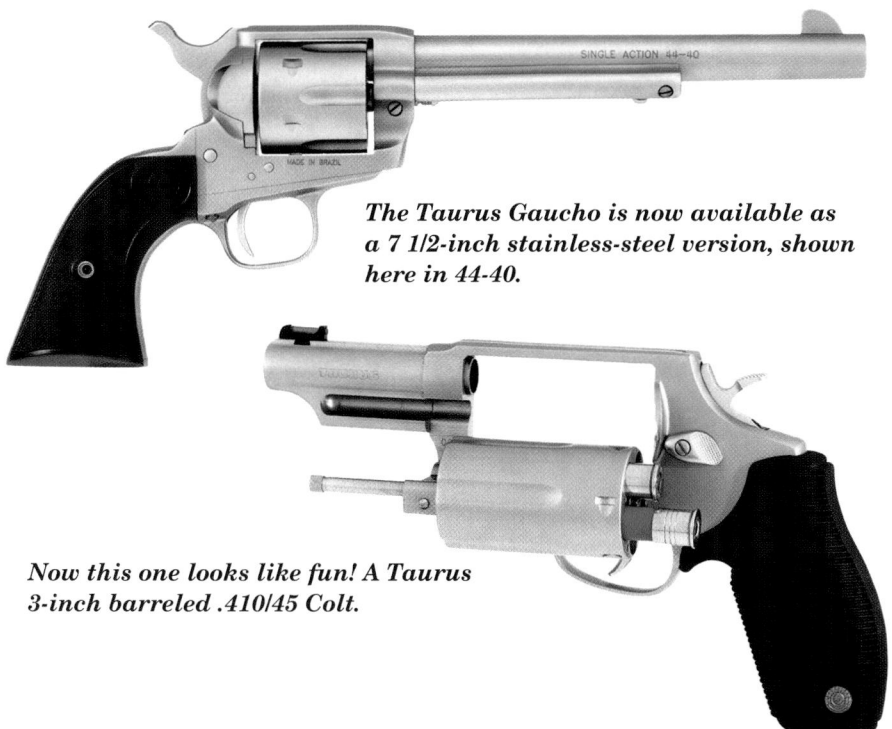

The Taurus Gaucho is now available as a 7 1/2-inch stainless-steel version, shown here in 44-40.

Now this one looks like fun! A Taurus 3-inch barreled .410/45 Colt.

offered as this year's Anniversary Model. The 44 Magnum Blackhawk was slightly larger than the 357 Magnum Blackhawk that preceded it which was a mite small in cylinder and frame —both were enlarged to house the 44 Magnum in 1956.

Just as with the 50th anniversary 357, this 44 Magnum is in the original barrel length (6-1/2 inches), carries a Micro rear sight on a flat-top frame, plus a ramp front sight and is built on the New Model action. The top of the barrel as on the 357 version has gold-filled lettering identifying this as a special anniversary model. The grip frame is steel and the grips, instead of the walnut found on most of the Flat-Top Blackhawks, is the checkered black rubber with black eagle insert found on the very first run of the 44 Blackhawks. Just before Skeeter Skelton died in 1988, Ruger was working on a custom 44 Blackhawk for him using the New Model action. We can consider that the prototype of the 50th Anniversary Model. I hope Ruger keeps the Anniversary Model 44 Magnum in the line after the anniversary run is over.

Ruger has not announced any other new handguns this year but rather continues to concentrate on providing a large lineup chambered in everything from 17 HMR to 454 Casull and 480 Ruger. The latter chamberings are found in the Super Redhawk Alaskan, which was designed to be an easy-to-pack survival six-gun. On the Super Redhawk Alaskan, the end of the barrel is flush with the frame, with a deep inverted muzzle crown, and a serrated sloping-forward ramp front sight has been added to the flat-topped frame matched with a standard white outline rear sight adjustable for windage and elevation. To handle the heavy loads used in such a short-barreled six-gun, the Alaskan comes with Hogue's rubber cushioned, finger-grooved Tamer Monogrip. As one might expect, recoil is quite heavy. However, thanks to the Hogue Tamer grips, it does not reach the uncontrollable level.

Last year Ruger also introduced the New Vaquero, replacing the standard Vaquero. The new version is basically the same size as the Colt Single Action Army and has already become quite popular with both cowboy action shooters and anyone else desiring a sturdy and reliable single-action six-gun. The New Vaquero is offered in both blue and stainless, 357 Magnum and 45 Colt, and in barrel lengths of 4-5/8 and 5-

1/2 inches for both calibers, as well as 7-1/2 inches for the 45 Colt. For years several reloading manuals had a special 45 Colt section with heavy loads marked for Ruger Blackhawk only. The same loads could be used in the original Vaquero which was built on the same frame size as the 45 Colt Blackhawk. These loads are NOT to be used in the 45 Colt New Vaquero because it has a smaller cylinder and frame than the Blackhawk.

Ruger continues to offer four of the most popular hunting six-guns: the Super Blackhawk, the Hunter Model, and the Redhawk in 44 Magnum as well as the Super Redhawk chambered in 44 Magnum, 454 Casull and 480 Ruger.

Taurus

As usual Taurus has a large lineup of revolvers for this year. The single-action Gaucho is now readily available in several versions. Four finishes are offered: blue steel, blue steel with a case-hardened frame, polished stainless steel and matte stainless steel. Calibers are 45 Colt, 357 Magnum and now 44-40. The first three traditional standard barrel lengths: 4-3/4, 5-1/2 and 7-1/2 inches, have been joined by a 12-inch "Buntline Special." The Gaucho is basically the same size as the Colt Single Action Army, and replicas thereof. It has a transfer bar safety, making it safe to carry fully loaded with six rounds.

It did not take long for Taurus to chamber their revolvers in both 500 and 460 S&W Magnums. This year they have gone both directions, offering a 10-inch and a 2 1/2-inch version in both calibers. All wear the soft rubber finger-groove grip that goes a long way to tame felt recoil. These are serious six-guns for serious purposes.

Another offering from Taurus with both a serious and a fun purpose is the five-shot .410/45 Colt. The cylinder is long enough to accept both .410 shotshell loads and 45 Colt cartridges. This Model 4410 is offered with both 3- and 6-inch barrels. It looks like a fun six-gun for clay pigeons or tin cans, and could also serve for dispatching snakes and varmints up close.

Taurus's medium-frame Tracker models are very popular in several calibers and this year's version is a five-shot 10mm-chambered revolver with a 4-inch ported barrel and Ribber grips, as well as a 6-inch vent-ribbed barreled option with finger-groove rubber grips. Both models have adjustable sights and Taurus now provides a plastic snap-on sight protector for the rear sight of all of their revolvers. Taurus also offers the Tracker in a five-shot 44 Magnum; the 44 Magnum chambering is also found in the 444 UltraLite with an alloy frame and titanium cylinder with either 2 1/4- or 4-inch barrel lengths.

One of Taurus's most popular offering is the Raging Bull, offered in 44 and 41 Magnum with six-shot cylinders, 454 with a five-shot cylinder and both the 460 and 500 S&W Magnums *(mentioned above)* with a longer five-shot cylinder and a longer frame.

Thompson/Center

For more than three decades, Thompson/Center has dominated the single-shot market for both silhouette shooters and handguns hunters. The original Contender was chambered in 38 Special and 22RF; however, it did not take long to discover the real potential of the Contender pistol. Basically stated, the Contender is a single-shot, break-open action pistol built to accept interchangeable barrels in a wide variety of chamberings, including both rimfire and centerfire cartridges, made possible by a rotating firing pin in the frame.

The original Contender has been replaced by the G2, which opens much easier and is available in blue with walnut grips and forearm, weighs approximately 3-3/4 pounds, and is offered in both 12- and 14-inch versions. Current factory chamberings include 17 HMR, 17 Mach II, 22 Long Rifle Match, 22 Hornet, 204 Ruger, 223 Remington, 6.8 Remington, 7-30 Waters, 30-30 Winchester, 357 Magnum, 375 JDJ, 44 Magnum and 45-70.

As strong as it is, the Contender is basically limited to those same cartridges found in lever-action rifles; the answer for higher pressure bolt-action rifle cartridges is the Thompson/Center Encore. The Encore is the same basic break-open, single-action pistol as the Contender, but is built for greater strength and weighs nearly one pound more. The Encore is offered in both 12- and 15-inch models, blued with walnut grip and forearm or stainless steel with rubber grip and forearm. Both the Contender and Encore are equipped with an adjustable rear sight and ramp front sight, triggers adjustable for over-travel, and drilled and tapped for scope mount bases. The Encore is factory chambered in 204 Ruger, 22-250, 223, 243 Winchester, 6.8 Remington, 7-08, 25-06, .270 Winchester, 30-06, 308 Winchester, 375 JDJ, 44 Magnum, 45-70, and 460 and 500 S&W Magnums. My favorite chamberings are the 22-250, 7-08, 308, and 500 Magnum. With these cartridges I can handle anything in any hunting situation.

United States Firearms (USFA)

"They don't make them like they used to!" Those of us who have been around long enough have said this many times when talking about cars, firearms —just about anything factory-produced. Times have changed, and production methods have changed However, there is one company still making them like they used to and that company is United State Firearms. USFA specializes in single-action six-guns ... and not just any single actions, but those built like they were from the 1870s up to the eve of World War II. In fact, USFA even started building revolvers under the old Blue Dome in Hartford, Connecticut. They have now moved into a thoroughly modern factory and the Blue Dome serves as office space.

The standard offering from USFA is the Single Action which is available in the same chamberings as in the "good old days" —the 45 Colt, 44-40, 44 Special, 44 Russian, 41 Long Colt, 38-40 and 32-20.

The first thing one notices about the USFA Single Action is the beautiful finish. The main frame and hammer are beautifully case-colored in what is described as Armory Bone Case, while the balance of the six-gun is finished in a deep, dark Dome Blue. Grips furnished as standard are checkered hard rubber with a "US" molded into the top part of the grip. Normally, I prefer to fit favored single-action six-guns with custom grips made of ivory, stag or some exotic wood. However, in the case of USFA Single Action Army six-guns, the grips are so perfectly fitted to the frame and feel so good that

&:&●&:&●&:&●&:&●&:&

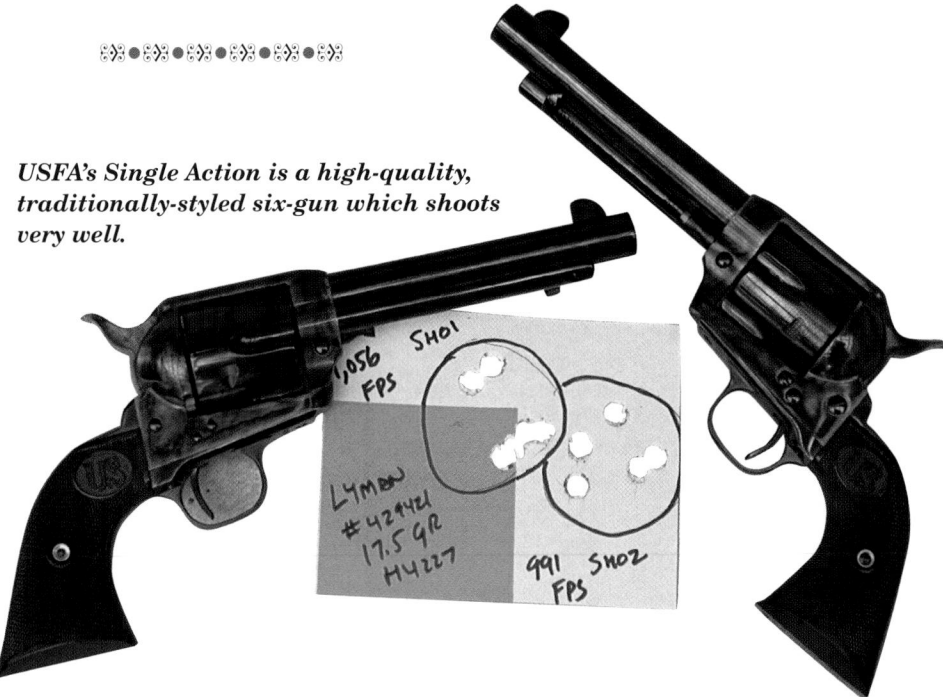

USFA's Single Action is a high-quality, traditionally-styled six-gun which shoots very well.

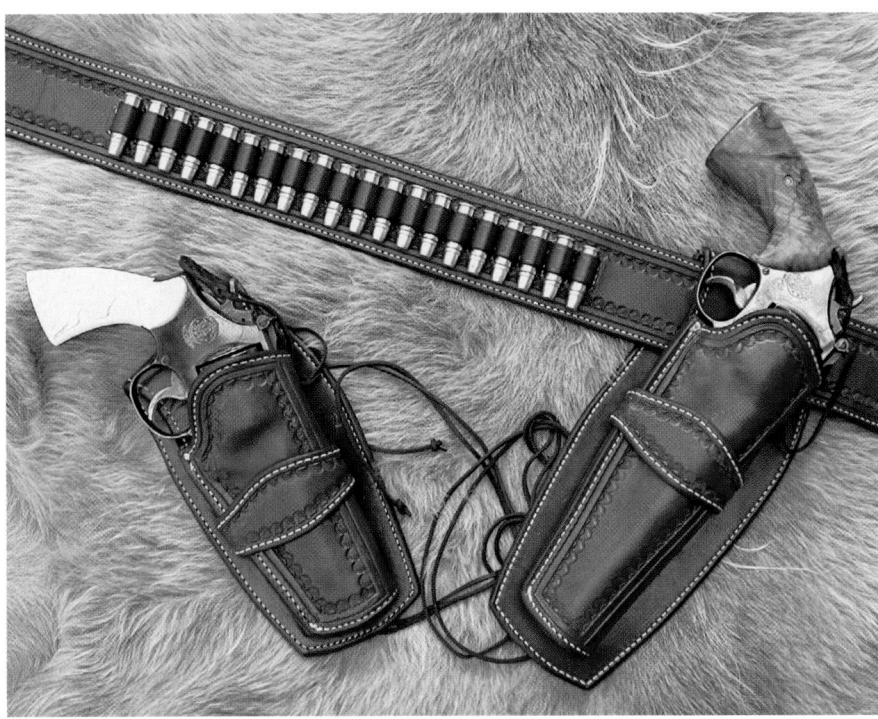

The Taffin Triple-Lock holster and belt is now available from www.sixgunner.com.

I am very hesitant to change them. If one looks at the grips on most single-action six-guns the fitting leaves a lot to be desired; not so here. These grips have been fitted to the grip frame on a factory-built revolver as carefully as custom grips by a master gripmaker.

The Single Action is available with barrel lengths of 4-3/4, 5-1/2, and 7-1/2 inches, and is joined by several other models such as the matte-blue finish Rodeo, the high-polish Dome Blued Cowboy and the antique patina-finished Gunslinger. Just as in the 1890s, one can also have a Flat-Top Target Single Action or a Bisley Model. Special versions include the Omnipotent with a grip frame reminiscent of the 1878 Double Action, the Snub Nose having the same grip frame but with a 2-, 3- or 4-inch barrel, and the Sheriff's Model offered in several barrel lengths without an ejector rod assembly. The Sheriff's Model is now up and running, and our version is a 2 1/2-inch nickel-plated 45 Colt.

United States Firearms Single Actions are not what you would call inexpensive. These revolvers are not assembly line mass-produced, and it is obvious the gunsmiths at

United States Firearms are a whole lot more than parts assemblers. It takes a lot of expensive hand-fitting to produce a single-action six-gun of this quality. This six-gunner, and a lot of others think they are worth it.

In addition to their standard line of single-action six-guns, USFA also has a complete custom shop offering many features found more than a century ago. For example, there is the famous 1902 Sears Gun duplicated in 45 Colt with a 4 3/4-inch barrel, full coverage engraving and full blue with gold accents and pearl grips. Then, the equally famous —if not more so —Theodore Roosevelt's 7 1/2-inch 44-40 Frontier Six Shooter with full engraving, silver- and gold-plated and ivory grips carved with TR's initials. Next, the Frontier Six-Shooter: another 7 1/2-inch 44-40 with full "C" engraving and scrimshawed pearl grips.

On any of their single-action six-guns, USFA offers a choice of A, B, C, or D engraving as well as a complete line of custom grips in ivory, stag, pearl, and fancy walnut.

When I was recently contacted by Joel Cosby of www.six-gunner.com to design a holster for marketing at his

website, I pulled out my cardboard patterns from the 1960s and sent them off. The result is the Taffin Triple-Lock holster and matching 2 1/2-inch cartridge belt, fully lined with suede leather to help keep it from slipping while being worn, and the holsters are also fully lined with smooth leather. Both belt and holster are crafted of premium leather with decorative border stamping; and the holster gets its name from the fact the body proper is locked to the back flap in three places, a wraparound loop in the middle, tie-down thong at the bottom and —most importantly —two Chicago screws that allow the holster to be tightly fitted to the belt. Each holster is fitted with a hammer thong with an easy-to-grasp release. By the way, any money I might make from the sale of this rig goes directly to the NRA. Check the web site for more details on availability for different revolvers.

Thanks to the efforts of Cimarron, EMF, Navy Arms and Taylor's & Co. it is now possible to shoot and enjoy quality replicas of almost every single-action six-gun available during the last three decades of the 19th century, including the Colt Richards Mason, Open-Top, Single Action Army and Bisley Model; the Remington 1875 and 1890 and the S&W Schofield and Model #3 Russian. This year the newest offerings from these importers are rifles —the 1876 Winchester and 1892 Takedown, as well as replicas of the Colt Lightning pump-action rifle. Colt is still producing only one revolver, the Single Action Army in 45 Colt, 44-40, 38-40, 357 Magnum, and 32-20. Rumors continue about their future; we will just have to wait and see what transpires.

I expect to spend another great six-gunning year shooting the 50th Anniversary 44 Magnum Models from Ruger and Smith & Wesson, a pair of 44 Specials from USFA, several custom 44s on Ruger Old Models, and a pair of AWA's octagon-barreled Ultimates set up with two cylinders for both 44 Special and 44 Magnum. All of this will just work in fine with my latest project —a book titled *44 Six-guns, Leverguns, Cartridges, and Loads.* May you have as much fun as I do.

RIFLES TODAY ✦

RIFLE REVIEW

by Layne Simpson

Gun Digest Tidbits From The Past

How far back does your collection of Gun Digest go? I have all the years back to 1963 (17th Edition) but I am missing several before that. I have edition numbers 2, 5, 7, 8, 12, 13, 14, and 15 but am missing the eight remaining editions.

Gun Digest has long had a reputation for accuracy but a glitch or two has managed to escape the editor's red pen through the years. Page 15 of the 2nd Edition is always worth a chuckle. The story on big-game rifles was written by Elmer Keith but the lead photo has Jack O'Connor sitting on a rock with his trusty 270 resting across his lap. Considering how those two felt about each other, you can bet that mix-up went over like a foreign object in the Governor's punch bowl.

Firearms manufacturers were still gearing down from war production so there were no prices in that issue but a few years later the Model 94 Winchester was $62.45 and a box of 30-30s went for $2.50. Price of the standard-grade Model 94 had increased to about $450 when it was dropped from production during early 2006 and a box of cartridges was just over 12 bucks. An automobile

that sold in the neighborhood of $1000 back then will set you back at least 30 times that today. A gallon of gas now costs about 30 times what it did back then. Who says today's rifles are not bargains?

Under the "so what's new?" category, turn to page 172 of the 1992 edition and read what I had to say under the Precision Imports heading about the Mauser Model 210 rifle chambered for a prototype cartridge under development at Federal. It was the 22 WMR case necked down to 17-caliber and they called it the 17 FMR. Sound familiar?

Now let us take a look at what actually is new and exciting for 2006.

Anschutz

In 1856 Julius Gottfried Anschutz founded the company to manufacture shotguns and pocket pistols and five generations later Jochen Anschutz is running the company that builds what many consider to be the most consistently accurate 22 rimfire rifles in the world. Other chambering options include 17 Mach 2, 17 HMR and 22 Hornet. New additions to the rifle lineup are Classic Beavertail variants of the Model 1416 in 22 Long Rifle, Model 1502 in 17 Mach 2 and Model 1517 in 17 HMR. As you might expect, the shape of the stock makes this one ideal for

shooting over a sandbag. The heavy barrel is 23 inches long and the rifle weighs just over six pounds.

Benelli USA

These days, Benelli is about much more than shotguns. Possibilities for the R1 autoloading centerfire rifle keep growing in number with a ComforTech recoil-dampening stock being the latest addition. Made of a black synthetic material (as is the forearm) the buttstock is easily adjusted for lengths of pull ranging from 13-1/2 inches to 14-3/8 inches by choosing among interchangeable, quick-switch recoil pad of three different thicknesses. Three gel-pad style inserts allow comb height to be varied and protect the cheek from recoil as well. Also available with its original wood stock, the R1 is offered in 270 WSM, 308 Winchester, 300 Winchester Magnum, 30-06 and 300 WSM.

Benelli USA is also the importer of Uberti-manufactured reproductions of various famous American firearms, including the Model 1860 Henry in 44-40 and 45 Colt; the Winchester 1886 Yellowboy in those two chamberings plus 38 Special; the Winchester 1873 in 357 Magnum, 44-40 and 45 Colt; the 1874 Sharps and Trapdoor Springfield in 45-70 Government; the Winchester 1885

High Wall in 45-70, 45-90 and 45-120 and the Colt Lightning in 357 Magnum and 45 Colt. From what I have seen, quality is at least as good as in the originals.

Beretta USA

Everybody who is anybody (and a few who are not) is now offering a reproduction of the Colt Lightning pump gun and one of the best I have examined is imported by Beretta USA. Called the Gold Rush, it is available in carbine and rifle versions in 38 Special and 45 Colt. Everything––including stock finish, receiver case-coloring and barrel bluing––on the rifle I examined was very nice. In fact, if I were to come down with a burning desire to trade my LeMond Crox de Fer for a four-legged mount, dress up like a cowpoke and arm myself with an affordable Colt Lightning, this is the one I would ride off into the sunset with.

Browning

One of the highlights for me during 2005 was a fabulous elk hunt in southern New Mexico and the rifle and bullet I used absolutely won my heart. I already own far more rifles than I actually need and seldom even think about adding another to my battery but the Browning A-Bolt Mountain Ti is surely tempting. As you have probably already guessed, its receiver is titanium and its stock is synthetic. Chambered to 300 WSM, the one I bumped off an elk with weighs exactly 7-1/2 pounds with three cartridges, a Zeiss 3-9X scope and a lightweight nylon carrying sling on board. The ammo I used was the new Supreme Elite loading with the equally new 180-grain XP3 bullet. Back home, prior to the hunt, I checked the 100-yard accuracy of that load along with Winchester's four other 180-grain loadings of the 300 WSM and not a single one exceeded two inches for three-shot averages; depending on the load, muzzle velocity averaged from 2879 to 2931 fps. Other chambering options for the A-Bolt Mountain Ti

To take this elk in New Mexico, I used a Browning A-Bolt Mountain Ti in 300 WSM and Winchester ammo loaded with the 180-grain XP3 bullet. Both rifle and bullet worked perfectly.

are 243 Winchester, 7mm-08, 308 Winchester, 270 Winchester, 270 WSM, 7mm WSM and 325 WSM.

Remember the Browning T-Bolt of the 1970s? Mine was the T-2 deluxe version with cut checkering on its stock and back then it sold for $97.50 or $25 more than the T-1 version. The latter actually sold for about two bucks less than the Remington Model 591 and that made it a genuine bargain in anybody's book. At the time, the T-Bolt was the most accurate rifle in 22 rimfire I had ever fired; the one I foolishly traded away would consistently average less than half an inch for five shots at 50 yards with Winchester Super Match ammo. After several decades of absence, the

T-Bolt is back and while it differs from the original in several ways, its straight-pull bolt locks up the same. The big difference is in the double helix magazine of the new rifle. It is a 10-round rotary magazine but since it has a slimmer profile than the rotary magazine designed by Ruger, it allows the midsection of the rifle to be slimmer. Very nice rifle.

Ed Brown Products

All of Ed Brown's rifles are now built around his new Model 704 action with controlled cartridge feeding; his old push-feed action is no longer being produced. Seven different rifle variations are available, five for big-game hunting and varmint shooting

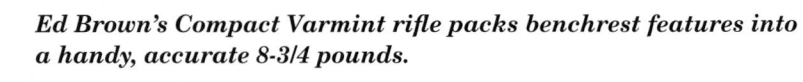

Ed Brown's Compact Varmint rifle packs benchrest features into a handy, accurate 8-3/4 pounds.

New for 2006 is The Express, built on Brown's new M-704 controlled-feed bolt action. Chamberings include 375 H&H, 416 Remington Magnum and 458 Lott.

At the heart of Brown's new M-704 controlled-feed action is this bolt with integral spring-loaded extractor.

⬨●⬨●⬨●⬨●⬨●⬨

(Savannah, Damara, Bushveld, Express and Compact Varmint) and two (Marine and Tactical) for everything else. Chambering options range from 223 Remington to 458 Lott with (oddly enough) not a single one of the super-short magnums included in the list. On the other hand, the complete line of Remington Ultra Mags from 7mm to 375 are offered. Standard barrel length for all calibers is 24 inches with the exceptions of 26 inches for the Tactical rifle and 22 inches for the Compact Varmint. The latter rifle, by the way, is available in 17 Remington, 204 Ruger, 223 Remington, 22-250, 243 Winchester, 6mm Remington, 260 Remington and 6.5-284 Norma.

Chipmunk Rifle Company

Some little girls love to shoot as much as some little boys and this is why Chipmunk introduced a pink laminated stock last year. It obviously was not pink enough to suit plinkers who wear pretty dresses and long curls and you really should wear sunshades when looking at this year's version. It's really cute and that's important to cute little girls. For the benefit of those who don't already know I will mention that the Chipmunk rifle is a single-shot and to make it as safe as possible in little hands, the firing pin has to be manually cocked after a round is chambered. Other features include a rebounding firing pin and a fully adjustable aperture-style rear sight. A scope mounting base is included with rifles wearing bull barrels. The barrel is 16 inches long and nominal rifle weights are 2-1/2 pounds for the standard barrel and 3-1/2 pounds for the bull barrel. Overall length is 30 inches. The Chipmunk is available in stainless or blued steel and with several stock options.

Cimarron Firearms

Lots of interesting rifles from this company for 2006. For starters there are reproductions of the Winchester Model 1892 in both solid-frame and takedown styles. Caliber options are 357 Magnum, 44-40 and 45 Colt. Magazine capacities are 12 rounds for the 24-inch barrel and 10 rounds for the 20-inch barrel. Then we have the Model 1885 Low Wall (thick-side version) with 30-inch octagon barrel in 22 LR, 22 Hornet, 30-30, 32-20, 32-40, 357 Magnum, 44-40 or 44

Magnum. Moving on to fans of the old Colt slide-action rifle, the Lightning is available in three variations, carbine in 32-20 with 20-inch barrel, sporting rifle with 24- or 26-inch round barrel in 38-40 and the same rifle with octagon barrel in 44-40. Moving back to single-shots, there is the "Adobe Walls" reproduction of the Remington Block in 45-70, a rifle that just about anybody including Billy Dixon would probably be proud to own. Among other nice things it has a 30-inch octagon barrel, Creedmore-style sights, case-colored receiver and hand-checkered walnut stock with German silver nose cap. Equally interesting is the Spencer Repeating Rifle in 56-50.

Cooper Arms

Dan Cooper says orders for his new repeating rifle have already far exceeded his expectations and shipment should commence sometime during late 2006. From what I have seen, it will be worth the wait. Mine will be in 25-06 and I promise to tell you all about it next time we meet.

CZ-USA

Chambered to 300 Winchester Magnum, the new Model 550 bolt gun comes with a minute-of-angle accuracy guarantee. On top of that, it has a very nice walnut stock replete with cut checkering. If that's not enough, the craftsmen in CZ's new custom shop will build one your way with the list of options including a McMillan synthetic stock. As centerfire rifles go, my favorite CZ is the custom grade Safari Classic with its fancy walnut stock, express-style rear sight and barrel-mounted front carrying sling swivel post. My pick would be 404 Jeffery but it is also available in 450 Rigby and 505 Gibbs.

GAMO

I don't often include air guns in this report but the new Viper Express from GAMO is so interesting I could not resist. Of spring piston design, it is both a shotgun and a rifle. When loaded with a reusable "shotshell" containing No. 9 lead shot, it shoots a 12-inch pattern at 10 yards, making it just the ticket for ridding the barn of rats and thinning out the gophers and starlings in your vegetable garden. Slide an adaptor into its chamber and it will fire a 22-caliber lead pellet at 850 fps. Very interesting. Fastest airgun in the GAMO lineup is the 17-caliber Viper with a muzzle velocity of 1200 fps. For several years now I have been using the 17-caliber Stutezen model (1150 fps) to control the gray squirrel population around my home and it sits ready and waiting in the corner beside my desk as I write this.

Just as interesting as the airguns is the new MTS 1000 Moving Target System. Set up the six-foot target, drop in the motorized carriage and a steel deer silhouette travels back and forth nonstop until you run out of pellets and switch it off. Designed for backyard shooting, it can be set at various distances to simulate shooting an actual deer-size target at various ranges. For example, when the target is 10 yards away, it simulates shots at a real running deer at about 90 yards. What fun!

Kimber

If any company builds a more handsome big-game rifle than Kimber, I have not discovered it and the new Model 8400 Classic is more of the same. Among other nice things, it has a lightly figured walnut stock with hand-rubbed finish and cut checkering, a Pachmayr Decelerator pad, steel grip cap and matte-finished metal. The rifle also has a Model 70-type three-position safety and hinged floorplate with

My new Cooper repeating rifle will be in 25-06 and it will look a lot like this one.

❊❊ ● ❊❊ ● ❊❊ ● ❊❊ ● ❊❊ ● ❊❊

its release tab located inside the trigger guard. Barrel lengths and calibers are 24 inches in 25-06, 270 Winchester and 30-06 Springfield and 26 inches in 300 Winchester Magnum and 338 Winchester Magnum. Nominal weights are 7-1/4 pounds for the magnums and seven pounds for the standards.

The Kimber family of 22 rimfire rifles keeps growing as well. I recently shot a couple of Pro Varmint rifles in 22 Long Rifle and 17 Mach 2 and both would consistently keep five bullets inside half an inch at 50 yards. Like all Kimber rimfires, those two have a three-position, Model 70-style safety, a free-floated, match-grade barrel replete with target-dimension chamber and hand-lapped bore.

Lapua

This Finnish company does not build rifles but it does make some of the world's best ammunition and I found out some of the things they do to make it that way during a recent visit to the factory. I kicked things off with a bang by heading to the woods where I took a moose with a Sako rifle

Regardless of the distance, no steel target was safe from me and this rifle in 338 Lapua.

❊❊ ● ❊❊ ● ❊❊ ● ❊❊ ● ❊❊ ● ❊❊

in one of my favorite chamberings, 9.3x62mm Mauser. It was the second moose I have taken in Finland with that cartridge. And yes, I used Lapua ammo. It just happened to be loaded with the recently-introduced Naturalis lead-free bullet and it worked quite nicely on moose. Then it was onward to the Lapua test range where I tried unsuccessfully to shoot up ammo of various calibers faster than they could make it. Most fun of all was shooting steel targets that had been torched from the body of an old Russian armored vehicle (or so they told me). For that I used an extremely accurate rifle in 338 Lapua. The armor-piercing load zipped right through out to 600 yards. I then switched to a match load with the Scenar match bullet (which is Lapua's answer to our Sierra MatchKing) and no paper target inside 1000 yards was safe. To cap it all off, I rode as navigator in a rally car driven by one of Europe's top drivers and just before I closed my eyes the speedometer read 120 and we had just become airborne after topping a hill. I'd love to do that again, too.

Legacy Sports International

The Howa family of rifles imported from Japan by Legacy Sports gets bigger every year. One recent addition is the Ultralight Mountain Rifle at 6-1/2 pounds in 243 Winchester, 7mm-08 and 308. Moving from one weight extreme to another we have the Thumbhole Varminter Extreme with thumbhole-style laminated stock and a variety of calibers ranging from 204 Ruger to 308 Winchester.

Marlin

With the Winchester Model 94 no longer in production, Marlin now owns the entire the lever-action deer rifle market among American manufacturers, rather than just most of it as has been the case during these past few years. Latest version of the unsinkable Model 336 is the XLR with stainless steel barreled action and black/gray laminated woods stock. Regardless of whether you buy one in 30-30, 444 Marlin, 45-70 or 450 Marlin, barrel length will be 24 inches, as it should be on a rifle of its style. Nominal weight is seven pounds. And while I am on the subject of American-built firearms (which seems to mean less and less as the years

go by) the Marlin 39A in 22 Rimfire is still available and still made just like it was when I bought my first one during the 1950s. Also still alive and well is the Marlin 1894 in 32 H&R Magnum, 32-20, 357 Magnum/38 Special and 44 Magnum/44 Special.

Mossberg

There are two new options in the Model 100 ATR rifle lineup for 2006. One is a short-action version with wood or synthetic stock in 243 Winchester and 308 Winchester. Another is the Combo with wood or synthetic stock in 270 Winchester or 30-06; both wearing a Bushnell 3-9X scope. Also new from Mossberg is the 802 Plinkster (where do they get these names?), a bolt-action rifle in 22 Long Rifle with an 18-inch barrel and a black synthetic stock. It is available with or without a 4x scope.

Navy Arms

If you have enjoyed watching the 1960s movie "Zulu" as many times as I have you know that in 1879, 139 British soldiers armed with Martini Henry rifles successfully defended their position at Rorke's Drift from 4000 Zulu warriors. Well, the staff at Navy Arms recently discovered a

cache of those rifles. After 100 years of storage, they are now for sale. Listed in the Navy Arms catalog as "British P-1871 Short Lever Martini Henry" rifles, they are chambered to 577-450, are complete with their original parts, and are classified as "NRA Good". Having one of these laying across your lap as you watch the movie yet another time will put you a wee bit closer to the action.

New England Firearms

The absolutely affordable break-action Handi-Rifle is now available with three interchangeable barrels in six different combinations: Sportster Combo with barrels in 223 Remington, 17 HMR and 22 Long Rifle; Pardner 20-gauge in 243 Winchester, 22 Long Rifle and 20-gauge; Pardner 12-gauge No. 1 in 270 Winchester, 22 Long Rifle and 12-gauge and Pardner 12-gauge No. 2 in 30-06, 22 Long Rifle and 12-gauge. Also available are a couple of youth versions with shortened buttstocks in 243, 22 LR and 20- or 12-gauge. Nominal weights run from five to seven pounds and barrel lengths range from 20 to 28 inches. Stocks and forearms are black synthetic. New chambering options for the wood-stocked version are 7.62x39mm Russian and 35 Whelen.

NoslerCustom

If you read my report last year, you know that only 500 rifles from NoslerCustom were to be built during 2005, all chambered to 300 WSM. Production will be limited to the same number of rifles in 2006 but the chambering is 280 Ackley Improved. The rifle will wear a Vari-X-III scope from the Leupold custom shop in the magnification range of your choice, 2.5-8X, 3.5-10X or 4.5-14X. Regardless of which scope you decide on, its range-compensation style of reticle will be calibrated for dead-on holds out to 500 yards with NoslerCustom ammo loaded with the 140-grain AccuBond bullet (40 rounds are included with the rifle). The scope will bear the same serial number as the rifle, as will the airline-approved travel case it will come in.

The Sako Quad I took on a Wyoming prairie dog shoot is now available with wood or synthetic stock.

Also new from NoslerCustom is a less expensive version of the limited-edition rifle called Model 48. About the only difference I see in their actions is the receiver of the Model 48 is drilled and tapped for a standard scope-mounting base while the base of the limited-edition rifle is an integral part of its receiver. The new rifle also wears a synthetic stock and is rated at 5-3/4 pounds. All metal wears a gray protective coating described by Nosler as MicroSlick. The rust-resistant finish is also applied to the inside of the bolt body and on the firing pin and its spring, making this the kind of rifle you want to have hanging from your shoulder when the weather turns nasty. The rifling of the match-grade, 24-inch stainless steel barrel is hand-lapped for smoothness. Only the 270 WSM chambering will be offered during 2006 and accuracy is guaranteed at 3/4-MOA for three shots with NoslerCustom ammo loaded with the 140-grain AccuBond bullet.

Remington

Believe it or not, our oldest firearms manufacturer who builds the world's most popular centerfire rifle (the Model 700) is now importing bolt-action rifles from other countries and they are built around the 1898 Mauser action. Two versions are slated for introduction. The Model 798 in 243 Winchester, 270 Winchester, 308 Winchester 30-06, 7mm Remington Magnum, 300 Winchester Mangnum, 375 H&H Magnum and 458 Winchester Magnum has Paul Mauser's non-rotating outside extractor. The Model 799 Mini in 22 Hornet, 222 Remington, 223 Remington, 22-250 and 7.62x39mm Russian looks like a Mauser but it has a Sako-style extractor. Barrel lengths are 20 inches for the Mini, 22 inches for the Model 798 in standard chamberings and 24 inches for magnum cartridges. Plinkers and small-game hunters are not being neglected either. Another bolt-action rifle is available in 22 Long Rifle and 22 WMR. Among other things, it has a 22-inch barrel and a brown stock of laminated wood.

Remington's Model 7400 autoloader (which began life many years ago as the Model 742) has an improved gas

system and is now called Model 750 Woodsmaster. The Woodsmaster moniker, by the way, has been around for a very long time and my 1940s vintage Remington Model 81 in 300 Savage goes by the same name. At any rate, the new Model 750 is slated for availability in a rifle version with 22-inch barrel and as a carbine with 18 1/2-inch barrel. Both have a Monte Carlo style walnut stock with cut checkering and R3 recoil pad. Caliber options are 243 Winchester, 308 Winchester, 270 Winchester, 30-06 and 35 Whelen.

Then we have the new Classic Deluxe version of the Model Seven. Barrel lengths are 22 inches in 300 WSM and 20 inches in 204 Ruger, 223 Remington and 350 Remington Magnum. This would also be the perfect candidate for the 338 Federal.

Rossi

The break-action, single shot rifle from Rossi is available in combo sets with a variety of interchangeable barrels and most are available with two types of buttstocks, standard for grownups and shortened for youngsters. To name but a couple of the combinations available—243 Winchester, 22 Rimfire and 20-gauge smoothbore or 12-gauge slug barrel and 50-caliber muzzleloader barrel.

Ruger

The new Compact version of the ever-popular 10/22 autoloader from

Ruger has a barrel length of 16-1/4 inches and its stock is shortened to a 12 3/4-inch pull. Nominal weight is 4-1/2 pounds, making this the perfect partner for running the old trap line. Other features include full-adjustable rear and fiber-optic front sights, birch stock and Weaver-style scope mounting base. To raise support funds for the USA Shooting Team's trip to the 2008 Summer Games in Beijing, Ruger and TALO Distributors have joined forces to come up with a special edition of the 10/22. Its features include a 20-inch heavy barrel, barracuda-style stock of red, white and blue laminated wood and two magazines. The equally new Stainless Frontier version of the Model 77 with its barrel-attached scope mounting rib has a stainless steel barreled action, a gray/black laminated wood stock, weighs 6-3/4 pounds and is available in several chamberings, including 323 WSM. I won't be surprised to see Ruger add the 338 Federal chambering to its list of options for the Model 77 rifle. If it becomes available in the Model 77RSI International I will most certainly have to have one.

Sako

The new single-set trigger now available on Sako varmint rifles works quite similar to the Canjar trigger I had years ago on a Model 70 in 220 Swift. Pull weight in its standard mode is adjustable from two to four

A wonderful small-game rifle, the T/C R-55 is now available in four versions and in 22 Long Rifle or in 17 Mach 2, the latter used to harvest these fox squirrels.

The smallest five-shot group I have fired at 100 yards with this Volquartsen autoloader in 17 Mach 2 measured well under half an inch.

pounds. Pushing forward on the fingerpiece reduces weight to nine ounces, or so says the owner's manual; when in its set mode, the trigger on my rifle breaks at a crisp two ounces. While using a couple of rifles in 223 Remington to thin out the prairie dog and coyote population I concluded that it is the best trigger available on a standard-production rifle. To answer another of your questions—yes it can be installed on any Model 75 rifle.

The Sako Quad with its four interchangeable barrels is the most interesting rifle I have shot in a very long time. Before using one to shoot prairie dogs for several days (the .22 Mac 2 barrel was the most fun), I spent some time shooting groups at 100 yards from a benchrest. I used a Burris Quad scope in the field, but when punching paper the little rifle wore a Bushnell Elite 4200 with a 4-16x magnification range. I shot five different loads in each of the four barrels and the one in 17 Mach 2 proved to be the most accurate with an overall average of 1.12 inches. Of the five loads fired, CCI and Remington were most accurate with respective averages of 0.79- and 0.83-inch. Virtually tied for second place in accuracy were the 17 HMR and 22 WMR barrels with

averages of 1.20 and 1.26 inches. The .22 Long Rifle barrel averaged 0.88-inch with Federal Classic and 0.91-inch with Remington Eley but its overall average was dead last at 1.45 inches. The Quad is now available in two versions, the original with synthetic stock and the new Hunter with walnut stock.

The Sako rifle I used to take an elk in Colorado during 2005 had been rebarreled to 338 Federal because the factory could not get one ready in time for my hunt. That cartridge is the same as the old 33-08 wildcat and I used to own a Remington Model 600 in that caliber. I no longer have the rifle but I still have reloading dies and was prepared to put them to use in case factory ammo did not arrive in time from Federal. But it did and I used it to take a young bull at just over 300 yards. The first shot through the lungs would have done it but I've learned to take no chances with elk and quickly followed up with a second shot. The animal took about half a dozen steps and piled up. Great little cartridge! It is kind to the shoulder and yet powerful enough any game up to elk and moose.

Savage

Savage has borrowed an idea

that I believe originated among benchrest shooters—a single-shot rifle with a right-hand bolt and left-hand ejection port. A rifle of this type can be fired quite rapidly since the shooter's left hand feeds cartridges while his right hand operates the bolt. This is important among benchrest shooters who try to get off five or 10 shots before range conditions change. An increase in firepower is not all that important to a varmint shooter but the fact that both hands share the loading and shooting chores is something to take note of. The new Model 12 Long Range Precision Varminter from Savage has this type of receiver and that along with an oversized knob on the bolt handle, a sandbag-friendly synthetic stock and the AccuTrigger add up to make it one serious varmint rifle. Chamberings are 204 Ruger, 223 Remington and 22-250.

Steyr Arms, Inc.

The 338 Federal chambering is a new addition to various Mannlicher rifles from Steyr. They include the Fullstock, Halfstock and Mountain versions of the Classic as well as the Pro Hunter and Ultra Light models. Weights vary from six to 7-1/2 pounds depending on model and barrel lengths range from 19 to 25-1/2 inches.

Also new is the 450 Marlin chambering in the Big Bore ProHunter with a 22-inch barrel. I examined one of these in early February and it took me back to the old days of rebarreling short-action bolt guns for Frank Barnes' 458 American. That's the 458 Winchester Magnum case shortened to two inches and, in case you haven't noticed, the 450 Marlin is the same except for a thicker headspacing belt on its case. At any rate, the Steyer rifle allows the use of pointed X-Bullets from Barnes in the Marlin cartridge and magazine length allows them to be seated out to an overall length of about three inches for an increase in useable case capacity over what is possible in a Marlin lever-action. Steyr is claiming muzzle velocities of 2450, 2300 and 2100 fps with Barnes

X-Bullets weighing 300, 350 and 400 grains, respectively. This is treading quite closely on the heels of the 458 Winchester Magnum in performance.

Taylor's & Company, Inc.

This company is known for its good-quality, imported reproductions of American-designed rifles of yesteryear, including the Model 1860 Henry in 44-40 and 45 Colt; the Model 1885 Winchester single-shot in 38-55 and 45-70; the Winchester 1866 in 32-20, 38 Special, 44-40 and 45 Colt, and the Model 1873 in the same chamberings. Or if your taste in rifles leans toward the Spencer 1865 repeater, you can get one here in 44-40, 45 Schofield or 56-50. Same goes for the 1874 Sharps in 45-70 and 45-120. Latest additions are a Winchester 1892 takedown rifle with 20- or 24-inch barrel in 357 Magnum, 38-40, 44-40 and 45 Colt and a lightweight, break-action single-shot rifle in 223 Remington and 243 Winchester called (oddly enough) the Spirit Overtop. How do they come up with these names?

Thompson/Center

Two of the best whitetail bucks I have taken during close to a half century of hunting them fell victim to the same rifle. I took one of the bucks in South Carolina with a rifle in 6mm-06 and took the other in Iowa with a 50-caliber muzzleloader. I have also used that same rifle in 204 Ruger and 223 Remington to bump off a varmint or two. I managed to accomplish all of that with a single rifle because it is a T/C Encore. The new ProHunter version of that rifle has what T/C describes as a Swing Hammer; by rotating the hammer spur left for a left-handed and right for a right-handed shooter, the need for a separate offset hammer spur is eliminated when a low-mounted scope is used. When used in its middle position the hammer is like any other. Once the spur is moved to your chosen position it is locked into place with a screw. Equally new is the FlexTech stock, said to reduce perceived recoil by as much

as 40 percent. Four rubber arches are incorporated into the buttstock just forward of a rather thick recoil pad and they all add up to ease the pain from hard-kicking cartridges.

I have been having a ball with a Thompson/Center R-55 in 22 Mach 2. Incredibly accurate, it is one of the most fun small-game rifles I have ever carried in the woods. The R-55 is now available in four variations: Classic with walnut stock and blued steel; All Weather in synthetic and stainless steel; Benchmark with laminated wood stock and bull barrel, and a light-barrel version of that rifle called Sporter. All models are also available in 22 Long Rifle.

Tikka

Where can you find better accuracy for your money than in a Tikka T3? Every single one I've worked with shot the way some writers say all rifles shoot. Latest variations are the Deluxe with walnut stock and Camo Stainless with (I'll let you guess). Chambering options range from 223 Remington to 338 Winchester Magnum with the 6.5x55mm Swedish somewhere in between those two.

U.S. Repeating Arms Co.

By the time you read this, U.S. Repeating Arms Company will have ceased production of three Winchester firearms, the Model 70 and Model 94 rifles and the Model 1300 Shotgun. The New Haven, Connecticut factory closed its doors on March 31, 2006. Incredibly sad, but true. So, if you have been putting off the purchase of one of those rifles in a particular caliber you'd better move quickly before they disappear from the shelves of dealers forever. I rushed out and latched onto a Model 94 in 25-35 I had been considering and am glad I did for several reasons, not the least of which it has proven to be a very nice 100-yard deer rifle and quite accurate to boot.

What it all boils down to is USRAC has ceased to be a manufacturer of firearms and has become an importer of firearms manufactured in other countries. An example of things to come is a new knockabout-quality bolt-action rifle in 22 rimfire called the Wildcat. Made is Russia, it weighs 4-1/2 pounds, has a five- or ten-shot detachable magazine and a barrel length of 21 inches. Another foreign-built rifle to be initially sold under the USRAC banner is the equally new SXR gas-operated autoloader in 270 WSM, 30-06, 300 WSM and 300 Winchester Magnum, replete

The Winchester Model 94 in 25-35 I used to take this Texas whitetail was one of the last built before U. S. Repeating Arms ceased production.

In the "So what's new? department", the Mannlicher-Schoenauer rifle I used to take this chamois in the Austrian Alps was chambered to 7x64mm Brenneke. Introduced in 1917, it duplicates the performance of the 280 Remington, which came along 40 years later.

with racy European styling. Last but not least in the guns-made-somewhere-else department is the "High Wall" Hunter single-shot in 223 Remington, 22-250, 270 WSM, 7mm WSM, 300 WSM and 325 WSM.

Volquartsen Custom

As sometimes happens with totally new firearms, the production of Tom Volquartsen's new match-grade autoloader in 223 Remington and 204 Ruger has been delayed a bit, but judging by the level of accuracy being produced by the prototypes, I'd say it will be well worth the wait. Tom hopes to deliver the first rifles during late 2006 and if he does I will let you know how mine shoots next year. A Volquartsen rifle I have been shooting a lot is a little autoloader in 17 Mach 2. The more I shoot that rifle and its cartridge the more fond I become of both. Last spring I took

it to a ranch in California and no ground squirrel or crow within 150 yards was safe. The smallest five-shot, 100-yard group I have fired on paper with that rifle measured 0.322-inch center-to-center. I used Federal ammo to shoot that group.

Weatherby

According to the 2006 Weatherby catalog, the Mark V Ultramark bridges the gap in features between the Mark V Deluxe and a budget-busting Mark V from Weatherby's custom shop. They start with a hand-selected blank of highly-figured walnut and give it a high-gloss finish replete with 20-line cut checkering. Add maple spacers between the solid recoil pad at the rear and a rosewood forearm tip up front, along with Monte Carlo styling and highly polished metal that would make Roy Weatherby proud and you have a Weatherby rifle that looks the way a Weatherby rifle is supposed to look. I don't care what they say about the advantages of stainless steel and plastic stocks––I still love blued steel and a good piece of walnut. Fact of the matter is, not long ago I started itching all over for another Weatherby Mark V and I chose the Deluxe grade in 240 Weatherby Magnum. Built around the standard-size Mark V receiver rather than the original magnum version, it is a wonderful little deer rifle. Back to the Ultramark, it is available in Roy's two favorite magnum cartridges, the 257 and the 300.

While I am on the subject of Deluxe rifles, you can also choose one from the Vanguard rifle lineup. From a distance you might mistake it for a Mark V Deluxe but upon closer examination you will discover about $1200 difference in its price. This is, without doubt, the most handsome Vanguard ever offered by Weatherby. It's got the right chamberings

too—270 Winchester, 30-06, 300 Weatherby Magnum and my favorite, the 257 Weatherby Magnum. I have a Vanguard Custom in that caliber and it just might be the best pronghorn antelope rifle I have ever owned. When zeroed three inches high with Weatherby ammo loaded with the 115-grain Ballistic Tip, the bullet is dead on point of aim at 300 yards and only half an antelope low at 400 yards.

Off and on through the years Weatherby has built a few pistols on the small Mark V action and the latest version is called Short Firing Platform or CFP for short (where do they get these names?). Of rear-grip design (as opposed to the center-grip design of the original Remington XP-100), it has a synthetic stock, a 16-inch barrel and is rated at 5-1/4 pounds. Chambering options are 223 Remington, 22-250, 243 Winchester and 7mm-08 Remington. The grip is ambidextrous so nobody can complain about being not being invited to the party.

So What's New?

A few months back I hunted chamois in the Austrian Alps. The rifle I used was a Mannlicher-Schoenauer built during the late 1940s and wearing a Kahles scope of the same vintage. While visiting the Kahles factory in Vienna I compared that scope with those being made today and was surprised to see very little difference in their optical quality. The fact that Kahles builds some of the clearest and brightest scopes in the world is not something that only recently happened—they have been doing it for a very long time. The Mannlicher-Schoenauer I used to bump off a chamois was chambered to 7x64mm Brenneke. Introduced in 1917, it duplicates the performance of the 280 Remington, which did not come along until 40 years later. So what's new?

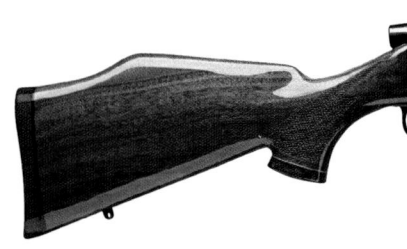

At first glance you'll think the new Weatherby Vanguard Deluxe with its handsome Mark V style stock actually is a Mark V rifle.

RIFLES TODAY ✧
SINGLE-SHOT RIFLE REVIEW

by John Campbell

It's hard to believe the range of classic single-shot rifles that has evolved in recent years. It seems American shooters just can't get enough of them, especially some form of the storied Sharps rifle. And what's especially encouraging is the number of highly skilled and specialized riflemakers that are cropping up. From their small shops come some of the most perfectly made and unusual single-shot rifles and actions you can imagine. One such maker is Joe Lozito. He not only makes an incredible version of the Sharps-Borchardt action, but will soon offer (probably by the time you read this) a recreation of the rare and mysterious Sharps 1875. If you have a hankering for a left-hand Sharps 1874, that's no problem. John Mitchell at Classic Rifle Co. can fix you up right quick. And Steve Earle is planning on introducing the coveted Wesson mid-range action. The list goes on. But that's the beauty of single-shot rifles: they're an alluring basis for beautiful, individual and accurate shooting instruments. But most importantly, single-shots are fun. Lots of fun. So, let's take a look at what's new this year.

Axtell Rifle Co.

Axtell Rifle is introducing the latest of its Native American Sharps Shooters of The Northern Plains series. These are Model 1877 Sharps rifles, with each limited series honoring a native American Indian tribe of the plains. The first was the Crow series, then the Nez Perce. Now Axtell is working on the Sioux tribute. Others will follow.

Each special edition series is *very* limited and is comprised of only *five* 1877 heavy-barrel Sporting rifles. Calibers will be 45-70 unless special ordered for another 45-caliber cartridge such as the 45-90 or 45-110. Along with their rifle, customers will get a traditional beaded scabbard, par flech cartridge bag, a knife with beaded sheath and a framed print of an art work by Gloria D'. The central idea of this series is to create rifles that an American Indian may have actually owned. Thus, there's no engraving and no fancy wood on these Sharps 77s.

"They will look old, but they will be new rifles," said Carmen Axtell. If you think you might be interested in one of these, my advice is to act quickly. All previous series have sold out almost immediately.

Axtell actually makes six versions of the 1877, sometimes known as the "English model." This was a sleek evolution of the Sharps 1874, and a very rare iteration of the Sharps "side-hammer" rifles.

Altogether, Axtell offers a Custom Express, No. 1 Creedmoor, No. 2 Long Range, Lower Sporter, Lower Business Rifle and an Overbaugh Schuetzen version of their Model 1877. Each rifle features cut rifled and hand-lapped Badger barrels, plus appropriate features for its application ... including a set of renowned Axell iron sights. If you like fine engraving, exhibition English or American black walnut, flawless checkering, or any other custom touch, all you need do is inquire. The sky's the limit at Axtell. Calibers are also appropriate to a rifle's use, and range from the irresistible little 40-50 Sharps bottleneck to the 45-100 ... although Axtell unequivocally recommends the 45-70. For any practical use, I wholeheartedly agree. Axtell always carries a backlog of orders, but the rifle or sight you get is more than worth it. Find out why at www.riflesmith.com.

Ballard Rifle & Cartridge Co.

The good news from Cody is that "Ballard is Back!" The great news is that the company's new owner, Bill Northrup, is putting things back together the way they used to be ... only this time even better. Bill even has old-time Ballard hands, Ron Long and Steve Garbe, along as consultants.

Northrup himself is a Wyoming native, degreed engineer, former

This great Ballard Long Range is specially designed for engaging targets between 200 and 1,000 yards. It's a favorite with silhouette and BPCR riflemen.

If you're a blackpowder cartridge aficionado, the Ballard #1 Silhouette rifle is your huckleberry. It has double-set triggers, ring lever and a recoil-spreading shotgun butt.

airline pilot, businessman and, most importantly, an avid shooter and hunter. There's nowhere to go but up with credentials like that, and the team that Northrup's put together.

As proof of that resurgence, I offer up four words: High-wall take-down. Yes, it's true. Ballard now offers its reproduction of the famous Winchester Model 1885 in the coveted take-down configuration. And make no mistake; Ballard's take-down system is a precise recreation of the original Winchester design. Open the lever, push the catch forward, rotate the barrel and forearm 90 degrees, and you have a two-piece rifle. This allows you to easily swap in barrels of another caliber ... or conveniently package

the rifle for carrying or shipping.

And as with other Ballard High-Walls, you can order the new take-down 85 in a range of calibers. The cognoscente will choose these carefully so that the rifle's switch-barrel capability will optimize its versatility. For example, how about a 30-40 Krag/ 405 Winchester two-barrel set? You could hunt everything from whitetails to lion with that one.

Ballard's new product line is still in development, and they no longer list rolling block rifles. But there's still the company's namesake: The Ballard. It's available in a dozen versions including the #1 Hunter, #1 Far West, #3 Gallery, # 5 Montana, #8 Union Hill, #7 Long Range, #6

Schuetzen, #5 Pacific, #4 Midrange, #4 Perfection, #3 Fine Gallery and #1 Silhouette (not an original Ballard style, of course). Specifications and calibers vary by model.

And to flesh out the 1885 story, Ballard still makes its all-parts-interchange-with-originals reproduction of the classic Winchester Single-Shot in seven variations. These include the Standard Sporter, Special Sporting, Helm Schuetzen, and 1885 Express (an attractive sporter rendition). Again, calibers vary by model ... but you'll have a virtually unlimited choice. Bill Northrup tells me he's willing to chamber the 1885 in just about any safe caliber. For example, Ballard is getting a bunch of new orders for rifles in 500 NE. That should give you an idea of top end possibilities.

Ballard also offers a wide array of parts and restoration services for original rifles, too. What's more, the Ballard restoration craftsmen will gladly tackle most any classic rifle. This includes old lever actions of most any make or model, German Schuetzens, etc. And in my opinion, Ballard's in-house color case-work is some of the finest in America. So if you have a well-worn rifle that's in

A specialty of Ballard Rifle craftsmen is beautiful color case-hardening. And this Long Range receiver shows it off beautifully. Need color case work for restoration? Call Ballard.

need of some quality work, it would be wise to check with Ballard. You can start by checking Ballard's web site at www.ballardrifles.com.

Borchardt Rifle Co.

Al Story's a busy man. He's still turning out one of the best Sharps-Borchardt Model 1878 rifles in North America plus his own action/rifle for the authoritative 50 BMG cartridge.

But the news this year from Al Story's Silver City, New Mexico, company is an all-new version of the German Lechner action.

This was one of the classic German Schuetzen actions and features an angled falling breechblock with a striker ignition system (the Sharps-Borchardt is similar), double set triggers and Teutonic style lever. Frank de Haas considered it one of the strongest of the German actions … if not the strongest.

The creator of the original action was Hans Lechner of Nurnberg, Germany, and many of his rifles were barreled for the 8.15x46R German Schuetzen cartridge. Al Story's actions will be available in more common American rimmed cartridges.

In general, Al will also update the mechanics of the action as well as recontour the back of the original deeply-concave frame in order to make the rifle easier to stock. If you're interested in one of these Lechner actions, contact Borchardt Rifle Co. for full details. They'll sure bring the spirit of real "German Schuetzen" back to any match.

But remember, Story's Sharps-Borchardt 1878 rifles remain a standard for the single-shot crowd, and most of the parts will interchange with the originals. For information on all rifles, call Al Story at Borchardt Rifle Co., 505-535-2923.

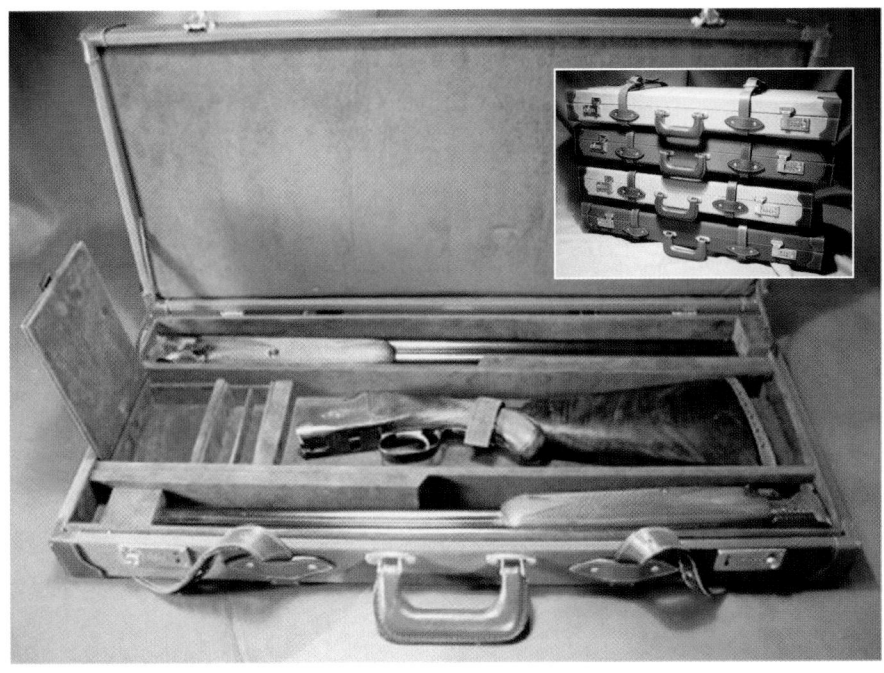

Brooks & Thomas Inc.

I really don't have to make a case for this new company. They do that themselves. In fact, fine English-style trunk cases are the proud product of Brooks & Thomas.

While a B&T case would be exquisite for any take-down single-shot, they can also be ordered for full-length rifles such as the Sharps 1874, Remington rolling block, etc. Call Brooks & Thomas at 719-574-4407 or visit their web site at www.brooksandthomas.com.

Cimarron

If there's one outfit that really caters to aficionados of the Old West, it's Cimarron. And as part of that effort, Cimarron offers no less than eight variants of the Sharps 1874. There's a Billy Dixon model that commemorates this buffalo hunter's famous long shot at the battle of Adobe Walls, as well as a Quigley model that recreates the Sharps rifle used by Tom Selleck in the movie "Quigley Down Under."

The interior of Brooks & Thomas cases is covered in modern billiard-type cloth and can be custom-compartmented to most any gun or single-shot rifle.

From there, you can move on to the 34-inch barreled Big 50 Sharps (in 50-90), the No. 1 Sporting, the option-laden Pride of The Plains, Texas Ranger Carbine, the Quigley II, or a more austere version of the Billy Dixon. Depending on model, the Cimarron Sharps is available in 45-70, 45-90, 45-120, 45-110, 50-90 and 50-70.

Cimarron also offers an Adobe Walls rolling block with double-set trigger in 45-70 … this to recognize the actual rifle that Billy Dixon owned and used on a daily basis (he made his famous 1583-yard shot with a borrowed Sharps).

More recently, Cimarron entered the market with a reproduction of the renowned Winchester Model 1885 Single-Shot; a subject with which I have some passing familiarity.

For those who seek the ultimate power, there is the Cimarron Big 50 Sharps in 50-90 with 34-inch barrel.

This beautiful Classic Rifle Co. Sharps 1877 was made up with shotgun butt, Rigby flats on the barrel, and a wedge-attached forearm with ebony tip.

The Cimarron 1885 can be had with either a straight grip or checkered pistol grip buttstock. There is also a Schuetzen double-set trigger available with the early Helm Schuetzen spur lever. These high-walls are available in 45-70, 45-90, 40-65, 38-55, 348 Winchester, and 30-40 Krag.

Finally, Cimarron's line includes the 1885 flat-side low-wall. It is a fine-looking rifle, and available in 22 LR, 22 Hornet, 30-30 Winchester, 32-20, 38-40, 357 Magnum, 44-40 and 44 Magnum.

For the coming year, Cimarron also offers some upscale single-shots, including the low-wall, engraved in authentic 19th century patterns. And believe me, these styles just "look right" on rifles that harken back to the Old West. Check it all out at www.cimarron-firearms.com.

Classic Rifle Company

Some shooters aren't satisfied with "production rifles," no matter how well they're made. These persnickety types insist on a completely custom arm, crafted individually just for them. For these folks, there is the Classic Rifle Company, of Bend, Oregon.

Here, bespoken Sharps 1874 rifles are built to order by master machinist and gunsmith, John Mitchell. And even if you're a lefty, there's no problem. Classic can deliver *a true left hand 1874* in any configuration you'd like. Classic also makes the Sharps 1877 model.

All actions are milled from 8620 steel, using original Sharps parts as patterns. Barrels are all match quality, with weight and length completely at the customer's discretion. Classic also offers tang sights machined from the same high quality steel as the rifle actions. They are precision instruments ... just as you'd expect from a master machinist.

For more information on Classic's rifles, visit www.classicrifles.

net. For a quote, phone 503-789-0227 and talk to John Mitchell personally. It'll be worth it.

Cornell Publications

Half of the fun in owning a classic single-shot rifle is discovering more about its history. And while there are many books out there on the Sharps, Ballard, Winchester and other single shots, there aren't too many catalogs. And it's the *catalogs* that really reveal the details of each model, options and other juicy facts.

However, original arms company catalogs from the 1800s are scarce as hen's teeth, and very expensive when you do find them—which isn't often. But all of that has changed now.

Cornell Publications of Brighton, Michigan, offers a bewildering selection of reproduction sporting arms catalogs that are targeted toward the shooter ... not the book collector. To put it another way, Cornell has taken original catalogs, scanned in every page, and reprinted them just as they were originally. High-quality modern paper is used, and sometimes the catalog covers are "recreated" in color. This is done when the original cover is missing or severely damaged. Still, the inside material is all original and unaltered. It is just published on new paper and saddle-stitched back into a catalog format.

For example, you can choose from a wide array of Sharps, Remington, Winchester, Ballard and other obscure single-shot catalogs at Cornell. The great part is that prices are mostly in the $10 to $15 range, so you can

Cornell Publications old single-shot catalog reproductions are targeted toward the shooter ... not the book collector. It's all-original content, but on modern paper with some "recreated" covers.

feel empowered to stock up on a number of oldies that will reveal an incredible amount of information.

But the Cornell selection is just too huge to be confined here. It's best to visit their web site at www.cornellpubs.com and surf through the massive number of options. You can also phone Cornell at 810-225-3075. They're nice people to talk to.

CPA Rifles

They say good things come in small packages. Well, CPA is a small company, but they've been making some terrific Stevens 44 1/2 reproductions since 1986.

Another good thing about CPA is that their rifles are even better than the originals. In every case, CPA actions are superior to the originals in

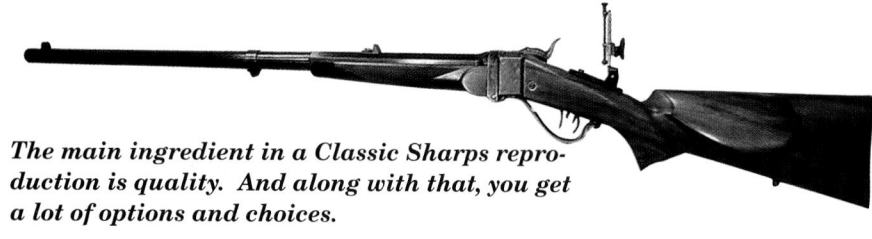

The main ingredient in a Classic Sharps reproduction is quality. And along with that, you get a lot of options and choices.

The name Creedmoor means long-range accuracy, and this C. Sharps Creedmoor delivers it... plus an incredibly sleek long barrel look.

Whether you prefer to take the 1874 Sharps afield or to the BPCR matches, this C. Sharps Sporter is an ideal choice in most any caliber.

One of the first applications of the Sharps action was military and that included handy and powerful carbines, like this one from C. Sharps.

material quality and heat treatment.

Since CPA makes virtually all of its rifles to custom order, there's not much you could call a "standard" CPA 44 1/2. But there are three basic models: The Schuetzen, Silhouette, and the Sporting/Varmint Rifle. A host of standard features come with every one. These include a color-cased action, double-set triggers, oil-finished semi-fancy pistol grip stock, a take-down system, and your choice of most any barrel contour in most any chambering from 22 Short to 45-110. Options include additional barrels, checkering, engraving, fancy wood and more. Once you submit a modest deposit, you'll have to wait from six to 12 months to have your CPA rifle delivered. But the quality of these CPA Stevens is worth the wait.

In addition to rifles, CPA offers a large selection of "single-shot stuff" for Stevens, Sharps, Ballard, Remington, Winchester and other classic single-shots. This includes semi-inletted stocks, buttplates, levers, palm rests, scope bases and a whole bunch more. It's worth a trip to the CPA web site just to find out, too. That's www.singleshotrifles.com.

C. Sharps Arms Co.

Back in 1975, this was the first company to reproduce the Sharps 1874 rifle. They also offer reproductions of the 1875 and 1877 Sharps, as well as their own recreation of the Winchester Model 1885 high-wall.

The heart of C. Sharps' business is five models of the classic 1874 "sidehammer" Sharps. First, there's the 10.5-pound Hartford Sporting Model with 26-, 28- or 30-inch tapered octagon barrel, double-set triggers, crescent butt and a silver nose-capped forearm. In contrast, the Bridgeport Sporting Rifle has a plain schnabel forend, wider "Bridgeport" steel butt and color-cased receiver. For something really special, there's the Boss Gun upgrade of the Hartford Sporting Rifle. It features a 34-inch barrel, engraved French grey receiver, XXX-figured wood, Hartford style forend with German silver nose cap, globe front sight, long-range tang rear sight and a lot more. It's available in Grades I, II or III, depending upon your taste and pocketbook. In these, you can choose from a raft of custom features, including a cut-rifled and hand-lapped barrel —plus lots of engraving. The Model 1874 is available in 19 calibers from 22 LR to 50-140.

C. Sharps also offers its interpretation of the 1875 Sharps in a Sporting Rifle and Classic Rifle configuration. Both have plain trigger and straight-grip stock with an optional pistol grip available. Pick from 19 calibers here, too.

The elegant 1877 "Custom Long Range Target" Sharps is also available

from C. Sharps. This one is custom production only and comes with a 32- or 34-inch tapered round barrel with Rigby flats at the breech. Calibers are 44-90 Sharps or Remington, 45-70, 45-90 and 45-100 Sharps. It comes with long-range sights, presentation-grade wood, checkering and more. Weight is about 10 lbs.

C. Sharps also introduced one of the first reproductions of the Winchester Model 1885. They still make them in four versions: The Sporting Rifle with single trigger, shotgun butt, straight grip and 26-, 28- or 30-inch tapered octagon barrel; the Highwall Classic with crescent butt, pistol-grip stock and a silver inlay in the forend, or the custom-order Highwall Schuetzen. You can choose from 20 calibers, now including the 38-40, 44-40 and 45 Colt. A Short Classic Highwall is available with an 18-, 20-, 22- or 24-inch tapered octagon barrel at no additional cost.

If you prefer to build your own rifle, C. Sharps has you covered there, too. Model 1874 Sharps or Model 1885 high-wall actions and barreled actions are also available.

For the full story on C. Sharps, visit their web site at www.csharpsarms.com.

Dakota Arms Inc.

To commemorate the 100th anniversary of the 30-06 Springfield cartridge, Dakota is doing something very special, exactly 101 times. For 2006, Dakota will create that many very Limited Edition Model 10 rifles chambered for the 30-06.

These rifles will have a 100-year banner on the sideplate with gold wire border, special wood, stocks, checkering, engraving, a color-cased receiver and jeweled block, Dakota scope bases and Talley rings, a hooded front sight, barrel band for the front sling swivel and more. Custom checkering and engraving, plus a matching serial number Swarovski scope, are optional. Serial numbers will run from 10-1906 to 10-2006. And each rifle comes with three boxes of Dakota 30-06 collector's ammunition and an autographed copy of J. Y. Jones' book *One Man, One Rifle, One Land.* For 101 lucky owners, this will be a once-in-a-lifetime opportunity.

Dakota's Model 10 falling-block action is fully machined from steel with a remarkably crisp trigger and fast lock time. The upper and lower tangs are short and straight, allowing for a wide range of stock design. Like the Ruger No. 1 (to which the Model 10 bears a superficial resemblance) the Dakota action is attached to the buttstock with a strong through-bolt. Other standard features include XX wood with hand-rubbed oil finish and checkering, mounts for Talley scope rings and a 23-inch barrel available in most any chambering from 22 LR to 300 Winchester Mag. The Model 10 Magnum takes you from there all the way up to the 338 Winchester, 375 H&H and 45-70. And because virtually no Model 10 is a "standard" Model 10, you can order any custom feature you want.

Dakota's "other single-shot" is the famous Miller. Since the early 1970s, this action has been well known to schuetzen rifleman, and is now part of the Dakota line. But the Miller is also one of the best single-shots for a custom sporter. Either way, each Miller is custom-built to your specifications. Sporter features include a hand-checkered English style buttstock with XXX wood and recoil pad. You also get the Miller action with jeweled block and 24-inch round barrel in just about any caliber up to 375 H&H. The Miller

Low Boy has a case-colored receiver, half-octagon barrel and more. The Model F is Anglo-inspired with English walnut perch-belly buttstock, Queen Anne grip, stainless receiver, globe front sight and Soule-type rear, plus a 26-inch octagon barrel chambered for any rimmed cartridge up to 45-110.

Many do not know it, but Dakota also makes a Sharps rifle. Only the Dakota Sharps is a scaled-down version of the famous Model 1874 long-range rifle. In conjunction with the Little Sharps Rifle Co., of Big Sandy, Montana, Dakota reduced the size of the action by 20 percent to provide a rifle capable of shooting smaller rimmed handgun and hunting cartridges. Standard features include a 26-inch octagonal barrel, steel buttplate, single blade rear sight with front bead, matte blue metal finish, and an optional half-octagonal barrel. Extras abound with a double-set trigger, pewter forend tip, French grey receiver finish, engraving, a wedding ring on half-octagon barrels and more.

Go to www.dakotaarms.com and delve into some of the finest single shots you will ever see.

Dixie Gun Works

This year, Dixie turns to the roots of the Confederacy by offering its reproduction of the 1862 Confederate Sharps Carbine, made by Pedersoli. The gun is 54-caliber, with a 22-inch browned, tapered round barrel with 1:48 twist and percussion ignition. Sights are browned steel base with integral blade front sight. The rear sight is blued steel, and the rifle has a single trigger. The butt and forestock are satin-finished American walnut, with the receiver, lock, lever, triggerplate and saddle bar and ring color case-hardened. Lockplate markings read **S.C. Robinson, Arms Manufactory, Richmond, VA 1862**.

In addition to the Carbine, Dixie has a new Malcolm-style scope for this year. This scope is a replica of the scope made by William Malcolm of Syracuse, New York, in the late 1800s. It has a period-correct 3/4-inch steel tube and is 29-1/2 inches long. This 6x instrument is made with high quality light-correcting

achromatic lenses with an adjustable focus eyepiece. It also employs fog-free nitrogen-filled technology. It has knurled brass fittings at the eyepiece and objective lens. The bases are made to be installed in the existing 3/8-inch sight dovetails on your rifle. External windage and elevation adjustments are made at the rear mount. Lens covers are included. The scope comes with a 5-inch extension/sunshade, which will allow it to fit a 30-inch barrel, but tube extensions are available to allow attachment to barrel lengths from 25 to 34 inches.

Dixie also offers Steve Meacham's Winchester High-Wall reproductions in Silhouette and Schuetzen configurations. There is also a selection of five Uberti high-walls. From the famous Italian maker, Pedersoli, Dixie offers no less than 16 variations of the Sharps Model 1874 "sidehammer." Pedersoli rolling blocks are also available from Dixie in eight different models. Dixie's Pedersoli line also includes reproductions of the famous Springfield "trapdoor" in rifle, carbine and deluxe "Officer's Model" trim. And, to be perfectly honest, Dixie prices are some of the best I've seen on any single-shots. So, you'd be wise to check into www.dixiegunworks.com.

Steve Earle

It has been a few years, but Steve Earle is still supplying his incredibly precise reproduction of the famous Wesson No. 1 action to a host of discriminating riflemen.

In fact, these classic actions are so popular that every Wesson Steve will be working on this year is already spoken for.

But before the year is out, Steve will be introducing something "completely different." This will be a recreation of the Wesson mid-range single-shot. It's a falling block action that has a central hammer. They only made seven originals and only four of those have survived as far as we know. Steve has one of those four on his bench.

From this historic action, Steve will be back-engineering a modern day Wesson mid-range. And he hopes to have the first prototypes

If you need a scope block, Steve Earl has one for you. Virtually any size, shape, or configuration is available.

⌘ ● ⌘ ● ⌘ ● ⌘ ● ⌘ ● ⌘

out of his shop by the end of the year. It will be something that's more than worth the wait.

As I've said, Steve still offers a fully CNC-machined reproduction of the classic Wesson No. 1 action. Each Earle-made Wesson No. 1 is cut from a solid block of 8620 steel and is fit and finished to tolerances that old man Wesson could only hope to achieve. And when you open the box, you'll be delighted with an impressively smooth 400 grit exterior polish.

Earle has made only two significant changes from the original: The first is a Mann-Niedner style small-diameter firing pin arrangement that's front-loaded into the breechblock. Secondly, Earle eliminated the original Wesson's sear adjustment screw and replaced it with an adjustment screw in the tumbler that allows reliable sear engagement and elimination of most

trigger "creep." While this approach does not strictly allow for trigger pull adjustment, Steve Earle's triggers commonly break at 2 to 2.5 lbs. As for chambering options, Earle's Wesson No. 1 is suitable for any rimmed cartridge with a smaller rim diameter than that of the 577 Nitro Express. And that's a lot of cartridges.

Steve Earle also makes scope blocks. All kinds of scope blocks. So if you want to mount an old Unertl or Lyman … or one of the new Malcolms, etc., Steve has the blocks you need. In fact, he's supplying one form of scope block to our Army ordnance command in Iraq.

So, if you're looking for exotic Wesson actions, scope blocks and more, Steve Earle is your man. Contact him directly at 781-585-6504, e-mail him at ssmugwump@adelphia. net, or drop him a note at 24 Palmer Rd., Plympton, MA 02367.

Jeff's Outfitters

To the relief of many shooters, the cases and accoutrements aspect of the old Cape Outfitters just didn't disappear. It became Jeff's Outfitters and it's doing a gangbusters business out of the old stomping grounds around Cape Girardeau, Missouri.

The bread-and-butter of this firm are classic trunk-type hard cases made along the lines of those common in the late 19th and early 20th centuries. They're leather or canvas-and-leather covered with partitioned felt-lined internal compartments for your rifle

and accessories. Cases are available for Sharps, Remington rolling block, Springfield trapdoor and similarly-shaped rifles. And if you want to make the kit look right, Jeff's even has the classic accessories to go along with these cases, including turnscrews, square or round nickel-plated oil cans and "Buffalo Hunter" cartridge belts.

But the single-shot stuff doesn't stop there at Jeff's. They also offer Pope or Winchester-style 'tuning fork' palm rests, steel trigger guards for imported rolling blocks, plus a huge selection of sights. These range from reproductions of the standard factory sights of the era to globe and windgauge front sights, Vernier tang sights for Winchesters, Ballards, Stevens and more. There's even an adjustable Hadley eyecup on tap.

I should also point out that you'll find all of this stuff is most affordably priced. Check it all out at www.jeffsoutfitters.com.

Krieghoff

For those who appreciate life's finer things, there is the Krieghoff Hubertus. This is a break-open single shot made in the finest Old World tradition. It comes with automatic safety, iron-sighted express style quarter-rib milled for scope mounts, a 23.5-inch or 21.5-inch barrel, hand-checkered European walnut stock with right- or left-hand cheekpiece, and a steel or Dural receiver that's nickel-plated for protection. A total of 18 calibers are available from the 222 to the 9.3x74R. From there, your options are virtually wide open.

For example, you can add a set trigger, wood upgrades, custom shaped receiver, sideplates, octagon barrel,

⌘ ● ⌘ ● ⌘ ● ⌘ ● ⌘ ● ⌘

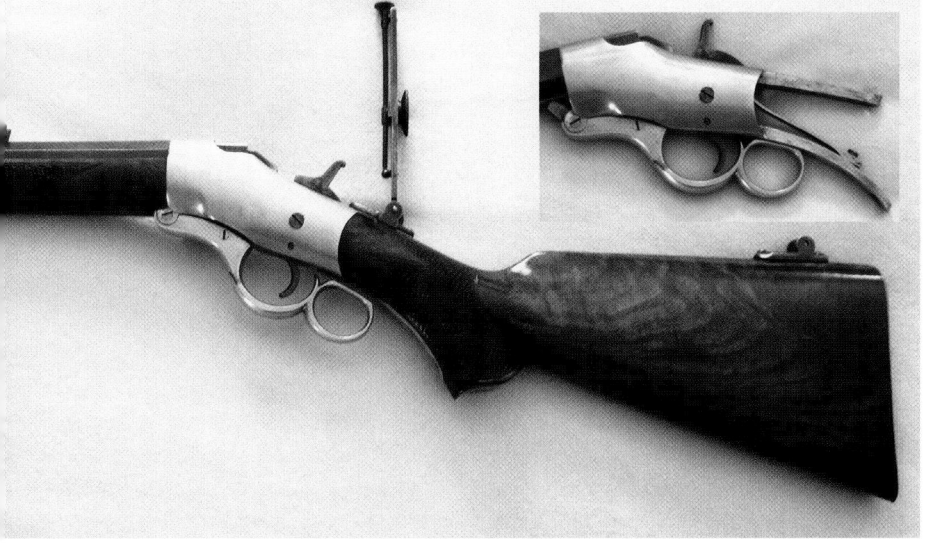

Inset: Metalsmith Steve Earl will have his own version of this original Wesson mid-range falling-block action only late in 2006. Steve's version will have some minor mechanical updates internally.

Only seven of these Wesson mid-range rifles are known to exist... and Steve Earl has access to one of them to reproduce.

a recoil reducer, a bewildering range of engraving and receiver finishes, the 7mm Remington Mag. or 300 Winchester Mag. chamberings, and a lot more. In fact, the Hubertus Custom Grade S is one of the finest examples of gunmaking art anywhere ... and good reason to consider a home equity loan.

Leatherwood Optics

There's no definite proof, but the telescopic rifle sight has been around since about 1830. They were used in the American Civil War, and made their way onto the Great Plains with the buffalo hunters.

One of the most popular scopes of that Western era was the Malcolm. It was long, but it was sharp, sturdy and precisely adjustable. Original Malcolms command a king's ransom today... if you can find one at all. But now, thanks to Jim Leatherwood, you can get a Malcolm scope that is, by virtually all measures, superior to the original.

Leatherwood's 6x Malcolm comes in a short and long tube version with precision-adjustable mounts that affix to any 28- to 34-inch barrel. The scope has multi-coated lenses, a 3/4-inch tube, crosshair reticule and is nitrogen-filled.

This scope is also incredibly rugged. If you're a blackpowder shooter with a 45-120 in the rack, there's no problem. The Leatherwood Malcolm will take the recoil in stride. And for matches that allow optical sights, this scope not only looks right, but

will be hard to beat for clanging iron or punching paper that's posted out there on the distant horizon. Learn more at www.leatherwoodoptics.com.

Lone Star Rifle Co., Inc.

The next best thing to a rolling block that was made in Ilion, New York, is one that's made in Conroe, Texas ... by Lone Star Rifle Co., of course. Years ago, Dave Higginbotham decided to recreate this classic Remington single-shot with exceptional precision and true-to-the-originals dimensions. The subsequent fame of both Lone Star and Higginbotham testify to the success of it all.

Lone Star offers seven models. The first is their Sporting Rifle, which is an exact recreation of the original Remington sporter. The second is their Target Rifle, which can be ordered in Target or Silhouette configurations. The Big 50 Buffalo Rifle is truly a big piece. It has to be since it's chambered for the 50-90. The Custer Rifle is another custom-order proposition, and is an authentic reproduction of the rifle actually used by Lt. Col. Custer on the Great Plains. In fact, one of Lone Star's Custer rifles is on display in the Living History Center at the Little Big Horn Battlefield.

For lightweight hunting rifles, there is Lone Star's No. 5, weighing about 6 lbs., and chambered in 24-35, 30-30, 30-40 Krag or 33 Winchester.

The No. 2 & 7 rifles are limited offerings and available

Frontier gunsmith Carlos Gove modified the Remington rolling block for side lever operation. Lone Star offers the same conversion.

in 17 HMR, 22 LR, 25-20 WCF, 32-20 WCF and 44-40 WCF.

And finally, the Gove side-lever "conversion" is a most elegant rendition of frontier gunsmith Carlos Gove's adaptation of the classic rolling-block action. Of course, the Lone Star rifle isn't a conversion of a previously existing rifle at all, but a rifle made from the ground up. It's just true to the Gove conversion's mechanics.

The option list for Lone Star Rifles is delightfully bewildering. But anyone considering a rifle for target competition should seriously consider the set trigger option for any rifle. Calibers? Pick your favorite from 22 RF to 50-140.

Another great part about Lone Star is that they deliver. Literally. Most orders take less than a year from placement to delivery. And such alacrity cannot be found everywhere.

In addition, Lone Star offers an outstanding restoration service for rolling blocks. They can even "antique" certain parts to make them match the patina and color that may already exist on an old firearm. So whether you're interested in a factory-new roller, or the restoration of an original, you'll find a great resource at www.lonestarrifle.com.

Lozito-Wolf Sharps, Sights and Accessories

It's a good thing that gunsmith Joe Lozito gets bored easily. Otherwise, he wouldn't have gone from one skill to another, and then put them all together in some of the most

If the beauty, simplicity and heritage of the classic rolling block appeals to you, then a Lone Star rolling block will overwhelm you. This one was made for gun writer Mike Venturino.

amazing single-shot actions and accoutrements that I've ever seen.

In partnership with master machinist and designer, Don Wolf, of nearby Huntington, NY, Lozito makes the most amazing Sharps actions I've ever seen!

The standard Lozito-Wolf Sharps Borchardt action sets the baseline for astonishment. And it gets better from there. This action is cut from a block of 4130, or other chrome-moly steel, to tolerances that the original Borchardts cannot match. Everything is perfect, including the finish polish. And, as with the original Sharps 1878, the Lozito-Sharps will accommodate virtually any rimmed or rimless cartridge. Want one with recessed wood panels? No problem. Want one with Zischang double set triggers? Just ask. Engraving, integral tang sight bases and more are also available. All from the skilled hands of Joe Lozito.

Remember I used the word "astonishment" above? That description comes into play with full force when you realize that Lozito-Wolf plans to introduce an improved 1878 with completely contained springs, improved striker arrangement, double-set triggers, integral tang sight base and an ambidextrous safety located in the forward lever loop that's automatically set when you open the action. In addition, you can choose between a single hunting trigger or double-set arrangement. To say it trumps Hugo Borchardt's mechanical design is an understatement. However, it does keep the sleek design shape of the original. That's hard to improve upon.

But the *piece de resistance* is yet to come. Lozito-Wolf plans to offer their own recreation of the mysterious Sharps 1875 action. Only two originals were ever made, and only one is known to still exist. And through careful research and study, Lozito and Wolf have made a perfectly functioning reproduction. The absolutely fascinating aspect of this action is that by moving a kidney-shaped button at the back of the hammer axle you can engage (or disengage) an internal mechanism that automatically re-cocks the hammer as the action's lever is closed. It is unbelievably neat. In fact, people who have seen the original Sharps 1875 think that the Lozito-Wolf action is a bit *too* close of a copy! So, if you'd like one for yourself, don't wait. Contact Lozito-Wolf ASAP. There's going to be a long line-up for these actions.

But Joe Lozito's skills and products don't stop with the Sharps. He also makes precision-machined Soule-style tang sights, globe and windgauge front sights, wood and ivory handled turnscrews, oil bottles, ball-and-needle-bearing cleaning rods and more. Each item is made with a precision and finish quality that simply befuddles the mind.

And if you think I'm being just a little too generous with my praise for Lozito-Wolf, I encourage you to visit their web site at www.lozito-wolf.com, e-mail them at requestinfo@lozito-wolf.com or phone them at 631-242-9782. The address is Lozito-Wolf, 51 Garden City St., Bay Shore, NY 11706. The color brochure they send you will prove that I've been quite restrained here. And believe me, it wasn't easy.

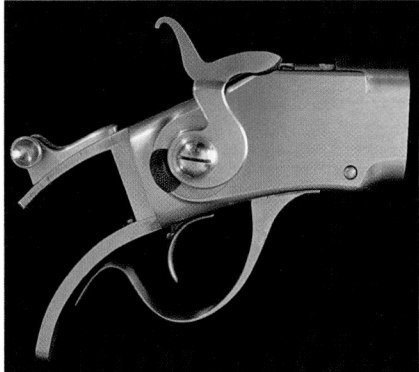

Top: Lozito-Wolf makes this beautiful reproduction of the famous and mysterious Sharps 75 action. The kidney-shaped button behind the hammer axle activates the auto re-cock mechanism.

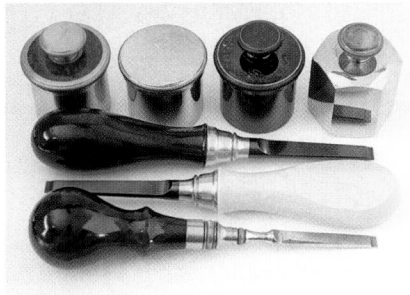

Bottom: A proper component of every fine cased rifle is a custom set of turnscrews and oil/grease bottles. These are also available, custom-order from Lozito-Wolf.

Lyman

This company is almost as old as breech-loading single-shots themselves. And all through its history, Lyman has been the "go-to source" for equipment to keep these great rifles shooting.

With the revival of the 405 Winchester (essentially a nitro powder version of the 40-70 Sharps Straight), there has been a collateral need for an appropriate cast bullet. To fill that

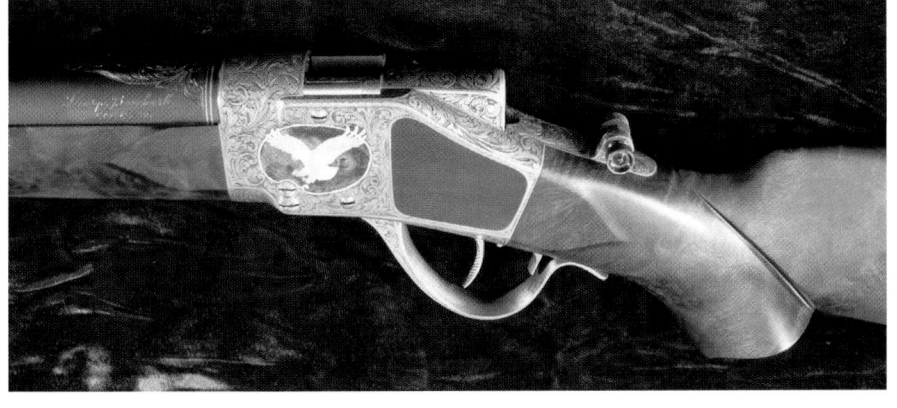

This is Joe Lozito's personal Sharps-Borchardt rifle. He made the action, the stock, engraved it, and even color-cased the inset on the frame with the inlaid gold eagle.

Single-Shot Rifle Review

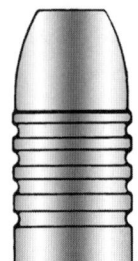
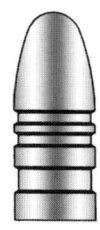

Left: Lyman has also brought back the #515142 mould for 50-caliber rifles. As its number suggests, this one weighs about 515 grs. in No. 2 alloy. It will handle anything.

Right: Lyman has re-introduced its #412263 mould. This 288-gr. bullet was especially designed for the 405 Winchester, but it works well in most any 40-caliber single-shot.

void, Lyman has re-introduced its #412263 bullet mould. This 288-grain bullet was especially designed for the 405 in the early 20th century, and it's still one of the best 405 designs going. But just because it is "for the 405," you shouldn't pigeonhole this mould at all. It works very well in most any 40-caliber single-shot when sized to the appropriate diameter for your rifle. So whether you have a 405 or not, this mould's worth a try.

Another revival from Lyman's classic mould list is the #515142 mould for 50-caliber rifles. As its number suggests, this one weighs about 515 grains in No. 2 alloy, and is a flying locomotive against wind, targets, bison —or just about anything that walks the North American continent. If you own, or plan on owning, a "Big 50" single-shot of any sort, this is the Big Bullet that goes with it.

But these new moulds don't even scratch the surface of all the great stuff Lyman has to offer the single-shot aficionado. See it all at www.Lymanproducts.com.

Meacham Tool & Hardware

Meacham continues to make some of the best Winchester Model 1885 repros going. Not only in terms of the metal, but the wood as well.

Meacham's period stocks are virtual copies of the classic Winchester profiles. In fact, it's very hard to tell they weren't made in New Haven.

This year, Meacham has two new items of special interest. The first is a benchrest version of the 1885 that's targeted (no pun intended) to the experimenter or serious hole-punching shooter. The Benchrest 85 features a 28-inch barrel that's drilled and tapped for scope mounts and can be chambered for virtually any rimmed cartridge. The forearm is flat-bottomed and 2 inches wide for a steady interface with the benchrest sandbags. In addition, the rifle has a traditional, wide Niedner buttplate to handle the recoil of shot after shot. Winchester never made one like this ... but accuracy buffs are going to love it.

Meacham hasn't overlooked the genius of Harry Pope in their new products either. Steve Meacham now offers a Pope-style bullet lubricator that pushes bullets into the lube chamber base-first. This approach eliminates the need for specific top punches to conform to the bullet nose, reduces deformation and thus enhances accuracy. This tool is a great update of the classic Pope design, and can be used right at the bench if you want ... which is a big reason why Harry designed it that way. In addition, Meacham has its own version of the unbeatable Pope re-decap tool. This is a hand-operated gizmo that knocks out spent primers and seats new ones in a cartridge case. It's pretty much indispensable for the breech-seating schuetzen enthusiast.

Meacham's list of traditional shooting goodies goes on. They have Unertl style scope bases, straight-line bullet seater dies, blackpowder compression dies, neck sizer dies and more. And it's all made to the famous Meacham quality standards.

But Winchester-style single-shot rifles are the mainstay of the Meacham operation. Meacham makes these in low-wall or high-wall style, and in five basic configurations: Helm Schuetzen, Special Target, Special Sporting,

Benchrest and Silhouette (high-wall only). Every Meacham receiver and block is CNC-machined. Each block is hand-lapped into the frame. Barrels are hand-fitted; wood is the best American black walnut ... and accuracy is outstanding.

Meacham also offers a plethora of options and special features, including your choice of Winchester-style plain, single-set or double-set Schuetzen triggers. So check Meacham's web site for one of the best Winchester single-shot repros available: www.meachamrifles.com.

Montana Vintage Arms

Without MVA sights, a lot of single-shot rifles couldn't exhibit the accuracy that they do.

This company's mainstay is a host of traditional tang sights based on the windage-adjustable Soule design.

Now MVA is making a series of classic 6x scopes with 3/4-inch tubes, parallax adjustment, Pope-style rib and battery stop, adjustable eyepiece and external adjustable Malcolm-type mounts. Lengths range from 23 inches on up to fit barrels as long as 34 inches.

There are also Sharps tang sights and a hunting-style Marble's configuration. In front sights, MVA offers Sharps, Stevens and Winchester-style globe sights, many with "windgauge" adjustment.

And great sights aren't all that you can get from MVA. They also have a Stevens-Pope-style palm rest, wooden scope cases, Winchester sight base screws (who hasn't needed these at least once?), crush-proof blackpowder cartridge blow tubes and an MVA powder measure that's the Rolls Royce of its kind for the blackpowder shooter. Peruse it all at www.montanavintagearms.com.

Navy Arms

You may have heard about that fabulous cache of antique firearms that was recently uncovered in Nepal. Well, Navy Arms managed to get a share of that terrific stuff, along with some good luck in other parts of the world. The result is probably a last-chance-in-a-lifetime opportunity to snag some incredible single-shots.

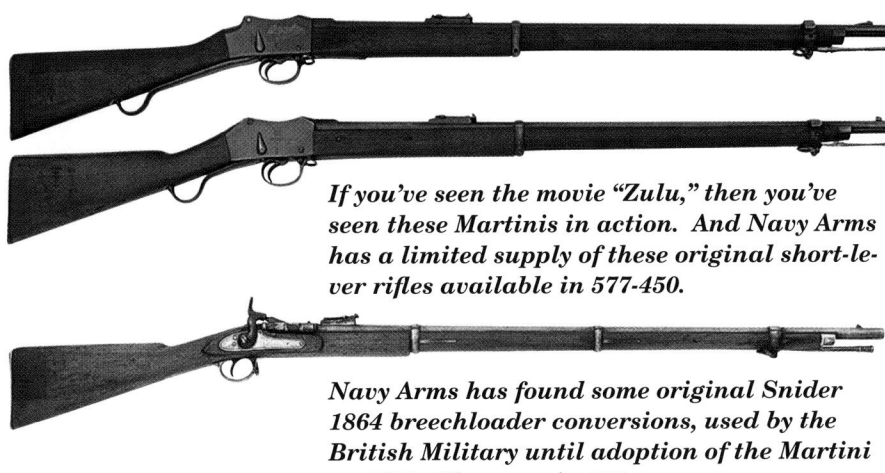

If you've seen the movie "Zulu," then you've seen these Martinis in action. And Navy Arms has a limited supply of these original short-lever rifles available in 577-450.

Navy Arms has found some original Snider 1864 breechloader conversions, used by the British Military until adoption of the Martini in 1871. These are in 577.

For example, Navy has found a limited supply of original short-lever Martinis which may actually have been used in the famous "Zulu Wars." These guns aren't talking, but your imagination will. They're in original used condition, which varies, and they're chambered for the 577-450.

From the Nepal horde, Navy has the Martini Gahendra, rarest of all Martinis. It was based on a Westley Richards design, produced in the 1880s in Nepal and issued to their famous Ghurka regiments. Caliber for these rifles is also 577-450.

Navy has also turned up some original Snider 1864 breechloader conversions, used by the British Military until adoption of the Martini in 1871. These rifles were first issued in 1865, and featured a system conceived by Jacob Snider to convert the British P-1853 Enfield to breech-loading. These Sniders are in caliber 577.

Finally, Navy also offers a very good selection of imported rolling-block rifles, 1885 Winchester reproductions, 1873 trapdoor Springfield repros and nine Sharps 1874 model rifles.

Check out these rifles and a lot more at Navy Arms' web site, www.navyarms.com. Just don't wait. You'll kick yourself if you miss your chance at those great antique single-shots.

Remington

If the term "elegantly simple," applies to any single-shot rifle, it's the Remington Rolling Block.

These rifles were used in virtually every corner of the world, especially as a military rifle. Remington still offers the rolling block today through its custom shop.

The No. 1 rolling block is available in two models. The first is the Mid-Range Sporter with pistol-grip buttstock and blued receiver. The 30-inch round barrel has a 1:18 twist and is chambered for the 45-70 Govt. cartridge. This rifle also has a set trigger, figured wood and color-cased receiver. Other options are available. The Mid-Range is ready to go for BPCR shooting and meets all criteria.

Remington's rolling block Silhouette Target rifle is also built to meet all NRA BPCR competition requirements as-delivered. The barrel is heavy, straight, 30 inches long and chambered for the 45-70 Govt. A color-cased receiver and single-set trigger are standard equipment, as is a pistol grip, checkering and a recoil-absorbing shotgun style butt. No sights are furnished since many BPCR shooters prefer to choose their own. Remember, these rifles are the real McCoy: *Remington* rolling blocks. Get the details at www.remington.com.

Shiloh Sharps Rifle Co.

Since they made the famous rifle that Tom Selleck used in the movie "Quigley Down Under," the folks at Shiloh have had a philosophy. And now they've put it down into one succinct phrase: "From Foundry to Finish."

This means that if a company can have control and oversight over every aspect of the product they produce, that product can be made with exceptional quality and consistency. Shiloh is structured to do just that because it is a vertically integrated concern, and they make virtually all of the components that go into a Shiloh Sharps right there at their own facilities. Like they say, quality from foundry to the finish. And that even includes engraving.

For example, many Shiloh rifles are embellished by Shiloh's noted in-house engraver, Suzi Bradley. Her work is some of the best in the business. You can also choose your action's metal finish at Shiloh. This includes antique, French grey, plus bone charcoal or pack-hardened color case. Personally, I prefer the understated values of the antique finish and bone charcoal hardening, especially with the deeper engraving.

Other custom Shiloh features include your choice of buttplates (important for silhouette shooters), cheekpieces, forend tips, grip styles, barrel contours (for most models), iron sights, scopes and more. Shiloh also offers a range of shooting accessories that are bound to tempt your budget.

But the rifles are the real seduction! Shiloh's 1863 rifles are a recreation of the earliest Sharps design that used combustible paper cartridges. They're all offered in 50 or 54 caliber. The Sporting Rifle features a 30-inch octagon barrel with buckhorn rear sight and blade front, plus double-set triggers. The Military Rifle has a 30-inch round barrel and includes a ladder rear sight, military style iron block front sight and single trigger. The Carbine has a 22-inch round barrel, ladder rear sight and iron block front sight.

As drawn metallic cartridge cases came into widespread use shortly after the Civil War, Sharps adapted the 1863 to handle them and created the Model 1874. This

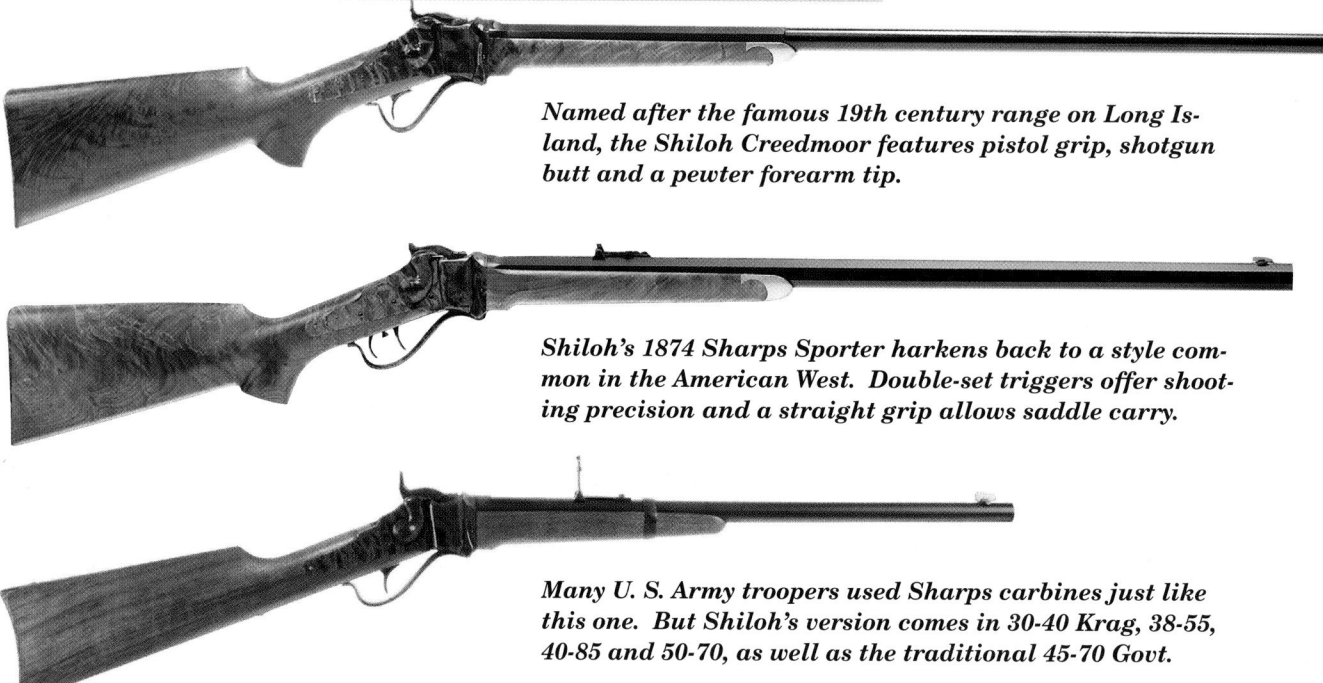

Named after the famous 19th century range on Long Island, the Shiloh Creedmoor features pistol grip, shotgun butt and a pewter forearm tip.

Shiloh's 1874 Sharps Sporter harkens back to a style common in the American West. Double-set triggers offer shooting precision and a straight grip allows saddle carry.

Many U. S. Army troopers used Sharps carbines just like this one. But Shiloh's version comes in 30-40 Krag, 38-55, 40-85 and 50-70, as well as the traditional 45-70 Govt.

became the classic "buffalo rifle" of the Great Plains, and is the mainstay of Shiloh's business today.

Shiloh makes no less than a dozen variants of the 1874, including the Creedmoor Silhouette Rifle, the Carbine, Hartford Model and more. This year, there's a new Carbine with a 22-inch round barrel, ladder rear sight and iron block front sight. Just pick one up and you instantly feel like a cavalryman of the 1870s. There's also a Military musket. Calibers range from 30-40 Krag to 50-90 2.5-inch.

One of Shiloh's newest offerings is a 6x scope with 3/4-inch tube. It has a blued steel finish with Malcolm-style mounts, Pope rib, parallax adjustment, four reticle options and comes in four lengths. Get the whole story of Shiloh products, plus some music you'll recognize, at www.shilohrifle.com.

Savage

Almost universally known for its classic Model 99 lever action, the Savage Arms Company's heritage reaches back to 1894 when Arthur Savage established the firm in Utica, New York. Since then, Savage has had its ups and downs, but is now on solid footing.

In fact, the ground is firm enough for Savage to re-introduce the Steven Favorite 30G single-shot ... although this rifle is made in Canada. I'm not reaching for a pun (at least deliberately) when I say the Favorite has been a real favorite with youngsters since it first appeared around the turn of the 20th century.

Today, the Stevens Favorite comes in 22 LR or 17 HMR, has a 20-inch half-octagon barrel with walnut-finished stocks and a schnable forend. The rear sight is adjustable and there's a post front sight ... pretty much the way great grandpa knew his Favorite. You can even get the Favorite in a take-down version for a few dollars more. This might be something to think about. Original Favorite take-downs command a very respectable price.

For more information, visit www.savagearms.com. It's a trip down memory lane.

Taylor & Co.

While you may not have been aware of this fine outfit, many shooters are. They've been around for 18 years, importing and selling a host of classic rifles.

In our prevue, that includes reproduction 1885 single shots

in both high-wall and low-wall configuration. These are made for Taylor in Italy. High-walls come in straight or pistol grip style in either 45-70 or 38-55. The low-walls are pistol grip only and can be ordered in 17 HM2, 17 HMR, 22 LR, 32-20 or 38-40.

Taylor also offers a broad selection of Italian-made Sharps rifles in 1859, 1863 and 1874 models. There is an especially impressive hand-engraved and gold-inlaid 1874 Deluxe that will tempt you to own just one more Sharps. These rifles are available in 45-70, 45-90 or 45-120. It all depends on how much "bang" you want for your buck.

Check out the whole Taylor line at www.taylorsfirearms.com.

Traditions

This outfit isn't just about blackpowder anymore. They sell Pedersoli single-shots, too: a rolling block repro in 45-70 with a brass barrel band, or five iterations of the 1874 Sharps rifle, all in 45-70. These are made by Pedersoli, so you know they're great quality. All models except the Standard 1874 come with double set triggers and target sights. The Deluxe is hand-engraved with satin-finished frame. You can also obtain some very

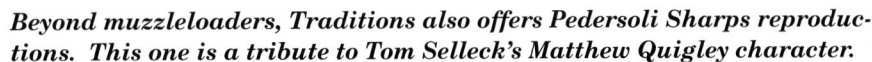

Beyond muzzleloaders, Traditions also offers Pedersoli Sharps reproductions. This one is a tribute to Tom Selleck's Matthew Quigley character.

nice tang and globe front sights from Traditions. Just visit their website at www.traditionsfirearms.com.

Treebone Carving

Show me a single-shot aficionado who doesn't have at least one "project gun" in the works, and I'll show you someone who really isn't serious about single-shots. Well, for everyone who needs a stock for whatever single-shot they're working on, there's Treebone Carving of Cimarron, New Mexico.

At Treebone, George Petersen has over 200 patterns and 4000 stock blanks to help make your project dreams come true. I know from personal experience that Treebone pre-turned stocks are precisely made and require only a minimum of final inletting to snug up to an action. What's more, they're carefully turned "on-center" which is a big help for any amateur craftsman. Patterns are available for the Remington rolling block, Winchester Single-Shot, Ballard, Sharps, Ruger, Trapdoor, Hepburn, Marlin and Winchester lever-guns, and more. Treebone also offers buttplates, traditional buttplate screws and forearm lugs.

George Petersen is a stand-up guy and prides himself on honest and responsible dealing. Proof of that comes through loud and clear on the Treebone web site, which has very valuable tutorial sections on how to fit stocks, with *lots* of pictures and great information. Check it out at www.treebonecarving.com or phone George at 505-376-2145.

Uberti

This Italian manufacturer was one of the first to offer a new version of the Winchester Model 1885 Single-Shot. And while the Uberti design has certain internal differences from the original Winchester "high-wall," it's

still a sound and well-made rifle that offers a lot of value for the money.

The foundation of the Uberti High-Wall line is the Sporting and Special Sporting single-shots. They're offered in 45-70 Govt., 45-90, and the bison-blasting 45-120 with 30 or 32-inch tapered octagon barrels that approximate the old Winchester No. 3 contour. The steel frame and lever are color case-hardened. Walnut stocks for the Sporting rifle feature a straight-grip buttstock with curved steel buttplate and traditional Schnabel forend. The Special Sporting version has a buttstock with a checkered pistol grip.

Those who prefer a slightly more compact rifle can choose Uberti's High-Wall Carbine in 45-70, but with a 28-inch tapered round barrel and a flat, shotgun style buttplate. Check Uberti's web site, www.uberti.com to see the design for yourself.

You can also get a reproduction No. 4 rolling block from Uberti with a 26-inch round or octagon barrel. The carbine model checks in with a round barrel at 22 inches in length. The forged steel frames are color case-hardened, trigger guards and buttplates are brass, and stocks are straight-grip walnut. Calibers available are 22 LR and 22 Mag. There's even a rolling block pistol available in the same calibers. And the price is a whole lot more reasonable than any original you might find.

Winchester

To paraphrase Mark Twain, "reports of Winchester's death are greatly exaggerated." That's especially true for rifles made outside of New Haven, Conn. One proof of this is Winchester's Model 1885.

While this Japanese-made version of the original Winchester Model 1885 is mechanically different than

John Browning's classic, it is still a mighty fine rifle. And it will continue to be available from U. S. Repeating Arms Co., current licensee of the Winchester name for firearms.

This year, the Winchester 1885 will be made in three versions. The specially engraved and gold-inlaid Centennial rifle will commemorate the 100th anniversary of the great .30-06 cartridge. The High-Wall Hunter will, once again, be available in a range of effective chamberings from 223 to 325 WSM. But you can also have a new low-wall 1885 with color-cased receiver and 24-inch sporter weight barrel in 22 LR or 17 Mach 2. See them all – alive and well – at www.winchesterguns.com.

Friends of Billy Dixon

This is not about single-shots or their accoutrements. It's about where you can put them to the ultimate test.

Once a year in June, at Scenic Mesa Ranch, Hotchkiss, Colorado (near Grand Junction), The Friends of Billy Dixon hold a match in commemoration of Dixon's famous 1538-yard shot at the Battle of Adobe Walls. Billy made his storied shot on June 29th, 1874.

To characterize this new match as ultra-long range target-shooting is an understatement. Target placement *starts* at 1000 yards, and extends out to 2000 yards.

The scaled steel targets are either animal silhouettes by artist David Torkelson or round gongs. But one solid hit at ranges like this is worth 20 at any shorter distance. For the long-range shootist, this will be the supreme challenge. For more information on dates and the shoot program, e-mail Mic McPherson at micmac@fone.net , Dave Torkelson at shevid@i70west.com or phone Scenic Ranch at 970-872-3078.

SHOTGUNS TODAY:

SHOTGUN REVIEW

by John Haviland

More and more shotguns are being imported into America. Marlin firearms justified having their new L.C. Smith guns made in Italy because: "Manufacturing costs prevent them from being American-made." Several American companies still haven't admitted defeat. Ruger makes all its guns in America and its Gold Label side-by-side sells very well. Remington, for the most part, fills its green boxes with American-made shotguns. Time will tell whether its new Model 105 Cti autoloader will put a dent in the popularity of Italian-made autoloaders.

Let's see what's new in shotguns, both imported and those made in America:

Benelli

The Nova pump is the gun many hunters carry when the mud's deep and the geese fly high. This year the Nova's one-piece buttstock and receiver separate at the head of the grip and the new gun is called the SuperNova. This allows the choice of several different buttstocks: the SteadyGrip vertical grip; camo and black ComforTech with gel inserts to reduce recoil and the ComforTech with an extra high comb for using a scope and a collapsible stock.

The Ultra Light 12 gauge is the

M2 autoloader slimmed down to six pounds. The Ultra Light loses a pound of weight with a shorter forearm, a 24-inch barrel and rib made of carbon fiber. The gun's walnut stock is coated with a "WeatherCoat" finish that Benelli states is impervious to any kind of weather. The gun comes with a set of shims to adjust cast and comb height, and five screw-in chokes. Everything fits in a hard case.

The M2 Field 20 gauge now has the ComforTech system in its buttstock. The gel buttpad spreads recoil over a wide area to reduce felt recoil. The gel inserts in the stock also flex during recoil to absorb some of the recoil's bite, and the soft comb insert is gentle to the cheek.

A dressed up Montefeltro is now called the Montefeltro Silver. The 12- or 20-gauge guns wear fancy walnut. The nickel-plated receiver is engraved with a pair of quail and a pointing setter in gold.

Beretta

There are four new Beretta shotguns: the 682 LTD, AL391 Teknys Gold Target featuring two interchangeable vent ribs, the 3901 Rifled Slug Shotgun for the American big-game hunter, and the 3901 Target RL created especially for new shooters, women and youth. The Target RL 12-gauge shotgun

The Blaser F3 12 gauge.

The Blaser F3's steel receiver measurers slightly less than 2.5 inches tall to make a very low profile gun.

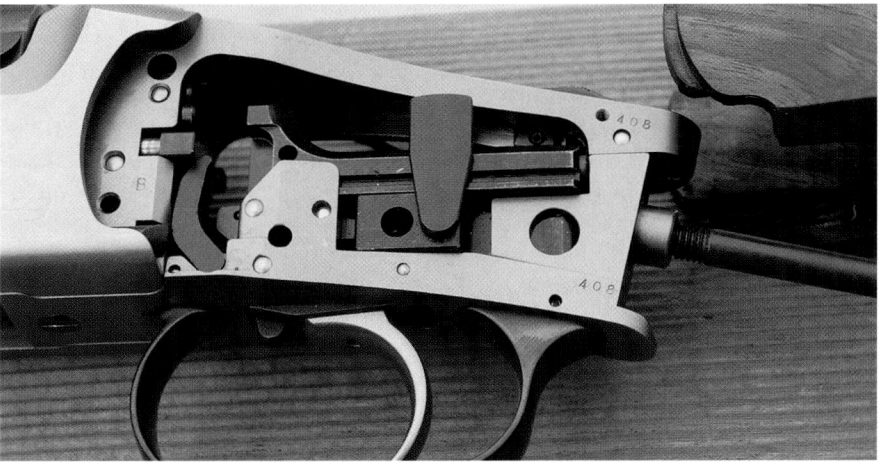

The inner workings of the Blaser F3.

is for smaller-stature shooters with an adjustable length of pull from 12 to 13 inches. The stock is also adjustable for cast on/off and comes equipped with Beretta's Memory System II to adjust the parallel comb. Magazine plugs can limit the gun to a single shot. This semiautomatic comes with either 26- or 28-inch barrels, a flat rib and a white mid and front bead. The stock and forearm are walnut finished in satin matte.

The 682 LTD is limited to 400 guns and has oil-finished expensive walnut stocks and hand checkering. Gold-filled engraving accents the sides and bottom of the matte-silver receiver. The gun is available in Sporting and Trap models.

The AL391 Teknys Gold Target has a 30-inch barrel with two interchangeable ribs. One is a flat rib for sporting, Skeet and the field that shoots flat patterns. A second is a stepped rib for trap shooting that shoots 70 percent of patterns above the point of aim. An 8.5-ounce recoil reducer in the stock cuts kick. A weighted magazine cap is also available to move balance forward.

The 3901 Rifled Slug Shotgun is a 12-gauge, gas-operated semiautomatic gun with a three-inch chamber. Its rifled 24-inch barrel has a cantilever rail to mount either sights or a scope. The stock is black synthetic, with pressed-in checkering.

Blaser

Because of Blaser's new F3 over/under, I cannot go back to South Dakota. During a pheasant hunt there last season I missed only three shots with the F3 the whole trip. While I

stood on top of a dirt bank a rooster flushed behind me and I turned and killed it. Another rooster flew far to my left and I killed it with the second barrel. A third cock jumped up 35 yards out as I closed the gun on two new shells. I knocked it out of the air. That went on the whole trip.

I was shooting way over my head. But I'm not going to tell that to Scott Mathews and his guides at Bad River Bucks & Birds (www.badriverhunts.com), in order to keep my reputation intact.

The new F3 had a lot to do with my above-average shooting. The gun weighed about eight pounds and its 28-inch barrels kept the gun's balance about in the middle of the gun. That worked well for point-and-shoot-shots and swinging the gun on crossing pheasants.

The F3 is made in Germany by Blaser Jagdwaffen and imported by Sigarms. The 12-gauge gun comes in Game and Competition Sporting and Trap models and guns with extensive engraving and high dollar wood.

The F3's steel receiver measures slightly less than 2.5 inches tall to make a very low profile gun. An underlug engages a recess in the bottom of the receiver to lock up the gun. The front of this lock is adjustable and can be replaced, if it wears over time. The hinge pins on both sides of the receiver that the barrels pivot on, the face of the breech and the firing pins can also be easily replaced.

The trigger assembly has what Blaser calls the Inertia Block System to prevent the hammers from striking forward unless the trigger is pulled and to prevent double firing. The trigger blade is also adjustable for length and angle. A barrel selection button is located inside the trigger guard ahead of the trigger and the safety on the tang is not automatic. All barrel sets weigh the same, no matter if they are 27 to 32 inches, because contours are changed slightly.

The Game model I shot in South Dakota had a full forearm and both barrels fit in my forward hand. The right side of the grip had a slight swell. My hands and my eyes worked together and the pheasants never had a chance.

Kevin Wistner, Sigarms national manager, said the German engineers listened to what Americans wanted in an over/under shotgun. "I think they got it right," Wistner said.

Browning

The Gold Superlite Micro shotgun promises to be a favorite among smaller-stature shooters. Weighing 6 pounds, 6 ounces, this little 20 gauge has a back-bored barrel, speed loading and soft shooting gas-operated system. Add to that a three-inch chamber in its 26-inch barrel and the Superlite can handle everything from dove to waterfowl.

The limited edition Browning NRA Gold Sporting shotgun represents the latest collaboration between Browning and the National Rifle Association. This model features a gold-filled NRA Heritage mark and motto on the left side of the receiver. With every gun sold, Browning will make a donation to the NRA Basic Firearms Training Program to help folks learn to enjoy firearms safely. The gun is available

Dave Henderson with his buck taken with a Remington BuckHammer 20-gauge slug fired from a Remington Sportsman 11-87 20-gauge slug gun.

in 12-gauge with a 2 3/4-inch chamber and a 28 or 30-inch barrel.

The Gold Evolve has taken on a new configuration in the Gold Evolve Sporting. This sleek version of the Gold has an alloy receiver, ported and back-bored barrel and 2 3/4-inch chamber. Five Invector-Plus choke tubes and a Hi Viz Tri-comp fiber-optic front sight round out the gun.

Evidently more than one shooter likes the Browning Cynergy over/under shotguns, but not its lines and strange-looking recoil pad. For those, Browning has made the Cynergy Classic Field and Sporting. These guns have traditional shotgun lines and a conventional butt stock configuration and silver nitride receiver.

The Browning Silver autoloading shotgun comes in three styles with a slight hump at the back of its receiver reminiscent of the old Browning A-5. The gas-operated gun is being promoted as a slightly less expensive gun than the Gold.

The Silver Hunter has a silver finish on the receiver and a checkered walnut stock and forearm. The gun comes in 3 or 3 1/2-inch 12 gauge with a 26-, 28- or 30-inch barrel. The Silver Stalker has a matte black finish and a composite stock and forearm. The Silver Camo is covered with either Mossy Oak Break-Up or Shadow Grass.

Ithaca

For the last 20-some years Ithaca has gone through financial difficulties. When the company closed its doors in 2005 nearly everyone thought that would be the end of the Ithaca. But Floyd and Craig Marshall had other ideas and bought the company in late 2005 and moved it to their MoldCraft mold and tool manufacturing plant in Upper Sandusky, Ohio.

In early 2006 the new Ithaca company concentrated on assembling guns from Model 37 parts on hand. In March of this year the Marshalls produced their first batch of Model 37 receivers and barrels. "First we're making a Turkey Slayer gun and then a police gun," Craig Marshall said. "A lot of people got stiffed

by the old company on the 125th anniversary (Model 37) guns, so we'll also be making what I call the 125th-plus one anniversary gun."

In the near future Marshall hopes to introduce more Model 37 guns. One is a small-bore gun for skeet shooters and young hunters. "There's a lot of interest," Marshall said. "The phone has been just ringing off the hook."

Remington

Remington has gone all out with its completely new CTi autoloader. The most notable feature is its skeleton receiver of titanium with a carbon-fiber housing. The gun feeds and ejects from the bottom of the receiver. A speed-loader system feeds the first shell into the chamber. The shell in the chamber and in the magazine can be quickly unloaded. The 12-gauge gun with a three-inch chamber weighs seven pounds.

Other features include a rotating, locking bolt head, Remington's TriNyte coating to protect the receiver, a trigger with a pull of 3-1/2 to 4 pounds and a cross-bolt safety that can be switched for a left-hand shooter.

Remington states four features in the CTi reduces felt recoil by half:

* An oil-filled cylinder in the stock regulates bolt speed.

* An R3 recoil pad absorbs recoil.

* A gas system spreads recoil over a longer time.

* An overbored barrel and a lengthened forcing cone provide less resistance to the shot column.

The Model 1100 G3 is said to have an enhanced gas-operating system that will handle 2-3/4 and 3-inch shells, keep the gun cleaner and reduce wear. The G3 comes in 12 and 20 gauge and the receiver wears Remington's Titanium PVD coating to guard against handling and the weather. All internal operating parts are nickel-plated and Teflon coated.

The Model 1100 Competition 12-gauge has an extended carrier release and a 30-inch barrel with a wide ten millimeter rib. The barrel bore is overbored and its forcing cone is lengthened. Five ProBore choke tubes are standard. A trap

Tes Salb with her buck taken with a Remington BuckHammer 20-gauge slug fired from a Remington Sportsman 11-87 20-gauge slug gun.

This Remington BuckHammer 20-gauge slug was retrieved from a dead Alabama buck.

⏩ • ⏩ • ⏩ • ⏩ • ⏩ • ⏩

version has an adjustable comb. All internal operating parts are nickel-plated and Teflon-coated.

The Special Purpose shotguns have received some enhancements. The 11-87 and 870 SPS-Turkey Super Magnum Camos are covered with Mossy Oak Obsession and their receivers are drilled and tapped for scope mounts. The 11-87 Turkey and Slug guns also have the option of a thumbhole stock.

The 11-87 Sportsman line now includes a 20-gauge slug gun. This synthetic stocked gun has a matching black matte finish on its metal. A cantilever scope base is mounted on its 21-inch rifled barrel. With a scope locked onto the barrel, instead of the

receiver, a slug gun seems to shoot much more precisely. That is certainly the case with one of these 20-gauge 11-87s I used deer hunting last fall. The gun punched out groups from two to three inches at 100 yards time after time with Remington's 2-3/4 and 3-inch BuckHammer slugs. I shot one whitetail doe with the 2 3/4-inch BuckHammer slug at about 80 yards. The slug went through both shoulders and the deer was dead right there.

The whole idea of the 11-87 20-gauge is a light-recoiling slug gun. The Sportsman 11-87 does that with a gas system that spreads recoil over a longer period and a R3 recoil pad thick as a pillow. The new Managed-Recoil BuckHammer slugs make the

gun even gentler on the shoulder.

The Model 870 pump continues to add models and features:

* This is the last year for the Dale Earnhardt Tribute shotguns. This year's gun is an 870 Wingmaster 20 gauge. Earnhardt's likeness and signature are engraved on the left side of the receiver.

* The 870 Express line has the option of a brown laminate stock and forearm.

* The 870 Express synthetic versions are offered in Mossy Oak Break-Up and Shadow Grass camo patterns.

* A Super Magnum Turkey barrel is available for 870s. The barrel comes with TruGlo fiber optic sights and a super-Full Hevi-Shot Choke Tube.

* The well-worn term "Tactical" has been applied to 870. The Tactical Speedfeed and SpecOps 870s have 18-inch barrels, olive drab finishes and pistol grip stocks.

* The NRA Edition Wingmaster is a 12 gauge with the NRA logo engraved on the right side of the receiver and the NRA Heritage logo on the left side.

Remington has given up on making an over/under shotgun and instead put its name on an Italian gun, the Premier Over &

Under. Models available include the Competition in 12-gauge and the Field and Upland in 12, 20 and 28 gauge.

The Competition has 28 or 30-inch barrels with a wide rib and white mid and front beads. The walnut stock has a slight swell on the right of the grip. The forearm has a Schnabel tip. The barrel selector is located on the tang safety and the receiver has a titanium coating.

The Field and Upland share most of the same features. But the Field has 26 or 28-inch barrels and a nickel-finished receiver. The Upland has a case-colored receiver with game scene engraving accented with gold.

Remington's Spartan line of imported guns continues to grow. The SPR453 autoloader handles all 12-gauge shells up to 3-1/2 inches. The gun's bolt face has dual extractors and its gas system is adjustable for smooth cycling. Barrel lengths are 24, 26 or 28 inches and include four screw-in choke tubes.

Marlin

Back in 1945, Marlin bought The Hunter Arms Company, of Fulton, New York, maker of the L.C. Smith side-by-side shotgun. Nicknamed the "Elsie", this sidelock double gun was made for a few years in the Marlin plant before being phased out.

To bring back the name, Marlin is importing an Italian gun and calling it the L.C. Smith. The new side-by-side wears side plates to echo the look of the original Smith guns. Although there was no over-and-under L.C. Smith, Marlin is offering 12 and 20-gauge over-and-under models.

The LC12-DB 12-gauge double barrel has three-inch chambers, a single trigger and selective automatic ejectors. The 28-inch barrels have a solid rib, and come with three screw-in choke tubes. Its walnut stock is checkered and the forearm has a beavertail shape. The 20-gauge version is similar, with 26-inch barrels.

The LC12-OU over/under wears 28-inch barrels with a ventilated rib, three-inch chambers and comes with three screw-in choke tubes. The 20 gauge has 26-inch barrels.

Mossberg

The Tactical Turkey Hunting Series features a polymer stock with a length of pull that is easily adjusted with a push of a button from 10-3/4 to 14-5/8 inches. The forend strap provides a stable resting position for the shooter's hand. These features are on the 835 Ulti-Mag, 535 ATS and 500 pumps. The guns include 20-inch ventilated rib barrels with adjustable fiber-optic sights and the new X-Factor ported Turkey choke tubes. The same setup is on the Special Purpose 500 Tactical, although in all black or Marinecote metal finish and black stock and forearm.

Savage

Savage is also importing Italian over/under shotguns. The Milano guns come in 12, 20, 28 gauges and .410-bore. Savage states the receivers of the guns are scaled to fit each gauge. However, the 12 gauge weighs 7-1/4 pounds, the 20 and 28 6 pounds and the .410 6-1/4 pounds. The guns have walnut stocks and firearms with modest point checkering patterns. The guns have automatic ejectors, a single selective trigger and a manual safety on the tang.

Winchester

Winchester has upgraded its Super X2 autoloader to the Super X3. The new gun's stock, grip and forearm are slimmer. An alloy magazine tube and a lightweight barrel with a narrow profile further reduce weight. The barrel bore is backbored to .742-inch and the new gunmetal gray Perma-Cote is more durable than traditional bluing. The X3's self-adjusting Active Valve ensures recoil reduction and durability in all conditions with all 12-gauge shells.

The SX3 comes in four models. The SX3 Field weighs only 6-1/2 pounds. A Pachmayr Decelerator recoil pad takes the sting out of three-inch magnum shells. A hard heel insert provides a slick surface on the pad that won't grab clothing when shouldering the gun. Spacers between the pad and stock are easily added or removed to adjust length of pull. The composite synthetic stock wears a Dura-Touch

Armor Coating ensuring a sure grip on the gun. Its metal wears a Perma-Cote finish on its metal. The Cantilever Deer is similar to the Composite, but wears a 22-inch rifled barrel. The barrel has a TRUGLO fiber optic front sight and a cantilever base to accept sights and scopes. The Waterfowl and Camo Field chambers 12-gauge 3-1/2 shells and wears Mossy Oak camo from muzzle to butt.

Winchester has added three models to its Select over/unders. The Midnight has high gloss bluing on its metal, and engraving of game birds accented with gold on both sides of the receiver. The White Field Extreme has an engraved silver nitrate receiver with oval pattern checkering on its grip and forearm. The White Field Traditional has more customary point pattern checkering.

Here's a wrap-up of new guns—

* The CZ Ringneck and Bobwhite side-by-sides are now chambered in 16 gauge. The Ringneck has a round knob grip and semi-beavertail forearm. It has a single trigger and 28-inch barrels choked Improved Cylinder and Modified. The Bobwhite has 26-inch barrels with the same chokes, double triggers and a straight grip and splinter forearm.

* New England Firearms' Partner pump line has been expanded to include walnut stocks in 12 and 20 gauge. A 12 gauge with a 3 1/2-inch chamber has also been added as well as a slug gun in 12 and 20, with rifled barrels and adjustable sights.

* SKB has an adjustable rib for its 85TSS trap over/unders. Patterns can be adjusted from flat-shooting to placing 90 percent of the pattern above the point of aim.

* Weatherby's Athena D'Italia Deluxe Shotgun is available in 12, 20 and 28 gauge. The side-by-side has extensive engraving, a single trigger and a wide choice of screw-in chokes. The Turkish walnut stock has a straight grip and a splinter forearm. Checkering is 24 lines per inch.

* Zoli of Italy Columbus target and game guns are aimed at the American market. The guns have titanium choke tubes, easy trigger assembly removal and extensive engraving on the receiver.

TODAY'S MUZZLELOADING ✛ BLACKPOWDER REVIEW

by Doc Carlson

There is no doubt the modern inline has taken over as the foremost rifle for muzzleloading hunters. Since its introduction in the mid-1980s this style of muzzleloader has taken the hunting market by storm. Many of the older muzzleloading manufacturers have dropped the majority of their traditional models in favor of the faster-selling inline rifle. There are still some, however, that like the style, beauty and nostalgia of a traditional muzzleloading rifle. These guns are still a large part of the hunting scene and prized family heirlooms, in many cases. And while there are still a wide range of models and styles available, many are turning to custom, hand-built guns that combine artistry with practical function in a gun to be used for hunting, target shooting, display as an art object—or all three.

Jim Chambers is a well-known contemporary gunmaker who made his reputation building fine Kentucky-style rifles. A few years back, he began assembling kits that could be sold to amateur gunmakers. The kit is a way for those who don't feel they can afford the services of a custom maker to acquire a top quality rifle. They also appeal to those who get a lot of satisfaction creating a finished rifle from the various parts. Many of the well-known custom makers often

start with one of the Chambers kits also, as they take a lot of the drudgery and sweat out of the building process, leaving more time for the artistry of carving, engraving and inlay work.

Chambers' kits start with top quality parts, using components that represent the epitome of 18th century rifle-making technology. He starts with locks that he produces himself. These are patterned after period locks and made from high carbon steel. The lock is carefully assembled and fitted, with all parts hardened and tempered where required. These locks would be right at home on the bench of the finest English or American gunbuilders of yesteryear. All that is required of the home builder is to polish and finish the outside of the lock, which is ready to go as furnished with the kit.

Stocks supplied as standard with the kits are nicely-figured hard maple. More highly figured wood can be ordered if one wishes, or cherry or walnut can be specified. The hard grunt work has been done on the stock wood. The stock, as supplied, is 95 percent shaped to the style of the rifle ordered, and inletting for the lock and barrel are 95 percent complete. Buttplate (always an inletting challenge), trigger guard, patch box and side plate are all 95 percent inletted. The machining of

the stock is held to a few thousands of an inch tolerance, and the final fitting of parts is well within the capabilities of anyone with even marginal tool savvy. The ramrod hole is drilled and the groove in the forend is machined. Stocks can be ordered with either a sliding wood patch box or a brass one—whichever catches your fancy. There is enough wood left on the stock so that any carving or individual decoration that the builder wishes can be done.

Barrels are top quality and supplied by Getz Barrel Company, Rice Barrel Company, Long Hammock Barrels and W.E. Rayl, Inc.—all well-known for fine-shooting barrels. You can specify which barrel company you want, if you have a preference. Barrels come with the barrel tennons installed, the front sight dovetail cut and the breech plug fitted. The breech plug carries a long tang that allows the builder to shape it, or cut it back to his preference. All screws and pins required for installation of the barrel and other parts are included with the kit.

The brass fittings—the buttplate, trigger guard, ramrod thimbles, end cap, etc.—are all easily worked soft yellow brass. This material finishes and polishes well and doesn't have any of the off-red color of the more common bronze.

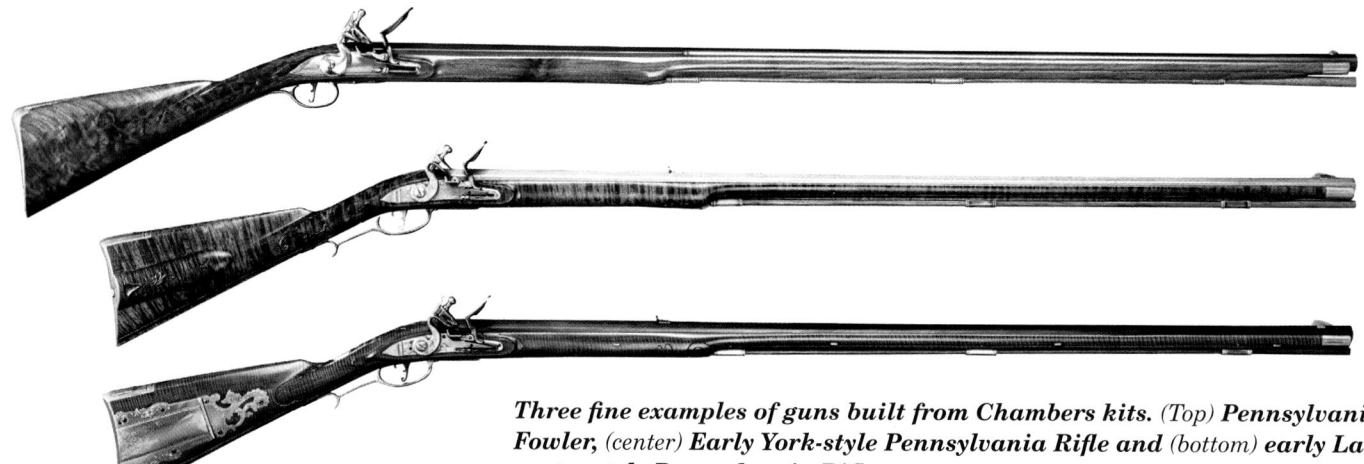

*Three fine examples of guns built from Chambers kits. (Top) **Pennsylvania Fowler**, (center) **Early York-style Pennsylvania Rifle** and (bottom) **early Lancaster-style Pennsylvania Rifle**.*

The kits can be ordered in several styles including Early Lancaster, Early York, Isaac Haines, Edward Marshall or Virginia-style Kentucky rifles. An early smooth-bored "rifle," New England colonial fowler and English fowler styles are also offered. Recently added is a nicely designed English Gentleman's Sporting Rifle in English walnut. There is also a Kentucky-style American pistol, if you are so inclined.

While these kits have most of the difficult fitting and shaping done, they still require some familiarity with working wood and metal. The components are of the best quality but, of course, the look and quality of the finished gun will depend upon your skills in finishing etc. If, on receiving the kit, it appears to be beyond what you can handle, Jim

Chambers will either set you up with a professional gun builder who can put it together for you—or he'll take it back for a full refund, no questions asked, if the kit parts are unaltered.

The Chambers kits are an excellent starting place for the creation of a top-quality functional firearm that can become a family heirloom. They allow the part-time hobby gun builder to produce a rifle of which he can be justly proud. The parts supplied are of the best quality and prices are well within the reach of the Average Joe. As stated before, many well-known custom rifle builders start with a Chambers kit. That tells you something about the quality that is in the box you receive.

If you are just getting your feet wet in gun-building, there are several good books that will lead you through

the process. A couple that come to mind are *The Art of Building the Pennsylvania Longrifle* by Dixon and *The Gunsmith of Greenville* by Peter Alexander; either or both will give step-by-step building directions and get you into carving and engraving. Both books are readily available from various muzzleloading suppliers.

American Pioneer Powder

American Pioneer Powder has added a premium-grade powder called Jim Shockey's Gold to their blackpowder substitute line of products. This new powder has one extra step added to the production process to give gilt-edged accuracy to the hunter. Available in either 50-grain premeasured compressed charge sticks for 45- or 50-caliber, or as loose powder in 2Fg or 3Fg granulations, the new powder is said to be even cleaner-burning and to give higher velocities with less variance shot-to-shot. As with other American Pioneer products, the powder contains no sulfur and

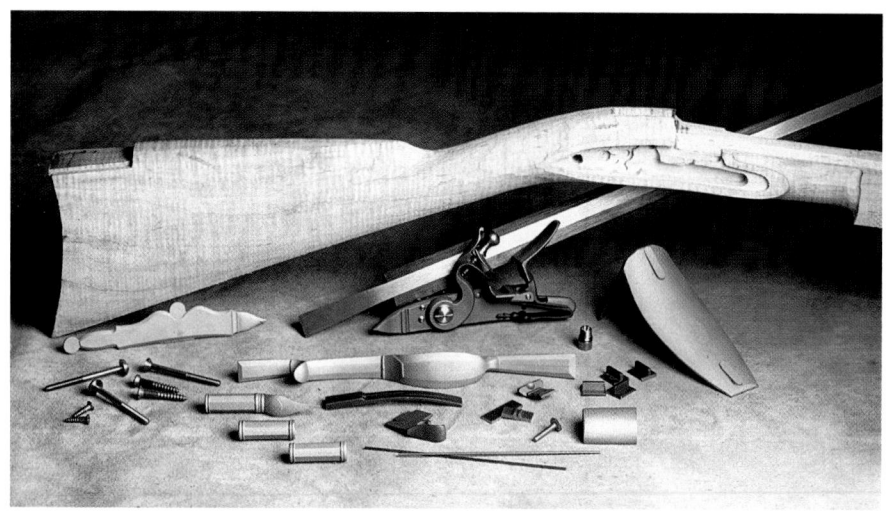

The kit comes with everything required to build a fine firearm except tools, finish and elbow grease.

The Gun Works English 4-bore rifle is one massive gun!

is recommended for sidelock guns in flint or percussion, inlines or cartridges for hunting or cowboy action shooting. It is easily ignited with a standard #11 percussion cap.

The Gun Works Muzzleloading Emporium

If building your own rifle isn't your cup of tea, there are many folks out there building top-quality traditional firearms. There is a wide variety of period correct, custom and semi-custom-made guns available to delight the heart of the shooter, hunter or collector who appreciates the guns of our forefathers.

During the time when the sun never set on the British Empire, English gunmakers were making beautiful hunting guns of large caliber for use in India and Africa. These guns were designed to take the largest and most dangerous animals on the face of the earth, and reliably served the hunter and explorer of the day. There are a few folks still producing these fine firearms today.

One of these is The Gun Works Muzzleloading Emporium, owned and operated by Joe and Suzi Williams. It is located in the Willamette Valley of Oregon, the destination of the Oregon Trail in days gone by. While the Williams offer all kinds of parts, etc., in their catalog, they also offer custom traditional muzzleloading arms: the Hawken, Pennsylvania and American Fowler-type guns (the Fowler available in both smoothbore and rifled versions). The Northwest Trade Gun is also available.

The gun that really caught my eye, however, was their English Sporting Rifle. The English gunmakers brought the muzzleloading hunting rifle to the peak of its development as a fast-handling well-fitting rifle that handled the recoil of big bores and heavy charges. Most English rifles that one handles are truly fine examples of the gunmakers' art; they literally ask to be taken hunting.

The English sporting rifles offered by The Gun Works are available in calibers from .45 to .69 as a normal thing. However, part of The Gun Works is the Oregon Barrel Company, and they make the barrels for the guns that they offer. The Oregon Barrel Company makes barrels from 32-caliber up to 2-bore. For those who are not up on the British designation of bore size, it is based upon the number of bore-sized lead round balls in a pound. Our modern shotgun gauges are based upon that same measure. Therefore, a 12-bore gun ran 12 balls to the pound—about a 72-caliber. The 2-bore would run two balls to the pound (an 8-ounce lead ball); about 1 1/4-inch bore diameter. There are very few barrel makers that make anything near that size. The fact that Oregon Barrel Co. does allows them to offer a real, honest-to-gosh large-bore elephant gun of the type used by Baker, Selous and the other famous ivory hunters of the mid-1800s.

The rifle in question is a 4-bore, English Sporting Rifle, typical of the highest development of the very large bore muzzle-loading African rifle. The pistol grip half-stock is walnut, with ebony grip cap and nose cap. The grip and forend are nicely checkered, as was typical on these guns. The Davis percussion lock is patterned after Alexander Henry locks. Alexander Henry was one of the better known makers of this type of rifle in the 1800s. The lock is a massive bar type that fits well on a gun of this size. The Oregon Barrel Company rifled barrel is octagon and tapers from 1-3/4 inches at the breech to 1-1/2 inches at the muzzle. It is 31-1/2 inches long and features a snail-type breech. Sights are the adjustable California type.

This massive gun weighs 18 pounds. The standard load is 250 grains of 1Fg or 2 Fg blackpowder behind a round ball that weighs around 1700 grains—about 1/4 of a pound! Suffice to say that this is not a rifle you shoot off a bench all day. Surprisingly, the big heavy rifles with English-styled stocks handle the heavy recoil very well. While they are not comparable to a 32-caliber squirrel rifle, the big guns are not seriously uncomfortable to shoot. The Brits definitely knew what they were about when they built guns.

In addition to the massive English sporting rifle, The Gun Works also offers custom rifles and smoothbores in about any style that one could wish for. So, if you are looking for a gun for any type of hunting or target shooting, or a serious rifle for dangerous game—or just want to have something that your hunting buddies will be impressed by—this is the outfit to contact.

Pacific Rifle Company

It appears Oregon is the place for the big-bore aficionado. Pacific Rifle Company, also based in Oregon, makes a large-bore rifle they call the 1837 Zephyr. This rifle is a little different than the average traditional gun. The rifle is based on the proven under-hammer action. This action has been around for well over a hundred years and offers several advantages. It is very simple, utilizing two moving parts: the trigger and the hammer. The mainspring is also the trigger guard.

The geometry of the trigger/hammer system delivers a very good trigger pull, one reason that many of this type action are seen on target rifles. The nipple is threaded directly into the bottom of the barrel, delivering the cap flame directly to the powder charge, similar to the modern in-line guns. The cap is protected from weather by being under the barrel, and the shooter is protected from flying cap parts upon firing. As the hammer is on the bottom of the gun, there is nothing to clutter the sight picture. The top of the barrel is clean, with no distractions. The barrel is seated into the steel receiver and the buttstock is held to the back side of the receiver with a through-bolt, a very stiff and solid setup. Hammer and trigger pivot on hardened steel pins. All-in-all, the under-hammer system is solid and relatively problem-free.

Pacific Rifle Company utilizes the Forsyth style of rifling with narrow lands and shallow grooves and very slow twist. This type of rifling was developed by a British officer in the mid-1800s for use with large-caliber round balls. It works very well and allows the ubiquitous round ball to be launched at higher velocities for flatter trajectories.

Pacific offers three major models of the Zephyr. All use musket caps for sure ignition of large powder charges. They all can be had with an integral recoil reduction system. Sights are buckhorn rear with German silver front blade, with other sight options available. The guns are supplied with browned barrels and receivers but engraving and optional finishes are available. Stocks are fancy American walnut finished with an oil and beeswax, hand rubbed finish. The buttplate is a wide, modified crescent style that handles recoil well. Hardware and fittings are browned steel.

The standard 1837 Zephyr is offered in a 62-caliber (20-bore) 30-inch tapered octagon barrel. It is intended for charges in the 175-grain range giving pretty much a flat trajectory out to 125 yards or so. It is recommended for any

Western game, up to and including smaller bears.

The Alaskan Zephyr is the same as the standard except the 28-inch tapered octagon barrel is 72-caliber (12-bore) and the ignition system utilizes two musket caps on side-by-side nipples that are fired simultaneously to ignite the 300-grain charges this big-game rifle is capable of digesting. At the 250-grain charge level, the gun shoots reasonably flat to 100 yards, and the blow from the 72-caliber round ball is sufficient to handle anything on the American continents, and most African game.

The largest-caliber Zephyr is called the African. The 26-inch barrel on this one is made in a 84-caliber (8-bore). The receiver on this gun is color-case hardened and the caliber designation and legend on the barrel are gold-filled. The receiver is tastefully engraved, the barrel sports English-type sights, and the stock utilizes a shotgun-type buttplate. This one is intended to be adequate for the largest game on the planet.

North Star West

One of the most popular guns among reenactors—at least the pre-1840 crowd, the buck skinners—is the Northwest Trade

North Star's Trade Pistol is representative of pistols imported from England during the North American fur trade

Gun. These smooth-bore flintlock firearms were a fixture of the fur trade in America from the mid-1600s to the 1860s. They were somewhat standardized, varying slightly depending upon the company that ordered them and the gunsmiths who made them. They all shared basically the same look and style.

In the 1970s, when the buckskinning hobby was really taking off, Curly Gostomski, a Dayton, Ohio tool and die maker, began to reproduce both French and British trade guns. He used guns in his collection for patterns, and refined the reproductions during correspondence with Charles Hanson, curator of The Museum of the Fur Trade in Chadron, Nebraska. What he put on the market was a reproduction of the original Fur Trade guns that would fool experts.

Curly sold the business, called North Star Enterprises, in the early 1990s and, after another sale, it is now owned by Matt and Mary Denison as

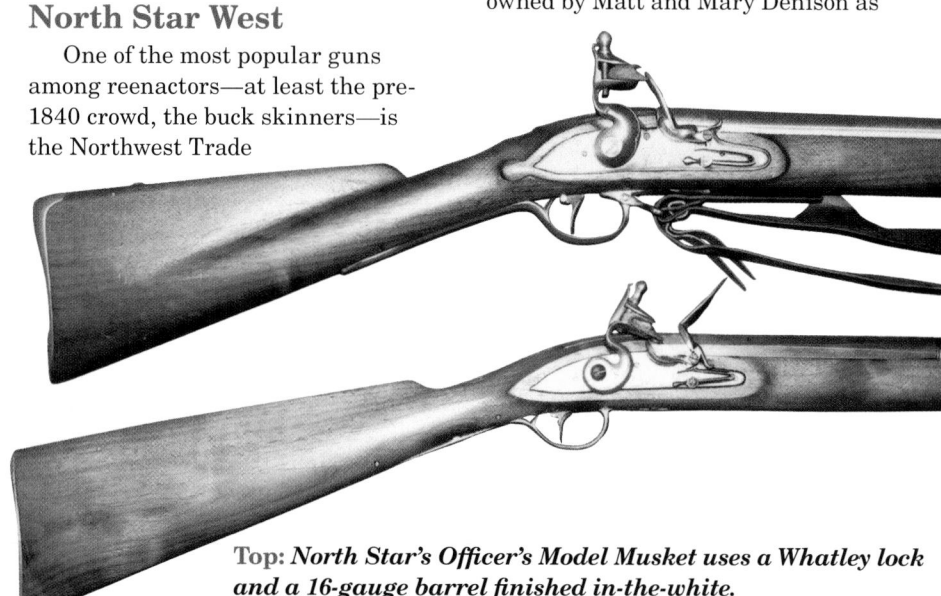

Top: *North Star's Officer's Model Musket uses a Whatley lock and a 16-gauge barrel finished in-the-white.*
Bottom: *The Chief's Trade Gun is a higher-grade model featuring a Ketland lock, blued finish and a walnut stock.*

North Star West based in Montana. They are continuing to produce exact copies of the Northwest Trade Gun.

North Star West produces five different long guns and a pistol; all flintlock and smoothbore, as were the originals. The models offered cover the various styles offered by fur-trading outfits—French, English and American—over a span of a couple of hundred years. The guns were in general use clear up to the early 1900s. No wonder they are so popular with the reenactment folks.

North Star West make their own locks, utilizing patterns by Barnett, Ketland and Whately—all well-known English makers of trade guns. All the iron hardware used on the guns is from molds designed and owned by the company. The guns are supplied in three ways—as a kit with a 95 percent inletted stock, completed lock, all hardware, and a set of instructions; as a completed gun "in the white," that is, completely assembled and shootable but with no finish on either barrel or stock, and as a complete, finished gun. This allows the buyer to tailor the order to match his pocketbook and gunsmithing ability.

The five long guns include, first, the Northwest Trade gun which is typical of the guns handled by Hudson Bay Company, the Northwest Company, and the American Fur Company, John Jacob Astor's outfit. They were in common use and trade from around 1770 until 1860 or so when percussion guns came into common use. It has the brass serpent sideplate and the proper sitting fox logo that the Indians looked for to ensure they were getting a good quality gun.

Next is an Early English-style gun, typical of those sold by English traders prior to the French and Indian War. It follows the typical trade gun style etc...but is an earlier style, typical of what the Hudson Bay Company traded before the French and Indian War. There were never a lot of these made and they are quite rare today.

The third type is a Chief's Grade Gun. These guns were a bit fancier than the standard trade gun. They were produced during a 20-year span, from 1790 to 1810. They were used by the British military as gifts to prominent Indian leaders to induce them to join the British against the Americans during the War of 1812.

The fourth type is an Officers Model Musket of the type that would have been typically carried by Rogers Rangers or high-ranking British officers during the French and Indian War. The gun would be quite correct for the period of the American Revolution, for that matter. It is copied from an original gun in the collection of the Smithsonian Institution in Washington, D.C. While this one is not technically a trade gun, it fits into the period quite nicely. A wide range of accoutrements are available for this gun: a bayonet & tomahawk, leather belt with cartridge box for paper cartridges, leather sling, leather frog scabbard for the bayonet and tomahawk, worm for the ramrod and instructions for making paper cartridges. The French and Indian War reenactors will be very interested in this one.

The fifth long gun is a Blanket Gun; basically a Northwest Trade

Gun that has had the barrel cut back to 18 inches and the buttstock shortened 6 inches or so. This is to reproduce a common modification that Indians performed on their guns to make them shorter and easier to handle while hunting, especially on horseback. It also made the gun easy to carry under a blanket—an early "concealed carry option."

The Trade Pistol offered by North Star West is a copy of the flintlock smoothbore pistol that was typically used by traders, trappers and factors of trading posts. These were imported in large numbers during the entire period of the North American fur trade.

All the guns are offered in a choice of 24- or 20-gauge, and in a variety of barrel lengths—with the exception of the Officer's Model Musket which is 66-caliber with a 37 1/2-inch barrel, like the original.

An interesting sidelight, the price of a typical trade gun during the heyday of the trade was 20 or so beaver pelts. With the price of beaver today, prices of the North Star West guns are pretty close to an equivalent with the fur trade prices. These guns are very nicely made and very period-correct. They fit perfectly in the hands of a reenactor, a primitive season hunter—or on the wall over the fireplace.

Remington

A couple of years ago Remington dropped their Model 700 ML bolt-action muzzleloading rifle, and many thought Remington was out of the muzzleloading business.

Remington's new rifle, the Genesis, with standard synthetic stock.

The Remington Genesis with the thumbhole-style stock and the camo option.

Not so. They are back with a new muzzleloading rifle called the Genesis.

This new rifle uses a side-rotating block that pivots to the left, exposing the breech of the barrel which takes the popular 209 shotgun primer. When rotated back in position, the block, called the Torch Cam action, seals the 209 into a weather-resistant package. The primer is fired by an external center-hung hammer that strikes a firing pin that extends through the block. There is no blow-back of fouling to bother the shooter, or get into the trigger group. After firing, the Torch Cam breech block is pivoted to the side, exposing the fired primer which can then be removed easily without the use of tools, something that is important in the hunting field. The 28-inch barrel utilizes a 1:28-inch twist and is capable of handling loads of 150 grains of black powder or black powder equivalent. Sights are fiber optic and the ramrod is aluminum for durability. The stock sports swivel studs, of course, and the barrel is drilled and tapped for scope mounting.

The gun features a dual safety, consisting of a traditional cross-bolt safety at the rear of the trigger guard and a rebounding hammer that locks in the cocked position, holding it away from the firing pin. Bumping the hammer accidentally will not fire the rifle. The breechplug is easily removed for cleaning, and the gun can be torn completely down in a few minutes for a thorough cleaning.

The new rifle is available in a variety of configurations and finishes. The metal can be had in blued steel, stainless or camouflage and the stock is available in either synthetic or laminated wood, in either thumb-hole or standard styles. Stocks can be had in a camo design also.

It's good to see Remington back in the muzzleloading market. After all, the company had its origin some 190 years ago as a maker of muzzleloading firearms and barrels. This new, very affordable rifle should be a good addition to the Remington line.

The Winchester 209 primer was developed specifically for Pyrodex and Triple 7 and the other substitutes, as well as black-powder.

There are a couple of new items in the muzzleloading ammunition department that will be available to hunters and shooters.

Traditions Performance Firearms

A problem often facing muzzleloading hunters is a fast second shot. There are many different things on the market to facilitate a relatively quick reload, but even the most efficient and fast reloading accessory can take too long to accomplish its purpose if an animal is bent on leaving the vicinity.

Traditions Performance Firearms has the answer. They are marketing their Express Double Shot double-barrel muzzleloader. This over-under rifle offers two shots as quick as you can pull the trigger. Looking very much like a 20-gauge O/U shotgun, the Express utilizes two 50-caliber 24-inch barrels with a 1:28 twist for the popular sabot, or slug-type bullets. The barrels are factory set to shoot to point of aim at 75 yards. The barrels have a screw-adjusted "barrel jack" system for fine-tuning the shot placement for different loads and bullets.

The gun features a top-break lever, similar to a shotgun, which allows access to the breech end of the barrels for the installation of 209 primers. The gun is rated for loads up to 150 grains; its four locking lugs give a great deal of strength. Double triggers allow for a quick second shot by merely pulling the other trigger.

Other features include fiber optic sights, sling swivels, rubber recoil pad, top tang safety and an aluminum ramrod. The top barrel is drilled and tapped for scope mounting, if you are so inclined.

The gun points and handles well, given its rather heavy 12 1/2-pound weight. The overall length is 41-1/2 inches. It features a walnut stock and forend, and blued steel receiver and barrels. In states where "two-shoot" guns are legal, this one should be very popular.

Winchester/ Hodgdon Powder Company

Winchester has partnered with Hodgdon Powder Company to produce a new 209 primer called the Winchester Triple 7. This primer is specifically designed for Hodgdon's Triple 7, and Pyrodex powders and pellets. The primer is formulated to give clean-burning of the propellant, and eliminate the ring that often forms just ahead of the chamber portion of the barrel. This has been a recurring problem with the 209 shotgun primer in in-lines for some time.

Muzzleloading hunters and shooters truly live in the best possible time, it would appear. There is a virtual cornucopia of powders, bullets, primers, accessories and guns available to delight the heart of any shooter—whether his interest is in hunting with the latest modern inline, or target-shooting with accurate reproductions of the guns of our forefathers. Something for everybody. ❀

2006
OPTICS FOR SHOOTERS

by Wayne Van Zwoll

*T*his is not the place to say it, but I'm going to anyway. I'm tired of new stuff. In fact, I'm in favor of everyone in the optics business taking a year off in Provence and mellowing out. There will still be an optics market when you get back. You might even find the customers will like you better. A line unchanged for a year will give everyone time to figure out what your company makes before half of it is supplanted by new models. A year over good French wine might convince you that old is not all that bad. Indeed, why not age scopes and binoculars? You could charge most for optics that sat in storage longest.

"I'd like that 4x32 – 1976 vintage, please." You applaud the customer's sophistication as you hand him the scope, nestled in a wooden box with delicate curls of sisal and aromatic cedar chips.

"A fine choice," you say smugly. "Delicate but cleanly formed. Bold, but with a satin finish. You can see through it too."

Actually, that's all we have to do with a sight or a binocular: see through it. Anything that helps us see through it quickly and shows us a bright, crisp image is good. Anything that distorts or dulls the image or makes the instrument hard to use fast is bad. You must be able

to adjust a scope so it looks where you're looking, and a binocular so the image is focused. Beyond that, you're just spending more money.

The binocular I bought 30 years ago is still a good binocular. It has cost me $2.50 a year to own.

A season in Provence would also help customers, come to think of it. There's not much to kill in that part of the world, so the need for multiple scopes and binoculars would vanish as quickly as memories of Mogan David. You might, as a customer, decide that funneling more money into gaping objective bells is a cruel injustice. Better those funds help resurrect vintage names in optics: Ajax, Pecar, Noske, Litschert, Wollensak …. OK, how about Lyman and Bausch & Lomb?

It's heart-warming that Meade is bringing back the Redfield brand. I saw a prototype this winter. Naturally, some refinements are on the way, not all of them useful. I told the Redfield team to leave well enough alone for now – at least reflect on proposed changes over a glass of port on a cottage veranda.

But they won't. How much reflection can you expect in a state where automobiles clog 10-lane freeways before sunup and film-makers cast gay cowboys?

Even north of the border in

Oregon, new products trump tradition. In 2007, its 100th year, Leupold is as committed as ever to innovation. Its 2006 VX-L scope, with a crescent-shaped objective, facilitates the mounting of big front glass low over the barrel. The advantage of a whopping exit pupil apparently justifies the objective's perpetual frown. It *is* an engineering marvel – not only the construction of such a lens, but its seal. You cannot thread in a crescent-shaped lens mount or a crescent-shaped retaining ring. The notion that round is no longer relevant crossed my mind, but only briefly.

Leupold can well afford to celebrate its century of service to shooters. The company has a fiercely loyal constituency. It showed up in my latest survey of elk hunters for the Rocky Mountain Elk Foundation.

As was the case a decade ago, Leupold buried the competition. The 220 Leupolds named outnumbered all other scope brands combined! Incidentally, almost all the scopes reported were variables, with 147 hunters favoring 3-9x models. That is consistent with preferences recorded in the '90s, when Leupold's Vari-X II 3-9x proved far more popular than any other single scope. Next closest tallies this year went to 2-7x, 4-12x and 2 1/2-8x sights. Despite my perennial stumping for low-power scopes, only 11 respondents used glass with top-end magnification of less than 7x. And much to my dismay, the 4x fixed-power sights that once graced *most* scoped elk rifles were mentioned just a dozen times. Only two hunters used 6x fixed-powers, while 22 carried variables of 14x to 20x on the top end!

Why so much power? Asked to list the shortest and longest shot distances at which they killed elk, respondents in my survey reported ranges of 1 to 925 yards. The mean for *shortest* shots came to 55 yards, a little farther than the *average* shot distance for my last four elk – 47 yards. The longest shots averaged 263 yards, which some shooters would say is not far. However, I have shot only one elk farther than 263 yards. Most surprising were claims of kills at extremely long range: nine between 600 and 750 yards and six more from 800 to 925! I wasn't there so can't confirm the shooting. I *have* riddled enough paper at 600 yards to know that first-round hits even that far away are hard to guarantee under field conditions.

At this year's SHOT Show Zeiss announced a new range-finding riflescope. More streamlined and lighter in weight than the Swarovski that preceded it, it is better suited to big game hunting. As surprising was a new Zeiss 4x32 scope. It's been years since the company has fielded such a sight. The future belongs to the variable – we all know that. But the old Zeiss 4x, and Swarovski's, with the Leupold 3x and Schmidt & Bender 4x36, rank among the greatest hunting sights ever, and sad was I to see them pass! This season's predictable proliferation of hulking variables excites me less than does the rare introduction of high-quality fixed-power sights.

This year's list of new optics is long indeed. Unless scope-makers relax for a season in Provence, we can expect the same next year

❈●❈●❈●❈●❈●❈

Wayne installs an Aimpoint tactical sight on a Smith & Wesson M&P 15. Note q-d lever.

– while sights we're just getting to know pass into obsolescence.

Aimpoint

The first red dot sight dates back to 1975. Inventor Gunnar Sandberg came up with what he called the single-point sight. You saw the dot with one eye, the target with the other. You couldn't look *through* the sight at all! Kenneth Mardklint told me on a visit to Sweden some years ago that Sandberg's invention soon evolved into a series of electronic sights that anchored a company: Aimpoint.

I've twice used Aimpoint sights on moose hunts. Both times, I could not have been better served. The Model 7000, mounted on a Blaser rifle, not only gave me fast aim in dark, thick cover; it helped me shoot 1 1/2-inch groups at the range. You needn't relinquish precision to get shotgun-quick sight pictures. Just keep dot brightness at its lowest practical setting for the sharpest sight picture.

Aimpoint red dot sights with no magnification offer unlimited eye relief, a real boon for us stock-

crawlers. You can point as with a shotgun bead, both eyes open. Models with magnification have generous eye relief. The latest Aimpoints feature ACET. Advanced Circuit Efficiency Technology reduces power demand, boosting battery life on the new Aimpoint 9000s to 50,000 hours! That's with the brightness set on 7. The highest setting is 10. The 9000 series comprises three models, and you get a choice of 2-minute or 4-minute dot. They're more rugged than ever, submersible to 15 meters.

Aimpoint's American representative Mike Kingston says the company supplies military sights to U.S. and French armies, and hunting models in 40 countries. "Our sights aren't cheap," says Mike. "They are simply the best red dot sights around. For most hunting, they're more effective than traditional scopes." One of every 10 Swedish hunters using optical sights carries an Aimpoint. Learn more at aimpoint.com.

Adirondack Optics

A couple of years ago, a small company from upstate New York

made headlines with a scope that could photograph an animal in the sight picture just as you pull the trigger! SmartScope was designed by Terry Gordon, a young entrepreneur who knew that producing the instrument would be an ambitious and costly project. "But we had help from fine and talented people," he says, "even the state of New York!"

Three SmartScopes now comprise the line All have 30mm tubes, and there's a parallax adjustment on the 3-10x44 and 6-16x44. At 22 ounces, the 1.5-6x40 is only a quarter-pound lighter than the others. A standard mil dot reticle lies in the front focal plane, so apparent reticle dimensions vary with magnification but not in relation to your target. This arrangement reflects European preferences and matches the design of other high-quality scopes in the Czech factory that builds the sight for ADK.

With quarter-minute adjustments and 3 inches of eye relief SmartScope incorporates some of the features of conventional sights, like fully multi-coated lenses. A Picatinny rail increases mounting latitude for the SmartScope, which has short free tube sections between bells and turret.

The internal digital camera is what makes this product unique. It's powered by a pair of 1.5-volt AA batteries housed in a turret compartment. A small screen atop the ocular bell has the on-off switch and a button that lets you take photos through the scope. The camera uses standard digital cards.

A SmartScope can tell you a lot about your shooting! For prices and specifications, telephone Adirondack Optics at 800-815-6814.

Alpen

Since its 1997 inception, Alpen Optics has imported binoculars and rifle scopes priced for value-conscious hunters. The latest Alpen catalog lists nearly four dozen binoculars, plus a dozen rifle-scopes – including a 4x32 and a 3-9x32 Kodiak that perform above their prices. Alpen's new 15-45x60 and 12-36x50 Compact spotting scopes should interest hunters. The 12-36x50 weighs just 20 ounces. Details at alpenoutdoor.com.

Barska

A relative newcomer to the sports optics industry, Barska scopes include Swat-line tacticals in 10-40x50, 6-24x44 and 8-32x44. All carry the IR, or "illuminated reticle" designation; all have turret AO dials and 30mm tubes. The Excavator line features 1-inch IR scopes: 4-16x50, 6-24x50 and 8-32x50. The Huntmaster Pro, Huntmaster and Cougar series have the variables most big game hunters want, from 1.5-6x42 to 4-14x50 AO. Some models offer illuminated reticles. The 4x32 and 6x42 mollify fixed-power fans. Euro-30 Pro and Euro-30 scopes have steel tubes; an additional feature of the Pro (3-12x50) is a center-lighted reticle. Varmint scopes are built on 1-inch tubes with front AO sleeves. They're available in 4-16x50, 6-24x42, 6-24x50 and 6.5-20x50.

Barska's short-coupled Contour 3-9x42 scopes feature a range/trajectory-compensating drum and switchable colored reticles. There's an Electro Sight resembling Bushnell's HoloSight, with four reticles and seven brightness settings. Red dot, air gun and rimfire models round out the Barska rifle scope lines.

The company also markets spotting scopes, from a 18-36x50 to a 22-67x100. For more on these and other Barska products, go to barska.com.

Browning

Bushnell produces the Browning line of optics under license. It's still a young stable, with just six hunting scopes: 2-7x32, 3-9x40, 3-9x50 and 5-15x40. There's also a 4-12x40 and an 8-24x40 (at $450 and $590) for varmint shooters. The Browning 15-45x65 spotting scope weighs 48 ounces. Its power range suits it well to western big game hunting. Browning also markets roof prism binoculars: 8x32, 8x42 and 10x42. Complete specifications are available at browningsportsoptics.com.

Brunton

Brunton's optics line now includes rifle scopes. In early 2006 the Riverton, Wyoming firm trotted out its NRA series of sports optics. Fixed-power 4x32 and 6x42 hunting scopes sell for only $179 each. FV variables range from a 1.5-5x20 to a 1.5-6x40 to a 3-9x40, all priced at $229. A 3.5-10x50 costs $60 more. At the low end is an SV 3-9x40 for $99. Find out more at brunton.com and nrasportsoptics.com.

Mike Jordan fires a new Browning autoloading rifle with one of Browning's variable scopes.

BSA

Sweet 17 Mach II rifle scopes made news last year as trajectory-compensated models for the 17 HMR cartridge. BSA's John Schild explains: "A trajectory drum on the elevation dial is calibrated for the 17 Mach II bullet, so you can zero for 50 yards, then dial up zero out to 175 yards." Sweet 17s come in 2-7x32, 3-12x40 and 6-18x40 versions, all with adjustable objectives. This year they're joined by 22 models in 2-7x32, 3-9x40 and 6-18x40 (all AO) configurations. Each comes with three interchangeable drums to give you accurate reads with 36-, 38- and 40-grain bullets, again to 175 yards.

Also for 2006, BSA is marketing a Varmint Hunter LLCP Combination. It includes a 4x32 scope, mounting hardware, laser sight and tactical light in one package. A bracket holds the light and laser sight on the scope. Equipped with a 650nm laser diode and a dot that subtends 11mm at 10 yards, the laser sight can be adjusted 5 MOA vertically and horizontally. There's both an on/off switch and a pressure-sensitive switch. The metal flashlight features a 3-volt bulb that delivers 34 lumens at 40 yards. It too offers a choice of standard and pressure-sensitive switches.

BSA's line includes 6-24x and 8-32x target scopes with dot and mil-dot reticles. You'll also find scopes for pistols, rimfire rifles and air guns. A series of red dot sights includes two with interchangeable reticles. The complete story is at bsaoptics.com.

Burris

The Short Mag scopes Burris announced last year augmented an already-complete line. The 1x, 4x, 2-7x, 3-9x and 4.5-14x are short-coupled sights with 3 1/2- to 5-inch eye relief and resettable windage and elevation dials. Retail prices range from $316 to $581, and all variables can be ordered with Ballistic Plex reticles. Burris also overhauled its flagship Signature series to produce Signature Select scopes, with more convenient turret location, index-matched lenses, rubber grips on power and AO rings. LRS versions (1.5-

Bushnell has a huge stable of sights, like the 4-12 Trophy Wayne is using here.

6x, 3-10x and 4-16x) offer resettable windage and elevation dials and lighted reticles. While the Short Mag and Signature Select scopes have 1-inch tubes, 30mm scopes have proliferated. Mounting these tight to the receiver is easier now with medium-height Burris Zee Rings. Signature Zee Rings now have double the original number of attaching screws, to secure scopes on big-bore rifles that jar your molars.

Burris is courting the tactical market with XTR (Xtreme Tactical Rifle) scopes in 1.5-6x, 10x, 3-12x and now 6-24x. They feature 30mm tubes with side-mounted parallax adjustments and steel-on-steel windage and elevation knobs. All models feature illuminated reticles but without the bubble of the LRS ocular housings. The Burris Tactical series includes a SpeedDot sight and Laser flashlight you can mount on Picatinny rails. For 2006, Burris is also marketing tactical scopes under the Fullfield II banner. Choose a 3-9x40, a 4.5-14x42 or a 6.5-20x50. All have TAC-2 adjustment knobs and AO collars up front.

Big news at Burris this year is the LaserScope, a sight with a laser-rangefinding unit built in. It's a 4-12x42 with ranging capabilities to 800 yards on reflective targets. At 26 ounces, the scope weighs

only a little more than standard models. The integral mount allows the scope to hug a Picatinny rail.

Also new this year: three 30mm Euro Diamond scopes with a 3P#4 E-Dot reticle. The 1-4x24, 2.5-10x50 and 3-12x56 offer eight light settings on a turret-mounted dial. Lighter scopes for short shooting and fast-handling firearms now include a 2-7x35 Fullfield II sight for shotguns and muzzleloading rifles. You'll find a 2-7x32 handgun scope with illuminated reticle too. For more information key up burrisoptics.com.

Bushnell

There's reorganization at Bushnell, even as the industry mourns the passing of its founder, Dave Bushnell (1913-2005). Bushnell now owns Michael's of Oregon and has grouped its merchandise under the Outdoor Products Division. There's a Technology Division for GPS and other electronic gear. The Premium Eyewear Division markets Serengeti sunglasses and related items. Bushnell, Tasco and Browning products for shooters fall into the Sports Optics Division.

The recognized leader in laser rangefinders, Bushnell now has an Elite 2500 with an "ARC" feature, which compensates for vertical angle. That is, the instrument will tell you not only the distance to an object, but the effective shot distance. If you shoot horizontally at a target 300 yards away, the actual and effective ranges are the same. But if the target is 300 yards away at a 45-degree vertical angle, the rifle will have to be aimed at a different place. Gravity affects only the horizontal component of the bullet's flight, which in this case is less than 300 yards. Bushnell's Elite 1500 has an internal device that instantly gives you the horizontal component of the actual yardage. It has 7x magnification and a 26mm objective. Retail price: $499.

The biggest news in rangefinding at Bushnell is the company's new 4-12x42 riflescope. It weighs 25 ounces, costs $900 and accurately reads the range from 30 to 800 yards. You'll get up to 8,000 ranges on its 3-volt lithium battery, partly because the switch is programmed to shut off automatically after 30 seconds of non-use. This scope comes with a BDC mil dot reticle and five dials to match the arch of your specific bullet.

In other scope news, there's an illuminated red dot reticle for the Elite 4200 2.5-10x50. Like other Elite scopes, this one features a fast-focus eyepiece and RainGuard lens coating. It weighs 22 ounces and lists for $549. For 2006, there's also an Elite 3200 3-9x40 with Ballistic reticle that helps you hit at extreme distance and even to compensate for wind. A new 6-24x40 Elite 4200 scope wears an adjustable objective dial on the turret, where focusing is most convenient. It features a mil dot reticle calibrated for use at 12x.

Shooters who enjoy changing reticle colors will appreciate three new Banner scopes: 3-9x40, 3-9x50 and 4-16x40. Choose a red reticle when light is dim, green when it's brighter. Priced at $135, $175 and $175, these scopes have one-piece bodies and battery cups on top of the fast-focus eyepieces. Another new sight with a color-choice reticle is the Trophy MP red dot scope designed for tactical rifles. It's a 1x32 sight with unlimited eye relief and an integral Weaver-style mount. The MP features quarter-minute clicks and sells for $229. If you hunt whitetails with shotgun or handgun, consider also the new HoloSight. It now uses AAA batteries. Lighter in weight and lower in profile than previous models, it costs $300 less as well!

Last year Bushnell trotted out three Trail Scout trail cameras you set up in the woods to get photos of those bucks that never come out in daylight. Fueled by four D batteries, all three came with 32 MB SD cards. This year, the series is getting 64 MB cards. Bushnell's tech wizards point out that though the camera does not include a screen, a compact screen is now available that can accept cards. So you can buy several cameras and view all their images on the 1.8-inch flat screen. The Camera Viewer has a USB port, operates on AA batteries and is small enough to tuck in a pocket. It lists for $100.

Bushnell has also announced an innovative spotting scope. The Image View 15-45x50 features a digital camera with VGA resolution and 16 MB of internal memory. It comes with shutter cable and tripod, hard case and PhotoSuite software for a modest $240. This season there's a new spotting scope *series*, the Legend. The 20-60x60 and 20-60x80 feature RainGuard lens coatings and long (1-inch) eye relief. Both come with tripods and hard and soft carrying cases. They weigh 34 and 55 ounces, list for $398 and $519. Bushnell has also upgraded its Spacemaster line with RainGuard coatings. See them all at bushnell.com.

Elcan

Rusty Maulden, whose company is the first to offer a digital rifle scope, emphasizes that "Elcan isn't new to optics. In fact, we've been building infrared scopes for military use since the late 1970s." The firm's name dates *way* back, to 1849 and Ernst Leitz. Elcan is an abbreviation, for Ernst Leitz of Canada. Rusty works from Elcan's U.S. digs in Richardson, Texas, near Dallas. But this subsidiary of Raytheon is multi-national, with offices in Midland, Ontario on Lake Huron, and in Malaga, Spain.

The technology to construct a digital scope has been around for some time, but not until recently was the project economically feasible. "We can now offer the scope for under $2,000 retail," smiles Rusty.

To understand the price, you need to know what's in an Elcan scope. Some features, like coated lenses, appear in most high-quality sights. The power range of 2.5x to 13.5x is broader than normal. Beyond that you have to think digitally. You don't look *through* this scope; rather, you see a digital display. Electronic buttons with arrows replace mechanical windage and elevation dials. Reticles? Choose one of four you can download from Elcan's website. "Or build your own," says Rusty. Specify zeroes, even reticle color. The SD card with that information can also install the ballistic properties of your favorite load. Once you install the data and zero the rifle, you can hold center by keying in the range on the scope's keyboard. Software automatically adjusts to compensate for bullet drop." This scope does not have a laser rangefinder. Rusty says it would have upped the cost too much and hiked weight well above an already hefty 28 ounces.

A unique feature of the DigitalHunter is its ability to record up to five seconds of video during a shooting sequence. The scope operates as a still camera, too. A port allows you to attach a remote screen so if you're coaching a shooter, you can see exactly what he or she sees in the sight picture. Or you can turn on the video and get up to seven five-second clips on a standard 64-mb SD card. A monitor on the top of the sight lets you review images after you record them. Explore DigitalHunter at elkcansportsoptics.com.

Famous Maker

China is earning market share in optics. Much in the manner of Japan's ascendancy, it is courting customers at the lowest price-points, offering good buys if not the best glass. Chinese manufacturers supply some well-known brand names. They've also fielded their own. For instance, "Famous Maker" catalogs a broad selection of sights at budget-friendly prices. Fogproof and waterproof, the scopes feature fully multi-coated lens systems. Choose from fixed-power 4x32s to 8-32x44 variables. There are specialty scopes for the SKS, slug guns, air rifles and handguns, plus red dot sights. Imported by sister company DKG Trading, Famous Maker scopes are available from Zander's Sporting Goods of Baldwin, IL (gzanders.com)

Kahles

A company that dates to the 19th century, Kahles can claim many milestones. In 1959 Kahles was the first company to use multi-coated lenses. In 1972, it was the first to employ an 0-ring to seal the turret. Kahles has pioneered lightweight, short-coupled 30mm scopes. The brilliant images in Kahles sights owe a lot to lens coatings that transmit 99.8 percent of incident light in green/yellow bands (500-540 nanometers). The coatings screen a little red (400 nanometers) to improve viewing at dawn and dusk.

The 30mm CSX Helia is the Kahles flagship line. It includes 1.1-4x24, 1.5-6x42, 2.5-10x50 and now 3-12x56 scopes. A battery-saving digital mechanism leaves the illuminated reticle in stand-by mode. Touch the dial and the reticle instantly brightens to the level you set before. "The CSX was designed for the American market, with the reticle in the second image plane," explains Karen Lutto, whose firm represents Kahles in the U.S. Even more popular Stateside is Kahles's newest 1-inch scope, the Helia CL (Compact Light). With 4 inches of eye relief, these sights deliver 10 percent more than the earlier AVs. A turret-mounted "AO" dial refines focus and eliminates parallax error. Parallax correction is particularly useful on high-power scopes; but Kahles is offering this feature on *every* CL sight – the 3-9x42, 3-10x50 and 4-12x52.

Multi-Zero is one feature of CL scopes you won't find elsewhere. It allows you to lock in up to five resettable zeroes. A miniature clutch

Chris Ellis sights through a Kahles Multi-Zero scope. Note the compact mechanism on the turret.

engages to give you normal quarter-minute adjustments; but once you've set a zero, you can disengage it to set another. Each is easily recorded. Once you've finished, all that's needed to change from one zero to the next is a twist of the elevation knob to another detent. Find out more at Kahles.com.

Kaps

For half a century, Kaps has been building scopes for soldiers and sportsmen from that legendary center of optical excellence, Wetzlar, Germany. The company's line of eight 30mm scopes include three fixed-power models: 4x36, 6x42, 8x56, 10x50 and 10x56. Variables range from a 1-4x22 to a 2.5-10x56. These are all high-quality sights, with hard-anodized alloy tubes housing multi-coated optics. Choose from eight reticles, and an illuminated reticle in some models. Retail prices begin at $699. Search kaps-optik.de.

Leatherwood

The Leatherwood ART (Auto-Ranging Telescope) got its field baptism largely on sniper rifles, but the company has since marketed sporting models under the Leatherwood Hi-Lux Optics brand. The M1200 features the trademark cam at the rear of the scope where it engages the special mount. Fit

an 18-inch target between stadia wires by adjusting the magnification, then shoot! This 6-24x50 scope automatically ranges the target and adjusts scope angle (zero) from 300 to 1200 meters. Of course, your bullet must track a pre-determined trajectory if the scope is to give you center hits. The M1200 is calibrated for flat-shooting rifles. It will work for most hunting-weight spitzers launched above 3000 fps. An M600 3-9x40 adjusts to bring bullets to point of aim to 600 meters.

Another venture at Leatherwood is the resurrection of the Malcomb telescopic sight used on long-range hunting rifles of the late 1800s. The 6x reproduction is faithful in profile and features to the original, though it has modern coated optics and is nitrogen-filled to prevent fogging. The 3/4-inch tube is fitted with external adjustments on barrel mounts and, with front tube extensions, can be adapted to almost any period rifle. The scope would look good on the 1874 Sharps, Remington Rolling Block or Winchester High Wall.

Get additional information at leatherwoodoptics.com.

Legacy Sports International

Known best for its Howa and Mauser rifles, Legacy Sports is

trying to make American hunters more aware of its Nikko-Sterling scopes, according to Janet Davis. Its Gold Crown rifle scopes come in Tactical and sporting configurations. The Tactical versions include 3-9x42, 4-12x50 and 6-24x50 sights with illuminated reticles. More choices are available in the sporting line. There's a 4x42 and a 4x32 AO – the latter for rimfire riflemen who want to zero out parallax at short ranges but demand a scope with slim profile and light weight. For big game hunting, choose a 3-9x42, a 3-9x42AO, a 4-12x42AO or the 4-12x50AO. Varmint hunters might prefer the 30mm Diamond Sportsman stable, with its 6-24x42 and 10-50x60 scopes, or the Target Master 6-24x44AO and 8-32x44AO. All scopes feature multi-coated lenses and fast-focus eyepieces. Most models have 1-inch tubes. Two Reflex Red Dot sights from Nikko-Sterling feature integral mounts and 11 brightness settings. For the latest from LSI, type legacysports.com.

Leica

New in 2006, Leica's CRF1200 rangefinder is just 4.5 inches long, 2.3 inches high and 1.3 inches wide. It weighs less than 8 ounces with battery and is waterproof to 3 feet. A scan mode allows periodic reads as you follow a moving target.

The CRF 1200 lists for $834. Key up leicacamerausa.com.

Leupold

For 2006, the biggest news from Leupold's Beaverton, Oregon office is the VX-L, a scope with an oversize objective bell grooved so it can be mounted low on the rifle. The idea is to increase objective and exit pupil size to transmit more light to the eye at dawn and dusk – without forcing the use of high rings. A 50mm VX-L mounts as low as you can seat a traditional 36mm objective. The 56mm VX-L snugs as close as a 40mm round front end. This scope is surely an engineering marvel! Just forming the objective bell and shaping the lenses must be dark magic indeed! You can't screw in the lens retainers, but these scopes are fog-proof! They have the Index Matched Lens System developed for Leupold's best sights. VX-Ls come in three models with 1-inch tubes: 3.5-10x50, 4.5-14x50 and 3.5-10x56. Also available: 4.5-14x56 and 6.5-20x56 with 30mm tubes. No, the view is not crescent-shaped!

Beyond VX-L, Leupold has been busy filling orders for the recently introduced VX-I, VX-II and VX-III scopes. These, and their fixed-power counterparts in the FX-II line, incorporate improvements like adjustments with positive

clicks under finger-friendly dials and upgraded lens coatings.

Tactical sights from Leupold now include two 1.5-5x20 variables. The 1-inch "Precision" scope weighs less than 10 ounces; the 30mm Mid Range / Tactical balances out at 15. A new reticle is designed to permit fine aim at long range but with the up-close-and-urgent speed of a Circle Dot. The 3.5-10x40 Long Range / Tactical Mark 4 gives you a front-plane reticle and the choice of target knobs with quarter-minute clicks or compact M3 (bullet drop compensating) dials. The M3's 1-minute elevation clicks allow quicker sight adjustment to extreme range. Windage is still split into half-minute clicks.

Pat Mundy notes that Leupold has an extensive line of thread-on accessories to improve the target image. There's a lens to coax warm colors out of foliage, so you can better spot game. Others function like tinted shooting glasses to cut glare or brighten sight pictures. These lenses come in diameters to fit most objectives of current Leupold scopes. If your tube isn't threaded, Leupold will thread it at half the list price.

Leupold's new-product list is long. It includes a 12-40x60HD (fluorite) spotting scope that adapts to most digital cameras. The 2.5-8x32 Leupold VX-III pistol scope weighs just 6 ounces, has 18 inches of eye relief. For more on these and other Leupold products, investigate the company website, leupold.com.

Meade

A few years ago, Meade Optical Company of Irvine, California built only astronomical telescopes. Now it also designs and builds rifle scopes. After ATK sold the Redfield, Simmons and Weaver brands to Meade, the company charted improvements, bringing in consultants Mark Thomas and Forrest Babcock to overhaul the Simmons line from the inside out. The Master Series Simmons with improved erector system debuted at the 2004 SHOT Show. Last year Master Series construction appeared in other Simmons models.

Leupold manufactures tactical sights for use on sniper rifles like this super-accurate 308.

This year it was adapted to a new Redfield scope. The Weaver line has remained as is for now, but there's no doubt that Meade CEO Steve Murdock wants to give all three brands higher profile. Visit meade.com.

Millett

The 30mm scopes anchoring Millett's Buck Gold series include Varmint/Target 4-16x56 and 6-25x56 variables. Choose a front-sleeve or turret-dial parallax adjustment. The 1-inch Buck Gold stable comprises six models, from 2-8x40 to 6-24x44. There are two Buck Gold Lightnings with electronically lit reticle center: a 1.5-6x44 and a 3-9x44. Penny-pinchers can find almost as many options in Millett's Buck Silver selection. The 3-9x40 and 6x40 offer two reticle choices. There's a 4-12x40 AO, with your pick of front or side focus. A 6-18x40 rounds out the line, along with an LER 2x20 pistol scope. Six models of red dot sights appear in Millett's catalog, all lithium-powered and, according to the company, parallax-free. Millett sells a 4-16x50 TRS-1 Tactical scope with one-piece 30mm tube. It has 1/8-minute elevation clicks and a green illuminated mil-dot reticle, a side-focus parallax knob and lockable adjustment dials.

Pistol sights have been a Millett mainstay for years. In 2006 there's a wide array for revolvers and autoloaders. Choose white bar, orange bar, 3-dot – any popular combination of front and rear profiles and colors. Also at Millett you'll find one- and two-piece steel scope mount bases, dovetail and Weaver-style. They're lighter in weight than most other steel bases and a perfect match for the scope rings Millett sells. The company offers see-through mounts and shooting accessories: pistol and rifle rests, flush-mount sling swivels and sight installation tools. Learn more at millettsights.com.

Nightforce

Dunk it in a pressure tank simulating submersion in 100 feet of water for 24 hours. Freeze it in a box cooled to a minus 80 degrees F, then heat it within an hour to 250 degrees F. Slam it in a recoil device delivering

Wayne likes this five-shot group from a Dakota Predator in 20 Tactical, with Nightforce scope.

1,250 Gs – both ways. Life is tough for scopes in north-central Idaho.

Nightforce NXS rifle scopes all endure that treatment so shooters can be assured they will perform reliably in the field. This relatively small line is big on quality. Nightforce makes no apology for steep price – it's unavoidable if you want the very best. Details like the use of dissimilar alloys in the erector assembly to ensure repeatable movement year after year, and lens coatings that weather mil-spec abrasion tests, make these scopes the choice of long-range enthusiasts, benchrest shooters and law enforcement marksmen. The 3.5-15x50 and 3.5-15x56 are typical – big 30mm scopes, and brilliant, with signature Nightforce reticles that appear only in the center of the field. Four-times magnification complements other models too: the 5.5-22x50, 5.5-22x56 and 8-32x56. There's a super-high-power 12-43x56 – but also hunting-size compacts: a 1-4x24 and a 2.5-10x24 (yes, a straight front end on a 2.5-10!) All Nightforce models have turret-mounted parallax knobs – save two benchrest scopes, an 8-32x56 and a 12-42x56, which carry front-

sleeve parallax adjustments. Precision Benchrest scopes feature resettable 1/8-minute windage and elevation dials.

The company also supplies machined rings and Picatinny rails for mounting, and mil-radian knobs for NXS scopes so you can adjust in mils (.1 mil per click, 5 per revolution). You'll find ballistic software with the Nightforce label. For more, key up NightforceOptics.com.

Nikon

There's not much to improve on the superb Nikon Monarch sights, so the firm has wisely limited recent changes to the lower-priced Buckmasters. Even there, new rounded objective housings and a quick-focus eyepiece have less to do with improved function than with cosmetics. Long-range shooters will like the more convenient turret-mounted dial on AO models. Get all the details at nikonusa.com.

Pentax

Last hunting season was the first for Pentax's PF-65ED, a top-quality spotting scope with straight and angled eyepieces. Waterproof and lightweight, it accepts 32x, 46x and 20-60x eyepieces. The 37-ounce scope is also compatible with XW telescope eyepieces and the PF-CA35 camera adapter for 35mm SLRs.

Pat Lytle of Pentax acknowledges that the company's new subcompact binoculars may not be as useful to riflemen as the proven PCF porro prism glasses in 8x40, 10x50, 12x50 and 20x60 versions. XCF porros in 8x40, 10x50, 12x50 and 16x50 offer most of the PCF features at lower cost. As with most firms marketing complete binocular lines, Pentax has committed to roof prism glasses for its top-end product. The DCF series, in 8x or 10x with 33- 36- or 42mm objectives, offers phase-corrected prisms in aluminum and polycarbonate shells. The flagship DCF SP comes in 8x32, 8x43, 10x43, 10x50 and 12.5x50 versions.

In rifle scopes, the Lightseeker series has been broadened, and new price points added. For 2006 there's a top-end Lightseeker 3-9x40 XL, and a compact Lightseeker 3-9x32 SL. The big Lightseeker 30 series now includes a 3-10x40, 4-16x50, 6-24x50 and 8.5-32x50. Whitetail and Pioneer variables serve the big game hunter on a budget. New this year is the Gameseeker clan, including six 1-inch variable models and 4x32 and 6x42 fixed-power scopes. This line features a 14-ounce 4-12x40 and a 20-ounce 2.5-10x56.

Review all the specifications at pentaximaging.com.

Redfield

Borrowing from the technology that enabled it to overhaul its Simmons line, Meade Optical has re-introduced Redfield optics. Born before World War I, Redfield turned belly up a few years ago. Those of us who remember Redfield as a premier scope brand were saddened indeed. New owner ATK did nothing to resurrect the label, but when it was sold, with Simmons and Weaver, hope revived. That hope now has substance, in Meade's new line of Redfield variable scopes.

All five models boast an amazing five-times magnification. That is, the top power is five times the lowest power. For years, three-times magnification was the practical limit. Bigger tubes allowed engineers to quadruple power with the magnification ring. But five times? "Mark Thomas deserves a lot of credit for these scopes," says Sherry Kerr, whose company represents the Meade scope brands. "Nobody else has a five-times hunting scope."

The 3-15x52 and 5-25x52 Redfields sport 1-inch tubes. The 1.5-7x42, 4-20x56 and 6-30x56 are built on 30mm pipes. The three most powerful variables have turret-dial adjustable objectives. Power rings and fast-focus eyepieces feature click detents for easy reference and sure stops. Windage and elevation dials can be reset by pushing down on the knobs and turning to zero. They're offered in both 1/4- and 1/8-minute versions. An apochromatic objective lens of ED glass increases light transmission and reduces color fringing. Hydrophobic lens coatings on exterior glass bead water so you see clearly in the rain. The optical design delivers a constant 4 inches of eye relief and a big eye-box for quick sighting. For more information on the rebirth of Redfield, go to redfieldusa.com.

Schmidt & Bender

Fifty years ago, a couple of German instrument makers got together to produce hunting sights. On the cusp now of third-generation management, the firm is still a family business, modest in scale compared to better-known German and Japanese-based concerns. But S&B optics are renowned for their high quality.

At the top of Schmidt & Bender's line are Zenith 30mm variables in power ranges 1.1-4x24, 1.5-6x42, 2.5-6x56 and 3-12x50. They feature resettable windage and elevation dials, with gauges on the dial faces to show where in the range of adjustment you are.

Schmidt & Bender variables and fixed-power sights have reticles installed in the first and second focal planes, depending on model. You can order lens filters and hoods. S&B offers a retrofitting service to fit new illuminated reticles on selected S&B scopes already afield. Learn more at schmidt-bender.de.

Shepherd

Waterloo, Nebraska is a small town. And Shepherd is by most standards a small company. But the 3-10x40 and 6-18x40 scopes from the Shepherd shop do what other scopes cannot. Shepherd scopes have two reticles, one in the front focal plane and one in the rear. They are superimposed, appearing as one. You get an aiming

Dan O'Connell bears down with a Remington 700 and Shepherd range-compensating 6-18x scope.

reticle that doesn't change size with power changes, but a range-finding reticle that varies in dimension as you turn the magnification ring. The range-finding reticle comprises a series of circles spaced on a vertical stem. Top to bottom, they're of decreasing diameter to match the diminishing apparent size of a deer as the distance increases. To use the scope, just fit a deer-size target in a circle. Correct holdover has already been factored in because no matter what the scope power, the 18-inch circle appears the same size in relation to the target. Choose from three range-finding reticles calibrated to match the trajectories of most popular big-game cartridges. Vertical and horizontal scales in the scope image field are marked in minutes of angle so you can compensate for wind and differences in drop between actual range and the nearest 100-yard mark indicated by the circles. The company also markets 8x42, 10x42 and 12x50 binoculars. Read more at shepherdscopes.com.

Sightron

With 51 rifle and pistol scopes in its current line, Sightron has a sight for almost every application. This year there's not much new, though three variable "SS" scopes with side-mounted parallax adjustments have just seen their first hunting season. The 3.5-10x44, 4.5-14x44 and 6.5-20x50 are fully multi-coated, waterproof and shipped with sunshades and dust covers. Plex, Dot and Mil Dot reticles are cataloged for the high-power models; the 3.5-10x comes with Plex or Mil Dot.

Sightron's 30mm S III-series includes 1.5-6x50 and 3.5-10x44 hunting scopes, plus three 6-24x50 models. Choose Plex, Dot or Mil Dot reticle. Fixed-power aficionados will appreciate the modestly priced SII 4x32 and 6x42 scopes. Whitetail and turkey hunters can well use the broad field and 4 inches of eye relief in the newest shotgun scope, the 2.5x32SG. Two lightweight red-dot sights feature 1x magnification and 33mm tubes. Last year Sightron announced a hunting-weight spotting scope with 25x *and* 20-60x eyepieces,

and a Cordura soft case zippered to allow quick access to the ends. That 20-60x63 spotter joins a 20-50x65 and a 20-50x80. But the company is still best known for its sights. See them in detail at sightron.com

Simmons

When Mead Optical acquired Simmons, Redfield and Weaver, it immediately began to overhaul the Simmons line, starting inside. The heart of each Simmons Master Series scope is a slotted beryllium-and-copper coil fitted to the rear of the erector assembly. It holds that tube tight against the windage and elevation adjustment pegs. Traditionally, the front of the erector assembly is pressed against the pegs by a biasing spring on the other side of the tube. The new rear-mounted biasing coil eliminates the need for a biasing spring. Result: smoother, more predictable point of impact shift as you turn the dials, and no drag from a forward spring. This arrangement now has a name: TrueZero. The new gimbal joint (the fitting that allows the erector tube 360-degree movement up front) is simple and sturdy. You get as much as 17 percent greater windage and elevation range, longer eye relief and a bigger, more forgiving eyebox. A fast-focus ocular housing helps deliver a sharp image of target and reticle.

The Master Series internal design is now available in several Simmons scopes, from the top-end Aetec to value-priced ProSport models. The 2.8-10x44 Aetec sits low on many rifles, as does the 4-14x44, which has a turret-mounted parallax dial. Both feature fast-focus eyepieces. Lower price-points distinguish the Prohunter, Prodiamond and Prosport models, and specialty scopes for rimfire rifles, handguns and crossbows. Simmons red dot sights are available with 30- and 42mm tubes. Look up simmonsoptics.com

Springfield

Known for its M1A rifles and XD and 1911 pistols, Springfield Armory has committed to selling a line of 13 tactical scopes. These include 3-9x42 and 3.5-10x50 hunting sights with

30mm tubes and turret-mounted AO dials. An internal bubble level at 6 o'clock helps prevent canting. You can specify illuminated reticles on most models. Their gear-driven power-change mechanism is 34 times as stout as a slot-and-pin arrangement, according to the firm's Bill Dermody. Learn about these scopes at springfield-armory.com.

Swarovski

The last couple of years have been quiet ones at Swarovski – at least as regards new product. The company has undergone significant organization changes Stateside but retains its base in Cranston RI. One of the most notable recent scope developments was last year's SR rail. This toothed rail on PH 1.25x24, PH 1-6x42 and PH 3-12x50 models eliminates the ring/tube juncture. With rail scopes, you get no ring scars, and no internal damage from tight rings. The scope cannot slip during heavy recoil. Tubes with rails must be machined from bar stock, so the rail actually strengthens the tube. Long popular in Europe, the rail scope is just now making headway in the U.S. It will not, I'm afraid, replace tubes made for rings anytime soon.

Mounts for the rail are expensive and not yet commonplace. But one mount that *can* fix a rail to any Picatinny or Weaver-style base is available for Swarovski SR scopes. It's stout, simple and easy to install. The front mates with the rail teeth; the rear clamp is allowed to float so you can position it just where you want it.

Primary 2006 offerings from Swarovski are its PVI-2 variable scopes with rear-focal-plane reticles that won't change apparent size as you dial magnification up or down. Europeans typically prefer front-plane reticles that stay the same size in relation to the target during power changes. The advantage is that you can use the reticle as a rangefinder without checking magnification. The disadvantage is that at high magnification, which you want for small targets far away, the enlarged reticle can obscure the target. When you dial the power down for fast shots in close cover, the reticle diminishes in size to the point that it can be hard to pick up. The PV1-2 series of Swarovski variables features five illuminated reticles that combine lines, bars and circles with dots to provide aiming devices that are easy to see quickly but permit precise aim at distance. The 1.25-4x24, 1.5-6x42, 2.5-10x56, 3-12x50, 4-16x50 and 6-24x50 are all equipped with the new BE-4 Digital Illuminator unit in the turret. High-power scopes have AO sleeves up front.

For more, key up swarovskioptik.com.

Swift

Founded in 1926, Swift Optics is still a family-owned company. It is headquartered in San Jose, California, from where the imported rifle scopes are shipped to 3000 dealers in 20 countries worldwide. The line includes pistol and rimfire scopes and two centerfire rifle series: the Premier and the Standard. A list of features includes those shared by most scope lines today. From 1.5-4.5x32 to 8-32x50, the 25 sights in Swift's line cover all hunting and target applications. You'll find particulars at swiftoptics.com.

Tasco

New 8x42 and 10x42 roof prism binoculars with BaK4 prisms and multi-coated lenses indicated a new direction for Tasco last year. Though the 26-ounce binoculars list for only

$70 and $80 and are built to sell in volume, they are, well, pretty good values. Such Tasco products always got grudging approval from sportsmen; but the line had become bloated with less worthy optics. When it acquired the brand a few years ago, Bushnell sifted through it, retaining only the best items – an $84 illuminated 3-9x40 rifle scope, for example. Tasco's 18-36x50 World Class spotting scope, with window mount and tripod, lists for just $132.

Despite rigorous culling, the current Tasco line encompasses many dozens of products. Compact and full-size binoculars range from 8x21 to 9x63. Choose roof or Porro prism models, even variable power. Tasco offers four spotting scopes for shooters. The line of rifle scopes spans fixed and variable power, in magnifications from 1.5x to 40x. Tasco's ProPoint red dot sights with 30mm tubes complement the Red Dot series with 38mm tubes. Scopes for rimfire rifles include versions with 1-inch and 3/4-inch tubes. The company also offers scope rings. Become fully informed at tasco.com.

Trijicon

Tritium-illuminated iron sights help you aim in dim light – even in the dark. Trijicon is one of the largest suppliers of these sights, which contain tiny cylinders of tritium gas with sapphire windows that distribute

the light from the tritium. The company also manufactures optical sights that use both tritium and fiber optic strands to brighten the reticle. The TR22 2.5-10x56 AccuPoint is a battery-free illuminated scope with 30mm tube and tritium-lit reticle. The ACOG (Advanced Combat Optical Gunsight) is another recent offering, in 3.5x35, 4x32 and 5.5x50 versions. It's adjustable for zero, like an ordinary scope. The Trijicon TriPower relies as well on a fluorescent collector. Like the ACOG, it has the profile of a red dot sight. Trijicon also makes a compact Reflex sight that hugs a handgun. The firm's AccuPoint scope series comprises 1.25-4x24, 3-9x40 and 2.5-10x56 models, all with red or yellow illuminated pyramid-on-post reticles. Go to trijicon.com for specifications.

TruGlo

Aiming an iron-sighted muzzleloader toward the sun, I figured I'd have no chance at all. But the sights on that rifle showed up just fine on the buck's shoulder, and he dropped to my shot. The TruGlo sights so effective at milking more minutes of hunting at day's end had given me the definition I needed in sunshine too bright for ordinary sights. TruGlo's fiber-optic bars concentrate light to give you a bright red or green dot that grabs your eye. Available for most rifles, pistols and shotguns, the firm's iron

This Weatherby Mark V wears a Weaver Grand Slam scope. The Grand Slam is a premier line.

The Zeiss 6-24x Diavari, among Wayne's favorite sights, graces a Savage rifle with AccuTrigger.

sights were joined in 2005 by rifle scopes – a 4x32 and three variables – with illuminated reticles. There are red dot optical sights with 25-, 30-, 36-, 40- and 45mm tubes. A new 2x30mm red dot sight features an 11-position rheostat. The company's Tru-Point Open Red Dot sight has a low-slung profile and a screen, per Bushnell's HoloSight. There's more, including scopes and red dot sights for crossbows, in the 2006 catalog, available on-screen at truglo.com.

Weaver

The Grand Slam scopes comprising Weaver's top line of sights are unchanged for 2006. In fact, they've been left alone since the brandwas bought by Meade Optical a few years back. Six models, from 1.5-5x32 to 6-20x40, cover any field application. Classic K- and V-series scopes, and Classic Handgun scopes, round out the selection of hunting optics. The newest model is a K-6 EER (extended eye relief) at $250. This isn't for Scout Rifle mounting or handguns; it's a scope designed for traditional rifles. The 4.6 inches of eye relief help stock-crawlers with hard-kicking rifles avoid half-moon scars.

Also new on the rifle scope front are two T-24s, one of the most popular target scopes Weaver has produced. The new scopes are identical save for the reticles: a 1/2-minute dot and a 1/8-minute dot. Their 1/4-minute windage and elevation target-style adjustments allow for fast zeroing or compensating for wind and range. Micro-Trac's dual-spring, two-contact adjustment mechanism ensures repeatability. The new T-series scopes come with extra oversized adjustment knobs, a sunshade and screw-in steel lens caps.

Weaver Grand Slam binoculars have been trimmed for 2006, and two models have been added to the line, a 7x42 and a 10x42. Not that Meade hasn't left its mark on the Weaver line as well. ETX spotting scopes, 48x90 and 73x125, look suspiciously like Meade telescopes.

Classic 20x50 and 15-40x60 spotting scopes remain in production. To get the inside scoop, key up weaveroptics.com.

XS Sights

Given the propensity of modern shooters to use optical sights, you might wonder how a company can make money marketing iron sights. But since its inception a little over a decade ago, XS Sight Systems has done just that. The firm has indeed changed in name and form over the years, but its mainstay products have always been "irons." The ghost ring receiver sight earned public acclaim at XS. It's tritium rifle and pistol sights are the choice of law enforcement officers as well as hunters. You'll find sights for shotguns and AR rifles, even the M1A. View the iron stable at xssights.com.

Zeiss

Traditionally conservative, Zeiss has made a push for more U.S. market share among hunters. It currently offers the popularly priced, American-style Conquest scope in 3-9x, 3.5-10x, 4.5-14x and 6.5-20x variations. All have 1-inch tubes. New for 2006 are 4x32, 2.5-8x32 and 1.8-5.5x38 models. The first two of these weigh less than 14 ounces and complement slim hunting rifles. There's no more useful fixed-power scope than a 4x32, and

in the crowded field of variables, you won't find a more versatile power range than 2.5-8x. A wonderful feature of both scopes is 4 inches of eye relief.

Zeiss has renamed the top-end Diavari scope line Victory to match the moniker of the company's best binoculars. A couple of new Victory Diavaris have appeared recently: the 2.5-10x42 and 6-24x72. They have 30mm and 34mm tubes, respectively. An illuminated reticle is standard on the big 6-24x72, as is a turret-mounted parallax adjustment. The mil dot reticle option is calibrated at 12x. The Zeiss Varipoint reticle is available in the 2.5-10x scope; so is a rail version of the tube. These are costly scopes, but if you want the best the world has to offer, you must keep them on your list.

Incidentally, Zeiss also has a Classic Diavari/Diatal series (variable/fixed-power) that can cause some confusion if you're trying to track name changes. These scopes are marketed in Europe but are not available in the U.S. What *is* new for Zeiss Stateside is a range-finding rifle scope, a 3-12x56 with a laser rangefinder built in. This Zeiss 30mm scope is optically superb and carries the rangefinder and illuminated reticle in a slim 35-ounce package. The rangefinder reads reflective objects to 1000 yards. ✦

HANDLOADING UPDATE

by Larry S. Sterett

*H*andloading for handgun, rifle, and shotgun cartridges is alive and doing well. In fact, with the retail price of loaded ammunition increasing, more shooters seem to be getting into handloading for their favorite calibers and gauges. This results in new equipment and components being introduced.

Remington introduced the 6.8mm SPC cartridge for the military back in 2004, but sporting rifles and ammunition were slow in getting into the hands of civilians. However,

reloading dies, unprimed brass and reloading data are now available. Hornady, Silver State and Barrett (and possibly others) have brass, and Remington should have bullets. Reloading dies are available from Hornady, Lee Precision, Huntington and Redding, and Hodgdon's has reloading data in their *2006 Annual* (page 83) and so does IMR in their basic manual; others will no doubt feature such data in their updated manuals. Suitable primers, powders, and bullets are available for most dealers handling handloading supplies.

Ballistic Products Inc.

Ballistic Products Inc. advertises it has everything for shotgunners, and there's not much the firm does not carry, at least for shotshell handloaders. Hulls, primers, powder, wads, presses, buffer, manuals, 'load log systems,' measures, loading blocks, shell boxes, roll-crimp tools and much more. Currently there are at least sixteen special loading manuals by Ballistic Products, and a baker's dozen 'Technical Guides.' Loading 16-gauge shells, and need more data? Try *The Sixteen Gauge Manual*. Thinking

Ballistic Products Inc. carries just about everything a handloading shotgunner needs––equipment, components and data.

A box of 70-grain .224 Hevi-Shot hollowpoint bullets have a core which is heavier than lead, thus producing a bullet with an overall length shorter than usual 70-grain .224-inch bullets.

about loading Hevi-Shot? Check out *Handloading Hevi-Shot*. For those whose favorite shotgun is a fine double, maybe chambered for 2-inch shells, there's *Care and Feeding of Fine Doubles*' with loads for 2, 2-1/4 and 2-1/2 inch, plus regular shells, and lots of useful information. BP has roll crimpers in seven sizes: 8, 10, 12, 16, 20, 28 gauges, plus .410-bore. For neatly packaging those reloads, the firm has 25-round boxes to fit most shotshells except the 8-gauge, 3-inch .410 and the 12-gauge hulls measuring 3-1/2 inches. They have 5- and 10-round boxes to fit the 12 gauge in 2-3/4, 3 and 3-1/2 inches length, the 10 gauge, and the 3-inch .410-bore. Other hard-to-find items include Mica Wad-Slick to dust plastic wad column, hull Shape-Up tools, and a Shot & Powder Separator capable of separating size 6 through 9 shot from the powder charge for those times when you forgot to put in the wad column. (You've never done that? Never? Well ... hardly ever.)

Berry's Manufacturing

Berry's Manufacturing produces a wide variety of copper-plated swaged bullets and plastic cartridge boxes in a wide variety of sizes for handloaders. New is an improved formula case lube, a 10-round slip-top box to handle 50 BMG cartridges, a 20-round slip-top box for 416 Rigby and 338 Lapua cartridges, and 50-round hinged-top boxes to handle 45-70 Gov't., Remington Ultra and Winchester WSM cartridges. Their 350-grain 50-caliber Blue Diamond Ballistic Tipped bullets are intended for muzzleloaders, but they might be a surprise in some of the handgun cartridges, such as the 500 Smith & Wesson, 50 Action Express, and even rifles, such as the 502 Thunder Sabre.

Brooks' Tru-Bore Moulds

Another source of moulds for cast bullet users is Brooks' Tru-Bore Moulds. The cast-iron blocks are lathe-bored in calibers from .320 to .600, and the blocks will fit Saeco handles. Almost any bullet nose design and groove layout can be produced, in a bullet length up to 1-1/2 inches.

Caldwell Shooting Supplies

Reloaders need to check out the end product, especially if it's a new load, prior to loading several hundred rounds. Caldwell Shooting Supplies has just what's needed, a Lead Sled DFT and ZeroMax shooting rest, both for rifles. The ZeroMax is a no-frills full-length rest of steel construction. It permits adjustment for windage and elevation, and comes with an unfilled medium-size varmint bag front rest. The Lead Sled DFT is five inches longer than the original Lead Sled, permitting 22 inches of adjustment, and features a dual frame to help absorb recoil, has 2.5 inches of elevation adjustment on the front rest and two inches of elevation adjustment on the rear rest. The baffled forward tray will hold up to 100 pounds of lead shot, and rubber-tipped feet reduce any tendency of the sled to slide. For handgunners, Caldwell has a new HAMMR rest with built-in windage and elevation adjustments and a hydraulic cylinder that absorbs recoil and resets the handgun. Inserts are available to fit M-1911s, Ruger single actions and S&W K-Frame square-butt handguns, and a universal handgun grip casting kit is available. It's also compatible with Ransom Rest grip inserts.

Colorado Shooter's Supply

Colorado Shooter's Supply has been turning out Hoch custom bullet moulds for a number of years. The moulds are custom-made, lathe-bored, in from one to four cavities. (No moulds are carried in stock.) They are made to the customer's design, are nose-pour, with plain or gascheck base, and can be produced in single cavity up to 75-caliber, and up to 45-caliber in the four-cavity version. (Minimum size is 25-caliber for rifle moulds, and 35 for base-pour handgun moulds. Moulds for handgun bullets contain two, three, or four cavities.) Weights of the cast bullets depend on the alloy used and the design of the mould, but an 875-grain gas-check bullet for the 50 Sharps or one of

the modern firearms with a 1/2-inch bore is possible, and even larger for the really big bores. You design the bullet and Colorado Shooter's Supply will produce the mould for it.

In the 2006 GUN DIGEST, mention was made of the 510 DTC EUROP cartridge as an answer to those states, such as California, where shooting 50 BMG cartridges was nixed. Now there's another new cartridge, the 416 Barrett, which is even better, with a flatter trajectory. Based on a necked-down and shortened 50 BMG case, the 416 Barrett is capable of sending a 400-grain grain bullet downrange at 3250 fps; the bullet is still supersonic at 2500 yards. Currently the only rifle so chambered is the single-shot Barrett Model 99 from Barrett

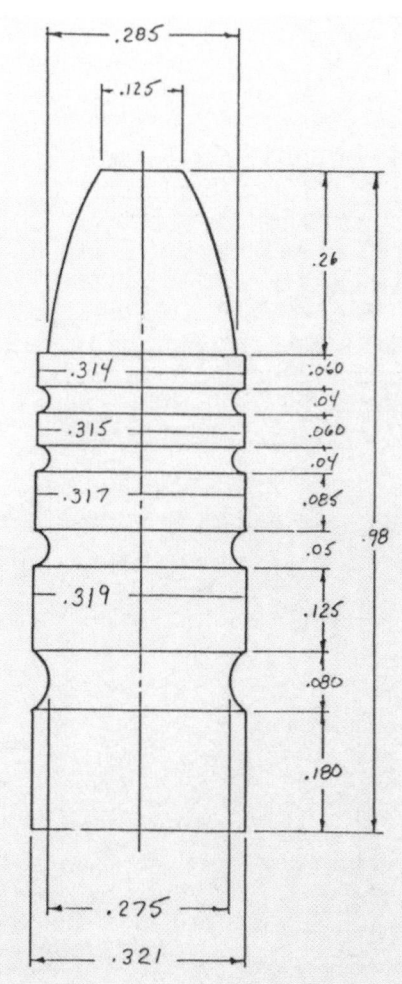

This drawing illustrates the type of bullet design for which Colorado Shooter's Supply can produce bullet moulds.

Firearms Manufacturing, but Lee Precision has loading dies for the cartridge. Regular 416 bullets should function in the new cartridge, but the two-inch long solid brass 416-size bullets with a ballistic coefficient of 0.943 will be necessary to achieve the desired downrange trajectory. They should be available by the time you read this, along with suggested loading data. (The 1000-yard shooters may enjoy shooting this new gem even more than the 50 BMG.)

Dillon Precision Products

Dillon Precision Products introduced an electric case feeder for the Dillon RL 550 press. It can be retrofitted to all RL 550 presses, and features technology used in the Dillon Super 1050 press. (Use of the case feeder increases productivity by at least 25 percent by reducing hand movements.) It comes with all necessary hardware and step-by-step instructions to make the conversion, and separate conversion kits can be purchased separately for most popular handgun calibers.

Forster

Forster Precision Products has new benchrest dies sets for the 6mm Dasher (BRImp), 6mm XC, 6.8mm SPC, and 325 Winchester Short Magnum (SWM) cartridges. All are available with full-length sizing dies, and the 6.8 SPC may be obtained with a neck-sizing die. Seating dies are available in original Bench Rest Ultra-Micrometer versions. Owners of a Forster Co-Ax reloading press who may have found the standard handle provides more leverage than they require can now order a new shorter handle with a comfortable ball fitting on the end. Another handy item is the stuck case remover for those times you forgot to lube the case prior to resizing and it became stuck in the die. Forster does not produce dies for the 50 BMG cartridge, but the firm does produce a case trimmer especially for this cartridge. The trimmer comes with a .510 pilot and a rim holder; no collet is required as the trimmer is for use only on the 50 BMG case. (An optional .505 pilot is available, if needed.)

Frankford Arsenal

Frankford Arsenal has a new electronic Micro Reloading Scale with a capacity of 750 grains ± .1 grain. (It can weigh in grains, grams and ounces.) Complete with battery, powder tray, cover, case, and calibration weight, the scale is small enough to fit in a shirt pocket. Other handy Frankford products for handloaders include corncob and walnut hull polishing media in treated and untreated grades, overall cartridge length gages, a Vibra-Prime Primer Tube Filler and, for bullet casters, Bullet Mould Cleaner, CleanCast Fluxing Compound and Drop Out, a way to "smoke" your bullet moulds.

GSI International

GSI has a new rotary bullet feeder and feed system to fit the Dillon RL 1050 progressive reloaders. The GSI toolhead features an integrated feed system that delivers bullets to the seating station. Every cycle of the handle feeds and seats a bullet in true progressive fashion.

Bob Hayley

Another source of loading tools, dies, and loaded ammunition and components for obsolete and odd-ball cartridges is Bob Hayley in Seymour, Texas. Need 8.15x46R bullets with central driving band, six-sided Metford bullets, pinfire cartridges, 577 Snider brass, or cartridges or brass for the 401 Winchester Self-Loader? Hayley may have them, and the necessary reloading dies.

Hodgdon

Handloaders can never have enough reloading data, and every new manual is worth having for reference. Hodgdon's *2006 Annual Manual* contains 202 pages of useful information, including ten interesting articles. There are 140 pages of loading data covering nearly 140 rifle cartridges from the 17 Ackley Hornet to the 50 BMG, and including the 6.8mm SPC and 325 WSM; 80 handgun cartridges from the 17 Bumble Bee to the 500 Smith & Wesson, and shotshells from the 10 gauge down to the .410-bore. Data for 17 of the rifle and handgun cartridges has been updated from previous manuals, and five new cartridges have been included, although the 5.7x28mm and 460 Smith & Wesson cartridges are not among them. (All told, this manual features more than 5000 loads.)

Some specialty rifle and handgun bullets for handloading by Northwest Custom Projectiles. Upper row (L/R): 90-grain bonded core .224, 160-grain .284 with rebated boattail base and work-hardened tip, 140-grain .284 with open tip and rebated boattail base, 140-grain .284 with flat base and open tip, 177-grain .308 with rebated base and work-hardened tip, 300 grain .338 with open tip and rebated boattail base. Lower row (L/R): 180-grain 10mm with rebated boattail base and truncated open nose, 260-grain .452 with rebated boat-tail base and truncated flat-tip nose, 300-grain .452 with rebated boattail base and truncated flat-tip nose, 350 grain .500 with flat base and flat base and pointed nose, 450-grain .500 with flat base and pointed nose, and 600-grain .510 with flat base and pointed tip for varmint hunting using the 50 BMG or similar cartridge. Other weights are possible.

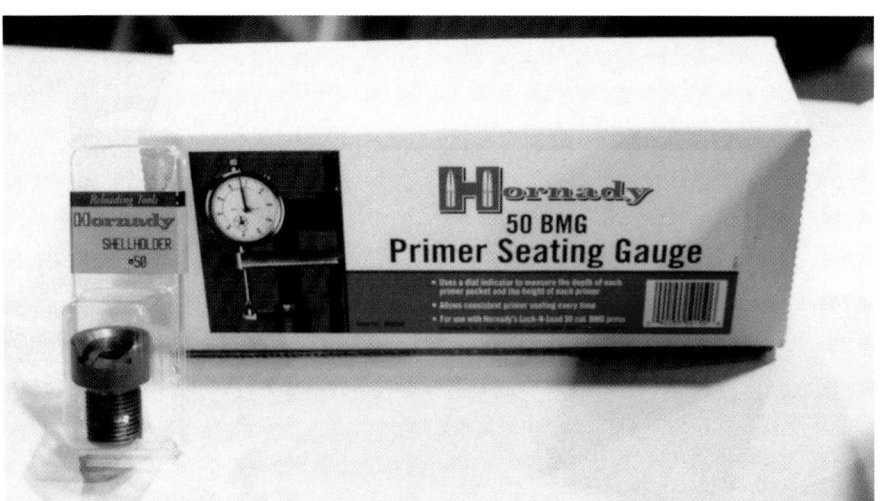

Hornady's new Primer Seating Gauge for the 50 BMG cartridge uses a dial indicator. The 50 BMG cartridge needs a #50 shellholder, shown on the left.

Hornady Mfg. Company

Hornady Mfg. Company has gone all out for handloaders in recent years. The Case Activated Powder Drop has been improved for smoother operation, quick change-overs, and to drop powder only when a case is present. The Quick Change Powder Die can now be preset to permit rapid caliber conversions, and to work with the new Powder Through Expanders. (The new expanders (PTX), available in seven sizes: .355, .357, .400, .430, .451/452, .475, and .500––eliminate the need for a separate case mouth expander die.) The Shell Holders have been improved by widening the mouth and rounding the edges, and five new sizes––455 Webley, 460 S&W, 8x56R H-M, 7.5mm Swiss Ordnance and 8x50R––have been introduced. The Shell Plates have also been improved with bevels and a radius at the mouth to provide smooth functioning.

Hornady has improved the Handheld Priming Tool with a new one-piece primer tray and improved lid retaining system. The body has been modified to permit shellholders and primer trays to be changed without removing the spring and punch.

A Pistol Rotor with standard metering insert is now available for use in the L-N-L Powder Measures, and a micrometer metering insert

can be obtained. Hornady has a 50 BMG Powder Measure, and a high-capacity metering kit is an option. (The 50 BMG measure can drop up to 265 grains of powder at a time, and the kit, which comes with a large hopper and a clear drop lube, and two metering units, will allow dropping 80 to 180 grains or 165 to 265 grains.)

Handloaders turning out a lot of 50 BMG, 50 Spotter, 510 DTC EUROP or 416 Barrett ammunition, may find the Hornady 50 BMG Primer Seating Gauge useful. It uses a dial indicator to measure the depth of each primer pocket and the height of each primer to permit the anvil to just touch the bottom of the primer pocket every single time. Thousand-yard shooters may find the bit of added effort pays off in small group sizes.

Hornady now features new and improved zip spindles on their die sets, and has added an even dozen new calibers to the die sets available. These include the 25 WSSM, 6.8mm Rem. SPC, 20 VT, 5.7x28mm FN, 22/250 Ackley Improved, 22x6mm, 280 Ackley Improved, 30-30 Ackley Improved 325 WSM, 7.92x33mm Kurz and the 8x50Rmm. The Ackley Improved cartridges are becoming popular again after more than four decades of seeming decline. (Maybe the 228 Ackley will even gain a new following.)

Another new Hornady die is one for loading blank cartridges for cowboy action shooting. Fitting any standard press that will accept 7/8x14 TPI dies, the 'blank dies' will handle cartridges from the 32-20 Winchester to the 45-70 Government.

Huntington Reloading Products

If a handloader ever needs a piece of equipment; dies, scales, presses, trimmers powder measures, empty brass, bullets, moulds, etc., Huntington in Oroville, California, either has it in stock or can supply it in short order. In 2006 the firm added more than 125 new products

The Hornady Case Activated Powder Drop has been improved for smoother operation, and quick changeovers. One of the new Hornady power-through expander dies can be seen below the Powder Measure.

for handloaders, including new Norma-produced brass cases for the 303 Savage cartridge. (The 303 Savage seems to be enjoying an increase in popularity and good brass for handloading has been difficult to find. The case can be formed from other calibers, with a bit of work, but Huntington had Norma produce new brass in this caliber.) The firm stocks the RCBS line, including the new Universal Hand Priming Tool, which features an ergonomic grip comfortable for use by right or left-hand users, and it will accept cases from the 32 ACP to the 45-70 Gov't. Two other new RCBS items are the Quick Change Powder Funnel and the Pan Scale Powder Funnel. Constructed of anti-static polymers, the QC funnel comes with five adapters and one drop tube, while the QC Pan Funnel will accommodate cases from 22 to 50-caliber. Huntington has more reloading and case-forming dies than any firm in the U. S., and probably worldwide. (The smallest forming dies are the 17s, and the largest are for the 585 Nyati.) Case brands available include Bertram, Magtech, Jamison, Norma, Starline, Winchester, Weatherby, HDS, Remington, Graf, Hornady, Horneber, Bell, Buffalo Bore, Federal, Lapua, Hirtenberger, Howell, RWS and Walter Gehmann brands. (Single cases can be purchased for many of the calibers, at prices ranging from sixteen cents each (Starline 9mm Makarov) to thirty-five dollars each (700 NE and 4-Bore).

Lee Precision

Lee Precision has new Bottleneck Crimp Dies for the 30 (7.65mm) Luger, 30 Tokarev (7.62mm), 30 Mauser (7.63mm), 357 SIG, and 400 Cor-Bon cartridges, and EasyX reloading dies from the 17 Remington to the 458 Winchester Magnum, including the 6.8mm Remington SPC. Lee also produces dies for the 50 BMG cartridge, and has a case length gauge for the 50 BMG cartridge. The Lee Turret Press (3 die), and the Lee Classic Turret Press (4 die), which is large enough to handle the 50 BMG case––with the Auto-Index disconnected––are fitted with the Lever Prime System.

Load Data

More and more loading data is available through computer programs and via the net. Purchasing the programs or subscribing to the service is the only requirement (read, *get out your credit card*.) One such service, Load Data, at www.loaddata.com, allows access to over 35 years of information from the pages of *Rifle* and *Handloader* magazines for one year.

LR Books

I have always had a fondness for wildcat cartridges, both for handguns and rifles. Finding loading data for such cartridges is not always easy, as many manuals do not provide such data. One of the newest sources for wildcat loading data can be found in *Wildcat Cartridges* by Fred Zeglin and published by LR Books. This 292-page hardbound volume doesn't cover every wildcat cartridge ever produced, but it covers many of both the older and newer designs, plus contains some good information on cartridges such as the 400 Whelen. (Chamber dimensions for the Whelen are included, along with a number of loads featuring modern bullet designs.) Chapter 18 is devoted to today's popular wildcats, from the 10 Eichelberger Squirrel, which can push a 7.2 grain bullet past 4000 fps, to the 50 BMD Short which is capable of sending a 750-grain A-MAX downrange at 1250 fps. (The 458 SOCOM is covered, but not the 500 Phantom, a design capable of pushing a 900-grain bullet out the muzzle at over 1100 fps. Loading data accompanies most of the wildcats discussed, along with a dimensioned case drawing, and background text. Data for the Rocky

J & J Products has a couple of new plastic cases for ammunition. This one will accept almost all cases from the 45-70 Gov't. to the 600 Nitro Express. It will not accept the 50 BMG or the 50-140 Express, but the cartridges shown are the 50-110, 338 Lapua, 416 Rigby, 408 CheyTac (This particular bullet is just a bit too long for the lid to fit properly.), 500 Jeffery, 400 A-Square and 500 Phantom.

Wildcat Cartridges contains hand-loading data on many of the newer wildcat cartridges, and a number of the older designs.

Gibbs cartridges is provided in a separate chapter, as are the designs of Charles Newton and other earlier experimenters. Anyone handloading for a wildcat cartridge will find this a useful reference volume.

Lyman Products Corporation

Lyman Products Corporation has new die sets for the 6.8mm SPC and the 405 Winchester cartridges, and new bullet moulds for the 405 and for 50-caliber shooters. The 405 Winchester mould will cast a 288-grain round-nose bullet, while the 50 mould will cast a 515-grain flat nose design. Both designs are originals from the heyday of these cartridges, and have been returned to production status.

The 48th edition of the *Lyman Reloading Handbook* and the third edition of the *Pistol & Revolver Handbook* need to be on every handloader's reference shelf. The *Reloading Handbook* features pressure-tested reloading data for all but the very latest rifle cartridges, plus an expanded handgun section. It includes some smokeless powder loads for modern blackpowder guns. Most powders, from Alliant to VihtaVuori and Winchester, are covered, along with most modern jacketed bullet brands, and many cast bullets. (No loading data for the 6.8mm SPC, 5.7x28mm, etc. cartridges in this edition.) The *Pistol & Revolver Handbook* covers the majority of current production handgun cartridges, with the exception on the 460 Smith & Wesson cartridge. Loading data is provided for the 45 GAP, 480 Ruger and 500 Smith & Wesson cartridges, with updating on the 'Cowboy' cartridges such as the 38-40, 44-40, 44 Russian, 45 Schofield and 45 Colt.

Magma Engineering Company

Magma Engineering Company, manufacturer of the Mark 7 Bullet Master, the Master Caster, Masterpot and other equipment for turning out cast bullets in quantity, has several new items. The firm has more than 200 styles of bullet moulds available, which can be machine-ready or fitted with RCBS or Lyman handles. A new Multi-Impact System is available for the Bullet Master, and so is a Bullet Separator System. The Multi-Impact provides multiple taps to the bullet mould to aid in releasing large and/ or sticking bullets, and the Bullet Separator separates the bullets into trays for easy inspection. (Both systems can be retrofitted to earlier Bullet Masters.) New conversions to handle longer rifle bullets are standard on current production Lube Master machines, and they can be retrofitted to earlier models.

Montana Vintage Arms

MVA has a new visible powder measure with a micrometer-adjustable scale. Intended for use when loading blackpowder cartridges, the measure comes with a brass hopper of choice, holding 1/4, 1/2 or a full pound of powder. (The scale holds approximately 125 grains of FFg powder.) Extra hopper and scale are available.

NECO

NECO is distributing a new German-manufactured chronograph––the PVN-21. Based on a quarter-century of experimental engineering ballistic velocity measurement systems, the PVN-21 can handle calibers from the 17 to 50 and velocities from 280 to 6500 fps. It features a daylight-independent infrared light-screen for indoor or outdoor use with a 4 x 8-inch sensor, and an accuracy of ±1 percent. It has a 250-shot memory, and a power consumption of 2.1 watts.

NECO is a source of computer-based handloading data. The firm will even provide a free demo disk for their QuickDesign and QuickLoad programs. These computer-aided cartridge design and viewer software, and interior and exterior ballistics programs require MS-Windows versions 98SE, ME, 2000 SP3 and XP SP1 systems to operate. Such programs may not provide all the answers, but it's another method of obtaining desired data.

Norma Precision

Over a century ago in Amotfors, Sweden, the firm of Norma Precision AB (www.norma.cc) got its start. Set up to produce 6.5x55mm bullets for Swedish Mauser rifle cartridges, the firm gained a reputation for producing top quality ammunition and reloading components, including powders for reloading. Yet, during that time the firm never published a loading manual––until now.

The Norma manual includes loading data for over six dozen cartridges, from the 222 Remington to the 505 Gibbs. Norma cases, powders and bullets are featured, coupled with Winchester primers. (Data is provided for some other bullet brands, including Hornady, Sierra, Nosier, Swift A-Frame and Woodleigh.) For each cartridge, a dimensioned drawing is provided, along with specs of the test barrel, the case brand and primer used. A short history of the cartridge is presented, and an illustration of each bullet for which loading data is listed precedes the actual data, along with the ballistic coefficient, overall cartridge length and bullet number. Minimum and maximum powder charges are listed for each bullet weight, along with

Norma's **Reloading Manual** *is the first in the history of the century-old firm, and it is excellent.*

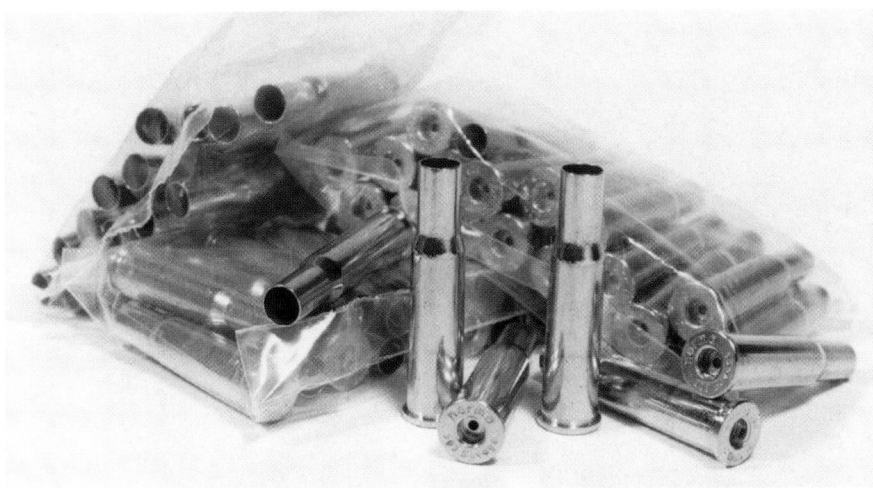

Unprimed Norma brass available from Huntington for the 303 Savage cartridge. Huntington also has loading dies for the 303 Savage, an early cartridge equal to the 30-30 Winchester and claimed by some riflemen to be even better.

the muzzle velocity in feet/second (fps) and meters/second (m/s).

No data is provided for handgun cartridges such as the 44 AutoMag and 44 Remington Magnum, both of which Norma produced, or for the 7x61mm Sharpe & Hart rifle cartridge. Data is included for the 308 and 358 Norma Magnum cartridges, plus a number of the military cartridges for which Norma produces brass.

Other material in this manual include the history of the Norma firm, descriptions of the Norma bullets, powder production, how to make a cartridge, a discussion of primers, step-by-step reloading, and much more. Loading data

for cartridges such as the 6.8mm SPC and 50 BMG is missing.

Nosler

Nosler, a leading name in bullet manufacturing, has been in business since 1948, and now builds bolt-action rifles––the Model 48 Sporter and the 2006 NoslerCustom––loads ammunition, and features a line of premium brass cartridge cases for handloaders in thirteen calibers, in addition to the regular bullet line. (The unprimed cases range from the 204 Ruger to the 300 Weatherby Magnum, and include the 6.5-284 Norma. The loaded ammunition covers more than forty different

cartridges from the 204 Ruger to the 416 Weatherby Magnum, and the *Nosler Reloading Guide No. 5* provides the data for reloading the empties after you've fired the ammunition.

Oehler Research

Every handloader should have access to a chronograph and Ken Oehler's are among the best available. However, production of the excellent Model 35 was suspended on January 1, 2006, although tech support and spare parts are still available. The Model 43 chronograph with SS3 and Windows Software is available. Acoustic targets, strain gages, pressure starter kit and other accessories are also available from Oehler Research in Austin, Texas.

Power Aisle, Inc.

Power Aisle, Inc. has several items handloaders can use, including the Precision Sighting Rest, Back Pack Varmint Bench, Pivoting Pistol Rest, Pivoting Varmint Rest, and the new Danger Game Machine Rest. This latter item, which should be available by the time you read this, rigidly holds a rifle or shotgun in firing position, is fully adjustable for leveling, windage and elevation, and is hydraulically fired. It eliminates the human error, and provides a look at exactly what the cartridge (handload or factory) will do in that particular firearm. It's a worthwhile investment for anyone doing much handloading.

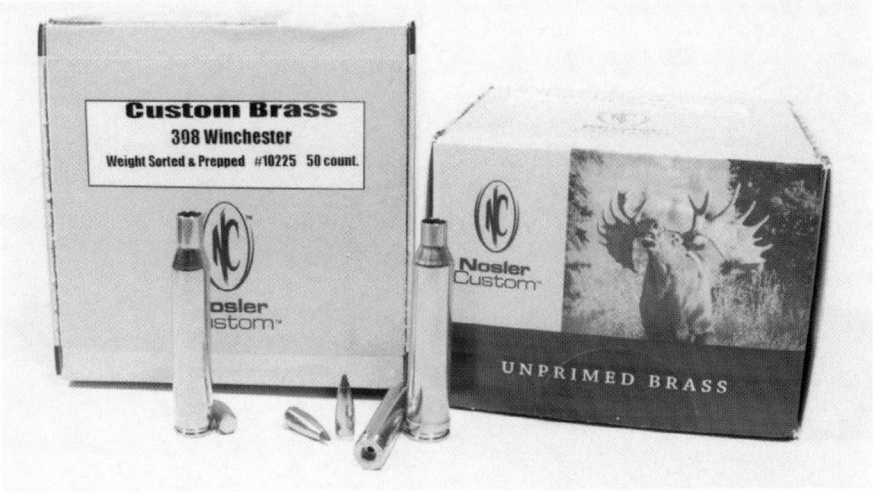

A 'demo' QuickDesign and Quick-Load CD available from Nostalgia Enterprises Co.

Nosler's unprimed brass for handloaders is available for cartridges ranging from the 204 Ruger to the 300 Weatherby Magnum.

RCE Co.

RCE Co. produces a full line of swaging gear for bullet production, plus a couple of special bullet jacket drawing presses. Swaged bullets can be turned out in sizes from 12-caliber to 37mm. RCE presses include the heavy-duty Walnut Hill hand press, a small MultiSwage hydraulic press for home or light commercial use and the larger Benchmaster and HydraSwage presses intended for continuous commercial use. With a background of more than thirty years in the business, RCE swaging equipment is time-tested.

Not everything new for handloaders has been covered. No doubt something has been missed, but a good majority has been touched on. What's been missed will hopefully be covered in the next edition, along with more new products.

RCBS

RCBS has a new 284-page *Handbook of Shotshell Reloading*, featuring over 2000 loads. It also contains a color identification photo of plastic wad columns, a tear-out safety wall chart, 56 separate reference notes on shotshell hulls, color identification photos of external and sectioned views of various hulls currently available, a section showing parts and drawings of RCBS shotshell presses, and much more.

For shooters reloading for handgun and rifle cartridges, there's a new 325 SWM Precision Mic for headspace measurement, two new deburring tools: one to handle deburring and outside chamfering of cases from 17 to 60 caliber, and a second for use when loading VLD-style bullets, a Hand Case Neck Turner, a Universal Hand Priming Tool with a shellholder that will accept cases from the 32 ACP to the 45-70 Government, and several new reloading die calibers. (New dies are available for the 5.7x28mm FN, 325 WSM, 338 Federal, and 460 Smith & Wesson cartridges, with the 460 S&W available in the 3-Die Carbide Roll Crimp set and the 325 WSM available in full length and X-Die sets.) For bullet casters, RCBS has over forty mould designs

A few of the big-bore cartridges for which reloading dies are available from various die manufacturers, such as Hornady, Lee Precision, and RCBS, or dealers handling their products. (Huntington and The Old Western Scrounger are also good sources for such dies.) (L/R): 50 BMG, 510 DTC EUROP, 50 Spotter, 416 Rigby, 408 CheyTac and the 416 Barrett.

for handgun bullets, including one for a 400-grain SWC intended for use in the 500 Smith & Wesson.

RCBS has two new quick-change powder measures, one regular and one high capacity. This latter one can drop up to 240 grains of smokeless powder at a time, and will accommodate two pounds of powder in the hopper. Each measure comes with drop tubes, metering assembly, and quick-drain attachment. (These qc attachments are also available

separately to permit upgrading existing Uniflow power measures.)

Redding

Redding Reloading Equipment celebrated its 60th anniversary in 2006 with the introduction of a considerable number of new products for handloaders. The Model 2400 Match Precision Case Trimming Lathe features micrometer adjustment to 0.001-inch, and will handle cases up to 3-1/4 inches in length. The

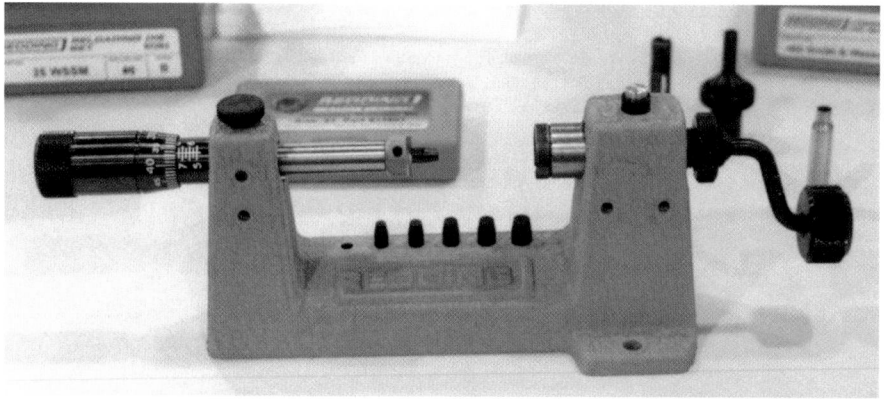

Redding's Model 2400 Match Precision Case Trimming Lathe, with some of the new Redding reloading die sets on the sides in the background—6.8mm Remington SPC, 460 Smith & Wesson, 30 B.R. Remington, etc.

cutter is titanium nitride-coated, and is replaceable, if necessary. The frame is cast iron with storage holes for extra pilots. (Primer pocket cleaners and neck-cleaning brushes can be mounted on the frame, if desired.) A universal collet, with push-button chuck lock, will handle most cases, and an optional power adapter with 1/4-inch hex is available to permit powering with a cordless screwdriver.

Other new Redding products include the "E-Z Feed" shellholders to permit easier case head entry, and a shellholder set containing six of the most popular shellholders––#1, #6, #10, #12, #18, and #19. These six shellholders will accommodate the most common (popular) rifle and handgun cartridges; examples include 30-06 Springfield, 7mm Remington Magnum, 223 Remington, 7.62x39mm, 45-70 Gov't. and 44 Magnum, plus those cartridges with similar rim sizes. Shellholders are available to fit most other cartridges, except the 50 BMG.

New Redding Competition Handgun Seating Dies and Competition Pro Series Die Sets are now available for the 460 and 500 Smith & Wesson Magnum cartridges. Other new die sets are available for the 338 Federal and 5.7x28mm FN cartridges in Type S, Match Die, and Competition Seating Dies. In addition, Bushing Style dies are available for the 20 Vartarg, 20 PPC, 20 BR, 6mm XC, and 30 BR Remington cartridges, plus in the regular die sets. Special small base, full length sizing dies are available to size 22 PPC, 6mm PPC, and 6mm BR Remington cases. Universal Decapping Die in small and large sizes can be obtained to deprime cases prior to resizing for those reloaders desiring to do so. The small die will handle cases from 22 through 50 caliber up to 2.625 inches in length, while the large die will do those cases from 25 through 50 caliber up to 3.00 inches in length. An optional 17-caliber decapping rod is available.

Imperial Sizing Die Wax has been available for a number of years, but Redding is now producing it, along with an Action Wax for use on autoloading pistol slides, bolt ways, etc. The paraffin-based Imperial Wax is excellent for sizing cases; it does the job without the mess and sticking of some lubricants used for sizing.

The Shiloh Sharps Rifle Mfg. Co.

Shiloh has an inline seater press that fits into the top of a regular press. Coupled with a Shiloh inline-seating die it seats bullets without distortion. Made specifically for 40- and 45-caliber Sharps cartridges, such as the 40-60, 40-90, 45-70, 45-100 and 45-120; nose punches are available for specific designs. Shiloh also has 20- and 50-hole loading blocks available to fit the large 40- and 45-caliber cartridges, and a 24-hole version for the rimmed 50-calibers (not the 50 BMG). For those handloaders with a preference for long drop tubes, Shiloh has one mounted on an oak base. Useful for a single case or with cases in a loading block, the tube and funnel are of polished brass.

VihtaVuori

Lapua ammunition, primers, bullets and VihtaVuori powders from Finland have been available for more than seven decades, and the excellent VihtaVuori Reloading Manual has gone through three editions. The loading data section includes loads for some cartridges not always found in other manuals. Among such cartridges are the 5.6x35R Vierling, 220 Russian, 5.6x50 and 5.6x50R Magnum, 5.7x57, 6.5x53R Finnish, 7x33 SAKO, and 8.2x53R Finnish. Loading data for handgun cartridges ranges from the 25 ACP to the 50 Action Express, including a few of the lesser known designs, such as the 7x49 GJW. (The 7x49 GJW is based on the 5.6x50 Magnum case with expanded neck to use in silhouette shooting.) Lapua has introduced a new 6.5x47 cartridge with a head diameter and overall length similar to that of the 308 Winchester (7.62 NATO). Loading data was not available as this is being written, but should be in the new, expanded fourth edition of the VihtaVuori

A video Reloading With the Master *is available through dealers handling VihtaVuori smokeless powder and Lapua bullets and/or ammunition.*

Manual, available at your local dealer about the time you read this.

Not everything new for handloaders has been covered. No doubt something has been missed, but a good majority has been touched on. What's been missed will hopefully be covered in the next edition, along with more new products. ✲

THE GUNS OF EUROPE
2007
WONDERNINES

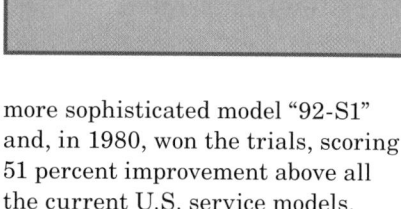

by Raymond Caranta

Fifty years ago, during the Cold War era, the Belgian thirteen-shot 9mm Luger Browning "Hi-Power" was in service with one hundred nations and universally considered, in Europe, as the pattern of the modern practical high-capacity handgun. Since 1935, production of this prestigious model exceeded one and a half million units.

The first generation of "Wondernines"

Unquestionably, the first commercial synthesis of the selective double-action trigger mechanism with a high-capacity 9mm Luger magazine came in 1971, with the Smith & Wesson model 59 fourteen-shot pistol. However, like many forerunners, its success was quite limited in our countries, as, on the one hand, there were no established requirements for such a feature and, on the other hand, our minds were not ready to accept its sophistication.

Nevertheless, as far as I was concerned, the light came on in 1975, at the Madrid European Gun Show, with the 15-shot CZ-75! Perhaps because its safety devices consisted only of a conventional sear thumb-safety and a hammer safety notch, it seemed more familiar to me.

Also, it was truly a beautiful and perfectly proportioned handgun: highly reliable, pleasant to shoot and extremely accurate.

In Italy the next year, I became acquainted with the first version of the Beretta 92, soon to be adopted by the Brazilian army, as well as Italy's military services. This gun also featured a plain thumb-safety and hammer safety notch, like the CZ-75. Italy was then facing "Red Brigades" and "Prima Linea" terrorism and the government "Carabinieri" were allowed to carry their service pistols with a round chambered.

As you can imagine, with more than 90,000 people frequently operating the slide of these guns, chambering a round, then manually decocking the hammer, the automatic hammer-dropping device became an essential requirement. In 1979 Beretta went to that configuration with their "92-S" version.

Moreover, that same year, following ballistic experiments at the Aberdeen Edgewood Arsenal, the U.S. Army determined the efficiency of the NATO 9mm Luger ammunition was equivalent to that of their 45 ACP hardball service round, which enabled the JSSAP (Joint Service Small Arms Program) committee to charge the U.S. Air Force A.F.A.L. Laboratory to develop the specifications for an up-to-date 9mm service pistol.

To make the story short, Beretta improved their "92-S" pistol into a more sophisticated model "92-S1" and, in 1980, won the trials, scoring 51 percent improvement above all the current U.S. service models.

Due to internal controversies, a new "XM9" test schedule was arranged by the JSSAP in 1981 and the U.S. Army was put in charge of its application.

In December 1984, in direct competition with the Smith & Wesson model "459", Heckler & Koch "P7-M13," Sig Sauer "P226," Browning HP "DA," Steyr "GB" and Walther "P-88," (1) Beretta won again with its improved "92-SB" pistol.

The offspring of this Homeric selection process, which lasted five years, are still the Beretta "M9" and its variations.

Concerning the Sig Sauer "P226" which finished second: it is still in production in a number of versions, such as the U.S. Army "M11 Compact" and the current British service models.

Smith & Wesson's extensive line of 9mm pistols is more than ever in production.

The Browning HP "DA," after several evolutions, recently gave birth to the new "Pro-9," made in U.S.A.

The Heckler & Koch "P7-M13" is still listed as a military model in some catalogs and its German Police 8-shot counterpart, the

"P7-M8," is currently exported on the international market. However, a more conventional line, the "USP" (listed in our table), has taken the baton.

The Walther "P-88" was adopted nowhere for different reasons (2), but it is listed (2006) in several variations, mostly for competitive shooting, as the "P-88 Champion" and "Competition".

The Steyr "GB" has disappeared following its 1984 failure because of reliability problems. It is now replaced in their line by the "M9" and "S"––entirely different models.

While all these champions were fighting for the honor of becoming the new U.S. service pistol, the small Austrian army released, in 1980, its own military specification for a national service model (3).

As none of the existing designs met its specific requirements, and the 25,000 units quantity required was quite small, a new contender, Mr. Gaston Glock, had to patent his own design in 1981––the "Glock 17"––adopted in 1983 by the Austrian services as the "Model 1980 Pistol." Since then, Glock pistols have conquered the world, with more than two million in service everywhere.

And the previously-mentioned "CZ-75"?

Czechoslovakia, part of the Soviet bloc, did not participate in the Free World activities and, therefore, was excluded from major Western commercial agreements until 1992. Meanwhile, their firearms were internationally distributed by the Merkuria concern to Europe, Africa, South America and Middle East.

Therefore, the "CZ-75" and "CZ-85" were "dream guns" for the U.S. *aficionados* during this 17-year period, particularly for their excellent compatibility to IPSC competition. In 1981 these guns inspired the late American 10mm "Bren Ten", without actually reaching industry production status.

When Czechoslovakia became the Czech Republic in 1994, Ceska Zbrojovka, the "CZ-75" and "CZ-85" manufacturer, became an independent gun company and was able to arrange the distribution of its products under its own trade mark.

The New Generation of "Wondernines"

The adoption of the fifteen-shot double-action "M9" pistol in 1984 made quite a stir among the U.S. security agencies already in turmoil over the unfavorable comparison of their traditional six-shot revolvers––though loaded with the new +P hollowpoint ammunition––to the thirteen-shot 9mm Brownings of South American cocaine smugglers.

Soon, everybody was wishing for his own "Wondernine!"

For us, America is the leading country in terms of technical progress. Soon, clever gun manufacturers introduced new designs––or clones of those already successful.

In Italy, the old Bernardelli firm tried to compete with Beretta with their "P-018/9" fifteen-shot model. In Spain, Astra, Llama and Star designed their own high-capacity 9mm pistols. In Hungary, Fegarmy first made a Browning "Hi-Power" clone and, later, fitted it with a selective double-action mechanism.

From Brazil, Taurus exported their "PT-92" licensed and improved version of the Beretta 92 and, later, designed original pistols.

By now, the original Bernardelli "P-018/9", Astra and Star designs have disappeared, but new models came from Israel (Bul and IMI), Czech Republic (Alfa and Moravia), Croatia (XD), Italy (Tanfoglio), Switzerland (Sphinx), Yugoslavia (Zastava) and, more recently, Turkey (Sarsilmaz). Another major producer of high-capacity 9mm Luger pistols is Russia, with their own Baïkal brand.

All these models in current production appear in the attached table, and most of them are described in the "Handguns" catalog section of the GUN DIGEST.

The 9mm Luger, 357 Sig, 40 S&W and 45 ACP chamberings

Since the general acceptance of these "Wondernines" twenty years ago, the 9mm Luger, their original chambering, has been challenged: first, by the 40 S&W in 1990; then by the 357 Sig in 1995; and, most recently, by the current 45 craze (45 ACP and 45 GAP in 2003).

Remember, in Europe, all government agencies are compelled to use full-jacketed bullets (FMJs), in accordance with the Hague Convention requirements, with few possible concessions (i.e. the "Action" special loading).

Bis. Russian compact pistol Baïkal MP-446P "Mini-Viking" was the new star at the 2004 SHOT Show.

Therefore, the stopping power is necessarily limited to the values mentioned for the applicable cartridges in the book reference (4), with which I entirely agree, considering my own experience as a national forensic expert.

In simplifying these statistics, a torso first hit can reasonably be expected to incapacitate an opponent in approximately two-thirds of cases, both with NATO 9mm Luger or 45 "hardball" ammunition. Such results can be increased up to 70 percent with the 40 S&W FMJ ammunition, indicating significant progress in this field.

Now, why is the 9mm Luger still––fifteen years after the appearance of the 40 S&W––the international military and police standard?

For several reasons.

1) This stopping power matter is seriously investigated and given due consideration only in the United States.

2) The 9mm Luger cartridge is lighter, smaller, cheaper––and manufactured and stored in such huge quantities that nobody wishes to change.

3) When the 9mm Luger was standardized as the NATO service cartridge fifty years ago, it was considered major progress by nations formerly using 32 ACP, 380 ACP and 7.65mm Long. Today, everybody is still satisfied, and doesn't feel a real need for change.

4) In Europe, handguns are treated as secondary weapons by the military, and the 9mm Luger is generally considered as efficient for submachine gun use.

5) As Russia has only recently joined the club, it is not time to change.

Concerning the 357 Sig cartridge, its main capability with FMJ bullets lies in its increased capability to pierce light body armor. Therefore, its introduction in European government supply systems is not considered worth the expense and complications it would introduce, contrasted to 9mm Luger high-velocity military loadings of similar potential that don't require a new gun.

For the 45-calibers, the 45 ACP is heavier, bulkier and more expensive than the 9mm Luger, with less penetration and a similar stopping power (4).

Then, why change?

The 45 GAP cartridge is too new to formulate an opinion but, up to now, it does not seems that it should, in the near term, dislodge the 9mm Luger from it's entrenched position. Moreover, most "Wondernine" models have an equivalent 40 S&W chambering for export.

The Current Families of European "Wondernines"

Twenty years after their introduction, the seven following general families can be discerned (in alphabetical order):

1 – The Russian Baïkals

They are all 15- or 17-shot conventional short-recoil models with tilting barrels and selective double-action triggers.

The MP446 "Viking," with its polymer frame, is the new service pistol since 2003, when it replaced the former MP443 "Grach" featuring a steel frame (weight savings = 5.6 oz.).

The MP446P "Mini-Viking" is the short 15-shot police version, introduced in 2004. An ambidextrous sear thumb-safety acts as a decocking lever when fully raised.

2 – The Berettas

The Beretta 92 is the oldest, with its models 96 (40) and 98 (9x21 IMI) descendants. This line consists of six basic variations, including the "Compacts" and "Centurions" (13-shot/L overall = 7.75"/Barrel = 4.29"). The "Combat" and "Vertec" are sporting variations. They are all short axial barrel-recoil pistols with lower swinging lock and selective double action (*a la* P-38).

The Beretta "90-Two", chambered both in 9mm Luger (17 + 1-shot) and 40 S&W (10 + 1-shot), is a new sporting development of the basic model 92, measuring L 8.5" x H 5.5" x W 1.5" and weighing 32.5 oz. It is available in "F" (drop hammer safety), "G" (decocking lever) and "D" (DAO) variations with a new receiver, modular grip unit, redesigned slide and slide stop and integral accessory rail with cover. It will supersede the "Centurion", "Combat" and "Vertec" models in 2007.

The 8000 "Cougar" is a rotating-barrel 15-shot pistol with a 3.62-inch barrel, also available with a short grip and a 10-shot magazine (weight savings = 6.43 oz.). It is being superseded, in 2006, by the new "PX4 Storm".

The "PX4 Storm," released in 2005, is a compact pistol (L overall = 7.6"/ Barrel = 4.00"/Weight = 28 oz), featuring a polymer receiver, a rotating barrel and a modular interchangeable trigger mechanism.

Without doubt, the new Beretta "PX4 Storm F" 9mm pistol is, by far, one of the best guns of the year. The grip, with interchangeable backs is super; both the single and double action pulls at, respectively, 4.7 and 10 pounds, are excellent and our best 25-meter offhand 10-shot groupings measure 2.36x2.36" and 2.28X2.64," with Winchester 115-grain FMJ ammunition.

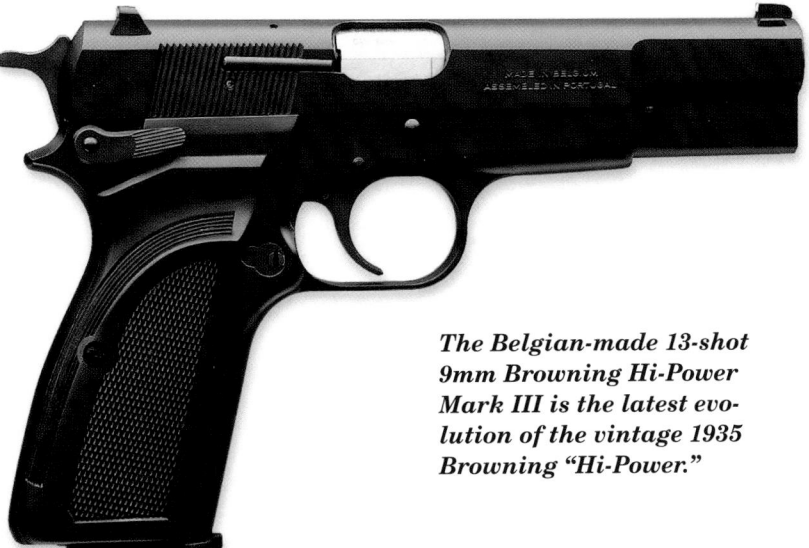

The Belgian-made 13-shot 9mm Browning Hi-Power Mark III is the latest evolution of the vintage 1935 Browning "Hi-Power."

It is intended to replace, in due time, both the "Cougar" and the 9000F/D. According to our recent tests, the "PX4 Storm" seems to be one of the best in its class for practical use.

The "9000F/SD" is a compact model with polymer receiver introduced in 2000 (L overall = 6.6"/ Barrel = 3.4"/Weight = 26.8 oz).

3 – The Browning Hi-Power and its clones

The Belgian "Hi-Power Mark III" is the latest evolution (1993) of the basic "Hi-Power" released in 1935. These pistols are tilting barrel single-action designs. According to some Middle East military men, the Browning "Hi-Power" is still the most reliable pistol they have used in their often-sandy environment.

The Hungarian Fegarmy "P9M" thirteen-shot single-action pistol is a clone of the original Browning "Hi-Power." It has been used as a base for developing two similar selective double-action models: the "P9R" (L overall = 8.00"/Barrel = 4.66"/Weight = 35.7 oz); "P9KK" (L overall = 7.48"/Barrel = 4.15"/Weight = 34.6 oz.), and a small one, the "P9RZ" (10-shot/L overall = 7"/Height = 4.56"/Barrel = 3.63"/Weight = 32.5 oz). This design includes a drop-hammer safety; for the "P9RZ," a polymer receiver would be welcome! The two samples tested were accurate and reliable with NATO-standard full jacketed ammunition.

4 - The CZ-75, CZ-85 and their clones

The original CZ-75 pistol is of all-steel construction and features a tilting barrel on a dual ramp, with inverted bolt and receiver sliding rails. Trigger pull is selective double action. The safety can be either a plain sear thumb-safety or, on recent models, a thumb-actuated drop hammer device.

The current Ceska Zbrojovka variations of the "CZ-75" and "CZ-85" pistols are very popular in Europe as they are sturdy, well made and particularly cost-effective! According to the "Handguns" section of the GUN DIGEST catalog, the situation looks very similar in America...

During the last thirty years, I have seen, handled, field-stripped and shot many Czech CZ-75s and found only one with a poor trigger pull. But, was it in its original condition?

The first clones to appear were the Italian Tanfoglios in 1983. At the beginning, they could only be described as "fair" but, soon, the Tanfoglio brothers properly tooled up and efficiently organized their factory so that, now, their catalog lists 34 models and variations! Moreover, being specialized in sophisticated IPSC target guns, their guns have won many trophies, while their champion, the Frenchman Eric Grauffel, has won several gold medals in the "Open" class.

The situation is similar for "Sphinx," having significantly improved their workmanship since the '80s. Today, the samples of their series 3000 I see at the international gun shows look very nice.

The IMI "Jericho" is another clone made in Israel for many years. In Europe, they are called "Samson." Their new SP21 "Barak" was introduced in 2002. It is a promising original design with dual recoil springs.

The Czech Alfa pistols are CZ-75 plain variations with polymer receivers, which recently appeared at the IWA European gun show.

The Israeli Bul "Cherokee", "Impact" and "Storm" are other CZ-75 clones.

The current "CZ-75 B" version of the original CZ-75 of yesteryear, with the plain sear thumb-safety, is still a beautiful gun with many, many fans!

SERVICE MODELS -EUROPEAN 9mm LUGER AUTOMATIC PISTOLS AS OF JANUARY 31, 2006

TRADE MARK	MODEL	MAGAZINE CAPACITY	LENGTH OVERALL in.	BARREL LENGTH in.	EMPTY WEIGHT oz.	LOADED WEIGHT oz.	ACTION	RECEIVER MATERIAL	OBSERVATIONS
ALFA	COMBAT*	16	8.27	4.45	30.3	37.2	OH/SDA/AFPS	P	CZECH.
ALFA	DEFENDER*	13	7.48	3.66	26.8	32.3	OH/SDA/AFPS	P	CZECH.
BAÏKAL	VIKING MP-446	17	7.67	4.43	29.6	36.9	OH/SDA/DHS	P	RUSSIA SM
BAÏKAL	MINI-VIKING # MP-446P	15	7.28	4.23	27.1	33.6	OH/SDA/DHS	P	RUSSIA
BAÏKAL	MP-444 BAGHIRA	15	7.32	3.97	26.2	32.6	H/SDA/DHS/SMS	P	RUSSIA
BAÏKAL	MP-445C VARYAG	15	7.4	4.37	29.6	36	OH/SDA/SSOH	P	RUSSIA
BAÏKAL	MP-445	17	8.26	4.92	31	38.3	OH/SDA/SSOH	P	RUSSIA
BERETTA	PX4-STORM*	17	7.6	4	28	35.3	DHS/OH/SDA/ DAO/DAOPA	P	ITALY CONVERTIBLE
BERETTA	92 FS	15	8.54	4.92	35.7	42	OH/SDA/DHS	LA	ITALY SM
BERETTA	8000F COUGAR*	15	7.08	3.62	33	39.4	OH/SDA/DHS	LA	ITALY OTHER CALIBERS
BERETTA	8000L COUGAR*	13	7.08	3.62	28.5	34.1	OA/SDA/DHS/PAO	LA	ITALY
BERETTA	9000F/D*	12	6.64	3.46	27.1	32.2	OA/SDA/SSOH/ DAO/DAOPS	P	ITALY
BERNARDELLI	2000	15	8.26	4.68	27.5	33.9	OA/SDA/SMS/AFPS	P	ITALY
BERNARDELLI	2000 BABY	13	7.46	3.89	25	30.6	OA/SDA/SMS/AFPS	P	ITALY
BROWNING	HI-POWER MK III	13	7.75	4.6	32.1	37.7	OA/SA/SMS	S	BELGIUM
BUL	CHEROKEE	17	8.26	4.45	27.5	34.8	OA/SDA/SMS/AFPS NEW RECEIVER	P	ISRAEL
BUL	COMPACT CHER.	17	7.48	3.66	25	32.3	OA/SDA/SMS/AFPS NEW RECEIVER	P	ISRAEL
BUL	IMPACT*	13	7.48	3.85	26.8	32.3	OA/SDA/SMS/AFPS NEW RECEIVER	P	ISRAEL OTHER CALIBERS
BUL	MINI-CHEROKEE	13	7.48	3.66	24.7	30.3	OA/SDA/SMS/AFPS NEW RECEIVER	P	ISRAEL
BUL	STORM*	16	8.07	4.76	37.5	44.3	OA/SDA/SMS/AFPS NEW RECEIVER	S	OTHER CALIBERS
CZ	75 B	16	8.11	4.72	37.5	44.3	OA/SDA/SMS/AFPS NEW RECEIVER	SS-A	CZECH
CZ	75 D COMPACT P-01	15	7.2	3.87	27.8	34.3	OA/SDA/DHS/AFPS	AL	CZECH
CZ	75 PCR COMPACT	13	7.2	3.87	27.8	33.4	OA/SDA/DHS/AFPS	AL	CZECH
CZ	2075 RAMI*	10	6.57	3	24.8	29	OA/SDA/SMS	AL	CZECH
CZ	110*	13	7.08	3.85	23.9	29.5	H/SDA/AFPS/DHS	P	CZECH
FEGARMY	F9 PR/F9 PRK	14	8.00/7.48	4.66/4.15	35.7/34.6	41.8/40.7	OH/SDA/DHS	S	HUNGARY
FEGARMY	F9 RZ*	10	7	3.63	32.1	36.8	OA/SDA/DHS/DAO	S	HUNGARY
GLOCK	17*	17	7.99	4.49	25	32.39	H/DAOPS/ATS	P	AUSTRIA
GLOCK	19*	15	6.81	4	23.7	30.2	H/DAOPS/ATS	P	AUSTRIA
GLOCK	26*	10	6.81	3.42	22.1	26.4	H/DAOPS/ATS	P	AUSTRIA
H&K	USP9	15	7.64	4.25	26.6	33.1	OH/SDA/DHS/DAO (9 OPTIONS)	P	OTHER CALIBERS GERMANY
H&K	USP9 SD	15	7.94	4.56	27.5	33.9	OH/SDA/DHS/DAO (9 OPTIONS)	P	GERMANY OTHER CALIBERS
H&K	USP9 COMPACT	13	6.81	3.58	25.5	31.1	OH/SDA/DHS/DAO (9 OPTIONS)	P	GERMANY SM
iMi	SP21 BARAK*	16	7.4	3.89	29.46	36.3	OH/SDA/DHS/AFPS	P	ISRAEL SM
iMi	JERICHO STANDARD*	15	8.25	4.52	39	45.43	OH/SDA/DHS/AFPS	S	OTHER CALIBERS ISRAEL
iMi	JERICHO SEMI COMPACT*	15	7.75	3.93	38	44.43	OH/SDA/DHS/AFPS	S	ISRAEL
iMi	JERICHO COMPACT*	12	7.25	3.64	34.3	39.44	OH/SDA/DHS/AFPS	S	ISRAEL
iMi	JERICHO SEMI COM POLYMER*	15	7.75	3.93	31	37.43	OH/SDA/DHS/AFPS	P	ISRAEL

9mm LUGER AUTOMATIC PISTOLS *(CONTINUED)*

TRADE MARK	MODEL	MAGAZINE CAPACITY	LENGTH OVERALL in.	BARREL LENGTH in.	EMPTY WEIGHT oz.	LOADED WEIGHT oz.	ACTION	RECEIVER MATERIAL	OBSERVATIONS
iMi	JERICHO COM POLYMER*	12	7.25	3.64	30	35.14	OH/SDA/DHS/AFPS	P	ISRAEL
MORAVIA	CZ-62000*	15	7.28	4	27.8	34.3	OH/SDA/DHS/AFPS	P	CZECH.
SARSILMAZ	KILINE 2000	15	8.18	4.47	42.7	49.1	OH/SDA/SMS	S	TURKISH
SARSILMAZ	KILINE 2000 LIGHT	15	8.18	4.47	35.7	42.1	OH/SDA/SMS	LA	TURKISH
SARSILMAZ	HANCER 2000	13	7.46	3.89	35.7	41.28	OH/SDA/SMS	S	TURKISH
SARSILMAZ	HANCER 2000 LIGHT	13	7.46	3.89	25.7	31.28	OH/SDA/SMS	LA	TURKISH
SIG SAUER	P226*	15	7.7	4.4	31.8 (AL) 42.14 (SS)	38.2(AL) 48.6 (SS)	OH/SDA/DHS/ DAK/DAO/ ALSO/SL/SO	AL or SS	OTHER CALIBERS GERMANY SM SEVERAL VERSIONS
SIG SAUER	P228	13	7.09	3.85	29.46	35	OH/SDA/DHS/AFPS	AL	GERMANY SM
SIG SAUER	P229*	13	7.09	3.85	30.09	36.46	OH/SDA/DHS/AFPS SOLID STEEL SLIDE	AL	GERMANY OTHER CALIBERS
SIG SAUER	P239*	8	6.61	3.58	27.5	30.92	OH/SDA/DHS/ AFPS/DAK	AL	GERMANY OTHER CALIBERS
SIG SAUER	P250 DCC*	15	7.09	4	25.71	32.14	OH/DAOPS/DHS/ AFPS	P	GERMANY SM
SIG SAUER	SPC 2009	15	7.09	3.58	25.46	31.9	OH/SDA/DHS/ AFPS	P	GERMANY
SIG SAUER	SP 2009 SP2022*	15	7.36	3.86	28.64	35	OH/SDA/DHS/ AFPS	P	GERMANY SM
SPHINX	3000*	15	8.46	4.53	37.1	43.6	OH/SDA/SMS/ AFPS/DAO	T	OTHER CALIBERS SWITZERLAND
SPHINX	3000 TACTICAL*	15	7.67	3.74	33.9	40.35	OH/SDA/SMS/ AFPS/DAO	T	SWITZERLAND
SPRINGFIELD ARMORY	5"XD TACTICAL*	15	8.07	5	31	37.5	H/DAOPS/ATS	P	OTHER CALIBERS CROATIA
SPRINGFIELD ARMORY	4"XD SERVICE*	15	7.08	4	23.2	29.64	H/DAOPS/ATS	P	OTHER CALIBERS CROATIA
SPRINGFIELD ARMORY	SUB-COMPACT*	10	6.1	3	20.5	24.8	H/DAOPS/ATS	P	CROATIA
STEYR	M9*	14	7.08	4	27.8	33.85	H/DAO/DAOPS	P	AUSTRIA
STEYR	S*	10	6.61	3.58	25	29.3	H/DAO/DAOPS	P	AUSTRIA
TANFOGLIO	COMBAT AND STAINLESS*	16	8.26	4.44	41.07	47.9	OH/SDA/SMS/AFPS	S and SS	OTHER CALIBERS ITALY
TANFOGLIO	COMPACT AND COMP. STANDARD	13	7.48	3.66	35.7	41.3	OH/SDA/SMS/AFPS	S	OTHER CALIBERS ITALY
TANFOGLIO	FORCE	16	8.26	4.44	30.35	37.2	OH/SDA/SMS/AFPS	P	OTHER CALIBERS ITALY
TANFOGLIO	FORCE COMPACT	13	7.67	3.66	26.8	32.35	OH/SDA/SMS/AFPS	P	OTHER CALIBERS ITALY
WALTHER	P99 (AS-QA-DAO)*	15	7.12	4	24.64	31.07	H/SDA/DHS/SAD/ DAO and DAOPA	P	GERMANY
WALTHER	P99 C*	10	6.6	3.5	20.5	26.8	H/SDA/DHS/SAD/ DAO and DAOPA	P	GERMANY
ZASTAVA	CZ 99	15	7.68	4.25	30.71	37.16	OH/SDA/DHS/AFPS	LA	JUGO-SLAVIA
ZASTAVA	CZ 99 COMPACT	15	7.08	3.85	28.75	35.2	OH/SDA/DHS/ AFPS	LA	JUGO-SLAVIA

Key to abbreviations: DHS=Drop hammer safety, SA=Single action, T=Titanium, AFPS=Automatic firing pin safety, H=Hammerless, SDA=Selective double action, TMS=Trigger manual safety, ATS=Automatic trigger safety, LA=Light alloy, SMS=Sear manual safety, # =New since 2002, DAK=Sig. Sauer DAO device at 7.7lbs., OH=External hammer, SM=Service model, * =Also available in .40SW, DAO=Double action only, P=Polymere, SS=Stainless steel, DAOPS=Pre-cocked striker DAO, S=Steel, carbon, SSOH=Sear safety with external hammer

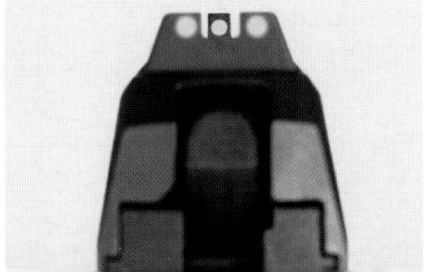

The pre-production CZ-85 with ambidextrous controls is one of my pet guns for the past twenty years!

All have polymer receivers, with the exception of the "Storm" which is of all-steel construction.

This line of double-action pistols was introduced in 1999. In view of their manufacturer's high repute, they cannot be otherwise than good, which is substantiated by the success of its "Cherokee" brand introduced in 2002.

The Moravia is a new version of the elegant Brno ZBF 99 prototype featuring a polymer receiver, displayed at the IWA gun show in 1998.

It looks good, but is not yet available, several years after its introduction.

The Sarsilmaz are Turkish clones of the same CZ-75, with steel or light alloy receivers, introduced in 1999 by an important shotgun manufacturer.

The Norinco NZ 85 B, chambered in 9mm Luger and NZ 98, chambered in 40 S&W, are Chinese imitations of the CZ-85, with ambidextrous sear safeties, shown this year (2006) at the IWA Norconia booth.

Concerning the technical evaluation of all these clones: provided they are made of good materials and well-fitted, they should be accurate and reliable, as their basic design is very sound and well-tried. The most critical point to check is the trigger pull, both in single and double action,

as according to my experience, if you start with a good trigger pull, you will have an excellent gun for many years but, if it is sluggish and creepy, your gunsmith has to be a wizard to obtain a decent let-off.

5 - The Glock family and its competitors

In 2006, Gaston Glock is at the apex of his glory, with a range of twenty-six models available in seven different chamberings (3): the 380 ACP, 9mm Luger, 357 Sig, 40 S&W, 10 mm Auto, 45 ACP and 45 GAP.

All these guns are based on the same action: a short-recoil ramped tilting barrel, with a polymer receiver and a hammerless striker mechanism featuring a pre-cocked double action trigger with the same finger pressure for all shots.

Their success induced some competitors to work on similar ideas.

The first European competition came in 1996 from Walther, in Germany, with their "P-99" model featuring either an "anti-stress" selective double-action trigger ("AS"), a "DAO" trigger or a pre-cocked double-action trigger ("QA" for "Quick Action"). These guns are made in Europe at a brand new (March 2006) Ulm Factory, or assembled and produced by Smith & Wesson in America. Then, in 2002, Springfield Armory

disclosed a new line of Croatian pistols of similar inspiration they are distributing exclusively: the "XD" brand, now available in 9mm Luger, 40 S&W and 45 GAP.

This writer has handled these enigmatic pistols several times at the SHOT Show, but never had the opportunity to shoot them, as they are not sold in Europe. They are attractive and seem to be very well made. According to the known sale figures, their popularity is fast increasing on the American market.

The last of these competitors are also Austrian products, the Steyr "M9" and "S" pistols, which firstly appeared in 1999, then were modified further and, since 2004, feature a new receiver.

Only recently, a prototype replica of the Glock G-19 was seen at the Pakistani Daudsons Industries IWA 2006 booth.

6 - The Heckler & Koch "USP" family

In 1990, the U.S. Navy JSOC (Joint Special Operations Command) issued a specification for an OHWS (Offensive Handgun Weapon System) in 45 ACP, and the subsequent selection was awarded to Heckler & Koch in 1993.

Conscious that the specific characteristics of their former P7 and P9S models required special training limiting their sales, they accordingly designed

The Glock "G 17," offered since 1983, is the basic model of this extraordinarily popular line. It is simple (34 components) and accurate with its 17-shot 9mm magazine

The brand new Heckler-und-Koch "P30" fifteen-shot 9mm pistol is a technical masterpiece featuring the most sophisticated improvements.

a new line of "USP" pistols, available in 9mm Luger, 40 S&W and 45 ACP, introduced in 1993 and completed them by an "USP Compact" version, in 1996.

These "USP" pistols feature ramped tilting barrels, polymer receivers, a recoil reducing system, a single control lever and a modular firing mechanism offering ten different options. They are among the most sophisticated of the market.

This superb line has been completed, this year, by a new fifteen-shot 9mm Luger model "P30" featuring ambidextrous controls, automatic hammer and firing pin safety, loaded indicator, luminous contrast sights and interchangeable backstraps (7 x 5.3 x 1.35"/Empty weight = 23.4 oz).

7 - Sig Sauer, Zastava and Norinco

The Sig Sauer line of selective double-action, light alloy-receiver pistols with ramped tilting barrel and side decocking lever started in 1971 in Switzerland, as the single–stack multi-caliber "P220" (5).

In accordance with the U.S. "XM9" specification of 1981, Sig Sauer designed the 15-shot "P226" model,

based on the "P220" action, in 1983. It finished technically first *ex aequo* with the Beretta 92 the next year, the latter being selected on price criterion. Later, this pistol was highly successful on the international market and became in 1990, with the "P228," one of the two British service pistols.

Since then, the Sig Sauer line of pistols, sold under the "Sigarms" trade mark in America, expanded a great deal and, in 2006, consists of thirty-six offsprings of the "P220" original model.

As the penalty for its success, the "P226" attracted a clone in 1990, the Zastava "CZ 99" made in Yugoslavia, now Serbia. After a suspension of exports resulting from the Balkan hostilities, this pistol was again offered by Zastava in 1999, together with a shorter compact model.

Finally, in 2006, the Chinese Norinco Company offers also two new high-capacity Sig clones chambered in 9mm Parabellum: the larger NP22 and smaller NP34, plus a 9mm variation of their original compact model "77", the "77 B."

My personal selection?

After several Browning "Hi-Powers", my first modern

"Wondernines" were a Beretta 92 and a pre-production "CZ-85" (s/n 00031), in 1985. Both were highly accurate and very reliable, even with French army ammunition, which was often of poor quality.

My pet gun was the Beretta, through which I have fired 15,000 rounds in fifteen years, as it made a good companion to a burst-firing model "93R" I liked to shoot for fun. The "CZ-85" is still in my possession and I would not dispose of it at any price.

Currently, I also use an eighteen-shot 9mm Luger Bul "M5," which is not a true "Wondernine" but, thanks to its adjustable rear sight, is very pleasant to shoot. However, it does not like our military ammunition...

My dream 9mm pistols?

Since last December, I have been vacillating between a Walther "P-99AS" and the new Beretta "PX4 Storm." At the moment, the Beretta has a slight edge, in remembrance of my old model 92... ✪

BIBLIOGRAPHY

Pistolets A Grande Puissance De Feu , by Raymond Caranta. Crépin-Leblond Publishers, 52902 CHAUMONT CEDEX 9, France. 1985. (in French).

The Walther Handgun Story, by Gene Gangarosa Jr. Stoeger Publishing Co, Wayne, NJ 07470.

Glock, Un Monde Technologique Nouveau, by Raymond Caranta. Crépin-Leblond Publishers, 52902 CHAUMONT CEDEX 9, France. 2005. (in French).

Street Stoppers, by Evan P. Marshall and Edwin J. Sanow. Paladin Press, Boulder, Colorado 80301.

Sig-Sauer, Une Epopée Technologique Européenne, by Raymond Caranta. Crépin-Leblond Publishers, 52902 CHAUMONT CEDEX 9, France. 2003. (in French)

AMMUNITION, BALLISTICS & COMPONENTS

by Holt Bodinson

*J*ust when you begin to feel there's just not room for another commercially viable cartridge, the manufacturers surprise us again and again with some great new offerings.

Who would have thought the venerable 308 Winchester case that has been around since 1952 would be morphed into yet another successful cartridge? This year Federal did it and names the case after the company--the 338 Federal. A-Square unleashes the 400 Dual Purpose Magnum. Freedom Arms comes roaring in with their belted 500 Wyoming Express. Hornady pumps new power into the 30-30, 35 Rem., 444 Rem., 45-70 and 450 Marlin lever-gun cartridges under the catchy banner of "LeverEvolution."

And new high-tech game bullets! Winchester engineers the XP3 and Barnes comes across with the MRX.

And high-tech shot! Remington stops loading Hevi-Shot and launches Wingmaster HD across the line while Winchester ramps up their Xtended Range Hi-Density shot offerings for waterfowl and turkey.

Industry shifts go on. Hodgdon seems to have a magic touch. Two years ago it acquired IMR Powder. This year Winchester Ammunition licenses Hodgdon to take over all their canister sales of the

Winchester powder line. Meanwhile, Hodgdon even has time to come to the table with a new magnum powder of their own—US869.

The ammunition, ballistic and components markets just get more interesting with every passing year.

A-Square Company

A-Square's founder, Arthur Alphin, has resumed management of the company. Well known for its unique cartridge offerings, A-Square hasn't disappointed us for 2007. The new member of the lineup is the 400 A-Square Dual Purpose Magnum. Dual purpose? Based on the belted H&H case, the new 400 is loaded with either the company's "Triad" of 400-grain big game bullets or lighter .410-inch pistol bullets for medium-size game and varmints. Velocity of the 400- and 210-grain pills is 2400 fps while the 170-grain pistol bullet steps out at 2980 fps. Intriguing, to say the least. www.a-squarecompany.com

Alliant Powder

Alliant has a new target shotgun powder. It's Clay Dot and appears to have a loading equivalence and burning rate similar to Hodgdon's Clays. Look

for it, and its loading data, at your dealer. www.alliantpowder.com

Ballistic Products

Here's the one-stop store for all your shotgun shell reloading and component needs bound in one of the most entertaining and informative catalogs ever fielded.

The best of their new products this year are their new publications. The shotshell reloader's bible is their "Advantages IV," that chronicles everything you need to know to build a better shell. "Dove & Pigeon

Ballistic Products'
"Shotshell Reloaders Log" provides
a permanent record of personal
handloads and their performance.

Magic" serves up some natural history and the most effective recipes for bagging and eating our most common avian fauna.

There's a brand-new *Shotshell Reloading Log*, and don't pass up their informative "Ballistic Products Technical Brochures." Need a deadly 20-gauge load for late-season pheasants, or a light load for directing the mighty 10-gauge toward crows and clays? Ballistic Products is the mother lode. www.ballisticproducts.com

Barnes Bullets

The highly successful Triple-Shock bullet has been morphed into the MRX bullet, standing for "Maximum-Range X-Bullet." As a cooperative venture with Federal, that will be loading the new bullet in its Premium line, the MRX bullet features a tungsten-alloy core and a polymer tip in the familiar Triple-Shock platform. Field reports indicate the MRX performs well on light game as well as heavy game—and at both close and distant ranges. Available as a reloading component from Barnes, the MRX will initially be offered in 20-bullet packs in 270, 7mm, 30 and 338 calibers in a variety of bullet weights. Also new to the line this year is a new solid copper, 50-caliber muzzleloading bullet featuring a boattail base and

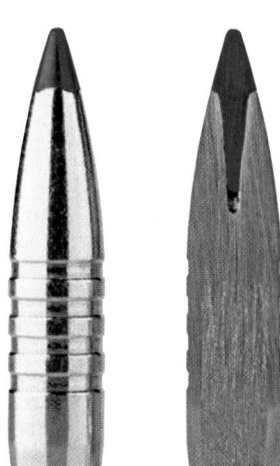

Barnes' technologically crafted MRX and Spit-Fire TMZs are among the most advanced bullets ever produced.

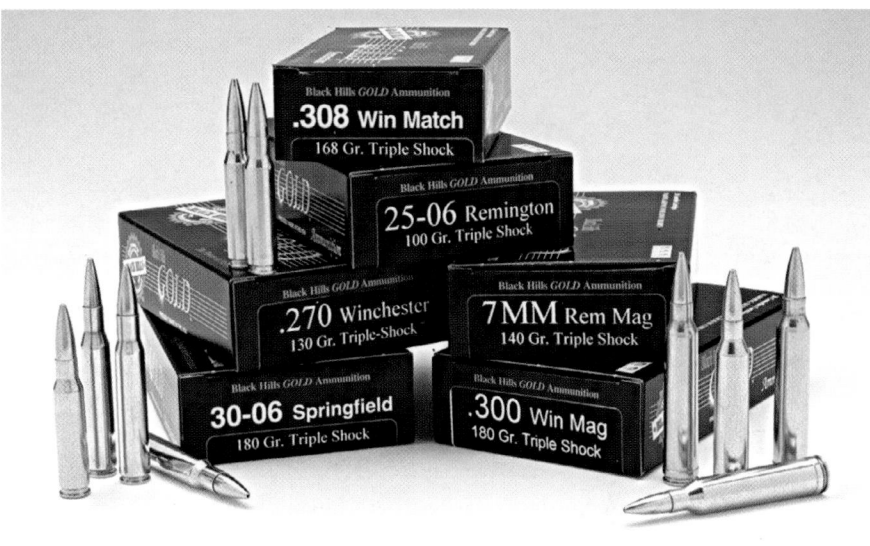

Black Hills offers a full ammunition line spiked with Barnes Triple-Shock bullets.

polymer tip for exceptional ballistic performance. Labeled the "Spit-Fire TMZ," it is available in 250- and 290-grain weights in 15- and 24-bullet packs. www.barnesbullets.com

Berger Bullets

Designed for long-range varminting, hot 22-caliber cf rifles, and fast twist barrels, Berger is now offering a 90-grain VLD hunting bullet with a BC of .517 and a 77-grain boattail with a BC of .387. Both new bullets are available with either conventional or moly-coated jackets. www.bergerbullets.com

Black Hills Ammunition

When our armed services go shopping for match- and sniper-grade ammunition, where do they go? They go to Black Hills, which now holds the 5.56mm contracts for the USMC rifle team, the Army's Marksmanship Unit, and the Navy's Surface Warfare Center. In fact, Black Hills offers more loads for the 223 Rem. than any other manufacturer, ranging from a 40-grain V-MAX at 3600 fps to a 77-grain Sierra MatchKing at 2750 fps. Lots of new hunting loads this year feature Barnes Triple-Shock and

Hornady A-MAX and V-MAX bullets. See them at www.black-hills.com

Brenneke USA

Wilhelm Brenneke invented the composite shotgun slug in 1898. The classic Brenneke was just redesigned, or tweaked a bit, with supporting plastic disks on both ends of the attached wad and a new H-wad between the powder and the slug. Brenneke USA indicates the new "Classic" 12-gauge, 2 3/4-inch slug is delivering groups under two inches at 50 yards and is suitable for either smooth or rifled bores. www.brennekeusa.com

CCI

CCI's Green Tag 22 LR match cartridge has an enviable record on the target range. Well, Green Tag has now been joined by a new match load specifically tuned to

The classic Brenneke slug has been updated and is proving more accurate than ever.

target-grade semi-auto rifles. The new "22 LR Select" features a 40-grain bullet at 1200 fps to keep those semi-autos functioning reliably in a competitive environment. The 22 Win. Mag. has been given a 21st century face lift with a new load featuring a 40-grain GamePoint controlled expansion softpoint at 1875 fps. The bullet is designed to hold together and mushroom, not fragment. It is proving effective on larger varmints like coyotes, while not destroying meat and hides on small species. Speaking of limiting tissue destruction in game, CCI is also fielding a new 20-grain FMJ loading for the 17 HMR at 2375 fps. www.cci-ammunition.com

CheyTac

Designed to fill the gap between the 338 Lapua and the 50 BMG, while outperforming the 50 BMG downrange, the 408 CheyTac cartridge features a 419-grain, lathe-turned, copper nickel alloy bullet manufactured by Lost River Ballistic Technologies. The long, pointy bullet has an average BC of .945 with a muzzle velocity of 2900 fps.

The CheyTac sniping system—which consists of a rifle, sound moderator, ballistics calculator linked to a weather sensor and a variety of sighting devices—is designed to neutralize soft targets to a distance of 2500 yards. www.cheytac.com

Cor-Bon

It's taken Cor-Bon many years to offer a premium line of rifle

CCI and Federal both offer a new 22 LR match cartridge for semi-autos.

⁅⁆●⁅⁆●⁅⁆

ammunition, but 2007 changes that. Their new DPX line of hunting ammunition is based on loading the Barnes Triple-Shock bullet in calibers from 223 Rem. through 45-70. The company continues to offer their original high performance handgun ammunition line as well as their Glaser Safety Slug, Pow'R Ball, Cowboy Action and DPX pistol lines. www.corbon.com

Federal

Do you know that Federal has never launched a cartridge that carries its name? Now they have! The new 338 Federal is based on a necked-up 308 Win. case and the ballistic performance it offers is impressive, especially when chambered in the short, light, handy rifles of today. The factory loads consist of a 180-grain Nosler AccuBond at 2830 fps; a 185-grain Barnes Triple-Shock at 2750 fps and a 210-grain Nosler Partition at 2630 fps. Excellent game loads all!

The big news in the Premium rifle ammunition line is the addition of the new Barnes MRX bullet as a 180-grain loading for the 308 Win., 30-06, 300 WSM and 300 Win. Mag. Look for the addition of Barnes Triple-Shock bullets to the 375 H&H, 416 Rem. Mag

⁅⁆●⁅⁆●⁅⁆

Federal finally has a cartridge that carries its name—the 338 Federal.

and Rigby and 458 Win. Mag. loadings that are now appropriately labeled "Cape.Shok." Federal's "Fusion" line, which features hunting bullets with the jacket plated to the core, has been expanded to include handgun calibers, specifically the 357 Mag., 41 Mag., 44 Mag. and 454 Casull, as well as a number of new rifle calibers. Federal's tight patterning "Flitecontrol" wad that first appeared in their turkey loads is now being employed in their 12-gauge 00 buckshot loads to improve pattern density at all ranges.

Recognizing that shooters are increasingly using computer-based ballistics programs, Federal now offers its own version, either online or as a download. See it at www.federalpremium.com

Fiocchi

Fiocchi introduced some interesting new ammunition lines being produced at their Ozark, Missouri plant. Loaded with Sierra MatchKing bullets, there's an Exacta Rifle Match line composed of the 223 Rem., 30-06 and 308 Win. cartridges as well as an Exacta Pistol IPSC Match line covering the 38 Super, 40 S&W, 45 Auto and 9mm Luger. Then there's an Extrema Rifle Hunting line featuring Hornady SST and Sierra GameKing bullets, and also an Extrema Pistol line based around the Hornady XTPHP bullets. www.fiocchiusa.com

Freedom Arms

Searching for a way to chamber a 50-caliber cartridge in their Model 83 series revolvers, Bob Baker, president of Freedom Arms, created an entirely new case that headspaces on a belt rather than a conventional rim. Named the Freedom Arms 500 Wyoming express (500WE), the 1.37-inch case is designed for .500-inch diameter bullets in the 350-450-grain range. Baker writes that "the cartridge was designed to not only get outstanding and predictable ballistic performance but to minimize forcing cone erosion, thereby extending the useful life of your Freedom Arms revolver. This is done by matching powder column length, powder volume, and bullet diameter to an expected range of bullet weights, velocity ranges and pressure levels." Brass and handloading data are available at the web site. Factory loaded ammunition should be available later in the year. There's something new at www.freedomarms.com

Hevi-Shot

Look out pheasants! Hevi-Shot has come up with two pheasant loads packing #5 Hevi-Shot. There's a 2-3/4-inch/12-ga. loading consisting of 1-1/8 oz. at 1350 fps and a 2 3/4-inch/20-ga. load with 1 oz. at 1250 fps. Speaking about the 20 gauge, there are three, exciting, new 3-inch/20-ga. waterfowl loads consisting of 1-1/4 oz. of #2, 4, and 6 Hevi-Shot at 1250 fps. The licensing agreement with Remington has expired so Hevi-Shot has launched its own independent ammunition company using the trademarks Hevi-Steel, Hevi-13, and Dead Coyote. Look for their new ammo on your dealer's shelves. www.hevishot.com

Hodgdon

Here's an interesting development. Hodgdon will now handle all of Winchester Ammunition's canister

Hornady's "LeverEvolution" loads put some snap into our woods rifles.

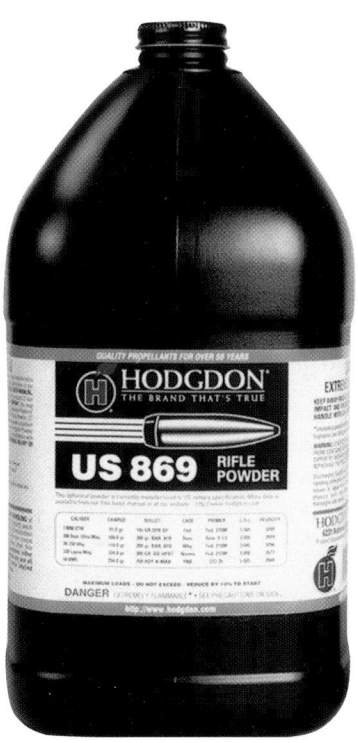

50 BMG shooters will find Hodgdon's new US 869 the perfect companion.

powder sales and distribution. Under their own labels, Hodgdon is introducing a super magnum spherical rifle powder, US869, designed for the 50 BMG—but equally useful in cartridges like the 300 Rem. Ultra-Mag. and the 30-378 Weatherby. New in the IMR powder line is "Trail Boss," a light, fluffy, high-bulk powder designed for the reduced loads commonly used in cowboy action events. Offering excellent ballistic uniformity, it occupies so much case volume that it is difficult to double-charge a case. The

new Hodgdon manual is out, and it's a dilly, covering over 5000 loads and new cartridges like the 325 WSM and the 204 Ruger. www.hodgdon.com

Hornady

Who would have thought that lever-action ammunition would get a major work over in the 21st century? It did. Hornady's "LeverEvolution" ammo for the 30-30, 35 Rem., 444 Marlin, 45-70 and 450 Marlin has set new performance benchmarks for trajectory, energy and expansion. The secret is a newly-designed series of sleek spitzer boattail bullets that are safe when stacked in a tubular magazine—thanks to their soft elastomer tips. The new loads are fast, too. The 30-30 ammunition carries a 160-grain bullet with a velocity of 2400 fps. Sighted in 3 inches high at 100 yards, the new 30-30 round is on at 200 yards and 12 inches low at 300.

That's flat. Other new ammunition offerings include the 416 Rigby, 338 Lapua, spitzer loads for the 460 S&W and 500 S&W, a 250-grain/20-gauge SST shotgun slug at 1800 fps and a 45-grain loading for the 204 Ruger at 3625 fps. New components? There's a 25-grain/17-caliber V-MAX, an 80-grain/224-caliber A-MAX and a 250-grain/338 BTHP. Big Red has been busy. www.hornady.com

Huntington

Buzz Huntington scours the globe for hard-to-find reloading components. If it's not catalogued, he can usually find it. Looking for a 500-grain bullet for your 50-110 Win. or 50 Alaskan? Huntington's has it under the excellent Woodleigh "Weldcore" label. In fact, Huntington's is the U.S. importer for the complete Woodleigh bullet line. Look for a wide selection of Jamison-made brass this year, including the 404 Jeffrey, 500 Jeffrey, 577-450 MH, 45-110/2 7/8-inch SS, 50-140/3 1/4-inch, 256 Win., and 351 WSL. Huntington's is also the place to shop for RCBS tooling and parts, both old and new. Try www.huntingtons.com. You'll be amazed what's there.

Lapua

The Finns have cooked up a new 6.5mm match cartridge, the 6.5x47 Lapua. The 6.5x47 case has been optimized for powder efficiency and match bullets. It has the same base

NobelSports' Sporting Clays pro-vide 1300 fps of performance.

diameter and a slightly shorter case than the 308 Win. so that it will function in 308 Win.-length actions. With a working pressure of 63,090 psi, it's a high-intensity cartridge offering 3084 fps with the 108-grain Scenar bullet, 2887 fps with the 123-grain Scenar and 2288 fps with the 139-grain Scenar. www.lapua.com

Magkor

Makers of that blackpowder substitute, Black Mag'3, Magkor is introducing the "Thundercharge." Thundercharge is a 45- or 50-caliber bullet wedded to a rigid column of Black Mag'3. They're calling it a "caseless cartridge for in-line muzzleloaders" and they're right. See it at www.magkor.com

Magtech Ammunition

When I went looking for a basic brass case to form into a 577 Snider, Magtech came to the rescue with their imported 24-gauge, brass shotshells. In fact, they offer brass shells designed to accept Large Pistol primers for the 9.1, 36, 32, 28, 24, 20, 16 and 12 gauges. In their popular handgun cartridge lines, they've added solid copper hollowpoint (SCHP) bullets across the board, to include the 454 Casull and 500 S&W. www.magtechammunition.com

Midway

Check out Midway's new on-line "GunTec Dictionary." It contains 5,300 firearm terms and definitions. If you want a short, concise definition for a complex term like "ballistic coefficient," visit www.midwayusa.com/dictionary for an answer.

NobelSport

Look for NobelSpeed Sporting Clays 12-gauge shotshells this year. Speedy they are. With 1 or 1-1/8 oz. of # 7.5 or 8, the new NobelSpeed shells are ripping out there at 1300 fps. www.nobelsportammo.com

Norma

Here's one for that special shooter who has everything. It's the "Norma Special Edition" set. Norma will engrave his or

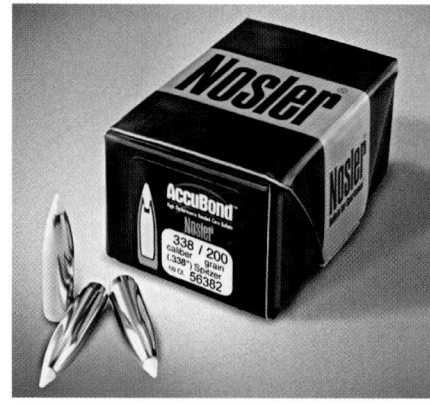

Nosler's 338-caliber/200-grain AccuBond complements cartridges like the new 338 Federal.

her name on thirty handloaded cartridges in either 9.3x74R or 300 Win. Mag. The cartridges feature gold-plated bullets and black ruthenium-plated cases, and are neatly displayed in a deluxe locking case. There's even a personalized certificate of authenticity included with the set. www.norma.cc

Nosler

Interesting line extensions. New this year in the AccuBond line are a 165-grain/308-caliber and a 200-grain/338-caliber bullet. The increasingly popular 204 Ruger got some attention with the introduction of the 40-grain/204-caliber Ballistic Tip Varmint pill, while in Nosler's Custom Competition line, there's a new 52-grain/.224-inch HPBT. www.nosler.com

Polywad

Hold on to those beautiful, vintage shotguns. Ever-innovative Polywad has designed two shotshells that keep pressures low, recoil mild while delivering great patterns. The "Vintager" comes as a 2-inch/12-gauge shell loaded with 24 grams of #6, 7.5 or 8 shot or as a 2 1/2-inch/20-gauge shell with a 3/4-oz. shot load. The companion shell is called the "DoubleWide," which carries the shot charge in Polywad's famous "Spred-R" wad. www.polywad.com

Prvi Partizan

Located in Serbia, Prvi Partizan has become a significant force in the international ammunition market, supplying not only loaded ammunition but component brass and bullets. One of its specialties is making runs of difficult-to-find and obsolete ammunition and brass which this year includes the 22 Rem. Jet Magnum, 7.92x33 Kurz, 8x50R Lebel, 7.5x55 Swiss, 6.5 Grendel and 7.62 Nagant. See www.prvipartizan.com and www.grafs.com

Puff-Lon

Puff-Lon is a new lubricating granulated filler that eliminates air space inside cartridge cases, isolates the base of the bullet from hot gases, and lubricates the barrel when fired. It's made from 100% pure cellulose blended with a mix of dry, synthetic lubricants. Those who've tried it, like it. www.pufflon.com

Remington

The big news at Big Green is Wingmaster HD, a proprietary shot composed of tungsten, bronze and iron with a density of 12 grams/cc that will replace the company's use of Hevi-Shot. The new shot is round, smooth and consistent in size—which translates into equal energy in every pellet and dense, efficient patterns without troublesome flyers. Having a hardness rating similar to steel, Wingmaster HD responds well to

similar choke settings. Approved for waterfowling, Wingmaster HD will be loaded across-the-board from the 3 1/2-inch /10-gauge to the 3-inch /20-gauge. The new loads are fast, too, ranging from 1300-1450 fps. The company slogan for Wingmaster HD is "Drop-Dead-Better." In the rifle ammunition lines, the 7mm Rem. Ultra Mag and the 300 WSM are being upgraded with Swift Scirocco Bonded bullets; the 270 WSM, 7mm Rem. Mag., 30-06, and 300 WSM are now offered with the AccuTip bullets; and the 7mm Rem. Ultra Mag and 300 Rem. Ultra Mag are being topped off with Swift's stout A-Frame projectiles. Managed recoil is still in, with two new STS target loads for the 2-3/4-inch/12 and 20 gauges consisting of 7/8-oz. of #8-1/2s at 1100 fps as well as a 7/8-oz. "Buckhammer" slug in the 20 gauge at 1275 fps. www.remington.com

Schroeder Bullets

Steve Schroeder is known for his 5mm conversion kits for the 5mm Remington Models 591/592, as well as for one of the most comprehensive offerings of difficult-to-find bullets and formed cases. Here's the place to find 130-grain/8mm bullets for the 7.92x33, or 10 bullet designs for the 8mm Nambu, or .351-inch diameter bullets for the 351 Win., or cases for Herter's 401 Powermag. You can reach him in San Diego at (619) 423-3523.

Sierra

The Bulletsmiths have been busy. Imagine a 90-grain/.224-inch HPBT match bullet requiring a 1x6.5" twist or faster for the 223 Rem/5.56x45 cartridge. The BC of this long, snaky, new pill is .504 at 2200 fps or faster! Then there's a 115-grain/.277-inch HPBT MatchKing aimed at the 6.8mm SPC market but equally useful in any 270-caliber gun. For those 1000-yard matches, there's a new 210-grain/.308-inch MatchKing that has been optimized with a longer ogive, smaller meplat,

◈ ● ◈ ● ◈ ● ◈ ● ◈ ● ◈

Puff-Lon is a new 100 percent cellulose, lubricating case filler for reduced loads.

Remington continues to upgrade its big-game loads with bullets like the Swift Scirocco.

◈ ● ◈ ● ◈ ● ◈ ● ◈ ● ◈

and improved boattail for downrange efficiency. www.sierrabullets.com

SinterFire

The leading industry supplier of lead-free, powdered copper/tin bullets, SinterFire has now developed its own lines of loaded ammunition. Its "Reduced Hazard Ammunition" offers two bullet weights in each of the following calibers: 9mm, 40 S&W, and 45 ACP. It's designed for reduced "splash-back" range training. The "GreenLine" adds a lead-free primer to the load. "Special Duty" law enforcement ammunition features a hollowpoint bullet that will fragment upon any object harder than the bullet itself, making it ideal for urban environments. SinterFire also offers a full line of its frangible bullets as components. www.sinterfire.com

Sisk Rifles

Sisk has taken the 325 WSM case, necked it up to 416-caliber and produced a proprietary 416-caliber

Look for a lot more component bullets from Speer.

Sisk Rifles took the 325 WSM, necked it up to 416, and created a short magnum that equals the 404 Jeffrey.

cartridge that offers full 404 Jeffery ballistic performance in a short-action rifle. www.siskguns.com

Speer

Look for a whole lot of component Trophy Bonded Sledgehammer Solids in 375, 416, 458 and 474-calibers ... plus a new 350-grain/500-caliber Uni-Cor soft point for the 500 S&W and 500 WE. www.speer-bullets.com

(L-R) SSK's new creations: 6.5 MPC/120-grain BT; 5.56 Ball; 6.5 MPC/100-grain SP; and 300 Whisper/240-grain SP.

SSK

JD Jones' newest creation is the 6.5 MPC (Multi-Purpose Cartridge). Based on a shortened 223 case, the cartridge is designed for close combat and designed to function in a 12-inch-barreled AR. The 6.5 is super-efficient, producing 2600 fps with a 95-grain solid in a 12-inch barrel and 2803 fps in a 20-inch barrel. SSK has also gone into the "machine-turned" bullet business, using both copper and brass alloys.

SSK offers a line of its own bullets, ranging in caliber from 6.5mm to 14.5mm, and will custom-turn small lots of bullets for experimenters for a nominal fee. www.sskindustries.com

Winchester

Winchester Ammunition has licensed Hodgdon its Winchester-branded reloading powders. Under the agreement, Hodgdon will be responsible for all orders, shipments, customer and technical service, and reloading data. On another cooperative front, Winchester has developed a new in-line primer designed specifically for Hodgdon's Triple Se7en and Pyrodex powders. The Winchester Triple Se7en primer reduces the classic fouling ring build-up that has plagued in-line muzzleloaders when using standard 209 shotgun primers. Searching for

the perfect hunting bullet that would be suitable for all sizes of big game, Winchester has developed the XP3. The XP3 combines a solid copper HP bullet with a bonded lead core and a polycarbonate tip. Available in 270, 7mm and 30-calibers, the new bullet retains 100 percent of its weight upon impact and will be incorporated into the Supreme Elite ammunition line. I shot Winchester's Xtended Range Hi-Density turkey loads for the 2005 Spring season and can attest to their lethality at ranges out to 50 yards. Now the new High-Density shot (55 percent more dense than steel) has been approved for waterfowl and will be introduced in the 3-inch/20 gauge, and the 3- and 3 1/2-inch/12 gauge. Twenty-gauge shotgun slug shooters will be pleased to see a new 260-grain Partition Gold 3-inch sabot load being offered with a muzzle velocity of 2000 fps as well as a 3/4 oz. Foster slug moving out at 1800 fps for the smooth bores. Pheasants watch out! The Super-Pheasant has been expanded to include a 2-3/4-inch /12-gauge loading of 1-3/8 oz. of # 4, 5, and 6 plated lead shot sizzling out at 1450 fps. And for fields where non-toxic shot must be used, there's a new 3-inch/12-gauge load using 1-1/4 oz. of #4 steel shot at 1400 fps. Big Red's been busy! www.winchester.com

Winchester's highly effective Xtended Range shot has been extended to their waterfowling line.

Average Centerfire Rifle Cartridge Ballistics and Prices

Many manufacturers do not supply suggested retail prices. Others did not get their pricing to us before press time. All pricing can vary dependent on the exact brand and style of ammo selected and/or the retail outlet from which you make your purchase. Pricing has been rounded to the nearest dollar and represents our best estimate of average pricing. An * after the cartridge means these loads are available with Nosler Partition or Swift A-Frame bullets. Listed pricing may or may not reflect this bullet type. ** = these are packed 50 to box, all others are 20 to box. Wea. Mag.= Weatherby Magnum. Spfd. = Springfield. A-A-Sq. = A-Square. N.E.=Nitro Express.

Cartridge	Bullet Wgt. Grs.	VELOCITY (fps)					ENERGY (ft. lbs.)					TRAJ. (in.)				Est. Price/ box
		Muzzle	100 yds.	200 yds.	300 yds.	400 yds.	Muzzle	100 yds.	200 yds.	300 yds.	400 yds.	100 yds.	200 yds.	300 yds.	400 yds.	
17, 22																
17 Remington	25	4040	3284	2644	2086	1606	906	599	388	242	143	+2.0	+1.7	-4.0	-17.0	$17
204 Ruger	32	4225	3632	3114	2652	2234	1268	937	689	500	355	.6	0.0	-4.2	-13.4	NA
204 Ruger	40	3900	3451	3046	2677	2336	1351	1058	824	636	485	.7	0.0	-4.5	-13.9	NA
204 Ruger	45	3625	3188	2792	2428	2093	1313	1015	778	589	438	1.00	0.0	-5.5	-16.9	NA
221 Fireball	50	2800	2137	1580	1180	988	870	507	277	155	109	+0.0	-7.0	-28.0	0.0	$14
22 Hornet	34	3050	2132	1415	1017	852	700	343	151	78	55	+0.0	-6.6	-15.5	-29.9	NA
22 Hornet	35	3100	2278	1601	1135	929	747	403	199	100	67	+2.75	0.0	-16.9	-60.4	NA
22 Hornet	45	2690	2042	1502	1128	948	723	417	225	127	90	+0.0	-7.7	-31.0	0.0	$27**
218 Bee	46	2760	2102	1550	1155	961	788	451	245	136	94	+0.0	-7.2	-29.0	0.0	$46**
222 Remington	40	3600	3117	2673	2269	1911	1151	863	634	457	324	+1.07	0.0	-6.13	-18.9	NA
222 Remington	50	3140	2602	2123	1700	1350	1094	752	500	321	202	+2.0	-0.4	-11.0	-33.0	$11
222 Remington	55	3020	2562	2147	1773	1451	1114	801	563	384	257	+2.0	-0.4	-11.0	-33.0	$12
22 PPC	52	3400	2930	2510	2130	NA	1335	990	730	525	NA	+2.0	1.4	-5.0	0.0	NA
223 Remington	40	3650	3010	2450	1950	1530	1185	805	535	340	265	+2.0	+1.0	-6.0	-22.0	$14
223 Remington	40	3800	3305	2845	2424	2044	1282	970	719	522	371	0.84	0.0	-5.34	-16.6	NA
223 Remington	50	3300	2874	2484	2130	1809	1209	917	685	504	363	1.37	0.0	-7.05	-21.8	NA
223 Remington	52/53	3330	2882	2477	2106	1770	1305	978	722	522	369	+2.0	+0.6	-6.5	-21.5	$14
223 Remington	55	3240	2748	2305	1906	1556	1282	922	649	444	296	+2.0	-0.2	-9.0	-27.0	$12
223 Remington	60	3100	2712	2355	2026	1726	1280	979	739	547	397	+2.0	+0.2	-8.0	-24.7	$16
223 Remington	64	3020	2621	2256	1920	1619	1296	977	723	524	373	+2.0	-0.2	-9.3	-23.0	$14
223 Remington	69	3000	2720	2460	2210	1980	1380	1135	925	750	600	+2.0	+0.8	-5.8	-17.5	$15
223 Remington	75	2790	2554	2330	2119	1926	1296	1086	904	747	617	2.37	0.0	-8.75	-25.1	NA
223 Remington	77	2750	2584	2354	2169	1992	1293	1110	948	804	679	1.93	0.0	-8.2	-23.8	NA
223 WSSM	55	3850	3438	3064	2721	2402	1810	1444	1147	904	704	0.7	0.0	-4.4	-13.6	NA
223 WSSM	64	3600	3144	2732	2356	2011	1841	1404	1061	789	574	1.0	0.0	-5.7	-17.7	NA
222 Rem. Mag.	55	3240	2748	2305	1906	1556	1282	922	649	444	296	+2.0	-0.2	-9.0	-27.0	$14
225 Winchester	55	3570	3066	2616	2208	1838	1556	1148	836	595	412	+2.0	+1.0	-5.0	-20.0	$19
224 Wea. Mag.	55	3650	3192	2780	2403	2057	1627	1244	943	705	516	+2.0	+1.2	-4.0	-17.0	$32
22-250 Rem.	40	4000	3320	2720	2200	1740	1420	980	660	430	265	+2.0	+1.8	-3.0	-16.0	$14
22-250 Rem.	50	3725	3264	2641	2455	2103	1540	1183	896	669	491	0.89	0.0	-5.23	-16.3	NA
22-250 Rem.	52/55	3680	3137	2656	2222	1832	1654	1201	861	603	410	+2.0	+1.3	-4.0	-17.0	$13
22-250 Rem.	60	3600	3195	2826	2485	2169	1727	1360	1064	823	627	+2.0	+2.0	-2.4	-12.3	$19
220 Swift	40	4200	3678	3190	2739	2329	1566	1201	904	666	482	+0.51	0.0	-4.0	-12.9	NA
220 Swift	50	3780	3158	2617	2135	1710	1586	1107	760	506	325	+2.0	+1.4	-4.4	-17.9	$20
220 Swift	50	3850	3396	2970	2576	2215	1645	1280	979	736	545	0.74	0.0	-4.84	-15.1	NA
220 Swift	55	3800	3370	2990	2630	2310	1765	1390	1090	850	650	0.8	0.0	-4.7	-14.4	NA
220 Swift	55	3650	3194	2772	2384	2035	1627	1246	939	694	506	+2.0	+2.0	-2.6	-13.4	$19
220 Swift	60	3600	3199	2824	2475	2156	1727	1364	1063	816	619	+2.0	+1.6	-4.1	-13.1	$19
22 Savage H.P.	71	2790	2340	1930	1570	1280	1225	860	585	390	190	+2.0	-1.0	-10.4	-35.7	NA
6mm (24)																
6mm BR Rem.	100	2550	2310	2083	1870	1671	1444	1185	963	776	620	+2.5	-0.6	-11.8	0.0	$22
6mm Norma BR	107	2822	2667	2517	2372	2229	1893	1690	1506	1337	1181	+1.73	0.0	-7.24	-20.6	NA
6mm PPC	70	3140	2750	2400	2070	NA	1535	1175	895	665	NA	+2.0	+1.4	-5.0	0.0	NA
243 Winchester	55	4025	3597	3209	2853	2525	1978	1579	1257	994	779	+0.6	0.0	-4.0	-12.2	NA
243 Winchester	60	3600	3110	2660	2260	1890	1725	1285	945	680	475	+2.0	+1.8	-3.3	-15.5	$17
243 Winchester	70	3400	3040	2700	2390	2100	1795	1435	1135	890	685	1.1	0.0	-5.9	-18.0	NA
243 Winchester	75/80	3350	2955	2593	2259	1951	1993	1551	1194	906	676	+2.0	+0.9	-5.0	-19.0	$16
243 Winchester	85	3320	3070	2830	2600	2380	2080	1770	1510	1280	1070	+2.0	+1.2	-4.0	-14.0	$18
243 Winchester	90	3120	2871	2635	2411	2199	1946	1647	1388	1162	966	1.4	0.0	-6.4	-18.8	NA
243 Winchester*	100	2960	2697	2449	2215	1993	1945	1615	1332	1089	882	+2.5	+1.2	-6.0	-20.0	$16
243 Winchester	105	2920	2689	2470	2261	2062	1988	1686	1422	1192	992	+2.5	+1.6	-5.0	-18.4	$21
243 Light Mag.	100	3100	2839	2592	2358	2138	2133	1790	1491	1235	1014	+1.5	0.0	-6.8	-19.8	NA
243 WSSM	55	4060	3628	3237	2880	2550	2013	1607	1280	1013	794	0.6	0.0	-3.9	-12.0	NA
243 WSSM	95	3250	3000	2763	2538	2325	2258	1898	1610	1359	1140	1.2	0.0	-5.7	-16.9	NA
243 WSSM	100	3110	2838	2583	2341	2112	2147	1789	1481	1217	991	1.4	0.0	-6.6	-19.7	NA
6mm Remington	80	3470	3064	2694	2352	2036	2139	1667	1289	982	736	+2.0	+1.1	-5.0	-17.0	$16
6mm Remington	100	3100	2829	2573	2332	2104	2133	1777	1470	1207	983	+2.5	+1.6	-5.0	-17.0	$16
6mm Remington	105	3060	2822	2596	2381	2177	2105	1788	1512	1270	1059	+2.5	+1.1	-3.3	-15.0	$21
6mm Rem. Light Mag.	100	3250	2997	2756	2528	2311	2345	1995	1687	1418	1186	1.59	0.0	-6.33	-18.3	NA
6.17(.243) Spitfire	100	3350	3122	2905	2698	2501	2493	2164	1874	1617	1389	2.4	3.20	0.0	-8.0	NA
240 Wea. Mag.	87	3500	3202	2924	2663	2416	2366	1980	1651	1370	1127	+2.0	+2.0	-2.0	-12.0	$32
240 Wea. Mag.	100	3395	3106	2835	2581	2339	2559	2142	1785	1478	1215	+2.5	+2.8	-2.0	-11.0	$43
25																
25-20 Win.	86	1460	1194	1030	931	858	407	272	203	165	141	0.0	-23.5	0.0	0.0	$32**
25-35 Win.	117	2230	1866	1545	1282	1097	1292	904	620	427	313	+2.5	-4.2	-26.0	0.0	$24
250 Savage	100	2820	2504	2210	1936	1684	1765	1392	1084	832	630	+2.5	+0.4	-9.0	-28.0	$17
257 Roberts	100	2980	2661	2363	2085	1827	1972	1572	1240	965	741	+2.5	-0.8	-5.2	-21.6	$20

Many manufacturers do not supply suggested retail prices. Others did not get their pricing to us before press time. All pricing can vary dependent on the exact brand and style of ammo selected and/or the retail outlet from which you make your purchase. Pricing has been rounded to the nearest dollar and represents our best estimate of average pricing. An * after the cartridge means these loads are available with Nosler Partition or Swift A-Frame bullets. Listed pricing may or may not reflect this bullet type. ** = these are packed 50 to box, all others are 20 to box. Wea. Mag.= Weatherby Magnum. Spfd. = Springfield. A-A-Sq. = A-Square. N.E.=Nitro Express.

Cartridge	Bullet Wgt. Grs.	VELOCITY (fps)					ENERGY (ft. lbs.)					TRAJ. (in.)				Est. Price/ box
		Muzzle	100 yds.	200 yds.	300 yds.	400 yds.	Muzzle	100 yds.	200 yds.	300 yds.	400 yds.	100 yds.	200 yds.	300 yds.	400 yds.	
257 Roberts+P	117	2780	2411	2071	1761	1488	2009	1511	1115	806	576	+2.5	-0.2	-10.2	-32.6	$18
257 Roberts+P	120	2780	2560	2360	2160	1970	2060	1750	1480	1240	1030	+2.5	+1.2	-6.4	-23.6	$22
257 Roberts	122	2600	2331	2078	1842	1625	1831	1472	1169	919	715	+2.5	0.0	-10.6	-31.4	$21
257 Light Mag.	117	2940	2694	2460	2240	2031	2245	1885	1572	1303	1071	+1.7	0.0	-7.6	-21.8	NA
25-06 Rem.	87	3440	2995	2591	2222	1884	2286	1733	1297	954	686	+2.0	+1.1	-2.5	-14.4	$17
25-06 Rem.	90	3440	3043	2680	2344	2034	2364	1850	1435	1098	827	+2.0	+1.8	-3.3	-15.6	$17
25-06 Rem.	100	3230	2893	2580	2287	2014	2316	1858	1478	1161	901	+2.0	+0.8	-5.7	-18.9	$17
25-06 Rem.	117	2990	2770	2570	2370	2190	2320	2000	1715	1465	1246	+2.5	+1.0	-7.9	-26.6	$19
25-06 Rem.*	120	2990	2730	2484	2252	2032	2382	1985	1644	1351	1100	+2.5	+1.2	-5.3	-19.6	$17
25-06 Rem.	122	2930	2706	2492	2289	2095	2325	1983	1683	1419	1189	+2.5	+1.8	-4.5	-17.5	$23
25 WSSM	85	3470	3156	2863	2589	2331	2273	1880	1548	1266	1026	1.0	0.0	-5.2	-15.7	NA
25 WSSM	115	3060	284	2639	2442	2254	2392	2066	1778	1523	1398	1.4	0.0	-6.4	-18.6	NA
25 WSSM	120	2990	2717	2459	2216	1987	2383	1967	1612	1309	1053	1.6	0.0	-7.4	-21.8	NA
257 Wea. Mag.	87	3825	3456	3118	2805	2513	2826	2308	1870	1520	1220	+2.0	+2.7	-0.3	-7.6	$32
257 Wea. Mag.	100	3555	3237	2941	2665	2404	2806	2326	1920	1576	1283	+2.5	+3.2	0.0	-8.0	$32
257 Scramjet	100	3745	3450	3173	2912	2666	3114	2643	2235	1883	1578	+2.1	+2.77	0.0	-6.93	NA
6.5																
6.5x47 Lapua	123	2887	NA	2554	NA	2244	2285	NA	1788	NA	1380	NA	4.53	0.00	-10.7	NA
6.5x50mm Jap.	139	2360	2160	1970	1790	1620	1720	1440	1195	985	810	+2.5	-1.0	-13.5	0.0	NA
6.5x50mm Jap.	156	2070	1830	1610	1430	1260	1475	1155	900	695	550	+2.5	-4.0	-23.8	0.0	NA
6.5x52mm Car.	139	2580	2360	2160	1970	1790	2045	1725	1440	1195	985	+2.5	0.0	-9.9	-29.0	NA
6.5x52mm Car.	156	2430	2170	1930	1700	1500	2045	1630	1285	1005	780	+2.5	-1.0	-13.9	0.0	NA
6.5x52mm Carcano	160	2250	1963	1700	1467	1271	1798	1369	1027	764	574	+3.8	0.0	-15.9	-48.1	NA
6.5x55mm Light Mag.	129	2750	2549	2355	2171	1994	2166	1860	1589	1350	1139	+2.0	0.0	-8.2	-23.9	NA
6.5x55mm Swe.	140	2550	NA	NA	NA	NA	2020	NA	NA	NA	NA	0.0	0.0	0.0	0.0	$18
6.5x55mm Swe.*	139/140	2850	2640	2440	2250	2070	2525	2170	1855	1575	1330	+2.5	+1.6	-5.4	-18.9	$18
6.5x55mm Swe.	156	2650	2370	2110	1870	1650	2425	1950	1550	1215	945	+2.5	0.0	-10.3	-30.6	NA
260 Remington	125	2875	2669	2473	2285	2105	2294	1977	1697	1449	1230	1.71	0.0	-7.4	-21.4	NA
260 Remington	140	2750	2544	2347	2158	1979	2351	2011	1712	1448	1217	+2.2	0.0	-8.6	-24.6	NA
6.5-284 Norma	142	3025	2890	2758	2631	2507	2886	2634	2400	2183	1982	1.13	0.0	-5.7	-16.4	NA
6.71 (264) Phantom	120	3150	2929	2718	2517	2325	2645	2286	1969	1698	1440	+1.3	0.0	-6.0	-17.5	NA
6.5 Rem. Mag.	120	3210	2905	2621	2353	2102	2745	2248	1830	1475	1177	+2.5	+1.7	-4.1	-16.3	Disc.
264 Win. Mag.	140	3030	2782	2548	2326	2114	2854	2406	2018	1682	1389	+2.5	+1.4	-5.1	-18.0	$24
6.71 (264) Blackbird	140	3480	3261	3053	2855	2665	3766	3307	2899	2534	2208	+2.4	+3.1	0.0	-7.4	NA
6.8mm Rem.	115	2775	2472	2190	1926	1683	1966	1561	1224	947	723	+2.1	0.0	-3.7	-9.4	NA
27																
270 Winchester	100	3430	3021	2649	2305	1988	2612	2027	1557	1179	877	+2.0	+1.0	-4.9	-17.5	$17
270 Win. (Rem.)	115	2710	2482	2265	2059	NA	1875	1485	1161	896	NA	0.0	4.8	-17.3	0.0	NA
270 Winchester	130	3060	2776	2510	2259	2022	2702	2225	1818	1472	1180	+2.5	+1.4	-5.3	-18.2	$17
270 Win. Supreme	130	3150	2881	2628	2388	2161	2865	2396	1993	1646	1348	1.3	0.0	-6.4	-18.9	NA
270 Winchester	135	3000	2780	2570	2369	2178	2697	2315	1979	1682	1421	+2.5	+1.4	-6.0	-17.6	$23
270 Winchester*	140	2940	2700	2480	2260	2060	2685	2270	1905	1590	1315	+2.5	+1.8	-4.6	-17.9	$20
270 Win. Light Magnum	130	3215	2998	2790	2590	2400	2983	2594	2246	1936	1662	1.21	0.0	-5.83	-17.0	NA
270 Winchester*	150	2850	2585	2336	2100	1879	2705	2226	1817	1468	1175	+2.5	+1.2	-6.5	-22.0	$17
270 Win. Supreme	150	2930	2693	2468	2254	2051	2860	2416	2030	1693	1402	1.7	0.0	-7.4	-21.6	NA
270 WSM	130	3275	3041	2820	2609	2408	3096	2669	2295	1564	1673	1.1	0.0	-5.5	-16.1	NA
270 WSM	140	3125	2865	2619	2386	2165	3035	2559	2132	1769	1457	1.4	0.0	-6.5	-19.0	NA
270 WSM	150	3120	2923	2734	2554	2380	3242	2845	2490	2172	1886	1.3	0.0	-5.9	-17.2	NA
270 Wea. Mag.	100	3760	3380	3033	2712	2412	3139	2537	2042	1633	1292	+2.0	+2.4	-1.2	-10.1	$32
270 Wea. Mag.	130	3375	3119	2878	2649	2432	3287	2808	2390	2026	1707	+2.5	-2.9	-0.9	-9.9	$32
270 Wea. Mag.*	150	3245	3036	2837	2647	2465	3507	3070	2681	2334	2023	+2.5	+2.6	-1.8	-11.4	$47
7mm																
7mm BR	140	2216	2012	1821	1643	1481	1525	1259	1031	839	681	+2.0	-3.7	-20.0	0.0	$23
7mm Mauser*	139/140	2660	2435	2221	2018	1827	2199	1843	1533	1266	1037	+2.5	0.0	-9.6	-27.7	$17
7mm Mauser	145	2690	2442	2206	1985	1777	2334	1920	1568	1268	1017	+2.5	+0.1	-9.6	-28.3	$18
7mm Mauser	154	2690	2490	2300	2120	1940	2475	2120	1810	1530	1285	+2.5	+0.8	-7.5	-23.5	$17
7mm Mauser	175	2440	2137	1857	1603	1382	2313	1774	1340	998	742	+2.5	-1.7	-16.1	0.0	$17
7x57 Light Mag.	139	2970	2730	2503	2287	2082	2722	2301	1933	1614	1337	+1.6	0.0	-7.2	-21.0	NA
7x30 Waters	120	2700	2300	1930	1600	1330	1940	1405	990	685	470	+2.5	-0.2	-12.3	0.0	$18
7mm-08 Rem.	120	3000	2725	2467	2223	1992	2398	1979	1621	1316	1058	+2.0	0.0	-7.6	-22.3	$18
7mm-08 Rem.*	140	2860	2625	2402	2189	1988	2542	2142	1793	1490	1228	+2.5	+0.8	-6.9	-21.9	$18
7mm-08 Rem.	154	2715	2510	2315	2128	1950	2520	2155	1832	1548	1300	+2.5	+1.0	-7.0	-22.7	$23
7mm-08 Light Mag.	139	3000	2790	2590	2399	2216	2777	2403	2071	1776	1515	+1.5	0.0	-6.7	-19.4	NA
7x64mm Bren.	140				Not Yet Announced											$17
7x64mm Bren.	154	2820	2610	2420	2230	2050	2720	2335	1995	1695	1430	+2.5	+1.4	-5.7	-19.9	NA
7x64mm Bren.*	160	2850	2669	2495	2327	2166	2885	2530	2211	1924	1667	+2.5	+1.6	-4.8	-17.8	$24
7x64mm Bren.	175				Not Yet Announced											$17
284 Winchester	150	2860	2595	2344	2108	1886	2724	2243	1830	1480	1185	+2.5	+0.8	-7.3	-23.2	$24

Many manufacturers do not supply suggested retail prices. Others did not get their pricing to us before press time. All pricing can vary dependent on the exact brand and style of ammo selected and/or the retail outlet from which you make your purchase. Pricing has been rounded to the nearest dollar and represents our best estimate of average pricing. An * after the cartridge means these loads are available with Nosler Partition or Swift A-Frame bullets. Listed pricing may or may not reflect this bullet type. ** = these are packed 50 to box, all others are 20 to box. Wea. Mag.= Weatherby Magnum. Spfd. = Springfield. A-A-Sq. = A-Square. N.E.=Nitro Express.

Cartridge	Bullet Wgt. Grs.	VELOCITY (fps) Muzzle	100 yds.	200 yds.	300 yds.	400 yds.	ENERGY (ft. lbs.) Muzzle	100 yds.	200 yds.	300 yds.	400 yds.	TRAJ. (in.) 100 yds.	200 yds.	300 yds.	400 yds.	Est. Price/ box
280 Remington	120	3150	2866	2599	2348	2110	2643	2188	1800	1468	1186	+2.0	+0.6	-6.0	-17.9	$17
280 Remington	140	3000	2758	2528	2309	2102	2797	2363	1986	1657	1373	+2.5	+1.4	-5.2	-18.3	$17
280 Remington*	150	2890	2624	2373	2135	1912	2781	2293	1875	1518	1217	+2.5	+0.8	-7.1	-22.6	$17
280 Remington	160	2840	2637	2442	2556	2078	2866	2471	2120	1809	1535	+2.5	+0.8	-6.7	-21.0	$20
280 Remington	165	2820	2510	2220	1950	1701	2913	2308	1805	1393	1060	+2.5	+0.4	-8.8	-26.5	$17
7x61mm S&H Sup.	154	3060	2720	2400	2100	1820	3200	2520	1965	1505	1135	+2.5	+1.8	-5.0	-19.8	NA
7mm Dakota	160	3200	3001	2811	2630	2455	3637	3200	2808	2456	2140	+2.1	+1.9	-2.8	-12.5	NA
7mm Rem. Mag. (Rem.)	140	2710	2482	2265	2059	NA	2283	1915	1595	1318	NA	0.0	-4.5	-1.57	0.0	NA
7mm Rem. Mag.*	139/140	3150	2930	2710	2510	2320	3085	2660	2290	1960	1670	+2.5	+2.4	-2.4	-12.7	$21
7mm Rem. Hvy Mag	139	3250	3044	2847	2657	2475	3259	2860	2501	2178	1890	1.1	0.0	-5.5	-16.2	NA
7mm Rem. Mag.	150/154	3110	2830	2568	2320	2085	3221	2667	2196	1792	1448	+2.5	+1.6	-4.6	-16.5	$21
7mm Rem. Mag.*	160/162	2950	2730	2520	2320	2120	3090	2650	2250	1910	1600	+2.5	+1.8	-4.4	-17.8	$34
7mm Rem. Mag.	165	2900	2699	2507	2324	2147	3081	2669	2303	1978	1689	+2.5	+1.2	-5.9	-19.0	$28
7mm Rem Mag.	175	2860	2645	2440	2244	2057	3178	2718	2313	1956	1644	+2.5	+1.0	-6.5	-20.7	$21
7mm Rem. SA ULTRA MAG	140	3175	2934	2707	2490	2283	3033	2676	2277	1927	1620	1.3	0.0	-6	-17.7	NA
7mm Rem. SA ULTRA MAG	150	3110	2828	2563	2313	2077	3221	2663	2188	1782	1437	2.5	2.1	-3.6	-15.8	NA
7mm Rem. SA ULTRA MAG	160	2960	2762	2572	2390	2215	3112	2709	2350	2029	1743	2.6	2.2	-3.6	-15.4	NA
7mm Rem. WSM	140	3225	3008	2801	2603	2414	3233	2812	2438	2106	1812	1.2	0.0	-5.6	-16.4	NA
7mm Rem. WSM	160	2990	2744	2512	2081	1883	3176	2675	2241	1864	1538	1.6	0.0	-7.1	-20.8	NA
7mm Wea. Mag.	140	3225	2970	2729	2501	2283	3233	2741	2315	1943	1621	+2.5	+2.0	-3.2	-14.0	$35
7mm Wea. Mag.	154	3260	3023	2799	2586	2382	3539	3044	2609	2227	1890	+2.5	+2.8	-1.5	-10.8	$32
7mm Wea. Mag.*	160	3200	3004	2816	2637	2464	3637	3205	2817	2469	2156	+2.5	+2.7	-1.5	-10.6	$47
7mm Wea. Mag.	165	2950	2747	2553	2367	2189	3188	2765	2388	2053	1756	+2.5	+1.8	-4.2	-16.4	$43
7mm Wea. Mag.	175	2910	2693	2486	2288	2098	3293	2818	2401	2033	1711	+2.5	+1.2	-5.9	-19.4	$35
7.21(.284) Tomahawk	140	3300	3118	2943	2774	2612	3386	3022	2693	2393	2122	2.3	3.20	0.0	-7.7	NA
7mm STW	140	3325	3064	2818	2585	2364	3436	2918	2468	2077	1737	+2.3	+1.8	-3.0	-13.1	NA
7mm STW Supreme	160	3150	2894	2652	2422	2204	3526	2976	2499	2085	1727	1.3	0.0	-6.3	-18.5	NA
7mm Rem. Ultra Mag.	140	3425	3184	2956	2740	2534	3646	3151	2715	2333	1995	1.7	1.60	-2.6	-11.4	NA
7mm Firehawk	140	3625	3373	3135	2909	2695	4084	3536	3054	2631	2258	+2.2	+2.9	0.0	-7.03	NA
30																
7.21 (.284) Firebird	140	3750	3522	3306	3101	2905	4372	3857	3399	2990	2625	1.6	2.4	0.0	-6.0	NA
30 Carbine	110	1990	1567	1236	1035	923	977	600	373	262	208	0.0	-13.5	0.0	0.0	$28**
303 Savage	190	1890	1612	1327	1183	1055	1507	1096	794	591	469	+2.5	-7.6	0.0	0.0	$24
30 Remington	170	2120	1822	1555	1328	1153	1696	1253	913	666	502	+2.5	-4.7	-26.3	0.0	$20
7.62x39mm Rus.	123/125	2300	2030	1780	1550	1350	1445	1125	860	655	500	+2.5	-2.0	-17.5	0.0	$13
30-30 Win.	55	3400	2693	2085	1570	1187	1412	886	521	301	172	+2.0	0.0	-10.2	-35.0	$18
30-30 Win.	125	2570	2090	1660	1320	1080	1830	1210	770	480	320	-2.0	-2.6	-19.9	0.0	$13
30-30 Win.	150	2390	1973	1605	1303	1095	1902	1296	858	565	399	+2.5	-3.2	-22.5	0.0	$13
30-30 Win. Supreme	150	2480	2095	1747	1446	1209	2049	1462	1017	697	487	0.0	-6.5	-24.5	0.0	NA
30-30 Win.	160	2300	1997	1719	1473	1268	1879	1416	1050	771	571	+2.5	-2.9	-20.2	0.0	$18
30-30 Win. Lever Evolution	160	2400	2150	1916	1699	NA	2046	1643	1304	1025	NA	3.00	0.20	-12.1	NA	NA
30-30 PMC Cowboy	170	1300	1198	1121			638	474				0.0	-27.0	0.0	0.0	NA
30-30 Win.*	170	2200	1895	1619	1381	1191	1827	1355	989	720	535	+2.5	-5.8	-23.6	0.0	$13
300 Savage	150	2630	2354	2094	1853	1631	2303	1845	1462	1143	886	+2.5	-0.4	-10.1	-30.7	$17
300 Savage	180	2350	2137	1935	1754	1570	2207	1825	1496	1217	985	+2.5	-1.6	-15.2	0.0	$17
30-40 Krag	180	2430	2213	2007	1813	1632	2360	1957	1610	1314	1064	+2.5	-1.4	-13.8	0.0	$18
7.65x53mm Arg.	180	2590	2390	2200	2010	1830	2685	2280	1925	1615	1345	+2.5	0.0	-27.6	0.0	NA
7.5x53mm Argentine	150	2785	2519	2269	2032	1814	2583	2113	1714	1376	1096	+2.0	0.0	-8.8	-25.5	NA
307 Winchester	150	2760	2321	1924	1575	1289	2530	1795	1233	826	554	+2.5	-1.5	-13.6	0.0	Disc.
307 Winchester	180	2510	2179	1874	1599	1362	2519	1898	1404	1022	742	+2.5	-1.6	-15.6	0.0	$20
7.5x55 Swiss	180	2650	2450	2250	2060	1880	2805	2390	2020	1700	1415	+2.5	+0.6	-8.1	-24.9	NA
7.5x55mm Swiss	165	2720	2515	2319	2132	1954	2710	2317	1970	1665	1398	+2.0	0.0	-8.5	-24.6	NA
308 Winchester	55	3770	3215	2726	2286	1888	1735	1262	907	638	435	-2.0	+1.4	-3.8	-15.8	$22
308 Winchester	150	2820	2533	2263	2009	1774	2648	2137	1705	1344	1048	+2.5	+0.4	-8.5	-26.1	$17
308 Winchester	165	2700	2440	2194	1963	1748	2670	2180	1763	1411	1199	+2.5	0.0	-9.7	-28.5	$20
308 Winchester	168	2680	2493	2314	2143	1979	2678	2318	1998	1713	1460	+2.5	0.0	-8.9	-25.3	$18
308 Win. (Fed.)	170	2000	1740	1510	NA	NA	1510	1145	860	NA	NA	0.0	0.0	0.0	0.0	NA
308 Winchester	178	2620	2415	2220	2034	1857	2713	2306	1948	1635	1363	+2.5	0.0	-9.6	-27.6	$23
308 Winchester*	180	2620	2393	2178	1974	1782	2743	2288	1896	1557	1269	+2.5	-0.2	-10.2	-28.5	$17
308 Light Mag.*	150	2980	2703	2442	2195	1964	2959	2433	1986	1606	1285	+1.6	0.0	-7.5	-22.2	NA
308 Light Mag.	165	2870	2658	2456	2263	2078	3019	2589	2211	1877	1583	+1.7	0.0	-7.5	-21.8	NA
308 High Energy	165	2870	2600	2350	2120	1890	3020	2485	2030	1640	1310	+1.8	0.0	-8.2	-24.0	NA
308 Light Mag.	168	2870	2658	2456	2263	2078	3019	2589	2211	1877	1583	+1.7	0.0	-7.5	-21.8	NA
308 High Energy	180	2740	2550	2370	2200	2030	3000	2600	2245	1925	1645	+1.9	0.0	-8.2	-23.5	NA
30-06 Spfd.	55	4080	3485	2965	2502	2083	2033	1483	1074	764	530	+2.0	+1.9	-2.1	-11.7	$22
30-06 Spfd. (Rem.)	125	2660	2335	2034	1757	NA	1964	1513	1148	856	NA	0.0	-5.2	-18.9	0.0	$17
30-06 Spfd.	125	3140	2780	2447	2138	1853	2736	2145	1662	1279	953	+2.0	+1.0	-6.2	-21.0	$17
30-06 Spfd.	150	2910	2617	2342	2083	1853	2820	2281	1827	1445	1135	+2.5	+0.8	-7.2	-23.4	$17

Many manufacturers do not supply suggested retail prices. Others did not get their pricing to us before press time. All pricing can vary dependent on the exact brand and style of ammo selected and/or the retail outlet from which you make your purchase. Pricing has been rounded to the nearest dollar and represents our best estimate of average pricing.
An * after the cartridge means these loads are available with Nosler Partition or Swift A-Frame bullets. Listed pricing may or may not reflect this bullet type.
** = these are packed 50 to box, all others are 20 to box. Wea. Mag.= Weatherby Magnum. Spfd. = Springfield. A-A-Sq. = A-Square. N.E.=Nitro Express.

Cartridge	Bullet Wgt. Grs.	VELOCITY (fps)					ENERGY (ft. lbs.)					TRAJ. (in.)				Est. Price/ box
		Muzzle	100 yds.	200 yds.	300 yds.	400 yds.	Muzzle	100 yds.	200 yds.	300 yds.	400 yds.	100 yds.	200 yds.	300 yds.	400 yds.	
30-06 Spfd.	152	2910	2654	2413	2184	1968	2858	2378	1965	1610	1307	+2.5	+1.0	-6.6	-21.3	$23
30-06 Spfd.*	165	2800	2534	2283	2047	1825	2872	2352	1909	1534	1220	+2.5	+0.4	-8.4	-25.5	$17
30-06 Spfd.	168	2710	2522	2346	2169	2003	2739	2372	2045	1754	1497	+2.5	+0.4	-8.0	-23.5	$18
30-06 Spfd. (Fed.)	170	2000	1740	1510	NA	NA	1510	1145	860	NA	NA	0.0	0.0	0.0	0.0	NA
30-06 Spfd.	178	2720	2511	2311	2121	1939	2924	2491	2111	1777	1486	+2.5	+0.4	-8.2	-24.6	$23
30-06 Spfd.*	180	2700	2469	2250	2042	1846	2913	2436	2023	1666	1362	-2.5	0.0	-9.3	-27.0	$17
30-06 Spfd.	220	2410	2130	1870	1632	1422	2837	2216	1708	1301	988	+2.5	-1.7	-18.0	0.0	$17
30 Mag.																
30-06 Light Mag.	150	3100	2815	2548	2295	2058	3200	2639	2161	1755	1410	+1.4	0.0	-6.8	-20.3	NA
30-06 Light Mag.	180	2880	2676	2480	2293	2114	3316	2862	2459	2102	1786	+1.7	0.0	-7.3	-21.3	NA
30-06 High Energy	180	2880	2690	2500	2320	2150	3315	2880	2495	2150	1845	+1.7	0.0	-7.2	-21.0	NA
300 REM SA ULTRA MAG	150	3200	2901	2622	2359	2112	3410	2803	2290	1854	1485	1.3	0.0	-6.4	-19.1	NA
300 REM SA ULTRA MAG	165	3075	2792	2527	2276	2040	3464	2856	2339	1898	1525	1.5	0.0	-7	-20.7	NA
300 REM SA ULTRA MAG	180	2960	2761	2571	2389	2214	3501	3047	2642	2280	1959	2.6	2.2	-3.6	-15.4	NA
7.82 (308) Patriot	150	3250	2999	2762	2537	2323	3519	2997	2542	2145	1798	+1.2	0.0	-5.8	-16.9	NA
300 WSM	150	3300	3061	2834	2619	2414	3628	3121	2676	2285	1941	1.1	0.0	-5.4	-15.9	NA
300 WSM	180	2970	2741	2524	2317	2120	3526	3005	2547	2147	1797	1.6	0.0	-7.0	-20.5	NA
300 WSM	180	3010	2923	2734	2554	2380	3242	2845	2490	2172	1886	1.3	0	-5.9	-17.2	NA
308 Norma Mag.	180	3020	2820	2630	2440	2270	3645	3175	2755	2385	2050	+2.5	+2.0	-3.5	-14.8	NA
300 Dakota	200	3000	2824	2656	2493	2336	3996	3542	3131	2760	2423	+2.2	+1.5	-4.0	-15.2	NA
300 H&H Magnum*	180	2880	2640	2412	2196	1990	3315	2785	2325	1927	1583	+2.5	+0.8	-6.8	-21.7	$24
300 H&H Magnum	220	2550	2267	2002	1757	NA	3167	2510	1958	1508	NA	-2.5	-0.4	-12.0	0.0	NA
300 Win. Mag.	150	3290	2951	2636	2342	2068	3605	2900	2314	1827	1424	+2.5	+1.9	-3.8	-15.8	$22
300 Win. Mag.	165	3100	2877	2665	2462	2269	3522	3033	2603	2221	1897	+2.5	+2.4	-3.0	-16.9	$24
300 Win. Mag.	178	2900	2760	2568	2375	2191	3509	3030	2606	2230	1897	+2.5	+1.4	-5.0	-17.6	$29
300 Win. Mag.*	180	2960	2745	2540	2344	2157	3501	3011	2578	2196	1859	+2.5	+1.2	-5.5	-18.5	$22
300 W.M. High Energy	180	3100	2830	2580	2340	2110	3840	3205	2660	2190	1790	+1.4	0.0	-6.6	-19.7	NA
300 W.M. Light Mag.	180	3100	2879	2668	2467	2275	3840	3313	2845	2431	2068	+1.39	0.0	-6.45	-18.7	NA
300 Win. Mag.	190	2885	1691	2506	2327	2156	3511	3055	2648	2285	1961	+2.5	+1.2	-5.0	-19.0	$26
300 W.M. High Energy	200	2930	2740	2550	2370	2200	3810	3325	2885	2495	2145	+1.6	0.0	-6.9	-20.1	NA
300 Win. Mag.*	200	2825	2595	2376	2167	1970	3545	2991	2508	2086	1742	-2.5	+1.6	-4.7	-17.2	$36
300 Win. Mag.	220	2680	2448	2228	2020	1823	3508	2927	2424	1993	1623	+2.5	0.0	-9.5	-27.5	$23
300 Rem. Ultra Mag.	150	3450	3208	2980	2762	2556	3964	3427	2956	2541	2175	1.7	1.5	-2.6	-11.2	NA
300 Rem. Ultra Mag.	180	3250	3037	2834	2640	2454	4221	3686	3201	2786	2407	2.4	0.0	-3.0	-12.7	NA
300 Wea. Mag.	100	3900	3441	3038	2652	2305	3714	2891	2239	1717	1297	+2.0	+2.6	-0.6	-8.7	$32
300 Wea. Mag.	150	3600	3307	3033	2776	2533	4316	3642	3064	2566	2137	+2.5	+3.2	0.0	-8.1	$32
300 Wea. Mag.	165	3450	3210	3000	2792	2593	4360	3796	3297	2855	2464	+2.5	+3.2	0.0	-7.8	NA
300 Wea. Mag.	178	3120	2902	2695	2497	2308	3847	3329	2870	2464	2104	+2.5	-1.7	-3.6	-14.7	$43
300 Wea. Mag.	180	3330	3110	2910	2710	2520	4430	3875	3375	2935	2540	+1.0	0.0	-5.2	-15.1	NA
300 Wea. Mag.	190	3030	2830	2638	2455	2279	3873	3378	2936	2542	2190	+2.5	+1.6	-4.3	-16.0	$38
300 Wea. Mag.	220	2850	2541	2283	1964	1736	3967	3155	2480	1922	1471	+2.5	+0.4	-8.5	-26.4	$35
300 Warbird	180	3400	3180	2971	2772	2582	4620	4042	3528	3071	2664	+2.59	+3.25	0.0	-7.95	NA
300 Pegasus	180	3500	3319	3145	2978	2817	4896	4401	3953	3544	3172	+2.28	+2.89	0.0	-6.79	NA
31																
32-20 Win.	100	1210	1021	913	834	769	325	231	185	154	131	0.0	-32.3	0.0	0.0	$23**
303 British	150	2685	2441	2210	1992	1787	2401	1984	1627	1321	1064	+2.5	+0.6	-8.4	-26.2	$18
303 British	180	2460	2124	1817	1542	1311	2418	1803	1319	950	687	+2.5	-1.8	-16.8	0.0	$18
303 Light Mag.	150	2830	2570	2325	2094	1884	2667	2199	1800	1461	1185	+2.0	0.0	-8.4	-24.6	NA
7.62x54mm Rus.	146	2950	2730	2520	2320	NA	2820	2415	2055	1740	NA	+2.5	+2.0	-4.4	-17.7	NA
7.62x54mm Rus.	180	2580	2370	2180	2000	1820	2650	2250	1900	1590	1100	+2.5	0.0	-9.8	-28.5	NA
7.7x58mm Jap.	150	2640	2399	2170	1954	1752	2321	1916	1568	1271	1022	+2.3	0.0	-9.7	-28.5	NA
7.7x58mm Jap.	180	2500	2300	2100	1920	1750	2490	2105	1770	1475	1225	+2.5	0.0	-10.4	-30.2	NA
8x56 R	205	2400	2188	1987	1797	1621	2621	2178	1796	1470	1196	+2.9	0.0	-11.7	-34.3	NA
8mm																
8x57mm JS Mau.	165	2850	2520	2210	1930	1670	2965	2330	1795	1360	1015	+2.5	+1.0	-7.7	0.0	NA
32 Win. Special	170	2250	1921	1626	1372	1175	1911	1393	998	710	521	+2.5	-3.5	-22.9	0.0	$14
8mm Mauser	170	2360	1969	1622	1333	1123	2102	1464	993	671	476	+2.5	-3.1	-22.2	0.0	$18
325 WSM	180	3060	2841	2632	2432	2242	3743	3226	2769	2365	2009	+1.4	0.0	-6.4	-18.7	NA
325 WSM	200	2950	2753	2565	2384	2210	3866	3367	2922	2524	2170	+1.5	0.0	-6.8	-19.8	NA
325 WSM	220	2840	2605	2382	2169	1968	3941	3316	2772	2300	1893	+1.8	0.0	-8.0	-23.3	NA
8mm Rem. Mag.	185	3080	2761	2464	2186	1927	3896	3131	2494	1963	1525	+2.5	+1.4	-5.5	-19.7	$30
8mm Rem. Mag.	220	2830	2581	2346	2123	1913	3912	3254	2688	2201	1787	+2.5	+0.6	-7.6	-23.5	Disc.
33																
338 Federal	180	2830	2590	2350	2130	1930	3200	2670	2215	1820	1480	1.80	0.00	-8.2	-23.9	NA
338 Federal	185	2750	2550	2350	2160	1980	3105	2660	2265	1920	1615	1.90	0.00	-8.3	-24.1	NA
338 Federal	210	2630	2410	2200	2010	1820	3225	2710	2265	1880	1545	2.30	0.00	-9.4	-27.3	NA
338-06	200	2750	2553	2364	2184	2011	3358	2894	2482	2118	1796	+1.9	0.00	-8.22	-23.6	NA

Many manufacturers do not supply suggested retail prices. Others did not get their pricing to us before press time. All pricing can vary dependent on the exact brand and style of ammo selected and/or the retail outlet from which you make your purchase. Pricing has been rounded to the nearest dollar and represents our best estimate of average pricing.
An * after the cartridge means these loads are available with Nosler Partition or Swift A-Frame bullets. Listed pricing may or may not reflect this bullet type.
** = these are packed 50 to box, all others are 20 to box. Wea. Mag.= Weatherby Magnum. Spfd. = Springfield. A-A-Sq. = A-Square. N.E.=Nitro Express.

Cartridge	Bullet Wgt. Grs.	VELOCITY (fps)					ENERGY (ft. lbs.)					TRAJ. (in.)				Est. Price/ box
		Muzzle	100 yds.	200 yds.	300 yds.	400 yds.	Muzzle	100 yds.	200 yds.	300 yds.	400 yds.	100 yds.	200 yds.	300 yds.	400 yds.	
330 Dakota	250	2900	2719	2545	2378	2217	4668	4103	3595	3138	2727	+2.3	+1.3	-5.0	-17.5	NA
338 Lapua	250	2963	2795	2640	2493	NA	4842	4341	3881	3458	NA	+1.9	0.0	-7.9	0.0	NA
338 Win. Mag.	200	2960	2658	2375	2110	1862	3890	3137	2505	1977	1539	+2.5	+1.0	-6.7	-22.3	$27
338 Win. Mag.*	210	2830	2590	2370	2150	1940	3735	3130	2610	2155	1760	+2.5	+1.4	-6.0	-20.9	$33
338 Win. Mag.*	225	2785	2517	2266	2029	1808	3871	3165	2565	2057	1633	+2.5	+0.4	-8.5	-25.9	$27
338 W.M. Heavy Mag.	225	2920	2678	2449	2232	2027	4259	3583	2996	2489	2053	+1.75	0.0	-7.65	-22.0	NA
338 W.M. High Energy	225	2940	2690	2450	2230	2010	4320	3610	3000	2475	2025	+1.7	0.0	-7.5	-22.0	NA
338 Win. Mag.	230	2780	2573	2375	2186	2005	3948	3382	2881	2441	2054	+2.5	+1.2	-6.3	-21.0	$40
338 Win. Mag.*	250	2660	2456	2261	2075	1898	3927	3348	2837	2389	1999	+2.5	+0.2	-9.0	-26.2	$27
338 W.M. High Energy	250	2800	2610	2420	2250	2080	4350	3775	3260	2805	2395	+1.8	0.0	-7.8	-22.5	NA
338 Ultra Mag.	250	2860	2645	2440	2244	2057	4540	3882	3303	2794	2347	1.7	0.0	-7.6	-22.1	NA
8.59(.338) Galaxy	200	3100	2899	2707	2524	2347	4269	3734	3256	2829	2446	3	3.80	0.0	-9.3	NA
340 Wea. Mag.*	210	3250	2991	2746	2515	2295	4924	4170	3516	2948	2455	+2.5	+1.9	-1.8	-11.8	$56
340 Wea. Mag.*	250	3000	2806	2621	2443	2272	4995	4371	3812	3311	2864	+2.5	+2.0	-3.5	-14.8	$56
338 A-Square	250	3120	2799	2500	2220	1958	5403	4348	3469	2736	2128	+2.5	+2.7	-1.5	-10.5	NA
338-378 Wea. Mag.	225	3180	2974	2778	2591	2410	5052	4420	3856	3353	2902	3.1	3.80	0.0	-8.9	NA
338 Titan	225	3230	3010	2800	2600	2409	5211	4524	3916	3377	2898	+3.07	+3.80	0.0	-8.95	NA
338 Excalibur	200	3600	3361	3134	2920	2715	5755	5015	4363	3785	3274	+2.23	+2.87	0.0	-6.99	NA
338 Excalibur	250	3250	2922	2618	2333	2066	5863	4740	3804	3021	2370	+1.3	0.0	-6.35	-19.2	NA
34, 35																
348 Winchester	200	2520	2215	1931	1672	1443	2820	2178	1656	1241	925	+2.5	-1.4	-14.7	0.0	$42
357 Magnum	158	1830	1427	1138	980	883	1175	715	454	337	274	0.0	-16.2	-33.1	0.0	$25**
35 Remington	150	2300	1874	1506	1218	1039	1762	1169	755	494	359	+2.5	-4.1	-26.3	0.0	$16
35 Remington	200	2080	1698	1376	1140	1001	1921	1280	841	577	445	+2.5	-6.3	-17.1	-33.6	$16
35 Rem. Lever Evolution	200	2225	1963	1721	1503	NA	2198	1711	1315	1003	NA	3.00	-1.30	-17.5	NA	NA
356 Winchester	200	2460	2114	1797	1517	1284	2688	1985	1434	1022	732	+2.5	-1.8	-15.1	0.0	$31
356 Winchester	250	2160	1911	1682	1476	1299	2591	2028	1571	1210	937	+2.5	-3.7	-22.2	0.0	$31
358 Winchester	200	2490	2171	1876	1619	1379	2753	2093	1563	1151	844	+2.5	-1.6	-15.6	0.0	$31
358 STA	275	2850	2562	2292	2039	NA	4958	4009	3208	2539	NA	+1.9	0.0	-8.6	0.0	NA
350 Rem. Mag.	200	2710	2410	2130	1870	1631	3261	2579	2014	1553	1181	+2.5	-0.2	-10.0	-30.1	$33
35 Whelen	200	2675	2378	2100	1842	1606	3177	2510	1958	1506	1145	+2.5	-0.2	-10.3	-31.1	$20
35 Whelen	225	2500	2300	2110	1930	1770	3120	2650	2235	1870	1560	+2.6	0.0	-10.2	-29.9	NA
35 Whelen	250	2400	2197	2005	1823	1652	3197	2680	2230	1844	1515	+2.5	-1.2	-13.7	0.0	$20
358 Norma Mag.	250	2800	2510	2230	1970	1730	4350	3480	2750	2145	1655	+2.5	+1.0	-7.6	-25.2	NA
358 STA	275	2850	2562	229*2	2039	1764	4959	4009	3208	2539	1899	+1.9	0.0	-8.58	-26.1	NA
9.3mm																
9.3x57mm Mau.	286	2070	1810	1590	1390	1110	2710	2090	1600	1220	955	+2.5	-2.6	-22.5	0.0	NA
9.3x62mm Mau.	286	2360	2089	1844	1623	NA	3538	2771	2157	1670	1260	+2.5	-1.6	-21.0	0.0	NA
9.3x64mm	286	2700	2505	2318	2139	1968	4629	3984	3411	2906	2460	+2.5	+2.7	-4.5	-19.2	NA
9.3x74Rmm	286	2360	2089	1844	1623	NA	3538	2771	2157	1670	NA	+2.5	-2.0	-11.0	0.0	NA
375																
38-55 Win.	255	1320	1190	1091	1018	963	987	802	674	587	525	0.0	-23.4	0.0	0.0	$25
375 Winchester	200	2200	1841	1526	1268	1089	2150	1506	1034	714	527	+2.5	-4.0	-26.2	0.0	$27
375 Winchester	250	1900	1647	1424	1239	1103	2005	1506	1126	852	676	+2.5	-6.9	-33.3	0.0	$27
376 Steyr	225	2600	2331	2078	1842	1625	3377	2714	2157	1694	1319	2.5	0.0	-10.6	-31.4	NA
376 Steyr	270	2600	2372	2156	1951	1759	4052	3373	2787	2283	1855	2.3	0.0	-9.9	-28.9	NA
375 Dakota	300	2600	2316	2051	1804	1579	4502	3573	2800	2167	1661	+2.4	0.0	-11.0	-32.7	NA
375 N.E. 2-1/2"	270	2000	1740	1507	1310	NA	2398	1815	1362	1026	NA	+2.5	-6.0	-30.0	0.0	NA
375 Flanged	300	2450	2150	1886	1640	NA	3998	3102	2369	1790	NA	+2.5	-2.4	-17.0	0.0	NA
375 H&H Magnum	250	2670	2450	2240	2040	1850	3955	3335	2790	2315	1905	+2.5	-0.4	-10.2	-28.4	$28
375 H&H Magnum	270	2690	2420	2166	1928	1707	4337	3510	2812	2228	1747	+2.5	0.0	-10.0	-29.4	$28
375 H&H Magnum*	300	2530	2245	1979	1733	1512	4263	3357	2608	2001	1523	+2.5	-1.0	-10.5	-33.6	$28
375 H&H Hvy. Mag.	270	2870	2628	2399	2182	1976	4937	4141	3451	2150	1845	+1.7	0.0	-7.2	-21.0	NA
375 H&H Hvy. Mag.	300	2705	2386	2090	1816	1568	4873	3793	2908	2195	1637	+2.3	0.0	-10.4	-31.4	NA
375 Rem. Ultra Mag.	270	2900	2558	2241	1947	1678	5041	3922	3010	2272	1689	1.9	2.7	-8.9	-27	NA
375 Rem. Ultra Mag.	300	2760	2505	2263	2035	1822	5073	4178	3412	2759	2210	2.0	0.0	-8.8	-26.1	NA
375 Wea. Mag.	300	2700	2420	2157	1911	1685	4856	3901	3100	2432	1891	+2.5	-.04	-10.7	0.0	NA
378 Wea. Mag.	270	3180	2976	2781	2594	2415	6062	5308	4635	4034	3495	+2.5	+2.6	-1.8	-11.3	$71
378 Wea. Mag.	300	2929	2576	2252	1952	1680	5698	4419	3379	2538	1881	+2.5	+1.2	-7.0	-24.5	$77
375 A-Square	300	2920	2626	2351	2093	1850	5679	4594	3681	2917	2281	+2.5	+1.4	-6.0	-21.0	NA
38-40 Win.	180	1160	999	901	827	764	538	399	324	273	233	0.0	-33.9	0.0	0.0	$42**
40, 41																
400 A-Square DPM	400	2400	2146	1909	1689	NA	5116	2092	3236	2533	NA	2.98	0.00	-10.0	NA	NA
400 A-Square DPM	170	2980	2463	2001	1598	NA	3352	2289	1512	964	NA	2.16	0.00	-11.1	NA	NA
408 CheyTac	419	2850	2752	2657	2562	2470	7551	7048	6565	6108	5675	-1.02	0.00	1.9	4.2	NA
405 Win.	300	2200	1851	1545	1296		3224	2282	1589	1119		4.6	0.0	-19.5	0.0	NA
450/400-3"	400	2150	1932	1730	1545	1379	4105	3316	2659	2119	1689	+2.5	-4.0	-9.5	-30.0	NA

Many manufacturers do not supply suggested retail prices. Others did not get their pricing to us before press time. All pricing can vary dependent on the exact brand and style of ammo selected and/or the retail outlet from which you make your purchase. Pricing has been rounded to the nearest dollar and represents our best estimate of average pricing.
An * after the cartridge means these loads are available with Nosler Partition or Swift A-Frame bullets. Listed pricing may or may not reflect this bullet type.
** = these are packed 50 to box, all others are 20 to box. Wea. Mag.= Weatherby Magnum. Spfd. = Springfield. A-A-Sq. = A-Square. N.E.=Nitro Express.

Cartridge	Bullet Wgt. Grs.	VELOCITY (fps)					ENERGY (ft. lbs.)					TRAJ. (in.)				Est. Price/ box
		Muzzle	100 yds.	200 yds.	300 yds.	400 yds.	Muzzle	100 yds.	200 yds.	300 yds.	400 yds.	100 yds.	200 yds.	300 yds.	400 yds.	
416 Dakota	400	2450	2294	2143	1998	1859	5330	4671	4077	3544	3068	+2.5	-0.2	-10.5	-29.4	NA
416 Taylor	400	2350	2117	1896	1693	NA	4905	3980	3194	2547	NA	+2.5	-1.2	15.0	0.0	NA
416 Hoffman	400	2380	2145	1923	1718	1529	5031	4087	3285	2620	2077	+2.5	-1.0	-14.1	0.0	NA
416 Rigby	350	2600	2449	2303	2162	2026	5253	4661	4122	3632	3189	+2.5	-1.8	-10.2	-26.0	NA
416 Rigby	400	2370	2210	2050	1900	NA	4990	4315	3720	3185	NA	+2.5	-0.7	-12.1	0.0	NA
416 Rigby	410	2370	2110	1870	1640	NA	5115	4050	3165	2455	NA	+2.5	-2.4	-17.3	0.0	$110
416 Rem. Mag.*	350	2520	2270	2034	1814	1611	4935	4004	3216	2557	2017	+2.5	-0.8	-12.6	-35.0	$82
416 Rem. Mag.*	400	2400	2175	1962	1763	1579	5115	4201	3419	2760	2214	+2.5	-1.5	-14.6	0.0	$80
416 Wea. Mag.*	400	2700	2397	2115	1852	1613	6474	5104	3971	3047	2310	+2.5	0.0	-10.1	-30.4	$96
10.57 (416) Meteor	400	2730	2532	2342	2161	1987	6621	5695	4874	4147	3508	+1.9	0.0	-8.3	-24.0	NA
404 Jeffrey	400	2150	1924	1716	1525	NA	4105	3289	2614	2064	NA	+2.5	-4.0	-22.1	0.0	NA
425, 44																
425 Express	400	2400	2160	1934	1725	NA	5115	4145	3322	2641	NA	+2.5	-1.0	-14.0	0.0	NA
44-40 Win.	200	1190	1006	900	822	756	629	449	360	300	254	0.0	-33.3	0.0	0.0	$36**
44 Rem. Mag.	210	1920	1477	1155	982	880	1719	1017	622	450	361	0.0	-17.6	0.0	0.0	$14
44 Rem. Mag.	240	1760	1380	1114	970	878	1650	1015	661	501	411	0.0	-17.6	0.0	0.0	$13
444 Marlin	240	2350	1815	1377	1087	941	2942	1753	1001	630	472	+2.5	-15.1	-31.0	0.0	$22
444 Marlin	265	2120	1733	1405	1160	1012	2644	1768	1162	791	603	+2.5	-6.0	-32.2	0.0	Disc.
444 Marlin Light Mag	265	2335	1913	1551	1266		3208	2153	1415	943		2.0	-4.90	-26.5	0.0	NA
444 Mar. Lever Evolution	265	2325	1971	1652	1380	NA	3180	2285	1606	1120	NA	3.00	-1.40	-18.6	NA	NA
45																
45-70 Govt.	300	1810	1497	1244	1073	969	2182	1492	1031	767	625	0.0	-14.8	0.0	0.0	$21
45-70 Govt. Supreme	300	1880	1558	1292	1103	988	2355	1616	1112	811	651	0.0	-12.9	-46.0	-105.0	NA
45-70 Lever Evolution	325	2050	1729	1450	1225	NA	3032	2158	1516	1083	NA	3.00	-4.10	-27.8	NA	NA
45-70 Govt. CorBon	350	1800	1526	1296			2519	1810	1307			0.0	-14.6	0.0	0.0	NA
45-70 Govt.	405	1330	1168	1055	977	918	1590	1227	1001	858	758	0.0	-24.6	0.0	0.0	$21
45-70 Govt. PMC Cowboy	405	1550	1193				1639	1280				0.0	-23.9	0.0	0.0	NA
45-70 Govt. Garrett	415	1850					3150					3.0	-7.0	0.0	0.0	NA
45-70 Govt. Garrett	530	1550	1343	1178	1062	982	2828	2123	1633	1327	1135	0.0	-17.8	0.0	0.0	NA
450 Marlin	350	2100	1774	1488	1254	1089	3427	2446	1720	1222	922	0.0	-9.7	-35.2	0.0	NA
450 Mar. Lever Evolution	325	2225	1887	1585	1331	NA	3572	2569	1813	1278	NA	3.00	-2.20	-21.3	NA	NA
458 Win. Magnum	350	2470	1990	1570	1250	1060	4740	3065	1915	1205	870	+2.5	-2.5	-21.6	0.0	$43
458 Win. Magnum	400	2380	2170	1960	1770	NA	5030	4165	3415	2785	NA	+2.5	-0.4	-13.4	0.0	$73
458 Win. Magnum	465	2220	1999	1791	1601	NA	5088	4127	3312	2646	NA	+2.5	-2.0	-17.7	0.0	NA
458 Win. Magnum	500	2040	1823	1623	1442	1237	4620	3689	2924	2308	1839	+2.5	-3.5	-22.0	0.0	$61
458 Win. Magnum	510	2040	1770	1527	1319	1157	4712	3547	2640	1970	1516	+2.5	-4.1	-25.0	0.0	$41
450 Dakota	500	2450	2235	2030	1838	1658	6663	5544	4576	3748	3051	+2.5	-0.6	-12.0	-33.8	NA
450 N.E. 3-1/4"	465	2190	1970	1765	1577	NA	4952	4009	3216	2567	NA	+2.5	-3.0	-20.0	0.0	NA
450 N.E. 3-1/4"	500	2150	1920	1708	1514	NA	5132	4093	3238	2544	NA	+2.5	-4.0	-22.9	0.0	NA
450 No. 2	465	2190	1970	1765	1577	NA	4952	4009	3216	2567	NA	+2.5	-3.0	-20.0	0.0	NA
450 No. 2	500	2150	1920	1708	1514	NA	5132	4093	3238	2544	NA	+2.5	-4.0	-22.9	0.0	NA
458 Lott	465	2380	2150	1932	1730	NA	5848	4773	3855	3091	NA	+2.5	-1.0	-14.0	0.0	NA
458 Lott	500	2300	2062	1838	1633	NA	5873	4719	3748	2960	NA	+2.5	-1.6	-16.4	0.0	NA
450 Ackley Mag.	465	2400	2169	1950	1747	NA	5947	4857	3927	3150	NA	+2.5	-1.0	-13.7	0.0	NA
450 Ackley Mag.	500	2320	2081	1855	1649	NA	5975	4085	3820	3018	NA	+2.5	-1.2	-15.0	0.0	NA
460 Short A-Sq.	500	2420	2175	1943	1729	NA	6501	5250	4193	3319	NA	+2.5	-0.8	-12.8	0.0	NA
460 Wea. Mag.	500	2700	2404	2128	1869	1635	8092	6416	5026	3878	2969	+2.5	+0.6	-8.9	-28.0	$72
475																
500/465 N.E.	480	2150	1917	1703	1507	NA	4926	3917	3089	2419	NA	+2.5	-4.0	-22.2	0.0	NA
470 Rigby	500	2150	1940	1740	1560	NA	5130	4170	3360	2695	NA	+2.5	-2.8	-19.4	0.0	NA
470 Nitro Ex.	480	2190	1954	1735	1536	NA	5111	4070	3210	2515	NA	+2.5	-3.5	-20.8	0.0	NA
470 Nitro Ex.	500	2150	1890	1650	1440	1270	5130	3965	3040	2310	1790	+2.5	-4.3	-24.0	0.0	$177
475 No. 2	500	2200	1955	1728	1522	NA	5375	4243	3316	2573	NA	+2.5	-3.2	-20.9	0.0	NA
50, 58																
505 Gibbs	525	2300	2063	1840	1637	NA	6166	4922	3948	3122	NA	+2.5	-3.0	-18.0	0.0	NA
500 N.E.-3"	570	2150	1928	1722	1533	NA	5850	4703	3752	2975	NA	+2.5	-3.7	-22.0	0.0	NA
500 N.E.-3"	600	2150	1927	1721	1531	NA	6158	4947	3944	3124	NA	+2.5	-4.0	-22.0	0.0	NA
495 A-Square	570	2350	2117	1896	1693	NA	5850	4703	3752	2975	NA	+2.5	-1.0	-14.5	0.0	NA
495 A-Square	600	2280	2050	1833	1635	NA	6925	5598	4478	3562	NA	+2.5	-2.0	-17.0	0.0	NA
500 A-Square	600	2380	2144	1922	1766	NA	7546	6126	4920	3922	NA	+2.5	-3.0	-17.0	0.0	NA
500 A-Square	707	2250	2040	1841	1567	NA	7947	6530	5318	4311	NA	+2.5	-2.0	-17.0	0.0	NA
500 BMG PMC	660	3080	2854	2639	2444	2248	13688		500 yd. zero			+3.1	+3.9	+4.7	+2.8	NA
577 Nitro Ex.	750	2050	1793	1562	1360	NA	6990	5356	4065	3079	NA	+2.5	-5.0	-26.0	0.0	NA
577 Tyrannosaur	750	2400	2141	1898	1675	NA	9591	7633	5996	4671	NA	+3.0	0.0	-12.9	0.0	NA
600, 700																
600 N.E.	900	1950	1680	1452	NA	NA	7596	5634	4212	NA	NA	+5.6	0.0	0.0	0.0	NA

Notes: Blanks are available in 32 S&W, 38 S&W and 38 Special. "V" after barrel length indicates test barrel was vented to produce ballistics similar to a revolver with a normal barrel-to-cylinder gap. Ammo prices are per 50 rounds except when marked with an ** which signifies a 20 round box; *** signifies a 25-round box. Not all loads are available from all ammo manufacturers. Listed loads are those made by Remington, Winchester, Federal, and others. DISC. is a discontinued load. Prices are rounded to nearest whole dollar and will vary with brand and retail outlet. † = new bullet weight this year; "c" indicates a change in data.

Cartridge	Bullet Wgt. Grs.	VELOCITY (fps)			ENERGY (ft. lbs.)			Mid-Range Traj. (in.)		Bbl. Lgth. (in.)	Est. Price/ box
		Muzzle	50 yds.	100 yds.	Muzzle	50 yds.	100 yds.	50 yds.	100 yds.		
22, 25											
221 Rem. Fireball	50	2650	2380	2130	780	630	505	0.2	0.8	10.5"	$15
25 Automatic	35	900	813	742	63	51	43	NA	NA	2"	$18
25 Automatic	45	815	730	655	65	55	40	1.8	7.7	2"	$21
25 Automatic	50	760	705	660	65	55	50	2.0	8.7	2"	$17
30											
7.5mm Swiss	107	1010	NA	NA	240	NA	NA	NA	NA	NA	NEW
7.62mmTokarev	87	1390	NA	NA	365	NA	NA	0.6	NA	4.5"	NA
7.62 Nagant	97	790	NA	NA	134	NA	NA	NA	NA	NA	NEW
7.63 Mauser	88	1440	NA	NA	405	NA	NA	NA	NA	NA	NEW
30 Luger	93†	1220	1110	1040	305	255	225	0.9	3.5	4.5"	$34
30 Carbine	110	1790	1600	1430	785	625	500	0.4	1.7	10"	$28
30-357 AeT	123	1992	NA	NA	1084	NA	NA	NA	NA	10"	NA
32											
32 S&W	88	680	645	610	90	80	75	2.5	10.5	3"	$17
32 S&W Long	98	705	670	635	115	100	90	2.3	10.5	4"	$17
32 Short Colt	80	745	665	590	100	80	60	2.2	9.9	4"	$19
32 H&R Magnum	85	1100	1020	930	230	195	165	1.0	4.3	4.5"	$21
32 H&R Magnum	95	1030	940	900	225	190	170	1.1	4.7	4.5"	$19
32 Automatic	60	970	895	835	125	105	95	1.3	5.4	4"	$22
32 Automatic	60	1000	917	849	133	112	96			4"	NA
32 Automatic	65	950	890	830	130	115	100	1.3	5.6	NA	NA
32 Automatic	71	905	855	810	130	115	95	1.4	5.8	4"	$19
8mm Lebel Pistol	111	850	NA	NA	180	NA	NA	NA	NA	NA	NEW
8mm Steyr	112	1080	NA	NA	290	NA	NA	NA	NA	NA	NEW
8mm Gasser	126	850	NA	NA	200	NA	NA	NA	NA	NA	NEW
9mm, 38											
380 Automatic	60	1130	960	NA	170	120	NA	1.0	NA	NA	NA
380 Automatic	85/88	990	920	870	190	165	145	1.2	5.1	4"	$20
380 Automatic	90	1000	890	800	200	160	130	1.2	5.5	3.75"	$10
380 Automatic	95/100	955	865	785	190	160	130	1.4	5.9	4"	$20
38 Super Auto +P	115	1300	1145	1040	430	335	275	0.7	3.3	5"	$26
38 Super Auto +P	125/130	1215	1100	1015	425	350	300	0.8	3.6	5"	$26
38 Super Auto +P	147	1100	1050	1000	395	355	325	0.9	4.0	5"	NA
9x18mm Makarov	95	1000	NA	NA	NA	NA	NA	NA	NA	NA	NEW
9x18mm Ultra	100	1050	NA	NA	240	NA	NA	NA	NA	NA	NEW
9x23mm Largo	124	1190	1055	966	390	306	257	0.7	3.7	4"	NA
9x23mm Win.	125	1450	1249	1103	583	433	338	0.6	2.8	NA	NA
9mm Steyr	115	1180	NA	NA	350	NA	NA	NA	NA	NA	NEW
9mm Luger	88	1500	1190	1010	440	275	200	0.6	3.1	4"	$24
9mm Luger	90	1360	1112	978	370	247	191	NA	NA	4"	$26
9mm Luger	95	1300	1140	1010	350	275	215	0.8	3.4	4"	NA
9mm Luger	100	1180	1080	NA	305	255	NA	0.9	NA	4"	NA
9mm Luger	115	1155	1045	970	340	280	240	0.9	3.9	4"	$21
9mm Luger	123/125	1110	1030	970	340	290	260	1.0	4.0	4"	$23
9mm Luger	140	935	890	850	270	245	225	1.3	5.5	4"	$23
9mm Luger	147	990	940	900	320	290	265	1.1	4.9	4"	$26
9mm Luger +P	90	1475	NA	NA	437	NA	NA	NA	NA	NA	NA
9mm Luger +P	115	1250	1113	1019	399	316	265	0.8	3.5	4"	$27
9mm Federal	115	1280	1130	1040	420	330	280	0.7	3.3	4"V	$24
9mm Luger Vector	115	1155	1047	971	341	280	241	NA	NA	4"	NA
9mm Luger +P	124	1180	1089	1021	384	327	287	0.8	3.8	4"	NA
38											
38 S&W	146	685	650	620	150	135	125	2.4	10.0	4"	$19
38 Short Colt	125	730	685	645	150	130	115	2.2	9.4	6"	$19
39 Special	100	950	900	NA	200	180	NA	1.3	NA	4"V	NA
38 Special	110	945	895	850	220	195	175	1.3	5.4	4"V	$23
38 Special	110	945	895	850	220	195	175	1.3	5.4	4"V	$23
38 Special	130	775	745	710	175	160	120	1.9	7.9	4"V	$22

Notes: Blanks are available in 32 S&W, 38 S&W and 38 Special. "V" after barrel length indicates test barrel was vented to produce ballistics similar to a revolver with a normal barrel-to-cylinder gap. Ammo prices are per 50 rounds except when marked with an ** which signifies a 20 round box; *** signifies a 25-round box. Not all loads are available from all ammo manufacturers. Listed loads are those made by Remington, Winchester, Federal, and others. DISC. is a discontinued load. Prices are rounded to nearest whole dollar and will vary with brand and retail outlet. † = new bullet weight this year; "c" indicates a change in data.

Cartridge	Bullet Wgt. Grs.	VELOCITY (fps)			ENERGY (ft. lbs.)			Mid-Range Traj. (in.)		Bbl. Lgth. (in).	Est. Price/ box
		Muzzle	50 yds.	100 yds.	Muzzle	50 yds.	100 yds.	50 yds.	100 yds.		
38 Special Cowboy	140	800	767	735	199	183	168			7.5" V	NA
38 (Multi-Ball)	140	830	730	505	215	130	80	2.0	10.6	4"V	$10**
38 Special	148	710	635	565	165	130	105	2.4	10.6	4"V	$17
38 Special	158	755	725	690	200	185	170	2.0	8.3	4"V	$18
38 Special +P	95	1175	1045	960	290	230	195	0.9	3.9	4"V	$23
38 Special +P	110	995	925	870	240	210	185	1.2	5.1	4"V	$23
38 Special +P	125	975	929	885	264	238	218	1	5.2	4"	NA
38 Special +P	125	945	900	860	250	225	205	1.3	5.4	4"V	#23
38 Special +P	129	945	910	870	255	235	215	1.3	5.3	4"V	$11
38 Special +P	130	925	887	852	247	227	210	1.3	5.50	4"V	NA
38 Special +P	147/150(c)	884	NA	NA	264	NA	NA	NA	NA	4"V	$27
38 Special +P	158	890	855	825	280	255	240	1.4	6.0	4"V	$20
357											
357 SIG	115	1520	NA	NA	593	NA	NA	NA	NA	NA	NA
357 SIG	124	1450	NA	NA	578	NA	NA	NA	NA	NA	NA
357 SIG	125	1350	1190	1080	510	395	325	0.7	3.1	4"	NA
357 SIG	150	1130	1030	970	420	355	310	0.9	4.0	NA	NA
356 TSW	115	1520	NA	NA	593	NA	NA	NA	NA	NA	NA
356 TSW	124	1450	NA	NA	578	NA	NA	NA	NA	NA	NA
356 TSW	135	1280	1120	1010	490	375	310	0.8	3.50	NA	NA
356 TSW	147	1220	1120	1040	485	410	355	0.8	3.5	5"	NA
357 Mag., Super Clean	105	1650									NA
357 Magnum	110	1295	1095	975	410	290	230	0.8	3.5	4"V	$25
357 (Med.Vel.)	125	1220	1075	985	415	315	270	0.8	3.7	4"V	$25
357 Magnum	125	1450	1240	1090	585	425	330	0.6	2.8	4"V	$25
357 (Multi-Ball)	140	1155	830	665	420	215	135	1.2	6.4	4"V	$11**
357 Magnum	140	1360	1195	1075	575	445	360	0.7	3.0	4"V	$25
357 Magnum	145	1290	1155	1060	535	430	360	0.8	3.5	4"V	$26
357 Magnum	150/158	1235	1105	1015	535	430	360	0.8	3.5	4"V	$25
357 Mag. Cowboy	158	800	761	725	225	203	185				NA
357 Magnum	165	1290	1189	1108	610	518	450	0.7	3.1	8-3/8"	NA
357 Magnum	180	1145	1055	985	525	445	390	0.9	3.9	4"V	$25
357 Magnum	180	1180	1088	1020	557	473	416	0.8	3.6	8"V	NA
357 Mag. CorBon F.A.	180	1650	1512	1386	1088	913	767	1.66	0.0		NA
357 Mag. CorBon	200	1200	1123	1061	640	560	500	3.19	0.0		NA
357 Rem. Maximum	158	1825	1590	1380	1170	885	670	0.4	1.7	10.5"	$14**
40, 10mm											
40 S&W	135	1140	1070	NA	390	345	NA	0.9	NA	4"	NA
40 S&W	155	1140	1026	958	447	362	309	0.9	4.1	4"	$14***
40 S&W	165	1150	NA	NA	485	NA	NA	NA	NA	4"	$18***
40 S&W	180	985	936	893	388	350	319	1.4	5.0	4"	$14***
40 S&W	180	1015	960	914	412	368	334	1.3	4.5	4"	NA
400 Cor-Bon	135	1450	NA	NA	630	NA	NA	NA	NA	5"	NA
10mm Automatic	155	1125	1046	986	436	377	335	0.9	3.9	5"	$26
10mm Automatic	170	1340	1165	1145	680	510	415	0.7	3.2	5"	$31
10mm Automatic	175	1290	1140	1035	650	505	420	0.7	3.3	5.5"	$11**
10mm Auto. (FBI)	180	950	905	865	361	327	299	1.5	5.4	4"	$16**
10mm Automatic	180	1030	970	920	425	375	340	1.1	4.7	5"	$16**
10mm Auto H.V.	180†	1240	1124	1037	618	504	430	0.8	3.4	5"	$27
10mm Automatic	200	1160	1070	1010	495	510	430	0.9	3.8	5"	$14**
10.4mm Italian	177	950	NA	NA	360	NA	NA	NA	NA	NA	NEW
41 Action Exp.	180	1000	947	903	400	359	326	0.5	4.2	5"	$13**
41 Rem. Magnum	170	1420	1165	1015	760	515	390	0.7	3.2	4"V	$33
41 Rem. Magnum	175	1250	1120	1030	605	490	410	0.8	3.4	4"V	$14**
41 (Med. Vel.)	210	965	900	840	435	375	330	1.3	5.4	4"V	$30
41 Rem. Magnum	210	1300	1160	1060	790	630	535	0.7	3.2	4"V	$33
41 Rem. Magnum	240	1250	1151	1075	833	706	616	0.8	3.3	6.5V	NA

Notes: Blanks are available in 32 S&W, 38 S&W and 38 Special. "V" after barrel length indicates test barrel was vented to produce ballistics similar to a revolver with a normal barrel-to-cylinder gap. Ammo prices are per 50 rounds except when marked with an ** which signifies a 20 round box; *** signifies a 25-round box. Not all loads are available from all ammo manufacturers. Listed loads are those made by Remington, Winchester, Federal, and others. DISC. is a discontinued load. Prices are rounded to nearest whole dollar and will vary with brand and retail outlet. † = new bullet weight this year; "c" indicates a change in data.

Cartridge	Bullet Wgt. Grs.	VELOCITY (fps)			ENERGY (ft. lbs.)			Mid-Range Traj. (in.)		Bbl. Lgth. (in.)	Est. Price/ box
		Muzzle	50 yds.	100 yds.	Muzzle	50 yds.	100 yds.	50 yds.	100 yds.		
44											
44 S&W Russian	247	780	NA	NA	335	NA	NA	NA	NA	NA	NA
44 S&W Special	180	980	NA	NA	383	NA	NA	NA	NA	6.5"	NA
44 S&W Special	180	1000	935	882	400	350	311	NA	NA	7.5"V	NA
44 S&W Special	200†	875	825	780	340	302	270	1.2	6.0	6"	$13**
44 S&W Special	200	1035	940	865	475	390	335	1.1	4.9	6.5"	$13**
44 S&W Special	240/246	755	725	695	310	285	265	2.0	8.3	6.5"	$26
44-40 Win. Cowboy	225	750	723	695	281	261	242				NA
44 Rem. Magnum	180	1610	1365	1175	1035	745	550	0.5	2.3	4"V	$18**
44 Rem. Magnum	200	1400	1192	1053	870	630	492	0.6	NA	6.5"	$20
44 Rem. Magnum	210	1495	1310	1165	1040	805	635	0.6	2.5	6.5"	$18**
44 (Med. Vel.)	240	1000	945	900	535	475	435	1.1	4.8	6.5"	$17
44 R.M. (Jacketed)	240	1180	1080	1010	740	625	545	0.9	3.7	4"V	$18**
44 R.M. (Lead)	240	1350	1185	1070	970	750	610	0.7	3.1	4"V	$29
44 Rem. Magnum	250	1180	1100	1040	775	670	600	0.8	3.6	6.5"V	$21
44 Rem. Magnum	250	1250	1148	1070	867	732	635	0.8	3.3	6.5"V	NA
44 Rem. Magnum	275	1235	1142	1070	931	797	699	0.8	3.3	6.5"	NA
44 Rem. Magnum	300	1200	1100	1026	959	806	702	NA	NA	7.5"	$17
44 Rem. Magnum	330	1385	1297	1220	1406	1234	1090	1.83	0.00	NA	NA
440 CorBon	260	1700	1544	1403	1669	1377	1136	1.58	NA	10"	NA
45, 50											
450 Short Colt/450 Revolver	226	830	NA	NA	350	NA	NA	NA	NA	NA	NEW
45 S&W Schofield	180	730	NA	NA	213	NA	NA	NA	NA	NA	NA
45 S&W Schofield	230	730	NA	NA	272	NA	NA	NA	NA	NA	NA
45 G.A.P.	185	1090	970	890	490	385	320	1	4.7	5	NA
45 G.A.P.	230	880	842	NA	396	363	NA	NA	NA	NA	NA
45 Automatic	165	1030	930	NA	385	315	NA	1.2	NA	5"	NA
45 Automatic	185	1000	940	890	410	360	325	1.1	4.9	5"	$28
45 Auto. (Match)	185	770	705	650	245	204	175	2.0	8.7	5"	$28
45 Auto. (Match)	200	940	890	840	392	352	312	2.0	8.6	5"	$20
45 Automatic	200	975	917	860	421	372	328	1.4	5.0	5"	$18
45 Automatic	230	830	800	675	355	325	300	1.6	6.8	5"	$27
45 Automatic	230	880	846	816	396	366	340	1.5	6.1	5"	NA
45 Automatic +P	165	1250	NA	NA	573	NA	NA	NA	NA	NA	NA
45 Automatic +P	185	1140	1040	970	535	445	385	0.9	4.0	5"	$31
45 Automatic +P	200	1055	982	925	494	428	380	NA	NA	5"	NA
45 Super	185	1300	1190	1108	694	582	504	NA	NA	5"	NA
45 Win. Magnum	230	1400	1230	1105	1000	775	635	0.6	2.8	5"	$14**
45 Win. Magnum	260	1250	1137	1053	902	746	640	0.8	3.3	5"	$16**
45 Win. Mag. CorBon	320	1150	1080	1025	940	830	747	3.47			NA
455 Webley MKII	262	850	NA	NA	420	NA	NA	NA	NA	NA	NA
45 Colt	200	1000	938	889	444	391	351	1.3	4.8	5.5"	$21
45 Colt	225	960	890	830	460	395	345	1.3	5.5	5.5"	$22
45 Colt + P CorBon	265	1350	1225	1126	1073	884	746	2.65	0.0		NA
45 Colt + P CorBon	300	1300	1197	1114	1126	956	827	2.78	0.0		NA
45 Colt	250/255	860	820	780	410	375	340	1.6	6.6	5.5"	$27
454 Casull	250	1300	1151	1047	938	735	608	0.7	3.2	7.5"V	NA
454 Casull	260	1800	1577	1381	1871	1436	1101	0.4	1.8	7.5"V	NA
454 Casull	300	1625	1451	1308	1759	1413	1141	0.5	2.0	7.5"V	NA
454 Casull CorBon	360	1500	1387	1286	1800	1640	1323	2.01	0.0		NA
460 S&W	200	2300	2042	1801	2350	1851	1441	0	-1.60	NA	NA
460 S&W	250	1900	1640	1412	2004	1494	1106	0	-2.75	NA	NA
460 S&W	395	1550	1389	1249	2108	1691	1369	0	-4.00	NA	NA
475 Linebaugh	400	1350	1217	1119	1618	1315	1112	NA	NA	NA	NA
480 Ruger	325	1350	1191	1076	1315	1023	835	2.6	0.0	7.5"	NA
50 Action Exp.	325	1400	1209	1075	1414	1055	835	0.2	2.3	6"	$24**
500 S&W	275	1665	1392	1183	1693	1184	854	1.5	NA	8.375	NA
500 S&W	400	1675	1472	1299	2493	1926	1499	1.3	NA	8.375	NA
500 S&W	440	1625	1367	1169	2581	1825	1337	1.6	NA	8.375	NA

Note: The actual ballistics obtained with your firearm can vary considerably from the advertised ballistics.
Also, ballistics can vary from lot to lot with the same brand and type load.

Cartridge	Bullet Wt. Grs.	Velocity (fps) 22-1/2" Bbl.		Energy (ft. lbs.) 22-1/2" Bbl.		Mid-Range Traj. (in.)	Muzzle Velocity
		Muzzle	100 yds.	Muzzle	100 yds.	100 yds.	6" Bbl.
17 Aguila	20	1850	1267	NA	NA	NA	NA
17 Hornady Mach 2	17	2100	1530	166	88	0.7	NA
17 HMR	17	2550	1902	245	136	NA	NA
17 HMR	20	2375	1776	250	140	NA	NA
22 Short Blank	—	—	—	—	—	—	—
22 Short CB	29	727	610	33	24	NA	706
22 Short Target	29	830	695	44	31	6.8	786
22 Short HP	27	1164	920	81	50	4.3	1077
22 Colibri	20	375	183	6	1	NA	NA
22 Super Colibri	20	500	441	11	9	NA	NA
22 Long CB	29	727	610	33	24	NA	706
22 Long HV	29	1180	946	90	57	4.1	1031
22 LR Pistol Match	40	1070	890	100	70	4.6	940
22 LR Sub Sonic HP	38	1050	901	93	69	4.7	NA
22 LR Standard Velocity	40	1070	890	100	70	4.6	940
22 LR AutoMatch	40	1200	990	130	85	NA	NA
22 LR HV	40	1255	1016	140	92	3.6	1060
22 LR Silhoutte	42	1220	1003	139	94	3.6	1025
22 SSS	60	950	802	120	86	NA	NA
22 LR HV HP	40	1280	1001	146	89	3.5	1085
22 Velocitor GDHP	40	1435	0	0	0	NA	NA
22 LR Hyper HP	32/33/34	1500	1075	165	85	2.8	NA
22 LR Stinger HP	32	1640	1132	191	91	2.6	1395
22 LR Hyper Vel	30	1750	1191	204	93	NA	NA
22 LR Shot #12	31	950	NA	NA	NA	NA	NA
22 WRF LFN	45	1300	1015	169	103	3	NA
22 Win. Mag.	30	2200	1373	322	127	1.4	1610
22 Win. Mag. V-Max BT	33	2000	1495	293	164	0.60	NA
22 Win. Mag. JHP	34	2120	1435	338	155	1.4	NA
22 Win. Mag. JHP	40	1910	1326	324	156	1.7	1480
22 Win. Mag. FMJ	40	1910	1326	324	156	1.7	1480
22 Win. Mag. Dyna Point	45	1550	1147	240	131	2.60	NA
22 Win. Mag. JHP	50	1650	1280	300	180	1.3	NA
22 Win. Mag. Shot #11	52	1000	—	NA	—	—	NA

SHOTSHELL LOADS & PRICES

NOTES: * = 10 rounds per box. ** = 5 rounds per box. Pricing variations and number of rounds per box can occur with type and brand of ammunition. Listed pricing is the average nominal cost for load style and box quantity shown. Not every brand is available in all shot size variations. Some manufacturers do not provide suggested list prices. All prices rounded to nearest whole dollar. The price you pay will vary dependent upon outlet of purchase. # = new load spec this year; "C" indicates a change in data.

Dram Equiv.	Shot Ozs.	Load Style	Shot Sizes	Brands	Avg. Price/box	Velocity (fps)
10 Gauge 3-1/2" Magnum						
4-1/2	2-1/4	premium	BB, 2, 4, 5, 6	Win., Fed., Rem.	$33	1205
Max	2	premium	4, 5, 6	Fed., Win.	NA	1300
4-1/4	2	high velocity	BB, 2, 4	Rem.	$22	1210
Max	18 pellets	premium	00 buck	Fed., Win.	$7**	1100
Max	1-7/8	Bismuth	BB, 2, 4	Bis.	NA	1225
Max	1-3/4	high density	BB, 2	Rem.	NA	1300
4-1/4	1-3/4	steel	TT, T, BBB, BB, 1, 2, 3	Win., Rem.	$27	1260
Mag	1-5/8	steel	T, BBB, BB, 2	Win.	$27	1285
Max	1-5/8	Bismuth	BB, 2, 4	Bismuth	NA	1375
Max	1-1/2	steel	T, BBB, BB, 1, 2, 3	Fed.	NA	1450
Max	1-3/8	steel	T, BBB, BB, 1, 2, 3	Fed., Rem.	NA	1500
Max	1-3/8	steel	T, BBB, BB, 2	Fed., Win.	NA	1450
Max	1-3/4	slug, rifled	slug	Fed.	NA	1280
Max	24 pellets	Buckshot	1 Buck	Fed.	NA	1100
Max	54 pellets	Super-X	4 Buck	Win.	NA	1150
12 Gauge 3-1/2" Magnum						
Max	2-1/4	premium	4, 5, 6	Fed., Rem., Win.	$13*	1150
Max	2	Lead	4, 5, 6	Fed.	NA	1300
Max	2	Copper plated turkey	4, 5	Rem.	NA	1300
Max	18 pellets	premium	00 buck	Fed., Win., Rem.	$7**	1100
Max	1-7/8	heavyweight	5, 6	Fed.	NA	1300
Max	1-3/4	high density	BB, 2, 4	Rem.	NA	1300
Max	1-7/8	Bismuth	BB, 2, 4	Bis.	NA	1225
Max	1-5/8	Hevi-shot	T	Hevi-shot	NA	1350
Max	1-5/8	high density	BB, 2	Fed.	NA	1450
Max	1-3/8	steel	T, BBB, BB, 2, 4	Fed., Win., Rem.	NA	1450
Max	1-1/2	Supreme H-V	BBB, BB, 2, 3	Win.	NA	1475
Max	1-3/8	H-speed steel	BB, 2	Rem.	NA	1550
Max	24 pellets	Premium	1 Buck	Fed.	NA	1100
Max	54 pellets	Super-X	4 Buck	Win.	NA	1050
12 Gauge 3" Magnum						
4	2	premium	BB, 2, 4, 5, 6	Win., Fed., Rem.	$9*	1175
4	1-7/8	premium	BB, 2, 4, 6	Win., Fed., Rem.	$19	1210
4	1-7/8	duplex	4x6	Rem.	$9*	1210
Max	1-3/4	turkey	4, 5, 6	Fed., Fio., Win., Rem.	NA	1300
Max	1-3/4	high density	BB, 2, 4	Rem.	NA	1450
Max	1-5/8	high density	BB, 2	Fed.	NA	1450
Max	1-5/8	high velocity	4, 5, 6	Fed.	NA	1350
4	1-5/8	premium	2, 4, 5, 6	Win., Fed., Rem.	$18	1290
Max	1-1/2	Hevi-shot	T	Hevi-shot	NA	1300
Max	1-1/2	high density	BB, 2, 4	Rem.	NA	1300
Max	1-5/8	Bismuth	BB, 2, 4, 5, 6	Bis.	NA	1250
4	24 pellets	buffered	1 buck	Win., Fed., Rem.	$5**	1040
4	15 pellets	buffered	00 buck	Win., Fed., Rem.	$6**	1210
4	10 pellets	buffered	000 buck	Win., Fed., Rem.	$6**	1225
4	41 pellets	buffered	4 buck	Win., Fed., Rem.	$6**	1210
Max	1-3/8	heavyweight	5, 6	Fed.	NA	1300
Max	1-3/8	high density	B, 2, 4, 6	Rem. Win.	NA	1450
Max	1-3/8	slug	slug	Bren.	NA	1476
Max	1-1/4	slug, rifled	slug	Fed.	NA	1600
Max	1-3/16	saboted slug	copper slug	Rem.	NA	1500
Max	7/8	slug, rifled	slug	Rem.	NA	1875
12 Gauge 3" Magnum (cont.)						
Max	1-1/8	low recoil	BB	Fed.	NA	850
Max	1-1/8	steel	BB, 2, 3, 4	Fed., Win., Rem.	NA	1550
Max	1-1/16	high density	2, 4	Win.	NA	1400
Max	1	steel	4, 6	Fed.	NA	1330
Max	1-3/8	buckhammer	slug	Rem.	NA	1500
Max	1	slug, rifled	slug, magnum	Win., Rem.	$5**	1760
Max	1	saboted slug	slug	Rem., Win., Fed.	$10**	1550
Max	385 grs.	partition gold	slug	Win.	NA	2000
3-5/8	1-3/8	steel	BBB, BB, 1, 2, 3, 4	Win., Fed., Rem.	$19	1275
Max	1-1/8	steel	BB, 2, 4	Rem.	NA	1500
Max	1-1/8	steel	T, BBB, BB, 2, 4, 5, 6	Fed., Win.	NA	1450
Max	1-1/8	steel	BB, 2	Fed.	NA	1400
4	1-1/4	steel	T, BBB, BB, 1, 2, 3, 4, 6	Win., Fed., Rem.	$18	1400
12 Gauge 2-3/4"						
Max	1-5/8	magnum	4, 5, 6	Win., Fed.	$8*	1250
Max	1-3/8	lead	4, 5, 6	Fiocchi	NA	1485
Max	1-3/8	turkey	4, 5, 6	Fio.	NA	1250
Max	1-3/8	steel	4, 5, 6	Fed.	NA	1400
Max	1-3/8	Bismuth	BB, 2, 4, 5, 6	Bis.	NA	1300
3-3/4	1-1/2	magnum	BB, 2, 4, 5, 6	Win., Fed., Rem.	$16	1260
Max	1-1/4	Supreme H-V	4, 5, 6, 7-1/2	Win. Rem.	NA	1400
3-3/4	1-1/4	high velocity	BB, 2, 4, 5, 6, 7-1/2, 8, 9	Win., Fed., Rem., Fio.	$13	1330
Max	1-1/4	high density	B, 2, 4	Win.	NA	1450
Max	1-1/4	high density	4, 6	Win.	NA	1325
3-1/4	1-1/4	standard velocity	6, 7-1/2, 8, 9	Win., Fed., Rem., Fio.	$11	1220
Max	1-1/8	Hevi-shot	5	Hevi-shot	NA	1350
3-1/4	1-1/8	standard velocity	4, 6, 7-1/2, 8, 9	Win., Fed., Rem., Fio.	$9	1255
Max	1-1/8	steel	2, 4	Rem.	NA	1390
Max	1	steel	BB, 2	Fed.	NA	1450
3-1/4	1	standard velocity	6, 7-1/2, 8	Rem., Fed., Fio., Win.	$6	1290
3-1/4	1-1/4	target	7-1/2, 8, 9	Win., Fed., Rem.	$10	1220
3	1-1/8	spreader	7-1/2, 8, 8-1/2, 9	Fio.	NA	1200
3	1-1/8	target	7-1/2, 8, 9, 7-1/2x8	Win., Fed., Rem., Fio.	$7	1200
2-3/4	1-1/8	target	7-1/2, 8, 8-1/2, 9, 7-1/2x8	Win., Fed., Rem., Fio.	$7	1145
2-3/4	1-1/8	low recoil	7-1/2, 8	Rem.	NA	1145
2-1/2	26 grams	low recoil	8	Win.	NA	980
2-1/4	1-1/8	target	7-1/2, 8, 8-1/2, 9	Rem., Fed.	$7	1080
Max	1	spreader	7-1/2, 8, 8-1/2, 9	Fio.	NA	1300
3-1/4	28 grams (1 oz)	target	7-1/2, 8, 9	Win., Fed., Rem., Fio.	$8	1290
3	1	target	7-1/2, 8, 8-1/2, 9	Win., Fio.	NA	1235
2-3/4	1	target	7-1/2, 8, 8-1/2, 9	Fed., Rem., Fio.	NA	1180
3-1/4	24 grams	target	7-1/2, 8, 9	Win., Fed., Fio.	NA	1325
3	7/8	light	8	Fio.	NA	1200
3-3/4	8 pellets	buffered	000 buck	Win., Fed., Rem.	$4**	1325
4	12 pellets	premium	00 buck	Win., Fed., Rem.	$5**	1290
3-3/4	9 pellets	buffered	00 buck	Win., Fed., Rem., Fio.	$19	1325
3-3/4	12 pellets	buffered	0 buck	Win., Fed., Rem.	$4**	1275

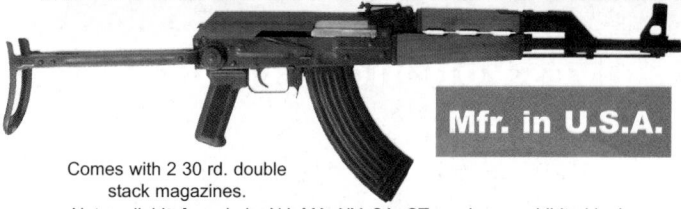

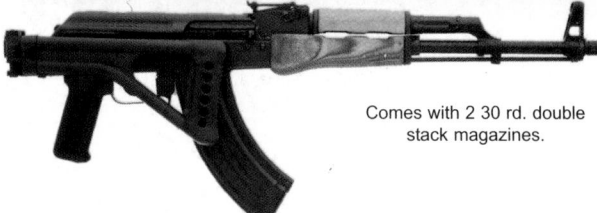

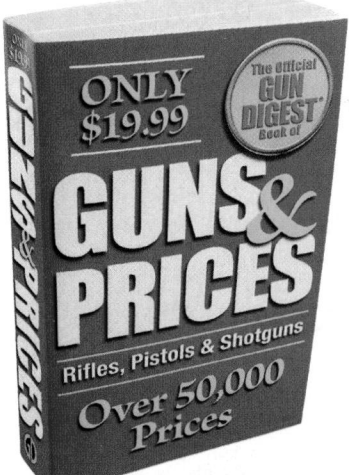
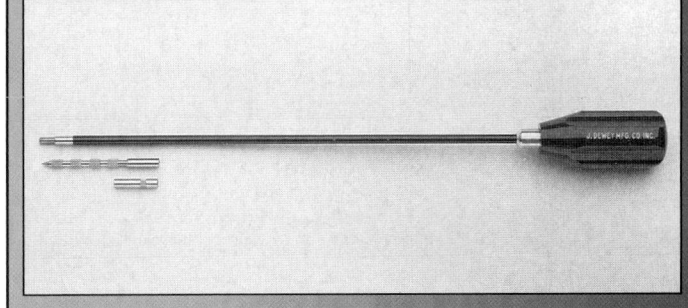
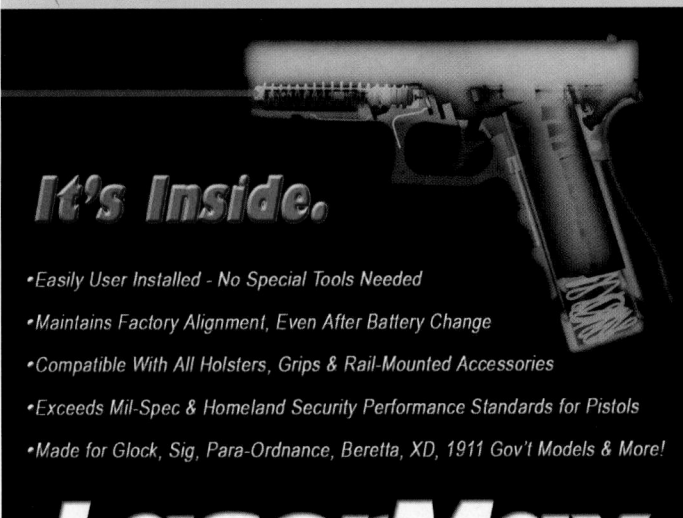

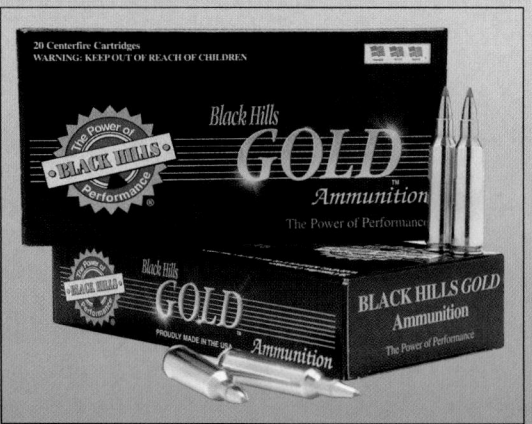
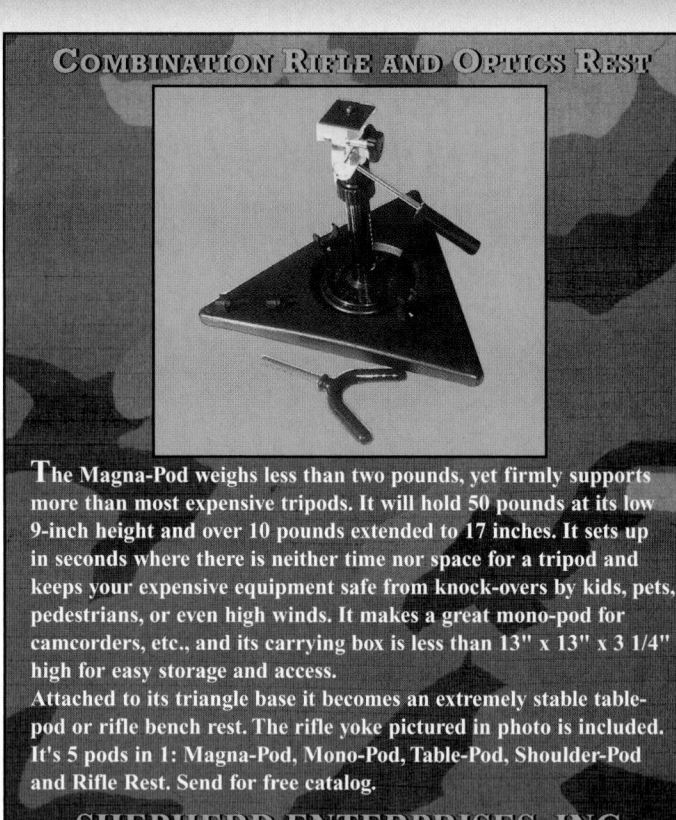

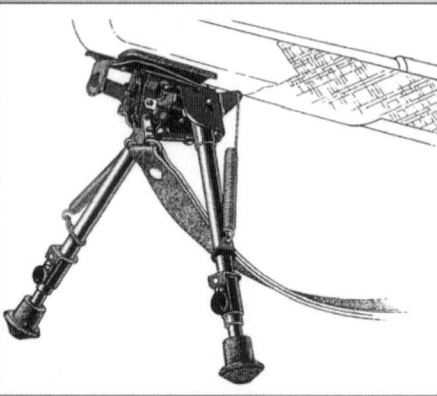

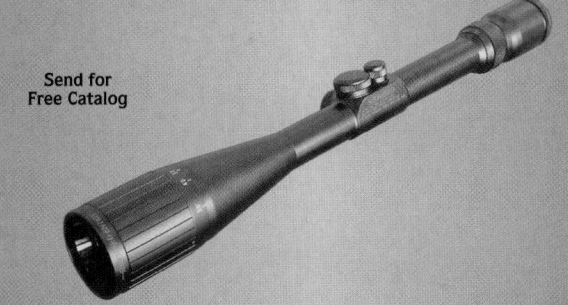

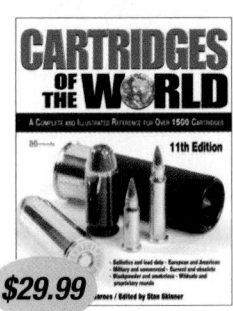
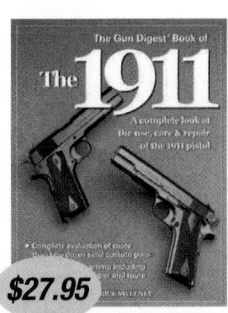

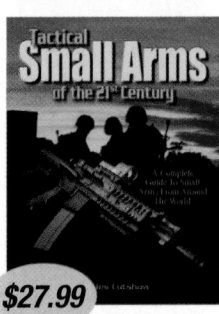

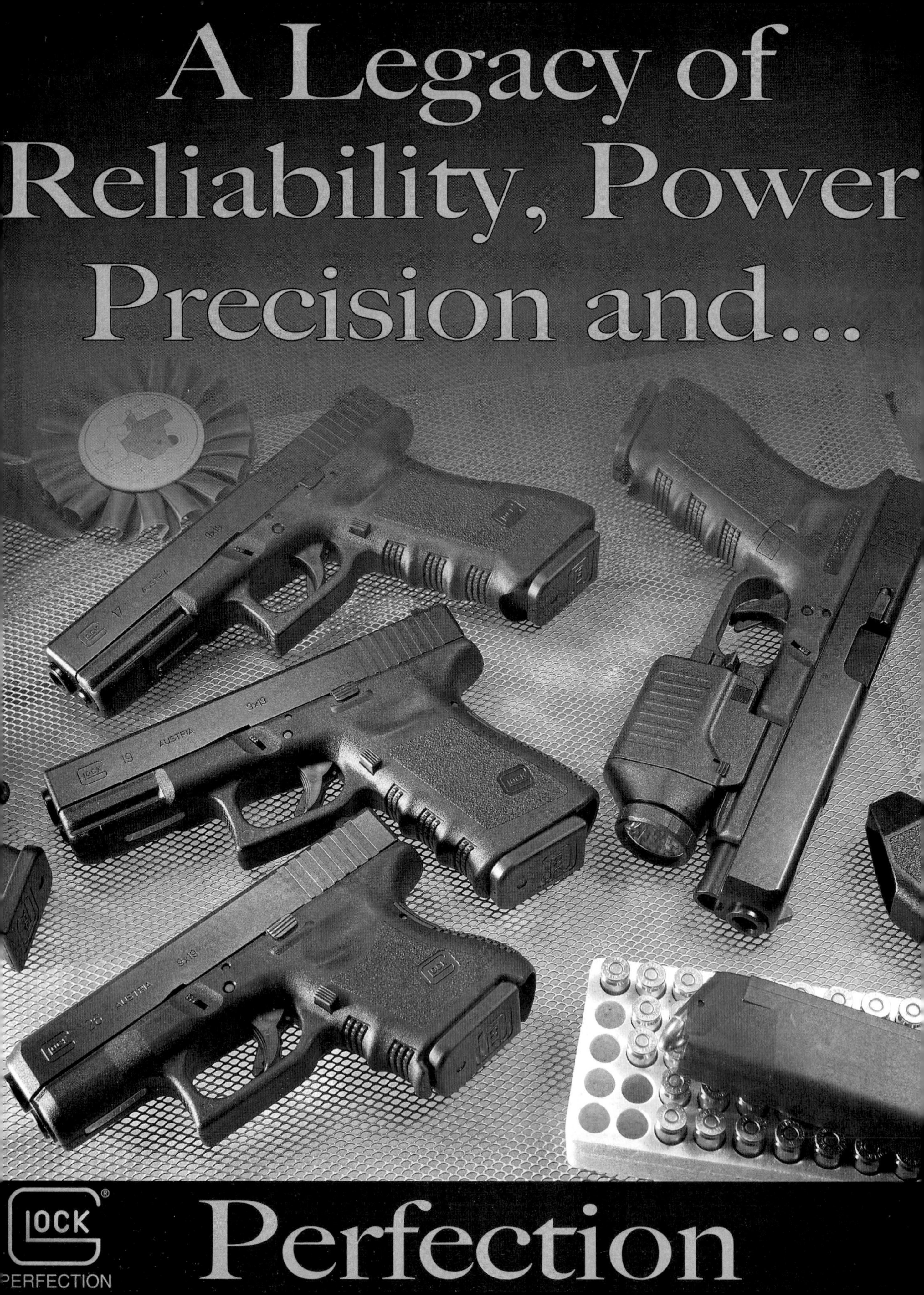
A Legacy of
Reliability, Power
Precision and...
GLOCK
PERFECTION
Perfection

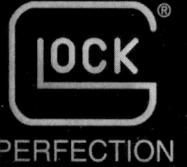

EYES-OPEN TARGETING
THE NEW RUGER M77® MARK II
STAINLESS STEEL FRONTIER RIFLE

Ruger Target Grey® Stainless M77 Mark II Frontier Rifle
KM77FRTG MKII
.243 Win., 7mm-08 Rem., .300 WSM, .308 Win., .325 WSM
Suggested retail price of $900.00
(rings included, scope not included)

Warner Glenn
Rancher & Professional Hunter
Douglas, Arizona

A lightweight, fast-handling, compact rifle offers a welcome edge when tracking game in difficult terrain. Sturm, Ruger gives you that edge with the M77 Mark II Frontier Rifle. We've taken our popular Ruger M77 Mark II Compact bolt action rifle and added a medium-weight, 16 1/2" precision hammer-forged barrel and a new, fast-handling forward scope mounting barrel rib. Chambered in a range of today's most popular cartridges, including the powerful .300 WSM and the new .325 WSM, the Ruger M77 Mark II Frontier Rifle gives new meaning to the word "handy."

The Ruger M77 Mark II Frontier Rifle features a black laminated-wood stock, stainless steel action, and stainless steel one-piece bolt. It includes patented Ruger scope rings to securely mount an intermediate-eye-relief scope on the barrel rib. It also comes with a Weaver-style scope base adapter, providing even more options to mount today's advanced optics.

You'll be amazed at how fast "eyes-open" target acquisition can be through a front-mounted intermediate-eye-relief scope, and how easy it is to carry your compact new rifle "at the balance," an impossibility with conventionally mounted scopes. Shoulder a Ruger M77 Mark II Frontier Rifle at your local retailer and see for yourself.

www.ruger.com

★★★★★
MADE
IN USA

Sturm, Ruger & Company, Inc.
Southport, CT 06890 U.S.A.
FREE Instruction Manuals are available
online at www.ruger.com

RUGER
ARMS MAKERS FOR RESPONSIBLE CITIZENS

2007
GUN DIGEST
Complete Compact
CATALOG

 GUNDEX

 HANDGUNS

 RIFLES

 SHOTGUNS

 BLACKPOWDER

 AIRGUNS

 ACCESSORIES

 REFERENCE

 DIRECTORY OF THE ARMS TRADE

GUNDEX

GUNDEX

GUNDEX

GUNDEX

GUNDEX

GUNDEX

GUNDEX

Includes models suitable for several forms of competition and other sporting purposes.

Accu-Tek AT-380 II 380 ACP

Auto-Ordnance 1911A1 Standard

Baer Custom Carry

Auto-Ordnance Deluxe

Baer Premium II

ACCU-TEK AT-380 II 380 ACP PISTOL

Caliber: 380 ACP, 6-shot magazine. **Barrel:** 2.8". **Weight:** 23.5 oz. **Length:** 6.125" overall. **Grips:** Textured black composition. **Sights:** Blade front, rear adjustable for windage. **Features:** Made from 17-4 stainless steel, has an exposed hammer, manual firing-pin safety block and trigger disconnect. Magazine release located on the bottom of the grip. American made, lifetime warranty. Comes with two 6-round stainless steel magazines and a California-approved cable lock. Introduced 2006. Made in U.S.A. by Accu-Tek.
Price: Satin stainless **$249.00**

AMERICAN DERRINGER LM5 AUTOMATIC PISTOL

Caliber: 25 ACP, 5-shot magazine; 32 Mag., 4-shot magazine. **Barrel:** 2". **Weight:** 15 oz. **Length:** 4". **Grips:** Wood. **Sights:** Fixed. **Features:** Compact, stainless, semi-auto, double-action hammerless design.
Price: **$2,660.00**

AMERICAN DERRINGER LM SIMMERLING AUTOMATIC PISTOL

Caliber: 45 ACP, 5-shot magazine. **Barrel:** 2". **Weight:** 24 oz. **Length:** 5". **Grips:** Polymer. **Sights:** Fixed. **Features:** Compact, stainless, semi-auto, double-action hammerless design.
Price: **$358.00**

AUTO-ORDNANCE 1911A1 AUTOMATIC PISTOL

Caliber: 45 ACP, 7-shot magazine. **Barrel:** 5". **Weight:** 39 oz. **Length:** 8.5" overall. **Grips:** Brown checkered plastic with medallion. **Sights:** Blade front, rear drift-adjustable for windage. **Features:** Same specs as 1911A1 military guns-parts interchangeable. Frame and slide blued; each radius has non-glare finish. Made in U.S.A. by Kahr Arms.
Price: 1911SE Standard, blued **$609.00**
Price: 1911WGSE Deluxe, black textured wraparound grips **$615.00**
Price: 1911PKZ Parkerized, lanyard loop, military rollstamp **$598.00**

BAER 1911 CUSTOM CARRY AUTO PISTOL

Caliber: 45 ACP, 7- or 10-shot magazine. **Barrel:** 5". **Weight:** 37 oz. **Length:** 8.5" overall. **Grips:** Checkered walnut. **Sights:** Baer improved ramp-style dovetailed front, Novak low-mount rear. **Features:** Baer forged NM frame, slide and barrel with stainless bushing. Baer speed trigger with 4-lb. pull. Partial listing shown. Made in U.S.A. by Les Baer Custom, Inc.
Price: Standard size, blued **$1,640.00**
Price: Standard size, stainless **$1,690.00**
Price: Comanche size, blued **$1,640.00**
Price: Comanche size, stainless **$1,690.00**
Price: Comanche size, aluminum frame, blued slide **$1,923.00**
Price: Comanche size, aluminum frame, stainless slide **$1,995.00**

BAER 1911 ULTIMATE RECON PISTOL

Caliber: 45 ACP, 7- or 10-shot magazine. **Barrel:** 5". **Weight:** 37 oz. **Length:** 8.5" overall. **Grips:** Checkered cocobolo. **Sights:** Baer improved ramp-style dovetailed front, Novak low-mount rear. **Features:** NM Caspian frame, slide and barrel with stainless bushing. Baer speed trigger with 4-lb. pull. Includes integral Picatinny rail and Sure-Fire X-200 light. Made in U.S.A. by Les Baer Custom, Inc. Introduced 2006.
Price: Bead blast blued **$2,988.00**
Price: Bead blast chrome **$3,230.00**

BAER 1911 PREMIER II AUTO PISTOL

Caliber: 38 Super, 400 Cor-Bon, 45 ACP, 7- or 10-shot magazine. **Barrel:** 5". **Weight:** 37 oz. **Length:** 8.5" overall. **Grips:** Checkered rosewood, double diamond pattern. **Sights:** Baer dovetailed front, low-mount Bo-Mar rear with hidden leaf. **Features:** Baer NM forged steel frame and barrel with stainless bushing, deluxe Commander hammer and sear, beavertail grip safety with pad, extended ambidextrous safety; flat mainspring housing; 30 lpi checkered front strap. Made in U.S.A. by Les Baer Custom, Inc.
Price: 5" 45 ACP **$1,598.00**
Price: 5" 400 Cor-Bon **$1,645.00**
Price: 5" 38 Super **$1,789.00**
Price: 6" 45 ACP (400 Cor-Bon and 38 Super available) **$1,755.00**
Price: Super-Tac 45 ACP (400 Cor-Bon and 38 Super available) **$2,098.00**

Baer 1911 Stinger   Beretta 92FS   Beretta Model 80 Cheetah

Beretta Bobcat

Beretta Tomcat

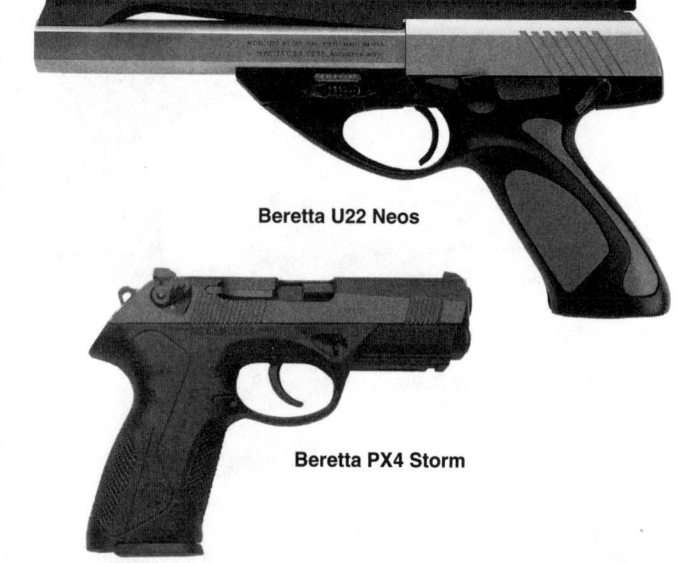

Beretta U22 Neos

Beretta PX4 Storm

BAER 1911 S.R.P. PISTOL

Caliber: 45 ACP. **Barrel:** 5". **Weight:** 37 oz. **Length:** 8.5" overall. **Grips:** Checkered walnut. **Sights:** Trijicon night sights. **Features:** Similar to the F.B.I. contract gun except uses Baer forged steel frame. Has Baer match barrel with supported chamber, Complete tactical action. Has Baer Ultra Coat finish. Introduced 1996. Made in U.S.A. by Les Baer Custom, Inc.
Price: Government or Comanche length **$2,339.00**

BAER 1911 STINGER PISTOL

Caliber: 45 ACP, 7-round magazine. **Barrel:** 5". **Weight:** 34 oz. **Length:** 8.5" overall. **Grips:** Checkered cocobolo. **Sights:** Baer dovetailed front, low-mount Bo-Mar rear with hidden leaf. **Features:** Baer NM frame. Baer Commanche slide, Officer's style grip frame, beveled mag well. Made in U.S.A. by Les Baer Custom, Inc.
Price: Blued **$1,666.00**
Price: Stainless **$1,675.00**

BAER 1911 PROWLER III PISTOL

Caliber: 45 ACP, 8-round magazine. **Barrel:** 5". **Weight:** 34 oz. **Length:** 8.5" overall. **Grips:** Checkered cocobolo. **Sights:** Baer dovetailed front, low-mount Bo-Mar rear with hidden leaf. **Features:** Similar to Premier II with tapered cone stub weight, rounded corners. Made in U.S.A. by Les Baer Custom, Inc.
Price: Blued **$2,215.00**

BERETTA MODEL 92FS PISTOL

Caliber: 9mm Para., 10-shot magazine. **Barrel:** 4.9". **Weight:** 34 oz. **Length:** 8.5" overall. **Grips:** Checkered black plastic. **Sights:** Blade front, rear adjustable for windage. Tritium night sights available. **Features:** Double action. Extractor acts as chamber loaded indicator, squared trigger guard, grooved front and backstraps, inertia firing pin. Matte or blued finish. Introduced 1977. Made in U.S.A.
Price: With plastic grips **$650.00**

BERETTA MODEL 80 CHEETAH SERIES DA PISTOLS

Caliber: 380 ACP, 10-shot magazine (M84); 8-shot (M85); 22 LR, 7-shot (M87). **Barrel:** 3.82". **Weight:** About 23 oz. (M84/85); 20.8 oz. (M87). **Length:** 6.8" overall. **Grips:** Glossy black plastic (wood optional at extra cost). **Sights:** Fixed front, drift-adjustable rear. **Features:** Double action, quick takedown, convenient magazine release. Introduced 1977. Made in U.S.A.
Price: Model 84 Cheetah, plastic grips **$625.00**
Price: Model 85 Cheetah, plastic grips, 8-shot **$575.00**
Price: Model 87 Cheetah, wood, 22 LR, 7-shot **$625.00**
Price: Model 87 Target, plastic grips **$698.00**

BERETTA MODEL 21 BOBCAT PISTOL

Caliber: 22 LR or 25 ACP. Both double action. **Barrel:** 2.4". **Weight:** 11.5 oz.; 11.8 oz. **Length:** 4.9" overall. **Grips:** Plastic. **Features:** Available in nickel, matte, engraved or blue finish. Introduced in 1985.

Price: Bobcat, 22 or 25, blue **$275.00**
Price: Bobcat, 22, stainless **$325.00**
Price: Bobcat, 22 or 25, matte **$250.00**

BERETTA MODEL 3032 TOMCAT PISTOL

Caliber: 32 ACP, 7-shot magazine. **Barrel:** 2.45". **Weight:** 14.5 oz. **Length:** 5" overall. **Grips:** Checkered black plastic. **Sights:** Blade front, drift-adjustable rear. **Features:** Double action with exposed hammer; tip-up barrel for direct loading/unloading; thumb safety; polished or matte blue finish. Made in U.S.A. Introduced 1996.
Price: Blue **$375.00**
Price: Matte **$350.00**
Price: Stainless **$450.00**
Price: With Tritium sights **$425.00**

BERETTA MODEL U22 NEOS

Caliber: 22 LR, 10-shot magazine. **Barrel:** 4.5"; 6". **Weight:** 32 oz.; 36 oz. **Length:** 8.8"; 10.3". **Sights:** Target. **Features:** Integral rail for standard scope mounts, light, perfectly weighted, 100% American made by Beretta.
Price: **$250.00**
Price: Inox **$325.00**
Price: DLX **$350.00**
Price: Inox **$375.00**

BERETTA MODEL PX4 STORM

Caliber: 9mm, 40 S&W. **Capacity:** 17 (9mm); 14 (40 S&W). **Barrel:** 4". **Weight:** 27.5 oz. **Grips:** Black checkered w/3 interchangeable backstraps. **Sights:** 3-dot ystems coated in Superluminova; removable front and rear sights. **Features:** DA/SA, manual safety/hammer decocking lever (ambi) and automatic firing pin block safety. Picatinny rail. Comes with two magazines (17/10 in 9mm and 14/10 in 40 S&W). Removable hammer unit. American made by Beretta. Introduced 2005.
Price: **$598.00**

Beretta Model M9

Beretta Model M9A1

Bersa Thunder 380

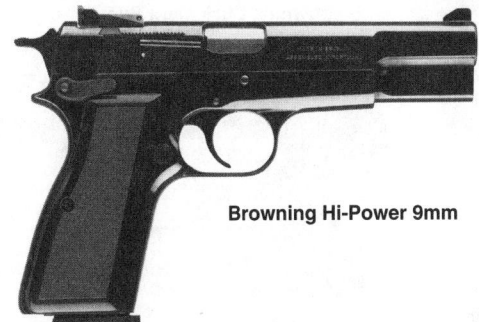

Browning Hi-Power 9mm

BERETTA MODEL M9

Caliber: 9mm. **Capacity:** 15. **Barrel:** 4.9". **Weight:** 32.2-35.3 oz. **Grips:** Plastic. **Sights:** Dot and post, low profile, windage adjustable rear. **Features:** DA/SA, forged aluminum alloy frame, delayed locking-bolt system, manual safety doubles as decocking lever, combat-style trigger guard, loaded chamber indicator. Comes with two magazines (15/10). American made by Beretta. Introduced 2005.
Price: **$650.00**

Beretta Model M9A1

Caliber: 9mm. **Capacity:** 15. **Barrel:** 4.9". **Weight:** 32.2-35.3 oz. **Grips:** Plastic. **Sights:** Dot and post, low profile, windage adjustable rear. **Features:** Same as M9, but also includes integral Mil-Std-1913 Picatinny rail, has checkered frontstrap and backstrap. Comes with two magazines (15/10). American made by Beretta. Introduced 2005.
Price: **$650.00**

BERSA THUNDER 45 ULTRA COMPACT PISTOL

Caliber: 45 ACP. **Barrel:** 3.6". **Weight:** 27 oz. **Length:** 6.7" overall. **Grips:** Anatomicaly designed polymer. **Sights:** White outline rear. **Features:** Double action; firing pin safeties, integral locking system. Available in matte, satin nickel, gold, or duo-tone. Introduced 2003. Imported from Argentina by Eagle Imports, Inc.
Price: Thunder 45, matte blue **$424.95**
Price: Thunder 45, duo-tone **$449.95**
Price: Thunder 45, Satin nickel **$466.95**

Bersa Thunder 380 Series Pistols

Caliber: 380 Auto, 7 rounds **Barrel:** 3.5". **Weight:** 23 oz. **Length:** 6.6" overall. **Features:** Otherwise similar to Thunder 45 Ultra Compact. 380 DLX has 9-round capacity. 380 Concealed Carry has 8 round capacity. Imported from Argentina by Eagle Imports, Inc.
Price: Thunder 380 Matte **$274.95**
Price: Thunder 380 Satin Nickle **$299.95**
Price: Thunder 380 Blue DLX **$308.95**
Price: Thunder 380 Matte CC (2006) **$291.95**

Bersa Thunder 9 Ultra Compact/40 Series Pistols

Caliber: 9mm, 40 S&W. **Barrel:** 3.5". **Weight:** 24.5 oz. **Length:** 6.6" overall. **Features:** Otherwise similar to Thunder 45 Ultra Compact. 9mm High Capacity model has 17-round capacity. 40 High Capacity model has 13-round capacity. Imported from Argentina by Eagle Imports, Inc.
Price: Thunder 9mm Matte **$424.95**
Price: Thunder 9mm High Capacity Satin Nickel **$466.95**
Price: Thunder 40 High Capacity Satin Nickel **$466.95**

BROWNING HI-POWER 9mm AUTOMATIC PISTOL

Caliber: 9mm Para., 13-round magazine; 40 S&W, 10-round magazine. **Barrel:** 4-5/8". **Weight:** 32 to 39 oz. **Overall length:** 7-3/4". **Metal Finishes:** Blued (Standard); black-epoxy/silver-chrome (Practical); black-epoxy (Mark III). **Grips:** Molded (Mark III); wraparound Pachmayr (Practical); or walnut grips (Standard). **Sights:** Fixed (Practical, Mark III, Standard); low-mount adjustable rear (Standard). Cable lock supplied. **Features:** External hammer with half-cock and thumb safeties. Fixed rear sight model available. Commander-style (Practical) or spur-type hammer, single action. Includes gun lock. Imported from Belgium by Browning.
Price: Practical **$846.00**
Price: Mark III **$781.00**
Price: Standard, fixed sights **$804.00**
Price: Standard, adjustable sights **$861.00**

BROWNING BUCK MARK PISTOLS

Common Features: **Caliber:** 22 LR, 10-shot magazine. **Action:** Blowback semi-auto. **Trigger:** Wide grooved style. **Sights:** Ramp front, Browning Pro-Target rear adjustable for windage and elevation. **Features:** Machined aluminum frame. Includes gun lock. Introduced 1985. Hunter, Camper Stainless, STD Stainless, 5.5 Target, 5.5 Field all introduced 2005. 18 variations, as noted below. **Grips:** Cocobolo, target-style (Hunter, 5.5 Target, 5.5 Field); polymer (Camper, Camper Stainless, Micro Nickel, Standard, STD Stainless); checkered walnut (Challenge); laminated (Plus and Plus Nickel); laminated rosewood (Bullseye Target, FLD Plus); rubber (Bullseye Standard). **Metal finishes:** Matte blue (Hunter, Camper, Challenge, Plus, Bullseye Target, Bullseye Standard, 5.5 Target, 5.5 Field, FLD Plus); matte stainless (Camper Stainless, STD Stainless, Micro Standard); nickel-plated (Micro Nickel, Plus Nickel, and Nickel). Made in U.S.A. From Browning.
Price: Hunter, 7.25" heavy barrel, 38 oz., Truglo sight **$360.00**
Price: Camper, 5.5" heavy barrel, 34 oz. **$287.00**
Price: Camper Stainless, 5.5" tapered bull barrel, 34 oz **$310.00**
Price: Camper Nickel, 5.5" tapered bull barrel, 34 oz **$320.00**
Price: Micro Nickel, 4" bull barrel, 32 oz. **$377.00**
Price: Nickel, 5.5" bull barrel, 34 oz **$377.00**
Price: Standard, 5.5" flat-side bull barrel, 34 oz. **$319.00**
Price: Standard Stainless, 5.5" flat-side bull barrel, 34 oz **$345.00**
Price: Micro Standard, 4" flat-side bull barrel, 32 oz **$319.00**
Price: Micro Standard Stainless, 4" flat-side bull barrel, 32 oz **$345.00**
Price: Plus Nickel, 5.5" flat-side bull barrel, 34 oz **$427.00**
Price: Plus, 5.5" flat-side bull barrel, 34 oz. **$390.00**
Price: Challenge, 5.5" lightweight taper barrel, 25 oz **$356.00**
Price: Bullseye Standard, 7.25" fluted bull barrel, 36 oz **$468.00**
Price: Bullseye Target, 7.25" fluted bull barrel, 36 oz.......... **$604.00**
Price: 5.5 Target, 5.5" round bull barrel, target sights, 35.5 oz **$511.00**
Price: 5.5 Field, 5.5" round bull barrel, 35 oz.................. **$511.00**
Price: FLD Plus, 5.5" flat-side bull barrel, 34 oz, Truglo sights **$390.00**

BROWNING PRO-9, PRO-40 PISTOLS

Caliber: 9mm Luger, 16-round magazine; 40 S&W, 14-round magazine. **Barrel:** 4". **Weight:** 30-33 oz. **Overall length:** 7.25". **Features:** Polymer frame, stainless-steel frames and barrels, double-action, ambidextrous decocker and safety. Fixed, 3-dot-style sights, 6" sight radius. Molded composite grips with interchangeable backstrap inserts. Cable lock supplied.
Price: **$628.00**

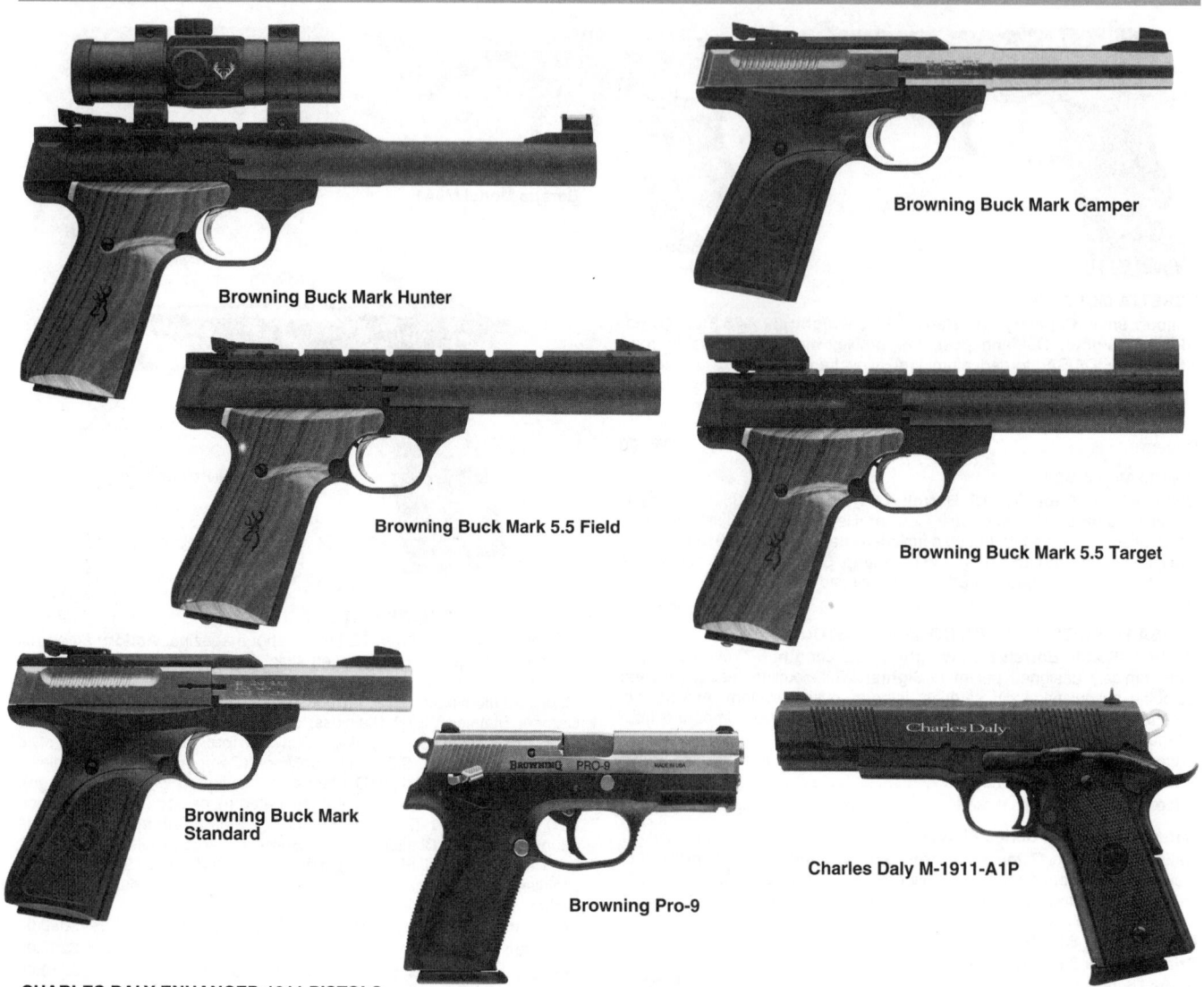

Browning Buck Mark Hunter

Browning Buck Mark Camper

Browning Buck Mark 5.5 Field

Browning Buck Mark 5.5 Target

Browning Buck Mark Standard

Browning Pro-9

Charles Daly M-1911-A1P

CHARLES DALY ENHANCED 1911 PISTOLS

Caliber: 45 ACP. **Barrel:** 5". **Weight:** 38 oz. **Length:** 8-3/4" overall. **Grips:** Checkered double diamond hardwood. **Sights:** Dovetailed front and dovetailed snag-free low profile rear sights, 3-dot system. **Features:** Extended high-rise beavertail grip safety, combat trigger, combat hammer, beveled magazine well, flared and lowered ejection port. Field Grade models are satin-finished blued steel. EMS series includes an ambidextrous safety, 4" barrel, 8-shot magazine. ECS series has a contoured left hand safety, 3.5" barrel, 6-shot magazine Two magazines, lockable carrying case. Introduced 1998. Empire series are stainless versions. Imported from the Philippines by K.B.I., Inc.

Price: EFS, blued, 39.5 oz., 5" barrel **$529.00**
Price: EMS, blued, 37 oz., 4" barrel **$529.00**
Price: ECS, blued, 34.5 oz., 3.5" barrel **$529.00**
Price: EFS Empire, stainless, 38.5 oz., 5" barrel **$629.00**
Price: EMS Empire, matte stainless, 36.5 oz., 4" barrel **$619.00**
Price: ECS Empire, matte stainless, 33.5 oz., 3.5" barrel **$619.00**

Charles Daly Enhanced Target 1911 Pistols

Caliber: 45 ACP. **Barrel:** 5". **Weight:** 38.5 oz. **Length:** 8-3/4" overall. **Features:** Similar to Daly Field and Empire models but with dovetailed front and fully adjustable rear target sights. Imported from the Philippines by K.B.I., Inc.

Price: EFS Target, stainless, 38.5 oz., 5" barrel **$724.00**
Price: EFS Custom Match Target, high-polish stainless **$799.00**

CHARLES DALY HP 9MM SINGLE-ACTION PISTOL

Caliber: 9mm, 10 round magazine. **Barrel:** 4.6". **Weight:** 34.5 oz. **Length:** 7-3/8" overall. **Grips:** Uncle Mike's padded rubber grip panels. **Sights:** XS Express Sight system set into front and rear dovetails. **Features:** John Browning design. Matte-blued steel frame and slide, thumb safety. Made in the U.S. by K.B.I., Inc.

Price: Hi-Power w/XS Sights **$549.00**

CHARLES DALY M-5 POLYMER-FRAMED HI-CAP 1911 PISTOL

Caliber: 9mm, 12-round magazine; 40 S&W 17-round magazine; 45 ACP, 13-round magazine. **Barrel:** 5". **Weight:** 33.5 oz. **Length:** 8.5" overall. **Grips:** Checkered polymer. **Sights:** Blade front, adjustable low-profile rear. **Features:** Stainless steel beaver-tail grip safety, rounded trigger-guard, tapered bull barrel, full-length guide rod, matte blue finish on frame and slide. 40 S&W models in M-5 Govt. 1911, M-5 Commander, and M-5 IPSC introduced 2006; M-5 Ultra X Compact in 9mm and 45 ACP introduced 2006; M-5 IPSC .45 ACP introduced 2006. Made in Israel by BUL, imported by K.B.I., Inc.

Price: M-5 Govt. 1911, 40 S&W/45 ACP, matte blue **$719.00**
Price: M-5 Commander, 40 S&W/45 ACP, matte blue **$719.00**
Price: M-5 Ultra X Compact, 9mm, 3.1" barrel, 7" OAL, 28 oz. **$719.00**
Price: M-5 Ultra X Compact, 45 ACP, 3.1" barrel, 7" OAL, 28 oz. . . . **$719.00**
Price: M-5 IPSC, 40 S&W/45 ACP, 5" barrel, 8.5" OAL, 33.5 oz. . **$1,499.00**

Cobra FS380

Cobra CA32

Colt Model 1991 Model O

Colt XSE
Lightweight
Commander

Colt XSE Government

Colt 38 Super

Colt Defender

COBRA ENTERPRISES FS380 AUTO PISTOL
Caliber: 380 ACP, 7-shot magazine. **Barrel:** 3.5". **Weight:** 2.1 lbs. **Length:** 6-3/8" overall. **Grips:** Black composition. **Sights:** Fixed. **Features:** Choice of bright chrome, satin nickel or black finish. Introduced 2002. Made in U.S.A. by Cobra Enterprises, Inc.
Price: $130.00

COBRA ENTERPRISES FS32 AUTO PISTOL
Caliber: 32 ACP, 8-shot magazine. **Barrel:** 3.5". **Weight:** 2.1 lbs. **Length:** 6-3/8" overall. **Grips:** Black composition. **Sights:** Fixed. **Features:** Choice of black, satin nickel or bright chrome finish. Introduced 2002. Made in U.S.A. by Cobra Enterprises, Inc.
Price: $130.00

COBRA INDUSTRIES PATRIOT PISTOL
Caliber: 380 ACP, 9mm Luger, 10-shot magazine. **Barrel:** 3.3". **Weight:** 20 oz. **Length:** 6" overall. **Grips:** Checkered polymer. **Sights:** Fixed. **Features:** Stainless steel slide with load indicator; double-action-only trigger system. Introduced 2002. Made in U.S.A. by Cobra Enterprises, Inc.
Price: $279.00

COBRA INDUSTRIES CA32, CA380
Caliber: 32 ACP, 380 ACP. **Barrel:** 2.8" **Weight:** 22 oz. **Length:** 5.4". **Grips:** Laminated wood (CA32); Black molded synthetic (CA380). **Sights:** Fixed. **Features:** True pocket pistol size. Made in U.S.A. by Cobra Enterprises, Inc.
Price: $110.00

COLT MODEL 1991 MODEL O AUTO PISTOL
Caliber: 45 ACP, 7-shot magazine. **Barrel:** 5". **Weight:** 38 oz. **Length:** 8.5" overall. **Grips:** Checkered black composition. **Sights:** Ramped blade front, fixed square notch rear, high profile. **Features:** Matte finish. Continuation of serial number range used on original G.I. 1911A1 guns. Comes with one magazine and molded carrying case. Introduced 1991.
Price: Blue $764.00
Price: Stainless $814.00

COLT XSE SERIES MODEL O AUTO PISTOLS
Caliber: 45 ACP, 8-shot magazine. **Barrel:** 4.25", 5". **Grips:** Checkered, double diamond rosewood. **Sights:** Drift-adjustable 3-dot combat. **Features:** Brushed stainless finish; adjustable, two-cut aluminum trigger; extended ambidextrous thumb safety; upswept beavertail with palm swell; elongated slot hammer. Introduced 1999. From Colt's Mfg. Co., Inc.
Price: XSE Government (5" bbl.) $917.00
Price: XSE Government (4.25" bbl.) $917.00

COLT XSE LIGHTWEIGHT COMMANDER AUTO PISTOL
Caliber: 45 ACP, 8-shot. **Barrel:** 4-1/4". **Weight:** 26 oz. **Length:** 7-3/4" overall. **Grips:** Double diamond checkered rosewood. **Sights:** Fixed, glare-proofed blade front, square notch rear; 3-dot system. **Features:** Brushed stainless slide, nickeled aluminum frame; McCormick elongated slot enhanced hammer, McCormick two-cut adjustable aluminum hammer. Made in U.S.A. by Colt's Mfg. Co., Inc.
Price: Stainless $917.00

COLT DEFENDER
Caliber: 45 ACP, 7-shot magazine. **Barrel:** 3". **Weight:** 22-1/2 oz. **Length:** 6-3/4" overall. **Grips:** Pebble-finish rubber wraparound with finger grooves. **Sights:** White dot front, snag-free Colt competition rear. **Features:** Stainless finish; aluminum frame; combat-style hammer; Hi Ride grip safety, extended manual safety, disconnect safety. Introduced 1998. Made in U.S.A. by Colt's Mfg. Co., Inc.
Price: $860.00

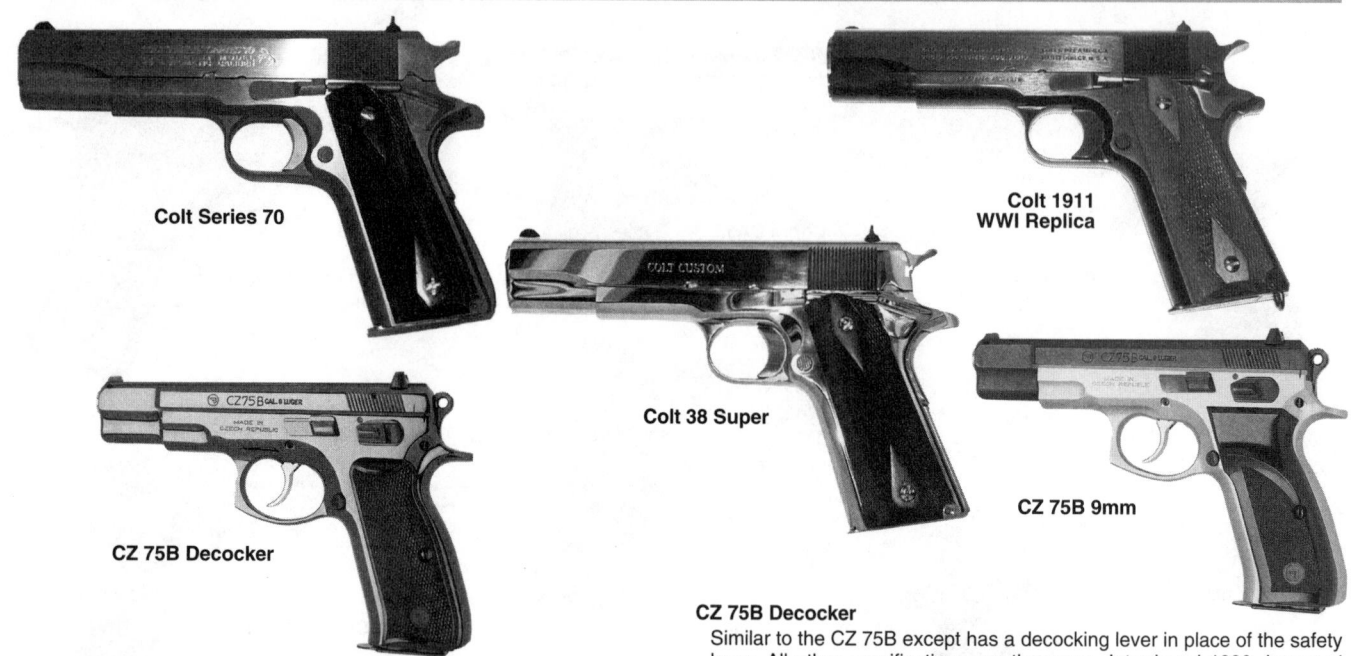

Colt Series 70

Colt 1911 WWI Replica

Colt 38 Super

CZ 75B Decocker

CZ 75B 9mm

COLT SERIES 70

Caliber: 45 ACP. **Barrel:** 5". **Weight:** NA. **Length:** NA. **Grips:** Rosewood with double diamond checkering pattern. **Sights:** Fixed. **Features:** Custom replica of the Original Series 70 pistol with a Series 70 firing system, original rollmarks. Introduced 2002. Made in U.S.A. by Colt's Mfg. Co., Inc.

Price: Blued **$919.00**
Price: Stainless **$950.00**

COLT 38 SUPER

Caliber: 38 Super. **Barrel:** 5" **Weight:** NA. **Length:** 8-1/2" **Grips:** Checkered rubber (stainless and blue models); wood with double diamond checkering pattern (bright stainless model). **Sights:** 3-dot. **Features:** Beveled magazine well, standard thumb safety and service-style grip safety. Introduced 2003. Made in U.S.A. by Colt's Mfg. Co., Inc.

Price: Blued **$837.00**
Price: Stainless **$866.00**
Price: Bright Stainless **$1,058.00**

COLT 1911 WWI REPLICA

Caliber: 45 ACP, 2 7-round magazines. **Barrel:** 5" **Weight:** 38 oz. **Length:** 8.5". **Grips:** Checkered walnut with double diamond checkering pattern. **Sights:** Tapered blade front sight, U-shaped rear notch. **Features:** Reproduction based on original 1911 blueprints. Original rollmarks and inspector marks. Smooth mainspring housing with lanyard loop, WWI-style manual thumb and grip safety, Carbonia blued finish. Introduced 2005. Made in U.S.A. by Colt's Mfg. Co., Inc.

Price: Blued **$990.00**

CZ 75B AUTO PISTOL

Caliber: 9mm Para., 40 S&W, 10-shot magazine. **Barrel:** 4.7". **Weight:** 34.3 oz. **Length:** 8.1" overall. **Grips:** High impact checkered plastic. **Sights:** Square post front, rear adjustable for windage; 3-dot system. **Features:** Single action/double action design; firing pin block safety; choice of black polymer, matte or high-polish blue finishes. All-steel frame. B-SA is a single action with a drop-free magazine. Imported from the Czech Republic by CZ-USA.

Price: 75B, black polymer, 16-shot magazine. **$509.00**
Price: 75B, glossy blue, dual-tone or satin nickel **$525.00**
Price: 40 S&W, black polymer, 12-shot magazine, ... **$525.00**
Price: 75B SA, 9mm/40 S&W, single action . . . . **$518.00/$535.00**
Price: 75 Stainless 9mm (2006), 16-shot magazine. **$565.00**

CZ 75B Decocker

Similar to the CZ 75B except has a decocking lever in place of the safety lever. All other specifications are the same. Introduced 1999. Imported from the Czech Republic by CZ-USA.

Price: 9mm, black polymer **$518.00**

CZ 75B Compact Auto Pistol

Similar to the CZ 75 except has 14-shot magazine in 9mm, 3.9" barrel and weighs 32 oz. Has removable front sight, non-glare ribbed slide top. Trigger guard is squared and serrated; combat hammer. Introduced 1993. Imported from the Czech Republic by CZ-USA.

Price: 9mm, black polymer **$539.00**
Price: 9mm, dual tone or satin nickel **$554.00**
Price: 9mm D PCR Compact, alloy frame **$554.00**
Price: 40 S&W, black polymer, 10+1, 37.8 oz. (2006) **$594.00**

CZ 75 Champion Pistol

Similar to the CZ 75B except has a longer frame and slide, rubber grip to accommodate new heavy-duty magazine. Ambidextrous thumb safety, extended magazine release; three-port compensator. Blued slide and stain nickel frame finish. Introduced 2005. Imported from the Czech Republic by CZ USA.

Price: 9mm, 16-shot mag. **$1,646.00**

CZ 75 Tactical Sport

Similar to the CZ 75B except the CZ 75 TS is a competition ready pistol designed for IPSC standard division (USPSA limited division). Fixed target sights, tuned single-action operation, lightweight polymer match trigger with adjustments for take-up and overtravel, competition hammer, extended magazine catch, ambidextrous manual safety, checkered walnut grips, polymer magazine well, two tone finish. Introduced 2005. Imported from the Czech Republic by CZ USA.

Price: 9mm, 20-shot mag. **$1,152.00**
Price: 40 S&W, 16-shot mag. **$1,152.00**

CZ 75 SP-01 Pistol

Similar to NATO-approved CZ 75 Compact P-01 model. Features an integral 1913 accessory rail on the dust cover, rubber grip panels, black polycoat finish, extended beavertail, new grip geometry with checkering on front and back straps, and double or single action operation. Introduced 2005. The Shadow variant designed as an IPSC "production" division competition firearm. Includes competition hammer, competition rear sight and fiber-optic front sight, modified slide release, lighter recoil and main spring for use with "minor power factor" competition ammunition. Includes polycoat finish and slim walnut grips. Finished by CZ Custom Shop. Imported from the Czech Republic by CZ-USA.

Price: SP-01 9mm, black polymer, 19+1 . . . . **$595.00**
Price: SP-01 Shadow **$615.00**

CZ 85

CZ 97B

CZ 75/85 Kadet

CZ 100

CZ 85B/85 Combat Auto Pistol

Same gun as the CZ 75 except has ambidextrous slide release and safety levers; non-glare, ribbed slide top; squared, serrated trigger guard; trigger stop to prevent overtravel. Introduced 1986. The CZ 85 Combat features a fully adjustable rear sight, extended magazine release, ambidextrous slide stop and safety catch, drop free magazine and overtravel adjustment. Imported from the Czech Republic by CZ-USA.
Price: 9mm, Black polymer **$536.00**
Price: Combat, black polymer **$599.00**
Price: Combat, dual-tone, glossy blue, satin nickel **$623.00**

CZ 83B DOUBLE-ACTION PISTOL

Caliber: 32 ACP, 380 ACP, 12-shot magazine. **Barrel:** 3.8". **Weight:** 26.2 oz. **Length:** 6.8" overall. **Grips:** High impact checkered plastic. **Sights:** Removable square post front, rear adjustable for windage; 3-dot system. **Features:** Single action/double action; ambidextrous magazine release and safety. Blue finish; non-glare ribbed slide top. Imported from the Czech Republic by CZ-USA.
Price: Glossy blue, 32 ACP or 380 ACP **$420.00**
Price: Satin Nickel **$420.00**

CZ 97B AUTO PISTOL

Caliber: 45 ACP, 10-shot magazine. **Barrel:** 4.85". **Weight:** 40 oz. **Length:** 8.34" overall. **Grips:** Checkered walnut. **Sights:** Fixed. **Features:** Single action/double action; full-length slide rails; screw-in barrel bushing; linkless barrel; all-steel construction; chamber loaded indicator; dual transfer bars. Introduced 1999. Imported from the Czech Republic by CZ-USA.
Price: Black polymer **$663.00**
Price: Glossy blue **$680.00**

CZ 75 KADET AUTO PISTOL

Caliber: 22 LR, 10-shot magazine. **Barrel:** 4.88". **Weight:** 36 oz. **Grips:** High impact checkered plastic. **Sights:** Blade front, fully adjustable rear. **Features:** Single action/double action mechanism; all-steel construction. Introduced 1999. Kadet conversion kit consists of barrel, slide, adjustable sights, and magazine to convert the centerfire 75 to rimfire. Imported from the Czech Republic by CZ-USA.
Price: Black polymer **$510.00**
Price: Kadet conversion kit **$299.00**

CZ 100 B AUTO PISTOL

Caliber: 9mm Para., 40 S&W. **Barrel:** 3.7". **Weight:** 24 oz. **Length:** 6.9" overall. **Grips:** Grooved polymer. **Sights:** Blade front with dot, white outline rear drift adjustable for windage. **Features:** Double action only with firing pin block; polymer frame, steel slide; has laser sight mount. Introduced 1996. Imported from the Czech Republic by CZ-USA.
Price: 9mm Para, 12-shot magazine **$449.00**
Price: 40 S&W, 10-shot magazine **$449.00**

CZ 2075 RAMI AUTO PISTOL

Caliber: 9mm Para., 40 S&W. **Barrel:** 3". **Weight:** 25 oz. **Length:** 6.5" overall. **Grips:** Rubber. **Sights:** Blade front with dot, white outline rear drift adjustable for windage. **Features:** Single-action/double-action; alloy or polymer frame, steel slide; has laser sight mount. Imported from the Czech Republic by CZ-USA.
Price: 9mm Para, alloy frame, 10 and 14-shot magazines **$576.00**
Price: 40 S&W, alloy frame, 8-shot magazine **$576.00**
Price: 9mm Para, polymer frame, 10 and 14-shot magazines **$510.00**
Price: 40 S&W, alloy frame, 8-shot magazine **$510.00**

CZ P-01 AUTO PISTOL

Caliber: 9mm Para. **Barrel:** 3.85". **Weight:** 27 oz. **Length:** 7.2" overall. **Grips:** Checkered rubber. **Sights:** Blade front with dot, white outline rear drift adjustable for windage. **Features:** Based on the CZ 75, except with forged aircraft-grade aluminum alloy frame. Hammer forged barrel, decocker, firing-pin block, M3 rail, dual slide serrations, squared triggerguard, re-contoured trigger, lanyard loop on butt. Serrated front- and back-strap. Introduced 2006. Imported from the Czech Republic by CZ-USA.
Price: 9mm Para, 14-shot magazines **$586.00**

DAN WESSON FIREARMS POINTMAN SEVEN AUTO PISTOL

Caliber: 10mm, 45 ACP. **Barrel:** 5". **Grips:** Diamond checkered cocobolo. **Sights:** Bo-Mar style adjustable target sight. **Weight:** 38 oz. **Features:** Stainless-steel frame and serrated slide. Series 70-style 1911, stainless-steel frame, forged stainless-steel slide. One-piece match-grade barrel and bushing. 20-LPI checkered mainspring housing, front and rear slide cocking serrations, beveled magwell, dehorned by hand. Lowered and flared ejection port, Ed Brown slide stop and memory groove grip safety, tactical extended thumb safety. Commander-style match hammer, match grade sear, aluminum trigger with stainless bow, Wolff springs. Introduced 2000. Made in U.S.A. by Dan Wesson Firearms, distributed by CZ-USA.
Price: 45 ACP, 7+1 . . . . **$1,079.00**
Price: 10mm, 8+1 . . . . **$1,079.00**

Dan Wesson Commander Classic Bobtail Auto Pistols

Similar to Pointman Seven, a Commander-sized frame with 4.25" barrel. Available with stainless finish, fixed night sights. Introduced 2005. Made in U.S.A. by Dan Wesson Firearms, distributed by CZ-USA.
Price: 45 ACP, 7+1, 34 oz. **$1,169.00**
Price: 10mm, 8+1, 34 oz. **$1,179.00**

DAN WESSON DW RZ-10 AUTO PISTOL

Caliber: 10mm. **Barrel:** 5". **Grips:** Diamond checkered cocobolo. **Sights:** Bo-Mar style adjustable target sight. **Weight:** 38.3 oz. **Features:** Stainless-steel frame and serrated slide. Series 70-style 1911, stainless-steel frame, forged stainless-steel slide. Commander-style match hammer. Reintroduced 2005. Made in U.S.A. by Dan Wesson Firearms, distributed by CZ-USA.
Price: 10mm, 8+1 . . . . **$1,089.00**

Desert Eagle Mark XIX

Desert Baby Eagle

EAA Witness

Ed Brown
Commander Bobtail

Ed Brown Classic Custom

Ed Brown Kobra
Executive Carry

DESERT EAGLE MARK XIX PISTOL

Caliber: 357 Mag., 9-shot; 44 Mag., 8-shot; 50 AE, 7-shot. **Barrel:** 6", 10", interchangeable. **Weight:** 357 Mag.-62 oz.; 44 Mag.-69 oz.; 50 AE-72 oz. **Length:** 10-1/4" overall (6" bbl.). **Grips:** Polymer; rubber available. **Sights:** Blade on ramp front, combat-style rear. Adjustable available. **Features:** Interchangeable barrels; rotating three-lug bolt; ambidextrous safety; adjustable trigger. Military epoxy finish. Satin, bright nickel, chrome, brushed, matte or black finishes available. 10" barrel extra. Imported from Israel by Magnum Research, Inc.

Price: 357, 6" bbl., standard pistol **$1,299.00**
Price: 44 Mag., 6", standard pistol **$1,299.00**
Price: 50 Magnum, 6" bbl., standard pistol **$1,299.00**

DESERT BABY EAGLE PISTOLS

Caliber: 9mm Para., 40 S&W, 45 ACP, 10-round magazine. **Barrel:** 3.5", 3.7", 4.72". **Weight:** 26.8-39.8 oz. **Length:** 7.25" to 8.25" overall. **Grips:** Polymer. **Sights:** Drift-adjustable rear, blade front. **Features:** Steel frame and slide; slide safety; decocker. Reintroduced in 1999. Imported from Israel by Magnum Research, Inc.

Price: Standard (9mm or 40 cal.; 4.72" barrel, 8.25" overall) **$549.00**
Price: Semi-Compact (9mm, 40 or 45 cal.; 3.7" barrel, 7.75" overall) **$549.00**
Price: Compact (9mm or 40 cal.; 3.5" barrel, 7.25" overall) **$549.00**
Price: Polymer (9mm or 40 cal; polymer frame; 3.25" barrel, 7.25" overall) . **$549.00**

EAA WITNESS FULL SIZE AUTO PISTOL

Caliber: 9mm Para., 38 Super, 18-shot magazine; 40 S&W, 10mm, 15-shot magazine; 45 ACP, 10-shot magazine. **Barrel:** 4.50". **Weight:** 35.33 oz. **Length:** 8.10" overall. **Grips:** Checkered rubber. **Sights:** Undercut blade front, open rear adjustable for windage. **Features:** Double-action/single-action trigger system; round trigger guard; frame-mounted safety. Introduced 1991. Polymer frame introduced 2005. Imported from Italy by European American Armory.

Price: 9mm, 38 Super, 10mm, 40 S&W, 45 ACP, full-size steel frame, Wonder finish **$459.00**
Price: 45/22 22 LR, full-size steel frame, blued **$429.00**
Price: 9mm, 40 S&W, 45 ACP, full-size polymer frame **$429.00**

EAA WITNESS COMPACT AUTO PISTOL

Caliber: 9mm Para., 40 S&W, 10mm, 12-shot magazine; 45 ACP, 8-shot magazine. **Barrel:** 3.6". **Weight:** 30 oz. **Length:** 7.3" overall. Otherwise similar to Full Size Witness. Polymer frame introducted 2005. Imported from Italy by European American Armory.

Price: 9mm, 10mm, 40 S&W, 45 ACP, steel frame, Wonder finish . **$459.00**
Price: 9mm, 40 S&W, 45 ACP, polymer frame **$429.00**

EAA WITNESS-P CARRY AUTO PISTOL

Caliber: 10mm, 15-shot magazine; 45 ACP, 10-shot magazine. **Barrel:** 3.6". **Weight:** 27 oz. **Length:** 7.5" overall. Otherwise similar to Full Size Witness. Polymer frame introduced 2005. Imported from Italy by European American Armory.

Price: 10mm, 45 ACP, polymer frame . . . . from **$469.00**

ED BROWN CLASSIC CUSTOM

Caliber: 45 ACP, 7 shot. **Barrel:** 5". **Weight:** 39 oz. **Stocks:** Cocobolo wood. **Sights:** Bo-Mar adjustable rear, dovetail front. **Features:** Single-action, M1911 style, custom made to order, stainless frame and slide available.

Price: Model CC-BB, blued. **$2,895.00**
Price: Model CC-SB, blued and stainless **$2,995.00**
Price: Model CC-SS, stainless **$3,095.00**

ED BROWN KOBRA CARRY BOBTAIL

Caliber: 45 ACP, 400 Cor-Bon, 40 S&W, 357 SIG, 38 Super, 9mm Luger, 7-shot magazine. **Barrel:** 4.25". **Weight:** 34 oz. **Grips:** Hogue exotic wood. **Sights:** Customer preference front; fixed Novak low mount rear. Optional night inserts available. **Features:** Checkered forestrap and bobtailed mainspring housing.

Price: Executive Carry . . . . **$2,195.00 to $2,370.00**

ED BROWN KOBRA AND KOBRA CARRY

Caliber: 45 ACP, 7-shot magazine. **Barrel:** 5" (Kobra); 4.25" (Kobra Carry). **Weight:** 39 oz. (Kobra); 34 oz. (Kobra Carry). **Grips:** Hogue exotic wood. **Sights:** Ramp, front; fixed Novak low-mount night sights, rear. **Features:** Has snakeskin pattern serrations on forestrap and mainspring housing, dehorned edges, beavertail grip safety.

Price: Kobra K-BB, blued **$1,995.00**
Price: Kobra K-SB, stainless and blued **$2,095.00**
Price: Kobra K-SS, stainless **$2,195.00**
Price: Kobra Carry KC-BB, blued **$2,095.00**

Ed Brown Kobra Carry

Ed Brown Kobra Carry K-SB

Ed Brown Executive Elite

Ed Brown Special Forces

Entréprise Boxer P500

Entréprise Tactical 500

Entréprise Elite P500

Excel Arms Accelerator MP-22

Ed Brown Executive Pistols
Similar to other Ed Brown products, but with 25-lpi checkered frame and mainspring housing.
Price: Elite blued, blued/stainless, or stainless, from **$2,195.00**
Price: Carry blued, blued/stainless, or stainless, from **$2,295.00**
Price: Target blued, blued/stainless, or stainless, intr. 2006, from **$2,470.00**

Ed Brown Special Forces Pistol
Similar to other Ed Brown products, but with ChainLink treatment on forestrap and mainspring housing. Slide coated with Gen III finish. "Square cut" serrations on rear of slide only. Dehorned. Introduced 2006.
Price: SF-BB blued **$1,995.00**

ENTRÉPRISE ELITE P500 AUTO PISTOL
Caliber: 45 ACP, 10-shot magazine. **Barrel:** 3.25", 4.25", 5". **Weight:** 36-40 oz. **Length:** 7.25-8.5" overall. **Grips:** Black ultra-slim, double diamond, checkered synthetic. **Sights:** Dovetailed blade front, rear adjustable for windage; 3-dot system. **Features:** Reinforced dust cover; lowered and flared ejection port; squared trigger guard; adjustable match trigger; bolstered front strap; high grip cut; high ride beavertail grip safety; steel flat mainspring housing; extended thumb lock; skeletonized hammer; match grade sear, disconnector; Wolff springs. Introduced 1998. Made in U.S.A. by Entréprise Arms.
Price: P500, P425, P325 models **$699.90**

Entréprise Medalist P500 Auto Pistol
Similar to the Elite model except has adjustable rear sight with dovetailed Patridge front; machined slide parallel rails; front and rear slide serrations; lowered and flared ejection port; full-length one-piece guide rod with plug; National Match barrel and bushing; stainless firing pin; tuned match extractor; oversize firing pin stop; slide lapped to frame. Introduced 1998. Made in U.S.A. by Entréprise Arms.
Price: 45 ACP **$979.00**
Price: 40 S&W **$1,099.00**

Entréprise Boxer P500 Auto Pistol
Similar to the Medalist model except has adjustable Competizione "melted" rear sight with dovetailed Patridge front; high mass chiseled slide with sweep cut; machined slide parallel rails; polished breech face and barrel channel. Introduced 1998. Made in U.S.A. by Entréprise Arms.
Price: 45 ACP **$1,399.00**
Price: 40 S&W intr. 2005 . . . . **$1,499.00**

Entréprise Tactical P500 Auto Pistol
Similar to the Elite model except has Tactical2 Ghost Ring sight or Novak low-mount sight; ambidextrous thumb safety; front and rear slide serrations; full-length guide rod; throated barrel; tuned match extractor; fitted barrel and bushing; stainless firing pin; slide lapped to frame. Introduced 1998. Made in U.S.A. by Entréprise Arms.
Price: **$979.90**

EXCEL ARMS ACCELERATOR MP-17/MP-22 PISTOLS
Caliber: 17HMR, 22WMR, 9-shot magazine. **Barrel:** 8.5" bull barrel. **Weight:** 54 oz. **Length:** 12.875" overall. **Grips:** Textured black composition. **Sights:** Fully adjustable target sights. **Features:** Made from 17-4 stainless steel, comes with aluminum rib, integral Weaver base, internal hammer, firing-pin block. American made, lifetime warranty. Comes with two 9-round stainless steel magazines and a California-approved cable lock. 22 WMR Introduced 2006. Made in U.S.A. by Excel Arms.
Price: **$412.00**
Price: SP-17 17 Mach 2 . . . . **$412.00**
Price: SP-22 22LR **$412.00**

Firestorm Mini

Firestorm 45 Gov't

Glock 17C

Glock 26

Glock 22

FIRESTORM AUTO PISTOLS

Caliber: 22LR, 32 ACP, 10-shot magazine; 380 ACP, 7-shot magazine; 9mm, 40 S&W, 10-shot magazine; 45 ACP, 7-shot magazine. **Barrel:** 3.5". **Weight:** from 23 oz. **Length:** from 6.6" overall. **Grips:** Rubber. **Sights:** 3-dot. **Features:** Double action. Distributed by SGS Importers International.

Price: 22LR, matte or duotone, from **$241.95**
Price: 380, matte or duotone, from **$241.95**
Price: Mini Firestorm 32 ACP, intr. 2006 . . . . **$358.95**
Price: Mini Firestorm 9mm, matte, duotone, nickel, from **$358.95**
Price: Mini Firestorm 40 S&W, matte, duotone, nickel, from **$358.95**
Price: Mini Firestorm 45 ACP, matte, duotone, chrome, from **$308.95**

GLOCK 17/17C AUTO PISTOL

Caliber: 9mm Para., 17/19/33-shot magazines. **Barrel:** 4.49". **Weight:** 22.04 oz. (without magazine). **Length:** 7.32" overall. **Grips:** Black polymer. **Sights:** Dot on front blade, white outline rear adjustable for windage. **Features:** Polymer frame, steel slide; double-action trigger with "Safe Action" system; mechanical firing pin safety, drop safety; simple takedown without tools; locked breech, recoil operated action. ILS designation refers to Internal Locking System. Adopted by Austrian armed forces 1983. NATO approved 1984. Imported from Austria by Glock, Inc.

Price: Fixed sight **$599.00**
Price: Fixed sight w/ILS. **$624.00**
Price: Adjustable sight **$617.00**
Price: Adjustable sight w/ILS. **$642.00**
Price: Night sight **$646.00**
Price: Night sight w/ILS. **$671.00**
Price: 17C Compensated (fixed sight) **$621.00**
Price: 17C Compensated (fixed sight) w/ILS **$646.00**

GLOCK 19/19C AUTO PISTOL

Caliber: 9mm Para., 15/17/19/33-shot magazines. **Barrel:** 4.02". **Weight:** 20.99 oz. (without magazine). **Length:** 6.85" overall. Compact version of Glock 17. Pricing the same as Model 17. Imported from Austria by Glock, Inc.

Price: Fixed sight **$599.00**
Price: 19C Compensated (fixed sight) **$621.00**

GLOCK 26 AUTO PISTOL

Caliber: 9mm Para. 10/12/15/17/19/33-shot magazines. **Barrel:** 3.46". **Weight:** 19.75 oz. **Length:** 6.29" overall. Subcompact version of Glock 17. Pricing the same as Model 17. Imported from Austria by Glock, Inc.
Price: Fixed sight **$599.00**

GLOCK 34 AUTO PISTOL

Caliber: 9mm Para. 17/19/33-shot magazines. **Barrel:** 5.32". **Weight:** 22.9 oz. **Length:** 8.15" overall. Competition version of Glock 17 with

extended barrel, slide, and sight radius dimensions. Imported from Austria by Glock, Inc.
Price: Adjustable sight **$679.00**
Price: Adjustable sight w/ILS **$704.00**

GLOCK 22/22C AUTO PISTOL

Caliber: 40 S&W, 15/17-shot magazines. **Barrel:** 4.49". **Weight:** 22.92 oz. (without magazine). **Length:** 7.32" overall. **Features:** Otherwise similar to Model 17, including pricing. Imported from Austria by Glock, Inc. Introduced 1990.

Price: Fixed sight **$599.00**
Price: Fixed sight w/ILS **$624.00**
Price: Adjustable sight **$617.00**
Price: Adjustable sight w/ILS **$642.00**
Price: Night sight **$646.00**
Price: Night sight w/ILS **$671.00**
Price: 22C Compensated (fixed sight) **$621.00**
Price: 22C Compensated (fixed sight) w/ILS **$646.00**

GLOCK 23/23C AUTO PISTOL

Caliber: 40 S&W, 13/15/17-shot magazines. **Barrel:** 4.02". **Weight:** 21.16 oz. (without magazine). **Length:** 6.85" overall. **Features:** Otherwise similar to Model 22, including pricing. Compact version of Glock 22. Imported from Austria by Glock, Inc. Introduced 1990.
Price: Fixed sight **$599.00**
Price: 23C Compensated (fixed sight) **$621.00**

GLOCK 27 AUTO PISTOL

Caliber: 40 S&W, 9/11/13/15/17-shot magazines. **Barrel:** 3.46". **Weight:** 19.75 oz. (without magazine). **Length:** 6.29" overall. **Features:** Otherwise similar to Model 22, including pricing. Subcompact version of Glock 22. Imported from Austria by Glock, Inc. Introduced 1996.
Price: Fixed sight **$599.00**

GLOCK 35 AUTO PISTOL

Caliber: 40 S&W, 15/17-shot magazines. **Barrel:** 5.32". **Weight:** 24.52 oz. (without magazine). **Length:** 8.15" overall. **Features:** Otherwise similar to Model 22. Competition version of Glock 22 with extended barrel, slide, and sight radius dimensions. Imported from Austria by Glock, Inc. Introduced 1996.
Price: Fixed sight **$679.00**
Price: Adjustable sight w/ILS **$704.00**

Glock 35

Glock 30

Glock 31

GLOCK 20/20C 10MM AUTO PISTOL

Caliber: 10mm, 15-shot magazines. **Barrel:** 4.6". **Weight:** 27.68 oz. (without magazine). **Length:** 7.59" overall. **Features:** Otherwise similar to Model 17. Imported from Austria by Glock, Inc. Introduced 1990.
Price: Fixed sight **$637.00**
Price: Fixed sight w/ILS. **$662.00**
Price: Adjustable sight **$655.00**
Price: Adjustable sight w/ILS. **$680.00**
Price: Night sight **$684.00**
Price: Night sight w/ILS. **$709.00**
Price: 20C Compensated (fixed sight) **$676.00**
Price: 20C Compensated (fixed sight) w/ILS **$701.00**

GLOCK 29 AUTO PISTOL

Caliber: 10mm, 10/15-shot magazines. **Barrel:** 3.78". **Weight:** 24.69 oz. (without magazine). **Length:** 6.77" overall. **Features:** Otherwise similar to Model 20, including pricing. Subcompact version of Glock 20. Imported from Austria by Glock, Inc. Introduced 1997.
Price: Fixed sight **$637.00**

GLOCK 21/21C AUTO PISTOL

Caliber: 45 ACP, 13-shot magazines. **Barrel:** 4.6". **Weight:** 26.28 oz. (without magazine). **Length:** 7.59" overall. **Features:** Otherwise similar to Model 17. Imported from Austria by Glock, Inc. Introduced 1991.
Price: Fixed sight **$637.00**
Price: Fixed sight w/ILS. **$662.00**
Price: Adjustable sight **$655.00**
Price: Adjustable sight w/ILS. **$680.00**
Price: Night sight **$684.00**
Price: Night sight w/ILS. **$709.00**
Price: 21C Compensated (fixed sight) **$676.00**
Price: 21C Compensated (fixed sight) w/ILS **$701.00**

GLOCK 30 AUTO PISTOL

Caliber: 45 ACP, 9/10/13-shot magazines. **Barrel:** 3.78". **Weight:** 23.99 oz. (without magazine). **Length:** 6.77" overall. **Features:** Otherwise similar to Model 21, including pricing. Subcompact version of Glock 21. Imported from Austria by Glock, Inc. Introduced 1997.
Price: Fixed sight **$637.00**

GLOCK 36 AUTO PISTOL

Caliber: 45 ACP, 6-shot magazines. **Barrel:** 3.78". **Weight:** 20.11 oz. (without magazine). **Length:** 6.77" overall. **Features:** Single-stack magazine, slimmer grip than Glock 21/30. Subcompact. Imported from Austria by Glock, Inc. Introduced 1997.
Price: Fixed sight **$637.00**

GLOCK 37 AUTO PISTOL

Caliber: 45 GAP, 10-shot magazines. **Barrel:** 4.49". **Weight:** 25.95 oz. (without magazine). **Length:** 7.32" overall. **Features:** Otherwise similar to Model 17. Imported from Austria by Glock, Inc. Introduced 2005.
Price: Fixed sight **$614.00**
Price: Fixed sight w/ILS. **$639.00**
Price: Adjustable sight **$632.00**
Price: Adjustable sight w/ILS. **$657.00**
Price: Night sight **$661.00**
Price: Night sight w/ILS. **$686.00**

GLOCK 38 AUTO PISTOL

Caliber: 45 GAP, 8/10-shot magazines. **Barrel:** 4.02". **Weight:** 24.16 oz. (without magazine). **Length:** 6.85" overall. **Features:** Otherwise similar to Model 37. Compact. Imported from Austria by Glock, Inc.
Price: Fixed sight **$614.00**

GLOCK 39 AUTO PISTOL

Caliber: 45 GAP, 6/8/10-shot magazines. **Barrel:** 3.46". **Weight:** 19.33 oz. (without magazine). **Length:** 6.3" overall. **Features:** Otherwise similar to Model 37. Subcompact. Imported from Austria by Glock, Inc.
Price: Fixed sight **$614.00**

GLOCK 25 AUTO PISTOL

Caliber: 380 ACP, 15/17/19-shot magazines. **Barrel:** 4.02". **Weight:** 20.11 oz. (without magazine). **Length:** 6.85" overall. **Features:** Otherwise similar to Model 17. Compact. Made in Austria by Glock, Inc. Not imported to U.S.
Price: . . . . **NA**

GLOCK 28 AUTO PISTOL

Caliber: 380 ACP, 10/12/15/17/19-shot magazines. **Barrel:** 3.46". **Weight:** 18.66 oz. (without magazine). **Length:** 6.29" overall. **Features:** Otherwise similar to Model 25. Subcompact. Made in Austria by Glock, Inc. Not imported to U.S.
Price: . . . . **NA**

GLOCK 31/31C AUTO PISTOL

Caliber: 357 Auto, 15/17-shot magazines. **Barrel:** 4.49". **Weight:** 23.28 oz. (without magazine). **Length:** 7.32" overall. **Features:** Otherwise similar to Model 17. Imported from Austria by Glock, Inc.
Price: Fixed sight **$599.00**
Price: Fixed sight w/ILS **$624.00**
Price: Adjustable sight **$617.00**
Price: Adjustable sight w/ILS **$642.00**
Price: Night sight **$646.00**
Price: Night sight w/ILS **$671.00**
Price: 31C Compensated (fixed sight) **$621.00**
Price: 31C Compensated (fixed sight) w/ILS **$646.00**

GLOCK 32/32C AUTO PISTOL

Caliber: 357 Auto, 13/15/17-shot magazines. **Barrel:** 4.02". **Weight:** 21.52 oz. (without magazine). **Length:** 6.85" overall. **Features:** Otherwise similar to Model 31. Compact. Imported from Austria by Glock, Inc.
Price: Fixed sight **$599.00**
Price: 32C Compensated (fixed sight) **$621.00**

GLOCK 33 AUTO PISTOL

Caliber: 357 Auto, 9/11/13/15/17-shot magazines. **Barrel:** 3.46". **Weight:** 19.75 oz. (without magazine). **Length:** 6.29" overall. **Features:** Otherwise similar to Model 31. Subcompact. Imported from Austria by Glock, Inc.
Price: Fixed sight **$599.00**

HAMMERLI "TRAILSIDE" TARGET PISTOL

Caliber: 22 LR. **Barrel:** 4.5", 6". **Weight:** 28 oz. **Grips:** Synthetic. **Sights:** Fixed. **Features:** 10-shot magazine. Imported from by Larry's Guns of Maine.
Price: **$579.00**

Hammerli Trailside

Heckler & Koch USP45

Heckler & Koch
USP Compact

Heckler & Koch
USP45 Tactical

Heckler & Koch
USP45 Compact

Heckler & Koch
Mark 23 Special Operations

HECKLER & KOCH USP AUTO PISTOL

Caliber: 9mm Para., 15-shot magazine; 40 S&W, 13-shot magazine; 45 ACP, 12-shot magazine. **Barrel:** 4.25-4.41". **Weight:** 1.65 lbs. **Length:** 7.64-7.87" overall. **Grips:** Non-slip stippled black polymer. **Sights:** Blade front, rear adjustable for windage. **Features:** New HK design with polymer frame, modified Browning action with recoil reduction system, single control lever. Special "hostile environment" finish on all metal parts. Available in SA/ DA, DAO, left- and right-hand versions. Introduced 1993. 45 ACP Introduced 1995. Imported from Germany by Heckler & Koch, Inc.
Price: USP 45 . . . . **$839.00**
Price: USP 40 and USP 9mm **$769.00**

Heckler & Koch USP Compact Auto Pistol

Caliber: 9mm Para., 13-shot magazine; 40 S&W and .357 SIG, 12-shot magazine; 45 ACP, 8-shot magazine. Similar to the USP except the 9mm Para., 357 SIG, and 40 S&W have 3.58" barrels, measure 6.81" overall, and weigh 1.47 lbs. (9mm). Introduced 1996. 45 ACP measures 7.09" overall. Introduced 1998. Imported from Germany by Heckler & Koch, Inc.
Price: USP Compact 45 . . . . **$874.00**
Price: USP Compact 9mm Para., 357 SIG, and 40 S&W **$799.00**

HECKLER & KOCH USP45 TACTICAL PISTOL

Caliber: 40 S&W, 13-shot magazine; 45 ACP, 12-shot magazine. **Barrel:** 4.90-5.09". **Weight:** 1.9 lbs. **Length:** 8.64" overall. **Grips:** Non-slip stippled polymer. **Sights:** Blade front, fully adjustable target rear. **Features:** Has extended threaded barrel with rubber O-ring; adjustable trigger; extended magazine floorplate; adjustable trigger stop; polymer frame. Introduced 1998. Imported from Germany by Heckler & Koch, Inc.
Price: USP Tactical 45. . . . . **$1,115.00**
Price: USP Tactical 40. . . . . **$1,019.00**

Heckler & Koch USP Compact Tactical Pistol

Caliber: 45 ACP, 8-shot magazine. Similar to the USP Tactical except measures 7.72" overall, weighs 1.72 lbs. Introduced 2006. Imported from Germany by Heckler & Koch, Inc.
Price: USP Compact Tactical **$1,115.00**

HECKLER & KOCH MARK 23 SPECIAL OPERATIONS PISTOL

Caliber: 45 ACP, 12-shot magazine. **Barrel:** 5.87". **Weight:** 2.42 lbs. **Length:** 9.65" overall. **Grips:** Integral with frame; black polymer. **Sights:** Blade front, rear drift adjustable for windage; 3-dot. **Features:** Civilian version of the SOCOM pistol. Polymer frame; double action; exposed hammer; short recoil, modified Browning action. Introduced 1996. Imported from Germany by Heckler & Koch, Inc.
Price: **$2,412.00**

HECKLER & KOCH P2000 AUTO PISTOL

Caliber: 9mm Para., 13-shot magazine; 40 S&W and .357 SIG, 12-shot magazine. **Barrel:** 3.62". **Weight:** 1.5 lbs. **Length:** 7" overall. **Grips:** Interchangeable panels. **Sights:** Fixed Patridge style, drift adjustable for windage, standard 3-dot. Incorporates features of HK USP Compact pistol, including Law Enforcement Modification (LEM) trigger, double-action hammer system, ambidextrous magazine release, dual slide-release levers, accessory mounting rails, recurved, hook trigger guard, fiber-reinforced polymer frame, modular grip with exchangeable back straps, nitro-carburized finish, lock-out safety device. Introduced 2003. Imported from Germany by Heckler & Koch, Inc.
Price: **$887.00**
Price: P2000 LEM DAO, 357 SIG, intr. 2006 . . . . **$887.00**
Price: P2000 SA/DA, , 357 SIG, intr. 2006. . . . . **$887.00**

HECKLER & KOCH P2000 SK AUTO PISTOL

Caliber: 9mm Para., 10-shot magazine; 40 S&W and .357 SIG, 9-shot magazine. **Barrel:** 3.27". **Weight:** 1.3 lbs. **Length:** 6.42" overall. **Sights:** Fixed Patridge style, drift adjustable. **Features:** Standard accessory rails, ambidextrous slide release, polymer frame, polygonal bore profile. Smaller version of P2000. Introduced 2005. Imported from Germany by Heckler & Koch, Inc.
Price: **$929.00**

Hi-Point 9MM Comp

Hi-Point C-9

Kahr K9

HI-POINT FIREARMS MODEL 9MM COMPACT PISTOL

Caliber: 9mm Para., 8-shot magazine. **Barrel:** 3.5". **Weight:** 25 oz. **Length:** 6.75" overall. **Grips:** Textured plastic. **Sights:** Combat-style adjustable 3-dot system; low profile. **Features:** Single-action design; frame-mounted magazine release; polymer frame. Scratch-resistant matte finish. Introduced 1993. Comps are similar except they have a 4" barrel with muzzle brake/compensator. Compensator is slotted for laser or flashlight mounting. Introduced 1998. Made in U.S.A. by MKS Supply, Inc.

Price: C-9 9mm **$140.00**
Price: C-9 Comp **$169.00**
Price: C-9 Comp-L w/laser sight **$219.00**

Hi-Point Firearms Model 380 Polymer Pistol

Similar to the 9mm Compact model except chambered for 380 ACP, 8-shot magazine, adjustable 3-dot sights. Weighs 25 oz. Polymer frame. Action locks open after last shot. Includes 10-shot and 8-shot magazine; trigger lock. Introduced 1998. Comps are similar except they have a 4" barrel with muzzle compensator. Introduced 2001. Made in U.S.A. by MKS Supply, Inc.

Price: CF-380 . . . . **$120.00**
Price: 380 Comp **$120.00**
Price: 380 Comp-L w/laser sight **$190.00**

HI-POINT FIREARMS 40SW/POLY AND 45 AUTO PISTOLS

Caliber: 40 S&W, 8-shot magazine; 45 ACP (9-shot). **Barrel:** 4.5". **Weight:** 32 oz. **Length:** 7.72" overall. **Sights:** Adjustable 3-dot. **Features:** Polymer frames, last round lock-open, grip mounted magazine release, magazine disconnect safety, integrated accessory rail, trigger lock. Introduced 2002. Made in U.S.A. by MKS Supply, Inc.

Price: 40SW Poly **$179.00**
Price: 40SW Poly w/laser **$239.00**
Price: 45 ACP **$179.00**
Price: 45 ACP w/laser **$239.00**

KAHR K SERIES AUTO PISTOLS

Caliber: K9: 9mm Para., 7-shot; K40: 40 S&W, 6-shot magazine. **Barrel:** 3.5". **Weight:** 25 oz. **Length:** 6" overall. **Grips:** Wraparound textured soft polymer. **Sights:** Blade front, rear drift adjustable for windage; bar-dot combat style. **Features:** Trigger-cocking double-action mechanism with passive firing pin block. Made of 4140 ordnance steel with matte black finish. Contact maker for complete price list. Introduced 1994. Made in U.S.A. by Kahr Arms.

Price: K9093C K9, matte stainless steel **$741.00**
Price: K9093NC K9, matte stainless steel w/tritium night sights . . . **$853.00**
Price: K9094C K9 matte blackened stainless steel **$772.00**
Price: K9098 K9 Elite 2003, stainless steel **$806.00**
Price: K4043 K40, matte stainless steel **$741.00**
Price: K4043N K40, matte stainless steel w/tritium night sights **$853.00**
Price: K4044 K40, matte blackened stainless steel **$772.00**
Price: K4048 K40 Elite 2003, stainless steel **$806.00**

Kahr MK Series Micro Pistols

Similar to the K9/K40 except is 5.35" overall, 4" high, with a 3.08" barrel. Weighs 23.1 oz. Has snag-free bar-dot sights, polished feed ramp, dual recoil spring system, DA-only trigger. Comes with 5-round flush baseplate and 6-shot grip extension magazine. Introduced 1998. Made in U.S.A. by Kahr Arms.

Price: M9093 MK9, matte stainless steel **$741.00**
Price: M9093N MK9, matte stainless steel, tritium night sights **$853.00**
Price: M9093-BOX MK9, matte stainless steel frame,
matte black slide **$475.00**
Price: M9098 MK9 Elite 2003, stainless steel **$806.00**
Price: M4043 MK40, matte stainless steel **$741.00**
Price: M4043N MK40, matte stainless steel, tritium night sights . . . **$853.00**
Price: M4048 MK40 Elite 2003, stainless steel **$806.00**

Kahr P Series Pistols

Caliber: 9x19, 40 S&W. Similar to K9/K40 steel frame pistol except has polymer frame, matte stainless steel slide. Barrel length 3.5"; overall length 5.8"; weighs 17 oz. Includes two 7-shot magazines, hard polymer case, trigger lock. Introduced 2000. Made in U.S.A. by Kahr Arms.

Price: KP9093 P9 . . . . **$697.00**
Price: KP9093N P9, tritium night sight **$808.00**
Price: KPS9093 P9 Covert, shortened grip, 15 oz., 6+1 . . . . **$697.00**
Price: KP4043 P40 . . . . **$697.00**
Price: KPS4043N P40 Covert, shortened grip, tritium night sights . **$697.00**

Kahr PM Series Pistols

Caliber: 9x19, 40 S&W. Similar to P-Series pistols except has smaller polymer frame (Polymer Micro). Barrel length 3.08"; overall length 5.35"; weighs 17 oz. Includes two 7-shot magazines, hard polymer case, trigger lock. Introduced 2000. Made in U.S.A. by Kahr Arms.

Price: PM9093 PM9 . . . . **$728.00**
Price: PM9093N PM9, tritium night sight **$839.00**
Price: PM4043 PM40 . . . . **$728.00**
Price: PM4044N PM40, Tungsten DLC finish, tritium night sights . . **$870.00**

KAHR T SERIES PISTOLS

Caliber: T9: 9mm Para., 8-shot magazine; T40: 40 S&W, 7-shot magazine. **Barrel:** 4". **Weight:** 28.1-29.1 oz. **Length:** 6.5" overall. **Grips:** Checkered Hogue Pau Ferro wood grips. **Sights:** Rear: Novak low profile 2-dot tritium night sight, front tritium night sight. **Features:** Similar to other Kahr makes, but with longer slide and barrel upper, longer butt. Trigger cocking DAO; lock breech; "Browning-type" recoil lug; passive striker block; no magazine disconnect. Comes with two magazines. Introduced 2004. Made in U.S.A. by Kahr Arms.

Price: KT9093 T9 matte stainless steel **$741.00**
Price: KT9093-NOVAK T9, "Tactical 9," Novak night sight. **$860.00**
Price: KT4093 T40 matte stainless steel **$741.00**

KAHR TP SERIES PISTOLS

Caliber: TP9: 9mm Para., 7-shot magazine; TP40: 40 S&W, 6-shot magazine. **Barrel:** 4". **Weight:** 19.1-20.1 oz. **Length:** 6.5-6.7" overall. **Grips:** Textured polymer. Similar to T-series guns, but with polymer frame, matte stainless slide. Comes with two magazines. TP40s introduced 2006. Made in U.S.A. by Kahr Arms.

Price: TP9093 TP9 . . . . **$697.00**
Price: TP9093-Novak TP9 . . . . **$839.00**
Price: TP4043 TP40 . . . . **$697.00**
Price: TP4043-Novak TP40, Novak night sights **$839.00**

Kel-Tec P-32   **Kel-Tec P-3AT**   **Kimber Pro Carry II**   **Kimber Ultra Carry II**

Kimber Ten II High Capacity Polymer

KAHR CW SERIES PISTOL
Caliber: 9mm Para., 7-shot magazine; 40 S&W, 6-shot magazine. **Barrel:** 3.5-3.6". **Weight:** 17.7-18.7 oz. **Length:** 5.9-6.36" overall. **Grips:** Textured polymer. Similar to P-Series, but CW Series have conventional rifling, metal-injection-molded slide stop lever, no front dovetail cut, one magazine. CW40 introduced 2006. Made in U.S.A. by Kahr Arms.
Price: CW9093 CW9 . . . . **$533.00**
Price: CW4043 CW40 . . . . **$533.00**

KEL-TEC P-11 AUTO PISTOL
Caliber: 9mm Para., 10-shot magazine. **Barrel:** 3.1". **Weight:** 14 oz. **Length:** 5.6" overall. **Grips:** Checkered black polymer. **Sights:** Blade front, rear adjustable for windage. **Features:** Ordnance steel slide, aluminum frame. Double-action-only trigger mechanism. Introduced 1995. Made in U.S.A. by Kel-Tec CNC Industries, Inc.
Price: Blue/Hard Chrome/Parkerized . . . . **$320 /$375 / $362**

KEL-TEC PF-9 PISTOL
Caliber: 9mm Luger; 7 rounds. **Weight:** 12.7 oz. **Sights:** Rear sight adjustable for windage and elevation. **Barrel Length:** 3.1". **Length:** 5.85". **Features:** Barrel, locking system, slide stop, assembly pin, front sight, recoil springs and guide rod adapted from P-11. Trigger system with integral hammer block and the extraction system adapted from P-3AT. MIL-STD-1913 Picatinny rail. Made in U.S.A. by Kel-Tec CNC Industries, Inc.
Price: Blue/ Parkerized/Hard Chrome. . . . . **$314/ $355 / $368**

KEL-TEC P-32 AUTO PISTOL
Caliber: 32 ACP, 7-shot magazine. **Barrel:** 2.68". **Weight:** 6.6 oz. **Length:** 5.07" overall. **Grips:** Checkered composite. **Sights:** Fixed. **Features:** Double-action-only mechanism with 6-lb. pull; internal slide stop. Textured composite grip/frame. Now available in 380 ACP. Made in U.S.A. by Kel-Tec CNC Industries, Inc.
Price: Blue/Hard Chrome/Parkerized . . . . **$300 / $355 / $340**

KEL-TEC P-3AT PISTOL
Caliber: 380 Auto; 7-rounds. **Weight:** 7.2 oz. **Length:** 5.2". **Features:** Lightest 380 auto made; aluminum frame, steel barrel.
Price: Blue/Hard Chrome/Parkerized . . . . **$300 / $355 / $340**

KEL-TEC PLR-16 PISTOL
Caliber: 5.56mm NATO; 10-round magazine. **Weight:** 51 oz. **Sights:** Rear sight adjustable for windage, front sight is M-16 blade. **Barrel Length:** 9.2". **Length:** 18.5". **Features:** Muzzle is threaded 1/2"-28 to accept standard attachments such as a muzzle brake. Except for the barrel, bolt, sights, and mechanism, the PLR-16 pistol is made of high-impact glass fiber reinforced polymer. Gas-operated semi-auto. Conventional gas-piston operation with M-16 breech locking system. MIL-STD-1913 Picatinny rail. Made in U.S.A. by Kel-Tec CNC Industries, Inc.
Price: Blued. **$640.00**

KIMBER CUSTOM II AUTO PISTOL
Caliber: 45 ACP, 40 S&W, 38 Super, 9mm, 10mm. **Barrel:** 5", match grade; 9mm, 10mm, 40 S&W, 38 Super barrels ramped. **Weight:** 38 oz. **Length:** 8.7" overall. **Grips:** Checkered black rubber, walnut, rosewood. **Sights:** Dovetailed front and rear, Kimber low profile adj. or fixed sights. **Features:** Slide, frame and barrel machined from steel or stainless steel. Match grade barrel, chamber and trigger group. Extended thumb safety, beveled magazine well, beveled front and rear slide serrations, high ride beavertail grip safety, checkered flat mainspring housing, kidney cut under trigger

guard, high cut grip, match grade stainless steel barrel bushing, polished breech face, Commander-style hammer, lowered and flared ejection port, Wolff springs, bead blasted black oxide or matte stainless finish. Introduced in 1996. Made in U.S.A. by Kimber Mfg., Inc.
Price: Custom II **$768.00**
Price: Custom II Walnut (double-diamond walnut grips) **$775.00**
Price: Stainless II **$865.00**
Price: Stainless II 40 S&W **$884.00**
Price: Stainless II Target 45 ACP (stainless, adj. sight) **$983.00**
Price: Stainless II Target 38 Super **$1,014.00**

Kimber Compact Stainless II Auto Pistol
Similar to Pro Carry II except has stainless steel frame, 4-inch bbl., grip is .400" shorter than standard, no front serrations. Weighs 34 oz. 45 ACP only. Introduced in 1998. Made in U.S.A. by Kimber Mfg., Inc.
Price: **$907.00**

Kimber Pro Carry II Auto Pistol
Similar to Custom II, has aluminum frame, 4" bull barrel fitted directly to the slide without bushing. HD with stainless steel frame. Introduced 1998. Made in U.S.A. by Kimber Mfg., Inc.
Price: Pro Carry II **$779.00**
Price: Pro Carry II w/night sights **$902.00**
Price: Pro Carry II Stainless w/night sights **$985.00**
Price: Pro Carry HD II **$906.00**

Kimber Ultra Carry II Auto Pistol
Lightweight aluminum frame, 3" match grade bull barrel fitted to slide without bushing. Grips .4" shorter. Low effort recoil. Weighs 25 oz. Introduced in 1999. Made in U.S.A. by Kimber Mfg., Inc.
Price: **$791.00**
Price: Ultra Carry II Stainless **$875.00**
Price: Ultra Carry II Stainless 40 S&W **$921.00**

Kimber Ten II High Capacity Polymer Pistol
Similar to Custom II, Pro Carry II and Ultra Carry II depending on barrel length. Thirteen-round magazine capacity (double stack and flush fitting). Polymer grip frame molded over stainless steel or aluminum (BP Ten pistols only) frame insert. Checkered front strap and belly of trigger guard. All models have fixed sights except Gold Match Ten II, which has adjustable sight. Frame grip dimensions approximately that of the standard 1911. **Weight:** 24 to 34 oz. Improved version of the Kimber Polymer series. Made in U.S.A. by Kimber Mfg., Inc.
Price: Pro Carry Ten II **$794.00**
Price: Stainless Ten II **$786.00**

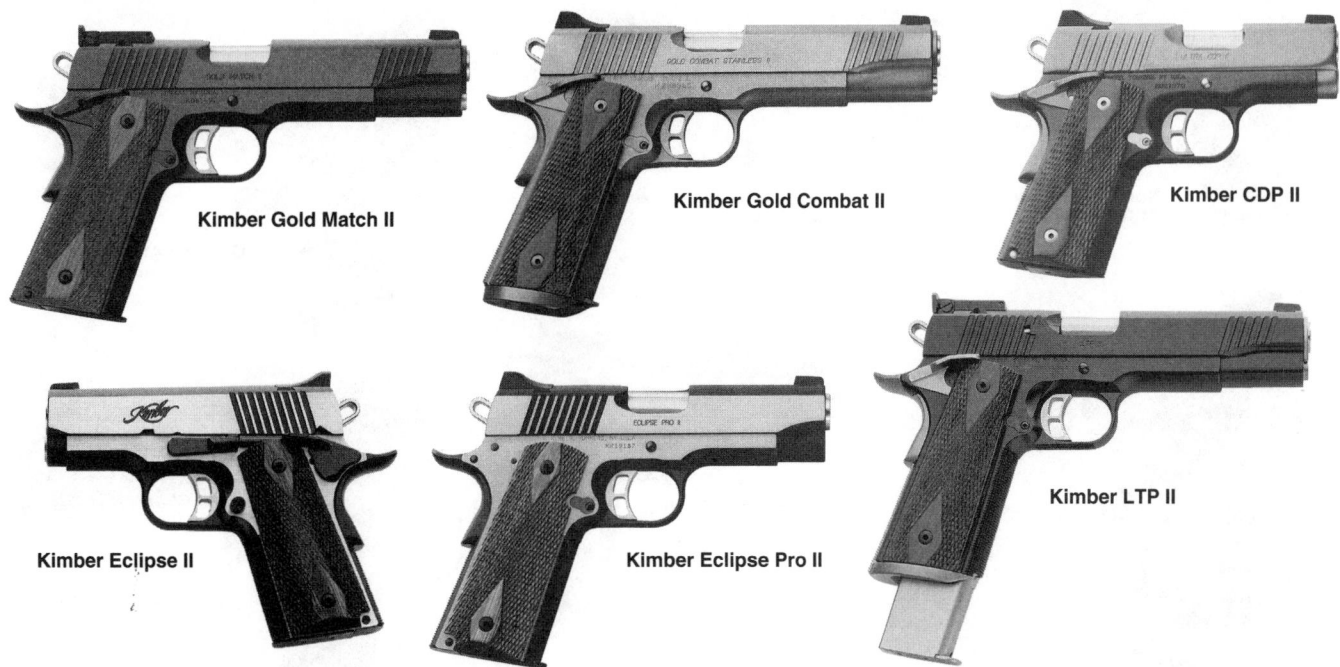

Kimber Gold Match II

Kimber Gold Combat II

Kimber CDP II

Kimber Eclipse II

Kimber Eclipse Pro II

Kimber LTP II

Kimber Gold Match II Auto Pistol

Similar to Custom II models. Includes stainless steel barrel with match grade chamber and barrel bushing, ambidextrous thumb safety, adjustable sight, premium aluminum trigger, hand-checkered double diamond rosewood grips. Barrel hand-fitted for target accuracy. Made in U.S.A. by Kimber Mfg., Inc.

Price: Gold Match II **$1,204.00**
Price: Gold Match Stainless II 45 ACP **$1,369.00**
Price: Gold Match Stainless II 40 S&W **$1,400.00**

Kimber Gold Match Ten II Polymer Auto Pistol

Similar to Stainless Gold Match II. High capacity polymer frame with 13-round magazine. Thumb safety. Introduced 1999. Made in U.S.A. by Kimber Mfg., Inc.

Price: **$1,072.00**

Kimber Gold Combat II Auto Pistol

Similar to Gold Match II except designed for concealed carry. Extended and beveled magazine well, Meprolight Tritium night sights; premium aluminum trigger; 30 lpi front strap checkering; extended magazine well. Introduced 1999. Made in U.S.A. by Kimber Mfg., Inc.

Price: Gold Combat II **$1,733.00**
Price: Gold Combat Stainless II **$1,674.00**

Kimber CDP II Series Auto Pistol

Similar to Custom II, but designed for concealed carry. Aluminum frame. Standard features include stainless steel slide, fixed Meprolight tritium 3-dot (green) dovetail-mounted night sights, match grade barrel and chamber, 30 LPI front strap checkering, two-tone finish, ambidextrous thumb safety, hand-checkered double diamond rosewood grips. Introduced in 2000. Made in U.S.A. by Kimber Mfg., Inc.

Price: Ultra CDP II 40 S&W **$1,215.00**
Price: Ultra CDP II (3" barrel, short grip) **$1,177.00**
Price: Compact CDP II (4" barrel, short grip) **$1,177.00**
Price: Pro CDP II (4" barrel, full length grip) **$1,177.00**
Price: Custom CDP II (5" barrel, full length grip) **$1,177.00**

Kimber Eclipse II Series Auto Pistol

Similar to Custom II and other stainless Kimber pistols. Stainless slide and frame, black oxide, two-tone finish. Gray/black laminated grips. 30 lpi front strap checkering. All models have night sights; Target versions have Meprolight adjustable Bar/Dot version. Made in U.S.A. by Kimber Mfg., Inc.

Price: Eclipse Ultra II (3" barrel, short grip) **$1,085.00**
Price: Eclipse Pro II (4" barrel, full length grip) **$1,085.00**
Price: Eclipse Pro Target II (4" barrel, full length grip, adjustable sight) **$1,189.00**
Price: Eclipse Custom II (5" barrel, full length grip) **$1,105.00**
Price: Eclipse Target II (5" barrel, full length grip, adjustable sight) **$1,189.00**
Price: Eclipse Custom II (10mm) **$1,220.00**

Kimber LTP II Auto Pistol

Similar to Gold Match II. Built for Limited Ten competition. First Kimber pistol with new, innovative Kimber external extractor. KimPro premium finish. Stainless steel match grade barrel. Extended and beveled magazine well. Checkered front strap and trigger guard belly. Tungsten full length guide rod. Premium aluminum trigger. Ten-round single stack magazine. Wide ambidextrous thumb safety. Made in U.S.A. by Kimber Mfg., Inc.

Price: **$2,099.00**

Kimber Super Match II Auto Pistol

Similar to Gold Match II. Built for target and action shooting competition. Tested for accuracy, target included. Stainless steel barrel and chamber. KimPro finish on stainless steel slide. Stainless steel frame. 30 lpi checkered front strap, premium aluminum trigger, Kimber adjustable sight. Introduced in 1999.

Price: **$1,986.00**

KORTH PISTOL

Caliber: 40 S&W, 357 SIG (9-shot); 9mm Para, 9x21 (10-shot). **Barrel:** 4" (standard), 5" (optional). **Weight:** 3.3 lbs. (single action), 11 lbs. (double action). **Sights:** Fully adjustable. **Features:** Recoil-operated action, mechanically-locked via large pivoting bolt block. Accessories include sound suppressor for qualified buyers. Imported by Korth U.S.A.

Price: **$7,578.00**

NORTH AMERICAN ARMS GUARDIAN DAO PISTOL

Caliber: 25 NAA, 32 ACP, 380 ACP, 32NAA, 6-shot magazine. **Barrel:** 2.49". **Weight:** 20.8 oz. **Length:** 4.75" overall. **Grips:** Black polymer. **Sights:** Low profile fixed. **Features:** Double-action only mechanism. All stainless steel construction. Introduced 1998. Made in U.S.A. by North American Arms.

Price: .... **$402.00 to $479.00**

North American Arms Guardian

Olympic Arms Matchmaster 5 1911

Olympic Arms Matchmaster 6 1911

Olympic Arms Enforcer 1911

Olympic Arms Cohort

Olympic Arms Big Deuce

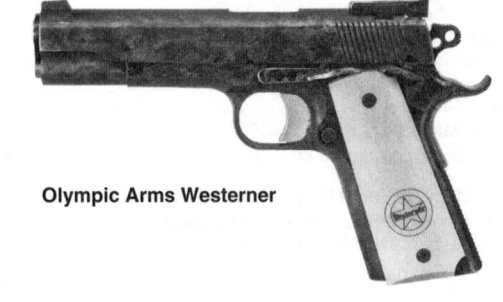

Olympic Arms Westerner

OLYMPIC ARMS MATCHMASTER 5 1911 PISTOL

Caliber: 45 ACP, 7-shot magazine. **Barrel:** 5" stainless steel. **Weight:** 40 oz. **Length:** overall. **Grips:** Smooth walnut with laser etched scorpion logo. **Sights:** Ramped blade, LPA adjustable rear. **Features:** Matched frame and slide, fitted and head-spaced barrel, complete ramp and throat jobs, lowered and widened ejection port, beveled mag well, hand-stoned-to-match hammer and sear, lightweight long-shoe over-travel adjusted trigger, shaped and tensioned extractor, extended thumb safety, wide beavertail grip safety and full length guide rod. Made in U.S.A. by Olympic Arms, Inc.
Price: **$714.00**

OLYMPIC ARMS MATCHMASTER 6 1911 PISTOL

Caliber: 45 ACP, 7-shot. **Barrel:** 6" stainless steel. **Weight:** 44 oz. **Length:** 9.75" overall. **Grips:** Smooth walnut. **Sights:** Ramped blade, LPA adjustable rear. **Features:** Matched frame and slide, fitted and head-spaced barrel, complete ramp and throat jobs, lowered and widened ejection port, beveled mag well, hand-stoned-to-match hammer and sear, lightweight long-shoe over-travel adjusted trigger, shaped and tensioned extractor, extended thumb safety, wide beavertail grip safety and full length guide rod. Made in U.S.A. by Olympic Arms, Inc.
Price: **$774.00**

OLYMPIC ARMS ENFORCER 1911 PISTOL

Caliber: 45 ACP, 6-shot magazine. **Barrel:** 4" bull barrel stainless steel. **Weight:** 35 oz. **Length:** 7.75" overall. **Grips:** Smooth walnut with etched black widow spider logo. **Sights:** Ramped blade front, LPA adjustable rear. **Features:** Similar to Matchmaster, but adds a bushingless bull barrel and a triplex counter-wound self-contained spring recoil system. Matched frame and slide, fitted and head-spaced barrel, complete ramp and throat jobs, lowered and widened ejection port, beveled mag well, hand-stoned-to-match hammer and sear, lightweight longshoe over-travel adjusted trigger, shaped and tensioned extractor, extended thumb safety, wide beavertail grip safety and full length guide rod. Made in U.S.A. by Olympic Arms.
Price: **$750.00**

OLYMPIC ARMS COHORT PISTOL

Caliber: 45 ACP, 7-shot magazine. **Barrel:** 4", bull barrel stainless steel. **Weight:** 36 oz. **Length:** 7.75" overall. **Grips:** Smooth walnut with laser-etched black widow logo. **Sights:** Ramped blade front, LPA adjustable rear. **Features:** Combines short Enforcer top end and recoil system with full-sized Matchmaster round-trigger-guard M-3 frame. Matched frame

and slide, fitted and head-spaced barrel, complete ramp and throat jobs, lowered and widened ejection port, beveled mag well, hand-stoned-to-match hammer and sear, lightweight long-shoe over-travel adjusted trigger, shaped and tensioned extractor, extended thumb safety, wide beavertail grip safety and full length guide rod. Made in U.S.A. by Olympic Arms.
Price: **$779.00**

OLYMPIC ARMS BIG DEUCE PISTOL

Caliber: 45 ACP, 7-shot magazine. **Barrel:** 6", 416 stainless steel. **Weight:** 40.3 oz. **Length:** 9.5" overall. **Grips:** Smooth walnut. **Sights:** Ramped blade front, LPA adjustable rear. **Features:** Beavertail grip safety; extended thumb safety and slide release; Commander-style hammer. Throated, polished and tuned. Parkerized matte black slide with satin stainless steel frame. Introduced 1995. Made in U.S.A. by Safari Arms, Inc.
Price: **$834.00**

OLYMPIC ARMS WESTERNER SERIES PISTOLS

Caliber: 45 ACP, 7-round magazine. **Barrel:** 4", 5", 6". **Grips:** Smooth ivory style. **Weight:** 35-43 oz. **Length:** 7.75". **Sights:** Adjustable rear, fixed front blade. **Features:** Similar to Matchmaster, parts numbered to the frame, color case hardening finish. Made in U.S.A. by Olympic Arms, Inc.
Price: Westerner, 5" barrel, 39 oz. **$834.00**
Price: Trail Boss, 6" barrel, 43 oz.. . . . . **$959.00**
Price: Constable, 4" barrel, 35 oz. **$935.00**

Olympic Arms Constable

Olympic Arms Trail Boss

Olympic Arms OA-93

Olympic Arms OA-98

Para-Ordnance SSP-SE1

Para-Ordnance P12-45

Para-Ordnance Todd Jarrett

OLYMPIC ARMS BLACK-TAC PISTOL
Caliber: 45 ACP, 7-round magazine. **Barrel:** 5". **Weight:** 40 oz. **Length:** 8.75". **Sights:** Low-profile adjustable rear, fixed front blade. **Features:** Blak-Tac finish process also used on AR/M-16 bolt carriers. Made in U.S.A. by Olympic Arms, Inc.
Price: **$834.00**

OLYMPIC ARMS OA-93 AR PISTOL
Caliber: 5.56 NATO. **Barrel:** 6.5", chrome-moly steel. **Weight:** 4.46 lbs. **Length:** 26.5". **Sights:** None. **Features:** Black matte finish; flash suppressor; flat-top upper, tubular handguard. Introduced 2005. Made in U.S.A. by Olympic Arms, Inc.
Price: $1,020.00

Olympic Arms OA-98 AR Pistol
Similar to the OA-93. **Weight:** 49 oz. Skeletonized version of OA-93, conforms to the AWB, uses standard AR15 magazines. Introduced 1998. Made in U.S.A. by Olympic Arms, Inc.
Price: $1,020.00

PARA-ORDNANCE PXT 1911 SINGLE-ACTION SINGLE-STACK AUTO PISTOLS
Caliber: 38 Super, 45 ACP. **Barrel:** 3.5", 4.25", 5". **Weight:** 28-40 oz. **Length:** 7.1-8.5" overall. **Grips:** Checkered cocobolo, textured composition, Mother of Pearl synthetic. **Sights:** Blade front, low-profile Novak Extreme Duty adjustable rear. High visibility 3-dot system. **Features:** Available with alloy, steel or stainless steel frames. Skeletonized trigger, spurred hammer. Manual thumb, grip and firing pin lock safeties. Full-length guide rod. PXT designates new Para Power

Extractor throughout the line. Introduced 2004. Made in Canada by Para-Ordnance.
Price: SSP-SE1 (2006), midnight blue, 7+1, 5" barrel $1,094.00
Price: OPS, stainless, Griptor grooves front strap (2006) $1,043.00
Price: LTC, blued or stainless, 7+1, 4.25" barrel . . . . . **$884.00 to 1,043.00**
Price: SSP, blued or stainless, 7+1, 4.25" barrel . . . . . **$884.00 to 1,043.00**

PARA-ORDNANCE PXT 1911 SINGLE-ACTION HIGH-CAPACITY AUTO PISTOLS
Caliber: 9mm, 45 ACP, 10//14/18-shot magazines. **Barrel:** 3", 5". **Weight:** 34-40 oz. **Length:** 7.1-8.5" overall. **Grips:** Textured composition. **Sights:** Blade front, low-profile Novak Extreme Duty adjustable rear or fixed sights. High visibility 3-dot system. **Features:** Available with alloy, steel or stainless steel frames. Skeletonized match trigger, spurred hammer, flared ejection port. Manual thumb, grip and firing pin lock safeties. Full-length guide rod. Introduced 2004. Made in Canada by Para-Ordnance.
Price: P14-45MB (2006), midnight blue, 14+1, 5" barrel $899.00
Price: P14-45 stainless, 14+1, 5" barrel $998.00
Price: P18-9 stainless,18+1 9mm, 5" barrel $1,049.00

Para-Ordnance PXT Limited Pistols
Similar to the PXT-Series pistols except with full-length recoil guide system; fully adjustable rear sight; tuned trigger with over-travel stop; beavertail grip safety; competition hammer; front and rear slide serrations; ambidextrous safety; lowered ejection port; ramped match-grade barrel; dove-tailed front sight. Introduced 2004. Made in Canada by Para-Ordnance.
Price: S12-45 LTD, 45 ACP, 12+1, stainless, Novak sights $1,163.00
Price: Todd Jarrett 40 S&W, 16+1, stainless $1,163.00

Para-Ordnance LDA

Para-Ordnance Carry

Para-Ordnance CCO

Para-Ordnance Tac-Four

Para-Ordnance Tac-S

Para-Ordnance Limited

Para-Ordnance Colonel

Para-Ordnance Nite-Trac

Para-Ordnance Slim Hawg

Para-Ordnance LDA Single-Stack Carry Auto Pistols
Similar to PXT-series except has double-action trigger mechanism, flush hammers, brushed stainless finish, checkered composition grips. Available in 45 ACP. Introduced 1999. Made in Canada by Para-Ordnance.
Price: Carry, 6+1, 3" barrel, stainless **$1,049.00**
Price: Carry, 6+1, 3" barrel, covert black. **$1,133.00**
Price: CCO, 7+1, 3.5" barrel **$1, 049.00**
Price: CCW, 7+1, 4.5" barrel **$1, 049.00**

Para-Ordnance LDA High-Cap Carry Auto Pistols
Similar to LDA-series with double-action trigger mechanism. Also, bobbed beavertail, high-cap mags. Available in 9mm Para., 45 ACP. Introduced 1999. Made in Canada by Para-Ordnance.
Price: Carry 12, 12+1, 3.5" barrel, stainless **$1,133.00**
Price: Tac-Four, 13+1, 4.5" barrel, stainless **$1,028.00**
Price: C TX189B, 18+1, 5" barrel, covert black, Novak sights . . . **$1,163.00**

Para-Ordnance LDA Single-Stack Auto Pistols
Similar to LDA-series with double-action trigger mechanism. Cocobolo and polymer grips. Available in 45 ACP. Introduced 1999. Made in Canada by Para-Ordnance.
Price: Black Watch Companion, 7+1, 3.5" barrel **$1,133.00**
Price: Tac-S, 7+1, 4.5" barrel, Spec Ops matte finish. **$944.00**
Price: Tac-S, 7+1, 4.5" barrel, stainless **$1,028.00**
Price: Limited, 7+1, 5" barrel, stainless. **$1,193.00**

Para-Ordnance LDA Hi-Capacity Auto Pistols
Similar to LDA-series with double-action trigger mechanism. Polymer grips. Available in 9mm, 40 S&W, 45 ACP. Introduced 1999. Made in Canada by Para-Ordnance.
Price: Colonel, 14+1, 4.25" barrel **$944.00**
Price: Hi-Cap 45, 14+1, 5" barrel, stainless **$1,028.00**
Price: Hi-Cap 9, 18+1, 5" barrel, covert black finish. **$944.00**
Price: Hi-Cap LTD 45 45 ACP, 14+1, 5" barrel, stainless. **$1,193.00**
Price: Hi-Cap LTD 40 40 S&W, 15+1, 5" barrel, stainless **$1,193.00**
Price: Hi-Cap LTD 9 9mm, 18+1, 5" barrel, stainless **$1,193.00**

Para-Ordnance LDA Light Rail Pistols
Similar to PXT and LDA-series above, with built-in light rail. Polymer grips. Available in 9mm, 40 S&W, 45 ACP. Made in Canada by Para-Ordnance.
Price: Nite-Tac 45, 14+1 45 ACP, 5" barrel, covert black **$1,034.00**
Price: Nite-Tac 40, 16+1 40S&W, 5" barrel, stainless (2006) **$1,103.00**
Price: Nite-Tac 9, 16+1 9mm, 5" barrel, stainless (2006) **$1,103.00**

PARA-ORDNANCE WARTHOG
Caliber: 9mm, 45 ACP, 6, 10, or 12-shot magazines. **Barrel:** 3". **Weight:** 24 to 31.5 oz. **Length:** 6.5". **Grips:** Varies by model. **Features:** Single action. Made in Canada by Para-Ordnance.
Price: Slim Hawg (2006) single stack .45 ACP, stainless, 6+1. . . . **$1,043.00**
Price: Nite Hawg .45 ACP, black finish, 10+1 . . . . **$1,013.00**
Price: Warthog .45 ACP, Regal finish, 10+1 . . . . **$884.00**
Price: Stainless Warthog .45 ACP (2006), brushed finish, 10+1 . . . **$989.00**
Price: Hawg 9 9mm Regal finish, alloy frame, 12+1 . . . . **$884.00**
Price: Lite Hawg 9 9mm (2006) black finish, alloy frame, 12+1. . . **$1,049.00**

Para-Ordnance Nite Hawg

Para-Ordnance Warthog

Para-Ordnance Lite Hawg

Phoenix Arms HP22

Ruger P89

Ruger P90

Ruger KP944D

PHOENIX ARMS HP22, HP25 AUTO PISTOLS

Caliber: 22 LR, 10-shot (HP22), 25 ACP, 10-shot (HP25). **Barrel:** 3". **Weight:** 20 oz. **Length:** 5-1/2" overall. **Grips:** Checkered composition. **Sights:** Blade front, adjustable rear. **Features:** Single action, exposed hammer; manual hold-open; button magazine release. Available in satin nickel, matte blue finish. Introduced 1993. Made in U.S.A. by Phoenix Arms.

Price: With gun lock **$130.00**
Price: HP Range kit with 5" bbl.,
locking case and accessories (1 Mag) **$171.00**
Price: HP Deluxe Range kit with 3" and 5" bbls.,
2 mags., case **$210.00**

ROCK RIVER ARMS BASIC CARRY AUTO PISTOL

Caliber: 45 ACP. **Barrel:** NA. **Weight:** NA. **Length:** NA. **Grips:** Rosewood, checkered. **Sights:** dovetail front sight, Heinie rear sight. **Features:** NM frame with 20-, 25- or 30-LPI checkered front strap, 5-inch slide with double serrations, lowered and flared ejection port, throated NM Kart barrel with NM bushing, match Commander hammer and match sear , aluminum speed trigger, dehorned, Parkerized finish, one magazine, accuracy guarantee. 3.5 lb. Trigger pull. Introduced 2006. Made in U.S.A. From Rock River Arms.

Price: PS2700 . . . . **$1,540.00**

RUGER P89 AUTOLOADING PISTOL

Caliber: 9mm Para., 15-shot magazine. **Barrel:** 4.50". **Weight:** 32 oz. **Length:** 7.84" overall. **Grips:** Grooved black synthetic composition. **Sights:** Square post front, square notch rear adjustable for windage, both with white dot inserts. **Features:** Double action, ambidextrous slide-mounted safety-levers. Slide 4140 chrome-moly steel or 400-series stainless steel, frame lightweight aluminum alloy. Ambidextrous magazine release. Blue, stainless steel. Introduced 1986; stainless 1990.

Price: P89, blue, extra mag and mag loader, plastic case locks . . . **$475.00**
Price: KP89, stainless, extra mag and mag loader,
plastic case locks **$525.00**

Ruger P89D Decocker Autoloading Pistol

Similar to standard P89 except has ambidextrous decocking levers in place of regular slide-mounted safety. Decocking levers move firing pin inside slide where hammer cannot reach it. Blue, stainless steel. Introduced 1990.

Price: P89D, blue, extra mag and mag loader, plastic case locks . . **$475.00**
Price: KP89D, stainless, extra mag and mag loader,
plastic case locks **$525.00**

RUGER P90 MANUAL SAFETY MODEL AUTOLOADING PISTOL

Caliber: 45 ACP, 8-shot magazine. **Barrel:** 4.50". **Weight:** 33.5 oz. **Length:** 7.75" overall. **Grips:** Grooved black synthetic composition. **Sights:** Square post front, square notch rear adjustable for windage, both with white dot. **Features:** Double action; ambidextrous slide-mounted safety-levers. Stainless steel only. Introduced 1991.

Price: KP90 with extra mag, loader, case and gunlock **$565.00**
Price: P90 (blue) **$525.00**

Ruger KP90 Decocker Autoloading Pistol

Similar to the P90 except has a manual decocking system. Ambidextrous decocking levers move the firing pin inside the slide where the hammer cannot reach it. Available only in stainless steel. Overall length 7.75", weighs 33.5 oz. Introduced 1991.

Price: KP90D with case, extra mag and mag loading tool **$565.00**

Ruger KP94 Autoloading Pistol

Sized midway between full-size P-Series and compact KP94. 4.25" barrel, 7.5" overall length, weighs about 33 oz. KP94 manual safety model; KP94D is decocker-only in 40-caliber with 10-shot magazine. Slide gripping grooves roll over top of slide. KP94 has ambidextrous safety-levers; KP944D has ambidextrous decocking levers. Matte finish stainless slide, barrel, alloy frame. Also blue. Includes hard case and lock. Introduced 1994. Made in U.S.A. by Sturm, Ruger & Co.

Price: P944, blue (manual safety) **$495.00**
Price: KP944 (40-caliber) (manual safety-stainless) **$575.00**
Price: KP944D (40-caliber)-decocker only **$575.00**

Ruger KP512 MKIII

Ruger Mark III Hunter

Ruger KP9515

Sigarms Revolution

RUGER P95 AUTOLOADING PISTOL

Caliber: 9mm Para., 15-shot magazine. **Barrel:** 3.9". **Weight:** 27 oz. **Length:** 7.25" overall. **Grips:** Grooved; integral with frame. **Sights:** Blade front, rear drift adjustable for windage; 3-dot system. **Features:** Molded polymer grip frame, stainless steel or chrome-moly slide. Suitable for +P+ ammunition. Safety model, decocker. Introduced 1996. Made in U.S.A. by Sturm, Ruger & Co. Comes with lockable plastic case, spare magazine, loader and lock, Picatinny rails.

Price: P95D15 decocker only **$425.00**
Price: P9515 stainless steel decocker only **$475.00**
Price: KP9515 safety model, stainless steel **$475.00**
Price: P9515 safety model, blued finish **$425.00**

RUGER MARK III STANDARD AUTOLOADING PISTOL

Caliber: 22 LR, 10-shot magazine. **Barrel:** 4-3/4", 5-1/2", 6", or 6-7/8". **Weight:** 35 oz. (4-3/4" bbl.). **Length:** 9" (4-3/4" bbl.). **Grips:** Checkered composition grip panels. **Sights:** Fixed, wide blade front, fixed rear. **Features:** Updated design of original Standard Auto and Mark II series. Standard models have lighter barrels. Target models have cocobolo grips; bull, target, competition, and hunter barrels; and adjustable sights. Introduced 2005.

Price: MKIII4, MKIII6 (blued) **$322.00**
Price: MKIII512 (blued) **$382.00**
Price: KMKIII512 (stainless) **$483.00**
Price: MKIII678 (blued) **$382.00**
Price: KMKIII678GC (stainless slabside barrel) **$555.00**
Price: KMKIII678GH (stainless fluted barrel) **$567.00**

Ruger 22/45 Mark III Pistol

Similar to other 22 Mark III autos except has Zytel grip frame that matches angle and magazine latch of Model 1911 45 ACP pistol. Available in 4" standard, 4-1/2" and 5-1/2" bull barrels. Comes with extra magazine, plastic case, lock. Introduced 1992. Hunter introduced 2006.

Price: P4MKIII, 4" bull barrel, adjustable sights **$307.00**
Price: P45GCMKIII, 4.5" bull barrel, fixed sights **$305.00**
Price: P512MKIII (5-1/2" bull blued barrel, adj. Sights) **$307.00**
Price: KP512MKIII (5-1/2" stainless bull barrel, adj. sights **$398.00**
Price: Hunter KP678HMKIII, 6-7/8" stainless fluted bull barrel, adj. sights **$487.00**

SEECAMP LWS 32 STAINLESS DA AUTO

Caliber: 32 ACP Win. Silvertip, 6-shot magazine. **Barrel:** 2", integral with frame. **Weight:** 10.5 oz. **Length:** 4-1/8" overall. **Grips:** Glass-filled nylon. **Sights:** Smooth, no-snag, contoured slide and barrel top. **Features:** Aircraft quality 17-4 PH stainless steel. Inertia-operated firing pin.

Hammer fired double-action-only. Hammer automatically follows slide down to safety rest position after each shot, no manual safety needed. Magazine safety disconnector. Polished stainless. Introduced 1985. From L.W. Seecamp.

Price: **$425.00**

SEMMERLING LM-4 SLIDE-ACTION PISTOL

Caliber: 45 ACP, 4-shot magazine. **Barrel:** 2". **Weight:** 24 oz. **Length:** NA. **Grips:** NA. **Sights:** NA. **Features:** The Semmerling LM-4 is a super compact pistol employing a thumb activated slide mechanism (the slide is manually retracted between shots). From American Derringer Corp.

Price: **$2,635.00**

SIGARMS REVOLUTION PISTOLS

Caliber: 45 ACP, 8-shot magazine. **Barrel:** 5". **Weight:** 40.3 oz. **Length:** 8.65" overall. **Grips:** Checkered wood grips. **Sights:** Novak night sights. Blade front, drift adjustable rear for windage. **Features:** Single-action 1911. Hand-fitted dehorned stainless-steel frame and slide; match-grade barrel, hammer/sear set and trigger; 25-lpi front strap checkering, 20-lpi mainspring housing checkering. Beavertail grip safety with speed bump, extended thumb safety, firing pin safety and hammer intercept notch. Introduced 2005. XO series has contrast sights, Ergo Grip XT textured polymer grips. Target line features adjustable target night sights, match barrel, custom wood grips, non-railed frame in stainless or Nitron finishes. TTT series is two-tone 1911 with Nitron slide and black controls on stainless frame. Includes burled maple grips, adjustable combat night sights. STX line available from SIGARMS Custom Shop; two-tone 1911, non-railed, Nitron slide, stainless frame, burled maple grips. Polished cocking serrations, flat-top slide, magwell. Carry line has Novak night sights, lanyard attachment point, gray diamondwood or rosewood grips, 8+1 capacity. Compact series has 6+1 capacity, 7.7" OAL, 4.25" barrel, slim-profile wood grips, weighs 30.3 oz. RCS line (Revolution Compact SAS) is Customs Shop version with anti-snag dehorning. Stainless or Nitron finish, Novak night sights, slim-profile gray diamondwood or rosewood grips. 6+1 capacity. Imported from Germany by SIGARMS, Inc.

Price: Revolution Nitron finish, w/or w/o Picatinny rail **$1,069.00**
Price: Revolution Stainless, w/or w/o Picatinny rail **$1,050.00**
Price: Revolution XO Black **$890.00**
Price: Revolution XO Stainless, intr. 2006 . . . . **$860.00**
Price: Revolution Target Nitron, intr. 2006 . . . . **$1,100.00**
Price: Revolution TTT, intr. 2006 . . . . **$1,070.00**
Price: Revolution STX, intr. 2006 . . . . **$1,300.00**
Price: Revolution Carry Nitron, 4.25" barrel, intr. 2006 . . . . **$1,070.00**
Price: Revolution Compact, Nitron finish **$1,080.00**
Price: Revolution RCS, Nitron finish. **$1,150.00**

SIG-Sauer P245 Compact

SIG-Sauer P220

SIG-Sauer Pro 2009

SIG-Sauer P229 Sport

SIG-Sauer P232

SIGARMS P220 AUTO PISTOLS

Caliber: 45 ACP, (7- or 8-shot magazine). **Barrel:** 4.4". **Weight:** 27.8 oz. **Length:** 7.8" overall. **Grips:** Checkered black plastic. **Sights:** Blade front, drift adjustable rear for windage. Optional Siglite night sights. **Features:** Double action. Stainless-steel slide, Nitron finish, alloy frame, M1913 Picatinny rail; safety system of decocking lever, automatic firing pin safety block, safety intercept notch, and trigger bar disconnector. Squared combat-type trigger guard. Slide stays open after last shot. Introduced 1976. P220 SAS Anti-Snag has dehorned stainless steel slide, front Siglite Night Sight, rounded trigger guard, dust cover, Custom Shop wood grips. Equinox line is Custom Shop product with Nitron stainless-steel slide with a black hard-anodized alloy frame, brush-polished flats and nickel accents. Truglo tritium fiber-optic front sight, rear Siglite night sight, gray laminated wood grips with checkering and stippling. Imported from Germany by SIGARMS, Inc.

Price: P220R **$840.00**
Price: P220R Two-Tone, matte-stainless slide, black alloy frame. . . **$840.00**
Price: P220 Stainless **$935.00**
Price: P220 Crimson Trace, w/lasergrips **$1150.00**
Price: P220 SAS Anti-Snag **$1,000.00**
Price: P220 Two-Tone SAO, single action, , intr. 2006, from. **$929.00**
Price: P220R DAK (intr. 2006). **$840.00**
Price: P220R Equinox (intr. 2006). **$1,070.00**

SIGARMS P220 CARRY AUTO PISTOLS

Caliber: 45 ACP, 8-shot magazine. **Barrel:** 3.9". **Weight:** NA. **Length:** 7.1" overall. **Grips:** Checkered black plastic. **Sights:** Blade front, drift adjustable rear for windage. Optional Siglite night sights. **Features:** Similar to full-size P220, except is "Commander" size. Single stack, DA/SA operation, Nitron finish, Picatinny rail, and either post and dot contrast or 3-dot Siglite night sights. Introduced 2005. Imported from Germany by SIGARMS, Inc.

Price: P220 Carry, from **$840.00**
Price: P220 Carry Two-Tone, from **$915.00**
Price: P220 Carry Equinox, wood grips, two tone, from **$1,070.00**

SIG-Sauer P229 DA Auto Pistol

Similar to the P228 except chambered for 9mm Para. (10- or 15-round magazines), 40 S&W, 357 SIG (10- or 12-round magazines). Has 3.86" barrel, 7.1" overall length and 3.35" height. Weight is 32.4 oz. Introduced 1991. Frame made in Germany, stainless steel slide assembly made in U.S.; pistol assembled in U.S. From SIGARMS, Inc.

Price: P229R, from **$840.00**
Price: P229R Crimson Trace, w/lasergrips, from **$1,150.00**

SIG SAUER SP2022 PISTOLS

Caliber: 9mm Para., 357 SIG, 40 S&W, 10-, 12-, or 15-shot magazines. **Barrel:** 3.9". **Weight:** 30.2 oz. **Length:** 7.4" overall. **Grips:** Composite and rubberized one-piece. **Sights:** Blade front, rear adjustable for windage. Optional Siglite night sights. **Features:** Polymer frame, stainless steel slide; integral frame accessory rail; replaceable steel frame rails; left- or right-handed magazine release, two interchangeable grips . From SIGARMS, Inc.

Price: SP2009, Nitron finish, from **$640.00**

SIG-Sauer P226 Pistols

Similar to the P220 pistol except has 4.4" barrel, measures 7.7" overall, weighs 34 oz. Chambered in 9mm, 357 SIG, or 40 S&W. X-Five series has factory tuned single-action trigger, 5" slide and barrel, ergonomic wood Nill grips with beavertail, ambidextrous thumb safety and stainless slide and frame with magwell, low-profile adjustable target sights, front cocking serrations and a 25-meter factory test target. Imported from Germany by SIGARMS, Inc.

Price: P226R, Nitron finish, night sights. **$915.00**
Price: P226R Two Tone, Nitron/stainless finish **$969.00**
Price: P226 Stainless, from **$935.00**
Price: P226 X-Five **$2,500.00**
Price: P226 X-Five Tactical, Ilaflon finish, high cap, from **$1,500.00**

SIG-SAUER P232 PERSONAL SIZE PISTOL

Caliber: 380 ACP, 7-shot. **Barrel:** 3.6". **Weight:** 17.6-22.4 oz. **Length:** 6.6" overall. **Grips:** Checkered black composite. **Sights:** Blade front, rear adjustable for windage. **Features:** Double action/single action or DAO. Blowback operation, stationary barrel. Introduced 1997. Imported from Germany by SIGARMS, Inc.

Price: P232, blued **$519.00**
Price: P232 Stainless **$709.00**
Price: P232 Two-Tone. **$539.00**

SIG-SAUER P239 PISTOL

Caliber: 9mm Para., 8-shot, 357 SIG 40 S&W, 7-shot magazine. **Barrel:** 3.6". **Weight:** 25.2 oz. **Length:** 6.6" overall. **Grips:** Checkered black composite. **Sights:** Blade front, rear adjustable for windage. Optional Siglite night sights. **Features:** SA/DA or DAO; blackened stainless steel slide, aluminum alloy frame. Introduced 1996. Made in U.S.A. by SIGARMS, Inc.

Price: P239 . . . . **$739.00**
Price: P239 Two-Tone, w/night sights, ... **$895.00**
Price: P239 DAK, double action **$739.00**

SIG-SAUER Mosquito

Smith & Wesson M&P

Smith & Wesson 457 TDA

Smith & Wesson 908

Smith & Wesson 4013 TSW

Smith & Wesson 410 DA

Smith & Wesson 910 DA

SIG-SAUER MOSQUITO PISTOL

Caliber: 22LR, 10-shot magazine. **Barrel:** 3.9". **Weight:** 24.6 oz. **Length:** 7.2" overall. **Grips:** Checkered black composite. **Sights:** Blade front, rear adjustable for windage. **Features:** Blowback operated, fixed barrel, polymer frame, slide-mounted ambidextrous safety. Introduced 2005. Made in U.S.A. by SIGARMS, Inc.
Price: Mosquito, blued **$390.00**
Price: Mosquito w/threaded barrel, intr. 2006 . . . . **$500.00**
Price: Mosquito Combat Green. **$460.00**

SMITH & WESSON M&P AUTO PISTOLS

Caliber: 9mm, 40 S&W, 357 SIG. **Barrel:** 4.25". **Weight:** 24.25 oz. **Length:** 7.5" overall. **Grips:** One-piece Xenoy, wraparound with straight backstrap. **Sights:** Ramp dovetail mount front; tritium sights optional; Novak Lo-mount Carry rear. **Features:** Zytel polymer frame, embedded stainless steel chassis; stainless steel slide and barrel, stainless steel structural components, black Melonite finish, reversible magazine catch, 3 interchangeable palmswell grip sizes, universal rail, sear deactivation lever, internal lock system, magazine disconnect. Ships with 2 magazines. Internal lock models available. Overall height: 5.5"; width: 1.2"; sight radius: 6.4". Introduced 2006. Made in U.S.A. by Smith & Wesson.
Price: M&P 40 S&W, 15+1 . . . . **$695.00**
Price: M&P 9mm, 17+1 . . . . **NA**
Price: M&P 357 SIG, 15+1 . . . . **NA**

SMITH & WESSON MODEL 457 TDA AUTO PISTOL

Caliber: 45 ACP, 7-shot magazine. **Barrel:** 3-3/4". **Weight:** 29 oz. **Length:** 7-1/4" overall. **Grips:** One-piece Xenoy, wraparound with straight backstrap. **Sights:** Post front, fixed rear, 3-dot system. **Features:** Aluminum alloy frame, matte blue carbon steel slide; bobbed hammer; smooth trigger. Introduced 1996. Made in U.S.A. by Smith & Wesson.
Price: Model 457, black matte finish **$681.00**
Price: Model 457S, matte finish stainless **$710.00**

SMITH & WESSON MODEL 908 AUTO PISTOL

Caliber: 9mm Para., 8-shot magazine. **Barrel:** 3-1/2". **Weight:** 24 oz. **Length:** 6-13/16". **Grips:** One-piece Xenoy, wraparound with straight backstrap. **Sights:** Post front, fixed rear, 3-dot system. **Features:** Aluminum alloy frame, matte blue carbon steel slide; bobbed hammer; smooth trigger. Introduced 1996. Made in U.S.A. by Smith & Wesson.
Price: Model 908, black matte finish **$617.00**
Price: Model 908S, stainless matte finish **$642.00**
Price: Model 908S Carry Combo, with holster **$656.00**

SMITH & WESSON MODEL 4013 TSW AUTO

Caliber: 40 S&W, 9-shot magazine. **Barrel:** 3-1/2". **Weight:** 26.8 oz. **Length:** 6 3/4" overall. **Grips:** Xenoy one-piece wraparound. **Sights:** Novak 3-dot system. **Features:** Traditional double-action system; stainless slide, alloy frame; fixed barrel bushing; ambidextrous decocker; reversible magazine catch, equipment rail. Introduced 1997. Made in U.S.A. by Smith & Wesson.
Price: Model 4013 TSW **$1,021.00**

SMITH & WESSON MODEL 410 DA AUTO PISTOL

Caliber: 40 S&W, 10-shot magazine. **Barrel:** 4". **Weight:** 28.5 oz. **Length:** 7.5". **Grips:** One-piece Xenoy, wraparound with straight backstrap. **Sights:** Post front, fixed rear; 3-dot system. **Features:** Aluminum alloy frame; blued carbon steel slide; traditional double action with left-side slide-mounted decocking lever; Introduced 1996. Made in U.S.A. by Smith & Wesson.
Price: Model 410, blued/black matte finish **$681.00**
Price: Model 410, blued/black matte finish **$681.00**
Price: Model 410S, stainless matte finish **$702.00**
Price: Model 410S, w/Crimson Trace lasergrips **$938.00**

SMITH & WESSON MODEL 910 DA AUTO PISTOL

Caliber: 9mm Para., 10-shot magazine. **Barrel:** 4". **Weight:** 28 oz. **Length:** 7-3/8" overall. **Grips:** One-piece Xenoy, wraparound with straight backstrap. **Sights:** Post front with white dot, fixed 2-dot rear. **Features:** Alloy frame, blue carbon steel slide. Slide-mounted decocking lever. Introduced 1995.
Price: Model 910, black matte frame **$617.00**
Price: Model 910S, stainless matte frame **$632.00**

**Smith & Wesson
3913 LadySmith**

Springfield Armory XD

Springfield Armory XD

SMITH & WESSON MODEL 3913 TRADITIONAL DOUBLE ACTIONS

Caliber: 9mm Para., 8-shot magazine. **Barrel:** 3-1/2". **Weight:** 24.8 oz. **Length:** 6-3/4" overall. **Grips:** One-piece Delrin wraparound, textured surface. **Sights:** Post front with white dot, Novak LoMount Carry with two dots. **Features:** TSW has aluminum alloy frame, stainless slide. Bobbed hammer with no half-cock notch; smooth .304" trigger with rounded edges. Straight backstrap. Equipment rail. Extra magazine included. Introduced 1989. The 3913-LS Ladysmith has frame that is upswept at the front, rounded trigger guard. Comes in frosted stainless steel with matching gray grips. Grips are ergonomically correct for a woman's hand. Novak LoMount Carry rear sight adjustable for windage. Extra magazine included. Introduced 1990.

Price: 3913TSW **$876.00**
Price: 3913-LS **$901.00**

SMITH & WESSON MODEL SW1911 PISTOLS

Caliber: 45 ACP, 8 rounds. **Barrel:** 5". **Weight:** 39 oz. **Length:** 8.7". **Grips:** Wood or rubber. **Sights:** Novak Lo-Mount Carry, white dot front. **Features:** Large stainless frame and slide with matte finish, single-side external safety. **No. 108284** has adjustable target rear sight, ambidextrous safety levers, 20-lpi checkered front strap, comes with two 8-round magazines. **DK** model (Doug Koenig) also has oversized magazine well, Doug Koenig speed hammer, flat competition speed trigger with overtravel stop, rosewood grips with Smith & Wesson silver medallions, oversized magazine well, special serial number run. **No. 108295** has olive drab Crimson Trace lasergrips. **No. 108299** has carbon-steel frame and slide with polished flats on slide, standard GI recoil guide, laminated double-diamond walnut grips with silver Smith & Wesson medallions, adjustable target sights. **Tactical Rail No. 108293** has a Picatinny rail, black Melonite finish, Novak Lo-Mount Carry Sights, scandium alloy frame. **Tactical Rail Stainless** introduced 2006. **SW1911PD** gun is Commander size, scandium-alloy frame, 4.25" barrel, 8" OAL, 28.0 oz., non-reflective black matte finish. **Gunsite** edition has scandium alloy frame, beveled edges, solid match aluminum trigger, Herrett's logoed tactical oval walnut stocks, special serial number run, brass bead Novak front sight. **SC** model has 4.25" barrel, scandium alloy frame, stainless-steel slide, non-reflective matte finish.

Price: SW1911 No. 108282............................. **$1,008.00**
Price: SW1911 No. 108284............................. **$1,101.00**
Price: SW1911 DK **$1,274.00**
Price: SW1911 No. 108295............................. **$1,248.00**
Price: SW1911 No. 108299............................. **$1,047.00**
Price: SW1911PD Tactical Rail No. 108293, scandium frame ... **$1,120.00**
Price: SW1911PD Tactical Rail No. 108303, stainless frame.... **$1,057.00**
Price: SW1911PD, scandium frame **$1,080.00**
Price: SW1911PD Gunsite, intr. 2006..................... **$1,204.00**
Price: SW1911SC...................................... **$1,080.00**

SMITH & WESSON MODEL 4040PD

Caliber: 40 S&W, 7 rounds. **Barrel:** 3.5". **Weight:** 25.6 oz. **Length:** 6.9". **Grips:** Rubber. **Sights:** Novak Lo-Mount Carry, white dot front.
Price: Scandium alloy frame **$840.00**

SMITH & WESSON ENHANCED SIGMA SERIES DAO PISTOLS

Caliber: 9mm Para., 40 S&W; 10-, 16-shot magazine. **Barrel:** 4". **Weight:** 24.7 oz. **Length:** 7-1/4" overall. **Grips:** Integral. **Sights:** White dot front, fixed rear; 3-dot system. Tritium night sights available. **Features:** Ergonomic polymer frame; low barrel centerline; internal striker firing system; corrosion-resistant slide; Teflon-filled, electroless-nickel coated magazine, equipment rail. Introduced 1994. Made in U.S.A. by Smith & Wesson.
Price: **$409.00**

SMITH & WESSON MODEL CS9 CHIEF'S SPECIAL AUTO

Caliber: 9mm Para., 7-shot magazine. **Barrel:** 3". **Weight:** 20.8 oz. **Length:** 6-1/4" overall. **Grips:** Hogue wraparound rubber. **Sights:** White dot front, fixed 2-dot rear. **Features:** Traditional double-action trigger mechanism. Alloy frame, stainless slide. Ambidextrous safety. Introduced 1999. Made in U.S.A. by Smith & Wesson.
Price: Stainless **$777.00**

SMITH & WESSON MODEL CS45 CHIEF'S SPECIAL AUTO

Caliber: 45 ACP, 6-shot magazine. **Weight:** 23.9 oz. **Features:** Introduced 1999. Made in U.S.A. by Smith & Wesson.
Price: Stainless **$825.00**

SMITH & WESSON MODEL SW990L

Caliber: 9mm Para. 4" barrel, (10 rounds); 40 S&W 4-1/8" barrel; 45 ACP 4.25" barrel; adj. sights. **Features:** Traditional double action satin stainless, black polymer frame, equipment rail, Saf-T-Trigger, interchangeable backstrap.
Price: 9mm, 40 S&W **$729.00**
Price: 45 ACP **$773.00**
Price: Compact: 9mm, 40 S&W, 3.5" barrel, 23 oz.............. **$729.00**

SPRINGFIELD ARMORY XD POLYMER AUTO PISTOLS

Caliber: 9mm Para., 357 SIG, 40 S&W, 45 ACP, 45 GAP. **Barrel:** 3", 4", 5". **Weight:** 20.5-31 oz. **Length:** 6.26-8" overall. **Grips:** Textured polymer. **Sights:** Varies by model; Fixed sights are dovetail front and rear steel 3-dot units. **Features:** Three sizes in X-Treme Duty (XD) line: Sub-Compact (3" barrel), Service (4" barrel), Tactical (5" barrel). Three ported models available. Ergonomic polymer frame, hammer-forged barrel, no-tool disassembly, ambidextrous magazine release, visual/tactile loaded chamber indicator, visual/tactile striker status indicator, grip safety, XD gear system included. Introduced 2004. XD 45 introduced 2006. From Springfield Armory.

Price: Sub-Compact Black 9mm, fixed sights **$536.00**
Price: Sub-Compact Black 9mm/40 S&W, Neinie night sights **$626.00**
Price: Sub-Compact Bi-Tone 9mm/40 S&W, fixed sights **$566.00**
Price: Sub-Compact OD Green 9mm/40 S&W, fixed sights **$536.00**
Price: Service Black 9mm/40 S&W/357 SIG, fixed sights **$536.00**
Price: Service Black 45 ACP, fixed sights.................... **$559.00**
Price: Service Black 45 GAP, fixed sights **$536.00**
Price: Service Black 9mm/40 S&W, Neinie night sights **$626.00**
Price: Service Bi-Tone 9mm/40 S&W/357 SIG/45 GAP, fixed sights **$566.00**
Price: Service Bi-Tone 45 ACP, fixed sights.................... **$595.00**
Price: Service OD Green 9mm/40 S&W/357 SIG/45 GAP,
fixed sights **$536.00**
Price: V-10 Ported Black 9mm/40 S&W/357 SIG.............. **$566.00**
Price: Tactical Black 45 ACP, fixed sights................... **$595.00**
Price: Tactical Black 9mm/40 S&W/357 SIG, fixed sights **$566.00**
Price: Tactical Bi-Tone 45 ACP/45 GAP, fixed sights **$626.00/ $595.00**
Price: Tactical OD Green 9mm/40 S&W/357 SIG/45 GAP,
fixed sights **$566.00**
Price: Tactical OD Green 45 ACP, fixed sights................ **$595.00**

Springfield Armory 1911A1 Standard

Springfield Armory Full-Size 1911A1

Springfield Armory Micro-Compact

Springfield Armory TRP

SPRINGFIELD ARMORY CUSTOM LOADED FULL-SIZE 1911A1 AUTO PISTOL

Caliber: 9mm Para., 9-shot; 45 ACP, 7-shot. **Barrel:** 5". **Weight:** 30-42 oz. **Length:** 8.5" overall. **Grips:** Cocobolo, polymer. **Sights:** Fixed 3-dot system or adjustable. **Features:** Beveled magazine well; lowered and flared ejection port. All forged parts, including frame, barrel, slide. All new production. Introduced 1990. From Springfield Armory.

Price: Tactical Combat Black Stainless Steel, fixed sights **$904.00**
Price: Stainless Steel, fixed sights **$902.00**
Price: Service Model 5" Lightweight, bi-tone finish. **$934.00**
Price: Stainless Steel, adjustable target sights. **$966.00**
Price: Black Stainless, adjustable Bo-Mar rear, 3-dot tritium **$1,124.00**
Price: Stainless Steel 9mm, fixed combat sights **$976.00**

SPRINGFIELD ARMORY GI .45 1911-A1 AUTO PISTOLS

Caliber: 45 ACP; 6-, 7-, 13-shot magazines. **Barrel:** 3", 4", 5". **Weight:** 28-36 oz. **Length:** 5.5-8.5" overall. **Grips:** Checkered double-diamond walnut, "U.S" logo. **Sights:** Fixed GI style. **Features:** Similar to WWII GI-issue 45s at hammer, beavertail, mainspring housing. From Springfield Armory.

Price: GI .45 4" Lightweight Champion, 7+1, 28 oz. **$564.00**
Price: GI .45 5" High Capacity, 13+1, 36 oz. **$617.00**
Price: GI .45 5" OD Green, 7+1, 36 oz. **$564.00**
Price: GI .45 3" Micro Compact, 6+1, 32 oz. **$608.00**

SPRINGFIELD ARMORY MIL-SPEC 1911-A1 AUTO PISTOLS

Caliber: 38 Super, 9-shot magazines; 45 ACP, 7-shot magazines. **Barrel:** 5". **Weight:** 35.6-39 oz. **Length:** 8.5-8.625" overall. **Features:** Similar to GI 45s. From Springfield Armory.

Price: Mil-Spec Parkerized, 7+1, 35.6 oz. **$660.00**
Price: Mil-Spec Stainless Steel, 7+1, 36 oz. **$724.00**
Price: Mil-Spec 38 Super, Nickel finish, 9+1, 39 oz. **$1,254.00**

Springfield Armory Custom Loaded Champion 1911-A1 Pistol

Similar to standard 1911A1, slide and barrel are 4". 7.5" OAL. Available in 45 ACP only. Novak Night Sights. Delta hammer and cocobolo grips. Parkerized or stainless. Introduced 1989.

Price: Stainless, 34 oz. **$952.00**
Price: Lightweight, 28 oz **$913.00**

Springfield Armory Custom Loaded Ultra Compact Pistol

Similar to 1911A1 Compact, shorter slide, 3.5" barrel, 6+1, 7" OAL. Beavertail grip safety, beveled magazine well, fixed sights. Videki speed trigger, flared ejection port, stainless steel frame, blued slide, match grade barrel, rubber grips. Introduced 1996. From Springfield Armory.

Price: Stainless Steel **$952.00**

SPRINGFIELD ARMORY CUSTOM LOADED MICRO-COMPACT 1911A1 PISTOL

Caliber: 45 ACP, 6+1 capacity. **Barrel:** 3" 1:16 LH. **Weight:** 24-32 oz. **Length:** 4.7". **Grips:** Slimline cocobolo. **Sights:** Novak LoMount tritium. Dovetail front. **Features:** Aluminum hard-coat anodized alloy frame, forged steel slide, forged barrel, ambi-thumb safety, Extreme Carry Bevel dehorning. Lockable plastic case, 2 magazines.

Price: Bi-Tone Operator w/light rail. **$1,284.00**
Price: Lightweight Bi-Tone **$1,220.00**

SPRINGFIELD ARMORY CUSTOM LOADED LONG SLIDE 1911A1 PISTOL

Caliber: 45 ACP, 7+1 capacity. **Barrel:** 6" 1:16 LH. **Weight:** 41 oz. **Length:** 9.5". **Grips:** Slimline cocobolo. **Sights:** Dovetail front; fully adjustable target rear. **Features:** Longer sight radius, 7.9".

Price: Bi-Tone Operator w/light rail. **$1,097.00**

Springfield Armory TRP Pistols

Similar to 1911A1 except 45 ACP only, checkered front strap and main-spring housing, Novak Night Sight combat rear sight and matching dove-tailed front sight, tuned, polished extractor, oversize barrel link; lightweight speed trigger and combat action job, match barrel and bushing, extended ambidextrous thumb safety and fitted beavertail grip safety. Checkered cocobolo wood grips, comes with two Wilson 7-shot magazines. Frame is engraved "Tactical," both sides of frame with "TRP". Introduced 1998. TRP-Pro Model meets FBI specifications for SWAT Hostage Rescue Team. From Springfield Armory.

Price: Standard with Armory Kote finish **$1,606.00**
Price: Standard, stainless steel **$1,606.00**
Price: Standard with Operator Light Rail Armory Kote **$1,689.00**
Price: TRP-Pro, Armory Kote finish **$2,395.00**

Springfield Armory Loaded Operator 1911-A1 Pistol

Similar to Full-Size 1911A1, except light-mounting rail is forged into frame. From Springfield Armory.

Price: Loaded Full-Size MC Operator, 42 oz., 8.5" OAL **$1,254.00**
Price: TRP Light Rail Armory Kote, 42 oz. **$1,689.00**
Price: Micro Compact LW, w/XML Mini Light , 32 oz., 6.7 OAL . . **$1,284.00**

Springfield Armory Trophy Match 1911A1 Pistol

Similar to Full Size model, 5" match barrel and slide, fully adjustable sights. From Springfield Armory.

Price: Trophy Match 45 ACP, stainless **$1,452.00**

Taurus PT-22

Taurus PT-24

Taurus PT-92

Taurus PT-100

Taurus PT-132
Millennium Pro

Taurus PT-138
Millennium Pro

TAURUS MODEL PT1911 PISTOLS

Caliber: 45 ACP. **Barrel:** 5". **Weight:** 32 oz. **Length:** 8.75". **Grips:** Checkered wood. **Sights:** Adjustable Heinie rear, blade front. **Features:** SA/DA; Steel slide, alloy frame, ventilated trigger. Bumper pads on magazines. Introduced 2005. Imported from Brazil by Taurus International.
Price: Blued, 8+1 . . . . **$599.00**
Price: Stainless **$619.00**

TAURUS MODEL PT-22/PT-25 AUTO PISTOLS

Caliber: 22 LR, 8-shot (PT 22); 25 ACP, 9-shot (PT 25). **Barrel:** 2.75". **Weight:** 12.3 oz. **Length:** 5.25" overall. **Grips:** Smooth rosewood or mother-of-pearl. **Sights:** Fixed. **Features:** Double action. Tip-up barrel for loading, cleaning. Blue, nickel, duo-tone or blue with gold accents. Introduced 1992. Made in U.S.A. by Taurus International.
Price: 22 LR, 25 ACP, blue, nickel or with duo-tone finish with rosewood grips **$227.00**
Price: 22 LR, 25 ACP, blue with gold trim, rosewood grips **$242.00**
Price: 22 LR, 25 ACP, blue, nickel or duo-tone finish with checkered wood grips **$227.00**
Price: 22 LR, 25 ACP, blue with gold trim, mother-of-pearl grips . . **$258.00**

TAURUS MODEL PT-24/7

Caliber: 9mm, 40 S&W, 45 ACP. **Barrel:** 4". **Weight:** 27.2 oz. **Length:** 7-1/8". **Grips:** "Ribber" rubber-finned overlay on polymer. **Sights:** Adjustable. **Features:** SA/DA; accessory rail, four safeties, blue or stainless finish. One-piece guide rod, flush-fit magazine, flared bushingless barrel, Picatinny accessory rail, manual safety, user changeable sights, loaded chamber indicator, tuned ejector and lowered port, one piece guide rod and flat wound captive spring. Introduced 2003. Long Slide models have 5" barrels, measure 8-1/8" overall, weigh 27.2 oz. Imported from Brazil by Taurus International.
Price: 9BP, 9mm, blued, 10+1 or 17+1 . . . . **$485.00**
Price: 40BP, 40 S&W, blued, 10+1 or 15+1 . . . . **$485.00**
Price: 40SSP, 40 S&W, stainless slide, 10+1 or 15+1 . . . . **$499.00**
Price: 45BP, 45 ACP, blued, 10+1 or 12+1 . . . . **$485.00**
Price: Long Slide 40B, 40 S&W, blued, 10+1 or 15+1 . . . . **$485.00**
Price: Long Slide 45B, 45 ACP, blued, 10+1 or 12+1 . . . . **$485.00**
Price: Long Slide 9SS, 9mm, stainless, 10+1 or 17+1 . . . . **$499.00**

TAURUS MODEL PT-92 AUTO PISTOL

Caliber: 9mm Para., 10- or 17-shot mags. **Barrel:** 5". **Weight:** 34 oz. **Length:** 8.5" overall. **Grips:** Checkered rubber, rosewood, mother-of-pearl. **Sights:** Fixed notch rear. 3-dot sight system. Also offered with micrometer-click adjustable night sights. **Features:** Double action,
ambidextrous 3-way hammer drop safety, allows cocked & locked carry. Blue, stainless steel, blue with gold highlights, stainless steel with gold highlights, forged aluminum frame, integral key-lock. .22 LR conversion kit available. Imported from Brazil by Taurus International.
Price: Blued or Stainless . . . . **$602.00 to $664.00**

Taurus Model PT-99 Auto Pistol

Similar to PT-92, fully adjustable rear sight.
Price: Blue . . . . **$617.00 to $633.00**
Price: 22 Conversion kit for PT 92 and PT99
(includes barrel and slide) **$266.00**

TAURUS MODEL PT-100/101 AUTO PISTOL

Caliber: 40 S&W, 10- or 11-shot mags. **Barrel:** 5". **Weight:** 34 oz. **Length:** 8-1/2". **Grips:** Checkered rubber, rosewood, mother-of-pearl. **Sights:** 3-dot fixed or adjustable; night sights available. **Features:** Single/double action with three-position safety/decocker. Reintroduced in 2001. Imported by Taurus International.
Price: PT100 . . . . **$602.00 to $664.00**
Price: PT101, adjustable rear sight . . . . **$617.00 to $633.00**

TAURUS MODEL PT-111 MILLENNIUM PRO AUTO PISTOL

Caliber: 9mm Para., 10- or 12-shot mags. **Barrel:** 3.25". **Weight:** 18.7 oz. **Length:** 6-1/8" overall. **Grips:** Checkered polymer. **Sights:** 3-dot fixed; night sights available. Low profile, 3-dot combat. **Features:** Double action only, polymer frame, matte stainless or blue steel slide, manual safety, integral key-lock. Deluxe models with wood grip inserts.
Price: . . . . **$395.00 to $410.00**
Price: Titanium Slide. **$499.00**

TAURUS PT-132 MILLENNIUM PRO AUTO PISTOL

Caliber: 32 ACP, 10-shot mag. **Barrel:** 3.25". **Weight:** 18.7 oz. **Grips:** Polymer. **Sights:** 3-dot fixed; night sights available. **Features:** Double-action-only, polymer frame, matte stainless or blue steel slide, manual safety, integral key-lock action. Introduced 2001.
Price: . . . . **$395.00 to $410.00**

TAURUS PT-138 MILLENNIUM PRO SERIES

Caliber: 380 ACP, 10- or 12-shot mags. **Barrel:** 3.25". **Weight:** 18.7 oz. **Grips:** Polymer. **Sights:** Fixed 3-dot fixed. **Features:** Double-action-only, polymer frame, matte stainless or blue steel slide, manual safety, integral key-lock.
Price: . . . . **$395.00 to $410.00**

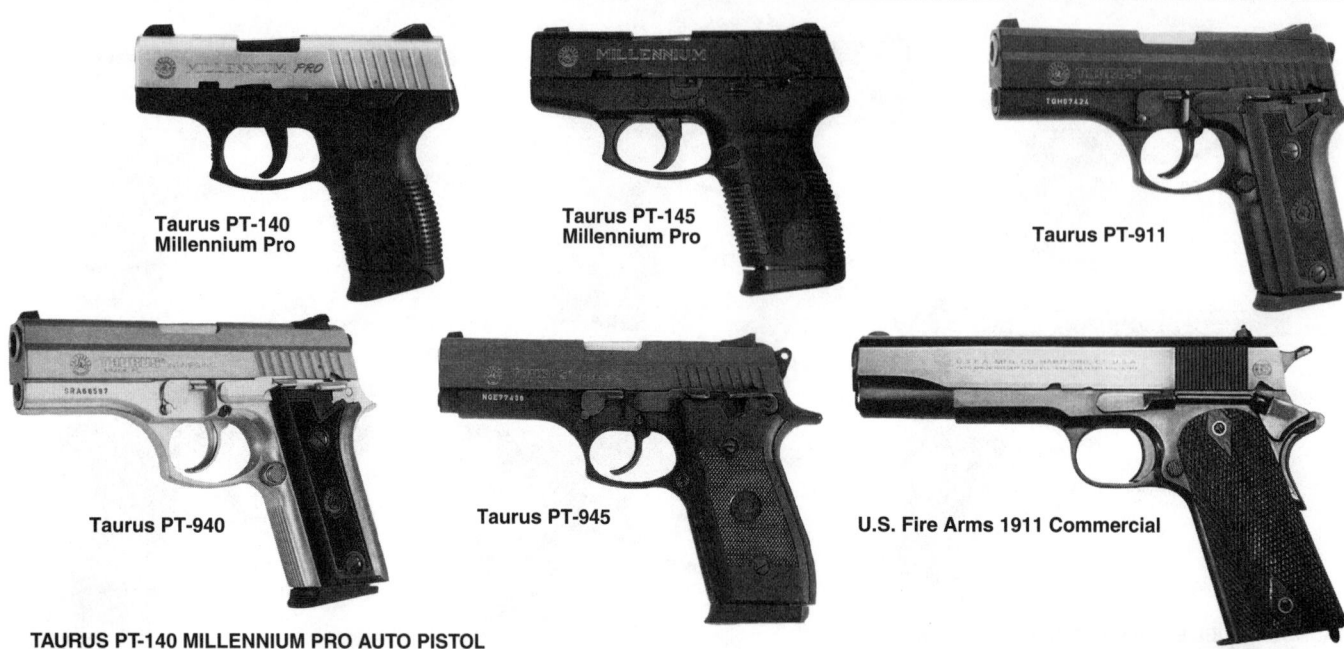

Taurus PT-140
Millennium Pro

Taurus PT-145
Millennium Pro

Taurus PT-911

Taurus PT-940

Taurus PT-945

U.S. Fire Arms 1911 Commercial

U.S. Fire Arms 1911 Military

TAURUS PT-140 MILLENNIUM PRO AUTO PISTOL

Caliber: 40 S&W, 10-shot mag. **Barrel:** 3.25". **Weight:** 18.7 oz. **Grips:** Checkered polymer. **Sights:** 3-dot fixed; night sights available. **Features:** Double action only; matte stainless or blue steel slide, black polymer frame, manual safety, integral key-lock action. From Taurus International.
Price: . . . . $410.00 to $425.00

TAURUS PT-145 MILLENNIUM AUTO PISTOL

Caliber: 45 ACP, 10-shot mag. **Barrel:** 3.27". **Weight:** 23 oz. **Stock:** Checkered polymer. **Sights:** 3-dot fixed; night sights available. **Features:** Double-action only, matte stainless or blue steel slide, black polymer frame, manual safety, integral key-lock. Compact model is 6+1 with a 3.25" barrel, weighs 20.8 oz. From Taurus International.
Price: PT-145, blued or stainless. . . . . $410.00 to $425.00
Price: PT-745 Compact, blued or stainless, intr. 2005 . . $410.00 to $425.00

TAURUS MODEL PT-911 AUTO PISTOL

Caliber: 9mm Para., 10-shot mag. **Barrel:** 4". **Weight:** 28.2 oz. **Length:** 7" overall. **Grips:** Checkered rubber, rosewood, mother-of-pearl. **Sights:** Fixed, 3-dot blue or stainless; night sights optional. **Features:** Double action, semi-auto ambidextrous 3-way hammer drop safety, allows cocked & locked carry. Blue, stainless steel, blue with gold highlights, or stainless steel with gold highlights, forged aluminum frame, integral key-lock.
Price: . . . . $547.00 to $625.00

TAURUS MODEL PT-940 AUTO PISTOL

Caliber: 40 S&W, 10-shot mag. **Barrel:** 3-5/8". **Weight:** 28.2 oz. **Length:** 7" overall. **Grips:** Checkered rubber, rosewood or mother-of-pearl. **Sights:** Fixed, 3-dot blue or stainless; night sights optional. **Features:** Double action, semi-auto ambidextrous 3-way hammer drop safety, allows cocked & locked carry. Blue, stainless steel, blue with gold highlights, or stainless steel with gold hightlights, forged aluminum frame, integral key-lock.
Price: . . . . $547.00 to $609.00

TAURUS MODEL PT-945/PT38S SERIES

Caliber: 45 ACP, 8-shot mag. **Barrel:** 4.25". **Weight:** 28.2/29.5 oz. **Length:** 7.48" overall. **Grips:** Checkered rubber, rosewood or mother-of-pearl. **Sights:** Fixed, 3-dot; night sights optional. **Features:** Double-action with ambidextrous 3-way hammer drop safety allows cocked & locked carry. Forged aluminum frame, PT-945C has ported barrel/slide. Blue, stainless, blue with gold highlights, stainless with gold highlights, integral key-lock. Introduced 1995. 38 Super line based on PT-945 frame introduced 2005. PT38S series is 10+1, 30 oz., 7.5" overall. Imported by Taurus International.
Price: PT-945. . . . . $586.00 to $648.00
Price: PT-38S . . . . $586.00 to $664.00

THOMPSON CUSTOM 1911A1 AUTOMATIC PISTOL

Caliber: 45 ACP, 7-shot magazine. **Barrel:** 4.3". **Weight:** 34 oz. **Length:** 8" overall. **Grips:** Checkered laminate grips with a Thompson bullet logo inlay. **Sights:** Front and rear sights are black with serrations and are dovetailed into the slide. **Features:** Machined from 420 stainless steel, matte finish. Thompson bullet logo on slide. Flared ejection port, angled front and rear serrations on slide, 20-lpi checkered mainspring housing and frontstrap. Adjustable trigger, combat hammer, stainless steel full-length recoil guide rod, extended beavertail grip safety; extended magazine release; checkered slide-stop lever. Made in U.S.A. by Kahr Arms.
Price: 1911CC (2006), stainless frame $775.00
Price: 1911TC, 5", 39 oz., 8.5" overall, stainless frame. $775.00
Price: 1911CCF (2006), 27 oz., aluminum frame $775.00
Price: 1911CAF, 5", 31.5 oz., 8.5" overall, aluminum frame $775.00

U.S. FIRE ARMS 1910 COMMERCIAL MODEL AUTOMATIC PISTOL

Caliber: 45 ACP, 7-shot magazine. **Barrel:** 5". **Weight:** NA. **Length:** NA. **Grips:** Browning original wide design, full checkered diamond walnut grips. **Sights:** Fixed. **Features:** High polish Armory Blue, fire blue appointments, 1905 patent dates, grip safety, small contoured checkered thumb safety and round 1905 fire blue hammer with hand cut checkering. Introduced 2006. Made in U.S.A. by United States Fire Arms Mfg. Co.
Price: $1,895.00

U.S. FIRE ARMS 1911 MILITARY MODEL AUTOMATIC PISTOL

Caliber: 45 ACP, 7-shot magazine. **Barrel:** 5". **Weight:** NA. **Length:** NA. **Grips:** Browning original wide design, full checkered diamond walnut grips. **Sights:** Fixed. **Features:** Military polish Armory Blue, fire blue appointments, 1905 patent dates, grip safety, small contoured checkered thumb safety and round 1905 fire blue hammer with hand cut checkering. Introduced 2006. Made in U.S.A. by United States Fire Arms Mfg. Co.
Price: $1,895.00

U.S. Fire Arms Super 38

U.S. Fire Arms Ace 22 LR

Walther PPK/S

Walther PPK

Walther P99

Walther P22

Wilkinson
Sherry

U.S. FIRE ARMS SUPER 38 AUTOMATIC PISTOL

Caliber: 38 Auto, 9-shot magazine. **Barrel:** 5". **Weight:** NA. **Length:** NA. **Grips:** Browning original wide design, full checkered diamond walnut grips. **Sights:** Fixed. **Features:** Armory blue, fire blue appointments, 1913 patent date, grip safety, small contoured checkered thumb safety and spur 1911 hammer with hand cut checkering. Supplied with two Super 38 Auto. mags. Super .38 roll mark on base. Introduced 2006. Made in U.S.A. by United States Fire Arms Mfg. Co.
Price: **$1,995.00**

U.S. FIRE ARMS ACE .22 LONG RIFLE AUTOMATIC PISTOL

Caliber: 22 LR, 10-shot magazine. **Barrel:** 5". **Weight:** NA. **Length:** NA. **Grips:** Browning original wide design, full checkered diamond walnut grips. **Sights:** Fixed. **Features:** Armory blue commercial finish, fire blue appointments, 1913 patent date, grip safety, small contoured checkered thumb safety and spur 1911 hammer with hand cut checkering. Supplied with two magazines. Ace roll mark on base. Introduced 2006. Made in U.S.A. by United States Fire Arms Mfg. Co.
Price: **$1,995.00**

WALTHER PPK/S AMERICAN AUTO PISTOL

Caliber: 380 ACP, 7-shot magazine. **Barrel:** 3.27". **Weight:** 23-1/2 oz. **Length:** 6.1" overall. **Stocks:** Checkered plastic. **Sights:** Fixed, white markings. **Features:** Double action; manual safety blocks firing pin and drops hammer; chamber loaded indicator on 32 and 380; extra finger rest magazine provided. Made in the United States. Introduced 1980.
Price: 380 ACP only, blue **$563.00**
Price: As above, 32 ACP or 380 ACP, stainless **$543.00**

Walther PPK American Auto Pistol

Similar to Walther PPK/S except weighs 21 oz., has 6-shot capacity. Made in the U.S. Introduced 1986.
Price: Stainless, 32 ACP or 380 ACP **$543.00**
Price: Blue, 380 ACP only **$543.00**

WALTHER P99 AUTO PISTOL

Caliber: 9mm Para., 9x21, 40 S&W,10-shot magazine. **Barrel:** 4". **Weight:** 25 oz. **Length:** 7" overall. **Grips:** Textured polymer. **Sights:** Blade front (comes with three interchangeable blades for elevation adjustment), micrometer rear adjustable for windage. **Features:** Double-action mechanism with trigger safety, decock safety, internal striker safety; chamber loaded indicator; ambidextrous magazine release levers; polymer frame with interchangeable backstrap inserts. Comes with two

magazines. Introduced 1997. Imported from Germany by Smith & Wesson U.S.A.
Price: **$665.00**

WALTHER P22 PISTOL

Caliber: 22 LR. **Barrel:** 3.4", 5". **Weight:** 19.6 oz. (3.4"), 20.3 oz. (5"). **Length:** 6.26", 7.83". **Grips:** NA. **Sights:** Interchangeable white dot, front, 2-dot adjustable, rear. **Features:** A rimfire version of the Walther P99 pistol, available in nickel slide with black frame, or green frame with black slide versions. Made in Germany and distributed in the U.S. by Smith & Wesson.
Price: From **$295.00**

WILKINSON SHERRY AUTO PISTOL

Caliber: 22 LR, 8-shot magazine. **Barrel:** 2-1/8". **Weight:** 9-1/4 oz. **Length:** 4-3/8" overall. **Grips:** Checkered black plastic. **Sights:** Fixed, groove. **Features:** Crossbolt safety locks the sear into the hammer. Available in all-blue finish or blue slide and trigger with gold frame. Introduced 1985.
Price: **$280.00**

WILKINSON LINDA AUTO PISTOL

Caliber: 9mm Para. **Barrel:** 8-5/16". **Weight:** 4 lbs., 13 oz. **Length:** 12-1/4" overall. **Grips:** Checkered black plastic pistol grip, walnut forend. **Sights:** Protected blade front, aperture rear. **Features:** Semi-auto only. Straight blowback action. Crossbolt safety. Removable barrel. From Wilkinson Arms.
Price: **$675.00**

Includes models suitable for several forms of competition and other sporting purposes.

Baer 1911 Ultimate Master

Baer 1911 Bullseye Wadcutter

Colt Gold Cup Trophy

Colt Special Combat Government

BAER 1911 ULTIMATE MASTER COMBAT PISTOL

Caliber: 38 Super, 400 Cor-Bon 45 ACP (others available), 10-shot magazine. **Barrel:** 5", 6"; Baer NM. **Weight:** 37 oz. **Length:** 8.5" overall. **Grips:** Checkered cocobolo. **Sights:** Baer dovetail front, low-mount Bo-Mar rear with hidden leaf. **Features:** Full-house competition gun. Baer forged NM blued steel frame and double serrated slide; Baer triple port, tapered cone compensator; fitted slide to frame; lowered, flared ejection port; Baer reverse recoil plug; full-length guide rod; recoil buff; beveled magazine well; Baer Commander hammer, sear; Baer extended ambidextrous safety, extended ejector, checkered slide stop, beavertail grip safety with pad, extended magazine release button; Baer speed trigger. Made in U.S.A. by Les Baer Custom, Inc.

Price: 45 ACP Compensated	**$2,599.00**
Price: 38 Super Compensated	**$2,789.00**
Price: 6" 45 ACP	**$2,586.00**
Price: 6" 38 Super	**$2,780.00**
Price: 6" 400 Cor-Bon	**$2,668.00**
Price: 5" 45 ACP	**$2,540.00**
Price: 5" 38 Super	**$2,699.00**
Price: 5" 400 Cor-Bon	**$2,589.00**

BAER 1911 NATIONAL MATCH HARDBALL PISTOL

Caliber: 45 ACP, 7-shot magazine. **Barrel:** 5". **Weight:** 37 oz. **Length:** 8.5" overall. **Grips:** Checkered walnut. **Sights:** Baer dovetail front with undercut post, low-mount Bo-Mar rear with hidden leaf. **Features:** Baer NM forged steel frame, double serrated slide and barrel with stainless bushing; slide fitted to frame; Baer match trigger with 4-lb. pull; polished feed ramp, throated barrel; checkered front strap, arched mainspring housing; Baer beveled magazine well; lowered, flared ejection port; tuned extractor; Baer extended ejector, checkered slide stop; recoil buff. Made in U.S.A. by Les Baer Custom, Inc.

Price: **$1,689.00**

Baer 1911 Bullseye Wadcutter Pistol

Similar to National Match Hardball except designed for wadcutter loads only. Polished feed ramp and barrel throat; Bo-Mar rib on slide; full length recoil rod; Baer speed trigger with 3-1/2-lb. pull; Baer deluxe hammer and sear; Baer beavertail grip safety with pad; flat mainspring housing checkered 20 lpi. Blue finish; checkered walnut grips. Made in U.S.A. by Les Baer Custom, Inc.

Price: From **$1,710.00**
Price: With 6" barrel, from **$1,865.00**

BF CLASSIC PISTOL

Caliber: Customer orders chamberings. **Barrel:** 8-15" Heavy Match Grade with 11-degree target crown. **Weight:** Approx 3.9 lbs. **Length:** from 16" overall. **Grips:** Thumbrest target style. **Sights:** Bo-Mar/Bond ScopeRib I Combo with hooded post front adjustable for height and width, rear notch available in .032", .062", .080" and .100" widths; 1/2-MOA clicks. **Features:** Hand fitted and headspaced, drilled and tapped for scope mount. Etched receiver; gold-colored trigger. Introduced 1988. Made in U.S.A. by E. Arthur Brown Co. Inc.

Price: **$789.00**

COLT GOLD CUP

Caliber: 45 ACP. **Barrel:** 5". **Weight:** 39 oz. **Sights:** Dovetail front, BoMar-style rear; or Colt adjustable staked front. **Features:** Stainless or blue finish; adjustable trigger; furnished with 7- and 8-round magazines.

Price: Blued **$1,300.00**
Price: Stainless **$1,400.00**

COLT MODEL 1991/2991

Caliber: 45 ACP, 38 Super. **Barrel:** 5". **Weight:** 39 oz. **Sight:** Fixed white dot style. **Features:** Stainless or blue finish; furnished with 7-round magazines.

Price: . . . . **$764.00 to $866.00**

COLT GOLD CUP MODEL O PISTOL

Caliber: 45 ACP, 8-shot magazine. **Barrel:** 5", with new design bushing. **Weight:** 39 oz. **Length:** 8-1/2". **Grips:** Checkered rubber composite with silver-plated medallion. **Sights:** Patridge-style front, Bo-Mar-style rear adjustable for windage and elevation, sight radius 6-3/4". **Features:** Arched or flat housing; wide, grooved trigger with adjustable stop; ribbed-top slide, hand fitted, with improved ejection port.

Price: Blue **$992.00**
Price: Stainless **$1,039.00**

COLT SPECIAL COMBAT GOVERNMENT

Caliber: 45 ACP, 38 Super. **Barrel:** 5". **Weight:** 39 oz. **Length:** 8-1/2". **Grips:** Rosewood w/double diamond checkering pattern. **Sights:** Clark dovetail, front; Bo-Mar adjustable, rear. **Features:** A competition-ready pistol with enhancements such as skeletonized trigger, upswept grip safety, custom tuned action, polished feed ramp. Blue or satin nickel finish. Introduced 2003. Made in U.S.A. by Colt's Mfg. Co.

Price: **$1,498.00**

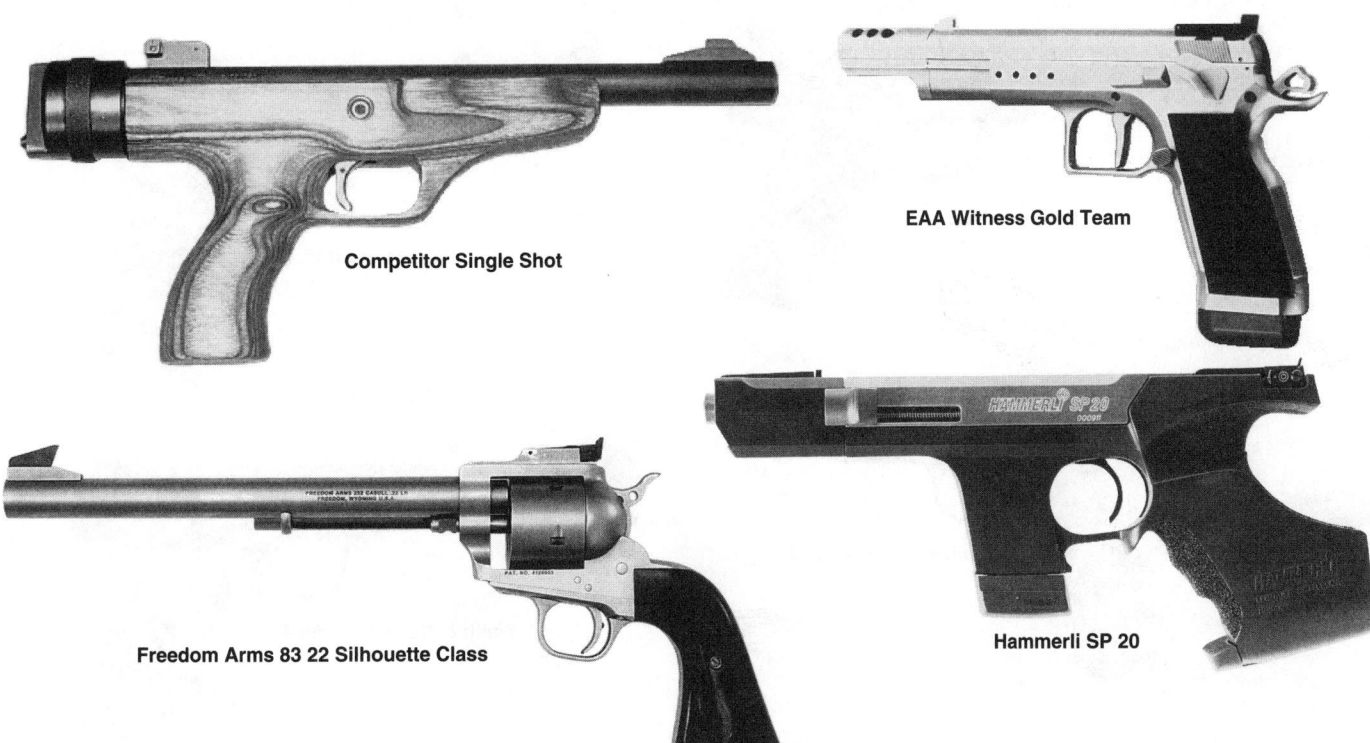

Competitor Single Shot

EAA Witness Gold Team

Freedom Arms 83 22 Silhouette Class

Hammerli SP 20

COMPETITOR SINGLE SHOT PISTOL

Caliber: 22 LR through 50 Action Express, including belted magnums. **Barrel:** 14" standard; 10.5" silhouette; 16" optional. **Weight:** About 59 oz. (14" bbl.). **Length:** 15.12" overall. **Grips:** Ambidextrous; synthetic (standard) or laminated or natural wood. **Sights:** Ramp front, adjustable rear. **Features:** Rotary canon-type action cocks on opening; cammed ejector; interchangeable barrels, ejectors. Adjustable single stage trigger, sliding thumb safety and trigger safety. Matte blue finish. Introduced 1988. From Competitor Corp., Inc.

Price: 14", standard calibers, synthetic grip **$480.00**

CZ 75 CHAMPION COMPETITION PISTOL

Caliber: 9mm Para., 40 S&W, 16-shot mag. **Barrel:** 4.4". **Weight:** 2.5 lbs. **Length:** 9.4" overall. **Grips:** Black rubber. **Sights:** Blade front, fully adjustable rear. **Features:** Single-action trigger mechanism; three-port compensator (40 S&W, 9mm have two port) full-length guide rod; extended magazine release; ambidextrous safety; flared magazine well; fully adjustable match trigger. Introduced 1999. Imported from the Czech Republic by CZ-USA.

Price: Dual-tone finish **$1,646.00**

EAA WITNESS GOLD TEAM AUTO

Caliber: 9mm Para., 9x21, 38 Super, 40 S&W, 45 ACP. **Barrel:** 5.1". **Weight:** 44 oz. **Length:** 10.5" overall. **Grips:** Checkered walnut, competition-style. **Sights:** Square post front, fully adjustable rear. **Features:** Triple-chamber cone compensator; competition SA trigger; extended safety and magazine release; competition hammer; beveled magazine well; beavertail grip. Hand-fitted major components. Hard chrome finish. Match-grade barrel. From E.A.A. Custom Shop. Introduced 1992. From European American Armory.

Price: **$1,699.00**

ENTRÉPRISE TOURNAMENT SHOOTER MODEL I

Caliber: 45 ACP, 10-shot mag. **Barrel:** 6". **Weight:** 40 oz. **Length:** 8.5" overall. **Grips:** Black ultra-slim double diamond checkered synthetic. **Sights:** Dovetailed Patridge front, adjustable rear. **Features:** Oversized magazine release button; flared magazine well; fully machined parallel slide rails; front and rear slide serrations; serrated top of slide; stainless ramped bull barrel with fully supported chamber; full-length guide rod

with plug; stainless firing pin; match extractor; polished ramp; tuned match extractor; black oxide. Introduced 1998. Made in U.S.A. by Entréprise Arms.

Price: **$2,300.00**
Price: TSMIII (Satin chrome finish, two-piece guide rod) **$2,700.00**

FREEDOM ARMS MODEL 83 22 FIELD GRADE SILHOUETTE CLASS

Caliber: 22 LR, 5-shot cylinder. **Barrel:** 10". **Weight:** 63 oz. **Length:** 15.5" overall. **Grips:** Black Micarta. **Sights:** Removable Patridge front blade; Iron Sight Gun Works silhouette rear, click adjustable for windage and elevation (optional adj. front sight and hood). **Features:** Stainless steel, matte finish, manual sliding-bar safety system; dual firing pins, lightened hammer for fast lock time, pre-set trigger stop. Introduced 1991. Made in U.S.A. by Freedom Arms.

Price: Silhouette Class **$1,913.95**

FREEDOM ARMS MODEL 83 CENTERFIRE SILHOUETTE MODELS

Caliber: 357 Mag., 41 Mag., 44 Mag.; 5-shot cylinder. **Barrel:** 10", 9" (357 Mag. only). **Weight:** 63 oz. (41 Mag.). **Length:** 15.5", 14-1/2" (357 only). **Grips:** Pachmayr Presentation. **Sights:** Iron Sight Gun Works silhouette rear sight, replaceable adjustable front sight blade with hood. **Features:** Stainless steel, matte finish, manual sliding-bar safety system. Made in U.S.A. by Freedom Arms.

Price: Silhouette Models **$1,683.95**

HAMMERLI SP 20 TARGET PISTOL

Caliber: 22 LR, 32 S&W. **Barrel:** 4.6". **Weight:** 34.6-41.8 oz. **Length:** 11.8" overall. **Grips:** Anatomically shaped synthetic Hi-Grip available in five sizes. **Sights:** Integral front in three widths, adjustable rear with changeable notch widths. **Features:** Extremely low-level sight line; anatomically shaped trigger; adjustable JPS buffer system for different recoil characteristics. Receiver available in red, blue, gold, violet or black. Introduced 1998. Imported from Switzerland by Larry's Guns of Maine.

Price: Hammerli 22 LR **$1,450.00**
Price: Hammerli 32 S&W **$1,560.00**

HAMMERLI X-ESSE SPORT PISTOL

An all-steel .22 LR target pistol with a Hi-Grip in a new anatomical shape and an adjustable hand rest. Made in Switzerland. Introduced 2003.

Price: **$750.00**

High Standard Trophy

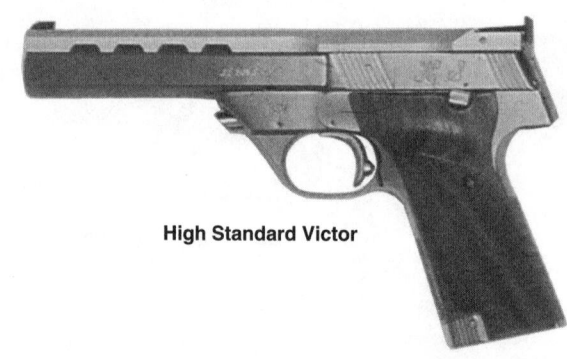

High Standard Victor

Kimber Super Match II

Smith & Wesson Model 41

HIGH STANDARD SUPERMATIC TROPHY TARGET PISTOL

Caliber: 22 LR, 9-shot mag. **Barrel:** 5.5" bull or 7.25" fluted. **Weight:** 44-46 oz. **Length:** 9.5-11.25" overall. **Stock:** Checkered hardwood with thumbrest. **Sights:** Undercut ramp front, frame-mounted micro-click rear adjustable for windage and elevation; drilled and tapped for scope mounting. **Features:** Gold-plated trigger, slide lock, safety-lever and magazine release; stippled front grip and backstrap; adjustable trigger and sear. Barrel weights optional. From High Standard Manufacturing Co., Inc.

Price: 5.5" barrel, adjustable sights. **$795.00**
Price: 7.25", adjustable sights. **$845.00**

HIGH STANDARD VICTOR TARGET PISTOL

Caliber: 22 LR, 10-shot magazine. **Barrel:** 4-1/2" or 5-1/2"; push-button takedown. **Weight:** 46 oz. **Length:** 9.5" overall. **Stock:** Checkered hardwood with thumbrest. **Sights:** Undercut ramp front, micro-click rear adjustable for windage and elevation. Also available with scope mount, rings, no sights. **Features:** Full-length vent rib. Gold-plated trigger, slide lock, safety-lever and magazine release; stippled front grip and backstrap; polished slide; adjustable trigger and sear. Comes with barrel weight. From High Standard Manufacturing Co., Inc.

Price: 4.5" or 5.5" barrel, universal scope base **$745.00**

KIMBER SUPER MATCH II

Caliber: 45 ACP, 8-shot magazine. **Barrel:** 5". **Weight:** 38 oz. **Length:** 8.7" overall. **Grips:** Rosewood double diamond. **Sights:** Blade front, Kimber fully adjustable rear. **Features:** Guaranteed shoot 1" group at 25 yards. Stainless steel frame, black KimPro slide; two-piece magazine well; premium aluminum match-grade trigger; 30 lpi front strap checkering; stainless match-grade barrel; ambidextrous safety; special Custom Shop markings. Introduced 1999. Made in U.S.A. by Kimber Mfg., Inc.

Price: **$1,994.00**

KORTH MATCH REVOLVER

Caliber: 357 Mag., 38 Special, 32 S&W Long, 9mm Para., 22 WMR, 22 LR. **Barrel:** 5-1/4", 6". **Grips:** Adjustable match of oiled walnut with matte finish. **Sights:** Fully adjustable rear sight leaves (width of sight notch: 3.4mm, 3.5mm, 3.6mm); undercut Patridge, front. **Trigger:** Equipped with machined trigger shoe. Interchangeable caliber cylinders available as well as a variety of finishes. Made in Germany.

Price: From **$7,650.00**

RUGER MARK III STANDARD AUTOLOADING PISTOL

Caliber: 22 LR, 10-shot magazine. **Barrel:** 4-3/4", 5-1/2", 6", or 6-7/8". **Weight:** 35 oz. (4-3/4" bbl.). **Length:** 9" (4-3/4" bbl.). **Grips:** Checkered composition grip panels. **Sights:** Fixed, wide blade front, fixed rear. **Features:** Updated design of original Standard Auto and Mark II series. Standard models have lighter barrels. Target models have cocobolo grips; bull, target, competition, and hunter barrels; and adjustable sights. Introduced 2005.

Price: MKIII4, MKIII6 (blued) **$322.00**
Price: MKIII512 (blued) **$382.00**
Price: KMKIII512 (stainless) **$483.00**
Price: MKIII678 (blued) **$382.00**
Price: KMKIII678GC (stainless slabside barrel) **$555.00**
Price: KMKIII678GH (stainless fluted barrel) **$567.00**

RUGER MARK III TARGET MODEL AUTOLOADING PISTOL

Caliber: 22 LR, 10-shot magazine. **Barrel:** 5-1/2" to 6-7/8". **Weight:** 41 to 45 oz. **Length:** 9.75" to 11-1/8" overall. **Grips:** Checkered cocobolo. **Sights:** .125" blade front, micro-click rear, adjustable for windage and elevation, loaded chamber indicator; integral lock, magazine disconnect. Plastic case with lock included. Mark II series introduced 1982, discontinued 2004. Mark III introduced 2005.

Price: MKIII512 (bull barrel, blued) **$382.00**
Price: KMKIII512 (bull barrel, stainless) **$483.00**
Price: MKIII678 (blued Target barrel, 6-7/8") **$382.00**
Price: KMKIII678GC (stainless slabside barrel) **$555.00**
Price: KMKIII678GH (stainless fluted barrel) **$567.00**

SMITH & WESSON MODEL 41 TARGET

Caliber: 22 LR, 10-shot clip. **Barrel:** 5.5", 7". **Weight:** 41 oz. (5-1/2" barrel). **Length:** 10-1/2" overall (5-1/2" barrel). **Grips:** Checkered walnut with modified thumbrest, usable with either hand. **Sights:** 1/8" Patridge on ramp base; micro-click rear adjustable for windage and elevation. **Features:** 3/8" wide, grooved trigger; adjustable trigger stop drilled and tapped.

Price: S&W Bright Blue, either barrel **$1,115.00**

Smith & Wesson Model 22A

Smith & Wesson Model 22S

Springfield Armory 1911A1 Trophy Match

STI Executive

STI Eagle 5.0

STI Trojan 6-inch

SMITH & WESSON MODEL 22A PISTOLS

Caliber: 22 LR, 10-shot magazine. **Barrel:** 4", 5.5" bull. **Weight:** 28-39 oz. **Length:** 9-1/2" overall. **Grips:** Dymondwood® with ambidextrous thumbrests and flared bottom or rubber soft touch with thumbrest. **Sights:** Patridge front, fully adjustable rear. **Features:** Sight bridge with Weaver-style integral optics mount; alloy frame, stainless barrel and slide; blue/black finish. Introduced 1997. The **22S** is similar to the Model 22A except has stainless steel frame. Introduced 1997. Made in U.S.A. by Smith & Wesson.

Price: No. 107400, 4" light barrel, 28 oz.. . . . . **$308.00**
Price: No. 107410, 5.5" bull barrel, 32 oz.. . . . . **$340.00**
Price: No. 107412, 5.5" bull barrel, 32 oz., rubber grips **$249.00**
Price: No. 107426, 5.5" barrel, HiViz front sight, 39 oz. **$429.00**
Price: No. 107430, 7" light barrel, HiViz front sight, 39 oz.. . . . . . . **$386.00**
Price: No. 107431, 5.5" bull barrel, target wood grip, 39 oz.. . . . . . . **$407.00**
Price: No. 107435, 5.5" barrel, camo finish. **$386.00**
Price: 22S No. 107300, 5.5" light barrel **$416.00**

SPRINGFIELD ARMORY LEATHAM LEGEND TGO SERIES PISTOLS

Three models of 5" barrel, 45 ACP 1911 pistols built for serious competition. TGO 1 has deluxe low mount Bo-Mar rear sight, Dawson fiber optics front sight, 3.5 lb. trigger pull.
Price: TGO 1 . . . . **$2,999.00**

Springfield Armory Trophy Match Pistol

Similar to Springfield Armory's Full Size model, but designed for bullseye and action shooting competition. Available with a Service Model 5" frame with matching slide and barrel in 5" and 6" lengths. Fully adjustable sights, checkered frame front strap, match barrel and bushing. In 45 ACP only. From Springfield Inc.
Price: **$1,248.00**

STI EAGLE 5.0, 6.0 PISTOL

Caliber: 9mm, 9x21, 38 & 40 Super, 40 S&W, 10mm, 45 ACP, 10-shot magazine. **Barrel:** 5", 6" bull. **Weight:** 34.5 oz. **Length:** 8.62" overall. **Grips:** Checkered polymer. **Sights:** STI front, Novak or Heine rear. **Features:** Standard frames plus 7 others; adjustable match trigger; skeletonized hammer; extended grip safety with locator pad. Introduced 1994. Made in U.S.A. by STI International.
Price: . . . . (5.0 Eagle) **$1,794.00**, (6.0 Eagle) **$1,894.00**

STI EXECUTIVE PISTOL

Caliber: 40 S&W. **Barrel:** 5" bull. **Weight:** 39 oz. **Length:** 8-5/8". **Grips:** Gray polymer. **Sights:** Dawson fiber optic, front; STI adjustable rear. **Features:** Stainless mag. well, front and rear serrations on slide. Made in U.S.A. by STI.
Price: **$2,389.00**

STI TROJAN

Caliber: 9mm, 38 Super, 40S&W, 45 ACP. **Barrel:** 5", 6". **Weight:** 36 oz. **Length:** 8.5". **Grips:** Rosewood. **Sights:** STI front with STI adjustable rear. **Features:** Stippled front strap, flat top slide, one-piece steel guide rod.
Price: (Trojan 5") **$1,024.00**
Price: (Trojan 6", not available in 38 Super) **$1,344.00**

Includes models suitable for hunting and competitive courses of fire, both police and international.

Charter Arms Bulldog

Charter Arms Off Duty

Charter Arms Undercover

Charter Arms Mag Pug

Comanche III

Dan Wesson Firearms Alaskan Guide Special

ARMSPORT MODEL 4540 REVOLVER
Caliber: 38 Special. **Barrel:** 4". **Weight:** 32 oz. **Length:** 9" overall. **Sights:** Fixed rear, blade front. **Features:** Ventilated rib; blued finish. Imported from Argentina by Armsport Inc.
Price: **$140.00**

CHARTER ARMS BULLDOG REVOLVER
Caliber: 44 Special. **Barrel:** 2.5". **Weight:** NA. **Sights:** Blade front, notch rear. **Features:** 6-round cylinder, soft-rubber pancake-style grips, shrouded ejector rod, wide trigger and hammer spur. American made by Charter Arms, distributed by MKS Supply.
Price: Blued **$324.00**
Price: Stainless **$347.00**
Price: Police Bulldog, .38 Special, 4" barrel, 24 oz. **$299.00**

CHARTER ARMS OFF DUTY REVOLVER
Caliber: 38 Special. **Barrel:** 2". **Weight:** 12.5 oz. **Sights:** Blade front, notch rear. **Features:** 5-round cylinder, aluminum casting, DAO. American made by Charter Arms, distributed by MKS Supply.
Price: Aluminum **$353.00**

CHARTER ARMS UNDERCOVER REVOLVER
Caliber: 38 Special. **Barrel:** 2". **Weight:** 16 oz. **Sights:** Blade front, notch rear. **Features:** 6-round cylinder. American made by Charter Arms, distributed by MKS Supply.
Price: Blued **$279.00**
Price: Blued DAO **$279.00**
Price: Stainless **$299.00**
Price: Stainless DAO **$299.00**

CHARTER ARMS MAG PUG REVOLVER
Caliber: 357 Magnum. **Barrel:** 2.2". **Weight:** 23 oz. **Sights:** Blade front, notch rear. **Features:** 5-round cylinder. American made by Charter Arms, distributed by MKS Supply.
Price: Blued **$325.00**
Price: Stainless **$335.00**

COLT SINGLE-ACTION ARMY
Caliber: 32-20, 38 Special, 357 Magnum, 38-40, 44-4-, 44 Special, 45 Long Colt. **Barrel:** 4.7 5", 5.5", 7.5". **Weight:** 40-44 oz. **Sights:** Blade front, notch rear. **Features:** Available in black powder and sheriff's models; nickel, blued or case-hardened frame; 6-round cylinder.
Price: . . . . (Blued) **$1,380.00**; (Stainless) **$1,530.00**

COMANCHE I, II, III DA REVOLVERS
Features: Adjustable sights. Blue or stainless finish. Distributed by SGS Importers.
Price: I 22 LR, 6" bbl., 9-shot, blue **$249.95**
Price: I 22LR, 6" bbl., 9-shot, stainless **$274.95**
Price: II 38 Special, 2" bbl., 6-shot, blue, intr. 2006 . . . . **$258.95**
Price: II 38 Special, 4" bbl., 6-shot, stainless **$249.95**
Price: III 357 Mag, 3" bbl., 6-shot, blue **$266.95**
Price: III 357 Mag. 2" bbl., 6-shot, blue **$274.95**
Price: II 38 Special, 3" bbl., 6-shot, stainless steel **$266.95**

DAN WESSON FIREARMS ALASKAN GUIDE SPECIAL
Caliber: 445 SuperMag; also chambers and fires 44 Magnum, 44 Special, 6 shots. **Sights:** Blade front, adjustable rear. **Barrel:** Compensated 4" vent heavy barrel assembly. **Weight:** 54.4 oz. **Length:** 11.7". **Features:** Stainless steel with baked on, non-glare, matte black coating, special laser engraving. Made in U.S.A. by Dan Wesson Firearms, distributed by CZ-USA.
Price: **$1,295.00**

DAN WESSON FIREARMS VH8 445 SUPERMAG
Caliber: 445 SuperMag; also chambers and fires 44 Magnum, 44 Special, 6 shots. **Sights:** Blade front, adjustable rear. **Barrel:** 8" full-length underlug. **Weight:** 54.4 oz. **Length:** 14.6". **Features:** Stainless-steel frame and barrel. Interchangeable barrels. Made in U.S.A. by Dan Wesson Firearms, distributed by CZ-USA.
Price: **$1,070.00**

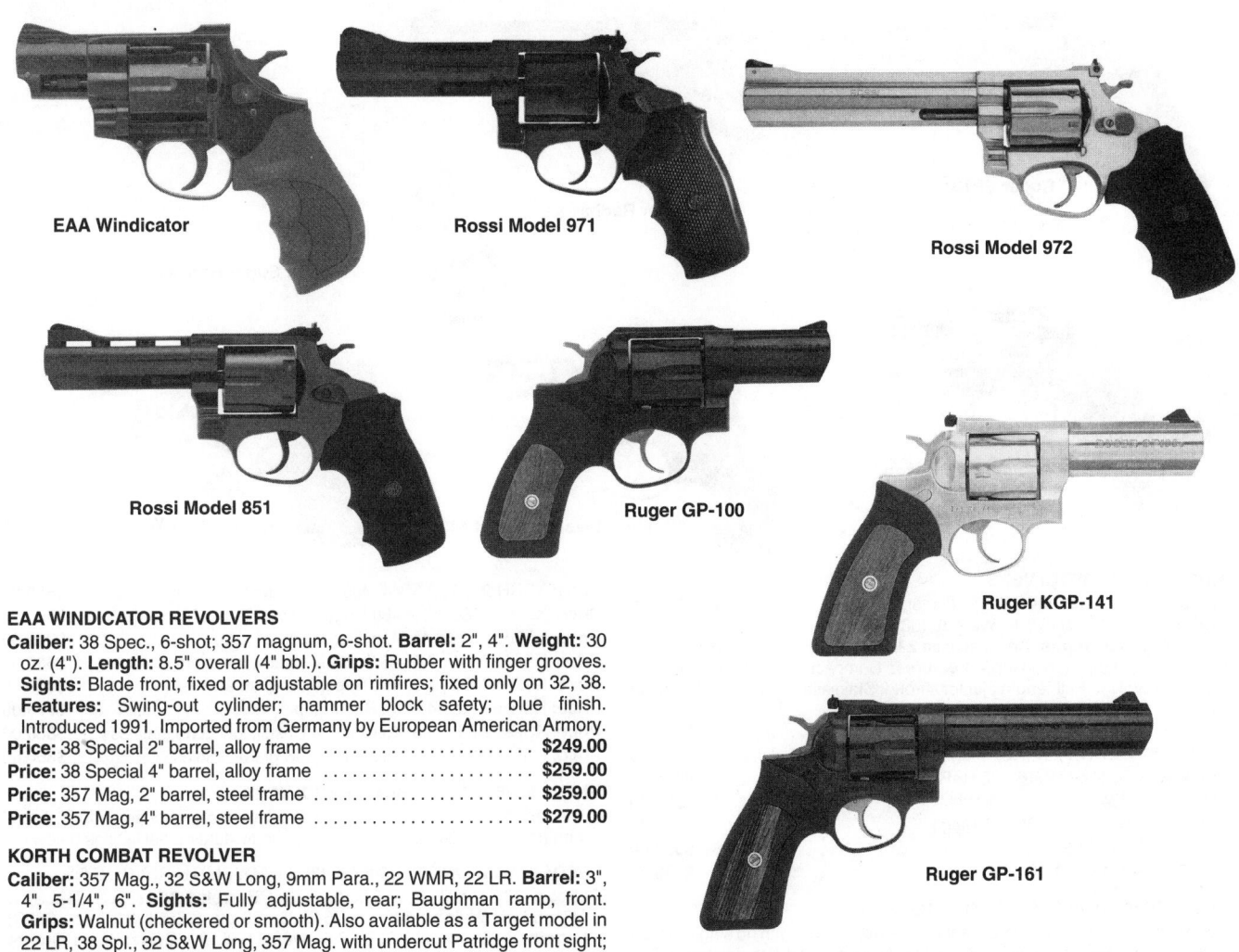

EAA Windicator

Rossi Model 971

Rossi Model 972

Rossi Model 851

Ruger GP-100

Ruger KGP-141

Ruger GP-161

EAA WINDICATOR REVOLVERS
Caliber: 38 Spec., 6-shot; 357 magnum, 6-shot. **Barrel:** 2", 4". **Weight:** 30 oz. (4"). **Length:** 8.5" overall (4" bbl.). **Grips:** Rubber with finger grooves. **Sights:** Blade front, fixed or adjustable on rimfires; fixed only on 32, 38. **Features:** Swing-out cylinder; hammer block safety; blue finish. Introduced 1991. Imported from Germany by European American Armory.
Price: 38 Special 2" barrel, alloy frame **$249.00**
Price: 38 Special 4" barrel, alloy frame **$259.00**
Price: 357 Mag, 2" barrel, steel frame **$259.00**
Price: 357 Mag, 4" barrel, steel frame **$279.00**

KORTH COMBAT REVOLVER
Caliber: 357 Mag., 32 S&W Long, 9mm Para., 22 WMR, 22 LR. **Barrel:** 3", 4", 5-1/4", 6". **Sights:** Fully adjustable, rear; Baughman ramp, front. **Grips:** Walnut (checkered or smooth). Also available as a Target model in 22 LR, 38 Spl., 32 S&W Long, 357 Mag. with undercut Patridge front sight; fully adjustable rear. Made in Germany. Imported by Korth USA.
Price: From **$7,203.00**

KORTH TROJA REVOLVER
Caliber: .357 Mag. **Barrel:** 6". **Finish:** Matte blue. **Grips:** Smooth, oversized finger contoured walnut. Introduced 2003. Imported from Germany by Korth USA.
Price: From **$5,593.00**

ROSSI MODEL 351/352 REVOLVERS
Caliber: 38 Special +P, 5-shot. **Barrel:** 2". **Weight:** 24 oz. **Length:** 6-1/2" overall. **Grips:** Rubber. **Sights:** Blade front, notch rear. **Features:** Patented key-lock Taurus Security System; forged steel frame. Introduced 2001. Made in Brazil by Amadeo Rossi. Imported by BrazTech/Taurus.
Price: Model 351 (blued finish) **$313.00**
Price: Model 352 (stainless finish) **$362.00**

ROSSI MODEL 461/462 REVOLVERS
Caliber: 357 Magnum +P, 6-shot. **Barrel:** 2". **Weight:** 26 oz. **Length:** 6.5" overall. **Grips:** Rubber. **Sights:** Fixed. **Features:** Single/ double action. Patented key-lock Taurus Security System; forged steel frame. Introduced 2001. Made in Brazil by Amadeo Rossi. Imported by BrazTech/Taurus.
Price: Model 461 (blued finish) **$313.00**
Price: Model 462 (stainless finish) **$362.00**

ROSSI MODEL 971/972 REVOLVERS
Caliber: 357 Magnum +P, 6-shot. **Barrel:** 4", 6". **Weight:** 32 oz. **Length:** 8.5" or 10.5" overall. **Grips:** Rubber. **Sights:** Blade front, adjustable rear.

Features: Single/double action. Patented key-lock Taurus Security System; forged steel frame. Introduced 2001. Made in Brazil by Amadeo Rossi. Imported by BrazTech/Taurus.
Price: Model 971 (blued finish, 4" bbl.) **$362.00**
Price: Model 972 (stainless steel finish, 6" bbl.). **$410.00**

Rossi Model 851
Similar to Model 971/972, chambered for 38 Special +P. Blued finish, 4" barrel. Introduced 2001. Made in Brazil by Amadeo Rossi. From BrazTech/Taurus.
Price: **$313.00**

RUGER GP-100 REVOLVERS
Caliber: 38 Spec. +P, 357 Mag., 6-shot. **Barrel:** 3", 3" full shroud, 4", 4" full shroud, 6", 6" full shroud. **Weight:** 3" barrel-35 oz., 3" full shroud-36 oz., 4" barrel-37 oz., 4" full shroud-38 oz. **Sights:** Fixed; adjustable on 4" full shroud, all 6" barrels. **Grips:** Ruger Santoprene Cushioned Grip with Goncalo Alves inserts. **Features:** Uses action, frame features of both the Security-Six and Redhawk revolvers. Full length, short ejector shroud. Satin blue and stainless steel.
Price: GPF-141 (357, 4" full shroud, adj. sights, blue) **$557.00**
Price: GPF-161 (357, 6" full shroud, adj. sights, blue), 46 oz. **$557.00**
Price: GPF-840 (38 Special, 4" half shroud, blued) **$552.00**
Price: GPF-841 38 Special, 4" full shroud) **$552.00**
Price: KGP-141 (357, 4" full shroud, adj. sights, stainless) **$615.00**
Price: KGP-161 (357, 6" full shroud, adj. sights, stainless) 46 oz. . . **$615.00**
Price: KGPF-331 (357, 3" full shroud, stainless) **$597.00**

Ruger SP101

Ruger Redhawk

Ruger Super Redhawk

Smith & Wesson Model 36LS

Smith & Wesson Model 442

Smith & Wesson Model 638

RUGER SP101 REVOLVERS

Caliber: 22 LR, 32 H&R Mag., 6-shot; 38 Spec. +P, 357 Mag., 5-shot. **Barrel:** 2-1/4", 3-1/16", 4". **Weight:** (38 & 357 mag models) 2-1/4"-25 oz.; 3-1/16"-27 oz. **Sights:** Adjustable on 22, 32, fixed on others. **Grips:** Ruger Cushioned Grip with inserts. **Features:** Compact, small frame, double-action revolver. Full-length ejector shroud. Stainless steel only. Introduced 1988.

Price: KSP-241X (4" heavy bbl., 22 LR), 34 oz. **$505.00**
Price: KSP-321X (2-1/4", 357 Mag.) **$530.00**
Price: KSP-3231X (3-1/16", 32 H&R), 30 oz. **$530.00**
Price: KSP-3241X (32 Mag., 4" bbl.) **$530.00**
Price: KSP-331X (3-1/16", 357 Mag.) **$495.00**
Price: KSP-821X (2-1/4", 38 Spec.) **$530.00**
Price: KSP-831X (3-1/16", 38 Spec.) **$530.00**

Ruger SP101 Double-Action-Only Revolver

Similar to standard SP101 except double-action-only with no single-action sear notch. Spurless hammer, floating firing pin and transfer bar safety system. Available with 2-1/4" barrel in 357 Magnum. Weighs 25 oz., overall length 7.06". Natural brushed satin, high-polish stainless steel. Introduced 1993.
Price: KSP321XL (357 Mag.) **$495.00**

RUGER REDHAWK

Caliber: 44 Rem. Mag., 6-shot. **Barrel:** 5-1/2", 7-1/2". **Weight:** About 54 oz. (7-1/2" bbl.). **Length:** 13" overall (7-1/2" barrel). **Grips:** Square butt cushioned grip panels. **Sights:** Interchangeable Patridge-type front, rear adjustable for windage and elevation. **Features:** Stainless steel, brushed satin finish, blued ordnance steel. 9-1/2" sight radius. Introduced 1979.
Price: KRH-44, stainless, 7-1/2" barrel **$730.00**
Price: KRH-44R, stainless, 7-1/2" barrel w/scope mount **$779.00**
Price: KRH-445, stainless, 5-1/2" barrel **$730.00**
Price: RH-445, blued, 5-1/2" barrel **$730.00**

RUGER SUPER REDHAWK REVOLVER

Caliber: 44 Rem. Mag., 45 Colt, 454 Casull, 480 Ruger 6-shot. **Barrel:** 2.5", 5.5", 7.5", 9.5". **Weight:** About 54 oz. (7.5" bbl.). **Length:** 13" overall (7.5" barrel). **Grips:** Square butt cushioned grip panels, Hogue Tamer Monogrip. **Features:** Similar to standard Redhawk except has heavy extended frame with Ruger Integral Scope Mounting System on wide topstrap. Wide hammer spur lowered for better scope clearance. Incorporates mechanical design features and improvements of GP-100. Ramp front sight base has Redhawk-style Interchangeable Insert sight blades, adjustable rear sight. Satin stainless steel and low-glare stainless finishes. Introduced 1987.

Price: KSRH-2454 , 2.5" 44 Mag, Hogue Tamer Monogrip **$860.00**
Price: KSRH-2480 , 2.5" 480 Ruger, Hogue Tamer Monogrip **$860.00**
Price: KSRH-7, 7.5" 44 Mag, Ruger grip **$779.00**
Price: KSRH-7454 , 7.5" 45 Colt/454 Casull, low glare stainless . . **$860.00**
Price: KSRH-7480 , 7.5" 480 Ruger, low glare stainless **$860.00**
Price: KSRH-9 , 9" 44 Mag, Ruger grip **$779.00**
Price: KSRH-9454 , 9.5" 45 Colt/454 Casull, low glare stainless . . **$860.00**
Price: KSRH-9480 , 9.5" 480 Ruger, low glare stainless **$860.00**

SMITH & WESSON J-FRAME REVOLVERS

The smallest S&W wheelguns come in a variety of chamberings, barrel lengths, and materials, as noted in the individual model listings below.

SMITH & WESSON 36LS/60LS/642LS LADYSMITH REVOLVERS

Caliber: .38 Special +P, 357 Mag., 5-shot. **Barrel:** 1-7/8" (36LS, 642LS); 2-1/8" (60LS) **Weight:** 14.5 oz. (642LS); 20 oz. (36LS); 21.5 oz. (60LS); **Length:** 6.25" overall (36LS); 6.6" overall (60LS); . **Grips:** Wood. **Sights:** Black blade, serrated ramp front, fixed notch rear. **Features:** 36/60LS models have a Chiefs Special-style frame. 642LS has Centennial-style frame, frosted matte finish, smooth combat wood grips. Introduced 1996. Comes in a fitted carry/storage case. Introduced 1989. Made in U.S.A. by Smith & Wesson.

Price: Model 36LS, 38+P, carbon steel frame **$596.00**
Price: Model 60LS, 357 Mag, matte stainless frame **$652.00**
Price: Model 642LS, 38+P, alloy frame, titanium cylinder **$664.00**

SMITH & WESSON MODEL 37/442/637/638/642 AIRWEIGHT REVOLVERS

Caliber: 38 Special +P, 5-shot. **Barrel:** 1-7/8". **Weight:** 15 oz. (37, 442); 20 oz. (3); 21.5 oz. (); **Length:** 6-3/8" overall. **Grips:** Soft rubber. **Sights:** Fixed, serrated ramp front, square notch rear. **Features:** Aluminum-alloy frames. Models 37, 637; Chiefs Special-style frame with exposed hammer. Introduced 1996. Models 442, 642; Centennial-style frame, enclosed hammer. Model 638, Bodyguard style, shrouded hammer. Comes in a fitted carry/storage case. Introduced 1989. Made in U.S.A. by Smith & Wesson.

Price: Model 37, glass-beaded black finish **$573.00**
Price: Model 442, blue/black finish, enclosed hammer, DA only . . . **$480.00**
Price: Model 637, matte silver finish **$457.00**
Price: Model 637 Carry Combo, with holster **$470.00**
Price: Model 637 w/Crimson Trace Lasergrip **$706.00**
Price: Model 638, matte silver finish, shrouded hammer **$480.00**
Price: Model 642, matte silver finish, DA only, introduced 1996 . . . **$476.00**
Price: Model 642 w/Crimson Trace Lasergrip **$706.00**

**Smith & Wesson
Model 60 Chief's Special**

**Smith & Wesson
Model 317 AirLite**

Smith & Wesson Model 340

**Smith & Wesson
Model 340 PD Airlite Sc**

**Smith & Wesson Model 360 PD
Airlite SC Chief's Special**

Smith & Wesson Model 386

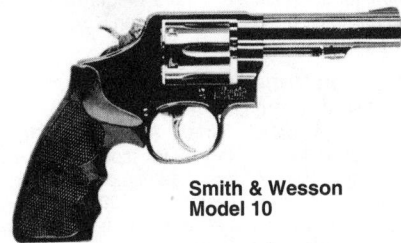

**Smith & Wesson
Model 10**

SMITH & WESSON MODEL 60 CHIEF'S SPECIAL

Caliber: 357 Magnum, 38 Special +P, 5-shot. **Barrel:** 2-1/8", 3" or 5". **Weight:** 22.5 oz. (2-1/8" barrel). **Length:** 6-5/8 overall (2-1/8" barrel). **Grips:** Rounded butt synthetic grips. **Sights:** Fixed, serrated ramp front, square notch rear. **Features:** Stainless steel construction, satin finish, internal lock. Introduced 1965. The 5-inch-barrel model has target semi-lug barrel, rosewood grip, red ramp front sight, adjustable rear sight. Made in U.S.A. by Smith & Wesson.
Price: 2-1/8" barrel, intr. 2005 . . . . **$623.00**
Price: 3" barrel, 7.5" OAL, 24 oz. **$661.00**
Price: 5" semi-lug barrel, 9-3/8" OAL, 30.5 oz. **$704.00**

SMITH & WESSON MODEL 317 AIRLITE REVOLVERS

Caliber: 22 LR, 8-shot. **Barrel:** 1-7/8", 3". **Weight:** 10.5 oz. **Length:** 6.25" overall (1-7/8" barrel). **Grips:** Rubber. **Sights:** Serrated ramp front, fixed notch rear. **Features:** Aluminum alloy, carbon and stainless steels, Chiefs Special-style frame with exposed hammer. Smooth combat trigger. Clear Cote finish. Introduced 1997. Made in U.S.A. by Smith & Wesson.
Price: Model 317, 1-7/8" barrel **$633.00**
Price: Model 317 w/HiViz front sight, 3" barrel, 7.25 OAL **$691.00**

SMITH & WESSON MODEL 340/340PD AIRLITE SC CENTENNIAL

Caliber: 357 Magnum, 38 Spec. +P, 5-shot. **Barrel:** 1-7/8". **Weight:** 12 oz. **Length:** 6-3/8" overall (1-7/8" barrel). **Grips:** Rounded butt rubber. **Sights:** Black blade front, rear notch **Features:** Centennial-style frame, enclosed hammer. Internal lock. Matte silver finish. Scandium alloy frame, titanium cylinder, stainless steel barrel liner. Made in U.S.A. by Smith & Wesson.
Price: Model 340 . . . . **$879.00**
Price: Model 340PD, red ramp front **$905.00**
Price: Model 340PD, HiViz front **$921.00**

SMITH & WESSON MODEL 351PD REVOLVER

Caliber: 22 Mag., 7-shot. **Barrel:** 1-7/8". **Weight:** 10.6 oz. **Length:** 6.25" overall (1-7/8" barrel). **Sights:** HiViz front sight, rear notch. **Grips:** Wood. **Features:** Seven-shot, aluminum-alloy frame. Chiefs Special-style frame with exposed hammer. Nonreflective matte-black finish. Internal lock. Made in U.S.A. by Smith & Wesson.
Price: **$679.00**

SMITH & WESSON MODEL 360/360PD AIRLITE CHIEF'S SPECIAL

Caliber: 357 Magnum, 38 Spec. +P, 5-shot. **Barrel:** 1-7/8". **Weight:** 12 oz. **Length:** 6-3/8" overall (1-7/8" barrel). **Grips:** Rounded butt rubber. **Sights:** Black blade front, fixed rear notch. **Features:** Chiefs Special-style frame with exposed hammer. Internal lock. Scandium alloy frame, titanium cylinder, stainless steel barrel. Made in U.S.A. by Smith & Wesson.
Price: Model 360 . . . . **$858.00**
Price: Model 360PD, red ramp front sight **$885.00**
Price: Model 360PD w/HiViz front sight **$901.00**

SMITH & WESSON MODEL 640 CENTENNIAL DA ONLY

Caliber: 357 Mag., 38 Spec. +P, 5-shot. **Barrel:** 2-1/8". **Weight:** 23 oz. **Length:** 6-3/4 overall. **Grips:** Uncle Mike's Boot grip. **Sights:** Serrated ramp front, fixed notch rear. **Features:** Stainless steel. Fully concealed hammer, snag-proof smooth edges. Internal lock. Introduced 1995 in 357 Magnum.
Price: **$690.00**

SMITH & WESSON MODEL 649 BODYGUARD REVOLVER

Caliber: 357 Mag., 38 Spec. +P, 5-shot. **Barrel:** 2-1/8". **Weight:** 23 oz. **Length:** 6-5/8" overall. **Grips:** Uncle Mike's Combat. **Sights:** Black pinned ramp front, fixed notch rear. **Features:** Stainless steel construction, satin finish. Internal lock. Bodyguard style, shrouded hammer. Made in U.S.A. by Smith & Wesson.
Price: **$684.00**

SMITH & WESSON K-FRAME/L-FRAME REVOLVERS

These mid-size S&W wheelguns come in a variety of chamberings, barrel lengths, and materials, as noted in the individual model listings below. 17 variations for 2006.

SMITH & WESSON MODEL 10 REVOLVER

Caliber: 38 Spec.+P, 6-shot. **Barrel:** 4". **Weight:** 36 oz. **Length:** 8-7/8" overall. **Grips:** Soft rubber; square butt. **Sights:** Fixed; black blade front, square notch rear. Blued carbon steel frame.
Price: Blue **$572.00**

SMITH & WESSON MODEL 64/67 REVOLVERS

Caliber: 38 Spec. +P, 6-shot. **Barrel:** 3". **Weight:** 33 oz. **Length:** 8-7/8" overall. **Grips:** Soft rubber. **Sights:** Fixed, 1/8" serrated ramp front, square notch rear. Model 67 (**Weight:** 36 oz. **Length:** 8-7/8") similar to Model 64 except for adjustable sights. **Features:** Satin finished stainless steel, square butt.
Price: Model 64, 3" barrel **$612.00**
Price: Model 64, 4" barrel, Uncle Mike's rubber grip, 36 oz. **$583.00**
Price: Model 67, 4" barrel, adjustable rear sight, red ramp front . . . **$674.00**

Smith & Wesson Model 21

Smith & Wesson Model 625

SMITH & WESSON MODEL 386

Caliber: 357 Magnum, 38 Spec. +P, 7-shot. **Barrel:** 3-1/8". **Weight:** 18.5 oz. **Length:** 8-1/8" overall. **Grips:** Rubber. **Sights:** Adjustable, HiViz front. **Features:** Scandium alloy frame, titanium cylinder, stainless steel barrel liner. Internal lock. Made in U.S.A. by Smith & Wesson.
Price: Matte silver finish **$920.00**

SMITH & WESSON MODEL 520

Caliber: 357 Magnum, 38 Spec. +P, 7-shot. **Barrel:** 4". **Weight:** 37.9 oz. **Length:** 8-7/8". **Grips:** Wood. **Sights:** Adjustable target rear, HiViz front. **Features:** Carbon steel frame, titanium cylinder. Updated L-frame replacement for discontinued K-frame Model 19. Internal lock. Introduced 2005. Made in U.S.A. by Smith & Wesson.
Price: Blue/black finish **$731.00**

SMITH & WESSON MODEL 617 REVOLVERS

Caliber: 22 LR, 6- or 10-shot. **Barrel:** 4". **Weight:** 41 oz. (4" barrel). **Length:** 9-1/8" (4" barrel). **Grips:** Soft rubber. **Sights:** Patridge front, adjustable rear. Drilled and tapped for scope mount. **Features:** Stainless steel with satin finish; 4" has .312" smooth trigger, .375" semi-target hammer; 6" has either .312" combat or .400" serrated trigger, .375" semi-target or .500" target hammer; 8-3/8" with .400" serrated trigger, .500" target hammer. Introduced 1990.
Price: 4" barrel, ... **$742.00**
Price: 6" barrel, 11-1/8" overall length, 45 oz.. . . . . **$751.00 to $770.00**

SMITH & WESSON MODELS 619/620 REVOLVERS

Caliber: 38 Special +P; 357 Mag., 7 rounds. **Barrel:** 4". **Weight:** 37.5 oz. **Length:** 9-1/2". **Grips:** Rubber. **Sights:** Integral front blade, fixed rear notch on the 619; adjustable white-outline target style rear, red ramp front on 620. **Features:** Replaces Models 65 and 66. Two-piece semi-lug barrel. Satin stainless frame and cylinder. Made in U.S.A. by Smith & Wesson.
Price: **$646.00**
Price: **$703.00**

SMITH & WESSON MODEL 686/686 PLUS REVOLVERS

Caliber: 357 Mag., 38 S&W Special; 6 rounds. **Barrel:** 2.5", 4", 6". **Weight:** 35 oz. (2.5" barrel). **Length:** 7-1/2", (2.5" barrel). **Grips:** Rubber. **Sights:** White outline adjustable rear, red ramp front. **Features:** Satin stainless frame and cylinder. Plus series guns have 7-shot cylinders. Introduced 1996. Powerport (PP) has Patridge front, adjustable rear sight. Introduced early 1980s. Made in U.S.A. by Smith & Wesson.
Price: 2.5" barrel, 6 rounds **$700.00**
Price: 4" barrel, 40 oz., 9-5/8" OAL. **$728.00**
Price: 6" barrel, 44 oz., 12" OAL. **$735.00**
Price: Plus, 2.5" barrel, 7 rounds **$727.00**
Price: Plus, 4" barrel, 7 rounds, 9-5/8" OAL **$752.00**
Price: Plus, 6" barrel, 7 rounds, 12" OAL **$764.00**
Price: PP, 6" barrel, 6 rounds, 11-3/8" OAL **$784.00**

SMITH & WESSON N-FRAME REVOLVERS

These large-frame S&W wheelguns come in a variety of chamberings, barrel lengths, and materials, as noted in the individual model listings below. 18 major variations for 2006.

SMITH & WESSON MODEL 21

Caliber: 44 Special, 6-round. **Barrel:** 4" tapered. **Weight:** NA. **Length:** NA. **Grips:** Smooth wood. **Sights:** Pinned half-moon service front; service rear. **Features:** Carbon steel frame, blued finish.
Price: **$855**

SMITH & WESSON MODEL 29 50TH ANNIVERSARY REVOLVER

Caliber: 44 Mag, 6-round. **Barrel:** 6.5". **Weight:** 48.5 oz. **Length:** 12". **Grips:** Cocobolo. **Sights:** Adjustable white-outline rear, red ramp front. **Features:** Carbon steel frame, polished-blued finish. Introduced 2005. Includes 24 carat gold-plated anniversary logo on frame, cleaning kit with screwdriver, mahogany presentation case, square-butt frame, serrated trigger. Original Model 29 made famous by "Dirty Harry" character created in 1971 by Clint Eastwood.
Price: Dealer pricing, no MSRP . . . . **NA**

SMITH & WESSON MODEL 325PD/329PD/357PD AIRLITE REVOLVERS

Caliber: 41 Mag. (357PD); 44 Spec., 44 Mag. (329PD); 45 ACP (325PD); 6-round. **Barrel:** 2-3/4" (325PD). **Weight:** 21.5 oz. (325PD, 2-3/4" barrel). **Length:** 7-1/4" (325PD, 2-3/4" barrel). **Grips:** Wood. **Sights:** Adj. rear, HiViz orange-dot front. **Features:** Scandium alloy frame, titanium cylinder. 4" model has HiViz green front sight and Ahrends finger-groove wood grips. Weighs 26.5 oz.
Price: 325PD, 2-3/4" barrel. **$986.00**
Price: 325PD , 4" barrel, Ahrends wood grips **$1,008.00**
Price: 329PD, 4" barrel, 9.5" OAL, 26 oz.. . . . . **$1,008.00**
Price: 357PD, 4" barrel, 9.5" OAL, 27.5 oz. **$1,008.00**

SMITH & WESSON MODEL 625 REVOLVERS

Caliber: 45 ACP, 6-shot. **Barrel:** 4", 5". **Weight:** 43 oz. (4" barrel). **Length:** 9-3/8" overall (4" barrel). **Grips:** Soft rubber; wood optional. **Sights:** Patridge front on ramp, S&W micrometer click rear adjustable for windage and elevation. **Features:** Stainless steel construction with .400" semi-target hammer, .312" smooth combat trigger; full lug barrel. Glass beaded finish. Introduced 1989. "Jerry Miculek" Professional (JMP) Series has .265"-wide grooved trigger, special wooden Miculek Grip, five full moon clips, gold bead Patridge front sight on interchangeable front sight base, bead blast finish. Unique serial number run. Mountain Gun has 4" tapered barrel, drilled and tapped, Hogue Rubber Monogrip, pinned black ramp front sight, micrometer click-adjustable rear sight, satin stainless frame and barrel, weighs 39.5 oz.
Price: 625, 4" or 5" barrel **$858.00**
Price: 625 JMP, 4" barrel, 9-3/9" OAL, 43 oz. **$887.00**
Price: 625 Mountain Gun, dealer pricing, no MSRP . . . . **NA**

SMITH & WESSON MODEL 629 REVOLVERS

Caliber: 44 Magnum, 44 S&W Special, 6-shot. **Barrel:** 4", 5", 6-1/2". **Weight:** 41.5 oz. (4" bbl.). **Length:** 9-5/8" overall (4" bbl.). **Grips:** Soft rubber; wood optional. **Sights:** 1/8" red ramp front, white outline rear, internal lock, adjustable for windage and elevation. Classic similar to standard Model 629, except Classic has full-lug 5" barrel, chamfered front of cylinder, interchangeable red ramp front sight with adjustable white outline rear, Hogue grips with S&W monogram, drilled and tapped for scope mounting. Factory accurizing and endurance packages. Introduced 1990. Classic Power Port has Patridge front sight and adjustable rear sight. Model 629CT has 5" barrel, Crimson Trace Hoghunter Lasergrips, 10.5" OAL, 45.5 oz. weight. Introduced 2006.
Price: 629, 4" **$826.00**
Price: 629, 6" barrel, 11-5/8" OAL, 45 oz. **$851.00**
Price: 629 Classic, 5" full lug barrel, 45.5 oz.. . . . . **$885.00**
Price: 629 Classic, 6-1/2" full lug barrel, 49.5 oz. **$912.00**
Price: 629 Classic, 6-1/2" full lug barrel, HiViz front sight **$939.00**
Price: 629 Classic Power Port, 6-1/2" full lug barrel. **$885.00**
Price: 629 Classic, 8-3/8" full lug barrel, 53.5 oz **$914.00**
Price: 629CT. . . . . **NA**

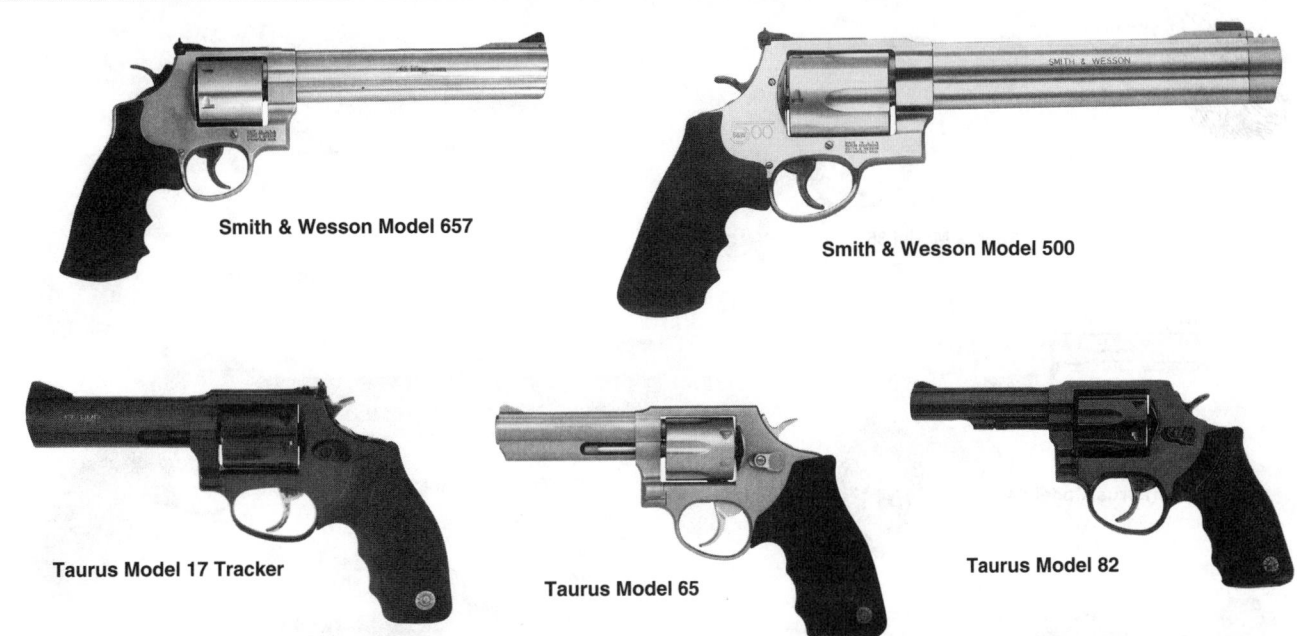

Smith & Wesson Model 657

Smith & Wesson Model 500

Taurus Model 17 Tracker

Taurus Model 65

Taurus Model 82

SMITH & WESSON MODEL 657 REVOLVER

Caliber: 41 Mag., 6-shot. **Barrel:** 7-1/2" full lug. **Weight:** 52 oz. **Grips:** Soft rubber. **Sights:** Pinned 1/8" red ramp front, micro-click rear adjustable for windage and elevation. Target hammer, drilled and tapped, unfluted cylinder. **Features:** Stainless steel construction.
Price: **$813.00**

SMITH & WESSON N-FRAME REVOLVERS

These extra-large X-frame S&W wheelguns come in a variety of chamberings, barrel lengths, and materials, as noted in the individual model listings below. 7 variations for 2006.

SMITH & WESSON MODEL 460V REVOLVERS

Caliber: 460 S&W Mag., 5-shot. Also chambers 454 Casull, 45 Colt. **Barrel:** 8-3/8" gain-twist rifling. **Weight:** 62.5 oz. **Length:** 11.25". **Grips:** Rubber. **Sights:** Adj. rear, red ramp front. **Features:** Satin stainless steel frame and cylinder, interchangeable compensator. 460XVR (X-treme Velocity Revolver) has black blade front sight with interchangeable green Hi-Viz tubes, adjustable rear sight. 7.5"-barrel version has Lothar-Walther barrel, 360-degree recoil compensator, tuned Performance Center action, pinned sear, integral Weaver base, non-glare surfaces, scope mount accessory kit for mounting full-size scopes, flashed-chromed hammer and trigger, Performance Center gun rug and shoulder sling. Interchangeable Hi-Viz green dot front sight, adjustable black rear sight, Hogue Dual Density Monogrip, matte-black frame and shroud finish with glass-bead cylinder finish, 72 oz. Compensated Hunter has tear drop chrome hammer, .312 chrome trigger, Hogue Dual Density Monogrip, satin/matte stainless finish, HiViz interchangeable front sight, adjustable black rear sight. XVR introduced 2006.
Price: 460V . . . . **NA**
Price: 460XVR, 8-3/8" barrel, 15" OAL, 72.5 oz. **$1,313.00**
Price: 460XVR, 7.5" barrel **$1,401.00**
Price: 460XVR, 3.5" barrel, 11" OAL, 59.5 oz. . . . . **NA**
Price: 460XVR Comp. Hunter, 10.5" barrel, 18" OAL, 82.5 oz. **$1,472**

SMITH & WESSON MODEL 500 REVOLVERS

Caliber: 500 S&W Mag., 5 rounds. **Barrel:** 4", 8-3/8". **Weight:** 72.5 oz. **Length:** 15" (8-3/8" barrel). **Grips:** Hogue Sorbothane Rubber. **Sights:** Interchangeable blade, front, adjustable rear. **Features:** Recoil compensator, ball detent cylinder latch, internal lock. 6 1/2"-barrel model has orange-ramp dovetail Millett front sight, adjustable black rear sight, Hogue Dual Density Monogrip, .312" chrome trigger with over-travel stop, chrome tear-drop hammer, glassbead finish. 10-1/2"-barrel model has red ramp front front sight, adjustable rear sight, .312 chrome trigger with overtravel stop, chrome tear drop hammer with pinned sear, hunting sling. Compensated Hunter has .400 orange ramp dovetail front sight, adjustable black blade rear sight, Hogue Dual Density Monogrip, glassbead finish w/black passivate clear coat. Made in U.S.A. by Smith & Wesson.
Price: 4" barrel, 10.25" OAL, 56 oz. **$1,256.00**
Price: 8-3/8" barrel **$1,186.00**
Price: 6.5" barrel, 14" OAL, 70 oz. **$1,460.00**
Price: 8-3/8" barrel w/HiViz front sight **$1,296.00**
Price: 10.5" barrel, 82 oz., with sling **$1,460.00**
Price: Compensated Hunter, 7.5" barrel, 71 oz. . . . . **NA**

TAURUS MODEL 17 "TRACKER"

Caliber: 17 HMR, 7-shot. **Barrel:** 6-1/2". **Weight:** 45.8 oz. **Grips:** Rubber. **Sights:** Adjustable. **Features:** Double action, matte stainless, integral key-lock.
Price: . . . . **$430.00 to $438.00**

Taurus Model 17-C Series

Similar to the Model 17 Tracker series but 8-shot cylinder, 2", 4" or 5" barrel, blue or stainless finish and regular (24 oz.) or UltraLite (18.5 oz.) versions available.
Price: . . . . **$359.00 to $391.00**

TAURUS MODEL 65 REVOLVER

Caliber: 357 Mag., 6-shot. **Barrel:** 4". **Weight:** 38 oz. **Length:** 10-1/2" overall. **Grips:** Soft rubber. **Sights:** Fixed. **Features:** Double action, integral key-lock. Seven models for 2006 Imported by Taurus International.
Price: Blue or matte stainless . . . . **$383.00 to $484.00**

Taurus Model 66 Revolver

Similar to Model 65, 4" or 6" barrel, 7-shot cylinder, adjustable rear sight. Integral key-lock action. Imported by Taurus International.
Price: Blue or matte stainless . . . . **$438.00 to $484.00**

TAURUS MODEL 82 HEAVY BARREL REVOLVER

Caliber: 38 Spec., 6-shot. **Barrel:** 4", heavy. **Weight:** 36.5 oz. **Length:** 9-1/4" overall (4" bbl.). **Grips:** Soft black rubber. **Sights:** Serrated ramp front, square notch rear. **Features:** Double action, solid rib, integral key-lock. Imported by Taurus International.
Price: Blue or matte stainless . . . . **$375.00 to $422.00**

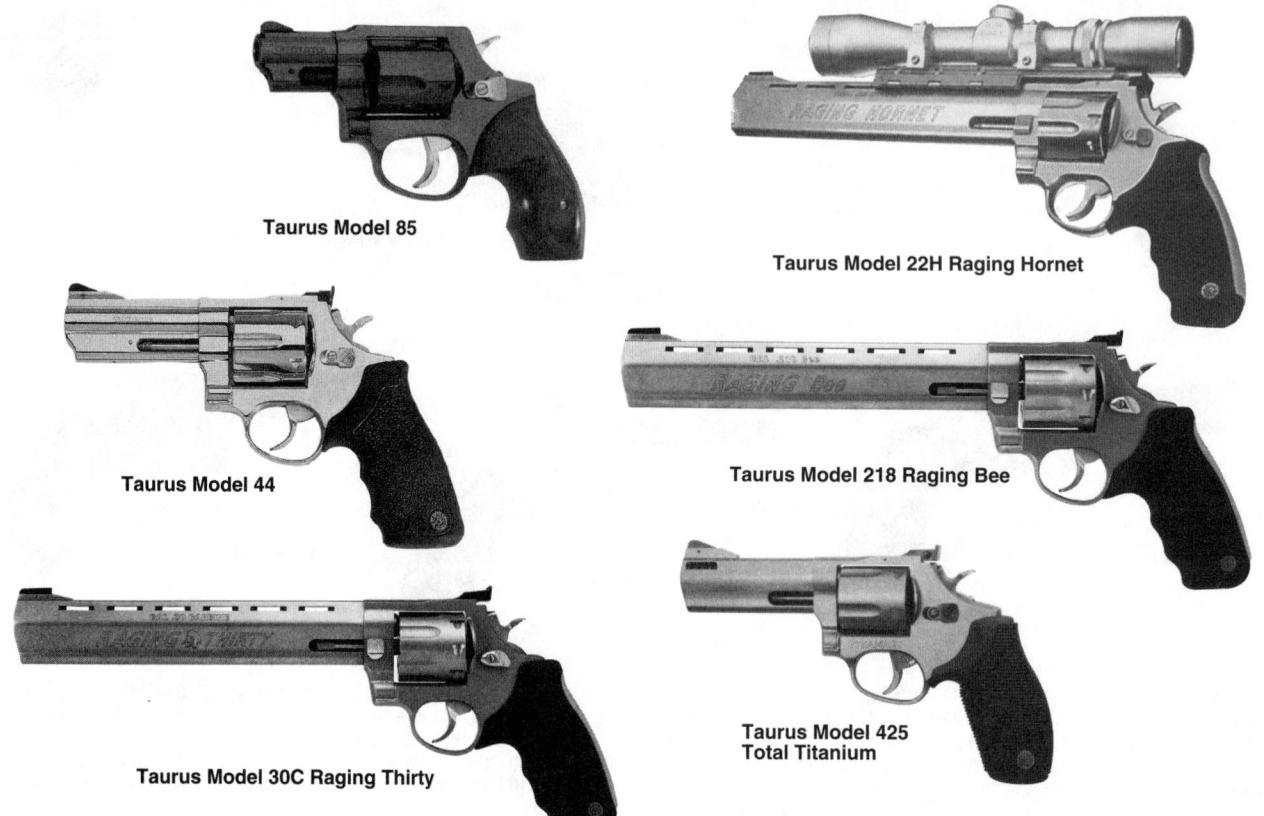

Taurus Model 85

Taurus Model 22H Raging Hornet

Taurus Model 44

Taurus Model 218 Raging Bee

Taurus Model 30C Raging Thirty

Taurus Model 425
Total Titanium

TAURUS MODEL 85 REVOLVER

Caliber: 38 Spec., 5-shot. **Barrel:** 2". **Weight:** 17-24.5 oz., titanium 13.5-15.4 oz. **Grips:** Rubber, rosewood or mother-of-pearl. **Sights:** Ramp front, square notch rear. **Features:** Blue, matte stainless, blue with gold accents, stainless with gold accents; rated for +P ammo. Integral keylock. Some models have titantium frame. Introduced 1980. Imported by Taurus International.
Price: . . . . **$383.00 to $548.00**

TAURUS IB INSTANT BACKUP REVOLVER

Caliber: 17 HMR, 8 shot. Barrel: 2". Weight: 17-24.5 oz., titanium 13.5-15.4 oz. Grips: Rubber, rosewood or mother-of-pearl. Sights: Notched rear sight with fixed front blade. Features: Miniaturized Model 85 design with concealed hammer. Dual lock cylinder latch. Blue or stainless. Introduced 2005. Imported by Taurus International.
Price: . . . . **$359.00 to $406.00**

TAURUS MODEL 94 REVOLVER

Caliber: 22 LR, 9-shot cylinder; 22 Mag, 8-shot cylinder **Barrel:** 2", 4", 5". **Weight:** 18.5-27.5 oz. **Grips:** Soft black rubber. **Sights:** Serrated ramp front, click-adjustable rear. **Features:** Double action, integral key-lock. Introduced 1989. Imported by Taurus International.
Price: . . . . **$359.00 to $406.00**

TAURUS MODEL 22H RAGING HORNET REVOLVER

Caliber: 22 Hornet, 8-shot. **Barrel:** 10". **Weight:** 50 oz. **Length:** 6.5" overall. **Grips:** Soft black rubber. **Sights:** Fully adjustable, scope mount base included. **Features:** Ventilated rib, stainless steel construction with matte finish. Double-action, integral key-lock. Introduced 1999. Imported by Taurus International.
Price: **$898.00**

TAURUS MODEL 30C RAGING THIRTY

Caliber: 30 Carbine, 8-shot. **Barrel:** 10". **Weight:** 72.3 oz. **Grips:** Soft black rubber. **Sights:** Adjustable. **Features:** Double-action, ventilated rib, matte stainless, comes with five "Stellar" full-moon clips, integral key-lock.
Price: **$898.00**

TAURUS MODEL 44 REVOLVER

Caliber: 44 Mag., 6-shot. **Barrel:** 4", 6-1/2", 8-3/8". **Weight:** 44-3/4 oz. **Grips:** Rubber. **Sights:** Adjustable. **Features:** Double-action. Integral key-lock. Introduced 1994. New Model 44S12 has 12" vent rib barrel. Imported from Brazil by Taurus International Manufacturing, Inc.
Price: Blue or stainless steel . . . . **$445.00 to $602.00**

TAURUS MODEL 217 TARGET "SILHOUETTE"

Caliber: 218 Bee, 8-shot. **Barrel:** 12". **Weight:** 52.3 oz. **Grips:** Rubber. **Sights:** Adjustable. **Features:** Double-action, ventilated rib, adjustable mainspring and trigger stop, matte stainless, integral key-lock.
Price: **$461.00**

TAURUS MODEL 218 RAGING BEE

Caliber: 218 Bee, 7-shot. **Barrel:** 10". **Weight:** 74.9 oz. **Grips:** Rubber. **Sights:** Adjustable rear. **Features:** Ventilated rib, adjustable action, matte stainless, integral key-lock. Also available as Model 218SS6 Tracker with 6-1/2" vent rib barrel.
Price: (Raging Bee) **$898.00**

TAURUS MODEL 425/627 TRACKER REVOLVERS

Caliber: 357 Mag., 7-shot; 41 Mag., 5-shot. **Barrel:** 4" and 6". **Weight:** 28.8-40 oz. (titanium) 24.3-28. (6"). **Grips:** Rubber. **Sights:** Fixed front, adjustable rear. **Features:** Double-action stainless steel, Shadow Gray or Total Titanium; vent rib (steel models only); integral key-lock action. Imported by Taurus International.
Price: . . . . **$531.00 to $766.00**
Price: Total Titanium **$766.00**

TAURUS MODEL 444 ULTRALIGHT

Caliber: 44 Mag, 5-shot. **Barrel:** 4". **Weight:** 28.3 oz. **Length:** 9.8" overall. **Grips:** Cushioned inset rubber. **Sights:** Fixed red-fiber optic front, adjustable rear. **Features:** UltraLite titanium blue finish, titanium/alloy frame built on Raging Bull design. Smooth trigger shoe, 1.760" wide, 6.280" tall. Barrel rate of twist 1:16", 6 grooves. Introduced 2005. Imported by Taurus International.
Price: **$650.00**

Taurus Model 445

Taurus Model 605

Taurus Model 731

Taurus Model 608

Taurus Model 450

Taurus Model 454 Raging Bull

Taurus Raging Bull Model 416

Taurus Model 617

TAURUS MODEL 445

Caliber: 44 Special, 5-shot. **Barrel:** 2". **Weight:** 20.3-28.25 oz. **Length:** 6-3/4" overall. **Grips:** Rubber. **Sights:** Ramp front, notch rear. **Features:** Blue or stainless steel. Standard or DAO concealed hammer, optional porting. Introduced 1997. Imported by Taurus International.
Price: . . . . **$345.00 to $500.00**
Price: Total Titanium 19.8 oz. **$600.00**

TAURUS MODEL 605 REVOLVER

Caliber: 357 Mag., 5-shot. **Barrel:** 2". **Weight:** 24 oz. **Grips:** Rubber. **Sights:** Fixed. **Features:** Double-action, blue or stainless or titanium, concealed hammer models DAO, porting optional, integral key-lock. Introduced 1995. Imported by Taurus International.
Price: **$625.00**

Taurus Model 731 Revolver

Similar to the Taurus Model 605, except in .32 Magnum.
Price: . . . . **$438.00 to $531.00**

TAURUS MODEL 608 REVOLVER

Caliber: 357 Mag. 38 Spec., 8-shot. **Barrel:** 4", 6-1/2", 8-3/8". **Weight:** 44-57 oz. **Length:** 9-3/8" overall. **Grips:** Soft black rubber. **Sights:** Adjustable. **Features:** Double-action, integral key-lock action. Available in blue or stainless. Introduced 1995. Imported by Taurus International.
Price: . . . . **$547.00 to $570.00**

Taurus Model 44 Series Revolver

Similar to Taurus Model 60 series, but in .44 Rem. Mag. With six-shot cylinder, blue and matte stainless finishes.
Price: . . . . **$500.00 to $578.00**

TAURUS MODEL 650CIA REVOLVER

Caliber: 357 Magnum, 5-shot. **Barrel:** 2". **Weight:** 24.5 oz. **Grips:** Rubber. **Sights:** Ramp front, square notch rear. **Features:** Double-action only, blue or matte stainless steel, integral key-lock, internal hammer. Introduced 2001. From Taurus International.
Price: . . . . **$383.00 to $430.00**

TAURUS MODEL 651 PROTECTOR REVOLVER

Caliber: 357 Magnum, 5-shot. **Barrel:** 2". **Weight:** 17-24.5 oz. **Grips:** Rubber. **Sights:** Fixed. **Features:** Concealed single-action/ double-action design. Shrouded cockable hammer, blue, matte stainless, Shadow Gray, Total Titanium, integral key-lock. Made in Brazil. Imported by Taurus International Manufacturing, Inc.
Price: . . . . **$383.00 to $430.00**

TAURUS MODEL 450 REVOLVER

Caliber: 45 Colt, 5-shot. **Barrel:** 2". **Weight:** 21.2-22.3 oz. **Length:** 6-5/8" overall. **Grips:** Rubber. **Sights:** Ramp front, notch rear. **Features:** Double-action, blue or stainless, ported, integral key-lock. Introduced 1999. Imported from Brazil by Taurus International.
Price: . . . . **$523.00 to $600.00**

TAURUS MODEL 444/454/480 RAGING BULL REVOLVERS

Caliber: 44 Mag., 45 LC, 454 Casull, 480 Ruger, 5-shot. **Barrel:** 5", 6-1/2", 8-3/8". **Weight:** 53-63 oz. **Length:** 12" overall (6-1/2" barrel). **Grips:** Soft black rubber. **Sights:** Patridge front, adjustable rear. **Features:** Double-action, ventilated rib, ported, integral key-lock. Introduced 1997. Imported by Taurus International.
Price: Blue . . . . **$602.00 to $797.00**

TAURUS RAGING BULL MODEL 416

Caliber: 41 Magnum, 6-shot. **Barrel:** 6-1/2". **Weight:** 61.9 oz. **Grips:** Rubber. **Sights:** Adjustable. **Features:** Double-action, ported, ventilated rib, matte stainless, integral key-lock.
Price: **$664.00**

TAURUS MODEL 617 REVOLVER

Caliber: 357 Magnum, 7-shot. **Barrel:** 2". **Weight:** 28.3 oz. **Length:** 6-3/4" overall. **Grips:** Soft black rubber. **Sights:** Fixed. **Features:** Double-action, blue, Shadow Gray, bright spectrum blue or matte stainless steel, integral key-lock. Available with porting, concealed hammer. Introduced 1998. Imported by Taurus International.
Price: . . . . **$391.00 to $453.00**
Price: Total Titanium, 19.9 oz. **$602.00**

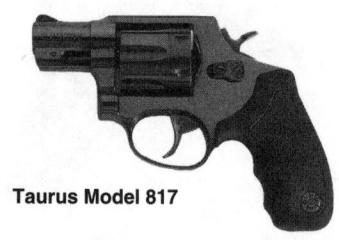

Taurus Model 817

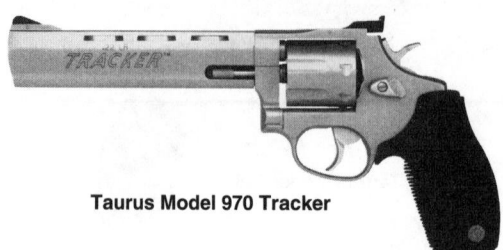

Taurus Model 970 Tracker

Taurus Model 905

TAURUS MODEL 817 ULTRA-LITE REVOLVER

Caliber: 38 Spec., 7-shot. **Barrel:** 2". **Weight:** 21 oz. **Length:** 6-1/2" overall. **Grips:** Soft rubber. **Sights:** Fixed. **Features:** Double-action, integral key-lock. Rated for +P ammo. Introduced 1999. Imported from Brazil by Taurus International.
Price: Blue $406.00

TAURUS MODEL 850CIA REVOLVER

Caliber: 38 Special, 5-shot. **Barrel:** 2". **Weight:** 17-24.5 oz. **Grips:** Rubber, mother-of-pearl. **Sights:** Ramp front, square notch rear. **Features:** Double-action only, blue or matte stainless steel, rated for +P ammo, integral key-lock, internal hammer. Introduced 2001. From Taurus International.
Price: . . . . $383.00 to $672.00
Price: Total Titanium $578.00

TAURUS MODEL 94, 941 REVOLVER

Caliber: 22 LR (Mod. 94), 22 WMR (Mod. 941), 8-shot. **Barrel:** 2", 4", 5". **Weight:** 27.5 oz. (4" barrel). **Grips:** Soft black rubber. **Sights:** Serrated

ramp front, rear adjustable. **Features:** Double-action, integral key-lock. Introduced 1992. Imported by Taurus International.
Price: . . . . $344.00 to $406.00

TAURUS MODEL 970/971 TRACKER REVOLVERS

Caliber: 22 LR (Model 970), 22 Magnum (Model 971); 7-shot. **Barrel:** 6". **Weight:** 53.6 oz. **Grips:** Rubber. **Sights:** Adjustable. **Features:** Double barrel, heavy barrel with ventilated rib; matte stainless finish, integral key-lock. Introduced 2001. From Taurus International.
Price: $422.00

TAURUS MODEL 905, 405, 455 PISTOL CALIBER REVOLVERS

Caliber: 9mm, .40, .45 ACP, 5-shot. **Barrel:** 2", 4", 6-1/2". **Weight:** 21 oz. to 40.8 oz. **Grips:** Rubber. **Sights:** Fixed, adjustable on Model 455SS6 in .45 ACP. **Features:** Produced as a backup gun for law enforcement officers. Introduced 2003. Imported from Brazil by Taurus International.
Price: . . . . $383.00 to $523.00

HANDGUNS — Single-Action Revolvers

Both classic six-shooters and modern adaptations for hunting and sport.

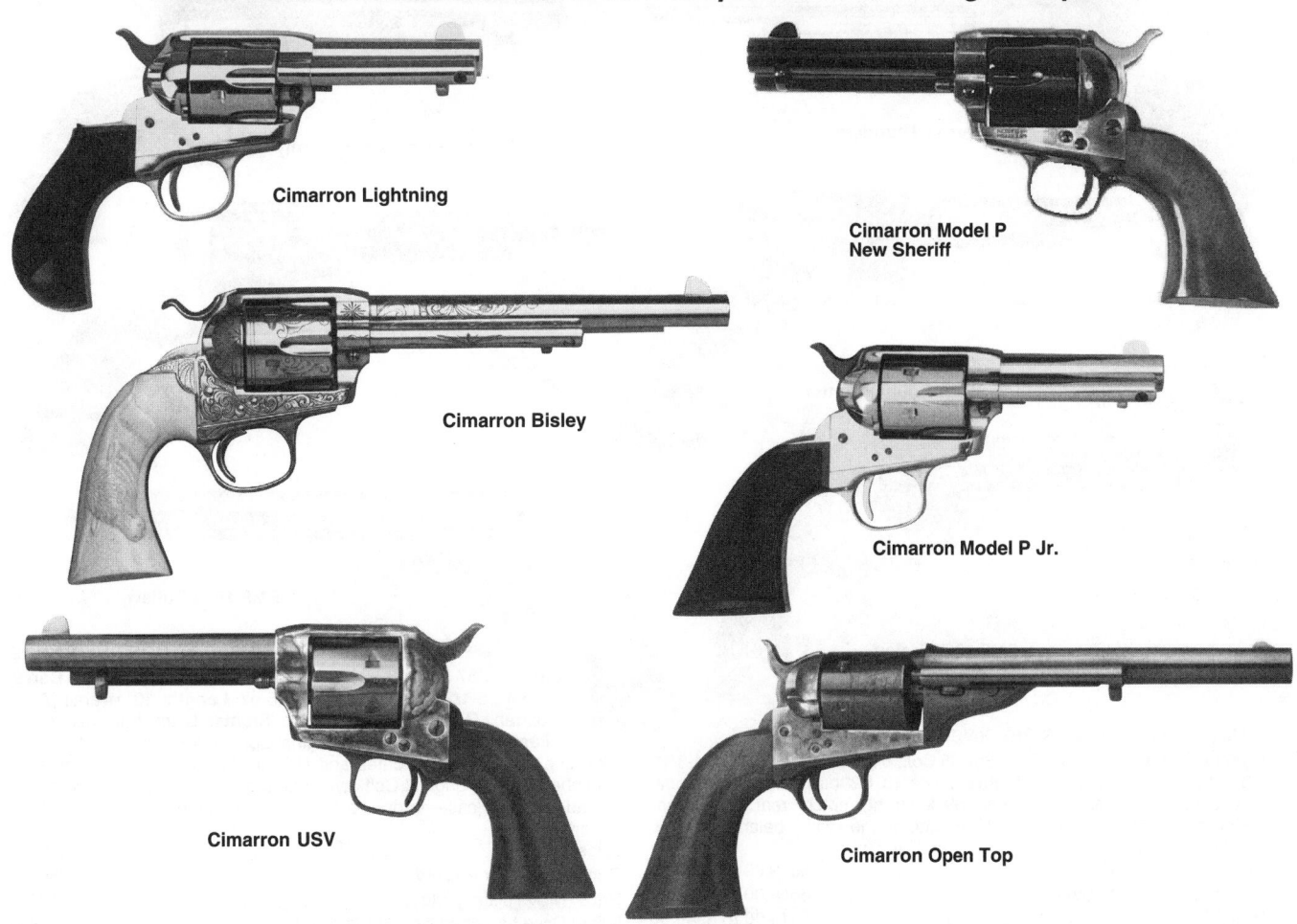

Cimarron Lightning

Cimarron Model P New Sheriff

Cimarron Bisley

Cimarron Model P Jr.

Cimarron USV

Cimarron Open Top

CHARLES DALY 1873 SINGLE-ACTION REVOLVER
Caliber: 357 Mag., 45 Colt, 6-shot. **Barrel:** 4.75", 5.5", 7.5". **Weight:** 36 oz. (4.75" barrel). **Length:** 10" overall (4.75" barrel). **Grips:** Hardwood with company logo near tang. **Sights:** Blade front, notch rear. **Features:** Stainless steel and color case hardened finishes. From K.B.I., Inc.
Price: 1873 Steel, 45 Colt, 4.75", 5.5", 7.5" barrel, brass frame.... **$449.00**
Price: 1873 Steel, 357 Mag, 4.75", 5.5", 7.5" barrel, brass frame .. **$479.00**
Price: 1873 Steel, 45 Colt, 4.75", 5.5", 7.5" barrel, steel frame **$449.00**
Price: 1873 Stainless Steel, 357 Mag, 4.75", 5.5", 7.5" barrel **$659.00**
Price: 1873 Stainless Steel, 45 Colt, 4.75", 5.5", 7.5" barrel **$659.00**

CIMARRON LIGHTNING SA
Caliber: 32-20, 32 H&R, 38 Colt, 38 Special. **Barrel:** 3-1/2", 4-3/4", 5-1/2". **Grips:** Smooth or checkered walnut. **Sights:** Blade front. **Features:** Replica of the Colt 1877 Lightning DA. Similar to Cimarron Thunderer™, except smaller grip frame to fit smaller hands. Standard blue, charcoal blue or nickel finish with forged, old model, or color case hardened frame. Introduced 2001. From Cimarron F.A. Co.
Price: .... **$499.00 to $559.00**

CIMARRON MODEL P
Caliber: 32 WCF, 38 WCF, 357 Mag., 44 WCF, 44 Spec., 45 Colt, 45 LC and 45 ACP. **Barrel:** 4-3/4", 5-1/2", 7-1/2". **Weight:** 39 oz. **Length:** 10" overall (4" barrel). **Grips:** Walnut. **Sights:** Blade front, fixed or adjustable rear. **Features:** Uses "old model" black powder frame with "Bullseye" ejector or New Model frame. Imported by Cimarron F.A. Co.
Price: .... **$499.00 to $559.00**
Price: New Sheriff .... **$499.00 to $559.00**

Cimarron Bisley Model Single-Action Revolvers
Similar to 1873 Model P, special grip frame and trigger guard, knurled wide-spur hammer, curved trigger. Available in 357 Mag., 44 WCF, 44 Spl., 45 Colt. Introduced 1999. Imported by Cimarron F.A. Co.
Price: **$525.00**

CIMARRON MODEL "P" JR.
Caliber: 32-20, 32 H&R, 38 Special. **Barrel:** 3-1/2", 4-3/4", 5-1/2". **Grips:** Checkered walnut. **Sights:** Blade front. **Features:** Styled after 1873 Colt Peacemaker, except 20 percent smaller. Blue finish with color case-hardened frame; Cowboy Comp® action. Introduced 2001. From Cimarron F.A. Co.
Price: .... **$489.00 to $529.00**

CIMARRON U. S. VOLUNTEER ARTILLERY MODEL SINGLE-ACTION
Caliber: 45 Colt. **Barrel:** 5-1/2". **Weight:** 39 oz. **Length:** 11-1/2" overall. **Grips:** Walnut. **Sights:** Fixed. **Features:** U.S. markings and cartouche, case-hardened frame and hammer; 45 Colt only. Imported by Cimarron F.A. Co.
Price: .... **$549.00 to $599.00**

CIMARRON 1872 OPEN TOP REVOLVER
Caliber: 38, 44 Special, 44 Colt, 44 Russian, 45LC, 45 S&W Schofield. **Barrel:** 5-1/2" and 7-1/2". **Grips:** Walnut. **Sights:** Blade front, fixed rear. **Features:** Replica of first cartridge-firing revolver. Blue, charcoal blue, nickel or Original® finish; Navy-style brass or steel Army-style frame. Introduced 2001 by Cimarron F.A. Co.
Price: .... **$529.00 to $599.00**

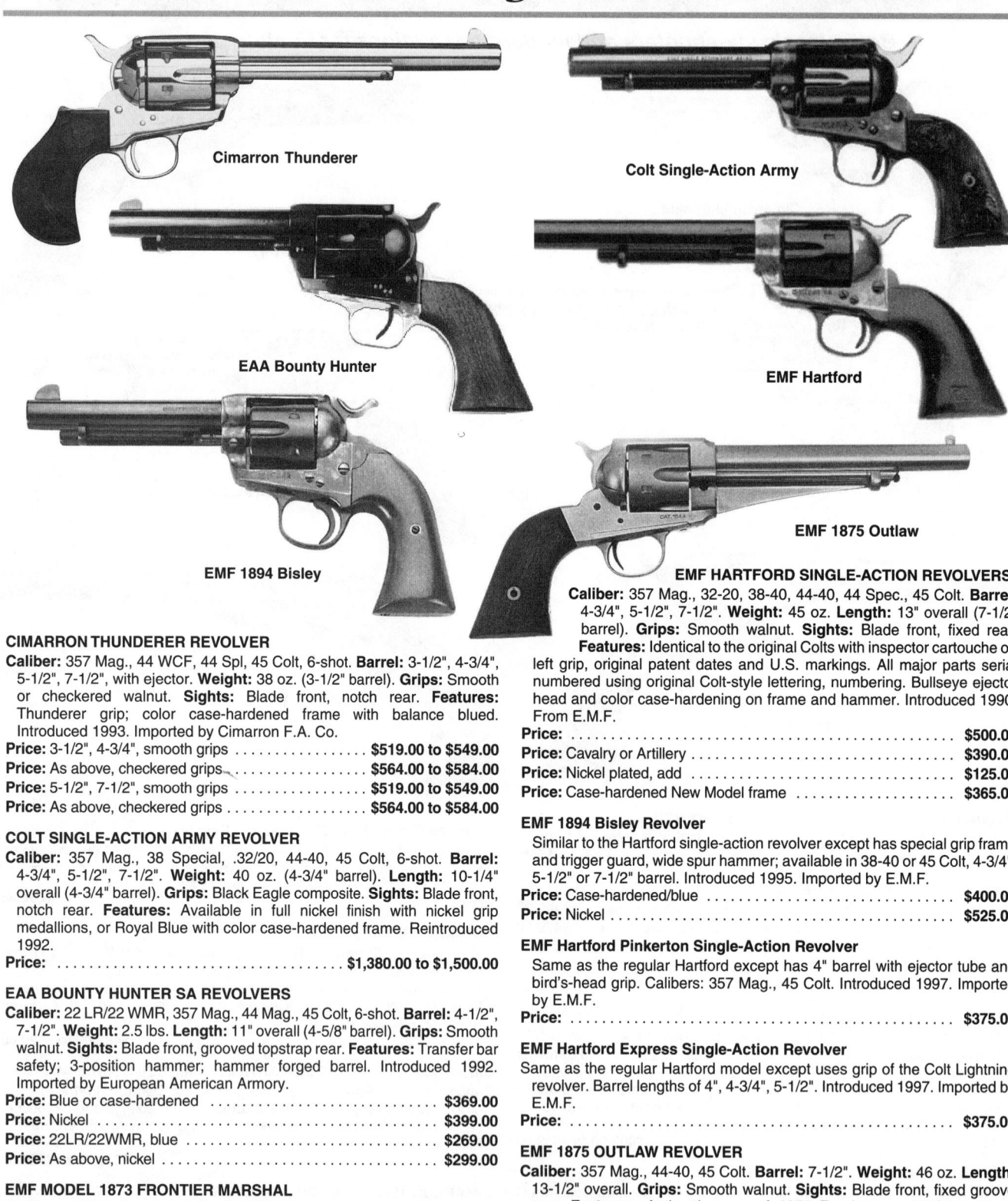

Cimarron Thunderer

Colt Single-Action Army

EAA Bounty Hunter

EMF Hartford

EMF 1894 Bisley

EMF 1875 Outlaw

CIMARRON THUNDERER REVOLVER

Caliber: 357 Mag., 44 WCF, 44 Spl, 45 Colt, 6-shot. **Barrel:** 3-1/2", 4-3/4", 5-1/2", 7-1/2", with ejector. **Weight:** 38 oz. (3-1/2" barrel). **Grips:** Smooth or checkered walnut. **Sights:** Blade front, notch rear. **Features:** Thunderer grip; color case-hardened frame with balance blued. Introduced 1993. Imported by Cimarron F.A. Co.

Price: 3-1/2", 4-3/4", smooth grips .... **$519.00 to $549.00**
Price: As above, checkered grips .... **$564.00 to $584.00**
Price: 5-1/2", 7-1/2", smooth grips .... **$519.00 to $549.00**
Price: As above, checkered grips .... **$564.00 to $584.00**

COLT SINGLE-ACTION ARMY REVOLVER

Caliber: 357 Mag., 38 Special, .32/20, 44-40, 45 Colt, 6-shot. **Barrel:** 4-3/4", 5-1/2", 7-1/2". **Weight:** 40 oz. (4-3/4" barrel). **Length:** 10-1/4" overall (4-3/4" barrel). **Grips:** Black Eagle composite. **Sights:** Blade front, notch rear. **Features:** Available in full nickel finish with nickel grip medallions, or Royal Blue with color case-hardened frame. Reintroduced 1992.

Price: .... **$1,380.00 to $1,500.00**

EAA BOUNTY HUNTER SA REVOLVERS

Caliber: 22 LR/22 WMR, 357 Mag., 44 Mag., 45 Colt, 6-shot. **Barrel:** 4-1/2", 7-1/2". **Weight:** 2.5 lbs. **Length:** 11" overall (4-5/8" barrel). **Grips:** Smooth walnut. **Sights:** Blade front, grooved topstrap rear. **Features:** Transfer bar safety; 3-position hammer; hammer forged barrel. Introduced 1992. Imported by European American Armory.

Price: Blue or case-hardened **$369.00**
Price: Nickel **$399.00**
Price: 22LR/22WMR, blue **$269.00**
Price: As above, nickel **$299.00**

EMF MODEL 1873 FRONTIER MARSHAL

Caliber: 357 Mag., 45 Colt. **Barrel:** 4-3/4", 5-1/2, 7-1/2". **Weight:** 39 oz. **Length:** 10-1/2" overall. **Grips:** One-piece walnut. **Sights:** Blade front, notch rear. **Features:** Bright brass trigger guard and backstrap, color case-hardened frame, blued barrel and cylinder. Introduced 1998. Imported from Italy by IAR, Inc.

Price: **$395.00**

EMF HARTFORD SINGLE-ACTION REVOLVERS

Caliber: 357 Mag., 32-20, 38-40, 44-40, 44 Spec., 45 Colt. **Barrel:** 4-3/4", 5-1/2", 7-1/2". **Weight:** 45 oz. **Length:** 13" overall (7-1/2" barrel). **Grips:** Smooth walnut. **Sights:** Blade front, fixed rear. **Features:** Identical to the original Colts with inspector cartouche on left grip, original patent dates and U.S. markings. All major parts serial numbered using original Colt-style lettering, numbering. Bullseye ejector head and color case-hardening on frame and hammer. Introduced 1990. From E.M.F.

Price: **$500.00**
Price: Cavalry or Artillery **$390.00**
Price: Nickel plated, add **$125.00**
Price: Case-hardened New Model frame **$365.00**

EMF 1894 Bisley Revolver

Similar to the Hartford single-action revolver except has special grip frame and trigger guard, wide spur hammer; available in 38-40 or 45 Colt, 4-3/4", 5-1/2" or 7-1/2" barrel. Introduced 1995. Imported by E.M.F.

Price: Case-hardened/blue **$400.00**
Price: Nickel **$525.00**

EMF Hartford Pinkerton Single-Action Revolver

Same as the regular Hartford except has 4" barrel with ejector tube and bird's-head grip. Calibers: 357 Mag., 45 Colt. Introduced 1997. Imported by E.M.F.

Price: **$375.00**

EMF Hartford Express Single-Action Revolver

Same as the regular Hartford model except uses grip of the Colt Lightning revolver. Barrel lengths of 4", 4-3/4", 5-1/2". Introduced 1997. Imported by E.M.F.

Price: **$375.00**

EMF 1875 OUTLAW REVOLVER

Caliber: 357 Mag., 44-40, 45 Colt. **Barrel:** 7-1/2". **Weight:** 46 oz. **Length:** 13-1/2" overall. **Grips:** Smooth walnut. **Sights:** Blade front, fixed groove rear. **Features:** Authentic copy of 1875 Remington with firing pin in hammer; color case-hardened frame, blue cylinder, barrel, steel backstrap and brass trigger guard. Also available in nickel, factory engraved. Imported by E.M.F.

Price: All calibers **$575.00**
Price: Nickel **$735.00**

EMF 1890 Police

Freedom Arms Model 83 Premier Grade

Freedom Arms Model 83 475 Linebaugh

Freedom Arms Model 83 Field Grade

Freedom Arms Model 97 Premier Grade

EMF 1890 Police Revolver
Similar to the 1875 Outlaw except has 5-1/2" barrel, weighs 40 oz., with 12-1/2" overall length. Has lanyard ring in butt. No web under barrel. Calibers 357, 44-40, 45 Colt. Imported by E.M.F.
Price: All calibers **$590.00**
Price: Nickel **$750.00**

FREEDOM ARMS MODEL 83 PREMIER GRADE REVOLVER
Caliber: 357 Mag., 41 Mag., 44 Mag., 454 Casull, 475 Linebaugh, 500 Wyo. Exp., 5-shot. **Barrel:** 4-3/4", 6", 7-1/2", 9" (357 Mag. only), 10" (except 357 Mag. and 500 Wyo. Exp. **Weight:** 53 oz. (7-1/2" bbl. In 454 Casull). **Length:** 13" (7-1/2" bbl.). **Grips:** Impregnated hardwood. **Sights:** Adjustable rear with replaceable front sight. Fixed rear notch and front blade. **Features:** Stainless steel construction with brushed finish; manual sliding safety bar. Micarta grips optional. 500 Wyo. Exp. Introduced 2006. Lifetime warranty. Made in U.S.A. by Freedom Arms, Inc.
Price: 500 WE, 454 Casull, 475 Linebaugh, 454 Casull **$2,120.00**
Price: 454 Casull, fixed sight. **$2,038.00**
Price: 357 Mag., 41 Mag., 44 Mag. **$2,035.00**

FREEDOM ARMS MODEL 83 FIELD GRADE REVOLVER
Caliber: 22 LR, 357 Mag., 41 Mag., 44 Mag., 454 Casull, 475 Linebaugh, 500 Wyo. Exp., 5-shot. **Barrel:** 4-3/4", 6", 7-1/2", 9" (357 Mag. only), 10" (except 357 Mag. and 500 Wyo. Exp.) **Weight:** 56 oz. (7-1/2" bbl. In 454 Casull). **Length:** 13.1" (7-1/2" bbl.). **Grips:** Pachmayr standard, impregnated hardwood or Micarta optional. **Sights:** Adjustable rear with

replaceable front sight. Model 83 frame. All stainless steel. Introduced 1988. Made in U.S.A. by Freedom Arms Inc.
Price: 454 Casull, 475 Linebaugh, 500 WE adj. sights **$1,639.00**
Price: 357 Mag., 41 Mag., 44 Mag. **$1,573.00**
Price: 22 LR with match chambers and 10" barrel. **$1,803.00**

FREEDOM ARMS MODEL 97 PREMIER GRADE REVOLVER
Caliber: 17HMR, 22 LR, 32 H&R, 357 Mag., 6-shot; 41 Mag., 44 Special, 45 Colt, 5-shot. **Barrel:** 4-1/4", 5-1/2", 7-1/2", 10" (17 HMR, 22LR & 32 H&R). **Weight:** 40 oz. (5-1/2" 357 Mag.). **Length:** 10-3/4" (5-1/2" bbl.). **Grips:** Impregnated hardwood; Micarta optional. **Sights:** Adjustable rear, replaceable blade front. Fixed rear notch and front blade. **Features:** Stainless steel construction, brushed finish, automatic transfer bar safety system. Introduced in 1997. Lifetime warranty. Made in U.S.A. by Freedom Arms.
Price: Centerfire cartridges, adjustable sights **$1,718.00**
Price: Rimfire cartridges. **$1,784.00**
Price: 32 H&R, 357 Mag., 6-shot; 45 Colt, fixed sights **$1,624.00**
Price: Extra fitted cylinders, centerfire, 22 WMR, 17 Mach II. **$272.00**
Price: Extra fitted 22 LR match grade cylinder. **$404.00**
Price: 22 LR match cylinder in place of 22 LR sporting cylinder . . . **$132.00**
Price: 357 Mag., 45 Colt, fixed sight **$1,576.00**
Price: Extra fitted cylinders 38 Special, 45 ACP **$264.00**
Price: 22 LR with sporting chambers **$1,732.00**
Price: Extra fitted 22 WMR cylinder **$264.00**
Price: Extra fitted 22 LR match grade cylinder **$476.00**
Price: 22 match grade chamber instead of 22 LR sport chamber . **$214.00**

HERITAGE ROUGH RIDER REVOLVER
Caliber: 17HMR, 17LR, 32 H&R, 32 S&W, 32 S&W Long, 357 Mag, 44-40, 45 LC, 22 LR, 22 LR/22 WMR combo, 6-shot. **Barrel:** 2-3/4", 3-1/2", 4-3/4", 6-1/2", 9". **Weight:** 31 to 38 oz. **Length:** NA. **Grips:** Exotic cocobolo laminated wood or mother-of-pearl; bird's-head models offered. **Sights:** Blade front, fixed rear. Adjustable sight on 4", 6" and 9" models. **Features:** Hammer block safety. High polish blue, black satin, silver satin, case-hardened and stainless finish. Introduced 1993. Made in U.S.A. by Heritage Mfg., Inc.
Price: . . . . **$159.95 to $499.95**

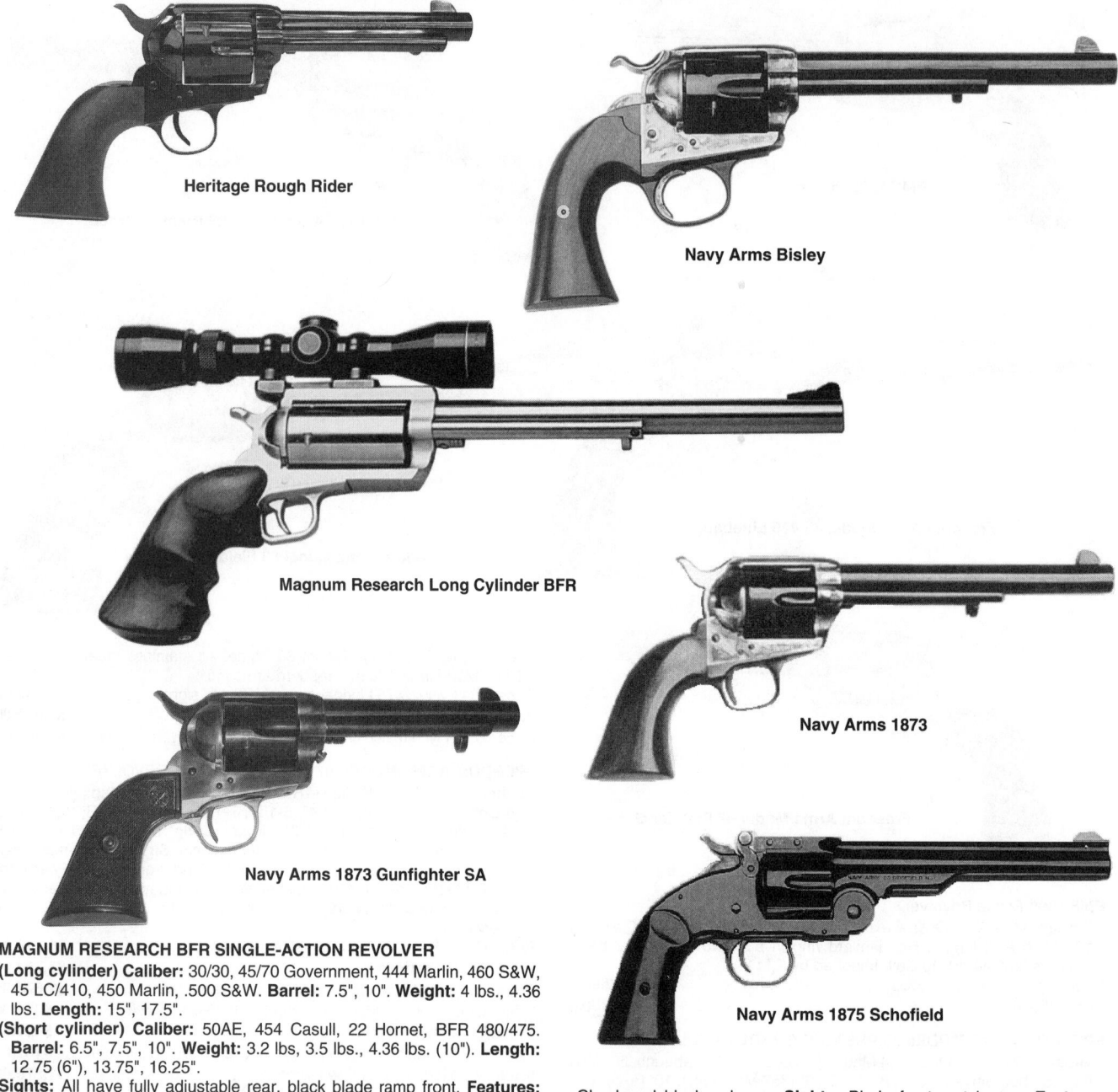

Heritage Rough Rider

Navy Arms Bisley

Magnum Research Long Cylinder BFR

Navy Arms 1873

Navy Arms 1873 Gunfighter SA

Navy Arms 1875 Schofield

MAGNUM RESEARCH BFR SINGLE-ACTION REVOLVER
(Long cylinder) Caliber: 30/30, 45/70 Government, 444 Marlin, 460 S&W, 45 LC/410, 450 Marlin, .500 S&W. **Barrel:** 7.5", 10". **Weight:** 4 lbs., 4.36 lbs. **Length:** 15", 17.5".
(Short cylinder) Caliber: 50AE, 454 Casull, 22 Hornet, BFR 480/475. **Barrel:** 6.5", 7.5", 10". **Weight:** 3.2 lbs, 3.5 lbs., 4.36 lbs. (10"). **Length:** 12.75 (6"), 13.75", 16.25".
Sights: All have fully adjustable rear, black blade ramp front. **Features:** Stainless steel construction, rubber grips, all 5-shot capacity. Barrels are stress-relieved and cut rifled. Made in U.S.A. From Magnum Research, Inc.
Price: **$899.00**

NAVY ARMS BISLEY MODEL SINGLE-ACTION REVOLVER
Caliber: 44-40 or 45 Colt, 6-shot cylinder. **Barrel:** 4-3/4", 5-1/2", 7-1/2". **Weight:** 40 oz. **Length:** 12-1/2" overall (7-1/2" barrel). **Grips:** Smooth walnut. **Sights:** Blade front, notch rear. **Features:** Replica of Colt's Bisley Model. Polished blue finish, color case-hardened frame. Introduced 1997. Imported by Navy Arms.
Price: **$511.00**

NAVY ARMS 1873 GUNFIGHTER SINGLE-ACTION REVOLVER
Caliber: 357 Mag., 44-40, 45 Colt, 6-shot cylinder. **Barrel:** 4-3/4", 5-1/2", 7-1/2". **Weight:** 37 oz. **Length:** 10-1/4" overall (4-3/4" barrel). **Grips:**

Checkered black polymer. **Sights:** Blade front, notch rear. **Features:** Blued with color case-hardened receiver, trigger and hammer; German Silver backstrap and triggerguard. American made Wolff trigger and mainsprings installed. Introduced 2005. Imported by Navy Arms.
Price: **$511.00**
Price: Stainless steel **$608.00**

NAVY ARMS 1875 SCHOFIELD REVOLVER
Caliber: 44-40, 45 Colt, 6-shot cylinder. **Barrel:** 3-1/2", 5", 7". **Weight:** 39 oz. **Length:** 10-3/4" overall (5" barrel). **Grips:** Smooth walnut. **Sights:** Blade front, notch rear. **Features:** Replica of Smith & Wesson Model 3 Schofield. Single-action, top-break with automatic ejection. Polished blue finish. Introduced 1994. Imported by Navy Arms.
Price: Hideout Model, 3-1/2" barrel **$849.00**
Price: Wells Fargo, 5" barrel **$849.00**
Price: U.S. Cavalry model, 7" barrel, military markings **$849.00**

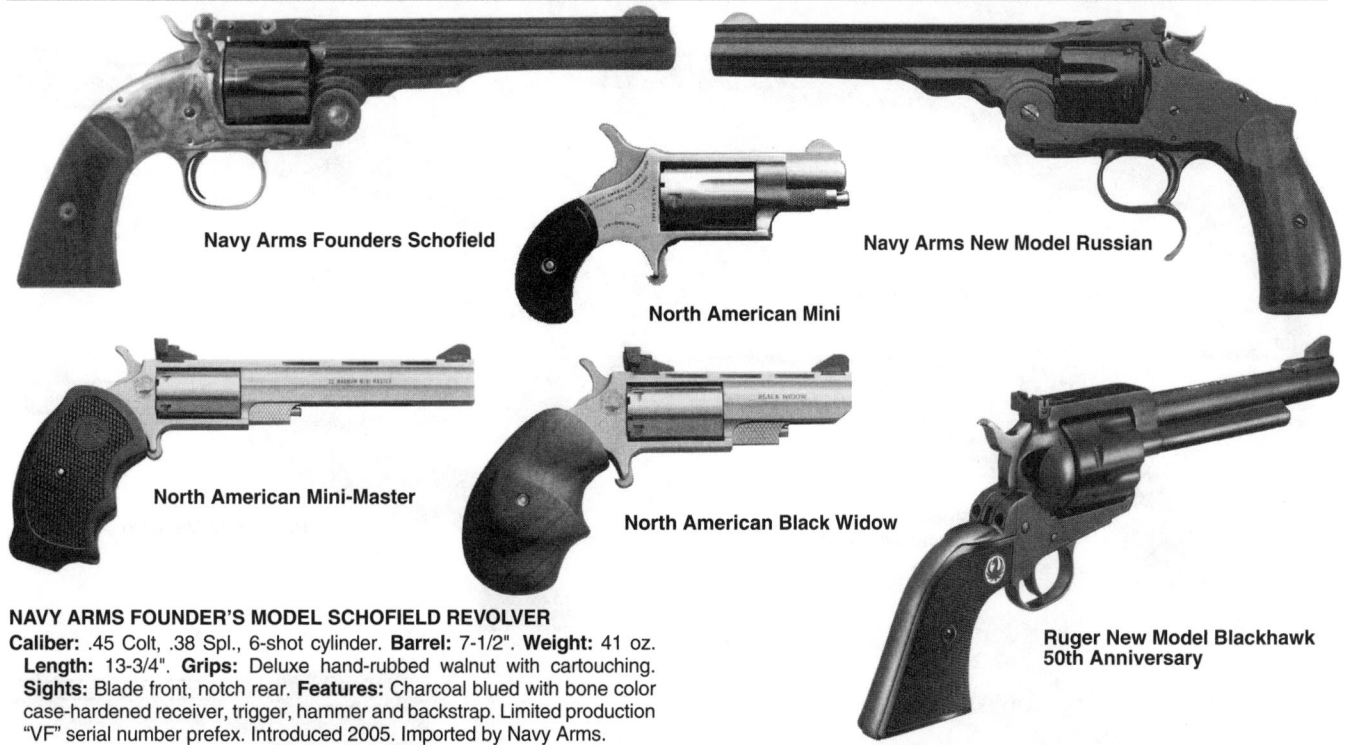

Navy Arms Founders Schofield

North American Mini

Navy Arms New Model Russian

North American Mini-Master

North American Black Widow

Ruger New Model Blackhawk
50th Anniversary

NAVY ARMS FOUNDER'S MODEL SCHOFIELD REVOLVER

Caliber: .45 Colt, .38 Spl., 6-shot cylinder. **Barrel:** 7-1/2". **Weight:** 41 oz. **Length:** 13-3/4". **Grips:** Deluxe hand-rubbed walnut with cartouching. **Sights:** Blade front, notch rear. **Features:** Charcoal blued with bone color case-hardened receiver, trigger, hammer and backstrap. Limited production "VF" serial number prefex. Introduced 2005. Imported by Navy Arms.
Price: **$946.00**

NAVY ARMS NEW MODEL RUSSIAN REVOLVER

Caliber: 44 Russian, 6-shot cylinder. **Barrel:** 6-1/2". **Weight:** 40 oz. **Length:** 12" overall. **Grips:** Smooth walnut. **Sights:** Blade front, notch rear. **Features:** Replica of the S&W Model 3 Russian Third Model revolver. Spur trigger guard, polished blue finish. Introduced 1999. Imported by Navy Arms.
Price: **$908.00**

NAVY ARMS SCOUT SMALL FRAME SINGLE ACTION REVOLVER

Caliber: .38 Spl., 6-shot cylinder. **Barrel:** 4-3/4", 5-1/2". **Weight:** 37 oz. **Length:** 10-3/4" overall (5-1/2" barrel). **Grips:** Checkered black polymer. **Sights:** Blade front, notch rear. **Features:** Blued with color case-hardened receiver, trigger and hammer; German Silver backstrap and triggerguard. Introduced 2005. Imported by Navy Arms.
Price: **$511.00**

NORTH AMERICAN MINI REVOLVERS

Caliber: 22 Short, 22 LR, 22 WMR, 5-shot. **Barrel:** 1-1/8", 1-5/8". **Weight:** 4 to 6.6 oz. **Length:** 3-5/8" to 6-1/8" overall. **Grips:** Laminated wood. **Sights:** Blade front, notch fixed rear. **Features:** All stainless steel construction. Polished satin and matte finish. Engraved models available. From North American Arms.
Price: 22 Short, 22 LR **$193.00**
Price: 22 WMR, 1-1/8" or 1-5/8" bbl. **$193.00**
Price: 22 WMR, 1-1/8" or 1-5/8" bbl. with extra 22 LR cylinder **$193.00**

NORTH AMERICAN MINI-MASTER

Caliber: 22 LR, 22 WMR, 17 HMR, 5-shot cylinder. **Barrel:** 4". **Weight:** 10.7 oz. **Length:** 7.75" overall. **Grips:** Checkered hard black rubber. **Sights:** Blade front, white outline rear adjustable for elevation, or fixed. **Features:** Heavy vented barrel; full-size grips. Non-fluted cylinder. Introduced 1989.
Price: Adjustable sight, 22 WMR, 17 HMR or 22 LR **$301.00**
Price: As above with extra WMR/LR cylinder **$330.00**
Price: Fixed sight, 22 WMR, 17 HMR or 22 LR **$272.00**
Price: As above with extra WMR/LR cylinder **$330.00**

North American Black Widow Revolver

Similar to Mini-Master, 2" heavy vent barrel. Built on 22 WMR frame. Non-fluted cylinder, black rubber grips. Available with Millett Low Profile fixed sights or Millett sight adjustable for elevation only. Overall length 5-7/8", weighs 8.8 oz. From North American Arms.
Price: Adjustable sight, 22 LR, 17 HMR or 22 WMR **$287.00**
Price: As above with extra WMR/LR cylinder **$316.00**
Price: Fixed sight, 22 LR, 17 HMR or 22 WMR **$287.00**
Price: As above with extra WMR/LR cylinder **$287.00**

REPLICA ARMS 1873 SINGLE ACTION REVOLVER

Caliber: .357 Magnum, 6-shot cylinder. **Barrel:** 4-3/4". **Weight:** 32 oz. **Length:** 10-1/4" overall. **Grips:** Walnut finished. **Sights:** Blade front, notch rear. **Features:** bead blue matte finish, matte brass trigger guard and backstrap. Introduced 2005. Imported by Navy Arms.
Price: **$334.95**

RUGER NEW MODEL SINGLE SIX & NEW MODEL .32 H&R SINGLE SIX REVOLVERS

Caliber: 17HMR, 17 Mach 2, 22LR, 22 Mag, 32 H&R. **Barrel:** 4-5/8", 5-1/2", 6-1/2", 7-1/2", 9-1/2". 6-shot. **Grips:** Rosewood, black laminate, simulated ivory. **Sights:** Adjustable or fixed. **Features:** Blued or stainless metalwork, short grips available, convertible models available. Introduced 2003 in 17HMR .
Price: 17 HMR/17 Mach 2 (blued and satin stainless).. **$411.00 to $695.00**
Price: 22 LR /22 Mag. (blued and satin stainless) ..... **$399.00 to $650.00**
Price: 32 H&R (blued and gloss stainless).......... **$535.00 to $576.00**

RUGER NEW MODEL BLACKHAWK/BLACKHAWK CONVERTIBLE

Caliber: 30 Carbine, 357 Mag./38 Spec., 41 Mag., 45 Colt, 6-shot. **Barrel:** 4-5/8", 5-1/2", 6-1/2", 7-1/2" (30 carbine and 45 Colt). **Weight:** 38 to 45 oz. **Lengths:** 10-3/8" to 13-3/8". **Grips:** American walnut. **Sights:** 1/8" ramp front, micro-click rear adjustable for windage and elevation. **Features:** Rosewood grips, Ruger transfer bar safety system, independent firing pin, hardened chrome-moly steel frame, music wire springs through-out. Case and lock included. Convertibles come with extra cylinder.
Price: 30 Carbine, 7-1/2" (BN31, blued) **$482.00**
Price: 357 Mag. (blued or satin stainless) .... **$482.00 to $589.00**
Price: 41 Mag. (blued) **$482.00**
Price: 45 Colt (blued or satin stainless) .... **$482.00 to $589.00**
Price: 357 Mag./9mm Convertible (BN34X, BN36X)........... **$546.00**
Price: 45 Colt/45 ACP Convertible (BN44X, BN455X).......... **$546.00**
Price: 50th Anniversary 44 Mag (S465N-50)................. **$605.00**

Ruger Bisley Single-Action

Ruger Blackhawk

Ruger Super Blackhawk Hunter

Ruger New Vaquero

Ruger New Bearcat

Taurus Gaucho

Ruger Bisley Single-Action Revolver

Similar to standard Blackhawk, hammer is lower with smoothly curved, deeply checkered wide spur. The trigger is strongly curved with wide smooth surface. Longer grip frame. Adjustable rear sight, ramp-style front. Unfluted cylinder and roll engraving, adjustable sights. Chambered for 22 LR, 357 Mag, 44 Mag. and 45 Colt; 6-1/2" to 7-1/2" barrel; overall length of 11-1/2" to 13-1/2"; weighs 43-51 oz. Plastic lockable case. Orig. fluted cylinder introduced 1985; discontinued 1991. Unfluted cylinder introduced 1986.
Price: RB35W (357Mag) RB-44W (44 Mag), RB45W (45 Colt).... **$597.00**
Price: RB22AW (22LR) **$475.00**

RUGER NEW MODEL SUPER BLACKHAWK

Caliber: 44 Mag., 6-shot. Also fires 44 Spec. **Barrel:** 4-5/8", 5-1/2", 7-1/2", 10-1/2" bull. **Weight:** 45-55 oz. **Length:** 10.5" to 16.5" overall. **Grips:** Rosewood or black laminate. **Sights:** 1/8" ramp front, micro-click rear adjustable for windage and elevation. **Features:** Ruger transfer bar safety system, fluted or unfluted cylinder, steel grip and cylinder frame, round or square back trigger guard, wide serrated trigger, wide spur hammer. With case and lock.
Price: Blue, 4-5/8", 5-1/2", 7-1/2" (S458N, S45N, S47N) **$579.00**
Price: Blue, 10-1/2" bull barrel (S411N) **$589.00**
Price: Stainless, 4-5/8", 5-1/2", 7-1/2" (KS458N, KS45N, KS47N) . **$594.00**
Price: Stainless, 10-1/2" bull barrel (KS411N) **$617.00**
Price: Hunter model, satin stainless, 7-1/2" (KS47NHNN) **$696.00**
Price: Hunter model, Bisley frame, satin stainless 7-1/2"
(KS47NHB) **$696.00**

RUGER NEW MODEL SUPER BLACKHAWK HUNTER

Caliber: 44 Mag., 6-shot. **Barrel:** 7-1/2", full-length solid rib, unfluted cylinder. **Weight:** 52 oz. **Length:** 13-5/8". **Grips:** Black laminated wood. **Sights:** Adjustable rear, replaceable front blade. **Features:** Reintroduced Ultimate SA revolver. Includes instruction manual, high-impact case, set 1" medium scope rings, gun lock, ejector rod as standard.
Price: **$639.00**

RUGER NEW VAQUERO SINGLE-ACTION REVOLVER

Caliber: 357 Mag., 45 Colt, 6-shot. **Barrel:** 4-5/8", 5-1/2", 7-1/2". **Weight:** 39-45 oz. **Length:** 10-1/2" overall (4-5/8" barrel). **Grips:** Rubber with Ruger medallion. **Sights:** Blade front, fixed notch rear. **Features:** Transfer bar safety system and loading gate interlock. Blued model color case-hardened finish on frame, rest polished and blued. Engraved model available. Gloss stainless. Introduced 2005.
Price: 357 Mag., blued or stainless **$590.00**
Price: 45 Colt, blued or stainless **$590.00**

RUGER NEW BEARCAT SINGLE-ACTION

Caliber: 22 LR, 6-shot. **Barrel:** 4". **Weight:** 24 oz. **Length:** 9" overall. **Grips:** Smooth rosewood with Ruger medallion. **Sights:** Blade front, fixed notch rear. **Features:** Reintroduction of the Ruger Bearcat with slightly lengthened frame, Ruger transfer bar safety system. Available in blue only. Rosewood grips. Introduced 1996 (blued), 2003 (stainless). With case and lock.
Price: SBC4, blued **$410.00**
Price: KSBC-4, satin stainless **$464.00**

TAURUS SINGLE-ACTION GAUCHO REVOLVERS

Caliber: 38 Spl, 357 Mag, 44-40, 45 Colt, 6-shot. **Barrel:** 4.75", 5.5", 7.5", 12". **Weight:** 36.7-37.7 oz. **Length:** 13". **Grips:** Checkered black polymer. **Sights:** Blade front, fixed notch rear. Integral transfer bar; blue, blue with case hardened frame, matte stainless and the hand polished "Sundance" stainless finish. Removable cylinder, half-cock notch. Introduced 2005. Imported from Brazil by Taurus International.
Price: S/A-357-B, 357 Mag., Sundance blue finish, 5.5" barrel.... **$499.00**
Price: S/A-357-S/S7, 357 Mag., polished stainless, 7.5" barrel.... **$510.00**
Price: S/A-4440-CHSA4, 44-40, case-hardened, 4.75" barrel **$510.00**
Price: S/A-45B12, 45 Colt, Buntline, 12" barrel **$525.00**

Tristar Regulator

Uberti 1873 Cattleman

Uberti 1870 Schofield

Uberti Bisley

U.S. Fire Arms Single Action Army Revolver

TRISTAR/UBERTI REGULATOR REVOLVER

Caliber: 45 Colt. **Barrel:** 4-3/4", 5.5". **Weight:** 32-38 oz. **Length:** 8-1/4" overall (4-3/4" bbl.) **Grips:** One-piece walnut. **Sights:** Blade front, notch rear. **Features:** Uberti replica of 1873 Colt Model "P" revolver. Color-case hardened steel frame, brass backstrap and trigger guard, hammer-block safety. Imported from Italy by Tristar Sporting Arms.
Price: Regulator. **$455.00**
Price: Regulator Deluxe (blued backstrap, trigger guard) **$489.00**
Price: Stallion (.17 HMR and .17 M2 Cylinders) **$459.00**

UBERTI 1873 CATTLEMAN SINGLE-ACTION

Caliber: 45 Colt; 6-shot fluted cylinder **Barrel:** 4-3/4", 5-1/2", 7-1/2". **Weight:** 2.3 lbs. (5-1/2" bbl.). **Length:** 11" overall (5-1/2" bbl.). **Grips:** Styles: Frisco (pearl styled); Desperado (buffalo horn styled); Chisholm (checkered walnut); Gunfighter (black checkered), Cody (ivory styled), one-piece walnut. **Sights:** Blade front, groove rear. **Features:** Steel or brass backstrap, trigger guard; color case-hardened frame, blued barrel, cylinder. NM designates New Model plunger style frame; OM designates Old Model screw cylinder pin retainer. Imported from Italy by Uberti U.S.A.
Price: 1873 Cattleman Frisco **$635.00**
Price: 1873 Cattleman Desperado (2006) **$635.00**
Price: 1873 Cattleman Chisholm (2006). **$385.00**
Price: 1873 Cattleman NM, blued 4-3/4" barrel **$385.00**
Price: 1873 Cattleman NM, stainless steel 7-1/2" barrel **$530.00**
Price: 1873 Cattleman OM, Old West finish, 5-1/2" barrel **$525.00**
Price: 1873 Cattleman NM, Nickel finish, 7-1/2" barrel. **$545.00**

UBERTI 1873 CATTLEMAN BIRD'S HEAD SINGLE ACTION

Caliber: 357 Mag., 45 Colt; 6-shot fluted cylinder **Barrel:** 3-1/2", 4", 4-3/4", 5-1/2". **Weight:** 2.3 lbs. (5-1/2" bbl.). **Length:** 10.9" overall (5-1/2" bbl.). **Grips:** One-piece walnut. **Sights:** Blade front, groove rear. **Features:** Steel or brass backstrap, trigger guard; color case-hardened frame, blued barrel, cylinder. Imported from Italy by Uberti U.S.A.
Price: 1873 Cattleman Bird's Head OM 3-1/2" barrel **$500.00**

UBERTI 1873 BUNTLINE AND REVOLVER CARBINE SINGLE ACTION

Caliber: 357 Mag., 44-40, 45 Colt; 6-shot fluted cylinder **Barrel:** 18". **Length:** 22.9" to 34". **Grips:** Walnut pistol grip or rifle stock. **Sights:** Fixed or adjustable. **Features:** Imported from Italy by Uberti U.S.A.
Price: 1873 Revolver Carbine, 18" barrel, 34" OAL **$585.00**
Price: 1873 Cattleman Buntline Target, 18" barrel, 22.9" OAL **$520.00**

UBERTI OUTLAW, FRONTIER, AND POLICE REVOLVERS

Caliber: 45 Colt, 6-shot fluted cylinder. **Barrel:** 5-1/2", 7-1/2". **Weight:** 2.5 to 2.8 lbs. **Length:** 10.8" to 13.6" overall. **Grips:** Two-piece smooth walnut. **Sights:** Blade front, notch rear. **Features:** Cartridge version of 1858 Remington percussion revolver. Nickel and blued finishes. Imported by Uberti U.S.A.
Price: 1875 Outlaw nickel finish **$515.00**
Price: 1875 Frontier, blued finish **$435.00**
Price: 1890 Police, blued finish **$440.00**

UBERTI 1870 SCHOFIELD-STYLE BREAK-TOP REVOLVER

Caliber: 38, 44 Russian, 44-40, 45 Colt, 6-shot cylinder. **Barrel:** 3-1/2", 5", 7". **Weight:** 2.4 lbs. (5" barrel) **Length:** 10.8" overall (5" barrel). **Grips:** Two-piece smooth walnut or pearl. **Sights:** Blade front, notch rear. **Features:** Replica of Smith & Wesson Model 3 Schofield. Single-action, top-break with automatic ejection. Polished blue finish (first model). Introduced 1994. Imported by Uberti U.S.A.
Price: No. 3-2nd Model, nickel finish **$925.00**

UBERTI BISLEY AND STALLION MODELS SINGLE-ACTION REVOLVERS

Caliber: 357 Mag., 45 Colt (Bisley); 22LR and 38 Special (Stallion), both with 6-shot fluted cylinder. **Barrel:** 4-3/4", 5-1/2", 7-1/2". **Weight:** 2 to 2.5 lbs. **Length:** 12.7" overall (7-1/2" barrel). **Grips:** Two-piece walnut. **Sights:** Blade front, notch rear. **Features:** Replica of Colt's Bisley Model. Polished blue finish, color case-hardened frame. Introduced 1997. Imported by Uberti U.S.A.
Price: 1873 Stallion, 5-1/2" barrel. **$425.00**
Price: 1873 Bisley, 7-1/2" barrel **$500.00**

U.S. Fire Arms Single Action Flattop Target

U.S. Fire Arms Single Action Omni-Potent

U.S. Fire Arms Single Action Bisley

U.S. Fire Arms Rodeo Cowboy Action

U.S. Firearms United States Pre-War

U.S. FIRE ARMS SINGLE ACTION REVOLVER

Caliber: 45 Colt (standard); 32 WCF, 38 WCF, 38 Special, 44 WCF, 44 Special, 6-shot cylinder. **Barrel:** 4-3/4", 5-1/2", 7-1/2". **Weight:** 37 oz. **Length:** NA. **Grips:** Hard rubber. **Sights:** Blade front, notch rear. **Features:** Recreation of original guns; 3" and 4" have no ejector. Available with all-blue, blue with color case-hardening, or full nickel-plate finish. Other models include Government Inspector Series ($1,485, walnut grips), Custer Battlefield Gun ($1,485, 7-1/2" barrel), Patriot Series ($1,280, lanyard loop in 30 Carbine), Flattop Target ($1,495), Sheriff's Model ($1,085, with barrel lengths starting at 2"), Snubnose ($1,295, barrel lengths 2", 3", 4"), Omni-Potent Six-Shooter and Omni-Target Six-Shooter (from $1,485), Bisley and Bisley Target (from $1,485, introduced 2006). Made in U.S.A. by United States Fire Arms Mfg. Co.
Price: Blue/cased-colors **$1,085.00**
Price: Nickel **$1,485.00**

U.S. FIRE ARMS RODEO COWBOY ACTION REVOLVER

Caliber: 45 Colt, 38 Special. **Barrel:** 4-3/4", 5-1/2". **Grips:** Rubber. **Features:** Historically correct Armory bone case hammer, blue satin finish, transfer bar safety system, correct solid firing pin. Entry level basic cowboy SASS gun. Other models include Cowboy ($945) and Gunslinger ($1,045). 2006 version includes brown-rubber stocks.
Price: **$649.00**

U.S. FIRE ARMS U.S. PRE-WAR

Caliber: 45 Colt (standard); 32 WCF, 38 WCF, 38 Special, 44 WCF, 44 Special. **Barrel:** 4-3/4", 5-1/2", 7-1/2". **Grips:** Hard rubber. **Features:** Armory bone case/Armory blue finish standard, cross-pin or black powder frame. Introduced 2002. Made in U.S.A. by United States Firearms Mfg. Co.
Price: **$1,345.00**

Specially adapted single-shot and multi-barrel arms.

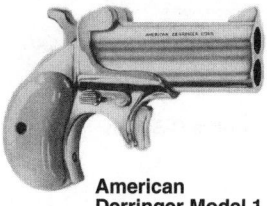

American Derringer Model 1

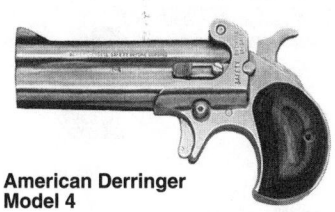

American Derringer Model 4

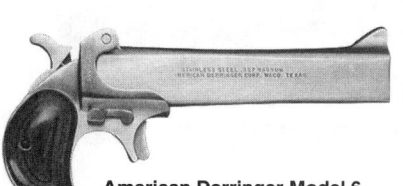

American Derringer Model 6

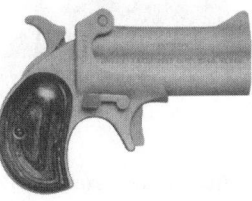

American Derringer Model 7

American Derringer Lady Derringer

American Derringer DA 38

AMERICAN DERRINGER MODEL 1

Caliber: 22 LR, 22 WMR, 30 Carbine, 30 Luger, 30-30 Win., 32 H&R Mag., 32-20, 380 ACP, 38 Super, 38 Spec., 38 Spec. shotshell, 38 Spec. +P, 9mm Para., 357 Mag., 357 Mag./45/410, 357 Maximum, 10mm, 40 S&W, 41 Mag., 38-40, 44-40 Win., 44 Spec., 44 Mag., 45 Colt, 45 Win. Mag., 45 ACP, 45 Colt/410, 45-70 single shot. **Barrel:** 3". **Weight:** 15-1/2 oz. (38 Spec.). **Length:** 4.82" overall. **Grips:** Rosewood, Zebra wood. **Sights:** Blade front. **Features:** Made of stainless steel with high-polish or satin finish. Two-shot capacity. Manual hammer block safety. Introduced 1980. Available in most pistol calibers. From American Derringer Corp.

Price: 22 LR . . . . **CALL**
Price: 38 Spec. . . . . **CALL**
Price: 357 Maximum . . . . **CALL**
Price: 357 Mag. . . . . **CALL**
Price: 9mm, 380 . . . . **CALL**
Price: 40 S&W . . . . **CALL**
Price: 44 Spec. . . . . **CALL**
Price: 44-40 Win. . . . . **CALL**
Price: 45 Colt . . . . **CALL**
Price: 30-30, 45 Win. Mag. . . . . **CALL**
Price: 41, 44 Mags. . . . . **CALL**
Price: 45-70, single shot . . . . **CALL**
Price: 45 Colt, 410, 2-1/2" . . . . **CALL**
Price: 45 ACP, 10mm Auto . . . . **CALL**

American Derringer Model 4

Similar to the Model 1 except has 4.1" barrel, overall length of 6", and weighs 16-1/2 oz.; chambered for 357 Mag., 357 Maximum, 45-70, 3" 410-bore shotshells or 45 Colt or 44 Mag. Made of stainless steel. Manual hammer block safety. Introduced 1980.

Price: 3" 410/45 Colt **$425.00**
Price: 45-70 . . . . **$560.00**
Price: 44 Mag. with oversize grips **$515.00**
Price: Alaskan Survival model
(45-70 upper barrel, 410 or 45 Colt lower) **$475.00**

American Derringer Model 6

Similar to the Model 1 except has 6" barrel chambered for 3" 410 shotshells or 22 WMR, 357 Mag., 45 ACP, 45 Colt; rosewood stocks; 8.2" o.a.l. and weighs 21 oz. Manual hammer block safety. Introduced 1980.

Price: 22 WMR **$440.00**
Price: 357 Mag. **$440.00**
Price: 45 Colt/410 . . . . **$450.00**
Price: 45 ACP **$440.00**

American Derringer Model 7 Ultra Lightweight

Similar to Model 1 except made of high strength aircraft aluminum. Weighs 7-1/2 oz., 4.82" o.a.l., rosewood stocks. Available in 22 LR, 22 WMR, 32 H&R Mag., 380 ACP, 38 Spec., 44 Spec. Introduced 1980.

Price: 22 LR, WMR **$325.00**
Price: 38 Spec. **$325.00**
Price: 380 ACP **$325.00**
Price: 32 H&R Mag/32 S&W Long **$325.00**
Price: 44 Spec. **$565.00**

American Derringer Model 10 Ultra Lightweight

Similar to the Model 1 except frame is aluminum, giving weight of 10 oz. Stainless barrels. Available in 38 Spec., 45 Colt or 45 ACP only. Matte gray finish. Introduced 1980.

Price: 45 Colt **$385.00**
Price: 45 ACP **$330.00**
Price: 38 Spec. **$305.00**

American Derringer Lady Derringer

Same as the Model 1 except has tuned action, is fitted with scrimshawed synthetic ivory grips; chambered for 32 H&R Mag. and 38 Spec.; 357 Mag., 45 Colt, 45/410. Deluxe Grade is highly polished; Deluxe Engraved is engraved in a pattern similar to that used on 1880s derringers. All models come in a French-fitted jewelry box. Introduced 1989.

Price: 32 H&R Mag. **$375.00**
Price: 357 Mag. **$405.00**
Price: 38 Spec. **$360.00**
Price: 45 Colt, 45/410 . . . . **$435.00**

American Derringer Texas Commemorative

Model 1 Derringer with solid brass frame, stainless steel barrel and rosewood grips. Available in 38 Spec., 44-40 Win., or 45 Colt. Introduced 1980.

Price: 38 Spec. **$365.00**
Price: 44-40 . . . . **$420.00**
Price: Brass frame, 45 Colt **$450.00**

AMERICAN DERRINGER DA 38 MODEL

Caliber: 22 LR, 9mm Para., 38 Spec., 357 Mag., 40 S&W. **Barrel:** 3". **Weight:** 14.5 oz. **Length:** 4.8" overall. **Grips:** Rosewood, walnut or other hardwoods. **Sights:** Fixed. **Features:** Double-action only; two shots. Manual safety. Made of satin-finished stainless steel and aluminum. Introduced 1989. From American Derringer Corp.

Price: 22 LR **$435.00**
Price: 38 Spec. **$460.00**
Price: 9mm Para. **$445.00**
Price: 357 Mag. **$450.00**
Price: 40 S&W **$475.00**

ANSCHUTZ MODEL 64P SPORT/TARGET PISTOL

Caliber: 22 LR, 22 WMR, 5-shot magazine. **Barrel:** 10". **Weight:** 3 lbs. 8 oz. **Length:** 18-1/2" overall. **Stock:** Choate Rynite. **Sights:** None furnished; grooved for scope mounting. **Features:** Right-hand bolt; polished blue finish. Introduced 1998. Imported from Germany by AcuSport.

Price: 22 LR **$455.95**
Price: 22 WMR **$479.95**

HANDGUNS — Miscellaneous

Bond Arms Texas Defender

Bond Arms Century 2000 Defender

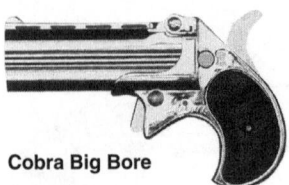

Cobra Big Bore

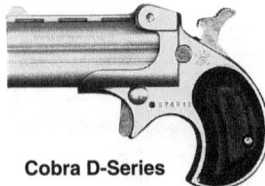

Cobra D-Series

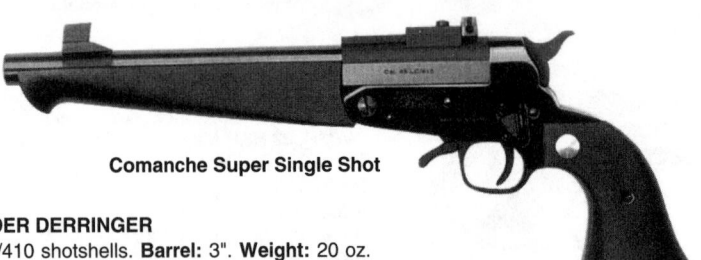

Comanche Super Single Shot

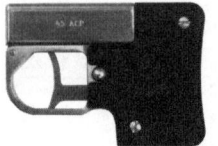

Downsizer WSP Single Shot

BOND ARMS TEXAS DEFENDER DERRINGER

Caliber: From 22 LR to 45 LC/410 shotshells. **Barrel:** 3". **Weight:** 20 oz. **Length:** 5". **Grips:** Rosewood. **Sights:** Blade front, fixed rear. **Features:** Interchangeable barrels, stainless steel firing pins, cross-bolt safety, automatic extractor for rimmed calibers. Stainless steel construction, brushed finish. Right or left hand.

Price: **$389.00**
Price: Interchangeable barrels, 22 LR thru 45 LC, 3".......... **$139.00**
Price: Interchangeable barrels, 45 LC, 3.5" **$159.00**

BOND ARMS CENTURY 2000 DEFENDER

Caliber: 45LC/410 shotshells. **Barrel:** 3.5". **Weight:** 21 oz. **Length:** 5.5". **Features:** Similar to Defender series.

Price: **$404.00**

BOND ARMS COWBOY DEFENDER

Caliber: From 22 LR to 45 LC/410 shotshells. **Barrel:** 3". **Weight:** 19 oz. **Length:** 5.5". **Features:** Similar to Defender series. No trigger guard.

Price: **$389.00**

BOND ARMS SNAKE SLAYER

Caliber: 45 LC/410 shotshell (2-1/2" or 3"). **Barrel:** 3.5". **Weight:** 21 oz. **Length:** 5.5". **Grips:** Extended rosewood. **Sights:** Blade front, fixed rear. **Features:** Single-action; interchangeable barrels; stainless steel firing pin. Introduced 2005.

Price: **$455.00**

BOND ARMS SNAKE SLAYER IV

Caliber: 45 LC/410 shotshell (2-1/2" or 3"). **Barrel:** 4.25". **Weight:** 22 oz. **Length:** 6.25". **Grips:** Extended rosewood. **Sights:** Blade front, fixed rear. **Features:** Single-action; interchangeable barrels; stainless steel firing pin. Introduced 2006.

Price: **$475.00**

BROWN CLASSIC SINGLE SHOT PISTOL

Caliber: 17 Ackley Hornet through 375x444. **Barrel:** 15" air-gauged match grade. **Weight:** About 3 lbs. 7 oz. **Grips:** Walnut; thumb rest target-style. **Sights:** None furnished; drilled and tapped for scope mounting. **Features:** Falling block action gives rigid barrel-receiver mating; hand fitted and headspaced. Introduced 1998. Made in U.S.A. by E.A. Brown Mfg.

Price: **$589.00**

CHARTER ARMS DIXIE DERRINGERS

Caliber: 22 LR, 22 WMR. **Barrel:** 1.125". **Weight:** 5-6 oz. **Length:** 4" overall. **Grips:** Black polymer **Sights:** Blade front, fixed notch rear. **Features:** Stainless finish. Introduced 2006. Made in U.S.A. by Charter Arms, distributed by MKS Supply.

Price: **$112.00**

COBRA BIG BORE DERRINGERS

Caliber: 22 WMR, 32 H&R Mag., 38 Spec., 9mm Para. **Barrel:** 2.75". **Weight:** 11.5 oz. **Length:** 4.65" overall. **Grips:** Textured black synthetic.

Sights: Blade front, fixed notch rear. **Features:** Alloy frame, steel-lined barrels, steel breech block. Plunger-type safety with integral hammer block. Chrome or black Teflon finish. Introduced 2002. Made in U.S.A. by Cobra Enterprises.

Price: **$98.00**
Price: 9mm Para **$136.00**

COBRA LONG-BORE DERRINGERS

Caliber: 22 WMR, 38 Spec., 9mm Para. **Barrel:** 3.5". **Weight:** 13 oz. **Length:** 5.65" overall. **Grips:** Textured black synthetic. **Sights:** Fixed. **Features:** Chrome or black Teflon finish. Larger than Davis D-Series models. Introduced 2002. Made in U.S.A. by Cobra Enterprises.

Price: **$136.00**
Price: 9mm Para. **$136.00**
Price: Big-Bore models (same calibers, 3/4" shorter barrels) **$136.00**

COBRA STARBIRD-SERIES DERRINGERS

Caliber: 22 LR, 22 WMR, 25 ACP, 32 ACP. **Barrel:** 2.4". **Weight:** 9.5 oz. **Length:** 4" overall. **Grips:** Laminated wood or pearl. **Sights:** Blade front, fixed notch rear. **Features:** Choice of black powder coat, satin nickel or chrome finish; spur trigger. Introduced 2002. Made in U.S.A. by Cobra Enterprises.

Price: **$112.00**

COMANCHE SUPER SINGLE SHOT PISTOL

Caliber: 45 LC, 410 ga. **Barrel:** 10". **Sights:** Adjustable. **Features:** Blue finish, not available for sale in CA, MA. Distributed by SGS Importers International, Inc.

Price: **$183.95**
Price: Satin nickel **$199.95**
Price: Camo, intr. 2006 .... **$216.95**

DOWNSIZER WSP SINGLE SHOT PISTOL

Caliber: 357 Magnum, 45 ACP, 38 Special. **Barrel:** 2.10". **Weight:** 11 oz. **Length:** 3.25" overall. **Grips:** Black polymer. **Sights:** None. **Features:** Single shot, tip-up barrel. Double action only. Stainless steel construction. Measures .900" thick. Introduced 1997. From Downsizer Corp.

Price: **$499.00**

GAUCHER GN1 SILHOUETTE PISTOL

Caliber: 22 LR, single shot. **Barrel:** 10". **Weight:** 2.4 lbs. **Length:** 15.5" overall. **Grips:** European hardwood. **Sights:** Blade front, open adjustable rear. **Features:** Bolt action, adjustable trigger. Introduced 1990. Imported from France by Mandall Shooting Supplies.

Price: About **$525.00**
Price: Model GP Silhouette **$425.00**

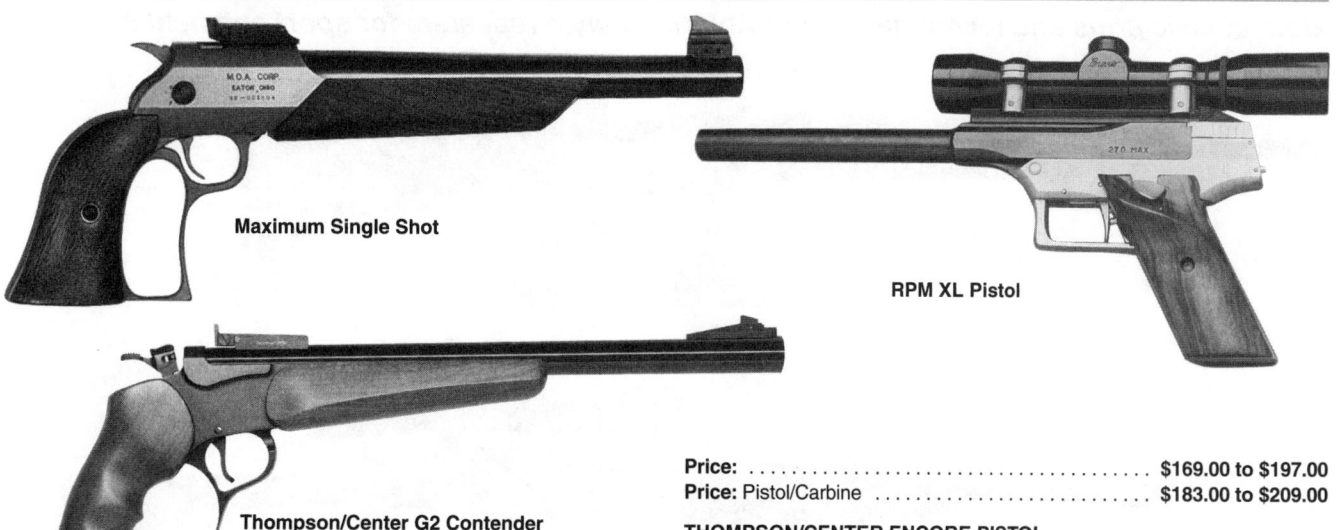

Maximum Single Shot

RPM XL Pistol

Thompson/Center G2 Contender

MAXIMUM SINGLE SHOT PISTOL
Caliber: 22 LR, 22 Hornet, 22 BR, 22 PPC, 223 Rem., 22-250, 6mm BR, 6mm PPC, 243, 250 Savage, 6.5mm-35M, 270 MAX, 270 Win., 7mm TCU, 7mm BR, 7mm-35, 7mm INT-R, 7mm-08, 7mm Rocket, 7mm Super-Mag., 30 Herrett, 30 Carbine, 30-30, 308 Win., 30x39, 32-20, 350 Rem. Mag., 357 Mag., 357 Maximum, 358 Win., 375 H&H, 44 Mag., 454 Casull. **Barrel:** 8-3/4", 10-1/2", 14". **Weight:** 61 oz. (10-1/2" bbl.); 78 oz. (14" bbl.). **Length:** 15", 18-1/2" overall (with 10-1/2" and 14" bbl., respectively). **Grips:** Smooth walnut stocks and forend. Also available with 17" finger groove grip. **Sights:** Ramp front, fully adjustable open rear. **Features:** Falling block action; drilled and tapped for M.O.A. scope mounts; integral grip frame/receiver; adjustable trigger; Douglas barrel (interchangeable). Introduced 1983. Made in U.S.A. by M.O.A. Corp.
Price: Stainless receiver, blue barrel **$799.00**
Price: Stainless receiver, stainless barrel **$883.00**
Price: Extra blued barrel **$254.00**
Price: Extra stainless barrel **$317.00**
Price: Scope mount **$60.00**

RPM XL SINGLE SHOT PISTOL
Caliber: 22 LR through 45-70. **Barrel:** 8", 10-3/4", 12", 14". **Weight:** About 60 oz. **Grips:** Smooth Goncalo Alves with thumb and heel rests. **Features:** Barrel drilled and tapped for scope mount. Visible cocking indicator. Spring-loaded barrel lock, positive hammer-block safety. Trigger adjustable for weight of pull and over-travel. Contact maker for complete price list. Made in U.S.A. by RPM.
Price: XL Hunter model (action only) **$1,045.00**
Price: Extra barrel . . . . **$250.00 to $300.00**

SPRINGFIELD M6 SCOUT PISTOL
Caliber: 22 LR/45 LC/410, 22 Hornet, 45 LC/410. **Barrel:** 10". **Weight:** NA. **Length:** NA. **Grips:** NA. **Sights:** NA. **Features:** Adapted from the U.S. Air Force M6 Survival Rifle, also available as a carbine with 16" barrel.

Price: . . . . **$169.00 to $197.00**
Price: Pistol/Carbine . . . . **$183.00 to $209.00**

THOMPSON/CENTER ENCORE PISTOL
Caliber: 22-250, 223, 204 Ruger, 6.8 Rem., 260 Rem., 7mm-08, 243, 308, 270, 30-06, 375 JDJ, 204 Ruger, 44 Mag., 454 Casull, 480 Ruger, 444 Marlin single shot, 450 Marlin with muzzle tamer, no sights. **Barrel:** 12", 15", tapered round. **Weight:** NA. **Length:** 21" overall with 12" barrel. **Grips:** American walnut with finger grooves, walnut forend. **Sights:** Blade on ramp front, adjustable rear, or none. **Features:** Interchangeable barrels; action opens by squeezing the trigger guard; drilled and tapped for scope mounting; blue finish. Announced 1996. Made in U.S.A. by Thompson/Center Arms.
Price: . . . . **$589.00 to $592.00**
Price: Extra 12" barrels **$262.00**
Price: Extra 15" barrels **$270.00**
Price: 45 Colt/410 barrel, 12" **$292.00**
Price: 45 Colt/410 barrel, 15" **$299.00**

Thompson/Center Stainless Encore Pistol
Similar to blued Encore, made of stainless steel, available with 15" barrel in 223, 22-250, 243 Win., 7mm-08, 308, 30/06 Sprgfld., 45/70 Gov't., 45/410 VR. With black rubber grip and forend. Made in U.S.A. by Thompson/Center Arms.
Price: . . . . **$636.00 to $644.00**

Thompson/Center G2 Contender Pistol
A second generation Contender pistol maintaining the same barrel interchangeability with older Contender barrels and their corresponding forends (except Herrett forend). The G2 frame will not accept old-style grips due to the change in grip angle. Incorporates an automatic hammer block safety with built-in interlock. Features include trigger adjustable for overtravel, adjustable rear sight; ramp front sight blade, blued steel finish.
Price: **$570.00**

UBERTI ROLLING BLOCK TARGET PISTOL
Caliber: 22LR, 22 Mag., single shot. **Barrel:** 9.5". **Weight:** 2.8 lbs. **Length:** 14". **Stocks:** Walnut grip and forend. **Sights:** Adjustable rear, blade front. **Features:** Replica of the 1871 rolling block target pistol. Case-hardened frame and backstrap, blued barrel and trigger guard. Made in Italy by Uberti, imported by Benelli USA.
Price: **$480.00**

Both classic arms and recent designs in American-style repeaters for sport and field shooting.

Armalite M15A2

Armalite AR-10A4

Armalite AR-180B

ARMALITE M15A2 CARBINE

Caliber: 223, 30-round magazine. **Barrel:** 16" heavy chrome lined; 1:9" twist. **Weight:** 7 lbs. **Length:** 35-11/16" overall. **Stock:** Green or black composition. **Sights:** Standard A2. **Features:** Upper and lower receivers have push-type pivot pin; hard coat anodized; A2-style forward assist; M16A2-type raised fence around magazine release button. Made in U.S.A. by ArmaLite, Inc.
Price: Green **$1,100.00**
Price: Black **$1,100.00**

ARMALITE AR-10A4 SPECIAL PURPOSE RIFLE

Caliber: 308 Win., 10- and 20-round magazine. **Barrel:** 20" chrome-lined, 1:11.25" twist. **Weight:** 9.6 lbs. **Length:** 41" overall. **Stock:** Green or black composition. **Sights:** Detachable handle, front sight, or scope mount available; comes with international style flattop receiver with Picatinny rail. **Features:** Forged upper receiver with case deflector. Receivers are hard-coat anodized. Introduced 1995. Made in U.S.A. by ArmaLite, Inc.
Price: Green **$1,506.00**
Price: Black **$1,506.00**

ArmaLite AR-10(T)

Similar to the ArmaLite AR-10A4 but with stainless steel, barrel, machined tool steel, two-stage National Match trigger group and other features.
Price: AR-10(T) rifle **$2,126.00**

ArmaLite AR-10A2

Utilizing the same 20" double-lapped, heavy barrel as the ArmaLite AR-10A4 Special Purpose Rifle. Offered in 308 caliber only. Made in U.S.A. by ArmaLite, Inc.
Price: AR-10A2 rifle or carbine **$1,506.00**

ARMALITE AR-180B RIFLE

Caliber: 223, 10-shot magazine. **Barrel:** 19.8". **Weight:** 6 lbs. **Length:** 38". **Stock:** Synthetic. **Sights:** Rear sight adjustable for windage, small and large apertures. **Features:** Lower receiver made of polymer, upper formed of sheet metal. Uses standard AR-15 magazines. Made in U.S.A. by Armalite.
Price: **$750.00**

ARSENAL USA SSR-56

Caliber: 7.62x39mm. **Barrel:** 16.25". **Weight:** 7.4 lbs. **Length:** 35.5" **Stock:** Black polymer. **Sights:** Adjustable rear. **Features:** An AK-47-style rifle built on a hardened Hungarian FEG receiver with the required six U.S.-made parts to make it legal for use with all extra-capacity magazines. From Arsenal I, LLC.
Price: **$565.00**

ARSENAL USA SSR-74-2

Caliber: 5.45x39mm **Barrel:** 16.25" **Weight:** 7 lbs. **Length:** 36.75" **Stock:** Polymer or wood. **Sights:** Adjustable. **Features:** Built with parts from an unissued Bulgarian AK-47 rifle, it has a Buffer Technologies recoil buffer, enough U.S.-made parts to allow pistol grip stock and use with all extra-capacity magazines. Assembled in U.S.A. From Arsenal I, LLC.
Price: **$499.00**

ARSENAL USA SSR-85C-2

Caliber: 7.62x39mm. **Barrel:** 16.25". **Weight:** 7.1 lbs. **Length:** 35.5". **Stock:** Polymer or wood. **Sights:** Adjustable rear calibrated to 800 meters. **Features:** Built from parts obtained from unissued Polish AK-47 rifles, the gas tube is vented and the receiver cover is plain. Rifle contains enough U.S.-sourced parts to allow pistol grip stock and use with all extra-capacity magazines. Assembled in U.S.A. by Arsenal I, LLC.
Price: **$499.00**

Auto-Ordnance 1927 A-1 Thompson

Barrett Model 82A-1

Beretta CX4 Carbine

AUTO-ORDNANCE 1927 A-1 THOMPSON
Caliber: 45 ACP. **Barrel:** 16-1/2". **Weight:** 13 lbs. **Length:** About 41" overall (Deluxe). **Stock:** Walnut stock and vertical forend. **Sights:** Blade front, open rear adjustable for windage. **Features:** Recreation of Thompson Model 1927. Semi-auto only. Deluxe model has finned barrel, adjustable rear sight and compensator; Standard model has plain barrel and military sight. From Auto-Ordnance Corp.
Price: Deluxe **$950.00**
Price: 1927A1C lightweight model (9-1/2 lbs.) **$950.00**

Auto-Ordnance Thompson M1/M1-C
Similar to the 1927 A-1 except is in the M-1 configuration with side cocking knob, horizontal forend, smooth unfinned barrel, sling swivels on butt and forend. Matte black finish. Introduced 1985.
Price: M1 semi-auto carbin **$950.00**
Price: M1-C lightweight semi-auto **$925.00**

Auto-Ordnance 1927 A-1 Commando
Similar to the 1927 A-1 except has Parkerized finish, black-finish wood butt, pistol grip, horizontal forend. Comes with black nylon sling. Introduced 1998. Made in U.S.A. by Auto-Ordnance Corp.
Price: **$950.00**

BARRETT MODEL 82A-1 SEMI-AUTOMATIC RIFLE
Caliber: 50 BMG, 10-shot detachable box magazine. **Barrel:** 29". **Weight:** 28.5 lbs. **Length:** 57" overall. **Stock:** Composition with energy-absorbing recoil pad. **Sights:** Scope optional. **Features:** Semi-automatic, recoil operated with recoiling barrel. Three-lug locking bolt; muzzle brake. Adjustable bipod. Introduced 1985. Made in U.S.A. by Barrett Firearms.
Price: From **$7,200.00**

BENELLI R1 RIFLE
Caliber: 300 Win. Mag., 300 WSM, 270 WSM (24" barrel); 30-06, 308 (22" barrel); 300 Win. Mag., 30-06, (20" barrel). **Weight:** 7.1 lbs. **Length:** 43.75" to 45.75" **Stock:** Select satin walnut or synthetic. **Sights:** None. **Features:** Auto-regulating gas-operated system, three-lug rotary bolt, interchangeable barrels, optional recoil pads. Introduced 2003. Imported from Italy by Benelli USA.
Price: Synthetic with ComforTech gel recoil pad **$1,365.00**
Price: Satin walnut **$1,200.00**

BERETTA CX4/PX4 STORM CARBINE
Caliber: 9mm Para, 40 S&W, 45 ACP. **Weight:** 5.75 lbs. **Barrel Length:** 16.6", chrome lined, rate of twist 1:16 (40 S&W) or 1:10 (9mm). **Length:** NA. **Stock:** Black synthetic. **Sights:** NA. **Features:** Introduced 2005. Imported from Italy by Beretta USA.
Price: Cx4 Carbine, 40 S&W, 10+1 . . . . **$800.00**
Price: Cx4 Carbine, 8000 Series, 9mm, 10+1 . . . . **$775.00**
Price: Cx4 Carbine, 8045 Series,45 ACP, 8+1 . . . . **$800.00**
Price: Cx4 Px4 Carbine, 40 S&W, 14+1. . . . . **$850.00**
Price: Cx4 Px4 Carbine, 9mm, 17+1 . . . . **$850.00**

BROWNING BAR SAFARI AND SAFARI W/BOSS SEMI-AUTO RIFLES
Caliber: Safari: 243, 25-06, 270, 7mm Rem Mag., 30-06, 308, 300 Win. Mag., 338 Win Mag. Safari w/BOSS: 270, 7mm Rem Mag., 30-06, 300 Win. Mag., 338 Win Mag., plus 270 WSM, 7mm WSM, 300 WSM. **Barrel:** 22-24" round tapered. **Weight:** 7.4-8.2 lbs. **Length:** 43-45" overall. **Stock:** French walnut pistol grip stock and forend, hand checkered. **Sights:** No sights. **Features:** Has new bolt release lever; removable trigger assembly with larger trigger guard; redesigned gas and buffer systems. Detachable 4-round box magazine. Scroll-engraved receiver is tapped for scope mounting. BOSS barrel vibration modulator and muzzle brake system available. Mark II Safari introduced 1993. Imported from Belgium by Browning.
Price: BAR Safari, 22" barrel, standard cartridge chamberings . . . **$889.00**
Price: BAR Safari, 24" barrel, magnum cartridge chamberings . . . **$972.00**
Price: BAR Safari w/BOSS, standard chamberings. **$988.00**
Price: BAR Safari w/BOSS, WSM and magnum chamberings . . . **$1,071.00**

Browning Mark II Safari

Browning Lightweight Stalker

Bushmaster M17S Bullpup

Bushmaster XM15 E2S Carbine

BROWNING BAR SHORTTRAC/LONGTRAC AUTO RIFLES

Caliber: (ShortTrac models) 270 WSM, 7mm WSM, 300 WSM, 243 Win., 308 Win.; (Long Trac models) 270 Win., 30-06 Sprfld., 7mm Rem. Mag., 300 Win. Mag. **Barrel:** 23". **Weight:** 6 lbs. 10 oz. to 7 lbs. 4 oz. **Length:** 41-1/2" to 44". **Stock:** Satin-finish walnut, pistol-grip, fluted forend. **Sights:** Adj. rear, bead front standard, no sights on BOSS models (optional). **Features:** Designed to handle new WSM chamberings. Gas-operated, blued finish, rotary bolt design (Long Trac models). Introduced 2001. Imported by Browning.

Price: BAR ShortTrac, 243 Win., 308 Win. **$885.00**
Price: BAR ShortTrac WSM, 270 WSM, 7mm WSM, 300 WSM, . . . **$965.00**
Price: BAR LongTrac, 270 Win., 30-06 Sprfld. **$885.00**
Price: BAR LongTrac, 7mm Rem. Mag., 300 Win. Mag. **$965.00**

BROWNING BAR LIGHTWEIGHT STALKER AUTO RIFLE

Caliber: 243, 308, 270, 30-06, 270 WSM, 7mm WSM, 300 WSM, 300 Win. Mag., 338 Win. Mag. **Barrel:** 20-24". **Weight:** 7.1-7.75 LBS. **Length:** 41-45" overall. **Stock:** Black composite stock and forearm. **Sights:** Hooded front and adjustable rear. **Features:** Gas-operated action with seven-lug rotary bolt; dual action bars; 2-, 3- or 4-shot magazine (depending on cartridge). Introduced 2001. Imported by Browning.

Price: BAR Lightweight Stalker, 243, 308, 270, 30-06 . . . . **$883.00**
Price: BAR Lightweight Stalker, WSM and magnums **$964.00**

BUSHMASTER M17S BULLPUP RIFLE

Caliber: 223, 10-shot magazine. **Barrel:** 21.5", chrome lined; 1:9" twist. **Weight:** 8.2 lbs. **Length:** 30" overall. **Stock:** Fiberglass-filled nylon. **Sights:** Designed for optics-carrying handle incorporates scope mount rail for Weaver-type rings; also includes 25-meter open iron sights. **Features:** Gas-operated, short-stroke piston system; ambidextrous magazine release. Introduced 1993. Made in U.S.A. by Bushmaster Firearms, Inc./Quality Parts Co.

Price: **$765.00**

BUSHMASTER SHORTY XM15 E2S CARBINE

Caliber: 223,10-shot magazine. **Barrel:** 16", heavy; 1:9" twist. **Weight:** 7.2 lbs. **Length:** 34.75" overall. **Stock:** A2 type; fixed black composition. **Sights:** Fully adjustable M16A2 sight system. **Features:** Patterned after Colt M-16A2. Chrome-lined barrel with manganese phosphate finish. "Shorty" handguards. Has forged aluminum receivers with pushpin. Made in U.S.A. by Bushmaster Firearms, Inc.

Price: (A2). **$985.00**
Price: (A3) **$1,085.00**

Bushmaster XM15 E2S Dissipator Carbine

Similar to the XM15 E2S Shorty carbine except has full-length "Dissipator" handguards. Weighs 7.6 lbs.; 34.75" overall; forged aluminum receivers with push-pin style takedown. Made in U.S.A. by Bushmaster Firearms, Inc.

Price: (A2 type). **$995.00**
Price: (A3 type) **$1,095.00**

Bushmaster XM15 E25 AK Shorty Carbine

Similar to the XM15 E2S Shorty except has 14.5" barrel with an AK muzzle brake permanently attached giving 16" barrel length. Weighs 7.3 lbs. Introduced 1999. Made in U.S.A. by Bushmaster Firearms, Inc.

Price: (A2 type). **$1,005.00**
Price: (A3 type). **$1,105.00**

Bushmaster M4/M4A3 Post-Ban Carbine

Similar to the XM15 E2S except has 14.5" barrel with Mini Y compensator, and fixed telestock. MR configuration has fixed carry handle; M4A3 has removeable carry handle.

Price: (M4) **$1,065.00**
Price: (M4A3) **$1,165.00**

Bushmaster Varminter

Colt Match Target Lightweight

BUSHMASTER VARMINTER RIFLE
Caliber: 223 Rem., 5-shot. **Barrel:** 24", 1:9" twist, fluted, heavy, stainless. **Weight:** 8-3/4 lbs. **Length:** 42-1/4". **Stock:** Rubberized pistol grip. **Sights:** 1/2" scope risers. **Features:** Gas-operated, semi-auto, two-stage trigger, slotted free floater forend, lockable hard case.
Price: **$1,245.00**

CENTURY INTERNATIONAL AES-10 HI-CAP RIFLE
Caliber: 7.62x39mm. 30-shot magazine. **Barrel:** 23.2". **Weight:** NA. **Length:** 41.5" overall. **Stock:** Wood grip, forend. **Sights:** Fixed-notch rear, windage-adjustable post front. **Features:** RPK-style, accepts standard double-stack AK-type mags. Side-mounted scope mount, integral carry handle, bipod. Imported by Century Arms Int'l.
Price: AES-10, from **$550.00**

CENTURY INTERNATIONAL GP WASR-10 HI-CAP RIFLE
Caliber: 7.62x39mm. 30-shot magazine. **Barrel:** 16.25", 1:10 rh twist. **Weight:** 7.5 lbs. **Length:** 34.25" overall. **Stock:** Wood laminate or composite, grip, forend. **Sights:** Fixed-notch rear, windage-adjustable post front. **Features:** Two 30-rd. detachable box magazines, cleaning kit, bayonet. Version of AKM rifle; U.S.-parts added for BATFE compliance. Threaded muzzle, folding stock, bayonet lug, compensator, Dragunov stock available. Made in Romania by Cugir Arsenal. Imported by Century Arms Int'l.
Price: GP WASR-10, from. **$450.00**

CENTURY INTERNATIONAL WASR-2 HI-CAP RIFLE
Caliber: 5.45x39mm. 30-shot magazine. **Barrel:** 16.25". **Weight:** 7.5 lbs. **Length:** 34.25" overall. **Stocks:** Wood laminate. **Sights:** Fixed-notch rear, windage-adjustable post front. **Features:** 1 30-rd. detachable box magazine, cleaning kit, sling. WASR-3 HI-CAP chambered in 223 Rem. Imported by Century Arms Int'l.
Price: GP WASR-2/3, from **$450.00**

CENTURY INTERNATIONAL WASR 22 RIFLE
Caliber: 22 LR. 10-shot magazine. **Barrel:** 16.25". **Weight:** 7.5 lbs. **Length:** 34.25" overall. **Stocks:** Wood laminate. **Sights:** Fixed-notch rear, windage-adjustable post front. **Features:** 2 10-rd. magazine, cleaning kit, sling. Imported by Century Arms Int'l.
Price: GP WASR 22, from. **$325.00**

CENTURY INTERNATIONAL M70AB2 SPORTER RIFLE
Caliber: 7.62x39mm. 30-shot magazine. **Barrel:** 16.25". **Weight:** 7.5 lbs. **Length:** 34.25" overall. **Stocks:** Metal grip, wood forend. **Sights:** Fixed-notch rear, windage-adjustable post front. **Features:** 2 30-rd. double-stack magazine, cleaning kit, compensator, bayonet lug and bayonet.

Paratrooper-style Kalashnikov with under-folding stock. Imported by Century Arms Int'l.
Price: M70AB2, from **$475.00**

COLT MATCH TARGET MODEL RIFLE
Caliber: 223 Rem., 5-shot magazine. **Barrel:** 16.1" or 20". **Weight:** 7.1 to 8-1/2 lbs. **Length:** 34-1/2" to 39" overall. **Stock:** Composition stock, grip, forend. **Sights:** Post front, rear adjustable for windage and elevation. **Features:** 5-round detachable box magazine, flash suppressor, sling swivels. Forward bolt assist included. Introduced 1991. Made in U.S.A. by Colt's Mfg. Co., Inc.
Price: Match Target HBAR, from **$1,300.00**

DPMS PANTHER ARMS AR-15 RIFLES
Caliber: 223 Rem., 7.62x39. **Barrel:** 16" to 24". **Weight:** 7-3/4 to 11-3/4 lbs. **Length:** 34-1/2" to 42-1/4" overall. **Stock:** Black Zytel® composite. **Sights:** Square front post, adjustable A2 rear. **Features:** Steel or stainless steel heavy or bull barrel; hardcoat anodized receiver; aluminum free-float tube handguard; many options. From DPMS Panther Arms.
Price: Panther Bull A-15 (20" stainless bull bbl.) **$915.00**
Price: Panther Bull Twenty-Four (24" stainless bull bbl.) **$945.00**
Price: Bulldog (20" stainless fluted bbl., flattop receiver) **$1,219.00**
Price: Panther Bull Sweet Sixteen (16" stainless bull bbl.) **$885.00**
Price: DCM Panther (20" stainless heavy bbl., n.m. sights) **$1,099.00**
Price: Panther 7.62x39 (20" steel heavy bbl.) **$849.00**

DSA Z4 GTC CARBINE WITH C.R.O.S.
Caliber: 5.56 NATO **Barrel:** 16" 1:9 twist M4 profile fluted chrome lined heavy barrel with threaded Vortec flash hider. **Weight:** 7.6 lbs. **Stock:** 6 position collapsible M4 stock, Predator P4X free float tactical rail. **Sights:** Chrome lined Picatinny gas block w/removable front sight. **Features:** The Corrosion Resistant Operating System incorporates the new P.O.F. Gas Trap System which removable gas plug eliminates problematic features of standard AR gas system, Forged 7075T6 DSA lower receiver. Introduced 2006. Made in U.S.A. by DSA, Inc.
Price:. **$1,700.00**

DSA CQB MRP, STANDARD MRP
Caliber: 5.56 NATO **Barrel:** 16" or 18" 1:7 twist chrome-lined or stainless steel barrel with A2 flash hider **Stock:** 6 position collapsible M4 stock. **Features:** LMT 1/2" MRP upper receiver with 20-1/2" Standard quad rail or 16 1/2" CQB quad rail, LMT enhanced bolt with dual extractor springs, free float barrel, quick change barrel system, forged 7075T6 DSA lower receiver. EOTech and vertical grip additional. Introduced 2006. Made in U.S.A. by DSA, Inc.
Price: CQB MRP w/16" chrome lined barrel **$2,420.00**
Price: CQB MRP w/16" stainless steel barrel **$2,540.00**
Price: Standard MRP w/16" chrome lined barrel **$2,620.00**
Price: Standard MRP w/16" or 18"stainless steel barrel **$2,720.00**

DSA SA58 Congo

DSA SA58 Para Congo

DSA SA58 Gray Wolf

DSA STD CARBINE

Caliber: 5.56 NATO. **Barrel:** 16" 1:9 twist D4 w/A2 flash hider. **Weight:** 6.25 lbs. **Length:** 31". **Stock:** A2 buttstock, D4 handguard w/heatshield. **Sights:** Forged A2 front sight with lug. **Features:** Forged 7075T6 DSA lower receiver, forged A2 or flattop upper receiver. Introduced 2006. Made in U.S.A. by DSA, Inc.

Price: A2 or Flattop STD Carbine **$1,025.00**
Price: w/LMT SOPMOD stock. **$1,267.00**

DSA 1R CARBINE

Caliber: 5.56 NATO. **Barrel:** 16" 1:9 twist D4 w/A2 flash hider. **Weight:** 6.25 lbs. **Length:** Variable. **Stock:** 6 position collapsible M4 stock, D4 handguard w/heatshield. **Sights:** Forged A2 front sight with lug. **Features:** Forged 7075T6 DSA lower receiver, forged A2 or flattop upper receiver. Introduced 2006. Made in U.S.A. by DSA, Inc.

Price: A2 or Flattop 1R Carbine **$1,055.00**
Price: w/VLTOR ModStock **$1,175.00**

DSA XM CARBINE

Caliber: 5.56 NATO. **Barrel:** 11-1/2" 1:9 twist D4 with 5-1/2" permanently attached flash hider. **Weight:** 6.25 lbs. **Length:** Variable. **Stock:** Collapsible, Handguard w/heatshield. **Sights:** Forged A2 front sight with lug. **Features:** Forged 7075T6 DSA lower receiver, forged A2 upper receiver. Introduced 2006. Made in U.S.A. by DSA, Inc.

Price: **$1,055.00**

DSA STANDARD

Caliber: 5.56 NATO. **Barrel:** 20" 1:9 twist heavy barrel w/A2 flash hider. **Weight:** 6.25 lbs. **Length:** 38-7/16". **Stock:** A2 buttstock, A2 handguard w/heatshield. **Sights:** Forged A2 front sight with lug. **Features:** Forged 7075T6 DSA lower receiver, forged A2 or flattop upper receiver. Introduced 2006. Made in U.S.A. by DSA, Inc.

Price: A2 or Flattop Standard **$1,025.00**

DSA DCM Rifle

Caliber: .223 Wylde Chamber. **Barrel:** 20" 1:8 twist chrome moly match grade Badger Barrel. **Weight:** 10 lbs. **Length:** 39.5". **Stock:** DCM freefloat handguard system, A2 buttstock. **Sights:** Forged A2 front sight with lug. **Features:** NM two stage trigger, NM rear sight, forged 7075T6 DSA lower receiver, forged A2 upper receiver. Introduced 2006. Made in U.S.A. by DSA, Inc.

Price: **$1,520.00**

DSA S1

Caliber: .223 Match Chamber. **Barrel:** 16", 20" or 24" 1:8 twist stainless steel bull barrel. **Weight:** 8.0, 9.5 and 10 lbs. **Length:** 34.25", 38.25" and 42.25". **Stock:** A2 buttstock with free float aluminum handguard. **Sights:** Picatinny gas block sight base. **Features:** Forged 7075T6 DSA lower receiver, Match two stage trigger, forged flattop upper receiver, fluted barrel optional. Introduced 2006. Made in U.S.A. by DSA, Inc.

Price: **$1,155.00**

DSA SA58 CONGO, PARA CONGO

Caliber: 308 Win. **Barrel:** 18" w/short Belgian short flash hider. **Weight:** 8.6 lbs. (Congo); 9.85 lbs. (Para Congo). **Length:** 39.75" **Stock:** Synthetic w/military grade furniture (Congo); Synthetic with non-folding steel para stock (Para Congo). **Sights:** Elevation adjustable protected post front sight, windage adjustable rear peep (Congo); Belgian type Para Flip Rear (Para Congo). **Features:** Fully-adjustable gas system, high-grade steel upper receiver with carry handle. Made in U.S.A. by DSA, Inc.

Price: Congo. **$1,695.00**
Price: Para Congo **$1,995.00**

DSA SA58 GRAY WOLF

Caliber: 308 Win. **Barrel:** 21" match-grade bull w/target crown. **Weight:** 13 lbs. **Length:** 41.75". **Stock:** Synthetic. **Sights:** Elevation-adjustable post front sight, windage-adjustable match rear peep. **Features:** Fully-adjustable gas system, high-grade steel upper receiver, Picatinny scope mount, DuraCoat finish. Made in U.S.A. by DSA, Inc.

Price: **$2,120.00**

DSA SA58 Predator

DSA SA58 T48

DSA SA58 G1

DSA SA58 Standard

DSA SA58 Carbine

DSA SA58 PREDATOR

Caliber: 243 Win., 260 Rem., 308 Win. **Barrel:** 16" and 19" w/target crown. **Weight:** 9 to 9.3 lbs. **Length:** 36.25" to 39.25". **Stock:** Green synthetic. **Sights:** Elevation-adjustable post front; windage-adjustable match rear peep. **Features:** Fully-adjustable gas system, high-grade steel upper receiver, Picatinny scope mount, DuraCoat solid and camo finishes. Made in U.S.A. by DSA, Inc.
Price: 243 Win., 260 Rem. **$1,695.00**
Price: 308 Win. **$1,640.00**

DSA SA58 T48

Caliber: 308 Win. **Barrel:** 21" with Browning long flash hider. **Weight:** 9.3 lbs. **Length:** 44.5". **Stock:** European walnut. **Sights:** Elevation-adjustable post front, windage adjustable rear peep. **Features:** Gas-operated semi-auto with fully adjustable gas system, high grade steel upper receiver with carry handle. DuraCoat finishes. Made in U.S.A. by DSA, Inc.
Price: **$1,995.00**

DSA SA58 G1

Caliber: 308 Win. **Barrel:** 21" with quick-detach flash hider. **Weight:** 10.65 lbs. **Length:** 44". **Stock:** Steel bipod cut handguard with hardwood stock and synthetic pistol grip. **Sights:** Elevation-adjustable post front, windage adjustable rear peep. **Features:** Gas-operated semi-auto with fully

adjustable gas system, high grade steel upper receiver with carry handle, original GI steel lower receiver with GI bipod. DuraCoat finishes. Made in U.S.A. by DSA, Inc.
Price: **$1,850.00**

DSA SA58 STANDARD

Caliber: 308 Win. **Barrel:** 21" bipod cut w/threaded flash hider. **Weight:** 8.75 lbs. **Length:** 43". **Stock:** Synthetic, X-Series or optional folding para stock. **Sights:** Elevation-adjustable post front, windage-adjustable rear peep. **Features:** Fully adjustable short gas system, high grade steel or 416 stainless upper receiver. Made in U.S.A. by DSA, Inc.
Price: High-grade steel. **$1,595.00**
Price: Folding para stock **$1,845.00**

DSA SA58 CARBINE

Caliber: 308 Win. **Barrel:** 16.25" bipod cut w/threaded flash hider. **Weight:** 8.35 lbs. **Length:** 37.5". **Stock:** Synthetic, X-Series or optional folding para stock. **Sights:** Elevation-adjustable post front, windage-adjustable rear peep. **Features:** Fully adjustable short gas system, high grade steel or 416 stainless upper receiver. Made in U.S.A. by DSA, Inc.
Price: High-grade steel. **$1,595.00**
Price: Stainless steel **$1,850.00**

DSA SA58 Medium Contour Tactical

DSA SA58 Medium Contour

DSA SA58 Bull

DSA SA58 OSW

EAA/Saiga 308

DSA SA58 TACTICAL CARBINE

Caliber: 308 Win. **Barrel:** 16.25" fluted with A2 flash hider. **Weight:** 8.25 lbs. **Length:** 36.5". **Stock:** Synthetic, X-Series or optional folding para stock. **Sights:** Elevation-adjustable post front, windage-adjustable match rear peep. **Features:** Shortened fully adjustable short gas system, high grade steel or 416 stainless upper receiver. Made in U.S.A. by DSA, Inc.
Price: High-grade steel **$1,595.00**
Price: Stainless steel. **$1,850.00**

DSA SA58 MEDIUM CONTOUR

Caliber: 308 Win. **Barrel:** 21" w/threaded flash hider. **Weight:** 9.75 lbs. **Length:** 43". **Stock:** Synthetic military grade. **Sights:** Elevation-adjustable post front, windage-adjustable match rear peep. **Features:** Gas-operated semi-auto with fully adjustable gas system, high grade steel receiver. Made in U.S.A. by DSA, Inc.
Price: **$1,595.00**

DSA SA58 BULL BARREL RIFLE

Caliber: 308 Win. **Barrel:** 21". **Weight:** 11.1 lbs. **Length:** 41.5". **Stock:** Synthetic, free floating handguard. **Sights:** Elevation-adjustable windage-

adjustable post front, match rear peep. **Features:** Gas-operated semi-auto with fully adjustable gas system, high grade steel or stainless upper receiver. Made in U.S.A. by DSA, Inc.
Price: **$1,745.00**
Price: Stainless steel **$1,995.00**

DSA SA58 MINI OSW

Caliber: 308 Win. **Barrel:** 11" or 13" w/A2 flash hider. **Weight:** 9 to 9.35 lbs. **Length:** 32.75" to 35". **Stock:** Fiberglass reinforced short synthetic handguard, para folding stock and synthetic pistol grip. **Sights:** Adjustable post front, para rear sight. **Features:** Semi-auto or select fire with fully adjustable short gas system, optional FAL rail handguard, SureFire Vertical Foregrip System, EOTech HOLOgraphic Sight and ITC cheekrest. Made in U.S.A. by DSA, Inc.
Price: **$1,845.00**

EAA/SAIGA SEMI-AUTO RIFLE

Caliber: 7.62x39, 308, 223. **Barrel:** 20.5", 22", 16.3". **Weight:** 7 to 8-1/2 lbs. **Length:** 43". **Stock:** Synthetic or wood. **Sights:** Adjustable, sight base. **Features:** Based on AK Combat rifle by Kalashnikov. Imported from Russia by EAA Corp.
Price: 7.62x39 (syn.). **$239.00**
Price: 308 (syn. or wood) **$429.00**
Price: 223 (syn.) **$389.00**

Excel Arms Accelerator

Heckler & Koch USC

Hi-Point Carbine

Les Baer Flattop

EXCEL ARMS ACCELERATOR RIFLES
Caliber: 17HMR, 22WMR, 17M2, 22LR, 9-shot magazine. **Barrel:** 18" fluted stainless steel bull barrel. **Weight:** 8 lbs. **Length:** 32.5" overall. **Grips:** Textured black polymer. **Sights:** Fully adjustable target sights. **Features:** Made from 17-4 stainless steel, aluminum shroud w/Weaver rail, manual safety, firing-pin block, last-round bolt-hold-open feature. Four packages with various equipment available. American made, lifetime warranty. Comes with one 9-round stainless steel magazine and a California-approved cable lock. Introduced 2006. Made in U.S.A. by Excel Arms.
Price: MR-17 17HMR **$498.00**
Price: MR-22 22WMR **$498.00**
Price: SR-17 17 Mach 2 .... **$498.00**
Price: SR-22 22LR **$498.00**

HECKLER & KOCH USC CARBINE
Caliber: 45 ACP, 10-shot magazine. **Barrel:** 16". **Weight:** 8.6 lb. **Length:** 35.4" overall. **Stock:** Skeletonized polymer thumbhole. **Sights:** Blade front with integral hood, fully adjustable diopter. **Features:** Based on German UMP submachine gun. Blowback operation; almost entirely constructed of carbon fiber-reinforced polymer. Free-floating heavy target barrel. Introduced 2000. From H&K.
Price: **$1,249.00**

HI-POINT 9MM CARBINE
Caliber: 9mm Para., 40 S&W, 10-shot magazine. **Barrel:** 16-1/2" (17-1/2" for 40 S&W). **Weight:** 4-1/2 lbs. **Length:** 31-1/2" overall. **Stock:** Black polymer, camouflage. **Sights:** Protected post front, aperture rear. Integral scope mount. **Features:** Grip-mounted magazine release. Black or

chrome finish. Sling swivels. Available with laser or red dot sights. Introduced 1996. Made in U.S.A. by MKS Supply, Inc.
Price: Black or chrome, 9mm **$199.00**
Price: 40 S&W **$225.00**
Price: Camo stock **$210.00**

IAI M-333 M1 GARAND
Caliber: 30-06, 8-shot clip. **Barrel:** 24". **Weight:** 9-1/2 lbs. **Length:** 43.6" overall. **Stock:** Hardwood. **Sights:** Blade front, aperture adjustable rear. **Features:** Parkerized finish; gas-operated semi-automatic; remanufactured to military specifications. From Intrac Arms International, Inc.
Price: **$971.75**

IAI M-888 M1 CARBINE SEMI-AUTOMATIC RIFLE
Caliber: 22, 30 carbine. **Barrel:** 18"-20". **Weight:** 5-1/2 lbs. **Length:** 35"-37" overall. **Stock:** Laminate, walnut or birch. **Sights:** Blade front, adjustable rear. **Features:** Gas-operated, air cooled, manufactured to military specifications. 10/15/30 rnd. mag. scope available. From Intrac Arms International, Inc.
Price: 30 cal. .... **$556.00 to $604.00**
Price: 22 cal. .... **$567.00 to $654.00**

IAI-65 Rifle
A civilian-legal version of the original HKM rifle manufactured in Hungary. Manufactured by Gordon Technologies using an original AMD-65 matching parts kit built on an AKM receiver. The original wire stock is present, but it is welded in the open position as per BATF regulations. Furnished with a 12.6" barrel with large weld-in-place muzzle brake to bring its length over the 16" federal minimum. This rifle accepts all 7.62x39mm magazines and drums. Introduced 2002. From Intrac Arms International, Inc.
Price: **$799.00**

LES BAER CUSTOM ULTIMATE AR 223 RIFLES
Caliber: 223. **Barrel:** 18", 20", 22", 24". **Weight:** 7-3/4 to 9-3/4 lb. **Length:** NA. **Stock:** Black synthetic. **Sights:** None furnished; Picatinny-style flattop rail for scope mounting. **Features:** Forged receiver; Ultra single-stage trigger (Jewell two-stage trigger optional); titanium firing pin; Versa-Pod bipod; chromed National Match carrier; stainless steel, hand-lapped and cryo-treated barrel; guaranteed to shoot 1/2 or 3/4 MOA, depending on model. Made in U.S.A. by Les Baer Custom Inc.
Price: Super Varmint Model **$1,989.00**
Price: Super Match Model (introduced 2006) **$2,144.00**
Price: M4 flattop model **$2,195.00**
Price: IPSC action model **$2,310.00**

Les Baer IPSC

Olympic Arms K9 Carbine

Olympic Arms K3B

LR 300 SR LIGHT SPORT RIFLE
Caliber: 223. **Barrel:** 16-1/4"; 1:9" twist. **Weight:** 7.2 lbs. **Length:** 36" overall (extended stock), 26-1/4" (stock folded). **Stock:** Folding, tubular steel, with thumbhole-type grip. **Sights:** Trijicon post front, Trijicon rear. **Features:** Uses AR-15 type upper and lower receivers; flattop receiver with weaver base. Accepts all AR-15/M-16 magazines. Introduced 1996. Made in U.S.A. from Z-M Weapons.
Price: **$2,550.00**

OLYMPIC ARMS K9, K10, K40, K45 PISTOL CALIBER RIFLES
Caliber: 9mm, 10mm, 40 S&W, 45 ACP; 32/10 shot magazines. **Barrel:** 16", button rifled, 416 stainless steel, 1x16 twist rate. **Weight:** 6.73 lbs. **Length:** 31.625" overall. **Stock:** A2 grip, 6-point collapsible stock. **Features:** Threaded muzzle, flash suppressor, front post with bayonet lug, A2 upper, includes one appropriately modified magazine.
Price: .... **NA**

OLYMPIC ARMS K3B RIFLE
Caliber: 5.56 NATO, 30-shot magazines. **Barrel:** 16", button rifled, 4140 chrome-moly steel, 1x9 twist rate. **Weight:** 6.77 lbs. **Length:** 31.75" overall. **Stock:** A2 grip, 6-point collapsible buttstock. **Sights:** post front, A2 adjustable rear. **Features:** Threaded muzzles, flash suppressors, bayonet lugs, A2 uppers. Available as A3 which adds flat top upper and detachable carry handle. Available as M4 which adds M4 contoured barrel and M4 handguards. Available as CAR which adds 5.5" permanently attached A2 flash suppressor. Available as FAR, which adds featherweight contoured barrel.
Price: K3B **$780.00**
Price: K3B-A3 .... **$875.00**

Price: K3B-M4 .... **$839.00**
Price: K3B-CAR **$810.00**
Price: K3B-FAR **$822.00**

PANTHER ARMS CLASSIC AUTO RIFLE
Caliber: 5.56x45mm. **Barrel:** Heavy 16" to 20" w/flash hider. **Weight:** 7 to 9 lbs. **Length:** 34-11/16" to 38-7/16". **Sights:** Adj. rear and front. **Stock:** Black Zytel w/trap door assembly. **Features:** Gas operated rotating bolt, mil spec or Teflon black finish.
Price: **$809.00**
Price: Stainless, match sights **$1,099.00**
Price: Southpaw **$875.00**
Price: 16" bbl. **$799.00**
Price: Panther Lite, 16" bbl. **$720.00**
Price: Panther carbine .... **$799.00 to $989.00**
Price: Panther bull bbl .... **$885.00 to $1,199.00**

REMINGTON MODEL 7400 AUTO RIFLE
Caliber: 243 Win., 270 Win., 308 Win., 30-06, 4-shot magazine. **Barrel:** 22" round tapered. **Weight:** 7-1/2 lbs. **Length:** 42-5/8" overall. **Stock:** Walnut, deluxe cut checkered pistol grip and forend. Satin or high-gloss finish. **Sights:** Gold bead front sight on ramp; step rear sight with windage adjustable. **Features:** Redesigned and improved version of the Model 742. Positive cross-bolt safety. Receiver tapped for scope mount. Introduced 1981.
Price: **$624.00**
Price: Carbine (18-1/2" bbl., 30-06 only) **$624.00**
Price: With black synthetic stock, matte black metal, rifle or carbine **$520.00**
Price: Weathermaster, nickel-plated w/synthetic stock and forend, 270, 30-06 .... **$624.00**

Remington Model 7400

Ruger Deerfield 99/44 Carbine

Ruger PC4 Carbine

Ruger Ranch Mini 14/5R

ROCK RIVER ARMS STANDARD A2 RIFLE
Caliber: 45 ACP. **Barrel:** NA. **Weight:** 8.2 lbs. **Length:** NA. **Stock:** Thermoplastic. **Sights:** Standard AR-15 style sights. **Features:** Two-stage, national match trigger; optional muzzle brake. Made in U.S.A. From Rock River Arms.
Price: $925.00

RUGER DEERFIELD 99/44 CARBINE
Caliber: 44 Mag., 4-shot rotary magazine. **Barrel:** 18-1/2". **Weight:** 6-1/4 lbs. **Length:** 36-7/8" overall. **Stock:** Hardwood. **Sights:** Gold bead front, folding adjustable aperture rear. **Features:** Semi-automatic action; dual front-locking lugs lock directly into receiver; integral scope mount; push-button safety; includes 1" rings and gun lock. Introduced 2000. Made in U.S.A. by Sturm, Ruger & Co.
Price: $675.00

RUGER PC4, PC9 CARBINES
Caliber: 9mm Para., 40 cal., 10-shot magazine. **Barrel:** 16.25". **Weight:** 6 lbs., 4 oz. **Length:** 34.75" overall. **Stock:** Black high impact synthetic checkered grip and forend. **Sights:** Blade front, open adjustable rear; integral Ruger scope mounts. **Features:** Delayed blowback action; manual push-button cross bolt safety and internal firing pin block safety automatic slide lock. Introduced 1997. Made in U.S.A. by Sturm, Ruger & Co.
Price: PC9, PC4, (9mm, 40 cal.). $623.00
Price: PC4GR, PC9GR, (40 auto, 9mm, post sights, ghost ring) . . $647.00

RUGER RANCH RIFLE AUTOLOADING RIFLE
Caliber: 223 Rem., 5-shot detachable box magazine. **Barrel:** 18-1/2". Rifling twist 1:9". **Weight:** 6.4 lbs. **Length:** 37-1/4" overall. **Stock:**

American hardwood, steel reinforced. **Sights:** Ramp front, fully adjustable rear. **Features:** Fixed piston gas-operated, positive primary extraction. New buffer system, redesigned ejector system. Ruger S100RM scope rings included on Ranch Rifle.
Price: Mini-14/5R, Ranch Rifle, blued, scope rings $750.00
Price: K-Mini-14/5R, Ranch Rifle, stainless, scope rings $809.00
Price: K-Mini-14/5RP, Ranch Rifle, stainless, synthetic stock $809.00

Ruger Mini Thirty Rifle
Similar to the Mini-14 Ranch Rifle except modified to chamber the 7.62x39 Russian service round. Weight is about 6-7/8 lbs. Has 6-groove barrel with 1:10" twist, Ruger Integral Scope Mount bases and folding peep rear sight. Detachable 5-shot staggered box magazine. Stainless w/synthetic stock. Introduced 1987.
Price: Stainless, scope rings $809.00

SIG 556 AUTOLOADING RIFLE
Caliber: 223 Rem., 30-shot detachable box magazine. **Barrel:** 16". Rifling twist 1:9". **Weight:** 6.8 lbs. **Length:** 36.5" overall. **Stock:** Polymer, folding style. **Sights:** Flip-up front combat sight, adjustable for windage and elevation. **Features:** Based on SG 550 series rifle. Two-position adjustable gas piston operating rod system, accepts standard AR magazines. Polymer forearm, three integrated Picatinny rails, forward mount for right- or left-side sling attachment. Aircraft-grade aluminum alloy trigger housing, hard-coat anodized finish; two-stage trigger, ambidextrous safety, 30-round polymer magazine, battery compartments, pistol-grip rubber-padded watertight adjustable butt stock with sling-attachment points. SIG 556 SWAT model has flat-top Picatinny railed receiver, tactical quad rail. Imported by Sigarms, Inc.
Price: SIG 556 .... $1,300.00

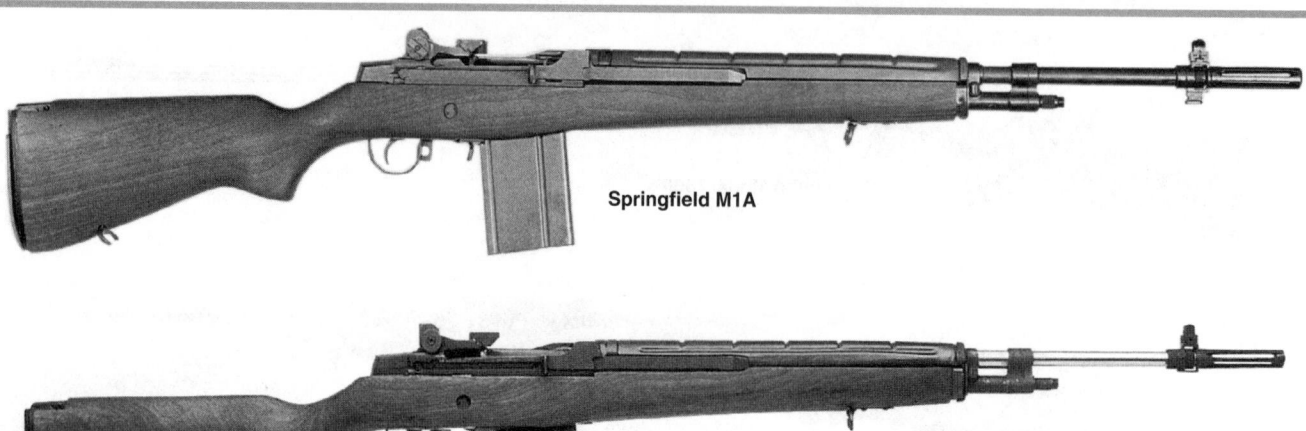

Springfield M1A

Springfield National Match M1A

Springfield Super Match with Camo M1A

SPRINGFIELD ARMORY M1A RIFLE

Caliber: 7.62mm NATO (308), 5- or 10-shot box magazine. **Barrel:** 25-1/16" with flash suppressor, 22" without suppressor. **Weight:** 9-3/4 lbs. **Length:** 44-1/4" overall. **Stock:** American walnut with walnut-colored heat-resistant fiberglass handguard. Matching walnut handguard available. Also available with fiberglass stock. **Sights:** Military, square blade front, full click-adjustable aperture rear. **Features:** Commercial equivalent of the U.S. M-14 service rifle with no provision for automatic firing. From Springfield Armory

Price: Standard M1A, black fiberglass stock. $1,498.00
Price: Standard M1A, black fiberglass stock, stainless $1,727.00
Price: Standard M1A, black stock, carbon barrel $1,379.00
Price: Standard M1A, Mossy Oak stock, carbon barrel $1,507.00
Price: Scout Squad M1A . . . . $1,653.00 to $1,727.00
Price: National Match . . . . $2,049.00 to $2,098.00
Price: Super Match (heavy premium barrel) . . . . about $3,149.00
Price: M1A SOCOM II rifle $1,948.00
Price: M25 White Feather Tactical rifle $4,648.00

SPRINGFIELD M1 GARAND RIFLE

Caliber: 308, 30-06. **Barrel:** 24". **Weight:** 9.5 lbs. **Length:** 43-3/5". **Stock:** Walnut. **Sights:** Military aperture with MOA adjustments for both windage and elevation, rear; military square post, front. **Features:** Original U.S. government-issue parts on a new walnut stock.

Price: . . . . $1,348.00 to $1,378.00

STONER SR-15 M-5 RIFLE

Caliber: 223. **Barrel:** 20". **Weight:** 7.6 lbs. **Length:** 38" overall. **Stock:** Black synthetic. **Sights:** Post front, fully adjustable rear (300-meter sight). **Features:** Modular weapon system; two-stage trigger. Black finish. Introduced 1998. Made in U.S.A. by Knight's Mfg.

Price: $1,650.00
Price: M-4 Carbine (16" barrel, 6.8 lbs) $1,555.00

STONER SR-25 CARBINE

Caliber: 7.62 NATO, 10-shot steel magazine. **Barrel:** 16" free-floating **Weight:** 7-3/4 lbs. **Length:** 35.75" overall. **Stock:** Black synthetic. **Sights:** Integral Weaver-style rail. Scope rings, iron sights optional. **Features:** Shortened, non-slip handguard; removable carrying handle. Matte black finish. Introduced 1995. Made in U.S.A. by Knight's Mfg. Co.

Price: $3,345.00

SMITH & WESSON M&P15 RIFLES

Caliber: 5.56mm NATO/223, 30-shot steel magazine. **Barrel:** 16", 1:9 **Weight:** 6.74 lbs., w/o magazine. **Length:** 32-35" overall. **Stock:** Black synthetic. **Sights:** Adjustable post front sight, adjustable dual aperture rear sight. **Features:** 6-position telescopic stock, thermo-set M4 handguard. 14.75" sight radius. 7-lbs. (approx.) trigger pull. 7075 T6 aluminum upper, 4140 steel barrel. Chromed barrel bore, gas key, bolt carrier. Hard-coat black-anodized receiver and barrel finish. Introduced 2006. Made in U.S.A. by Smith & Wesson.

Price: M&P15 No. 811000 . . . . $1,200.00
Price: M&P15T No. 811001, free float modular rail forend $1,700.00
Price: M&P15A No. 811002, folding battle rear sight. $1,300.00

WILKINSON LINDA CARBINE

Caliber: 9mm Para. **Barrel:** 16-3/16". **Weight:** 7 lbs. **Stocks:** Fixed tubular with wood pad. **Sights:** Aperture rear sight. **Features:** Aluminum receiver, pre-ban configuration (limited supplies), vent. barrel shroud, small wooden forearm, 18 or 31 shot mag. Many accessories.

Price: $1,800.00

Wilkinson Linda L2 Limited Edition

Manufactured from the last 600 of the original 2,200 pre-ban Linda carbines, includes many upgrades and accessories. New in 2002.

Price: $4,800.00

WILKINSON TERRY CARBINE

Caliber: 9mm Para. **Barrel:** 16-3/16". **Weight:** 7 lbs. **Stocks:** Black or maple. **Sights:** Adjustable. **Features:** Blowback semi-auto action, 31-shot mag., closed breech.

Price:. . . . . NA

Both classic arms and recent designs in American-style repeaters for sport and field shooting.

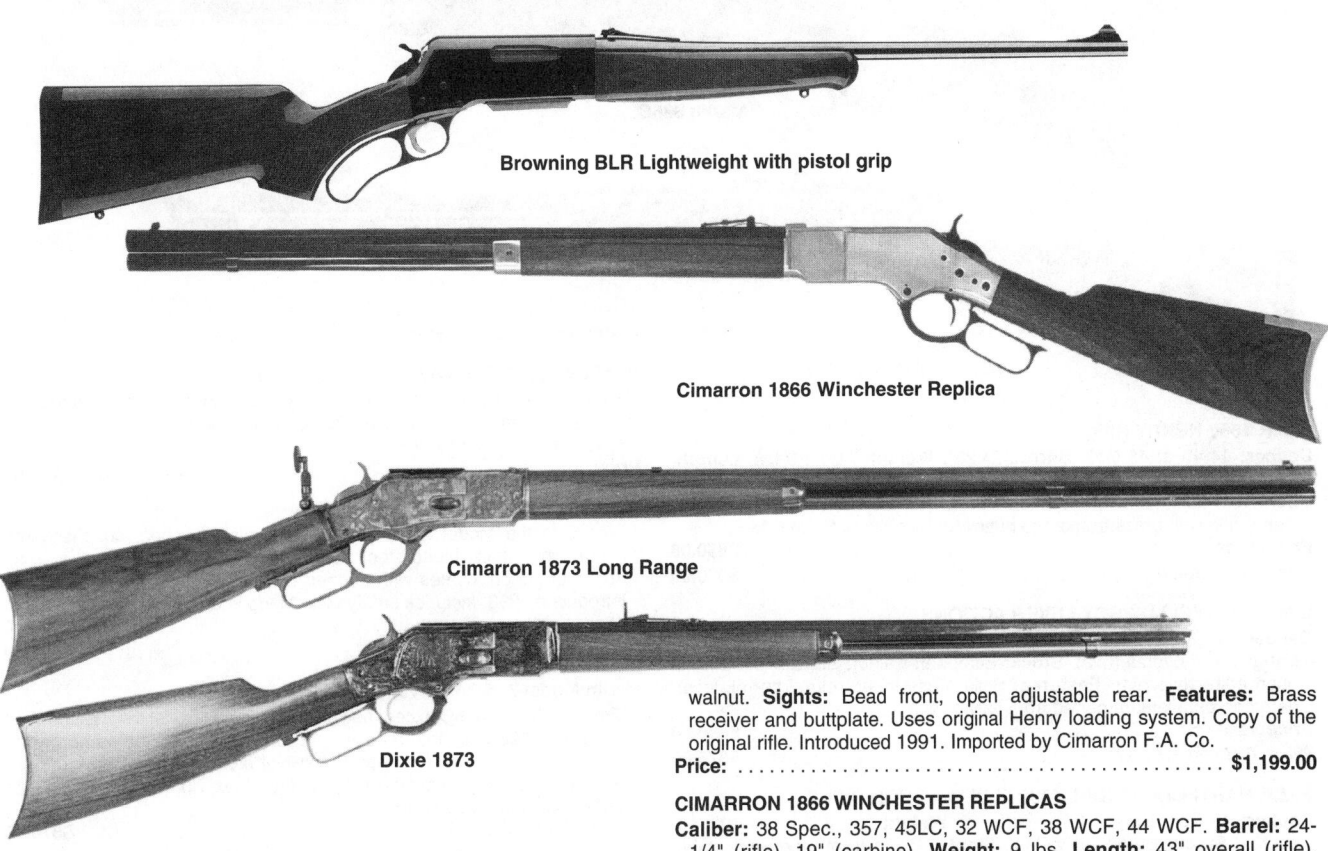

Browning BLR Lightweight with pistol grip

Cimarron 1866 Winchester Replica

Cimarron 1873 Long Range

Dixie 1873

BROWNING BLR RIFLES

Action: Lever action with rotating bolt head, multiple-lug breech bolt with recessed bolt face, side ejection. Rack-and-pinion lever. Flush-mounted detachable magazines, with 4+1 capacity for magnum cartridges, 5+1 for standard rounds. **Barrel:** Button-rifled chrome-moly steel with crowned muzzle. **Stock:** Buttstocks and forends are American walnut with grip and forend checkering. Recoil pad installed. **Trigger:** Wide-groove design, trigger travels with lever. Half-cock hammer safety; fold-down hammer. **Sights:** Gold bead on ramp front; low-profile square-notch adjustable rear. **Features:** Blued barrel and receiver, high-gloss wood finish. Receivers are drilled and tapped for scope mounts, swivel studs included. Action lock provided. Introduced 1996. Four model name variations for 2006, as noted below. Imported from Japan by Browning.

BROWNING BLR LIGHTWEIGHT W/PISTOL GRIP, SHORT AND LONG ACTION; LIGHTWEIGHT '81, SHORT AND LONG ACTION

Calibers, Short Action, 20" barrel: 22-250, 243, 7mm-08, 308, 358, 450 Marlin. **Calibers, Short Action, 22" barrel:** 270 WSM, 7mm WSM, 300 WSM, 325 WSM. **Calibers, Long Action 22" barrel:** 270, 30-06. **Calibers, Long Action 24" barrel:** 7mm Rem. Mag., 300 Win. Mag. **Weight:** 6.5-7.75 lbs. **Length:** 40-45" overall. **Stock:** New checkered pistol grip and Schnabel forearm. Lightweight '81 differs from Pistol Grip models with a Western-style straight grip stock and banded forearm. Lightweight w/Pistol Grip Short Action and Long Action introduced 2005. Model '81 Lightning Long Action introduced 1996.
Price: Lightweight w/Pistol Grip Short Action . . . . **$765.00 to $836.00**
Price: Lightweight w/Pistol Grip Long Action **$809.00**
Price: Lightweight '81 Short Action . . . . **$731.00 to $802.00**
Price: Lightweight '81 Long Action **$775.00**

CIMARRON 1860 HENRY REPLICA

Caliber: 44 WCF, 45LC; 13-shot magazine. **Barrel:** 24-1/4" (rifle), 22" (carbine). **Weight:** 9-1/2 lbs. **Length:** 43" overall (rifle). **Stock:** European walnut. **Sights:** Bead front, open adjustable rear. **Features:** Brass receiver and buttplate. Uses original Henry loading system. Copy of the original rifle. Introduced 1991. Imported by Cimarron F.A. Co.
Price: **$1,199.00**

CIMARRON 1866 WINCHESTER REPLICAS

Caliber: 38 Spec., 357, 45LC, 32 WCF, 38 WCF, 44 WCF. **Barrel:** 24-1/4" (rifle), 19" (carbine). **Weight:** 9 lbs. **Length:** 43" overall (rifle). **Stock:** European walnut. **Sights:** Bead front, open adjustable rear. **Features:** Solid brass receiver, buttplate, forend cap. Octagonal barrel. Copy of the original Winchester '66 rifle. Introduced 1991. Imported by Cimarron F.A. Co.
Price: Rifle **$965.00**
Price: Carbine **$950.00**

CIMARRON 1873 SHORT RIFLE

Caliber: 357 Mag., 38 Spec., 32 WCF, 38 WCF, 44 Spec., 44 WCF, 45 Colt. **Barrel:** 20" tapered octagon. **Weight:** 7.5 lbs. **Length:** 39" overall. **Stock:** Walnut. **Sights:** Bead front, adjustable semi-buckhorn rear. **Features:** Has half "button" magazine. Original-type markings, including caliber, on barrel and elevator and "Kings" patent. From Cimarron F.A. Co.
Price: **$1,149.00**

Cimarron 1873 Sporting Rifle

Similar to the 1873 Short Rifle except has 24" barrel with half-magazine.
Price: **$1,149.00**

CIMARRON 1873 LONG RANGE RIFLE

Caliber: 44 WCF, 45 Colt. **Barrel:** 30", octagonal. **Weight:** 8-1/2 lbs. **Length:** 48" overall. **Stock:** Walnut. **Sights:** Blade front, semi-buckhorn ramp rear. Tang sight optional. **Features:** Color case-hardened frame; choice of modern blue-black or charcoal blue for other parts. Barrel marked "Kings Improvement." From Cimarron F.A. Co.
Price: **$1,199.00**

DIXIE ENGRAVED 1873 RIFLE

Caliber: 44-40, 11-shot magazine. **Barrel:** 20", round. **Weight:** 7-3/4 lbs. **Length:** 39" overall. **Stock:** Walnut. **Sights:** Blade front, adjustable rear. **Features:** Engraved and case-hardened frame. Replica of Winchester 1873. Made in Italy. From 21 Gun Works.
Price: **$1,425.00**
Price: Plain, blued carbine **$1,015.00**

Marlin 336C

Marlin 1894 Cowboy

E.M.F. 1860 HENRY RIFLE
Caliber: 44-40 or 45 Colt. **Barrel:** 24.25". **Weight:** About 9 lbs. **Length:** About 43.75" overall. **Stock:** Oil-stained American walnut. **Sights:** Blade front, rear adjustable for elevation. **Features:** Reproduction of the original Henry rifle with brass frame and buttplate, rest blued. From E.M.F.
Price: Brass frame................................... $850.00
Price: Steel frame $950.00

E.M.F. 1866 YELLOWBOY LEVER ACTIONS
Caliber: 38 Spec., 44-40. **Barrel:** 19" (carbine), 24" (rifle). **Weight:** 9 lbs. **Length:** 43" overall (rifle). **Stock:** European walnut. **Sights:** Bead front, open adjustable rear. **Features:** Solid brass frame, blued barrel, lever, hammer, buttplate. Imported from Italy by E.M.F.
Price: Rifle.. $690.00
Price: Carbine $675.00

E.M.F. HARTFORD MODEL 1892 LEVER-ACTION RIFLE
Caliber: 45 Colt. **Barrel:** 24", octagonal. **Weight:** 7-1/2 lbs. **Length:** 43" overall. **Stock:** European walnut. **Sights:** Blade front, open adjustable rear. **Features:** Color case-hardened frame, lever, trigger and hammer with blued barrel, or overall blue finish. Introduced 1998. Imported by E.M.F.
Price: Standard $590.00

E.M.F. MODEL 1873 LEVER-ACTION RIFLE
Caliber: 32/20, 357 Mag., 38/40, 44-40, 44 Spec., 45 Colt. **Barrel:** 24". **Weight:** 8 lbs. **Length:** 43-1/4" overall. **Stock:** European walnut. **Sights:** Bead front, rear adjustable for windage and elevation. **Features:** Color case-hardened frame (blue on carbine). Imported by E.M.F.
Price: Rifle.. $865.00
Price: Carbine, 19" barrel $865.00

E.M.F. MODEL 1873 REVOLVER CARBINE
Caliber: 357 Mag., 45 Colt. **Barrel:** 18". **Weight:** 4 lbs., 8 oz. **Length:** 34" overall. **Stock:** One-piece walnut. **Sights:** Blade front, notch rear. **Features:** Color case-hardened frame, blue barrel, backstrap and trigger guard. Introduced 1998. Imported from Italy by IAR, Inc.
Price: Standard $490.00

MARLIN MODEL 336C LEVER-ACTION CARBINE
Caliber: 30-30 or 35 Rem., 6-shot tubular magazine. **Barrel:** 20" Micro-Groove®. **Weight:** 7 lbs. **Length:** 38-1/2" overall. **Stock:** Checkered American black walnut, capped pistol grip. Mar-Shield® finish; rubber buttpad; swivel studs. **Sights:** Ramp front with Wide-Scan hood, semi-buckhorn folding rear adjustable for windage and elevation. **Features:** Hammer-block safety. Receiver tapped for scope mount, offset hammer spur; top of receiver sandblasted to prevent glare. Includes safety lock.
Price: $570.00

Marlin Model 336A Lever-Action Carbine
Same as the Marlin 336C except has cut-checkered, walnut-finished hardwood pistol grip stock with swivel studs, 30-30 only, 6-shot. Hammer-block safety. Adjustable rear sight, brass bead front. Includes safety lock.
Price: $477.00
Price: With 4x scope and mount $527.00

Marlin Model 336SS Lever-Action Carbine
Same as the 336C except receiver, barrel and other major parts are machined from stainless steel. 30-30 only, 6-shot; receiver tapped for scope. Includes safety lock.
Price: $692.00

Marlin Model 336W Lever-Action Rifle
Similar to the Model 336C except has walnut-finished, cut-checkered Maine birch stock; blued steel barrel band has integral sling swivel; no front sight hood; comes with padded nylon sling; hard rubber buttplate. Introduced 1998. Includes safety lock. Made in U.S.A. by Marlin.
Price: $482.00
Price: With 4x scope and mount $535.00

Marlin Model 336XLR Lever-Action Rifle
Similar to Model 336C except has an 24" stainless barrel with Ballard-type cut rifling, stainless steel receiver and other parts, laminated hardwood stock with pistol grip, nickel-plated swivel studs. Chambered for 30-30 Win. with Hornady Evolution spire-pointed Flex-Tip cartridges. Includes safety lock. Introduced 2006.
Price: (Model 336XLR) $874.00

MARLIN MODEL 444 LEVER-ACTION SPORTER
Caliber: 444 Marlin, 5-shot tubular magazine. **Barrel:** 22" deep cut Ballard rifling. **Weight:** 7-1/2 lbs. **Length:** 40-1/2" overall. **Stock:** Checkered American black walnut, capped pistol grip, rubber rifle buttpad. Mar-Shield® finish; swivel studs. **Sights:** Hooded ramp front, folding semi-buckhorn rear adjustable for windage and elevation. **Features:** Hammer-block safety. Receiver tapped for scope mount; offset hammer spur. Includes safety lock.
Price: $665.00

Marlin Model 444XLR Lever-Action Rifle
Similar to Model 444 except has an 24" stainless barrel with Ballard-type cut rifling, stainless steel receiver and other parts, laminated hardwood stock with pistol grip, nickel-plated swivel studs. Chambered for 444 Marlin with Hornady Evolution spire-pointed Flex-Tip cartridges. Includes safety lock. Introduced 2006.
Price: (Model 444XLR) $874.00

MARLIN MODEL 1894 LEVER-ACTION CARBINE
Caliber: 44 Spec./44 Mag., 10-shot tubular magazine. **Barrel:** 20" Ballard-type rifling. **Weight:** 6 lbs. **Length:** 37-1/2" overall. **Stock:** Checkered American black walnut, straight grip and forend. Mar-Shield® finish. Rubber rifle buttpad; swivel studs. **Sights:** Wide-Scan hooded ramp front, semi-buckhorn folding rear adjustable for windage and elevation. **Features:** Hammer-block safety. Receiver tapped for scope mount, offset hammer spur, solid top receiver sand blasted to prevent glare. Includes safety lock.
Price: $614.00

Marlin Model 1894C Carbine
Similar to the standard Model 1894 except chambered for 38 Spec./357 Mag. with full-length 9-shot magazine, 18-1/2" barrel, hammer-block safety, hooded front sight. Introduced 1983. Includes safety lock.
Price: $614.00

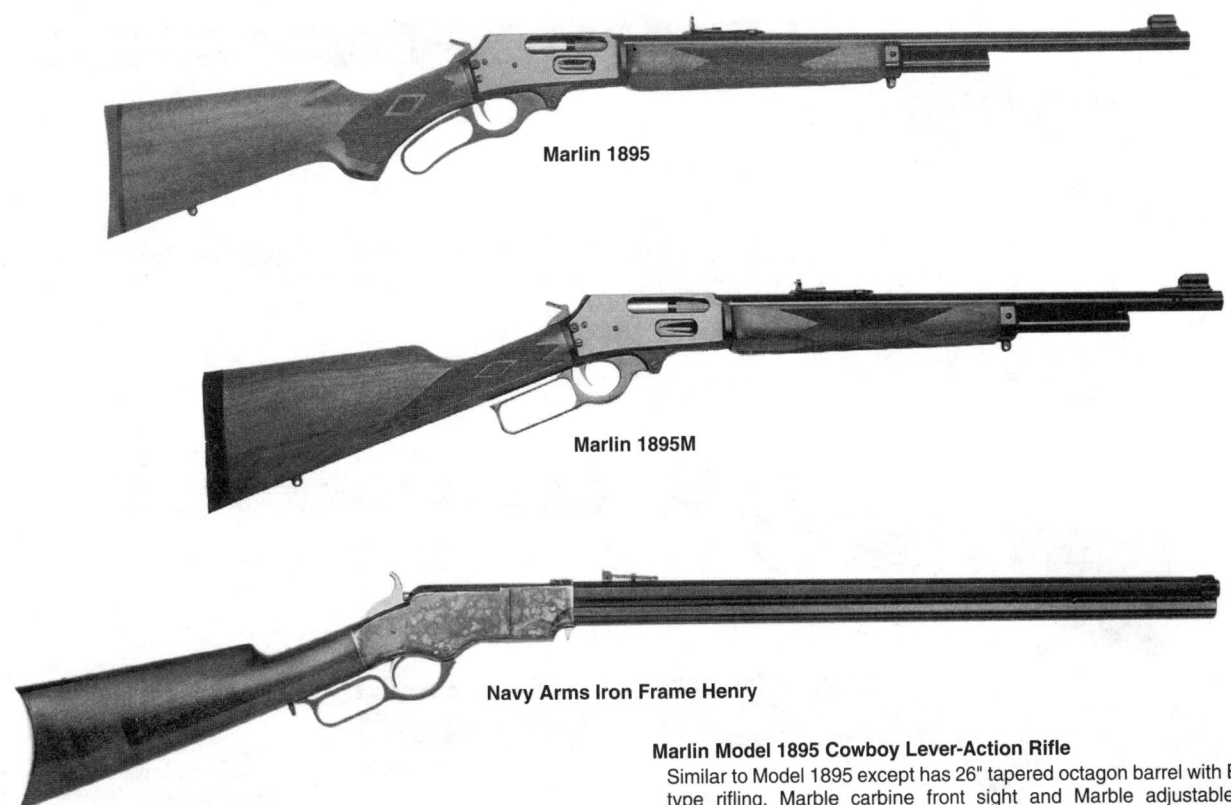

Marlin 1895

Marlin 1895M

Navy Arms Iron Frame Henry

MARLIN MODEL 1894 COWBOY

Caliber: 357 Mag., 44 Mag., 45 Colt, 10-shot magazine. **Barrel:** 20" tapered octagon, deep cut rifling. **Weight:** 7-1/2 lbs. **Length:** 41-1/2" overall. **Stock:** Straight grip American black walnut, hard rubber buttplate, Mar-Shield® finish. **Sights:** Marble carbine front, adjustable Marble semi-buckhorn rear. **Features:** Squared finger lever; straight grip stock; blued steel forend tip. Designed for Cowboy Shooting events. Introduced 1996. Includes safety lock. Made in U.S.A. by Marlin.
Price: **$889.00**

Marlin Model 1894SS

Similar to Model 1894 except has stainless steel barrel, receiver, lever, guard plate, magazine tube and loading plate. Nickel-plated swivel studs.
Price: **$752.00**

MARLIN MODEL 1895 LEVER-ACTION RIFLE

Caliber: 45-70, 4-shot tubular magazine. **Barrel:** 22" round. **Weight:** 7-1/2 lbs. **Length:** 40-1/2" overall. **Stock:** Checkered American black walnut, full pistol grip. Mar-Shield® finish; rubber buttpad; quick detachable swivel studs. **Sights:** Bead front with Wide-Scan hood, semi-buckhorn folding rear adjustable for windage and elevation. **Features:** Hammer-block safety. Solid receiver tapped for scope mounts or receiver sights; offset hammer spur. Includes safety lock.
Price: **$665.00**

Marlin Model 1895G Guide Gun Lever-Action Rifle

Similar to Model 1895 with deep-cut Ballard-type rifling; straight-grip walnut stock. Overall length is 37", weighs 7 lbs. Introduced 1998. Includes safety lock. Made in U.S.A. by Marlin.
Price: **$681.00**

Marlin Model 1895GS Guide Gun

Similar to Model 1895G except receiver, barrel and most metal parts are machined from stainless steel. Chambered for 45-70, 4-shot, 18-1/2" barrel. Overall length is 37", weighs 7 lbs. Introduced 2001. Includes safety lock. Made in U.S.A. by Marlin.
Price: **$805.00**

Marlin Model 1895 Cowboy Lever-Action Rifle

Similar to Model 1895 except has 26" tapered octagon barrel with Ballard-type rifling, Marble carbine front sight and Marble adjustable semi-buckhorn rear sight. Receiver tapped for scope or receiver sight. Overall length is 44-1/2", weighs about 8 lbs. Introduced 2001. Includes safety lock. Made in U.S.A. by Marlin.
Price: **$849.00**

Marlin Model 1895XLR Lever-Action Rifle

Similar to Model 1895 except has an 24" stainless barrel with Ballard-type cut rifling, stainless steel receiver and other parts, laminated hardwood stock with pistol grip, nickel-plated swivel studs. Chambered for 45-70 Government with Hornady Evolution spire-pointed Flex-Tip cartridges. Includes safety lock. Introduced 2006.
Price: (Model 1895MXLR) **$874.00**

Marlin Model 1895M Lever-Action Rifle

Similar to Model 1895G except has an 18-1/2" barrel with Ballard-type cut rifling. Chambered for 450 Marlin. Includes safety lock.
Price: (Model 1895M) **$733.00**

Marlin Model 1895MXLR Lever-Action Rifle

Similar to Model 1895M except has an 24" stainless barrel with Ballard-type cut rifling, stainless steel receiver and other parts, laminated hardwood stock with pistol grip, nickel-plated swivel studs. Chambered for 450 Marlin with Hornady Evolution spire-pointed Flex-Tip cartridges. Includes safety lock. Introduced 2006.
Price: (Model 1895MXLR) **$874.00**

NAVY ARMS MILITARY HENRY RIFLE

Caliber: 44-40 or 45 Colt, 12-shot magazine. **Barrel:** 24-1/4". **Weight:** 9 lbs., 4 oz. **Stock:** European walnut. **Sights:** Blade front, adjustable ladder-type rear. **Features:** Brass frame, buttplate, rest blued. Replica of the model used by cavalry units in the Civil War. Has full-length magazine tube, sling swivels; no forend. Imported from Italy by Navy Arms.
Price: **$1,199.00**

Navy Arms Iron Frame Henry

Similar to the Military Henry Rifle except receiver is blued or color case-hardened steel. Imported by Navy Arms.
Price: . . . . **$1,258.00-$1,275.00**

Navy Arms 1866 Yellow Boy

Navy Arms 1892 Rifle

Puma Model 92

Remington 7600 Rifle

NAVY ARMS 1866 YELLOW BOY RIFLE
Caliber: 38 Spec., 44-40, 45 Colt, 12-shot magazine. **Barrel:** 20" or 24", full octagon. **Weight:** 8-1/2 lbs. **Length:** 42-1/2" overall. **Stock:** Walnut. **Sights:** Blade front, adjustable ladder-type rear. **Features:** Brass frame, forend tip, buttplate, blued barrel, lever, hammer. Introduced 1991. Imported from Italy by Navy Arms.
Price: $942.00
Price: Carbine, 19" barrel $908.00

NAVY ARMS 1866 SPORTING YELLOW BOY RIFLES
Caliber: 45 Colt. **Barrel:** 24-1/4" octagonal; 1:16" twist. **Weight:** 8.16 lbs. **Length:** 43-3/4" overall. **Stock:** Walnut. **Sights:** Blade front, adjustable folding rear. **Features:** Brass receiver; blued or white barrel; 13-shot magazine. Introduced 2001. Imported from Uberti by Navy Arms.
Price: (blued barrel)................................... $942.00

NAVY ARMS 1873 WINCHESTER-STYLE RIFLE
Caliber: 357 Mag., 44-40, 45 Colt, 12-shot magazine. **Barrel:** 24-1/4". **Weight:** 8-1/4 lbs. **Length:** 43" overall. **Stock:** European walnut. **Sights:** Blade front, buckhorn rear. **Features:** Color case-hardened frame, rest blued. Full-octagon barrel. Imported by Navy Arms.
Price: $1,079.00
Price: 1873 Carbine, 19" barrel $1,054.00
Price: 1873 Sporting Rifle (full oct. bbl., checkered walnut stock and forend) $1,218.00
Price: 1873 Border Model, 20" octagon barrel $1,079.00
Price: 1873 Deluxe Border Model $1,218.00

NAVY ARMS 1892 RIFLE
Caliber: 357 Mag., 44-40, 45 Colt. **Barrel:** 24-1/4" octagonal. **Weight:** 7 lbs. **Length:** 42" overall. **Stock:** American walnut. **Sights:** Blade front, semi-buckhorn rear. **Features:** Replica of Winchester's early Model 1892

with octagonal barrel, forend cap and crescent buttplate. Blued or color case-hardened receiver. Introduced 1998. Imported by Navy Arms.
Price: $355.00

Navy Arms 1892 Stainless Carbine
Similar to the 1892 Rifle except stainless steel, has 20" round barrel, weighs 5-3/4 lbs., and is 37-1/2" overall. Introduced 1998. Imported by Navy Arms.
Price: $345.00

Navy Arms 1892 Short Rifle
Similar to the 1892 Rifle except has 20" octagonal barrel, weighs 6-1/4 lbs., and is 37-3/4" overall. Replica of the rare, special order 1892 Winchester nicknamed the "Texas Special." Blued or color case-hardened receiver and furniture. Introduced 1998. Imported by Navy Arms.
Price: $355.00

PUMA MODEL 92 RIFLES & CARBINES
Caliber: 38 Spec./357 Mag., 44 Mag., 45 Colt, 454 Casull, 480 Ruger. **Barrel:** 16". 18", 20" round, 24" octagonal; porting and large lever loop available. **Weight:** 6.1 to 7.7 lbs. **Stock:** Walnut-stained hardwood. **Sights:** Open, buckhorn front & rear; HiViz also available. **Features:** Blue, case-hardened, stainless steel and brass receivers, matching buttplates. Blued, stainless steel barrels, full-length magazines. Thumb safety. 45 Colt and 454 Casull carbine introduced in 2002. The 480 Ruger version introduced in 2003. Imported from Brazil by Legacy Sports International.
Price: .... $450.00 to $617.00

REMINGTON MODEL 7600 PUMP ACTION
Caliber: 243, 270, 30-06, 308. **Barrel:** 22" round tapered. **Weight:** 7-1/2 lbs. **Length:** 42-5/8" overall. **Stock:** Cut-checkered walnut pistol grip and forend, Monte Carlo with full cheekpiece. Satin or high-gloss finish. **Sights:** Gold bead front sight on matted ramp, open step adjustable sporting rear. **Features:** Redesigned and improved version of the Model 760. Detachable 4-shot clip. Cross-bolt safety. Receiver tapped for scope mount. Introduced 1981.
Price: $588.00
Price: Carbine (18-1/2" bbl., 30-06 only) $588.00
Price: With black synthetic stock, matte black metal, rifle or carbine $484.00

Ruger Model 96/44

Tristar 1873 Sporting Rifle

Tristar 1866 Yellowboy Carbine

Tristar 1860 Henry

Uberti 1873 Sport

RUGER MODEL 96/44 LEVER-ACTION RIFLE
Caliber: 44 Mag., 4-shot rotary magazine. **Barrel:** 18-1/2". **Weight:** 6 lbs. **Length:** 37.75" overall. **Stock:** American hardwood. **Sights:** Gold bead front, folding leaf rear. **Features:** Solid chrome-moly steel receiver. Manual cross-bolt safety, visible cocking indicator; short-throw lever action; integral scope mount; blued finish; color case-hardened lever. Introduced 1996. Made In U.S. by Sturm, Ruger & Co.
Price: 96/44M, 44 Mag $546.00

TRISTAR/SHARPS 1874 SPORTING RIFLE
Caliber: 45-70. **Barrel:** 28", 32", 34" octagonal. **Weight:** 9.75 lbs. **Length:** 44.5" overall. **Stock:** Walnut. **Sights:** Dovetail front, adjustable rear. **Features:** Cut checkering, case colored frame finish.
Price: $839.00
Price: Bridgeport Sharps $899.00

TRISTAR/UBERTI 1866 SPORTING RIFLE, CARBINE
Caliber: 45 Colt. **Barrel:** 24-1/4", octagonal. **Weight:** 8.1 lbs. **Length:** 43-1/4" overall. **Stock:** Walnut. **Sights:** Blade front adjustable for windage, rear adjustable for elevation. **Features:** Frame, buttplate, forend cap of polished brass, balance charcoal blued. Imported by Tristar Sporting Arms Ltd.

Price: $1,109.00
Price: Yellowboy carbine (19" round bbl.) $999.00

TRISTAR/UBERTI 1860 HENRY RIFLE
Caliber: 45 Colt. **Barrel:** 24-1/4", half-octagon. **Weight:** 9.2 lbs. **Length:** 43-3/4" overall. **Stock:** American walnut. **Sights:** Blade front, rear adjustable for elevation. **Features:** Frame, elevator, magazine follower, buttplate are brass, balance blue. Imported by Tristar Sporting Arms Ltd. Arms, Inc.
Price: $1,359.00

TRISTAR/UBERTI 1873 SPORTING RIFLE
Caliber: 45 Colt. **Barrel:** 24-1/4", 30", octagonal. **Weight:** 8.1 lbs. **Length:** 43-1/4" overall. **Stock:** Walnut. **Sights:** Blade front adjustable for windage, open rear adjustable for elevation. **Features:** Color case-hardened frame, blued barrel, hammer, lever, buttplate, brass elevator. Imported from Italy by Tristar Sporting Arms Ltd.
Price: 24-1/4" barrel $1,259.00

UBERTI 1873 SPORTING RIFLE
Caliber: 357 Mag., 44-40, 45 Colt. **Barrel:** 19", to 24-1/4". **Weight:** Up to 8.2 lbs. **Length:** Up to 43.3" overall. **Stock:** Walnut, straight grip and pistol grip. **Sights:** Blade front adjustable for windage, open rear adjustable for elevation. **Features:** Color case-hardened frame, blued barrel, hammer, lever, buttplate, brass elevator. Imported by Benelli USA.
Price: 1873 Carbine, 19" round barrel $945.00
Price: 1873 Short Rifle, 20" octagonal barrel $985.00
Price: 1873 Special Sporting Rifle, 24.25" octagonal barrel $1,100.00

Uberti 1866 Yellowboy

Uberti 1860 Henry

U.S. Fire Arms Lightning Premium Carbine

U.S. Fire Arms Standard Lightning

UBERTI 1866 YELLOWBOY CARBINE, SHORT RIFLE, RIFLE

Caliber: 38 Spec., 44-40, 45 Colt. **Barrel:** 24-1/4", octagonal. **Weight:** 8.2 lbs. **Length:** 43-1/4" overall. **Stock:** Walnut. **Sights:** Blade front adjustable for windage, rear adjustable for elevation. **Features:** Frame, buttplate, forend cap of polished brass, balance charcoal blued. Imported by Benelli USA.

Price: 1866 Yellowboy Carbine, 19" round barrel $885.00
Price: 1866 Yellowboy Short Rifle, 20" octagonal barrel $900.00
Price: 1866 Yellowboy Rifle, 24.25" octagonal barrel $900.00

UBERTI 1860 HENRY RIFLE

Caliber: 44-40, 45 Colt. **Barrel:** 24-1/4", half-octagon. **Weight:** 9.2 lbs. **Length:** 43-3/4" overall. **Stock:** American walnut. **Sights:** Blade front, rear adjustable for elevation. **Features:** Imported by Benelli USA.

Price: 1860 Henry Trapper, 18.5" barrel, brass frame $1,050.00
Price: 1860 Henry Rifle, 24.25" barrel, brass frame $1,050.00
Price: 1860 Henry Rifle steel, 24.25" barrel, case-hardened frame $1,150.00
Price: 1860 Henry Rifle Iron Frame, 24.25" barrel $1,050.00

Uberti 1860 Henry Trapper Carbine

Similar to the 1860 Henry Rifle except has 18-1/2" barrel, measures 37-3/4" overall, and weighs 8 lbs. Introduced 1999. Imported by Benelli USA.
Price: Brass frame, blued barrel $989.00

UBERTI LIGHTNING RIFLE

Caliber: 357 Mag., 45 Colt, 10+1. **Barrel:** 20" to 24.25". **Stock:** Walnut. **Finish:** Blue or case-hardened. Introduced 2006. Imported by Benelli USA.

Price: 1875 Lightning Rifle, 24.25" barrel $1,199.00
Price: 1875 Lightning Short Rifle, 20" barrel. $1,199.00
Price: 1875 Lightning Carbine, 20" barrel. $1,049.00

UBERTI SPRINGFIELD TRAPDOOR RIFLE

Caliber: 4-70, single shot. **Barrel:** 22" or 32.5". **Stock:** Walnut. **Finish:** Blue and case-hardened. Introduced 2006. Imported by Benelli USA.
Price: Springfield Trapdoor Carbine, 22" barrel $1,100.00
Price: Springfield Trapdoor Army, 32.5" barrel $1,295.00

U.S. FIRE ARMS STANDARD LIGHTNING MAGAZINE RIFLE

Caliber: 45 Colt, 44 WCF, 44 Spl., 38 WCF, 15-shot. **Barrel:** 26". **Stock:** Oiled walnut. **Finish:** High polish blue. Nickel finish also available. Introduced 2002. Made in U.S.A. by United States Fire-Arms Manufacturing Co.

Price: Round barrel. $1,480.00
Price: Octagonal barrel, checkered forend. $1,750.00
Price: Half-round barrel, checkered forend $1,999.00
Price: Premium Carbine, 20" round barrel $1,480.00
Price: Baby Carbine, 20" special taper barrel $1,999.00
Price: Trapper, 16" special taper barrel $2,155.00
Price: Cowboy Action Lightning $1,345.00
Price: Cowboy Action Lightning Carbine, 20" round barrel $1,345.00

WINCHESTER MODEL 1895 LEVER-ACTION RIFLE

Caliber: 405 Win, 4-shot magazine. **Barrel:** 24", round. **Weight:** 8 lbs. **Length:** 42" overall. **Stock:** American walnut. **Sights:** Gold bead front, buckhorn rear adjustable for elevation. **Features:** Re-creation of the original Model 1895. Polished blue finish. Two-piece cocking lever, Schnabel forend, straight-grip stock. Introduced 1995. From U.S. Repeating Arms Co., Inc.
Price: Grade I $1,116.00

Includes models for a wide variety of sporting and competitive purposes and uses.

Anschutz 1733D

Barrett Model 95

Blaser R93 Classic

ANSCHUTZ 1743D BOLT-ACTION RIFLE

Caliber: 222 Rem., 3-shot magazine. **Barrel:** 19.7". **Weight:** 6.4 lbs. **Length:** 39" overall. **Stock:** European walnut. **Sights:** Hooded blade front, folding leaf rear. **Features:** Receiver grooved for scope mounting; single stage trigger; claw extractor; sling safety; sling swivels. Imported from Germany by AcuSport Corp.

Price: **$1,588.95**

ANSCHUTZ 1740 MONTE CARLO RIFLE

Caliber: 22 Hornet, 5-shot clip; 222 Rem., 3-shot clip. **Barrel:** 24". **Weight:** 6-1/2 lbs. **Length:** 43.25" overall. **Stock:** Select European walnut. **Sights:** Hooded ramp front, folding leaf rear; drilled and tapped for scope mounting. **Features:** Uses Match 54 action. Adjustable single stage trigger. Stock has roll-over Monte Carlo cheekpiece, slim forend with Schnabel tip, Wundhammer palm swell on grip, rosewood gripcap with white diamond insert. Skip-line checkering on grip and forend. Introduced 1997. Imported from Germany by AcuSport Corp.

Price: From **$1,439.00**
Price: Model 1730 Monte Carlo, as above except in
22 Hornet **$1,439.00**

Anschutz 1733D Rifle

Similar to the 1740 Monte Carlo except has full-length, walnut, Mannlicher-style stock with skip-line checkering, rosewood Schnabel tip, and is chambered for 22 Hornet. Weighs 6.4 lbs., overall length 39", barrel length 19.7". Imported from Germany by AcuSport Corp.

Price: **$1,588.95**

BARRETT MODEL 95 BOLT-ACTION RIFLE

Caliber: 50 BMG, 5-shot magazine. **Barrel:** 29". **Weight:** 22 lbs. **Length:** 45" overall. **Stock:** Energy-absorbing recoil pad. **Sights:** Scope optional. **Features:** Bolt-action, bullpup design. Disassembles without tools; extendable bipod legs; match-grade barrel; muzzle brake. Introduced 1995. Made in U.S.A. by Barrett Firearms Mfg., Inc.

Price: From **$4,950.00**

BLASER R93 BOLT-ACTION RIFLE

Caliber: 22-250, 243, 6.5x55, 270, 7x57, 7mm-08, 308, 30-06, 257 Wby. Mag., 7mm Rem. Mag., 300 Win. Mag., 300 Wby. Mag., 338 Win Mag., 375 H&H, 416 Rem. Mag. **Barrel:** 22" (standard calibers), 26" (magnum). **Weight:** 7 lbs. **Length:** 40" overall (22" barrel). **Stock:** Two-piece European walnut. **Sights:** None furnished; drilled and tapped for scope mounting. **Features:** Straight pull-back bolt action with thumb-activated safety slide/cocking mechanism; interchangeable barrels and bolt heads. Introduced 1994. Imported from Germany by SIGARMS.

Price: R93 Classic **$3,680.00**
Price: R93 LX **$1,895.00**
Price: R93 Synthetic (black synthetic stock) **$1,595.00**
Price: R93 Safari Synthetic (416 Rem. Mag. only) **$1,855.00**
Price: R93 Grand Lux **$4,915.00**
Price: R93 Attaché **$5,390.00**

BRNO 98 BOLT-ACTION RIFLE

Caliber: 7x64, 243, 270, 308, 30-06, 300 Win. Mag., 9.3x62. **Barrel:** 23.6". **Weight:** 7.2 lbs. **Length:** 40.9" overall. **Stock:** European walnut. **Sights:** Blade on ramp front, open adjustable rear. **Features:** Uses Mauser 98-type action; polished blue. Announced 1998. Imported from the Czech Republic by Euro-Imports.

Price: Standard calibers **$507.00**
Price: Magnum calibers **$547.00**
Price: With set trigger, standard calibers **$615.00**
Price: As above, magnum calibers **$655.00**
Price: With full stock, set trigger, standard calibers ... **$703.00**
Price: As above, magnum calibers **$743.00**
Price: 300 Win. Mag., with BOSS **$933.00**

BROWNING A-BOLT RIFLES

Common Features: Short-throw (60°) fluted bolt, three locking lugs, plunger-type ejector; adjustable trigger is grooved. Chrome-plated trigger sear. Hinged floorplate, detachable box magazine. Slide tang safety. Receivers are drilled and tapped for scope mounts, swivel studs included. Barrel is free-floating and glass-bedded, recessed muzzle. Safety is top-tang sliding button. Engraving available for bolt sleeve or rifle body. Introduced 1985. 30 model name variations, as noted below. Imported from Japan by Browning.

Browning A-Bolt Hunter

Browning A-Bolt Medallion

Browning A-Bolt White Gold Medallion

BROWNING A-BOLT HUNTER

Calibers, 22" barrel: 223, 22-250, 243, 270 Win., 30-06, 7mm-08, 308. **Calibers, 23" barrel:** 270 WSM, 7mm WSM, 300 WSM, 325 WSM (intr. 2005). **Calibers, 24" barrel:** 25-06. **Calibers, 26" barrel:** 7mm Rem. Mag., 300 Win. Mag., 338 Win. Mag. **Weight:** 6.25-7.2 lbs. **Length:** 41.25-46.5" overall. **Stock:** Sporter-style walnut; checkered grip and forend. **Metal Finish:** Low-luster blueing.
Price: Hunter . . . . **$705.00 to $734.00**

Browning A-Bolt Hunter Left-Hand

Calibers, 22" barrel: 223 Rem.; 223 WSSM, 243 WSSM, 25 WSSM (WSSMs intr. 2005). **Calibers, 23" barrel:** 270 WSM, 7mm WSM, 300 WSM, 325 WSM (intr. 2005). **Weight:** 6.25-6.6 lbs. **Length:** 41.25-42.75" overall. **Features:** Otherwise similar to A-Bolt Hunter.
Price: Hunter, Left-Hand . . . . **$735.00 to $785.00**

BROWNING A-BOLT HUNTER FLD

Caliber, 23" barrel: 270 WSM, 7mm WSM, 300 WSM, 325 WSM (intr. 2005). **Weight:** 6.6 lbs. **Length:** 42.75" overall. **Features:** FLD has low-luster blueing and select Monte Carlo stock with right-hand palm swell, double-border checkering. Otherwise similar to A-Bolt Hunter.
Price: FLD **$808.00**

BROWNING A-BOLT HUNTER WSSM, FLD WSSM

Calibers, 22" barrel: 223 WSSM, 243 WSSM, 25 WSSM. **Weight:** 6.3 lbs. **Length:** 41.25" overall. **Features:** WSSM has classic walnut stock. FLD has low-luster blueing and select Monte Carlo stock with right-hand palm swell, double-border checkering. Otherwise similar to A-Bolt Hunter.
Price: WSSM **$755.00**
Price: FLD WSSM **$829.00**

BROWNING A-BOLT MOUNTAIN TI

Caliber: 223 WSSM, 243 WSSM, 25 WSSM (all added 2005); 270 WSM, 7mm WSM, 300 WSM. **Barrel:** 22" or 23". **Weight:** 5.25-5.5 lbs. **Length:** 41.25-42.75" overall. **Stock:** Lightweight fiberglass Bell & Carlson model in Mossy-Oak New Break Up camo. **Metal Finish:** Stainless barrel, titanium receiver. **Features:** Pachmayr Decelerator recoil pad. Introduced 1999.
Price: . . . . **$1,669.00 to $1,690.00**

Browning A-Bolt Micro Hunter and Micro Hunter Left-Hand

Calibers, 20" barrel: 22-250, 243, 308, 7mm-08. **Calibers, 22" barrel:** 22 Hornet, 270 WSM, 7mm WSM, 300 WSM, 325 WSM (2005). **Weight:** 6.25-6.4 lbs. **Length:** 39.5-41.5" overall. **Features:** Classic walnut stock with 13.3" LOP. Otherwise similar to A-Bolt Hunter.

Price: Micro Hunter. . . . . **$684.00 to $714.00**
Price: Micro Hunter Left-Hand . . . . **$714.00 to $744.00**

BROWNING A-BOLT MEDALLION

Calibers, 22" barrel: 223, 22-250, 243, 308, 270 Win., 280, 30-06. **Calibers, 23" barrel:** 270 WSM, 7mm WSM, 300 WSM, 325 WSM (intr. 2005). **Calibers, 24" barrel:** 25-06. **Calibers, 26" barrel:** 7mm Rem. Mag., 300 Win. Mag., 338 Win. Mag., 375 H&H. **Weight:** 6.25-7.1 lbs. **Length:** 41.25-46.5" overall. **Stock:** Select walnut stock, glossy finish, rosewood grip and forend caps, checkered grip and forend. **Metal Finish:** Engraved high-polish blued receiver.
Price: Medallion . . . . **$805.00 to $835.00**
Price: Medallion WSSM in 223/243/25 WSSM **$856.00**

BROWNING A-BOLT MEDALLION W/BOSS

Calibers, 22" barrel: 223 WSSM, 243 WSSM, 25 WSSM (intr. 2005), 270, 30-06. **Calibers, 23" barrel:** 270 WSM, 7mm WSM, 300 WSM. **Calibers, 24" barrel:** 375 H&H. **Calibers, 26" barrel:** 300 Win. Mag., 338 Win. Mag. Same as the Medallion model A-Bolt except has left-hand action. Introduced 1987.
Price: Medallion Left-Hand. . . . . **$885.00 to $936.00**

Browning A-Bolt Medallion Left-Hand

Calibers, 22" barrel: 223 Rem., 223 WSSM, 243 WSSM, 25 WSSM (all intr. 2005), 270, 30-06. **Calibers, 23" barrel:** 270 WSM, 7mm WSM, 300 WSM, 325 WSM (intr. 2005). **Calibers, 26" barrel:** 7mm Rem. Mag., 300 Win. Mag. Same as the Medallion model A-Bolt except has left-hand action. Introduced 1987.
Price: Medallion Left-Hand. . . . . **$837.00 to $886.00**

Browning A-Bolt Medallion Left-Hand w/BOSS

Calibers, 22" barrel: 270, 30-06. **Calibers, 26" barrel:** 7mm Rem. Mag., 300 Win. Mag. Same as the Medallion Left-Hand except has BOSS device.
Price: Medallion Left-Hand w/BOSS . . . . **$917.00 to $945.00**

BROWNING A-BOLT WHITE GOLD MEDALLION, RMEF WHITE GOLD, WHITE GOLD MEDALLION W/BOSS

Calibers, 22" barrel: 270 Win., 30-06. **Calibers, 23" barrel:** 270 WSM, 7mm WSM, 300 WSM, 325 WSM (intr. 2005). **Calibers, 26" barrel:** 7mm Rem. Mag., 300 Win. Mag. **Weight:** 6.4-7.7 lbs. **Length:** 42.75-46.5" overall. **Stock:** select walnut stock with brass spacers between rubber recoil pad and between the rosewood gripcap and forend tip; gold-filled barrel inscription; palm-swell pistol grip, Monte Carlo comb, 22 lpi checkering with double borders. **Metal Finish:** Engraved high-polish stainless receiver and barrel. BOSS version chambered in 270 Win. and 30-06 (22" barrel) and 7mm Rem. Mag. and 300 Win. Mag. (26" barrel) Introduced 1988. RMEF version has engraved gripcap, continental cheekpiece; gold engraved, stainless receiver and bbl. Introduced 2004.
Price: White Gold Medallion . . . . **$1,155.00 to $1,183.00**
Price: Rocky Mt. Elk Foundation White Gold, 7mm Rem. Mag., . . **$1,261.00**
Price: White Gold Medallion w/BOSS . . . . **$1,235.00 to $1,263.00**

Browning A-Bolt Stainless Stalker

Browning A-Bolt Varmint Stalker

Browning A-Bolt Composite Stalker

Browning A-Bolt Eclipse Hunter

Browning A-Bolt Eclipse M-1000

BROWNING A-BOLT STAINLESS STALKER, STAINLESS STALKER LEFT-HAND

Calibers, 22" barrel: 223, 243, 270, 280, 7mm-08, 30-06, 308. **Calibers, 23" barrel:** 270 WSM, 7mm WSM, 300 WSM, 325 WSM (intr. 2005). **Calibers, 24" barrel:** 25-06. **Calibers, 26" barrel:** 7mm Rem. Mag., 300 Win. Mag., 338 Win. Mag., 375 H&H. **Weight:** 6.1-7.2 lbs. **Length:** 40.9-46.5" overall. **Features:** Similar to the A-Bolt Hunter model except receiver and barrel are made of stainless steel; other exposed metal surfaces are finished silver-gray matte. Graphite-fiberglass composite textured stock. No sights are furnished, except on 375 H&H, which comes with open sights. Introduced 1987.
Price: Stainless Stalker . . . . **$897.00 to $926.00**
Price: Stainless Stalker Left-Hand . . . . **$925.00 to $954.00**
Price: Stainless Stalker WSSM, 223/243/25 WSSM **$808.00**

Browning A-Bolt Stainless Stalker, Stainless Stalker Left-Hand, w/BOSS

Calibers, 22" barrel: 223 WSSM, 243 WSSM, 25 WSSM, 270, 30-06. **Calibers, 23" barrel:** 270 WSM, 7mm WSM, 300 WSM, 325 WSM (intr. 2005). **Calibers, 24" barrel:** 375 H&H. **Calibers, 26" barrel:** 7mm Rem. Mag., 300 Win. Mag., 338 Win. Mag. **Features:** Similar to the A-Bolt Stainless Stalker, except includes BOSS.
Price: Stainless Stalker w/BOSS . . . . **$977.00 to $1,027.00**
Price: Stainless Stalker Left-Hand w/BOSS . . . . . . **$1,005.00 to $1,034.00**

BROWNING A-BOLT VARMINT STALKER, VARMINT STALKER WSSM

Calibers, 24" barrel: 223 Rem., 223 WSSM, 243 WSSM, 25 WSSM. **Calibers, 26" barrel:** 22-250. **Weight:** 7.8-8.2 lbs. **Length:** 42.75-45.75" overall. **Features:** Similar to the A-Bolt Stainless Stalker except has black graphite-fiberglass stock with textured finish and matte blue-finish on all exposed metal surfaces. Medium-heavy varmint barrel. No sights are furnished. Introduced 1987.
Price: Varmint Stalker **$860.00**
Price: Varmint Stalker WSSM **$913.00**

BROWNING A-BOLT COMPOSITE STALKER

Calibers, 22" barrel: 223, 22-250, 243, 270, 280, 7mm-08, 30-06, 308. **Calibers, 23" barrel:** 270 WSM, 7mm WSM, 300 WSM, 325 WSM (intr. 2005). **Calibers, 24" barrel:** 25-06. **Calibers, 26" barrel:** 7mm Rem. Mag., 300 Win. Mag., 338 Win. Mag. **Weight:** 6.1-7.2 lbs. **Length:** 40.75-46.5" overall. **Features:** Similar to the A-Bolt Stainless Stalker except has black composite stock with textured finish and matte-blued finish on all exposed metal surfaces except bolt sleeve. No sights are furnished.
Price: Composite Stalker . . . . **$705.00 to $735.00**

BROWNING A-BOLT ECLIPSE HUNTER W/BOSS, M-1000 ECLIPSE W/BOSS, M-1000 ECLIPSE WSM, STAINLESS M-1000 ECLIPSE WSM

Calibers, 22" barrel: 270, 30-06. **Calibers, 26" barrel:** 7mm Rem. Mag., 300 Win. Mag., 270 WSM, 7mm WSM, 300 WSM. **Weight:** 7.5-9.9 lbs. **Length:** 42.75-46.5" overall. **Features:** All models have gray/black laminated thumbhole stock. Introduced 1996. Two versions have BOSS barrel vibration modulator and muzzle brake. Hunter has sporter-weight barrel. M-1000 Eclipses have long actions and heavy target barrels, adjustable triggers, bench-style forends, 3-shot magazines. Introduced 1997.
Price: Eclipse Hunter w/BOSS . . . . **$1,134.00 to $1,162.00**
Price: M-1000 Eclipse w/BOSS, 300 Win. Mag. only **$1,168.00**
Price: M-1000 Eclipse WSM, 270 WSM, 7mm WSM, 300 WSM. . **$1,068.00**
Price: Stainless M-1000 Eclipse WSM **$1,292.00**

CENTERFIRE RIFLES — Bolt-Action

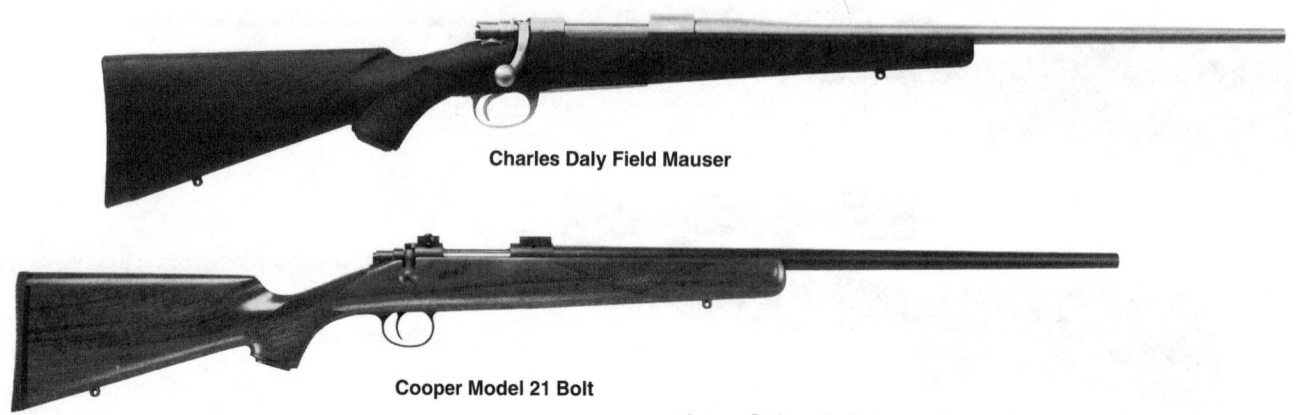

Charles Daly Field Mauser

Cooper Model 21 Bolt

CARBON ONE BOLT-ACTION RIFLE

Caliber: 22-250 to 375 H&H. **Barrel:** Up to 28". **Weight:** 5-1/2 to 7-1/4 lbs. **Length:** Varies. **Stock:** Synthetic or wood. **Sights:** None furnished. **Features:** Choice of Remington, Browning or Winchester action with free-floated Christensen graphite/epoxy/steel barrel, trigger pull tuned to 3 to 3-1/2 lbs. Made in U.S.A. by Christensen Arms.
Price: Carbon One Hunter Rifle, 6-1/2 to 7 lbs. $1,499.00
Price: Carbon One Custom, 5-1/2 to 6-1/2 lbs., Shilen trigger . . $2,750.00
Price: Carbon Ranger, 50 BMG, 5-shot repeater $4,750.00
Price: Carbon Ranger, 50 BMG, single shot $3,950.00

CENTURY INTERNATIONAL M70 SPORTER DOUBLE-TRIGGER BOLT-ACTION RIFLE

Caliber: 22-250, 270, 300 Win. Mag., 308 Win., 24" barrel. **Weight:** 7.95 lbs. **Length:** 44.5" **Sights:** Flip-up U-notch rear sight, hooded blade front sight. **Features:** Mauser M98-type action; 5-rd fixed box magazine. 22-250 has hinged floorplate. Monte Carlo stock, oil finish. Adjustable trigger on double-trigger models. 300 Win. Mag. Has 3-rd. fixed box magazine. 308 holds 5 rds. 300 and 308 have buttpads. Manufactured by Zastava in Yugoslavia, imported by Century International.
Price: M70 Sporter Double-Trigger $500.00
Price: M70 Sporter Double-Trigger 22-250 . . . . $475.00
Price: M70 Sporter Single-Trigger .300 Win. Mag. $475.00
Price: M70 Sporter Single/Double Trigger .308 Win. $500.00

CHARLES DALY FIELD MAUSER RIFLE

Caliber: 22-250, 243, 25-06, 270, 308, 30-06 (in 22" barrels); 7mm Rem. Mag. and 300 Win. Mag. in 24" barrels. **Weight:** NA. **Sights:** None; drilled and tapped for scope mounts. **Features:** Mauser Model 98-type action; carbon or stainless steel barrels; slide safety; polymer stock; fully adjustable trigger.
Price: Field Grade Mauser $459.00
Price: Mauser SS $549.00
Price: Magnum calibers. $579.00

COOPER MODEL 16 WSSM BOLT-ACTION RIFLE

Caliber: 223 WSSM, 25 WSSM, 243 WSSM. **Barrel:** 26" stainless match. **Weight:** 6.5-7.5 lbs. **Stock:** AA-AAA select Claro walnut, 22 lpi hand checkering. **Sights:** None furnished. **Features:** Three front locking-lug bolt-action.
Price: Varminter. $1,198.00
Price: Montana Varminter $1,459.00
Price: Varmint Extreme $1,895.00

COOPER MODEL 21 BOLT-ACTION RIFLE

Caliber: 17 Rem., 17 Mach IV, 19-223, Tactical 20, 204 Ruger, 20 VarTarg, 221 Fireball, 222 Rem, 222 Rem Mag, 223 Rem, 223 Rem AI, 22 PPC, 6mm PPC, 6x45, 6x47, 6.8 SPC. **Barrel:** 22" or 24" stainless match or 4140 blued. **Weight:** 6.5-7.5 lbs. **Stock:** AA-AAA select Claro walnut, 22 lpi hand checkering. **Sights:** None furnished. **Features:** Three front locking-lug bolt-action single shot. **Action:** 6.6" long, Sako style, modified for rimmed cases. Retractable tab ejector. Fully adjustable single-stage

trigger. Options include wood upgrades, case-color metalwork, barrel fluting, custom LOP, and many others.
Price: Phoenix. $1,298.00
Price: Varminter $1,198.00
Price: Montana Varminter. $1,459.00
Price: Varmint Extreme $1,895.00
Price: Classic (blued barrel) $1,398.00
Price: Custom Classic (blued barrel) $1,995.00
Price: Western Classic (case color, octagonal blued barrel) $2,698.00

COOPER MODEL 22 BOLT-ACTION RIFLE

Caliber: 22-250 Rem., 22-250 Rem. AI, 25-06 Rem., 25-06 Rem. AI, 243 Win., 243 Win. AI, 220 Swift, 250/3000 AI, 257 Roberts, 257 Roberts AI, 7mm-08, 6mm Rem., 260 Rem., 6 x 284, 6.5 x 284, 22 BR, 6mm BR, 308 Win. **Barrel:** 24" stainless match or 4140 blued. **Weight:** 7.5 lbs. **Stock:** AA-AAA select Claro walnut, 22 lpi hand checkering. **Sights:** None furnished. **Features:** Three front locking-lug bolt-action single shot. **Action:** 8.25" long, Sako style, plunger-style ejector. Fully adjustable single-stage trigger. Options include wood upgrades, case-color metalwork, barrel fluting, custom LOP, and many others.
Price: Phoenix. $1,398.00
Price: Varminter $1,349.00
Price: Montana Varminter. $1,459.00
Price: Varmint Extreme $1,995.00
Price: Classic (blued barrel) $1,398.00
Price: Custom Classic (blued barrel) $2,195.00
Price: Western Classic (case color, octagonal blued barrel) $2,896.00

COOPER MODEL 38 BOLT-ACTION RIFLE

Caliber: 17 Squirrel, 17 Hee Bee, 17 Ackley Hornet, 19 Calhoun, 22 Hornet, 22 K Hornet, 22 Squirrel, 218 Bee, 218 Mash Bee. **Barrel:** 24" stainless match. **Weight:** 6.5-7.5 lbs. **Stock:** AA-AAA select Claro walnut, 22 lpi hand checkering. **Sights:** None furnished. **Features:** Three front locking-lug mini bolt-action single shot. **Action:** 6.6" long, Sako style, modified for rimmed cases. Retractable tab ejector. Fully adjustable single-stage trigger. Options include wood upgrades, case-color metalwork, barrel fluting, custom LOP, and many others.
Price: Varminter $1,198.00
Price: Montana Varminter. $1,459.00
Price: Varmint Extreme $1,895.00
Price: Classic $1,398.00
Price: Custom Classic (blued barrel) $1,995.00
Price: Western Classic (case color, octagonal blued barrel) $2,698.00

CZ 527 LUX BOLT-ACTION RIFLE

Caliber: 22 Hornet, 222 Rem., 223 Rem., detachable 5-shot magazine. **Barrel:** 23-1/2"; standard or heavy barrel. **Weight:** 6 lbs., 1 oz. **Length:** 42-1/2" overall. **Stock:** European walnut with Monte Carlo. **Sights:** Hooded front, open adjustable rear. **Features:** Improved mini-Mauser action with non-rotating claw extractor; single set trigger; grooved receiver. Imported from the Czech Republic by CZ-USA.
Price: $566.00
Price: Model FS, full-length stock, cheekpiece $658.00

CZ 527 Lux

CZ 527 FS

CZ 527 American

CZ 550 Lux

CZ 550 Medium Magnum

CZ 550 American Classic Bolt-Action Rifle

Similar to CZ 550 Lux except has American classic-style stock with 18 lpi checkering; free-floating barrel; recessed target crown. Has 25.6" barrel; weighs 7.48 lbs. No sights furnished. Introduced 1999. Imported from the Czech Republic by CZ-USA.

Price: . . . . **$586.00 to $609.00**

CZ 550 Medium Magnum Bolt-Action Rifle

Similar to the CZ 550 Lux except chambered for the 300 Win. Mag. and 7mm Rem. Mag.; 5-shot magazine. Adjustable iron sights, hammer-forged barrel, single-set trigger, Turkish walnut stock. Weighs 7.5 lbs. Introduced 2001. Imported from the Czech Republic by CZ-USA.

Price: **$621.00**

CZ 550 Magnum Bolt-Action Rifle

Similar to CZ 550 Lux except has long action for 300 Win. Mag., 375 H&H, 416 Rigby, 458 Win. Mag. Overall length is 46.45"; barrel length 25"; weighs 9.24 lbs. Hooded front sight, express rear with one standing, two folding leaves. Imported from the Czech Republic by CZ-USA.

Price: 300 Win. Mag.. . . . . **$717.00**
Price: 375 H&H **$756.00**
Price: 416 Rigby **$809.00**
Price: 458 Win. Mag. **$744.00**

CZ 527 American Classic Bolt-Action Rifle

Similar to the CZ 527 Lux except has classic-style stock with 18 lpi checkering; free-floating barrel; recessed target crown on barrel. No sights furnished. Introduced 1999. Imported from the Czech Republic by CZ-USA.

Price: 22 Hornet, 222 Rem., 223 Rem.. . . . . **$586.00 to $609.00**

CZ 550 LUX BOLT-ACTION RIFLE

Caliber: 22-250, 243, 6.5x55, 7x57, 7x64, 308 Win., 9.3x62, 270 Win., 30-06. **Barrel:** 20.47". **Weight:** 7.5 lbs. **Length:** 44.68" overall. **Stock:** Turkish walnut in Bavarian style or FS (Mannlicher). **Sights:** Hooded front, adjustable rear. **Features:** Improved Mauser-style action with claw extractor, fixed ejector, square bridge dovetailed receiver; single set trigger. Imported from the Czech Republic by CZ-USA.

Price: Lux. . . . . **$566.00 to $609.00**
Price: FS (full stock) **$706.00**

CZ 550 Magnum

Dakota 76 Traveler

Dakota 76 Classic

Dakota 76 Safari

CZ 700 M1 SNIPER RIFLE

Caliber: 308 Winchester, 10-shot magazine. **Barrel:** 25.6". **Weight:** 11.9 lbs. **Length:** 45" overall. **Stock:** Laminated wood thumbhole with adjustable buttplate and cheekpiece. **Sights:** None furnished; permanently attached Weaver rail for scope mounting. **Features:** 60-degree bolt throw; oversized trigger guard and bolt handle for use with gloves; full-length equipment rail on forend; fully adjustable trigger. Introduced 2001. Imported from the Czech Republic by CZ-USA.
Price: **$2,097.00**

DAKOTA 76 TRAVELER TAKEDOWN RIFLE

Caliber: 257 Roberts, 25-06, 7x57, 270, 280, 30-06, 338-06, 35 Whelen (standard length); 7mm Rem. Mag., 300 Win. Mag., 338 Win. Mag., 416 Taylor, 458 Win. Mag. (short magnums); 7mm, 300, 330, 375 Dakota Magnums. **Barrel:** 23". **Weight:** 7-1/2 lbs. **Length:** 43-1/2" overall. **Stock:** Medium fancy-grade walnut in classic style. Checkered grip and forend; solid buttpad. **Sights:** None furnished; drilled and tapped for scope mounts. **Features:** Threadless disassembly. Uses modified Model 76 design with many features of the Model 70 Winchester. Left-hand model also available. Introduced 1989. Made in U.S.A. by Dakota Arms, Inc.
Price: Classic. **$4,495.00**
Price: Safari **$5,495.00**
Price: Extra barrels . . . . **$1,650.00 to $1,950.00**

DAKOTA 76 CLASSIC BOLT-ACTION RIFLE

Caliber: 257 Roberts, 270, 280, 30-06, 7mm Rem. Mag., 338 Win. Mag., 300 Win. Mag., 375 H&H, 458 Win. Mag. **Barrel:** 23". **Weight:** 7-1/2 lbs. **Length:** 43-1/2" overall. **Stock:** Medium fancy grade walnut in classic style. Checkered pistol grip and forend; solid buttpad. **Sights:** None furnished; drilled and tapped for scope mounts. **Features:** Has many features of the original Winchester Model 70. One-piece rail trigger guard assembly; steel gripcap. Model 70-style trigger. Many options available. Left-hand rifle available at same price. Introduced 1988. From Dakota Arms, Inc.
Price: **$3,595.00**

DAKOTA 76 SAFARI BOLT-ACTION RIFLE

Caliber: 270 Win., 7x57, 280, 30-06, 7mm Dakota, 7mm Rem. Mag., 300 Dakota, 300 Win. Mag., 330 Dakota, 338 Win. Mag., 375 Dakota, 458 Win. Mag., 300 H&H, 375 H&H, 416 Rem. **Barrel:** 23". **Weight:** 8-1/2 lbs. **Length:** 43-1/2" overall. **Stock:** XXX fancy walnut; point-pattern with wraparound forend checkering. **Sights:** Ramp front, standing leaf rear. **Features:** Has many features of the original Winchester Model 70. Barrel band front swivel, inletted rear. Cheekpiece with shadow line. Steel gripcap. Introduced 1988. From Dakota Arms, Inc.
Price: Wood stock. **$4,595.00**

Dakota African Grade

Similar to 76 Safari except chambered for 338 Lapua Mag., 404 Jeffery, 416 Rigby, 416 Dakota, 450 Dakota, 4-round magazine, select wood, two stock cross-bolts. 24" barrel, weighs 9-10 lbs. Ramp front sight, standing leaf rear. Introduced 1989.
Price: **$4,995.00**

Dakota Longbow

Dakota 97 Lightweight Hunter

Dakota Hunter

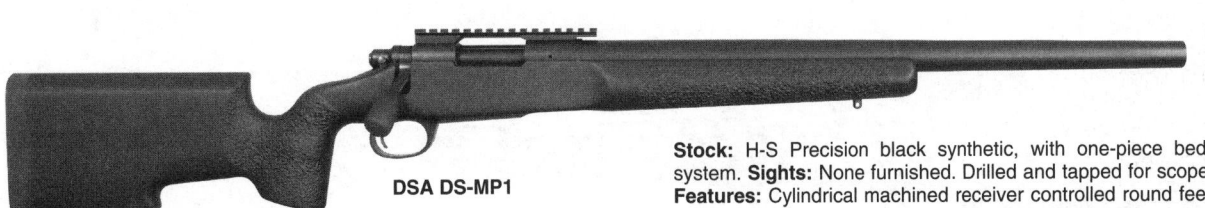

DSA DS-MP1

DAKOTA LONGBOW TACTICAL E.R. RIFLE

Caliber: 300 Dakota Magnum, 330 Dakota Magnum, 338 Lapua Magnum. **Barrel:** 28", .950" at muzzle **Weight:** 13.7 lbs. **Length:** 50" to 52" overall. **Stock:** Ambidextrous McMillan A-2 fiberglass, black or olive green color; adjustable cheekpiece and buttplate. **Sights:** None furnished. Comes with Picatinny one-piece optical rail. **Features:** Uses the Dakota 76 action with controlled-round feed; three-position firing pin block safety, claw extractor; Model 70-style trigger. Comes with bipod, case tool kit. Introduced 1997. Made in U.S.A. by Dakota Arms, Inc.
Price: **$4,250.00**

DAKOTA 97 LIGHTWEIGHT HUNTER

Caliber: 22-250 to 330. **Barrel:** 22" to 24". **Weight:** 6.1 to 6.5 lbs. **Length:** 43" overall. **Stock:** Fiberglass. **Sights:** Optional. **Features:** Matte blue finish, black stock. Right-hand action only. Introduced 1998. Made in U.S.A. by Dakota Arms, Inc.
Price: **$1,995.00**

DAKOTA LONG RANGE HUNTER RIFLE

Caliber: 25-06, 257 Roberts, 270 Win., 280 Rem., 7mm Rem. Mag., 7mm Dakota Mag., 30-06, 300 Win. Mag., 300 Dakota Mag., 338 Win. Mag., 330 Dakota Mag., 375 H&H Mag., 375 Dakota Mag. **Barrel:** 24", 26", match-quality; free-floating. **Weight:** 7.7 lbs. **Length:** 45" to 47" overall.

Stock: H-S Precision black synthetic, with one-piece bedding block system. **Sights:** None furnished. Drilled and tapped for scope mounting. **Features:** Cylindrical machined receiver controlled round feed; Mauser-style extractor; three-position striker blocking safety; fully adjustable match trigger. Right-hand action only. Introduced 1997. Made in U.S.A. by Dakota Arms, Inc.
Price: **$1,995.00**

DSA DS-MP1

Caliber: 308 Win. match chamber. **Barrel:** 22", 1:10 twist, hand-lapped stainless-steel match-grade Badger Barrel with recessed target crown. **Weight:** 11.5 lbs. **Length:** 41.75". **Stock:** Black McMillan A5 pillar bedded in Marine-Tex with 13.5" length of pull. **Sights:** Tactical Picatinny rail. **Features:** Action, action threads and action bolt locking shoulder completely trued, Badger Ordnance precision ground heavy recoil lug, machined steel Picatinny rail sight mount, trued action threads, action bolt locking shoulder, bolt face and lugs, 2.5-lb. trigger pull, barrel and action finished in Black DuraCoat, guaranteed to shoot 1/2 MOA at 100 yards with match-grade ammo. Introduced 2006. Made in U.S.A. by DSA, Inc.
Price: **$2,800.00**

ED BROWN SAVANNA RIFLE

Caliber: 30-06, 300 Win. Mag., 300 Weatherby, 338 Win. Mag. **Barrel:** 22", 23", 24". **Weight:** 8 to 8-1/2 lbs. **Stock:** Fully glass-bedded McMillan fiberglass sporter. **Sights:** None furnished. Talley scope mounts utilizing heavy duty 8-40 screws. **Features:** Custom action with machined steel trigger guard and hinged floor plate. Available in left-hand version.
Price: From . . . . **$2,795.00 to $2,895.00**

Ed Brown 702 Savanna

Ed Brown 702 Ozark

Ed Brown 702 Bushveld

Ed Brown 702 Varmint

Ed Brown Model 702 Denali, Ozark

Similar to the Ed Brown Model 702 Savanna but lighter weight, designed specifically for mountain hunting, especially suited to the 270 and 280 calibers. Right-hand only. Weighs about 7.75 lbs. The Model 702 Ozark is made on a short action with a lightweight stock. Ozark calibers are 223, 243, 6mm, 260 Rem., 7mm-08, 308. Weight 6.5 lbs.

Price: From **$2,800.00**

ED BROWN MODEL 702 BUSHVELD

Caliber: 338 Win. Mag., 375 H&H, 416 Rem. Mag., 458 Win. Mag., 458 Lott and all Ed Brown Savanna long action calibers. **Barrel:** 24" medium or heavy weight. **Weight:** 8.25 lbs. **Stock:** Fully bedded McMillan fiberglass with Monte Carlo style cheekpiece, Pachmayr Decelerator recoil pad. **Sights:** None furnished. Talley scope mounts utilizing heavy duty 8-40 screws. **Features:** Options include left-hand action, stainless steel barrel, additional calibers, iron sights.

Price: From . . . . **$2,895.00 to $3,195.00**

ED BROWN MODEL 702 VARMINT

Caliber: 223, 22-250, 220 Swift, 243, 6mm, 308. **Barrel:** Medium weight #5 contour 24"; heavyweight #17 contour 24"; 26" optional. **Weight:** 9 lbs. **Stock:** Fully glass-bedded McMillan fiberglass with recoil pad. **Sights:** None furnished. Talley scope mounts with heavy duty 8-40 screws. **Features:** Fully-adjustable trigger, steel trigger guard and floor plate, many options available.

Price: From **$2,495.00**

HOWA LIGHTNING BOLT-ACTION RIFLE

Caliber: 223, 22-250, 243, 204 Ruger, 270, 308, 30-06, 7mm Rem. Mag., 300 Win. Mag., 338 Win. Mag, 300 WSM, 7mm WSM, 270 WSM. **Barrel:** 22", 24" magnum calibers. **Weight:** 7-1/2 lbs. **Length:** 42-44" overall (22" barrel). **Stock:** Black Bell & Carlson Carbelite composite with Monte Carlo comb; checkered grip and forend; also Realtree camo available. **Sights:** None furnished. Drilled and tapped for scope mounting. **Features:** Three-position thumb safety; hinged floorplate; polished blue/black finish. Introduced 1993. From Legacy Sports International.

Price: Blue, standard calibers. **$439.00**
Price: Blue, magnum calibers. **$470.00**
Price: Stainless, standard calibers **$661.00**
Price: Stainless, magnum calibers **$690.00**

Howa Lightning

Howa M-1500 Hunter

Howa M-1500 Ultralight

Howa M-1500 Varmint Supreme

Howa M-1500 Hunter Bolt-Action Rifle

Similar to Lightning Model except has walnut-finished hardwood stock, three-position safety. Polished blue finish or stainless steel. Introduced 1999. From Legacy Sports International.

Price: Blue, standard calibers $574.00
Price: Stainless, standard calibers $682.00
Price: Blue, magnum calibers $595.00
Price: Stainless, magnum calibers $704.00
Price: Blued, camo stock. $545.00

Howa M-1500 Supreme Rifles

Similar to Howa M-1500 Lightning except stocked with JRS Classic or Thumbhole Sporter laminated wood stocks in Nutmeg (brown/black) or Pepper (gray/black) colors. Barrel: 22"; 24" magnum calibers. Weights are JRS stock 8 lbs., THS stock 8.3 lbs. Three-position safety. Introduced 2001. Imported from Japan by Legacy Sports International.

Price: Blue, standard calibers, JRS stock. $646.00
Price: Blue, standard calibers, THS stock $704.00
Price: Blue, magnum calibers, JRS stock $675.00
Price: Blue, magnum calibers, THS stock $733.00
Price: Stainless, standard calibers, JRS stock $755.00
Price: Stainless, standard calibers, THS stock $813.00
Price: Stainless, magnum calibers, JRS stock $784.00
Price: Stainless, magnum calibers, THS stock $842.00

Howa M-1500 Ultralight

Similar to Howa M-1500 Lightning except receiver milled to reduce weight; three-position safety; tapered 22" barrel; 1-10" twist. Chambered for 243 Win. Stocks are black texture-finished hardwood. Weighs 6.4 lbs. Length 40" overall.

Price: Blued $539.00
Price: Stainless model $658.00

Howa M-1500 Varmint and Varmint Supreme Rifles

Similar to M-1500 Lightning except has heavy 24" hammer-forged barrel. Chambered for 223, 22-250, 308. Weighs 9.3 lbs.; overall length 44.5". Introduced 1999. Imported from Japan by Interarms/Howa. Varminter Supreme has heavy barrel, target crown muzzle; three-position safety. Heavy 24" barrel, laminated wood with raised comb stocks, rollover cheekpiece, vented beavertail forearm; available in 223 Rem., 22-250 Rem., 204 Ruger, 308 Win. Weighs 9.9 lbs. Carbon fiber thumbhole stock option available. Introduced 2001. Imported from Japan by Legacy Sports International.

Price: Varminter, blue, polymer stock. $546.00
Price: Varminter, stainless, polymer stock $664.00
Price: Varminter, blue, wood stock $610.00
Price: Varminter, stainless, wood stock $719.00
Price: Varminter Supreme, blued . . . . $711.00 to $733.00
Price: Varminter Supreme, stainless . . . . $820.00 to $842.00
Price: Varminter, blued, camo stock $582.00
Price: Varminter, stainless, camo stock $704.00

Kimber 8400

Kimber 84M Classic

L.A.R. Grizzly

Magnum Research Tactical

KENNY JARRETT BOLT-ACTION RIFLE

Caliber: 223 Rem., 243 Improved, 243 Catbird, 7mm-08 Improved, 280 Remington, .280 Ackley Improved, 7mm Rem. Mag., 284 Jarrett, 30-06 Springfield, 300 Win. Mag., .300 Jarrett, 323 Jarrett, 338 Jarrett, 375 H&H, 416 Rem., 450 Rigby., other modern cartridges. **Barrel:** NA. **Weight:** NA. **Length:** NA. **Stock:** NA. **Features:** Tri-Lock receiver. Talley rings and bases. Accuracy guarantees and custom loaded ammunition.

Price: Signature Series	**$6,880.00**
Price: Wind Walker	**$6,650.00**
Price: Original Beanfield (customer's receiver)	**$4,850.00**
Price: Professional Hunter	**$9,390.00**

KIMBER MODEL 8400 BOLT-ACTION RIFLE

Caliber: 270, 7mm, 300 or 325 WSM, 4 shot. **Barrel:** 24". **Weight:** 6 lbs. 3 oz. to 6 lbs 10 oz. **Length:** 43.25". **Stock:** Claro walnut or Kevlar-reinforced fiberglass. **Sights:** None; drilled and tapped for bases. **Features:** Mauser claw extractor, two-position wing safety, action bedded on aluminum pillars and fiberglass, free-floated barrel, match grade adjustable trigger set at 4 lbs., matte or polished blue or matte stainless finish. Introduced 2003. Made in U.S.A. by Kimber Mfg. Inc.

Price: Classic.................................**$1,080.00 to $2,030.00**

KIMBER MODEL 84M BOLT-ACTION RIFLE

Caliber: 22-250, 204 Ruger, 223, 243, 260 Rem., 7mm-08, 308, 5-shot. **Barrel:** 22", 24", 26". **Weight:** 5 lbs., 10 oz. to 10 lbs. **Length:** 41" to 45". **Stock:** Claro walnut, checkered with steel gripcap; synthetic or gray laminate. **Sights:** None; drilled and tapped for bases. **Features:** Mauser claw extractor, three-position wing safety, action bedded on aluminum pillars, free-floated barrel, match-grade trigger set at 4 lbs., matte blue finish. Includes cable lock. Introduced 2001. Made in U.S.A. by Kimber Mfg. Inc.

Price: Classic (243, 260, 7mm-08, 308).......... **$945.00 to $1,828.00**
Price: Varmint (22-250)................................ **$1,038.00**

L.A.R. GRIZZLY 50 BIG BOAR RIFLE

Caliber: 50 BMG, single shot. **Barrel:** 36". **Weight:** 30.4 lbs. **Length:** 45.5" overall. **Stock:** Integral. Ventilated rubber recoil pad. **Sights:** None furnished; scope mount. **Features:** Bolt-action bullpup design, thumb and bolt stop safety. All-steel construction. Introduced 1994. Made in U.S.A. by L.A.R. Mfg., Inc.

Price: **$2,350.00**

MAGNUM RESEARCH MAGNUM LITE TACTICAL RIFLE

Caliber: 223 Rem., 22-250, 308 Win., 300 Win. Mag., 300 WSM. **Barrel:** 26" Magnum Lite™ graphite. **Weight:** 8.3 lbs. **Length:** NA. **Stock:** H-S Precision™ tactical black synthetic. **Sights:** None furnished; drilled and tapped for scope mount. **Features:** Accurized Remington 700 action; adjustable trigger; adjustable comb height. Tuned to shoot 1/2" MOA or better. Introduced 2001. From Magnum Research Inc.

Price: **$2,400.00**

Remington 673 Guide

Remington 700 Classic

Remington 700 ADL Synthetic

Remington 700 BDL

MOUNTAIN EAGLE MAGNUM LITE RIFLE

Caliber: 22-250, 223 Rem. (Varmint); 280, 30-06 (long action); 7mm Rem. Mag., 300 Win. Mag., (magnum action). **Barrel:** 24", 26", free floating. **Weight:** 7 lbs., 13 oz. **Length:** 44" overall (24" barrel). **Stock:** Kevlar-graphite with aluminum bedding block, high comb, recoil pad, swivel studs; made by H-S Precision. **Sights:** None furnished. **Features:** Special Sako action with one-piece forged bolt, hinged steel floorplate, lengthened receiver ring; adjustable trigger. Introduced 1996. From Magnum Research, Inc.
Price: Magnum Lite (graphite barrel) **$2,295.00**

REMINGTON MODEL 673 GUIDE RIFLE

Caliber: 65mm Rem. Mag., 308 Win., 300 Rem. SA Ultra Mag., 350 Rem. Mag. **Barrel:** 22". **Weight:** 7-1/2 lbs. **Length:** 41-3/16". **Stock:** Two-tone wide striped, laminated, weather resistant. **Features:** Magnum contour barrel with machined steel ventilated rib, iron sights.
Price: **$825.00**

REMINGTON MODEL 700 CLASSIC RIFLE

Caliber: 300 Savage. **Barrel:** 24". **Weight:** About 7-1/4 lbs. **Length:** 44-1/2" overall. **Stock:** American walnut, 20 lpi checkering on pistol grip and forend. Classic styling. Satin finish. **Sights:** None furnished. Receiver drilled and tapped for scope mounting. **Features:** A "classic" version of the BDL with straight comb stock. Fitted with rubber recoil pad. Sling swivel studs installed. Hinged floorplate. Limited production in 2003 only.
Price: **$683.00**
Price: Left-hand model . . . . **$769.00 to $796.00**

REMINGTON MODEL 700 ADL DELUXE RIFLE

Caliber: 270, 30-06. **Barrel:** 22" round tapered. **Weight:** 7-1/4 lbs. **Length:** 41-5/8" overall. **Stock:** Walnut. Satin-finished pistol grip stock with fine-line cut checkering, Monte Carlo. **Sights:** Gold bead ramp front; removable, step-adjustable rear with windage screw. **Features:** Side safety, receiver tapped for scope mounts.
Price: **$580.00**

Remington Model 700 ADL Synthetic

Similar to the 700 ADL except has a fiberglass-reinforced synthetic stock with straight comb, raised cheekpiece, positive checkering, and black rubber buttpad. Metal has matte finish. Available in 22-250, 223, 243, 270, 308, 30-06 with 22" barrel, 300 Win. Mag., 7mm Rem. Mag. with 24" barrel. Introduced 1996.
Price: From . . . . **$500.00 to $527.00**

Remington Model 700 ADL Synthetic Youth

Similar to the Model 700 ADL Synthetic except has 1" shorter stock, 20" barrel. Chambered for 243, 308. Introduced 1998.
Price: **$500.00**

Remington Model 700 BDL Custom Deluxe Rifle

Same as 700 ADL except chambered for 222, 223 (short action, 24" barrel), 7mm-08, 280, 22-250, 25-06, (short action, 22" barrel), 243, 270, 30-06, skip-line checkering, black forend tip and gripcap with white line spacers. Matted receiver top, quick-release floorplate. Hooded ramp front sight, quick detachable swivels.
Price: **$683.00**
Also available in 17 Rem., 7mm Rem. Mag., 7mm Rem. Ultra Mag., 300 Win. Mag. (long action, 24" barrel); 300 Rem. Ultra Mag. (26" barrel). Overall length 44-1/2", weight about 7-1/2 lbs.
Price: . . . . **$709.00 to $723.00**

Remington Model 700 BDL Left-Hand Custom Deluxe

Same as 700 BDL except mirror-image left-hand action, stock. Available in 270, 30-06, 7mm Rem. Mag., 300 Rem. Ultra Mag., 338 Rem. Ultra Mag., 7mm Rem. Ultra Mag.
Price: . . . . **$709.00 to $749.00**

Remington 700 BDL Left-Hand

Remington 700 BDL DM

Remington 700 BDL SS DM

Remington 700 Custom KS Mountain

Remington 700 LSS Mountain

Remington Model 700 BDL DM Rifle
Same as 700 BDL except detachable box magazine (4-shot, standard calibers, 3-shot for magnums). Glossy stock finish, open sights, recoil pad, sling swivels. Available in 270, 30-06, 7mm Rem. Mag., 300 Win. Mag. Introduced 1995.
Price: From . . . . **$749.00 to $776.00**

Remington Model 700 BDL SS Rifle
Similar to 700 BDL rifle except hinged floorplate, 24" standard weight barrel in all calibers; magnum calibers have magnum-contour barrel. No sights supplied, but comes drilled and tapped. Corrosion-resistant follower and fire control, stainless BDL-style barreled action with fine matte finish. Synthetic stock has straight comb and cheekpiece, textured finish, positive checkering, plated swivel studs. Calibers: 270, 30-06; magnums:7mm Rem. Mag., 7mm Rem. UltraMag., 300 Rem. Ultra Mag. (26" barrel) 300 Win. Mag., 338 Rem. Ultra Mag., 7mm Rem. SAUM, 300 Rem. SAUM. Weight: 7-3/8 to 7-1/2 lbs. Introduced 1993.
Price: From . . . . **$735.00 to $775.00**

Remington Model 700 BDL SS DM Rifle
Same as 700 BDL SS except detachable box magazine. Barrel, receiver and bolt made of #416 stainless steel; black synthetic stock, fine-line engraving. Available in 270, 30-06, 7mm Rem. Mag., 300 Win. Mag. Introduced 1995.
Price: From . . . . **$801.00 to $828.00**

Remington Model 700 Custom KS Mountain Rifle
Similar to 700 BDL except custom finished with aramid fiber reinforced resin synthetic stock. Available in left- and right-hand versions. Chambered 270 Win., 280 Rem., 30-06, 7mm Rem. Mag., 7mm STW, 300 Rem. Ultra Mag., 338 Rem. Ultra Mag., 300 Win. Mag., 300 Wby. Mag., 35 Whelen, 338 Win. Mag., 8mm Rem. Mag., 375 H&H, with 24" barrel (except 300 Rem. Ultra Mag., 26"), 7mm RUM, 375 RUM. Weighs 6 lbs., 6 oz. Introduced 1986.
Price: Right-hand **$1,314.00**
Price: Left-hand **$1,393.00**
Price: Stainless . . . . **$1,500.00 to $1,580.00**

Remington Model 700 LSS Mountain Rifle
Similar to Model 700 Custom KS Mountain Rifle except stainless steel 22" barrel and two-tone laminated stock. Chambered in 260 Rem., 7mm-08, 270 Winchester and 30-06. Overall length 42-1/2", weighs 6-5/8 oz. Introduced 1999.
Price: **$800.00**

Remington 700 Safari KS

Remington 700 AWR

Remington 700 APR African Plains

Remington 700 LSS

Remington 700 MTN DM

Remington Model 700 Safari Grade

Similar to 700 BDL aramid fiber reinforced fiberglass stock, blued carbon steel bbl. and action, or stainless, w/cheekpiece, custom finished and tuned. In 8mm Rem. Mag., 375 H&H, 416 Rem. Mag. or 458 Win. Mag. calibers only with heavy barrel. Right- and left-hand versions.

Price: Safari KS . . . . **$1,520.00 to $1,601.00**
Price: Safari KS (stainless right-hand only) **$1,697.00**

Remington Model 700 AWR Alaskan Wilderness Rifle

Similar to the 700 BDL except has stainless barreled action and black Teflon 24" bbl. 26" Ultra Mag raised cheekpiece, magnum-grade black rubber recoil pad. Chambered for 7mm RUM., 375 RUM, 7mm STW, 300 Rem. Ultra Mag., 300 Win. Mag., 300 Wby. Mag., 338 Rem. Ultra Mag., 338 Win. Mag., 375 H&H. Aramid fiber reinforced fiberglass stock. Introduced 1994.

Price: . . . . (right-hand) **$1,593.00**; (left-hand) **$1,673.00**

Remington Model 700 APR African Plains Rifle

Similar to Model 700 BDL except magnum receiver and specially contoured 26" Custom Shop barrel with satin blued finish, laminated wood stock with raised cheekpiece, satin finish, black buttpad, 20 lpi cut checkering. Chambered for 7mm Rem. Mag., 7mm RUM, 375 RUM, 300 Rem. Ultra Mag., 300 Win. Mag., 300 Wby. Mag., 338 Win. Mag., 338 Rem. Ultra Mag., 375 H&H. Introduced 1994.

Price: **$1,716.00**

Remington Model 700 LSS Rifle

Similar to 700 BDL except stainless steel barreled action, gray laminated wood stock with Monte Carlo comb and cheekpiece. No sights furnished. Available in (RH) 7mm Rem. Mag., 300 Win. Mag., 300 RUM, 338 RUM, 7mm Rem. Ultra Mag., 375 Rem. Ultra Mag., (LH) 7mm Rem. Ultra Mag., 300 Rem. Ultra Mag., and 338 RUM. Introduced 1996.

Price: From . . . . (Right-hand) **$820.00 to $840.00**; (left-hand) **$867.00**

Remington Model 700 MTN DM Rifle

Similar to 700 BDL except weighs 6-1/2 to 6-5/8 lbs., 22" tapered barrel. Redesigned pistol grip, straight comb, contoured cheekpiece, hand-rubbed oil stock finish, deep cut checkering, hinged floorplate and magazine follower, two-position thumb safety. Chambered for 260 Rem., 270 Win., 7mm-08, 25-06, 280 Rem., 30-06, 4-shot detachable box magazine. Overall length is 41-5/8" to 42-1/2". Introduced 1995.

Price: **$728.00**

Remington 700 Titanium

Remington 700 VLS

Remington 700 VS

Remington EtronX

Remington 700 Sendero SF

Remington Model 700 Titanium

Similar to 700 BDL except has titanium receiver, spiral-cut fluted bolt, skeletonized bolt handle and carbon-fiber and aramid fiber reinforced stock with sling swivel studs. Barrel 22"; weighs 5-1/4 lbs. (short action) or 5-1/2 lbs. (long action). Satin stainless finish. 260 Rem., 270 Win., 7mm-08, 30-06, 308 Win. Introduced 2001.

Price: **$1,239.00**

Remington Model 700 VLS Varmint Laminated Stock

Similar to 700 BDL except 26" heavy barrel without sights, brown laminated stock with beavertail forend, gripcap, rubber buttpad. Available in 223 Rem., 22-250, 6mm, 243, 308. Polished blue finish. Introduced 1995.

Price: From **$705.00**

Remington Model 700 VS Varmint Synthetic Rifles

Similar to 700 BDL Varmint Laminated except composite stock reinforced with aramid fiber reinforced, fiberglass and graphite. Aluminum bedding block that runs full length of receiver. Free-floating 26" barrel. Metal has black matte finish; stock has textured black and gray finish and swivel studs. Available in 223, 22-250, 308. Right- and left-hand. Introduced 1992.

Price: .... **$811.00 to $837.00**

Remington Model 700 VS SF Rifle

Similar to Model 700 Varmint Synthetic except satin-finish stainless barreled action with 26" fluted barrel, spherical concave muzzle crown. Chambered for 223, 220 Swift, 22-250 and 204 Ruger. Introduced 1994.

Price: **$1,025.00**

Remington Model 700 EtronX VSSF Rifle

Similar to Model 700 VS SF except features battery-powered ignition system for near-zero lock time and electronic trigger mechanism. Requires ammunition with EtronX electrically fired primers. Aluminum-bedded 26" heavy, stainless steel, fluted barrel; overall length 45-7/8"; weight 8 lbs., 14 oz. Black, Kevlar-reinforced composite stock. Light-emitting diode display on grip top indicates fire or safe mode, loaded or unloaded chamber, battery condition. Introduced 2000.

Price: 220 Swift, 22-250 or 243 Win. **$1,332.00**

Remington Model 700 XCR Rifle

Similar to standard Model 700 except 24" or 26" barrel; black matte finish; stainless steel barrel and receiver; comes in standard, magnum and short/long magnum calibers.

Price: .... **$867.00 to $893.00**

Remington 710

Remington Seven LS

Remington Model Seven LS Mag

Remington Model Seven SS Mag

Remington Model Seven Custom MS

REMINGTON MODEL 700 SENDERO SF RIFLE
Caliber: 7mm Rem. SAUM, 300 Rem. SAUM, 7mm Rem. Mag., 7mm STW, 300 Rem. Ultra Mag., 338 Rem. Ultra Mag., 300 Win. Mag., 7mm Rem. Ultra Mag. **Barrel:** 26". **Weight:** 8-1/2 lbs. **Length:** 45-3/4" to 46-5/8" overall. **Stock:** Aramid fiber refinforced fiberglass. **Sights:** NA. **Features:** Stainless steel action and fluted stainless barrel. Introduced 1996.
Price: . . . . $1,003.00 to $1,016.00

REMINGTON MODEL 710 BOLT-ACTION RIFLE
Caliber: 270 Win., 30-06. **Barrel:** 22". **Weight:** 7-1/8 lbs. **Length:** 42-1/2" overall. **Stock:** Gray synthetic. **Sights:** Bushnell Sharpshooter 3-9x scope mounted and bore-sighted. **Features:** Unique action locks bolt directly into barrel; 60-degree bolt throw; 4-shot dual-stack magazine; key-operated Integrated Security System locks bolt open. Introduced 2001. Made in U.S.A. by Remington Arms Co.
Price: $425.00

REMINGTON MODEL SEVEN LS
Caliber: 223 Rem., 243 Win., 7mm-08 Rem., 308 Win. **Barrel:** 20". **Weight:** 6-1/2 lbs. **Length:** 39-1/4" overall. **Stock:** Brown laminated, satin finished. **Features:** Satin finished carbon steel barrel and action, 4-round magazine, hinged magazine floorplate. Furnished with iron sights and sling swivel studs, drilled and tapped for scope mounts.
Price: $701.00
Price: 7mmRSAUM, 300RSAUM, LS Magnum, 22" bbl. $741.00
Price: AWR model $1,547.00

Remington Model Seven SS
Similar to Model Seven LS except stainless steel barreled action and black synthetic stock, 20" barrel. Chambered for 243, 260 Rem., 7mm-08, 308. Introduced 1994.
Price: $729.00
Price: 7mmRSAUM, 300RSAUM, Model Seven SS
Magnum, 22" bbl. $769.00

Remington Model Seven Custom MS Rifle
Similar to Model Seven LS except full-length Mannlicher-style stock of laminated wood with straight comb, solid black recoil pad, black steel forend tip, cut checkering, gloss finish. Barrel length 20", weighs 6-3/4 lbs. Available in 222 Rem., 223, 22-250, 243, 6mm Rem., 260 Rem., 7mm-08 Rem., 308, 350 Rem. Mag., 250 Savage, 257 Roberts, 35 Rem. Polished blue finish. Introduced 1993. From Remington Custom Shop.
Price: From $1,332.00

Remington Model Seven Youth Rifle
Similar to Model Seven LS except hardwood stock, 1" shorter length of pull, chambered for 223, 243, 260 Rem., 7mm-08. Introduced 1993.
Price: $547.00

Remington Model Seven Custom KS
Similar to Model Seven LS except gray aramid fiber reinforced stock with 1" black rubber recoil pad and swivel studs. Blued satin carbon steel barreled action. No sights on 223, 260 Rem., 7mm-08, 308; 35 Rem. and 350 Rem. have iron sights.
Price: $1,314.00

Ruger Magnum

Ruger 77/22 Hornet Varmint

Ruger M77 Mark II

Ruger KM77RLFP MKII

Ruger KM77RFP MKII

RUGER MAGNUM RIFLE

Caliber: 338 Lapua, 375 H&H, 416 Rigby, 458 Lott. **Barrel:** 23". **Weight:** 9-1/2 to 10-1/4 lbs. **Length:** 44". **Stock:** AAA Premium Grade Circassian walnut with live-rubber recoil pad, metal gripcap, and studs for mounting sling swivels. **Sights:** Blade, front; V-notch rear express sights (one stationary, two folding) drift-adjustable for windage. **Features:** Floorplate latch secures the hinged floorplate against accidental dumping of cartridges; one-piece bolt has a non-rotating Mauser-type controlled-feed extractor; fixed-blade ejector.
Price: M77RSMMKII **$1,975.00**

RUGER 77/22 HORNET BOLT-ACTION RIFLE

Caliber: 22 Hornet, 6-shot rotary magazine. **Barrel:** 20". **Weight:** About 6 lbs. **Length:** 39-3/4" overall. **Stock:** Checkered American walnut, black rubber buttpad. **Sights:** Brass bead front, open adjustable rear; also available without sights. **Features:** Same basic features as rimfire model except slightly lengthened receiver. Uses Ruger rotary magazine. Three-position safety. Comes with 1" Ruger scope rings. Introduced 1994.
Price: 77/22RH (rings only) **$649.00**
Price: K77/22VHZ Varmint, laminated stock, no sights **$685.00**

RUGER M77 MARK II RIFLE

Caliber: 223, 220 Swift, 22-250, 204 Ruger, 243, 6mm Rem., 257 Roberts, 25-06, 6.5x55 Swedish, 270, 260 Rem., 280 Rem., 308, 30-06, 7mm Rem. Mag., 7mm WSM, 7mm/08, 300 WSM, 300 Win. Mag., 338 Win. Mag., 4-shot magazine. **Barrel:** 20", 22"; 24" (magnums). **Weight:** About 7 lbs. **Length:** 39-3/4" overall. **Stock:** Synthetic American walnut; swivel studs, rubber buttpad. **Sights:** None furnished. Receiver has Ruger integral scope mount base, Ruger 1" rings. **Features:** Short action with new trigger, 3-position safety. Steel trigger guard. Left-hand available. Introduced 1989.

Price: M77RMKII (no sights) **$716.00**
Price: M77LRMKII (left-hand, 25/06, 270, 30-06, 7mm Rem.
Mag.,300 Win. Mag.) **$716.00**

Ruger M77RSI International Carbine

Same as standard Model 77 except 18" barrel, full-length International-style stock, steel forend cap, loop-type steel sling swivels. Integral base receiver, open sights, Ruger 1" steel rings. Improved front sight. Available in 243, 270, 308, 30-06. Weighs 7 lbs. Length overall is 38-3/8".
Price: M77RSIMKII **$819.00**

Ruger M77 Mark II All-Weather and Sporter Model Stainless Rifle

Similar to wood-stock M77 Mark II except all metal parts are stainless steel, has an injection-molded, glass-fiber-reinforced polymer stock. Laminated wood stock. Chambered for 223, 22/250, 25/06, 260 Rem., 7mm WSM, 7mm/08, 7mm SWM, 280 Rem., 300 WSM, 204 Ruger, 243, 270, 308, 30-06, 7mm Rem. Mag., 300 Win. Mag., 325 WSM, 338 Win. Mag. Fixed-blade-type ejector, three-position safety, new trigger guard with patented floorplate latch. Integral Scope Base Receiver, 1" Ruger scope rings, built-in sling swivel loops. Introduced 1990.
Price: K77RFPMKII **$716.00**
Price: K77RLFPMKII Ultra-Light, synthetic stock, rings, no sights . **$716.00**
Price: K77LRBBZMKII, left-hand bolt, rings, no sights, laminated
stock **$773.00**
Price: K77RBZMKII, no sights, laminated wood stock, 223,
22/250, 243, 270, 280 Rem., 7mm Rem. Mag., 30-06,
308, 300 Win. Mag., 338 Win. Mag. **$773.00**
Price: KM77RFPMKII, M77RMKII **$773.00**

Ruger M77RL Ultra Light

Similar to standard M77 except weighs 6 lbs., chambered for 223, 243, 308, 270, 30-06, 257 Roberts, barrel tapped for target scope blocks, 20" Ultra Light barrel. Overall length 40". Ruger's steel 1" scope rings supplied. Introduced 1983.
Price: M77RLMKII **$729.00**

Ruger M77VT Target

Ruger Frontier

Sako TRG-S

Sako 85 Grey Wolf

Sako 75 Hunter

Ruger M77 Mark II Compact Rifles

Similar to standard M77 except reduced 16-1/2" barrel, weighs 5-3/4 lbs. Chambered for 223, 243, 260 Rem., 308, and 7mm-08.
Price: M77CR MKII (blued finish, walnut stock) **$675.00**
Price: KM77CRBBZ MkII (stainless finish, black laminated stock) . **$729.00**

RUGER M77VT TARGET RIFLE

Caliber: 22-250, 220 Swift, 223, 204 Ruger, 243, 25-06, 308. **Barrel:** 26" heavy stainless steel with target gray finish. **Weight:** 9-3/4 lbs. **Length:** Approx. 44" overall. **Stock:** Laminated American hardwood with beavertail forend, steel swivel studs; no checkering or gripcap. **Sights:** Integral scope mount bases in receiver. **Features:** Ruger diagonal bedding system. Ruger steel 1" scope rings supplied. Fully adjustable trigger. Steel floorplate and trigger guard. New version introduced 1992.
Price: K77VTMKII **$870.00**

RUGER FRONTIER RIFLE

Caliber: 243, 7mm/08, 308, 300WSM, 325WSM. **Barrel:** 16-1/2". **Weight:** 6-1/4 lbs. **Stock:** Black laminate. **Features:** Front scope mounting rib, blued finish; overall length 35-1/2". Introduced 2005, stainless in 2006.
Price: **$799.00**

SAKO TRG-42 BOLT-ACTION RIFLE

Caliber: 338 Lapua Mag. and 300 Win. Mag. **Barrel:** 27-1/8". **Weight:** 11-1/4 lbs. **Length:** NA. **Stock:** NA. **Sights:** NA. **Features:** 5-shot magazine, fully adjustable stock and competition trigger. Imported from Finland by Beretta USA.
Price: **$3,525.00**

SAKO MODEL 85 BOLT-ACTION RIFLES

Caliber: 22-250, 243, 25-06, 260, 6.5x55mm, 270, 270 WSM, 7mm-08, 308, 30-06; 7mm WSM, 300 WSM, 338 Federal. **Barrel:** 22.4", 22.9", 24.4". **Weight:** 7.75 lbs. **Length:** NA. **Stock:** Polymer, laminated or high-grade walnut, straight comb, shadow-line cheekpiece. **Sights:** None furnished. **Features:** Controlled-round feeding, adjustable trigger, matte stainless or nonreflective satin blue. Quad model is polymer/stainless with four interchangeable barrels in 22LR, 22 WMR 17 HMR and 17 Mach 2; 50-degree bolt-lift, ambidextrous palm-swell, adjustable butt-pad. Introduced 2006. Imported from Finland by Beretta USA.
Price: Sako 85 Hunter, walnut/blued **$1,595.00**
Price: Sako 85 Grey Wolf, laminated/stainless. **$1,495.00**
Price: Sako 85 Quad, polymer/stainless **$925.00**
Price: Sako 85 Quad Combo, four barrels **$1,800.00**

SAKO 75 HUNTER BOLT-ACTION RIFLE

Caliber: 223, 22-250, 243, 25-06, 260, 270, 270 WSM, 280, 300 Win. Mag., 30-06; 7mm-08, 308 Win., 270 Wby. Mag., 7mm Rem. Mag., 7mm STW, 7mm Wby. Mag., 300 Wby. Mag., 338 Win. Mag., 340 Wby. Mag., 375 H&H. **Barrel:** 22", standard calibers; 24", 26" magnum calibers. **Weight:** About 6 lbs. **Length:** NA. **Stock:** European walnut with matte lacquer finish. **Sights:** None furnished; dovetail scope mount rails. **Features:** New design with three locking lugs and a mechanical ejector, key locks firing pin and bolt, cold hammer-forged barrel is free-floating, two-position safety, hinged floorplate or detachable magazine that can be loaded from the top, short 70-degree bolt lift. Five action lengths. Introduced 1997. Imported from Finland by Beretta USA.
Price: From **$1,375.00**

Sako 75 Stainless Hunter

Sako 75 Deluxe

Sako 75 Varmint

Savage 110GXP3

Sako 75 Stainless Synthetic Rifle

Similar to 75 Hunter except all metal is stainless steel, synthetic stock has soft composite panels molded into forend and pistol grip. Available in 22-250, 243, 308 Win., 25-06, 270, 30-06 with 22" barrel, 7mm Rem. Mag., 7mm STW, 300 Win. Mag., 338 Win. Mag. and 375 H&H Mag. with 24" barrel and 300 Wby. Mag., 300 Rem. Ultra Mag. with 26" barrel. Introduced 1997. Imported from Finland by Beretta USA.
Price: from **$1,495.00**

Sako 75 Deluxe Rifle

Similar to 75 Hunter except select wood rosewood gripcap and forend tip. Available in 17 Rem., 222, 223, 25-06, 243, 7mm-08, 308, 25-06, 270, 280, 30-06; 270 Wby. Mag., 7mm Rem. Mag., 7mm STW, 7mm Wby. Mag., 300 Win. Mag., 300 Wby. Mag., 338 Win. Mag., 340 Wby. Mag., 375 H&H, 416 Rem. Mag. Introduced 1997. Imported from Finland by Beretta USA.
Price: from **$2,050.00**

Sako 75 Varmint Stainless Laminated Rifle

Similar to Sako 75 Hunter except chambered only for 222, 223, 22-250, 22 PPC USA, 6mm PPC, heavy 24" barrel with recessed crown; set trigger; all metal is stainless steel, laminated wood stock with beavertail forend. Introduced 1999. Imported from Finland by Beretta USA.
Price: **$1,959.00**

Sako 75 Varmint Rifle

Similar to Model 75 Hunter except chambered only for 17 Rem., 222 Rem., 223 Rem., 22-250 Rem., 22 PPC and 6mm PPC, 24" heavy barrel with recessed crown; set trigger; beavertail forend. Introduced 1998. Imported from Finland by Beretta USA.
Price: **$1,850.00**

SAUER 202 BOLT-ACTION RIFLE

Caliber: Standard 243, 6.5x55, 270 Win., 308 Win., 30-06; magnum 7mm Rem. Mag., 300 Win. Mag., 300 Wby. Mag., 375 H&H. **Barrel:** 23.6" (standard), 26" (magnum). **Weight:** 7.7 lbs. (standard). **Length:** 44.3" overall (23.6" barrel). **Stock:** Select American Claro walnut with high-gloss epoxy finish, rosewood grip and forend caps; 22 lpi checkering. Synthetic also available. **Sights:** None furnished; drilled and tapped for scope mounting. **Features:** Short 60" bolt throw; detachable box magazine; six-lug bolt; quick-change barrel; tapered bore; adjustable two-stage trigger; firing pin cocking indicator. Introduced 1994. Imported from Germany by SIGARMS, Inc.
Price: Standard calibers, right-hand **$1,035.00**
Price: Magnum calibers, right-hand **$1,106.00**
Price: Standard calibers, synthetic stock **$985.00**
Price: Magnum calibers, synthetic stock **$1,056.00**

SAVAGE MODEL 10GXP3, 110GXP3 PACKAGE GUNS

Caliber: 223 Rem., 22-250 Rem., 243 Win., 7mm-08 Rem., 308 Win., 300 WSM (10GXP3). 25-06 Rem., 270 Win., 30-06 Spfld., 7mm Rem. Mag., 300 Win. Mag., 300 Rem. Ultra Mag. (110GXP3). **Barrel:** 22" 24", 26". **Weight:** 7.5 lbs. average. **Length:** 43" to 47". **Stock:** Walnut Monte Carlo with checkering. **Sights:** 3-9x40mm scope, mounted & bore sighted. **Features:** Blued, free floating and button rifled, internal box magazines, swivel studs, leather sling. Left-hand available.
Price: Accu-trigger **$539.00**

SAVAGE MODEL 11FXP3, 111FXP3, 111FCXP3, 11FYXP3 (Youth) PACKAGE GUNS

Caliber: 223 Rem., 22-250 Rem., 243 Win., 308 Win., 300 WSM (11FXP3). 270 Win., 30-06 Spfld., 25-06 Rem., 7mm Rem. Mag., 300 Win. Mag., 338 Win. Mag., 300 Rem. Ultra Mag. (11FCXPE & 111FXP3). **Barrel:** 22" to 26". **Weight:** 6.5 lbs. **Length:** 41" to 47". **Stock:** Synthetic checkering, dual pillar bed. **Sights:** 3-9X40mm scope, mounted & bore sighted. **Features:** Blued, free floating and button rifled, Top loading internal box mag (except 111FXCP3 has detachable box mag.). Nylon sling and swivel studs. Some left-hand available.
Price: Model 11FXP3 . . . . **$516.00**
Price: Model 111FCXP3 . . . . **$411.00**
Price: Model 11FYXP3, 243 Win., 12.5" pull (youth) **$501.00**

Savage Model 10FP

Savage Model 10FPLE1

Savage Model 10FPXP-LE

Savage Model 111F

SAVAGE MODEL 16FXP3, 116FXP3 SS ACTION PACKAGE GUNS

Caliber: 223 Rem., 243 Win., 308 Win., 300 WSM, 270 Win., 30-06 Spfld., 7mm Rem. Mag., 300 Win. Mag., 338 Win. Mag., 375 H&H, 7mm S&W, 7mm Rem. Ultra Mag., 300 Rem. Ultra Mag. **Barrel:** 22", 24", 26". **Weight:** 6.75 lbs. average. **Length:** 41" to 46". **Stock:** Synthetic checkering, dual pillar bed. **Sights:** 3-9X40mm scope, mounted & bore sighted. **Features:** Free floating and button rifled. Internal box mag., nylon sling and swivel studs.
Price: **$601.00**

SAVAGE MODEL 10FM SIERRA ULTRA LIGHT RIFLE

Caliber: 223, 243, 308. **Barrel:** 20". **Weight:** 6 lbs. **Length:** 41-1/2". **Stock:** "Dual Pillar" bedding in black synthetic stock with silver medallion in gripcap. **Sights:** None furnished; drilled and tapped for scope mounting. **Features:** True short action. Model 10FCM has detachable box magazine. Comes with sling and quick-detachable swivels. Introduced 1998. Made in U.S.A. by Savage Arms, Inc.
Price: **$552.00**

SAVAGE MODEL 10/110FP LONG RANGE RIFLE

Caliber: 223, 25-06, 308, 30-06, 300 Win. Mag., 7mm Rem. Mag., 4-shot magazine. **Barrel:** 24", heavy; recessed target muzzle. **Weight:** 8-1/2 lbs. **Length:** 45.5" overall. **Stock:** Black graphite/fiberglass composition; positive checkering. **Sights:** None furnished. Receiver drilled and tapped for scope mounting. **Features:** Pillar-bedded stock. Black matte finish on all metal parts. Double swivel studs on the forend for sling and/or bipod mount. Right- or left-hand. Introduced 1990. From Savage Arms, Inc.
Price: Right- or left-hand. **$601.00**

Savage Model 10FP Tactical Rifle

Similar to the Model 110FP except has true short action, chambered for 223, 308; black synthetic stock with "Dual Pillar" bedding. Introduced 1998. Made in U.S.A. by Savage Arms, Inc.
Price: **$601.00**
Price: Model 10FLP (left-hand) **$601.00**
Price: Model 10FP-LE1 (20"), 10FPLE2 (26") **$601.00**
Price: Model 10FPXP-LE w/Burris 3.5-10x50 scope,
Harris bipod package **$1,805.00**

Savage Model 10FP-LE1A Tactical Rifle

Similar to the Model 110FP except weighs 10.75 lbs. and has overall length of 39.75". Chambered for 223 Rem., 308 Win. Black synthetic Choate™ adjustable stock with accessory rail and swivel studs.
Price: **$729.00**

SAVAGE MODEL 111 CLASSIC HUNTER RIFLES

Caliber: 25-06 Rem., 270 Win., 30-06 Spfld., 7mm Rem. Mag., 300 Win. Mag., 7mm RUM, 300 RUM. **Barrel:** 22", 24", 26" (magnum calibers). **Weight:** 6.5 to 7.5 lbs. **Length:** 42.75" to 47.25". **Stock:** Walnut-finished hardwood (M111G, GC); graphite/fiberglass filled composite. **Sights:** Ramp front, open fully adjustable rear; drilled and tapped for scope mounting. **Features:** Three-position top tang safety, double front locking lugs, free-floated button-rifled barrel. Comes with trigger lock, target, ear puffs. Introduced 1994. Made in U.S.A. by Savage Arms, Inc.
Price: Model 111F (270 Win., 30-06 Spfld., 7mm Rem. Mag., 300 Win. Mag.). **$486.00**
Price: Model 111F (25-06 Rem., 338 Win. Mag., 7mm Rem. Ultra Mag, 300 Rem. Ultra Mag.) **$486.00**
Price: Model 111G
(wood stock, top-loading magazine, right- or left-hand) **$436.00**
Price: Model 111GNS (wood stock, detachable box magazine, no sights, right-hand only) **$518.00**

Savage Model 111F

Savage Model 11FCNS

Savage Model 11G

Savage Model 10GY

Savage Model 12FV

Savage Model 12VSS

Savage Model 11 Classic Hunter Rifles, Short Action

Similar to the Model 111F except has true short action, chambered for 22-250, Rem., 243 Win., 7mm-08 Rem., 308 Win.; black synthetic stock with "Dual Pillar" bedding, positive checkering. Introduced 1998. Made in U.S.A. by Savage Arms, Inc.

Price: Model 11F **$486.00**
Price: Model 11FL (left-hand) **$486.00**
Price: Model 11FCNS (right-hand, no sights) **$507.00**
Price: Model 11G (wood stock) **$496.00**
Price: Model 11GL (as above, left-hand) **$496.00**

Savage Model 10GY

Similar to the Model 111G except weighs 6.3 lbs., is 42-1/2" overall, and the stock is scaled for ladies, small-framed adults and youths. Chambered for 223, 243, 308. Ramp front sight, open adjustable rear; drilled and tapped for scope mounts. Made in U.S.A. by Savage Arms, Inc.

Price: Model 10GY (short action, calibers 223, 243, 308) **$496.00**

SAVAGE MODEL 112 LONG RANGE RIFLES

Caliber: 5-shot magazine. **Barrel:** 26" heavy. **Weight:** 8.8 lbs. **Length:** 47.5" overall. **Stock:** Black graphite/fiberglass filled composite with positive checkering. **Sights:** None furnished; drilled and tapped for scope mounting. **Features:** Pillar-bedded stock. Blued barrel with recessed target-style muzzle. Double front swivel studs for attaching bipod. Introduced 1991. Made in U.S.A. by Savage Arms, Inc.

Price: Model 112BVSS (heavy-prone laminated stock with high comb, Wundhammer swell, fluted stainless barrel, bolt handle, trigger guard) **$675.00**

Savage Model 12 Long Range Rifles

Similar to the Model 112 Long Range except with true short action, chambered for 223, 22-250, 308. Models 12FV, 12FVSS have black synthetic stocks with "Dual Pillar" bedding, positive checkering, swivel studs; Model 12BVSS has brown laminated stock with beavertail forend, fluted stainless barrel. Introduced 1998. Made in U.S.A. by Savage Arms, Inc.

Price: Model 12FV (223, 22-250, 243 Win., 308 Win., blue) **$549.00**
Price: Model 12FVSS (blue action, fluted stainless barrel) **$667.00**
Price: Model 12FLV (as above, left-hand) **$549.00**
Price: Model 12FVS (blue action, fluted stainless barrel, single shot) **$667.00**
Price: Model 12BVSS (laminated stock) **$721.00**
Price: Model 12BVSS-S (as above, single shot) **$721.00**

Savage Model 16FCSS

Savage Model 116FSAK

SIGARMS SHR 970

Steyr Mannlicher SBS

Steyr SBS Forester

Savage Model 12VSS Varminter Rifle

Similar to other Model 12s except blue/stainless steel action, fluted stainless barrel, Choate full pistol grip, adjustable synthetic stock, Sharp Shooter trigger. Overall length 47-1/2", weighs appx. 15 lbs. No sights; drilled and tapped for scope mounts. Chambered in 223, 22-250, 308 Win. Made in U.S.A. by Savage Arms, Inc.

Price: **$934.00**

SAVAGE MODEL 116 WEATHER WARRIORS

Caliber: 375 H&H, 300 Rem. Ultra Mag., 308 Win., 300 Rem. Ultra Mag., 300 WSM, 7mm Rem. Ultra Mag., 7mm Rem. Short Ultra Mag., 7mm S&W, 7mm-08 Rem. **Barrel:** 22", 24" for 7mm Rem. Mag., 300 Win. Mag., 338 Win. Mag. (M116FSS only). **Weight:** 6.25 to 6.5 lbs. **Length:** 41" to 47". **Stock:** Graphite/fiberglass filled composite. **Sights:** None furnished; drilled and tapped for scope mounting. **Features:** Stainless steel with matte finish; free-floated barrel; quick-detachable swivel studs; laser-etched bolt; scope bases and rings. Left-hand models available in all models, calibers at same price. Model 116FSS introduced 1991; 116FSAK introduced 1994. Made in U.S.A. by Savage Arms, Inc.

Price: Model 116FSS (top-loading magazine) **$520.00**
Price: Model 116FSAK (top-loading magazine,
Savage adjustable muzzle brake system) **$601.00**
Price: Model 16BSS (brown laminate, 24") **$668.00**
Price: Model 116BSS (brown laminate, 26") **$668.00**

Savage Model 16FCSS Rifle

Similar to Model 116FSS except true short action, chambered for 223, 243, 22" free-floated barrel; black graphite/fiberglass stock, "Dual Pillar" bedding. Also left-hand version available. Introduced 1998. Made in U.S.A. by Savage Arms, Inc.

Price: **$552.00**

SIGARMS SHR 970 SYNTHETIC RIFLE

Caliber: 270, 30-06. **Barrel:** 22". **Weight:** 7.2 lbs. **Length:** 41.9" overall. **Stock:** Textured black fiberglass or walnut. **Sights:** None furnished; drilled and tapped for scope mounting. **Features:** Quick takedown; interchangeable barrels; removable box magazine; cocking indicator; three-position safety. Introduced 1998. Imported by SIGARMS, Inc.

Price: Synthetic stock **$499.00**
Price: Walnut stock **$550.00**

STEYR CLASSIC MANNLICHER SBS RIFLE

Caliber: 243, 25-06, 308, 6.5x55, 6.5x57, 270, 7x64 Brenneke, 7mm-08, 7.5x55, 30-06, 9.3x62, 6.5x68, 7mm Rem. Mag., 300 Win. Mag., 8x68S, 4-shot magazine. **Barrel:** 23.6" standard; 26" magnum; 20" full stock standard calibers. **Weight:** 7 lbs. **Length:** 40.1" overall. **Stock:** Hand-checkered fancy European oiled walnut with standard forend. **Sights:** Ramp front adjustable for elevation, V-notch rear adjustable for windage. **Features:** Single adjustable trigger; 3-position roller safety with "safe-bolt" setting; drilled and tapped for Steyr factory scope mounts. Introduced 1997. Imported from Austria by GSI, Inc.

Price: Full-stock, standard calibers **$1,749.00**

STEYR SBS FORESTER RIFLE

Caliber: 243, 25-06, 270, 7mm-08, 308 Win., 30-06, 7mm Rem. Mag., 300 Win. Mag. Detachable 4-shot magazine. **Barrel:** 23.6", standard calibers; 25.6", magnum calibers. **Weight:** 7.5 lbs. **Length:** 44.5" overall (23.6" barrel). **Stock:** Oil-finished American walnut with Monte Carlo cheekpiece. Pachmayr 1" swivels. **Sights:** None furnished. Drilled and tapped for Browning A-Bolt mounts. **Features:** Three-position ambidextrous roller tang safety. Matte finish on barrel and receiver; adjustable trigger. Rotary cold-hammer forged barrel. Introduced 1997. Imported by GSI, Inc.

Price: Standard calibers **$799.00**
Price: Magnum calibers **$829.00**

Steyr SBS Prohunter

Steyr Scout Rifle

Tikka T-3 Hunter

Weatherby Mark V Lazermark

Steyr SBS Prohunter Rifle
Similar to the SBS Forester except has ABS synthetic stock with adjustable butt spacers, straight comb without cheekpiece, palm swell, Pachmayr 1" swivels. Special 10-round magazine conversion kit available. Introduced 1997. Imported by GSI.
Price: Standard calibers **$769.00**
Price: Magnum calibers **$799.00**

STEYR SCOUT BOLT-ACTION RIFLE
Caliber: 308 Win., 5-shot magazine. Barrel: 19", fluted. Weight: NA. Length: NA. Stock: Gray Zytel. Sights: Pop-up front & rear, Leupold M8 2.5x28 IER scope on Picatinny optic rail with Steyr mounts. Features: luggage case, scout sling, two stock spacers, two magazines. Introduced 1998. From GSI.
Price: From **$1,969.00**

STEYR SSG BOLT-ACTION RIFLE
Caliber: 308 Win., detachable 5-shot rotary magazine. Barrel: 26". Weight: 8.5 lbs. Length: 44.5" overall. Stock: Black ABS Cycolac with spacers for length of pull adjustment. Sights: Hooded ramp front adjustable for elevation, V-notch rear adjustable for windage. Features: Sliding safety; NATO rail for bipod; 1" swivels; Parkerized finish; single or double-set triggers. Imported from Austria by GSI, Inc.
Price: SSG-PI, iron sights **$1,699.00**
Price: SSG-PII, heavy barrel, no sights **$1,699.00**
Price: SSG-PIIK, 20" heavy barrel, no sights **$1,699.00**
Price: SSG-PIV, 16.75" threaded heavy barrel with flash hider . . **$2,659.00**

TIKKA T-3 BIG BOAR SYNTHETIC BOLT-ACTION RIFLE
Caliber: 308, 30-06, 300 WSM. Barrel: 19". Weight: 6 lbs. Length: 39.5" overall. Stock: Laminated. Sights: None furnished. Features:

Detachable, 3-round. Receiver dove-tailed for scope mounting. Reintroduced 1996. Imported from Finland by Beretta USA.
Price: Left-hand **$695.00**

Tikka T-3 Super Varmint Rifle
Similar to the standard T-3 rifle except has 23-3/8" heavy stainless barrel. Chambered for 22-250, 223, 308. Reintroduced 2005. Made in Finland by Sako. Imported by Beretta USA.
Price: **$1,425.00**

TIKKA T-3 HUNTER
Caliber: 223, 22-250, 243, 308, 25-06, 270, 30-06, 300 Win. Mag., 338 Win. Mag., 270 WSM, 300 WSM, 6.5x55 Swedish Mauser, 7mm Rem. Mag. Stock: Walnut. Sight: None furnished. Barrel: 22-7/16", 24-3/8". Features: Detachable magazine, aluminum scope rings. Introduced 2005. Imported from Finland by Beretta USA.
Price: **$695.00**

Tikka T-3 Stainless Synthetic
Similar to the T-3 Hunter except stainless steel, synthetic stock. Available in 243, 25-06, 270, 308, 30-06, 270 WSM, 300 WSM, 7mm Rem. Mag., 300 Win. Mag., 338 Win. Mag. Introduced 2005. Imported from Finland by Beretta USA.
Price: **$895.00**

ULTRA LIGHT ARMS BOLT-ACTION RIFLES
Caliber: 17 Rem. to 416 Rigby. Barrel: Douglas, length to order. Weight: 4-3/4 to 7-1/2 lbs. Length: Varies. Stock: Kevlar® graphite composite, variety of finishes. Sights: None furnished; drilled and tapped for scope mounts. Features: Timney trigger, hand-lapped action, button-rifled barrel, hand-bedded action, recoil pad, sling-swivel studs, optional Jewell trigger. Made in U.S.A. by New Ultra Light Arms.
Price: Model 20 (short action) **$2,800.00**
Price: Model 24 (long action) **$2,900.00**
Price: Model 28 (magnum action) **$3,200.00**
Price: Model 40 (300 Wby. Mag., 416 Rigby) **$3,200.00**
Price: Left-hand models, add **$100.00**

Weatherby Mark V Sporter

Weatherby Mark V Stainless

Weatherby Mark V Synthetic

Weatherby Mark V Accumark

WEATHERBY MARK V DELUXE BOLT-ACTION RIFLE

Caliber: All Weatherby calibers plus 22-250, 243, 25-06, 270 Win., 280 Rem., 7mm-08, 30-06, 308 Win. **Barrel:** 24" barrel on standard calibers. **Weight:** 8-1/2 to 10-1/2 lbs. **Length:** 46-5/8" to 46-3/4" overall. **Stock:** Walnut, Monte Carlo with cheekpiece; high luster finish; checkered pistol grip and forend; recoil pad. **Sights:** None furnished. **Features:** Cocking indicator; adjustable trigger; hinged floorplate, thumb safety; quick detachable sling swivels. Made in U.S.A. From Weatherby.

Price: 257, 270, 7mm. 300, 340 Wby. Mags., 26" barrel **$1,767.00**
Price: 416 Wby. Mag. with Accubrake, 28" barrel **$2,079.00**
Price: 460 Wby. Mag. with Accubrake, 28" barrel **$2,443.00**
Price: 24" barrel **$1,715.00**

Weatherby Mark V Lazermark Rifle

Same as Mark V Deluxe except stock has extensive oak leaf pattern laser carving on pistol grip and forend. Introduced 1981.

Price: 257, 270, 7mm Wby. Mag., 300, 340, 26". **$1,923.00**
Price: 378 Wby. Mag., 28"................................. **$2,266.00**
Price: 416 Wby. Mag., 28", Accubrake **$2,266.00**
Price: 460 Wby. Mag., 28", Accubrake **$2,661.00**

Weatherby Mark V Sporter Rifle

Same as the Mark V Deluxe without the embellishments. Metal has low-luster blue, stock is Claro walnut with matte finish, Monte Carlo comb, recoil pad. Introduced 1993. From Weatherby.

Price: 22-250, 243, 240 Wby. Mag., 25-06, 7mm-08,
270 WCF, 280, 30-06, 308; 24" **$1,091.00**
Price: 257 Wby., 270, 7 mm Wby., 7mm Rem., 300 Wby.,
300 Win., 340 Wby., 338 Win. Mag., 26" barrel for Wby. calibers;
24" for non-Wby. calibers **$1,143.00**

Weatherby Mark V Stainless Rifle

Similar to the Mark V Deluxe except made of 410-series stainless steel. Also available in 30-378 Wby. Mag. Has lightweight injection-molded synthetic stock with raised Monte Carlo comb, checkered grip and forend,

custom floorplate release. Right-hand only. Introduced 1995. Made in U.S.A. From Weatherby.

Price: 22-250 Rem., 243 Win., 240 Wby. Mag., 25-06 Rem.,
270 Win., 280 Rem., 7mm-08 Rem., 30-06 Spfld., 308 Win.,
24" barrel... **$1,018.00**
Price: 257, 270, 7mm, 300, 340 Wby. Mags., 26" barrel **$1,070.00**
Price: 7mm Rem. Mag., 300 Win. Mag., 338 Win. Mag.,
375 H&H Mag., 24" barrel **$1,070.00**

Weatherby Mark V Synthetic

Similar to the Mark V Stainless except made of matte finished blued steel. Injection molded synthetic stock. Weighs 6-1/2 lbs., 24" barrel. Available in 22-250, 240 Wby. Mag., 243, 25-06, 270, 7mm-08, 280, 30-06, 308. Introduced 1997. Made in U.S.A. From Weatherby.

Price: **$923.00**
Price: 257, 270, 7mm, 300, 340 Wby. Mags., 26" barrel **$975.00**
Price: 7mm STW, 7mm Rem. Mag., 300, 338 Win. Mags **$975.00**
Price: 375 H&H, 24" barrel **$975.00**
Price: 30-378 Wby. Mag., 338-378 Wby. 28" barrel **$1,151.00**

WEATHERBY MARK V ACCUMARK RIFLE

Caliber: 257, 270, 7mm, 300, 340 Wby. Mags., 338-378 Wby. Mag., 30-378 Wby. Mag., 7mm STW, 7mm Rem. Mag., 300 Win. Mag. **Barrel:** 26", 28". **Weight:** 8-1/2 lbs. **Length:** 46-5/8" overall. **Stock:** Bell & Carlson with full length aluminum bedding block. **Sights:** None furnished. Drilled and tapped for scope mounting. **Features:** Uses Mark V action with heavy-contour stainless barrel with black oxidized flutes, muzzle diameter of .705". Introduced 1996. Made in U.S.A. From Weatherby.

Price: 26" **$1,507.00**
Price: 30-378 Wby. Mag., 338-378 Wby. Mag., 28",
Accubrake **$1,724.00**
Price: 223, 22-250, 243, 240 Wby. Mag., 25-06, 270,
280 Rem., 7mm-08, 30-06, 308; 24" **$1,455.00**
Price: Accumark left-hand 257, 270, 7mm, 300, 340 Wby.
Mag., 7mm Rem. Mag., 7mm STW, 300 Win. Mag. **$1,559.00**
Price: Accumark left-hand 30-378, 333-378 Wby. Mags. **$1,788.00**

Weatherby Mark V SVR

Weatherby Mark V Dangerous Game Rifle

Wilderness Explorer

Weatherby Mark V Accumark Ultra Lightweight Rifles
Similar to the Mark V Accumark except weighs 5-3/4 lbs., 6-3/4 lbs. in Mag. calibers.; 24", 26" fluted barrel with recessed target crown; hand-laminated stock with CNC-machined aluminum bedding plate and faint gray "spider web" finish. Available in 257, 270, 7mm, 300 Wby. Mags. (26"); 243, 240 Wby. Mag., 25-06, 270 Win., 280 Rem., 7mm-08, 7mm Rem. Mag., 30-06, 338-06 A-Square, 308, 300 Win. Mag. (24"). Introduced 1998. Made in U.S.A. by Weatherby.
Price: .... $1,459.00 to $1,517.00
Price: Left-hand models $1,559.00

Weatherby Mark V SVM/SPM Rifles
Similar to the Mark V Accumark except has 26" fluted (SVM) or 24" fluted Krieger barrel, spiderweb-pattern tan laminated synthetic stock. SVM has a fully adjustable trigger. Chambered for 223, 22-250, 220 Swift (SVM only), 243, 7mm-08 and 308. Made in U.S.A. by Weatherby.
Price: SVM (Super VarmintMaster), repeater or single-shot $1,517.00
Price: SPM (Super Predator Master) $1,459.00

Weatherby Mark V Special Varmint Rifle (SVR)
Similar to the Super VarmintMaster and Accumark with 22", #3 contour chrome-moly 4140 steel Krieger Criterion button-rifled barrel with one-degree target crown and hand-laminated composite stock. Available in .223 Rem. (5+1 magazine capacity) and .22-250 Rem. (4+1 magazine capacity) in right-hand models only.
Price: $999.00

Weatherby Mark V Fibermark Rifles
Similar to other Mark V models except has black Kevlar® and fiberglass composite stock and bead-blast blue or stainless finish. Chambered for 19 standard and magnum calibers. Introduced 1983; reintroduced 2001. Made in U.S.A. by Weatherby.
Price: Fibermark .... $1,070.00 to $1,347.00
Price: Fibermark stainless .... $1,165.00 to $1,390.00

WEATHERBY MARK V DANGEROUS GAME RIFLE
Caliber: 375 H&H, 375 Wby. Mag., 378 Wby. Mag., 416 Rem. Mag., 416 Wby. Mag., 458 Win. Mag., .458 Lott, 460 Wby. Mag. 300 Win. Mag., 300 Wby., Mag., 338 Win. Mag., 340 Wby. Mag., 24" only **Barrel:** 24" or 26". **Weight:** 8-3/4 to 9-1/2 lbs. **Length:** 44-5/8" to 46-5/8" overall. **Stock:** Kevlar® and fiberglass composite. **Sights:** Barrel-band hooded front with large gold bead, adjustable ramp/shallow "V" rear. **Features:** Designed for dangerous game hunting. Black oxide matte finish on all metalwork; Pachmayr Decelerator™ recoil pad, short-throw Mark V action. Introduced 2001. Made in U.S.A. by Weatherby.
Price: .... $2,703.00 to $2,935.00

WEATHERBY MARK V SUPER BIG GAMEMASTER DEER RIFLE
Caliber: 240 Wby. Mag., 25-06 Rem., 270 Win., 280 Rem., 30-06 Spfld., 257 Wby. Mag., 270 Wby. Mag., 7mm Rem., Mag., 7mm Wby. Mag., 338-06 A-Square, 300 Win. Mag., 300 Wby. Mag. **Barrel:** 26", target crown. **Weight:** 5-3/4 lbs., (6-3/4 lbs. Magnum). **Stock:** Raised comb Monte Carlo composite. **Features:** Fluted barrel, aluminum bedding block, Pachmayr decelerator, 54-degree bolt lift, adj. trigger.
Price: $1,459.00
Price: Magnum $1,517.00

WEATHERBY MARK V ROYAL CUSTOM RIFLE
Caliber: 257, 270, 7mm, 300, 340 all Wby. Mags. Other calibers available upon request. **Barrel:** 26". **Stock:** Monte Carlo hand-checkered Claro walnut with high gloss finish. **Features:** Bolt and follower are damascened with checkered knob. Engraved receiver, bolt sleeve and floorplate sport scroll pattern. Animal images on floorplate optional. High gloss blue, 24-karat gold and nickel-plating. Made in U.S.A. From Weatherby.
Price: $5,831.00

WEATHERBY THREAT RESPONSE RIFLES (TRR) SERIES
Caliber: TRR 223 Rem., 300 Win. TRR Magnum and Magnum Custom 300 Win. Mag., 300 Wby. Mag., 30-378 Wby. Mag., 328-378 Wby. Mag. **Barrel:** 22", 26", target crown. **Stock:** Hand-laminated composite. TTR & TRR Magnum have raised comb Monte Carlo style. TRR Magnum Custom adjustable ergonomic stock. **Features:** Adjustable trigger, aluminum bedding block, beavertail forearms dual tapered, flat-bottomed. "Rocker Arm" lockdown scope mounting. 54 degree bolt. Pachmayr decelerator pad. Made in U.S.A.
Price: TRR Magnum Custom 300 .... $2,699.00
Price: 30-378, 338-378 with accubrake $2,861.00

WILDERNESS EXPLORER MULTI-CALIBER CARBINE
Caliber: 22 Hornet, 218 Bee, 44 Magnum, 50 A.E. (interchangeable). **Barrel:** 18", match grade. **Weight:** 5.5 lbs **Length:** 38-1/2" overall. **Stock:** Synthetic or wood. **Sights:** None furnished; comes with Weaver-style mount on barrel. **Features:** Quick-change barrel and bolt face for caliber switch. Removable box magazine; adjustable trigger with side safety; detachable swivel studs. Introduced 1997. Made in U.S.A. by Phillips & Rogers, Inc.
Price: $995.00

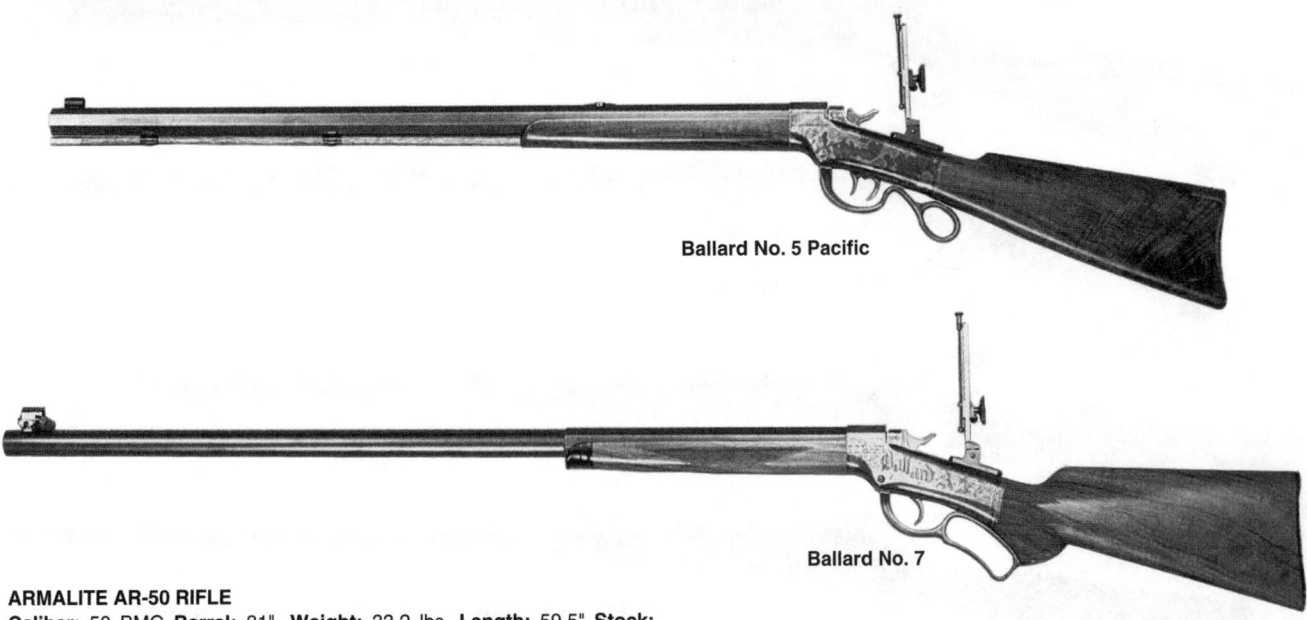

Ballard No. 5 Pacific

Ballard No. 7

ARMALITE AR-50 RIFLE
Caliber: 50 BMG **Barrel:** 31". **Weight:** 33.2 lbs. **Length:** 59.5" **Stock:** Synthetic. **Sights:** None furnished. **Features:** A single-shot bolt action rifle designed for long range shooting. Available in left-hand model. Made in U.S.A. by Armalite.
Price: $2,999.00

ARMSPORT 1866 SHARPS RIFLE, CARBINE
Caliber: 45-70. **Barrel:** 28", round or octagonal. **Weight:** 8.10 lbs. **Length:** 46" overall. **Stock:** Walnut. **Sights:** Blade front, folding adjustable rear. Tang sight set optionally available. **Features:** Replica of the 1866 Sharps. Color case-hardened frame, rest blued. Imported by Armsport.
Price: $865.00
Price: With octagonal barrel $900.00
Price: Carbine, 22" round barrel $850.00

BALLARD NO. 1 3/4 FAR WEST RIFLE
Caliber: 22 LR, 32-40, 38-55, 40-65, 40-70, 45-70, 45-110, 50-70, 50-90. **Barrel:** 30" std. or heavyweight. **Weight:** 10-1/2 lbs. (std.) or 11-3/4 lbs. (heavyweight bbl.) **Length:** NA. **Stock:** Walnut. **Sights:** Blade front, Rocky Mountain rear. **Features:** Single- or double-set triggers, S-lever or ring-style lever; color case-hardened finish; hand polished and lapped Badger barrel. Made in U.S.A. by Ballard Rifle & Cartridge Co.
Price: $2,250.00

BALLARD NO. 4 PERFECTION RIFLE
Caliber: 22 LR, 32-40, 38-55, 40-65, 40-70, 45-90, 45-110, 50-70, 50-90. **Barrel:** 30" or 32" octagon, standard or heavyweight. **Weight:** 10-1/2 lbs. (standard) or 11-3/4 lbs. (heavyweight bbl.). **Length:** NA. **Stock:** Smooth walnut. **Sights:** Blade front, Rocky Mountain rear. **Features:** Rifle or shotgun-style buttstock, straight grip action, single or double-set trigger, "S" or right lever, hand polished and lapped Badger barrel. Made in U.S.A. by Ballard Rifle & Cartridge Co.
Price: $2,250.00

BALLARD NO. 5 PACIFIC SINGLE-SHOT RIFLE
Caliber: 32-40, 38-55, 40-65, 40-90, 40-70 SS, 45-70 Govt., 45-110 SS, 50-70 Govt., 50-90 SS. **Barrel:** 30", or 32" octagonal. **Weight:** 10-1/2 lbs. **Length:** NA. **Stock:** High-grade walnut; rifle or shotgun style. **Sights:** Blade front, Rocky Mountain rear. **Features:** Standard or heavy barrel; double-set triggers; under-barrel wiping rod; ring lever. Introduced 1999. Made in U.S.A. by Ballard Rifle & Cartridge Co.
Price: $2,575.00

BALLARD NO. 7 LONG RANGE RIFLE
Caliber: 32-40, 38-55, 40-65, 40-70 SS, 45-70 Govt., 45-90, 45-110. **Barrel:** 32", 34" half-octagon. **Weight:** 11-3/4 lbs. **Length:** NA. **Stock:** Walnut; checkered pistol grip shotgun butt, ebony forend cap. **Sights:** Globe front. **Features:** Designed for shooting up to 1000 yards. Standard or heavy barrel; single or double-set trigger; hard rubber or steel buttplate. Introduced 1999. Made in U.S.A. by Ballard Rifle & Cartridge Co.
Price: From $2,475.00

BALLARD NO. 8 UNION HILL RIFLE
Caliber: 22 LR, 32-40, 38-55, 40-65 Win., 40-70 SS. **Barrel:** 30" half-octagon. **Weight:** About 10-1/2 lbs. **Length:** NA. **Stock:** Walnut; pistol grip butt with cheekpiece. **Sights:** Globe front. **Features:** Designed for 200-yard offhand shooting. Standard or heavy barrel; double-set triggers; full loop lever; hook Schuetzen buttplate. Introduced 1999. Made in U.S.A. by Ballard Rifle & Cartridge Co.
Price: From $2,500.00

BALLARD MODEL 1885 HIGH WALL SINGLE SHOT RIFLE
Caliber: 17 Bee, 22 Hornet, 218 Bee, 219 Don Wasp, 219 Zipper, 22 Hi-Power, 225 Win., 25-20 WCF, 25-35 WCF, 25 Krag, 7mmx57R, 30-30, 30-40 Krag, 303 British, 33 WCF, 348 WCF, 35 WCF, 35-30/30, 9.3x74R, 405 WCF, 50-110 WCF, 500 Express, 577 Express. **Barrel:** Lengths to 34". **Weight:** NA. **Length:** NA. **Stock:** Straight-grain American walnut. **Sights:** buckhorn or flattop rear, blade front. **Features:** Faithful copy of original Model 1885 High Wall; parts interchange with original rifles; variety of options available. Introduced 2000. Made in U.S.A. by Ballard Rifle & Cartridge LLC.
Price: From $2,313.00
Price: With single set trigger from $2,355.00

BARRETT MODEL 99 SINGLE SHOT RIFLE
Caliber: 50 BMG. **Barrel:** 33". **Weight:** 25 lbs. **Length:** 50.4" overall. **Stock:** Anodized aluminum with energy-absorbing recoil pad. **Sights:** None furnished; integral M1913 scope rail. **Features:** Bolt action; detachable bipod; match-grade barrel with high-efficiency muzzle brake. Introduced 1999. Made in U.S.A. by Barrett Firearms.
Price: From $3,000.00

BROWN MODEL 97D SINGLE SHOT RIFLE
Caliber: 17 Ackley Hornet through 45-70 Govt. **Barrel:** Up to 26", air gauged match grade. **Weight:** About 5 lbs., 11 oz. **Stock:** Sporter style with pistol grip, cheekpiece and Schnabel forend. **Sights:** None furnished; drilled and tapped for scope mounting. **Features:** Falling block action gives rigid barrel-receiver matting; polished blue/black finish. Hand-fitted action. Many options. Made in U.S.A. by E. Arthur Brown Co., Inc.
Price: From $699.00

CENTERFIRE RIFLES — Single Shot

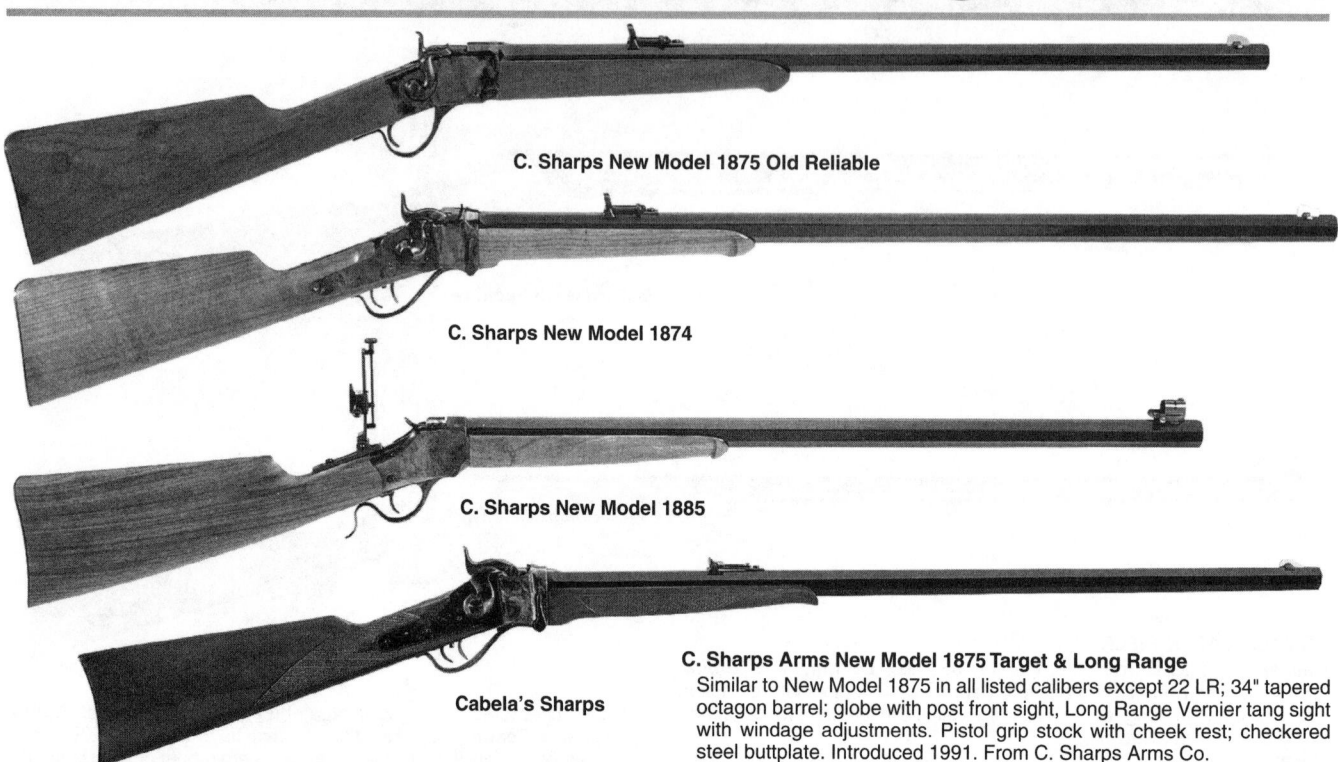

C. Sharps New Model 1875 Old Reliable

C. Sharps New Model 1874

C. Sharps New Model 1885

Cabela's Sharps

BROWNING MODEL 1885 HIGH WALL SINGLE SHOT RIFLE

Caliber: 22-250, 30-06, 270, 7mm Rem. Mag., 454 Casull, 45-70. **Barrel:** 28". **Weight:** 8 lbs., 12 oz. **Length:** 43-1/2" overall. **Stock:** Walnut with straight grip, Schnabel forend. **Sights:** None furnished; drilled and tapped for scope mounting. **Features:** Replica of J.M. Browning's high-wall falling block rifle. Octagon barrel with recessed muzzle. Imported from Japan by Browning. Introduced 1985.
Price: **$1,027.00**

BRNO ZBK 110 SINGLE SHOT RIFLE

Caliber: 222 Rem., 5.6x52R, 22 Hornet, 5.6x50 Mag., 6.5x57R, 7x57R, 8x57JRS. **Barrel:** 23.6". **Weight:** 5.9 lbs. **Length:** 40.1" overall. **Stock:** European walnut. **Sights:** None furnished; drilled and tapped for scope mounting. **Features:** Top tang opening lever; cross-bolt safety; polished blue finish. Announced 1998. Imported from The Czech Republic by Euro-Imports.
Price: Standard calibers **$223.00**
Price: 7x57R, 8x57JRS **$245.00**
Price: Lux model, standard calibers **$311.00**
Price: Lux model, 7x57R, 8x57JRS **$333.00**

C. SHARPS ARMS NEW MODEL 1875 OLD RELIABLE RIFLE

Caliber: 22LR, 32-40 & 38-55 Ballard, 38-56 WCF, 40-65 WCF, 40-90 3-1/4", 40-90 2-5/8", 40-70 2-1/10", 40-70 2-1/4", 40-70 2-1/2", 40-50 1-11/16", 40-50 1-7/8", 45-90, 45-70, 45-100, 45-110, 45-120. Also available on special order only in 50-70, 50-90, 50-140. **Barrel:** 24", 26", 30" (standard), 32", 34" optional. **Weight:** 8-12 lbs. **Stock:** Walnut, straight grip, shotgun butt with checkered steel buttplate. **Sights:** Silver blade front, Rocky Mountain buckhorn rear. **Features:** Recreation of the 1875 Sharps rifle. Production guns will have case-colored receiver. Available in Custom Sporting and Target versions upon request. Announced 1986. From C. Sharps Arms Co.
Price: 1875 Sporting Rifle (30" tapered oct. bbl.) **$1,185.00**

C. Sharps Arms 1875 Classic Sharps

Similar to New Model 1875 Sporting Rifle except 26", 28" or 30" full octagon barrel, crescent buttplate with toe plate, Hartford-style forend with cast German silver nose cap. Blade front sight, Rocky Mountain buckhorn rear. Weighs 10 lbs. Introduced 1987. From C. Sharps Arms Co.
Price: **$1,470.00**

C. Sharps Arms New Model 1875 Target & Long Range

Similar to New Model 1875 in all listed calibers except 22 LR; 34" tapered octagon barrel; globe with post front sight, Long Range Vernier tang sight with windage adjustments. Pistol grip stock with cheek rest; checkered steel buttplate. Introduced 1991. From C. Sharps Arms Co.
Price: **$1,549.50**

C. SHARPS ARMS NEW MODEL 1874 OLD RELIABLE

Caliber: 40-50, 40-70, 40-90, 45-70, 45-90, 45-100, 45-110, 45-120, 50-70, 50-90, 50-140. **Barrel:** 26", 28", 30" tapered octagon. **Weight:** About 10 lbs. **Length:** NA. **Stock:** American black walnut; shotgun butt with checkered steel buttplate; straight grip, heavy forend with Schnabel tip. **Sights:** Blade front, buckhorn rear. Drilled and tapped for tang sight. **Features:** Recreation of the Model 1874 Old Reliable Sharps Sporting Rifle. Double-set triggers. Reintroduced 1991. Made in U.S.A. by C. Sharps Arms.
Price: **$1,584.00**

C. SHARPS ARMS NEW MODEL 1885 HIGHWALL RIFLE

Caliber: 22 LR, 22 Hornet, 219 Zipper, 25-35 WCF, 32-40 WCF, 38-55 WCF, 40-65, 30-40 Krag, 40-50 ST or BN, 40-70 ST or BN, 40-90 ST or BN, 45-70 2-1/10" ST, 45-90 2-4/10" ST, 45-100 2-6/10" ST, 45-110 2-7/8" ST, 45-120 3-1/4" ST. **Barrel:** 26", 28", 30", tapered full octagon. **Weight:** About 9 lbs., 4 oz. **Length:** 47" overall. **Stock:** Oil-finished American walnut; Schnabel-style forend. **Sights:** Blade front, buckhorn rear. Drilled and tapped for optional tang sight. **Features:** Single trigger; octagonal receiver top; checkered steel buttplate; color case-hardened receiver and buttplate, blued barrel. Many options available. Made in U.S.A. by C. Sharps Arms Co
Price: From **$1,439.00**

C. SHARPS ARMS CUSTOM NEW MODEL 1877 LONG RANGE TARGET RIFLE

Caliber: 44-90 Sharps/Rem., 45-70, 45-90, 45-100 Sharps. **Barrel:** 32", 34" tapered round with Rigby flat. **Weight:** Appx. 10 lbs. **Stock:** Walnut checkered. Pistol grip/forend. **Sights:** Classic long range with windage. **Features:** Custom production only.
Price: .... **$5,550.00 and up**

CABELA'S SHARPS SPORTING RIFLE

Caliber: 45-70, 45-120, 45-110. **Barrel:** 32", tapered octagon. **Weight:** 9 lbs. **Length:** 47-1/4" overall. **Stock:** Checkered walnut. **Sights:** Blade front, open adjustable rear. **Features:** Color case-hardened receiver and hammer, rest blued. Introduced 1995. Imported by Cabela's.
Price: **$1199.99**
Price: (Heavy target Sharps, 45-70, 45-120, 50-70) **$1,399.99**
Price: (Quigley Sharps, 45-70, 45-120, 45-110) **$1,699.99**

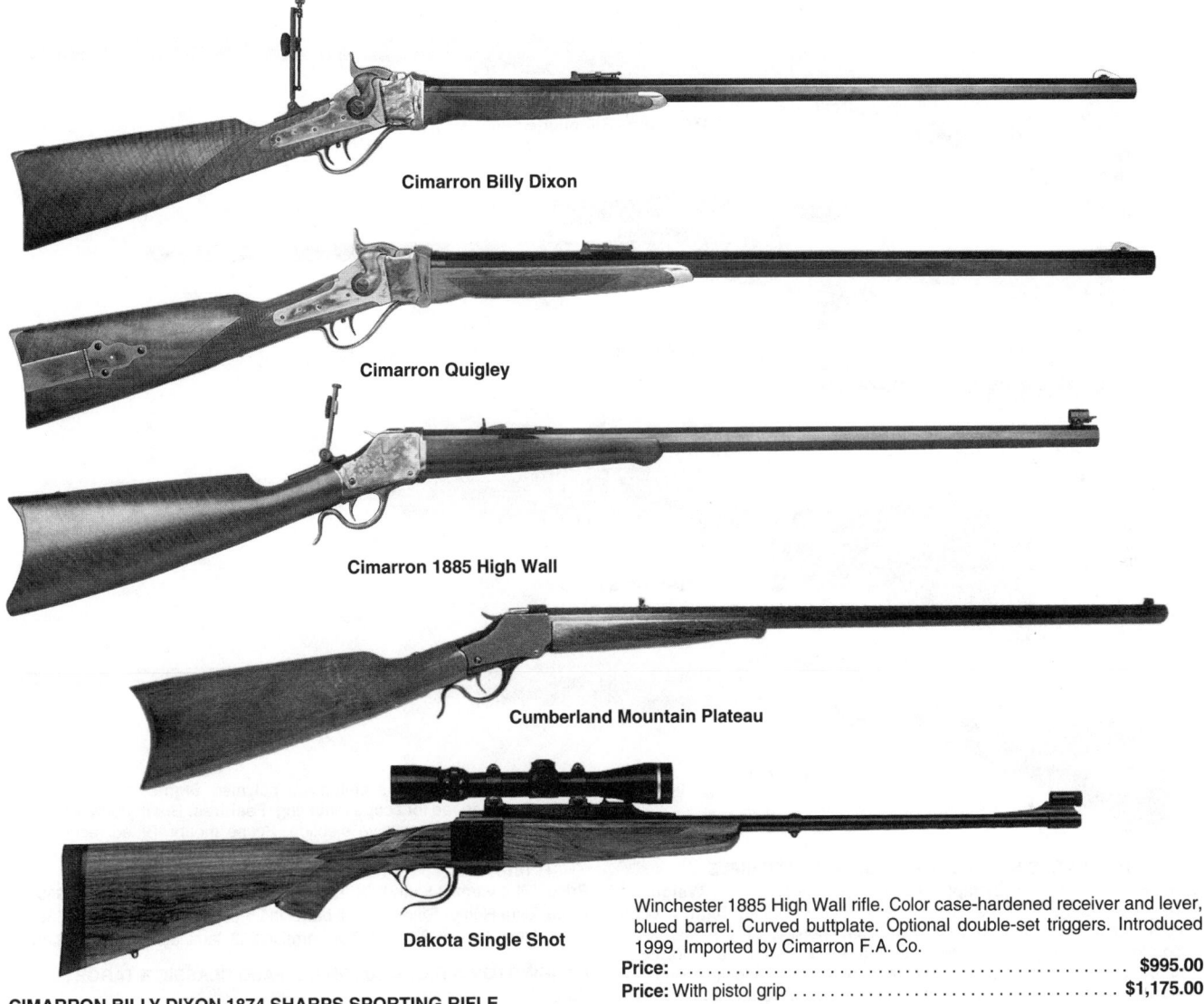

Cimarron Billy Dixon

Cimarron Quigley

Cimarron 1885 High Wall

Cumberland Mountain Plateau

Dakota Single Shot

CIMARRON BILLY DIXON 1874 SHARPS SPORTING RIFLE
Caliber: 40-40, 50-90, 50-70, 45-70. **Barrel:** 32" tapered octagonal. **Weight:** NA. **Length:** NA. **Stock:** European walnut. **Sights:** Blade front, Creedmoor rear. **Features:** Color case-hardened frame, blued barrel. Hand-checkered grip and forend; hand-rubbed oil finish. Introduced 1999. Imported by Cimarron F.A. Co.
Price: **$1,670.00**

CIMARRON QUIGLEY MODEL 1874 SHARPS SPORTING RIFLE
Caliber: 45-110, 50-70, 50-40, 45-70, 45-90, 45-120. **Barrel:** 34" octagonal. **Weight:** NA. **Length:** NA. **Stock:** Checkered walnut. **Sights:** Blade front, adjustable rear. **Features:** Blued finish; double-set triggers. From Cimarron F.A. Co.
Price: **$1,805.00**

CIMARRON SILHOUETTE MODEL 1874 SHARPS SPORTING RIFLE
Caliber: 45-70, 50-70. **Barrel:** 32" octagonal. **Weight:** NA. **Length:** NA. **Stock:** Walnut. **Sights:** Blade front, adjustable rear. **Features:** Pistol-grip stock with shotgun-style buttplate; cut-rifled barrel. From Cimarron F.A. Co.
Price: **$1,620.00**

CIMARRON MODEL 1885 HIGH WALL RIFLE
Caliber: 38-55, 40-65, 45-70, 45-90, 45-120, 30-40 Krag, 348 Winchester. **Barrel:** 30" octagonal. **Weight:** NA. **Length:** NA. **Stock:** European walnut. **Sights:** Bead front, semi-buckhorn rear. **Features:** Replica of the Winchester 1885 High Wall rifle. Color case-hardened receiver and lever, blued barrel. Curved buttplate. Optional double-set triggers. Introduced 1999. Imported by Cimarron F.A. Co.
Price: **$995.00**
Price: With pistol grip **$1,175.00**

CUMBERLAND MOUNTAIN PLATEAU RIFLE
Caliber: 40-65, 45-70. **Barrel:** Up to 32"; round. **Weight:** About 10-1/2 lbs. (32" barrel). **Length:** 48" overall (32" barrel). **Stock:** American walnut. **Sights:** Marble's bead front, Marble's open rear. **Features:** Falling block action with underlever. Blued barrel and receiver. Stock has lacquer finish, crescent buttplate. Introduced 1995. Made in U.S.A. by Cumberland Mountain Arms, Inc.
Price: **$1,085.00**

DAKOTA MODEL 10 SINGLE SHOT RIFLE
Caliber: Most rimmed and rimless commercial calibers. **Barrel:** 23". **Weight:** 6 lbs. **Length:** 39-1/2" overall. **Stock:** Medium fancy grade walnut in classic style. Checkered grip and forend. **Sights:** None furnished. Drilled and tapped for scope mounting. **Features:** Falling block action with underlever. Top tang safety. Removable trigger plate for conversion to single set trigger. Introduced 1990. Made in U.S.A. by Dakota Arms.
Price: **$3,595.00**
Price: Barreled action **$2,095.00**
Price: Action only **$1,850.00**
Price: Magnum calibers **$3,595.00**
Price: Magnum barreled action **$2,050.00**
Price: Magnum action only **$1,675.00**

Dixie 1874 Sharps Silhouette

H&R Ultra Varmint

H&R Ultra Hunter

H&R Buffalo

DIXIE 1874 SHARPS BLACK POWDER SILHOUETTE RIFLE

Caliber: 45-70. **Barrel:** 30"; tapered octagon; blued; 1:18" twist. **Weight:** 10 lbs., 3 oz. **Length:** 47-1/2" overall. **Stock:** Oiled walnut. **Sights:** Blade front, ladder-type hunting rear. **Features:** Replica of the Sharps #1 Sporter. Shotgun-style butt with checkered metal buttplate; color case-hardened receiver, hammer, lever and buttplate. Tang is drilled and tapped for tang sight. Double-set triggers. Meets standards for NRA blackpowder cartridge matches. Introduced 1995. Imported from Italy by Dixie Gun Works.
Price: **$1,075.00**

Dixie 1874 Sharps Lightweight Hunter/Target Rifle

Same as the Dixie 1874 Sharps Black Powder Silhouette model except has a straight-grip buttstock with military-style buttplate. Based on the 1874 military model. Introduced 1995. Imported from Italy by Dixie Gun Works.
Price: **$1,025.00**

E.M.F. 1874 METALLIC CARTRIDGE SHARPS RIFLE

Caliber: 45-70, 45/120. **Barrel:** 28", octagon. **Weight:** 10-3/4 lbs. **Length:** NA. **Stock:** Oiled walnut. **Sights:** Blade front, flip-up open rear. **Features:** Replica of the 1874 Sharps Sporting rifle. Color case-hardened lock; double-set trigger; blue finish. Imported by E.M.F.
Price: From **$700.00**
Price: With browned finish **$1,000.00**
Price: Military Carbine **$650.00**

HARRINGTON & RICHARDSON ULTRA VARMINT/ULTRA HUNTER RIFLES

Caliber: 204 Ruger, 22 WMR, 22-250, 223, 243, 25-06, 30-06. **Barrel:** 22" to 26" heavy taper. **Weight:** About 7.5 lbs. **Stock:** Laminated birch with Monte Carlo comb or skeletonized polymer. **Sights:** None furnished. Drilled and tapped for scope mounting. **Features:** Break-open action with side-lever release, positive ejection. Scope mount. Blued receiver and barrel. Swivel studs. Introduced 1993. Ultra Hunter introduced 1995. From H&R 1871, Inc.
Price: Ultra Varmint Fluted, 24" bull barrel, polymer stock **$406.00**
Price: Ultra Hunter Rifle, 26" bull barrel in 25-06, laminated stock . **$357.00**
Price: Ultra Varmint Rifle, 22" bull barrel in 223, laminated stock . . **$357.00**

HARRINGTON & RICHARDSON BUFFALO CLASSIC & TARGET RIFLES

Caliber: 45-70. **Barrel:** 32" heavy. **Weight:** 8 lbs. **Length:** 46" overall. **Stock:** Cut-checkered American black walnut. **Sights:** Williams receiver sight; Lyman target front sight with 8 aperture inserts. **Features:** Color case-hardened Handi-Rifle action with exposed hammer; color case-hardened crescent buttplate; 19th century checkering pattern. Introduced 1995. Target model (introduced 1998) is similar to the Buffalo Classic rifle except chambered for 38-55 Win., has 28" barrel. The barrel, steel trigger guard and forend spacer, are highly polished and blued. Color case-hardened receiver and buttplate. Made in U.S.A. by H&R 1871, LLC.
Price: Buffalo Classic Rifle **$449.00**
Price: Target Model Rifle. **$449.00**

HARRIS GUNWORKS ANTIETAM SHARPS RIFLE

Caliber: 40-65, 45-75. **Barrel:** 30", 32", octagon or round, hand-lapped stainless or chrome-moly. **Weight:** 11.25 lbs. **Length:** 47" overall. **Stock:** Choice of straight grip, pistol grip or Creedmoor with Schnabel forend; pewter tip optional. Standard wood is A Fancy; higher grades available. **Sights:** Montana Vintage Arms #111 Low Profile Spirit Level front, #108 mid-range tang rear with windage adjustments. **Features:** Recreation of the 1874 Sharps sidehammer. Action is color case-hardened, barrel satin black. Chrome-moly barrel optionally blued. Optional sights include #112 Spirit Level Globe front with windage, #107 Long Range rear with windage. Introduced 1994. Made in U.S.A. by Harris Gunworks.
Price: **$2,400.00**

Lone Star Silhouette

Model 1885 High Wall

Mossberg SSi-One Sporter

Mossberg SSi-One Varminter

KRIEGHOFF HUBERTUS SINGLE-SHOT RIFLE

Caliber: 222, 243, 270, 308, 30-06, 5.6x50R Mag., 5.6x52R, 6x62R Freres, 6.5x57R, 6.5x65R, 7x57R, 7x65R, 8x57JRS, 8x75RS, 9.3x74R, 7mm Rem. Mag., 300 Win. Mag. **Barrel:** 23-1/2". **Weight:** 6-1/2 lbs. **Length:** 40.5. **Stock:** High-grade walnut. **Sights:** Blade front, open rear. **Features:** Break-open loading with manual cocking lever on top tang; takedown; extractor; Schnabel forearm; many options. Imported from Germany by Krieghoff International Inc.
Price: Hubertus single shot, from **$5,995.00**
Price: Hubertus, magnum calibers **$6,995.00**

LONE STAR NO. 5 REMINGTON PATTERN ROLLING BLOCK RIFLE

Caliber: 25-35, 30-30, 30-40 Krag. **Barrel:** 26" to 34". **Weight:** NA. **Length:** NA. **Stock:** American walnut. **Sights:** Beech style, Marble bead, Rocky Mountain-style, front; Buckhorn, early or late combination, rear. **Features:** Round, tapered round, octagon, tapered octagon, half octagon-half round barrels; bone-pack color case-hardened actions; single, single set, or double-set triggers. Made in U.S.A. by Lone Star Rifle Co., Inc.
Price: **$1,995.00**

Lone Star Cowboy Action Rifle

Similar to the Lone Star No. 5 rifle, but designed for cowboy action shooting with 28-33" barrel, buckhorn rear sight.
Price: **$1,595.00**

Lone Star Custom Silhouette Rifle

Similar to the Lone Star No. 5 rifle but custom made in any caliber or barrel length.
Price: **$1,995.00**

MEACHAM HIGHWALL SILHOUETTE or SCHUETZEN RIFLE

Caliber: any rimmed cartridge. **Barrel:** 26-34". **Weight:** 7-15 lbs. **Sights:** none. Tang drilled for Win. base, 3/8 dovetail slot front. **Stock:** Fancy eastern walnut with cheekpiece; ebony insert in forearm tip. **Features:** Exact copy of 1885 Winchester. With most Winchester factory options

available including double set triggers. Introduced 1994. Made in U.S.A. by Meacham T&H Inc.
Price: . . . . from **$3,899.00**

MERKEL K-1 MODEL LIGHTWEIGHT STALKING RIFLE

Caliber: 243 Win., 270 Win., 7x57R, 308 Win., 30-06, 7mm Rem. Mag., 300 Win. Mag., 9.3x74R. **Barrel:** 23.6". **Weight:** 5.6 lbs. unscoped. **Stock:** Satin-finished walnut, fluted and checkered; sling-swivel studs. **Sights:** None (scope base furnished). **Features:** Franz Jager single-shot break-open action, cocking/uncocking slide-type safety, matte silver receiver, selectable trigger pull weights, integrated, quick detach 1" or 30mm optic mounts (optic not included). Imported from Germany by GSI.
Price: Standard, simple border engraving **$3,795.00**
Price: Premium, light arabesque scroll **$3,795.00**
Price: Jagd, fine engraved hunting scenes **$4,395.00**

MODEL 1885 HIGH WALL RIFLE

Caliber: 30-40 Krag, 32-40, 38-55, 40-65 WCF, 45-70. **Barrel:** 26" (30-40), 28" to 30" all others. Douglas Premium #3 tapered octagon. **Weight:** 9 lbs, 4 oz. **Length:** 47" overall. **Stock:** Premium American black walnut. **Sights:** Marble's standard ivory bead front, #66 long blade top rear with reversible notch and elevator. **Features:** Receiver with octagon top, thick-wall High Wall with coil spring action. Tang drilled, tapped for High Wall tang sight. Receiver, lever, hammer and breechblock color case-hardened. Available from Montana Armory, Inc.
Price: **$1,350.00**

MOSSBERG SSi-ONE SINGLE SHOT RIFLE

Caliber: 223 Rem., 22-250 Rem., 243 Win., 270 Win., 308 Rem., 30-06. **Barrel:** 24". **Weight:** 8 lbs. **Length:** 40". **Stock:** Satin-finished walnut, fluted and checkered; sling-swivel studs. **Sights:** None (scope base furnished). **Features:** Frame accepts interchangeable barrels including 12 gauge, fully rifled slug barrel and 12 ga., 3-1/2" chambered barrel with Ulti-Full Turkey choke tube. Lever-opening, break-action design; single-stage trigger; ambidextrous, top-tang safety; internal eject/extract selector. Introduced 2000. From Mossberg.
Price: SSi-One Sporter (standard barrel) or 12 ga., 3-1/2" chamber **$459.00**
Price: SSi-One Varmint (bull barrel, 22-250 Rem. only;
weighs 10 lbs.) **$480.00**
Price: SSi-One 12 gauge Slug (fully rifled barrel, no sights,
scope base) **$480.00**

Navy Arms #2 Creedmoor

Navy Arms 1874 Sharps Cavalry Carbine

Navy Arms 1874 Sharps Plains

Navy Arms 1874 Sharps Sporting

Navy Arms Sharps #2 Sporting

Navy Arms Sharps #2 Silhouette

Replica of the 1874 Sharps miltary carbine. Color case-hardened receiver and furniture. Imported by Navy Arms.

Price: **$1,245.00**

Navy Arms Sharps Sporting Rifle
Same as the Navy Arms Sharps Plains Rifle except has pistol grip stock. Introduced 1997. Imported by Navy Arms.

Price: 45-70 only. **$1,739.00**
Price: #2 Sporting with case-hardened receiver **$1,739.00**
Price: #2 Silhouette with full octagonal barrel **$1,739.00**

NAVY ARMS 1885 HIGH WALL RIFLE
Caliber: 45-70; others available on special order. **Barrel:** 28" round, 30" octagonal. **Weight:** 9.5 lbs. **Length:** 45-1/2" overall (30" barrel). **Stock:** Walnut. **Sights:** Blade front, vernier tang-mounted peep rear. **Features:** Replica of Winchester's High Wall designed by Browning. Color case-hardened receiver, blued barrel. Introduced 1998. Imported by Navy Arms.

Price: 28", round barrel, target sights. **$1,169.00**
Price: 30" octagonal barrel, target sights **$1,169.00**

NAVY ARMS 1873 SHARPS "QUIGLEY" RIFLE
Caliber: 45/70. **Barrel:** 34" heavy octagonal. **Stock:** Walnut. **Features:** Case-hardened receiver and military patchbox. Exact reproduction from "Quigley Down Under."

Price: **$1,826.00**

NAVY ARMS 1873 SHARPS NO. 2 CREEDMOOR RIFLE
Caliber: 45/70. **Barrel:** 30" tapered round. **Stock:** Walnut. **Sights:** Front globe, "soule" tang rear. **Features:** Nickel receiver and action. Lightweight sporting rifle.

Price: **$1,739.00**

NAVY ARMS 1874 SHARPS CAVALRY CARBINE
Caliber: 45-70. **Barrel:** 22". **Weight:** 7 lbs., 12 oz. **Length:** 39" overall. **Stock:** Walnut. **Sights:** Blade front, military ladder-type rear. **Features:**

Navy Arms 1873 Springfield

Navy Arms Rolling Block Buffalo

New England Firearms Handi-Rifle

New England Firearms Super Light

NAVY ARMS 1873 SPRINGFIELD CAVALRY CARBINE
Caliber: 45-70. **Barrel:** 22". **Weight:** 7 lbs. **Length:** 40-1/2" overall. **Stock:** Walnut. **Sights:** Blade front, military ladder rear. **Features:** Blued lockplate and barrel; color case-hardened breechblock; saddle ring with bar. Replica of 7th Cavalry gun. Imported by Navy Arms.
Price: **$1,195.00**

NAVY ARMS "JOHN BODINE" ROLLING BLOCK RIFLE
Caliber: 45-70. **Barrel:** 30" heavy octagonal. **Stock:** Walnut. **Sights:** Globe front, "soule" tang rear. **Features:** Double-set triggers.
Price: **$1,856.00**
Price: (#2 with deluxe nickel finished receiver) **$1,856.00**

NAVY ARMS SHARPS NO. 3 LONG RANGE RIFLE
Caliber: 45-70, 45-90. **Barrel:** 34" octagon. **Weight:** 10 lbs., 12 oz. **Length:** 51-1/2". **Stock:** Deluxe walnut. **Sights:** Globe target front and match grade rear tang. **Features:** Shotgun buttplate, German silver forend cap, color case hardenend receiver. Imported by Navy Arms.
Price: **$2,194.00**

NEW ENGLAND FIREARMS HANDI-RIFLE
Caliber: 204 Ruger, 22 Hornet, 223, 243, 30-30, 270, 280 Rem., 7mm-08, 308, 7.62x39 Russian, 30-06, 357 Mag., 35 Whelen, 44 Mag., 45-70, 500 S&W. **Barrel:** from 20" to 26", blued or stainless. **Weight:** 5.5 to 7 lbs. **Stock:** Walnut-finished hardwood or synthetic. **Sights:** Vary by model, but most have ramp front, folding rear, or are drilled and tapped for scope mount. **Features:** Break-open action with side-lever release. Swivel studs on all models. Blue finish. Introduced 1989. From New England Firearms.
Price: Various cartridges. **$292.00**
Price: 7.62x39 Russian, 35 Whelen, intr. 2006 .... **$292.00**
Price: Youth, 37" OAL, 11.75" LOP, 6.75 lbs. **$292.00**
Price: Handi-Rifle/Pardner combo, 20 ga. synthetic, intr. 2006 .... **$325.00**
Price: Handi-Rifle/Pardner Superlight, 20 ga., 5.5 lbs. , intr. 2006.. **$325.00**
Price: Synthetic. **$302.00**
Price: Stainless. **$364.00**
Price: Superlight, 20" barrel, 35.25" OAL, 5.5 lbs. **$302.00**

NEW ENGLAND FIREARMS SURVIVOR RIFLE
Caliber: 223, 308 Win., .410 shotgun, 45 Colt, single shot. **Barrel:** 20" to 22". **Weight:** 6 lbs. **Length:** 34.5" to 36" overall. **Stock:** Black polymer, thumbhole design. **Sights:** None furnished; scope mount provided. **Features:** Receiver drilled and tapped for scope mounting. Stock and forend have storage compartments for ammo, etc.; comes with integral swivels and black nylon sling. Introduced 1996. Made in U.S.A. by New England Firearms.
Price: Blue or nickel finish **$304.00**

New England Firearms Survivor

Remington No. 1 Mid-Range

Replica Arms Sharps "Quigley"

Ruger No. 1B

NEW ENGLAND FIREARMS SPORTSTER/VERSA PACK RIFLE

Caliber: 17M2, 17HMR, 22LR, 22 WMR, .410 bore single shot. **Barrel:** 20" to 22". **Weight:** 5.4 to 7 lbs. **Length:** 33" to 38.25" overall. **Stock:** Black polymer. **Sights:** Adjustable rear, ramp front. **Features:** Receiver drilled and tapped for scope mounting. Made in U.S.A. by New England Firearms.

Price: Sportster 17M2, 17HMR............................ **$193.00**
Price: Sportster **$161.00**
Price: Sportster Youth **$161.00**
Price: Sportster 22/410 Versa Pack **$176.00**

REMINGTON NO. 1 ROLLING BLOCK MID-RANGE SPORTER

Caliber: 45-70. **Barrel:** 30" round. **Weight:** 8-3/4 lbs. **Length:** 46-1/2" overall. **Stock:** American walnut with checkered pistol grip and forend. **Sights:** Beaded blade front, adjustable center-notch buckhorn rear. **Features:** Recreation of the original. Polished blue metal finish. Many options available. Introduced 1998. Made in U.S.A. by Remington.

Price: **$1,450.00**
Price: Silhouette model with single-set trigger, heavy barrel **$1,560.00**

REPLICA ARMS SHARPS "QUIGLEY" RIFLE

Caliber: .45-70. **Barrel:** 28" octagon. **Weight:** 10 lbs. **Length:** 47-1/4" overall. **Grips:** Walnut checkered at wrist and forend. **Sights:** High blade front, full buckhorn rear. **Features:** Color case-hardened receiver, trigger, patchbox, hammer and lever. Double-set triggers, German silver gripcap.

Price: **$1,241.95**

REPLICA ARMS SHARPS "BIG GAME" RIFLE

Caliber: .45-70. **Barrel:** 28" Deluxe Heavy Round. **Weight:** 8.8 lbs. **Length:** 44.8" overall. **Grips:** Walnut. **Sights:** Gold bead front, full buckhorn rear. **Features:** Color case-hardened receiver, trigger, hammer and lever. Double-set triggers.

Price: **$1,014.00**

ROSSI SINGLE SHOT CENTERFIRE RIFLE

Caliber: 308 Win., 270 Win., 30-06 Spfld., 223 Rem., 243 Win. **Barrel:** 23". **Weight:** 6 to 6.5 lbs. **Stock:** Monte Carlo, exotic woods, walnut finish & swivels with white line space and recoil pad. **Sights:** None, scope rails and hammer extension included. **Features:** Break-open, positive ejection, internal transfer bar mechanism and manual external safety. Trigger block system included.

Price: **$179.95**

ROSSI CENTERFIRE/SHOTGUN "MATCHED PAIRS"

Caliber: 12 ga./223 Rem., full size, 20 ga./223 Rem. full & youth, 12 ga./342 Win. full, 20 ga./243 Win., full & youth, 12 ga./308 Win. full, 20 ga./308 Win. full & youth, 12 ga./30-06 Spfld. full, 20 ga./30-06 Spfld. full, 12 ga./270 Win. full, 20 ga./270 Win. full. **Barrel:** 28"/23" full, 22"/22" youth. **Weight:** 5 to 7 lbs. **Stock:** Straight, exotic woods, walnut finish and swivels with white line spacer and recoil pad. **Sights:** Bead front shotgun, fully adjustable rifle, drilled and tapped. **Features:** Break-open, positive ejection, internal transfer bar mechanism and manual external safety. Trigger block system included.

Price:: **$350.00**

RUGER NO. 1B SINGLE SHOT

Caliber: 218 Bee, 22 Hornet, 220 Swift, 22-250, 223, 204 Ruger, 243, 25-06, 270, 30-06, 7mm Rem. Mag., 300 Win. Mag., 308 Win., 338 Win. Mag., 270 Wby., 300 Wby. **Barrel:** 26" round tapered with quarter-rib; with Ruger 1" rings. **Weight:** 8 lbs. **Length:** 42-1/4" overall. **Stock:** Walnut, two-piece, checkered pistol grip and semi-beavertail forend. **Sights:** None, 1" scope rings supplied for integral mounts. **Features:** Under-lever, hammerless falling block design has auto ejector, top tang safety.

Price: 1B.. **$1,000.00**
Price: K1-B-BBZ stainless steel, laminated stock 25-06, 7MM mag, 7MM STW, 300 Win Mag., 243 Win., 30-06, 308 Win. **$1,032.00**

Ruger K1-B-BBZ

Ruger No. 1A Light Sporter

Ruger No. 1V Varminter

Ruger No. 1 RSI

Ruger No. 1H Tropical

Ruger No. 1S Medium Sporter

Ruger No. 1A Light Sporter
Caliber: 204 Ruger, 243, 30-06, 270 and 7x57. **Weight**: About 7-1/4 lbs. Similar to the No. 1B Standard Rifle except has lightweight 22" barrel, Alexander Henry-style forend, adjustable folding leaf rear sight on quarter-rib, dovetailed ramp front with gold bead.
Price: No. 1A **$1,000.00**

Ruger No. 1V Varminter
Similar to the No. 1B Standard Rifle except has 24" heavy barrel. Semi-beavertail forend, barrel ribbed for target scope block, with 1" Ruger scope rings. Calibers 22-250, 220 Swift (w/26" bbl.), 223, 25-06, 6mm Rem. Weight about 9 lbs.
Price: No. 1V **$1,000.00**
Price: K1-V-BBZ stainless steel, laminated stock 22-250. . . . . . **$1,032.00**

Ruger No. 1 RSI International
Similar to the No. 1B Standard Rifle except has lightweight 20" barrel, full-length International-style forend with loop sling swivel, adjustable folding leaf rear sight on quarter-rib, ramp front with gold bead. Calibers 243, 30-06, 270 and 7x57. Weight is about 7-1/4 lbs.
Price: No. 1 RSI **$1,032.00**

Ruger No. 1H Tropical Rifle
Similar to the No. 1B Standard Rifle except has Alexander Henry forend, adjustable folding leaf rear sight on quarter-rib, ramp front with dovetail gold bead, 24" heavy barrel. Calibers 375 H&H, 416 Rigby, 458 Lott, 405 Win. and 458 Win. Mag. (weighs about 9 lbs.).
Price: No. 1H. **$1,000.00**
Price: K1-H-BBZ, S/S, 375 H&H, 416 Rigby **$1,032.00**

Ruger No. 1S Medium Sporter
Similar to the No. 1B Standard Rifle except has Alexander Henry-style forend, adjustable folding leaf rear sight on quarter-rib, ramp front sight base and dovetail-type gold bead front sight. Calibers: 9.3x74R, 45-70 with 22" barrel. Weighs about 7-1/2 lbs. In 45-70.
Price: No. 1S. **$1,000.00**
Price: K1-S-BBZ, S/S, 45-70 . . . . **$1032.00**

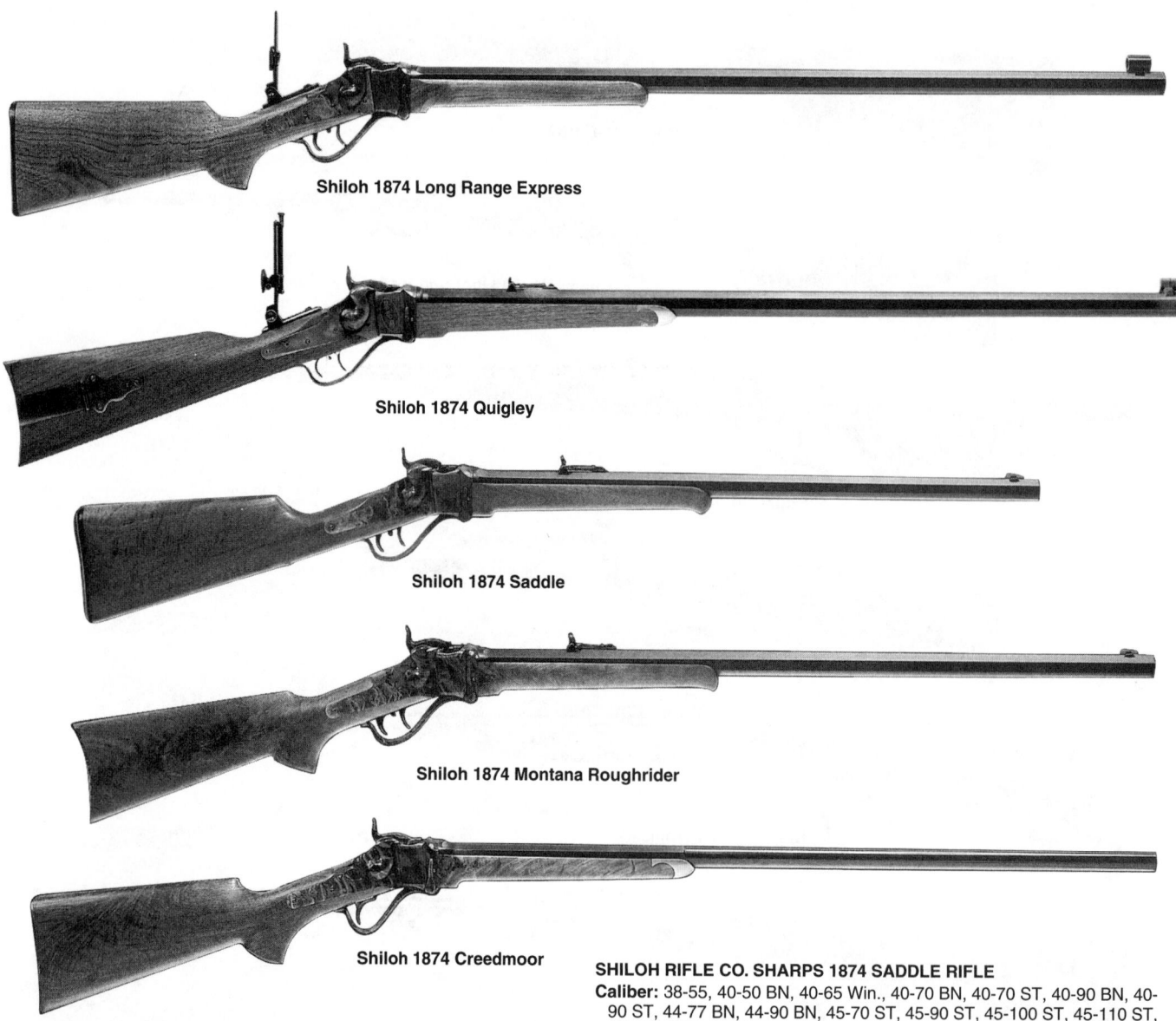

Shiloh 1874 Long Range Express

Shiloh 1874 Quigley

Shiloh 1874 Saddle

Shiloh 1874 Montana Roughrider

Shiloh 1874 Creedmoor

SHILOH RIFLE CO. SHARPS 1874 LONG RANGE EXPRESS
Caliber: 40-50 BN, 40-70 BN, 40-90 BN, 45-70 ST, 45-90 ST, 45-110 ST, 50-70 ST, 50-90 ST, 38-55, 40-70 ST, 40-90 ST. **Barrel:** 34" tapered octagon. **Weight:** 10-1/2 lbs. **Length:** 51" overall. **Stock:** Oil-finished walnut (upgrades available) with pistol grip, shotgun-style butt, traditional cheek rest, Schnabel forend. **Sights:** Customer's choice. **Features:** Re-creation of the Model 1874 Sharps rifle. Double-set triggers. Made in U.S.A. by Shiloh Rifle Mfg. Co.
Price: **$1,638.00**
Price: Sporting Rifle No. 1 (similar to above except with 30" bbl., blade front, buckhorn rear sight) **$1,638.00**
Price: Sporting Rifle No. 3 (similar to No. 1 except straight-grip stock, standard wood) **$1,547.00**

SHILOH RIFLE CO. SHARPS 1874 QUIGLEY
Caliber: 45-70, 45-110. **Barrel:** 34" heavy octagon. **Stock:** Military-style with patch box, standard grade American walnut. **Sights:** Semi buckhorn, interchangeable front and midrange vernier tang sight with windage. **Features:** Gold inlay initials, pewter tip, Hartford collar, case color or antique finish. Double-set triggers.
Price: **$2,903.00**

SHILOH RIFLE CO. SHARPS 1874 SADDLE RIFLE
Caliber: 38-55, 40-50 BN, 40-65 Win., 40-70 BN, 40-70 ST, 40-90 BN, 40-90 ST, 44-77 BN, 44-90 BN, 45-70 ST, 45-90 ST, 45-100 ST, 45-110 ST, 45-120 ST, 50-70 ST, 50-90 ST. **Barrel:** 26" full or half octagon. **Stock:** Semi fancy American walnut. Shotgun style with cheekrest. **Sights:** Buckhorn and blade. **Features:** Double-set trigger, numerous custom features can be added.
Price: **$1,594.00**

SHILOH RIFLE CO. SHARPS 1874 MONTANA ROUGHRIDER
Caliber: 38-55, 40-50 BN, 40-65 Win., 40-70 BN, 40-70 ST, 40-90 BN, 40-90 ST, 44-77 BN, 44-90 BN, 45-70 ST, 45-90 ST, 45-100 ST, 45-110 ST, 45-120 ST, 50-70 ST, 50-90 ST. **Barrel:** 30" full or half octagon. **Stock:** American walnut in shotgun or military style. **Sights:** Buckhorn and blade. **Features:** Double-set triggers, numerous custom features can be added.
Price: **$1,638.00**

SHILOH RIFLE CO. SHARPS CREEDMOOR TARGET
Caliber: 38-55, 40-50 BN, 40-65 Win., 40-70 BN, 40-70 ST, 40-90 BN, 40-90 ST, 44-77 BN, 44-90 BN, 45-70 ST, 45-90 ST, 45-100 ST, 45-110 ST, 45-120 ST, 50-70 ST, 50-90 ST. **Barrel:** 32", half round-half octagon. **Stock:** Extra fancy American walnut. Shotgun style with pistol grip. **Sights:** Customer's choice. **Features:** Single trigger, AA finish on stock, polished barrel and screws, pewter tip.
Price: **$2,485.00**

Thompson/Center Encore

Thompson/Center Encore "Katahdin"

Thompson/Center Contender

Traditions 1874 Sharps Deluxe

Traditions 1874 Sharps Sporting Deluxe

THOMPSON/CENTER ENCORE RIFLE
Caliber: 22-250, 223, 243, 204 Ruger, 6.8 Rem. Spec., 25-06, 270, 7mm-08, 308, 30-06, 7mm Rem. Mag., 300 Win. Mag. **Barrel:** 24", 26". **Weight:** 6 lbs., 12 oz. (24" barrel). **Length:** 38-1/2" (24" barrel). **Stock:** American walnut. Monte Carlo style; Schnabel forend or black composite. **Sights:** Ramp-style white bead front, fully adjustable leaf-type rear. **Features:** Interchangeable barrels; action opens by squeezing trigger guard; drilled and tapped for T/C scope mounts; polished blue finish. Introduced 1996. Made in U.S.A. by Thompson/Center Arms.
Price: . . . . **$604.00 to $663.00**
Price: Extra barrels **$277.00**

Thompson/Center Stainless Encore Rifle
Similar to blued Encore except stainless steel with blued sights, black composite stock and forend. Available in 22-250, 223, 7mm-08, 30-06, 308. Introduced 1999. Made in U.S.A. by Thompson/Center Arms.
Price: . . . . **$680.00 to $738.00**

THOMPSON/CENTER ENCORE "KATAHDIN" CARBINE
Caliber: 45-70 Gov't., 450 Marlin. **Barrel:** 18" with muzzle tamer. **Stock:** Composite.
Price: **$619.00**

Thompson/Center G2 Contender Rifle
Similar to the G2 Contender pistol, but in a compact rifle format. Weighs 5-1/2 lbs. Features interchangeable 23" barrels, chambered for 17 HMR, 22LR, 223 Rem., 30/30 Win. and 45/70 Gov't; plus a 45 Cal. Muzzleloading barrel. All of the 16-1/4" and 21" barrels made for the old-style Contender will fit. Introduced 2003. Made in U.S.A. by Thompson/Center Arms.
Price: . . . . **$622.00 to $637.00**

TRADITIONS 1874 SHARPS DELUXE RIFLE
Caliber: 45-70. **Barrel:** 32" octagonal; 1:18" twist. **Weight:** 11.67 lbs. **Length:** 48.8" overall. **Stock:** Checkered walnut with German silver nose cap and steel buttplate. **Sights:** Globe front, adjustable Creedmore rear with 12 inserts. **Features:** Color case-hardened receiver; double-set triggers. Introduced 2001. Imported from Pedersoli by Traditions.
Price: **$999.00**

Traditions 1874 Sharps Sporting Deluxe Rifle
Similar to Sharps Deluxe but custom silver engraved receiver, European walnut stock and forend, satin finish, set trigger, fully adjustable.
Price: **$1,999.00**

Traditions 1874 Sharps Standard Rifle
Similar to 1874 Sharps Deluxe except has blade front and adjustable buckhorn-style rear sight. Weighs 10.67 pounds. Introduced 2001. Imported from Pedersoli by Traditions.
Price: **$769.00**

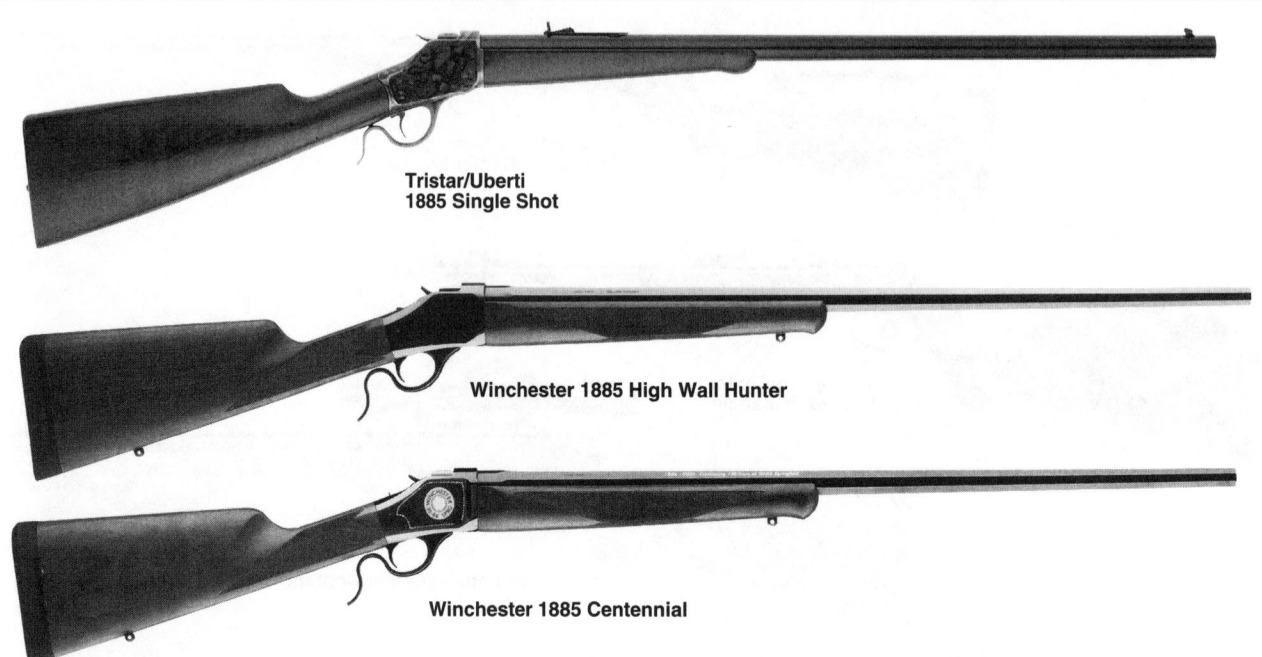

**Tristar/Uberti
1885 Single Shot**

Winchester 1885 High Wall Hunter

Winchester 1885 Centennial

TRADITIONS ROLLING BLOCK SPORTING RIFLE
Caliber: 45-70. **Barrel:** 30" octagonal; 1:18" twist. **Weight:** 11.67 lbs. **Length:** 46.7" overall. **Stock:** Walnut. **Sights:** Blade front, adjustable rear. **Features:** Antique silver, color case-hardened receiver, drilled and tapped for tang/globe sights; brass buttplate and trigger guard. Introduced 2001. Imported from Pedersoli by Traditions.
Price: **$769.00**

TRADITIONS ROLLING BLOCK SPORTING RIFLE
IN 30-30 WINCHESTER
Caliber: 30-30. **Barrel:** 28" round, blued. **Weight:** 8.25 lbs. **Stock:** Walnut. **Sights:** Fixed front, adjustable rear. **Features:** Steel buttplate, trigger guard, barrel band.
Price: **$769.00**

UBERTI 1874 SHARPS SPORTING RIFLE
Caliber: 45-70. **Barrel:** 30", 32", 34" octagonal. **Weight:** 10.57 lbs. with 32" barrel. **Length:** 48.9" with 32" barrel. **Stock:** Walnut. **Sights:** Dovetail front, Vernier tang rear. **Features:** Cut checkering, case-colored finish on frame, buttplate, and lever.
Price: Standard Sharps (2006), 30" barrel **$1,195.00**
Price: Special Sharps (2006) 32" barrel **$1,450.00**
Price: Deluxe Sharps (2006) 34" barrel **$2,200.00**
Price: Down Under Sharps (2006) 34" barrel **$1,799.00**
Price: Adobe Walls Sharps (2006) 32" barrel **$1,750.00**
Price: Longe Range Sharps (2006) 34" barrel **$1,799.00**

UBERTI ROLLING BLOCK CARBINE AND RIFLE
Caliber: 22 LR, 22 WMR, 22 Hornet, 357 Mag., single shot. **Barrel:** 22" to 26". **Weight:** 4.9 lbs. (Carbine) **Length:** 35.5" overall. **Stock:** Walnut stock and forend. **Sights:** Blade front, fully adjustable open rear. **Features:** Resembles Remington New Model No. 4 carbine. Brass trigger guard and buttplate; color case-hardened frame, blued barrel. Imported by Uberti USA Inc.
Price: Carbine, 22" barrel **$535.00**
Price: Rifle, 26" barrel **$600.00**

UBERTI HIGH-WALL RIFLE
Caliber: 45-70, 45-90, 45-120 single shot. **Barrel:** 28" to 23". **Weight:** 9.3 to 9.9 lbs. **Length:** 44.5" to 47" overall. **Stock:** Walnut stock and forend. **Sights:** Blade front, fully adjustable open rear. **Features:** Based on Winchester High-Wall design by John Browning. Color case-hardened frame and lever, blued barrel and buttplate. Imported by Uberti USA Inc.
Price: 1885 High-Wall, 28" round barrel **$850.00**
Price: 1885 High-Wall Sporting, 30" octagonal barrel **$850.00**
Price: 1885 High-Wall Special Sporting, 32" octagonal barrel. ... **$1,035.00**

WINCHESTER MODEL 1885 HIGH WALL HUNTER
Caliber: 22-250 Rem., 223 Rem., 270 WSM, 300 WSM, 7mm WSM, 325 WSM. **Barrel:** 28". **Weight:** 8.5 lbs. **Length:** 44". **Stock:** Walnut. **Features:** Single-shot, Pachmayr recoil pad.
Price: **$1,085.00**

Winchester Model 1885 30-06 Centennial High Wall Hunter
Similar to the Model 1885 High Wall Hunter except chambered 30-06 Springfield with satin finished checkered walnut stock.
Price: **$1,617.00**

Designs for sporting and utility purposes worldwide.

Beretta Express SSO

Beretta Model 455 SxS

Charles Daly Superior

Charles Daly Empire Combo

BERETTA EXPRESS SSO O/U DOUBLE RIFLES

Caliber: 375 H&H, 458 Win. Mag., 9.3x74R. **Barrel:** 25.5". **Weight:** 11 lbs. **Stock:** European walnut with hand-checkered grip and forend. **Sights:** Blade front on ramp, open V-notch rear. **Features:** Sidelock action with color case-hardened receiver (gold inlays on SSO6 Gold). Ejectors, double triggers, recoil pad. Introduced 1990. Imported from Italy by Beretta U.S.A.

Price: SSO6. . . . . **$21,000.00**
Price: SSO6 Gold **$23,500.00**

BERETTA MODEL 455 SxS EXPRESS RIFLE

Caliber: 375 H&H, 458 Win. Mag., 470 NE, 500 NE 3", 416 Rigby. **Barrel:** 23-1/2" or 25-1/2". **Weight:** 11 lbs. **Stock:** European walnut with hand-checkered grip and forend. **Sights:** Blade front, folding leaf V-notch rear. **Features:** Sidelock action with easily removable sideplates; color case-hardened finish (455), custom big game or floral motif engraving (455EELL). Double triggers, recoil pad. Introduced 1990. Imported from Italy by Beretta U.S.A.

Price: Model 455 . . . . **$36,000.00**
Price: Model 455EELL **$47,000.00**

BRNO 500 COMBINATION GUNS

Caliber/Gauge: 12 (2-3/4" chamber) over 5.6x52R, 5.6x50R, 222 Rem., 243, 6.x55, 308, 7x57R, 7x65R, 30-06. **Barrel:** 23.6". **Weight:** 7.6 lbs. **Length:** 40.5" overall. **Stock:** European walnut. **Sights:** Bead front, V-notch rear; grooved for scope mounting. **Features:** Boxlock action; double-set trigger; blue finish with etched engraving. Announced 1998. Imported from The Czech Republic by Euro-Imports.

Price: **$1,023.00**
Price: O/U double rifle, 7x57R, 7x65R, 8x57JRS **$1,125.00**

BRNO ZH 300 COMBINATION GUN

Caliber/Gauge: 22 Hornet, 5.6x50R Mag., 5.6x52R, 7x57R, 7x65R, 8x57JRS over 12, 16 (2-3/4" chamber). **Barrel:** 23.6". **Weight:** 7.9 lbs. **Length:** 40.5" overall. **Stock:** European walnut. **Sights:** Blade front, open adjustable rear. **Features:** Boxlock action; double triggers; automatic safety. Announced 1998. Imported from The Czech Republic by Euro-Imports.

Price: **$724.00**

BRNO ZH Double Rifles

Similar to ZH 300 Combination guns except double rifle barrels. Available in 7x65R, 7x57R and 8x57JRS. Announced 1998. Imported from The Czech Republic by Euro-Imports.

Price: **$1,125.00**

CHARLES DALY SUPERIOR COMBINATION GUN

Caliber/Gauge: 12 ga. over 22 Hornet, 223 Rem., 22-250, 243 Win., 270 Win., 308 Win., 30-06. **Barrel:** 23.5", shotgun choked Imp. Cyl. **Weight:** About 7.5 lbs. **Stock:** Checkered walnut pistol grip buttstock and semi-beavertail forend. **Features:** Silvered, engraved receiver; chrome-moly steel barrels; double triggers; extractors; sling swivels; gold bead front sight. Introduced 1997. Imported from Italy by K.B.I. Inc.

Price: **$1,479.00**

Charles Daly Empire Combination Gun

Same as the Superior grade except has deluxe wood with European-style comb and cheekpiece; slim forend. Introduced 1997. Imported from Italy by K.B.I., Inc.

Price: **$2,189.00**

CZ 584 SOLO COMBINATION GUN

Caliber/Gauge: 7x57R; 12, 2-3/4" chamber. **Barrel:** 24.4". **Weight:** 7.37 lbs. **Length:** 45.25" overall. **Stock:** Circassian walnut. **Sights:** Blade front, open rear adjustable for windage. **Features:** Kersten-style double lump locking system; double-trigger Blitz-type mechanism with drop safety and adjustable set trigger for the rifle barrel; auto safety, dual extractors; receiver dovetailed for scope mounting. Imported from the Czech Republic by CZ-USA.

Price: **$851.00**

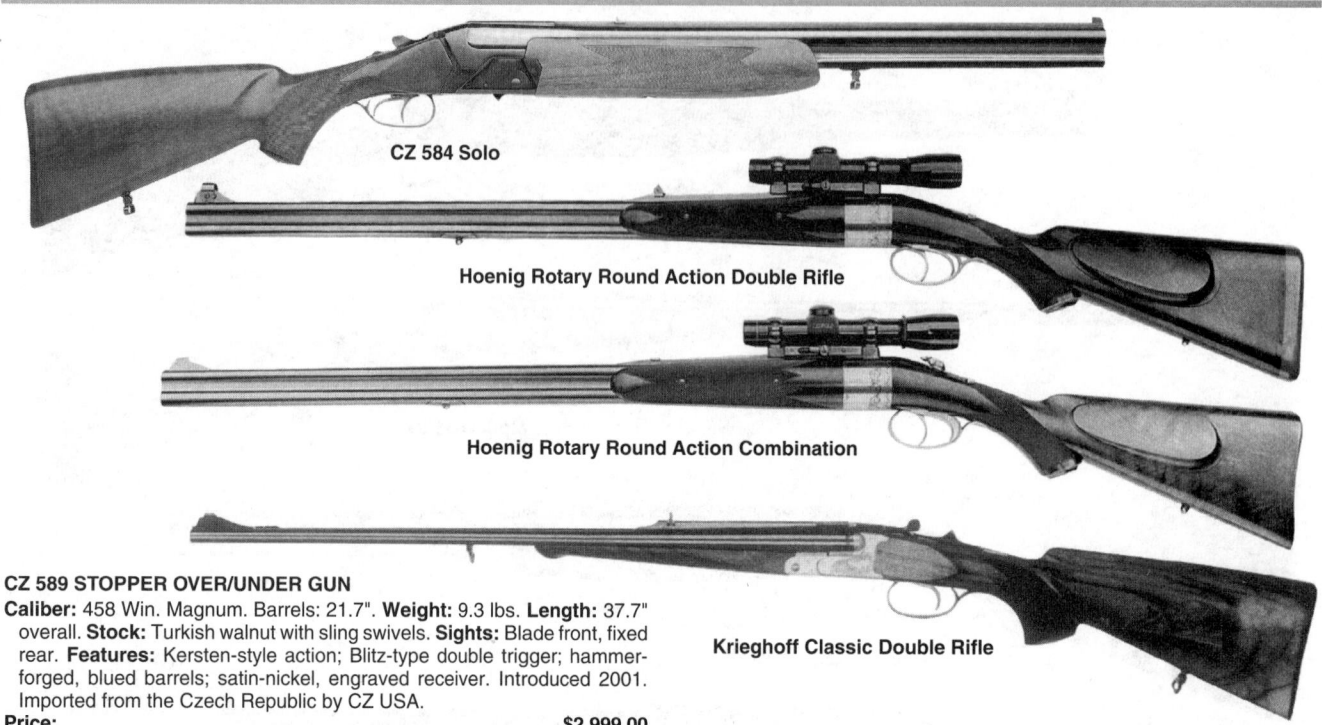

CZ 584 Solo

Hoenig Rotary Round Action Double Rifle

Hoenig Rotary Round Action Combination

Krieghoff Classic Double Rifle

CZ 589 STOPPER OVER/UNDER GUN
Caliber: 458 Win. Magnum. **Barrels:** 21.7". **Weight:** 9.3 lbs. **Length:** 37.7" overall. **Stock:** Turkish walnut with sling swivels. **Sights:** Blade front, fixed rear. **Features:** Kersten-style action; Blitz-type double trigger; hammer-forged, blued barrels; satin-nickel, engraved receiver. Introduced 2001. Imported from the Czech Republic by CZ USA.
Price: **$2,999.00**
Price: Fully engraved model **$3,999.00**

DAKOTA DOUBLE RIFLE
Caliber: 470 Nitro Express, 500 Nitro Express. **Barrel:** 25". **Stock:** Exhibition-grade walnut. **Sights:** Express-style. **Features:** Round action; selective ejectors; recoil pad; Americase. From Dakota Arms Inc.
Price: **$25,000.00**

EAA/BAIKAL IZH-94 COMBINATION GUN
Caliber/Gauge: 12, 3" chamber; 222 Rem., 223, 5.6x50R, 5.6x55E, 7x57R, 7x65R, 7.62x39, 7.62x51, 308, 7.62x53R, 7.62x54R, 30-06. **Barrel:** 24", 26"; imp., mod. and full choke tubes. **Weight:** 7.28 lbs. **Stock:** Walnut; rubber buttpad. **Sights:** Express-style. **Features:** Hammer-forged barrels with chrome-lined bores; machined receiver; single-selective or double triggers. Imported by European American Armory.
Price: Blued finish **$549.00**
Price: 20 ga./22 LR, 20/22 Mag, 3" **$629.00**

GARBI EXPRESS DOUBLE RIFLE
Caliber: 7x65R, 9.3x74R, 375 H&H. **Barrel:** 24-3/4". **Weight:** 7-3/4 to 8-1/2 lbs. **Length:** 41-1/2" overall. **Stock:** Turkish walnut. **Sights:** Quarter-rib with express sight. **Features:** Side-by-side double; H&H-pattern sidelock ejector with reinforced action, chopper lump barrels of Boehler steel; double triggers; fine scroll and rosette engraving, or full coverage ornamental; coin-finished action. Introduced 1997. Imported from Spain by Wm. Larkin Moore.
Price: **$19,900.00**

HOENIG ROTARY ROUND ACTION DOUBLE RIFLE
Caliber: Most popular calibers from 225 Win. to 9.3x74R. **Barrel:** 22" to 26". **Stock:** English Walnut; to customer specs. **Sights:** Swivel hood front with button release (extra bead stored in trap door gripcap), express-style rear on quarter-rib adjustable for windage and elevation; scope mount. **Features:** Round action opens by rotating barrels, pulling forward. Inertia extractor system, rotary safety blocks strikers. Single lever quick-detachable scope mount. Simple takedown without removing forend. Introduced 1997. Made in U.S.A. by George Hoenig.
Price: **$25,000.00**

HOENIG ROTARY ROUND ACTION COMBINATION
Caliber: 28 ga. **Barrel:** 26". **Weight:** 7 lbs. **Stock:** English Walnut to customer specs. **Sights:** Front ramp with button release blades. Foldable

aperture tang sight windage and elevation adjustable. Quarter-rib with scope mount. **Features:** Round action opens by rotating barrels, pulling forward. Inertia extractor; rotary safety blocks strikers. Simple takedown without removing forend. Made in U.S.A. by George Hoenig.
Price: **$25,000.00**

KRIEGHOFF CLASSIC DOUBLE RIFLE
Caliber: 7x57R, 7x65R, 308 Win., 30-06, 8x57 JRS, 8x75RS, 9.3x74R, 375NE, 500/416NE, 470NE, 500NE. **Barrel:** 23.5". **Weight:** 7.3 to 8 lbs; 10-11 lbs. Big 5. **Stock:** High grade European walnut. Standard model has conventional rounded cheekpiece, Bavaria model has Bavarian-style cheekpiece. **Sights:** Bead front with removable, adjustable wedge (375 H&H and below), standing leaf rear on quarter-rib. **Features:** Boxlock action; double triggers; short opening angle for fast loading; quiet extractors; sliding, self-adjusting wedge for secure bolting; Purdey-style barrel extension; horizontal firing pin placement. Many options available. Introduced 1997. Imported from Germany by Krieghoff International.
Price: With small Arabesque engraving **$8,950.00**
Price: With engraved sideplates **$12,300.00**
Price: For extra barrels **$5,450.00**
Price: Extra 20-ga., 28" shotshell barrels **$3,950.00**

Krieghoff Classic Big Five Double Rifle
Similar to the standard Classic except available in 375 Flanged Mag. N.E., 500/416 N.E., 470 N.E., 500 N.E. Has hinged front trigger, non-removable muzzle wedge (models larger than 375 caliber), Universal Trigger System, Combi Cocking Device, steel trigger guard, specially weighted stock bolt for weight and balance. Many options available. Introduced 1997. Imported from Germany by Krieghoff International. Imperial Model introduced 2006.
Price: **$11,450.00**
Price: With engraved sideplates **$14,800.00**

LEBEAU-COURALLY EXPRESS RIFLE SxS
Caliber: 7x65R, 8x57JRS, 9.3x74R, 375 H&H, 470 N.E. **Barrel:** 24" to 26". **Weight:** 7-3/4 to 10-1/2 lbs. **Stock:** Fancy French walnut with cheekpiece. **Sights:** Bead on ramp front, standing left express rear on quarter-rib. **Features:** Holland & Holland-type sidelock with automatic ejectors; double triggers. Built to order only. Imported from Belgium by Wm. Larkin Moore.
Price: **$41,000.00**

DRILLINGS, COMBINATION GUNS, DOUBLE GUNS

Merkel 96K Engraved

Merkel 140-1

Rizzini Express

Savage 24F Combination

Springfield M6 Scout

MERKEL DRILLINGS
Caliber/Gauge: 12, 20, 3" chambers, 16, 2-3/4" chambers; 22 Hornet, 5.6x50R Mag., 5.6x52R, 222 Rem., 243 Win., 6.5x55, 6.5x57R, 7x57R, 7x65R, 308, 30-06, 8x57JRS, 9.3x74R, 375 H&H. **Barrel:** 25.6". **Weight:** 7.9 to 8.4 lbs. depending upon caliber. **Stock:** Oil-finished walnut with pistol grip; cheekpiece on 12-, 16-gauge. **Sights:** Blade front, fixed rear. **Features:** Double barrel locking lug with Greener cross bolt; scroll-engraved, case-hardened receiver; automatic trigger safety; Blitz action; double triggers. Imported from Germany by GSI.
Price: Model 96K (manually cocked rifle system), from **$7,495.00**
Price: Model 96K Engraved (hunting series on receiver) **$8,595.00**

MERKEL BOXLOCK DOUBLE RIFLES
Caliber: 5.6x52R, 243 Winchester, 6.5x55, 6.5x57R, 7x57R, 7x65R, 308 Winchester, 30-06 Springfield, 8x57 IRS, 9.3x74R. **Barrel:** 23.6". **Weight:** 7.7 oz. **Length:** NA. **Stock:** Walnut, oil finished, pistol grip. **Sights:** Fixed 100 meter. **Features:** Anson & Deely boxlock action with cocking indicators, double triggers, engraved color case-hardened receiver. Introduced 1995. Imported from Germany by GSI.
Price: Model 140-1, from **$6,695.00**
Price: Model 140-1.1 (engraved silver-gray receiver), from **$7,795.00**

RIZZINI EXPRESS 90L DOUBLE RIFLE
Caliber: 30-06, 7x65R, 9.3x74R. **Barrel:** 24". **Weight:** 7-1/2 lbs. **Length:** 40" overall. **Stock:** Select European walnut with satin oil finish; English-style cheekpiece. **Sights:** Ramp front, quarter-rib with express sight. **Features:** Color case-hardened boxlock action; automatic ejectors; single selective trigger; polished blue barrels. Extra 20 gauge shotgun barrels available. Imported for Italy by Wm. Larkin Moore.
Price: With case **$3,850.00**

SAVAGE 24F PREDATOR O/U COMBINATION GUN
Caliber/Gauge: 22 Hornet, 223, 30-30 over 12 (24F-12) or 22 LR, 22 Hornet, 223, 30-30 over 20 ga. (24F-20); 3" chambers. **Action:** Takedown, low rebounding visible hammer. Single trigger, barrel selector spur on hammer. **Barrel:** 24" separated barrels; 12 ga. has mod. choke tubes, 20 ga. has fixed Mod. choke. **Weight:** 8 lbs. **Length:** 40-1/2" overall. **Stock:** Black Rynite composition. **Sights:** Blade front, rear open adjustable for elevation. **Features:** Introduced 1989.
Price: 24F-12 . . . . **$661.00**
Price: 24F-20 **$628.00**

SPRINGFIELD ARMORY M6 SCOUT RIFLE/SHOTGUN
Caliber/Gauge: 22 LR or 22 Hornet over 410 bore. **Barrel:** 18.25". **Weight:** 4 lbs. **Length:** 32" overall. **Stock:** Folding detachable with storage for 15 22 LR, four 410 shells. **Sights:** Blade front, military aperture for 22; V-notch for 410. **Features:** All metal construction. Designed for quick disassembly and minimum maintenance. Folds for compact storage. Introduced 1982; reintroduced 1996. Imported from the Czech Republic by Springfield Armory.
Price: Parkerized **$185.00**
Price: Stainless steel **$219.00**

Designs for hunting, utility and sporting purposes, including training for competition.

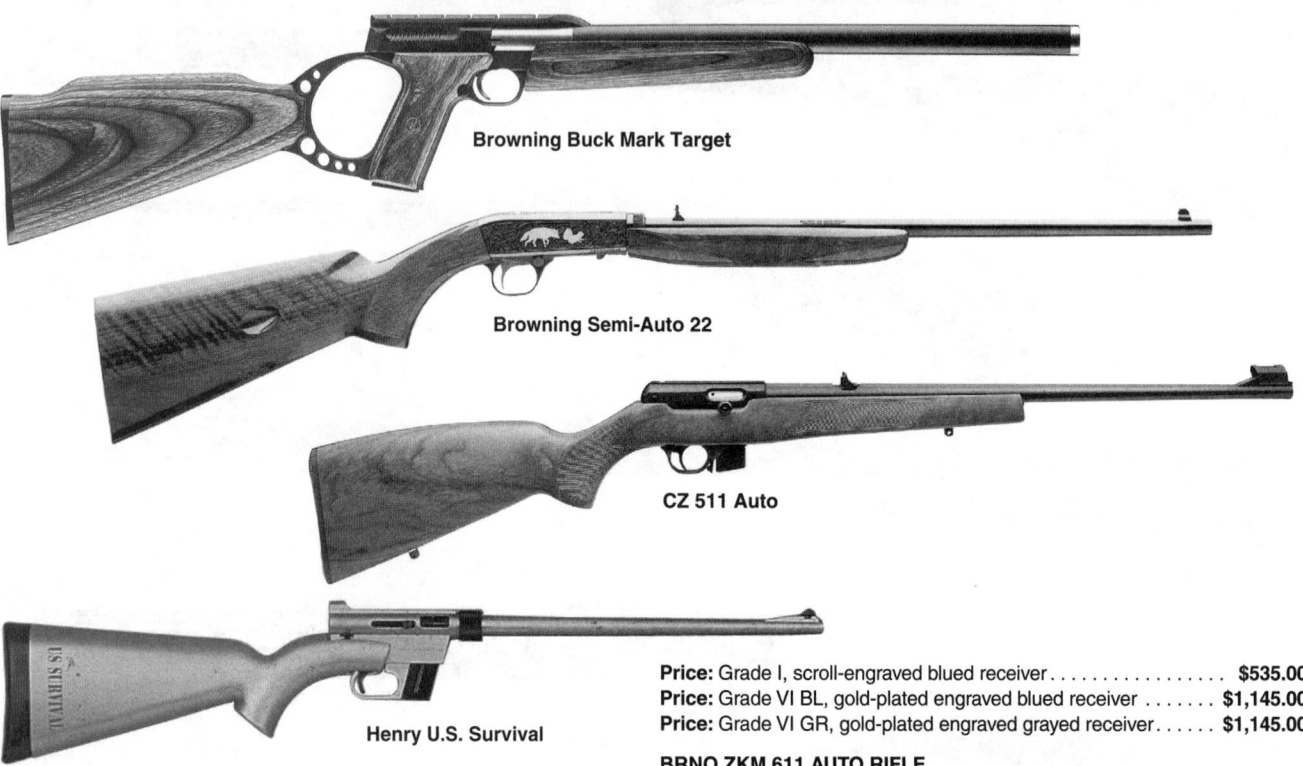

Browning Buck Mark Target

Browning Semi-Auto 22

CZ 511 Auto

Henry U.S. Survival

AR-7 EXPLORER CARBINE

Caliber: 22 LR, 8-shot magazine. **Barrel:** 16". **Weight:** 2-1/2 lbs. **Length:** 34-1/2", 16-1/2" stowed. **Stock:** Molded Cycolac; snap-on rubber buttpad. **Sights:** Square blade front, aperture rear. **Features:** Takedown design stores barrel and action in hollow stock. Light enough to float. Reintroduced 1999. From AR-7 Industries, LLC.
Price: Black matte finish $150.00
Price: AR-20 Sporter (tubular stock, barrel shroud) $200.00
Price: AR-7 camo- or walnut-finish stock $164.95

BROWNING BUCK MARK SEMI-AUTO RIFLES

Caliber: 22 LR, 10+1. **Action:** A rifle version of the Buck Mark Pistol; straight blowback action; machined aluminum receiver with integral rail scope mount; manual thumb safety. **Barrel:** Recessed crowns. **Stock:** Stock and forearm with full pistol grip. **Features:** Action lock provided. Introduced 2001. Four model name variations for 2006, as noted below. **Sights:** FLD Target, FLD Carbon, and Target models have integrated scope rails. Sporter has Truglo/Marble fiber optic sights. Imported from Japan by Browning.
Price: FLD Target, 5.5 lbs., bull barrel, laminated stock $589.00
Price: FLD Carbon, 3.6 lbs., carbon composite barrel $652.00
Price: Target, 5.4 lbs., blued bull barrel, wood stock............ $572.00
Price: Sporter, 4.4 lbs., blued sporter barrel w/sights........... $572.00

BROWNING SEMI-AUTO 22 RIFLE

Caliber: 22 LR, 11+1. **Barrel:** 16.25". **Weight:** 5.2 lbs. **Length:** 37" overall. **Stock:** Checkered select walnut with pistol grip and semi-beavertail forend. **Sights:** Gold bead front, folding leaf rear. **Features:** Engraved receiver with polished blue finish; cross-bolt safety; tubular magazine in buttstock; easy takedown for carrying or storage. The Grade VI is available with either grayed or blued receiver with extensive engraving with gold-plated animals: right side pictures a fox and squirrel in a woodland scene; left side shows a beagle chasing a rabbit. On top is a portrait of the beagle. Stock and forend are of high-grade walnut with a double-bordered cut checkering design. Introduced 1987. Imported from Japan by Browning.

Price: Grade I, scroll-engraved blued receiver $535.00
Price: Grade VI BL, gold-plated engraved blued receiver $1,145.00
Price: Grade VI GR, gold-plated engraved grayed receiver...... $1,145.00

BRNO ZKM 611 AUTO RIFLE

Caliber: 22 WMR, 6- or 10-shot magazine. **Barrel:** 20.4". **Weight:** 5.9 lbs. **Length:** 38.9" overall. **Stock:** European walnut. **Sights:** Hooded blade front, open adjustable rear. **Features:** Removable box magazine; polished blue finish; cross-bolt safety; grooved receiver for scope mounting; easy takedown for storage. Imported from The Czech Republic by Euro-Imports.
Price: $475.00

CZ 511 AUTO RIFLE

Caliber: 22 LR, 8-shot magazine. **Barrel:** 22.2". **Weight:** 5.39 lbs. **Length:** 38.6" overall. **Stock:** Walnut with checkered pistol grip. **Sights:** Hooded front, adjustable rear. **Features:** Polished blue finish; detachable magazine; sling swivel studs. Imported from the Czech Republic by CZ-USA.
Price: $351.00

HENRY U.S. SURVIVAL RIFLE .22

Caliber: 22 LR, 8-shot magazine. **Barrel:** 16" steel lined. **Weight:** 2.5 lbs. **Stock:** ABS plastic. **Sights:** Blade front on ramp, aperture rear. **Features:** Takedown design stores barrel and action in hollow stock. Light enough to float. Silver, black or camo finish. Comes with two magazines. Introduced 1998. From Henry Repeating Arms Co.
Price: $205.00

MARLIN MODEL 60 AUTO RIFLE

Caliber: 22 LR, 14-shot tubular magazine. **Barrel:** 19" round tapered. **Weight:** About 5-1/2 lbs. **Length:** 37-1/2" overall. **Stock:** Press-checkered, walnut-finished Maine birch with Monte Carlo, full pistol grip; Mar-Shield® finish. **Sights:** Ramp front, open adjustable rear. **Features:** Matted receiver is grooved for scope mount. Manual bolt hold-open; automatic last-shot bolt hold-open. Model 60C is similar except has hardwood Monte Carlo stock with Mossy Oak Break-Up camouflage pattern. From Marlin.
Price: $200.00
Price: With 4x scope $208.00
Price: (Model 60C camo) $236.00
Price: (Model 60DL walnut tone finish) $236.00

RIMFIRE RIFLES — Autoloaders

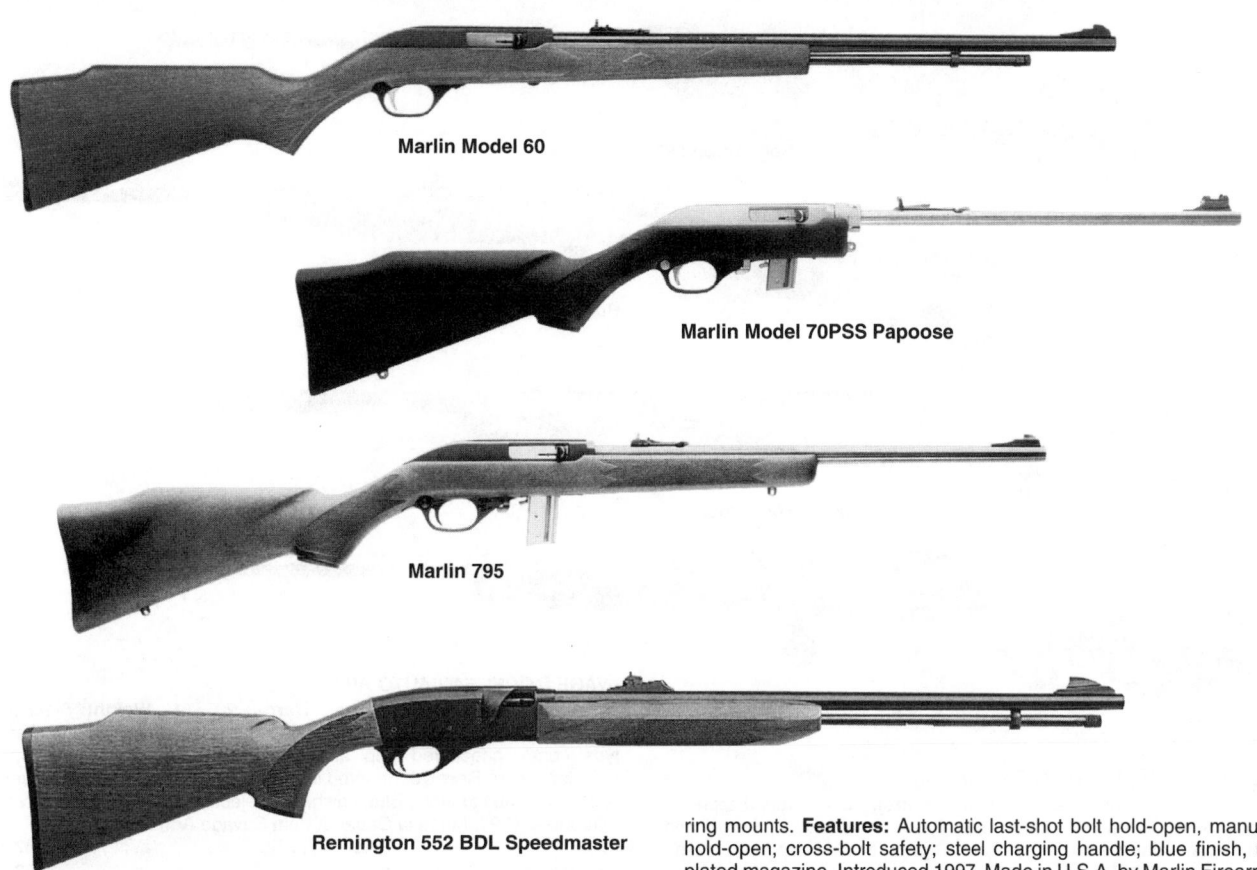

Marlin Model 60

Marlin Model 70PSS Papoose

Marlin 795

Remington 552 BDL Speedmaster

Marlin Model 60SS Self-Loading Rifle

Same as the Model 60 except breech bolt, barrel and outer magazine tube are made of stainless steel; most other parts are either nickel-plated or coated to match the stainless finish. Monte Carlo stock is of black/gray Maine birch laminate, and has nickel-plated swivel studs, rubber buttpad. Introduced 1993. From Marlin.

Price: **$318.00**
Price: Model 60SSK (black fiberglass-filled stock) **$269.00**
Price: Model 60SB (walnut-finished birch stock) **$235.00**
Price: Model 60SB with 4x scope **$270.00**

MARLIN 70PSS PAPOOSE STAINLESS RIFLE

Caliber: 22 LR, 7-shot magazine. **Barrel:** 16-1/4" stainless steel, Micro-Groove® rifling. **Weight:** 3-1/4 lbs. **Length:** 35-1/4" overall. **Stock:** Black fiberglass-filled synthetic with abbreviated forend, nickel-plated swivel studs, molded-in checkering. **Sights:** Ramp front with orange post, cut-away Wide Scan™ hood; adjustable open rear. Receiver grooved for scope mounting. **Features:** Takedown barrel; cross-bolt safety; manual bolt hold-open; last shot bolt hold-open; comes with padded carrying case. Introduced 1986. Made in U.S.A. by Marlin.

Price: **$318.00**

MARLIN MODEL 717M2 17 MACH 2 RIFLE

Caliber: 17 Mach 2, 7-shot. **Barrel:** 22" sporter. **Weight:** 5.5 lbs. **Length:** 37". **Stock:** Walnut-finished hardwood stock. **Sights:** Adjustable open rear, ramp front, grooved for scope mount. **Features:** Swivel studs, cross-bolt safety. Similar in design to 917 series bolt guns.

Price: 717M2 .... **$264.00**

MARLIN MODEL 7000 AUTO RIFLE

Caliber: 22 LR, 10-shot magazine **Barrel:** 18" heavy target with 12-groove Micro-Groove® rifling, recessed muzzle. **Weight:** 5-1/2 lbs. **Length:** 37" overall. **Stock:** Black fiberglass-filled synthetic with Monte Carlo combo, swivel studs, molded-in checkering. **Sights:** None furnished; comes with

ring mounts. **Features:** Automatic last-shot bolt hold-open, manual bolt hold-open; cross-bolt safety; steel charging handle; blue finish, nickel-plated magazine. Introduced 1997. Made in U.S.A. by Marlin Firearms Co.

Price: **$263.00**

MARLIN MODEL 795 AUTO RIFLE

Caliber: 22. **Barrel:** 18" with 16-groove Micro-Groove® rifling. Ramp front sight, adjustable rear. Receiver grooved for scope mount. **Stock:** Black synthetic. **Features:** 10-round magazine, last shot hold-open feature. Introduced 1997. SS is similar to Model 795 excapt stainless steel barrel. Most other parts nickel-plated. Adjustable folding semi-buckhorn rear sights, ramp front high-visibility post and removeable cutaway wide scan hood. Made in U.S.A. by Marlin Firearms Co.

Price: 795 .... **$172.00**
Price: 795SS **$255.00**

REMINGTON MODEL 552 BDL DELUXE SPEEDMASTER RIFLE

Caliber: 22 S (20), L (17) or LR (15) tubular mag. **Barrel:** 21" round tapered. **Weight:** 5-3/4 lbs. **Length:** 40" overall. **Stock:** Walnut. Checkered grip and forend. **Sights:** Big game. **Features:** Positive cross-bolt safety, receiver grooved for tip-off mount.

Price: **$393.00**

REMINGTON 597 AUTO RIFLE

Caliber: 22 LR, 10-shot clip. **Barrel:** 20". **Weight:** 5-1/2 lbs. **Length:** 40" overall. **Stock:** Black synthetic. **Sights:** Big game. **Features:** Matte black finish, nickel-plated bolt. Receiver is grooved and drilled and tapped for scope mounts. Introduced 1997. Made in U.S.A. by Remington.

Price: **$169.00**
Price: Model 597 Magnum, 22 WMR, 8-shot clip **$335.00**
Price: Model 597 LSS (laminated stock, stainless) **$279.00**
Price: Model 597 SS
(22 LR, stainless steel, black synthetic stock) **$224.00**
Price: Model 597 LS heavy barrel (22 LR, laminated stock) **$265.00**
Price: Model 597 Magnum LS heavy barrel
(22 WMR, lam. stock) **$399.00**
Price: Model 597 Magnum 17 HMR, 8-shot clip **$361.00**

Remington 597

Ruger 10/22 Deluxe Sporter

Ruger 10/22 Target

Savage Model 64FV

RUGER 10/22 AUTOLOADING CARBINE

Caliber: 22 LR, 10-shot rotary magazine. **Barrel:** 18-1/2" round tapered. **Weight:** 5 lbs. **Length:** 37-1/4" overall. **Stock:** American hardwood with pistol grip and barrel band or synthetic. **Sights:** Brass bead front, folding leaf rear adjustable for elevation. **Features:** Detachable rotary magazine fits flush into stock, cross-bolt safety, receiver tapped and grooved for scope blocks or tip-off mount. Scope base adaptor furnished with each rifle.
Price: Model 10/22 RB (blue) **$250.00**
Price: Model K10/22RB (bright finish stainless barrel) **$295.00**
Price: Model 10/22RPF (blue, synthetic stock) **$250.00**
Price: Model 10/22CRR Compact RB (blued), intr. 2006 . . . . **$275.00**

Ruger 10/22 Deluxe Sporter
Same as 10/22 Carbine except walnut stock with hand checkered pistol grip and forend; straight buttplate, no barrel band, has sling swivels.
Price: Model 10/22 DSP **$314.00**

Ruger 10/22T Target Rifle
Similar to the 10/22 except has 20" heavy, hammer-forged barrel with tight chamber dimensions, improved trigger pull, laminated hardwood stock dimensioned for optical sights. No iron sights supplied. Introduced 1996. Made in U.S.A. by Sturm, Ruger & Co.
Price: 10/22T **$432.00**
Price: K10/22T, stainless steel **$480.00**
Price: K10/22RR, 20" bbl. **$275.00**

Ruger K10/22RPF All-Weather Rifle
Similar to the stainless K10/22/RB except has black composite stock of thermoplastic polyester resin reinforced with fiberglass; checkered grip and forend. Brushed satin, natural metal finish with clear hardcoat finish. Weighs 5 lbs., measures 36-3/4" overall. Introduced 1997. From Sturm, Ruger & Co.
Price: **$295.00**

RUGER 10/22 MAGNUM AUTOLOADING CARBINE

Caliber: 22 WMR, 9-shot rotary magazine. **Barrel:** 18-1/2". **Weight:** 6 lbs. **Length:** 37-1/4" overall. **Stock:** Birch. **Sights:** Gold bead front, folding rear. **Features:** All-steel receiver has integral Ruger scope bases for the included 1" rings. Introduced 1999. Made in U.S.A. by Sturm, Ruger & Co.
Price: 10/22RBM **$536.00**

SAVAGE MODEL 64G AUTO RIFLE

Caliber: 22 LR, 10-shot magazine. **Barrel:** 20", 21". **Weight:** 5-1/2 lbs. **Length:** 40", 41". **Stock:** Walnut-finished hardwood with Monte Carlo-type comb, checkered grip and forend. **Sights:** Bead front, open adjustable rear. Receiver grooved for scope mounting. **Features:** Thumb-operated rotating safety. Blue finish. Side ejection, bolt hold-open device. Introduced 1990. Made in Canada, from Savage Arms.
Price: **$162.00**
Price: Model 64FSS, stainless **$202.00**
Price: Model 64F, black synthetic stock **$135.00**
Price: Model 64GXP package gun includes
4x15 scope and mounts **$171.00**
Price: Model 64FXP (black stock, 4x15 scope) **$142.00**
Price: Model 64F Camo **$135.00**

Savage Model 64FV Auto Rifle
Similar to the Model 64F except has heavy 21" barrel with recessed crown; no sights provided, comes with Weaver-style bases. Introduced 1998. Imported from Canada by Savage Arms, Inc.
Price: **$135.00**
Price: Model 64FSS, stainless **$202.00**

TAURUS MODEL 63 RIFLE

Caliber: 22 LR, 10-shot tube-fed magazine. **Barrel:** 23". **Weight:** 72 oz. **Length:** 32-1/2". **Stock:** Hand-fitted walnut-finished hardwood. **Sights:** Adjustable rear, fixed front. **Features:** Manual safety, metal buttplate, can accept Taurus tang sight. Charged and cocked with operating plunger at front of forend. Available in blue or polished stainless steel.
Price: 63 . . . . **$295.00**
Price: 63SS **$311.00**

THOMPSON/CENTER 22 LR CLASSIC RIFLE

Caliber: 22 LR, 8-shot magazine. **Barrel:** 22" match-grade. **Weight:** 5-1/2 pounds. **Length:** 39-1/2" overall. **Stock:** Satin-finished American walnut with Monte Carlo-type comb and pistol gripcap, swivel studs. **Sights:** Ramp-style front and fully adjustable rear, both with fiber optics. **Features:** All-steel receiver drilled and tapped for scope mounting; barrel threaded to receiver; thumb-operated safety; trigger guard safety lock included. New .22 Classic Benchmark TGT target rifle variant has 18" heavy barrel, brown laminated target stock, blued with matte finish, 10-shot magazine and no sights; drilled and tapped.
Price: T/C 22 LR Classic (blue) **$396.00**
Price: T/C 22 LR Classic Benchmark **$505.00**

Classic and modern models for sport and utility, including training.

Browning BL-22

Henry Lever-Action 22

Henry Golden Boy 22

Henry Pump-Action 22

Marlin Model 39A

BROWNING BL-22 and BL-17 RIFLES

Action: Short-throw lever action, side ejection. Rack-and-pinion lever. Tubular magazines, with 15+1 capacity for 22LR or 17M2. **Barrel:** Recessed muzzle. **Stock:** Walnut, two-piece straight grip Western style. **Trigger:** Half-cock hammer safety; fold-down hammer. **Sights:** Bead post front, folding-leaf rear. Steel receiver grooved for scope mount. **Weight:** 5-5.4 lbs. **Length:** 36.75-40.75" overall. **Features:** Action lock provided. Introduced 1996. FLD Grade II Octagon has octagonal 24" barrel, silver nitride receiver with scroll engraving, gold-colored trigger; 17M2 introduced 2005. FLD Grade I has satin-nickel receiver, blued trigger, no stock checkering. FLD Grade II has satin-nickel receivers with scroll engraving; gold-colored trigger, cut checkering. Both introduced 2005. Grade I has blued receiver and trigger, no stock checkering. Grade II has gold-colored trigger, cut checkering, blued receiver with scroll engraving. 17M2 models introduced 2005. Imported from Japan by Browning.

Price: BL-22 Grade I/II . . . . **$462.00 /$524.00**
Price: BL-22 FLD Grade I/II. . . . . **$494.00 /$555.00**
Price: BL-22 FLD, Grade II Octagon. **$726.00**
Price: BL-17 Grade I/II . . . . **$484.00 /$546.00**
Price: BL-17 FLD Grade I/II. . . . . **$516.00 /$577.00**
Price: BL-17 FLD, Grade II Octagon. **$748.00**

HENRY LEVER-ACTION 22

Caliber: 22 Long Rifle (15-shot). **Barrel:** 18-1/4" round. **Weight:** 5-1/2 lbs. **Length:** 34" overall. **Stock:** Walnut. **Sights:** Hooded blade front, open adjustable rear. **Features:** Polished blue finish; full-length tubular magazine; side ejection; receiver grooved for scope mounting. Introduced 1997. Made in U.S.A. by Henry Repeating Arms Co.

Price: **$279.95**
Price: Youth model (33" overall, 11-round 22 LR) **$279.95**

HENRY GOLDEN BOY 22 LEVER-ACTION RIFLE

Caliber: 22 LR, 22 Magnum, 16-shot. **Barrel:** 20" octagonal. **Weight:** 6.25 lbs. **Length:** 38" overall. **Stock:** American walnut. **Sights:** Blade front, open rear. **Features:** Brasslite receiver, brass buttplate, blued barrel and lever. Introduced 1998. Made in U.S.A. from Henry Repeating Arms Co.

Price: **$409.95**
Price: Magnum **$485.00**

HENRY PUMP-ACTION 22 PUMP RIFLE

Caliber: 22 LR, 15-shot. **Barrel:** 18.25". **Weight:** 5.5 lbs. **Length:** NA. **Stock:** American walnut. **Sights:** Bead on ramp front, open adjustable rear. **Features:** Polished blue finish; receiver groved for scope mount; grooved slide handle; two barrel bands. Introduced 1998. Made in U.S.A. from Henry Repeating Arms Co.

Price: **$309.95**

MARLIN MODEL 39A GOLDEN LEVER-ACTION RIFLE

Caliber: 22, S (26), L (21), LR (19), tubular mag. **Barrel:** 24" Micro-Groove®. **Weight:** 6-1/2 lbs. **Length:** 40" overall. **Stock:** Checkered American black walnut; Mar-Shield® finish. Swivel studs; rubber buttpad. **Sights:** Bead ramp front with detachable Wide-Scan™ hood, folding rear semi-buckhorn adjustable for windage and elevation. **Features:** Hammer block safety; rebounding hammer. Takedown action, receiver tapped for scope mount (supplied), offset hammer spur, gold-colored steel trigger. From Marlin Firearms.

Price: **$552.00**

Remington Model 572 BDL Deluxe Fieldmaster

Ruger Model 96/22

Ruger Model 96/17

Taurus 62R

Taurus 72C-SS

REMINGTON 572 BDL DELUXE FIELDMASTER PUMP RIFLE

Caliber: 22 S (20), L (17) or LR (15), tubular mag. **Barrel:** 21" round tapered. **Weight:** 5-1/2 lbs. **Length:** 40" overall. **Stock:** Walnut with checkered pistol grip and slide handle. **Sights:** Big game. **Features:** Cross-bolt safety; removing inner magazine tube converts rifle to single shot; receiver grooved for tip-off scope mount.
Price: **$407.00**

RUGER MODEL 96 LEVER-ACTION RIFLE

Caliber: 22 WMR, 9 rounds; 44 Magnum, 4 rounds; 17 HMR 9 rounds. **Barrel:** 18-1/2". **Weight:** 5-1/4 lbs. **Length:** 37-1/4" overall. **Stock:** Hardwood. **Sights:** Gold bead front, folding leaf rear. **Features:** Sliding cross button safety, visible cocking indicator; short-throw lever action. Introduced 1996. Made in U.S.A. by Sturm, Ruger & Co.
Price: 96/22M (22 WMR)...................................... **$390.00**
Price: 96/22M (44 Mag.)...................................... **$546.00**
Price: 96/17M (17 HMR) **$390.00**

TAURUS MODEL 62 PUMP RIFLE

Caliber: 22 LR, 12- or 13-shot. **Barrel:** 16-1/2" or 23" round. **Weight:** 72 oz. to 80 oz. **Length:** 39" overall. **Stock:** Premium hardwood. **Sights:** Adjustable rear, bead blade front, optional tang. **Features:** Blue, case hardened or stainless, bolt-mounted safety, pump action, manual firing pin block, integral security lock system. Imported from Brazil by Taurus International.
Price: M62C (blue) **$280.00**
Price: M62C-CH (case-hardened, blue) **$280.00**
Price: M62CCH-T (case-hardened, blue) **$358.00**
Price: M62C-SS (stainless steel) **$295.00**
Price: M62CSS-T (stainless steel) **$373.00**
Price: M62C-SS-Y (stainless steel) **$327.00**

Price: M62C-T (blue) **$358.00**
Price: M62C-Y (blue) **$311.00**
Price: M62R (blue) **$280.00**
Price: M62R-CH (case-hardened, blue) **$280.00**
Price: M62RCH-T (case-hardened, blue) **$358.00**
Price: M62R-SS (stainless steel) **$295.00**
Price: M62RSS-T (stainless steel) **$373.00**
Price: M62R-T (blue) **$358.00**

Taurus Model 72 Pump Rifle

Same as Model 62 except chambered in 22 Magnum or .17 HMR; 16-1/2" bbl. holds 10-12 shots, 23" bbl. holds 11-13 shots. Weighs 72 oz. to 80 oz. Introduced 2001. Imported from Brazil by Taurus International.
Price: M72C (blue) **$295.00**
Price: M72C-CH (case-hardened, blue) **$295.00**
Price: M72CCH-T (case-hardened, blue) **$373.00**
Price: M72C-SS (stainless steel) **$311.00**
Price: M72CSS-T (stainless steel) **$389.00**
Price: M72C-T (blue) **$373.00**
Price: M72R (blue) **$295.00**
Price: M72R-CH (case-hardened, blue) **$295.00**
Price: M72RCH-T (case-hardened, blue) **$373.00**
Price: M72R-SS (stainless steel) **$311.00**
Price: M72RSS-T (stainless steel) **$389.00**
Price: M72R-T (blue) **$373.00**

Includes models for a variety of sports, utility and competitive shooting.

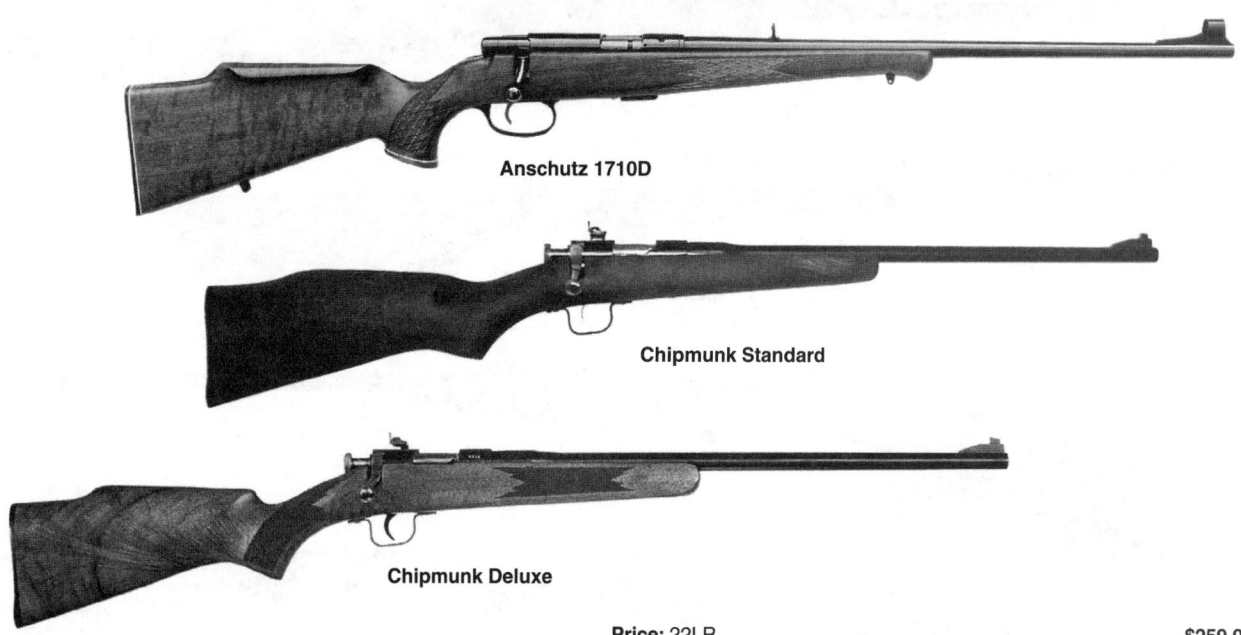

Anschutz 1710D

Chipmunk Standard

Chipmunk Deluxe

ANSCHUTZ 1416D/1516D CLASSIC RIFLES
Caliber: 22 LR (1416D), 5-shot clip; 22 WMR (1516D), 4-shot clip. **Barrel:** 22-1/2". **Weight:** 6 lbs. **Length:** 41" overall. **Stock:** European hardwood with walnut finish; classic style with straight comb, checkered pistol grip and forend. **Sights:** Hooded ramp front, folding leaf rear. **Features:** Uses Match 64 action. Adjustable single stage trigger. Receiver grooved for scope mounting. Imported from Germany by AcuSport Corp.
Price: 1416D, 22 LR **$755.95**
Price: 1516D, 22 WMR **$779.95**
Price: 1416D Classic left-hand **$679.95**

Anschutz 1416D/1516D Walnut Luxus Rifles
Similar to the Classic models except have European walnut stocks with Monte Carlo cheekpiece, slim forend with Schnabel tip, cut checkering on grip and forend. Introduced 1997. Imported from Germany by AcuSport Corp.
Price: 1416D (22 LR) **$755.95**
Price: 1516D (22 WMR) **$779.95**

ANSCHUTZ 1518D LUXUS BOLT-ACTION RIFLE
Caliber: 22 WMR, 4-shot magazine. **Barrel:** 19-3/4". **Weight:** 5-1/2 lbs. **Length:** 37-1/2" overall. **Stock:** European walnut. **Sights:** Blade on ramp front, folding leaf rear. **Features:** Receiver grooved for scope mounting; single stage trigger; skip-line checkering; rosewood forend tip; sling swivels. Imported from Germany by AcuSport Corp.
Price: **$1,186.95**

ANSCHUTZ 1710D CUSTOM RIFLE
Caliber: 22 LR, 5-shot clip. **Barrel:** 24-1/4". **Weight:** 7-3/8 lbs. **Length:** 42-1/2" overall. **Stock:** Select European walnut. **Sights:** Hooded ramp front, folding leaf rear; drilled and tapped for scope mounting. **Features:** Match 54 action with adjustable single-stage trigger; roll-over Monte Carlo cheekpiece, slim forend with Schnabel tip, Wundhammer palm swell on pistol grip, rosewood gripcap with white diamond insert; skip-line checkering on grip and forend. Introduced 1988. Imported from Germany by AcuSport Corp.
Price: **$1,289.95**

CHARLES DALY SUPERIOR II RIMFIRE RIFLE
Caliber: 22LR, 22MRF, 17HRM. **Barrel:** 22". **Weight:** 6 pounds. **Sights:** None. Drilled and tapped for scope mounts. **Features:** Manufactured by Zastava. Walnut stock, two-position safety; 5-round magazine capacity. Introduced 2005.

Price: 22LR **$259.00**
Price: 22WMR **$299.00**
Price: 17HMR **$334.00**

CHIPMUNK SINGLE SHOT RIFLE
Caliber: 22 LR, 22 WMR, single shot. **Barrel:** 16-1/8". **Weight:** About 2-1/2 lbs. **Length:** 30" overall. **Stocks:** American walnut. **Sights:** Post on ramp front, peep rear adjustable for windage and elevation. **Features:** Drilled and tapped for scope mounting using special Chipmunk base ($13.95). Engraved model also available. Made in U.S.A. Introduced 1982. From Rogue Rifle Co., Inc.
Price: Standard **$194.25**
Price: Standard 22 WMR **$209.95**
Price: Deluxe (better wood, checkering) **$246.95**
Price: Deluxe 22 WMR **$262.95**
Price: Laminated stock **$209.95**
Price: Laminated stock, 22 WMR **$225.95**
Price: Bull barrel models of above, add **$16.00**

CHIPMUNK TM (TARGET MODEL)
Caliber: 22 S, L, or LR. **Barrel:** 18" blue. **Weight:** 5 lbs. **Length:** 33". **Stocks:** Walnut with accessory rail. **Sights:** 1/4 minute micrometer adjustable. **Features:** Manually cocking single shot bolt action, blue receiver, adjustable buttplate and buttpad.
Price: **$329.95**

COOPER MODEL 57-M BOLT-ACTION RIFLE
Caliber: 22 LR, 22 WMR, 17 HMR, 17 Mach 2. **Barrel:** 22" or 24" stainless steel or 4140 match grade. **Weight:** 6.5-7.5 lbs. **Stock:** AA-AAA select Claro walnut, 22 lpi hand checkering. **Sights:** None furnished. **Features:** Three rear locking lug, repeating bolt-action with 5-shot mag. for 22 LR and 17M2; 4-shot mag for 22 WMR and 17 HMR. Fully adjustable trigger. Left-hand models add $150 to base rifle price. 1/4"-group rimfire accuracy guarantee at 50 yds.; 1/2"-group centerfire accuracy guarantee at 100 yds. Options include wood upgrades, case-color metalwork, barrel fluting, custom LOP, and many others.
Price: Classic **$1,349.00**
Price: LVT **$1,459.00**
Price: Custom Classic **$1,995.00**
Price: Western Classic **$2,698.00**
Price: TRP-3 (22 LR only, benchrest style) **$1,295.00**
Price: Jackson Squirrel Rifle **$1,498.00**
Price: Jackson Hunter (synthetic) **$1,298.00**

Cooper Model 57 Classic

Cooper Custom Classic

CZ 452 Lux

CZ 452 Varmint

CZ 452 American Classic

Henry "Mini" Bolt 22

CZ 452 LUX BOLT-ACTION RIFLE

Caliber: 22 LR, 22 WMR, 5-shot detachable magazine. **Barrel:** 24.8". **Weight:** 6.6 lbs. **Length:** 42.63" overall. **Stock:** Walnut with checkered pistol grip. **Sights:** Hooded front, fully adjustable tangent rear. **Features:** All-steel construction, adjustable trigger, polished blue finish. Imported from the Czech Republic by CZ-USA.
Price: 22 LR, 22 WMR. **$378.00**

CZ 452 Varmint Rifle

Similar to the Lux model except has heavy 20.8" barrel; stock has beavertail forend; weighs 7 lbs.; no sights furnished. Available only in 22 LR. Imported from the Czech Republic by CZ-USA.
Price: **$407.00**

CZ 452 American Classic Bolt-Action Rifle

Similar to the CZ 452 M 2E Lux except has classic-style stock of Circassian walnut; 22.5" free-floating barrel with recessed target crown;

receiver dovetail for scope mounting. No open sights furnished. Introduced 1999. Imported from the Czech Republic by CZ-USA.
Price: 22 LR, 22 WMR **$420.00**

HARRINGTON & RICHARDSON
ULTRA HEAVY BARREL 22 MAG RIFLE

Caliber: 22 WMR, single shot. **Barrel:** 22" bull. **Stock:** Cinnamon laminated wood with Monte Carlo cheekpiece. **Sights:** None furnished; scope mount rail included. **Features:** Hand-checkered stock and forend; deep-crown rifling; tuned trigger; trigger locking system; hammer extension. Introduced 2001. From H&R 1871 LLC.
Price: **$193.00**

HENRY ACU-BOLT RIFLE

Caliber: 22, 22 Mag., 17HMR; single shot. **Barrel:** 20". **Weight:** 4.15 lbs. **Length:** 36". **Stock:** One-piece fiberglass synthetic. **Sights:** Scope mount and 4x scope included. **Features:** Stainless barrel and receiver, bolt-action.
Price: **$325.00**

HENRY "MINI" BOLT ACTION 22 RIFLE

Caliber: 22 LR, single shot youth gun. **Barrel:** 16" stainless, 8-groove rifling. **Weight:** 3.25 lbs. **Length:** 30", LOP 11-1/2". **Stock:** Synthetic, pistol grip, wraparound checkering and beavertail forearm. **Sights:** William Fire sights. **Features:** One-piece bolt configuration manually operated safety.
Price: **$169.95**

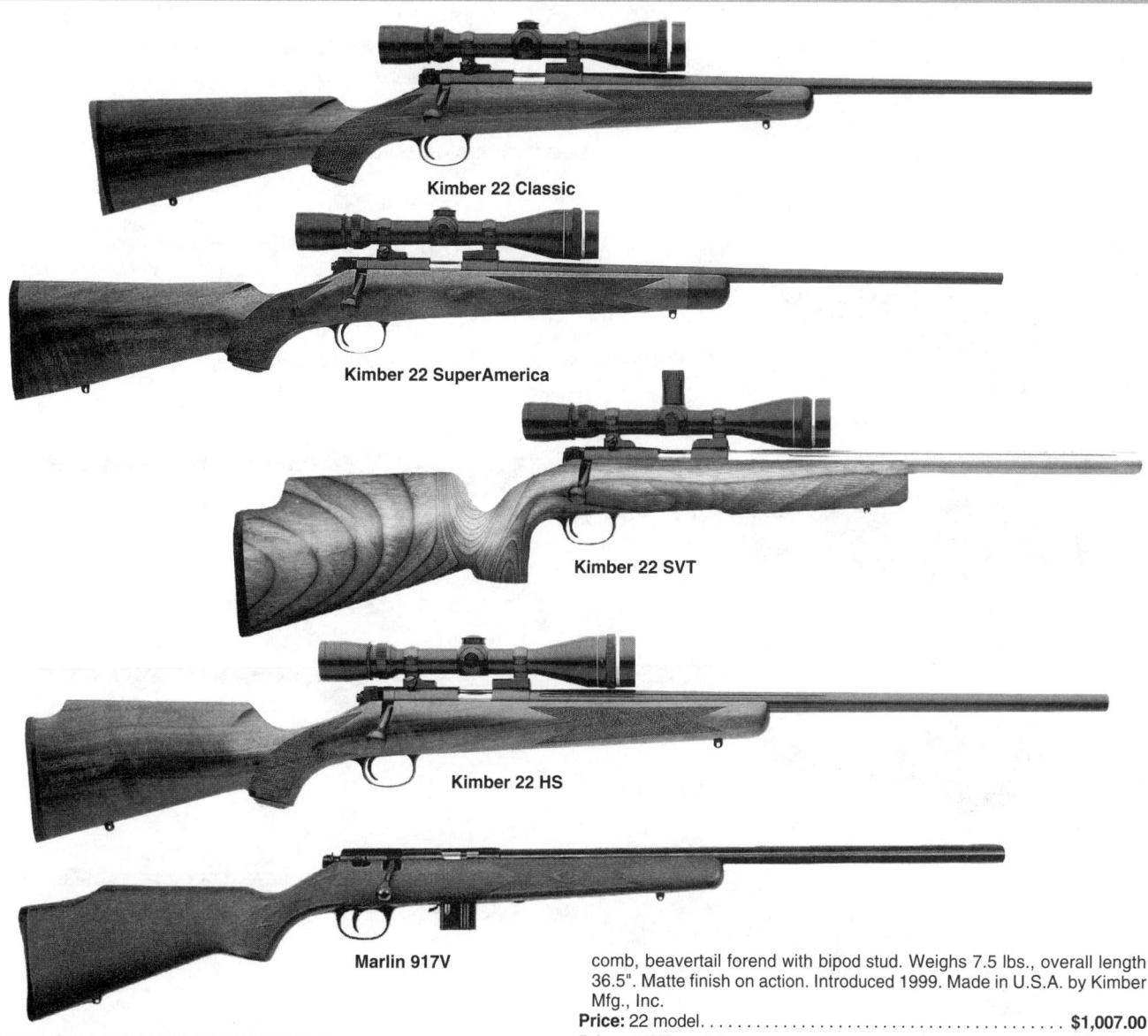

Kimber 22 Classic

Kimber 22 SuperAmerica

Kimber 22 SVT

Kimber 22 HS

Marlin 917V

KIMBER 22 CLASSIC BOLT-ACTION RIFLE

Caliber: 22 LR and 17 Mach 2, 5-shot magazine. **Barrel:** 18", 22", 24" match grade; 11-degree target crown. **Weight:** 5 to 8 lbs. **Length:** 35" to 43". **Stock:** Classic Claro walnut, hand-cut checkering, steel gripcap, swivel studs. **Sights:** None, drilled and tapped. **Features:** All-new action with Mauser-style full-length claw extractor, two-position wing safety, match trigger, pillar-bedded action with recoil lug. Introduced 1999. Made in U.S.A. by Kimber Mfg., Inc.

Price: Classic 22 . . . . $1,147.00
Price: Classic Varmint (22 or17M2) $1,055.00
Price: Hunter (22) $809.00
Price: Hunter (17M2) $846.00

Kimber 22 SuperAmerica Bolt-Action Rifle

Similar to 22 Classic except has AAA Claro walnut stock with wraparound 22 lpi hand-cut checkering, ebony forend tip, beaded cheekpiece. Introduced 1999. Made in U.S.A. by Kimber Mfg., Inc.
Price: $1,865.00

Kimber 22 SVT Bolt-Action Rifle

Similar to 22 Classic except has 18" stainless steel, fluted bull barrel, gray laminated, high-comb target-style stock with deep pistol grip, high comb, beavertail forend with bipod stud. Weighs 7.5 lbs., overall length 36.5". Matte finish on action. Introduced 1999. Made in U.S.A. by Kimber Mfg., Inc.
Price: 22 model $1,007.00
Price: 17M2 model $1,055.00

Kimber 22 HS (Hunter Silhouette) Bolt-Action Rifle

Similar to 22 Classic except 24" medium sporter match-grade barrel with half-fluting; high comb, walnut, Monte Carlo target stock with 18 lpi checkering; matte blue metal finish. Introduced 1999. Made in U.S.A. by Kimber Mfg., Inc.
Price: $915.00

MARLIN MODEL 917/717 17 HMR/17 MACH 2 BOLT-ACTION RIFLES

Caliber: 17 HMR, 17 Mach 2, 7-shot. **Barrel:** 22". **Weight:** 6 lbs., stainless 7 lbs. **Length:** 41". **Stock:** Checkered walnut Monte Carlo SS, laminated black/grey. **Sights:** No sights but receiver grooved. **Features:** Swivel studs, positive thumb safety, red cocking indicator, safety lock, SS 1" brushed aluminum scope rings.

Price: 917 (new version 17 HMR intr. 2006, black synthetic stock) . $269.00
Price: 917V (17 HMR, walnut-finished hardwood stock) $292.00
Price: 917VS (17 HMR, heavy stainless barrel) $433.00
Price: 917VR (17 HMR, intr. 2006, heavy barrel) $282.00
Price: 917VR (17 HMR, heavy stainless fluted barrel) $459.00
Price: 917M2 (17 Mach 2, walnut-finished hardwood stock) $274.00
Price: 917M2S (17 Mach 2, 22" heavy stainless barrel) $410.00

Marlin Model 15YN "Little Buckaroo"

Marlin Model 980S

Marlin 880V

Marlin 925

Marlin 925C

MARLIN MODEL 915YN "LITTLE BUCKAROO"
Caliber: 22 S, L, LR, single shot. **Barrel:** 16-1/4" Micro-Groove®. **Weight:** 4-1/4 lbs. **Length:** 33-1/4" overall. **Stock:** One-piece walnut-finished, press-checkered Maine birch with Monte Carlo; Mar-Shield® finish. **Sights:** Ramp front, adjustable open rear. **Features:** Beginner's rifle with thumb safety, easy-load feed throat, red cocking indicator. Receiver grooved for scope mounting. Introduced 1989.
Price: **$225.00**
Price: 915YS (stainless steel with fire sights) **$255.00**

MARLIN MODEL 980S BOLT-ACTION RIFLE
Caliber: 22 LR, 7-shot clip magazine. **Barrel:** 22" Micro-Groove®. **Weight:** 6 lbs. **Length:** 41" overall. **Stock:** Black fiberglass-filled synthetic with nickel-plated swivel studs and molded-in checkering. **Sights:** Ramp front with orange post and cutaway Wide-Scan™ hood, adjustable semi-buckhorn folding rear. **Features:** Stainless steel barrel, receiver, front breech bolt and striker; receiver grooved for scope mounting. Introduced 1994. Model 880SQ (Squirrel Rifle) is similar but has heavy 22" barrel. Made in U.S.A. by Marlin.
Price: 980S **$349.00**
Price: 980V, heavy target barrel, 7 lbs., no sights. **$349.00**

Marlin Model 981T Bolt-Action Rifle
Same as Marlin 980S except blued steel, tubular magazine, holds 17 Long Rifle cartridges. Weighs 6 lbs.
Price: **$229.00**

Marlin Model 925 Bolt-Action Repeater
Similar to Marlin 980S, except walnut-finished hardwood stock, adjustable open rear sight, ramp front. Weighs 5.5 lbs.
Price: **$229.00**
Price: With 4x scope and mount **$239.00**

Marlin Model 925R Bolt-Action Repeater
Similar to Marlin 925, except Monte Carlo black-fiberglass synthetic stock. Weighs 5.5 lbs. OAL: 41". Introduced 2006.
Price: **$229.00**
Price: With 4x scope and mount **$239.00**

Marlin Model 925C Bolt-Action Repeater
Same as Model 980S except Mossy Oak® Break-Up camouflage stock. Made in U.S.A. by Marlin. Weighs 5.5 lbs.
Price: **$268.00**

Marlin 983T

Ruger K77/22 Varmint

Ruger 77/22R

MARLIN MODEL 982 BOLT-ACTION RIFLE

Caliber: 22 WMR. **Barrel:** 22" Micro-Groove®. **Weight:** 6 lbs. **Length:** 41" overall. **Stock:** Walnut Monte Carlo genuine American black walnut with swivel studs; full pistol grip; classic cut checkering; rubber rifle butt pad; tough Mar-Shield® finish. **Sights:** Adjustable semi-buckhorn folding rear, ramp front sight with brass bead and Wide-Scan™ front sight hood. **Features:** 7-shot clip, thumb safety, red cocking indicator, receiver grooved for scope mount. 982S has stainless steel front breech bolt, barrel, receiver and bolt knob. All other parts are either stainless steel or nickel-plated. Has black Monte Carlo stock of fiberglass-filled polycarbonate with molded-in checkering, nickel-plated swivel studs. Introduced 2005. Model 982S has selected heavy 22" stainless steel barrel with recessed muzzle, and comes without sights; receiver is grooved for scope mount and 1" ring mounts are included. Weighs 7 lbs. Introduced 1997. Made in U.S.A. by Marlin Firearms Co.

Price: 982 . . . . **$341.00**
Price: 982L (laminated hardwood stock, 6.25 lbs). **$361.00**
Price: 982S (stainless parts, 6.25 lbs). **$377.00**
Price: 982VS (heavy stainless barrel, 7 lbs). **$357.00**

Marlin Model 925M/925MC Bolt-Action Rifles

Similar to the Model 982 except chambered for 22 WMR. Has 7-shot clip magazine, 22" Micro-Groove® barrel, checkered walnut-finished Maine birch stock. Introduced 1989.

Price: 925M **$260.00**
Price: 925MC (Mossy Oak Break-Up camouflage stock) **$300.00**

MARLIN MODEL 983 BOLT-ACTION RIFLE

Caliber: 22 WMR. **Barrel:** 22"; 1:16" twist. **Weight:** 6 lbs. **Length:** 41" overall. **Stock:** Walnut Monte Carlo with sling swivel studs, rubber buttpad. **Sights:** Ramp front with brass bead, removable hood; adjustable semi-buckhorn folding rear. **Features:** Thumb safety, red cocking indicator, receiver grooved for scope mount. 983S is same as the Model 983 except front breech bolt, striker knob, trigger stud, cartridge lifter stud and outer magazine tube are of stainless steel; other parts are nickel-plated. Introduced 1993. 983T has a black Monte Carlo fiberglass-filled synthetic stock with sling swivel studs. Introduced 2001.Made in U.S.A. by Marlin Firearms Co.

Price: 983 . . . . **$356.00**
Price: 983S (stainless barrel) **$377.00**
Price: 983T (fiberglass stock) **$273.00**

MEACHAM LOW-WALL RIFLE

Caliber: any rimfire cartridge. **Barrel:** 26-34". **Weight:** 7-15 lbs. **Sights:** none. Tang drilled for Win. base, 3/8 dovetail slot front. **Stock:** Fancy eastern walnut with cheekpiece; ebony insert in forearm tip. **Features:** Exact copy of 1885 Winchester. With most Winchester factory options available including double set triggers. Introduced 1994. Made in U.S.A. by Meacham T&H Inc.

Price: From **$3,899.00**

NEW ENGLAND FIREARMS SPORTSTER™ SINGLE-SHOT RIFLES

Caliber: 22 LR, 22 WMR, 17 HMR, single-shot. **Barrel:** 20". **Weight:** 5-1/2 lbs. **Length:** 36-1/4" overall. **Stock:** Black polymer. **Sights:** None furnished; scope mount included. **Features:** Break open, side-lever release; automatic ejection; recoil pad; sling swivel studs; trigger locking system. Introduced 2001. Made in U.S.A. by New England Firearms.

Price: **$149.00**
Price: Youth model (20" bbl., 33" overall, weighs 5-1/3 lbs.) **$149.00**
Price: Sportster 17 HMR **$180.00**

NEW ULTRA LIGHT ARMS 20RF BOLT-ACTION RIFLE

Caliber: 22 LR, single shot or repeater. **Barrel:** Douglas, length to order. **Weight:** 5-1/4 lbs. **Length:** Varies. **Stock:** Kevlar®/graphite composite, variety of finishes. **Sights:** None furnished; drilled and tapped for scope mount. **Features:** Timney trigger, hand-lapped action, button-rifled barrel, hand-bedded action, recoil pad, sling-swivel studs, optional Jewell trigger. Made in U.S.A. by New Ultra Light Arms.

Price: 20 RF single shot **$800.00**
Price: 20 RF repeater **$850.00**

ROSSI MATCHED PAIR SINGLE-SHOT RIFLE/SHOTGUN

Caliber: 22 LR or 22 Mag. **Barrel:** 18-1/2" or 23". **Weight:** 6 lbs. **Stock:** Hardwood (brown or black finish). **Sights:** Fully adjustable front and rear. **Features:** Break-open breech, transfer-bar manual safety, includes matched 410-, 20 or 12 gauge shotgun barrel with bead front sight. Introduced 2001. Imported by BrazTech/Taurus.

Price: Blue **$139.95**
Price: Stainless steel **$169.95**

RUGER K77/22 VARMINT RIFLE

Caliber: 22 LR, 10-shot, 22 WMR, 9-shot detachable rotary magazine. **Barrel:** 24", heavy. **Weight:** 6-7/8 lbs. **Length:** 43.25" overall. **Stock:** Laminated hardwood with rubber buttpad, quick-detachable swivel studs. **Sights:** None furnished. Comes with Ruger 1" scope rings. **Features:** Stainless steel or blued finish. Three-position safety, dual extractors. Stock has wide, flat forend. Introduced 1993.

Price: K77/22VBZ, 22 LR **$746.00**
Price: K77/22VMBZ, 22 WMR **$746.00**

RUGER 77/22 RIMFIRE BOLT-ACTION RIFLE

Caliber: 22 LR, 10-shot rotary magazine; 22 WMR, 9-shot rotary magazine. **Barrel:** 20". **Weight:** About 6 lbs. **Length:** 39-3/4" overall. **Stock:** Checkered American walnut, laminated hardwood, or synthetic stocks, stainless sling swivels. **Sights:** Plain barrel with 1" Ruger rings. **Features:** Mauser-type action uses Ruger's rotary magazine. Three-position safety, simplified bolt stop, patented bolt locking system. Uses the dual-screw barrel attachment system of the 10/22 rifle. Integral scope mounting system with 1" Ruger rings. Blued model introduced 1983. Stainless steel and blued with synthetic stock introduced 1989.

Price: 77/22R (no sights, rings, walnut stock) **$674.00**
Price: K77/22RP (stainless, no sights, rings, synthetic stock) **$674.00**
Price: 77/22RM (22 WMR, blue, walnut stock) **$674.00**
Price: K77/22RMP (22 WMR, stainless, synthetic stock) **$674.00**

Savage Mark I-G

Savage Mark II-BV

Savage Mark II-FXP

Savage Mark II-FSS

Savage Model 93G

RUGER 77/17 RIMFIRE BOLT-ACTION RIFLE

Caliber: 17HMR (9-shot rotary magazine); 17 Mach 2 (10-shot rotary magazine). **Barrel:** 20" to 24". **Weight:** 6-7.5 lbs. **Length:** 39"-to 41.75" overall. **Stock:** Checkered American walnut, laminated hardwood, or synthetic stocks, stainless sling swivels. **Sights:** Plain barrel with 1" Ruger rings. **Features:** Mauser-type action uses Ruger's rotary magazine. Three-position safety, simplified bolt stop, patented bolt locking system. Uses the dual-screw barrel attachment system of the 10/22 rifle. Integral scope mounting system with 1" Ruger rings. Introduced 2002.

Price: 77/17RM (no sights, rings, walnut stock) **$674.00**
Price: 77/17RMP (stainless, no sights, rings, synthetic stock) **$674.00**
Price: K77/17VMBBZ (Target grey bbl, black laminate stock) **$746.00**
Price: 77/17RMP (blued, walnut stock) **$674.00**
Price: K77/17VM2BBZ (Target grey bbl, black laminate stock) **$746.00**

SAVAGE MARK I-G BOLT-ACTION RIFLE

Caliber: 22 LR, single shot. **Barrel:** 20-3/4". **Weight:** 5-1/2 lbs. **Length:** 39-1/2" overall. **Stock:** Walnut-finished hardwood with Monte Carlo-type comb, checkered grip and forend. **Sights:** Bead front, open adjustable rear. Receiver grooved for scope mounting. **Features:** Thumb-operated rotating safety. Blue finish. Rifled or smooth bore. Introduced 1990. Made in Canada, from Savage Arms, Inc.

Price: Mark IG, rifled or smooth bore, right- or left-handed **$152.00**
Price: Mark I-GY (Youth), 19" bbl., 37" overall, 5 lbs. **$152.00**
Price: Mark I-LY (Youth), 19" bbl., color laminate **$187.00**
Price: Mark I-GSB (22 LR shot cartridge) **$152.00**

SAVAGE MARK II BOLT-ACTION RIFLE

Caliber: 22 LR, 10-shot magazine. **Barrel:** 20-1/2". **Weight:** 5-1/2 lbs. **Length:** 39-1/2" overall. **Stock:** Walnut-finished hardwood with Monte Carlo-type comb, checkered grip and forend. **Sights:** Bead front, open adjustable rear. Receiver grooved for scope mounting. **Features:** Thumb-operated rotating safety. Blue finish. Introduced 1990. Made in Canada, from Savage Arms, Inc.

Price: Mark II-BV **$264.00**
Price: Mark II Camo **$184.00**
Price: Mark II-GY (youth), 19" barrel, 37" overall, 5 lbs. **$169.00**
Price: Mark II-GL, left-hand **$169.00**
Price: Mark II-GLY (youth) left-hand **$169.00**
Price: Mark II-FXP (as above with black synthetic stock) **$158.00**
Price: Mark II-F (as above, no scope) **$151.00**

Savage Mark II-FSS Stainless Rifle

Similar to the Mark II except has stainless steel barreled action and black synthetic stock with positive checkering, swivel studs, and 20.75" free-floating and button-rifled barrel with detacheable magazine. Weighs 5.5 lbs. Introduced 1997. Imported from Canada by Savage Arms, Inc.
Price: **$213.00**

SAVAGE MODEL 93G MAGNUM BOLT-ACTION RIFLE

Caliber: 22 WMR, 5-shot magazine. **Barrel:** 20-3/4". **Weight:** 5-3/4 lbs. **Length:** 39-1/2" overall. **Stock:** Walnut-finished hardwood with Monte Carlo-type comb, checkered grip and forend. **Sights:** Bead front, adjustable open rear. Receiver grooved for scope mount. **Features:** Thumb-operated rotary safety. Blue finish. Introduced 1994. Made in Canada, from Savage Arms.

Price: **$195.00**
Price: Model 93F (as above with black graphite/fiberglass stock) . **$187.00**

Savage Model 93FSS

Savage Model 93FVSS

Savage Model 30G Stevens "Favorite"

Savage Cub G Youth

Winchester Model 1885 Low Wall

Savage Model 93FSS Magnum Rifle

Similar to Model 93G except stainless steel barreled action and black synthetic stock with positive checkering. Weighs 5-1/2 lbs. Introduced 1997. Imported from Canada by Savage Arms, Inc.

Price: $236.00

Savage Model 93FVSS Magnum Rifle

Similar to Model 93FSS Magnum except 21" heavy barrel with recessed target-style crown, satin-finished stainless barreled action, black graphite/fiberglass stock. Drilled and tapped for scope mounting; comes with Weaver-style bases. Introduced 1998. Imported from Canada by Savage Arms, Inc.

Price: $267.00
Price: With scope $305.00

SAVAGE MODEL 30G STEVENS "FAVORITE"

Caliber: 22 LR, 22WMR Model 30GM, 17 HMR Model 30R17. **Barrel:** 21". **Weight:** 4.25 lbs. **Length:** 36.75". **Stock:** Walnut, straight grip, Schnabel forend. **Sights:** Adjustable rear, bead post front. **Features:** Lever action falling block, inertia firing pin system, Model 30G half octagonal bbl. Model 30GM full octagonal bbl.

Price: Model 30G $228.00
Price: Model 30GM $266.00
Price: Model 30R17 . . . . $292.00

SAVAGE CUB G YOUTH

Caliber: 22 S, L, LR; 17 Mach 2. **Barrel:** 16.125" **Weight:** 3.3 lbs. **Length:** 33" **Stock:** Walnut finished hardwood. **Sights:** Bead post, front; peep, rear. **Features:** Mini single shot bolt action, free-floating button-rifled barrel, blued finish. From Savage Arms.

Price: 22 S, L, LR $156.00
Price: 17 Mach 2. . . . . $165.00

WINCHESTER MODEL 1885 LOW WALL RIMFIRE

Caliber: 17 Mach 2. **Barrel:** 24". **Weight:** 8 lbs. **Length:** 41" overall. **Stock:** Walnut. **Features:** Drilled and tapped for scope mount or tang sight. Case-colored receiver, buttplate and lever, fine-line checkering.

Price: Grade I $1,014.00

Includes models for classic American and ISU target competition and other sporting and competitive shooting.

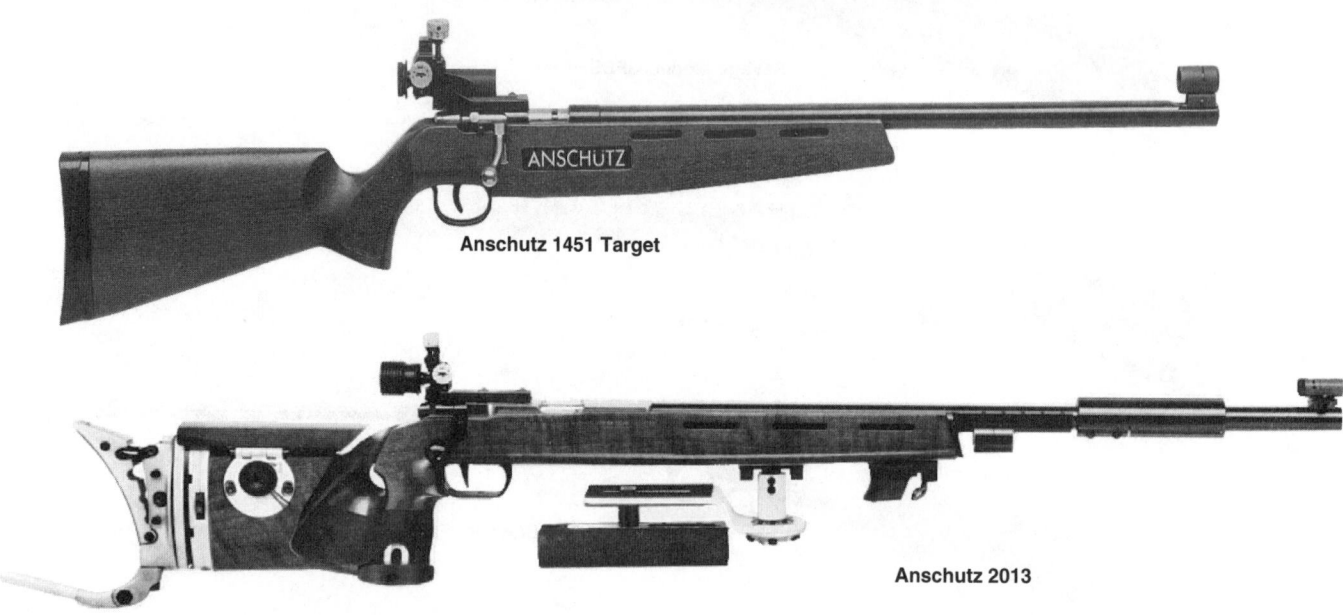

Anschutz 1451 Target

Anschutz 2013

ANSCHUTZ 1451R SPORTER TARGET RIFLE

Caliber: 22 LR, 5-shot magazine. **Barrel:** 22" heavy match. **Weight:** 6.4 lbs. **Length:** 39.75" overall. **Stock:** European hardwood with walnut finish. **Sights:** None furnished. Grooved receiver for scope mounting or Anschutz micrometer rear sight. **Features:** Sliding safety, two-stage trigger. Adjustable buttplate; forend slide rail to accept Anschutz accessories. Imported from Germany by GSI.
Price: **$549.00**

ANSCHUTZ 1451 TARGET RIFLE

Caliber: 22 LR. **Barrel:** 22". **Weight:** About 6.5 lbs. **Length:** 40". **Sights:** Optional. Receiver grooved for scope mounting. **Features:** Designed for the beginning junior shooter with adjustable length of pull from 13.25" to 14.25" via removable butt spacers. Two-stage trigger factory set at 2.6 lbs. Introduced 1999. Imported from Germany by Gunsmithing, Inc.
Price: **$347.00**
Price: #6834 Match Sight Set **$227.10**

ANSCHUTZ 1808D-RT SUPER RUNNING TARGET RIFLE

Caliber: 22 LR, single shot. **Barrel:** 32-1/2". **Weight:** 9 lbs. **Length:** 50" overall. **Stock:** European walnut. Heavy beavertail forend; adjustable cheekpiece and buttplate. Stippled grip and forend. **Sights:** None furnished. Grooved for scope mounting. **Features:** Designed for Running Target competition. Nine-way adjustable single-stage trigger, slide safety. Introduced 1991. Imported from Germany by Gunsmithing, Inc.
Price: Right-hand. **$1,364.10**

ANSCHUTZ 1903 MATCH RIFLE

Caliber: 22 LR, single shot. **Barrel:** 25.5", .75" diameter. **Weight:** 10.1 lbs. **Length:** 43.75" overall. **Stock:** Walnut-finished hardwood with adjustable cheekpiece; stippled grip and forend. **Sights:** None furnished. **Features:** Uses Anschutz Match 64 action and #5098 two-stage trigger. A medium weight rifle for intermediate and advanced Junior Match competition. Introduced 1987. Imported from Germany by Gunsmithing, Inc.
Price: Right-hand. **$720.40**
Price: Left-hand **$757.90**

ANSCHUTZ 64-MS R SILHOUETTE RIFLE

Caliber: 22 LR, 5-shot magazine. **Barrel:** 21-1/2", medium heavy; 7/8" diameter. **Weight:** 8 lbs. **Length:** 39.5" overall. **Stock:** Walnut-finished hardwood, silhouette-type. **Sights:** None furnished. **Features:** Uses

Match 64 action. Designed for metallic silhouette competition. Stock has stippled checkering, contoured thumb groove with Wundhammer swell. Two-stage #5098 trigger. Slide safety locks sear and bolt. Introduced 1980. Imported from Germany by AcuSport Corp., Gunsmithing, Inc.
Price: 64-MS R **$704.30**

ANSCHUTZ 2013 BENCHREST RIFLE

Caliber: 22 LR, single shot. **Barrel:** 19.6". **Weight:** About 10.3 lbs. **Length:** 37.75" to 42.5" overall. **Stock:** Benchrest style of European hardwood. Stock length adjustable via spacers and buttplate. **Sights:** None furnished. Receiver grooved for mounts. **Features:** Uses the Anschutz 2013 target action; two-stage adjustable target trigger factory set at 3.9 oz. Introduced 1994. Imported from Germany by Gunsmithing, Inc.
Price: **$1,757.20**

Anschutz 2007 Match Rifle

Uses same action as the Model 2013, but has a lighter barrel. European walnut stock in right-hand, true left-hand or extra-short models. Sights optional. Available with 19.6" barrel with extension tube, or 26", both in stainless or blue. Introduced 1998. Imported from Germany by Gunsmithing, Inc.
Price: Right-hand, blue, no sights **$1,766.60**
Price: Right-hand, blue, no sights, extra-short stock **$1,756.60**
Price: Left-hand, blue, no sights **$1,856.80**

ANSCHUTZ 1827 BIATHLON RIFLE

Caliber: 22 LR, 5-shot magazine. **Barrel:** 21-1/2". **Weight:** 8-1/2 lbs. with sights. **Length:** 42-1/2" overall. **Stock:** European walnut with cheekpiece, stippled pistol grip and forend. **Sights:** Optional globe front specially designed for Biathlon shooting, micrometer rear with hinged snow cap. **Features:** Uses Super Match 54 action and nine-way adjustable trigger; adjustable wooden buttplate, biathlon butthook, adjustable hand-stop rail. Introduced 1982. Imported from Germany by Gunsmithing, Inc.
Price: Right-hand, with sights, about . . . . **$1,500.50 to $1,555.00**

Anschutz 1827BT Fortner Biathlon Rifle

Similar to the Anschutz 1827 Biathlon rifle except uses Anschutz/Fortner system straight-pull bolt action, blued or stainless steel barrel. Introduced 1982. Imported from Germany by Gunsmithing, Inc.
Price: Right-hand, with sights. . . . . **$1,908.00 to $2,210.00**
Price: Left-hand, with sights . . . . **$2,099.20 to $2,395.00**
Price: Right-hand, sights, stainless barrel **$2,045.20**

Anschutz 54.18MS REP

Anschutz 20.12

ANSCHUTZ SUPER MATCH SPECIAL MODEL 2013 RIFLE

Caliber: 22 LR, single shot. **Barrel:** 25.9". **Weight:** 13 lbs. **Length:** 41.7" to 42.9". **Stock:** A thumbhole version made of European walnut, both the cheekpiece and buttplate are highly adjustable. **Sights:** None furnished. **Features:** Developed by Anschütz for women to shoot in the sport rifle category. Stainless or blue. Introduced in 1997.

Price: Right-hand, blue, no sights, walnut.................... **$2,219.30**

Price: Right-hand, stainless, no sights, walnut **$2,345.30**

Price: Left-hand, blue, no sights, walnut..................... **$2,319.50**

ANSCHUTZ 2012 SPORT RIFLE

Caliber: 22 LR, 5-shot magazine. **Barrel:** 22.4" match; detachable muzzle tube. **Weight:** 7.9 lbs. **Length:** 40.9" overall. **Stock:** European walnut, thumbhole design. **Sights:** None furnished. **Features:** Uses Anschutz 54.18 barreled action with two-stage match trigger. Introduced 1997. Imported from Germany by AcuSport Corp.

Price: .... **$1,425.00 to $2,219.95**

ANSCHUTZ 1911 PRONE MATCH RIFLE

Caliber: 22 LR, single shot. **Barrel:** 27-1/4". **Weight:** 11 lbs. **Length:** 46" overall. **Stock:** Walnut-finished European hardwood; American prone-style with adjustable cheekpiece, textured pistol grip, forend with swivel rail and adjustable rubber buttplate. **Sights:** None furnished. Receiver grooved for Anschutz sights (extra). **Features:** Two-stage trigger adjustable from 2.1 to 8.6 oz. Extremely fast lock time. Stainless or blue barrel. Imported from Germany by Gunsmithing, Inc.

Price: Right-hand, no sights **$1,714.20**

ANSCHUTZ 1912 SPORT RIFLE

Caliber: 22 LR, single shot. **Barrel:** 25.9". **Weight:** About 11.4 lbs. **Length:** 41.7 to 42.9". **Stock:** European walnut or aluminum. **Sights:** None furnished. **Features:** Lightweight sport rifle version of the 1913 but weighs 1.5 pounds less. Stainless or blue barrel. Introduced 1997.

Price: Right-hand, blue, no sights, walnut.................. **$1,789.50**

Price: Right-hand, blue, no sights, aluminum **$2,129.80**

Price: Right-hand, stainless, no sights, walnut **$1,910.30**

Price: Left-hand, blue, no sights, walnut **$1,879.00**

Anschutz 1913 Super Match Rifle

Same as the Model 1911 except European walnut International-type stock with adjustable cheekpiece, or color laminate, both available with straight or lowered forend, adjustable aluminum hook buttplate, adjustable hand stop, weighs 15.5 lbs., 46" overall. Stainless or blue barrel. Imported from Germany by Gunsmithing, Inc.

Price: Right-hand, blue, no sights, walnut stock.... **$2,139.00 to $2,175.00**

Price: Right-hand, blue, no sights, color laminate stock **$2,199.40**

Price: Right-hand, blue, no sights, walnut, lowered forend **$2,181.80**

Price: Right-hand, blue, no sights, color laminate, lowered forend **$2,242.20**

Price: Left-hand, blue, no sights, walnut stock .... **$2,233.10 to $2,275.00**

Anschutz 54.18MS REP Deluxe Silhouette Rifle

Same basic action and trigger specifications as the Anschutz 1913 Super Match but with removable 5-shot clip magazine, 22.4" barrel extendable to 30" using optional extension and weight set. Weight is 8.1 lbs. Receiver drilled and tapped for scope mounting. Stock is thumbhole silhouette version or standard silhouette version, both are European walnut. Introduced 1990. Imported from Germany by Gunsmithing, Inc.

Price: Thumbhole stock **$1,461.40**

Price: Standard stock **$1,212.10**

Anschutz 1907 Standard Match Rifle

Same action as Model 1913 but with 7/8" diameter 26" barrel (stainless or blue). Length is 44.5" overall, weighs 10.5 lbs. Choice of stock configurations. Vented forend. Designed for prone and position shooting ISU requirements; suitable for NRA matches. Also available with walnut flat-forend stock for benchrest shooting. Imported from Germany by Gunsmithing, Inc.

Price: Right-hand, blue, no sights, hardwood stock........................... **$1,253.40 to $1,299.00**

Price: Right-hand, blue, no sights, colored laminated stock .... **$1,316.10 to $1,375.00**

Price: Right-hand, blue, no sights, walnut stock **$1,521.10**

Price: Left-hand, blue barrel, no sights, walnut stock **$1,584.60**

Anschutz 1907

Armalite
AR-10(T)

Bushmaster A2

Bushmaster DCM

ARMALITE AR-10(T) RIFLE

Caliber: 308, 10-shot magazine. **Barrel:** 24" target-weight Rock 5R custom. **Weight:** 10.4 lbs. **Length:** 43.5" overall. **Stock:** Green or black compostion; N.M. fiberglass handguard tube. **Sights:** Detachable handle, front sight, or scope mount available. Comes with international-style flattop receiver with Picatinny rail. **Features:** National Match two-stage trigger. Forged upper receiver. Receivers hard-coat anodized. Introduced 1995. Made in U.S.A. by ArmaLite, Inc.
Price: Green **$2,126.00**
Price: Black **$2,126.00**

ARMALITE M15A4(T) EAGLE EYE RIFLE

Caliber: 223, 10-round magazine. **Barrel:** 24" heavy stainless; 1:8" twist. **Weight:** 9.2 lbs. **Length:** 42-3/8" overall. **Stock:** Green or black butt, N.M. fiberglass handguard tube. **Sights:** One-piece international-style flattop receiver with Weaver-type rail, including case deflector. **Features:** Detachable carry handle, front sight and scope mount (30mm or 1") available. Upper and lower receivers have push-type pivot pin, hard coat anodized. Made in U.S.A. by ArmaLite, Inc.
Price: Green **$1,378.00**
Price: Black **$1,504.00**

BLASER R93 LONG RANGE RIFLE

Caliber: 308 Win., 10-shot detachable box magazine. **Barrel:** 24". **Weight:** 10.4 lbs. **Length:** 44" overall. **Stock:** Aluminum with synthetic lining. **Sights:** None furnished; accepts detachable scope mount. **Features:** Straight-pull bolt action with adjustable trigger; fully adjustable stock; quick takedown; corrosion resistant finish. Introduced 1998. Imported from Germany by SIGARMS.
Price: **$2,360.00**

BUSHMASTER A2 RIFLE

Caliber: 308, 5.56mm. **Barrel:** 16", 20". **Weight:** 8.3 lbs. **Length:** 38.25" overall (20" barrel). **Stock:** Black composition; A2 type. **Sights:** Adjustable post front, adjustable aperture rear. **Features:** Patterned after Colt M-16A2. Chrome-lined barrel with manganese phosphate exterior. Forged aluminum receivers with push-pin takedown. Available in stainless barrel and camo stock versions. Made in U.S.A. by Bushmaster Firearms Co.
Price: 20" match heavy barrel (A2 type). . . . . **$1,025.00 to $1,185.00**
Price: (A3 type) **$1,135.00**

BUSHMASTER DCM COMPETITION RIFLE

Caliber: 223. **Barrel:** 20" extra-heavy (1" diameter) barrel with 1.8" twist for heavier competition bullets. **Weight:** Appx. 12 lbs. with balance weights. **Length:** NA. **Stock:** NA. **Sights:** A2 rear sight. **Features:** Has special competition rear sight with interchangeable apertures, extra-fine 1/2- or 1/4-MOA windage and elevation adjustments; specially ground front sight post in choice of three widths. Full-length handguards over free-floater barrel tube. Introduced 1998. Made in U.S.A. by Bushmaster Firearms, Inc.
Price: **$1,395.00**

Colt Accurized

Colt Match Target HBAR

Colt Match Target HBAR II

EAA/Izhmash URAL 5.1

BUSHMASTER VARMINTER RIFLE

Caliber: 5.56mm. **Barrel:** 24", fluted. **Weight:** 8.4 lbs. **Length:** 42.25" overall. **Stock:** Black composition, A2 type. **Sights:** None furnished; upper receiver has integral scope mount base. **Features:** Chrome-lined .950" extra heavy barrel with counter-bored crown, manganese phosphate finish, free-floating aluminum handguard, forged aluminum receivers with push-pin takedown, hard anodized mil-spec finish. Competition trigger optional. Made in U.S.A. by Bushmaster Firearms, Inc.

Price: 20" Match heavy barrel. **$1,265.00**
Price: Stainless barrel **$1,265.00**

COLT MATCH TARGET MODEL RIFLE

Caliber: 223 Rem., 8-shot magazine. **Barrel:** 20". **Weight:** 7.5 lbs. **Length:** 39" overall. **Stock:** Composition stock, grip, forend. **Sights:** Post front, aperture rear adjustable for windage and elevation. **Features:** Five-round detachable box magazine, standard-weight barrel, sling swivels. Has forward bolt assist. Military matte black finish. Introduced 1991.

Price: **$1,144.00**
Price: With compensator **$1,150.00**

Colt Accurized Rifle

Similar to the Match Target Model except has 24" barrel. Features flat-top receiver for scope mounting, stainless steel heavy barrel, tubular handguard, and free-floating barrel. Matte black finish. Weighs 9.25 lbs. Made in U.S.A. by Colt's Mfg. Co., Inc.

Price: Model CR6724 . . . . **$1,290.00 to $1,470.00**

Colt Match Target HBAR Rifle

Similar to the Target Model except has heavy barrel, 800-meter rear sight adjustable for windage and elevation, 9-round capacity. Weighs 8 lbs. Introduced 1991.

Price: Model MT6601, MT6601C **$1,300.00**

Colt Match Target Competition HBAR Rifle

Similar to the Match Target except has removeable carry handle for scope mounting, 1:9" rifling twist, 9-round magazine. Weighs 8.5 lbs. Introduced 1991.

Price: Model MT6700, MT6700C **$1,315.00**

Colt Match Target Competition HBAR II Rifle

Similar to the Match Target Competition HBAR except has 16:1" barrel, overall length 34.5", and weighs 7.1 lbs. Introduced 1995.

Price: Model MT6731 . . . . **$1,290.00**

EAA/HW 660 MATCH RIFLE

Caliber: 22 LR. **Barrel:** 26". **Weight:** 10.7 lbs. **Length:** 45.3" overall. **Stock:** Match-type walnut with adjustable cheekpiece and buttplate. **Sights:** Globe front, match aperture rear. **Features:** Adjustable match trigger; stippled pistol grip and forend; forend accessory rail. Introduced 1991. Imported from Germany by European American Armory.

Price: About **$999.00**
Price: With laminate stock **$1,159.00**

EAA/IZHMASH URAL 5.1 TARGET RIFLE

Caliber: 22 LR. **Barrel:** 26.5". **Weight:** 11.3 lbs. **Length:** 44.5". **Stock:** Wood, international style. **Sights:** Adjustable click rear, hooded front with inserts. **Features:** Forged barrel with rifling, adjustable trigger, aluminum rail for accessories, hooked adjustable buttplate. Adjustable comb, adjustable large palm rest. Hand stippling on grip area.

Price: . . . . **NA**

EAA/IZHMASH Biathlon Target

Ed Brown Model 702 Light Tactical

Ed Brown Model 702 Tactical

Ed Brown 702 Marine Sniper

Olympic Arms PCR-Servicematch

EAA/Izhmash Biathlon Target Rifle

Similar to URAL with addition of snow covers for barrel and sights, stock holding extra mags, round trigger block. Unique bolt utilizes toggle action. Designed to compete in 40 meter biathlon event. 22 LR, 19.5" bbl.

Price: **$979.00**

EAA/Izhmash Biathalon Basic Target Rifle

Same action as Biathlon but designed for plinking or fun. Beech stock, heavy barrel with Weaver rail for scope mount. 22 LR, 19.5" bbl.

Price: **$339.00**

ED BROWN MODEL 702 TACTICAL

Caliber: 308, 300 Win. Mag. **Barrel:** 26". **Weight:** 11.25 lbs. **Stock:** Hand bedded McMillan A-3 fiberglass tactical stock with recoil pad. **Sights:** None furnished. Leupold Mark 4 30mm scope mounts utilizing heavy-duty screws. **Features:** Custom short or long action, steel trigger guard, hinged floor plate, additional calibers available.

Price: From **$2,900.00**

ED BROWN MODEL 702, M40A2 MARINE SNIPER

Caliber: 308 Win., 30-06 Springfield. **Barrel:** Match-grade 24". **Weight:** 9.25 lbs. **Stock:** Hand bedded McMillan GP fiberglass tactical stock with

recoil pad in special Woodland Camo molded-in colors. **Sights:** None furnished. Leupold Mark 4 30mm scope mounts with heavy-duty screws. **Features:** Steel trigger guard, hinged floor plate, three position safety. Left-hand model available.

Price: From **$2,900.00**

OLYMPIC ARMS PCR-SERVICEMATCH RIFLE

Caliber: 223, 10-shot magazine. **Barrel:** 20", broach-cut 416 stainless steel. **Weight:** About 10 lbs. **Length:** 39.5" overall. **Stock:** A2 stowaway grip and trapdoor buttstock. **Sights:** Post front, E2-NM fully adjustable aperture rear. **Features:** Based on the AR-15. Conforms to all DCM standards. Free-floating 1:8.5" or 1:10" barrel; crowned barrel; no bayonet lug. Introduced 1996. Made in U.S.A. by Olympic Arms, Inc.

Price: **$1,062.00**

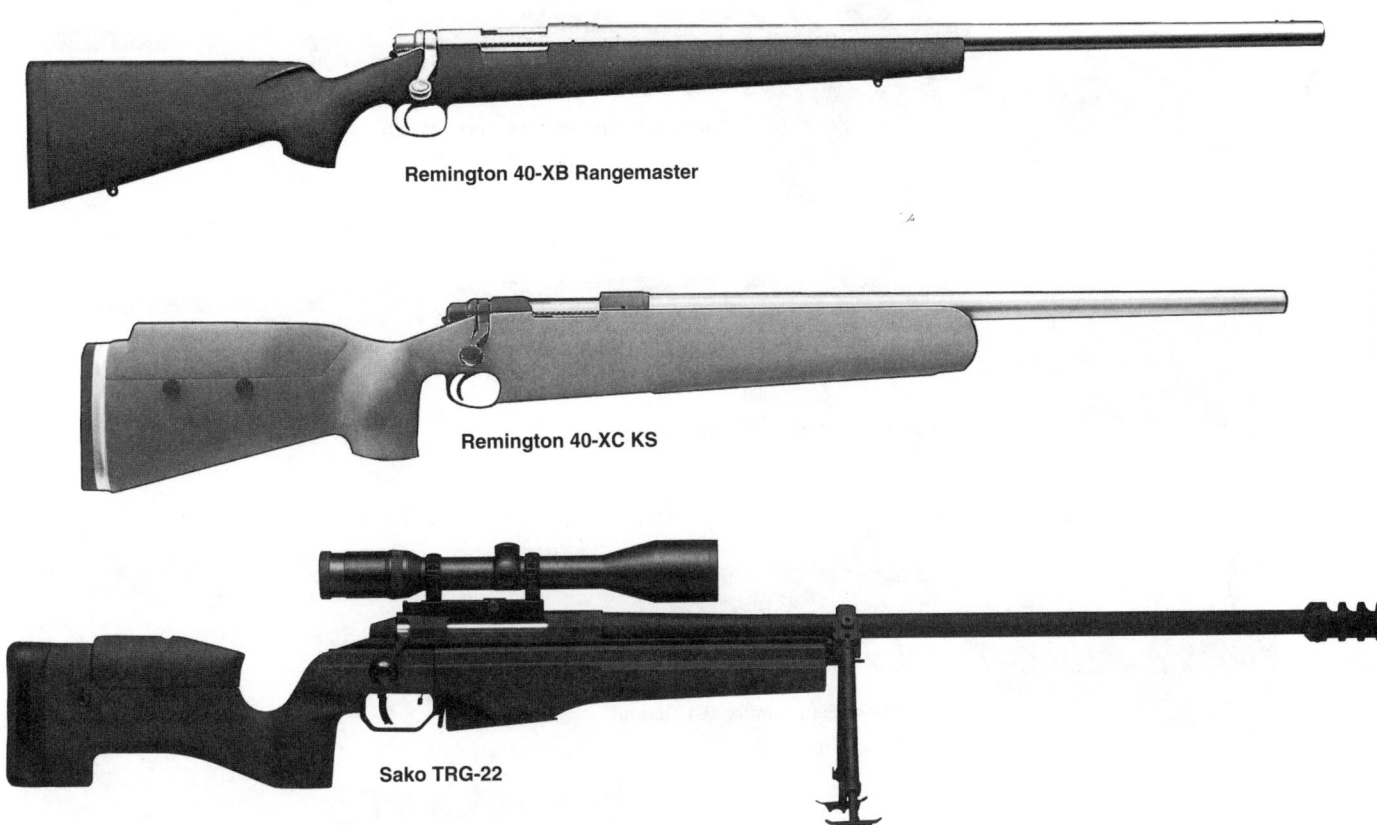

Remington 40-XB Rangemaster

Remington 40-XC KS

Sako TRG-22

OLYMPIC ARMS PCR-1 RIFLE

Caliber: 223, 10-shot magazine. **Barrel:** 20", 24"; 416 stainless steel. **Weight:** 10 lbs., 3 oz. **Length:** 38.25" overall with 20" barrel. **Stock:** A2 stowaway grip and trapdoor butt. **Sights:** None supplied; flattop upper receiver, cut-down front sight base. **Features:** Based on the AR-15 rifle. Broach-cut, free-floating barrel with 1:8.5" or 1:10" twist. No bayonet lug. Crowned barrel; fluting available. Introduced 1994. Made in U.S.A. by Olympic Arms, Inc.
Price: **$1,038.00**

Olympic Arms PCR-2, PCR-3 Rifles

Similar to the PCR-1 except has 16" barrel, weighs 8 lbs., 2 oz.; has post front sight, fully adjustable aperture rear. Model PCR-3 has flattop upper receiver, cut-down front sight base. Introduced 1994. Made in U.S.A. by Olympic Arms, Inc.
Price: **$958.00**

REMINGTON 40-XB RANGEMASTER TARGET CENTERFIRE

Caliber: 15 calibers from 220 Swift to 300 Win. Mag. **Barrel:** 27-1/4". **Weight:** 11-1/4 lbs. **Length:** 47" overall. **Stock:** American walnut, laminated thumbhole or Kevlar with high comb and beavertail forend stop. Rubber non-slip buttplate. **Sights:** None. Scope blocks installed. **Features:** Adjustable trigger. Stainless barrel and action. Receiver drilled and tapped for sights.
Price: Standard single shot . (right-hand) **$1,636.00**; (left-hand) **$1,761.00**
Price: Repeater **$1,734.00**

REMINGTON 40-XBBR KS

Caliber: Five calibers from 22 BR to 308 Win. **Barrel:** 20" (light varmint class), 24" (heavy varmint class). **Weight:** 7-1/4 lbs. (light varmint class); 12 lbs. (heavy varmint class). **Length:** 38" (20" bbl.), 42" (24" bbl.). **Stock:** Aramid fiber. **Sights:** None. Supplied with scope blocks. **Features:** Unblued benchrest with stainless steel barrel, trigger adjustable from 1-1/2 lbs. to 3-1/2 lbs. Special two-oz. trigger extra cost. Scope and mounts extra.
Price: Single shot **$1,876.00**

REMINGTON 40-XC KS TARGET RIFLE

Caliber: 7.62 NATO, 5-shot. **Barrel:** 24", stainless steel. **Weight:** 11 lbs. without sights. **Length:** 43-1/2" overall. **Stock:** Aramid fiber. **Sights:** None furnished. **Features:** Designed to meet the needs of competitive shooters. Stainless steel barrel and action.
Price: **$1,821.00**

REMINGTON 40-XR CUSTOM SPORTER

Caliber: 22 LR, 22 WM. **Features:** Model XR-40 Target rifle action. Many options available.
Price: Single shot **$3,383.00**

SAKO TRG-22/TRG-42 BOLT-ACTION RIFLE

Caliber: 308 Win., 10-shot magazine. **Barrel:** 26". **Weight:** 10-1/4 lbs. **Length:** 45-1/4" overall. **Stock:** Reinforced polyurethane with fully adjustable cheekpiece and buttplate. **Sights:** None furnished. Optional quick-detachable, one-piece scope mount base, 1" or 30mm rings. **Features:** Resistance-free bolt, free-floating heavy stainless barrel, 60-degree bolt lift. Two-stage trigger is adjustable for length, pull, horizontal or vertical pitch. Introduced 2000. Imported from Finland by Beretta USA.
Price: TRG-22 Green Folding Stock....................... **$4,525.00**
Price: TRG-22 Green or black stock....................... **$2,825.00**
Price: TRG-42 300 Win Mag., green stock....... **$2,825.00 to $3,525.00**
Price: TRG-42 338 Lapua Mag., green stock..... **$2,825.00 to $3,525.00**

SPRINGFIELD ARMORY M1A SUPER MATCH

Caliber: 308 Win. **Barrel:** 22", heavy Douglas Premium. **Weight:** About 11 lbs. **Length:** 44.31" overall. **Stock:** Heavy walnut competition stock with longer pistol grip, contoured area behind the rear sight, thicker butt and forend, glass bedded. **Sights:** National Match front and rear. **Features:** Has figure-eight-style operating rod guide. Introduced 1987. From Springfield Armory.
Price: About **$2,479.00**

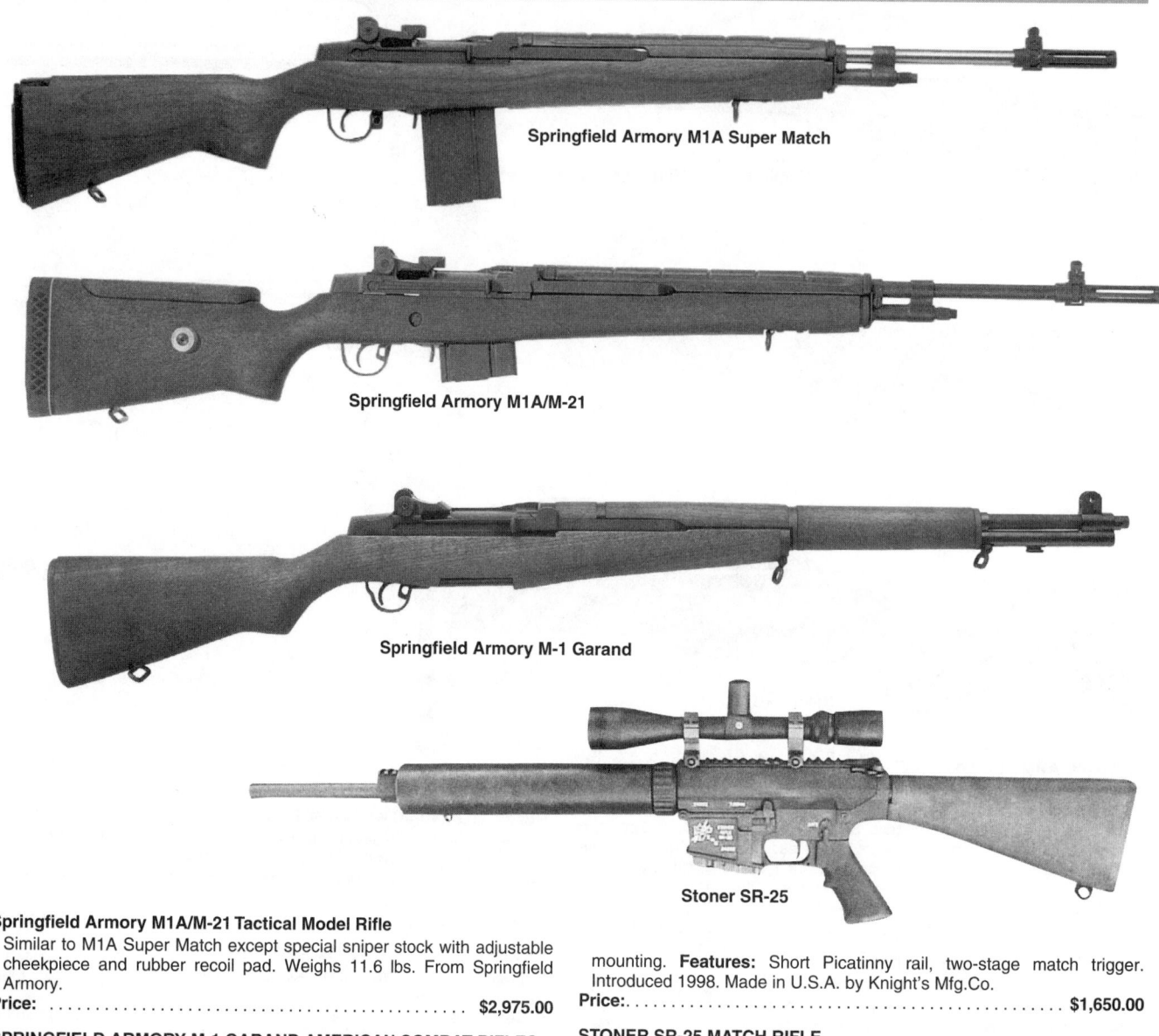

Springfield Armory M1A Super Match

Springfield Armory M1A/M-21

Springfield Armory M-1 Garand

Stoner SR-25

Springfield Armory M1A/M-21 Tactical Model Rifle

Similar to M1A Super Match except special sniper stock with adjustable cheekpiece and rubber recoil pad. Weighs 11.6 lbs. From Springfield Armory.

Price: **$2,975.00**

SPRINGFIELD ARMORY M-1 GARAND AMERICAN COMBAT RIFLES

Caliber: 30-06, 308 Win., 8-shot. **Barrel:** 24". **Weight:** 9.5 lbs. **Length:** 43.6". **Stock:** American walnut. **Sights:** Military square post front, military aperture, MOA adjustable rear. **Features:** Limited production, certificate of authenticity, all new receiver, barrel and stock with remaining parts USGI mil-spec. Two-stage military trigger.

Price: About.. **$2,479.00**

STONER SR-15 MATCH RIFLE

Caliber: 223. **Barrel:** 20". **Weight:** 7.9 lbs. **Length:** 38" overall. **Stock:** Black synthetic. **Sights:** None furnished; flattop upper receiver for scope mounting. **Features:** Short Picatinny rail, two-stage match trigger. Introduced 1998. Made in U.S.A. by Knight's Mfg.Co.

Price:.. **$1,650.00**

STONER SR-25 MATCH RIFLE

Caliber: 7.62 NATO, 10-shot steel magazine, 5-shot optional. **Barrel:** 24" heavy match; 1:11.25" twist. **Weight:** 10.75 lbs. **Length:** 44" overall. **Stock:** Black synthetic AR-15A2 design. Full floating forend of mil-spec synthetic attaches to upper receiver at a single point. **Sights:** None furnished. Has integral Weaver-style rail. Rings and iron sights optional. **Features:** Improved AR-15 trigger, AR-15-style seven-lug rotating bolt. Introduced 1993. Made in U.S.A. by Knight's Mfg. Co.

Price: **$3,345.00**

Price: SR-25 Lightweight Match (20" medium match target contour barrel, 9.5 lbs., 40" overall) **$3,345.00**

Includes a wide variety of sporting guns and guns suitable for various competitions.

Benelli Legacy

Beretta AL391
Urika Gold Sporting

Benelli M4

AYA MODEL 4/53 SHOTGUNS

Gauge: 12, 16, 20, 28, 410. **Barrel:** 27" (28 and 410) or 28". **Weight:** To customer specifications. **Length:** To customer specifications. **Features:** Hammerless boxlock action; double triggers; light scroll engraving; automatic safety; straight grip oil finish walnut stock; checkered butt.
Price: **$2,850.00**

BENELLI LEGACY SHOTGUN

Gauge: 12, 20, 2-3/4" and 3" chamber. **Barrel:** 24", 26", 28" (Full, Mod., Imp. Cyl., Imp. Mod., cylinder choke tubes). Mid-bead sight. **Weight:** 5.8 to 7.4 lbs. **Length:** 49-5/8" overall (28" barrel). **Stock:** Select European walnut with satin finish. **Features:** Uses the rotating bolt inertia recoil operating system with a two-piece steel/aluminum etched receiver (bright on lower, blue upper). Drop adjustment kit allows the stock to be custom fitted without modifying the stock. Introduced 1998. Imported from Italy by Benelli USA, Corp.
Price: **$1,435.00**

Benelli Sport II Shotgun

Similar to the Legacy model except has dual tone blue/silver receiver, two carbon fiber interchangeable vent ribs, adjustable butt pad, adjustable buttstock, and functions with ultra-light target loads. Walnut stock with satin finish. Introduced 1997. Imported from Italy by Benelli USA.
Price: **$1,470.00**

BENELLI M2 FIELD SHOTGUNS

Gauge: 12 ga., 3" chamber. **Barrel:** 21", 24", 26", 28". **Weight:** 6.9 to 7.2 lbs. **Length:** 42.5 to 49.5" overall. **Stock:** Synthetic, Advantage® Max-4 HD™, Advantage® Timber HD™. **Sights:** Red bar. **Features:** Uses the Inertia Driven™ bolt mechanism. Vent rib. Comes with set of five choke tubes. Imported from Italy by Benelli USA.
Price: Synthetic ComforTech gel recoil pad **$1,175.00**
Price: Camo ComforTech gel recoil pad **$1,295.00**
Price: Satin walnut. **$1,110.00**
Price: Rifled slug synthetic **$1,240.00**
Price: Timber HD turkey model w/SteadyGrip stock. **$1,335.00**

BENELLI M4 TACTICAL SHOTGUN

Gauge: 12 ga., 3" chamber. **Barrel:** 18.5". **Weight:** 7.8 lbs. **Length:** 40" overall. **Stock:** Synthetic. **Sights:** Ghost Ring rear, fixed blade front. **Features:** Auto-regulating gas-operated (ARGO) action, three choke tubes, Picatinny rail, standard and collapsible stocks available, optional tactical gun case. Introduced 2006. Imported from Italy by Benelli USA.
Price: Pistol grip stock **$1,535.00**

BENELLI MONTEFELTRO SHOTGUNS

Gauge: 12 and 20 ga. Full, Imp. Mod., Mod., Imp. Cyl. choke tubes. **Barrel:** 24", 26", 28". **Weight:** 5.3 to 7.1 lbs. **Stock:** Checkered walnut with satin finish. **Length of Pull:** 12-1/2 to 14-3/8" overall. **Length:** 43.6 to 49.5" overall. **Features:** Uses the Montefeltro rotating bolt system with a simple inertia recoil design. Finish is blue. Introduced 1987.
Price: 24", 26", 28" **$1,070.00**
Price: Grade II **$1,220.00**
Price: 20 ga. **$1,070.00**
Price: 20 ga. short stock (LOP: 12.5") **$1,080.00**

BENELLI SUPER BLACK EAGLE II SHOTGUNS

Gauge: 12, 3-1/2" chamber. **Barrel:** 24", 26", 28" (Cyl. Imp. Cyl., Mod., Imp. Mod., Full choke tubes). **Weight:** 7.1 to 7.3 lbs. **Length:** 45.6 to 49.6" overall. **Stock:** European walnut with satin finish, polymer, or camo. Adjustable for drop. **Sights:** Red bar front. **Features:** Uses Montefeltro inertia recoil bolt system. Vent rib. Advantage® Max-4 HD™, Advantage® Timber HD™ camo patterns. Minimum recommend load in all Benelli semi-autos: 3 dram, 1-1/8 oz. Introduced 1991. Left-hand models available. Imported from Italy by Benelli USA.
Price: Synthetic stock, ComforTech gel recoil pad **$1,515.00**
Price: Camo stock, ComforTech gel recoil pad **$1,635.00**
Price: Satin walnut stock **$1,450.00**
Price: Synthetic stock **$1,380.00**
Price: Camo stock **$1,500.00**
Price: Rifled slug synthetic **$1,580.00**
Price: Timber HD turkey model w/SteadyGrip stock **$1,535.00**

Benelli Ultra Light

Uses the inertia recoil bolt system. Gloss-blued finish receiver. Weight is 6.0 lbs., 24" barrel, 45.5 overall length. WeatherCoat walnut stock. Introduced 2006. Imported from Italy by Benelli USA.
Price: **$1,335.00**

Benelli Ultralight

Beretta 3901 Ambassador

Beretta 3901 Citizen

Beretta AL391 Urika Sporting

BENELLI CORDOBA HIGH-VOLUME SHOTGUN

Gauge: 12; 3" chamber. **Barrel:** 28" and 30", ported, 10mm sporting rib. **Weight:** 7.2 to 7.3 lbs. **Length:** 49.6 to 51.6". **Features:** Designed for high-volume sporting clays and Argentina dove shooting. Inertia-driven action, Extended Sport CrioChokes, 4+1 capacity. Imported from Italy by Benelli USA.
Price: **$1,665.00**

BERETTA 3901 SHOTGUNS

Gauge: 12, 20 gauge; 3" chamber, semi-auto. **Barrel:** 26", 28". **Weight:** 6.55 lbs. (20 ga.), 7.2 lbs. (12 ga.). **Length:** NA. **Stock:** Wood, X-tra wood (special process wood enhancement), and polymer. **Features:** Based on A390 shotgun introduced in 1996. Mobilchokes, removable trigger group. 3901 Target RL uses gas operating system; Sporting style flat rib with steel front bead and mid-bead, walnut stock and forearm, satin matte finish, adjustable LOP from 12–13", adjustable for cast on/off, Beretta's Memory System II to adjust the parallel comb. Weighs 7.2 lbs. 3901 Citizen has polymer stock. 3901 Statesman has basic wood and checkering treatment. 3901 Ambassador has X-tra wood stock and fore end; high-polished receiver with engraving, Gel-Tek recoil pad, optional TruGlo fiber-optic front sight. 3901 Rifled Slug Shotgun has black high-impact synthetic stock and fore end, 24" barrel,1:28 twist, Picatinny cantilever rail. Introduced 2006. Made in U.S. by Beretta USA.
Price: **$1,295.00**
Price: 3901 Target RL **$898.00**
Price: 3901 Citizen **$750.00**
Price: 3901 Citizen **$898.00**
Price: 3901 Ambassador............................... **$998.00**
Price: 3901 Rifled Slug Shotgun....................... **$799.00**

BERETTA UGB25 XCEL

Gauge: 12, 2-3/4" chambers. **Barrel:** 28", 30", 32"; competition-style interchangeable vent rib; Optima choke tubes. **Weight:** 7.7-9 lbs. **Stock:** High-grade walnut with oil finish; hand-checkered grip and forend, adjustable. **Features:** Break-open semiautomatic. High-resistance fiberglass-reinforced technopolymer trigger plate, self-lubricating firing mechanism. Rounded alloy receiver, polished sides, external cartridge carrier and feeding port, bottom eject. two technopolymer recoil dampers on breech bolt, double recoil dampers located in the receiver, Beretta Recoil Reduction System, recoil-absorbing Beretta Gel Tek recoil pad. Optima-Bore barrel with a lengthened forcing cone, Optimachoke and Extended Optimachoke tubes. Steel-shot capable, interchangeable aluminum alloy top rib. Introduced 2006. Imported from Italy by Beretta USA.
Price: **$3,275.00**

BERETTA AL391 TEKNYS SHOTGUNS

Gauge: 12, 20 gauge; 3" chamber, semi-auto. **Barrel:** 26", 28". **Weight:** 5.9 lbs. (20 ga.), 7.3 lbs. (12 ga.). **Length:** NA. **Stock:** X-tra wood (special process wood enhancement). **Features:** Flat 1/4 rib, TruGlo Tru-Bead sight, recoil reducer, stock spacers, overbored bbls., flush choke tubes. Comes with fitted, lined case.
Price: From **$1,425.00**

BERETTA AL391 URIKA AND URIKA OPTIMA AUTO SHOTGUNS

Gauge: 12, 20 gauge; 3" chamber. **Barrel:** 22", 24", 26", 28", 30"; five Mobilchoke choke tubes. **Weight:** 5.95 to 7.28 lbs. **Length:** Varies by model. **Stock:** Walnut, black or camo synthetic; shims, spacers and interchangeable recoil pads allow custom fit. **Features:** Self-compensating gas operation handles full range of loads; recoil reducer in receiver; enlarged trigger guard; reduced-weight receiver, barrel and forend; hard-chromed bore. Introduced 2000. Urika Gold and Gold Sporting models are similar to AL391 Urika except features deluxe wood, jewelled bolt and carrier, gold-inlaid receiver with black or silver finish. Introduced 2000. Urika Sporting models are similar to AL391 Urika except has competition sporting stock with rounded rubber recoil pad, wide vent rib with white front and mid-rib beads, satin-black receiver with silver markings. Available in 12 and 20 gauge. Introduced 2000. Urika Trap has wide vent rib with white front and mid-rib beads, Monte Carlo stock and special trap recoil pad. Gold Trap features highly figured walnut stock and forend, gold-filled Beretta logo and signature on receiver. Optima bore and Optima choke tubes. Introduced 2000. Urika Parallel Target RL and SL models have parallel comb, Monte Carlo stock with tighter grip radius and stepped vent rib. SL model has same features but with 13.5" length of pull stock. Introduced 2000. Urika Youth has a 24" or 26" barrel with 13.5" stock for youths and smaller shooters. Introduced 2000. Imported from Italy by Beretta USA.
Price: .... **$998.00 to $1,500**

Beretta A391 Xtrema2 3.5

Browning Gold Deer Hunter

Browning Gold Fusion

Browning Gold Superlite Micro

Browning NWTF Mossy Oak® Break-Up™

BERETTA A391 XTREMA2 3.5 AUTO SHOTGUNS

Gauge: 12 ga. 3.5" chamber. **Barrel:** 24", 26", 28". **Weight:** 7.8 lbs. **Stock:** Synthetic. **Features:** Semi-auto goes with two-lug rotating bolt and self-compensating gas valve, extended tang, cross bolt safety, self-cleaning, with case.

Price: From **$1,098.00**

BROWNING GOLD AUTO SHOTGUNS

Gauge: 12, 3" or 3-1/2" chamber; 20, 3" chamber. **Barrel:** 12 ga.-26", 28", 30", Invector Plus choke tubes; 20 ga.-26", 30", Invector choke tubes. **Weight:** 7 lbs., 9 oz. (12 ga.), 6 lbs., 12 oz. (20 ga.). **Length:** 46-1/4" overall (20 ga., 26" barrel). **Stock:** 14"x1-1/2"x2-1/3"; select walnut with gloss finish; palm swell grip. **Features:** Self-regulating, self-cleaning gas system shoots all loads; lightweight receiver with special non-glare deep black finish; large reversible safety button; large rounded trigger guard; gold trigger. The 20 gauge has slightly smaller dimensions; 12 gauge have back-bored barrels, Invector Plus tube system. Introduced 1994. Gold Evolve shotguns have new rib design, HiViz sights. Gold Micro has a 26" barrel, 13-7/8" pull length and smaller pistol grip for youths and other small shooters. Introduced 2001. Gold Fusion has front HiViz Pro-Comp and center bead on tapered vent rib; ported and back-bored Invector Plus barrel; 2-3/4" chamber; satin-finished stock with solid, radiused recoil pad with hard heel insert; non-glare black alloy receiver, shim-adj. stock. Imported by Browning.

Price: Gold Evolve, 12 or 20 ga., 3" chamber **$1,196.00**
Price: Gold Hunter, 12 or 20 ga., 3" or 3-1/2" chamber, from **$1,025.00**
Price: Gold FLD, 12 or 20 ga., semi-humpback receiver **$1,025.00**
Price: Gold Rifled Deer Hunter, 12 or 20 ga., scope mount **$1,131.00**
Price: Gold Upland Special, 12 or 20 ga., 24" or 26" barrel **$1,025.00**
Price: Gold Superlite Micro, 20 ga., 24" or 26" barrel, 6.6 lbs. **$1,025.00**
Price: Gold Fusion, 12 or 20 ga., 6.4 to 7 lbs., ... **$1,129.00**
Price: Gold Fusion High Grade, 12 or 20 ga., intr. 2005 . . . . **$2,095.00**

Browning Gold Stalker Auto Shotgun

Similar to the Gold Hunter except has black composite stock and forend. Chambered in 12 gauge, 3" or 3-1/2" chamber. Gold Deer Stalker has fully rifled barrel, cantilever scope mount. Introduced 1999. Imported by Browning.

Price: Gold Stalker, 3" or 3-1/2" chamber, 26" or 28" barrel, from . . **$981.00**
Price: Gold FLD Stalker, 3" chamber, semi-humpback receiver . . . **$981.00**
Price: Gold Rifled Deer Stalker, 12 ga. 3" chamber, 22" barrel **$981.00**

Browning Gold NWTF Turkey Series and Mossy Oak Shotguns

Similar to the Gold Hunter except has specialized camouflage patterns, including National Wild Turkey Federation design. Includes extra-full choke tube and HiViz fiber-optic sights on some models and Dura-Touch coating. Camouflage patterns include Mossy Oak New Break-Up (NBU) or Mossy Oak New Shadow Grass (NSG). NWTF models include NWTF logo on stock. Introduced 2001. From Browning.

Price: NWFT Gold Ultimate Turkey, 24" barrel, 3-1/2" chamber . . **$1,440.00**
Price: NWFT Gold Turkey, 24" barrel, 3" chamber **$1,202.00**
Price: Gold NSG, 26" or 28" barrel, 3" or 3-1/2" chamber, from . . **$1,127.00**
Price: Gold NBU, 26" barrel, 3" or 3-1/2" chamber, from **$1,127.00**
Price: Gold Rifle Deer NBU, 22" barrel, 3" chamber, from **$1,218.00**

Browning Gold Light 10 Gauge

Charles Daly Field Pump

Charles Daly Maxi-Mag Field Hunter VR-MC

Charles Daly Superior II

Escort Model AS

BROWNING GOLD "CLAYS" AUTO SHOTGUNS

Gauge: 12, 2-3/4" chamber. **Barrel:** 28", 30", Invector Plus choke tubes. **Weight:** about 7.75 lbs. **Length:** From 47.75 to 50.5". **Stock:** Select walnut with gloss finish; palm swell grip, shim adjustable. **Features:** Ported barrels, "Golden Clays" models feature gold inlays and engraving. Otherwise similar to Gold series guns. Imported by Browning.

Price: Gold "Golden Clays" Sporting Clays, intr. 2005	**$1,812.00**
Price: Gold Sporting Clays	**$1,105.00**
Price: Gold "Golden Clays" Ladies Sporting Clays, intr. 2005	**$1,812.00**
Price: Gold Ladies Sporting Clays	**$1,105.00**

Browning Gold Light 10 Gauge Auto Shotgun

Similar to the Gold Hunter except has an alloy receiver that is 1 lb. lighter than standard model. Offered in 26" or 28" bbls. With Mossy Oak® Break-Up™ or Shadow Grass coverage; 5-shot magazine. Weighs 9 lbs., 10 oz. (28" bbl.). Introduced 2001. Imported by Browning.

Price: Camo model only **$1,336.00**

CHARLES DALY FIELD SEMI-AUTO SHOTGUNS

Gauge: 12, 20, 28. **Barrel:** 22", 24", 26", 28" or 30". **Stock:** Synthetic black, Realtree Hardwoods or Advantage Timber. **Features:** Interchangeable

barrels handle all loads including steel shot. Slug model has adjustable sights. Maxi-Mag is 3.5" chamber.

Price: Field Hunter **$389.00**

CHARLES DALY SUPERIOR II SEMI-AUTO SHOTGUNS

Gauge: 12, 20, 28. **Barrel:** 26", 28" or 30". **Stock:** Select Turkish walnut. **Features:** Factory ported interchangeable barrels; wide vent rib on Trap and Sport models; fluorescent red sights.

Price: Superior Hunter VR-MC **$539.00**
Price: Superior Sport **$569.00**

ESCORT SEMI-AUTO SHOTGUNS

Gauge: 12, 20. **Barrel:** 22", 24", 26", 18" (AimGuard model); 3" chambers. **Weight:** 6 lbs, 4 0. to 7 lbs., 6 oz. **Stock:** Polymer, black, or camo finish; also Turkish walnut. **Features:** Black chrome finish; top of receiver dovetailed for sight mounting. Gold-plated trigger, trigger guard safety, magazine cut-off. Three choke tubes (IC, M, F — except AimGuard); 24" bbl. model comes with turkey choke tube. **Sights:** Optional HiViz Spark and TriViz fiber-optic sights. Introduced 2002. Camo model introduced 2003. Youth, Slug, Obsession Camo models introduced 2005. Three-barrel pumpset introduced 2006. Imported from Turkey by Legacy Sports International.

Price: From **$392.00**

Remington Model 105 CTI

Remington Model 1100 G3

Remington Model 11-87 Premier

FRANCHI INERTIA I-12 SHOTGUN

Gauge: 12, 3" chamber. **Barrel:** 24", 26", 28" (Cyl., IC, Mod., IM, F choke tubes). **Weight:** 7.5 to 7.7. lbs. **Length:** 45" to 49". **Stock:** 14-3.8" LOP, satin walnut with checkered grip and forend, synthetic, Advantage Timber HD or Max-4 camo patterns. **Features:** Inertia-Driven action. AA walnut stock. Red bar front sight, metal mid sight. Imported from Italy by Benelli USA.

Price: Synthetic **$679.00**
Price: Camo **$749.00**
Price: Satin walnut **$779.00**
Price: White Gold engraved receiver, hard case. **$1,399.00**

FRANCHI MODEL 712/720 RAPTOR SHOTGUNS

Gauge: 12, 20 3" chamber. **Barrel:** 28", 30". **Weight:** 6.2 to 7.1 lbs. **Length:** 50" to 52". **Stock:** Satin walnut, WeatherCoat finish. **Sights:** Front and mid metal beads. **Features:** Comes with custom-fitted hard case and cleaning kit, extended choke tubes. Made in Italy and imported by Benelli USA.

Price: Walnut **$899.00**

FRANCHI MODEL 720 SHOTGUNS

Gauge: 20, 3" chamber. **Barrel:** 24", 26", 28" w/(IC, Mod., F choke tubes). **Weight:** 5.9 to 6.1 lbs. **Length:** 43.25" to 49". **Stock:** WeatherCoat finish walnut, Max-4 and Timber HD camo. **Sights:** Front bead. **Features:** Made in Italy and imported by Benelli USA.

Price: Walnut **$749.00**
Price: Camo **$799.00**
Price: Walnut, 12.5" LOP, 43.25" OAL **$739.00**

FRANCHI 48AL FIELD AND DELUXE SHOTGUNS

Gauge: 20 or 28, 2-3/4" chamber. **Barrel:** 24", 26", 28" (Full, Cyl., Mod., choke tubes). **Weight:** 5.4 to 5.7 lbs. **Length:** 42.25" to 48". **Stock:** Walnut with checkered grip and forend. **Features:** Long recoil-operated action. Chrome-lined bore; cross-bolt safety. Imported from Italy by Benelli USA.

Price: 20 ga. **$749.00**
Price: 20 ga. Deluxe A grade walnut **$970.00**
Price: 28 ga. **$850.00**

FRANCHI RAPTOR SPORTING CLAYS SHOTGUN

Gauge: 12 and 20; 6-round capacity. **Barrel:** 30" (12 ga.) or 28" (20 ga.); ported; tapered target rib and bead front sight. **Weight:** 7.1 lbs. (Model 712) or 6.2 lbs. (Model 720). **Stock:** Walnut with WeatherCoat (impervious to weather). **Features:** Gas-operated, satin nickel receiver.

Price: **$850.00**

HARRINGTON & RICHARDSON EXCELL AUTO 5 SHOTGUNS

Gauge: 12, 3" chamber. **Barrel:** 22", 24", 28", four screw-in choke tubes (IC, M, IM, F). **Weight:** About 7 lbs. **Length:** 42.5" to 48.5" overall, depending on barrel length. **Stock:** American walnut with satin finish; cut checkering; ventilated buttpad. Synthetic stock or camo-finish. **Sights:** Metal bead front or fiber-optic front and rear. **Features:** Ventilated rib on all models except slug gun. Imported by H&R 1871, Inc.

Price: Synthetic, black, 28" barrel, 48.5" OAL **$415.00**
Price: Walnut, checkered grip/forend, 28" barrel, 48.5" OAL **$461.00**
Price: Waterfowl, camo finish **$521.00**
Price: Turkey, camo finish, 22" barrel, fiber optic sights **$521.00**
Price: Combo, synthetic black stock, with slug barrel **$583.00**

REMINGTON MODEL 105 CTI SHOTGUN

Gauge: 12, 3" chamber, 2-shot magazine. **Barrel:** 26", 28" (IC, Mod., Full ProBore chokes). **Weight:** 7 lbs. **Length:** 46.25" overall (26" barrel). **Stock:** Walnut with satin finish. Checkered grip and forend. **Sights:** Front bead. **Features:** Aircraft-grade titanium receiver body, skeletonized receiver with carbon fiber shell. Bottom feed and eject, target grade trigger, R3 recoil pad, FAA-approved lockable hard case, .735" overbored barrel with lengthened forcing cones. TriNyte coating; carbon/aramid barrel rib. Introduced 2006.

Price: **$1,332.00**

REMINGTON MODEL 1100 G3 SHOTGUN

Gauge: 20, 12; 3" chamber **Barrel:** 26", 28". **Weight:** 6.75-7.6 lbs. **Stock:** Realwood semi-Fancy carbon fiber laminate stock, high gloss finish, machine cut checkering. **Features:** Gas operating system, pressure compensated barrel, solid carbon-steel engraved receiver, titanium coating. Action bars, trigger and extended carrier release, action bar sleeve, action spring, locking block, hammer, sear and magazine tube have nickel-plated, Teflon coating. R3 recoil pad, overbored (.735" dia.) vent rib barrels, ProBore choke tubes. 20-gauges have Rem Chokes. Comes with lockable hard case. Introduced 2006. Competition model has overbored 30" barrel, 10mm target-style rib with twin beads. Optimized for 2 3/4" target and light field loads. Introduced 2006.

Price: 12 or 20 gauge **$1,065.00**

REMINGTON MODEL 11-87 PREMIER SHOTGUNS

Gauge: 12, 20, 3" chamber. **Barrel:** 26", 28", 30" RemChoke tubes. Light Contour barrel. **Weight:** About 7-3/4 lbs. **Length:** 46" overall (26" bbl.). **Stock:** Walnut with satin or high-gloss finish; cut checkering; solid brown buttpad; no white spacers. **Sights:** Bradley-type white-faced front, metal bead middle. **Features:** Pressure compensating gas system allows shooting 2-3/4" or 3" loads interchangeably with no adjustments. Stainless magazine tube; redesigned feed latch, barrel support ring on operating bars; pinned forend. Introduced 1987.

Price: From **$860.00**

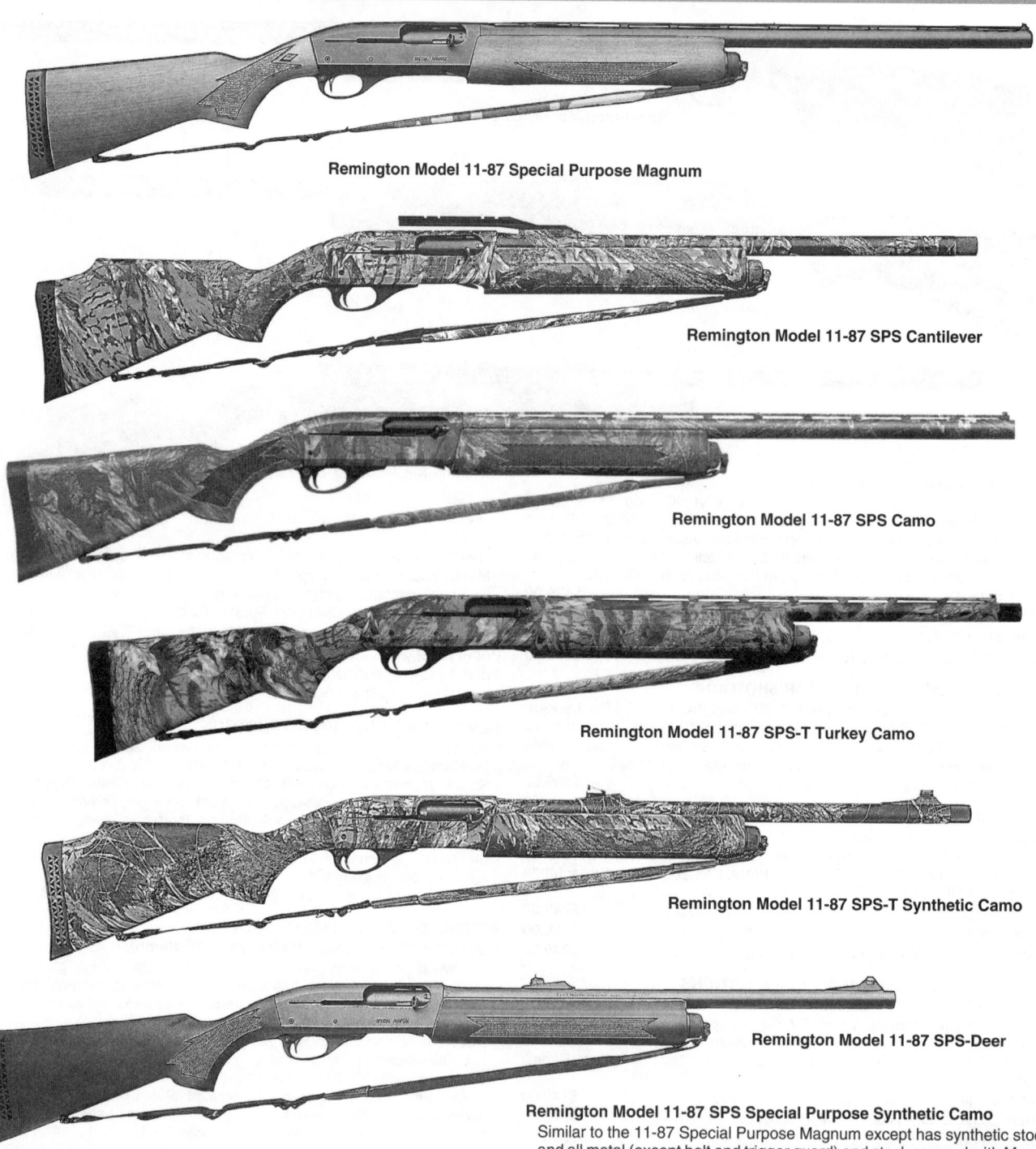

Remington Model 11-87 Special Purpose Magnum

Remington Model 11-87 SPS Cantilever

Remington Model 11-87 SPS Camo

Remington Model 11-87 SPS-T Turkey Camo

Remington Model 11-87 SPS-T Synthetic Camo

Remington Model 11-87 SPS-Deer

Remington Model 11-87 Special Purpose Magnum

Similar to the 11-87 Premier except has dull stock finish, Parkerized exposed metal surfaces. Bolt and carrier have dull blackened coloring. Comes with 26" or 28" barrel with RemChokes, padded Cordura nylon sling and quick detachable swivels. Introduced 1987. Thumbhole model available. Cantilever model has fully rifled barrel; synthetic stock with Monte Carlo comb; cantilever scope mount deer barrel. Comes with sling and swivels. Introduced 1994.

Price: With synthetic stock and forend (SPS) **$791.00**

Remington Model 11-87 SPS Special Purpose Synthetic Camo

Similar to the 11-87 Special Purpose Magnum except has synthetic stock and all metal (except bolt and trigger guard) and stock covered with Mossy Oak® Break-Up™ camo finish. In 12 gauge only, 26", RemChoke. Comes with camo sling, swivels. Introduced 1992. Turkey Camo model has 21" vent rib barrel with RemChoke tube. Completely covered with Mossy Oak® Break-Up™ Brown camouflage. Bolt body, trigger guard and recoil pad are non-reflective black. Super Magnum Synthetic Camo has 23" vent rib barrel with Turkey Super full choke tube, chambered for 12 ga., 3-1/2", TruGlo rifle sights. Version available without TruGlo sights. Introduced 2001. Special Purpose-Deer Shotgun has fully-rifled 21" barrel with rifle sights, black non-reflective, synthetic stock and forend, black carrying sling. Introduced 1993.

Price: From **$963.00**

Remington Model 11-87 SP

Remington Model 1100 Youth Turkey Camo

Remington 1100 LT-20 Deer

Remington Model 1100 Sporting 28

Remington Model 1100 Classic Trap

Remington Model 1100 Sporting 12

Remington Model 11-87 SP and SPS Super Magnum Shotguns

Similar to Model 11-87 Special Purpose Magnum except has 3-1/2" chamber. Available in flat finish American walnut or black synthetic stock, 26" or 28" black matte finished barrel and receiver; Imp. Cyl., Modified and Full RemChoke tubes. Overall length 45-3/4", weighs 8 lbs., 2 oz. Introduced 2000. From Remington Arms Co.

Price: From **$948.00**

Remington Model 11-87 Upland Special Shotgun

Similar to 11-87 Premier except has 23" vent rib barrel with straight grip, English-style walnut stock. Available in 12 or 20 gauge. Overall length 43-1/2", weighs 7-1/4 lbs. (6-1/2 lbs. in 20 ga.). Comes with Imp. Cyl., Modified and Full choke tubes. Introduced 2000.

Price: 12 or 20 gauge **$860.00**

REMINGTON MODEL 1100 CLASSIC FIELD SHOTGUN

Gauge: 12, 16, 20, 28 ga., 2-3/4" chamber; 410 bore; 3" chamber. **Barrel:** 25", 26", 28". **Weight:** 6.5-7.9 lbs. **Stock:** Semi-gloss American walnut stock and fore-end with cut checkering. **Features:** Gas operating system, pressure compensated barrel, machined steel receiver and barrel, high-polish blued finish.White diamond grip cap, white line spacers, butt plate, and Classic Field roll mark. Rem Chokes. Classic Trap model carries a 30" low-profile, light-target contoured vent rib barrel with standard .727" dimensions. Included are three specialized Rem Choke trap tubes: Singles (.027"), Mid Handicap (.034"), and Long Handicap (.041"). The fore-end and Monte Carlo stock are semi-fancy American walnut with deep-cut checkering and a high-gloss finish. Sporting line comes in 12, 20, and 28 gauges and .410 bore. Sporting models include semi-fancy American walnut stock and fore-end, cut checkering, high-gloss finish, 28-inch vent rib, Rem Choke barrel.

Price: Classic Field **$833.00**
Price: Classic Trap **$972.00**
Price: Sporting 12, 20, 28, .410 . . . . **$932.00 to $972.00**

Remington Model SP-10

Remington Model SP-10 Camo

Stoeger Model 2000

Traditions ALS 2100

REMINGTON MODEL SP-10 MAGNUM SHOTGUN

Gauge: 10, 3-1/2" chamber, 2-shot magazine. **Barrel:** 26", 30" (full and mod. RemChokes). **Weight:** 10-3/4 to 11 lbs. **Length:** 47-1/2" overall (26" barrel). **Stock:** Walnut with satin finish or black synthetic with 26" barrel. Checkered grip and forend. **Sights:** Twin bead. **Features:** Stainless steel gas system with moving cylinder; 3/8" vent rib. Receiver and barrel have matte finish. Brown recoil pad. Comes with padded Cordura nylon sling. Introduced 1989. SP-10 Magnum Camo has buttstock, forend, receiver, barrel and magazine cap covered with Mossy Oak® Break-Up™ camo finish; bolt body and trigger guard have matte black finish. RemChoke tube, 26" vent rib barrel with mid-rib bead and Bradley-style front sight, swivel studs and quick-detachable swivels, non-slip Cordura carrying sling in same camo pattern. Introduced 1993.

Price: . . . . **$1,484.00 to $1,627.00**

SARSILMAZ SEMI-AUTOMATIC SHOTGUN

Gauge: 12, 3" chamber. **Barrel:** 26" or 28"; fixed chokes. **Stock:** Walnut or synthetic. **Features:** Handles 2-3/4" or 3" magnum loads. Introduced 2000. Imported from Turkey by Armsport Inc.

Price: With walnut stock **$969.95**
Price: With synthetic stock **$919.95**

STOEGER MODEL 2000 SHOTGUNS

Gauge: 12, 3" chamber, set of five choke tubes (C, IC, M, F, XFT). **Barrel:** 24", 26", 28", 30". **Stock:** Walnut, synthetic, Timber HD, Max-4. **Sights:** Red bar front. **Features:** Inertia-recoil. Minimum recommended load: 3 dram, 1-1/8 oz. Imported by Benelli USA.

Price: Walnut **$435.00**
Price: Synthetic **$425.00**
Price: Max-4, Timber HD **$485.00**
Price: Field and slug barrel combo . . . . **$635.00 to $715.00**

TRADITIONS ALS 2100 SERIES SEMI-AUTOMATIC SHOTGUNS

Gauge: 12, 3" chamber; 20, 3" chamber. **Barrel:** 24", 26", 28" (Imp. Cyl., Mod. and Full choke tubes). **Weight:** 5 lbs., 10 oz. to 6 lbs., 5 oz. **Length:** 44" to 48" overall. **Stock:** Walnut or black composite. **Features:** Gas-operated; vent rib barrel with Beretta-style threaded muzzle. Introduced 2001 by Traditions.

Price: Field Model (12 or 20 ga., 26" or 28" bbl., walnut stock) **$479.00**
Price: Youth Model (12 or 20 ga., 24" bbl., walnut stock) **$479.00**
Price: (12 or 20 ga., 26" or 28" barrel, composite stock) **$459.00**

Traditions ALS 2100 Turkey Semi-Automatic Shotgun

Similar to ALS 2100 Field Model except chambered in 12 gauge, 3" only with 26" barrel and Mossy Oak® Break Up™ camo finish. Weighs 6 lbs.; 46" overall.

Price: **$519.00**

Traditions ALS 2100 Waterfowl Semi-Automatic Shotgun

Similar to ALS 2100 Field Model except chambered in 12 gauge, 3" only with 28" barrel and Advantage® Wetlands™ camo finish. Weighs 6.25 lbs.; 48" overall. Multi chokes.

Price: **$529.00**

Traditions ALS 2100 Hunter Combo

Similar to ALS 2100 Field Model except 2 barrels, 28" vent rib and 24" fully rifled deer. Weighs 6 to 6.5 lbs.; 48" overall. Choice TruGlo adj. sights or fixed cantilever mount on rifled barrel. Multi chokes.

Price: Walnut, rifle barrel **$609.00**
Price: Walnut, cantilever **$629.00**
Price: Synthetic **$579.00**

Traditions ALS 2100 Slug Hunter Shotgun

Similar to ALS 2100 Field Model, 12 ga., 24" barrel, overall length 44"; weighs 6.25 lbs. Designed specifically for the deer hunter. Rifled barrel has 1 in 36" twist. Fully adjustable fiber-optic sights.

Price: Walnut, rifle barrel **$529.00**
Price: Synthetic, rifle barrel **$499.00**
Price: Walnut, cantilever **$549.00**
Price: Synthetic, cantilever **$529.00**

Traditions ALS 2100 Home Security Shotgun

Similar to ALS 2100 Field Model, 12 ga., 20" barrel, overall length 40", weighs 6 lbs. Can be reloaded with one hand while shouldered and on-target. Swivel studs installed in stock.

Price: **$399.00**

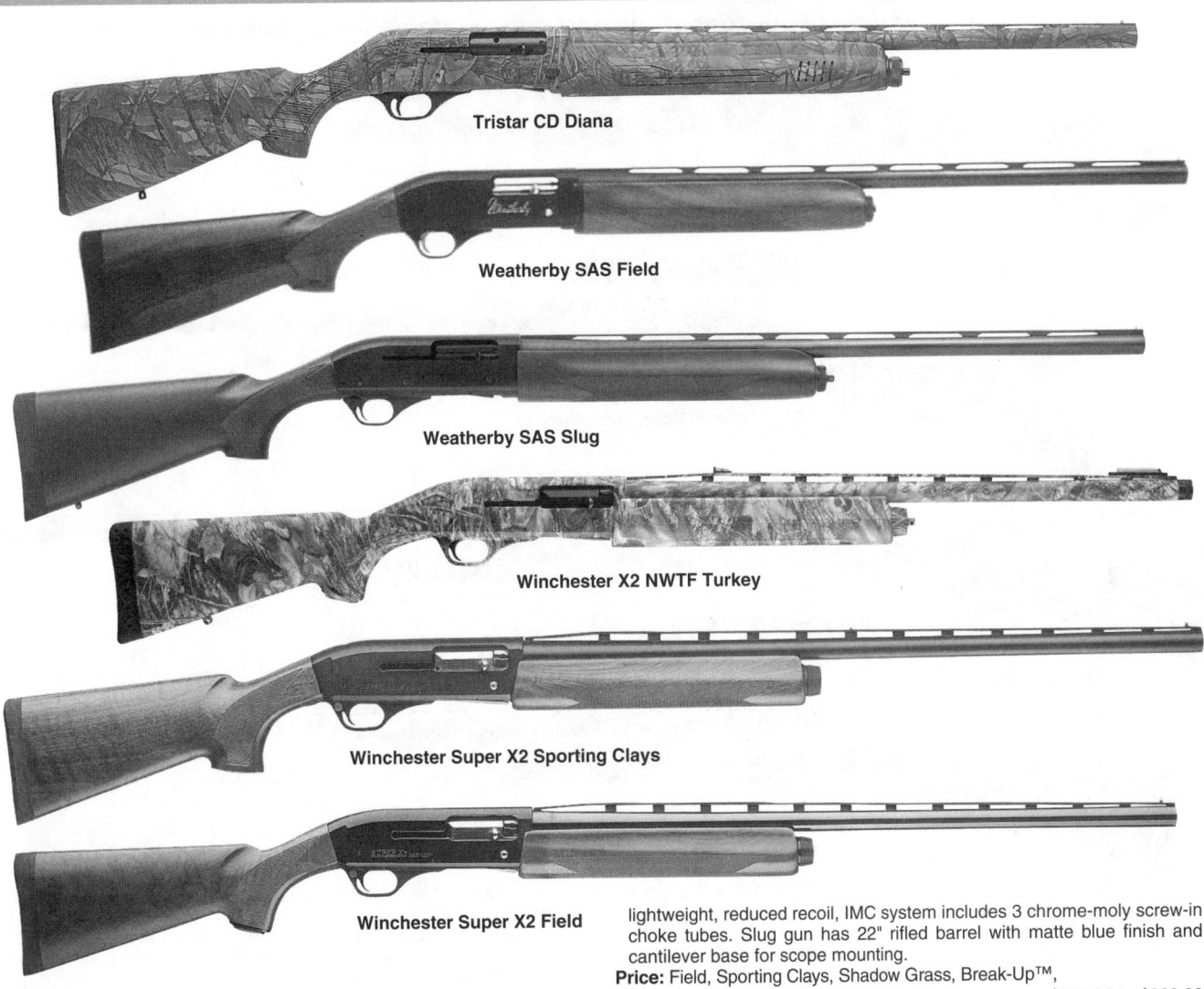

Tristar CD Diana

Weatherby SAS Field

Weatherby SAS Slug

Winchester X2 NWTF Turkey

Winchester Super X2 Sporting Clays

Winchester Super X2 Field

TRISTAR CD DIANA AUTO SHOTGUNS
Gauge: 12, shoots 2-3/4" or 3" interchangeably. **Barrel:** 24", 26", 28" (Imp. Cyl., Mod., Full choke tubes). **Stock:** European walnut or black synthetic. **Features:** Gas-operated action; blued barrel; checkered pistol grip and forend; vent rib barrel. Available with synthetic and camo stock and in slug model. First introduced 1999 under the name "Tristar Phantom." Imported by Tristar Sporting Arms Ltd.
Price: . . . . **$399.00 to $535.00**

VERONA MODEL SX400 SEMI AUTO SHOTGUNS
Gauge: 12. **Barrel:** 26", 30". **Weight:** 6-1/2 lbs. **Stock:** Walnut, black composite. **Sights:** Red dot. **Features:** Aluminum receivers, gas-operated, 2-3/4" or 3" Magnum shells without adj. or Mod., 4 screw-in chokes and wrench included. Sling swivels, gold trigger. Blued barrel. Imported from Italy by B.C. Outdoors.
Price: 401S, 12 ga. **$398.40**
Price: 405SDS, 12 ga. **$610.00**
Price: 405L, 12 ga. **$331.20**

WEATHERBY SAS (SEMI-AUTOMATIC SHOTGUNS)
Gauge: 12 ga. **Barrel:** Vent ribbed, 24" to 30". **Weight:** 7 lbs. to 7-3/4 lbs. **Stock:** SAS field and sporting clays, walnut. SAS Shadow Grass, Break-Up™, Synthetic, composite. **Sights:** SAS sporting clays, brass front and mid-point rear. SAS Shadow Grass and Break-Up™, HiViz front and brass mid. Synthetic has brass front. **Features:** Easy to shoot, load, clean;

lightweight, reduced recoil, IMC system includes 3 chrome-moly screw-in choke tubes. Slug gun has 22" rifled barrel with matte blue finish and cantilever base for scope mounting.
Price: Field, Sporting Clays, Shadow Grass, Break-Up™,
Synthetic, Slug Gun . . . . **$879.00 to $969.00**

WINCHESTER SUPER X2 AUTO SHOTGUNS
Gauge: 12, 3", 3-1/2" chamber. **Barrel:** Belgian, 24", 26", 28"; Invector Plus choke tubes. **Weight:** 7-1/4 to 7-1/2 lbs. **Stock:** 14-1/4"x1-3/4"x2". Walnut or black synthetic. **Features:** Gas-operated action shoots all loads without adjustment; vent rib barrels; 4-shot magazine. Introduced 1999. Assembled in Portugal by U.S. Repeating Arms Co.
Price: Magnum, 3-1/2", synthetic stock, 26" or 28" bbl. **$1,185.00**
Price: Camo Waterfowl, 3-1/2", Mossy Oak® Shadow Grass **$1,185.00**
Price: NWTF Turkey, 3-1/2", Mossy Oak® Break-Up™ camo **$1,236.00**
Price: Universal Hunter Model **$1,252.00**

Winchester Super X2 Sporting Clays Auto Shotguns
Similar to the Super X2 except has two gas pistons (one for target loads, one for heavy 3" loads), adjustable comb system and high-post rib. Back-bored barrel with Invector Plus choke tubes. Offered in 28" and 30" barrels. Introduced 2001. From U.S. Repeating Arms Co.
Price: Super X2 sporting clays **$1,015.00**
Price: Signature red stock **$976.00**

Winchester Super X2 Field 3" Auto Shotgun
Similar to the Super X2 except 3" chamber, walnut stock and forearm and high-profile rib. Back-bored barrel and Invector Plus choke tubes. Introduced 2001. From U.S. Repeating Arms Co.
Price: Super X2 Field 3", 26" or 28" bbl.. . . . . **$1,015.00**

Includes a wide variety of sporting guns and guns suitable for competitive shooting.

Benelli Nova Pump

Benelli Nova Pump Slug

Browning BPS 10 gauge

Browning BPS 10 gauge Mossy Oak® Shadow Grass

BENELLI NOVA PUMP SHOTGUNS
Gauge: 12, 20. **Barrel:** 24", 26", 28". **Stock:** Synthetic, Max-4 and Timber H-D (12 ga. and 20 ga). **Sights:** Red bar. **Features:** 2-3/ 4", 3" chamber (3-1/2" 12 ga. only). Montefeltro rotating bolt design with dual action bars, magazine cut-off, synthetic trigger assembly, 4-shot magazine. Introduced 1999. Imported from Italy by Benelli USA.
Price: Synthetic $360.00
Price: Timber HD $440.00
Price: Max-4 .... $440.00

BENELLI NOVA PUMP TACTICAL SHOTGUN
Similar to the Nova except has 18.5" barrel with adjustable rifle-type or ghost ring sights; weighs 7.2 lbs.; black synthetic stock. Introduced 1999. Imported from Italy by Benelli USA.
Price: With rifle sights $325.00
Price: With ghost-ring sights $360.00

BENELLI NOVA PUMP RIFLED SLUG GUN
Similar to Nova Pump Slug Gun except has 24" barrel and rifled bore; open rifle sights; synthetic stock; weighs 8.1 lbs.
Price: Synthetic $535.00
Price: Timber HD $625.00
Price: Field/Slug combo, synthetic $560.00

BROWNING BPS PUMP SHOTGUNS
Gauge: 10, 12, 3-1/2" chamber; 12 or 20, 3" chamber (2-3/4" in target guns), 28, 2-3/4" chamber, 5-shot magazine, .410, 3" chamber. **Barrel:** 10 ga.-24" Buck Special, 28", 30", 32" Invector; 12, 20 ga.-22", 24", 26", 28", 30", 32" (Imp. Cyl., Mod. or Full), .410-26" barrel. (Imp. Cyl., Mod. and Full

choke tubes.) Also available with Invector choke tubes, 12 or 20 ga.; Upland Special has 22" barrel with Invector tubes. BPS 3" and 3-1/2" have back-bored barrel. **Weight:** 7 lbs., 8 oz. (28" barrel). **Length:** 48-3/4" overall (28" barrel). **Stock:** 14-1/4"x1-1/2"x2-1/2". Select walnut, semi-beavertail forend, full pistol grip stock. **Features:** All 12 gauge 3" guns except Buck Special and game guns have back-bored barrels with Invector Plus choke tubes. Bottom feeding and ejection, receiver top safety, high post vent rib. Double action bars eliminate binding. Vent rib barrels only. All 12 and 20 gauge guns with 3" chamber available with fully engraved receiver flats at no extra cost. Each gauge has its own unique game scene. Introduced 1977. Imported from Japan by Browning.
Price: 12 ga., 3-1/2" Stalker (black syn. stock)............... $596.00
Price: 12, 20 ga., Hunter, Invector Plus $509.00
Price: 12 ga. Deer Hunter (22" rifled bbl., cantilever mount) $624.00
Price: 28 ga., Hunter, Invector $544.00
Price: .410, Hunter, Invector $544.00

BROWNING BPS 10 GAUGE CAMO PUMP SHOTGUN
Similar to the standard BPS except completely covered with Mossy Oak® Shadow Grass camouflage. Available with 24", 26", 28" barrel. Introduced 1999. Imported by Browning.
Price:... $709.00

BROWNING BPS GAME GUN DEER HUNTER
Similar to the standard BPS except has newly designed receiver/magazine tube/barrel mounting system to eliminate play, heavy 20.5" barrel with rifle-type sights with adjustable rear, solid receiver scope mount, "rifle" stock dimensions for scope or open sights, sling swivel studs. Gloss or matte finished wood with checkering, polished blue metal. Introduced 1992.
Price:... $624.00

Charles Daly Maxi-Mag Turkey

Escort AimGuard

Escort Field Hunter

BROWNING BPS STALKER PUMP SHOTGUN
Same gun as the standard BPS except all exposed metal parts have a matte blued finish and the stock has a durable black finish with a black recoil pad. Available in 10 ga. (3-1/2") and 12 ga. with 3" or 3-1/2" chamber, 22", 28", 30" barrel with Invector choke system. Introduced 1987.
Price: 12 ga., 3" chamber, Invector Plus..................... **$492.00**
Price: 10, 12 ga., 3-1/2" chamber **$596.00**

BROWNING BPS NWTF TURKEY SERIES PUMP SHOTGUN
Similar to the BPS Stalker except has full coverage Mossy Oak® Break-Up™ camo finish on synthetic stock, forearm and exposed metal parts. Offered in 10 and 12 gauge, 3" or 3-1/2" chamber; 24" bbl. has extra-full choke tube and HiViz fiber-optic sights. Introduced 2001. From Browning.
Price: 10 ga., 3-1/2" chamber............................. **$760.00**
Price: 12 ga., 3-1/2" chamber **$760.00**
Price: 12 ga., 3" chamber **$636.00**

BROWNING BPS MICRO PUMP SHOTGUN
Similar to the BPS Stalker except 20 ga. only, 22" Invector barrel, stock has pistol grip with recoil pad. Length of pull is 13-1/4"; weighs 6 lbs., 12 oz. Introduced 1986.
Price:... **$509.00**

CHARLES DALY FIELD PUMP SHOTGUNS
Gauge: 12, 20. **Barrel:** Interchangeable 18-1/2", 24", 26", 28", 30" multi-choked. **Weight:** NA. **Stock:** Synthetic, various finishes, recoil pad. **Receiver:** Machined aluminum. **Features:** Field Tactical and Slug models come with adustable sights; Youth models may be upgraded to full size. Imported from Akkar, Turkey.
Price: Field Tactical **$199.00**
Price: Field Hunter **$219.00**
Price: Field Hunter, Realtree Hardwood **$219.00**
Price: Field Hunter Advantage **$219.00**

CHARLES DALY MAXI-MAG PUMP SHOTGUNS
Gauge: 12 gauge, 3-1/2". **Barrel:** 24", 26", 28"; multi-choke system. **Weight:** NA. **Stock:** Synthetic black, Realtree Hardwoods, or Advantage Timber receiver, aluminum alloy. **Features:** Handles 2-3/4", 3" and 3-1/2" loads. Interchangeable ported barrels; Turkey package includes sling, HiViz sights, XX Full choke. Imported from Akkar, Turkey.
Price: Field Hunter **$259.00**
Price: Field Hunter Advantage **$319.00**
Price: Field Hunter Hardwoods **$319.00**
Price: Field Hunter Turkey **$389.00**

DIAMOND 12 GA. PUMP SHOTGUNS
Gauge: 12, 2-3/4" and 3" chambers. **Barrel:** 18"-30". **Weight:** 7 lbs. **Stock:** Walnut, synthetic. **Features:** Aluminum one-piece receiver sculpted for lighter weight. Double locking on fixed bolt. Gold, Elite and Panther series with vented barrels and 3 chokes. All series slug guns available (Gold and Elite with sights). Imported from Istanbul by ADCO Sales.
Price: Gold, 28" vent rib w/3 chokes, walnut **$359.00**
Price: Gold, 28", synthetic **$329.00**
Price: Gold Slug, 24" w/sights, walnut or synthetic .... **$329.00 to $359.00**
Price: Silver Mariner 18.5" Slug, synthetic **$399.00**
Price: Silver Mariner 22" vent rib w/3 chokes **$419.00**
Price: Elite, 22" slug w/sights; 24", 28" vent rib w/3 chokes, walnut .... **$329.00 to $349.00**
Price: Panther, 28", 30" vent rib w/3 chokes, synthetic **$279.00**
Price: Panther,18.5", 22" Slug, synthetic .... **$209.00 to $265.00**
Price: Imperial 12 ga., 28" vent rib w/3 chokes, 3.5" chamber, walnut **$399.00**

ESCORT PUMP SHOTGUNS
Gauge: 12, 20; 3" chamber. **Barrel:** 18" (AimGuard model); 22" (FH Slug model), 24", 26" and 28" (Field Hunter models), choke tubes (M, IC, F); turkey choke w/24" bbl. **Weight:** 6.4 to 7 lbs. **Stock:** Polymer, black chrome or camo finish. **Features:** Alloy receiver w/ dovetail for sight mounting. Two stock adjusting spacers included. Introduced 2003. From Legacy Sports International.
Price: Field Hunter, black stock **$247.00**
Price: Camo, 24" bbl. **$363.00**
Price: AimGuard, 20" bbl., black stock **$211.00**
Price: MarineGuard, nickel finish **$254.00**
Price: Combo (2 bbls.) **$270.00**

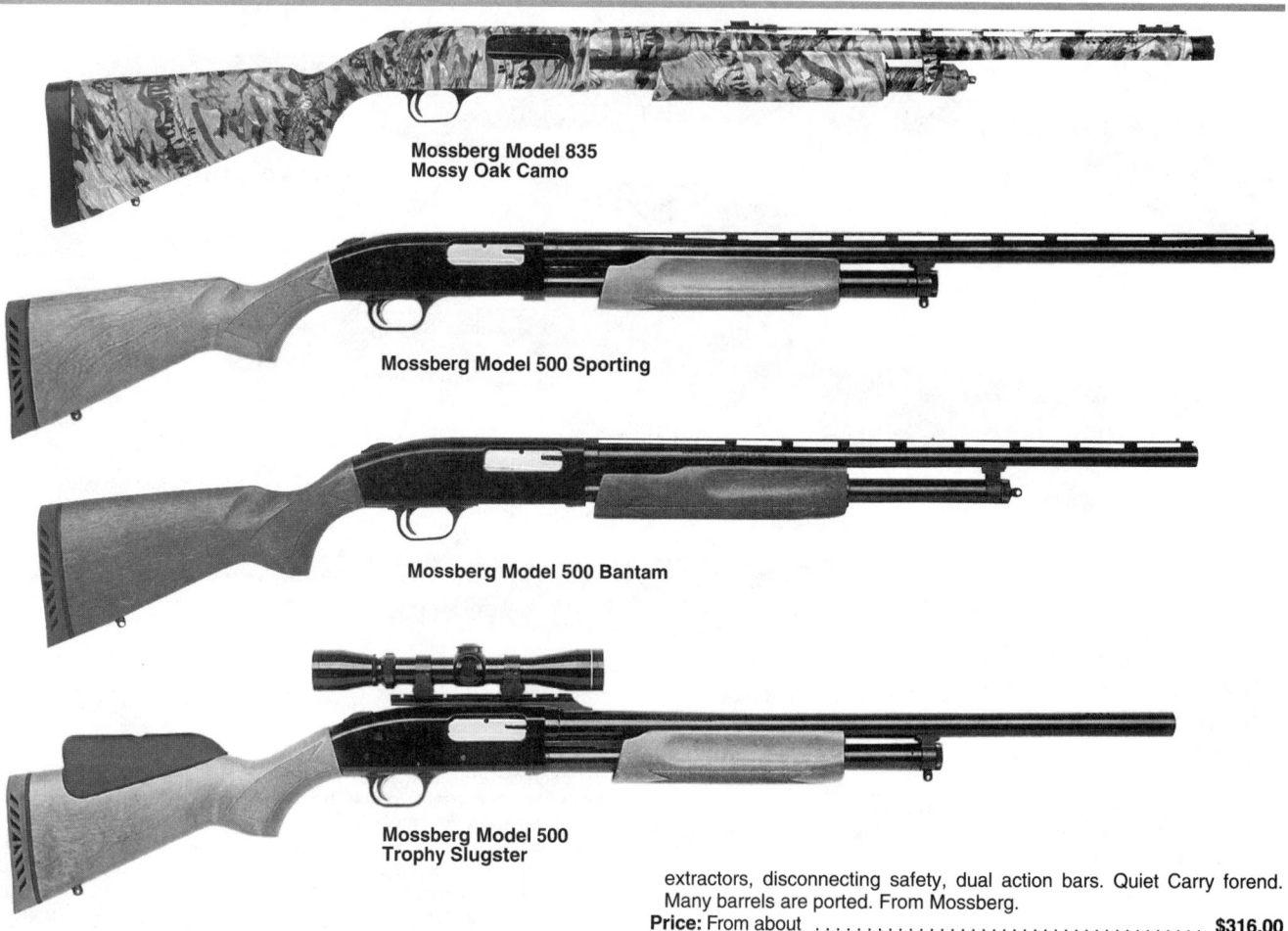

**Mossberg Model 835
Mossy Oak Camo**

Mossberg Model 500 Sporting

Mossberg Model 500 Bantam

**Mossberg Model 500
Trophy Slugster**

MOSSBERG MODEL 835 ULTI-MAG PUMP SHOTGUNS

Gauge: 12, 3-1/2" chamber. **Barrel:** Ported 24" rifled bore, 24", 28", Accu-Mag choke tubes for steel or lead shot. **Weight:** 7-3/4 lbs. **Length:** 48-1/2" overall. **Stock:** 14"x1-1/2"x2-1/2". Dual Comb. Cut-checkered hardwood or camo synthetic; both have recoil pad. **Sights:** White bead front, brass mid-bead; fiber-optic rear. **Features:** Shoots 2-3/4", 3" or 3-1/2" shells. Back-bored and ported barrel to reduce recoil, improve patterns. Ambidextrous thumb safety, twin extractors, dual slide bars. Mossberg Cablelock included. Introduced 1988.

Price: 28" vent rib, hardwood stock. $394.00
Price: Combos, 24" rifled or smooth bore, rifle sights, 24" vent rib
Accu-Mag Ulti-Full choke tube, Mossy Oak® camo finish $556.00
Price: RealTree Camo Turkey, 24" vent rib, Accu-Mag extra-full
tube, synthetic stock $574.00
Price: Mossy Oak® Camo, 28" vent rib, Accu-Mag tubes,
synthetic stock $574.00
Price: OFM Camo, 28" vent rib, Accu-Mag Mod. tube,
synthetic stock $438.00

Mossberg Model 835 Synthetic Stock Shotgun

Similar to the Model 835, except with 28" ported barrel with Accu-Mag Mod. choke tube, Parkerized finish, black synthetic stock and forend. Introduced 1998. Made in U.S. by Mossberg.
Price: $394.00

MOSSBERG MODEL 500 SPORTING PUMP SHOTGUNS

Gauge: 12, 20, .410, 3" chamber. **Barrel:** 18-1/2" to 28" with fixed or Accu-Choke, plain or vent rib. **Weight:** 6-1/4 lbs. (.410), 7-1/4 lbs. (12). **Length:** 48" overall (28" barrel). **Stock:** 14"x1-1/2"x2-1/2". Walnut-stained hardwood. Cut-checkered grip and forend. **Sights:** White bead front, brass mid-bead; fiber-optic. **Features:** Ambidextrous thumb safety, twin extractors, disconnecting safety, dual action bars. Quiet Carry forend. Many barrels are ported. From Mossberg.
Price: From about $316.00
Price: Sporting Combos (field barrel and Slugster barrel). From . . $381.00

Mossberg Model 500 Bantam Pump Shotgun

Same as the Model 500 Sporting Pump except 12 or 20 gauge, 22" vent rib Accu-Choke barrel with choke tube set; has 1" shorter stock, reduced length from pistol grip to trigger, reduced forend reach. Introduced 1992.
Price: $316.00
Price: With Realtree Hardwoods camouflage finish (20 ga. only) . . $364.00

Mossberg Model 500 Camo Pump Shotgun

Same as the Model 500 Sporting Pump except 12 gauge only and entire gun is covered with Mossy Oak® Advantage camouflage finish. Receiver drilled and tapped for scope mounting. Comes with quick detachable swivel studs, swivels, camouflage sling, Mossberg Cablelock.
Price: From about $364.00

Mossberg Model 500 Persuader/Cruiser Shotguns

Similar to Mossberg Model 500 except has 18-1/2" or 20" barrel with cylinder bore choke, synthetic stock and blue or Parkerized finish. Available in 12, 20 and .410 with bead or ghost ring sights, 6- or 8-shot magazines. From Mossberg.
Price: 12 gauge, 20" barrel, 8-shot, bead sight. $357.00
Price: 20 gauge or .410, 18-1/2" barrel, 6-shot, bead sight $357.00
Price: Home Security 410 (.410, 18-1/2" barrel
with spreader choke) $360.00

MOSSBERG MODEL 590 SPECIAL PURPOSE SHOTGUN

Similar to Model 500 except has Parkerized or Marinecote finish, 9-shot magazine and black synthetic stock (some models feature Speed Feed). Available in 12 gauge only with 20", cylinder bore barrel. Weighs 7-1/4 lbs. From Mossberg.
Price: Bead sight, heat shield over barrel $525.00

Remington 870 Wingmaster

Remington Model 870 50th Anniversary Classic Trap

Remington Model 870 Marine Magnum

Remington Model 870 Wingmaster LW

NEW ENGLAND PARDNER PUMP SHOTGUN

Gauge: 12 ga., 3". **Barrel:** 28" vent rib, screw-in Modified choke tube. **Weight:** 7-1/2 lbs. **Length:** 48-1/2". **Stock:** American walnut, grooved forend, ventilated recoil pad. **Sights:** Bead front. **Features:** Machined steel receiver, double action bars, five-shot magazine.
Price: $200.00

REMINGTON MODEL 870 WINGMASTER SHOTGUNS

Gauge: 12 ga., 16 ga., 3" chamber. **Barrel:** 26", 28", 30" (RemChokes). **Weight:** 7-1/4 lbs. **Length:** 46", 48". **Stock:** Walnut, hardwood, synthetic. **Sights:** Single bead (Twin bead Wingmaster). **Features:** Light contour barrel. Double action bars, cross-bolt safety, blue finish.
Price: Wingmaster, walnut, blued, 26", 28", 30" $665.00
Price: 870 Wingmaster Super Magnum, 3-1/2" chamber, 28" $732.00

Remington Model 870 Classic Trap Shotgun

Similar to Model 870 Wingmaster except has 30" vent rib, light contour barrel, singles, mid- and long-handicap choke tubes, semi-fancy American walnut stock, high-polish blued receiver with engraving. Chamber 2-1/2". From Remington Arms Co.
Price: $872.00

Remington Model 870 Marine Magnum Shotgun

Similar to 870 Wingmaster except all metal plated with electroless nickel, black synthetic stock and forend. Has 18" plain barrel (cyl.), bead front sight, 7-shot magazine. Introduced 1992.
Price: $647.00

Remington Model 870 Wingmaster LW Shotgun

Similar to Model 870 Wingmaster except in 28 gauge and .410-bore only, 25" vent rib barrel with RemChoke tubes, high-gloss wood finish.
Price: .410-bore $695.00
Price: 28 gauge $749.00

Remington Model 870 Express Shotguns

Similar to Model 870 Wingmaster except walnut-toned hardwood stock with solid, black recoil pad and pressed checkering on grip and forend. Outside metal surfaces have black oxide finish. Comes with 26" or 28" vent rib barrel with mod. RemChoke tube.
Price: 12 ga., 20 ga., 16 ga. (28") $345.00
Price: Express Combo, 12 ga., 26" vent rib with mod. RemChoke and 20" fully rifled barrel with rifle sights, or RemChoke . . . . . $469.00 to $503.00
Price: Express synthetic, 12-ga., 26" or 28" $345.00
Price: Express combo (20 ga.) with extra deer rifled barrel, fully rifled or RemChoke . . . . $469.00 to $503.00

Remington Model 870 Express Super Magnum Shotgun

Similar to Model 870 Express except 28" vent rib barrel with 3-1/2" chamber, vented recoil pad. Introduced 1998.
Price: $389.00
Price: Super Magnum synthetic, 26" $389.00
Price: Super Magnum turkey camo (full-coverage RealTree Advantage camo), 23" $513.00
Price: Super Magnum combo (26" with Mod. RemChoke and 20" fully rifled deer barrel with 3" chamber and rifle sights; wood stock) $536.00
Price: Super Magnum synthetic turkey, 23" (black) $403.00

Remington Model 870 Wingmaster Super Magnum Shotgun

Similar to Model 870 Express Super Magnum except high-polish blued finish, 28" ventilated barrel with Imp. Cyl., Modified and Full choke tubes, checkered high-gloss walnut stock. Overall length 48", weighs 7-1/2 lbs. Introduced 2000.
Price: 3-1/2" chamber $732.00

Remington Model 870 Sps Super Slug Deer Gun Shotgun

Similar to the Model 870 Express synthetic except has 23" rifled, modified contour barrel with cantilever scope mount. Comes with black synthetic stock and forend with swivel studs, black Cordura nylon sling. Fully rifled centilever barrel. Introduced 1999.
Price: $580.00

Remington Model 870 Express Super Magnum

Remington Model 870 Express Deer Gun

Remington Model 870 Express Turkey

Remington Model 870 SPS Super Slug Deer Gun

Remington Model 870 SPS-T Camo

Remington Model 870 SPS-T Super Magnum Camo Shotguns
Similar to the Model 870 Express synthetic, chambered for 12 ga., 3" shells, has Mossy Oak® Break-Up™ synthetic stock and metal treatment, TruGlo fiber-optic sights. Introduced 2001.
Price: 20" RS, Rem. choke **$653.00**

Remington Model 870 Express Deer Shotguns
Same as Model 870 Express except 20" barrel with fixed imp. cyl. choke, open iron sights, Monte Carlo stock. Introduced 1991.
Price: **$345.00**
Price: With fully rifled barrel **$385.00**

Remington Model 870 Express Turkey Shotguns
Same as Model 870 Express except 3" chamber, 21" vent rib turkey barrel and extra-full Rem. choke turkey tube; 12 ga. only. Introduced 1991.
Price: **$359.00**
Price: Express Turkey Camo stock has Skyline Excel camo, matte black metal **$412.00**

Remington Model 870 Express Synthetic 18" Shotgun
Similar to Model 870 Express with 18" barrel except synthetic stock and forend; 7-shot. Introduced 1994.
Price: **$332.00**

REMINGTON MODEL 870 SPS SUPER MAGNUM CAMO SHOTGUN
Gauge: 12, 3-1/2" chamber. **Barrel:** 26", 28", vent rib, with Full, Mod., Imp. Cyl. RemChoke. **Weight:** 7-1/4 lbs. to 7-1/2 lbs. **Length:** 46" to 481/2" overall. **Stock:** Mossy Oak® Break-Up™ camo finish. **Sights:** Metal bead front. **Features:** Synthetic stock and all metal (except bolt and trigger guard) and stock covered with Mossy Oak® Break-Up™ camo finish. Comes with camo sling, swivels.
Price: **$653.00**

WINCHESTER MODEL 9410 LEVER-ACTION SHOTGUN
Gauge: .410, 2-1/2" chamber. **Barrel:** 24" cyl. bore, also Invector choke system. **Weight:** 6-3/4 lbs. **Length:** 42-1/8" overall. **Stock:** Checkered walnut straight-grip; checkered walnut forearm. **Sights:** Adjustable "V" rear, TruGlo® front. **Features:** Model 94 rifle action (smoothbore) chambered for .410 shotgun. Angle Controlled Eject extractor/ejector; choke tubes; 9-shot tubular magazine; 13-1/2" length of pull. Introduced 2001. From U.S. Repeating Arms Co.
Price: 9410 fixed choke **$626.00**
Price: 9410 Packer w/chokes **$647.00**
Price: 9410 w/Invector, traditional model **$626.00**
Price: 9410 w/Invector, Packer model **$647.00**
Price: 9410 w/Invector, semi-fancy traditional **$626.00**

Includes a variety of game guns and guns for competitive shooting.

Beretta DT Trident Skeet

Beretta Series 682 Gold E Sporting

Beretta Series 682 Gold E Trap Combo

Beretta S687 EELL Combo

Beretta 686 Onyx

BERETTA DT10 TRIDENT SHOTGUNS

Gauge: 12, 2-3/4", 3" chambers. **Barrel:** 28", 30", 32", 34"; competition-style vent rib; fixed or Optima choke tubes. **Weight:** 7.9 to 9 lbs. **Stock:** High-grade walnut stock with oil finish; hand-checkered grip and forend, adjustable stocks available. **Features:** Detachable, adjustable trigger group, raised and thickened receiver, forend iron has adjustment nut to guarantee wood-to-metal fit. Introduced 2000. Imported from Italy by Beretta USA.
Price: DT10 Trident Trap (selective, lockable single trigger, adjustable stock. . . . . **$,8500.00**
Price: DT10 Trident Top Single **$10,790.00**
Price: DT10 Trident X Trap Combo (single and o/u barrels) **$11,040.00**
Price: DT10 Trident Skeet (skeet stock with rounded recoil pad, tapered rib) **$8,030.00**
Price: DT10 Trident Sporting (sporting clays stock with rounded recoil pad) **$7,850.00**
Price: DT10L Sporting **$8,475.00**

BERETTA SERIES 682 GOLD E SKEET, TRAP, SPORTING O/U SHOTGUNS

Gauge: 12, 2-3/4" chambers. **Barrel:** skeet-28"; trap-30" and 32", Imp. Mod. & Full and Mobilchoke; trap mono shotguns-32" and 34" Mobilchoke; trap top single guns-32" and 34" Full and Mobilchoke; trap combo sets-from 30" O/U, to 32" O/U, 34" top single. **Stock:** Close-grained walnut, hand checkered. **Sights:** White Bradley bead front sight and center bead. **Features:** Receiver has Greystone gunmetal gray finish with gold accents. Trap Monte Carlo stock has deluxe trap recoil pad. Various grades available. Imported from Italy by Beretta USA.
Price: 682 Gold E Trap with adjustable stock **$4,325.00**
Price: 682 Gold E Trap Top Combo **$5,475.00**
Price: 682 Gold E Sporting **$3,550.00**
Price: 682 Gold E skeet, adjustable stock **$4,325.00**

BERETTA 686 ONYX O/U SHOTGUNS

Gauge: 12, 20, 28; 3", 3.5" chambers. **Barrel:** 26", 28" (Mobilchoke tubes). **Weight:** 6.8-6.9 lbs. **Stock:** Checkered American walnut. **Features:** Intended for the beginning sporting clays shooter. Has wide, vented target rib, radiused recoil pad. Polished black finish on receiver and barrels. Introduced 1993. Imported from Italy by Beretta U.S.A.
Price: White Onyx. **$1,875.00**
Price: Onyx Pro **$1,875.00**
Price: Onyx Pro 3.5 . . . . **$1,975.00**

Beretta S686 Silver Pigeon

Beretta Over/Under Field Shotgun

Beretta S687 Silver Pigeon II Sporting

Beretta SO9

BERETTA SILVER PIGEON O/U SHOTGUNS

Gauge: 12, 20, 28, 3" chambers (2-3/4" 28 ga.). .410 bore, 3" chamber. **Barrel:** 26", 28". **Weight:** 6.8 lbs. **Stock:** Checkered walnut. **Features:** Interchangeable barrels (20 and 28 ga.), single selective gold-plated trigger, boxlock action, auto safety, Schnabel forend.

Price: Silver Pigeon S	**$2,150.00**
Price: Silver Pigeon S Combo	**$2,975.00**
Price: Silver Pigeon II	**$2,525.00**
Price: Silver Pigeon II, 28 ga.	**$3,475.00**
Price: Silver Pigeon III	**$2,650.00**
Price: Silver Pigeon IV	**$2,955.00**
Price: Silver Pigeon V	**$3,495.00**

BERETTA ULTRALIGHT O/U SHOTGUNS

Gauge: 12, 2-3/4" chambers. **Barrel:** 26", 28", Mobilchoke tubes. **Weight:** About 5 lbs., 13 oz. **Stock:** Select American walnut with checkered grip and forend. **Features:** Low-profile aluminum alloy receiver with titanium breech face insert. Electroless nickel receiver with game scene engraving. Single selective trigger; automatic safety. Introduced 1992. Ultralight Deluxe except has matte electroless nickel finish receiver with gold game scene engraving; matte oil-finished, select walnut stock and forend. Imported from Italy by Beretta U.S.A.

Price:	**$1,975.00**
Price: Ultralight Deluxe	**$2,350.00**

BERETTA COMPETITION SHOTGUNS

Gauge: 12, 20, 28, and .410 bore, 2-3/4", 3" and 3-1/2" chambers. **Barrel:** 26" and 28" (Mobilchoke tubes). **Stock:** Close-grained walnut. **Features:** Highly-figured, American walnut stocks and forends, and a unique, weather-resistant finish on barrels. Silver designates standard 686, 687 models with silver receivers; 686 Silver Pigeon has enhanced engraving pattern, Schnabel forend; Gold indicates higher grade 686EL, 687EL models with full sideplates; Diamond is for 687EELL models with highest grade wood, engraving. Case provided with Gold and Diamond grades. Imported from Italy by Beretta U.S.A.

Price: S687 Silver Pigeon II Sporting	**$2,850.00**
Price: S687 EL Gold Pigeon II (deep relief engraving)	**$5,095.00**
Price: S687 EL Gold Pigeon II combo, 20/28 or 28/.410	**$6,195.00**
Price: S687 EELL Gold Pigeon Sporting (D.R. engraving)	**$6,495.00**
Price: Gold Sporting Pigeon	**$4,971.00**
Price: 28 and 410 combo	**NA**

BERETTA MODEL SO5, SO6, SO9 SHOTGUNS

Gauge: 12, 2-3/4" chambers. **Barrel:** To customer specs. **Stock:** To customer specs. **Features:** SO5-trap, skeet and sporting clays models SO5; SO6-SO6 and SO6 EELL are field models. SO6 has a case-hardened or silver receiver with contour hand engraving. SO6 EELL has hand-engraved receiver in a fine floral or "fine English" pattern or game scene, with bas-relief chisel work and gold inlays. SO6 and SO6 EELL are available with sidelocks removable by hand. Imported from Italy by Beretta U.S.A.

Price: SO5 Trap, skeet, Sporting	**$13,000.00**
Price: SO6 Trap, skeet, Sporting	**$17,500.00**
Price: SO6 EELL Field, custom specs	**$28,000.00**
Price: SO9 (12, 20, 28, .410, 26", 28", 30", any choke)	**$31,000.00**

BRNO ZH 300 O/U SHOTGUNS

Gauge: 12, 2-3/4" chambers. **Barrel:** 26", 27-1/2", 29" (skeet, Imp. Cyl., Mod., Full). **Weight:** 7 lbs. **Length:** 44.4" overall. **Stock:** European walnut. **Features:** Double triggers; automatic safety; polished blue finish, engraved receiver. Announced 1998. Imported from the Czech Republic by Euro-Imports.

Price: ZH 301, field	**$594.00**
Price: ZH 302, skeet	**$608.00**
Price: ZH 303, 12 ga. trap	**$608.00**
Price: ZH 321, 16 ga.	**$595.00**

BRNO 501.2 O/U SHOTGUN

Gauge: 12, 2-3/4" chambers. **Barrel:** 27.5" (Full & Mod.). **Weight:** 7 lbs. **Length:** 44" overall. **Stock:** European walnut. **Features:** Boxlock action with double triggers; ejectors; automatic safety; hand-cut checkering. Announced 1998. Imported from the Czech Republic by Euro-Imports.

Price:	**$850.00**

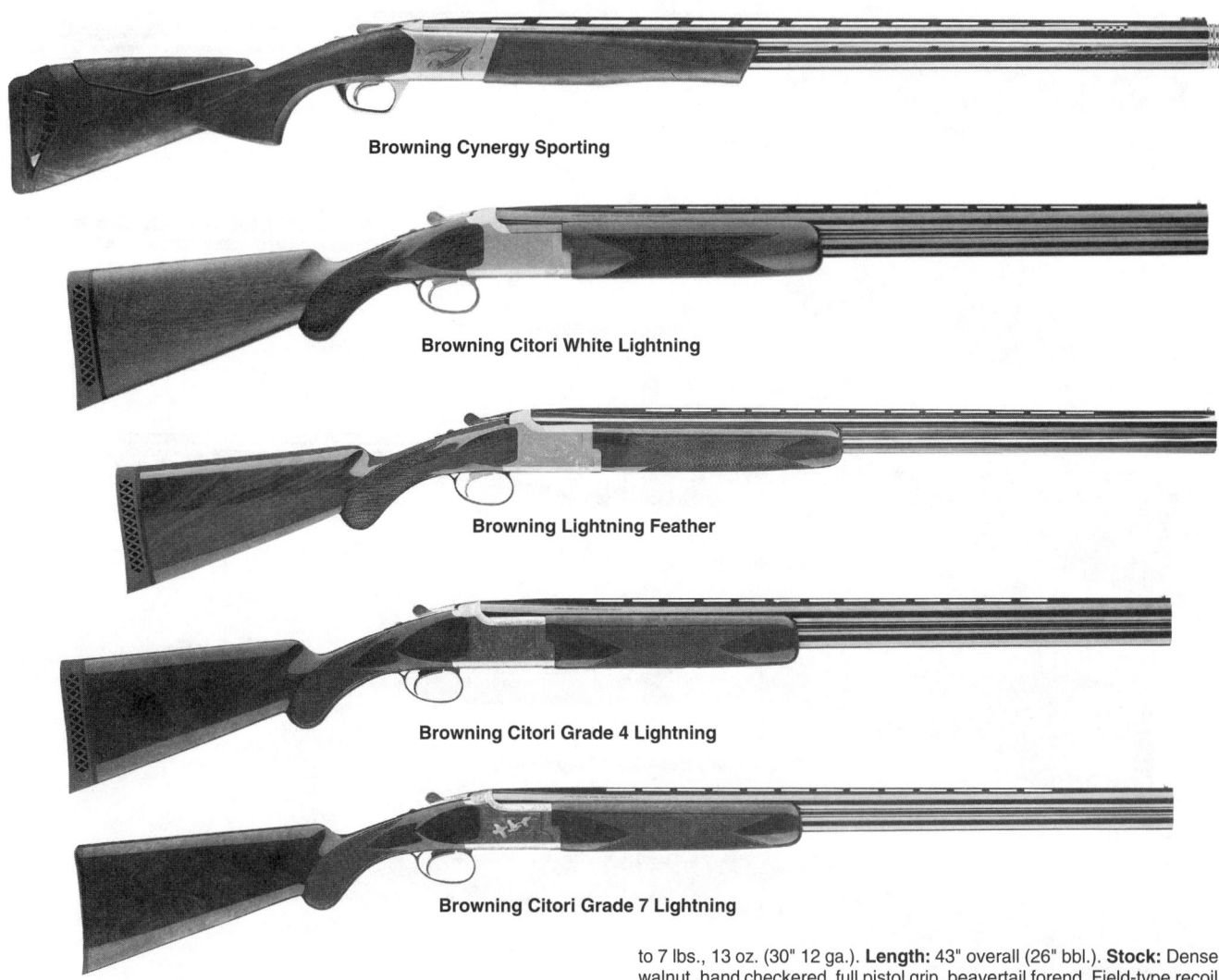

Browning Cynergy Sporting

Browning Citori White Lightning

Browning Lightning Feather

Browning Citori Grade 4 Lightning

Browning Citori Grade 7 Lightning

BROWNING CYNERGY O/U SHOTGUNS

Gauge: 12, 20, 28. **Barrel:** 26", 28", 30", 32". **Stock:** Walnut or composite. **Sights:** White bead front most models; HiViz Pro-Comp sight on some models; mid bead. **Features:** Mono-Lock hinge, recoil-reducing interchangeable Inflex recoil pad, silver nitride receiver; striker-based trigger, ported barrel option. 12 models cataloged for 2006. Nine new models introduced 2006: Cynergy Sporting, Adjustable Comb; Cynergy Sporting Composite with TopCote; Cynergy Sporting Composite CF; Cynergy Field, Composite; Cynergy Classic Sporting; Cynergy Classic Field; Cynergy Camo Mossy Oak New Shadow Grass; Cynergy Camo Mossy Oak New Break-Up; and Cynergy Camo Mossy Oak Brush. Imported from Japan by Browning.

Price: Cynergy Field, 12 ga., Grade 1 walnut, ... **$2,048.00**
Price: Cynergy Field Small Gauge, 20 /28 ga., intr. 2005 . . . . . . **$2,062.00**
Price: Cynergy Sporting Small Gauge, 20 /28 ga., intr. 2005 . . . **$3,080.00**
Price: Cynergy Field Composite, 12 ga., ... **$1,890.00**
Price: Cynergy Sporting, 12 ga.; 28", 30", or 32" barrels **$3,046.00**
Price: Cynergy Sporting Composite 12 ga. **$2,846.00**
Price: Cynergy Sporting, adjustable comb, intr. 2006. . . . . **$3,351.00**
Price: Cynergy Sporting Composite w/TopCote, intr. 2006. . . . . . **$2,979.00**

BROWNING CITORI O/U SHOTGUNS

Gauge: 12, 20, 28 and .410. **Barrel:** 26", 28" in 28 and .410. Offered with Invector choke tubes. All 12 and 20 gauge models have back-bored barrels and Invector Plus choke system. **Weight:** 6 lbs., 8 oz. (26" .410)

to 7 lbs., 13 oz. (30" 12 ga.). **Length:** 43" overall (26" bbl.). **Stock:** Dense walnut, hand checkered, full pistol grip, beavertail forend. Field-type recoil pad on 12 ga. field guns and trap and skeet models. **Sights:** Medium raised beads, German nickel silver. **Features:** Barrel selector integral with safety, automatic ejectors, three-piece takedown. 25 models cataloged for 2006. Two limited-run models reintroduced 2006: Citori 4-Barrel Skeet Set, Grade I; Citori 4-Barrel Skeet Set, Grade VII. Imported from Japan by Browning.

Price: Lightning, 12 and 20 ga.. . . . . **$1,645.00**
Price: Lightning, 28 ga. and .410 bore **$1,709.00**
Price: White Lightning, 12 and 20 ga. **$1,714.00**
Price: White Lightning, 28 ga. and .410 bore **$1,790.00**
Price: 525 Field, 12 and 20 ga.. . . . . **$1,981.00**
Price: 525 Field, 28 ga. and .410 bore. **$2,010.00**
Price: Superlight Feather, 12 and 20 ga. (2-3/4"), 6.25/5.7 lbs.. . . . **$1,938.00**
Price: Lightning Feather, 12 and 20 ga., ... **$1,869.00**
Price: Citori 4-Barrel Skeet Set, Grade I, intr. 2006 . . . . **$8,412.00**

Browning Citori High Grade Shotguns

Similar to standard Citori except has engraved hunting scenes and gold inlays, high-grade, hand-oiled walnut stock and forearm. Introduced 2000. From Browning.

Price: Gran Lightning, engraved receiver, from **$2,429.00**
Price: Grade IV Lightning, engraved gray receiver, introduced 2005, from. **$2,608.00**
Price: Grade VII Lightning, engraved gray or blue receiver, introduced 2005, from **$4,146.00**

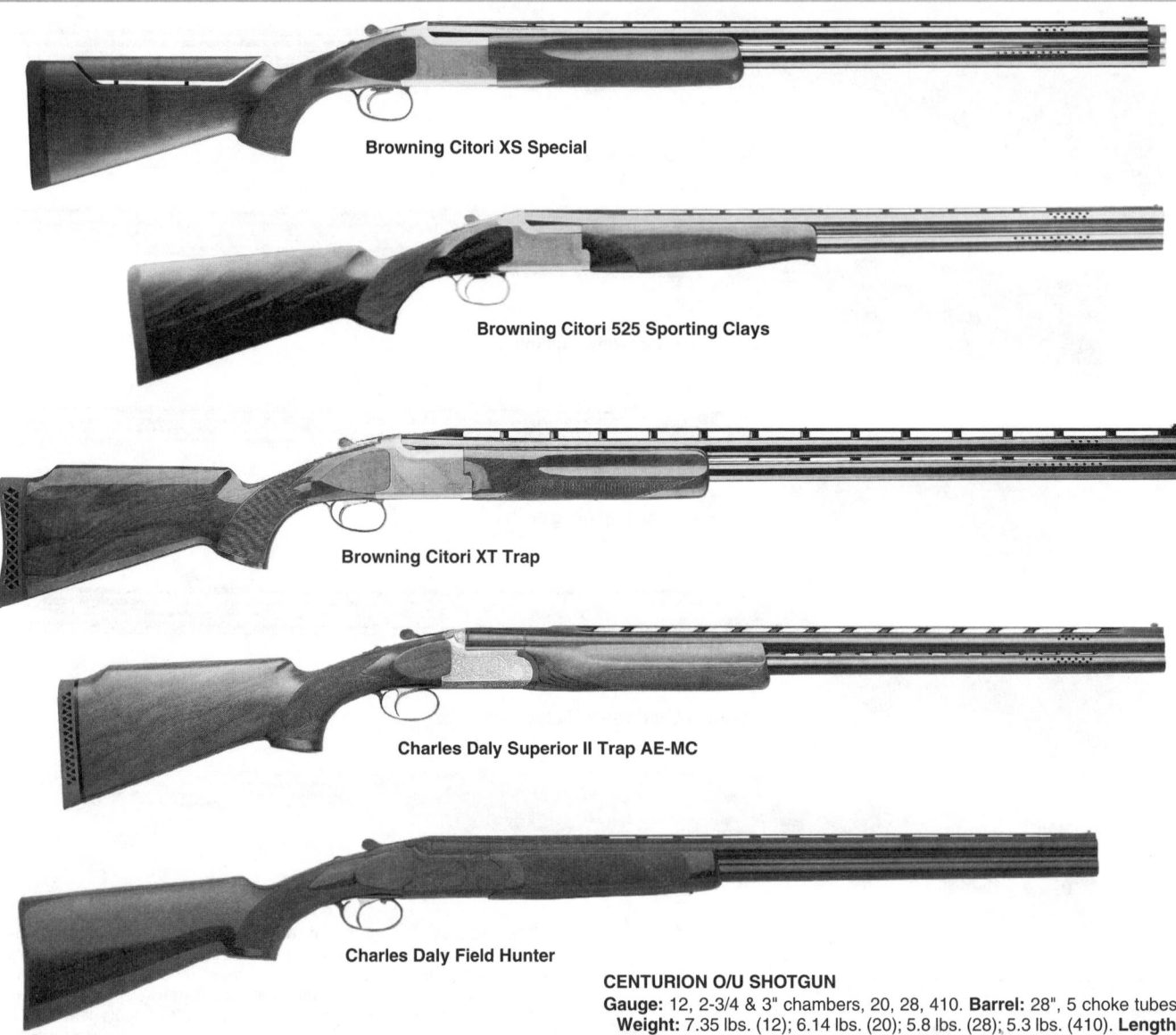

Browning Citori XS Special

Browning Citori 525 Sporting Clays

Browning Citori XT Trap

Charles Daly Superior II Trap AE-MC

Charles Daly Field Hunter

Browning Citori XS Sporting O/U Shotguns

Similar to the standard Citori except available in 12, 20, 28 or .410 with 28", 30", 32" ported barrels with various screw-in choke combinations: S (Skeet), C (Cylinder), IC (Improved Cylinder), M (Modified), and IM (Improved Modified). Has pistol grip stock, rounded or Schnabel forend. Weighs 7.1 lbs. to 8.75 lbs. Introduced 2004.

Price: XS Special, 12 ga.; 30", 32" barrels **$2,727.00**
Price: XS Sporting, 12 or 20 ga. **$2,472.00**
Price: XS Skeet, 12 or 20 ga. **$2,434.00**
Price: 525 Sporting Grade I, 12 ga. intr. 2005. . . . . **$2,319.00**
Price: 525 Golden Clays, 12 or 20 gauge **$3,058.00**
Price: 525 Golden Clays, 28 or .410 . . . . **$4,653.00**

Browning Citori XT Trap O/U Shotgun

Similar to the Citori XS Special except has engraved silver nitride receiver with gold highlights, vented side barrel rib. Available in 12 gauge with 30" or 32" barrels, Invector-Plus choke tubes, adjustable comb and buttplate. Introduced 1999. Imported by Browning.

Price: XT Trap **$2,275.00**
Price: XT Trap w/adjustable comb. **$2,549.00**
Price: XT Trap Gold w/adjustable comb, introduced 2005 . . . . . . **$4,221.00**

CENTURION O/U SHOTGUN

Gauge: 12, 2-3/4 & 3" chambers, 20, 28, 410. **Barrel:** 28", 5 choke tubes. **Weight:** 7.35 lbs. (12); 6.14 lbs. (20); 5.8 lbs. (28); 5.3 lbs. (410). **Length:** 45". **Stock:** Glossy Turkish walnut. **Features:** Single selective trigger, automatic safety, extractors, ventilated recoil pad, front bead sight. Manufactured by CFS in Turkey. Imported by Century International.
Price: **$470.00**

CHARLES DALY SUPERIOR II TRAP AE-MC O/U SHOTGUN

Gauge: 12, 2-3/4" chambers. **Barrel:** 30" choke tubes. **Weight:** About 7 lbs. **Length:** 47-3/8". **Stock:** Checkered walnut; pistol grip, semi-beavertail forend. **Features:** Silver engraved receiver, chrome-moly steel barrels; gold single selective trigger; automatic safety, automatic ejectors; red bead front sight, metal bead center; recoil pad. Introduced 1997. Imported from Italy by K.B.I., Inc.
Price: **$1,699.00**

CHARLES DALY FIELD II HUNTER O/U SHOTGUN

Gauge: 12, 20, 28 and .410 bore (3" chambers, 28 ga. has 2-3/4"). **Barrel:** 28" Mod & Full, 26" Imp. Cyl. & Mod (.410 is Full & Full). **Weight:** About 7 lbs. **Length:** 42-3/4" to 44-3/4". **Stock:** Checkered walnut pistol grip and forend. **Features:** Blued engraved receiver, chrome-moly steel barrels; gold single selective trigger; automatic safety; extractors; gold bead front sight. Introduced 1997. Imported from Italy by K.B.I., Inc.
Price: 12 or 20 ga. **$1,029.00**
Price: 28 ga., .410 bore **$1,129.00**

Charles Daly Superior Hunter

Charles Daly Empire II Mono Trap

Charles Daly Empire II EDL Hunter

Charles Daly Empire Sporting O/U

Charles Daly Superior II Hunter AE O/U Shotgun

Similar to the Field Hunter AE except has silvered, engraved receiver. Introduced 1997. Imported from Italy by F.B.I., Inc.

Price: 28 ga., .410 bore **$1,519.00**

Charles Daly Field Hunter AE-MC O/U Shotgun

Similar to the Field Hunter except in 12 or 20 only, 26" or 28" barrels with five multi-choke tubes; automatic ejectors. Introduced 1997. Imported from Italy by K.B.I., Inc.

Price: 12 or 20 ga. **$1,279.00**

Charles Daly Superior II Sporting O/U Shotgun

Similar to the Field Hunter AE-MC except 28" or 30" barrels; silvered, engraved receiver; five choke tubes; ported barrels; red bead front sight. Introduced 1997. Imported from Italy by K.B.I., Inc.

Price: **$1,659.00**

CHARLES DALY EMPIRE II EDL HUNTER AE, AE-MC O/U SHOTGUNS

Gauge: 12, 20, .410, 3" chambers, 28 ga., 2-3/4". **Barrel:** 26", 28" (12, 20, choke tubes), 26" (Imp. Cyl. & Mod., 28 ga.), 26" (Full & Full, .410). **Weight:** About 7 lbs. **Stocks:** Checkered walnut pistol grip buttstock, semi-beavertail forend; recoil pad. **Features:** Silvered, engraved receiver; chrome-moly barrels; gold single selective trigger; automatic safety; automatic ejectors; red bead front sight, metal bead middle sight. Introduced 1997. Imported from Italy by K.B.I., Inc.

Price: Empire II EDL AE-MC (dummy sideplates) 12 or 20 . . . . . **$2,029.00**
Price: Empire II EDL AE, 28 . . . . **$2,019.00**
Price: Empire II EDL AE, .410 . . . . **$2,019.00**

Charles Daly Empire II Sporting AE-MC O/U Shotgun

Similar to the Empire II EDL Hunter except 12 or 20 gauge only, 28", 30" barrels with choke tubes; ported barrels; special stock dimensions. Introduced 1997. Imported from Italy by K.B.I., Inc.

Price: **$2,049.00**

CHARLES DALY EMPIRE II TRAP AE-MC O/U SHOTGUNS

Gauge: 12, 2-3/4" chambers. **Barrel:** 30" choke tubes. **Weight:** About 7 lbs. **Stock:** Checkered walnut; pistol grip, semi-beavertail forend. **Features:** Silvered, engraved, reinforced receiver; chrome-moly steel barrels; gold single selective trigger; automatic safety, automatic ejector; red bead front sight, metal bead center; recoil pad. Imported from Italy by K.B.I., Inc.

Price: **$2,099.00**
Price: Mono AE-MC, adj. comb **$2,999.00**
Price: AE-MC combo set, adj. comb **$3,919.00**

CHARLES DALY DIAMOND REGENT GTX DL HUNTER O/U SHOTGUNS

Gauge: 12, 20, .410, 3" chambers, 28, 2-3/4" chambers. **Barrel:** 26", 28", 30" (choke tubes), 26" (Imp. Cyl. & Mod. in 28, 26" (Full & Full) in .410. **Weight:** About 7 lbs. **Stock:** Extra select fancy European walnut with 24" hand checkering, hand rubbed oil finish. **Features:** Boss-type action with internal side lumps. Deep cut hand-engraved scrollwork and game scene set in full sideplates. GTX detachable single selective trigger system with coil springs; chrome-moly steel barrels; automatic safety; automatic ejectors, white bead front sight, metal bead center sight. Introduced 1997. Imported from Italy by K.B.I., Inc.

Price: 12 or 20 . . . . **Special order only**
Price: 28 . . . . **Special order only**
Price: .410 bore . . . . **Special order only**
Price: Diamond Regent GTX EDL Hunter (as above with engraved scroll and birds, 10 gold inlays), 12 or 20 . . . . **Special order only**
Price: As above, 28 . . . . **Special order only**
Price: As above, .410 . . . . **Special order only**

CHARLES DALY DIAMOND GTX SPORTING O/U SHOTGUN

Gauge: 12, 20, 3" chambers. **Barrel:** 28", 30" with choke tubes. **Weight:** About 8.5 lbs. **Stock:** Checkered deluxe walnut; sporting clays dimensions. Pistol grip; semi-beavertail forend; hand rubbed oil finish. **Features:** Chromed, hand-engraved receiver; chrome-moly steel barrels; GTX detachable single selective trigger system with coil springs; automatic safety; automatic ejectors; red bead front sight; ported barrels. Introduced 1997. Imported from Italy by K.B.I., Inc.

Price: . . . . **Price on request**

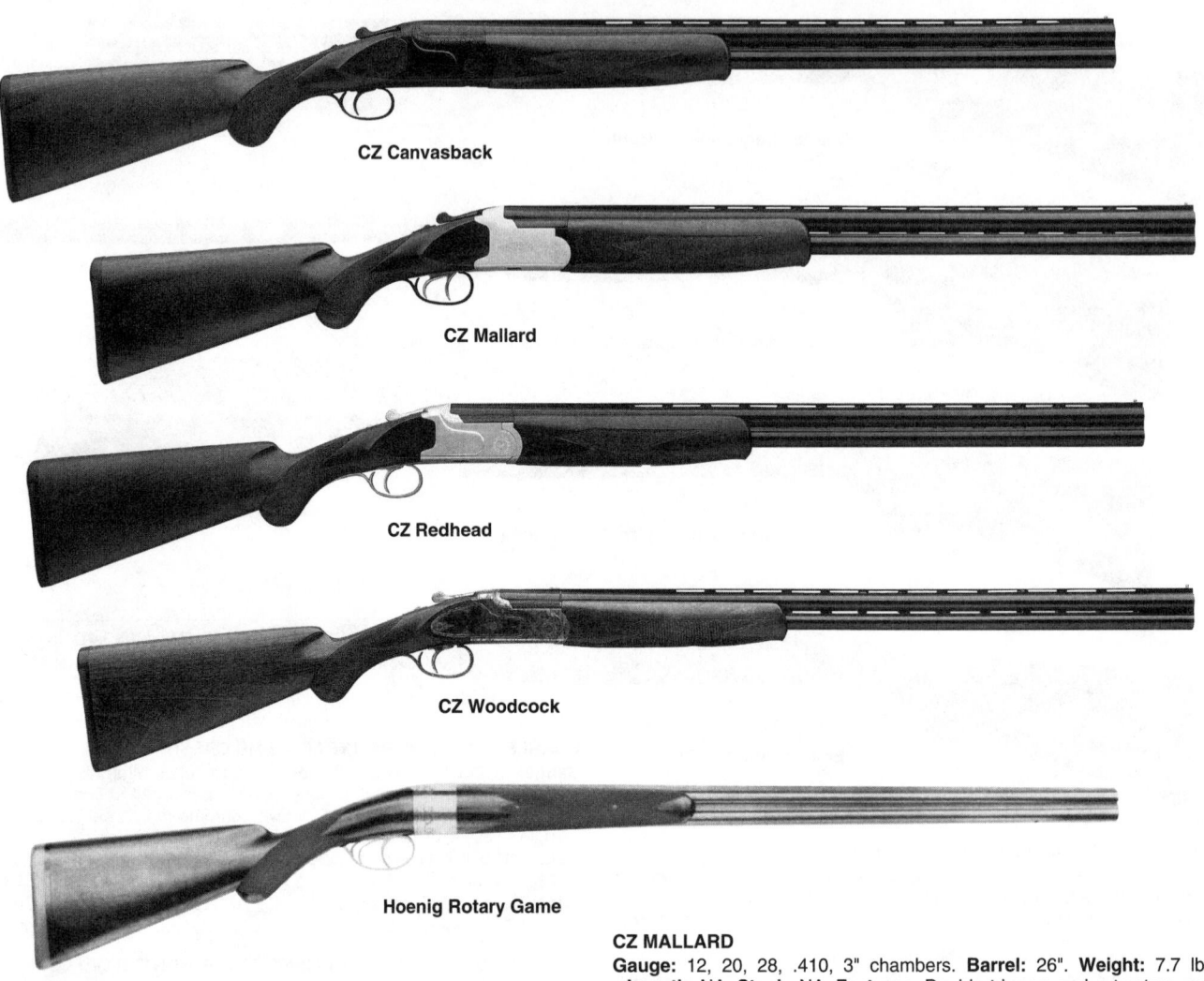

CZ Canvasback

CZ Mallard

CZ Redhead

CZ Woodcock

Hoenig Rotary Game

CHARLES DALY DIAMOND GTX TRAP AE-MC O/U SHOTGUN
Gauge: 12, 2-3/4" chambers. **Barrel:** 30" (Full & Full). **Weight:** About 8.5 lbs. **Stock:** Checkered deluxe walnut; pistol grip; trap dimensions; semi-beavertail forend; hand-rubbed oil finish. **Features:** Silvered, hand-engraved receiver; chrome-moly steel barrels; GTX detachable single selective trigger system with coil springs, automatic safety, automatic ejectors, red bead front sight, metal bead middle; recoil pad. Imported from Italy by K.B.I., Inc.
Price: . . . . **Price on request**

CHARLES DALY DIAMOND GTX DL HUNTER O/U SHOTGUN
Gauge: 12, 20, .410, 3" chambers, 28, 2-3/4" chambers. **Barrel:** 26", 28", choke tubes in 12 and 20 ga., 26" (Imp. Cyl. & Mod.), 26" (Full & Full) in .410-bore. **Weight:** About 8.5 lbs. **Stock:** Select fancy European walnut stock, with 24 lpi hand checkering; hand-rubbed oil finish. **Features:** Boss-type action with internal side lugs, hand-engraved scrollwork and game scene. GTX detachable single selective trigger system with coil springs; chrome-moly steel barrels, automatic safety, automatic ejectors, red bead front sight, recoil pad. Introduced 1997. Imported from Italy by K.B.I., Inc.
Price: . . . . **Special order only**

CZ CANVASBACK
Gauge: 12, 20, 3" chambers. **Barrel:** 26", 28". **Weight:** 7.3 lbs. **Length:** NA. **Stock:** NA. **Features:** Single selective trigger, set of 5 screw-in chokes, black chrome finished receiver, Schnable forend. From CZ-USA.
Price: **$708.00**

CZ MALLARD
Gauge: 12, 20, 28, .410, 3" chambers. **Barrel:** 26". **Weight:** 7.7 lbs. **Length:** NA. **Stock:** NA. **Features:** Double triggers and extractors, coin finished receiver, Schnable forend, multi chokes. From CZ-USA.
Price: **$487.00**

CZ REDHEAD
Gauge: 12, 20, 3" chambers. **Barrel:** 28". **Weight:** 7.4 lbs. **Length:** NA. **Stock:** NA. **Features:** Single selective triggers and extractors (12 & 20 ga.), screw-in chokes (12, 20, 28 ga.) choked IC and Mod (.410), coin finished receiver, Schnable forend, multi chokes. From CZ-USA.
Price: **$836.00**

CZ WOODCOCK
Gauge: 12, 20, 28, .410, 3" chambers. **Barrel:** 26". **Weight:** 7.7 lbs. **Length:** NA. **Stock:** NA. **Features:** Single selective triggers and extractors (auto ejectors on 12 & 20 ga.), screw-in chokes (12, 20, 28 ga.) choked IC and Mod (.410), coin finished receiver, Schnable forend, multi chokes. The sculptured frame incorporates a side plate, resembling a true side lock, embellished with hand engraving and finished wtih color casehardening. From CZ-USA.
Price: **$1,078.00**

HOENIG ROTARY ROUND ACTION GAME GUN O/U SHOTGUN
Gauge: 20, 28. **Barrel:** 26", 28", solid tapered rib. **Weight:** 6 lbs. and 6-1/4 lbs. **Stock:** English walnut to customer specifications. **Features:** Round action opens by rotating barrels, pulling forward. Inertia extraction system, rotary wing safety blocks strikers. Simple takedown without removing forend. Introduced 1997. Made in U.S.A. by George Hoenig.
Price: **$20,000.00**

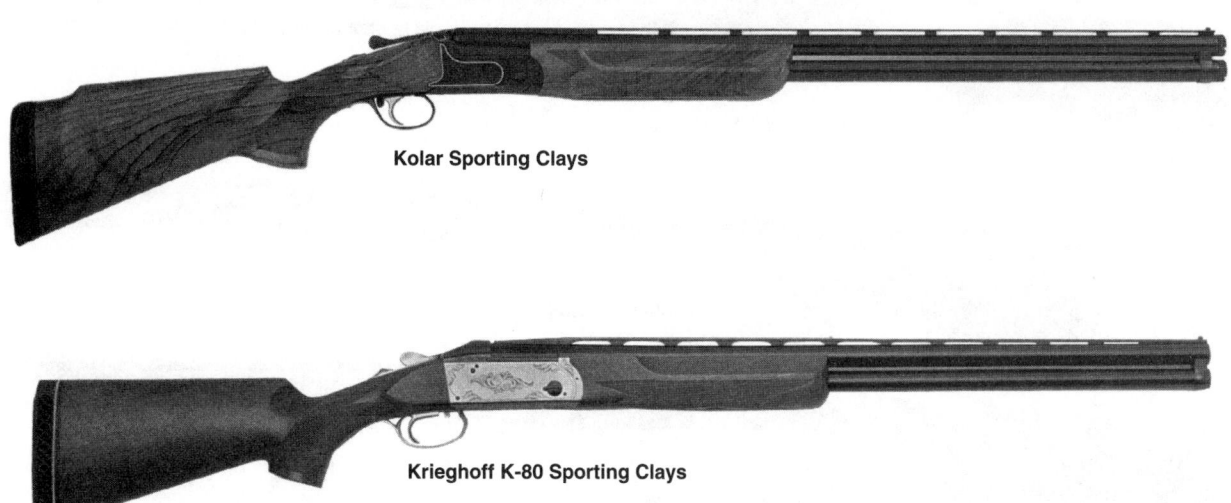

Kolar Sporting Clays

Krieghoff K-80 Sporting Clays

KIMBER MARIAS O/U SHOTGUNS
Gauge: 12, 20; 3". **Barrel:** 26", 28", 30". **Weight:** 7.4 lbs. **Length:** NA. **Stock:** Turkish walnut stocks, 24-lpi checkering, oil finish. LOP: 14.75 inches. **Features:** Hand-detachable back-action sidelock, bone-charcoal case coloring. Hand-engraving on receiver and locks, Belgian rust blue barrels, chrome lined. Five thinwall choke tubes, automatic ejectors, ventilated rib. Gold line cocking indicators on locks. Grade I has 28-inch barrels, Prince of Wales stock in grade three Turkish walnut in either 12 or 20 gauge. Grade II shas grade four Turkish walnut stocks, 12 gauge in Prince of Wales and 20 with either Prince of Wales or English profiles. Imported from Italy by Kimber Mfg., Inc.
Price: Grade I . . . . **NA**
Price: Grade II . . . . **NA**

KOLAR SPORTING CLAYS O/U SHOTGUNS
Gauge: 12, 2-3/4" chambers. **Barrel:** 30", 32", 34"; extended choke tubes. **Stock:** 14-5/8"x2-1/2"x1-7/8"x1-3/8". French walnut. Four stock versions available. **Features:** Single selective trigger, detachable, adjustable for length; overbored barrels with long forcing cones; flat tramline rib; matte blue finish. Made in U.S. by Kolar.
Price: Standard **$8,995.00**
Price: Elite **$12,495.00**
Price: Elite Gold **$15,295.00**
Price: Legend **$15,995.00**
Price: Select **$18,995.00**
Price: Custom . . . . **Price on request**

Kolar AAA Competition Trap O/U Shotgun
Similar to the Sporting Clays gun except has 32" O/U /34" Unsingle or 30" O/U /34" Unsingle barrels as an over/under, unsingle, or combination set. Stock dimensions are 14-1/2"x2-1/2"x1-1/2"; American or French walnut; step parallel rib standard. Contact maker for full listings. Made in U.S.A. by Kolar.
Price: Over/under, choke tubes, standard. **$9,595.00**
Price: Unsingle, choke tubes, standard **$10,195.00**
Price: Combo (30"/34", 32"/34"), standard **$12,595.00**

Kolar AAA Competition Skeet O/U Shotgun
Similar to the Sporting Clays gun except has 28" or 30" barrels with Kolarite AAA sub gauge tubes; stock of American or French walnut with matte finish; flat tramline rib; under barrel adjustable for point of impact. Many options available. Contact maker for complete listing. Made in U.S.A. by Kolar.
Price: Standard, choke tubes **$10,495.00**
Price: Standard, choke tubes, two-barrel set **$12,995.00**

KRIEGHOFF K-80 SPORTING CLAYS O/U SHOTGUN
Gauge: 12. **Barrel:** 28", 30", 32", 34" with choke tubes. **Weight:** About 8 lbs. **Stock:** #3 Sporting stock designed for gun-down shooting. **Features:** Standard receiver with satin nickel finish and classic scroll engraving. Selective mechanical trigger adjustable for position. Choice of tapered flat or 8mm parallel flat barrel rib. Free-floating barrels. Aluminum case. Imported from Germany by Krieghoff International, Inc.
Price: Standard grade with five choke tubes, from **$9,395.00**

KRIEGHOFF K-80 SKEET O/U SHOTGUNS
Gauge: 12, 2-3/4" chambers. **Barrel:** 28", 30", 32", (skeet & skeet), optional choke tubes). **Weight:** About 7-3/4 lbs. **Stock:** American skeet or straight skeet stocks, with palm-swell grips. Walnut. **Features:** Satin gray receiver finish. Selective mechanical trigger adjustable for position. Choice of ventilated 8mm parallel flat rib or ventilated 8-12mm tapered flat rib. Introduced 1980. Imported from Germany by Krieghoff International, Inc.
Price: Standard, skeet chokes **$8,375.00**
Price: Skeet Special (28", 30", 32" tapered flat rib,
skeet & skeet choke tubes) **$9,100.00**

KRIEGHOFF K-80 TRAP O/U SHOTGUNS
Gauge: 12, 2-3/4" chambers. **Barrel:** 30", 32" (Imp. Mod. & Full or choke tubes). **Weight:** About 8-1/2 lbs. **Stock:** Four stock dimensions or adjustable stock available; all have palm-swell grips. Checkered European walnut. **Features:** Satin nickel receiver. Selective mechanical trigger, adjustable for position. Ventilated step rib. Introduced 1980. Imported from Germany by Krieghoff International, Inc.
Price: K-80 O/U (30", 32", Imp. Mod. & Full), from **$8,850.00**
Price: K-80 Unsingle (32", 34", Full), standard, from **$10,080.00**
Price: K-80 Combo (two-barrel set), standard, from **$13,275.00**

Krieghoff K-20 O/U Shotgun
Similar to the K-80 except built on a 20-gauge frame. Designed for skeet, sporting clays and field use. Offered in 20, 28 and .410; 28", 30" and 32" barrels. Imported from Germany by Krieghoff International Inc.
Price: K-20, 20 gauge, from **$9,575.00**
Price: K-20, 28 gauge, from **$9,725.00**
Price: K-20, .410, from **$9,725.00**

LEBEAU-COURALLY BOSS-VEREES O/U SHOTGUN
Gauge: 12, 20, 2-3/4" chambers. **Barrel:** 25" to 32". **Weight:** To customer specifications. **Stock:** Exhibition-quality French walnut. **Features:** Boss-type sidelock with automatic ejectors; single or double triggers; chopper lump barrels. A custom gun built to customer specifications. Imported from Belgium by Wm. Larkin Moore.
Price: From **$96,000.00**

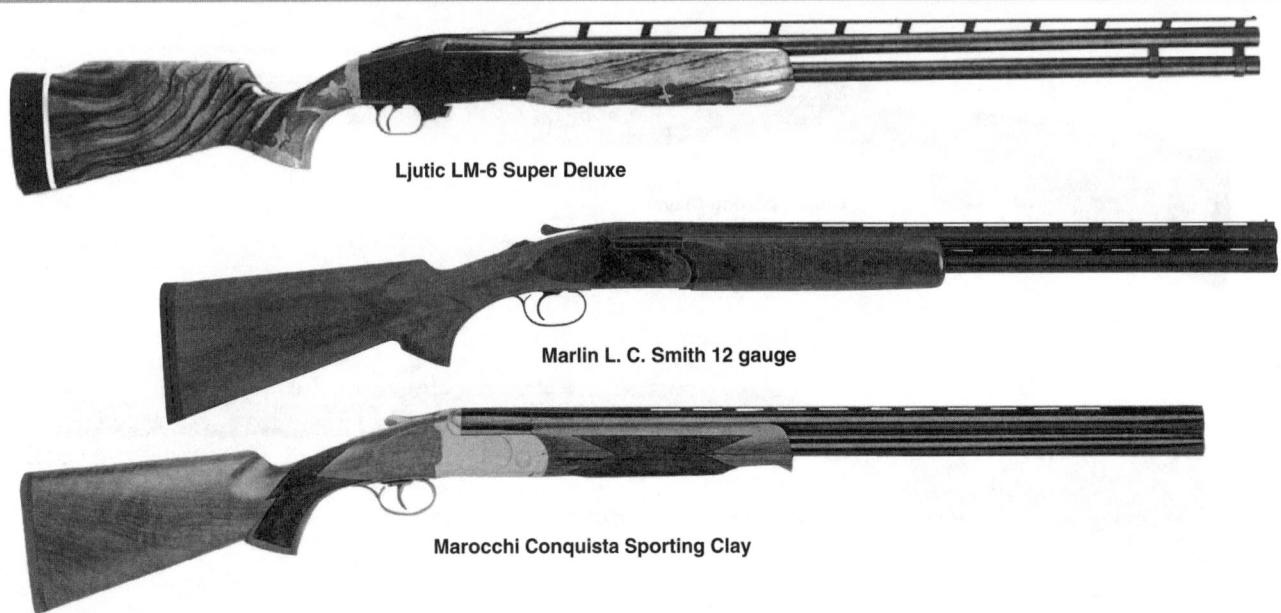

Ljutic LM-6 Super Deluxe

Marlin L. C. Smith 12 gauge

Marocchi Conquista Sporting Clay

LJUTIC LM-6 SUPER DELUXE O/U SHOTGUNS

Gauge: 12. **Barrel:** 28" to 34", choked to customer specs for live birds, trap, international trap. **Weight:** To customer specs. **Stock:** To customer specs. Oil finish, hand checkered. **Features:** Custom-made gun. Hollow-milled rib, pull or release trigger, push-button opener in front of trigger guard. From Ljutic Industries.

Price: Super Deluxe LM-6 O/U **$19,995.00**
Price: Over/Under combo (interchangeable single barrel,
two trigger guards, one for single trigger, one for doubles) ... **$27,995.00**
Price: Extra over/under barrel sets, 29"-32" **$6,995.00**

LUGER CLASSIC O/U SHOTGUNS

Gauge: 12, 3" and 3-1/2" chambers. **Barrel:** 26", 28", 30"; Imp. Cyl. Mod. and Full choke tubes. **Weight:** 7-1/2 lbs. **Length:** 45" overall (28" barrel) **Stock:** Select-grade European walnut, hand-checkered grip and forend. **Features:** Gold, single selective trigger; automatic ejectors. Introduced 2000.

Price: Classic (26", 28" or 30" barrel; 3-1/2" chambers)......... **$919.00**
Price: Classic Sporting (30" barrel; 3" chambers) **$964.00**

MARLIN L. C. SMITH O/U SHOTGUNS

Gauge: 12, 20. **Barrel:** 26", 28". **Stock:** Checkered walnut w/recoil pad. **Length:** 45". **Weight:** 7.25 lbs. **Features:** 3" chambers; 3 choke tubes (IC, Mod., Full), single selective trigger, selective automatic ejectors; vent rib; bead front sight. Imported from Italy by Marlin. Introduced 2005.

Price: LC12-OU (12 ga., 28" barrel) **$1,416.00**
Price: LC20-OU (20 ga., 26" barrel, 6.25 lbs., OAL 43") **$1,416.00**

MAROCCHI CONQUISTA SPORTING CLAYS O/U SHOTGUNS

Gauge: 12, 2-3/4" chambers. **Barrel:** 28", 30", 32" (ContreChoke tubes); 10mm concave vent rib. **Weight:** About 8 lbs. **Stock:** 14-1/2"-14-7/8"x2-3/16"x1-7/16"; American walnut with checkered grip and forend; sporting clays butt pad. **Sights:** 16mm luminescent front. **Features:** Lower mono-block and frame profile. Fast lock time. Ergonomically-shaped trigger adjustable for pull length. Automatic selective ejectors. Coin-finished receiver, blued barrels. Five choke tubes, hard case. Available as true left-hand model, opening lever operates from left to right; stock has left-hand cast. Introduced 1994. Imported from Italy by Precision Sales International.

Price: Grade I, right-hand **$1,490.00**
Price: Grade I, left-hand **$1,615.00**
Price: Grade II, right-hand **$1,828.00**
Price: Grade II, left-hand **$2,180.00**
Price: Grade III, right-hand, from **$3,093.00**
Price: Grade III, left-hand, from **$3,093.00**

Marocchi Conquista Trap O/U Shotguns

Similar to Conquista Sporting Clays model except 30" or 32" barrels choked Full & Full, stock dimensions of 14-1/2"-14-7/8"x1-11/ 16"x1-9/32"; weighs about 8-1/4 lbs. Introduced 1994. Imported from Italy by Precision Sales International.

Price: Grade I, right-hand............................... **$1,490.00**
Price: Grade II, right-hand **$1,828.00**
Price: Grade III, right-hand, from **$3,093.00**

Marocchi Conquista Skeet O/U Shotguns

Similar to Conquista Sporting Clays model except 28" (skeet & skeet) barrels, stock dimensions of 14-3/8"-14-3/4"x2-3/16"x1-1/2". Weighs about 7-3/4 lbs. Introduced 1994. Imported from Italy by Precision Sales International.

Price: Grade I, right-hand............................... **$1,490.00**
Price: Grade II, right-hand **$1,828.00**
Price: Grade III, right-hand, from **$3,093.00**

MAROCCHI MODEL 99 SPORTING TRAP AND SKEET O/U SHOTGUNS

Gauge: 12, 2-3/4", 3" chambers. **Barrel:** 28", 30", 32". **Stock:** French walnut. **Features:** Boss Locking system, screw-in chokes, low recoil, lightweight Monoblock barrels and ribs. Imported from Italy by Precision Sales International.

Price: Grade I **$2,350.00**
Price: Grade II **$2,870.00**
Price: Grade II Gold **$3,025.00**
Price: Grade III **$3,275.00**
Price: Grade III Gold **$3,450.00**
Price: Blackgold **$4,150.00**
Price: Lodestar **$5,125.00**
Price: Brittania **$5,125.00**
Price: Diana **$6,350.00**

MAROCCHI CONQUISTA USA MODEL 92 SPORTING CLAYS O/U SHOTGUN

Gauge: 12, 3" chambers. **Barrel:** 30"; back-bored, ported (ContreChoke Plus tubes); 10 mm concave ventilated top rib, ventilated middle rib. **Weight:** 8 lbs. 2 oz. **Stock:** 14-1/4"-14-5/8"x 2-1/8"x1-3/8"; American walnut with checkered grip and forend; sporting clays butt pad. **Features:** Low profile frame; fast lock time; automatic selective ejectors; blued receiver and barrels. Comes with three choke tubes. Ergonomically shaped trigger adjustable for pull length without tools. Barrels are back-bored and ported. Introduced 1996. Imported from Italy by Precision Sales International.

Price: **$1,490.00**

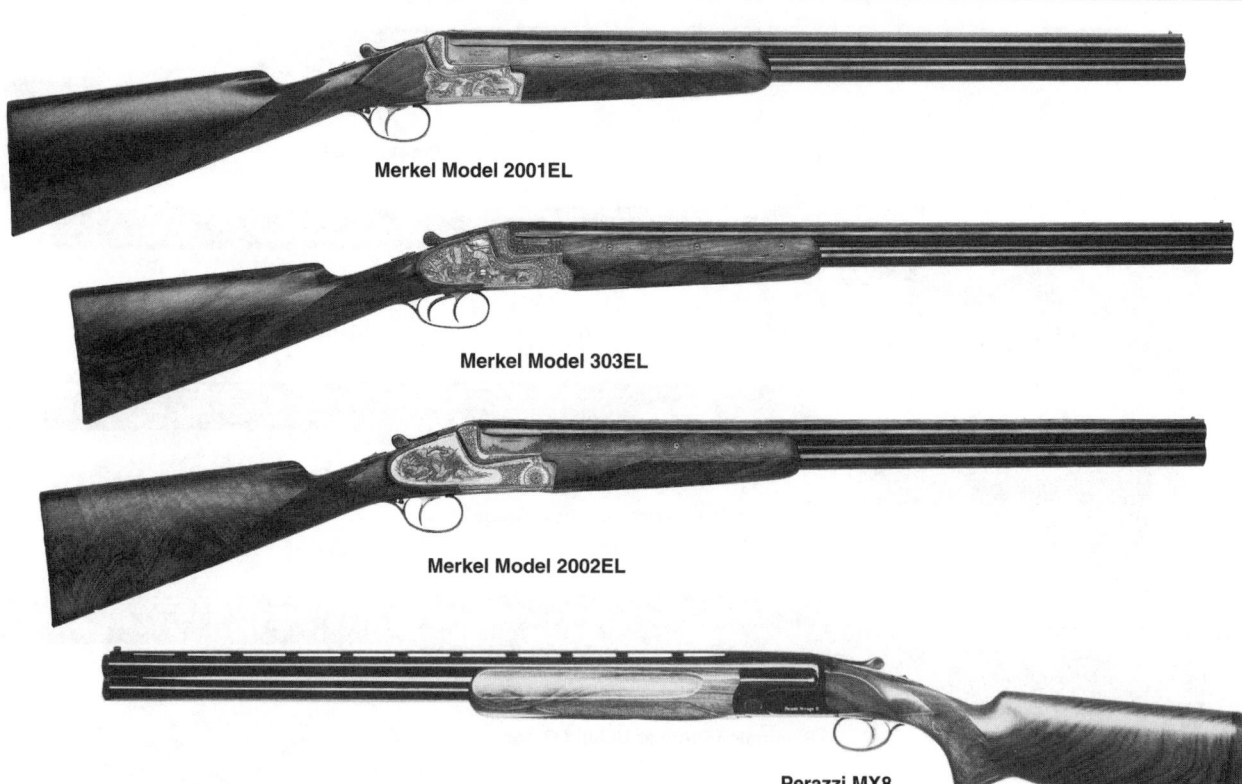

Merkel Model 2001EL

Merkel Model 303EL

Merkel Model 2002EL

Perazzi MX8

MERKEL MODEL 2001EL O/U SHOTGUN

Gauge: 12, 20, 3" chambers, 28, 2-3/4" chambers. **Barrel:** 12-28"; 20, 28 ga.-26-3/4". **Weight:** About 7 lbs. (12 ga.). **Stock:** Oil-finished walnut; English or pistol grip. **Features:** Self-cocking Blitz boxlock action with cocking indicators; Kersten double cross-bolt lock; silver-grayed receiver with engraved hunting scenes; coil spring ejectors; single selective or double triggers. Imported from Germany by GSI, Inc.
Price: 12, 20 . . . . **$7,295.00**
Price: 28 ga. **$7,295.00**
Price: Model 2000EL (scroll engraving, 12, 20 or 28) **$5,795.00**

Merkel Model 303EL O/U Shotgun

Similar to Model 2001EL except Holland & Holland-style sidelock action with cocking indicators; English-style arabesque engraving. Available in 12, 20, 28 gauge. Imported from Germany by GSI, Inc.
Price: **$19,995.00**

Merkel Model 2002EL O/U Shotgun

Similar to Model 2001EL except dummy sideplates, arabesque engraving with hunting scenes; 12, 20, 28 gauge. Imported from Germany by GSI, Inc.
Price: **$10,995.00**

PERAZZI MX8/MX8 SPECIAL TRAP, SKEET O/U SHOTGUNS

Gauge: 12, 2-3/4" chambers. **Barrel:** Trap: 29-1/2" (Imp. Mod. & Extra Full), 31-1/2" (Full & Extra Full). Choke tubes optional. Skeet: 27-5/8" (skeet & skeet). **Weight:** About 8-1/2 lbs. (trap); 7 lbs., 15 oz. (skeet). **Stock:** Interchangeable and custom made to customer specs. **Features:** Has detachable and interchangeable trigger group with flat V springs. Flat 7/16" vent rib. Many options available. Imported from Italy by Perazzi U.S.A., Inc.
Price: From **$12,756.00**
Price: MX8 Special (adj. four-position trigger). From **$11,476.00**
Price: MX8 Special combo (o/u and single barrel sets). From . . **$15,127.00**

Perazzi MX8 Special Skeet O/U Shotgun

Similar to the MX8 Skeet except has adjustable four-position trigger, skeet stock dimensions. Imported from Italy by Perazzi U.S.A., Inc.
Price: From **$11,166.00**

PERAZZI MX8 O/U SHOTGUNS

Gauge: 12, 2-3/4" chambers. **Barrel:** 28-3/8" (Imp. Mod. & Extra Full), 29-1/2" (choke tubes). **Weight:** 7 lbs., 12 oz. **Stock:** Special specifications. **Features:** Has single selective trigger; flat 7/16" x 5/16" vent rib. Many options available. Imported from Italy by Perazzi U.S.A., Inc.
Price: Standard **$12,532.00**
Price: Sporting **$11,166.00**
Price: Trap Double Trap (removable trigger group) **$15,581.00**
Price: Skeet **$12,756.00**
Price: SC3 grade (variety of engraving patterns) . . . . **$23,000.00+**
Price: SCO grade (more intricate engraving, gold inlays) . . . . . **$39,199.00+**

Perazzi MX8/20 O/U Shotgun

Similar to the MX8 except has smaller frame and has a removable trigger mechanism. Available in trap, skeet, sporting or game models with fixed chokes or choke tubes. Stock is made to customer specifications. Introduced 1993. Imported from Italy by Perazzi U.S.A., Inc.
Price: From **$11,166.00**

PERAZZI MX12 HUNTING O/U SHOTGUNS

Gauge: 12, 2-3/4" chambers. **Barrel:** 26-3/4", 27-1/2", 28-3/8", 29-1/2" (Mod. & Full); choke tubes available in 27-5/8", 29-1/2" only (MX12C). **Weight:** 7 lbs., 4 oz. **Stock:** To customer specs; interchangeable. **Features:** Single selective trigger; coil springs used in action; Schnabel forend tip. Imported from Italy by Perazzi U.S.A., Inc.
Price: From **$11,166.00**
Price: MX12C (with choke tubes). From **$11,960.00**

Perazzi MX20 Hunting O/U Shotguns

Similar to the MX12 except 20 ga. frame size. Non-removable trigger group. Available in 20, 28, .410 with 2-3/4" or 3" chambers. 26" standard, and choked Mod. & Full. Weight is 6 lbs., 6 oz. Imported from Italy by Perazzi U.S.A., Inc.
Price: From **$11,166.00**
Price: MX20C (as above, 20 ga. only, choke tubes). From . . . **$11,960.00**

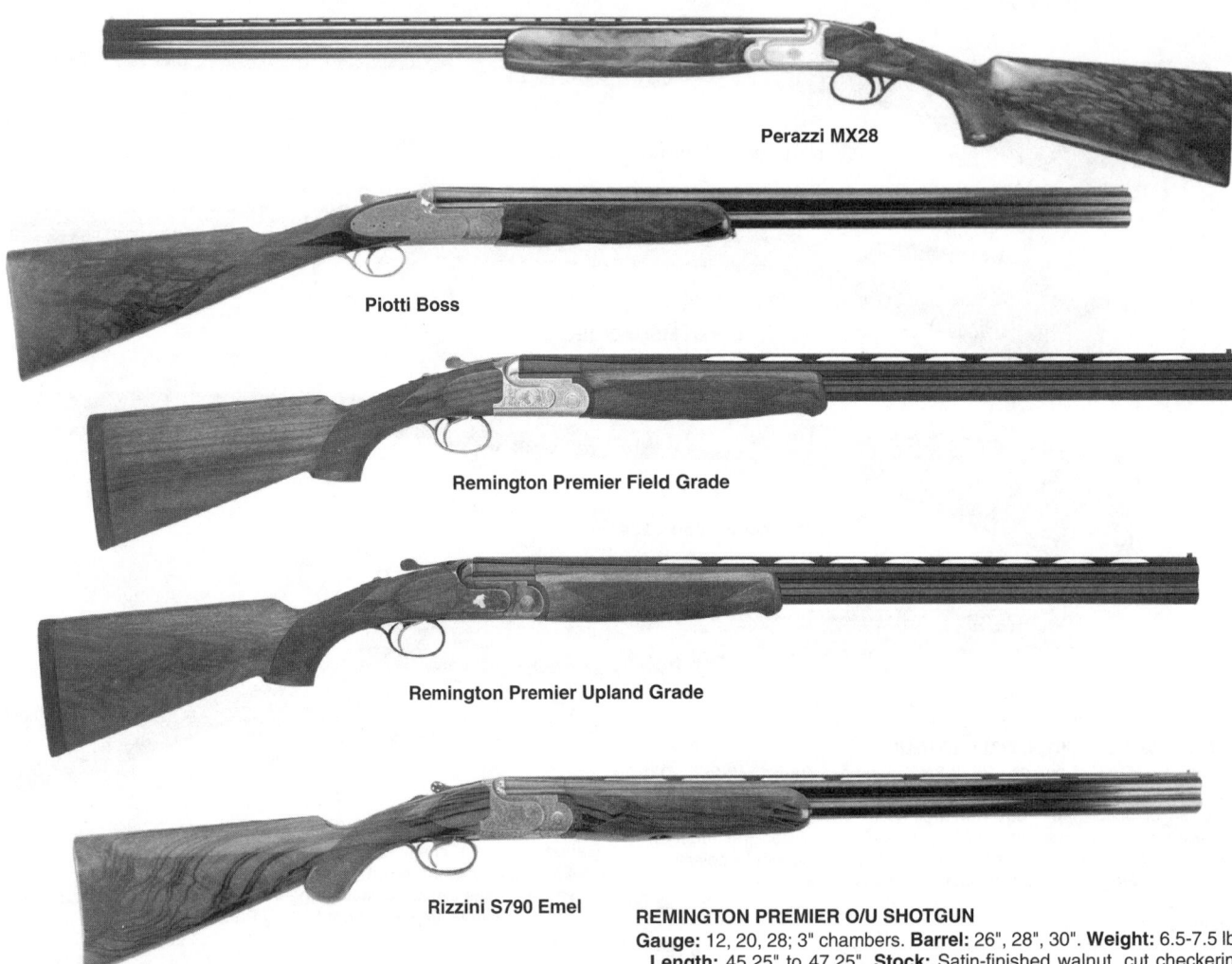

Perazzi MX28

Piotti Boss

Remington Premier Field Grade

Remington Premier Upland Grade

Rizzini S790 Emel

PERAZZI MX10 O/U SHOTGUN

Gauge: 12, 2-3/4" chambers. **Barrel:** 29.5", 31.5" (fixed chokes). **Weight:** NA. **Stock:** Walnut; cheekpiece adjustable for elevation and cast. **Features:** Adjustable rib; vent side rib. Externally selective trigger. Available in single barrel, combo, over/under trap, skeet, pigeon and sporting models. Introduced 1993. Imported from Italy by Perazzi U.S.A., Inc.
Price: MX200410. . . . . **$18,007.00**

PERAZZI MX28, MX410 GAME O/U SHOTGUN

Gauge: 28, 2-3/4" chambers, .410, 3" chambers. **Barrel:** 26" (Imp. Cyl. & Full). **Weight:** NA. **Stock:** To customer specifications. **Features:** Made on scaled-down frames proportioned to the gauge. Introduced 1993. Imported from Italy by Perazzi U.S.A., Inc.
Price: From **$22,332.00**

PIOTTI BOSS O/U SHOTGUN

Gauge: 12, 20. **Barrel:** 26" to 32", chokes as specified. **Weight:** 6.5 to 8 lbs. **Stock:** Dimensions to customer specs. Best quality figured walnut. **Features:** Essentially a custom-made gun with many options. Introduced 1993. Imported from Italy by Wm. Larkin Moore.
Price: From **$48,000.00**

POINTER O/U SHOTGUN

Gauge: 12. **Barrel:** 28". **Stock:** Walnut. **Features:** Kickeez buttpad, Tru-Glo sight, extractors, barrel selector, engraved receiver, gold trigger and 5 choke tubes. Introduced 2006. Imported by Legacy Sports Int.
Price: **$599.00**

REMINGTON PREMIER O/U SHOTGUN

Gauge: 12, 20, 28; 3" chambers. **Barrel:** 26", 28", 30". **Weight:** 6.5-7.5 lbs. **Length:** 45.25" to 47.25". **Stock:** Satin-finished walnut, cut checkering, Schnabel forends. **Sights:** 10mm target-style rib, ivory front bead and steel midpost. **Features:** Competition STS has Titanium PVD-finished receiver, right-hand palm swell, gold-colored trigger, engraved receiver, 12-gauge overbored barrel (0.735") with lengthened forcing cones. Includes five ProBore choke tubes w/knurled extensions. Field Grade has nickel-finished receiver with game scene engraving, 5 flush-mount ProBore choke tubes; 28-gauge equipped with 3 tubes. 7mm rib. Upland Grade has oil-finished walnut stock and forend, case-colored receiver with gold-accent game-scene engraving. Hard case included for all models. Introduced 2006. Imported from Italy by Remington.
Price: Field Grade, from **$1,840.00**
Price: Upland Grade, from **$1,920.00**
Price: Competition STS **$2,240.00**
Price: Field Grade, from **$1,840.00**

RIZZINI S790 EMEL O/U SHOTGUN

Gauge: 20, 28, .410. **Barrel:** 26", 27.5" (Imp. Cyl. & Imp. Mod.). **Weight:** About 6 lbs. **Stock:** 14"x1-1/2"x2-1/8". Extra fancy select walnut. **Features:** Boxlock action with profuse engraving; automatic ejectors; single selective trigger; silvered receiver. Comes with Nizzoli leather case. Introduced 1996. Imported from Italy by Wm. Larkin Moore & Co.
Price: From **$9,725.00**

Rizzini S792 EMEL O/U Shotgun

Similar to S790 EMEL except dummy sideplates with extensive engraving coverage. Nizzoli leather case. Introduced 1996. Imported from Italy by Wm. Larkin Moore & Co.
Price: From **$9,075.00**

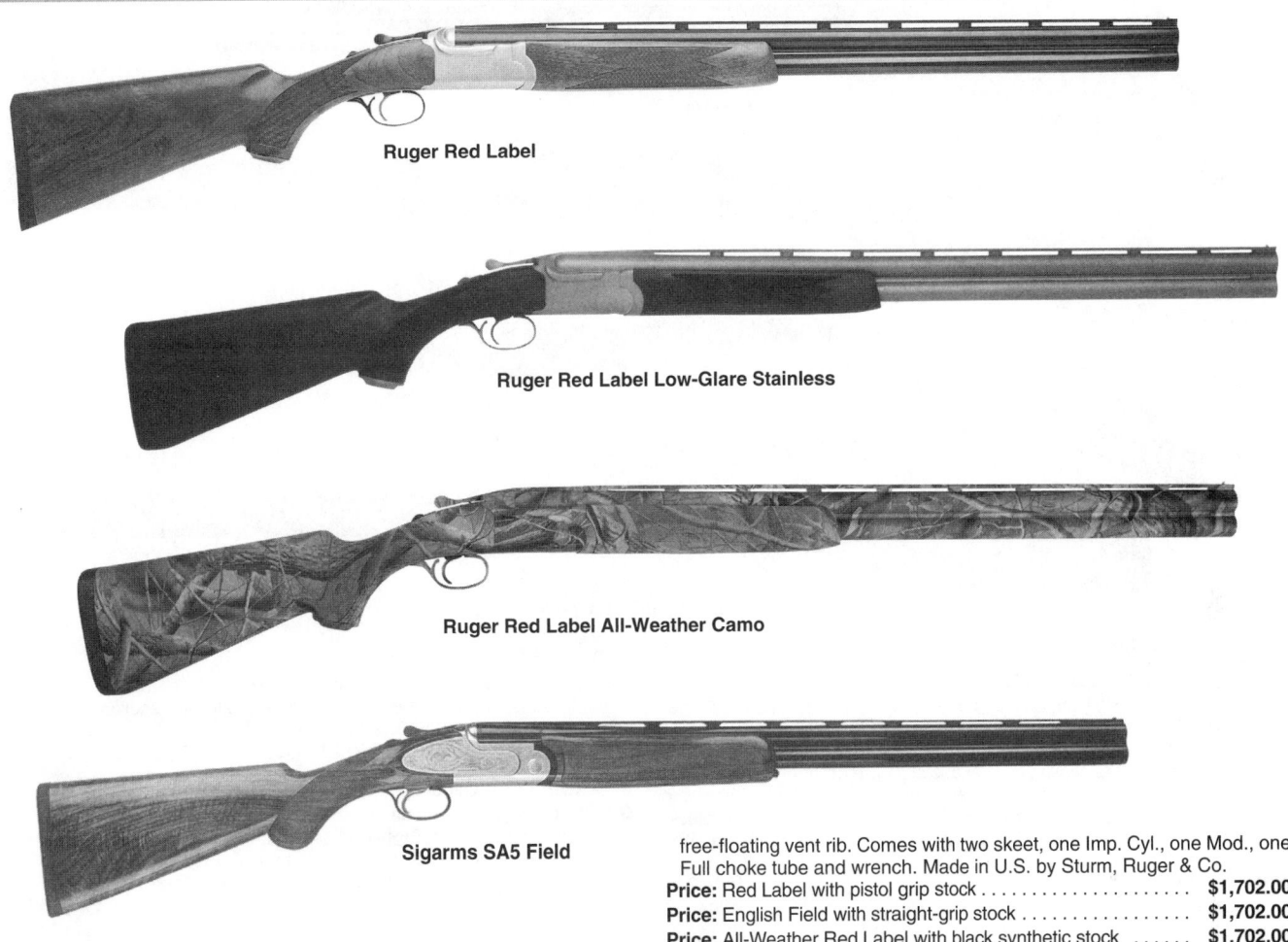

Ruger Red Label

Ruger Red Label Low-Glare Stainless

Ruger Red Label All-Weather Camo

Sigarms SA5 Field

RIZZINI UPLAND EL O/U SHOTGUN

Gauge: 12, 16, 20, 28, .410. **Barrel:** 26", 27-1/2", Mod. & Full, Imp. Cyl. & Imp. Mod. choke tubes. **Weight:** About 6.6 lbs. **Stock:** 14-1/ 2"x1-1/2"x2-1/4". **Features:** Boxlock action; single selective trigger; ejectors; profuse engraving on silvered receiver. Comes with fitted case. Introduced 1996. Imported from Italy by Wm. Larkin Moore & Co.
Price: From **$3,350.00**

Rizzini Artemis O/U Shotgun

Same as Upland EL model except dummy sideplates with extensive game scene engraving. Fancy European walnut stock. Fitted case. Introduced 1996. Imported from Italy by Wm. Larkin Moore & Co.
Price: From **$2,100.00**

RIZZINI S782 EMEL O/U SHOTGUN

Gauge: 12, 2-3/4" chambers. **Barrel:** 26", 27.5" (Imp. Cyl. & Imp. Mod.). **Weight:** About 6.75 lbs. **Stock:** 14-1/2"x1-1/2"x2-1/4". Extra fancy select walnut. **Features:** Boxlock action with dummy sideplates, extensive engraving with gold inlaid game birds, silvered receiver, automatic ejectors, single selective trigger. Nizzoli leather case. Introduced 1996. Imported from Italy by Wm. Larkin Moore & Co.
Price: From **$11,450.00**

RUGER RED LABEL O/U SHOTGUNS

Gauge: 12, 20, 3" chambers; 28 2-3/4" chambers. **Barrel:** 26", 28", 30" in 12 and 20 gauge (skeet [two], Imp. Cyl., Full, Mod. screw-in choke tubes). Proved for steel shot. **Weight:** About 7 lbs. (20 ga.); 7-1/2 lbs. (12 ga.). **Length:** 43" overall (26" barrels). **Stock:** 14"x1-1/2"x2-1/2". Straight grain American walnut or black synthetic. Checkered pistol grip or straight grip, checkered forend, rubber butt pad. **Features:** Stainless steel receiver. Single selective mechanical trigger, selective automatic ejectors; serrated

free-floating vent rib. Comes with two skeet, one Imp. Cyl., one Mod., one Full choke tube and wrench. Made in U.S. by Sturm, Ruger & Co.
Price: Red Label with pistol grip stock **$1,702.00**
Price: English Field with straight-grip stock **$1,702.00**
Price: All-Weather Red Label with black synthetic stock **$1,702.00**
Price: Sporting clays (30" bbl.) **$1,702.00**

Ruger Engraved Red Label O/U Shotgun

Similar to Red Label except scroll engraved receiver with 24-carat gold game bird (pheasant in 12 gauge, grouse in 20 gauge, woodcock in 28 gauge). Introduced 2000.
Price: Engraved Red Label
(12, 20 and 28 gauge in 26" and 28" barrels) **$1,902.00**

SARSILMAZ O/U SHOTGUNS

Gauge: 12, 3" chambers. **Barrel:** 26", 28"; fixed chokes or choke tubes. **Weight:** NA. **Length:** NA. **Stock:** Oil-finished hardwood. **Features:** Double or single selective trigger, wide vent rib, chrome-plated parts, blued finish. Introduced 2000. Imported from Turkey by Armsport Inc.
Price: Double triggers; mod. and full or imp. cyl.
and mod. fixed chokes **$499.95**
Price: Single selective trigger; imp. cyl. and mod. or mod.
and full fixed chokes **$575.00**
Price: Single selective trigger; five choke tubes and wrench **$695.00**

SIGARMS SA5 O/U SHOTGUNS

Gauge: 12, 20, 3" chamber. **Barrel:** 26-1/2", 27" (Full, Imp. Mod., Mod., Imp. Cyl., Cyl. choke tubes). **Weight:** 6.9 lbs. (12 gauge), 5.9 lbs. (20 gauge). **Stock:** 14-1/2" x 1-1/2" x 2-1/2". Select grade walnut; checkered 20 lpi at grip and forend. **Features:** Single selective trigger, automatic ejectors; hand engraved detachable side plate; matte nickel receiver, rest blued; tapered bolt lock-up. Introduced 1997. Imported by SIGARMS, Inc.
Price: Field, 12 gauge **$2,670.00**
Price: Sporting clays **$2,800.00**
Price: Field 20 gauge **$2,670.00**

Stoeger Condor

Traditions Classic Field Hunter

Traditions Classic Field III

Traditions Classic Upland II

SKB MODEL 85TSS O/U SHOTGUNS

Gauge: 12, 20, .410: 3"; 28, 2-3/4". **Barrel:** Chrome lined 26", 28", 30", 32" (w/choke tubes). **Weight:** 7 lbs., 7 oz. to 8 lbs., 14 oz. **Stock:** Hand-checkered American walnut with matte finish, Schnabel or grooved forend. Target stocks available in various styles. **Sights:** Metal bead front or HiViz competition sights. **Features:** Low profile boxlock action with Greener-style cross bolt; single selective trigger; manual safety. Back-bored barrels with lengthened forcing cones. Introduced 2004. Imported from Japan by G.U. Inc.

Price: Sporting clays, 12 or 20 . . . . **$1,949.00**
Price: Sporting clays, 28 . . . . **$1,949.00**
Price: Sporting clays set, 12 and 20 . . . . **$3,149.00**
Price: Skeet, 12 or 20 . . . . **$1,949.00**
Price: Skeet, 28 or .410 . . . . **$2,129.00 to $2,179.00**
Price: Skeet, three-barrel set, 20, 28, .410 . . . . **$4,679.00**
Price: Trap, standard or Monte Carlo **$1,499.00**
Price: Trap adjustable comb **$2,129.00**

SKB MODEL 585 O/U SHOTGUNS

Gauge: 12 or 20, 3"; 28, 2-3/4"; .410, 3". **Barrel:** 12 ga.-26", 28", 30", 32", 34" (InterChoke tubes); 20 ga.-26", 28" (InterChoke tubes); 28-26", 28" (InterChoke tubes); .410-26", 28" (InterChoke tubes). Ventilated side ribs. **Weight:** 6.6 to 8.5 lbs. **Length:** 43" to 51-3/8" overall. **Stock:** 14-1/8"x1-1/2"x2-3/16". Hand checkered walnut with high-gloss finish. Target stocks available in standard and Monte Carlo. **Sights:** Metal bead front (field), target style on skeet, trap, sporting clays. **Features:** Boxlock action; silver nitride finish with field or target pattern engraving; manual safety, automatic ejectors, single selective trigger. All 12 gauge barrels are back-bored, have lengthened forcing cones and longer choke tube system. Sporting clays models in 12 gauge with 28" or 30" barrels available with optional 3/8" step-up target-style rib, matte finish, nickel center bead, white front bead. Introduced 1992. Imported from Japan by G.U., Inc.

Price: Field. **$1,499.00**
Price: Two-barrel field set, 12 & 20 . . . . **$2,399.00**
Price: Two-barrel field set, 20 & 28 or 28 & .410 . . . . **$2,469.00**

SKB Model 585 Gold Package

Similar to Model 585 Field except gold-plated trigger, two gold-plated game inlays, Schnabel forend. Silver or blue receiver. Introduced 1998. Imported from Japan by G.U. Inc.

Price: 12, 20 ga. **$1,689.00**
Price: 28, .410 . . . . **$1,749.00**

SKB Model 505 O/U Shotgun

Similar to Model 585 except blued receiver, standard bore diameter, standard InterChoke system on 12, 20, 28, different receiver engraving. Imported from Japan by G.U. Inc.

Price: Field, 12 (26", 28"), 20 (26", 28") **$1,229.00**

STOEGER CONDOR SPECIAL O/U SHOTGUNS

Gauge: 12, 20, 2-3/4" 3" chambers; 16, .410. **Barrel:** 22", 24", 26", 28", 30". **Weight:** 5.5 to 7.8 lbs. **Sights:** Brass bead. **Features:** IC, M, or F screw-in choke tubes with each gun. Oil finished hardwood with pistol grip and forend. Auto safety, single trigger, automatic extractors.

Price: Condor, 12, 20, 16 ga. or .410 . . . . **$350.00**
Price: Condor Supreme (w/mid bead), 12 or 20 ga. **$539.00**
Price: Condor Combo, 12 and 20 ga. barrels. . . . . . . **$550.00 to $650.00**
Price: Condor Youth, 20 ga. or .410 . . . . **$350.00**
Price: Condor Competition, 12 or 20 ga. **$599.00**

TRADITIONS CLASSIC SERIES O/U SHOTGUNS

Gauge: 12, 3"; 20, 3"; 16, 2-3/4"; 28, 2-3/4"; .410, 3". **Barrel:** 26" and 28". **Weight:** 6 lbs., 5 oz. to 7 lbs., 6 oz. **Length:** 43" to 45" overall. **Stock:** Walnut. **Features:** Single-selective trigger; chrome-lined barrels with screw-in choke tubes; extractors (Field Hunter and Field I models) or automatic ejectors (Field II and Field III models); rubber butt pad; top tang safety. Imported from Fausti of Italy by Traditions.

Price: Field Hunter: Blued receiver; 12 or 20 ga.; 26" bbl. has IC and Mod. tubes, 28" has mod. and full tubes **$669.00**
Price: Field I: Blued receiver; 12, 20, 28 ga. or .410; fixed chokes (26" has I.C. and mod., 28" has mod. and full) **$619.00**
Price: Field II: Coin-finish receiver; 12, 16, 20, 28 ga. or .410; gold trigger; choke tubes **$789.00**
Price: Field III: Coin-finish receiver; gold engraving and trigger; 12 ga.; 26" or 28" bbl.; choke tubes **$999.00**
Price: Upland II: Blued receiver; 12 or 20 ga.; English-style straight walnut stock; choke tubes **$839.00**
Price: Upland III: Blued receiver, gold engraving; 20 ga.; high-grade pistol grip walnut stock; choke tubes **$1,059.00**
Price: Upland III: Blued, gold engraved receiver, 12 ga. Round pistol grip stock, choke tubes **$1,059.00**
Price: Sporting Clay II: Silver receiver; 12 ga.; ported barrels with skeet, i.c., mod. and full extended tubes **$959.00**
Price: Sporting Clay III: Engraved receivers, 12 and 20 ga., walnut stock, vent rib, extended choke tubes **$1,189.00**

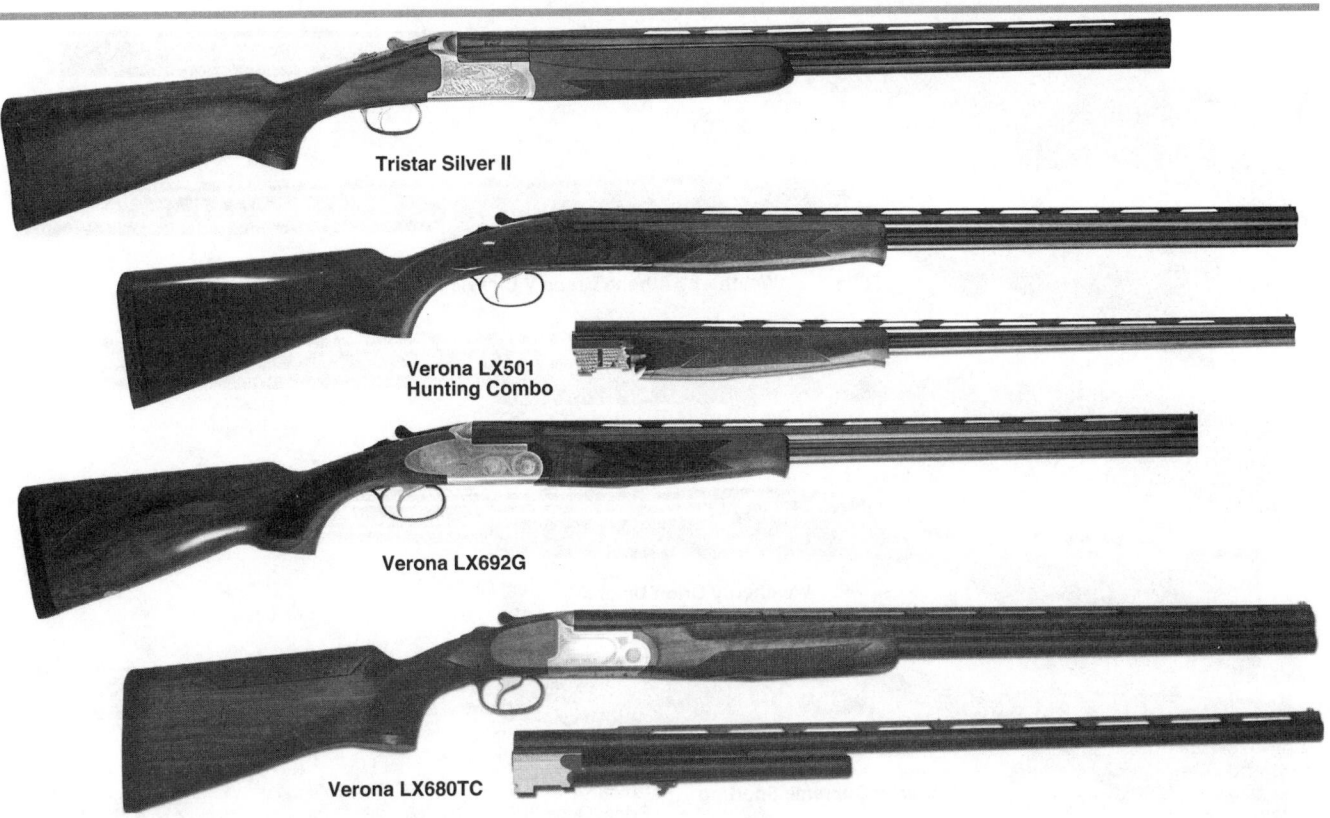

Tristar Silver II

Verona LX501 Hunting Combo

Verona LX692G

Verona LX680TC

TRADITIONS MAG 350 SERIES O/U SHOTGUNS

Gauge: 12, 3-1/2". **Barrel:** 24", 26" and 28". **Weight:** 7 lbs. to 7 lbs., 4 oz. **Length:** 41" to 45" overall. **Stock:** Walnut or composite with Mossy Oak® Break-Up™ or Advantage® Wetlands ™ camouflage. **Features:** Black matte, engraved receiver; vent rib; automatic ejectors; single-selective trigger; three screw-in choke tubes; rubber recoil pad; top tang safety. Imported from Fausti of Italy by Traditions.

Price: (Mag Hunter II: 28" black matte barrels, walnut stock, includes I.C.,
Mod. and Full tubes) **$799.00**

Price: (Turkey II: 24" or 26" camo barrels, Break-Up™ camo stock, includes
Mod., Full and X-Full tubes) **$889.00**

Price: (Waterfowl II: 28" camo barrels, Advantage Wetlands camo stock,
includes IC, Mod. and Full tubes) **$899.00**

TRISTAR SILVER II O/U SHOTGUN

Gauge: 12, 20, .410. **Barrel:** 26" barrel (Imp. Cyl., Mod., Full choke tubes, 12 and 20 ga.), 28" (Imp. Cyl., Mod., Full choke tubes, 12 ga. only), 26" (Imp. Cyl. & Mod. fixed chokes, 28 and .410) automatic selective ejectors. **Weight:** 6 lbs., 15 oz. (12 ga., 26"). **Length:** 45-1/2" overall. **Stock:** 14-3/8"x1-1/2"x2-3/8". Figured walnut, cut checkering; sporting clays quick-mount buttpad. **Sights:** Target bead front. **Features:** Boxlock action with single selective trigger, automatic selective ejectors; special broadway channeled rib; vented barrel rib; chrome bores. Chrome-nickel finish on frame, with engraving. Imported from Italy by Tristar Sporting Arms Ltd.

Price: **$669.00**

VERONA LX501 HUNTING O/U SHOTGUNS

Gauge: 12, 20, 28, .410 (2-3/4", 3" chambers). **Barrel:** 28"; 12, 20 ga. have Interchoke tubes, 28 ga. and .410 have fixed Full & Mod. **Weight:** 6-7 lbs. **Stock:** Matte-finished walnut with machine-cut checkering. **Features:** Gold-plated single-selective trigger; ejectors; engraved, blued receiver; non-automatic safety; coil spring-operated firing pins. Introduced 1999. Imported from Italy by B.C. Outdoors.

Price: 12 and 20 ga. **$878.08**
Price: 28 ga. and .410 . . . . **$926.72**
Price: .410 . . . . **$907.01**
Price: Combos 20/28, 28/.410 . . . . **$1,459.20**

Verona LX692 Gold Hunting O/U Shotguns

Similar to Verona LX501 except engraved, silvered receiver with false sideplates showing gold inlaid bird hunting scenes on three sides; Schnabel forend tip; hand-cut checkering; black rubber butt pad. Available in 12 and 20 gauge only, five Interchoke tubes. Introduced 1999. Imported from Italy by B.C. Outdoors.

Price: **$1,295.00**
Price: LX692G Combo 28/.410 . . . . **$2,192.40**

Verona LX680 Sporting O/U Shotgun

Similar to Verona LX501 except engraved, silvered receiver; ventilated middle rib; beavertail forend; hand-cut checkering; available in 12 or 20 gauge only with 2-3/4" chambers. Introduced 1999. Imported from Italy by B.C. Outdoors.

Price: **$1,159.68**

Verona LX680 Skeet/Sporting/Trap O/U Shotgun

Similar to Verona LX501 except skeet or trap stock dimensions; beavertail forend, palm swell on pistol grip; ventilated center barrel rib. Introduced 1999. Imported from Italy by B.C. Outdoors.

Price: **$1,736.96**

Verona LX692 Gold Sporting O/U Shotgun

Similar to Verona LX680 except false sideplates have gold-inlaid bird hunting scenes on three sides; red high-visibility front sight. Introduced 1999. Imported from Italy by B.C. Outdoors.

Price: Skeet/sporting **$1,765.12**
Price: Trap (32" barrel, 7-7/8 lbs.) **$1,594.80**

VERONA LX680 COMPETITION TRAP O/U SHOTGUNS

Gauge: 12. **Barrel:** 30" O/U, 32" single bbl. **Weight:** 8-3/8 lbs. combo, 7 lbs. single. **Stock:** Walnut. **Sights:** White front, mid-rib bead. **Features:** Interchangeable barrels switch from o/u to single configurations. 5 Briley chokes in combo, 4 in single bbl. extended forcing cones, ported barrels 32" with raised rib. By B.C. Outdoors.

Price: Trap Single (LX680TGTSB) **$1,736.96**
Price: Trap Combo (LX680TC) **$2,553.60**

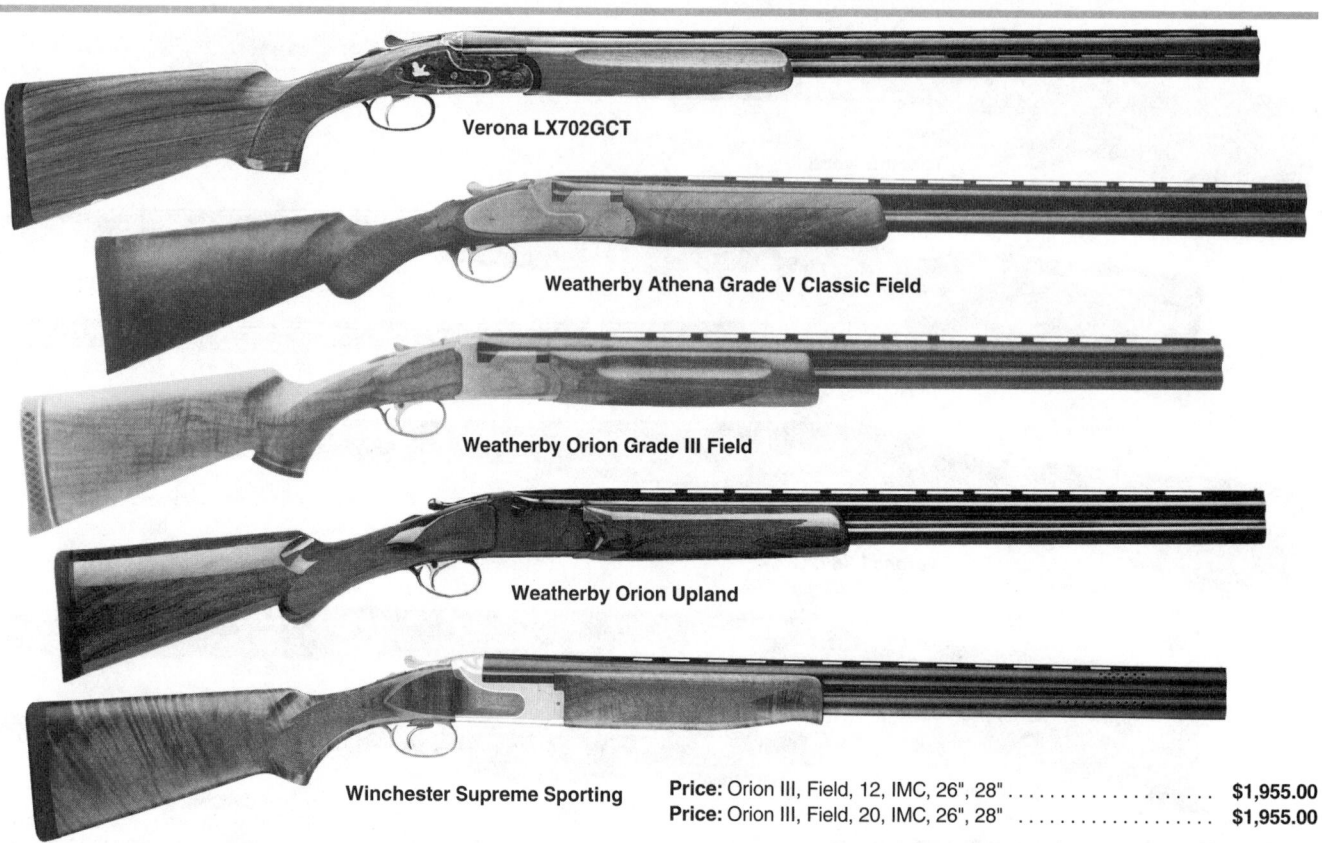

Verona LX702GCT

Weatherby Athena Grade V Classic Field

Weatherby Orion Grade III Field

Weatherby Orion Upland

Winchester Supreme Sporting

VERONA LX702 GOLD TRAP COMBO O/U SHOTGUNS

Gauge: 20/28, 2-3/4" chamber. **Barrel:** 30". **Weight:** 7 lbs. **Stock:** Turkish walnut with beavertail forearm. **Sights:** White front bead. **Features:** 2-barrel competition gun. Color case-hardened side plates and receiver with gold inlaid pheasant. Vent rib between barrels. 5 Interchokes. Imported from Italy by B.C. Outdoors.
Price: Combo **$2,467.84**
Price: 20 ga. **$1,829.12**

Verona LX702 Skeet/Trap O/U Shotguns

Similar to Verona LX702. Both are 12 gauge and 2-3/4" chamber. Skeet has 28" barrel and weighs 7-3/4 lbs. Trap has 32" barrel and weighs 7-7/8 lbs. By B.C. Outdoors.
Price: Skeet **$1,829.12**
Price: Trap **$1,829.12**

WEATHERBY ATHENA GRADE V CLASSIC FIELD O/U SHOTGUN

Gauge: 12, 20, 3" chambers. **Barrel:** 26", 28", IMC multi-choke tubes. **Weight:** 12 ga., 7-1/4 to 8 lbs.; 20 ga. 6-1/2 to 7-1/4 lbs. **Stock:** Oil-finished American Claro walnut with fine-line checkering, rounded pistol grip and slender forend. **Features:** Old English recoil pad. Sideplate receiver has rose and scroll engraving.
Price: **$3,037.00**

Weatherby Athena Grade III Classic Field O/U Shotgun

Similar to Athena Grade V, has Grade III Claro walnut with oil finish, rounded pistol grip, slender forend; silver nitride/gray receiver has rose and scroll engraving with gold-overlay upland game scenes. Introduced 1999. Imported from Japan by Weatherby.
Price: 12, 20, 28 ga. **$2,173.00**

WEATHERBY ORION GRADE III FIELD O/U SHOTGUNS

Gauge: 12, 20, 3" chambers. **Barrel:** 26", 28", IMC multi-choke tubes. **Weight:** 6-1/2 to 8 lbs. **Stock:** 14-1/4"x1-1/2"x2-1/2". American walnut, checkered grip and forend. Rubber recoil pad. **Features:** Selective automatic ejectors, single selective inertia trigger. Top tang safety, Greener cross bolt. Has silver-gray receiver with engraving and gold duck/pheasant. Imported from Japan by Weatherby.

Price: Orion III, Field, 12, IMC, 26", 28" **$1,955.00**
Price: Orion III, Field, 20, IMC, 26", 28" **$1,955.00**

Weatherby Orion Grade II Classic Field O/U Shotgun

Similar to Orion Grade III Field except stock has high-gloss finish, and bird on receiver is not gold. Available in 12 gauge, 26", 28", 30" barrels, 20 gauge, 26" 28", both with 3" chambers, 28 gauge, 26", 2-3/4" chambers. All have IMC choke tubes. Imported from Japan by Weatherby.
Price: **$1,622.00**

Weatherby Orion Upland O/U Shotgun

Similar to Orion Grade III Field. Plain blued receiver, gold W on trigger guard; rounded pistol grip, slender forend of Claro walnut with high-gloss finish; black butt pad. Available in 12 and 20 gauge with 26" and 28" barrels. Introduced 1999. Imported from Japan by Weatherby.
Price: **$1,299.00**

WEATHERBY ORION SSC O/U SHOTGUN

Gauge: 12, 3" chambers. **Barrel:** 28", 30", 32" (skeet, SC1, Imp. Cyl., SC2, Mod. IMC choke tubes). **Weight:** About 8 lbs. **Stock:** 14-3/ 4"x2-1/4"x1-1/2". Claro walnut with satin oil finish; Schnabel forend tip; sporter-style pistol grip; Pachmayr Decelerator recoil pad. **Features:** Designed for sporting clays competition. Has lengthened forcing cones and back-boring; ported barrels with 12mm grooved rib with mid-bead sight; mechanical trigger is adjustable for length of pull. Introduced 1998. Imported from Japan by Weatherby.
Price: SSC (Super Sporting Clays) **$2,059.00**

WINCHESTER SELECT O/U SHOTGUNS

Gauge: 12, 2-3/4", 3" chambers. **Barrel:** 28", 30", Invector Plus choke tubes. **Weight:** 7 lbs. 6 oz. to 7 lbs. 12. oz. **Length:** 45" overall (28" barrel). **Stock:** Checkered walnut stock. **Features:** Chrome-plated chambers; back-bored barrels; tang barrel selector/safety; deep-blued finish. Introduced 2000. From U.S. Repeating Arms. Co.
Price: Select Field (26" or 28" barrel, 6mm vent rib) **$1,498.00**
Price: Select Energy **$1,950.00**
Price: Select Elegance **$2,320.00**
Price: Select Energy Trap **$1,871.00**
Price: Select Energy Trap adjustable **$2,115.00**
Price: Select Energy Sporting adjustable **$2,115.00**

Variety of models for utility and sporting use, including some competitive shooting.

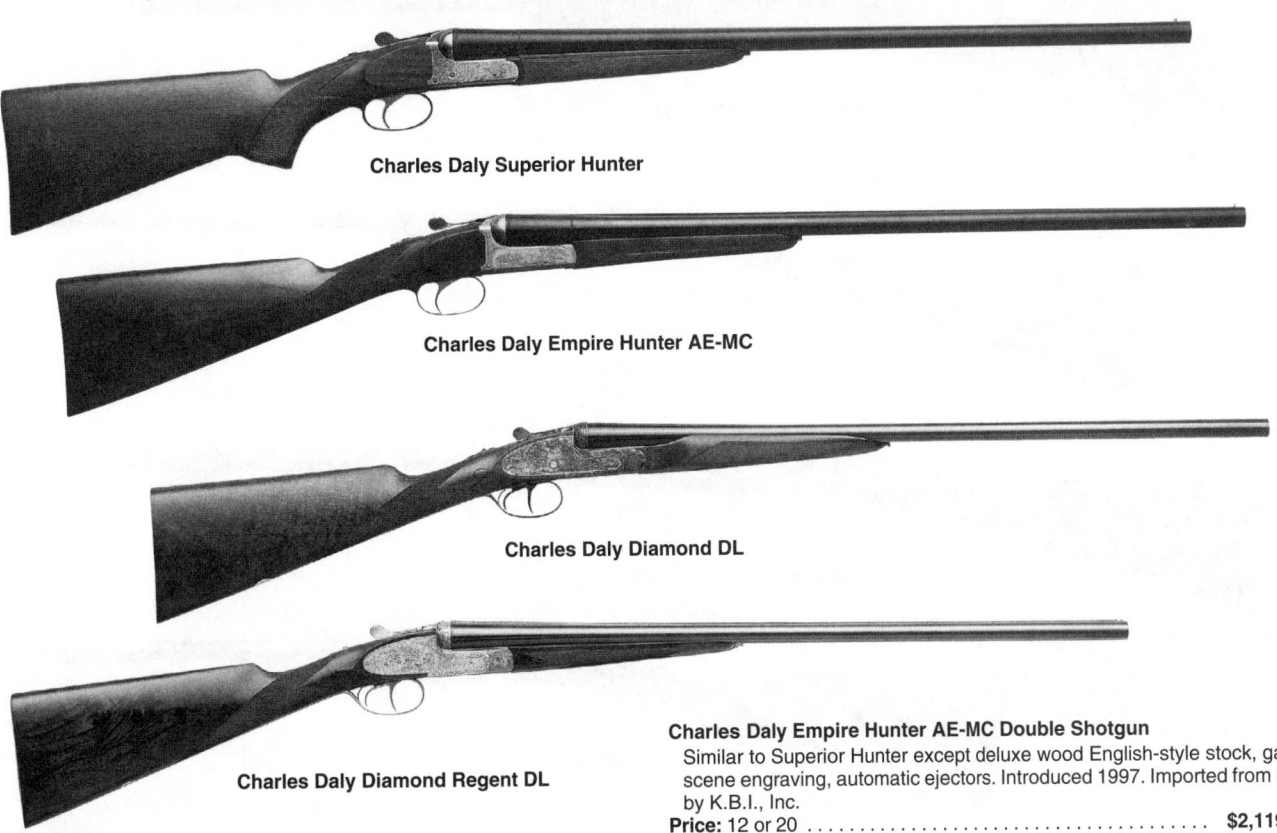

Charles Daly Superior Hunter

Charles Daly Empire Hunter AE-MC

Charles Daly Diamond DL

Charles Daly Diamond Regent DL

ARRIETA SIDELOCK DOUBLE SHOTGUNS

Gauge: 12, 16, 20, 28, .410. **Barrel:** Length and chokes to customer specs. **Weight:** To customer specs. **Stock:** To customer specs. Straight English with checkered butt (standard), or pistol grip. Select European walnut with oil finish. **Features:** Essentially custom gun with myriad options. H&H pattern hand-detachable sidelocks, selective automatic ejectors, double triggers (hinged front) standard. Some have self-opening action. Finish and engraving to customer specs. Imported from Spain by Wingshooting Adventures.

Price: Model 557, auto ejectors. From	$3,250.00
Price: Model 570, auto ejectors. From	$3,950.00
Price: Model 578, auto ejectors. From	$4,350.00
Price: Model 600 Imperial, self-opening. From	$6,050.00
Price: Model 601 Imperial Tiro, self-opening. From	$6,950.00
Price: Model 801. From	$9,135.00
Price: Model 802. From	$9,135.00
Price: Model 803. From	$6,930.00
Price: Model 871, auto ejectors. From	$5,060.00
Price: Model 872, self-opening. From	$12,375.00
Price: Model 873, self-opening. From	$8,200.00
Price: Model 874, self-opening. From	$9,250.00
Price: Model 875, self-opening. From	$14,900.00

CHARLES DALY SUPERIOR HUNTER AND SUPERIOR MC DOUBLE SHOTGUNS

Gauge: 12, 20, 3" chambers, 28, 2-3/4" chambers. **Barrel:** 28" (Mod. & Full) 26" (Imp. Cyl. & Mod.). **Weight:** About 7 lbs. **Stock:** Checkered walnut pistol grip buttstock, splinter forend. **Features:** Silvered, engraved receiver; chrome-lined barrels; gold single trigger; automatic safety; extractors; gold bead front sight. Introduced 1997. Imported from Italy by K.B.I., Inc.

Price: Superior Hunter, 28 gauge and .410	$1,659.00
Price: Superior Hunter MC 26"-28"	$1,629.00

CHARLES DALY EMPIRE HUNTER AE-MC Double Shotgun

Similar to Superior Hunter except deluxe wood English-style stock, game scene engraving, automatic ejectors. Introduced 1997. Imported from Italy by K.B.I., Inc.

Price: 12 or 20 . . . . **$2,119.00**

CHARLES DALY DIAMOND DL DOUBLE SHOTGUN

Gauge: 12, 20, .410, 3" chambers, 28, 2-3/4" chambers. **Barrel:** 28" (Mod. & Full), 26" (Imp. Cyl. & Mod.), 26" (Full & Full, .410). **Weight:** From 5 lbs. to 7 lbs. **Stock:** Select fancy European walnut, English-style butt, beavertail forend; hand-checkered, hand-rubbed oil finish. **Features:** Drop-forged action with gas escape valves; demi-block barrels with concave rib; selective automatic ejectors; hand-detachable double safety sidelocks with hand-engraved rose and scrollwork. Hinged front trigger. Color case-hardened receiver. Introduced 1997. Imported from Spain by K.B.I., Inc.

Price: . . . . **Special order only**

CHARLES DALY DIAMOND REGENT DL DOUBLE SHOTGUN

Gauge: 12, 20, .410, 3" chambers, 28, 2-3/4" chambers. **Barrel:** 28" (Mod. & Full), 26" (Imp. Cyl. & Mod.), 26" (Full & Full, .410). **Weight:** About 5-7 lbs. **Stock:** Special select fancy European walnut, English-style butt, splinter forend; hand-checkered; hand-rubbed oil finish. **Features:** Drop-forged action with gas escape valves; demi-block barrels of chrome-nickel steel with concave rib; selective automatic-ejectors; hand-detachable, double-safety H&H sidelocks with demi-relief hand engraving; H&H pattern easy-opening feature; hinged trigger; coin finished action. Introduced 1997. Imported from Spain by K.B.I., Inc.

Price: Special Custom Order . . . . **NA**

CHARLES DALY FIELD II, AE-MC HUNTER DOUBLE SHOTGUN

Gauge: 12, 20, 28, .410 (3" chambers; 28 has 2-3/4"). **Barrel:** 32" (Mod. & Mod.), 28, 30" (Mod. & Full), 26" (Imp. Cyl. & Mod.) .410 (Full & Full). **Weight:** 6 lbs. to 11.4 lbs. **Stock:** Checkered walnut pistol grip and forend. **Features:** Silvered, engraved receiver; gold single selective trigger in 10, 12, and 20 ga.; double triggers in 28 and .410; automatic safety; extractors; gold bead front sight. Introduced 1997. Imported from Spain by K.B.I., Inc.

Price: 28 ga., .410-bore	$1,189.00
Price: 12 or 20 AE-MC	$1,099.00

Charles Daly Field II Hunter

CZ Bobwhite

CZ Ringneck

CZ Durango

CZ Hammer Coach

CZ BOBWHITE AND RINGNECK SHOTGUNS
Gauge: 12, 20, 28, .410. (5 screw-in chokes in 12 and 20 ga. and fixed chokes in IC and Mod in .410). **Barrel:** 20". **Weight:** 6.5 lbs. **Length:** NA. **Stock:** Sculptured Turkish walnut with straight English-style grip and double triggers (Bobwhite) or conventional American pistol grip with a single trigger (Ringneck). Both are hand checkered 20 lpi. **Features:** Both color case-hardened shotguns are hand engraved.
Price: Bobwhite $695.00
Price: Ringneck $912.00

CZ DURANGO AND AMARILLO SHOTGUNS
Gauge: 12, 3" chambers. **Barrel:** 20". **Weight:** 6.7 lbs. **Length:** NA. **Stock:** Hand checkered walnut with old style round knob pistol grip. **Features:** The Durango comes with a single trigger, while the Amarillo is a double trigger shotgun The receiver, trigger guard, and forend metal are finished in 19th century color case-hardening.
Price: $795.00

CZ HAMMER COACH SHOTGUNS
Gauge: 12, 3" chambers. **Barrel:** 20". **Weight:** 6.7 lbs. **Length:** NA. **Stock:** NA. **Features:** Following in the tradition of the guns used by the stagecoach guards of the 1880's, this cowboy gun features double triggers, 19th century color case-hardening and fully functional external hammers.
Price: $795.00

DAKOTA PREMIER GRADE SHOTGUN
Gauge: 12, 16, 20, 28, .410. **Barrel:** 27". **Weight:** NA. **Length:** NA. **Stock:** Exhibition-grade English walnut, hand-rubbed oil finish with straight grip and splinter forend. **Features:** French grey finish; 50 percent coverage engraving; double triggers; selective ejectors. Finished to customer specifications. Made in U.S. by Dakota Arms.
Price: 12, 16, 20 gauge $13,950.00
Price: 28 gauge and .410 . . . . $15,345.00

Dakota Legend Shotgun
Similar to Premier Grade except has special selection English walnut, full-coverage scroll engraving, oak and leather case. Made in U.S. by Dakota Arms.
Price: 12, 16, 20 gauge $18,000.00
Price: 28 gauge and .410 . . . . $19,800.00

E.M.F. HARTFORD MODEL COWBOY SHOTGUN
Gauge: 12. **Barrel:** 20". **Weight:** NA. **Length:** NA. **Stock:** Checkered walnut. **Sights:** Center bead. **Features:** Exposed hammers; color case-hardened receiver; blued barrel. Introduced 2001. Imported from Spain by E.M.F. Co. Inc.
Price: $625.00

SHOTGUNS — Side-by-Side

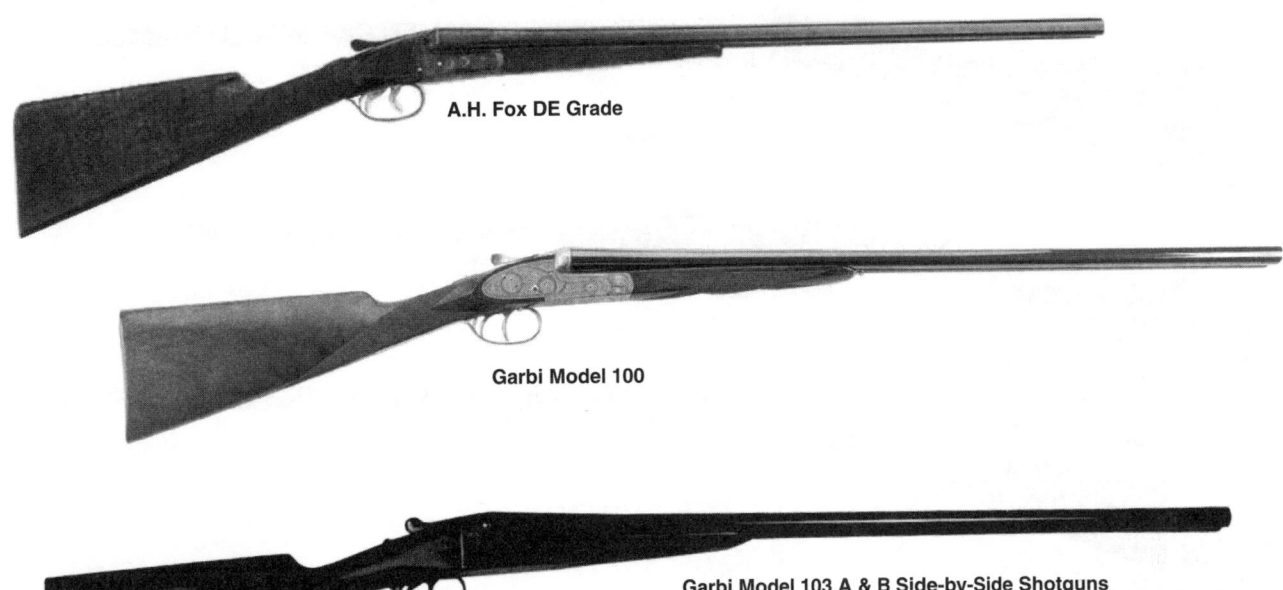

A.H. Fox DE Grade

Garbi Model 100

Bill Hanus Birdgun

FOX, A.H., SIDE-BY-SIDE SHOTGUNS

Gauge: 16, 20, 28, .410. **Barrel:** Length and chokes to customer specifications. Rust-blued Chromox or Krupp steel. **Weight:** 5-1/2 to 6-3/4 lbs. **Stock:** Dimensions to customer specifications. Hand-checkered Turkish Circassian walnut with hand-rubbed oil finish. Straight, semi or full pistol grip; splinter, Schnabel or beavertail forend; traditional pad, hard rubber buttplate or skeleton butt. **Features:** Boxlock action with automatic ejectors; double or Fox single selective trigger. Scalloped, rebated and color case-hardened receiver; hand finished and hand-engraved. Grades differ in engraving, inlays, grade of wood, amount of hand finishing. Introduced 1993. Made in U.S. by Connecticut Shotgun Mfg.

Price: CE Grade	**$11,000.00**
Price: XE Grade	**$12,500.00**
Price: DE Grade	**$15,000.00**
Price: FE Grade	**$20,000.00**
Price: Exhibition Grade	**$30,000.00**
Price: 28/.410 CE Grade	**$12,500.00**
Price: 28/.410 XE Grade	**$14,000.00**
Price: 28/.410 DE Grade	**$16,500.00**
Price: 28/.410 FE Grade	**$21,500.00**
Price: 28/.410 Exhibition Grade	**$30,000.00**
Price: 28 or .410-bore	**$1,500.00**

GARBI MODEL 100 DOUBLE SHOTGUN

Gauge: 12, 16, 20, 28. **Barrel:** 26", 28", choked to customer specs. **Weight:** 5-1/2 to 7-1/2 lbs. **Stock:** 14-1/2"x2-1/4"x1-1/2". European walnut. Straight grip, checkered butt, classic forend. **Features:** Sidelock action, automatic ejectors, double triggers standard. Color case-hardened action, coin finish optional. Single trigger; beavertail forend, etc. optional. Five additional models available. Imported from Spain by Wm. Larkin Moore.

Price: From **$4,850.00**

Garbi Model 101 Side-by-Side Shotgun

Similar to the Garbi Model 100 except hand engraved with scroll engraving; select walnut stock; better overall quality than the Model 100. Imported from Spain by Wm. Larkin Moore.

Price: From **$6,250.00**

Garbi Model 103 A & B Side-by-Side Shotguns

Similar to the Garbi Model 100 except has Purdey-type fine scroll and rosette engraving. Better overall quality than the Model 101. Model 103B has nickel-chrome steel barrels, H&H-type easy opening mechanism; other mechanical details remain the same. Imported from Spain by Wm. Larkin Moore.

Price: Model 103A. From **$8,000.00**
Price: Model 103B. From **$11,800.00**

Garbi Model 200 Side-by-Side Shotgun

Similar to the Garbi Model 100 except has heavy-duty locks, magnum proofed. Very fine Continental-style floral and scroll engraving, well figured walnut stock. Other mechanical features remain the same. Imported from Spain by Wm. Larkin Moore.

Price: **$11,200.00**

HANUS BIRDGUN SHOTGUN

Gauge: 16, 20, 28. **Barrel:** 27", 20 and 28 ga.; 28", 16 ga. (skeet 1 & skeet 2). **Weight:** 5 lbs., 4 oz. to 6 lbs., 4 oz. **Stock:** 14-3/8"x1-1/2"x2-3/8", with 1/4" cast-off. Select walnut. **Features:** Boxlock action with ejectors; splinter forend, straight English grip; checkered butt; English leather-covered handguard and AyA snap caps included. Made by AyA. Introduced 1998. Imported from Spain by Bill Hanus Birdguns.

Price: **$2,995.00**

KIMBER VALIER GRADE I and II SHOTGUN

Gauge: 20, 3" chambers. **Barrels:** 26" or 28", IC and M. **Weight:** 6 lbs. 8 oz. **Stock:** Turkish walnut, English style. **Features:** Sidelock design, double triggers, 50-percent engraving; 24 lpi checkering; auto-ejectors (extractors only on Grade I). Color case-hardened sidelocks, rust blue barrels. Imported from Turkey by Kimber Mfg., Inc.

Price: Grade I **$3,879.00**
Price: Grade II **$4,480.00**

LEBEAU — COURALLY BOXLOCK SIDE-BY-SIDE SHOTGUN

Gauge: 12, 16, 20, 28, .410-bore. **Barrel:** 25" to 32". **Weight:** To customer specifications. **Stock:** French walnut. **Features:** Anson & Deely-type action with automatic ejectors; single or double triggers. Custom gun built to customer specifications. Imported from Belgium by Wm. Larkin Moore.

Price: From **$25,500.00**

LEBEAU-COURALLY SIDELOCK SIDE-BY-SIDE SHOTGUN

Gauge: 12, 16, 20, 28, .410-bore. **Barrel:** 25" to 32". **Weight:** To customer specifications. **Stock:** Fancy French walnut. **Features:** Holland & Holland-type action with automatic ejectors; single or double triggers. Custom gun built to customer specifications. Imported from Belgium by Wm. Larkin Moore.

Price: From **$56,000.00**

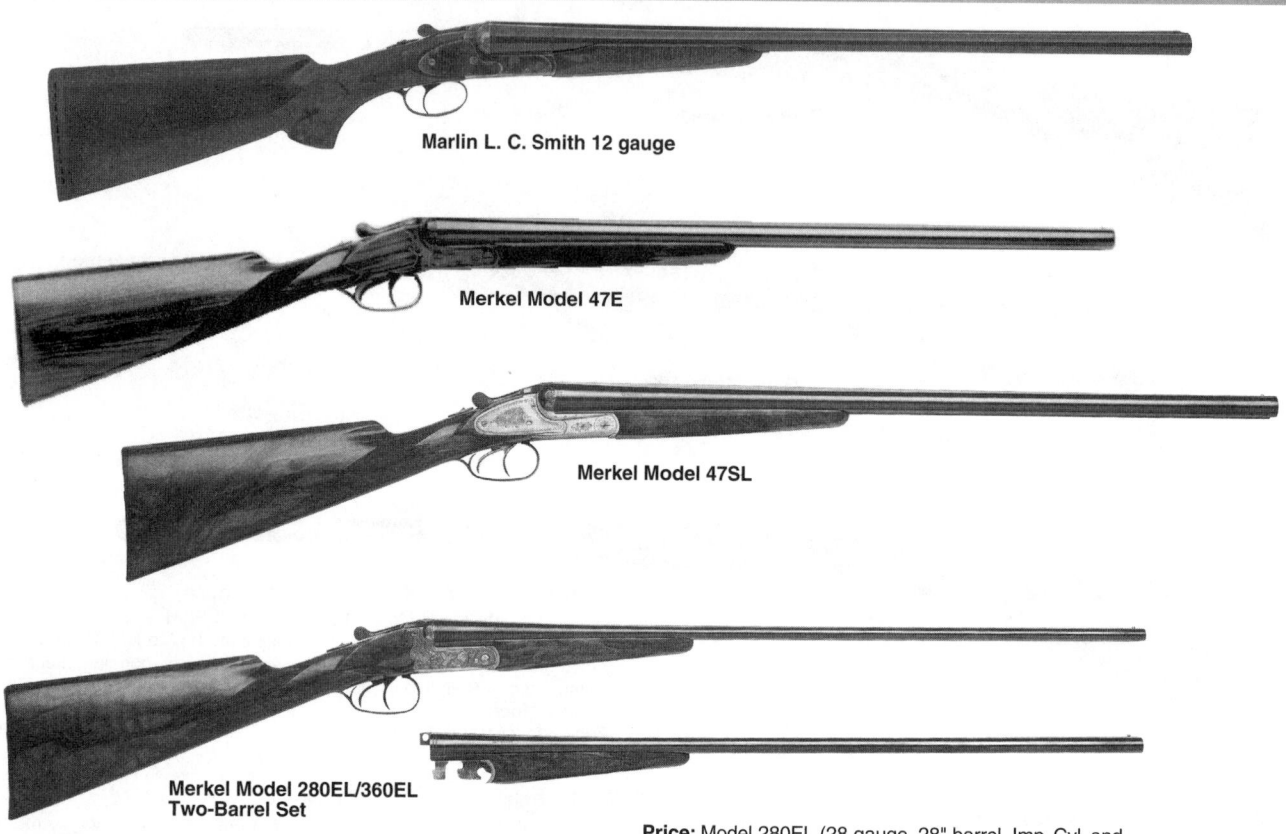

Marlin L. C. Smith 12 gauge

Merkel Model 47E

Merkel Model 47SL

Merkel Model 280EL/360EL Two-Barrel Set

MARLIN L. C. SMITH SIDE-BY-SIDE SHOTGUN

Gauge: 12, 20. **Stock:** Checkered walnut w/recoil pad. **Features:** 3" chambers, single trigger, selective automatic ejectors; 3 choke tubes (IC, Mod., Full); solid rib, bead front sight. Imported from Italy by Marlin. Introduced 2005.
Price: LC12-DB (28" barrel, 43" OAL, 6.25 lbs) **$2,109.00**
Price: LC20-DB (26" barrel, 41" OAL, 6 lbs) **$2,109.00**

MERKEL MODEL 47E, 147E SIDE-BY-SIDE SHOTGUNS

Gauge: 12, 3" chambers, 16, 2-3/4" chambers, 20, 3" chambers. **Barrel:** 12, 16 ga.-28"; 20 ga.-26-3/4" (Imp. Cyl. & Mod., Mod. & Full). **Weight:** About 6-3/4 lbs. (12 ga.). **Stock:** Oil-finished walnut; straight English or pistol grip. **Features:** Anson & Deeley-type boxlock action with single selective or double triggers, automatic safety, cocking indicators. Color case-hardened receiver with standard arabesque engraving. Imported from Germany by GSI.
Price: Model 47E (H&H ejectors) **$3,295.00**
Price: Model 147E (as above with ejectors) **$3,995.00**

Merkel Model 47SL, 147SL Side-by-Side Shotguns

Similar to Model 47E except H&H style sidelock action with cocking indicators, ejectors. Silver-grayed receiver and sideplates have arabesque engraving, engraved border and screws (Model 47S), or fine hunting scene engraving (Model 147S). Imported from Germany by GSI.
Price: Model 47SL **$5,995.00**
Price: Model 147SL **$7,995.00**
Price: Model 247SL (English-style engraving, large scrolls) **$7,995.00**
Price: Model 447SL (English-style engraving, small scrolls) **$9,995.00**

Merkel Model 280EL, 360EL Shotguns

Similar to Model 47E except smaller frame. Greener cross bolt with double under-barrel locking lugs, fine engraved hunting scenes on silver-grayed receiver, luxury-grade wood, Anson and Deely box-lock action. H&H ejectors, single-selective or double triggers. Introduced 2000. From Merkel.

Price: Model 280EL (28 gauge, 28" barrel, Imp. Cyl. and
Mod. chokes) **$5,795.00**
Price: Model 360EL (.410, 28" barrel, Mod. and
Full chokes) **$5,795.00**
Price: Model 280/360EL two-barrel set (28 and .410 gauge
as above) **$8,295.00**

Merkel Model 280SL and 360SL Shotguns

Similar to Model 280EL and 360EL except has sidelock action, double triggers, English-style arabesque engraving. Introduced 2000. From Merkel.
Price: Model 280SL (28 gauge, 28" barrel, Imp. Cyl. and
Mod. chokes) **$8,495.00**
Price: Model 360SL (.410, 28" barrel, Mod. and
Full chokes) **$8,495.00**
Price: Model 280/360SL two-barrel set **$11,995.00**

PIOTTI KING NO. 1 SIDE-BY-SIDE SHOTGUN

Gauge: 12, 16, 20, 28, .410. **Barrel:** 25" to 30" (12 ga.), 25" to 28" (16, 20, 28, .410). To customer specs. Chokes as specified. **Weight:** 6-1/2 lbs. to 8 lbs. (12 ga. to customer specs.). **Stock:** Dimensions to customer specs. Finely figured walnut; straight grip with checkered butt with classic splinter forend and hand-rubbed oil finish standard. Pistol grip, beavertail forend. **Features:** Holland & Holland pattern sidelock action, automatic ejectors. Double trigger; non-selective single trigger optional. Coin finish standard; color case-hardened optional. Top rib; level, file-cut; concave, ventilated optional. Very fine, full coverage scroll engraving with small floral bouquets. Imported from Italy by Wm. Larkin Moore.
Price: From **$29,600.00**

Piotti King Extra Side-by-Side Shotgun

Similar to the Piotti King No. 1 except with upgraded engraving. Choice of any type of engraving, including bulino game scene engraving and game scene engraving with gold inlays. Engraved and signed by a master engraver. Other mechanical specifications remain the same. Imported from Italy by Wm. Larkin Moore.
Price: From **$35,000.00**

Piotti Lunik

Rizzini Sidelock

Ruger Gold Label

Stoeger Uplander

Stoeger Silverado Coach

Price: 12, 20 ga. From	**$66,900.00**
Price: 28, .410 bore. From	**$75,500.00**

RUGER GOLD LABEL SIDE-BY-SIDE SHOTGUN
Gauge: 12, 3" chambers. **Barrel:** 28" with skeet tubes. **Weight:** 6-1/2 lbs. **Length:** 45". **Stock:** American walnut straight or pistol grip. **Sights:** Gold bead front, full length rib, serrated top. **Features:** Spring-assisted break-open, SS trigger, auto eject. Five interchangeable screw-in choke tubes, combination safety/barrel selector with auto safety reset.

Price:	**$2,050.00**

STOEGER UPLANDER SIDE-BY-SIDE SHOTGUNS
Gauge: 16, 28, 2-3/4 chambers. 12, 20, .410, 3" chambers. **Barrel:** 22", 24", 26", 28". **Weight:** 7.3 lbs. **Sights:** Brass bead. **Features:** Double trigger, IC & M fixed choke tubes with gun.

Price: With fixed or screw-in chokes	**$350.00**
Price: Supreme, screw-in chokes, 12 or 20 ga.	**$475.00**
Price: Youth, 20 ga. or .410, 22" barrel, double trigger	**$350.00**
Price: Combo, 20/28 ga. or 12/20 ga.	**$629.00**

STOEGER COACH GUN SIDE-BY-SIDE SHOTGUNS
Gauge: 12, 20, 2-3/4", 3" chambers. **Barrel:** 20". **Weight:** 6-1/2 lbs. **Stock:** Brown hardwood, classic beavertail forend. **Sights:** Brass bead. **Features:** IC & M fixed chokes, tang auto safety, auto extractors, black plastic buttplate. Imported by Benelli USA.

Price: Supreme blued finish	**$410.00**
Price: Supreme blued barrel, stainless receiver.	**$420.00**
Price: Supreme polished nickel receiver	**$440.00**
Price: Coach Gun synthetic stock, stainless receiver/barrel	**$340.00**
Price: Nickel Coach Gun synthetic stock, stainless	**$400.00**
Price: Silverado Coach Gun with English synthetic stock	**$400.00**

Piotti Lunik Side-by-Side Shotgun
Similar to the Piotti King No. 1 in overall quality. Has Renaissance-style large scroll engraving in relief. Best quality Holland & Holland-pattern sidelock ejector double with chopper lump (demi-bloc) barrels. Other mechanical specifications remain the same. Imported from Italy by Wm. Larkin Moore.

Price: From	**$30,900.00**

PIOTTI PIUMA SIDE-BY-SIDE SHOTGUN
Gauge: 12, 16, 20, 28, .410. **Barrel:** 25" to 30" (12 ga.), 25" to 28" (16, 20, 28, .410). **Weight:** 5-1/2 to 6-1/4 lbs. (20 ga.). **Stock:** Dimensions to customer specs. Straight grip stock with walnut checkered butt, classic splinter forend, hand-rubbed oil finish are standard; pistol grip, beavertail forend, satin luster finish optional. **Features:** Anson & Deeley boxlock ejector double with chopper lump barrels. Level, file-cut rib, light scroll and rosette engraving, scalloped frame. Double triggers; single non-selective optional. Coin finish standard, color case-hardened optional. Imported from Italy by Wm. Larkin Moore.

Price: From	**$14,800.00**

RIZZINI SIDELOCK SIDE-BY-SIDE SHOTGUN
Gauge: 12, 16, 20, 28, .410. **Barrel:** 25" to 30" (12, 16, 20 ga.), 25" to 28" (28, .410). To customer specs. Chokes as specified. **Weight:** 6-1/2 lbs. to 8 lbs. (12 ga. to customer specs). **Stock:** Dimensions to customer specs. Finely figured walnut; straight grip with checkered butt with classic splinter forend and hand-rubbed oil finish standard. Pistol grip, beavertail forend. **Features:** Sidelock action, auto ejectors. Double triggers or non-selective single trigger standard. Coin finish standard. Imported from Italy by Wm. Larkin Moore.

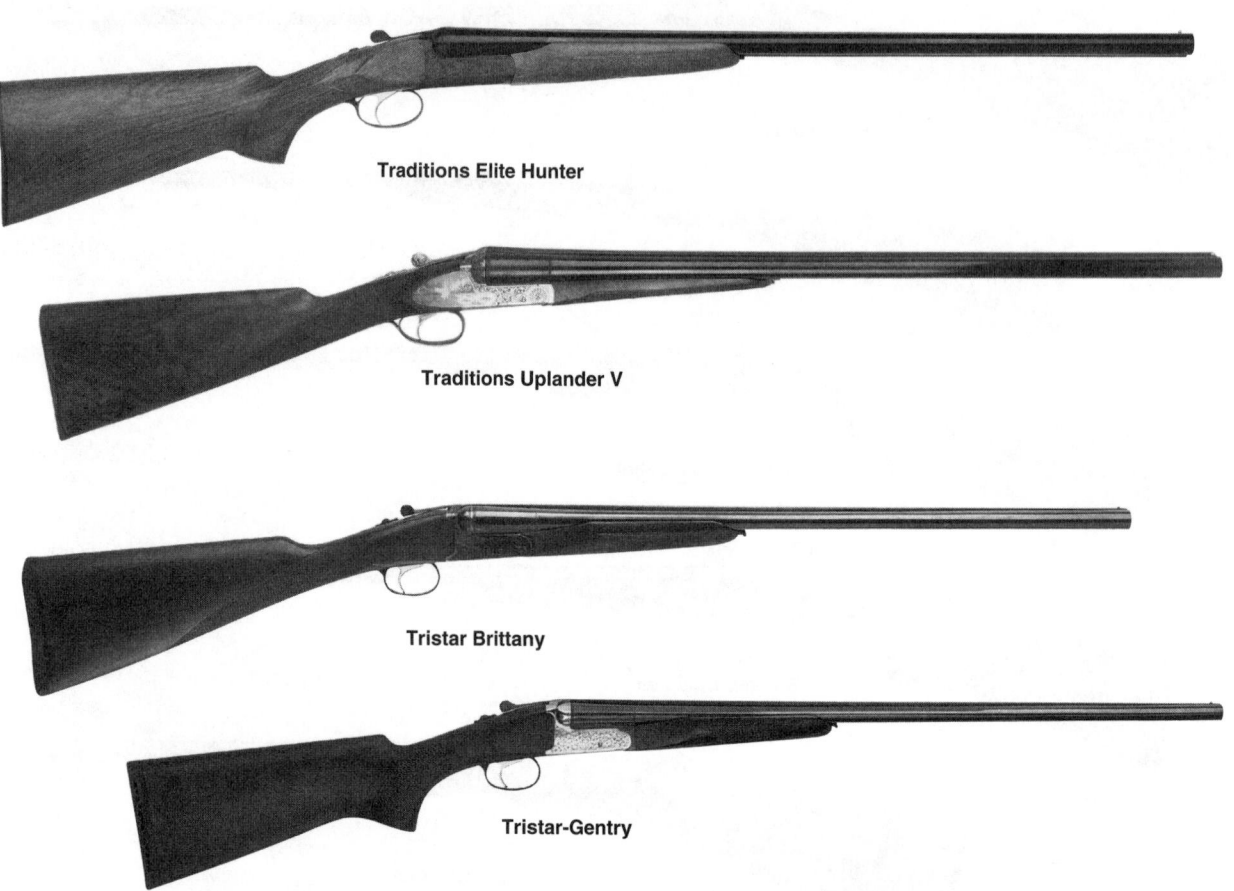

Traditions Elite Hunter

Traditions Uplander V

Tristar Brittany

Tristar-Gentry

TRADITIONS ELITE SERIES SIDE-BY-SIDE SHOTGUNS

Gauge: 12, 3"; 20, 3"; 28, 2-3/4"; .410, 3". **Barrel:** 26". **Weight:** 5 lbs., 12 oz. to 6-1/2 lbs. **Length:** 43" overall. **Stock:** Walnut. **Features:** Chrome-lined barrels; fixed chokes (Elite Field III ST, Field I DT and Field I ST) or choke tubes (Elite Hunter ST); extractors (Hunter ST and Field I models) or automatic ejectors (Field III ST); top tang safety. Imported from Fausti of Italy by Traditions.
Price: Elite Field I DT — 12, 20, 28 ga. or .410; IC and Mod. fixed chokes (F and F on .410); double triggers . . . . **$789.00 to $969.00**
Price: Elite Field I ST — 12, 20, 28 ga. or .410; same as DT but with single trigger . . . . **$969.00 to $1,169.00**
Price: Elite Field III ST — 28 ga. or .410; gold-engraved receiver; high-grade walnut stock **$2,099.00**
Price: Elite Hunter ST — 12 or 20 ga.; blued receiver; IC and Mod. choke tubes **$999.00**

TRADITIONS UPLANDER SERIES SIDE-BY-SIDE SHOTGUNS

Gauge: 12, 3"; 20, 3". **Barrel:** 26", 28". **Weight:** 6-1/4 lbs. to 6-1/2 lbs. **Length:** 43" to 45" overall. **Stock:** Walnut. **Features:** Barrels threaded for choke tubes (Improved Cylinder, Modified and Full); top tang safety, extended trigger guard. Engraved silver receiver with side plates and lavish gold inlays. Imported from Fausti of Italy by Traditions.
Price: Uplander III Silver 12, 20 ga. **$2,699.00**
Price: Uplander V Silver 12, 20 ga. **$3,199.00**

TRISTAR BRITTANY SIDE-BY-SIDE SHOTGUN

Gauge: 12, 16, 20, 28, .410, 3" chambers. **Barrel:** 12 ga., 20 ga., 26", 28"; 16 ga., 27", 28 ga., 27", 410 ga., 27". All have CT-3 Chokes. **Weight:** 6.2 to 7.2 lbs. **Stock:** Walnut English-style, semi-beavertail forearm with cut checkering, standard semi-gloss finish. **Features:** Boxlock action, engraved case colored frame, auto selective ejectors, single selective trigger.
Price: . . . . **$1,050.00 to $1,069.00**

TRISTAR GENTRY SIDE-BY-SIDE SHOTGUN

Gauge: 12, 16, 20, 28, .410, 3" chambers (16 and 28-ga. @ 2 3/4"). **Barrel:** 12 ga., 27", 20 ga., 28"; 28 ga., 26", 410 ga., 26". All have CT-3 Chokes. **Weight:** 6.2 to 6.8 lbs. **Stock:** Walnut pistol grip stock, semi-beavertail forearm with cut checkering, standard semi-gloss finish. **Features:** Boxlock action, engraved antique silver frame, extractors, single selective trigger with top tang selector.
Price: . . . . **$929.00 to $945.00**

Variety of designs for utility and sporting purposes, as well as for competitive shooting.

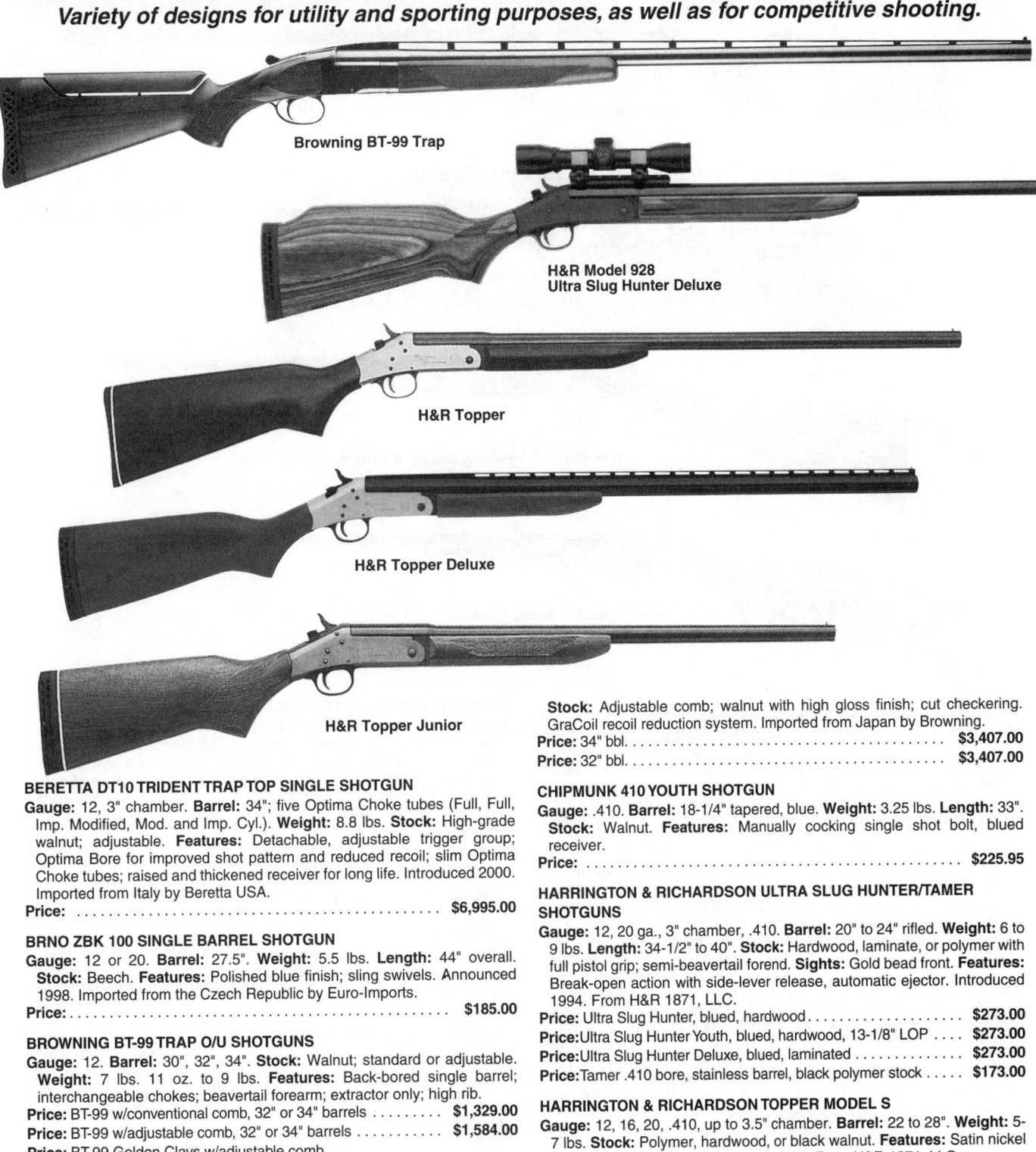

Browning BT-99 Trap

H&R Model 928 Ultra Slug Hunter Deluxe

H&R Topper

H&R Topper Deluxe

H&R Topper Junior

BERETTA DT10 TRIDENT TRAP TOP SINGLE SHOTGUN
Gauge: 12, 3" chamber. **Barrel:** 34"; five Optima Choke tubes (Full, Full, Imp. Modified, Mod. and Imp. Cyl.). **Weight:** 8.8 lbs. **Stock:** High-grade walnut; adjustable. **Features:** Detachable, adjustable trigger group; Optima Bore for improved shot pattern and reduced recoil; slim Optima Choke tubes; raised and thickened receiver for long life. Introduced 2000. Imported from Italy by Beretta USA.
Price: **$6,995.00**

BRNO ZBK 100 SINGLE BARREL SHOTGUN
Gauge: 12 or 20. **Barrel:** 27.5". **Weight:** 5.5 lbs. **Length:** 44" overall. **Stock:** Beech. **Features:** Polished blue finish; sling swivels. Announced 1998. Imported from the Czech Republic by Euro-Imports.
Price: **$185.00**

BROWNING BT-99 TRAP O/U SHOTGUNS
Gauge: 12. **Barrel:** 30", 32", 34". **Stock:** Walnut; standard or adjustable. **Weight:** 7 lbs. 11 oz. to 9 lbs. **Features:** Back-bored single barrel; interchangeable chokes; beavertail forearm; extractor only; high rib.
Price: BT-99 w/conventional comb, 32" or 34" barrels **$1,329.00**
Price: BT-99 w/adjustable comb, 32" or 34" barrels **$1,584.00**
Price: BT-99 Golden Clays w/adjustable comb,
32" or 34" barrels **$3,509.00**
Price: BT-99 Micro w/conventional comb, 30" or 32" barrels **$1,329.00**

BROWNING GOLDEN CLAYS SHOTGUN
Gauge: 12, 3" chamber. **Barrel:** 32", 34" with Full, Improved Modified, Modified tubes. **Weight:** 8 lbs. 14 oz. to 9 lbs. **Length:** 49" to 51" overall.

Stock: Adjustable comb; walnut with high gloss finish; cut checkering. GraCoil recoil reduction system. Imported from Japan by Browning.
Price: 34" bbl. **$3,407.00**
Price: 32" bbl. **$3,407.00**

CHIPMUNK 410 YOUTH SHOTGUN
Gauge: .410. **Barrel:** 18-1/4" tapered, blue. **Weight:** 3.25 lbs. **Length:** 33". **Stock:** Walnut. **Features:** Manually cocking single shot bolt, blued receiver.
Price: **$225.95**

HARRINGTON & RICHARDSON ULTRA SLUG HUNTER/TAMER SHOTGUNS
Gauge: 12, 20 ga., 3" chamber, .410. **Barrel:** 20" to 24" rifled. **Weight:** 6 to 9 lbs. **Length:** 34-1/2" to 40". **Stock:** Hardwood, laminate, or polymer with full pistol grip; semi-beavertail forend. **Sights:** Gold bead front. **Features:** Break-open action with side-lever release, automatic ejector. Introduced 1994. From H&R 1871, LLC.
Price: Ultra Slug Hunter, blued, hardwood **$273.00**
Price: Ultra Slug Hunter Youth, blued, hardwood, 13-1/8" LOP **$273.00**
Price: Ultra Slug Hunter Deluxe, blued, laminated **$273.00**
Price: Tamer .410 bore, stainless barrel, black polymer stock **$173.00**

HARRINGTON & RICHARDSON TOPPER MODEL S
Gauge: 12, 16, 20, .410, up to 3.5" chamber. **Barrel:** 22 to 28". **Weight:** 5-7 lbs. **Stock:** Polymer, hardwood, or black walnut. **Features:** Satin nickel frame, blued barrel. Reintroduced 1992. From H&R 1871, LLC.
Price: Deluxe Classic, 12/20 ga., 28" barrel w/vent rib **$225.00**
Price: Topper Deluxe 12 ga., 28" barrel, black hardwood **$179.00**
Price: Topper 12, 16, 20 ga., .410, 26" to 28", black hardwood.... **$153.00**
Price: Topper Junior 20 ga., .410, 22" barrel, hardwood **$160.00**
Price: Topper Junior Classic, 20 ga., .410, checkered hardwood .. **$160.00**

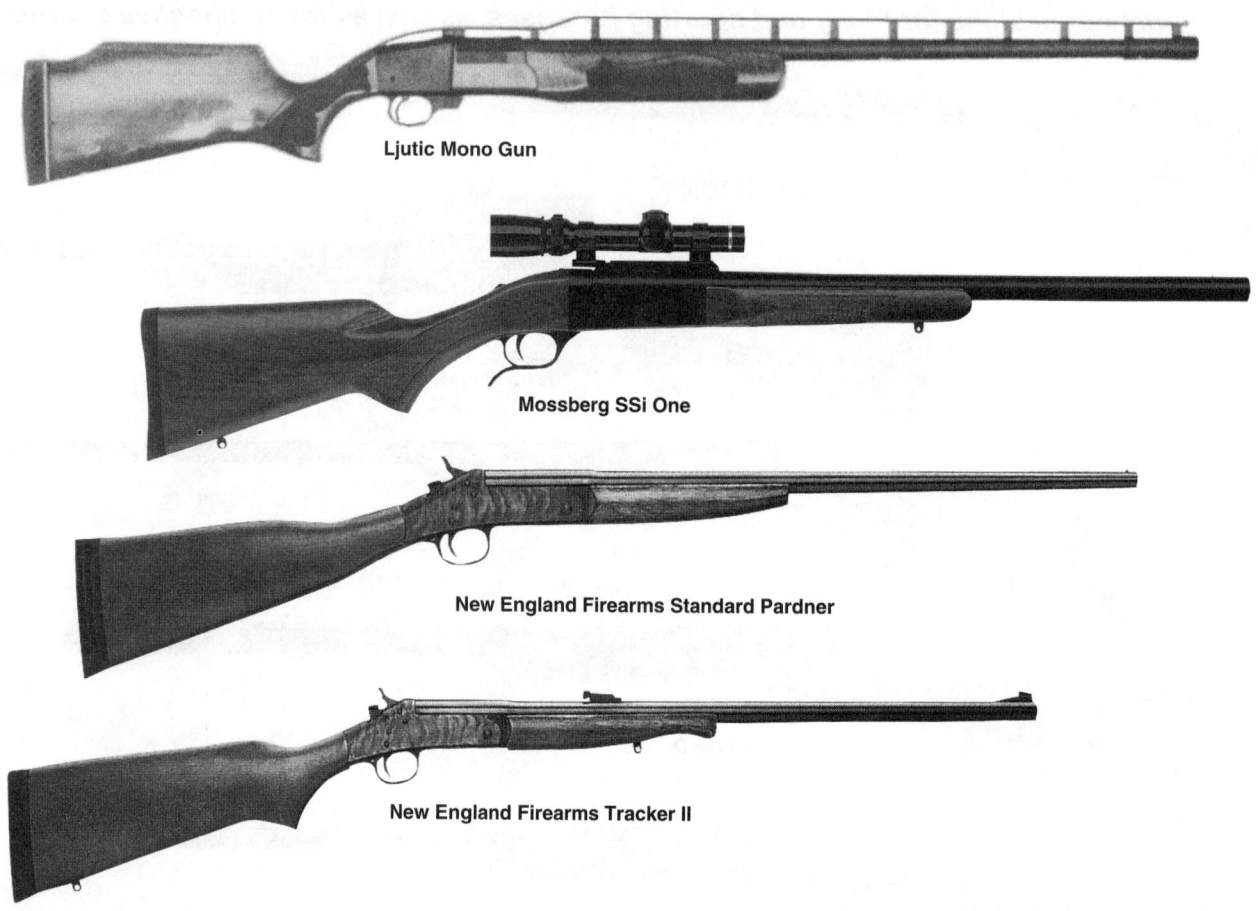

Ljutic Mono Gun

Mossberg SSi One

New England Firearms Standard Pardner

New England Firearms Tracker II

KRIEGHOFF K-80 SINGLE BARREL TRAP GUN

Gauge: 12, 2-3/4" chamber. **Barrel:** 32" or 34" Unsingle. Fixed Full or choke tubes. **Weight:** About 8-3/4 lbs. **Stock:** Four stock dimensions or adjustable stock available. All hand-checkered European walnut. **Features:** Satin nickel finish. Selective mechanical trigger adjustable for finger position. Tapered step vent rib. Adjustable point of impact.
Price: Standard grade Full Unsingle, from **$10,080.00**

KRIEGHOFF KX-5 TRAP GUN

Gauge: 12, 2-3/4" chamber. **Barrel:** 32", 34"; choke tubes. **Weight:** About 8-1/2 lbs. **Stock:** Factory adjustable stock. European walnut. **Features:** Ventilated tapered step rib. Adjustable position trigger, optional release trigger. Fully adjustable rib. Satin gray electroless nickel receiver. Fitted aluminum case. Imported from Germany by Krieghoff International, Inc.
Price: **$5,395.00**

LJUTIC MONO GUN SINGLE BARREL SHOTGUN

Gauge: 12 only. **Barrel:** 34", choked to customer specs; hollow-milled rib, 35-1/2" sight plane. **Weight:** Approx. 9 lbs. **Stock:** To customer specs. Oil finish, hand checkered. **Features:** Custom gun. Pull or release trigger; removable trigger guard contains trigger and hammer mechanism; Ljutic pushbutton opener on front of trigger guard. From Ljutic Industries.
Price: Std., med. or Olympic rib, custom bbls., fixed choke. **$6,995.00**
Price: As above with screw-in choke barrel **$7,395.00**
Price: Stainless steel mono gun **$7,995.00**

Ljutic LTX Pro 3 Deluxe Mono Gun

Deluxe, lightweight version of the Mono gun with high quality wood, upgrade checkering, special rib height, screw-in chokes, ported and cased.
Price: **$8,995.00**
Price: Stainless steel model **$9,995.00**

MOSSBERG SSi-ONE 12 GAUGE SLUG SHOTGUN

Gauge: 12, 3" chamber. **Barrel:** 24", fully rifled. **Weight:** 8 lbs. **Length:** 40" overall. **Stock:** Walnut, fluted and cut checkered; sling-swivel studs; drilled and tapped for scope base. **Sights:** None (scope base supplied). **Features:** Frame accepts interchangeable rifle barrels (see Mossberg SSi-One rifle listing); lever-opening, break-action design; ambidextrous, top-tang safety; internal eject/extract selector. Introduced 2000. From Mossberg.
Price: **$480.00**

Mossberg SSi-One Turkey Shotgun

Similar to SSi-One 12 gauge slug shotgun, but chambered for 12 ga., 3-1/2" loads. Includes Accu-Mag Turkey Tube. Introduced 2001. From Mossberg.
Price: **$459.00**

NEW ENGLAND FIREARMS PARDNER AND TRACKER II SHOTGUNS

Gauge: 10, 12, 16, 20, 28, .410, up to 3.5" chamber for 10 and 12 ga. 16, 28, 2-3/4" chamber. **Barrel:** 24" to 30". **Weight:** Varies from 5 to 9.5 lbs. **Length:** Varies from 36" to 48". **Stock:** Walnut-finished hardwood with full pistol grip, synthetic, or camo finish. **Sights:** Bead front on most. **Features:** Transfer bar ignition; break-open action with side-lever release. Introduced 1987. From New England Firearms.
Price: Pardner, all gauges, hardwood stock, 26" to 32" blued barrel, Mod. or Full choke, ... **$140.00**
Price: Pardner Youth, hardwood stock, straight grip, 22" blued barrel **$149.00**
Price: Pardner Screw-In Choke model, intr. 2006 . . . . **$164.00**
Price: Turkey model, 10/12 ga., camo finish or black. . . **$192.00 to $259.00**
Price: Youth Turkey, 20 ga., camo finish or black **$192.00**
Price: Waterfowl, 10 ga., camo finish or hardwood **$227.00**
Price: Tracker II slug gun, 12/20 ga., hardwood **$196.00**

SHOTGUNS — Bolt Actions & Single Shot

Rossi Single-Shot

Rossi Matched Pair

Savage 210F Slug Warrior

Stoeger Single-Shot

Tar-Hunt RSG-20 Mountaineer

ROSSI SINGLE-SHOT SHOTGUN

Gauge: 12, 20, 2-3/4" chamber; .410, 3" chamber. **Barrel:** 28" full, 22" Youth. **Weight:** 5 lbs. **Stock:** Stained hardwood. **Sights:** Bead. **Features:** Break-open, positive ejection, internal transfer bar, trigger block.
Price: $101.00

ROSSI MATCHED PAIR SINGLE-SHOT SHOTGUN/RIFLE

Gauge: .410, 20 or 12. **Barrel:** 22" (18.5" Youth), 28" (23" full). **Weight:** 4-6 lbs. **Stock:** Hardwood (brown or black finish). **Sights:** Bead front. **Features:** Break-open internal transfer bar manual external safety; blued or stainless steel finish; sling-swivel studs; includes matched 22 LR or 22 mag. barrel with fully adjustable front and rear sight. Trigger block system. Introduced 2001. Imported by BrazTech/Taurus.
Price: Blue $139.95
Price: Stainless steel $169.95

SAVAGE MODEL 210F SLUG WARRIOR SHOTGUN

Gauge: 12, 3" chamber; 2-shot magazine. **Barrel:** 24" 1:35" rifling twist. **Weight:** 7-1/2 lbs. **Length:** 43.5" overall. **Stock:** Glass-filled polymer with positive checkering. **Features:** Based on the Savage Model 110 action; 60-degree bolt lift; controlled round feed; comes with scope mount. Introduced 1996. Made in U.S. by Savage Arms.
Price: $475.00
Price: (Camo) $513.00

STOEGER SINGLE-SHOT SHOTGUN

Gauge: 12, 20, .410, 2-3/4", 3" chambers. **Barrel:** 26", 28". **Weight:** 5.4 lbs. **Length:** 40-1/2" to 42-1/2" overall. **Sights:** Brass bead. **Features:** .410, Full fixed choke tubes, screw-in. .410 12 ga. hardwood pistol-grip stock and forend. 20 ga. 26" bbl., hardwood forend.
Price: Blue; Youth $109.00
Price: Youth with English stock $119.00

TAR-HUNT RSG-12 PROFESSIONAL RIFLED SLUG GUN

Gauge: 12, 2-3/4" or 3" chamber, 1-shot magazine. **Barrel:** 23", fully rifled with muzzle brake. **Weight:** 7-3/4 lbs. **Length:** 41-1/2" overall. **Stock:** Matte black McMillan fiberglass with Pachmayr Decelerator pad. **Sights:** None furnished; comes with Leupold windage or Weaver bases. **Features:** Uses rifle-style action with two locking lugs; two-position safety; Shaw barrel; single-stage, trigger; muzzle brake. Many options available. Right- and left-hand models at same prices. Introduced 1991. Made in U.S. by Tar-Hunt Custom Rifles, Inc.
Price: 12 ga. Professional model, right- or left-hand; $2,585.00

Tar-Hunt RSG-16 Elite Shotgun

Similar to RSG-12 Professional except 16 gauge; right- or left-hand versions.
Price: $2,585.00

Tar-Hunt RSG-20 Mountaineer Slug Gun

Similar to the RSG-12 Professional except chambered for 20 gauge (2-3/4" and 3" shells); 23" Shaw rifled barrel, with muzzle brake; two-lug bolt; one-shot blind magazine; matte black finish; McMillan fiberglass stock with Pachmayr Decelerator pad; receiver drilled and tapped for Rem. 700 bases. Right- or left-hand versions. Weighs 6-1/2 lbs. Introduced 1997. Made in U.S. by Tar-Hunt Custom Rifles, Inc.
Price: $2,585.00

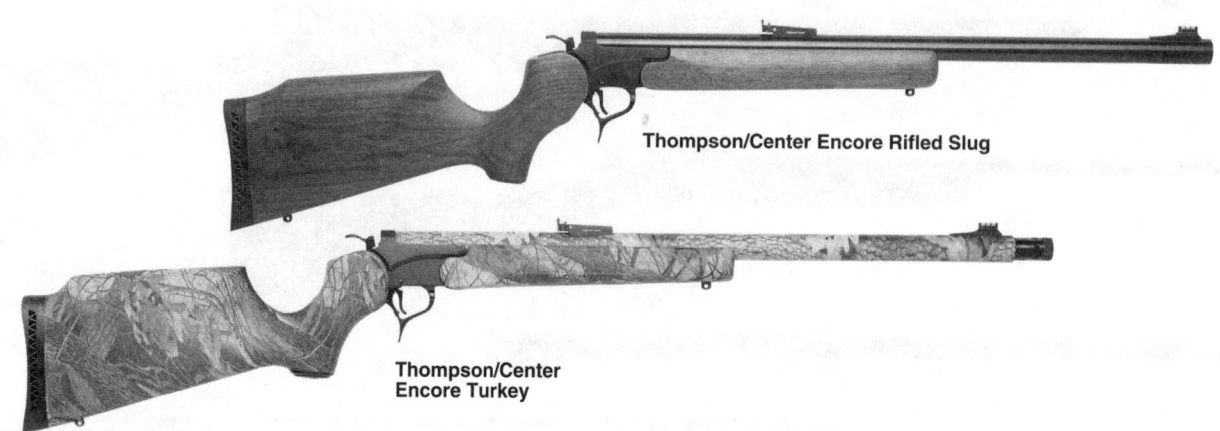

Thompson/Center Encore Rifled Slug

Thompson/Center
Encore Turkey

THOMPSON/CENTER ENCORE RIFLED SLUG GUN
Gauge: 20, 3" chamber. **Barrel:** 26", fully rifled. **Weight:** About 7 lbs. **Length:** 40-1/2" overall. **Stock:** Walnut with walnut forearm. **Sights:** Steel; click-adjustable rear and ramp-style front, both with fiber optics. **Features:** Encore system features a variety of rifle, shotgun and muzzle-loading rifle barrels interchangeable with the same frame. Break-open design operates by pulling up and back on trigger guard spur. Composite stock and forearm available. Introduced 2000.
Price: **$684.00**

THOMPSON/CENTER ENCORE TURKEY GUN
Gauge: 12 ga. **Barrel:** 24". **Features:** All-camo finish, high definition Realtree Hardwoods HD camo.
Price: **$763.00**

Designs for utility, suitable for and adaptable to competitions and other sporting purposes.

Benelli M3 Convertible

Mossberg Model 500 Persuader

Mossberg Ghost Ring

BENELLI M3 CONVERTIBLE SHOTGUN

Gauge: 12, 2-3/4", 3" chambers, 5-shot magazine. **Barrel:** 19-3/4" (Cyl.). **Weight:** 7 lbs., 4oz. **Length:** 41" overall. **Stock:** High-impact polymer with sling loop in side of butt; rubberized pistol grip on stock. **Sights:** Open rifle, fully adjustable. Ghost ring and rifle type. **Features:** Combination pump/auto action. Alloy receiver with inertia recoil rotating locking lug bolt; matte finish; automatic shell release lever. Introduced 1989. Imported by Benelli USA. Price with pistol grip, open rifle sights.

Price: With standard stock, open rifle sights **$1,235.00**
Price: With ghost ring sight system, standard stock **$1,185.00**
Price: With ghost ring sights, pistol grip stock **$1,165.00**

BENELLI M2 TACTICAL SHOTGUN

Gauge: 12, 2-3/4", 3" chambers, 5-shot magazine. **Barrel:** 18.5" IC, M, F choke tubes. **Weight:** 6.7 lbs. **Length:** 39.75" overall. **Stock:** Black polymer. **Sights:** Rifle type with ghost ring system, tritium night sights optional. **Features:** Semi-auto intertia recoil action. Cross-bolt safety; bolt release button; matte-finish metal. Introduced 1993. Imported from Italy by Benelli USA.

Price: With rifle sights, standard stock **$1,000.00**
Price: With ghost ring rifle sights, standard stock **$1,065.00**
Price: With ghost ring sights, pistol grip stock **$1,065.00**
Price: With rifle sights, pistol grip stock **$1,000.00**
Price: ComforTech stock, rifle sights **$1,135.00**
Price: Comfortech Stock, Ghost-Ring **$1,185.00**

Benelli M2 Practical Shotgun

Similar to M2 Tactical shotgun, Picatinny receiver rail for scope mounting, nine-round magazine, 26" compensated barrel and ghost ring sights. Designed for IPSC competition.
Price: **$1,335.00**

CROSSFIRE SHOTGUN/RIFLE

Gauge/Caliber: 12, 2-3/4" Chamber: 4-shot/223 Rem. (5-shot). **Barrel:** 20" (shotgun), 18" (rifle). **Weight:** About 8.6 lbs. **Length:** 40" overall. **Stock:** Composite. **Sights:** Meprolight night sights. Integral Weaver-style scope rail. **Features:** Combination pump-action shotgun, rifle; single selector, single trigger; dual action bars for both upper and lower actions; ambidextrous selector and safety. Introduced 1997. Made in U.S. From Hesco.
Price: About **$1,895.00**
Price: With camo finish **$1,995.00**

FABARM TACTICAL SEMI-AUTOMATIC SHOTGUN

Gauge: 12, 3" chamber. **Barrel:** 20". **Weight:** 6.6 lbs. **Length:** 41.2" overall. **Stock:** Polymer or folding. **Sights:** Ghost ring (tritium night sights optional). **Features:** Gas operated; matte receiver; twin forged action bars; over-sized bolt handle and safety button; Picatinny rail; includes cylinder bore choke tube. New features include polymer pistol grip stock. Introduced 2001. Imported from Italy by Heckler & Koch Inc.
Price: $999.00

FABARM FP6 PUMP SHOTGUN

Gauge: 12, 3" chamber. **Barrel:** 20" (Cyl.); accepts choke tubes. **Weight:** 6.6 lbs. **Length:** 41.25" overall. **Stock:** Black polymer with textured grip, grooved slide handle. **Sights:** Blade front. **Features:** Twin action bars; anodized finish; free carrier for smooth reloading. Introduced 1998. New features include ghost-ring sighting system, low profile Picatinny rail, and pistol grip stock. Imported from Italy by Heckler & Koch, Inc.
Price: (Carbon fiber finish) $499.00
Price: With flip-up front sight, Picatinny rail with rear sight, oversize safety button $499.00

MOSSBERG MODEL 500 PERSUADER SECURITY SHOTGUNS

Gauge: 12, 20, .410, 3" chamber. **Barrel:** 18-1/2", 20" (Cyl.). **Weight:** 7 lbs. **Stock:** Walnut-finished hardwood or black synthetic. **Sights:** Metal bead front. **Features:** Available in 6- or 8-shot models. Top-mounted safety, double action slide bars, swivel studs, rubber recoil pad. Blue, Parkerized, Marinecote finishes. Mossberg Cablelock included. From Mossberg.
Price: 12 ga., 18-1/2", blue, wood or synthetic stock,
6-shot $353.00
Price: Cruiser, 12 ga., 18-1/2", blue, pistol grip, heat shield $357.00
Price: As above, 20 ga. or .410 bore $345.00

Mossberg Model 500, 590 Mariner Pump Shotgun

Similar to the Model 500 or 590 Persuader except all metal parts finished with Marinecote metal finish to resist rust and corrosion. Synthetic field stock; pistol grip kit included. Mossberg Cablelock included.
Price: 6-shot, 18-1/2" barrel $497.00
Price: 9-shot, 20" barrel **$513.00**

Mossberg Model 500, 590 Ghost-Ring Shotgun

Similar to the Model 500 Persuader except has adjustable blade front, adjustable Ghost-Ring rear sight with protective "ears." Model 500 has 18.5" (Cyl.) barrel, 6-shot capacity; Model 590 has 20" (Cyl.) barrel, 9-shot capacity. Both have synthetic field stock. Mossberg Cablelock included. Introduced 1990. From Mossberg.
Price: 500 Parkerized $468.00
Price: 590 Parkerized $543.00
Price: 590 Parkerized Speedfeed stock $586.00

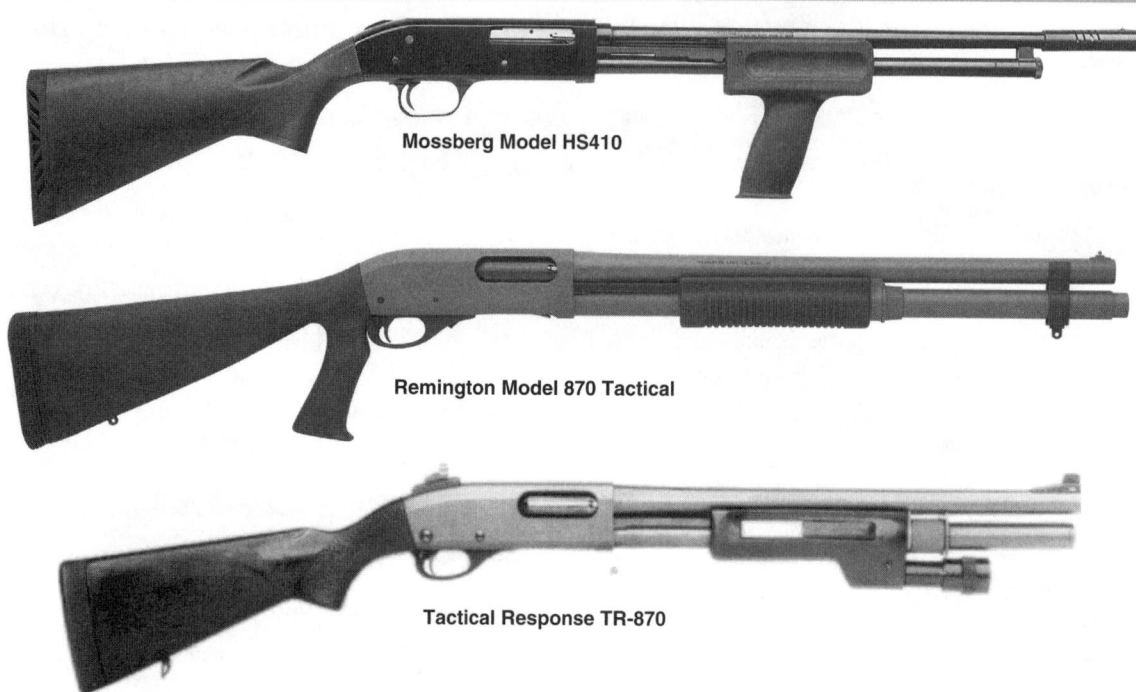

Mossberg Model HS410

Remington Model 870 Tactical

Tactical Response TR-870

Mossberg Model HS410 Shotgun

Similar to the Model 500 Persuader pump except chambered for 20 gauge or .410 with 3" chamber; has pistol grip forend, thick recoil pad, muzzle brake and has special spreader choke on the 18.5" barrel. Overall length is 37.5", weight is 6.25 lbs. Blue finish; synthetic field stock. Mossberg Cablelock and video included. Introduced 1990.

Price: HS 410 . . . . **$355.00**

MOSSBERG MODEL 590 SHOTGUN

Gauge: 12, 3" chamber. **Barrel:** 20" (Cyl.). **Weight:** 7-1/4 lbs. **Stock:** Synthetic field or Speedfeed. **Sights:** Metal bead front. **Features:** Top-mounted safety, double slide action bars. Comes with heat shield, bayonet lug, swivel studs, rubber recoil pad. Blue, Parkerized or Marinecote finish. Mossberg Cablelock included. From Mossberg.

Price: Blue, synthetic stock **$417.00**
Price: Parkerized, synthetic stock **$476.00**
Price: Parkerized, Speedfeed stock **$519.00**

REMINGTON MODEL 870 AND MODEL 1100 TACTICAL SHOTGUNS

Gauge: 12, 2-3/4 or 3" chamber, 7-shot magazine. **Barrel:** 18", 20", 22" (Cyl or IC). **Weight:** 7.5-7.75 lbs. **Length:** 38.5-42.5" overall. **Stock:** Black synthetic, synthetic Speedfeed IV full pistol-grip stock, or Knoxx Industries SpecOps stock w/recoil-absorbing spring-loaded cam and adjustable length of pull (12" to 16", 870 only). **Sights:** Front post w/dot only on 870; rib and front dot on 1100. **Features:** R3 recoil pads, LimbSaver technology to reduce felt recoil, 2-, 3- or 4-shot extensions based on barrel length; matte-olive-drab barrels and receivers. Model 1100 Tactical is available with Speedfeed IV pistol grip stock or standard black synthetic stock and forend. Speedfeed IV model has an 18" barrel with two-shot

extension. Standard synthetic-stocked version is equipped with 22" barrel and four-shot extension. Introduced 2006. From Remington Arms Co.

Price: 870, Speedfeed IV stock, 3" chamber, 38.5" overall **$599.00**
Price: 870, SpecOps stock, 3" chamber, 38.5" overall **$625.00**
Price: 1100, synthetic stock, 2-3/4" chamber, 42.5" overall **$759.00**

TACTICAL RESPONSE TR-870 STANDARD MODEL SHOTGUNS

Gauge: 12, 3" chamber, 7-shot magazine. **Barrel:** 18" (Cyl.). **Weight:** 9 lbs. **Length:** 38" overall. **Stock:** Fiberglass-filled polypropolene with non-snag recoil absorbing butt pad. Nylon tactical forend houses flashlight. **Sights:** Trak-Lock ghost ring sight system. Front sight has Tritium insert. **Features:** Highly modified Remington 870P with Parkerized finish. Comes with nylon three-way adjustable sling, high visibility non-binding follower, high performance magazine spring, Jumbo Head safety, and Side Saddle extended 6-shot shell carrier on left side of receiver. Introduced 1991. From Scattergun Technologies, Inc.

Price: Standard model **$815.00**
Price: FBI model **$770.00**
Price: Patrol model **$595.00**
Price: Border Patrol model **$605.00**
Price: K-9 model (Rem. 11-87 action) **$995.00**
Price: Urban Sniper, Rem. 11-87 action **$1,290.00**
Price: Louis Awerbuck model **$705.00**
Price: Practical Turkey model **$725.00**
Price: Expert model **$1,350.00**
Price: Professional model **$815.00**
Price: Entry model **$840.00**
Price: Compact model **$635.00**
Price: SWAT model **$1,195.00**

BLACKPOWDER PISTOLS — Single Shot, Flint & Percussion

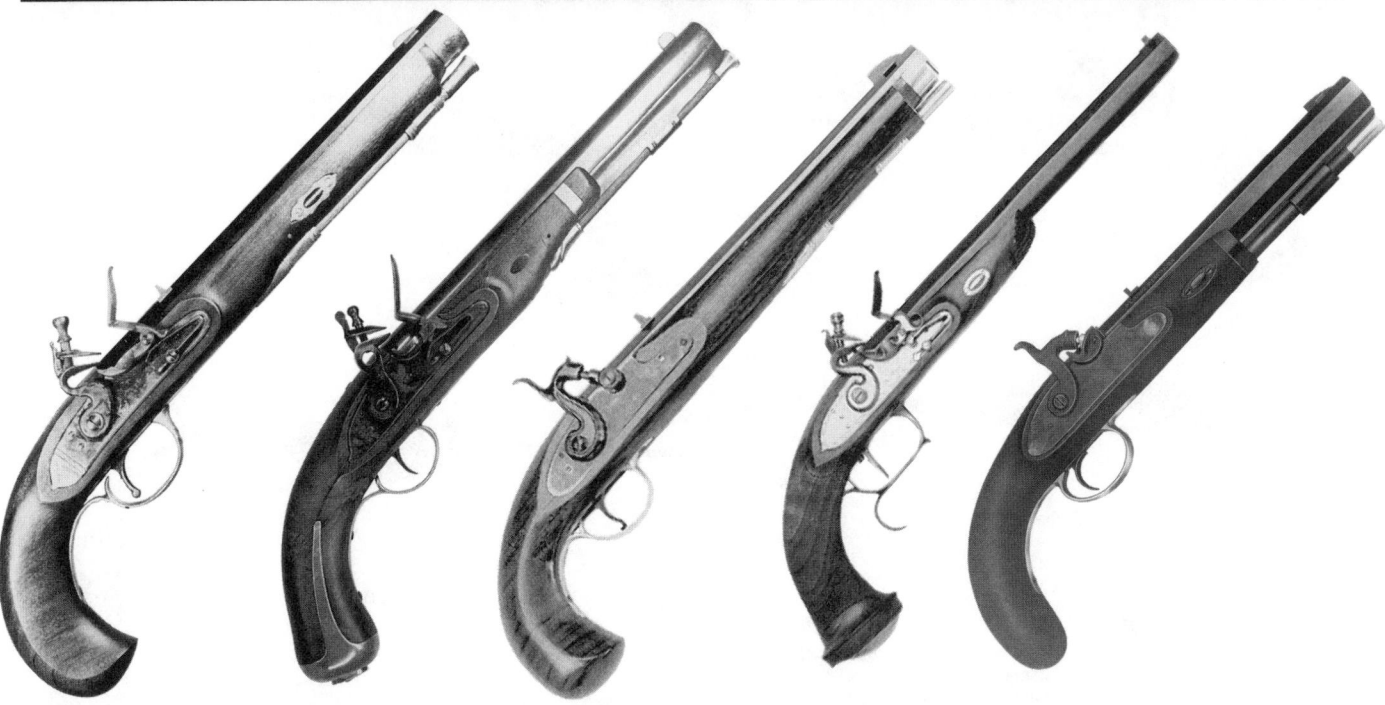

Dixie Pennsylvania   Harper's Ferry   Kentucky   Le Page   Lyman Plains Pistol

DIXIE PENNSYLVANIA PISTOL

Caliber: 44 (.430" round ball). **Barrel:** 10", (7/8" octagon). **Weight:** 2-1/2 lbs. **Stocks:** Walnut-stained hardwood. **Sights:** Blade front, open rear drift-adjustable for windage; brass. **Features:** Flintlock only. Brass trigger guard, thimbles, instep, wedge plates; high-luster blue barrel. Imported from Italy by Dixie Gun Works.
Price: Finished $215.00
Price: Kit $195.00

FRENCH-STYLE DUELING PISTOL

Caliber: 44. **Barrel:** 10". **Weight:** 35 oz. **Length:** 15-3/4" overall. **Stocks:** Carved walnut. **Sights:** Fixed. **Features:** Comes with velvet-lined case and accessories. Imported by Mandall Shooting Supplies.
Price: $295.00

HARPER'S FERRY 1806 PISTOL

Caliber: 58 (.570" round ball). **Barrel:** 10". **Weight:** 40 oz. **Length:** 16" overall. **Stocks:** Walnut. **Sights:** Fixed. **Features:** Case-hardened lock, brass-mounted browned barrel. Replica of the first U.S. gov't.-made flintlock pistol. Imported by Navy Arms, Dixie Gun Works.
Price: . . . . $275.00 to $405.00
Price: Kit (Dixie) $295.00

KENTUCKY FLINTLOCK PISTOL

Caliber: 44, 45. **Barrel:** 10-1/8". **Weight:** 32 oz. **Length:** 15-1/2" overall. **Stocks:** Walnut. **Sights:** Fixed. **Features:** Specifications, including caliber, weight and length may vary with importer. Case-hardened lock, blued barrel; available also as brass barrel flintlock Model 1821. Imported by Navy Arms, The Armoury, Dixie Gun Works.
Price: $300.00
Price: In kit form. From . . . . $90.00 to $112.00
Price: Single cased set (Navy Arms) $360.00
Price: Double cased set (Navy Arms) $590.00

Kentucky Percussion Pistol

Similar to Flint version but percussion lock. Imported by The Armoury, Navy Arms, CVA (50-cal.).
Price: . . . . $129.95 to $225.00
Price: Steel barrel (Armoury) $179.00
Price: Single cased set (Navy Arms) $355.00
Price: Double cased set (Navy Arms) $600.00

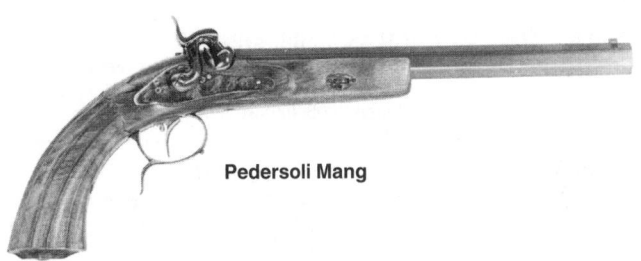

Pedersoli Mang

LE PAGE PERCUSSION DUELING PISTOL

Caliber: 44. **Barrel:** 10", rifled. **Weight:** 40 oz. **Length:** 16" overall. **Stocks:** Walnut, fluted butt. **Sights:** Blade front, notch rear. **Features:** Double-set triggers. Blued barrel; trigger guard and buttcap are polished silver. Imported by Dixie Gun Works.
Price: $470.00

LYMAN PLAINS PISTOL

Caliber: 50 or 54. **Barrel:** 8"; 1:30" twist, both calibers. **Weight:** 50 oz. **Length:** 15" overall. **Stocks:** Walnut half-stock. **Sights:** Blade front, square notch rear adjustable for windage. **Features:** Polished brass trigger guard and ramrod tip, color case-hardened coil spring lock, spring-loaded trigger, stainless steel nipple, blackened iron furniture. Hooked patent breech, detachable belt hook. Introduced 1981. From Lyman Products.
Price: Finished $244.95
Price: Kit $189.95

PEDERSOLI MANG TARGET PISTOL

Caliber: 38. **Barrel:** 10.5", octagonal; 1:15" twist, **Weight:** 2.5 lbs. **Length:** 17.25" overall. **Stocks:** Walnut with fluted grip. **Sights:** Blade front, open rear adjustable for windage. **Features:** Browned barrel, polished breech plug, remainder color case-hardened. Imported from Italy by Dixie Gun Works.
Price: $1,100.00

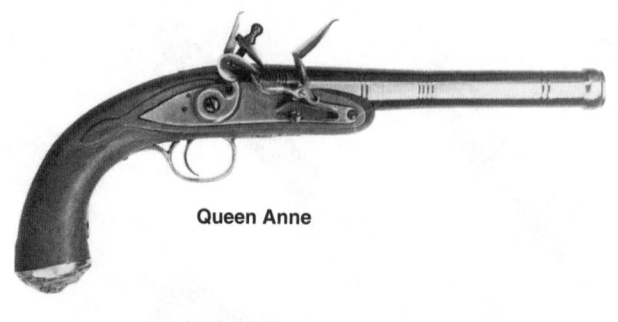

Queen Anne

Traditions Pioneer

Traditions William Parker

Traditions Buckhunter Pro

QUEEN ANNE FLINTLOCK PISTOL
Caliber: 50 (.490" round ball). **Barrel:** 7-1/2", smoothbore. **Stocks:** Walnut. **Sights:** None. **Features:** Browned steel barrel, fluted brass trigger guard, brass mask on butt. Lockplate left in the white. Made by Pedersoli in Italy. Introduced 1983. Imported by Dixie Gun Works.
Price: **$290.00**
Price: Kit **$195.00**

REPLICA ARMS "SEVEN SEAS" DERRINGER
Caliber: 36 cal., smoothbore percussion. **Barrel:** 4-5/8". **Weight:** 21 oz. **Length:** 11" overall. **Grips:** Walnut finished. **Features:** All steel barrel with brass accents. Introduced 2005. Imported by Navy Arms.
Price: **$99.95**

TRADITIONS BUCKHUNTER PRO IN-LINE PISTOL
Caliber: 50. **Barrel:** 9-1/2", round. **Weight:** 48 oz. **Length:** 14" overall. **Stocks:** Smooth walnut or black epoxy-coated hardwood grip and forend. **Sights:** Beaded blade front, folding adjustable rear. **Features:** Thumb safety; removable stainless steel breech plug; adjustable trigger; barrel drilled and tapped for scope mounting. From Traditions.
Price: With walnut grip. **$229.00**
Price: Nickel with black grip **$239.00**
Price: With walnut grip and 12-1/2" barrel **$239.00**
Price: Nickel with black grip, muzzle brake and 14-3/4"
fluted barrel **$289.00**
Price: 45 cal. nickel w/bl. grip,
muzzle brake and 14-3/4" fluted bbl. **$289.00**

TRADITIONS KENTUCKY PISTOL
Caliber: 50. **Barrel:** 10"; octagon with 7/8" flats; 1:20" twist. **Weight:** 40 oz. **Length:** 15" overall. **Stocks:** Stained beech. **Sights:** Blade front, fixed rear. **Features:** Bird's-head grip; brass thimbles; color case-hardened lock. Percussion only. Introduced 1995. From Traditions.
Price: Finished. **$139.00**
Price: Kit **$109.00**

TRADITIONS PIONEER PISTOL
Caliber: 45. **Barrel:** 9-5/8"; 13/16" flats, 1:16" twist. **Weight:** 31 oz. **Length:** 15" overall. **Stocks:** Beech. **Sights:** Blade front, fixed rear. **Features:** V-type mainspring. Single trigger. German silver furniture, blackened hardware. From Traditions.
Price:. **$139.00**
Price: Kit **$119.00**

TRADITIONS TRAPPER PISTOL
Caliber: 50. **Barrel:** 9-3/4"; 7/8" flats; 1:20" twist. **Weight:** 2-3/4 lbs. **Length:** 16" overall. **Stocks:** Beech. **Sights:** Blade front, adjustable rear. **Features:** Double-set triggers; brass buttcap, trigger guard, wedge plate, forend tip, thimble. From Traditions.
Price: Percussion **$189.00**
Price: Flintlock **$209.00**
Price: Kit **$149.00**

TRADITIONS VEST-POCKET DERRINGER
Caliber: 31. **Barrel:** 2-1/4"; brass. **Weight:** 8 oz. **Length:** 4-3/4" overall. **Stocks:** Simulated ivory. **Sights:** Bead front. **Features:** Replica of riverboat gamblers' derringer; authentic spur trigger. From Traditions.
Price: **$109.00**

TRADITIONS WILLIAM PARKER PISTOL
Caliber: 50. **Barrel:** 10-3/8"; 15/16" flats; polished steel. **Weight:** 37 oz. **Length:** 17-1/2" overall. **Stocks:** Walnut with checkered grip. **Sights:** Brass blade front, fixed rear. **Features:** Replica dueling pistol with 1:20" twist, hooked breech. Brass wedge plate, trigger guard, cap guard; separate ramrod. Double-set triggers. Polished steel barrel, lock. Imported by Traditions.
Price:. **$269.00**

Army 1860

Baby Dragoon 1848

Dixie Wyatt Earp

Le Mat Revolver

ARMY 1860 PERCUSSION REVOLVER

Caliber: 44, 6-shot. **Barrel:** 8". **Weight:** 40 oz. **Length:** 13-5/8" overall. **Stocks:** Walnut. **Sights:** Fixed. **Features:** Engraved Navy scene on cylinder; brass trigger guard; case-hardened frame, loading lever and hammer. Some importers supply pistol cut for detachable shoulder stock, have accessory stock available. Imported by Cabela's (1860 Lawman), E.M.F., Navy Arms, The Armoury, Cimarron, Dixie Gun Works (half-fluted cylinder, not roll engraved), Euroarms of America (brass or steel model), Armsport, Traditions (brass or steel), Uberti U.S.A. Inc., United States Patent Fire-Arms.

Price: About **$232.00**
Price: Hartford model, steel frame, German silver trim,
    cartouches (E.M.F.) **$215.00**
Price: Single cased set (Navy Arms) **$300.00**
Price: Double cased set (Navy Arms) **$490.00**
Price: 1861 Navy: Same as Army except 36-cal., 7-1/2" bbl.,
    weighs 41 oz., cut for shoulder stock; round cylinder
    (fluted available), from Cabela's, CVA (brass frame, 44 cal.),
    United States Patent Fire-Arms . . . . **$99.95 to $385.00**
Price: Steel frame kit (E.M.F., Euroarms) . . . . **$125.00 to $216.25**
Price: Colt Army Police, fluted cyl., 5-1/2", 36-cal. (Cabela's) **$124.95**
Price: With nickeled frame, barrel and backstrap, gold-tone fluted cylinder,
    trigger and hammer, simulated ivory grips (Traditions) **$199.00**

BABY DRAGOON 1848, 1849 POCKET, WELLS FARGO

Caliber: 31. **Barrel:** 3", 4", 5", 6"; seven-groove; RH twist. **Weight:** About 21 oz. **Stocks:** Varnished walnut. **Sights:** Brass pin front, hammer notch rear. **Features:** No loading lever on Baby Dragoon or Wells Fargo models. Unfluted cylinder with stagecoach holdup scene; cupped cylinder pin; no grease grooves; one safety pin on cylinder and slot in hammer face; straight (flat) mainspring. From Armsport, Cimarron F.A. Co., Dixie Gun Works, Uberti U.S.A. Inc.

Price: 6" barrel, with loading lever (Dixie Gun Works) **$232.00**
Price: 4" (Uberti USA Inc.) **$275.00**

DIXIE WYATT EARP REVOLVER

Caliber: 44. **Barrel:** 12", octagon. **Weight:** 46 oz. **Length:** 18" overall. **Stocks:** Two-piece walnut. **Sights:** Fixed. **Features:** Highly polished brass frame, backstrap and trigger guard; blued barrel and cylinder; case-hardened hammer, trigger and loading lever. Navy-size shoulder stock ($45) requires minor fitting. From Dixie Gun Works.

Price: **$180.00**

LE MAT REVOLVER

Caliber: 44/65. **Barrel:** 6-3/4" (revolver); 4-7/8" (single shot). **Weight:** 3 lbs., 7 oz. **Stocks:** Hand-checkered walnut. **Sights:** Post front, hammer notch rear. **Features:** Exact reproduction with all-steel construction; 44-cal. 9-shot cylinder, 65-cal. single barrel; color case-hardened hammer with selector; spur trigger guard; ring at butt; lever-type barrel release. From Navy Arms and Dixie Gun Works.

Price: Cavalry model (lanyard ring, spur trigger guard) **$645.00**
Price: Army model (round trigger guard, pin-type barrel release) . **$645.00**
Price: Naval-style (thumb selector on hammer) **$645.00**

NEW MODEL 1858 ARMY PERCUSSION REVOLVER

Caliber: 36 or 44, 6-shot. **Barrel:** 6-1/2" or 8". **Weight:** 38 oz. **Length:** 13-1/2" overall. **Stocks:** Walnut. **Sights:** Blade front, groove-in-frame rear. **Features:** Replica of Remington Model 1858. Also available from some importers as Army Model Belt Revolver in 36-cal., a shortened and lightened version of the 44. Target Model (Uberti U.S.A. Inc., Navy Arms) has fully adjustable target rear sight, target front, 36 or 44. Imported by Cabela's, Cimarron F.A. Co., CVA (as 1858 Army, brass frame, 44 only), Dixie Gun Works, Navy Arms, The Armoury, E.M.F., Euroarms of America (engraved, stainless and plain), Armsport, Traditions (44 only), Uberti U.S.A. Inc.

Price: Steel frame, about . . . . **$99.95 to $280.00**
Price: Steel frame kit (Euroarms, Navy Arms) . . . . **$115.95 to $150.00**
Price: Stainless steel Model 1858 (Euroarms, Uberti U.S.A. Inc., Cabela's,
    Navy Arms, Armsport, Traditions) . . . . **$169.95 to $380.00**
Price: Target Model, adjustable rear sight (Cabela's, Euroarms, Uberti
    U.S.A. Inc., Stone Mountain Arms) . . . . **$95.95 to $399.00**
Price: Brass frame (CVA, Cabela's, Traditions, Navy
    Arms) . . . . **$79.95 to $187.000**
Price: As above, kit (Dixie Gun Works) . . . . **$145.00 to $188.95**
Price: Buffalo model, 44-cal. (Cabela's) **$119.99**
Price: Hartford model, steel frame, German silver trim,
    cartouche (E.M.F.) **$215.00**

NAVY ARMS NEW MODEL POCKET REVOLVER

Caliber: 31, 5-shot. **Barrel:** 3-1/2", octagon. **Weight:** 15 oz. **Length:** 7-3/4". **Stocks:** Two-piece walnut. **Sights:** Fixed. **Features:** Replica of the Remington New Model Pocket. Available with polished brass frame or nickel-plated finish. Introduced 2000. Imported by Navy Arms.

Price: **$300.00**

BLACKPOWDER REVOLVERS

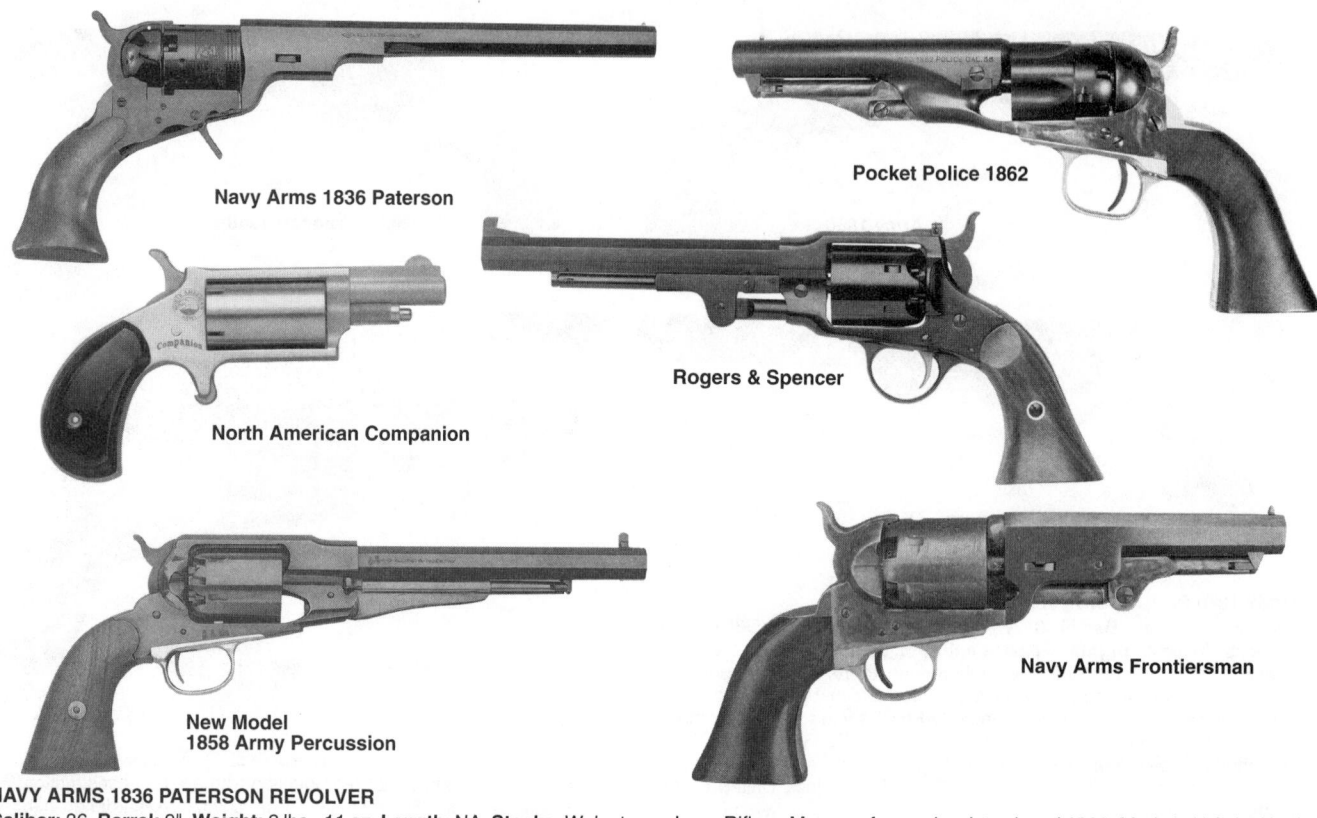

Navy Arms 1836 Paterson

North American Companion

Pocket Police 1862

Rogers & Spencer

New Model 1858 Army Percussion

Navy Arms Frontiersman

NAVY ARMS 1836 PATERSON REVOLVER
Caliber: 36. **Barrel:** 9". **Weight:** 2 lbs., 11 oz. **Length:** NA. **Stocks:** Walnut. **Sights:** NA. **Features:** Hidden trigger, blued barrel, replica of 5-shooter, roll-engraved with stagecoach holdup scene.
Price: . . . . $425.00 to $461.00

NAVY ARMS 1851 NAVY "FRONTIERSMAN" REVOLVER
Caliber: .36, 6-shot cylinder. **Barrel:** 5". **Weight:** 32 oz. **Length:** 10-1/2" overall . **Grips:** One piece walnut. **Sights:** Post front, notch rear. **Features:** Blued with color case-hardened receiver, trigger and hammer; German Silver backstrap and triggerguard. Introduced 2005. Imported by Navy Arms.
Price: $315.00

NAVY MODEL 1851 PERCUSSION REVOLVER
Caliber: 36, 44, 6-shot. **Barrel:** 7-1/2". **Weight:** 44 oz. **Length:** 13" overall. **Stocks:** Walnut finish. **Sights:** Post front, hammer notch rear. **Features:** Brass backstrap and trigger guard; some have 1st Model squareback trigger guard, engraved cylinder with navy battle scene; case-hardened frame, hammer, loading lever. Imported by The Armoury, Cabela's, Cimarron F.A. Co., Navy Arms, E.M.F., Dixie Gun Works, Euroarms of America, Armsport, CVA (44-cal. only), Traditions (44 only), Uberti U.S.A. Inc., United States Patent Fire-Arms.
Price: Brass frame. . . . . $99.95 to $385.00
Price: Steel frame . . . . $130.00 to $285.00
Price: Kit form . . . . $110.00 to $142.50
Price: Engraved model (Dixie Gun Works) $190.00
Price: Single cased set, steel frame (Navy Arms) $280.00
Price: Double cased set, steel frame (Navy Arms) $455.00
Price: Confederate Navy (Cabela's) $89.99
Price: Hartford model, steel frame, German silver trim,
cartouche (E.M.F.) $190.00

NORTH AMERICAN COMPANION PERCUSSION REVOLVER
Caliber: 22. **Barrel:** 1-1/8". **Weight:** 5.1 oz. **Length:** 4-1/2" overall. **Stocks:** Laminated wood. **Sights:** Blade front, notch fixed rear. **Features:** All stainless steel construction. Uses standard #11 percussion caps. Comes with bullets, powder measure, bullet seater, leather clip holster, gun rag.

Long Rifle or Magnum frame size. Introduced 1996. Made in U.S. by North American Arms.
Price: Long Rifle frame. $156.00

North American Magnum Companion Percussion Revolver
Similar to the Companion except has larger frame. Weighs 7.2 oz., has 1-5/8" barrel, measures 5-7/16" overall. Comes with bullets, powder measure, bullet seater, leather clip holster, gun rag. Introduced 1996. Made in U.S. by North American Arms.
Price: $215.00

POCKET POLICE 1862 PERCUSSION REVOLVER
Caliber: 36, 5-shot. **Barrel:** 4-1/2", 5-1/2", 6-1/2", 7-1/2". **Weight:** 26 oz. **Length:** 12" overall (6-1/2" bbl.). **Stocks:** Walnut. **Sights:** Fixed. **Features:** Round tapered barrel; half-fluted and rebated cylinder; case-hardened frame, loading lever and hammer; silver or brass trigger guard and backstrap. Imported by Dixie Gun Works, Navy Arms (5-1/2" only), Uberti U.S.A. Inc. (5-1/2", 6-1/2" only), United States Patent Fire-Arms and Cimarron F.A. Co.
Price: About . . . . $139.95 to $335.00
Price: Single cased set with accessories (Navy Arms) $365.00
Price: Hartford model, steel frame, German silver trim,
cartouche (E.M.F.) $215.00

ROGERS & SPENCER PERCUSSION REVOLVER
Caliber: 44. **Barrel:** 7-1/2". **Weight:** 47 oz. **Length:** 13-3/4" overall. **Stocks:** Walnut. **Sights:** Cone front, integral groove in frame for rear. **Features:** Accurate reproduction of a Civil War design. Solid frame; extra large nipple cut-out on rear of cylinder; loading lever and cylinder easily removed for cleaning. From Dixie Gun Works, Euroarms of America (standard blue, engraved, burnished, target models), Navy Arms.
Price: . . . . $160.00 to $299.95
Price: Nickel-plated. $215.00
Price: Engraved (Euroarms) $287.00
Price: Kit version . . . . $245.00 to $252.00
Price: Target version (Euroarms) . . . . $239.00 to $270.00
Price: Burnished London Gray (Euroarms) . . . . $245.00 to $270.00

BLACKPOWDER REVOLVERS

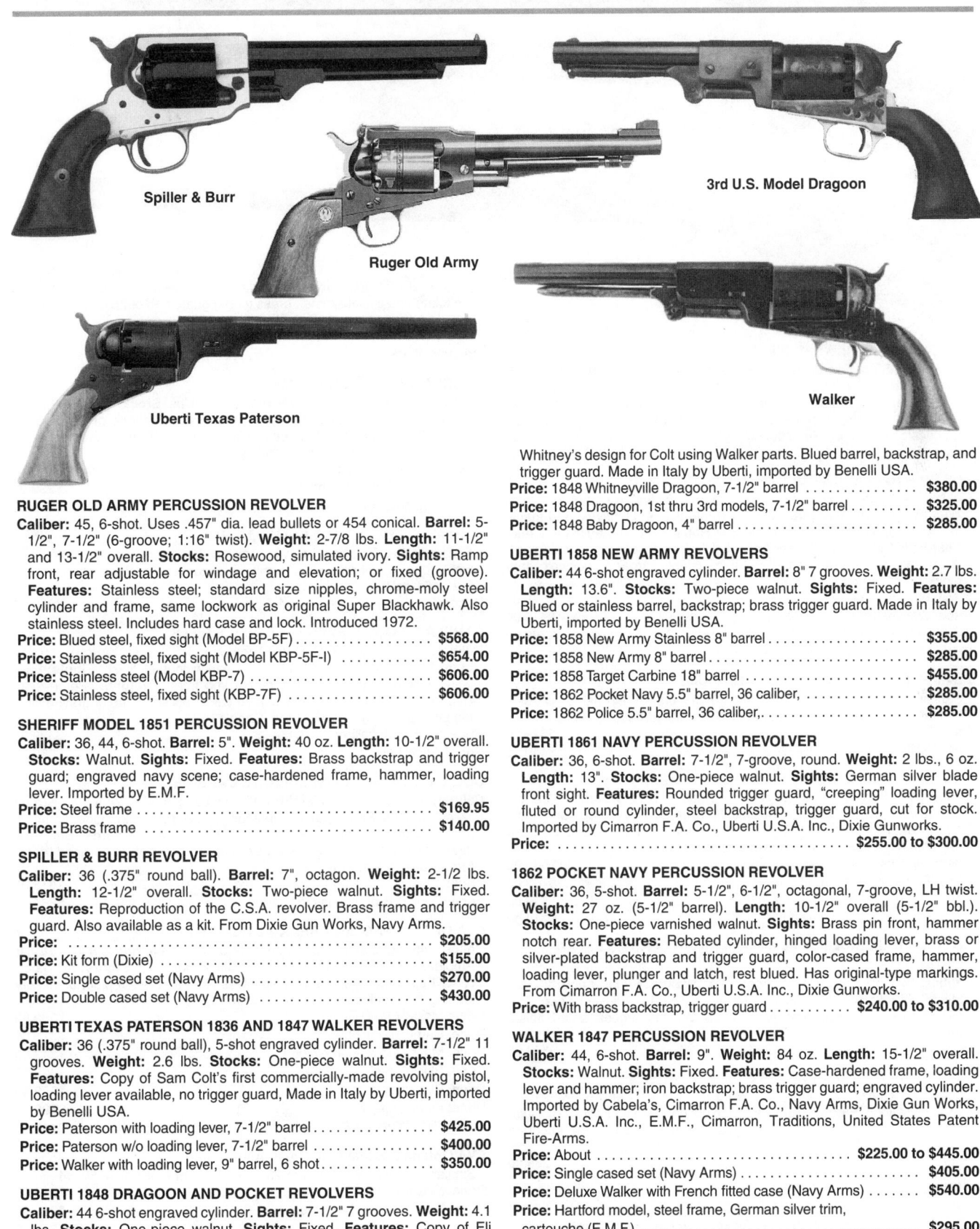

Spiller & Burr

Ruger Old Army

3rd U.S. Model Dragoon

Uberti Texas Paterson

Walker

RUGER OLD ARMY PERCUSSION REVOLVER
Caliber: 45, 6-shot. Uses .457" dia. lead bullets or 454 conical. **Barrel:** 5-1/2", 7-1/2" (6-groove; 1:16" twist). **Weight:** 2-7/8 lbs. **Length:** 11-1/2" and 13-1/2" overall. **Stocks:** Rosewood, simulated ivory. **Sights:** Ramp front, rear adjustable for windage and elevation; or fixed (groove). **Features:** Stainless steel; standard size nipples, chrome-moly steel cylinder and frame, same lockwork as original Super Blackhawk. Also stainless steel. Includes hard case and lock. Introduced 1972.
Price: Blued steel, fixed sight (Model BP-5F) $568.00
Price: Stainless steel, fixed sight (Model KBP-5F-I) $654.00
Price: Stainless steel (Model KBP-7) $606.00
Price: Stainless steel, fixed sight (KBP-7F) $606.00

SHERIFF MODEL 1851 PERCUSSION REVOLVER
Caliber: 36, 44, 6-shot. **Barrel:** 5". **Weight:** 40 oz. **Length:** 10-1/2" overall. **Stocks:** Walnut. **Sights:** Fixed. **Features:** Brass backstrap and trigger guard; engraved navy scene; case-hardened frame, hammer, loading lever. Imported by E.M.F.
Price: Steel frame $169.95
Price: Brass frame $140.00

SPILLER & BURR REVOLVER
Caliber: 36 (.375" round ball). **Barrel:** 7", octagon. **Weight:** 2-1/2 lbs. **Length:** 12-1/2" overall. **Stocks:** Two-piece walnut. **Sights:** Fixed. **Features:** Reproduction of the C.S.A. revolver. Brass frame and trigger guard. Also available as a kit. From Dixie Gun Works, Navy Arms.
Price: $205.00
Price: Kit form (Dixie) $155.00
Price: Single cased set (Navy Arms) $270.00
Price: Double cased set (Navy Arms) $430.00

UBERTI TEXAS PATERSON 1836 AND 1847 WALKER REVOLVERS
Caliber: 36 (.375" round ball), 5-shot engraved cylinder. **Barrel:** 7-1/2" 11 grooves. **Weight:** 2.6 lbs. **Stocks:** One-piece walnut. **Sights:** Fixed. **Features:** Copy of Sam Colt's first commercially-made revolving pistol, loading lever available, no trigger guard, Made in Italy by Uberti, imported by Benelli USA.
Price: Paterson with loading lever, 7-1/2" barrel $425.00
Price: Paterson w/o loading lever, 7-1/2" barrel $400.00
Price: Walker with loading lever, 9" barrel, 6 shot $350.00

UBERTI 1848 DRAGOON AND POCKET REVOLVERS
Caliber: 44 6-shot engraved cylinder. **Barrel:** 7-1/2" 7 grooves. **Weight:** 4.1 lbs. **Stocks:** One-piece walnut. **Sights:** Fixed. **Features:** Copy of Eli Whitney's design for Colt using Walker parts. Blued barrel, backstrap, and trigger guard. Made in Italy by Uberti, imported by Benelli USA.
Price: 1848 Whitneyville Dragoon, 7-1/2" barrel $380.00
Price: 1848 Dragoon, 1st thru 3rd models, 7-1/2" barrel $325.00
Price: 1848 Baby Dragoon, 4" barrel $285.00

UBERTI 1858 NEW ARMY REVOLVERS
Caliber: 44 6-shot engraved cylinder. **Barrel:** 8" 7 grooves. **Weight:** 2.7 lbs. **Length:** 13.6". **Stocks:** Two-piece walnut. **Sights:** Fixed. **Features:** Blued or stainless barrel, backstrap; brass trigger guard. Made in Italy by Uberti, imported by Benelli USA.
Price: 1858 New Army Stainless 8" barrel $355.00
Price: 1858 New Army 8" barrel $285.00
Price: 1858 Target Carbine 18" barrel $455.00
Price: 1862 Pocket Navy 5.5" barrel, 36 caliber, ... $285.00
Price: 1862 Police 5.5" barrel, 36 caliber, ... $285.00

UBERTI 1861 NAVY PERCUSSION REVOLVER
Caliber: 36, 6-shot. **Barrel:** 7-1/2", 7-groove, round. **Weight:** 2 lbs., 6 oz. **Length:** 13". **Stocks:** One-piece walnut. **Sights:** German silver blade front sight. **Features:** Rounded trigger guard, "creeping" loading lever, fluted or round cylinder, steel backstrap, trigger guard, cut for stock. Imported by Cimarron F.A. Co., Uberti U.S.A. Inc., Dixie Gunworks.
Price: . . . . $255.00 to $300.00

1862 POCKET NAVY PERCUSSION REVOLVER
Caliber: 36, 5-shot. **Barrel:** 5-1/2", 6-1/2", octagonal, 7-groove, LH twist. **Weight:** 27 oz. (5-1/2" barrel). **Length:** 10-1/2" overall (5-1/2" bbl.). **Stocks:** One-piece varnished walnut. **Sights:** Brass pin front, hammer notch rear. **Features:** Rebated cylinder, hinged loading lever, brass or silver-plated backstrap and trigger guard, color-cased frame, hammer, loading lever, plunger and latch, rest blued. Has original-type markings. From Cimarron F.A. Co., Uberti U.S.A. Inc., Dixie Gunworks.
Price: With brass backstrap, trigger guard . . . . $240.00 to $310.00

WALKER 1847 PERCUSSION REVOLVER
Caliber: 44, 6-shot. **Barrel:** 9". **Weight:** 84 oz. **Length:** 15-1/2" overall. **Stocks:** Walnut. **Sights:** Fixed. **Features:** Case-hardened frame, loading lever and hammer; iron backstrap; brass trigger guard; engraved cylinder. Imported by Cabela's, Cimarron F.A. Co., Navy Arms, Dixie Gun Works, Uberti U.S.A. Inc., E.M.F., Cimarron, Traditions, United States Patent Fire-Arms.
Price: About . . . . $225.00 to $445.00
Price: Single cased set (Navy Arms) $405.00
Price: Deluxe Walker with French fitted case (Navy Arms) $540.00
Price: Hartford model, steel frame, German silver trim,
cartouche (E.M.F.) $295.00

Austin & Halleck 420 LR In-Line

Cabela's Traditional Hawken

ARMOURY R140 HAWKEN RIFLE

Caliber: 45, 50 or 54.**Barrel:** 29". **Weight:** 8-3/4 to 9 lbs. **Length:** 45-3/4" overall. **Stock:** Walnut, with cheekpiece. **Sights:** Dovetailed front, fully adjustable rear. **Features:** Octagon barrel, removable breech plug; double set triggers; blued barrel, brass stock fittings, color case-hardened percussion lock. From Armsport, The Armoury.
Price: . . . . **$225.00 to $245.00**

AUSTIN & HALLECK MODEL 420 LR IN-LINE RIFLE

Caliber: 45 and 50. **Barrel:** 26", 1" octagon to 3/4" round; 1:28" twist. **Weight:** 7-7/8 lbs. **Length:** 47-1/2" overall. **Stock:** Lightly figured maple in Classic or Monte Carlo style. **Sights:** Ramp front, fully adjustable rear. **Features:** Blue or electroless nickel finish; in-line percussion action with removable weather shroud; Timney adjustable target trigger with sear block safety. Introduced 1998.
Price: Blue. **$549.00**
Price: Stainless steel **$579.00**
Price: Blue, hand-select highly figured stock **$709.00**
Price: Stainless steel, select stock **$739.00**

Austin & Halleck Model 320 LR In-Line Rifle

Similar to the Model 420 LR (45 and 50 calibers) except has black resin synthetic stock with checkered grip and forend. Introduced 1998.
Price: Blue. **$419.00**
Price: Stainless steel **$449.00**

AUSTIN & HALLECK MOUNTAIN RIFLE

Caliber: 50. **Barrel:** 32"; 1:28" or 1:66" twist; 1" flats. **Weight:** 7-1/2 lbs. **Length:** 49" overall. **Stock:** Curly maple. **Sights:** Silver blade front, buckhorn rear. **Features:** Available in percussion or flintlock; double throw adjustable set triggers; rust brown finish.
Price: Flintlock, fancy wood **$589.00**
Price: Flintlock, select wood **$769.00**
Price: Percussion, fancy wood **$539.00**
Price: Percussion, select wood **$719.00**

AUSTIN & HALLECK MODEL 649 AMERICAN CLASSIC LEVER ACTION

Caliber: 45 or 50. **Barrel:** 22" Krieger, 1:24". **Weight:** 6.7 lbs. **Length:** 39.5" overall. **Stock:** Boyd's walnut or curly maple. **Sights:** Adjustable rear, Tru-Glo front blade. **Features:** A&H Brush Country trigger; blued finish. Introduced 2006.
Price: **$599.00**

BOSTONIAN PERCUSSION RIFLE

Caliber: 45. **Barrel:** 30", octagonal. **Weight:** 7-1/4 lbs. **Length:** 46" overall. **Stock:** Walnut. **Sights:** Blade front, fixed notch rear. **Features:** Color case-hardened lock, brass trigger guard, buttplate, patchbox. Imported from Italy by E.M.F.
Price: **$285.00**

CABELA'S BLUE RIDGE RIFLE

Caliber: 32, 36, 45, 50, .54. **Barrel:** 39", octagonal. **Weight:** About 7-3/4 lbs. **Length:** 55" overall. **Stock:** American black walnut. **Sights:** Blade front, rear drift adjustable for windage. **Features:** Color case-hardened lockplate and cock/hammer, brass trigger guard and buttplate, double set, double-phased triggers. From Cabela's.
Price: Percussion **$459.99**
Price: Flintlock **$489.99**

CABELA'S TRADITIONAL HAWKEN

Caliber: 50, 54. **Barrel:** 29". **Weight:** About 9 lbs. **Stock:** Walnut. **Sights:** Blade front, open adjustable rear. **Features:** Flintlock or percussion. Adjustable double-set triggers. Polished brass furniture, color case-hardened lock. Imported by Cabela's.
Price: Percussion, right-hand **$299.99**
Price: Percussion, left-hand **$299.99**
Price: Flintlock, right-hand **$339.99**

Cabela's Sporterized Hawken Hunter Rifle

Similar to the Traditional Hawken except has more modern stock style with rubber recoil pad, blued furniture, sling swivels. Percussion only, in 50- or 54-caliber.
Price: Carbine or rifle, right-hand **$369.99**

CABELA'S KODIAK EXPRESS DOUBLE RIFLE

Caliber: 50, 54, 58, 72. **Barrel:** Length NA; 1:48" twist. **Weight:** 9.3 lbs. **Length:** 45-1/4" overall. **Stock:** European walnut, oil finish. **Sights:** Fully adjustable double folding-leaf rear, ramp front. **Features:** Percussion. Barrels regulated to point of aim at 75 yards; polished and engraved lock, top tang and trigger guard. From Cabela's.
Price: 50, 54, 58 calibers **$829.99**
Price: 72 caliber **$859.99**

COOK & BROTHER CONFEDERATE CARBINE

Caliber: 58. **Barrel:** 24". **Weight:** 7-1/2 lbs. **Length:** 40-1/2" overall. **Stock:** Select walnut. **Features:** Re-creation of the 1861 New Orleans-made artillery carbine. Color case-hardened lock, browned barrel. Buttplate, trigger guard, barrel bands, sling swivels and nosecap of polished brass. From Euroarms of America.
Price: **$513.00**
Price: Cook & Brother rifle (33" barrel) **$552.00**

CVA OPTIMA PRO 209 BREAK-ACTION RIFLE

Caliber: 45, 50. **Barrel:** 29" fluted, blue or nickel. **Weight:** 8.8 lbs. **Stock:** Ambidextrous Mossy Oak® Camo or black FiberGrip. **Sights:** Adj. fiber-optic. **Features:** Break-action, stainless No. 209 breech plug, aluminum loading rod, cocking spur, lifetime warranty.
Price: Mossy Oak® Camo **$399.95**
Price: Camo, nickel bbl. **$379.95**
Price: Mossy Oak® Camo/blued **$349.95**
Price: Black/nickel **$329.95**
Price: Black/blued **$299.95**
Price: Blued fluted bbl. **$99.95**
Price: Nickel fluted bbl. **$115.95**

CVA Optima 209 Magnum Break-Action Rifle

Similar to Optima Pro but with 26" bbl., nickel or blue finish, 50 cal.
Price: Mossy Oak® Camo/nickel **$310.00**
Price: Mossy Oak® Camo/blue **$290.00**
Price: Black/blued **$235.00**

BLACKPOWDER MUSKETS & RIFLES

Dixie Sharps New Model 1859 Military

Euroarms 1861 Springfield

CVA Optima Elite

Similar to Optima Pro but chambered for 45, 50 black powder plus 243, 270, 30-06 centerfire cartridges.
Price: Hardwoods Green HD/blue $415.00
Price: Black Fleck/blue $355.00

CVA BUCKHORN 209 MAGNUM

Caliber: 50. **Barrel:** 24". **Weight:** 6.3 lbs. **Sights:** Illuminator fiber-optic. **Features:** Grip-dot stock, thumb-actuated safety; drilled and tapped for scope mounts.
Price: Black stock, blue barrel $145.00

CVA KODIAK MAGNUM RIFLE

Caliber: 50. No. 209 primer ignition. **Barrel:** 28"; 1:28" twist. **Stock:** Ambidextrous black or Mossy Oak® camo. **Sights:** Fiber-optic. **Features:** Blue or nickel finish, recoil pad, lifetime warranty. From CVA.
Price: Mossy Oak® camo; nickel barrel $300.00
Price: Black stock; nickel barrel $255.00
Price: Black stock; blued barrel $225.00

DIXIE EARLY AMERICAN JAEGER RIFLE

Caliber: 54. **Barrel:** 27-1/2" octagonal; 1:24" twist. **Weight:** 8-1/4 lbs. **Length:** 43-1/2" overall. **Stock:** American walnut; sliding wooden patchbox on butt. **Sights:** Notch rear, blade front. **Features:** Flintlock or percussion. Browned steel furniture. Imported from Italy by Dixie Gun Works.
Price: Flintlock or percussion $825.00

DIXIE DELUXE CUB RIFLE

Caliber: 40. **Barrel:** 28". **Weight:** 6-1/2 lbs. **Stock:** Walnut. **Sights:** Fixed. **Features:** Short rifle for small game and beginning shooters. Brass patchbox and furniture. Flint or percussion. From Dixie Gun Works.
Price: Finished $575.00
Price: Kit $500.00
Price: Super Cub (50-caliber) $550.00

DIXIE 1863 SPRINGFIELD MUSKET

Caliber: 58 (.570" patched ball or .575" Minie). **Barrel:** 50", rifled. **Stock:** Walnut stained. **Sights:** Blade front, adjustable ladder-type rear. **Features:** Bright-finish lock, barrel, furniture. Reproduction of the last of the government regulation muzzleloaders. Imported from Japan by Dixie Gun Works.
Price: Finished $650.00
Price: Kit $575.00

DIXIE PEDERSOLI 1857 MAUSER RIFLE

Caliber: 54. **Barrel:** 39-3/8". **Weight:** NA. **Length:** 52" overall. **Stock:** European walnut with oil finish, sling swivels. **Sights:** Fully adjustable rear, lug front. **Features:** Percussion (musket caps). Armory bright finish with color case-hardened lock and barrel tang, engraved lockplate, steel ramrod. Introduced 2000. Imported from Italy by Dixie Gun Works.
Price: $1,025.00

DIXIE PEDERSOLI 1766 CHARLEVILLE MUSKET

Caliber: 69. **Barrel:** 44-3/4". **Weight:** 10-1/2 lbs. **Length:** 57-1/2" overall. **Stock:** European walnut with oil finish. **Sights:** Fixed rear, lug front.

Features: Smoothbore flintlock. Armory bright finish with steel furniture and ramrod. Introduced 2000. Imported from Italy by Dixie Gun Works.
Price: $1,025.00

DIXIE SHARPS NEW MODEL 1859 MILITARY RIFLE

Caliber: 54. **Barrel:** 30", 6-groove; 1:48" twist. **Weight:** 9 lbs. **Length:** 45-1/2" overall. **Stock:** Oiled walnut. **Sights:** Blade front, ladder-style rear. **Features:** Blued barrel, color case-hardened barrel bands, receiver, hammer, nosecap, lever, patchbox cover and buttplate. Introduced 1995. Imported from Italy by Dixie Gun Works.
Price: $1,025.00

DIXIE U.S. MODEL 1816 FLINTLOCK MUSKET

Caliber: 69. **Barrel:** 42", smoothbore. **Weight:** 9.75 lbs. **Length:** 56.5" overall. **Stock:** Walnut with oil finish. **Sights:** Blade front. **Features:** All metal finished "National Armory Bright;" three barrel bands with springs; steel ramrod with button-shaped head. Imported by Dixie Gun Works.
Price: $1,025.00

DIXIE U.S. MODEL 1861 SPRINGFIELD

Caliber: 58. **Barrel:** 40". **Weight:** About 8 lbs. **Length:** 55-13/16" overall. **Stock:** Oil-finished walnut. **Sights:** Blade front, step adjustable rear. **Features:** Exact recreation of original rifle. Sling swivels attached to trigger guard bow and middle barrel band. Lockplate marked "1861" with eagle motif and "U.S. Springfield" in front of hammer; "U.S." stamped on top of buttplate. From Dixie Gun Works.
Price: Kit $575.00

E.M.F. 1863 SHARPS MILITARY CARBINE

Caliber: 54. **Barrel:** 22", round. **Weight:** 8 lbs. **Length:** 39" overall. **Stock:** Oiled walnut. **Sights:** Blade front, military ladder-type rear. **Features:** Color case-hardened lock, rest blued. Imported by E.M.F.
Price: $600.00

EUROARMS VOLUNTEER TARGET RIFLE

Caliber: 451. **Barrel:** 33" (two-band), 36" (three-band). **Weight:** 11 lbs. (two-band). **Length:** 48.75" overall (two-band). **Stock:** European walnut with checkered wrist and forend. **Sights:** Hooded bead front, adjustable rear with interchangeable leaves. **Features:** Alexander Henry-type rifling with 1:20" twist. Color case-hardened hammer and lockplate, brass trigger guard and nosecap, remainder blued. Imported by Euroarms of America, Dixie Gun Works.
Price: Two-band $828.00

EUROARMS 1861 SPRINGFIELD RIFLE

Caliber: 58. **Barrel:** 40". **Weight:** About 10 lbs. **Length:** 55.5" overall. **Stock:** European walnut. **Sights:** Blade front, three-leaf military rear. **Features:** Reproduction of the original three-band rifle. Lockplate marked "1861" with eagle and "U.S. Springfield." White metal. Imported by Euroarms of America.
Price: $579.00

EUROARMS ZOUAVE RIFLE

Caliber: 58 percussion. **Barrel:** 33". **Overall length:** 49".
Price: $469.00

EUROARMS HARPERS FERRY RIFLE

Caliber: 54 flintlock. **Barrel:** 35". **Overall length:** 50-1/2".
Price: $735.00

EUROARMS RICHMOND RIFLE

Caliber: 58 percussion. **Barrel:** 40". **Overall length:** 49".
Price: $579.00

BLACKPOWDER MUSKETS & RIFLES

Gonic Model 93 Thumbhole

Harper's Ferry 1803

J.P. Murray

Kentucky Flintlock

GONIC MODEL 93 M/L RIFLE
Caliber: 45, 50. **Barrel:** 26"; 1:24" twist. **Weight:** 6-1/2 to 7 lbs. **Length:** 43" overall. **Stock:** American hardwood with black finish. **Sights:** Adjustable or aperture rear, hooded post front. **Features:** Adjustable trigger with side safety; unbreakable ramrod; comes with A. Z. scope bases installed. Introduced 1993. Made in U.S. by Gonic Arms, Inc.
Price: Model 93 Standard (blued barrel)....................... **$720.00**
Price: Model 93 Standard (stainless brl., 50 cal. only) **$782.00**

Gonic Model 93 Deluxe M/L Rifle
Similar to the Model 93 except has classic-style walnut or gray laminated wood stock. Introduced 1998. Made in U.S. by Gonic Arms, Inc.
Price: Blue barrel, sights, scope base, choice of stock........... **$902.00**
Price: Stainless barrel, sights, scope base, choice of stock
(50 cal. only) **$964.00**

Gonic Model 93 Mountain Thumbhole M/L Rifles
Similar to the Model 93 except has high-grade walnut or gray laminate stock with extensive hand-checkered panels, Monte Carlo cheekpiece and beavertail forend; integral muzzle brake. Introduced 1998. Made in U.S. by Gonic Arms, Inc.
Price: Blued or stainless **$2,700.00**

HARPER'S FERRY 1803 FLINTLOCK RIFLE
Caliber: 54 or 58. **Barrel:** 35". **Weight:** 9 lbs. **Length:** 59-1/2" overall. **Stock:** Walnut with cheekpiece. **Sights:** Brass blade front, fixed steel rear. **Features:** Brass trigger guard, sideplate, buttplate; steel patchbox. Imported by Euroarms of America, Navy Arms (54-cal. only), Cabela's, and Dixie Gun Works.
Price:................................... **$495.95 to $995.00**
Price: 54-cal. (Navy Arms) **$625.00**
Price: 54-cal. (Cabela's) **$599.99**
Price: 54-cal. (Dixie Gun Works) **$995.00**
Price: 54-cal. (Euroarms) **$575.00**

HAWKEN RIFLE
Caliber: 45, 50, 54 or 58. **Barrel:** 28", blued, 6-groove rifling. **Weight:** 8-3/4 lbs. **Length:** 44" overall. **Stock:** Walnut with cheekpiece. **Sights:** Blade front, fully adjustable rear. **Features:** Coil mainspring, double-set triggers, polished brass furniture. From Armsport and E.M.F.
Price:....................................... **$220.00 to $345.00**

J.P. HENRY TRADE RIFLE
Caliber: 54. **Barrel:** 34"; 1" flats. **Weight:** 8-1/2 lbs. **Length:** 45" overall. **Stock:** Premium curly maple. **Sights:** Silver blade front, fixed buckhorn rear. **Features:** Brass buttplate, side plate, trigger guard and nosecap; browned barrel and lock; L&R Large English percussion lock; single trigger. Made in U.S. by J.P. Gunstocks, Inc.
Price:.. **$965.50**

J.P. MURRAY 1862-1864 CAVALRY CARBINE
Caliber: 58 (.577" Minie). **Barrel:** 23". **Weight:** 7 lbs., 9 oz. **Length:** 39" overall. **Stock:** Walnut. **Sights:** Blade front, rear drift adjustable for windage. **Features:** Browned barrel, color case-hardened lock, blued swivel and band springs, polished brass buttplate, trigger guard, barrel bands. From Euroarms of America.
Price:.. **$521.00**

KENTUCKY FLINTLOCK RIFLE
Caliber: 44, 45, or 50. **Barrel:** 35". **Weight:** 7 lbs. **Length:** 50" overall. **Stock:** Walnut stained, brass fittings. **Sights:** Fixed. **Features:** Available in carbine model also, 28" bbl. Some variations in detail, finish. Kits also available from some importers. Imported by The Armoury.
Price: About .... **$217.95 to $345.00**

Kentucky Percussion Rifle
Similar to Flintlock except percussion lock. Finish and features vary with importer. Imported by The Armoury and CVA.
Price: About **$259.95**
Price: 45 or 50 cal. (Navy Arms) **$425.00**
Price: Kit, 50 cal. (CVA) **$189.95**

KNIGHT 50 CALIBER DISC IN-LINE RIFLE
Caliber: 50. **Barrel:** 24", 26". **Weight:** 7 lbs., 14 oz. **Length:** 43" overall (24" barrel). **Stock:** Checkered synthetic with palm swell grip, rubber recoil pad, swivel studs; black, Advantage or Mossy Oak® Break-Up camouflage. **Sights:** Bead on ramp front, fully adjustable open rear. **Features:** Bolt-action in-line system uses #209 shotshell primer for ignition; primer is held in plastic drop-in Primer Disc. Available in blued or stainless steel. Made in U.S. by Knight Rifles (Modern Muzzleloading).
Price:....................................... **$439.95 to $632.45**

BLACKPOWDER MUSKETS & RIFLES

Knight 50 Caliber DISC In-Line

Knight Master Hunter DISC Extreme

London Armory 1861

Knight Master Hunter II DISC In-Line Rifle

Similar to Knight 50 caliber DISC rifle except features premium, wood laminated two-tone stock, gold-plated trigger and engraved trigger guard, jeweled bolt and fluted, air-gauged Green Mountain 26" barrel. Length 45" overall, weighs 7 lbs., 7 oz. Includes black composite thumbhole stock. Introduced 2000. Made in U.S. by Knight Rifles (Modern Muzzleloading).
Price: **$1,099.95**

KNIGHT MUZZLELOADER DISC EXTREME

Caliber: 45 fluted, 50. **Barrel:** 26". **Stock:** Stainless steel laminate, blued walnut, black composite thumbhole with blued or SS. **Sights:** Fully adjustable metallic. **Features:** New full plastic jacket ignition system.
Price: 50 SS laminate **$703.95**
Price: 45 SS laminate **$769.95**
Price: 50 blue walnut **$626.95**
Price: 45 blue walnut **$703.95**
Price: 50 blue composite **$549.95**
Price: 45 blue composite **$632.45**
Price: 50 SS composite **$632.45**
Price: 45 SS composite **$703.95**

Knight Master Hunter DISC Extreme

Similar to DISC Extreme except fluted barrel, two-tone laminated thumbhole Monte Carlo-style stock, black composite thumbhole field stock included. Jeweled bolt, adjustable premium trigger.
Price: 50 .... **$1,044.95**

KNIGHT AMERICAN KNIGHT M/L RIFLE

Caliber: 50. **Barrel:** 22"; 1:28" twist. **Weight:** 6 lbs. **Length:** 41" overall. **Stock:** Black composite. **Sights:** Bead on ramp front, open fully adjustable rear. **Features:** Double safety system; one-piece removable hammer assembly; drilled and tapped for scope mounting. Introduced 1998. Made in U.S. by Knight Rifles.
Price: blued, black comp **$197.95**
Price: blued, black comp VP **$225.45**

KNIGHT WOLVERINE 209

Caliber: 50. **Barrel:** 22". **Stock:** HD stock with SS barrel, break-up stock blued, black composite thumbhole with stainless steel, standard black composite with blued or SS. **Sights:** Metallic with fiber-optic. **Features:** Double safety system, adjustable match grade trigger, left-hand model available. Full plastic jacket ignition system.
Price: Starting at **$302.45**

KNIGHT REVOLUTION

Caliber: 50, 209 primer ignition. **Barrel:** Stainless, 27". **Weight:** 7 lbs., 14 oz. **Stock:** Walnut, laminated, black composite, Mossy Oak® Break-Up™ or Hardwoods Green finish. **Features:** Blued or stainless finish, adjustable trigger and sights.
Price: .... **NA**

LONDON ARMORY 1861 ENFIELD MUSKETOON

Caliber: 58, Minie ball. **Barrel:** 24", round. **Weight:** 7 to 7-1/2 lbs. **Length:** 40-1/2" overall. **Stock:** Walnut, with sling swivels. **Sights:** Blade front, graduated military-leaf rear. **Features:** Brass trigger guard, nosecap, buttplate; blued barrel, bands, lockplate, swivels. Imported by Euroarms of America, Navy Arms.
Price: .... **$300.00 to $475.00**
Price: Kit .... **$365.00 to $367.00**

LONDON ARMORY 2-BAND 1858 ENFIELD

Caliber: .577" Minie, .575" round ball. **Barrel:** 33". **Weight:** 10 lbs. **Length:** 49" overall. **Stock:** Walnut. **Sights:** Folding leaf rear adjustable for elevation. **Features:** Blued barrel, color case-hardened lock and hammer, polished brass buttplate, trigger guard, nosecap. From Navy Arms, Euroarms of America, Dixie Gun Works.
Price: .... **$385.00 to $513.00**

LONDON ARMORY 3-BAND 1853 ENFIELD

Caliber: 58 (.577" Minie, .575" round ball, .580" maxi ball). **Barrel:** 39". **Weight:** 9-1/2 lbs. **Length:** 54" overall. **Stock:** European walnut. **Sights:** Inverted "V" front, traditional Enfield folding ladder rear. **Features:** Recreation of the famed London Armory Company Pattern 1853 Enfield Musket. One-piece walnut stock, brass buttplate, trigger guard and nosecap. Lockplate marked "London Armoury Co." and with a British crown. Blued Baddeley barrel bands. From Dixie Gun Works, Euroarms of America, Navy Arms.
Price: About .... **$350.00 to $528.00**
Price: Assembled kit (Dixie, Euroarms of America) **$469.00**

LYMAN TRADE RIFLE

Caliber: 50, 54. **Barrel:** 28" octagon;1:48" twist. **Weight:** 8-3/4 lbs. **Length:** 45" overall. **Stock:** European walnut. **Sights:** Blade front, open rear adjustable for windage or optional fixed sights. **Features:** Fast twist rifling for conical bullets. Polished brass furniture with blue steel parts, stainless steel nipple. Hook breech, single trigger, coil spring percussion lock. Steel barrel rib and ramrod ferrules. Introduced 1980. From Lyman.
Price: 50 cal. percussion................................. **$581.80**
Price: 50 cal. flintlock **$652.80**
Price: 54 cal. percussion **$581.80**
Price: 54 cal. flintlock **$652.80**

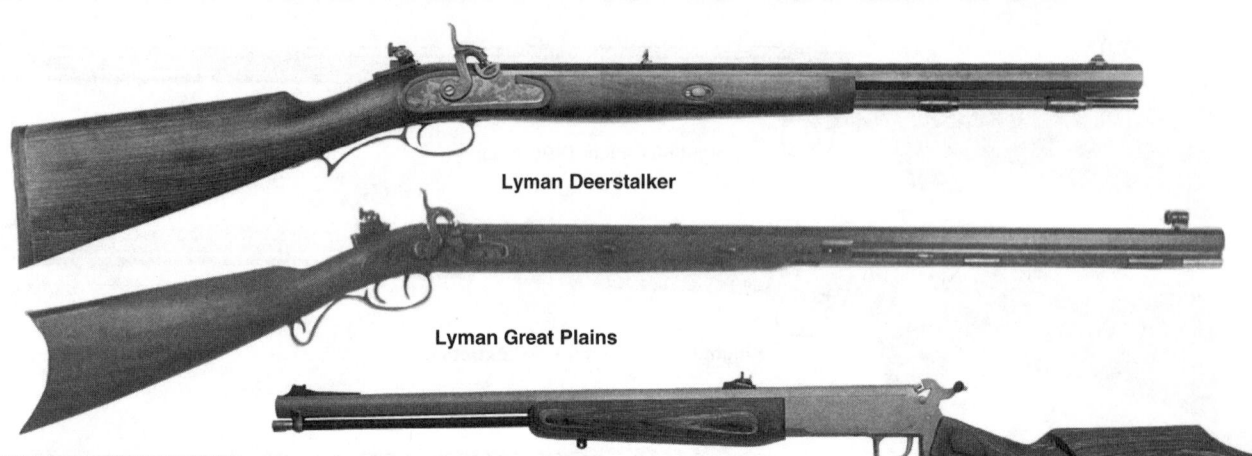

Lyman Deerstalker

Lyman Great Plains

Markesbery KM Colorado

LYMAN DEERSTALKER RIFLE

Caliber: 50, 54. **Barrel:** 24", octagonal; 1:48" rifling. **Weight:** 7-1/2 lbs. **Stock:** Walnut with black rubber buttpad. **Sights:** Lyman #37MA beaded front, fully adjustable fold-down Lyman #16A rear. **Features:** Stock has less drop for quick sighting. All metal parts are blackened, with color case-hardened lock; single trigger. Comes with sling and swivels. Available in flint or percussion. Introduced 1990. From Lyman.

Price: 50 cal. flintlock $652.80
Price: 50 or 54 cal., percussion, left-hand, carbine $695.40
Price: 50 or 54 cal., flintlock, left-hand $645.00
Price: 54 cal. flintlock $780.50
Price: 54 cal. percussion $821.80
Price: Stainless steel $959.80

LYMAN GREAT PLAINS RIFLE

Caliber: 50, 54. **Barrel:** 32"; 1:60" twist. **Weight:** 9 lbs. **Stock:** Walnut. **Sights:** Steel blade front, buckhorn rear adjustable for windage and elevation and fixed notch primitive sight included. **Features:** Blued steel furniture. Stainless steel nipple. Coil spring lock, Hawken-style trigger guard and double-set triggers. Round thimbles recessed and sweated into rib. Steel wedge plates and toe plate. Introduced 1979. From Lyman.

Price: Percussion $469.95
Price: Flintlock $494.95
Price: Percussion kit $359.95
Price: Flintlock kit $384.95
Price: Left-hand percussion $474.95
Price: Left-hand flintlock $499.95

Lyman Great Plains Hunter Model

Similar to Great Plains model except 1:32" twist shallow-groove barrel and comes drilled and tapped for Lyman 57GPR peep sight.
Price: $959.80

MARKESBERY KM BLACK BEAR M/L RIFLE

Caliber: 36, 45, 50, 54. **Barrel:** 24"; 1:26" twist. **Weight:** 6-1/2 lbs. **Length:** 38-1/2" overall. **Stock:** Two-piece American hardwood, walnut, black laminate, green laminate, black composition, X-Tra or Mossy Oak® Break-Up™ camouflage. **Sights:** Bead front, open fully adjustable rear. **Features:** Interchangeable barrels; exposed hammer; Outer-Line Magnum ignition system uses small rifle primer or standard No. 11 cap and nipple. Blue, black matte, or stainless. Made in U.S. by Markesbery Muzzle Loaders.

Price: American hardwood walnut, blue finish $536.63
Price: American hardwood walnut, stainless $553.09
Price: Black laminate, blue finish $539.67
Price: Black laminate, stainless $556.27
Price: Camouflage stock, blue finish $556.46
Price: Camouflage stock, stainless $573.73
Price: Black composite, blue finish $532.65
Price: Black composite, stainless $549.93
Price: Green laminate, blue finish $539.00
Price: Green laminate, stainless $556.27

Markesbery KM Brown Bear Rifle

Similar to KM Black Bear except one-piece thumbhole stock with Monte Carlo comb. Stock in Crotch Walnut composite, green or black laminate, black composite or X-Tra or Mossy Oak® Break-Up™ camouflage. Made in U.S. by Markesbery Muzzle Loaders, Inc.

Price: Black composite, blue finish $658.83
Price: Crotch Walnut, blue finish $658.83
Price: Camo composite, blue finish $682.64
Price: Walnut wood $662.81
Price: Black wood $662.81
Price: Black laminated wood $662.81
Price: Green laminated wood $662.81
Price: Camo wood $684.69
Price: Black composite, stainless $676.11
Price: Crotch Walnut composite, stainless $676.11
Price: Camo composite, stainless $697.69
Price: Walnut wood, stainless $680.07
Price: Black wood, stainless $680.07
Price: Black laminated wood, stainless $680.07
Price: Green laminate, stainless $680.07
Price: Camo wood, stainless $702.76

Markesbery KM Grizzly Bear Rifle

Similar to KM Black Bear except thumbhole buttstock with Monte Carlo comb. Stock in Crotch Walnut composite, green or black laminate, black composite or X-Tra or Mossy Oak® Break-Up camouflage. Made in U.S. by Markesbery Muzzle Loaders, Inc.

Price: Black composite, blue finish $642.96
Price: Crotch Walnut, blue finish $642.96
Price: Camo composite, blue finish $666.67
Price: Walnut wood $646.93
Price: Black wood $646.93
Price: Black laminate wood $646.93
Price: Green laminate wood $646.93
Price: Camo wood $670.74
Price: Black composite, stainless $660.98
Price: Crotch Walnut composite, stainless $660.98
Price: Black laminate wood, stainless $664.20
Price: Green laminate, stainless $664.20
Price: Camo wood, stainless $685.74
Price: Camo composite, stainless $684.04
Price: Walnut wood, stainless $664.20
Price: Black wood, stainless $664.20

BLACKPOWDER MUSKETS & RIFLES

Mississippi 1841

Navy Arms 1763 Charleville

Navy Arms Berdan

Markesbery KM Polar Bear Rifle

Similar to KM Black Bear except one-piece stock with Monte Carlo comb. Stock in American Hardwood walnut, green or black laminate, black composite, or X-Tra or Mossy Oak® Break-Up™ camouflage. Interchangeable barrel system, Outer-Line ignition system, cross-bolt double safety. Available in 36, 45, 50, 54 caliber. Made in U.S. by Markesbery Muzzle Loaders, Inc.

Price: American Hardwood walnut, blue finish **$539.01**
Price: Black composite, blue finish **$536.63**
Price: Black laminate, blue finish **$541.17**
Price: Green laminate, blue finish **$541.17**
Price: Camo, blue finish **$560.43**
Price: American Hardwood walnut, stainless **$556.27**
Price: Black composite, stainless **$556.04**
Price: Black laminate, stainless **$570.56**
Price: Green laminate, stainless **$570.56**
Price: Camo, stainless **$573.94**

MARKESBERY KM COLORADO ROCKY MOUNTAIN RIFLE

Caliber: 36, 45, 50, 54. **Barrel:** 24"; 1:26" twist. **Weight:** 6-1/2 lbs. **Length:** 38-1/2" overall. **Stock:** American hardwood walnut, green or black laminate. **Sights:** Firesight bead on ramp front, fully adjustable open rear. **Features:** Replicates Reed/Watson rifle of 1851. Straight grip stock with or without two barrel bands, rubber recoil pad, large-spur hammer. Made in U.S. by Markesbery Muzzle Loaders, Inc.

Price: American hardwood walnut, blue finish **$545.92**
Price: Black or green laminate, blue finish **$548.30**
Price: American hardwood walnut, stainless **$563.17**
Price: Black or green laminate, stainless **$566.34**

MDM BUCKWACKA IN-LINE RIFLES

Caliber: 45, 50. **Barrel:** 23", 25". **Weight:** 7 to 7-3/4 lbs. **Stock:** Black, walnut, laminated and camouflage finishes. **Sights:** Williams Fire Sight blade front, Williams fully adjustable rear with ghost-ring peep aperture. **Features:** Break-open action; Incinerating Ignition System incorporates 209 shotshell primer directly into breech plug; 50-caliber models handle up to 150 grains of Pyrodex; synthetic ramrod; transfer bar safety; stainless or blued finish. Made in U.S. by Millennium Designed Muzzleloaders Ltd.

Price: 50 cal., blued finish **$309.95**
Price: 50 cal., stainless **$339.95**
Price: Camouflage stock . . . . **$359.95 to $389.95**

MDM M2K In-Line Rifle

Similar to Buckwacka except adjustable trigger and double-safety mechanism designed to prevent misfires. Made in U.S. by Millennium Designed Muzzleloaders Ltd.

Price: . . . . **$529.00 to $549.00**

MISSISSIPPI 1841 PERCUSSION RIFLE

Caliber: 54, 58. **Barrel:** 33". **Weight:** 9-1/2 lbs. **Length:** 48-5/8" overall. **Stock:** One-piece European walnut full stock with satin finish. **Sights:** Brass blade front, fixed steel rear. **Features:** Case-hardened lockplate marked "U.S." surmounted by American eagle. Two barrel bands, sling swivels. Steel ramrod with brass end, browned barrel. From Navy Arms, Dixie Gun Works, E.M.F., Cabela's, Euroarms of America.

Price: About **$575.00**

NAVY ARMS 1763 CHARLEVILLE

Caliber: 69. **Barrel:** 44-5/8". **Weight:** 8 lbs., 12 oz. **Length:** 59-3/8" overall. **Stock:** Walnut. **Sights:** Brass blade front. **Features:** Replica of French musket used by American troops during the American Revolution. Imported by Navy Arms.

Price: **$1,020.00**

NAVY ARMS BERDAN 1859 SHARPS RIFLE

Caliber: 54. **Barrel:** 30". **Weight:** 8 lbs., 8 oz. **Length:** 46-3/4" overall. **Stock:** Walnut. **Sights:** Blade front, folding military ladder-type rear. **Features:** Replica of the Union sniper rifle used by Berdan's 1st and 2nd Sharpshooter regiments. Color case-hardened receiver, patchbox, furniture. Double-set triggers. Imported by Navy Arms.

Price: **$1,165.00**
Price: 1859 Sharps Infantry Rifle (three-band) **$1,100.00**

NAVY ARMS 1859 SHARPS CAVALRY CARBINE

Caliber: 54. **Barrel:** 22". **Weight:** 7-3/4 lbs. **Length:** 39" overall. **Stock:** Walnut. **Sights:** Blade front, military ladder-type rear. **Features:** Color case-hardened action, blued barrel. Has saddle ring. Introduced 1991. Imported from Navy Arms.

Price: **$1,000.00**

NAVY ARMS 1861 SPRINGFIELD RIFLE

Caliber: 58. **Barrel:** 40". **Weight:** 10 lbs., 4 oz. **Length:** 56" overall. **Stock:** Walnut. **Sights:** Blade front, military leaf rear. **Features:** Steel barrel, lock and all furniture have polished bright finish. Has 1855-style hammer. Imported by Navy Arms.

Price: **$590.00**

NAVY ARMS 1863 C.S. RICHMOND RIFLE

Caliber: 58. **Barrel:** 40". **Weight:** 10 lbs. **Length:** NA. **Stocks:** Walnut. **Sights:** Blade front, adjustable rear. **Features:** Copy of three-band rifle musket made at Richmond Armory for the Confederacy. All steel polished bright. Imported by Navy Arms.

Price: **$590.00**

NAVY ARMS 1863 SPRINGFIELD

Caliber: 58, uses .575 Minie. **Barrel:** 40", rifled. **Weight:** 9-1/2 lbs. **Length:** 56" overall. **Stock:** Walnut. **Sights:** Open rear adjustable for elevation. **Features:** Full-size, three-band musket. Polished bright metal, including lock. From Navy Arms.

Price: Finished rifle **$590.00**

BLACKPOWDER MUSKETS & RIFLES

Navy Arms Whitworth

New England Firearms Huntsman

Peifer TS-93

NAVY ARMS PARKER-HALE VOLUNTEER RIFLE
Caliber: .451. **Barrel:** 32". **Weight:** 9-1/2 lbs. **Length:** 49" overall. **Stock:** Walnut, checkered wrist and forend. **Sights:** Globe front, adjustable ladder-type rear. **Features:** Recreation of the type of gun issued to volunteer regiments during the 1860s. Rigby-pattern rifling, patent breech, detented lock. Stock is glass bedded for accuracy. Imported by Navy Arms.
Price: **$905.00**

NAVY ARMS PARKER-HALE WHITWORTH MILITARY TARGET RIFLE
Caliber: 45. **Barrel:** 36". **Weight:** 9-1/4 lbs. **Length:** 52-1/2" overall. **Stock:** Walnut. Checkered at wrist and forend. **Sights:** Hooded post front, open step-adjustable rear. **Features:** Faithful reproduction of Whitworth rifle. Trigger has detented lock, capable of fine adjustments without risk of the sear nose catching on the half-cock notch and damaging both parts. Introduced 1978. Imported by Navy Arms.
Price: **$930.00**

NAVY ARMS SMITH CARBINE
Caliber: 50. **Barrel:** 21-1/2". **Weight:** 7-3/4 lbs. **Length:** 39" overall. **Stock:** American walnut. **Sights:** Brass blade front, folding ladder-type rear. **Features:** Replica of breech-loading Civil War carbine. Color case-hardened receiver, rest blued. Cavalry model has saddle ring and bar, Artillery model has sling swivels. Imported by Navy Arms.
Price: Cavalry model **$645.00**
Price: Artillery model **$645.00**

NEW ENGLAND FIREARMS SIDEKICK
Caliber: 50, 209 primer ignition. **Barrel:** 26" (magnum). **Weight:** 6.5 lbs. **Length:** 41.25". **Stock:** Black matte polymer or hardwood. **Sights:** Adjustable fiber-optic open, tapped for scope mounts. **Features:** Single-shot based on H&R break-open action. Uses No. 209 shotgun primer held in place by special primer carrier. Telescoping brass ramrod. Introduced 2004.
Price: Wood stock, blued frame, black-oxide barrel) **$216.00**
Price: Stainless barrel and frame, synthetic stock) **$310.00**

NEW ENGLAND FIREARMS HUNTSMAN
Caliber: 50, 209 primer ignition. **Barrel:** 22" to 26". **Weight:** 5.25 to 6.5 lbs. **Length:** 40" to 43". **Stock:** Black matte polymer or hardwood. **Sights:** Fiber-optic open sights, tapped for scope mounts. **Features:** Break-open action, transfer-bar safety system, breech plug removable for cleaning. Introduced 2004.
Price: Stainless Huntsman **$306.00**
Price: Huntsman **$212.00**
Price: Pardner Combo 12 ga./50 cal muzzleloader **$259.00**
Price: Tracker II Combo 12 ga. rifled slug barrel /50 cal. **$288.00**
Price: Handi-Rifle Combo 243/50 cal **$405.00**

New England Firearms Stainless Huntsman
Similar to Huntsman, but with matte nickel finish receiver and stainless bbl. Introduced 2003. From New England Firearms.
Price: **$81.00**

PACIFIC RIFLE MODEL 1837 ZEPHYR
Caliber: 62. **Barrel:** 30", tapered octagon. **Weight:** 7-3/4 lbs. **Length:** NA. **Stock:** Oil-finished fancy walnut. **Sights:** German silver blade front, semi-buckhorn rear. Options available. **Features:** Improved underhammer action. First production rifle to offer Forsyth rifle, with narrow lands and shallow rifling with 1:14" pitch for high-velocity round balls. Metal finish is slow rust brown with nitre blue accents. Optional sights, finishes and integral muzzle brake available. Introduced 1995. Made in U.S. by Pacific Rifle Co.
Price: From **$995.00**

Pacific Rifle Big Bore African Rifles
Similar to the 1837 Zephyr except in 72-caliber and 8-bore. The 72-caliber is available in standard form with 28" barrel, or as the African with flat buttplate, checkered upgraded wood; weight is 9 lbs. The 8-bore African has dual-cap ignition, 24" barrel, weighs 12 lbs., checkered English walnut, engraving, gold inlays. Introduced 1998. Made in U.S. by Pacific Rifle Co.
Price: 72-caliber, from **$1,150.00**
Price: 8-bore, from **$2,500.00**

PEIFER MODEL TS-93 RIFLE
Caliber: 45, 50. **Barrel:** 24" Douglas premium; 1:20" twist in 45; 1:28" in 50. **Weight:** 7 lbs. **Length:** 43-1/4" overall. **Stock:** Bell & Carlson solid composite, with recoil pad, swivel studs. **Sights:** Williams bead front on ramp, fully adjustable open rear. Drilled and tapped for Weaver scope mounts with dovetail for rear peep. **Features:** In-line ignition uses #209 shotshell primer; fast lock time; fully enclosed breech; adjustable trigger; automatic safety; removable primer holder. Blue or stainless. Made in U.S. by Peifer Rifle Co. Introduced 1996.
Price: Blue, black stock. **$730.00**
Price: Blue, wood or camouflage composite stock, or stainless with black composite stock **$803.00**
Price: Stainless, wood or camouflage composite stock **$876.00**

PRAIRIE RIVER ARMS PRA BULLPUP RIFLE
Caliber: 50. **Barrel:** 28"; 1:28" twist. **Weight:** 7-1/2 lbs. **Length:** 31-1/2" overall. **Stock:** Hardwood or black all-weather. **Sights:** Blade front, open adjustable rear. **Features:** Bullpup design thumbhole stock. Patented internal percussion ignition system. Left-hand model available. Dovetailed for scope mount. Introduced 1995. Made in U.S. by Prairie River Arms, Ltd.
Price: 4140 alloy barrel, hardwood stock **$199.00**
Price: All Weather stock, alloy barrel **$205.00**

REPLICA ARMS 1863 SHARPS SPORTING RIFLE
Caliber: .54 cal percussion. **Barrel:** 28" Octagonal. **Weight:** 8.82 lbs. **Length:** 45" overall. **Grips:** Walnut checkered at wrist and forend. **Sights:** Blade front, full buckhorn rear. **Features:** Color case-hardened receiver, trigger, hammer and lever. Double-set triggers.
Price: **$939.00**

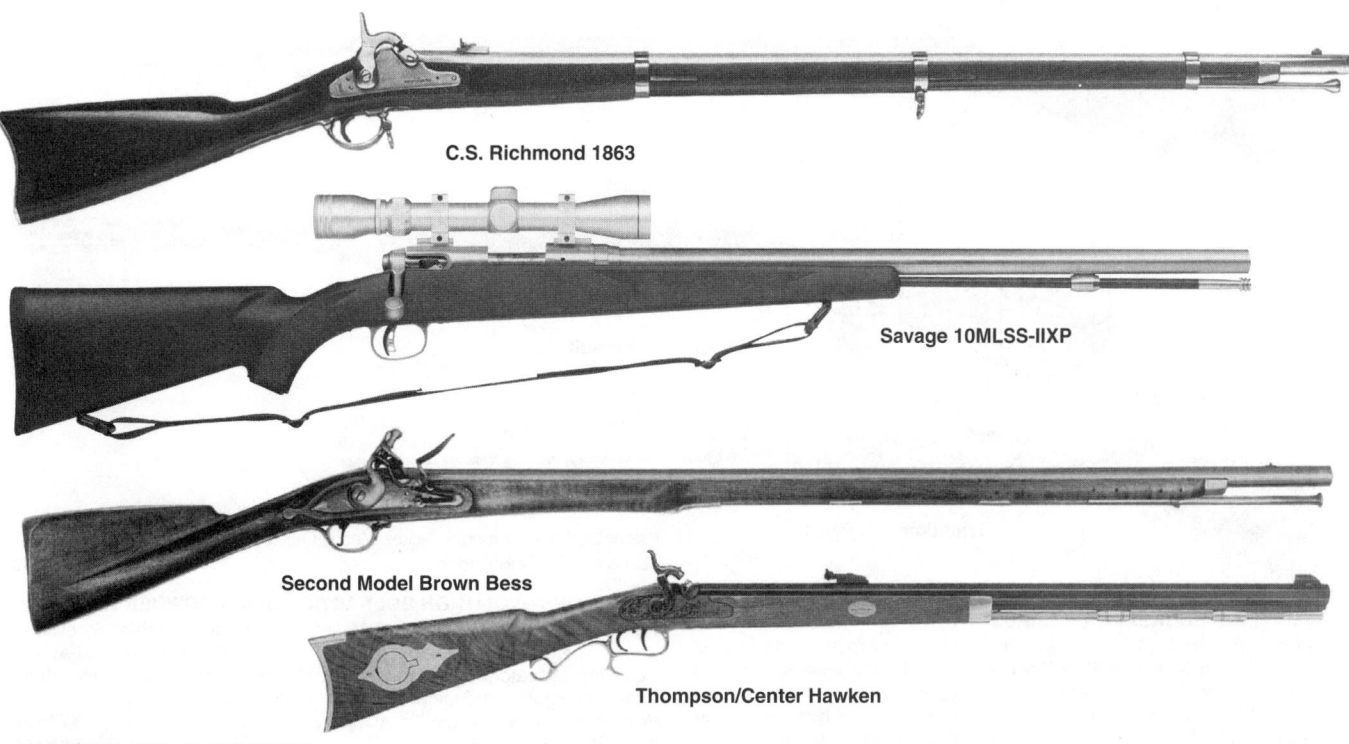

C.S. Richmond 1863

Savage 10MLSS-IIXP

Second Model Brown Bess

Thompson/Center Hawken

RICHMOND, C.S., 1863 MUSKET

Caliber: 58. **Barrel:** 40". **Weight:** 11 lbs. **Length:** 56-1/4" overall. **Stock:** European walnut with oil finish. **Sights:** Blade front, adjustable folding leaf rear. **Features:** Reproduction of the three-band Civil War musket. Sling swivels attached to trigger guard and middle barrel band. Lockplate marked "1863" and "C.S. Richmond." All white metal. Brass buttplate and forend cap. Imported by Euroarms of America, Navy Arms, and Dixie Gun Works.

Price: Euroarms $530.00
Price: Dixie Gun Works $1,025.00

SAVAGE MODEL 10ML MUZZLELOADER RIFLE SERIES

Caliber: 50. **Barrel:** 24", 1:24 twist, blue or stainless. **Weight:** 7.75 lbs. **Stock:** Black synthetic, Realtree Hardwood JD Camo, brown laminate. **Sights:** Green adjustable rear, Red FiberOptic front. **Features:** XP Models scoped, no sights, designed for smokeless powder, #209 primer ignition. Removeable breech plug and vent liner.

Price: Model 10ML-II. $531.00
Price: Model 10ML-II Camo $569.00
Price: Model 10MLSS-II Camo $628.00
Price: Model 10MLBSS-II $667.00
Price: Model 10ML-IIXP $569.00
Price: Model 10MLSS-IIXP $628.00

SECOND MODEL BROWN BESS MUSKET

Caliber: 75, uses .735" round ball. **Barrel:** 42", smoothbore. **Weight:** 9-1/2 lbs. **Length:** 59" overall. **Stock:** Walnut (Navy); walnut-stained hardwood (Dixie). **Sights:** Fixed. **Features:** Polished barrel and lock with brass trigger guard and buttplate. Bayonet and scabbard available. From Navy Arms, Dixie Gun Works, Cabela's.

Price: Finished. . . . . $475.00 to $950.00
Price: Kit (Dixie Gun Works, Navy Arms) . . . . $575.00 to $775.00
Price: Carbine (Navy Arms) $835.00
Price: Dixie Gun Works $950.00

THOMPSON/CENTER BLACK DIAMOND RIFLE XR

Caliber: 50. **Barrel:** 26" with QLA; 1:28" twist. **Weight:** 6 lbs., 9 oz. **Length:** 41-1/2" overall. **Stock:** Black Rynite with molded-in checkering and gripcap, or walnut. **Sights:** TruGlo fiber-optic ramp-style front, TruGlo fiber-optic open rear. **Features:** In-line ignition system for musket cap, No.

11 cap, or 209 shotshell primer; removable universal breech plug; stainless steel construction. Selected models available in .45 cal. Made in U.S. by Thompson/Center Arms.

Price: With composite stock, blued $337.00
Price: With walnut stock $412.00

THOMPSON/CENTER ENCORE 209x50 MAGNUM

Caliber: 50. **Barrel:** 26"; interchangeable with centerfire calibers. **Weight:** 7 lbs. **Length:** 40-1/2" overall. **Stock:** American walnut butt and forend, or black composite. **Sights:** TruGlo fiber-optic front and rear. **Features:** Blue or stainless steel. Uses the stock, frame and forend of the Encore centerfire pistol; break-open design using trigger guard spur; stainless steel universal breech plug; uses #209 shotshell primers. Introduced 1998. Made in U.S. by Thompson/Center Arms.

Price: Stainless wtih camo stock $772.00
Price: Blue, walnut stock and forend $678.00
Price: Blue, composite stock and forend $637.00
Price: Stainless, composite stock and forend $713.00
Price: All camo Realtree Hardwoods $729.00

THOMPSON/CENTER FIRE STORM RIFLE

Caliber: 50. **Barrel:** 26"; 1:28" twist. **Weight:** 7 lbs. **Length:** 41-3/4" overall. **Stock:** Black synthetic with rubber recoil pad, swivel studs. **Sights:** Click-adjustable steel rear and ramp-style front, both with fiber-optic inserts. **Features:** Side hammer lock is the first designed for up to three 50-grain Pyrodex pellets; patented Pyrodex Pyramid breech directs ignition fire 360 degrees around base of pellet. Quick Load Accurizor Muzzle System; aluminum ramrod. Flintlock only. Introduced 2000. Made in U.S. by Thompson/Center Arms.

Price: Blue finish, flintlock model with 1:48" twist for round balls,
conicals $436.00
Price: SST, flintlock $488.00

THOMPSON/CENTER HAWKEN RIFLE

Caliber: 50. **Barrel:** 28" octagon, hooked breech. **Stock:** American walnut. **Sights:** Blade front, rear adjustable for windage and elevation. **Features:** Solid brass furniture, double-set triggers, button rifled barrel, coil-type mainspring. From Thompson/Center Arms.

Price: Percussion model $590.00
Price: Flintlock model $615.00

BLACKPOWDER MUSKETS & RIFLES

Traditions Deerhunter

Traditions Pursuit

Traditions PA Pellet

TRADITIONS BUCKSKINNER CARBINE
Caliber: 50. **Barrel:** 21"; 15/16" flats, half octagon, half round; 1:20" or 1:66" twist. **Weight:** 6 lbs. **Length:** 37" overall. **Stock:** Beech or black laminated. **Sights:** Beaded blade front, fiber-optic open rear click adjustable for windage and elevation or fiber-optics. **Features:** Uses V-type mainspring, single trigger. Non-glare hardware; sling swivels. From Traditions.
Price: Flintlock **$249.00**
Price: Flintlock, laminated stock **$303.00**

TRADITIONS DEERHUNTER RIFLE SERIES
Caliber: 32, 50 or 54. **Barrel:** 24", octagonal; 15/16" flats; 1:48" or 1:66" twist. **Weight:** 6 lbs. **Length:** 40" overall. **Stock:** Stained hardwood or All-Weather composite with rubber buttpad, sling swivels. **Sights:** Lite Optic blade front, adjustable rear fiber-optics. **Features:** Flint or percussion with color case-hardened lock. Hooked breech, oversized trigger guard, blackened furniture, PVC ramrod. All-Weather has composite stock and C-nickel barrel. Drilled and tapped for scope mounting. Imported by Traditions, Inc.
Price: Percussion, 50; blued barrel; 1:48" twist **$189.00**
Price: Percussion, 54 . . . . **$169.00**
Price: Flintlock, 50 caliber only; 1:48" twist **$179.00**
Price: Flintlock, All-Weather, 50-cal. **$239.00**
Price: Redi-Pak, 50 cal. flintlock **$219.00**
Price: Flintlock, left-handed hardwood, 50 cal. **$209.00**
Price: Percussion, All-Weather, 50 or 54 cal. **$179.00**
Price: Percussion, 32 cal. **$199.00**

Traditions Panther Sidelock Rifle
Similar to Deerhunter rifle, but has blade front and windage-adjustable-only rear sights, black composite stock.
Price: **$129.00**

TRADITIONS PURSUIT BREAK-OPEN MUZZLELOADER
Caliber: 45, 54 and 12 gauge. **Barrel:** 28", tapered, fluted; blued, stainless or Hardwoods Green camo. **Weight:** 8-1/4 lbs. **Length:** 44" overall. **Stock:** Synthetic black or Hardwoods Green. **Sights:** Steel fiber-optic rear, bead front. Introduced 2004 by Traditions, Inc.
Price: Steel, blued, 45 or 50 cal., synthetic stock **$279.00**
Price: Steel, nickel, 45 or 50 cal., synthetic stock **$309.00**
Price: Steel, nickel w/Hardwoods Green stock **$359.00**
Price: Matte blued; 12 ga., synthetic stock **$369.00**
Price: Matte blued; 12 ga. w/Hardwoods Green stock **$439.00**
Price: Lightweight model, blued, synthetic stock **$199.00**
Price: Lightweight model, blued, Mossy Oak®
Break-Up™ Camo stock **$239.00**

Price: Lightweight model, nickel, Mossy Oak®
Break-Up™ Camo stock **$279.00**

TRADITIONS EVOLUTION BOLT-ACTION BLACKPOWDER RIFLE
Caliber: 50 percussion. **Barrel:** 26", fluted with porting. **Sights:** Steel fiber-optic. **Weight:** 7 to 7-1/4 lbs. **Length:** 45" overall. **Features:** Bolt-action, cocking indicator, thumb safety, aluminum ramrod, sling studs. Wide variety of stocks and metal finishes. Introduced 2004 by Traditions, Inc.
Price: Synthetic stock **$279.00**
Price: Walnut X-wood **$349.00**
Price: Brown laminated. **$469.00**
Price: Advantage Timber **$369.00**
Price: Synthetic, TruGlo sights **$249.00**
Price: Mossy Oak® Break-up™ **$279.00**
Price: Nickel finish **$309.00**
Price: Beech/nickel, Advantage/nickel, Advantage 54 cal. **$289.00**

TRADITIONS PA PELLET FLINTLOCK
Caliber: 50. **Barrel:** 26", blued, nickel. **Weight:** 7 lbs. **Stock:** Hardwood, synthetic and synthetic break-up. **Sights:** Fiber-optic. **Features:** Removeable breech plug, left-hand model with hardwood stock. 1:48" twist.
Price: Hardwood, blued **$259.00**
Price: Hardwood left, blued **$269.00**

TRADITIONS HAWKEN WOODSMAN RIFLE
Caliber: 50 and 54. **Barrel:** 28"; 15/16" flats. **Weight:** 7 lbs., 11 oz. **Length:** 44-1/2" overall. **Stock:** Walnut-stained hardwood. **Sights:** Beaded blade front, hunting-style open rear adjustable for windage and elevation. **Features:** Percussion only. Brass patchbox and furniture. Double triggers. From Traditions.
Price: 50 or 54 . . . . **$299.00**
Price: 50-cal., left-hand. **$279.00**
Price: 50-cal., flintlock. **$299.00**

TRADITIONS KENTUCKY RIFLE
Caliber: 50. **Barrel:** 33-1/2"; 7/8" flats; 1:66" twist. **Weight:** 7 lbs. **Length:** 49" overall. **Stock:** Beech; inletted toe plate. **Sights:** Blade front, fixed rear. **Features:** Full-length, two-piece stock; brass furniture; color case-hardened lock. From Traditions.
Price: **$279.00**

TRADITIONS PENNSYLVANIA RIFLE
Caliber: 50. **Barrel:** 40-1/4"; 7/8" flats; 1:66" twist, octagon. **Weight:** 9 lbs. **Length:** 57-1/2" overall. **Stock:** Walnut. **Sights:** Blade front, adjustable rear. **Features:** Brass patchbox and ornamentation. Double-set triggers. From Traditions.
Price: Flintlock **$529.00**
Price: Percussion **$519.00**

BLACKPOWDER MUSKETS & RIFLES

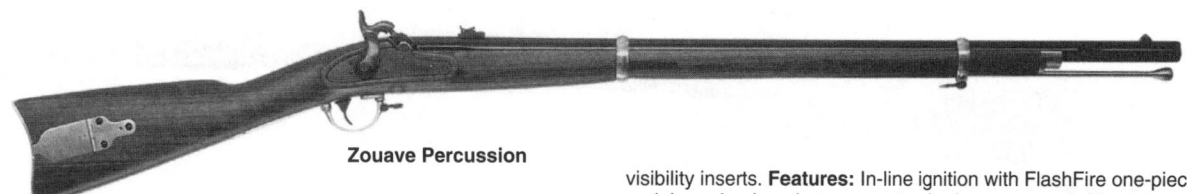

Zouave Percussion

TRADITIONS SHENANDOAH RIFLE
Caliber: 36, 50. **Barrel:** 33-1/2" octagon; 1:66" twist. **Weight:** 7 lbs., 3 oz. **Length:** 49-1/2" overall. **Stock:** Walnut. **Sights:** Blade front, buckhorn rear. **Features:** V-type mainspring; double-set trigger; solid brass buttplate, patchbox, nosecap, thimbles, trigger guard. Introduced 1996. From Traditions.
Price: Flintloc **$419.00**
Price: Percussion **$399.00**
Price: 36 cal. flintlock, 1:48" twist **$419.00**
Price: 36 cal. percussion, 1:48" twist **$449.00**

TRADITIONS TENNESSEE RIFLE
Caliber: 50. **Barrel:** 24", octagon; 15/16" flats; 1:66" twist. **Weight:** 6 lbs. **Length:** 40-1/2" overall. **Stock:** Stained beech. **Sights:** Blade front, fixed rear. **Features:** One-piece stock has inletted brass furniture, cheekpiece; double-set trigger; V-type mainspring. Flint or percussion. From Traditions.
Price: Flintlock **$339.00**
Price: Percussion **$329.00**

TRADITIONS TRACKER 209 IN-LINE RIFLES
Caliber: 45, 50. **Barrel:** 22" blued or C-nickel finish; 1:28" twist, 50 cal. 1:20" 45 cal. **Weight:** 6 lbs., 4 oz. **Length:** 41" overall. **Stock:** Black, Advantage Timber® composite, synthetic. **Sights:** Lite Optic blade front, adjustable rear. **Features:** Thumb safety; adjustable trigger; rubber butt pad and sling swivel studs; takes 150 grains of Pyrodex pellets; one-piece breech system takes 209 shotshell primers. Drilled and tapped for scope. From Traditions.
Price: (Black composite or synthetic stock, 22" blued barrel) **$129.00**
Price: (Black composite or synthetic stock, 22" C-nickel barrel) . . . **$139.00**
Price: (Advantage Timber® stock, 22" C-nickel barrel) **$189.00**
Price: (Redi-Pak, black stock and blued barrel, powder flask, capper, ball starter, other accessories) **$179.00**
Price: (Redi-Pak, synthetic stock and blued barrel, with scope) **$229.00**

ULTRA LIGHT ARMS MODEL 209 MUZZLELOADER
Caliber: 45 or 50. **Barrel:** 24" button rifled; 1:32" twist. **Weight:** Under 5 lbs. **Stock:** Kevlar/Graphite. **Features:** Recoil pad, sling swivels included. Some color options available. Adj. Timney trigger, positive primer extraction.
Price: **$1,100.00**

WHITE MODEL 97 WHITETAIL HUNTER RIFLE
Caliber: 45, 50. **Barrel:** 22", 1:20 twist (45 cal.); 1:24 twist (50 cal.). **Weight:** 7.7 lbs. **Length:** 40" overall. **Stock:** Black laminated or black composite. **Sights:** Marble TruGlo fully adjustable, steel rear with white diamond, red bead front with high-visibility inserts. **Features:** In-line ignition with FlashFire one-piece nipple and breech plug that uses standard or magnum No. 11 caps, fully adjustable trigger, double safety system, aluminum ramrod; drilled and tapped for scope. Hard case. Made in U.S.A. by Split Fire Sporting Goods.
Price: Whitetail w/laminated or composite stock. **$499.95**
Price: Adventurer w/26" stainless barrel & thumbhole stock) **$699.95**
Price: Odyssey w/24" carbon fiber wrapped barrel & thumbhole stock **$1,299.95**

WHITE MODEL 98 ELITE HUNTER RIFLE
Caliber: 45, 50. **Barrel:** 24", 1:24 twist (50 cal). **Weight:** 8.6 lbs. **Length:** 43-1/2" overall. **Stock:** Black laminate wtih swivel studs. **Sights:** TruGlo fully adjustable, steel rear with white diamond, red bead front with high-visibility inserts. **Features:** In-line ignition with FlashFire one-piece nipple and breech plug that uses standard or magnum No. 11 caps, fully adjustable trigger, double safety system, aluminum ramrod, drilled and tapped for scope, hard gun case. Made in U.S.A. by Split Fire Sporting Goods.
Price: Composite or laminate wood stock **$499.95**

White Thunderbolt Rifle
Similar to the Elite Hunter but is designed to handle 209 shotgun primers only. Has 26" stainless steel barrel, weighs 9.3 lbs. and is 45-1/2" long. Composite or laminate stock. Made in U.S.A. by Split Fire Sporting Goods.
Price: **$599.95**

WHITE MODEL 2000 BLACKTAIL HUNTER RIFLE
Caliber: 50. **Barrel:** 22", 1:24" twist (50 cal.). **Weight:** 7.6 lbs. **Length:** 39-7/8" overall. **Stock:** Black laminated with swivel studs with laser engraved deer or elk scene. **Sights:** TruGlo fully adjustable, steel rear with white diamond, red bead front with high-visibility inserts. **Features:** Teflon finished barrel, in-line ignition with FlashFire one-piece nipple and breech plug that uses standard or magnum No. 11 caps, fully adjustable trigger, double safety system, aluminum ramrod, drilled and tapped for scope. Hard gun case. Made in U.S.A. by Split Fire Sporting Goods.
Price: Laminate wood stock, w/laser engraved game scene **$599.95**

WHITE LIGHTNING II RIFLE
Caliber: 45 and 50 percussion. **Barrel:** 24", 1:32 twist. **Sights:** Adj. rear. **Stock:** Black polymer. **Weight:** 6 lbs. **Features:** In-line, 209 primer ignition system, blued or nickel-plated bbl., adj. trigger, Delrin ramrod, sling studs, recoil pad. Made in U.S.A. by Split Fire Sporting Goods.
Price: **$299.95**

WHITE ALPHA RIFLE
Caliber: 45, 50 percussion. **Barrel:** 27" tapered, stainless. **Sights:** Marble TruGlo rear, fiber-optic front. **Stock:** Laminated. **Features:** Lever action rotating block, hammerless; adj. trigger, positive safety. All stainless metal, including trigger. Made in U.S.A. by Split Fire Sporting Goods.
Price: **$449.95**

WINCHESTER APEX SWING-ACTION MAGNUM RIFLE
Caliber: 45, 50. **Barrel:** 28". **Stock:** Mossy Oak® Camo, Black Fleck. **Sights:** Adj. fiber-optic. **Weight:** 7 lbs., 12 oz. **Overall length:** 42". **Features:** Monte Carlo cheekpiece, swing-action design, external hammer.
Price: Mossy Oak®/stainless **$489.95**
Price: Black Fleck/stainless **$449.95**
Price: Full Mossy Oak® **$469.95**
Price: Black Fleck/blued **$364.95**

WINCHESTER X-150 BOLT-ACTION MAGNUM RIFLE
Caliber: 45, 50. **Barrel:** 26". **Stock:** Hardwoods or Timber HD, Black Fleck, Break-Up™. **Weight:** 8 lbs., 3 oz. **Sights:** Adj. fiber-optic. **Features:** No. 209 shotgun primer ignition, stainless steel bolt, stainless fluted bbl.
Price: Mossy Oak®, Timber, Hardwoods/stainless **$349.95**
Price: Black Fleck/stainless **$299.95**
Price: Mossy Oak®, Timber, Hardwoods/blued **$279.95**
Price: Black Fleck/blued **$229.95**

ZOUAVE PERCUSSION RIFLE
Caliber: 58, 59. **Barrel:** 32-1/2". **Weight:** 9-1/2 lbs. **Length:** 48-1/2" overall. **Stock:** Walnut finish, brass patchbox and buttplate. **Sights:** Fixed front, rear adjustable for elevation. **Features:** Color case-hardened lockplate, blued barrel. From Navy Arms, Dixie Gun Works, E.M.F., Cabela's, Euroarms of America.
Price: . . . . **$415.00 to $625.00**

Knight TK2000

AUSTIN & HALLECK MODEL 520 LR MUZZLELOADING SHOTGUN

Caliber: 12. **Barrel:** 26" w/screw-in chokes. **Weight:** 6.5 lbs. **Length:** 47-1/2" overall. **Stock:** Lightly figured maple in Classic or Monte Carlo style. **Sights:** Rib with Tru-Glo front dot. **Features:** In-line percussion action with removable weather shroud; Timney adjustable target trigger with sear block safety. Introduced 2006.
Price: Blue **$549.00**

CABELA'S BLACKPOWDER SHOTGUNS

Gauge: 10, 12, 20. **Barrel:** 10-ga., 30"; 12-ga., 28-1/2" (Extra-Full, Mod., Imp. Cyl. choke tubes); 20-ga., 27-1/2" (Imp. Cyl. & Mod. fixed chokes). **Weight:** 6-1/2 to 7 lbs. **Length:** 45" overall (28-1/2" barrel). **Stock:** American walnut with checkered grip; 12- and 20-gauge have straight stock, 10-gauge has pistol grip. **Features:** Blued barrels, engraved, color case-hardened locks and hammers, brass ramrod tip. From Cabela's.
Price: 10-gauge **$759.99**
Price: 12-gauge **$649.99**
Price: 20-gauge **$599.99**

DIXIE MAGNUM PERCUSSION SHOTGUN

Gauge: 10, 12, 20. **Barrel:** 30" (Imp. Cyl. & Mod.) in 10-gauge; 28" in 12-gauge. **Weight:** 6-1/4 lbs. **Length:** 45" overall. **Stock:** Hand-checkered walnut, 14" pull. **Features:** Double triggers; light hand engraving; case-hardened locks in 12-gauge, polished steel in 10-gauge; sling swivels. From Dixie Gun Works.
Price: 12 ga. **$685.00**
Price: 12-ga. kit **$500.00**
Price: 20-ga. **$685.00**
Price: 10-ga. **$685.00**
Price: 10-ga. kit **$500.00**
Price: Coach Gun, 12 ga. 20" bbl **$625.00**

KNIGHT TK2000 MUZZLELOADING SHOTGUN (209)

Gauge: 12. **Barrel:** 26", extra-full choke tube. **Weight:** 7 lbs., 9 oz. **Length:** 45" overall. **Stock:** Synthetic black or Advantage Timber HD; recoil pad; swivel studs. **Sights:** Fully adjustable rear, blade front with fiber-optics. **Features:** Receiver drilled and tapped for scope mount; in-line ignition; adjustable trigger; removable breech plug; double safety system; Imp. Cyl. choke tube available. Made in U.S. by Knight Rifles.
Price: . . . . **$349.95 to $399.95**

KNIGHT VERSATILE TK2002

Gauge: 12. **Stock:** Black composite, blued, Advantage Timber HD finish. Both with sling swivel studs installed. **Sights:** Adjustable metallic TruGlo fiber-optic. **Features:** Full plastic jacket ignition system, screw-on choke tubes, load without removing choke tubes, jug-choked barrel design. Improved cylinder and modified choke tubes available.
Price: . . . . **$349.95 to $399.95**

NAVY ARMS STEEL SHOT MAGNUM SHOTGUN

Gauge: 10. **Barrel:** 28" (Cyl. & Cyl.). **Weight:** 7 lbs., 9 oz. **Length:** 45-1/2" overall. **Stock:** Walnut, with cheekpiece. **Features:** Designed specifically for steel shot. Engraved, polished locks; sling swivels; blued barrels. Imported by Navy Arms.
Price: **$605.00**

NAVY ARMS T&T SHOTGUN

Gauge: 12. **Barrel:** 28" (Full & Full). **Weight:** 7-1/2 lbs. **Stock:** Walnut. **Sights:** Bead front. **Features:** Color case-hardened locks, double triggers, blued steel furniture. From Navy Arms.
Price: **$580.00**

WHITE TOMINATOR SHOTGUN

Caliber: 12. **Barrel:** 25" blue, straight, tapered stainless steel. **Weight:** NA. **Length:** NA. **Stock:** Black laminated or black wood. **Sights:** Drilled and tapped for easy scope mounting. **Features:** Interchangeable choke tubes. Custom vent rib with high visibility front bead. Double safeties. Fully adjustable custom trigger. Recoil pad and sling swivel studs. Made in U.S.A. by Split Fire Sporting Goods.
Price: **$349.95**

AIRGUNS — Handguns

ARS HUNTING MASTER AR6 AIR PISTOL
Caliber: .22 (177 +20 special order). **Barrel:** 12" rifled. **Weight:** 3 lbs. **Length:** 18.25 overall. **Power:** NA. **Grips:** Indonesian walnut with checkered grip. **Sights:** Adjustable rear, blade front. **Features:** 6 shot repeater with rotary magazine, single or double action, receiver grooved for scope, hammer block and trigger block safeties.
Price: .... **NA**

BEEMAN P1 MAGNUM AIR PISTOL
Caliber: .177, .20. **Barrel:** 8.4". **Weight:** 2.5 lbs. **Length:** 11" overall. **Power:** Top lever cocking; spring-piston. **Grips:** Checkered walnut. **Sights:** Blade front, square notch rear with click micrometer adjustments for windage and elevation. Grooved for scope mounting. **Features:** Dual power for 177 and 20 cal.: low setting gives 350-400 fps; high setting 500-600 fps. All Colt 45 auto grips fit gun. Dry-firing feature for practice. Optional wood shoulder stock. Imported by Beeman.
Price: **$430.00**

BEEMAN P3 PNEUMATIC AIR PISTOL
Caliber: .177. **Barrel:** NA. **Weight:** 1.7 lbs. **Length:** 9.6" overall. **Power:** Single-stroke pneumatic; overlever barrel cocking. **Grips:** Reinforced polymer. **Sights:** Adjustable rear, blade front. **Features:** Velocity 410 fps. Polymer frame; automatic safety; two-stage trigger; built-in muzzle brake.
Price: **$200.00**
Price: Combo **$315.00**

BEEMAN/FWB 103 AIR PISTOL
Caliber: .177. **Barrel:** 10.1", 12-groove rifling. **Weight:** 2.5 lbs. **Length:** 16.5" overall. **Power:** Single-stroke pneumatic, underlever cocking. **Grips:** Stippled walnut with adjustable palm shelf. **Sights:** Blade front, open rear adjustable for windage and elevation. Notch size adjustable for width. Interchangeable front blades. **Features:** Velocity 510 fps. Fully adjustable trigger. Cocking effort 2 lbs. Imported by Beeman.
Price: Right-hand **$1,750.00**
Price: Left-hand **$1,865.00**

BEEMAN HW70A AIR PISTOL
Caliber: .177. **Barrel:** 6-1/4", rifled. **Weight:** 38 oz. **Length:** 12-3/4" overall. **Power:** Spring, barrel cocking. **Grips:** Plastic, with thumbrest. **Sights:** Hooded post front, square notch rear adjustable for windage and elevation. Comes with scope base. **Features:** Adjustable trigger, 31-lb. cocking effort, 440 fps MV; automatic barrel safety. Imported by Beeman.
Price: **$220.00**

BEEMAN/WEBLEY TEMPEST AIR PISTOL
Caliber: .177. **Barrel:** 6-7/8". **Weight:** 32 oz. **Length:** 8.9" overall. **Power:** Spring-piston, break barrel. **Grips:** Checkered black plastic with thumbrest. **Sights:** Blade front, adjustable rear. **Features:** Velocity to 500 fps (177), 400 fps (22). Aluminum frame; black epoxy finish; manual safety. Imported from England by Beeman.
Price: **$235.00**

Beeman/Webley Hurricane Air Pistol
Similar to the Tempest except has extended frame in the rear for a click-adjustable rear sight; hooded front sight; comes with scope mount. Imported from England by Beeman.
Price: **$275.00**

BENJAMIN & SHERIDAN CO2 PISTOLS
Caliber: .177, .22, single shot. **Barrel:** 6-3/8", brass. **Weight:** 1 lb. 12 oz. **Length:** 9" overall. **Power:** 12-gram CO2 cylinder. **Grips:** American Hardwood. **Sights:** High ramp front, fully adjustable notched rear. **Features:** Velocity to 500 fps. Turnbolt action with cross-bolt safety. Gives about 40 shots per CO2 cylinder. Black or nickel finish. Made in U.S. by Crosman Corp.
Price: EB17 (.177), EB22 (.22) **$185.00**

BENJAMIN & SHERIDAN PNEUMATIC PELLET PISTOLS
Caliber: .177, .22, single shot. **Barrel:** 9-3/8", rifled brass. **Weight:** 2 lbs., 8 oz. **Length:** 12.25" overall. **Power:** Underlever pnuematic, hand pumped. **Grips:** American Hardwood. **Sights:** High ramp front, fully adjustable notch rear. **Features:** Velocity to 525 fps (variable). Bolt action with cross-

bolt safety. Choice of black or nickel finish. Made in U.S. by Crosman Corp.
Price: Black finish, HB17 (.177), HB22 (.22) **$115.00**

BRNO TAU-7 CO2 MATCH AIR PISTOL
Caliber: 177. **Barrel:** 10.25". **Weight:** 2.31 lbs. **Length:** 15.75" overall. **Power:** 12-gram CO2 cartridge. **Grips:** Stippled hardwood with adjustable palm rest. **Sights:** Blade front, open fully adjustable rear. **Features:** Comes with extra seals and counterweight. Blue finish.
Price: **$500.00**

CROSMAN AUTO AIR II RED DOT PISTOLS
Caliber: BB, 17-shot magazine; .177 pellet, single shot. **Barrel:** 8-5/8" steel, smooth-bore. **Weight:** 13 oz. **Length:** 10-3/4" overall. **Power:** CO2 Powerlet. **Grips:** NA. **Sights:** Blade front, adjustable rear; highlighted system. **Features:** Velocity to 480 fps (BBs), 430 fps (pellets). Semi-automatic action with BBs, single shot with pellets. Black. From Crosman.
Price: AAIIB **$38.00**

CROSMAN MODEL 1008 REPEAT AIR PISTOL
Caliber: .177, 8-shot pellet clip. **Barrel:** 4.25", rifled steel. **Weight:** 17 oz. **Length:** 8.625" overall. **Power:** CO2 Powerlet. **Grips:** Checkered black plastic. **Sights:** Post front, adjustable rear. **Features:** Velocity about 430 fps. Break-open barrel for easy loading; single or double semi-automatic action; two 8-shot clips included. Optional carrying case available. From Crosman.
Price: **$60.00**

CROSMAN MAGNUM AIR PISTOLS
Caliber: .177, pellets. **Barrel:** Rifled steel. **Weight:** 2 lbs. **Length:** 9.38". **Power:** CO2. **Grips:** NA. **Sights:** Blade front, rear adjustable. **Features:** Single/double action accepts sights and scopes with standard 3/8" dovetail mount. Model 3576W features 6" barrel for increased accuracy. From Crosman.
Price: 3576W **$50.00**

DAISY/POWERLINE MODEL 15XT AIR PISTOL
Caliber: 177 BB, 15-shot built-in magazine. **Barrel:** NA. **Weight:** NA. **Length:** 7.21". **Power:** CO2. **Grips:** NA. **Sights:** NA. **Features:** Velocity 425 fps. Made in the U.S.A. by Daisy Mfg. Co.
Price: **$47.99**
Price: With electronic point sight **$57.99**

DAISY MODEL 717 AIR PISTOL
Caliber: 177, single shot. **Weight:** 2.25 lbs. **Length:** 13-1/2" overall. **Grips:** Molded checkered woodgrain with contoured thumbrest. **Sights:** Blade and ramp front, open rear with windage and elevation adjustments. **Features:** Single pump pneumatic pistol. Rifled steel barrel. Crossbolt trigger block. Muzzle velocity 360 fps. From Daisy Mfg. Co.
Price: **$152.99**

DAISY MODEL 747 TRIUMPH AIR PISTOL
Caliber: .177, single shot. **Weight:** 2.35 lbs. **Length:** 13-1/2" overall. **Grips:** Molded checkered woodgrain with contoured thumbrest. **Sights:** Blade and ramp front, open rear with windage and elevation adjustments. **Features:** Single pump pneumatic pistol. Lothar Walther rifled high-grade steel barrel; crowned 12 lands and grooves, right-hand twist. Precision bore sized for match pellets. Muzzle veocity 360 fps. From Daisy Mfg. Co.
Price: **$203.99**

DAISY/POWERLINE 693 AIR PISTOL
Caliber: .177, single shot. **Weight:** 1.10 lbs. **Length:** 7.9" overall. **Grips:** Molded brown checkered. **Sights:** Blade and ramp front, fixed open rear. **Features:** Semi-automatic BB pistol with a nickel finish and smooth bore steel barrel. Muzzle veocity 400 fps. From Daisy Mfg. Co.
Price: **$66.99**

EAA/BAIKAL IZH-M46 TARGET AIR PISTOL
Caliber: .177, single shot. **Barrel:** 10". **Weight:** 2.4 lbs. **Length:** 16.8" overall. **Power:** Underlever single-stroke pneumatic. **Grips:** Adjustable wooden target. **Sights:** Micrometer fully adjustable rear, blade front. **Features:** Velocity about 440 fps. Hammer-forged, rifled barrel. Imported from Russia by European American Armory.
Price: **$349.00**

EAA MP651K

Gamo PT-80

GAMO P-23, P-23 LASER PISTOL

Caliber: .177, 12-shot. **Barrel:** 4.25". **Weight:** 1 lb. **Length:** 7.5". **Power:** CO2 cartridge, semi-automatic, 410 fps. **Grips:** Plastic. **Sights:** NA. **Features:** Walther PPK cartridge pistol copy, optional laser sight. Imported from Spain by Gamo.
Price: . . . . $89.95, (with laser) $129.95

GAMO PT-80, PT-80 LASER PISTOL

Caliber: .177, 8-shot. **Barrel:** 4.25". **Weight:** 1.2 lbs. **Length:** 7.2". **Power:** CO2 cartridge, semi-automatic, 410 fps. **Grips:** Plastic. **Sights:** 3-dot. **Features:** Optional laser sight and walnut grips available. Imported from Spain by Gamo.
Price: . . . . $108.95, (with laser) $129.95, (with walnut grip) $119.95

HAMMERLI AP-40 AIR PISTOL

Caliber: .177. **Barrel:** 10". **Weight:** 2.2 lbs. **Length:** 15.5". **Power:** NA. **Grips:** Adjustable orthopedic. **Sights:** Fully adjustable micrometer. **Features:** Sleek, light, well balanced and accurate.
Price: $1,400.00

MORINI CM 162 EL MATCH AIR PISTOLS

Caliber: .177, single shot. **Barrel:** 9.4". **Weight:** 32 oz. **Length:** 16.1" overall. **Power:** Scuba air. **Grips:** Adjustable match type. **Sights:** Interchangeable blade front, fully adjustable match-type rear. **Features:** Power mechanism shuts down when pressure drops to a preset level. Adjustable electronic trigger.
Price: $1,075.00

PARDINI K58 MATCH AIR PISTOLS

Caliber: .177, single shot. **Barrel:** 9". **Weight:** 37.7 oz. **Length:** 15.5" overall. **Power:** Precharged compressed air; single-stroke cocking. **Grips:** Adjustable match type; stippled walnut. **Sights:** Interchangeable post front, fully adjustable match rear. **Features:** Fully adjustable trigger. Short version K-2 available. Imported from Italy by Larry's Guns.
Price: $819.00

RWS 9B/9N AIR PISTOLS

Caliber: .177, single shot. **Barrel:** 8". **Weight:** 2.38 lbs. **Length:** 10.4". **Power:** 550 fps. **Grips:** Right hand with thumbrest. **Sights:** Adjustable. **Features:** Spring-piston powered; Black or nickel finish.
Price: 9B/9N $150.00

STEYR LP10P MATCH AIR PISTOL

Caliber: .177, single shot. **Barrel:** 9". **Weight:** 38.7 oz. **Length:** 15.3" overall. **Power:** Scuba air. **Grips:** Adjustable Morini match, palm shelf, stippled walnut. **Sights:** Interchangeable blade in 4mm, 4.5mm or 5mm widths, adjustable open rear, interchangeable 3.5mm or 4mm leaves. **Features:** Velocity about 500 fps. Adjustable trigger, adjustable sight radius from 12.4" to 13.2". With compensator. Recoil elimination.
Price: $1,400.00

TECH FORCE SS2 OLYMPIC COMPETITION AIR PISTOL

Caliber: .177 pellet, single shot. **Barrel:** 7.4". **Weight:** 2.8 lbs. **Length:** 16.5" overall. **Power:** Spring piston, sidelever. **Grips:** Hardwood. **Sights:** Extended adjustable rear, blade front accepts inserts. **Features:** Velocity 520 fps. Recoilless design; adjustments allow duplication of a firearm's feel. Match-grade, adjustable trigger; includes carrying case. Imported from China by Compasseco, Inc.
Price: $295.00

TECH FORCE 35 AIR PISTOL

Caliber: 177 pellet, single shot. **Weight:** 2.86 lbs. **Length:** 14.9" overall. **Power:** Spring-piston, underlever. **Grips:** Hardwood. **Sights:** Micrometer adjustable rear, blade front. **Features:** Velocity 400 fps. Grooved for scope mount; trigger safety. Imported from China by Compasseco, Inc.
Price: $39.95

TECH FORCE S2-1 AIR PISTOL

Similar to Tech Force 8 except basic grips and sights for plinking.
Price: $29.95

WALTHER LP300 MATCH PISTOL

Caliber: 177. **Barrel:** 236mm. **Weight:** 1.018g. **Length:** NA. **Power:** NA. **Grips:** NA. **Sights:** Integrated front with three different widths, adjustable rear. **Features:** Adjustable grip and trigger.
Price: $1,800.00

AIRGUNS — Long Guns

AIRFORCE CONDOR RIFLE
Caliber: .177, .22. **Barrel:** 24" rifled. **Weight:** 6.5 lbs. **Length:** 38.75" overall. **Power:** NA. **Grips:** NA. **Sights:** None, integral mount supplied. **Features:** 600-1,300 fps. 3,000 psi fill pressure. Automatic safety. Air tank volume: 490cc.
Price: Gun only (22 or 177) **$569.95**

AIRFORCE TALON AIR RIFLE
Caliber: 177, 22, single-shot. **Barrel:** 18". **Weight:** 5.5 lbs. **Length:** 32.6". **Power:** Precharged pneumatic. **Stock:** NA. **Sights:** Intended for scope use, fiber-optic open sights optional. **Features:** Lothar Walther match barrel, adjustable power levels from 400-1000 FPS, operates on high pressure air from scuba tank or hand pump. Accessories attach to multiple dovetailed mounting rails. Manufactured in the U.S.A. by AirForce Airguns.
Price: **$459.95**

AIRFORCE TALON SS AIR RIFLE
Caliber: 177, 22, single-shot. **Barrel:** 12". **Weight:** 5.25 lbs. **Length:** 32.75". **Power:** Precharged pneumatic. **Stock:** NA. **Sights:** Intended for scope use, fiber-optic open sights optional. **Features:** Lothar Walther match barrel, adjustable power levels from 400-1000 FPS. Chamber in front of barrel strips away air turbulence, protects muzzle and reduces firing report. Operates on high pressure air from scuba tank or hand pump. Accessories attach to multiple dovetailed mounting rails. Manufactured in the U.S.A. by AirForce Airguns.
Price: **$459.95**

AIRROW MODEL A-8SRB STEALTH AIR RIFLE
Caliber: 177, 22, 25, 9-shot. **Barrel:** 20"; rifled. **Weight:** 6 lbs. **Length:** 34" overall. **Power:** CO2 or compressed air; variable power. **Stock:** Telescoping CAR-15-type. **Sights:** Variable 3.5-10x scope. **Features:** Velocity 1100 fps in all calibers. Pneumatic air trigger. All aircraft aluminum and stainless steel construction. Mil-spec materials and finishes. From Swivel Machine Works, Inc.
Price: About **$2,299.00**

AIRROW MODEL A-8S1P STEALTH AIR RIFLE
Caliber: #2512 16" arrow. **Barrel:** 16". **Weight:** 4.4 lbs. **Length:** 30.1" overall. **Power:** CO2 or compressed air; variable power. **Stock:** Telescoping CAR-15-type. **Sights:** Scope rings only. 7 oz. rechargeable cylinder and valve. **Features:** Velocity to 650 fps with 260-grain arrow. Pneumatic air trigger. Broadhead guard. All aircraft aluminum and stainless steel construction. Mil-spec materials and finishes. A-8S Models perform to 2,000 PSIG above or below water levels. Waterproof case. From Swivel Machine Works, Inc.
Price: **$1,699.00**

ANSCHÜTZ 2002 MATCH AIR RIFLES
Caliber: .177, single shot. **Barrel:** 25.2". **Weight:** 10.8 lbs. **Length:** 42.5" overall. **Stock:** European walnut, blonde hardwood or colored laminated hardwood; stippled grip and forend. Also available with flat-forend walnut stock for benchrest shooting and aluminum. **Sights:** Optional sight set #6834. **Features:** Muzzle velocity 575 fps. Balance, weight match the 1907 ISU smallbore rifle. Uses #5021 match trigger. Recoil and vibration free. Fully adjustable cheekpiece and buttplate; accessory rail under forend. Available in pneumatic and compressed air versions. Imported from Germany by Gunsmithing, Inc., Accuracy International, Champion's Choice.
Price: Right-hand, blonde hardwood stock, with sights **$1,275.00**
Price: Right-hand, walnut stock **$1,275.00**
Price: Right-hand, color laminate stock **$1,300.00**
Price: Right-hand, aluminum stock, butt plate **$1,495.00**
Price: Left-hand, color laminate stock **$1,595.00**
Price: Model 2002D-RT Running Target, right-hand, no sights .. **$1,248.90**
Price: #6834 Sight Set **$227.10**

ARS HUNTING MASTER AR6 AIR RIFLE
Caliber: .22, 6-shot repeater. **Barrel:** 25-1/2". **Weight:** 7 lbs. **Length:** 41-1/4" overall. **Power:** Precompressed air from 3000 psi diving tank. **Stock:** Indonesian walnut with checkered grip; rubber buttpad. **Sights:** Blade front, adjustable peep rear. **Features:** Velocity over 1000 fps with 32-grain

pellet. Receiver grooved for scope mounting. Has 6-shot rotary magazine. Imported by Air Rifle Specialists.
Price: **$580.00**

BEEMAN KODIAK AIR RIFLE
Caliber: .25, single shot. **Barrel:** 17.6". **Weight:** 9 lbs. **Length:** 45.6" overall. **Power:** Spring-piston, barrel cocking. **Stock:** Stained hardwood. **Sights:** Blade front, open fully adjustable rear. **Features:** Velocity to 820 fps. Up to 30 foot pounds muzzle energy. Imported by Beeman.
Price: **$725.00**

BEEMAN R1 AIR RIFLE
Caliber: .177, .20 or .22, single shot. **Barrel:** 19.6", 12-groove rifling. **Weight:** 8.5 lbs. **Length:** 45.2" overall. **Power:** Spring-piston, barrel cocking. **Stock:** Walnut-stained beech; cut-checkered pistol grip; Monte Carlo comb and cheekpiece; rubber buttpad. **Sights:** Tunnel front with interchangeable inserts, open rear click-adjustable for windage and elevation. Grooved for scope mounting. **Features:** Velocity 940-1000 fps (177), 860 fps (20), 800 fps (22). Non-drying nylon piston and breech seals. Adjustable metal trigger. Milled steel safety. Right- or left-hand stock. Adjustable cheekpiece and buttplate at extra cost. Custom and Super Laser versions available. Imported by Beeman.
Price: Right-hand **$665.00**
Price: Left-hand **$720.00**

BEEMAN R7 AIR RIFLE
Caliber: .177, .20, single shot. **Barrel:** 17". **Weight:** 6.1 lbs. **Length:** 40.2" overall. **Power:** Spring-piston. **Stock:** Stained beech. **Sights:** Hooded front, fully adjustable micrometer click open rear. **Features:** Velocity to 700 fps (177), 620 fps (20). Receiver grooved for scope mounting; double-jointed cocking lever; fully adjustable trigger; checkered grip. Imported by Beeman.
Price: **$350.00**

BEEMAN R9 AIR RIFLE
Caliber: .177, .20, single shot. **Barrel:** NA. **Weight:** 7.3 lbs. **Length:** 43" overall. **Power:** Spring-piston, barrel cocking. **Stock:** Stained hardwood. **Sights:** Tunnel post front, fully adjustable open rear. **Features:** Velocity to 1000 fps (177), 800 fps (20). Adjustable Rekord trigger; automatic safety; receiver dovetailed for scope mounting. Imported from Germany by Beeman Precision Airguns.
Price: **$420.00**

BEEMAN R11 MKII AIR RIFLE
Caliber: .177, single shot. **Barrel:** 19.6". **Weight:** 8.6 lbs. **Length:** 43.5" overall. **Power:** Spring-piston, barrel cocking. **Stock:** Walnut-stained beech; adjustable buttplate and cheekpiece. **Sights:** None furnished. Has dovetail for scope mounting. **Features:** Velocity 910-940 fps. All-steel barrel sleeve. Imported by Beeman.
Price: **$650.00**

BEEMAN RX-2 GAS-SPRING MAGNUM AIR RIFLE
Caliber: .177, .20, .22, .25, single shot. **Barrel:** 19.6", 12-groove rifling. **Weight:** 8.8 lbs. **Power:** Gas-spring piston air; single stroke barrel cocking. **Stock:** Walnut-finished hardwood, hand checkered, with cheekpiece. Adjustable cheekpiece and buttplate. **Sights:** Tunnel front, click-adjustable rear. **Features:** Velocity adjustable to about 1200 fps. Imported by Beeman.
Price: .177, .20, .22 or .25 regular, right-hand **$750.00**

BEEMAN R1 CARBINE
Caliber: .177, .20, .22, .25, single shot. **Barrel:** 16.1". **Weight:** 8.6 lbs. **Length:** 41.7" overall. **Power:** Spring-piston, barrel cocking. **Stock:** Stained beech; Monte Carlo comb and checkpiece; cut checkered pistol grip; rubber buttpad. **Sights:** Tunnel front with interchangeable inserts, open adjustable rear; receiver grooved for scope mounting. **Features:** Velocity up to 1000 fps (177). Non-drying nylon piston and breech seals. Adjustable metal trigger. Machined steel receiver end cap and safety. Right- or left-hand stock. Imported by Beeman.
Price: 177, 20, 22, 25, right-hand .... **$665.00**; left-hand **$720.00**

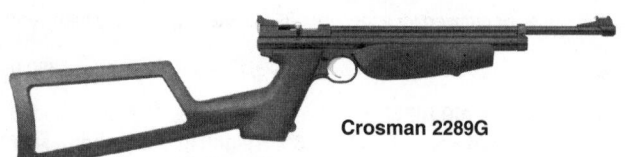

Crosman 2289G

BEEMAN/FEINWERKBAU 603 AIR RIFLE

Caliber: .177, single shot. **Barrel:** 16.6". **Weight:** 10.8 lbs. **Length:** 43" overall. **Power:** Single stroke pneumatic. **Stock:** Special laminated hardwoods and hard rubber for stability. Multi-colored stock also available. **Sights:** Tunnel front with interchangeable inserts, click micrometer match aperture rear. **Features:** Velocity to 570 fps. Recoilless action; double supported barrel; special, short rifled area frees pellet from barrel faster. Fully adjustable match trigger with separately adjustable trigger and trigger slack weight. Trigger and sights blocked when loading latch is open. Imported by Beeman.
Price: Right-hand. **$2,395.00**
Price: Left-hand **$2,495.00**
Price: Junior **$2,095.00**

BEEMAN/FEINWERKBAU P70 AND P70 JUNIOR AIR RIFLE

Caliber: .177, single shot. **Barrel:** 16.6". **Weight:** 10.6 lbs. **Length:** 42.6" overall. **Power:** Precharged pneumatic. **Stock:** Laminated hardwoods and hard rubber for stability. Multi-colored stock also available. **Sights:** Tunnel front with interchangeable inserts, click micrometer match aperture rear. **Features:** Velocity to 570 fps. Recoilless action; double supported barrel; special short rifled area frees pellet from barrel faster. Fully adjustable match trigger with separately adjustable trigger and trigger slack weight. Trigger and sights blocked when loading latch is open. Imported by Beeman.
Price: P70, precharged, right-hand **$2,825.00**
Price: P70, precharged, left-hand **$2,925.00**
Price: P70, precharged, Junior **$2,150.00**

BEEMAN/HW 97 AIR RIFLE

Caliber: .177, .20, single shot. **Barrel:** 17.75". **Weight:** 9.2 lbs. **Length:** 44.1" overall. **Power:** Spring-piston, underlever cocking. **Stock:** Walnut-stained beech; rubber buttpad. **Sights:** None. Receiver grooved for scope mounting. **Features:** Velocity 830 fps (177). Fixed barrel with fully opening, direct loading breech. Adjustable trigger. Imported by Beeman Precision Airguns.
Price: Right-hand only. **$595.00**

BENJAMIN & SHERIDAN PNEUMATIC (PUMP-UP) AIR RIFLE

Caliber: .177 or .22, single shot. **Barrel:** 19-3/8", rifled brass. **Weight:** 5-1/2 lbs. **Length:** 36-1/4" overall. **Power:** Underlever pneumatic, hand pumped. **Stock:** American walnut stock and forend. **Sights:** High ramp front, fully adjustable notched rear. **Features:** Variable velocity to 800 fps. Bolt action with ambidextrous push-pull safety. Black or nickel finish. Made in the U.S. by Benjamin Sheridan Co.
Price: **$140.95**

BRNO TAU-200 AIR RIFLES

Caliber: .177, single shot. **Barrel:** 19", rifled. **Weight:** 7-1/2 lbs. **Length:** 42" overall. **Power:** 6-oz. CO2 cartridge. **Stock:** Wood match style with adjustable comb and buttplate. **Sights:** Globe front with interchangeable inserts, fully adjustable open rear. **Features:** Adjustable trigger. Comes with extra seals, large CO2 bottle, counterweight. Imported by Pyramyd Air.
Price: **$495.00**

BSA SUPERTEN MK3 AIR RIFLE

Caliber: .177, .22 10-shot repeater. **Barrel:** 17-1/2". **Weight:** 7 lbs., 8 oz. **Length:** 37" overall. **Power:** Precharged pneumatic via buddy bottle. **Stock:** Oil-finished hardwood; Monte Carlo with cheekpiece, cut checkered grip; adjustable recoil pad. **Sights:** No sights; intended for scope use. **Features:** Velocity 1000+ fps (177), 1000+ fps (22). Patented 10-shot indexing magazine, bolt-action loading. Left-hand version also available. Imported from U.K.
Price: **$599.95**

BSA SUPERTEN MK3 BULLBARREL

Caliber: .177,. 22, .25, single shot. **Barrel:** 18-1/2". **Weight:** 8 lbs., 8 oz. **Length:** 43" overall. **Power:** Spring-air, underlever cocking. **Stock:** Oil-finished hardwood; Monte Carlo with cheekpiece, checkered at grip; recoil pad. **Sights:** Ramp front, micrometer adjustable rear. Maxi-Grip scope rail. **Features:** Velocity 950 fps (177), 750 fps (22), 600 fps (25). Patented rotating breech design. Maxi-Grip scope rail protects optics from recoil; automatic anti-beartrap plus manual safety. Imported from U.K.
Price: Rifle, MKII Carbine (14" barrel, 39-1/2" overall) **$349.95**

BSA MAGNUM SUPERSPORT™ AIR RIFLE, CARBINE

Caliber: .177, .22, .25, single shot. **Barrel:** 18-1/2". **Weight:** 6 lbs., 8 oz. **Length:** 41" overall. **Power:** Spring-air, barrel cocking. **Stock:** Oil-finished hardwood; Monte Carlo with cheekpiece, recoil pad. **Sights:** Ramp front, micrometer adjustable rear. Maxi-Grip scope rail. **Features:** Velocity 950 fps (177), 750 fps (22), 600 fps (25). Patented Maxi-Grip scope rail protects optics from recoil; automatic anti-beartrap plus manual tang safety. Muzzle brake standard. Imported for U.K.
Price: **$194.95**
Price: Carbine, 14" barrel, muzzle brake **$214.95**

BSA METEOR AIR RIFLE

Caliber: .177, .22, single shot. **Barrel:** 18-1/2". **Weight:** 6 lbs. **Length:** 41" overall. **Power:** Spring-air, barrel cocking. **Stock:** Oil-finished hardwood. **Sights:** Ramp front, micrometer adjustable rear. **Features:** Velocity 650 fps (177), 500 fps (22). Automatic anti-beartrap; manual tang safety. Receiver grooved for scope mounting. Imported from U.K.
Price: Rifle **$144.95**
Price: Carbine **$164.95**

CROSMAN MODEL POWERMASTER 664SBAIR RIFLES

Caliber: .177 (single shot pellet) or BB, 200-shot reservoir. **Barrel:** 20", rifled steel. **Weight:** 2 lbs. 15 oz. **Length:** 38-1/2" overall. **Power:** Pneumatic; hand-pumped. **Stock:** Wood-grained ABS plastic; checkered pistol grip and forend. **Sights:** Fiber-optic front, fully adjustable open rear. **Features:** Velocity about 645 fps. Bolt action, cross-bolt safety. From Crosman.
Price: **$65.00**

CROSMAN MODEL PUMPMASTER 760AIR RIFLES

Caliber: .177 pellets (single shot) or BB (200-shot reservoir). **Barrel:** 19-1/2", rifled steel. **Weight:** 2 lbs., 12 oz. **Length:** 33.5" overall. **Power:** Pneumatic, hand-pump. **Stock:** Walnut-finished ABS plastic stock and forend. **Features:** Velocity to 590 fps (BBs, 10 pumps). Short stroke, power determined by number of strokes. Fiber-optic front sight and adjustable rear sight. Cross-bolt safety. From Crosman.
Price: Model 760 . . . . **$40.00**

CROSMAN MODEL REPEATAIR 1077 RIFLES

Caliber: .177 pellets, 12-shot clip. **Barrel:** 20.3", rifled steel. **Weight:** 3 lbs., 11 oz. **Length:** 38.8" overall. **Power:** CO2 Powerlet. **Stock:** Textured synthetic or hardwood. **Sights:** Blade front, fully adjustable rear. **Features:** Velocity 590 fps. Removable 12-shot clip. True semi-automatic action. From Crosman.
Price: **$68.00**
Price: 1077W (walnut stock) **$100.00**

CROSMAN 2260 AIR RIFLE

Caliber: .22, single shot. **Barrel:** 24". **Weight:** 4 lbs., 12 oz. **Length:** 39.75" overall. **Power:** CO2 Powerlet. **Stock:** Hardwood. **Sights:** Blade front, adjustable rear open or peep. **Features:** About 600 fps. Made in U.S. by Crosman Corp.
Price: **$80.00**

CROSMAN MODEL CLASSIC 2100 AIR RIFLE

Caliber: 177 pellets (single shot), or BB (200-shot BB reservoir). **Barrel:** 21", rifled. **Weight:** 4 lbs., 13 oz. **Length:** 39-3/4" overall. **Power:** Pump-up, pneumatic. **Stock:** Wood-grained checkered ABS plastic. **Features:** Three pumps give about 450 fps, 10 pumps about 755 fps (BBs). Cross-bolt safety; concealed reservoir holds over 200 BBs. From Crosman.
Price: Model 2100B **$55.00**

AIRGUNS — Long Guns

CROSMAN MODEL 2260 AIR RIFLE
Caliber: 22, single shot. **Barrel:** 19", rifled steel. **Weight:** 4 lbs., 12 oz. **Length:** 39.75" overall. **Stock:** Full-size, American hardwood. **Features:** Variable pump power; three pumps give 395 fps, six pumps 530 fps, 10 pumps 600 fps (average). Full-size adult air rifle. From Crosman.
Price: **$80.00**

DAISY 1938 RED RYDER AIR RIFLE
Caliber: BB, 650-shot repeating action. **Barrel:** Smoothbore steel with shroud. **Weight:** 2.2 lbs. **Length:** 35.4" overall. **Stock:** Walnut stock burned with Red Ryder lariat signature. **Sights:** Post front, adjustable V-slot rear. **Features:** Walnut forend. Saddle ring with leather thong. Lever cocking. Gravity feed. Controlled velocity. From Daisy Mfg. Co.
Price: **$44.95**

DAISY MODEL 840B GRIZZLY AIR RIFLE
Caliber: .177 pellet single shot; or BB 350-shot. **Barrel:** 19", smoothbore, steel. **Weight:** 2.25 lbs. **Length:** 36.8" overall. **Power:** Single pump pneumatic. **Stock:** Molded wood-grain stock and forend. **Sights:** Ramp front, open, adjustable rear. **Features:** Muzzle velocity 320 fps (BB), 300 fps (pellet). Steel buttplate; straight pull bolt action; cross-bolt safety. Forend forms pump lever. From Daisy Mfg. Co.
Price: **$47.99**
Price: (840C in Mossy Oak Breakup Camo) **$54.99**

DAISY MODEL 105 BUCK AIR RIFLE
Caliber: .177 or BB. **Barrel:** Smoothbore steel. **Weight:** 1.6 lbs. **Length:** 29.8" overall. **Power:** Lever cocking, spring air. **Stock:** Stained solid wood. **Sights:** TruGlo fiber-optic, open fixed rear. **Features:** Velocity to 275. Cross-bolt trigger block safety. From Daisy Mfg. Co.
Price: **$35.99**

DAISY/POWERLINE TARGET PRO 953 AIR RIFLE
Caliber: .177 pellets, single shot. **Weight:** 6.40 lbs. **Length:** 39.75" overall. **Power:** Pneumatic single-pump cocking lever; straight-pull bolt. **Stock:** Full-length, match-style black composite. **Sights:** Front and rear fiber optic. **Features:** Rifled high-grade steel barrel with 1:15 twist. Max. Muzzle Velocity of 560 fps. From Daisy Mfg. Co
Price: **$89.99**

DAISY/POWERLINE 880 AIR RIFLE
Caliber: .177 pellet or BB, 50-shot BB magazine, single shot for pellets. **Barrel:** Rifled steel. **Weight:** 3.7 lbs. **Length:** 37.6" overall. **Power:** Multi-pump pneumatic. **Stock:** Molded wood grain; Monte Carlo comb. **Sights:** Hooded front, adjustable rear. **Features:** Velocity to 685 fps. (BB). Variable power (velocity, range) increase with pump strokes; resin receiver with dovetailed scope mount. Made in U.S.A. by Daisy Mfg. Co.
Price: **$60.99**

DAISY/POWERLINE 901 AIR RIFLE
Caliber: .177. **Barrel:** Rifled steel. **Weight:** 3.7 lbs. **Length:** 37.5" overall. **Power:** Multi-pump pneumatic. **Stock:** Advanced composite. **Sights:** Fiber-optic front, adjustable rear. **Features:** Velocity to 750 fps. (BB); advanced composite receiver with dovetailed mounts for optics. Made in U.S.A. by Daisy Mfg. Co.
Price: **$66.99**

EAA/BAIKAL MP-512 AIR RIFLE
Caliber: 177, single shot. **Barrel:** 17.7". **Weight:** 6.2 lbs. **Length:** 41.3" overall. **Power:** Spring-piston, single stroke. **Stock:** Black synthetic. **Sights:** Adjustable rear, hooded front. **Features:** Velocity 490 fps. Hammer-forged, rifled barrel; automatic safety; scope mount rail. Imported from Russia by European American Armory.
Price: 177 caliber. **$49.00**

EAA/BAIKAL IZH-61 AIR RIFLE
Caliber: 177 pellet, 5-shot magazine. **Barrel:** 17.8". **Weight:** 6.4 lbs. **Length:** 31" overall. **Power:** Spring-piston, side-cocking lever. **Stock:** Black plastic. **Sights:** Adjustable rear, fully hooded front. **Features:** Velocity 490 fps. Futuristic design with adjustable stock. Imported from Russia by European American Armory.
Price: **$99.00**

EAA/BAIKAL IZHMP-532 AIR RIFLE
Caliber: 177 pellet, single shot. **Barrel:** 15.8". **Weight:** 9.3 lbs. **Length:** 46.1" overall. **Power:** Single-stroke pneumatic. **Stock:** One- or two-piece competition-style stock with adjustable buttpad, pistol grip. **Sights:** Fully adjustable rear, hooded front. **Features:** Velocity 460 fps. Five-way adjustable trigger. Imported from Russia by European American Armory.
Price: **$599.00**

GAMO DELTA AIR RIFLE
Caliber: 177. **Barrel:** 15.7". **Weight:** 4.2 lbs. **Length:** 37.8". **Power:** Single-stroke pneumatic, 525 fps. **Stock:** Synthetic. **Sights:** TruGlo fiber-optic.
Price: **$89.95**

GAMO SPORTER AIR RIFLE
Caliber: 177. **Barrel:** NA. **Weight:** 5.5 lbs. **Length:** 42.5". **Power:** Single-stroke pneumatic, 760 fps. **Stock:** Wood. **Sights:** Adjustable TruGlo fiber-optic. **Features:** Intended to bridge the gap between Gamo's Young Hunter model and the adult-sized Hunter 440. Imported from Spain by Gamo.
Price: **$159.95**

GAMO HUNTER 440 AIR RIFLES
Caliber: 177, 22. **Barrel:** NA. **Weight:** 6.6 lbs. **Length:** 43.3". **Power:** Single-stroke pneumatifc, 1,000 fps (177), 750 fps (22). **Stock:** Wood. **Sights:** Adjustable TruGlo fiber-optic. **Features:** Adjustable two-stage trigger, rifled barrel, raised scope ramp on receiver. Realtree camo model available.
Price: **$229.95**
Price: Hunter 440 Combo with BSA 4x32mm scope **$259.95**

HAMMERLI AR 50 AIR RIFLE
Caliber: 177. **Barrel:** 19.8". **Weight:** 10 lbs. **Length:** 43.2" overall. **Power:** Compressed-air. **Stock:** Anatomically-shaped universal and right-hand; match style; multi-colored laminated wood. **Sights:** Interchangeable element tunnel front, adjustable Hammerli peep rear. **Features:** Vibration-free firing release; adjustable match trigger and trigger stop; stainless air tank, built-in pressure gauge. Gives 270 shots per filling. Imported from Switzerland by SIGARMS, Inc.
Price: **$1,653.00**

HAMMERLI MODEL 450 MATCH AIR RIFLE
Caliber: 177, single shot. **Barrel:** 19.5". **Weight:** 9.8 lbs. **Length:** 43.3" overall. **Power:** Pneumatic. **Stock:** Match style with stippled grip, rubber buttpad. Beech or walnut. **Sights:** Match tunnel front, Hammerli diopter rear. **Features:** Velocity about 560 fps. Removable sights; forend sling rail; adjustable trigger; adjustable comb. Imported from Switzerland by SIGARMS, Inc.
Price: Beech stock **$1,355.00**
Price: Walnut stock **$1,395.00**

RWS/DIANA MODEL 24 AIR RIFLES
Caliber: 177, 22, single shot. **Barrel:** 17", rifled. **Weight:** 6 lbs. **Length:** 42" overall. **Power:** Spring-air, barrel cocking. **Stock:** Beech. **Sights:** Hooded front, adjustable rear. **Features:** Velocity of 700 fps (177). Easy cocking effort; blue finish. Imported from Germany by Dynamit Nobel-RWS, Inc.
Price: 24, 24C **$215.00**

RWS/Diana Model 34 Air Rifles
Similar to the Model 24 except has 19" barrel, weighs 7.5 lbs. Gives velocity of 1000 fps (177), 800 fps (22). Adjustable trigger, synthetic seals. Comes with scope rail.
Price: 177 or 22 .... **$290.00**
Price: Model 34N (nickel-plated metal, black epoxy-coated wood stock) **$350.00**
Price: Model 34BC (matte black metal, black stock, 4x32 scope, mounts) **$510.00**

RWS/DIANA MODEL 36 AIR RIFLES
Caliber: 177, 22, single shot. **Barrel:** 19", rifled. **Weight:** 8 lbs. **Length:** 45" overall. **Power:** Spring-air, barrel cocking. **Stock:** Beech. **Sights:** Hooded front (interchangeable inserts available), adjustable rear. **Features:** Velocity of 1000 fps (177-cal.). Comes with scope mount; two-stage adjustable trigger. Imported from Germany by Dynamit Nobel-RWS, Inc.
Price: 36, 36C **$435.00**

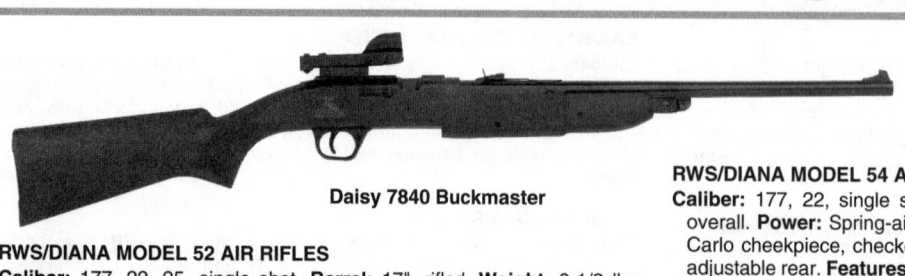

Daisy 7840 Buckmaster

RWS/DIANA MODEL 52 AIR RIFLES

Caliber: 177, 22, 25, single shot. **Barrel:** 17", rifled. **Weight:** 8-1/2 lbs. **Length:** 43" overall. **Power:** Spring-air, sidelever cocking. **Stock:** Beech, with Monte Carlo, cheekpiece, checkered grip and forend. **Sights:** Ramp front, adjustable rear. **Features:** Velocity of 1100 fps (177). Blue finish. Solid rubber buttpad. Imported from Germany by Dynamit Nobel-RWS, Inc.

Price: 177, 22 . . . . **$565.00**
Price: 25 . . . . **$605.00**
Price: Model 52 Deluxe (177) **$810.00**

RWS/DIANA MODEL 45 AIR RIFLE

Caliber: 177, single shot. **Weight:** 8 lbs. **Length:** 45" overall. **Power:** Spring-air, barrel cocking. **Stock:** Walnut-finished hardwood with rubber recoil pad. **Sights:** Globe front with interchangeable inserts, micro. click open rear with four-way blade. **Features:** Velocity of 820 fps. Dovetailed base for either micrometer peep sight or scope mounting. Automatic safety. Imported from Germany by Dynamit Nobel-RWS, Inc.

Price: **$350.00**

RWS/DIANA MODEL 46 AIR RIFLES

Caliber: 177, 22, single shot. **Barrel:** 18". **Weight:** 8.2 lbs. **Length:** 45" overall. **Stock:** Hardwood; Monte Carlo. **Sights:** Blade front, adjustable rear. **Features:** Underlever cocking spring-air (950 fps in 177, 780 fps in 22); extended scope rail, automatic safety, rubber buttpad, adjustable trigger. Imported from Germany by Dynamit Nobel-RWS, Inc.

Price: **$470.00**
Price: Model 46E (as above except matte black metal, black stock)
. . . . **$430.00**

RWS/DIANA MODEL 54 AIR RIFLE

Caliber: 177, 22, single shot. **Barrel:** 17". **Weight:** 9 lbs. **Length:** 43" overall. **Power:** Spring-air, sidelever cocking. **Stock:** Walnut with Monte Carlo cheekpiece, checkered grip and forend. **Sights:** Ramp front, fully adjustable rear. **Features:** Velocity to 1000 fps (177), 900 fps (22). Totally recoilless system; floating action absorbs recoil. Imported from Germany by Dynamit Nobel-RWS, Inc.

Price: **$785.00**

RWS/DIANA MODEL 350 MAGNUM AIR RIFLE

Caliber: 177, 22, single shot. **Barrel:** 19-1/2". **Weight:** 8 lbs. **Length:** 48". **Stock:** Beechwood; Monte Carlo. **Sights:** Hooded front, fully adjustable rear. **Features:** Break-barrel, spring-air; 1,250 fps. Imported from Germany by Dynamit Nobel-RWS, Inc.

Price: . . . . **NA**

TECH FORCE 6 AIR RIFLE

Caliber: 177 pellet, single shot. **Barrel:** 14". **Weight:** 6 lbs. **Length:** 35.5" overall. **Power:** Spring-piston, sidelever action. **Stock:** Paratrooper-style folding, full pistol grip. **Sights:** Adjustable rear, hooded front. **Features:** Velocity 800 fps. All-metal construction; grooved for scope mounting. Imported from China by Compasseco, Inc.

Price: **$69.95**

TECH FORCE 25 AIR RIFLE

Caliber: 177, 22 pellet; single shot. **Barrel:** NA. **Weight:** 7.5 lbs. **Length:** 46.2" overall. **Power:** Spring piston, break-action barrel. **Stock:** Oil-finished wood; Monte Carlo stock with recoil pad. **Sights:** Adjustable rear, hooded front with insert. **Features:** Velocity 1,000 fps (177); grooved receiver and scope stop for scope mounting; adjustable trigger; trigger safety. Imported from China by Compasseco, Inc.

Price: 177 or 22 caliber **$125.00**
Price: Includes rifle and Tech Force 96 red dot point sight **$164.95**

METALLIC CARTRIDGE PRESSES

CH4D Heavyduty Champion

Frame: Cast iron
Frame Type: O-frame
Die Thread: 7/8-14 or 1-14
Avg. Rounds Per Hour: NA
Ram Stroke: 3-1/4"
Weight: 26 lbs.
Features: 1.185" diameter ram with 16 square inches of bearing surface; ram drilled to allow passage of spent primers; solid steel handle; toggle that slightly breaks over the top dead center. Includes universal primer arm with large and small punches. From CH Tool & Die/4D Custom Die.
Price: **$261.98**

CH4D No. 444 4-Station "H" Press

Frame: Aluminum alloy
Frame Type: H-frame
Die Thread: 7/8-14
Avg. Rounds Per Hour: 200
Ram Stroke: 3-3/4"
Weight: 21 lbs.
Features: Two 7/8" solid steel shaft "H" supports; platen rides on permanently lubed bronze bushings; loads smallest pistol to largest magnum rifle cases and has strength to full-length resize. Includes four rams, large and small primer arm and primer catcher. From CH Tool & Die/4D Custom Die, Co.
Price: **$235.46**

CH4D No. 444-X Pistol Champ

Frame: Aluminum alloy
Frame Type: H-frame
Die Thread: 7/8-14
Avg. Rounds Per Hour: 200
Ram Stroke: 3-3/4"
Weight: 12 lbs.
Features: Tungsten carbide sizing die; Speed Seater seating die with tapered entrance to automatically align bullet on case mouth; automatic primer feed for large or small primers; push-button powder measure with easily changed bushings for 215 powder/load combinations; taper crimp die. Conversion kit for caliber changeover available. From CH Tool & Die/4D Custom Die, Co.
Price: . . . . **$292.00 to $316.50**

CORBIN CSP-2 Mega Mite

Frame: Steel
Frame Type: H-Frame
Die Thread: 1.5x12
Avg. Rounds Per Hour: NA
Ram Stroke: 6"
Weight: 80 lbs.
Features: Handles 50 BMG and 20mm, smaller calibers wtih standard reloading adapter kit included. Die adapters for all threads available. Side- roller handle or extra long power handle, left- or right-hand operation. Ram is bearing guided. Uses standard Corbin-H swaging, drawing and jacket-making dies. Cold-forms lead bullets up to 12 gauge. Optional floor stand available.
Price: **$750.00**

CORBIN CSP-2 Hydro Mite Hyrdraulic Drawing/Swaging Press

Frame: Steel
Frame Type: Cabinet Mtg.
Die Thread: 1.5x12
Avg. Rounds Per Hour: NA
Ram Stroke: NA
Weight: 300 lbs.
Features: Reloads standard calibers, swages bullets up to 458 caliber, draws jackets and extrudes small diameter lead wire. Optional speed and thrust control unit available. Uses Corbin-S swaging and drawing dies. Comes with T- slot ram adapter for standard shell holders. Make free 22 and 6mm jackets from fired 22 cases using optional Corbin kit.
Price: **$2,995.00**

CORBIN CSP-1 S-Press Benchrest Reloading/Swaging Tool

Frame: Steel
Frame Type: O-frame
Die Thread: 7/8-14
Avg. Rounds Per Hour: NA
Ram Stroke: 4"
Weight: 22 lbs.
Features: Handles standard calibers and swages bullets up to 458 caliber. Hand built. All moving parts run in bearings. Industrial hard-chromed ram, left- or right-hand operation. Quick stroke change doubles power for bullet swaging. Roller bearing links, expanded neoprene foam grip. Comes with reloading adapter kit for standard T-slot shell holders.
Price: **$329.00**

FORSTER Co-Ax Press B-2

Frame: Cast iron
Frame Type: Modified O-frame
Die Thread: 7/8-14
Avg. Rounds Per Hour: 120
Ram Stroke: 4"
Weight: 18 lbs.
Features: Snap in/snap out die change; spent primer catcher with drop tube threaded into carrier below shellholder; automatic, handle-activated, cammed shellholder with opposing spring-loaded jaws to contact extractor groove; floating guide rods for alignment and reduced friction; no torque on the head due to design of linkage and pivots; shellholder jaws that float with die permitting case to center in the die; right- or left-hand operation; priming device for seating to factory specifications. "S" shellholder jaws included. From Forster Products.
Price: **$336.30**
Price: Extra LS shellholder jaws **$29.00**

CH4D No. 444

CH4D 444-X Pistol Champ

Forster Co-Ax

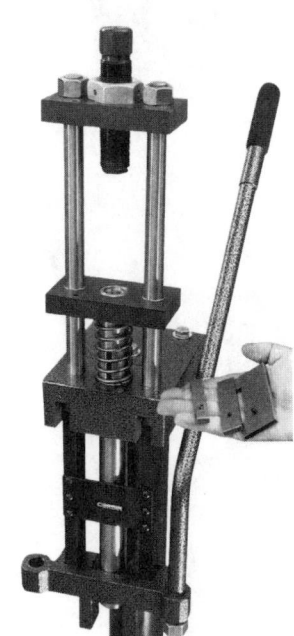

Corbin CSP-2

METALLIC CARTRIDGE PRESSES

HOLLYWOOD Senior Press

Frame: Ductile iron
Frame Type: O-frame
Die Thread: 7/8-14
Avg. Rounds Per Hour: 50-100
Ram Stroke: 6-1/2"
Weight: 50 lbs.
Features: Leverage and bearing surfaces ample for reloading cartridges or swaging bullets. Precision ground one-piece 2-1/2" pillar with base; operating handle of 3/4" steel and 15" long; 5/8" steel tie-down rod for added strength when swaging; heavy steel toggle and camming arms held by 1/2" steel pins in reamed holes. The 1-1/2" steel die bushing takes standard threaded dies; removed, it allows use of Hollywood shotshell dies. From Hollywood Engineering.
Price: $900.00

Hollywood Senior Turret

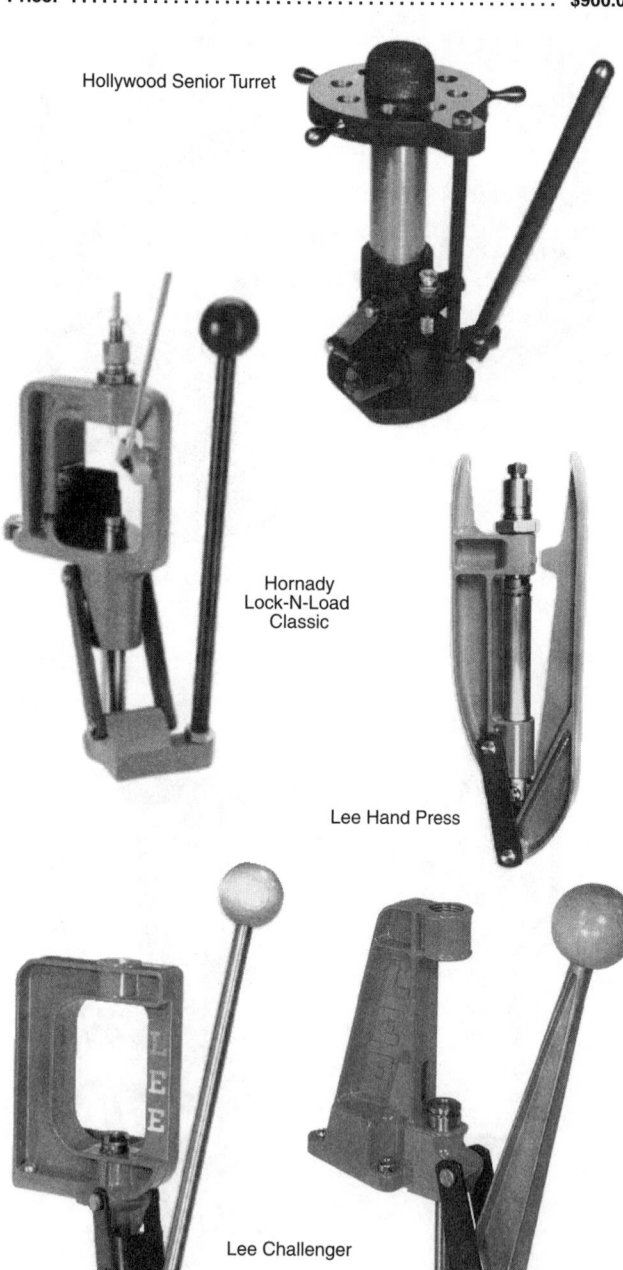

Hornady
Lock-N-Load
Classic

Lee Hand Press

Lee Challenger

Lee Reloader

HOLLYWOOD Senior Turret Press

Frame: Ductile iron
Frame Type: H-frame
Die Thread: 7/8-14
Avg. Rounds Per Hour: 50-100
Ram Stroke: 6-1/2"
Weight: 50 lbs.
Features: Same features as Senior press except has three-position turret head; holes in turret may be tapped 1-1/2" or 7/8" or four of each. Height 15". Comes complete with one turret indexing handle; one operating handle and three turret indexing handles; one 5/8" tie down bar for swaging. From Hollywood Engineering.
Price: $1,000.00

HORNADY Lock-N-Load Classic

Frame: Die cast heat-treated aluminum alloy
Frame Type: O-frame
Die Thread: 7/8-14
Avg. Rounds Per Hour: NA
Ram Stroke: 3-5/8"
Weight: 14 lbs.
Features: Features Lock-N-Load bushing system that allows instant die changeovers. Solid steel linkage arms that rotate on steel pins; 30° angled frame design for improved visibility and accessibility; primer arm automatically moves in and out of ram for primer pickup and solid seating; two primer arms for large and small primers; long offset handle for increased leverage and unobstructed reloading; lifetime warranty. Comes as a package with primer catcher, PPS automatic primer feed and three Lock-N-Load die bushings. Dies and shellholder available separately or as a kit with primer catcher, positive priming system, automatic primer feed, three die bushings and reloading accessories. From Hornady Mfg. Co.
Price: Press and Three Die Bushings $129.44
Price: Classic Reloading Kit $347.06

LEE Hand Press

Frame: ASTM 380 aluminum
Frame Type: NA
Die Thread: 7/8-14
Avg. Rounds Per Hour: 100
Ram Stroke: 3-1/4"
Weight: 1 lb., 8 oz.
Features: Small and lightweight for portability; compound linkage for handling up to 375 H&H and case forming. Dies and shellholder not included. From Lee Precision, Inc.
Price: $28.98

LEE Challenger Press

Frame: ASTM 380 aluminum
Frame Type: O-frame
Die Thread: 7/8-14
Avg. Rounds Per Hour: 100
Ram Stroke: 3-1/2"
Weight: 4 lbs., 1 oz.
Features: Larger than average opening with 30° offset for maximum hand clearance; steel connecting pins; spent primer catcher; handle adjustable for start and stop positions; handle repositions for left- or right-hand use; shortened handle travel to prevent springing the frame from alignment. Dies and shellholders not included. From Lee Precision, Inc.
Price: $49.00

LEE Classic Cast

Features: Cast iron, O-type. Adjustable handle moves from right to left, start and stop position is adjustable. Large 1-1/8" diameter hollow ram catches primers for disposal. Automatic primer arm with bottom of stroke priming. Two assembled primer arms included. From Lee Precision, Inc.
Price: $105.00

LEE Reloader Press

Frame: ASTM 380 aluminum
Frame Type: C-frame
Die Thread: 7/8-14
Avg. Rounds Per Hour: 100
Ram Stroke: 3"
Weight: 1 lb., 12 oz.
Features: Balanced lever to prevent pinching fingers; unlimited hand clearance; left- or right-hand use. Dies and shellholders not included. From Lee Precision, Inc.
Price: $28.98

LEE Turret Press

Frame: ASTM 380 aluminum
Frame Type: O-frame
Die Thread: 7/8-14
Avg. Rounds Per Hour: 300
Ram Stroke: 3"
Weight: 7 lbs., 2 oz.
Features: Replaceable turret lifts out by rotating 30°; T-primer arm reverses for large or small primers; built-in primer catcher; adjustable handle for right- or left-hand use or changing angle of down stroke; accessory mounting hole for Lee Auto-Disk powder measure. Optional Auto-Index rotates die turret to next station for semi-progressive use. Safety override prevents overstressing should turret not turn. From Lee Precision, Inc.
Price: $71.98
Price: With Auto-Index $85.98
Price: Four-Hole Turret with Auto-Index $87.98
Price: Lee Classic Turret Press 90064 (2006) $120.00
Price: Lee Classic Cast 50 Cal BMG 90859 (2006) $231.00

METALLIC CARTRIDGE PRESSES

LYMAN 310 Tool

Frame: Stainless steel
Frame Type: NA
Die Thread: .609-30
Avg. Rounds Per Hour: NA
Ram Stroke: NA
Weight: 10 oz.
Features: Compact, portable reloading tool for pistol or rifle cartridges. Adapter allows loading rimmed or rimless cases. Die set includes neck resizing/decapping die, primer seating chamber; neck expanding die; bullet seating die; and case head adapter. From Lyman Products Corp.
Price: Dies $45.00
Price: Handles $47.50
Price: Carrying pouch $9.95

LYMAN AccuPress

Frame: Die cast
Frame Type: C-frame
Die Thread: 7/8-14
Avg. Rounds Per Hour: 75
Ram Stroke: 3.4"
Weight: 4 lbs.
Features: Reversible, contoured handle for bench mount or hand-held use; for rifle or pistol; compound leverage; Delta frame design. Accepts all standard powder measures. From Lyman Products Corp.
Price: $34.95

LYMAN Crusher II

Frame: Cast iron
Frame Type: O-frame
Die Thread: 7/8-14
Avg. Rounds Per Hour: 75
Ram Stroke: 3-7/8"
Weight: 19 lbs.
Features: Reloads both pistol and rifle cartridges; 1" diameter ram; 4-1/2" press opening for loading magnum cartridges; direct torque design; right- or left-hand use. New base design with 14 square inches of flat mounting surface with three bolt holes. Comes with priming arm and primer catcher. Dies and shellholders not included. From Lyman Products Corp.
Price: $116.50

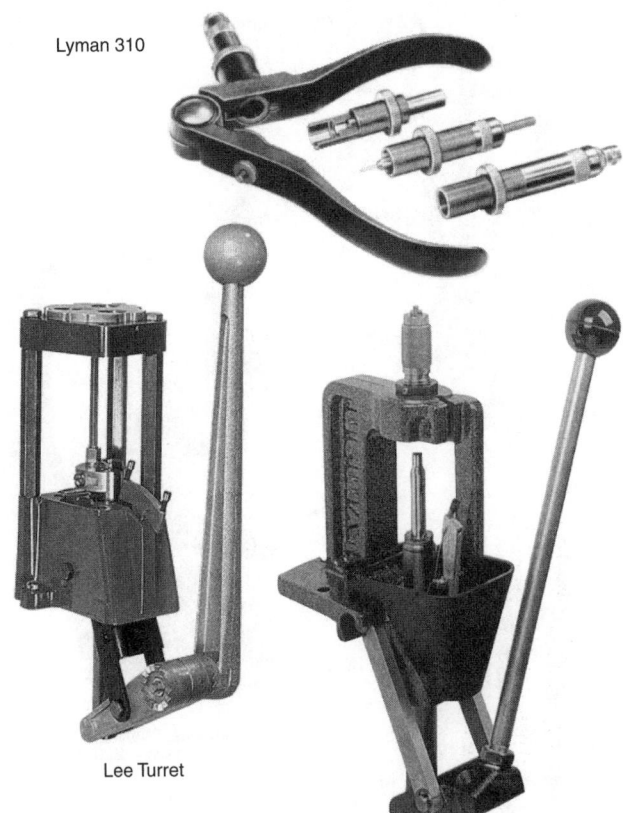

Lyman 310

Lee Turret

Lyman Crusher II

LYMAN T-Mag II

Frame: Cast iron with silver metalflake powder finish
Frame Type: Turret
Die Thread: 7/8-14
Avg. Rounds Per Hour: 125
Ram Stroke: 3-13/16"
Weight: 18 lbs.
Features: Re-engineered and upgraded with new turret system for ease of indexing and tool-free turret removal for caliber changeover; new flat machined base for bench mounting; new nickel-plated non-rust handle and links; and new silver hammertone powder coat finish for durability. Right- or left-hand operation; handles all rifle or pistol dies. Comes with priming arm and primer catcher. Dies and shellholders not included. From Lyman Products Corp.
Price: $164.95
Price: Extra turret $37.50

MEACHAM Anywhere Portable Reloading Press

Frame: Anodized 6061 T6 aircraft aluminum
Frame Type: Cylindrical
Die Thread: 7/8-14
Avg. Rounds Per Hour: NA
Ram Stroke: 2.7"
Weight: 2 lbs. (hand held); 5 lbs. (with docking kit)
Features: A lightweight portable press that can be used hand-held, or with a docking kit, can be clamped to a table top up to 9.75" thick. Docking kit includes a powder measure mount that clamps to the press body and a holder for the other die. Designed for neck sizing and bullet seating of short action cartridges, it can be used for long action cartridges with the addition of an Easy Seater straight line seating die. Dies not included.
Price: $99.95
Price: (with docking kit) $144.95
Price: Easy Seater $114.95
Price: Bushing type Neck Sizer $74.95

PONSNESS/WARREN Metal-Matic P-200

Frame: Die cast aluminum
Frame Type: Unconventional
Die Thread: 7/8-14
Avg. Rounds Per Hour: 200+
Weight: 18 lbs.
Features: Designed for straight-wall cartridges; die head with 10 tapped holes for holding dies and accessories for two calibers at one time; removable spent primer box; pivoting arm moves case from station to station. Comes with large and small primer tool. Optional accessories include primer feed, extra die head, primer speed feeder, powder measure extension and dust cover. Dies, powder measure and shellholder not included. From Ponsness/Warren.
Price: $215.00
Price: Extra die head $44.95
Price: Powder measure extension $29.95
Price: Primer feed $44.95
Price: Primer speed feed $14.50
Price: Dust cover $21.95

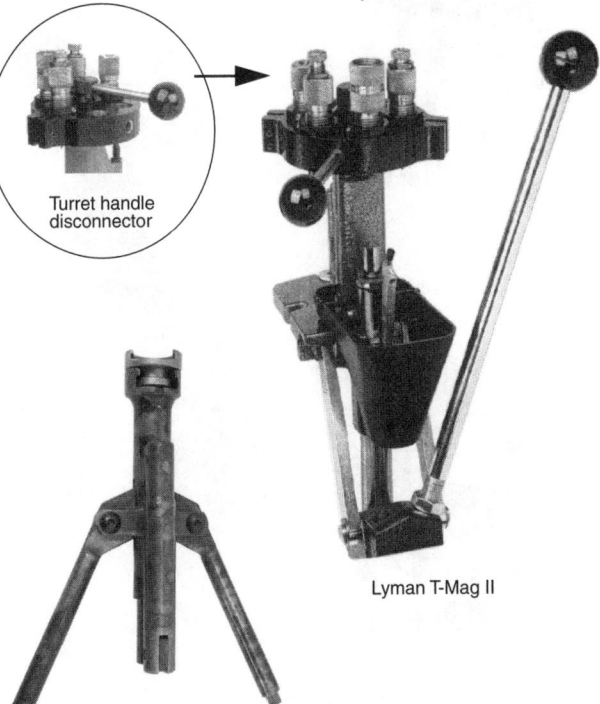

Turret handle disconnector

Lyman T-Mag II

Meacham Re-De-Capper

METALLIC CARTRIDGE PRESSES

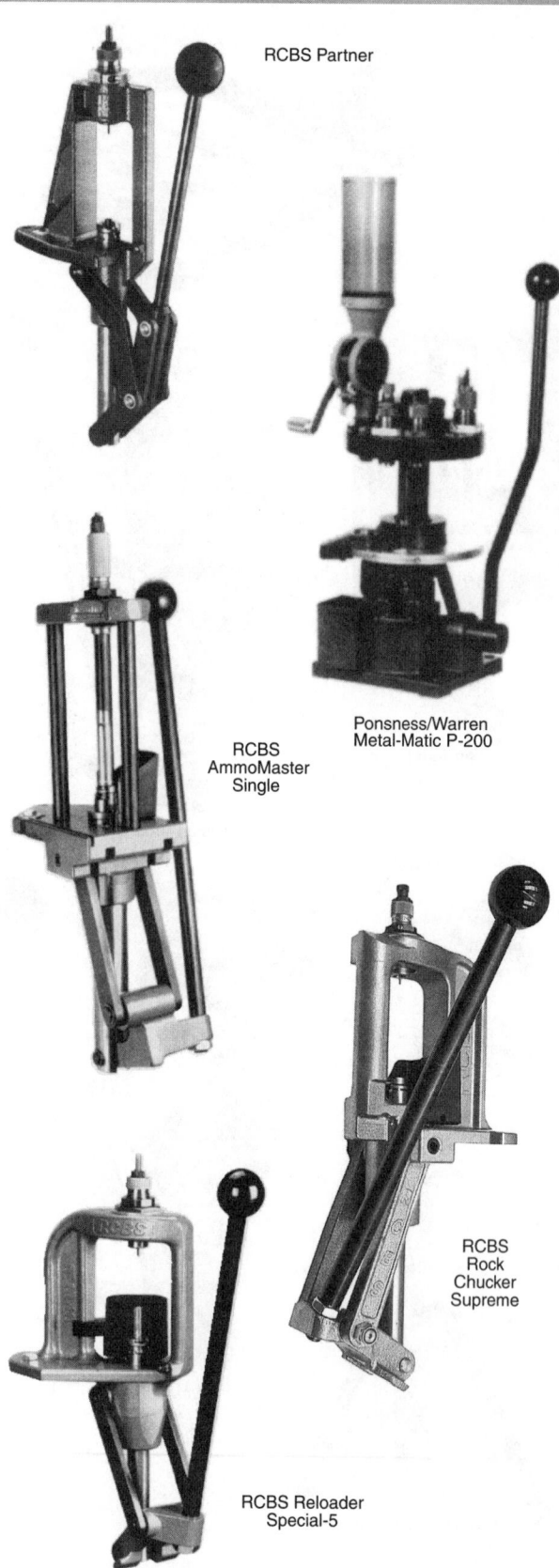

RCBS Partner

Ponsness/Warren
Metal-Matic P-200

RCBS
AmmoMaster
Single

RCBS
Rock
Chucker
Supreme

RCBS Reloader
Special-5

RCBS Partner

Frame: Aluminum   **Avg. Rounds Per Hour:** 50-60
Frame Type: O-frame   **Ram Stroke:** 3-5/8"
Die Thread: 7/8-14   **Weight:** 5 lbs.
Features: Designed for the beginning reloader. Comes with primer arm equipped with interchangeable primer plugs and sleeves for seating large and small primers. Shellholder and dies not included. Available in kit form (see Metallic Presses-Accessories). From RCBS.
Price: **$69.95**

RCBS AmmoMaster-2 Single Stage Press

Frame: Aluminum base; cast iron top plate connected by three steel posts.   **Die Thread:** 1-1/4"-12 bushing; 7/8"-14 threads
Frame Type: NA   **Avg. Rounds Per Hour:** 50-60
     Ram Stroke: 5-1/4"
     Weight: 19 lbs.
Features: Single-stage press convertible to progressive. Will form cases or swage bullets. Case detection system to disengage powder measure when no case is present in powder charging station; five-station shellplate; Uniflow Powder measure with clear powder measure adaptor to make bridged powders visible and correctable. 50-cal. conversion kit allows reloading 50 BMG. Kit includes top plate to accommodate either 1-3/8" x 12 or 1-1/2" x 12 reloading dies. Piggyback die plate for quick caliber change-overs available. Reloading dies not included. From RCBS.
Price: AmmoMaster-2 No. 88703 .... **$265.95**
Price: 50 BMG 1-1/2" die kit No. 88705 .... **$397.95**
Price: 50 BMG 1-1/2" press conversion kit No. 88709 .... **$128.95**
Price: Piggyback/AmmoMaster die plate **$23.95**
Price: Piggyback/AmmoMaster shellplate **$31.95**
Price: Dust cover **$16.95**

RCBS Reloader Special-5

Frame: Aluminum   **Avg. Rounds Per Hour:** 50-60
Frame Type: 30° offset O-frame   **Ram Stroke:** 3-1/16"
Die Thread: 1-1/4"-12 bushing; 7/8-14 threads   **Weight:** 7.5 lbs.
Features: Single-stage press convertible to progressive with RCBS Piggyback II or 3. Primes cases during resizing operation. Will accept RCBS shotshell dies. From RCBS.
Price: **$130.95**

RCBS Rock Chucker Supreme

Frame: Cast iron   **Avg. Rounds Per Hour:** 50-60
Frame Type: O-frame   **Ram Stroke:** 4.25"
Die Thread: 1-1/4"-12 bushing; 7/8-14 threads   **Weight:** 17 lbs.
Features: Redesigned to allow loading of longer cartridge cases. Made for heavy-duty reloading, case forming and bullet swaging. Provides 4" of ram-bearing surface to support 1" ram and ensure alignment; ductile iron toggle blocks; hardened steel pins. Comes standard with Universal Primer Arm and primer catcher. Can be converted from single-stage to progressive with Piggyback II conversion unit. From RCBS.
Price: **$159.95**

REDDING T-7 Turret Press

Frame: Cast iron   **Avg. Rounds Per Hour:** NA
Frame Type: Turret   **Ram Stroke:** 3.4"
Die Thread: 7/8-14   **Weight:** 23 lbs., 2 oz.
Features: Strength to reload pistol and magnum rifle, linkage pins heat-treated, precision ground and in double shear; hollow ram to collect spent primers; removable turret head for caliber changes; progressive linkage for increased power as ram nears die; rear turret support for stability and precise alignment; 7-station turret head; priming arm for both large and small primers. Also available in kit form with shellholder and one die set. From Redding Reloading Equipment.
Price: **$345.00**
Price: Kit **$393.00**

REDDING Boss

Frame: Cast iron   **Avg. Rounds Per Hour:** NA
Frame Type: O-frame   **Ram Stroke:** 3.4"
Die Thread: 7/8-14   **Weight:** 11 lbs., 8 oz.
Features: 36° frame offset for visibility and accessibility; primer arm positioned at bottom ram travel; positive ram travel stop machined to hit exactly top-dead-center. Also available in kit form with shellholder and set of Redding A dies. From Redding Reloading Equipment.
Price: **$159.00**
Price: Kit **$207.00**
**Price: Big Boss Press (heavier frame,
     longer stroke for mag. cartridges)** .... **$199.50 to $247.50**

METALLIC CARTRIDGE PRESSES

REDDING Ultramag

Frame: Cast iron
Frame Type: Non-conventional
Die Thread: 7/8-14
Avg. Rounds Per Hour: NA
Ram Stroke: 4-1/8"
Weight: 23 lbs., 6 oz.
Features: Unique compound leverage system connected to top of press for tons of ram pressure for case forming and bullet swaging; large 4-3/4" frame opening for loading oversized cartridges; hollow ram for spent primers. Kit available with shellholder and one set Redding A dies. From Redding Reloading Equipment.
Price: **$351.00**
Price: Kit **$396.00**

ROCK CRUSHER Press

Frame: Cast iron
Frame Type: O-frame
Die Thread: 2-3/4"-12 with bushing reduced to 1-1/2"-12
Avg. Rounds Per Hour: 50
Ram Stroke: 6"
Weight: 67 lbs.
Features: Designed to load and form ammunition from 50 BMG up to 23x115 Soviet. Frame opening of 8-1/2" x 3-1/2"; 1-1/2" x 12"; bushing can be removed and bushings of any size substituted; ram pressure can exceed 10,000 lbs. with normal body weight; 40mm diameter ram. Angle block for bench mounting and reduction bushing for RCBS dies available. Accessories for Rock Crusher include powder measure, dies, shellholder, bullet puller, priming tool, case gauge and others. From The Old Western Scrounger.
Price: **$795.00**
Price: Angle block **$57.95**
Price: Reduction bushing **$21.00**
Price: Shellholder **$47.25**
Price: Priming tool, 50 BMG, 20 Lahti **$65.10**

Progressive Presses

CORBIN Benchrest S-Press

Frame: All steel
Frame Type: O-Frame
Die Thread: 7/8-14 and T-slot adapter
Avg. Rounds Per Hour: NA
Ram Stroke: 4" and 2"
Weight: 22 lbs.
Features: Roller bearing linkage, removeable head, right- or left-hand mount.
Price: **$329.00**

DILLON RL 550B

Frame: Aluminum alloy
Frame Type: NA
Die Thread: 7/8-14
Avg. Rounds Per Hour: 500-600
Ram Stroke: 3-7/8"
Weight: 25 lbs.
Features: Four stations; removable tool head to hold dies in alignment and allow caliber changes without die adjustment; auto priming system that emits audible warning when primer tube is low; a 100-primer capacity magazine contained in DOM steel tube for protection; new auto powder measure system with simple mechanical connection between measure and loading platform for positive powder bar return; a separate station for crimping with star-indexing system; 220 ejected-round capacity bin; 3/4-lb. capacity powder measure. Height above bench, 35"; requires 3/4" bench overhang. Will reload 120 different rifle and pistol calibers. Comes with one caliber conversion kit. Dies not included. From Dillon Precision Products, Inc.
Price: **$349.95**

DILLON Super 1050

Frame: Ductile iron
Frame Type: Platform type
Die Thread: 7/8-14
Avg. Rounds Per Hour: 1000-1200
Ram Stroke: 2-5/16"
Weight: 62 lbs.
Features: Eight stations; auto case feed; primer pocket swager for military cartridge cases; auto indexing; removable tool head; auto prime system with 100-primer capacity; low primer supply alarm; positive powder bar return; auto powder measure; 515 ejected round bin capacity; 500-600 case feed capacity; 3/4-lb. capacity powder measure. Has lengthened frame and short-stroke crank to accommodate long calibers. Loads all pistol rounds as well as 30 M1 Carbine, 223, and 7.62x39 rifle rounds. Height above the bench, 43". Dies not included. From Dillon Precision Products, Inc.
Price: **$1,449.95**

DILLON Square Deal B

Frame: Zinc alloy
Frame Type: NA
Die Thread: None (unique Dillon design)
Avg. Rounds Per Hour: 400-500
Ram Stroke: 2-5/16"
Weight: 17 lbs.
Features: Four stations; auto indexing; removable tool head; auto prime system with 100-primer capacity; low primer supply alarm; auto powder measure; positive powder bar return; 170 ejected round capacity bin; 3/4-lb. capacity

powder measure. Height above the bench, 34". Comes complete with factory adjusted carbide die set. From Dillon Precision Products, Inc.
Price: **$289.95**

DILLON XL 650

Frame: Aluminum alloy
Frame Type: NA
Die Thread: 7/8-14
Avg. Rounds Per Hour: 800-1000
Ram Stroke: 4-9/16"
Weight: 46 lbs.
Features: Five stations; auto indexing; auto case feed; removable tool head; auto prime system with 100-primer capacity; low primer supply alarm; auto powder measure; positive powder bar return; 220 ejected round capacity bin; 3/4-lb. capacity powder measure. 500-600 case feed capacity with optional auto case feed. Loads all pistol/rifle calibers less than 3-1/2" in length. Height above the bench, 44"; 3/4" bench overhang required. From Dillon Precision Products, Inc.
Price: Less dies **$459.95**

HORNADY Lock-N-Load AP

Frame: Die cast heat-treated aluminum alloy
Frame Type: O-frame
Die Thread: 7/8-14
Avg. Rounds Per Hour: NA
Ram Stroke: 3-3/4"
Weight: 26 lbs.
Features: Features Lock-N-Load bushing system that allows instant die changeovers; five-station die platform with option of seating and crimping separately or adding taper-crimp die; auto prime with large and small primer tubes with 100-primer capacity and protective housing; brass kicker to eject loaded rounds into 80-round capacity cartridge catcher; offset operating handle for leverage and unobstructed operation; 2" diameter ram driven by heavy-duty cast linkage arms rotating on steel pins. Comes with five Lock-N- Load die bushings, shellplate, deluxe powder measure, auto powder drop, and auto primer feed and shut-off, brass kicker and primer catcher. Lifetime warranty. From Hornady Mfg. Co.
Price: **$416.38**

Redding
Turret Press

Redding
Boss

Redding
Ultramag

Dillon RL 550B

METALLIC CARTRIDGE PRESSES

LEE Load-Master

Frame: ASTM 380 aluminum
Frame Type: O-frame
Die Thread: 7/8-14

Avg. Rounds Per Hour: 600
Ram Stroke: 3-1/4"
Weight: 8 lbs., 4 oz.

Features: Available in kit form only. A 1-3/4" diameter hard chrome ram for han-dling largest magnum cases; loads rifle or pistol rounds; five station press to fac-tory crimp and post size; auto indexing with wedge lock mechanism to hold one ton; auto priming; removable turrets; four-tube case feeder with optional case collator and bullet feeder (late 1995); loaded round ejector with chute to optional loaded round catcher; quick change shellplate; primer catcher. Dies and shell-holder for one caliber included. From Lee Precision, Inc.
Price: Rifle $320.00
Price: Pistol $330.00
Price: Extra turret $14.98
Price: Adjustable charge bar $9.98

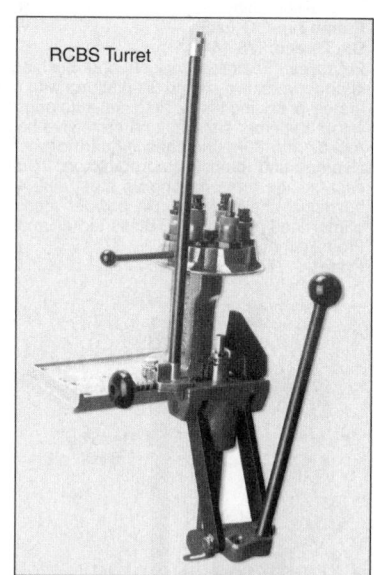

RCBS Turret

Lee Load-Master

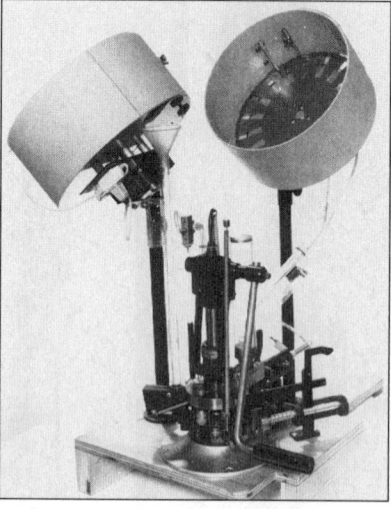

Fully-automated
Star Universal

LEE Pro 1000

Frame: ASTM 380 aluminum and steel
Frame Type: O-frame
Die Thread: 7/8-14

Avg. Rounds Per Hour: 600
Ram Stroke: 3-1/4"
Weight: 8 lbs., 7 oz.

Features: Optional transparent large/small or rifle case feeder; deluxe auto-disk case-activated powder measure; case sensor for primer feed. Comes complete with carbide die set (steel dies for rifle) for one caliber. Optional accessories include: case feeder for large/small pistol cases or rifle cases; shell plate carrier with auto prime, case ejector, auto-index and spare parts; case collator for case feeder. From Lee Precision, Inc.
Price: $201.98

PONSNESS/WARREN Metallic II

Frame: Die cast aluminum
Frame Type: H-frame
Die Thread: 7/8-14

Avg. Rounds Per Hour: 150+
Ram Stroke: NA
Weight: 32 lbs.

Features: Die head with five tapped 7/8-14 holes for dies, powder measure or other accessories; pivoting die arm moves case from station to station; depriming tube for removal of spent primers; auto primer feed; interchangeable die head. Optional accessories include additional die heads, powder measure extension tube to accommodate any standard powder measure, primer speed feeder to feed press primer tube without disassembly. Comes with small and large primer seating tools. Dies, powder measure and shellholder not included. From Ponsness/Warren.
Price: $375.00
Price: Extra die head $56.95
Price: Primer speed feeder $14.50
Price: Powder measure extension $29.95
Price: Dust cover $27.95

RCBS Pro 2000™

Frame: Cast iron
Frame Type: H-Frame
Die Thread: 7/8-14

Avg. Rounds Per Hour: 500-600
Ram Stroke: NA
Weight: NA

Features: Five-station manual indexing; full-length sizing; removable die plate; fast caliber conversion. Uses APS Priming System. From RCBS.
Price: $587.95

RCBS Turret Press

Frame: Cast iron
Frame Type: NA
Die Thread: 7/8-14

Avg. Rounds Per Hour: 50 to 200
Ram Stroke: NA
Weight: NA

Features: Six-station turret head; positive alignment; on-press priming.
Price: $231.95

STAR Universal Pistol Press

Frame: Cast iron w/aluminum base
Frame Type: Unconventional
Die Thread: 11/16-24 or 7/8-14

Avg. Rounds Per Hour: 300
Ram Stroke: NA
Weight: 27 lbs.

Features: Four or five-station press depending on need to taper crimp; handles all popular handgun calibers from 32 Long to 45 Colt. Comes completely assembled and adjusted with carbide dies (except 30 Carbine) and shellholder to load one caliber. Prices slightly higher for 9mm and 30 Carbine. From Star Machine Works.
Price: With taper crimp $1,055.00
Price: Without taper crimp $1,025.00
Price: Extra tool head, taper crimp $425.00
Price: Extra tool head, w/o taper crimp $395.00

DILLON SL 900

Press Type: Progressive
Avg. Rounds Per Hour: 700-900
Weight: 51 lbs.
Features: 12-ga. only; factory adjusted to load AA hulls; extra large 25-pound capacity shot hopper; fully-adjustable case-activated shot system; hardened steel starter crimp die; dual-action final crimp and taper die; tilt-out wad guide; auto prime; auto index; strong mount machine stand. From Dillon Precision Products.
Price: **$844.90**

HOLLYWOOD Automatic Shotshell Press

Press Type: Progressive
Avg. Rounds Per Hour: 1,800
Weight: 100 lbs.
Features: Ductile iron frame; fully automated press with shell pickup and ejector; comes completely set up for one gauge; one starter crimp; one finish crimp; wad guide for plastic wads; decap and powder dispenser unit; one wrench for inside die lock screw; one medium and one large spanner wrench for spanner nuts; one shellholder; powder and shot measures. Available for 10, 12, 20, 28 or 410. From Hollywood Engineering.
Price: **$5,000.00**

HOLLYWOOD Senior Turret Press

Press Type: Turret
Avg. Rounds Per Hour: 200
Weight: 50 lbs.
Features: Multi-stage press constructed of ductile iron comes completely equipped to reload one gauge; one starter crimp; one finish crimp; wad guide for plastic wads; decap and powder dispenser unit; one wrench for inside die lock screw; one medium and one large spanner wrench for spanner nuts; one shellholder; powder and shot measures. Available for 10, 12, 16, 20, 28 or 410. From Hollywood Engineering.
Price: Press only **$1,000.00**
Price: Dies **$200.00**

HORNADY 366 Auto

Press Type: Progressive
Avg. Rounds Per Hour: NA
Weight: 25 lbs.
Features: Heavy-duty die cast and machined steel body and components; auto primer feed system; large capacity shot and powder tubes; adjustable for right- or left-hand use; automatic charge bar with shutoff; swing-out wad guide; primer catcher at base of press; interchangeable shot and powder bushings; life-time warranty. Available for 12, 20, 28 2-3/4" and 410 2-1/2". From Hornady Mfg. Co.
Price: **$575.05**
Price: Die set, 12, 20, 28 . . . . **$202.77**
Price: Magnum conversion dies, 12, 20 . . . . **$43.25**

LEE Load-All II

Press Type: Single stage
Avg. Rounds Per Hour: 100
Weight: 3 lbs. 3 oz.
Features: Loads steel or lead shot; built-in primer catcher at base with door in front for emptying; recesses at each station for shell positioning; optional primer feed. Comes with safety charge bar with 24 shot and powder bushings. Available for 12-, 16- or 20-gauge. From Lee Precision, Inc.
Price: **$52.98**

MEC 600 Jr. Mark V

Press Type: Single stage
Avg. Rounds Per Hour: 150
Weight: 16 lbs.
Features: Spindex crimp starter for shell alignment during crimping; a cam-action crimp die; Pro-Check to keep charge bar properly positioned; adjustable for three shells. Available in 10, 12, 16, 20, 28 gauges and 410 bore. Die set not included. From Mayville Engineering Company, Inc.
Price: **$120.32**
Price: Die set **$67.27**

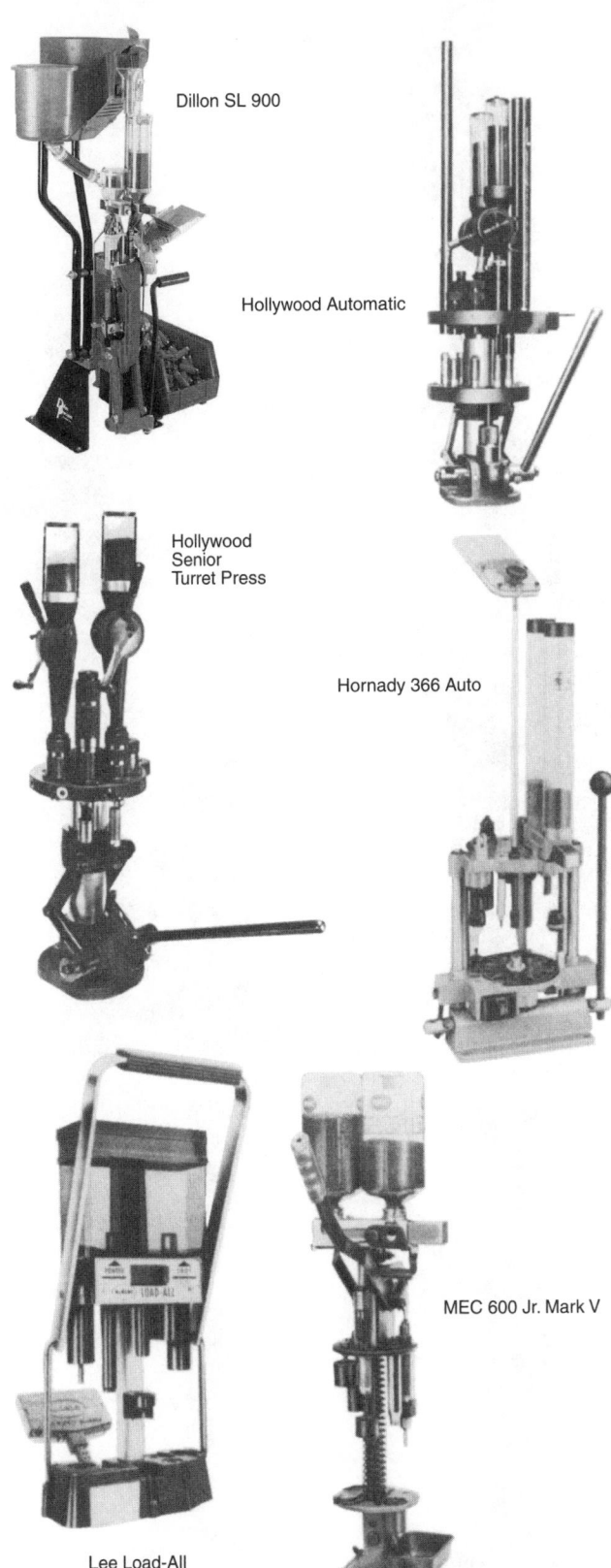

Dillon SL 900

Hollywood Automatic

Hollywood Senior Turret Press

Hornady 366 Auto

MEC 600 Jr. Mark V

Lee Load-All

SHOTSHELL RELOADING PRESSES

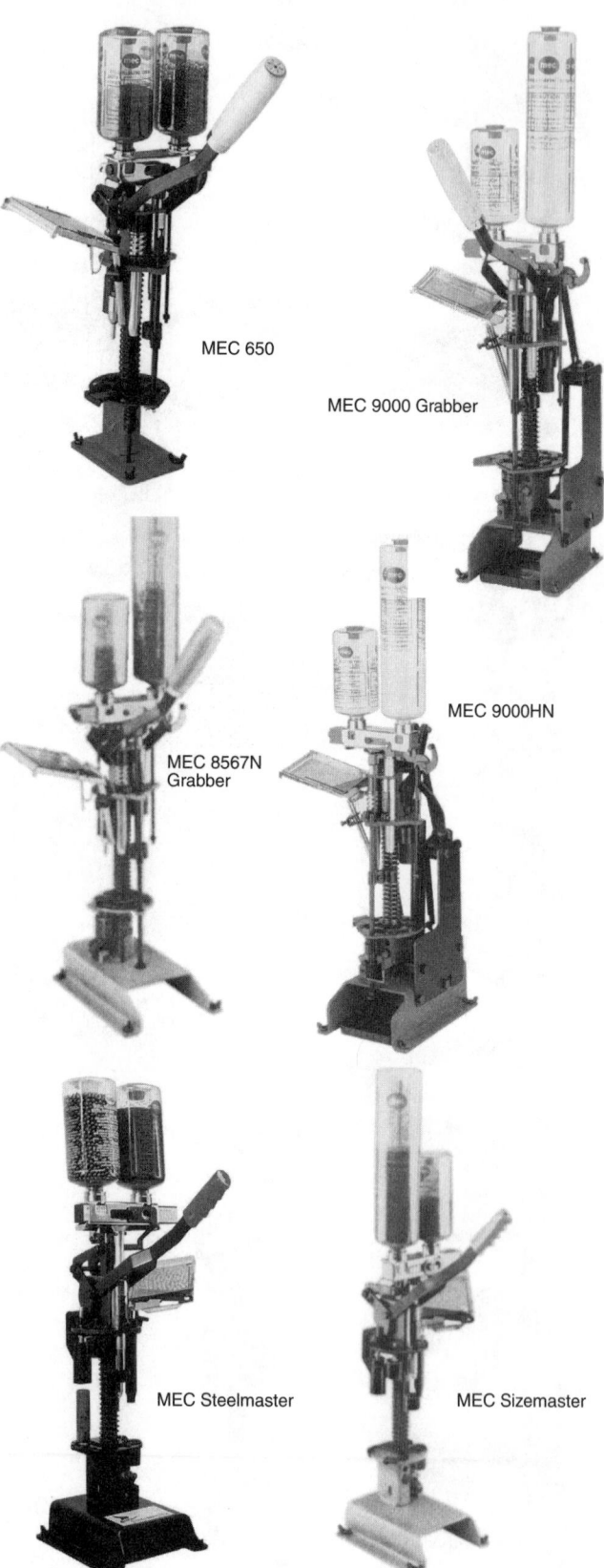

MEC 650

MEC 9000 Grabber

MEC 8567N Grabber

MEC 9000HN

MEC Steelmaster

MEC Sizemaster

MEC 650N

Press Type: Progressive
Avg. Rounds Per Hour: 400
Weight: 19 lbs.
Features: Six-station press; does not resize except as separate operation; auto primer feed standard; three crimping stations for starting, closing and tapering crimp. Die sets not available. Available in 12, 16, 20, 28 and 410. From Mayville Engineering Company, Inc.
Price: **$240.00**

MEC 8567N Grabber

Press Type: Progressive
Avg. Rounds Per Hour: 400
Weight: 22 lbs.
Features: Six-station press; auto primer feed; auto-cycle charging; three-stage crimp; power ring resizer returns base to factory specs; resizes high and low base shells; optional kits to reload three shells and steel shot. Available in 12, 16, 20, 28 gauge and 410 bore. From Mayville Engineering Company, Inc.
Price: **$338.00**
Price: 3" kit, 12-ga. **$79.32**
Price: 3" kit, 20-ga. **$45.32**
Price: Steel shot kit **$39.65**

MEC 9000GN

Press Type: Progressive
Avg. Rounds Per Hour: 400
Weight: 27 lbs.
Features: All same features as the MEC Grabber but with auto-indexing and auto-eject. Finished shells automatically ejected from shell carrier to drop chute for boxing. Available in 12, 16, 20, 28 and 410. From Mayville Engineering Company, Inc.
Price: **$407.00**

MEC 9000HN

Press Type: Progressive
Avg. Rounds Per Hour: 400
Weight: 31 lbs.
Features: Same features as 9000GN with addition of foot pedal-operated hydraulic system for complete automation. Operates on standard 110V household current. Comes with bushing-type charge bar and three bushings. Available in 12, 16, 20, 28 gauge and 410 bore. From Mayville Engineering Company, Inc.
Price: **$958.00**

MEC 8120 Sizemaster

Press Type: Single stage
Avg. Rounds Per Hour: 150
Weight: 20 lbs.
Features: Power ring eight-fingered collet resizer returns base to factory specs; handles brass or steel, high or low base heads; auto primer feed; adjustable for three shells. Available in 10, 12, 16, 20, 28 gauges and 410 bore. From Mayville Engineering Company, Inc.
Price: **$182.18**
Price: Die set, 12, 16, 20, 28, 410 . . . . **$100.47**
Price: Die set, 10-ga. **$117.92**

MEC Steelmaster

Press Type: Single stage
Avg. Rounds Per Hour: 150
Weight: 20 lbs.
Features: Same features as Sizemaster except can load steel shot. Press is available for 3-1/2" 10-ga. and 12-ga. 2-3/4", 3" or 3-1/2". For loading lead shot, die sets available in 10, 12, 16, 20, 28 and 410. From Mayville Engineering Company, Inc.
Price: **$196.79**
Price: 12 ga. 3-1/2" **$220.41**

SHOTSHELL RELOADING PRESSES

PONSNESS/WARREN Du-O-Matic 375C

Press Type: Progressive
Avg. Rounds Per Hour: NA
Weight: 31 lbs.
Features: Steel or lead shot reloader; large shot and powder reservoirs; bushing access plug for dropping in shot buffer or buckshot; positive lock charging ring to prevent accidental flow of powder; double-post construction for greater leverage; removable spent primer box; spring-loaded ball check for centering size die at each station; tip-out wad guide; two-gauge capacity tool head. Available in 10 (extra charge), 12, 16, 20, 28 and 410 with case lengths of 2-1/2", 2-3/4", 3" and 3-1/2". From Ponsness/ Warren.
Price: 12-, 20-, and 28-ga., 2-3/4" and 410, 2-1/2" **$289.00**
Price: 12-ga. 3-1/2"; 3" 12, 20, 410 . . . . **$305.00**
Price: 12, 20 2-3/4" **$383.95**
Price: 10-ga. press **$315.00**

PONSNESS/WARREN Hydro-Multispeed

Hydraulic system developed for Ponsness/Warren L/S-1000. Usable for the 950, 900 and 800 series presses. Three reloading speed settings operated with variable foot pedal control. Features stop/reverse at any station; automatic shutdown with pedal control release; fully adjustable hydraulic cylinder rod to prevent racking or bending of machine; quick disconnect hoses for ease of installation. Preassembled with step-by-step instructions. From Ponsness/Warren.
Price: **$879.00**
Price: Cylinder kit **$399.95**

PONSNESS/WARREN L/S-1000

Frame: Die cast aluminum
Avg. Rounds Per Hour: NA
Weight: 55 lbs.
Features: Fully progressive press to reload steel, bismuth or lead shot. Equipped with new Uni-Drop shot measuring and dispensing system which allows the use of all makes of shot in any size. Shells automatically resized and deprimed with new Auto-Size and De-Primer system. Loaded rounds drop out of shellholders when completed. Each shell pre-crimped and final crimped with Tru- Crimp system. Available in 10-gauge 3-1/2" or 12-gauge 2-3/4" and 3". 12-gauge 3-1/2" conversion kit also available. 20-gauge 2-3/4" and 3" special order only. From Ponsness/Warren.
Price: 12 ga. **$849.00**
Price: 10 ga. **$895.00**
Price: Conversion kit **$199.00**

PONSNESS/WARREN Size-O-Matic 900 Elite

Press Type: Progressive
Avg. Rounds Per Hour: 500-800
Weight: 49 lbs.
Features: Progressive eight-station press; frame of die-cast aluminum; center post design index system ensures positive indexing; timing factory set, drilled and pinned. Automatic features include index, deprime, reprime, powder and shot drop, crimp start, tapered final crimp, finished shell ejection. Available in 12, 20, 28 and 410. 16-ga. special order. Kit includes new shellholders, seating port, resize/primer knockout assembly, new crimp assembly. From Ponsness/Warren.
Price: **$749.00**
Price: Conversion tooling, 12, 20, 28, 410 . . . . **$189.00**

PONSNESS/WARREN Platinum 2000

Press Type: Progressive
Avg. Rounds Per Hour: 500-800
Weight: 52 lbs.
Features: Progressive eight-station press, similar to 900 and 950 except has die removal system that allows removal of any die component during reloading cycle. Comes standard with 25-lb. shot tube, 19" powder tube, brass adjustable priming feed allows adjustment of primer seating depth. From Ponsness/Warren.
Price: **$889.00**

RCBS The Grand

Press Type: Progressive
Avg. Rounds Per Hour: NA
Weight: NA
Features: Constructed from a high-grade aluminum casting, allows complete resizing of high and low base hulls. Available for 12 and 20 gauge.
Price: **$812.95**

Ponsness/Warren
Du-O-Matic 375C

Ponsness/Warren
Hydro-Multispeed

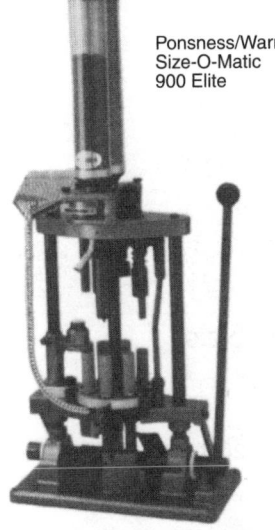

Ponsness/Warren
Size-O-Matic
900 Elite

Ponsness/Warren
Platinum 2000

RCBS The Grand

Maker and Model	Magn.	Field at 100 Yds. (feet)	Eye Relief (in.)	Length (in.)	Tube Dia. (in.)	W & E Adjustments	Weight (ozs.)	Price	Other Data
ADCO									
Magnum 50 mm[5]	0			4.1	45mm	Int.	6.8	$269.00	[1]Multi-Color Dot system changes from red to green. [2]For airguns, paint ball, rimfires. Uses common lithium water battery. [3]Comes with standard dovetail mount. [4].75" dovetail mount; poly body; adj. intensity diode. [5]10 MOA dot; black or nickel. [6]Square format; with mount battery. From ADCO Sales.
MIRAGE Ranger 1"	0			5.2	1	Int.	3.9	159.00	
MIRAGE Ranger 30mm	0			5.5	30mm	Int.	5	159.00	
MIRAGE Competitor	0			5.5	30mm	Int.	5.5	229.00	
IMP Sight[2]	0			4.5		Int.	1.3	17.95	
Square Shooter 2[3]	0			5		Int.	5	99.00	
MIRAGE Eclipse[1]	0			5.5	30mm	Int.	5.5	229.00	
Champ Red Dot	0			4.5		Int.	2	33.95	
Vantage 1"	0			3.9	1	Int.	3.9	129.00	
Vantage 30mm	0			4.2	30mm	Int.	4.9	159.00	
Vision 2000[6]	0	60		4.7		Int.	6.2	79.00	
e-dot ESB[1]	0			4.12	1	Int.	3.7	139.00	
e-dot E1B	0			4.12	1	Int.	3.7	99.00	
e-dot ECB	0			3.8	30mm	Int.	6.4	99.00	
e-dot E30B	0			4.3	30mm	Int.	4.6	99.00	
AIMPOINT									
Comp M2	0			5.1	30mm	Int.	7.8	471.00	Illuminates red dot in field of view. Noparallax (dot does not need to be centered). Unlimited field of view and eye relief. On/off, adj. intensity. Comp M2 Series: Standard CQB sight for Special Forces. CET tachnology. Rings–SRP-L and QRP fit Picatinny rails. QRW fits Weaver mount. QR = Quick Release. Comp M3 Series: Compact for bows, pistols. Black matte and silver metallic finishes (SM). Rings– SRW-L, SRP-M, SRW-M. 9000 Series: Matte black and camo finishes. ACET technology. 30mm rings fit on Weaver rail, No 11286. [1]Comes with 30mm rings, battery, lense cloth. [2] Requires 1" rings. Black finish. AP Comp avail. in black, blue, SS, camo.
Comp ML2	0			5.1	30mm	Int.	7.8	422.00	
Comp ML2 2X	2			6.5	30mm	Int.	10.3	551.00	
Comp M3	0			5.1	30mm	Int.	7.8	535.00	
Comp ML3	0			5.1	30mm	Int.	7.8	480.00	
9000L	0			7.9	30mm	Int.	8.1	370.00	
9000L 2X	2			9.3	30mm	Int.	8.1	470.00	
9000SC	0			6.3	30mm	Int.	7.4	370.00	
9000SC Camo	0			6.3	30mm	Int.	7	390.00	
9000SC 2X	2			7.7	30mm	Int.	9.9	470.00	
Comp C3	0			4.9	30mm	Int.	7.1	399.00	
Comp C3 2X	2			6.1	30mm	Int.	9.5	507.00	
Comp SM	0			4.9	30mm	Int.	7.1	372.00	
Comp M[2]	0			5	30mm	Int.	6.1	409.00	
	0			6	30mm	Int.	6	297.00	
Series 3000 Universal[2]	0			6.25	1	Int.	6	232.00	
Series 5000/2x[1]	2			7	30mm	Int.	9	388.00	
APEX									
Model 4030		3-9x		40/14	42mm	Int.		250.00	
Model 4035		3.5-10x		28/10	50mm	Int.		285.00	
Model 4040		4-16x		23.6/6.2	50mm	Int.		300.00	
Model 4045		6-24x		15/4	50mm	Int.		310.00	
ARMSON O.E.G.									
Standard	0			5.125	1	Int.	4.3	202.00	Shown red dot aiming point. No batteries needed. Standard model fits 1" ring mounts (not incl.). Other O.E.G. models for shotguns and rifles can be special ordered. [1]Daylight Only Sight with .375" dovetail mount for 22s. Does not contain tritium. From Trijicon, Inc.
22 DOS[1]	0			3.75		Int.	3	127.00	
22 Day/Night	0			3.75		Int.	3	169.00	
M16/AR-15	0			5.125		Int.	5.5	226.00	
ARTEMIS 2000									
4x32	4	34.4	3.15	10.7	1	Int.	17.5	215.00	Click-stop windage and elevation adjustments; constantly centered reticle; rubber eyepiece ring; nitrogen filled. Imported from the Czech Republic by CZ-USA.
6x42	6	23	3.15	13.7	1	Int.	17.5	317.00	
7x50	7	18.7	3.15	13.9	1	Int.	17.5	329.00	
1.5-6x42	1.5-6	40-12.8	2.95	12.4	30mm	Int.	19.4	522.00	
2-8x42	2-8	31-9.5	2.95	13.1	30mm	Int.	21.1	525.00	
3-9x42	3-9	24.6-8.5	2.95	12.4	30mm	Int.	19.4	466.00	
3-12x50	3-12	20.6-6.2	2.95	14	30mm	Int.	22.9	574.00	
BEC									
EuroLux									
EL2510x56	2.5-10	39.4-11.5	3.25-2	15.1	30mm	Int.	25.4	249.90	Black matte finish. Multi-coated lenses; 1/4-MOA click adjustments (1/2- MOA on EL4x25, AR4x22WA); fog and water-proof. [1]For AR-15; bullet drop compensator; q.d. mount. [2]Rubber armored. Imported by BEC Inc. Partial listing shown. Contact BEC for complete details. [3]All Goldlabel scopes feature lighted reticles and finger-adjustable windage and elevation adjustments. [4]Bullet-drop compensator system for Mini-14 and AR-15 rifles.
EL39x42	3-9	34.1-13.2	3.5-3	12.3	30mm	Int.	17.7	99.80	
EL28x36	2-8	44.9-11.5	3.8-3	12.2	30mm	Int.	15.9	149.50	
ELA39x40RB[2]	3-9	39-13	3	12.7	30mm	Int.	14.3	95.95	
EL6x42	6	21	3	12.6	30mm	Int.	14.8	69.00	
EL4x42	4	29	3	12.6	30mm	Int.	14.8	59.60	
EL4x36	4	29	3	12	30mm	Int.	14	49.90	
EL4x25	4	26	3	7	30mm	Int.	7.6	37.00	
AR4x22WA[1]	4	24	3	7	34mm	Int.	13.6	109.97	
Goldlabel[3]									
GLI 624x50	6-24	16-4	3.5-3	15.3	1	Int.	22.5	139.00	
GLI 416x50	4-16	25-6	3.5-3	13.5	1	Int.	21.8	135.00	
GLI 39x40R[2]	3-9	39-13	3.5-3	12.7	28mm	Int.	18.5	99.00	
GLC 5x42BD[4]	5	24	3.5	8.7	1	Int.	16.5	79.00	
BEEMAN									
Rifle Scopes									
5045[1]	4-12	26.9-9	3	13.2	1	Int.	15	275.00	All scopes have 5 point reticle, all glass fully-coated lenses. [1]Parallel adjustable. [2]Reticle lighted by ambient light. [3]Available with lighted Electro-Dot reticle. Imported by Beeman.
5046[1]	6-24	18-4.5	3	16.9	1	Int.	20.2	395.00	
5050[1]	4	26	3.5	11.7	1	Int.	11	80.00	
5055[1]	3-9	38-13	3.5	10.75	1	Int.	11.2	90.00	
5060[1]	4-12	30-10	3	12.5	1	Int.	16.2	210.00	
5065[1]	6-18	17-6	3	14.7	1	Int.	17.3	265.00	
5066RL[2]	2-7	58-15	3	11.4	1	Int.	17	380.00	
5047L[2]	4	25	3.5	7	1	Int.	13.7	NA	

Maker and Model	Magn.	Field at 100 Yds. (feet)	Eye Relief (in.)	Length (in.)	Tube Dia. (in.)	W & E Adjustments	Weight (ozs.)	Price	Other Data
BEEMAN *(cont.)*									
Pistol Scopes									
5021	2	19	10-24	9.1	1	Int.	7.4	85.50	
5020	1.5	14	11-16	8.3	.75	Int.	3.6	NA	
BROWNING									
882732M	2-7	42.5-12.1	3.7	11.6	1	Int.	11.7	335.95	
883940M	3-9	32-11	3.4	12.4	1	Int.	13.1	351.95	
883950M	3-9	30-10	3.4	15.7	1	Int.	18.9	419.95	
88412M	4-12	26.8-8.8	3.4	13.4	1	Int.	18.3	449.95	
885154M	5-15	20.9-7	3.4	14.4	1	Int.	19.1	489.95	
888244M	8-24	12-4	3.4	14.2	1	Int.	19.6	589.95	
BSA									
Catseye[1]									[1]Waterproof, fogproof; multi-coated lenses; finger-adjustable knobs.
CE1545x32	1.5-4.5	78-23	4	11.25	1	Int.	12	91.95	[2]Waterproof, fogproof; matte black finish. [3]With 4" sunshade; target
CE310x44	3-10	39-12	3.25	12.75	1	Int.	16	151.95	knobs; 1/8-MOA click adjustments. [4]Adjustable for parallax; with sun
CE3510x50	3.5-10	30-10.5	3.25	13.25	1	Int.	17.25	171.95	shades; target knobs, 1/8-MOA adjustments. Imported by BSA.
CE416x50	4-16	25-6	3	15.25	1	Int.	22	191.95	[5]Illuminated reticle model; also available in 3-10x, 3.5-10x, and 3-9x.
CE624x50	6-24	16-3	3	16	1	Int.	23	222.95	[6]Red dot sights also available in 42mm and 50mm versions. [7]Includes
CE1545x32IR	1.5-4.5	78-23	5	11.25	1	Int.	12	121.95	Universal Bow Mount. [8]Five other models offered. From BSA.
Deer Hunter[2]									
DH25x20	2.5	72	6	7.5	1	Int.	7.5	59.95	
DH4x32	4	32	3	12	1	Int.	12.5	49.95	
DH39x32	3-9	39-13	3	12	1	Int.	11	69.95	
DH39x40	3-9	39-13	3	13	1	Int.	12.1	89.95	
DH39x50	3-9	41-15	3	12.75	1	Int.	13	109.95	
DH2510x44	2.5-10	42-12	3	13	1	Int.	12.5	99.95	
DH1545x32	1.5-4.5	78-23	5	11.25	1	Int.	12	79.95	
Contender[3]									
CT24x40TS	24	6	3	15	1	Int.	18	129.95	
CT36x40TS	36	3	3	15.25	1	Int.	19	139.95	
CT312x40TS	3-12	28-7	3	13	1	Int.	17.5	129.95	
CT416x40TS	4-16	21-5	3	13.5	1	Int.	18	131.95	
CT624x40TS	6-24	16-4	3	15.5	1	Int.	20	149.95	
CT832x40TS	8-32	11-3	3	15.5	1	Int.	20	171.95	
CT312x50TS	3-12	28-7	3	13.75	1	Int.	21	131.95	
CT416x50TS	4-16	21-5	3	15.25	1	Int.	22	151.95	
CT624x50TS	6-24	16-4	3	16	1	Int.	23	171.95	
CT832x50TS	8-32	11-3	3	16.5	1	Int.	24	191.95	
Pistol									
P52x20	2	NA	NA	NA	NA	Int.	NA	89.95	
Platinum[4]									
PT24x44TS	24	4.5	3	16.25	1	Int.	17.9	189.55	
PT36x44TS	36	3	3	14.9	1	Int.	17.9	199.95	
PT624x44TS	6-24	15-4.5	3	15.25	1	Int.	18.5	221.95	
PT832x44TS	8-32	11-3.5	3	17.25	1	Int.	19.5	229.95	
.22 Special									
S39x32WR	3-9	37.7-14.1	3	12	1	Int.	12.3	89.95	
S4x32WR	4	26	3	10.75	1	Int.	9	39.95-44.95	
Air Rifle									
AR4x32	4	33	3	13	1	Int.	14	69.95	
AR27x32	2-7	48	3	12.25	1	Int.	14	79.95	
AR312x44	3-12	36	3	12.25	1	Int.	15	109.95	
Red Dot									
RD30[6]	0			3.8	30mm	Int.	5	59.95	
PB30[6]	0			3.8	30mm	Int.	4.5	79.95	
Bow30[7]	0			NA	30mm	Int.	5	89.95	
Big Cat									
BIgCat[8]	3.5-10	30-11	5	9.7	1	Int.	16.8	219.95	
BURRIS									
Mr. T Black Diamond Titanium									Available in Carbon Black, Titanium Gray and Autumn Gold finishes.
2.5-10x50A	2.5-10	4.25-4.75		13.6			29	1,518.00	**Black Diamond & Fullfield:** All scopes avail. with Plex reticle. Steel-
4-16x50	4-16	27-7.5	3.3-3.8	13.6	30mm	Int.	27	1,594.00	on- steel click adjustments. [1]Dot reticle on some models. [2]Post
Black Diamond									crosshair reticle extra. [3]Matte satin finish. [4]Available with parallax
3-12x50[3, 4, 6]	3.2-11.9	34-12	3.5-4	13.8	30mm	Int.	25	974.00	adjustment (standard on 10x, 12x, 4-12x, 6-12x, 6-18x, 6x HBR and
6-24x50	6-24	18-6	3.5-4	16.2	30mm	Int.	25	1,046.00	3-12x Signature). [5]Silver matte finish extra. [6]Target knobs extra, stan-
Fullfield II									dard on silhouette models. LER and XER with P.A., 6x HBR.
2.5x9	2.5	55	3.5-3.75	10.25	1	Int.	9	307.00	[7]Sunshade avail. [8]Avail. with Fine Plex reticle. [9]Available with Heavy
1.75-5x[1, 2, 9, 10]	1.7-4.6	66-25	3.5-3.75	10.875	1	Int.	13	400.00	Plex reticle. [10]Available with Posi- Lock. [11]Available with Peep Plex
3-9x40[1, 2, 3, 10]	3.3-8.7	38-15	3.5-3.75	12.625	1	Int.	15	336.00	reticle. [12]Also avail. for rimfires, airguns. [13]Selected models available
3-9x50	3-9	35-15	3.5-3.75	13	1	Int.	18	481.00	with camo finish.
3.5-10x50mm[3, 5, 10]	3.7-9.7	29.5-11	3.5-3.75	14	1	Int.	19	542.00	**Signature Series:** LER=Long Eye Relief; IER=Intermediate Eye
4.5-14x[1, 4, 8, 11]	4.4-11.8	27-10	3.5-3.75	15	1	Int.	18	585.00	Relief; XER=Extra Eye Relief.
6.5-20x[1, 3, 4, 6, 7, 8]	6.5-17.6	16.7	3.5-3.75	15.8	1	Int.	18.5	656.00	**Speeddot 135:** [14]Waterproof, fogproof, coated lenses, 11 bright ness
Compact Scopes									set tings; 3-MOA or 11-MOA dot size; includes Weaver-style rings
1x XER[3]	1	51	4.5-20	8.8	1	Int.	7.9	320.00	and battery. **Partial listing shown.** Contact Burris for complete
4x[4, 5]	3.6	24	3.75-5	8.25	1	Int.	7.8	397.00	details.
6x[1, 4]	5.5	17	3.75-5	9	1	Int.	8.2	397.00	
6x HBR[1, 5, 8]	6	13	4.5	11.25	1	Int.	13	415.00	
1-4x XER[3]	1-3.8	53-15	4.25-30	8.8	1	Int.	10.3	467.00	
3-9x[4, 5]	3.6-8.8	25-11	3.75-5	12.625	1	Int.	11.5	442.00	

Maker and Model	Magn.	Field at 100 Yds. (feet)	Eye Relief (in.)	Length (in.)	Tube Dia. (in.)	W & E Adjustments	Weight (ozs.)	Price	Other Data
BURRIS *(cont.)*									
4-12x[1, 4, 6]	4.5-11.6	19-8	3.75-4	15	1	Int.	15	534.00	
Signature Series									
1.5-6x[2, 3, 5, 9, 10]	1.7-5.8	70-20	3.5-4	10.8	1	Int.	13	601.00	
8x3[2, 5, 11]	2.1-7.7	53-17	3.5-4	11.75	1	Int.	14	840.00	
3-10x[3, 5, 10, 13]	3.3-8.8	36-14	3.5-4	12.875	1	Int.	15.5	665.00	
3-12x[3, 10]	3.3-11.7	34-9	3.5-4	14.25	1	Int.	21	701.00	
4-16x[1, 3, 5, 6, 8, 10]	4.3-15.7	33-9	3.5-4	15.4	1	Int.	23.7	760.00	
6-24x[1, 3, 5, 6, 8, 10, 13]	6.6-23.8	17-6	3.5-4	16	1	Int.	22.7	787.00	
8-32x[8,10,12]	8.6-31.4	13-3.8	3.5-4	17	1	Int.	24	840.00	
Speeddot 135[14]									
Red Dot	1			4.85	35mm	Int.	5	291.00	
Handgun									
1.50-4x LER[1, 5, 10]	1.6-3	16-11	11-25	10.25	1	Int.	11	411.00	
2-7x LER[3, 4, 5, 10]	2-6.5	21-7	7-27	9.5	1	Int.	12.6	458.00	
2x LER[4, 5, 6]	1.7	21	10-24	8.75	1	Int.	6.8	286.00	
4x LER[1, 4, 5, 6, 10]	3.7	11	10-22	9.625	1	Int.	9	338.00	
3x12x LER[1, 4, 6]	9.5	4	8-12	13.5	1	Int.	14	558.00	
Scout Scope									
1xXER[3,9]	1.5	32	4-24	9	1	Int.	7.0	320.00	
2.75x3[.9]	2.7	15	7-14	9.375	1	Int.	7.0	356.00	
BUSHNELL (Bausch & Lomb Elite rifle scopes sold under Bushnell brand)									
Elite 4200 RainGuard									
42-6244M[1]	6-24	18-6	3	16.9	1	Int.	20.2	671.95	(Bushnell)
42-2104G[2]	2.5-10	41.5-10.8	3	13.5	1	Int.	16	579.95	[1]Wide Angle. [2]Also silver finish.
42-2152	2.5-10	40.3-10.8	3.3	14.3	1	Int.	18	740.95	
42-1636M	1.5-6	61.8-16.1	3	12.8	1	Int.	15.4	559.95	
42-4164M	4-16	26-7	3.5	18.6	1	Int.	18.6	593.95	
42-4165M	4-16	26-7	3	15.6	1	Int.	22	767.95	
42-8324M	8-32	14-3.75	3.3	18	1	Int.	22	739.95	
Elite 3200 RainGuard									
32-5155M	5-15	21-7	3	15.9	1	Int.	19	463.95	(Bushnell Elite)
32-4124A[1]	4-12	26.9-9	3	13.2	1	Int.	15	411.95	[1]Adj. objective, sunshade; with 1/4-MOA dot or Mil Dot reticle. [2]Also
32-1040M	10	11	3.5	11.7	1	Int.	15.5	279.95	in matte and silver finish. [3]Only in matte finish. [4]Also in matte and
32-3940G[4]	3-9	33.8-11.5	3	12.6	1	Int.	13	279.95	silver finish. [5]Adjustable objective. [6]50mm objective; also in matte
32-2732M	2-7	44.6-12.7	3	11.6	1	Int.	12	265.95	finish. [7]Also in silver finish. [8]40mm. [9]Ill. dot reticle. **Partial listings**
32-39544G[6]	3-9	31.5-10.5	3	15.7	1	Int.	19	335.95	**shown. Contact Bushnell Performance Optics for details.**
32-3955E	3-9	31.5-10.5	3	15.6	30mm	Int.	22	561.95	
Elite 3200 Handgun RainGuard									
32-2632M[7]	2-6	10-4	20	9	1	Int.	10	389.95	A reticle is the crosshair or pattern placed in the eyepiece
32-2636[10]	2-6	10-4	20	9	1	Int.	10	431.95	of the scope which establishes the gun's position on the target.
Holosight									
.51-0021	1x	Unlimited	6"/10'	4.1	NA	Int.	6.4	389.95	
.53-0021	1x	Unlimited	Unlimited	6	NA	Int.	12	350.95	
.53-0027	1x	Unlimited	Unlimited	6	NA	Int.	12	370.95	
Legend									
.75-2732M	2-7	56-16	3.5	11.6	1	Int.	11.6	187.95	
.75-3940M	3-9	36-13	3.5	13.1	1	Int.	14.6	207.95	
.75-3950M	3-9	36-13	3.5	13.1	1	Int.	16	227.95	
.75-4124M	4-12	30.9-10.1	3.5	14.4	1	Int.	17.3	265.95	
.75-5154M	5-15	23.8	3.5	14.6	1	Int.	17.7	277.95	
Trophy									
73-0134	1	68	Unlimited	5.5	1	Int.	6	119.95	
73-1500[1]	1.75-5	68-23	3.5	10.8	1	Int.	12.3	155.95	
73-4124[1]	4-12	32-11	3	12.5	1	Int.	16.1	263.95	
73-3940[2]	3-9	42-14	3	11.7	1	Int.	13.2	139.95	
73-6184[7]	6-18	17.3-6	3	14.8	1	Int.	17.9	331.95	
Turkey & Brush									
73-142[11]	1.75-4	73-30	3.5	10.8	32mm	Int.	10.9	149.95	
Trophy Handgun									
73-2632[3]	2-6	21-7	9-26	9.1	1	Int.	10.9	251.95	
Banner									
71-1545	1.5-4.5	67-23	3.5	10.5	1	Int.	10.5	101.95	
71-3944[9]	3-9	36-13	4	11.5	1	Int.	12.5	109.95	
71-3950[10]	3-9	26-10	3	16	1	Int.	19	163.95	
71-4124[7]	4-12	29-11	3	12	1	Int.	15	138.95	
71-6185[10]	6-18	17-6	3	16	1	Int.	18	183.95	
Sportsman									
72-0038	3-9	37-14	3.5	12	1	Int.	6	69.95	
72-0039	3-9	38-13	3.5	10.75	1	Int.	11.2	101.95	
72-0412[7]	4-12	27-9	3.2	13.1	1	Int.	14.6	123.95	
72-1393[6]	3-9	35-12	3.5	11.75	1	Int.	10	59.95	
72-1548[9]	1.5-4.5	71-25	3.5	10.4	1	Int.	11.8	95.95	
72-1403	4	29	4	11.75	1	Int.	9.2	49.95	
72-3940M	3-9	42-14	3	12.7	1	Int.	12.5	83.95	
22 Rimfire									
76-2239	3-9	40-13	3	11.75	1	Int.	11.2	53.95	
76-2243	4	30	3	11.5	1	Int.	10	45.95	

Plex   Fine Plex   Peep Plex   Target Dot

Heavy Plex & Electro-Dot Plex   Ballistic Mil-Dot   Mil-Dot

MULTI-X   CIRCLE-X

MIL DOT   3-2-1 LOW-LIGHT

¼ M.O.A.   EUROPEAN

SCOPES / Hunting, Target & Varmint

Maker and Model	Magn.	Field at 100 Yds. (feet)	Eye Relief (in.)	Length (in.)	Tube Dia. (in.)	W & E Adjustments	Weight (ozs.)	Price	Other Data
EUROPTIK SUPREME									
4x36K	4	39	3.5	11.6	26mm	Int.	14	795.00	[1]Military scope with adjustable parallax. Fixed powers have 26mm tubes, variables have 30mm tubes. Some models avail. with steel tubes. All lenses multi-coated. Dust and water tight. From Europtik.
6x42K	6	21	3.5	13	26mm	Int.	15	875.00	
8x56K	8	18	3.5	14.4	26mm	Int.	20	925.00	
1.5-6x42K	1.5-6	61.7-23	3.5	12.6	30mm	Int.	17	1,095.00	
2-8x42K	2-8	52-17	3.5	13.3	30mm	Int.	17	1,150.00	
2.5-10x56K	2.5-10	40-13.6	3.5	15	30mm	Int.	21	1,295.00	
3-12x56 Super	3-12	10.8-34.7	3.5-2.5	15.2	30mm	Int.	24	1,495.00	
4-16x56 Super	4-16	9.8-3.9	3.1	18	30mm	Int.	26	1,575.00	
3-9x40 Micro	3-9	3.2-12.1	2.7	13	1	Int.	14	1,450.00	
2.5-10x46 Micro	2.5-10	13.7-33.4	2.7	14	30mm	Int.	20	1,395.00	
4-16x56 EDP[1]	4-16	22.3-7.5	3.1	18	30mm	Int.	29	1,995.00	
7-12x50 Target	7-12	8.8-5.5	3.5	15	30mm	Int.	21	1,495.00	
JAEGER									
ST-10		10, 17	Varies	13	30mm, 35mm		34	895.00	All scopes available w/standard and extra-long eye relief eyepiece. Variable power military and police tactical scope systems are also available. Offers scope rings and bases. By U.S.O. Jaeger.
SN-1 Long Range		17, 22, 42	12.35 (10x)	Varies	30mm, 35mm, 40mm		36	2,395.00	
SN6 2d Perimeter		10, 17, 22	12.35 (10x)	Varies	30mm, 35mm, 40mm		34	1,295.00	
SN-9 Extreme Range		22, 42	6.2 (22x)	Varies			62.4	2,600.00	
SN-12 CQB		3, 4	38 (3x)	7.5	1		34	865.00	
USMC 10x Sniper		10	10.36	12.5	1		34	2,500.00	
USMC M40A3		10	10.36	12.5	1		34	NA	
JH-4 Safari		1-4	119-34	9.25	30mm		31	1,195.00	
JH-3 Denali		1.8-10x	48.7-12.35	13	30mm		32	1,695.00	
JH-3 Serengeti		3.2-17x		14.5	30mm		33	1,895.00	
JH-T-PAL Chucker		3.8-22x	30-6.2	17.5	30mm		34	1,995.00	
KAHLES									
C-1 Series									
C1-4	1-1.4	108-31.8	3.55	10.83	30mm	Int.	14.6	943.33	Aluminum tube. Multi-coated, waterproof. [1]Also available with illuminated reticle. Imported from Austria by Swarovski Optik.
C5-6x42	1.5-6	72-21.3	3.55	12.01	30mm	Int.	16.4	1,043.33	
C2.5-10	2.5-10	43.5-12.9	3.55	12.8	30mm	Int.	17.3	1,187.76	
C3-12	3-12	37.5-10.8	3.55	13.98	30mm	Int.	19.4	1,332.22	
American Hunter Riflescopes									
2-7x36	2-7	48-27.3	3.35	11.06	1	Int.	12.2	621.11	
3-9	3-9	39-14.5	3.35	12.09	1	Int.	13.1	732.22	
Compact Fixed Power									
4x36	4	34.5	3.15	11.22	1	Int.	12.7	665.56	
6x42	6	23.4	3.15	12.4	1	Int.	14.5	854.44	
Compact 30mm Riflescopes w/Illuminated Reticle									
CSX 1-4	1.1-4	110.94-31.78	3.55	11.04	30mm	Int.	15.4	1,476.00	
CSX 2.5-10	1.5-6	74.96-21.29	3.55	12.2	30mm	Int.	17.15	1,665.55	
CSX 2.5-10	2.5-10	43.5-12.9	3.55	12.8	30mm	Int.	18.3	1,743.00	
Compact 30mm Riflescopes, Illumited									
CB 1.5-6	1.5-6	72-21.3	3.55	12.01	30mm	Int.	16.4	1,498.89	
CB 2.5-10	2.5-10'	43.5-12.9	3.55	12.8	30mm	Int.	17.3	965.55	
CB 3-12	3-12	37.5-10.8	3.55	13.98	30mm	Int.	19.4	1,743.33	
CL 1" Riflescopes									
CL3-9x42	3-9	39-15	3.60	12.09	1	Int.	14.46	887.78	
CL3-10	3-10	34-12	3.60	12.59	1	Int.	16.4	965.55	
CL4-12	4-12	29-10	3.60	12.59	1	Int.	18.34	998.89	
CL 1" Riflescopes with Multizer									
CL3-9x42	3-9	39-15	3.60	12.09	1	Int.	14.99	1,076.67	
CL3-10x50	3-10	34-12	3.60	12.59	1	Int.	16.93	1,110.00	
CL4-12x52	4-12	29-10	3.60	12.59	1	Int.	18.87	1,176.67	
LEATHERWOOD									
Uni-Dial*									
U3510x50 3.5-10	50	36.7-12.8	3.25	13.11			18.7	335.50	*Elevation adjustment is 1/8" and windage adjustment is 1/4". All air-glass surfaces are fully multi-coated to maximize light transmission.
U412-50 4-12	50	30.6-10.2	3.25	14.53			22.1	385.00	
U618-50 6-18	50	20.4-7.5	3.25	15.35			22	418.50	
U6520x50 6.5-20	50	18.8-6.3	3.25	15.43			23.5	437.50	
U3501x50MD 3.5-10	50	36.7-12.8	3.25	13.11			18.7	475.00	
Distinguished									
D3510x50 3.5-10	50	36.7-12.8	3.25	13.11			17.2	199.00	
D412x50 4-12	50	30.6-10.2	3.25	14.53			20.6	239.00	
D618x5- 6-18	50	20.4-7.5	3.25	15.35			21.5	267.50	
D6520x50 6.5-20	50	18.8-6.3	3.35	15.43			22	275.00	
D3510x50MD 3.5-10	50	36.7-12.8	3.25	13.11			17.2	399.00	
Expert									
E412x44 4-12	44	30.6-10.7	3.25	14.53			19.7	149.00	
E618x44 6-18	44	20.4-6.8	3.25	15.35			20.2	159.00	
E6520x44 6.5-20	44	18.8-6.28	3.25	15.43			21.2	223.50	
Sharpshooter									
S39x40 3-9	40	41-15	3.25	13			13.5	95.00	
S39x40IR 3-9	40	39-13	3.25	12.75			14	105.00	
S39x50 3-9	50	41-13	3.25	12.75			14.5	112.00	
S3510x50 3.5-10	50	36.7-12.8	3.25	13.11			16.2	119.00	
S310x44 3-10	44	40.8-12.8	3.25	13.11			15.2	107.00	

Maker and Model	Magn.	Field at 100 Yds. (feet)	Eye Relief (in.)	Length (in.)	Tube Dia. (in.)	W & E Adjustments	Weight (ozs.)	Price	Other Data
LEATHERWOOD (cont.)									
S55-16x44 5.5-16	44	21.9-7.5	3.25	14.41			19.9	149.00	
S6520x44 6.5-20	44	18.8-6.28	3.25	15.43			21.7	145.00	
Long Eye Relief									
LER2732 2-7	32	18.88-6.28	11.2-8.7	11.08			11.57	185.00	
Double-Duce Rimfire									
RF4x32 4	32	26	3	12			11	49.50	
RF39x32 3-9	32	38.5-13	3	12.5			12	69.50	
LEICA									
Ultravid 1.75-6x32	1.75-6	47-18	4.8-3.7	11.25	30mm	Int.	14	749.00	Aluminum tube with hard anodized matte black finish with titanium
Ultravid 3.5-10x42	3.5-10	29.5-10.7	4.6-3.6	12.62	30mm	Int.	16	849.00	accents; finger-adjustable windage and elevation with 1/4-MOA
Ultravid 4.5-14x42	4.5-14	20.5-7.4	5-3.7	12.28	30mm	Int.	18	949.00	clicks. Made in U.S. From Leica.

Leicaplex Standard Leica Dot Standard Dot Crosshair Euro Post & Plex

Maker and Model	Magn.	Field at 100 Yds. (feet)	Eye Relief (in.)	Length (in.)	Tube Dia. (in.)	W & E Adjustments	Weight (ozs.)	Price	Other Data
LEUPOLD									
M8-3.5x10	3.2-9.5	29.9	4.7	13.5	30mm	Int.	19.5	1,124.99	Constantly centered reticles, choice of Duplex, tapered CPC, Leupold
M8-2.7-28	2.66	41	3.8	9.9	1	Int.	8.2	299.99	Dot, Crosshair and Dot. CPC and Dot reticles extra. [1]2x and 4x
M8-4X Compact RF	3.6	25.5	4.5	9.2	1	Int.	7.5	289.99	scopes have from 12"-24" of eye relief and are suitable for handguns,
Vari-X 2-7x	2.5-6.5	41.7-17.3	4.2	10.8	1	Int.	10	299.99	top ejection arms and muzzleloaders. [2]3x9 Compact, 6x Compact,
Vari-X 3-9x	3.3-8.5	32-13.1	4.2	12.2	1	Int.	12	314.99	12x, 3x9, and 6.5x20 come with adjustable objective. Sunshade avail-
M8-4X	4	24	4	10.5	1	Int.	9.3	249.99	able for all adjustable objective scopes, **$23.20-$41.10.** [3]Long Range
M8-6x36mm	5.9	17.7	4.3	11.3	1	Int.	10	469.99	scopes have side focus parallax adjustment, additional windage and
M8-6x42mm	6	17	4.5	11.9	1	Int.	11.3	424.99	elevation travel. Partial listing shown. **Contact Leupold for com-**
M8-12x40	11.6	9.1	4.2	13	1	Int.	13.5	474.99	**plete details.**
Vari-X 3-9x	3.5-8.6	32.9-13.1	4-2	12.2	1	Int.	12	454.99	
Vari-X-III 1.5-5x20	1.5-4.5	65-17	4.4-3.6	9.4	1	Int.	9.7	499.99	
Vari-X-III 1.75-6x32	1.9-5.6	51	4.4-3.2	11.4	1	Int.	11.6	499.99	
Vari-X-III 2.5x8	2.6-7.8	37-13.5	4.4-3.5	11.4	1	Int.	11.6	499.99	
Vari-X-III 3.5-10x40	3.9-9.6	29.7-11	4.4-3.5	12.6	1	Int.	13	549.99	
Vari-X-III 3.5-10x50	3.3-9.5	29.8-11	4.4-3.5	12.2	1	Int.	15.1	624.99	
Vari-X-III 4.5-14x40	4.8-14.2	19.9	4.4-3.6	12.6	1	Int.	13.2	699.99	
*Vari-X-III 4.5-14x50	4.9-14.4	19.1	4.4-3.6	12.6	1	Int.	16	789.99	
Vari-X III 4.5-14x50 LRT[4]	4.9-14.3	19-6	5-3.7	12.1	30mm	Int.	17.5	999.00	
Vari-X III 6.5-20 A.O.	6.5-19.2	14.3-5.6	5-3.6	14.3	1	Int.	16	749.99	
Vari-X III 6.5-20xLRT	6.5-19.2	14.3-5.5	4.4	14.2	1	Int.	21	974.99	
Vari-X III 8.5-25x40 LRT	8.3-24.3	11.3-4.3	5.2	14.3	1	Int.	21	1,039.99	
Vari-X III 8.5-25x 50 LRT[4]	8.3-24.3	11.3-4.3	5.2-7	14.4	30mm	Int.	21	1,149.99	
Mark 4 M1-10x40	10	11.1	3.6	13.125	30mm	Int.	21	1,124.99	
Mark 4 M1-16x40	16	6.6	4.1	12.875	30mm	Int.	22	1,509.99	
Mark 4 M3-10x40LRT	10	13.1	3.4	13.125	30mm	Int.	21	939.99	
Mark 4 6.5x20[2]	6.5-19.5	14.3-5.5	5.5-3.8	11.2	30mm	Int.	16	1,198.99	
LPS 1.5-6x42	1.5-6	58.7-15.7	4	11.2	30mm	Int.	16	1,198.99	
LPS 2.5-10x45	2.6-9.8	37.2	4.5-3.8		1	Int.	17.2	1,119.99	
LPS 3.5-14x52	3.5-14	28-7.2	4	13.1	30mm	Int.	22	1,249.99	
Rimfire									
Vari-X 2-7x RF Special	3.6	25.5	4.5	9.2	1	Int.	7.5	299.99	
Shotgun									
M8 2.5x20	2.3	39.5	4.9	8.4	1	Int.	6	249.99	
LYMAN									
Super TargetSpot[1]	10, 12, 15, 20, 25, 30	5.5	2	24.3	.75	Int.	27.5	685.00	Made under license from Lyman to Lyman's orig. specs. Blue steel. Threepoint suspension rear mount with .25-min. click adj. Data listed for 20x model. [1]Price appx. Made in U.S. by Parsons Optical Mfg. Co.
McMILLAN									
Vision Master 2.5-10x	2.5-10	14.2-4.4	4.3-3.3	13.3	30mm	Int.	17	1,250.00	42mm obj. lens; .25-MOA clicks; nitrogen filled, fogproof, waterproof;
Vision Master Model 1[1]	2.5-10	14.2-4.4	4.3-3.3	13.3	30mm	Int.	17	1,250.00	etched duplex-type reticle. [1]Tactical Scope with external adj. knobs, military reticle; 60+ min. adj.
MEOPTA									
Artemis									
4x32A[1]	4	34	3.15	11	1	Int.	14.7	194.00	Steel tubes are waterproof, dustproof, and shockproof; nitrogen filled.
6x42A[1]	6	23	3.15	13.6	1	Int.	18.2	267.00	Anti-reflective coatings, protective rubber eye piece, clear caps.
7x50A[1]	7	18	3.15	14.1	1	Int.	19	278.00	Made in Czech Replublic by Meopta. [1]Range finder reticles available. Partial listing shown.
MEPROLIGHT									
Meprolight Reflex Sights 14-21 5.5 MOA 1x30[1]	1			4.4	30mm	Int.	5.2	335.00	[1]Also available with 4.2 MOA dot. Uses tritium and fiber-optics, no batteries required. From Hesco, Inc.
MILLETT									
Buck 3-9x44	3-9	38-14	3.25-4	13	1	Int.	16.2	249.65	[1]3-MOA dot. 25-MOA dot. 33-, 5-, 8-, 10-MOA dots. 410-MOA dot.
Buck 3.5-10x50	3.5-10	NA	NA	NA	1	NA	NA	270.65	All have click adjustments; waterproof, shockproof; 11 dot intensity
Buck 3-12x44 A/O	3-12	NA	NA	NA	1	NA	NA	270.65	settings. All avail. in matte/black or silver finish. From Millett Sights.
Buck 4-16x44 A/O	4-16	NA	NA	NA	1	NA	NA	290.00	
Buck Varmint 4-16x56	4-16	NA	NA	NA	30mm	NA	NA	380.00	
Buck Varmint 6-25x56	6-25	NA	NA	NA	30mm	NA	NA	405.00	
Buck Varmint 6-25x56	6-25	NA	NA	NA	30mm	NA	NA	431.00	

Duplex CPC Post & Duplex

Leupold Dot Dot

Maker and Model	Magn.	Field at 100 Yds. (feet)	Eye Relief (in.)	Length (in.)	Tube Dia. (in.)	W & E Adjustments	Weight (ozs.)	Price	Other Data
MILLETT *(cont.)*									
Buck Lightning 1.5-6x44	1.5-6	NA	NA	NA	1	NA	NA	323.00	
Buck Lightning 3-9x44	3-9	NA	NA	NA	1	NA	NA	323.00	
Buck Silver 3-9x40	3-9	NA	NA	NA	1	NA	NA	135.95	
Buck Silver 4-12x40 A/O	4-12	NA	NA	NA	1	NA	NA	170.00	
Buck Silver 6-18x40 A/O	6-18	NA	NA	NA	1	NA	NA	170.00	
Buck Silver Compact 2x20	2	NA	NA	NA	1	NA	NA	104.48	
Buck Silver Compact 4x32	4	NA	NA	NA	1	NA	NA	109.60	
Buck Silver Compact 1.5-4x32	1.5-4	NA	NA	NA	1	NA	NA	142.80	
SP-1 Compact[1] Red Dot	1	36.65		4.1	1	Int.	3.2	137.77	
SP-2 Compact[2] Red Dot	1	58		4.5	30mm	Int.	4.3	137.77	
MultiDot SP[3]	1	50		4.8	30mm	Int.	5.3	205.90	
MIRADOR									
RXW 4x40[1]	4	37	3.8	12.4	1	Int.	12	179.95	[1]Wide angle scope. Multi-coated objective lens. Nitrogen filled; water-
RXW 1.5-5x20[1]	1.5-5	46-17.4	4.3	11.1	1	Int.	10	188.95	proof; shockproof. From Mirador Optical Corp.
RXW 3-9x40	3-9	43-14.5	3.1	12.9	1	Int.	13.4	251.95	
NIGHTFORCE									
3.5-15x50	3.5-15	27.6-9.7.3		14.7	30mm		30	1,278.90	Lighted reticles with eleven intensity levels. Most scopes have choice
3.5-15x56	3.5-15	27.6-7	3	14.8	30mm	Int.	31	1,309.77	of reticles. From Lightforce U.S.A.
5.5-22x56	5.5-22	17.5-4.47		15	30mm	Int.	31	1,385.90	
5.5-22x56	5.5-22	17.5-4.7		15.2	30mm	Int.	32	1,300.18	
8-32x56	8-32	12.1-3.1		15.9	30mm	Int.	34	1,519.25	
12-42x56	12-42	8.2-2.4		16.1	30mm	Int.	34	1,648.24	
3.5-15x36	3.5-15	24.5-6.9		15.8	30mm	Int.	32	1,000.83	
8-32x56	8-32	9.4-3.1	3	16.6	30mm	Int.	36	997.90	
12-42x56	12-42	6.7-2.3	3	17	30mm	Int.	36	1,053.64	
NIKON									
Buckmasters									
4x40	4	30.4	3.3	12.7	1	Int.	11.8	159.95	Super multi-coated lenses and blackening of all internal metal parts
3-9x40[4]	3.3-8.6	33.8-11.3	3.5-3.4	12.7	1	Int.	13.4	209.95	for maximum light gathering capability; positive .25-MOA; fogproof;
3-9x50	3.3-8.6	33.8-11.3	3.5-3.4	12.9	1	Int.	18.2	299.95	waterproof; shockproof; luster and matte finish. [1]Also available in
4-12x50	4-12	24.3-8.0	3.7	13.9	1	Int.	20.6	349.95	matte silver finish. [2]Available in silver matte finish. [3]Available with
Monarch UCC									TurkeyPro or Nikoplex reticle. [4]Silver Shadow finish; black matte
4x40[2]	4	26.7	3.5	11.7	1	Int.	11.7	229.95	**$296.95**. Partial listing shown. From Nikon, Inc.
1.5-4.5x20[3]	1.5-4.5	67.8-22.5	3.7-3.2	10.1	1	Int.	9.5	239.95	
2-7x32	2-7	46.7-13.7	3.9-3.3	11.3	1	Int.	11.3	269.95	
3-9x40[1]	3-9	33.8-11.3	3.6-3.2	12.5	1	Int.	12.5	299.95	
3.5-10x50	3.5-10	25.5-8.9	3.9-3.8	13.7	1	Int.	15.5	439.95	
4-12x40 A.O.	4-12	25.7-8.6	3.6-3.2	14	1	Int.	16.6	369.95	
6.5-20x44	6.5-19.4	16.2-5.4	3.5-3.1	14.8	1	Int.	19.6	469.95	
2x20 EER	2	22	26.4	8.1	1	Int.	6.3	169.95	
NORINCO									
N2520	2.5	44.1	4		1	Int.		52.28	Partial listing shown. Some with Ruby Lens coating, blue/black and
N420	4	29.3	3.7		1	Int.		52.70	matte finish. Imported by Nic Max, Inc.
N640	6	20	3.1		1	Int.		67.88	
N154520	1.5-4.5	63.9-23.6	4.1-3.2			Int.		80.14	
N251042	2.5-10	27-11	3.5-2.8		1	Int.		206.60	
N3956	3-9	35.1-6.3	3.7-2.6		1	Int.		231.88	
N31256	3-12	26-10	3.5-2.8		1	Int.		290.92	
NC2836M	2-8	50.8-14.8	3.6-2.7		1	Int.		255.60	
PARSONS									
Parsons Long Scope	6	10	2	28-34+	.75	Ext.	13	475.00- 525.00	Adj. for parallax, focus. Micrometer rear mount with .25-min. click adjust ments. Price is approximate. Made in U.S. by Parsons Optical Mfg. Co.
PENTAX									
Lightseeker 1.75-6x[1]	1.75-6	71-20	3.5-4	10.8	1	Int.	13	546.00	[1]Glossy finish; Matte finish, Heavy Plex or Penta-Plex, **$546.00**.
Lightseeker 2-8x[2]	2-8	53-17	3.5-4	11.7	1	Int.	14	594.00	[2]Glossy finish; Matte finish, **$594.00**. [3]Glossy finish; Matte finish,
Lightseeker 3-9x[3, 4, 10, 11]	3-9	36-14	3.5-4	12.7	1	Int.	15	594.00	**$628.00**; Heavy Plex, add **$20.00**. [4]Matte finish; Mil-Dot, **$798.00**.
Lightseeker 3.5-10x[5]	3.5-10	29.5-11	3.5-4	14	1	Int.	19.5	630.00	[5]Glossy finish; Matte finish, **$652.00**; Heavy Plex, add **$10.00**.
Lightseeker 4-16x[6,9]	4-16	33-9	3.5-4	15.4	1	Int.	22.7	888.00	[6]Glossy finish; Matte finish, **$816.00**; with Heavy Plex, **$830.00**; with
Lightseeker 6-24x[7, 12]	6-24	18-5.5	3.5-4	16	1	Int.	23.7	1,028.00	Mil-Dot, **$978.00**. [7]Matte finish; with Mil-Dot, **$1,018.00**. [8]Matte finish,
Lightseeker 8.5-32x[8]	8.5-32	13-3.8	3.5-4	17.2	1	Int.	24	968.00	with Mil-Dot, **$1098.00**. [9]Lightseeker II, Matte finish, **$844.00**.
Shotgun									[10]Lightseeker II, Glossy finish, **$636.00**. [11]Lightseeker II, Matte finish,
Lightseeker 2.5x1[3]	2.5	55	3.5-4	10	1	Int.	9	398.00	**$660.00**. [12]Lightseeker II, Matte finish, **$878.00**. [13]Matte finish;
Lightseeker Zero-X SG Plus	0	51	4.5-15	8.9	1	Int.	7.9	372.00	Advantage finish, Break-up Mossy Oak finish, Treestand Mossy Oak
Lightseeker Zero-X/ V Still-Target	0-4	53.8-15	3.5-7	8.9	1	Int.	10.3	476.00	finish, **$364.00**. From Pentax Corp.
Lightseeker Zero X/ V	0-4	53.8-15	3.5-7	8.9	1	Int.	10.3	454.00	
Pentax Reticles									

Heavy Plex   Fine Plex   Penta-Plex   Deepwoods Plex   Comp-Plex   Mil-dot

Maker and Model	Magn.	Field at 100 Yds. (feet)	Eye Relief (in.)	Length (in.)	Tube Dia. (in.)	W & E Adjustments	Weight (ozs.)	Price	Other Data
RWS									
300	4	36	3.5	11.75	1	Int.	13.2	170.00	
450	3-9	43-14	3.5	12	1	Int.	14.3	215.00	
SCHMIDT & BENDER									
Fixed									All scopes have 30-yr. warranty, click adjustments, centered reticles, rotation indicators. [1]Glass reticle; aluminum. Available in aluminum with mounting rail. [2]Aluminum only. [3]Aluminum tube. Choice of two bullet drop compensators, choice of two sunshades, two range finding reticles. From Schmidt & Bender, Inc. [4]Parallax adjustment in third turret; extremely fine crosshairs. [5]Available with illuminated reticle that glows red; third turret houses on/off switch, dimmer and battery. [6]4-16x50/Long Range. [7]Also with Long Eye Relief. From Schmidt & Bender, Inc. Available with illuminated crosshairs and parallax adjustment.
4x36	4	30	3.25	11	1	Int.	14	979.00	
6x42	6	21	3.25	13	1	Int.	17	1,069.00	
8x56	8	16.5	3.25	14	1	Int.	22	1,299.00	
Variables									
2.5-10x56[1, 5]	2.5-10	37.5-12	3.90	14	30mm	Int.	24.6	1,659.00	
3-12x42[2]	3-12	34.5-11.5	3.90	13.5	30mm	Int.	19	2,059.00	
3-12x50[1, 5]	3-12	33.3-12.6	3.90	13.5	30mm	Int.	22.9	2,059.00	
4-16x50 Varmint[4, 6]	4-16	22.5-7.5	3.90	14	30mm	Int.	26	1,979.00	
Police/Marksman II									
3-12x50[7]	3-12	33.3-12.6	3.74	13.9	34mm	Int.	18.5	2,799.00	
SCHMIDT & BENDER ZENITH SERIES									
3-12x50	3-12	33.3-11.4	3.70	13.71	NA	NA	23.4	1,795.00	
2.5-10x56	2.5-10	39.6-12	3.70	14.81	NA	NA	24	2,089.00	

| No 1 (fixed) | No. 1 variable | No. 2 | No. 3 | No. 4 | No. 6 | No. 7 | No. 8 | No. 8 Dot | No. 9 |

Maker and Model	Magn.	Field at 100 Yds. (feet)	Eye Relief (in.)	Length (in.)	Tube Dia. (in.)	W & E Adjustments	Weight (ozs.)	Price	Other Data
SIGHTRON									
Variables									[1]Adjustable objective. [2]3MOA dot; also with 5 or 10 MOA dot. [3]Variable 3, 5, 10 MOA dot; black finish; also stainless. [4]Satin black; also stainless. Electronic Red Dot scopes come with ring mount, front and rear extension tubes, polarizing filter, battery, haze filter caps, wrench. Rifle, pistol, shotgun scopes have aluminum tubes, Exac Trak adjustments. Lifetime warranty. From Sightron, Inc. 53" sun shade. [6]Mil-Dot or Plex reticle. [7]Dot or Plex reticle. [8]Double Diamond reticle.
SII 1.56x42	1.5-6	50-15	3.8-4	11.69	1	Int.	15.35	372.25	
SII 2.58x42	2.5-8	36-12	3.6-4.2	11.89	1	Int.	12.82	338.40	
SII 39x42[4, 6, 7]	3-9	34-12	3.6-4.2	12.00	1	Int.	13.22	356.22	
SII 312x42[6]	3-12	32-9	3.6-4.2	11.89	1	Int.	12.99	421.55	
SII 3.510x42	3.5-10	32-11	3.6	11.89	1	Int.	13.16	421.01	
SII 4.514x42[1]	4.5-14	22-7.9	3.6	13.88	1	Int.	16.07	481.14	
Target									
SII 24x44	24	4.1	4.33	13.30	1	Int.	15.87	441.82	
SII 416x42[1, 4, 5, 6, 7]	4-16	26-7	3.6	13.62	1	Int.	16	481.11	
SII 624-42[1, 4, 5, 7]	6-24	16-5	3.6	14.6	1	Int.	18.7	562.96	
Compact									
SII 4x32	4	25	4.5	9.69	1	Int.	9.34	266.86	
SII2.5-10x32	2.5-10	41-10.5	3.75-3.5	10.9	1	Int.	10.39	338.40	
Shotgun									
SII 2.5x20SG	2.5	41	4.3	10.28	1	Int.	8.46	266.88	
Pistol									
SII 1x28P[4]	1	30	9-24	9.49	1	Int.	8.46	314.79	
SII 2x28P[4]	2	16-10	9-24	9.49	1	Int.	8.28	314.79	
SIMMONS									
22 Mag.									[1]Matte; also polished finish. [2]Silver; also black matte or polished. [3]Black matte finish. [4]Granite finish. [5]Camouflage. [6]Black polish. [7]With ring mounts. [8]Silver; black polish avail. [10]50mm obj.; black matte. [11]Black or silver matte. [12]75-yd. parallax; black or silver matte. [13]TV view. [14]Adj. obj. [15]Silver matte. [16]Adj. objective; 4" sunshade; black matte. [17]Octagon body; rings included; black matte or silver finish. [18]Black matte finish; also available in silver. [19]Smart reticle. [20]Target turrets. [21]With dovetail rings. [23]With 3V lithium battery, extension tube, polarizing filter, Weaver rings. **Only selected models shown.** Contact Simmons Outdoor Corp. for complete details.
801102[2]	4	29.5	3	11.75			11	49.99	
801103[1]	4	23.5	3	7.25			8.25	49.99	
801103[7]	3-9	29.5	3.3	11.5			10	59.99	
AETEC									
2100[8]	2.8-10	44-14	5	11.9	1	Int.	15.5	189.99	
21041[6]	3.8-12	33-11	4	13.5	1	Int.	20	199.99	
44 Mag									
M-1044[3]	3-10	34-10.5	3	12.75	1	Int.	15.5	149.99	
M-1045[3]	4-12	29.5-9.5	3	13.2	1	Int.	18.25	169.99	
M-1047[3]	6.5-20	14-.5	2.6-3.4	12.8	1	Int.	19.5	199.99	
1048[3, 20] (3)	6.5-20	16-5.5	2.6-3.4	14.5	1	Int.	20	219.99	
M-1050DM[3, 19]	3.8-12	26-9	3	13.08	1	Int.	16.75	189.99	
8-Point									
4-12x40mm AO[3]	4-12	29-10	3-2 7/8	13.5	1	Int.	15.75	99.99	
4x32mm[3]	4	28.75	3	11.625	1	Int.	14.25	34.99	
3-9x32mm[3]	3-9	37.5-13	3-2 7/8	11.875	1	Int.	11.5	39.99	
3-9x40mm[18]	3-9	37-13	3-2 7/8	12.25	1	Int.	12.25	49.99-79.99	
3-9x50mm[3]	3-9	32-11.75	3-2 7/8	13	1	Int.	15.25	79.99	
Prohunter									
7700	2-7	53-16.25	3	11.5	1	Int.	12.5	79.99	
7710[2]	3-9	36-13	3	12.6	1	Int.	13.5	89.99	
7716	4-12	26-9	3	12.6	1	Int.	16.75	129.99	
7721	6-18	18.5-6	3	13.75	1	Int.	16	144.99	
7740[3]	6	21.75	3	12.5	1	Int.	12	99.99	
Prohunter Handgun									
7732[18]	2	22	9-17	8.75	1	Int.	7	109.99	
7738[18]	4	15	11.8-17.6	8.5	1	Int.	8	129.99	
82200[9]	2-6							159.99	

Truplex™   Smart   ProDiamond®   Crossbow

Maker and Model	Magn.	Field at 100 Yds. (feet)	Eye Relief (in.)	Length (in.)	Tube Dia. (in.)	W & E Adjustments	Weight (ozs.)	Price	Other Data
SIMMONS (cont.)									
Whitetail Classic									
WTC 11[4]	1.5-5	75-23	3.4-3.2	9.3	1	Int.	9.7	184.99	
WTC 12[4]	2.5-8	45-14	3.2-3	11.3	1	Int.	13	199.99	
WTC 13[4]	3.5-10	30-10.5	3.2-3	12.4	1	Int.	13.5	209.99	
WTC 15[4]	3.5-10	29.5-11.5	3.2	12.75	1	Int.	13.5	289.99	
WTC 45[4]	4.5-14	22.5-8.6	3.2	13.2	1	Int.	14	265.99	
Whitetail Expedition									
1.5-6x32mm[3]	1.5-6	72-19	3	11.16	1	Int.	15	259.99	
3-9x42mm[3]	3-9	40-13.5	3	13.2	1	Int.	17.5	269.99	
4-12x42mm[3]	4-12	29-9.6	3	13.46	1	Int.	21.25	299.99	
6-18x42mm[3]	6-18	18.3-6.5	3	15.35	1	Int.	22.5	319.99	
Pro50									
8800[10]	4-12	27-9	3.5	13.2	1	Int.	18.25	179.99	
8810[10]	6-18	17-5.8	3.6	13.2	1	Int.	18.25	174.99	
808825	3.5-10	32-8.75	3.5	3.25	1	Int.	14.5	179.99	
808830	2.5-10	39-12.2	2.75	12.75	1	Int.	15.9	179.99	
Shotgun									
2100[4]	4	16	5.5	8.8	1	Int.	9.1	84.99	
2100[5]	2.5	24	6	7.4	1	Int.	7	59.99	
7789D	2	31	5.5	8.8	1	Int.	8.75	99.99	
7790D	4	17	5.5	8.5	1	Int.	8.75	114.99	
7791D	1.5-5	76-23.5	3.4	9.5	1	Int.	10.75	138.99	
Blackpowder									
BP0420M17	4	19.5	4	7.5	1	Int.	8.3	59.99	
BP2732M12	2-7	57.7-16.6	3	11.6	1	Int.	12.4	129.99	
Red Dot									
5100421	1			4.8	30mm	Int.	4.7	44.99	
5111222	1			5.25	42mm	Int.	6	49.99	
Pro Air Gun									
21608 A.O.	4	25	3.5	12	1	Int.	11.3	99.99	
21613 A.O.	4-12	25-9	3.1-2.9	13.1	1	Int.	15.8	179.99	
21619 A.O.	6-18	18-7	2.9-2.7	13.8	1	Int.	18.2	189.99	
SPRINGFIELD ARMORY									
	6		3.5	13	1	Int.	14.7	379.00	[1]Range finding reticle with automatic bullet drop compensator for 308 match ammo to 700 yds. [2]Range finding reticle with automatic bullet drop compensator for 223 match ammo to 700 yds. [3]Also avail. as 2nd Gen. with target knobs and adj. obj., **$549.00**; as 3rd Gen. with illuminated reticle, **$749.00**; as Mil-Dot model with illuminated Target Tracking reticle, target knobs, adj. obj., **$698.00**. [4]Unlimited range finding, target knobs, adj. obj., illuminated Target Tracking green reticle. All scopes have matte black finish, internal bubble level, 1/4-MOA clicks. From Springfield, Inc.
4-14x70 Tactical Government Model[2]	4-14		3.5	14.25	1	Int.	15.8	395.00	
4-14x56 1st Gen. Government Model[3]	4-14		3.5	14.75	30mm	Int.	23	480.00	
10x56 Mil-Dot Government Model[4]	10		3.5	14.75	30mm	Int.	28	672.00	
6-20x56 Mil-Dot Government Model	6-20		3.5	18.25	30mm	Int.	33	899.00	
SWAROVSKI OPTIK									
PH Series									
1.25-4x24[1]	1.25-4	98.4-31.2	3.15	10.63	30mm	Int.	16.2	1,333.23	
1.5-6x42[1]	1.5-6	65.4-21	3.15	12.99	30mm	Int.	20.8	1,483.34	
2.5-10x42[1, 2]	2.5-10	39.6-12.6	3.15	13.23	30mm	Int.	19.8	1,705.56	
3-12x50[1]	3-12	33-10.5	3.15	14.33	30mm	Int.	22.4	1,727.78	
4-16x50	4-16	30-8.5	3.15	14.22	30mm	Int.	22.3	1,754.44	
6-24x50	6-24	18.6-5.4	3.15	15.4	30mm	Int.	23.6	1,976.67	
AV Series									
3-9x36	3-9	39-13.5	3.35	11.8	1	Int.	11.7	854.44	
3-10x42AV[4]	3-10	33-11.7	3.35	12.44	1	Int.	12.7	943.33	
4-12x50AV[4]	4-12	29.1-9.9	3.35	13.5	1	Int.	13.9	987.78	
6-18x50	6-18	17.4-6.6	3.5	14.84	1	Int.	20.3	1,065.56	
SWIFT									
600 4x15	4	17	2.8	10.6	.75	Int.	3.5	15.00	All Swift scopes, with the exception of the 4x15, have Quadraplex reticles and are fogproof and waterproof. The 4x15 has crosshair reticle and is non-waterproof. [1]Available in regular matte black or silver finish. [2]Comes with ring mounts, wrench, lens caps, extension tubes, filter, battery. [3]Regular and matte black finish. [4]Speed Focus scopes. Partial listing shown. From Swift Instruments.
601 3-7x20	3-7	25-12	3-2.9	11	.75	Int.	5.6	35.00	
650 4x32	4	26	4	12	1	Int.	9.1	75.00	
653 4x40WA[1]	4	35	4	12.2	1	Int.	12.6	125.00	
654 3-9x32	3-9	35-12	3.4-2.9	12	1	Int.	9.8	125.00	
656 3-9x40WA[1]	3-9	40-14	3.4-2.8	12.6	1	Int.	12.3	140.00	
657 6x40	6	28	4	12.6	1	Int.	10.4	125.00	
658 2-7x40WA[3]	2-7	55-18	3.3-3	11.6	1	Int.	12.5	160.00	
659 3.5-10x44WA	3.5-10	34-12	3-2.8	12.8	1	Int.	13.5	230.00	
665 1.5-4.5x21	1.5-4.5	69-24.5	3.5-3	10.9	1	Int.	9.6	125.00	
665M 1.5-4.5x21	1.5-4.5	69-24.5	3.5-3	10.9	1	Int.	9.6	125.00	
666M Shotgun 1x20	1	113	3.2	7.5	1	Int.	9.6	130.00	
667 Fire-Fly[2]	1	40		5.4	30mm	Int.	5	220.00	
668M 4x32	4	25	4	10	1	Int.	8.9	120.00	
669M 6-18x44	6-18	18-6.5	2.8	14.5	1	Int.	17.6	220.00	
680M	3.9	43-14	4	18	40mm	Int.	17.5	399.95	
681M	1.5-6	56-13	4	11.8	40mm	Int.	17.5	399.95	
682M	4-12	33-11	4	15.4	50mm	Int.	21.7	499.95	
683M	2-7	55-17	3.3	11.6	32mm	Int.	10.6	499.95	
Premier Rifle Scopes									
648M[1] 1.5-4.5	32	71-25	3.05-3.27	10.41	1	Int.	12.7	179.95	

TDS   No. 4   No. 4A   No. 7A   Plex   No. 24

Maker and Model	Magn.	Field at 100 Yds. (feet)	Eye Relief (in.)	Length (in.)	Tube Dia. (in.)	W & E Adjustments	Weight (ozs.)	Price	Other Data
SWIFT *(cont.)*									
649R 4-12	50	29.5-9.5	3.3-3	13.8	1	Int.	15.8	245.00	
658M 2-7	40	55-18	3.3-3	11.6	1	Int.	12.5	175.00	
659S 3.5-10	44	34-12	3-2.8	12.8	1	Int.	13.5	215.00	
669M 6-18	44	18-6.5	2.8	14.5	1	Int.	17.6	230.00	
671M 3-9	50	35-25	3.24- 3.12	15.5	1	Int.	18.2	250.00	
672M 6-18	50	19-6.7	3.25-3	15.8	1	Int.	20.9	260.00	
674M 3-9	40	40-14.2	3.6-2.9	12	1	Int.	13.1	170.00	
676S 4-12	40	29.3-10.5	3.15-2.9	12.4	1	Int.	15.4	180.00	
677M 6-24	50	18-5	3.1-3.2	15.9	1	Int.	20.8	280.00	
678M 8-32	50	13-3.5	3.13-2.94	16.9	1	Int.	21.5	290.00	
685M[3] 3-9	40	39-13.5	3.7-2.8	12.4	1	Int.	20.5	189.95	
686M[3] 6.5-20	44	19-6.5	2.7	15.6	1	Int.	23.6	249.95	
687M[2] 4.5-14	44	25.5-8.5	3.2	14.1	1	Int.	21.5	220.00	
688M[2] 6-18	44	19.597	2.8	15.4	1	Int.	22.6	240.00	
Standard Rifle Scopes									
587[5] 4	32	25	3.1	11.7	1	Int.	13	50.00	
653M 4	40	35	4	12.2	1	Int.	12.6	128.00	
654M 3-9	32	35-12	3.4-2.9	12	1	Int.	9.8	125.00	
656 3-9	40	40-14	3.4-2.8	12.6	1	Int.	12.3	140.00	
657M 6	40	28	4	12.6	1	Int.	10.4	125.00	
660M[4] 2-6	32	14-4.5	20-12.6	5.5	1	Int.	10.6	241.80	
661M[4] 4	32	6.6	13.8	9.4	1	Int.	9.9	130.00	
663S[4] 4	32	9.8	7.3	7.2	1	Int.	8.5	130.00	
665M 1.5-4.5	21	69-24.5	3.5-3	10.8	1	Int.	9.6	125.00	
668M 4	32	25	4	10	1	Int.	8.9	120.00	
TASCO									
Target & Varmint									
VAR211042M	1.5-10	35.9	3	14	1	Int.	19.1	89.95	
MAG624X40	6-24	17-4	3	16	1	Int.	19.1	113.95	
VAR624X42M	6-24	13-3.7	7	16	1	Int.	19.6	113.95	
TG624X44DS	15-4.5	15-4.5	3	16.5	1	Int.	19.6	199.95	
TG832X44DS	8-32	11-3.5	3.25	17	1	Int.	20	219.95	
World Class									
BA1545X32	1.5-4.5	77-23	4	11.25	1	Int.	12	59.95	
DWC28x32	2-8	50-17	4	10.5	1	Int.	12.5	69.96	
DWC39X40N	3-9	41-15	3.5	12.75	1	Int.	13	73.95	
WA39X40N	3-9	41-15	3.5	12.75	1	Int.	13	73.95	
WA39X40STN	3-9	41-15	3.5	12.75	1	Int.	13	73.95	
DWC39X50N	3-9	41-13	3	12.5	1	Int.	15.8	87.95	
DWC39X40M	3-9	41-15	3.5	12.75	1	Int.	13	73.95	
DWC416X40	4-16	22.5-5-9	3.7	14	1	Int.	16	103.95	
DWC416X50	4-16	28-7	3	16	1	Int.	20.5	123.95	
ProPoint									
PDP2	1	40	Un.	5	1	Int.	5.5	117.95	
PDP3CMP	1	68	Un.	4.75	1	Int.	5.4	157.95	
PDP3	1	52	Un.	5	1	Int.	5.5	137.95	
PD3ST1	1	52	Un.	5	1	Int.	5.5	143.95	
PDPRGD	1	60	Un.	5.4	1	Int.	5.7	91.95	
Golden Antler									
DMGA4X32T	4	32	3	13.25	1	Int.	11	37.95	
GA3940	3-9	41-15	3	12.75	1	Int.	13	57.95	
GA2532CB	2.5	43	3.2	11.4	1	Int.	10.1	43.95	
GA3932AGD	3-9	39	3	13.25	1	Int.	12	43.95	
Pronghorn									
PH39X40D	3-9	39-13	3	13	1	Int.	12.1	47.95	
PH4X32D	4	32	3	12	1	Int.	11	32.95	
PH2533	2.5	43	3.2	11.4	1	Int.	10.1	32.95	
PH3950D	3-9	33	3.3	13	1	Int.	14.8	57.95	
.22 Riflescopes									
MAG39X32D	3-9	17.75-6	3	12.75	1	Int.	11.3	55.95	
MAG4X32SD	4	13.5	3	12.75	1	Int.	12.1	43.95	
Rimfire									
EZ01D	1	35	Un.	4.75	1	Int.	2.5	17.95	
RF37X20D	3-7	24	2.5	11.5	1	Int.	5.7	29.95	
RF4X15D	4	20.5	2.5	11	1	Int.	3.8	7.95	
RF4X20WAD	4	23	2.5	10.5	1	Int.	3.8	9.95	
Red Dot									
BKR30	1	57	Un.	3.75	1	Int.	6	45.95	
BKR3022* (22 rimfire)	1	57	Un.	3.75	1	Int.	6	45.95	
BKR42	1	62	Un.	3.75	1	Int.	6.7	57.95	
THOMPSON/CENTER RECOIL PROOF SERIES									
Pistol Scopes									
8315[2]	2.5-7	15-5	8-21, 8-11	9.25	1	Int.	9.2	364.00	[1]Black finish; silver optional. [2]Black; lighted reticle. From Thompson/Center Arms.
8326[4]	2.5-7	15-5	8-21, 8-11	9.25	1	Int.	10.5	432.00	
Muzzleloader Scopes									
8658	1	60	3.8	9.125	1	Int.	10.2	146.00	
8662	4	16	3	8.8	1	Int.	9.1	141.00	

SCOPES / Hunting, Target & Varmint

Maker and Model	Magn.	Field at 100 Yds. (feet)	Eye Relief (in.)	Length (in.)	Tube Dia. (in.)	W & E Adjustments	Weight (ozs.)	Price	Other Data
TRIJICON									
Reflex II 1x24	1			4.25		Int.	4.2	425.00	[1]Advanced Combat Optical Gunsight for AR-15, M16, with integral mount. Other mounts available. All models feature tritium and fiber optics dual-lighting system that requires no batteries. From Trijicon, Inc.
TA44 1.5x16[1]	1.5	39	2.4	5.34		Int.	5.31	895.00	
TA45 1.5x24[1]	1.5	25.6	3.6	5.76		Int.	5.92	950.00	
TA47 2x20[1]	2	33.1	2.1	5.3		Int.	5.82	950.00	
TA50 3x24[1]	3	29.5	1.4	5		Int.	5.89	950.00	
TA11 3.5x35[1]	3.5	25.6	2.4	8		Int.	14	1,295.00	
TA01 4x32[1]	4	36.8	1.5	5.8		Int.	9.9	950.00	
Variable AccuPoint									
3-9x40	3-9	33.8-11.3	3.6-3.2	12.2	1	Int.	12.8	720.00	
1.25-4x24	1.25-4	61.6-20.5	4.8-3.4	10.2	1	Int.	11.4	700.00	
ULTRA DOT									
Micro-Dot Scopes[1]									
1.5-4.5x20 Rifle	1.5-4.5	80-26	3	9.8	1	Int.	10.5	297.00	[1]Brightness-adjustable fiber optic red dot reticle. Waterproof, nitrogen-filled one-piece tube. Tinted see-through lens covers and battery included. [2]Parallax adjustable. [3]Ultra Dot sights include rings, battery, polarized filter, and 5-year warranty. All models available in black or satin finish. [4]Illuminated red dot has eleven brightness settings. Shock-proof aluminum tube. From Ultra Dot Distribution.
2-7x32	2-7	54-18	3	11	1	Int.	12.1	308.00	
3-9x40	3-9	40-14	3	12.2	1	Int.	13.3	327.00	
4x-12x56[2]	4-12	30-10	3	14.3	1	Int.	18.3	417.00	
Ultra-Dot Sights[3]									
Ultra-Dot 25[4]	1			5.1	1	Int.	3.9	159.00	
Ultra-Dot 30[4]	1			5.1	30mm	Int.	4	179.00	
UNERTL									
1" Target	6, 8, 10	16-10	2	21.5	.75	Ext.	21	675.00	[1]Dural .25-MOA click mounts. Hard coated lenses. Non-rotating objective lens focusing. [2].25-MOA click mounts. [3]With target mounts. [4]With calibrated head. [5]Same as 1" Target but without objective lens focusing. [6]With new Posa mounts. [7]Range focus unit near rear of tube. Price is with Posa or standard mounts. Magnum clamp. From Unertl.
10X	10	10.3	3	12.5	1	Ext.	35	2,500.00	
1.25" Target[1]	8, 10, 12, 14	12-16	2	25	.75	Ext.	21	715.00	
1.5" Target	10, 12, 14, 16, 18, 20	11.5-3.2	2.25	25.5	.75	Ext.	31	753.50	
2" Target[2]	10, 12, 14, 16, 18, 24, 30, 32, 36	8	2.25	26.25	1	Ext.	44	918.50	
Varmint, 1.25"[3] 3" Ultra Varmint, 2"[4]	15	12.6-7	2.25	24	1	Ext.	34	918.50	
Small Game[5]	3, 4, 6	25-17	2.25	18	.75	Ext.	16	550.00	
Programmer 200[7]	10, 12, 14, 16, 18, 20, 24, 30, 36	11.3-4		26.5	1	Ext.	45	1,290.00	
B8									
Tube Sight				17		Ext.		420.00	
U.S. OPTICS									
SN-1/TAR Fixed Power System									
16.2x	15	8.6	4.3	16.5	30mm	Int.	27	1,700.00	Prices shown are estimates; scopes built to order; choice of reticles; choice of front or rear focal plane; extra-heavy MIL-SPEC construction; extra-long turrets; individual W&E rebound springs; up to 100mm dia. objectives; up to 50mm tubes; all lenses multi-coated. Other magnifications available. [1]Modular components allow a variety of fixed or variable magnifications, night vision, etc. Made in U.S. by U.S. Optics.
22.4x	20	5.8	3.8	18	30mm	Int.	29	1,800.00	
26x	24	5	3.4	18	30mm	Int.	31	1,900.00	
31x	30	4.6	3.5	18	30mm	Int.	32	2,100.00	
37x	36	4	3.6	18	30mm	Int.	32	2,300.00	
48x	50	3	3.8	18	30mm	Int.	32	2,500.00	
Variables									
SN-2	4-22	26.8-5.8	5.4-3.8	18	30mm	Int.	24	1,762.00	
SN-3	1.6-8		4.4-4.8	18.4	30mm	Int.	36	1,435.00	
SN-4	1-4	116-31.2	4.6-4.9	18	30mm	Int.	35	1,065.00	
Fixed Power									
SN-6	8, 10, 17, 22	14-8.5	3.8-4.8	9.2	30mm	Int.	18	1,195.00	
SN-8 Modular[1]	4, 10, 20, 40	32	3.3	7.5	30mm	Int.	11.1	890.00-4,000.00	
WEAVER									
Riflescopes									
K2.5[1]	2.5	35	3.7	9.5	1	Int.	7.3	132.86	[1]Gloss black. [2]Matte black. [3]Silver. [4]Satin. [5]Silver and black (slightly higher in price). [6]Field of view measured at 18" eye relief. .25 MOA click adjustments, except T-Series which vary from .125 to .25 clicks. One-piece tubes with multi-coated lenses. All scopes are shock-proof, waterproof, and fogproof. Dual-X reticle available in all except V24 which has a fine X-hair and dot; T-Series in which certain models are available in fine X-hair and dots; Qwik-Point red dot scopes which are available in fixed 4 or 12 MOA, or variable 4-8-12 MOA. V16 also available with fine X-hair, dot or Dual-X reticle. T-Series scopes have Micro-Trac® adjustments. From Weaver Products.
K4[1,2]	3.7	26.5	3.3	11.3	1	Int.	10	149.99	
K6[1]	5.7	18.5	3.3	11.4	1	Int.	10	154.99	
KT15[1]	14.6	7.5	3.2	12.9	1	Int.	14.7	281.43	
V3[1,2]	1.1-2.8	88-32	3.9-3.7	9.2	1	Int.	8.5	189.99	
V9[1,2]	2.8-8.7	33-11	3.5-3.4	12.1	1	Int.	11.1	249.99-299.99	
V9x50[1,2]	3-9	29.4-9.9	3.6-3	13.1	1	Int.	14.5	239.99	
V10[1-3]	2.2-9.6	38.5-9.5	3.4-3.3	12.2	1	Int.	11.2	259.99-269.99	
V10-50[1-3]	2.3-9.7	40.2-9.2	2.9-2.8	13.75	1	Int.	15.2	279.99	
V16 MDX[2,3]	3.8-15.5	26.8-6.8	3.1	13.9	1	Int.	16.5	329.99	
V16 MFC[2,3]	3.8-15.5	26.8-6.8	3.1	13.9	1	Int.	16.5	329.99	
V16 MDT[2,3]	3.8-15.5	26.8-6.8	3.1	13.9	1	Int.	16.5	329.99	
V24 Varmint[2]	6-24	15.3-4	3.15	14.3	1	Int.	17.5	379.99-399.99	
Handgun									
H2[1-3]	2	21	4-29	8.5	1	Int.	6.7	161.43	
H4[1-3]	4	18	11.5-18	8.5	1	Int.	6.7	175.00	
VH4[1-3]	1.5-4	13.6-5.8	11-17	8.6	1	Int.	8.1	215.71	
VH8[1-3]	2.5-8	8.5-3.7	12.16	9.3	1	Int.	8.3	228.57	
Rimfire									
RV7[2]	2.5-7	37-13	3.7-3.3	10.75	1	Int.	10.7	148.57	

Maker and Model	Magn.	Field at 100 Yds. (feet)	Eye Relief (in.)	Length (in.)	Tube Dia. (in.)	W & E Adjustments	Weight (ozs.)	Price	Other Data
WEAVER (cont.)									
Grand Slam									
6-20x40mm Varminter Reticle[2]	6-20X	16.5-5.25	2.75-3	14.48	1	Int.	17.75	**419.99**	
6-20x40mm Fine Crosshairs w/Dot[2]	6-20X	16.5-5.25	2.75-3	14.48	1	Int.	17.75	**419.99**	
1.5-5x32mm[2]	1.5-5X	71-21	3.25	10.5	1	Int.	10.5	**349.99**	
4.75x40mm[2]	4.75X	14.75	3.25	11	1	Int.	10.75	**299.99**	
3-10x40mm[2]	3-10X	35-11.33	3.5-3	12.08	1	Int.	12.08	**329.99**	
3.5-10x50mm[2]	3.5-10X	30.5-10.8	3.5-3	12.96	1	Int.	16.25	**389.99**	
4.5-14x40mm	4.5-14X	22.5-10.5	3.5-3	14.48	1	Int.	17.5	**399.99**	
T-Series									
T-64	614	14	3.58	12.75	1	Int.	14.9	**424.95**	
T-36[3-4]	36	3	3	15.1	1	Int.	16.7	**489.99**	
ZEISS									
ZM/Z									
6x42MC	6	22.9	3.2	12.7	1	Int.	13.4	**749.00**	[1]Also avail. with illuminated reticle. [2]Illuminated Vari-point reticle. Black matte finish. All scopes have .25-min. click-stop adjustments. Choice of Z-Plex or fine crosshair reticles. Rubber armored objective bell, rubber eyepiece ring. Lenses have T-Star coating for highest light transmission. VM/V scopes avail. with rail mount. Partial listing shown. From Carl Zeiss Optical, Inc.
8x56MC	8	18	3.2	13.8	1	Int.	17.6	**829.00**	
1.25-4x24MC	1.25-4	105-33	3.2	11.46	30mm	Int.	17.3	**779.00**	
1.5-6x42MC	1.5-6	65.5-22.9	3.2	12.4	30mm	Int.	18.5	**899.00**	
2.5-10x48MC[1]	2.5-10	33-11.7	3.2	14.5	30mm	Int.	24	**1,029.00**	
3-12x56MC	3-12	27.6-9.9	3.2	15.3	30mm	Int.	25.8	**1,099.00**	
Conquest									
3-9x40MC[3]	3-9	37.5	3.34	12.36	1	Int.	17.28	**499.99**	[1]Stainless. [2]Turkey reticle. [3]Black matte finish. All scopes have .25-min. click-stop adjustments. Choice of Z-Plex, Turkey or fine crosshair reticles. Coated lenses for highest light transmisison. Partial listing shown. From Carl Zeiss Optical, Inc.
3-9x40MC[1]	3-9	37.5	3.34	12.36	1	Int.	17.28	**529.99**	
3-9x40S[3]	3-9	37.5	3.34	12.36	1	Int.	17.28	**499.99**	
3-9x40S[2,3]	3-9	37.5	3.34	12.36	1	Int.	17.28	**529.99**	
3-12x56MC[3]	2.5-10	27.6	3.2	15.3	30mm	Int.	25.8	**1,049.00**	
3-12x56MC[1]	3-12	27.6	3.2	15.3	30mm	Int.	25.8	**1,079.00**	
VM/V									
1.1-4x24 VariPoint T[2]	1.1-4	120-34	3.5	11.8	30mm	Int.	15.8	**1,699.00**	
1.5-6x42T*	1.5-6	65.5-22.9	3.2	12.4	30mm	Int.	18.5	**1,299.00**	
2.5-10x50T*[1]	2.5-10	47.1-13	3.5	12.5	30mm	Int.	16.25	**1,499.00**	
3-12x56T*	3-12	37.5-10.5	3.5	13.5	30mm	Int.	19.5	**1,499.00**	
3-9x42T*	3-9	42-15	3.74	13.3	1	Int.	15.3	**1,999.00**	
5-15x42T*	5-15	25.7-8.5	3.74	13.3	1	Int.	15.4	**1,399.00**	

Hunting scopes in general are furnished with a choice of reticlecrosshairs, post with crosshairs, tapered or blunt post, or dot crosshairs, etc.
The great majority of target and varmint scopes have medium or fine crosshairs but post or dot reticles may be ordered.
W=windage; E=Elevation; MOA=Minute of Angle or 1" (approx.) at 100 yards.

LASER SIGHTS

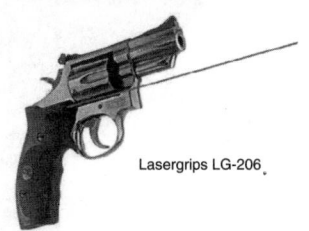

Lasergrips LG-206

Alpec Mini Shot

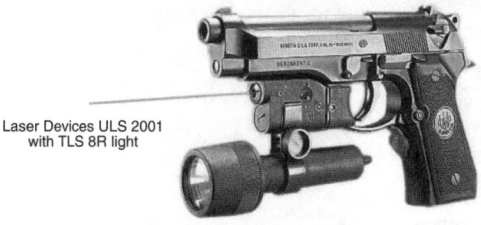

Laser Devices ULS 2001
with TLS 8R light

Maker and Model	Wave length (nm)	Beam Color	Lens	Operating Temp. (degrees F.)	Weight (ozs.)	Price	Other Data
ALPEC							[1]Range 1000 yards. [2]Range 300 yards. Mini Shot II range 500 yards, output 650mm, **$129.95**. [3]Range 300 yards; Laser Shot II 500 yards; Super Laser Shot 1000 yards. Black or stainless finish aluminum; removable pressure or push-button switch. Mounts for most handguns, many rifles and shotguns. From Alpec Team, Inc.
Power Shot[1]	635	Red	Glass	NA	2.5	**$199.95**	
Mini Shot[2]	670	Red	Glass	NA	2.5	**$99.95**	
Laser Shot[3]	670	Red	Glass	NA	3.0	**$99.95**	
BEAMSHOT							[1]Black or silver finish; adj. for windage and elevation; 300-yd. range; also M1000/S (500-yd. range), M1000/u (800-yd.). [2]Black finish; 300-, 500-, 800-yd. models. All come with removable touch pad switch, 5" cable. Mounts to fit virtually any firearm. From Quarton USA Co.
1000[1]	670	Red	Glass	NA	3.8	**NA**	
3000[2]	635/670	Red	Glass	NA	2.0	**NA**	
1001/u	635	Red	Glass	NA	3.8	**NA**	
780	780	Red	Glass	NA	3.8	**NA**	
BSA							[1]Comes with mounts for 22/air rifle and Weaver-style bases.
LS650[1]	N/A	Red	NA	NA	NA	**$49.95**	
LASERAIM							[1]Red dot/laser combo; 300-yd. range; LA3xHD Hotdot has 500-yd. range **$249.00**; [4] MOA dot size, laser gives 2" dot size at 100 yds. 230mm obj. lens; [4]MOA dot at 100 yds: fits Weaver base. 3300-yd range; 2" dot at 100 yds.; rechargeable Nicad battery 41.5-mile range; 1" dot at 100 yds.; 20+ hrs. batt. life. [5]1.5-mile range; 1" dot at 100 yds; rechargeable Nicad battery (comes with in-field charger); [6]Black or satin finish. With mount, **$169.00**. [7]Laser projects 2" dot at 100 yds.: with rotary switch; with Hotdot **$237.00**; with Hotdot touch switch **$357.00**. [8]For Glock 17-27; G1 Hotdot **$299.00**; price installed. 10Fits std. Weaver base, no rings required; 6-MOA dot; seven brightness settings. All have W&E adj.; black or satin silver finish. From Laseraim Technologies, Inc.
LRS-0650-SSW	650	Red	Glass	NA	1.2	**$96.00**	
LRS-0650-SCS	650	Red	Glass	NA	1.2	**$96.00**	
LRS-0650-CCW	650	Red	Glass	NA	1.2	**$96.00**	
LRS-0635-SSW	635	Red	Glass	NA	1.2	**$112.00**	
LRS-0635-SCS	635	Red	Glass	NA	1.2	**$112.00**	
LRS-0635-CCW	635	Red	Glass	NA	1.2	**$112.00**	
QDL-65GB-730	650	Red	Glass	NA	1.8	**$119.95**	
QDL-65SW-730	650	Red	Glass	NA	1.8	**$119.95**	
QDL-63GB-730	635	Red	Glass	NA	1.8	**$147.95**	
QDL-63SW-730	635	Red	Glass	NA	1.8	**$147.95**	
PLR-0006-140	650	Red	Glass	NA	1.8	**$78.95**	
PLW-0006-140	635	Red	Glass	NA	1.8	**$78.95**	
BLS-0650/0635-140	650/635	Red	Glass	NA	NA	**$78.95**	
Lasers							
MA-35RB Mini Aimer[7]				NA	1.0	**$129.00**	
G1 Laser[8]				NA	2.0	**$229.00**	
LASER DEVICES							[1]For S&W P99 semi-auto pistols; also BA-2, 5 oz., **$339.00**. [2]For revolvers. [3]For HK, Walther P99. [4]For semi-autos. [5]For rifles; also FA-4/ULS, 2.5 oz., **$325.00**. [6]For HK sub guns. [7]For military rifles. [8]For shotguns. [9]For SIG-Pro pistol. [10]Universal, semi-autos. [11]For AR-15 variants. All avail. with Magnum Power Point (650nM) or daytime-visible Super Power Point (632nM) diode. Infrared diodes avail. for law enforcement. From Laser Devices, Inc.
BA-1[1]	632	Red	Glass	NA	2.4	**$372.00**	
BA-3[2]	632	Red	Glass	NA	3.3	**$332.50**	
BA-5[3]	632	Red	Glass	NA	3.2	**$372.00**	
Duty-Grade[4]	632	Red	Glass	NA	3.5	**$372.00**	
FA-4[5]	632	Red	Glass	NA	2.6	**$358.00**	
LasTac[1]	632	Red	Glass	NA	5.5	**$298.00 to 477.00**	
MP-5[6]	632	Red	Glass	NA	2.2	**$495.00**	
MR-2[7]	632	Red	Glass	NA	6.3	**$485.00**	
SA-2[8]	632	Red	Glass	NA	3.0	**$360.00**	
SIG-Pro[9]	632	Red	Glass	NA	2.6	**$372.00**	
ULS-2001[10]	632	Red	Glass	NA	4.5	**$210.95**	
Universal AR-2A	632	Red	Glass	NA	4.5	**$445.00**	
LASERGRIPS							Replaces existing grips with built-in laser high in the right grip panel. Integrated pressure sensi tive pad in grip activates the laser. Also has master on/off switch. [1]For Colt 1911/Commander. [2]For all Glock models. Option on/off switch. Requires factory installation. [3]For S&W K, L, N frames, round or square butt (LG-207); [4]For Taurus small-frame revolvers. [5]For Ruger SP-101. [6]For SIG Sauer P226. From Crimson Trace Corp. [7]For Beretta 92/96. [8]For Ruger MK II. [9]For S&W J-frame. [10]For Sig Sauer P228/229. [11]For Colt 1911 full size, wraparound. [12]For Beretta 92/96, wraparound. [13]For Colt 1911 compact, wraparound. [14]For S&W J-frame, rubber.
LG-301/401/401-P1[1]	633	Red-Orange	Glass	NA		**$299.00**	
LG-304/404/404-P1[2]	633	Red-Orange	Glass	NA		**$229.00**	
LG-302/312[3]	633	Red-Orange	Glass	NA		**$229.00**	
LG-617[4]	633	Red-Orange	Glass	NA		**$229.00**	
LG-619[5]	633	Red-Orange	Glass	NA		**$229.00**	
LG-626[6]	633	Red-Orange	Glass	NA		**$595.00**	
LG-629[7]	633	Red-Orange	Glass	NA		**$299.00**	

LASER SIGHTS

Lasermax Glock 23 Lasers

Lasermax Glock 35

Lasermax SIG 228 two-tone

Maker and Model	Wave length (nm)	Beam Color	Lens	Operating Temp. (degrees F.)	Weight (ozs.)	Price	Other Data
LASERGRIPS *(cont.)*							
LG-203[8]	633	Red-Orange	Glass	NA		$299.00	
LG-389[9]	633	Red-Orange	Glass	NA		$299.00	
LG-320[10]	633	Red-Orange	Glass	NA		$299.00	
LG-326[11]	633	Red-Orange	Glass	NA		$329.00	
LG-329[12]	633	Red-Orange	Glass	NA		$329.00	
LG-359[13]	633	Red-Orange	Glass	NA		$329.00	
LG-101[14]	633	Red-Orange	Glass	NA		$299.00	
LASERLYTE							[1]Dot/circle or dot/crosshair projection; black or stainless. [2]Also 635/645mm model. From Tac Star Laserlyte. in grip activates the laser. Also has master on/off switch.
LLX-0006-140/090[1]	635/645	Red		NA	1.4	$159.95	
WPL-0004-140/090[2]	670	Red		NA	1.2	$109.95	
TPL-0004-140/090[2]	670	Red		NA	1.2	$109.95	
T7S-0004-140[2]	670	Red		NA	0.8	$109.95	
LASERMAX							Internal Laser Sights: Replace the recoil spring/guide rod assembly and include a customized takedown lever that serves as the laser on/off switch. For Glock, Sigarms, Beretta, Springfield and 1911 Gov't models and more. Easy installation - no gunsmithing necessary. Laser/Tactical Lights: LaserMax's distinctive pulsing beam combines with a 60 Lumen Tactical Light in the integrated LMS-1202 shotgun unit. Compatability:
LMS-1131P[1]	635	Red-Orange	Glass	15° F - 120° F	.6	$339.00	
LMS-1141P[2]	635	Red-Orange	Glass	15° F - 120° F	.6	$339.00	
LMS-1141LP[3]	635	Red-Orange	Glass	15° F - 120° F	.6	$339.00	
LMS-1151P[4]	635	Red-Orange	Glass	15° F - 120° F	.6	$339.00	[1]Glock 19, 23, 32, 38
LMS-1151PFGR[5]	635	Red-Orange	Glass	15° F - 120° F	.6	$339.00	[2]Glock 17, 22, 31, 37
LMS-1161[6]	635	Red-Orange	Glass	15° F - 120° F	.6	$339.00	[3]Glock 34, 35, 17L, 24, 37L
LMS-1171[7]	635	Red-Orange	Glass	15° F - 120° F	.6	$339.00	[4]Glock 20, 21
LMS-1181[8]	635	Red-Orange	Glass	15° F - 120° F	.6	$339.00	[5]Glock 20, 21 FG/R
LMS-1191[9]	635	Red-Orange	Glass	15° F - 120° F	.6	$339.00	[6]Glock 26, 27, 33
LMS-2201[10]	635	Red-Orange	Glass	15° F - 120° F	.6	$399.00	[7]Glock 39
LMS-2251[11]	635	Red-Orange	Glass	15° F - 120° F	.6	$399.00	[8]Glock 36
LMS-2261[12]	635	Red-Orange	Glass	15° F - 120° F	.6	$399.00	[9]Glock 29, 30
LMS-2261S[13]	635	Red-Orange	Glass	15° F - 120° F	.6	$399.00	[10]SIG P220, .45 ACP
LMS-2263[14]	635	Red-Orange	Glass	15° F - 120° F	.6	$399.00	[11]SIG P225
LMS-2281[15]	635	Red-Orange	Glass	15° F - 120° F	.6	$399.00	[12]SIG P226, 9mm
LMS-2291[16]	635	Red-Orange	Glass	15° F - 120° F	.6	$399.00	[13]SIG P226, 9mm*
LMS-2391[17]	635	Red-Orange	Glass	15° F - 120° F	.6	$399.00	[14]SIG P226 .357/.40
LMS-2451[18]	635	Red-Orange	Glass	15° F - 120° F	.6	$399.00	[15]SIG P228
LMS-1911M[19]	635	Red-Orange	Glass	15° F - 120° F	.6	$399.00	[16]SIG P229
LMS-1911S[20]	635	Red-Orange	Glass	15° F - 120° F	.6	$399.00	[17]SIG P239, .357, .40
LMS-1911B[21]	635	Red-Orange	Glass	15° F - 120° F	.6	$399.00	[18]SIG P245
LMS-PARA1911M[22]	635	Red-Orange	Glass	15° F - 120° F	.6	$399.00	[19]1911 Gov't, matte
LMS-PARA1911S[23]	635	Red-Orange	Glass	15° F - 120° F	.6	$399.00	[20]1911 Gov't, stainless
LMS-PARA1911B[24]	635	Red-Orange	Glass	15° F - 120° F	.6	$399.00	[21]1911 Gov't, blued
LMS-3XD[25]	635	Red-Orange	Glass	15° F - 120° F	.6	$399.00	[22]Para 1911, matte
LMS-4XD9/357[26]	635	Red-Orange	Glass	15° F - 120° F	.6	$399.00	[23]Para 1911, stainless
LMS-4XD40[27]	635	Red-Orange	Glass	15° F - 120° F	.6	$399.00	[24]Para 1911, blued
LMS-5XD[28]	635	Red-Orange	Glass	15° F - 120° F	.6	$399.00	[25]Springfield XD, 3"
LMS-1431[29]	635	Red-Orange	Glass	15° F - 120° F	.6	$399.00	[26]Springfield XD, 4", 9mm, .357
LMS-1441[30]	635	Red-Orange	Glass	15° F - 120° F	.6	$399.00	[27]Springfield XD, 4", .40
LMS-591S[31]	635	Red-Orange	Glass	15° F - 120° F	.6	$399.00	[28]Springfield XD, 5"
LMS-591B[32]	635	Red-Orange	Glass	15° F - 120° F	.6	$399.00	[29]Beretta 92/96 Centurion
LMS-1202[33]	635	Red-Orange	Glass	15° F - 120° F	.6	$399.00	[30]Beretta 92/96 full-size [31]S&W 5906-type, stainless [32]S&W, full-size [33]Remington 870, 1100, 11-87; Benelli M1014 12-gauge semi-auto combat shotguns

SCOPE RINGS & BASES

Maker, Model, Type	Adjust.	Scopes	Price
ADCO			
Std. Black or nickel		1"	$13.95
Std. Black or nickel		30mm	$13.95
Rings Black or nickel		30mm with 3/8" grv.	$13.95
Rings Black or nickel		1" raised 3/8" grv.	$13.95
AIMTECH			
AMT Auto Mag II .22 Mag.	No	Weaver rail	$56.99
Astra .44 Mag Revolver	No	Weaver rail	$63.25
Beretta/Taurus 92/99	No	Weaver rail	$63.25
Browning Buckmark/Challenger II	No	Weaver rail	$56.99
Browning Hi-Power	No	Weaver rail	$63.25
Glock 17, 17L, 19, 23, 24 etc. no rail	No	Weaver rail	$63.25
Glock 20, 21 no rail	No	Weaver rail	$63.25
Glock 9mm and .40 with access. rail	No	Weaver rail	$74.95
Govt. 45 Auto/.38 Super	No	Weaver rail	$63.25
Hi-Standard (Mitchell version) 107	No	Weaver rail	$63.25
H&K USP 9mm/40 rail mount	No	Weaver rail	$74.95
Rossi 85/851/951 Revolvers	No	Weaver rail	$63.25
Ruger Mk I, Mk II	No	Weaver rail	$49.95
Ruger P85/P89	No	Weaver rail	$63.25
S&W K, L, N frames	No	Weaver rail	$63.25
S&W K, L, N with tapped top strap*	No	Weaver rail	$69.95
S&W Model 41 Target 22	No	Weaver rail	$63.25
S&W Model 52 Target 38	No	Weaver rail	$63.25
S&W Model 99 Walther frame rail mount	No	Weaver rail	$74.95
S&W 2nd Gen. 59/459/659 etc.	No	Weaver rail	$56.99
S&W 3rd Gen. full size 5906 etc.	No	Weaver rail	$69.95
S&W 422, 622, 2206	No	Weaver rail	$56.99
S&W 645/745	No	Weaver rail	$56.99
S&W Sigma	No	Weaver rail	$64.95
Taurus PT908	No	Weaver rail	$63.25
Taurus 44 6.5" bbl.	No	Weaver rail	$69.95
Walther 99	No	Weaver rail	$74.95
Shotguns			
Benelli M-1 Super 90	No	Weaver rail	$44.95
Benelli Montefeltro	No	Weaver rail	$44.95
Benelli Nova	No	Weaver rail	$69.95
Benelli Super Black Eagle	No	Weaver rail	$49.95
Browning A-5 12-ga.	No	Weaver rail	$40.95
Browning BPS 12-ga.	No	Weaver rail	$40.95
Browning Gold Hunter 12-ga.	No	Weaver rail	$44.95
Browning Gold Hunter 20-ga.	No	Weaver rail	$49.95
Browning Gold Hunter 10-ga.	No	Weaver rail	$49.95
Beretta 303 12-ga.	No	Weaver rail	$44.95
Beretta 390 12-ga.	No	Weaver rail	$44.95
Beretta Pintail	No	Weaver rail	$44.95
H&K Fabarms Gold/Silver Lion	No	Weaver rail	$49.95
Ithaca 37/87 12-ga.	No	Weaver rail	$40.95
Ithaca 37/87 20-ga.	No	Weaver rail	$40.95
Mossberg 500/Maverick 12-ga.	No	Weaver rail	$40.95
Mossberg 500/Maverick 20-ga.	No	Weaver rail	$40.95
Mossberg 835 3.5" Ulti-Mag	No	Weaver rail	$40.95
Mossberg 5500/9200	No	Weaver rail	$40.95
Remington 1100/1187 12-ga.	No	Weaver rail	$42.80
Remington 1100/1187 12-ga. LH	No	Weaver rail	$42.80
Remington 1100/1187 20-ga.	No	Weaver rail	$40.95
Remington 1100/1187 20-ga. LH	No	Weaver rail	$40.95
Remington 870 12-ga.	No	Weaver rail	$40.95
Remington 870 12-ga. LH	No	Weaver rail	$40.95
Remington 870 20-ga.	No	Weaver rail	$42.80
Remington 870 20-ga. LH	No	Weaver rail	$42.80
Remington 870 Express Magnum	No	Weaver rail	$40.95
Remington SP-10 10-ga.	No	Weaver rail	$49.95
Winchester 1300 12-ga.	No	Weaver rail	$40.95
Winchester 1400 12-ga.	No	Weaver rail	$40.95
Winchester Super X2	No	Weaver rail	$44.95
"Rib Rider" Ultra Low Profile Mounts **Non See-Through 2-piece rib attached**			
Mossberg 500/835/9200	No	Weaver rail	$29.95
Remington 1100/1187/870	No	Weaver rail	$29.95
Winchester 1300	No	Weaver rail	$29.95
1-Piece Rib Rider Low Rider Mounts			
Mossberg 500/835/9200	No	Weaver rail	$29.95
Remington 1100/1187/870	No	Weaver rail	$29.95
Winchester 1300	No	Weaver rail	$29.95
2-Piece Rib Rider See-Through			
Mossberg 500/835/9200	No	Weaver rail	$29.95
Remington 1100/1187/870	No	Weaver rail	$29.95
Winchester 1300	No	Weaver rail	$29.95

Maker, Model, Type	Adjust.	Scopes	Price
AIMTECH (cont.)			
1-Piece Rib Rider See-Through			
Mossberg 500/835/9200	No	Weaver rail	$29.95
Remington 1100/1187/870	No	Weaver rail	$29.95
Winchester 1300	No	Weaver rail	$29.95
Rifles			
AR-15/M16	No	Weaver rail	$21.95
Browning A-Bolt	No	Weaver rail	$21.95
Browning BAR	No	Weaver rail	$21.95
Browning BLR	No	Weaver rail	$21.95
CVA Apollo	No	Weaver rail	$21.95
Marlin 336	No	Weaver rail	$21.95
Mauser Mark X	No	Weaver rail	$21.95
Modern Muzzleloading	No	Weaver rail	$21.95
Remington 700 Short Action	No	Weaver rail	$21.95
Remington 700 Long Action	No	Weaver rail	$21.95
Remington 7400/7600	No	Weaver rail	$21.95
Ruger 10/22	No	Weaver rail	$21.95
Ruger Mini 14 Scout Rail**	No	Weaver rail	$89.50
Savage 110, 111, 113, 114, 115, 116	No	Weaver rail	$21.95
Thompson Center Thunderhawk	No	Weaver rail	$21.95
Traditions Buckhunter	No	Weaver rail	$21.95
White W Series	No	Weaver rail	$21.95
White G Series	No	Weaver rail	$21.95
White WG Series	No	Weaver rail	$21.95
Winchester Model 70	No	Weaver rail	$21.95
Winchester 94 AE	No	Weaver rail	$21.95

All mounts no-gunsmithing, iron sight usable. Rifle mounts are solid see-through bases. All mounts accommodate standard Weaver-style rings of all makers. From Aimtech division, L&S Technologies, Inc. *3-blade sight mount combination. **Replacement handguard and mounting rail.

Maker, Model, Type	Adjust.	Scopes	Price
A.R.M.S.			
M16A1, A2, AR-15	No	Weaver rail	$59.95
Multibase	No	Weaver rail	$59.95
#19 ACOG Throw Lever Mt.	No	Weaver rail	$150.00
#19 Weaver/STANAG Throw Lever Rail	No	Weaver rail	$140.00
STANAG Rings	No	30mm	$75.00
Throw Lever Rings	No	Weaver rail	$99.00
Ring Inserts	No	1", 30mm	$29.00
#22M68 Aimpoint Comp Ring Throw Lever	No	Weaver rail	$99.00
#38 Std. Swan Sleeve[1]	No		$180.00
#39 A2 Plus Mod. Mt.	No	#39T rail	$125.00

[1]Avail. in three lengths. From A.R.M.S., Inc.

Maker, Model, Type	Adjust.	Scopes	Price
ARMSON			
AR-15[1]	No	1"	$45.00
Mini-14[2]	No	1"	$66.00
H&K[3]	No	1"	$82.00

[1]Fastens with one nut. [2]Models 181, 182, 183, 184, etc. [3]Claw mount. From Trijicon, Inc.

Maker, Model, Type	Adjust.	Scopes	Price
AO			
AO/Lever Scout Scope	No	Weaver rail	$50.00

No gunsmithing required for lever-action rifles with 8" Weaver-style rails; surrounds barrel shank; 6" long; low profile. AO Sight Systems Inc.

Maker, Model, Type	Adjust.	Scopes	Price
B-SQUARE			
Pistols (centerfire)			
Colt M1911	E only	Weaver rail	$79.30
H&K USP, 9mm and 40 S&W	No	Weaver rail	$79.30
Pistols (rimfire)			
Browning Buck Mark	No	Weaver rail	$39.10
Ruger Mk I/II, bull or taper	No	Weaver rail	$44.56-48.02
Revolvers			
Colt Anaconda/Python/Taurus 689	No	Weaver rail	$70.36-79.30
Ruger Single-Six	No	Weaver rail	$66.50-74.94
Ruger GP-100	No	Weaver rail	$70.36-79.30
Ruger Blackhawk, Super	No	Weaver rail	$70.36-79.30
Ruger Redhawk, Super	No	Weaver rail	$70.36-79.30
Smith & Wesson K, L, N	No	Weaver rail	$66.50-74.94
Taurus 66, 669, 607, 608	No	Weaver rail	$66.50-74.94
InterLock Rings (sporting rifles)			
1" Standard Dovetail (w/recoil blade)	No	Weaver rail	$31.94-$36.34
30mm Stand. Dovetail (w/recoil blade)	No	Weaver rail	$36.34
1"x11mm Dovetail	No	Weaver rail	$34.14
1"x.22 Dovetail	No	Weaver rail	$31.94

SCOPE RINGS & BASES

Maker, Model, Type	Adjust.	Scopes	Price
B-SQUARE (cont.)			
InterLock Adjustable Rings (sporting rifles)			
1" Standard Dovetail (w/recoil blade)	Yes	Weaver rail	$60.55
30mm Stand. Dovetail (w/recoil blade)	Yes	Weaver rail	$64.96
1"x11mm Dovetail	Yes	Weaver rail	$60.56
1"x.22 Dovetail	Yes	Weaver rail	$64.96
InterLock One-Piece Bases			
Most models			$5.50
Modern Military (rings incl.)			
AK-47/MAC 90	No	Weaver rail	$70.36
Colt AR-15	No	Weaver rail	$72.60
FN/FAL/LAR (See-Thru rings)	No	Weaver rail	$99.40
Classic Military (rings incl.)			
H&K 91	No	Weaver rail	$110.56
Mauser 38, 94, 96, 98	E only	Weaver rail	$79.30
Mosin-Nagant (all)	E only	Weaver rail	$79.30
Air Rifles			
RWS, Diana, BSA, Gamo	W&E	11mm rail	$49.95-59.95
Weihrauch, Anschutz, Beeman, Webley	W&E	11mm rail	$59.95-69.95
Shotgun Saddle Mounts			
Benelli Super 90 (See-Thru)	No	Weaver rail	$61.86
Browning BPS, A-5 9 (See-Thru)	No	Weaver rail	$61.86
Browning Gold 10/12/20-ga. (See- Thru)	No	Weaver rail	$61.86
Ithaca 37, 87	No	Weaver rail	$61.86
Mossberg 500/Mav. 88	No	Weaver rail	$61.86
Mossberg 835/Mav. 91	No	Weaver rail	$61.86
Remington 870/1100/11-87	No	Weaver rail	$61.86
Remington SP10	No	Weaver rail	$61.86
Winchester 1200-1500	No	Weaver rail	$61.86

Prices shown for anodized black finish; add $10 for stainless finish. Partial listing of mounts shown here. Contact B-Square for complete listing and details.

Maker, Model, Type	Adjust.	Scopes	Price
BEEMAN			
Two-Piece, Med.	No	1"	$31.50
Deluxe Two-Piece, High	No	1"	$33.00
Deluxe Two-Piece	No	30mm	$41.00
Deluxe One-Piece	No	1"	$50.00
Dampa Mount	No	1"	$120.00

All grooved receivers and scope bases on all known air rifles and 22-cal. rimfire rifles (1/2" to 5/8" 6mm to 15mm).

Maker, Model, Type	Adjust.	Scopes	Price
BOCK			
Swing ALK[1]	W&E	1", 26mm, 30mm	$349.00
Safari KEMEL[2]	W&E	1", 26mm, 30mm	$149.00
Claw KEMKA[3]	W&E	1", 26mm, 30mm	$224.00
ProHunter Fixed[4]	No	1", 26mm, 30mm	$95.00

[1]Q.D.: pivots right for removal. For Steyr-Mannlicher, Win. 70, Rem. 700, Mauser 98, Dakota, Sako, Sauer 80, 90. Magnum has extra-wide rings, same price. [2]Heavy-duty claw-type reversible for front or rear removal. For Steyr-Mannlicher rifles. [3]True claw mount for bolt-action rifles. Also in extended model. For Steyr-Mannlicher, Win. 70, Rem. 700. Also avail. as Gunsmith Bases, not drilled or contoured same price. [4]Extra-wide rings. Imported from Germany by GSI, Inc.

Maker, Model, Type	Adjust.	Scopes	Price
BSA			
AA Airguns	Yes	Super Ten, 240 Magnum, Maxi gripped scope rail equipped air rifles	$59.99 (adj). $29.99 (fixed)

Maker, Model, Type	Adjust.	Scopes	Price
BURRIS			
Supreme (SU) One-Piece (T)[1]	W only	1" split rings, 3 heights	1-piece base - $23.00-27.00
Trumount (TU) Two-Piece (T)	W only	1" split rings, 3 heights	2-piece base - $21.00-30.00
Trumount (TU) Two-Piece Ext.	W only	1" split rings	$26.00
Browning 22-cal. Auto Mount[2]	No	1" split rings	$20.00
1" 22-cal. Ring Mounts[3]	No	1" split rings	$24.00-41.00
L.E.R. (LU) Mount Bases[4]	W only	1" split rings	$24.00-52.00
L.E.R. No Drill-No Tap Bases[4,7,8]	W only	1" split rings	$48.00-52.00
Extension Rings[5]	No	1" scopes	$28.00-46.00
Ruger Ring Mount[6,9]	W only	1" split rings	$50.00-68.00
Std. 1" Rings[9]		Low, medium, high heights	$29.00-43.00
Zee Rings[9]		Fit Weaver bases; medium and high heights	$29.00-44.00
Signature Rings	No	30mm split rings	$68.00
Rimfire/Airgun Rings	W only	1" split rings, med. & high	$24.00-41.00

Maker, Model, Type	Adjust.	Scopes	Price
BURRIS (cont.)			
Double Dovetail (DD) Bases	No	30mm Signature	$23.00-26.00

[1]Most popular rifles. Universal rings, mounts fit Burris, Universal, Redfield, Leupold and Browning bases. Comparable prices. [2]Browning Standard 22 Auto rifle. [3]Grooved receivers. [4]Universal dovetail; accepts Burris, Universal, Redfield, Leupold rings. For Dan Wesson, S&W, Virginian, Ruger Blackhawk, Win. 94. [5]Medium standard front, extension rear, per pair. Low standard front, extension rear per pair. [6]Compact scopes, scopes with 2" bell for M77R. [7]Selected rings and bases available with matte Safari or silver finish. [8]For S&W K, L, N frames, Colt Python, Dan Wesson with 6" or longer barrels. [9]Also in 30mm.

Maker, Model, Type	Adjust.	Scopes	Price
CATCO			
Enfield Drop-In	No	1"	$39.95

Uses Weaver-style rings (not incl.). No gunsmithing required. See-Thru design. From CATCO.

Maker, Model, Type	Adjust.	Scopes	Price
CLEAR VIEW			
Universal Rings, Mod. 101[1]	No	1" split rings	$21.95
Standard Model[2]	No	1" split rings	$21.95
Broad View[3]	No	1"	$21.95
22 Model[4]	No	3/4", 7/8", 1"	$13.95
SM-94 Winchester[5]	No	1" split rings	$23.95
94 EJ[6]	No	1" split rings	$21.95

[1]Most rifles by using Weaver-type base; allows use of iron sights. [2]Most popular rifles; allows use of iron sights. [3]Most popular rifles; low profile, wide field of view. [4]22 rifles with grooved receiver. [5]Side mount. [6]For Win. A.E. From Clear View Mfg.

Maker, Model, Type	Adjust.	Scopes	Price
CONETROL			
Huntur[1] (base & rings)	W only	1", split rings, 3 heights	$119.88
Gunnur[2] (base & rings)	W only	1", split rings, 3 heights	$149.88
Custum[3] (base & rings)	W only	1", split rings, 3 heights	$179.88
One-Piece Side Mount Base[4]	W only		
DapTar Bases[5]	W only		
Pistol Bases, 2- or 3-ring[6]	W only		
Fluted Bases[7]	W only		$179.88
Metric Rings[8]	W only	26mm, 26.5mm, 30mm	$119.96-179.88

[1]All popular rifles, including metric-drilled foreign guns. Price shown for base, two rings. Matte finish. [2]Gunnur grade has mirror-finished rings to match scopes. Satin-finish base to match guns. Price shown for base, two rings. [3]Custom grade has mirror-finished rings and streamlined, streamlined base. Price shown for base, two rings. [4]Win. 94, Krag, older split-bridge Mannlicher-Schoenauer, Mini-14, etc. Prices same as above. [5]For all popular guns with integral mounting provision, including Sako, BSA Ithacagun, Ruger, Tikka, H&K, BRNO and many others. Also for grooved-receiver rimfires and air rifles. Prices same as above. [6]For XP-100, T/C Contender, Colt SAA, Ruger Blackhawk, S&W and others. [7]Sculptured two-piece bases as found on fine custom rifles. Price shown is for base alone. Also available unfinished $99.96, or finished but unblued $119.88. [8]26mm, 26.5mm, and 30mm rings made in projectionless style, in three heights. Three-ring mount for T/C Contender and other pistols in Conetrol's three grades. Any Conetrol mount available in stainless steel add 50 percent. Adjust-Quik-Detach (AQD) mounting is now available from Conetrol. Jam screws return the horizontal-split rings to zero. Adjustable for windage. AQD bases $89.94. AQD rings $99.96. (Total cost of complete setup, rings and two-piece base, is $179.88).

Maker, Model, Type	Adjust.	Scopes	Price
EAW			
Quick-Loc Mount	W&E	1", 26mm	$345.00
	W&E	30mm	$360.00
Magnum Fixed Mount	W&E	1", 26mm	$305.00
	W&E	30mm	$320.00

Fit most popular rifles. Available in 4 heights, 4 extensions. Reliable return to zero. Stress-free mounting. Imported by New England Custom Gun Svc.

Maker, Model, Type	Adjust.	Scopes	Price
GENTRY			
Feather-Light Rings and Bases	No	1", 30mm	$90.00-125.00

Bases for Rem. Seven, 700, Mauser 98, Browning A-Bolt, Weatherby Mk. V, Win. 70, HVA, Dakota. Two-piece base for Rem. Seven, chrome-moly or stainless. Rings in matte, regular blue, or stainless gray; four heights. From David Gentry.

Maker, Model, Type	Adjust.	Scopes	Price
GRIFFIN & HOWE			
Topmount[1]	No	1", 30mm	$625.00
Sidemount[2]	No	1", 30mm	$255.00
Garand Mount[3]	No	1"	$255.00

[1]Quick-detachable, double-lever mount with 1" rings, installed; with 30mm rings $875.00. [2]Quick-detachable, double-lever mount with 1" rings; with 30mm rings $375.00; installed, 1" rings. $405.00; installed, 30mm rings $525.00. [3]Price installed, with 1" rings $405.00. From Griffin & Howe.

Maker, Model, Type	Adjust.	Scopes	Price
G. G. & G.			
Remington 700 Rail	No	Weaver base	$135.00
Sniper Grade Rings	No	30mm	$159.95
M16/AR15 F.I.R.E. Std.[1]	No	Weaver rail	$75.00
M16/AR15 F.I.R.E. Scout	No	Weaver rail	$82.95
Aimpoint Standard Ring	No		$164.95
Aimpoint Cantilever Ring	No	Weaver rail	$212.00

[1]For M16/A3, AR15 flat top receivers; also in extended length. [2]For Aimpoint 5000 and Comp; quick detachable; spare battery compartment. [3]Low profile; quick release. From G. G. & G.

SCOPE RINGS & BASES

Maker, Model, Type	Adjust.	Scopes	Price
IRONSIGHTER			
Ironsighter See-Through Mounts[1]	No	1" split rings	$29.40-64.20
Ironsighter S-9[4]	No	1" split rings	$45.28
Ironsighter AR-15/M-16[8]	No	1", 30mm	$70.10
Ironsighter 22-Cal.Rimfire[2]	No	1"	$18.45
Model #570[9]	No	1" split rings	$29.40
Model #573[9]	No	30mm split rings	$45.28
Model #727[3]	No	.875" split rings	$18.45
Blackpowder Mount[7]	No	1"	$34.20-78.25

[1]Most popular rifles. Rings have oval holes to permit use of iron sights. [2]For 1" dia. scopes. [3]For .875 dia. scopes. [4]For 1" dia. extended eye relief scopes. [7]Fits most popular blackpowder rifles; two-piece (CVA, Knight, Marlin and Austin & Halleck) and one-piece integral (T/C). [8]Model 716 with 1" #540 rings; fits Weaver-style bases. Some models in stainless finish. [9]New detachable Weaver-style rings fit all Weaver-style bases. **Price: $26.95.** From Ironsighter Co.

Maker, Model, Type	Adjust.	Scopes	Price
K MOUNT by KENPATABLE			
Shotgun Mount	No	1", laser or red dot device	$49.95
SKS1	No	1"	$39.95

Wrap-around design; no gunsmithing required. Models for Browning BPS, A-5 12-ga., Sweet 16, 20, Rem. 870/1100 (LTW, and L.H.), S&W 916, Mossberg 500, Ithaca 37 & 51 12-ga., S&W 1000/3000, Win. 1400. [1]Requires simple modification to gun. From KenPatable Ent.

Maker, Model, Type	Adjust.	Scopes	Price
KRIS MOUNTS			
Side-Saddle[1]	No	1", 26mm split rings	$12.98
Two-Piece (T)[2]	No	1", 26mm split rings	$8.98
One Piece (T)[3]	No	1", 26mm split rings	$12.98

[1]One-piece mount for Win. 94. [2]Most popular rifles and Ruger. [3]Blackhawk revolver. Mounts have oval hole to permit use of iron sights.

Maker, Model, Type	Adjust.	Scopes	Price
KWIK-SITE			
Adapter	No	1"	$27.95-57.95
KS-W2[2]	No	1"	$21.95
KS-W94[3]	No	1"	$42.95
KS-WEV (Weaver-style rings)	No	1"	$19.95
KS-WEV-HIGH	No	1"	$19.95
KS-T22 1"[4]	No	1"	$17.95
KS-FL Flashlite[5]	No	Mini or C cell flash light	$37.95
KS-T88[6]	No	1"	$21.95
KS-T89	No	30mm	$21.95
KSN 22 See-Thru	No	1", 7/8"	$17.95
KSN-T22	No	1", 7/8"	$17.95
KSN-M-16 See-Thru (for M16 + AR-15)	No	1"	$49.95
KS-202[1]	No	1"	$27.97
KS-203	No	30mm	$42.95
KSBP[7]	No	Integral	$76.95
KSB Base Set			$5.95
Combo Bases & Rings	No	1"	$21.95

Bases interchangeable with Weaver bases. [1]Most rifles. Allows use of iron sights. [2]22-cal. rifles with grooved receivers. Allows use of iron sights. [3]Model 94, 94 Big Bore. No drilling or tapping. Also in adjustable model **$57.95.** [4]Non-See-Thru model for grooved receivers. [5]Allows C-cell or Mini Mag Lites to be mounted atop See-Thru mounts. [6]Fits any Redfield, Tasco, Weaver or Universal-style Kwik-Site dovetail base. [7]Blackpowder mount with integral rings and sights. [8]Shotgun side mount. Bright blue, black matte or satin finish. Standard, high heights.

Maker, Model, Type	Adjust.	Scopes	Price
LASER AIM	No	Laser Aim	$19.99-69.00

Mounts Laser Aim above or below barrel. Available for most popular hand guns, rifles, shotguns, including militaries. From Laser Aim Technologies, Inc.

Maker, Model, Type	Adjust.	Scopes	Price
LEUPOLD			
STD Bases[1]	W only	One- or two-piece bases	$25.40
STD Rings[2]		1" super low, low, medium, high	$33.60
DD RBH Handgun Mounts[2]	No		$34.00
Dual Dovetail Bases[3]	No		$25.40
Dual Dovetail Rings[8]		1", low, med, high	$33.60
Ring Mounts[4,5,6]	No	7/8", 1"	$102.80
22 Rimfire[8]	No	7/8", 1"	$73.60
Gunmaker Base[7]	W only	1"	$73.60
Quick Release Rings		1", low, med., high	$43.00-81.00
Quick Release Bases[9]	No	1", one- or two- piece	$73.60

[1]Base and two rings; Casull, Ruger, S&W, T/C; add $5.00 for silver finish. [2]Rem. 700, Win. 70-type actions. For Ruger No. 1, 77, 77/22; interchangeable with Ruger units. For dovetailed rimfire rifles. Sako; high, medium, low. [7]Must be drilled, tapped for each action. [8]13mm dovetail receiver. [9]BSA Monarch, Rem. 40x, 700, 721, 725, Ruger M77, S&W 1500, Weatherby Mark V, Vanguard, Win. M70.

Maker, Model, Type	Adjust.	Scopes	Price
MARLIN			
One-Piece QD (T)	No	1" split rings	$10.10

Most Marlin lever actions.

Maker, Model, Type	Adjust.	Scopes	Price
MILLETT RINGS			
One-Piece Bases[6]	Yes	1"	$26.41
Universal Two-Piece Bases			
700 Series	W only	Two-piece bases	$26.41
FN Series	W only	Two-piece bases	$26.41
70 Series[1]	W only	1", two-piece bases	$26.41
Angle-Loc Rings[2]	W only	1", low, medium, high	$35.49
Ruger 77 Rings[3]		1"	$38.14
Shotgun Rings[4]		1"	$32.55
Handgun Bases, Rings[5]		1"	$36.07-80.38
30mm Rings[7]		30mm	$20.95-41.63
Extension Rings[8]		1"	$40.43-56.44
See-Thru Mounts[9]	No	1"	$29.35-31.45
Shotgun Mounts[10]	No	1"	$52.45
Timber Mount	No	1"	$81.90

BRNO, Rem. 40x, 700, 722, 725, 7400 Ruger 77 (round top), Marlin, Weatherby, FN Mauser, FN Brownings, Colt 57, Interarms Mark X, Parker-Hale, Savage 110, Sako (round receiver); many others. [1]Fits Win. M70 70XTR, 670, Browning BBR, BAR, BLR, A-Bolt, Rem. 7400/7600, Four, Six, Marlin 336, Win. 94 A. E., Sav. 110. [2]To fit Weaver-type bases. [3]Engraved. Smooth **$34.60.** [4]For Rem. 870, 1100; smooth. [5]Two- and three-ring sets for Colt Python, Trooper, Diamondback, Peacekeeper, Dan Wesson, Ruger Redhawk, Super Redhawk. [6]Turn-in bases and Weaver-style for most popular rifles and T/C Contender, XP-100 pistols. [7]Both Weaver and turn-in styles; three heights. [8]Med. or high; ext. front std. rear, ext. rear std. front, ext. front ext. rear; **$40.90** for double extension. [9]Many popular rifles, Knight MK-85, T/C Hawken, Renegade, Mossberg 500 Slugster, 835 slug. [10]For Rem. 879/1100, Win. 1200, 1300/1400, 1500, Mossberg 500. Some models available in nickel at extra cost. New Angle-Loc two-piece bases fit all Weaver-style rings. In smooth, matte and nickel finishes, they are available for Browning A-Bolt, Browning BAR/BLR, Interarms MK X, FN, Mauser 98, CVA rifles with octagon barrels, CVA rifles with round receiver, Knight MK-85, Knight Wolverine, Remington 700, Sauer SHR 970, Savage 110, Winchester 70 **$24.95 to $28.95.** From Millett Sights.

Maker, Model, Type	Adjust.	Scopes	Price
MMC			
AK[1]	No		$39.95
FN FAL/LAR[2]	No		$59.95

[1]Fits all AK derivative receivers; Weaver-style base; low-profile scope position. [2]Fits all FAL versions; Weaver-style base. From MMC.

Maker, Model, Type	Adjust.	Scopes	Price
REDFIELD			
JR-SR (T)1. One/two-piece bases.	W only	3/4", 1", 26mm, 30mm	JR: $15.99-46.99 SR:15.99-33.49
Ring (T)[2]	No	3/4" and 1"	$27.95-29.95
Widefield See-Thru Mounts	No	1"	$15.95
Ruger Rings[4]	No	1", med., high	$30.49-36.49
Ruger 30mm[5]	No	1"	$37.99-40.99

[1]Low, med. & high, split rings. Reversible extension front rings for 1". Two-piece bases for Sako. Colt Sauer bases **$39.95.** Med. Top Access JR rings nickel-plated **$28.95.** SR two-piece ABN mount nickel-plated **$22.95.** [2]Split rings for grooved 22s; 30mm, black matte **$42.95.** [3]Used with MP scopes for S&W K, L or N frame, XP-100, T/C Contender, Ruger receivers. [4]For Ruger Model 77 rifles, medium and high; medium only for M77/22. [5]For Model 77. Also in matte finish **$45.95.** [6]Aluminun 22 groove mount **$14.95**, base and medium rings **$18.95.** Scout mounts available for Mosin Nagant, Schmidt Rubin K-31, 98K Mauser, Husqvarna Mauser, Persian Mauser, Turkish Mauser.

Maker, Model, Type	Adjust.	Scopes	Price
S&K			
Insta-Mount (T) Bases and Rings[1]	W only	Uses S&K rings only	$47.00-117.00
Conventional Rings and Bases[2]	W only	1" split rings	From $65.00
Sculptured Bases, Rings[2]	W only	1", 26mm, 30mm	From $65.00
Smooth Contoured Rings[3]	Yes	1", 26mm, 30mm	$90.00-120.00

[1]1903, A3, M1 Carbine, Lee Enfield #1. MkIII, #4, #5, M1917, M98 Mauser, AR-15, AR-180, M-14, M-1, Ger. K-43, Mini-14, M1-A, Krag, AKM, Win. 94, SKS Type 56, Daewoo, H&K. [2]Most popular rifles already drilled and tapped and Sako, Tikka dovetails. [3]No projections; weigh 1/2-oz. each; matte or gloss finish. Horizontally and vertically split rings, matte or high gloss.

Maker, Model, Type	Adjust.	Scopes	Price
SAKO			
QD Dovetail	W only	1"	$70.00-155.00

Sako, or any rifle using Sako action, 3 heights available. Stoeger, importer.

Maker, Model, Type	Adjust.	Scopes	Price
SPRINGFIELD, INC.			
M1A Third Generation	No	1" or 30mm	$123.00
M1A Standard	No	1" or 30mm	$77.00
M6 Scout Mount	No		$29.00

Weaver-style bases. From Springfield, Inc.

Maker, Model, Type	Adjust.	Scopes	Price
TALBOT			
QD Bases	No		$180.00-190.00
Rings	No	1", 30mm	$50.00-70.00

Blue or stainless steel; standard or extended bases; rings in three heights. For most popular rifles. From Talbot QD Mounts.

SCOPE RINGS & BASES

Maker, Model, Type	Adjust.	Scopes	Price
TASCO			
Centerfire rings	Integral	1", 30mm, matte black	**$5.95**
High centerfire rings	Special high	1", matte black aluminum	**$5.95**
.22/airgun rings	Yes	1", matte black aluminum	**$5.95**
.22/airgun "Quick Peep" rings	Yes	1", matte black aluminum	**$5.95**
THOMPSON/CENTER			
Duo-Ring Mount[1]	No	1"	**$78.00**
Weaver-Style Bases	No		**$14.00–28.50**
Weaver-Style Rings[2]	No	1"	**$36.00**

[1]Attaches directly to T/C Contender bbl., no drilling/tapping; also for T/C M/L rifles, needs base adapter; blue or stainless. [2]Medium and high; blue or silver finish. From Thompson/Center.

Maker, Model, Type	Adjust.	Scopes	Price
UNERTL			
1/4 Click[1]	Yes	3/4", 1" target scopes	**Per set $285.00**

[1]Unertl target or varmint scopes. Posa or standard mounts, less bases. From Unertl.

Maker, Model, Type	Adjust.	Scopes	Price
WARNE			
Premier Series (all steel)			
T.P.A. (Permanently Attached)	No	1", 4 heights 30mm, 2 heights	**$87.75-98.55**
Premier Series Rings fit Premier Series Bases			
Premier Series (all-steel Q.D. rings)			
Premier Series (all steel) Quick detachable lever	No	1", 4 heights 26mm, 2 heights 30mm, 3 heights	**$129.95-131.25 $142.00**
BRNO 19mm	No	1", 3 heights 30mm, 2 heights	**$125.00-136.70**
BRNO 16mm		1", 2 heights	**$125.00**
Ruger	No	1", 4 heights 30mm, 3 heights	**$125.00-136.70**
Ruger M77	No	1", 3 heights 30mm, 2 heights	**$125.00-136.70**
Sako Medium & Long Action	No	1", 4 heights 30mm, 3 heights	**$125.00-136.70**
Sako Short Action	No	1", 3 heights	**$125.00**
All-Steel One-Piece Base, ea.			**$38.50**
All-Steel Two-Piece Base, ea.			**$14.00**
Maxima Series (fits all Weaver-style bases)			
Permanently Attached[1]	No	1", 3 heights 30mm, 3 heights	**$25.50 $36.00**
Adjustable Double Lever[2]	No	1", 3 heights 30mm, 3 heights	**$72.60 $80.75**
Thumb Knob	No	1", 3 heights 30mm, 3 heights	**$59.95 $68.25**
Stainless-Steel Two-Piece Base, ea.			**$15.25**

Vertically split rings with dovetail clamp, precise return to zero. Fit most popular rifles, handguns. Regular blue, matte blue, silver finish. [1]All-Steel, non-Q.D. rings. [2]All-steel, Q.D. rings. From Warne Mfg. Co.

Maker, Model, Type	Adjust.	Scopes	Price
WEAVER			
Top Mount	No	7/8", 1", 30mm, 33mm	**$24.95-38.95**
Side Mount	No	1", 1" long	**$14.95-34.95**
Tip-Off Rings	No	7/8", 1"	**$24.95-32.95**
Pivot Mounts	No	1"	**$38.95**
Complete Mount Systems			
Pistol	No	1"	**$75.00-105.00**
Rifle	No	1"	**$32.95**
SKS Mount System	No	1"	**$49.95**
Pro-View (no base required)	No	1"	**$13.95-15.95**
Converta-Mount, 12-ga. (Rem. 870, Moss. 500)	No	1", 30mm	**$74.95**
See-Thru Mounts			
Detachable	No	1"	**$27.00-32.00**
System (no base required)	No	1"	**$15.00-35.00**
Tip-Off	No	1"	**$15.00**

Maker, Model, Type	Adjust.	Scopes	Price
WEAVER (cont.)			

Nearly all modern rifles, pistols, and shotguns. Detachable rings in standard, See-Thru, and extension styles, in Low, Medium, High or X-High heights; gloss (blued), silver and matte finishes to match scopes. Extension rings are only available in 1" High style and See-Thru X-tensions only in gloss finish. Tip-Off rings only for 3/8" grooved receivers or 3/8" grooved adaptor bases; no base required. See-Thru & Pro-View mounts for most modern big bore rifles, some in silver. No Drill & Tap Pistol systems in gloss or silver for Colt Python, Trooper, 357, Officer's Model, Ruger Single-Six, Security-Six (gloss finish only), Blackhawk, Super Blackhawk, Blackhawk SRM 357, Redhawk, Mini-14 Series (not Ranch), Ruger 22 Auto Pistols, Mark II, Smith & Wesson I- and current K-frames with adj. rear sights. Converta-Mount Systems in Standard and See-Under for Mossberg 500 (12- and 20-ga.), Remington 870, 11-87 (12- and 20- ga. lightweight), Winchester 1200, 1300, 1400, 1500. Converta-Brackets, bases, rings also available for Beretta A303 and A390, Browning A-5, BPS Pump, Ithaca 37, 87. From Weaver.

Maker, Model, Type	Adjust.	Scopes	Price
WEIGAND			
Browning Buck Mark[1]	No		**$29.95**
Integra Mounts[2]	No		**$39.95-69.00**
S&W Revolver[3]	No		**$29.95**
Ruger 10/22[4]	No		**$14.95-39.95**
Ruger Revolver[5]	No		**$29.95**
Taurus Revolver[4]	No		**$29.95-65.00**
Lightweight Rings	No	1", 30mm	**$29.95-39.95**
1911			
SM3[6]	No	Weaver rail	**$99.95**
APCMNT[7]	No		**$69.95**

[1]No gunsmithing. [2]S&W K, L, N frames, Taurus vent rib models, Colt Anaconda/Python, Ruger Redhawk, Ruger 10/22. [3]K, L, N frames. [4]Three models. [5]Redhawk, Blackhawk, GP-100. [6]3rd Gen., drill and tap, without slots **$59.95**. [7]For Aimpoint Comp. Red Dot scope, silver only. From Weigand Combat Handguns, Inc.

Maker, Model, Type	Adjust.	Scopes	Price
WIDEVIEW			
Premium 94 Angle Eject and side mount	No	1"	**$22.44**
Premium See-Thru	No	1"	**$22.44**
22 Premium See-Thru	No	3/4", 1"	**$16.47**
Universal Ring Angle Cut	No	1"	**$31.28**
Universal Ring Straight Cut	No	1"	**$18.70**
Solid Mounts			
Lo Ring Solid[1]	No	1"	**$22.44**
Hi Ring Solid[1]	No	1"	**$18.14**
SR Rings		1", 30mm	**$16.32**
22 Grooved Receiver	No	1"	**$16.32**
Blackpowder Mounts[2]	No	1"	**$22.44**
High, extra-high ring mounts with base	No	up to 60mm	**$30.16**
AR15 and M16	No		**$32.92**

[1]For Weaver-type base. Models for many popular rifles. Low ring, high ring and grooved receiver types. [2]No drilling, tapping, for T/C Renegade, Hawken, CVA, Knight Traditions guns. From Wideview Scope Mount Corp.

Maker, Model, Type	Adjust.	Scopes	Price
WILLIAMS			
Side Mount with HCO Rings[1]	No	1", split or extension rings	**$74.35**
Side Mount, Offset Rings[2]	No	Same	**$61.45**
Sight-Thru Mounts[3]	No	1", 7/8" sleeves	**$19.50**
Streamline Mounts	No	1" (bases form rings)	**$26.50**

[1]Most rifles, Br. S.M.L.E. (round rec.) **$14.41** extra. [2]Most rifles including Win. 94 Big Bore. [3]Many modern rifles, including CVA Apollo, others with 1" octagon barrels.

Maker, Model, Type	Adjust.	Scopes	Price
YORK			
M-1 Garand	Yes	1"	**$39.95**

Centers scope over the action. No drilling, tapping or gunsmithing. Uses standard dovetail rings. From York M-1 Conversions.

NOTES

(S) Side Mount; (T) Top Mount; 22mm=.866"; 25.4mm=1.024"; 26.5mm=1.045"; 30mm=1.81".

Sporting Leaf and Open Sights

AUTOMATIC DRILLING REAR SIGHT Most German and Austrian drillings have this kind of rear sight. When rifle barrel is selected, the rear sight automatically comes to the upright position. Base length 2.165", width .472", folding leaf height .315". From New England Custom Gun Service.
Price: $48.50

CLASSIC MARBLE/WILLIAMS STYLE FULLY ADJUSTABLE REAR SPORTING SIGHTS Screw-on attachment. Dovetailed graduated windage and elevation adjustment. Elevation and windage lock with set screws. Available in steel or lightweight alloy construction. From Sarco, Inc.
Price: $13.50

ERA MASTERPIECE ADJUSTABLE REAR SIGHTS Precision-machined, all-steel, polished and blued. Attaches with 8-36 socket head screw. Use small screwdriver to adjust windage and elevation. Available for various barrel widths. From New England Custom Gun Service.
Price: $82.00

ERA CLASSIC ADJUSTABLE REAR SIGHT Similar to the Masterpiece unit except windage is adjusted by pushing sight sideways, then locking it with a reliable clamp. Precision machined all steel construction, polished, with 6-48 fastening screw and Allen wrench. Shallow "V" and "U" notch. Length 2.170", width .550". From New England Custom Gun Service.
Price: $55.00

ERA EXPRESS SIGHTS A wide variety of open sights and bases for custom installation. Partial listing shown. From New England Custom Gun Service.
Price: One-leaf express $66.00
Price: Two-leaf express $71.50
Price: Three-leaf express $77.00
Price: Bases for above $27.50
Price: Standing rear sight, straight $13.25
Price: Base for above $16.50

ERA CLASSIC EXPRESS SIGHTS Standing or folding leaf sights are securely locked to the base with the ERA Magnum Clamp, but can be loosened for sighting in. Base can be attached with two socket-head cap screws or soldered. Finished and blued. Barrel diameters from .600" to .930". From New England Custom Gun Service.
Price: Standing leaf $54.00
Price: One-leaf express $96.00
Price: Two-leaf express $101.00
Price: Three-leaf express $120.00

ERA MASTERPIECE REAR SIGHT Adjustable for windage and elevation, and adjusted and locked with a small screwdriver. Comes with 8-36 socket-head cap screw and wrench. Barrel diameters from .600" to .930".
Price: $75.00

G.G. & G. SAME PLANE APERTURE M-16/AR-15 A2-style dual aperture rear sight with both large and small apertures centered on the same plane.
Price: $45.00

LYMAN No.16 Middle sight for barrel dovetail slot mounting. Folds flat when scope or peep sight is used. Sight notch plate adjustable for elevation. White triangle for quick aiming. Designed to fit 3/8" dovetail slots. Three heights: A-.400" to.500", B-.345" to .445", C-.500" to .600". A slot blank designed to fill dovetail notch when sight is removed is available
Price: $5.00
Price: $13.25

MARBLE FALSE BASE #76, #77, #78 New screw-on base for most rifles replaces factory base. 3/8" dovetail slot permits installation of any folding rear sight. Can be had in sweat-on models also.
Price: $8.00

MARBLE FOLDING LEAF Flattop or semi-buckhorn style. Folds down when scope or peep sights are used. Reversible plate gives choice of "U" or "V" notch. Adjustable for elevation.
Price: $16.00
Price: Also available with both windage and elevation adjustment $18.00

MARBLE SPORTING REAR With white enamel diamond, gives choice of two "U" and two "V" notches or different sizes. Adjustment in height by means of double step elevator and sliding notch piece. For all rifles; screw or dovetail installation.
Price: .... $16.00 to $17.00

MARBLE #20 UNIVERSAL New screw or sweat-on base. Both have .100" elevation adjustment. In five base sizes. Three styles of U-notch, square notch, peep. Adjustable for windage and elevation.
Price: Screw-on. $23.00
Price: Sweat-on $21.00

MILLETT SPORTING & BLACKPOWDER RIFLE Open click adjustable rear fits 3/8" dovetail cut in barrel. Choice of white outline, target black or open express V rear blades. Also available is a replacement screw-on sight with express V, .562" hole centers. Dovetail fronts in white or blaze orange in seven heights (.157"-.540").
Price: Dovetail or screw-on rear. $58.38
Price: Front sight $12.96

MILLETT SCOPE-SITE Open, adjustable or fixed rear sights dovetail into a base integral with the top scope-mounting ring. Blaze orange front ramp sight is integral with the front ring half. Rear sights have white outline aperture. Provides fast, short-radius, Patridge-type open sights on the top of the scope. Can be used with all Millett rings, Weaver-style bases, Ruger 77 (also fits Redhawk), Ruger Ranch Rifle, No. 1, No. 3, Rem. 870, 1100; Burris, Leupold and Redfield bases.
Price: Scope-Site top only, windage only. $31.15
Price: As above, fully adjustable $66.10
Price: Scope-Site Hi-Turret, fully adjustable, low, medium, high $66.10

RUGER WINDAGE ADJUSTABLE FOLDING REAR SIGHT Fits all Ruger rifles produced with standard folding rear sights. Available in low (.480"), medium (.503") and high (.638") heights. From Sturm, Ruger & Co., Inc.
Price: $19.80

TRIJICON 3-DOT NIGHT SIGHTS Self-luminous and machined from steel. Available for the M16/AR-15, H&K rifles. Front and rear sets and front only.
Price: .... $50.00 to $84.00

WHITWORTH STYLE ENGLISH 3 LEAF EXPRESS SIGHTS Folding leafs marked in 100, 200 and 300 yard increments. Slide assembly is dovetailed in base. Available in four different styles: 3 folding leaves, flat bottom; 1 fixed, 2 folding leaves, flat bottom; 3 folding leaves, round bottom; 1 fixed, 2 folding leaves, round bottom. Available from Sarco, Inc.
Price: $49.95

WICHITA MULTI RANGE SIGHT SYSTEM Designed for silhouette shooting. System allows you to adjust the rear sight to four repeatable range settings, once it is pre-set. Sight clicks to any of the settings by turning a serrated wheel. Front sight is adjustable for weather and light conditions with one adjustment. Specify gun when ordering.
Price: Rear sight. $145.00
Price: Front sight $110.00

WILLIAMS DOVETAIL OPEN SIGHT (WDOS) Open rear sight with windage and elevation adjustment. Furnished "U" notch or choice of blades. Slips into dovetail and locks with gib lock. Heights from .281" to .531".
Price: With blade. $19.50
Price: Less blade $12.45
Price: Rear sight blades, each $7.05

WILLIAMS GUIDE OPEN SIGHT (WGOS) Open rear sight with windage and elevation adjustment. Bases to fit most military and commercial barrels. Choice of square "U" or "V" notch blade, 3/16", 1/4", 5/16", or 3/8" high.
Price: Less blade. $19.50
Price: Extra blades, each $7.05

WILLIAMS WGOS OCTAGON Open rear sight for 1" octagonal barrels. Installs with two 6-48 screws and uses same hole spacing as most T/C muzzleloading rifles. Four heights, choice of square, U, V, or B blade.
Price: $26.55

WILLIAMS WSKS, WAK47 Replaces original military-type rear sight. Adjustable for windage and elevation. No drilling or tapping. Peep aperture or open. For SKS carbines, AK-47-style rifles.
Price: Aperture. $25.95
Price: Open $24.95

WILLIAMS WM-96 Fits Mauser 96-type military rifles. Replaces original rear sight with open blade or aperture. Fully adjustable for windage and elevation. No drilling or tapping.
Price: Aperture. $25.95
Price: Open $24.95

WILLIAMS FIRE RIFLE SETS Replacement front and rear fiber optic sights. Red bead front, two green elements in the fully-adjustable rear. Made of CNC-machined metal.
Price: For Ruger 10/22. .... $24.95
Price: For most Marlin and Win. (3/8" dovetail) $34.95
Price: For Remington (newer style sight base) $28.95

Aperture and Micrometer Receiver Sights

A2 REAR SIGHT KIT Featuring an exclusive numbered windage knob. For .223 AR-style rifles. From ArmaLite, Inc.
Price: $55.00

AO GHOST RING HUNTING SIGHT Fully adjustable for windage and elevation. Available for most rifles, including blackpowder guns. Minimum gunsmithing required for most installations; matches most mounting holes. From AO Sight Systems, Inc.
Price: $90.00

AO AR-15/M-16 APERTURE Drop-in replacement of factory sights. Both apertures are on the same plane. Large ghost ring has .230" inside diameter; small ghost ring has .100" inside diameter. From AO Sight Systems, Inc.
Price: $30.00

AO BACKUP GHOST RING SIGHTS Mounts to scope base and retains zero when reinstalled in the field. Affords same elevation/windage adjustability as AO Hunting Ghost Rings. Included are both .191" and .230" apertures and test posts. Available for Ruger, Sako, Remington 700 and other rifles. From AO Sight Systems, Inc.
Price: $65.00

AO TACTICAL SIGHTS For HK UMP/USC/G36/SL8/M P5. The Big Dot Tritium or standard dot tritium is mated with a large .300" diameter rear ghost ring. The "same plane" rear aperture flips from the .300" to a .230" diameter ghost ring. From AO Sight Systems, Inc.
Price: .... $90.00 to $120.00

AO Ghost Ring

BEEMAN/FEINWERKBAU 5454 MATCH APERTURE SIGHT Small size, new-design sight uses constant-pressure flat springs to eliminate point of impact shifts.
Price: $350.00

METALLIC SIGHTS

BEEMAN SPORT APERTURE SIGHT Positive click micrometer adjustments. Standard units with flush surface screwdriver adjustments. Deluxe version has target knobs. For air rifles with grooved receivers.
Price: Standard **$40.00**
Price: Deluxe **$50.00**

BUSHMASTER COMPETITION A2 REAR SIGHT ASSEMBLY Elevation and windage mechanism feature either 1/2 or 1/4 minute of adjustment. Long distance aperture allows screw-in installation of any of four interchangeable micro-apertures.
Price: 1/2 M.O.A. **$109.95**
Price: 1/4 M.O.A. **$114.95**

DPMS NATIONAL MATCH Replaces the standard A2 rear sight on M16/AR-15 rifles. Has 1/4-minute windage and 1/2-minute elevation adjustments. Includes both a .052" and .200" diameter aperture.
Price: **$92.99**

ENFIELD No. 4 TARGET/MATCH SIGHT Originally manufactured by Parker-Hale, has adjustments up to 1,300 meters. Micrometer click adjustments for windage. Adjustable aperture disc has six different openings from .030" to .053". From Sarco, Inc.
Price: **$49.95**

EAW RECEIVER SIGHT A fully adjustable aperture sight that locks securely into the EAW quick-detachable scope mount rear base. Made by New England Custom Gun Service.
Price: **$80.00**

ERA SEE-THRU Contains fiber optic center dot. Fits standard 3/8" American dovetails. Locks in place with set screw. Ideal for use on moving targets. Width 19.5mm. Available in low (.346", medium .425" and high .504" models. From New England Custom Gun Service.
Price: **$27.50**

G. G.& G. MAD IRIS Multiple Aperture Device is a four sight, rotating aperture disk with small and large apertures on the same plane. Mounts on M-16/ AR-15 flattop receiver. Fully adjustable.
Price: **$141.95**
Price: A2 IRIS, two apertures, full windage adjustments **$124.95**

KNIGHT'S ARMAMENT 600 METER FOLDING REAR SIGHT Click adjustable from 200 to 600 meters with clearly visible range markings. Intermediate clicks allows for precise zero at known ranges. Allows use of optical scopes by folding don. Mounts on rear of upper receiver rail on SR-25 and similar rifles. From Knight's Armament Co.
Price: **$181.00**

KNIGHT'S ARMAMENT FOLDING 300M SIGHT Mounts on flat-top upper receivers on SR-25 and similar rifles. May be used as a back-up iron sight for a scoped rifle/carbine or a primary sight. Peep insert may be removed to expose the 5mm diameter ghost ring aperture. From Knight's Armament Co.
Price: **$144.00**

LYMAN NO. 2 TANG SIGHT Designed for the Winchester Model 94. Has high index marks on aperture post; comes with both .093" quick sighting aperture, .040" large disk aperture, and replacement mounting screws.
Price: **$76.00**
Price: For Marlin lever actions **$76.00**

LYMAN No. 57 1/4-minute clicks. Stayset knobs. Quick-release slide, adjustable zero scales. Made for almost all modern rifles.
Price: **$67.50**
Price: No. 57SME, 57SMET (for White Systems Model 91 and Whitetail rifles) **$62.50**

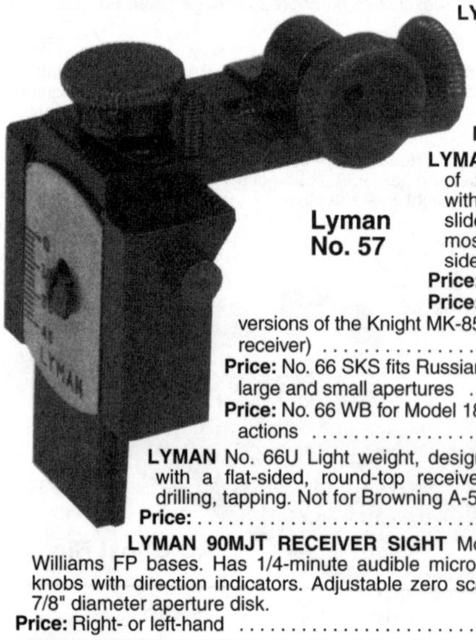

Lyman No. 57

LYMAN 57GPR Designed especially for the Lyman Great Plains Rifle. Mounts directly onto the tang of the rifle and has 1/4-minute micrometer click adjustments.
Price: **$62.50**

LYMAN No. 66 Fits close to the rear of flat-sided receivers, furnished with Stayset knobs. Quick-release slide, 1/4-min. adjustments. For most lever or slide action or flat-sided automatic rifles.
Price: **$67.50**
Price: No. 66MK (for all current versions of the Knight MK-85 in-line rifle with flat-sided receiver) **$67.50**
Price: No. 66 SKS fits Russian and Chinese SKS rifles; large and small apertures **$67.50**
Price: No. 66 WB for Model 1886 Winchester lever actions **$67.50**

LYMAN No. 66U Light weight, designed for most modern shotguns with a flat-sided, round-top receiver. 1/4-minute clicks. Requires drilling, tapping. Not for Browning A-5, Rem. M11.
Price: **$71.50**

LYMAN 90MJT RECEIVER SIGHT Mounts on standard Lyman and Williams FP bases. Has 1/4-minute audible micrometer click adjustments, target knobs with direction indicators. Adjustable zero scales, quick-release slide. Large 7/8" diameter aperture disk.
Price: Right- or left-hand **$74.95**

LYMAN RECEIVER SIGHT Audible-click adjustments for windage and elevation, coin-slotted "stayset" knobs and two interchangeable apertures. For Mauser, Springfield, Sako, T/C Hawken, Rem. 700, Win. 70, Savage 110, SKS, Win. 94, Marlin 336 and 1894.
Price: **$53.99**

LYMAN 1886 #2 TANG SIGHT Fits the Winchester 1886 lever action rifle and replicas thereof not containing a tang safety. Has height index marks on the aperture post and an .800" maximum elevation adjustment. Included is a .093" x 1/2" quick-sighting aperture and .040 x 5/8" target disk.
Price: **$76.00**

MARBLE PEEP TANG SIGHT All-steel construction. Micrometer-like click adjustments for windage and elevation. For most popular old and new lever-action rifles.
Price: **$125.00**

MILLETT PEEP RIFLE SIGHTS Fully adjustable, heat-treated nickel steel peep aperture receiver sight for the Mini-14. Has fine windage and elevation adjustments; replaces original.
Price: Rear sight, Mini-14 .... **$68.95**
Price: Front sight, Mini-14 .... **$37.95**
Price: Front and rear combo with hood **$89.95**

NATIONAL MATCH REAR SIGHT KIT For AR-15 style rifles. From Armalite, Inc.
Price: 1/2 W, 1/2E **$80.00**
Price: 1/4 W, 1/2 E **$80.00**

NECG PEEP SIGHT FOR WEAVER SCOPE MOUNT BASES Attaches to Weaver scope mount base. Windage adjusts with included Allen wrenches, elevation with a small screwdriver. Furnished with two apertures (.093" and .125" diameter hole) and two interchangeable elevation slides for high or low sight line. From New England Custom Gun Service.
Price: **$85.00**

NECG PEEP SIGHT FOR GROOVED MOUNT BASES Windage adjusts with included Allen wrenches, elevation with a small screwdriver. Furnished with two apertures (.093" and .125" diameter hole) and two interchangeable elevation slides for high or low sight line. From New England Custom Gun Service.
Price: **$85.00**

NECG RUGER PEEP SIGHT Made for Ruger M-77 and No. 1 rifles, it is furnished with .093" and .125" opening apertures. Can be installed on a standard Ruger rear mount base or quarter rib. Tightening the aperture disk will lock the elevation setting in place. From New England Custom Gun Service.
Price: **$85.00**

T/C HUNTING STYLE TANG PEEP SIGHT Compact, all steel construction, with locking windage and elevation adjustments. For use with "bead style" and fiber optic front sights. Models available to fit all traditional T/C muzzleloading rifles. From Thompson/Center Arms.
Price: **$58.00**

T/C CONTENDER CARBINE PEEP SIGHT All-steel, low profile, click-adjustable unit mounting on the pre-drilled tapped scope mount holes on the T/C Contender Carbine. From Thompson/Center Arms.
Price: **$56.00**

WILLIAMS APERTURE SIGHT Made to fit SKS rifles.
Price: **$23.49**

WILLIAMS FIRE SIGHT PEEP SETS Combines the Fire Sight front bead with Williams fully adjustable metallic peep rear.
Price: For SKS **$39.95**
Price: For Ruger 10/22, 99/44, 96/22, 96/22 Mag. **$47.95**
Price: For Marlin or Winchester lever actions .... **$50.95 to $80.95**

WILLIAMS FP Internal click adjustments. Positive locks. For virtually all rifles, T/C Contender, Heckler & Koch HK-91, Ruger Mini-14, plus Win., Rem., and Ithaca shotguns.
Price: From **$69.95**
Price: With Target Knobs **$81.50**
Price: FP-GR (for dovetail-grooved receivers, .22s and air guns) **$69.95**

WILLIAMS TARGET FP Similar to the FP series but developed for most bolt-action rimfire rifles. Target FP High adjustable from 1.250" to 1.750" above centerline of bore; Target FP Low adjustable from .750" to 1.250". Attaching bases for Rem. 540X, 541-S, 580, 581, 582 (#540); Rem. 510, 511, 512, 513-T, 521-T (#510); Win. 75 (#75); Savage/ Anschutz 64 and Mark 12 (#64). Some rifles require drilling, tapping.
Price: High or Low **$77.95**
Price: Base only **$18.95**
Price: Mount holes **$59.95**

WILLIAMS 5-D SIGHT Low cost sight for shotguns, 22s and the more popular big game rifles. Adjustment for windage and elevation. Fits most guns without drilling and tapping. Also for British SMLE, Winchester M94 Side Eject.
Price: From **$36.95**
Price: With Shotgun Aperture **$36.95**

WILLIAMS 5D RECEIVER SIGHT Alloy construction and similar design to the FP model except designed to fit Win. 94, Marlin 336, Marlin 1895, Mauser 98.
Price: **$34.50**

WILLIAMS GUIDE (WGRS) Receiver sight for 30 M1 Carbine, M1903A3 Springfield, Savage 24s, Savage-Anschutz and Weatherby XXII. Utilizes military dovetail; no drilling. Double-dovetail windage adjustment, sliding dovetail adjustment for elevation.
Price: .... **$34.95 to $47.95**

Vernier Tang Sights

BALLARD TANG SIGHTS Available in variety of models including short & long staff hunter, Pacific & Montana, custom units allowing windage & elevation adjustments. Uses 8x40 base screws with screw spacing of 1.120". From Axtell Rifle Co.
Price: .... **$175.00 to $325.00**

LYMAN TANG SIGHT Made for Win. 94, 1886, Marlin 30, 336 and 1895.
Price: .... **$59.99 to $64.99**

MARLIN TANG SIGHTS Available in short and long staff hunter models using 8x40 base screws and screw spacing of 1.120". From Axtell Rifle Co.
Price: .... **$170.00 to $180.00**

PEDERSOLI CREEDMORE Adjustable for windage and elevation, fits Traditions by Pedersoli rifles and other brands. From Dixie Gun Works.
Price: **$110.00**

REMINGTON TANG SIGHTS Available in short-range hunter and vernier, mid- and long-range vernier and custom models with windage and elevation adjustments. Uses 10x28 base screws, with screw spacing of 1.940". Eye disk has .052" hole with 10x40 thread. From Axtell Rifle Co.
Price: .... **$175.00 to $325.00**

SHARPS TANG SIGHTS Reproduction tang sights as manufactured for various Sharps rifles through the years 1859-1878. Wide variety of models available including Standard Issue Sporting Peep, Hartford Transition Mid and Long Range, and Custom Express Sights. From Axtell Rifle Co.
Price: .... **$150.00 to $340.00**

STEVENS CUSTOM Available in thin base short and long staff hunter, mid and long range sporting vernier, custom mid and long range (custom models allow windage and elevation adjustments) models. Uses 5x40 base screws with screw spacing of 1.485". From Axtell Rifle Co.
Price: .... **$170.00 to $325.00**

TAURUS TANG SIGHT Made of blue steel, available for Taurus Models 62, 72, 172, 63, 73 and 173. Folds down, aperture disk sight, height index marks on aperture post.
Price: **$77.00**

WINCHESTER & BROWNING TANG SIGHTS Available in variety of models, including thin & thick base short & long staff hunter, mid & long range sporting vernier and custom units. Screw spacing of 2.180" on all models. From Axtell Rifle Co.
Price: .... **$170.00 to $325.00**

Globe Target Front Sights

AXTELL CUSTOM GLOBE Designed similar to the original Winchester #35 sight, it contains five inserts. Also available with spirit level. From Axtell Rifle Co.
Price: .... **$125.00 to $175.00**

BALLARD FRONT SIGHTS Available in windgauge with spirit level, globe with clip, and globe with spirit level (all with five inserts) and beach combination with gold plated rocker models. Dovetail of .375" for all. From Axtell Rifle Co.
Price: .... **$125.00 to $240.00**

LYMAN 20 MJT TARGET FRONT Has 7/8" diameter, one-piece steel globe with 3/8" dovetail base. Height is .700" from bottom of dovetail to center of aperture; height on 20 LJT is .750". Comes with seven Anschutz-size steel inserts-two posts and five apertures .126" through .177".
Price: 20 MJT or 20 LJT **$33.75**

Lyman No. 17A Target

LYMAN No. 17A TARGET Includes seven interchangeable inserts: four apertures, one transparent amber and two posts .50" and .100" in width.
Price: **$28.25**
Price: Insert set **$13.25**

LYMAN 17AEU Similar to the Lyman 17A except has a special dovetail design to mount easily onto European muzzleloaders such as CVA, Traditions and Investarm. All steel, comes with eight inserts.
Price: **$26.00**

LYMAN No. 93 MATCH Has 7/8" diameter, fits any rifle with a standard dovetail mounting block. Comes with seven target inserts and accepts most Anschutz accessories. Hooked locking bolt and nut allows quick removal, installation. Base available in .860" (European) and .562" (American) hole spacing.
Price: **$45.00**

MAYNARD FRONT SIGHTS Custom globe with five inserts and clip. Also available with spirit level bracket and windgauge styles. From Axtell Rifle Co.
Price: .... **$125.00 to $240.00**

PEDERSOLI GLOBE A tunnel front sight with 12 interchangeable inserts for high precision target shooting. Fits Traditions by Pedersoli and other rifles.
Price: **$69.95**

REMINGTON FRONT SIGHTS Available in windgauge with spirit level, custom globe with clip and custom globe with spirit level (all with five inserts) and beach combination with gold plated rocker models. Dovetail .460". From Axtell Rifle Co.
Price: .... **$125.00 to $250.00**

SHARPS FRONT SIGHTS Original-style globe with non-moveable post and pinhead. Also available with windgauge and spirit level. From Axtell Rifle Co.
Price: .... **$100.00 to $265.00**

WILLIAMS TARGET GLOBE FRONT Adapts to many rifles. Mounts to the base with a knurled locking screw. Height is .545" from center, not including base. Comes with inserts.
Price: **$47.95**
Price: Dovetail base (low) .220" **$18.95**
Price: Dovetail base (high) .465" **$18.95**
Price: Screw-on base, .300" height, .300" radius **$16.95**
Price: Screw-on base, .450" height, .350" radius **$16.95**
Price: Screw-on base, .215" height, .400" radius **$16.95**

WINCHESTER & BROWNING FRONT SIGHTS Available in windgauge with spirit level, globe with clip, globe with spirit level (all with five inserts) and beach combination with gold plated rocker models. From Axtell Rifle Co.
Price: .... **$125.00 to $240.00**

Front Sights

AO TACTICAL SIGHTS Three types of drop-in replacement front posts–round top or square top night sight posts in standard and Big Dot sizes, or white stripe posts in .080 and .100 widths. For AR15 and M16 rifles. From AO Sight Systems, Inc.
Price: .... **$30.00 to $90.00**

AO RIFLE TEST POSTS Allows easy establishment of correct front post height. Provides dovetail post with .050" segments to allow shooter to "shoot-n-snip", watching point-of-impact walk into point of aim. Available for 3/8" standard dovetail, Ruger-style or Mauser. From AO Sight Systems, Inc.
Price: **$5.00**

AR-10 DETACHABLE FRONT SIGHT Allows use of the iron rear sight, but are removable for use of telescopic sights with no obstruction to the sight line, For AR-style rifles. From ArmaLite, Inc.
Price: .... **$50.00 to $70.00**

ASHLEY AR-15/M-16 FRONT SIGHTS Drop-in replacement sight post. Double faced so it can be rotated 180 degrees for 2.5 MOA elevation adjustment. Available in .080" width with .030" white stripe, or .100" with .040" stripe. From Ashley Outdoors, Inc.
Price: **$30.00**
Price: Tritium Dot Express **$60.00**

BUSHMASTER FLIP-UP FRONT SIGHT Made for V Match AR-style rifles, this sight unit slips over milled front sight bases and clamps around barrel. Locks with the push of a button. For use with flip-up style rear sights or the A3 removable carry handle. From Bushmaster Firearms.
Price: **$99.95**

BUSHMASTER A2 COMPETITION FRONT SIGHT POST Surface ground on three sides for optimum visual clarity. Available in two widths: .052"; and .062". From Bushmaster Firearms.
Price: **$12.95**

CLASSIC STREAMLINED FRONT SPORTER RAMP SIGHT Comes with blade and sight cover. Serrated and contoured ramp. Screw-on attachment. Slide-on sight cover is easily detachable. Gold bead. From Sarco, inc.
Price: **$13.50**

ERA BEADS FOR RUGER RIFLES White bead and fiber optic front sights that replace the standard sights on M-77 and No. 1 Ruger rifles. Using 3/32" beads, they are available in heights of .330", .350", .375", .415" and .435". From New England Custom Gun Service.
Price: .... **$16.00 to $24.00**

ERA FRONT SIGHTS European-type front sights inserted from the front. Various heights available. From New England Custom Gun Service.
Price: 1/16" silver bead. **$11.50**
Price: 3/32" silver bead **$16.00**
Price: Sourdough bead **$14.50**
Price: Fiber optic **$24.00**
Price: Folding night sight with ivory bead **$39.50**

Knight's Armament

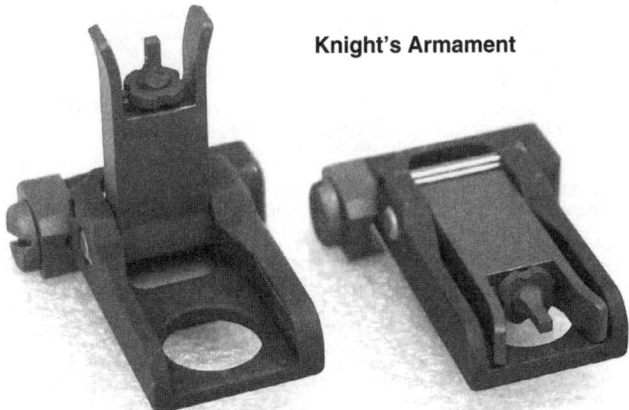

KNIGHT'S ARMAMENT FRONT STANDING/FOLDING SIGHT Mounts to the SR-25 rifle barrel gas block's MilStd top rail. Available in folding sight model. From Knight's Armament Co.
Price: .... **$145.00 to $175.00**

KNIGHT'S ARMAMENT CARRYING HANDLE SIGHT Rear sight and carry handle for the SR-25 rifle. Has fixed range and adjustable windage. From Knight's Armament Co.
Price: **$181.15**

KNIGHT'S ARMAMENT MK II FOLDING FRONT SIGHT For the SR-25 rifle. Requires modified handguard. From Knight's Armament Co.
Price: **$175.00**

KNIGHT'S ARMAMENT FOR FREE-FLOATING RAS Mounts to free-floating SR-25 and SR-15 RAS (rail adapter system) rifle forends. Adjustable for elevation. Made of aluminum. From Knight's Armament Co.
Price: **$155.25**

KNS PRECISION SYSTEMS SIGHT Screws into front base. Hooded for light consistency; precision machined with fine wire crosshairs measuring .010-inches thick. Aperture measures .240-inches diameter. Standard and duplex reticles. Available for AK-47, MAK-90, AR-15, M16, FN-FAL, H&K 91, 93, 94, MP5, SP89, L1A1, M1 Garand.
Price: **$25.99**

LYMAN HUNTING SIGHTS Made with gold or white beads 1/16" to 3/32" wide and in varying heights for most military and commercial rifles. Dovetail bases.
Price: **$8.95**

MARBLE STANDARD Ivory, red, or gold bead. For all American-made rifles, 1/16" wide bead with semi-flat face that does not reflect light. Specify type of rifle when ordering.
Price: **$10.00**

MARBLE CONTOURED Has 3/8" dovetail base, .090" deep, is 5/8" long. Uses standard 1/16" or 3/32" bead, ivory, red, or gold. Specify rifle type.
Price: **$11.50**

NATIONAL MATCH FRONT SIGHT POST Has .050" blade. For AR-style rifle. From ArmaLite, Inc.
Price: **$12.00**

T/C FIBER OPTIC FRONT MUZZLELOADER SIGHT Ramp-style steel with fiber optic bead for all tradition cap locks, both octagonal and round barrels with dovetail, and most T/C rifles. From Thompson/Center Arms.
Price: .... **$16.95 to $36.00**

TRIJICON NIGHT SIGHT Self-luminous tritium gas-filled front sight for the M16/AR-15 series.
Price: **$60.00**

WILLIAMS GOLD BEAD Available in .312", .343", and .406" high models all with 3/32" bead.
Price: **$10.95**

WILLIAMS RISER BLOCKS For adding .250" height to front sights when using a receiver sight. Two widths available: .250" for Williams Streamlined Ramp or .340" on all standard ramps having this base width. Uses standard 3/8" dovetail.
Price: **$5.46**

WILLIAMS AR-15 FIRESIGHT Fiber optic unit attaches to any standard AR-15-style front sight assembly. From Williams Gun Sight Co.
Price: **$41.95**

Ramp Sights

ERA MASTERPIECE Banded ramps; 21 sizes; hand-detachable beads and hood; beads inserted from the front. Various heights available. From New England Custom Gun Service.
Price: Banded ramp **$54.00**
Price: Hood **$10.50**
Price: 1/16" silver bead **$11.50**
Price: 3/32" silver bead **$16.00**
Price: Sourdough bead **$14.50**
Price: Fiber optic **$22.00**
Price: Folding night sight with ivory bead **$39.50**

HOLLAND & HOLLAND STYLE FRONT SIGHT RAMPS Banded and screw-on models in the Holland & Holland-style night sight. Flips forward to expose a .0781" silver bead. Flip back for use of the .150" diameter ivory bead for poor light or close-up hunting. Band thickness .040", overall length 3.350", band length 1.180". From New England Custom Gun Service.
Price: .... **$90.00 to $115.00**

LYMAN NO. 18 SCREW-ON RAMP Used with 8-40 screws but may also be brazed on. Heights from .10" to .350". Ramp without sight.
Price: **$13.75**

MARBLE FRONT RAMPS Available in polished or dull matte finish or serrated style. Standard 3/8x.090" dovetail slot. Made for MR-width (.340") front sights. Can be used as screw-on or sweat-on. Heights: .100", .150", .300".
Price: Polished or matte **$14.00**
Price: Serrated **$10.00**

NECG UNIVERSAL FRONT SIGHTS Available in five ramp heights and three front sight heights. Sights can be adjusted up or down .030" with an Allen wrench. Slips into place and then locks into position with a set screw. Six different front sight shapes are offered, including extra large and fiber optic. All hoods except the extra low ramp slide on from the rear and click in place. Extra low ramp has spring-loaded balls to lock hood. Choose from three hood sizes. From New England Custom Gun Service.
Price: **$25.50**

T/C TARGET SIGHT FOR OCTAGON BARREL MUZZLELOADERS A precision rear sight with click adjustments (via knurled knobs) for windage and elevation. Available for 15/16-inch and 1-inch octagon barrels with a screw hole spacing of .836-inch between centers. From Thompson/Center Arms.
Price: **$56.00**

T/C FIBER OPTIC MUZZLELOADER SIGHT Click adjustable for windage and elevation. Steel construction fitted with Tru-Glo™ fiber optics. Models available for most T/C muzzleloading rifles. Fits others with 1-inch and 15/16-inch octagon barrels with a hole spacing of .836-inch between screws. From Thompson/Center Arms.
Price: **$36.00**

WILLIAMS SHORTY RAMP Companion to "Streamlined" ramp, about 1/2" shorter. Screw-on or sweat-on. It is furnished in 1/8", 3/16", 9/32", and 3/8" heights without hood only. Also for shotguns.
Price: **$18.25**
Price: With dovetail lock **$20.35**

WILLIAMS STREAMLINED RAMP Available in screw-on or sweat-on models. Furnished in 9/16", 7/16", 3/8", 5/16", 3/16" heights.
Price: **$21.95**
Price: Sight hood **$4.95**

WILLIAMS STREAMLINED FRONT SIGHTS Narrow (.250" width) for Williams Streamlined ramps and others with 1/4" top width; medium (.340" width) for all standard factory ramps. Available with white, gold or fluorescent beads, 1/16" or 3/32".
Price: .... **$10.50 to $10.95**

Handgun Sights

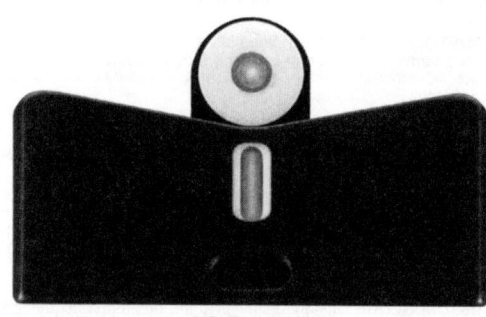

AO Express

AO EXPRESS SIGHTS Low-profile, snag-free express-type sights. Shallow V rear with white vertical line, white dot front. All-steel, matte black finish. Rear is available in different heights. Made for most pistols, many with double set-screws. From AO Sight Systems, Inc.
Price: Standard Set, front and rear **$60.00**
Price: Big Dot Set, front and rear **$60.00**
Price: Tritium Set, Standard or Big Dot **$90.00**
Price: 24/7 Pro Express, Std. or Big Dot Tritium **$120.00**

BO-MAR DELUXE BMCS Gives 3/8" windage and elevation adjustment at 50 yards on Colt Gov't 45; sight radius under 7". For GM and Commander models only. Uses existing dovetail slot. Has shield-type rear blade.
Price: **$65.95**
Price: BMCS-2 (for GM and 9mm) **$68.95**
Price: Flat bottom **$65.95**
Price: BMGC (for Colt Gold Cup), angled serrated blade, rear **$68.95**
Price: BMGC front sight **$12.95**
Price: BMCZ-75 (for CZ-75, TZ-75, P-9 and most clones).
Works with factory front **$68.95**

BO-MAR FRONT SIGHTS Dovetail style for S&W 4506, 4516, 1076; undercut style (.250", .280", 5/16" high); Fast Draw style (.210", .250", .230" high).
Price: **$12.95**

BO-MAR BMU XP-100/T/C CONTENDER No gunsmithing required; has .080" notch.
Price: **$77.00**

BO-MAR BMML For muzzleloaders; has .062" notch, flat bottom.
Price: **$65.95**
Price: With 3/8" dovetail **$65.95**

BO-MAR RUGER "P" ADJUSTABLE SIGHT Replaces factory front and rear sights.
Price: Rear sight **$65.95**
Price: Front sight **$12.00**

BO-MAR BMR Fully adjustable rear sight for Ruger MKI, MKII Bull barrel autos.
Price: Rear **$65.95**
Price: Undercut front sight **$12.00**

BO-MAR GLOCK Fully adjustable, all-steel replacement sights. Sight fits factory dovetail. Longer sight radius. Uses Novak Glock .275" high, .135" wide front, or similar.
Price: Rear sight **$68.95**
Price: Front sight **$20.95**

BO-MAR LOW PROFILE RIB & ACCURACY TUNER Streamlined rib with front and rear sights; 7 1/8" sight radius. Brings sight line closer to the bore than standard or extended sight and ramp. Weight 5 oz. Made for Colt Gov't 45, Super 38, and Gold Cup 45 and 38.
Price: **$140.00**

BO-MAR COMBAT RIB For S&W Model 19 revolver with 4" barrel. Sight radius 5 3/4", weight 5 1/2 oz.
Price: **$127.00**

BO-MAR WINGED RIB For S&W 4" and 6" length barrels-K-38, M10, HB 14 and 19. Weight for the 6" model is about 7 1/4 oz.
Price: **$140.00**

BO-MAR COVER-UP RIB Adjustable rear sight, winged front guards. Fits right over revolver's original front sight. For S&W 4" M-10HB, M-13, M-58, M-64 & 65, Ruger 4" models SDA-34, SDA-84, SS-34, SS-84, GF-34, GF-84.
Price: **$130.00**

CHIP MCCORMICK "DROP-IN" A low mount sight that fits any 1911-style slide with a standard military-type dovetail sight cut (60x.290"). Dovetail front sights also available. From Chip McCormick Corp.
Price: **$47.95**

CHIP MCCORMICK FIXED SIGHTS Same sight picture (.110" rear, 110" front) that's become the standard for pro combat shooters. Low mount design with rounded edges. For 1911-style pistols. May require slide machining for installation. From Chip McCormick Corp.
Price: **$24.95**

C-MORE SIGHTS Replacement front sight blades offered in two types and five styles. Made of Du Pont Acetal, they come in a set of five high-contrast colors: blue, green, pink, red and yellow. Easy to install. Patridge style for Colt Python (all barrels), Ruger Super Blackhawk (7 1/2"), Ruger Blackhawk (4 5/8"); ramp style for Python (all barrels), Blackhawk (4 5/8"), Super Blackhawk (7 1/2" and 10 1/2"). From C-More Systems.
Price: Per set **$19.95**

G.G. & G. GHOST RINGS Replaces the factory rear sight without gunsmithing. Black phosphate finish. Available for Colt M1911 and Commander, Beretta M92F, Glock, S&W, SIG Sauer.
Price: **$65.00**

Heinie Slant Pro

HEINIE SLANT PRO Made with a slight forward slant, the unique design of these rear sights is snag free for unimpeded draw from concealment. The combination of the slant and the rear serrations virtually eliminates glare. Made for most popular handguns. From Heinie Specialty Products.
Price: .... **$50.35 to $122.80**

HEINIE STRAIGHT EIGHT SIGHTS Consists of one tritium dot in the front sight and a slightly smaller Tritium dot in the rear sight. When aligned correctly, an elongated 'eight' is created. The Tritium dots are green in color. Designed with the belief that the human eye can correct vertical alignment faster than horizontal. Available for most popular handguns. From Heinie Specialty Products.
Price: .... **$104.95 to $122.80**

HEINIE CROSS DOVETAIL FRONT SIGHTS Made in a variety of heights, the standard dovetail is 60 degrees x .305" x .062" with a .002 taper. From Heinie Specialty Products.
Price: .... **$20.95 to $47.20**

JP GHOST RING Replacement bead front, ghost rear for Glock and M1911 pistols. From JP Enterprises.
Price: **$79.95**
Price: Bo-Mar replacement leaf with JP dovetail front bead **$99.95**

LES BAER CUSTOM ADJUSTABLE LOW MOUNT REAR SIGHT Considered one of the top adjustable sights in the world for target shooting with 1911-style pistols. Available with Tritium inserts. From Les Baer Custom.
Price: .... **$49.00** (standard); **$99.00** (tritium)

LES BAER DELUXE FIXED COMBAT SIGHT A tactical-style sight with a very low profile. Incorporates a no-snag design and has serrations on sides. For 1911-style pistols. Available with Tritium inserts for night shooting. From Les Baer Custom.
Price: .... **$26.00** (standard); **$67.00** (with Tritium)

LES BAER DOVETAIL FRONT SIGHT Blank dovetail sight machined from bar stock. Can be contoured to many different configurations to meet user's needs. Available with Tritium insert. From Les Baer Custom.
Price: .... **$17.00** (standard); **$47.00** (with Tritium insert)

LES BAER FIBER OPTIC FRONT SIGHT Dovetail .330x65 degrees, .125" wide post, .185" high, .060" diameter. Red and green fiber optic. From Les Baer Custom.
Price: **$24.00**

LES BAER PPC-STYLE ADJUSTABLE REAR SIGHT Made for use with custom built 1911-style pistols, allows the user to preset three elevation adjustments for PPC-style shooting. Milling required for installation. Made from 4140 steel. From Les Baer Custom.
Price: **$120.00**

LES BAER DOVETAIL FRONT SIGHT WITH TRITIUM INSERT This fully contoured and finished front sight comes ready for gunsmith installation. From Les Baer Custom.
Price: **$47.00**

MMC TACTICAL ADJUSTABLE SIGHTS Low-profile, snag free design. Twenty-two click positions for elevation, drift adjustable for windage. Machined from 4140 steel and heat treated to 40 RC. Tritium and non-tritium. Ten different configurations and colors. Three different finishes. For 1911s, all Glock, HK USP, S&W, Browning Hi-Power.
Price: Sight set, tritium **$144.92**
Price: Sight set, white outline or white dot **$99.90**
Price: Sight set, black **$93.90**

MEPROLIGHT TRITIUM NIGHT SIGHTS Replacement sight assemblies for low-light conditions. Available for pistols (fixed and adj.),rifles, shotguns. 12-year warranty for useable illumination, while non-TRU-DOT have a 5-year warranty. Distributed in American by Kimber.
Price: Kahr K9, K40, fixed, TRU-DOT **$100.00**
Price: Ruger P85, P89, P94, adjustable, TRU-DOT **$156.00**
Price: Ruger Mini-14R sights **$140.00**
Price: SIG Sauer P220, P225, P226, P228, adjustable, TRU-DOT **$156.00**

Price: Smith&Wesson autos, fixed or adjustable, TRU-DOT **$100.00**
Price: Taurus PT92, PT100, adjustable, TRU-DOT **$156.00**
Price: Walther P-99, fixed, TRU-DOT **$100.00**
Price: Shotgun bead **$32.00**
Price: Beretta M92, Cougar, Brigadier, fixed, TRU-DOT **$100.00**
Price: Browning Hi-Power, adjustable, TRU-DOT **$156.00**
Price: Colt M1911 Govt., adjustable, TRU-DOT **$156.00**

MILLETT SERIES 100 REAR SIGHTS All-steel highly visible, click adjustable. Blades in white outline, target black, silhouette, 3-dot. Fit most popular revolvers and autos.
Price: .... **$54.95 to $88.95**

MILLETT BAR/DOT Made with orange or white bar or dot for increased visibility. Available for Beretta 84, 85, 92S, 92SB, Browning, Colt Python & Trooper, Ruger GP 100, P85, Redhawk, Security Six.
Price: .... **$14.99 to $24.99**

MILLETT 3-DOT SYSTEM SIGHTS The 3-Dot System sights use a single white dot on the front blade and two dots flanking the rear notch. Fronts available in Dual-Crimp and Wide Stake-On styles, as well as special applications. Adjustable rear sight available for most popular auto pistols and revolvers including Browning Hi-Power, Colt 1911 Government and Ruger P85.
Price: Front, from **$18.00**
Price: Adjustable rear **$63.95**

MILLETT REVOLVER FRONT SIGHTS All-steel replacement front sights with either white or orange bar. Easy to install. For Ruger GP-100, Redhawk, Security-Six, Police-Six, Speed-Six, Colt Trooper, Diamondback, King Cobra, Peacemaker, Python, Dan Wesson 22 and 15-2.
Price: .... **$15.20 to $18.00**

MILLETT DUAL-CRIMP FRONT SIGHT Replacement front sight for automatic pistols. Dual-Crimp uses an all-steel two-point hollow rivet system. Available in eight heights and four styles. Has a skirted base that covers the front sight pad. Easily installed with the Millett Installation Tool Set. Available in Blaze Orange Bar, White Bar, Serrated Ramp, Plain Post. Available in heights of .185", .200", .225", .275", .312", .340" and .410".
Price: **$18.00**

MILLETT STAKE-ON FRONT SIGHT Replacement front sight for automatic pistols. Stake-On sights have skirted base that covers the front sight pad. Easily installed with the Millet Installation Tool Set. Available in seven heights and four styles-Blaze Orange Bar, White Bar, Serrated Ramp, Plain Post. Available for Glock 17L and 24, others.
Price: **$18.00**

MILLETT ADJUSTABLE TARGET Positive light-deflection serration and slant to eliminate glare and sharp edge sight notch. Audible "click" adjustments. For AMT Hardballer, Beretta 84, 85, 92S, 92SB, Browning Hi-Power, Colt 1911 Government and Gold Cup, Colt revolvers, Dan Wesson 15, 41, 44, Ruger revolvers, Glock 17, 17L, 19, 20, 21, 22, 23.
Price: **$63.95**

MILLETT ADJUSTABLE WHITE OUTLINE Similar to the Target sight, except has a white outline on the blade to increase visibility. Available for the same handguns as the Target model, plus BRNO CZ-75/TZ-75/TA-90 without pin on front sight, and Ruger P85.
Price: Each **$63.95**

OMEGA OUTLINE SIGHT BLADES Replacement rear sight blades for Colt and Ruger single action guns and the Interarms Virginian Dragoon. Standard Outline available in gold or white notch outline on blue metal. From Omega Sales, Inc.
Price: **$10.00**

OMEGA MAVERICK SIGHT BLADES Replacement "peep-sight" blades for Colt, Ruger SAs, Virginian Dragoon. Three models available-No. 1, Plain; No. 2, Single Bar; No. 3, Double Bar Rangefinder. From Omega Sales, Inc.
Price: Each **$10.00**

ONE RAGGED HOLE Replacement rear sight ghost ring sight for Ruger handguns. Fits Blackhawks, Redhawks, Super Blackhawks, GP series and Mk. II target pistols with adjustable sights. From One Ragged Hole, Tallahassee, Florida.
Price: .... **NA**

PACHMAYR ACCU-SET Low-profile, fully adjustable rear sight to be used with existing front sight. Available with target, white outline or 3-dot blade. Blue finish. Uses factory dovetail and locking screw. For Browning, Colt, Glock, SIG Sauer, S&W and Ruger autos. From Pachmayr.
Price: **$59.98**

P-T TRITIUM NIGHT SIGHTS Self-luminous tritium sights for most popular handguns, Colt AR-15, H&K rifles and shotguns. Replacement handgun sight sets available in 3-Dot style (green/green, green/yellow, green/orange) with bold outlines around inserts; Bar-Dot available in green/green with or without white outline rear sight. Functional life exceeds 15 years. From Innovative Weaponry, Inc.
Price: Handgun sight sets **$99.95**
Price: Rifle sight sets **$99.95**
Price: Rifle, front only **$49.95**
Price: Shotgun, front only **$49.95**

T/C ENCORE FIBER OPTIC SIGHT SETS Click adjustable, steel rear sight and ramp-style front sight, both fitted with Tru-GloTM fiber optics. Specifically-designed for the T/C Encore pistol series. From Thompson/Center Arms.
Price: **$49.35**

T/C ENCORE TARGET REAR SIGHT Precision, steel construction with click adjustments (via knurled knobs) for windage and elevation. Models available with low, medium and high blades. From Thompson/Center Arms.
Price: **$54.00**

METALLIC SIGHTS

TRIJICON NIGHT SIGHTS Three-dot night sight system uses tritium lamps in the front and rear sights. Tritium "lamps" are mounted in silicone rubber inside a metal cylinder. A polished crystal sapphire provides protection and clarity. Inlaid white outlines provide 3-dot aiming in daylight also. Available for most popular handguns including Glock 17, 19, 20, 21, 23, 24, 25, 26, 29, 30, H&K USP, Ruger P94, SIG P220, P225, 226, Colt 1911. Front and rear sets available. From Trijicon, Inc.
Price: . . . . **$80.00 to $299.00**

TRIJICON 3-DOT Self-luminous front iron night sight for the Ruger SP101.
Price: **$50.00**

WICHITA SERIES 70/80 SIGHT Provides click windage and elevation adjustments with precise repeatability of settings. Sight blade is grooved and angled back at the top to reduce glare. Available in Low Mount Combat or Low Mount Target styles for Colt 45s and their copies, S&W 645, Hi-Power, CZ 75 and others.
Price: Rear sight, target or combat **$80.00**
Price: Front sight, Patridge or ramp **$18.00**

WICHITA GRAND MASTER DELUXE RIBS Ventilated rib has wings machined into it for better sight acquisition and is relieved for Mag-Na-Porting. Milled to accept Weaver see-thru-style rings. Made of stainless; front and rear sights blued. Has Wichita Multi-Range rear sight system, adjustable front sight. Made for revolvers with 6" barrel.
Price: Model 301S, 301B (adj. sight K frames with custom bbl. of 1" to 1.032" dia. L and N frame with 1.062" to 1.100" dia. bbl.) **$250.00**
Price: Model 303S, 303B (adj. sight K, L, N frames with factory barrel) **$250.00**

WICHITA MULTI-RANGE QUICK CHANGE SIGHTING SYSTEM Multi-range rear sight can be pre-set to four positive repeatable range settings. Adjustable front sight allows compensation for changing lighting and weather conditions with just one front sight adjustment. Front sight comes with Lyman 17A Globe and set of apertures.
Price: Rear sight **$145.00**
Price: Front, sight **$110.00**

WILLIAMS FIRE SIGHT SETS Red fiber optic metallic sight replaces the original. Rear sight has two green fiber optic elements. Made of CNC-machined aluminum. Fits all Glocks, Ruger P-Series (except P-85), S&W 910, Colt Gov't. Model Series 80, Ruger GP 100 and Redhawk, and SIG Sauer (front only).
Price: Front and rear set **$45.95**
Price: SIG Sauer front **$22.95**
Price: Ruger P345/KP345 (2006) **$45.95**
Price: Taurus PT111, PT140, PT145, PT1232, PT138 . . . . **$44.95**

WILSON ADJUSTABLE REAR SIGHTS Machined from steel, the click adjustment design requires simple cuts and no dovetails for installation. Available in several configurations: matte black standard blade with .128" notch; with .110" notch; with Tritium dots and .128" square or "U" shaped notch; and Combat Pyramid. From Wilson Combat.
Price: . . . . **$24.95 to $69.95**

WILSON NITE-EYES SIGHTS Low-profile, snag free design with green and yellow Tritium inserts. For 1911-style pistols. From Wilson Combat.
Price: **$119.95**

WILSON TACTICAL COMBAT SIGHTS Low-profile and snag-free in design, the sight employs the Combat Pyramid shape. For many 1911-style pistols and some Glock models. From Wilson Combat.
Price: **$139.95**

Shotgun Sights

AO SHOTGUN SIGHTS 24/7 Pro Express sights fit Remington rifle sighted barrels. Front sight divetails into existing ramp, rear installs on Remington rear ramp. Available in Big Dot Tritium or Standard Dot Tritium. Three other styles (for pedestal base, beaded, and ribbed barrels) provide a Big Dot Tritium front that epoxies over the existing bead front sight. From AO Sight Systems, Inc.
Price: 24/7 Tritium Sets.. . . . . **$90.00 to $120.00**
Price: Big Dot Tritium (front only) **$60.00**

BRADLEY SHOTGUN SIGHTS Front beads available in sizes of 1/8" and 5/32" in thread sizes of #3-56, #6-48, and #8-40. From 100 Straight Products.
Price: **$5.00**

BRADLEY CENTER SIGHTS Available in 1/16" bead size and #3-56 thread or taper. Plain brass, bright silver and white finishes. From 100 Straight Products.
Price: . . . . **$2.50 to $6.00 each**

BRADLEY SHOTGUN SIGHT ASSORTMENT An assortment of the most frequently used sights including six each of 18-3, 18-6,532-3, 532-7, 532-9, MB-01 and MB-11. From 100 Straight Products.
Price: **$119.95**

CARLSON SHOTGUN SIGHT A brilliant orange bead securely held by two bands. Used for low light conditions. Bead size .150", thread size 6-48. From Carlson's and 100 Straight Products.
Price: **$7.50**

FIRE FLY EM-109 SL SHOTGUN SIGHT Made of aircraft-grade aluminum, this 1/4-oz. "channel" sight has a thick, sturdy hollowed post between the side rails to give a Patridge sight picture. All shooting is done with both eyes open, allowing the shooter to concentrate on the target, not the sights. The hole in the sight post gives reduced-light shooting capability and allows for fast, precise aiming. For sport or combat shooting. Model EM-109 fits all vent. rib and double barrel shotguns and muzzleloaders with octagon barrel. Model MOC-110 fits all plain barrel shotguns without screw-in chokes. From JAS, Inc.
Price: **$35.00**

LYMAN Three sights of over-sized ivory beads. No. 10 Front (press fit) for double barrel or ribbed single barrel guns **$4.50**; No. 10D Front (screw fit) for non-ribbed single barrel guns (comes with wrench) **$5.50**; No. 11 Middle (press fit) for double and ribbed single barrel guns
Price: **$4.75**

MMC M&P COMBAT SHOTGUN SIGHT SET A durable, protected ghost ring aperture, combat sight made of steel. Fully adjustable for windage and elevation.
Price: M&P Sight Set (front and rear). **$73.45**
Price: As above, installed **$83.95**

MMC TACTICAL GHOST RING SIGHT Click adjustable for elevation with 30 MOA total adjustment in 3 MOA increments. Click windage adjustment. Machined from 4140 steel, heat-treated to 40 RC. Front sight available in banded tactical or serrated ramp. Front and rear sights available with or without tritium. Available in three different finishes.
Price: Rear Ghost Ring with tritium. **$119.95**
Price: Rear Ghost Ring without tritium **$99.95**
Price: Front Banded Tactical with tritium **$59.95**
Price: Front Banded Tactical without tritium **$39.95**
Price: Front serrated ramp **$24.95**

MARBLE SHOTGUN BEAD SIGHTS No. 214-Ivory front bead, 11/64", tapered shank **$4.40**; No. 223-Ivory rear bead, .080", tapered shank **$4.40**; No. 217-Ivory front bead, 11/64", threaded shank **$4.75**; No. 223-T-Ivory rear bead, .080, threaded shank **$5.95**. Reamers, taps and wrenches available from Marble Arms.

MEPROLIGHT Ghost ring sight set for Benelli tactical shotguns. From Meprolight, Inc.
Price: **$100.00**

MILLETT SHURSHOT SHOTGUN SIGHT A sight system for shotguns with ventilated rib. Rear sight attaches to the rib, front sight replaces the front bead. Front has an orange face, rear has two orange bars. For 870, 1100 or other models.
Price: Rear, fixed. **$14.95**
Price: Adjustable front and rear set **$35.95**
Price: Front **$14.95**

NECG IVORY SHOTGUN BEAD Genuine ivory shotgun beads with 6-48 thread. Available in heights of .157" and .197". From New England Custom Gun Service.
Price: **$9.00**

POLY-CHOKE Replacement front shotgun sights in four styles-Xpert, Poly Bead, Xpert Mid Rib sights, and Bev-L-Block. Xpert Front available in 3x56, 6x48 thread, 3/32" or 5/32" shank length, gold, ivory **$4.70**; or Sun Spot orange bead **$5.95**; Poly Bead is standard replacement 1/8" bead, 6x48 **$2.95**; Xpert Mid Rib in tapered carrier (ivory only) **$5.95**; or 3x56 threaded shank (gold only) **$2.95**; Hi and Lo Blok sights with 6x48 thread, gold or ivory **$5.25**. From Marble Arms.

SLUG SIGHTS Made of non-marring black nylon, front and rear sights stretch over and lock onto barrel. Sights are low profile with blaze orange front blade. Adjustable for windage and elevation. For plain-barrel (non-ribbed) guns in 12-, 16- and 20-gauge, and for shotguns with 5/16" and 3/8" ventilated ribs. From Innovision Ent.
Price: **$11.95**

TRIJICON 3-DOT NIGHT SIGHTS Self-luminous and machined from steel. Available for Remington 870, 1100, 1187.
Price: . . . . **$75.00 to $175.00**

WILLIAMS GUIDE BEAD SIGHT Fits all shotguns, 1/8" ivory, red or gold bead. Screws into existing sight hole. Various thread sizes and shank lengths.
Price: **$4.77**

WILLIAMS SLUGGER SIGHTS Removable aluminum sights attach to the shotgun rib. High profile front, fully adjustable rear. Fits 1/4", 5/16" or 3/8" (special) ribs.
Price: **$34.95**

WILLIAMS UNIVERSAL SLUGGER shotgun fire sight set. Fiber optic, front and rear metallic sights attach to most vent ribs. Adjustable for windage and elevation. No gunsmithing required.
Price: **$39.95**

WILLIAMS FIRE SIGHTS Fiber optic light gathering front sights in red or yellow, glow with natural light. Fit 1/4", 5/16" or 3/8" vent. ribs, most popular shotguns.
Price: **$13.95**

WILLIAMS SIGHT KITS Contains over 36 beads to fit any shotgun (with drills and taps).
Price: **$102.99**

Sight Attachments

MERIT ADJUSTABLE APERTURES Eleven clicks give 12 different apertures. No. 3 Disc and Master, primarily target types, 0.22" to .125"; No. 4, 1/2" dia. hunting type, .025" to .155". Available for all popular sights. The Master, with flexible rubber light shield, is particularly adapted to extension, scope height, and tang sights. All models have internal click springs; are hand fitted to minimum tolerance.
Price: No. 3 Master Disk. **$66.00**
Price: No. 3 Target Disc (Plain Face) **$56.00**
Price: No. 4 Hunting Disc **$48.00**

MERIT LENS DISC Similar to Merit Iris Shutter (Model 3 or Master) but incorporates provision for mounting prescription lens integrally. Lens may be obtained locally from your optician. Sight disc is 7/16" wide (Model 3), or 3/4" wide (Master).
Price: No. 3 Target Lens Disk. **$68.00**
Price: No. 3 Master Lens Disk **$78.00**

MERIT OPTICAL ATTACHMENT For iron sight shooting with handgun or rifle. Instantly attached by rubber suction cup to prescription or shooting glasses. Swings aside. Aperture adjustable from .020" to .156".
Price: **$65.00**

WILLIAMS APERTURES Standard thread, fits most sights. Regular series 3/8" to 1/2" O.D., .050" to .125" hole. "Twilight" series has white reflector ring.
Price: Regular series **$4.97**
Price: Twilight series **$6.79**
Price: Wide open 5/16" aperture for shotguns fits 5-D or Foolproof sights (specify model) **$8.77**

Bushnell Collapsible
Spotting Scope

ALPEN MODEL 711 20x50 mini-scope, 20x, 50mm eyepiece, field of view at 1,000 yds. 147 ft., multi-coated lens, weighs 10 oz., waterproof.
Price: **$60.97**

ALPEN MODEL 722 12-36x compact, 50mm eyepiece, field of view at 1,000 yds: 115 ft. (12x); 59 ft. (36x); multi-coated lens, weighs 27 oz., waterproof.
Price: **$124.20**

ALPEN MODEL 725 and 728 Compact 15-45x60, 60mm obj., center focus, multi-coated lens, field of view at 1,000 yds: 136 ft. (15x); 107 ft. (45x); weighs 27 oz., waterproof.
Price: .... **$151.62 and $154.85**

ALPEN MODEL 730 15-30x50, 60mm obs., field of view at 1,000 yds: 136 ft. (15x); 99 ft. (50x); multi-coated lens, weighs 28 oz., waterproof.
Price: **$116.14**

ALPEN MODEL 788 20-60x80, 80mm obj., field of view at 1,000 yds: 93 ft. (20x); 47 ft. (60x); multi-coated lens, weighs 64 oz., waterproof.
Price: **$404.69**

BROWNING 15-45x zoom, 65mm objective lens. Weighs 48 oz. Waterproof, fogproof. Tripod, soft and hard cases included.
Price: **$559.95**

BUSHNELL DISCOVERER, 15x to 60x zoom, 60mm objective. Constant focus throughout range. Field of view at 1,000 yds. 38 ft. (60x), 150 ft. (15x). Comes with lens caps. Length: 17-1/2"; weighs 48.5 oz.
Price: **$342.95**

BUSHNELL ELITE 15x to 45x zoom, 60mm objective. Field of view (1,000 yards) 125 yds.@15X, 65 yds.@45X. Length: 12.2"; weighs 26.5 oz. Waterproof, armored. Tripod mount. Comes with black case and rainguard.
Price: **$586.95**

BUSHNELL ELITE ZOOM 20x-60x, 70mm objective. Roof prism. Field of view at 1,000 yds. 90-50 ft. Length: 16"; weighs 40 oz. Waterproof, armored. Tripod mount. Comes with black case.
Price: **$806.95**

BUSHNELL 80MM ELITE 20x-60x zoom, 80mm objective. Field of view at 1,000 yds. 98-50 ft. (zoom). Weighs 53 oz. Length: 17". Interchangeable bayonet-style eyepieces. Built-in peep sight.
Price: With EDPrime Glass **$1,173.95**

BUSHNELL TROPHY 65mm objective, 20x-60x zoom. Field of view at 1,000 yds. 90 ft. (20x), 45 ft. (60x). Length: 12.7"; weighs 20 oz. Black rubber armored, waterproof. Case included.
Price: **$297.95**

BUSHNELL COMPACT TROPHY 50mm objective, 20x-50x zoom. Field of view at 1,000 yds. 92 ft. (20x), 52 ft. (50x). Length: 12.2"; weighs 17 oz. Black rubber armored, waterproof. Case included.
Price: **$257.95**

BUSHNELL COMPACT SENTRY 18-36x50mm objective. Field of view at 1,000 yds. 115 ft. (80x), 75 ft. (36x). Length: 8.7", weighs 21.5 oz. With tripod and hard case. Waterproof.
Price: **$157.95**

BUSHNELL SPACEMASTER 20x-45x zoom. Long eye relief. Rubber armored, prismatic. 60mm objective. Field of view at 1,000 yds. 90-58 ft. Minimum focus 20 ft. Length: 12.7"; weighs 43 oz.
Price: With tripod, carrying case and 20x-45x LER eyepiece. **$502.95**

BUSHNELL SPACEMASTER COLLAPSIBLE 15-45x zoom, 50mm objective lens. Field of view at 1,000 yds., 113 ft. (15x), 52 ft. (45x). Length: 8". Weighs 22.8 oz. Comes with tripod, window mount and case.
Price: **$209.95**

BUSHNELL SPORTVIEW 15x-45x zoom, 50mm objective. Field of view at 1,000 yds. 103 ft. (15x), 35 ft. (45x). Length: 17.4"; weighs 34.4 oz.
Price: With tripod and carrying case **$91.95**

BUSHNELL LEGEND 20x-60x zoom, 60mm objective. Field of view at 1,000 yds. 138 ft. (20x), 68 ft. (60x). Length: 14.3"; weighs 34.3 oz.
Price: With carrying case **$398.95**

CELESTRON MINI 50MM ZOOM Offset 45° or straight body. Comes with 12x36x eyepiece. 50mm obj. Field of view at 1,000 yds. 160 (or 82), waterproof. Length: 8.5", weighs 1.4 lbs.
Price: .... **NA**

CELESTRON ULTIMA SERIES Offset 45° or straight body. 18x55, 20-60 zoom or 22-60 zoom. Aperture: 65mm, 80mm or 100mm, field of view at 1,000 yds., 89' at 18x, 38' at 55x, 105' at 20x, 95' at 22x, 53' at 66x. Length: 13", 16" or 19". Weighs 2.3 to 4.5 lbs.
Price: Body. .... **NA**

HERMES 1 70mm objective, 16x, 25x, 40x. Field of view at 1,000 meters 160 ft. (16x), 75 ft. (40x). Length: 12.2"; weighs 33 oz. From CZ-USA.
Price: Body. **$359.00**
Price: 25x eyepiece **$86.00**
Price: 40x eyepiece **$128.00**

KOWA TS-500 SERIES Offset 45° or straight body. Comes with 20-40x zoom eyepiece or 20x fixed eyepiece. 50mm obj. Field of view at 1,000 yds.: 171 ft. (20x fixed), 132-74 ft. (20-40x zoom). Length: 8.9-10.4", weighs 13.4-14.8 oz.
Price: TS-501 (offset 45° body w/20x fixed eyepiece) **$258.00**
Price: TS-502 (straight body w/20x fixed eyepiece) **$231.00**
Price: TS-501Z (offset 45° body w/20-40x zoom eyepiece) **$321.00**
Price: TS-502Z (straight body w/20-40x zoom eyepiece) **$290.00**

KOWA TS-660 SERIES Offset 45° or straight body. Fully waterproof. Available with ED lens.Sunshade and rotating tripod mount. 66mm obj. Field of view at 1,000 yds.: 177 ft. (20xW), 154 ft. (27xW), 131 ft. (30xW), 102 ft. (25x), 92 ft. (25xLER), 108-79 ft. (20-40x multi-coated zoom), 98-62 ft. (20-60x high grade zoom). Length: 12.3"; weighs 34.9-36.7 oz.
Price: TSN-662 body (straight) **$610.00**
Price: TSN-663 body (45 offset, ED lens) **$1,070.00**
Price: TSN-664 body (straight, ED lens) **$1,010.00**
Price: TSE-Z6 (20-40x multi-coatedzoom eyepiece) **$378.00**
Price: TSE-17HB (25x long eye relief eyepiece) **$240.00**
Price: TSE-14W (30x wide angle high-grade eyepiece) **$288.00**
Price: TSE-21WB (20x wide-angle eyepiece) **$230.00**
Price: TSE-15 WM (27x wide-angle eyepiece) **$182.00**
Price: TSE-16 PM (25x eyepiece) **$108.00**
Price: TSN-DA1 digital photo adapter **$105.00**
Price: DA1 adapter rings **$43.00**
Price: TSN-PA2 (800mm photo adapter) **$269.00**
Price: TSN-PA4 (1200mm photo adapter) **$330.00**
Price: Camera mounts (for use with photo adapter) **$30.00**
Price Eyepieces for TSN 77mm series,
TSN-660 series, 661 body (45° offset) **$660.00**

KOWA TSN-660 SERIES Offset 45° or straight body. Fully waterproof. Available with fluorite lens. Sunshade and rotating tripod mount. 66mm obj., field of view at 1,000 yds.: 177 ft. (20x), 154 ft. (27xW), 131 ft. (30xW), 102 ft. (25x), 92 ft. (25xLER), 62 ft. (40x), 108-79 ft. (20-40x Multi-Coated Zoom), 102-56 ft. (20-60x zoom), 98-62 ft. (20-60x High Grade Zoom). Length: 12.3"; weighs 34.9-36.7 oz. Note: Eyepieces for TSN 77mm Series, TSN-660 Series, and TSN610 Series are interchangeable.
Price: TSN-661 body (45° offset) **$660.00**
Price: TSN-662 body (straight) **$610.00**
Price: TSN-663 body (45° offset, fluorite lens) **$1,070.00**
Price: TSN-664 body (straight, fluorite lens) **$1,010.00**
Price: TSE-Z4 (20-60x high-grade zoom eyepiece) **$378.00**
Price: TSE-Z6 (20-40x multi-coated zoom eyepiece) **$250.00**
Price: TSE-17HB (25x long eye relief eyepiece) **$240.00**
Price: TSE-14W (30x wide angle eyepiece) **$288.00**
Price: TSE-21WB (20x wide angle eyepiece) **$230.00**
Price: TSE-15PM (27x wide angle eyepiece) **$182.00**
Price: TSE-10PM (40x eyepiece) **$108.00**
Price: TSE-16PM (25x eyepiece) **$105.00**
Price: TSN-DA1 (digital photo adapter) **$105.00**
Price: Adapter rings for DA1 .... **$43.00**
Price: TSN-PA2 (800mm photo adapter) **$269.00**
Price: TSN-PA4 (1200mm photo adapter) **$330.00**
Price: Camera mounts (for use with photo adapter) **$30.00**

KOWA TSN-820M SERIES Offset 45° or straight body. Fully waterproof. Available with fluorite lens. Sunshade and rotating tripod mount. 82mm obj., field of view at 1,000 yds: 75 ft. (27xLER, 50xW), 126 ft. (32xW), 115-58 ft. (20-60xZoom). Length: 15"; weighs 49.4-52.2 oz.
Price: TSN-821M body (45° offset) **$850.00**
Price: TSN-822M body (straight) **$770.00**
Price: TSN-823M body (45° offset, fluorite lens) **$1,850.00**
Price: TSN-824M body (straight, fluorite lens) **$1,730.00**
Price: TSE-Z7 (20-60x zoom eyepiece) **$433.00**
Price: TSE-9W (50x wide angle eyepiece) **$345.00**
Price: TSE-14WB (32x wide angle eyepiece) **$366.00**
Price: TSE-17HC (27x long eye relief eyepiece) **$248.00**
Price: TSN-DA1 (digital photo adapter) **$105.00**
Price: Adapter rings for DA1 .... **$43.00**
Price: TSN-PA2C (850mm photo adapter) **$300.00**
Price: Camera mounts (for use with photo adapter) **$30.00**

LEUPOLD 10-20x40mm COMPACT 40mm objective, 10-20x. Field of view at 100 yds. 19.9-13.6 ft.; eye relief 18.5mm (10x). Overall length: 7.5", weighs 15.8 oz. Rubber armored.
Price: **$439.95**

LEUPOLD 55-30x50 COMPACT 50mm objective, 15-30x. Field of view at 100 yds. 13.6 ft.; eye relief 17.5mm; Overall length: 11"; weighs 1.5 oz.
Price: **$564.99**

LEUPOLD Wind River Sequoia 15-30x60mm, 60mm objective, 15-30x. Field of view at 100 yds.: 13.1 ft.; eye relief: 16.5mm. Overall length: 13". Weighs 35.1 oz.
Price: **$294.99**

SPOTTING SCOPES

LEUPOLD Wind River Sequoia 15-45x60mm Angled. Armored, 15-45x. Field of view at 100 yds.: 13.1-6.3 ft.; eye relief: 16.5-13.0. Overall length: 12.5". Weighs 35.1 oz.
Price: **$309.99**

LEUPOLD Golden Ring 12-40x60mm; 12.7x38.1x. Field of view at 100 yds.: 16.8-5.2 ft.; eye relief: 30.0; Overall length: 12.4". Weighs 37.0 oz.
Price: **$1,124.99**

LEUPOLD Golden Ring 15-30x50mm Compact Armored; 15.2-30.4x; field of view at 100 yds.: 13.6-8.9 ft.; eye relief: 17.5-17.1; overall length: 11.0". Weighs 21.5 oz.
Price: **$564.99**

MIRADOR TTB SERIES Draw tube armored spotting scopes. Available with 75mm or 80mm objective. Zoom model (28x-62x, 80mm) is 11-7/8" (closed), weighs 50 oz. Field of view at 1,000 yds. 70-42 ft. Comes with lens covers.
Price: 28-62x80mm **$1,133.95**
Price: 32x80mm **$971.95**
Price: 26-58x75mm **$989.95**
Price: 30x75mm **$827.95**

MIRADOR SSD SPOTTING SCOPES 60mm objective, 15x, 20x, 22x, 25x, 40x, 60x, 20-60x; field of view at 1,000 yds. 37 ft.; length: 10 1/4"; weighs 33 oz.
Price: 25x **$575.95**
Price: 22x Wide Angle **$593.95**
Price: 20-60x Zoom **$746.95**
Price: As above, with tripod, case **$944.95**

MIRADOR SIA SPOTTING SCOPES Similar to the SSD scopes except with 45° eyepiece. Length: 12-1/4"; weighs 39 oz.
Price: 25x **$809.95**
Price: 22x Wide Angle **$827.95**
Price: 20-60x Zoom **$980.95**

MIRADOR SSR SPOTTING SCOPES 50mm or 60mm objective. Similar to SSD except rubber armored in black or camouflage. Length: 11-1/8"; weighs 31 oz.
Price: Black, 20x **$521.95**
Price: Black, 18x Wide Angle **$539.95**
Price: Black, 16-48x Zoom **$692.95**
Price: Black, 20x, 60mm, EER **$692.95**
Price: Black, 22x Wide Angle, 60mm **$701.95**
Price: Black, 20-60x Zoom **$854.95**

MIRADOR SSF FIELD SCOPES Fixed or variable power, choice of 50mm, 60mm, 75mm objective lens. Length: 9-3/4"; weighs 20 oz. (15-32x50).
Price: 20x50mm **$359.95**
Price: 25x60mm **$440.95**
Price: 30x75mm **$584.95**
Price: 15-32x50mm Zoom **$548.95**
Price: 18-40x60mm Zoom **$629.95**
Price: 22-47x75mm Zoom **$773.95**

MIRADOR SRA MULTI ANGLE SCOPES Similar to SSF Series except eyepiece head rotates for viewing from any angle.
Price: 20x50mm **$503.95**
Price: 25x60mm **$647.95**
Price: 30x75mm **$764.95**
Price: 15-32x50mm Zoom **$692.95**
Price: 18-40x60mm Zoom **$836.95**
Price: 22-47x75mm Zoom **$953.95**

MIRADOR SIB FIELD SCOPES Short-tube, 45° scopes with porro prism design. 50mm and 60mm objective. Length: 10 1/4"; weighs 18.5 oz. (15-32x50mm); field of view at 1,000 yds. 129-81 ft.
Price: 20x50mm **$386.95**
Price: 25x60mm **$449.95**
Price: 15-32x50mm Zoom **$575.95**
Price: 18-40x60mm Zoom **$638.95**

NIKON FIELDSCOPES 60mm and 78mm lens. Field of view at 1,000 yds. 105 ft. (60mm, 20x), 126 ft. (78mm, 25x). Length: 12.8" (straight 60mm), 12.6" (straight 78mm); weighs 34.5 to 47.5 oz. Eyepieces available separately.
Price: 60mm straight body **$499.99**
Price: 60mm angled body **$519.99**
Price: 60mm straight ED body **$779.99**
Price: 60mm angled ED body **$849.99**
Price: 78mm straight ED body **$899.99**
Price: 78mm angled ED body **$999.99**
Price: Eyepieces (15x to 60x) .... **$146.95 to $324.95**
Price: 20-45x eyepiece (25-56x for 78mm) **$320.55**

NIKON 60mm objective, 20x fixed power or 15-45x zoom. Field of view at 1,000 yds. 145 ft. (20x). Gray rubber armored. Straight or angled eyepiece. Weighs 44.2 oz., length: 12.1" (20x).
Price: 20x60 fixed (with eyepiece) **$290.95**
Price: 15-45x zoom (with case, tripod, eyepiece) **$578.95**

PENTAX PF-80ED 80mm objective lens available in 18x, 24x, 36x, 48x, 72x and 20-60x. Length: 15.6", weighs 11.9 to 19.2 oz.
Price: **$1,320.00**

SIGHTRON SII 2050X63 63mm objective lens, 20x-50x zoom. Field of view at 1,000 yds 91.9 ft. (20x), 52.5 ft. (50x). Length: 14"; weighs 30.8 oz. Black rubber finish. Also available with 80mm objective lens.
Price: 63mm or 80mm **$339.95**

SIMMONS 1280 50mm objective, 15-45x zoom. Black matte finish. Ocular focus. Peep finder sight. Waterproof. Field of view at 95-51 ft. 1,000 yds. Weights 33.5 oz., length: 12".
Price: With tripod **$189.99**

SIMMONS 1281 60mm objective, 20-60x zoom. Black matte finish. Ocular focus. Peep finder sight. Waterproof. Field of view at 78-43 ft. 1,000 yds. Weights 34.5 oz. Length: 12".
Price: With tripod **$209.99**

SIMMONS 77206 PROHUNTER 50mm objectives, 25x fixed power. Field of view at 1,000 yds. 113 ft.; length: 10.25"; weighs 33.25 oz. Black rubber armored.
Price: With tripod case **$160.60**

SIMMONS 41200 REDLINE 50mm objective, 15x-45x zoom. Field of view at 1,000 yds. 104-41 ft.; length: 16.75"; weighs 32.75 oz.
Price: With hard case and tripod **$74.99**
Price: 20-60x, 60mm objective **$99.99**

SWAROVSKI ATS-STS 65mm or 80mm objective, 20-60x zoom, or fixed 20x, 30x 45x eyepieces. Field of view at 1,000 yds. 180 ft. (20xSW), 126 ft. (30xSW), 84 ft. (45xSW), 108-60 ft. (20-60xS) for zoom. Length: 13.98" (ATS/STS 80), 12.8" (ATS/STS 65); weighs 45.93 oz. (ATS 80), 47.70 oz. (ATS 80HD), 45.23 oz. (STS 80), 46.91 oz. (STS 80 HD), 38.3 oz. (ATS 65), 39.9 oz. (ATS 65HD) 38.1 oz. (STS 65), 39.2 oz. (STS 65 HD).
Price: ATS 65 (angled eyepiece) **$1,254.45**
Price: STS 65 (straight eyepiece) **$1,254.45**
Price: ATS-80/STS 80 .... **$1,565.57**
Price: ATS/STS 80 (HD) **$2,110.01**
Price: 20xSW **$372.23**
Price: 30xSW **$388.90**
Price: 45xSW **$432.23**

SWIFT LYNX M836 15x-45x zoom, 60mm objective. Weighs 7 lbs., length: 14". Has 45° eyepiece, sunshade.
Price: **$315.00**

SWIFT NIGHTHAWK M849U 80mm objective, 20x-60x zoom, or fixed 19, 25x, 31x, 50x, 75x eyepieces. Has rubber armored body, 1.8x optical finder, retractable lens hood, 45° eyepiece. Field of view at 1,000 yds. 60 ft. (28x), 41 ft. (75x). Length: 13.4 oz.; weighs 39 oz.
Price: Body only **$870.00**
Price: 20-68x eyepiece **$370.00**
Price: Fixed eyepieces .... **$130.00 to $240.00**
Price: Model 849 (straight) body **$795.00**

SWIFT LYNX 60mm objective, 15-45x zoom, 45° inclined roof prism, magenta coated on all air-to-glass surfaces, rubber armored body, length: 14", weighs 30 oz. Equipped with sun shade, threaded dust covers and low level tripod.
Price: complete **$330.00**

SWIFT TELEMASTER M841 60mm objective. 15x to 60x variable power. Field of view at 1,000 yds. 160 feet (15x) to 40 feet (60x). Weighs 3.25 lbs.; length: 18" overall.
Price: **$399.50**

SWIFT PANTHER M844 15x-45x zoom or 22x WA, 15x, 20x, 40x. 60mm objective. Field of view at 1,000 yds. 141 ft. (15x), 68 ft. (40x), 95-58 ft. (20x-45x).
Price: Body only **$380.00**
Price: 15x-45x zoom eyepiece **$120.00**
Price: 20x-45x zoom (long eye relief) eyepiece **$140.00**
Price: 15x, 40x eyepiece **$65.00**
Price: 22x WA eyepiece **$80.00**

SWIFT M700T 12x-36x, 50mm objective. Field of view at 100 yds. 16 ft. (12x), 9 ft. (36x). Length: 14"; weighs 3.22 lbs. (with tripod).
Price: **$30.00**

TASCO 15-45x zoom, 50mm objective lens, Field of view at 1000 yds: 115 ft. (15x), Length: 13.8". Weighs 24 oz. Matte black finish.
Price: **$128.95**

TASCO 20-50x zoom, 50mm objective. Field of view at 1000 yds: 147 ft. (20x). Length: 7.5". Weighs 10.6 oz. Black finish.
Price: **$80.95**

TASCO 20-60x zoom, 60mm objective. Field of view at 1000 yds: 91 ft. (20x). Length: 13.8". Weighs 30 oz. Black finish.
Price: **$138.95**

TASCO 12-36x zoom 50mm objective. Field of view at 1000 yds. 144 ft. (12x). Length: 7.8". Weighs 17 oz. Black rubber armor. Includes carrying case.
Price: **$118.95**

UNERTL "FORTY-FIVE" 54mm objective. 20x (single fixed power). Field of view at 100 yds. 10',10"; eye relief 1"; focusing range infinity to 33 ft. Weighs about 32 oz.; overall length: 15-3/4". With lens covers.
Price: With mono-layer magnesium coating **$810.00**

UNERTL STRAIGHT PRISMATIC 24x63. 63.5mm objective, 24x. Field of view at 100 yds., 7 ft. Relative brightness, 6.96. Eye relief 1/2". Weighs 40 oz.; length: closed 19". Push-pull and screw-focus eyepiece. 16x and 32x eyepieces **$125.00 each.**
Price: **$786.00**

UNERTL 20x STRAIGHT PRISMATIC 54mm objective, 20x. Field of view at 100 yds. 8.5 ft. Relative brightness 6.1. Eye relief 1/2". Weighs 36 oz.; length: closed 13-1/2". Complete with lens covers.
Price: **$695.00**

UNERTL TEAM SCOPE 100mm objective. 15x, 24x, 32x eyepieces. Field of view at 100 yds. 13 to 7.5 ft. Relative brightness, 39.06 to 9.79. Eye relief 2" to 1-1/2". Weighs 13 lbs.; length: 29-7/8" overall. Metal tripod, yoke and wood carrying case furnished (total weighs 80 lbs.).
Price: **$3,624.50**

WEAVER 20x50 50mm objective. Field of view 124 ft. at 100 yds. Eye relief .85"; weighs 21 oz.; overall length: 10". Waterproof, armored.
Price: **$249.99**

WEAVER 15-40x60 ZOOM 60mm objective. 15x-40x zoom. Field of view at 100 yds. 119 ft. (15x), 66 ft. (60x). Overall length: 12.5", weighs 26 oz. Waterproof, armored.
Price: **$399.99**

Briley Screw-In Chokes

Installation of these choke tubes requires that all traces of the original choking be removed, the barrel threaded internally with square threads and then the tubes are custom fitted to the specific barrel diameter. The tubes are thin and, therefore, made of stainless steel. Cost of installation for single-barrel guns (pumps, autos), lead shot, 12-gauge, **$149.00**, 20-gauge **$159.00**; steel shot **$179.00** and **$189.00**, all with three chokes; un-single target guns run **$219.00**; over/unders and side-by-sides, lead shot, 12-gauge **$369.00**, 20-gauge **$389.00**; steel shot **$469.00** and **$489.00**, all with five chokes. For 10-gauge auto or pump with two steel shot chokes, **$189.00**; over/unders, side-by-sides with three steel shot chokes, **$349.00**. For 16-gauge auto or pump, three lead shot chokes, **$179.00**; over/unders, side-by-sides with five lead shot chokes, **$449.00**. The 28 and 410-bore run **$179.00** for autos and pumps with three lead shot chokes, **$449.00** for over/unders and side-by-sides with five lead shot chokes.

Carlson's Choke Tubes

Manufactures choke tubes for Beretta, Benelli, Remington, Winchester, Browning Invector and Invector Plus, TruChokes, FranChokes, American Arms, Ruger and more. All choke tubes are manufactured from corrosion resistant stainless steel. Most tubes are compatible with lead, steel, Hevi-shot, etc. Available in flush mount, extended sporting clay and extended turkey designs, ported and non-ported. Also offers sights, rifled choke tubes and other accessories for most shotgun models. Prices range from **$18.95** to **$36.95**.

Cutts Compensator

The Cutts Compensator is one of the oldest variable choke devices available. Manufactured by Lyman Gunsight Corporation, it is available with a steel body. A series of vents allows gas to escape upward and downward. For the 12-ga. Comp body, six fixed-choke tubes are available: the Spreader–popular with skeet shooters; Improved Cylinder; Modified; Full; Superfull, and Magnum Full. Full, Modified and Spreader tubes are available for 12 or 20. Cutts Compensator, complete with wrench, adaptor and any single tube **$87.50**. All single choke tubes **$26.00** each. No factory installation available.

Dayson Automatic Brake System

This system fits most single barrel shotguns threaded for choke tubes, and cuts away 30 grooves on the exterior of a standard one-piece wad as it exits the muzzle. This slows the wad, allowing shot and wad to separate faster, reducing shot distortion and tightening patterns. The A.B.S. choke tube is claimed to reduce recoil by about 25 percent, and with the muzzle brake up to 60 percent. Ventilated choke tubes available from .685" to .725", in .005" increments. Model I ventilated choke tube for use with A.B.S. muzzle brake, **$49.95**; for use without muzzle brake, **$52.95**; A.B.S. muzzle brake, from **$69.95**. Contact Dayson Arms for more data.

Gentry Quiet Muzzle Brake

Developed by gunmaker David Gentry, the "Quiet Muzzle Brake" is said to reduce recoil by up to 85 percent with no loss of accuracy or velocity. There is no increase in noise level because the noise and gases are directed away from the shooter. The barrel is threaded for installation and the unit is blued to match the barrel finish. Price, installed, is **$150.00**. Add **$15.00** for stainless steel, **$45.00** for knurled cap to protect threads. Shipping extra.

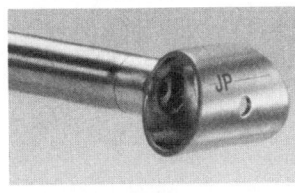

JP Muzzle Brake

JP Muzzle Brake

Designed for single shot handguns, AR-15, Ruger Mini-14, Ruger Mini Thirty and other sporting rifles, the JP muzzle brake redirects high pressure gases against a large frontal surface which applies forward thrust to the gun. All gases are directed up, rearward and to the sides. Priced at **$79.95** (AR-15 or sporting rifles), **$89.95** (bull barrel and SKS, AK models), **$89.95** (Ruger Minis), dual chamber model **$79.95**. From JP Enterprises, Inc.

KDF Slim Line Muzzle Brake

This threaded muzzle brake has 30 pressure ports that direct combustion gases in all directions to reduce felt recoil up to a claimed 80 percent without affecting accuracy or ballistics. Reduces felt recoil of a 30-06 to that of a 243. Price, installed, is **$199.00**. From KDF, Inc.

KDF Kick Arrestor

This mercury-filled, inertia-type recoil reducer is installed in the butt of a wood or synthetic stock (rifle or shotgun) to reduce recoil up to 20 percent. Adds 16 oz. ot the weight of the gun Measures 6.25; L x .75" in diameter. Price, installed, is **$165.00**. From KDF, Inc.

Laseraim

Simple, no-gunsmithing compensator reduces felt recoil and muzzle flip by up to 30 percent. Machined from single piece of stainless steel (Beretta/Taurus model made of aircraft aluminum). In black and polished finish. For Colt Government/Commander and Beretta/Taurus full-size pistols. Weighs 1 ounce. **$49.00**. From Laseraim Arms Inc.

Mag-Na-Port

Electrical Discharge Machining works on any firearm except those having non-conductive shrouded barrels. EDM is a metal erosion technique using carbon electrodes that control the area to be processed. The Mag-Na-Port venting process utilizes small trapezoidal openings to direct powder gases upward and outward to reduce recoil. No effect is had on bluing or nickeling outside the Mag-Na-Port area so no refinishing is needed. Rifle-style porting on single shot or large caliber handguns with barrels 7-1/2" or longer is **$115.00**; Dual Trapezoidal porting on most handguns with minimum barrel length of 3", **$115.00**; standard revolver porting, **$88.50**; Scandium/titanium-sleeved barrels **$139.50** (2 ports) or **$195.00** (4 ports); porting through the slide and barrel for semi-autos, **$129.50**; traditional rifle porting, **$135.00**. Prices do not include shipping, handling and insurance. From Mag-Na-Port International.

Mag-Na-Brake

A screw-on brake under 2" long with progressive integrated exhaust chambers to neutralize expanding gases. Gases dissipate with an opposite twist to prevent the brake from unscrewing, and with a 5° forward angle to minimize sound pressure level. Available in blue, satin blue, bright or satin stainless. Standard and Light Contour installation cost **$195.00** for bolt-action rifles, many single action and single shot handguns. A knurled thread protector supplied at extra cost. Also available in Varmint-style with exhaust chambers covering 220° for prone-position shooters. From Mag-Na-Port International.

Poly-Choke

Marble Arms Corp., manufacturer of the Poly-Choke adjustable shotgun choke, now offers two models in 12-, 16-, 20-, and 28-gauge–the ventilated and standard-style chokes. Each provides nine choke settings including Xtra-Full and Slug. The ventilated model reduces 20 percent of a shotgun's recoil, the company claims, and is priced at **$135.00**. The standard model is **$125.00**. Postage not included. Contact Marble Arms for more data.

Pro-port

A compound ellipsoid muzzle venting process similar to Mag-Na-Porting, only exclusively applied to shotguns. Like Mag-Na-Porting, this system reduces felt recoil, muzzle jump, and shooter fatigue. Pro-Port is a patented process and installation is available in both the U.S. and Canada. Cost for the Pro-Port process is **$139.00** for over/unders (both barrels); **$110.00** for only the top or bottom barrel; and **$88.50** for single-barrel shotguns. Optional pigeon porting costs **$25.00** extra per barrel. Prices do not include shipping and handling. From Magnaport International.

Que Industries Adjustable Muzzle Brake

The Que Brake allows for fine-tuning of a rifle's accuracy by rotating the brake to one of 100 indexed stops. Mounts in minutes without barrel modification with heat-activated tensioning ring. The slotted exhaust ports reduce recoil by venting gases sideways, away from rifle. **$189.50**. From Que Industries.

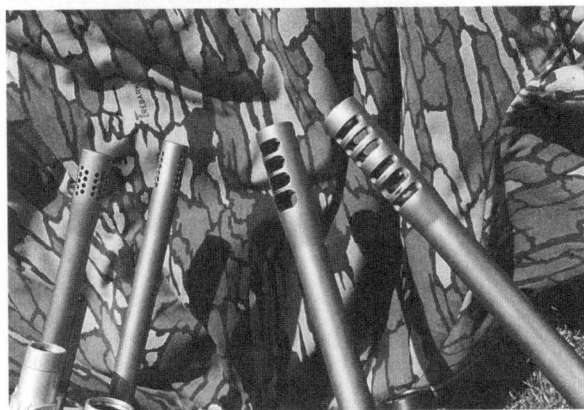

SSK Arrestor muzzle brakes

SSK Arrestor Brake

This is a true muzzle brake with an expansion chamber. It takes up about 1" of barrel and reduces velocity accordingly. Some Arrestors are added to a barrel, increasing its length. Said to reduce the felt recoil of a 458 to that approaching a 30-06. Can be set up to give zero muzzle rise in any caliber, and can be added to most guns. For handgun or rifle. Prices start at **$95.00**. Contact SSK Industries for full data.

THE 2007 Gun Digest WEB DIRECTORY

by Holt Bodinson

"Home is where you hang your @" is latest slogan of the e-commerce world, and who would have ever guessed that the word "blog" would be the most looked-up word last year on the Merriman-Webster Dictionary Web site.

What's a blog? According to Merriman Webster, Inc., it's "a Web site that contains an online personal journal with reflections, comments, and often hyperlinks." There are a lot of gunny blogs out there.

The other Internet terms we've added to our dictionary are worms, viruses, adware, spyware, hackers and malicious software. There are dangers lurking in today's cyberspace, and you need a full battery of firewall, antivirus, spyware and adware programs for protection when romping around on the Web.

Major corporate advertising is moving aggressively on the Web, and why not? More than half of American households have some form of Broadband connection with the average U.S. Internet user spending 3 hours a day online. On a daily basis, AOL, MSN and Yahoo report a combined use by some 50 million customers

That universal auction site, eBay, has over a 150 million registered users. In fact, eBay.com has become such a significant resource for buying or selling gun parts, accessories and tools, we're adding it to our Gun Digest Web Directory this year.

And the person who fathered the World Wide Web in 1991, Timothy J. Berners-Lee, is plowing ahead to create the Semantic Web—a place where computers will understand and communicate with each other, searching out each other's data bases without our having to coax them along. Stay tuned.

The firearms industry has done a remarkably good job of adapting to e-commerce. More and more firearm related businesses are striking out and creating their own discrete web pages. It's never been easier with the inexpensive software programs now available.

The Gun Digest Web Directory is now in its eighth year of publication. The Internet is a dynamic environment and since our last edition, there have been numerous changes. Companies have consolidated and adopted a new owner's web site address. New companies have appeared and old companies and discussion groups have disappeared. Search engines are now more powerful than ever and seem to root out even the most obscure reference to a product name or manufacturer.

The following index of web addresses is offered to our readers as a convenient jumping-off point. Half the fun is just exploring what's out there. Considering that most of the web pages have hot links to other firearm-related web pages, the Internet trail just goes on-and-on once you've taken the initial step to go online.

Here are a few pointers:

If the web site you desire is not listed, try using the full name of the company or product, typed without spaces, between www.-and-.com, for example, www.krause.com. Probably 95 percent of current Web sites are based on this simple, self-explanatory format.

Try a variety of search engines like Microsoft Internet Explorer, Metacrawler, GoTo.com, Yahoo, HotBot, AltaVista, Lycos, Excite, InfoSeek, Looksmart, Google, and WebCrawler while using key words such as gun, firearm, rifle, pistol, blackpowder, shooting, hunting— frankly, any word that relates to the sport. Each search engine combs through the World Wide Web in a different fashion and produces different results. We find Google to be among the best. Accessing the various search engines is simple. Just type www.google.com for example, and you're on your way.

Welcome to the digital world of firearms. "A journey of a thousand sites begins with a single click."

WEB DIRECTORY

Ammunition and Components

A-Square Co. www.a-squarecompany.com
3-D Ammunition www.3dammo.com
Accurate Arms Co. Inc www.accuratepowder.com
ADCO/Nobel Sport Powder www.adcosales.com
Aguila Ammunition www.aguilaammo.com
Alliant Powder www.alliantpowder.com
American Ammunition www.a-merc.com
American Derringer Co. www.amderringer.com
American Pioneer Powder www.americanpioneerpowder.com
Ammo Depot www.ammodepot.com
Arizona Ammunition, Inc. www.arizonaammunition.com
A-Zoom Ammo www.a-zoom.com
Ballistic Products,Inc. www.ballisticproducts.com
Barnaul Cartridge Plant www.ab.ru/~stanok
Barnes Bullets www.barnesbullets.com
Baschieri & Pellagri www.baschieri-pellagri.com
Beartooth Bullets www.beartoothbullets.com
Bell Brass www.bellbrass.com
Berger Bullets, Ltd. www.bergerbullets.com
Berry's Mfg., Inc. www.berrysmfg.com
Big Bore Bullets of Alaska www.awloo.com/bbb/index.htm
Big Bore Express www.powerbeltbullets.com
Bismuth Cartridge Co. www.bismuth-notox.com
Black Dawge Cartridge www.blackdawgecartridge.com
Black Hills Ammunition, Inc. www.black-hills.com
Brenneke of America Ltd. www.brennekeusa.com
Buffalo Arms www.buffaloarms.com
Calhoon, James, Bullets www.jamescalhoon.com
Cartuchos Saga www.saga.es
Cast Performance Bullet www.castperformance.com
CCI www.cci-ammunition.com
Century International Arms www.centuryarms.com
Cheaper Than Dirt www.cheaperthandirt.com
Cheddite France www.cheddite.com
Claybuster Wads www.claybusterwads.com
Clean Shot Powder www.cleanshot.com
Cole Distributing www.cole-distributing.com
Combined Tactical Systems www.less-lethal.com
Cor-Bon/Glaser www.cor-bon.com
Cowboy Bullets www.cowboybullets.com
Denver Bullet Co. denbullets@aol.com
Dillon Precision www.dillonprecision.com
Dionisi Cartridge www.dionisi.com
DKT, Inc. www.dktinc.com
Down Range Mfg. www.downrangemfg.com
Dynamit Nobel RWS Inc. www.dnrws.com
Elephant/Swiss Black Powder www.elephantblackpowder.com
Eley Ammunition www.eleyusa.com
Eley Hawk Ltd. www.eleyhawk.com
Environ-Metal www.hevishot.com
Estate Cartridge www.estatecartridge.com
Extreme Shock Munitions www.extremeshockusa.com
Federal Cartridge Co. www.federalpremium.com
Fiocchi of America www.fiocchiusa.com
Fowler Bullets www.benchrest.com/fowler
Garrett Cartridges www.garrettcartridges.com
Gentner Bullets www.benchrest.com/gentner/
Glaser Safety Slug, Inc. www.corbon.com
GOEX Inc. www.goexpowder.com
GPA www.cartouchegpa.com
Graf & Sons www.grafs.com
Hawk Bullets www.hawkbullets.com
Hevi.Shot www.hevishot.com
Hi-Tech Ammunition www.iidbs.com/hitech
Hodgdon Powder www.hodgdon.com
Hornady www.hornady.com
Hull Cartridge www.hullcartridge.com
Huntington Reloading Products www.huntingtons.com
Impact Bullets www.impactbullets.com
IMR Smokeless Powders www.imrpowder.com
International Cartridge Corp www.internationalcartridgecorp.com
Israel Military Industries www.imisammo.co.il
ITD Enterprise www.itdenterpriseinc.com
Kent Cartridge America www.kentgamebore.com
Knight Bullets www.benchrest.com/knight/
Kynoch Ammunition www.kynochammunition.com
Lapua www.lapua.com
Lawrence Brand Shot www.metalico.com
Lazzeroni Arms Co. www.lazzeroni.com
Leadheads Bullets www.proshootpro.com
Liberty Shooting Supplies www.libertyshootingsupplies.com
Lightfield Ammunition Corp www.lightfieldslugs.com
Lomont Precision Bullets www.klomont.com/kent
Lost River Ballistic Technologies,Inc. www.lostriverballistic.com
Lyman www.lymanproducts.com
Magkor Industries. www.magkor.com
Magnum Muzzleloading Products www.mmpsabots.com
Magnus Bullets www.magnusbullets.com
MagSafe Ammunition www.realpages.com/magsafeammo
Magtech www.magtechammunition.com

Masterclass Bullet Co. www.mastercast.com
Meister Bullets www.meisterbullets.com
Midway USA www.midwayusa.com
Miltex,Inc. www.miltexusa.com
Mitchell Mfg. Co. www.mitchellsales.com
MK Ballistic Systems www.mkballistics.com
Mullins Ammunition www.mullinsammunition.com
National Bullet Co. www.nationalbullet.com
Nobel Sport www.nobelsportammo.com
Norma www.norma.cc
North Fork Technologies www.northforkbullets.com
Nosler Bullets, Inc. www.nosler.com
Old Western Scrounger www.ows-ammunition.com
Oregon Trail/Trueshot Bullets www.trueshotbullets.com
Pattern Control www.patterncontrol.com
PMC-Eldorado Cartridge www.pmcammo.com
Polywad www.polywad.com
PowerBelt Bullets www.powerbeltbullets.com
Precision Ammunition www.precisionammo.com
Precision Reloading www.precisionreloading.com
Pro Load Ammunition www.proload.com
Rainier Ballistics www.rainierballistics.com
Ram Shot Powder www.ramshot.com
Reloading Specialties Inc. www.reloadingspecialties.com
Remington www.remington.com
Rocky Mountain Cartridge www.rockymountaincartridge.com
RWS/RUAG Ammotec USA www.ruagammotecusa.com
Schuetzen Powder www.schuetzenpowder.com
Sellier & Bellot USA inc. www.sb-usa.com
Shilen www.shilen.com
Sierra www.sierrabullets.com
Simunition. www.simunition.com
Speer Bullets www.speer-bullets.com
Sporting Supplies Int'l Inc. www.ssiintl.com
Starline www.starlinebrass.com
Swift Bullets Co. www.swiftbullet.com
Top Brass www.top-brass.com
Triton Cartridge www.a-merc.com
Trueshot Bullets www.trueshotbullets.com
Tru-Tracer www.trutracer.com
Ultramax Ammunition www.ultramaxammunition.com
Vihtavuori Lapua www.vihtavuori-lapua.com
West Coast Bullets www.westcoastbullet.com
Western Powders Inc. www.westernpowders.com
Widener's Reloading & Shooters Supply www.wideners.com
Winchester Ammunition www.winchester.com
Windjammer Tournament Wads. www.windjammer-wads.com
Wolf Ammunition www.wolfammo.com
Woodleigh Bullets www.woodleighbullets.com.au
Zanders Sporting Goods www.gzanders.com

CASES, SAFES, GUN LOCKS, AND CABINETS

Ace Case Co. www.acecase.com
AG English Sales Co. www.agenglish.com
All Americas' Outdoors www.innernet.net/gunsafe
Alpine Cases www.alpinecases.com
Aluma Sport by Dee Zee www.deezee.com
American Security Products www.amsecusa.com
Americase www.americase.com
Avery Outdoors, Inc. www.averyoutdoors.com
Bear Track Cases www.beartrackcases.com
Boyt Harness Co. www.boytharness.com
Bulldog Gun Safe Co. www.gardall.com
Cannon Safe Co. www.cannonsafe.com
CCL Security Products www.cclsecurity.com
Concept Development Corp. www.saf-t-blok.com
Doskocil Mfg. Co. www.doskocilmfg.com
Fort Knox Safes www.ftknox.com
Franzen Security Products www.securecase.com
Frontier Safe Co. www.frontiersafe.com
Granite Security Products www.granitesafe.com
Gunlocker Phoenix USA Inc. www.gunlocker.com
GunVault www.gunvault.com
Hakuba USA Inc. www.hakubausa.com
Heritage Safe Co. www.heritagesafecompany.com
Hide-A-Gun www.hide-a-gun.com
Homak Safes www.homak.com
Hunter Company www.huntercompany.com
Kalispel Case Line www.kalispelcaseline.com
Knouff & Knouff, Inc. www.kkair.com
Knoxx Industries www.knoxx.com
Kolpin Mfg. Co. www.kolpin.com
Liberty Safe & Security www.libertysafe.com
New Innovative Products www.starlightcases
Noble Security Systems Inc. www.noble.co.ll
Phoenix USA Inc. www.gunlocker.com
Plano Molding Co. www.planomolding.com
Rhino Gun Cases www.rhinoguns.com
Rhino Safe www.rhinosafe.com
Safe Tech, Inc. www.safrgun.com
Saf-T-Hammer www.saf-t-hammer.com

WEB DIRECTORY

Saf-T-Lok Corp. www.saf-t-lok.com
San Angelo All-Aluminum Products Inc. sasptuld@x.netcom.com
Securecase www.securecase.com
Shot Lock Corp. www.shotlock.com
Smart Lock Technology Inc. www.smartlock.com
Sportsmans Steel Safe Co. www.sportsmansteelsafes.com
Stack-On Products Co. www.stack-on.com
Sun Welding www.sunwelding.com
T.Z. Case Int'l www.tzcase.com
Versatile Rack Co. www.versatilegunrack.com
V-Line Industries www.vlineind.com
Winchester Safes www.fireking.com
Ziegel Engineering www.ziegeleng.com
Zonetti Armor www.zonettiarmor.com

CHOKE DEVICES, RECOIL REDUCERS, AND ACCURACY DEVICES

100 Straight Products www.100straight.com
Answer Products Co. www.answerrifles.com
Briley Mfg www.briley.com
Carlson's www.choketube.com
Colonial Arms www.colonialarms.com
Comp-N-Choke www.comp-n-choke.com
Hastings www.hastingsbarrels.com
Kick's Industries www.kicks-ind.com
Mag-Na-Port Int'l Inc. www.magnaport.com
Metro Gun www.metrogun.com
Patternmaster Chokes www.patternmaster.com
Poly-Choke www.poly-choke.com
Sims Vibration Laboratory www.limbsaver.com
Teague Precision Chokes www.teague.ca
Truglo www.truglo.com

CHRONOGRAPHS AND BALLISTIC SOFTWARE

Barnes Ballistic Program www.barnesbullets.com
Ballisticard Systems www.ballisticards.com
Competition Electronics www.competitionelectronics.com
Competitive Edge Dynamics www.cedhk.com
Hodgdon Shotshell Program www.hodgdon.com
Lee Shooter Program www.leeprecision.com
Load From A Disk www.loadammo.com
Oehler Research Inc. www.oehler-research.com
PACT www.pact.com
ProChrony www.competitionelectronics.com
Quickload www.neconos.com
RCBS Load www.rcbs.com
Shooting Chrony Inc www.shootingchrony.com
Sierra Infinity Ballistics Program www.sierrabullets.com

CLEANING PRODUCTS

Accupro www.accupro.com
Ballistol USA www.ballistol.com
Birchwood Casey www.birchwoodcasey.com
Blue Wonder www.bluewonder.com
Bore Tech www.boretech.com
Break-Free, Inc. www.break-free.com
Bruno Shooters Supply www.brunoshooters.com
Butch's Bore Shine www.lymanproducts.com
C.J. Weapons Accessories www.cjweapons.com
Clenzoil www.clenzoil.com
Corrosion Technologies www.corrosionx.com
Dewey Mfg. www.deweyrods.com
Eezox Inc. www.xmission.com
G 96 www.g96.com
Gunzilla www.topduckproducts.com
Hollands Shooters Supply www.hollandgun.com
Hoppes www.hoppes.com
Hydrosorbent Products www.dehumidify.com
Inhibitor VCI Products www.theinhibitor.com
Iosso Products www.iosso.com
KG Industries www.kgcoatings.com
Kleen-Bore Inc. www.kleen-bore.com
L&R Mfg. www.lrultrasonics.com
Lyman www.lymanproducts.com
Mil-Comm Products www.mil-comm.com
Militec-1 www.militec-1.com
Mpro7 Gun Care www.mp7.com
Otis Technology, Inc. www.otisgun.com
Outers www.outers-guncare.com
Ox-Yoke Originals Inc. www.oxyoke.com
Parker-Hale Ltd. www.parker-hale.com
Prolix Lubricant www.prolixlubricant.com
ProShot Products www.proshotproducts.com
ProTec Lubricants www.proteclubricants.com
Rusteprufe Labs www.rusteprufe.com
Sagebrush Products www.sagebrushproducts.com
Sentry Solutions Ltd. www.sentrysolutions.com
Shooters Choice Gun Care www.shooters-choice.com
Silencio www.silencio.com
Slip 2000 www.slip2000.com

Stony Point Products www.uncle-mikes.com
Tetra Gun www.tetraproducts.com
The TM Solution thetmsolution@comsast.net
World's Fastest Gun Bore Cleaner www.michaels-oregon.com

FIREARM MANUFACTURERS AND IMPORTERS

AAR, Inc. www.iar-arms.com
Accuracy Int'l North America www.accuracyinternational.org
Accuracy Rifle Systems www.mini-14.net
Ace Custom 45's www.acecustom45.com
Advanced Weapons Technology www.AWT-Zastava.com
AIM www.aimsurplus.com
AirForce Airguns www.airforceairguns.com
Airguns of Arizona www.airgunsofarizona.com
Airgun Express www.airgunexpress.com
Alchemy Arms www.alchemyltd.com
Alexander Arms www.alexanderarms.com
American Derringer Corp. www.amderringer.com
American Spirit Arms Corp. www.gunkits.com
American Western Arms www.awaguns.com
Anics Corp. www.anics.com
Answer Products Co. www.answerrifles.com
AR-7 Industries,LLC www.ar-7.com
Ares Defense Systems www.aresdefense.com
Armalite www.armalite.com
Armi Sport www.armisport.com
Armory USA www.globaltraders.com
Armsco www.armsco.net
Armscorp USA Inc. www.armscorpusa.com
Arnold Arms www.arnoldarms.com
Arsenal Inc. www.arsenalinc.com
Arthur Brown Co. www.eabco.com
Austin & Halleck www.austinhalleck.com
Autauga Arms,Inc. www.autaugaarms.com
Auto-Ordnance Corp. www.tommygun.com
AWA Int'l www.awaguns.com
Axtell Rifle Co. www.riflesmith.com
Aya www.aya-fineguns.com
Baikal www.baikalinc.ru/eng/
Ballard Rifles,LLC www.ballardrifles.com
Barrett Firearms Mfg. www.barrettrifles.com
Beeman Precision Airguns www.beeman.com
Benelli USA Corp. www.benelliusa.com
Benjamin Sheridan www.crosman.com
Beretta U.S.A. Corp. www.berettausa.com
Bernardelli www.bernardelli.com
Bersa www.bersa-llama.com
Bill Hanus Birdguns www.billhanusbirdguns.com
Bleiker www.bleiker.ch
Bluegrass Armory www.bluegrassarmory.com
Bond Arms www.bondarms.com
Borden's Rifles, Inc. www.bordensrifles.com
Boss & Co. www.bossguns.co.uk
Bowen Classic Arms www.bowenclassicarms.com
Briley Mfg www.briley.com
BRNO Arms www.zbrojovka.com
Brown, David McKay www.mckaybrown.com
Brown, Ed Products www.brownprecision.com
Browning www.browning.com
BSA Guns www.bsaguns.com
BUL Ltd. www.bultransmark.com
Bushmaster Firearms/Quality Parts www.bushmaster.com
BWE Firearms www.bwefirearms.com
Caesar Guerini USA www.gueriniusa.com
Cape Outfitters www.doublegun.com
Carbon 15 www.professional-ordnance.com
Caspian Arms, Ltd. www.caspianarmsltd.8m.com
Casull Arms Corp. www.casullarms.com
CDNN Investments, Inc. www.cdnninvestments.com
Century Arms www.centuryarms.com
Chadick's Ltd. www.chadicks-ltd.com
Champlin Firearms www.champlinarms.com
Chapuis Arms www.doubleguns.com/chapuis.htm
Charles Daly www.charlesdaly.com
Charter Arms www.charterfirearms.com
Christensen Arms www.christensenarms.com
Cimarron Firearms Co. www.cimarron-firearms.com
Clark Custom Guns www.clarkcustomguns.com
Cobra Enterprises www.cobrapistols.com
Cogswell & Harrison www.cogswell.co.uk/home.htm
Colt's Mfg Co. www.colt.com
Compasseco, Inc. www.compasseco.com
Connecticut Valley Arms www.cva.com
Cooper Firearms www.cooperfirearms.com
Corner Shot www.cornershot.com
Crosman www.crosman.com
Crossfire, L.L.C. www.crossfirelle.com
C.Sharp Arms Co. www.csharparms.com
CZ USA www.cz-usa.com
Daisy Mfg Co. www.daisy.com
Dakota Arms Inc. www.dakotaarms.com

WEB DIRECTORY

Dan Wesson Firearms www.danwessonfirearms.com
Davis Industries www.davisindguns.com
Detonics USA www.detonicsusa.com
Dixie Gun Works www.dixiegunworks.com
Dlask Arms Corp. www.dlask.com
D.P.M.S., Inc. www.dpmsinc.com
D.S.A, Inc. www.dsarms.com
Dumoulin www.dumoulin-herstal.com
Dynamit Noble www.dnrws.com
Eagle Imports,Inc. www.bersa-llama.com
EDM Arms www.edmarms.com
E.M.F. Co. www.emf-company.com
Enterprise Arms www.enterprise.com
European American Armory Corp. www.eaacorp.com
Evans, William www.williamevans.com
Excel Arms www.excelarms.com
Fabarm www.fabarm.com
FAC-Guns-N-Stuff www.gunsnstuff.com
Falcon Pneumatic Systems www.falcon-airguns.com
Fausti Stefano www.faustistefanoarms.com
Firestorm www.firestorm-sgs.com
Flodman Guns www.flodman.com
FN Herstal www.fnherstal.com
FNH USA www.fnhusa.com
Franchi www.franchiusa.com
Freedom Arms www.freedomarms.com
Galazan www.connecticutshotgun.com
Gambo Renato www.renatogamba.it
Gamo www.gamo.com
Gary Reeder Custom Guns www.reeder-customguns.com
Gazelle Arms www.gazellearms.com
Gibbs Rifle Company www.gibbsrifle.com
Glock www.glock.com
Griffin & Howe www.griffinhowe.com
Grizzly Big Boar Rifle www.largrizzly.com
GSI Inc. www.gsifirearms.com
Guerini www.gueriniusa.com
Hammerli www.hammerli.com
Hatfield Gun Co. www.hatfield-usa.com
Hatsan Arms Co. www.hatsan.com.tr
Heckler and Koch www.hk-usa.com
Henry Repeating Arms Co. www.henryrepeating.com
Heritage Mfg. www.heritagemfg.com
Heym www.heym-waffenfabrik.de
High Standard Mfg. www.highstandard.com
Hi-Point Firearms www.hi-pointfirearms.com
Holland & Holland www.hollandandholland.com
H&R Firearms www.marlinfirearms.com
H-S Precision www.hsprecision.com
Hunters Lodge Corp. www.hunterslodge.com
IAR Inc. www.iar-arms.com
Imperial Miniature Armory www.1800miniature.com
Interarms www.interarms.com
International Military Antiques, Inc. www.ima-usa.com
Inter Ordnance www.interordnance.com
Intrac Arms International LLC www.hsarms.com
Israel Arms www.israelarms.com
Izhevsky Mekhanichesky Zavod www.baikalinc.ru
Jarrett Rifles,Inc. www.jarrettrifles.com
J&G Sales, Ltd. www.jgsales.com
Johannsen Express Rifle www.johannsen-jagd.de
JP Enterprises, Inc. www.jprifles.com
Kahr Arms/Auto-Ordnance www.kahr.com
K.B.I. www.kbi-inc.com
Kel-Tec CNC Ind., Inc. www.kel-tec.com
Kifaru www.kifaru.net
Kimber www.kimberamerica.com
Knight's Mfg. Co. www.knightsarmco.com
Knight Rifles www.knightrifles.com
Korth www.korthwaffen.de
Krieghoff GmbH www.krieghoff.de
KY Imports, Inc. www.kyimports.com
Krieghoff Int'l www.krieghoff.com
L.A.R Mfg www.largrizzly.com
Lazzeroni Arms Co. www.lazzeroni.com
Legacy Sports International www.legacysports.com
Les Baer Custom, Inc. www.lesbaer.com
Lewis Machine & Tool Co. www.lewismachine.net
Linebaugh Custom Sixguns www.sixgunner.com/linebaugh
Ljutic www.ljuticgun.com
Llama www.bersa-llama.com
Lone Star Rifle Co. www.lonestarrifle.com
Magnum Research www.magnumresearch.com
Markesbery Muzzleloaders www.markesbery.com
Marksman Products www.marksman.com
Marlin www.marlinfirearms.com
Mauser www.mauserwaffen.de
McMillan Bros Rifle Co. www.mcfamily.com
Meacham Rifles www.meachamrifles.com
Merkel www.hk-usa.com
Miller Arms www.millerarms.com

Miltech www.miltecharms.com
Miltex, Inc. www.miltexusa.com
Mitchell's Mausers www.mitchellsales.com
MK Ballistic Systems www.mkballistics.com
M-Mag www.mmag.com
Montana Rifle Co. www.montanarifleman.com
Navy Arms www.navyarms.com
Nesika www.nesika.com
New England Arms Corp. www.newenglandarms.com
New England Custom Gun Svc, Ltd. www.newenglandcustomgun.com
New England Firearms www.hr1871.com
New Ultra Light Arms www.newultralight.com
North American Arms www.northamericanarms.com
Nosler Bullets,Inc. www.nosler.com
Nowlin Mfg. Inc. www.nowlinguns.com
O.F. Mossberg & Sons www.mossberg.com
Ohio Ordnance Works www.ohioordnanceworks.com
Olympic Arms www.olyarms.com
Panther Arms www.dpmsinc.com
Para-Ordnance www.paraord.com
Pedersoli Davide & Co. www.davide-pedersoli.com
Perazzi www.perazzi.com
Pietta www.pietta.it
PKP Knife-Pistol www.sanjuanenterprise.com
Power Custom www.powercustom.com
Purdey & Sons www.purdey.com
Remington www.remington.com
Republic Arms Inc. www.republicarmsinc.com
Rhineland Arms, Inc. www.rhinelandarms.com
Rigby www.johnrigbyandco.com
Rizzini USA www.rizziniusa.com
Robar Companies, Inc. www.robarguns.com
Robinson Armament Co. www.robarm.com
Rock River Arms, Inc. www.rockriverarms.com
Rogue Rifle Co. Inc. www.chipmunkrifle.com
Rohrbaugh Firearms www.rohrbaughfirearms.com
Rossi Arms www.rossiusa.com
RPM www.rpmxlpistols.com
RWS/RUAG Ammotec USA www.ruagammotecusa.com
Sabatti SPA www.sabatti.com
Saco Defense www.sacoinc.com
Safari Arms www.olyarms.com
Sako www.berettausa.com
Samco Global Arms Inc. www.samcoglobal.com
Sarco Inc. www.sarcoinc.com
Savage Arms Inc. www.savagearms.com
Scattergun Technologies Inc. www.wilsoncombat.com
Searcy Enterprises www.searcyent.com
Shiloh Rifle Mfg. www.shilohrifle.com
SIGARMS,Inc. www.sigarms.com
Simpson Ltd. www.simpsonltd.com
SKB Shotguns www.skbshotguns.com
Smith & Wesson www.smith-wesson.com
SOG International, Inc. soginc@go-concepts.com
Sphinx System www.sphinxarms.com
Springfield Armory www.springfield-armory.com
SSK Industries www.sskindustries.com
Stag Arms www.stagarms.com
Steyr Arms, Inc. www.steyrarms.com
Strayer-Voigt Inc. www.sviguns.com
Sturm,Ruger & Company www.ruger-firearms.com
Tactical Solutions www.tacticalsol.com
Tar-Hunt Slug Guns, Inc. www.tar-hunt.com
Taser Int'l www.taser.com
Taurus www.taurususa.com
Taylor's & Co., Inc. www.taylorsfirearms.com
Tennessee Guns www.tennesseeguns.com
The 1877 Sharps Co. www.1877sharps.com
Thompson Center Arms www.tcarms.com
Tikka www.berettausa.com
TNW, Inc. tncorp@aol.com
Traditions www.traditionsfirearms.com
Tristar Sporting Arms www.tristarsportingarms.com
Uberti www.ubertireplicas.com
U.S. Firearms Mfg. Co. www.usfirearms.com
U.S. Repeating Arms Co. www.winchester-guns.com
Ultra Light Arms www.newultralight.com
Valkyrie Arms www.valkyriearms.com
Vektor Arms www.vektorarms.com
Volquartsen Custom Ltd. www.volquarsen.com
Vulcan Armament www.vulcanarmament.com
Walther USA www.waltheramerica.com
Weatherby www.weatherby.com
Webley and Scott Ltd. www.webley.co.uk
Westley Richards www.westleyrichards.com
Widley www.widleyguns.com
Wild West Guns www.wildwestguns.com
William Larkin Moore & Co. www.doublegun.com
Wilson Combat www.wilsoncombat.com
Winchester Firearms www.winchester-guns.com

WEB DIRECTORY

GUN PARTS, BARRELS, AFTER-MARKET ACCESSORIES

300 Below www.300below.com
Accuracy International of North America www.accuracyinternational.org
Accuracy Speaks, Inc. www.accuracyspeaks.com
Advanced Barrel Systems www.carbonbarrels.com
Advantage Arms www.advantagearms.com
AK-USA www.ak-103.com
American Spirit Arms Corp. www.gunkits.com
AMT Gun Parts www.amt-gunparts.com
Badger Barrels, Inc. www.badgerbarrels.com
Bar-Sto Precision Machine www.barsto.com
Battenfeld Technologies www.battenfeldtechnologies.com
Bellm TC's www.bellmtcs.com
Belt Mountain Enterprises www.beltmountain.com
Briley www.briley.com
Brownells www.brownells.com
B-Square www.b-square.com
Buffer Technologies www.buffertech.com
Bullberry Barrel Works www.bullberry.com
Bushmaster Firearms/Quality Parts www.bushmaster.com
Butler Creek Corp www.butler-creek.com
Cape Outfitters Inc. www.capeoutfitters.com
Caspian Arms Ltd. www.caspianarms.com
Cheaper Than Dirt www.cheaperthandirt.com
Chesnut Ridge www.chestnutridge.com/
Chip McCormick Corp www.chipmccormickcorp.com
Choate Machine & Tool Co. www.riflestock.com
Cierner, Jonathan Arthur www.22lrconversions.com
CJ Weapons Accessories www.cjweapons.com
Clerke International Arms (Bo Clerke) www.clerkebarrels.com
Colonial Arms www.colonialarms.com
Comp-N-Choke www.comp-n-choke.com
Cylinder & Slide Shop www.cylinder-slide.com
Digi-Twist www.fmtcorp.com
Dixie Gun Works www.dixiegun.com
Douglas Barrels www.benchrest.com/douglas/
DPMS www.dpmsinc.com
D.S.Arms,Inc. www.dsarms.com
eBay www.ebay.com
Ed Brown Products www.edbrown.com
EFK Marketing/Fire Dragon Pistol Accessories www.flmfire.com
E.R. Shaw www.ershawbarrels.com
Federal Arms www.fedarms.com
Forrest Inc. www.gunmags.com
Fulton Armory www.fulton-armory.com
Galazan www.connecticutshotgun.com
Gemtech www.gem-tech.com
Gentry, David www.gentrycustom.com
GG&G www.gggaz.com
Green Mountain Rifle Barrels www.gmriflebarrel.com
Gun Parts Corp. www.e-gunparts.com
Harris Engineering www.harrisbipods.com
Hart Rifle Barrels www.hartbarrels.com
Hastings Barrels www.hastingsbarrels.com
Heinie Specialty Products www.heinie.com
Holland Shooters Supply www.hollandgun.com
100 Straight Products www.100straight.com
I.M.A. www.ima-usa.com
Jarvis, Inc. www.jarvis-custom.com
J&T Distributing www.jtdistributing.com
John's Guns www.johnsguns.com
John Masen Co. www.johnmasen.com
Jonathan Arthur Ciener, Inc. www.22lrconversions.com
JP Enterprises www.jpar15.com
Keng's Firearms Specialities www.versapod.com
KG Industries www.kgcoatings.com
Kick Eez www.kickeez.com
Kidd Triggers www.coolguyguns.com
King's Gunworks www.kingsgunworks.com
Knoxx Industries www.knoxx.com
Krieger Barrels www.kriegerbarrels.com
K-VAR Corp. www.k-var.com
Les Baer Custom, Inc. www.lesbaer.com
Lilja Barrels www.riflebarrels.com
Lone Star Rifle Co. www.lonestarrifles.com
Lone Wolf Dist. www.lonewolfdist.com
Lothar Walther Precision Tools Inc. www.lothar-walther.de
M&A Parts, Inc. www.m-aparts.com
MAB Barrels www.mab.com.au
Majestic Arms www.majesticarms.com
Marvel Products, Inc. www.marvelprod.com
MEC-GAR SrL www.mec-gar.com
Mesa Tactical www.mesatactical.com
Michaels of Oregon Co. www.michaels-oregon.com
North Mfg. Co. www.rifle-barrels.com
Numrich Gun Parts Corp. www.e-gunparts.com
Pachmayr www.pachmayr.com
Pac-Nor Barrels www.pac-nor.com
Para Ordinance Pro Shop www.ltms.com
Point Tech Inc. pointec@ibm.net
Promag Industries www.promagindustries.com

Power Custom, Inc. www.powercustom.com
Red Star Arms www.redstararms.com
Rocky Mountain Arms www.rockymountainarms.com
Royal Arms Int'l www.royalarms.com
R.W. Hart www.rwhart.com
Sarco Inc. www.sarcoinc.com
Scattergun Technologies Inc. www.wilsoncombat.com
Schuemann Barrels www.schuemann.com
Seminole Gunworks Chamber Mates www.chambermates.com
Shilen www.shilen.com
Sims Vibration Laboratory www.limbsaver.com
Smith & Alexander Inc. www.smithandalexander.com
Speed Shooters Int'l www.shooternet.com/ssi
Sprinco USA Inc. sprinco@primenet.com
STI Int'l www.stiguns.com
S&S Firearms www.ssfirearms.com
SSK Industries www.sskindustries.com
Sunny Hill Enterprises www.sunny-hill.com
Tactical Innovations www.tacticalinc.com
Tapco www.tapco.com
Trapdoors Galore www.trapdoors.com
Triple K Manufacturing Co. Inc. www.triplek.com
U.S.A. Magazines Inc. www.usa-magazines.com
Verney-Carron SA www.verney-carron.com
Volquartsen Custom Ltd. www.volquartsen.com
W.C. Wolff Co. www.gunsprings.com
Waller & Son www.wallerandson.com
Weigand Combat Handguns www.weigandcombat.com
Western Gun Parts www.westerngunparts.com
Wilson Arms www.wilsonarms.com
Wilson Combat www.wilsoncombat.com
Wisner's Inc. www.gunpartsspecialist.com
Z-M Weapons www.zmweapons.com/home.htm

GUNSMITHING SUPPLIES AND INSTRUCTION

American Gunsmithing Institute www.americangunsmith.com
Battenfeld Technologies www.battenfeldtechnologies.com
Bellm TC's www.bellmtcs.com
Brownells, Inc. www.brownells.com
B-Square Co. www.b-square.com
Clymer Mfg. Co. www.clymertool.com
Craftguard Metal Finishing crftgrd@aol.com
Dem-Bart www.dembartco.com
Doug Turnbull Restoration www.turnbullrestoration.com
Du-Lite Corp. www.dulite.com
Dvorak Instruments www.dvorakinstruments.com
Gradiant Lens Corp. www.gradientlens.com
Grizzly Industrial www.grizzly.com
Gunline Tools www.gunline.com
Harbor Freight www.harborfreight.com
JGS Precision Tool Mfg. LLC www.jgstools.com
Mag-Na-Port International www.magnaport.com
Manson Precision Reamers www.mansonreamers.com
Midway www.midwayusa.com
Murray State College www.mscok.edu
Olympus America Inc. www.olympus.com
Pacific Tool & Gauge www.pacifictoolandgauge.com
Trinidad State Junior College www.trinidadstate.edu

HANDGUN GRIPS

Ajax Custom Grips, Inc. www.ajaxgrips.com
Altamont Co. www.altamontco.com
Aluma Grips www.alumagrips.com
Badger Grips www.pistolgrips.com
Barami Corp. www.hipgrip.com
Blu Magnum Grips www.blumagnum.com
Buffalo Brothers www.buffalobrothers.com
Crimson Trace Corp. www.crimsontrace.com
Eagle Grips www.eaglegrips.com
Falcon Industries www.ergogrips.net
Herrett's Stocks www.herrettstocks.com
Hogue Grips www.getgrip.com
Kirk Ratajesak www.kgratajesak.com
Lett Custom Grips www.lettgrips.com
N.C. Ordnance www.gungrip.com
Nill-Grips USA www.nill-grips.com
Pachmayr www.pachmayr.com
Pearce Grips www.pearcegrip.com
Trausch Grips Int.Co. www.trausch.com
Tyler-T Grips www.t-grips.com
Uncle Mike's: www.uncle-mikes.com

HOLSTERS AND LEATHER PRODUCTS

Akah www.akah.de
Aker Leather Products www.akerleather.com
Alessi Distributor R&F Inc. www.alessiholsters.com
Alfonso's of Hollywood www.alfonsogunleather.com
Armor Holdings www.holsters.com
Bagmaster www.bagmaster.com
Bianchi International www.bianchi-intl.com
Blackhills Leather www.blackhillsleather.com

WEB DIRECTORY

BodyHugger Holsters www.nikolais.com
Boyt Harness Co. www.boytharness.com
Brigade Gun Leather www.brigadegunleather.com
Chimere www.chimere.com
Classic Old West Styles www.cows.com
Conceal It www.conceal-it.com
Concealment Shop Inc. www.theconcealmentshop.com
Coronado Leather Co. www.coronadoleather.com
Creedmoor Sports, Inc. www.creedmoorsports.com
Custom Leather Wear www.customleatherwear.com
Defense Security Products www.thunderwear.com
Dennis Yoder www.yodercustomleather.com
DeSantis Holster www.desantisholster.com
Dillon Precision www.dillonprecision.com
Don Hume Leathergoods, Inc. www.donhume.com
Ernie Hill International www.erniehill.com
Fist www.fist-inc.com
Fobus USA www.fobusholster.com
Front Line Ltd. frontlin@internet-zahav.net
Galco www.usgalco.com
Gilmore's Sports Concepts www.gilmoresports.com
Gould & Goodrich www.goulduse.com
Gunmate Products www.gun-mate.com
Hellweg Ltd. www.hellwegltd.com
Hide-A-Gun www.hide-a-gun.com
Holsters.Com www.holsters.com
Horseshoe Leather Products www.horseshoe.co.uk
Hunter Co. www.huntercompany.com
Kirkpatrick Leather Company www.kirkpatrickleather.com
KNJ www.knjmfg.com
Kramer Leather www.kramerleather.com
Law Concealment Systems www.handgunconcealment.com
Levy's Leathers Ltd. www.levysleathers.com
Michaels of Oregon Co. www.michaels-oregon.com
Milt Sparks Leather www.miltsparks.com
Mitch Rosen Extraordinary Gunleather www.mitchrosen.com
Old World Leather www.gun-mate.com
Pacific Canvas & Leather Co. paccanadleather@directway.com
Pager Pal www.pagerpal.com
Phalanx Corp. www.smartholster.com
PWL www.pwlusa.com
Rumanya Inc. www.rumanya.com
S.A. Gunleather www.elpasoleather.com
Safariland Ltd. Inc. www.safariland.com
Shooting Systems Group Inc. www.shootingsystems.com
Strictly Anything Inc. www.strictlyanything.com
Strong Holster Co. www.strong-holster.com
The Belt Co. www.conceal-it.com
The Leather Factory Inc. lflandry@flash.net
The Outdoor Connection www.outdoorconnection.com
Top-Line USA inc. www.toplineusa.com
Triple K Manufacturing Co. www.triplek.com
Wilson Combat www.wilsoncombat.com

MISCELLANEOUS SHOOTING PRODUCTS

10X Products Group www.10Xwear.com
Aero Peltor www.aearo.com
American Body Armor www.americanbodyarmor.com
Armor Holdings Products www.armorholdings.com
Battenfeld Technologies www.battenfeldtechnologies.com
Beamhit www.beamhit.com
Beartooth www.beartoothproducts.com
Bodyguard by S&W www.yourbodyguard.com
Burnham Brothers www.burnhambrothers.com
Collectors Armory www.collectorsarmory.com
Dalloz Safety www.cdalloz.com
Deben Group Industries Inc. www.deben.com
Decot Hy-Wyd Sport Glasses www.sportyglasses.com
E.A.R., Inc. www.earinc.com
First Choice Armor www.firstchoicearmor.com
Gunstands www.gunstands.com
Howard Leight Hearing Protectors www.howardleight.com
Hunters Specialities www.hunterspec.com
Johnny Stewart Wildlife Calls www.hunterspec.com
Merit Corporation www.meritcorporation.com
Michaels of Oregon www.michaels-oregon.com
MPI Outdoors www.mpioutdoors.com
MTM Case-Gard www.mtmcase-gard.com
North Safety Products www.northsafety-brea.com
Plano Molding www.planomolding.com
Pro-Ears www.pro-ears.com
Second Chance Body Armor Inc. www.secondchance.com
Silencio www.silencio.com
Smart Lock Technologies www.smartlock.com
Surefire www.surefire.com
Taser Int'l www.taser.com
Walker's Game Ear Inc. www.walkersgameear.com

MUZZLELOADING FIREARMS AND PRODUCTS

American Pioneer Powder www.americanpioneerpowder.com
Armi Sport www.armisport.com

Austin & Halleck, Inc. www.austinhalleck.com
Barnes Bullets www.barnesbullets.com
Black Powder Products www.bpiguns.com
Buckeye Barrels wwwbuckeyebarrels.com
CVA www.cva.com
Davide Perdsoli & co. www.davide-pedersoli.com
Dixie Gun Works, Inc. www.dixiegun.com
Elephant/Swiss Black Powder www.elephantblackpowder.com
Goex Black Powder www.goexpowder.com
Green Mountain Rifle Barrel Co. www.gmriflebarrel.com
Harvester Bullets www.harvesterbullets.com
Hornady www.hornady.com
Jedediah Starr Trading Co. www.jedediah-starr.com
Jim Chambers Flintlocks www.flintlocks.com
Kahnke Gunworks www.powderandbow.com/kahnke/
Knight Rifles www.knightrifles.com
L&R Lock Co. www.lr-rpl.com
Log Cabin Shop www.logcabinshop.com
Lyman www.lymanproducts.com
Magkor Industries www.magkor.com
Millennium Designed Muzzleloaders www.mdm-muzzleloaders.com
MSM, Inc. www.msmfg.com
Muzzleload Magnum Products www.mmpsabots.com
Muzzleloading Technologies, Inc. www.mtimuzzleloading.com
Navy Arms www.navyarms.com
Northwest Trade Guns www.northstarwest.com
Nosler, Inc. www.nosler.com
October Country Muzzleloading www.oct-country.com
Ox-Yoke Originals Inc. www.oxyoke.com
Pacific Rifle Co. pacificrifle@aol.com
Palmetto Arms www.palmetto.it
Pietta www.pietta.it
Precision Rifle Dead Center Bullets www.prbullet.com
R.E. Davis Co. www.redaviscompany.com
Remington www.remington.com
Rightnour Mfg. Co. Inc. www.rmcsports.com
The Rifle Shop trshoppe@aol.com
Savage Arms, Inc. www.savagearms.com
Schuetzen Powder www.schuetzenpowder.com
TDC www.tdcmfg.com
Thompson Center Arms www.tcarms.com
Traditions Performance Muzzleloading www.traditionsfirearms.com

PUBLICATIONS, VIDEOS, AND CD'S

A&J Arms Booksellers www.ajarmsbooksellers.com
Airgun Letter www.airgunletter.com
American Cop www.americancopmagazine.com
American Firearms Industry www.amfire.com
American Handgunner www.americanhandgunner.com
American Hunter www.nrapublications.org
American Rifleman www.nrapublications.org
American Shooting Magazine www.americanshooting.com
Blacksmith sales@blacksmithcorp.com
Blackpowder Hunting www.blackpowderhunting.org
Black Powder Cartridge News www.blackpowderspg.com
Black Powder Journal www.blackpowderjournal.com
Blue Book Publications www.bluebookinc.com
Combat Handguns www.combathandguns.com
Concealed Carry www.uscca.us
Countrywide Press www.countrysport.com
DBI Books/Krause Publications www.krause.com
Delta Force www.infogo.com/delta
Gun List www.gunlist.com
Gun Video www.gunvideo.com
GUNS Magazine www.gunsmagazine.com
Guns & Ammo www.gunsandammomag.com
Gunweb Magazine WWW Links www.imags.com
Gun Week www.gunweek.com
Gun World www.gunworld.com
Harris Publications www.harrispublications.com
Heritage Gun Books www.gunbooks.com
Krause Publications www.krause.com
Law and Order www.hendonpub.com
Moose Lake Publishing MooselakeP@aol.com
Munden Enterprises Inc. www.bob-munden.com
Outdoor Videos www.outdoorvideos.com
Precision Shooting www.precisionshooting.com
Predator Extreme www.predatorextreme.com
Predator & Prey www.predatorandpreymag.com
Ray Riling Arms Books www.rayrilingarmsbooks.com
Rifle and Handloader Magazines www.riflemagazine.com
Safari Press Inc. www.safaripress.com
Shoot! Magazine www.shootmagazine.com
Shooters News www.shootersnews.com
Shooting Illustrated www.nrapublications.org
Shooting Industry www.shootingindustry.com
Shooting Sports Retailer www.shootingsportsretailer.com
Shooting Sports USA www.nrapublications.org
Shotgun News www.shotgunnews.com
Shotgun Report www.shotgunreport.com
Shotgun Sports Magazine www.shotgun-sports.com

WEB DIRECTORY

Small Arms Review www.smallarmsreview.com
Small Caliber News www.smallcaliber.com
Sporting Clays Web Edition www.sportingclays.net
Sports Afield www.sportsafield.comm
Sports Trend www.sportstrend.com
Sportsmen on Film www.sportsmenonfilm.com
The Gun Journal www.shooters.com
The Shootin Iron www.off-road.com/4x4web/si/si.html
The Single Shot Exchange Magazine singleshot@earthlink.net
The Sixgunner www.sskindustries.com
Voyageur Press www.voyageurpress.com
VSP Publications www.gunbooks.com
Vulcan Outdoors Inc. www.vulcanpub.com

RELOADING TOOLS AND SUPPLIES

Ballisti-Cast Mfg. www.ballisti-cast.com
Battenfeld Technologies www.battenfeldtechnologies.com
Bruno Shooters Supply www.brunoshooters.com
CH/4D Custom Die www.ch4d.com
Colorado Shooters Supply www.hochmoulds.com
Corbin Mfg & Supply Co. www.corbins.com
Dillon Precision www.dillonprecision.com
Forster Precision Products www.forsterproducts.com
Hanned Line www.hanned.com
Harrell's Precision www.harrellsprec.com
Holland's Shooting Supplies www.hollandgun.com
Hornady www.hornady.com
Huntington Reloading Products www.huntingtons.com
J & J Products Co. www.jandjproducts.com
Lead Bullet Technology LBTisaccuracy@lmbris.net
Lee Precision, Inc. www.leeprecision.com
Littleton Shotmaker www.leadshotmaker.com
Load Data www.loaddata.com
Lyman www.lymanproducts.com
Magma Engineering www.magmaengr.com
Mayville Engineering Co. (MEC) www.mecreloaders.com
Midway www.midwayusa.com
Moly-Bore www.molybore.com
MTM Case-Guard www.mtmcase-guard.com
NECO www.neconos.com
NEI www.neihandtools.com
Neil Jones Custom Products www.neiljones.com
Ponsness/Warren www.reloaders.com
Ranger Products www.pages.prodigy.com/rangerproducts.home.htm
Rapine Bullet Mold Mfg Co. www.bulletmoulds.com
RCBS www.rcbs.com
Redding Reloading Equipment www.redding-reloading.com
Russ Haydon's Shooting Supplies www.shooters-supply.com
Sinclair Int'l Inc. www.sinclairintl.com
Stoney Point Products Inc www.stoneypoint.com
Thompson Bullet Lube Co. www.thompsonbulletlube.com
Vickerman Seating Die www.castingstuff.com
Wilson (L.E. Wilson) www.lewilson.com

RESTS — BENCH, PORTABLE, ATTACHABLE

Battenfeld Technolgies www.battenfeldtechnologies.com
Bench Master www.bench-master.com
B-Square www.b-square.com
Bullshooter www.bullshooterssightingin.com
Desert Mountain Mfg. www.bench-master.com
Harris Engineering Inc. www.harrisbipods.com
Kramer Designs www.snipepod.com
L Thomas Rifle Support www.ltsupport.com
Level-Lok www.levellok.com
Midway www.midwayusa.com
Predator Sniper Styx www.predatorsniperstyx.com
Ransom International www.ransom-intl.com
R.W. Hart www.rwhart.com
Sinclair Intl, Inc. www.sinclairintl.com
Stoney Point Products www.uncle-mikes.com
Target Shooting www.targetshooting.com
Varmint Masters www.varmintmasters.com
Versa-Pod www.versa-pod.com

SCOPES, SIGHTS, MOUNTS AND ACCESSORIES

Accusight www.accusight.com
ADCO www.shooters.com/adco/index/htm
Adirondack Opitcs www.adkoptics.com
Aimpoint www.aimpoint.com
Aim Shot, Inc. www.miniosprey.com
Aimtech Mount Systems www.aimtech-mounts.com
Alpec Team, Inc. www.alpec.com
Alpen Outdoor Corp. www.alpenoutdoor.com
American Technologies Network, Corp. www.atncorp.com
AmeriGlo, LLC www.ameriglo.net
AO Sight Systems Inc. www.aosights.com
Ashley Outdoors, Inc. www.ashleyoutdoors.com
ATN www.atncorp.com
Badger Ordnance www.badgerordnance.com
Beamshot-Quarton www.beamshot.com

BSA Optics www.bsaoptics.com
B-Square Company, Inc. www.b-square.com
Burris www.burrisoptics.com
Bushnell Performance Optics www.bushnell.com
Carl Zeiss Optical Inc. www.zeiss.com
Carson Optical www.carson-optical.com
C-More Systems www.cmore.com
Conetrol Scope Mounts www.conetrol.com
Crimson Trace Corp. www.crimsontrace.com
Crossfire L.L.C. www.amfire.com/hesco/html
DCG Supply Inc. www.dcgsupply.com
D&L Sports www.dlsports.com
EasyHit, Inc. www.easyhit.com
EAW www.eaw.de
Elcan Optical Technologies www.armament.com, www.elcan.com
Electro-Optics Technologies www.eotechmdc.com/holosight
Europtik Ltd. www.europtik.com
Fujinon, Inc. www.fujinon.com
Gilmore Sports www.gilmoresports.com
Hakko Co. Ltd. www.hakko-japan.co.jp
Hesco www.hescosights.com
Hitek Industries www.nightsight.com
HIVIZ www.hivizsights.com
Horus Vision www.horusvision.com
Hunter Co. www.huntercompany.com
Innovative Weaponry, Inc. www.ptnightsights.com
Ironsighter Co. www.ironsighter.com
ITT Night Vision www.ittnightvision.com
Kahles www.kahlesoptik.com
Kowa Optimed Inc. www.kowascope.com
Kwik-Site Co. www.kwiksitecorp.com
Laser Bore Sight www.laserboresight.com
Laser Devices Inc. www.laserdevices.com
Lasergrips www.crimsontrace.com
LaserLyte www.laserlytesights.com
LaserMax Inc. www.lasermax.com
Laser Products www.surefire.com
Leapers, Inc. www.leapers.com
Leatherwood www.leatherwoodoptics.com
Leica Camera Inc. www.leica-camera.com/usa
Leupold www.leupold.com
LightForce/NightForce USA www.nightforcescopes.com
Lyman www.lymanproducts.com
Lynx www.b-square.com
Marble's Outdoors www.marblesoutdoors.com
MDS,Inc. www.mdsincorporated.com
Meopta www.meopta.com
Meprolight www.kimberamerica.com
Micro Sight Co. www.microsight.com
Millett www.millettsights.com
Miniature Machine Corp. www.mmcsight.com
Montana Vintage Arms www.montanavintagearms.com
Mounting Solutions Plus www.mountsplus.com
NAIT www.nait.com
Newcon International Ltd. newconsales@newcon-optik.com
Night Force Optics www.nightforcescopes.com
Night Owl Optics www.nightowloptics.com
Nikon Inc. www.nikonusa.com
North American Integrated Technologies www.nait.com
O.K. Weber, Inc. www.okweber.com
Optolyth-Optic www.optolyth.de
Pentax Corp. www.pentaxlightseeker.com
Premier Reticle www.premierreticles.com
Redfield www.redfieldoptics.com
R&R Int'l Trade www.nightoptic.com
Schmidt & Bender www.schmidt-bender.com
Scopecoat www.scopecoat.com
Scopelevel www.scopelevel.com
Segway Industries www.segway-industries.com
Shepherd Scope Ltd. www.shepherdscopes.com
Sightron www.sightron.com
Simmons www.simmonsoptics.com
S&K www.scopemounts.com
Springfield Armory www.springfield-armory.com
Sure-Fire www.surefire.com
Swarovski/Kahles www.swarovskioptik.com
Swift Optics www.swiftoptics.com
Talley Mfg. Co. www.talleyrings.com
Tasco www.tascosales.com
Trijicon Inc. www.trijicon.com
Truglo Inc. www.truglo.com
UltraDot www.ultradotusa.com
Unertl Optical Co. www.unertloptics.com
US Night Vision www.usnightvision.com
U.S. Optics Technologies Inc. www.usoptics.com
Valdada-IOR Optics www.valdada.com
Warne www.warnescopemounts.com
Weaver Scopes www.weaveroptics.com
Wilcox Industries Corp www.wilcoxind.com
Williams Gun Sight Co. www.williamsgunsight.com
Zeiss www.zeiss.com

WEB DIRECTORY

SHOOTING ORGANIZATIONS, SCHOOLS AND RANGES

Amateur Trapshooting Assoc. www.shootata.com
American Custom Gunmakers Guild www.acgg.org
American Gunsmithing Institute www.americangunsmith.com
American Pistolsmiths Guild www.americanpistol.com
American Shooting Sports Council www.assc.com
American Single Shot Rifle Assoc. www.assra.com
Antique Shooting Tool Collector's Assoc. www.oldshootingtools.org
Assoc. of Firearm & Tool Mark Examiners www.afte.org
BATF www.atf.ustreas.gov
Blackwater Lodge and Training Center www.blackwaterlodge.com
Boone and Crockett Club www.boone-crockett.org
Buckmasters, Ltd. www.buckmasters.com
Cast Bullet Assoc. www.castbulletassoc.org
Citizens Committee for the Right to Keep & Bear Arms www.ccrkba.org
Civilian Marksmanship Program www.odcmp.com
Colorado School of Trades www.gunsmith-school.com
Ducks Unlimited www.ducks.org
Fifty Caliber Institute www.fiftycal.org
Fifty Caliber Shooters Assoc. www.fcsa.org
Firearms Coalition www.nealknox.com
Front Sight Firearms Training Institute www.frontsight.com
German Gun Collectors Assoc. www.germanguns.com
Gun Clubs www.associatedgunclubs.com
Gun Owners' Action League www.goal.org
Gun Owners of America www.gunowners.org
Gun Trade Asssoc. Ltd. www.brucepub.com/gta
Gunsite Training Center, Inc. www.gunsite.com
Handgun Hunters International www.sskindustries.com
Hunting and Shooting Sports Heritage Fund www.hsshf.org
International Defense Pistol Assoc. www.idpa.com
International Handgun Metallic Silhouette Assoc. www.ihmsa.org
International Hunter Education Assoc. www.ihea.com
International Single Shot Assoc. www.issa-schuetzen.org
Jews for the Preservation of Firearms Ownership www.jpfo.org
Mule Deer Foundation www.muledeer.org
Muzzle Loaders Assoc. of Great Britain www.mlagb.com
National 4-H Shooting Sports www.4-hshootingsports.org
National Benchrest Shooters Assoc. www.benchrest.com
National Muzzle Loading Rifle Assoc. www.nmlra.org
National Reloading Manufacturers Assoc www.reload-nrma.com
National Rifle Assoc. www.nra.org
National Rifle Assoc. ILA www.nraila.org
National Shooting Sports Foundation www.nssf.org
National Skeet Shooters Association www.nssa-nsca.com
National Sporting Clays Assoc. www.nssa-nsca.com
National Wild Turkey Federation www.nwtf.com
NICS/FBI www.fbi.gov
North American Hunting Club www.huntingclub.com
Order of Edwardian Gunners (Vintagers) www.vintagers.org
Pennsylvania Gunsmith School www.pagunsmith.com
Quail Unlimited www.qu.org
Right To Keep and Bear Arms www.rkba.org
Rocky Mountain Elk Foundation www.rmef.org
SAAMI www.saami.org
Safari Club International www.scifirstforhunters.org
Second Amendment Foundation www.saf.org
Second Amendment Sisters www.2asisters.org
Shooting Ranges Int'l www.shootingranges.com
Single Action Shooting Society www.sassnet.com
Students for Second Amendment www.sf2a.org
S&W Academy and Nat'l Firearms Trng. Center www.sw-academy.com
Tactical Defense Institute www.tdiohio.com
Ted Nugent United Sportsmen of America www.tnugent.com
Thunder Ranch www.thunderranchinc.com
Trapshooters Homepage www.trapshooters.com
Trinidad State Junior College www.trinidadstate.edu
U.S. Concealed Carry Association www.uscca.us
U.S. Int'l Clay Target Assoc. www.usicta.com
United States Fish and Wildlife Service www.fws.gov
U.S. Practical Shooting Assoc. www.uspsa.org
USA Shooting www.usashooting.com
Varmint Hunters Assoc. www.varminthunter.org
U.S. Sportsmen's Alliance www.ussportsmen.org
Women Hunters www.womanhunters.com
Women's Shooting Sports Foundation www.wssf.org

STOCKS

Advanced Technology www.atigunstocks.com
Battenfeld Technologies www.battenfeldtechnologies.com
Bell & Carlson, Inc. www.bellandcarlson.com
Boyd's Gunstock Industries, Inc. www.boydgunstocks.com
Butler Creek Corp www.butler-creek.com
Calico Hardwoods, Inc. www.calicohardwoods.com
Choate Machine www.riflestock.com
Elk Ridge Stocks www.reamerrentals.com/elk_ridge.htm
Fajen www.battenfeldtechnologies.com
Great American Gunstocks www.gunstocks.com
Herrett's Stocks www.herrettstocks.com
High Tech Specialties www.bansnersrifle.com/hightech
Holland's Shooting Supplies www.hollandgun.com

Knoxx Industries www.knoxx.com
Lone Wolf www.lonewolfriflestocks.com
McMillan Fiberglass Stocks www.mcmfamily.com
MPI Stocks www.mpistocks.com
Precision Gun Works www.precisiongunstocks.com
Ram-Line www.outers-guncare.com
Rimrock Rifle Stock www.rimrockstocks.com
Royal Arms Gunstocks www.imt.net/~royalarms
S&K Industries www.sandkgunstocks.com
Speedfeed, Inc. www.speedfeedinc.com
Tiger-Hunt Curly Maple Gunstocks www.gunstockwood.com
Wenig Custom Gunstocks Inc. www.wenig.com

TARGETS AND RANGE EQUIPMENT

Action Target Co. www.actiontarget.com
Advanced Interactive Systems www.ais-sim.com
Birchwood Casey www.birchwoodcasey.com
Caswell Meggitt Defense Systems www.mds-caswell.com
Champion Traps & Targets www.championtarget.com
Just Shoot Me Products www.ballistictec.com
Laser Shot www.lasershot.com
MTM Products www.mtmcase-gard.com
Natiional Target Co. www.nationaltarget.com
Newbold Target Systems www.newboldtargets.com
Porta Target, Inc. www.portatarget.com
Range Management Services Inc. www.casewellintl.com
Range Systems www.shootingrangeproducts.com
Reactive Target Systems Inc. chrts@primenet.com
ShatterBlast Targets www.daisy.com
Super Trap Bullet Containment Systems www.supertrap.com
Thompson Target Technology www.thompsontarget.com
Tombstone Tactical Targets www.tttargets.com
Visible Impact Targets www.crosman.com
White Flyer www.whiteflyer.com

TRAP AND SKEET SHOOTING EQUIPMENT AND ACCESSORIES

Auto-Sporter Industries www.auto-sporter.com
10X Products Group www.10Xwear.com
Claymaster Traps www.claymaster.com
Do-All Traps, Inc. www.do-alltraps.com
Laporte USA www.laporte-shooting.com
Outers www.blount.com
Trius Products Inc. www.triustraps.com
White Flyer www.whiteflyer.com

TRIGGERS

Brownells www.brownells.com
Chip McCormick Corp. www.chipmccormickcorp.com
Huber Concepts www.huberconcepts.com
Kidd Triggers. www.coolguyguns.com
Shilen www.shilen.com
Timney Triggers www.timneytrigger.com

MAJOR SHOOTING WEB SITES AND LINKS

24 Hour Campfire www.24hourcampfire.com
Alphabetic Index of Links www.gunsgunsguns.com
Auction Arms www.auctionarms.com
Benchrest Central www.benchrest.com
Big Game Hunt www.biggamehunt.net
Bullseye Pistol www.bullseyepistol.com
Firearms History www.researchpress.co.uk/firearms
Firearm News www.firearmnews.com
Gun Broker Auctions www.gunbroker.com
Gun Index www.gunindex.com
Gun Industry www.gunindustry.com
Gun Blast www.gunblast.com
Gun Boards www.gunboards.com
Gun Broker www.gunbroker.com
Gun Law www.gunlaw.com
Gun Manuals www.gunmanuals.ch/manuals.htm
Gun Nuts Firearm Schematics www.gunuts.com
Guns For Sale www.gunsamerica.com
Guns Unified Nationally Endorsing Dignity www.guned.com
Gun Shop Finder www.gunshopfinder.com
Hunting Information (NSSF) www.huntinfo.org
Hunting Net www.hunting.net
Hunting Network www.huntingnetwork.com
Keep and Bear Arms www.keepandbeararms.com
Leverguns www.leverguns.com
Outdoor Press Room www.outdoorpressroom.com
Outdoor Yellow Pages www.outdoorsyp.com
Real Guns www.realguns.com
Rec.Guns www.recguns.com
Shooter's Online Services www.shooters.com
Shotgun Sports Resource Guide www.shotgunsports.com
Sixgunner www.sixgunner.com
Sportsman's Web www.sportsmansweb.com
Surplus Rifles www.surplusrifle.com
Wing Shooting USA www.wingshootingusa.org

PERIODICAL PUBLICATIONS

AAFTA News (M)
5911 Cherokee Ave., Tampa, FL 33604. Official newsletter of the American Airgun Field Target Assn.

The Accurate Rifle
Precisions Shooting, Inc., 222 Mckee Street, Manchester CT 06040. $37 yr. Dedicated to the rifle accuracy enthusiast.

Action Pursuit Games Magazine (M)
CFW Enterprises, Inc., 4201 W. Vanowen Pl., Burbank, CA 91505 818-845-2656. $4.99 single copy U.S., $5.50 Canada. Editor: Dan Reeves. World's leading magazine of paintball sports.

Air Gunner Magazine
4 The Courtyard, Denmark St., Wokingham, Berkshire RG11 2AZ, England/011-44-734-771677. $U.S. $44 for 1 yr. Leading monthly airgun magazine in U.K.

Airgun Ads
Box 33, Hamilton, MT 59840/406-363-3805; Fax: 406-363-4117. $35 1 yr. (for first mailing; $20 for second mailing; $35 for Canada and foreign orders.) Monthly tabloid with extensive For Sale and Wanted airgun listings.

The Airgun Letter
Gapp, Inc., 4614 Woodland Rd., Ellicott City, MD 21042-6329/410-730-5496; Fax: 410-730-9544; e-mail: staff@airgnltr.net; http://www.airgunletter.com. $21 U.S., $24 Canada, $27 Mexico and $33 other foreign orders, 1 yr. Monthly newsletter for airgun users and collectors.

Airgun World
4 The Courtyard, Denmark St., Wokingham, Berkshire RG40 2AZ, England/011-44-734-771677. Call for subscription rates. Oldest monthly airgun magazine in the U.K., now a sister publication to *Air Gunner.*

Alaska Magazine
Morris Communications, 735 Broad Street, Augusta, GA 30901/706-722-6060. Hunting, Fishing and Life on the Last Frontier articles of Alaska and western Canada.

American Firearms Industry
Nat'l. Assn. of Federally Licensed Firearms Dealers, 2455 E. Sunrise Blvd., Suite 916, Ft. Lauderdale, FL 33304. $35.00 yr. For firearms retailers, distributors and manufacturers.

American Guardian
NRA, 11250 Waples Mill Rd., Fairfax, VA 22030. Publications division. $15.00 1 yr. Magazine features personal protection; home-self-defense; family recreation shooting; women's issues; etc.

American Gunsmith
Belvoir Publications, Inc., 75 Holly Hill Lane, Greenwich, CT 06836-2626/203-661-6111. $49.00 (12 issues). Technical journal of firearms repair and maintenance.

American Handgunner*
Publisher's Development Corp., 591 Camino de la Reina, Suite 200, San Diego, CA 92108/800-537-3006 $16.95 yr. Articles for handgun enthusiasts, competitors, police and hunters.

American Hunter (M)
National Rifle Assn., 11250 Waples Mill Rd., Fairfax, VA 22030 (Same address for both.) Publications Div. $35.00 yr. Wide scope of hunting articles.

American Rifleman (M)
National Rifle Assn., 11250 Waples Mill Rd., Fairfax, VA 22030 (Same address for both). Publications Div. $35.00 yr. Firearms articles of all kinds.

American Survival Guide
McMullen Angus Publishing, Inc., 774 S. Placentia Ave., Placentia, CA 92670-6846. 12 issues $19.95/714-572-2255; FAX: 714-572-1864.

Armes & Tir*
c/o FABECO, 38, rue de Trévise 75009 Paris, France. Articles for hunters, collectors, and shooters. French text.

Arms Collecting (Q)
Museum Restoration Service, P.O. Box 70, Alexandria Bay, NY 13607-0070. $22.00 yr.; $62.00 3 yrs.; $112.00 5 yrs.
Australian Shooter (formerly Australian Shooters Journal)
Sporting Shooters' Assn. of Australia, Inc., P.O. Box 2066, Kent Town SA 5071, Australia. $60.00 yr. locally; $65.00 yr. overseas surface mail. Hunting and shooting articles.

The Backwoodsman Magazine
P.O. Box 627, Westcliffe, CO 81252. $16.00 for 6 issues per yr.; $30.00 for 2 yrs.; sample copy $2.75. Subjects include muzzle-loading, woodslore, primitive survival, trapping, homesteading, blackpowder cartridge guns, 19th century how-to.

Black Powder Cartridge News (Q)
SPG, Inc., P.O. Box 761, Livingston, MT 59047/Phone/Fax: 406-222-8416. $17 yr. (4 issues) ($6 extra 1st class mailing). For the blackpowder cartridge enthusiast.

Blackpowder Hunting (M)
Intl. Blackpowder Hunting Assn., P.O. Box 1180Z, Glenrock, WY 82637/307-436-9817. $20.00 1 yr., $36.00 2 yrs. How-to and where-to features by experts on hunting; shooting; ballistics; traditional and modern blackpowder rifles, shotguns, pistols and cartridges.

Black Powder Times
P.O. Box 234, Lake Stevens, WA 98258. $20.00 yr.; add $5 per year for Canada, $10 per year other foreign. Tabloid newspaper for blackpowder activities; test reports.

Blade Magazine
Krause Publications, 700 East State St., Iola, WI 54990-0001. $25.98 for 12 issues. Foreign price (including Canada-Mexico) $50.00. A magazine for all enthusiasts of handmade, factory and antique knives.

Caliber
GFI-Verlag, Theodor-Heuss Ring 62, 50668 Koln, Germany. For hunters, target shooters and reloaders.

The Caller (Q) (M)
National Wild Turkey Federation, P.O. Box 530, Edgefield, SC 29824. Tabloid newspaper for members; 4 issues per yr. (membership fee $25.00)

Cartridge Journal (M)
Robert Mellichamp, 907 Shirkmere, Houston, TX 77008/713-869-0558. Dues $12 for U.S. and Canadian members (includes the newsletter); 6 issues.

The Cast Bullet*(M)
Official journal of The Cast Bullet Assn. Director of Membership, 203 E. 2nd St., Muscatine, IA 52761. Annual membership dues $14, includes 6 issues.

Cibles
14, rue du Patronage-Laique, BP 2057, 52902 Chaumont, cedex 9, France. French-language arms magazine also carries a small amount of arms-related and historical content. 12 issues per year. Tel/03-25-03-87-47/Email cibeles@graphycom.com; Website: www.graphycom.com

COLTELLI, che Passione (Q)
Casella postale N.519, 20101 Milano, Italy/Fax:02-48402857. $15 1 yr., $27 2 yrs. Covers all types of knives—collecting, combat, historical. Italian text.

Combat Handguns*
Harris Publications, Inc., 1115 Broadway, New York, NY 10010.

Deer & Deer Hunting Magazine
Krause Publications, 700 E. State St., Iola, WI 54990-0001. $19.95 yr. (9 issues). For the serious deer hunter. Website: www.krause.com

The Derringer Peanut (M)
The National Association of Derringer Collectors, P.O. Box 20572, San Jose, CA 95160. A newsletter dedicated to developing the best derringer information. Write for details.

Deutsches Waffen Journal
Journal-Verlag Schwend GmbH, Postfach 100340, D-74503 Schwäbisch Hall, Germany/0791-404-500; FAX:0791-404-505 and 404-424. DM102 p. yr. (interior); DM125.30 (abroad), postage included. Antique and modern arms and equipment. German text.

Double Gun Journal
P.O. Box 550, East Jordan, MI 49727/800-447-1658. $35 for 4 issues.

Ducks Unlimited, Inc. (M)
1 Waterfowl Way, Memphis, TN 38120

The Engraver (M) (Q)
P.O. Box 4365, Estes Park, CO 80517/970-586-2388; Fax: 970-586-0394. Mike Dubber, editor. The journal of firearms engraving.

The Field
King's Reach Tower, Stamford St., London SE1 9LS England. £36.40 U.K. 1 yr.; 49.90 (overseas, surface mail) yr.; £82.00 (overseas, air mail) yr. Hunting and shooting articles, and all country sports.

Field & Stream
Time4 Media, Two Park Ave., New York, NY 10016/212-779-5000. 12 issues/$19.97. Monthly shooting column. Articles on hunting and fishing.

Field Tests
Belvoir Publications, Inc., 75 Holly Hill Lane; P.O. Box 2626, Greenwich, CT 06836-2626/203-661-6111; 800-829-3361 (subscription line). U.S. & Canada $29 1 yr., $58 2 yrs.; all other countries $45 1 yr., $90 2 yrs. (air).

Fur-Fish-Game
A.R. Harding Pub. Co., 2878 E. Main St., Columbus, OH 43209. $15.95 yr. Practical guidance regarding trapping, fishing and hunting.

The Gottlieb-Tartaro Report
Second Amendment Foundation, James Madison Bldg., 12500 NE 10th Pl., Bellevue, WA 98005/206-454-7012;Fax:206-451-3959. $30 for 12 issues. An insiders guide for gun owners.

Gray's Sporting Journal
Gray's Sporting Journal, P.O. Box 1207, Augusta, GA 30903. $36.95 per yr. for 6 issues. Hunting and fishing journals. Expeditions and Guides Book (Annual Travel Guide).

Gun List†
700 E. State St., Iola, WI 54990. $37.98 yr. (26 issues); $66.98 2 yrs. (52 issues). Indexed market publication for firearms collectors and active shooters; guns, supplies and services. Website: www.krause.com

Gun News Digest (Q)
Second Amendment Fdn., P.O. Box 488, Station C, Buffalo, NY 14209/716-885-6408; Fax:716-884-4471. $10 U.S.; $20 foreign.

The Gun Report
World Wide Gun Report, Inc., Box 38, Aledo, IL 61231-0038. $33.00 yr. For the antique and collectable gun dealer and collector.

Gunmaker (M) (Q)
ACGG, P.O. Box 812, Burlington, IA 52601-0812. The journal of custom gunmaking.

The Gunrunner
Div. of Kexco Publ. Co. Ltd., Box 565G, Lethbridge, Alb., Canada T1J 3Z4. $23.00 yr., sample $2.00. Monthly newspaper, listing everything from antiques to artillery.

Gun Show Calendar (Q)
700 E. State St., Iola, WI 54990. $14.95 yr. (4 issues). Gun shows listed; chronologically and by state. Website: www.krause.com

Gun Tests
11 Commerce Blvd., Palm Coast, FL 32142. The consumer resource for the serious shooter. Write for information.

Gun Trade News
Bruce Publishing Ltd., P.O. Box 82, Wantage, Ozon OX12 7A8, England/44-1-235-771770; Fax: 44-1-235-771848. Britain's only "trade only" magazine exclusive to the gun trade.

Gun Week†
Second Amendment Foundation, P.O. Box 488, Station C, Buffalo, NY 14209. $35.00 yr. U.S. and possessions; $45.00 yr. other countries. Tabloid paper on guns, hunting, shooting and collecting (36 issues).

Gun World
Y-Visionary Publishing, LP 265 South Anita Drive, Ste. 120, Orange, CA 92868. $21.97 yr.; $34.97 2 yrs. For the hunting, reloading and shooting enthusiast.

Guns & Ammo
Primedia, 6420 Wilshire Blvd., Los Angeles, CA 90048/213-782-2780. $23.94 yr. Guns, shooting, and technical articles.

Guns
Publishers Development Corporation, P.O. Box 85201, San Diego, CA 92138/800-537-3006. $19.95 yr. In-depth articles on a wide range of guns, shooting equipment and related accessories for gun collectors, hunters and shooters.

Guns Review
Ravenhill Publishing Co. Ltd., Box 35, Standard House, Bonhill St., London EC 2A 4DA, England. £20.00 sterling (approx. U.S. $38 USA & Canada) yr. For collectors and shooters.

H.A.C.S. Newsletter (M)
Harry Moon, Pres., P.O. Box 50117, South Slope RPO, Burnaby BC, V5J 5G3, Canada/604-438-0950; Fax:604-277-3646. $25 p. yr. U.S. and Canada. Official newsletter of The Historical Arms Collectors of B.C. (Canada).

Handgunner*
Richard A.J. Munday, Seychelles house, Brightlingsen, Essex CO7 ONN, England/012063-305201. £18.00 (sterling).

Handguns*
Primedia, 6420 Wilshire Blvd., Los Angeles, CA 90048/323-782-2868. For the handgunning and shooting enthusiast.

Handloader*
Wolfe Publishing Co., 2626 Stearman Road, Ste. A, Prescott, AZ 86301/520-445-7810;Fax:520-778-5124. $22.00 yr. The journal of ammunition reloading.

INSIGHTS*
NRA, 11250 Waples Mill Rd., Fairfax, VA 22030. Editor, John E. Robbins. $15.00 yr., which includes NRA junior membership; $10.00 for adult subscriptions (12 issues). Plenty of details for the young hunter and target shooter; emphasizes gun safety, marksmanship training, hunting skills.

International Arms & Militaria Collector (Q)
Arms & Militaria Press, P.O. Box 80, Labrador, Qld. 4215, Australia. A$39.50 yr. (U.S. & Canada), 2 yrs. A$77.50; A$37.50 (others), 1 yr., 2 yrs. $73.50 all air express mail; surface mail is less. Editor: Ian D. Skennerton.

International Shooting Sport*/UIT Journal
International Shooting Union (UIT), Bavariaring 21, D-80336 Munich, Germany. Europe: (Deutsche Mark) DM44.00 yr., 2 yrs. DM83.00; outside Europe: DM50.00 yr., 2 yrs. DM95.00 (air mail postage included.) For international sport shooting.

Internationales Waffen-Magazin
Habegger-Verlag Zürich, Postfach 9230, CH-8036 Zürich, Switzerland. SF 105.00 (approx. U.S. $73.00) surface mail for 10 issues. Modern and antique arms, self-defense. German text; English summary of contents.

The Journal of the Arms & Armour Society (M)
A. Dove, P.O. Box 10232, London, SW19 2ZD England. £15.00 surface mail; £20.00 airmail sterling only yr. Articles for the historian and collector.

Journal of the Historical Breechloading Smallarms Assn.
Published annually. P.O. Box 12778, London, SE1 6XB, England. $21.00 yr. Articles for the collector plus mailings of short articles on specific arms, reprints, newsletters, etc.

Knife World
Knife World Publications, P.O. Box 3395, Knoxville, TN 37927. $15.00 yr.; $25.00 2 yrs. Published monthly for knife enthusiasts and collectors. Articles on custom and factory knives; other knife-related interests, monthly column on knife identification, military knives.

Man At Arms*
P.O. Box 460, Lincoln, RI 02865. $27.00 yr., $52.00 2 yrs. plus $8.00 for foreign subscribers. The N.R.A. magazine of arms collecting-investing, with excellent articles for the collector of antique arms and militaria.

The Mannlicher Collector (Q)(M)
Mannlicher Collectors Assn., Inc., P.O. Box 7144, Salem Oregon 97303. $20/ yr. subscription included in membership.

MAGNUM
Rua Madre Rita Amada de Jesus, 182 , Granja Julieta, Sao Paulo – SP – 04721-050 Brazil. No details.

*Published bi-monthly
† Published weekly
‡Published three times per month. All others are published monthly.

M=Membership requirements; write for details.
Q=Published Quarterly.

PERIODICAL PUBLICATIONS

MAN/MAGNUM
S.A. Man (Pty) Ltd., P.O. Box 35204, Northway, Durban 4065, Republic of South Africa. SA Rand 200.00 for 12 issues. Africa's only publication on hunting, shooting, firearms, bushcraft, knives, etc.

The Marlin Collector (M)
R.W. Paterson, 407 Lincoln Bldg., 44 Main St., Champaign, IL 61820.

Muzzle Blasts (M)
National Muzzle Loading Rifle Assn., P.O. Box 67, Friendship, IN 47021/812-667-5131. $35.00 yr. annual membership. For the blackpowder shooter.

Muzzleloader Magazine*
Scurlock Publishing Co., Inc., Dept. Gun, Route 5, Box 347-M, Texarkana, TX 75501. $18.00 U.S.; $22.50 U.S./yr. for foreign subscribers. The publication for blackpowder shooters.

National Defense (M)*
American Defense Preparedness Assn., Two Colonial Place, Suite 400, 2101 Wilson Blvd., Arlington, VA 22201-3061/703-522-1820; FAX: 703-522-1885. $35.00 yr. Articles on both military and civil defense field, including weapons, materials technology, management.

National Knife Magazine (M)
Natl. Knife Coll. Assn., 7201 Shallowford Rd., P.O. Box 21070, Chattanooga, TN 37424-0070. Membership $35 yr.; $65.00 International yr.

National Rifle Assn. Journal (British) (Q)
Natl. Rifle Assn. (BR.), Bisley Camp, Brookwood, Woking, Surrey, England. GU24, OPB. £24.00 Sterling including postage.

National Wildlife*
Natl. Wildlife Fed., 1400 16th St. NW, Washington, DC 20036, $16.00 yr. (6 issues); *International Wildlife*, 6 issues, $16.00 yr. Both, $22.00 yr., includes all membership benefits. Write attn.: Membership Services Dept., for more information.

New Zealand GUNS*
Waitekauri Publishing, P.O. 45, Waikino 3060, New Zealand. $NZ90.00 (6 issues) yr. Covers the hunting and firearms scene in New Zealand.

New Zealand Wildlife (Q)
New Zealand Deerstalkers Assoc., Inc., P.O. Box 6514, Wellington, N.Z. $30.00 (N.Z.). Hunting, shooting and firearms/game research articles.

North American Hunter* (M)
P.O. Box 3401, Minnetonka, MN 55343/612-936-9333; e-mail: huntingclub@pclink.com. $18.00 yr. (7 issues). Articles on all types of North American hunting.

Outdoor Life
Time4 Media, Two Park Ave., New York, NY 10016. $14.97/10 issues. Extensive coverage of hunting and shooting. Shooting column by Jim Carmichel.

La Passion des Courteaux (Q)
Phenix Editions, 25 rue Mademoiselle, 75015 Paris, France. French text.

Paintball Games International Magazine
Aceville Publications, Castle House, 97 High St., Colchester, Essex, England CO1 1TH/011-44-206-564840. Write for subscription rates. Leading magazine in the U.K. covering competitive paintball activities.

Paintball News
PBN Publishing, P.O. Box 1608, 24 Henniker St., Hillsboro, NH 03244/603-464-6080. $35 U.S. 1 yr. Bi-weekly. Newspaper covering the sport of paintball, new product reviews and industry features.

Paintball Sports (Q)
Paintball Publications, Inc., 540 Main St., Mount Kisco, NY 10549/941-241-7400. $24.75 U.S. 1 yr., $32.75 foreign. Covering the competitive paintball scene.

Performance Shooter
Belvoir Publications, Inc., 75 Holly Hill Lane, Greenwich, CT 06836-2626/203-661-6111. $45.00 yr. (12 issues). Techniques and technology for improved rifle and pistol accuracy.

Petersen's HUNTING Magazine
Primedia, 6420 Wilshire Blvd., Los Angeles, CA 90048. $19.94 yr.; Canada $29.34 yr.; foreign countries $29.94 yr. Hunting articles for all game; test reports.

P.I. Magazine
America's Private Investigation Journal, 755 Bronx Dr., Toledo, OH 43609. Chuck Klein, firearms editor with column about handguns.

Pirsch
BLV Verlagsgesellschaft GmbH, Postfach 400320, 80703 Munich, Germany/089-12704-0;Fax:089-12705-354. German text.

Point Blank
Citizens Committee for the Right to Keep and Bear Arms (sent to contributors), Liberty Park, 12500 NE 10th Pl., Bellevue, WA 98005

POINTBLANK (M)
Natl. Firearms Assn., Box 4384 Stn. C, Calgary, AB T2T 5N2, Canada. Official publication of the NFA.

The Police Marksman*
6000 E. Shirley Lane, Montgomery, AL 36117. $17.95 yr. For law enforcement personnel.

Police Times (M)
3801 Biscayne Blvd., Miami, FL 33137/305-573-0070.

Popular Mechanics
Hearst Corp., 224 W. 57th St., New York, NY 10019. Firearms, camping, outdoor oriented articles.

Precision Shooting
Precision Shooting, Inc., 222 McKee St., Manchester, CT 06040. $37.00 yr. U.S. Journal of the International Benchrest Shooters, and target shooting in general. Also considerable coverage of varmint shooting, as well as big bore, small bore, schuetzen, lead bullet, wildcats and precision reloading.

Rifle*
Wolfe Publishing Co., 2626 Stearman Road, Ste. A, Prescott, AZ 86301/520-445-7810; Fax: 520-778-5124. $19.00 yr. The sporting firearms journal.

Rifle's Hunting Annual
Wolfe Publishing Co., 2626 Stearman Road, Ste. A, Prescott, AZ 86301/520-445-7810; Fax: 520-778-5124. $4.99 Annual. Dedicated to the finest pursuit of the hunt.

Rod & Rifle Magazine
Lithographic Serv. Ltd., P.O. Box 38-138, Wellington, New Zealand. $50.00 yr. (6 issues). Hunting, shooting and fishing articles.

Safari* (M)
Safari Magazine, 4800 W. Gates Pass Rd., Tucson, AZ 85745/602-620-1220. $55.00 (6 times). The journal of big game hunting, published by Safari Club International. Also publish *Safari Times*, a monthly newspaper, included in price of $55.00 national membership.

Second Amendment Reporter
Second Amendment Foundation, James Madison Bldg., 12500 NE 10th Pl., Bellevue, WA 98005. $15.00 yr. (non-contributors).

Shoot! Magazine*
Shoot! Magazine Corp., 1770 West State Stret PMB 340, Boise ID 83702/208-368-9920; Fax: 208-338-8428. Website: www.shootmagazine.com; $32.95 (6 times/yr.). Articles of interest to the cowboy action shooter, or others interested the Western-era firearms and ammunition.

Shooter's News
23146 Lorain Rd., Box 349, North Olmsted, OH 44070/216-979-5258;Fax:216-979-5259. $29 U.S. 1 yr., $54 2 yrs.; $52 foreign surface. A journal dedicated to precision riflery.

Shooting Industry
Publisher's Dev. Corp., 591 Camino de la Reina, Suite 200, San Diego, CA 92108. $50.00 yr. To the trade. $25.00.

Shooting Sports USA
National Rifle Assn. of America, 11250 Waples Mill Road, Fairfax, VA 22030. Annual subscriptions for NRA members are $5 for classified shooters and $10 for non-classified shooters. Non-NRA member subscriptions are $15. Covering events, techniques and personalities in competitive shooting.

Shooting Sportsman*
P.O. Box 11282, Des Moines, IA 50340/800-666-4955 (for subscriptions). Editorial: P.O. Box 1357, Camden, ME 04843. $19.95 for six issues. The magazine of wingshooting and fine guns.

The Shooting Times & Country Magazine (England)†
IPC Magazines Ltd., King's Reach Tower, Stamford St, 1 London SE1 9LS, England/0171-261-6180;Fax:0171-261-7179. £65 (approx. $98.00) yr.; £79 yr. overseas (52 issues). Game shooting, wild fowling, hunting, game fishing and firearms articles. Britain's best selling field sports magazine.

Shooting Times
Primedia, 2 News Plaza, P.O. Box 1790, Peoria, IL 61656/309-682-6626. $16.97 yr. Guns, shooting, reloading; articles on every gun activity.

The Shotgun News‡
Primedia, 2 News Plaza, P.O. Box 1790, Peoria, IL 61656/800-495-8362. 36 issues/ yr. @ $28.95; 12 issues/yr. @ $19.95. foreign subscription call for rates. Sample copy $4.00. Gun ads of all kinds.

SHOT Business
National Shooting Sports Foundation, Flintlock Ridge Office Center, 11 Mile Hill Rd., Newtown, CT 06470-2359/203-426-1320; FAX: 203-426-1087. For the shooting, hunting and outdoor trade retailer.

Shotgun Sports
P.O. Box 6810, Auburn, CA 95604/916-889-2220; FAX:916-889-9106. $31.00 yr. Trapshooting how-to's, shotshell reloading, shotgun patterning, shotgun tests and evaluations, Sporting Clays action, waterfowl/upland hunting. Call 1-800-676-8920 for a free sample copy.

The Single Shot Exhange Magazine
PO box 1055, York SC 29745/803-628-5326 phone/fax. $31.50/yr., monthly. Articles of interest to the blackpowder cartridge shooter and antique arms collector.

Single Shot Rifle Journal* (M)
Editor John Campbell, PO Box 595, Bloomfield Hills, MI 48303/248-458-8415. Email: jcampbel@dmbb.com Annual dues $35 for 6 issues. Journal of the American Single Shot Rifle Assn.

The Sixgunner (M)
Handgun Hunters International, P.O. Box 357, MAG, Bloomingdale, OH 43910

The Skeet Shooting Review
National Skeet Shooting Assn., 5931 Roft Rd., San Antonio, TX 78253. $20.00 yr. (Assn. membership includes mag.) Competition results, personality profiles of top Skeet shooters, how-to articles, technical, reloading information.

Soldier of Fortune
Subscription Dept., P.O. Box 348, Mt. Morris, IL 61054. $29.95 yr.; $39.95 Canada; $50.95 foreign.
Sporting Classics

Sporting Classics, Inc.
PO Box 23707, Columbia, SC 29223/1-800-849-1004. 1 yr./6 issues/$23.95; 2 yrs./12 issues/$38.95; 3 yrs./18 issues/$47.95. Firearms & outdoor articles and columns.

Sporting Clays Magazine
Patch Communications, 5211 South Washington Ave., Titusville, FL 32780/407-268-5010; FAX: 407-267-7216. $29.95 yr. (12 issues). Official publication of the National Sporting Clays Association.

Sporting Goods Business
Miller Freeman, Inc., One Penn Plaza, 10th Fl., New York, NY 10119-0004. Trade journal.

Sporting Goods Dealer
Two Park Ave., New York, NY 10016. $100.00 yr. Sporting goods trade journal.

Sporting Gun
Bretton Court, Bretton, Peterborough PE3 8DZ, England. £27.00 (approx. U.S. $36.00), airmail £35.50 yr. For the game and clay enthusiasts.

Sports Afield
15621 Chemical Lane, Huntington Beach CA 92648. U.S./800-234-3537. International/714-894-9080. Nine issues for $29.97. Website: www.sportsafield.com. America's oldest outdoor publication is now devoted to high-end sporting pursuits, especially in North America and Africa.

The Squirrel Hunter
P.O. Box 368, Chireno, TX 75937. $14.00 yr. Articles about squirrel hunting.

Stott's Creek Calendar
Stott's Creek Printers, 2526 S 475 W, Morgantown, IN 46160/317-878-5489. 1 yr (3 issues) $11.50; 2 yrs. (6 issues) $20.00. Lists all gun shows everywhere in convenient calendar form; call for information.

Super Outdoors
2695 Aiken Road, Shelbyville, KY 40065/502-722-9463; 800-404-6064; Fax: 502-722-8093. Mark Edwards, publisher. Contact for details.

TACARMI
Via E. De Amicis, 25; 20123 Milano, Italy. $100.00 yr. approx. Antique and modern guns. (Italian text.)

Territorial Dispatch—1800s Historical Publication (M)
National Assn. of Buckskinners, 4701 Marion St., Suite 324, Livestock Exchange Bldg., Denver, CO 80216. Michael A. Nester & Barbara Wyckoff, editors. 303-297-9671.

Trap & Field
1000 Waterway Blvd., Indianapolis, IN 46202. $25.00 yr. Official publ. Amateur Trapshooting Assn. Scores, averages, trapshooting articles.

Turkey Call* (M)
Natl. Wild Turkey Federation, Inc., P.O. Box 530, Edgefield, SC 29824. $25.00 with membership (6 issues per yr.)

Turkey & Turkey Hunting*
Krause Publications, 700 E. State St., Iola, WI 54990-0001. $13.95 (6 issue p. yr.). Magazine with leading-edge articles on all aspects of wild turkey behavior, biology and the successful ways to hunt better with that info. Learn the proper techniques to calling, the right equipment, and more.

The U.S. Handgunner* (M)
U.S. Revolver Assn., 40 Larchmont Ave., Taunton, MA 02780. $10.00 yr. General handgun and competition articles. Bi-monthly sent to members.

U.S. Airgun Magazine
P.O. Box 2021, Benton, AR 72018/800-247-4867; Fax: 501-316-8549. 10 issues a yr. Cover the sport from hunting, 10-meter, field target and collecting. Write for details.

The Varmint Hunter Magazine (Q)
The Varmint Hunters Assn., Box 759, Pierre, SD 57501/800-528-4868. $24.00 yr.

Waffenmarkt-Intern
GFI-Verlag, Theodor-Heuss Ring 62, 50668 K"ln, Germany. Only for gunsmiths, licensed firearms dealers and their suppliers in Germany, Austria and Switzerland.

Wild Sheep (M) (Q)
Foundation for North American Wild Sheep, 720 Allen Ave., Cody, WY 82414. Website: http://iigi.com/os/non/fnaws/fnaws.htm; e-mail: fnaws@wyoming.com. Official journal of the foundation.

Wisconsin Outdoor Journal
Krause Publications, 700 E. State St., Iola, WI 54990-0001. $17.97 yr. (8 issues). For Wisconsin's avid hunters and fishermen, with features from all over that state with regional reports, legislative updates, etc. Website: www.krause.com

Women & Guns
P.O. Box 488, Sta. C, Buffalo, NY 14209. $24.00 yr. U.S.; $72.00 foreign (12 issues). Only magazine edited by and for women gun owners.

World War II*
Cowles History Group, 741 Miller Dr. SE, Suite D-2, Leesburg, VA 20175-8920. Annual subscriptions $19.95 U.S.; $25.95 Canada; 43.95 foreign. The title says it—WWII; good articles, ads, etc.

---

*Published bi-monthly
† Published weekly
‡Published three times per month. All others are published monthly.

M=Membership requirements; write for details.
Q=Published Quarterly.

THE ARMS LIBRARY

FOR COLLECTOR ◆ HUNTER ◆ SHOOTER ◆ OUTDOORSMAN

IMPORTANT NOTICE TO BOOK BUYERS

Books listed here may be bought from **Ray Riling Arms Books Co.**, 6844 Gorsten St., Philadelphia, PA 19119, Phone 215-438-2456; FAX: 215-438-5395. E-mail: sales@rayrilingarmsbooks.com. Larry Riling is the researcher and compiler of "The Arms Library" and a seller of gun books for over 32 years. The Riling stock includes books classic and modern, many hard-to-find items, and many not obtainable elsewhere. These pages list a portion of the current stock. They offer prompt, complete service, with delayed shipments occurring only on out-of-print or out-of-stock books.

Visit our Web site at **www.rayrilingarmsbooks.com** and order all of your favorite titles online from our secure site.

NOTICE FOR ALL CUSTOMERS: Remittance in U.S. funds must accompany all orders. For your convenience we accept VISA, MasterCard, Discover & American Express. For shipments in the U.S., add $7.00 for the 1st book and $2.00 for each additional book for postage and insurance. Min-

imum order $10.00. International Orders add $13.00 for the 1st book and $5.00 for each additional book. All International orders are shipped at the buyer's risk unless an additional $5 for insurance is included. USPS does not offer insurance to all countries unless shipped Air-Mail. Please e-mail or call for pricing.

Payments in excess of order or for "Backorders" are credited or fully refunded at request. Books "As-Ordered" are not returnable except by permission and a handling charge on these of 10% or $2.00 per book, whichever is greater, is deducted from refund or credit. Only Pennsylvania customers must include current sales tax.

A full variety of arms books also available from **Rutgers Book Center**, 127 Raritan Ave., Highland Park, NJ 08904/908-545-4344; FAX: 908-545-6686 or **I.D.S.A. Books**, 1324 Stratford Drive, Piqua, OH 45356/937-773-4203; FAX: 937-778-1922.

BALLISTICS AND HANDLOADING

ABC's of Reloading, 7th Edition, by Bill Chevalier, Iola, WI, Krause Publications, 2005. 288 pp., illustrated with 550 b&w photos. Softcover. NEW. $21.95

The American Cartridge, by Charles Suydam, Borden Publishing Co. Alhambra, CA, 1986. 184 pp., illus. Softcover $24.95
An illustrated study of the rimfire cartridge in the United States.

Ammo and Ballistics II, by Robert W. Forker, Safari Press, Inc., Huntington Beach, CA, 2002. 298 pp., illus. Paper covers. $19.95
Ballistic data on 125 calibers and 1,400 loads out to 500 yards.

Barnes Bullets Reloading Manual Number 3, Barnes Bullets, American Fork, UT, 2003. 668 pp., illus. $29.95
Features data and trajectories on the new weight X, XBT and Solids in calibers from .22 to .50 BMG.

Black Powder, Pig Lead and Steel Silhouettes, by Paul A. Matthews, Prescott, AZ, Wolfe Publishing, 2002. 132 pp., illustrated with b&w photographs and detailed drawings and diagrams. Softcover. NEW. $16.95

Cartridge Reloading Tools of the Past, by R.H. Chamberlain, and Tom Quigley, Castle Rock, WA, 1998. 167 pp., illus. Paper covers. $25.00
A detailed treatment of the extensive Winchester and Ideal line of handloading tools and bullet molds, plus Remington, Marlin, Ballard, Browning, Maynard, and many others.

Cast Bullets for the Black Powder Rifle, by Paul A. Matthews, Wolfe Publishing Co., Prescott, AZ, 1996. 133 pp., illus. Paper covers. $22.50
The tools and techniques used to make your cast bullet shooting a success.

Complete Blackpowder Handbook, 4th Edition, by Sam Fadala, DBI Books, a division of Krause Publications, Iola, WI, 2001. 400 pp., illus. Paper covers. $22.95
Expanded and completely rewritten edition of the definitive book on the subject of blackpowder.

Complete Reloading Manual, One Book / One Caliber, CA, Load Books USA, 2000. $7.95 each
Contains unabridged information from U.S. bullet and powder makers. With thousands of proven and tested loads, plus dozens of various bullet designs and different powders. Spiral bound. Available in all calibers.

Designing and Forming Custom Cartridges for Rifles and Handguns, by Ken Howell. Precision Shooting, Manchester, CT. 2002. 600 pp., illus. $59.95
The classic work in its field, out of print for the last few years and virtually unobtainable on the used book market, now returns in an exact reprint of the original. Full size (8-1/2" x 11"), hardcovers. Dozens of cartridge drawings never published anywhere before—dozens you've never heard of (guaranteed!). Precisely drawn to the dimensions specified by the men who designed them, the factories that made them, and the authorities that set the standards. All drawn to the same format and scale (1.5x) for most, how to form them from brass. Other practical information included.

Early Gunpowder Artillery 1300-1600 by John Norris, London, The Crowood Press, 2003. 1st edition. 141 pp., with 160 b&w photos. Hardcover. New in new dust jacket. $34.95

Early Loading Tools & Bullet Molds, Pioneer Press, 1988. 88 pp., illus. Softcover. $7.50

Handbook for Shooters and Reloaders, by P.O. Ackley, Salt Lake City, UT, 1998, (Vol. I), 567 pp., illus. Includes a separate exterior ballistics chart. $24.95; (Vol. II), a new printing with specific new material. 495 pp., illus. $21.95

Handgun Stopping Power; The Definitive Study, by Marshall & Sandow. Boulder, CO, Paladin Press, 1992. 240 pp. $45.00
Offers accurate predictions of the stopping power of specific loads in calibers from 380 Auto to 45 ACP, as well as such specialty rounds as the Glaser Safety Slug, Federal Hydra-Shok, MagSafe, etc. This is the definitive methodology for predicting the stopping power of handgun loads, the first to take into account what really happens when a bullet meets a man.

Handloader's Digest: 18th Edition edited by Ken Ramage, Iola, WI, Krause Publications, 2003. 300 b&w photos, 256 pp. Softcover. NEW. $19.95

Handloader's Manual of Cartridge Conversions, Revised 3rd edition, by John Donnelly, and Bryce Towsley, Accokeek, MD, Stoeger Publications, 2004. 609 pp. Hardcover. NEW $39.95
Over 900 cartridges described in detail, complete with dimensions, and accurate drawings. Includes case capacities and all physical data.

Hatcher's Notebook, by S. Julian Hatcher, Stackpole Books, Harrisburg, PA, 1992. 488 pp., illus. $39.95
A reference work for shooters, gunsmiths, ballisticians, historians, hunters and collectors.

Headstamped Cartridges and Their Variations; Volume 1 by Daniel L. Shuey, W.R.A. Co., Rockford, IL, WCF Publications, 2003. 351 pp. illustrated with b&w photos. Hardcover. NEW. $55.00

Headstamped Cartridges and Their Variations; Volume 2 by Daniel L. Shuey, W.R.A. Co., Rockford, IL, WCF Publications, 2003. 351 pp. illustrated with b&w photos. Hardcover. NEW. $55.00

History & Development of Small Arms Ammunition, Volume 1, Second Edition– With A Value Guide, Martial Long Arms, Flintlock through Rimfire, by George A. Hoyem, Missoula, MI, Armory Publications, 2005. Hardcover. New in new dust jacket. $60.00

History & Development of Small Arms Ammunition, Volume 3, Second Edition– With A Value Guide, Martial Long Arms, Flintlock through Rimfire, by George A. Hoyem, Missoula, MI, Armory Publications, 2006. Hardcover. New in new dust jacket. $60.00

Hornady Handbook of Cartridge Reloading, 6th Edition, Vol. I and II, edited by Larry Steadman, Hornady Mfg. Co., Grand Island, NE, 2003., illus. $49.95
Two volumes; Volume 1, 773 pp.; Volume 2, 717 pp. New edition of this famous reloading handbook covers rifle and handgun reloading data and ballistic tables. Latest loads, ballistic information, etc.

How-To's for the Black Powder Cartridge Rifle Shooter, by Paul A. Matthews, Wolfe Publishing Co., Prescott, AZ, 1995. 45 pp. Paper covers. $22.50
Covers lube recipes, good bore cleaners and over-powder wads. Tips include compressing powder charges, combating wind resistance, improving ignition and much more.

The Hunter's Guide to Accurate Shooting, by Wayne van Zwoll, Guilford, CT, Lyons Press, 2002. 1st edition. 288 pp. Hardcover. New in new dust jacket. $29.95

The Illustrated Reference of Cartridge Dimensions, edited by Dave Scovill, Wolfe Publishing Co., Prescott, AZ, 1994. 343 pp., illus. Paper covers. $19.00
A comprehensive volume with over 300 cartridges. Standard and metric dimensions have been taken from SAAMI drawings and/or fired cartridges.

Loading the Black Powder Rifle Cartridge, by Paul A. Matthews, Wolfe Publishing Co., Prescott, AZ, 1993. 121 pp., illus. Paper covers. $22.50
Author Matthews brings the blackpowder cartridge shooter valuable information on the basics, including cartridge care, lubes and moulds, powder charges and developing and testing loads in his usual authoritative style.

Lyman 48th Reloading Handbook, No. 48. Connecticut, Lan Publishing Corporation, 2003. 48th edition. 480 pp. Softcover. NEW. $26.95

Lyman Cast Bullet Handbook, 3rd Edition, edited by C. Kenneth Ramage, Lyman Publications, Middlefield, CT, 1980. 416 pp., illus. Paper covers. $19.95
Information on more than 5000 tested cast bullet loads and 19 pages of trajectory and wind drift tables for cast bullets.

Lyman Black Powder Handbook, 2nd Edition, edited by Sam Fadala, Lyman Products for Shooters, Middlefield, CT, 2000. 239 pp., illus. Paper covers. $19.95
Comprehensive load information for the modern blackpowder shooter.

Lyman Shotshell Handbook, 4th Edition, edited by Edward A. Matunas, Lyman Products Co., Middlefield, CT, 1996. 330 pp., illus. Paper covers. $24.95
Has 9,000 loads, including slugs and buckshot, plus feature articles and a full color I.D. section. Superb reference text.

Make It Accurate–Get the Maximum Performance from Your Hunting Rifle, by Craig Boddington, Long Beach, CA, Safari Press, 1999. Hardcover. New in new dust jacket. $24.95

Metallic Cartridge Conversions: The History of the Guns and Modern Reproductions, by Dennis Adler, Foreword by R. L. Wilson, Iola, WI, Krause Publications, 2003. 1st edition. 208 pp. 250 color photos. Hardcover. New in new dust jacket. $39.95

Modern Exterior Ballistics, by Robert L. McCoy, Schiffer Publishing Co., Atglen, PA, 1999. 128 pp. $95.00
Advanced students of exterior ballistics and flight dynamics will find this comprehensive textbook on the subject a useful addition to their libraries.

Modern Reloading 2nd Edition, by Richard Lee, Inland Press, 2003. 623 pp., illus. $29.95
The how-to's of rifle, pistol and shotgun reloading plus load data for rifle and pistol calibers.

Modern Reloading Manual, 2nd Edition by Richard Lee, privately printed, 2003. 510 pp., illus. Hardcover. NEW. $24.95

Mr. Single Shot's Cartridge Handbook, by Frank de Haas, Mark de Haas, Orange City, IA, 1996. 116 pp., illus. Paper covers. $22.50
This book covers most of the cartridges, both commercial and wildcat, that the author has known and used.

Norma Reloading Manual, by Norma Precision AB, 2004, 1st edition. Data for over 2,000 loads in 73 calibers. 432 pp. Hardcover, NEW. $34.95

Nosler Reloading Manual #5, edited by Gail Root, Nosler Bullets, Inc., Bend, OR, 2002. 516 pp., illus. $29.99
Combines information on their ballistic tip, partition and handgun bullets with traditional powders and new powders never before used, plus trajectory information from 100 to 500 yards.

The Paper Jacket, by Paul Matthews, Wolfe Publishing Co., Prescott, AZ, 1991. Paper covers. $14.50
Up-to-date and accurate information about paper-patched bullets.

Reloading for Shotgunners, 4th Edition, by Kurt D. Fackler, and M.L. McPherson, DBI Books, a division of Krause Publications, Iola, WI, 1997. 320 pp., illus. Paper covers. $19.95
Expanded reloading tables with over 11,000 loads. Bushing charts for every major press and component maker. All new presentation on all aspects of shotshell reloading by two of the top experts in the field.

Reloading Tools, Sights and Telescopes for S/S Rifles, by Gerald O. Kelver, Brighton, CO, 1982. 163 pp., illus. Softcover. $15.00
A listing of most of the famous makers of reloading tools, sights and telescopes with a brief description of the products they manufactured.

The Rimfire Cartridge in the United States and Canada, Illustrated History of Rimfire Cartridges, Manufacturers, and the Products Made from 1857-1984, by John L. Barber, Thomas Publications, Gettysburg, PA 2000. 1st edition. Profusely illus. 221 pp. $50.00
The author has written an encyclopedia of rimfire cartridges from the 22 to the massive 1.00 in. Gatling. Fourteen chapters, six appendices and an excellent bibliography.

Round Ball to Rimfire: A History of Civil War Small Arms Ammunition, Vol. 1, by Dean S. Thomas, Gettysburg, PA, Thomas Publications, 2003. 488 pp. Hardcover. $40.00
Federal pistols, revolvers and miscellaneous essays.

Round Ball to Rimfire: A History of Civil War Small Arms Ammunition, Vol. 2, by Dean S. Thomas, Gettysburg, PA, Thomas Publications, 2003. 488 pp. Hardcover. NEW. $49.95
Federal pistols, revolvers and miscellaneous essays.

Round Ball to Rimfire: A History of Civil War Small Arms Ammunition, Vol. 3, by Dean S. Thomas, Gettysburg, PA, Thomas Publications, 2003. 488 pp. Hardcover. $49.95
Federal pistols, revolvers and miscellaneous essays.

Shotshells & Ballistics, Safari Press, 2002. 275 pp., photos. Softcover, $19.95
Accentuated with photos from the field and the range, this is a reference book unlike any other.

Sierra Reloading Manual, 5th Edition: Rifle and Handgun Manual of Reloading Data. Sedalia, MO, Sierra Bullets, 2003. Hardcover. NEW. $39.95

Sixgun Cartridges and Loads, by Elmer Keith, The Gun Room Press, Highland Park, NJ, 1986. 151 pp., illus. $24.95
A manual covering the selection, uses and loading of the most suitable and popular revolver cartridges. Originally published in 1936. Reprint.

Speer Reloading Manual No. 13, edited by members of the Speer research staff, Omark Industries, Lewiston, ID, 1999. 621 pp., illus. $24.95
With 13 new sections containing the latest technical information and reloading trends for both novice and expert in this latest edition. More than 9,300 loads are listed, including new propellant powders from Accurate Arms, Alliant, Hodgdon and Vihtavuori.

Stopping Power: A Practical Analysis of the Latest Handgun Ammunition, by Marshall & Sanow, Boulder, CO, Paladin Press, 2002. 1st edition. 600+ photos, 360 pp. Softcover. $49.95
If you want to know how handgun ammunition will work against human targets in the future, you must look at how similar ammo has worked against human targets in the past. Stopping Power bases its conclusions on real-world facts from real-world gunfights. It provides the latest street results of actual police and civilian shootings in all of the major handgun calibers, from 22 LR to 45 ACP, plus more than 30 chapters of vital interest to all gun owners.

Street Stoppers, The Latest Handgun Stopping Power Street Results, by Marshall & Lanow, Boulder, CO, Paladin Press, 1996. 374 pp., illus. Softcover. $42.95
Street Stoppers is the long-awaited sequel to Handgun Stopping Power. It provides the latest results of real-life shootings in all of the major handgun calibers, plus more than 25 thought- provoking chapters that are vital to anyone interested in firearms, wound ballistics, and combat shooting. This book also covers the street results of the hottest new caliber to hit the shooting world in years, the 40 Smith & Wesson. Updated street results of the latest exotic ammunition including Remington Golden Saber and CCI-Speer Gold Dot, plus the venerable offerings from MagSafe, Glaser, Cor-Bon and others. A fascinating look at the development of Hydra-Shok ammunition is included.

Understanding Firearm Ballistics, 6th Edition by Robert A. Rinker, Mulberry House Publishing Co., Corydon, IN, 2005. 437 pp., illus. Paper covers. New, revised and expanded. $24.95
Explains basic to advanced firearm ballistics in understandable terms.

Why Not Load Your Own?, by Col. T. Whelen, Gun Room Press, Highland Park, NJ 1996, 4th ed., rev. 237 pp., illus. $20.00
A basic reference on handloading, describing each step, materials and equipment. Includes loads for popular cartridges.

Wildcat Cartridges, "Reloader's Handbook of Wildcat Cartridge Design", by Fred Zeglin, privately printed, 2005. 1st edition. 287 Pages, hardback book. Forward by Wayne van Zwoll. Pictorial hardcover. NEW. $39.95
22 chapters cover wildcatting from every possible angle. History, dimensions, load data, and how to make or use reloading tool and reamers. If you're interested in reloading or wildcatting this is a must have book.

Wildcat Cartridges Volumes 1 & 2 Combination, by the editors of Handloaders magazine, Wolfe Publishing Co., Prescott, AZ, 1997. 350 pp., illus. Paper covers. $39.95
A profile of the most popular information on wildcat cartridges that appeared in the *Handloaders* magazine.

W.R.A. Co.; Headstamped Cartridges and their Variations; Volume 1, by Daniel Shuey, Rockford, IL, WCF Publications, 2001. 298pp illustrated with b&w photos, Hardcover, NEW. $55.00

W.R.A. Co.; Headstamped Cartridges and their Variations; Volume 2, by Daniel Shuey, Rockford, IL, WCF Publications, 2003. 351pp illustrated with b&w photos, Hardcover, NEW. $50.00

COLLECTORS

The 1 October 1934 SS Dienstalterliste, by the Ulric of England Research Unit San Jose, CA, R. James Bender Publishing, 1994. Reprint softcover. NEW. $29.95

The 10. Panzer Division: In Action in the East, West and North Africa 1939-1943, by Jean Resta and N. Moller, Canada, J.J. Fedorowicz Publishing Inc., 2003. 1st edition. Hardcover. NEW. $89.95

18th Century Weapons of the Royal Welsh Fuziliers from Flixton Hall, by Erik Goldstein, Thomas Publications, Gettysburg, PA, 2002. 1st edition. 126 pp., illustrated with b&w photos. Softcover. $19.95

The .45-70 Springfield Book I, by Albert Frasca and Robert Hill, Frasca Publishing, 2000. Memorial edition. Hardback with gold embossed cover and spine. $95.00
The Memorial edition reprint of the 45-70 Springfield was done to honor Robert H. Hill who was an outstanding Springfield collector, historian, researcher, and gunsmith. Only 1,000 of these highly regarded books were printed, using the same binding and cover material as the original 1980 edition. The book is considered the bible for 45-70 Springfield Trapdoor collectors.

The .45-70 Springfield Book II 1865-1893, by Albert Frasca, Frasca Publishing, Springfield, Ohio 1997 Hardback with gold embossed cover and spine. 400+ pp. and 400+ photographs which cover ALL the trapdoor Springfield models. Hardback with gold embossed cover and spine. $85.00
A MUST for the trapdoor collector!

The .45-70 Springfield, by Joe Poyer and Craig Riesch, North Cape Publications, Tustin, CA, 1996. 150 pp., illus. Paper covers. $16.95
A revised and expanded edition of a best-selling reference work organized by serial number and date of production to aid the collector in identifying popular "Trapdoor" rifles and carbines.

'51 Colt Navies, by Nathan L. Swayze, The Gun Room Press, Highland Park, NJ, 1993. 243 pp., illus. $59.95
The Model 1851 Colt Navy, its variations and markings.

The 1862 U.S. Cavalry Tactics, by Philip St. George Cooke, Mechanicsburg, PA, Stackpole Books, 2004. 416 pp. Hardcover. New in new dust jacket. $19.89

A Collector's Guide to the '03 Springfield, by Bruce N. Canfield, Andrew Mowbray Inc., Lincoln, RI, 2004. 160 pp., illus. Paper covers. $22.00
A comprehensive guide follows the '03 through its unparalleled tenure of service. Covers all of the interesting variations, modifications and accessories of this highly collectible military rifle.

A Collector's Guide to United States Combat Shotguns, by Bruce N. Canfield, Andrew Mowbray Inc., Lincoln, RI, 1992. 184 pp., illus. Paper covers. $24.00

This book provides full coverage of combat shotguns, from the earliest examples right up to the Gulf War and beyond.

A Collector's Guide to Winchester in the Service, by Bruce N. Canfield, Andrew Mowbray, Inc., Lincoln, RI, 1991. 192 pp., illus. Paper covers. $24.00

The firearms produced by Winchester for the national defense. From Hotchkiss to the M14, each firearm is illustrated and illustrated.

A Concise Guide to the Artillery at Gettysburg, by Gregory Coco, Thomas Publications, Gettysburg, PA, 1998. 96 pp., illus. Paper covers. $10.00

Coco's 10 book on Gettysburg is a beginner's guide to artillery and its use at the battle. It covers the artillery batteries describing the types of cannons, shells, fuses, etc. using interesting narrative and human interest stories.

A Glossary of the Construction, Decoration and Use of Arms and Armor in All Countries and in All Times, by George Cameron Stone, Dover Publishing, New York 1999. Softcover. $39.95

An exhaustive study of arms and armor in all countries through recorded history—from the Stone Age up to WWII. With over 4,500 b&w illustrations, this Dover edition is an unabridged republication of the work originally published in 1934 by the Southworth Press, Portland, MA. A new introduction has been specially prepared for this edition.

A Guide to American Trade Catalogs 1744-1900, by Lawrence B. Romaine, Dover Publications, New York, NY. 422 pp., illus. Paper covers. $12.95

A Guide to Ballard Breechloaders, by George J. Layman, Pioneer Press, Union City, TN, 1997. 261 pp., illus. Paper covers. $19.95

Documents the saga of this fine rifle from the first models made by Ball & Williams of Worchester, to its production by the Marlin Firearms Co., to the cessation of 19th century manufacture in 1891, and finally to the modern reproductions made in the 1990s.

A Guide to the Maynard Breechloader, by George J. Layman, George J. Layman, Ayer, MA, 1993. 125 pp., illus. Paper covers. $11.95

The first book dedicated entirely to the Maynard family of breech-loading firearms. Coverage of the arms is given from the 1850s through the 1880s.

A Guide to U. S. Army Dress Helmets 1872-1904, by Kasal and Moore, North Cape Publications, 2000. 88 pp., illus. Paper covers. $15.95

This thorough study provides a complete description of the Model 1872 and 1881 dress helmets worn by the U.S. Army.

A Study of Remington's Smoot Patent and Number Four Revolvers, by Parker Harry, Parker Ora Lee, and Joan Reisch, Foreword by Roy M. Marcot, Santa Ana, CA, Armslore Press, Graphic Publishers, 2003. 1st edition. 120 pp., profusely illus., plus 8-page color section. Softcover. $17.95

A detailed, pictorial essay on Remington's early metallic cartridge-era pocket revolvers: their design, development, patents, models, identification and variations. Includes the biography of arms inventor Wm. S. Smoot, for the first time ever, as well as a mini-history of the Remington Arms Company.

Accoutrements of the United States Infantry, Riflemen, and Dragoons 1834-1839, by R.T. Huntington, Historical Arms Series No. 20. Canada, Museum Restoration. 58 pp. illus. Softcover. $8.95

Although the 1841 edition of the U.S. Ordnance Manual provides ample information on the equipment that was in use during the 1840s, it is evident that the patterns of equipment that it describes were not introduced until 1838 or 1839. This guide is intended to fill this gap in our knowledge by providing an overview of what we now know about the accoutrements that were issued to the regular infantryman, rifleman, and dragoon, in the 1830s with excursions into earlier and later years.

Ackermann Military Prints: Uniforms of the British and Indian Armies 1840-1855, by William Y. Carman with Robert W. Kenny Jr., Schiffer Publications, Atglen, PA, 2002. 1st edition. 176 pp., with over 160 color images. $69.95

Afrikakorps: Rommel's Tropical Army in Original Color, by Bernd Peitz, Gary Wilkins. Atglen, PA, Schiffer Publications, 2004. 1st edition. 192 pp., with over 200 color and b&w photographs. Hardcover. New in new dust jacket. $59.95

Air Guns, by Eldon G. Wolff, Duckett's Publishing Co., Tempe, AZ, 1997. 204 pp., illus. Paper covers. $35.00

Historical reference covering many makers, European and American guns, canes and more.

All About Southerners, including a detailed look at the characteristics and design of the "Best Little Pistol in the World," by Lionel J. Bogut, Sun City, CA, White Star, Inc., 2002. A limited edition of 1,000 copies. Signed and numbered. 114 pp., including bibliography, and plenty of b&w photographs and detailed drawings. Hardcover. $29.95

Allgemeine-SS The Commands, Units and Leaders of the General SS, by Mark C. Yerger, Atglen, PA, Schiffer Publications, 1997. 1st edition. Hardcover. New in new dust jacket. $49.95

Allied and Enemy Aircraft: May 1918; Not to be Taken from the Front Lines, Historical Arms Series No. 27. Canada, Museum Restoration. Softcover. $8.95

The basis for this title is a very rare identification manual published by the French government in 1918 that illustrated 60 aircraft with three or more views: French, English American, German, Italian, and Belgian, which might have been seen over the trenches of France. Each is described in a text translated from the original French. This is probably the most complete collection of illustrations of WWI aircraft that has survived.

American Beauty; The Prewar Colt National Match Government Model Pistol, by Timothy J. Mullin, Collector Grade Publications, Cobourg, Ontario, Canada. 72 pp., illus. $34.95

Includes over 150 serial numbers, and 20 spectacular color photos of factory engraved guns and other authenticated upgrades, including rare "double-carved" ivory grips.

American Civil War Artillery 1861-65: Field Artillery, by Philip Oxford Katcher, United Kingdom, Osprey Publishing, 2001. 1st edition. 48 pp. Softcover. $14.95

Perhaps the most influential arm of either army in the prosecution of the American Civil War, the artillery of both sides grew to be highly professional organizations. This book covers all the major artillery pieces employed, including the Napoleon, Parrott Rifle and Mountain Howitzer.

American Military and Naval Belts, 1812-1902, by R. Stephen Dorsey, Eugene, OR, Collectors Library, 2002. 1st edition. Hardcover. $80.00

With introduction by Norm Flayderman, this massive work is the NEW key reference on sword belts, waist belts, sabre belts, shoulder belts and cartridge belts (looped and non-looped). At over 460 pp., this 8-1/2" x 11" book offers over 840 photos (primarily in color) and original period drawings. In addition, this work offers the first, comprehensive research on the Anson Mills woven cartridge belts: the man, the company and its personalities, the belt-related patents and the government contracts from 1880 through 1902. This book is a "must" for all accoutrements collectors, military historians and museums.

American Military Belt Plates, by Michael J. O'Donnell and J. Duncan Campbell. Alexandria, VA, O'Donnell Publishing, 2000. 2nd edition. 614 pp., illus. Hardcover $49.00

At last available and well worth the wait! This massive study encompasses all the known plates from the Revolutionary War through the Spanish-American conflict. A sweeping, handsomely presented study that covers 1776 through 1910. Over 1,025 specimens are illustrated front and back along with many images of soldiers wearing various plates.

American Military Headgear Insignia, by Michael J. O'Donnell and J. Duncan Campbell, Alexandria, VA, O'Donnell Publishing, 2004. 1st edition. 311 pp., 703 photo figures, 4 sketches. Hardcover. New in new dust jacket. $89.95

The American Military Saddle, 1776-1945, by R. Stephen Dorsey and Kenneth L. McPheeters, Collector's Library, Eugene, OR, 1999. 400 pp., illus. $67.00

The most complete coverage of the subject ever written on the American Military Saddle. Nearly 1,000 actual photos and official drawings, from the major public and private collections in the U.S. and Great Britain.

American Police Collectibles; Dark Lanterns and Other Curious Devices, by Matthew G. Forte, Turn of the Century Publishers, Upper Montclair, NJ, 1999. 248 pp., illus. $24.95

For collectors of police memorabilia (handcuffs, police dark lanterns, mechanical and chain nippers, rattles, billy clubs and nightsticks) and police historians.

American Thunder II: The Military Thompson Submachine Guns, by Frank Iannamico, Harmony, ME, Moose Lake Publishing, 2004, 2nd edition. 536 pp., Soft cover, NEW. $29.95

Many great photographs that show detail markings and features of the various models, as well as vintage WW11 photographs showing the Thompson in action.

An Introduction to the Civil War Small Arms, by Earl J. Coates and Dean S. Thomas, Thomas Publishing Co., Gettysburg, PA, 1990. 96 pp., illus. Paper covers. $10.00

The small arms carried by the individual soldier during the Civil War.

Arming the Glorious Cause; Weapons of the Second War for Independence, by James B. Whisker, Daniel D. Hartzler and Larry W. Tantz, Old Bedford Village Press, Bedford, PA., 1998. 175 pp., illus. $45.00

A photographic study of Confederate weapons.

Arms & Accoutrements of the Mounted Police 1873-1973, by Roger F. Phillips, and Donald J. Klancher, Museum Restoration Service, Ont., Canada, 1982. 224 pp., illus. $49.95

A definitive history of the revolvers, rifles, machine guns, cannons, ammunition, swords, etc. used by the NWMP, the RNWMP and the RCMP during the first 100 years of the Force.

Arms & Accoutrements of the Mounted Police 1873-1973, by Roger F. Phillips, and Donald J. Klancher, Museum Restoration Service, Ont., Canada, 2005. 224 pp., illus. Softcover. NEW. $29.50

A definitive history of the revolvers, rifles, machine guns, cannons, ammunition, swords, etc. used by the NWMP, the RNWMP and the RCMP during the first 100 years of the Force.

Arms and Armor in Colonial America 1526-1783, by Harold Peterson, Dover Publishing, New York, 2000. 350 pp. with over 300 illustrations, index, bibliography and appendix. Softcover. $34.95

Over 200 years of firearms, ammunition, equipment and edged weapons.

Arms and Armor in the Art Institute of Chicago, by Waltler J. Karcheski, Bulfinch, New York 1999. 128 pp., 103 color photos, 12 b&w illustrations. $50.00

The George F. Harding Collection of arms and armor is the most visited installation at the Art Institute of Chicago—a testament to the enduring appeal of swords, muskets and the other paraphernalia of medieval and early modern war. Organized both chronologically and by type of weapon, this book captures the best of this astonishing collection in 115 striking photographs—most in color—accompanied by illuminating text. Here are intricately filigreed breastplates and ivory-handled crossbows, samurai katana and Toledo-steel scimitars, elaborately decorated maces and beautifully carved flintlocks—a treat for anyone who has ever been beguiled by arms, armor and the age of chivalry.

Arms Makers of Maryland, by Daniel D. Hartzler, George Shumway, York, PA, 1975. 200 pp., illus. $50.00

A thorough study of the gunsmiths of Maryland who worked during the late 18th and early 19th centuries.

Arms Makers of Western Pennsylvania, by James B. Whisker, Old Bedford Village Press. 1st edition. Deluxe hardbound edition, 176 pp., illus. $50.00

Printed on fine coated paper with many large photographs and detailed text describing the period, lives, tools, and artistry of the Arms Makers of Western Pennsylvania.

ARMS LIBRARY

Arsenal of Freedom: The Springfield Armory 1890-1948, by Lt. Col. William Brophy, Andrew Mowbray, Inc., Lincoln, RI,1997. 20 pp. of photos. 400 pp. As new, Softcover. $29.95

A year-by-year account drawn from offical records. Packed with reports, charts, tables and line drawings.

The Art of Gun Engraving, by Claude Gaier and Pietro Sabatti, Knickerbocker Press, N.Y., 1999. 160 pp., illus. $34.95

The richness and detail lavished on early firearms represents a craftmanship nearly vanished. Beginning with crossbows, hunting scenes, portraits, or mythological themes are intricately depicted within a few square inches of etched metal. The full-color photos contained herein recaptures this lost art with exquisite detail.

The Art of Remington Arms, by Tom Davis, Sporting Classics, 2004, 1st edition. Large format book, featuring 200 paintings by Remington Arms over the years on its calendars, posters, shell boxes, etc. 50 full-color by Bob Kuhn alone. Hardcover. NEW $54.95

Astra Automatic Pistols, by Leonardo M. Antaris, FIRAC Publishing Co., Sterling, CO, 1989. 248 pp., illus. $55.00

Charts, tables, serial ranges, etc. The definitive work on Astra pistols.

Ballard: The Great American Single Shot Rifle, by John T. Dutcher. Denver, CO, privately printed, 2002. 1st edition. 380 pp., illustrated with b&w photos, with 8- page color insert. Hardcover. New in new dust jacket. $79.95

Basic Documents on U.S. Martial Arms, commentary by Col. B.R. Lewis, reissue by Ray Riling, Phila., PA, 1956 and 1960. Rifle Musket Model 1855. Each $10.00

The first issue rifle of musket caliber, a muzzleloader equipped with the Maynard Primer, 32 pp. Rifle Musket Model 1863. The typical Union muzzleloader of the Civil War, 26 pp. Breech- Loading Rifle Musket Model 1866. The first of our 50-caliber breechloading rifles, 12 pp. Remington Navy Rifle Model 1870. A commercial type breech-loader made at Springfield, 16 pp. Lee Straight Pull Navy Rifle Model 1895. A magazine cartridge arm of 6mm caliber, 23 pp. Breech-Loading Arms (five models) 27 pp. Ward-Burton Rifle Musket 1871, 16 pp.

Battle Colors: Insignia and Aircraft Markings of the Eighth Air Force in World War II, by Robert A. Watkins, Atglen, PA, Schiffer Publications, 2004. 1st edition. Softcover. $45.00

Battle Weapons of the American Revolution, by George C. Neuman, Scurlock Publishing Co., Texarkana, TX, 2001. 400 pp. Illus. Softcovers. $44.95

The most extensive photographic collection of Revolutionary War weapons ever in one volume. More than 1,600 photos of over 500 muskets, rifles, swords, bayonets, knives and other arms used by both sides in America's War for Independence.

The Bedford County Rifle and Its Makers, by Calvin Hetrick, Introduction by George Shumway, George Shumway Pub., 1975. 40 pp. illus. Softcover. $10.00

The author's study of the graceful and distinctive muzzle-loading rifles made in Bedford County, Pennsylvania, stands as a milestone on the long path to the understanding of America's longrifles.

The Belgian Rattlesnake; The Lewis Automatic Machine Gun, by William M. Easterly, Collector Grade Publications, Cobourg, Ontario, Canada, 1998. 584 pp., illus. $79.95

The most complete account ever published on the life and times of Colonel Isaac Newton Lewis and his crowning invention, the Lewis Automatic machine gun.

Best of Holland & Holland, England's Premier Gunmaker, by Michael McIntosh and Jan G. Roosenburg. Safari Press, Inc., Long Beach, CA, 2002. 1st edition. 298 pp. Profuse color illustrations. $69.95

Holland & Holland has had a long history of not only building London's "best" guns but also providing superior guns–the ultimate gun in finish, engraving, and embellishment. From the days of old in which a maharaja would order 100 fancifully engraved H&H shotguns for his guests to use at his duck shoot, to the recent elaborately decorated sets depicting the Apollo 11 moon landing or the history of the British Empire, all of these guns represent the zenith in the art and craft of gunmaking and engraving. These and other H&H guns in the series named "Products of Excellence" are a cut above the ordinary H&H gun and hark back to a time when the British Empire ruled over one-third of the globe–a time when rulers, royalty, and the rich worldwide came to H&H for a gun that would elevate them above the crowd.

The Big Guns, Civil War Siege, Seacoast, and Naval Cannon, by Edwin Olmstead, Wayne E. Stark, and Spencer C. Tucker, Museum Restoration Service, Bloomfield, Ontario, Canada, 1997. 360 pp., illus. $80.00

This book is designed to identify and record the heavy guns available to both sides by the end of the Civil War.

Blue Book of Air Guns, 4th Edition, edited by S.P. Fjestad, Blue Book Publications, Inc. Minneapolis, MN 2005. $24.95

This new edition simply contains more airgun values and information than any other single publication.

Blue Book of Gun Values, 26th Edition, edited by S.P. Fjestad, Blue Book Publications, Inc. Minneapolis, MN 2005. $39.95

This new edition simply contains more firearm values and information than any other single publication. Expanded to over 1,600 pages featuring over 100,000 firearms prices.

Blue Book of Modern Black Powder Values, 4th Edtion by Dennis Adler, Blue Book Publications, Inc. Minneapolis, MN 2005. 271 pp., illus. 41 color photos. Softcover. $24.95

This new title contains more up-to-date blackpowder values and related information than any other single publication. This new book will keep you up-to-date on modern blackpowder models and prices, including most makes and models introduced this year!

The Blunderbuss 1500-1900, by James D. Forman, Historical Arms Series No. 32. Canada, Museum Restoration, 1994. 40 pp., illus. Softcover. $8.95

An excellent and authoritative booklet giving tons of information on the Blunderbuss, a very neglected subject.

Boarders Away Volume I: With Steel-Edged Weapons & Polearms, by William Gilkerson, Andrew Mowbray, Inc. Publishers, Lincoln, RI, 1993. 331 pp. $48.00

Contains the essential 24-page chapter "War at Sea" which sets the historical and practical context for the arms discussed. Includes chapters on Early Naval Weapons, Boarding Axes, Cutlasses, Officers Fighting Swords and Dirks, and weapons at hand of Random Mayhem.

Boarders Away, Volume II: Firearms of the Age of Fighting Sail, by William Gilkerson, Andrew Mowbray, Inc. Publishers, Lincoln, RI, 1993. 331 pp., illus. $65.00

Covers the pistols, muskets, combustibles and small cannons used aboard American and European fighting ships, 1626-1826.

Boston's Gun Bible, by Boston T. Party, Ignacio, CO, Javelin Press, August 2000. Expanded edition. Softcover. $28.00

This mammoth guide for gun owners everywhere is a completely updated and expanded edition (more than 500 new pages!) of Boston T. Party's classic Boston on Guns and Courage. Boston gives new advice on which shoulder weapons and handguns to buy and why, before exploring such topics as why you should consider not getting a concealed carry permit, what guns and gear will likely be outlawed next, how to spend within your budget, why you should go to a quality defensive shooting academy now, which guns and gadgets are inferior and why, how to spot off illegal government gun registration lists, how to spot an undercover agent trying to entrap law- abiding gun owners and much more.

The Bren Gun Saga, by Thomas B. Dugelby, Collector Grade Publications, Cobourg, Ontario, Canada, 1999, revised and expanded edition. 406 pp., illus. $65.95

A modern, definitive book on the Bren in this revised expanded edition, which in terms of numbers of pages and illustrations is nearly twice the size of the original.

British Board of Ordnance Small Arms Contractors 1689-1840, by De Witt Bailey, Rhyl, England, W. S. Curtis, 2000. 150 pp. $18.00

Thirty years of research in the Archives of the Ordnance Board in London has identified more than 600 of these suppliers. The names of many can be found marking the regulation firearms of the period. In the study, the contractors are identified both alphabetically and under a combination of their date period together with their specialist trade.

The British Enfield Rifles, Volume 1, The SMLE MK I and MK III Rifles, by Charles R. Stratton, North Cape Pub., Tustin, CA, 1997. 150 pp., illus. Paper covers. $16.95

A systematic and thorough examination on a part-by-part basis of the famous British battle rifle that endured for nearly 70 years as the British Army's number one battle rifle.

The British Enfield Rifles, Volume 2, No. 4 and No. 5 Rifles, by Charles R. Stratton, North Cape Publications, Tustin, CA, 1999. 150 pp., illus. Paper covers. $16.95

The historical background for the development of both rifles describing each variation and an explanation of all the marks, numbers and codes found on most parts.

The British Enfield Rifles, Volume 4, The Pattern 1914 and U. S. Model 1917 Rifles, by Charles R. Stratton, North Cape Publications, Tustin, CA, 2000. Paper covers. $16.95

One of the least known American and British collectible military rifles is analyzed on a part by part basis. All markings and codes, refurbishment procedures and WWII upgrade are included as are the various sniper rifle versions.

The British Falling Block Breechloading Rifle from 1865, by Jonathan Kirton, Tom Rowe Books, Maynardsville, TN, 2nd edition, 1997. 380 pp., illus. $70.00

Expanded edition of a comprehensive work on the British falling block rifle.

British Gun Engraving, by Douglas Tate, Safari Press, Inc., Huntington Beach, CA, 1999. 240 pp., illus. Limited, signed and numbered edition, in a slipcase. $80.00

A historic and photographic record of the last two centuries.

British Gunmakers: Volume One – London, by Nigel Brown, London, Quiller, 2004. 1st edition 280 pp., 33 colour, 43 b&w photographs, line drawings. Hardcover.] $99.95

] **British Gunmakers: Volume Two-Birmingham, Scotland, And the Regions,** by Nigel Brown, London, Quiller,2005. 1st edition. With this book, read in conjunction with Volume One, the reader or scholar should be able to trace the history and likely age of any shotgun or rifle made in this region since 1800. 439 pp., hardcover. NEW. $99.95

British Military Flintlock Rifles 1740-1840, With a Remarkable Wealth of Data about the Riflemen and Regiments that Carried These Weapons, by De Witt Bailey, Andrew Mowbray, Inc. Lincoln, RI, 2002. 1st edition. 264 pp. with over 320 photographs. Hardcover. $47.95

Pattern 1776 Rifles, the Ferguson Breechloader, the famous Baker Rifle, rifles of the Hessians and other German Mercenaries, American Loyalist rifles, rifles given to Indians, Cavalry rifles and rifled carbines, bayonets, accoutrements, ammunition and more.

British Service Rifles and Carbines 1888-1900, by Alan M. Petrillo, Excaliber Publications, Latham, NY, 1994. 72 pp., illus, Paper covers. $11.95

A complete review of the Lee-Metford and Lee-Enfield rifles and carbines.

British Single Shot Rifles, Volume 1, Alexander Henry, by Wal Winfer, Tom Rowe, Maynardsville, TN, 1998, 200 pp., illus. $50.00

Detailed study of the single shot rifles made by Henry. Illustrated with hundreds of photographs and drawings.

British Single Shot Rifles Volume 2, George Gibbs, by Wal Winfer, Tom Rowe, Maynardsville, TN, 1998. 177 pp., illus. $50.00

Detailed study of the Farquharson as made by Gibbs. Hundreds of photos.

British Single Shot Rifles, Volume 3, Jeffery, by Wal Winfer, Rowe Publications, Rochester, N.Y., 1999. 260 pp., illus. $60.00

The Farquharsen as made by Jeffery and his competitors, Holland & Holland, Bland, Westley, Manton. Large section on the development of nitro cartridges including the 600.

British Single Shot Rifles, Vol. 4; Westley Richards, by Wal Winfer, Rowe Publications, Rochester, N.Y., 2000. 265 pp., photos. $60.00

In this 4th volume, Winfer covers a detailed study of the Westley Richards single shot rifles, including Monkey Tails, Improved Martini, 1872,1873, 1878,1881, 1897 Falling Blocks. He also covers Westley Richards cartridges, history and reloading information.

]British Single Shot Rifles, Vol. 5; Holland & Holland, by Winfer, Wal, Rochester, NY: Rowe Publications, 2004. 1st edition. ISBN: 097076085X. Volume 5 of the never ending study of the British single shot. One of the rarest and finest quality single shots made by any British firm is described. A large section is devoted to the cartridge developments carried on by Hollands with a large section on their Paradox cartridges. One of the rarest and finest quality single shots made by any British firm is described. 218 pages. Hardcover. New in new dust jacket. (12063)

Broad Arrow: British & Empire Factory Production, Proof, Inspection, Armourers, Unit & Issue Markings, by Ian Skennerton. Australia, Arms & Militaria Press, 2001. 140 pp., circa 80 illus. Stiff paper covers. $29.95

Thousands of service markings are illustrated and their applications described. Invaluable reference on units, also ideal for medal collectors.

Browning Dates of Manufacture, compiled by George Madis, Art and Reference House, Brownsboro, TX, 1989. 48 pp. $7.50

Gives the date codes and product codes for all models from 1824 to the present.

The Browning Machine Gun Volume 1-Rifle Caliber Brownings in U.S. Service, by Dolf Goldsmith, Canada: Collector Grade Publications, 2005. 1st Edition, This profusely illustrated history covers all models of the U.S. Browning, from the first "gas hammer" Model 1895 and the initial recoil-operated Models of 1901 and 1910, through the adoption and manufacture of the famous water-cooled heavy Model 1917 during World War I and the numerous Interwar experimental tank and aircraft guns, most of which were built up on surplus M1917 receivers. 552 pp., 568 illustrations. Hardcover. New in new dust jacket. $79.95

Browning–Sporting Arms of Distinction 1903-1992, by Matt Eastman, Long Beach, CA, Safari Press, 2004. 428 pp., profuse illus. Hardcover. New in new dust jacket. $50.00

Browning Sporting Firearms: Dates of Manufacture, by D. R. Morse. Phoenix, AZ, Firing Pin Enterpizes, 2003. 37 pp. Softcover. New. $6.95

Covers their pistols, revolvers, rifles, shotguns and commemoratives, plus, models and serial numbers.

Bullard Firearms, by G. Scott Jamieson, Schiffer Publications, Atglen, PA 2002. 1st edition. 400 pp., with over 1100 color and b&w photographs, charts, diagrams. Hardcover. $100.00

Bullard Firearms is the story of a mechanical genius whose rifles and cartridges were the equal of any made in America in the 1880s, yet little of substance had been written about James H. Bullard or his arms prior to 1988 when the first edition, called Bullard Arms, was published. This greatly expanded volume answers many of the questions posed in the first edition. The final chapter outlines, in chart form, almost 500 Bullard rifles by serial number, caliber and type. Quick and easy to use, this book is a real benefit for collectors and dealers alike.

Burning Powder, compiled by Major D.B. Wesson, Wolfe Publishing Company, Prescott, AZ, 1992. 110 pp. Soft cover. $10.95

A rare booklet from 1932 for Smith & Wesson collectors.

The Burnside Breech Loading Carbines, by Edward A. Hull, Andrew Mowbray, Inc., Lincoln, RI, 1986. 95 pp., illus. $16.00

No. 1 in the "Man at Arms Monograph Series." A model-by-model historical/technical examination of one of the most widely used cavalry weapons of the American Civil War based upon important and previously unpublished research.

C.S. Armory Richmond: History of the Confederate States Armory, Richmond, VA and the Stock Shop at the C.S. Armory, Macon, GA., by Paul Davies, privately printed, 2000. 368 pp., illustrated with b&w photos. Hardcover. $75.00

The American Society of Arms Collectors is pleased to recommend C.S. Armory Richmond as a useful and valuable reference for collectors and scholars in the field of antique firearms. Gives fantastic explanations of machinery, stocks, barrels, and every facet of the production process during the timeframe covered in this book.

Cacciare A Palla: Uso E Tecnologia Dell'arma Rigata, by Marco E. Nobili, Italy, Il Volo Srl, 1994. 4th Edition–1st printing. 397 pp., illustrated with b&w photographs. Hardcover. New in new dust jacket. $75.00

The Call of Duty; Military Awards and Decorations of the United States of America, by John E. Strandberg, LTC and Roger James Bender, San Jose, CA, R. James Bender Publishing, 2005. (New expanded edition). 559 pp. illustrated with 1,293 photos (most in color). Hardcover. NEW. $67.95

Camouflage Uniforms of European and NATO Armies; 1945 to the Present, by J. F. Borsarello, Atglen, PA, Schiffer Publications. Over 290 color and b&w photographs, 120 pp. Softcover. $29.95

This full-color book covers nearly all of the NATO, and other European armies' camouflaged uniforms, and not only shows and explains the many patterns, but also their efficacy of design. Described and illustrated are the variety of materials tested in over 40 different armies, and includes the history of obsolete trial tests

from 1945 to the present time. This book provides a superb reference for the historian, reenactor, designer, and modeler.

Camouflage Uniforms of the Waffen-SS A Photographic Reference, by Michael Beaver, Schiffer Publishing, Atglen, PA. Over 1,000 color and b&w photographs and illustrations, 296 pp. $69.95

This book unveils the shroud of mystery surrounding Waffen-SS camouflage clothing. Illustrated here, both in color and b&w photographs, this unparalleled look at Waffen-SS combat troops and their camouflage clothing will benefit both the historian and collector.

Canadian Colts for the Boer War, by Col. Robert D. Whittington III. Hooks, TX, Brownlee Books, 2003. A limited edition of 1,000 copies. Numbered. 5 pp. Paper covers. New. $15.00

A study of Colt Revolvers issued to the First and Second Canadian Contingents Special Service Force.

Canadian Colts for the Boer War, Part 2, Col. Robert D. by Whittington III, Hooks, TX, Brownlee Books, 2005. A limited edition of 1,000 copies. Numbered. 5 pp. Paper covers, NEW. $5.00

Canadian Gunsmiths from 1608: A Checklist of Tradesmen, by John Belton, Historical Arms Series No. 29. Canada, Museum Restoration, 1992. 40 pp., 17 illustrations. Softcover. $8.95

This checklist is a greatly expanded version of HAS No. 14, listing the names, occupation, location, and dates of more than 1,500 men and women who worked as gunmakers, gunsmiths, armorers, gun merchants, gun patent holders, and a few other gun related trades. A collection of contemporary gunsmiths' letterhead have been provided to add color and depth to the study.

Canadian Miliitaria Directory & Sourcebook Second Edition, by Clive M. Law, Ont. Canada, Service Publications, 1998. pp. 90. Softcover. NEW. $14.95

Cap Guns, by James Dundas, Schiffer Publishing, Atglen, PA, 1996. 160 pp., illus. Paper covers. $29.95

Over 600 full-color photos of cap guns and gun accessories with a current value guide.

Carbines of the Civil War, by John D. McAulay, Pioneer Press, Union City, TN, 1981. 123 pp., illus. Paper covers. $12.95

A guide for the student and collector of the colorful arms used by the Federal cavalry.

Carbines of the U.S. Cavalry 1861-1905, by John D. McAulay, Andrew Mowbray Publishers, Lincoln, RI, 1996. $35.00

Covers the crucial use of carbines from the beginning of the Civil War to the end of the cavalry horse era in 1905.

Cartridge Carbines of the British Army, by Alan M. Petrillo, Excalibur Publications, Latham, NY, 1998. 72 pp., illus. Paper covers. $11.95

Begins with the Snider-Enfield which was the first regulation cartridge carbine introduced in 1866 and ends with the 303 caliber No.5, Mark 1 Enfield.

Cartridge Reloading Tools of the Past, by R.H. Chamberlain and Tom Quigley, Castle Rock, WA, 1998. 167 pp., illus. Paper covers. $25.00

A detailed treatment of the extensive Winchester and Ideal lines of handloading tools and bulletmolds plus Remington, Marlin, Ballard, Browning and many others.

Cartridges for Collectors, by Fred Datig, Pioneer Press, Union City, TN, 1999. Three volumes of 176 pp. each. Vol. 1 (Centerfire); Vol. 2 (Rimfire and Misc.) types. Volume 1, softcover only, $19.95. Volumes 2 and 3, hardcover. $19.95

Vol. 3 (Additional Rimfire, Centerfire, and Plastic.). All illustrations are shown in full-scale drawings.

Civil War Arms Makers and Their Contracts, edited by Stuart C. Mowbray and Jennifer Heroux, Andrew Mowbray Publishing, Lincoln, RI, 1998. 595 pp. $39.50

A facsimile reprint of the Report by the Commissioner of Ordnance and Ordnance Stores, 1862.

Civil War Arms Purchases and Deliveries, edited by Stuart C. Mowbray, Andrew Mowbray Publishing, Lincoln, RI, 1998. 300pp., illus. $39.50

A facsimile reprint of the master list of Civil War weapons purchases and deliveries including Small Arms, Cannon, Ordnance and Projectiles.

Civil War Battles of the Western Theatre, by Walter Crutcher (Foreword), Bryan S. Bush. Paducah, KY, Turner Publishing, 2000. 204 pp. Hardcover. New in new dust jacket. $39.89

Civil War Cartridge Boxes of the Union Infantryman, by Paul Johnson, Andrew Mowbray, Inc., Lincoln, RI, 1998. 352 pp., illus. $45.00

There were four patterns of infantry cartridge boxes used by Union forces during the Civil War. The author describes the development and subsequent pattern changes to these cartridge boxes. All updated prices, scores of new listings, and hundreds of new pictures!

Civil War Collector's Price Guide; 30th Anniversary 10th Edition, Orange, VA, Publisher's Press, 2003. All 260 pps., illus. Softcover. NEW. $34.95

Civil War Commanders, by Dean Thomas, Thomas Publications, Gettysburg, PA. 1998. 72 pp., illus., photos. Paper covers. $9.95

138 photographs and capsule biographies of Union and Confederate officers. A convenient personalities reference guide.

Civil War Heavy Explosive Ordnance: A Guide to Large Artillery Projectiles, Torpedoes, and Mines, by Jack Bell, Denton, TX, University of North Texas Press, 2003. 1,016 b&w photos. 537 pp. Hardcover. New in new dust jacket. $50.00

Civil War Infantryman: In Camp, on the March, and in Battle, by Dean Thomas, Thomas Publications, Gettysburg, PA. 1998. 72 pp., illus. Softcovers. $12.95

Uses first-hand accounts to shed some light on the "common soldier" of the Civil War from enlistment to muster-out, including camp, marching, rations, equipment, fighting, and more.

Civil War Pistols, by John D. McAulay, Andrew Mowbray Inc., Lincoln, RI, 1992. 166 pp., illus. $38.50

A survey of the handguns used during the American Civil War.

Civil War Relic Hunting A to Z, by Robert Buttafuso, Sheridan Books, 2000. 1st edition. illus., 91 pp., b&w illustrations. Softcover. NEW. $21.95

Civil War Sharps Carbines and Rifles, by Earl J. Coates and John D. McAulay, Thomas Publications, Gettysburg, PA, 1996. 108 pp., illus. Paper covers. $12.95

Traces the history and development of the firearms including short histories of specific serial numbers and the soldiers who received them.

Civil War Small Arms of the U.S. Navy and Marine Corps, by John D. McAulay, Mowbray Publishing, Lincoln, RI, 1999. 186 pp., illus. $39.00

The first reliable and comprehensive guide to the firearms and edged weapons of the Civil War Navy and Marine Corps.

Col. Burton's Spiller & Burr Revolver, by Matthew W. Norman, Mercer University Press, Macon, GA, 1997. 152 pp., illus. $22.95

A remarkable archival research project on the arm together with a comprehensive story of the establishment and running of the factory.

Cole Agee: Texas Engraver, by Howard Jink, Texas, Privately Printed, 2004. 1st Edition, SIGNED by the author. Hardcover. New in new dust jacket. $44.99

A compilation of pictures and stories about one of America's famous gun engravers who worked from the 1920s to 1955. Many fine examples of his work are pictured in this volume, with a strong emphasis on the Colt Single Action Army Revolver. A great book for the collector, historian, and firearms engraver.

Collecting Military Headgear; A Guide to 5000 Years of Helmet History, by Robert Atglen Attard, PA, Schiffer Publications, 2004. 1st edition. Hardcover. New in new dust jacket. $69.95

Collecting Third Reich Recordings, by Stuart McKenzie, San Jose, CA, R. James Bender Publishing, 2001. 1st edition. Softcover. NEW. $29.95

Collector's Illustrated Encyclopedia of the American Revolution, by George C. Neumann and Frank J. Kravic, Rebel Publishing Co., Inc., Texarkana, TX, 1989. 286 pp., illus. $42.95

A showcase of more than 2,300 artifacts made, worn, and used by those who fought in the War for Independence.

Colonel Thomas Claiborne Jr. and the Colt Whitneyville-Walker Pistol, by Col. Robert D. Whittington III, Hooks, TX, Brownlee Books, 2005. A limited edition of 1,000 copies. Numbered. 8 pp. Paper covers, NEW. $7.50

Colonels in Blue: Union Army Colonels of the Civil War, by Roger Hunt, New York, Atglen, PA, Schiffer Publications, 2003. 1st edition. 288 pp., with over 640 b&w photographs. Hardcover. New in new dust jacket. $59.95

Colonial Frontier Guns, by T.M. Hamilton, Pioneer Press, Union City, TN, 1988. 176 pp., illus. Paper covers. $17.50

A complete study of early flint muskets of this country.

The Colt 1909 Military Revolvers; The 1904 Thompson-Lagarde Report, and General John J. Pershing, by Col. Robert D. Whittington III, Hooks, TX, Brownlee Books, 2005. A limited edition of 1,000 copies. Numbered. 10 pp. Paper covers. NEW. $10.00

Colt and Its Collectors Exhibition Catalog for Colt: The Legacy of A Legend, Buffalo Bill Historical Center, Cody, Wyoming. Colt Collectors Association, 2003. 1st edition. Hardcover. New in new dust jacket. $125.00

Colt and Its Collectors accompanies the upcoming special exhibition, Colt: The Legacy of a Legend, opening at the Buffalo Bill Historical Center in May 2003. Numerous essays, over 750 color photographs by Paul Goodwin.

The Colt Armory, by Ellsworth Grant, Man-at-Arms Bookshelf, Lincoln, RI, 1996. 232 pp., illus. $35.00

A history of Colt's Manufacturing Company.

The Colt Engraving Book, Volumes I & II, by R. L. Wilson. Privately printed, 2001. Each volume is appx. 500 pp., with 650 illustrations, most in color. $390.00

This third edition from the original texts of 1974 and 1982 has been fine-tuned and dramatically expanded, and is by far the most illuminating and complete. With over 1,200 illustrations, more than 2/3 of which are in color, this book joins the author's The Book of Colt Firearms, and Fine Colts as companion volumes. Approximately 1,000 pages in two volumes, each signed by the author, serial numbered, and strictly limited to 3000 copies. Volume I covers from the Paterson and pre-Paterson period through c.1921 (end of the Helfricht period). Volume II commences with Kornbrath and Glahn, and covers Colt embellished arms from c.1919 through 2000.

The Colt Model 1905 Automatic Pistol, by John Potocki, Andrew Mowbray Publishing, Lincoln, RI, 1998. 191 pp., illus. $28.00

Covers all aspects of the Colt Model 1905 Automatic Pistol, from its invention by the legendary John Browning to its numerous production variations.

Colt Peacemaker British Model, by Keith Cochran, Cochran Publishing Co., Rapid City, SD, 1989. 160 pp., illus. $35.00

Covers those revolvers Colt squeezed in while completing a large order of revolvers for the U.S. Cavalry in early 1874, to those magnificent cased target revolvers used in the pistol competitions at Bisley Commons in the 1890s.

Colt Peacemaker Encyclopedia, by Keith Cochran, Cochran Publishing Co., Rapid City, SD, 1986. 434 pp., illus. $60.00

A must-have book for the Peacemaker collector.

Colt Peacemaker Encyclopedia, Volume 2, by Keith Cochran, Cochran Publishing Co., SD, 1992. 416 pp., illus. $60.00

Included in this volume are extensive notes on engraved, inscribed, historical and noted revolvers, as well as those revolvers used by outlaws, lawmen, movie and television stars.

Colt Pistols, Texas, and the U.S. Army 1847-1861, by Col. Robert D. Whittington III, Hooks, TX, Brownlee Books, 2005. A limited edition of 1,000 copies. Numbered. 8 pp. Paper covers, NEW. $7.50

Colt Presentations: From the Factory Ledgers 1856-1869, by Herbert G. Houze. Lincoln, RI, Andrew Mowbray, Inc., 2003. 112 pp., 45 b&w photos. Softcover. $21.95

Samuel Colt was a generous man. He also used gifts to influence government decision makers. But after Congress investigated him in 1854, Colt needed to hide the gifts from prying eyes, which makes it very difficult for today's collectors to document the many revolvers presented by Colt and the factory. Using the original account journals of the Colt's Patent Fire Arms Manufacturing Co., renowned arms authority Herbert G. Houze finally gives us the full details behind hundreds of the most exciting Colts ever made.

Colt Revolvers and the Tower of London, by Joseph G. Rosa, Royal Armouries of the Tower of London, London, England, 1988. 72 pp., illus. Softcover. $15.00

Details the story of Colt in London through the early cartridge period.

Colt Single Action Army Revolver Study: New Discoveries, by Kenneth Moore, Lincoln, RI, Andrew Mowbray, Inc., 2003. 1st edition. 200 pp., with 77 photos and illustrations. Hardcover. New. $49.95

25 years after co-authoring the classic Study of the Colt Single Action Army Revolver, Ken fills in the gaps and sets the record straight. Decades in the making, this impressive new study brings us entirely up to date, including all the new research that the author has painstakingly gathered over the years. The serial number data alone will astound you. Includes, ejector models, special section on low serial numbers, U.S. Army testing data, new details about militia S.A.A.'s plus a true wealth of cartridge info.

Colt Single Action Army Revolvers: The Legend, the Romance and the Rivals, by "Doc" O'Meara, Krause Publications, Iola, WI, 2000. 160 pp., illustrated with 250 photos in b&w and a 16-page color section. $22.95

Production figures, serial numbers by year, and rarities.

Colt Single Action Army Revolvers and Alterations, by C. Kenneth Moore, Mowbray Publishers, Lincoln, RI, 1999. 112 pp., illus. $35.00

A comprehensive history of the revolvers that collectors call "Artillery Models." These are the most historical of all S.A.A. Colts, and this new book covers all the details.

Colt Single Action Army Revolvers and the London Agency, by C. Kenneth Moore, Andrew Mowbray Publishers, Lincoln, RI, 1990. 144 pp., illus. $35.00

Drawing on vast documentary sources, this work chronicles the relationship between the London Agency and the Hartford home office.

Colt Sporting Firearms: Dates of Manufacture, by D.R. Morse, Phoenix, AZ, Firing Pin Enterprizes, 2003. 82 pp. Softcover. New. $6.95

Covers their pistols, revolvers, rifles, shotguns and commemoratives, plus models and serial numbers.

The Colt U.S. General Officers' Pistols, by Horace Greeley IV, Andrew Mowbray Inc., Lincoln, RI, 1990. 199 pp., illus. $38.00

These unique weapons, issued as a badge of rank to General Officers in the U.S. Army from WWII onward, remain highly personal artifacts of the military leaders who carried them. Includes serial numbers and dates of issue.

Colts from the William M. Locke Collection, by Frank Sellers, Andrew Mowbray Publishers, Lincoln, RI, 1996. 192 pp., illus. $55.00

This important book illustrates all of the famous Locke Colts, with captions by arms authority Frank Sellers.

Colt's Dates of Manufacture 1837-1978, by R.L. Wilson, published by Maurie Albert, Coburg, Australia; N.A. distributor Madis Books, TX, 1997. 61 pp. $7.50

An invaluable pocket guide to the dates of manufacture of Colt firearms up to 1978.

Colt's Pocket '49: Its Evolution Including the Baby Dragoon and Wells Fargo, by Robert Jordan and Darrow Watt, privately printed, Loma Mar, CA 2000. 304 pp., with 984 color photos, illus. Beautifully bound in a deep blue leather-like case. $125.00

Detailed information on all models and covers engaving, cases, accoutrements, holsters, fakes, and much more. Included is a summary booklet containing information such as serial numbers, production ranges and identifing photos. This book is a masterpiece on its subject.

Colt's SAA Post War Models, by George Garton, The Gun Room Press, Highland Park, NJ, 1995. 166 pp., illus. $39.95

Complete facts on the post-war Single Action Army revolvers. Information on calibers, production numbers and variations taken from factory records.

Combat Helmets of the Third Reich: A Study in Photographs, by Thomas Kibler, Pottsboro, TX, Reddick Enterprises, 2003. 1st edition. 96 pp., illustrated in full color. Pictorial softcover. NEW. $19.95

The Combat Perspective The Thinking Man's Guide to Self-Defense, by Gabriel Suarez, Boulder, CO, Paladin Press, 2003. 1st edition. 112 pp. Softcover. NEW. $15.00

Complete Guide to all United States Military Medals 1939 to Present, by Colonel Frank C. Foster, Medals of America Press, Fountain Inn, SC, 2000. 121 pp., illus., photos. $29.95

Complete criteria for every Army, Navy, Marine, Air Force, Coast Guard, and Merchant Marine award since 1939. All decorations, service medals, and ribbons shown in full color and accompanied by dates and campaigns, as well as detailed descriptions on proper wear and display.

Complete Guide to the M1 Garand and the M1 Carbine, by Bruce N. Canfield, 2nd printing, Andrew Mowbray Inc., Lincoln, RI, 1999. 296 pp., illus. $39.50

Expanded and updated coverage of both the M1 Garand and the M1 Carbine, with more than twice as much information as the author's previous book on this topic.

The Complete Guide to U.S. Infantry Weapons of the First War, by Bruce Canfield, Andrew Mowbray, Publisher, Lincoln, RI, 2000. 304 pp., illus. $39.95

The definitive study of the U.S. Infantry weapons used in WWI.

The Complete Guide to U.S. Infantry Weapons of World War Two, by Bruce Canfield, Andrew Mowbray, Publisher, Lincoln, RI, 1995. 303 pp., illus. $39.95

A definitive work on the weapons used by the United States Armed Forces in WWII.

Confederate Belt Buckles & Plates by Steve E. Mullinax, O'Donnell Publishing, Alexandria, VA, 1999. Expanded edition. 247 pp., illus. Hardcover. $34.00

Hundreds of crisp photographs augment this classic study of Confederate accoutrement plates.

Confederate Carbines & Musketoons Cavalry Small Arms Manufactured in and for the Southern Confederacy 1861-1865. by John M. Murphy, Santa Ana, CA, privately printed, 2002. Reprint. Hardcover. New in new dust jacket. $79.95

Confederate Rifles & Muskets: Infantry Small Arms Manufactured in the Southern Confederacy 1861-1865, by John M. Murphy. Santa Ana, CA, privately printed, 1996. Reprint. 768 pp., 8 pp. color plates, profusely illustrated. Hardcover. $119.95

The first in-depth and academic analysis and discussion of the "long" longarms produced in the South by and for the Confederacy during the American Civil War. The collection of Dr. Murphy is doubtless the largest and finest grouping of Confederate longarms in private hands today.

Confederate Saddles & Horse Equipment, by Ken R. Knopp, Orange, VA, Publisher's Press, 2002. 194 pps., illus. Hardcover. $39.95

Confederate Saddles & Horse Equipment is a pioneer work on the subject. After 10 years of research Ken Knopp has compiled a thorough and fascinating study of the little-known field of Confederate saddlery and equipment. His analysis of ordnance operations coupled with his visual presentation of surviving examples offers an indispensable source for collectors and historians.

Cooey Firearms, Made in Canada 1919-1979, by John A. Belton, Museum Restoration, Canada, 1998. 36pp., with 46 illus. Paper covers. $8.95

More than 6 million rifles and at least 67 models were made by this small Canadian riflemaker. They have been identified from the first 'Cooey Canuck' through the last variations made by the 'Winchester-Cooey'. Each is descibed and most are illustrated in this first book on the Cooey.

Cougar Attacks: Encounters of the Worst Kind, by Kathy Etling, New York, Lyons Press, 2004. 1st edition. Softcover. NEW. $14.95

Cowboy and Gunfighter Collectible, by Bill Mackin, Mountain Press Publishing Co., Missoula, MT, 1995. 178 pp., illus. Paper covers. $25.00

A photographic encyclopedia with price guide and makers' index.

Cowboy Collectibles and Western Memorabilia, by Bob Bell and Edward Vebell, Schiffer Publishing, Atglen, PA, 1992. 160 pp., illus. Paper covers. $29.95

The exciting era of the cowboy and the wild west collectibles including rifles, pistols, gun rigs, etc.

Cowboy Culture: The Last Frontier of American Antiques, by Michael Friedman, Schiffer Publishing, Ltd., West Chester, PA, 2002. 300 pp., illus. $89.95

Covers the artful aspects of the old west, the antiques and collectibles. Illustrated with clear color plates of over 1,000 items such as spurs, boots, guns, saddles, etc.

Cowboys and the Trappings of the Old West, by William Manns and Elizabeth Clair Flood, Zon International Publishing Co., Santa Fe, NM, 1997, 1st edition. 224 pp., illus. $45.00

A pictorial celebration of the cowboy dress and trappings.

Custer & His Wolverines: The Michigan Cavalry Brigade, 1861-1865, by Edward G. Longacre, Cambridge, MA, Da Capo Press, 2004. 2nd edition, 24 b&w photos, 5 maps; 6" x 9", 352 pp. Softcover. NEW. $18.00

Custom Firearms Engraving, by Tom Turpin, Krause Publications, Iola, WI, 1999. 208 pp., illus. $49.95

Over 200 four-color photos with more than 75 master engravers profiled. Engravers directory with addresses in the U.S. and abroad.

Daisy Air Rifles & BB Guns: The First 100 Years, by Neal Punchard. St. Paul, MN, Motorbooks, 2002. 1st edition. 10" x 10", 156 pp., 300 color. Hardcover. $29.95

Flash back to the days of your youth and recall fond memories of your Daisy. Daisy Air Rifles and BB Guns looks back fondly on the first 100 years of Daisy BB rifles and pistols, toy and cork guns, accessories, packaging, period advertising and literature.

The Decorations, Medals, Ribbons, Badges and Insignia of the United States Army; World War II to Present, by Col. Frank C. Foster, Medals of America Press, Fountain Inn, SC. 2001. 145 pp., illus. $29.95

The most complete guide to United States Army medals, ribbons, rank, insignia and patches from WWII to the present day. Each medal and insignia shown in full color. Includes listing of respective criteria and campaigns.

The Decorations, Medals, Ribbons, Badges and Insignia of the United States Navy; World War II to Present, by James G. Thompson, Medals of America Press, Fountain Inn, SC. 2000. 123 pp., illus. $29.95

The most complete guide to United States Army medals, ribbons, rank, insignia and patches from WWII to the present day. Each medal and insignia shown in full color. Includes listing of respective criteria and campaigns.

Defending the Dominion, Canadian Military Rifles, 1855-1955, by David Edgecombe. Service Publications, Ont., Canada, 2003. 168 pp., with 60+ illustrations. Hardcover. $39.95

This book contains much new information on the Canadian acquisition, use and disposal of military rifles during the most significant century in the development of small arms. In addition to the venerable Martini-Henry, there are chapters on the Winchester, Snider, Starr, Spencer, Peabody, Enfield rifles and others.

The Derringer in America, Volume 1, The Percussion Period, by R.L. Wilson and L.D. Eberhart, Andrew Mowbray Inc., Lincoln, RI, 1985. 271 pp., illus. $48.00

A long awaited book on the American percussion derringer.

The Derringer in America, Volume 2, the Cartridge Period, by L.D. Eberhart and R.L. Wilson, Andrew Mowbray Inc., Publishers, Lincoln, RI, 1993. 284 pp., illus. $65.00

Comprehensive coverage of cartridge derringers organized alphabetically by maker. Includes all types of derringers known by the authors to have been offered in the American market.

The Devil's Paintbrush: Sir Hiram Maxim's Gun, by Dolf Goldsmith, 3rd Edition, expanded and revised, Collector Grade Publications, Toronto, Canada, 2002. 384 pp., illus. $79.95

The classic work on the world's first true automatic machine gun.

Die Wehrmacht, Volume One, by Uwe Feist, Ryton Publications, Bellingham, WA, 2000. Large format (8-3/4" x 11-1/2") hardbound book with over 250 b&w photos and 240 color prints, all on high quality coated paper. Hardcover. $65.00

This is a great reference book, the first in a new series dedicated to the weapons, uniforms and equipment of the German Wehrmacht in WWII. Includes color photos of each weapon, plus hundreds of wartime photos.

Dressed For Duty: America's Women in Uniform, 1898-1973 Volume II, by Jill Halcomb Smith, San Nose, CA, Bender Publishing,2004. 1st edition. 44 pp., 1,300 photos & illustrations (many in color), deluxe binding. Hardcover. NEW. $59.95

Dr. Josephus Requa Civil War Dentist and the Billinghurst-Requa Volley Gun, by John M. Hyson Jr., and Margaret Requa DeFrancisco, Museum Restoration Service, Bloomfield, Ont., Canada, 1999. 36 pp., illus. Paper covers. $8.95

The story of the inventor of the first practical rapid-fire gun to be used during the American Civil War.

The Dutch Luger (Parabellum) A Complete History, by Bas J. Martens and Guus de Vries, Ironside International Publishers, Inc., Alexandria, VA, 1995. 268 pp., illus. $49.95

The history of the Luger in the Netherlands. An extensive description of the Dutch pistol and trials and the different models of the Luger in the Dutch service.

E.C. Prudhomme's Gun Engraving Review, by E. C. Prudhomme, R&R Books, Livonia, NY, 1994. 164 pp., illus. $60.00

As a source for engravers and collectors, this book is an indispensable guide to styles and techniques of the world's foremost engravers.

The Eagle on U.S. Firearms, by John W. Jordan, Pioneer Press, Union City, TN, 1992. 140 pp., illus. Paper covers. $17.50

Stylized eagles have been stamped on government owned or manufactured firearms in the U.S. since the beginning of our country. This book lists and illustrates these various eagles in an informative and refreshing manner.

Emblems of Honor; Patches and Insignia of the U.S. Army from the Great War to the Early Cold War Vol. IV Armor–Cavalry–Tank Destroyer, by Kurt Keller, Constabulary, PA, privately printed, 2005. 1st edition, signed. 232 pp., with over 600 color photos. Hardcover. New in new dust jacket. $59.95

The Emma Gees, by Capt. Herbert W. McBride, Mt. Ida, AR, Lancer Publishing, 2003. 224 pp., b&w photos. Softcover. NEW. $19.95

Encyclopedia of Rifles & Handguns; A Comprehensive Guide to Firearms, edited by Sean Connolly, Chartwell Books, Inc., Edison, NJ., 1996. 160 pp., illus. $26.00

Encyclopedia of United States Army Insignia and Uniforms, by William Emerson, OK, University of Oklahoma Press, 1996. Hardcover. NEW. $134.95

Enemies Foreign and Domestic, by Matthew Bracken, San Diego, CA, Steelcutter Publishing, 2003. Softcover. NEW. $19.89

Eprouvettes: A Comprehensive Study of Early Devices for the Testing of Gunpowder, by R.T.W. Kempers, Royal Armouries Museum, Leeds, England, 1999. 352 pp., illustrated with 240 b&w and 28 color plates. $125.00

Equipment of the WWII Tommy, by David Gordon, Missoula, MT, Pictorial Histories Publishing, 2004. 1st edition. Softcover. NEW. $24.95

Fifteen Years in the Hawken Lode, by John D. Baird, The Gun Room Press, Highland Park, NJ, 1976. 120 pp., illus. $24.95

A collection of thoughts and observations gained from many years of intensive study of the guns from the shop of the Hawken brothers.

Fighting Colors: The Creation of Military Aircraft Nose Art, by Gary Velasco, Paducah, KY, Turner Publishing, 2005. 1st edition. Hardcover. New in new dust jacket. $57.95

Fighting Iron, by Art Gogan, Andrew Mowbray, Inc., Lincoln, R.I., 2002. 176 pp., illus. $28.00

It doesn't matter whether you collect guns, swords, bayonets or accoutrement–sooner or later you realize that it all comes down to the metal. If you don't understand the metal, you don't understand your collection.

Fine Art of the West, by Byron Price, New York, Abbeville Press, 2004, 2nd revised edition. A glossary and bibliography complete this first comprehensive look at one of America's most fascinating forms of artistic expression.

276 pages illustrated with color photos. Hardcover . NEW. $75.00

Firearm Suppressor Patents; Volume 1: United States Patents, by N.R. Parker, Foreword by Alan C. Paulson, Boulder, CO, Paladin Press, 2004. 392 pp., illus. Softcover. NEW. $45.00

Firearms, by Derek Avery, Desert Publications, El Dorado, AR, 1999. 95 pp., illus. $9.95

The firearms included in this book are by necessity only a selection, but nevertheless one that represents the best and most famous weapons seen since the WWII.

ARMS LIBRARY

Firearms and Tackle Memorabilia, by John Delph, Schiffer Publishing, Ltd., West Chester, PA, 1991. 124 pp., illus. $39.95

A collector's guide to signs and posters, calendars, trade cards, boxes, envelopes, and other highly sought after memorabilia. With a value guide.

Firearms from Europe, 2nd Edition, by David Noe, Larry W. Yantz, Dr. James B. Whisker, Rowe Publications, Rochester, N.Y., 2002. 192 pp., illus. $45.00

A history and description of firearms imported during the American Civil War by the United States of America and the Confederate States of America.

Firearms of the American West 1803-1865, Volume 1, by Louis A. Garavaglia and Charles Worman, University of Colorado Press, Niwot, CO, 1998. 402 pp., illus. $79.95

Traces the development and uses of firearms on the frontier during this period.

Firearms of the American West 1866-1894, Volume 2, by Louis A. Garavaglia and Charles G. Worman, University of Colorado Press, Niwot, CO, 1998. 416 pp., illus. $79.95

A monumental work that offers both technical information on all of the important firearms used in the West during this period and a highly entertaining history of how they were used, who used them, and why.

Firepower from Abroad, by Wiley Sword, Andrew Mowbray Publishing, Lincoln, R.I., 2000. 120 pp., illus. $23.00

The Confederate Enfield and the LeMat revolver and how they reached the Confederate market.

Flayderman's Guide to Antique American Firearms and Their Values, 8th Edition, edited by Norm Flayderman, Krause Publications, Iola, WI, 2001. 692 pp., illus. Paper covers. $34.95

A completely updated and new edition with more than 3,600 models and variants extensively described with all marks and specifications necessary for quick identification.

Flintlock Fowlers: The First Guns Made in America, by Tom Grinslade, Texarkana, TX: Scurlock Publishing Co., 2005. 1st edition. 248 pages. Hardcover. New in new dust jacket. $75.00

The most complete compilation of fowlers ever in one book. Essential resource for collectors, builders and flintlock enthusiasts!

The FN-FAL Rifle, et al, by Duncan Long, Paladin Press, Boulder, CO, 1999. 144 pp., illus. Paper covers. $18.95

Detailed descriptions of the basic models produced by Fabrique Nationale and the myriad variants that evolved as a result of the firearms' universal acceptance.

Freund & Bro. Pioneer Gunmakers to the West, by F.J. Pablo Balentine, Graphic Publishers, Newport Beach, CA, 1997. 380 pp., illus. $69.95

The story of Frank W. and George Freund, skilled German gunsmiths who plied their trade on the Western American frontier during the final three decades of the nineteenth century.

The Fusil de Tulole in New France, 1691-1741, by Russel Bouchard, Museum Restorations Service, Bloomfield, Ontario, Canada, 1997. 36 pp., illus. Paper covers. $8.95

The development of the company and the identification of their arms.

The Gas Trap Garand, by Billy Pyle, Collector Grade Publications, Cobourg, Ontario, Canada, 1999 316 pp., illus. $59.95

The in-depth story of the rarest Garands of them all, the initial 80 Model Shop rifles made under the personal supervision of John Garand himself in 1934 and 1935, and the first 50,000 plus production "gas trap" M1's manufactured at Springfield Armory between August, 1937 and August, 1940.

George Schreyer, Sr. and Jr., Gunmakers of Hanover, Pennsylvania, by George Shumway, George Shumway Publishers, York, PA, 1990. 160pp., illus. $50.00

This monograph is a detailed photographic study of almost all known surviving longrifles and smoothbore guns made by highly regarded gunsmiths George Schreyer, Sr. and George Schreyer Jr.

German and Austrian Gunmakers Trade Catalogs, by George Hoyem, Jaeger Press, 2002. 252 pp. 8-1/2" x 11" case bound book with a four color dust jacket. Hardcover. New in new dust jacket. $60.00

Compiled by Hans E. Pfingsten and George A. Hoyem, containing five illustrated trade catalogues dating from 1914 to 1935, three of them export issues in German, English, French and Spanish.

German Anti-Tank Weapons–Panzerbuchse, Panzerfaust and Panzerschrek: Propaganda Series Volume 5, by DeVries and Martens. Alexandria,VA, Ironside Intl., 2005. 1st edition. 152 pp., illustrated with 200 high quality b&w photos, mot never published before. Hardcover, NEW. $38.95

The German Assault Rifle 1935-1945, by Peter R. Senich, Paladin Press, Boulder, CO, 1987. 328 pp., illus. $60.00

A complete review of machine carbines, machine pistols and assault rifles employed by Hitler's Wehrmacht during WWII.

German Belt Buckles 1845-1945: Buckles of the Enlisted Soldiers, by Peter Nash Atglen, PA, Schiffer Publications, 2003. 1st edition. Hardcover. New in new dust jacket. $59.95

German Camouflaged Helmets of the Second World War; Volume 1: Painted and Textured Camouflage, by Branislav Atglen Radovic, PA, Schiffer Publications, 2004. 1st edition. Hardcover. New in new dust jacket. $79.95

German Camouflaged Helmets of the Second World War; Volume 2: Wire, Netting, Covers, Straps, Interiors, Miscellaneous, by Branislav Atglen Radovic, PA, Schiffer Publications, 2004. 1st edition. Hardcover. New in new dust jacket. $79.95

German Cross in Gold–Holders of the SS and Police, by Mark Yerger, San Jose, CA, Bender Publishing, 2004. 1st edition. 432 pp., 295 photos and illustrations, deluxe binding. Hardcover. NEW. $44.95

German Cross in Gold–Holders of the SS and Police Volume 2-"Das Reich", by Mark Yerger, San Jose, CA, Bender Publishing, 2005. 1st edition. 432 pp., 295 photos and illustrations, deluxe binding. Hardcover. NEW. $44.95

The German K98k Rifle, 1934-1945: The Backbone of the Wehrmacht, by Richard D. Law, Collector Grade Publications, Toronto, Canada, 1993. 336 pp., illus. $69.95

The most comprehensive study ever published on the 14,000,000 bolt-action K98k rifles produced in Germany between 1934 and 1945.

German Machine Guns, by Daniel D. Musgrave, revised edition, Ironside International Publishers, Inc. Alexandria, VA, 1992. 586 pp., 650 illus. $49.95

The most definitive book ever written on German machine guns. Covers the introduction and development of machine guns in Germany from 1899 to the rearmament period after WWII.

German Military Abbreviations, by Military Intelligence Service, Canada, Service Publications. 268 pp. Stiff paper covers. NEW. $16.95

German Military Rifles and Machine Pistols, 1871-1945, by Hans Dieter Gotz, Schiffer Publishing Co., West Chester, PA, 1990. 245 pp., illus. $35.00

This book portrays, in words and pictures, the development of the modern German weapons and their ammunition, including the scarcely known experimental types.

German Paratroops: Uniforms, Insignia & Equipment of the Fallschirmjager in World War II, by Robert Atglen Kurtz, PA, Schiffer Publications, 2003. 1st edition. Hardcover. New in new dust jacket. $59.95

German Tanks of World War II in Color, by Michael Green; Thomas Anderson; Frank Schultz, St. Paul, MN, MBI Publishing Company, 2000. 1st edition. Softcover. NEW. $14.95

Gods and Generals Photographic Companion, by Rob Gibson and Dennis Frye. Gettysburg, PA, Thomas Publications, 2003. 1st edition. 88 pp. Softcover. NEW. $19.95

Gold Dust & Gunsmoke, by John Boessenecker, New York, John Wiley & Sons, 2000. 370 pp. Softcover. NEW. $10.00

Government Issue: U.S. Army European Theater of Operations Collector Guide, by Henry-Paul Enjames, Philippe Charbonnier, France, Histoire & Collections, 2004. Hardcover, NEW. $49.89

The Government Models, by William H.D. Goddard, Andrew Mowbray Publishing, Lincoln, RI, 1998. 296 pp., illus. $58.50

The most authoritative source on the development of the Colt model of 1911.

Grasshoppers and Butterflies, by Adrian B. Caruana, Museum Restoration Service, Alexandria Bay, N.Y., 1999. 32 pp., illus. Paper covers. $8.95

No.39 in the Historical Arms Series. The light 3 pounders of Pattison and Townsend.

The Greener Story, by Graham Greener, Quiller Press, London, England, 2000. 256 pp., illustrated with 32 pp. of color photos. $69.95

W.W. Greener, his family history, inventions, guns, patents, and more.

The Greenhill Dictionary of Guns and Gunmakers: From Colt's First Patent to the Present Day, 1836-2001, by John Walter, Greenhill Publishing, 2001, 1st edition, 576 pp., illustrated with 200 photos, 190 trademarks and 40 line drawings, Hardcover. $59.95

Covers military small arms, sporting guns and rifles, air and gas guns, designers, inventors, patentees, trademarks, brand names and monograms.

Grenade–British and Commonwealth Hand and Rifle Grenades, by Rick Landers, Norman Bonney and Gary Oakley. Australia, privately printed, 2001. 1st edition. 294 pp., illustrated with b&w photos drawings. Hardcover. New in new dust jacket. $69.95

Covers from Type No.1 to No. 95 includes dischargers, fuzes, markings, equipment.

The Gun and Its Development, by W.W. Greener, New York, Lyons Press, 2002. 9th Edition. Rewritten, and with many additional illustrations. 804 pp. plus advertising section. Contains over 700 illustrations plus many tables. Softcover. $19.95

A famed book of great value, truly encyclopedic in scope and sought after by firearms collectors.

Gun Powder Cans & Kegs, by Ted and David Bacyk and Tom Rowe, Rowe Publications, Rochester, NY, 1999. 150 pp., illus. $65.00

The first book devoted to powder tins and kegs. All cans and kegs in full color. With a price guide and rarity scale.

Gun Tools, Their History and Identification by James B. Shaffer, Lee A. Rutledge and R. Stephen Dorsey, Collector's Library, Eugene, OR, 1992. 375 pp., illus. $30.00

Written history of foreign and domestic gun tools from the flintlock period to WWII.

Gun Tools, Their History and Identifications, Volume 2, by Stephen Dorsey and James B. Shaffer, Collectors' Library, Eugene, OR, 1997. 396 pp., illus. Paper covers. $30.00

Gun tools from the Royal Armouries Museum in England, Pattern Room, Royal Ordnance Reference Collection in Nottingham and from major private collections.

Gunmakers of London 1350-1850 with Supplement, by Howard L. Blackmore, Museum Restoration Service, Alexandria Bay, NY, 1999. 222 pp., illus. Two volumes. Slipcased. $135.00

A listing of all the known workmen of gun making in the first 500 years, plus a history of the guilds, cutlers, armourers, founders, blacksmiths, etc. 260 gunmarks are illustrated. Supplement is 156 pages, and begins with an introductory chapter on "foreign" gunmakers followed by records of all the new information found about previously unidentified armourers, gunmakers and gunsmiths.

ARMS LIBRARY

The Guns of Dagenham: Lanchester, Patchett, Sterling, by Peter Laidler and David Howroyd, Collector Grade Publications, Inc., Cobourg, Ont., Canada, 1995. 310 pp., illus. $39.95

An in-depth history of the small arms made by the Sterling Company of Dagenham, Essex, England, from 1940 until Sterling was purchased by British Aerospace in 1989 and closed.

The Guns of Remington: Historic Firearms Spanning Two Centuries, compiled by Howard M. Madaus, Biplane Productions, Publisher, in cooperation with Buffalo Bill Historical Center, Cody, WY, 1998. 352 pp., illustrated with over 800 color photos. $79.95

A complete catalog of the firearms in the exhibition, "It Never Failed Me: The Arms & Art of Remington Arms Company" at the Buffalo Bill Historical Center, Cody, Wyoming.

Guns of the Third Reich, by John Walter, Pennsylvania, Stackpole Books, 2004. 1st edition. 256 pp., 60 illust. Hardcover. New in new dust jacket. $34.95

John Walter examines the full range of guns used by the Third Reich from the commercially successful Walter PP and PPK, to the double-action, personal defense pistols Mauser HSc and Sauer M38.

Guns of the Western Indian War, by R. Stephen Dorsey, Collector's Library, Eugene, OR, 1997. 220 pp., illus. Paper covers. $30.00

The full story of the guns and ammunition that made western history in the turbulent period of 1865-1890.

The Guns that Won the West: Firearms of the American Frontier, 1865-1898, by John Walter, Stackpole Books, Inc., Mechanicsburg, PA., 1999. 256 pp., illus. $34.95

Here is the story of the wide range of firearms from pistols to rifles used by plainsmen and settlers, gamblers, native Americans and the U.S. Army.

Gunsmiths of Illinois, by Curtis L. Johnson, George Shumway Publishers, York, PA, 1995. 160 pp., illus. $50.00

Genealogical information is provided for nearly 1,000 gunsmiths. Contains hundreds of illustrations of rifles and other guns, of handmade origin, from Illinois.

The Gunsmiths of Manhattan, 1625-1900: A Checklist of Tradesmen, by Michael H. Lewis, Museum Restoration Service, Bloomfield, Ont., Canada, 1991. 40 pp., illus. Paper covers. $8.95

This listing of more than 700 men in the arms trade in New York City prior to about the end of the 19th century will provide a guide for identification and further research.

Gunsmiths of Maryland, by Daniel D. Hartzler and James B. Whisker, Old Bedford Village Press, Bedford, PA, 1998. 208 pp., illus. $45.00

Covers firelock Colonial period through the breech-loading patent models. Featuring longrifles.

Gunsmiths of the Carolinas 1660-1870, by Daniel D. Hartzler and James B. Whisker, Old Bedford Village Press, Bedford, PA, 1998. 176 pp., illus. $40.00

This deluxe hard bound edition is printed on fine coated paper, with about 90 pages of large photographs of fine longrifles from the Carolinas, and about 90 pages of detailed research on the gunsmiths who created the highly prized and highly collectable longrifles.

Gunsmiths of Virginia, by Daniel D. Hartzler and James B. Whisker, Old Bedford Village Press, Bedford, PA, 1992. 206 pp., illus. $40.00

A photographic study of American longrifles.

Gunsmiths of West Virginia, by Daniel D. Hartzler and James B. Whisker, Old Bedford Village Press, Bedford, PA, 1998. 176 pp., illus. $40.00

A photographic study of American longrifles.

Gunsmiths of York County, Pennsylvania, by Daniel D. Hartzler and James B. Whisker, Old Bedford Village Press, Bedford, PA, 1998. 160 pp., illus. $40.00

Photographs and research notes on the longrifles and gunsmiths of York County, Pennsylvania.

Hand Forged for Texas Cowboys, by Kurt House, an Antonio, TX, Three Rivers Publishing, 2005. 160 pp. Hardcover. New in new dust jacket. $69.95

Harrington & Richardson Sporting Firearms: Dates of Manufacture 1871-1991, by D.R. Morse. Phoenix, AZ, Firing Pin Enterprizes, 2003. 14 pp. Softcover. NEW. $6.95

Covers their pistols, revolvers, rifles, shotguns and commemoratives, plus models.

The Hawken Rifle: Its Place in History, by Charles E. Hanson Jr., The Fur Press, Chadron, NE, 1979. 104 pp., illus. Paper covers. $15.00

A definitive work on this famous rifle.

Hi-Standard Sporting Firearms: Dates of Manufacture, by D.R. Morse. 1926-1992. Phoenix, AZ, Firing Pin Enterprizes, 2003. 22 pp. Softcover. New. $6.95

Covers their pistols, revolvers, rifles, shotguns and commemoratives, plus models and serial numbers.

High Standard: A Collector's Guide to the Hamden & Hartford Target Pistols, by Tom Dance, Andrew Mowbray, Inc., Lincoln, RI, 1991. 192 pp., illus. Paper covers. $24.00

From Citation to Supermatic, all of the production models and specials made from 1951 to 1984 are covered according to model number or series.

Historical Hartford Hardware, by William W. Dalrymple, Colt Collector Press, Rapid City, SD, 1976. 42 pp., illus. Paper covers. $10.00

Historically associated Colt revolvers.

The History of Colt Firearms, by Dean Boorman, Lyons Press, New York, NY, 2001. 144 pp., illus. $29.95

Discover the fascinating story of the world's most famous revolver, complete with more than 150 stunning full-color photographs.

History of Modern U.S. Military Small Arms Ammunition, Volume 1, 1880-1939, revised by F.W. Hackley, W.H. Woodin and E.L. Scranton, Thomas Publications, Gettysburg, PA, 1998. 328 pp., illus. $49.95

This revised edition incorporates all publicly available information concerning military small arms ammunition for the period 1880 through 1939 in a single volume.

The History of Smith & Wesson Firearms, by Dean Boorman, Lyons Press, New York, NY, 2002. 44 pp., illustrated in full color. Hardcover. New in new dust jacket. $29.95

The definitive guide to one of the world's best-known firearms makers. Takes the story through the years of the Military and Police 38 and of the Magnum cartridge, to today's wide range of products for law-enforcement customers.

The History of Winchester Rifles, by Dean Boorman, Lyons Press, New York, NY, 2001. 144 pp., illus. 150 full-color photos. $29.95

A captivating and wonderfully photographed history of one of the most legendary names in gun lore.

Holsters and Shoulder Stocks of the World, by Anthony Vanderlinden, Greensboro, NC, Wet Dog Publications, 2005. 1st edition. 204 pp., with over 1000 b&w photos. Hardcover. New in new dust jacket. $45.95

About 500 holsters and shoulder-stocks will be documented in this first edition. Pistols are listed by make and model. The user guide references the countries which used the holsters so that collectors can instantly refer to either a pistol model or country or use.

Honour Bound: The Chauchat Machine Rifle, by Gerard Demaison and Yves Buffetaut, Collector Grade Publications, Inc., Cobourg, Ont., Canada, 1995. $39.95

The story of the CSRG (Chauchat) machine rifle, the most manufactured automatic weapon of WWI.

Hunting Weapons from the Middle Ages to the Twentieth Century, by Howard L. Blackmore, Dover Publications, Meneola, NY, 2000. 480 pp., illus. Paper covers. $16.95

Dealing mainly with the different classes of weapons used in sport–swords, spears, crossbows, guns, and rifles–from the Middle Ages until the present day.

Identification Handbook of British Grenades 1900-1960 (Numerical Series), by Rick Landers, Norman Bonney and Gary Oakley. Australia. Privately printed, 2001. 1st edition. 48 pp., illustrated with b&w photos and drawings. Softcover. New. $10.95

Description, illustration and identification details of all British grenades in the numerical series.

Illustrations of United States Military Arms 1776-1903 and Their Inspector's Marks, compiled by Turner Kirkland, Pioneer Press, Union City, TN, 1988. 37 pp., illus. Paper covers. $7.00

Reprinted from the 1949 Bannerman catalog. Valuable information for both the advanced and beginning collector.

Imperial German Military Officers' Helmets and Headdress 1871-1918, by Thomas N.G. Stubbs, Atglen, PA, Schiffer Publications, 2003. 1st edition. Hardcover. New in new dust jacket. $79.95

Imperial Japanese Grenade Rifles and Launchers, by Gregory A. Babich and Thomas A. Keep Lemont, PA, Dutch Harlow Publishing, 2004. 1st edition. Hardcover. New in new dust jacket. $75.00

Indian Trade Relics, by Lar Hothem, Paducah, KY, Collector Books, 2003. 1st edition. 320pp. Pictorial Hardcover. NEW. $29.95

Indian War Cartridge Pouches, Boxes and Carbine Boots, by R. Stephen Dorsey, Collector's Library, Eugene, OR, 1993. 156 pp., illus. Paper covers. $20.00

The key reference work to the cartridge pouches, boxes, carbine sockets and boots of the Indian War period 1865-1890.

Individual Gear and Personal Items of the GI in Europe 1942-1945; From Pro-Kits to Pin-Up, by James Klokner, Atglen., PA, Schiffer Publications, 2005. 1st edition. 224 pages with over 470 color and b&w photographs. Hardcover. New in new dust jacket. $59.95

This book is by far the best and most complete study available of personal items of the American soldier during World War II and truly an indispensable resource.

International Armament, with History, Data, Technical Information and Photographs of Over 800 Weapons, 2nd edition, new printing, by George B. Johnson, Alexandria, VA, Ironside International, 2002. Hardcover. New in new dust jacket. $59.95

The development and progression of modern military small arms. All significant weapons have been included and examined in depth. Over 800 photographs and illustrations with both historical and technical data. Two volumes are now bound into one book.

Jaeger Rifles, Collected Articles Published in Muzzle Blasts, by George Shumway, York PA, 2003. Reprint. 108 pp., illus. Stiff paper covers. New. $30.00

Thirty-six articles previously published in Muzzle Blasts are reproduced here.

Japanese Rifles of World War Two, by Duncan O. McCollum, Excalibur Publications, Latham, NY, 1996. 64 pp., illus. Paper covers. $18.95

A sweeping view of the rifles and carbines that made up Japan's arsenal during the conflict.

Kalashnikov "Machine Pistols, Assault Rifles, and Machine Guns, 1945 to the Present", by John Walter, Stackpole Books, Mechanicsburg, PA 1999, hardcover, photos, illus., 146 pp. $22.95

This exhaustive work published by Greenhill Military Manuals features a gun-by-gun directory of Kalashnikov variants. Technical specifications and illustrations are provided throughout, along with details of sights, bayonets, markings and ammunition. A must for the serious collector and historian.

ARMS LIBRARY

The Kentucky Rifle, by Captain John G.W. Dillin, George Shumway Publisher, York, PA, 1993. 221 pp., illus. $50.00
  This well-known book was the first attempt to tell the story of the American longrifle. This edition retains the original text and illustrations with supplemental footnotes provided by Dr. George Shumway.
Legends and Reality of the AK, by Val Shilin and Charlie Cutshaw, Paladen Press, Boulder, CO, 2000. 192 pp., illus. Paper covers. $35.00
  A behind-the-scenes look at history, design and impact of the Kalashnikov family of weapons.
The Light 6-Pounder Battalion Gun of 1776, by Adrian Caruana, Museum Restoration Service, Bloomfield, Ontario, Canada, 2001. 76 pp., illus. Paper covers. $8.95
The London Gun Trade, 1850-1920, by Joyce E. Gooding, Museum Restoration Service, Bloomfield, Ontario, Canada, 2001. 48 pp., illus. Paper covers. $8.95
  Names, dates and locations of London gunmakers working between 1850 and 1920 are listed. Compiled from the original Kelly's post office directories of the City of London.
The London Gunmakers and the English Duelling Pistol, 1770-1830, by Keith R. Dill, Museum Restoration Service, Bloomfield, Ontario, Canada, 1997. 36 pp., illus. Paper covers. $8.95
  Ten gunmakers made London one of the major gunmaking centers of the world. This book examines how the design and construction of their pistols contributed to that reputation and how these characteristics may be used to date flintlock arms.
Longrifles of Pennsylvania, Volume 1, Jefferson, Clarion & Elk Counties, by Russel H. Harringer, George Shumway Publisher, York, PA, 1984. 200 pp., illus. $50.00
  First in series that will treat in great detail the longrifles and gunsmiths of Pennsylvania.
Lugers at Random, by Charles Kenyon Jr., Handgun Press, Glenview, IL, 1990. 420 pp., illus. $59.95
  A new printing of this classic, comprehensive reference for all Luger collectors.
The M-1 Carbine: A Revolution in Gun-Stocking, by Grafton H. Cook II and Barbara W. Cook, Lincoln, RI, Andrew Mowbray, Inc., 2002. 1st edition. 208 pp., heavily illustrated with 157 rare photographs of the guns and the men and women who made them. Softcover $29.95
  Shows you, step by step, how M1 carbine stocks were made, right through to assembly with the hardware. Learn about M1 Carbine development, and how the contracting and production process actually worked. Also contains lots of detailed information about other military weapons, like the M1A1, the M1 Garand, the M14 and much, much more.
M1 Carbine: Design, Development, and Production, by Larry Ruth, Gun Room Press, Highland Park, NJ, 1987. 291 pp., illus. Paper $19.95
  The origin, development, manufacture and use of this famous carbine of WWII.
The M1 Carbine Owner's Guide, by Larry Ruth and Scott A. Duff, Scott A. Duff Publications, Export, PA, 1997. 126 pp., illus. Paper covers. $21.95
  This book answers the questions M1 owners most often ask concerning maintenance activities not encountered by military users.
The M1 Garand: Owner's Guide, by Scott A. Duff, Scott A. Duff Publications, Export, PA, 1998. 132 pp., illus. Paper covers. $21.95
  This book answers the questions M1 owners most often ask concerning maintenance activities not encountered by military users.
The M1 Garand: Post World War, by Scott A. Duff, Scott A. Duff Publications, Export, PA, 1990. 139 pp., illus. Softcover. $21.95
  A detailed account of the activities at Springfield Armory through this period. International Harvester, H&R, Korean War production and quantities delivered. Serial numbers.
The M1 Garand: World War II, by Scott A. Duff, Scott A. Duff Publications, Export, PA, 2001. 210 pp., illus. Paper covers. $34.95
  The most comprehensive study available to the collector and historian on the M1 Garand of WWII.
The M1 Garand 1936 to 1957, by Joe Poyer and Craig Riesch, North Cape Publications, Tustin, CA, 1996. 216 pp., illus. Paper covers. $19.95
  Describes the entire range of M1 Garand production in text and quick-scan charts.
The M1 Garand Serial Numbers and Data Sheets, by Scott A. Duff, Scott A. Duff Publications, Export, PA, 1995. 101 pp., illus. Paper covers. $11.95
  Provides the reader with serial numbers related to dates of manufacture and a large sampling of data sheets to aid in identification or restoration.
Machine Guns, by Ian V. Hogg, Iola, WI, Krause Publications, 2002. 1st edition. 336 pp., illustrated with b&w photos with a 16-page color section. Softcover $29.95
  A detailed history of the rapid-fire gun, 14th Century to present. Covers the development, history and specifications.
Made in the C.S.A.: Saddle Makers of the Confederacy, by Ken R. Knopp, Hattiesburg, MS, privately printed, 2003. 1st edition signed. 205 pp., illus., signed by the author. Softcover. NEW. $30.00
Maine Made Guns and Their Makers, by Dwight B. Demeritt Jr., Maine State Museum, Augusta, ME, 1998. 209 pp., illus. $55.00
  An authoritative, biographical study of Maine gunsmiths.
Marksmanship in the U.S. Army, by William Emerson, Oklahoma, Univ. of Oklahoma Press, 2004 256 pages Illustrated with b&w photos. Hardcover. NEW $64.95
Marlin Firearms: A History of the Guns and the Company That Made Them, by Lt. Col. William S. Brophy, USAR, Ret., Stackpole Books, Harrisburg, PA, 1989. 672 pp., illus. $80.00
  The definitive book on the Marlin Firearms Co. and their products.

Martini-Henry .450 Rifles & Carbines, by Dennis Lewis, Excalibur Publications, Latham, NY, 1996. 72 pp., illus. Paper covers. $11.95
  The stories of the rifles and carbines that were the mainstay of the British soldier through the Victorian wars.
Mauser Bolt Rifles, by Ludwig Olson, F. Brownell & Son, Inc., Montezuma, IA, 1999. 364 pp., illus. $64.95
  The most complete, detailed, authoritative and comprehensive work ever done on Mauser bolt rifles. Completely revised deluxe 3rd edition.
Mauser Military Rifle Markings, by Terence W. Lapin, Arlington, VA, Hyrax Publishers, LLC, 2001. 167 pp., illus. 2nd edition. Revised and expanded. Softcover. $22.95
  A general guide to reading and understanding the often mystifying markings found on military Mauser rifles. Includes German Regimental markings as well as German police markings and WWII German Mauser subcontractor codes. A handy reference to take to gun shows.
Military Holsters of World War II, by Eugene J. Bender, Rowe Publications, Rochester, NY, 1998. 200 pp., illus. $45.00
  A revised edition with a new price guide of the most definitive book on this subject.
The Military Remington Rolling Block Rifle, by George Layman, Pioneer Press, TN, 1998. 146 pp., illus. Paper covers. $24.95
  A standard reference for those with an interest in the Remington rolling block family of firearms.
Military Rifles of Japan, 5th Edition, by F.L. Honeycutt, Julin Books, Lake Park, FL, 1999. 208 pp., illus. $42.00
  A new revised and updated edition. Includes the early Murata-period markings, etc.
Mortimer, the Gunmakers, 1753-1923, by H. Lee Munson, Andrew Mowbray Inc., Lincoln, RI, 1992. 320 pp., illus. $65.00
  Seen through a single, dominant, English gunmaking dynasty, this fascinating study provides a window into the classical era of firearms artistry.
The Mosin-Nagant Rifle, by Terence W. Lapin, North Cape Publications, Tustin, CA, 1998. 30 pp., illus. Paper covers. $19.95
  The first ever complete book on the Mosin-Nagant rifle written in English. Covers every variation.
Mossberg Sporting Firearms: Dates of Manufacture, by D.R. Morse, Phoenix, AZ, Firing Pin Enterprizes, 2003. Softcover. NEW. $6.95
  Covers their pistols, revolvers, rifles, shotguns and commemoratives, plus models and serial numbers.
The MP38, 40, 40/1 & 41 Submachine Gun, by de Vries & Martens. Propaganda Photo Series, Volume II. Alexandria, VA, Ironside International, 2001. 1st edition. 150 pp., illustrated with 200 high quality b&w photos. Hardcover. $34.95
  Covers all essential information on history and development, ammunition and accessories, codes and markings, and contains photos of nearly every model and accessory. Includes a unique selection of original German WWII propaganda photos, most never published before.
The Navy Luger, by Joachim Gortz and John Walter, Handgun Press, Glenview, IL, 1988. 128 pp., illus. $24.95
  The 9mm Pistole 1904 and the Imperial German Navy. A concise illustrated history.
The New World of Russian Small Arms and Ammunition, by Charlie Cutshaw, Paladin Press, Boulder, CO, 1998. 160 pp., illus. $42.95
  Detailed descriptions, specifications and first-class illustrations of the AN-94, PSS silent pistol, Bizon SMG, Saifa-12 tactical shotgun, the GP-25 grenade launcher and more cutting edge Russian weapons.
The Number 5 Jungle Carbine, by Alan M. Petrillo, Excalibur Publications, Latham, NY, 1994. 32 pp., illus. Paper covers. $7.95
  A comprehensive treatment of the rifle that collectors have come to call the "Jungle Carbine"– the Lee-Enfield Number 5, Mark 1.
Observations on Colt's Second Contract, November 2, 1847, by G. Maxwell Longfield and David T. Basnett, Museum Restoration Service, Bloomfield, Ontario, Canada, 1997. 36 pp., illus. Paper covers. $6.95
  This study traces the history and the construction of the Second Model Colt Dragoon supplied in 1848 to the U.S. Cavalry.
The Official Soviet SVD Manual, by Major James F. Gebhardt (Ret.), Paladin Press, Boulder, CO, 1999. 112 pp., illus. Paper covers. $22.00
  Operating instructions for the 7.62mm Dragunov, the first Russian rifle developed from scratch specifically for sniping.
Orders, Decorations and Badges of the Socialist Republic of Vietnam and the National Front for the Liberation of South Vietnam, by Edward J. Emering, Schiffer Publications, Atglen, PA. 2000. 96 pp., 190 color and b&w photographs, line drawings. $24.95
  The Orders and Decorations of the "enemy" during the Vietnam War have remained shrouded in mystery for many years. References to them are scarce and interrogations of captives during the war often led to the proliferation of misinformation concerning them. Includes value guide.
Ordnance Tools, Accessories & Appendages of the M1 Rifle, by Billy Pyle. Houston, TX, privately printed, 2002. 2nd edition. 206 pp., illustrated with b&w photos. Softcover $40.00
OSS Special Weapons II, by John Brunner, Williamstown, NJ, Phillips Publications, 2005, 2nd edition. 276pp. profusely illustrated with photos, some in color. Hardcover, New in New DJ. $59.95
The P-08 Parabellum Luger Automatic Pistol, edited by J. David McFarland, Desert Publications, Cornville, AZ, 1982. 20 pp., illus. Paper covers. $11.95
  Covers every facet of the Luger, plus a listing of all known Luger models.
Packing Iron, by Richard C. Rattenbury, Zon International Publishing, Millwood, NY, 1993. 216 pp., illus. $45.00
  The best book yet produced on pistol holsters and rifle scabbards. Over 300 variations of holster and scabbards are illustrated in large, clear plates.

Painted Steel, Steel Pots Volume 2, by Chris Armold, Bender Publishing, San Jose, CA, 2001. 384 pp., 1,053 photos, hundreds in color. $57.95

From the author of "Steel Pots: The History of America's Steel Combat Helmets" comes "Painted Steel: Steel Pots, Vol. II." This companion volume features detailed chapters on painted and unit marked helmets of WWI and WWII, plus a variety of divisional, regimental and subordinate markings. Special full-color plates detail subordinate unit markings such as the tactical markings used by the U.S. 2nd Division in WWI.

The Parker Gun Catalog 1900, by Parker Brothers, Davis, IL: Old Reliable Publishing, 1996. Reprint. Deluxe reprint, 15pp., illustrated. Stiff paper covers. $10.00

One of the most attractive and sought-after of the Parker gun catalogs, this one shows the complete Parker line circa 1900. This is the only catalog which pictures EH and NH grades, and is the first to picture $50.00 VH grade.

The Parker Gun Catalog 1910, by Parker Brothers, Davis, IL: Old Reliable Publishing, 1996. Reprint. Deluxe reprint, 20 pp., illustrated. Stiff paper covers. $10.00

One of the most attractive and sought-after of the Parker gun catalogs, this one shows the complete Parker line circa 1910.

The Parker Gun Catalog 1913 (Flying Ducks), by Parker Brothers, Davis, IL: Old Reliable Publishing, 1996. 36 pp., illustrated. Stiff paper covers. $20.00

One of the most attractive and sought-after of the Parker gun catalogs, this one shows the complete Parker line circa 1913. A deluxe reprint, it has the same embossed cover as the original "Flying Ducks" catalog.

Pattern Dates for British Ordnance Small Arms, 1718-1783, by DeWitt Bailey, Thomas Publications, Gettysburg, PA, 1997. 116 pp., illus. Paper covers. $20.00

The weapons discussed in this work are those carried by troops sent to North America between 1737 and 1783, or shipped to them as replacement arms while in America.

Percussion Ammunition Packets 1845-1888 Union, Confederate & European, by John J. Malloy, Dean S. Thomas and Terry A. White with Foreward by Norm Flayderman. Gettysburg, PA, Thomas Publications, 2003. 1st edition. 134 pp., illustrated with color photos. Hardcover. New. $75.00

Finally a means to recognize the untold variety of labeled types of ammunition box labels.

Peters & King, by Thomas D. Schiffer. Krause Publications, Iola, WI 2002. 1st edition. 256 pp., 200+ b&w photos with a 32-page color section. Hardcover. $44.95

Discover the history behind Peters Cartridge and King Powder and see how they shaped the arms industry into what it is today and why their products fetch hundreds, even thousands of dollars at auctions. Current values are provided for their highly collectible product packaging and promotional advertising premiums such as powder kegs, tins, cartridge boxes, and calendars.

Plates and Buckles of the American Military 1795-1874, by Sydney C. Kerksis, Orange, VA, Publisher's Press, 1998. 5th edition. 568 pp., illustrated with hundreds of b&w photos. Hardcover. $39.00

The single most comprehensive reference for U.S. and Confederate plates.

The Presentation and Commercial Colt Walker Pistols, by Col. Robert D. Whittington III, Hooks, TX, Brownlee Books, 2003. A limited edition of 1,000 copies. Numbered. 21 pp. Paper covers. New. $15.00

A study of events at the Whitneyville Armoury and Samuel Colt's Hartford Factory from 1 June 1847 to 29 November 1848.

Price Guide: Orders and Decorations Germany, 1871-1945, Second Edition, by Klaus Lubbe, Germany, Niemann,2004. 2nd edition. German and English text. 817 pp., over 2,000 photos. Hardcover. NEW. $104.95

It is a reference for prices as well as on the differences between the various orders, decorations, award documents, award cases of issue, and miniatures. No fantasy pieces are included, or projected orders which were never realized.

Production Statistics U.S. Arms Makers From Armalite to Winchester, by Phoenix, AZ, Firing Pin Enterprizes, 1997. 262 pp. Softcover. NEW. $19.95

Proud Promise: French Autoloading Rifles, 1898-1979, by Jean Huon, Collector Grade Publications, Inc., Cobourg, Ont., Canada, 1995. 216 pp., illus. $39.95

The author has finally set the record straight about the importance of French contributions to modern arms design.

Purdey Gun and Rifle Makers: The Definitive History, by Donald Dallas, Quiller Press, London, 2000. 245 pp., illus. Color throughout. A limited edition of 3,000 copies. Signed and numbered. With a PURDEY book plate. $99.95

The Queen Anne Pistol, 1660-1780: A History of the Turn-Off Pistol, by John W. Burgoyne, Bloomfield, Ont., Canada, Museum Restoration Service, 2002. 1st edition–Historical Arms New Series No. 1. 120 pp., a detailed, fast moving, thoroughly researched text and almost 200 cross-referenced illustrations. Pictorial hardcover. $35.00

This distinctive breech-loading arm was developed in the middle years of the 17th century but found popularity during the reign of the monarch (1702-1714), by whose name it is known.

Recreating the 18th Century Powder Horn, by Scott and Cathy Sibley, Texarcana, TX, Scurlock Publishing, 2005. 1st edition. 91 pp. Softcover. NEW. $19.95

Scott and Cathy Sibley demonstrates every detail and secret of recreating an 18th century powder horn. New and experienced horn makers will enjoy this how-to book. Lavishly illustrated with full-color photos and step-by-step illustrations.

Red Shines The Sun: A Pictorial History of the Fallschirm-Infantrie, by Eric Queen. San Jose, CA, R. James Bender Publishing, 2003. 1st edition. Hardcover. $69.95

A culmination of 12 years of research, this reference work traces the history of the Army paratroopers of the Fallschirm-Infanterie from their origins in 1937, to the

expansion to battalion strength in 1938, then on through operations at Wola Gulowska (Poland), and Moerdijk (Holland). This 240-page comprehensive look at their history is supported by 600 images, many of which are in full color, and nearly 90% are previously unpublished.

Reloading Tools, Sights and Telescopes for Single Shot Rifles, by Gerald O. Kelver, Brighton, CO, 1982. 163 pp., illus. Paper covers. $13.95

A listing of most of the famous makers of reloading tools, sights and telescopes with a brief description of the products they manufactured.

The Remington-Lee Rifle, by Eugene F. Myszkowski, Excalibur Publications, Latham, NY, 1995. 100 pp., illus. Paper covers. $22.50

Features detailed descriptions, including serial number ranges, of each model from the first Lee magazine rifle produced for the U.S. Navy to the last Remington-Lee small bore shipped to the Cuban Rural Guard.

Remington 'America's Oldest Gunmaker', The Official Authorized History of the Remington Arms Company, by Roy Marcot. Madison, NC, Remington Arms Company, 1999. 1st edition. 312 pp., with 167 b&w illustrations, plus 291 color plates. $79.95

This is without a doubt the finest history of that firm ever to have been compiled. Based on firsthand research in the Remington company archives, it is extremely well written.

Remington Sporting Firearms: Dates of Manufacture, by D.R. Morse, Phoenix, AZ, Firing Pin Enterprizes, 2003. 43 pp. Softcover. New. $6.95

Covers their pistols, revolvers, rifles, shotguns and commemoratives, plus models and serial numbers.

Remington's Vest Pocket Pistols, by Robert E. Hatfield, Lincoln, RI, Andrew Mowbray, Inc., 2002. 117 pp. Hardcover. $29.95

While Remington Vest Pocket pistols have always been popular with collectors, very little solid information has been available about them. Inside you will find 100+ photographs, serial number data, exploded views of all four Remington Vest Pocket pistol sizes, component parts lists and a guide to disassembly and reassembly. Also includes a discussion of Vest Pocket Wire-Stocked Buggy/Bicycle rifles, plus the documented serial number story.

Revolvers of the British Services 1854-1954, by W.H.J. Chamberlain and A.W.F. Taylerson, Museum Restoration Service, Ottawa, Canada, 1989. 80 pp., illus. $27.50

Covers the types issued among many of the United Kingdom's naval, land or air services.

Rifles of the U.S. Army 1861-1906, by John D. McAulay, Andrew Mowbray, Inc., Lincoln, RI, 2003. 1st edition. Over 40 rifles covered, 278 pp., illus. Hardcover. New. $47.95

There have been several excellent books written about the manufacture of rifles for the U.S. Army from the time of the Civil War to the early 20th century. However, few of these books have focused upon what happened to these rifles after they were issued. This exciting new book by renowned authority John McAulay fills this gap. It gives the reader detailed coverage of the issue and actual field service of America's fighting rifles, both in peacetime and in war, including their military service with the infantry, artillery, cavalry and engineers.

One feature that all readers will value is the impressive number of historical photos, taken during the Civil War, the Mexican War, the Indian Wars, the Spanish-American War, the Philippine Insurrection and more, showing these rifles in the hands of the men who fought with them. Procurement information, issue details and historical background.

Ruger and his Guns, by R.L. Wilson, Simon & Schuster, New York, NY, 1996. 358 pp., illus. $29.95

A history of the man, the company and their firearms.

Running Recon: A Photo Jorney with SOG Special Ops Along the Ho Chi Minh Trail, by Frank Grecco. Boulder, CO: Paladin Press, 2004. 1st edition.

Running Recon is a combination of military memoir and combat photography book. It reflects both the author's experience in Kontum, Vietnam, from April 1969 to April 1970 as part of the top-secret Studies and Observation Group (SOG) and the collective experience of SOG veterans in general. Hardcover. NEW. $79.95

Russell M. Catron and His Pistols, by Warren H. Buxton, Ucross Books, Los Alamos, NM, 1998. 224 pp., illus. Paper covers. $49.50

An unknown American firearms inventor and manufacturer of the mid-twentieth century. Military, commerical, ammunition.

The SAFN-49 and the FAL, by Joe Poyer and Dr. Richard Feirman, North Cape Publications, Tustin, CA, 1998. 160 pp., illus. Paper covers. $14.95

The first complete overview of the SAFN-49 battle rifle, from its pre-WWII beginnings to its military service in countries as diverse as the Belgian Congo and Argentina. The FAL was a "light" version of the SAFN-49 and it became the Free World's most adopted battle rifle.

Savage Sporting Firearms: Dates of Manufacture 1907-1997, by D.R. Morse. Phoenix, AZ, Firing Pin Enterprizes, 2003. 22 pp. Softcover. New. $6.95

Covers their pistols, revolvers, rifles, shotguns and commemoratives, plus models and serial numbers.

Scale Model Firearms, by Joseph D. Kramer. Pittsburgh, PA, privately printed, 1999. 1st edition. 136 pp., oversize, many color photos, index. Softcover. New. $35.00

Each of the models, which are nearly all in one-half scale, require a year or more to complete and in most cases only one example was made. Mr. R. E. Hutchen's uncompromising devotion to the production of these models, is a tribute to a man who is known internationally to be the finest maker of model firearms in the world.

Scottish Firearms, by Claude Blair and Robert Woosnam-Savage, Museum Restoration Service, Bloomfield, Ont., Canada, 1995. 52 pp., illus. Paper covers. $8.95

This revision of the first book devoted entirely to Scottish firearms is supplemented by a register of surviving Scottish long guns.

Sharps Firearms, by Frank Seller, Denver, CO, 1998. 358 pp., illus. $59.95

Traces the development of Sharps firearms with full range of guns made including all martial variations.

The Sight Book; Winchester, Lyman, Marble, and Other Companies, by George Madis, Borwsboro,TX, Art & Reference House, 2005. 1st edition. 183 page, with over 350 illustrations. Hardcover. NEW. $26.95

Silk and Steel: Women at Arms, by R. L. Wilson, New York, Random House, 2003. 1st edition. 300+ Striking four-color images; 8-1/2" x 11", 320 pp. Hardcover. New in new dust jacket. (9775). $65.00

Beginning with Artemis and Diana, goddesses of hunting, evolving through modern times, here is the first comprehensive presentation on the subject of women and firearms. No object has had a greater impact on world history over the past 650 years than the firearm, and a surprising number of women have been keen on the subject, as shooters, hunters, collectors, engravers, and even gunmakers.

The SKS Carbine, by Steve Kehaya and Joe Poyer, North Cape Publications, Tustin, CA, 1997. 150 pp., illus. Paper covers. $16.95

The first comprehensive examination of a major historical firearm used through the Vietnam conflict to the diamond fields of Angola.

The SKS Type 45 Carbines, by Duncan Long, Desert Publications, El Dorado, AZ, 1992. 110 pp., illus. Paper covers. $19.95

Covers the history and practical aspects of operating, maintaining and modifying this abundantly available rifle.

Slave Badges and the Slave-Hire System in Charleston, South Carolina, 1783- 1865, by Harlan Greene, Harry S. Hutchins Jr., Brian E. Hutchins. Jefferson, NC, McFarland & Company, 2004. 152 pp. Hardcover, NEW. $35.00

Smith & Wesson 1857-1945, by Robert J. Neal and Roy G. Jinks, R&R Books, Livonia, NY, 1996. 434 pp., illus. $50.00

The bible for all existing and aspiring Smith & Wesson collectors.

Smith & Wesson Sporting Firearms: Dates of Manufacture, by D.R. Morse, Phoenix, AZ, Firing Pin Enterprizes, 2003. 76 pp. Softcover. NEW. $6.95

Covers their pistols, revolvers, rifles, shotguns and commemoratives, plus models and serial numbers.

Sniper Variations of the German K98k Rifle, by Richard D. Law, Collector Grade Publications, Ontario, Canada, 1997. 240 pp., illus. $47.50

Volume 2 of "Backbone of the Wehrmacht" the author's in-depth study of the German K98k rifle. This volume concentrates on the telescopic-sighted rifle of choice for most German snipers during WWII.

Southern Derringers of the Mississippi Valley, by Turner Kirkland, Pioneer Press, Tenn., 1971. 80 pp., illus., paper covers. $4.00

A guide for the collector and a much-needed study.

Soviet Russian Tokarev "TT" Pistols and Cartridges 1929-1953, by Fred Datig, Graphic Publishers, Santa Ana, CA, 1993. 168 pp., illus. $39.95

Details of rare arms and their accessories are shown in hundreds of photos. It also contains a complete bibliography and index.

Spencer Repeating Firearms, by Roy M. Marcot, New York, Rowe Publications, 2002. 316 pp.; numerous b&w photos and illustrations. Hardcover. $65.00

Sporting Collectibles, by Jim and Vivian Karsnitz, Schiffer Publishing Ltd., West Chester, PA, 1992. 160 pp., illus. Paper covers. $29.95

The fascinating world of hunting related collectibles presented in an informative text.

The Springfield 1903 Rifles, by Lt. Col. William S. Brophy, USAR, Ret., Stackpole Books Inc., Harrisburg, PA, 1985. 608 pp., illus. $75.00

The illustrated, documented story of the design, development, and production of all the models, appendages, and accessories.

SS Headgear, by Kit Wilson. Johnson Reference Books, Fredericksburg, VA. 72 pp., 15 full-color plates and over 70 b&w photos. $16.50

An excellent source of information concerning all types of SS headgear, to include Allgemeine- SS, Waffen-SS, visor caps, helmets, overseas caps, M-43's and miscellaneous headgear. Also includes a guide on the availability and current values of SS headgear. This guide was compiled from auction catalogs, dealer price lists, and input from advanced collectors in the field.

SS Helmets: A Collector's Guide, Vol 1, by Kelly Hicks, Johnson Reference Books, Fredericksburg, VA. 96 pp., illus. $17.50

Deals only with SS helmets and features some very nice color close-up shots of the different SS decals used. Over 85 photographs, 27 in color. The author has documented most of the known types of SS helmets, and describes in detail all of the vital things to look for in determining the originality, style type, and finish.

SS Helmets: A Collector's Guide, Vol 2, by Kelly Hicks. Johnson Reference Books, Fredericksburg, VA. 2000. 128 pp. 107 full-color photos, 14 period photos. $25.00

Volume II contains dozen of highly detailed, full-color photos of rare and original SS and Field Police helmets, featuring both sides as well as interior view. The outstanding decal section offers detailed close-ups of original SS and Police decals, and in conjunction with Volume I, completes the documentation of virtually all types of original decal variations used between 1934 and 1945.

SS Steel; Parade and Combat Helmets of Germany's Third Reich Elite, by Kelly Hicks, San Jose, CA, Bender Publishing, 2004. 1st edition. 241 pp., 400 photos and illustrations in color, deluxe binding. Hardcover. NEW. $44.95

SS Uniforms, Insignia and Accoutrements, by A. Hayes. Schiffer Publications, Atglen, PA. 1996. 248 pp., with over 800 color and b&w photographs. $69.95

This new work explores in detailed color the complex subject of Allgemeine and Waffen-SS uniforms, insignia, and accoutrements. Hundreds of authentic items are extensively photographed in close-up to enable the reader to examine and study.

Sturmgewehr! From Firepower to Striking Power, by Hans-Dieter Handrich. Canada, Collector Grade, 2004. 1st edition. 600 pp., 392 illustrations. Hardcover. New in new dust jacket. $77.50

Hans-Dieter Handrich, prize winning German military historian, has spent years researching original documentation held in the military archives of Germany and elsewhere to produce the entire technical and tactical history of the design, development and fielding of the world's first mass-produced assault rifle and the revolutionary 7.92x33mm kurz cartridge.

Sturm Ruger Sporting Firearms: Dates of Manufacture, by D.R. Morse, Phoenix, AZ, Firing Pin Enterprizes, 2003. 22 pp. Softcover, NEW. $6.95

Covers their pistols, revolvers, rifles, shotguns and commemoratives, plus models and serial numbers.

The Sumptuous Flaske, by Herbert G. Houze, Andrew Mowbray, Inc., Lincoln, RI, 1989. 158 pp., illus. Softcover. $35.00

Catalog of a recent show at the Buffalo Bill Historical Center bringing together some of the finest European and American powder flasks of the 16th to 19th centuries.

The Swedish Mauser Rifles, by Steve Kehaya and Joe Poyer, North Cape Publications, Tustin, CA, 1999. 267 pp., illus. Paper covers. $19.95

Every known variation of the Swedish Mauser carbine and rifle is described, all match and target rifles and all sniper versions. Includes serial number and production data.

System Lefaucheaux: Continuing the Study of Pinfire Cartridge Arms Including Their Role in the American Civil War, by Chris C. Curtis, Foreword by Norm Flayderman, Armslore Press, 2002. 1st edition. 312 pp., heavily illustrated with b&w photos. Hardcover. New in new dust jacket. $44.95

Tombstone-The Guns and Gear, by Peter Sherayko, Boise, ID, Shoot Magazine Corp., 2004. 248 pp. Hardcover. New in new dust jacket. $39.50

Written by Peter Sherayko (Texas Jack Vermillion in the film), this book answers the questions that gun enthusiasts have asked since the film's release, and is designed to be a guide to functional originals and quality reproductions for moviemakers, reenactors, and collectors alike. This is a hardbound book with over 400 color pictures of original and replica guns, holsters, saddles, knives, spurs and clothing.

Thompson: The American Legend, by Tracie L. Hill, Collector Grade Publications, Ontario, Canada, 1996. 584 pp., illus. $85.00

The story of the first American submachine gun. All models are featured and discussed.

Thoughts on the Kentucky Rifle in its Golden Age, by Joe K. Kindig, III. York, PA, George Shumway Publisher, 2002. Annotated second edition. 561 pp.; Illustrated. This scarce title, long out of print, is once again available. Hardcover. $85.00

The definitive book on the Kentucky Rifle, illustrating 266 of these guns in 856 detailed photographs.

Tin Lids–Canadian Combat Helmets, #2 in "Up Close" Series, by Roger V. Lucy, Ottawa, Ontario, Service Publications, 2000. 2nd edition. 48 pp. Softcover. NEW. $17.95

Toys That Shoot and Other Neat Stuff, by James Dundas, Schiffer Books, Atglen, PA, 1999. 112 pp., illus. Paper covers. $24.95

Shooting toys from the twentieth century, especially 1920s to 1960s, in over 420 color photographs of BB guns, cap shooters, marble shooters, squirt guns and more. Complete with a price guide.

Trade Guns of the Hudson's Bay Company 1670-1970, Historical Arms New Series No. 2. by S. James Gooding, Bloomfield, Ont. Canada, Museum Restoration Service, 2003. 1st edition. 158 pp., thoroughly researched text. Includes bibliographical references. Pictorial hardcover. NEW. $35.00

The Trapdoor Springfield, by M.D. Waite and B.D. Ernst, The Gun Room Press, Highland Park, NJ, 1983. 250 pp., illus. $39.95

The first comprehensive book on the famous standard military rifle of the 1873-92 period.

Treasures of the Moscow Kremlin: Arsenal of the Russian Tsars, A Royal Armories and the Moscow Kremlin exhibition, HM Tower of London 13, June 1998 to 11 September, 1998. BAS Printers, Over Wallop, Hampshire, England. xxii plus 192 pp. over 180 color illustrations. Text in English and Russian. $65.00

For this exhibition catalog, each of the 94 objects on display are photographed and described in detail to provide the most informative record of this important exhibition.

U.S. Army Headgear 1812-1872, by John P. Langellier and C. Paul Loane. Atglen, PA, Schiffer Publications, 2002. 167 pp., with over 350 color and b&w photos. Hardcover. $69.95

This profusely illustrated volume represents more than three decades of research in public and private collections by military historian John P. Langellier and Civil War authority C. Paul Loane.

U.S. Army Rangers & Special Forces of World War II Their War in Photographs, by Robert Todd Ross, Atglen, PA, Schiffer Publications, 2002. 216 pp., over 250 b&w and color photographs. Hardcover. $59.95

Never before has such an expansive view of WWII elite forces been offered in one volume. An extensive search of public and private archives unearthed an astonishing number of rare and never before seen images, including color. Most notable are the nearly 20 exemplary photographs of Lieutenant Colonel William O. Darby's Ranger Force in Italy, taken by Robert Capa, considered by many to be the greatest combat photographer of all time.

U.S. Guns of World War II, by Paul Davies, Gettysburg, PA, Thomas Publications, 2004. 1st edition. 144 pp., Softcover. NEW. $17.95

A record of army ordnance research and the development of small arms. Hundreds of photos.

U.S. Handguns of World War II: The Secondary Pistols and Revolvers, by Charles W. Pate, Andrew Mowbray, Inc., Lincoln, RI, 1998. 515 pp., illus. $39.00
This indispensable new book covers all of the American military handguns of WWII except for the M1911A1 Colt automatic.

U.S. Martial Single Shot Pistols, by Daniel D. Hartzler and James B. Whisker, Old Bedford Village Press, Bedford, PA, 1998. 128 pp., illus. $45.00
A photographic chronicle of military and semi-martial pistols supplied to the U.S. Government and the several States.

U.S. Military Arms Dates of Manufacture from 1795, by George Madis, Dallas, TX, 1995. 64 pp. Softcover. $9.95
Lists all U.S. military arms of collector interest alphabetically, covering about 250 models.

U.S. M1 Carbines: Wartime Production, by Craig Riesch, North Cape Publications, Tustin, CA, 1994. 72 pp., illus. Paper covers. $16.95
Presents only verifiable and accurate information. Each part of the M1 Carbine is discussed fully in its own section; including markings and finishes.

U.S. Naval Handguns, 1808-1911, by Fredrick R. Winter, Andrew Mowbray Publishers, Lincoln, RI, 1990. 128 pp., illus. $26.00
The story of U.S. Naval handguns spans an entire century–included are sections on each of the important naval handguns within the period.

U.S. Silent Service–Dolphins & Combat Insignia 1924-1945, by David Jones. Bender Publishing, San Jose, CA, 2001. 224 pp., 532 photos (most in full color). $39.95
After eight years of extensive research, the publication of this book is a submarine buff and collector's dream come true. This beautiful full-color book chronicles, with period letters and sketches, the developmental history of U.S. submarine insignia prior to 1945. It also contains many rare and never before published photographs, plus interviews with WWII submarine veterans, from enlisted men to famous skippers. All known contractors are covered plus embroidered versions, mess dress variations, the Roll of Honor, submarine combat insignia, battleflags, launch memorabilia and related submarine collectibles (postal covers, match book covers, jewelry, posters, advertising art, postcards, etc.).

Uniform and Dress Army and Navy of the Confederate States of America (Official Regulations), by Confederate States of America., Ray Riling Arms Books, Philadelphia, PA, 1960. $20.00
A portfolio containing a complete set of nine color plates especially prepared for framing, reproduced in exactly 200 sets from the very rare Richmond, VA., 1861 regulations.

Uniforms & Equipment of the Austro-Hungarian Army in World War One, by Spencer A. Coil, Atglen, PA, Schiffer Publications, 2003. 1st edition. 352 pp., with over 550 b&w and color photographs. Hardcover. New in new dust jacket. $69.95

Uniforms and Insignia of the Cossacks in the German Wehrmacht in World War II, by Peter Schuster and Harald Tiede, Atglen, PA, Schiffer Publications, 2003. 1st edition. 160 pp., illustrated with over 420 b&w and color photographs. Hardcover. New in new dust jacket. $49.95

Uniforms & Equipment of the Imperial German Army 1900-1918: A Study in Period Photographs, by Charles Woolley, Schiffer Publications, Atglen, PA, 2000. 375 pp., over 500 b&w photographs and 50 color drawings. Fully illustrated. $69.95
Features formal studio portraits of pre-war dress and wartime uniforms of all arms. Also contains photo postal cards taken in the field of Infantry, Pionier, Telegraph-Signal, Landsturm, and Mountain Troops, vehicles, artillery, musicians, the Bavarian Leib Regiment, specialized uniforms and insignia, small arms close-ups, unmotorized transport, group shots and Balloon troops and includes a 60-page full-color uniform section reproduced from rare 1914 plates.

Uniforms of the Third Reich: A Study in Photographs, by Maguire Hayes, Schiffer Publications, Atglen, PA, 1997. 200 pp., with over 400 color photographs. $69.95
This new book takes a close look at a variety of authentic WWII era German uniforms including examples from the Army, Luftwaffe, Kriegsmarine, Waffen-SS, Allgemeine-SS, Hitler youth and political leaders. The pieces are shown in large full frame front and rear shots, and in painstaking detail to show tailors' tags, buttons, insignia detail etc. and allow the reader to see what the genuine article looks like. Various accoutrements worn with the uniforms are also included to aid the collector.

Uniforms of the United States Army, 1774-1889, by Henry Alexander Ogden, Dover Publishing, Mineola, NY. 1998. 48 pp. of text plus 44 color plates. Softcover. $9.95
A republication of the work published by the quarter-master general, United States army in 1890. A striking collection of lithographs and a marvelous archive of military, social, and costume history portraying the gamut of U.S. Army uniforms from fatigues to full dress, between 1774 and 1889.

Uniforms of the Waffen-SS; Black Service Uniform–LAH Guard Uniform–SS Earth-Grey Service Uniform–Model 1936 Field Service Uniform–1939-1940–1941 Volume 1, by Michael D. Beaver, Schiffer Publications, Atglen, PA, 2002. 272 pp., with 500 color, and b&w photos. $79.95
This spectacular work is a heavily documented record of all major clothing articles of the Waffen- SS. Hundreds of unpublished photographs were used in production. Original and extremely rare SS uniforms of various types are carefully photographed and presented here. Among the subjects covered in this multi volume series are field-service uniforms, sports, drill, dress, armored personnel, tropical, and much more. This book is indispensable and an absolute must- have for any serious historian of WWII German uniforms.

Uniforms of the Waffen-SS; Sports and Drill Uniforms–Black Panzer Uniform–Camouflage–Concentration Camp Personnel-SD-SS Female Auxiliaries, Volume 3, by Michael D. Beaver, Schiffer Publications, Atglen, PA, 2002. 272 pp., with 500 color, and b&w photos. $79.95

Uniforms of the Waffen-SS; 1942-1943–1944-1945–Ski Uniforms–Overcoats–White Service Uniforms–Tropical Clothing, Volume 2, by Michael D. Beaver, Schiffer Publications, Atglen, PA, 2002. 272 pp., with 500 color, and b&w photos. $79.95

Uniforms, Organization, and History of the German Police, Volume I, by John R. Angolia and Hugh Page Taylor, San Jose, CA, R. James Bender Publishing, 2004. 704 pp. illustrated with b&w and color photos. Hardcover. NEW. $59.95

Uniforms, Organization, and History of the NSKK/NSFK, by John R. Angolia and David Littlejohn, Bender Publishing, San Jose, CA, 2000. $44.95
This work is part of the on-going study of political organizations that formed the structure of the Hitler hierarchy, and is authored by two of the most prominent authorities on the subject of uniforms and insignia of the Third Reich. This comprehensive book covers details on the NSKK and NSFK such as history, organization, uniforms, insignia, special insignia, flags and standards, gorgets, daggers, awards, "day badges," and much more!

United States Marine Corps Uniforms, Insignia, and Personal Items of World War II by Harlan Glenn Atglen, PA: Schiffer Publications, 2005. 1st edition. 272 pp. Hardcover. NEW $79.95
Covering in detail the combat and dress uniforms of the United States Marine in World War II, this new volume is destined to become the World War II Marine Corps collector's reference! Shown in detail are the herringbone utilities that Marines wore from Guadalcanal to Okinawa, as well as Summer Service, Winter Service and Dress (Blues) uniforms.

United States Martial Flintlocks, by Robert M. Reilly, Mowbray Publishing Co., Lincoln, RI, 1997. 264 pp., illus. $40.00
A comprehensive history of American flintlock longarms and handguns (mostly military) c. 1775 to c. 1840.

United States Submachine Guns: From the American 180 to the ZX-7, by Frank Iannamico, Harmony, ME, Moose Lake Publishing, 2004. 1st edition. Soft cover. NEW. $29.95
This profusely illustrated new book covers the research and development of the submachine gun in the U.S. from World War I to the present. Many photos and charts, nearly 500 pages!

Variations of Colt's New Model Police and Pocket Breech Loading Pistols, by John D. Breslin, William Q. Pirie and David E. Price, Lincoln, RI, Andrew Mowbray Publishers, 2002. 1st edition. 158 pp., heavily illustrated with over 160 photographs and superb technical detailed drawings and diagrams. Pictorial hardcover. $37.95
A type-by-type guide to what collectors call small frame conversions.

Vietnam Order of Battle, by Shelby L. Stanton, William C. Westmoreland. Mechanicsburg, PA, Stackpole Books, 2003. 1st edition. 416 pp., 32 in full color, 101 pp. halftones. Hardcover. New in new dust jacket. $69.95

Visor Hats of the United States Armed Forces 1930-1950, by Joe Tonelli, Atglen, PA, Schiffer Publications, 2003. 1st edition. Hardcover. New in new dust jacket. $79.95

The W.F. Cody Buffalo Bill Collector's Guide with Values, by James W. Wojtowicz, Collector Books, Paducah, KY, 1998. 271 pp., illus. $24.95
A profusion of colorful collectibles including lithographs, programs, photographs, books, medals, sheet music, guns, etc. and today's values.

The Walker's Walkers Controversy is Solved, by Col. Robert D. Whittington III, Hooks, TX, Brownlee Books, 2003. A limited edition of 1,000 copies. Numbered. 17 pp. Paper covers. New. $15.00
The truth about serial numbers on the Colt Whitneyville-Walker pistols presented to Captain Samuel Hamilton Walker by Sam Colt and J. B. Colt on July 28th, 1847.

Walther: A German Legend, by Manfred Kersten, Safari Press, Inc., Huntington Beach, CA, 2000. 400 pp., illus. $85.00
This comprehensive book covers, in rich detail, all aspects of the company and its guns, including an illustrious and rich history, the WWII years, all the pistols (models 1 through 9), the P-38, P-88, the long guns, 22 rifles, centerfires, Wehrmacht guns, and even a gun that could shoot around a corner.

The Walther Handgun Story: A Collector's and Shooter's Guide, by Gene Gangarosa, Steiger Publications, 1999. 300 pp., illus. Paper covers. $21.95
Covers the entire history of the Walther empire. Illustrated with over 250 photos.

Walther Models PP & PPK, 1929-1945 – Volume 1, by James L. Rankin, Coral Gables, FL, 1974. 142 pp., illus. $40.00
Complete coverage on the subject as to finish, proofmarks and Nazi Party inscriptions.

Walther P-38 Pistol, by Maj. George Nonte, Desert Publications, Cornville, AZ, 1982. 100 pp., illus. Paper covers. $12.95
Complete volume on one of the most famous handguns to come out of WWII. All models covered.

Walther Pistols: Models 1 Through P99, Factory Variations and Copies, by Dieter H. Marschall, Ucross Books, Los Alamos, NM. 2000. 140 pp., with 140 b&w illustrations, index. Paper covers. $19.95
This is the English translation, revised and updated, of the highly successful and widely acclaimed German language edition. This book provides the collector with a reference guide and overview of the entire line of the Walther military, police, and self-defense pistols from the very first to the very latest. Models 1-9, PP, PPK, MP, AP, HP, P.38, P1, P4, P38K, P5, P88, P99 and the Manurhin models. Variations, where issued, serial ranges, calibers, marks, proofs, logos, and design aspects in an astonishing quantity and variety are crammed into this very well researched and highly regarded work.

Walther Volume II, Engraved, Presentation and Standard Models, by James L. Rankin, J.L. Rankin, Coral Gables, FL, 1977. 112 pp., illus. $40.00
The new Walther book on embellished versions and standard models. Has 88 photographs, including many color plates.

Walther, Volume III, 1908-1980, by James L. Rankin, Coral Gables, FL, 1981. 226 pp., illus. $40.00

Covers all models of Walther handguns from 1908 to date, includes holsters, grips and magazines.

Winchester an American Legend, by R.L. Wilson, New York, Book Sales, 2004. Reprint. Hardcover. New in new dust jacket. $29.95

Winchester Bolt Action Military & Sporting Rifles 1877 to 1937, by Herbert G. Houze, Andrew Mowbray Publishing, Lincoln, RI, 1998. 295 pp., illus. $45.00

Winchester was the first American arms maker to commercially manufacture a bolt action repeating rifle, and this book tells the exciting story of these Winchester bolt actions.

The Winchester Book, by George Madis, David Madis Gun Book Distributor, Dallas, TX, 2000. 650 pp., illus. $54.50

A new, revised 25th anniversary edition of this classic book on Winchester firearms. Complete serial ranges have been added.

Winchester Dates of Manufacture 1849-1984, by George Madis, Art & Reference House, Brownsboro, TX, 1984. 59 pp. $9.50

A most useful work, compiled from records of the Winchester factory.

Winchester Engraving, by R.L. Wilson, Beinfeld Books, Springs, CA, 1989. 500 pp., illus. $135.00

A classic reference work of value to all arms collectors.

The Winchester Handbook, by George Madis, Art & Reference House, Lancaster, TX, 1982. 287 pp., illus. $26.95

The complete line of Winchester guns, with dates of manufacture, serial numbers, etc.

Winchester Lever Action Repeating Firearms, Vol. 1, The Models of 1866, 1873 and 1876, by Arthur Pirkle, North Cape Publications, Tustin, CA, 1995. 112 pp., illus. Paper covers. $19.95

Complete, part-by-part description, including dimensions, finishes, markings and variations throughout the production run of these fine, collectible guns.

Winchester Lever Action Repeating Rifles, Vol. 2, The Models of 1886 and 1892, by Arthur Pirkle, North Cape Publications, Tustin, CA, 1996. 150 pp., illus. Paper covers. $19.95

Describes each model on a part-by-part basis by serial number range complete with finishes, markings and changes.

Winchester Lever Action Repeating Rifles, Vol. 3, The Model of 1894, by Arthur Pirkle, North Cape Publications, Tustin, CA, 1998. 150 pp., illus. Paper covers. $19.95

The first book ever to provide a detailed description of the Model 1894 rifle and carbine.

The Winchester Lever Legacy, by Clyde "Snooky" Williamson, Buffalo Press, Zachary, LA, 1988. 664 pp., illus. $75.00

A book on reloading for the different calibers of the Winchester lever action rifle.

The Winchester Model 1876 "Centennial" Rifle, by Herbert G. Houze. Lincoln, RI, Andrew Mowbray, Inc., 2001. Illustrated with over 180 b&w photographs. 192 pp. Hardcover. $45.00

The first authoritative study of the Winchester Model 1876 written using the company's own records. This book dispels the myth that the Model 1876 was merely a larger version of the Winchester company's famous Model 1873 and instead traces its true origins to designs developed immediately after the American Civil War. The specifics of the model–such as the numbers made in its standard calibers, barrel lengths, finishes and special order features–are fully listed here for the first time. For Winchester collectors, and those interested in the mechanics of the 19th-century arms industry, this book provides a wealth of previously unpublished information.

Winchester Pocket Guide: Identification & Pricing for 50 Collectible Rifles and Shotguns, by Ned Schwing, Iola, WI, Krause Publications, 2004. 1st edition. 224 pp., illus. Softcover. NEW. $12.95

Winchester Repeating Arms Company Its History & Development from 1865 to 1981, by Herbert G. Houze, Iola, WI, Krause Publications, 2004. 1st edition. Softcover. NEW. $34.98

The Winchester Single-Shot, Volume 1; A History and Analysis, by John Campbell, Andrew Mowbray, Inc., Lincoln, RI, 1995. 272 pp., illus. $55.00

Covers every important aspect of this highly-collectible firearm.

The Winchester Single-Shot, Volume 2; Old Secrets and New Discoveries, by John Campbell, Andrew Mowbray, Inc., Lincoln, RI, 2000. 280 pp., illus. $55.00

An exciting follow-up to the classic first volume.

Winchester Sporting Firearms: Dates of Manufacture, by D.R. Morse, Phoenix, AZ, Firing Pin Enterprizes, 2003. 45 pp. Softcover. NEW. $6.95

Covers their pistols, revolvers, rifles, shotguns and commemoratives, plus models and serial numbers.

The Winchester-Lee Rifle, by Eugene Myszkowski, Excalibur Publications, Tucson, AZ 2000. 96 pp., illus. Paper covers. $22.95

The development of the Lee Straight Pull, the cartridge and the approval for military use. Covers details of the inventor and memorabilia of Winchester-Lee related material.

World War One Collectors Handbook Volumes 1 and 2, by Paul Schulz, Hayes Otoupalik and Dennis Gordon, Missoula, MT, privately printed, 2002. Two volumes in one edition. 110 pp., loaded with b&w photos. Softcover. NEW. $21.95

Covers, uniforms, insignia, equipment, weapons, souvenirs and miscellaneous. Includes price guide. For all of you Doughboy collectors, this is a must.

World War II German War Booty, A Study in Photographs, by Thomas M. Johnson, Atglen, PA, Schiffer Publications, 2003. 1st edition. 368 pp. Hardcover. New in new dust jacket. $79.95

Worldwide Webley and the Harrington and Richardson Connection, by Stephen Cuthbertson, Ballista Publishing and Distributing Ltd., Gabriola Island, Canada, 1999. 259 pp., illus. $50.00

A masterpiece of scholarship. Over 350 photographs plus 75 original documents, patent drawings, and advertisements accompany the text.

The World's Great Handguns: From 1450 to the Present Day, by Roger Ford, Secaucus, NJ, Chartwell Books, Inc., 1997. 1st edition. 176 pp. Hardcover. New in new dust jacket. $19.95

EDGED WEAPONS

A Guide to Military Dress Daggers, Volume 1, by Kurt Glemser, Johnson Reference Books, Fredericksburg, VA, 1991. 160 pp., illus. Softcover. $26.50

Very informative guide to dress daggers of foreign countries, to include an excellent chapter on DDR daggers. There is also a section on reproduction Third Reich period daggers. Provides, for the first time, identification of many of the war-time foreign dress daggers.

A Guide to Military Dress Daggers, Volume 2, by Kurt Glemser, Johnson Reference Books, Fredericksburg, VA, 1993. 160 pp., illus. $32.50

As in the first volume, reproduction daggers are covered in depth (Third Reich, East German, Italian, Polish and Hungarian). American Navy dirks are featured for the first time. Bulgarian Youth daggers, Croatian daggers and Imperial German Navy dagger scabbards all have chapters devoted to them. Continues research initiated in Volume I on such subjects as dress daggers, Solingen export daggers, East German daggers and Damascus Smith Max Dinger.

A Photographic Supplement of Confederate Swords, with addendum, by William A. Albaugh III, Broadfoot Publishing, Wilmington, NC. 1999. 205 plus 54 pp. of the addendum, illustrated with b&w photos. $45.00

Advanced Bowie Techniques: The Finer Points of Fighting with a Large Knife, by Dwight McLemore, Boulder, CO, Paladin Press, 2005. 1st edition.

Progressive drills combine techniques into sequences designed to show you how to maximize time, distance and movement to create openings for attacking or defending yourself against one or more opponents. 248 pp. Soft cover. NEW. $35.00

Advertising Cutlery; With Values, by Richard White, Schiffer Publishing, Ltd., Atglen, PA, 176 pp., with over 400 color photos. Softcover. $29.95

Advertising Cutlery is the first-ever publication to deal exclusively with the subject of promotional knives. Containing over 400 detailed color photographs, this book explores over 100 years of advertisements stamped into the sides of knives. In addition to the book's elegant photographic presentation, extensive captions and text give the reader the background information necessary for evaluating collectible advertising knives.

Allied Military Fighting Knives; And the Men Who Made Them Famous, by Robert A. Buerlein, Paladin Press, Boulder, CO, 2001. 185 pp., illustrated with b&w photos. Softcover. $35.00

The American Eagle Pommel Sword: The Early Years 1794-1830, by Andrew Mowbray, Manrat Arms Publications, Lincoln, RI, 1997. 244 pp., illus. $65.00

The standard guide to the most popular style of American sword.

American Knives; The First History and Collector's Guide, by Harold L. Peterson, The Gun Room Press, Highland Park, NJ, 1980. 178 pp., illus. $24.95

A reprint of this 1958 classic. Covers all types of American knives.

American Military Bayonets of the 20th Century, by Gary M. Cunningham, Scott A. Duff Publications, Export, PA, 1997. 116 pp., illus. Paper covers. $21.95

A guide for collectors, including notes on makers, markings, finishes, variations, scabbards, and production data.

American Premium Guide To Knives & Razors; Identification and Value Guide 6th Edition, by Jim Sargent, Iola, WI, Krause Publications, 2004. 504 pp. plus 2,500 b&w photos. Softcover. NEW. $24.99

American Primitive Knives 1770-1870, by G.B. Minnes, Museum Restoration Service, Ottawa, Canada, 1983. 112 pp., illus. $24.95

Origins of the knives, outstanding specimens, structural details, etc.

American Socket Bayonets and Scabbards, by Robert M. Reilly, 2nd printing, Andrew Mowbray, Inc., Lincoln, RI, 1998. 208 pp., illus. $45.00

Full coverage of the socket bayonet in America, from Colonial times through the post-Civil War.

The American Sword, 1775-1945, by Harold L. Peterson, Ray Riling Arms Books, Co., Phila., PA, 2001. 286 pp. plus 60 pp. of illus. $49.95

1977 reprint of a survey of swords worn by U.S. uniformed forces, plus the rare "American Silver Mounted Swords, (1700-1815)."

American Swords and Sword Makers, by Richard H. Bezdek, Paladin Press, Boulder, CO, 1994. 648 pp., illus. $79.95

The long-awaited definitive reference volume to American swords, sword makers and sword dealers from Colonial times to the present.

American Swords & Sword Makers Volume 2, by Richard H. Bezdek, Paladin Press, Boulder, CO, 1999. 376 pp., illus. $69.95

More than 400 stunning photographs of rare, unusual and one-of-a-kind swords from the top collections in the country.

American Swords from the Philip Medicus Collection, edited by Stuart C. Mowbray, with photographs and an introduction by Norm Flayderman, Andrew Mowbray Publishers, Lincoln, RI, 1998. 272 pp., with 604 swords illustrated. $55.00

Covers all areas of American sword collecting.

The Ames Sword Company Catalog: An Exact Reprint of the Original 19th Century Military and Fraternal Sword Catalog, by Stuart C. Mowbray, Lincoln,

RI, Andrew Mowbray, Inc., 2003. 1st edition. 200 pp., 541 swords illustrated with original prices and descriptions. Pictorial hardcover. $37.50

The level of detail in these original catalog images will surprise you. Dealers who sold Ames swords used this catalog in their stores, and every feature is clearly shown. Reproduced directly from the incredibly rare originals, military, fraternal and more! The key to identifying hundreds of Ames swords! Shows the whole Ames line, including swords from the Civil War and even earlier. Lots of related military items like belts, bayonets, etc.

The Ames Sword Company, 1829-1935, by John D. Hamilton, Andrew Mowbray Publisher, Lincoln, RI, 1995. 255 pp., illus. $45.00

An exhaustively researched and comprehensive history of America's foremost sword manufacturer and arms supplier during the Civil War.

Antique American Switchblades; Identification & Value Guide, by Mark Erickson, Iola, WI, Krause Publications, 2004. 1st edition. Softcover. NEW. $19.95

Antlers & Iron II, by Krause Publications, Iola, WI, 1999. 40 pp., illustrated with 100 photos. Paper cover. $12.00

Lays out actual plans so you can build your mountain man folding knife using ordinary hand tools. Step-by-step instructions, with photos, design, antler slotting and springs.

The Art of Throwing Weapons, by James W. Madden, Paladin Press, Boulder, CO, 1993. 102 pp., illus. $14.00

This comprehensive manual covers everything from the history and development of the five most common throwing weapons–spears, knives, tomahawks, shurikens and boomerangs–to their selection or manufacture, grip, distances, throwing motions and advanced combat methods.

Arte of Defence an Introduction to the Use of the Rapier, by William E. Wilson, Union City, CA, Chivalry Bookshelf, 2002. 1st edition. 167 pp., illustrated with over 300 photographs. Softcover $24.95

Axes of War and Power, by James Gamble, Douglas, CA, privately printed, 2002. 1st edition. Softcover. NEW. $19.95

Battle Blades: A Professional's Guide to Combat Fighting Knives, by Greg Walker; Foreword by Al Mar, Paladin Press, Boulder, CO, 1993. 168 pp., illus. $40.95

The author evaluates daggers, Bowies, switchblades and utility blades according to their design, performance, reliability and cost.

The Bayonet in New France, 1665-1760, by Erik Goldstein, Museum Restoration Service, Bloomfield, Ontario, Canada, 1997. 36 pp., illus. Paper covers. $8.95

Traces bayonets from the recently developed plug bayonet, through the regulation socket bayonets, which saw service in North America.

Bayonets from Janzen's Notebook, by Jerry Jansen, Cedar Ridge Publications, Tulsa, OK, 2000. 6th printing. 258 pp., illus. Hardcover. $45.00

This collection of over 1,000 pieces is one of the largest in the U.S.

Bayonets: An Illustrated History, by Martin J. Brayley, Iola, WI, Krause Publications, 2004. 1st edition 256 pp., illus. Softcover. NEW. $29.95

Bayonets, Knives & Scabbards; United States Army Weapons Report 1917 Thru 1945, edited by Frank Trzaska, Knife Books, Deptford, NJ, 1999. 80 pp., illus. Paper covers. $15.95

Follows the United States edged weapons from the close of WWI through the end of WWII. Manufacturers involved, dates, numbers produced, problems encountered, and production data.

The Best of U.S. Military Knives, Bayonets & Machetes, by M.H. Cole, edited by Michael W. Silvey. Privately printed, 2002. Hardcover. New in new dust jacket. $59.95

Blade's Guide to Making Knives, by Joe Kertzman, Iola,WI, Krause Publications,2005. 1st edition. Techniques for everything from forging steel to making a tomahawk are covered for the diverse population of knife makers. 160 pp., 250 color illustrations demonstrate expert techniques. Soft cover. $24.89

Book of Edged Weapons, Ephrata, Pennsylvania, Science Press Division, 2004. 351 pp. illustrated with b&w photos. Hardcover. NEW. $40.00

The Book of the Sword, by Richard F. Burton, Dover Publications, New York, NY, 1987. 199 pp., illus. Paper covers. $12.95

Traces the sword's origin from its birth as a charged and sharpened stick through diverse stages of development.

Borders Away, Volume 1: With Steel, by William Gilkerson, Andrew Mowbray, Inc., Lincoln, RI, 1991. 184 pp., illus. $48.00

A comprehensive study of naval armament under fighting sail. This first volume covers axes, pikes and fighting blades in use from 1626 to 1826.

Borders Away, Volume 2: Firearms of the Age of Fighting Sail, by William Gilkerson, Andrew Mowbray, Inc., Lincoln, RI, 1999. 331 pp., illus. with 200 photos, 16-color plates. $65.00

Completing a two-volume set, this impressive work covers the pistols, muskets, combustibles, and small cannons once employed aboard American and European fighting ships.

Bowie and Big-Knife Fighting System, by Dwight C. McLemore, Boulder, CO, Paladin Press, 2003. 240 pp., illus. Softcover. NEW. $35.00

The Bowie Knife: Unsheathing an American Legend, by Norm Flayderman, Lincoln, RI, Andrew Mowbray, Inc., 2004. 1st edition. New in new dust jacket. $79.95

Bowie Knives and Bayonets of the Ben Palmer Collection, 2nd Edition, by Ben Palmer, Bill Moran and Jim Phillips. Williamstown, NJ, Phillips Publications, 2002. 224 pp. Illustrated with photos. Hardcover $49.95

Vastly expanded with more than 300 makers, distributors and dealers added to the makers list; chapter on the Bowie knife photograph with 50 image photo gallery of

knife holders from the Mexican War, Civil War, and the West; contains a chapter on Bowie Law; includes several unpublished Bowie documents, including the first account of the Alamo. As things stand, it is a 'must' read for collectors, particularly if you're looking for photos of some knives not often seen, or curious about what Bill Moran might have to say about some of the old Bowie designs.

Bowies, Big Knives, and the Best of Battle Blades, by Bill Bagwell, Paladin Press, Boulder, CO. 2001. 184 pp., illus. Paper covers. $30.00

This book binds the timeless observations and invaluable advice of master bladesmith and blade combat expert Bill Bagwell under one cover for the first time. Here, you'll find all of Bagwell's classic SOF columns, plus all-new material linking his early insights with his latest conclusions.

British & Commonwealth Bayonets, by Ian D. Skennerton and Robert Richardson, I.D.S.A. Books, Piqua, OH, 1986. 404 pp., 1300 illus. $40.00

The Case Cutler Dynasty, by Brad Lockwood, Paducah,KY, Collector Books, 2005. 1st edition. 320 pages. Pictorial hardcover. NEW. $19.95

The Case Cutlery Dynasty shows how history becomes mythology over time, money is sometimes thicker than blood, and how a single family from humble beginnings came to dominate an important American industry.

Civil War Cavalry & Artillery Sabers, 1833-1865, by John H. Thillmann, Andrew Mowbray, Inc. Lincoln, RI, 2002. 1st edition. 500+ pp., over 50 color photographs, 1,373 b&w illustrations, coated paper, dust jacket, premium hardcover binding. Hardcover. $79.95

Clandestine Edged Weapons, by William Windrum, Phillips Publications, Williamstown, NJ, 2001. 74 pp., illustrated with b&w photographs. Pictorial softcover. $9.95

Collecting the Edged Weapons of Imperial Germany, by Johnson & Wittmann, Johnson Reference Books, Fredericksburg, VA, 1989. 363 pp., illus. $39.50

An in-depth study of the many ornate military, civilian, and government daggers and swords of the Imperial era.

Collector's Guide to Ames U.S. Contract Military Edged Weapons: 1832-1906, by Ron G. Hickox, Pioneer Press, Union City, IN, 1993. 70 pp., illus. Paper covers. $17.50

While this book deals primarily with edged weapons made by the Ames Manufacturing Company, this guide refers to other manufacturers of United States swords.

Collector's Guide to E.C. Simmons Keen Kutter Cutlery Tools, by Jerry and Elaine Heuring, Paducah, KY, Collector Books, 2000. 1st edition. 192 pp. Softcover. $19.95

Collector's Guide to Switchblade Knives, an Illustrated Historical and Price Reference, by Richard V. Langston, Paladin Press, Boulder, CO. 2001. 224 pp., illus. $49.95

It has been more than 20 years since a major work on switchblades has been published, and never has one showcased as many different types as Rich Langston's new book. The Collector's Guide to Switchblade Knives contains a history of the early cutlery industry in America; a detailed examination of the evolution of switchblades; and a user-friendly, up-to-the-minute, illustrated reference section that helps collectors and novices alike identify all kinds of knives, from museum-quality antiques to Granddad's old folder that's been hidden in the attic for decades.

The Complete Bladesmith: Forging Your Way to Perfection, by Jim Hrisoulas, Paladin Press, Boulder, CO, 1987. 192 pp., illus. $42.95

Novices as well as the experienced bladesmith will benefit from this definitive guide to smithing world-class blades.

The Complete Book of Pocketknife Repair, by Ben Kelly Jr., Krause Publications, Iola, WI, 1995. 130 pp., illus. Paper covers. $10.95

Everything you need to know about repairing knives can be found in this step-by-step guide to knife repair.

The Complete Encyclopedia to Knives, by A.E. Hartink, NJ, Chartwell, 2005. More than 600 superb illustrations. 448 pages. Hardcover. New in new dust jacket. $19.95

Confederate Edged Weapons, by W.A. Albaugh, R&R Books, Lavonia, NY, 1994. 198 pp., illus. $40.00

The master reference to edged weapons of the Confederate forces. Features precise line drawings and an extensive text.

The Connoisseur's Book of Japanese Swords, by Kodauska Nagayama, International, Tokyo, Japan, 1997. 348 pp., illus. $75.00

Translated by Kenji Mishina. A comprehensive guide to the appreciation and appraisal of the blades of Japanese swords. The most informative guide to the blades of Japanese swords ever to appear in English.

Counterfeiting Antique Cutlery, by Gerald Witcher, National Brokerage and Sales, Inc., Brentwood, TN. 1997. 512 pp., illustrated with 1,500-2,000 b&w photographs. $24.95

Cutting Edge: Japanese Swords in the British Museum, by Victor Harris, VT, Tuttle Publishing, 2005. 1st edition. It includes hundreds of photos, with 16 pages in full color. 160 pp., illustrated with 320 b&w photos; 34 color photos; and a 2-page spread of line art. Hardcover. New in new dust jacket. $40.00

Daggers and Fighting Knives of the Western World: From the Stone Age til 1900, by Harold Peterson, Dover Publishing, Mineola, NY, 2001. 96 pp., plus 32 pp. of matte stock. Over 100 illustrations. Softcover. $9.95

The only full-scale reference book devoted entirely to the subject of fighting knives, flint knives, daggers of all sorts, scramasaxes, hauswehren, dirks and more. 108 plates, bibliography and Index.

The Earliest Commando Knives, by William Windrum. Phillips Publications, Williamstown, NJ. 2001. 74 pp., illus. Softcover. $9.95

ARMS LIBRARY

Edged Weapon Accouterments of Germany 1800-1945, Kreutz, Hofmann, Johnson, Reddick, Pottsboro, TX, Reddick Enterprises, 2002. 1st edition. Hardcover. NEW. $49.00

Eickhorn Edged Weapons Exports, Vol. 1: Latin America, by A.M. de Quesada Jr. and Ron G. Hicock, Pioneer Press, Union City, TN, 1996. 120 pp., illus. Softcovers. $15.00

This research studies the various Eickhorn edged weapons and accessories manufactured for various countries outside of Germany.

Exploring the Dress Daggers and Swords of the SS, by Thomas T. Wittmann, Johnson Reference Books, Fredericksburg, VA, 2003. 1st edition. 750 pp., illustrated with nearly 1000 photographs, many in color. $150.00

Covers all model SS Service Daggers, Chained SS Officer Daggers, Himmler & Rohm Inscriptions, Damascus presentations, SS Officer Degen, Himmler Birthday Degen, Silver Lionhead Swords, Blade etch study & much more. Profusely illustrated with historically important period in-wear photographs. Most artifacts appearing for the first time in reference.

Exploring the Dress Daggers of the German Army, by Thomas T. Wittmann, Johnson Reference Books, Fredericksburg, VA, 1995. 350 pp., illus. $69.95

The first in-depth analysis of the dress daggers worn by the German Army.

Exploring the Dress Daggers of the German Luftwaffe, by Thomas T. Wittmann, Johnson Reference Books, Fredericksburg, VA, 1998. 350 pp., illus. $79.95

Examines the dress daggers and swords of the German Luftwaffe. The designs covered include the long DLV patterns, the Glider Pilot designs of the NSFK and DLV, 1st and 2nd model Luftwaffe patterns, the Luftwaffe sword and the General Officer Degen. Many are pictured for the first time in color.

Exploring The Dress Daggers of the German Navy, by Thomas T. Wittmann, Johnson Reference Books, Fredericksburg, VA, 2000. 560 pp., illus. $89.95

Explores the dress daggers and swords of the Imperial, Weimar, and Third Reich eras, from 1844-1945. Provides detailed information, as well as many superb b&w and color photographs of individual edged weapons. Many are pictured for the first time in full color.

Fighting Tomahawk: An Illustrated Guide to Using the Tomahawk and Long Knife as Weapons, by Dwight C. McLemore, Boulder, CO, Paladin Press, 2004. 1st edition. 296 pp. Softcover. NEW. $39.95

The First Commando Knives, by Prof. Kelly Yeaton and Col. Rex Applegate, Phillips Publications, Williamstown, NJ, 1996. 115 pp., illus. Paper covers. $12.95

Here is the full story of the Shanghai origins of the world's best known dagger.

George Schrade and His Accomplishments, by George Schrade, privately printed, 2004. 84 pp. Softcover. NEW. $25.00

German Clamshells and Other Bayonets, by G. Walker and R.J. Weinard, Johnson Reference Books, Fredericksburg, VA, 1994. 157 pp., illus. $22.95

Includes unusual bayonets, many of which are shown for the first time. Current market values are listed.

German Etched Dress Bayonets (Extra-Seitengewehr) 1933-1945, by Wayne H. Techet. Printed by the author, Las Vegas, NV. 2002. Color section and value guide. 262 pp. Limited edition of 1,300 copies. Signed and numbered. $55.00

Photographs of over 200 obverse and reverse motifs. Rare SS and Panzer patterns pictured for the first time, with an extensive chapter on reproductions and Red Flags.

German Swords and Sword Makers: Edged Weapons Makers from the 14th to the 20th Centuries, by Richard H. Bezdek, Paladin Press, Boulder, CO, 2000. 248 pp., illus. $59.95

This book contains the most information ever published on German swords and edged weapons makers from the Middle Ages to the present.

Greenhill Military Manual: Combat Knives, by Leroy Thompson, London, Greenhill Publishing, 2004. 1st edition. Hardcover. NEW. $24.00

The Halberd and other European Polearms 1300-1650, by George Snook, Museum Restoration Service, Bloomfield, Ontario, Canada, 1998. 40 pp., illus. Paper covers. $8.95

A comprehensive introduction to the history, use, and identification of the staff weapons of Europe.

Highland Swordsmanship: Techniques of the Scottish Swordmasters, edited by Mark Rector. Chivalry Bookshelf, Union City, CA, 2001. 208 pp., Includes more than 100 illustrative photographs. Softcover $29.95

Rector has done a superb job at bringing together two influential yet completely different 18th century fencing manuals from Scotland. Adding new interpretive plates, Mark offers new insights and clear presentations of many useful techniques. With contributions by Paul MacDonald and Paul Wagner, this book promises to be a treat for students of historical fencing, Scottish history and reenactors.

How to Make a Tactical Folder, by Bob Tetzuola, Krause Publications, Iola, WI, 2000. 160 pp., illus. Paper covers. $16.95

Step-by-step instructions and outstanding photography guide the knifemaker from start to finish.

How to Make Folding Knives, by Ron Lake, Frank Centofante and Wayne Clay, Krause Publications, Iola, WI, 1995. 193 pp., illus. Paper covers. $13.95

With step-by-step instructions, learn how to make your own folding knife from three top custom makers.

How to Make Knives, by Richard W. Barney and Robert W. Loveless, Krause Publications, Iola, WI, 1995. 182 pp., illus. Paper covers. $13.95

Complete instructions from two premier knife makers on making high-quality, handmade knives.

How to Make Multi-Blade Folding Knives, by Eugene Shadley & Terry Davis, Krause Publications, Iola, WI, 1997. 192 pp., illus. Paper covers. $19.95

This step-by-step instructional guide teaches knifemakers how to craft these complex folding knives.

KA-BAR: The Next Generation of the Ultimate Fighting Knife, by Greg Walker, Paladin Press, Boulder, CO, 2001. 88 pp., illus. Softcover. $16.00

The KA-BAR fighting/utility knife is the most widely recognized and popular combat knife ever to be produced in the United States. Since its introduction on 23 November 1942, the KA-BAR has performed brilliantly on the battlefields of Europe, the South Pacific, Korea, Southeast Asia, Central America and the Middle East, earning its moniker as the "ultimate fighting knife."

Kalashnikov Bayonets: The Collector's Guide to Bayonets for the AK and its Variations, by Martin D. Ivie, Texas, Diamond Eye Publications, 2002. 1st edition. 220 pp., with over 250 color photos and illustrations. Hardcover. $59.95

Knife and Tomahawk Throwing: The Art of the Experts, by Harry K. McEvoy, Charles E. Tuttle, Rutland, VT, 1989. 150 pp., illus. Softcover. $8.95

The first book to employ side-by-side the fascinating art and science of knives and tomahawks.

The Knife in Homespun America and Related Items: Its Construction and Material, as used by Woodsmen, Farmers, Soldiers, Indians and General Population, by Madison Grant, York, PA, privately printed, 1984. 1st edition. 187 pp., profusely illustrated. $45.00

Shows over 300 examples of knives and related items made and used by woodsmen, farmers, soldiers, Indians and the general frontier population.

Knife Talk, The Art and Science of Knifemaking, by Ed Fowler, Krause Publications, Iola, WI, 1998. 158 pp., illus. Paper covers. $14.95

Valuable how-to advice on knife design and construction plus 20 years of memorable articles from the pages of "Blade" Magazine.

Knifemakers of Old San Francisco, by Bernard Levine, 2nd edition, Paladin Press, Boulder, CO, 1998. 150 pp., illus. $39.95

The definitive history of the knives and knife-makers of 19th century San Francisco.

Knives 2006 26th Anniversary Edition, edited by Joe Kertzman, Iola, WI, Krause Publications, 2004. Softcover. NEW. $24.99

Knives of the United States Military–World War II, by Michael W. Silvey, privately printed, Sacramento, CA 1999. 250 pp., illustrated with full color photos. $60.00

240 full-page color plates depicting the knives of WWII displayed against a background of wartime accoutrements and memorabilia. The book focuses on knives and their background.

Knives of the United States Military in Vietnam: 1961-1975, by Michael W. Silvey, privately printed, Sacramento, CA., 139 pp. Hardcover. $45.00

A beautiful color celebration of the most interesting and rarest knives of the Vietnam War, emphasizing SOG knives, Randalls, Gerbers, Eks, and other knives of this era. Shown with these knives are the patches and berets of the elite units who used them.

Les Baionnettes Reglementaires Francises de 1840 a 1918 "The Bayonets; Military Issue 1840-1918", by French Assoc. of Bayonet Collectors, 2000. 77 pp. illus. $24.95

Profusely illustrated. By far the most comprehensive guide to French military bayonets done for this period. Includes hundreds of illustrations. 77 large 8-1/4" x 11-1/2" pages. French text. Color photos are magnificent!

The Master Bladesmith: Advanced Studies in Steel, by Jim Hrisoulas, Paladin Press, Boulder, CO, 1990. 296 pp., illus. $49.95

The author reveals the forging secrets that for centuries have been protected by guilds.

Medieval Swordsmanship, Illustrated Methods and Techniques, by John Clements, Paladin Press, Boulder, CO, 1998. 344 pp., illus. $40.00

The most comprehensive and historically accurate view ever written of the lost fighting arts of Medieval knights.

The Military Knife & Bayonet Book, by Homer Brett, World Photo Press, Japan. 2001. 392 pp., illus. $69.95

Professional studio color photographs with more than 1,000 military knives and knife-bayonets illustrated. Both the U.S. and foreign sections are extensive, and includes standard models, prototypes and experimental models. Many of the knives and bayonets photographed have never been previously illustrated in any other book. The U.S. section also includes the latest developments in military Special Operations designs. Written in Japanese and English.

Military Knives: A Reference Book, by Frank Trzaska (editor), Knife Books, Deptford, NJ, 2001. 255 pp., illus. Softcover. $17.95

A collection of your favorite Military Knife articles from the pages of Knife World magazine. 67 articles ranging from the Indian Wars to the present day modern military knives.

Modern Combat Blades, by Duncan Long, Paladin Press, Boulder, CO, 1993. 128 pp., illus. $30.00

Long discusses the pros and cons of bowies, bayonets, commando daggers, kukris, switchblades, butterfly knives, belt-buckle blades and many more.

Modern Fencing: A Comprehensive Manual for the Foil, The Epee, The Sabre, by Clovis Deladrier, Boulder, CO, Paladin Press, 2005. 312pp. Soft cover. NEW. $35.00

Though long out of print, Modern Fencing is still considered one of the best fencing manuals ever written and is often cited by modern fencing masters for its concise lessons and excellent photos.

The Modern Swordsman, by Fred Hutchinson, Paladin Press, Boulder, CO, 1999. 80 pp., illus. Paper covers. $22.00

Realistic training for serious self-defense.

Moran, 50 Years Anniversary Knives: The Complete History of Their Making, by Dominique Beaucant, privately printed, 1998, signed by the publisher. Soft cover, 108 pp. Soft cover. NEW. $20.00

Includes photos and descriptions of the 50 knives Moran made to celebrate his golden anniversary as a knife maker, and much more.

Officer Swords of the German Navy 1806-1945, Claus P. Stefanski & Dirk, Schiffer Publications, Atglen, PA, 2002. 1st edition. 176 pp., with over 250 b&w and color photos. Hardcover. $59.95

Official Price Guide to Collector Knives; 14th Edition, by C. Houston Price, New York, House of Collectibles, 2004. 500 photos, 8 pp. in color. 497 pp. Softcover. NEW. $17.95

Official Scout Blades with Prices, by Ed Holbrook, privately printed, 2004. Softcover. NEW. $25.00

On Damascus Steel, by Dr. Leo S. Figiel, Atlantis Arts Press, Atlantis, FL, 1991. 145 pp., illus. $65.00

The historic, technical and artistic aspects of Oriental and mechanical Damascus. Persian and Indian sword blades, from 1600-1800, which have never been published, are illustrated.

The Pattern-Welded Blade: Artistry in Iron, by Jim Hrisoulas, Paladin Press, Boulder, CO, 1994. 120 pp., illus. $44.95

Reveals the secrets of this craft–from the welding of the starting billet to the final assembly of the complete blade.

Pocket Knives of the United States Military, by Michael W. Silvey, Sacramento, CA, privately printed, 2002. 135 pp. Hardcover. $34.95

This beautiful new full color book is the definitive reference on U.S. military folders. Pocket Knives of the United States Military is organized into the following sections: Introduction, The First Folders, WWI, WWII, and Postwar (which covers knives up through the late 1980s). Essential reading for pocketknife and military knife collectors alike!

The Randall Chronicles, by Pete Hamilton, privately printed, 2002. 160 pp., profusely illustrated in color. Hardcover in dust jacket. $79.95

Randall Fighting Knives In Wartime: WWII, Korea, and Vietnam, by Robert E. Hunt. Sacramento, CA, privately printed, 2002. 1st edition. 192 pp. Hardcover. $44.95

While other books on Randall knives have been published, this new title is the first to focus specifically on Randalls with military ties. There are three main sections, containing more than 80 knives from the WWII, Korea, and Vietnam War periods. Each knife is featured in a high quality, full page, full color photograph, with the opposing page carrying a detailed description of the knife and its history or other related information.

Randall Made Knives, by Robert L. Gaddis, Paladin Press, Boulder, CO, 2000. 292 pp., illus. $59.95

Plots the designs of all 24 of Randall's unique knives. This step-by-step book, seven years in the making, is worth every penny and moment of your time.

Randall Made Knives- A Timeline, The Quick Reference Guide, by Edna and Sheldon Wickersham, privately printed, 2005. Stiff paper covers. $20.00

This 12x25" two-sided laminated reference sheet folds neatly into a back pants pocket, and allows you to date any given Randall knife with a good degree of confidence, wherever you need it. A great resource for all Randall fans!

Randall Military Models; Fighters, Bowies and Tang Knives, by Robert E. Hunt, Sacramento, CA, privately printed, 2004. 1st edition. Hardcover. New in new dust jacket. $74.95

Remington Knives–Past & Present, by Ron Stewart and Roy Ritchie, Paducah, KY, Collector Books, 2005. 1st edition. 288 pp. Softcover. NEW. $16.95

Renaissance Swordsmanship, by John Clements, Paladin Press, Boulder, CO, 1997. 152 pp., illus. Paper covers. $25.00

The illustrated use of rapiers and cut-and-thrust swords.

Rice's Trowel Bayonet, reprinted by Ray Riling Arms Books Co., Philadelphia, PA, 1968. 8 pp., illus. Paper covers. $3.00

A facsimile reprint of a rare circular originally published by the U.S. government in 1875 for the information of U.S. troops.

The Scottish Dirk, by James D. Forman, Museum Restoration Service, Bloomfield, Ont., Canada, 1991. 60 pp., illus. Paper covers. $8.95

More than 100 dirks are illustrated with a text that sets the dirk and Sgian Dubh in their socio- historic content following design changes through more than 300 years of evolution.

Seitengewehr: History of the German Bayonet, 1919-1945, by George T. Wheeler, Johnson Reference Books, Fredericksburg, VA, 2000. 320 pp., illus. $44.95

Provides complete information on Weimar and Third Reich bayonets, as well as their accompanying knots and frogs. Illustrates re-issued German and foreign bayonets utilized by both the Reichswehr and the Wehrmacht, and details the progression of newly manufactured bayonets produced after Hitler's rise to power. Photos illustrate rarely seen bayonets worn by the Polizei, Reichsbahn, Postschutz, Hitler Jugend, and other civil and political organizations. German modified bayonets from other countries are pictured and described. Book contains an up-to-date price guide including current valuations.

Silver Mounted Swords: The Lattimer Family Collection; Featuring Silver Hilts Through the Golden Age, by Daniel Hartzler, Rowe Publications, New York, 2000. 300 pp., with over 1,000 illustrations and 1,350 photos. Oversize 9" x12". $75.00

The world's largest Silver Hilt collection.

Small Arms Identification Series, No. 6. British Service Sword & Lance Patterns, by Ian Skennerton, I.D.S.A. Books, Piqua, OH, 1994. 48 pp. $12.50

Small Arms Series, No. 2. The British Spike Bayonet, by Ian Skennerton, I.D.S.A. Books, Piqua, OH, 1982. 32 pp., 30 illus. $9.00

Socket Bayonets of the Great Powers, by Robert W. Shuey, Excalibur Publications, Tucson, AZ, 2000 96 pp., illus. Paper covers $22.95

With 175 illustrations, the author brings together, in one place, many of the standard socket arrangements used by some of the " Great Powers." With an illustrated glossary of blade shape and socket design.

The Socket in the British Army 1667-1783, by Erik Goldstein, Andrew Mowbray, Inc., Lincoln, RI, 2001. 136 pp., illus. $23.00

The spectacle of English "redcoats" on the attack, relentlessly descending upon enemy lines with fixed bayonets, is one of the most chilling images from European history and the American Revolution. Drawing upon new information from archaeological digs and archival records, the author explains how to identify each type of bayonet and shows which bayonets were used where and with which guns.

Standard Guide to Razors, 2nd Edition, by Roy Ritchie and Ron Stewart. Paducah, KY, Collector Books, 1999 values. 224 pp. Softcover. NEW. $9.95

Switchblade: The Ace of Blades, Revised and Updated, by Ragnar Benson and edited by Michael D. Janich, Boulder, CO, Paladin Press, 2004. 104 pp. Softcover. $16.00

Switchblades of Italy, by Tim Zinser, Dan Fuller and Neal Punchard. Paducah, KY, Turner Publishing, 2002. 128 pp. Hardcover. New in new dust jacket. $39.89

Swords and Blades of the American Revolution, by George C. Neumann, Rebel Publishing Co., Inc., Texarkana, TX, 1991. 288 pp., illus. $36.95

The encyclopedia of bladed weapons–swords, bayonets, spontoons, halberds, pikes, knives, daggers, axes–used by both sides, on land and sea, in America's struggle for independence.

Swords and Sabers of the Armory at Springfield, by Burton A. Kellerstedt, New Britain, CT, 1998. 121 pp., illus. Softcover. $29.95

The basic and most important reference for its subject, and one that is unlikely to be surpassed for comprehensiveness and accuracy.

Swords and Sword Makers of England and Scotland, by Richard H. Bezdek, Boulder, CO, Paladin Press, 2003. 1st edition. 424 pp., illus. Hardcover. New in new dust jacket. $69.95

Covers English sword makers from the 14th century and Scottish makers from the 16th century all the way through the renowned Wilkinson Sword Company and other major sword manufacturers of today. The important early English sword- and blade-making communities of Hounslow Heath and Shotley Bridge, and the influential Cutlers Company of London. The book concludes with dozens of beautiful illustrations of hilt designs taken directly from famed sword hilt maker Matthew Boulton's 18th-century pattern book and more than 450 spectacular photographs of English and Scottish swords of every type and era from some of the world's major collections.

Tactical Folding Knife; A Study of the Anatomy and Construction of the Liner- Locked Folder, by Bob Terzuola, Krause Publications, Iola, WI. 2000. 160 pp., 200 b&w photos, illus. Paper covers. $16.00

Step-by-step instructions and outstanding photography guide the knifemaker from start to finish. This book details everything from the basic definition of a tactical folder to the final polishing as the knife is finished.

Tactical Knives, by Dietmar Pohl, Iola, WI, Krause Publications, 2003. 1st edition. Softcover. NEW. $24.95

Travels for Daggers, Historic Edged Weaponry, by Eiler R. Cook, Hendersonville, NC, 2004. 1st edition. Hardcover. New in new dust jacket. $38.95

The U.S. M-3 Trench Knife of World War Two, by Vincent J. Coniglio and Robert S. Laden. Matamoras, PA, privately printed, 2003. 2nd printing. Softcover. NEW. $18.00

U.S. Military Knives, Bayonets and Machetes Price Guide, 5th Edition, by Frank Trzaska (editor), Knife Books, Deptford, NJ, 2006. 80 pp., illus. Softcover. $9.95

This volume follows in the tradition of the previous three versions of using major works on the subject as a reference to keep the price low to you.

U.S. Naval Officers; Their Swords and Dirks Featuring the Collection of the United States Naval Academy Museum, by Peter Tuite, Lincoln, RI, Andrew Mowbray, Inc., 2005. 1st edition. 240 pp., illustrated with over 500 color photos. Pictorial hardcover. NEW. $75.00

Wayne Goddard's $50 Knife Shop, by Wayne Goddard, Krause Publications, Iola, WI, 2000. 160 pp., illus. Softcover. $19.95

This book expands on information from Goddard's popular column in *Blade* magazine to show knifemakers of all skill levels how to create helpful gadgets and supply their shop on a shoestring.

The Wittmann German Dagger Price Guide for 2004, by David Hohaus and Thomas Wittmann, Moorestown, NJ, privately printed, 2004. 1st edition. Stiff paper covers. NEW. $11.95

Wonder of Knifemaking, by Wayne Goddard, Krause Publications, Iola, WI. 2000. 160 pp., illustrated with 150 b&w photos and 16-page color section. Softcover. $19.95

Master bladesmith Wayne Goddard draws on his decades of experience to answer questions of knifemakers at all levels. As a columnist for *Blade* magazine, Goddard has been answering real questions from real knifemakers for the past eight years. Now, all the details are compiled in one place as a handy reference for every knifemaker, amateur or professional.

GENERAL

331+ Essential Tips and Tricks; A How-To Guide for the Gun Collector, by Stuart Mowbray, Lincoln, RI, 2006. 1st edition. FULL COLOR, 272 pp., 357 photographs. Soft cover. NEW. $35.99

Everything from gun photography to detecting refinishes can be found in this comprehensive new reference book.

Action Shooting: Cowboy Style, by John Taffin, Krause Publications, Iola, WI, 1999. 320 pp., illus. $39.95

Details on the guns and ammunition. Explanations of the rules used for many events.

ARMS LIBRARY

Advanced Muzzleloader's Guide, by Toby Bridges, Stoeger Publishing Co., So. Hackensack, NJ, 1985. 256 pp., illus. Paper covers. $14.95
The complete guide to muzzle-loading rifles, pistols and shotguns–flintlock and percussion.

Aids to Musketry for Officers & NCOs, by Capt. B.J. Friend, Excalibur Publications, Latham, NY, 1996. 40 pp., illus. Paper covers. $7.95
A facsimile edition of a pre-WWI British manual filled with useful information for training the common soldier.

Airgun Odyssey, by Steve Hanson, Manchester, CT, Precision Shooting, Inc., 2004. 1st edition. 175 pp. Pictorial softcover. $27.95

America's Great Gunmakers, by Wayne van Zwoll, Stoeger Publishing Co., So. Hackensack, NJ, 1992. 288 pp., illus. Paper covers. $16.95
This book traces in great detail the evolution of guns and ammunition in America and the men who formed the companies that produced them.

American Air Rifles, by James E. House. Krause Publications, Iola, WI, 2002. 1st edition. 208 pp., with 198 b&w photos. Softcover. $22.95
Air rifle ballistics, sights, pellets, games, and hunting caliber recommendations are thoroughly explained to help shooters get the most out of their American air rifles. Evaluation of more than a dozen American-made and American-imported air rifle models.

American and Imported Arms, Ammunition and Shooting Accessories, Catalog No. 18 of the Shooter's Bible, Stoeger, Inc., reprinted by Fayette Arsenal, Fayetteville, NC, 1988. 142 pp., illus. Paper covers. $10.95
A facsimile reprint of the 1932 Stoeger's Shooter's Bible.

The American B.B. Gun: A Collector's Guide, by Arni T. Dunathan. A.S. Barnes and Co., Inc., South Brunswick, 2001. 154 pp., illustrated with nearly 200 photographs, drawings and detailed diagrams. Hardcover. $35.00

Annie Oakley of the Wild West, by Walter Havighurst, New York, Castle Books, 2000. 246 pp. Hardcover. New in new dust jacket. $10.00

Antique Guns; The Collector's Guide, by Steve Carpenteri, Accokeek, MD: Stoeger Publications, 2005. Revised edition. 260 pp., illus. plus 32-page color section. Soft cover. New. $22.95
Covers a vast spectrum of pre-1900 firearms: those manufactured by U.S. gun makers as well as Canadian, French, German, Belgian, Spanish and other foreign firms.

Armed and Female, by Paxton Quigley, E.P. Dutton, New York, NY, 2001. 237 pp., illus. Softcover $9.95
The first complete book on one of the hottest subjects in the media today, the arming of the American woman.

Armed Response, by Massad Ayoob, and David Kenik, NY, Merril Press, 2005. 179 pp., with b&w photos. Forward by Massad Ayoob. Soft cover. NEW. $19.95
These are valuable real-life lessons about preparing to face a lethal threat, winning a gun fight, and surviving the ensuing court battle that can not be found outside of expensive tactical schools.

Arming & Equipping the United States Cavalry 1865-1902, by Dusan Farrington, Lincoln, RI: Andrew Mowbray, Inc., 2005. 1st edition. Hardcover. New in new dust jacket. $68.95
Simply packed with serial numbers, issue information, reports from the field and more! Meticulously researched and absolutely up-to-date. A complete reference to all the arms and accoutrements.

Arming the Glorious Cause: Weapons of the Second War for Independence, by James B. Whisker, Daniel D. Hartzler and Larry W. Yantz, R & R Books, Livonia, NY, 1998. 175 pp., illus. $45.00
A photographic study of Confederate weapons.

Arms & Armor in the Art Institute of Chicago, by Walter J. Karcheski Jr., Bulfinch Press, Boston, MA, 1995. 128 pp., illus. $35.00
Now, for the first time, the Art Institute of Chicago's arms and armor collection is presented in the visual delight of 103 color illustrations.

Arms for the Nation: Springfield Longarms, edited by David C. Clark, Scott A. Duff, Export, PA, 1994. 73 pp., illus. Paper covers. $9.95
A brief history of the Springfield Armory and the arms made there.

Arrowmaker Frontier Series Volume 1, by Roy Chandler, Jacksonville, NC, Ron Brigade Armory, 2000. 390 pp. Hardcover. New in new dust jacket. $38.95

Arsenal of Freedom, The Springfield Armory, 1890-1948: A Year-by-Year Account Drawn from Official Records, compiled and edited by Lt. Col. William S. Brophy, USAR Ret., Andrew Mowbray, Inc., Lincoln, RI, 1991. 400 pp., illus. Softcover. $29.95
A "must buy" for all students of American military weapons, equipment and accoutrements.

The Art of American Arms Makers Marketing Guns, Ammunition, and Western Adventure During the Golden Age of Illustration, by Richard C., Rattenbury, Oklahoma City, OK, National Cowboy Museum, 2004. 132 pp. of color photos. Softcover. NEW. $29.95

The Art of American Game Calls, by Russell E. Lewis, Paducah, KY, Collector Books, 2005. 1st edition. 176 pp. Pictorial hardcover. NEW. $24.95

The Art of Blacksmithing, by Alex W. Bealer, New York, Book Sales, 1996. Revised edition. 440 pp. Hardcover. New in new dust jacket. $10.00

The Art of Remington Arms, Sporting Classics, 2004, by Tom Davis. 1st edition. Hardcover. NEW. $60.00

Battle of the Bulge: Hitler's Alternate Scenarios, by Peter Tsouras, Mechanicsburg, PA, Stackpole Books, 2004. 1st edition. 256 pp., 24 b&w photos, 10 maps. Hardcover. NEW. $34.95

The Belgian Rattlesnake: The Lewis Automatic Machine Gun, by William M. Easterly, Collector Grade Publications, Inc., Cobourg, Ont. Canada, 1998. 542 pp., illus. $79.95
A social and technical biography of the Lewis automatic machine gun and its inventors.

The Benchrest Shooting Primer, edited by Dave Brennan, Precision Shooting, Inc., Manchester, CT, 2000. 2nd edition. 420 pp., illustrated with b&w photographs, drawings and detailed diagrams. Pictorial softcover. $24.95
The very best articles on shooting and reloading for the most challenging of all the rifle accuracy disciplines…benchrest shooting.

The Black Rifle Frontier Series Volume 2, by Roy Chandler, Jacksonville, NC, Iron Brigade Armory, 2002. 226 pp. Hardcover. New in new dust jacket. $42.95
In 1760, inexperienced Jack Elan settles in Sherman's Valley, suffers tragedy, is captured by hostiles, escapes, and fights on. This is the "2nd" book in the Frontier Series.

Blue Book of Airguns 5th Edition, by Robert Beeman and John Allen, Minneapolis, MN, Blue Book Publications, Inc., 2005. Softcover. NEW. $24.95

Blue Book of Gun Values, 27th Edition (2006 Edition), by S.P. Fjestad, Minneapolis, MN, Blue Book Publications, Inc., 1,800 pp., illus. Paper covers. $39.50

Blue Book of Modern Black Powder Values, 4th Edition, by Dennis Adler, John Allen, Minneapolis, MN, Blue Book Publications, Inc., 2004. Softcover. NEW. $24.95

Bodyguard Manual, by Leroy Thompson, Mechanicsburg, PA. Greenhill Books, 2005. 208 pp., 16 pages of plates. Soft cover. NEW. $23.95
Bodyguard Manual details the steps a protective team takes to prevent attack as well as the tactics employed when it is necessary to counter one.

British Small Arms of World War II, by Ian D. Skennerton, Arms & Militaria Press, Australia, 1988. 110 pp., 37 illus. $25.00

C Stories, by Jeff Cooper, Sycamore Island Books, 2005. 1st edition. 316 pp. Hardcover. New in new dust jacket. $49.95
Quite simply, C Stories is Jeff Cooper at his best.

Carbine and Shotgun Speed Shooting: How to Hit Hard and Fast in Combat, by Steve Moses. Paladin Press, Boulder, CO. 2002. 96 pp., illus. Softcover $18.00
In this groundbreaking book, he breaks down the mechanics of speed shooting these weapons, from stance and grip to sighting, trigger control and more, presenting them in a concise and easily understood manner.

Cavalry Raids of the Civil War, by Col. Robert W. Black, Mechanicsburg, PA, Stackpole Books, 2004. 1st edition. 288 pp., 30 b&w drawings. Softcover. NEW. $17.95

CO2 Pistols and Rifles, by James E. House, Iola, WI, Krause Publications, 2004. 1st edition 240 pp., with 198 b&w photos. Softcover. NEW. $24.95

Combatives FM-3-25.150, by US Army, Boulder,CO, Paladin Press, 2004. Photos, illus., 272 pp. Soft cover. NEW. $19.95
This exact reprint of the U.S. Army's most current field manual on hand-to-hand combat (FM 3-25.150) reflects the first major revision to the Army's close-quarters combat program in a decade. This field manual shows them how.

The Complete .50-caliber Sniper Course, by Dean Michaelis, Paladin Press, Boulder, CO, 2000. 576 pp., illus., $60.00
The history from German Mauser T-Gewehr of WWI to the Soviet PTRD and beyond. Includes the author's Program of Instruction for Special Operations Hard-Target Interdiction Course.

The Complete Guide to Game Care and Cookery, 4th Edition, by Sam Fadala, Krause Publications, Iola, WI, 2003. 320 pp., illus. Paper covers. $21.95
Over 500 photos illustrating the care of wild game in the field and at home with a separate recipe section providing over 400 tested recipes.

The Concealed Handgun Manual, 4th Edition, by Chris Bird, San Antonio, TX, Privateer Publications, 2004. 332 pp., illus. Softcover, NEW. $21.95

Cowboys & the Trappings of the Old West, by William Manns & Elizabeth Clair Flood, Santa Fe, NM, ZON International Publishing Company, 1997. 224 pp., 550 colorful photos. Foreword by Roy Rogers. Hardcover. $45.00
Big & beautiful book covering: Hats, boots, spurs, chaps, guns, holsters, saddles and more. It's really a pictorial cele bration of the old time buckaroo. This exceptional book presents all the accoutrements of the cowboy life in a comprehensive tribute to the makers. The history of the craftsmen and the evolution of the gear are lavishly illustrated.

Cowgirls, Revised and Expanded 2nd Edition Early Images and Collectibles Price Guide, by Judy Crandall, Atglen, PA, Schiffer Publications, 2005. 2nd edition. Soft cover. NEW. $24.95
The First Ladies from the Great American West live again in this comprehensive pictorial chronicle.

Cowgirls: Women of the Wild West, by Elizabeth Clair Flood and William Maims, edited by Helene Helene, Santa Fe, NM, ZON International Publishing Company, 2000. 1st edition. Hardcover. New in new dust jacket. $45.00

Custom Firearms Engraving, by Tom Turpin, Krause Publications, Iola, WI, 1999. 208 pp., illus. $49.95
Provides a broad and comprehensive look at the world of firearms engraving. The exquisite styles of more than 75 master engravers are shown on beautiful examples of handguns, rifles, shotguns, and other firearms, as well as knives.

Custom Gunmakers of the 20th Century, by Michael Pretov, Manchester, CT, Precision Shooting, 2005. 168 pp., illustrated with photos. Hardcover. $24.95 NEW.

Daisy Air Rifles & BB Guns: The First 100 Years, by Neal Punchard, St. Paul, MN, Motorbooks, 2002. 1st edition. Hardcover, 10" x 10", 156 pp., 300 color. Hardcover. $29.95

Dead On, by Tony Noblitt and Warren Gabrilska, Paladin Press, Boulder, CO, 1998. 176 pp., illus. Paper covers. $22.00

The long-range marksman's guide to extreme accuracy.

Defensive Use of Firearms, by Stephen Wenger, Boulder,CO, Paladin Press, 2005. 5-1/2" x 8-1/2", soft cover, illus., 120 pp. Soft cover. NEW. $20.00

This concise and affordable handbook offers the reader a set of common-sense principles, tactics and techniques distilled from hundreds of hours of the author's training, which includes certification as a law-enforcement handgun, shotgun, patrol rifle and tactical shooting instructor.

Do or Die A Supplementary Manual on Individual Combat, by Lieut. Col. A.J. Drexel Biddle, U.S.M.C.R., Boulder, CO, Paladin Press, 2004. 80 pp., illus. Softcover, $15.00

Down to Earth: The 507th Parachute Infantry Regiment in Normandy: June 6-july 11 1944, by Martin Morgan ICA, Atglen, PA, Schiffer Publishing, 2004. 1st edition. 304 pp., color and b&w photos. Hardcover. New in new dust jacket. $69.95

Early American Flintlocks, by Daniel D. Hartzler and James B. Whisker, Bedford Valley Press, Bedford, PA 2000. 192 pp., Illustrated. $45.00

Covers early Colonial guns, New England guns, Pennsylvania Guns and Southern guns.

Effective Defense: The Woman, the Plan, the Gun, by Gila Hayes, Onalaska, WA, Police Bookshelf, 2000. 2nd edition. Photos, 264 pp. Softcover. NEW. $16.95

Elmer Keith: The Other Side of a Western Legend, by Gene Brown., Precision Shooting, Inc., Manchester, CT 2002. 1st edition. 168 pp., illustrated with b&w photos. Softcover. $19.95

An updated and expanded edition of his original work, incorporating new tales and information that have come to light in the past six years. Gene Brown was a long time friend of Keith, and today is unquestionably the leading authority on Keith's books.

Encyclopedia of Native American Bows, Arrows and Quivers, by Steve Allely and Jim Hamm, The Lyons Press, N.Y., 1999. 160 pp., illus. $29.95

A landmark book for anyone interested in archery history, or Native Americans.

The Exercise of Armes, by Jacob de Gheyn, Dover Publications, Inc., Mineola, NY, 1999. 144 pp., illus. Paper covers. $14.95

Republications of all 117 engravings from the 1607 classic military manual. A meticulously accurate portrait of uniforms and weapons of the 17th century Netherlands.

Fighting Iron: A Metals Handbook for Arms Collectors, by Art Gogan, Mowbray Publishers, Inc., Lincoln, RI, 2002. 176 pp., illus. $28.00

A guide that is easy to use, explains things in simple English and covers all of the different historical periods that we are interested in.

FBI Guide to Concealable Weapons, by the FBI, Boulder, Co, Paladin Press, 2005. Photos, 88 pp. Soft cover. NEW. $15.00

As citizens responsible for our own safety, we must know everything possible about the dangers that face us, and awareness is the first, vital step in this direction.

The Filipino Fighting Whip: Advanced Training Methods and Combat Applications, by Tom Meadows, Boulder, CO, Paladin Press, 2005. This book is a comprehensive guide for advanced training methods and combat applications as practiced and taught by the best fighters and whip practitioners in the world. 216pp. Soft cover. NEW. $20.00

Fine Art of the West, by Byron B. Price and Christopher Lyon, New York, Abbeville Press, 2004. Hardcover. NEW. $75.00

Firearm Suppressor Patents, Volume One: United States Patents, by N.R. Parker, Boulder, CO, Paladin Press, 2004. 392 pp., illustrated. Soft cover. NEW. $45.00

This book provides never-before-published interviews with three of today's top designers as well as a special section on the evolution of cutting-edge silencer mounting systems.

Firearms Assembly Disassembly; Part 4: Centerfire Rifles (2nd Edition), by J. B. Wood, Iola, WI, Krause Publications, 2004. 2nd edition. 576 pp., 1,750 b&w photos. Softcover. NEW. $24.95

Fireworks: A Gunsight Anthology, by Jeff Cooper, Paladin Press, Boulder, CO, 1998. 192 pp., illus. Paper cover. $27.00

A collection of wild, hilarious, shocking and always meaningful tales from the remarkable life of an American firearms legend.

Force-On-Force Gunfight Training: The Interactive, Reality Based Solution, by Gabriel Suarez, Boulder,CO, Paladin Press, 2005. 105 pp., illustrated with photos. Soft cover. NEW. $15.00

Fort Robinson, Frontier Series, Volume 4, by Roy Chandler, Jacksonville, NC, Ron Brigade Armory, 2003. 1st edition. 560 pp. Hardcover. New in new dust jacket. $39.95

Frederic Remington: The Color of Night, by Nancy Anderson, Princeton University Press, 2003. 1st edition. 136 color illus, 24 halftones; 10" x 11", 208 pp. Hardcover, New in new dust jacket. $49.95; UK $52.49

From a Stranger's Doorstep to the Kremlin Gate, by Mikhail Kalashnikov, Ironside International Publishers, Inc., Alexandria, VA, 1999. 460 pp., illus. $34.95

A biography of the most influential rifle designer of the 20th century. His AK-47 assault rifle has become the most widely used (and copied) assault rifle of this century.

The Frontier Rifleman, by H.B. LaCrosse Jr., Pioneer Press, Union City, TN, 1989. 183 pp., illus. Softcover. $17.50

The Frontier rifleman's clothing and equipment during the era of the American Revolution, 1760- 1800.

Galloping Thunder: The Stuart Horse Artillery Battalion, by Robert Trout, Mechanicsburg, PA, Stackpole Books, 2002. 1st edition. Hardcover, NEW. $39.95

The Gatling Gun: 19th Century Machine Gun to 21st Century Vulcan, by Joseph Berk, Paladin Press, Boulder, CO, 1991. 136 pp., illus. $34.95

Here is the fascinating on-going story of a truly timeless weapon, from its beginnings during the Civil War to its current role as a state-of-the-art modern combat system.

German Artillery of World War Two, by Ian V. Hogg, Stackpole Books, Mechanicsburg, PA, 1997. 304 pp., illus. $44.95

Complete details of German artillery use in WWII.

Gone Diggin: Memoirs of a Civil War Relic Hunter, by Toby Law, Orange, VA, Publisher's Press, 2002. 1st edition signed. 151 pp., illustrated with b&w photos. $24.95

The true story of one relic hunter's life–The author kept exacting records of every relic hunt and every relic hunter he was with working with.

Grand Old Lady of No Man's Land: The Vickers Machine Gun, by Dolf L. Goldsmith, Collector Grade Publications, Cobourg, Canada, 1994. 600 pp., illus. $79.95

Goldsmith brings his years of experience as a U.S. Army armourer, machine gun collector and shooter to bear on the Vickers, in a book sure to become a classic in its field.

Greenhill Military Manuals; Small Arms: Pistols and Rifles, by Ian Hogg; London, Greenhill Press, 2003. Revised. 160 pp., illus. Hardcover. $24.00

This handy reference guide, by the leading small arms author, provides descriptions, technical specifications and illustrations of 75 of the most important pistols and rifles, including the Heckler & Koch USP/SOCOM pistols, the FN Five-seven 5.7mm pistol, the Heckler & Koch G36 rifle and much more.

Gun Digest 2006, 60th Annual Edition, edited by Ken Ramage, Iola, WI, Krause Publications, 2005. Softcover. NEW. $24.95

This all new 59th edition continues the editorial excellence, quality, content and comprehensive cataloguing that firearms enthusiasts have come to know and expect. The most read gun book in the world for the last half century.

The Gun Digest Book of Cowboy Action Shooting: Gear, Guns,

Tactics, edited by Kevin Michalowski, Iola, WI, Krause Publications, 2005. 1st edition Softcover. NEW. $24.99

The Gun Digest Book of Exploded Firearms Drawings: 975 Isometric Views, by Harold Murtz, Iola,WI, Krause Publications, 2005, 3rd edition. 1032 pp., 975 photos, soft cover. NEW. $34.95

This book is sure to become a must-have for gunsmiths, shooters and law enforcement officials!

Gun Digest Blackpowder Loading Manual New 4th Edition, by Sam Fadala, Iola, WI, Krause Publications, 2004. 352 pp., illus. Softcover. NEW. $27.95

The Gun Digest Book of Deer Guns, edited by Dan Shideler, Iola, WI, Krause Publications, 2004. 1st edition Softcover, NEW. $14.99

The Gun Digest Book of Guns for Personal Defense Arms & Accessories for Self- Defense, edited by Kevin Michalowski, Iola, WI, Krause Publications, 2004. 1st edition Softcover. NEW. $14.99

The Gun Digest Book of Sporting Clays, 3rd edition, edited by Rick Sapp, Iola, WI, Krause Publications, 2005. 1st edition Softcover, NEW. $19.95

The Gun Digest Book of Trap & Skeet Shooting, 4th edition, edited by Rick Sapp, Iola, WI, Krause Publications, 2004. 1st edition Softcover, NEW. $22.95

Gun Engraving, by C. Austyn, Safari Press Publication, Huntington Beach, CA, 1998. 128 pp., plus 24 pp. of color photos. $50.00

A well-illustrated book on fine English and European gun engravers. Includes a fantastic pictorial section that lists types of engravings and prices.

Gun Notes, Volume 1, by Elmer Keith, Safari Press, Huntington Beach, CA, 2002. 219 pp., illus. Softcover. $24.95

A collection of Elmer Keith's most interesting columns and feature stories that appeared in "Guns & Ammo" magazine from 1961 to the late 1970's.

Gun Notes, Volume 2, by Elmer Keith, Safari Press, Huntington Beach, CA, 2002. 292 pp., illus. Softcover. $24.95

Covers articles from Keith's monthly column in "Guns & Ammo" magazine during the period from 1971 through Keith's passing in 1982.

Guns & Shooting: A Selected Bibliography, by Ray Riling, Ray Riling Arms Books Co., Phila., PA, 1982. 434 pp., illus. Limited, numbered edition. $75.00

A limited edition of this superb bibliographical work, the only modern listing of books devoted to guns and shooting.

Guns Illustrated 2006: 38th Edition, edited by Ken Ramage, Iola, WI, Krause Publications, 2005. Softcover. NEW. $21.95

Highly informative, technical articles on a wide range of shooting topics by some of the top writers in the industry. A catalog section lists more than 3,000 firearms currently manufactured in or imported to the U.S.

The Guns of the Gunfighters: Lawmen, Outlaws & TV Cowboys, by Doc O'Meara, Iola, WI, Krause Publications, 2003. 1st edition. 16-page color section, 225 b&w photos. Hardcover. $34.95

Explores the romance of the Old West, focusing on the guns that the good guys & bad guys, real & fictional characters, carried with them. Profiles of more than 50 gunslingers, half from the Old West and half from Hollywood, include a brief biography of each gunfighter, along with the guns they carried. Fascinating stories about the TV and movie celebrities of the 1950s and 1960s detail their guns and the skill–or lack thereof–they displayed.

Guns, Bullets, and Gunfighters, by Jim Cirillo, Paladin Press, Boulder, CO, 1996. 119 pp., illus. Paper covers. $16.00

Lessons and tales from a modern-day gunfighter.

ARMS LIBRARY

Gunstock Carving: A Step-by-Step Guide to Engraving Rifles and Shotguns, by Bill Janney, East Pertsburg, PA, Fox Chapel Publishing, October 2002. 89 pp., illustrated in color. Softcover. $19.95

Learn gunstock carving from an expert. Includes step-by-step projects and instructions, patterns, tips and techniques.

Hands Off! Self Defense for Women, by Maj. Fairbairn, Boulder, CO: Paladin Press, 2004. 56 pp. Soft cover. NEW. $15.00

Paladin Press is proud to bring back a work by the inimitable self-defense master W.E. Fairbairn so that a new generation of Americans can enjoy his teachings.

Hand-To-Hand Combat: United States Naval Institute, by U.S. Navy Boulder, CO, Paladin Press, 2003. 1st edition. 240 pp. Softcover. $25.00

Now you can own one of the classic publications in the history of U.S. military close-quarters combat training. In 11 photo-heavy chapters, Hand-to-Hand Combat covers training tips; vulnerable targets; the brutal fundamentals of close-in fighting; frontal and rear attacks; prisoner search and control techniques; disarming pistols, rifles, clubs and knives; offensive means of "liquidating an enemy"; and much more. After reading this book (originally published by the United States Naval Institute in 1943), you will see why it has long been sought by collectors and historians of hand-to-hand combat.

Hidden in Plain Sight, "A Practical Guide to Concealed Handgun Carry" (Revised 2nd Edition), by Trey Bloodworth and Mike Raley, Paladin Press, Boulder, CO, 1997, softcover, photos, 176 pp. $20.00

Concerned with how to comfortably, discreetly and safely exercise the privileges granted by a CCW permit? This invaluable guide offers the latest advice on what to look for when choosing a CCW, how to dress for comfortable, effective concealed carry, traditional and more unconventional carry modes, accessory holsters, customized clothing and accessories, accessibility data based on draw-time comparisons and new holsters on the market. Includes 40 new manufacturer listings.

HK Assault Rifle Systems, by Duncan Long, Paladin Press, Boulder, CO, 1995. 110 pp., illus. Paper covers. $27.95

The little known history behind this fascinating family of weapons tracing its beginnings from the ashes of WWII to the present time.

Holsters for Combat and Concealed Carry, by R.K. Campbell, Boulder, CO, Paladin Press, 2004. 1st edition. 144 pp. Softcover. NEW. $22.00

Hostage Rescue Manual; Tactics of the Counter-Terrorist Professionals, by Leroy Thompson, Mechanicsburg,PA. Greehhill Books, 2005. Incorporating vivid photographs and diagrams of rescue units in action, the Hostage Rescue Manual is the complete reference work on counter-terrorist procedures all over the world. 208 pp., with 16 pages of photos. Soft cover. NEW. $23.95

The Hunter's Guide to Accurate Shooting, by Wayne van Zwoll, Guilford, CT, Lyons Press, 2002. 1st edition. 288 pp. Hardcover. $29.95

Firearms expert van Zwoll explains exactly how to shoot the big-game rifle accurately. Taking into consideration every pertinent factor, he shows a step-by-step analysis of shooting and hunting with the big-game rifle.

The Hunting Time: Adventures in Pursuit of North American Big Game: A Forty-Year Chronicle, by John E. Howard, Deforest, WI, Saint Huberts Press, 2002. 1st edition. 537 pp., illustrated with drawings. Hardcover. $29.95

From a novice's first hunt for whitetailed deer in his native Wisconsin, to a seasoned hunter's pursuit of a Boone and Crockett Club record book caribou in the northwest territories, the author carries the reader along on his forty year journey through the big game fields of North America.

Instinct Combat Shooting; Defensive Handgunning for Police, by Chuck Klein, Flushing, NY, Looseleaf Law, 2004. 54 pages. Soft cover. NEW. $22.95

Tactical tips for effective armed defense, helpful definitions and court-ready statements that help you clearly articulate and competently justify your deadly force decision-making.

Jack O'Connor Catalogue of Letters, by Ellen Enzler Herring, Agoura, CA, Trophy Room Books, 2002. 1st edition. Hardcover. NEW. $55.00

Jack O'Connor—The Legendary Life of America's Greatest Gunwriter, by R. Anderson, Long Beach, CA, Safari Press, 2002. 1st edition. 240 pp., profuse photos. Hardcover. $29.95

This is the book all hunters in North America have been waiting for—the long-awaited biography on Jack O'Connor! Jack O'Connor was the preeminent North American big-game hunter and gunwriter of the twentieth century, and Robert Anderson's masterfully written new work is a blockbuster filled with fascinating facts and stories about this controversial character. O'Connor's lifelong friend Buck Buckner has contributed two chapters on his experiences with the master of North American hunting.

Jane's Guns Recognition Guide: 4th Edition, by Ian Hogg, Terry Gander, NY, Harper Collins, 2005. 464 pp., illustrated. Soft cover. NEW. $24.95

This book will help you identify them all. Jane's, always known for meticulous detail in the information of military equipment, aircraft, ships and much more!

Joe Rychertinik Reflects on Guns, Hunting, and Days Gone By, by Joe Rychertinik, Precision Shooting, Inc., Manchester, CT, 1999. 281 pp., illus. Thirty articles by a master story-teller. Paper covers. $16.95

Kill or Get Killed, by Col. Rex Applegate, Paladin Press, Boulder, CO, 1996. 400 pp., illus. $49.95

The best and longest-selling book on close combat in history.

Living With Terrorism; Survival Lessons from the streets of Jerusalem, by Howard Linett, Boulder, CO, Paladin Press, 2005. 277 pp., illustrated with photos. Soft cover. NEW. $20.00

Before these dangers become a reality in your life, read this book.

The Lost Classics of Jack O'Connor, edited by Jim Casada, Columbia, SC, Live Oak Press, 2004. 1st edition. Hardcover. New in new dust jacket. $35.00

Manual for H&R Reising Submachine Gun and Semi-Auto Rifle, edited by George P. Dillman, Desert Publications, El Dorado, AZ, 1994. 81 pp., illus. Paper covers. $14.95

A reprint of the Harrington & Richardson 1943 factory manual and the rare military manual on the H&R submachine gun and semi-auto rifle.

The Manufacture of Gunflints, by Sydney B.J. Skertchly, facsimile reprint with new introduction by Seymour de Lotbiniere, Museum Restoration Service, Ontario, Canada, 1984. 90 pp., illus. $24.50

Limited edition reprinting of the very scarce London edition of 1879.

Master Tips, by J. Winokur, Potshot Press, Pacific Palisades, CA, 1985. 96 pp., illus. Paper covers. $11.95

Basics of practical shooting.

The Military and Police Sniper, by Mike R. Lau, Precision Shooting, Inc., Manchester, CT, 1998. 352 pp., illus. Paper covers. $44.95

Advanced precision shooting for combat and law enforcement.

Military Small Arms of the 20th Century, 7th Edition, by Ian V. Hogg and John Weeks, DBI Books, a division of Krause Publications, Iola, WI, 2000. 416 pp., illus. Paper covers. Over 800 photographs and illustrations. $24.95

Covers small arms of 46 countries.

Modern Guns Identification and Values, 15th edition, by Steve and Russell Quertermous, Paducah, KY, Collector's Books, 2004. 1800+ illus; 8.5x11", 544 pp. Soft cover. NEW. $16.95

Updated edition features current market values for over 2,500 models of rifles, shotguns, & handguns. Contains model name, gauge or caliber, action, finish or stock & forearm, barrel, cylinder or magazine, sights, weight & length, & comments.

Modern Gun Values: 13th Edition, edited by Ken Ramage, Krause Publications, Iola, WI, 2006. Softcover. NEW. $24.95

Modern Law Enforcement Weapons & Tactics, 3rd edition, by Patrick Sweeney, Iola, WI, Krause Publications, 2004. Illustrated, b&w photos, 256 pages. $22.99

Sweeney walks you through the latest gear and tactics employed by American law enforcement officers.

Modern Sporting Guns, by Christopher Austyn, Safari Press, Huntington Beach, CA, 1994. 128 pp., illus. Hardcover. $40.00

A discussion of the "best" English guns; round action, over-and-under, boxlocks, hammer guns, bolt action and double rifles as well as accessories.

More Tactical Reality; Why There's No Such Thing as an Advanced Gunfight, by Louis Awerbuck, Boulder, CO, Paladin Press, 2004. 144 pp. Softcover. NEW. $25.00

The MP-40 Machine Gun, Desert Publications, El Dorado, AZ, 1995. 32 pp., illus. Paper covers. $11.95

A reprint of the hard-to-find operating and maintenance manual for one of the most famous machine guns of WWII.

Naval Percussion Locks and Primers, by Lt. J. A. Dahlgren, Museum Restoration Service, Bloomfield, Canada, 1996. 140 pp., illus. $35.00

First published as an Ordnance Memoranda in 1853, this is the finest existing study of percussion locks and primers origin and development.

The Official Soviet AKM Manual, translated by Maj. James F. Gebhardt (Ret.), Paladin Press, Boulder, CO, 1999. 120 pp., illus. Paper covers. $18.00

This official military manual, available in English for the first time, was originally published by the Soviet Ministry of Defence. Covers the history, function, maintenance, assembly and disassembly, etc. of the 7.62mm AKM assault rifle.

The One-Round War: U.S.M.C. Scout-Snipers in Vietnam, by Peter Senich, Paladin Press, Boulder, CO, 1996. 384 pp., illus. Paper covers $59.95

Sniping in Vietnam focusing specifically on the Marine Corps program.

Optics Digest: Scopes, Binoculars, Rangefinders, and Spotting Scopes, by Clair Rees, Long Beach, CA, Safari Press, 2005. 1st edition. 189 pp. Softcover. NEW. $24.95

OSS Special Operations in China, by Col. F. Mills and John W. Brunner, Williamstown, NJ, Phillips Publications, 2003. 1st edition. 550 pp., illustrated with photos. Hardcover. New in new dust jacket. $34.95

Paintball Digest The Complete Guide to Games, Gear, and Tactics, by Richard Sapp, Iola, WI, Krause Publications, 2004. 1st edition. 272 pp. Softcover. NEW. $19.99

Paleo-Indian Artifacts: Identification & Value Guide, by Lar Hothem, Paducah, KY, Collector Books, 2005. 1st edition. 379 pp. Pictorial hardcover. NEW. $29.95

Panzer Aces German Tank Commanders of WWII, by Franz Kurowski, translated by David Johnston, Mechanicsburg, PA, Stackpole Books, 2004. 1st edition. 448 pp., 50 b&w photos Softcover. NEW. $19.95

Parker Brothers: Knight of the Trigger, by Ed Muderlak, Davis, IL, Old Reliable Publishing, 2002. 223 pp. $25.00

Knight of the Trigger tells the story of the Old West when Parker's most famous gun saleman traveled the country by rail, competing in the pigeon ring, hunting with the rich and famous, and selling the "Old Reliable" Parker shotgun. The life and times of Captain Arthur William du Bray, Parker Brothers' on-the-road sales agent from 1884 to 1926, is described in a novelized version of his interesting life.

Peril in the Powder Mills: Gunpowder & Its Men, by David McMahon & Anne Kelly Lane, West Conshohocken, PA, privately printed, 2004. 1st edition. 118 pp. Softcover. NEW. $18.95

Powder Horns and their Architecture; And Decoration as Used by the Soldier, Indian, Sailor and Traders of the Era, by Madison Grant, York, PA, privately printed, 1987. 165 pp., profusely illustrated. Hardcover. $45.00

Covers homemade pieces from the late eighteenth and early nineteenth centuries.

Practically Speaking: An Illustrated Guide–The Game, Guns and Gear of the International Defensive Pistol Association, by Walt Rauch, Lafayette Hills, PA, privately printed, 2002. 1st edition. 79 pp., illustrated with drawings and color photos. Softcover. $24.95

The game, guns and gear of the International Defensive Pistol Association with real-world applications.

Present Sabers: A Popular History of the U.S. Horse Cavalry, by Allan T. Heninger, Tucson, AZ, Excalibur Publications, 2002. 1st edition. 160 pp., with 148 photographs, 45 illustrations and 4 charts. Softcover. $24.95

An illustrated history of America's involvement with the horse cavalry, from its earliest beginnings during the Revolutionary War through its demise in WWII. The book also contains several appendices, as well as depictions of the regular insignia of all the U.S. Cavalry units.

Principles of Personal Defense, by Jeff Cooper, Paladin Press, Boulder, CO, 2006. 80 pp., illus. Paper covers. $14.00

This revised edition of Jeff Cooper's classic on personal defense offers great new illustrations and a new preface while retaining the theory of individual defense behavior presented in the original book.

Queen's Rook: A Soldier's Story, by Croft Barker, Flatonia,TX, Cistern Publishing, 2004. Limited edition of 500 copies. 177 pp., with 50 never before published photographs. Soft cover. NEW. $35.00

Men of the U.S. Army were assigned to South Vietnamese Infantry companies and platoons. Many of these men were lost in a war that is still misunderstood. This is their story, written in their own words. These Americans, and the units they lived with, engaged in savage fights against Viet Cong guerillas and North Vietnamese Army Regulars in the dark, deadly jungles north of Saigon.

The Quotable Hunter, edited by Jay Cassell and Peter Fiduccia, The Lyons Press, N.Y., 1999. 224 pp., illus. $20.00

This collection of more than three hundred memorable quotes from hunters through the ages captures the essence of the sport, with all its joys idiosyncrasies, and challenges.

Real World Self-Defense by Jerry Vancook, Boulder, CO, Paladin Press, 1999. Illus., 224 pp. Soft cover. NEW. $20.00

Presenting tactics and techniques that are basic, easy to learn and proven effective under the stress of combat, he covers unarmed defense, improvised weapons, edged weapons, firearms and more.

Renaissance Drill Book, by Jacob de Gheyn, edited by David J. Blackmore, Mechanicsburg, PA, Greenhill Books, 2003. 1st edition. 248 pp., 117 illustrations. Hardcover. $24.95

Jacob de Gheyn's Exercise of Armes was an immense success when first published in 1607. It is a fascinating 17th-century military manual, designed to instruct contemporary soldiers how to handle arms effectively, and correctly, and it makes for a unique glimpse into warfare as waged in the Thirty Years War and the English Civil War. In addition, detailed illustrations show the various movements and postures to be adopted during use of the pike.

A Rifleman Went to War, by H. W. McBride, Lancer Militaria, Mt. Ida, AR, 1987. 398 pp., illus. $29.95

The classic account of practical marksmanship on the battlefields of WWI.

Running Recon, A Photo Journey with SOG Special Ops Along the Ho Chi Minh Trail, by Frank Greco, Boulder, CO, Paladin Press, 2004. 1st edition. Hardcover. $79.95

Running Recon is a combination of military memoir and combat photography book. It reflects both the author's experience in Kontum, Vietnam, from April 1969 to April 1970 as part of the top-secret Studies and Observation Group (SOG) and the collective experience of SOG veterans in general. What sets it apart from other Vietnam books is its wealth of more than 700 photographs, many never before published, from the author's personal collection and those of his fellow SOG veterans.

Sharpshooting for Sport and War, by W.W. Greener, Wolfe Publishing Co., Prescott, AZ, 1995. 192 pp., illus. $30.00

This classic reprint explores the *first* expanding bullet; service rifles; shooting positions; trajectories; recoil; external ballistics; and other valuable information.

Shooter's Bible 2006 No. 97, by Wayne Van Zwoll, Stoeger Publishing, 2005. 576 pages. Soft cover. NEW. $21.95

New for this edition is a special Web Directory designed to complement the regular Reference section, including the popular Gun finder index.

Shooting Buffalo Rifles of the Old West, by Mike Venturino, MLV Enterprises, Livingston, MT, 2002. 278 pp., illustrated with b&w photos. Softcover. $30.00

This tome will take you through the history, the usage, the many models, and the actual shooting (and how to's) of the many guns that saw service on the Frontier and are lovingly called "Buffalo Rifles" today. If you love to shoot your Sharps, Ballards, Remingtons, or Springfield "Trapdoors" for hunting or competition, or simply love Old West history, your library WILL NOT be complete without this latest book from Mike Venturino!

Shooting Colt Single Actions, by Mike Venturino, MLV Enterprises, Livingston, MT, 1997. 205 pp., illus. Softcover. $25.00

A complete examination of the Colt Single Action including styles, calibers and generations, b&w photos throughout.

Shooting Lever Guns of the Old West, by Mike Venturino, MLV Enterprises, Livingston, MT, 1999. 300 pp., illus. Softcover. $27.95

Shooting the lever action type repeating rifles of our American West.

Shooting Sixguns of the Old West, by Mike Venturino, MLV Enterprises, Livingston, MT, 1997. 221 pp., illus. Paper covers. $26.50

A comprehensive look at the guns of the early West: Colts, Smith & Wesson and Remingtons, plus blackpowder and reloading specs.

Shooting to Live, by Capt. W.E. Fairbairn and Capt. E.A. Sykes, Paladin Press, Boulder, CO, 1997, 4-1/2" x 7", soft cover, illus., 112 pp. $14.00

This is the product of Fairbairn's and Sykes' practical experience with the handgun. Hundreds of incidents provided the basis for the first true book on life-or-death shootouts with the pistol. Shooting to Live teaches all concepts, considerations and applications of combat pistol craft.

Small Arms of World War II, by Chris Chant, St. Paul, MN, MBI Publishing Company, 2001. 1st edition. 96 pp., single page on each weapon with photograph, description, and a specifications table. Hardcover. New. $13.95

Detailing the design and development of each weapon, this book covers the most important infantry weapons used by both Allied and Axis soldiers between 1939 and 1945. These include both standard infantry bolt-action rifles, such as the German Kar 98 and the British Lee-Enfield, plus the automatic rifles that entered service toward the end of the war, such as the Stg 43. As well as rifles, this book also features submachine guns, machine guns and handguns and a specifications table for each weapon.

Sniper Training, FM 23-10, Reprint of the U.S. Army field manual of August, 1994, Paladin Press, Boulder, CO, 1995. 352 pp., illus. Paper covers. $30.00

The most up-to-date U.S. military sniping information and doctrine.

Song of Blue Moccasin, by Roy Chandler, Jacksonville, NC, Ron Brigade Armory, 2004. 231 pp. Hardcover. New in new dust jacket. $45.00

Speak Like a Native; Professional Secrets for Mastering Foreign Languages, by Michael Janich, Boulder CO, Paladin Press, 2005. 136 pages. Soft cover. NEW. $19.00

No matter what language you wish to learn or the level of fluency you need to attain, this book can help you learn to speak like a native.

Special Operations: Weapons and Tactics, by Timothy Mullin, London, Greenhill Press, 2003. 1st edition. 176 pp., with 189 illustrations. $39.95

The tactics and equipment of Special Forces explained in full, Contains 200 images of weaponry and training. This highly illustrated guide covers the full experience of special operations training from every possible angle. There is also considerable information on nonfirearm usage, such as specialized armor and ammunition.

2006 Standard Catalog of Firearms, 16th Edition, by Ned Schwing, Iola, WI, Krause Publications, 2006. 1504 pp., illus. 7,000 b&w photos plus a 16-page color section. Paper covers. $34.95

This is the largest, most comprehensive and best-selling firearm book of all time! And this year's edition is a blockbuster for both shooters and firearm collectors. More than 14,000 firearms are listed and priced in up to six grades of condition. That's almost 100,000 prices! Gun enthusiasts will love the new full-color section of photos highlighting the finest firearms sold at auction this past year.

Standard Catalog of Military Firearms 3rd Edition: The Collector's Price & Reference Guide, by Ned Schwing, Iola, WI, Krause Publications, 2005. 480 pp. Softcover. $29.99

A companion volume to Standard Catalog of Firearms, this revised and expanded second edition comes complete with all the detailed information readers found useful and more. Listings beginning with the early cartridge models of the 1870s to the latest high-tech sniper rifles have been expanded to include more models, variations, historical information, and data, offering more detail for the military firearms collector, shooter, and history buff. Identification of specific firearms is easier with nearly 250 additional photographs. Plus, readers will enjoy "snap shots," small personal articles from experts relating real-life experiences with exclusive models. Revised to include every known military firearm available to the U.S. collector. Special feature articles on focused aspects of collecting and shooting.

Street Tough, Hard Core, Anything Goes, Street Fighting Fundamentals, by Phil Giles, Boulder, CO, Paladin Press, 2004. 176 pages. Soft cover. NEW. $25.00

A series of intense training drills performed at full power and full speed sets the Street Tough program apart from all other self-defense regimens.

Stress Fire, Vol. 1: Stress Fighting for Police, by Massad Ayoob, Police Bookshelf, Concord, NH, 1984. 149 pp., illus. Paper covers. $11.95

Gunfighting for police, advanced tactics and techniques.

Survival Guns, by Mel Tappan, Desert Publications, El Dorado, AZ, 1993. 456 pp., illus. Paper covers. $25.00

Discusses in a frank and forthright manner which handguns, rifles and shotguns to buy for personal defense and securing food, and the ones to avoid.

The Tactical Advantage, by Gabriel Suarez, Paladin Press, Boulder, CO, 1998. 216 pp., illus. Paper covers. $22.00

Learn combat tactics that have been tested in the world's toughest schools.

Tactical Marksman, by Dave M. Lauch, Paladin Press, Boulder, CO, 1996. 165 pp., illus. Paper covers. $35.00

A complete training manual for police and practical shooters.

Tim Murphy Rifleman Frontier Series Volume 3, by Roy Chandler, Jacksonville, NC, Iron Brigade Armory, 2003. 1st edition. 396 pp. Hardcover. $39.95

Tim Murphy may be our young nation's earliest recognized hero. Murphy was seized by Seneca Tribesmen during his infancy. Traded to the Huron, he was renamed and educated by Sir William Johnson, a British colonial officer. Freed during the prisoner exchange of 1764, Murphy discovered his superior ability with a Pennsylvania longrifle. An early volunteer in the Pennsylvania militia, Tim Murphy served valiantly in rifle companies including the justly famed Daniel Morgan's Riflemen. This is Murphy's story.

To Ride, Shoot Straight, and Speak the Truth, by Jeff Cooper, Paladin Press, Boulder, CO, 1997, 5-1/2" x 8-1/2", soft-cover, illus., 384 pp. $32.00

Combat mind-set, proper sighting, tactical residential architecture, nuclear war–these are some of the many subjects explored by Jeff Cooper in this illustrated anthology. The author discusses various arms, fighting skills and the importance of knowing how to defend oneself, and one's honor, in our rapidly changing world.

Trailriders Guide to Cowboy Action Shooting, by James W. Barnard, Pioneer Press, Union City, TN, 1998. 134 pp., plus 91 photos, drawings and charts. Paper covers. $24.95

Covers the complete spectrum of this shooting discipline, from how to dress to authentic leather goods, which guns are legal, calibers, loads and ballistics.

Traveler's Guide to the Firearms Laws of the Fifty States, 2006 edition., by Scott Kappas, KY, Traveler's Guide, 2006, 64 pp. Softcover, NEW. $12.95

U.S. Army Hand-to-Hand Combat: FM 21-150, 1954 edition. Boulder, CO, Paladin Press, 2005. 192 pp. illus. Soft cover. NEW. $20.00

U.S. Infantry Weapons in Combat: Personal Experiences from Wolrd War II and Korea, by Mark Goodwin w/ forward by Scott Duff, Export, PA, Scott Duff Pub., 2005. 237 pp., over 50 Photos and drawings. Soft cover. NEW. $23.50

The stories about US infantry weapons contained in this book are the real hands-on experiences of the men who actually used them for their intended purposes.

U.S. Marine Corp Rifle and Pistol Marksmanship, 1935, reprinting of a government publication, Lancer Militaria, Mt. Ida, AR, 1991. 99 pp., illus. Paper covers. $11.95

The old corps method of precision shooting.

U.S. Marine Corps Scout/Sniper Training Manual, Lancer Militaria, Mt. Ida, AR, 1989. Softcover. $27.95

Reprint of the original sniper training manual used by the Marksmanship Training Unit of the Marine Corps Development and Education Command in Quantico, Virginia.

U.S. Marine Corps Scout-Sniper, World War II and Korea, by Peter R. Senich, Paladin Press, Boulder, CO, 1994. 236 pp., illus. $44.95

The most thorough and accurate account ever printed on the training, equipment and combat experiences of the U.S. Marine Corps Scout-Snipers.

U.S. Marine Corps Sniping, Lancer Militaria, Mt. Ida, AR, 1989. Irregular pagination. Softcover. $18.95

A reprint of the official Marine Corps FMFM1-3B.

U.S. Marine Uniforms-1912-1940, by Jim Moran, Williamstown, NJ, Phillips Publications, 2001. 174 pp., illustrated with b&w photographs. Hardcover. $49.95

The Ultimate Sniper: An Advanced Training Manual for Military and Police Snipers by Major John L. Plaster, Paladin Press, Boulder, CO, 2006. 572 pp., illus. Paper covers. $49.95

Uniforms And Equipment of the Imperial Japanese Army in World War II, by Mike Hewitt, Atglen, PA, Schiffer Publications, 2002. 176 pp., with over 520 color and b&w photos. Hardcover. $59.95

Unrepentant Sinner, by Col. Charles Askins, Paladin Press, Boulder, CO, 2000. 322 pp., illus. $29.95

The autobiography of Colonel Charles Askins.

Vietnam Order of Battle, by Shelby L. Stanton, William C. Westmoreland, Mechanicsburg, PA, Stackpole Books, 2003. 1st edition. 416 pp., 32 in full color, 101 halftones. Hardcover. $69.95

A monumental, encyclopedic work of immense detail concerning U.S. Army and allied forces that fought in the Vietnam War from 1962 through 1973. Extensive lists of units providing a record of every Army unit that served in Vietnam, down to and including separate companies, and also including U.S. Army aviation and riverine units. Shoulder patches and distinctive unit insignia of all divisions and battalions. Extensive maps portraying unit locations at each six-month interval. Photographs and descriptions of all major types of equipment employed in the conflict. Plus much more!

Warriors; On living with Courage, Discipline, and Honor, by Loren Christensen, Boulder, CO, Paladin Press, 2004. 376 pages. Soft cover. NEW. $20.00

The "Walking Stick" Method of Self-Defence, by an officer of the indian police, Boulder, CO: Paladin Press, 2004. 1st edition. 112 pages. Soft cover. NEW. $15.00

The entire range of defensive and offensive skills is discussed and demonstrated, including guards, strikes, combinations, counterattacks, feints and tricks, double-handed techniques and training drills.

Weapons of Delta Force, by Fred Pushies, St. Paul, MN, MBI Publishing Company, 2002. 1st edition. 128 pp., 100 b&w and 100 color illustrated. Hardcover. $24.95

America's elite counter-terrorist organization, Delta Force, is a handpicked group of the U.S. Army's finest soldiers. Delta uses some of the most sophisticated weapons in the field today, and all are detailed in this book. Pistols, sniper rifles, special mission aircraft, fast attack vehicles, SCUBA and paratrooper gear, and more are presented in this fully illustrated account of our country's heroes and their tools of the trade.

Weapons of the Waffen-SS, by Bruce Quarrie, Sterling Publishing Co., Inc., 1991. 168 pp., illus. $24.95

An in-depth look at the weapons that made Hitler's Waffen-SS the fearsome fighting machine it was.

Weatherby: The Man, The Gun, The Legend, by Grits and Tom Gresham, Cane River Publishing Co., Natchitoches, LA, 1992. 290 pp., illus. $24.95

A fascinating look at the life of the man who changed the course of firearms development in America.

The Winchester Era, by David Madis, Art & Reference House, Brownsville, TX, 1984. 100 pp., illus. $19.95

Story of the Winchester company, management, employees, etc.

Winchester Pocket Guide; Identification and Pricing for 50 Collectible Rifles and Shotguns, by Ned Schwing, Iola,WI, Krause Publications, 2004. 224 pp., illustrated. Soft cover. NEW. $12.95

The Winchester Pocket Guide also features advice on collecting, grading and pricing the collectible firearms.

With British Snipers to the Reich, by Capt. C. Shore, Lander Militaria, Mt. Ida, AR, 1948. 420 pp., illus. $29.95

One of the greatest books ever written on the art of combat sniping.

The World's Machine Pistols and Submachine Guns–Vol. 2a 1964 to 1980, by Nelson & Musgrave, Ironside International, Alexandria, VA, 2000. 673 pp. $59.95

Containing data, history and photographs of over 200 weapons. With a special section covering shoulder stocked automatic pistols, 100 additional photos.

The World's Sniping Rifles, by Ian V. Hogg, Stackpole Books, Mechanicsburg, 1998. 144 pp., illus. $24.00

A detailed manual with descriptions and illustrations of more than 50 high-precision rifles from 14 countries and a complete analysis of sights and systems.

Wyatt Earp: A Biography of the Legend: Volume 1: The Cowtown Years, by Lee A. Silva, Santa Ana, CA, privately printed, 2002. 1st edition signed. Hardcover. New in new dust jacket. $86.95

GUNSMITHING

Accurizing the Factory Rifle, by M.L. McPhereson, Precision Shooting, Inc., Manchester, CT, 1999. 335 pp., illus. Paper covers. $44.95

A long-awaited book, which bridges the gap between the rudimentary (mounting sling swivels, scope blocks and that general level of accomplishment) and the advanced (precision chambering, barrel fluting, and that general level of accomplishment) books that are currently available today.

Antique Firearms Assembly Disassembly: The Comprehensive Guide to Pistols, Rifles, & Shotguns, by David Chicoine, Iola,WI, Krause Publications, 2005. 528 pages. 600 b&w photos & illus. Soft cover. NEW. $29.95

Create a resource unequaled by any. Features over 600 photos of antique and rare firearms for quick identification.

The Art of Engraving, by James B. Meek, F. Brownell & Son, Montezuma, IA, 1973. 196 pp., illus. $42.95

A complete, authoritative, imaginative and detailed study in training for gun engraving. The first book of its kind–and a great one.

Checkering and Carving of Gun Stocks, by Monte Kennedy, Stackpole Books, Harrisburg, PA, 1962. 175 pp., illus. $39.95

Revised, enlarged cloth-bound edition of a much sought-after, dependable work.

Firearms Assembly/Disassembly, Part I: Automatic Pistols, 2nd Revised Edition, The Gun Digest Book of, by J.B. Wood, DBI Books, a division of Krause Publications, Iola, WI, 1999. 480 pp., illus. Paper covers. $24.95

Covers 58 popular autoloading pistols plus nearly 200 variants of those models integrated into the text and completely cross-referenced in the index.

Firearms Assembly/Disassembly Part II: Revolvers, Revised Edition, The Gun Digest Book of, by J.B. Wood, DBI Books, a division of Krause Publications, Iola, WI, 1997. 480 pp., illus. Paper covers. $27.95

Covers 49 popular revolvers plus 130 variants. The most comprehensive and professional presentation available to either hobbyist or gunsmith.

Firearms Assembly/Disassembly Part III: Rimfire Rifles 2nd Edition, The Gun Digest Book of, by J. B. Wood, Krause Publications, Iola, WI, 2006. 480 pp., illus. Paper covers. $24.95

Greatly expanded edition covering 65 popular rimfire rifles plus over 100 variants all completely cross-referenced in the index.

Firearms Assembly/Disassembly Part IV: Centerfire Rifles, 3rd Revised Edition, The Gun Digest Book of, by J.B. Wood, Krause Publications, Iola, WI, 2004. 480 pp., illus. Paper covers. $24.95

Covers 54 popular centerfire rifles plus 300 variants. The most comprehensive and professional presentation available to either hobbyist or gunsmith.

Firearms Assembly/Disassembly, Part V: Shotguns, Revised Edition, The Gun Digest Book of, by J.B. Wood, Krause Publications, Iola, WI, 2002. 480 pp., illus. Paper covers. $24.95

Covers 46 popular shotguns plus over 250 variants with step-by-step instructions on how to dismantle and reassemble each. The most comprehensive and professional presentation available to either hobbyist or gunsmith.

Firearms Assembly 3: The NRA Guide to Rifle and Shotguns, NRA Books, Wash., DC, 1980. 264 pp., illus. Paper covers. $14.95

Text and illustrations explaining the takedown of 125 rifles and shotguns, domestic and foreign.

Firearms Assembly 4: The NRA Guide to Pistols and Revolvers, NRA Books, Wash., DC, 1980. 253 pp., illus. Paper covers. $14.95

Text and illustrations explaining the takedown of 124 pistol and revolver models, domestic and foreign.

Firearms Bluing and Browning, by R.H. Angier, Stackpole Books, Harrisburg, PA. 151 pp., illus. $19.95

A world master gunsmith reveals his secrets of building, repairing and renewing a gun, quite literally, lock, stock and barrel. A useful, concise text on chemical coloring methods for the gunsmith and mechanic.

Guns and Gunmaking Tools of Southern Appalachia, by John Rice Irwin, Schiffer Publishing Ltd., 1983. 118 pp., illus. Paper covers. $9.95

The story of the Kentucky rifle.

Gunsmith Kinks, by F.R. (Bob) Brownell, F. Brownell & Son, Montezuma, IA, 1st ed., 1969. 496 pp., well illus. $22.98

A widely useful accumulation of shop kinks, short cuts, techniques and pertinent comments by practicing gunsmiths from all over the world.

Gunsmith Kinks 2, by Bob Brownell, F. Brownell & Son, Publishers, Montezuma, IA, 1983. 496 pp., illus. $22.95

A collection of gunsmithing knowledge, shop kinks, new and old techniques, shortcuts and general know-how straight from those who do them best–the gunsmiths.

Gunsmith Kinks 3, edited by Frank Brownell, Brownells Inc., Montezuma, IA, 1993. 504 pp., illus. $24.95

Tricks, knacks and "kinks" by professional gunsmiths and gun tinkerers. Hundreds of valuable ideas are given in this volume.

Gunsmith Kinks 4, edited by Frank Brownell, Brownells Inc., Montezuma, IA, 2001. 564 pp., illus. $27.75

332 detailed illustrations. 560+ pages with 706 separate subject headings and over 5000 cross- indexed entries. An incredible gold mine of information.

The Gunsmith Machinist, by Steve Acker, Village Press Publications Inc, Michigan. 2001. Hardcover, New in new dust jacket. $69.95

The Gunsmith of Grenville County: Building the American Longrifle, by Peter Alexander, Texarkana, TX, Scurlock Publishing Co., 2002. 400 pp.in, with hundreds of illustrations, and six color photos of original rifles. Stiff paper covers. $45.00

The most extensive how-to book on building longrifles ever published. Takes you through every step of building your own longrifle, from shop set up and tools to engraving, carving and finishing.

Gunsmithing, by Roy F. Dunlap, Stackpole Books, Harrisburg, PA, 1990. 742 pp., illus. $44.95

A manual of firearm design, construction, alteration and remodeling. For amateur and professional gunsmiths and users of modern firearms.

Gunsmithing at Home: Lock, Stock and Barrel, by John Traister, Stoeger Publishing Co., Wayne, NJ, 1997. 320 pp., illus. Paper covers. $19.95

A complete step-by-step fully illustrated guide to the art of gunsmithing.

Gunsmithing Shotguns: The Complete Guide to Care & Repair, by David Henderson, New York, Globe Pequot, 2003. 1st edition. Hardcover. NEW. $24.95

Gunsmithing Tips and Projects, a collection of the best articles from the *Handloader* and *Rifle* magazines, by various authors, Wolfe Publishing Co., Prescott, AZ, 1992. 443 pp., illus. Paper covers. $25.00

Includes such subjects as shop, stocks, actions, tuning, triggers, barrels, customizing, etc.

Gunsmithing: Guns of the Old West: Expanded 2nd Edition, by David Chicoine, Iola, WI, Krause Publications, 2004. 446 pp.in, illus. Softcover. NEW. $29.95

Gunsmithing: Pistols & Revolvers: Expanded 2nd Edition, by Patrick Sweeney, Iola, WI, Krause Publications, 2004. Softcover, NEW. $19.99

Gunsmithing: Rifles, by Patrick Sweeney, Krause Publications, Iola, WI, 1999. 352 pp., illus. Paper covers. $24.95

Tips for lever-action rifles. Building a custom Ruger 10/22. Building a better hunting rifle.

Home Gunsmithing the Colt Single Action Revolvers, by Loren W. Smith, Ray Riling Arms Books, Co., Phila., PA, 2001. 119 pp., illus. $29.95

Affords the Colt Single Action owner detailed, pertinent information on the operating and servicing of this famous and historic handgun.

How to Convert Military Rifles, Williams Gun Sight Co., Davision, MI, new and enlarged seventh edition, 1997. 76 pp., illus. Paper covers. $13.95

This latest edition updated the changes that have occured over the past thirty years. Tips, instructions and illustratons on how to convert popular military rifles as the Enfield, Mauser 96 and SKS just to name a few are presented.

Mauser M98 & M96, by R.A. Walsh, Wolfe Publishing Co., Prescott, AR, 1998. 123 pp., illus. Paper covers. $32.50

How to build your own favorite custom Mauser rifle from two of the best bolt action rifle designs ever produced–the military Mauser Model 1898 and Model 1896 bolt rifles.

Mr. Single Shot's Gunsmithing-Idea-Book, by Frank de Haas, Mark de Haas, Orange City, IA, 1996. 168 pp., illus. Paper covers. $22.50

Offers easy to follow, step-by-step instructions for a wide variety of gunsmithing procedures all reinforced by plenty of photos.

Recreating the American Longrifle, by William Buchele, et al, George Shumway Publisher, York, Pa, 5th edition, 1999. 175 pp., illus. $40.00

Includes full size plans for building a Kentucky rifle.

The Story of Pope's Barrels, by Ray M. Smith, R&R Books, Livonia, NY, 1993. 203 pp., illus. $39.00

A reissue of a 1960 book whose author knew Pope personally. It will be of special interest to Schuetzen rifle fans, since Pope's greatest days were at the height of the Schuetzen-era before WWI.

Survival Gunsmithing, by J.B. Wood, Desert Publications, Cornville, AZ, 1986. 92 pp., illus. Paper covers. $11.95

A guide to repair and maintenance of the most popular rifles, shotguns and handguns.

The Tactical 1911, by Dave Lauck, Paladin Press, Boulder, CO, 1998. 137 pp., illus. Paper covers. $20.00

Here is the only book you will ever need to teach you how to select, modify, employ and maintain your Colt.

HANDGUNS

.22 Caliber Handguns; A Shooter's Guide, by D.F. Geiger, Lincoln, RI, Andrew Mowbray, Inc., 2003. 1st edition. Softcover. $21.95

The .380 Enfield No. 2 Revolver, by Mark Stamps and Ian Skennerton, I.D.S.A. Books, Piqua, OH, 1993. 124 pp., 80 illus. Paper covers. $19.95

9mm Parabellum; The History & Development of the World's 9mm Pistols & Ammunition, by Klaus-Peter Konig and Martin Hugo, Schiffer Publishing Ltd., Atglen, PA, 1993. 304 pp., illus. $39.95

Detailed history of 9mm weapons from Belguim, Italy, Germany, Israel, France, U.S.A., Czechoslovakia, Hungary, Poland, Brazil, Finland and Spain.

Advanced Master Handgunning, by Charles Stephens, Paladin Press, Boulder, CO, 1994. 72 pp., illus. Paper covers. $14.00

Secrets and surefire techniques for winning handgun competitions.

A Study of Colt New Army and Navy Pattern Double action Revolvers 1889-1908, by Robert Best. Privately Printed, 2005, 2nd Printing. "A Study…" is a detailed

look into Colt's development and production of the Double Action Swing Out Cylinder New Army and Navy series revolvers. Civilian model production, U.S. Army and Navy models and contracts, and other Government organizations using these revolvers are all covered in this book. In depth research by the author into Colt's shipping records, and the Government Archives is used to document the material presented. Model variations and serial number ranges are also presented in six color charts and a complete listing of all variations. There are over 150 photographs with 24 pages of color photos to show specific markings and manufacturing changes. Fully documented. 276 pages. Hardcover. NEW. $62.00

Advanced Tactical Marksman More High Performance Techniques for Police, Military, and Practical Shooters, by Dave M. Lauck. Paladin Press, Boulder, CO, 2002. 1st edition. 232 pp., photos, illus. Softcover $35.00

Lauck, one of the most respected names in high-performance shooting and gunsmithing, refines and updates his 1st book. Dispensing with overcomplicated mil-dot formulas and minute-of- angle calculations, Lauck shows you how to achieve superior accuracy and figure out angle shots, train for real-world scenarios, choose optics and accessories.

American Beauty: The Prewar Colt National Match Government Model Pistol, by Timothy Mullin, Collector Grade Publications, Canada, 1999. 72 pp., 69 illus. $34.95

69 illustrations, 20 in full color photos of factory engraved guns and other authenticated upgrades, including rare 'double-carved' ivory grips.

The Automatic Pistol, by J.B.L. Noel, Foreword by Timothy J. Mullin, Boulder, CO, Paladin Press, 2004. 128 pp., illus. Softcover. NEW. $14.00

The Ayoob Files: The Book, by Massad Ayoob, Police Bookshelf, Concord, NH, 1995. 223 pp., illus. Paper covers. $14.95

The best of Massad Ayoob's acclaimed series in *American Handgunner* magazine.

Big Bore Handguns, by John Taffin, Krause Publications, Iola, WI, 2002. 1st edition. 352 pp., 320 b&w photos with a 16-page color section. Hardcover. $39.95

Gives honest reviews and an inside look at shooting, hunting, and competing with the biggest handguns around. Covers handguns from major gunmakers, as well as handgun customizing, accessories, reloading, and cowboy activities. Significant coverage is also given to handgun customizing, accessories, reloading, and popular shooting hobbies including hunting and cowboy activities.

Bill Ruger's .22 Pistol: A Photographic Essay of the Ruger Rimfire Pistol, by Don Findlay, New York, Simon & Schuster, 2000. 2nd printing.Limited edition of 100 copies, signed and numbered. Hardcover, NEW. $100.00

The Browning High Power Automatic Pistol (Expanded Edition), by Blake R. Stevens, Collector Grade Publications, Canada, 1996. 310 pp., with 313 illus. $49.95

An in-depth chronicle of seventy years of High Power history, from John M. Browning's original 16-shot prototypes to the present. Profusely illustrated with rare original photos and drawings from the FN Archive to describe virtually every sporting and military version of the High Power. The Expanded Edition contains 30 new pages on the interesting Argentine full-auto High Power, the latest FN 'MK3' and BDA9 pistols, plus FN's revolutionary P90 5.7x28mm Personal Defense Weapon, and more!

Browning Hi-Power Pistols, Desert Publications, Cornville, AZ, 1982. 20 pp., illus. Paper covers. $11.95

Covers all facets of the various military and civilian models of the Browning Hi-Power pistol.

Canadian Military Handguns 1855-1985, by Clive M. Law, Museum Restoration Service, Bloomfield, Ont., Canada, 1994. 130pp., illus. $40.00

A long-awaited and important history for arms historians and pistol collectors.

Classic Handguns of the 20th Century, By David Arnold. Iola, WI, Krause Publications, 2004. You'll need this book to find out what qualities,

contributions and characteristics made each of the twenty handguns found within a "classic" in the eyes of noted gun

historian and author, David W. Arnold. Join him on this most fascinating visual walk through the most significant and prolific

handguns of the 20th century. From the Colt Single-Action Army Revolver and the German P08 Luger to the Walther P-38

and Beretta Model 92. 144 pp., color photos. Softcover. NEW. $24.99

Collecting U. S. Pistols & Revolvers, 1909-1945, by J. C. Harrison. The Arms Chest, Oklahoma City, OK, 1999. 2nd edition (revised). 185 pp., illus. Spiral bound. $35.00

Valuable and detailed reference book for the collector of U.S. pistols & revolvers. Identifies standard issue original military models of the M1911, M1911A1 and M1917 Cal .45 pistols and revolvers as produced by all manufacturers from 1911 through 1945. Plus .22 Ace models, National Match models, and similar foreign military models produced by Colt or manufactured under Colt license, plus arsenal repair, refinish and lend-lease models.

ARMS LIBRARY

The Colt .45 Auto Pistol, compiled from U.S. War Dept. Technical Manuals, and reprinted by Desert Publications, Cornville, AZ, 1978. 80 pp., illus. Paper covers. $12.95

Covers every facet of this famous pistol from mechanical training, manual of arms, disassembly, repair and replacement of parts.

Colt Single Action Army Revolver Study: New Discoveries, by Kenneth Moore, Lincoln, RI, Andrew Mowbray, Inc., 2003. 1st edition. Hardcover. NEW. $47.95

The Combat Perspective; The Thinking Man's Guide to Self-Defense, by Gabriel Suarez, Boulder, CO, Paladin Press, 2003. 1st edition. 112 pp. Softcover. $15.00

In The Combat Perspective, Suarez keys in on developing your knowledge about and properly organizing your mental attitude toward combat to improve your odds of winning – not just surviving – such a fight. The principles are as applicable to the bladesman as they are to the rifleman, to the unarmed fighter as they are to the sniper. In this book he examines each in a logical and scientific manner, demonstrating why, when it comes to defending your life, the mental edge is at least as critical to victory as the tactical advantage.

Complete Encyclopedia of Pistols & Revolvers, by A.E. Hartnik, Knickerbocker Press, New York, NY, 2003. 272 pp., illus. $19.95

A comprehensive encyclopedia specially written for collectors and owners of pistols and revolvers.

Concealable Pocket Pistols: How to Choose and Use Small-Caliber Handguns, by Terence McLeod, Paladin Press, 2001. 1st edition. 80 pp. Softcover. $14.00

Small-caliber handguns are often maligned as too puny for serious self-defense, but millions of Americans own and carry these guns and have used them successfully to stop violent assaults. This is the first book ever devoted to eliminating the many misconceptions about the usefulness of these popular guns. Find out what millions of Americans already know about these practical self-defense tools.

The Concealead Handgun Manual, 4th Edition, by Chris Bird. San Antonio, Privateer Publications, 2004. If you carry a gun for personal protection, or plan to, you need to read this book. You will learn whether carrying a gun is for you, what gun to choose and how to carry it, how to stay out of trouble, when to shoot and how to shoot, gunfighting tactics, what to expect after you have shot someone, and how to apply for a concealed-carry license in 30 states, plus never-before published details of actual shooting incidents. 332 pp., illus. Softcover. NEW. $21.95

The Confederate Lemat Revolver; Secret Weapon of the Confederacy?, by Doug Adams, Lincoln, RI, Andrew Mowbray, Inc.,2005. 1st edition. This exciting new book describes LeMat's wartime adventures aboard blockade runners and alongside the famous leaders of the Confederacy, as well as exploring, as never before, the unique revolvers that he manufactured for the Southern Cause. Nearly 200 spectacular, FULL-COLOR, illustrations and over 70 black & white period

photos, illustrations and patent drawings. 112 pages. Softcover. NEW. $29.95

The Custom Revolver, by Hamilton S. Bowen, Foreword by Ross Seyfried. Louisville, TN, privately printed, 2001. 1st edition. New in new dust jacket. $49.95

The Darling Pepperbox: The Story of Samuel Colt's Forgotten Competitors in Bellingham, Mass. and Woonsocket, RI, by Stuart C. Mowbray, Lincoln, RI, Andrew Mowbray, Inc., 2004. 1st edition. 104 pp. Softcover. NEW. $19.95

Developmental Cartridge Handguns of .22 Calibre, as Produced in the United States & Abroad from 1855 to 1875, by John S. Laidacker, Atglen, PA, Schiffer Publications, 2003. Reprint. 597 pp., with over 860 b&w photos, drawings, and charts. Hardcover. $100.00

This book is a reprint edition of the late John Laidacker's personal study of early .22 Cartridge Handguns from 1855-1875. Laidacker's primary aim was to offer a quick reference to the collector, and his commentary on the wide variety of types, variations and makers, as well as detailed photography, make this a superb addition to any firearm library.

Effective Handgun Defense, by Frank James, Iola, WI, Krause Publications, 2004. 1st edition. 223 pp., illustated, softcover. NEW $19.95

Engraved Handguns of .22 Calibre, by John S. Laidacker, Atglen, PA, Schiffer Publications, 2003. 1st edition. 192 pp., with over 400 color and b&w photos. $69.95

Essential Guide to Handguns: Firearms Instruction for Personal Defense and Protection, by Stephen Rementer and Brian Eimer, Phd., Flushing, NY, Looseleaf law Publications, 2005. 1st edition. Over 300 pages plus illustrations. Softcover. NEW. $24.89

The Farnam Method of Defensive Handgunning, by John S. Farnam, Police Bookshelf, 1999. 191 pp., illus. Paper covers. $24.00

A book intended to not only educate the new shooter, but also to serve as a guide and textbook for his and his instructor's training courses.

Fast and Fancy Revolver Shooting, by Ed McGivern, Anniversary Edition, Winchester Press, Piscataway, NJ, 1984. 484 pp., illus. $19.95

A fascinating volume, packed with handgun lore and solid information by the acknowledged dean of revolver shooters.

Fench Service Handguns: 1858-2004, by Eugene Medlin & Jean Huon, Tommy Gun Publications, 2004. 1st edition. Over 10 years in the making, this book offers in-depth coverage on everything from the 11mm Pinfire to the 9mm Parabellum– including various Lefaucheux revolvers, MAB's, Spanish pistols, and revolvers

used in WWI, Uniques, plus, many photos of one of a kind prototypes of the French contract

Browning, Model 1935s, and 35a pistols used in WWII. Beautiful b&w full shot photos of the guns, and close ups of markings and numbers, not to mention numerous drawings, lists of production numbers, graphs, and exploded views of the guns. Over 200 pages and more than 125 photographs. Hardcover, NEW. $44.95

German Handguns: The Complete Book of the Pistols and Revolvers of Germany, 1869 to the Present, by Ian Hogg, Greenhill Publishing, 2001. 320 pp., 270 illustrations. Hardcover. $49.95

Ian Hogg examines the full range of handguns produced in Germany from such classics as the Luger M1908, Mauser HsC and Walther PPK, to more unusual types such as the Reichsrevolver M1879 and the Dreyse 9mm. He presents the key data (length, weight, muzzle velocity, and range) for each weapon discussed and also gives its date of introduction and service record, evaluates and discusses peculiarities, and examines in detail particular strengths and weaknesses.

The Glock in Competition, by Robin Taylor, Spokane, WA, Taylor Press, 2006, 2nd edition. Covered topics include reloading, trigger configurations, recalls, and refits, magazine problems, modifying the Glock, choosing factory ammo, and a host of others. 248 pp., Softcover. NEW $19.95

Glock: The New Wave in Combat Handguns, by Peter Alan Kasler, Paladin Press, Boulder, CO, 1993. 304 pp., illus. $27.00

Kasler debunks the myths that surround what is the most innovative handgun to be introduced in some time.

Glock's Handguns, by Duncan Long, Desert Publications, El Dorado, AR, 1996. 180 pp., illus. Paper covers. $19.95

An outstanding volume on one of the world's newest and most successful firearms of the century.

Greenhill Military Manual: Combat Handguns, by Leroy Thompson, London, Greenhill Publishing, 2004. 1st edition Hardcover. $24.00

Gun Digest Book of Beretta Pistols, by Massad Ayoob, Iola, WI, Krause Publications, 2005. 1st edition. 288 pp., 300+ photos help with identification. Softcover. NEW. $24.89

This new release from the publishers of Gun Digest, readers get information including caliber, weight and barrel lengths for modern pistols. A review of the accuracy and function of all models of modern Beretta pistolsgive active shooters details needed to make the most of this popular firearm. More than 300 photographs, coupled witharticles detailing the development of design and style of these handguns, create a comprehensive must-have resource.

Gun Digest Book of Combat Handgunnery 5th Edition, Complete Guide to Combat Shooting, by Massad Ayoob, Iola, WI, Krause Publications, 2002. Softcover. NEW. $19.95

The Gun Digest Book of the 1911, by Patrick Sweeney, Krause Publications, Iola, WI, 2002. 336 pp., with 700 b&w photos. Softcover. $27.95

Complete guide of all models and variations of the Model 1911. The author also includes repair tips and information on buying a used 1911.

The Gun Digest Book of the 1911 2nd Edition, by Patrick Sweeney, Krause Publications, Iola, WI, 2006. 336 pp., with 700 b&w photos. Softcover. $27.95

Complete guide of all models and variations of the Model 1911. The author also includes repair tips and information on buying a used 1911.

Gun Digest Book of the Glock; A Comprehensive Review, Design, History and Use, Iola, WI, Krause Publications, 2003. 1st edition. 303 pp., with 500 b&w photos. Softcover. 24.95

Examine the rich history and unique elements of the most important and influential firearms design of the past 50 years, the Glock autoloading pistol. This comprehensive review of the revolutionary pistol analyzes the performance of the various models and chamberings and features a complete guide to available accessories and little-known factory options. You'll see why it's the preferred pistol for law enforcement use and personal protection.

Gun Digest Book of the Sig-Sauer, by Massad Ayoob, Iola, WI, Krause Publications, 2005. 1st edition. 304pp. Softcover. NEW. $27.99

Noted firearms training expert Massad Ayoob takes an in- depth look at some of the finest pistols on the market. If you own a SIG-Sauer pistol, have consdered buying one or just appreciate the fine quality of these pistols, this is the book for you. Ayoob takes a practical look at each of the SIG-Sauer pistols including handling characteristics, and design and performance. Each gun in every caliber is teSted and evaluated, giving you all the details you need as you choose and use YOUR SIG-Sauer pistol.

Gun Digest Book of Smith & Wesson, by Patrick Sweeney, Iola, WI, Krause Publications, 2005. 1st edition. Covers all categories of Smith & Wesson Guns in both competition and law enforcement. 312 pp., 500 b&w photos. Softcover. NEW. $19.99

Hand Cannons: The World's Most Powerful Handguns, by Duncan Long, Paladin Press, Boulder, CO, 1995. 208 pp., illus. Paper covers. $22.00

Long describes and evaluates each powerful gun according to their features.

Handgun Combatives, by Dave Spaulding, Flushing, NY, Looseleaf Law Publications,2005. 212 pp., with 60 plus photos, softcover. NEW $22.95

Handgun Stopping Power "The Definitive Study," by Evan P. Marshall & Edwin J. Sanow, Paladin Press, Boulder, CO, 1997. 240 pp. photos. Softcover. $45.00

Dramatic first-hand accounts of the results of handgun rounds fired into criminals by cops, storeowners, cabbies and others are the heart and soul of this long-awaited book. This is the definitive methodology for predicting the stopping power of handgun loads, the first to take into account what really happens when a bullet meets a man.

ARMS LIBRARY

Handguns 2006, 19th Edition, Ken Ramage, Iola WI, Gun Digest Books, 2006 19thh edition 320 pp., 500 b&w photos, Softcover. NEW. $24.99

Target shooters, handgun hunters, collectors and those who rely upon handguns for self- defense will want to pack this value-loaded and entertaining volume in their home libraries. Shooters will find the latest pistol and revolver designs and accessories, plus test reports on several models. The handgun becomes an artist's canvas in a showcase of engraving talents. The catalog section–with comprehensive specs on every known handgun in production–includes a new display of semi-custom handguns, plus an expanded, illustrated section on the latest grips, sights, scopes and other aiming devices. Offer easy access to products, services and manufacturers.

Handguns of the Armed Organizations of the Soviet Occupation Zone and German Democratic Republic, by Dieter H. Marschall, Los Alamos, NM, Ucross Books, 2000. Softcover. NEW. $29.95

Translated from German this groundbreaking treatise covers the period from May 1945 through 1996. The organizations that used these pistols are described along with the guns and holsters. Included are the P08, P38, PP, PPK, P1001, PSM, Tokarev, Makarov, (including .22 LR, cutaway, silenced, Suhl marked), Stechlin, plus Hungarian, Romanian and Czech pistols.

Heckler & Koch's Handguns, by Duncan Long, Desert Publications, El Dorado, AR, 1996. 142 pp., illus. Paper covers. $19.95

Traces the history and the evolution of H&K's pistols from the company's beginning at the end of WWII to the present.

Hidden in Plain Sight, by Trey Bloodworth & Mike Raley, Paladin Press, Boulder, CO, 2003. Paper covers. $20.00

A practical guide to concealed handgun carry.

High Standard: A Collectors Guide to the Hamden & Hartford Target Pistols, by Tom Dance, Andrew Mowbray, Inc., Lincoln, RI, 1999. 192 pp., heavily illustrated with b&w photographs and technical drawings. $24.00

From Citation to Supermatic, all of the production models and specials made from 1951 to 1984 are covered according to model number or series, making it easy to understand the evolution to this favorite of shooters and collectors.

High Standard Automatic Pistols 1932-1950, by Charles E. Petty, The Gun Room Press, Highland Park, NJ, 1989. 124 pp., illus. $14.95

A definitive source of information for the collector of High Standard arms.

Hi-Standard Pistols and Revolvers, 1951-1984, by James Spacek, Chesire, CT, 1998. 128 pp., illus. Paper covers. $14.95

Technical details, marketing features and instruction/parts manual of every model High Standard pistol and revolver made between 1951 and 1984. Most accurate serial number information available.

History of Smith & Wesson Firearms, by Dean Boorman, New York, Lyons Press, 2002. 1st edition. 144 pp., illustrated in full color. Hardcover. $29.95

The definitive guide to one of the world's best-known firearms makers. Takes the story through the years of the Military & Police .38 & of the Magnum cartridge, to today's wide range of products for law-enforcement customers.

How to Become a Master Handgunner: The Mechanics of X-Count Shooting, by Charles Stephens, Paladin Press, Boulder, CO, 1993. 64 pp., illus. Paper covers. $14.00

Offers a simple formula for success to the handgunner who strives to master the technique of shooting accurately.

How to Customize Your Glock: Step-By-Step Modifications You Can Do at Little Cost, by Robert and Morgan Boatman, Paladin Press, Boulder, CO, 2005, 1st edition. 8-1/2" x 11", softcover, photos, 72 pp. Softcover. NEW. $20.00

This mini-"Glocksmithing" course by Glock enthusiasts Robert and Morgan Boatman first explains why you would make a specific modification and what you gain in terms of improved performance. The workbook format makes the manual simple to follow as you work on your Glock, andhigh-resolution photos illustrate each part and step precisely.

The Inglis Diamond: The Canadian High Power Pistol, by Clive M. Law, Collector Grade Publications, Canada, 2001. 312 pp., illus. $49.95

This definitive work on Canada's first and indeed only mass produced handgun, in production for a very brief span of time and consequently made in relatively few numbers, the venerable Inglis-made Browning High Power covers the pistol's initial history, the story of Chinese and British adoption, use post-war by Holland, Australia, Greece, Belgium, New Zealand, Peru, Brasil and other countries. All new information on the famous light-weights and the Inglis Diamond variations. Completely researched through official archives in a dozen countries. Many of the bewildering variety of markings have never been satisfactorily explained until now

Japanese Military Cartridge Handguns 1893-1945, A Revised and Expanded Edition of Hand Cannons of Imperial Japan, by Harry L. Derby III and James D. Brown, Atglen, PA, Schiffer Publications, 2003. 1st edition. Hardcover. New in new dust jacket. $79.95

When originally published in 1981, The Hand Cannons of Imperial Japan was heralded as one of the most readable works on firearms ever produced. To arms collectors and scholars, it remains a prized source of information on Japanese handguns, their development, and their history. In this new Revised and Expanded edition, original author Harry Derby has teamed with Jim Brown to provide a thorough update reflecting 20 years of additional research. An appendix on valuation has also been added, using a relative scale that should remain relevant despite inflationary pressures. For the firearms collector, enthusiast, historian or dealer, this is the most complete and up-to-date work on Japanese military handguns ever written.

Living with Glocks: The Complete Guide to the New Standard in Combat Handguns, by Robert H. Boatman, Boulder, CO, Paladin Press, 2002. 1st edition. 184 pp., illus. Hardcover. $29.95

In addition to demystifying the enigmatic Glock trigger, Boatman describes and critiques each Glock model in production. Separate chapters on the G36, the enhanced G20 and the full-auto G18 emphasize the job-specific talents of these

standout models for those seeking insight on which Glock pistol might best meet their needs. And for those interested in optimizing their Glock's capabilities, this book addresses all the peripherals–holsters, ammo, accessories, silencers, modifications and conversions, training programs and more.

Living With the 1911, by Robert Boatman, Boulder, CO, paladin Press, 2005. 144 pp., softcover. NEW $25.00

The Luger Handbook, by Aarron Davis, Krause Publications, Iola, WI, 1997. 112 pp., illus. Paper covers. $9.95

Now you can identify any of the legendary Luger variations using a simple decision tree. Each model and variation includes pricing information, proof marks and detailed attributes in a handy, user-friendly format. Plus, it's fully indexed. Instantly identify that Luger!

The Luger Story, by John Walter, Stackpole Books, Mechanicsburg, PA, 2001. 256 pp., illus. Paper covers. $19.95

The standard history of the world's most famous handgun.

Lugers at Random (Revised Format Edition), by Charles Kenyon Jr., Handgun Press, Glenview, IL, 2000. 420 pp., illus. $59.95

A new printing of this classic, comprehensive reference for all Luger collectors.

Lyman Pistol and Revolver Handbook, 3rd edition, by Lyman. Middletown,CT, Lyman Products Corp, 2005. 3rd edition. 272 pp., Softcover. NEW $22.95

The Mauser Self-Loading Pistol, by Belford & Dunlap, Borden Publishing Co., Alhambra, CA. Over 200 pp., 300 illus., large format. $29.95

The long-awaited book on the "Broom Handles," covering their inception in 1894 to the end of production. Complete and in detail: pocket pistols, Chinese and Spanish copies.

Mental Mechanics of Shooting: How to Stay Calm at the Center, by Vishnu Karmakar and Thomas Whitney, Littleton, CO, Center Vision, Inc., 2001. 144 pp. Softcover. $19.95

Not only will this book help you stay free of trigger jerk, it will help you in all areas of your shooting.

Model 1911 Automatic Pistol, by Robert Campbell, Accokeek, Maryland, Stoeger Publications, 2004. Hardcover. NEW. $24.95

Modern Law Enforcement Weapons & Tactics, 3rd Edition, by Patrick Sweeney, Iola, WI, Krause Publications, 2004. 256 pp. Softcover. NEW. $22.99

The Official 9mm Markarov Pistol Manual, translated into English by Major James Gebhardt, U.S. Army (Ret.), Desert Publications, El Dorado, AR, 1996. 84 pp., illus. Paper covers. $14.95

The information found in this book will be of enormous benefit and interest to the owner or a prospective owner of one of these pistols.

The Operator's Tactical Pistol Shooting Manual; A Practical Guide to Combat Marksmanship, by Erik Lawrence, Linesville, PA, Blackheart Publishing, 2003. 1st edition. 233 pp. Softcover. $24.50

This manual-type book begins with the basics of safety with a pistol and progresses into advanced pistol handling. A self-help guide for improving your capabilities with a pistol at your own pace.

The P08 Luger Pistol, by de Vries & Martens, Alexandria, VA, Ironside International, 2002. 152 pp., illustrated with 200 high quality b&w photos. Hardcover. $34.95

Covers all essential information on history and development, ammunition and accessories, codes and markings, and contains photos of nearly every model and accessory. Includes a unique selection of original German WWII propoganda photos, most never published before.

The P-08 Parabellum Luger Automatic Pistol, edited by J. David McFarland, Desert Publications, Cornville, AZ, 1982. 20 pp., illus. Paper covers. $14.95

Covers every facet of the Luger, plus a listing of all known Luger models.

The P-38 Pistol: Postwar Distributions, 1945-1990. Volume 3, by Warren Buxton, Ucross Books, Los Alamos, MN 1999, plus an addendum to Volumes 1 & 2. 272 pp. with 342 illustrations. $68.50

The P-38 Pistol: The Contract Pistols, 1940-1945. Volume 2., by Warren Buxton, Ucross Books, Los Alamos, MN 1999. 256 pp. with 237 illustrations. $68.50

The P-38 Pistol: The Walther Pistols, 1930-1945. Volume 1, by Warren Buxton, Ucross Books, Los Alamos, MN 1999. $68.50

A limited run reprint of this scarce and sought-after work on the P-38 Pistol. 328 pp. with 160 illustrations.

The Peacemakers:Arms and Adventure in the American West, by RL Wilson. New York, Book Sales, 2004, reprint. 392pp. colored endpapers, 320 full color illustrations. Hardcover in New DJ, NEW. $24.89

Percussion Pistols and Revolvers: History, Performance and Practical Use, by Mike Cumpston and Johnny Bates, Texas, Iunivers, Inc, 2005. 1st edition. With the advent of the revolving pistols, came patents that created monopolies in revolver production and the through-bored cylinder necessary for self-contained metallic cartridges. The caplock revolvers took on a separate evolution and remained state of the art long after the widespread appearance of cartridge firing rifles and shotguns. 208 pages. Softcover. $19.95

Pistol as a Weapon of Defence in the House and on the Road, by Jeff Cooper, Boulder, CO, Paladin Press, 2004. 1st edition. Penned in 1875 and recently discovered collecting dust on a library bookshelf, this primer for the pistol is remarkably timely in its insights and observations. From a historical perspective, it contains striking parallels to the thinking and controversy that swirl about the practical use of the pistol today. 48pp. Softcover. NEW. $9.00

ARMS LIBRARY

Pistols of the World ; Fully Revised, 4th edition. Iola, WI, Krause Publications, 2005. 4th edition. 432 pp., chronicles 2,500 handguns made from 1887-2004. Stiff Paper Covers, NEW. $22.95

More than 1,000 listings and 20 years of coverage were added since the previous edition.

Pistols of World War I, by Robert J. Adamek, Pittsburgh, Pentagon Press, 2001. 1st edition signed and numbered. Over 90 pistols illustrated, technical data, designers, history, proof marks. 296 pp. with illustrations and photos. Softcover. $45.00

Over 25 pistol magazines illustrated with dimensions, serial number ranges. Over 35 cartridges illustrated with dimensions, manufactures, year of introduction. Weapons from 16 countries involved in WWI, statistics, quantities made, identification.

Remington Large-Bore Conversion Revolvers, by R. Phillips. Canada, Prately printed, 2005. Limited printing of 250 signed and numbered copies.in leather hardcover. 126 pp., with 200 illustrations. NEW $55.00

The Ruger .22 Automatic Pistol, Standard/Mark I/Mark II Series, by Duncan Long, Paladin Press, Boulder, CO, 1989. 168 pp., illus. Paper covers. $16.00

The definitive book about the pistol that has served more than 1 million owners so well.

Ruger .22 Automatic Pistols: The Complete Guide for all Models from 1947 to 2003, Grand Rapids, MI, The Ruger Store, 2004. 74 pp., 66 high-resolution grayscale images. Printed in the U.S.A. with card stock cover and bright white paper. Softcover. NEW. $12.95

Includes 'rare' complete serial numbers and manufacturing dates from 1949-2004.

The Ruger "P" Family of Handguns, by Duncan Long, Desert Publications, El Dorado, AZ, 1993. 128 pp., illus. Paper covers. $14.95

A full-fledged documentary on a remarkable series of Sturm Ruger handguns.

Ruger Pistol Reference Booklet 1949-1982 (Pocket Guide to Ruger Rimfire Pistols Standard and Mark I), by Don Findlay. Lubbock Tx, Privately Printed, 2005. 1st edition. Designed for the professional un dealer as well as the collector. Complete list of serial numbers as well as production dates. Also, includes photos of the

original boxes the guns came in. 24 pp., illustrated with b&w photos. Softcover. NEW. $9.95

The Semi-automatic Pistols in Police Service and Self Defense, by Massad Ayoob, Police Bookshelf, Concord, NH, 1990. 25 pp., illus. Softcover. $11.95

First quantitative, documented look at actual police experience with 9mm and 45 police service automatics.

Shooting Colt Single Actions, by Mike Venturino, Livingston, MT, 1997. 205 pp., illus. Paper covers. $25.00

A definitive work on the famous Colt SAA and the ammunition it shoots.

Sig Handguns, by Duncan Long, Desert Publications, El Dorado, AZ, 1995. 150 pp., illus. Paper covers. $19.95

The history of Sig/Sauer handguns, including Sig, Sig-Hammerli and Sig/Sauer variants.

Sixgun Cartridges and Loads, by Elmer Keith, reprint edition by The Gun Room Press, Highland Park, NJ, 1984. 151 pp., illus. $24.95

A manual covering the selection, use and loading of the most suitable and popular revolver cartridges.

Smith & Wesson's Automatics, by Larry Combs, Desert Publications, El Dorado, AZ, 1994. 143 pp., illus. Paper covers. $19.95

A must for every S&W auto owner or prospective owner.

Smith & Wesson: Sixguns of the Old West, by David Chicoine. Lincoln, RI., Andrew Mowbray, Inc., 2004. 1st edition. 480 pp., countless photos and detailed technical drawings. The Schofields, The Americans, The Russians, The New Model #3s, and The DAs. Hardcover. New in new dust jacket. $69.49

Spanish Handguns: The History of Spanish Pistols and Revolvers, by Gene Gangarosa Jr., Stoeger Publishing Co., Accokeek, MD, 2001. 320 pp., illustrated, b&w photos. Paper covers. $21.95

Star Firearms, by Leonardo M. Antaris, Davenport, TA, Firac Publications Co., 2002. 1st edition. Hardcover. New in new dust jacket. $119.95

The Tactical 1911, by Dave Lauck, Paladin Press, Boulder, CO, 1999. 152 pp., illus. Paper covers. $22.00

The cop's and SWAT operator's guide to employment and maintenance.

The Tactical Pistol, by Gabriel Suarez, Foreword by Jeff Cooper, Paladin Press, Boulder, CO, 1996. 216 pp., illus. Paper covers. $25.00

Advanced gunfighting concepts and techniques.

Tactical Pistol Shooting; Your Guide to Tactics that Work, by Erik Lawrence. Iola, WI, Krause Publications,2005. 1st edition. More than 250 step-by-step photos to illustrate techniques. 233 pp. Softcover. NEW $18.95

The Thompson/Center Contender Pistol, by Charles Tephens, Paladin Press, Boulder, CO, 1997. 58 pp., illus. Paper covers. $14.00

How to tune and time, load and shoot accurately with the Contender pistol.

The Truth About Handguns, by Duane Thomas, Paladin Press, Boulder, CO, 1997. 136 pp., illus. Paper covers. $18.00

Exploding the myths, hype, and misinformation about handguns.

U.S. Handguns of World War II, The Secondary Pistols and Revolvers, by Charles W. Pate, Mowbray Publishers, Lincoln, RI, 1997. 368 pp., illus. $39.00

This indispensable new book covers all of the American military handguns of WWII except for the M1911A1.

The Model 35 Radom Pistol, by Terence Lapin, Hyrax Publishers, 2004. 95 pages with b &w photos, Stiff paper Covers. NEW. $18.95

Walther Pistols: Models 1 Through P99, Factory Variations and Copies, by Dieter H. Marschall, Ucross Books, Los Alamos, NM. 2000. 140 pp., with 140 b&w illustrations, index. Paper covers. $19.95

This is the English translation, revised and updated, of the highly successful and widely acclaimed German language edition. This book provides the collector with a reference guide and overview of the entire line of the Walther military, police, and self-defense pistols from the very first to the very latest Variations, where issued, serial ranges, calibers, marks, proofs, logos, and design aspects in an astonishing quantity and variety are crammed into this very well researched and highly regarded work.

HUNTING

NORTH AMERICA

A Pheasant Hunter's Notebook: Revised Second Edition, by Larry Brown, Camden, ME, Country Sport Press, 2003. 1st edition. 266 pp. Hardcover. $26.95

Larry Brown has spent a lifetime pursuing America's most colorful and raucous upland game bird, and the advice he presents here, based on written records of his hunts over the decades, is priceless. Particularly valuable are his strategies for hunting different kinds of cover in varying types of weather.

A Varmint Hunter's Odyssey, by Steve Hanson with guest chapter by Mike Johnson, Precision Shooting, Inc. Manchester, CT, 1999. 279 pp., illus. Paper covers. $39.95

A new classic by a writer who eats, drinks and sleeps varmint hunting and varmint rifles.

Advanced Black Powder Hunting, by Toby Bridges, Stoeger Publishing Co., Wayne, NJ, 1998. 288 pp., illus. Paper covers. $21.95

The first modern day publication to be filled from cover to cover with guns, loads, projectiles, accessories and the techniques to get the most from today's front loading guns.

Adventures of an Alaskan–You Can Do, by Dennis W. Confer, Foreword by Craig Boddington. Anchorage, AK, Wiley Ventures, 2003. 1st edition. 279 pp., illus. Softcover. $24.95

This book is about 45% fishing, 45% hunting, & 10% related adventures; travel, camping and boating. It is written to stimulate, encourage and motivate readers to make happy memories that they can do on an average income and to entertain, educate and inform readers of outdoor opportunities.

Aggressive Whitetail Hunting, by Greg Miller, Krause Publications, Iola, WI, 1995. 208 pp., illus. Paper covers. $14.95

Learn how to hunt trophy bucks in public forests, private farmlands and exclusive hunting grounds from one of America's foremost hunters.

Alaska Safari, by Harold Schetzle & Sam Fadala, Anchorage, AK, Great Northwest Publishing, 2002. Revised 2nd edition. 366 pp., illus. with b&w photos. Softcover. $29.95

The author has brought a wealth of information to the hunter and anyone interested in Alaska. Harold Schetzle is a great guide and has also written another book called "Alaska Wilderness Hunter" which is a wonderful book of stories of Alaska hunting taken from many, many years of hunting and guiding. The most comprehensive guide to Alaska hunting.

Alaskan Adventures-Volume I-The Early Years, by Russell Annabel, Long Beach, CA, Safari Press, 2005, 2nd printing. 453 pp., illus. Hardcover. New in new dust jacket. $35.00

No other writer has ever been able to capture the spirit of adventure and hunting in Alaska like Russell Annabel.

Alaskan Yukon Trophies Won and Lost, by G.O. Young, Wolfe Publishing, Prescott, AZ, 2002. 273 pp. with b&w photographs and a five-page epilogue by the publisher. Softcover. $35.00

A classic big game hunting tale.

American Duck Shooting, by George Bird Grinnell, Stackpole Books, Harrisburg, PA, 1991. 640 pp., illus. Paper covers. $19.95

First published in 1901 at the height of the author's career. Describes 50 species of waterfowl, and discusses hunting methods common at the turn of the century.

Antlers: A Guide to Collecting, Scoring, Mounting, and Carving by Dennis Walrod, Stackpole Books, 2005. 256 pp., 76 b&w photos, 13 illustrations; 27 charts. Soft cover. NEW. $16.95

The book is also loaded with practical information and step-by-step instructions for collectors and craftsmen, designed to maximize the use you can get out of your antlers.

Autumn Passages, compiled by the editors of Ducks Unlimited magazine, Willow Creek Press, Minocqua, WI, 1997. 320 pp. $27.50

An exceptional collection of duck hunting stories. Reminiscences of a hunter's life in rural America.

Bare November Days, by George Bird Evans et al, Down East Books, Camden, MA 2002. 136 pp., illus. $39.50

A new, original anthology, a tribute to ruffed grouse, king of upland birds.

Bear Hunting in Alaska: How to Hunt Brown and Grizzly Bears, by Tony Russ, Northern Publishing, 2004. 116 b&w photos, illus. 256 pp. Soft cover. $22.95

Teaches every skill you will need to prepare for, scout, find, select, stalk, shoot and care for one of the most sought-after trophies on earth – the Alaskan brown bear and the Alaskan Grizzly.

Bears of Alaska, by Erwin Bauer, Sasquatch Books, 2002. Soft cover. $15.95

The Best of Babcock, by Havilah Babcock, Introduction by Hugh Grey, The Gunnerman Press, Auburn Hills, MI, 1985. 262 pp., illus. $19.95

A treasury of memorable pieces, 21 of which have never before appeared in book form.

ARMS LIBRARY

Blacktail Trophy Tactics, by Boyd Iverson, Stoneydale Press, Stevensville, MI, 1992. 166 pp., illus. Paper covers. $14.95

A comprehensive analysis of blacktail deer habits, describing a deer's and man's use of scents, still hunting, tree techniques, etc.

Bowhunter's Handbook, Expert Strategies and Techniques, by M.R. James with Fred Asbell, Dave Holt, Dwight Schuh and Dave Samuel, DBI Books, a division of Krause Publications, Iola, WI, 1997. 256 pp., illus. Paper covers. $19.95

Tips from the top on taking your bowhunting skills to the next level.

The Buffalo Harvest, by Frank Mayer as told to Charles Roth, Pioneer Press, Union City, TN, 1995. 96 pp., illus. Paper covers. $12.50

The story of a hide hunter during his buffalo hunting days on the plains.

Call of the Quail: A Tribute to the Gentleman Game Bird, by Michael McIntosh, et al., Countrysport Press, Traverse City, MI, 1990. 175 pp., illus. $35.00

A new anthology on quail hunting.

Calling All Elk, by Jim Zumbo, Cody, WY, 1989. 169 pp., illus. Paper covers. $14.95

The only book on the subject of elk hunting that covers every aspect of elk vocalization.

The Complete Book of Grouse Hunting, by Frank Woolner, The Lyons Press, New York, NY, 2000. 192 pp., illus. Paper covers. $24.95

The history, habits, and habitat of one of America's great game birds—and the methods used to hunt it.

The Complete Book of Mule Deer Hunting, by Walt Prothero, The Lyons Press, New York, NY, 2000. 192 pp., illus. Paper covers. $24.95

Field-tested practical advice on how to bag the trophy buck of a lifetime.

The Complete Book of Wild Turkey Hunting, by John Trout Jr., The Lyons Press, New York, NY, 2000. 192 pp., illus. Paper covers. $24.95

An illustrated guide to hunting for one of America's most popular game birds.

The Complete Book of Woodcock Hunting, by Frank Woolner, The Lyons Press, New York, NY, 2000. 192 pp., illus. Paper covers. $24.95

A thorough, practical guide to the American woodcock and to woodcock hunting.

The Complete Guide To Hunting Wild Boar in California, by Gary Kramer, Safari Press, 2002. 1st edition. 127 pp., 37 photos. Softcover. $15.95

Gary Kramer takes the hunter all over California, from north to south and east to west. He discusses natural history, calibers, bullets, rifles, pistols, shotguns, black powder, and bow and arrows—even recipes.

The Complete Venison Cookbook from Field to Table, by Jim & Ann Casada, Krause Publications, Iola, WI, 1996. 208 pp., Comb-bound. $12.95

More than 200 kitchen-tested recipes make this book the answer to a table full of hungry hunters or guests.

Cougar Attacks: Encounters of the Worst Kind, by Kathy Etling, NY, Lyons Press, 2004. 1st edition. 256 pp., illustrated with b&w photos. Soft cover. NEW. $14.95

Blood-curdling encounters between the big cats of North America and their most reluctant prey, humans.

Coveys and Singles: The Handbook of Quail Hunting, by Robert Gooch, A.S. Barnes, San Diego, CA, 1981. 196 pp., illus. $11.95

The story of the quail in North America.

Coyote Hunting, by Phil Simonski, Stoneydale Press, Stevensville, MT, 1994. 126 pp., illus. Paper covers. $12.95

Probably the most thorough "how-to-do-it" book on coyote hunting ever written.

Dabblers & Divers: A Duck Hunter's Book, compiled by the editors of Ducks Unlimited magazine, Willow Creek Press, Minocqua, WI, 1997. 160 pp., illus. $39.95

A word-and-photographic portrayal of waterfowl hunter's singular intimacy with, and passion for, watery haunts and wildfowl.

Deer & Deer Hunting, by Al Hofacker, Krause Publications, Iola, WI, 1993. 208 pp., illus. $34.95

Coffee-table volume packed full of how-to-information that will guide hunts for years to come.

The Deer Hunters: The Tactics, Lore, Legacy and Allure of American Deer Hunting, edited by Patrick Durkin, Krause Publications, Iola, WI, 1997. 208 pp., illus. $29.95

More than 20 years of research from America's top whitetail hunters, researchers, and photographers have gone into the making of this book.

Dreaming the Lion, by Thomas McIntyre, Countrysport Press, Traverse City, MI, 1994. 309 pp., illus. $35.00

Reflections on hunting, fishing and a search for the wild. Twenty-three stories by *Sports Afield* editor, Tom McIntyre.

Eastern Cougar: Historic Accounts, Scientific Investigations, and New Evidence, by Chris Bolgiano, Mechanicsburg,PA, Stackpole Books, 2005. Soft cover. NEW. $19.95

This fascinating anthology probes America's troubled history with large predators and makes a vital contribution to the wildlife management debates of today.

Elk and Elk Hunting, by Hart Wixom, Stackpole Books, Harrisburg, PA, 1986. 288 pp., illus. $34.95

Your practical guide to fundamentals and fine points of elk hunting.

Elk Hunting Guide: Skills, Gear, and Insight. By Tom Airhart, Stackpole Books, 2005. 432 pp., 71 b&w photos, 38 illus. $19.95

A thorough, informative guide to the growing sport of elk hunting with in-depth coverage of current equipment and gear, techniques for tracking elk and staying safe in the wilderness and advice on choosing guides and outfitters.

Elk Hunting in the Northern Rockies, by Ed Wolff, Stoneydale Press, Stevensville, MT, 1984. 162 pp., illus. $18.95

Helpful information about hunting the premier elk country of the northern Rocky Mountain states—Wyoming, Montana and Idaho.

Elk Hunting with the Experts, by Bob Robb, Stoneydale Press, Stevensville, MT, 1992. 176 pp., illus. Paper covers. $15.95

A complete guide to elk hunting in North America by America's top elk hunting expert.

Encyclopedia of Buffalo Hunters and Skinners Volume 1 A-D, by Gilbert Reminger, Pioneer Press, 2003. Hardcover. NEW. $35.00

The first volume in the series. 286 pp., acknowledgements, introduction, preface, illustrated, maps, plates, portraits, appendices, bibliography, index.

Fair Chase in North America, by Craig Boddington, Long Beach, CA, Safari Press, 2004. 1st edition. Hardcover. New in new dust jacket. $39.95

Firelight, by Burton L. Spiller, Gunnerman Press, Auburn Hills, MI, 1990. 196 pp., illus. $19.95

Enjoyable tales of the outdoors and stalwart companions.

Getting a Stand, by Miles Gilbert, Pioneer Press, Union City, TN, 1993. 204 pp., illus. Paper covers. $13.95

An anthology of 18 short personal experiences by buffalo hunters of the late 1800s, specifically from 1870-1882.

Greatest Elk; The Complete Historical and Illustrated Record of North America's Biggest Elk, by R. Selner, Safari Press, Huntington Beach, CA, 2000. 209 pp., profuse color illus. $39.95

Here is the book all elk hunters have been waiting for! This oversized book holds the stories and statistics of the biggest bulls ever killed in North America. Stunning, full-color photographs highlight over 40 world-class heads, including the old world records!

Grouse and Woodcock, A Gunner's Guide, by Don Johnson, Krause Publications, Iola, WI, 1995. 256 pp., illus. Paper covers. $14.95

Find out what you need in guns, ammo, equipment, dogs and terrain.

Gunning for Sea Ducks, by George Howard Gillelan, Tidewater Publishers, Centreville, MD, 1988. 144 pp., illus. $14.95

A book that introduces you to a practically untouched arena of waterfowling.

Head Fer the Hills-Volume VI (1934-1960), by Russell Annabel, Long Beach, CA, Safari Press, 2005, Deluxe, Limited, Signed edition. 312 pp., photos, drawings. Hardcover in a Slipcase. NEW. $60.00

As Tex Cobb, Russell Annabel's famous mentor and eternal companion, was famous for saying, "Head fer the hills," which is exactly what Rusty did.

The Heck with Moose Hunting, by Jim Zumbo, Wapiti Valley Publishing Co., Cody, WY, 1996. 199 pp., illus. $17.95

Jim's hunts around the continent including encounters with moose, caribou, sheep, antelope and mountain goats.

High Pressure Elk Hunting, by Mike Lapinski, Stoneydale Press Publishing Co., Stevensville, MT, 1996. 192 pp., illus. $19.95

The secrets of hunting educated elk revealed.

Horns in the High Country, by Andy Russell, Alfred A. Knopf, NY, 1973. 259 pp., illus. Paper covers. $12.95

A many-sided view of wild sheep and their natural world.

How to Hunt, by Dave Bowring, Winchester Press, Piscataway, NJ, 1982. 208 pp., illus. Hardcover $15.00

A basic guide to hunting big game, small game, upland birds, and waterfowl.

Hunt High for Rocky Mountain Goats, Bighorn Sheep, Chamois & Tahr, by Duncan Gilchrist, Stoneydale Press, Stevensville, MT, 1992. 192 pp., illus. Paper covers. $19.95

The source book for hunting mountain goats.

The Hunter's Alaska, by Roy F. Chandler, Iron Brigade, 2005. Hardcover. NEW. $49.95

This is a book written by Roy F. Chandler (Rocky). Rocky's Alaskan travels span half a century. Hunters hoping to hunt the "Great Land" will read exactly how it is done and what they can hope for if they ever make it into the Alaskan wilderness. The is a new publication; 2500 signed and numbered copies. Previous books, by Rocky, about hunting Alaska have become collectors items. This book has information from the prior books and much more "added" information.

Hunting Adventure of Me and Joe, by Walt Prothero, Safari Press, Huntington Beach, CA, 1995. 220 pp., illus. $22.50

A collection of the author's best and favorite stories.

Hunting America's Wild Turkey, by Toby Bridges, Stoeger Publishing Company, Pocomoke, MD, 2001. 256 pp., illus. $16.95

The techniques and tactics of hunting North America's largest, and most popular, woodland game bird.

Hunting Hard in Alaska, by Marc Taylor, Anchorage, AK, Biblio Distribution, 2003 Softcover. $19.95

Hunting In Alaska: A Comprehensive Guide, by Christopher Batin, Alaska Angler Pubs., 2002. 430 pages. Soft cover. NEW. $29.95

Hunting the Land of the Midnight Sun, by Alaska Professional Hunters Assoc., Safari Press, 2005. Hardcover. New in new dust jacket. $29.95

Contains contributions from Rob Holt, Gary King, Gary LaRose, Garth Larsen, Jim Shockey, Jeff Davis, and many others.

Hunting Mature Bucks, by Larry L. Weishuhn, Krause Publications, Iola, WI, 1995. 256 pp., illus. Paper covers. $14.95

One of North America's top white-tailed deer authorities shares his expertise on hunting those big, smart and elusive bucks.

Hunting Open-Country Mule Deer, by Dwight Schuh, Sage Press, Nampa, ID, 1989. 180 pp., illus. $18.95

A guide taking Western bucks with rifle and bow.

ARMS LIBRARY

Hunting the Rockies, Home of the Giants, by Kirk Darner, Marceline, MO, 1996. 291 pp., illus. $25.00

Understand how and where to hunt Western game in the Rockies.

Hunting Western Deer, by Jim and Wes Brown, Stoneydale Press, Stevensville, MT, 1994. 174 pp., illus. Paper covers. $14.95

A pair of expert Oregon hunters provide insight into hunting mule deer and blacktail deer in the western states.

Hunting Wild Turkeys in the West, by John Higley, Stoneydale Press, Stevensville, MT, 1992. 154 pp., illus. Paper covers. $12.95

Covers the basics of calling, locating and hunting turkeys in the western states.

Hunting with the Twenty-Two, by Charles Singer Landis, R&R Books, Livonia, NY, 1994. 429 pp., illus. $35.00

A miscellany of articles touching on the hunting and shooting of small game.

I Don't Want to Shoot an Elephant, by Havilah Babcock, The Gunnerman Press, Auburn Hills, MI, 1985. 184 pp., illus. $19.95

Eighteen delightful stories that will enthrall the upland gunner for many pleasurable hours.

In Search of the Buffalo, by Charles G. Anderson, Pioneer Press, Union City, TN, 1996. 144 pp., illus. Paper covers. $13.95

The primary study of the life of J. Wright Mooar, one of the few hunters fortunate enough to kill a white buffalo.

In the Turkey Woods, by Jerome B. Robinson, The Lyons Press, N.Y., 1998. 207 pp., illus. $24.95

Practical expert advice on all aspects of turkey hunting–from calls to decoys to guns.

Jaybirds Go to Hell on Friday, by Havilah Babcock, The Gunnerman Press, Auburn Hills, MI, 1985. 149 pp., illus. $19.95

Sixteen jewels that reestablish the lost art of good old-fashioned yarn telling.

Kodiak Island and its Bears, by Harry Dodge, Anchorage, Great Northwest Publishing, 2004. 364 pp., carefully indexed, thoughtfully footnoted, and lavishly illustrated. $27.50

This is the most significant volume about Kodiak Island and its bears that has been published in at least 20 years. This book now stands to become a new classic for all time.

The Lost Classics of Jack O'Connor, by Jim Casada, Live Oak Press, 2004. 33 photos, 40 illus. by Dan Burr; 376 pp., with illustrations and photos. Hardcover. New in new dust jacket. $35.00

Exciting tales with a twist of humor.

Montana–Land of Giant Rams, Volume 2, by Duncan Gilchrist, Outdoor Expeditions and Books, Corvallis, MT, 1992. 208 pp., illus. $34.95

The reader will find stories of how many of the top-scoring trophies were taken.

Montana–Land of Giant Rams, Volume 3, by Duncan Gilchrist, Outdoor Expeditions and Books, Corvallis, MT, 1999. 224 pp., illus. Paper covers. $19.95

All new sheep information including over 70 photos. Learn about how Montana became the "Land of Giant Rams" and what the prospects of the future are.

More Tracks: 78 Years of Mountains, People & Happiness, by Howard Copenhaver, Stoneydale Press, Stevensville, MT, 1992. 150 pp., illus. $18.95

A collection of stories by one of the back country's best storytellers about the people who shared with Howard his great adventure in the high places and wild Montana country.

Mostly Huntin', by Bill Jordan, Everett Publishing Co., Bossier City, LA, 1987. 254 pp., illus. $21.95

Jordan's hunting adventures in North America, Africa, Australia, South America and Mexico.

Mule Deer: Hunting Today's Trophies, by Tom Carpenter and Jim Van Norman, Krause Publications, Iola, WI, 1998. 256 pp., illus. Paper covers. $19.95

A tribute to both the deer and the people who hunt them. Includes info on where to look for big deer, prime mule deer habitat and effective weapons for the hunt.

Muzzleloading for Deer and Turkey, by Dave Ehrig, Stackpole Books, 2005. 475 pp., 293 b&w photos. Hardcover. New in new dust jacket. $29.95

My Health is Better in November, by Havilah Babcock, University of S. Carolina Press, Columbia, SC, 1985. 284 pp., illus. $24.95

Adventures in the field set in the plantation country and backwater streams of SC.

The North American Waterfowler, by Paul S. Bernsen, Superior Publ. Co., Seattle, WA, 1972. 206 pp. Paper covers. $9.95

The complete inside and outside story of duck and goose shooting. Big and colorful, illustrations by Les Kouba.

The Old Man and the Boy, by Robert Ruark, Henry Holt & Co., New York, NY, 303 pp., illus. $24.95

A timeless classic, telling the story of a remarkable friendship between a young boy and his grandfather as they hunt and fish together.

The Old Man's Boy Grows Older, by Robert Ruark, Henry Holt & Co., Inc., New York, NY, 1993. 300 pp., illus. $24.95

The heartwarming sequel to the best-selling The Old Man and the Boy.

One Man, One Rifle, One Land; Hunting all Species of Big Game in North America, by J.Y. Jones, Safari Press, Huntington Beach, CA, 2000. 400 pp., illus. $59.95

Journey with J.Y. Jones as he hunts each of the big-game animals of North America–from the polar bear of the high Arctic to the jaguar of the low-lands of Mexico–with just one rifle.

Outdoor Pastimes of an American Hunter, by Theodore Roosevelt, Stackpole Books, Mechanicsburg, PA, 1994. 480 pp., illus. Paper covers. $18.95

Stories of hunting big game in the West and notes about animals pursued and observed.

The Outlaw Gunner, by Harry M. Walsh, Tidewater Publishers, Cambridge, MD, 1973. 178 pp., illus. $22.95

A colorful story of market gunning in both its legal and illegal phases.

Pheasant Days, by Chris Dorsey, Voyageur Press, Stillwater, MN, 1992. 233 pp., illus. $24.95

The definitive resource on ringnecks. Includes everything from basic hunting techniques to the life cycle of the bird.

Pheasant Hunter's Harvest, by Steve Grooms, Lyons & Burford Publishers, New York, NY, 1990. 180 pp. $22.95

A celebration of pheasant, pheasant dogs and pheasant hunting. Practical advice from a passionate hunter.

Pheasant Tales, by Gene Hill et al, Countrysport Press, Traverse City, MI, 1996. 202 pp., illus. $39.00

Charley Waterman, Michael McIntosh and Phil Bourjaily join the author to tell some of the stories that illustrate why the pheasant is America's favorite game bird.

Pheasants of the Mind, by Datus Proper, Wilderness Adventures Press, Bozeman, MT, 1994. 154 pp., illus. $25.00

No single title sums up the life of the solitary pheasant hunter like this masterful work.

Portraits of Elk Hunting, by Jim Zumbo, Safari Press, Huntington Beach, CA, 2001. 222 pp. illus. $39.95

Zumbo has captured in photos as well as in words the essence, charisma, and wonderful components of elk hunting: back-country wilderness camps, sweaty guides, happy hunters, favorite companions, elk woods, and, of course, the majestic elk. Join Zumbo in the uniqueness of the pursuit of the magnificent and noble elk.

Precision Bowhunting: A Year-Round approach to taking Mature Whitetails, by John and Chrs Eberhart, Stackpole Books, 2005. 214 pp., b&w photos. Soft cover. NEW. $16.95

Packed with vital information and fresh insights, Precision Bow hunting belongs on the bookshelf of every serious bow hunter.

Proven Whitetail Tactics, by Greg Miller, Krause Publications, Iola, WI, 1997. 224 pp., illus. Paper covers. $19.95

Proven tactics for scouting, calling and still-hunting whitetail.

Quest for Dall Rams, by Duncan Gilchrist, Duncan Gilchrist Outdoor Expeditions and Books, Corvallis, MT, 1997. 224 pp., illus. Paper covers. $19.95

The most complete book of Dall sheep ever written. Covers information on Alaska and provinces with Dall sheep and explains hunting techniques, equipment, etc.

Quest for Giant Bighorns, by Duncan Gilchrist, Outdoor Expeditions and Books, Corvallis, MT, 1994. 224 pp., illus. Paper covers. $19.95

How some of the most successful sheep hunters hunt and how some of the best bighorns were taken.

Radical Elk Hunting Strategies, by Mike Lapinski, Stoneydale Press Publishing Co., Stevensville, MT, 1988. 161 pp., illus. $18.95

Secrets of calling elk in close.

Rattling, Calling & Decoying Whitetails, by Gary Clancy, edited by Patrick Durkin, Krause Publications, Iola, WI, 2000. 208 pp., illus. Paper covers. $19.95

How to consistently coax big bucks into range.

Records of North American Caribou and Moose, Craig Boddington et al, The Boone & Crockett Club, Missoula, MT, 1997. 250 pp., illus. $24.95

More than 1,800 caribou listings and more than 1,500 moose listings, organized by the state or Canadian province where they were taken.

Records of North American Elk and Mule Deer, 2nd Edition, edited by Jack and Susan Reneau, The Boone & Crockett Club, Missoula, MT, 1996. 360 pp., illus. Paper cover, $18.95; hardcover $24.95

Updated and expanded edition featuring more than 150 trophy, field and historical photos of the finest elk and mule deer trophies ever recorded.

Records of North American Sheep, Rocky Mountain Goats and Pronghorn, edited by Jack and Susan Reneau, The Boone & Crockett Club, Missoula, MT, 1996. 400 pp., illus. Paper cover, $18.95; hardcover, $24.95

The first B&C Club records book featuring all 3941 accepted wild sheep, Rocky Mountain goats and pronghorn trophies.

Reflections on Snipe, by Worth Mathewson, illustrated by Eldridge Hardie, Camden, ME, Country Sport Press, 2003. Hardcover. 144 pp. $25.00

Reflections on Snipe is a delightful compendium of information on snipe behavior and habitats; gunning history; stories from the field; and the pleasures of hunting with good companions, whether human or canine.

Return of Royalty; Wild Sheep of North America, by Dr. Dale E. Toweill and Dr. Valerius Geist, The Boone and Crockett Club, Missoula, MT, 1999. 224 pp., illus. $59.95

A celebration of the return of the wild sheep to many of its historical ranges.

Ringneck; A Tribute to Pheasants and Pheasant Hunting, by Steve Grooms, Russ Sewell and Dave Nomsen, The Lyons Press, New York, NY, 2000. 120 pp., illus. $40.00

A glorious full-color coffee-table tribute to the pheasant and those who hunt them.

Rooster! A Tribute to Pheasant Hunting, by Dale C. Spartas, Riverbend Publishing, 2003. 1st edition. 150+ glorious photos of pheasants, hunting dogs and hunting trips with family and friends. 128 pp. Hardcover. $39.95

A very special, must-have book for the 2.3 million pheasant hunters across the country!

Rub-Line Secrets, by Greg Miller, edited by Patrick Durkin, Krause Publications, Iola, WI, 1999. 208 pp., illus. Paper covers. $19.95

Based on nearly 30 years' experience. Proven tactics for finding, analyzing and hunting big bucks' rub-lines.

The Season, by Tom Kelly, Lyons & Burford, New York, NY, 1997. 160 pp., illus. $22.95

The delight and challenges of a turkey hunter's spring season.

Secret Strategies from North America's Top Whitetail Hunters, compiled by Nick Sisley, Krause Publications, Iola, WI, 1995. 256 pp., illus. Paper covers. $14.95

Bow and gun hunters share their success stories.

Sheep Hunting in Alaska–The Dall Sheep Hunter's Guide, by Tony Russ, Outdoor Expeditions and Books, Corvallis, MT, 1994. 160 pp., illus. Paper covers. $19.95

A how-to guide for the Dall sheep hunter.

Southern Deer & Deer Hunting, by Larry Weishuhn and Bill Bynum, Krause Publications, Iola, WI, 1995. 256 pp., illus. Paper covers. $14.95

Mount a trophy southern whitetail on your wall with this firsthand account of stalking big bucks below the Mason-Dixon line.

Spring Gobbler Fever, by Michael Hanback, Krause Publications, Iola, WI, 1996. 256 pp., illus. Paper covers. $15.95

Your complete guide to spring turkey hunting.

Stand Hunting for Whitetails, by Richard P. Smith, Krause Publications, Iola, WI, 1996. 256 pp., illus. Paper covers. $14.95

The author explains the tricks and strategies for successful stand hunting.

Successful Black Bear Hunting, by Bill Vaznis, Iola, WI, Krause Publications, 2004. 214 pp., b&w photos. Soft cover. NEW. $16.95

The Sultan of Spring: A Hunter's Odyssey Through the World of the Wild Turkey, by Bob Saile, The Lyons Press, New York, NY, 1998. 176 pp., illus. $22.95

A literary salute to the magic and mysticism of spring turkey hunting.

Taking Big Bucks, by Ed Wolff, Stoneydale Press, Stevensville, MT, 1987. 169 pp., illus. $18.95

Solving the whitetail riddle.

Tales of Quails 'n Such, by Havilah Babcock, University of S. Carolina Press, Columbia, SC, 1985. 237 pp. $19.95

A group of hunting stories, told in informal style, on field experiences in the South in quest of small game.

They Left Their Tracks, by Howard Coperhaver, Stoneydale Press Publishing Co., Stevensville, MT, 1990. 190 pp., illus. $18.95

Recollections of 60 years as an outfitter in the Bob Marshall Wilderness.

To Heck with Moose Hunting, by Jim Zumbo, Wapiti Publishing Co., Cody, WY, 1996. 199 pp., illus. $17.95

Jim's hunts around the continent and even an African adventure.

Track Pack: Animal Tracks In Full Life Size, by Ed Gray, Mechanicsburg, PA, Stackpole Books, 2003. 1st edition. Spiral-bound, 34 pp. $7.95

An indispensable reference for hunters, trackers, and outdoor enthusiasts. This handy guide features the tracks of 38 common North American animals, from squirrels to grizzlies.

The Trickiest Thing in Feathers, by Corey Ford, compiled and edited by Laurie Morrow, illustrated by Christopher Smith, Wilderness Adventures, Gallatin Gateway, MT, 1998. 208 pp., illus. $29.95

Here is a collection of Corey Ford's best wing-shooting stories, many of them previously unpublished.

The Upland Equation: A Modern Bird-Hunter's Code, by Charles Fergus, Lyons & Burford Publishers, New York, NY, 1996. 86 pp. $18.00

A book that deserves space in every sportsman's library. Observations based on firsthand experience.

Upland Tales, edited by Worth Mathewson, Sand Lake Press, Amity, OR, 1996. 271 pp., illus. $29.95

A collection of articles on grouse, snipe and quail.

Waterfowler's World, by Bill Buckley, Ducks Unlimited, Inc., Memphis, TN, 1999. 192 pp., illustrated in color. $37.50

An unprecedented pictorial book on waterfowl and waterfowlers.

When the Duck Were Plenty, by Ed Muderlak, Safari Press, Inc., Huntington Beach, CA, 2000. 300 pp., illus. $29.95

The golden age of waterfowling and duck hunting from 1840 until 1920. An anthology.

Whitetail: Behavior Through the Seasons, by Charles J. Alsheimer, Krause Publications, Iola, WI, 1996. 208 pp., illus. $34.95

In-depth coverage of whitetail behavior presented through striking portraits of the whitetail in every season.

Whitetail: The Ultimate Challenge, by Charles J. Alsheimer, Krause Publications, Iola, WI, 1995. 228 pp., illus. Paper covers. $14.95

Learn deer hunting's most intriguing secrets–fooling deer using decoys, scents and calls–from America's premier authority.

Whitetails by the Moon, by Charles J. Alsheimer, edited by Patrick Durkin, Krause Publications, Iola, WI, 1999. 208 pp., illus. Paper covers. $19.95

Predict peak times to hunt whitetails. Learn what triggers the rut.

Wildfowler's Season, by Chris Dorsey, Lyons & Burford Publishers, New York, NY, 1998. 224 pp., illus. $37.95

Modern methods for a classic sport.

Wildfowling Tales, by William C. Hazelton, Wilderness Adventures Press, Belgrade, MT, 1999. 117 pp., illustrated with etchings by Brett Smith. In a slipcase. $50.00

Tales from the great ducking resorts of the continent.

Windward Crossings: A Treasury of Original Waterfowling Tales, by Chuck Petrie et al, Willow Creek Press, Minocqua, WI, 1999. 144 pp., 48 color art and etching reproductions. $35.00

An illustrated, modern anthology of previously unpublished waterfowl hunting (fiction and creative nonfiction) stories by America's finest outdoor journalists.

Wings of Thunder: New Grouse Hunting Revisited, by Steven Mulak, Countrysport Books, Selma, AL, 1998. 168 pp. illus. $30.00

The author examines every aspect of New England grouse hunting as it is today–the bird and its habits, the hunter and his dog, guns and loads, shooting and hunting techniques, practice on clay targets, clothing and equipment.

The Woodchuck Hunter, by Paul C. Estey, R&R Books, Livonia, NY, 1994. 135 pp., illus. $25.00

This book contains information on woodchuck equipment, the rifle, telescopic sights and includes interesting stories.

AFRICA/ASIA/ELSEWHERE

A Bullet Well Placed; One Hunter's Adventures Around the World, by Johnny Chilton, Safari Press, 2004. 245 pages. Hardcover. New in new dust jacket. $34.95

Painting a picture of what it is actually like to be there and do it, this well-written book captures the excitement and emotions of each journey.

A Country Boy in Africa, by George Hoffman, Trophy Room Books, Agoura, CA, 1998. 267 pp., illustrated with over 100 photos. Limited, numbered edition signed by the author. $85.00

In addition to the author's long and successful hunting career, he is known for developing a most effective big game cartridge, the .416 Hoffman.

A Hunter's Africa, by Gordon Cundill, Trophy Room Books, Agoura, CA, 1998. 298 pp., over 125 photographic illustrations. Limited numbered edition signed by the author. $125.00

A good look by the author at the African safari experience–elephant, lion, spiral-horned antelope, firearms, people and events, as well as the clients that make it worthwhile.

A Hunter's Wanderings in Africa, by Frederick Courteney Selous, Alexanders Books, Alexander, NC, 2003. 504 pp., illus. $28.50

A reprinting of the 1920 London edition. A narrative of nine years spent amongst the game of the far interior of South Africa.

A Pioneering Hunter, by B Marsh, Safari Press, 2006. A limited edition of 1,000 copies. Signed and numbered. 247 pp., color photos. Hardcover in a Slipcase. NEW. $65.00

Elephant cropping, buffalo tales, and colorful characters–this book has it all.

A Professional Hunter's Journey of Discovery, by Alec McCallum, Agoura, CA, Trophy Room Books, 2003. Limited edition of 1,000. Signed and numbered. 132 pp. Hardcover. New in new dust jacket. $125.00

A View From A Tall Hill: Robert Ruark in Africa, by Terry Wieland, Bristol, CT, Country Sport Press, 2004. Reprint. 432 pp., Hardcover New in new dust jacket $45.00

African Adventures and Misadventures: Escapades in East Africa with Mau Mau and Giant Forest Hogs, by William York, Long Beach, CA, Safari Press, 2003. A limited edition of 1,000 copies. Signed and numbered. 250 pp., color and b&w photos. Hardcover in a slipcase. $70.00

From his early days in Kenya when he and a companion trekked alone through the desert of the NFD and had to fend off marauding lions that ate his caravan ponies to encountering a Mau Mau terrorist who took potshots at his victims with a stolen elephant gun, the late Bill York gives an entertaining account of his life that will keep you turning the pages. As with York's previous book, the pages are loaded with interesting anecdotes, fascinating tales, and well-written prose that give insight into East Africa and its more famous characters.

African Game Trails, by Theodore Roosevelt, Peter Capstick, Series Editor, St. Martin's Press, New York, NY 1988. 583 pp., illus. $24.95

The famed safari of the noted sportsman, conservationist, and President.

African Hunter, by James Mellon, Safari Press, Huntington Beach, CA, 1996. 522 pp., illus. Paper covers, $75.00

Regarded as the most comprehensive title ever published on African hunting.

African Hunter II, edited by Craig Boddington and Peter Flack, Foreword by Robin Hurt, Introduction by James Mellon, Long Beach, CA, Safari Press, 2004. 1st edition. 606 pp., profuse color and b&w photos. Hardcover. $135.00

James Mellon spent five years hunting in every African country open to hunting during the late 1960s and early 1970s, making him uniquely qualified to write a book. Because so much has changed in today's Africa, however, it was necessary to update the original. With over 500 full-color pp., hundreds of photographs, and updated tables on animals and where they are available, this is THE book to consult for the information on Africa today.

African Rifles & Cartridges, by John Taylor, The Gun Room Press, Highland Park, NJ, 1977. 431 pp., illus. $35.00

Experiences and opinions of a professional ivory hunter in Africa describing his knowledge of numerous arms and cartridges for big game. A reprint.

African Twilight, by Robert F. Jones, Wilderness Adventure Press, Bozeman, MT, 1994. 208 pp., illus. $36.00

Details the hunt, danger and changing face of Africa over a span of three decades.

Atkin, Grant & Lang: A Detailed History of Enduring Gunmakers (trade edition), by Don Masters, Safari Press, 2005. 316 pp., color and b&w photos. Hardcover. New in new dust jacket. $69.89

The history of three makers and their several relatives making guns under their own names. In the pages of this book you can learn all the details of the gun makers: dates, premises, main employees, rises and declines in sales fortunes, as well as the many interesting historical anecdotes and insights we have come to expect from Don Masters.

ARMS LIBRARY

Baron in Africa; The Remarkable Adventures of Werner von Alvensleben, by Brian Marsh, Foreword by Ian Player, Safari Press, Huntington Beach, CA, 2001. 288 pp., illus. $35.00

Follow his career as he hunts lion, goes after large kudu, kills a full-grown buffalo with a spear, and hunts for elephant and ivory in some of the densest brush in Africa. The adventure and the experience were what counted to this fascinating character, not the money or fame; indeed, in the end he left Mozambique with barely more than the clothes on his back. This is a must-read adventure story of one of the most interesting characters to have come out of Africa after WWII.

Big Game and Big Game Rifles, by John "Pondoro" Taylor, Safari Press, Huntington Beach, CA, 1999. 215 pp., illus. $24.95

Covers rifles and calibers for elephant, rhino, hippo, buffalo and lion.

Buffalo!, by Craig Boddington, Safari Books, 2006. 256 pp., color photos, Hardcover. NEW. $39.95

Craig tells his readers where to hunt, how and when to hunt, and what will happen when they do hunt. He describes what it means to rush the herd, one of his favorite methods of hunting these worthy opponents. He tells of the great bull in Masailand that he almost got, of the perfect hunt he had in Zambia, and of the charge he experienced in Tanzania.

Buffalo, Elephant, & Bongo (Trade Edition): Alone in the Savannas and Rain Forests of the Cameroon, by Reinald Von Meurers, Long Beach, CA, Safari Press, 2004. Hardcover. New in new dust jacket. $39.50

Cottar: The Exception was the Rule, by Pat Cottar, Trophy Room Books, Agoura, CA, 1999. 350 pp., illus. Limited, numbered and signed edition. $135.00

The remarkable big game hunting stories of one of Kenya's most remarkable pioneers.

The Dangerous Game, True Stories of Dangerous Hunting on Three Continents. Safari Press, 2006. A limited edition of 500 copies. Signed and numbered. 225 pp., photos. Hardcover in a Slipcase. NEW. $70.00

Death and Double Rifles, by Mark Sullivan, Nitro Express Safaris, Phoenix, AZ, 2000. 295 pp., illus. $85.00

Sullivan has captured every thrilling detail of hunting dangerous game in this lavishly illustrated book. Full of color pictures of African hunts & rifles.

Death in a Lonely Land, by Peter Capstick, St. Martin's Press, New York, NY, 1990. 284 pp., illus. $22.95

Twenty-three stories of hunting as only the master can tell them.

Death in the Dark Continent, by Peter Capstick, St. Martin's Press, New York, NY, 1983. 238 pp., illus. $22.95

A book that brings to life the suspense, fear and exhilaration of stalking ferocious killers under primitive, savage conditions, with the ever present threat of death.

Death in the Long Grass, by Peter Hathaway Capstick, St. Martin's Press, New York, NY, 1977. 297 pp., illus. $22.95

A big game hunter's adventures in the African bush.

Death in the Silent Places, by Peter Capstick, St. Martin's Press, New York, NY, 1981. 243 pp., illus. $23.95

The author recalls the extraordinary careers of legendary hunters such as Corbett, Karamojo Bell, Stigand and others.

Elephant Hunters, Men of Legend, by Tony Sanchez-Arino, Safari Press, 2005. A limited edition of 1,000 copies. Signed and numbered. 240 pp. Hardcover in a Slipcase. NEW. $100.00

This newest book from Tony Sanchez is the most interesting ever to emerge on that intrepid and now finished breed of man: Elephant Hunters, Men of Legend.

Encounters with Lions, by Jan Hemsing, Trophy Room Books, Agoura, CA, 1995. 302 pp., illus. $75.00

Some stories fierce, fatal, frightening and even humorous of when man and lion meet.

Fodor's African Safari, From Budget to Big Spending Where and How to Find the Best Big Game Adventure In Southern and Eastern Africa, by David Bristow, Julian Harrison, Chris Swiac, New York, Fodor's, 2004. 1st edition. 190 pp. Softcover. NEW. $9.95

Frederick Selous: A Hunting Legend-Recollections By and About the Great Hunter (trade edition), by F.C. Selous (edited by James Casada), Safari Press, 2005. 187 pp., illus. Hardcover. $34.95

This second book on Selous, edited by Africana expert Dr. James Casada, completes the work on the lost writings by Selous begun in Africa's Greatest Hunter.

From Mt Kenya to the Cape: Ten Years of African Hunting, by Craig Boddington, Long Beach, CA, Safari Press, 2005. Hardcover. New in new dust jacket. $39.95

This wealth of information makes not only great reading, but the appendixes also provide tips on rifles, cartridges, equipment, and how to plan a safari.

From Sailor to Professional Hunter: The Autobiography of John Northcote, Trophy Room Books, Agoura, CA, 1997. 400 pp., illus. Limited edition, signed and numbered. $125.00

Only a handful of men can boast of having a 50-year professional hunting career throughout Africa as John Northcote has had.

Gone are the Days; Jungle Hunting for Tiger and other Game in India and Nepal 1953-1969, by Peter Byrne, Safari Press, Inc., Huntington Beach, CA, 2001. 225 pp., illus. Limited signed, numbered, slipcased. $70.00

Great Hunters: Their Trophy Rooms and Collections, Volume 1, compiled and published by Safari Press, Inc., Huntington Beach, CA, 1997. 172 pp., illustrated in color. $60.00

A rare glimpse into the trophy rooms of top international hunters. A few of these trophy rooms are museums.

Great Hunters: Their Trophy Rooms & Collections, Volume 2, compiled and published by Safari Press, Inc., Huntington Beach, CA, 1998. 224 pp., illustrated with 260 full-color photographs. $60.00

Volume two of the world's finest, best produced series of books on trophy rooms and game collections. 46 sportsmen sharing sights you'll never forget on this guided tour.

Great Hunters: Their Trophy Rooms & Collections, Volume 3, compiled and published by Safari Press, Inc., Huntington Beach, CA, 2000. 204 pp., illustrated with 260 full-color photographs. $60.00

At last, the long-awaited third volume in the best photographic series ever published of trophy room collections is finally available. Unbelievable as it may sound, this book tops all previous volumes. Besides some of the greatest North American trophy rooms ever seen, an extra effort was made to include European collections. As before, each trophy room is accompanied by an informative text explaining the collection and giving you insights into the hunters who went to such great efforts to create their trophy rooms. All professionally photographed in the highest quality possible.

Great Hunters: Their Trophy Rooms & Collections, Volume 4, compiled and published by Safari Press, Inc., Huntington Beach, CA, 2005. 204 pp., illustrated with 260 full-color photographs. $60.00

At last, the long-awaited fourth volume in the best photographic series ever published of trophy room collections is finally available. Unbelievable as it may sound, this book tops all previous volumes. Besides some of the greatest North American trophy rooms ever seen, an extra effort was made to include European collections. As before, each trophy room is accompanied by an informative text explaining the collection and giving you insights into the hunters who went to such great efforts to create their trophy rooms. All professionally photographed in the highest quality possible.

Heart of an African Hunter, by Peter Flack, Long Beach, CA, Safari Press, 2005. 266 pp. illustrated with b&w photos. Hardcover. NEW. $35.00

Hemingway in Africa: The Last Safari, by Christopher Ondaatje, Overlook Press, 2004. 1st edition. 240 pp. Hardcover. New in new dust jacket. $37.50

Horn of the Hunter, by Robert Ruark, Safari Press, Long Beach, CA, 1987. 315 pp., illus. $35.00

Ruark's most sought-after title on African hunting, here in reprint.

Horned Death, by John F. Burger, Safari Press, Huntington Beach, CA, 1992. 343 pp. illus. $35.00

The classic work on hunting the African buffalo.

Hunter's Tracks, by J.A. Hunter, Safari Press Publications, Huntington Beach, CA, 1999. 240 pp., illus. $24.95

This is the exciting story of John Hunter's efforts to capture the shady head man of a gang of ivory poachers and smugglers. The story is interwoven with the tale of one of East Africa's most grandiose safaris taken with an Indian maharaja.

Hunting in Ethiopia, An Anthology, by Tony Sanchez-Arino, Safari Press, Huntington Beach, CA, 1996. 350 pp., illus. Limited, signed and numbered edition. $135.00

The finest selection of hunting stories ever compiled on hunting in this great game country.

Hunting in Kenya, by Tony Sanchez-Arino, Safari Press, Inc., Huntington Beach, CA, 2000. 350 pp., illus. Limited, signed and numbered edition in a slipcase. $135.00

The finest selection of hunting stories ever compiled on hunting in this great game country make up this anthology.

Hunting in the Sudan, An Anthology, compiled by Tony Sanchez-Arino, Safari Press, Huntington Beach, CA, 1992. 350 pp., illus. Limited, signed and numbered edition in a slipcase. $125.00

The finest selection of hunting stories ever compiled on hunting in this great game country.

The Hunting Instinct, by Phillip D. Rowter, Safari Press, Inc., Huntington Beach, CA, 1999. Limited edition signed and numbered and in a slipcase. $50.00

Safari chronicles from the Republic of South Africa and Namibia 1990-1998.

The Hunting Instinct,, by Phillip D. Rowter, Safari Press, Inc., Huntington Beach, CA, 2005, trade edition. Hardcover. New in new dust jacket. $29.95

Safari chronicles from the Republic of South Africa and Namibia 1990-1998.

Hunting the Dangerous Game of Africa, by John Kingsley-Heath, Sycamore Island Books, Boulder, CO, 1998. 477 pp., illus. $95.00

Written by one of the most respected, successful, and ethical P.H.'s to trek the sunlit plains of Botswana, Kenya, Uganda, Tanganyika, Somaliland, Eritrea, Ethiopia, and Mozambique. Filled with some of the most gripping and terrifying tales ever to come out of Africa.

Hunting, Settling and Remembering, by Philip H. Percival, Trophy Room Books, Agoura, CA, 1997. 230 pp., illus. Limited, numbered and signed edition. $85.00

If Philip Percival is to come alive again, it will be through this, the first edition of his easy, intricate and magical book illustrated with some of the best historical big game hunting photos ever taken.

Hunting Trips in The Land of the Dragon; Anglo and American Sportsmen in Old China, 1870-1940, by Kenneth Czech, Safari Press, 2005. Hardcover. New in new dust jacket. $34.95

The first part of this anthology takes the reader after duck, pheasant, and other upland game while the second part focuses on the large game of China and the border regions. The latter includes hunts for Manchurian tiger, tufted deer, goral, wild goat, wild yak, antelope, takin, wild sheep in the Mongolian Altai, wapiti, blue sheep, ibex, Ovis poli of the Pamir, wild sheep of the Tian Shan, brown bear, and panda–all written by such famous names as Major General Kinloch, St. George Littledale, Kermit Roosevelt, and Roy Chapman Andrews.

ARMS LIBRARY

In the Salt, by Lou Hallamore, Trophy Room Books, Agoura, CA, 1999. 227 pp., illustrated in b&w and full color. Limited, numbered and signed edition. $125.00

A book about people, animals and the big game hunt, about being outwitted and outmaneuvered. It is about knowing that sooner or later your luck will change and your trophy will be "in the salt."

International Hunter 1945-1999, Hunting's Greatest Era, by Bert Klineburger, Sportsmen on Film, Kerrville, TX, 1999. 400 pp., illus. A limited, numbered and signed edition. $125.00

The most important book of the greatest hunting era by the world's preeminent International hunter.

The Jim Corbett Collection, by Jim Corbett, Safari press, 2005. 1124 pp., illus, 5 volumes. Hardcover in a Slipcase. NEW. $100.00

The complete set of Jim Corbett's works, housed in a printed slipcase and feature the work of the internationally famous wildlife artist Guy Coheleach.

King of the Wa-Kikuyu, by John Boyes, St. Martin Press, New York, NY, 1993. 240 pp., illus. $19.95

In the 19th and 20th centuries, Africa drew to it a large number of great hunters, explorers, adventurers and rogues. Many have become legendary, but John Boyes (1874-1951) was the most legendary of them all.

Kwaheri! On the Spoor of Big Game in East Africa, by Robert von Reitnauer, Long beach, CA, Safari Press, 2005. Limited edition of 1,000 copies. Signed and numbered. 285 pp., illustrated with photos. Hardcover in a Slipcase. NEW. $75.00

This is the story of an immense land in the days before the truly big tuskers all but disappeared. A very good read.

Last Horizons: Hunting, Fishing and Shooting on Five Continents, by Peter Capstick, St. Martin's Press, New York, NY, 1989. 288 pp., illus. $19.95

The first in a two-volume collection of hunting, fishing and shooting tales from the selected pages of *The American Hunter, Guns & Ammo* and *Outdoor Life.*

Last of the Ivory Hunters, by John Taylor, Safari Press, Long Beach, CA, 1990. 354 pp., illus. $29.95

Reprint of the classic book "Pondoro" by one of the most famous elephant hunters of all time.

Legends of the Field: More Early Hunters in Africa, by W.R. Foran, Trophy Room Press, Agoura, CA, 1997. 319 pp., illus. Limited edition. $100.00

This book contains the biographies of some very famous hunters: William Cotton Oswell, F.C. Selous, Sir Samuel Baker, Arthur Neumann, Jim Sutherland, W.D.M. Bell and others.

Lives of A Professional Hunting Family, by Gerard Agoura Miller, Trophy Room Books, 2003. A limited edition of 1,000 copies. Signed and numbered. 303 pp., 230 b&w photographic illustrations. Hardcover. $135.00

The Lost Classics, by Robert Ruark, Safari Press, Huntington Beach, CA, 1996. 260 pp., illus. $35.00

The magazine stories that Ruark wrote in the 1950s and 1960s finally in print in book form.

The Lost Wilderness; True Accounts of Hunters and Animals in East Africa, by Mohamed Ismail and Alice Pianfetti, Safari Press, Inc., Huntington Beach, CA, 2000. 216 pp., photos, illus. Limited edition signed, numbered and slipcased. $60.00

Mahonhboh, by Ron Thomson, Hartbeesport, South Africa, 1997. 312 pp., illus. Limited signed and numbered edition. $50.00

Elephants and elephant hunting in South Central Africa.

The Man-Eaters of Tsavo, by Lt. Colonel J.H. Patterson, Peter Capstick, series editor, St. Martin's Press, New York, NY, 1986, 5th printing. 346 pp., illus. $14.95

Maneaters and Marauders, by John "Pondoro" Taylor, Long Beach, CA, Safari Press, 2005. 1st edition, Safari edition. Hardcover. New in new dust jacket. $29.95

McElroy Hunts Asia, by C.J. McElroy, Safari Press, Inc., Huntington Beach, CA, 1989. 272 pp., illus. $50.00

From the founder of SCI comes a book on hunting the great continent of Asia for big game: tiger, bear, sheep and ibex. Includes the story of the all-time record Altai Argali as well as several markhor hunts in Pakistan.

Memoirs of a Sheep Hunter, by Rashid Jamsheed, Safari Press, Inc., Huntington Beach, CA, 1996. 330 pp., illus. $70.00

The author reveals his exciting accounts of obtaining world-record heads from his native Iran, and his eventual move to the U.S. where he procured a grand-slam of North American sheep.

Memoirs of An African Hunter (trade Edition), by Terry Irwin, Safari Press, 2005. 411 pp., 95 color and 20 b&w photos, large format. Hardcover $70.00

Memories of Africa; Hunting in Zambia and Sudan, by W. Brach, Safari Press, 2005. Limited edition of 1,000 copies. Signed and numbered. 285 pp., illustrated with photos. Hardcover in a Slipcase. NEW. $85.00

Written with an interesting flair and a true graphic perspective of the animals, people, and the hunt, this is a realistic portrayal, not Hollywood-style swaggering and gun-slinging, of hunting the magnificent wildlife of Zambia and Sudan over the last three decades.

Mundjamba: The Life Story of an African Hunter, by Hugo Seia, Trophy Room Books, Agoura, CA, 1996. 400 pp., illus. Limited, numbered and signed by the author. $125.00

An autobiography of one of the most respected and appreciated professional African hunters.

My Africa: A Professional Hunter's Journey of Discovery, by Alec McCallum, Trouphy Room Books, 2003. Limited edition of 1000. Signed and numbered. hunting. 232 pp. Hardcover. New in new dust jacket. $125.00

My Wanderings Though Africa: The Life and Times of a Professional Hunter, by Mike and James Cameron, Safari Press, 2004. Deluxe, limited, signed edition. 208 pp., b&w photos. Hardcover in a Slipcase. NEW. $75.00

This is a book for readers whose imagination carries them into a world where reality means starry skies, the call of a jackal and the moan of a lion, the smell of gun oil, and smoke from a cooking fire rising into the African night.

The Nature of the Game, by Ben Hoskyns, Quiller Press, Ltd., London, England, 1994. 160 pp., illus. $37.50

The first complete guide to British, European and North American game.

On Safari with Bwana Game–Trade Edition, by Eric Balson, Long Beach, CA, Safari Press, 2004. 1st edition. Hardcover. New in new dust jacket. $39.95

On Target, by Christian Le Noel, Trophy Room Books, Agoura, CA, 1999. 275 pp., illus. Limited, numbered and signed edition. $85.00

History and hunting in Central Africa.

One Long Safari, by Peter Hay, Trophy Room Books, Agoura, CA, 1998. 350 pp., with over 200 photographic illustrations and 7 maps. Limited numbered edition signed by the author. $100.00

Contains hunts for leopards, sitatunga, hippo, rhino, snakes and, of course, the general African big game bag.

Optics for the Hunter, by John Barsness, Safari Press, Inc., Huntington Beach, CA, 1999. 236 pp., illus. $24.95

An evaluation of binoculars, scopes, range finders, spotting scopes for use in the field.

Out in the Midday Shade, by William York, Safari Press, Inc., Huntington Beach, CA, 1999. Limited, signed and numbered edition in a slipcase. $70.00

Memoirs of an African hunter 1949-1968.

Out in the Midday Shade, by William York, Safari Press, Inc., Huntington Beach, CA, 2005. Trade Edition. Hardcover. New in new dust jacket. $35.00

The Path of a Hunter, by Gilles Tre-Hardy, Trophy Room Books, Agoura, CA, 1997. 318 pp., illus. Limited Edition, signed and numbered. $85.00

A most unusual hunting autobiography with much about elephant hunting in Africa.

The Perfect Shot: Mini Edition for Africa, by Kevin Robertson, Long Beach, CA, Safari Press, 2004. 2nd printing Softcover. NEW. $17.95

The Perfect Shot: Shot Placement for African Big Game, by Kevin "Doctari" Robertson, Safari Press, Inc., Huntington Beach, CA, 1999. 230 pp., illus. $65.00

The most comprehensive work ever undertaken to show the anatomical features for all classes of African game. Includes caliber and bullet selection, rifle selection and trophy handling.

Peter Capstick's Africa: A Return to the Long Grass, by Peter Hathaway Capstick, St. Martin's Press, N. Y., NY, 1987. 213 pp., illus. $35.00

A first-person adventure in which the author returns to the long grass for his own dangerous and very personal excursion.

Pondoro, by John Taylor, Safari Press, Inc., Huntington Beach, CA, 1999. 354 pp., illus. $29.95

The author is considered one of the best storytellers in the hunting book world, and Pondoro is highly entertaining. A classic African big-game hunting title.

The Quotable Hunter, by Jay Cassell and Peter Fiduccia, The Lyons Press, N.Y., 1999. 288 pp., illus. $20.00

This collection of more than three hundred quotes from hunters through the ages captures the essence of the sport, with all its joys, idosyncrasies, and challenges.

Return to Toonaklut–The Russell Annabel Story, by Jeff Davis, Long Beach, CA, Safari Press, 2002. 248 pp., photos, illus. $34.95

Those of us who grew up after WW II cannot imagine the Alaskan frontier that Rusty Annabel walked into early in the twentieth century. The hardships, the resourcefulness, the natural beauty, not knowing what lay beyond the next horizon, all were a part of his existence. This is the story of the man behind the legend, and it is as fascinating as any of the tales Rusty Annabel ever spun for the sporting magazines.

Rifles and Cartridges for Large Game–From Deer to Bear–Advice on the Choice of A Rifle, by Layne Simpson, Long Beach, CA, Safari Press, 2002. Illustrated with 100 color photos, oversize book. 225 pp., color illus. $39.95

Layne Simpson, who has been field editor for *Shooting Times* magazine for 20 years, draws from his hunting experiences on five continents to tell you what rifles, cartridges, bullets, loads, and scopes are best for various applications, and he explains why in plain English. Developer of the popular 7mm STW cartridge, Simpson has taken big game with rifle cartridges ranging in power from the .220 Swift to the .460 Weatherby Magnum, and he pulls no punches when describing their effectiveness in the field.

Rifles for Africa; Practical Advice on Rifles and Ammunition for an African Safari, by Gregor Woods, Long Beach, CA, Safari Press, 2002. 1st edition. 430 pp., illus., photos. $39.95

Invaluable to the person who seeks advice and information on what rifles, calibers, and bullets work on African big game, be they the largest land mammals on earth or an antelope barely weighing in at 20 lbs.!

Robert Ruark's Africa, by Robert Ruark, edited by Michael McIntosh, Countrysport Press, Selma, AL, 1999. 256 pp. illustrated with 19 original etchings by Bruce Langton. $32.00

These previously uncollected works of Robert Ruark make this a classic big-game hunting book.

Safari: The Last Adventure, by Peter Capstick, St. Martin's Press, New York, NY, 1984. 291 pp., illus. $22.95

A modern comprehensive guide to the African Safari.

Safari Rifles: Double, Magazine Rifles and Cartridges for African Hunting, by Craig Boddington, Safari Press, Huntington Beach, CA, 1990. 416 pp., illus. $37.50

A wealth of knowledge on the safari rifle. Historical and present double-rifle makers, ballistics for the large bores, and much, much more.

Sands of Silence, by Peter H. Capstick, Saint Martin's Press, New York, NY, 1991. 224 pp., illus. $35.00

Join the author on safari in Nambia for his latest big-game hunting adventures.

Song of the Summits–Hunting Sheep, Ibex, and Markhor in Asia, Europe, and North America, Limited Edition by Jesus Yurén, Long Beach, CA, Safari Press, 2003. Hardcover in a slipcase. NEW. $75.00

Sunset Tales of Safariland, by Stan Bleazard, Trophy Room Books, 2006. Deluxe, Limited, Signed edition. Large 8-1/2" x 11" format, bound in sumptuous forest green gilt stamped suede binding. 274 pages. 113 b&w photographic illustrations and index. NEW. $125.00

Sunset Tales of Safariland will be of considerable interest to anyone interested in big game hunting.

Tales of the African Frontier, by J.A. Hunter, Safari Press Publications, Huntington Beach, CA, 1999. 308 pp., illus. $24.95

The early days of East Africa is the subject of this powerful John Hunter book.

Tanzania Safari: Hei Safari, by Robert DePole, Trophy Room Books, 2004. Sumptuous burgundy gilt stamped faux suede binding, 343 pages plus 12-page index of people and places. 32 pages of b&w photographic illustrations. Hardcover. NEW. $125.00

The reader will "see" the animals on the pages long enough to remember them forever.

To Heck With It–I'm Going Hunting–My First Eighteen Years as an International Big-Game Hunter–Limited Edition, by Arnold Alward with Bill Quimby, Long Beach, CA, Safari Press, 2003. Deluxe, 1st edition, limited to 1,000 signed copies. NEW. $80.00

Uganda Safaris, by Brian Herne, Winchester Press, Piscataway, NJ, 1979. 236 pp., illus. $24.95

The chronicle of a professional hunter's adventures in Africa.

Under the African Sun, by Dr. Frank Hibben, Safari Press, Inc., Huntington Beach, CA, 1999. Limited edition signed, numbered and in a slipcase. $85.00

Forty-eight years of hunting the African continent.

Under the African Sun, by Dr. Frank Hibben, Safari Press, Inc., Huntington Beach, CA, 2005. Trade edition. 305 pages illustrated with b&w and color photos. Hardcover . New in new dust jacket. $39.95

Under the Shadow of Man Eaters, by Jerry Jaleel, The Jim Corbett Foundation, Edmonton, Alberta, Canada, 1997. 152 pp., illus. A limited, numbered and signed edition. Paper covers. $35.00

The life and legend of Jim Corbett of Kumaon.

Use Enough Gun, by Robert Ruark, Safari Press, Huntington Beach, CA, 1997. 333 pp., illus. $35.00

Robert Ruark on big game hunting.

Warrior: The Legend of Col. Richard Meinertzhagen, by Peter H. Capstick, St. Martins Press, New York, NY, 1998. 320 pp., illus. $23.95

A stirring and vivid biography of the famous British colonial officer Richard Meinertzhagen, whose exploits earned him fame and notoriety as one of the most daring and ruthless men to serve during the glory days of the British Empire.

The Waterfowler's World, by Bill Buckley, Willow Creek Press, Minocqua, WI, 1999. 176 pp., 225 color photographs. $37.50

Waterfowl hunting from Canadian prairies, across the U.S. heartland, to the wilds of Mexico, from the Atlantic to the Pacific coasts and the Gulf of Mexico.

The Weatherby: Stories From the Premier Big-Game Hunters of the World, 1956- 2002, edited by Nancy Vokins, Long Beach, CA, Safari Press, 2004. Deluxe, limited, signed edition. 434 pp., profuse color and b&w illus. Hardcover in a slipcase. $200.00

The Wheel of Life–Bunny Allen, A Life of Safaris and Sex, by Bunny Allen, Long Beach, CA, Safari Press, 2004. 1st edition. 300 pp., illus, photos. Hardcover. $34.95

Where Lions Roar: Ten More Years of African Hunting, by Craig Boddington, Safari Press, Huntington Beach, CA, 1997. 250 pp., $35.00

The story of Boddington's hunts in the Dark Continent during the last ten years.

White Hunter, by J.A. Hunter, Safari Press Publications, Huntington Beach, CA, 1999. 282 pp., illus. $24.95

This book is a seldom-seen account of John Hunter's adventures in pre-WWII Africa.

Wind, Dust and Snow, by Robert M. Anderson, Safari Press, Inc., Huntington Beach, CA, 1997. 240 pp., illus. $65.00

A complete chronology of modern exploratory and pioneering Asian sheep-hunting expeditions from 1960 until 1996, with wonderful background history and previously untold stories.

With a Gun in Good Country, by Ian Manning, Trophy Room Books, Agoura, CA, 1996. Limited, numbered and signed by the author. $85.00

A book written about that splendid period before the poaching onslaught which almost closed Zambia and continues to the granting of her independence. It then goes on to recount Manning's experiences in Botswana, Congo, and briefly in South Africa.

Yoshi–The Life and Travels of an International Trophy Hunter, by W. Yoshimoto with Bill Quimby, Long Beach, CA, Safari Press, Inc., 2002. A limited edition of 1,000 copies, signed and numbered. 298 pp., color and b&w photos. Hardcover in a slipcase. $85.00

Watson T. Yoshimoto, a native Hawaiian, collected all 16 major varieties of the world's wild sheep and most of the many types of goats, ibex, bears, antelopes, and antlered game of Asia, Europe, North America, South America, and the South Pacific...as well as the African Big Five. Along the way he earned the respect of his peers and was awarded hunting's highest achievement, the coveted Weatherby Award.

RIFLES

.577 Snider-Enfield Rifles & Carbines; British Service Longarms, by Ian Skennerton. 1866-C.1880. Australia, Arms & Militaria Press, 2003. 1st edition. 240 pp. plus 8 color plates, 100 illustrations. Marking Ribbon. Hardcover. $39.50

The definitive study of Britain's first breech-loading rifle, at first converted from Enfield muskets, then newly made with Mk III breech. The trials, development, rifle and carbine models are detailed; new information along with descriptions of the cartridges.

The '03 Springfield Rifles Era, by Clark S. Campbell, Richmond, VA, privately printed, 2003. 1st edition. 368 pp., 146 illustrations, drawn to scale by author. Hardcover. $58.00

A much-expanded version of this author's famous The '03 Springfield (1957) and The '03 Springfields (1971), representing 40 years of research into all things '03. Part I is a complete and verifiably correct study of all standardized and special-purpose models of the U.S. M1903 Springfield rifle, in both .22 and .30 calibers, including those prototypes which led to standard models, and also all standardized .30 caliber cartridges, including National and International Match, and caliber .22. Part II is the result of the author's five years as a Research and Development Engineer with Remington Arms Co., and will be of inestimable value to anyone planning a custom sporter, whether or not based on the '03.

A Master Gunmaker's Guide to Building Bolt-Action Rifles, by Bill Holmes, Boulder, CO, Paladin Press, 2003. Photos, illus., 152 pp. Softcover. $25.00

Many people today call themselves gunmakers, but very few have actually made a gun. Most buy parts wherever available and simply assemble them. During the past 50 years Bill Holmes has built from scratch countless rifles, shotguns and pistols of amazing artistry, ranging in caliber from .17 to .50.

A Question of Confidence–The Ross Rifle in the Trenches #4 in "Up Close" Series, by Col. A.F. Duguid, Ottawa, Ontario, Service Publications, 2000. 1st edition. 48 pp., 19 illustrations. Softcover, NEW. $29.95

The Accurate Rifle, by Warren Page, Claymore Publishing, Ohio, 1997. 254 pp., illus. Revised edition. Paper covers. $17.95

Provides hunters & shooters alike with detailed practical information on the whole range of subjects affecting rifle accuracy, he explains techniques in ammo, sights & shooting methods. With a 1996 equipment update from Dave Brennan.

The Accurate Varmint Rifle, by Boyd Mace, Precision Shooting, Inc., Whitehall, NY, 1991. 184 pp., illus. $15.00

A long overdue and long needed work on what factors go into the selection of components for and the subsequent assembly of...the accurate varmint rifle.

Accurizing & Shooting Lee-Enfields, by Ian Skennerton, Australia, Arms & Militaria Press, 2005. This new full color heavily illustrated work by Ian Skennerton answers all those questions regarding the use of the Lee Enfield Rifles. Packed with detailed information covering the guns, the armourer's tools, and the sighting options for this fascinating series. 35 pp., saddle-stitched laminated covers. ALL Color photos and illustrations. Stiff Paper Covers. NEW. $15.00

The AK-47 and AK-74 Kalashnikov Rifles and Their Variations, by Joe Poyer, Tustin, CA, North Cape Publications, 2004. 1st edition. Softcover, NEW. $22.95

The AK-47 Assault Rifle, Desert Publications, Cornville, AZ, 1981. 150 pp., illus. Paper covers. $15.95

Complete and practical technical information on the only weapon in history to be produced in an estimated 30,000,000 units.

American Hunting Rifles: Their Application in the Field for Practical Shooting, by Craig Boddington, Safari Press, Huntington Beach, CA, 1996. 446 pp., illus. Second printing trade edition. Softcover $24.95

Covers all the hunting rifles and calibers that are needed for North America's diverse game.

The American Krag Rifle and Carbine, by Joe Poyer, North Cape Publications, Tustin, CA, 2002. 1st edition. 317 pp., illustrated with hundreds of b&w drawings and photos. Softcover. $19.95

Provides the arms collector, historian and target shooter with a part-by-part analysis of what has been called the rifle with the smoothest bolt action ever designed. Changes to all parts are analyzed in detail and matched to serial number ranges. Monthly serial number chart by production year has been devised that will provide the collector with the year and month in which his gun was manufactured. New and complete exploded view was produced for this book.

The American Percussion Schuetzen Rifle, by J. Hamilton and T. Rowe, Rochester, NY, Rowe Publications, 2005. 1st edition. 388 pp. Hardcover. New in new dust jacket. $89.95

An Illustrated Guide to the '03 Springfield Service Rifle, by Bruce Canfield, Lincoln, RI, Andrew Mowbray, 2005. 240 pp., illustrated with over 450 photos. Pictorial Hardcover. NEW. $49.95

Your ultimate guide to the military '03 Springfield! Covers all models, all manufacturers and all conflicts, including WWI, WWII and beyond. Heavily illustrated with professional photography showing the details that separate a great collectible rifle from the rest. Serial number tables, combat photos, sniper rifles and more!

The AR-15 Complete Assembly Guide, Volume 2, by Walt Kuleck and Clint McKee. Export, PA, Scott A. Duff Publications, 2002. 1st edition. 155 pp., 164 photographs & line drawings. Softcover. $19.95

This book goes beyond the military manuals in depth and scope, using words and pictures to clearly guide the reader through every operation required to assemble their AR-15-type rifle. You'll learn the best and easiest ways to build your rifle. It won't make you an AR-15 armorer, but it will make you a more knowledgeable owner. You'll be able to do more with (and to) your rifle. You'll also be able to better judge the competence of those whom you choose to work on your rifle, and to discuss your needs more intelligently with them. In short, if you build it, you'll know how to repair it.

The AR-15 Complete Owner's Guide, Volume 1, 2nd Edition, by Walt Kuleck and Scott Duff, Export, PA, Scott A. Duff Publications, 2002. 224 pp., 164 photographs & line drawings. Softcover. $21.95

This book provides the prospective, new or experienced AR-15 owner with the in-depth knowledge he or she needs to select, configure, operate, maintain and troubleshoot his or her rifle. The Guide covers history, applications, details of components and subassemblies, operating, cleaning, maintenance, and future of perhaps the most versatile rifle system ever produced. A comprehensive Colt model number table and pre-/post-ban serial number information are included. This is the book I wish had existed prior to buying my first AR-15!

The AR-15/M16, A Practical Guide, by Duncan Long, Paladin Press, Boulder, CO, 1985. 168 pp., illus. Paper covers. $22.00

The definitive book on the rifle that has been the inspiration for so many modern assault rifles.

Argentine Mauser Rifles 1871-1959, by Colin Atglen, Webster, PA, Schiffer Publications, 2003. 1st edition. 304 pp., over 400 b&w and color photographs, drawings, and charts. Hardcover. $79.95

This is the complete story of Argentina's contract Mauser rifles from the purchase of their first Model 1871s to the disposal of the last shipment of surplus rifles received in the United States in May 2002. The Argentine Commission's relentless pursuit of tactical superiority resulted in a major contribution to the development of Mauser's now famous bolt-action system. The combined efforts of the Belgian, Turkish and Argentine arms commissions between 1889 and 1892 produced the origins of what became the Model 98 bolt-action system that is still in use today over 110 years later.

The Art of Shooting with the Rifle, by Col. Sir H. St. John Halford, Excalibur Publications, Latham, NY, 1996. 96 pp., illus. Paper covers. $12.95

A facsimile edition of the 1888 book by a respected rifleman providing a wealth of detailed information.

The Art of the Rifle, by Jeff Cooper, Paladin Press, Boulder, CO, 1997. 104 pp., illus. $29.95

Everything you need to know about the rifle whether you use it for security, meat or target shooting.

Assault Rifle, by Maxim Popenker, and Anthony Williams, London, Crowood Press, 2005. 224 pp. Hardcover. New in new dust jacket. $34.95

Includes: Brief historical summary of the assault rifle, its origins and development; Gun design including operating mechanisms and weapon configuration; ammunition design and performance; Ballistics, especially the balance between recoil and effectiveness; and a history of the assault rifle cartridge. The second part includes: National military rifle programs since the end of WWII; history of developments in each country including experimental programs; and detailed descriptions of the principal service and experimental weapons.

Ballard: The Great American Single Shot Rifle, by John T. Dutcher, Denver, CO, privately printed, 2002. 1st edition. 380 pp., illustrated with b&w photos, with an 8- page color insert. Hardcover. $79.95

Benchrest Actions and Triggers, by Stuart Otteson. Rohnert Park, CA, Adams-Kane Press, July 2003. Limited edition. 64 pp. Softcover. $27.95

Stuart Otteson's Benchrest Actions and Triggers is truly a lost classic. Benchrest Actions and Triggers is a compilation of 17 articles Mr. Otteson wrote. The articles contained are of particular interest to the benchrest crowd. Reprinted by permission of Wolfe Publishing.

Black Magic: The Ultra Accurate AR-15, by John Feamster, Precision Shooting, Manchester, CT, 1998. 300 pp., illus. $29.95

The author has compiled his experiences pushing the accuracy envelope of the AR-15 to its maximum potential. A wealth of advice on AR-15 loads, modifications and accessories for everything from NRA Highpower and Service Rifle competitions to benchrest and varmint shooting.

The Black Rifle, M16 Retrospective, R. Blake Stevens and Edward C. Ezell, Collector Grade Publications, Toronto, Canada, 1987. 400 pp., illus. $42.95

Black Rifle II: The M16 into the 21st Century, by Christopher R. Bartocci, Canada, Collector Grade Publications, 2004. 1st edition. 408 pp., 626 illustrations. Hardcover. New in new dust jacket. $69.95

Blitzkrieg!–The MP40 Maschinenpistole of WWII, by Frank Iannamico, Harmony, ME, Moose Lake Publishing, 2003. 1st edition. Over 275 pp., 280 photos and documents. Softcover. $29.95

It's back, now in a new larger 8" x11" format. Lots of new information and many unpublished photos. This book includes the history and development of the German machine pistol from the MP18.I to the MP40.

Bolt Action Rifles, Expanded 4th Edition, by Frank de Haas and Wayne van Zwoll, Krause Publications, Iola, WI 2003. 696 pp., illustrated with 615 b&w photos. Softcover. $29.95

Boss & Co. Builders of the Best Guns Only, 2nd Edition., Donald Dallas, London, Quiller Press, 2006. 272 pp., color and b&w photos. Hardcover. New in new dust jacket. $95.00

This second edition brings the history of the firm up-to-date, with over 100 new photos, freshly researched material, new appendixes, and serial numbers to the present day. The new appendix on all the engravers who worked for Boss will prove of great interest to Boss owners, for now the engraver particular to each gun can be ascertained. By giving serial numbers up to the present day, guns can now be dated precisely and pairs long since parted can be re-united. This definitive history of Boss & Co was fully authorized by the firm.

British .22RF Training Rifles, by Dennis Lewis and Robert Washburn, Excalibur Publications, Latham, NY, 1993. 64 pp., illus. Paper covers. $10.95

The story of Britain's training rifles from the early Aiming Tube models to the post-WWII trainers.

Building Double Rifles on Shotgun Actions, by W. Ellis Brown, Ft. Collins, CO, Bunduki Publishing, 2001. 1st edition. 187 pp., including index and b&w photographs. Hardcover. $55.00

Classic Sporting Rifles, by Christopher Austyn, Safari Press, Huntington Beach, CA, 1997. 128 pp., illus. $50.00

As the head of the gun department at Christie's Auction House the author examines the "best" rifles built over the last 150 years.

The Collectable '03, by J.C. Harrison, The Arms Chest, Oklahoma City, OK. 1999. 2nd edition (revised). 234 pp., illustrated with drawings, Spiral bound. $35.00

Valuable and detailed reference book for the collector of the Model 1903 Springfield rifle.

Collecting Classic Bolt Action Military Rifles, by Paul S. Scarlata, Andrew Mowbray, Inc., Lincoln, RI, 2001. 280 pp., illus. $39.95

Over 400 large photographs detail key features you will need to recognize in order to identify guns for your collection. Learn the original military configurations of these service rifles so you can tell them apart from altered guns and bad restorations. The historical sections are particularly strong, giving readers a clear understanding of how and why these rifles were developed, and which troops used them.

Collecting the Garand, by J.C. Harrison, The Arms Chest, Oklahoma City, OK. 2001. 2nd edition (revised). 198 pp., illus. with pictures and drawings. Spiral bound. $35.00

Valuable and detailed reference book for the collector of the Garand.

Collecting the M1 Carbine, by J.C. Harrison, The Arms Chest, Oklahoma City, OK. 2000. 2nd edition (revised). 247 pp., illustrated with pictures and drawings. Spiral bound. $35.00

Valuable and detailed reference book for the collector of the M1 Carbine. Identifies standard issue original military models of M1 and M1A1 Models of 1942, '43, '44, and '45 carbines as produced by each manufacturer, plus arsenal repair, refinish and lend-lease.

The Competitive AR15: The Mouse That Roared, by Glenn Zediker, Zediker Publishing, Oxford, MS, 1999. 286 pp., illus. Paper covers. $29.95

A thorough and detailed study of the newest precision rifle sensation.

The Complete AR15/M16 Sourcebook, Revised and Updated Edition, by Duncan Long, Paladin Press, Boulder, CO, 2002. 336 pp., illus. Paper covers. $39.95

The latest development of the AR15/M16 and the many spin-offs now available, selective-fire conversion systems for the 1990s, the vast selection of new accessories.

The Complete Book of the .22: A Guide to the World's Most Popular Guns, by Wayne van Zwoll, Lyons Press, 2004. 1st edition. 336 pp. Hardcover. NEW. $26.95

Complete Guide to the M1 Garand and the M1 Carbine, by Bruce Canfield, Andrew Mowbray, Inc., Lincoln, RI, 1999. 296 pp., illus. $39.50

Covers all of the manufacturers of components, parts, variations and markings. Learn which parts are proper for which guns. The total story behind these guns, from their invention through WWII, Korea, Vietnam and beyond! 300+ photos show you features, markings, overall views and action shots. Thirty-three tables and charts give instant reference to serial numbers, markings, dates of issue and proper configurations. Special sections on sniper guns, National Match rifles, exotic variations, and more!

The Complete M1 Garand, by Jim Thompson, Paladin Press, Boulder, CO, 1998. 160 pp., illus. Paper cover. $24.00

A guide for the shooter and collector, heavily illustrated.

Crown Jewels: The Mauser In Sweden; A Century of Accuracy and Precision, by Dana Jones, Canada, Collector Grade Publications, 2003. 1st edition. 312 pp., 691 illustrations. Hardcover. $49.95

Here is the first in-depth study of all the Swedish Mausers: the 6.5mm M/94 carbines, M/96 long rifles, M/38 short rifles, Swedish K98Ks (called the M/39 in 7.92x57mm, then, after rechambering to fire the 8x63mm machine gun cartridge, the M/40); sniper rifles, and other military adaptations such as grenade launchers and artillery simulators. Also covers a wide variety of the micrometer-adjustment rear sight inserts and "diopter" receiver sights which were produced in order to allow shooters to take full advantage of the accuracy and precision of the Swedish Mauser. Full chapters on bayonets and the many accessories, both military and civilian.

Defending the Dominion, Canadian Military Rifles, 1855-1955, by David Edgecombe, Ont. Canada, Service Publications, 2003. 1st edition. 168 pp., with 60+ illustrations. Hardcover. NEW. $39.95

Desperate Measures-The Last Ditch Weapons of the Nazi Voksstrurm, by Darrin Weaver, Canada, Collector Grade Publications, 2005. All are covered in detail, and the book includes many previously unpublished photographs of original Volkssturm weapons, including prototypes and rare presentation examples. Other Volkssturm weapons included the anti-tank Panzerfaust ("tank fist"), a single-shot, rocket-propelled shaped-charge device capable of defeating any Allied tank then in existence, and numerous "clones" of the British Sten machine carbine, which were hastily manufactured by a considerable number of German firms (a memorandum speaks of "30 subcontractors and 14 assembly points"). Programs were also begun to develop special Volkspistolen, made largely from stamped sheet metal. 424

pp., 558 illustrations. Hardcover. New in new dust jacket. $69.50

The Emma Gees, by Capt. Herbert W McBride, Mt. Ida, AR, Lancer Publishing, 2003. Reprint. 224 pp., b&w photos. Softcover. $19.95

The Emma Gees is the rest of McBride's story. First published in 1918, this was McBride's first book about his service with the machine gun section in WWI. The Emma Gees was even rarer than *A Rifleman Went to War* until this reprint that

ARMS LIBRARY

includes new biographical information from the National Archives of Canada. With chapters such as "A Fine Day for Murder" and "Sniper Barn," this is an excellent companion to his other book.

F.N.-F.A.L. Auto Rifles, Desert Publications, Cornville, AZ, 1981. 130 pp., illus. Paper covers. $18.95

A definitive study of one of the free world's finest combat rifles.

The FAL Rifle, by R. Blake Stevens and Jean van Rutten, Collector Grade Publications, Cobourg, Canada, 1993. 848 pp., illus. $129.95

Originally published in three volumes, this classic edition covers North American, UK and Commonwealth and the metric FAL's.

The Fighting Rifle, by Chuck Taylor, Paladin Press, Boulder, CO, 1983. 184 pp., illus. Paper covers. $25.00

The difference between assault and battle rifles and auto and light machine guns.

The FN-49; Last Elegant Old-World Military Rifle, by Wayne Johnson., Greensboro, NC, Wet Dog Publications, 2004. 200 pages with over 300 quality b&w photographs. Hardcover. NEW. $45.95

The FN-49 The Last Elegant old World Military Rifle book contains both information on the SAFN as well as the AFN rifle.

The FN-FAL Rifle, et al, by Duncan Long, Delta Press, El Dorado, AR, 1998. 148 pp., illus. Paper covers. $18.95

A comprehensive study of one of the classic assault weapons of all times. Detailed descriptions of the basic models plus the myriad of variants that evolved as a result of its universal acceptance.

Forty Years with the .45-70, Second edition, revised and expanded, by Paul A. Matthews, Wolfe Publishing Co., Prescott, AZ, 1997. 184 pp., illus. Paper covers. $17.95

This book is pure gun lore of the .45-70. It not only contains a history of the cartridge, but also years of the author's personal experiences.

German Sniper 1914-1945, by Peter R. Senich, Paladin Press, Boulder, CO, 1997 8-1/2" x 11", hardcover, photos, 468 pp. $69.95

The complete story of Germany's sniping arms development through both world wars. Presents more than 600 photos of Mauser 98's, Selbstladegewehr 41s and 43s, optical sights by Goerz, Zeiss, etc., plus German snipers in action. An exceptional hardcover collector's edition for serious military historians everywhere.

The Great Remington 8 and Model 81 Autoloading Rifles, by John Henwood, Canada, Collector Grade Publications, 2003. 1st edition. 304 pp., 291 illustrations, 31 in color. Hardcover. $59.95

Greenhill Military Manual: Military Rifles of Two World Wars, by John Walter, London, Greenhill Publishing, 2003. 1st edition. 144 pp., illus. Hardcover. $24.00

Handbook of Military Rifle Marks 1866-1950 (Third Edition), by Richard A. Hoffman and Noel P. Schott, St. Louis, MO, Mapleleaf Militaria Publications, 2002. 3rd edition. NEW. $30.00

The Gun Digest Book of the.22 Rimfire, by James House, Iola,WI, Krause Publications, 2005. 250 b&w photos; 288 pp. Soft cover. NEW. $24.99

Gun-Guides, AK-47 AKM All Variants, Disassembly and Reassembly Guide, by Gun Guides, 2005. 16 pp., illustrations, Cardstock cover. Bright white paper. Soft cover. NEW. $6.50

The complete guide for ALL models.

Gun-Guides, Colt AR15 and All Variants, Disassembly and Reassembly Guide, by Gun Guides, 2005. 16 pp., illustrations, Cardstock cover. Bright white paper. Soft cover. NEW. $6.50

The complete guide for ALL models.

Gun-Guides, Ruger 10/22 & 10/17 Carbines Complete Guide to all Models from 1964-2004, by Gun Guides, 2005. 16 pp., illustrations, Cardstock cover. Bright white paper. Soft cover. NEW. $6.50

The complete guide for ALL models.

Gun-Guides, Ruger Mini-14 Complete Guide to all Models from 1972-2003, by Gun Guides, 2005. 52 pp., illustrations, Cardstock cover. Bright white paper. Soft cover. NEW. $11.95

The complete guide for ALL models.

Gun-Guides, SKS Semi-Automatic Rifles, Disassembly and Reassembly Guide, by Gun Guides, 2005. 16 pp., illustrations, Cardstock cover. Bright white paper. Soft cover. NEW. $6.50

The complete guide for ALL models.

Handbook of Military Rifle Marks 1866-1950 (third edition), by Richard Hoffman, and Noel Schott, Maple leaf Militaria Publications, 2002. An illustrated military rifles and marks. Officially being used as a reference tool by many law enforcement agencies including BATF, the St Louis and Philadelphia Police Departments and the Illinois State Police. 66 pp., with illustrations, signed by the authors. Stiff Paper Covers. NEW. $20.00

High Performance Muzzle Loading Big Game Rifles, by Toby Bridges, Maryland, Stoeger Publications, 2004. Covers all aspects of in-lines including getting top performance, working up loads, choosing projectiles, scope selection, coping with muzzleloader trajectory, tips for maintaining accuracy, plus much, much more. 160 pages. Pictorial Hardcover. NEW. $24.95

The Historic Henry Rifle: Oliver Winchester's Famous Civil War Repeater, by Wiley Sword, Andrew Mowbray, Inc., Lincoln, RI. 2002. Softcover. $29.95

Perhaps the most important firearm of its era. Tested and proved in the fiery crucible of the Civil War, the Henry Rifle became the forerunner of the famous line of Winchester Repeating Rifles that "Won the West." Here is the fascinating story from the frustrations of early sales efforts aimed at the government to the inspired purchase of the Henry Rifle by veteran soldiers who wanted the best weapon.

Hitler's Garands: German Self-Loading Rifles of World War II, by Darrin W. Weaver, Collector Grade Publications, Canada, 2001. 392 pp., 590 illustrations. $69.95

Hitler's Wehrmacht began WWII armed with the bolt-action K98k, a rifle only cosmetically different from that with which Imperial Germany had fought the Great War a quarter-century earlier. Then in 1940, the Heereswaffenamt (HWaA, the Army Weapons Office) issued a requirement for a new self-loading rifle. Taking their lead from the Russians, Walther copied (and patented) the gas system of the Tokarev SVT self-loader, grafting it onto the flap-locked bolt of the G41 to create the G43, which was only produced during the last nineteen desperate months of WWII.

How-To's for the Black Powder Cartridge Rifle Shooter, by Paul A. Matthews, Wolfe Publishing Co., Prescott, AZ, 1996. 136 pp., illus. Paper covers. $22.50

Practices and procedures used in the reloading and shooting of blackpowder cartridges.

How to Convert Military Rifles, Davidson, MI, Williams Gun Sight Company, 1998. New revised enlarged seventh edition. 76 pp., illus. Softcover. $13.95

Explains the features that make certain models more desirable for conversion. Covers the steps to proper scope mounting, installing triggers and safeties; restocking and finishing. The exploded parts drawings are extremely useful and sight fitting charts can save hours of frustration. Revised and enlarged edition presents information on 14 military and civilian rifles.

The Hunter's Guide to Accurate Shooting, by Wayne van Zwoll, Guilford, CT, Lyons Press, 2002. 1st edition. 288 pp. Hardcover. $29.95

Firearms expert van Zwoll explains exactly how to shoot the big-game rifle accurately. Taking into consideration every pertinent factor, he shows a step-by-step analysis of shooting and hunting with the big-game rifle.

Imperial Japanese Grenade Rifles and Launchers, by Greg Babisch and Thomas Keep, Lemont, PA, Dutch Harlow Publishing, 2004. 247 pp., illustrated with numerous b&w and color photos throughout. Hardcover. New in new dust jacket. $75.00

This book is a must for museums, military historians, and collectors of Imperial Japanese rifles, rifle cartridges, and ordnance.

Jaeger Rifles Collected Articles Published in Muzzle Blasts, by George Shumway, York, PA, George Shumway, 2003. 108 pp., illus. Stiff paper covers. NEW. $30.00

Johnson Rifles and Machine Guns: The Story of Melvin Maynard Johnson Jr. and his Guns, by Bruce N. Canfield, Lincoln, RI, Andrew Mowbray, Inc., 2002. 1st edition. 272 pp. with over 285 photographs. Hardcover. $49.95

The M1941 Johnson rifle is the hottest WWII rifle on the collector's market today. From invention and manufacture through issue to the troops, this book covers them all!

Kalashnikov: The Arms and the Man, A Revised and Expanded Edition of the AK47 Story, by Edward C. Ezell, Canada, Collector Grade Publications, 2002. 312 pp., 356 illustrations. Hardcover. $59.95

The original edition of The AK47 Story was published in 1986, and the events of the intervening 15 years have provided much fresh new material. Beginning with an introduction by Dr. Kalashnikov, this is a most comprehensive study of the "life and times" of the AK, starting with the early history of small arms manufacture in Czarist Russia and then the Soviet Union.

The Last Enfield: SA80—The Reluctant Rifle, by Steve Raw, Collector Grade Publications, Canada 2003. 1st edition. 360 pp., with 382 illustrations. Hardcover. $49.95

This book presents the entire, in-depth story of its subject firearm, in this case the controversial British SA80, right from the founding of what became the Royal Small Arms Factory (RSAF) Enfield in the early 1800s; briefly through two world wars with Enfield at the forefront of small arms production for British forces; and covering the adoption of the 7.62mm NATO cartridge in 1954 and the L1A1 rifle in 1957.

The Last Steel Warrior: The U.S. M14 Rifle, by Frank Iannamico, Moose Lake Pub., 2006. Over 400 pp. and 537 photos and illustrations. Soft cover. NEW. $29.95

Acclaimed gun author Frank Iannamico's latest book covers history, development and deployment of the influential M14 rifle.

The Lee Enfield No. 1 Rifles, by Alan M. Petrillo, Excaliber Publications, Latham, NY, 1992. 64 pp., illus. Paper covers. $10.95

Highlights the SMLE rifles from the Mark 1-VI.

The Lee Enfield Number 4 Rifles, by Alan M. Petrillo, Excalibur Publications, Latham, NY, 1992. 64 pp., illus. Paper covers. $10.95

A pocket-sized, bare-bones reference devoted entirely to the .303 WWII and Korean War vintage service rifle.

Legendary Sporting Rifles, by Sam Fadala, Stoeger Publishing Co., So. Hackensack, NJ, 1992. 288 pp., illus. Paper covers. $16.95

Covers a vast span of time and technology beginning with the Kentucky longrifle.

The Li'l M1 .30 Cal. Carbine, by Duncan Long, Desert Publications, El Dorado, AZ, 1995. 203 pp., illus. Paper covers. $19.95

Traces the history of this little giant from its original creation.

Living With the Big .50, The Shooter's Guide to the World's Most Powerful Rifle, Robert Boatman, Boulder, CO, Paladin Press, 2004. 176 pp. Soft cover. NEW. $29.00

Living with the Big .50 is the most thorough book ever written on this powerhouse rifle.

M1 Carbine Owner's Manual, M1, M2 & M3 .30 Caliber Carbines, Firepower Publications, Cornville, AZ, 1984. 102 pp., illus. Paper covers. $9.95

The complete book for the owner of an M1 carbine.

The M1 Garand Complete Assembly Guide, Vol 2, by Walt Kuleck, and Clint McKee, Export, PA, Scott Duff Publications, 2004. 162 pp. $21.95

You'll learn the best and easiest ways to build your rifle. It won't make you a Garand armorer, but it will make you a more knowledgeable owner. You'll be able to do more with (and to) your rifle.

The M1903 Springfield Rifle and It's Variations, by Joe Poyer, Tustin, CA, North Cape Publications, 2004. 466 pp., illustrated with hundreds of color and b&w drawings and photos. Soft cover. NEW. $22.95

It covers the entire spectrum of the Model 1903 rifle.

The M1 Garand Serial Numbers & Data Sheets, by Scott A. Duff, Scott A. Duff, Export, PA, 1995. 101 pp. Paper covers. $11.95

This pocket reference book includes serial number tables and data sheets on the Springfield Armory, gas trap rifles, gas port rifles, Winchester Repeating Arms, International Harvester and H&R Arms Co. and more.

The M1 Garand: Post World War, by Scott A. Duff, Scott A. Duff Publications, Export, PA, 1990. 139 pp., illus. Softcover. $21.95

A detailed account of the activities at Springfield Armory through this period. International Harvester, H&R, Korean War production and quantities delivered. Serial numbers.

The M1 Garand: World War 2, by Scott A. Duff, Scott A. Duff Publications, Export, PA, 1993. 210 pp., illus. Paper covers. $34.95

The most comprehensive study available to the collector and historian on the M1 Garand of WWII.

The M14 Owner's Guide and Match Conditioning Instructions, by Scott A. Duff and John M. Miller, Duff Publications, Export, PA, 1996. 180 pp., illus. Paper covers. $19.95

Traces the history and development from the T44 through the adoption and production of the M14 rifle.

The M14 Rifle, facsimile reprint of FM 23-8, Desert Publications, Cornville, AZ, 50 pp., illus. Paper $11.95

Well illustrated and informative reprint covering the M-14 and M-14E2.

The M14-Type Rifle: A Shooter's and Collector's Guide, by Joe Poyer, North Cape Publications, Tustin, CA, 1997. 82 pp., illus. Paper covers. $14.95

Covers the history and development, commercial copies, cleaning and maintenance instructions, and targeting and shooting.

M14/M14A1 Rifles and Rifle Marksmanship, Desert Publications, El Dorado, AZ, 1995. 236 pp., illus. Paper covers. $19.95

Contains a detailed description of the M14 and M14A1 rifles and their general characteristics, procedures for disassembly & assembly, operating and functioning of the rifles.

The M16/AR15 Rifle, by Joe Poyer, North Cape Publications, Tustin, CA, 1998. 150 pp., illus. Paper covers. $14.95

From its inception as the first American assault battle rifle to the firing lines of the National Matches, the M16/AR15 rifle in all its various models and guises has made a significant impact on the American rifleman.

Major Ned H. Roberts and the Schuetzen Rifle, edited by Gerald O. Kelver, Brighton, CO, 1998. 3rd edition. 122 pp., illus. $13.95

A compilation of the writings of Major Ned H. Roberts which appeared in various gun magazines.

Mannlicher Military Rifles: Straight Pull and Turn Bolt Designs, Paul Scarlata, Lincoln, RI, Andrew Mowbray, 2004 Profusely illustrated with close-up photos, drawings and diagrams, this book is the most detailed examination of Mannlicher military rifles ever produced in the English language. Inside these pages, you will understand the genius behind Mannlicher's magazine systems, straight-pull and turn bolt military rifles. And you will learn why they became the standard by which all others were judged. Hardcover, 168 pages 8.5 x 11, filled with black & white photos. Hardcover. NEW $32.49

Mauser Smallbore Sporting, Target and Training Rifles, by Jon Speed, Collector Grade Publications, Inc., Cobourg, Ont., Canada, 1998. 372 pp., illus. $67.50

The history of all the smallbore sporting, target and training rifles produced by the legendary Mauser-Werke of Obendorf am Neckar.

Mauser: Original-Oberndorf Sporting Rifles, by Jon Speed, Collector Grade Publications, Inc., Cobourg, Ont., Canada, 1997. 508 pp., illus. $89.95

The most exhaustive study ever published of the design origins and manufacturing history of the original Oberndorf Mauser Sporter.

MG34-MG42 German Universal Machineguns, by Folke Myrvang, Collector Grade Publications, Canada. 2002. 496 pp., 646 illustrations. $79.95

This is the first-ever COMPETE study of the MG34 & MG42. Here the author presents in-depth coverage of the historical development, fielding, tactical use of and modifications made to these remarkable guns and their myriad accessories and ancillaries, plus authoritative tips on troubleshooting.

Military Bolt Action Rifles, 1841-1918, by Donald B. Webster, Museum Restoration Service, Alexander Bay, NY, 1993. 150 pp., illus. $34.50

A photographic survey of the principal rifles and carbines of the European and Asiatic powers of the last half of the 19th century and the first years of the 20th century.

The Mini-14, by Duncan Long, Paladin Press, Boulder, CO, 1987. 120 pp., illus. Paper covers. $17.00

History of the Mini-14, the factory-produced models, specifications, accessories, suppliers, and much more.

The MKB 42, MP43, MP44 and the Sturmgewehr 44, by de Vries & Martens. Alexandria, VA, Ironside International, 2003. 1st edition. 152 pp., illustrated with 200 high quality b&w photos. Hardcover. $39.95

Covers all essential information on history and development, ammunition and accessories, codes and markings, and contains photos of nearly every model and accessory. Includes a unique selection of original German WWII propaganda photos, most never published before.

Modern Guns: Fred Adolph Genoa, by Fred Adolph, Oceanside, CA, Armory Publications, 2003. 68 pp., illustrated. Stiff Paper Covers. New. $19.95

One of only a few catalogs that list 2, 3 and 4 barrel guns.

Modern Sniper Rifles, by Duncan Long, Paladin Press, Boulder, CO, 1997, 8-1/2" x 11", soft cover, photos, illus., 120 pp. $20.00

Noted weapons expert Duncan Long describes the .22 LR, single-shot, bolt-action, semiautomatic and large-caliber rifles that can be used for sniping purposes, including the U.S. M21, Ruger Mini-14, AUG and HK-94SG1. These and other models are evaluated on the basis of their features, accuracy, reliability and handiness in the field. The author also looks at the best scopes, ammunition and accessories.

More Single Shot Rifles and Actions, by Frank de Haas and Mark de Haas, Orange City, IA, 1996. 146 pp., illus. Paper covers. $22.50

Covers 45 different single shot rifles. Includes the history plus photos, drawings and personal comments.

Mr. Single Shot's Book of Rifle Plans, by Frank de Haas and Mark de Haas, Orange City, IA, 1996. 85 pp., illus. Paper covers. $22.50

Contains complete and detailed drawings, plans and instructions on how to build four different and unique breech-loading single shot rifles of the author's own proven design.

Muskets of the Revolution and the French & Indian Wars; The Smoothbore Longarm in Early America, Including British, French, Dutch, German, Spanish, and American Weapons, by Bill Ahearn, Lincoln, RI, Andrew Mowbray, 2005. 248 pp., illustrated. Pictorial Hardcover. NEW. $49.95

Not just a technical study of old firearms, this is a tribute to the bravery of the men who fought on both sides of that epic conflict and a celebration of the tools of freedom that have become so much a part of our national character. Includes many never-before published photos!

Neutrality Through Marksmanship: A Collector's and Shooter's Guide to Swedish Army Rifles 1867-1942, by Doug Bowser, Camellia City Military Publications, 1996. 1st edition. Stiff paper covers. NEW. $20.00

The No. 4 (T) Sniper Rifle: An Armourer's Perspective, by Peter Laidler with Ian Skennerton, I.D.S.A. Books, Piqua, OH, 1993. 125 pp., 75 illus. Paper covers. $19.95

A reprint of the 1864 London edition. Captain Heaton was one of the great rifle shots from the earliest days of the Volunteer Movement.

The Official SKS Manual, Translation by Major James F. Gebhardt (Ret.), Paladin Press, Boulder, CO, 1997. 96 pp., illus. Paper covers. $16.00

This Soviet military manual covering the widely distributed SKS is now available in English.

Official Soviet AK-47 Manual: Operating Instructions For the 5.45MM Kalashnikov Assault Rifle, and Kalashnikov Light Machine Gun, by James Gebhardt, Boulder, CO, Paladin Press, 2006. 8-1/2" x 11", illus., 150 pp. Soft cover. NEW. $25.00

Written to teach Russian soldiers every detail of the operation and maintenance of the Kalashnikov Assault Rifle (AK-74) and Kalashnikov Light Machine Gun (RPK-74), this manual includes ballistic tables, zeroing information, combat firing instructions, data for the 5.45mm service cartridge and more.

Old German Target Arms: Alte Schiebenwaffen, by Jesse Thompson, C. Ron Dillon, Allen Hallock and Bill Loos, Rochester, NY, Tom Rowe Publications, 2003. 1st edition. 392 pp. Hardcover. $98.00

History of Schueten shooting from the middle ages through WWII. Hundreds of illustrations, most in color. History & Memorabilia of the Bundesschiessen (State or National Shoots), Bird Target rifles, American shooters in Germany. Schutzen rifles such as matchlocks, wheellocks, flintlocks, percussion, bader, bornmuller, rifles by Buchel and more.

Old German Target Arms: Alte Schiebenwaffen Volume 2, by Jesse Thompson, C. Ron Dillon, Allen Hallock and Bill Loos, Rochester, NY, Tom Rowe Publications, 2004. 1st edition. 392 pp. Hardcover. $98.00

Old German Target Arms: Alte Schiebenwaffen Volume 3, by Jesse Thompson, C. Ron Dillon, Allen Hallock and Bill Loos, Rochester, NY, Tom Rowe Publications, 2005. 1st edition. 392 pp. Hardcover. $98.00

Ordnance Tools, Accessories & Appendages of the M1 Rifle, by Billy Pyle, Houston, TX, privately printed, 2002. 2nd edition. 206 pp., illustrated with b&w photos. Softcover. $40.00

This is the new updated edition with over 350 pictures and drawings, of which 30 are new. Part I contains accessories, appendages, and equipment including such items as bayonets, blank firing attachments, cheek pads, cleaning equipment, clips, flash hiders, grenade launchers, scabbards, slings, telescopes and mounts, winter triggers, and much more. Part II covers ammunition, grenades, and pyrotechnics. Part III shows the inspection gages. Part IV presents the ordnance tools, fixtures, and assemblies. Part V contains miscellaneous items related to the M1 Rifle such as arms racks, rifle racks, clip loading machine, and other devices.

Police Rifles, by Richard Fairburn, Paladin Press, Boulder, CO, 1994. 248 pp., illus. Paper covers. $35.00

Selecting the right rifle for street patrol and special tactical situations.

The Poor Man's Sniper Rifle, by D. Boone, Paladin Press, Boulder, CO, 1995. 152 pp., illus. Paper covers. $18.95

Here is a complete plan for converting readily available surplus military rifles to high- performance sniper weapons.

A Potpourri of Single Shot Rifles and Actions, by Frank de Haas and Mark de Haas, Ridgeway, MO, 1993. 153 pp., illus. Paper covers. $22.50

The author's 6th book on non-bolt-action single shots. Covers more than 40 single-shot rifles in historical and technical detail.

Precision Shooting with the M1 Garand, by Roy Baumgardner, Precision Shooting, Inc., Manchester, CT, 1999. 142 pp., illus. Paper covers. $12.95

Starts off with the ever popular ten-article series on accurizing the M1 that originally appeared in Precision Shooting in the 1993-95 era. There follows nine more Baumgardner-authored articles on the M1 Garand and finally a 1999 updating chapter.

The Remington 700, by John F. Lacy, Taylor Publishing Co., Dallas, TX, 2002. 208 pp., illus. $49.95

Covers the different models, limited editions, chamberings, proofmarks, serial numbers, military models, and much more.

Remington Autoloading And Pump Action Rifles, by Eugene Myszkowski, Tucson, AZ, Excalibur Publications, 2002. 132 pp., with 162 photographs, 6 illustrations and 18 charts. Softcover. $20.95

An illustrated history of Remington's centerfire Models 760, 740, 742, 7400 and 7600. The book is thoroughly researched and features many previously unpublished photos of the rifles, their accessories and accoutrements. Also covers high grade, unusual and experimental rifles. Contains information on collecting, serial numbers and barrel codes.

The Rifle Rules: Magic for the Ultimate Rifleman, by Don Paul, Kaua'i, HI, Pathfinder Publications, 2003. 1st edition. 116 pp., illus. Softcover. $14.95

A new method that shows you how to add hundreds of yards to your effective shooting ability. Ways for you to improve your rifle's accuracy which no factory can do. Illustrations & photos added to make new concepts easy.

The Rifle Shooter, by G. David Tubb, Oxford, MS, Zediker Publishing, 2004. 1st edition. 416 pp softcover, 7x10 size, 400 photos and illustrations, very high quality printing. Softcover. $34.95

This is not just a revision of his landmark "Highpower Rifle" but an all-new, greatly expanded work that reveals David's thoughts and recommendations on all aspects of precision rifle shooting. Each shooting position and event is dissected and taken to extreme detail, as are the topics of ammunition, training, rifle design, event strategies, and wind shooting. You will learn the secrets of perhaps the greatest rifleman ever, and you'll learn how to put them to work for you!

Rifles of the U.S. Army 1861-1906, by John D. McAulay, Lincoln, RI, Andrew Mowbray, Inc., 2003. 1st edition. 278 pp., illus. Hardcover. $45.89

Rifles of the White Death (Valkoisen Kuoleman Kivaarit) A Collector's and Shooter's Guide to Finnish Military Rifles 1918-1944, by Doug Bowser, MS, Camellia City Military Publications, 1998. 1st edition. Stiff paper covers. NEW. $35.00

Rock Island Rifle Model 1903, by C.S. Ferris, Export, PA, Scott A. Duff Publications, 2002. 177 pp., illustrated with b&w photographs. Foreword by Scott A. Duff. Softcover. $22.95

S.L.R.–Australia's F.N. F.A.L., by Ian Skennerton and David Balmer, Arms & Militaria Press, 1989. 124 pp., 100 illus. Paper covers. $24.50

Schuetzen Rifles, History and Loading, by Gerald O. Kelver, Pioneer Press, Union City, TN, 1998. 3rd edition. Illus. $13.95

Reference work on these rifles, their bullets, loading, telescopic sights, accuracy, etc. A limited, numbered ed.

Serbian And Yugoslav Mauser Rifles, by Banko Bogdanovich, Tustin, CA, North Cape Publications, 2005. 278 pp. Soft cover. NEW. $19.95

In Serbian and Yugoslav Mauser Rifles, each model is discussed in its own chapter. All serial numbers are presented by year. All markings are presented and translated and all finishes and changes to all models are described in text and charts and well illustrated with both photographs and excellent drawings for clarity.

Shooting Lever Guns of the Old West, by Mike Venturino, MLV Enterprises, Livingston, MT, 1999. 300 pp., illus. Paper covers. $27.95

Shooting the lever action type repeating rifles of our American west.

Shooting the .43 Spanish Rolling Block, by Croft Barker, Flatonia, TX, Cistern Publishing, 2003. 1st edition. 137 pp. Softcover. $25.50

The SOURCE for information on .43 caliber rolling blocks. Lots of photos and text covering Remington & Oveido actions, antique cartridges, etc. Features smokless & black powder loads, rifle disassembly and maintenance, 11 mm bullets. Required reading for the rolling block owner.

Shooting the Blackpowder Cartridge Rifle, by Paul A. Matthews, Wolfe Publishing Co., Prescott, AZ, 1994. 129 pp., illus. Paper covers. $22.50

A general discourse on shooting the blackpowder cartridge rifle and the procedure required to make a particular rifle perform.

The Single Shot Military Rifle Handbook, by Croft Barker, Flatonia, TX, Cistern Publishing, 2005. 130 pp., b&w photos. Soft cover. NEW. $25.50

Contains instruction on preparing authentic ammunition, shooting techniques, the uses of vintage military sights, rifle refurbishing, etc. Evolution of the single shot military rifle and the center fire cartridge is described. Includes over 40 new high quality photos of vintage rifles, antique cartridges and related equipment.

Single Shot Rifles and Actions, by Frank de Haas, Orange City, IA, 1990. 352 pp., illus. Softcover. $27.00

The definitive book on over 60 single shot rifles and actions.

Small Arms Identification Series, No. 1–.303 Rifle, No. 1 S.M.L.E. Marks III and III*, by Ian Skennerton, I.D.S.A. Books, Piqua, OH, 1981. 48 pp. $10.50

Small Arms Identification Series, No. 2–.303 Rifle, No. 4 Marks I, & I*, Marks 1/2, 1/3 & 2, by Ian Skennerton, I.D.S.A. Books, Piqua, OH, 1994. 48 pp. $10.50

Small Arms Identification Series, No. 3–9mm Austen Mk I & 9mm Owen Mk I Sub- Machine Guns, by Ian Skennerton, I.D.S.A. Books, Piqua, OH, 1994. 48 pp. $10.50

Small Arms Identification Series, No. 4–.303 Rifle, No. 5 Mk I, by Ian Skennerton, I.D.S.A. Books, Piqua, OH, 1994. 48 pp. $10.50

Small Arms Identification Series, No. 5–.303-in. Bren Light Machine Gun, by Ian Skennerton, I.D.S.A. Books, Piqua, OH, 1994. 48 pp. $10.50

The Springfield Rifle M1903, M1903A1, M1903A3, M1903A4, Desert Publications, Cornville, AZ, 1982. 100 pp. Paper covers. $14.95

Covers every aspect of disassembly and assembly, inspection, repair and maintenance.

Still More Single Shot Rifles, by James J. Grant, Pioneer Press, Union City, TN, 1995. 211 pp., illus. $29.95

This is Volume Four in a series of single shot rifles by America's foremost authority. It gives more in-depth information on those single shot rifles presented in the first three books.

The Sturm, Ruger 10/22 Rifle and .44 Magnum Carbine, by Duncan Long, Paladin Press, Boulder, CO, 1988. 108 pp., illus. Paper covers. $15.00

An in-depth look at both weapons detailing the elegant simplicity of the Ruger design. Offers specifications, troubleshooting procedures and ammunition recommendations.

Swedish Mauser Rifles, by Steve Kehaya and Joe Poyer, Tustin, CA, North Cape Publications, 2004. 2nd edition, revised. 267 pp., illus. Softcover. $19.95

Every known variation of the Swedish Mauser carbine and rifle is described including all match and target rifles and all sniper versions. Includes serial number and production data.

Swiss Magazine Loading Rifles 1869 to 1958, by Joe Poyer, Tustin, CA, North Cape Publications, 2003. 1st edition. 317 pp., illustrated with hundreds of b&w drawings and photos. Softcover. $19.95

It covers the K-31 on a part-by-part basis, as well as its predecessor models of 1889 and 1911, and the first repeating magazine rifle ever adopted by a military, the Model 1869 Vetterli rifle and its successor models. Also includes a history of the development and use of these fine rifles. Details regarding their ammunition, complete assembly/disassembly instructions as well as sections on cleaning, maintenance and trouble shooting.

The Tactical Rifle, by Gabriel Suarez, Paladin Press, Boulder, CO, 1999. 264 pp., illus. Paper covers. $25.00

The precision tool for urban police operations.

Target Rifle in Australia, by J.E. Corcoran, R&R, Livonia, NY, 1996. 160 pp., illus. $40.00

A most interesting study of the evolution of these rifles from 1860-1900. British rifles from the percussion period through the early smokeless era are discussed.

Total Airguns; The Complete Guide to Huting with Air Rifles, by Peter Wadeson, London, Swan Hill Press, 2005. 300 pp., b&w photos. Hardcover. NEW. $29.95

This book covers every aspect from choosing a rifle and scope to field craft and hunting techniques, camouflage, decoys, night shooting, and equipment maintenance. Extensive details on all air gun shooting techniques.

U.S. Marine Corps AR15/M16 A2 Manual, reprinted by Desert Publications, El Dorado, AZ, 1993. 262 pp., illus. Paper covers. $16.95

A reprint of TM05538C-23&P/2, August, 1987. The A-2 manual for the Colt AR15/M16.

U.S. Marine Corps Rifle Marksmanship, by U.S. Marine Corps, Boulder, CO, Paladin Press, 2002. Photos, illus., 120 pp. Softcover. $20.00

This manual is the very latest Marine doctrine on the art and science of shooting effectively in battle. Its 10 chapters teach the versatility, flexibility and skills needed to deal with a situation at any level of intensity across the entire range of military operations. Topics covered include the proper combat mindset; cleaning your rifle under all weather conditions; rifle handling and marksmanship the Marine way; engaging targets from behind cover; obtaining a battlefield zero; engaging immediate threat, multiple and moving targets; shooting at night and at unknown distances; and much more.

U.S. Rifle M14–From John Garand to the M21, by R. Blake Stevens, Collector Grade Publications, Inc., Toronto, Canada, revised second edition, 1991. 350 pp., illus. $49.50

A classic, in-depth examination of the development, manufacture and fielding of the last wood- and-metal ("lock, stock, and barrel") battle rifle to be issued to U.S. troops.

United States Rifle Model of 1917, by CS Ferris, Export, PA, Scott Duff Pubs., 2004. 213 pp., illustrated with b&w photographs. Foreword by Scott A. Duff. Soft cover. NEW. $23.95

If you are interested in the study of the United States Rifle Model of 1917 and have been disappointed by the lack of information available, then this book is for you!

The Ultimate in Rifle Accuracy, by Glenn Newick, Stoeger Publishing Co., Wayne, NJ, 1999. 205 pp., illus. Paper covers. $11.95

This handbook contains the information you need to extract the best performance from your rifle.

War Baby! The U.S. Caliber 30 Carbine, Volume 1, by Larry Ruth, Collector Grade Publications, Toronto, Canada, 1992. 512 pp., illus. $69.95

Volume 1 of the in-depth story of the phenomenally popular U.S. caliber 30 carbine. Concentrates on design and production of the military 30 carbine during WWII.

War Baby Comes Home: The U.S. Caliber 30 Carbine, Volume 2, by Larry Ruth, Collector Grade Publications, Toronto, Canada, 1993. 386 pp., illus. $49.95

The triumphant completion of Larry Ruth's two-volume, in-depth series on the most popular U.S. military small arm in history.

The Winchester Model 52, Perfection in Design, by Herbert G. Houze, Krause Publications, Iola, WI, 2005. Softcover, 192 pp., illus. $24.95

This book covers the complete story of this technically superior gun.

Winchester: An American Legend, by R.L. Wilson, NY, Book Sales, 2004. reprint. 404 pp., illustrated with color and b&w photographs. Hardcover. New in new dust jacket. $29.95

The Winchester Model 52: Perfection in Design, by Herbert Houze. Iola,WI, Krause Publications, 2006. Soft cover. NEW. $19.95

Herbert Houze unravels the mysteries surrounding the development of what many consider the most perfect rifle ever made. The book covers the rifle's improvements through five modifications. Users, collectors and marksmen will appreciate each variation's history, serial number sequences and authentic photos.

Winchester Slide-Action Rifles, Models 61, 62, 1890 & 1906, by Ned Schwing, Iola, WI, Krause Publications, 2004. 456 Pages, illustrated, 300 b&w photos.

Take a complete historical look at the favorite slide-action guns of America through Ned Schwing's eyes. Explore receivers, barrels, markings, stocks, stampings and engraving in complete detail. Soft cover. NEW. $39.95

The Workbench AR-15 Project; A Step by Step Guide to Building Your Own Legal AR-15 Without Paperwork, by D.A. Hanks, Boulder, CO, Paladin Press, 2004. 80 pp., photos. Soft cover. NEW. $18.89

Hänks walks you through the entire process with clear text and detailed photos–staying legal, finishing the lower receiver, assembling all the parts and test-firing your completed rifle. For academic study only.

SHOTGUNS

75 Years with the Shotgun, by C.T. (Buck) Buckman, Valley Publishers, Fresno, CA, 1974. 141 pp., illus. $10.00

An expert hunter and trapshooter shares experiences of a lifetime.

A Collector's Guide to United States Combat Shotguns, by Bruce N. Canfield, Andrew Mowbray Inc., Publishers, Lincoln, RI, 1993. 184 pp., illus. Paper covers. $24.00

Full coverage of the combat shotgun, from the earliest examples to the Gulf War and beyond.

A.H. Fox: "The Finest Gun in the World," revised and enlarged edition, by Michael McIntosh, Countrysport, Inc., New Albany, OH, 1995. 408 pp., illus. $60.00

The first detailed history of one of America's finest shotguns.

Advanced Combat Shotgun: Stress Fire 2, by Massad Ayoob, Police Bookshelf, Concord, NH, 1993. 197 pp., illus. Paper covers. $14.95

Advanced combat shotgun fighting for police.

Best Guns, by Michael McIntosh, Countrysport Press, Selma, AL, 1999, revised edition. 418 pp. $45.00

Combines the best shotguns ever made in America with information on British and Continental makers.

The Best of Holland & Holland, England's Premier Gunmaker, by Michael McIntosh and Jan G. Roosenburg. Long Beach, CA, Safari Press, Inc., 2002. 1st edition. 298 pp., profuse color illustrations. Hardcover. $69.95

Holland & Holland has had a long history of not only building London's "best" guns but also providing superior guns–the ultimate gun in finish, engraving, and embellishment. From the days of old in which a maharaja would order 100 fancifully engraved H&H shotguns for his guests to use at his duck shoot to the recent elaborately decorated sets depicting the Apollo 11 moon landing or the history of the British Empire, all of these guns represent the zenith in the art and craft of gunmaking and engraving. Never before have so many superlative guns from H&H– or any other maker for that matter–been displayed in one book. In addition, many interesting details and a general history of H&H are provided.

The Better Shot, by Ken Davies, Quiller Press, London, England, 1992. 136 pp., illus. $39.95

Step-by-step shotgun techniques with Holland and Holland.

Black's Buyer's Directory 2006 Wing & Clay, by James Black, Grand View Media, 2005. Soft cover. NEW. $14.95

1,637 companies in 62 sections providing shotgun related products and services worldwide. Destinations: 1,412 hunting, 1,279 sporting clays, trap and skeet clubs state by state.

Breaking Clays, Chris Batha, Mechanicsburg, A, Stackpole Books, 2005. Hardcover. New in new dust jacket. $29.95

This clear and concise book offers a distillation of the best tips and techniques that really work to improve your scores and give you the knowledge to develop to your full shooting potential.

Browning Auto-5 Shotguns: The Belgian FN Production, by H. M. Shirley Jr. and Anthony Vanderlinden, Geensboro, NC, Wet Dog Publications, 2003. Limited edition of 2,000 copies, signed by the author. 233 pp., plus index. Over 400 quality b&w photographs and 24 color photographs. Hardcover $59.95

This is the first book devoted to the history, model variations, accessories and production dates of this legendary gun. This publication is to date the only reference book on the Auto-5 (A-5) shotgun prepared entirely with the extensive cooperation and support of Browning, FN Herstal, the Browning Firearms Museum and the Liege Firearms Museum.

Browning-Sporting Arms of Distinction 1903-1992, by Matt Eastman, Safari Press, 2005. Hardcover. New in new dust jacket. $50.00

Finally, the history of the Browning family, the inventions, the company, and Browning's association with Colt, Winchester, Savage, and others is detailed in this all-inclusive book, which is profusely illustrated with hundreds of pictures and charts.

Cogswell & Harrison; Two Centuries of Gunmaking, by G. Cooley and J. Newton, Safari Press, Long Beach, CA, 2000. 128 pp., 30 color photos, 100 b&w photos. $39.95

The authors have gathered a wealth of fascinating historical and technical material that will make the book indispensable, not only to many thousands of "Coggie" owners worldwide, but also to anyone interested in the general history of British gunmaking.

The Defensive Shotgun, by Louis Awerbuck, S.W.A.T. Publications, Cornville, AZ, 1989. 77 pp., illus. Softcover. $14.95

Cuts through the myths concerning the shotgun and its attendant ballistic effects.

The Ducks Unlimited Guide to Shotgunning, by Don Zutz, Willow Creek Press, Minocqua, WI, 2000. 166 pg. Illustrated. $24.50

This book covers everything from the grand old guns of yesterday to today's best shotguns and loads, from the basic shotgun fit and function to expert advice on ballistics, chocks, and shooting techniques.

Fine European Gunmakers: Best Continental European Gunmakers & Engravers, by M. Nobili, Long Beach, CA, Safari Press, 2002. 250 pp., illustated in color. $69.95

Many experts argue that Continental gunmakers produce guns equally as good or better than British makers. Marco Nobili's new work showcases the skills of the best craftsmen from continental Europe, and the author brings to life in words and pictures their finest sporting guns. The book covers the histories of the individual firms and looks at the guns they currently build, tracing the developments of their most influential models.

Firearms Assembly/Disassembly, Part V: Shotguns, 2nd Edition, The Gun Digest Book of, by J.B. Wood, Krause Publications, Iola, WI, 2002. 560 pp., illus. $24.95

Covers 54 popular shotguns plus over 250 variants. The most comprehensive and professional presentation available to either hobbyist or gunsmith.

Game Shooting, by Robert Churchill, Countrysport Press, Selma, AL, 1998. 258 pp., illus. $30.00

The basis for every shotgun instructional technique devised and the foundation for all wingshooting and the game of sporting clays.

The Greatest Hammerless Repeating Shotgun Ever Built: The Model 12 Winchester 1912-1964 by David Riffle, 1995. Color illustrations. 195 large detailed b&w photos, 298 pp. Pictorial Hardcover. NEW. $54.95

This offers an extremely well written and detailed year by year study of the gun, its details, inventors, makers, engravers, and star shooters.

The Greener Story, by Graham Greener, Safari Press, Long Beach, CA, 2000. 231 pp., color and b&w illustrations. $69.95

The history of the Greener gunmakers and their guns.

Greenhill Military Manual: Combat Shotguns, by Leroy Thompson, London, Greenhill Publishing, 2002. 1st edition. 144 pp., illus. Hardcover. $24.00

The combat shotgun is one of the most devastating yet most misunderstood close-combat weapons. A great intimidator, the combat shotgun is widely used by military and police units for crowd control. This book traces the history of the combat shotgun, specialized tactics for its usage, the myriad ammunition choices, and the wealth of combat shotguns available to the military or police operator.

The Gun Review Book, by Michael McIntosh, Countrysport Press, Camden, MA, 1997. Paper covers. $19.95

Compiled here for the first time are McIntosh's popular gun reviews from *"Shooting Sportsman; The Magazine of Wingshooting and Fine Shotguns."* The author traces the history of gunmakes, then examines, analyzes, and critiques the fine shotguns of England, Continental Europe and the United States.

Gunsmithing Shotguns: The Complete Guide to Care & Repair, by David Henderson, New York, Globe Pequot, 2003. 1st edition, b&w photos & illus; 6" x 9", 256 pp., illus. Hardcover. $24.95

An overview designed to provide insight, ideas and techniques that will give the amateur gunsmith the confidence and skill to work on his own guns. General troubleshooting, common problems, stocks and woodworking, soldering and brazing, barrel work and more.

The Heyday of the Shotgun, by David Baker, Safari Press, Inc., Huntington Beach, CA, 2000. 160 pp., illus. $39.95

The art of the gunmaker at the turn of the last century when British craftsmen brought forth the finest guns ever made.

Holland & Holland: The "Royal" Gunmaker, by Donald Dallas, London, Safari Press, 2004. 1st edition. 311 pp. Hardcover. $75.00

Donald Dallas tells the fascinating story of Holland & Holland from its very beginnings, and the history of the family is revealed for the first time. The terrific variety of the firm's guns and rifles is described in great detail and set within the historical context of their eras. From punt gun to boy's gun, from rook rifle to elephant gun, Holland & Holland supplied sporting firearms to every corner of the world. The book is profusely illustrated with color and b&w photographs, mostly unpublished. In addition many rare guns and rifles are described and illustrated.

The House of Churchill, by Don Masters, Safari Press, Long Beach, CA, 2002. 512 pp., profuse color and b&w illustrations. $79.95

This marvelous work on the house of Churchill contains serial numbers and dates of manufacture of its guns from 1891 forward, price lists from 1895 onward, a complete listing of all craftsmen employed at the company, as well as the prices realized at the famous Dallas auction where the "last" production guns were sold. It was written by Don Masters, a long-time Churchill employee, who is keeping the flame of Churchill alive.

The Italian Gun, by Steve Smith and Laurie Morrow, Wilderness Adventures, Gallatin Gateway, MT, 1997. 325 pp., illus. $49.95

The first book ever written entirely in English for American enthusiasts who own, aspire to own, or simply admire Italian guns.

The Ithaca Featherlight Repeater; The Best Gun Going, by Walter C. Snyder, Southern Pines, NC, 1998. 300 pp., illus. $89.95

Describes the complete history of each model of the legendary Ithaca Model 37 and Model 87 Repeaters from their conception in 1930 throught 1997.

ARMS LIBRARY

The Ithaca Gun Company from the Beginning, by Walter C. Snyder, Cook & Uline Publishing Co., Southern Pines, NC, 2nd edition, 1999. 384 pp., illustrated in color and b&w. $90.00

The entire family of Ithaca Gun Company products is described along with new historical information and the serial number/date of manufacturing listing has been improved.

The Little Trapshooting Book, by Frank Little, Shotgun Sports Magazine, Auburn, CA, 1994. 168 pp., illus. Paper covers. $19.95

Packed with know-how from one of the greatest trapshooters of all time.

Lock, Stock, and Barrel, by C. Adams and R. Braden, Safari Press, Huntington Beach, CA, 1996. 254 pp., illus. $24.95

The process of making a best grade English gun from a lump of steel and a walnut tree trunk to the ultimate product plus practical advice on consistent field shooting with a double gun.

Mental Training for the Shotgun Sports, by Michael J. Keyes, Shotgun Sports, Auburn, CA, 1996. 160 pp., illus. Paper covers. $29.95

The most comprehensive book ever published on what it takes to shoot winning scores at trap, skeet and sporting clays.

More Shotguns and Shooting, by Michael McIntosh, Countrysport Books, Selma, AL, 1998. 256 pp., illus. $30.00

From specifics of shotguns to shooting your way out of a slump, it's McIntosh at his best.

Mossberg Shotguns, by Duncan Long, Delta Press, El Dorado, AR, 2000. 120 pp., illus. $24.95

This book contains a brief history of the company and its founder, full coverage of the pump and semiautomatic shotguns, rare products and a care and maintenance section.

The Mysteries of Shotgun Patterns, by George G. Oberfell and Charles E. Thompson, Oklahoma State University Press, Stillwater, OK, 2005. 164 pp., illus. Paper covers. $25.00

Shotgun ballistics for the hunter in non-technical language.

The Parker Gun, by Larry Baer, Gun Room Press, Highland Park, NJ, 1993. 195 pp., illustrated with b&w and color photos. $35.00

Covers in detail, production of all models on this classic gun. Many fine specimens from great collections are illustrated.

Parker Guns 'The Old Reliable'- A Concise History of the Famous American Shotgun Manufacturing Co., by Ed Muderlak, Long Beach, CA, Safari Press, 2004. Hardcover. New in new dust jacket. $48.50

A must-have for the American shotgun enthusiast.

Parker Gun Identification & Serialization, by S.P. Fjestad, Minneapolis, MN, Blue Book Publications, 2002. 1st edition. Softcover. $34.95

This new 608-page publication is the only book that provides an easy reference for Parker shotguns manufactured between 1866-1942. Included is a comprehensive 46-page section on Parker identification, with over 100 detailed images depicting serialization location and explanation, various Parker grades, extra features, stock configurations, action types, and barrel identification.

The Parker Story: Volumes 1 & 2, by Bill Mullins, "et al." The Double Gun Journal, East Jordan, MI, 2000. 1,025 pp. of text and 1,500 color and monochrome illustrations. Hardbound in a gold-embossed cover. $295.00

The most complete and attractive "last word" on America's preeminent double gun maker. Includes tables showing the number of guns made by gauge, barrel length and special features for each grade.

Pigeon Shooter: The Complete Guide to Modern Pigeon Shooting, by Jon Batley, London, Swan Hill press, 2005. Hardcover. NEW. $29.95

Covering everything from techniques to where and when to shoot. This updated edition contains all the latest information on decoys, hides, and the new pigeon magnets as well as details on the guns and equipment required and invaluable hands-on instruction.

Purdey Gun and Rifle Makers: The Definitive History, by Donald Dallas, Quiller Press, London 2000. 245 pp., illus. Signed and numbered. Limited edition of 3,000 copies. With a PURDEY bookplate. $100.00

Re-creating the Double Barrel Muzzle Loading Shotgun, by William R. Brockway, York, PA, George Shumway, 2003. Revised 2nd edition. 175 pp., illus. Includes full size drawings. Softcover. $40.00

This popular book, first published in 1985 and out of print for over a decade, has been updated by the author. This book treats the making of double guns of classic style, and is profusely illustrated, showing how to do it all. Many photos of old and contemporary shotguns.

Reloading for Shotgunners, 4th Edition, by Kurt D. Fackler and M.L. McPherson, DBI Books, a division of Krause Publications, Iola, WI, 1997. 320 pp., illus. Paper covers. $19.95

Expanded reloading tables with over 11,000 loads. Bushing charts for every major press and component maker. All new presentation on all aspects of shotshell reloading by two of the top experts in the field.

Remington Double Shotguns, by Charles G. Semer, Denver, CO, 1997. 617 pp., illus. $60.00

This book deals with the entire production and all grades of double shotguns made by Remington during the period of their production 1873-1910.

The Shotgun Encyclopedia, by John Taylor, Safari Press, Inc., Huntington Beach, CA, 2000. 260 pp., illus. $34.95

A comprehensive reference work on all aspects of shotguns and shotgun shooting.

Shotgun Technicana, by Michael McIntosh and David Trevallion, Camden, ME, Down East Books, 2002. 272 pp., with 100 illustrations. Hardcover $28.00

Everything you wanted to know about fine double shotguns by the nation's foremost experts.

The Shotgun–A Shooting Instructor's Handbook, by Michael Yardley, Long Beach, CA, Safari Press, 2002. 272 pp., b&w photos, line drawings. Hardcover. $29.95

This is one of the very few books intended to be read by shooting instructors and other advanced shooters. He analyzes the components and development of shooting techniques by pointing out the styles of great instructors such as Percy Stanbury and Robert Churchill, as well as the shooting techniques of some of the best-known modern competitors. There is practical advice on gun fit, and on gun and cartridge selection.

Shotgunning: The Art and the Science, by Bob Brister, Winchester Press, Piscataway, NJ, 1976. 321 pp., illus. $18.95

Hundreds of specific tips and truly novel techniques to improve the field and target shooting of every shotgunner.

Shotguns and Shooting, by Michael McIntosh, Countrysport Press, New Albany, OH, 1995. 258 pp., illus. $30.00

The art of guns and gunmaking, this book is a celebration no lover of fine doubles should miss.

Shotguns & Shotgunning, by Layne Simpson, Iola, WI, Krause Publications, 2003. 1st edition. High-quality color photography 224 pp., color illus. Hardcover. $36.95

This is the most comprehensive and valuable guide on the market devoted exclusively to shotguns. Part buyer's guide, part technical manual, and part loving tribute, shooters and hunters of all skill levels will enjoy this comprehensive reference tool. Excellent resource for shooters, hunters, and collectors. Comprehensive guide covers the technical aspects of shotguns, hunting with shotguns, the evolution of shotguns, and popular shooting games.

Spanish Best: The Fine Shotguns of Spain, 2nd Edition, by Terry Wieland, Down East Books, Traverse City, MI, 2001. 364 pp., illus. $60.00

A practical source of information for owners of Spanish shotguns and a guide for those considering buying a used shotgun.

Streetsweepers: The Complete Book of Combat Shotguns, Revised and Updated edition, by Duncan Long, Boulder Co, Paladin Press, 2004. 224 pp. Soft cover. NEW. $29.95

Including how to choose the right gauge and shot, decipher the terminology and use special-purpose rounds such as flechettes and tear-gas projectiles; and gives expert instruction on customizing shotguns, telling you what you must know about the assault weapon ban before you choose or modify your gun.

Successful Shotgunning; How to Build Skill in the Field and Take More Birds in Competition, by Peter F. Blakeley, Mechanicsburg, PA, Stackpole Books, 2003. 1st edition. 305 pp., illustrated with 119 b&w photos & 4-page color section with 8 photos. Hardcover. $24.95

Successful Shotgunning focuses on wing-shooting and sporting clays techniques.

The Tactical Shotgun, by Gabriel Suzrez, Paladin Press, Boulder, CO, 1996. 232 pp., illus. Paper covers. $25.00

The best techniques and tactics for employing the shotgun in personal combat.

Trap & Skeet Shooting, 4th Edition, by Chris Christian, DBI Books, a division of Krause Publications, Iola, WI, 1994. 288 pp., illus. Paper covers. $21.95

A detailed look at the contemporary world of trap, skeet and sporting clays.

Trapshooting is a Game of Opposites, by Dick Bennett, Shotgun Sports, Inc., Auburn, CA, 1996. 129 pp., illus. Paper covers. $19.95

Discover everything you need to know about shooting trap like the pros.

U.S. Shotguns, All Types, reprint of TM9-285, Desert Publications, Cornville, AZ, 1987. 257 pp., illus. Paper covers. $18.95

Covers operation, assembly and disassembly of nine shotguns used by the U.S. armed forces.

U.S. Winchester Trench and Riot Guns and Other U.S. Military Combat Shotguns, by Joe Poyer, North Cape Publications, Tustin, CA, 1992. 124 pp., illus. Paper covers. $15.95

A detailed history of the use of military shotguns, and the acquisition procedures used by the U.S. Army's Ordnance Department in both world wars.

Uncle Dan Lefever, Master Gunmaker: Guns of Lasting Fame, by Robert W. Elliott, privately printed, 2002. Profusely illustrated with b&w photos, with a 45-page color section. 239 pp. Handsomely bound, with gilt titled spine and top cover. Hardcover. $60.00

The Winchester Model Twelve, by George Madis, Art and Reference House, Dallas, TX, 1982. 176 pp., illus. $26.95

A definitive work on this famous American shotgun.

The World's Fighting Shotguns, by Thomas F. Swearengen, T.B.N. Enterprises, Alexandria, VA, 1998. 500 pp., illus. $59.95

The complete military and police reference work from the shotgun's inception to date, with up-to-date developments.

ARMS ASSOCIATIONS

UNITED STATES

ALABAMA
Alabama Gun Collectors Assn.
Secretary, P.O. Box 70965, Tuscaloosa, AL 35407

ALASKA
Alaska Gun Collectors Assn., Inc.
C.W. Floyd, Pres., 5240 Little Tree, Anchorage, AK 99507

ARIZONA
Arizona Arms Assn.
Don DeBusk, President, 4837 Bryce Ave., Glendale, AZ 85301

CALIFORNIA
California Cartridge Collectors Assn.
Rick Montgomery, 1729 Christina, Stockton, CA 95204
209-463-7216 eves.
California Waterfowl Assn.
4630 Northgate Blvd., #150, Sacramento, CA 95834
Greater Calif. Arms & Collectors Assn.
Donald L. Bullock, 8291 Carburton St., Long Beach, CA 90808-3302
Los Angeles Gun Ctg. Collectors Assn.
F.H. Ruffra, 20810 Amie Ave., Apt. #9, Torrance, CA 90503
Stock Gun Players Assn.
6038 Appian Way, Long Beach, CA, 90803

COLORADO
Colorado Gun Collectors Assn.
L.E.(Bud) Greenwald, 2553 S. Quitman St., Denver, CO 80219/303-935-3850
Rocky Mountain Cartridge Collectors Assn.
John Roth, P.O. Box 757, Conifer, CO 80433

CONNECTICUT
Ye Connecticut Gun Guild, Inc.
Dick Fraser, P.O. Box 425, Windsor, CT 06095

FLORIDA
Unified Sportsmen of Florida
P.O. Box 6565, Tallahassee, FL 32314

GEORGIA
Georgia Arms Collectors Assn., Inc.
Michael Kindberg, President, P.O. Box 277, Alpharetta, GA 30239-0277

ILLINOIS
Illinois State Rifle Assn.
P.O. Box 637, Chatsworth, IL 60921
Mississippi Valley Gun & Cartridge Coll. Assn.
Bob Filbert, P.O. Box 61, Port Byron, IL 61275/309-523-2593
Sauk Trail Gun Collectors
Gordell M. Matson, P.O. Box 1113, Milan, IL 61264
Wabash Valley Gun Collectors Assn., Inc.
Roger L. Dorsett, 2601 Willow Rd., Urbana, IL 61801
217-384-7302

INDIANA
Indiana State Rifle & Pistol Assn.
Thos. Glancy, P.O. Box 552, Chesterton, IN 46304
Southern Indiana Gun Collectors Assn., Inc.
Sheila McClary, 309 W. Monroe St., Boonville, IN 47601/812-897-3742

IOWA
Beaver Creek Plainsmen Inc.
Steve Murphy, Secy., P.O. Box 298, Bondurant, IA 50035
Central States Gun Collectors Assn.
Dennis Greischar, Box 841, Mason City, IA 50402-0841

KANSAS
Kansas Cartridge Collectors Assn.
Bob Linder, Box 84, Plainville, KS 67663

KENTUCKY
Kentuckiana Arms Collectors Assn.
Charles Billips, President, Box 1776, Louisville, KY 40201
Kentucky Gun Collectors Assn., Inc.
Ruth Johnson, Box 64, Owensboro, KY 42302/502-729-4197

LOUISIANA
Washitaw River Renegades
Sandra Rushing, P.O. Box 256, Main St., Grayson, LA 71435

MARYLAND
Baltimore Antique Arms Assn.
Mr. Cillo, 1034 Main St., Darlington, MD 21304

MASSACHUSETTS
Bay Colony Weapons Collectors, Inc.
John Brandt, Box 111, Hingham, MA 02043
Massachusetts Arms Collectors
Bruce E. Skinner, P.O. Box 31, No. Carver, MA 02355/508-866-5259

MICHIGAN
Association for the Study and Research of .22 Caliber Rimfire Cartridges
George Kass, 4512 Nakoma Dr., Okemos, MI 48864

MINNESOTA
Sioux Empire Cartridge Collectors Assn.
Bob Cameron, 14597 Glendale Ave. SE, Prior Lake, MN 55372

MISSISSIPPI
Mississippi Gun Collectors Assn.
Jack E. Swinney, P.O. Box 16323, Hattiesburg, MS 39402

MISSOURI
Greater St. Louis Cartridge Collectors Assn.
Don MacChesney, 634 Scottsdale Rd., Kirkwood, MO 63122-1109
Mineral Belt Gun Collectors Assn.
D.F. Saunders, 1110 Cleveland Ave., Monett, MO 65708
Missouri Valley Arms Collectors Assn., Inc.
L.P Brammer II, Membership Secy., P.O. Box 33033, Kansas City, MO 64114

MONTANA
Montana Arms Collectors Assn.
Dean E. Yearout, Sr., Exec. Secy., 1516 21st Ave. S., Great Falls, MT 59405
Weapons Collectors Society of Montana
R.G. Schipf, Ex. Secy., 3100 Bancroft St., Missoula, MT 59801 406-728-2995

NEBRASKA
Nebraska Cartridge Collectors Club
Gary Muckel, P.O. Box 84442, Lincoln, NE 68501

NEW HAMPSHIRE
New Hampshire Arms Collectors, Inc.
James Stamatelos, Secy., P.O. Box 5, Cambridge, MA 02139

NEW JERSEY
Englishtown Benchrest Shooters Assn.
Michael Toth, 64 Cooke Ave., Carteret, NJ 07008
Jersey Shore Antique Arms Collectors
Joe Sisia, P.O. Box 100, Bayville, NJ 08721-0100
New Jersey Arms Collectors Club, Inc.
Angus Laidlaw, Vice President, 230 Valley Rd., Montclair, NJ 07042/201-746-0939; e-mail: acclaidlaw@juno.com

NEW YORK
Iroquois Arms Collectors Assn.
Bonnie Robinson, Show Secy., P.O. Box 142, Ransomville, NY 14131/716-791-4096
Mid-State Arms Coll. & Shooters Club
Jack Ackerman, 24 S. Mountain Terr., Binghamton, NY 13903

NORTH CAROLINA
North Carolina Gun Collectors Assn.
Jerry Ledford, 3231-7th St. Dr. NE, Hickory, NC 28601

OHIO
Ohio Gun Collectors Assn.
P.O. Box 9007, Maumee, OH 43537-9007/419-897-0861; Fax: 419-897-0860
Shotshell Historical and Collectors Society
Madeline Bruemmer, 3886 Dawley Rd., Ravenna, OH 44266
The Stark Gun Collectors, Inc.
William I. Gann, 5666 Waynesburg Dr., Waynesburg, OH 44688

OREGON
Oregon Arms Collectors Assn., Inc.
Phil Bailey, P.O. Box 13000-A, Portland, OR 97213-0017
503-281-6864; off.: 503-281-0918
Oregon Cartridge Collectors Assn.
Boyd Northrup, P.O. Box 285, Rhododendron, OR 97049

PENNSYLVANIA
Presque Isle Gun Collectors Assn.
James Welch, 156 E. 37 St., Erie, PA 16504

SOUTH CAROLINA
Belton Gun Club, Inc.
Attn. Secretary, P.O. Box 126, Belton, SC 29627/864-369-6767

Gun Owners of South Carolina
Membership Div.: William Strozier, Secretary, P.O. Box 70, Johns Island, SC 29457-0070/803-762-3240; Fax: 803-795-0711; e-mail: 76053.222@compuserve. com

SOUTH DAKOTA
Dakota Territory Gun Coll. Assn., Inc.
Curt Carter, Castlewood, SD 57223

TENNESSEE
Smoky Mountain Gun Coll. Assn., Inc.
Hugh W. Yabro, President, P.O. Box 23225, Knoxville, TN 37933

Tennessee Gun Collectors Assn., Inc.
M.H. Parks, 3556 Pleasant Valley Rd., Nashville, TN 37204-3419

TEXAS
Houston Gun Collectors Assn., Inc.
P.O. Box 741429, Houston, TX 77274-1429
Texas Gun Collectors Assn.
Bob Eder, Pres., P.O. Box 12067, El Paso, TX 79913/915-584-8183
Texas State Rifle Assn.
1131 Rockingham Dr., Suite 101, Richardson, TX 75080-4326

VIRGINIA
Virginia Gun Collectors Assn., Inc.
Addison Hurst, Secy., 38802 Charlestown Height, Waterford, VA 20197/540-882-3543

WASHINGTON
Association of Cartridge Collectors on the Pacific Northwest
Robert Jardin, 14214 Meadowlark Drive KPN, Gig Harbor, WA 98329
Washington Arms Collectors, Inc.
Joyce Boss, P.O. Box 389, Renton, WA, 98057-0389/206-255-8410

WISCONSIN
Great Lakes Arms Collectors Assn., Inc.
Edward C. Warnke, 2913 Woodridge Lane, Waukesha, WI 53188
Wisconsin Gun Collectors Assn., Inc.
Lulita Zellmer, P.O. Box 181, Sussex, WI 53089

WYOMING
Wyoming Weapons Collectors
P.O. Box 284, Laramie, WY 82073/307-745-4652 or 745-9530

NATIONAL ORGANIZATIONS

Amateur Trapshooting Assn.
David D. Bopp, Exec. Director, 601 W. National Rd., Vandalia, OH 45377/937-898-4638; Fax: 937-898-5472
American Airgun Field Target Assn.
5911 Cherokee Ave., Tampa, FL 33604
American Coon Hunters Assn.
Opal Johnston, P.O. Cadet, Route 1, Box 492, Old Mines, MO 63630
American Custom Gunmakers Guild
Jan Billeb, Exec. Director, 22 Vista View Drive, Cody, WY 82414-9606 (307) 587-4297 (phone/fax) Email: acgg@acgg.org Website: www.acgg.org
American Defense Preparedness Assn.
Two Colonial Place, 2101 Wilson Blvd., Suite 400, Arlington, VA 22201-3061
American Paintball League
P.O. Box 3561, Johnson City, TN 37602/800-541-9169
American Pistolsmiths Guild
Alex B. Hamilton, Pres., 1449 Blue Crest Lane, San Antonio, TX 78232/210-494-3063
American Police Pistol & Rifle Assn.
3801 Biscayne Blvd., Miami, FL 33137

American Single Shot Rifle Assn.
Gary Staup, Secy., 709 Carolyn Dr., Delphos, OH 45833
419-692-3866.
Website: www.assra.com
American Society of Arms Collectors
George E. Weatherly, P.O. Box 2567, Waxahachie, TX 75165
American Tactical Shooting Assn.(A.T.S.A.)
c/o Skip Gochenour, 2600 N. Third St., Harrisburg, PA 17110
717-233-0402;
Fax: 717-233-5340
Association of Firearm and Tool Mark Examiners
Lannie G. Emanuel, Secy., Southwest Institute of Forensic Sciences, P.O. Box 35728, Dallas, TX 75235/214-920-5979; Fax: 214-920-5928; Membership Secy., Ann D. Jones, VA Div. of Forensic Science, P.O. Box 999, Richmond, VA 23208 804-786-4706; Fax: 804-371-8328
Boone & Crockett Club
250 Station Dr., Missoula, MT 59801-2753
Browning Collectors Assn.
Secretary:Scherrie L. Brennac, 2749 Keith Dr., Villa Ridge, MO 63089/314-742-0571
The Cast Bullet Assn., Inc.
Ralland J. Fortier, Editor, 4103 Foxcraft Dr., Traverse City, MI 49684
Citizens Committee for the Right to Keep and Bear Arms
Natl. Hq., Liberty Park, 12500 NE Tenth Pl., Bellevue, WA 98005
Colt Collectors Assn.
25000 Highland Way, Los Gatos, CA 95030/408-353-2658
Contemporary Longrifle Association
P.O. Box 2097, Staunton, VA 24402/540-886-6189
Website: www.CLA@longrifle.ws
Ducks Unlimited, Inc.
Natl. Headquarters, One Waterfowl Way, Memphis, TN 38120
901-758-3937
Fifty Caliber Shooters Assn.
PO Box 111, Monroe UT 84754-0111
Firearms Coalition/Neal Knox Associates
Box 6537, Silver Spring, MD 20906 301-871-3006
Firearms Engravers Guild of America
Rex C. Pedersen, Secy., 511 N. Rath Ave., Lundington, MI 49431 616-845-7695 (Phone/Fax)
Foundation for North American Wild Sheep
720 Allen Ave., Cody, WY 82414-3402; web site: iigi.com/os/non/fnaws/fnaws.htm; e-mail: fnaws@wyoming.com
Freedom Arms Collectors Assn.
P.O. Box 160302, Miami, FL 33116-0302
Garand Collectors Assn.
P.O. Box 181, Richmond, KY 40475
Glock Collectors Assn.
P.O. Box 1063, Maryland Heights, MO 63043
314-878-2061 Phone/Fax
Glock Shooting Sports Foundation
BO Box 309, Smyrna GA 30081
770-432-1202
Website: www.gssfonline.com

ARMS ASSOCIATIONS

Golden Eagle Collectors Assn. (G.E.C.A.)
Chris Showler, 11144 Slate Creek Rd., Grass Valley, CA 95945

Gun Owners of America
8001 Forbes Place, Suite 102, Springfield, VA 22151/703-321-8585

Handgun Hunters International
J.D. Jones, Director, P.O. Box 357 MAG, Bloomingdale, OH 43910

Harrington & Richardson Gun Coll. Assn.
George L. Cardet, 330 S.W. 27th Ave., Suite 603, Miami, FL 33135

High Standard Collectors' Assn.
John J. Stimson, Jr., Pres., 540 W. 92nd St., Indianapolis, IN 46260
Website: www.highstandard.org

Hopkins & Allen Arms & Memorabilia Society (HAAMS)
P.O. Box 187, 1309 Pamela Circle, Delphos, OH 45833

International Ammunition Association, Inc.
C.R. Punnett, Secy., 8 Hillock Lane, Chadds Ford, PA 19317
610-358-1285; Fax: 610-358-1560

International Benchrest Shooters
Joan Borden, RR1, Box 250BB, Springville, PA 18844
717-965-2366

International Blackpowder Hunting Assn.
P.O. Box 1180, Glenrock, WY 82637/307-436-9817

IHMSA (Intl. Handgun Metallic Silhouette Assn.)
PO Box 368, Burlington, IA 52601
Website: www.ihmsa.org

International Society of Mauser Arms Collectors
Michael Kindberg, Pres., P.O. Box 277, Alpharetta, GA 30239-0277

Jews for the Preservation of Firearms Ownership (JPFO) 501(c)(3)
2872 S. Wentworth Ave., Milwaukee, WI 53207
414-769-0760; Fax: 414-483-8435

The Mannlicher Collectors Assn.
Membership Office: P.O. Box 1249, The Dalles, Oregon 97058

Marlin Firearms Collectors Assn., Ltd.
Dick Paterson, Secy., 407 Lincoln Bldg., 44 Main St., Champaign, IL 61820

Merwin Hulbert Association,
2503 Kentwood Ct., High Point, NC 27265

Miniature Arms Collectors/Makers Society, Ltd.
Ralph Koebbeman, Pres., 4910 Kilburn Ave., Rockford, IL 61101
815-964-2569

M1 Carbine Collectors Assn. (M1-CCA)
623 Apaloosa Ln., Gardnerville, NV 89410-7840

National Association of Buckskinners (NAB)
Territorial Dispatch—1800s Historical Publication, 4701 Marion St., Suite 324, Livestock Exchange Bldg., Denver, CO 80216
303-297-9671

The National Association of Derringer Collectors
P.O. Box 20572, San Jose, CA 95160

National Assn. of Federally Licensed Firearms Dealers
Andrew Molchan, 2455 E. Sunrise, Ft. Lauderdale, FL 33304

National Association to Keep and Bear Arms
P.O. Box 78336, Seattle, WA 98178

National Automatic Pistol Collectors Assn.
Tom Knox, P.O. Box 15738, Tower Grove Station, St. Louis, MO 63163

National Bench Rest Shooters Assn., Inc.
Pat Ferrell, 2835 Guilford Lane, Oklahoma City, OK 73120-4404
405-842-9585; Fax: 405-842-9575

National Muzzle Loading Rifle Assn.
Box 67, Friendship, IN 47021
812-667-5131
Website: www.nmlra@nmlra.org

National Professional Paintball League (NPPL)
540 Main St., Mount Kisco, NY 10549/914-241-7400

National Reloading Manufacturers Assn.
One Centerpointe Dr., Suite 300, Lake Oswego, OR 97035

National Rifle Assn. of America
11250 Waples Mill Rd., Fairfax, VA 22030/703-267-1000
Website: www.nra.org

National Shooting Sports Foundation, Inc.
Doug Painter, President, Flintlock Ridge Office Center, 11 Mile Hill Rd., Newtown, CT 06470-2359
203-426-1320; Fax: 203-426-1087

National Skeet Shooting Assn.
Dan Snyuder, Director, 5931 Roft Road, San Antonio, TX 78253-9261/800-877-5338
Website: nssa-nsca.com

National Sporting Clays Association
Ann Myers, Director, 5931 Roft Road, San Antonio, TX 78253-9261/800-877-5338
Website: nssa-nsca.com

National Wild Turkey Federation, Inc.
P.O. Box 530, 770 Augusta Rd., Edgefield, SC 29824

North American Hunting Club
P.O. Box 3401, Minnetonka, MN 55343/612-936-9333;
Fax: 612-936-9755

North American Paintball Referees Association (NAPRA)
584 Cestaric Dr., Milpitas, CA 95035

North-South Skirmish Assn., Inc.
Stevan F. Meserve, Exec. Secretary, 507 N. Brighton Court, Sterling, VA 20164-3919

Old West Shooter's Association
712 James Street, Hazel TX 76020
817-444-2049

Remington Society of America
Gordon Fosburg, Secretary, 11900 North Brinton Road, Lake, MI 48623

Rocky Mountain Elk Foundation
P.O. Box 8249, Missoula, MT 59807-8249/406-523-4500;
Fax: 406-523-4581
Website: www.rmef.org

Ruger Collector's Assn., Inc.
P.O. Box 240, Greens Farms, CT 06436

Safari Club International
4800 W. Gates Pass Rd., Tucson, AZ 85745/520-620-1220

Sako Collectors Assn., Inc.
Jim Lutes, 202 N. Locust, Whitewater, KS 67154

Second Amendment Foundation
James Madison Building, 12500 NE 10th Pl., Bellevue, WA 98005

Single Action Shooting Society (SASS)
23255-A La Palma Avenue, Yorba Linda, CA 92887/714-694-1800;
Fax: 714-694-1815
email: sasseot@aol.com
Website: www.sassnet.com

Smith & Wesson Collectors Assn.
Cally Pletl, Admin. Asst.,PO Box 444, Afton, NY 13730

The Society of American Bayonet Collectors
P.O. Box 234, East Islip, NY 11730-0234

Southern California Schuetzen Society
Dean Lillard, 34657 Ave. E., Yucaipa, CA 92399

Sporting Arms and Ammunition Manufacturers' Institute (SAAMI)
Flintlock Ridge Office Center, 11 Mile Hill Rd., Newtown, CT 06470-2359/203-426-4358;
Fax: 203-426-1087

Sporting Clays of America (SCA)
Ron L. Blosser, Pres., 9257 Buckeye Rd., Sugar Grove, OH 43155-9632/614-746-8334;
Fax: 614-746-8605

Steel Challenge
23234 Via Barra, Valencia CA 91355
Website: www.steelchallenge.com

The Thompson/Center Assn.
Joe Wright, President, Box 792, Northboro, MA 01532/508-845-6960

U.S. Practical Shooting Association/IPSC
Dave Thomas, P.O. Box 811, Sedro Woolley, WA 98284/360-855-2245
Website: www.uspsa.org

U.S. Revolver Assn.
Brian J. Barer, 40 Larchmont Ave., Taunton, MA 02780/508-824-4836

U.S.A. Shooting
U.S. Olympic Shooting Center, One Olympic Plaza, Colorado Springs, CO 80909/719-578-4670
Website: wwwusashooting.org

The Varmint Hunters Assn., Inc.
Box 759, Pierre, SD 57501
Member Services 800-528-4868

Weatherby Collectors Assn., Inc.
P.O. Box 478, Pacific, MO 63069
Website:
www.weatherbycollectors.com
Email: WCAsecretary@aol.com

The Wildcatters
P.O. Box 170, Greenville, WI 54942

Winchester Arms Collectors Assn.
P.O. Box 230, Brownsboro, TX 75756/903-852-4027

The Women's Shooting Sports Foundation (WSSF)
4620 Edison Avenue, Ste. C, Colorado Springs, CO 80915
719-638-1299; Fax: 719-638-1271
email: wssf@worldnet.att.net

ARGENTINA

Asociacion Argentina de Coleccionistas de Armes y Municiones
Castilla de Correos No. 28, Succursal I B, 1401 Buenos Aires, Republica Argentina

AUSTRALIA

Antique & Historical Arms Collectors of Australia
P.O. Box 5654, GCMC Queensland 9726, Australia

The Arms Collector's Guild of Queensland, Inc.
Ian Skennerton, P.O. Box 433, Ashmore City 4214, Queensland, Australia

Australian Cartridge Collectors Assn., Inc.
Bob Bennett, 126 Landscape Dr., E. Doncaster 3109, Victoria, Australia

Sporting Shooters Assn. of Australia, Inc.
P.O. Box 2066, Kent Town, SA 5071, Australia

BRAZIL

Associaçao de Armaria Coleçao e Tiro (ACOLTI)
Rua do Senado, 258 - 2 andar, Centro, Rio de Janeiro - RJ - 20231-002 Brazil / tel: 0055-21-31817989

CANADA

ALBERTA

Canadian Historical Arms Society
P.O. Box 901, Edmonton, Alb., Canada T5J 2L8

National Firearms Assn.
Natl. Hq: P.O. Box 1779, Edmonton, Alb., Canada T5J 2P1

BRITISH COLUMBIA

The Historical Arms Collectors of B.C. (Canada)
Harry Moon, Pres., P.O. Box 50117, South Slope RPO, Burnaby, BC V5J 5G3, Canada
604-438-0950; Fax: 604-277-3646

ONTARIO

Association of Canadian Cartridge Collectors
Monica Wright, RR 1, Millgrove, ON, LOR IVO, Canada

Tri-County Antique Arms Fair
P.O. Box 122, RR #1, North Lancaster, Ont., Canada K0C 1Z0

EUROPE

BELGIUM

European Cartridge Research Association
Graham Irving, 21 Rue Schaltin, 4900 Spa, Belgium
32.87.77.43.40;
Fax: 32.87.77.27.51

CZECHOSLOVAKIA

Spolecnost Pro Studium Naboju (Czech Cartridge Research Association)
JUDr. Jaroslav Bubak, Pod Homolko 1439, 26601 Beroun 2, Czech Republic

DENMARK

Aquila Dansk Jagtpatron Historic Forening (Danish Historical Cartridge Collectors Club)
Steen Elgaard Møller, Ulriksdalsvej 7, 4840 Nr. Alslev, Denmark 10045-53846218;
Fax: 00455384 6209

ENGLAND

Arms and Armour Society
Hon. Secretary A. Dove, P.O. Box 10232, London, 5W19 2ZD, England

Dutch Paintball Federation
Aceville Publ., Castle House 97 High Street, Colchester, Essex C01 1TH, England/011-44-206-564840

European Paintball Sports Foundation
c/o Aceville Publ., Castle House 97 High St., Colchester, Essex, C01 1TH, England

Historical Breechloading Smallarms Assn.
D.J. Penn M.A., Secy., P.O. Box 12778, London SE1 6BX, England

National Rifle Assn.
(Great Britain) Bisley Camp, Brookwood, Woking Surrey GU24 OPB, England/01483.797777;
Fax: 014730686275

United Kingdom Cartridge Club
Ian Southgate, 20 Millfield, Elmley Castle, Nr. Pershore, Worcestershire, WR10 3HR, England

FRANCE

STAC-Western Co.
3 Ave. Paul Doumer (N.311); 78360 Montesson, France 01.30.53-43-65;
Fax: 01.30.53.19.10

GERMANY

Bund Deutscher Sportschützen e.v. (BDS)
Borsigallee 10, 53125 Bonn 1, Germany

Deutscher Schützenbund
Lahnstrasse 120, 65195 Wiesbaden, Germany

NORWAY

Scandinavian Ammunition Research Association
c/o Morten Stoen, Annerudstubben 3, N-1383 Asker, Norway

NEW ZEALAND

New Zealand Cartridge Collectors Club
Terry Castle, 70 Tiraumea Dr., Pakuranga, Auckland, New Zealand

New Zealand Deerstalkers Association
P.O. Box 6514 TE ARO, Wellington, New Zealand

SOUTH AFRICA

Historical Firearms Soc. of South Africa
P.O. Box 145, 7725 Newlands, Republic of South Africa

Republic of South Africa Cartridge Collectors Assn.
Arno Klee, 20 Eugene St., Malanshof Randburg, Gauteng 2194, Republic of South Africa

**S.A.A.C.A.
(Southern Africa Arms and Ammunition Assn.)**
Gauteng office:
P.O. Box 7597, Weltevreden Park, 1715, Republic of South Africa/ 011-679-1151; Fax: 011-679-1131;
e-mail: saaaca@iafrica.com
Kwa-Zulu Natal office:
P.O. Box 4065, Northway, Kwazulu-Natal 4065, Republic of South Africa

SAGA (S.A. Gunowners' Assn.)
P.O. Box 35203, Northway, Kwazulu-Natal 4065, Republic of South Africa

SPAIN

Asociacion Espanola de Colleccionistas de Cartuchos (A.E.C.C.)
Secretary: Apdo. Correos No. 1086, 2880-Alcala de Henares (Madrid), Spain. President: Apdo. Correos No. 682, 50080 Zaragoza, Spain

2007
GUN DIGEST
DIRECTORY OF THE
ARMS TRADE

The **Product Directory** contains 84 product categories. The **Manufacturer's Directory** alphabetically lists the manufacturers with their addresses, phone numbers, FAX numbers and Internet addresses, if available.

DIRECTORY OF THE ARMS TRADE INDEX

AMMUNITION COMPONENTS, SHOTSHELL

A.W. Peterson Gun Shop, Inc., The
Ballistic Products, Inc.
Blount, Inc., Sporting Equipment Div.
CCI/Speer Div of ATK
Cheddite, France S.A.
Claybuster Wads & Harvester Bullets
Dina Arms Corporation
Garcia National Gun Traders, Inc.
Gentner Bullets
Guncrafter Industries
Magtech Ammunition Co. Inc.
Peterson Gun Shop, Inc., A.W.
Precision Reloading, Inc.
Ravell Ltd.
Tar-Hunt Custom Rifles, Inc.
Vitt/Boos

AMMUNITION COMPONENTS – BULLETS, POWDER, PRIMERS, CASES

A.W. Peterson Gun Shop, Inc., The
Acadian Ballistic Specialties
Accuracy Unlimited
Accurate Arms Co., Inc.
Action Bullets & Alloy Inc.
ADCO Sales, Inc.
Alaska Bullet Works, Inc.
Alex, Inc.
Alliant Techsystems, Smokeless Powder Group
Allred Bullet Co.
Alpha LaFranck Enterprises
American Products, Inc.
Arizona Ammunition, Inc.
Armfield Custom Bullets
A-Square Co.
Austin Sheridan USA, Inc.
Baer's Hollows
Ballard Rifle & Cartridge Co., LLC
Barnes
Barnes Bullets, Inc.
BC-Handmade Bullets
Beartooth Bullets
Bell Reloading, Inc.
Berger Bullets Ltd.
Berry's Mfg., Inc.
Big Bore Bullets of Alaska
Big Bore Express
Bitterroot Bullet Co.
Black Belt Bullets (See Big Bore Express)
Black Hills Shooters Supply
Black Powder Products
Blount, Inc., Sporting Equipment Div.
Blue Mountain Bullets
Brenneke GmbH
Briese Bullet Co., Inc.
BRP, Inc. High Performance Cast Bullets
Buck Stix-SOS Products Co.
Buckeye Custom Bullets
Buckskin Bullet Co.
Buffalo Arms Co.
Buffalo Bullet Co., Inc.
Buffalo Rock Shooters Supply
Bull-X, Inc.
Butler Enterprises
Cain's Outdoors, Inc.
Cambos Outdoorsman
Canyon Cartridge Corp.
Cast Performance Bullet Company
Casull Arms Corp.
CCI/Speer Div of ATK
Champion's Choice, Inc.
Cheddite, France S.A.

CheVron Bullets
Chuck's Gun Shop
Clean Shot Technologies
Competitor Corp., Inc.
Cook Engineering Service
Cummings Bullets
Curtis Cast Bullets
Curtis Gun Shop (See Curtis Cast Bullets)
Custom Bullets by Hoffman
D.L. Unmussig Bullets
Dakota Arms, Inc.
Davide Pedersoli and Co.
Dina Arms Corporation
DKT, Inc.
Dohring Bullets
Eichelberger Bullets, Wm.
Federal Cartridge Co.
Fiocchi of America, Inc.
Firearm Brokers
Forkin Custom Classics
Fowler, Bob (See Black Powder Products)
Freedom Arms, Inc.
Garcia National Gun Traders, Inc.
Gehmann, Walter (See Huntington Die Specialties)
GOEX, Inc.
Golden Bear Bullets
Gotz Bullets
Grayback Wildcats
Gun City
Gun Works, The
Harris Enterprises
Harrison Bullets
Hart & Son, Inc.
Hawk Laboratories, Inc. (See Hawk, Inc.)
Hawk, Inc.
Heidenstrom Bullets
Hercules, Inc. (See Alliant Techsystems Smokeless Powder Group)
Hi-Performance Ammunition Company
Hirtenberger AG
Hobson Precision Mfg. Co.
Hodgdon Powder Co.
Hornady Mfg. Co.
HT Bullets
Hunters Supply, Inc.
Huntington Die Specialties
Impact Case & Container, Inc.
Imperial Magnum Corp.
IMR Powder Co.
Intercontinental Distributors, Ltd.
J&D Components
J&L Superior Bullets (See Huntington Die Specialties)
J.R. Williams Bullet Co.
James Calhoon Mfg.
Jamison International
Jensen Bullets
Jensen's Firearms Academy
Jericho Tool & Die Co., Inc.
Jester Bullets
JLK Bullets
JRP Custom Bullets
Kaswer Custom, Inc.
Keith's Bullets
Keng's Firearms Specialty, Inc./US Tactical Systems
Ken's Kustom Kartridges
Knight Rifles
Knight Rifles (See Modern Muzzleloading, Inc.)
Lawrence Brand Shot (See Precision Reloading, Inc.)
Liberty Shooting Supplies
Lightning Performance Innovations, Inc.
Lindsley Arms Cartridge Co.
Littleton, J. F.
Lomont Precision Bullets
Lyman Products Corp.

Magnus Bullets
MagSafe Ammo, Inc.
Magtech Ammunition Co. Inc.
Marchmon Bullets
Markesbery Muzzle Loaders, Inc.
Marshall Fish Mfg. Gunsmith Sptg. Co.
McMurdo, Lynn
Meister Bullets (See Gander Mountain)
Men-Metallwerk Elisenhuette GmbH
Midway Arms, Inc.
MI-TE Bullets
Montana Precision Swaging
Mulhern, Rick
Murmur Corp.
Nagel's Custom Bullets
Nammo Lapua Oy
National Bullet Co.
Naval Ordnance Works
North American Shooting Systems
North Devon Firearms Services
Northern Precision
Northwest Custom Projectile
Nosler, Inc.
OK Weber, Inc.
Oklahoma Ammunition Co.
Old Wagon Bullets
Old Western Scrounger LLC
Ordnance Works, The
Oregon Trail Bullet Company
Pacific Rifle Co.
Page Custom Bullets
Penn Bullets
Peterson Gun Shop, Inc., A.W.
Petro-Explo Inc.
Phillippi Custom Bullets, Justin
Pinetree Bullets
PMC/Eldorado Cartridge Corp.
Polywad, Inc.
Pony Express Reloaders
Power Plus Enterprises, Inc.
Precision Delta Corp.
Prescott Projectile Co.
Price Bullets, Patrick W.
PRL Bullets, c/o Blackburn Enterprises
Professional Hunter Supplies
Proofmark Corp.
PWM Sales Ltd.
Quality Cartridge
Quarton Beamshot
Rainier Ballistics
Ramon B. Gonzalez Guns
Ramon B. Gonzalez Guns
Ravell Ltd.
Redwood Bullet Works
Reloading Specialties, Inc.
Remington Arms Co., Inc.
Rhino
Robinson H.V. Bullets
Rubright Bullets
Russ Haydon's Shooters' Supply
SAECO (See Redding Reloading Equipment)
Scharch Mfg., Inc.-Top Brass
Schneider Bullets
Schroeder Bullets
Schumakers Gun Shop
Seebeck Assoc., R.E.
Shappy Bullets
Sharps Arms Co., Inc., C.
Shilen, Inc.
Sierra Bullets
SOS Products Co. (See Buck Stix-SOS Products Co.)
Southern Ammunition Co., Inc.
Specialty Gunsmithing
Speer Bullets
Spencer's Rifle Barrels, Inc.
SSK Industries
Stanley Bullets
Star Ammunition, Inc.
Star Custom Bullets

Starke Bullet Company
Starline, Inc.
Stewart's Gunsmithing
Swift Bullet Co.
T.F.C. S.p.A.
Taracorp Industries, Inc.
Tar-Hunt Custom Rifles, Inc.
TCCI
TCSR
Thompson Bullet Lube Co.
Thompson Precision
Traditions Performance Firearms
True Flight Bullet Co.
Tucson Mold, Inc.
USAC
Vann Custom Bullets
Vihtavuori Oy/Kaltron-Pettibone
Vincent's Shop
Viper Bullet and Brass Works
Walters Wads
Watson Bullets
Western Nevada West Coast Bullets
Widener's Reloading & Shooting Supply, Inc.
Wildey F. A., Inc.
Winchester Div. Olin Corp.
Woodleigh (See Huntington Die Specialties)
Worthy Products, Inc.
Wyant Bullets
Wyoming Custom Bullets
Zero Ammunition Co., Inc.

AMMUNITION, COMMERCIAL

3-Ten Corp.
A.W. Peterson Gun Shop, Inc., The
Ad Hominem
Air Arms
American Ammunition
Arizona Ammunition, Inc.
Arms Corporation of the Philippines
A-Square Co.
Austin Sheridan USA, Inc.
Ballistic Products, Inc.
Benjamin/Sheridan Co., Crosman
Black Hills Ammunition, Inc.
Blammo Ammo
Blount, Inc., Sporting Equipment Div.
Brenneke GmbH
Buchsenmachermeister
Buffalo Arms Co.
Buffalo Bullet Co., Inc.
Bull-X, Inc.
Cabela's
Cambos Outdoorsman
Casull Arms Corp.
CBC
CCI/Speer Div of ATK
Champion's Choice, Inc.
Cor-Bon Inc./Glaser LLC
Crosman Airguns
Cubic Shot Shell Co., Inc.
Dan Wesson Firearms
Dead Eye's Sport Center
Delta Arms Ltd.
Delta Frangible Ammunition LLC
Dynamit Nobel-RWS, Inc.
Effebi SNC-Dr. Franco Beretta
Eley Ltd.
Ellett Bros.
Estate Cartridge, Inc.
Federal Cartridge Co.
Fiocchi of America, Inc.
Firearm Brokers
Garcia National Gun Traders, Inc.
Garrett Cartridges, Inc.
Garthwaite Pistolsmith, Inc., Jim
Gibbs Rifle Co., Inc.
Gil Hebard Guns, Inc.
Glaser LLC

Glaser Safety Slug, Inc. (see CorBon/Glaser)
GOEX, Inc.
Goodwin's Guns
Grayback Wildcats
Gun City
Gun Room Press, The
Gun Works, The
Guncrafter Industries
Hansen & Co.
Hart & Son, Inc.
Hastings
Hi-Performance Ammunition Company
Hirtenberger AG
Hofer Jagdwaffen, P.
Hornady Mfg. Co.
Hunters Supply, Inc.
Intercontinental Distributors, Ltd.
Ion Industries, Inc.
Keng's Firearms Specialty, Inc./US Tactical Systems
Kent Cartridge America, Inc.
Knight Rifles
Lethal Force Institute (See Police Bookshelf)
Lock's Philadelphia Gun Exchange
Lomont Precision Bullets
Magnum Research, Inc.
MagSafe Ammo, Inc.
Magtech Ammunition Co. Inc.
Markell, Inc.
Marshall Fish Mfg. Gunsmith Sptg. Co.
Men-Metallwerk Elisenhuette GmbH
Mullins Ammunition
Nammo Lapua Oy
New England Ammunition Co.
Oklahoma Ammunition Co.
Old Western Scrounger LLC
Outdoor Sports Headquarters, Inc.
P.S.M.G. Gun Co.
Paragon Sales & Services, Inc.
Parker & Sons Shooting Supply
Peterson Gun Shop, Inc., A.W.
PMC/Eldorado Cartridge Corp.
Police Bookshelf
Polywad, Inc.
Pony Express Reloaders
Precision Delta Corp.
Pro Load Ammunition, Inc.
Quality Cartridge
R.E.I.
Ravell Ltd.
Remington Arms Co., Inc.
Rucker Dist. Inc.
RWS (See U.S. Importer-Dynamit Nobel-RWS, Inc.)
Sellier & Bellot, USA, Inc.
Southern Ammunition Co., Inc.
Speer Bullets
Starr Trading Co., Jedediah
TCCI
Thompson Bullet Lube Co.
USAC
VAM Distribution Co. LLC
Victory USA
Vihtavuori Oy/Kaltron-Pettibone
Visible Impact Targets
Voere-KGH GmbH
Weatherby, Inc.
Westley Richards & Co. Ltd.
Whitestone Lumber Corp.
Widener's Reloading & Shooting Supply, Inc.
Wildey F. A., Inc.
William E. Phillips Firearms
Winchester Div. Olin Corp.
Zero Ammunition Co., Inc.

AMMUNITION, CUSTOM

3-Ten Corp.
A.W. Peterson Gun Shop, Inc., The

PRODUCT & SERVICE DIRECTORY

Accuracy Unlimited
AFSCO Ammunition
Allred Bullet Co.
American Derringer Corp.
American Products, Inc.
Arizona Ammunition, Inc.
Arms Corporation of the
  Philippines
Ballard Rifle & Cartridge Co., LLC
Bear Arms
Belding's Custom Gun Shop
Berger Bullets Ltd.
Big Bore Bullets of Alaska
Black Hills Ammunition, Inc.
Blue Mountain Bullets
Brynin, Milton
Buckskin Bullet Co.
Buffalo Arms Co.
CBC
CFVentures
Champlin Firearms, Inc.
Country Armourer, The
Cubic Shot Shell Co., Inc.
Custom Tackle and Ammo
D.L. Unmussig Bullets
Dakota Arms, Inc.
Dead Eye's Sport Center
Delta Frangible Ammunition LLC
DKT, Inc.
Estate Cartridge, Inc.
GDL Enterprises
Gentner Bullets
GOEX, Inc.
Grayback Wildcats
Hawk, Inc.
Hirtenberger AG
Hobson Precision Mfg. Co.
Horizons Unlimited
Hornady Mfg. Co.
Hunters Supply, Inc.
Jensen Bullets
Jensen's Custom Ammunition
Jensen's Firearms Academy
Kaswer Custom, Inc.
L. E. Jurras & Assoc.
L.A.R. Mfg., Inc.
Lethal Force Institute (See Police
  Bookshelf)
Lindsley Arms Cartridge Co.
Linebaugh Custom Sixguns
MagSafe Ammo, Inc.
Magtech Ammunition Co. Inc.
McMurdo, Lynn
Men-Metallwerk Elisenhuette
  GmbH
Milstor Corp.
Mullins Ammunition
Oklahoma Ammunition Co.
P.S.M.G. Gun Co.
Peterson Gun Shop, Inc., A.W.
Phillippi Custom Bullets, Justin
Power Plus Enterprises, Inc.
Precision Delta Corp.
Professional Hunter Supplies
Quality Cartridge
R.E.I.
Ramon B. Gonzalez Guns
Sandia Die & Cartridge Co.
SOS Products Co. (See Buck Stix-
  SOS Products Co.)
Specialty Gunsmithing
Spencer's Rifle Barrels, Inc.
SSK Industries
Star Custom Bullets
Stewart's Gunsmithing
TCCI
Vitt/Boos
Vulpes Ventures, Inc., Fox
  Cartridge Division
Watson Bullets
Worthy Products, Inc.
Zero Ammunition Co., Inc.

AMMUNITION, FOREIGN

A.W. Peterson Gun Shop, Inc., The
Ad Hominem
AFSCO Ammunition
Air Arms
Armscorp USA, Inc.
B&P America
Cape Outfitters
CBC
Cheddite, France S.A.
Cubic Shot Shell Co., Inc.
Dead Eye's Sport Center
DKT, Inc.
Dynamit Nobel-RWS, Inc.
E. Arthur Brown Co. Inc.
Fiocchi of America, Inc.
Gamebore Division, Polywad, Inc.
Gibbs Rifle Co., Inc.
GOEX, Inc.
Gunsmithing, Inc.
Hansen & Co.
Heidenstrom Bullets
Hirtenberger AG
Hornady Mfg. Co.
International Shooters Service
Intrac Arms International
Jack First, Inc.
K.B.I. Inc.
MagSafe Ammo, Inc.
Magtech Ammunition Co. Inc.
Marksman Products
Mullins Ammunition
Navy Arms Company
Oklahoma Ammunition Co.
P.S.M.G. Gun Co.
Paragon Sales & Services, Inc.
Paul Co., The
Peterson Gun Shop, Inc., A.W.
Petro-Explo Inc.
Precision Delta Corp.
R.E.T. Enterprises
Ramon B. Gonzalez Guns
RWS (See U.S. Importer-Dynamit
  Nobel-RWS, Inc.)
Samco Global Arms, Inc.
Sentinel Arms
Southern Ammunition Co., Inc.
Speer Bullets
Stratco, Inc.
T.F.C. S.p.A.
Vector Arms, Inc.
Victory Ammunition
Vihtavuori Oy/Kaltron-Pettibone
Wolf Performance Ammunition

ANTIQUE ARMS DEALER

Ackerman & Co.
Ad Hominem
Antique American Firearms
Antique Arms Co.
Aplan Antiques & Art
Ballard Rifle & Cartridge Co., LLC
Bear Mountain Gun & Tool
Bob's Tactical Indoor Shooting
  Range & Gun Shop
Buffalo Arms Co.
Cape Outfitters
CBC-BRAZIL
Chadick's Ltd.
Chambers Flintlocks Ltd., Jim
Champlin Firearms, Inc.
Chuck's Gun Shop
Cleland's Outdoor World, Inc.
Clements' Custom Leathercraft,
  Chas
Cole's Gun Works
Cousin Bob's Mountain Products
D&D Gunsmiths, Ltd.
David R. Chicoine
Dixie Gun Works
Dixon Muzzleloading Shop, Inc.
Duffy, Charles E. (See Guns
  Antique & Modern DBA)

Ed's Gun House
Enguix Import-Export
Fagan Arms
Flayderman & Co., Inc.
Getz Barrel Company
Glass, Herb
Goergen's Gun Shop, Inc.
Golden Age Arms Co.
Goodwin's Guns
Gun Hunter Books (See Gun
  Hunter Trading Co.)
Gun Hunter Trading Co.
Gun Room Press, The
Gun Room, The
Gun Works, The
Guns Antique & Modern DBA /
  Charles E. Duffy
Hallowell & Co.
Hammans, Charles E.
HandCrafts Unltd. (See Clements'
  Custom Leathercraft)
Handgun Press
Hansen & Co.
Hunkeler, A. (See Buckskin
  Machine Works)
Imperial Miniature Armory
James Wayne Firearms for
  Collectors and Investors
Kelley's
Knight's Manufacturing Co.
Ledbetter Airguns, Riley
LeFever Arms Co., Inc.
Lever Arms Service Ltd.
Lock's Philadelphia Gun Exchange
Log Cabin Sport Shop
Logdewood Mfg.
Marshall Fish Mfg. Gunsmith
  Sptg. Co.
Martin B. Retting Inc.
Martin's Gun Shop
Michael's Antiques
Mid-America Recreation, Inc.
Montana Outfitters, Lewis E.
  Yearout
Muzzleloaders Etcetera, Inc.
Navy Arms Company
New England Arms Co.
Olathe Gun Shop
P.S.M.G. Gun Co.
Peter Dyson & Son Ltd.
Pony Express Sport Shop
Powder Horn Ltd.
Ravell Ltd.
Reno, Wayne
Retting, Inc., Martin B.
Robert Valade Engraving
Rutgers Book Center
Samco Global Arms, Inc.
Sarco, Inc.
Scott Fine Guns Inc., Thad
Shootin' Shack
Sportsmen's Exchange & Western
  Gun Traders, Inc.
Steves House of Guns
Stott's Creek Armory, Inc.
Track of the Wolf, Inc.
Turnbull Restoration, Doug
Vic's Gun Refinishing
Wallace, Terry
Westley Richards & Co. Ltd.
Wild West Guns
Winchester Consultants
Winchester Sutler, Inc., The
Yearout, Lewis E. (See Montana
  Outfitters)

APPRAISER – GUNS, ETC.

A.W. Peterson Gun Shop, Inc., The
Ackerman & Co.
Antique Arms Co.
Barta's Gunsmithing
Beitzinger, George
Blue Book Publications, Inc.

Bob's Tactical Indoor Shooting
  Range & Gun Shop
Bonham's & Butterfields
Bullet N Press
Cape Outfitters
Chadick's Ltd.
Champlin Firearms, Inc.
Christie's East
Clark Firearms Engraving
Cleland's Outdoor World, Inc.
Clements' Custom Leathercraft,
  Chas
Cole's Gun Works
Colonial Arms, Inc.
Colonial Repair
Corry, John
Custom Tackle and Ammo
D&D Gunsmiths, Ltd.
David R. Chicoine
DGR Custom Rifles
Dietz Gun Shop & Range, Inc.
Dixie Gun Works
Dixon Muzzleloading Shop, Inc.
Duane's Gun Repair (See DGR
  Custom Rifles)
Ed's Gun House
Eversull Co., Inc.
Fagan Arms
Ferris Firearms
Firearm Brokers
Flayderman & Co., Inc.
Forty-Five Ranch Enterprises
Frontier Arms Co., Inc.
Gene's Custom Guns
Getz Barrel Company
Gillmann, Edwin
Goergen's Gun Shop, Inc.
Golden Age Arms Co.
Griffin & Howe, Inc.
Griffin & Howe, Inc.
Gun City
Gun Hunter Books (See Gun
  Hunter Trading Co.)
Gun Hunter Trading Co.
Gun Room Press, The
Gun Shop, The
Gun Works, The
Guncraft Books (See Guncraft
  Sports, Inc.)
Guncraft Sports, Inc.
Guncraft Sports, Inc.
Gunsmithing, Inc.
Hallowell & Co.
Hammans, Charles E.
HandCrafts Unltd. (See Clements'
  Custom Leathercraft)
Handgun Press
Hank's Gun Shop
Hansen & Co.
Irwin, Campbell H.
Ithaca Classic Doubles
J.W. Wasmundt-Gunsmith
Jackalope Gun Shop
James Wayne Firearms for
  Collectors and Investors
Jensen's Custom Ammunition
JG Airguns, LLC
Kelley's
Ken Eyster Heritage Gunsmiths,
  Inc.
L.L. Bean, Inc.
Lampert, Ron
LaRocca Gun Works
Ledbetter Airguns, Riley
LeFever Arms Co., Inc.
Lock's Philadelphia Gun Exchange
Log Cabin Sport Shop
Logdewood Mfg.
Long, George F.
Marshall Fish Mfg. Gunsmith
  Sptg. Co.
Martin B. Retting Inc.
Martin's Gun Shop
Mathews Gun Shop &
  Gunsmithing, Inc.

McCann Industries
Mercer Custom Guns
Montana Outfitters, Lewis E.
  Yearout
Muzzleloaders Etcetera, Inc.
Navy Arms Company
New England Arms Co.
Nu Line Guns
Olathe Gun Shop
Orvis Co., The
P&M Sales & Services, LLC
P.S.M.G. Gun Co.
Pasadena Gun Center
Pentheny de Pentheny
Perazone-Gunsmith, Brian
Peterson Gun Shop, Inc., A.W.
Pettinger Books, Gerald
Pony Express Sport Shop
Powder Horn Ltd.
R.A. Wells Custom Gunsmith
R.E.T. Enterprises
Ramon B. Gonzalez Guns
Retting, Inc., Martin B.
Robert Valade Engraving
Russ Haydon's Shooters' Supply
Rutgers Book Center
Scott Fine Guns Inc., Thad
Shootin' Shack
Sportsmen's Exchange & Western
  Gun Traders, Inc.
Steven Dodd Hughes
Stott's Creek Armory, Inc.
Stratco, Inc.
Swampfire Shop, The (See
  Peterson Gun Shop, Inc., A.W.)
Ten-Ring Precision, Inc.
Vic's Gun Refinishing
Walker Arms Co., Inc.
Wallace, Terry
Weber & Markin Custom
  Gunsmiths
Werth, T. W.
Whitestone Lumber Corp.
Wild West Guns
Williams Shootin' Iron Service,
  The Lynx-Line
Winchester Consultants
Winchester Sutler, Inc., The
Yearout, Lewis E. (See Montana
  Outfitters)

AUCTIONEER – GUNS, ETC.

"Little John's" Antique Arms
Bonham's & Butterfields
Buck Stix-SOS Products Co.
Christie's East
Fagan Arms
Pete de Coux Auction House
Sotheby's

BOOKS & MANUALS (PUBLISHERS & DEALERS)

A.W. Peterson Gun Shop, Inc., The
Alpha 1 Drop Zone
American Gunsmithing Institute
American Handgunner Magazine
Armory Publications
Arms & Armour Press
Austin Sheridan USA, Inc.
Ballistic Products, Inc.
Ballistic Products, Inc.
Barnes Bullets, Inc.
Beartooth Bullets
Beeman Precision Airguns
Blacksmith Corp.
Blacktail Mountain Books
Blue Book Publications, Inc.
Blue Ridge Machinery & Tools,
  Inc.
Boone's Custom Ivory Grips, Inc.

PRODUCT & SERVICE DIRECTORY

Brownells, Inc.
Buchsenmachermeister
Bullet N Press
C. Sharps Arms Co. Inc./Montana
Armory
Cain's Outdoors, Inc.
Cape Outfitters
Cheyenne Pioneer Products
Collector's Armoury, Ltd.
Colonial Repair
Crit' R Calls
David R. Chicoine
deHaas Barrels
Dixon Muzzleloading Shop, Inc.
Excalibur Publications
Executive Protection Institute
F+W Publications, Inc.
Fulton Armory
Galati International
GAR
Golden Age Arms Co.
Gun City
Gun Hunter Books (See Gun
Hunter Trading Co.)
Gun Hunter Trading Co.
Gun List (See F+W Publications)
Gun Room Press, The
Gun Works, The
Guncraft Books (See Guncraft
Sports, Inc.)
Guncraft Sports, Inc.
Gunnerman Books
GUNS Magazine
Gunsmithing, Inc.
H&P Publishing
Handgun Press
Harris Publications
Hawk Laboratories, Inc. (See
Hawk, Inc.)
Hawk, Inc.
Heritage/VSP Gun Books
Hodgdon Powder Co.
Hofer Jagdwaffen, P.
Hornady Mfg. Co.
Huntington Die Specialties
I.D.S.A. Books
Info-Arm
Ironside International Publishers,
Inc.
Jantz Supply, Inc.
Jeff's Outfitters
JG Airguns, LLC
Kelley's
King & Co.
Koval Knives
KP Books Division of F+W
Publications
L.B.T.
Lebeau-Courally
Lethal Force Institute (See Police
Bookshelf)
Lyman Products Corp.
Machinist's Workshop-Village
Press
Madis Books
Magma Engineering Co.
Marshall Fish Mfg. Gunsmith
Sptg. Co.
Montana Armory, Inc.
Montana Precision Swaging
Mulberry House Publishing
Nammo Lapua Oy
Navy Arms Company
NgraveR Co., The
Numrich Gun Parts Corporation
OK Weber, Inc.
Outdoor Sports Headquarters, Inc.
Paintball Games International
Magazine Aceville
Pansch, Robert F
Pejsa Ballistics
Pettinger Books, Gerald
PFRB Co.
Police Bookshelf
Precision Reloading, Inc.

Precision Shooting, Inc.
Primedia Publishing Co.
Professional Hunter Supplies
Ravell Ltd.
Ray Riling Arms Books Co.
Remington Double Shotguns
Russ Haydon's Shooters' Supply
Rutgers Book Center
S&S Firearms
Safari Press, Inc.
Saunders Gun & Machine Shop
Scharch Mfg., Inc.-Top Brass
Scharch Mfg., Inc.-Top Brass
Semmer, Charles (See Remington
Double Shotguns)
Sharps Arms Co., Inc., C.
Shotgun Sports Magazine, dba
Shootin' Accessories Ltd.
Sierra Bullets
Speer Bullets
SPG, Inc.
Stackpole Books
Star Custom Bullets
Stoeger Industries
Stoeger Publishing Co. (See
Stoeger Industries)
Swift Bullet Co.
Thomas, Charles C.
Track of the Wolf, Inc.
Trafalgar Square
Trotman, Ken
Tru-Balance Knife Co.
Vega Tool Co.
VSP Publishers (See Heritage/VSP
Gun Books)
W.E. Brownell Checkering Tools
WAMCO-New Mexico
Wells Creek Knife & Gun Works
Wilderness Sound Products Ltd.
Williams Gun Sight Co.
Winchester Consultants
Winfield Galleries LLC
Wolfe Publishing Co.

BULLET CASTING, ACCESSORIES

A.W. Peterson Gun Shop, Inc., The
Ballisti-Cast, Inc.
Buffalo Arms Co.
Bullet Metals
Cast Performance Bullet Company
CFVentures
Cooper-Woodward Perfect Lube
Davide Pedersoli and Co.
Ferguson, Bill
Fluoramics, Inc.
Hanned Line, The
Huntington Die Specialties
L.B.T.
Lee Precision, Inc.
Lithi Bee Bullet Lube
Lyman Products Corp.
MA Systems, Inc.
Magma Engineering Co.
Ox-Yoke Originals, Inc.
Rapine Bullet Mould Mfg. Co.
Redding Reloading Equipment
SPG, Inc.

BULLET CASTING, FURNACES & POTS

A.W. Peterson Gun Shop, Inc., The
Ballisti-Cast, Inc.
Buffalo Arms Co.
Bullet Metals
Ferguson, Bill
GAR
Gun Works, The
Lee Precision, Inc.
Lyman Products Corp.
Magma Engineering Co.

Rapine Bullet Mould Mfg. Co.
Thompson Bullet Lube Co.

BULLET CASTING, LEAD

A.W. Peterson Gun Shop, Inc., The
Action Bullets & Alloy Inc.
Ames Metal Products Co.
Buckskin Bullet Co.
Buffalo Arms Co.
Bullet Metals
Gun Works, The
Hunters Supply, Inc.
Jericho Tool & Die Co., Inc.
Lee Precision, Inc.
Lithi Bee Bullet Lube
Magma Engineering Co.
Montana Precision Swaging
Ox-Yoke Originals, Inc.
Penn Bullets
Proofmark Corp.
SPG, Inc.
Splitfire Sporting Goods, L.L.C.
Walters Wads

BULLET PULLERS

A.W. Peterson Gun Shop, Inc., The
Battenfeld Technologies, Inc.
Davide Pedersoli and Co.
Gun Works, The
Howell Machine, Inc.
Huntington Die Specialties
Royal Arms Gunstocks

BULLET TOOLS

A.W. Peterson Gun Shop, Inc., The
Brynin, Milton
Camdex, Inc.
Corbin Mfg. & Supply, Inc.
Cumberland Arms
Eagan Gunsmiths
Hanned Line, The
Holland's Gunsmithing
Lee Precision, Inc.
Niemi Engineering, W. B.
North Devon Firearms Services
Rorschach Precision Products
Sport Flite Manufacturing Co.
WTA Manufacturing

BULLET, CASE & DIE LUBRICANTS

Beartooth Bullets
Bonanza (See Forster Products)
Buckskin Bullet Co.
Buffalo Arms Co.
Camp-Cap Products
CFVentures
Cooper-Woodward Perfect Lube
CVA
E-Z-Way Systems
Ferguson, Bill
Forster Products, Inc.
GAR
Guardsman Products
Hanned Line, The
Heidenstrom Bullets
Hornady Mfg. Co.
Imperial (See E-Z-Way Systems)
Knoell, Doug
L.B.T.
Le Clear Industries (See E-Z-Way
Systems)
Lee Precision, Inc.
Lithi Bee Bullet Lube
MI-TE Bullets
RCBS Operations/ATK
Reardon Products
Rooster Laboratories
Shay's Gunsmithing

Uncle Mike's (See Michaels of
Oregon, Co.)
Widener's Reloading & Shooting
Supply, Inc.
Young Country Arms

CARTRIDGES FOR COLLECTORS

Ackerman & Co.
Ad Hominem
Armory Publications
Cameron's
Campbell, Dick
Cole's Gun Works
Colonial Repair
Country Armourer, The
Cubic Shot Shell Co., Inc.
Duane's Gun Repair (See DGR
Custom Rifles)
Ed's Gun House
Ed's Gun House
Enguix Import-Export
Forty-Five Ranch Enterprises
Goergen's Gun Shop, Inc.
Gun City
Gun Hunter Books (See Gun
Hunter Trading Co.)
Gun Hunter Trading Co.
Gun Room Press, The
Jack First, Inc.
Kelley's
Liberty Shooting Supplies
Michael's Antiques
Montana Outfitters, Lewis E.
Yearout
Numrich Gun Parts Corporation
Pasadena Gun Center
Pete de Coux Auction House
Samco Global Arms, Inc.
SOS Products Co. (See Buck Stix-
SOS Products Co.)
Stone Enterprises Ltd.
Ward & Van Valkenburg
Winchester Consultants
Yearout, Lewis E. (See Montana
Outfitters)

CASE & AMMUNITION PROCESSORS, INSPECTORS, BOXERS

A.W. Peterson Gun Shop, Inc., The
Ammo Load Worldwide, Inc.
Hafner World Wide, Inc.
Scharch Mfg., Inc.-Top Brass

CASE CLEANERS & POLISHING MEDIA

A.W. Peterson Gun Shop, Inc., The
Battenfeld Technologies, Inc.
Buffalo Arms Co.
G96 Products Co., Inc.
Gun Works, The
Huntington Die Specialties
Lee Precision, Inc.
Penn Bullets
Tru-Square Metal Products, Inc.
VibraShine, Inc.

CASE PREPARATION TOOLS

A.W. Peterson Gun Shop, Inc., The
Battenfeld Technologies, Inc.
Forster Products, Inc.
High Precision
Huntington Die Specialties
J. Dewey Mfg. Co., Inc.
K&M Services
Lee Precision, Inc.
Match Prep-Doyle Gracey

Plum City Ballistic Range
PWM Sales Ltd.
RCBS Operations/ATK
Redding Reloading Equipment
Russ Haydon's Shooters' Supply
Sinclair International, Inc.
Six Enterprises
Stoney Point Products, Inc.

CASE TRIMMERS, TRIM DIES & ACCESSORIES

A.W. Peterson Gun Shop, Inc., The
Buffalo Arms Co.
Creedmoor Sports, Inc.
Forster Products, Inc.
Fremont Tool Works
K&M Services
Lyman Products Corp.
Match Prep-Doyle Gracey
OK Weber, Inc.
PWM Sales Ltd.
Redding Reloading Equipment

CASE TUMBLERS, VIBRATORS, MEDIA & ACCESSORIES

4-D Custom Die Co.
A.W. Peterson Gun Shop, Inc., The
Battenfeld Technologies, Inc.
Berry's Mfg., Inc.
Dillon Precision Products, Inc.
Penn Bullets
Raytech Div. of Lyman Products
Corp.
Tru-Square Metal Products, Inc.
VibraShine, Inc.

CASES, CABINETS, RACKS & SAFES – GUN

All Rite Products, Inc.
Allen Co., Inc.
Alumna Sport by Dee Zee
American Display Co.
American Security Products Co.
Americase
Art Jewel Enterprises Ltd.
Bagmaster Mfg., Inc.
Barramundi Corp.
Berry's Mfg., Inc.
Big Spring Enterprises "Bore
Stores"
Bison Studios
Black Sheep Brand
Brauer Bros.
Browning Arms Co.
Bushmaster Hunting & Fishing
Cannon Safe, Inc.
Chipmunk (See Oregon Arms,
Inc.)
Connecticut Shotgun Mfg. Co.
D&L Industries (See D.J.
Marketing)
D.J. Marketing
Dara-Nes, Inc. (See Nesci
Enterprises, Inc.)
Deepeeka Exports Pvt. Ltd.
Doskocil Mfg. Co., Inc.
DTM International, Inc.
EMF Co. Inc.
English, Inc., A.G.
Enhanced Presentations, Inc.
Eversull Co., Inc.
Flambeau, Inc.
Fort Knox Security Products
Freedom Arms, Inc.
Galati International
GALCO International Ltd.
Gun-Ho Sports Cases
Hall Plastics, Inc., John
Homak

61ST EDITION, 2007 ⊕ **535**

PRODUCT & SERVICE DIRECTORY

Hoppe's Div. Penguin Industries, Inc.
Hunter Co., Inc.
Hydrosorbent Products
Impact Case & Container, Inc.
Jeff's Outfitters
Johanssons Vapentillbehor, Bert
Kalispel Case Line
KK Air International (See Impact Case & Container Co., Inc.)
Knock on Wood Antiques
Kolpin Outdoors, Inc.
Lakewood Products LLC
Liberty Safe
Marsh, Mike
McWelco Products
Morton Booth Co.
MPC
MTM Molded Products Co., Inc.
Nalpak
Necessary Concepts, Inc.
Nesci Enterprises Inc.
Oregon Arms, Inc. (See Rogue Rifle Co., Inc.)
Outa-Site Gun Carriers
Outdoor Connection, Inc., The
Pflumm Mfg. Co.
Poburka, Philip (See Bison Studios)
Powell & Son (Gunmakers) Ltd., William
Prototech Industries, Inc.
Rogue Rifle Co., Inc./Chipmunk Rifles
S.A.R.L. G. Granger
Schulz Industries
Silhouette Leathers
Southern Security
Sportsman's Communicators
Sun Welding Safe Co.
Surecase Co., The
Sweet Home, Inc.
Tinks & Ben Lee Hunting Products (See Wellington Outdoors)
Trulock Tool
Universal Sports
W. Waller & Son, Inc.
Whitestone Lumber Corp.
Wilson Case, Inc.
Woodstream
Zanotti Armor, Inc.
Ziegel Engineering

CHOKE DEVICES, RECOIL ABSORBERS & RECOIL PADS

3-Ten Corp.
A.W. Peterson Gun Shop, Inc., The
Action Products, Inc.
Answer Products Co.
Bansner's Ultimate Rifles, LLC
Bartlett Engineering
Battenfeld Technologies, Inc.
Bob Allen Sportswear
Briley Mfg. Inc.
Brooks Tactical Systems-Agrip
Brownells, Inc.
Buffer Technologies
Bull Mountain Rifle Co.
C&H Research
Cation
Chicasaw Gun Works
Clearview Products
Colonial Arms, Inc.
Connecticut Shotgun Mfg. Co.
CRR, Inc./Marble's Inc.
Danuser Machine Co.
Dina Arms Corporation
Gentry Custom LLC
Graybill's Gun Shop
Gruning Precision, Inc.
Harry Lawson Co.
Hastings
Haydel's Game Calls, Inc.

Hogue Grips
Holland's Gunsmithing
I.N.C. Inc. (See Kickeez I.N.C., Inc.)
Jackalope Gun Shop
Jenkins Recoil Pads
JP Enterprises, Inc.
KDF, Inc.
Kickeez I.N.C., Inc.
Lawson Co., Harry
London Guns Ltd.
Lyman Products Corp.
Mag-Na-Port International, Inc.
Marble Arms (See CRR, Inc./Marble's Inc.)
Menck, Gunsmith Inc., T.W.
Middlebrooks Custom Shop
Mobile Area Networks, Inc.
Morrow, Bud
Nu Line Guns
One Of A Kind
P.S.M.G. Gun Co.
Palsa Outdoor Products
Parker & Sons Shooting Supply
Pro-Port Ltd.
Que Industries, Inc.
Shotguns Unlimited
Simmons Gun Repair, Inc.
Stan Baker Sports
Stone Enterprises Ltd.
Time Precision
Truglo, Inc.
Trulock Tool
Uncle Mike's (See Michaels of Oregon, Co.)
Universal Sports
Virgin Valley Custom Guns
Williams Gun Sight Co.
Wilsom Combat
Wise Guns, Dale

CHRONOGRAPHS & PRESSURE TOOLS

C.W. Erickson's Mfg., L.L.C.
Clearview Products
Competition Electronics, Inc.
Hege Jagd-u. Sporthandels GmbH
Hutton Rifle Ranch
Mac-1 Airgun Distributors
Oehler Research, Inc.
PACT, Inc.
Romain's Custom Guns, Inc.
Savage Arms, Inc.
Stratco, Inc.
Tepeco

CLEANERS & DEGREASERS

A.W. Peterson Gun Shop, Inc., The
Barnes Bullets, Inc.
Camp-Cap Products
G96 Products Co., Inc.
Gun Works, The
Hafner World Wide, Inc.
Half Moon Rifle Shop
Kleen-Bore, Inc.
Modern Muzzleloading, Inc.
Northern Precision
Parker & Sons Shooting Supply
Parker Gun Finishes
PJL Industries/ProChemCo/PrOlixr
R&S Industries Corp.
Rusteprufe Laboratories
Sheffield Knifemakers Supply, Inc.
Shooter's Choice Gun Care
Sierra Specialty Prod. Co.
Spencer's Rifle Barrels, Inc.
United States Products Co.

CLEANING & REFINISHING SUPPLIES

A.W. Peterson Gun Shop, Inc., The
AC Dyna-tite Corp.
Alpha 1 Drop Zone
American Gas & Chemical Co., Ltd.,
Answer Products Co.
Armite Laboratories Inc.
Atlantic Mills, Inc.
Atsko/Sno-Seal, Inc.
Barnes Bullets, Inc.
Battenfeld Technologies, Inc.
Beeman Precision Airguns
Bill's Gun Repair
Birchwood Casey
Blount, Inc., Sporting Equipment Div.
Blount/Outers ATK
Blue and Gray Products Inc. (See Ox-Yoke Originals)
Break-Free, Inc.
Brownells, Inc.
C.S. Van Gorden & Son, Inc.
Cain's Outdoors, Inc.
Cambos Outdoorsman
Cambos Outdoorsman
Camp-Cap Products
CCI/Speer Div of ATK
Connecticut Shotgun Mfg. Co.
Creedmoor Sports, Inc.
CRR, Inc./Marble's Inc.
Custom Products (See Jones Custom Products)
Cylinder & Slide, Inc., William R. Laughridge
Dara-Nes, Inc. (See Nesci Enterprises, Inc.)
Deepeeka Exports Pvt. Ltd.
Dem-Bart Checkering Tools, Inc.
Desert Mountain Mfg.
Du-Lite Corp.
Dykstra, Doug
E&L Mfg., Inc.
Effebi SNC-Dr. Franco Beretta
Faith Associates
Flitz International Ltd.
Fluoramics, Inc.
Frontier Products Co.
G96 Products Co., Inc.
Golden Age Arms Co.
Guardsman Products
Gunsmithing, Inc.
Hafner World Wide, Inc.
Half Moon Rifle Shop
Hammans, Charles E.
Hoppe's Div. Penguin Industries, Inc.
Hornady Mfg. Co.
Hydra-Tone Chemicals, Inc.
Hydrosorbent Products
Iosso Products
J. Dewey Mfg. Co., Inc.
Jantz Supply, Inc.
Jonad Corp.
K&M Industries, Inc.
Kellogg's Professional Products
Kesselring Gun Shop
Kleen-Bore, Inc.
Knight Rifles
Laurel Mountain Forge
Lee Supplies, Mark
Lewis Lead Remover, The (See Brownells, Inc.)
List Precision Engineering
LPS Laboratories, Inc.
Lyman Products Corp.
Mac-1 Airgun Distributors
Marble Arms (See CRR, Inc./Marble's Inc.)
Mark Lee Supplies
Micro Sight Co.
Minute Man High Tech Industries
MTM Molded Products Co., Inc.

Muscle Products Corp.
Nesci Enterprises Inc.
Northern Precision
October Country Muzzleloading
Otis Technology, Inc.
Outers Laboratories Div. of ATK
Ox-Yoke Originals, Inc.
Parker & Sons Shooting Supply
Parker Gun Finishes
Paul Co., The
Pete Rickard, Inc.
PJL Industries/ProChemCo/PrOlixr
Precision Airgun Sales, Inc.
Precision Reloading, Inc.
Pro-Shot Products, Inc.
R&S Industries Corp.
Radiator Specialty Co.
Richards MicroFit Stocks, Inc.
Rooster Laboratories
Rusteprufe Laboratories
Saunders Gun & Machine Shop
Schumakers Gun Shop
Shooter's Choice Gun Care
Shotgun Sports Magazine, dba Shootin' Accessories Ltd.
Silencio/Safety Direct
Sinclair International, Inc.
Sno-Seal, Inc. (See Atsko/Sno-Seal, Inc.)
Southern Bloomer Mfg. Co.
Splitfire Sporting Goods, L.L.C.
Stoney Point Products, Inc.
Svon Corp.
T.F.C. S.p.A.
Tennessee Valley Mfg.
Tetra Gun Care
Texas Platers Supply Co.
Tru-Square Metal Products, Inc.
United States Products Co.
Van Gorden & Son Inc., C. S.
Venco Industries, Inc. (See Shooter's Choice Gun Care)
VibraShine, Inc.
Watson Bullets
WD-40 Co.
Wick, David E.
Willow Bend
Young Country Arms

COMPUTER SOFTWARE – BALLISTICS

Action Target, Inc.
AmBr Software Group Ltd.
Arms, Programming Solutions (See Arms Software)
Ballistic Program Co., Inc., The
Barnes Bullets, Inc.
Corbin Mfg. & Supply, Inc.
Country Armourer, The
Data Tech Software Systems
Gun Works, The
Hodgdon Powder Co.
J.I.T. Ltd.
Jensen Bullets
Oehler Research, Inc.
Outdoor Sports Headquarters, Inc.
PACT, Inc.
Pejsa Ballistics
Powley Computer (See Hutton Rifle Ranch)
RCBS Operations/ATK
Sierra Bullets
Tioga Engineering Co., Inc.
W. Square Enterprises

CUSTOM GUNSMITH

A&W Repair
A.A. Arms, Inc.
A.W. Peterson Gun Shop, Inc., The
Acadian Ballistic Specialties
Accuracy Unlimited
Acra-Bond Laminates

Actions by "T" Teddy Jacobson
Adair Custom Shop, Bill
Ahlman Guns
Aldis Gunsmithing & Shooting Supply
Alpha Precision, Inc.
Alpine Indoor Shooting Range
Amrine's Gun Shop
Answer Products Co.
Antique Arms Co.
Armament Gunsmithing Co., Inc.
Arms Craft Gunsmithing
Armscorp USA, Inc.
Artistry in Wood
Art's Gun & Sport Shop, Inc.
Baelder, Harry
Bain & Davis, Inc.
Bansner's Ultimate Rifles, LLC
Barnes Bullets, Inc.
Baron Technology
Barrel & Gunworks
Barta's Gunsmithing
Bauska Barrels
Bear Arms
Bear Mountain Gun & Tool
Behlert Precision, Inc.
Beitzinger, George
Belding's Custom Gun Shop
Bengtson Arms Co., L.
Bill Adair Custom Shop
Billings Gunsmiths
BlackStar AccuMax Barrels
BlackStar Barrel Accurizing (See BlackStar AccuMax)
Bob Rogers Gunsmithing
Bond Custom Firearms
Borden Ridges Rimrock Stocks
Borovnik K.G., Ludwig
Bowen Classic Arms Corp.
Brace, Larry D.
Briese Bullet Co., Inc.
Briganti Custom Gunsmith
Briley Mfg. Inc.
Broad Creek Rifle Works, Ltd.
Brockman's Custom Gunsmithing
Broken Gun Ranch
Brown Precision, Inc.
Buchsenmachermeister
Buckhorn Gun Works
Budin, Dave
Buehler Custom Sporting Arms
Bull Mountain Rifle Co.
Bullberry Barrel Works, Ltd.
Burkhart Gunsmithing, Don
Cambos Outdoorsman
Cambos Outdoorsman
Campbell, Dick
Carolina Precision Rifles
Carter's Gun Shop
Caywood, Shane J.
CBC-BRAZIL
Chambers Flintlocks Ltd., Jim
Champlin Firearms, Inc.
Chicasaw Gun Works
Chuck's Gun Shop
Clark Custom Guns, Inc.
Clark Firearms Engraving
Classic Arms Company
Classic Arms Corp.
Clearview Products
Cleland's Outdoor World, Inc.
Coffin, Charles H.
Cogar's Gunsmithing
Cole's Gun Works
Colonial Arms, Inc.
Colonial Repair
Colorado Gunsmithing Academy
Colorado School of Trades
Colt's Mfg. Co., Inc.
Competitive Pistol Shop, The
Conrad, C. A.
Corkys Gun Clinic
Cullity Restoration
Custom Shop, The
Custom Single Shot Rifles

D&D Gunsmiths, Ltd.
D.L. Unmussig Bullets
Dangler, Homer L.
D'Arcy Echols & Co.
Darlington Gun Works, Inc.
Dave's Gun Shop
David Miller Co.
David R. Chicoine
David W. Schwartz Custom Guns
Davis, Don
Delorge, Ed
Del-Sports, Inc.
DGR Custom Rifles
DGS, Inc., Dale A. Storey
Dietz Gun Shop & Range, Inc.
Dilliott Gunsmithing, Inc.
Don Klein Custom Guns
Donnelly, C. P.
Duane A. Hobbie Gunsmithing
Duane's Gun Repair (See DGR Custom Rifles)
Duffy, Charles E. (See Guns Antique & Modern DBA)
Duncan's Gun Works, Inc.
E. Arthur Brown Co. Inc.
Eckelman Gunshop
Ed Brown Products, Inc.
Ed Brown Products, Inc.
Eggleston, Jere D.
Entreprise Arms, Inc.
Erhardt, Dennis
Eversull Co., Inc.
Evolution Gun Works, Inc.
FERLIB
Ferris Firearms
Fisher, Jerry A.
Fisher Custom Firearms
Fleming Firearms
Flynn's Custom Guns
Forkin Custom Classics
Forster, Kathy (See Custom Checkering)
Forster, Larry L.
Forthofer's Gunsmithing & Knifemaking
Fred F. Wells/Wells Sport Store
Frontier Arms Co., Inc.
Fullmer, Geo. M.
Fulton Armory
G.G. & G.
Galaxy Imports Ltd., Inc.
Garthwaite Pistolsmith, Inc., Jim
Gary Reeder Custom Guns
Gator Guns & Repair
Genecco Gun Works
Gene's Custom Guns
Gentry Custom LLC
George Hoenig, Inc.
Gillmann, Edwin
Gilmore Sports Concepts, Inc.
Goens, Dale W.
Goodling's Gunsmithing
Grace, Charles E.
Graybill's Gun Shop
Greg Gunsmithing Repair
Gre-Tan Rifles
Griffin & Howe, Inc.
Griffin & Howe, Inc.
Gruning Precision, Inc.
Gun Doc, Inc.
Gun Shop, The
Gun Works, The
Guncraft Books (See Guncraft Sports, Inc.)
Guncraft Sports, Inc.
Guncraft Sports, Inc.
Guns Antique & Modern DBA / Charles E. Duffy
Gunsite Training Center
Gunsmithing Ltd.
Hamilton, Alex B. (See Ten-Ring Precision, Inc.)
Hammans, Charles E.
Hammerli Service-Precision Mac
Hammond Custom Guns Ltd.

Hank's Gun Shop
Hanson's Gun Center, Dick
Harry Lawson Co.
Hart & Son, Inc.
Hart Rifle Barrels, Inc.
Hartmann & Weiss GmbH
Hawken Shop, The (See Dayton Traister)
Hecht, Hubert J., Waffen-Hecht
Heilmann, Stephen
Heinie Specialty Products
Hensley, Gunmaker, Darwin
High Bridge Arms, Inc.
High Performance International
High Precision
High Standard Mfg. Co./F.I., Inc.
Highline Machine Co.
Hill, Loring F.
Hiptmayer, Armurier
Hiptmayer, Klaus
Hoag, James W.
Hodgson, Richard
Hofer Jagdwaffen, P.
Holland's Gunsmithing
Huebner, Corey O.
Hunkeler, A. (See Buckskin Machine Works)
Imperial Magnum Corp.
Irwin, Campbell H.
Israel Arms Inc.
Ivanoff, Thomas G. (See Tom's Gun Repair)
J&S Heat Treat
J.J. Roberts / Engraver
J.W. Wasmundt-Gunsmith
Jack Dever Co.
Jackalope Gun Shop
James Calhoon Mfg.
Jamison's Forge Works
Jarrett Rifles, Inc.
Jarvis, Inc.
Jay McCament Custom Gunmaker
Jensen's Custom Ammunition
Jim Norman Custom Gunstocks
Jim's Precision, Jim Ketchum
John Rigby & Co.
John's Custom Leather
Jones Custom Products, Neil A.
Juenke, Vern
K. Eversull Co., Inc.
KDF, Inc.
Keith's Custom Gunstocks
Ken Eyster Heritage Gunsmiths, Inc.
Ken Starnes Gunmaker
Ketchum, Jim (See Jim's Precision)
Kilham & Co.
King's Gun Works
Kleinendorst, K. W.
KOGOT
Korzinek Riflesmith, J.
L. E. Jurras & Assoc.
LaFrance Specialties
Lampert, Ron
LaRocca Gun Works
Larry Lyons Gunworks
Lathrop's, Inc.
Laughridge, William R. (See Cylinder & Slide, Inc.)
Lawson Co., Harry
Lazzeroni Arms Co.
LeFever Arms Co., Inc.
Les Baer Custom, Inc.
Linebaugh Custom Sixguns
List Precision Engineering
Lock's Philadelphia Gun Exchange
Lone Star Rifle Company
Long, George F.
Mag-Na-Port International, Inc.
Mahovsky's Metalife
Makinson, Nicholas
Marshall Fish Mfg. Gunsmith Sptg. Co.
Martini & Hagn, Ltd.

Martin's Gun Shop
Martz, John V.
Mathews Gun Shop & Gunsmithing, Inc.
Mazur Restoration, Pete
McCann, Tom
McCluskey Precision Rifles
McGowen Rifle Barrels
McMillan Rifle Barrels
MCS, Inc.
Mercer Custom Guns
Michael's Antiques
Mid-America Recreation, Inc.
Middlebrooks Custom Shop
Miller Arms, Inc.
Miller Custom
Mills Jr., Hugh B.
Moeller, Steve
Monell Custom Guns
Morrison Custom Rifles, J. W.
Morrow, Bud
Mo's Competitor Supplies (See MCS, Inc.)
Mowrey's Guns & Gunsmithing
Mullis Guncraft
Muzzleloaders Etcetera, Inc.
NCP Products, Inc.
Neil A. Jones Custom Products
Nelson's Custom Guns, Inc.
Nettestad Gun Works
New England Arms Co.
New England Custom Gun Service
Newman Gunshop
Nicholson Custom
Nickels, Paul R.
North American Shooting Systems
Nu Line Guns
Olson, Vic
Orvis Co., The
Ottmar, Maurice
Ox-Yoke Originals, Inc.
Ozark Gun Works
P&M Sales & Services, LLC
P.S.M.G. Gun Co.
PAC-NOR Barreling
Pagel Gun Works, Inc.
Parker & Sons Shooting Supply
Parker Gun Finishes
Pasadena Gun Center
Paterson Gunsmithing
Paulsen Gunstocks
Peacemaker Specialists
Pence Precision Barrels
Pennsylvania Gunsmith School
Penrod Precision
Pentheny de Pentheny
Perazone-Gunsmith, Brian
Performance Specialists
Pete Mazur Restoration
Peterson Gun Shop, Inc., A.W.
Piquette's Custom Engraving
Plum City Ballistic Range
Powell & Son (Gunmakers) Ltd., William
Power Custom, Inc.
Professional Hunter Supplies
Quality Custom Firearms
R&J Gun Shop
R.A. Wells Custom Gunsmith
Ramon B. Gonzalez Guns
Ray's Gunsmith Shop
Renfrew Guns & Supplies
Ridgetop Sporting Goods
Ries, Chuck
RMS Custom Gunsmithing
Robar Co., Inc., The
Robert Valade Engraving
Robinson, Don
Romain's Custom Guns, Inc.
Ron Frank Custom Classic, Inc.
Royal Arms Gunstocks
Ruger's Custom Guns
Rupert's Gun Shop
Savage Arms, Inc.
Schiffman, Mike

Schumakers Gun Shop
Score High Gunsmithing
Sharp Shooter Supply
Shaw, Inc., E. R. (See Small Arms Mfg. Co.)
Shay's Gunsmithing
Shooters Supply
Shootin' Shack
Shotguns Unlimited
Silver Ridge Gun Shop (See Goodwin Guns)
Simmons Gun Repair, Inc.
Singletary, Kent
Siskiyou Gun Works (See Donnelly, C. P.)
Skeoch, Brian R.
Sklany's Machine Shop
Small Arms Mfg. Co.
Small Arms Specialists
Smith, Art
Snapp's Gunshop
Speiser, Fred D.
Spencer Reblue Service
Spencer's Rifle Barrels, Inc.
Splitfire Sporting Goods, L.L.C.
Sportsmen's Exchange & Western Gun Traders, Inc.
Spradlin's
Springfield Armory
Springfield, Inc.
SSK Industries
Star Custom Bullets
Steelman's Gun Shop
Steffens, Ron
Steven Dodd Hughes
Stiles Custom Guns
Stott's Creek Armory, Inc.
Sturgeon Valley Sporters
Sullivan, David S. (See Westwind Rifles, Inc.)
Swampfire Shop, The (See Peterson Gun Shop, Inc., A.W.)
Swann, D. J.
Swenson's 45 Shop, A. D.
Swift River Gunworks
Szweda, Robert (See RMS Custom Gunsmithing)
Taconic Firearms Ltd., Perry Lane
Tank's Rifle Shop
Tar-Hunt Custom Rifles, Inc.
Tarnhelm Supply Co., Inc.
Taylor & Robbins
Tennessee Valley Mfg.
Ten-Ring Precision, Inc.
Terry K. Kopp Professional Gunsmithing
Terry Theis-Engraver
Time Precision
Tom's Gun Repair, Thomas G. Ivanoff
Tom's Gunshop
Trevallion Gunstocks
Trulock Tool
Tucker, James C.
Turnbull Restoration, Doug
Upper Missouri Trading Co.
Van Horn, Gil
Van Patten, J. W.
Vest, John
Vic's Gun Refinishing
Virgin Valley Custom Guns
Walker Arms Co., Inc.
Wallace, Terry
Wardell Precision
Weatherby, Inc.
Weber & Markin Custom Gunsmiths
Weems, Cecil
Werth, T. W.
Wessinger Custom Guns & Engraving
Westley Richards & Co. Ltd.
Westwind Rifles, Inc., David S. Sullivan
White Barn Wor

White Rifles, Inc.
Wichita Arms, Inc.
Wiebe, Duane
Wild West Guns
William E. Phillips Firearms
Williams Gun Sight Co.
Williams Shootin' Iron Service, The Lynx-Line
Williamson Precision Gunsmithing
Wilsom Combat
Winter, Robert M.
Wise Guns, Dale
Wiseman and Co., Bill
Wright's Gunstock Blanks
Zeeryp, Russ

CUSTOM METALSMITH

A&W Repair
A.W. Peterson Gun Shop, Inc., The
Ackerman & Co.
Ahlman Guns
Alaskan Silversmith, The
Aldis Gunsmithing & Shooting Supply
Alpha Precision, Inc.
Amrine's Gun Shop
Answer Products Co.
Antique Arms Co.
Artistry in Wood
Baron Technology
Barrel & Gunworks
Bauska Barrels
Bear Mountain Gun & Tool
Behlert Precision, Inc.
Beitzinger, George
Bengtson Arms Co., L.
Bill Adair Custom Shop
Billings Gunsmiths
Billingsley & Brownell
Bob Rogers Gunsmithing
Bowen Classic Arms Corp.
Brace, Larry D.
Briganti Custom Gunsmith
Broad Creek Rifle Works, Ltd.
Brown Precision, Inc.
Buckhorn Gun Works
Buehler Custom Sporting Arms
Bull Mountain Rifle Co.
Bullberry Barrel Works, Ltd.
Campbell, Dick
Carter's Gun Shop
Caywood, Shane J.
Checkmate Refinishing
Colonial Repair
Colorado Gunsmithing Academy
Craftguard
Crandall Tool & Machine Co.
Cullity Restoration
Custom Shop, The
Custom Single Shot Rifles
D&D Gunsmiths, Ltd.
D'Arcy Echols & Co.
Dave's Gun Shop
Delorge, Ed
DGS, Inc., Dale A. Storey
Dietz Gun Shop & Range, Inc.
Dilliott Gunsmithing, Inc.
Don Klein Custom Guns
Duane's Gun Repair (See DGR Custom Rifles)
Duncan's Gun Works, Inc.
Erhardt, Dennis
Eversull Co., Inc.
Ferris Firearms
Fisher, Jerry A.
Forster, Larry L.
Forthofer's Gunsmithing & Knifemaking
Fred F. Wells/Wells Sport Store
Fullmer, Geo. M.
Genecco Gun Works
Gentry Custom LLC
Grace, Charles E.

PRODUCT & SERVICE DIRECTORY

Graybill's Gun Shop
Gun Shop, The
Gunsmithing Ltd.
Hamilton, Alex B. (See Ten-Ring
  Precision, Inc.)
Harry Lawson Co.
Hartmann & Weiss GmbH
Hecht, Hubert J., Waffen-Hecht
Heilmann, Stephen
High Precision
Highline Machine Co.
Hiptmayer, Armurier
Hiptmayer, Klaus
Hoag, James W.
Holland's Gunsmithing
Ivanoff, Thomas G. (See Tom's
  Gun Repair)
J J Roberts Firearm Engraver
J&S Heat Treat
J.J. Roberts / Engraver
Jackalope Gun Shop
Jamison's Forge Works
Jay McCament Custom Gunmaker
KDF, Inc.
Ken Eyster Heritage Gunsmiths,
  Inc.
Ken Starnes Gunmaker
Kilham & Co.
Kleinendorst, K. W.
Lampert, Ron
LaRocca Gun Works
Larry Lyons Gunworks
Lawson Co., Harry
Les Baer Custom, Inc.
List Precision Engineering
Lock's Philadelphia Gun Exchange
Mahovsky's Metalife
Makinson, Nicholas
Martini & Hagn, Ltd.
Mazur Restoration, Pete
McCann Industries
Mid-America Recreation, Inc.
Miller Arms, Inc.
Morrison Custom Rifles, J. W.
Morrow, Bud
Mullis Guncraft
Nelson's Custom Guns, Inc.
Nettestad Gun Works
New England Custom Gun Service
Nicholson Custom
Noreen, Peter H.
Nu Line Guns
Olson, Vic
Ozark Gun Works
P.S.M.G. Gun Co.
Pagel Gun Works, Inc.
Parker & Sons Shooting Supply
Parker Gun Finishes
Pasadena Gun Center
Penrod Precision
Pete Mazur Restoration
Precision Specialties
Quality Custom Firearms
R.A. Wells Custom Gunsmith
Rice, Keith (See White Rock Tool
  & Die)
Robar Co., Inc., The
Robinson, Don
Romain's Custom Guns, Inc.
Ron Frank Custom Classic, Inc.
Score High Gunsmithing
Simmons Gun Repair, Inc.
Singletary, Kent
Skeoch, Brian R.
Sklany's Machine Shop
Small Arms Specialists
Smith, Art
Smith, Sharmon
Snapp's Gunshop
Spencer Reblue Service
Spencer's Rifle Barrels, Inc.
Sportsmen's Exchange & Western
  Gun Traders, Inc.
Spradlin's
SSK Industries

Steffens, Ron
Stiles Custom Guns
Taylor & Robbins
Ten-Ring Precision, Inc.
Tom's Gun Repair, Thomas G.
  Ivanoff
Turnbull Restoration, Doug
Van Horn, Gil
Van Patten, J. W.
Vic's Gun Refinishing
Waldron, Herman
Wallace, Terry
Weber & Markin Custom
  Gunsmiths
Werth, T. W.
Wessinger Custom Guns &
  Engraving
White Rock Tool & Die
Wiebe, Duane
Wild West Guns
Williams Shootin' Iron Service,
  The Lynx-Line
Williamson Precision
  Gunsmithing
Winter, Robert M.
Wise Guns, Dale
Wright's Gunstock Blanks

DECOYS

A.W. Peterson Gun Shop, Inc., The
Ad Hominem
Belding's Custom Gun Shop
Bill Russ Trading Post
Boyds' Gunstock Industries, Inc.
Carry-Lite, Inc.
Farm Form Decoys, Inc.
Feather, Flex Decoys
Flambeau, Inc.
G&H Decoys, Inc.
Grand Slam Hunting Products
Klingler Woodcarving
Kolpin Outdoors, Inc.
L.L. Bean, Inc.
Murphy, R.R. Co., Inc.
Original Deer Formula Co., The
Quack Decoy & Sporting Clays
Tanglefree Industries
Tru-Nord Compass
Woods Wise Products

DIE ACCESSORIES, METALLIC

A.W. Peterson Gun Shop, Inc., The
High Precision
Howell Machine, Inc.
King & Co.
Rapine Bullet Mould Mfg. Co.
Redding Reloading Equipment
Sinclair International, Inc.
Sport Flite Manufacturing Co.

DIES, METALLIC

4-D Custom Die Co.
A.W. Peterson Gun Shop, Inc., The
Austin Sheridan USA, Inc.
Bald Eagle Precision Machine Co.
Buffalo Arms Co.
Competitor Corp., Inc.
Dakota Arms, Inc.
Dillon Precision Products, Inc.
Dixie Gun Works
Fremont Tool Works
Gruning Precision, Inc.
Hollywood Engineering
Jones Custom Products, Neil A.
King & Co.
Lee Precision, Inc.
MEC-Gar S.R.L.
Montana Precision Swaging
Neil A. Jones Custom Products
Ozark Gun Works
PWM Sales Ltd.

Rapine Bullet Mould Mfg. Co.
RCBS Operations/ATK
Romain's Custom Guns, Inc.
Sinclair International, Inc.
Six Enterprises
Spencer's Rifle Barrels, Inc.
Sport Flite Manufacturing Co.
SSK Industries
Vega Tool Co.

DIES, SHOTSHELL

A.W. Peterson Gun Shop, Inc., The
Hollywood Engineering
Lee Precision, Inc.
MEC, Inc.

DIES, SWAGE

4-D Custom Die Co.
A.W. Peterson Gun Shop, Inc., The
Bullet Swaging Supply, Inc.
Competitor Corp., Inc.
Corbin Mfg. & Supply, Inc.
D.L. Unmussig Bullets
Hollywood Engineering
Howell Machine, Inc.
Montana Precision Swaging
Sport Flite Manufacturing Co.

ENGRAVER, ENGRAVING TOOLS

Ackerman & Co.
Adair Custom Shop, Bill
Ahlman Guns
Alaskan Silversmith, The
Allard, Gary/Creek Side Metal &
  Woodcrafters
Allen Firearm Engraving
Altamont Co.
American Pioneer Video
Baron Technology
Barraclough, John K.
Bates Engraving, Billy
Bill Adair Custom Shop
Billy Bates Engraving
Boessler, Erich
Brooker, Dennis
Buchsenmachermeister
Churchill, Winston G.
Clark Firearms Engraving
Collings, Ronald
Creek Side Metal & Woodcrafters
Cullity Restoration
Cupp, Alana, Custom Engraver
Dayton Traister
Delorge, Ed
Dolbare, Elizabeth
Dremel Mfg. Co.
Dubber, Michael W.
Engraving Artistry
Eversull Co., Inc.
Firearms Engraver's Guild of
  America
Forty-Five Ranch Enterprises
Fountain Products
Frank Knives
Fred F. Wells/Wells Sport Store
Gary Reeder Custom Guns
Gene's Custom Guns
Glimm's Custom Gun Engraving
Golden Age Arms Co.
Gournet Artistic Engraving
Grant, Howard V.
GRS/Glendo Corp.
Gun Room, The
Gurney, F. R.
Half Moon Rifle Shop
Harris Hand Engraving, Paul A.
Hawken Shop, The (See Dayton
  Traister)
Hiptmayer, Armurier
Hiptmayer, Heidemarie
Hofer Jagdwaffen, P.

J J Roberts Firearm Engraver
J.J. Roberts / Engraver
Jeff Flannery Engraving
Jim Blair Engraving
John J. Adams & Son Engravers
Kane, Edward
Kehr, Roger
Kelly, Lance
Ken Eyster Heritage Gunsmiths,
  Inc.
Kenneth W. Warren Engraver
Klingler Woodcarving
Koevenig's Engraving Service
Larry Lyons Gunworks
LeFever Arms Co., Inc.
Lindsay Engraving & Tools
McCombs, Leo
McDonald, Dennis
McKenzie, Lynton
Mele, Frank
Mid-America Recreation, Inc.
Nelson, Gary K.
New Orleans Jewelers Supply Co.
NgraveR Co., The
Oker's Engraving
Pedersen, C. R.
Pedersen, Rex C.
Peter Hale/Engraver
Piquette's Custom Engraving
Quality Custom Firearms
Rabeno, Martin
Ralph Bone Engraving
Reed, Dave
Reno, Wayne
Riggs, Jim
Robert Evans Engraving
Robert Valade Engraving
Robinson, Don
Rohner, Hans
Rohner, John
Rosser, Bob
Rundell's Gun Shop
Sam Welch Gun Engraving
Sampson, Roger
Schiffman, Mike
Sheffield Knifemakers Supply, Inc.
Sherwood, George
Singletary, Kent
Smith, Mark A.
Smith, Ron
Smokey Valley Rifles
SSK Industries
Steve Kamyk Engraver
Swanson, Mark
Terry Theis-Engraver
Thiewes, George W.
Thirion Gun Engraving, Denise
Viramontez Engraving
Vorhes, David
W.E. Brownell Checkering Tools
Wagoner, Vernon G.
Wallace, Terry
Warenski Engraving
Weber & Markin Custom
  Gunsmiths
Wells, Rachel
Wessinger Custom Guns &
  Engraving
Winchester Consultants

GAME CALLS

A.W. Peterson Gun Shop, Inc., The
African Import Co.
Bill Russ Trading Post
Bostick Wildlife Calls, Inc.
Cedar Hill Game Calls, LLC
Crit' R Calls
Crit'R Call (See Rocky Mountain
  Wildlife Products)
Custom Calls
D-Boone Ent., Inc.
Deepeeka Exports Pvt. Ltd.
DJ Illinois River Valley Calls, Inc.
Dr. O's Products Ltd.

Faulhaber Wildlocker
Faulk's Game Call Co., Inc.
Flambeau, Inc.
Glynn Scobey Duck & Goose Calls
Grand Slam Hunting Products
Green Head Game Call Co.
Hally Caller
Haydel's Game Calls, Inc.
Hunter's Specialties Inc.
Keowee Game Calls
Kolpin Outdoors, Inc.
Lohman Mfg. Co., Inc.
Mallardtone Game Calls
Moss Double Tone, Inc.
Oakman Turkey Calls
Original Deer Formula Co., The
Outdoor Sports Headquarters, Inc.
Pete Rickard, Inc.
Primos Hunting Calls
Protektor Model
Quaker Boy, Inc.
Sceery Game Calls
Sure-Shot Game Calls, Inc.
Tanglefree Industries
Tinks & Ben Lee Hunting Products
  (See Wellington Outdoors)
Tink's Safariland Hunting Corp.
Wellington Outdoors
Wilderness Sound Products Ltd.
Woods Wise Products

GAUGES, CALIPERS & MICROMETERS

Blue Ridge Machinery & Tools,
  Inc.
Gruning Precision, Inc.
Huntington Die Specialties
JGS Precision Tool Mfg., LLC
K&M Services
King & Co.
Spencer's Rifle Barrels, Inc.
Starrett Co., L. S.
Stoney Point Products, Inc.

GUN PARTS, U.S. & FOREIGN

"Su-Press-On", Inc.
A.A. Arms, Inc.
A.W. Peterson Gun Shop, Inc., The
Ahlman Guns
Amherst Arms
Antique Arms Co.
Armscorp USA, Inc.
Auto-Ordnance Corp.
B.A.C.
Ballard Rifle & Cartridge Co., LLC
Bar-Sto Precision Machine
Bear Mountain Gun & Tool
Billings Gunsmiths
Bill's Gun Repair
Bob's Gun Shop
Briese Bullet Co., Inc.
Brownells, Inc.
Bryan & Assoc.
Buffer Technologies
Cambos Outdoorsman
Cambos Outdoorsman
Cape Outfitters
Caspian Arms, Ltd.
CBC-BRAZIL
Century International Arms, Inc.
Chicasaw Gun Works
Chip McCormick Corp.
Cleland's Outdoor World, Inc.
Cole's Gun Works
Colonial Arms, Inc.
Colonial Repair
Colt's Mfg. Co., Inc.
Cylinder & Slide, Inc., William R.
  Laughridge
David R. Chicoine
Delta Arms Ltd.

PRODUCT & SERVICE DIRECTORY

DGR Custom Rifles
Dibble, Derek A.
Dixie Gun Works
Duane's Gun Repair (See DGR Custom Rifles)
Duffy, Charles E. (See Guns Antique & Modern DBA)
E.A.A. Corp.
Ed Brown Products, Inc.
EMF Co. Inc.
Enguix Import-Export
Entreprise Arms, Inc.
European American Armory Corp. (See E.A.A. Corp.)
Evolution Gun Works, Inc.
Falcon Industries, Inc.
Fleming Firearms
Fulton Armory
Gentry Custom LLC
Glimm's Custom Gun Engraving
Granite Mountain Arms, Inc.
Greider Precision
Gre-Tan Rifles
Gun Doc, Inc.
Gun Hunter Books (See Gun Hunter Trading Co.)
Gun Hunter Trading Co.
Gun Room Press, The
Gun Shop, The
Gun Works, The
Guns Antique & Modern DBA / Charles E. Duffy
Gunsmithing, Inc.
Hawken Shop, The (See Dayton Traister)
High Performance International
High Standard Mfg. Co./F.I., Inc.
Irwin, Campbell H.
Jack First, Inc.
Jamison's Forge Works
JG Airguns, LLC
Jonathan Arthur Ciener, Inc.
Kimber of America, Inc.
Knight's Manufacturing Co.
Krico Deutschland GmbH
LaFrance Specialties
Lampert, Ron
LaPrade
Laughridge, William R. (See Cylinder & Slide, Inc.)
Leapers, Inc.
List Precision Engineering
Lodewick, Walter H.
Logdewood Mfg.
Lomont Precision Bullets
Long, George F.
Markell, Inc.
Martin's Gun Shop
MCS, Inc.
Mid-America Recreation, Inc.
Mobile Area Networks, Inc.
Morrow, Bud
Mo's Competitor Supplies (See MCS, Inc.)
North Star West
Nu Line Guns
Numrich Gun Parts Corporation
Olathe Gun Shop
Olympic Arms Inc.
P.S.M.G. Gun Co.
Pacific Armament Corp
Peacemaker Specialists
Perazone-Gunsmith, Brian
Performance Specialists
Peter Dyson & Son Ltd.
Peterson Gun Shop, Inc., A.W.
Ranch Products
Randco UK
Ravell Ltd.
Retting, Inc., Martin B.
Romain's Custom Guns, Inc.
Ruger (See Sturm Ruger & Co., Inc.)
Rutgers Book Center
S&S Firearms

Sabatti SPA
Samco Global Arms, Inc.
Sarco, Inc.
Scherer Supplies
Shootin' Shack
Silver Ridge Gun Shop (See Goodwin Guns)
Simmons Gun Repair, Inc.
Smires, C. L.
Smith & Wesson
Southern Ammunition Co., Inc.
Southern Armory, The
Sportsmen's Exchange & Western Gun Traders, Inc.
Springfield Sporters, Inc.
Springfield, Inc.
Steyr Mannlicher GmbH & Co. KG
STI International
Strayer-Voigt, Inc.
Sturm Ruger & Co. Inc.
Sunny Hill Enterprises, Inc.
Swampfire Shop, The (See Peterson Gun Shop, Inc., A.W.)
T&S Industries, Inc.
Tank's Rifle Shop
Tarnhelm Supply Co., Inc.
Taylor's & Co., Inc.
Terry K. Kopp Professional Gunsmithing
Tom Forrest, Inc.
VAM Distribution Co. LLC
W. Waller & Son, Inc.
W.C. Wolff Co.
Walker Arms Co., Inc.
Wescombe, Bill (See North Star West)
Wild West Guns
Williams Mfg. of Oregon
Wilsom Combat
Winchester Sutler, Inc., The
Wise Guns, Dale
Wisners, Inc.

GUNS & GUN PARTS, REPLICA & ANTIQUE

A.W. Peterson Gun Shop, Inc., The
Ackerman & Co.
Ahlman Guns
Armi San Paolo
Auto-Ordnance Corp.
Ballard Rifle & Cartridge Co., LLC
Bear Mountain Gun & Tool
Billings Gunsmiths
Bob's Gun Shop
Buffalo Arms Co.
Cache La Poudre Rifleworks
Cash Mfg. Co./ TDC
CBC-BRAZIL
CCL Security Products
Chambers Flintlocks Ltd., Jim
Chicasaw Gun Works
Cimarron F.A. Co.
Cogar's Gunsmithing
Cole's Gun Works
Colonial Repair
Colt Blackpowder Arms Co.
Colt's Mfg. Co., Inc.
Custom Single Shot Rifles
Delhi Gun House
Delta Arms Ltd.
Dilliott Gunsmithing, Inc.
Dixie Gun Works
Dixon Muzzleloading Shop, Inc.
Ed's Gun House
Euroarms of America, Inc.
Flintlocks, Etc.
Getz Barrel Company
Golden Age Arms Co.
Gun Doc, Inc.
Gun Hunter Books (See Gun Hunter Trading Co.)
Gun Hunter Trading Co.
Gun Room Press, The
Gun Works, The

Hastings
Heidenstrom Bullets
Hunkeler, A. (See Buckskin Machine Works)
IAR Inc.
Imperial Miniature Armory
Ithaca Classic Doubles
Jack First, Inc.
JG Airguns, LLC
Ken Starnes Gunmaker
L&R Lock Co.
Leonard Day
List Precision Engineering
Lock's Philadelphia Gun Exchange
Logdewood Mfg.
Lone Star Rifle Company
Lucas, Edward E
Martin's Gun Shop
Mathews Gun Shop & Gunsmithing, Inc.
Mid-America Recreation, Inc.
Mowrey Gun Works
Navy Arms Company
Neumann GmbH
North Star West
Nu Line Guns
Numrich Gun Parts Corporation
Olathe Gun Shop
Parker & Sons Shooting Supply
Pasadena Gun Center
Peacemaker Specialists
Pecatonica River Longrifle
Peter Dyson & Son Ltd.
Pony Express Sport Shop
R.A. Wells Custom Gunsmith
Randco UK
Ravell Ltd.
Retting, Inc., Martin B.
Rutgers Book Center
S&S Firearms
Samco Global Arms, Inc.
Sarco, Inc.
Shootin' Shack
Silver Ridge Gun Shop (See Goodwin Guns)
Simmons Gun Repair, Inc.
Sklany's Machine Shop
Southern Ammunition Co., Inc.
Starr Trading Co., Jedediah
Stott's Creek Armory, Inc.
Taylor's & Co., Inc.
Tennessee Valley Mfg.
Tiger-Hunt Longrifle Gunstocks
Tristar Sporting Arms, Ltd.
Turnbull Restoration, Doug
Upper Missouri Trading Co.
VTI Gun Parts
Weber & Markin Custom Gunsmiths
Wescombe, Bill (See North Star West)
Whitestone Lumber Corp.
Winchester Sutler, Inc., The

GUNS, AIR

A.W. Peterson Gun Shop, Inc., The
Air Arms
Air Venture Airguns
AirForce Airguns
Airrow
Allred Bullet Co.
Arms Corporation of the Philippines
BEC, Inc.
Beeman Precision Airguns
Benjamin/Sheridan Co., Crosman
Bryan & Assoc.
BSA Guns Ltd.
Compasseco, Ltd.
Component Concepts, Inc.
Crosman Airguns
Daisy Outdoor Products
Daystate Ltd.
Domino

Dynamit Nobel-RWS, Inc.
Effebi SNC-Dr. Franco Beretta
European American Armory Corp. (See E.A.A. Corp.)
Feinwerkbau Westinger & Altenburger
Gamo USA, Inc.
Gaucher Armes, S.A.
Gun Room Press, The
Hammerli Service-Precision Mac
IAR Inc.
International Shooters Service
J.G. Anschutz GmbH & Co. KG
JG Airguns, LLC
Labanu Inc.
Leapers, Inc.
List Precision Engineering
Mac-1 Airgun Distributors
Marksman Products
Maryland Paintball Supply
Nationwide Airgun Repair
Olympic Arms Inc.
Pardini Armi Srl
Park Rifle Co., Ltd., The
Precision Airgun Sales, Inc.
Ripley Rifles
Robinson, Don
RWS (See U.S. Importer-Dynamit Nobel-RWS, Inc.)
Safari Arms/Schuetzen Pistol Works
Savage Arms, Inc.
Smith & Wesson
Steyr Mannlicher GmbH & Co. KG
Stone Enterprises Ltd.
Tippman Sports, LLC
Tristar Sporting Arms, Ltd.
Trooper Walsh
Visible Impact Targets
Walther GmbH, Carl
Webley and Scott Ltd.
Weihrauch KG, Hermann

GUNS, FOREIGN MANUFACTURER U.S. IMPORTER

A.W. Peterson Gun Shop, Inc., The
Accuracy Internationl Precision Rifles (See U.S.)
Accuracy Int'l. North America, Inc.
Ad Hominem
Air Arms
Armas Garbi, S.A.
Armas Kemen S. A. (See U.S. Importers)
Armi Perazzi S.P.A.
Armi San Marco (See Taylor's & Co.)
Armi Sport (See Cape Outfitters)
Arms Corporation of the Philippines
Armscorp USA, Inc.
Arrieta S.L.
Astra Sport, S.A.
Atamec-Bretton
AYA (See U.S. Importer-New England Custom Gun Serv
B.A.C.
B.C. Outdoors
BEC, Inc.
Benelli Armi S.P.A.
Benelli USA Corp.
Beretta Pietro S.P.A.
Beretta U.S.A. Corp.
Bernardelli, Vincenzo
Bersa S.A.
Bertuzzi (See U.S. Importer-New England Arms Co.)
Bill Hanus Birdguns, LLC
Blaser Jagdwaffen GmbH
Borovnik K.G., Ludwig
Bosis (See U.S. Importer-New England Arms Co.)
Brenneke GmbH

Browning Arms Co.
Bryan & Assoc.
BSA Guns Ltd.
Buchsenmachermeister
Cabanas (See U.S. Importer-Mandall Shooting Supply
Cabela's
Cache La Poudre Rifleworks
Cape Outfitters
CBC
Champlin Firearms, Inc.
Chapuis Armes
Churchill (See U.S. Importer-Ellett Bros.)
Collector's Armoury, Ltd.
Cosmi Americo & Figlio S.N.C.
Crucelegui, Hermanos (See U.S. Importer-Mandall)
Dakota (See U.S. Importer-EMF Co., Inc.)
Dakota Arms, Inc.
Daly, Charles/KBI
Davide Pedersoli and Co.
Domino
Dumoulin, Ernest
Eagle Imports, Inc.
EAW (See U.S. Importer-New England Custom Gun Serv
Ed's Gun House
Effebi SNC-Dr. Franco Beretta
EMF Co. Inc.
Euro-Imports
Eversull Co., Inc.
F.A.I.R.
Fabarm S.p.A.
FEG
Feinwerkbau Westinger & Altenburger
FERLIB
Fiocchi Munizioni S.A. (See U.S. Importer-Fiocch
Firearms Co. Ltd. / Alpine (See U.S. Importer-Mandall
Flintlocks, Etc.
Galaxy Imports Ltd., Inc.
Gamba Renato Bremec Srl
Gamo (See U.S. Importers-Arms United Corp., Daisy M
Gaucher Armes, S.A.
Gibbs Rifle Co., Inc.
Glock GmbH
Goergen's Gun Shop, Inc.
Griffin & Howe, Inc.
Griffin & Howe, Inc.
Grulla Armes
Hammerli AG
Hammerli USA
Hartford (See U.S. Importer-EMF Co. Inc.)
Hartmann & Weiss GmbH
Heckler & Koch, Inc.
Hege Jagd-u. Sporthandels GmbH
Helwan (See U.S. Importer-Interarms)
Hofer Jagdwaffen, P.
Holland & Holland Ltd.
Howa Machinery, Ltd.
I.A.B. (See U.S. Importer-Taylor's & Co., Inc.)
IAR Inc.
IGA (See U.S. Importer-Stoeger Industries)
Imperial Magnum Corp.
Imperial Miniature Armory
Inter Ordnance of America LP
International Shooters Service
Intrac Arms International
J.G. Anschutz GmbH & Co. KG
JSL (See U.S. Importer-Specialty Shooters Supply)
K. Eversull Co., Inc.
Kimar (See U.S. Importer-IAR, Inc.)
Korth Germany GmbH
Krico Deutschland GmbH

PRODUCT & SERVICE DIRECTORY

Krieghoff Gun Co., H.
Lakefield Arms Ltd. (See Savage Arms, Inc.)
Laurona Armas Eibar, S.A.L.
Lebeau-Courally
Lever Arms Service Ltd.
Lomont Precision Bullets
London Guns Ltd.
Marocchi F.lli S.p.A
Mauser Werke Oberndorf Waffensysteme GmbH
McCann Industries
MEC-Gar S.R.L.
Merkel
Mitchell's Mauser
Morini (See U.S. Importers-Mandall Shooting Supplies, Inc.)
Nammo Lapua Oy
New England Custom Gun Service
New SKB Arms Co.
Norica, Avnda Otaola
Norinco
Norma Precision AB (See U.S. Importers-Dynamit)
OK Weber, Inc.
Para-Ordnance Mfg., Inc.
Pardini Armi Srl
Perugini Visini & Co. S.r.l.
Peters Stahl GmbH
Pietta (See U.S. Importers-Navy Arms Co, Taylor's
Piotti (See U.S. Importer-Moore & Co., Wm. Larkin)
PMC/Eldorado Cartridge Corp.
Powell & Son (Gunmakers) Ltd., William
Prairie Gun Works
Rizzini F.lli (See U.S. Importers-Wm. Larkin Moore & Co., N.E. Arms Corp.)
Rizzini SNC
Robinson Armament Co.
Rossi Firearms
Rottweil Compe
Rutten (See U.S. Importer-Labanu Inc.)
RWS (See U.S. Importer-Dynamit Nobel-RWS, Inc.)
S.A.R.L. G. Granger
S.I.A.C.E. (See U.S. Importer-IAR Inc.)
Sabatti SPA
Sako Ltd. (See U.S. Importer-Stoeger Industries)
San Marco (See U.S. Importers-Cape Outfitters-EMF Co., Inc.
Sarsilmaz Shotguns-Turkey (see B.C. Outdoors)
Sauer (See U.S. Importers-Paul Co., The Sigarms Inc.)
Savage Arms (Canada), Inc.
SGS Importer's International, Inc.
SIG
Sigarms Inc.
SIG-Sauer (See U.S. Importer-Sigarms, Inc.)
SKB Shotguns
Small Arms Specialists
Societa Armi Bresciane Srl (See U.S. Importer-Cape Outfitters)
Sphinx Systems Ltd.
Springfield Armory
Springfield, Inc.
Steyr Mannlicher GmbH & Co. KG
T.F.C. S.p.A.
Tanfoglio Fratelli S.r.l.
Tanner (See U.S. Importer-Mandall Shooting Supplies, Inc.)
Taurus International Firearms (See U.S. Importer Taurus Firearms, Inc.)
Taurus S.A. Forjas

Techno Arms (See U.S. Importer-Auto-Ordnance Corp.)
Tikka (See U.S. Importer-Stoeger Industries)
TOZ (See U.S. Importer-Nygord Precision Products, Inc.)
Ugartechea S. A., Ignacio
Ultralux (See U.S. Importer-Keng's Firearms Specialty, Inc.)
Valtro USA, Inc.
Verney-Carron
Voere-KGH GmbH
Walther GmbH, Carl
Webley and Scott Ltd.
Weihrauch KG, Hermann
Westley Richards & Co. Ltd.
Yankee Gunsmith "Just Glocks"
Zabala Hermanos S.A.

GUNS, FOREIGN-IMPORTER

A.W. Peterson Gun Shop, Inc., The
Accuracy International
AcuSport Corporation
Auto-Ordnance Corp.
B.A.C.
B.C. Outdoors
Bell's Legendary Country Wear
Benelli USA Corp.
Bill Hanus Birdguns, LLC
Bridgeman Products
British Sporting Arms
Browning Arms Co.
Caesar Guerini USA, Inc.
Cape Outfitters
Century International Arms, Inc.
Champion Shooters' Supply
Champion's Choice, Inc.
Cimarron F.A. Co.
CVA
CZ USA
Dixie Gun Works
Dynamit Nobel-RWS, Inc.
E&L Mfg., Inc.
E.A.A. Corp.
Eagle Imports, Inc.
Ellett Bros.
EMF Co. Inc.
Euroarms of America, Inc.
Eversull Co., Inc.
Fiocchi of America, Inc.
Flintlocks, Etc.
Franzen International, Inc. (See U.S. Importer-Importer Co.)
G.U., Inc. (See U.S. Importer-New SKB Arms Co.)
Galaxy Imports Ltd., Inc.
Gamba, USA
Gamo USA, Inc.
Giacomo Sporting USA
Glock, Inc.
GSI, Inc.
Gun Shop, The
Guncraft Books (See Guncraft Sports, Inc.)
Guncraft Sports, Inc.
Gunsite Training Center
Hammerli USA
IAR Inc.
Imperial Magnum Corp.
Imperial Miniature Armory
Intrac Arms International
K. Eversull Co., Inc.
K.B.I. Inc.
Kemen America
Keng's Firearms Specialty, Inc./US Tactical Systems
Krieghoff International, Inc.
Labanu Inc.
Legacy Sports International
Lion Country Supply
London Guns Ltd.
Magnum Research, Inc.
Marlin Firearms Co.

Marx, Harry (See U.S. Importer for FERLIB)
MCS, Inc.
MEC-Gar U.S.A., Inc.
Mitchell Mfg. Corp.
Navy Arms Company
New England Arms Co.
OK Weber, Inc.
Orvis Co., The
P.S.M.G. Gun Co.
Para-Ordnance, Inc.
Paul Co., The
Perazone-Gunsmith, Brian
Perazzi U.S.A. Inc.
Powell Agency, William
Quality Arms, Inc.
Rocky Mountain Armoury
S.D. Meacham
Safari Arms/Schuetzen Pistol Works
Samco Global Arms, Inc.
Savage Arms, Inc.
Scott Fine Guns Inc., Thad
SGS Importer's International, Inc.
Sigarms Inc.
SKB Shotguns
Small Arms Specialists
Southern Ammunition Co., Inc.
Specialty Shooters Supply, Inc.
Springfield, Inc.
Stoeger Industries
Stone Enterprises Ltd.
Swarovski Optik North America Ltd.
Taurus Firearms, Inc.
Taylor's & Co., Inc.
Track of the Wolf, Inc.
Traditions Performance Firearms
Tristar Sporting Arms, Ltd.
Trooper Walsh
U.S. Importer-Wm. Larkin Moore
VAM Distribution Co. LLC
Vector Arms, Inc.
VTI Gun Parts
Westley Richards Agency USA (See U.S. Importer
Wingshooting Adventures
Yankee Gunsmith "Just Glocks"

GUNS, SURPLUS, PARTS & AMMUNITION

A.W. Peterson Gun Shop, Inc., The
Ahlman Guns
Alpha 1 Drop Zone
Armscorp USA, Inc.
B.A.C.
Bob's Gun Shop
Cambos Outdoorsman
Century International Arms, Inc.
Cole's Gun Works
Delta Arms Ltd.
Ed's Gun House
Firearm Brokers
Fleming Firearms
Fulton Armory
Garcia National Gun Traders, Inc.
Gun City
Gun Hunter Books (See Gun Hunter Trading Co.)
Gun Hunter Trading Co.
Gun Room Press, The
Hank's Gun Shop
Hege Jagd-u. Sporthandels GmbH
Ken Starnes Gunmaker
LaRocca Gun Works
Lever Arms Service Ltd.
Log Cabin Sport Shop
Martin B. Retting Inc.
Martin's Gun Shop
Navy Arms Company
Numrich Gun Parts Corporation
Oil Rod and Gun Shop
Olathe Gun Shop
Paragon Sales & Services, Inc.

Pasadena Gun Center
Power Plus Enterprises, Inc.
Ravell Ltd.
Retting, Inc., Martin B.
Rutgers Book Center
Samco Global Arms, Inc.
Sarco, Inc.
Shootin' Shack
Silver Ridge Gun Shop (See Goodwin Guns)
Simmons Gun Repair, Inc.
Sportsmen's Exchange & Western Gun Traders, Inc.
Springfield Sporters, Inc.
T.F.C. S.p.A.
Tarnhelm Supply Co., Inc.
Taylor's & Co., Inc.
Whitestone Lumber Corp.
Williams Shootin' Iron Service, The Lynx-Line

GUNS, U.S. MADE

3-Ten Corp.
A.A. Arms, Inc.
A.W. Peterson Gun Shop, Inc., The
Accu-Tek
Acra-Bond Laminates
Ad Hominem
Airrow
Allred Bullet Co.
American Derringer Corp.
AR-7 Industries, LLC
ArmaLite, Inc.
Armscorp USA, Inc.
A-Square Co.
Austin & Halleck, Inc.
Auto-Ordnance Corp.
Ballard Rifle & Cartridge Co., LLC
Barrett Firearms Manufacturer, Inc.
Bar-Sto Precision Machine
Benjamin/Sheridan Co., Crosman
Beretta Pietro S.P.A.
Beretta U.S.A. Corp.
Bill Hanus Birdguns, LLC
Bill Russ Trading Post
Bond Arms, Inc.
Borden Ridges Rimrock Stocks
Borden Rifles Inc.
Brockman's Custom Gunsmithing
Browning Arms Co.
Bryan & Assoc.
Bushmaster Firearms, Inc.
C. Sharps Arms Co. Inc./Montana Armory
Cabela's
Cache La Poudre Rifleworks
Cambos Outdoorsman
Cape Outfitters
Casull Arms Corp.
CCL Security Products
Champlin Firearms, Inc.
Charter 2000
Cobra Enterprises, Inc.
Colt's Mfg. Co., Inc.
Competitor Corp., Inc.
Competitor Corp., Inc.
Conetrol Scope Mounts
Connecticut Shotgun Mfg. Co.
Connecticut Valley Classics (See CVC, BPI)
Cooper Arms
Crosman Airguns
Cumberland Arms
CVA
Dakota Arms, Inc.
Dan Wesson Firearms
Dayton Traister
Detonics USA
Dixie Gun Works
Downsizer Corp.
DS Arms, Inc.
DunLyon R&D, Inc.
E&L Mfg., Inc.

E. Arthur Brown Co. Inc.
Eagle Arms, Inc. (See ArmaLite, Inc.)
Ed Brown Products, Inc.
Ed Brown Products, Inc.
Ellett Bros.
Emerging Technologies, Inc. (See Laseraim Technologies, Inc.)
Empire Rifles
Entreprise Arms, Inc.
Essex Arms
Excel Industries, Inc.
Firearm Brokers
Fletcher-Bidwell, LLC
FN Manufacturing
Freedom Arms, Inc.
Fulton Armory
Galena Industries AMT
Garcia National Gun Traders, Inc.
Gary Reeder Custom Guns
Genecco Gun Works
Gentry Custom LLC
George Hoenig, Inc.
Gibbs Rifle Co.
Gil Hebard Guns, Inc.
Gilbert Equipment Co., Inc.
Goergen's Gun Shop, Inc.
Granite Mountain Arms, Inc.
Gun Room Press, The
Gun Works, The
Guncrafter Industries
H&R 1871.LLC
Hammans, Charles E.
Hammerli USA
Harrington & Richardson (See H&R 1871, Inc.)
Hart & Son, Inc.
Hatfield Gun
Hawken Shop, The (See Dayton Traister)
Heritage Firearms (See Heritage Mfg., Inc.)
Heritage Manufacturing, Inc.
Hesco-Meprolight
High Precision
High Standard Mfg. Co./F.I., Inc.
Hi-Point Firearms/MKS Supply
HJS Arms, Inc.
Hoehn Sales, Inc.
H-S Precision, Inc.
Hutton Rifle Ranch
IAR Inc.
Imperial Miniature Armory
Israel Arms Inc.
Ithaca Classic Doubles
Ithaca Gun Company LLC
Ithaca Guns USA, LLC
Jim Norman Custom Gunstocks
John Rigby & Co.
John's Custom Leather
JP Enterprises, Inc.
K.B.I. Inc.
Kahr Arms
Kehr, Roger
Kelbly, Inc.
Kel-Tec CNC Industries, Inc.
Keystone Sporting Arms, Inc. (Crickett Rifles)
Kimber of America, Inc.
Knight Firearms
Knight's Manufacturing Co.
Kolar
L.A.R. Mfg., Inc.
LaFrance Specialties
Lakefield Arms Ltd. (See Savage Arms, Inc.)
Laseraim Technologies, Inc.
Les Baer Custom, Inc.
Lever Arms Service Ltd.
Ljutic Industries, Inc.
Lock's Philadelphia Gun Exchange
Lomont Precision Bullets
Lone Star Rifle Company
Mag-Na-Port International, Inc.
Magnum Research, Inc.

Marlin Firearms Co.
Marshall Fish Mfg. Gunsmith Sptg. Co.
Mathews Gun Shop & Gunsmithing, Inc.
Maverick Arms, Inc.
McCann Industries
Meacham Tool & Hardware Co., Inc.
Mid-America Recreation, Inc.
Miller Arms, Inc.
MKS Supply, Inc. (See Hi-Point Firearms)
MOA Corporation
Montana Armory, Inc.
MPI Stocks
Navy Arms Company
NCP Products, Inc.
New Ultra Light Arms, LLC
Noreen, Peter H.
North American Arms, Inc.
North Star West
Nowlin Mfg. Co.
Olympic Arms Inc.
Oregon Arms, Inc. (See Rogue Rifle Co., Inc.)
P&M Sales & Services, LLC
Parker & Sons Shooting Supply
Parker Gun Finishes
Phoenix Arms
Police Bookshelf
Precision Small Arms Inc.
ProWare, Inc.
Rapine Bullet Mould Mfg. Co.
Remington Arms Co., Inc.
Rifles, Inc.
Robinson Armament Co.
Rock River Arms
Rogue Rifle Co., Inc./Chipmunk Rifles
Rogue River Rifleworks
Rohrbaugh
Romain's Custom Guns, Inc.
RPM
Ruger (See Sturm Ruger & Co., Inc.)
Safari Arms/Schuetzen Pistol Works
Savage Arms (Canada), Inc.
Schumakers Gun Shop
Searcy Enterprises
Sharps Arms Co., Inc., C.
Sigarms Inc.
Sklany's Machine Shop
Small Arms Specialists
Smith & Wesson
Sound Tech
Spencer's Rifle Barrels, Inc.
Springfield Armory
Springfield, Inc.
SSK Industries
STI International
Stoeger Industries
Strayer-Voigt, Inc.
Sturm Ruger & Co. Inc.
Sunny Hill Enterprises, Inc.
T&S Industries, Inc.
Taconic Firearms Ltd., Perry Lane
Tank's Rifle Shop
Tar-Hunt Custom Rifles, Inc.
Taurus Firearms, Inc.
Taylor's & Co., Inc.
Texas Armory (See Bond Arms, Inc.)
Thompson/Center Arms
Time Precision
Tippman Sports, LLC
Tristar Sporting Arms, Ltd.
U.S. Repeating Arms Co., Inc.
Uselton/Arms, Inc.
Vector Arms, Inc.
Visible Impact Targets
Volquartsen Custom Ltd.
Wallace, Terry
Weatherby, Inc.

Wescombe, Bill (See North Star West)
Wessinger Custom Guns & Engraving
Whitestone Lumber Corp.
Wichita Arms, Inc.
Wildey F. A., Inc.
Wilsom Combat
Winchester Consultants
Z-M Weapons

GUNSMITH SCHOOL

American Gunsmithing Institute
Colorado Gunsmithing Academy
Colorado School of Trades
Cylinder & Slide, Inc., William R. Laughridge
Gun Doc, Inc.
Lassen Community College, Gunsmithing Dept.
Laughridge, William R. (See Cylinder & Slide, Inc.)
Log Cabin Sport Shop
Modern Gun Repair School
Murray State College
North American Correspondence Schools, The Gun Pro
Nowlin Mfg. Co.
NRI Gunsmith School
Pennsylvania Gunsmith School
Piedmont Community College
Pine Technical College
Professional Gunsmiths of America
Smith & Wesson
Southeastern Community College
Spencer's Rifle Barrels, Inc.
Trinidad St. Jr. Col. Gunsmith Dept.
Wright's Gunstock Blanks
Yavapai College

GUNSMITH SUPPLIES, TOOLS & SERVICES

A.W. Peterson Gun Shop, Inc., The
Alaskan Silversmith, The
Aldis Gunsmithing & Shooting Supply
Alley Supply Co.
Allred Bullet Co.
Alpec Team, Inc.
American Gunsmithing Institute
Ballard Rifle & Cartridge Co., LLC
Bar-Sto Precision Machine
Battenfeld Technologies, Inc.
Bauska Barrels
Bear Mountain Gun & Tool
Bengtson Arms Co., L.
Bill's Gun Repair
Blue Ridge Machinery & Tools, Inc.
Boyds' Gunstock Industries, Inc.
Briley Mfg. Inc.
Brockman's Custom Gunsmithing
Brownells, Inc.
Bryan & Assoc.
B-Square Company, Inc.
Buffer Technologies
Bushmaster Firearms, Inc.
C.S. Van Gorden & Son, Inc.
Cain's Outdoors, Inc.
Carbide Checkering Tools (See J&R Engineering)
Caywood, Shane J.
CBC-BRAZIL
Chapman Manufacturing Co.
Chicasaw Gun Works
Chip McCormick Corp.
Choate Machine & Tool Co., Inc.
Colonial Arms, Inc.
Colorado School of Trades
Colt's Mfg. Co., Inc.
Conetrol Scope Mounts

Cousin Bob's Mountain Products
CRR, Inc./Marble's Inc.
Cumberland Arms
Custom Checkering Service, Kathy Forster
Dan's Whetstone Co., Inc.
D'Arcy Echols & Co.
Dem-Bart Checkering Tools, Inc.
Dem-Bart Checkering Tools, Inc.
Dixie Gun Works
Dixie Gun Works
Dremel Mfg. Co.
Du-Lite Corp.
Ed Brown Products, Inc.
Entreprise Arms, Inc.
Evolution Gun Works, Inc.
Faith Associates
FERLIB
Fisher, Jerry A.
Forgreens Tool & Mfg., Inc.
Forster, Kathy (See Custom Checkering)
Forster Products, Inc.
Gentry Custom LLC
Gilmore Sports Concepts, Inc.
Grace Metal Products
Gre-Tan Rifles
Gruning Precision, Inc.
Gun Works, The
Gunline Tools
Half Moon Rifle Shop
Hammond Custom Guns Ltd.
Hastings
Henriksen Tool Co., Inc.
High Performance International
High Precision
Holland's Gunsmithing
Ironsighter Co.
Israel Arms Inc.
Ivanoff, Thomas G. (See Tom's Gun Repair)
J&R Engineering
J&S Heat Treat
J. Dewey Mfg. Co., Inc.
Jack First, Inc.
Jantz Supply, Inc.
Jenkins Recoil Pads
JGS Precision Tool Mfg., LLC
Jonathan Arthur Ciener, Inc.
Jones Custom Products, Neil A.
Kailua Custom Guns Inc.
Kasenit Co., Inc.
Kleinendorst, K. W.
Korzinek Riflesmith, J.
L. E. Jurras & Assoc.
LaBounty Precision Reboring, Inc
LaFrance Specialties
Laurel Mountain Forge
Lee Supplies, Mark
List Precision Engineering
Lock's Philadelphia Gun Exchange
London Guns Ltd.
Mahovsky's Metalife
Marble Arms (See CRR, Inc./Marble's Inc.)
Mark Lee Supplies
Marsh, Mike
Martin's Gun Shop
McFarland, Stan
Menck, Gunsmith Inc., T.W.
Metalife Industries (See Mahovsky's Metalife)
Micro Sight Co.
Midway Arms, Inc.
MMC
Mo's Competitor Supplies (See MCS, Inc.)
Mowrey's Guns & Gunsmithing
Neil A. Jones Custom Products
New England Custom Gun Service
NgraveR Co., The
Ole Frontier Gunsmith Shop
Olympic Arms Inc.
Parker & Sons Shooting Supply
Parker Gun Finishes

Parker Gun Finishes
Paulsen Gunstocks
Perazone-Gunsmith, Brian
Peter Dyson & Son Ltd.
Power Custom, Inc.
Practical Tools, Inc.
Precision Specialties
R.A. Wells Custom Gunsmith
Ranch Products
Ransom International Corp.
Reardon Products
Rice, Keith (See White Rock Tool & Die)
Richards MicroFit Stocks, Inc.
Robar Co., Inc., The
Romain's Custom Guns, Inc.
Royal Arms Gunstocks
Rusteprufe Laboratories
Score High Gunsmithing
SGS Importer's International, Inc.
Sharp Shooter Supply
Shooter's Choice Gun Care
Simmons Gun Repair, Inc.
Smith Abrasives, Inc.
Southern Bloomer Mfg. Co.
Spencer's Rifle Barrels, Inc.
Spradlin's
Starrett Co., L. S.
Stiles Custom Guns
Stoney Point Products, Inc.
Sullivan, David S. (See Westwind Rifles, Inc.)
Sunny Hill Enterprises, Inc.
T&S Industries, Inc.
T.W. Mench Gunsmith, Inc.
Tank's Rifle Shop
Tar-Hunt Custom Rifles, Inc.
Terry Theis-Engraver
Texas Platers Supply Co.
Tom's Gun Repair, Thomas G. Ivanoff
Track of the Wolf, Inc.
Trinidad St. Jr. Col. Gunsmith Dept.
Trulock Tool
Turnbull Restoration, Doug
United States Products Co.
Van Gorden & Son Inc., C. S.
Venco Industries, Inc. (See Shooter's Choice Gun Care)
Volquartsen Custom Ltd.
W.C. Wolff Co.
Warne Manufacturing Co.
Washita Mountain Whetstone Co.
Weigand Combat Handguns, Inc.
Wessinger Custom Guns & Engraving
White Rock Tool & Die
Wilcox All-Pro Tools & Supply
Wild West Guns
Will-Burt Co.
Williams Gun Sight Co.
Williams Shootin' Iron Service, The Lynx-Line
Willow Bend
Windish, Jim
Wise Guns, Dale
Wright's Gunstock Blanks
Yavapai College
Ziegel Engineering

HANDGUN ACCESSORIES

A.A. Arms, Inc.
A.W. Peterson Gun Shop, Inc., The
Action Direct, Inc.
ADCO Sales, Inc.
Advantage Arms, Inc.
Aimtech Mount Systems
Ajax Custom Grips, Inc.
Alpha 1 Drop Zone
American Derringer Corp.
Arms Corporation of the Philippines

Astra Sport, S.A.
Bagmaster Mfg., Inc.
Bar-Sto Precision Machine
Behlert Precision, Inc.
Berry's Mfg., Inc.
Blue and Gray Products Inc. (See Ox-Yoke Originals)
Bond Custom Firearms
Bowen Classic Arms Corp.
Bridgeman Products
Broken Gun Ranch
Brooks Tactical Systems-Agrip
Bushmaster Hunting & Fishing
Butler Creek Corp.
Cannon Safe, Inc.
Centaur Systems, Inc.
Central Specialties Ltd. (See Trigger Lock Division)
Charter 2000
Cheyenne Pioneer Products
Chicasaw Gun Works
Clark Custom Guns, Inc.
Classic Arms Company
Concealment Shop, Inc., The
Conetrol Scope Mounts
Crimson Trace Lasers
CRR, Inc./Marble's Inc.
Cylinder & Slide, Inc., William R. Laughridge
D&L Industries (See D.J. Marketing)
D.J. Marketing
Dade Screw Machine Products
Dan Wesson Firearms
Delhi Gun House
DeSantis Holster & Leather Goods, Inc.
Dina Arms Corporation
Dixie Gun Works
Doskocil Mfg. Co., Inc.
E&L Mfg., Inc.
E. Arthur Brown Co. Inc.
E.A.A. Corp.
Eagle Imports, Inc.
Ed Brown Products, Inc.
Ed Brown Products, Inc.
Essex Arms
European American Armory Corp. (See E.A.A. Corp.)
Evolution Gun Works, Inc.
Falcon Industries, Inc.
Feinwerkbau Westinger & Altenburger
Fisher Custom Firearms
Fleming Firearms
Freedom Arms, Inc.
G.G. & G.
Galati International
GALCO International Ltd.
Garcia National Gun Traders, Inc.
Garthwaite Pistolsmith, Inc., Jim
Gil Hebard Guns, Inc.
Gilmore Sports Concepts, Inc.
Glock, Inc.
Gould & Goodrich Leather, Inc.
Gun Works, The
Gun-Alert
Gun-Ho Sports Cases
H.K.S. Products
Hafner World Wide, Inc.
Hammerli USA
Heinie Specialty Products
Henigson & Associates, Steve
High Standard Mfg. Co./F.I., Inc.
Hill Speed Leather, Ernie
HIP-GRIP Barami Corp.
Hi-Point Firearms/MKS Supply
Hobson Precision Mfg. Co.
Hoppe's Div. Penguin Industries, Inc.
H-S Precision, Inc.
Hume, Don
Hunter Co., Inc.
Impact Case & Container, Inc.
Jarvis, Inc.

PRODUCT & SERVICE DIRECTORY

JB Custom
Jim Noble Co.
John's Custom Leather
Jonathan Arthur Ciener, Inc.
JP Enterprises, Inc.
Kalispel Case Line
KeeCo Impressions, Inc.
Keller Co., The
King's Gun Works
KK Air International (See Impact Case & Container Co., Inc.)
Kolpin Outdoors, Inc.
L&S Technologies Inc. (See Aimtech Mount Systems)
Lakewood Products LLC
LaserMax
Les Baer Custom, Inc.
Lock's Philadelphia Gun Exchange
Lohman Mfg. Co., Inc.
Mag-Na-Port International, Inc.
Mag-Pack Corp.
Marble Arms (See CRR, Inc./Marble's Inc.)
Markell, Inc.
MEC-Gar S.R.L.
Menck, Gunsmith Inc., T.W.
Middlebrooks Custom Shop
Millett Sights
Mogul Co./Life Jacket
MTM Molded Products Co., Inc.
No-Sho Mfg. Co.
Numrich Gun Parts Corporation
Outdoor Sports Headquarters, Inc.
Ox-Yoke Originals, Inc.
Pachmayr Div. Lyman Products
Pager Pal
Parker & Sons Shooting Supply
Pearce Grip, Inc.
Phoenix Arms
Police Bookshelf
Practical Tools, Inc.
Precision Small Arms Inc.
Protector Mfg. Co., Inc., The
Ram-Line ATK
Ranch Products
Ransom International Corp.
RPM
SGS Importer's International, Inc.
Simmons Gun Repair, Inc.
Southern Bloomer Mfg. Co.
Springfield Armory
Springfield, Inc.
SSK Industries
Sturm Ruger & Co. Inc.
T.F.C. S.p.A.
Tactical Defense Institute
Tanfoglio Fratelli S.r.l.
Thompson/Center Arms
Trigger Lock Division / Central Specialties Ltd.
Trijicon, Inc.
Triple-K Mfg. Co., Inc.
Truglo, Inc.
United States Products Co.
Universal Sports
Volquartsen Custom Ltd.
W. Waller & Son, Inc.
W.C. Wolff Co.
Warne Manufacturing Co.
Weigand Combat Handguns, Inc.
Wessinger Custom Guns & Engraving
Whitestone Lumber Corp.
Wichita Arms, Inc.
Wild West Guns
Williams Gun Sight Co.
Wilsom Combat
Yankee Gunsmith "Just Glocks"
Ziegel Engineering

HANDGUN GRIPS

A.A. Arms, Inc.
A.W. Peterson Gun Shop, Inc., The
African Import Co.

Ahrends Grips
Ajax Custom Grips, Inc.
Altamont Co.
American Derringer Corp.
Arms Corporation of the Philippines
Art Jewel Enterprises Ltd.
Baelder, Harry
Bob's Gun Shop
Boone Trading Co., Inc.
Boone's Custom Ivory Grips, Inc.
Boyds' Gunstock Industries, Inc.
Brooks Tactical Systems-Agrip
Clark Custom Guns, Inc.
Claro Walnut Gunstock Co.
Cole-Grip
Colonial Repair
Crimson Trace Lasers
Cylinder & Slide, Inc., William R. Laughridge
Dan Wesson Firearms
Dixie Gun Works
Dolbare, Elizabeth
E.A.A. Corp.
Eagle Imports, Inc.
Ed Brown Products, Inc.
EMF Co. Inc.
Essex Arms
European American Armory Corp. (See E.A.A. Corp.)
Falcon Industries, Inc.
Feinwerkbau Westinger & Altenburger
Fisher Custom Firearms
Garthwaite Pistolsmith, Inc., Jim
Goodwin's Guns
Herrett's Stocks, Inc.
High Standard Mfg. Co./F.I., Inc.
HIP-GRIP Barami Corp.
Hogue Grips
H-S Precision, Inc.
Huebner, Corey O.
International Shooters Service
Israel Arms Inc.
John Masen Co. Inc.
KeeCo Impressions, Inc.
Korth Germany GmbH
Les Baer Custom, Inc.
Lett Custom Grips
Linebaugh Custom Sixguns
Lyman Products Corp.
Michaels of Oregon Co.
Millett Sights
Mobile Area Networks, Inc.
N.C. Ordnance Co.
Newell, Robert H.
Northern Precision
Pachmayr Div. Lyman Products
Pardini Armi Srl
Parker & Sons Shooting Supply
Pearce Grip, Inc.
Precision Small Arms Inc.
Radical Concepts
Robinson, Don
Rosenberg & Son, Jack A.
Roy's Custom Grips
Spegel, Craig
Stoeger Industries
Sturm Ruger & Co. Inc.
Sunny Hill Enterprises, Inc.
Tactical Defense Institute
Taurus Firearms, Inc.
Tirelli
Tom Forrest, Inc.
Triple-K Mfg. Co., Inc.
Uncle Mike's (See Michaels of Oregon, Co.)
Volquartsen Custom Ltd.
Western Mfg. Co.
Whitestone Lumber Corp.
Wright's Gunstock Blanks

HEARING PROTECTORS

A.W. Peterson Gun Shop, Inc., The

Aero Peltor
Ajax Custom Grips, Inc.
Browning Arms Co.
Creedmoor Sports, Inc.
David Clark Co., Inc.
Dillon Precision Products, Inc.
Dixie Gun Works
E-A-R, Inc.
Electronic Shooters Protection, Inc.
Gentex Corp.
Gun Room Press, The
Gunsmithing, Inc.
Hoppe's Div. Penguin Industries, Inc.
Kesselring Gun Shop
Parker & Sons Shooting Supply
Paterson Gunsmithing
Peltor, Inc. (See Aero Peltor)
Police Bookshelf
R.E.T. Enterprises
Ridgeline, Inc.
Rucker Dist. Inc.
Silencio/Safety Direct
Tactical Defense Institute
Triple-K Mfg. Co., Inc.
Watson Bullets
Whitestone Lumber Corp.

HOLSTERS & LEATHER GOODS

A.A. Arms, Inc.
A.W. Peterson Gun Shop, Inc., The
Action Direct, Inc.
Action Products, Inc.
Aker International, Inc.
AKJ Concealco
Alessi Holsters, Inc.
Arratoonian, Andy (See Horseshoe Leather Products)
Bagmaster Mfg., Inc.
Bandcor Industries, Div. of Man-Sew Corp.
Bang-Bang Boutique (See Holster Shop, The)
Beretta Pietro S.P.A.
Bianchi International, Inc.
Bond Arms, Inc.
Brooks Tactical Systems-Agrip
Browning Arms Co.
Bull-X, Inc.
Cape Outfitters
Cathey Enterprises, Inc.
Chace Leather Products
Churchill Glove Co., James
Cimarron F.A. Co.
Classic Old West Styles
Clements' Custom Leathercraft, Chas
Cobra Sport S.R.I.
Collector's Armoury, Ltd.
Colonial Repair
Counter Assault
Delhi Gun House
DeSantis Holster & Leather Goods, Inc.
Dillon Precision Products, Inc.
Dixie Gun Works
Eagle Imports, Inc.
El Paso Saddlery Co.
Ellett Bros.
EMF Co. Inc.
Faust Inc., T. G.
Freedom Arms, Inc.
Gage Manufacturing
GALCO International Ltd.
Garcia National Gun Traders, Inc.
Gil Hebard Guns, Inc.
Gilmore Sports Concepts, Inc.
GML Products, Inc.
Gould & Goodrich Leather, Inc.
Gun Leather Limited
Gun Works, The
Hafner World Wide, Inc.

HandCrafts Unltd. (See Clements' Custom Leathercraft)
Hank's Gun Shop
Heinie Specialty Products
Henigson & Associates, Steve
Hill Speed Leather, Ernie
HIP-GRIP Barami Corp.
Hobson Precision Mfg. Co.
Hogue Grips
Horseshoe Leather Products
Hume, Don
Hunter Co., Inc.
Jeff's Outfitters
Jim Noble Co.
John's Custom Leather
Keller Co., The
Kirkpatrick Leather Co.
Kolpin Outdoors, Inc.
Korth Germany GmbH
Kramer Handgun Leather
L.A.R. Mfg., Inc.
Lawrence Leather Co.
Lock's Philadelphia Gun Exchange
Lone Star Gunleather
Markell, Inc.
Marksman Products
Michaels of Oregon Co.
Minute Man High Tech Industries
Navy Arms Company
No-Sho Mfg. Co.
Null Holsters Ltd. K.L.
October Country Muzzleloading
Oklahoma Leather Products, Inc.
Old West Reproductions, Inc. R.M. Bachman
Outdoor Connection, Inc., The
Pager Pal
Parker & Sons Shooting Supply
Pathfinder Sports Leather
Protektor Model
PWL Gunleather
Ramon B. Gonzalez Guns
Renegade
Ringler Custom Leather Co.
Rogue Rifle Co., Inc./Chipmunk Rifles
S&S Firearms
Safariland Ltd., Inc.
Scharch Mfg., Inc.-Top Brass
Schulz Industries
Second Chance Body Armor
SGS Importer's International, Inc.
Silhouette Leathers
Smith Saddlery, Jesse W.
Sparks, Milt
Stalker, Inc.
Starr Trading Co., Jedediah
Strong Holster Co.
Stuart, V. Pat
Tabler Marketing
Tactical Defense Institute
Ted Blocker Holsters
Tex Shoemaker & Sons, Inc.
Thad Rybka Custom Leather Equipment
Torel, Inc./Tandy Brands Outdoors/AA & E
Triple-K Mfg. Co., Inc.
Tristar Sporting Arms, Ltd.
Uncle Mike's (See Michaels of Oregon, Co.)
Venus Industries
W. Waller & Son, Inc.
Walt's Custom Leather, Walt Whinnery
Watson Bullets
Westley Richards & Co. Ltd.
Whinnery, Walt (See Walt's Custom Leather)
Wild Bill's Originals
Wilsom Combat

HUNTING & CAMP GEAR, CLOTHING, ETC.

A.W. Peterson Gun Shop, Inc., The
Action Direct, Inc.
Action Products, Inc.
Adventure 16, Inc.
All Rite Products, Inc.
Alpha 1 Drop Zone
Armor (See Buck Stop Lure Co., Inc.)
Atlanta Cutlery Corp.
Atsko/Sno-Seal, Inc.
Bagmaster Mfg., Inc.
Barbour, Inc.
Bauer, Eddie
Bear Archery
Beaver Park Product, Inc.
Beretta Pietro S.P.A.
Better Concepts Co.
Bill Russ Trading Post
Bob Allen Sportswear
Boonie Packer Products
Boss Manufacturing Co.
Browning Arms Co.
Buck Stop Lure Co., Inc.
Bushmaster Hunting & Fishing
Cambos Outdoorsman
Cambos Outdoorsman
Camp-Cap Products
Carhartt, Inc.
Churchill Glove Co., James
Clarkfield Enterprises, Inc.
Classic Old West Styles
Clements' Custom Leathercraft, Chas
Coghlan's Ltd.
Cold Steel Inc.
Coleman Co., Inc.
Coulston Products, Inc.
Counter Assault
Dakota Corp.
Danner Shoe Mfg. Co.
Deepeeka Exports Pvt. Ltd.
Dr. O's Products Ltd.
Duofold, Inc.
Dynalite Products, Inc.
E-A-R, Inc.
Flambeau, Inc.
Forrest Tool Co.
Fox River Mills, Inc.
Frontier
G&H Decoys, Inc.
Gerber Legendary Blades
Glacier Glove
Grand Slam Hunting Products
HandCrafts Unltd. (See Clements' Custom Leathercraft)
High North Products, Inc.
Hinman Outfitters, Bob
Hodgman, Inc.
Houtz & Barwick
Hunter's Specialties Inc.
James Churchill Glove Co.
John's Custom Leather
K&M Industries, Inc.
Kamik Outdoor Footwear
Kolpin Outdoors, Inc.
L.L. Bean, Inc.
LaCrosse Footwear, Inc.
Leapers, Inc.
MAG Instrument, Inc.
Mag-Na-Port International, Inc.
McCann Industries
Murphy, R.R. Co., Inc.
Original Deer Formula Co., The
Orvis Co., The
Palsa Outdoor Products
Partridge Sales Ltd., John
Pointing Dog Journal, Village Press Publications
Powell & Son (Gunmakers) Ltd., William
Pro-Mark Div. of Wells Lamont
Ringler Custom Leather Co.

Rocky Shoes & Boots
Scansport, Inc.
Sceery Game Calls
Schaefer Shooting Sports
Servus Footwear Co.
Simmons Outdoor Corp.
Sno-Seal, Inc. (See Atsko/Sno-
    Seal, Inc.)
Swanndri New Zealand
TEN-X Products Group
Tink's Safariland Hunting Corp.
Torel, Inc./Tandy Brands
    Outdoors/AA & E
Triple-K Mfg. Co., Inc.
Tru-Nord Compass
United Cutlery Corp.
Venus Industries
Walls Industries, Inc.
Wideview Scope Mount Corp.
Wilderness Sound Products Ltd.
Winchester Sutler, Inc., The
Wolverine Footwear Group
Woolrich, Inc.
Wyoming Knife Corp.
Yellowstone Wilderness Supply

KNIVES & KNIFEMAKER'S SUPPLIES

A.G. Russell Knives, Inc.
A.W. Peterson Gun Shop, Inc., The
Action Direct, Inc.
Adventure 16, Inc.
African Import Co.
Aitor-Berrizargo S.L.
American Target Knives
Art Jewel Enterprises Ltd.
Atlanta Cutlery Corp.
B&D Trading Co., Inc.
Barteaux Machete
Benchmark Knives (See Gerber
    Legendary Blades)
Beretta Pietro S.P.A.
Beretta U.S.A. Corp.
Bill Russ Trading Post
Boker USA, Inc.
Boone Trading Co., Inc.
Boone's Custom Ivory Grips, Inc.
Bowen Knife Co.
Brooks Tactical Systems-Agrip
Browning Arms Co.
Buck Knives, Inc.
Buster's Custom Knives
Cain's Outdoors, Inc.
Camillus Cutlery Co.
Campbell, Dick
Case & Sons Cutlery Co., W R
Chicago Cutlery Co.
Claro Walnut Gunstock Co.
Clements' Custom Leathercraft,
    Chas
Cold Steel Inc.
Coleman Co., Inc.
Collector's Armoury, Ltd.
Compass Industries, Inc.
Creative Craftsman, Inc., The
Crosman Blades (See Coleman
    Co., Inc.)
CRR, Inc./Marble's Inc.
Cutco Cutlery
damascususa@inteliport.com
Dan's Whetstone Co., Inc.
Deepeeka Exports Pvt. Ltd.
Delhi Gun House
DeSantis Holster & Leather
    Goods, Inc.
Diamond Machining Technology
    Inc. (See DMT)
Dixie Gun Works
Dolbare, Elizabeth
EdgeCraft Corp., S. Weiner
Empire Cutlery Corp.
Eze-Lap Diamond Prods.
Flitz International Ltd.

Forrest Tool Co.
Forthofer's Gunsmithing &
    Knifemaking
Fortune Products, Inc.
Frank Knives
Frost Cutlery Co.
Galati International
George Ibberson (Sheffield) Ltd.
Gerber Legendary Blades
Glock, Inc.
Golden Age Arms Co.
Gun Room, The
Gun Works, The
H&B Forge Co.
Hafner World Wide, Inc.
Hammans, Charles E.
HandCrafts Unltd. (See Clements'
    Custom Leathercraft)
Harris Publications
High North Products, Inc.
Hoppe's Div. Penguin Industries,
    Inc.
Hunter Co., Inc.
J.A. Blades, Inc. (See Christopher
    Firearms Co.)
J.A. Henckels Zwillingswerk Inc.
Jantz Supply, Inc.
Jenco Sales, Inc.
Jim Blair Engraving
Johnson Wood Products
KA-BAR Knives
Kasenit Co., Inc.
Kershaw Knives
Knifeware, Inc.
Koval Knives
Lamson & Goodnow Mfg. Co.
Lansky Sharpeners
Leapers, Inc.
Leatherman Tool Group, Inc.
Lethal Force Institute (See Police
    Bookshelf)
Linder Solingen Knives
Marble Arms (See CRR,
    Inc./Marble's Inc.)
Marshall Fish Mfg. Gunsmith
    Sptg. Co.
Matthews Cutlery
McCann Industries
Normark Corp.
October Country Muzzleloading
Outdoor Edge Cutlery Corp.
Plaza Cutlery, Inc.
Queen Cutlery Co.
R&C Knives & Such
R. Murphy Co., Inc.
Randall-Made Knives
Robert Valade Engraving
Scansport, Inc.
Schiffman, Mike
Sheffield Knifemakers Supply, Inc.
Smith Saddlery, Jesse W.
Springfield Armory
Spyderco, Inc.
Starr Trading Co., Jedediah
T.F.C. S.p.A.
Terry Theis-Engraver
Traditions Performance Firearms
Traditions Performance Firearms
Tru-Balance Knife Co.
Tru-Nord Compass
United Cutlery Corp.
Utica Cutlery Co.
Venus Industries
W.R. Case & Sons Cutlery Co.
Washita Mountain Whetstone Co.
Wells Creek Knife & Gun Works
Wenger North America/Precise
    Int'l.
Western Cutlery (See Camillus
    Cutlery Co.)
Whinnery, Walt (See Walt's
    Custom Leather)
Wideview Scope Mount Corp.
Wyoming Knife Corp.

LABELS, BOXES & CARTRIDGE HOLDERS

Ballistic Products, Inc.
Berry's Mfg., Inc.
Cabinet Mtn. Outfitters Scents &
    Lures
Cheyenne Pioneer Products
Del Rey Products
DeSantis Holster & Leather
    Goods, Inc.
Flambeau, Inc.
Hafner World Wide, Inc.
J&J Products, Inc.
Kolpin Outdoors, Inc.
Liberty Shooting Supplies
Midway Arms, Inc.
MTM Molded Products Co., Inc.
Outdoor Connection, Inc., The
Walt's Custom Leather, Walt
    Whinnery
Ziegel Engineering

LEAD WIRES & WIRE CUTTERS

Ames Metal Products Co.
Big Bore Express
Bullet Swaging Supply, Inc.
Corbin Mfg. & Supply, Inc.
D.L. Unmussig Bullets
Liberty Mfg., Inc.
Lightning Performance
    Innovations, Inc.
Montana Precision Swaging
Northern Precision
Sport Flite Manufacturing Co.
Star Ammunition, Inc.

LOAD TESTING & PRODUCT TESTING

Ballistic Research
Bridgeman Products
Briese Bullet Co., Inc.
Buckskin Bullet Co.
Claybuster Wads & Harvester
    Bullets
Clearview Products
Dead Eye's Sport Center
Defense Training International,
    Inc.
Duane's Gun Repair (See DGR
    Custom Rifles)
Gruning Precision, Inc.
H.P. White Laboratory, Inc.
Hank's Gun Shop
Henigson & Associates, Steve
Hutton Rifle Ranch
J&J Sales
Jensen Bullets
Jonathan Arthur Ciener, Inc.
L. E. Jurras & Assoc.
L.B.T.
Liberty Shooting Supplies
Linebaugh Custom Sixguns
Lomont Precision Bullets
McMurdo, Lynn
Middlebrooks Custom Shop
Modern Gun Repair School
Multiplex International
Oil Rod and Gun Shop
Plum City Ballistic Range
R.A. Wells Custom Gunsmith
Rupert's Gun Shop
SOS Products Co. (See Buck Stix-
    SOS Products Co.)
Spencer's Rifle Barrels, Inc.
Tar-Hunt Custom Rifles, Inc.
Trinidad St. Jr. Col. Gunsmith
    Dept.
Vulpes Ventures, Inc., Fox
    Cartridge Division

W. Square Enterprises
X-Spand Target Systems

LOADING BLOCKS, METALLIC & SHOTSHELL

A.W. Peterson Gun Shop, Inc., The
Battenfeld Technologies, Inc.
Buffalo Arms Co.
Huntington Die Specialties
Jericho Tool & Die Co., Inc.
Sinclair International, Inc.

LUBRISIZERS, DIES & ACCESSORIES

A.W. Peterson Gun Shop, Inc., The
Ballisti-Cast, Inc.
Buffalo Arms Co.
Cast Performance Bullet Company
Cooper-Woodward Perfect Lube
Eagan Gunsmiths
GAR
Hart & Son, Inc.
Javelina Lube Products
Lee Precision, Inc.
Lithi Bee Bullet Lube
Lyman Products Corp.
Magma Engineering Co.
PWM Sales Ltd.
RCBS Operations/ATK
S&S Firearms
SPG, Inc.
Thompson Bullet Lube Co.
United States Products Co.
WTA Manufacturing

MOULDS & MOULD ACCESSORIES

A.W. Peterson Gun Shop, Inc., The
Ad Hominem
American Products, Inc.
Ballisti-Cast, Inc.
Buffalo Arms Co.
Bullet Swaging Supply, Inc.
Cast Performance Bullet Company
Davide Pedersoli and Co.
Eagan Gunsmiths
GAR
Gun Works, The
Huntington Die Specialties
L.B.T.
Lee Precision, Inc.
Lyman Products Corp.
Magma Engineering Co.
MEC-Gar S.R.L.
Old West Bullet Moulds
Pacific Rifle Co.
Penn Bullets
Peter Dyson & Son Ltd.
Rapine Bullet Mould Mfg. Co.
RCBS Operations/ATK
S&S Firearms

MUZZLE-LOADING GUNS, BARRELS & EQUIPMENT

A.W. Peterson Gun Shop, Inc., The
Accuracy Unlimited
Ackerman & Co.
Allen Mfg.
Armi San Paolo
Austin & Halleck, Inc.
Bentley, John
Big Bore Express
Birdsong & Assoc., W. E.
Black Powder Products
Blount/Outers ATK
Blue and Gray Products Inc. (See
    Ox-Yoke Originals)

Buckskin Bullet Co.
Bullberry Barrel Works, Ltd.
Butler Creek Corp.
Cabela's
Cache La Poudre Rifleworks
Cain's Outdoors, Inc.
California Sights (See Fautheree,
    Andy)
Cash Mfg. Co./ TDC
Caywood Gunmakers
CBC-BRAZIL
Chambers Flintlocks Ltd., Jim
Chicasaw Gun Works
Cimarron F.A. Co.
Claybuster Wads & Harvester
    Bullets
Cogar's Gunsmithing
Colonial Repair
Colt Blackpowder Arms Co.
Cousin Bob's Mountain Products
Cumberland Arms
Curly Maple Stock Blanks (See
    Tiger-Hunt)
CVA
Dangler, Homer L.
Davide Pedersoli and Co.
Dayton Traister
deHaas Barrels
Delhi Gun House
Dixie Gun Works
Dixie Gun Works
Dixon Muzzleloading Shop, Inc.
Dolbare, Elizabeth
Ellett Bros.
EMF Co. Inc.
Euroarms of America, Inc.
Flintlocks, Etc.
Fort Hill Gunstocks
Fowler, Bob (See Black Powder
    Products)
Frontier
Getz Barrel Company
Goergen's Gun Shop, Inc.
Golden Age Arms Co.
Green Mountain Rifle Barrel Co.,
    Inc.
Gun Works, The
H&R 1871.LLC
Hastings
Hawken Shop, The
Hawken Shop, The (See Dayton
    Traister)
Hege Jagd-u. Sporthandels GmbH
Hodgdon Powder Co.
Hoppe's Div. Penguin Industries,
    Inc.
Hornady Mfg. Co.
House of Muskets, Inc., The
Hunkeler, A. (See Buckskin
    Machine Works)
Hydra-Tone Chemicals, Inc.
IAR Inc.
Impact Case & Container, Inc.
Ironsighter Co.
J. Dewey Mfg. Co., Inc.
Jamison's Forge Works
K&M Industries, Inc.
Kalispel Case Line
Kennedy Firearms
Knight Rifles
Knight Rifles (See Modern
    Muzzleloading, Inc.)
Kolar
L&R Lock Co.
L&S Technologies Inc. (See
    Aimtech Mount Systems)
Lakewood Products LLC
Lodgewood Mfg.
Log Cabin Sport Shop
Lothar Walther Precision Tool Inc.
Lyman Products Corp.
Markesbery Muzzle Loaders, Inc.
Mathews Gun Shop &
    Gunsmithing, Inc.
McCann, Tom

Michaels of Oregon Co.
Millennium Designed
  Muzzleloaders
Modern Muzzleloading, Inc.
Mowrey Gun Works
Navy Arms Company
Newman Gunshop
North Star West
October Country Muzzleloading
Oklahoma Leather Products, Inc.
Olson, Myron
Orion Rifle Barrel Co.
Ox-Yoke Originals, Inc.
Pacific Rifle Co.
Parker & Sons Shooting Supply
Parker Gun Finishes
Pecatonica River Longrifle
Peter Dyson & Son Ltd.
Pioneer Arms Co.
Rossi Firearms
S&S Firearms
Selsi Co., Inc.
Simmons Gun Repair, Inc.
Sklany's Machine Shop
Smokey Valley Rifles
South Bend Replicas, Inc.
Southern Bloomer Mfg. Co.
Splitfire Sporting Goods, L.L.C.
Starr Trading Co., Jedediah
Stone Mountain Arms
Sturm Ruger & Co. Inc.
Taylor's & Co., Inc.
Tennessee Valley Mfg.
Thompson Bullet Lube Co.
Thompson/Center Arms
Track of the Wolf, Inc.
Traditions Performance Firearms
Truglo, Inc.
Uncle Mike's (See Michaels of
  Oregon, Co.)
Universal Sports
Upper Missouri Trading Co.
Venco Industries, Inc. (See
  Shooter's Choice Gun Care)
Village Restorations & Consulting,
  Inc.
Virgin Valley Custom Guns
Voere-KGH GmbH
W.E. Birdsong & Assoc.
Warne Manufacturing Co.
Wescombe, Bill (See North Star
  West)
White Rifles, Inc.
William E. Phillips Firearms
Woodworker's Supply
Wright's Gunstock Blanks
Young Country Arms
Ziegel Engineering

PISTOLSMITH

A.W. Peterson Gun Shop, Inc., The
Acadian Ballistic Specialties
Accuracy Unlimited
Adair Custom Shop, Bill
Ahlman Guns
Aldis Gunsmithing & Shooting
  Supply
Alpha Precision, Inc.
Alpine Indoor Shooting Range
Armament Gunsmithing Co., Inc.
Bain & Davis, Inc.
Bar-Sto Precision Machine
Behlert Precision, Inc.
Bengtson Arms Co., L.
Bill Adair Custom Shop
Billings Gunsmiths
Bowen Classic Arms Corp.
Broken Gun Ranch
Caraville Manufacturing
Chicasaw Gun Works
Chip McCormick Corp.
Clark Custom Guns, Inc.
Colonial Repair
Colorado School of Trades

Colt's Mfg. Co., Inc.
Corkys Gun Clinic
Cylinder & Slide, Inc., William R.
  Laughridge
D&D Gunsmiths, Ltd.
D&L Sports
David R. Chicoine
Dayton Traister
Dilliott Gunsmithing, Inc.
Ellicott Arms, Inc. / Woods
  Pistolsmithing
Evolution Gun Works, Inc.
Ferris Firearms
Firearm Brokers
Fisher Custom Firearms
Forkin Custom Classics
G.G. & G.
Garthwaite Pistolsmith, Inc., Jim
Gary Reeder Custom Guns
Genecco Gun Works
Gentry Custom LLC
Greider Precision
Gun Doc, Inc.
Gun Works, The
Guncraft Sports, Inc.
Guncraft Sports, Inc.
Gunsite Training Center
Hamilton, Alex B. (See Ten-Ring
  Precision, Inc.)
Hammerli Service-Precision Mac
Hammond Custom Guns Ltd.
Hank's Gun Shop
Hanson's Gun Center, Dick
Hawken Shop, The (See Dayton
  Traister)
Heinie Specialty Products
High Bridge Arms, Inc.
High Standard Mfg. Co./F.I., Inc.
Highline Machine Co.
Hoag, James W.
Irwin, Campbell H.
Ivanoff, Thomas G. (See Tom's
  Gun Repair)
J&S Heat Treat
Jackalope Gun Shop
Jarvis, Inc.
Jensen's Custom Ammunition
Jungkind, Reeves C.
Kaswer Custom, Inc.
Ken Starnes Gunmaker
Kilham & Co.
King's Gun Works
La Clinique du .45
LaFrance Specialties
LaRocca Gun Works
Lathrop's, Inc.
Lawson, John G. (See Sight Shop,
  The)
Leckie Professional Gunsmithing
Les Baer Custom, Inc.
Linebaugh Custom Sixguns
List Precision Engineering
Long, George F.
Mag-Na-Port International, Inc.
Mahovsky's Metalife
Marvel, Alan
Mathews Gun Shop &
  Gunsmithing, Inc.
MCS, Inc.
Middlebrooks Custom Shop
Miller Custom
Mitchell's Accuracy Shop
MJK Gunsmithing, Inc.
Modern Gun Repair School
Mo's Competitor Supplies (See
  MCS, Inc.)
Mowrey's Guns & Gunsmithing
Mullis Guncraft
NCP Products, Inc.
Novak's, Inc.
Nowlin Mfg. Co.
Nu Line Guns
Olathe Gun Shop
Paris, Frank J.
Pasadena Gun Center

Peacemaker Specialists
Performance Specialists
Peterson Gun Shop, Inc., A.W.
Piquette's Custom Engraving
Power Custom, Inc.
Precision Specialties
Ramon B. Gonzalez Guns
Randco UK
Ries, Chuck
Rim Pac Sports, Inc.
Robar Co., Inc., The
RPM
Ruger's Custom Guns
Score High Gunsmithing
Shooters Supply
Shootin' Shack
Sight Shop, The
Singletary, Kent
Spradlin's
Springfield, Inc.
SSK Industries
Swenson's 45 Shop, A. D.
Swift River Gunworks
Ten-Ring Precision, Inc.
Terry K. Kopp Professional
  Gunsmithing
Time Precision
Tom's Gun Repair, Thomas G.
  Ivanoff
Turnbull Restoration, Doug
Vic's Gun Refinishing
Volquartsen Custom Ltd.
Walker Arms Co., Inc.
Walters Industries
Wardell Precision
Wessinger Custom Guns &
  Engraving
White Barn Wor
Wichita Arms, Inc.
Wild West Guns
Williams Gun Sight Co.
Williamson Precision
  Gunsmithing
Wilsom Combat
Wright's Gunstock Blanks

POWDER MEASURES, SCALES, FUNNELS & ACCESSORIES

4-D Custom Die Co.
A.W. Peterson Gun Shop, Inc., The
Battenfeld Technologies, Inc.
Buffalo Arms Co.
Cain's Outdoors, Inc.
Davide Pedersoli and Co.
Dillon Precision Products, Inc.
Fremont Tool Works
Frontier
GAR
High Precision
Hoehn Sales, Inc.
Jones Custom Products, Neil A.
Modern Muzzleloading, Inc.
Neil A. Jones Custom Products
Pacific Rifle Co.
Precision Reloading, Inc.
Ramon B. Gonzalez Guns
RCBS Operations/ATK
Redding Reloading Equipment
Saunders Gun & Machine Shop
Schumakers Gun Shop
Spencer's Rifle Barrels, Inc.
Vega Tool Co.
VibraShine, Inc.
VTI Gun Parts

PRESS ACCESSORIES, METALLIC

A.W. Peterson Gun Shop, Inc., The
Buffalo Arms Co.
Hollywood Engineering
Huntington Die Specialties

MA Systems, Inc.
R.E.I.
Redding Reloading Equipment
Thompson Tool Mount
Vega Tool Co.

PRESS ACCESSORIES, SHOTSHELL

A.W. Peterson Gun Shop, Inc., The
Hollywood Engineering
Lee Precision, Inc.
MEC, Inc.
Precision Reloading, Inc.
R.E.I.

PRESSES, ARBOR

A.W. Peterson Gun Shop, Inc., The
Blue Ridge Machinery & Tools,
  Inc.
Hoehn Sales, Inc.
K&M Services
RCBS Operations/ATK
Spencer's Rifle Barrels, Inc.

PRESSES, METALLIC

4-D Custom Die Co.
A.W. Peterson Gun Shop, Inc., The
Austin Sheridan USA, Inc.
Battenfeld Technologies, Inc.
Dillon Precision Products, Inc.
Fremont Tool Works
Hornady Mfg. Co.
Huntington Die Specialties
Lee Precision, Inc.
Meacham Tool & Hardware Co.,
  Inc.
Midway Arms, Inc.
R.E.I.
Ramon B. Gonzalez Guns
RCBS Operations/ATK
Spencer's Rifle Barrels, Inc.

PRESSES, SHOTSHELL

A.W. Peterson Gun Shop, Inc., The
Ballistic Products, Inc.
Dillon Precision Products, Inc.
Hornady Mfg. Co.
MEC, Inc.
Precision Reloading, Inc.
Spolar Power Load, Inc.

PRESSES, SWAGE

A.W. Peterson Gun Shop, Inc., The
Bullet Swaging Supply, Inc.
Corbin Mfg. & Supply, Inc.
Howell Machine, Inc.

PRIMING TOOLS & ACCESSORIES

A.W. Peterson Gun Shop, Inc., The
Bald Eagle Precision Machine Co.
GAR
Hart & Son, Inc.
Huntington Die Specialties
K&M Services
RCBS Operations/ATK
Simmons, Jerry
Sinclair International, Inc.

REBORING & RERIFLING

Ahlman Guns
Barrel & Gunworks
Bauska Barrels
BlackStar AccuMax Barrels
BlackStar Barrel Accurizing (See
  BlackStar AccuMax)
Buffalo Arms Co.

Champlin Firearms, Inc.
Ed's Gun House
Fred F. Wells/Wells Sport Store
Ivanoff, Thomas G. (See Tom's
  Gun Repair)
Jonathan Arthur Ciener, Inc.
LaBounty Precision Reboring, Inc
NCP Products, Inc.
Pence Precision Barrels
Redman's Rifling & Reboring
Rice, Keith (See White Rock Tool
  & Die)
Ridgetop Sporting Goods
Savage Arms, Inc.
Shaw, Inc., E. R. (See Small Arms
  Mfg. Co.)
Siegrist Gun Shop
Simmons Gun Repair, Inc.
Stratco, Inc.
Terry K. Kopp Professional
  Gunsmithing
Time Precision
Tom's Gun Repair, Thomas G.
  Ivanoff
Turnbull Restoration, Doug
Van Patten, J. W.
White Rock Tool & Die

RELOADING TOOLS AND ACCESSORIES

4-D Custom Die Co.
Advance Car Mover Co., Rowell
  Div.
American Products, Inc.
Ammo Load Worldwide, Inc.
Armfield Custom Bullets
Armite Laboratories Inc.
Arms Corporation of the
  Philippines
Atsko/Sno-Seal, Inc.
Bald Eagle Precision Machine Co.
Ballistic Products, Inc.
BC-Handmade Bullets
Berger Bullets Ltd.
Berry's Mfg., Inc.
Blount, Inc., Sporting Equipment
  Div.
Blue Mountain Bullets
Blue Ridge Machinery & Tools,
  Inc.
Bonanza (See Forster Products)
BRP, Inc. High Performance Cast
  Bullets
Brynin, Milton
Buck Stix-SOS Products Co.
Buffalo Arms Co.
C&D Special Products (See
  Claybuster Wads & Harvester
  Bullets)
Camdex, Inc.
Canyon Cartridge Corp.
Case Sorting System
CCI/Speer Div of ATK
CH Tool & Die Co. (See 4-D
  Custom Die Co.)
CheVron Bullets
Claybuster Wads & Harvester
  Bullets
Cook Engineering Service
Cumberland Arms
Curtis Cast Bullets
Custom Products (See Jones
  Custom Products)
CVA
D.C.C. Enterprises
Davide Pedersoli and Co.
Davis, Don
Davis Products, Mike
Denver Instrument Co.
Dillon Precision Products, Inc.
Dropkick
E&L Mfg., Inc.
Eagan Gunsmiths
Eichelberger Bullets, Wm.

Enguix Import-Export
Euroarms of America, Inc.
E-Z-Way Systems
Federated-Fry (See Fry Metals)
Ferguson, Bill
Fisher Custom Firearms
Flambeau, Inc.
Flitz International Ltd.
Forster Products, Inc.
Fremont Tool Works
Fry Metals
Gehmann, Walter (See Huntington Die Specialties)
Graf & Sons
Graphics Direct
Graves Co.
Green, Arthur S.
Greenwood Precision
Gun City
Hanned Line, The
Hanned Precision (See The Hanned Line)
Harrell's Precision
Harris Enterprises
Harrison Bullets
Heidenstrom Bullets
High Precision
Hirtenberger AG
Hodgdon Powder Co.
Holland's Gunsmithing
Hornady Mfg. Co.
Howell Machine, Inc.
Hunters Supply, Inc.
Hutton Rifle Ranch
Image Ind. Inc.
Imperial Magnum Corp.
INTEC International, Inc.
Iosso Products
J&L Superior Bullets (See Huntington Die Specialties)
Jack First, Inc.
Javelina Lube Products
JLK Bullets
Jonad Corp.
Jones Custom Products, Neil A.
Jones Moulds, Paul
K&M Services
Kapro Mfg. Co. Inc. (See R.E.I.)
Knoell, Doug
Korzinek Riflesmith, J.
L.A.R. Mfg., Inc.
L.E. Wilson, Inc.
Le Clear Industries (See E-Z-Way Systems)
Lee Precision, Inc.
Liberty Mfg., Inc.
Liberty Shooting Supplies
Lightning Performance Innovations, Inc.
Lithi Bee Bullet Lube
Littleton, J. F.
Lock's Philadelphia Gun Exchange
Lortone Inc.
Lyman Instant Targets, Inc. (See Lyman Products Corp.)
Lyman Products Corp.
MA Systems, Inc.
Magma Engineering Co.
Match Prep-Doyle Gracey
Mayville Engineering Co. (See MEC, Inc.)
MCS, Inc.
MEC, Inc.
Midway Arms, Inc.
MI-TE Bullets
Montana Armory, Inc.
Mo's Competitor Supplies (See MCS, Inc.)
MTM Molded Products Co., Inc.
MWG Co.
Nammo Lapua Oy
Navy Arms Company
Newman Gunshop
North Devon Firearms Services
Old West Bullet Moulds

Outdoor Sports Headquarters, Inc.
Paragon Sales & Services, Inc.
Pinetree Bullets
Ponsness, Warren
Professional Hunter Supplies
Pro-Shot Products, Inc.
Protector Mfg. Co., Inc., The
R.A. Wells Custom Gunsmith
R.E.I.
Rapine Bullet Mould Mfg. Co.
Redding Reloading Equipment
Reloading Specialties, Inc.
Rice, Keith (See White Rock Tool & Die)
Rochester Lead Works
Rooster Laboratories
Rorschach Precision Products
SAECO (See Redding Reloading Equipment)
Sandia Die & Cartridge Co.
Saunders Gun & Machine Shop
Saville Iron Co. (See Greenwood Precision)
Seebeck Assoc., R.E.
Sharp Shooter Supply
Sharps Arms Co., Inc., C.
Sierra Specialty Prod. Co.
Silver Eagle Machining
Skip's Machine
Sno-Seal, Inc. (See Atsko/Sno-Seal, Inc.)
SOS Products Co. (See Buck Stix-SOS Products Co.)
Spencer's Rifle Barrels, Inc.
SPG, Inc.
SSK Industries
Stalwart Corporation
Star Custom Bullets
Stillwell, Robert
Stoney Point Products, Inc.
Stratco, Inc.
Taracorp Industries, Inc.
TCCI
TCSR
Tetra Gun Care
Thompson/Center Arms
Vega Tool Co.
Venco Industries, Inc. (See Shooter's Choice Gun Care)
VibraShine, Inc.
Vibra-Tek Co.
Vihtavuori Oy/Kaltron-Pettibone
Vitt/Boos
W.B. Niemi Engineering
W.J. Riebe Co.
WD-40 Co.
Webster Scale Mfg. Co.
White Rock Tool & Die
Widener's Reloading & Shooting Supply, Inc.
Wise Custom Guns
Woodleigh (See Huntington Die Specialties)
Yesteryear Armory & Supply
Young Country Arms

RESTS BENCH, PORTABLE AND ACCESSORIES

A.W. Peterson Gun Shop, Inc., The
Adventure 16, Inc.
Armor Metal Products
B.M.F. Activator, Inc.
Bald Eagle Precision Machine Co.
Bald Eagle Precision Machine Co.
Bartlett Engineering
Battenfeld Technologies, Inc.
Blount/Outers ATK
Browning Arms Co.
B-Square Company, Inc.
Clift Mfg., L. R.
Desert Mountain Mfg.
Greenwood Precision
Harris Engineering Inc.

Hart & Son, Inc.
Hidalgo, Tony
Hoehn Sales, Inc.
Hoppe's Div. Penguin Industries, Inc.
J&J Sales
Keng's Firearms Specialty, Inc./US Tactical Systems
Kolpin Outdoors, Inc.
Kramer Designs
Midway Arms, Inc.
Millett Sights
Outdoor Connection, Inc., The
Protektor Model
Ransom International Corp.
Russ Haydon's Shooters' Supply
Saville Iron Co. (See Greenwood Precision)
Sinclair International, Inc.
Six Enterprises
Stoney Point Products, Inc.
Tonoloway Tack Drives
Torel, Inc./Tandy Brands Outdoors/AA & E
Varmint Masters, LLC
Wichita Arms, Inc.
York M-1 Conversion
Zanotti Armor, Inc.
Ziegel Engineering

RIFLE BARREL MAKER

Airrow
American Safe Arms, Inc.
Barrel & Gunworks
Bauska Barrels
BlackStar AccuMax Barrels
BlackStar Barrel Accurizing (See BlackStar AccuMax)
Border Barrels Ltd.
Buchsenmachermeister
Bullberry Barrel Works, Ltd.
Bushmaster Firearms, Inc.
Carter's Gun Shop
Christensen Arms
Cincinnati Swaging
D.L. Unmussig Bullets
deHaas Barrels
Dilliott Gunsmithing, Inc.
Dina Arms Corporation
DKT, Inc.
Donnelly, C. P.
Douglas Barrels, Inc.
Fred F. Wells/Wells Sport Store
Gaillard Barrels
Getz Barrel Company
Getz Barrel Company
Granite Mountain Arms, Inc.
Green Mountain Rifle Barrel Co., Inc.
Gruning Precision, Inc.
Gun Works, The
Half Moon Rifle Shop
Hart Rifle Barrels, Inc.
Hastings
Hofer Jagdwaffen, P.
H-S Precision, Inc.
Krieger Barrels, Inc.
Les Baer Custom, Inc.
Lilja Precision Rifle Barrels
Lothar Walther Precision Tool Inc.
Martini & Hagn, Ltd.
McGowen Rifle Barrels
McMillan Rifle Barrels
Mid-America Recreation, Inc.
Modern Gun Repair School
Morrison Precision
Obermeyer Rifled Barrels
Olympic Arms Inc.
Orion Rifle Barrel Co.
PAC-NOR Barreling
Pence Precision Barrels
Perazone-Gunsmith, Brian
Rogue Rifle Co., Inc./Chipmunk Rifles

Sabatti SPA
Savage Arms, Inc.
Schneider Rifle Barrels, Inc.
Shaw, Inc., E. R. (See Small Arms Mfg. Co.)
Shilen, Inc.
Siskiyou Gun Works (See Donnelly, C. P.)
Small Arms Mfg. Co.
Specialty Shooters Supply, Inc.
Spencer's Rifle Barrels, Inc.
Steyr Mannlicher GmbH & Co. KG
Strutz Rifle Barrels, Inc., W. C.
Swift River Gunworks
Terry K. Kopp Professional Gunsmithing
Turnbull Restoration, Doug
Verney-Carron
Virgin Valley Custom Guns
William E. Phillips Firearms
Wilson Arms Co., The
Wiseman and Co., Bill

SCOPES, MOUNTS, ACCESSORIES, OPTICAL EQUIPMENT

A.R.M.S., Inc.
A.W. Peterson Gun Shop, Inc., The
Accu-Tek
Ackerman, Bill (See Optical Services Co.)
Action Direct, Inc.
ADCO Sales, Inc.
Aimpoint, Inc.
Aimtech Mount Systems
Air Venture Airguns
All Rite Products, Inc.
Alpec Team, Inc.
Apel GmbH, Ernst
ArmaLite, Inc.
B.A.C.
B.M.F. Activator, Inc.
Bansner's Ultimate Rifles, LLC
Barrett Firearms Manufacturer, Inc.
Beaver Park Product, Inc.
BEC, Inc.
Beeman Precision Airguns
Benjamin/Sheridan Co., Crosman
Bill Russ Trading Post
BKL Technologies
Blount, Inc., Sporting Equipment Div.
Blount/Outers ATK
Borden Rifles Inc.
Broad Creek Rifle Works, Ltd.
Brockman's Custom Gunsmithing
Brownells, Inc.
Brunton U.S.A.
BSA Optics
B-Square Company, Inc.
Bull Mountain Rifle Co.
Burris Co., Inc.
Bushmaster Firearms, Inc.
Bushnell Outdoor Products
Butler Creek Corp.
Cabela's
Carl Zeiss Inc.
Center Lock Scope Rings
Chuck's Gun Shop
Clark Custom Guns, Inc.
Clearview Mfg. Co., Inc.
Compass Industries, Inc.
Compasseco, Ltd.
Concept Development Corp.
Conetrol Scope Mounts
Creedmoor Sports, Inc.
Crimson Trace Lasers
Crosman Airguns
D.C. Engineering, Inc.
D.C.C. Enterprises
D.L. Unmussig Bullets
Daisy Outdoor Products
Del-Sports, Inc.

DHB Products
Dolbare, Elizabeth
E. Arthur Brown Co. Inc.
Eagle Imports, Inc.
Edmund Scientific Co.
Eggleston, Jere D.
Ellett Bros.
Emerging Technologies, Inc. (See Laseraim Technologies, Inc.)
Entreprise Arms, Inc.
Evolution Gun Works, Inc.
Excalibur Electro Optics, Inc.
Excel Industries, Inc.
Falcon Industries, Inc.
Farr Studio, Inc.
Freedom Arms, Inc.
Fujinon, Inc.
G.G. & G.
Galati International
Gentry Custom LLC
Gil Hebard Guns, Inc.
Gilmore Sports Concepts, Inc.
Goodwin's Guns
GSI, Inc.
Gun South, Inc. (See GSI, Inc.)
Gunsmithing, Inc.
Hakko Co. Ltd.
Hammerli USA
Hart & Son, Inc.
Harvey, Frank
Highwood Special Products
Hiptmayer, Armurier
Hiptmayer, Klaus
Hoehn Sales, Inc.
Holland's Gunsmithing
Hunter Co., Inc.
Impact Case & Container, Inc.
Ironsighter Co.
Jantz Supply, Inc.
Jena Eur
Jerry Phillips Optics
Jewell Triggers, Inc.
John Masen Co. Inc.
John's Custom Leather
Kahles A. Swarovski Company
Kalispel Case Line
KDF, Inc.
Keng's Firearms Specialty, Inc./US Tactical Systems
Kesselring Gun Shop
Kimber of America, Inc.
Knight's Manufacturing Co.
Kowa Optimed, Inc.
KVH Industries, Inc.
Kwik-Site Co.
L&S Technologies Inc. (See Aimtech Mount Systems)
L.A.R. Mfg., Inc.
Laser Devices, Inc.
Laseraim Technologies, Inc.
LaserMax
Leapers, Inc.
Leica USA, Inc.
Les Baer Custom, Inc.
Leupold & Stevens, Inc.
List Precision Engineering
Lohman Mfg. Co., Inc.
Lomont Precision Bullets
London Guns Ltd.
Mac-1 Airgun Distributors
Mag-Na-Port International, Inc.
Marksman Products
Maxi-Mount Inc.
McMillan Optical Gunsight Co.
MCS, Inc.
MDS
Meopta USA, LLC
Merit Corp.
Military Armament Corp.
Millett Sights
Mirador Optical Corp.
Mitchell Optics, Inc.
MMC
Mo's Competitor Supplies (See MCS, Inc.)

PRODUCT & SERVICE DIRECTORY

MWG Co.
Navy Arms Company
New England Custom Gun Service
Nikon, Inc.
Norincoptics (See BEC, Inc.)
Olympic Optical Co.
Op-Tec
Optical Services Co.
Orchard Park Enterprise
Oregon Arms, Inc. (See Rogue Rifle Co., Inc.)
Outdoor Connection, Inc., The
Parker & Sons Shooting Supply
Parsons Optical Mfg. Co.
PECAR Herbert Schwarz GmbH
Pentax U.S.A., Inc.
PMC/Eldorado Cartridge Corp.
Precision Sport Optics
Premier Reticles
Quarton Beamshot
R.A. Wells Custom Gunsmith
Ram-Line ATK
Ramon B. Gonzalez Guns
Ranch Products
Randolph Engineering, Inc.
Rice, Keith (See White Rock Tool & Die)
Robinson Armament Co.
Rogue Rifle Co., Inc./Chipmunk Rifles
Romain's Custom Guns, Inc.
RPM
S&K Scope Mounts
Saunders Gun & Machine Shop
Schmidt & Bender, Inc.
Schumakers Gun Shop
Scope Control, Inc.
Score High Gunsmithing
Segway Industries
Selsi Co., Inc.
Sharp Shooter Supply
Shepherd Enterprises, Inc.
Sightron, Inc.
Simmons Outdoor Corp.
Six Enterprises
Southern Bloomer Mfg. Co.
Spencer's Rifle Barrels, Inc.
Splitfire Sporting Goods, L.L.C.
Sportsmatch U.K. Ltd.
Spradlin's
Springfield Armory
Springfield, Inc.
SSK Industries
Stiles Custom Guns
Stoeger Industries
Stoney Point Products, Inc.
Sturm Ruger & Co. Inc.
Sunny Hill Enterprises, Inc.
Swarovski Optik North America Ltd.
Swift Instruments
T.K. Lee Co.
Talley, Dave
Tasco Sales, Inc.
Tele-Optics
Thompson/Center Arms
Traditions Performance Firearms
Trijicon, Inc.
Truglo, Inc.
U.S. Optics, A Division of Zeitz Optics U.S.A.
Ultra Dot Distribution
Uncle Mike's (See Michaels of Oregon, Co.)
Unertl Optical Co., Inc.
United Binocular Co.
Virgin Valley Custom Guns
Visible Impact Targets
Voere-KGH GmbH
Warne Manufacturing Co.
Watson Bullets
Weaver Products ATK
Weaver Scope Repair Service
Webley and Scott Ltd.
Weigand Combat Handguns, Inc.

Wessinger Custom Guns & Engraving
Westley Richards & Co. Ltd.
White Rifles, Inc.
White Rock Tool & Die
Whitestone Lumber Corp.
Wideview Scope Mount Corp.
Wilcox Industries Corp.
Wild West Guns
Williams Gun Sight Co.
York M-1 Conversion
Zanotti Armor, Inc.

SHELLHOLDERS

A.W. Peterson Gun Shop, Inc., The
Fremont Tool Works
GAR
Hart & Son, Inc.
Huntington Die Specialties
K&M Services
King & Co.
Protektor Model
PWM Sales Ltd.
RCBS Operations/ATK
Redding Reloading Equipment
Vega Tool Co.

SHOOTING/TRAINING SCHOOL

Alpine Indoor Shooting Range
American Gunsmithing Institute
American Small Arms Academy
Auto Arms
Beretta U.S.A. Corp.
Bob's Tactical Indoor Shooting Range & Gun Shop
Bridgeman Products
Chapman Academy of Practical Shooting
Chelsea Gun Club of New York City Inc.
Cleland's Outdoor World, Inc.
CQB Training
Defense Training International, Inc.
Executive Protection Institute
Ferris Firearms
Front Sight Firearms Training Institute
G.H. Enterprises Ltd.
Gene's Custom Guns
Gentner Bullets
Gilmore Sports Concepts, Inc.
Griffin & Howe, Inc.
Griffin & Howe, Inc.
Gun Doc, Inc.
Guncraft Books (See Guncraft Sports, Inc.)
Guncraft Sports, Inc.
Guncraft Sports, Inc.
Gunsite Training Center
Henigson & Associates, Steve
High North Products, Inc.
Jensen's Custom Ammunition
Jensen's Firearms Academy
Kemen America
L.L. Bean, Inc.
Lethal Force Institute (See Police Bookshelf)
Long, George F.
McMurdo, Lynn
Mendez, John A.
Midwest Shooting School, The
NCP Products, Inc.
North American Shooting Systems
North Mountain Pine Training Center (See Executive Protection Institute)
Nowlin Mfg. Co.
Paxton Quigley's Personal Protection Strategies
Pentheny de Pentheny
Performance Specialists

Protektor Model
SAFE
Shoot Where You Look
Shooter's World
Shooters, Inc.
Shooting Gallery, The
Sigarms Inc.
Smith & Wesson
Specialty Gunsmithing
Starlight Training Center, Inc.
Tactical Defense Institute
Thunder Ranch
Western Missouri Shooters Alliance
Yankee Gunsmith "Just Glocks"
Yavapai Firearms Academy Ltd.

SHOTSHELL MISCELLANY

A.W. Peterson Gun Shop, Inc., The
American Products, Inc.
Ballistic Products, Inc.
Bridgeman Products
Gun Works, The
Lee Precision, Inc.
MEC, Inc.
Precision Reloading, Inc.
R.E.I.
RCBS Operations/ATK
T&S Industries, Inc.
Vitt/Boos
Ziegel Engineering

SIGHTS, METALLIC

100 Straight Products, Inc.
A.W. Peterson Gun Shop, Inc., The
Accura-Site (See All's, The Jim Tembelis Co., Inc.)
Ad Hominem
Alley Supply Co.
Alpec Team, Inc.
Andela Tool & Machine, Inc.
AO Sight Systems
ArmaLite, Inc.
Aspen Outfitting Co.
Axtell Rifle Co.
B.A.C.
Ballard Rifle & Cartridge Co., LLC
BEC, Inc.
Bob's Gun Shop
Bo-Mar Tool & Mfg. Co.
Bond Custom Firearms
Bowen Classic Arms Corp.
Brockman's Custom Gunsmithing
Brooks Tactical Systems-Agrip
Brownells, Inc.
Buffalo Arms Co.
Bushmaster Firearms, Inc.
C. Sharps Arms Co. Inc./Montana Armory
California Sights (See Fautheree, Andy)
Campbell, Dick
Cape Outfitters
Cape Outfitters
Cash Mfg. Co./ TDC
Center Lock Scope Rings
Champion's Choice, Inc.
Chip McCormick Corp.
C-More Systems
Colonial Repair
CRR, Inc./Marble's Inc.
D.C. Engineering, Inc.
Davide Pedersoli and Co.
DHB Products
Dixie Gun Works
DPMS (Defense Procurement Manufacturing Services, Inc.)
Duffy, Charles E. (See Guns Antique & Modern DBA)
E. Arthur Brown Co. Inc.
Effebi SNC-Dr. Franco Beretta
Evolution Gun Works, Inc.

Farr Studio, Inc.
G.G. & G.
Garthwaite Pistolsmith, Inc., Jim
Goergen's Gun Shop, Inc.
Gun Doctor, The
Guns Antique & Modern DBA / Charles E. Duffy
Gunsmithing, Inc.
Hank's Gun Shop
Heidenstrom Bullets
Heinie Specialty Products
Hesco-Meprolight
Hiptmayer, Armurier
Hiptmayer, Klaus
Innovative Weaponry Inc.
International Shooters Service
J.G. Anschutz GmbH & Co. KG
Jeff's Outfitters
JP Enterprises, Inc.
Keng's Firearms Specialty, Inc./US Tactical Systems
Knight Rifles
Knight's Manufacturing Co.
L.P.A. Inc.
Leapers, Inc.
Les Baer Custom, Inc.
List Precision Engineering
London Guns Ltd.
Lyman Instant Targets, Inc. (See Lyman Products Corp.)
Marble Arms (See CRR, Inc./Marble's Inc.)
MCS, Inc.
MEC-Gar S.R.L.
Meprolight (See Hesco-Meprolight)
Merit Corp.
Mid-America Recreation, Inc.
Middlebrooks Custom Shop
Millett Sights
MMC
Modern Muzzleloading, Inc.
Montana Armory, Inc.
Montana Vintage Arms
Mo's Competitor Supplies (See MCS, Inc.)
Navy Arms Company
New England Custom Gun Service
Newman Gunshop
Novak's, Inc.
OK Weber, Inc.
One Ragged Hole
Parker & Sons Shooting Supply
Perazone-Gunsmith, Brian
RPM
Sharps Arms Co., Inc., C.
Slug Site
STI International
T.F.C. S.p.A.
Talley, Dave
Tank's Rifle Shop
Trijicon, Inc.
Truglo, Inc.
U.S. Optics, A Division of Zeitz Optics U.S.A.
Warne Manufacturing Co.
Weigand Combat Handguns, Inc.
Wichita Arms, Inc.
Wild West Guns
Williams Gun Sight Co.
Wilsom Combat
Wilsom Combat
XS Sight Systems

STOCK MAKER

Acra-Bond Laminates
Amrine's Gun Shop
Antique Arms Co.
Artistry in Wood
Aspen Outfitting Co.
Bain & Davis, Inc.
Bansner's Ultimate Rifles, LLC
Baron Technology
Belding's Custom Gun Shop

Billings Gunsmiths
Boltin, John M.
Borden Ridges Rimrock Stocks
Bowerly, Kent
Boyds' Gunstock Industries, Inc.
Brace, Larry D.
Briganti Custom Gunsmith
Broad Creek Rifle Works, Ltd.
Brown Precision, Inc.
Buehler Custom Sporting Arms
Bullberry Barrel Works, Ltd.
Burkhart Gunsmithing, Don
Cambos Outdoorsman
Cambos Outdoorsman
Campbell, Dick
Caywood, Shane J.
Chicasaw Gun Works
Chuck's Gun Shop
Claro Walnut Gunstock Co.
Coffin, Charles H.
Colorado Gunsmithing Academy
Custom Shop, The
Custom Single Shot Rifles
D&D Gunsmiths, Ltd.
Dangler, Homer L.
D'Arcy Echols & Co.
David W. Schwartz Custom Guns
DGR Custom Rifles
DGR Custom Rifles
DGS, Inc., Dale A. Storey
Don Klein Custom Guns
Erhardt, Dennis
Eversull Co., Inc.
Fieldsport Ltd.
Fisher, Jerry A.
Forster, Larry L.
Fred F. Wells/Wells Sport Store
Gary Goudy Classic Stocks
Genecco Gun Works
Gene's Custom Guns
Gillmann, Edwin
Grace, Charles E.
Great American Gunstock Co.
Gruning Precision, Inc.
Gunsmithing Ltd.
Hank's Gun Shop
Harper's Custom Stocks
Harry Lawson Co.
Heilmann, Stephen
Hensley, Gunmaker, Darwin
Heydenberk, Warren R.
High Tech Specialties, Inc.
Huebner, Corey O.
Jack Dever Co.
Jackalope Gun Shop
Jamison's Forge Works
Jay McCament Custom Gunmaker
Jim Norman Custom Gunstocks
John Rigby & Co.
K. Eversull Co., Inc.
Keith's Custom Gunstocks
Ken Eyster Heritage Gunsmiths, Inc.
Larry Lyons Gunworks
Lawson Co., Harry
Marshall Fish Mfg. Gunsmith Sptg. Co.
Martini & Hagn, Ltd.
Mathews Gun Shop & Gunsmithing, Inc.
McGowen Rifle Barrels
Mercer Custom Guns
Mid-America Recreation, Inc.
Mike Yee Custom Stocking
Mitchell, Jack
Mobile Area Networks, Inc.
Modern Gun Repair School
Morrow, Bud
Nelson's Custom Guns, Inc.
Nettestad Gun Works
Nickels, Paul R.
Paul and Sharon Dressel
Paul D. Hillmer Custom Gunstocks
Paulsen Gunstocks
Pawling Mountain Club

Pecatonica River Longrifle
Pentheny de Pentheny
Quality Custom Firearms
R&J Gun Shop
R.A. Wells Custom Gunsmith
Ralph Bone Engraving
Richards MicroFit Stocks, Inc.
RMS Custom Gunsmithing
Robinson, Don
Ron Frank Custom Classic, Inc.
Royal Arms Gunstocks
Ruger's Custom Guns
Skeoch, Brian R.
Smith, Art
Smith, Sharmon
Speiser, Fred D.
Steven Dodd Hughes
Stott's Creek Armory, Inc.
Sturgeon Valley Sporters
Taylor & Robbins
Tennessee Valley Mfg.
Tiger-Hunt Longrifle Gunstocks
Treebone Carving
Tucker, James C.
Turnbull Restoration, Doug
Vest, John
Walker Arms Co., Inc.
Weber & Markin Custom
 Gunsmiths
Wenig Custom Gunstocks
Werth, T. W.
Wiebe, Duane
Wild West Guns
Williamson Precision
 Gunsmithing
Winter, Robert M.

STOCKS (COMMERCIAL)

A.W. Peterson Gun Shop, Inc., The
Accuracy Unlimited
Acra-Bond Laminates
African Import Co.
Ahlman Guns
Aspen Outfitting Co.
B.A.C.
Baelder, Harry
Balickie, Joe
Bansner's Ultimate Rifles, LLC
Barnes Bullets, Inc.
Battenfeld Technologies, Inc.
Beitzinger, George
Belding's Custom Gun Shop
Bell & Carlson, Inc.
Blount, Inc., Sporting Equipment
 Div.
Blount/Outers ATK
Bob's Gun Shop
Borden Ridges Rimrock Stocks
Borden Rifles Inc.
Bowerly, Kent
Boyds' Gunstock Industries, Inc.
Brockman's Custom Gunsmithing
Buckhorn Gun Works
Bull Mountain Rifle Co.
Butler Creek Corp.
Cali'co Hardwoods, Inc.
Cape Outfitters
Caywood, Shane J.
Chambers Flintlocks Ltd., Jim
Chicasaw Gun Works
Claro Walnut Gunstock Co.
Coffin, Charles H.
Colonial Repair
Colorado Gunsmithing Academy
Colorado School of Trades
Conrad, C. A.
Curly Maple Stock Blanks (See
 Tiger-Hunt)
Custom Checkering Service, Kathy
 Forster
D&D Gunsmiths, Ltd.
D&G Precision Duplicators (See
 Greenwood Precision)
D.C. Engineering, Inc.

Davide Pedersoli and Co.
DGR Custom Rifles
Duane's Gun Repair (See DGR
 Custom Rifles)
Duncan's Gun Works, Inc.
Effebi SNC-Dr. Franco Beretta
Eggleston, Jere D.
Eversull Co., Inc.
Falcon Industries, Inc.
Falcon Industries, Inc.
Fieldsport Ltd.
Fisher, Jerry A.
Folks, Donald E.
Forster, Kathy (See Custom
 Checkering)
Forthofer's Gunsmithing &
 Knifemaking
Game Haven Gunstocks
George Hoenig, Inc.
Gervais, Mike
Gillmann, Edwin
Goens, Dale W.
Golden Age Arms Co.
Great American Gunstock Co.
Greenwood Precision
Gun Shop, The
Hammerli USA
Hanson's Gun Center, Dick
Harper's Custom Stocks
Harry Lawson Co.
Hecht, Hubert J., Waffen-Hecht
Hensley, Gunmaker, Darwin
High Tech Specialties, Inc.
Hiptmayer, Armurier
Hiptmayer, Klaus
Hogue Grips
H-S Precision, Inc.
Huebner, Corey O.
Israel Arms Inc.
Ivanoff, Thomas G. (See Tom's
 Gun Repair)
Jarrett Rifles, Inc.
Jeff's Outfitters
Jim Norman Custom Gunstocks
John Masen Co. Inc.
Johnson Wood Products
KDF, Inc.
Keith's Custom Gunstocks
Kelbly, Inc.
Kilham & Co.
Klingler Woodcarving
Lawson Co., Harry
McDonald, Dennis
McMillan Fiberglass Stocks, Inc.
Michaels of Oregon Co.
Mid-America Recreation, Inc.
Miller Arms, Inc.
Mitchell, Jack
Mobile Area Networks, Inc.
Morrison Custom Rifles, J. W.
MPI Stocks
MWG Co.
NCP Products, Inc.
Nelson's Custom Guns, Inc.
New England Arms Co.
New England Custom Gun Service
Newman Gunshop
Oil Rod and Gun Shop
One Of A Kind
Orvis Co., The
Ottmar, Maurice
Pagel Gun Works, Inc.
Paragon Sales & Services, Inc.
Parker & Sons Shooting Supply
Paul and Sharon Dressel
Paul D. Hillmer Custom Gunstocks
Paulsen Gunstocks
Pawling Mountain Club
Pecatonica River Longrifle
Perazone-Gunsmith, Brian
Powell & Son (Gunmakers) Ltd.,
 William
Precision Gun Works
R&J Gun Shop
R.A. Wells Custom Gunsmith

Ram-Line ATK
Rampart International
Richards MicroFit Stocks, Inc.
RMS Custom Gunsmithing
Robinson, Don
Robinson Armament Co.
Robinson Firearms Mfg. Ltd.
Romain's Custom Guns, Inc.
Ron Frank Custom Classic, Inc.
Royal Arms Gunstocks
Saville Iron Co. (See Greenwood
 Precision)
Schiffman, Mike
Score High Gunsmithing
Simmons Gun Repair, Inc.
Six Enterprises
Speiser, Fred D.
Stan De Treville & Co.
Stiles Custom Guns
Swann, D. J.
Swift River Gunworks
Szweda, Robert (See RMS Custom
 Gunsmithing)
T.F.C. S.p.A.
Tecnolegno S.p.A.
Tirelli
Tom's Gun Repair, Thomas G.
 Ivanoff
Track of the Wolf, Inc.
Treebone Carving
Trevallion Gunstocks
Tuttle, Dale
Vic's Gun Refinishing
Virgin Valley Custom Guns
Volquartsen Custom Ltd.
Walker Arms Co., Inc.
Weber & Markin Custom
 Gunsmiths
Weems, Cecil
Wenig Custom Gunstocks
Werth, T. W.
Western Mfg. Co.
Wild West Guns
Williams Gun Sight Co.
Windish, Jim
Wright's Gunstock Blanks
Zeeryp, Russ

STUCK CASE REMOVERS

A.W. Peterson Gun Shop, Inc., The
GAR
Huntington Die Specialties
Redding Reloading Equipment
Tom's Gun Repair, Thomas G.
 Ivanoff

TARGETS, BULLET & CLAYBIRD TRAPS

A.W. Peterson Gun Shop, Inc., The
Action Target, Inc.
Air Arms
American Target
Beeman Precision Airguns
Benjamin/Sheridan Co., Crosman
Birchwood Casey
Blount, Inc., Sporting Equipment
 Div.
Blount/Outers ATK
Blue and Gray Products Inc. (See
 Ox-Yoke Originals)
Brown Precision, Inc.
Bull-X, Inc.
Caswell International
Champion Target Co.
Creedmoor Sports, Inc.
Crosman Airguns
D.C.C. Enterprises
Daisy Outdoor Products
Diamond Mfg. Co.
Federal Champion Target Co.
G.H. Enterprises Ltd.

H-S Precision, Inc.
Hunterjohn
J.G. Dapkus Co., Inc.
Kennebec Journal
Kleen-Bore, Inc.
Lakefield Arms Ltd. (See Savage
 Arms, Inc.)
Leapers, Inc.
Littler Sales Co.
Lyman Instant Targets, Inc. (See
 Lyman Products Corp.)
Marksman Products
Mendez, John A.
Mountain Plains Industries
MSR Targets
N.B.B., Inc.
National Target Co.
North American Shooting Systems
Outers Laboratories Div. of ATK
Ox-Yoke Originals, Inc.
Palsa Outdoor Products
Passive Bullet Traps, Inc. (See
 Savage Range Systems, Inc.)
PlumFire Press, Inc.
Precision Airgun Sales, Inc.
Protektor Model
Quack Decoy & Sporting Clays
Remington Arms Co., Inc.
Rockwood Corp.
Rocky Mountain Target Co.
Savage Range Systems, Inc.
Schaefer Shooting Sports
Seligman Shooting Products
Shooters Supply
Shoot-N-C Targets (See
 Birchwood Casey)
SPG, Inc.
Target Shooting, Inc.
Thompson Target Technology
Trius Traps, Inc.
Universal Sports
Visible Impact Targets
Watson Bullets
Woods Wise Products
World of Targets (See Birchwood
 Casey)
X-Spand Target Systems

TAXIDERMY

African Import Co.
Bill Russ Trading Post
Kulis Freeze Dry Taxidermy
World Trek, Inc.

TRAP & SKEET SHOOTER'S EQUIPMENT

American Products, Inc.
Bagmaster Mfg., Inc.
Ballistic Products, Inc.
Beretta Pietro S.P.A.
Blount/Outers ATK
Bob Allen Sportswear
Bridgeman Products
C&H Research
Cape Outfitters
Claybuster Wads & Harvester
 Bullets
Danuser Machine Co.
Fiocchi of America, Inc.
G.H. Enterprises Ltd.
Gun Works, The
Hoppe's Div. Penguin Industries,
 Inc.
Jamison's Forge Works
Jenkins Recoil Pads
Jim Noble Co.
Kalispel Case Line
Kolar
Lakewood Products LLC
Ljutic Industries, Inc.
Mag-Na-Port International, Inc.
MEC, Inc.
Moneymaker Guncraft Corp.

MTM Molded Products Co., Inc.
NCP Products, Inc.
Pachmayr Div. Lyman Products
Palsa Outdoor Products
Pro-Port Ltd.
Protektor Model
Quack Decoy & Sporting Clays
Remington Arms Co., Inc.
Rhodeside, Inc.
Shotgun Sports Magazine, dba
 Shootin' Accessories Ltd.
Stan Baker Sports
T&S Industries, Inc.
TEN-X Products Group
Torel, Inc./Tandy Brands
 Outdoors/AA & E
Trius Traps, Inc.
Truglo, Inc.
Universal Sports
Warne Manufacturing Co.
Weber & Markin Custom
 Gunsmiths
X-Spand Target Systems
Ziegel Engineering

TRIGGERS, RELATED EQUIPMENT

A.W. Peterson Gun Shop, Inc., The
B&D Trading Co., Inc.
B.M.F. Activator, Inc.
Behlert Precision, Inc.
Bond Custom Firearms
Boyds' Gunstock Industries, Inc.
Broad Creek Rifle Works, Ltd.
Bull Mountain Rifle Co.
Chicasaw Gun Works
Dayton Traister
Dolbare, Elizabeth
Eversull Co., Inc.
Feinwerkbau Westinger &
 Altenburger
Gentry Custom LLC
Gun Works, The
Hart & Son, Inc.
Hastings
Hawken Shop, The (See Dayton
 Traister)
High Performance International
Holland's Gunsmithing
Impact Case & Container, Inc.
Jewell Triggers, Inc.
John Masen Co. Inc.
Jones Custom Products, Neil A.
JP Enterprises, Inc.
K. Eversull Co., Inc.
Kelbly, Inc.
KK Air International (See Impact
 Case & Container Co., Inc.)
Knight's Manufacturing Co.
L&R Lock Co.
Les Baer Custom, Inc.
List Precision Engineering
London Guns Ltd.
M.H. Canjar Co.
Master Lock Co.
Miller Single Trigger Mfg. Co.
NCP Products, Inc.
Neil A. Jones Custom Products
Nowlin Mfg. Co.
Penrod Precision
Perazone-Gunsmith, Brian
Robinson Armament Co.
Sharp Shooter Supply
Shilen, Inc.
Simmons Gun Repair, Inc.
Spencer's Rifle Barrels, Inc.
Tank's Rifle Shop
Target Shooting, Inc.
Watson Bullets
York M-1 Conversion

A Zone Bullets, 2039 Walter Rd., Billings, MT 59105 / 800-252-3111; FAX: 406-248-1961

A&W Repair, 2930 Schneider Dr., Arnold, MO 63010 / 617-287-3725

A.A. Arms, Inc., 4811 Persimmont Ct., Monroe, NC 28110 / 704-289-5356 or 800-935-1119; FAX: 704-289-5859

A.B.S. III, 9238 St. Morritz Dr., Fern Creek, KY 40291

A.G. Russell Knives, Inc., 2900 S. 26th St., Rogers, AR 72758 / 800-255-9034; FAX: 479-636-8493 ag@agrussell.com www.agrussell.com

A.R.M.S., Inc., 230 W. Center St., West Bridgewater, MA 02379-1620 / 508-584-7816; FAX: 508-588-8045

A.W. Peterson Gun Shop, Inc., The, 4255 West Old U.S. 441, Mount Dora, FL 32757-3299 / 352-383-4258; FAX: 352-735-1001

AC Dyna-tite Corp., 155 Kelly St., P.O. Box 0984, Elk Grove Village, IL 60007 / 847-593-5566; FAX: 847-593-1304

Acadian Ballistic Specialties, P.O. Box 787, Folsom, LA 70437 / 504-796-0078 gunsmith@neasolft.com

Accuracy Den, The, 25 Bitterbrush Rd., Reno, NV 89523 / 702-345-0225

Accuracy International, Foster, P.O. Box 111, Wilsall, MT 59086 / 406-587-7922; FAX: 406-585-9434

Accuracy Internationl Precision Rifles (See U.S.)

Accuracy Int'l. North America, Inc., P.O. Box 5267, Oak Ridge, TN 37831 / 423-482-0330; FAX: 423-482-0336

Accuracy Unlimited, 7479 S. DePew St., Littleton, CO 80123

Accuracy Unlimited, 16036 N. 49 Ave., Glendale, AZ 85306 / 602-978-9089; FAX: 602-978-9089 fglenn@cox.net www.glenncustom.com

Accura-Site (See All's, The Jim Tembelis Co., Inc.)

Accurate Arms Co., Inc., 5891 Hwy. 230 West, McEwen, TN 37101 / 931-729-4207; FAX: 931-729-4211 burrensburg@aac-ca.com www.accuratepowder.com

Accu-Tek, 4510 Carter Ct., Chino, CA 91710

Ackerman & Co., Box 133 U.S. Highway Rt. 7, Pownal, VT 05261 / 802-823-9874 muskets@togsther.net

Ackerman, Bill (See Optical Services Co.)

Acra-Bond Laminates, 134 Zimmerman Rd., Kalispell, MT 59901 / 406-257-9003; FAX: 406-257-9003 merlins@digisys.net www.acrabondlaminates.com

Action Bullets & Alloy Inc., RR 1, P.O. Box 189, Quinter, KS 67752 / 785-754-3609; FAX: 785-754-3629 bullets@ruraltel.net

Action Direct, Inc., 14285 SW 142nd St., Miami, FL 33186-6720 / 800-472-2388; FAX: 305-256-3541 info@action-direct.com www.action-direct.com

Action Products, Inc., 22 N. Mulberry St., Hagerstown, MD 21740 / 301-797-1414; FAX: 301-733-2073

Action Target, Inc., P.O. Box 636, Provo, UT 84603 / 801-377-8033; FAX: 801-377-8096 www.actiontarget.com

Actions by "T" Teddy Jacobson, 16315 Redwood Forest Ct., Sugar Land, TX 77478 / 281-565-6977 or 281-277-4008 tjacobson@houston.rr.com www.actionsbyt.blogspot.com

AcuSport Corporation, William L. Fraim, One Hunter Place, Bellefontaine, OH 43311-3001 / 937-593-7010; FAX: 937-592-5625 www.acusport.com

Ad Hominem, 3130 Gun Club Lane, RR #3, Orillia, ON L3V 6H3 CANADA / 705-689-5303; FAX: 705-689-5303

Adair Custom Shop, Bill, 2886 Westridge, Carrollton, TX 75006

ADCO Sales, Inc., 4 Draper St. #A, Woburn, MA 01801 / 781-935-1799; FAX: 781-935-1011

Advance Car Mover Co., Rowell Div., P.O. Box 1, 240 N. Depot St., Juneau, WI 53039 / 414-386-4464; FAX: 414-386-4416

Advantage Arms, Inc., 25163 W. Ave. Stanford, Valencia, CA 91355 / 661-257-2290

Adventure 16, Inc., 4620 Alvarado Canyon Rd., San Diego, CA 92120 / 619-283-6314

Aero Peltor, 90 Mechanic St., Southbridge, MA 01550 / 508-764-5500; FAX: 508-764-0188

African Import Co., 22 Goodwin Rd., Plymouth, MA 02360 / 508-746-8552; FAX: 508-746-0404 africanimport@aol.com

AFSCO Ammunition, 731 W. Third St., P.O. Box L, Owen, WI 54460 / 715-229-2516 sailers@webtv.net

Ahlman Guns, 9525 W. 230th St., Morristown, MN 55052 / 507-685-4243; FAX: 507-685-4280 www.ahlmans.com

Ahrends Grips, Box 203, Clarion, IA 50525 / 515-532-3449; FAX: 515-532-3926 ahrends@goldfieldaccess.net www.ahrendsgripsusa.com

Aimpoint, Inc., 14103 Mariah Ct., Chantilly, VA 20151-2113 / 877-246-7668; FAX: 703-263-9463 info@aimpoint.com www.aimpoint.com

Aimtech Mount Systems, P.O. Box 223, Thomasville, GA 31799 / 229-226-4313; FAX: 229-227-0222 mail@aimtech-mounts.com www.aimtech-mounts.com

Air Arms, Hailsham Industrial Park, Diplocks Way, Hailsham, E. Sussex, BN27 3JF ENGLAND / 011-0323-845853; FAX: 1323 440573 general.air-arms@ukcom www.air-arms.co.uk.

Air Venture Airguns, 9752 E. Flower St., Bellflower, CA 90706 / 562-867-6355

AirForce Airguns, P.O. Box 2478, Fort Worth, TX 76113 / 817-451-8966; FAX: 817-451-1613 www.airforceairguns.com

Airrow, 11 Monitor Hill Rd., Newtown, CT 06470 / 203-270-6343

Aitor-Berrizargo S.L., Eitua 15 P.O. Box 26, 48240, Berriz (Viscaya), SPAIN / 43-17-08-50 info@aitor.com www.ailor.com

Ajax Custom Grips, Inc., 9130 Viscount Row, Dallas, TX 75247 / 214-630-8893; FAX: 214-630-4942

Aker International, Inc., 2248 Main St., Suite 6, Chula Vista, CA 91911 / 619-423-5182; FAX: 619-423-1363 aker@akerleather.com www.akerleather.com

AKJ Concealco, P.O. Box 871596, Vancouver, WA 98687-1596 / 360-891-8222; FAX: 360-891-8221 Concealco@aol.com www.greatholsters.com

Alana Cupp Custom Engraver, P.O. Box 207, Annabella, UT 84711 / 801-896-4834

Alaska Bullet Works, Inc., 9978 Crazy Horse Drive, Juneau, AK 99801 / 907-789-3834; FAX: 907-789-3433

Alaskan Silversmith, The, 2145 Wagner Hollow Rd., Fort Plain, NY 13339 / 518-993-3983 sidbell@capital.net www.sidbell.cizland.com

Aldis Gunsmithing & Shooting Supply, 502 S. Montezuma St., Prescott, AZ 86303 / 602-445-6723; FAX: 602-445-6763

Alessi Holsters, Inc., 2465 Niagara Falls Blvd., Amherst, NY 14228-3527 / 716-691-5615

Alex, Inc., 3420 Cameron Bridge Rd., Manhattan, MT 59741-8523 / 406-282-7396; FAX: 406-282-7396

All American Lead Shot Corp., P.O. Box 224566, Dallas, TX 75062

All Rite Products, Inc., 9554 Wells Circle, Suite D, West Jordan, UT 84088-6226 / 800-771-8471; FAX: 801-280-8302 info@allriteproducts.com www.allriteproducts.com

Allard, Gary/Creek Side Metal & Woodcrafters, Fishers Hill, VA 22626 / 540-465-3903

Allen Co., Inc., 525 Burbank St., Broomfield, CO 80020 / 303-469-1857 or 800-876-8600; FAX: 303-466-7437

Allen Firearm Engraving, P.O. Box 155, Camp Verde, AZ 86322 / 928-567-6711 rosebudmulgco@netzero.com rosebudmulgco@netzero.com

Allen Mfg., 6449 Hodgson Rd., Circle Pines, MN 55014 / 612-429-8231

Alley Supply Co., P.O. Box 848, Gardnerville, NV 89410 / 775-782-3800; FAX: 775-782-3827 jetalley@aol.com www.alleysupplyco.com

Alliant Techsystems, Smokeless Powder Group, P.O. Box 6, Rt. 114, Bldg. 229, Radford, VA 24141-0096 www.alliantpowder.com

Allred Bullet Co., 932 Evergreen Drive, Logan, UT 84321 / 435-752-6983; FAX: 435-752-6983

Alpec Team, Inc., 201 Rickenbacker Cir., Livermore, CA 94550 / 510-606-8245; FAX: 510-606-4279

Alpha 1 Drop Zone, 2121 N. Tyler, Wichita, KS 67212 / 316-729-0800; FAX: 316-729-4262 www.alpha1dropzone.com

Alpha LaFranck Enterprises, P.O. Box 81072, Lincoln, NE 68501 / 402-466-3193

Alpha Precision, Inc., 3238 Della Slaton Rd., Comer, GA 30629-2212 / 706-783-2131 jim@alphaprecisioninc.com www.alphaprecisioninc.com

Alpine Indoor Shooting Range, 2401 Government Way, Coeur d'Alene, ID 83814 / 208-676-8824; FAX: 208-676-8824

Altamont Co., 901 N. Church St., P.O. Box 309, Thomasboro, IL 61878 / 217-643-3125 or 800-626-5774; FAX: 217-643-7973

Alumna Sport by Dee Zee, 1572 NE 58th Ave., P.O. Box 3090, Des Moines, IA 50316 / 800-798-9899

Amadeo Rossi S.A., Rua: Amadeo Rossi, 143, Sao Leopoldo, RS 93030-220 BRAZIL / 051-592-5566 rossi.firearms@pnet.com.br

Amato, Jeff. See: J&M PRECISION MACHINING

AmBr Software Group Ltd., P.O. Box 301, Reisterstown, MD 21136-0301 / 800-888-1917; FAX: 410-526-7212

American Ammunition, 3545 NW 71st St., Miami, FL 33147 / 305-835-7400; FAX: 305-694-0037

American Derringer Corp., 127 N. Lacy Dr., Waco, TX 76705 / 800-642-7817 or 254-799-9111; FAX: 254-799-7935

American Display Co., 55 Cromwell St., Providence, RI 02907 / 401-331-2464; FAX: 401-421-1264

American Gas & Chemical Co., Ltd.,, 220 Pegasus Ave., Northvale, NJ 07647 / 201-767-7300

American Gunsmithing Institute, 1325 Imola Ave. #504, Napa, CA 94559 / 707-253-0462; FAX: 707-253-7149 www.americangunsmith.com

American Handgunner Magazine, 12345 World Trade Dr., San Diego, CA 92128 / 800-537-3006; FAX: 858-605-0204 www.americanhandgunner.com

American Pioneer Video, P.O. Box 50049, Bowling Green, KY 42102-2649 / 800-743-4675

American Products, Inc., 14729 Spring Valley Road, Morrison, IL 61270 / 815-772-3336; FAX: 815-772-8046

American Safe Arms, Inc., 1240 Riverview Dr., Garland, UT 84312 / 801-257-7472; FAX: 801-785-8156

American Security Products Co., 11925 Pacific Ave., Fontana, CA 92337 / 909-685-9680 or 800-421-6142; FAX: 909-685-9685

American Small Arms Academy, P.O. Box 12111, Prescott, AZ 86304 / 602-778-5623

American Target, 1328 S. Jason St., Denver, CO 80223 / 303-733-0433; FAX: 303-777-0311

American Target Knives, 1030 Brownwood NW, Grand Rapids, MI 49504 / 616-453-1998

Americase, P.O. Box 271, 1610 E. Main, Waxahachie, TX 75165 / 800-880-3629; FAX: 214-937-8373

Ames Metal Products Co., 4323 S. Western Blvd., Chicago, IL 60609 / 773-523-3230 or 800-255-6937; FAX: 773-523-3854 amesmetal@webtv.net

Amherst Arms, P.O. Box 1457, Englewood, FL 34295 / 941-475-2020; FAX: 941-473-1212

Ammo Load Worldwide, Inc., 815 D St., Lewiston, ID 83501 / 800-528-5610; FAX: 208-746-1730 info@ammoload.com www.ammoload.com

Amrine's Gun Shop, 937 La Luna, Ojai, CA 93023 / 805-646-2376

Amsec, 11925 Pacific Ave., Fontana, CA 92337

Analog Devices, Box 9106, Norwood, MA 02062

Andela Tool & Machine, Inc., RD3, Box 246, Richfield Springs, NY 13439

Anderson Manufacturing Co., Inc., 22602 53rd Ave. SE, Bothell, WA 98021 / 206-481-1858; FAX: 206-481-7839

Andres & Dworsky KG, Bergstrasse 18, A-3822 Karlstein, Thaya, AUSTRIA / 0 28 44-285; FAX: 0 28 44-28619 andres.dnorsky@wvnet.as

Angelo & Little Custom Gun Stock Blanks, P.O. Box 240046, Dell, MT 59724-0046

Answer Products Co., 1519 Westbury Drive, Davison, MI 48423 / 810-653-2911

Antique American Firearms, P.O. Box 71035, Dept. GD, Des Moines, IA 50325 / 515-224-6552

Antique Arms Co., 1110 Cleveland Ave., Monett, MO 65708 / 417-235-6501

AO Sight Systems, 2401 Ludelle St., Fort Worth, TX 76105 / 888-744-4880; or 817-536-0136; FAX: 817-536-3517

Apel GmbH, Ernst, Am Kirschberg 3, D-97818, Gerbrunn, GERMANY / 0 (931) 707192 info@eaw.de www.eaw.de

Aplan Antiques & Art, James O., HC 80, Box 793-25, Piedmont, SD 57769 / 605-347-5016

AR-7 Industries, LLC, 998 N. Colony Rd., Meriden, CT 06450 / 203-630-3536; FAX: 203-630-3637

Arizona Ammunition, Inc., 21421 No. 14th Ave., Suite E, Phoenix, AZ 85027 / 623-516-9004; FAX: 623-516-9012 www.azammo.com

ArmaLite, Inc., P.O. Box 299, Geneseo, IL 61254 / 800-336-0184 or 309-944-6939; FAX: 309-944-6949

Armament Gunsmithing Co., Inc., 525 Rt. 22, Hillside, NJ 07205 / 908-686-0960; FAX: 718-738-5019 armamentgunsmithing@worldnet.att.net

Armas Garbi, S.A., 12-14 20.600 Urki, 12, Eibar (Guipuzcoa), SPAIN / 943 20 3873; FAX: 943 20 3873 armosgarbi@euskalnet.n

Armas Kemen S. A. (See U.S. Importers)

Armfield Custom Bullets, 10584 County Road 100, Carthage, MO 64836 / 417-359-8480; FAX: 417-359-8497

Armi Perazzi S.P.A., Via Fontanelle 1/3, I-25080, Botticino Mattina, ITALY / 030-2692591; FAX: 030-2692594

Armi San Marco (See Taylor's & Co.)

MANUFACTURER'S DIRECTORY

Armi San Paolo, 172-A, I-25062, via Europa, ITALY / 030-2751725

Armi Sport (See Cape Outfitters)

Armite Laboratories Inc., 1560 Superior Ave., Costa Mesa, CA 92627 / 949-646-9035; FAX: 949-646-8319 armite@pacbell.net www.armitelahs.com

Armoloy Co. of Ft. Worth, 204 E. Daggett St., Fort Worth, TX 76104 / 817-332-5604; FAX: 817-335-6517 info@armoloyftworth.com www.armoloyftworth.com

Armor (See Buck Stop Lure Co., Inc.)

Armor Metal Products, P.O. Box 4609, Helena, MT 59604 / 406-442-5560; FAX: 406-442-5650

Armory Publications, 2120 S. Reserve St., PMB 253, Missoula, MT 59801 / 406-549-7670; FAX: 406-728-0597 armorypub@aol.com www.armorypub.com

Arms & Armour Press, Wellington House, 125 Strand, London, WC2R 0BB ENGLAND / 0171-420-5555; FAX: 0171-240-7265

Arms Corporation of the Philippines, Armscor Ave. Brgy. Fortune, Marikina City, PHILIPPINES / 632-941-6243 or 632-941-6244; FAX: 632-942-0682 info@armscor.com.ph www.armscor.com.ph

Arms Craft Gunsmithing, 1106 Linda Dr., Arroyo Grande, CA 93420 / 805-481-2830

Arms, Programming Solutions (See Arms Software)

Armscor Precision, 5740 S. Arville St. #219, Las Vegas, NV 89118 / 702-362-7750

Armscorp USA, Inc., 4424 John Ave., Baltimore, MD 21227 / 301-775-8134 info@armscorpusa.com www.armscorpusa.com

Arratoonian, Andy (See Horseshoe Leather Products)

Arrieta S.L., Morkaiko 5, 20870, Elgoibar, SPAIN / 34-43-743150; FAX: 34-43-743154

Art Jewel Enterprises Ltd., Eagle Business Ctr., 460 Randy Rd., Carol Stream, IL 60188 / 708-260-0400

Artistry in Wood, 134 Zimmerman Rd., Kalispell, MT 59901 / 406-257-9003; FAX: 406-257-9167 merlins@digisys.net www.acrabondlaminates.com

Art's Gun & Sport Shop, Inc., 6008 Hwy. Y, Hillsboro, MO 63050

Aspen Outfitting Co., Jon Hollinger, 9 Dean St., Aspen, CO 81611 / 970-925-3406

A-Square Co., 205 Fairfield Ave., Jeffersonville, IN 47130 / 812-283-0577; FAX: 812-283-0375

Astra Sport, S.A., Apartado 3, 48300 Guernica, Espagne, SPAIN / 34-4-6250100; FAX: 34-4-6255186

Atamec-Bretton, 19 rue Victor Grignard, F-42026, St.-Etienne (Cedex 1, FRANCE / 33-77-93-54-69; FAX: 33-77-93-57-98

Atlanta Cutlery Corp., 2143 Gees Mill Rd., Box 839 CIS, Conyers, GA 30207 / 800-883-0300; FAX: 404-388-0246

Atlantic Mills, Inc., 1295 Towbin Ave., Lakewood, NJ 08701-5934 / 800-242-7374

Atsko/Sno-Seal, Inc., 2664 Russell St., Orangeburg, SC 29115 / 803-531-1820; FAX: 803-531-2139 info@atsko.com www.atsko.com

Austin & Halleck, Inc., 2150 South 950 East, Provo, UT 84606-6285 / 877-543-3256 or 801-374-9990; FAX: 801-374-9998 www.austinhallek.com

Austin Sheridan USA, Inc., 490 Main St., Middlefield, CT 06455 / 860-349-1772; FAX: 860-349-1771 asusa@sbcglobal.net

Auto Arms, 738 Clearview, San Antonio, TX 78228 / 512-434-5450

Auto-Ordnance Corp., P.O. Box 220, Blauvelt, NY 10913 / 914-353-7770

Autumn Sales, Inc. (Blaser), 1320 Lake St., Fort Worth, TX 76102 / 817-335-1634; FAX: 817-338-0119

Avnda Otaola Norica, 16 Apartado 68, 20600, Eibar, SPAIN

AWC Systems Technology, P.O. Box 41938, Phoenix, AZ 85080-1938 / 623-780-1050; FAX: 623-780-2967 awc@awcsystech.com www.awcsystech.com

Axtell Rifle Co., 353 Mill Creek Road, Sheridan, MT 59749 / 406-842-5814

AYA (See U.S. Importer-New England Custom Gun Serv

B

B&D Trading Co., Inc., 3935 Fair Hill Rd., Fair Oaks, CA 95628 / 800-334-3790 or 916-967-9366; FAX: 916-967-4873

B&P America, 12321 Brittany Cir., Dallas, TX 75230 / 972-726-9069

B.A.C., 17101 Los Modelos St., Fountain Valley, CA 92708 / 435-586-3286

B.C. Outdoors, Larry McGhee, PO Box 61497, Boulder City, NV 89006 / 702-294-3056; FAX: 702-294-0413 jdalton@pmcammo.com www.pmcammo.com

B.M.F. Activator, Inc., 12145 Mill Creek Run, Plantersville, TX 77363 / 936-894-2397; FAX: 936-894-2397 bmf25years@aol.com

Baelder, Harry, Alte Goennebeker Strasse 5, 24635, Rickling, GERMANY / 04328-722732; FAX: 04328-722733

Baer's Hollows, P.O. Box 603, Taft, CA 93268 / 719-438-5718

Bagmaster Mfg., Inc., 2731 Sutton Ave., St. Louis, MO 63143 / 314-781-8002; FAX: 314-781-3363 sales@bagmaster.com www.bagmaster.com

Bain & Davis, Inc., 307 E. Valley Blvd., San Gabriel, CA 91776-3522 / 626-573-4241; FAX: 323-283-7449 baindavis@aol.com

Baker, Stan. See: STAN BAKER SPORTS

Bald Eagle Precision Machine Co., 101 Allison St., Lock Haven, PA 17745 / 570-748-6772; FAX: 570-748-4443 bepmachine@aol.com baldeaglemachine.com

Balickie, Joe, 408 Trelawney Lane, Apex, NC 27502 / 919-362-5185

Ballard, Donald. See: BALLARD INDUSTRIES

Ballard Industries, Donald Ballard Sr., P.O. Box 2035, Arnold, CA 95223 / 408-996-0957; FAX: 408-257-6828

Ballard Rifle & Cartridge Co., LLC, 113 W. Yellowstone Ave., Cody, WY 82414 / 307-587-4914; FAX: 307-527-6097 ballard@wyoming.com www.ballardrifles.com

Ballistic Products, Inc., 20015 75th Ave. North, Corcoran, MN 55340-9456 / 763-494-9237; FAX: 763-494-9236 info@ballisticproducts.com www.ballisticproducts.com

Ballistic Program Co., Inc., The, 2417 N. Patterson St., Thomasville, GA 31792 / 912-228-5739 or 800-368-0835

Ballistic Research, 1108 W. May Ave., McHenry, IL 60050 / 815-385-0037

Ballisti-Cast, Inc., P.O. Box 1057, Minot, ND 58702-1057 / 701-497-3333; FAX: 701-497-3335

Bandcor Industries, Div. of Man-Sew Corp., 6108 Sherwin Dr., Port Richey, FL 34668 / 813-848-0432

Bang-Bang Boutique (See Holster Shop, The)

Bansner's Ultimate Rifles, LLC, P.O. Box 839, 261 E. Main St., Adamstown, PA 19501 / 717-484-2370; FAX: 717-484-0523 bansner@aol.com www.bansnersrifle.com

Barbour, Inc., 55 Meadowbrook Dr., Milford, NH 03055 / 603-673-1313; FAX: 603-673-6510

Barnes, 4347 Tweed Dr., Eau Claire, WI 54703-6302

Barnes Bullets, Inc., P.O. Box 215, American Fork, UT 84003 / 801-756-4222 or 800-574-9200; FAX: 801-756-2465 email@barnesbullets.com www.barnesbullets.com

Baron Technology, 62 Spring Hill Rd., Trumbull, CT 06611 / 203-452-0515; FAX: 203-452-0663 dbaron@baronengraving.com www.baronengraving.com

Barraclough, John K., 55 Merit Park Dr., Gardena, CA 90247 / 310-324-2574 jbarraclough@sbcglobal.net

Barramundi Corp., P.O. Drawer 4259, Homosassa Springs, FL 32687 / 904-628-0200

Barrel & Gunworks, 2601 Lake Valley Rd., Prescott Valley, AZ 86314 / 928-772-4060 www.cutrifle.com

Barrett Firearms Manufacturer, Inc., P.O. Box 1077, Murfreesboro, TN 37133 / 615-896-2938; FAX: 615-896-7313

Bar-Sto Precision Machine, 73377 Sullivan Rd., P.O. Box 1838, Twentynine Palms, CA 92277 / 760-367-2747; FAX: 760-367-2407 barsto@eee.org www.barsto.com

Barta's Gunsmithing, 10231 U.S. Hwy. 10, Cato, WI 54230 / 920-732-4472

Barteaux Machete, 1916 SE 50th Ave., Portland, OR 97215-3238 / 503-233-5880

Bartlett Engineering, 40 South 200 East, Smithfield, UT 84335-1645 / 801-563-5910

Bates Engraving, Billy, 2302 Winthrop Dr. SW, Decatur, AL 35603 / 256-355-3690 bbrn@aol.com www.angelfire.com/al/billybates

Battenfeld Technologies, Inc., 5885 W. Van Horn Tavern Rd., Columbia, MO 65203 / 573-445-9200; FAX: 573-447-4158 battenfeldtechnologies.com

Bauer, Eddie, 15010 NE 36th St., Redmond, WA 98052

Baumgartner Bullets, 3011 S. Alane St., W. Valley City, UT 84120

Bauska Barrels, 105 9th Ave. W., Kalispell, MT 59901 / 406-752-7706

BC-Handmade Bullets, 482 Comerwood Court, S. San Francisco, CA 94080 / 650-583-1550; FAX: 650-583-1550

Bear Archery, RR 4, 4600 Southwest 41st Blvd., Gainesville, FL 32601 / 904-376-2327

Bear Arms, 374-A Carson Rd., St. Mathews, SC 29135

Bear Mountain Gun & Tool, 120 N. Plymouth, New Plymouth, ID 83655 / 208-278-5221; FAX: 208-278-5221

Beartooth Bullets, P.O. Box 491, Dept. HLD, Dover, ID 83825-0491 / 208-448-1865 bullets@beartoothbullets.com beartoothbullets.com

Beaver Park Product, Inc., 840 J St., Penrose, CO 81240 / 719-372-6744

BEC, Inc., 1227 W. Valley Blvd., Suite 204, Alhambra, CA 91803 / 626-281-5751; FAX: 626-293-7073

Beeks, Mike. See: GRAYBACK WILDCATS

Beeman Precision Airguns, 5454 Argosy Dr., Huntington Beach, CA 92649 / 714-890-4808; FAX: 714-890-4808

Behlert Precision, Inc., P.O. Box 288, 7067 Easton Rd., Pipersville, PA 18947 / 215-766-8681 or 215-766-7301; FAX: 215-766-8681

Beitzinger, George, 116-20 Atlantic Ave., Richmond Hill, NY 11419 / 718-847-7661

Belding's Custom Gun Shop, 10691 Sayers Rd., Munith, MI 49259 / 517-596-2388

Bell & Carlson, Inc., Dodge City Industrial Park, 101 Allen Rd., Dodge City, KS 67801 / 800-634-8586 or 620-225-6688; FAX: 620-225-6688 email@bellandcarlson.com www.bellandcarlson.com

Bell Reloading, Inc., 1725 Harlin Lane Rd., Villa Rica, GA 30180

Bell's Gun & Sport Shop, 3309-19 Mannheim Rd., Franklin Park, IL 60131

Bell's Legendary Country Wear, 22 Circle Dr., Bellmore, NY 11710 / 516-679-1158

Benchmark Knives (See Gerber Legendary Blades)

Benelli Armi S.P.A., Via della Stazione, 61029, Urbino, ITALY / 39-722-307-1; FAX: 39-722-327427

Benelli USA Corp., 17603 Indian Head Hwy., Accokeek, MD 20607 / 301-283-6981; FAX: 301-283-6988 benelliusa.com

Bengtson Arms Co., L., 6345-B E. Akron St., Mesa, AZ 85205 / 602-981-6375

Benjamin/Sheridan Co., Crosman, Rts. 5 and 20, E. Bloomfield, NY 14443 / 716-657-6161; FAX: 716-657-5405 www.crosman.com

Bentley, John, 128-D Watson Dr., Turtle Creek, PA 15145

Beretta Pietro S.P.A., Via Beretta, 18, 25063, Gardone Valtrompia, ITALY / 39-30-8341-1 info@beretta.com www.beretta.com

Beretta U.S.A. Corp., 17601 Beretta Dr., Accokeek, MD 20607 / 301-283-2191; FAX: 301-283-0435

Berger Bullets Ltd., 5443 W. Westwind Dr., Glendale, AZ 85310 / 602-842-4001; FAX: 602-934-9083

Bernardelli, Vincenzo, P.O. Box 460243, Houston, TX 77056-8243 www.bernardelli.com

Bernardelli, Vincenzo, Via Grande, 10, Sede Legale Torbole Casaglia, Brescia, ITALY / 39-30-8912851-2-3; FAX: 39-030-2150963 bernardelli@bernardelli.com www.bernardelli.com

Berry's Mfg., Inc., 401 North 3050 East St., St. George, UT 84770 / 435-634-1682; FAX: 435-634-1683 sales@berrysmfg.com www.berrysmfg.com

Bersa S.A., Benso Bonadimani, Magallanes 775 B1704 FLC, Ramos Mejia, ARGENTINA / 011-4656-2377; FAX: 011-4656-2093+ info@bersa-sa.com.dr www.bersa-sa.com.ar

Bert Johanssons Vapentillbehor, S-430 20 Veddige, SWEDEN.

Bertuzzi (See U.S. Importer-New England Arms Co.)

Better Concepts Co., 663 New Castle Rd., Butler, PA 16001 / 412-285-9000

Beverly, Mary, 3201 Horseshoe Trail, Tallahassee, FL 32312

Bianchi International, Inc., 100 Calle Cortez, Temecula, CA 92590 / 909-676-5621; FAX: 909-676-6777

Big Bore Bullets of Alaska, P.O. Box 521455, Big Lake, AK 99652 / 907-373-2673; FAX: 907-373-2673 doug@mtaonline.net ww.awloo.com/bbb/index.

Big Bore Express, 2316 E. Railroad St., Nampa, ID 83651 / 800-376-4010 FAX: 208-466-6927 info@powerbeltbullets.com bigbore

MANUFACTURER'S DIRECTORY

Big Spring Enterprises "Bore Stores", P.O. Box 1115, Big Spring Rd., Yellville, AR 72687 / 870-449-5297; FAX: 870-449-4446

Bilal, Mustafa. See: TURK'S HEAD PRODUCTIONS

Bilinski, Bryan. See: FIELDSPORT LTD.

Bill Adair Custom Shop, 2886 Westridge, Carrollton, TX 75006 / 972-418-0950

Bill Austin's Calls, Box 284, Kaycee, WY 82639 / 307-738-2552

Bill Hanus Birdguns, LLC, P.O. Box 533, Newport, OR 97365 / 541-265-7433; FAX: 541-265-7400 www.billhanusbirdguns.com

Bill Russ Trading Post, William A. Russ, 25 William St., Addison, NY 14801-1326 / 607-359-3896

Bill Wiseman and Co., P.O. Box 3427, Bryan, TX 77805 / 409-690-3456; FAX: 409-690-0156

Billeb, Stephen. See: QUALITY CUSTOM FIREARMS

Billings Gunsmiths, 1841 Grand Ave., Billings, MT 59102 / 406-256-8390; FAX: 406-256-6530 blgsgunsmiths@msn.com www.billingsgunsmiths.net

Billingsley & Brownell, P.O. Box 25, Dayton, WY 82836 / 307-655-9344

Bill's Gun Repair, 1007 Burlington St., Mendota, IL 61342 / 815-539-5786

Billy Bates Engraving, 2302 Winthrop Dr. SW, Decatur, AL 35603 / 256-355-3690 bbrn@aol.com www.angelfire.com/al/billybates

Birchwood Casey, 7900 Fuller Rd., Eden Prairie, MN 55344 / 800-328-6156 or 612-937-7933; FAX: 612-937-7979

Birdsong & Assoc., W. E., 1435 Monterey Rd., Florence, MS 39073-9748 / 601-366-8270

Bismuth Cartridge Co., 3500 Maple Ave., Suite 1650, Dallas, TX 75219 / 214-521-5880; FAX: 214-521-9035

Bison Studios, 1409 South Commerce St., Las Vegas, NV 89102 / 702-388-2891; FAX: 702-383-9967

Bitterroot Bullet Co., 2001 Cedar Ave., Lewiston, ID 83501-0412 / 208-743-5635 brootbld@lewiston.com

BKL Technologies, P.O. Box 5237, Brownsville, TX 78523

Black Belt Bullets (See Big Bore Express)

Black Hills Ammunition, Inc., P.O. Box 3090, Rapid City, SD 57709-3090 / 605-348-5150; FAX: 605-348-9827

Black Hills Shooters Supply, P.O. Box 4220, Rapid City, SD 57709 / 800-289-2506

Black Powder Products, 67 Township Rd. 1411, Chesapeake, OH 45619 / 614-867-8047

Black Sheep Brand, 3220 W. Gentry Pkwy., Tyler, TX 75702 / 903-592-3853; FAX: 903-592-0527

Blacksmith Corp., P.O. Box 280, North Hampton, OH 45349 / 937-969-8389; FAX: 937-969-8399 sales@blacksmithcorp.com www.blacksmithcorp.com

BlackStar AccuMax Barrels, 11501 Brittmoore Park Drive, Houston, TX 77041 / 281-721-6040; FAX: 281-721-6041

BlackStar Barrel Accurizing (See BlackStar AccuMax)

Blacktail Mountain Books, 42 First Ave. W., Kalispell, MT 59901 / 406-257-5573

Blammo Ammo, P.O. Box 1677, Seneca, SC 29679 / 803-882-1768

Blaser Jagdwaffen GmbH, D-88316, Isny Im Allgau, GERMANY

Blount, Inc., Sporting Equipment Div., 2299 Snake River Ave., P.O. Box 856, Lewiston, ID 83501 / 800-627-3640 or 208-746-2351; FAX: 208-799-3904

Blount/Outers ATK, P.O. Box 39, Onalaska, WI 54650 / 608-781-5800; FAX: 608-781-0368

Blue and Gray Products Inc. (See Ox-Yoke Originals)

Blue Book Publications, Inc., 8009 34th Ave. S., Ste. 175, Minneapolis, MN 55425 / 952-854-5229; FAX: 952-853-1486 bluebook@bluebookinc.com www.bluebookinc.com

Blue Mountain Bullets, 64146 Quail Ln., Box 231, John Day, OR 97845 / 541-820-4594; FAX: 541-820-4594

Blue Ridge Machinery & Tools, Inc., P.O. Box 536-GD, Hurricane, WV 25526 / 800-872-6500; FAX: 304-562-5311 blueridgemachine@worldnet.att.net www.blueridgemachinery.com

BMC Supply, Inc., 26051 - 179th Ave. SE, Kent, WA 98042

Bob Allen Co., P.O. Box 477, 214 SW Jackson, Des Moines, IA 50315 / 800-685-7020; FAX: 515-283-0779

Bob Allen Sportswear, 220 S. Main St., Osceola, IA 50213 / 210-344-8531; FAX: 210-342-2703 sales@bob-allen.com www.bob-allen.com

Bob Rogers Gunsmithing, P.O. Box 305, 344 S. Walnut St., Franklin Grove, IL 61031 / 815-456-2685; FAX: 815-456-2685 3006bud@netscape.comm

Bob's Gun Shop, P.O. Box 200, Royal, AR 71968 / 501-767-1970; FAX: 501-767-1970 gunparts@hsnp.com www.gun-parts.com

Bob's Tactical Indoor Shooting Range & Gun Shop, 90 Lafayette Rd., Salisbury, MA 01952 / 508-465-5561

Boessler, Erich, Am Vogeltal 3, 97702, Munnerstadt, GERMANY

Boker USA, Inc., 1550 Balsam Street, Lakewood, CO 80214 / 303-462-0662; FAX: 303-462-0668 sales@bokerusa.com bokerusa.com

Boltin, John M., P.O. Box 644, Estill, SC 29918 / 803-625-2185

Bo-Mar Tool & Mfg. Co., 6136 State Hwy. 300, Longview, TX 75604 / 903-759-4784; FAX: 903-759-9141 marykor@earthlink.net bo-mar.com

Bonadimani, Benso. See: BERSA S.A.

Bonanza (See Forster Products), 310 E. Lanark Ave., Lanark, IL 61046 / 815-493-6360; FAX: 815-493-2371

Bond Arms, Inc., P.O. Box 1296, Granbury, TX 76048 / 817-573-4445; FAX: 817-573-5636 www.bondarms.com

Bond Custom Firearms, 8954 N. Lewis Ln., Bloomington, IN 47408 / 812-332-4519

Bonham's & Butterfields, 220 San Bruno Ave., San Francisco, CA 94103 / 415-861-7500; FAX: 415-861-0183 arms@butterfields.com www.butterfields.com

Boone Trading Co., Inc., P.O. Box 669, Brinnon, WA 98320 / 800-423-1945 or 360-796-4330; FAX: 360-796-4511 sales@boonetrading.com boonetrading.com

Boone's Custom Ivory Grips, Inc., 562 Coyote Rd., Brinnon, WA 98320 / 206-796-4330

Boonie Packer Products, P.O. Box 12517, Salem, OR 97309-0517 / 800-477-3244 or 503-581-3244; FAX: 503-581-3191 customerservice@booniepacker.com www.booniepacker.com

Borden Ridges Rimrock Stocks, RR 1 Box 250 BC, Springville, PA 18844 / 570-965-2505; FAX: 570-965-2328

Borden Rifles Inc., RD 1, Box 250 #BC, Springville, PA 18844 / 717-965-2505; FAX: 717-965-2328

Border Barrels Ltd., Riccarton Farm, Newcastleton, SCOTLAND UK

Borovnik K.G., Ludwig, 9170 Ferlach, Bahnhofstrasse 7, AUSTRIA / 042 27 24 42; FAX: 042 26 43 49

Bosis (See U.S. Importer-New England Arms Co.)

Boss Manufacturing Co., 221 W. First St., Kewanee, IL 61443 / 309-852-2131 or 800-447-4581; FAX: 309-852-0848

Bostick Wildlife Calls, Inc., P.O. Box 728, Estill, SC 29918 / 803-625-2210; or 803-625-4512

Bowen Classic Arms Corp., P.O. Box 67, Louisville, TN 37777 / 865-984-3583 www.bowenclassicarms.com

Bowen Knife Co., Inc., P.O. Box 802, Magnolia, AR 71754 / 800-397-4794; FAX: 870-234-9005 info@bowen.com www.bowenknife.com

Bowerly, Kent, 710 Golden Pheasant Dr., Redmond, OR 97756 / 541-923-3501 bowerly@bendbroadband.com

Boyds' Gunstock Industries, Inc., 25376 403 Rd. Ave., Mitchell, SD 57301 / 605-996-5011; FAX: 605-996-9878 www.boydsgunstocks.com

Brace, Larry D., 771 Blackfoot Ave., Eugene, OR 97404 / 541-688-1278; FAX: 541-607-5833

Brauer Bros., 345 Industrial Blvd., Ste. B, McKinney, TX 75069 / 976-548-8881; FAX: 972-548-8886 www.brauerbros.com

Break-Free, Inc., 13386 International Pkwy., Jacksonville, FL 32218 / 800-428-0588; FAX: 904-741-5407 contactus@armorholdings.com www.break-free.com

Brenneke GmbH, P.O. Box 1646, 30837, Langenhagen, GERMANY / +49-511-97262-0; FAX: +49-511-97262-62 info@brenneke.de brenneke.com

Bridgeman Products, Harry Jaffin, 153 B Cross Slope Ct., Englishtown, NJ 07726 / 732-536-3604; FAX: 732-972-1004

Briese Bullet Co., Inc., 3442 42nd Ave. SE, Tappen, ND 58487 / 701-327-4578; FAX: 701-327-4579

Brigade Quartermasters, 1025 Cobb International Blvd., Dept. VH, Kennesaw, GA 30144-4300 / 404-428-1248 or 800-241-3125; FAX: 404-426-7726

Briganti, A.J. See: BRIGANTI CUSTOM GUNSMITH

Briganti Custom Gunsmith, A.J. Briganti, 512 Rt. 32, Highland Mills, NY 10930 / 845-928-9573

Briley Mfg. Inc., 1230 Lumpkin, Houston, TX 77043 / 800-331-5718 or 713-932-6995; FAX: 713-932-1043

Brill, R. See: ROYAL ARMS INTERNATIONAL

British Sporting Arms, RR 1, Box 193A, Millbrook, NY 12545 / 845-677-8303; FAX: 845-677-5756 info@bsaltd.com www.bsaltd.com

Broad Creek Rifle Works, Ltd., 120 Horsey Ave., Laurel, DE 19956 / 302-875-5446; FAX: 302-875-1448 bcrw4guns@aol.com

Brockman's Custom Gunsmithing, P.O. Box 357, Gooding, ID 83330 / 208-934-5050

Broken Gun Ranch, 10739 126 Rd., Spearville, KS 67876 / 316-385-2587; FAX: 316-385-2597 nbowlin@ucom.net www.brokengunranch

Brooker, Dennis, Rt. 1, Box 12A, Derby, IA 50068 / 515-533-2103

Brooks Tactical Systems-Agrip, 279-C Shorewood Ct., Fox Island, WA 98333 / 253-549-2866 FAX: 253-549-2703 brooks@brookstactical.com www.brookstactical.com

Brown Precision, Inc., 7786 Molinos Ave., Los Molinos, CA 96055 / 530-384-2506; FAX: 916-384-1638 www.brownprecision.com

Brownells, Inc., 200 S. Front St., Montezuma, IA 50171 / 800-741-0015; FAX: 800-264-3068 orderdesk@brownells.com www.brownells.com

Browning Arms Co., One Browning Place, Morgan, UT 84050 / 801-876-2711; FAX: 801-876-3331 www.browning.com

Browning Arms Co. (Parts & Service), 3005 Arnold Tenbrook Rd., Arnold, MO 63010 / 617-287-6800; FAX: 617-287-9751

BRP, Inc. High Performance Cast Bullets, 1210 Alexander Rd., Colorado Springs, CO 80909 / 719-633-0658

Brunton U.S.A., 620 E. Monroe Ave., Riverton, WY 82501 / 307-856-6559; FAX: 307-857-4702 info@brunton.com www.brunton.com

Bryan & Assoc., R. D. Sauls, P.O. Box 5772, Anderson, SC 29623-5772 / 864-261-6810 bryanandac@aol.com www.huntersweb.com/bryanandac

Brynin, Milton, P.O. Box 383, Yonkers, NY 10710 / 914-779-4333

BSA Guns Ltd., Armoury Rd. Small Heath, Birmingham B11 2PP, ENGLAND / 011-021-772-8543; FAX: 011-021-773-0845 sales@bsagun.com www.bsagun.com

BSA Optics, Inc., 3911 SW 47th Ave., Ste. 914, Ft. Lauderdale, FL 33314 / 954-581-2144; FAX: 954-581-3165 4info@basaoptics.com www.bsaoptics.com

B-Square Company, Inc., 8909 Forum Way, Ft. Worth, TX 76140 / 800-433-2909; FAX: 817-926-7012 bsquare@b-square.com www.b-square.com

Buchsenmachermeister, Peter Hofer Jagdwaffen, A-9170 Ferlach, Kirchgasse 24, Kirchgasse, AUSTRIA / 43 4227 3683; or 43 664 3200216; FAX: 43 4227 368330 peterhofer@hoferwaffen.com www.hoferwaffen.com

Buck Knives, Inc., 1900 Weld Blvd., P.O. Box 1267, El Cajon, CA 92020 / 619-449-1100 or 800-326-2825; FAX: 619-562-5774

Buck Stix-SOS Products Co., Box 3, Neenah, WI 54956

Buck Stop Lure Co., Inc., 3600 Grow Rd. NW, P.O. Box 636, Stanton, MI 48888 / 989-762-5091; FAX: 989-762-5124 buckstop@nethawk.com www.buckstopscents.com

Buckeye Custom Bullets, 6490 Stewart Rd., Elida, OH 45807 / 419-641-4463

Buckhorn Gun Works, 8109 Woodland Dr., Black Hawk, SD 57718 / 605-787-6472

Buckskin Bullet Co., P.O. Box 1893, Cedar City, UT 84721 / 435-586-3286

Budin, Dave, 817 Main St., P.O. Box 685, Margaretville, NY 12455 / 914-568-4103; FAX: 914-586-4105

Budin, Dave. See: DEL-SPORTS, INC.

Buehler Custom Sporting Arms, P.O. Box 4096, Medford, OR 97501 / 541-664-9109 rbrifle@earthlink.net

Buenger Enterprises/Goldenrod Dehumidifier, 3600 S. Harbor Blvd., Oxnard, CA 93035 / 800-451-6797 or 805-985-5828; FAX: 805-985-1534

Buffalo Arms Co., 660 Vermeer Ct., Ponderay, ID 83852 / 208-263-6953; FAX: 208-265-2096 www.buffaloarms.com

Buffalo Bullet Co., Inc., 12637 Los Nietos Rd., Unit A, Santa Fe Springs, CA 90670 / 800-423-8069; FAX: 562-944-5054 rdanlitz@verizon.net

Buffalo Gun Center, 3385 Harlem Rd., Buffalo, NY 14225 / 716-833-2581; FAX: 716-833-2265 www.buffaloguncenter.com

Buffalo Rock Shooters Supply, R.R. 1, Ottawa, IL 61350 / 815-433-2471

550 ✦ *GUN DIGEST*®

Buffer Technologies, P.O. Box 105047, Jefferson City, MO 65110 / 573-634-8529; FAX: 573-634-8522 sales@buffertech.com buffertech.com

Bull Mountain Rifle Co., 6327 Golden West Terrace, Billings, MT 59106 / 406-656-0778

Bullberry Barrel Works, Ltd., 2430 W. Bullberry Ln., Hurricane, UT 84737 / 435-635-9866; FAX: 435-635-0348 fred@bullberry.com www.bullberry.com

Bullet Metals, Bill Ferguson, P.O. Box 1238, Sierra Vista, AZ 85636 / 520-458-5321; FAX: 520-458-1421 info@theantimonyman.com www.bullet-metals.com

Bullet N Press, 1210 Jones St., Gastonia, NC 28052 / 704-853-0265 bnpress@quik.com www.oldwestgunsmith.com

Bullet Swaging Supply, Inc., P.O. Box 1056, 303 McMillan Rd., West Monroe, LA 71291 / 318-387-3266; FAX: 318-387-7779 leblackmon@colla.com

Bull-X, Inc., 411 E. Water St., Farmer City, IL 61842-1556 / 309-928-2574 or 800-248-3845; FAX: 309-928-2130

Burkhart Gunsmithing, Don, P.O. Box 852, Rawlins, WY 82301 / 307-324-6007

Burnham Bros., P.O. Box 1148, Menard, TX 78659 / 915-396-4572; FAX: 915-396-4574

Burris Co., Inc., P.O. Box 1747, 331 E. 8th St., Greeley, CO 80631 / 970-356-1670; FAX: 970-356-8702

Bushmaster Firearms, Inc., 999 Roosevelt Trail, Windham, ME 04062 / 800-998-7928; FAX: 207-892-8068 info@bushmaster.com www.bushmaster.com

Bushmaster Hunting & Fishing, 451 Alliance Ave., Toronto, ON M6N 2J1 CANADA / 416-763-4040; FAX: 416-763-0623

Bushnell Outdoor Products, 9200 Cody, Overland Park, KS 66214 / 913-752-3400 or 800-423-3537; FAX: 913-752-3550

Buster's Custom Knives, P.O. Box 214, Richfield, UT 84701 / 435-896-5319; FAX: 435-896-8333 www.warenskiknives.com

Butler Creek Corp., 9200 Cody St., Overland Park, KS 66214 / 800-845-2444 or 406-388-1356; FAX: 406-388-7204

Butler Enterprises, 834 Oberting Rd., Lawrenceburg, IN 47025 / 812-537-3584

Buzz Fletcher Custom Stockmaker, 117 Silver Road, P.O. Box 189, Taos, NM 87571 / 505-758-3486

C

C&D Special Products (See Claybuster Wads & Harvester Bullets)

C&H Research, 115 Sunnyside Dr., Box 351, Lewis, KS 67552 / 316-324-5445 or 888-324-5445; FAX: 620-324-5984 info@mercuryrecoil.com www.mercuryrecoil.com

C. Sharps Arms Co. Inc./Montana Armory, 100 Centennial Dr., P.O. Box 885, Big Timber, MT 59011 / 406-932-4353; FAX: 406-932-4443

C.S. Van Gorden & Son, Inc., 1815 Main St., Bloomer, WI 54724 / 715-568-2612 vangorden@bloomer.net

C.W. Erickson's Mfg., L.L.C., P.O. Box 522, Buffalo, MN 55313 / 763-682-3665; FAX: 763-682-4328 cwerickson@archerhunter.com www.archerhunter.com

Cabanas (See U.S. Importer-Mandall Shooting Supply

Cabela's, One Cabela Drive, Sidney, NE 69160 / 308-254-5505; FAX: 308-254-8420

Cabinet Mtn. Outfitters Scents & Lures, P.O. Box 766, Plains, MT 59859 / 406-826-3970

Cache La Poudre Rifleworks, 140 N. College, Ft. Collins, CO 80524 / 920-482-6913

Caesar Guerini USA, Inc., 700 Lake St., Cambridge, MD 21613 / 410-901-1131; FAX: 410-901-1137 info@gueriniusa.com www.gueriniusa.com

Cain's Outdoors, Inc., 1832 Williams Hwy., Williamstown, WV 26187 / 304-375-7842; FAX: 304-375-7842 muzzleloading@cainsoutdoor.com www.cainsoutdoor.com

Cali'co Hardwoods, Inc., 3580 Westwind Blvd., Santa Rosa, CA 95403 / 707-546-4045; FAX: 707-546-4027 calicohardwoods@msn.com

California Sights (See Fautheree, Andy)

Cambos Outdoorsman, 532 E. Idaho Ave., Ontario, OR 97914 / 541-889-3135; FAX: 541-889-2633

Cambos Outdoorsman, Fritz Hallberg, 532 E. Idaho Ave., Ontario, OR 97914 / 541-889-3135; FAX: 541-889-2633

Camdex, Inc., 2330 Alger, Troy, MI 48083 / 810-528-2300; FAX: 810-528-0989

Cameron's, 16690 W. 11th Ave., Golden, CO 80401 / 303-279-7365; FAX: 303-568-1009 ncnoremac@aol.com

Camillus Cutlery Co., 54 Main St., Camillus, NY 13031 / 315-672-8111; FAX: 315-672-8832

Campbell, Dick, 196 Garden Homes Dr., Colville, WA 99114 / 509-684-6080; FAX: 509-684-6080 dicksknives@aol.com

Camp-Cap Products, P.O. Box 3805, Chesterfield, MO 63006 / 866-212-4639; FAX: 636-536-6320 mandrytrc@sbcglobal.net www.langenberghats.com

Cannon Safe, Inc., 216 S. 2nd Ave. #BLD-932, San Bernardino, CA 92400 / 310-692-0636 or 800-242-1055; FAX: 310-692-7252

Canyon Cartridge Corp., P.O. Box 152, Albertson, NY 11507 FAX: 516-294-8946

Cape Outfitters, 599 County Rd. 206, Cape Girardeau, MO 63701 / 573-335-4103; FAX: 573-335-1555

Caraville Manufacturing, P.O. Box 4545, Thousand Oaks, CA 91359 / 805-499-1234

Carbide Checkering Tools (See J&R Engineering)

Carhartt, Inc., 5750 Mercury Dr., Dearborn, MI 48126 / 800-833-3118 www.carhartt.com

Carl Walther GmbH, B.P. 4325, D-89033, Ulm, GERMANY

Carl Zeiss Inc., 13005 N. Kingston Ave., Chester, VA 23836 / 800-338-2984; FAX: 804-530-8481

Carolina Precision Rifles, 1200 Old Jackson Hwy., Jackson, SC 29831 / 803-827-2069

Carrell, William. See: CARRELL'S PRECISION FIREARMS

Carrell's Precision Firearms, William Carrell, 1952 W.Silver Falls Ct., Meridian, ID 83642-3837

Carry-Lite, Inc., P.O. Box 1587, Fort Smith, AR 72902 / 479-782-8971; FAX: 479-783-0234

Carter's Gun Shop, 225 G St., Penrose, CO 81240 / 719-372-6240 rlewiscarter@msn.com

Case & Sons Cutlery Co., W R, Owens Way, Bradford, PA 16701 / 814-368-4123 or 800-523-6350; FAX: 814-768-5369

Case Sorting System, 12695 Cobblestone Creek Rd., Poway, CA 92064 / 619-486-9340

Cash Mfg. Co./ TDC, P.O. Box 130, 201 S. Klein Dr., Waunakee, WI 53597-0130 / 608-849-5664; FAX: 608-849-5664 office@tdcmfg.com www.tdcmfg.com

Caspian Arms, Ltd., 14 North Main St., Hardwick, VT 05843 / 802-472-6454; FAX: 802-472-6709

Cast Bullet Association, The, 12857 S. Road, Hoyt, KS 66440-9116 cbamemdir@castbulletassoc.org www.castbulletassoc.org

Cast Performance Bullet Company, P.O. Box 153, Riverton, WY 82501 / 307-857-2940; FAX: 307-857-3132 castperform@wyoming.com castperformance.com

Casull Arms Corp., P.O. Box 1629, Afton, WY 83110 / 307-886-0200

Caswell International, 720 Industrial Dr. No. 112, Cary, IL 60013 / 847-639-7666; FAX: 847-639-7694 www.caswellintl.com

Cathey Enterprises, Inc., P.O. Box 2202, Brownwood, TX 76804 / 915-643-2553; FAX: 915-643-3653

Cation, 2341 Alger St., Troy, MI 48083 / 810-689-0658; FAX: 810-689-7558

Caywood, Shane J., P.O. Box 321, Minocqua, WI 54548 / 715-277-3866

Caywood Gunmakers, 18 Kings Hill Estates, Berryville, AR 72616 / 870-423-4741 www.caywoodguns.com

CBC, Avenida Humberto de Campos 3220, 09400-000, Ribeirao Pires, SP, BRAZIL / 55 11 4822 8378; FAX: 55 11 4822 8323 export@cbc.com.bc www.cbc.com.bc

CBC-BRAZIL, 3 Cuckoo Lane, Honley, Yorkshire HD7 2BR, ENGLAND / 44-1484-661062; FAX: 44-1484-663709

CCG Enterprises, 5217 E. Belknap St., Halton City, TX 76117 / 800-819-7464

CCI/Speer Div of ATK, P.O. Box 856, 2299 Snake River Ave., Lewiston, ID 83501 / 800-627-3640 or 208-746-2351

CCL Security Products, 199 Whiting St., New Britain, CT 06051 / 800-733-8588

Cedar Hill Game Calls, LLC, 238 Vic Allen Rd., Downsville, LA 71234 / 318-982-5632; FAX: 318-982-2031

Centaur Systems, Inc., 1602 Foothill Rd., Kalispell, MT 59901 / 406-755-8609; FAX: 406-755-8609

Center Lock Scope Rings, 9901 France Ct., Lakeville, MN 55044 / 952-461-2114; FAX: 952-461-2194 marklee55044@usfamily.net

Central Specialties Ltd. (See Trigger Lock Division)

Century International Arms, Inc., 430 S. Congress Ave. Ste. 1, Delray Beach, FL 33445-4701 / 800-527-1252; FAX: 561-998-1993 support@centuryarms.com www.centuryarms.com

CFVentures, 509 Harvey Dr., Bloomington, IN 47403-1715 paladinwilltravel@yahoo.com www.caversam16.freeserve.co.uk

CH Tool & Die Co. (See 4-D Custom Die Co.), 711 N Sandusky St., P.O. Box 889, Mt. Vernon, OH 43050-0889 / 740-397-7214; FAX: 740-397-6600

Chace Leather Products, 507 Alden St., Fall River, MA 02722 / 508-678-7556; FAX: 508-675-9666 chacelea@aol.com www.chaceleather.com

Chadick's Ltd., P.O. Box 100, Terrell, TX 75160 / 214-563-7577

Chambers Flintlocks Ltd., Jim, 116 Sams Branch Rd., Candler, NC 28715 / 828-667-8361; FAX: 828-665-0852 www.flintlocks.com

Champion Shooters' Supply, P.O. Box 303, New Albany, OH 43054 / 614-855-1603; FAX: 614-855-1209

Champion Target Co., 232 Industrial Parkway, Richmond, IN 47374 / 800-441-4971

Champion's Choice, Inc., 201 International Blvd., LaVergne, TN 37086 / 615-793-4066; FAX: 615-793-4070 champ.choice@earthlink.net www.champchoice.com

Champlin Firearms, Inc., P.O. Box 3191, Woodring Airport, Enid, OK 73701 / 580-237-7388; FAX: 580-242-6922 info@champlinarms.com www.champlinarms.com

Chapman Academy of Practical Shooting, 4350 Academy Rd., Hallsville, MO 65255 / 573-696-5544; FAX: 573-696-2266 hq@chapmanacademy.com chapmanacademy.com

Chapman, J. Ken. See: OLD WEST BULLET MOULDS

Chapman Manufacturing Co., 471 New Haven Rd., P.O. Box 250, Durham, CT 06422 / 860-349-9228; FAX: 860-349-0084 sales@chapmanmfg.com www.chapmanmfg.com

Chapuis Armes, Z1 La Gravoux, BP15, 42380 P.O. Box 15, St. Bonnet-le-Chatea, FRANCE / (33)477.50.06.96; FAX: (33)477 50 10 70 info@chapuis.armes.com www.chapuis-armes.com

Charter 2000, 273 Canal St., Shelton, CT 06484 / 203-922-1652

Checkmate Refinishing, 370 Champion Dr., Brooksville, FL 34601 / 352-799-5774; FAX: 352-799-2986 checkmatecustom.com

Cheddite, France S.A., 99 Route de Lyon, F-26501, Bourg-les-Valence, FRANCE / 33-75-56-4545; FAX: 33-75-56-3587 export@cheddite.com

Chelsea Gun Club of New York City Inc., 237 Ovington Ave., Apt. D53, Brooklyn, NY 11209 / 718-836-9422; or 718-833-2704

CheVron Bullets, RR1, Ottawa, IL 61350 / 815-433-2471

Cheyenne Pioneer Products, P.O. Box 28425, Kansas City, MO 64188 / 816-413-9196; FAX: 816-455-2859 cheyennepp@aol.com www.cartridgeboxes.com

Chicago Cutlery Co., 5500 N. Pearl St., Ste. 400, Rosemont, IL 60018 / 847-678-8600 www.chicagocutlery.com

Chicasaw Gun Works, 4 Mi. Mkr., Pluto Rd., Box 2024, Shady Spring, WV 25918-0868 / 304-763-2848; FAX: 304-763-3725

Chip McCormick Corp., P.O. Box 694, Spicewood, TX 78669 / 800-328-2447; FAX: 830-693-4975 www.chipmccormickcorp.com

Chipmunk (See Oregon Arms, Inc.)

Choate Machine & Tool Co., Inc., P.O. Box 218, 116 Lovers Ln., Bald Knob, AR 72010 / 501-724-6193; or 800-972-6390; FAX: 501-724-5873

Christensen Arms, 192 East 100 North, Fayette, UT 84630 / 435-528-7999; FAX: 435-528-7494 www.christensenarms.com

Christie's East, 20 Rockefeller Plz., New York, NY 10020-1902 / 212-606-0406 christics.com

Chu Tani Ind., Inc., P.O. Box 2064, Cody, WY 82414-2064

Chuck's Gun Shop, P.O. Box 597, Waldo, FL 32694 / 904-468-2264

Churchill (See U.S. Importer-Ellett Bros.)

Churchill, Winston G., 2838 20 Mile Stream Rd., Proctorville, VT 05153 / 802-226-7772

Churchill Glove Co., James, P.O. Box 298, Centralia, WA 98531 / 360-736-2816; FAX: 360-330-0151

CIDCO, 21480 Pacific Blvd., Sterling, VA 22170 / 703-444-5353

Cimarron F.A. Co., P.O. Box 906, Fredericksburg, TX 78624-0906 / 830-997-9090; FAX: 830-997-0802 cimgraph@koc.com www.cimarron-firearms.com

Cincinnati Swaging, 2605 Marlington Ave., Cincinnati, OH 45208

Clark Custom Guns, Inc., 336 Shootout Lane, Princeton, LA 71067 / 318-949-9884; FAX: 318-949-9829

Clark Firearms Engraving, 6347 Avon Ave., San Gabriel, CA 91775-1801 / 818-287-1652

Clarkfield Enterprises, Inc., 1032 10th Ave., Clarkfield, MN 56223 / 612-669-7140

Claro Walnut Gunstock Co., 1235 Stanley Ave., Chico, CA 95928 / 530-342-5188; FAX: 530-342-5199 wally@clarowalnutgunstocks.com www.clarowalnutgunstocks.com

Classic Arms Company, Rt 1 Box 120F, Burnet, TX 78611 / 512-756-4001

Classic Arms Corp., P.O. Box 106, Dunsmuir, CA 96025-0106 / 530-235-2000

Classic Old West Styles, 1060 Doniphan Park Circle C, El Paso, TX 79936 / 915-587-0684

Claybuster Wads & Harvester Bullets, 309 Sequoya Dr., Hopkinsville, KY 42240 / 800-922-6287; or 800-284-1746; FAX: 502-885-8088

Clean Shot Technologies, 21218 St. Andrews Blvd. Ste 504, Boca Raton, FL 33433 / 888-866-2532

Clearview Mfg. Co., Inc., 413 S. Oakley St., Fordyce, AR 71742 / 870-352-8557; FAX: 870-352-7120

Clearview Products, 3021 N. Portland, Oklahoma City, OK 73107

Cleland's Outdoor World, Inc., 10306 Airport Hwy., Swanton, OH 43558 / 419-865-4713; FAX: 419-865-5865 hasresa@cieiancs.com www.clelands.com

Clements' Custom Leathercraft, Chas, 1741 Dallas St., Aurora, CO 80010-2018 / 303-364-0403; FAX: 303-739-9824 gryphons@home.com kuntaoslcat.com

Clenzoil Worldwide Corp., Jack Fitzgerald, 25670 1st St., Westlake, OH 44145-1430 / 440-899-0482; FAX: 440-899-0483

Clift Mfg., L. R., 3821 Hammonton Rd., Marysville, CA 95901 / 916-755-3390; FAX: 916-755-3393

Clymer Mfg. Co., 1645 W. Hamlin Rd., Rochester Hills, MI 48309-3312 / 248-853-5555; FAX: 248-853-1530

C-More Systems, P.O. Box 1750, 7553 Gary Rd., Manassas, VA 20108 / 703-361-2663; FAX: 703-361-5881

Cobra Enterprises, Inc., 1960 S. Milestone Drive, Suite F, Salt Lake City, UT 84104 FAX: 801-908-8301 www.cobrapistols@networld.com

Cobra Sport S.R.I., Via Caduti Nei Lager No. 1, 56020 San Romano, Montopoli v/Arno Pi, ITALY / 0039-571-450490; FAX: 0039-571-450492

Coffin, Charles H., 3719 Scarlet Ave., Odessa, TX 79762 / 915-366-4729; FAX: 915-366-4729

Cogar's Gunsmithing, 206 Redwine Dr., Houghton Lake, MI 48629 / 517-422-4591 ecogar@peoplepc.com

Coghlan's Ltd., 121 Irene St., Winnipeg, MB R3T 4C7 CANADA / 204-284-9550; FAX: 204-475-4127

Cold Steel Inc., 3036 Seaborg Ave. Ste. A, Ventura, CA 93003 / 800-255-4716; or 800-624-2363; FAX: 805-642-9727

Cole-Grip, 16135 Cohasset St., Van Nuys, CA 91406 / 818-782-4424

Coleman Co., Inc., 3600 N. Hydraulic, Wichita, KS 67219 / 800-835-3278 www.coleman.com

Cole's Gun Works, Old Bank Building, Rt. 4 Box 250, Moyock, NC 27958 / 919-435-2345

Collector's Armoury, Ltd., Tom Nelson, 9404 Gunston Cove Rd., Lorton, VA 22079 / 703-493-9120; FAX: 703-493-9424 www.collectorsarmoury.com

Collings, Ronald, 1006 Cielta Linda, Vista, CA 92083

Colonial Arms, Inc., P.O. Box 636, Selma, AL 36702-0636 / 334-872-9455; FAX: 334-872-9540 colonialarms@mindspring.com www.colonialarms.com

Colonial Repair, 47 Navarre St., Roslindale, MA 02131-4725 / 617-469-4951

Colorado Gunsmithing Academy, RR 3 Box 79B, El Campo, TX 77437 / 719-336-4099 or 800-754-2046; FAX: 719-336-9642

Colorado School of Trades, 1575 Hoyt St., Lakewood, CO 80215 / 800-234-4594; FAX: 303-233-4723

Colt Blackpowder Arms Co., 110 8th Street, Brooklyn, NY 11215 / 718-499-4678; FAX: 718-768-8056

Colt's Mfg. Co., Inc., P.O. Box 1868, Hartford, CT 06144-1868 / 800-962-COLT or 860-236-6311; FAX: 860-244-1449

Compass Industries, Inc., 104 East 25th St., New York, NY 10010 / 212-473-2614 or 800-221-9904; FAX: 212-353-0826

Compasseco, Ltd., 151 Atkinson Hill Ave., Bardstown, KY 40004 / 502-349-0910

Competition Electronics, Inc., 3469 Precision Dr., Rockford, IL 61109 / 815-874-8001; FAX: 815-874-8181

Competitive Pistol Shop, The, 5233 Palmer Dr., Fort Worth, TX 76117-2433 / 817-834-8479

Competitor Corp., Inc., 26 Knight St. Unit 3, P.O. Box 352, Jaffrey, NH 03452 / 603-532-9483; FAX: 603-532-8209 competitorcorp@aol.com competitor-pistol.com

Component Concepts, Inc., 530 S. Springbrook Road, Newberg, OR 97132 / 503-554-8095; FAX: 503-554-9370 cci@cybcon.com www.phantomonline.com

Concealment Shop, Inc., The, 3550 E. Hwy. 80, Mesquite, TX 75149 / 972-289-8997 or 800-444-7090; FAX: 972-289-4410 info@theconcealmentshop.com www.theconcealmentshop.com

Concept Development Corp., 16610 E. Laser Drive, Suite 5, Fountain Hills, AZ 85268-6644

Conetrol Scope Mounts, 10225 Hwy. 123 S., Seguin, TX 78155 / 830-379-3030 or 800-CONETROL; FAX: 830-379-3030 email@conetrol.com www.conetrol.com

Connecticut Shotgun Mfg. Co., P.O. Box 1692, 35 Woodland St., New Britain, CT 06051 / 860-225-6581; FAX: 860-832-8707

Connecticut Valley Classics (See CVC, BPI)

Conrad, C. A., 3964 Ebert St., Winston-Salem, NC 27127 / 919-788-5469

Cook Engineering Service, 891 Highbury Rd., Vict 3133, 3133 AUSTRALIA

Cooper Arms, P.O. Box 114, Stevensville, MT 59870 / 406-777-0373; FAX: 406-777-0228

Cooper-Woodward Perfect Lube, 4120 Oesterle Rd., Helena, MT 59602 / 406-459-2287 cwperfectlube@mt.net cwperfectlube.com

Corbin Mfg. & Supply, Inc., 600 Industrial Circle, P.O. Box 2659, White City, OR 97503 / 541-826-5211; FAX: 541-826-8669 sales@corbins.com www.corbins.com

Cor-Bon Inc./Glaser LLC, P.O. Box 173, 1311 Industry Rd., Sturgis, SD 57785 / 605-347-4544 or 800-221-3489; FAX: 605-347-5055 email@corbon.com www.corbon.com

Corkys Gun Clinic, 4401 Hot Springs Dr., Greeley, CO 80634-9226 / 970-330-0516

Corry, John, 861 Princeton Ct., Neshanic Station, NJ 08853 / 908-369-8019

Cosmi Americo & Figlio S.N.C., Via Flaminia 307, Ancona, ITALY / 071-888208; FAX: 39-071-887008

Coulston Products, Inc., P.O. Box 30, 201 Ferry St. Suite 212, Easton, PA 18044-0030 / 215-253-0167 or 800-445-9927; FAX: 215-252-1511

Counter Assault, 120 Industrial Court, Kalispell, MT 59901 / 406-257-4740; FAX: 406-257-6674

Country Armourer, The, P.O. Box 308, Ashby, MA 01431-0308 / 508-827-6797; FAX: 508-827-4845

Cousin Bob's Mountain Products, 7119 Ohio River Blvd., Ben Avon, PA 15202 / 412-766-5114; FAX: 412-766-9354

CP Bullets, 1310 Industrial Hwy #5-6, Southhampton, PA 18966 / 215-953-7264; FAX: 215-953-7275

CQB Training, P.O. Box 1739, Manchester, MO 63011

Craftguard, 3624 Logan Ave., Waterloo, IA 50703 / 319-232-2959; FAX: 319-234-0804

Crandall Tool & Machine Co., 19163 21 Mile Rd., Tustin, MI 49688 / 616-829-4430

Creative Craftsman, Inc., The, 95 Highway 29 N., P.O. Box 331, Lawrenceville, GA 30246 / 404-963-2112; FAX: 404-513-9488

Creedmoor Sports, Inc., 3052 Industry St. #103, Oceanside, CA 92054 / 767-757-5529; FAX: 760-757-5558 shoot@creedmoorsports.com www.creedmoorsports.com

Creek Side Metal & Woodcrafters, Fishers Hill, VA 22626 / 703-465-3903

Creighton Audette, 19 Highland Circle, Springfield, VT 05156 / 802-885-2331

Crimson Trace Lasers, 8090 S.W. Cirrus Dr., Beverton, OR 97008 / 800-442-2406; FAX: 503-627-0166 travis@crimsontrace.com www.crimsontrace.com

Crit' R Call, P.O. Box 999, La Porte, CO 80535 / 970-484-2768; FAX: 970-484-0807 critrcall@larinet.net www.critrcall.com

Crit'R Call (See Rocky Mountain Wildlife Products)

Crosman Airguns, Rts. 5 and 20, E. Bloomfield, NY 14443 / 716-657-6161; FAX: 716-657-5405

Crosman Blades (See Coleman Co., Inc.)

CRR, Inc./Marble's Inc., 420 Industrial Park, P.O. Box 111, Gladstone, MI 49837 / 906-428-3710; FAX: 906-428-3711

Crucelegui, Hermanos (See U.S. Importer-Mandall)

Cubic Shot Shell Co., Inc., 98 Fatima Dr., Campbell, OH 44405 / 330-755-0349

Cullity Restoration, 209 Old Country Rd., East Sandwich, MA 02537 / 508-888-1147

Cumberland Arms, 514 Shafer Road, Manchester, TN 37355 / 800-797-8414

Cummings Bullets, 1417 Esperanza Way, Escondido, CA 92027

Cupp, Alana, Custom Engraver, P.O. Box 207, Annabella, UT 84711 / 801-896-4834

Curly Maple Stock Blanks (See Tiger-Hunt)

Curtis Cast Bullets, 527 W. Babcock St., Bozeman, MT 59715 / 406-587-8117; FAX: 406-587-8117

Curtis Gun Shop (See Curtis Cast Bullets)

Custom Bullets by Hoffman, 2604 Peconic Ave., Seaford, NY 11783

Custom Calls, 607 N. 5th St., Burlington, IA 52601 / 319-752-4465

Custom Checkering Service, Kathy Forster, 2124 S.E. Yamhill St., Portland, OR 97214 / 503-236-5874

Custom Products (See Jones Custom Products)

Custom Shop, The, 890 Cochrane Crescent, Peterborough, ON K9H 5N3 CANADA / 705-742-6693

Custom Single Shot Rifles, 9651 Meadows Lane, Guthrie, OK 73044 / 405-282-3634

Custom Tackle and Ammo, P.O. Box 1886, Farmington, NM 87499 / 505-632-3539

Cutco Cutlery, P.O. Box 810, Olean, NY 14760 / 716-372-3111

CVA, 5988 Peachtree Corners East, Norcross, GA 30071 / 770-449-4687; FAX: 770-242-8546 info@cva.com www.cva.com

Cylinder & Slide, Inc., William R. Laughridge, 245 E. 4th St., Fremont, NE 68025 / 402-721-4277; FAX: 402-721-0263 bill@cylinder-slide.com www.clinder-slide.com

CZ USA, P.O. Box 171073, Kansas City, KS 66117 / 913-321-1811; FAX: 913-321-4901

D

D&D Gunsmiths, Ltd., 363 E. Elmwood, Troy, MI 48083 / 248-583-1512; FAX: 248-583-1524

D&G Precision Duplicators (See Greenwood Precision)

D&L Industries (See D.J. Marketing)

D&L Sports, P.O. Box 651, Gillette, WY 82717 / 307-686-4008

D.C. Engineering, Inc., 8633 Southfield Fwy., Detroit, MI 48228-1975 / 248-634-0941 guns@rifletech.com www.rifletech.com

D.C.C. Enterprises, 259 Wynburn Ave., Athens, GA 30601

D.J. Marketing, 10602 Horton Ave., Downey, CA 90241 / 310-806-0891; FAX: 310-806-6231

D.L. Unmussig Bullets, 7862 Brentford Dr., Richmond, VA 23225 / 804-320-1165; FAX: 804-320-4587

Dade Screw Machine Products, 2319 N.W. 7th Ave., Miami, FL 33127 / 305-573-5050

Daisy Outdoor Products, P.O. Box 220, Rogers, AR 72757 / 479-636-1200; FAX: 479-636-0573 www.daisy.com

Dakota (See U.S. Importer-EMF Co., Inc.)

Dakota Arms, Inc., 130 Industry Road, Sturgis, SD 57785 / 605-347-4686; FAX: 605-347-4459 info@dakotaarms.com www.dakotaarms.com

Dakota Corp., 77 Wales St., P.O. Box 543, Rutland, VT 05701 / 802-775-6062 or 800-451-4167; FAX: 802-773-3919

Daly, Charles/KBI, P.O. Box 6625, Harrisburg, PA 17112 / 866-DALY GUN

Da-Mar Gunsmith's, Inc., 102 1st St., Solvay, NY 13209

damascususa@inteliport.com, 149 Deans Farm Rd., Tyner, NC 27980 / 252-221-2010; FAX: 252-221-2010 damascususa@inteliport.com www.damascususa.com

Dan Wesson Firearms, 5169 Rt. 12 South, Norwich, NY 13815 / 607-336-1174; FAX: 607-336-2730 dwservice@cz-usa.com dz-usa.com

Dangler, Homer L., 2870 Lee Marie Dr., Adrian, MI 49221 / 517-266-1997

Danner Shoe Mfg. Co., 12722 N.E. Airport Way, Portland, OR 97230 / 503-251-1100 or 800-345-0430; FAX: 503-251-1119

Dan's Whetstone Co., Inc., 418 Hilltop Rd., Pearcy, AR 71964 / 501-767-1616; FAX: 501-767-9598 questions@danswhetstone.com www.danswhetstone.com

MANUFACTURER'S DIRECTORY

Danuser Machine Co., 550 E. Third St., P.O. Box 368, Fulton, MO 65251 / 573-642-2246; FAX: 573-642-2240 sales@danuser.com www.danuser.com

Dara-Nes, Inc. (See Nesci Enterprises, Inc.)

D'Arcy Echols & Co., P.O. Box 421, Millville, UT 84326 / 435-755-6842

Darlington Gun Works, Inc., P.O. Box 698, 516 S. 52 Bypass, Darlington, SC 29532 / 803-393-3931

Darwin Hensley Gunmaker, P.O. Box 329, Brightwood, OR 97011 / 503-622-5411

Data Tech Software Systems, 19312 East Eldorado Drive, Aurora, CO 80013

Dave Norin Schrank's Smoke & Gun, 2010 Washington St., Waukegan, IL 60085 / 708-662-4034

Dave's Gun Shop, P.O. Box 2824, Casper, WY 82602-2824 / 307-754-9724

David Clark Co., Inc., P.O. Box 15054, Worcester, MA 01615 / 508-756-6216; FAX: 508-753-5827 sales@davidclark.com www.davidclark.com

David Condon, Inc., 109 E. Washington St., Middleburg, VA 22117 / 703-687-5642

David Miller Co., 3131 E. Greenlee Rd., Tucson, AZ 85716 / 520-326-3117

David R. Chicoine, 1210 Jones Street, Gastonia, NC 28052 / 704-853-0265 bnpress@quik.com www.oldwestgunsmith.com

David W. Schwartz Custom Guns, 2505 Waller St., Eau Claire, WI 54703 / 715-832-1735

Davide Pedersoli and Co., Via Artigiani 57, Gardone VT, Brescia 25063, ITALY / 030-8915000; FAX: 030-8911019 info@davide-pedersoli.com www.davide_pedersoli.com

Davis, Don, 1619 Heights, Katy, TX 77493 / 713-391-3090

Davis Industries (See Cobra Enterprises, Inc.)

Davis Products, Mike, 643 Loop Dr., Moses Lake, WA 98837 / 509-765-6178 or 509-766-7281

Daystate Ltd., Birch House Lanee, Cotes Heath Staffs, ST15.022, ENGLAND / 01782-791755; FAX: 01782-791617

Dayton Traister, 4778 N. Monkey Hill Rd., P.O. Box 593, Oak Harbor, WA 98277 / 360-679-4657; FAX: 360-675-1114

D-Boone Ent., Inc., 5900 Colwyn Dr., Harrisburg, PA 17109

Dead Eye's Sport Center, 76 Baer Rd., Shickshinny, PA 18655 / 570-256-7432 deadeyeprizz@aol.com

Deepeeka Exports Pvt. Ltd., D-78, Saket, Meerut-250-006, INDIA / 011-91-121-640363 or ; FAX: 011-91-121-640988 deepeeka@poboxes.com www.deepeeka.com

Defense Training International, Inc., 749 S. Lemay, Ste. A3-337, Ft. Collins, CO 80524 / 303-482-2520; FAX: 303-482-0548

deHaas Barrels, 20049 W. State Hwy. Z, Ridgeway, MO 64481 / 660-872-6308

Del Rey Products, P.O. Box 5134, Playa Del Rey, CA 90296-5134 / 213-823-0494

Delhi Gun House, 1374 Kashmere Gate, New Delhi 110 006, INDIA / 2940974; or 394-0974; FAX: 2917344 dgh@vsnl.com

Delorge, Ed, 6734 W. Main, Houma, LA 70360 / 985-223-0206 delorge@triparish.net www.eddelorge.com

Del-Sports, Inc., Dave Budin, P.O. Box 685, 817 Main St., Margaretville, NY 12455 / 845-586-4103; FAX: 845-586-4105

Delta Arms Ltd., P.O. Box 1000, Delta, VT 84624-1000

Delta Enterprises, 284 Hagemann Drive, Livermore, CA 94550

Delta Frangible Ammunition LLC, P.O. Box 2350, Stafford, VA 22555-2350 / 540-720-5778 or 800-339-1933; FAX: 540-720-5667 dfa@dfanet.com www.dfanet.com

Dem-Bart Checkering Tools, Inc., 1825 Bickford Ave., Snohomish, WA 98290 / 360-568-7356 walt@dembartco.com www.dembartco.com

Denver Instrument Co., 6542 Fig St., Arvada, CO 80004 / 800-321-1135; or 303-431-7255; FAX: 303-423-4831

DeSantis Holster & Leather Goods, Inc., 431 Bayview Ave., Amityville, NY 11701 / 631-841-6300; FAX: 631-841-6320 www.desantisholster.com

Desert Mountain Mfg., P.O. Box 130184, Coram, MT 59913 / 800-477-0762 or 406-387-5361; FAX: 406-387-5361

Detonics USA, 53 Perimeter Center East #200, Atlanta, GA 30346 / 866-759-1169

DGR Custom Rifles, 4191 37th Ave. SE, Tappen, ND 58487 / 701-327-8135

DGS, Inc., Dale A. Storey, 1117 E. 12th, Casper, WY 82601 / 307-237-2414; FAX: 307-237-2414 dalest@trib.com www.dgsrifle.com

DHB Products, 336 River View Dr., Verona, VA 24482-2547 / 703-836-2648

Diamond Machining Technology Inc. (See DMT)

Diamond Mfg. Co., P.O. Box 174, Wyoming, PA 18644 / 800-233-9601

Dibble, Derek A., 555 John Downey Dr., New Britain, CT 06051 / 203-224-2630

Dietz Gun Shop & Range, Inc., 421 Range Rd., New Braunfels, TX 78132 / 830-885-4662

Dilliott Gunsmithing, Inc., 657 Scarlett Rd., Dandridge, TN 37725 / 865-397-9204 gunsmithd@aol.com dilliottgunsmithing.com

Dillon Precision Products, Inc., 8009 East Dillon's Way, Scottsdale, AZ 85260 / 480-948-8009 or 800-762-3845; FAX: 480-998-2786 sales@dillonprecision.com www.dillonprecision.com

Dina Arms Corporation, P.O. Box 46, Royersford, PA 19468 / 610-287-0266; FAX: 610-287-0266 dinaarms@erols.com www.users.erds.com/dinarms

Dixie Gun Works, P.O. Box 130, Union City, TN 38281 / 731-885-0700; FAX: 731-885-0440 info@dixiegunworks.com www.dixiegunworks.com

Dixon Muzzleloading Shop, Inc., 9952 Kunkels Mill Rd., Kempton, PA 19529 / 610-756-6271

DJ Illinois River Valley Calls, Inc., P.O. Box 370, S. Pekin, IL 61564-0370 / 866-352-2557; FAX: 309-348-3987 djcalls@grics.net www.djcalls.com

DKT, Inc., 14623 Vera Dr., Union, MI 49130-9744 / 800-741-7083 orders; FAX: 616-641-2015

DLO Mfg., 10807 SE Foster Ave., Arcadia, FL 33821-7304

DMT-Diamond Machining Technology, Inc., 85 Hayes Memorial Dr., Marlborough, MA 01752 FAX: 508-485-3924

Dohring Bullets, 100 W. 8 Mile Rd., Ferndale, MI 48220

Dolbare, Elizabeth, P.O. Box 502, Dubois, WY 82513-0502 / 307-450-7500 edolbare@hotmail.com www.scrimshaw-engraving.com

Domino, P.O. Box 108, 20019 Settimo Milanese, Milano, ITALY / 1-39-2-33512040; FAX: 1-39-2-33511587

Don Klein Custom Guns, 433 Murray Park Dr., Ripon, WI 54971 / 920-748-2931 daklein@charter.net www.donkleincustomguns.com

Donnelly, C. P., 405 Kubli Rd., Grants Pass, OR 97527 / 541-846-6604

Doskocil Mfg. Co., Inc., P.O. Box 1246, 4209 Barnett, Arlington, TX 76017 / 817-467-5116; FAX: 817-472-9810

Douglas Barrels, Inc., 5504 Big Tyler Rd., Charleston, WV 25313-1398 / 304-776-1341; FAX: 304-776-8560 www.benchrest.com/douglas

Downsizer Corp., P.O. Box 710316, Santee, CA 92072-0316 / 619-448-5510 www.downsizer.com

DPMS (Defense Procurement Manufacturing Services, Inc.), 13983 Industry Ave., Becker, MN 55308 / 800-578-DPMS or 763-261-5600; FAX: 763-261-5599

Dr. O's Products Ltd., P.O. Box 111, Niverville, NY 12130 / 518-784-3333; FAX: 518-784-2800

Dremel Mfg. Co., 4915-21st St., Racine, WI 53406

Dri-Slide, Inc., 411 N. Darling, Fremont, MI 49412 / 616-924-3950

Dropkick, 1460 Washington Blvd., Williamsport, PA 17701 / 717-326-6561; FAX: 717-326-4950

DS Arms, Inc., P.O. Box 370, 27 West 990 Industrial Ave., Barrington, IL 60010 / 847-277-7258; FAX: 847-277-7259 www.dsarms.com

DTM International, Inc., 40 Joslyn Rd., P.O. Box 5, Lake Orion, MI 48362 / 313-693-6670

Duane A. Hobbie Gunsmithing, 2412 Pattie Ave., Wichita, KS 67216 / 316-264-8266

Duane's Gun Repair (See DGR Custom Rifles)

Dubber, Michael W., P.O. Box 312, Evansville, IN 47702 / 812-424-9000; FAX: 812-424-6551

Duffy, Charles E. (See Guns Antique & Modern DBA), 224 Williams Ln., P.O. Box 2, West Hurley, NY 12491 / 845-679-2997 ceo1923@prodigy.net

Du-Lite Corp., 171 River Rd., Middletown, CT 06457 / 203-347-2505; FAX: 203-347-9404

Dumoulin, Ernest, Rue Florent Boclinville 8-10, 13-4041, Votten, BELGIUM / 41 27 78 92

Duncan's Gun Works, Inc., 1619 Grand Ave., San Marcos, CA 92078 / 760-727-0515

DunLyon R&D, Inc., 52151 E. U.S. Hwy. 60, Miami, AZ 85539 / 928-473-9027

Duofold, Inc., RD 3 Rt. 309, Valley Square Mall, Tamaqua, PA 18252 / 717-386-2666; FAX: 717-386-3652

Dybala Gun Shop, P.O. Box 1024, FM 3156, Bay City, TX 77414 / 409-245-0866

Dykstra, Doug, 411 N. Darling, Fremont, MI 49412 / 616-924-3950

Dynalite Products, Inc., 215 S. Washington St., Greenfield, OH 45123 / 513-981-2124

Dynamit Nobel-RWS, Inc., 81 Ruckman Rd., Closter, NJ 07624 / 201-767-7971; FAX: 201-767-1589

E

E&L Mfg., Inc., 4177 Riddle Bypass Rd., Riddle, OR 97469 / 541-874-2137; FAX: 541-874-3107

E. Arthur Brown Co. Inc., 4353 Hwy. 27 E., Alexandria, MN 56308 / 320-762-8847; FAX: 320-763-4310 www.eabco.com

E.A.A. Corp., P.O. Box 1299, Sharpes, FL 32959 / 407-639-4842 or 800-536-4442; FAX: 407-639-7006

Eagan, Donald. See: EAGAN GUNSMITHS

Eagan Gunsmiths, Donald V. Eagan, P.O. Box 196, Benton, PA 17814 / 570-925-6134

Eagle Arms, Inc. (See ArmaLite, Inc.)

Eagle Grips, Eagle Business Center, 460 Randy Rd., Carol Stream, IL 60188 / 800-323-6144 or 708-260-0400; FAX: 708-260-0486

Eagle Imports, Inc., 1750 Brielle Ave., Unit B1, Wanamassa, NJ 07712 / 732-493-0333; FAX: 732-493-0301 gsodini@aol.com www.bersafirearmsusa.com

E-A-R, Inc., Div. of Cabot Safety Corp., 5457 W. 79th St., Indianapolis, IN 46268 / 800-327-3431; FAX: 800-488-8007

EAW (See U.S. Importer-New England Custom Gun Serv

Eckelman Gunshop, CR 215, Brainerd, MN 56401 / 218-829-3176

Ed Brown Products, Inc., P.O. Box 492, Perry, MO 63462 / 573-565-3261; FAX: 573-565-2791 edbrown@edbrown.com www.edbrown.com

Ed Brown Products, Inc., 43825 Muldrow Trl., P.O. Box 492, Perry, MO 63462 / 573-565-3261; FAX: 573-565-2791 edbrown@edbrown.com www.edbrown.com

Edenpine, Inc. c/o Six Enterprises, Inc., 320 D Turtle Creek Ct., San Jose, CA 95125 / 408-999-0201; FAX: 408-999-0216

EdgeCraft Corp., S. Weiner, 825 Southwood Rd., Avondale, PA 19311 / 610-268-0500 or 800-342-3255; FAX: 610-268-3545 www.edgecraft.com

Edmisten Co., P.O. Box 1293, Boone, NC 28607

Edmund Scientific Co., 101 E. Gloucester Pike, Barrington, NJ 08033 / 609-543-6250

Ed's Gun House, Ed Kukowski, P.O. Box 62, Minnesota City, MN 55959 / 507-689-2925

Effebi SNC-Dr. Franco Beretta, via Rossa, 4, 25062, ITALY / 030-2751955; FAX: 030-2180414

Eggleston, Jere D., 400 Saluda Ave., Columbia, SC 29205 / 803-799-3402

Eichelberger Bullets, Wm., 158 Crossfield Rd., King Of Prussia, PA 19406

El Paso Saddlery Co., P.O. Box 27194, El Paso, TX 79926 / 915-544-2233; FAX: 915-544-2535 info@epsaddlery.com www.epsaddlery.com

Electro Prismatic Collimators, Inc., 1441 Manatt St., Lincoln, NE 68521

Electronic Shooters Protection, Inc., 15290 Gadsden Ct., Brighton, CO 80603 / 800-797-7791; FAX: 303-659-8668 esp@usa.net espamerican.com

Eley Ltd., Selco Way Minworth Industrial Estate, Minworth Sutton Coldfield, West Midlands, B76 1BA ENGLAND / 44 0 121-313-4567; FAX: 44 0 121-313-4568 www.eley.co.uk

Ellett Bros., 267 Columbia Ave., P.O. Box 128, Chapin, SC 29036 / 803-345-3751 or 800-845-3711; FAX: 803-345-1820 www.ellettbrothers.com

Ellicott Arms, Inc. / Woods Pistolsmithing, 8390 Sunset Dr., Ellicott City, MD 21043 / 410-465-7979

EMAP USA, 6420 Wilshire Blvd., Los Angeles, CA 90048 / 213-782-2000; FAX: 213-782-2867

Emerging Technologies, Inc. (See Laseraim Technologies, Inc.)

EMF Co. Inc., 1900 E. Warner Ave., Suite 1-D, Santa Ana, CA 92705 / 949-261-6611; FAX: 949-756-0133

Empire Cutlery Corp., 12 Kruger Ct., Clifton, NJ 07013 / 201-472-5155; FAX: 201-779-0759

Empire Rifles, P.O. Box 406, Meriden, NH 03770 / info@empirerifles.com www.empirerifles.com

English, Inc., A.G., 708 S. 12th St., Broken Arrow, OK 74012 / 918-251-3399 info@agenglish.com www.agenglish.com

Engraving Artistry, 36 Alto Rd., Burlington, CT 06013 / 860-673-6837 bobburt44@hotmail.com

Enguix Import-Export, Alpujarras 58, Alzira, Valencia, SPAIN / (96) 241 43 95; FAX: (96) 241 43 95

Enhanced Presentations, Inc., 5929 Market St., Wilmington, NC 28405 / 910-799-1622; FAX: 910-799-5004

Ensign-Bickford Co., The, 660 Hopmeadow St., Simsbury, CT 06070

Entreprise Arms, Inc., 5321 Irwindale Ave., Irwindale, CA 91706-2025 / 626-962-8712; FAX: 626-962-4692 www.entreprise.com

EPC, 1441 Manatt St., Lincoln, NE 68521 / 402-476-3946

Erhardt, Dennis, 4508 N. Montana Ave., Helena, MT 59602 / 406-442-4533

Essex Arms, P.O. Box 363, Island Pond, VT 05846 / 802-723-6203; FAX: 802-723-6203

Estate Cartridge, Inc., 900 Bob Ehlen Dr., Anoka, MN 55303-7502 / 409-856-7277; FAX: 409-856-5486

Euber Bullets, No. Orwell Rd., Orwell, VT 05760 / 802-948-2621

Euroarms of America, Inc., P.O. Box 3277, Winchester, VA 22604 / 540-662-1863; FAX: 540-662-4464 tell-us@euroarms.net www.euroarms.net

Euro-Imports, George Tripes, 412 Slayden St., Yoakum, TX 77995 / 361-293-9353; FAX: 361-293-9353 mrbrno@yahoo.com

European American Armory Corp. (See E.A.A. Corp.)

Eversull Co., Inc., 1 Tracemont, Boyce, LA 71409 / 318-793-8728; FAX: 318-793-5483 bestguns@aol.com

Evolution Gun Works, Inc., 48 Belmont Ave., Quakertown, PA 18951-1347 www.egw-guns.com

Excalibur Electro Optics, Inc., P.O. Box 400, Fogelsville, PA 18051-0400 / 610-391-9105; FAX: 610-391-9220

Excalibur Publications, P.O. Box 89667, Tucson, AZ 85752 / 520-575-9057 excalibureditor@earthlink.net

Excel Industries, Inc., 4510 Carter Ct., Chino, CA 91710 / 909-627-2404; FAX: 909-627-7817

Executive Protection Institute, P.O. Box 802, Berryville, VA 22611 / 540-554-2540; FAX: 540-554-2558 ruk@crosslink.net www.personalprotecion.com

Eze-Lap Diamond Prods., P.O. Box 2229, 15164 W. State St., Westminster, CA 92683 / 714-847-1555; FAX: 714-897-0280

E-Z-Way Systems, P.O. Box 4310, Newark, OH 43058-4310 / 614-345-6645 or 800-848-2072; FAX: 614-345-6600

F

F.A.I.R., Via Gitti, 41, 25060 Marcheno (BS), 25060 Marcheno Bresc, ITALY / 030 861162-8610344; FAX: 030 8610179 info@fair.it www.fair.it

F+W Publications, Inc., 700 E. State St., Iola, WI 54990 / 715-445-2214; FAX: 715-445-4087

Fabarm S.p.A., Via Averolda 31, 25039 Travagliato, Brescia, ITALY / 030-6863629; FAX: 030-6863684 info@fabarm.com www.fabarm.com

Fagan Arms, 22952 15 Mile Rd., Clinton Township, MI 48035 / 810-465-4637; FAX: 810-792-6996

Faith Associates, P.O. Box 549, Flat Rock, NC 28731-0549 FAX: 828-697-6827

Falcon Industries, Inc., P.O. Box 1690, Edgewood, NM 87015 / 505-281-3783; FAX: 505-281-3991 shines@ergogrips.net www.ergogrips.com

Far North Outfitters, Box 1252, Bethel, AK 99559

Farm Form Decoys, Inc., 1602 Biovu, P.O. Box 748, Galveston, TX 77553 / 409-744-0762 or 409-765-6361; FAX: 409-765-8513

Farr Studio, Inc., 17149 Bournbrook Ln., Jeffersonton, VA 22724-1796 / 615-638-8825

Farrar Tool Co., Inc., 11855 Cog Hill Dr., Whittier, CA 90601-1902 / 310-863-4367; FAX: 310-863-5123

Faulhaber Wildlocker, Dipl.-Ing. Norbert Wittasek, Seilergasse 2, A-1010 Wien, AUSTRIA / 43-1-5137001; FAX: 43-1-5137001 faulhaber1@utanet.at

Faulk's Game Call Co., Inc., 616 18th St., Lake Charles, LA 70601 / 337-436-9726; FAX: 337-494-7205

Faust Inc., T. G., 544 Minor St., Reading, PA 19602 / 610-375-8549; FAX: 610-375-4488

Fautheree, Andy, P.O. Box 4607, Pagosa Springs, CO 81157 / 970-731-5003; FAX: 970-731-5009

Feather, Flex Decoys, 4500 Doniphan Dr., Neosho, MO 64850 / 318-746-8596; FAX: 318-742-4815

Federal Cartridge Co., 900 Ehlen Dr., Anoka, MN 55303 / 612-323-2300; FAX: 612-323-2506

Federal Champion Target Co., 232 Industrial Pkwy., Richmond, IN 47374 / 800-441-4971; FAX: 317-966-7747

Federated-Fry (See Fry Metals)

FEG, Budapest, Soroksariut 158, H-1095, HUNGARY

Feinwerkbau Westinger & Altenburger, Neckarstrasse 43, 78727, Oberndorf a. N., GERMANY / 07423-814-0; FAX: 07423-814-200 info@feinwerkbau.de www.feinwerkbau.de

Ferguson, Bill, P.O. Box 1238, Sierra Vista, AZ 85636 / 520-458-5321; FAX: 520-458-9125

Ferguson, Bill. See: BULLET METALS

FERLIB, Via Parte 33 Marcheno/BS, Marcheno/BS, ITALY / 00390308610191; FAX: 00390308966882 info@ferlib.com www.ferlib.com

Ferris Firearms, 7110 F.M. 1863, Bulverde, TX 78163 / 210-980-4424

Fieldsport Ltd., Bryan Bilinski, 3313 W. South Airport Rd., Traverse City, MI 49684 / 616-933-0767

Fiocchi Munizioni S.A. (See U.S. Importer-Fiocch

Fiocchi of America, Inc., 5030 Fremont Rd., Ozark, MO 65721 / 417-725-4118 or 800-721-2666; FAX: 417-725-1039

Firearm Brokers, 4143 Taylor Blvd., Louisville, KY 40215 / 502-366-0555 firearmbrokers@aol.com www.firearmbrokers.com

Firearms Co. Ltd. / Alpine (See U.S. Importer-Mandall

Firearms Engraver's Guild of America, 3011 E. Pine Dr., Flagstaff, AZ 86004 / 928-527-8427 fegainfo@fega.com

Fisher, Jerry A., 631 Crane Mt. Rd., Big Fork, MT 59911 / 406-837-2722

Fisher Custom Firearms, 2199 S. Kittredge Way, Aurora, CO 80013 / 303-755-3710

Fitzgerald, Jack. See: CLENZOIL WORLDWIDE CORP.

Flambeau, Inc., 15981 Valplast Rd., Middlefield, OH 44062 / 216-632-1631; FAX: 216-632-1581 www.flambeau.com

Flayderman & Co., Inc., P.O. Box 2446, Fort Lauderdale, FL 33303 / 954-761-8855 www.flayderman.com

Fleming Firearms, 7720 E. 126th St. N., Collinsville, OK 74021-7016 / 918-665-3624

Fletcher-Bidwell, LLC, 305 E. Terhune St., Viroqua, WI 54665-1631 / 866-637-1860 fbguns@netscape.net

Flintlocks, Etc., 160 Rossiter Rd., P.O. Box 181, Richmond, MA 01254 / 413-698-3822; FAX: 413-698-3866 flintetc@berkshire.rr.com

Flitz International Ltd., 821 Mohr Ave., Waterford, WI 53185 / 414-534-5898; FAX: 414-534-2991

Fluoramics, Inc., 18 Industrial Ave., Mahwah, NJ 07430 / 800-922-0075; FAX: 201-825-7035 pdouglas@fluoramics.com www.tufoil.com

Flynn's Custom Guns, P.O. Box 7461, Alexandria, LA 71306 / 318-455-7130

FN Manufacturing, P.O. Box 24257, Columbia, SC 29224 / 803-736-0522

Folks, Donald E., 205 W. Lincoln St., Pontiac, IL 61764 / 815-844-7901

Foredom Electric Co., Rt. 6, 16 Stony Hill Rd., Bethel, CT 06801 / 203-792-8622

Forgreens Tool & Mfg., Inc., P.O. Box 955, Robert Lee, TX 76945 / 915-453-2800; FAX: 915-453-2460

Forkin Custom Classics, 205 10th Ave. S.W., White Sulphur Spring, MT 59645 / 406-547-2344

Forrest Tool Co., P.O. Box 768, 44380 Gordon Ln., Mendocino, CA 95460 / 707-937-2141; FAX: 717-937-1817

Forster, Kathy (See Custom Checkering)

Forster, Larry L., Box 212, 216 Hwy. 13 E., Gwinner, ND 58040-0212 / 701-678-2475

Forster Products, Inc., 310 E. Lanark Ave., Lanark, IL 61046 / 815-493-6360; FAX: 815-493-2371 info@forsterproducts.com www.forsterproductscom

Fort Hill Gunstocks, 12807 Fort Hill Rd., Hillsboro, OH 45133 / 513-466-2763

Fort Knox Security Products, 1051 N. Industrial Park Rd., Orem, UT 84057 / 801-224-7233 or 800-821-5216; FAX: 801-226-5493

Forthofer's Gunsmithing & Knifemaking, 5535 U.S. Hwy. 93S, Whitefish, MT 59937-8411 / 406-862-2674

Fortune Products, Inc., 205 Hickory Creek Rd., Marble Falls, TX 78654 / 210-693-6111; FAX: 210-693-6394 randy@accusharp.com

Forty-Five Ranch Enterprises, Box 1080, Miami, OK 74355-1080 / 918-542-5875

Foster, . See: ACCURACY INTERNATIONAL

Fountain Products, 492 Prospect Ave., West Springfield, MA 01089 / 413-781-4651; FAX: 413-733-8217

Fowler, Bob (See Black Powder Products)

Fox River Mills, Inc., P.O. Box 298, 227 Poplar St., Osage, IA 50461 / 515-732-3798; FAX: 515-732-5128

Fraim, William. See: ACUSPORT CORPORATION

Frank Knives, 1147 SW Bryson Str. 1, Dallas, OR 97338 / 503-831-1489; FAX: 541-563-3041

Frank Mittermeier, Inc., P.O. Box 1, Bronx, NY 10465

Franzen International, Inc. (See U.S. Importer-Importer Co.)

Fred F. Wells/Wells Sport Store, 110 N. Summit St., Prescott, AZ 86301 / 928-445-3655 www.wellssportstore@cableone.net

Freedom Arms, Inc., P.O. Box 150, Freedom, WY 83120 / 307-883-2468; FAX: 307-883-2005

Fremont Tool Works, 1214 Prairie, Ford, KS 67842 / 316-369-2327

Front Sight Firearms Training Institute, P.O. Box 2619, Aptos, CA 95001 / 800-987-7719; FAX: 408-684-2137

Frontier, 2910 San Bernardo, Laredo, TX 78040 / 956-723-5409; FAX: 956-723-1774

Frontier Arms Co., Inc., 401 W. Rio Santa Cruz, Green Valley, AZ 85614-3932

Frontier Products Co., 2401 Walker Rd., Roswell, NM 88201-8950 / 505-627-0763

Frost Cutlery Co., P.O. Box 22636, Chattanooga, TN 37422 / 615-894-6079; FAX: 615-894-9576

Fry Metals, 4100 6th Ave., Altoona, PA 16602 / 814-946-1611

Fujinon, Inc., 10 High Point Dr., Wayne, NJ 07470 / 201-633-5600; FAX: 201-633-5216

Fullmer, Geo. M., 2499 Mavis St., Oakland, CA 94601 / 510-533-4193

Fulton Armory, 8725 Bollman Place No. 1, Savage, MD 20763 / 301-490-9485; FAX: 301-490-9547 www.fulton.armory.com

Furr Arms, 91 N. 970 West, Orem, UT 84057 / 801-226-3877; FAX: 801-226-3877

G

G&H Decoys, Inc., P.O. Box 1208, Hwy. 75 North, Henryetta, OK 74437 / 918-652-3314; FAX: 918-652-3400

G.C. Bullet Co., Inc., 40 Mokelumne River Dr., Lodi, CA 95240

G.G. & G., 3602 E. 42nd Stravenue, Tucson, AZ 85713 / 520-748-7167; FAX: 520-748-7583 ggg&3@aol.com www.ggg&3.com

G.H. Enterprises Ltd., Bag 10, Okotoks, AB T0L 1T0 CANADA / 403-938-6070

G.U., Inc. (See U.S. Importer-New SKB Arms Co.)

G96 Products Co., Inc., 85 5th Ave., Bldg. #6, Paterson, NJ 07544 / 973-684-4050; FAX: 973-684-3848 g96prod@aol

Gage Manufacturing, 663 W. 7th St., A, San Pedro, CA 90731 / 310-832-3546

Gaillard Barrels, Box 68, St. Brieux, SK S0K 3V0 CANADA / 306-752-3769; FAX: 306-752-5969

Galati International, P.O. Box 10, 616 Burley Ridge Rd., Wesco, MO 65586 / 636-584-0785; FAX: 573-775-4308 support@galatiinternational.com www.galatiinternational.com

Galaxy Imports Ltd., Inc., P.O. Box 3361, Victoria, TX 77903 / 361-573-4867; FAX: 361-576-9622 galaxy@cox-internet.com

GALCO International Ltd., 2019 W. Quail Ave., Phoenix, AZ 85027 / 623-474-7070; FAX: 623-582-6854 customerservice@usgalco.com www.usgalco.com

Galena Industries AMT, 5463 Diaz St., Irwindale, CA 91706 / 626-856-8883; FAX: 626-856-8878

Gamba Renato Bremec Srl, Via Artigiani 93, 25063 Gardone V.T. BS, ITALY / 30-8910264-5; FAX: 30-8912180 infocomm@renatogamba.it www.renatogamba.it

Gamba, USA, P.O. Box 60452, Colorado Springs, CO 80960 / 719-578-1145; FAX: 719-444-0731

Game Haven Gunstocks, 13750 Shire Rd., Wolverine, MI 49799 / 616-525-8257

Gamebore Division, Polywad, Inc., P.O. Box 7916, Macon, GA 31209 / 478-477-0669; or 800-998-0669

Gamo (See U.S. Importers-Arms United Corp., Daisy M

Gamo USA, Inc., 3911 SW 47th Ave., Suite 914, Fort Lauderdale, FL 33314 / 954-581-5822; FAX: 954-581-3165 gamousa@gate.net www.gamo.com

Gander Mountain, Inc., 12400 Fox River Rd., Wilmont, WI 53192 / 414-862-6848

GAR, 590 McBride Ave., West Paterson, NJ 07424 / 973-754-1114; FAX: 973-754-1114 garreloading@aol.com www.garreloading.com

Garcia National Gun Traders, Inc., 225 SW 22nd Ave., Miami, FL 33135 / 305-642-2355

Garrett Cartridges, Inc., P.O. Box 178, Chehalis, WA 98532 / 360-736-0702 www.garrettcartridges.com

Garthwaite Pistolsmith, Inc., Jim, 12130 State Route 405, Watsontown, PA 17777 / 570-538-1566 www.garthwaite.com

Gary Goudy Classic Stocks, 1512 S. 5th St., Dayton, WA 99328 / 509-382-2726 goudy@icehouse.net

Gary Reeder Custom Guns, 2601 7th Ave. E., Flagstaff, AZ 86004 / 928-526-3313; FAX: 928-527-0840 gary@reedercustomguns.com www.reedercustomguns.com

Gator Guns & Repair, 7952 Kenai Spur Hwy., Kenai, AK 99611-8311

Gaucher Armes, S.A., 46 rue Desjoyaux, 42000, Saint-Etienne, FRANCE / 04-77-33-38-92; FAX: 04-77-61-95-72

GDL Enterprises, 409 Le Gardeur, Slidell, LA 70460 / 504-649-0693

Gehmann, Walter (See Huntington Die Specialties)

Genco, P.O. Box 5704, Asheville, NC 28803

Genecco Gun Works, 10512 Lower Sacramento Rd., Stockton, CA 95210 / 209-951-0706; FAX: 209-931-3872

Gene's Custom Guns, P.O. Box 10534, White Bear Lake, MN 55110 / 651-429-5105; FAX: 651-429-7365

Gentex Corp., 5 Tinkham Ave., Derry, NH 03038 / 603-434-0311; FAX: 603-434-3002 sales@derry.gentexcorp.com www.derry.gentexcorp.com

Gentner Bullets, 109 Woodlawn Ave., Upper Darby, PA 19082 / 610-352-9396 dongentner@rcn.com www.gentnerbullets.com

Gentry Custom LLC, 314 N. Hoffman, Belgrade, MT 59714 / 406-388-GUNS gentryshop@earthlink.net www.gentrycustom.com

George & Roy's, P.O. Box 2125, Sisters, OR 97759-2125 / 503-228-5424 or 800-553-3022; FAX: 503-225-9409

George Hoenig, Inc., 6521 Morton Dr., Boise, ID 83704 / 208-375-1116; FAX: 208-375-1116

George Ibberson (Sheffield) Ltd., 25-31 Allen St., Sheffield, S3 7AW ENGLAND / 0114-2766123; FAX: 0114-2738465 sales@eggintongroup.co.uk www.eggintongroup.co.uk

Gerber Legendary Blades, 14200 SW 72nd Ave., Portland, OR 97223 / 503-639-6161 or 800-950-6161; FAX: 503-684-7008

Gervais, Mike, 3804 S. Cruise Dr., Salt Lake City, UT 84109 / 801-277-7729

Getz Barrel Company, P.O. Box 88, 426 E. Market St., Beavertown, PA 17813 / 570-658-7263; FAX: 570-658-4110 www.getzbrl.com

Giacomo Sporting USA, 6234 Stokes Lee Center Rd., Lee Center, NY 13363

Gibbs Rifle Co., Inc., 219 Lawn St., Martinsburg, WV 25401 / 304-262-1651; FAX: 304-262-1658 support@gibbsrifle.com www.gibbsrifle.com

Gil Hebard Guns, Inc., 125 Public Square, Knoxville, IL 61448 / 309-289-2700; FAX: 309-289-2233

Gilbert Equipment Co., Inc., 960 Downtowner Rd., Mobile, AL 36609 / 205-344-3322

Gillmann, Edwin, 33 Valley View Dr., Hanover, PA 17331 / 717-632-1662 gillmaned@superpa.net

Gilmore Sports Concepts, Inc., 5949 S. Garnett Rd., Tulsa, OK 74146 / 918-250-3810; FAX: 918-250-3845 info@gilmoresports.com www.gilmoresports.com

Glacier Glove, 4890 Aircenter Circle, Suite 210, Reno, NV 89502 / 702-825-8225; FAX: 702-825-6544

Glaser LLC, P.O. Box 173, Sturgis, SD 57785 / 605-347-4544 or 800-221-3489; FAX: 605-347-5055 email@corbon.com www.safetyslug.com

Glaser Safety Slug, Inc. (see CorBon/Glaser safetyslug.com)

Glass, Herb, P.O. Box 25, Bullville, NY 10915 / 914-361-3021

Glimm, Jerome. See: GLIMM'S CUSTOM GUN ENGRAVING

Glimm's Custom Gun Engraving, Jerome C. Glimm, 19 S. Maryland, Conrad, MT 59425 / 406-278-3574 lag@mcn.net www.gunengraver.biz

Glock GmbH, P.O. Box 50, A-2232, Deutsch, Wagram, AUSTRIA

Glock, Inc., P.O. Box 369, Smyrna, GA 30081 / 770-432-1202; FAX: 770-433-8719

Glynn Scobey Duck & Goose Calls, Rt. 3, Box 37, Newbern, TN 38059 / 731-643-6128

GML Products, Inc., 394 Laredo Dr., Birmingham, AL 35226 / 205-979-4867

Goens, Dale W., P.O. Box 224, Cedar Crest, NM 87008 / 505-281-5419

Goergen's Gun Shop, Inc., 17985 538th Ave., Austin, MN 55912 / 507-433-9280

GOEX, Inc., P.O. Box 659, Doyline, LA 71023-0659 / 318-382-9300; FAX: 318-382-9303 mfahringer@goexpowder.com www.goexpowder.com

Golden Age Arms Co., 115 E. High St., Ashley, OH 43003 / 614-747-2488

Golden Bear Bullets, 3065 Fairfax Ave., San Jose, CA 95148 / 408-238-9515

Goodling's Gunsmithing, 1950 Stoverstown Rd., Spring Grove, PA 17362 / 717-225-3350

Goodwin, Fred. See: GOODWIN'S GUNS

Goodwin's Guns, Fred Goodwin, Silver Ridge, ME 04776 / 207-365-4451

Gotz Bullets, 11426 Edgemere Ter., Roscoe, IL 61073-8232

Gould & Goodrich Leather, Inc., 709 E. McNeil St., Lillington, NC 27546 / 910-893-2071; FAX: 910-893-4742 info@gouldusa.com www.gouldusa.com

Gournet Artistic Engraving, Geoffroy Gournet, 820 Paxinosa Ave., Easton, PA 18042 / 610-559-0710 www.geoffroygournet.com

Gournet, Geoffroy. See: GOURNET ARTISTIC ENGRAVING

Grace, Charles E., 718 E. 2nd, Trinidad, CO 81082 / 719-846-9435 chuckgrace@sensonics.com

Grace Metal Products, P.O. Box 67, Elk Rapids, MI 49629 / 616-264-8133

Graf & Sons, 4050 S. Clark St., Mexico, MO 65265 / 573-581-2266; FAX: 573-581-2875 customerservice@grafs.com / www.grafs.com

Grand Slam Hunting Products, Box 121, 25454 Military Rd., Cascade, MD 21719 / 301-241-4900; FAX: 301-241-4900 rlj6call@aol.com

Granite Mountain Arms, Inc., 3145 W. Hidden Acres Trail, Prescott, AZ 86305 / 520-541-9758; FAX: 520-445-6826

Grant, Howard V., Hiawatha 15, Woodruff, WI 54568 / 715-356-7146

Graphics Direct, P.O. Box 372421, Reseda, CA 91337-2421 / 818-344-9002

Graves Co., 1800 Andrews Ave., Pompano Beach, FL 33069 / 800-327-9103; FAX: 305-960-0301

Grayback Wildcats, Mike Beeks, 5306 Bryant Ave., Klamath Falls, OR 97603 / 541-884-1072; FAX: 541-884-1072 graybackwildcats@aol.com

Graybill's Gun Shop, 1035 Ironville Pike, Columbia, PA 17512 / 717-684-2739

Great American Gunstock Co., 3420 Industrial Drive, Yuba City, CA 95993 / 800-784-4867; FAX: 530-671-3906 gunstox@hotmail.com www.gunstocks.com

Green, Arthur S., 485 S. Robertson Blvd., Beverly Hills, CA 90211 / 310-274-1283

Green Head Game Call Co., RR 1, Box 33, Lacon, IL 61540 / 309-246-2155

Green Mountain Rifle Barrel Co., Inc., P.O. Box 2670, 153 W. Main St., Conway, NH 03818 / 603-447-1095; FAX: 603-447-1099 info@gmriflebarrel.com www.gmriflebarrel.com

Greenwood Precision, P.O. Box 407, Rogersville, MO 65742 / 417-725-2330

Greg Gunsmithing Repair, 3732 26th Ave. N., Robbinsdale, MN 55422 / 612-529-8103

Greg's Superior Products, P.O. Box 46219, Seattle, WA 98146

Greider Precision, 431 Santa Marina Ct., Escondido, CA 92029 / 760-480-8892; FAX: 760-480-9800 greider@msn.com

Gre-Tan Rifles, 29742 W.C.R. 50, Kersey, CO 80644 / 970-353-6176; FAX: 970-356-5940 www.gtrtooling.com

Griffin & Howe, Inc., 340 W. Putnam Ave., Greenwich, CT 06830 / 203-618-0270 info@griffinhowe.com www.griffinhowe.com

Griffin & Howe, Inc., 33 Claremont Rd., Bernardsville, NJ 07924 / 908-766-2287; FAX: 908-766-1068 info@griffinhowe.com www.griffinhowe.com

Grifon, Inc., 58 Guinam St., Waltham, MS 02154

Groenewold, John. See: JG AIRGUNS, LLC

GRS/Glendo Corp., P.O. Box 1153, 900 Overlander St., Emporia, KS 66801 / 620-343-1084 or 800-836-3519; FAX: 620-343-9640 glendo@glendo.com www.glendo.com

Grulla Armes, Apartado 453, Avda Otaloa 12, Eiber, SPAIN

Gruning Precision, Inc., 7101 Jurupa Ave., No. 12, Riverside, CA 92504 / 909-289-4371; FAX: 909-689-7791 gruningprecision@earthlink.net www.gruningprecision.com

GSI, Inc., 7661 Commerce Ln., Trussville, AL 35173 / 205-655-8299

Guarasi, Robert. See: WILCOX INDUSTRIES CORP.

Guardsman Products, 411 N. Darling, Fremont, MI 49412 / 616-924-3950

Gun City, 212 W. Main Ave., Bismarck, ND 58501 / 701-223-2304

Gun Doc, Inc., 5405 NW 82nd Ave., Miami, FL 33166 / 305-477-2777; FAX: 305-477-2778 www.gundoc.com

Gun Doctor, The, P.O. Box 72817, Roselle, IL 60172 / 708-894-0668

Gun Hunter Books (See Gun Hunter Trading Co.), 5075 Heisig St., Beaumont, TX 77705 / 409-835-3006; FAX: 409-838-2266 gunhuntertrading@hotmail.com

Gun Hunter Trading Co., 5075 Heisig St., Beaumont, TX 77705 / 409-835-3006; FAX: 409-838-2266 gunhuntertrading@hotmail.com

Gun Leather Limited, 116 Lipscomb, Fort Worth, TX 76104 / 817-334-0225; FAX: 800-247-0609

Gun List (See F+W Publications), 700 E. State St., Iola, WI 54990 / 715-445-2214; FAX: 715-445-4087

Gun Room Press, The, 127 Raritan Ave., Highland Park, NJ 08904 / 732-545-4344; FAX: 732-545-6686 gunbooks@rutgersgunbooks.com www.rutgersgunbooks.com

Gun Room, The, 1121 Burlington, Muncie, IN 47302 / 765-282-9073; FAX: 765-282-5270 bshstleguns@aol.com

Gun Shop, The, 62778 Spring Creek Rd., Montrose, CO 81401

Gun Shop, The, 5550 S. 900 East, Salt Lake City, UT 84117 / 801-263-3633

Gun South, Inc. (See GSI, Inc.)

Gun Vault, 7339 E. Acoma Dr., Ste. 7, Scottsdale, AZ 85260 / 602-951-6855

Gun Works, The, 247 S. 2nd St., Springfield, OR 97477 / 541-741-4118; FAX: 541-988-1097 info@thegunworks.com www.thegunworks.com

Gun-Alert, 1010 N. Maclay Ave., San Fernando, CA 91340 / 818-365-0864; FAX: 818-365-1308

Guncraft Books (See Guncraft Sports, Inc.), 10737 Dutchtown Rd., Knoxville, TN 37932 / 865-966-4545; FAX: 865-966-4500 findit@guncraft.com www.guncraft.com

Guncraft Sports, Inc., 10737 Dutchtown Rd., Knoxville, TN 37932 / 865-966-4545; FAX: 865-966-4500 findit@guncraft.com www.usit.net/guncraft

Guncraft Sports, Inc., Marie C. Wiest, 10737 Dutchtown Rd., Knoxville, TN 37932 / 865-966-4545; FAX: 865-966-4500 findit@guncraft.com www.guncraft.com

Guncrafter Industries, 171 Madison 1510, Huntsville, AR 72740 / 479-665-2466 www.guncrafterindustries.com

Gun-Ho Sports Cases, 110 E. 10th St., St. Paul, MN 55101 / 612-224-9491

Gunline Tools, 2950 Saturn St., "O", Brea, CA 92821 / 714-993-5100; FAX: 714-572-4128

Gunnerman Books, P.O. Box 81697, Rochester Hills, MI 48308 / 248-608-2856 gunnermanbks@att.net

Guns Antique & Modern DBA / Charles E. Duffy, 224 Williams Lane, P.O. Box 2, West Hurley, NY 12491 / 845-679-2997 ceo1923@prodigy.net

GUNS Magazine, 12345 World Trade Dr., San Diego, CA 92128-3743 / 619-297-5350; FAX: 619-297-5353

Gunsight, The, 1712 N. Placentia Ave., Fullerton, CA 92631

Gunsite Training Center, P.O. Box 700, Paulden, AZ 86334 / 520-636-4565; FAX: 520-636-1236

Gunsmithing Ltd., 57 Unquowa Rd., Fairfield, CT 06824 / 203-254-0436; FAX: 203-254-1535

Gunsmithing, Inc., 30 W. Buchanan St., Colorado Springs, CO 80907 / 719-632-3795; FAX: 719-632-3493 www.nealsguns.com

Gurney, F. R., Box 13, Sooke, BC V0S 1N0 CANADA / 604-642-5282; FAX: 604-642-7859

H

H&B Forge Co., Rt. 2, Geisinger Rd., Shiloh, OH 44878 / 419-895-1856

H&P Publishing, 7174 Hoffman Rd., San Angelo, TX 76905 / 915-655-5953

H&R 1871.LLC, 60 Industrial Rowe, Gardner, MA 01440 / 508-632-9393; FAX: 508-632-2300 hr1871@hr1871.com www.hr1871.com

H. Krieghoff Gun Co., Boschstrasse 22, D-89079, Ulm, GERMANY / 731-401820; FAX: 731-4018270

H.K.S. Products, 7841 Founion Dr., Florence, KY 41042 / 606-342-7841 or 800-354-9814; FAX: 606-342-5865

H.P. White Laboratory, Inc., 3114 Scarboro Rd., Street, MD 21154 / 410-838-6550; FAX: 410-838-2802 info@hpwhite.com www.hpwhite.com

Hafner World Wide, Inc., P.O. Box 1987, Lake City, FL 32055 / 904-755-6481; FAX: 904-755-6595 hafner@isgroupe.net

Hakko Co. Ltd., 1-13-12, Narimasu, Itabashiku Tokyo, JAPAN / 03-5997-7870/2; FAX: 81-3-5997-7840

Half Moon Rifle Shop, 490 Halfmoon Rd., Columbia Falls, MT 59912 / 406-892-4409 halfmoonrs@centurytel.net

Hall Manufacturing, 142 CR 406, Clanton, AL 35045 / 205-755-4094

Hall Plastics, Inc., John, P.O. Box 1526, Alvin, TX 77512 / 713-489-8709

Hallberg, Fritz. See: CAMBOS OUTDOORSMAN

Hallowell & Co., P.O. Box 1445, Livingston, MT 59047 / 406-222-4770; FAX: 406-222-4792 morris@hallowellco.com www.hallowellco.com

Hally Caller, 443 Wells Rd., Doylestown, PA 18901 / 215-345-6354; FAX: 215-345-6354 info@hallycaller.com www.hallycaller.com

Hamilton, Alex B. (See Ten-Ring Precision, Inc.)

Hammans, Charles E., P.O. Box 788, 2022 McCracken, Stuttgart, AR 72160-0788 / 870-673-1388

Hammerli AG, Industrieplaz, a/Rheinpall, CH-8212 Neuhausen, SWITZERLAND info@hammerli.com www.haemmerliich.com

Hammerli Service-Precision Mac, Rudolf Marent, 9711 Tiltree St., Houston, TX 77075 / 713-946-7028 rmarent@webtv.net

Hammerli USA, 19296 Oak Grove Circle, Groveland, CA 95321 FAX: 209-962-5311

Hammond Custom Guns Ltd., 619 S. Pandora, Gilbert, AZ 85234 / 602-892-3437

HandCrafts Unltd. (See Clements' Custom Leathercraft), 1741 Dallas St., Aurora, CO 80010-2018 / 303-364-0403; FAX: 303-739-9824 gryphons@home.com kuntaoslcat.com

Handgun Press, P.O. Box 406, Glenview, IL 60025 / 847-657-6500; FAX: 847-724-8831 handgunpress@comcast.net

Hank's Gun Shop, Box 370, 50 W. 100 South, Monroe, UT 84754 / 435-527-4456 hanksgs@altazip.com

Hanned Line, The, 4463 Madoc Way, San Jose, CA 95130 smith@hanned.com www.hanned.com

Hanned Precision (See The Hanned Line)

Hansen & Co., 244-246 Old Post Rd., Southport, CT 06490 / 203-259-6222; FAX: 203-254-3832

Hanson's Gun Center, Dick, 233 Everett Dr., Colorado Springs, CO 80911

Harford (See U.S. Importer-EMF Co., Inc.)

Harper's Custom Stocks, 928 Lombrano St., San Antonio, TX 78207 / 210-732-7174

Harrell's Precision, 5756 Hickory Dr., Salem, VA 24153 / 540-380-2683

Harrington & Richardson (See H&R 1871, Inc.)

Harris Engineering Inc., Dept. GD54, 999 Broadway, Barlow, KY 42024 / 270-334-3633; FAX: 270-334-3000

Harris Enterprises, P.O. Box 105, Bly, OR 97622 / 503-353-2625

Harris Hand Engraving, Paul A., 113 Rusty Ln., Boerne, TX 78006-5746 / 512-391-5121

Harris Publications, 1115 Broadway, New York, NY 10010 / 212-807-7100; FAX: 212-627-4678

Harrison Bullets, 6437 E. Hobart St., Mesa, AZ 85205

Harry Lawson Co., 3328 N. Ricky Blvd., Tucson, AZ 85716 / 520-326-1117; FAX: 520-326-1117

Hart & Son, Inc., Robert W., 401 Montgomery St., Nescopeck, PA 18635 / 717-752-3655; FAX: 717-752-1088

Hart Rifle Barrels, Inc., P.O. Box 182, 1690 Apulia Rd., Lafayette, NY 13084 / 315-677-9841; FAX: 315-677-9610 hartrb@aol.com hartbarrels.com

Hartford (See U.S. Importer-EMF Co. Inc.)

Hartmann & Weiss GmbH, Rahlstedter Bahnhofstr. 47, 22143, Hamburg, GERMANY / (40) 677 55 85; FAX: (40) 677 55 92 hartmannundweiss@t-online.de

Harvey, Frank, 218 Nightfall, Terrace, NV 89015 / 702-558-6998

Hastings, P.O. Box 135, Clay Center, KS 67432 / 785-632-3169; FAX: 785-632-6554

Hatfield Gun, 224 N. 4th St., St. Joseph, MO 64501

Hawk Laboratories, Inc. (See Hawk, Inc.), 849 Hawks Bridge Rd., Salem, NJ 08079 / 609-299-2700; FAX: 609-299-2800

Hawk, Inc., 849 Hawks Bridge Rd., Salem, NJ 08079 / 609-299-2700; FAX: 609-299-2800 info@hawkbullets.com www.hawkbullets.com

Hawken Shop, The, P.O. Box 593, Oak Harbor, WA 98277 / 206-679-4657; FAX: 206-675-1114

Hawken Shop, The (See Dayton Traister)

Haydel's Game Calls, Inc., 5018 Hazel Jones Rd., Bossier City, LA 71111 / 318-746-3586; FAX: 318-746-3711 www.haydels.com

Hecht, Hubert J., Waffen-Hecht, P.O. Box 2635, Fair Oaks, CA 95628 / 916-966-1020

Heckler & Koch GmbH, P.O. Box 1329, 78722 Oberndorf, Neckar, GERMANY / 49-7423179-0; FAX: 49-7423179-2406

Heckler & Koch, Inc., 21480 Pacific Blvd., Sterling, VA 20166-8900 / 703-450-1900; FAX: 703-450-8160 www.hecklerkoch-usa.com

Hege Jagd-u. Sporthandels GmbH, P.O. Box 101461, W-7770, Ueberlingen a. Boden, GERMANY

Heidenstrom Bullets, Dalghte 86-3660 Rjukan, 35091818, NORWAY, olau.joh@online.tuo

Heilmann, Stephen, P.O. Box 657, Grass Valley, CA 95945 / 530-272-8758; FAX: 530-274-0285 sheilmann@jps.net www.metalwood.com

Heinie Specialty Products, 301 Oak St., Quincy, IL 62301-2500 / 217-228-9500; FAX: 217-228-9502 rheinie@heinie.com www.heinie.com

Helwan (See U.S. Importer-Interarms)

Henigson & Associates, Steve, P.O. Box 2726, Culver City, CA 90231 / 310-305-8288; FAX: 310-305-1905

Henriksen Tool Co., Inc., 8515 Wagner Creek Rd., Talent, OR 97540 / 541-535-2309; FAX: 541-535-2309

Henry Repeating Arms Co., 110 8th St., Brooklyn, NY 11215 / 718-499-5600; FAX: 718-768-8056 info@henryrepeating.com www.henryrepeating.com

Hensley, Gunmaker, Darwin, P.O. Box 329, Brightwood, OR 97011 / 503-622-5411

Heppler, Keith. See: KEITH'S CUSTOM GUNSTOCKS

Hercules, Inc. (See Alliant Techsystems Smokeless Powder Group)

Heritage Firearms (See Heritage Mfg., Inc.)

Heritage Manufacturing, Inc., 4600 NW 135th St., Opa Locka, FL 33054 / 305-685-5966; FAX: 305-687-6721 infohmi@heritagemfg.com www.heritagemfg.com

Heritage/VSP Gun Books, P.O. Box 887, McCall, ID 83638 / 208-634-4104; FAX: 208-634-3101 heritage@gunbooks.com www.gunbooks.com

Herrett's Stocks, Inc., P.O. Box 741, Twin Falls, ID 83303 / 208-733-1498

Hesco-Meprolight, 2139 Greenville Rd., LaGrange, GA 30241 / 706-884-7967; FAX: 706-882-4683

Hesse Arms, Robert Hesse, 1126 70th St. E., Inver Grove Heights, MN 55077-2416 / 651-455-5760; FAX: 612-455-5760

Hesse, Robert. See: HESSE ARMS

Heydenberk, Warren R., 1059 W. Sawmill Rd., Quakertown, PA 18951 / 215-538-2682

Hickman, Jaclyn, Box 1900, Glenrock, WY 82637

Hidalgo, Tony, 12701 SW 9th Pl., Davie, FL 33325 / 954-476-7645

High Bridge Arms, Inc., 3185 Mission St., San Francisco, CA 94110 / 415-282-8358

High North Products, Inc., P.O. Box 2, Antigo, WI 54409 / 715-627-2331; FAX: 715-623-5451

High Performance International, 5734 W. Florist Ave., Milwaukee, WI 53218 / 414-466-9040; FAX: 414-466-7050 mike@hpirifles.com www.hpirifles.com

High Precision, Bud Welsh, 80 New Road, E. Amherst, NY 14051 / 716-688-6344; FAX: 716-688-0425 welsh5168@aol.com www.high-precision.com

High Standard Mfg. Co./F.I., Inc., 5200 Mitchelldale St., Ste. E17, Houston, TX 77092-7222 / 713-462-4200 or 800-272-7816; FAX: 713-681-5665 info@highstandard.com www.highstandard.com

High Tech Specialties, Inc., P.O. Box 839, 293 E Main St., Rear, Adamstown, PA 19501 / 717-484-0405; FAX: 717-484-0523 bansner@aol.com www.bansmersrifle.com/hightech

Highline Machine Co., Randall Thompson, Randall Thompson, 654 Lela Place, Grand Junction, CO 81504 / 970-434-4971

Highwood Special Products, 1531 E. Highwood, Pontiac, MI 48340

Hill, Loring F., 304 Cedar Rd., Elkins Park, PA 19027

Hill Speed Leather, Ernie, 4507 N 195th Ave., Litchfield Park, AZ 85340 / 602-853-9222; FAX: 602-853-9235

Hinman Outfitters, Bob, 107 N Sanderson Ave., Bartonville, IL 61607-1839 / 309-691-8132

Hi-Performance Ammunition Company, 484 State Route 366, Apollo, PA 15613 / 304-674-9000; FAX: 304-675-6700

HIP-GRIP Barami Corp., P.O. Box 252224, West Bloomfield, MI 48325-2224 / 248-738-0462; FAX: 248-738-2542 hipgripja@aol.com www.hipgrip.com

Hi-Point Firearms/MKS Supply, 8611-A North Dixie Dr., Dayton, OH 45414 / 877-425-4867; FAX: 937-454-0503 www.hi-pointfirearms.com

Hiptmayer, Armurier, RR 112 750, P.O. Box 136, Eastman, PQ J0E 1P0 CANADA / 514-297-2492

Hiptmayer, Heidemarie, RR 112 750, P.O. Box 136, Eastman, PQ J0E 1P0 CANADA / 514-297-2492

Hiptmayer, Klaus, RR 112 750, P.O. Box 136, Eastman, PQ J0E 1P0 CANADA / 514-297-2492

Hirtenberger AG, Leobersdorferstrasse 31, A-2552, Hirtenberg, AUSTRIA / 43(0)2256 81184; FAX: 43(0)2256 81808 www.hirtenberger.ot

HJS Arms, Inc., P.O. Box 3711, Brownsville, TX 78523-3711 / 956-542-2767; FAX: 956-542-2767

Hoag, James W., 8523 Canoga Ave., Suite C, Canoga Park, CA 91304 / 818-998-1510

Hobson Precision Mfg. Co., 210 Big Oak Ln., Brent, AL 35034 / 205-926-4662; FAX: 205-926-3193 cahobbob@dbtech.net

Hodgdon Powder Co., 6231 Robinson, Shawnee Mission, KS 66202 / 913-362-9455; FAX: 913-362-1307

Hodgman, Inc., 1750 Orchard Rd., Montgomery, IL 60538 / 708-897-7555; FAX: 708-897-7558

Hodgson, Richard, 9081 Tahoe Lane, Boulder, CO 80301

Hoehn Sales, Inc., 2045 Kohn Road, Wright City, MO 63390 / 636-745-8144; FAX: 636-745-7868 hoehnsales@direcway.com

Hofer Jagdwaffen, P., A9170 Ferlach, Kirchgasse 24, Kirchgasse, AUSTRIA / 43 4227 3683; FAX: 43 4227 368330 peterhofer@hoferwaffen.com www.hoferwaffen.com

Hoffman New Ideas, 821 Northmoor Rd., Lake Forest, IL 60045 / 312-234-4075

Hogue Grips, P.O. Box 1138, Paso Robles, CA 93447 / 800-438-4747 or 805-239-1440; FAX: 805-239-2553

Holland & Holland Ltd., 33 Bruton St., London, ENGLAND / 44-171-499-4411; FAX: 44-171-408-7962

Holland's Gunsmithing, P.O. Box 69, Powers, OR 97466 / 541-439-5155; FAX: 541-439-5155

Hollinger, Jon. See: ASPEN OUTFITTING CO.

Hollywood Engineering, 10642 Arminta St., Sun Valley, CA 91352 / 818-842-8376; FAX: 818-504-4168 cadqueenel1@aol.com

Homak, 350 N. La Salle Dr. Ste. 1100, Chicago, IL 60610-4731 / 312-523-3100; FAX: 312-523-9455

Hoppe's Div. Penguin Industries, Inc., 9200 Cody St., Overland Park, KS 66214 / 800-845-2444

Horizons Unlimited, P.O. Box 426, Warm Springs, GA 31830 / 706-655-3603; FAX: 706-655-3603

Hornady Mfg. Co., P.O. Box 1848, Grand Island, NE 68802 / 800-338-3220 or 308-382-1390; FAX: 308-382-5761

Horseshoe Leather Products, Andy Arratoonian, The Cottage Sharow, Ripon, ENGLAND U.K. / 44-1765-605858 andy@horseshoe.co.uk www.holsters.org

House of Muskets, Inc., The, PO Box 4640, Pagosa Springs, CO 81157 / 970-731-2295

Houtz & Barwick, P.O. Box 435, W. Church St., Elizabeth City, NC 27909 / 800-775-0337 or 919-335-4191; FAX: 919-335-1152

Howa Machinery, Ltd., 1900-1 Sukaguchi Kiyosu, Aichi 452-8601, JAPAN / 81-52-408-1231; FAX: 81-52-401-4999 howa@howa.co.jp http://www.howa.cojpl

Howell Machine, Inc., 815 D St., Lewiston, ID 83501 / 208-743-7418; FAX: 208-746-1703 ammoload@microwavedsl.com www.ammoload.com

H-S Precision, Inc., 1301 Turbine Dr., Rapid City, SD 57701 / 605-341-3006; FAX: 605-342-8964

HT Bullets, 244 Belleville Rd., New Bedford, MA 02745 / 508-999-3338

Hubert J. Hecht Waffen-Hecht, P.O. Box 2635, Fair Oaks, CA 95628 / 916-966-1020

Huebner, Corey O., P.O. Box 564, Frenchtown, MT 59834 / 406-721-7168 bugsboys@hotmail.com

Huey Gun Cases, 820 Indiana St., Lawrence, KS 66044-2645 / 785-842-0062; FAX: 785-842-0062 hueycases@aol.com www.hueycases.com

Hume, Don, P.O. Box 351, Miami, OK 74355 / 800-331-2686; FAX: 918-542-4340 info@donhume.com www.donhume.com

Hunkeler, A. (See Buckskin Machine Works), 3235 S 358th St., Auburn, WA 98001 / 206-927-5412

Hunter Co., Inc., 3300 W. 71st Ave., Westminster, CO 80030 / 303-427-4626; FAX: 303-428-3980 debbiet@huntercompany.com www.huntercompany.com

Hunterjohn, P.O. Box 771457, St. Louis, MO 63177 / 314-531-7250 www.hunterjohn.com

Hunter's Specialties Inc., 6000 Huntington Ct. NE, Cedar Rapids, IA 52402-1268 / 319-395-0321; FAX: 319-395-0326

Hunters Supply, Inc., P.O. Box 313, Tioga, TX 76271 / 940-437-2458; FAX: 940-437-2228 hunterssupply@hotmail.com www.hunterssupply.net

Huntington Die Specialties, 601 Oro Dam Blvd., Oroville, CA 95965 / 530-534-1210 or 866-735-6237; FAX: 530-534-1212 buy@huntingtons.com www.huntingtons.com

Hutton Rifle Ranch, P.O. Box 170317, Boise, ID 83717 / 208-345-8781 www.martinbrevik@aol.com

Hydra-Tone Chemicals, Inc., 7785 Foundation Dr., Suite 6, Florence, KY 41042 / 859-342-5553; FAX: 859-342-2380 www.hydra-tone.com

Hydrosorbent Products, P.O. Box 437, Ashley Falls, MA 01222 / 800-448-7903; FAX: 413-229-8743 orders@dehumidify.com www.dehumidify.com

I

I.A.B. (See U.S. Importer-Taylor's & Co., Inc.)

I.D.S.A. Books, 1324 Stratford Drive, Piqua, OH 45356 / 937-773-4203; FAX: 937-778-1922

I.N.C. Inc. (See Kickeez I.N.C., Inc.)

I.S.W., 106 E. Cairo Dr., Tempe, AZ 85282

IAR Inc., 33171 Camino Capistrano, San Juan Capistrano, CA 92675 / 949-443-3642; FAX: 949-443-3647 sales@iar-arms.com iar-arms.com

Ide, Ken. See: STURGEON VALLEY SPORTERS

IGA (See U.S. Importer-Stoeger Industries)

Image Ind. Inc., 11220 E. Main St., Huntley, IL 60142-7369 / 630-766-2402; FAX: 630-766-7373

Impact Case & Container, Inc., P.O. Box 1129, Rathdrum, ID 83858 / 877-687-2452; FAX: 208-687-0632 bradk@icc-case.com www.icc-case.com

Imperial (See E-Z-Way Systems), P.O. Box 4310, Newark, OH 43058-4310 / 614-345-6645; FAX: 614-345-6600 ezway@infinet.com www.jcunald.com

Imperial Magnum Corp., P.O. Box 249, Oroville, WA 98844 / 604-495-3131; FAX: 604-495-2816

Imperial Miniature Armory, 1115 FM 359, Houston, TX 77035-3305 / 800-646-4288; FAX: 832-595-8787 miniguns@houston.rr.com www.1800miniature.com

IMR Powder Co., 1080 Military Turnpike, Suite 2, Plattsburg, NY 12901 / 518-563-2253; FAX: 518-563-6916

Info-Arm, P.O. Box 1262, Champlain, NY 12919 / 514-955-0355; FAX: 514-955-0357 infoarm@qc.aira.com

Innovative Weaponry Inc., 2513 E. Loop 820 N., Fort Worth, TX 76118 / 817-284-0099 or 800-334-3573

INTEC International, Inc., P.O. Box 5708, Scottsdale, AZ 85261 / 602-483-1708

Inter Ordnance of America LP, 3305 Westwood Industrial Dr., Monroe, NC 28110-5204 / 704-821-8337; FAX: 704-821-8523

Intercontinental Distributors, Ltd., P.O. Box 815, Beulah, ND 58523

International Shooters Service, P.O. Box 185234, Ft. Worth, TX 76181 / 817-595-2090; FAX: 817-595-2090 is_s_@sbcglobal.net www.iss-internationalshootersservice.com

Intrac Arms International, 5005 Chapman Hwy., Knoxville, TN 37920

Ion Industries, Inc., 3508 E Allerton Ave., Cudahy, WI 53110 / 414-486-2007; FAX: 414-486-2017

Iosso Products, 1485 Lively Blvd., Elk Grove Village, IL 60007 / 847-437-8400; FAX: 847-437-8478

Iron Bench, 12619 Bailey Rd., Redding, CA 96003 / 916-241-4623

Ironside International Publishers, Inc., P.O. Box 1050, Lorton, VA 22199

Ironsighter Co., P.O. Box 85070, Westland, MI 48185 / 734-326-8731; FAX: 734-326-3378 www.ironsighter.com

Irwin, Campbell H., 140 Hartland Blvd., East Hartland, CT 06027 / 203-653-3901

Israel Arms Inc., 5625 Star Ln. #B, Houston, TX 77057 / 713-789-0745; FAX: 713-914-9515 www.israelarms.com

Ithaca Classic Doubles, Stephen Lamboy, No. 5 Railroad St., Victor, NY 14564 / 716-924-2710; FAX: 716-924-2737 ithacadoubles.com

Ithaca Gun Company LLC, 901 Rt. 34 B, King Ferry, NY 13081 / 315-364-7171; FAX: 315-364-5134 info@ithacagun.com

Ithaca Guns USA, LLC, 420 N. Walpole St., Upper Sandusky, OH 43351 / 419-294-4113; FAX: 419-294-9433 service@ithacaguns.com www.ithacagunusa.com

Ivanoff, Thomas G. (See Tom's Gun Repair)

J

J J Roberts Firearm Engraver, 7808 Lake Dr., Manassas, VA 20111 / 703-330-0448; FAX: 703-264-8600 james.roberts@angelfire.com www.angelfire.com/va2/engraver

J&D Components, 75 East 350 North, Orem, UT 84057-4719 / 801-225-7007 www.jdcomponents.com

J&J Products, Inc., 9240 Whitmore, El Monte, CA 91731 / 818-571-5228; FAX: 800-927-8361

J&J Sales, 1501 21st Ave. S., Great Falls, MT 59405 / 406-727-9789 mtshootingbench@yahoo.com www.j&jsales.us

J&L Superior Bullets (See Huntington Die Specialties)

J&M Precision Machining, Jeff Amato, RR 1 Box 91, Bloomfield, IN 47424

J&R Engineering, P.O. Box 77, 200 Lyons Hill Rd., Athol, MA 01331 / 508-249-9241

J&R Enterprises, 4550 Scotts Valley Rd., Lakeport, CA 95453

J&S Heat Treat, 803 S. 16th St., Blue Springs, MO 64015 / 816-229-2149; FAX: 816-228-1135

J. Dewey Mfg. Co., Inc., P.O. Box 2014, Southbury, CT 06488 / 203-264-3064; FAX: 203-262-6907 deweyrods@worldnet.att.net www.deweyrods.com

J. Korzinek Riflesmith, RD 2, Box 73D, Canton, PA 17724 / 717-673-8512

J.A. Blades, Inc. (See Christopher Firearms Co.)

J.A. Henckels Zwillingswerk Inc., 9 Skyline Dr., Hawthorne, NY 10532 / 914-592-7370

J.G. Anschutz GmbH & Co. KG, Daimlerstr. 12, D-89079 Ulm, Ulm, GERMANY / 49 731 40120; FAX: 49 731 4012700 JGA-info@anschuetz-sport.com www.anschuetz-sport.com

J.G. Dapkus Co., Inc., Commerce Circle, P.O. Box 293, Durham, CT 06422 www.explodingtargets.com

J.I.T. Ltd., P.O. Box 230, Freedom, WY 83120 / 708-494-0937

J.J. Roberts / Engraver, 7808 Lake Dr., Manassas, VA 20111 / 703-330-0448 jjrengraver@aol.com www.angelfire.com/va2/engraver

J.R. Williams Bullet Co., 2008 Tucker Rd., Perry, GA 31069 / 912-987-0274

J.W. Morrison Custom Rifles, 4015 W. Sharon, Phoenix, AZ 85029 / 602-978-3754

J.W. Wasmundt-Gunsmith, Jim Wasmundt, P.O. Box 130, 140 Alder St., Powers, OR 97466-0130 / 541-439-2044 jwasm@juno.com

Jack A. Rosenberg & Sons, 12229 Cox Ln., Dallas, TX 75234 / 214-241-6302

Jack Dever Co., 8520 NW 90th St., Oklahoma City, OK 73132 / 405-721-6393 jbdever1@home.com

Jack First, Inc., 1201 Turbine Dr., Rapid City, SD 57703 / 605-343-9544; FAX: 605-343-9420

Jack Jonas Appraisals & Taki, 13952 E. Marina Dr., #604, Aurora, CO 80014

Jackalope Gun Shop, 1048 S. 5th St., Douglas, WY 82633 / 307-358-3441 wildcatoutfitters@msn.com www.jackalopegunshop.com

Jaffin, Harry. See: BRIDGEMAN PRODUCTS

Jagdwaffen, Peter. See: BUCHSENMACHERMEISTER

James Calhoon Mfg., 4343 U.S. Highway 87, Havre, MT 59501 / 406-395-4079 www.jamescalhoon.com

James Churchill Glove Co., PO Box 298, Centralia, WA 98531 / 360-736-2816; FAX: 360-330-0151 churchillglove@localaccess.com

James Wayne Firearms for Collectors and Investors, 2608 N. Laurent, Victoria, TX 77901 / 361-578-1258; FAX: 361-578-3559

Jamison International, Marc Jamison, 3551 Mayer Ave., Sturgis, SD 57785 / 605-347-5090; FAX: 605-347-4704 jbell2@masttechnology.com

Jamison, Marc. See: JAMISON INTERNATIONAL

Jamison's Forge Works, 4527 Rd. 6.5 NE, Moses Lake, WA 98837 / 509-762-2659

Jantz Supply, Inc., 309 West Main Dept HD, Davis, OK 73030-0584 / 580-369-2316; FAX: 580-369-3082 jantz@brightok.net www.knifemaking.com

Jarrett Rifles, Inc., 383 Brown Rd., Jackson, SC 29831 / 803-471-3616 www.jarrettrifles.com

Jarvis, Inc., 1123 Cherry Orchard Lane, Hamilton, MT 59840 / 406-961-4392

Javelina Lube Products, P.O. Box 337, San Bernardino, CA 92402 / 909-350-9556; FAX: 909-429-1211

Jay McCament Custom Gunmaker, Jay McCament, 1730-134th St. Ct. S., Tacoma, WA 98444 / 253-531-8832

JB Custom, P.O. Box 6912, Leawood, KS 66206 / 913-381-2329

Jeff Flannery Engraving, 11034 Riddles Run Rd., Union, KY 41091 / 859-384-3127; FAX: 859-384-2222 engraving@fuse.net http://home.fuse.net/engraving/

Jeff's Outfitters, 63F Sena Fawn, Cape Girardeau, MO 63701 / 573-651-3200; FAX: 573-651-3207 info@jeffsoutfitters.com www.jeffsoutfitters.com

Jena Eur, P.O. Box 319, Dunmore, PA 18512

Jenco Sales, Inc., P.O. Box 1000, Manchaca, TX 78652 / 800-531-5301; FAX: 800-266-2373 jencosales@sbcglobal.net

Jenkins Recoil Pads, 5438 E. Frontage Ln., Olney, IL 62450 / 618-395-3416

Jensen Bullets, RR 1 Box 187, Arco, ID 83213 / 208-785-5590

Jensen's Custom Ammunition, 5146 E. Pima, Tucson, AZ 85712 / 602-325-3346; FAX: 602-322-5704

Jensen's Firearms Academy, 1280 W. Prince, Tucson, AZ 85705 / 602-293-8516

Jericho Tool & Die Co., Inc., 121 W. Keech Rd., Bainbridge, NY 13733-3248 / 607-563-8222; FAX: 607-563-8560 jerichotool.com www.jerichotool.com

Jerry Phillips Optics, P.O. Box L632, Langhorne, PA 19047 / 215-757-5037; FAX: 215-757-7097

Jesse W. Smith Saddlery, 0499 County Road J, Pritchett, CO 81064 / 509-325-0622

Jester Bullets, Rt. 1 Box 27, Orienta, OK 73737

Jewell Triggers, Inc., 3620 Hwy. 123, San Marcos, TX 78666 / 512-353-2999; FAX: 512-392-0543

JG Airguns, LLC, John Groenewold, P.O. Box 830, Mundelein, IL 60060 / 847-566-2365; FAX: 847-566-4065 info@jgairguns.biz www.jgairguns.biz

JGS Precision Tool Mfg., LLC, 60819 Selander Rd., Coos Bay, OR 97420 / 541-267-4331; FAX: 541-267-5996 jgstools@harborside.com www.jgstools.com

Jim Blair Engraving, P.O. Box 64, Glenrock, WY 82637 / 307-436-8115 jblairengrav@msn.com

Jim Noble Co., 204 W. 5th St., Vancouver, WA 98660 / 360-695-1309; FAX: 360-695-6835 jnobleco@aol.com

Jim Norman Custom Gunstocks, 14281 Cane Rd., Valley Center, CA 92082 / 619-749-6252

Jim's Precision, Jim Ketchum, 1725 Moclips Dr., Petaluma, CA 94952 / 707-762-3014

JLK Bullets, 414 Turner Rd., Dover, AR 72837 / 501-331-4194

Johanssons Vapentillbehor, Bert, S-430 20, Veddige, SWEDEN

John Hall Plastics, Inc., P.O. Box 1526, Alvin, TX 77512 / 713-489-8709

John J. Adams & Son Engravers, 7040 VT Rt 113, Vershire, VT 05079 / 802-685-0019

John Masen Co. Inc., 1305 Jelmak, Grand Prairie, TX 75050 / 817-430-8732; FAX: 817-430-1715

John Partridge Sales Ltd., Trent Meadows Rugeley, Staffordshire, WS15 2HS ENGLAND

John Rigby & Co., 500 Linne Rd. Ste. D, Paso Robles, CA 93446 / 805-227-4236; FAX: 805-227-4723 jrigby@calinet www.johnrigbyandco.com

MANUFACTURER'S DIRECTORY

John's Custom Leather, 523 S. Liberty St., Blairsville, PA 15717 / 724-459-6802; FAX: 724-459-5996
Johnson Wood Products, 34897 Crystal Road, Strawberry Point, IA 52076 / 563-933-6504 johnsonwoodproducts@yahoo.com
Jonad Corp., 2091 Lakeland Ave., Lakewood, OH 44107 / 216-226-3161
Jonathan Arthur Ciener, Inc., 8700 Commerce St., Cape Canaveral, FL 32920 / 321-868-2200; FAX: 321-868-2201 www.22lrconversions.com
Jones Custom Products, Neil A., 17217 Brookhouser Rd., Saegertown, PA 16433 / 814-763-2769; FAX: 814-763-4228 njones@mdvl.net neiljones.com
Jones, J. See: SSK INDUSTRIES
Jones Moulds, Paul, 4901 Telegraph Rd., Los Angeles, CA 90022 / 213-262-1510
JP Enterprises, Inc., P.O. Box 378, Hugo, MN 55038 / 651-426-9196; FAX: 651-426-2472 www.jprifles.com
JP Sales, Box 307, Anderson, TX 77830
JRP Custom Bullets, RR2 2233 Carlton Rd., Whitehall, NY 12887 / 518-282-0084 or 802-438-5548
JSL Ltd. (See U.S. Importer-Specialty Shooters Supply)
Juenke, Vern, 25 Bitterbush Rd., Reno, NV 89523 / 702-345-0225
Jungkind, Reeves C., 509 E. Granite St., Llano, TX 78643-3055 / 325-247-1151
Jurras, L. See: L. E. JURRAS & ASSOC.
Justin Phillippi Custom Bullets, P.O. Box 773, Ligonier, PA 15658 / 412-238-9671

K

K&M Industries, Inc., Box 66, 510 S. Main, Troy, ID 83871 / 208-835-2281; FAX: 208-835-5211
K&M Services, 5430 Salmon Run Rd., Dover, PA 17315 / 717-292-3175; FAX: 717-292-3175
K. Eversull Co., Inc., 1 Tracemont, Boyce, LA 71409 / 318-793-8728; FAX: 318-793-5483 bestguns@aol.com
K.B.I. Inc., P.O. Box 6625, Harrisburg, PA 17112 / 717-540-8518; FAX: 717-540-8567
KA-BAR Knives, 200 Homer St., Olean, NY 14760 / 800-282-0130; FAX: 716-790-7188 info@ka-bar.com www.ka-bar.com
Kahles A. Swarovski Company, 2 Slater Rd., Cranston, RI 02920 / 401-946-2220; FAX: 401-946-2587
Kahr Arms, P.O. Box 220, 630 Route 303, Blauvelt, NY 10913 / 845-353-7770; FAX: 845-353-7833 www.kahr.com
Kailua Custom Guns Inc., 51 N. Dean Street, Coquille, OR 97423 / 541-396-5413 kailuacustom@aol.com www.kailuacustom.com
Kalispel Case Line, P.O. Box 267, Cusick, WA 99119 / 509-445-1121
Kamik Outdoor Footwear, 554 Montee de Liesse, Montreal, PQ H4T 1P1 CANADA / 514-341-3950; FAX: 514-341-1861
Kane, Edward, P.O. Box 385, Ukiah, CA 95482 / 707-462-2937
Kapro Mfg. Co. Inc. (See R.E.I.)
Kasenit Co., Inc., 39 Park Ave., Highland Mills, NY 10930 / 845-928-9595; FAX: 845-986-8038
Kaswer Custom, Inc., 13 Surrey Drive, Brookfield, CT 06804 / 203-775-0564; FAX: 203-775-6872
KDF, Inc., 2485 Hwy. 46 N., Seguin, TX 78155 / 830-379-8141; FAX: 830-379-5420
KeeCo Impressions, Inc., 346 Wood Ave., North Brunswick, NJ 08902 / 800-468-0546
Kehr, Roger, 2131 Agate Ct. SE, Lacy, WA 98503 / 360-491-0691
Keith's Bullets, 942 Twisted Oak, Algonquin, IL 60102 / 708-658-3520
Keith's Custom Gunstocks, Keith M. Heppler, 540 Banyan Circle, Walnut Creek, CA 94598 / 925-934-3509; FAX: 925-934-3143 kmheppler@hotmail.com
Kelbly, Inc., 7222 Dalton Fox Lake Rd., North Lawrence, OH 44666 / 216-683-4674; FAX: 216-683-7349
Keller Co., The, P.O. Box 4057, Port Angeles, WA 98363-0997 / 214-770-8585
Kelley's, P.O. Box 125, Woburn, MA 01801-0125 / 800-879-7273; FAX: 781-272-7077 kels@star.net www.kelsmilitary.com
Kellogg's Professional Products, 325 Pearl St., Sandusky, OH 44870 / 419-625-6551; FAX: 419-625-6167 skwigton@aol.com
Kelly, Lance, 1723 Willow Oak Dr., Edgewater, FL 32132 / 904-423-4933

Kel-Tec CNC Industries, Inc., P.O. Box 236009, Cocoa, FL 32923 / 321-631-0068; FAX: 321-631-1169 www.kel-tec.com
Kemen America, 2550 Hwy. 23, Wrenshall, MN 55797 / 218-384-3670 patrickl@midwestshootingschool.com midwestshootingschool.com
Ken Eyster Heritage Gunsmiths, Inc., 6441 Bisop Rd., Centerburg, OH 43011 / 740-625-6131; FAX: 740-625-7811
Ken Starnes Gunmaker, 15617 NE 324th Circle, Battle Ground, WA 98604 / 360-666-5025; FAX: 360-666-5024 kstarnes@kdsa.com
Keng's Firearms Specialty, Inc./US Tactical Systems, 875 Wharton Dr., P.O. Box 44405, Atlanta, GA 30336-1405 / 404-691-7611; FAX: 404-505-8445
Kennebec Journal, 274 Western Ave., Augusta, ME 04330 / 207-622-6288
Kennedy Firearms, 10 N. Market St., Muncy, PA 17756 / 717-546-6695
Kenneth W. Warren Engraver, P.O. Box 2842, Wenatchee, WA 98807 / 509-663-6123; FAX: 509-665-6123
Ken's Kustom Kartridges, 331 Jacobs Rd., Hubbard, OH 44425 / 216-534-4595
Kent Cartridge America, Inc., P.O. Box 849, 1000 Zigor Rd., Kearneysville, WV 25430
Keowee Game Calls, 608 Hwy. 25 North, Travelers Rest, SC 29690 / 864-834-7204; FAX: 864-834-7831
Kershaw Knives, 18600 SW Teton Ave., Tualatin, OR 97062 / 503-682-1966 or 800-325-2891; FAX: 503-682-7168
Kesselring Gun Shop, 4024 Old Hwy. 99N, Burlington, WA 98233 / 360-724-3113; FAX: 360-724-7003 info@kesselrings.com www.kesselrings.com
Ketchum, Jim (See Jim's Precision)
Keystone Sporting Arms, Inc. (Crickett Rifles), 8920 State Route 405, Milton, PA 17847 / 800-742-2777; FAX: 570-742-1455
Kickeez I.N.C., Inc., 301 Industrial Dr., Carl Junction, MO 64834-8806 / 419-649-2100; FAX: 417-649-2200 kickeez@sbcglobal.net www.kickeez.net
Kilham & Co., Main St., P.O. Box 37, Lyme, NH 03768 / 603-795-4112
Kimar (See U.S. Importer-IAR, Inc.)
Kimber of America, Inc., 1 Lawton St., Yonkers, NY 10705 / 800-880-2418; FAX: 914-964-9340
King & Co., P.O. Box 1242, Bloomington, IL 61702 / 309-473-3964 or 800-914-5464; FAX: 309-473-2161
King's Gun Works, 1837 W. Glenoaks Blvd., Glendale, CA 91201 / 818-956-6010; FAX: 818-548-8606
Kirkpatrick Leather Co., P.O. Box 677, Laredo, TX 78040 / 956-723-6631; FAX: 956-725-0672 mike@kirkpatrickleather.com www.kirkpatrickleather.com
KK Air International (See Impact Case & Container Co., Inc.)
Kleen-Bore, Inc., 8909 Forum Way, Ft. Worth, TX 76140 / 413-527-0300; FAX: 817-926-7012 info@kleen-bore.com www.kleen-bore.com
Kleinendorst, K. W., RR 1, Box 1500, Hop Bottom, PA 18824 / 570-289-4687; FAX: 570-289-8673
Klingler Woodcarving, P.O. Box 141, Thistle Hill, Cabot, VT 05647 / 802-426-3811 www.vermartcrafts.com
Knifeware, Inc., P.O. Box 3, Greenville, WV 24945 / 304-832-6878
Knight Rifles, 21852 Hwy. J46, P.O. Box 130, Centerville, IA 52544 / 515-856-2626; FAX: 515-856-2628 www.knightrifles.com
Knight Rifles (See Modern Muzzleloading, Inc.)
Knight's Manufacturing Co., 701 Columbia Blvd., Titusville, FL 32780 / 321-607-9900; FAX: 321-268-1498 civiliansales@knightarmco.com www.knightarmco.com
Knock on Wood Antiques, 355 Post Rd., Darien, CT 06820 / 203-655-9031
Knoell, Doug, 9737 McCardle Way, Santee, CA 92071 / 619-449-5189
Knopp, Gary. See: SUPER 6 LLC
Koevenig's Engraving Service, Box 55 Rabbit Gulch, Hill City, SD 57745 / 605-574-2239 ekoevenig@msn.com
KOGOT, 410 College, Trinidad, CO 81082 / 719-846-9406; FAX: 719-846-9406
Kolar, 1925 Roosevelt Ave., Racine, WI 53406 / 414-554-0800; FAX: 414-554-9093
Kolpin Outdoors, Inc., P.O. Box 107, 205 Depot St., Fox Lake, WI 53933 / 414-928-3118; FAX: 414-928-3687 cdutton@kolpin.com www.kolpin.com
Korth Germany GmbH, Robert Bosch Strasse, 11, D-23909, 23909 Ratzeburg, GERMANY / 4541-840363; FAX: 4541-84 05 35 info@korthwaffen.de www.korthwaffen.de

Korth USA, 437R Chandler St., Tewksbury, MA 01876 / 978-851-8656; FAX: 978-851-9462 info@kortusa.com www.korthusa.com
Korzinek Riflesmith, J., RD 2 Box 73D, Canton, PA 17724 / 717-673-8512
Koval Knives, 5819 Zarley St., Suite A, New Albany, OH 43054 / 614-855-0777; FAX: 614-855-0945 koval@kovalknives.com www.kovalknives.com
Kowa Optimed, Inc., 20001 S. Vermont Ave., Torrance, CA 90502 / 310-327-1913; FAX: 310-327-4177 scopekowa@kowa.com www.kowascope.com
KP Books Division of F+W Publications, 700 E. State St., Iola, WI 54990-0001 / 715-445-2214
Kramer Designs, P.O. Box 129, Clancy, MT 59634 / 406-933-8658; FAX: 406-933-8658
Kramer Handgun Leather, P.O. Box 112154, Tacoma, WA 98411 / 800-510-2666; FAX: 253-564-1214 www.kramerleather.com
Krico Deutschland GmbH, Nurnbergerstrasse 6, D-90602, Pyrbaum, GERMANY / 09180-2780; FAX: 09180-2661
Krieger Barrels, Inc., 2024 Mayfield Rd, Richfield, WI 53076 / 262-628-8558; FAX: 262-628-8748
Krieghoff Gun Co., H., Boschstrasse 22, D-89079 Elm, GERMANY / 731-4018270
Krieghoff International, Inc., 7528 Easton Rd., Ottsville, PA 18942 / 610-847-5173; FAX: 610-847-8691
Kukowski, Ed. See: ED'S GUN HOUSE
Kulis Freeze Dry Taxidermy, 725 Broadway Ave., Bedford, OH 44146 / 440-232-8352; FAX: 440-232-7305 jkulis@kastaway.com www.kastaway.com
KVH Industries, Inc., 110 Enterprise Center, Middletown, RI 02842 / 401-847-3327; FAX: 401-849-0045
Kwik-Site Co., 5555 Treadwell St., Wayne, MI 48184 / 734-326-1500; FAX: 734-326-4120 kwiksiteco@aol.com

L

L&R Lock Co., 2328 Cains Mill Rd., Sumter, SC 29154 / 803-481-5790; FAX: 803-481-5795
L&S Technologies Inc. (See Aimtech Mount Systems)
L. Bengtson Arms Co., 6345-B E. Akron St., Mesa, AZ 85205 / 602-981-6375
L. E. Jurras & Assoc., L. E. Jurras, P.O. Box 680, Washington, IN 47501 / 812-254-6170; FAX: 812-254-6170 jurras@sbcglobal.net www.leejurras.com
L.A.R. Mfg., Inc., 4133 W. Farm Rd., West Jordan, UT 84088 / 801-280-3505; FAX: 801-280-1972
L.B.T., Judy Smith, HCR 62, Box 145, Moyie Springs, ID 83845 / 208-267-3588 lbtisaccuracy@imbris.net
L.E. Wilson, Inc., Box 324, 404 Pioneer Ave., Cashmere, WA 98815 / 509-782-1328; FAX: 509-782-7200
L.L. Bean, Inc., Freeport, ME 04032 / 207-865-4761; FAX: 207-552-2802
L.P.A. Inc., Via Alfieri 26, Gardone V.T., Brescia, ITALY / 30-891-14-81; FAX: 30-891-09-51
L.R. Clift Mfg., 3821 Hammonton Rd., Marysville, CA 95901 / 916-755-3390; FAX: 916-755-3393
La Clinique du .45, 1432 Rougemont, Chambly, PQ J3L 2L8 CANADA / 514-658-1144
Labanu Inc., 2201-F Fifth Ave., Ronkonkoma, NY 11779 / 516-467-6197; FAX: 516-981-4112
LaBoone, Pat. See: MIDWEST SHOOTING SCHOOL, THE
LaBounty Precision Reboring, Inc, 7968 Silver Lake Rd., PO Box 186, Maple Falls, WA 98266 / 360-599-2047; FAX: 360-599-3018
LaCrosse Footwear, Inc., 18550 NE Riverside Parkway, Portland, OR 97230 / 503-766-1010 or 800-323-2668; FAX: 503-766-1015 customerservice@lacrossefootwear.com www.lacrossefootwear.com
LaFrance Specialties, P.O. Box 87933, San Diego, CA 92138 / 619-293-3373; FAX: 619-293-0819 timlafrance@att.net lafrancespecialties.com
Lake Center Marina, P.O. Box 670, St. Charles, MO 63302 / 314-946-7500
Lakefield Arms Ltd. (See Savage Arms, Inc.)
Lakewood Products LLC, 275 June St., Berlin, WI 54923 / 800-872-8458; FAX: 920-361-7719 lakewood@centurytel.net www.lakewoodproducts.com
Lamboy, Stephen. See: ITHACA CLASSIC DOUBLES
Lampert, Ron, Rt. 1, 44857 Schoolcraft Trl., Guthrie, MN 56461 / 218-854-7345
Lamson & Goodnow Mfg. Co., 45 Conway St., Shelburne Falls, MA 03170 / 413-625-6564 or 800-872-6564; FAX: 413-625-9816 www.lamsonsharp.com

Lansky Levine, Arthur. See: LANSKY SHARPENERS
Lansky Sharpeners, Arthur Lansky Levine, P.O. Box 50830, Las Vegas, NV 89016 / 702-361-7511; FAX: 702-896-9511
LaPrade, P.O. Box 250, Ewing, VA 24248 / 423-733-2615
LaRocca Gun Works, 51 Union Place, Worcester, MA 01608 / 508-754-2887; FAX: 508-754-2887 www.laroccagunworks.com
Larry Lyons Gunworks, 110 Hamilton St., Dowagiac, MI 49047 / 616-782-9478
Laser Devices, Inc., 2 Harris Ct. A-4, Monterey, CA 93940 / 831-373-0701; FAX: 831-373-0903 sales@laserdevices.com www.laserdevices.com
Laseraim Technologies, Inc., P.O. Box 3548, Little Rock, AR 72203 / 501-375-2227
Laserlyte, 2201 Amapola Ct., Torrance, CA 90501
LaserMax, 3495 Winton Place, Rochester, NY 14623-2807 / 800-527-3703; FAX: 585-272-5427 customerservice@lasermax-inc.com www.lasermax.com
Lassen Community College, Gunsmithing Dept., P.O. Box 3000, Hwy. 139, Susanville, CA 96130 / 916-251-8800; FAX: 916-251-8838 staylor@lassencollege.edu www.lassencommunitycollege.edu
Lathrop's, Inc., 5146 E. Pima, Tucson, AZ 85712 / 520-881-0266 or 800-875-4867; FAX: 520-322-5704
Laughridge, William R. (See Cylinder & Slide, Inc.)
Laurel Mountain Forge, P.O. Box 52, Crown Point, IN 46308 / 219-548-2950; FAX: 219-548-2950
Laurona Armas Eibar, S.A.L., Avenida de Otaola 25, P.O. Box 260, Eibar 20600, SPAIN / 34-43-700600; FAX: 34-43-700616
Lawrence Brand Shot (See Precision Reloading, Inc.)
Lawrence Leather Co., P.O. Box 1479, Lillington, NC 27546 / 910-893-2071; FAX: 910-893-4742
Lawson Co., Harry, 3328 N. Richey Blvd., Tucson, AZ 85716 / 520-326-1117; FAX: 520-326-1117
Lawson, John. See: SIGHT SHOP, THE
Lawson, John G. (See Sight Shop, The)
Lazzeroni Arms Co., P.O. Box 26696, Tucson, AZ 85726 / 888-492-7247; FAX: 520-624-4250
Le Clear Industries (See E-Z-Way Systems)
Leapers, Inc., 7675 Five Mile Rd., Northville, MI 48167 / 248-486-1231; FAX: 248-486-1430
Leatherman Tool Group, Inc., 12106 NE Ainsworth Cir., P.O. Box 20595, Portland, OR 97294 / 503-253-7826; FAX: 503-253-7830
Lebeau-Courally, Rue St. Gilles, 386 4000, Liege, BELGIUM / 042-52-48-43; FAX: 32-4-252-2008 info@lebeau-courally.com www.lebeau-courally.com
Leckie Professional Gunsmithing, 546 Quarry Rd., Ottsville, PA 18942 / 215-847-8594
Ledbetter Airguns, Riley, 1804 E Sprague St., Winston Salem, NC 27107-3521 / 919-784-0676
Lee Precision, Inc., 4275 Hwy. U, Hartford, WI 53027 / 262-673-3075; FAX: 262-673-9273 info@leeprecision.com www.leeprecision.com
Lee Supplies, Mark, 9901 France Ct., Lakeville, MN 55044 / 612-461-2114
LeFever Arms Co., Inc., 6234 Stokes, Lee Center Rd., Lee Center, NY 13363 / 315-337-6722; FAX: 315-337-1543
Legacy Sports International, 206 S. Union St., Alexandria, VA 22314 / 703-548-4837 www.legacysports.com
Leica USA, Inc., 156 Ludlow Ave., Northvale, NJ 07647 / 201-767-7500; FAX: 201-767-8666
Leonard Day, 3 Kings Hwy., West Hatfield, MA 01027-9506 / 413-337-8369
Les Baer Custom, Inc., 29601 34th Ave., Hillsdale, IL 61257 / 309-658-2716; FAX: 309-658-2610 www.lesbaer.com
LesMerises, Felix. See: ROCKY MOUNTAIN ARMOURY
Lethal Force Institute (See Police Bookshelf), P.O. Box 122, Concord, NH 03301 / 603-224-6814; FAX: 603-226-3554
Lett Custom Grips, 672 Currier Rd., Hopkinton, NH 03229-2652 / 800-421-5388; FAX: 603-226-4580 info@lettgrips.com www.lettgrips.com
Leupold & Stevens, Inc., 14400 NW Greenbrier Pky., Beaverton, OR 97006 / 503-646-9171; FAX: 503-526-1455
Lever Arms Service Ltd., 2131 Burrard St., Vancouver, BC V6J 3H7 CANADA / 604-736-2711; FAX: 604-738-3503 leverarms@leverarms.com www.leverarms.com
Lew Horton Dist. Co., Inc., 15 Walkup Dr., Westboro, MA 01581 / 508-366-7400; FAX: 508-366-5332
Lewis Lead Remover, The (See Brownells, Inc.)

Liberty Mfg., Inc., 2233 East 16th St., Los Angeles, CA 90021 / 323-581-9171; FAX: 323-581-9351 libertymfginc@aol.com
Liberty Safe, 999 W. Utah Ave., Payson, UT 84651-1744 / 800-247-5625; FAX: 801-489-6409
Liberty Shooting Supplies, P.O. Box 357, Hillsboro, OR 97123 / 503-640-5518; FAX: 503-640-5518 info@libertyshootingsupplies.com www.libertyshootingsupplies.com
Lightning Performance Innovations, Inc., RD1 Box 555, Mohawk, NY 13407 / 315-866-8819; FAX: 315-867-5701
Lilja Precision Rifle Barrels, P.O. Box 372, Plains, MT 59859 / 406-826-3084; FAX: 406-826-3083 lilja@riflebarrels.com www.riflebarrels.com
Lincoln, Dean, Box 1886, Farmington, NM 87401
Linder Solingen Knives, 4401 Sentry Dr. #B, Tucker, GA 30084 / 770-939-6915; FAX: 770-939-6738
Lindsay Engraving & Tools, Steve Lindsay, 3714 W. Cedar Hills, Kearney, NE 68845 / 308-236-7885 steve@lindsayengraving.com www.handgravers.com
Lindsay, Steve. See: LINDSAY ENGRAVING & TOOLS
Lindsley Arms Cartridge Co., P.O. Box 757, 20 College Hill Rd., Henniker, NH 03242 / 603-995-1267
Linebaugh Custom Sixguns, P.O. Box 455, Cody, WY 82414 / 307-645-3332 www.sixgunner.com
Lion Country Supply, P.O. Box 480, Port Matilda, PA 16870
List Precision Engineering, Unit 1 Ingley Works, 13 River Road, Barking, ENGLAND / 011-081-594-1686
Lithi Bee Bullet Lube, 1728 Carr Rd., Muskegon, MI 49442 / 616-788-4479 lithibee@att.net
"Little John's" Antique Arms, 1740 W. Laveta, Orange, CA 92668
Littler Sales Co., 20815 W. Chicago, Detroit, MI 48228 / 313-273-6889; FAX: 313-273-1099 littlersales@aol.com
Littleton, J. F., 275 Pinedale Ave., Oroville, CA 95966 / 916-533-6084
Ljutic Industries, Inc., 732 N. 16th Ave., Suite 22, Yakima, WA 98902 / 509-248-0476; FAX: 509-576-8233 ljuticgun@earthlink.net www.ljuticgun.com
Lock's Philadelphia Gun Exchange, 6700 Rowland Ave., Philadelphia, PA 19149 / 215-332-6225; FAX: 215-332-4800 locks.gunshop@verizon.net
Lodewick, Walter H., 2816 NE Halsey St., Portland, OR 97232 / 503-284-2554 wlodewick@aol.com
Lodgewood Mfg., P.O. Box 611, Whitewater, WI 53190 / 262-473-5444; FAX: 262-473-6448 lodgewd@idcnet.com www.lodgewood.com
Log Cabin Sport Shop, 8010 Lafayette Rd., Lodi, OH 44254 / 330-948-1082; FAX: 330-948-4307 logcabin@logcabinshop.com www.logcabinshop.com
Logdewood Mfg., P.O. Box 611, Whitewater, WI 53190 / 262-473-5444; FAX: 262-473-6448 lodgewd@idcnet.com www.lodgewood.com
Lohman Mfg. Co., Inc., 4500 Doniphan Dr., P.O. Box 220, Neosho, MO 64850 / 417-451-4438; FAX: 417-451-2576
Lomont Precision Bullets, 278 Sandy Creek Rd., Salmon, ID 83467 / 208-756-6819; FAX: 208-756-6824 www.klomont.com
London Guns Ltd., Box 3750, Santa Barbara, CA 93130 / 805-683-4141; FAX: 805-683-1712
Lone Star Gunleather, 1301 Brushy Bend Dr., Round Rock, TX 78681 / 512-255-1805
Lone Star Rifle Company, 11231 Rose Road, Conroe, TX 77303 / 936-856-3363; FAX: 936-856-3363 dave@lonestar.com
Long, George F., 1402 Kokanee Ln., Grants Pass, OR 97527 / 541-476-0836
Lortone Inc., 2856 NW Market St., Seattle, WA 98107
Lothar Walther Precision Tool Inc., 3425 Hutchinson Rd., Cumming, GA 30040 / 770-889-9998; FAX: 770-889-4919 lotharwalther@mindspring.com www.lothar-walther.com
LPS Laboratories, Inc., 4647 Hugh Howell Rd., P.O. Box 3050, Tucker, GA 30084 / 404-934-7800
Lucas, Edward E, 32 Garfield Ave., East Brunswick, NJ 08816 / 201-251-5526
Lupton, Keith. See: PAWLING MOUNTAIN CLUB
Lyman Instant Targets, Inc. (See Lyman Products Corp.)
Lyman Products Corp., 475 Smith St., Middletown, CT 06457-1541 / 800-423-9704; FAX: 860-632-1699 lymansales@cshore.com www.lymanproducts.com

M

M.H. Canjar Co., 6510 Raleigh St., Arvada, CO 80003 / 303-295-2638; FAX: 303-295-2638
MA Systems, Inc., P.O. Box 894, Pryor, OK 74362-0894 / 918-824-3705; FAX: 918-824-3710
Mac-1 Airgun Distributors, 13974 Van Ness Ave., Gardena, CA 90249-2900 / 310-327-3581; FAX: 310-327-0238 mac1@mac1airgun.com www.mac1airgun.com
Machinist's Workshop-Village Press, P.O. Box 1810, Traverse City, MI 49685 / 800-447-7367; FAX: 616-946-3289
Madis Books, 2453 West Five Mile Pkwy., Dallas, TX 75233 / 214-330-7168
Madis, George. See: WINCHESTER CONSULTANTS
MAG Instrument, Inc., 1635 S. Sacramento Ave., Ontario, CA 91761 / 909-947-1006; FAX: 909-947-3116
Magma Engineering Co., P.O. Box 161, 20955 E. Ocotillo Rd., Queen Creek, AZ 85242 / 602-987-9008; FAX: 602-987-0148
Mag-Na-Port International, Inc., 41302 Executive Dr., Harrison Twp., MI 48045-1306 / 586-469-6727; FAX: 586-469-0425 email@magnaport.com www.magnaport.com
Magnum Power Products, Inc., P.O. Box 17768, Fountain Hills, AZ 85268
Magnum Research, Inc., 7110 University Ave. NE, Minneapolis, MN 55432 / 800-772-6168 or 763-574-1868; FAX: 763-574-0109 info@magnumresearch.com
Magnus Bullets, P.O. Box 239, Toney, AL 35773 / 256-420-8359; FAX: 256-420-8360 bulletman@mchsi.com www.magnusbullets.com
Mag-Pack Corp., P.O. Box 846, Chesterland, OH 44026 / 440-285-9480 magpack@aol.com
MagSafe Ammo, Inc., 4700 S. US Highway 17/92, Casselberry, FL 32707-3814 / 407-834-9966; FAX: 407-834-8185 www.magsafeammo.com
Magtech Ammunition Co. Inc., 6845 20th Ave. S., Ste. 120, Centerville, MN 55038 / 651-762-8500; FAX: 651-429-9485 www.magtechammunition.com
Mahovsky's Metalife, R.D. 1, Box 149a Eureka Road, Grand Valley, PA 16420 / 814-436-7747
Makinson, Nicholas, RR 3, Komoka, ON N0L 1R0 CANADA / 519-471-5462
Mallardtone Game Calls, 10406 96th St., Court West, Taylor Ridge, IL 61284 / 309-798-2481; FAX: 309-798-2501
Marble Arms (See CRR, Inc./Marble's Inc.)
Marchmont Bullets, 6502 Riverdale Rd., Whitmore Lake, MI 48189
Marent, Rudolf. See: HAMMERLI SERVICE-PRECISION MAC
Mark Lee Supplies, 9901 France Ct., Lakeville, MN 55044 / 952-461-2114; FAX: 952-461-2194 marklee55044@usfamily.net
Markell, Inc., 422 Larkfield Center 235, Santa Rosa, CA 95403 / 707-573-0792; FAX: 707-573-9867
Markesbery Muzzle Loaders, Inc., 7065 Production Ct., Florence, KY 41042 / 859-342-5553; FAX: 859-342-2380 www.markesbery.com
Marksman Products, 5482 Argosy Dr., Huntington Beach, CA 92649 / 714-898-7535 or 800-822-8005; FAX: 714-891-0782
Marlin Firearms Co., 100 Kenna Dr., North Haven, CT 06473 / 203-239-5621; FAX: 203-234-7991 www.marlinfirearms.com
Marocchi F.lli S.p.A, Via Galileo Galilei 8, I-25068 Zanano, ITALY
Marsh, Mike, Croft Cottage, Main St., Derbyshire, DE4 2BY ENGLAND / 01629 650 669
Marshall Enterprises, 792 Canyon Rd., Redwood City, CA 94062
Marshall Fish Mfg. Gunsmith Sptg. Co., 87 Champlain Ave., Westport, NY 12993 / 518-962-4897; FAX: 518-962-4897
Martin B. Retting Inc., 11029 Washington, Culver City, CA 90232 / 213-837-2412 retting@retting.com
Martini & Hagn, Ltd., 1264 Jimsmith Lake Rd., Cranbrook, BC V1C 6V6 CANADA / 250-417-2926; FAX: 250-417-2928 martini-hagn@shaw.ca www.martiniandhagngunmakers.com
Martin's Gun Shop, 937 S. Sheridan Blvd., Lakewood, CO 80226 / 303-922-2184
Martz, John V., 8060 Lakeview Lane, Lincoln, CA 95648 FAX: 916-645-3815

Marvel, Alan, 3922 Madonna Rd., Jarretsville, MD 21084 / 301-557-6545

Marx, Harry (See U.S. Importer for FERLIB)

Maryland Paintball Supply, 8507 Harford Rd., Parkville, MD 21234 / 410-882-5607

Master Lock Co., 2600 N. 32nd St., Milwaukee, WI 53245 / 414-444-2800

Match Prep-Doyle Gracey, P.O. Box 155, Tehachapi, CA 93581 / 661-822-5383; FAX: 661-823-8680 gracenotes@csurpers.net www.matchprep.com

Mathews Gun Shop & Gunsmithing, Inc., 2791 S. Gaffey St., San Pedro, CA 90731-6515 / 562-928-2129; FAX: 562-928-8629

Matthews Cutlery, 4401 Sentry Dr. #B, Tucker, GA 30084 / 770-939-6915

Mauser Werke Oberndorf Waffensysteme GmbH, Postfach 1349, 78722, Oberndorf/N., GERMANY

Maverick Arms, Inc., 7 Grasso Ave., P.O. Box 497, North Haven, CT 06473 / 203-230-5300; FAX: 203-230-5420

Maxi-Mount Inc., P.O. Box 291, Willoughby Hills, OH 44096-0291 / 440-944-9456; FAX: 440-944-9456 maximount454@yahoo.com

Mayville Engineering Co. (See MEC, Inc.)

Mazur Restoration, Pete, 13083 Drummer Way, Grass Valley, CA 95949 / 530-268-2412

McCament, Jay. See: JAY MCCAMENT CUSTOM GUNMAKER

McCann, Tom, 14 Walton Dr., New Hope, PA 18938 / 215-862-2728

McCann Industries, P.O. Box 641, Spanaway, WA 98387 / 253-537-6919; FAX: 253-537-6919 mccann.machine@worldnet.att.net www.mccannindustries.com

McCluskey Precision Rifles, 10502 14th Ave. NW, Seattle, WA 98177 / 206-781-2776

McCombs, Leo, 1862 White Cemetery Rd., Patriot, OH 45658 / 740-256-1714

McDonald, Dennis, 8359 Brady St., Peosta, IA 52068 / 319-556-7940

McFarland, Stan, 2221 Idella Ct., Grand Junction, CO 81505 / 970-243-4704

McGhee, Larry. See: B.C. OUTDOORS

McGowen Rifle Barrels, 5961 Spruce Lane, St. Anne, IL 60964 / 815-937-9816; FAX: 815-937-4024

Mchalik, Gary. See: ROSSI FIREARMS

McKenzie, Lynton, 6940 N. Alvernon Way, Tucson, AZ 85718 / 520-299-5090

McMillan Fiberglass Stocks, Inc., 1638 W. Knudsen Dr. #102, Phoenix, AZ 85027 / 623-582-9635; FAX: 623-581-3825 mfsinc@mcmfamily.com www.mcmfamily.com

McMillan Optical Gunsight Co., 28638 N. 42nd St., Cave Creek, AZ 85331 / 602-585-7868; FAX: 602-585-7872

McMillan Rifle Barrels, P.O. Box 3427, Bryan, TX 77805 / 409-690-3456; FAX: 409-690-0156

McMurdo, Lynn, P.O. Box 404, Afton, WY 83110 / 307-886-5535

MCS, Inc., 166 Pocono Rd., Brookfield, CT 06804-2023 / 203-775-1013; FAX: 203-775-9462

McWelco Products, 6730 Santa Fe Ave., Hesperia, CA 92345 / 619-244-8876; FAX: 619-244-9398 products@mcwelco.com www.mcwelco.com

MDS, P.O. Box 1441, Brandon, FL 33509-1441 / 813-653-1180; FAX: 813-684-5953

Meacham Tool & Hardware Co., Inc., 37052 Eberhardt Rd., Peck, ID 83545 / 208-486-7171 smeacham@clearwater.net www.meachamrifles.com

Measures, Leon. See: SHOOT WHERE YOU LOOK

MEC, Inc., 715 South St., Mayville, WI 53050 reloaders@mayvl.com www.mecreloaders.com

MEC-Gar S.R.L., Via Madonnina 64, Gardone V.T. Brescia, ITALY / 39-030-3733668; FAX: 39-030-3733687 info@mec-gar.it www.mec-gar.it

MEC-Gar U.S.A., Inc., Hurley Farms Industr. Park, 115, Hurley Road 6G, Oxford, CT 06478 / 203-262-1525; FAX: 203-262-1719 mecgar@aol.com www.mec-gar.com

Mech-Tech Systems, Inc., 1602 Foothill Rd., Kalispell, MT 59901 / 406-755-8055

Meister Bullets (See Gander Mountain)

Mele, Frank, 201 S. Wellow Ave., Cookeville, TN 38501 / 615-526-4860

Menck, Gunsmith Inc., T.W., 5703 S 77th St., Ralston, NE 68127

Mendez, John A., 1309 Continental Dr., Daytona Beach, FL 32117-3807 / 407-344-2791

Men-Metallwerk Elisenhuette GmbH, P.O. Box 1263, Nassau/Lahn, D-56372 GERMANY / 2604-7819

Meopta USA, LLC, 50 Davids Dr., Hauppauge, NY 11788 / 631-436-5900 ussales@meopta.com www.meopta.com

Meprolight (See Hesco-Meprolight)

Mercer Custom Guns, 216 S. Whitewater Ave., Jefferson, WI 53549 / 920-674-3839

Merit Corp., P.O. Box 9044, Schenectady, NY 12309 / 518-346-1420 sales@meritcorporation.com www.meritcorporation.com

Merkel, Schutzenstrasse 26, D-98527 Suhl, Suhl, GERMANY FAX: 011-49-3681-854-203 www.merkel-waffen.de

Metal Merchants, P.O. Box 186, Walled Lake, MI 48390-0186

Metalife Industries (See Mahovsky's Metalife)

Michael's Antiques, Box 591, Waldoboro, ME 04572

Michaels of Oregon Co., 9200 Cody St., Overland Park, KS 66214 / 800-845-2444 www.michaels-oregon.com

Micro Sight Co., 502 May St., Arroyo Grande, CA 93420-2832

Microfusion Alfa S.A., Paseo San Andres N8, P.O. Box 271, Eibar 20600, 20600 SPAIN / 34-43-11-89-16; FAX: 34-43-11-40-38

Mid-America Recreation, Inc., 1328 5th Ave., Moline, IL 61265 / 309-764-5089; FAX: 309-764-5089 fmilcusguns@aol.com www.midamericarecreation.com

Middlebrooks Custom Shop, 7366 Colonial Trail East, Surry, VA 23883 / 757-357-0881; FAX: 757-365-0442

Midway Arms, Inc., 5875 W. Van Horn Tavern Rd., Columbia, MO 65203 / 800-243-3220; FAX: 800-992-8312 www.midwayusa.com

Midwest Gun Sport, 1108 Herbert Dr., Zebulon, NC 27597 / 919-269-5570

Midwest Shooting School, The, Pat LaBoone, 2550 Hwy. 23, Wrenshall, MN 55797 / 218-384-3670 shootingschool@starband.net

Midwest Sport Distributors, Box 129, Fayette, MO 65248

Mike Davis Products, 643 Loop Dr., Moses Lake, WA 98837 / 509-765-6178; or 509-766-7281

Mike Yee Custom Stocking, 29927 56 Pl. S., Auburn, WA 98001 / 253-839-3991 miknadyee@comcast.net

Military Armament Corp., P.O. Box 120, Mt. Zion Rd., Lingleville, TX 76461 / 817-965-3253

Millennium Designed Muzzleloaders, P.O. Box 536, Routes 11 & 25, Limington, ME 04049 / 207-637-2316

Miller Arms, Inc., 1310 Industry Rd., Sturgis, SD 57785-9129 / 605-642-5160; FAX: 605-642-5160

Miller Custom, 210 E. Julia, Clinton, IL 61727 / 217-935-9362

Miller Single Trigger Mfg. Co., 6680 Rt. 5-20, P.O. Box 471, Bloomfield, NY 14469 / 585-657-6338

Millett Sights, 7275 Murdy Circle, Adm. Office, Huntington Beach, CA 92647 / 714-842-5575 or 800-645-5388; FAX: 714-843-5707

Mills Jr., Hugh B., 3615 Canterbury Rd., New Bern, NC 28560 / 919-637-4631

Milstor Corp., 80-975 Indio Blvd. C-7, Indio, CA 92201 / 760-775-9998; FAX: 760-775-5229 milstor@webtv.net

Minute Man High Tech Industries, 10611 Canyon Rd. E., Suite 151, Puyallup, WA 98373 / 800-233-2734

Mirador Optical Corp., P.O. Box 11614, Marina Del Rey, CA 90295-7614 / 310-821-5587; FAX: 310-305-0386

Mitchell, Jack, c/o Geoff Gaebe, Addieville East Farm, 200 Pheasant Dr., Mapleville, RI 02839 / 401-568-3185

Mitchell Mfg. Corp., P.O. Box 9295, Fountain Valley, CA 92728 / 714-444-2220

Mitchell Optics, Inc., 2072 CR 1100 N, Sidney, IL 61877 / 217-688-2219 or 217-621-3018; FAX: 217-688-2505 mitchell@attglobal.net

Mitchell's Accuracy Shop, 68 Greenridge Dr., Stafford, VA 22554 / 703-659-0165

Mitchell's Mauser, P.O. Box 9295, Fountain Valley, CA 92728 / 714-979-7663; FAX: 714-899-3660

MI-TE Bullets, 1396 Ave. K, Ellsworth, KS 67439 / 785-472-4575; FAX: 785-472-5579

Mixson Corp., 7635 W. 28th Ave., Hialeah, FL 33016 / 305-821-5190 or 800-327-0078; FAX: 305-558-9318

MJK Gunsmithing, Inc., 417 N. Huber Ct., E. Wenatchee, WA 98802 / 509-884-7683

MKS Supply, Inc. (See Hi-Point Firearms)

MMC, 4430 Mitchell St., North Las Vegas, NV 89081 / 800-998-7483; FAX: 702-267-9463 info@mmcsight.com www.mmcsight.com

MOA Corporation, 285 Government Valley Rd., Sundance, WY 82729 / 307-283-3030 www.moaguns.com

Mobile Area Networks, Inc., 2772 Depot St., Sanford, FL 32773 / 407-333-2350; FAX: 407-333-9903 georgew@mobilan.com www.mobilan.com

Modern Gun Repair School, P.O. Box 846, Saint Albans, VT 05478 / 802-524-2223; FAX: 802-524-2053 jfwp@dlilearn.com www.mgsinfoadlifearn.com

Modern Muzzleloading, Inc., P.O. Box 130, Centerville, IA 52544 / 515-856-2626

Moeller, Steve, 1213 4th St., Fulton, IL 61252 / 815-589-2300

Mogul Co./Life Jacket, 500 N. Kimball Rd., Ste. 109, South Lake, TX 76092

Monell Custom Guns, 228 Red Mills Rd., Pine Bush, NY 12566 / 914-744-3021

Moneymaker Guncraft Corp., 1420 Military Ave., Omaha, NE 68131 / 402-556-0226

Montana Armory, Inc., 100 Centennial Dr., P.O. Box 885, Big Timber, MT 59011 / 406-932-4353; FAX: 406-932-4443

Montana Outfitters, Lewis E. Yearout, 308 Riverview Dr. E., Great Falls, MT 59404 / 406-761-0859; or 406-727-4560

Montana Precision Swaging, P.O. Box 4746, Butte, MT 59702 / 406-494-0600; FAX: 406-494-0600

Montana Rifleman, Inc., 2593A Hwy. 2 East, Kalispell, MT 59901 / 406-755-4867

Montana Vintage Arms, 2354 Bear Canyon Rd., Bozeman, MT 59715

Morini (See U.S. Importers-Mandall Shooting Supplies, Inc.)

Morrison Custom Rifles, J. W., 4015 W Sharon, Phoenix, AZ 85029 / 602-978-3754

Morrison Precision, 6719 Calle Mango, Hereford, AZ 85615 / 520-378-6207 morprec@c2i2.com

Morrow, Bud, 11 Hillside Lane, Sheridan, WY 82801-9729 / 307-674-8360

Morton Booth Co., P.O. Box 123, Joplin, MO 64802 / 417-673-1962; FAX: 417-673-3642

Mo's Competitor Supplies (See MCS, Inc.)

Moss Double Tone, Inc., P.O. Box 1112, 2101 S. Kentucky, Sedalia, MO 65301 / 816-827-0827

Mountain Plains Industries, 3720 Otter Place, Lynchburg, VA 24503 / 800-687-3000; FAX: 434-386-6217 MPI_targets@adelphia.net

Mowrey Gun Works, P.O. Box 246, Waldron, IN 46182 / 317-525-6181; FAX: 317-525-9595

Mowrey's Guns & Gunsmithing, 119 Fredericks St., Canajoharie, NY 13317 / 518-673-3483

MPC, P.O. Box 450, McMinnville, TN 37110-0450 / 615-473-5513; FAX: 615-473-5516 thebox@blomand.net www.mpc-thebox.com

MPI Stocks, P.O. Box 83266, Portland, OR 97283 / 503-226-1215; FAX: 503-226-2661

MSR Targets, P.O. Box 1042, West Covina, CA 91793 / 818-331-7840

MTM Molded Products Co., Inc., 3370 Obco Ct., Dayton, OH 45414 / 937-890-7461; FAX: 937-890-1747

Mulberry House Publishing, P.O. Box 2180, Apache Junction, AZ 85217 / 888-738-1567; FAX: 480-671-1015

Mulhern, Rick, Rt. 5, Box 152, Rayville, LA 71269 / 318-728-2688

Mullins Ammunition, Rt. 2 Box 304N, Clintwood, VA 24228 / 276-926-6772; FAX: 276-926-6092 mammo@extremeshockusa.com www.extremeshockusa.com

Mullis Guncraft, 3523 Lawyers Road E., Monroe, NC 28110 / 704-283-6683

Multiplex International, 26 S. Main St., Concord, NH 03301 FAX: 603-796-2223

Multipropulseurs, La Bertrandiere, 42580, FRANCE / 77 74 01 30; FAX: 77 93 19 34

Mundy, Thomas A., 69 Robbins Road, Somerville, NJ 08876 / 201-722-2199

Murmur Corp., 2823 N. Westmoreland Ave., Dallas, TX 75222 / 214-630-5400

Murphy, R.R. Murphy Co., Inc. See: MURPHY, R.R. CO., INC.

Murphy, R.R. Co., Inc., R.R. Murphy Co., Inc. Murphy, P.O. Box 102, Ripley, TN 38063 / 901-635-4003; FAX: 901-635-2320

Murray State College, 1 Murray Campus St., Tishomingo, OK 73460 / 508-371-2371 darnold@mscol.edu

Muscle Products Corp., 112 Fennell Dr., Butler, PA 16002 / 800-227-7049 or 724-283-0567; FAX: 724-283-8310 mpc@mpc_home.com www.mpc_home.com

MANUFACTURER'S DIRECTORY

Muzzleloaders Etcetera, Inc., 9901 Lyndale Ave. S., Bloomington, MN 55420 / 952-884-1161 www.muzzleloaders-etcetera.com
MWG Co., P.O. Box 971202, Miami, FL 33197 / 800-428-9394 or 305-253-8393; FAX: 305-232-1247

N

N.B.B., Inc., 24 Elliot Rd., Sterling, MA 01564 / 508-422-7538 or 800-942-9444
N.C. Ordnance Co., P.O. Box 3254, Wilson, NC 27895 / 919-237-2440; FAX: 919-243-9845 bharvey@nc.rr.com www.gungrip.com
Nagel's Custom Bullets, 100 Scott St., Baytown, TX 77520-2849
Nalpak, 1267 Vernon Way, El Cajon, CA 92020
Nammo Lapua Oy, P.O. Box 5, Lapua, FINLAND / 358-6-4310111; FAX: 358-6-4310317 info@nammo.ti www.lapua.com
Nastoff, Steve. See: NASTOFFS 45 SHOP, INC.
Nastoffs 45 Shop, Inc., Steve Nastoff, 1057 Laverne Dr., Youngstown, OH 44511
National Bullet Co., 1585 E. 361 St., Eastlake, OH 44095 / 216-951-1854; FAX: 216-951-7761
National Target Co., 3958-D Dartmouth Ct., Frederick, MD 21703 / 800-827-7060; FAX: 301-874-4764
Nationwide Airgun Repair, 2310 Windsor Forest Dr., Louisville, KY 40272 / 502-937-2614; FAX: 812-637-1463 shortshoestring@insightbb.com
Naval Ordnance Works, 467 Knott Rd., Sheperdstown, WV 25443 / 304-876-0998; FAX: 304-876-0998 nvordfdy@earthlink.net
Navy Arms Company, 219 Lawn St., Martinsburg, WV 25401 / 304-262-9870; FAX: 304-262-1658 info@navyarms.com www.navyarms.com
NCP Products, Inc., 3500 12th St. N.W., Canton, OH 44708 / 330-456-5130; FAX: 330-456-5234
Necessary Concepts, Inc., P.O. Box 571, Deer Park, NY 11729 / 516-667-8509; FAX: 516-667-8588
NEI Handtools, Inc., 10960 Gary Player Dr., El Paso, TX 79935
Neil A. Jones Custom Products, 17217 Brookhouser Road, Saegertown, PA 16433 / 814-763-2769; FAX: 814-763-4228
Nelson, Gary K., 975 Terrace Dr., Oakdale, CA 95361 / 209-847-4590
Nelson, Stephen. See: NELSON'S CUSTOM GUNS, INC.
Nelson's Custom Guns, Inc., Stephen Nelson, 7430 Valley View Dr. N.W., Corvallis, OR 97330 / 541-745-5232 nelsons-custom@attbi.com
Nesci Enterprises Inc., P.O. Box 119, Summit St., East Hampton, CT 06424 / 203-267-2588
Nesika Bay Precision, 22239 Big Valley Rd., Poulsbo, WA 98370 / 206-697-3830
Nettestad Gun Works, 38962 160th Avenue, Pelican Rapids, MN 56572 / 218-863-1338
Neumann GmbH, Am Galgenberg 6, 90575, GERMANY / 09101/8258; FAX: 09101/6356
New England Ammunition Co., 1771 Post Rd. East, Suite 223, Westport, CT 06880 / 203-254-8048
New England Arms Co., Box 278, Lawrence Lane, Kittery Point, ME 03905 / 207-439-0593; FAX: 207-439-0525 info@newenglandarms.com www.newenglandarms.com
New England Custom Gun Service, 438 Willow Brook Rd., Plainfield, NH 03781 / 603-469-3450; FAX: 603-469-3471 bestguns@adelphia.net www.newenglandcustom.com
New Orleans Jewelers Supply Co., 206 Charters St., New Orleans, LA 70130 / 504-523-3839; FAX: 504-523-3836
New SKB Arms Co., C.P.O. Box 1401, Tokyo, JAPAN / 81-3-3943-9550; FAX: 81-3-3943-0695
New Ultra Light Arms, LLC, P.O. Box 340, Granville, WV 26534
Newark Electronics, 4801 N. Ravenswood Ave., Chicago, IL 60640
Newell, Robert H., 55 Coyote, Los Alamos, NM 87544 / 505-662-7135
Newman Gunshop, 2035 Chester Ave. #411, Ottumwa, IA 52501-3715 / 515-937-5775
NgraveR Co., The, 67 Wawecus Hill Rd., Bozrah, CT 06334 / 860-823-1533; FAX: 860-887-6252 ngraver98@aol.com www.ngraver.com
Nicholson Custom, 17285 Thornlay Road, Hughesville, MO 65334 / 816-826-8746

Nickels, Paul R., 2216 Jacob Dr., Santa Clara, UT 84765-5399 / 435-652-1959
Niemi Engineering, W. B., Box 126 Center Rd., Greensboro, VT 05841 / 802-533-7180; FAX: 802-533-7141
Nighthawk Custom, 1306 W. Trimble, Berryville, AR 72616 / 877-268-GUNS; (4867) or 870-423-GUNS; FAX: 870-423-4230 www.nighthawkcustom.com
Nikon, Inc., 1300 Walt Whitman Rd., Melville, NY 11747 / 516-547-8623; FAX: 516-547-0309
Noreen, Peter H., 5075 Buena Vista Dr., Belgrade, MT 59714 / 406-586-7383
Norica, Avnda Otaola, 16 Apartado 68, Eibar, SPAIN
Norinco, 7A Yun Tan N, Beijing, CHINA
Norincoptics (See BEC, Inc.)
Norma Precision AB (See U.S. Importers-Dynamit)
Normark Corp., 10395 Yellow Circle Dr., Minnetonka, MN 55343-9101 / 612-933-7060; FAX: 612-933-0046
North American Arms, Inc., 2150 South 950 East, Provo, UT 84606-6285 / 800-821-5783 or 801-374-9990; FAX: 801-374-9998
North American Correspondence Schools, The Gun Pro, Oak & Pawney St., Scranton, PA 18515 / 717-342-7701
North American Shooting Systems, P.O. Box 306, Osoyoos, BC V0H 1V0 CANADA / 250-495-3131; FAX: 250-495-3131 rifle@cablerocket.com
North Devon Firearms Services, 3 North St., Braunton, EX33 1AJ ENGLAND / 01271 813624; FAX: 01271 813624
North Mountain Pine Training Center (See Executive Protection Institute)
North Star West, 20242 Smokey Rd., Frenchtown, MT 59834 / 406-626-4081 northstarwest.com
Northern Precision, 329 S. James St., Carthage, NY 13619 / 315-493-1711
Northside Gun Shop, 2725 NW 109th, Oklahoma City, OK 73120 / 405-840-2353
Northwest Custom Projectile, P.O. Box 127, Butte, MT 59703-0127 www.customprojectile.com
No-Sho Mfg. Co., 10727 Glenfield Ct., Houston, TX 77096 / 713-723-5332
Nosler, Inc., P.O. Box 671, Bend, OR 97709 / 800-285-3701 or 541-382-3921; FAX: 541-388-4667 www.nosler.com
Novak's, Inc., 1206 1/2 30th St., P.O. Box 4045, Parkersburg, WV 26101 / 304-485-9295; FAX: 304-428-6722 www.novaksights.com
Nowlin Mfg. Co., 20622 S 4092 Rd., Claremore, OK 74017 / 918-342-0689; FAX: 918-342-0624 nowlinguns@msn.com nowlinguns.com
NRI Gunsmith School, P.O. Box 182968, Columbus, OH 43218-2968
Nu Line Guns, 8150 CR 4055, Rhineland, MO 65069 / 573-676-5500; FAX: 314-447-5018 nlg@ktis.net
Null Holsters Ltd. K.L., 161 School St. N.W., Resaca, GA 30735 / 706-625-5643; FAX: 706-625-9392 ken@klnullholsters.com www.klnullholsters.com
Numrich Gun Parts Corporation, 226 Williams Lane, P.O. Box 299, West Hurley, NY 12491 / 866-686-7424; FAX: 877-GUNPART info@gunpartscorp.com www.@e-gunparts.com

O

O.F. Mossberg & Sons, Inc., 7 Grasso Ave., North Haven, CT 06473 / 203-230-5300; FAX: 203-230-5420
Oakman Turkey Calls, RD 1, Box 825, Harrisonville, PA 17228 / 717-485-4620
Obermeyer Rifled Barrels, 23122 60th St., Bristol, WI 53104 / 262-843-3537; FAX: 262-843-2129 www.obermeyerbarrels.com
October Country Muzzleloading, P.O. Box 969, Dept. GD, Hayden, ID 83835 / 208-772-2068; FAX: 208-772-9230 ocinfo@octobercountry.com www.octobercountry.com
Oehler Research, Inc., P.O. Box 9135, Austin, TX 78766 / 512-327-6900 or 800-531-5125; FAX: 512-327-6903 www.oehler-research.com
Oil Rod and Gun Shop, 69 Oak St., East Douglas, MA 01516 / 508-476-3687
OK Weber, Inc., P.O. Box 7485, Eugene, OR 97401 / 541-747-0458; FAX: 541-747-5927 okweber@pacinfo www.okweber.com
Oker's Engraving, P.O. Box 126, Shawnee, CO 80475 / 303-838-6042 engraver@netscape.com
Oklahoma Ammunition Co., 3701A S. Harvard Ave., No. 367, Tulsa, OK 74135-2265 / 918-396-3187; FAX: 918-396-4270
Oklahoma Leather Products, Inc., 500 26th NW, Miami, OK 74354 / 918-542-6651; FAX: 918-542-6653

Olathe Gun Shop, 716-A South Rogers Road, Olathe, KS 66062 / 913-782-6900; FAX: 913-782-6902 info@olathegunshop.com www.olathegunshop.com
Old Wagon Bullets, 32 Old Wagon Rd., Wilton, CT 06897
Old West Bullet Moulds, J. Ken Chapman, P.O. Box 519, Flora Vista, NM 87415 / 505-334-6970
Old West Reproductions, Inc. R.M. Bachman, 446 Florence S. Loop, Florence, MT 59833 / 406-273-2615; FAX: 406-273-2615 rick@oldwestreproductions.com www.oldwestreproductions.com
Old Western Scrounger LLC, 219 Lawn St., Martinsburg, NV 25401 / 304-262-9870; FAX: 304-262-1658 www.ows-ammo.com
Ole Frontier Gunsmith Shop, 2617 Hwy. 29 S., Cantonment, FL 32533 / 904-477-8074
Olson, Myron, 989 W. Kemp, Watertown, SD 57201 / 605-886-9787
Olson, Vic, 5002 Countryside Dr., Imperial, MO 63052 / 314-296-8086
Olympic Arms Inc., 620-626 Old Pacific Hwy. SE, Olympia, WA 98513 / 360-456-3471; FAX: 360-491-3447 info@olyarms.com www.olyarms.com
Olympic Optical Co., P.O. Box 752377, Memphis, TN 38175-2377 / 901-794-3890 or 800-238-7120; FAX: 901-794-0676
One Of A Kind, 15610 Purple Sage, San Antonio, TX 78255 / 512-695-3364
One Ragged Hole, P.O. Box 13624, Tallahassee, FL 32317-3624
Op-Tec, P.O. Box L632, Langhorn, PA 19047 / 215-757-5037; FAX: 215-757-7097
Optical Services Co., P.O. Box 1174, Santa Teresa, NM 88008-1174 / 505-589-3833
Orchard Park Enterprise, P.O. Box 563, Orchard Park, NY 14127 / 616-656-0356
Ordnance Works, The, 2969 Pigeon Point Rd., Eureka, CA 95501 / 707-443-3252
Oregon Arms, Inc. (See Rogue Rifle Co., Inc.)
Oregon Trail Bullet Company, P.O. Box 529, Dept. P, Baker City, OR 97814 / 800-811-0548; FAX: 514-523-1803
Original Deer Formula Co., The, P.O. Box 1705, Dickson, TN 37056 / 800-874-6965; FAX: 615-446-0646 deerformula1@aol.com www.deerformula.com
Orion Rifle Barrel Co., RR2, 137 Cobler Village, Kalispell, MT 59901 / 406-257-5649
Orvis Co., The, Rt. 7, Manchester, VT 05254 / 802-362-3622; FAX: 802-362-3525
Otis Technology, Inc., RR 1 Box 84, Boonville, NY 13309 / 315-942-3320
Ottmar, Maurice, Box 657, 113 E. Fir, Coulee City, WA 99115 / 509-632-5717
Outa-Site Gun Carriers, 219 Market St., Laredo, TX 78040 / 210-722-4678 or 800-880-9715; FAX: 210-726-4858
Outdoor Connection, Inc., The, 7901 Panther Way, Waco, TX 76712-6556 / 800-533-6076; FAX: 254-776-3553 info@outdoorconnection.com www.outdoorconnection.com
Outdoor Edge Cutlery Corp., 4699 Nautilus Ct. S. Ste. 503, Boulder, CO 80301-5310 / 303-530-7667; FAX: 303-530-7020 www.outdooredge.com
Outdoor Enthusiast, 3784 W. Woodland, Springfield, MO 65807 / 417-883-9841
Outdoor Sports Headquarters, Inc., 967 Watertower Ln., West Carrollton, OH 45449 / 513-865-5855; FAX: 513-865-5962
Outers Laboratories Div. of ATK, Route 2, P.O. Box 39, Onalaska, WI 54650 / 608-781-5800; FAX: 608-781-0368
Ox-Yoke Originals, Inc., 34 Main St., Milo, ME 04463 / 800-231-8313 or 207-943-7351; FAX: 207-943-2416
Ozark Gun Works, 11830 Cemetery Rd., Rogers, AR 72756 / 479-631-1024; FAX: 479-631-1024 ozarkgunworks@cox.net www.geocities.com

P

P&M Sales & Services, LLC, 4697 Tote Rd. Bldg. H-B, Comins, MI 48619 / 989-848-8364; FAX: 989-848-8364 info@pmsales-online.com
P.S.M.G. Gun Co., 10 Park Ave., Arlington, MA 02174 / 781-646-1699; FAX: 781-643-7212 psmg2@aol.com
Pachmayr Div. Lyman Products, 475 Smith St., Middletown, CT 06457 / 860-632-2020 or 800-225-9626; FAX: 860-632-1699 lymansales@cshore.com www.pachmayr.com

MANUFACTURER'S DIRECTORY

Pacific Armament Corp, 4813 Enterprise Way, Unit K, Modesto, CA 95356 / 209-545-2800 gunsparts@att.net
Pacific Rifle Co., P.O. Box 841, Carlton, OR 97111 / 503-852-6276 pacificrifle@aol.com
PAC-NOR Barreling, 99299 Overlook Rd., P.O. Box 6188, Brookings, OR 97415 / 503-469-7330; FAX: 503-469-7331 info@pac-nor.com www.pac-nor.com
PACT, Inc., P.O. Box 535025, Grand Prairie, TX 75053 / 972-641-0049; FAX: 972-641-2641
Page Custom Bullets, P.O. Box 25, Port Moresby, NEW GUINEA
Pagel Gun Works, Inc., 2 SE 1st St., Grand Rapids, MN 55744
Pager Pal, P.O. Box 54864, Hurst, TX 76054-4864 / 800-561-1603; FAX: 817-285-8769 info@pagerpal.com www.pagerpal.com
Paintball Games International Magazine Aceville, Castle House 97 High St., Essex, ENGLAND / 011-44-206-564840
Palsa Outdoor Products, P.O. Box 81336, Lincoln, NE 68501 / 402-488-5288; FAX: 402-488-2321
Pansch, Robert F, 1004 Main St. #10, Neenah, WI 54956 / 920-725-8175
Paragon Sales & Services, Inc., 2501 Theodore St., Crest Hill, IL 60435-1613 / 815-725-9212; FAX: 815-725-8974
Para-Ordnance Mfg., Inc., 980 Tapscott Rd., Scarborough, ON M1X 1E7 CANADA / 416-297-7855; FAX: 416-297-1289
Para-Ordnance, Inc., 1919 NE 45th St., Ste 215, Ft. Lauderdale, FL 33308 / 416-297-7855; FAX: 416-297-1289 info@paraord.com www.paraord.com
Pardini Armi Srl, Via Italica 154, 55043, Lido Di Camaiore Lu, ITALY / 584-90121; FAX: 584-90122
Paris, Frank J., 17417 Pershing St., Livonia, MI 48152-3822
Park Rifle Co., Ltd., The, Unit 6a Dartford Trade Park, Power Mill Lane, Dartford DA7 7NX, ENGLAND / 011-0322-222512
Parker & Sons Shooting Supply, 9337 Smoky Row Road, Strawberry Plains, TN 37871 / 865-933-3286; FAX: 865-932-8586
Parker Gun Finishes, 9337 Smokey Row Rd., Strawberry Plains, TN 37871 / 865-933-3286; FAX: 865-932-8586 parcraft7838@netzero.com
Parsons Optical Mfg. Co., PO Box 192, Ross, OH 45061 / 513-867-0820; FAX: 513-867-8380 psscopes@concentric.net
Partridge Sales Ltd., John, Trent Meadows, Rugeley, ENGLAND
Pasadena Gun Center, 206 E. Shaw, Pasadena, TX 77506 / 713-472-0417; FAX: 713-472-1322
Passive Bullet Traps, Inc. (See Savage Range Systems, Inc.)
Paterson Gunsmithing, 438 Main St., Paterson, NJ 07502 / 201-345-4100
Pathfinder Sports Leather, 2920 E. Chambers St., Phoenix, AZ 85040 / 602-276-0016
Patrick W. Price Bullets, 16520 Worthley Drive, San Lorenzo, CA 94580 / 510-278-1547
Pattern Control, 114 N. Third St., P.O. Box 462105, Garland, TX 75046 / 214-494-3551; FAX: 214-272-8447
Paul A. Harris Hand Engraving, 113 Rusty Lane, Boerne, TX 78006-5746 / 512-391-5121
Paul and Sharon Dressel, 209 N. 92nd Ave., Yakima, WA 98908 / 509-966-9233; FAX: 509-966-3365 dressels@nwinfo.net www.dressels.com
Paul Co., The, 27385 Pressonville Rd., Wellsville, KS 66092 / 785-883-4444; FAX: 785-883-2525
Paul D. Hillmer Custom Gunstocks, 7251 Hudson Heights, Hudson, IA 50643 / 319-988-3941
Paul Jones Moulds, 4901 Telegraph Rd., Los Angeles, CA 90022 / 213-262-1510
Paulsen Gunstocks, Rt. 71, Box 11, Chinook, MT 59523 / 406-357-3403
Pawling Mountain Club, Keith Lupton, P.O. Box 573, Pawling, NY 12564 / 914-855-3825
Paxton Quigley's Personal Protection Strategies, 9903 Santa Monica Blvd., 300, Beverly Hills, CA 90212 / 310-281-1762 www.defend-net.com/paxton
Payne Photography, Robert, Robert, P.O. Box 141471, Austin, TX 78714 / 512-272-4554
Peacemaker Specialists, 144 Via Fuchsia, Paso Robles, CA 93446 / 805-238-9100; FAX: 805-238-9100 www.peacemakerspecialists.com
Pearce Grip, Inc., P.O. Box 40367, Fort Worth, TX 76140 / 817-568-9704; FAX: 817-568-9707 info@pearcegrip.com www.pearcegrip.com

PECAR Herbert Schwarz GmbH, Kreuzbergstrasse 6, 10965, Berlin, GERMANY / 004930-785-7383; FAX: 004930-785-1934 michael.schwart@pecar-berlin.de www.pecar-berlin.de
Pecatonica River Longrifle, 5205 Nottingham Dr., Rockford, IL 61111 / 815-968-1995; FAX: 815-968-1996
Pedersen, C. R., 2717 S. Pere Marquette Hwy., Ludington, MI 49431 / 231-843-2061; FAX: 231-845-7695 fega@fega.com
Pedersen, Rex C., 2717 S. Pere Marquette Hwy., Ludington, MI 49431 / 231-843-2061; FAX: 231-845-7695 fega@fega.com
Peifer Rifle Co., P.O. Box 220, Nokomis, IL 62075
Pejsa Ballistics, 1314 Marquette Ave., Apt 906, Minneapolis, MN 55403 / 612-332-5073; FAX: 612-332-5204 pejsa@sprintmail.com pejsa.com
Peltor, Inc. (See Aero Peltor)
Pence Precision Barrels, 7567 E. 900 S., S. Whitley, IN 46787 / 219-839-4745
Pendleton Woolen Mills, P.O. Box 3030, 220 N.W. Broadway, Portland, OR 97208 / 503-226-4801
Penn Bullets, P.O. Box 756, Indianola, PA 15051
Pennsylvania Gun Parts Inc., RR 7 Box 150, Mount Pleasant, PA 15666
Pennsylvania Gunsmith School, 812 Ohio River Blvd., Avalon, Pittsburgh, PA 15202 / 412-766-1812; FAX: 412-766-0855 pgs@pagunsmith.com www.pagunsmith.com
Penrod, Mark. See: PENROD PRECISION
Penrod Precision, Mark Penrod, 312 College Ave., P.O. Box 307, N. Manchester, IN 46962 / 260-982-8385; FAX: 260-982-1819 markpenrod@kconline.com
Pentax U.S.A., Inc., 600 12th St. Ste. 300, Golden, CO 80401 / 303-799-8000; FAX: 303-460-1628 www.pentaxlightseeker.com
Pentheny de Pentheny, c/o H.P. Okelly, 321 S. Main St., Sebastopol, CA 95472 / 707-824-1637; FAX: 707-824-1637
Perazone-Gunsmith, Brian, Cold Spring Rd., Roxbury, NY 12474 / 607-326-4088; FAX: 607-326-3140 bpgunsmith@catskill.net www.bpgunsmith@catskill.net
Perazzi U.S.A. Inc., 1010 West Tenth, Azusa, CA 91702 / 626-334-1234; FAX: 626-334-0344 perazziusa@aol.com
Performance Specialists, 308 Eanes School Rd., Austin, TX 78746 / 512-327-0119
Perugini Visini & Co. S.r.l., Via Camprelle, 126, 25080 Nuvolera, ITALY / 30-6897535; FAX: 30-6897821 peruvisi@virgilia.it
Pete de Coux Auction House, 14940 Brenda Dr., Prescott, AZ 86305-7447 / 928-776-8285; FAX: 928-776-8276 pdbullets@commspeed.net
Pete Mazur Restoration, 13083 Drummer Way, Grass Valley, CA 95949 / 530-268-2412; FAX: 530-268-2412
Pete Rickard, Inc., 115 Roy Walsh Rd, Cobleskill, NY 12043 / 518-234-2731; FAX: 518-234-2454 rickard@telenet.net www.peterickard.com
Peter Dyson & Son Ltd., 3 Cuckoo Lane, Honley, Holmfirth, West Yorkshire, HD9 6AS ENGLAND / 44-1484-661062; FAX: 44-1484-663709 peter@peterdyson.co.uk www.peterdyson.co.uk
Peter Hale/Engraver, 997 Maple Dr., Spanish Fork, UT 84660-2524 / 801-798-8215
Peters Stahl GmbH, Stettiner Strasse 42, D-33106, Paderborn, GERMANY / 05251-750025; FAX: 05251-75611 info@peters-stahl.com www.peters-stahl.com
Peterson Gun Shop, Inc., A.W., 4255 W. Old U.S. 441, Mt. Dora, FL 32757-3299 / 352-383-4258; FAX: 352-735-1001
Petro-Explo Inc., 7650 U.S. Hwy. 287, Suite 100, Arlington, TX 76017 / 817-478-8888
Pettinger Books, Gerald, 47827 300th Ave., Russell, IA 50238 / 641-535-2239 gpettinger@lisco.com
Pflumm Mfg. Co., 10662 Widmer Rd., Lenexa, KS 66215 / 800-888-4867; FAX: 913-451-7857
PFRB Co., P.O. Box 1242, Bloomington, IL 61702 / 309-473-3964 or 800-914-5464; FAX: 309-473-2161
Phillippi Custom Bullets, Justin, P.O. Box 773, Ligonier, PA 15658 / 724-238-2962; FAX: 724-238-9671 jrp@wpa.net http://www.wpa.net~jrphil
Phoenix Arms, 4231 Brickell St., Ontario, CA 91761 / 909-937-6900; FAX: 909-937-0060
Piedmont Community College, P.O. Box 1197, Roxboro, NC 27573 / 336-599-1181; FAX: 336-597-3817 www.piedmont.cc.nc.us

Pietta (See U.S. Importers-Navy Arms Co, Taylor's
Pine Technical College, 1100 4th St., Pine City, MN 55063 / 800-521-7463; FAX: 612-629-6766
Pinetree Bullets, 133 Skeena St., Kitimat, BC V8C 1Z1 CANADA / 604-632-3768; FAX: 604-632-3768
Pioneer Arms Co., 355 Lawrence Rd., Broomall, PA 19008 / 215-356-5203
Piotti (See U.S. Importer-Moore & Co., Wm. Larkin)
Piquette, Paul. See: PIQUETTE'S CUSTOM ENGRAVING
Piquette's Custom Engraving, Paul R. Piquette, 511 Southwick St., Feeding Hills, MA 01030 / 413-789-4582 ppiquette@comcast.net www.pistoldynamics.com
PJL Industries/ProChemCo/PrOlixr, P.O. Box 1466, West Jordan, UT 84084-1466 / 801-569-2763 or 800-248-LUBE(5823); FAX: 801-569-8225 prolix@prolixlubricant.com www.prolixlubricant.com
Plaza Cutlery, Inc., 3333 Bristol, 161 South Coast Plaza, Costa Mesa, CA 92626 / 714-549-3932
Plum City Ballistic Range, N2162 80th St., Plum City, WI 54761 / 715-647-2539
PlumFire Press, Inc., 30-A Grove Ave., Patchogue, NY 11772-4112 / 800-695-7246; FAX: 516-758-4071
PMC/Eldorado Cartridge Corp., P.O. Box 62508, 12801 U.S. Hwy. 95 S., Boulder City, NV 89005 / 702-294-0025; FAX: 702-294-0121 kbauer@pmcammo.com www.pmcammo.com
Poburka, Philip (See Bison Studios)
Pointing Dog Journal, Village Press Publications, P.O. Box 968, Dept. PGD, Traverse City, MI 49685 / 800-272-3246; FAX: 616-946-3289
Police Bookshelf, P.O. Box 122, Concord, NH 03301 / 603-224-6814; FAX: 603-226-3554
Polywad, Inc., P.O. Box 7916, Macon, GA 31209 / 478-477-0669 or 800-998-0669 FAX: 478-477-0666 polywadmpb@aol.com www.polywad.com
Ponsness, Warren, 7634 W. Ohio St., Rathdrum, ID 83858 / 800-732-0706; FAX: 208-687-2233 www.reloaders.com
Pony Express Reloaders, 608 E. Co. Rd. D, Suite 3, St. Paul, MN 55117 / 612-483-9406; FAX: 612-483-9884
Pony Express Sport Shop, 23404 Lyons Ave., PMB 448, Newhall, CA 91321-2511 / 818-895-1231
Powder Horn Ltd., P.O. Box 565, Glenview, IL 60025 / 305-565-6060
Powell & Son (Gunmakers) Ltd., William, 35-37 Carrs Lane, Birmingham, B4 7SX ENGLAND / 121-643-0689; FAX: 121-631-3504 sales@william-powell.co.uk www.william-powell.co.uk
Powell Agency, William, 22 Circle Dr., Bellmore, NY 11710 / 516-679-1158
Power Custom, Inc., 29739 Hwy. J, Gravois Mills, MO 65037 / 573-372-5684; FAX: 573-372-5799 rwpowers@laurie.net www.powercustom.com
Power Plus Enterprises, Inc., P.O. Box 38, Warm Springs, GA 31830 / 706-655-2132
Powley Computer (See Hutton Rifle Ranch)
Practical Tools, Inc., 7067 Easton Rd., P.O. Box 133, Pipersville, PA 18947 / 215-766-7301; FAX: 215-766-8681
Prairie Gun Works, 1-761 Marion St., Winnipeg, MB R2J 0K6 CANADA / 204-231-2976; FAX: 204-231-8566
Pranger, Ed G., 1414 7th St., Anacortes, WA 98221 / 206-293-3488
Precision Airgun Sales, Inc., 5247 Warrensville Ctr. Rd., Maple Hts., OH 44137 / 216-587-5005; FAX: 216-587-5005
Precision Cast Bullets, 101 Mud Creek Lane, Ronan, MT 59864 / 406-676-5135
Precision Delta Corp., P.O. Box 128, Ruleville, MS 38771 / 662-756-2810; FAX: 662-756-2590
Precision Firearm Finishing, 25 N.W. 44th Avenue, Des Moines, IA 50313 / 515-288-8680; FAX: 515-244-3925
Precision Gun Works, 104 Sierra Rd., Dept. GD, Kerrville, TX 78028 / 830-367-4587
Precision Reloading, 124 S. Main St., Mitchell, SD 57301 / 605-996-9984
Precision Reloading, Inc., P.O. Box 122, Stafford Springs, CT 06076 / 860-684-7979; FAX: 860-684-6788 info@precisionreloading.com www.precisionreloading.com
Precision Shooting, Inc., 222 McKee St., Manchester, CT 06040 / 860-645-8776; FAX: 860-643-8215 www.precisionshooting.com
Precision Small Arms Inc., 9272 Jeronimo Rd., Ste. 121, Irvine, CA 92618 / 800-554-5515 or 949-768-3530; FAX: 949-768-4808 www.tcbebe.com

562 ⬧ *GUN DIGEST*®

MANUFACTURER'S DIRECTORY

Precision Specialties, 131 Hendom Dr., Feeding Hills, MA 01030 / 413-786-3365; FAX: 413-786-3365

Precision Sport Optics, 15571 Producer Lane, Unit G, Huntington Beach, CA 92649 / 714-891-1309; FAX: 714-892-6920

Premier Reticles, 920 Breckinridge Lane, Winchester, VA 22601-6707 / 540-722-0601; FAX: 540-722-3522

Prescott Projectile Co., 1808 Meadowbrook Road, Prescott, AZ 86303

Preslik's Gunstocks, 4245 Keith Ln., Chico, CA 95926 / 916-891-8236

Price Bullets, Patrick W., 16520 Worthley Dr., San Lorenzo, CA 94580 / 510-278-1547

Primedia Publishing Co., 6420 Wilshire Blvd., Los Angeles, CA 90048 / 213-782-2000; FAX: 213-782-2867

Primos Hunting Calls, 604 First St., Flora, MS 39071 / 601-879-9323; FAX: 601-879-9324 www.primos.com

PRL Bullets, c/o Blackburn Enterprises, 114 Stuart Rd., Ste. 110, Cleveland, TN 37312 / 423-559-0340

Pro Load Ammunition, Inc., 5180 E. Seltice Way, Post Falls, ID 83854 / 208-773-9444; FAX: 208-773-9441

Professional Gunsmiths of America, 1201 South 13 Hwy., Lexington, MO 64067 / 816-529-1337

Professional Hunter Supplies, P.O. Box 608, 468 Main St., Ferndale, CA 95536 / 707-786-9140; FAX: 707-786-9117 wmebride@humboldt.com

Pro-Mark Div. of Wells Lamont, 6640 W. Touhy, Chicago, IL 60648 / 312-647-8200

Proofmark Corp., P.O. Box 357, Burgess, VA 22432 / 804-453-4337; FAX: 804-453-4337 proofmark@direcway.com www.proofmarkbullets.com

Pro-Port Ltd., 41302 Executive Dr., Harrison Twp., MI 48045-1306 / 586-469-6727; FAX: 586-469-0425 e-mail@magnaport.com www.magnaport.com

Pro-Shot Products, Inc., P.O. Box 763, Taylorville, IL 62568 / 217-824-9133; FAX: 217-824-8861 www.proshotproducts.com

Protector Mfg. Co., Inc., The, 443 Ashwood Pl., Boca Raton, FL 33431 / 407-394-6011

Protektor Model, 1-11 Bridge St., Galeton, PA 16922 / 814-435-2442 mail@protektormodel.com www.protektormodel.com

Prototech Industries, Inc., 10532 E Road, Delia, KS 66418 / 785-771-3571 prototec@grapevine.net

ProWare, Inc., 15847 NE Hancock St., Portland, OR 97230 / 503-239-0159

PWL Gunleather, P.O. Box 450432, Atlanta, GA 31145 / 800-960-4072; FAX: 770-822-1704 covert@pwlusa.com www.pwlusa.com

PWM Sales Ltd., N.D.F.S., Gowdall Lane, Pollington DN14 0AU, ENGLAND / 01405862688; FAX: 01405862622 Paulwelburn9@aol.com

Pyramyd Stone Inter. Corp., 2447 Suffolk Lane, Pepper Pike, OH 44124-4540

Q

Quack Decoy & Sporting Clays, 4 Ann & Hope Way, P.O. Box 98, Cumberland, RI 02864 / 401-723-8202; FAX: 401-722-5910

Quaker Boy, Inc., 5455 Webster Rd., Orchard Parks, NY 14127 / 716-662-3979; FAX: 716-662-9426

Quality Arms, Inc., Box 19477, Dept. GD, Houston, TX 77224 / 281-870-8377 arrieta2@excite.com www.arrieta.com

Quality Cartridge, P.O. Box 445, Hollywood, MD 20636 / 301-373-3719 www.qual-cart.com

Quality Custom Firearms, Stephen Billeb, 22 Vista View Dr., Cody, WY 82414 / 307-587-4278; FAX: 307-587-4297 stevebilleb@wyoming.com

Quarton Beamshot, 4538 Centerview Dr., Ste. 149, San Antonio, TX 78228 / 800-520-8435; FAX: 210-735-1326 www.beamshot.com

Que Industries, Inc., P.O. Box 2471, Everett, WA 98203 / 425-303-9088; FAX: 206-514-3266 queinfo@queindustries.com

Queen Cutlery Co., P.O. Box 500, Franklinville, NY 14737 / 800-222-5233; FAX: 800-299-2618

R

R&C Knives & Such, 2136 Candy Cane Walk, Manteca, CA 95336-9501 / 209-239-3722; FAX: 209-825-6947

R&D Gun Repair, Kenny Howell, RR1 Box 283, Beloit, WI 53511

R&J Gun Shop, 337 S. Humbolt St., Canyon City, OR 97820 / 541-575-2130 rjgunshop@highdesertnet.com

R&S Industries Corp., 8255 Brentwood Industrial Dr., St. Louis, MO 63144 / 314-781-5169 ron@miraclepolishingcloth.com www.miraclepolishingcloth.com

R. Murphy Co., Inc., 13 Groton-Harvard Rd., P.O. Box 376, Ayer, MA 01432 / 617-772-3481 www.r.murphyknives.com

R.A. Wells Custom Gunsmith, 3452 1st Ave., Racine, WI 53402 / 414-639-5223

R.E. Seebeck Assoc., P.O. Box 59752, Dallas, TX 75229

R.E.I., P.O. Box 88, Tallevast, FL 34270 / 813-755-0085

R.E.T. Enterprises, 2608 S. Chestnut, Broken Arrow, OK 74012 / 918-251-GUNS; (4867) FAX: 918-251-0587

R.T. Eastman Products, P.O. Box 1531, Jackson, WY 83001 / 307-733-3217; or 800-624-4311

Rabeno, Martin, 530 The Eagle Pass, Durango, CO 81301 / 970-382-0353 fancygun@aol.com

Radack Photography, Lauren, 21140 Jib Court L-12, Aventura, FL 33180 / 305-931-3110

Radiator Specialty Co., 1900 Wilkinson Blvd., P.O. Box 34689, Charlotte, NC 28234 / 800-438-6947; FAX: 800-421-9525 tkrossell@gunk.com www.gunk.com

Radical Concepts, P.O. Box 1473, Lake Grove, OR 97035 / 503-538-7437

Rainier Ballistics, 4500 15th St. East, Tacoma, WA 98424 / 800-638-8722; FAX: 253-922-7854 sales@rainierballistics.com www.rainierballistics.com

Ralph Bone Engraving, 718 N. Atlanta St., Owasso, OK 74055 / 918-272-9745

Ram-Line ATK, P.O. Box 39, Onalaska, WI 54650

Ramon B. Gonzalez Guns, P.O. Box 370, Monticello, NY 12701 / 845-794-2510

Rampart International, 2781 W. MacArthur Blvd., B-283, Santa Ana, CA 92704 / 800-976-7240 or 714-557-6405

Ranch Products, P.O. Box 145, Malinta, OH 43535 / 313-277-3118; FAX: 313-565-8536 stevenacrawford@msn.com ranchproducts.com

Randall-Made Knives, P.O. Box 1988, Orlando, FL 32802 / 407-855-8075

Randco UK, 286 Gipsy Rd., Welling, DA16 1JJ ENGLAND / 44 81 303 4118

Randolph Engineering, Inc., Ranger Shooting Glasses, 26 Thomas Patten Dr., Randolph, MA 02368 / 800-541-1405; FAX: 781-986-0337 sales@randolphusa.com www.randolphusa.com

Range Brass Products Company, P.O. Box 218, Rockport, TX 78381

Ransom International Corp., P.O. Box 3845, Prescott, AZ 86302 / 928-778-7899; FAX: 928-778-7993 ransom@cableone.net www.ransomrest.com

Rapine Bullet Mould Mfg. Co., 9503 Landis Lane, East Greenville, PA 18041 / 215-679-5413; FAX: 215-679-9795

Ravell Ltd., 289 Diputacion St., 08009, Barcelona, SPAIN / 34(3) 4874486; FAX: 34(3) 4881394

Ray Riling Arms Books Co., 6844 Gorsten St., Philadelphia, PA 19119 / 215-438-2456; FAX: 215-438-5395 sales@rayrilingarmsbooks.com www.rayrilingarmsbooks.com

Ray's Gunsmith Shop, 3199 Elm Ave., Grand Junction, CO 81504 / 970-434-6162; FAX: 970-434-3452

Raytech Div. of Lyman Products Corp., 475 Smith Street, Middletown, CT 06457-1541 / 860-632-2020 or 800-225-9626; FAX: 860-632-1699 raysales@cshore.com www.raytech-ind.com

RCBS Operations/ATK, 605 Oro Dam Blvd., Oroville, CA 95965 / 800-533-5000; FAX: 530-533-1647 www.rcbs.com

Reardon Products, P.O. Box 126, Morrison, IL 61270 / 815-772-3155

Recoilless Technologies, Inc. (RTI), RTI/High-Low, 2141 E. Cedar #2, Tempe, AZ 85281 / 480-966-7051

Red Diamond Dist. Co., 1304 Snowdon Dr., Knoxville, TN 37912

Redding Reloading Equipment, 1089 Starr Rd., Cortland, NY 13045 / 607-753-3331; FAX: 607-756-8445 techline@redding-reloading.com www.redding-reloading.com

Redfield Media Resource Center, 4607 N.E. Cedar Creek Rd., Woodland, WA 98674 / 360-225-5000; FAX: 360-225-7616

Redman's Rifling & Reboring, 189 Nichols Rd., Omak, WA 98841 / 509-826-5512

Redwood Bullet Works, 3559 Bay Rd., Redwood City, CA 94063 / 415-367-6741

Reed, Dave, Rt. 1, Box 374, Minnesota City, MN 55959 / 507-689-2944

Reimer Johannsen, Inc., 438 Willow Brook Rd., Plainfield, NH 03781 / 603-469-3450; FAX: 603-469-3471

Reloaders Equipment Co., 4680 High St., Ecorse, MI 48229

Reloading Specialties, Inc., Box 1130, Pine Island, MN 55463 / 507-356-8500; FAX: 507-356-8800

Remington Arms Co., Inc., 870 Remington Drive, P.O. Box 700, Madison, NC 27025-0700 / 800-243-9700; FAX: 336-548-8700 info@remington.com www.remington.com

Remington Double Shotguns, 7885 Cyd Dr., Denver, CO 80221 / 303-429-6947

Renegade, P.O. Box 31546, Phoenix, AZ 85046 / 602-482-6777; FAX: 602-482-1952

Renfrew Guns & Supplies, R.R. 4, Renfrew, ON K7V 3Z7 CANADA / 613-432-7080

Reno, Wayne, 2808 Stagestop Road, Jefferson, CO 80456

Republic Arms, Inc. (See Cobra Enterprises, Inc.)

Retting, Inc., Martin B., 11029 Washington, Culver City, CA 90232 / 213-837-2412

RG-G, Inc., P.O. Box 935, Trinidad, CO 81082 / 719-845-1436

RH Machine & Consulting Inc., P.O. Box 394, Pacific, MO 63069 / 314-271-8465

Rhino, P.O. Box 787, Locust, NC 28097 / 704-753-2198

Rhodeside, Inc., 1704 Commerce Dr., Piqua, OH 45356 / 513-773-5781

Rice, Keith (See White Rock Tool & Die)

Richards MicroFit Stocks, Inc., P.O. Box 1066, Sun Valley, CA 91352 / 800-895-7420; FAX: 818-771-1242 sales@rifle-stocks.com www.rifle-stocks.com

Ridgeline, Inc., Bruce Sheldon, P.O. Box 930, Dewey, AZ 86327-0930 / 800-632-5900; FAX: 602-632-3980

Ridgetop Sporting Goods, P.O. Box 306, 42907 Hilligoss Ln. East, Eatonville, WA 98328 / 360-832-6422; FAX: 360-832-6422

Ries, Chuck, 415 Ridgecrest Dr., Grants Pass, OR 97527 / 503-476-5623

Rifles, Inc., 3580 Leal Rd., Pleasanton, TX 78064 / 830-569-2055; FAX: 830-569-2297

Riggs, Jim, 206 Azalea, Boerne, TX 78006 / 210-249-8567

Riley Ledbetter Airguns, 1804 E. Sprague St., Winston Salem, NC 27107-3521 / 919-784-0676

Rim Pac Sports, Inc., 1034 N. Soldano Ave., Azusa, CA 91702-2135

Ringler Custom Leather Co., 31 Shining Mtn. Rd., Powell, WY 82435 / 307-645-3255

Ripley Rifles, 42 Fletcher Street, Ripley, Derbyshire, DE5 3LP ENGLAND / 011-0773-748353

Rizzini F.lli (See U.S. Importers-Wm. Larkin Moore & Co., N.E. Arms Corp.)

Rizzini SNC, Via 2 Giugno, 7/7Bis-25060, Marcheno (Brescia), ITALY

RLCM Enterprises, 110 Hill Crest Drive, Burleson, TX 76028

RMS Custom Gunsmithing, 4120 N. Bitterwell, Prescott Valley, AZ 86314 / 520-772-7626 www.customstockmaker.com

Robar Co., Inc., The, 21438 N. 7th Ave., Suite B, Phoenix, AZ 85027 / 623-581-2648; FAX: 623-582-0059 info@robarguns.com www.robarguns.com

Robert Evans Engraving, 332 Vine St., Oregon City, OR 97045 / 503-656-5693

Robert Valade Engraving, 931 3rd Ave., Seaside, OR 97138 / 503-738-7672

Robinett, R. G., P.O. Box 72, Madrid, IA 50156 / 515-795-2906

Robinson, Don, Pennsylvania Hse, 36 Fairfax Crescent, W Yorkshire, ENGLAND / 0422-364458 donrobinsonuk@yahoo.co.uk www.guns4u2.co.uk

Robinson Armament Co., P.O. Box 16776, Salt Lake City, UT 84116 / 801-355-0401; FAX: 801-355-0402 zdf@robarm.com www.robarm.com

Robinson Firearms Mfg. Ltd., 1699 Blondeaux Crescent, Kelowna, BC V1Y 4J8 CANADA / 604-868-9596

Robinson H.V. Bullets, 3145 Church St., Zachary, LA 70791 / 504-654-4029

Rochester Lead Works, 76 Anderson Ave., Rochester, NY 14607 / 716-442-8500; FAX: 716-442-4712

Rock River Arms, 101 Noble St., Cleveland, IL 61241

Rockwood Corp., Speedwell Division, 136 Lincoln Blvd., Middlesex, NJ 08846 / 800-243-8274; FAX: 980-560-7475

MANUFACTURER'S DIRECTORY

Rocky Mountain Armoury, Mr. Felix LesMerises, 610 Main Street, P.O. Box 691, Frisco, CO 80443-0691 / 970-668-0136; FAX: 970-668-4484 felix@rockymountainarmoury.com

Rocky Mountain Target Co., 3 Aloe Way, Leesburg, FL 34788 / 352-365-9598

Rocky Shoes & Boots, 294 Harper St., Nelsonville, OH 45764 / 800-848-9452 or 614-753-1951; FAX: 614-753-4024

Rogue Rifle Co., Inc./Chipmunk Rifles, 1140 36th St. N., Ste. B, Lewiston, ID 83501 / 208-743-4355; FAX: 208-743-4163 customerservice@roguerifle.com www.roguerifle.com

Rogue River Rifleworks, 500 Linne Road #D, Paso Robles, CA 93446 / 805-227-4706; FAX: 805-227-4723 rrrifles@calinet.com

Rohner, Hans, 1148 Twin Sisters Ranch Rd., Nederland, CO 80466-9600

Rohner, John, 186 Virginia Ave., Asheville, NC 28806 / 828-281-3704

Rohrbaugh, P.O. Box 785, Bayport, NY 11705 / 631-363-2843; FAX: 631-363-2681 API380@aol.com

Romain's Custom Guns, Inc., RD 1, Whetstone Rd., Brockport, PA 15823 / 814-265-1948 romwhetstone@penn.com

Ron Frank Custom Classic, Inc., 7131 Richland Rd., Ft. Worth, TX 76118 / 817-284-9300; FAX: 817-284-9300 rfrank3974@aol.com

Rooster Laboratories, P.O. Box 414605, Kansas City, MO 64141 / 816-474-1622; FAX: 816-474-7622

Rorschach Precision Products, 417 Keats Cir., Irving, TX 75061 / 214-790-3487

Rosenberg & Son, Jack A., 12229 Cox Ln., Dallas, TX 75234 / 214-241-6302

Ross, Don, 12813 West 83 Terrace, Lenexa, KS 66215 / 913-492-6982

Rosser, Bob, 2809 Crescent Ave., Suite 20, Homewood, AL 35209 / 205-870-4422; FAX: 205-870-4421 www.hand-engravers.com

Rossi Firearms, Gary Mchalik, 16175 NW 49th Ave., Miami, FL 33014-6314 / 305-474-0401; FAX: 305-623-7506

Rottweil Compe, 1330 Glassell, Orange, CA 92667

Royal Arms Gunstocks, 919 8th Ave. NW, Great Falls, MT 59404 / 406-453-1149 royalarms@lmt.net www.lmt.net/~royalarms

Royal Arms International, R J Brill, P.O. Box 6083, Woodland Hills, CA 91365 / 818-704-5110; FAX: 818-887-2059 royalarms.com

Roy's Custom Grips, 793 Mt. Olivet Church Rd., Lynchburg, VA 24504 / 434-993-3470

RPM, 15481 N. Twin Lakes Dr., Tucson, AZ 85739 / 520-825-1233; FAX: 520-825-3333

Rubright Bullets, 1008 S. Quince Rd., Walnutport, PA 18088 / 215-767-1339

Rucker Dist. Inc., P.O. Box 479, Terrell, TX 75160 / 214-563-2094

Ruger (See Sturm Ruger & Co., Inc.)

Ruger, Chris. See: RUGER'S CUSTOM GUNS

Ruger's Custom Guns, Chris Ruger, 1050 Morton Blvd., Kingston, NY 12401 / 845-336-7106; FAX: 845-336-7106 rugerscustom@outdrs.net rugergunsmith.com

Rundell's Gun Shop, 6198 Frances Rd., Clio, MI 48420 / 313-687-0559

Rupert's Gun Shop, 2202 Dick Rd., Suite B, Fenwick, MI 48834 / 517-248-3252 17rupert@pathwaynet.com

Russ Haydon's Shooters' Supply, 15018 Goodrich Dr. NW, Gig Harbor, WA 98329 / 877-663-6249; FAX: 253-857-7884 info@shooters-supply.com www.shooters-supply.com

Russ, William. See: BILL RUSS TRADING POST

Rusteprufe Laboratories, 1319 Jefferson Ave., Sparta, WI 54656 / 608-269-4144; FAX: 608-366-1972 rusteprufe@centurytel.net www.rusteprufe.com

Rutgers Book Center, 127 Raritan Ave., Highland Park, NJ 08904 / 732-545-4344; FAX: 732-545-6686 gunbooks@rutgersgunbooks.com www.rutgersgunbooks.com

Rutten (See U.S. Importer-Labanu Inc.)

RWS (See U.S. Importer-Dynamit Nobel-RWS, Inc.), 81 Ruckman Rd., Closter, NJ 07624 / 201-767-7971; FAX: 201-767-1589

S

S&K Scope Mounts, RD 2 Box 21C, Sugar Grove, PA 16350 / 814-489-3091 or 800-578-9862; FAX: 814-489-5466

comments@scopemounts.com www.scopemounts.com

S&S Firearms, 74-11 Myrtle Ave., Glendale, NY 11385 / 718-497-1100; FAX: 718-497-1105 info@ssfirearms.com ssfirearms.com

S.A.R.L. G. Granger, 66 Cours Fauriel, 42100, Saint Etienne, FRANCE / 04 77 25 14 73; FAX: 04 77 38 66 99

S.C.R.C., P.O. Box 660, Katy, TX 77492-0660 FAX: 281-492-6332

S.D. Meacham, 1070 Angel Ridge, Peck, ID 83545

S.I.A.C.E. (See U.S. Importer-IAR Inc.)

Sabatti SPA, Via A Volta 90, 25063 Gandome V.T.(BS), Brescia, ITALY / 030-8912207-831312; FAX: 030-8912059 info@sabatti.it www.sabatti.com

SAECO (See Redding Reloading Equipment)

Safari Arms/Schuetzen Pistol Works, 620-626 Old Pacific Hwy. SE, Olympia, WA 98513 / 360-459-3471; FAX: 360-491-3447 info@olyarms.com www.olyarms.com

Safari Press, Inc., 15621 Chemical Lane B, Huntington Beach, CA 92649 / 714-894-9080; FAX: 714-894-4949 info@safaripress.com www.safaripress.com

Safariland Ltd., Inc., 3120 E. Mission Blvd., P.O. Box 51478, Ontario, CA 91761 / 909-923-7300; FAX: 909-923-7400

SAFE, P.O. Box 864, Post Falls, ID 83877 / 208-773-3624; FAX: 208-773-6819 staysafe@safe-llc.com www.safe-llc.com

Sako Ltd. (See U.S. Importer-Stoeger Industries)

Sam Welch Gun Engraving, Sam Welch, HC 64 Box 2110, Moab, UT 84532 / 435-259-8131

Samco Global Arms, Inc., 6995 NW 43rd St., Miami, FL 33166 / 305-593-9782; FAX: 305-593-1014 samco@samcoglobal.com www.samcoglobal.com

Sampson, Roger, 2316 Mahogany St., Mora, MN 55051 / 612-679-4868

San Marco (See U.S. Importers-Cape Outfitters-EMF Co., Inc.

Sandia Die & Cartridge Co., 37 Atancacio Rd. NE, Albuquerque, NM 87123 / 505-298-5729

Sarco, Inc., 323 Union St., Stirling, NJ 07980 / 908-647-3800; FAX: 908-647-9413

Sarsilmaz Shotguns-Turkey (see B.C. Outdoors)

Sauer (See U.S. Importers-Paul Co., The Sigarms Inc.)

Sauls, R. See: BRYAN & ASSOC.

Saunders Gun & Machine Shop, 145 Delhi Rd., Manchester, IA 52057 / 563-927-4026

Savage Arms (Canada), Inc., 248 Water St., P.O. Box 1240, Lakefield, ON K0L 2H0 CANADA / 705-652-8000; FAX: 705-652-8431 www.savagearms.com

Savage Arms, Inc., 100 Springdale Rd., Westfield, MA 01085 / 413-568-7001; FAX: 413-562-7764

Savage Range Systems, Inc., 100 Springdale Rd., Westfield, MA 01085 / 413-568-7001; FAX: 413-562-1152 snailtraps@savagearms.com www.snailtraps.com

Saville Iron Co. (See Greenwood Precision)

Scansport, Inc., P.O. Box 700, Enfield, NH 03748 / 603-632-7654

Sceery Game Calls, P.O. Box 6520, Sante Fe, NM 87502 / 505-471-9110; FAX: 505-471-3476

Schaefer Shooting Sports, P.O. Box 1515, Melville, NY 11747-0515 / 516-643-5466; FAX: 516-643-2426 robert@robertschaefer.com www.schaefershooting.com

Scharch Mfg., Inc.-Top Brass, 10325 Co. Rd. 120, Salida, CO 81201 / 800-836-4683; FAX: 719-539-3021 topbrass@scharch.com www.handgun-brass.com

Scherer, Liz. See: SCHERER SUPPLIES

Scherer Supplies, Liz Scherer, Box 250, Ewing, VA 24248 FAX: 423-733-2073

Schiffman, Mike, 8233 S. Crystal Springs, McCammon, ID 83250 / 208-254-9114

Schmidt & Bender, Inc., P.O. Box 134, Meriden, NH 03770 / 603-469-3565; FAX: 603-469-3471 scopes@adelphia.net www.schmidtbender.com

Schneider Bullets, 3655 West 214th St., Fairview Park, OH 44126

Schneider Rifle Barrels, Inc., 1403 W. Red Baron Rd., Payson, AZ 85541 / 602-948-2525

School of Gunsmithing, The, 6065 Roswell Rd., Atlanta, GA 30328 / 800-223-4542

Schroeder Bullets, 1421 Thermal Ave., San Diego, CA 92154 / 619-423-3523; FAX: 619-423-8124

Schulz Industries, 16247 Minnesota Ave., Paramount, CA 90723 / 213-439-5903

Schumakers Gun Shop, 512 Prouty Corner Lp. A, Colville, WA 99114 / 509-684-4848

Scope Control, Inc., 5775 Co. Rd. 23 SE, Alexandria, MN 56308 / 612-762-7295

Score High Gunsmithing, 9812-A, Cochiti SE, Albuquerque, NM 87123 / 800-326-5632 or 505-292-5532; FAX: 505-292-2592 scorehi@scorehi.com www.probed2000.com

Scott Fine Guns Inc., Thad, P.O. Box 412, Indianola, MS 38751 / 601-887-5929

Searcy Enterprises, P.O. Box 584, Boron, CA 93596 / 760-762-6771; FAX: 760-762-0191

Second Chance Body Armor, P.O. Box 578, Central Lake, MI 49622 / 616-544-5721; FAX: 616-544-9824

Seebeck Assoc., R.E., P.O. Box 59752, Dallas, TX 75229

Segway Industries, P.O. Box 783, Suffern, NY 10901-0783 / 914-357-5510

Seligman Shooting Products, Box 133, Seligman, AZ 86337 / 602-422-3607 shootssp@yahoo.com

Sellier & Bellot, USA, Inc., P.O. Box 27006, Shawnee Mission, KS 66225 / 913-685-0916; FAX: 913-685-0917

Selsi Co., Inc., P.O. Box 10, Midland Park, NJ 07432-0010 / 201-935-0388; FAX: 201-935-5851

Semmer, Charles (See Remington Double Shotguns), 7885 Cyd Dr., Denver, CO 80221 / 303-429-6947

Sentinel Arms, P.O. Box 57, Detroit, MI 48231 / 313-331-1951; FAX: 313-331-1456

Servus Footwear Co., 1136 2nd St., Rock Island, IL 61204 / 309-786-7741; FAX: 309-786-9808

SGS Importer's International, Inc., 1750 Brielle Ave., Unit B1, Wanamassa, NJ 07712 / 732-493-0302; FAX: 732-493-0301 gsodini@aol.com www.firestorm-sgs.com

Shappy Bullets, 76 Milldale Ave., Plantsville, CT 06479 / 203-621-3704

Sharp Shooter Supply, 4970 Lehman Road, Delphos, OH 45833 / 419-695-3179

Sharps Arms Co., Inc., C., 100 Centennial, Box 885, Big Timber, MT 59011 / 406-932-4353

Shaw, Inc., E. R. (See Small Arms Mfg. Co.)

Shay's Gunsmithing, 931 Marvin Ave., Lebanon, PA 17042

Sheffield Knifemakers Supply, Inc., P.O. Box 741107, Orange City, FL 32774-1107 / 386-775-6453; FAX: 386-774-5754

Sheldon, Bruce. See: RIDGELINE, INC.

Shepherd Enterprises, Inc., Box 189, Waterloo, NE 68069 / 402-779-2424; FAX: 402-779-4010 sshepherd@shepherdscopes.com www.shepherdscopes.com

Sherwood, George, 46 N. River Dr., Roseburg, OR 97470 / 541-672-3159

Shilen, Inc., 205 Metro Park Blvd., Ennis, TX 75119 / 972-875-5318; FAX: 972-875-5402

Shiloh Rifle Mfg., P.O. Box 279, Big Timber, MT 59011

Shoot Where You Look, Leon Measures, Dept GD, 408 Fair, Livingston, TX 77351

Shooters Arms Manufacturing, Inc., Rivergate Mall, Gen. Maxilom Ave., Cebu City 6000, PHILIPPINES / 6332-254-8478 www.shootersarms.com.ph

Shooter's Choice Gun Care, 15050 Berkshire Ind. Pkwy., Middlefield, OH 44062 / 440-834-8888; FAX: 440-834-3388 www.shooterschoice.com

Shooter's Edge Inc., 3313 Creekstone Dr., Fort Collins, CO 80525

Shooters Supply, 1120 Tieton Dr., Yakima, WA 98902 / 509-452-1181

Shooter's World, 3828 N. 28th Ave., Phoenix, AZ 85017 / 602-266-0170

Shooters, Inc., 5139 Stanart St., Norfolk, VA 23502 / 757-461-9152; FAX: 757-461-9155 gflocker@aol.com

Shootin' Shack, 357 Cypress Drive, No. 10, Tequesta, FL 33469 / 561-746-2731; FAX: 561-545-4861

Shooting Gallery, The, 8070 Southern Blvd., Boardman, OH 44512 / 216-726-7788

Shoot-N-C Targets (See Birchwood Casey)

Shotgun Sports, P.O. Box 6810, Auburn, CA 95604 / 530-889-2220; FAX: 530-889-9106 custsrv@shotgunsportsmagazine.com shotgunsportsmagazine.com

Shotgun Sports Magazine, dba Shootin' Accessories Ltd., P.O. Box 6810, Auburn, CA 95604 / 916-889-2220 custsrv@shotgunsportsmagazine.com shotgunspotsmagazine.com

Shotguns Unlimited, 2307 Fon Du Lac Rd., Richmond, VA 23229 / 804-752-7115

Siegrist Gun Shop, 8752 Turtle Road, Whittemore, MI 48770 / 989-873-3929

Sierra Bullets, 1400 W. Henry St., Sedalia, MO 65301 / 816-827-6300; FAX: 816-827-6300

Sierra Specialty Prod. Co., 1344 Oakhurst Ave., Los Altos, CA 94024 FAX: 415-965-1536

SIG, CH-8212 Neuhausen, SWITZERLAND

Sigarms Inc., 18 Industrial Dr., Exeter, NH 03833 / 603-772-2302; FAX: 603-772-9082 www.sigarms.com

Sight Shop, The, John G. Lawson, 1802 E. Columbia Ave., Tacoma, WA 98404 / 253-474-5465 parahellum9@aol.com www.thesightshop.org

Sightron, Inc., 1672B Hwy. 96, Franklinton, NC 27525 / 919-528-8783; FAX: 919-528-0995 info@sightron.com www.sightron.com

SIG-Sauer (See U.S. Importer-Sigarms, Inc.)

Silencio/Safety Direct, 56 Coney Island Dr., Sparks, NV 89431 / 800-648-1812 or 702-354-4451; FAX: 702-359-1074

Silent Hunter, 1100 Newton Ave., W. Collingswood, NJ 08107 / 609-854-3276

Silhouette Leathers, 8598 Hwy. 51 N. #4, Millington, TN 38053 silhouetteleathers@yahoo.com silhouetteleathers.com

Silver Eagle Machining, 18007 N. 69th Ave., Glendale, AZ 85308

Silver Ridge Gun Shop (See Goodwin Guns)

Simmons, Jerry, 715 Middlebury St., Goshen, IN 46528-2717 / 574-533-8546

Simmons Gun Repair, Inc., 700 S. Rogers Rd., Olathe, KS 66062 / 913-782-3131; FAX: 913-782-4189

Simmons Outdoor Corp., 6001 Oak Canyon, Irvine, CA 92618 / 949-451-1450; FAX: 949-451-1460 www.meade.com

Sinclair International, Inc., 2330 Wayne Haven St., Fort Wayne, IN 46803 / 260-493-1858 or 800-717-8211; FAX: 260-493-2530 sales@sinclairintl.com www.sinclairintl.com

Singletary, Kent, 4538 W. Carol Ave., Glendale, AZ 85302 / 602-526-6836 kent@kscustom www.kscustom.com

Siskiyou Gun Works (See Donnelly, C. P.)

Six Enterprises, 320-D Turtle Creek Ct., San Jose, CA 95125 / 408-999-0201; FAX: 408-999-0216

SKB Shotguns, 4325 S. 120th St., Omaha, NE 68137 / 800-752-2767; FAX: 402-330-8040 skb@skbshotguns.com www.skbshotguns.com

Skeoch, Brian R., P.O. Box 279, Glenrock, WY 82637 / 307-436-9655 skeochbrian@netzero.com

Skip's Machine, 364 29 Road, Grand Junction, CO 81501 / 303-245-5417

Sklany's Machine Shop, 566 Birch Grove Dr., Kalispell, MT 59901 / 406-755-4257

Slug Site, Ozark Wilds, 21300 Hwy. 5, Versailles, MO 65084 / 573-378-6430 john@ebeling.com john.ebeling.com

Small Arms Mfg. Co., 5312 Thoms Run Rd., Bridgeville, PA 15017 / 412-221-4343; FAX: 412-221-4303

Small Arms Specialists, 443 Firchburg Rd., Mason, NH 03048 / 603-878-0427; FAX: 603-878-3905 miniguns@empire.net miniguns.com

Smires, C. L., 5222 Windmill Lane, Columbia, MD 21044-1328

Smith & Wesson, 2100 Roosevelt Ave., Springfield, MA 01104 / 413-781-8300; FAX: 413-731-8980 qa@smith-wesson.com www.smith-wesson.com

Smith, Art, P.O. Box 645, Park Rapids, MN 56470 / 218-732-5333

Smith, Mark A., P.O. Box 182, Sinclair, WY 82334 / 307-324-7929

Smith, Michael, 2612 Ashmore Ave., Red Bank, TN 37415 / 615-267-8341

Smith, Ron, 5869 Straley, Fort Worth, TX 76114 / 817-732-6768

Smith, Sharmon, 4545 Speas Rd., Fruitland, ID 83619 / 208-452-6329 sharmon@fmtc.com

Smith Abrasives, Inc., 1700 Sleepy Valley Rd., Hot Springs, AR 71902-5095 / 501-321-2244; FAX: 501-321-9232 www.smithabrasives.com

Smith, Judy. See: L.B.T.

Smith Saddlery, Jesse W., 0499 County Road J, Pritchett, CO 81064 / 509-325-0622

Smokey Valley Rifles, E1976 Smokey Valley Rd., Scandinavia, WI 54977 / 715-467-2674

Snapp's Gunshop, 6911 E. Washington Rd., Clare, MI 48617 / 989-386-9226 snapp@glccomputers.com

Sno-Seal, Inc. (See Atsko/Sno-Seal, Inc.)

Societa Armi Bresciane Srl (See U.S. Importer-Cape Outfitters)

SOS Products Co. (See Buck Stix-SOS Products Co.), Box 3, Neenah, WI 54956

Sotheby's, 1334 York Ave. at 72nd St., New York, NY 10021 / 212-606-7260

Sound Tech, Box 738, Logan, NM 88426 / 205-999-0416; or 505-487-2277 silenceio@wmconnect.com www.soundtechsilencers.com

South Bend Replicas, Inc., 61650 Oak Rd., South Bend, IN 46614 / 574-289-4500

Southeastern Community College, 1015 S. Gear Ave., West Burlington, IA 52655 / 319-752-2731

Southern Ammunition Co., Inc., 4232 Meadow St., Loris, SC 29569-3124 / 803-756-3262; FAX: 803-756-3583

Southern Armory, The, 25 Millstone Rd., Woodlawn, VA 24381 / 703-238-1343; FAX: 703-238-1453

Southern Bloomer Mfg. Co., P.O. Box 1621, Bristol, TN 37620 / 615-878-6660; FAX: 615-878-8761

Southern Security, 1700 Oak Hills Dr., Kingston, TN 37763 / 423-376-6297; FAX: 800-251-9992

Sparks, Milt, 605 E. 44th St. No. 2, Boise, ID 83714-4800

Spartan-Realtree Products, Inc., 1390 Box Circle, Columbus, GA 31907 / 706-569-9101; FAX: 706-569-0042

Specialty Gunsmithing, Lynn McMurdo, P.O. Box 404, Afton, WY 83110 / 307-886-5535

Specialty Shooters Supply, Inc., 3325 Griffin Rd., Suite 9mm, Fort Lauderdale, FL 33317

Speer Bullets, P.O. Box 856, Lewiston, ID 83501 / 208-746-2351 www.speer-bullets.com

Spegel, Craig, P.O. Box 387, Nehalem, OR 97131 / 503-368-5653

Speiser, Fred D., 2229 Dearborn, Missoula, MT 59801 / 406-549-8133

Spencer Reblue Service, 1820 Tupelo Trail, Holt, MI 48842 / 517-694-7474

Spencer's Rifle Barrels, Inc., 4107 Jacobs Creek Dr., Scottsville, VA 24590 / 804-293-6836; FAX: 804-293-6836 www.spencersriflebarrels.com

SPG, Inc., P.O. Box 1625, Cody, WY 82414 / 307-587-7621; FAX: 307-587-7695 spg@cody.wtp.net www.blackpowderspg.com

Sphinx Systems Ltd., Gesteigtstrasse 12, CH-3800, Matten, BRNE, SWITZERLAND

Splitfire Sporting Goods, L.L.C., P.O. Box 1044, Orem, UT 84059-1044 / 801-932-7950; FAX: 801-932-7959 www.splitfireguns.com

Spolar Power Load, Inc., 17376 Filbert, Fontana, CA 92335 / 800-227-9667

Sport Flite Manufacturing Co., 637 Kingsley Trl., Bloomfield Hills, MI 48304-2320 / 248-647-3747

Sporting Clays Of America, 9257 Buckeye Rd., Sugar Grove, OH 43155-9632 / 740-746-8334 FAX: 740-746-8605

Sports Afield Magazine, 15621 Chemical Lane B, Huntington Beach, CA 92649 / 714-894-9080; FAX: 714-894-4949 info@sportsafield.com www.sportsafield.com

Sportsman Safe Mfg. Co., 6309-6311 Paramount Blvd., Long Beach, CA 90805 / 800-266-7150; or 310-984-5445

Sportsman's Communicators, 588 Radcliffe Ave., Pacific Palisades, CA 90272 / 800-538-3752

Sportsmatch U.K. Ltd., 16 Summer St. Leighton, Buzzard Beds, Bedfordshire, LU7 1HT ENGLAND / 4401525-381638; FAX: 4401525-851236 info@sportsmatch-uk.com www.sportsmatch-uk.com

Sportsmen's Exchange & Western Gun Traders, Inc., 813 Doris Ave., Oxnard, CA 93030 / 805-483-1917

Spradlin's, 457 Shannon Rd., Texas Creek Cotopaxi, CO 81223 / 719-275-7105; FAX: 719-275-3852 spradlins@prodigy.net www.spradlins.net

Springfield Armory, 420 W. Main St., Geneseo, IL 61254 / 309-944-5631; FAX: 309-944-3676 sales@springfield-armory.com www.springfieldarmory.com

Springfield Sporters, Inc., RD 1, Penn Run, PA 15765 / 412-254-2626; FAX: 412-254-9173

Springfield, Inc., 420 W. Main St., Geneseo, IL 61254 / 309-944-5631; FAX: 309-944-3676

Spyderco, Inc., 820 Spyderco Way, Golden, CO 80403 / 800-525-7770; FAX: 303-278-2229 sales@spyderco.com www.spyderco.com

SSK Industries, J. D. Jones, 590 Woodvue Lane, Wintersville, OH 43953 / 740-264-0176; FAX: 740-264-2257 www.sskindustries.com

Stackpole Books, 5067 Ritter Rd., Mechanicsburg, PA 17055-6921 / 717-796-0411 or 800-732-3669; FAX: 717-796-0412 tmanney@stackpolebooks.com www.stackpolebooks.com

Stalker, Inc., P.O. Box 21, Fishermans Wharf Rd., Malakoff, TX 75148 / 903-489-1010

Stalwart Corporation, P.O. Box 46, Evanston, WY 82931 / 307-789-7687; FAX: 307-789-7688

Stan Baker Sports, Stan Baker, 10000 Lake City Way, Seattle, WA 98125 / 206-522-4575

Stan De Treville & Co., 4129 Normal St., San Diego, CA 92103 / 619-298-3393

Stanley Bullets, 2085 Heatheridge Ln., Reno, NV 89509

Star Ammunition, Inc., 5520 Rock Hampton Ct., Indianapolis, IN 46268 / 800-221-5927; FAX: 317-872-5847

Star Custom Bullets, P.O. Box 608, 468 Main St., Ferndale, CA 95536 / 707-786-9140; FAX: 707-786-9117 wmebridge@humboldt.com

Star Machine Works, P.O. Box 1872, Pioneer, CA 95666 / 209-295-5000

Starke Bullet Company, P.O. Box 400, 605 6th St. NW, Cooperstown, ND 58425 / 888-797-3431

Starkey Labs, 6700 Washington Ave. S., Eden Prairie, MN 55344

Starkey's Gun Shop, 9430 McCombs, El Paso, TX 79924 / 915-751-3030

Starlight Training Center, Inc., Rt. 1, P.O. Box 88, Bronaugh, MO 64728 / 417-843-3555

Starline, Inc., 1300 W. Henry St., Sedalia, MO 65301 / 660-827-6640; FAX: 660-827-6650 info@starlinebrass.com http://www.starlinebrass.com

Starr Trading Co., Jedediah, P.O. Box 2007, Farmington Hills, MI 48333 / 877-857-8277; FAX: 248-683-3282 mtman1849@aol.com www.jedediah-starr.com

Starrett Co., L. S., 121 Crescent St., Athol, MA 01331 / 978-249-3551; FAX: 978-249-8495

Steelman's Gun Shop, 10465 Beers Rd., Swartz Creek, MI 48473 / 810-735-4884

Steffens, Ron, 18396 Mariposa Creek Rd., Willits, CA 95490 / 707-485-0873

Stegall, James B., 26 Forest Rd., Wallkill, NY 12589

Steve Henigson & Associates, P.O. Box 2726, Culver City, CA 90231 / 310-305-8288; FAX: 310-305-1905

Steve Kamyk Engraver, 9 Grandview Dr., Westfield, MA 01085-1810 / 413-568-0457 stevek201@comcast.net

Steven Dodd Hughes, P.O. Box 545, Livingston, MT 59047 / 406-222-9377; FAX: 406-222-9377

Steves House of Guns, Rt. 1, Minnesota City, MN 55959 / 507-689-2573

Stewart's Gunsmithing, P.O. Box 5854, Pietersburg North 0750, Transvaal, SOUTH AFRICA / 01521-89401

Steyr Arms, P.O. Box 2609, Cumming, GA 30028 / 770-888-4201 www.steyrarms.com

Steyr Mannlicher GmbH & Co. KG, Mannlicherstrasse 1, 4400 Steyr, Steyr, AUSTRIA / 0043-7252-896-0; FAX: 0043-7252-78620 office@steyr-mannlicher.com www.steyr-mannlicher.com

STI International, 114 Halmar Cove, Georgetown, TX 78628 / 800-959-8201; FAX: 512-819-0465 www.stiguns.com

Stiles Custom Guns, 76 Cherry Run Rd., Box 1605, Homer City, PA 15748 / 712-479-9945 glstiles@yourinter.net www.yourinter.net/glstiles

Stillwell, Robert, 421 Judith Ann Dr., Schertz, TX 78154

Stoeger Industries, 17603 Indian Head Hwy., Suite 200, Accokeek, MD 20607-2501 / 301-283-6300; FAX: 301-283-6986 www.stoegerindustries.com

Stoeger Publishing Co. (See Stoeger Industries)

Stone Enterprises Ltd., 426 Harveys Neck Rd., P.O. Box 335, Wicomico Church, VA 22579 / 804-580-5114; FAX: 804-580-8421

Stone Mountain Arms, 5988 Peachtree Corners E., Norcross, GA 30071 / 800-251-9412

Stoney Point Products, Inc., 9200 Cody St., Overland Park, KS 66214 / 800-845-2444; FAX: 507-354-7236 stoney@newulmtel.net www.stoneypoint.com

Storm, Gary, P.O. Box 5211, Richardson, TX 75083 / 214-385-0862

Stott's Creek Armory, Inc., 2526 S. 475W, Morgantown, IN 46160 / 317-878-5489 stottscrk@aol.com www.Sccalendar.aol.com

Stratco, Inc., P.O. Box 2270, Kalispell, MT 59901 / 406-755-1221; FAX: 406-755-1226

Strayer, Sandy. See: STRAYER-VOIGT, INC.

Strayer-Voigt, Inc., Sandy Strayer, 3435 Ray Orr Blvd., Grand Prairie, TX 75050 / 972-513-0575

Strong Holster Co., 39 Grove St., Gloucester, MA 01930 / 508-281-3300; FAX: 508-281-6321

Strutz Rifle Barrels, Inc., W. C., P.O. Box 611, Eagle River, WI 54521 / 715-479-4766

MANUFACTURER'S DIRECTORY

Stuart, V. Pat, Rt. 1, Box 447-S, Greenville, VA 24440 / 804-556-3845
Sturgeon Valley Sporters, Ken Ide, P.O. Box 283, Vanderbilt, MI 49795 / 989-983-4338 k.ide@mail.com
Sturm Ruger & Co. Inc., 200 Ruger Rd., Prescott, AZ 86301 / 928-541-8820; FAX: 520-541-8850 www.ruger.com
Sullivan, David S. (See Westwind Rifles, Inc.)
"Su-Press-On", Inc., P.O. Box 09161, Detroit, MI 48209 / 313-842-4222
Sun Welding Safe Co., 290 Easy St. No. 3, Simi Valley, CA 93065 / 805-584-6678; or 800-729-SAFE; (7233) FAX: 805-584-6169 sunwelding.com
Sunny Hill Enterprises, Inc., W1790 Cty. HHH, Malone, WI 53049 / 920-418-3906; FAX: 920-795-4822 triggerguard@sunny-hill.com www.sunny-hill.com
Super 6 LLC, Gary Knopp, 3806 W. Lisbon Ave., Milwaukee, WI 53208 / 414-344-3343; FAX: 414-344-0304
Surecase Co., The, 233 Wilshire Blvd., Ste. 900, Santa Monica, CA 90401 / 800-92ARMLOC
Sure-Shot Game Calls, Inc., P.O. Box 816, 6835 Capitol, Groves, TX 77619 / 409-962-1636; FAX: 409-962-5465
Svon Corp., 2107 W. Blue Heron Blvd., Riviera Beach, FL 33404 / 508-881-8852
Swampfire Shop, The (See Peterson Gun Shop, Inc., A.W.)
Swann, D. J., 5 Orsova Close, Eltham North Vic., 3095 AUSTRALIA / 03-431-0323
Swanndri New Zealand, 152 Elm Ave., Burlingame, CA 94010 / 415-347-6158
Swanson, Mark, 975 Heap Avenue, Prescott, AZ 86301 / 928-778-4423
Swarovski Optik North America Ltd., 2 Slater Rd., Cranston, RI 02920 / 401-946-2220 or 800-426-3089; FAX: 401-946-2587
Sweet Home, Inc., P.O. Box 900, Orrville, OH 44667-0900
Swenson's 45 Shop, A. D., 3839 Ladera Vista Rd., Fallbrook, CA 92028-9431
Swift Bullet Co., P.O. Box 27, 201 Main St., Quinter, KS 67752 / 913-754-3959; FAX: 913-754-2359
Swift Instruments, 2055 Gateway Place, Ste. 500, San Jose, CA 95110 / 800-523-4544; FAX: 408-292-7967 www.swiftoptics.com
Swift River Gunworks, 450 State St., Belchertown, MA 01007 / 413-323-4052
Szweda, Robert (See RMS Custom Gunsmithing)

T

T&S Industries, Inc., 1027 Skyview Dr., W. Carrollton, OH 45449 / 513-859-8414; FAX: 937-859-8404 keith.tomlinson@tandsshellcatcher.com www.tandsshellcatcher.com
T.F.C. S.p.A., Via G. Marconi 118, B, Villa Carcina 25069, ITALY / 030-881271; FAX: 030-881826
T.G. Faust, Inc., 544 Minor St., Reading, PA 19602 / 610-375-8549; FAX: 610-375-4488
T.K. Lee Co., 1282 Branchwater Ln., Birmingham, AL 35216 / 205-913-5222 odonmich@aol.com www.scopedot.com
T.W. Mench Gunsmith, Inc., 5703 S. 77th St., Ralston, NE 68127 guntools@cox.net http://llwww.members.cox.net/guntools
Tabler Marketing, 2554 Lincoln Blvd., Suite 555, Marina Del Rey, CA 90291 / 818-386-0373; FAX: 818-386-0373
Taconic Firearms Ltd., Perry Lane, P.O. Box 553, Cambridge, NY 12816 / 518-677-2704; FAX: 518-677-5974
Tactical Defense Institute, 2174 Bethany Ridges, West Union, OH 45693 / 937-544-7228; FAX: 937-544-2887 tdiohio@dragonbbs.com www.tdiohio.com
Talley, Dave, P.O. Box 369, Santee, SC 29142 / 803-854-5700 or 307-436-9315; FAX: 803-854-9315 talley@diretway www.talleyrings.com
Talon Industries Inc. (See Cobra Enterprises, Inc.)
Tanfoglio Fratelli S.r.l., via Valtrompia 39, 41, Brescia, ITALY / 011-39-030-8910361; FAX: 011-39-030-8910183 info@tanfoglio.it www.tanfoglio.it
Tanglefree Industries, 1261 Heavenly Dr., Martinez, CA 94553 / 800-982-4868; FAX: 510-825-3874
Tank's Rifle Shop, P.O. Box 474, Fremont, NE 68026-0474 / 402-727-1317 jtank@tanksrifleshop.com www.tanksrifleshop.com
Tanner (See U.S. Importer-Mandall Shooting Supplies, Inc.)
Taracorp Industries, Inc., 1200 Sixteenth St., Granite City, IL 62040 / 618-451-4400
Target Shooting, Inc., P.O. Box 773, Watertown, SD 57201 / 605-882-6955; FAX: 605-882-8840

Tar-Hunt Custom Rifles, Inc., 101 Dogtown Rd., Bloomsburg, PA 17815 / 570-784-6368; FAX: 570-389-9150 www.tar-hunt.com
Tarnhelm Supply Co., Inc., 431 High St., Boscawen, NH 03303 / 603-796-2551; FAX: 603-796-2918 info@tarnhelm.com www.tarnhelm.com
Tasco Sales, Inc., 2889 Commerce Pkwy., Miramar, FL 33025
Taurus Firearms, Inc., 16175 NW 49th Ave., Miami, FL 33014 / 305-624-1115; FAX: 305-623-7506
Taurus International Firearms (See U.S. Importer Taurus Firearms, Inc.)
Taurus S.A. Forjas, Avenida Do Forte 511, Porto Alegre, RS BRAZIL 91360 / 55-51-347-4050; FAX: 55-51-347-3065
Taylor & Robbins, P.O. Box 164, Rixford, PA 16745 / 814-966-3233
Taylor's & Co., Inc., 304 Lenoir Dr., Winchester, VA 22603 / 540-722-2017; FAX: 540-722-2018 info@taylorsfirearms.com www.taylorsfirearms.com
TCCI, P.O. Box 302, Phoenix, AZ 85001 / 602-237-3823; FAX: 602-237-3858
TCSR, 3998 Hoffman Rd., White Bear Lake, MN 55110-4626 / 800-328-5323; FAX: 612-429-0526
Techno Arms (See U.S. Importer- Auto-Ordnance Corp.)
Tecnolegno S.p.A., Via A. Locatelli, 6 10, 24019 Zogno, ITALY / 0345-55111; FAX: 0345-55155
Ted Blocker Holsters, 9438 SW Tigard St., Tigard, OR 97223 / 800-650-9742; FAX: 503-670-9692 www.tedblockerholsters.com
Tele-Optics, 630 E. Rockland Rd., P.O. Box 6313, Libertyville, IL 60048 / 847-362-7757; FAX: 847-362-7757
Tennessee Valley Mfg., 14 County Road 521, Corinth, MS 38834 / 601-286-5014 tvm@avsia.com www.avsia.com/tvm
Ten-Ring Precision, Inc., Alex B. Hamilton, 1449 Blue Crest Lane, San Antonio, TX 78232 / 210-494-3063; FAX: 210-494-3066
TEN-X Products Group, 1905 N. Main St., Suite 133, Cleburne, TX 76031-1305 / 972-243-4016 or 800-433-2225; FAX: 972-243-4112
Tepeco, P.O. Box 342, Friendswood, TX 77546 / 713-482-2702
Terry K. Kopp Professional Gunsmithing, 1201 South 13 Hwy., Lexington, MO 64067 / 816-529-1337
Terry Theis-Engraver, Terry Theis, 21452 FM 2093, Harper, TX 78631 / 830-864-4438
Testing Systems, Inc., 220 Pegasus Ave., Northvale, NJ 07647
Tetra Gun Care, 8 Vreeland Rd., Florham Park, NJ 07932 / 973-443-0004; FAX: 973-443-0263
Tex Shoemaker & Sons, Inc., 714 W. Cienega Ave., San Dimas, CA 91773 / 909-592-2071; FAX: 909-592-2378 texshoemaker@texshoemaker.com www.texshoemaker.com
Texas Armory (See Bond Arms, Inc.)
Texas Platers Supply Co., 2453 W. Five Mile Parkway, Dallas, TX 75233 / 214-330-7168
Thad Rybka Custom Leather Equipment, 2050 Canoe Creek Rd., Springvale, AL 35146-6709
Thad Scott Fine Guns, Inc., P.O. Box 412, Indianola, MS 38751 / 601-887-5929
Theis, Terry. See: TERRY THEIS-ENGRAVER
Thiewes, George W., 14329 W. Parada Dr., Sun City West, AZ 85375
Things Unlimited, 235 N. Kimbau, Casper, WY 82601 / 307-234-5277
Thirion Gun Engraving, Denise, P.O. Box 408, Graton, CA 95444 / 707-829-1876
Thomas, Charles C., 2600 S. First St., Springfield, IL 62704 / 217-789-8980; FAX: 217-789-9130 books@ccthomas.com ccthomas.com
Thompson Bullet Lube Co., P.O. Box 409, Wills Point, TX 75169 / 866-476-1500; FAX: 866-476-1500 thompsonbulletlube.com www.thompsonbulletlube.com
Thompson Precision, 110 Mary St., P.O. Box 251, Warren, IL 61087 / 815-745-3625
Thompson, Randall. See: HIGHLINE MACHINE CO.
Thompson Target Technology, 4804 Sherman Church Ave. S.W., Canton, OH 44710 / 330-484-6480; FAX: 330-491-1087 www.thompsontarget.com
Thompson Tool Mount, 1550 Solomon Rd., Santa Maria, CA 93455 / 805-934-1281 ttm@pronet.net www.thompsontoolmount.com

Thompson/Center Arms, P.O. Box 5002, Rochester, NH 03866 / 603-332-2394; FAX: 603-332-5133 tech@tcarms.com www.tcarms.com
Thunder Ranch, 96747 Hwy. 140 East, Lakeview, OR 97630 / 541-947-4104; FAX: 541-947-4105 troregon@centurytel.net www.thunderranchinc.com
Tiger-Hunt Longrifle Gunstocks, Box 379, Beaverdale, PA 15921 / 814-472-5161 tigerhunt4@aol.com www.gunstockwood.com
Tikka (See U.S. Importer-Stoeger Industries)
Time Precision, 4 Nicholas Sq., New Milford, CT 06776-3506 / 860-350-8343; FAX: 860-350-6343 timeprecision@aol.com www.benchrest.com/timeprecision
Tinks & Ben Lee Hunting Products (See Wellington Outdoors)
Tink's Safariland Hunting Corp., P.O. Box 244, 1140 Monticello Rd., Madison, GA 30650 / 706-342-4915; FAX: 706-342-7568
Tioga Engineering Co., Inc., P.O. Box 913, 13 Cone St., Wellsboro, PA 16901 / 570-724-3533; FAX: 570-724-3895 tiogaeng@epix.net
Tippman Sports, LLC, 2955 Adams Center Rd., Fort Wayne, IN 46803 / 260-749-6022; FAX: 260-441-8504 www.tippmann.com
Tirelli, Snc Di Tirelli Primo E.C., Via Matteotti No. 359, Gardone V.T. Brescia, ITALY / 0039-030-8912819; FAX: 0039-030-832240 tirelli@tirelli.it www.tirelli.it
TM Stockworks, 6355 Maplecrest Rd., Fort Wayne, IN 46835 / 219-485-5389
Tom Forrest, Inc., P.O. Box 326, Lakeside, CA 92040 / 619-561-5800; FAX: 888-GUN-CLIP info@gunmag.com www.gunmags.com
Tombstone Smoken' Deals, 4038 E. Taro Ln., Phoenix, AZ 85050
Tom's Gun Repair, Thomas G. Ivanoff, 76-6 Rt. Southfork Rd., Cody, WY 82414 / 307-587-6949
Tom's Gunshop, 3601 Central Ave., Hot Springs, AR 71913 / 501-624-3856
Tonoloway Tack Drives, HCR 81, Box 100, Needmore, PA 17238
Torel, Inc./Tandy Brands Outdoors/AA & E, 208 Industrial Loop, Yoakum, TX 77995 / 361-293-6366; FAX: 361-293-9127
TOZ (See U.S. Importer-Nygord Precision Products, Inc.)
Track of the Wolf, Inc., 18308 Joplin St. NW, Elk River, MN 55330-1773 / 763-633-2500; FAX: 763-633-2550 www.trackofthewolf.com
Traditions Performance Firearms, P.O. Box 776, 1375 Boston Post Rd., Old Saybrook, CT 06475 / 860-388-4656; FAX: 860-388-4657 info@traditionsfirearms.com www.traditionsfirearms.com
Trafalgar Square, P.O. Box 257, N. Pomfret, VT 05053 / 802-457-1911
Trail Visions, 5800 N. Ames Terrace, Glendale, WI 53209 / 414-228-1328
Treadlok Gun Safe, Inc., 1764 Granby St. NE, Roanoke, VA 24012 / 800-729-8732 or 703-982-6881; FAX: 703-982-1059
Treebone Carving, P.O. Box 551, Cimarron, NJ 87714 / 505-376-2145 treebonecarving.com
Treemaster, P.O. Box 247, Guntersville, AL 35976 / 205-878-3597
Trevallion Gunstocks, 9 Old Mountain Rd., Cape Neddick, ME 03902 / 207-361-1130
Trigger Lock Division / Central Specialties Ltd., 220-D Exchange Dr., Crystal Lake, IL 60014 / 847-639-3900; FAX: 847-639-3972
Trijicon, Inc., 49385 Shafer Ave., P.O. Box 930059, Wixom, MI 48393-0059 / 248-960-7700 or 800-338-0563
Trilby Sport Shop, 1623 Hagley Rd., Toledo, OH 43612-2024 / 419-472-6222
Trilux, Inc., P.O. Box 24608, Winston-Salem, NC 27114 / 910-659-9438; FAX: 910-768-7720
Trinidad St. Jr. Col. Gunsmith Dept., 600 Prospect St., Trinidad, CO 81082 / 719-846-5631; FAX: 719-846-5667
Tripes, George. See: EURO-IMPORTS
Triple-K Mfg. Co., Inc., 2222 Commercial St., San Diego, CA 92113 / 619-232-2066; FAX: 619-232-7675 sales@triplek.com www.triplek.com
Tristar Sporting Arms, Ltd., 1816 Linn St. #16, N. Kansas City, MO 64116-3627 / 816-421-1400; FAX: 816-421-4182 tristarsporting@sbcglobal.net www.tristarsportingarms

MANUFACTURER'S DIRECTORY

Trius Traps, Inc., P.O. Box 25, 221 S. Miami Ave., Cleves, OH 45002 / 513-941-5682; FAX: 513-941-7970 triustraps@fuse.net www.triustraps.com
Trooper Walsh, 2393 N. Edgewood St., Arlington, VA 22207
Trotman, Ken, P. O. Box 505, Huntingdon, PE 29 2XW ENGLAND / 01480 454292; FAX: 01480 384651 enquiries@kentrotman.com www.kentrotman.com
Tru-Balance Knife Co., P.O. Box 140555, Grand Rapids, MI 49514 / 616-647-1215
True Flight Bullet Co., 5581 Roosevelt St., Whitehall, PA 18052 / 610-262-7630; FAX: 610-262-7806
Truglo, Inc., P.O. Box 1612, McKinna, TX 75070 / 972-774-0300; FAX: 972-774-0323 www.truglosights.com
Trulock Tool, P.O. Box 530, Whigham, GA 31797 / 229-762-4678; FAX: 229-762-4050 trulockchokes@hotmail.com trulockchokes.com
Tru-Nord Compass, 1504 Erick Lane, Brainerd, MN 56401 / 218-829-2870; FAX: 218-829-2870 www.trunord.com
Tru-Square Metal Products, Inc., 640 First St. SW, P.O. Box 585, Auburn, WA 98071 / 253-833-2310 or 800-225-1017; FAX: 253-833-2349 t-tumbler@qwest.net
Tucker, James C., P.O. Box 366, Medford, OR 97501 / 541-664-9160 jctstocker@yahoo.com
Tucson Mold, Inc., 930 S. Plumer Ave., Tucson, AZ 85719 / 520-792-1075; FAX: 520-792-1075
Turk's Head Productions, Mustafa Bilal, 13545 Erickson Pl. NE, Seattle, WA 98125-3794 / 206-782-4164; FAX: 206-783-5677 info@turkshead.com www.turkshead.com
Turnbull Restoration, Doug, 6680 Rts. 5 & 20, P.O. Box 471, Bloomfield, NY 14469 / 585-657-6338; FAX: 585-657-6338 turnbullrest@mindspring.com www.turnbullrestoration.com
Tuttle, Dale, 4046 Russell Rd., Muskegon, MI 49445 / 616-766-2250

U

U.S. Importer-Wm. Larkin Moore, 8430 E. Raintree Ste. B-7, Scottsdale, AZ 85260
U.S. Optics, A Division of Zeitz Optics U.S.A., 5900 Dale St., Buena Park, CA 90621 / 714-994-4901; FAX: 714-994-4904 www.usoptics.com
U.S. Repeating Arms Co., Inc., 275 Winchester Ave., Morgan, UT 84050-9333 / 801-876-3440; FAX: 801-876-3737 www.winchester-guns.com
U.S. Tactical Systems (See Keng's Firearms Specialty, Inc.)
Ugartechea S. A., Ignacio, Chonta 26, Eibar, SPAIN / 43-121257; FAX: 43-121669
Ultra Dot Distribution, P.O. Box 362, 6304 Riverside Dr., Yankeetown, FL 34498 / 352-447-2255; FAX: 352-447-2266
Ultralux (See U.S. Importer-Keng's Firearms Specialty, Inc.)
Uncle Bud's, HCR 81, Box 100, Needmore, PA 17238 / 717-294-6000; FAX: 717-294-6005
Uncle Mike's (See Michaels of Oregon, Co.)
Unertl Optical Co., Inc., 103 Grand Avenue, P.O. Box 895, Mars, PA 16046-0895 / 724-625-3810; FAX: 724-625-3819 unertl@nauticom.net www.unertloptics.com
UniTec, 1250 Bedford SW, Canton, OH 44710 / 216-452-4017
United Binocular Co., 9043 S. Western Ave., Chicago, IL 60620
United Cutlery Corp., 1425 United Blvd., Sevierville, TN 37876 / 865-428-2532 or 800-548-0835; FAX: 865-428-2267 www.unitedcutlery.com
United States Products Co., 518 Melwood Ave., Pittsburgh, PA 15213-1136 / 412-621-2130; FAX: 412-621-8740 sales@us-products.com www.usporepaste.com
Universal Sports, P.O. Box 532, Vincennes, IN 47591 / 812-882-8680; FAX: 812-882-8680
Upper Missouri Trading Co., P.O. Box 100, 304 Harold St., Crofton, NE 68730-0100 / 402-388-4844 www.uppermotradingco.com
USAC, 4500-15th St. East, Tacoma, WA 98424 / 206-922-7589
Uselton/Arms, Inc., 842 Conference Dr., Goodlettsville, TN 37072 / 615-851-4919
Utica Cutlery Co., 820 Noyes St., Utica, NY 13503 / 315-733-4663; FAX: 315-733-6602

V

V. H. Blackinton & Co., Inc., 221 John L. Dietsch, Attleboro Falls, MA 02763-0300 / 508-699-4436; FAX: 508-695-5349
Valdada Enterprises, P.O. Box 773122, 31733 County Road 35, Steamboat Springs, CO 80477 / 970-879-2983; FAX: 970-879-0851 www.valdada.com
Valtro USA, Inc., 1281 Andersen Dr., San Rafael, CA 94901 / 415-256-2575; FAX: 415-256-2576
VAM Distribution Co. LLC, 1141-B Mechanicsburg Rd., Wooster, OH 44691 www.rex10.com
Van Gorden & Son Inc., C. S., 1815 Main St., Bloomer, WI 54724 / 715-568-2612
Van Horn, Gil, P.O. Box 207, Llano, CA 93544
Van Patten, J. W., P.O. Box 145, Foster Hill, Milford, PA 18337 / 717-296-7069
Vann Custom Bullets, 2766 N. Willowside Way, Meridian, ID 83642
Varmint Masters, LLC, Rick Vecqueray, P.O. Box 6724, Bend, OR 97708 / 541-318-7306; FAX: 541-318-7306 varmintmasters@bendcable.com www.varmintmasters.net
Vecqueray, Rick. See: VARMINT MASTERS, LLC
Vector Arms, Inc., 270 W. 500 N., North Salt Lake, UT 84054 / 801-295-1917; FAX: 801-295-9316 vectorarms@bbscmail.com www.vectorarms.com
Vega Tool Co., c/o T. R. Ross, 4865 Tanglewood Ct., Boulder, CO 80301 / 303-530-0174 clanlaird@aol.com www.vegatool.com
Venco Industries, Inc. (See Shooter's Choice Gun Care)
Venus Industries, P.O. Box 246, Sialkot-1, PAKISTAN FAX: 92 432 85579
Verney-Carron, 54 Boulevard Thiers-B.P. 72, 42002 St. Etienne Cedex 1, St. Etienne Cedex 1, FRANCE / 33-477791500; FAX: 33-477790702 email@verney-carron.com www.verney-carron.com
Vest, John, 1923 NE 7th St., Redmond, OR 97756 / 541-923-8898
VibraShine, Inc., P.O. Box 577, Taylorsville, MS 39168 / 601-785-9854; FAX: 601-785-9874 rdbeke@vibrashine.com www.vibrashine.com
Vibra-Tek Co., 1844 Arroya Rd., Colorado Springs, CO 80906 / 719-634-8611; FAX: 719-634-6886
Vic's Gun Refinishing, 6 Pineview Dr., Dover, NH 03820-6422 / 603-742-0013
Victory Ammunition, P.O. Box 1022, Milford, PA 18337 / 717-296-5768; FAX: 717-296-9298
Victory USA, P.O. Box 1021, Pine Bush, NY 12566 / 914-744-2060; FAX: 914-744-5181
Vihtavuori Oy, FIN-41330 Vihtavuori, FINLAND, / 358-41-3779211; FAX: 358-41-3771643
Vihtavuori Oy/Kaltron-Pettibone, 1241 Ellis St., Bensenville, IL 60106 / 708-350-1116; FAX: 708-350-1606
Viking Video Productions, P.O. Box 251, Roseburg, OR 97470
Village Restorations & Consulting, Inc., P.O. Box 569, Claysburg, PA 16625 / 814-239-8200; FAX: 814-239-2165 www.villagerestoration@yahoo.com
Vincent's Shop, 210 Antoinette, Fairbanks, AK 99701
Viper Bullet and Brass Works, 11 Brock St., Box 582, Norwich, ON N0J 1P0 CANADA
Viramontez Engraving, Ray Viramontez, 601 Springfield Dr., Albany, GA 31721 / 229-432-9683 sgtvira@aol.com
Viramontez, Ray. See: VIRAMONTEZ ENGRAVING
Virgin Valley Custom Guns, 450 E 800 N. #20, Hurricane, UT 84737 / 435-635-8941; FAX: 435-635-8943 vvcguns@infowest.com www.virginvalleyguns.com
Visible Impact Targets, Rts. 5 & 20, E. Bloomfield, NY 14443 / 716-657-6161; FAX: 716-657-5405
Vitt/Boos, 1195 Buck Hill Rd., Townshend, VT 05353 / 802-365-9232
Voere-KGH GmbH, Untere Sparchen 56, A-6330 Kufstein, Tirol, AUSTRIA / 0043-5372-62547; FAX: 0043-5372-65752 voere@aon.com www.voere.com
Volquartsen Custom Ltd., 24276 240th Street, P.O. Box 397, Carroll, IA 51401 / 712-792-4238; FAX: 712-792-2542 info@volquartsen.com www.volquartsen.com
Vorhes, David, 3042 Beecham St., Napa, CA 94558 / 707-226-9116; FAX: 707-253-7334
VSP Publishers (See Heritage/VSP Gun Books), P.O. Box 887, McCall, ID 83638 / 208-634-4104; FAX: 208-634-3101 heritage@gunbooks.com www.gunbooks.com

VTI Gun Parts, P.O. Box 509, Lakeville, CT 06039 / 860-435-8068; FAX: 860-435-8146 mail@vtigunparts.com www.vtigunparts.com
Vulpes Ventures, Inc., Fox Cartridge Division, P.O. Box 1363, Bolingbrook, IL 60440-7363 / 630-759-1229

W

W. Square Enterprises, 9826 Sagedale Dr., Houston, TX 77089 / 281-484-0935; FAX: 281-464-9940 lfdw@pdq.net www.loadammo.com
W. Waller & Son, Inc., 52 Coventry Dr., Sunapee, NH 03782 / 603-763-3320 or 800-874-2247 FAX: 603-763-3225; waller@wallerandson.com www.wallerandson.com
W.B. Niemi Engineering, Box 126 Center Road, Greensboro, VT 05841 / 802-533-7180 or 802-533-7141
W.C. Wolff Co., P.O. Box 458, Newtown Square, PA 19073 / 610-359-9600 or 800-545-0077 mail@gunsprings.com www.gunsprings.com
W.E. Birdsong & Assoc., 1435 Monterey Rd., Florence, MS 39073-9748 / 601-366-8270
W.E. Brownell Checkering Tools, 9390 Twin Mountain Cir., San Diego, CA 92126 / 858-695-2479; FAX: 858-695-2479
W.J. Riebe Co., 3434 Tucker Rd., Boise, ID 83703
W.R. Case & Sons Cutlery Co., Owens Way, Bradford, PA 16701 / 814-368-4123 or 800-523-6350; FAX: 814-368-1736 jsullivan@wrcase.com www.wrcase.com
Wagoner, Vernon G., 2325 E. Encanto St., Mesa, AZ 85213-5107 / 480-835-1307
Waldron, Herman, Box 475, 80 N. 17th St., Pomeroy, WA 99347 / 509-843-1404
Walker Arms Co., Inc., 499 County Rd. 820, Selma, AL 36701 / 334-872-6231; FAX: 334-872-6262
Wallace, Terry, 385 San Marino, Vallejo, CA 94589 / 707-642-7041
Walls Industries, Inc., P.O. Box 98, 1905 N. Main, Cleburne, TX 76033 / 817-645-4366; FAX: 817-645-7946 www.wallsoutdoors.com
Walters Industries, 6226 Park Lane, Dallas, TX 75225 / 214-691-6973
Walters, John. See: WALTERS WADS
Walters Wads, John Walters, 500 N. Avery Dr., Moore, OK 73160 / 405-799-0376; FAX: 405-799-7727 www.tinwadman@cs.com
Walther America, P.O. Box 22, Springfield, MA 01102 / 413-747-3443 www.walther-usa.com
Walther GmbH, Carl, B.P. 4325, D-89033 Ulm, GERMANY
Walt's Custom Leather, Walt Whinnery, 1947 Meadow Creek Dr., Louisville, KY 40218 / 502-458-4361
WAMCO-New Mexico, P.O. Box 205, Peralta, NM 87042-0205 / 505-869-0826
Ward & Van Valkenburg, 114 32nd Ave. N., Fargo, ND 58102 / 701-232-2351
Ward Machine, 5620 Lexington Rd., Corpus Christi, TX 78412 / 512-992-1221
Wardell Precision, P.O. Box 391, Clyde, TX 79510-0391 / 325-893-3763 fwardell@valornet.com
Warenski Engraving, Julie Warenski, 590 E. 500 N., Richfield, UT 84701 / 435-896-5319; FAX: 435-896-8333 julie@warenskiknives.com
Warenski, Julie. See: WARENSKI ENGRAVING
Warne Manufacturing Co., 9560 SW Herman Rd., Tualatin, OR 97062 / 503-657-5590 or 800-683-5590; FAX: 503-657-5695 info@warnescopemounts.com www.warnescopemounts.com
Washita Mountain Whetstone Co., P.O. Box 20378, Hot Springs, AR 71903 / 501-525-3914 www.@hsnp.com
Wasmundt, Jim. See: J.W. WASMUNDT-GUNSMITH
Watson Bros., 39 Redcross Way, London Bridge SE1 1H6, London, ENGLAND FAX: 44-171-403-336
Watson Bullets, 231 Allies Pass, Frostproof, FL 33843 / 863-635-7948 cbestbullet@aol.com
Wayne Specialty Services, 260 Waterford Drive, Florissant, MO 63033 / 413-831-7083
WD-40 Co., 1061 Cudahy Pl., San Diego, CA 92110 / 619-275-1400; FAX: 619-275-5823
Weatherby, Inc., 3100 El Camino Real, Atascadero, CA 93422 / 805-466-1767; FAX: 805-466-2527 www.weatherby.com
Weaver Products ATK, P.O. Box 39, Onalaska, WI 54650 / 800-648-9624 or 608-781-5800; FAX: 608-781-0368
Weaver Scope Repair Service, 1121 Larry Mahan Dr., Suite B, El Paso, TX 79925 / 915-593-1005 frank@weaver-scope-repair.com www.weaver-scope-repair.com

Webb, Bill, 6504 North Bellefontaine, Kansas City, MO 64119 / 816-453-7431

Weber & Markin Custom Gunsmiths, 4-1691 Powick Rd., Kelowna, BC V1X 4L1 CANADA / 250-762-7575; FAX: 250-861-3655 www.weberandmarkinguns.com

Webley and Scott Ltd., Frankley Industrial Park, Tay Rd., Birmingham, B45 0PA ENGLAND / 011-021-453-1864; FAX: 0121-457-7846 guns@webley.co.uk www.webley.co.uk

Webster Scale Mfg. Co., P.O. Box 188, Sebring, FL 33870 / 813-385-6362

Weems, Cecil, 510 W. Hubbard St., Mineral Wells, TX 76067-4847 / 817-325-1462

Weigand Combat Handguns, Inc., 1057 South Main Rd., Mountain Top, PA 18707 / 570-868-8358; FAX: 570-868-5218 sales@jackweigand.com www.jackweigand.com

Weihrauch KG, Hermann, Industriestrasse 11, 8744 Mellrichstadt, Mellrichstadt, GERMANY

Welch, Sam. See: SAM WELCH GUN ENGRAVING

Wellington Outdoors, P.O. Box 244, 1140 Monticello Rd., Madison, GA 30650 / 706-342-4915; FAX: 706-342-7568

Wells, Rachel, 110 N. Summit St., Prescott, AZ 86301 / 928-445-3655 wellssportstore@cableone.net

Wells Creek Knife & Gun Works, 32956 State Hwy. 38, Scottsburg, OR 97473 / 541-587-4202; FAX: 541-587-4223

Welsh, Bud. See: HIGH PRECISION

Wenger North America/Precise Int'l., 15 Corporate Dr., Orangeburg, NY 10962 / 800-431-2996; FAX: 914-425-4700

Wenig Custom Gunstocks, 103 N. Market St., P.O. Box 249, Lincoln, MO 65338 / 660-547-3334; FAX: 660-547-2881 gustock@wenig.com www.wenig.com

Werth, T. W., 1203 Woodlawn Rd., Lincoln, IL 62656 / 217-732-1300; FAX: 217-735-5106

Wescombe, Bill (See North Star West)

Wessinger Custom Guns & Engraving, 268 Limestone Rd., Chapin, SC 29036 / 803-345-5677

West, Jack L., 1220 W. Fifth, P.O. Box 427, Arlington, OR 97812

Western Cutlery (See Camillus Cutlery Co.)

Western Mfg. Co., 550 Valencia School Rd., Aptos, CA 95003 / 831-688-5884 lotsabears@eathlink.net

Western Missouri Shooters Alliance, P.O. Box 11144, Kansas City, MO 64119 / 816-597-3950; FAX: 816-229-7350

Western Nevada West Coast Bullets, P.O. Box 2270, Dayton, NV 89403-2270 / 702-246-3941; FAX: 702-246-0836

Westley Richards & Co. Ltd., 40 Grange Rd., Birmingham, ENGLAND / 010-214722953; FAX: 010-214141138 sales@westleyrichards.com www.westleyrichards.com

Westley Richards Agency USA (See U.S. Importer)

Westwind Rifles, Inc., David S. Sullivan, P.O. Box 261, 640 Briggs St., Erie, CO 80516 / 303-828-3823

Weyer International, 2740 Nebraska Ave., Toledo, OH 43607 / 419-534-2020; FAX: 419-534-2697

Whinnery, Walt (See Walt's Custom Leather)

White Barn Wor, 431 County Road, Broadlands, IL 61816

White Pine Photographic Services, Hwy. 60, General Delivery, Wilno, ON K0J 2N0 CANADA / 613-756-3452

White Rifles, Inc., 234 S. 1250 W., Linden, UT 84042 / 801-932-7950 www.whiterifles.com

White Rock Tool & Die, 6400 N. Brighton Ave., Kansas City, MO 64119 / 816-454-0478

Whitestone Lumber Corp., 148-02 14th Ave., Whitestone, NY 11357 / 718-746-4400; FAX: 718-767-1748 whstco@aol.com

Wichita Arms, Inc., 923 E. Gilbert, Wichita, KS 67211 / 316-265-0661; FAX: 316-265-0760 sales@wichitaarms.com www.wichitaarms.com

Wick, David E., 1504 Michigan Ave., Columbus, IN 47201 / 812-376-6960

Widener's Reloading & Shooting Supply, Inc., P.O. Box 3009 CRS, Johnson City, TN 37602 / 615-282-6786; FAX: 615-282-6651

Wideview Scope Mount Corp., 13535 S. Hwy. 16, Rapid City, SD 57702 / 605-341-3220; FAX: 605-341-9142 wvdon@rapidnet.com www.wideviewscopemount.com

Wiebe, Duane, 1111 157th St. Ct. E., Tacoma, WA 98445 / 530-344-1357; FAX: 530-344-1357 duane@directcom.net

Wiest, Marie. See: GUNCRAFT SPORTS, INC.

Wilcox All-Pro Tools & Supply, 4880 147th St., Montezuma, IA 50171 / 515-623-3138; FAX: 515-623-3104

Wilcox Industries Corp., Robert F. Guarasi, 53 Durham St., Portsmouth, NH 03801 / 603-431-1331; FAX: 603-431-1221

Wild Bill's Originals, P.O. Box 13037, Burton, WA 98013 / 206-463-5738; FAX: 206-465-5925 billcleaver@centurytel.net billcleaver@centurytel.net

Wild West Guns, 7100 Homer Dr., Anchorage, AK 99518 / 800-992-4570 or 907-344-4500; FAX: 907-344-4005 wwguns@ak.net www.wildwestguns.com

Wilderness Sound Products Ltd., 4015 Main St. A, Springfield, OR 97478

Wildey F. A., Inc., 45 Angevin Rd., Warren, CT 06754-1818 / 860-355-9000; FAX: 860-354-7759 wildeyfa@optonline.net www.wildeyguns.com

Wildlife Research Center, Inc., 1050 McKinley St., Anoka, MN 55303 / 763-427-3350 or 800-USE-LURE; (873-5873) FAX: 763-427-8354 www.wildlife.com

Will-Burt Co., 169 S. Main, Orrville, OH 44667

William E. Phillips Firearms, 38 Avondale Rd., Wigston, Leicester, ENGLAND / 0116 2886334; FAX: 0116 2810644 william.phillips2@tesco.net

William Powell Agency, 22 Circle Dr., Bellmore, NY 11710 / 516-679-1158

Williams Gun Sight Co., 7389 Lapeer Rd., Box 329, Davison, MI 48423 / 810-653-2131 or 800-530-9028; FAX: 810-658-2140 williamsgunsight.com

Williams Mfg. of Oregon, 110 East B St., Drain, OR 97435 / 503-836-7461; FAX: 503-836-7245

Williams Shootin' Iron Service, The Lynx-Line, Rt. 2 Box 223A, Mountain Grove, MO 65711 / 417-948-0902; FAX: 417-948-0902

Williamson Precision Gunsmithing, 117 W. Pipeline, Hurst, TX 76053 / 817-285-0064; FAX: 817-280-0044

Willow Bend, P.O. Box 203, Chelmsford, MA 01824 / 978-256-8508; FAX: 978-256-8508

Wilsom Combat, 2234 CR 719, Berryville, AR 72616-4573 / 800-955-4856; FAX: 870-545-3310 info@wilsoncombat.com www.wilsoncombat.com

Wilson Arms Co., The, 63 Leetes Island Rd., Branford, CT 06405 / 203-488-7297; FAX: 203-488-0135

Wilson Case, Inc., P.O. Box 1106, Hastings, NE 68902-1106 / 800-322-5493; FAX: 402-463-5276 sales@wilsoncase.com www.wilsoncase.com

Wilson Combat, 2234 CR 719, Berryville, AR 72616-4573 / 800-955-4856

Winchester Consultants, George Madis, P.O. Box 545, Brownsboro, TX 75756 / 903-852-6480; FAX: 903-852-5486 gmadis@earthlink.com www.georgemadis.com

Winchester Div. Olin Corp., 427 N. Shamrock, E. Alton, IL 62024 / 618-258-3566; FAX: 618-258-3599

Winchester Sutler, Inc., The, 270 Shadow Brook Lane, Winchester, VA 22603 / 540-888-3595; FAX: 540-888-4632

Windish, Jim, 2510 Dawn Dr., Alexandria, VA 22306 / 703-765-1994

Winfield Galleries LLC, 748 Hanley Industrial Ct., St. Louis, MO 63144 / 314-645-7636; FAX: 314-781-0224 info@winfieldgalleries.com www.winfieldgalleries.com

Wingshooting Adventures, 0-1845 W. Leonard, Grand Rapids, MI 49544 / 616-677-1980; FAX: 616-677-1986

Winter, Robert M., P.O. Box 484, 42975-287th St., Menno, SD 57045 / 605-387-5322

Wise Custom Guns, 1402 Blanco Rd., San Antonio, TX 78212-2716 / 210-828-3388

Wise Guns, Dale, 1402 Blanco Rd., San Antonio, TX 78212 / 210-734-9999

Wiseman and Co., Bill, P.O. Box 3427, Bryan, TX 77805 / 409-690-3456; FAX: 409-690-0156

Wisners, Inc., P.O. Box 58, Adna, WA 98522 / 360-748-4590; FAX: 360-748-6028 parts@wisnersinc.com www.wisnersinc.com

Wolf Performance Ammunition, 2201 E. Winston Rd., Ste. K, Anaheim, CA 92806-5537 / 702-837-8506; FAX: 702-837-9250

Wolfe Publishing Co., 2625 Stearman Rd., Ste. A, Prescott, AZ 86301 / 928-445-7810 or 800-899-7810; FAX: 928-778-5124 wolfepub@riflemag.com www.riflemagazine.com

Wolverine Footwear Group, 9341 Courtland Dr. NE, Rockford, MI 49351 / 616-866-5500; FAX: 616-866-5658

Woodleigh (See Huntington Die Specialties)

Woods Wise Products, P.O. Box 681552, Franklin, TN 37068 / 800-735-8182; FAX: 615-726-2637

Woodstream, P.O. Box 327, Lititz, PA 17543 / 717-626-2125; FAX: 717-626-1912

Woodworker's Supply, 1108 North Glenn Rd., Casper, WY 82601 / 307-237-5354

Woolrich, Inc., Mill St., Woolrich, PA 17701 / 800-995-1299; FAX: 717-769-6234/6259

World of Targets (See Birchwood Casey)

World Trek, Inc., 7170 Turkey Creek Rd., Pueblo, CO 81007-1046 / 719-546-2121; FAX: 719-543-6886

Worthy Products, Inc., RR 1, P.O. Box 213, Martville, NY 13111 / 315-324-5298

Wright's Gunstock Blanks, 8540 SE Kane Rd., Gresham, OR 97080 / 503-666-1705 doyal@wrightsguns.com www.wrightsguns.com

WTA Manufacturing, P.O. Box 164, Kit Carson, CO 80825 / 719-962-3570 or 719-962-3570 wta@rebeltec.net http://www.members.aol.com/ductman249/wta.html

Wyant Bullets, Gen. Del., Swan Lake, MT 59911

Wyoming Custom Bullets, 1626 21st St., Cody, WY 82414

Wyoming Knife Corp., 101 Commerce Dr., Fort Collins, CO 80524 / 303-224-3454

X

XS Sight Systems, 2401 Ludelle St., Fort Worth, TX 76105 / 888-744-4880; FAX: 800-734-7939

X-Spand Target Systems, 26-10th St. SE, Medicine Hat, AB T1A 1P7 CANADA / 403-526-7997; FAX: 403-528-2362

Y

Yankee Gunsmith "Just Glocks", 2901 Deer Flat Dr., Copperas Cove, TX 76522 / 817-547-8433; FAX: 254-547-8887 ed@justglocks.com www.justglocks.com

Yavapai College, 1100 E. Sheldon St., Prescott, AZ 86301 / 520-776-2353; FAX: 520-776-2355

Yavapai Firearms Academy Ltd., P.O. Box 27290, Prescott Valley, AZ 86312 / 928-772-8262; FAX: 928-772-0062 info@yfainc.com www.yfainc.com

Yearout, Lewis E. (See Montana Outfitters)

Yellowstone Wilderness Supply, P.O. Box 129, West Yellowstone, MT 59758 / 406-646-7613

Yesteryear Armory & Supply, P.O. Box 408, Carthage, TN 37030

York M-1 Conversion, 12145 Mill Creek Run, Plantersville, TX 77363 / 936-894-2397; FAX: 936-894-2397 bmf25years@aol.com

Young Country Arms, William, 1409 Kuehner Dr. #13, Simi Valley, CA 93063-4478

Z

Zabala Hermanos S.A., P.O. Box 97, Elbar Lasao, 6, Elgueta, Guipuzcoa, 20600 SPAIN / 34-943-768076; FAX: 34-943-768201 imanol@zabalahermanos.com www.zabalabermanos.com

Zander's Sporting Goods, 7525 Hwy. 154 West, Baldwin, IL 62217-9706 / 800-851-4373; FAX: 618-785-2320

Zanotti Armor, Inc., 123 W. Lone Tree Rd., Cedar Falls, IA 50613 / 319-232-9650 www.zanottiarmor.com

Zeeryp, Russ, 1601 Foard Dr., Lynn Ross Manor, Morristown, TN 37814 / 615-586-2357

Zero Ammunition Co., Inc., 1601 22nd St. SE, P.O. Box 1188, Cullman, AL 35056-1188 / 800-545-9376; FAX: 205-739-4683 zerobulletco@aoz.com www.zerobullets.com

Ziegel Engineering, 1390 E. Bunnett St. "F", Signal Hill, CA 90755 / 562-596-9481; FAX: 562-598-4734 ziegel@aol.com www.ziegeleng.com

Zim's, Inc., 4370 S. 3rd West, Salt Lake City, UT 84107 / 801-268-2505

Z-M Weapons, 203 South St., Bernardston, MA 01337 / 413-648-9501; FAX: 413-648-0219

NUMBERS

100 Straight Products, Inc., P.O. Box 6148, Omaha, NE 68106 / 402-556-1055; FAX: 402-556-1055

3-Ten Corp., P.O. Box 269, Feeding Hills, MA 01030 / 413-789-2086; FAX: 413-789-1549 www.3-ten.com

4-D Custom Die Co., 711 N. Sandusky St., P.O. Box 889, Mt. Vernon, OH 43050-0889 / 740-397-7214; FAX: 740-397-6600 info@ch4d.com ch4d.com

W9-BQS-724

Instructor's Manual

Electronic Health Records:

Understanding and Using Computerized Medical Records

Richard Gartee

PEARSON
Prentice
Hall

Upper Saddle River, New Jersey 07458

10 9 8 7 6 5 4 3 2 1
ISBN 0-13-232911-5

Table of Contents

Chapter 7 **Using the EHR to Improve Patient Care 97**

Chapter 8 **Privacy and Security of Health Records 110**

Chapter 9 **EHR and Technology 121**

Contents of Instructor's Resource CD

Readme.txt

Test Gen

PowerPoint Files

Chapter 1—presented in two parts, plus a chapter summary review and a post-test review (4 files)

Chapter 2—presented in two parts, plus a chapter summary review and a post-test review (4 files)

Chapter 3—presented in three parts, plus a chapter summary review and a post-test review (5 files)

Chapter 4—presented in four parts, plus a chapter summary review and a post-test review (6 files)

Chapter 5—presented in three parts, plus a chapter summary review and a post-test review (5 files)

Comprehensive Evaluation 1–5—post-test review presented in two files

Chapter 6—presented in four parts, plus a chapter summary review and a post-test review (6 files)

Chapter 7—presented in three parts, plus a chapter summary review and a post-test review (5 files)

Chapter 8—presented in three parts, plus a chapter summary review and a post-test review (5 files)

Chapter 9—presented in three parts, plus a chapter summary review and a post-test review (5 files)

Comprehensive Evaluation 6–9—post-test review presented in two files

Exercise Print To HTML Files

fig3–57_rosa_garcia.htm

fig4–14_harold_baker.htm

fig4–31_gary_yamamoto.htm

fig4–50_kerry_baker.htm

fig4–67_terry_chun.htm

fig5–33_m_williams.htm

fig5–37_m_williams_counseling.htm

fig5–55_gloria_natell.htm

fig5–56_exam_(c_brown).htm

fig6–24_juan_garcia.htm

fig6–44_greg_natell.htm

fig7–23_daniels.htm

fig7–49_t_williams.htm

fig9–40_greensher.htm

fig9–44_exam_green.htm

Preface

Thank you for teaching *Electronic Health Records: Understanding and Using Computerized Medical Records.* As you may be aware from the popular media or have read in the textbook introduction, there is a rapidly spreading push to adopt electronic health records (EHR) at every level of health care in America. I believe that you as a teacher, using this textbook, will contribute to our nation's transition to an EHR. Let me explain why I believe this is so.

Many medical practices and hospitals are in the process of evaluating, purchasing, or installing an EHR today or in the near future. There are a number of excellent books that provide advice on evaluating vendors, purchasing a system, and even training and implementation suggestions.

In the health care business world EHR decisions are being made from the top down. Typically, an organization forms a committee of doctors, computer professionals, and business managers to evaluate vendors and eventually recommend an EHR system. The most common implementation strategy is to identify enthusiastic doctors or nurses and make them team leaders as the organization sets about the task of training the rest of the employees. Numerous articles and books discuss the problems that practices encounter during implementation even with this approach.

The top-down approach to EHR training and implementation alone will not be sufficient. What is going to be required for the nation to succeed is for a large portion of the health care workforce to have experience with the general use, concepts, and principles of an EHR.

As teachers you have already experienced how varied the levels of computer proficiency can be in a class of new students. Therefore, it may not surprise you to learn that among health care professionals there are similar variances and a good deal of trepidation at the thought of using an EHR with their patients. Overcoming this is where I believe your course is going to have an impact on medicine.

The purpose of this book is not to train a particular brand of EHR system but rather to build, through practical experience, an understanding and a comfort with computerized medical records that can be directly applied in the clinical setting. Students who complete this course will more readily understand and be able to use whatever EHR they find in the workplace. Your students may very well lead the EHR implementation at their clinics.

This unique book may be the first of its kind for teaching electronic health records; as such this course may be new for you as well. In this manual, I have endeavored to provide you with tips and suggestions to make your task a little easier. The accompanying Instructor's Resource CD includes PowerPoint presentations for every chapter. TestGen, and a folder of files that are output by the Print to HTML feature of the software.

The HTML files have a two-fold purpose: first they can be used by instructors for comparison to student files, second they are used by the PowerPoint slides to display exercise output. (Note that links within the files are inactive and will report "Page not found" if clicked. See the section titled "Distance Learning Print To HTML Option" in the Installation chapter.) The "readme.txt" file on the Instructor's Resource CD contains a list of the HTML and PowerPoint files.

It is my hope that with your teaching skills, and the combination of the *Electronic Health Records* textbook and the Student Edition software, we will create thousands of doctors, nurses, medical assistants, and clinical staff who complement the top-down approach to EHR implementation at their facility by becoming the grassroots—individuals well grounded in understanding and using computerized medical records.

Richard Gartee

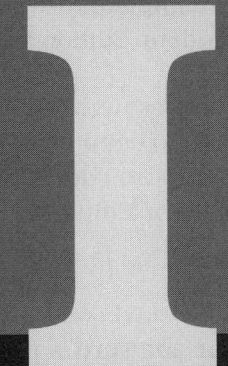

Installation of the Student Edition Software

Contents

This section contains the following information about installation:

Overview

The combination of the *Electronic Health Records* textbook and the Student Edition software provides a complete learning system. To complete the exercises in the textbook students will need to use the Medcin® Student Edition software.

There are two configurations for this software: client/server network installation and local installation on individual workstations. Instructions for both network and local installations are provided later. There are also copies of the installation instructions in two readme files on the Student Edition installation CD.

If you are teaching this course in a classroom with networked computers, the client/server network installation is recommended. The software is provided on a CD supplied to schools by Prentice Hall. Alternatively, schools that do not have networks may install the software on individual classroom workstations by following the instructions for local installation provided later.

If students are in a distance learning program or working independently, they will need to purchase the software CD (ISBN 0-13-178937-6) and follow the directions for local installation included with the CD.

When you insert the Medcin Student Edition software CD into the CD-ROM drive of the computer, the install program should run automatically. If it does not start up automatically, you can start it manually by clicking on the Windows Start button, then click on the Run option. Type "d:\autorun.exe" in the field that is displayed, then click OK. (Note that 'd:' should be replaced with the drive letter of your CD-ROM drive.)

Minimum Workstation Requirements

Processor: 200 mHz Pentium

Windows XP, Windows 2000 (or later) with MDAC component (2.6 or later) installed

CD-ROM drive

RAM: 64 megabytes (free not counting OS)

Number of colors: 256 (8 bit color)

Display size (pixels per inch): 800 × 600 (1024 × 768 recommended)

Mouse with at least two buttons (for left and right click)

Internet Explorer 5.5 or later

Microsoft.Net Framework version 1.1 or later

Before the installation, the install routine will verify the version of the Windows MDAC component. If it is not current, the installation will stop. You must update the operating system to continue. The update is available online from Microsoft.

During the installation, the install routine will also verify the version of Microsoft.Net Framework. If it is not current, an updated version will be installed from the CD.

Printers

The Student Edition software uses standard Windows print services and should be compatible with most printers.

Local Installation on Individual Workstations

Follow these instructions if you are a student installing the software on your own computer or a school using individual (nonnetworked) computers.

Step 1 Remove any previous installation of the Medcin Student Edition before reinstalling this software. Follow the steps in the section titled "Uninstalling the Medcin Server and Student Edition Software."

Step 2 Insert the Medcin Student Edition software CD into the CD drive of the computer. The install program will run automatically. When the screen shown in Figure I-1 is displayed, locate and click on the button labeled "Next."

▶ **Figure I-1 Medcin Student Edition Setup Wizard**

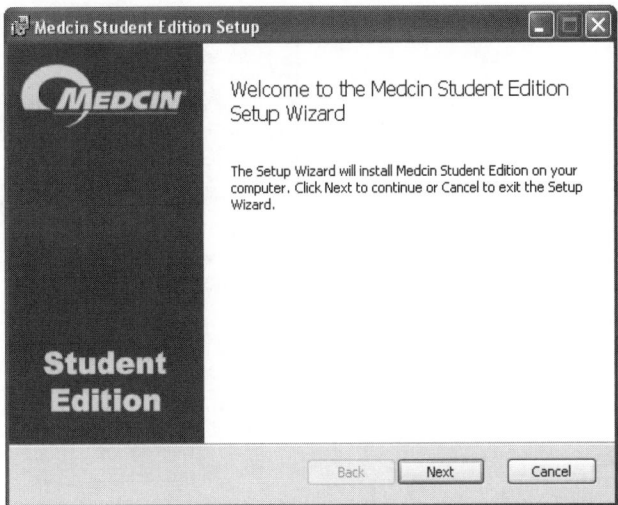

If instead of Figure I-1 you see the screen displayed in Figure I-15, you have not removed the previous installation. Refer to the section titled "Uninstalling the Medcin Server and Student Edition Software."

If instead of Figure I-1 you see the error message displayed in Figure I-18, your version of the Windows operating system is not up-to-date or is missing a required component. The installation will not proceed until you update the Windows component. Refer to the section titled "Updating Windows MDAC."

Step 3 Locate and click on the button labeled "Local" as shown in Figure I-2. The confirmation screen shown in Figure I-3 will be displayed.

Step 4 If you need to change your selection, click on the button labeled "Back." When you are ready to proceed, locate and click the button labeled "Install." The program will begin copying the files, as shown in Figure I-4.

► Figure I-2 Choose Setup
Type Local

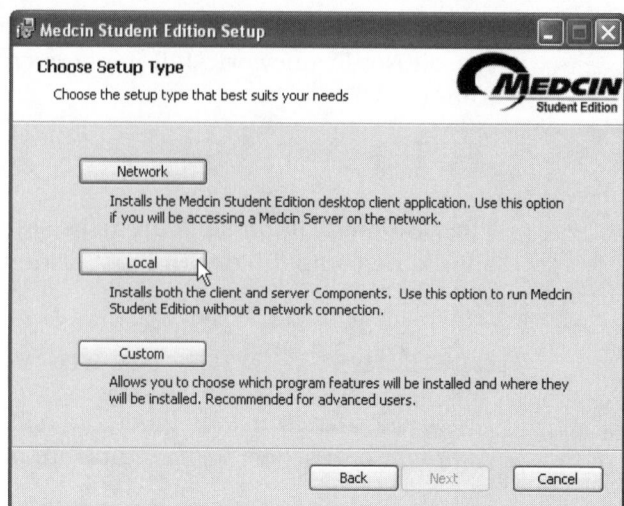

► Figure I-3 Installation
Confirmation Screen

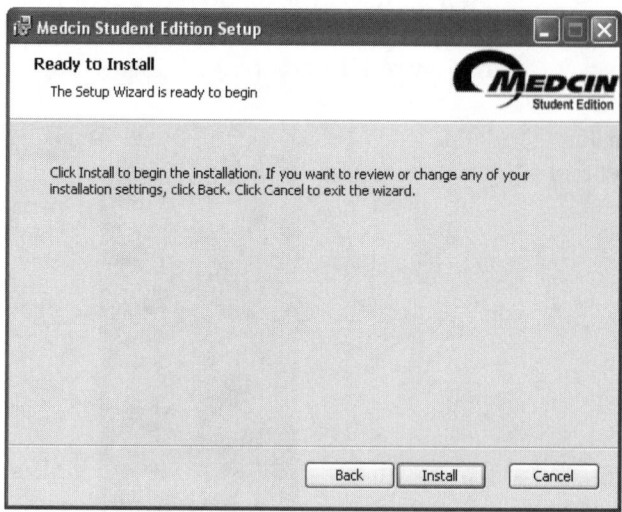

► Figure I-4 Green Bar in
Window Indicates Progress
of Installation

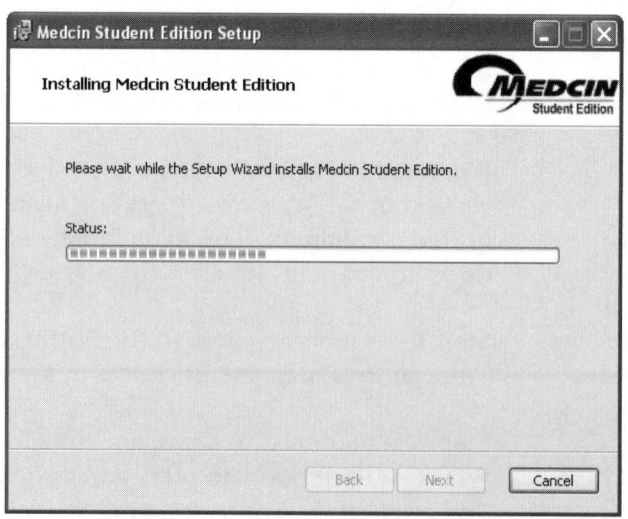

Note

If you have firewall software on your computer, during or after the installation of the Medcin Server component you may see a message from your firewall software similar to Figure I-5 If this occurs, select the option to Always Allow Connections to Medcinserv.exe.

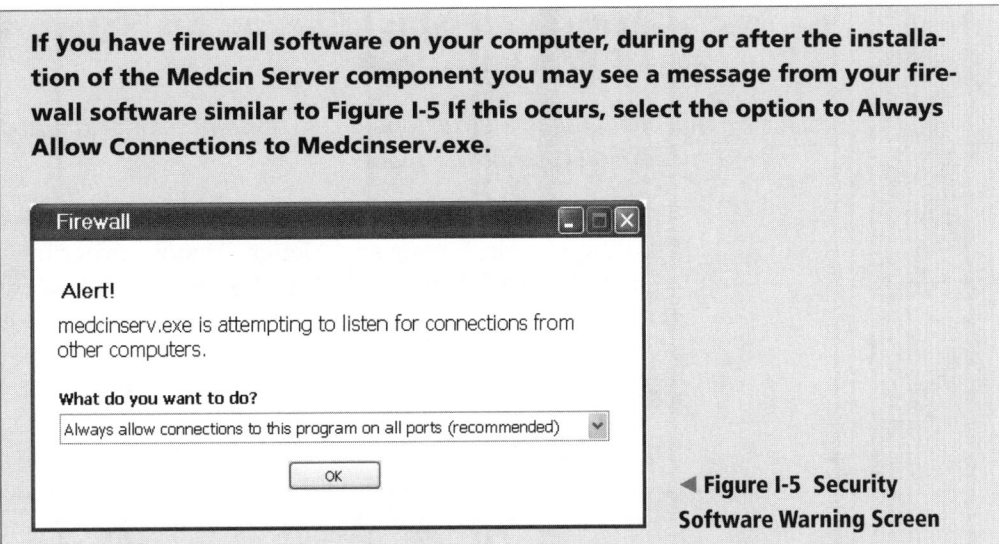

◀ **Figure I-5 Security Software Warning Screen**

Step 5 When installation has been completed, the screen shown in Figure I-6 will be displayed. Locate and click the button labeled "Finish."

When you install the Student Edition software, the Medcin Server will run automatically. The server should minimize itself. If it does not, you can click the button labeled "Hide" as shown in Figure I-7. The Medcin Server must be running to use the Student Edition software. You do not have to shut down the Medcin Server when you are through with your exercises.

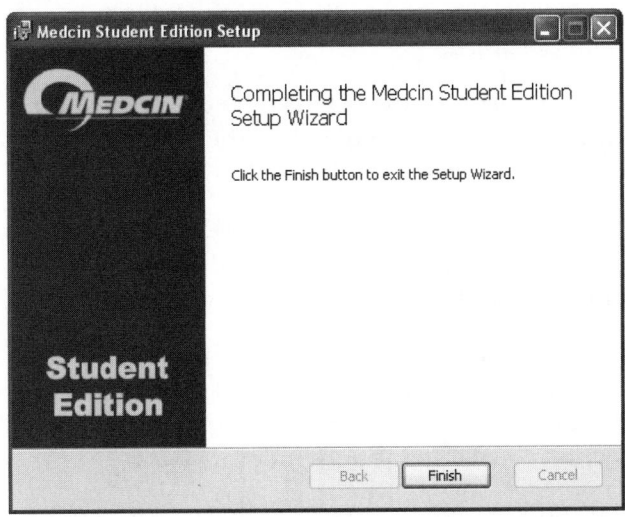

▲ **Figure I-6 Click the Button Labeled "Finish" to Complete Installation**

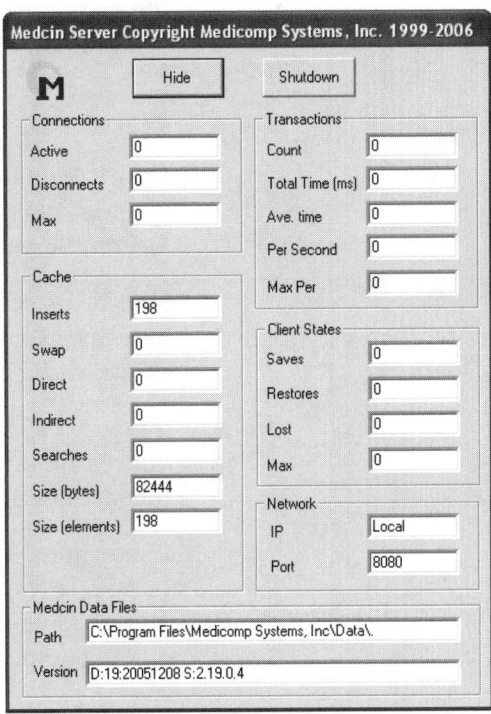

▲ **Figure I-7 Medcin Server**

Client/Server Installation on Network Server and Workstations

Follow these instructions if you are a network administrator installing the software on a school network.

The most efficient use of computer resources for classroom instruction is to install the Medcin Server and Medcin History programs on a network server and to install the Medcin Student Edition client on each workstation. Server installation should be installed by someone with network administrator privileges.

Technical Information

The Medcin Server installs and runs as a "service." It will automatically start anytime the server is booted. It has a shutdown procedure that may be used if necessary; however, the Medcin Server is required for all student exercises and should, therefore, be left running at all times.

The Medcin Server will default to use port 8080. You will have an option to change the port number. If you do so, you will need to know the new port number as you install each client workstation.

The Medcin History program is not a service and does not start automatically; however, it is required while students are working exercises in the last third of the book. Therefore, it is recommended that you add the program "Medcin History Pool Loader" to the list of programs that automatically start when the server boots.

The Student Edition software uses a standard Windows component MDAC to access its data. This component is part of the operating system and should already be on the server and all workstations. The installation routine will verify the component is up-to-date; if it is not, you will need to update the Windows component. Refer to the section titled "Updating Windows MDAC."

Installation of the Medcin Server

Step 1 Remove any previous installation of the Medcin Server before reinstalling this software. Follow the steps in the section titled "Uninstalling the Medcin Server and Student Edition Software."

Step 2 Insert the Medcin Student Edition software CD into the CD drive of the network server. The install program will run automatically. When the screen shown in Figure I-1 is displayed, locate and click on the button labeled "Next."

If instead of Figure I-1 you see the screen displayed in Figure I-15, you have not removed the previous installation. Refer to the section titled "Uninstalling the Medcin Server and Student Edition Software."

If instead of Figure I-1 you see the error message displayed in Figure I-18, your version of the Windows operating system is not up-to-date or is missing a required component. The installation will not proceed until you update the Windows component. Refer to the section titled "Updating Windows MDAC."

Step 3 Locate and click on the button labeled "Custom" as shown in Figure I-8. Note: The button labeled "Network" is used for installation of the Medcin Client (not the server).

▶ **Figure I-8 Choose Setup Type Custom to Install Network Server**

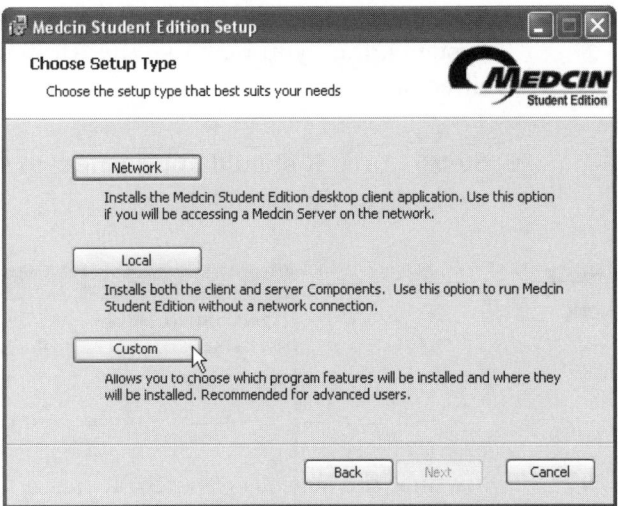

▶ **Figure I-9 Expand List and Select Student Edition Client to Modify**

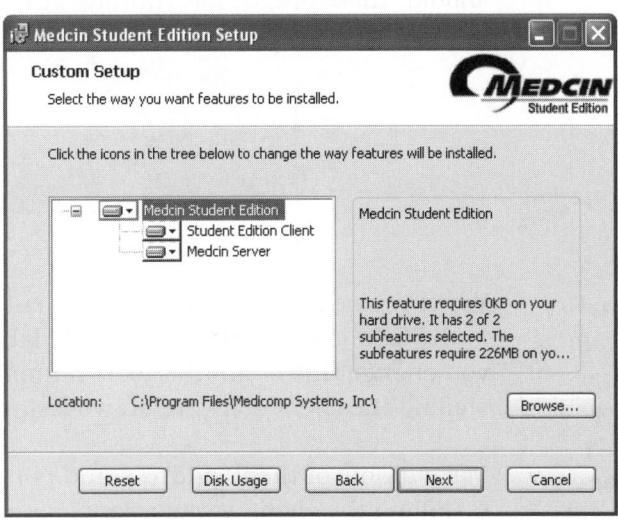

Step 4 Expand the selection components of the Student Edition by clicking on the plus sign. All components are selected. Locate and click on the drop-down arrow next to Student Edition Client and deselect it (as shown in Figure I-10).

▶ **Figure I-10 Click Down Arrow and Select "Entire Feature Will Be Unavailable"**

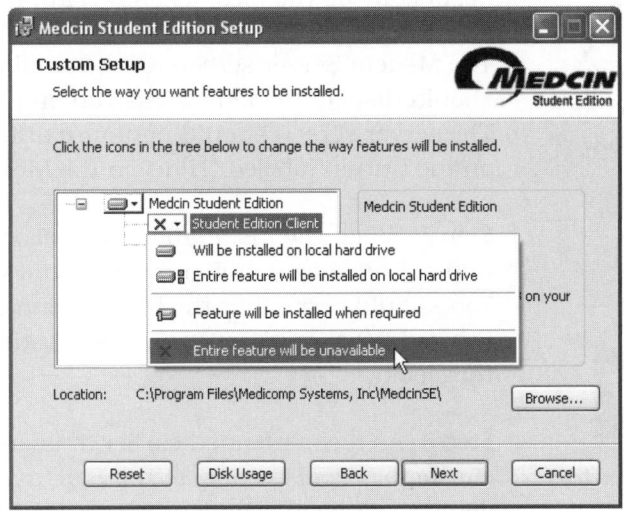

The installation will default the program path to "C:\program files\medicomp systems, inc"; you may use the "Browse" button to select an alternate directory.

Step 5 A red X should appear next to the Student Edition Client. Click "Next" to continue the installation.

▶ **Figure I-11 Enter the IP Address of the Network Server**

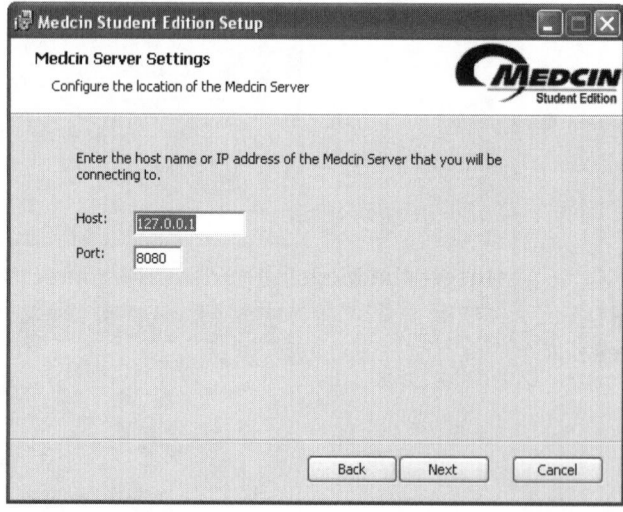

Note

During the installation, the install routine will register and attempt to start the Medcin Server. If you are running a firewall program, you may be prompted to create a rule to permit the program to run on the network (similar to the message shown Figure I-5). Set the firewall to Always Allow Connections to medcinserv.exe.

When the next screen is displayed, enter the IP address of the network server in the field labeled "Host." The field labeled "Port" will default to port 8080. If you change this to another port number, make a note of it for the persons installing the client software on workstations.

Make a note of the IP address and port number as they will be required when installing the client workstations.

Click on the "Next" button.

Step 6 A confirmation screen similar to Figure I-3 will be displayed. If you need to change your selection, click on the button labeled "Back"; when you are ready to proceed, locate and click the button labeled "Install." The program will begin copying the files, as shown in Figure I-4.

The Medcin Server screen will be similar to Figure I-7, except that the IP field should display the IP address you entered at Step 4 instead of the word "Local." The server screen should minimize automatically. If it does not, locate and click on the button labeled "Hide" in the Medcin Server window.

Step 7 When the installation has been completed, click the button labeled "Finish" as shown in Figure I-6. You do not have to reboot the network server. You should verify that the Medcin Server is running. A small icon similar to Figure I-12 should appear in the Windows Taskbar notification area (near the clock).

▲ **Figure I-12 Medcin Icon in Windows Taskbar**

Step 8 As recommended earlier, it is suggested that you add the program "Medcin History Pool Loader" to the Startup group. This program is required for students to perform exercises in the last half of the book. You will minimize hassles for the instructor if you set it up to auto start whenever the network reboots.

The program you want to add to Startup is located in the server directory below the program files directory selected in Step 4. The default directory is "C:\program files\medicomp systems, inc\server." The history program name is "MedcinHP.exe." Add a shortcut for the program to the Windows Startup group.

Installation of Workstation Client Software

Step 1 Proceed to each workstation and install the Student Edition Client software.

Installing the client requires the IP address of the network server and port number (which defaults to 8080).

Insert the Medcin Student Edition software CD into the CD drive of the workstation. The install program will run automatically. When the screen shown in Figure I-1 is displayed, locate and click on the button labeled "Next."

If instead of Figure I-1 you see the error message displayed in Figure I-18, the version of the Windows operating system on the workstation is not up-to-date or is missing a required component. Refer to the section titled "Updating Windows MDAC."

Note if workstations do not have CD drives a person with network access may be able to run the setup program remotely by leaving the CD on the main server and browsing to the network server.

Step 2 Locate and click on the button labeled "Network" as shown in Figure I-13.

▶ **Figure I-13 Choose Setup Type Network to Install Workstation Client**

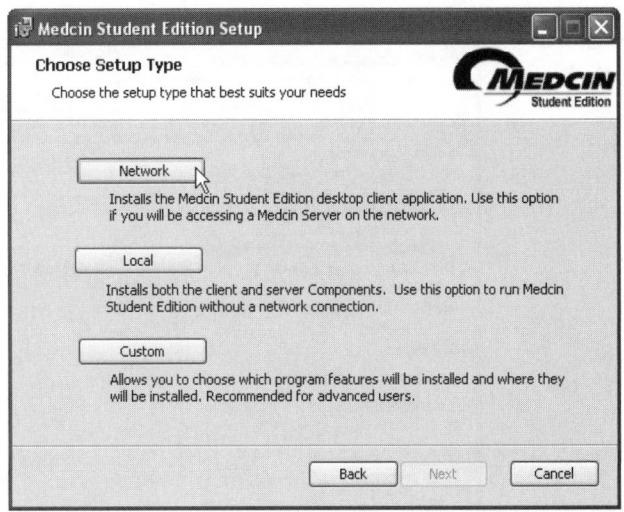

Step 3 When the next screen (similar to Figure I-11) is displayed, enter the IP address of the network server in the field labeled "Host" and enter the port number in the field labeled "Port." The default port is 8080.

The correct value for both of these fields will be provided by the network administrator who installed the Medcin Server on your network.

Note

During the installation, the install program will attempt to verify the connection to the Medcin Server via the network. If you have firewall software on the workstation computers, you may see a message from your firewall software similar to Figure I-5. If this occurs, select the option to Always Allow Connections to Medcinserv.exe.

Step 4 Click the button labeled "Next." A confirmation screen similar to Figure I-3 will be displayed.

If you need to change your selection, click on the button labeled "Back"; when you are ready to proceed, locate and click the button labeled "Install." The program will begin copying the files, as shown in Figure I-4.

Step 5 When the installation has been completed, click the button labeled "Finish" as shown in Figure I-6.

Step 6 Test the installation by locating and clicking on the Medcin icon on the desktop. When the login screen appears, enter your name and click the "OK" button. If the program starts without displaying an error, the server and client are installed correctly and communicating. Exit the program without printing or saving.

Distance Learning—Print to HTML Option

To allow students from multiple classes to share the same computer and to avoid complications caused by saving and backing up exercise data, no exercise in the Student Edition requires the students to save their work. All work is printed using the Windows standard; any Windows-compatible printer should work.

For distance learning or other situations when the instructor desires a file instead of a printout, the software will allow the student to "Print to HTML." This will output the exercise printout into a file that can be e-mailed or given to the instructor. The instructor will be able to open and view the student's work with an ordinary Web browser, such as Microsoft Internet Explorer as shown in Figure I-14.

▶ Figure I-14 Browser View of Patient Note Created with Print to HTML

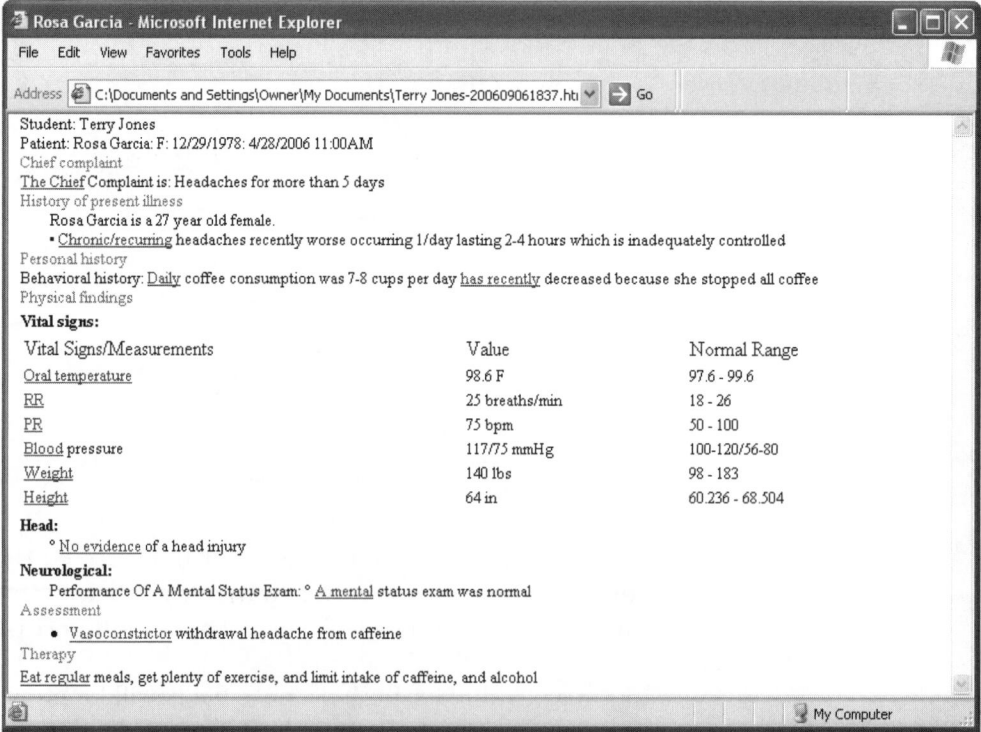

The files are always created in the directory "My Documents" of the currently logged on user. The file name is the student ID (as entered in the login screen) followed by a number representing the date and time of creation. The file extension is ".htm." If students are using "Print to HTML" on computers shared with other students, remember the files will accumulate and will eventually need to be deleted.

If you prefer to receive student work in the form of a file instead of a printout, please provide students with directions on how to transfer files to you and how to capture the graphic exercises. You may wish to establish a procedure or create a batch file for the transfer of student files to the instructor.

There are five exercises in the book in which the student prints a graph or picture. These can not print to the HTML file; thus, distance learning students will have to mail the printout or follow alternate directions from the instructor.

One alternative for printed graphs and annotated drawings is to have students capture the graph screen by using the Windows print screen feature and save it using the Windows Paint program. Sample instructions are as follows:

1. While the graph window is displaying the image, simultaneously press the keys on your keyboard marked [CTRL] and [PRT SCR].

2. Open the Windows Paint program.

3. Select the Edit Menu. Select Paste.

4. Select the File Menu. Select "Save As."

5. Enter your student ID and the exercise number in the field labeled "File Name," for example, "Terry Jones-43.bmp."

6. Take note of the directory you are about to save in, so you can find your file later; then click on the button labeled "Save."

7. Exit the Paint program.

8. Give the file to your instructor.

Tip! If students save files as a "JPG" type instead of a "BMP," you can view those files in a browser and they will be smaller to e-mail. This step requires extra instruction to the students.

The Student Edition History Program

The Student Edition software uses data from a patient history pool loaded in RAM on the server. The special program "MedcinHP.exe" that loads the history must remain running while students perform exercises in Chapter 6, Chapter 7, and the comprehensive evaluation exercise in Chapter 9.

Students working on local installations of the Student Edition must manually start the History program **before** starting the Student Edition software while working exercises in these chapters.

Network installations need run only one copy of the History Program, that is, the one on the network server that is running the Medcin Server. It is suggested that network installations add "Medcin History Pool Loader" to the Start group, so that Windows will automatically run the program whenever the server is rebooted. Once loaded, the program can be minimized. For further details on the Student Edition History program, see Appendix B.

Uninstalling or Repairing the Student Edition Software

Repairing an Installation

Follow these instructions if you have reason to believe program files of the software have been deleted or damaged or if you wish to modify the installation parameters.

Insert the Student Edition software CD in the CD drive of the computer. The screen shown in Figure I-15 will be displayed.

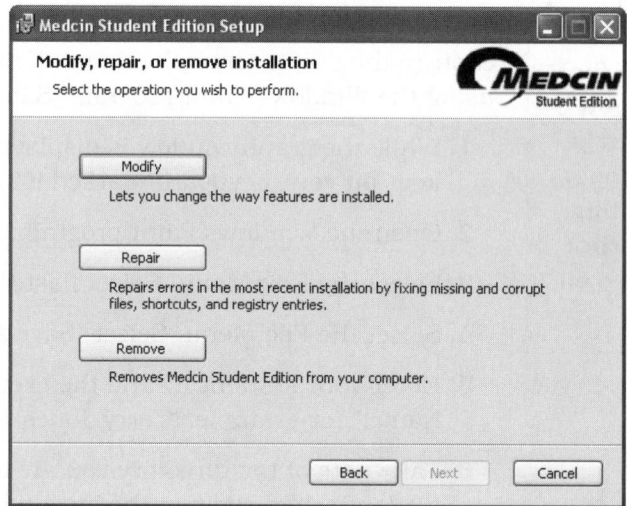

Select either the button labeled "Repair" or "Modify" depending on what you want to do.

"Repair" will rerun the installation using the same choices that the installer originally specified.

You must stop and uninstall the Medcin Server **before** removing or reinstalling the Student Edition software on a network server or a local installation.

You do not have to do this to remove the Student Edition Client from a workstation. Proceed to Step 4 if you are removing the client software from a workstation.

"Modify" will allow the user to change the settings and then rerun the installation. Selecting "Modify" will display the Custom installation screen shown in Figure I-9 and allow the user to proceed from there using the buttons labeled "Next" and "Back." Refer to figures earlier in this document to change a particular setting.

When the necessary changes have been made and/or the software has been reloaded, click on the button labeled "Finish."

Uninstalling the Medcin Server and Student Edition Software

Follow these instructions if you need to uninstall the Student Edition program files.

Step 1 Confirm that there are no copies of the Student Edition Client software running. (For a local installation, confirm that the Student Edition is not running.)

Step 2 Locate and click on the Medcin Server icon in the Windows Taskbar (shown in Figure I-12). The Medcin Server screen shown in Figure I-7 will be invoked.

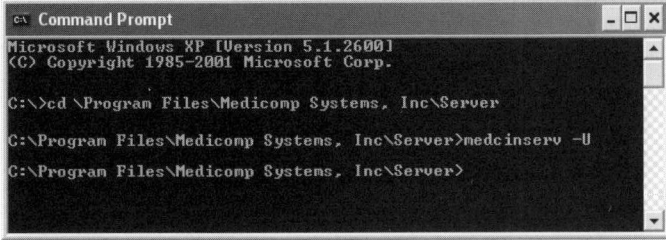

Locate and click on the button labeled "Shutdown." When the confirmation dialog window appears, confirm that you want to shut down the Medcin Server.

Step 3 Run the Windows command prompt. A window similar to Figure I-16 will be invoked.

▲ **Figure I-16 Windows Command Prompt Used to Uninstall Medcin Server**

Change directories to the directory in which the Medcin Server was installed. The default directory is "C:\program files\medicomp systems, inc\server."

When the correct directory name is displayed, type the following command. Make certain to use a capital "-U" at the end of the line.

Type: **medcinserv.exe -U**

Compare your screen to Figure I-16. If everything is typed correctly, press the Enter key.

Type: **exit** and press the Enter key to close the window.

Step 4 If the Student Edition CD is currently in the CD drive and a screen similar to Figure I-15 is displayed, locate and click on the button labeled "Remove." When the confirmation dialog window appears, confirm that you want to remove the Student Edition software.

Alternative Method

You can use the Windows "Add or Remove Software" program to perform this step if you do not have access to the Student Edition CD at this time.

▶ **Figure I-17 Windows Add or Remove Software Window**

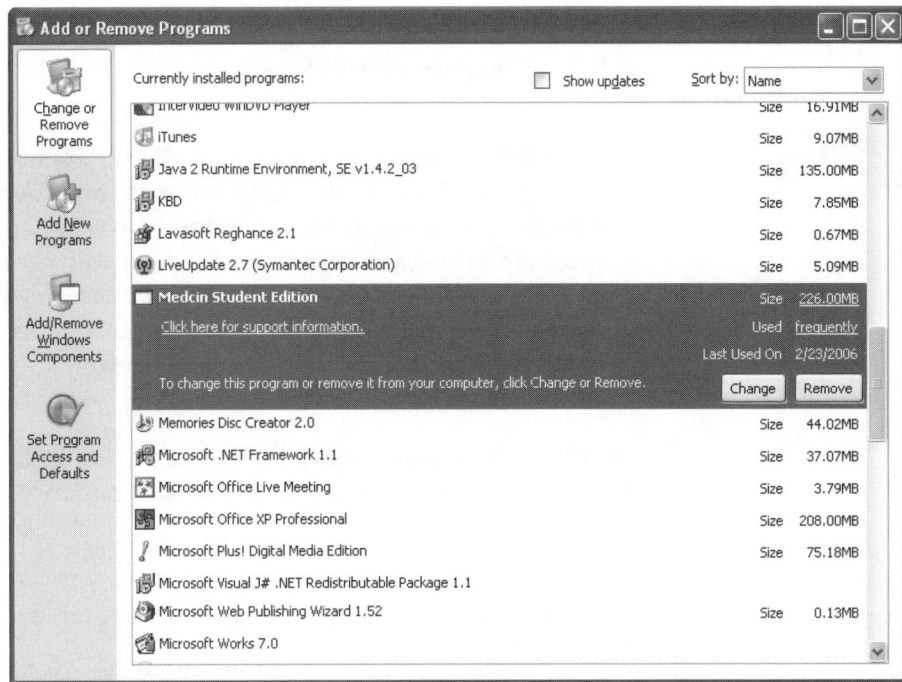

Click on the Windows Start button, click on Settings, and click on Control Panel, and click on "Add or Remove Software" option.

Locate the entry for Medcin Student Edition.

Locate and click on the button labeled "Remove." When the confirmation dialog window appears, confirm that you want to remove the Medcin software.

Updating Windows MDAC

The Student Edition software uses a standard component of the Windows operating system called MDAC to access its data. This component should have already been installed with the operating system.

At the beginning of the installation, the install routine will verify the version of the Windows MDAC component*. If it is not current, the installation will stop and display the warning shown in Figure I-18. You must update the operating system before installation can continue. The update is available online from Microsoft.

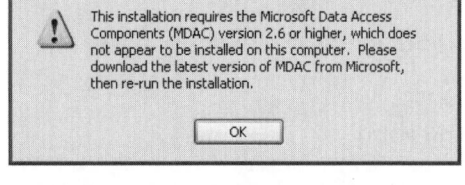

▲ **Figure I-18 Warning Message That MDAC Component Is Missing or Outdated**

Step 1 Connect to the Internet. Go to the Microsoft support Web site.

Step 2 Locate the download page for Microsoft Data Access Components. At the time of publication the URL was as follows:

http://msdn.microsoft.com/data/mdac/downloads

However, Microsoft may change the URL at some future date. If the download site is not at this URL, locate the Search field on the Microsoft page and type the keywords "MDAC downloads."

Step 3 Read and follow the download directions for your operating system provided on the Microsoft Web page.

> **Note**
>
> The Student Edition software (and all .Net applications) require at least version 2.6 of MDAC. However, different Microsoft operating systems typically have later versions in their updates. Also MDAC service packs are not incremental patches, as is the case with some Microsoft updates. Therefore, you do *not* need to install MDAC 2.6 and 2.7 before you install MDAC 2.8, for example. When choosing a download, always select the highest version number of MDAC available for your operating system.

Step 4 When the operating system has been updated, restart your computer and proceed with the installation of the Student Edition software.

Technical Note: The installation routine verifies the MDAC component by checking the value of the Windows registry key:
HKEY_LOCAL_MACHINE\Software\Microsoft\DataAccess\FullInstallVer

Technical Support

Follow these instructions if you experience technical difficulties with this product.

If you experience technical difficulties with this product, please fill out the Web form at:

http://247.prenhall.com/email/index.asp

Our technical support staff will need to know certain things about your system in order to help us solve your problems more quickly and efficiently. You should have the following information ready:

- Product title and product ISBN (you can find this information on the package or book)
- Computer make and model
- CD-ROM drive make and model
- Operating system (Windows version)
- RAM available
- Hard disk space available
- Graphics card type
- Sound card type
- Printer make and model
- Network connection
- Detailed description of the problem, including the exact wording of any error messages

1 Electronic Health Records— An Overview

Chapter 1 provides a foundation for student learning, introducing concepts and topics that are explained in depth in subsequent chapters. These include the eight core functions of an EHR described by the IOM, the three key criteria defined by the CPRI, and the four components of the patient chart referred to by the acronym SOAP.

The chapter begins with a definition of electronic health records, discusses why they are important, and explains the forces in our society driving their adoption. This includes government initiatives inaugurated by President George W. Bush, the creation of the Office of National Coordinator of Health Information Technology, and the goals and strategies outlined by that office.

In the context of this book, we use the following definition, derived from the combined work of IOM, CPRI, and HIPAA: **EHR— the portions of a patient's medical records that are stored in a computer system as well as the functional benefits derived from having an electronic health record.**

Workflow scenarios compare the flow of information into paper versus electronic charts, the workflow of physician lab orders, and differences between inpatient and outpatient settings. A comparison of electronic versus paper lab orders is reinforced in Chapter 6 and a discussion of inpatient nursing is reinforced with material in Chapter 2.

The vignette "Where's My Chart?" uses the real-life story of a patient to emphasize the need for readily accessible patient records and makes the point that the current state of health care is such that even when electronic health records exist they are not always available across disparate systems. This lays the groundwork for the conclusion of Chapter 1, which describes some of the communication standards used to exchange EHR data, and for Chapter 2, which describes why records need to be codified with standard codes.

Additional topics introduced in this chapter include the potential uses of EHR data for patient health management, decision support, and the electronic interchange of data between systems. These concepts are then covered further in Chapters 6, 7, and 9.

Learning Outcomes

After completing this chapter, students should be able to:

◆ Define electronic health records

◆ Explain why electronic health records are important

◆ Discuss the forces driving the adoption of electronic health records

◆ Describe the flow of medical information into the chart

◆ Describe different methods of capturing and recording data

◆ Understand levels of electronic health record implementations

◆ Describe workflow of physician orders and results

◆ Explain why systems and devices should be able to exchange electronic data

◆ Compare electronic health records in an inpatient versus outpatient setting

Teaching Recommendations

Electronic health records is currently the hot topic in health care. Supplement this chapter with class discussion of current news stories concerning the adoption of EHR. Stories are appearing regularly and frequently on TV and in newspapers and national magazines. You can also find updated items on the Web site of the Office of National Coordinator of Health Information Technology and various leading health care organizations. Here are three suggested sites:

http://www.hhs.gov/healthit (Office of National Coordinator of Health Information Technology)

http://www.himss.org (Healthcare Information Management Systems Society—click on Topics & Tools to find Electronic Health Records)

http://www.medrecinst.com (The Medical Records Institute)

Health care is far behind other industries in adoption of everyday computer technology. One startling example of this is demonstrated by having students examine the contents of their wallet. They might find a credit or debit card, student ID, driver license, library card, and health insurance card. Of all the cards in our wallets, typically the insurance card will be the one that doesn't have a magnetic strip or bar code.

In most areas of the country, even a library card has a bar code that allows the patron to be quickly identified by the library computer. Contrast this with the first visit to a medical office, which typically begins with the medical receptionist copying the insurance card and then keying the insurance subscriber information manually into the computer.

Another suggestion is to have students read the real-life story "Where's My Chart?" and then invite discussion of similar experiences from the students. Typically you can expect several students to know someone who had experiences like the patient in the story.

Acronyms are used extensively in both medicine and computers and, therefore, in this textbook. Students should learn the acronyms provided in the table at the beginning of each chapter. Familiarity with these terms will help the student understand and communicate effectively with others in the health care workplace.

Have students review the Chapter Summary and answer the 15 questions at the end of the chapter. The answer key for the questions is provided after the chapter outline. A bank of test questions to create your own chapter exam is also available on the Prentice Hall Health Instructor's Resource CD.

Chapter 1 Outline

I. What Are Electronic Health Records?
   A. Historical names for computerized patient medical records
   B. New name: Electronic Health Records.
   C. The IOM called for the creation of an electronic patient record
   D. IOM defined eight core functions:
      1. Health information and data
      2. Result management
      3. Order management
      4. Decision support
      5. Electronic communication and connectivity
      6. Patient support
      7. Administrative processes and reporting
      8. Reporting and population health

   E. CPRI identified three key criteria for an EHR:
      1. Capture data at the point of care
      2. Integrate data from multiple sources
      3. Provide decision support

   F. HIPAA Security Rule defined protection for health data
   G. EHR definition for textbook (based on IOM, CPRI, and HIPAA)

II. Why Electronic Health Records Are Important
   A. Drawbacks to paper records:
      1. Often abbreviated
      2. Cryptic
      3. Illegible
      4. Chart must be transported from one office to another
      5. Not easily searchable

B. Advantages of electronic health records

    1. Simultaneously accessible at multiple locations by multiple providers

    2. Searchable by computer

    3. Data are likely to be standard medical terms

    4. Capable of being transferred electronically to another system

    5. Health maintenance

    6. Trend analysis

    7. Alerts

    8. Decision support

        A) Prescriptions

        B) Drug formulary

        C) Medical references

        D) Protocols

III. Forces Driving the EHR

A. Health and safety

B. National Coordinator for Health Information Technology

C. Readiness for change

D. Vision for consumer-centric and information-rich care

E. Strategic framework—Goals and strategies

    1. Goal 1: Inform clinical practice

        a) Strategy 1. Incentivize EHR adoption

        b) Strategy 2. Reduce risk of EHR investment

        c) Strategy 3. Promote EHR diffusion in rural and underserved areas

    2. Goal 2: Interconnect clinicians

        a) Strategy 1. Foster regional collaborations

        b) Strategy 2. Develop a national health information network

        c) Strategy 3. Coordinate federal health information systems

    3. Goal 3: Personalize care

        a) Strategy 1. Encourage use of personal health records

        b) Strategy 2. Enhance informed consumer choice

        c) Strategy 3. Promote use of telehealth systems

    4. Goal 4: Improve population health

        a) Strategy 1. Unify public health surveillance architectures

        b) Strategy 2. Streamline quality and health status monitoring

        c) Strategy 3. Accelerate research and dissemination of evidence

F. Where's My Chart? A Real-Life Story

IV. Building the EHR

A. Medical vocabulary used in an EHR should be codified

B. Coding systems should use a national standard

C. EHR requires changes in the way providers work

V. Flow of Medical Information into the Chart

A. Four components of a chart:

    1. Subjective component

    2. Objective component

    3. Assessment

    4. Plan

VI. Flow of an Office Fully Using EHR

    A. Doctors say

VII. Transition to an EHR

    A. Determine if any of the information is already available electronically

    B. Determine how much can be implemented before impacting the provider workflow

VIII. Levels of EHR Implementation

    A. Building the EHR in steps

        1. Measure paper chart documents to predict how the chart can be computerized

        2. Comparison of papers in chart by provider type

IX. Comparing the EHR in an Inpatient versus Outpatient Setting

X. Methods of Capturing and Recording Data

XI. Workflow of Physician Orders and Results

    A. Lab Orders and results

    B. Comparison of lab order and results workflow

    C. Medication orders

    D. Radiology orders and reports

XII. Electronic Data Interchange Between Systems and Devices

    A. HL7

    B. CDISC

    C. DICOM

    D. Medical devices

XIII. Chapter Summary

Answer Key 1-1

Testing Your Knowledge of Chapter 1

1. What does the acronym EHR stand for?

ANSWER: Electronic Health Records

2. What is the definition of an EHR?

ANSWER: The working definition for this textbook is as follows:

The portions of a patient's medical records that are stored in a computer system as well as the functional benefits derived from having an electronic health record.

3. Explain the benefits of EHR over paper charts.

ANSWER: Acceptable answers include:

    Simultaneously accessible at multiple locations by multiple providers

    Searchable by computer

    Data are more likely to be standard medical terms

    Capable of being transferred electronically to another system

Additional benefits realized from having codified EHR data:

    Health maintenance

    Trend analysis

    Alerts

    Decision support

Give examples for the following terms:

4. Trend analysis

ANSWER: Acceptable answers include:

Graphs or comparison of data from different dates, tests, or events. Cumulative summary reports. Comparison of changes in medications or dosage to changes in blood tests.

5. Decision support

ANSWER: Providing reference information just when the clinician needs it. Examples from the text include prescription drugs, drug formularies, generic or therapeutically equivalents to brand-name drugs, evidence-based guidelines and online medical references. The text also describes protocols as standard plans of therapy that can be used for treatment of different conditions.

6. Alerts

ANSWER: Acceptable answers include:

A message or reminder that is automatically generated from the data. Students might also cite the example of two or more conflicting medications.

7. Health maintenance

ANSWER: Acceptable answers include:

Reminders to make the patient aware when it is time for a preventative procedure or a check-up, a flu shot, or other immunization. Some students may list specific items referenced in the textbook, such as mammograms or PSA screenings. The example of a reminder from the dentist was also used.

8. Describe what generally takes place from the time a patient checks in at a physician's office until the patient checks out.

ANSWER:

1. Patient checks in with the receptionist.
2. Patient updates his or her medical history and reason for visit in the waiting area.
3. Patient moves to exam room; nurse takes vitals and reviews symptoms and the reason for the visit.
4. Physician enters, reviews chart, and discusses symptoms and the reason for the visit. If it is necessary for the patient to disrobe, the doctor usually leaves to see another patient and then returns to perform the clinical exam.
5. Clinician performs a physical exam, assesses patient condition, writes orders for tests or prescription, provides education or counseling, and dictates or updates chart.
6. If tests have been ordered, a specimen is taken or the patient is given directions to an outside lab.
7. Patient is given educational material and prescriptions and then checks out.

9. Describe what points of the workflow are different between offices using a paper and electronic charts.

ANSWER: Figures 1-2 and 1-3 compared the workflow of offices using paper and electronic charts in 12 steps. Students should identify most of the differences. Any acceptable comparison of those figures should suffice. Here is a summary of key differences:

Both workflows started with the patient calling for an appointment. Astute students may point out that an alternative for some EHR offices is to allow scheduling over the Web; extra points for those students.

Paper: The night before the visit paper charts are pulled.

EHR: Pulling charts is not necessary; however, some EHR systems can automatically verify the patient's insurance eligibility.

Paper: The patient updates his or her history on a paper form.

EHR: The patient completes his or her medical history and reason for today's visit using a computer in a private area of waiting room.

Paper: The patient describes symptoms and reason for the visit to the nurse; vital signs are recorded in the paper chart by the nurse. The doctor enters and the patient repeats description of symptoms and reason for the visit.

EHR: The nurse reviews patient-entered data with the patient and edits for clarification if necessary. Vital signs can be electronically transferred from instruments into chart.

The clinician performs the physical exam and makes a clinical assessment and a plan of treatment.

Paper: The clinician makes a few notes and retains the observations and physical exam in his or her memory.

EHR: The clinician records the findings at the time of the exam or shortly thereafter; has access to previous problems and reviews those; makes the clinical assessment and plan of treatment.

Paper: The clinician handwrites prescriptions and orders, makes a note of them in the paper chart, and marks billing codes and diagnoses codes on the paper encounter form. The clinician creates the exam note from memory, either handwriting in the chart or dictating.

EHR: The clinician enters the findings directly into the EHR while the patient is still present. Orders create tasks for lab personnel to obtain a specimen, which is subsequently transmitted directly to the lab. Prescriptions are written as part of the chart and transmitted to the pharmacy.

Paper: Dictated notes must be transcribed and subsequently reviewed and signed by the clinician and then filed in the paper chart.

EHR: When the exam is finished, the note is finished. A copy of the completed note can be printed and given to the patient with other patient education materials.

Patient checks out.

Paper: Billing information is manually keyed into the computer from the encounter form. The codes circled by the clinician are only a best guess and may require a coding specialist to verify them.

EHR: The billing codes can be automatically calculated from the completed note and electronically transferred from the EHR into the billing system.

Paper: Results from tests are returned and the chart is pulled again. The doctor must review and sign the results, staff must notify the patient, and the chart must be refiled.

EHR: Results received electronically are merged directly into the patient chart and immediately available for clinician review and patient notification.

10. Describe at least three differences between inpatient and outpatient EHR systems.

ANSWER:

Outpatient	Inpatient
Most physician offices have a single chart for the patient. Notes for each visit, test results, and any other reports are added to the chart.	Most hospitals start a new chart each time a patient is admitted. Information from previous stays in the hospital is linked to the patient ID, but the current chart contains only information related to the current stay.
The quantity of data in an outpatient chart is relatively low by comparison.	The quantity of data in an inpatient chart is likely to be much larger. Vital signs are taken and nurse's notes are added numerous times per day; dietitians, respiratory therapists, and other providers add to the chart. There are typically many more orders for labs, medications, etc.
The central element in the chart is the physician's exam note.	Physician exams tend to be brief. The main focus of the chart is the physician orders and nurse's notes indicating the patient's response.

11. Describe the workflow associated with an electronic lab order.

ANSWER: (Note that the student is not asked to compare the paper and electronic workflow, just to describe the electronic.)

The clinician orders a blood test.

The electronic requisition is entered in a computer.

The patient's demographic and insurance information is populated automatically.

The electronic order system compares the test codes on the order to coverage rules for the patient's insurance and automatically alerts the user if a signed Advance Beneficiary Notice is required.

The specimen of the patient's blood is drawn.

Labels are generated by the computerized requisition system and are attached to the specimen.

The requisition is transmitted electronically to the lab system computer and contains the information required to process the test.

If the blood is drawn at the medical office but the test is not performed there, the sample is picked up by a courier and transported to the reference lab.

The tests are most often performed by automated equipment that communicates results to the lab information system assigning values to codes for each component of the test.

The results are returned electronically and merged into the patient's EHR.

The clinician will be alerted that the results are ready.

The clinician will review the results of the test and take appropriate action.

The clinician can then order the treatments or follow-up tests and send messages to the staff or the patient about the results.

Orders are tracked in an EHR from the moment they are entered in the system. A report of pending orders is always available.

12. Name at least three forces driving the change to EHR.

ANSWER: At least three of the following:

Medical specialization (patients no longer have just one doctor)

Increasingly mobile society (patients relocate and change doctors often)

Internet (patients are researching their conditions and demanding access to their own records)

New methods of diagnostic and preventative medicine require the ability to share exam records

Health safety (deaths as a result of medical errors that could have been prevented by electronic records)

Employers (The Leapfrog Group)

Government initiatives

13. What are the four goals of the Strategic Framework created by the Office of the National Coordinator for Health Information Technology?

ANSWER:

Inform clinical practice

Interconnect clinicians

Personalize care

Improve population health

14. Name some advantages of electronic prescriptions.

ANSWER:

The physician issues the prescription and records it in the chart in one step.

The prescription can be transmitted electronically from the physician's computer system to the pharmacy, saving time for the patient and eliminating the need for the doctor's staff to call in the prescription.

Reduces errors caused by handwritten prescriptions.

The DUR and formulary compliance checking can be performed by the doctor's computer at the time the prescription is written. This allows any problems with the prescription to be corrected prior to sending it to the pharmacy. This drastically reduces phone calls back to the prescribing physician from the pharmacy, saving everyone time.

Each medication is automatically recorded in the medication list as the prescription is created; a current and recent medications list is available to the clinician while writing the prescription. This reduces prescribing errors.

Electronic systems shorten the time it takes to write a prescription by maintaining a list of prescriptions the clinician writes frequently. Physicians of patients with chronic diseases frequently write renewals for existing prescriptions; with EHR systems they perform this task with a few clicks of the mouse.

All FDA-approved drugs are listed in the computer, eliminating the need to use a drug reference book to find an uncommon drug.

15. What is HL7?

ANSWER: Any of these:

A national communication standard for transferring health data between disparate systems.

HL7 is the primary standard for the communication of patient demographics, lab orders, results, radiology reports, clinical observations, and many other types of clinical data maintained in the EHR.

A nonprofit organization that developed and maintains the leading messaging standard used to exchange clinical and administrative data between different health care computer systems.

HL7 stands for Health Level Seven.

Coding Standards

2

In the previous chapter we defined the EHR as the portions of the patient's medical record stored in the computer system as well as the functional benefits derived from having an electronic health record. However, those benefits cannot be realized just by converting paper charts into computer records.

Chapter 2 describes the various forms of storing EHR data and the value of using standardized codes for those data. For the interchange of EHR data to occur, different computer systems must identify medical procedures and concepts in the same way. However, today there exist multiple coding standards. This leads to the key point of this chapter:

> **EHR data stored in a machine-readable, codified form add significant value, but using a national standard code set instead of proprietary codes to codify the data will better enable the exchange of medical records between systems, improve the accuracy of the content, and open the door to the functional benefits derived from having an electronic health record.**

This chapter covers each of the prominent standards, their history, purpose, and relationship to each other. It also describes the influence of the U.S. and U.K. governments on the adoption of standard coding systems.

In this chapter, the student acquires a knowledge of EHR coding systems and their history and then in subsequent chapters will also acquire firsthand experience using some of those nomenclatures with medical record software. The software used with this book is based on Medcin, one of the nationally accepted nomenclature standards described in this chapter. The Student Edition software contains the full Medcin nomenclature used in professional EHR systems.

Students who are familiar with billing codes will find it particularly interesting to discover that there are so many other coding systems in use today. The chapter explains and provides examples of why billing codes and EHR nomenclatures are different. This book does not endeavor to teach billing, but there is an important relationship between the information recorded in the patient exam note and the level of billing codes that can be used to bill for the visit. This chapter provides the history of the CPT-4 and ICD-9CM codes, which are subsequently utilized by the student in Chapter 5.

Nursing codes that are described in this chapter are an example of too many different standards trying to accomplish the same task. Nursing codes are frequently used in inpatient EHR systems. A registered nurse, with an additional degree in nursing informatics, provides a firsthand account of her fellow nurses' experiences when hospital systems transition to electronic records. Her observations about performing real-time data entry as opposed to "catching up" charts every couple of hours support the emphasis subsequent chapters place on entering EHR data at the time the patient is seen.

Learning Outcomes

After completing this chapter, students should be able to:

◆ Describe the importance of codified electronic health records
◆ Explain the government's influence on coding standards
◆ Have an understanding of prominent EHR code sets, such as SNOMED CT, MEDCIN, LOINC, as well as various nursing code sets
◆ Have an understanding of prominent billing code sets, such as CPT-4, ABC, ICD-9CM, and ICD-10
◆ Explain how EHR code sets differ from CPT-4, ICD-9CM, and NDC codes

Teaching Recommendations

Use this chapter to help the student understand that EHR systems are still evolving; decisions about clinical terminologies and discussions about mapping one code system to another are not uncommon in health care organizations. Students who have taken this course will find themselves more knowledgeable about code sets and nomenclatures than most employees in the health care workplace. Even a passing familiarity with the names and purpose of the various coding systems will help the student stand out in the medical office when these issues arise.

Instructors who have taught a billing or coding course may feel inclined to go into more depth in this chapter because CPT-4 and ICD-9CM codes are introduced here. However, it is better to wait until Chapter 5 to add that type of supplementary material. Review Chapter 5 yourself before making any decision about this.

Class discussions can begin by determining which of the code sets in this chapter students may have heard of or worked with previously. Have any of the students had previous courses in medical office coding, or are any of the students nurses?

Make certain the students understand what is meant by a codified medical record and how the use of standard codes allows diverse EHR systems to understand the data from another provider's system.

Chapter 1 set forth some key benefits that can be realized from using electronic health records; most of those rely on programs that find and match specific medical data. Discuss with the students how codified records can be used to generate alerts, promote health and preventative maintenance, or create graphs and charts from multiple instances of the same test result.

Make certain the students understand the concept of an EHR nomenclature as defined in this chapter. It is used here interchangeably with *clinical terminology* and *clinical vocabulary*. The term *nomenclature* is used extensively in the remainder of this book.

In Chapter 3 students will begin exercises with software that uses the Medcin nomenclature. To prepare students for the next chapter, go over the six broad categories into which Medcin findings are organized. The following table will help you correlate the categories with the four sections of a SOAP chart students learned in Chapter 1.

Medcin Category	SOAP Section
Symptoms	Subjective
History	
Physical Exam	Objective
Tests (performed)	
Diagnosis	Assessment
Therapy	Plan
Tests (ordered)	

Note that the Medcin "Tests" category applies to either "Objective" or "Plan," depending on whether the test was performed at the doctor's office or ordered to be done later.

Another key concept from this chapter that will be used throughout the remainder of the book is that of a *clinical finding*. Findings precorrelate individual medical terms into clinically relevant phrases that are medically meaningful to the clinician. Point out that most Medcin findings represent a meaningful clinical observation or term, as opposed to individual components of a term. You can supplement this with a discussion comparing Figures 2-5 and 2-6 in the textbook.

Findings differ from billing codes in that a billing code represents that an encounter or procedure has occurred or has been performed. A finding documents the details of that event.

Clinical terminologies are regularly updated. Information on new releases of the clinical nomenclatures discussed in this chapter may be available at the following three Web sites:

http://www.snomed.org (click on the tab labeled " SNOMED CT") *http://www.medicomp.com* (Medcin—also has a Flash presentation for high-speed connections)

http://www.regenstrief.org/loinc (LOINC information)

Have students review the Chapter Summary and answer the 15 questions at the end of the chapter. The answer key for the questions is provided after the chapter outline. A bank of test questions to create your own chapter exam is also available on the Prentice Hall Health Instructor's Resource CD.

Chapter 2 Outline

I. The Value of Codified Electronic Health Records
  A. Forms of EHR data
    1. Digital images
    2. Text
    3. Discrete data
      a) Fielded data
      b) Coded data

  B. Limitations of types of data
    1. Comparison of lab results
      a) Scanned image
      b) Text file
      c) Codified data

    2. Alerts
    3. Health maintenance
    4. Standard coding systems

II. Government Influence on Coding Standards
  A. CMS (HCFA)
  B. HIPAA
  C. Department of Health initiatives
  D. Department of Defense initiatives
  E. Indian Health Service
  F. United Kingdom National Health Service

III. Comparison of Prominent EHR Code Sets
  A. How EHR nomenclatures differ from other code sets
  B. SNOMED CT
  C. Medcin
  D. LOINC
  E. UMLS
  F. Nursing code sets
    1. NANDA Taxonomy II
    2. NIC
    3. NOC
    4. CCC
    5. Omaha System
    6. ICNP
    7. NMDS
    8. PNDS

9. PCDS
10. SNOMED CT

G. A Nurse's Notes—A Real-Life Story

IV. How EHR Code Sets Differ from Billing Code Sets

A. CPT-4
B. ABC
C. ICD-9CM
D. ICD-10
1. ICD-10PCS

E. NDC and other drug codes
1. RxNorm
2. NDF-RT

V. Conclusion

VI. Chapter Summary

Answer Key 2-1

Testing Your Knowledge of Chapter 2

1. Name three forms of EHR data.

ANSWER: Digital images, text data, discrete data
(Also acceptable answers: fielded data, coded data)

2. Name at least four medical code sets considered national standards.

ANSWER: Any four of the following:

SNOMED CT
Medcin
LOINC
NANDA Taxonomy II
NIC
NOC
CCC
Omaha System
ICNP
NMDS
PNDS
PCDS
CPT-4
HCPCS
ICD-9CM
NDC
RxNorm
NDF-RT

3. Describe what influence the government has on the selection of standard code sets.

ANSWER: CMS and its predecessor HCFA required the used of CPT-4, HCPCS, and ICD-9CM codes for billing; private insurance followed suit.

HIPAA authorized NCVHS to select national standards.

HHS established standards for federal agencies, leading by example.

4. What does the acronym HIPAA stand for?

ANSWER: Health Insurance Portability and Accountability Act

5. Which committee of the government has been designated to select national standards?

ANSWER: National Committee on Vital and Health Statistics (NCVHS)

6. What is a nomenclature?

ANSWER: Nomenclature is a system (or list) of names used in a field of science, typically created by a recognized group or authority. In an EHR the term is used for organized lists of medical phrases and codified data to help to standardize the way clinicians record information. EHR nomenclatures are also called clinical vocabularies or clinical terminologies.

7. In an EHR what is meant by the term *finding*?

ANSWER: Any answer similar to one of the following:

Findings are codified observations that are medically meaningful to the clinician.

Findings precorrelate individual medical terms into clinically relevant phrases.

Findings are less granular than individual terms.

8. Explain the difference between a finding and a billing code.

ANSWER: Any answer similar to one of the following:

Findings differ from billing codes in that a billing code represents that an encounter or procedure has occurred or has been performed. A finding documents the details of that event.

Findings are designed to codify the details and nuance of the patient–clinician encounter.

Findings describe what the clinician observed during the visit. Billing codes identify only the type and complexity of the exam.

Each code set that becomes a national standard does so because it is designed for a particular purpose. Give a brief description of the original purpose of each of the following coding systems:

9. SNOMED CT

ANSWER: A medical nomenclature developed by the College of American Pathologists and United Kingdom's National Health Service. It is a merger of two previous coding systems, SNOMED and the Read codes.

SNOMED CT is the general core terminology used to support the patient medical record information in both countries. Its origin in 1965 was to codify pathology studies.

10. Medcin

ANSWER: A medical nomenclature and knowledge base developed by Medicomp Systems, Inc., in 1978; selected by NCVHS as an enabling standard because it enables the physician to create a complete electronic record at the time of the exam.

11. LOINC

ANSWER: Created in 1995 and maintained by the Regenstrief Institute at the Indiana University School of Medicine; LOINC originated as a clinical terminology for laboratory test orders and results.

12. CPT-4

ANSWER: Created in 1966 by the American Medical Association to accurately identify medical, surgical, and diagnostic services performed. It is used for insurance billing.

13. ICD-9CM

ANSWER: A system of standardized codes developed collaboratively between the World Health Organization (WHO) and 10 international centers. The coding system today evolved from the International List of Causes of Death, which originated in 1900. In 1948, WHO expanded and renamed the system to make it useful for codifying patient medical conditions as well.

14. In the United States should ICD-9CM or ICD-10 be used for insurance claims?

ANSWER: ICD-9CM

(Note: ICD-10 is used in the United States only for death certificates at this time.)

15. Describe the difference between an EHR nomenclature and a billing code set.

ANSWER: The level of detail represented by the codes.

EHR nomenclatures have codes to represent not only procedures and diseases but also symptoms, observations, history, medications, and many other details.

EHR nomenclatures contain cross-references to other code sets, whereas billing codes sets do not.

Learning Medical Record Software

Chapter 3 introduces the Student Edition software, which will be used for the remainder of the book. In a series of brief hands on exercises the student becomes familiar with EHR concepts, learns to navigate the software, and creates an actual exam note.

About Medcin

Medcin is a medical nomenclature that is one of the leading national standards. The knowledge base is used in many EHR systems as well as the Department of Defense CHCS II system. We are fortunate that they have allowed us to use their knowledge base in the companion software for this book.

The purpose of the Student Edition software is to allow the student to learn by doing. This is not a tutorial for a particular commercial medical package. Medcin is not a brand of EHR, but rather the licensed core technology used by 10 of the top 15 EHR systems.

Because Medcin is widely adopted as the technology underlying commercial EHR systems, there is a high potential for students to apply skills they acquire in this course directly to an EHR application in their office. Due to unique software vendor designs, those systems will not be identical to the student software, but they will seem very familiar to someone who has completed this course.

Even EHR systems that may use proprietary or user-defined codes still behave in a conceptually similar manner to the student software. These facts increase the likelihood that the student's knowledge will transfer easily to a commercial medical record system in use at clinics in local areas.

The purpose of this book is to build, through practical experience, an understanding and a comfort with computerized medical records that can be directly applied in the clinical setting. Whether the clinic EHR uses Medcin or another nomenclature, the learner will be familiar with the concepts, terminology, and workings of an EHR. Students will have confidence in their ability and will approach the EHR without fear or trepidation.

In Chapter 3 students will learn the basic layout of the screen and the concepts of adding and editing findings, and adding details to findings. Detailed instructions for scrolling and navigating the lists are provided and the student actually completes and prints a finished exam note by the end of the chapter.

Since this will be many students' first experience using an EHR, the vignette selected for this chapter is the recollection by a practicing physician of his first day using an EHR in front of patients. Students will no doubt sympathize with his plight and be encouraged with his success at the conclusion.

Learning Outcomes

After completing this chapter, students should be able to:

♦ Start and stop the Student Edition software
♦ Navigate the screen
♦ Select a patient
♦ Create a new encounter
♦ Enter a chief complaint
♦ Enter vital signs
♦ Access the Symptoms, History, Physical Exam, Assessment, and Therapy tabs to select appropriate findings in each portion of the exam
♦ Add free text, prefixes, status, and results to findings
♦ Print a copy of the completed exam note

Teaching Recommendations

Software Tips That Apply to This and All Future Chapters

■ Run the exercises yourself beforehand. This may be a new course for you and you may have just received this manual and the software, but do not attempt to teach an exercise that you have not worked through yourself. Fortunately, Chapters 1 and 2 do not have exercises, so if you are trying to work ahead of the class, you should be able to stay a chapter or two ahead of the students.

■ The software login screen prompts students for their name or student ID. Instruct your students which one you prefer them to use. The login name or ID is printed on the student's work in most exercises. Caution: Because there is no validation of the student ID, it is possible for one student to do work for another student.

Note: Students should not type a period in the Student Name or ID field if they will be using the Print to HTML feature (discussed later).

■ To allow students from multiple classes to share the same computer and to avoid complications caused by saving and backing up student data, the Student Edition software does **not** use a save function. All work to be turned in is printed. The exercises have been designed to be completed and printed in a single class period.

Since the students cannot save their work to resume later, when students finish an exercise, consider the class time remaining before beginning the next exercise.

Alerts in the textbook remind the students to make sure they have their printout in hand before exiting the software. However, you should caution the students that network printers sometimes queue up multiple print jobs, and they should make sure they actually have the printout in hand before closing the program. The software also prompts the student who attempts to exit without printing.

If your school has a distance learning program or if you prefer to check students' work online, the software has a "Print to HTML" feature that will output the exam notes to a file that can be opened with a Web browser. For more information on this feature see the "Distance Learning" section in the chapter of this manual titled "Installing the Software."

■ The Student Edition software automatically calculates the patient's age based on the encounter date. Some of the features in the program use this information to present findings that are clinically relevant to the patient's age and sex or based on the patient's previous encounters. Remind students to be careful when creating new encounters to exactly match the date and time in the textbook exercises.

Note: There may be a difference in the age displayed in the window title and the one used in the encounter. We are interested in the age at the time of the encounter. This will remain the same from class to class as long as the students use the correct encounter date.

■ Weigh grading heavily toward correct completion of the exercises. Student printouts of patient notes compared to the samples printed in the textbook are used to evaluate the students' success. Because students will assume responsibility for producing accurate medical records in the clinic, accurately recording the findings in these exercises should be a primary goal.

Students who have incorrect or missing items on their patient exam notes should be required to repeat the exercise. Emphasize that accuracy is paramount in a medical record. An answer key for the patient exam note (at the end of this section) will allow you to help students find where they are making mistakes.

■ The exercises in this book are intended to provide conceptual learning experiences with EHR software. Although the exercises have been designed to produce medically accurate exam notes, the notes do not necessarily represent a thorough medical exam. In many cases the exam has been abridged to shorten the time it takes students to complete the exercise.

Exercises may omit certain routine elements of the exam that would normally be documented by a clinician. This is not a limitation of the Medcin knowledge base or of the physicians who reviewed the exercises for this book. This is done solely to facilitate completion of exercises in the allotted class time.

Students in your course who are already medical professionals may recognize that the exams are not complete. Do not allow them to become distracted by this. The purpose of each exercise is to explore some new aspect of the EHR within the normal class time. Eliminating some elements of a full exam was unavoidable to achieve the goals of the exercise.

Additional Tips for Chapter 3 Exercises

This chapter uses a series of 20 short exercises to allow students to explore and become comfortable with the Student Edition software. It may be possible to complete several of these exercises in a single class period. Some of the exercises simply allow students with less computer experience to come up to speed.

The purpose of this chapter is to become familiar with the software and EHR concepts through hands-on exercises. Students will not be able to complete all the exercises in this chapter in one class period. Therefore, in subsequent class periods, each time students resume work on this chapter they must repeat at least three steps:

1. Start the Medcin Student Edition software.

2. Select the patient **Rosa Garcia.**

3. Create a new encounter for a **10 Minute Visit, April 28, 2006 11:00 AM.**

With few exceptions that are clearly marked, students will be able to continue with the next hands-on exercise without repeating preceding ones. However, when students continue without repeating prior exercises, the exam note in the right pane of the window will not contain as much information as the figures printed in the textbook. This is to be expected.

Have students review the Chapter Summary and answer the 14 questions at the end of the chapter. The answer key for the questions is provided after the chapter outline. Students should also turn in a printout or file of their exam note for Rosa Garcia. An answer key showing the steps used to create the patient note is provided as well.

A bank of test questions to create your own chapter exam is also available on the Prentice Hall Health Instructor's Resource CD.

Chapter 3 Outline

I. Introducing the Medcin Student Edition Software
   A. Review of facts about Medcin nomenclature
   B. About the exercises in this book

II. Understanding the Software
   A. Hands-On Exercise 1: Starting Up the Medcin Software
   B. Navigating the screen
      1. The menu bar and toolbar
      2. The Medcin Nomenclature pane
      3. The Encounter View pane
      4. Entry details for a current finding
   C. Hands-On Exercise 2: Exiting and Restarting the Software
   D. Hands-On Exercise 3: Using the Menu to Select a Patient

Answer Key 3-1

Testing Your Knowledge of Chapter 3

Students should be permitted run the Student Edition software to answer the following questions:

1. Which menu did you use to select the patient?

ANSWER: Select.

2. Which menu did you use to start a new encounter?

ANSWER: Select.

3. Where did you set the label "10 Minute Visit," which appeared in the title of the window?

ANSWER: In the New Encounter window, the encounter reason field, just below the calendar.

The tabs on the left of the list of Medcin findings have medical abbreviations. Write the meaning of each of the following:

4. **Sx**

    ANSWER: Symptoms

5. **Hx**

    ANSWER: History

6. **Px**

    ANSWER: Physical exam

7. **Tx**

    ANSWER: Tests

8. **Dx**

    ANSWER: Diagnosis (Assessment is also acceptable.)

9. **Rx**

    ANSWER: Therapy (Plan is also acceptable.)

10. **How old is the patient?**

    ANSWER: Rosa Garcia is 27 years old. This is in the printed exam note and displayed in the right pane.

11. **How long had she been having headaches?**

    ANSWER: 5 days (or more than 5 days)

12. **What is the clinical assessment (her diagnosis)?**

    ANSWER: Vasoconstrictor withdrawal headache from caffeine. (Also acceptable: caffeine withdrawal headache.)

13. **How do you invoke the Vital Signs window?**

    ANSWER: Select the Active Forms tab at the bottom of the screen, click the button labeled "Forms" in the toolbar, select Vitals from the Form Manager window.

    (Also acceptable: From the Form Manager window.)

14. **Why is it important to make sure you have your printout before exiting the Student Edition?**

    ANSWER: Because you will lose your work when you exit.

15. **Students should have produced a narrative document of a patient encounter and handed it in to you.**

    Compare the contents of the student exam note to Answer Key 3-2. Mark off one point for each finding that is omitted or does not match the exam note shown in the answer key. Step numbers provided in the answer key will allow you to help students identify the point in the exercise where their error most likely occurred.

Answer Key 3-2

Evaluation of Printed Exam Note for Exercises 21–22: Documenting a Visit for Headaches

The following corresponds to Figure 3-57 in the textbook. A "Print to HTML" file named "fig3-57_rosa_garcia.htm" is available on the Instructor's Resource CD.

Student: *(name or ID)*	*Step 2*
Patient: Rosa Garcia: F: 12/29/1978: 4/28/2006 11:00AM	*Steps 3 and 4*

CHIEF COMPLAINT
The Chief Complaint is: Headaches for more than 5 days

Step 5

HISTORY OF PRESENT ILLNESS
Rosa Garcia is a 27-year-old female.
• Chronic/recurring headaches recently worse occurring 1/day
  lasting 2–4 hours, which is inadequately controlled

Steps 6–8

PERSONAL HISTORY
Behavioral history: Daily coffee consumption was 7–8 cups per day;
has recently decreased because she stopped all coffee

Steps 9–12

PHYSICAL FINDINGS

Vital signs:

Steps 14

Vital Signs/Measurements	Value	Normal Range
Oral temperature	98.6 F	97.6–99.6
RR	25 breaths/min	18–26
PR	75 bpm	50–100
Blood pressure	117/75 mmHg	100–120/56–80
Weight	140 lbs	98–183
Height	64 in	60.2–68.5

Head:
• No evidence of a head injury

Step 15

Neurological:
Performance of a Mental Status Exam: • A mental status exam was normal

Step 16

ASSESSMENT
• Vasoconstrictor withdrawal headache from caffeine

Step 17

THERAPY
Eat regular meals, get plenty of exercise, and limit intake of
caffeine and alcohol

Step 18

4

Data Entry at the Point of Care

Chapter 4 increases the students' core competency toward entry of EHR data in real time. Beginning with an exercise that reinforces the students' experience from Chapter 3, the text continues to build skills by exploring additional methods of locating findings and entering data. Hands-on exercises are used to teach each feature.

The conclusion of Dr. Wenner's real-life story in Chapter 3 leads us to the key point of this chapter and, in fact, to one of the key tenets of this book:

Documenting a visit at the point of care ensures a more accurate record, provides the most benefits from the system, and allows the note to be completed before the patient ever leaves the office.

To document in real time one must be able to quickly navigate and enter findings. Chapter 4 teaches students to use features that are standard in most EHR systems, such as Search, Prompt, Lists and Forms, to preload the findings that are likely to be needed for each type of patient. Students learn by documenting four patient visits differently. The concept of clinician orders is also introduced in this chapter.

The goals of this chapter are to increase familiarity with the software, thereby increasing speed of data entry, and to learn additional methods of data entry that enable a clinician to document the visit while the patient is still present.

Since this chapter expands the students' understanding of Forms and since form design tools are a part of almost every EHR system on the market, the vignette for this chapter is by a practicing physician who immediately understood the value of Forms for his practice and learned to create his own. The story includes an example of one of the forms he made. Also note that he mentions his staff still determines his billing codes for him, a topic discussed in depth in the next chapter.

Learning Outcomes

After completing this chapter, students should be able to:

◆ Use the Student Edition software to create exam notes for a variety of patients and conditions.

◆ Search for a finding using the "Search" button.

◆ Understand and use the Prompt feature.

◆ Load and use lists of findings to speed up data entry.

◆ Understand and use Forms.

◆ Record orders for tests and therapies.

◆ Record prescriptions.

Teaching Recommendations

■ The first exercise will allow you to evaluate the students' knowledge of the software so far. The exercise uses only the features they have learned in Chapter 3. Students who have any difficulty with this exercise should review and repeat the exercises in Chapter 3 before continuing with this chapter.

■ At this point the students should have mastered the basic layout of the screen and the concepts of adding and editing findings, and adding details to findings. Detailed instructions for scrolling and navigating the lists that were provided in the previous chapter should no longer be necessary. From this point forward, instructions are simplified in areas where the student should already be familiar with the program. This chapter also begins using red and blue bullets (typographic characters) to indicate findings where the student should click the red or blue button in the software.

■ Note that in most cases the screens in the figures are captured after the finding has been selected. The description of a finding often changes when it is selected. Because of this the text instructs students to locate a finding by the description before it is selected, as this is what students will see on their screen. The figures students use to compare their work show the description after the finding is selected.

■ As mentioned in the previous chapter, patient exam notes produced in the exercises are similar to notes created in a medical office; however, they are not intended to represent full and complete medical exams. Exercises in this and other chapters are abridged where necessary to provide conceptual learning experiences within the allotted class time.

■ In two places in this chapter an exercise is a continuation of a previous one and both must be completed before the note is printed. These are Exercises 24–25 and Exercises 26–27. Make certain there is sufficient class time remaining for two exercises before starting the first of the pair.

■ Exercise 24: Caution students who are unfamiliar with medical terms to use care to spell **angina pectoris** correctly when entering the search string. Also note that both words must be entered. (This keeps the search results from having too many findings for the exercise.)

■ Exercise 25 introduces students to lab orders. Although most commercial EHR systems offer laboratory interface systems that electronically send orders, receive results, and automatically populate the EHR with lab data, the Student Edition software does not. It would be inappropriate for student software to contain a true electronic lab order system.

In an EHR, a button similar to the "Lab Orders" button in the toolbar will typically invoke a window in which the clinician creates the actual electronic lab order and sends it to the lab. The importance of electronic lab order systems is covered in Chapter 6 and a pending test order window will be used in Chapter 7 as a simulation of ordering and tracking lab results on a computer. In this exercise students are only recording an order in the note.

■ Exercise 26, Figure 4-43 incorrectly show the red button selected for "Nasal Discharge"; the red button should be selected for "Nasal Discharge Purulent" instaed. However the instructions in the text correctly direct the student to select "Nasal Discharge Purulent".

■ Exercise 27 introduces students to medication orders. Although most commercial EHR systems offer sophisticated prescription writers that make extensive use of the patient's current and previous medications, allergy data, as well as insurance formulary and extensive drug databases, the Student Edition software does not contain those features.

It would be inappropriate to provide students with the capability of writing and sending actual drug prescriptions. The exercises in this and other chapters provide a simulation intended only to demonstrate the concept of writing a prescription on a computer. Similarly, the concepts of automatic drug utilization review and formulary compliance checking are explained but not performed by the software. However, these topics are discussed in several chapters of the book.

■ Exercise 28 is listed as optional, but it is recommended. The exercise reinforces a key concept that the ability to locate findings quickly will improve the speed at which an EHR can be entered. Since the exercise repeats steps with which the students are familiar, students should be able to complete the exercise quickly. This will result in increased confidence as they move forward in subsequent chapters. At the end of the exercise it is interesting to survey students as to the time it took most of them to complete the exercise.

■ Exercise 29: The EHR form has been abridged to shorten the time it takes students to complete the exercise; a full version of the form as it is used in a medical office would have much more detail. A short intake form might be used by a nurse or medical assistant for prescreening. The clinician would then complete the exam, following up on any abnormal findings.

Before beginning Exercise 29, ask students to look at the paper form represented in Figure 4-51 and think about similar forms they might have filled out during visits to their own doctors.

■ After completing this chapter, students should be comfortable with the general process of locating findings and expanding the tree to view additional findings, using Lists, Forms Search, and Prompt features to create patient exam notes. As discussed earlier, this chapter is fundamental to the remainder of the course. Students having difficulty with any area should repeat those exercises before proceeding.

■ Have students review the Chapter Summary and answer the 14 questions at the end of the chapter. The answer key for the questions is provided after the chapter outline. Students should also turn in a printout or file of their exam notes for each exercise. Answer keys showing the steps used to create the patient note are provided for each.

A bank of test questions to create your own chapter exam is also available on the Prentice Hall Health Instructor's Resource CD.

Chapter 4 Outline

I. Increased Familiarity with the Software

II. Documenting a Brief Patient Visit
  A. Hands-On Exercise 23: Documenting a Visit for a Common Cold

III. Why Speed of Entry Is Important in the EHR
  A. Document in real time
  B. Quickly navigate and enter findings

IV. Methods to Increase Speed of Entry
  A. Encounter Tab toolbar
  B. Search and Prompt features
  C. How Search works
    1. Hands-On Exercise 24: Using Search
    2. Hands-On Exercise 25: Ordering Diagnostic Tests

V. Shortcuts That Increase Speed for Routine Exams

VI. The Concept of Lists
  A. Hands-On Exercise 26: Using Adult URI List
  B. Hands-On Exercise 27: Writing Prescriptions in an EHR
  C. Hands-On Exercise 28: Timed Experiment for Extra Credit

VII. The Concept of Forms
  A. Comparison of lists and forms

VIII. Standard Initial Visit Intake for Adult
  A. Hand-On Exercise 29: Using Forms
    1. Left and right mouse buttons

IX. How I Learned to Stop Worrying and Love Forms—A Real-Life Story

X. Chapter Summary

Answer Key 4-1

Testing Your Knowledge of Chapter 4

Students should be permitted run the Medcin Student Edition software to answer the following questions:

1. How do you select a list?

ANSWER: Click on the "List" button in the toolbar to invoke the List Manager window. Locate and highlight the desired list, and then click on the button labeled "Load List." (Also acceptable: From the List Manager.)

2. How do you select Forms?

ANSWER: Select the Active Forms tab at the bottom of the screen. Click the button labeled "Forms" in the toolbar, and then locate and click on the desired form in the Form Manager window. (Also acceptable: From the Form Manager window.)

3. List three features Forms have that Lists do not.

ANSWER: Any three of the following:

Forms are static; findings have a fixed position on Forms and will consistently remain in that position every time the form is used.

Findings from multiple sections of the nomenclature can be mixed on the same page of the form in any way that will enable the quickest data entry. Findings in a list are always organized by category.

Forms may include check boxes, drop-down lists, the fields in the Entry Details section, the onset date, and free-text boxes to record comments.

Forms can control which findings are required and which are optional; every question on a form does not have to be answered for every visit.

4. Describe what the "Prompt" button on the toolbar does.

ANSWER: Generates a list of findings clinically related to the finding currently highlighted.

Write the meaning of each of the following medical abbreviations (as they were used in this chapter):

5. ROS

ANSWER: Review of Systems

6. HPI

ANSWER: History of Present Illness

7. HEENT

ANSWER: Head, Eyes, Ears, Nose, and Throat

8. URI

ANSWER: Upper Respiratory Infection

9. Sig

ANSWER: Instructions for labeling a prescription

(Also acceptable: The student may list the type of information that makes us the "Sig." This would include the quantity prescribed, the number of times per day, capsules to take each time, number of days to take the drug, the total quantity prescribed, the number of refills allowed, and any free-text instructions to the patient.)

10. How do you indicate a "possible" diagnosis?

ANSWER: Select the diagnosis. Then use the Prefix field in the Entry Details section to select "possible" from the drop-down list.

11. **Auto-Negative (the "Negs" button) functions on what two tabs?**

   ANSWER: Symptoms and Physical Exam (or Sx and Px)

12. **Describe how to record a test that was ordered and describe how to record a test that was performed.**

   ANSWER: On the Tx tab:

   Clicking on any test automatically records it as performed.

   Using the prefix "ordered" changes the test to ordered. Alternatively, highlighting a test description (without clicking the red or blue button) and then clicking the "Order" button in the toolbar orders the test.

13. **What Entry Details field is used with a finding to indicate the patient's fever was "mild"?**

   ANSWER: Entry Detail Field "Modifier"

14. **How do you change the numbers on the "List Size" button and what do the numbers do?**

   ANSWER: Clicking on the "List Size" button changes the number sequentially from 1–3 and then back to 1. The list size increases or decreases the quantity of findings listed in the nomenclature pane.

15. **Students should have produced four narrative documents of patient encounters and one optionally for extra credit.**

   Compare the contents of the student exam notes to Answer Keys 4-2 to 4-6. Mark off one point for each finding that is omitted or does not match the exam note shown in the answer key. Step numbers provided in the right column will allow you to help students identify the point in the exercise where their error most likely occurred.

Answer Key 4-2

Evaluation of Printed Exam Note for Exercise 23: Documenting a Visit for a Common Cold

The following corresponds to Figure 4-14 in the textbook. A "Print to HTML" file named "fig4-14_harold_baker.htm" is available on the Instructor's Resource CD.

Harold Baker Student: *(name or ID)*	Page 1 of 1	
Patient: Harold Baker: M: 1/18/1968: 5/01/2006 02:00PM		*Steps 1 and 2*
CHIEF COMPLAINT The Chief Complaint is: Cold or flu		*Step 3*
HISTORY OF PRESENT ILLNESS Harold Baker is a 38-year-old male.		
• Headache		*Step 4*
• Watery nasal discharge		*Step 5*
• Sneezing		*Step 6*
Personal history Behavioral history: No tobacco use		*Step 7*

PHYSICAL FINDINGS
Vital signs:

Vital Signs/Measurements Range	Value	Normal
Oral temperature	99.7 F	97.6–99.6
RR	25 breaths/min	18–26
PR	65 bpm	50–100
Blood pressure	120/80 mmHg	100–120/60–80
Weight	175 lbs	125–225
Height	72 in	65.4–74

Step 8

Head:
• No evidence of a head injury

Step 9

Eyes:

General/bilateral:
• Eyes: normal

Ears:

General/bilateral:
• Ears: normal

Nose:
• A nasal discharge was seen
• No tenderness of the sinus
• Upper Airway: normal

Oral cavity:
• Normal

Step 10

Lungs:
• Normal

Step 11

ASSESSMENT
• Common cold

Step 12

THERAPY
• Fluids
• Bed rest

Step 13

Answer Key 4-3

Evaluation of Printed Exam Note for Exercises 24–25: Using Search and Ordering Diagnostic Tests

The following corresponds to Figure 4-31 in the textbook. A "Print to HTML" file named "fig4-31_gary_yamamoto.htm" is available on the Instructor's Resource CD.

Gary Yamamoto Student: *(name or ID)*	Page 1 of 1	
Patient: Gary Yamamoto: M: 11/11/1956: 5/02/2006 02:45PM		*Steps 1 and 2*
CHIEF COMPLAINT The Chief Complaint is: Suspected Angina		*Step 3*

HISTORY OF PRESENT ILLNESS Gary Yamamoto is a 49-year-old male • Jaw pain during exercise. • No chest pain or discomfort • No dyspnea	*Step 9*
PAST MEDICAL/SURGICAL HISTORY **Diagnosis History:** No hypertension No diabetes mellitus **PERSONAL HISTORY** Behavioral history: Not smoking	*Step 10*

PHYSICAL FINDINGS *Step 4*

Vital signs:

Vital Signs/Measurements	Value	Normal Range
Oral temperature	98.6 F	97.6–99.6
RR 22 breaths/min	18–26	
PR 70 bpm	50–100	
Blood pressure	130/85 mmHg	100–120/60–80
Weight	138 lbs	125–225
Height	65 in	65–73.6

• Pulse rhythm was regular • No hypotension was observed **Cardiovascular system:** Heart Rate and Rhythm: • No bradycardia was observed Heart Sounds: • No S3 was heard • No S4 was heard • No gallop was heard **Skin:** • No generalized pallor	*Step 11*
TESTS **Electrocardiogram:** An ECG was performed	*Step 12*
ASSESSMENT • Possible angina pectoris	*Step 17*
PLAN • An electrolyte panel	*Steps 13 and 14*
• A lipid profile	*Step 15*
• Total plasma cholesterol level • A chest x-ray with posterior-anterior and lateral views	*Step 16*

Answer Key 4-4

Evaluation of Printed Exam Note for Exercises 26–27: Using Adult URI List and Writing Prescriptions in an EHR

The following corresponds to Figure 4-50 in the textbook. A "Print to HTML" file named "fig4-50_kerry_baker.htm" is available on the Instructor's Resource CD.

Patient: Kerry Baker: F: 5/08/1970: 5/03/2006 10:00AM		*Steps 1 and 2*

CHIEF COMPLAINT	*Step 3*
The Chief Complaint is: Patient reported cold or flu	

HISTORY OF PRESENT ILLNESS

Kerry Baker is a 35 year-old female

• Sinus pain • Nasal discharge • Nasal passage blockage	*Step 6*

PAST MEDICAL/SURGICAL HISTORY	
REPORTED HISTORY:	*Step 11*
Reported medications: Not taking medication Medical: A recent URI	

PERSONAL HISTORY

Behavioral history: Not smoking

REVIEW OF SYSTEMS	*Steps 8–9*
Systemic symptoms: Not feeling tired or poorly. Mild fever. No chills	*except "mild" fever*
Head symptoms:	*Step 10*
No headache	

Otolaryngeal symptoms:

No earache, no discharge from the ears, and no sore throat

Neck symptoms:

No swollen glands in the neck

Pulmonary symptoms:

No dyspnea, no cough, not coughing up sputum, and no hemoptysis

Musculoskeletal symptoms:

No muscle aches

PHYSICAL FINDINGS	
VITAL SIGNS:	*Step 4*

Vital Signs/Measurements Range	Value	Normal
Oral temperature	99 F	97.6–99.6
RR 23 breaths/min	18–26	
PR 78 bpm	50–100	
Blood pressure	120/80 mmHg	100–120/56–80
Weight	100 lbs	98–183
Height	60 in	60.2–68.5

Ears:	
General/bilateral: Tympanic Membrane: • Both tympanic membranes were normal	*Step 12*

Nose:

• A purulent nasal discharge was seen • Tenderness of the sinus
• Nasal septum showed no abnormalities • Nasal turbinate was not swollen.

Pharynx:

Oropharynx: • Tonsils showed no abnormalities
Mucosal Findings: • Pharynx was not inflamed

Lymph Nodes:

• Normal

Lungs:

• Respiratory movements were normal • Chest was normal to percussion
• No wheezing was heard • No rhonchi were heard
• No rales/crackles were heard

ASSESSMENT • Acute sinusitis	*Step 13*
ALLERGIES No allergies	*Step 11*
PLAN • Fluids	*Step 14*
• Amoxicillin 500 mg cap (1 po q8h 10) DISP: 30 Refill: 1 Generic: Y Using: Amoxil Mfg: SmithKline Beecham	*Steps 15–18*

Answer Key 4-5

Evaluation of Printed Exam Note for Exercise 28: Timed Experiment for Extra Credit

The student printout should correspond to Figure 4-50 in the textbook except for the time of the encounter entered in Step 2. If the time is not 10:15 AM, the student did not perform the exercise correctly.

Kerry Baker Student: *(name or ID)*	Page 1 of 1	
Patient: Kerry Baker: F: 5/08/1970: 5/03/2006 **10:15AM**		*Step 2*
Students were also instructed to write *their start and stop times on their printout* *to measure how long it took to complete the exercise*		*Step 19*

Answer Key 4-6

Evaluation of Printed Exam Note for Exercise 29: Using Forms

The following corresponds to Figure 4-67 in the textbook. A "Print to HTML" file named "fig4-67_terry_chun.htm" is available on the Instructor's Resource CD.

Terry Chun Student: *(name or ID)*	Page 1 of 2	
Patient: Terry Chun: F: 6/10/1974: 5/04/2006 09:45AM		*Steps 1 and 2*
CHIEF COMPLAINT The Chief Complaint is: New Patient Chart		*Step 3*
HISTORY OF PRESENT ILLNESS Terry Chun is a 31-year-old female		

• Sinus pain • Nasal discharge • Nasal passage blockage	*Step 6*
• Headache recurrent • Sleep disturbances	*Steps 7 and 8*
• No depression • No generalized pain • Not feeling tired or poorly • No fever • No eyesight problems • No hearing loss • No sore throat • No chest pain or discomfort • No palpitations • No dyspnea • Normal appetite • No nausea • No vomiting • No abdominal pain • No diarrhea • No dysuria • No changes in urinary habits • No dizziness	*Step 9*

PAST MEDICAL/SURGICAL HISTORY **Reported History:** Reported medications: Not taking medication **Diagnosis History:** No acute myocardial infarction No hypertension No esophageal reflux No peptic ulcer No diabetes mellitus Migraine headache No stroke syndrome No cancer **PERSONAL HISTORY** Behavioral history: No tobacco use Alcohol: Alcohol use Habits: No recent medical examination **FAMILY HISTORY** No diabetes mellitus Migraine headache No cancer	*Step 13*

REVIEW OF SYSTEMS Patient denies depression but seems very sad	*Step 10*

PHYSICAL FINDINGS

VITAL SIGNS:

Vital Signs/Measurements	Value	Normal Range	
Oral temperature	97 F	97.6–99.6	*Step 14*
RR 22 breaths/min	18–26		
PR 65 bpm	50–100		
Blood pressure	118/81 mmHg	100–120/56–80	
Weight	133 lbs	98–183	

General appearance: • Awake • Alert • Oriented to time, place, and person **Head:** • No evidence of a head injury **Eyes:** General/bilateral Pupils: • Normal **Ears:** General/bilateral Hearing: • Normal	*Step 15*

Nose:

• Tenderness of the sinus

Pharynx:

Oropharynx: • Tonsils showed no abnormalities

Neck:

• Pain was not elicited by motion

Breasts:

General/bilateral:
• No breast mass was found • No tenderness of the breast

Lungs:

• Respiration rhythm and depth were normal

Cardiovascular system:

Heart Rate and Rhythm: • Normal
Murmurs: • No murmurs were heard

Abdomen:

Palpation: • No abdominal tenderness • No mass was palpated in the abdomen
Hernia: • No hernia was discovered

Neurological:

• Speech was normal
Mental Status Findings: • Mental status was normal
Balance: • Normal
Reflexes: • Normal

ASSESSMENT	
• Normal examination	*Step 16*
ALLERGIES	
No allergies	*Step 13*

Electronic Coding from Medical Records

Chapter 5 expands on two of the standardized code sets typically used for billing that were introduced in Chapter 2. Obviously, a complete medical coding course cannot be taught in a single chapter and that is not the intent of this chapter. The purpose of this chapter is to help the student understand the relationship of a codified EHR nomenclature to the CPT-4 Evaluation and Management codes. Later the chapter explores the use of ICD-9CM codes as a key to protocols and (in Chapter 6 to problem lists.)

The CPT-4 Evaluation and Management (E&M) codes have fairly complicated billing rules and severe penalties that cause many providers to select E&M codes that are a level lower than is actually justified by the visit. This chapter explains the rules for E&M coding by analyzing the CMS guidelines in the context of an electronic health record of a visit.

This chapter discusses the elements of an E&M code and compares tables of key elements from the CMS guideline with corresponding key elements of the E&M calculation using the Student Edition software. Hands-on exercises display the findings relevant to a particular key element as the element is discussed in the text. This helps the learner visually understand the relationship of the exam note to the billing codes.

The real-life story demonstrates the relevancy of this chapter's material in the clinic. Dr. Phil Yount, M.D., a practicing physician, discusses the improvement an EHR had on the E&M coding at his group practice in North Carolina. He also discusses clinicians' tendency to undercode.

The chapter then transitions to ICD-9CM codes and discusses their effect on reimbursement, levels of specificity in diagnosis coding, use of multiple diagnosis codes per visit, and justification of the medical necessity of procedures by correct diagnosis coding.

Beyond billing, this chapter also explores the relationship of the diagnosis to patient care plans and orders as well as tests to rule out a diagnosis. This discussion of diagnosis codes is also foundational to Chapter 6, which introduces problem lists and discusses the relationship of diagnosis to codes to a problem list.

A key point for the chapter is that

> **EHR systems support accurate, complete, and consistent coding practices by documenting the encounter with codified nomenclature that can be analyzed and used to determine the level of billing justified and the correct coding of diagnosis.**

As discussed in the final exercise of Chapter 4, a fairly normal workflow in a medical office is to have a nurse or medical assistant start the EHR encounter and save it. Other medical staff members who interact with the patient during the visit retrieve the record, add to it, and save it again. In this chapter the student is taught how to retrieve an existing encounter. This skill will also be used in subsequent chapters.

Learning Outcomes

After completing this chapter, students should be able to:

- Explain why billing codes are important in an EHR system
- Show how evaluation and management codes are determined
- Name and describe key components of E&M codes
- Read and understand the tables used in CMS guidelines
- Explain how the level of key components determines the level of the E&M code
- Use E&M calculator software
- Correctly use and document the time factor to change the level of an E&M code
- Use a diagnosis to find protocols
- Order tests to confirm or rule out a diagnosis

Teaching Recommendations

■ This chapter uses a series of hands-on exercises to break up the fairly dry subject of E&M coding guidelines into digestible pieces. The chapter is not intended as a short course on billing as it does not cover any procedure codes except the evaluation and management codes. A brief history of the CPT-4, HCPCS, and ICD-9CM sets was provided in Chapter 2. If you feel students have forgotten it by Chapter 5, you may wish to have them review those code sets before beginning this chapter.

- If you have previously taught billing or coding classes, you may wish to supplement this chapter with your own lecture material.

- In order to focus strictly on the topic at hand the students do very little data entry. Exercises 30–32 may be stopped and restarted at any point so you can feel free to manage the class time as your students' grasp of the material dictates.

- Once the fundamentals of the E&M code calculations are explained, the chapter proceeds to show how additions to the exam findings alter the E&M code. These exercises are intended to provide an experiential understanding of concepts discussed in this chapter. They should not be construed by the students as a means to increase the E&M codes when it is not warranted.

  Students should not get the impression that it is OK to upcode to maximize reimbursement unless legally entitled by documentation and service provided. Remind students that it is unethical and **illegal** to maximize payment by means that contradict regulatory guidelines.

  Similarly, Exercise 33 demonstrates how time becomes a factor in determining the E&M code. Again, remind students a clinician cannot use time as a factor unless it is substantiated in the documentation.

  Diagnoses or procedures should not be inappropriately included or excluded because payment or the insurance policy coverage requirement will be affected. Medical coders must adhere to the coding conventions, official coding guidelines, and official rules and assign codes that are clearly and consistently supported by clinical documentation in the health record.

- The question may arise if this chapter is necessary for clinical students, such as those students involved in nursing programs. There are several reasons why including this chapter is a good idea:

  - Although some medical programs are uncomfortable discussing billing, the reality is that providers need to be paid for their work. The vast majority of those payments are the result of filing insurance claims that require CPT-4 and ICD-9CM codes. Those codes are derived from the medical records made during the course of the patient exam or treatment. Understanding the relationship of the exam note to those codes is fundamental to the financial success of the medical practice.

  - Nurses in particular need to recognize that later in their schooling they may choose to become licensed nurse practitioners (ARNP) who will apply what they learn here when documenting their own work as providers.

  - Even medical staff who will enter only a portion of data in the EHR need to understand the effect of the EHR on the E&M code so they will capture sufficient detail for the primary provider to bill. You can use the examples in this chapter of the levels of PFSH, which is one portion of the chart often entered by a nurse or medical assistant.

- Reviewers of this book found the table in Figure 5–17, Relationship of Key Component Levels Determine E&M Code, particularly useful for pulling all of the concepts of the key elements together to explain the resulting E&M code. You may find it helpful to use this figure in your lecture on the subject.

■ Areas where students may have trouble:

- Failure to click the "ROS" button will record findings under History of Present Illness instead of Review of Systems. (Solution: Delete the incorrectly recorded symptoms; then click the "ROS" button and reselect the symptoms or restart the exercise if very little data have been entered when the error is discovered.)

- Tests that appear under Tests instead of Plan indicate the student clicked the red button on the finding instead of the "Order" button on the toolbar. (Solution: Delete the finding and reselect it using the "Order" button or edit the finding and set the Prefix field to "ordered.")

- By this point in the exercises students are no longer given instructions when to expand the tree of findings. For example in Exercise 34 students are simply told to locate and click the red button for "Sedentary," which is located under "Exercise Habits."

■ Exercises 34 and 35 are completed together. Make sure there is sufficient class time remaining to complete the pair before starting Exercise 34.

■ Have students review the Chapter Summary and answer the 15 questions at the end of the chapter. The answer key for the questions is provided after the chapter outline. Students should also turn in three printouts or files of their exam notes for Exercises 32–34. Answer keys showing the steps used to create the patient note are provided for each.

A bank of test questions to create your own chapter exam is also available on the Prentice Hall Health Instructor's Resource CD.

Chapter 5 Outline

I. CPT-4 and ICD-9CM Codes for Billing

II. Understanding Evaluation and Management Codes

III. Using EHR Software to Calculate the Correct E&M Code
  A. Hands-On Exercise 30: Calculating E&M Codes from an Exam

IV. How the Level of an E&M Code Is Determined
  A. Key component: History
    1. Chief Complaint
    2. History of Present Illness
    3. Review of Systems
    4. Past, Family, and/or Social History
  B. How history may be documented
  C. Key component: Examination
  D. Key component: Medical Decision Making
    1. Number of diagnoses or management options
    2. Amount and/or complexity of data to be reviewed
    3. Risk of significant complications, morbidity, and/or mortality
  E. Determining the Level of Medical Decision Making
  F. Other components: Counseling, coordination of care, and time

V. Putting It All Together
    A. Evaluating key components

VI. Factors That Affect the E&M Code Set
    A. Hands-On Exercise 31: Exploring the E&M Calculator

VII. Factors That Increase the Level of Codes
    A. Fraud and abuse
    B. Hands-On Exercise 32: Calculating E&M for a More Complex Visit
        1. History
        2. Examination
        3. Medical Decision Making
        4. Time
    C. Hands-On Exercise 33: Counseling More Than 50% of Face-to-Face Time

VIII. A New Level of Efficiency in Addition to Improved E&M Coding—A Real-Life Story

IX. ICD-9CM Codes Justify Billing
    A. Determine the Level of specificity
    B. Multiple diagnosis codes per visit
    C. Primary and secondary diagnoses
    D. Medical necessity
    E. Ordering tests to confirm or rule out diagnosis

X. How the ICD-9 Code Influences Orders and Treatment
    A. Hands-On Exercise 34: Orders Based on Diagnosis
    B. Hands-On Exercise 35: Multiple Diagnoses

XI. Chapter Summary

Answer Key 5-1

Testing Your Knowledge of Chapter 5

Students do not have to run the software to complete these answers.

1. What does the acronym E&M stand for?

ANSWER: Evaluation and Management

2. How many levels are there for a category of E&M codes?

ANSWER: Four

3. Name the three key components of an E&M code:

ANSWER: History, Examination, Medical Decision Making

4. How many levels are there for each key component?

ANSWER: Four

5. How many key components determine the level of E&M code for an established patient?

ANSWER: Two of three

Write the definitions for the following History acronyms:

6. HPI

Answer: History of Present Illness

7. ROS

Answer: Review of Systems

8. PFSH

Answer: Past History, Family History, and Social History (or Past, Family, and Social History)

9. Explain how the level of a general multisystem exam is determined.

Answer: General answer: It is determined by the number of elements of the exam marked with bullets and the number of systems examined.

(Specific answer) Level 1 = 1–5 elements with bullets; Level 2 = 6 or more elements with bullets; Level 3 = at least 12 elements with bullets (2 in 6 different body systems or 12 elements in 2 systems); Level 4 = all elements with bullets in at least 9 systems.

10. What determines the level of risk?

Answer: The highest level of risk in any one category (presenting problems, diagnostic procedures, or management options) determines the overall risk.

11. How many subcomponents (elements) of Medical Decision Making determine its level?

Answer: Determined by the highest levels of any two of the three elements: number of diagnoses, amount or complexity of data, or the level of risk.

12. What makes up face-to-face time?

Answer: Face-to-face time incorporates the total time both before and after the visit, such as time taking patient history, performing the exam, reviewing lab results, planning for follow-up care, and communicating with other providers about the patient's case.

13. When does time become a factor in determining the level of E&M code?

Answer: When counseling and/or coordination of care is more than 50% of the face-to-face time or floor/unit time.

14. What does the "E&M" button on the toolbar do?

Answer: Invoke the Evaluation and Management Calculator window. (Also acceptable: Opens the E&M Calculator window.)

15. How do you record an E&M code in the patient exam note?

Answer: Click on the button labeled "Post to Encounter" in the E&M Calculator window.

Students should have produced and submitted three narrative documents of patient encounters.

Compare the contents of the student exam notes to Answer Keys 5-2, 5-3, and 5-4. Mark off one point for each finding that is omitted or does not match the exam note shown in the answer key. Step numbers provided in the right column will allow you to help students identify the point in the exercise where their error most likely occurred.

Answer Key 5-2

Evaluation of Printed Exam Note for Exercise 32: Calculating E&M for a More Complex Visit

The following corresponds to Figure 5-33 in the textbook. A "Print to HTML" file named "fig5-33_ m_williams.htm" is available on the Instructor's Resource CD.

Mary Williams Student: *(name or ID)*	Page 1 of 1
Patient: Mary Williams: F: 2/14/1980: 5/05/2006 10:45AM **CHIEF COMPLAINT** The Chief Complaint is: Patient reports stuffy sinus **HISTORY OF PRESENT ILLNESS** Mary Williams is a 26-year-old female • Sinus pain • Nasal discharge • Nasal passage blockage	*Step 1*
PERSONAL HISTORY Behavioral history: Smoking for 16 years	*Step 5*
REVIEW OF SYSTEMS **Systemic symptoms:** No fever	*Step 4*
PHYSICAL FINDINGS **Vital signs:**	*Step 7*

Vital Signs/Measurements Range	Value	Normal
Oral temperature	97.9 F	97.6–99.6
RR 25 breaths/min	18–26	
PR 65 bpm	50–100	
Blood pressure	128/90 mmHg	100–120/56–80
Weight	155 lbs	98–183
Height	65 in	60.2–68.5

Ears: General/bilateral: Tympanic Membrane: • Both tympanic membranes were normal **Nose:** • A purulent nasal discharge was seen • Nasal turbinate was swollen • Tenderness of the sinus **Pharynx:** Oropharynx: • Tonsils showed no abnormalities Mucosal Findings: • Pharynx was not inflamed **Lungs:** • Chest was normal to percussion	*Step 1*
• No wheezing was heard • No rhonchi were heard	*Step 6*
ASSESSMENT • Acute sinusitis **PLAN** • Fluids	*Step 1*
PRACTICE MANAGEMENT Estab outpatient expanded h&p - low complexity Fdecisions;	*Step 10*
Total face-to-face time 15 min	*Step 9*

Answer Key 5-3

Evaluation of Printed Exam Note for Exercise 33: Counseling More Than 50% of Face-to-Face Time

The following corresponds to Figure 5-37 in the textbook. A "Print to HTML" file named "fig5-37_ m_williams_counseling.htm" is available on the Instructor's Resource CD.

Mary Williams Student: *(name or ID)*	Page 1 of 1	
Patient: Mary Williams: F: 2/14/1980: 5/05/2006 10:45AM **CHIEF COMPLAINT** The Chief Complaint is: Patient reports stuffy sinus **HISTORY OF PRESENT ILLNESS** Mary Williams is a 26-year-old female • Sinus pain • Nasal discharge • Nasal passage blockage	*Step 1*	
PERSONAL HISTORY Behavioral history: Smoking for 16 years	*Step 3*	
PHYSICAL FINDINGS **Ears:** General/bilateral: Tympanic Membrane: • Both tympanic membranes were normal **Nose:** • A purulent nasal discharge was seen • Nasal turbinate was swollen • Tenderness of the sinus **Pharynx:** Oropharynx: • Tonsils showed no abnormalities Mucosal Findings: Pharynx was not inflamed **Lungs:** • Chest was normal to percussion **ASSESSMENT** • Acute sinusitis **PLAN** • Fluids	*Step 1*	
PRACTICE MANAGEMENT Estab outpatient expanded h&p - low complexity decisions; Total face to face time 15 min;	*Step 5*	
Counseling and coordination of care was more than 50% of encounter time 10 minutes of a 15 minute visit was spent counseling the patient on the risks of smoking and the very early age at which she started. We discussed the various aids to help her quit. She has agreed to try over-the-counter patches	*Step 6*	

Answer Key 5-4

Evaluation of Printed Exam Note for Exercises 34–35: Orders Based on Diagnosis and Multiple Diagnoses

The following corresponds to Figure 5-55 in the textbook. A "Print to HTML" file named "fig5-55_gloria_natell.htm" is available on the Instructor's Resource CD.

Gloria Natell Student: *(name or ID)*	Page 1 of 1	
Patient: Gloria Natell: F: 9/07/1953: 5/08/2006 01:30PM		*Steps 1 and 2*
CHIEF COMPLAINT The Chief Complaint is: Patient reports jaw pain		*Step 3*
PERSONAL HISTORY		*Step 8*
Behavioral history: Not smoking Habits: Sedentary		
Home environment: Housing has peeling lead-based paint		*Step 14*
REVIEW OF SYSTEMS		*Step 7*
Head symptoms: No headache		*Step 15*
Otolaryngeal symptoms:		*Step 7*
Jaw pain		
Cardiovascular symptoms:		
No chest pain or discomfort and no palpitations		
Gastrointestinal symptoms:		
No nausea, no vomiting,		*Step 15*
and no abdominal pain		*Step 7*
Endocrine symptoms:		
No excessive sweating		*Step 7*
Neurological symptoms:		
No dizziness		*Step 7*
and no generalized convulsions		*Step 15*
No fainting,		*Step 7*
no confusion, and no disorientation		*Step 15*
PHYSICAL FINDINGS **Vital signs:**		*Step 4*
Vital Signs/Measurements	Value	Normal Range
Oral temperature	99 F	97.6–99.6
RR 27 breaths/min	18–26	
PR 70 bpm	50–100	
Blood pressure	115/70 mmHg	100–120/56–80
Weight	150 lbs	98–183
Height	70 in	59.8–68.1
Oral cavity:		
Gums: • Showed no gingival line		*Step 16*

Cardiovascular system:	
Heart Sounds: • No S3 was heard • No S4 was heard • No gallop was heard	*Step 9*
Skin:	
• No generalized pallor	
ASSESSMENT	
• Angina pectoris	*Step 6*
• Possible poisoning by lead	*Step 13*
PLAN	
• A comprehensive metabolic panel	*Step 10*
• A hepatic function panel	*Step 17*
• A lipid profile	*Step 10*
• Serum lead level • Urine lead, 24 hr	*Step 17*
• An ECG • A cardiac stress test	*Step 10*
• Institute prescribed exercise program • Low-cholesterol diet • Low-fat cooking	*Step 11*
• Family screening	*Step 18*

Comprehensive Evaluation of Chapters 1–5

This comprehensive evaluation is at the midpoint of the book to help you measure your students' mastery of the material. Students complete both a written test and hands-on exercise. Answer keys are provided later.

Detailed steps guide the students through the hands-on exercise in the same manner as previous exercises except there are no figures to compare against. Figures 5-56 – 5-74 only appear in the instructor's materials and do not appear in the student text. Students must be able to follow directions and document the patient visit without visual cues. An illustrated, step-by-step walkthrough of the exercise is provided later in this chapter. A PowerPoint presentation of Exercise 36 included on the Instructor's Resource CD can be used for class review after the exams have been graded.

Students should be permitted to run the Student Edition software during both the written and practical exams.

Depending on the length of classes, it may be necessary to administer the written exam in one class period and the hands-on exercise in another so that there will be time to complete the hands-on exercise.

Answer Key 5-5

Part I—Written Exam

Give a brief description of the purpose of each of the following coding systems:

1. **Medcin**

   ANSWER: A medical nomenclature and knowledge base designed for point-of-care use. It is used to document the patient visit in a codified structure that generates a complete exam note. The nomenclature codifies findings. Each finding represents a meaningful clinical observation or term linked with other medically relevant findings.

2. **CPT-4**

   ANSWER: Current Procedural Terminology, Fourth Edition. CPT-4 is a billing code set that provides standardized codes for reporting medical services, procedures, and treatments performed for patients by the medical staff.

3. **ICD-9CM**

   ANSWER: International Classification of Diseases, Ninth Revision, Clinical Modifications is a system of standardized codes to classify mortality and morbidity. ICD-9CM diagnosis codes are required on insurance claims to justify the need for the procedure or service performed. ICD-9CM is also used to statistically track causes of death.

   Students might also remember that the first two volumes provide a listing and an index of diagnosis codes. The third volume, however, lists codes for hospital inpatient procedures. Also in Chapter 5, students learned that the codes could be used as keys to protocols and care plans.

4. Explain the difference between an EHR nomenclature and a billing code set.

ANSWER: EHR nomenclatures differ from billing codes in that they are designed to codify the details and nuance of the patient–clinician encounter. Billing codes are designed to represent the exam, service, or a medical supply.

5. Describe how to retrieve a previous patient encounter.

ANSWER: Click Select on the menu bar and then click Existing Encounter. A small window will open from which you may select the desired encounter.

6. Which screen do you use to set the reason for the visit?

ANSWER: The New Encounter window (where you set the date and time of the new encounter).

7. How do you load a list?

ANSWER: Click on the button on the toolbar labeled "Lists." This invokes the List Manager window. Highlight the desired list and click the button labeled "Load List." (Also acceptable: From the List Manager window.)

8. How do you enter vital signs?

ANSWER: The textbook teaches students to enter vital signs using the Vital Signs Form. They also used a Short Intake Form that included vital signs. Acceptable answer: Vitals signs are entered (in this text) through a form.

Write the meaning of each of the following medical abbreviations:

9. ROS

ANSWER: Review of Systems

10. Hx

ANSWER: History

11. HEENT

ANSWER: Head, Eyes, Ears, Nose and Throat (note that some medical texts include mouth). Do not mark off students who add mouth if the other body parts are listed correctly.

12. Dx

ANSWER: Diagnosis or diagnoses

13. PFSH

ANSWER: Past History, Family History, and Social History. (Also acceptable: Past, Family and Social History.)

14. URI

ANSWER: Upper Respiratory Infection

15. E&M

ANSWER: Evaluation and Management

16. Describe how to record a test that was performed.

ANSWER: Click the red or blue button for the test finding. (Note: The wrong answer is to click the "order" button. This will not record the test as performed.)

17. How many levels are there for a category of E&M codes?

ANSWER: Four

18. Name the key components of an E&M code.

ANSWER: History, Examination, Medical Decision Making

19. What Entry Details field is used with a finding to indicate a "possible" diagnosis?

ANSWER: The Prefix field

20. What determines the E&M level of risk?

ANSWER: Risk is determined by three factors: number of possible diagnoses and/or management options that must be considered; the amount and/or complexity of medical records, diagnostic tests, and/or other information that must be obtained, reviewed, and analyzed; and the risk of significant complications, morbidity, and/or mortality, as well as co-morbidities, associated with the patient's presenting problems, diagnostic procedures, and/or the possible management options. Each of these factors has four levels.

The short answer is the level of risk is determined by the factor with the highest level (most risk or complexity).

21. Where are "bullets" used in E&M calculation?

ANSWER: In the Examination component. They refer to specific items in various body systems marked with a typographic character called a "bullet" in the CMS guidelines.

Describe the purpose of the following buttons on the Medcin toolbar:

22. Prompt

ANSWER: "Prompt" with current finding dynamically generates a list of findings medically related to the finding that was highlighted at the time the "Prompt" button was clicked. All six tabs of the Nomenclature pane are populated with related findings (if any exist).

23. Order

ANSWER: Adds the prefix "Ordered" to a test finding. (Acceptable answer: Orders tests.)

24. List Size

ANSWER: Increases or decreases the number of findings displayed on a list in the Nomenclature pane.

25. Rx

ANSWER: Invokes prescription writer (Also acceptable: Orders medications.)

26. Search

ANSWER: Searches for a word or phrase; it is used to locate quickly all findings in the nomenclature containing either matching words or synonyms of the search word.

27. Negs

ANSWER: Auto-Negative; a button that will automatically set all the findings (that are not already set) to "normal." The "Negs" button is operative only on Symptom or Physical Exam findings.

28. ROS

ANSWER: The "ROS" button toggles off and on. When it is On, selecting findings in the History tab records them in the Review of Systems section of the note. When it is Off, findings selected in the History tab are recorded in the History of Present Illness section.

29. E&M

ANSWER: Invokes the E&M Calculator window.

30. Explain the difference in calculating the E&M level of a general multi-system exam and a single organ exam.

ANSWER: Both types of exams determine the level by the number of items examined that were marked with bullets in a particular CMS guideline. In the general multisystem exam there will be bullets in every body system, and generally all the bullets count toward the level. In a single organ exam, certain body systems are outlined with a shaded border and clinicians must perform the items in the shaded boxes to determine the level of the exam. Also certain body systems have no items marked with bullets in a single organ exam.

Carl Brown

Student: Terry Jones
Patient: Carl Brown: M: 10/11/1975: 5/09/2006 09:15AM
Chief complaint
The Chief Complaint is: Patient reports waking at night short of breath.
History of present illness
    Carl Brown is a 30 year old male.
    • Paroxysmal nocturnal dyspnea.
Past medical/surgical history
Reported History:
    Reported prior tests: No chest x-ray was performed and an ECG was not performed.
    Reported medications: Not taking medication.
    Medical: No previous hospitalization for a pulmonary problem.
    Exposure: No exposure to a contagious disease.
    Environmental exposure: Secondhand cigarette smoke exposure, exposure to dust mites, and animal dander.
Diagnosis History:
    No coronary artery disease
    No angina pectoris
    No acute myocardial infarction
    No congestive heart failure.
    No hypertension.
    Bronchitis
    Asthma.
    No esophageal reflux
    No peptic ulcer.
    No diabetes mellitus.
    No migraine headache
    No stroke syndrome.
    No cancer
Personal history
Behavioral history: No tobacco use.
Alcohol: Alcohol use.
Habits: A recent medical examination.
Travel history: Travel history was unknown.
Family history
No coronary artery disease
    No angina pectoris
    No acute myocardial infarction
    No congestive heart failure
    No hypertension
    No bronchitis
    No asthma
    No esophageal reflux
    No peptic ulcer
    No diabetes mellitus
    No migraine headache
    No stroke syndrome
    No cancer.

▲ **Figure 5-56a Printed Exam Note—Carl Brown Page 1 of 2**

Carl Brown

Review of systems
Systemic symptoms: Not feeling tired or poorly, no fever, and no recent weight loss.
Head symptoms: No headache and no sinus pain.
Eye symptoms: No watery discharge from eyes. No red eyes.
Otolaryngeal symptoms: No nasal passage blockage and no sore throat.
Cardiovascular symptoms: No chest pain or discomfort.
Pulmonary symptoms: Not feeling congested in the chest, no dyspnea, no cough, no hemoptysis, and no wheezing.
Physical findings
Vital signs:

Vital Signs/Measurements	Value	Normal Range
Oral temperature	98.6 F	97.6 - 99.6
RR	28 breaths/min	18 - 26
PR	78 bpm	50 - 100
Blood pressure	120/80 mmHg	100-120/60-80
Weight	175 lbs	125 - 225
Height	71 in	65.4 - 74

   ° No pulsus paradoxus was noted.
Eyes:
General/bilateral:
External Eye: ° No petechiae in the conjunctiva.
Nose:
   • An .2 cm intranasal polyp was found. ° No rhinorrhea was seen.
Lymph Nodes:
   ° Normal.
Lungs:
   ° Respiration rhythm and depth was normal. ° Respiratory movements were normal.
   ° Chest was normal to percussion. ° No wheezing was heard. ° No rhonchi were heard.
   ° No decrease in breath sounds was heard. ° No prolonged expiratory time.
   ° No rales/crackles were heard.
Cardiovascular system:
Murmurs: ° No murmurs were heard.
Abdomen:
Palpation: ° No abdominal tenderness.
Skin:
   ° No ordered cyanosis.
Assessment
   • Possible mild intermittent asthma
Therapy
   • Frequent vacuuming.
   • Avoid exposure to allergens.
   • Follow-up visit.
Allergies
An allergy. No known drug allergies.
Counseling/Education

   • Patient education about asthma
Plan
   • CBC with differential
   • Spirometry
   • Albuterol
   90 ug puffs (1 inh prn) DISP:1 inhal Refill:3 Generic:Y Using:Proventil Mfg: Schering
Practice Management
   Estab outpatient expanded h&p - low complexity decisions; Total face to face time ten min

▲ **Figure 5-56b Printed Exam Note—Carl Brown Page 2 of 2**

Answer Key 5-6

Part II—Evaluation of Printed Exam Note for Exercise 36: Examination of a Patient with Asthma

The following corresponds to Figure 5-56 in this Instructor's Manual. A "Print to HTML" file named "fig5-56_exam_(c_brown).htm" is available on the Instructor's Resource CD.

A PowerPoint file is also available for class review after the exam has been graded. The steps in the answer key that follows may be used by the instructor to help students find where they made any error.

Carl Brown Student: *(name or ID)*	Page 1 of 2	
Patient: Carl Brown: M: 10/11/1975: 5/09/2006 09:15AM		*Steps 1 and 2*
CHIEF COMPLAINT The Chief Complaint is: Patient reports waking at night short of breath.		*Step 3*
HISTORY OF PRESENT ILLNESS Carl Brown is a 30-year-old male. • Paroxysmal nocturnal dyspnea.		*Step 8*
PAST MEDICAL/SURGICAL HISTORY		*Step 6*
Reported History: Reported prior tests: No chest x-ray was performed and an ECG was not performed. Reported medications: Not taking medication.		
Medical: No previous hospitalization for a pulmonary problem.		*Step 10*
Exposure: No exposure to a contagious disease.		*Step 6*
Environmental exposure: Secondhand cigarette smoke exposure, exposure to dust mites, and animal dander.		*Step 10*
Diagnosis History: No coronary artery disease No angina pectoris No acute myocardial infarction No congestive heart failure No hypertension Bronchitis Asthma No esophageal reflux No peptic ulcer No diabetes mellitus No migraine headache No stroke syndrome No cancer **PERSONAL HISTORY** Behavioral history: No tobacco use Alcohol: Alcohol use Habits: A recent medical examination Travel history: Travel history was unknown		*Step 6*

FAMILY HISTORY

No coronary artery disease
No angina pectoris
No acute myocardial infarction
No congestive heart failure
No hypertension
No bronchitis
No asthma
No esophageal reflux
No peptic ulcer
No diabetes mellitus
No migraine headache
No stroke syndrome
No cancer

REVIEW OF SYSTEMS	*Step 9*
Systemic symptoms:	
Not feeling tired or poorly, no fever, and no recent weight loss	
Head symptoms:	
No headache and no sinus pain	
Eye symptoms:	
No watery discharge from eyes. No red eyes	
Otolaryngeal symptoms:	
No nasal passage blockage and no sore throat	
Cardiovascular symptoms:	
No chest pain or discomfort	
Pulmonary symptoms:	
Not feeling congested in the chest, no dyspnea, no cough, no hemoptysis, and no wheezing	

PHYSICAL FINDINGS — *Step 4*

Vital signs:

Vital Signs/Measurements Range	Value	Normal
Oral temperature	98.6 F	97.6–99.6
RR 28 breaths/min	18–26	
PR 78 bpm	50–100	
Blood pressure	120/80 mmHg	100–120/60–80
Weight	175 lbs	125–225
Height	71 in	65.4–74

• No pulsus paradoxus was noted	*Step 12*
Eyes:	
General/bilateral:	
External Eye: • No petechiae in the conjunctiva	

Nose:	*Step 11*
• An .2 cm intranasal polyp was found	

• No rhinorrhea was seen	*Step 12*
Lymph nodes:	
• Normal	
Lungs:	
• Respiration rhythm and depth were normal • Respiratory movements were normal • Chest was normal to percussion • No wheezing was heard • No rhonchi were heard • No decrease in breath sounds was heard • No prolonged expiratory time • No rales/crackles were heard	
Cardiovascular system:	
Murmurs: • No murmurs were heard	

Abdomen:	
Palpation: • No abdominal tenderness	
Skin:	
• No ordered cyanosis	

| **ASSESSMENT** | |
| • Possible mild intermittent asthma | *Step 14* |

THERAPY	
• Frequent vacuuming	*Step 15*
• Avoid exposure to allergens	
• Follow-up visit	

| **ALLERGIES** | |
| An allergy. No known drug allergies | *Step 6* |

| **COUNSELING/EDUCATION** | |
| • Patient education about asthma | *Step 15* |

PLAN	
• CBC with differential	*Step 13*
• Spirometry	

| • Albuterol | *Steps 16–17* |
| 90 ug puffs (1 inh prn) DISP:1 inhal Refill:3 Generic: Y Using:Proventil Mfg: Schering | |

| **PRACTICE MANAGEMENT** | |
| Estab outpatient expanded h&p - low complexity decisions; Total face-to-face time 10 min | *Step 19* |

Instructor's Illustrated Steps for Hands-On Exercise 36: Examination of a Patient with Asthma

Carl Brown is 30-year-old established patient with possible mild asthma who comes to the office complaining of awakening in the night short of breath. In this exercise you use the skills you have acquired to document this exam.

▶ **Figure 5-57 Selecting Carl Brown from the Patient Selection Window**

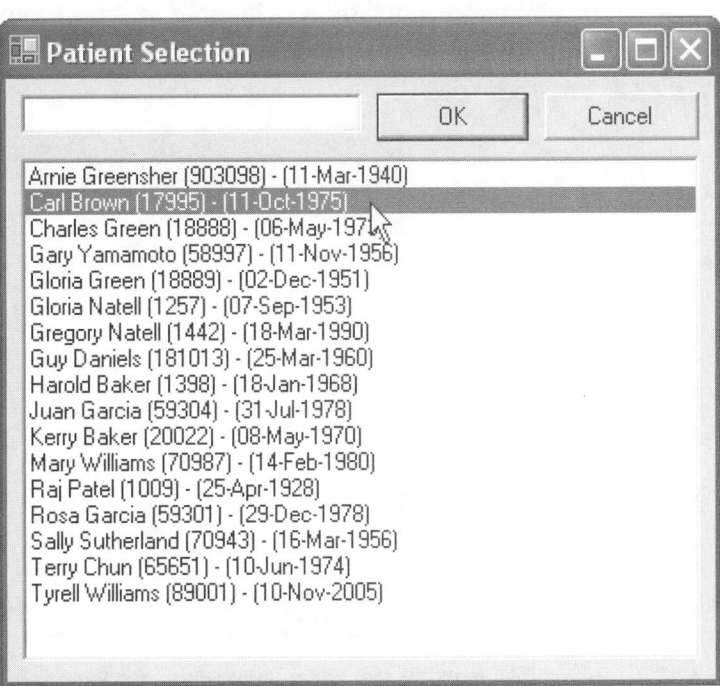

Step 1 If you have not already done so, start the Student Edition software.

Click Select on the menu bar, and then click Patient.

In the Patient Selection window, locate and click on **Carl Brown**.

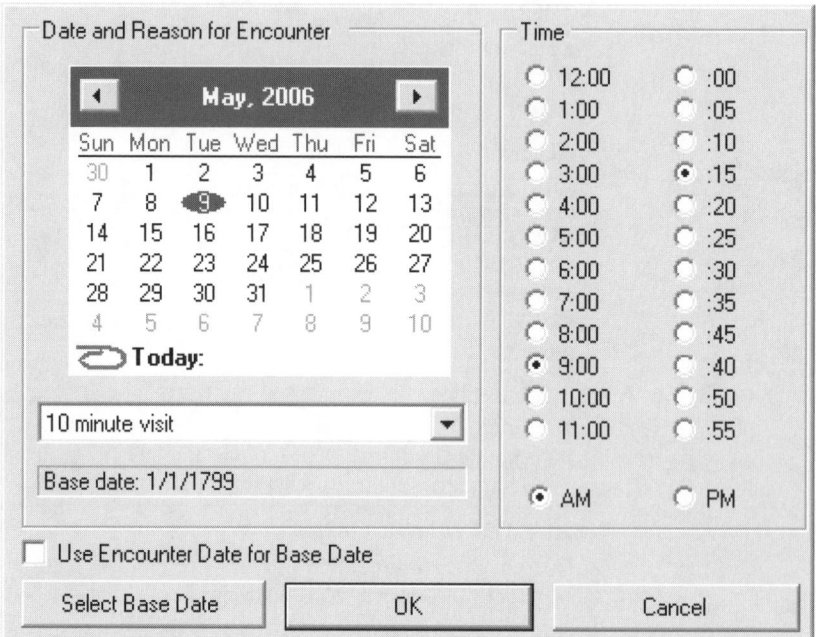

▲ Figure 5-58 New Encounter for a 10-Minute Visit, May 9, 2006, 9:15 AM

Step 2 Click Select on the menu bar, and then click New Encounter.

Select the date **May 9, 2006**, the time **9:15 AM**, and the reason **10 Minute Visit**.

Make certain you set the date and reason correctly. Compare your screen to the date, time, and reason printed in bold type before clicking on the "OK" button.

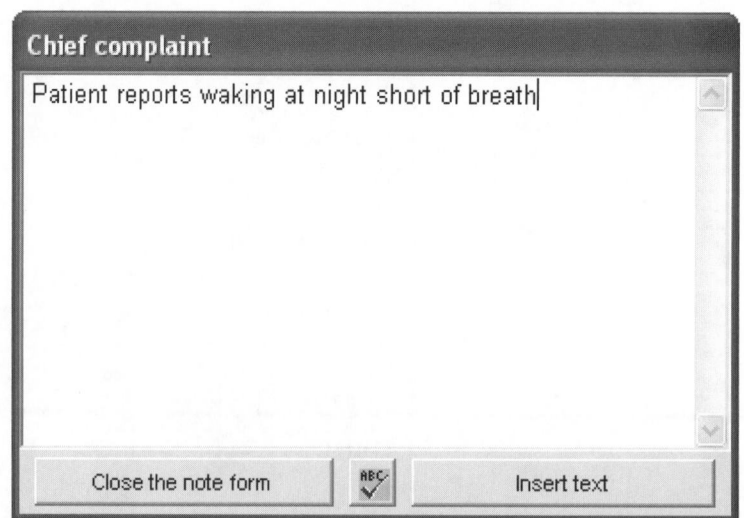

▲ Figure 5-59 Chief Complaint Dialog for Patient Reports Waking at Night Short of Breath

Step 3 Enter the Chief Complaint by locating the button in the toolbar labeled "Chief" and clicking on it.

In the dialog window that will open, type "**Patient reports waking at night short of breath.**"

When you have finished typing, click on the button labeled "Close the Note Dialog."

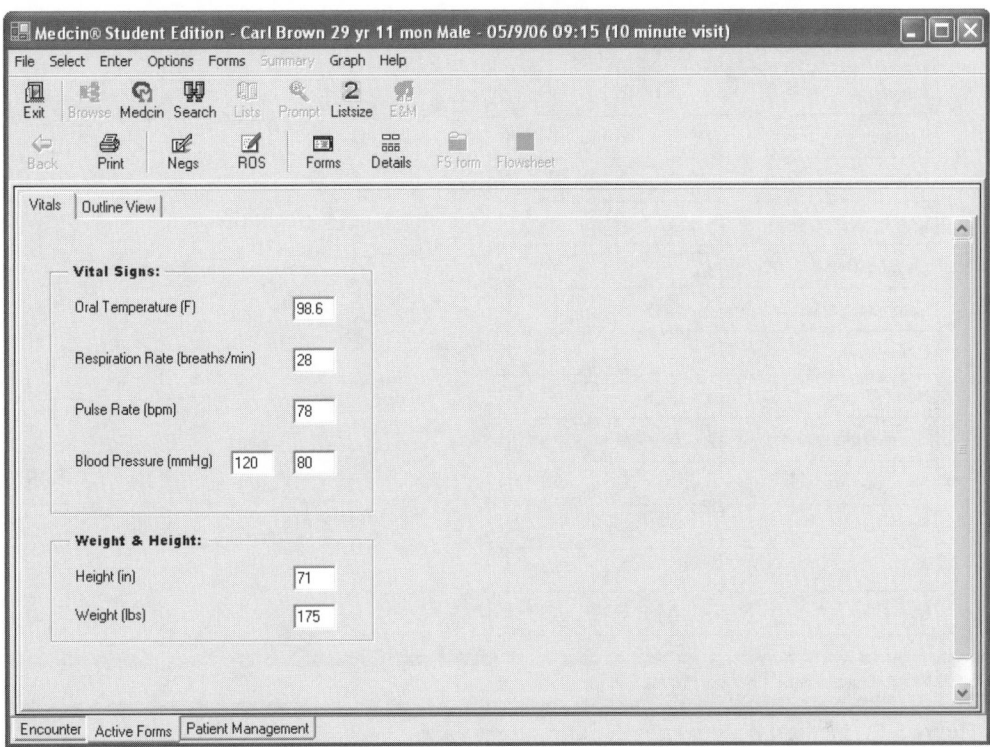

▲ **Figure 5-60 Vital Signs Form for Carl Brown**

Step 4 Begin the visit by taking Carl's vital signs and medical history.

Use the form labeled "Vitals," which you will select from the Forms Manager, invoked on the Active Forms tab (as you have done in previous exercises).

Enter Carl's vital signs in the corresponding fields on the form as follows:

Temperature:	**98.6**
Respiration:	**28**
Pulse:	**78**
BP:	**120/80**
Height:	**71**
Weight:	**175**

When you have finished, check your work. If it is correct, proceed to Step 5.

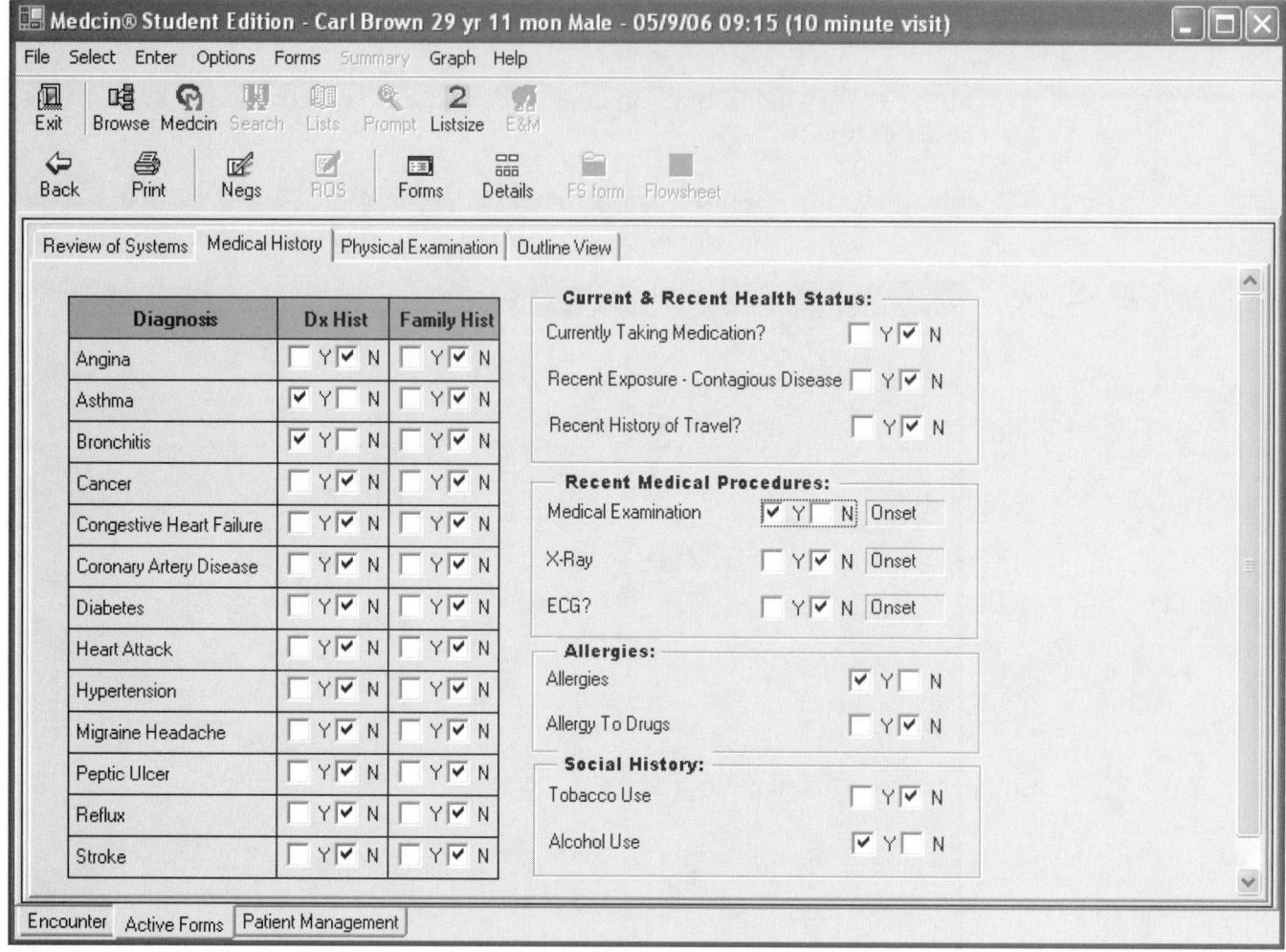

▲ **Figure 5-61 Medical History Page of Short Intake Form**

Step 5 Remain on the Active Forms tab. Take the patient's medical history by using the Short Intake Form.

Locate and click on the button labeled "Forms" in the toolbar at the top of your screen to invoke the Forms Manager window again.

Locate and click on the form labeled "Short Intake" as you have done in previous exercises.

Step 6 When the Short Intake Form is displayed, locate and click on the tab labeled "Medical History."

Enter the Dx History and Family History by clicking on the Y (yes) check box or the N check box for the following items:

Diagnosis	Dx Hist	Family Hist
Angina	✓ N	✓ N
Asthma	✓ Y	✓ N
Bronchitis	✓ Y	✓ N
Cancer	✓ N	✓ N
Congestive Heart Failure	✓ N	✓ N
Coronary Artery Disease	✓ N	✓ N
Diabetes	✓ N	✓ N
Heart Attack	✓ N	✓ N
Hypertension	✓ N	✓ N
Migraine Headache	✓ N	✓ N
Peptic Ulcer	✓ N	✓ N
Reflux	✓ N	✓ N
Stroke	✓ N	✓ N

Complete the rest of the patient's medical history in the right side of the form by locating and clicking on the check boxes as follows:

Currently Taking Medication	✓ N
Recent Exposure (Contagious Disease)	✓ N
Recent History of Travel	✓ N
Recent Medical Examination	✓ Y
Recent X-Ray	✓ N
Recent ECG	✓ N
Allergies	✓ Y
Allergy to Drugs	✓ N
Tobacco	✓ N
Alcohol	✓ Y

When you have finished, check your work. If it is correct, click on the Encounter tab at the bottom of the screen.

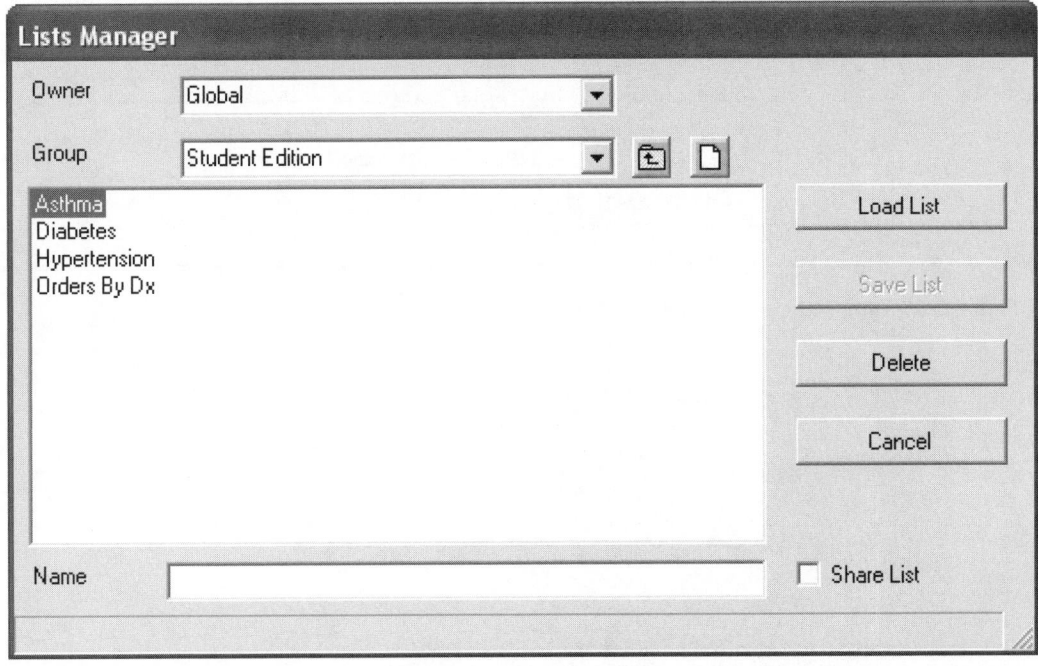

▶ **Figure 5-62 Select Asthma from Lists Manager Window**

Step 7 Locate and click on the "Lists" button in the toolbar at the top of your screen. The List Manager window will be invoked.

Two fields at the top of the List Manager window organize the display of list names, filtering them by Owner and Group. The Student Edition has two groups: "All" and "Student Edition."

Click on the down arrow in the Group field and select the group "Student Edition" as you have done previously in Chapter 5.

Locate and highlight the list named Asthma. Click your mouse on the button labeled "Load List."

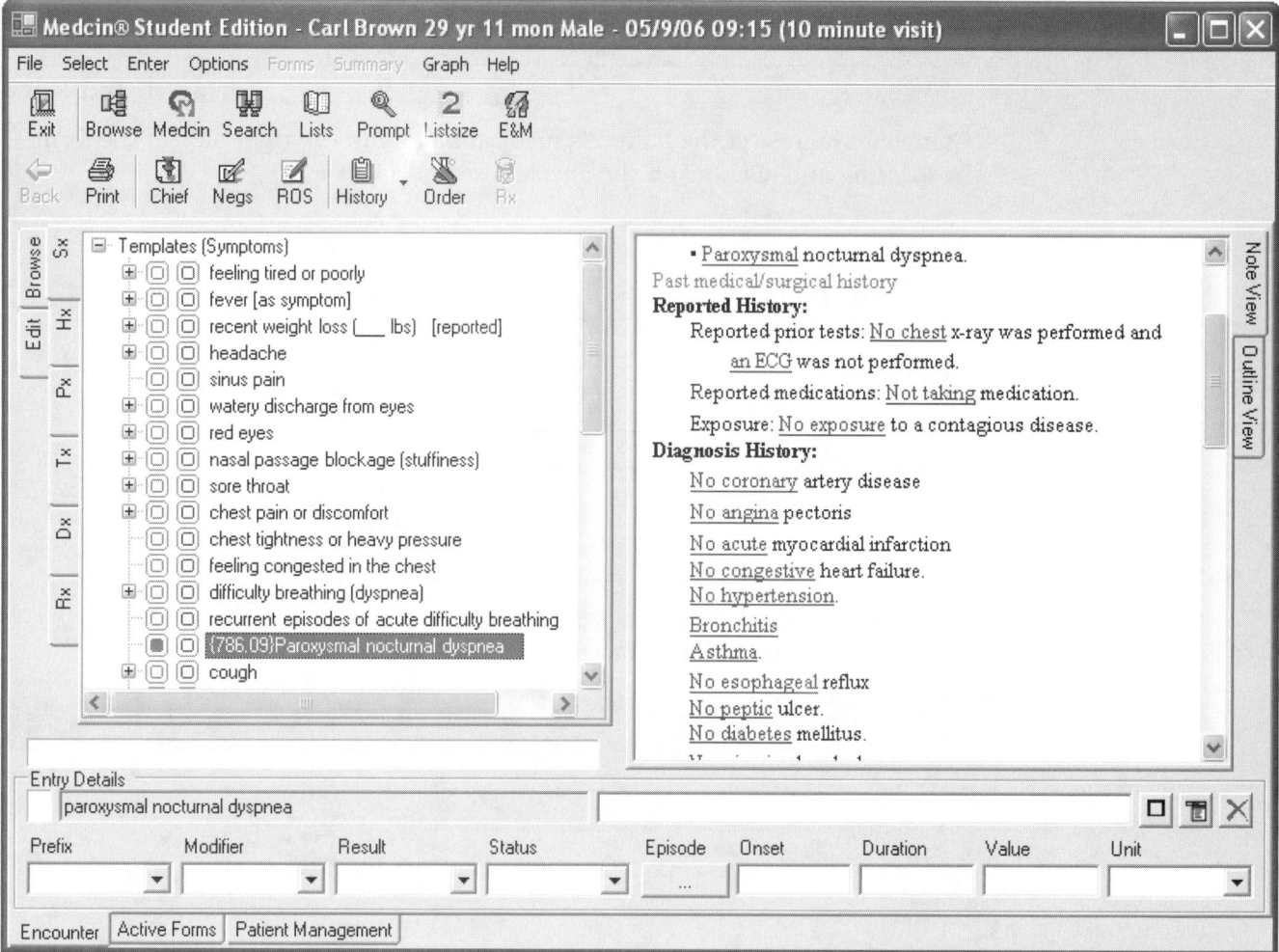

▲ **Figure 5-63 Symptoms on the Asthma List (Template)**

Step 8 The left pane should be on the Sx tab and the title of first line should be "Templates (Symptoms)." If it is not, click on the tab labeled "Sx."

Locate and click on the following symptom findings:

● (red button) awaking in night short of breath

The text will change to Paroxysmal Nocturnal Dyspnea.

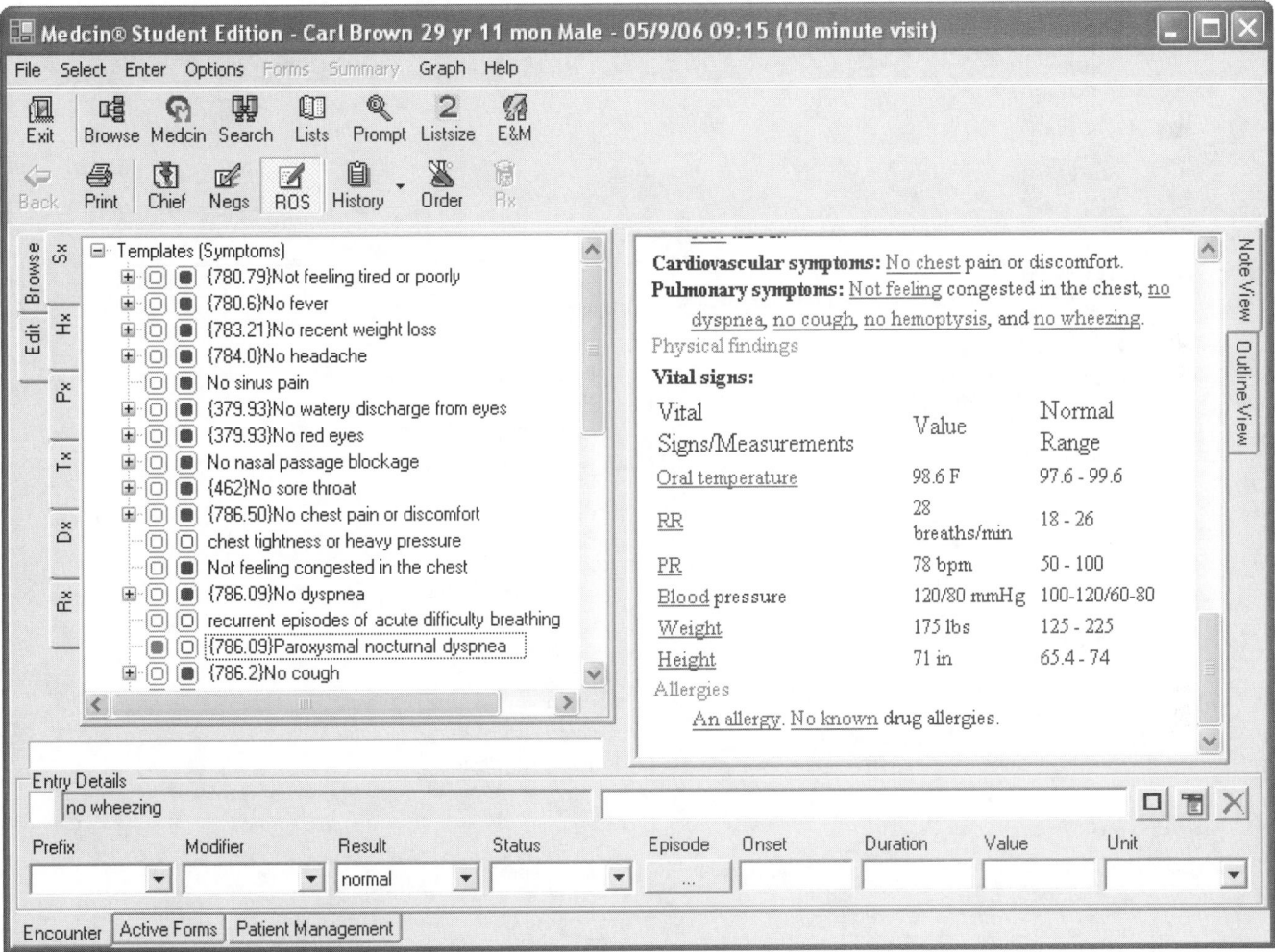

▲ **Figure 5-64 Auto Negative (Neg) and Review of Systems (ROS) Findings**

Step 9 Locate and click on the "ROS" button in the toolbar at the top of your screen.

Verify the "ROS" button is depressed.

Locate and click on the button labeled "Negs" in the toolbar at the top of your screen.

All unselected symptoms findings will be set by Auto Negative.

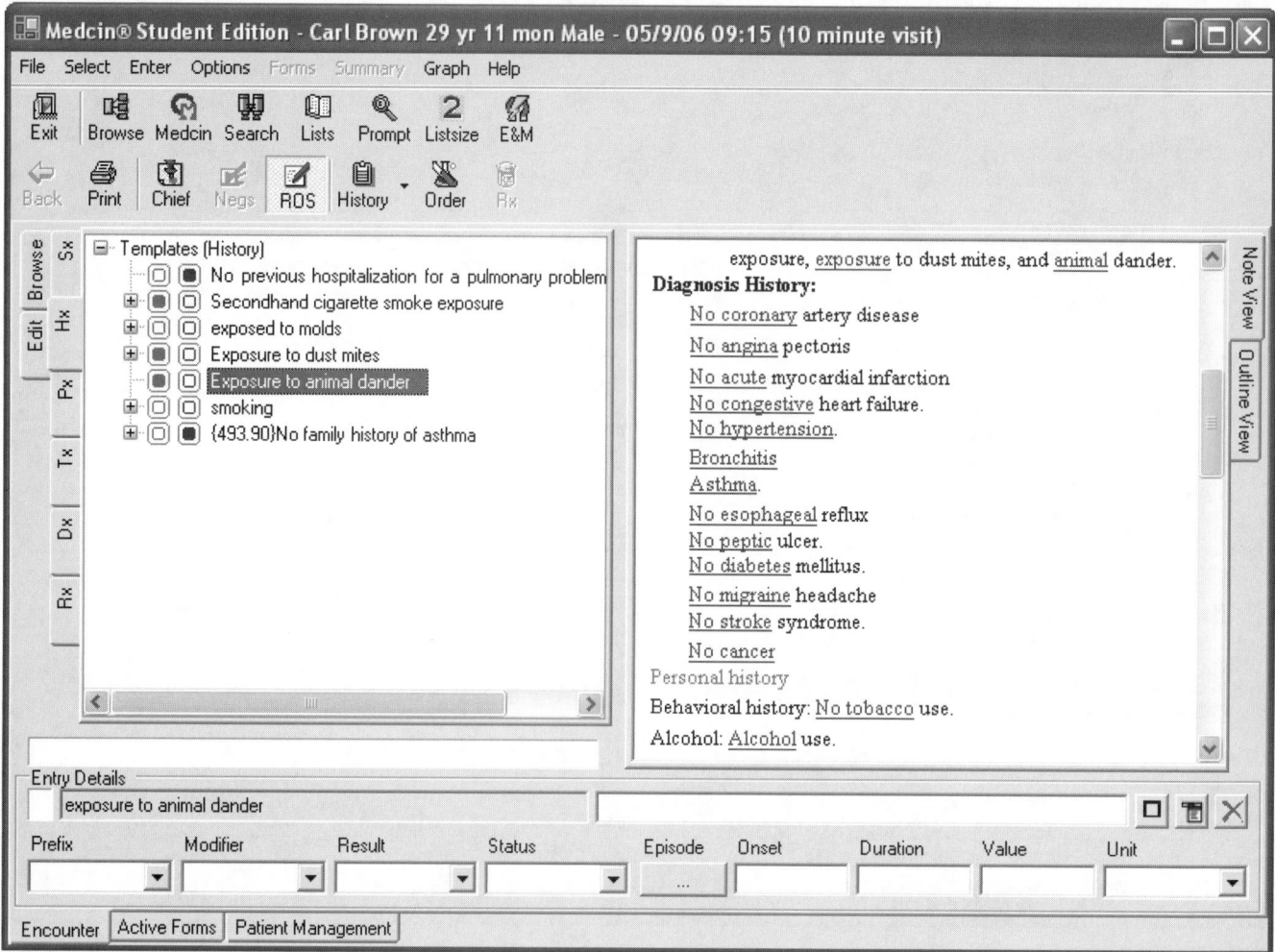

▲ **Figure 5-65 Hx Tab**

Step 10 Next click on the Hx tab to enter the patient's history. Note that "No family history of asthma" was already set via the Short Intake Form.

Locate and click on the following findings:

● (blue button) Previous hospitalization for pulmonary problem

● (red button) Exposure to secondhand cigarette smoke

● (red button) Exposure to dust mites

● (red button) Exposure to animal dander

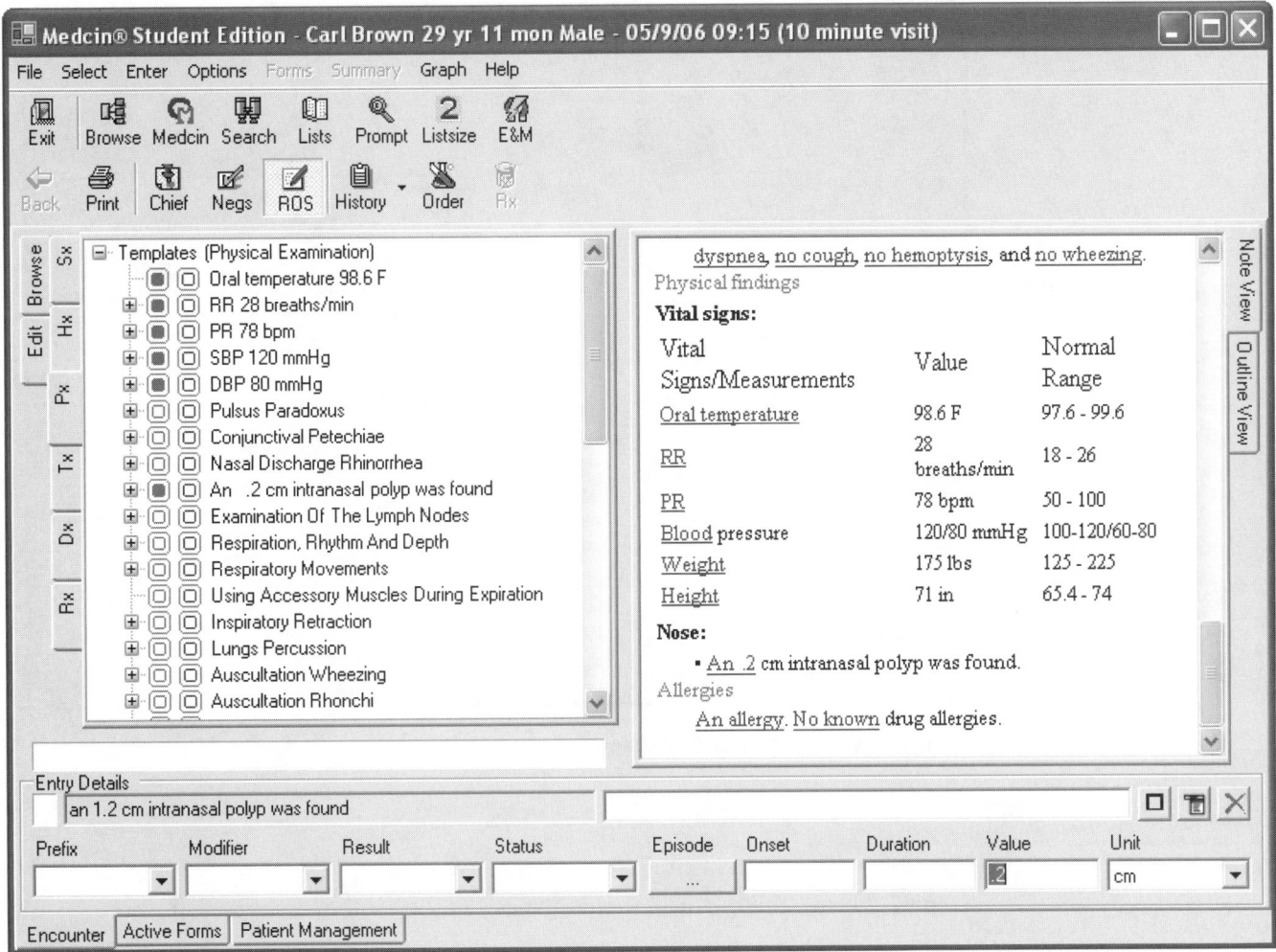

▲ **Figure 5-66 Px Tab with Finding: 1.2 cm Interstesal Polyp**

Step 11 Click on the Px tab to document the physical exam. Notice that the findings from the Vitals Form are already displayed.

Locate and highlight the finding: Intranasal polyp __ cm.

In the Entry Details section of your screen, locate the field labeled "Value." Enter the numeric value **0.2** (two tenths) and press the Enter key.

The finding text should change to read "An .2 cm intranasal polyp was found."

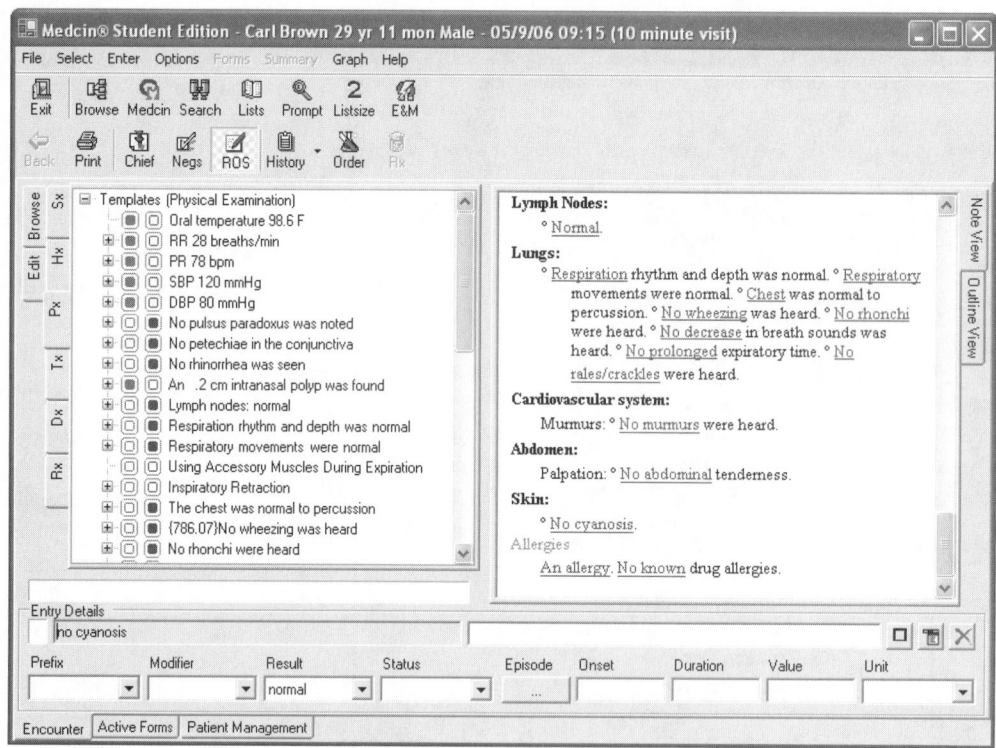

▲ **Figure 5-67 Px Tab After Auto-Negs**

Step 12 Locate the button labeled "Negs" in the toolbar and click it once.

Px findings not previously set will be set by Auto Negative.

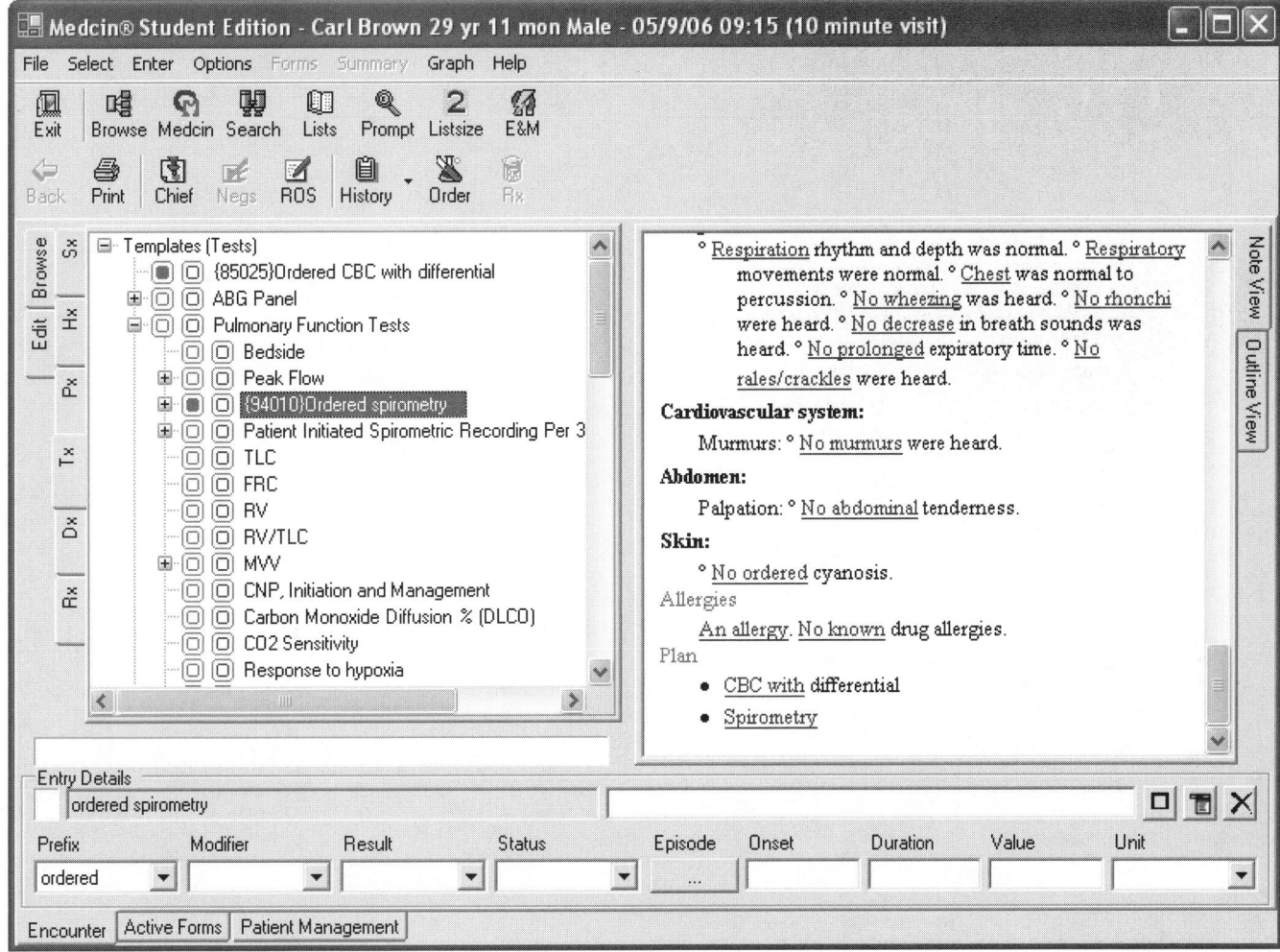

▲ **Figure 5-68 Order CBC and Spirometry**

Step 13 Click on Tx tab.

Locate and highlight **CBC with Differential;** click on the "Order" button.

Expand the tree of findings for Pulmonary Function Tests.

Locate and highlight **Spirometry** and click on the "Order" button.

Verify that both tests appear in the plan before proceeding.

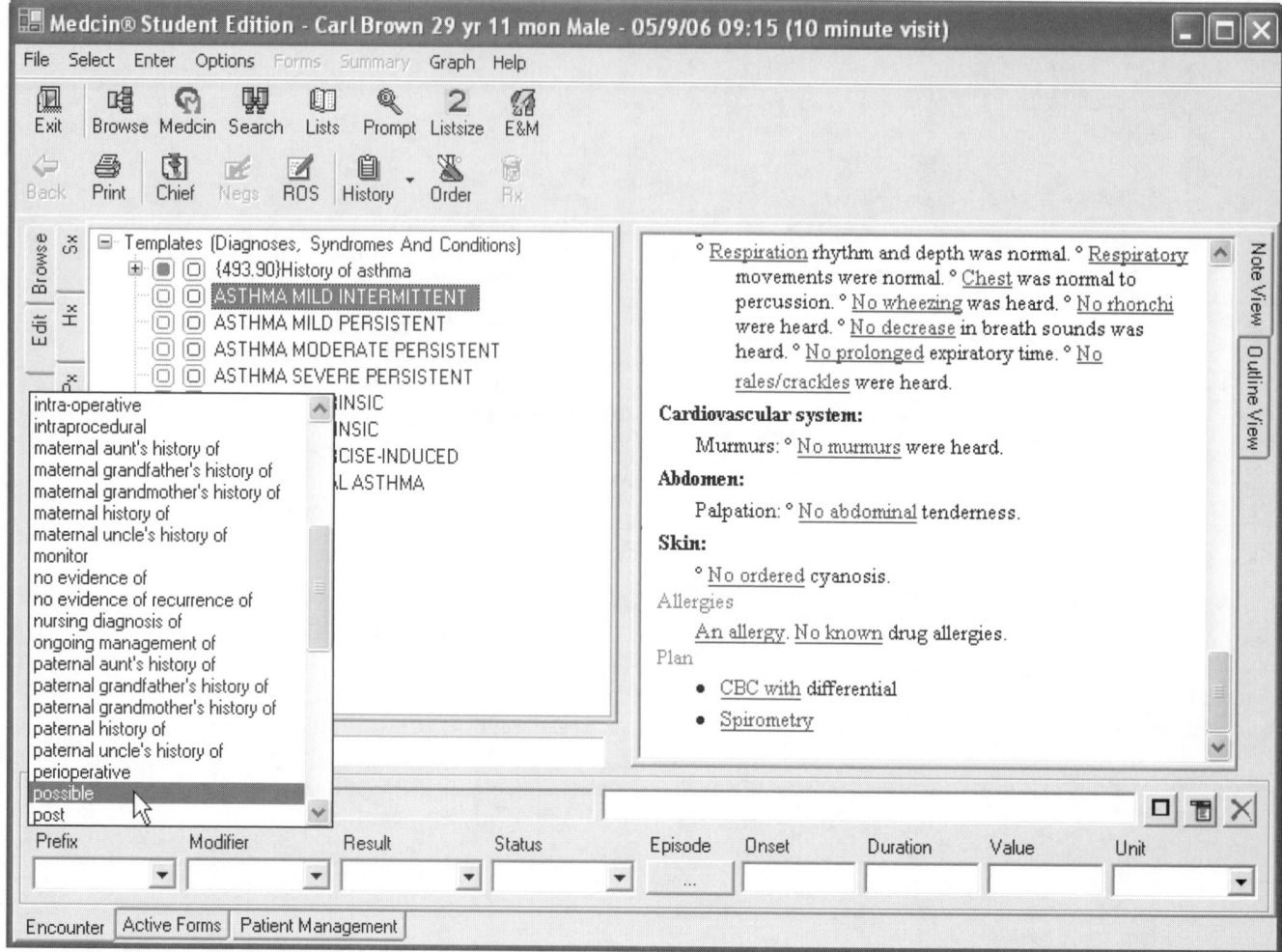

▲ **Figure 5-69 Assessment—Possible Asthma**

Step 14 Click on the Dx tab.

Locate and click on the following finding:

● (red button) Asthma mild intermittent

Click the down arrow button in the Prefix field. Select the prefix **"possible"** from the drop-down list displayed.

Step 15 Click on the Rx tab.

Expand the tree for Environmental Control Measures.

Locate and click on the following finding:

● (red button) Frequent vacuuming

● (red button) Avoid allergens

● (red button) Patient education—asthma

● (red button) Follow-up visit

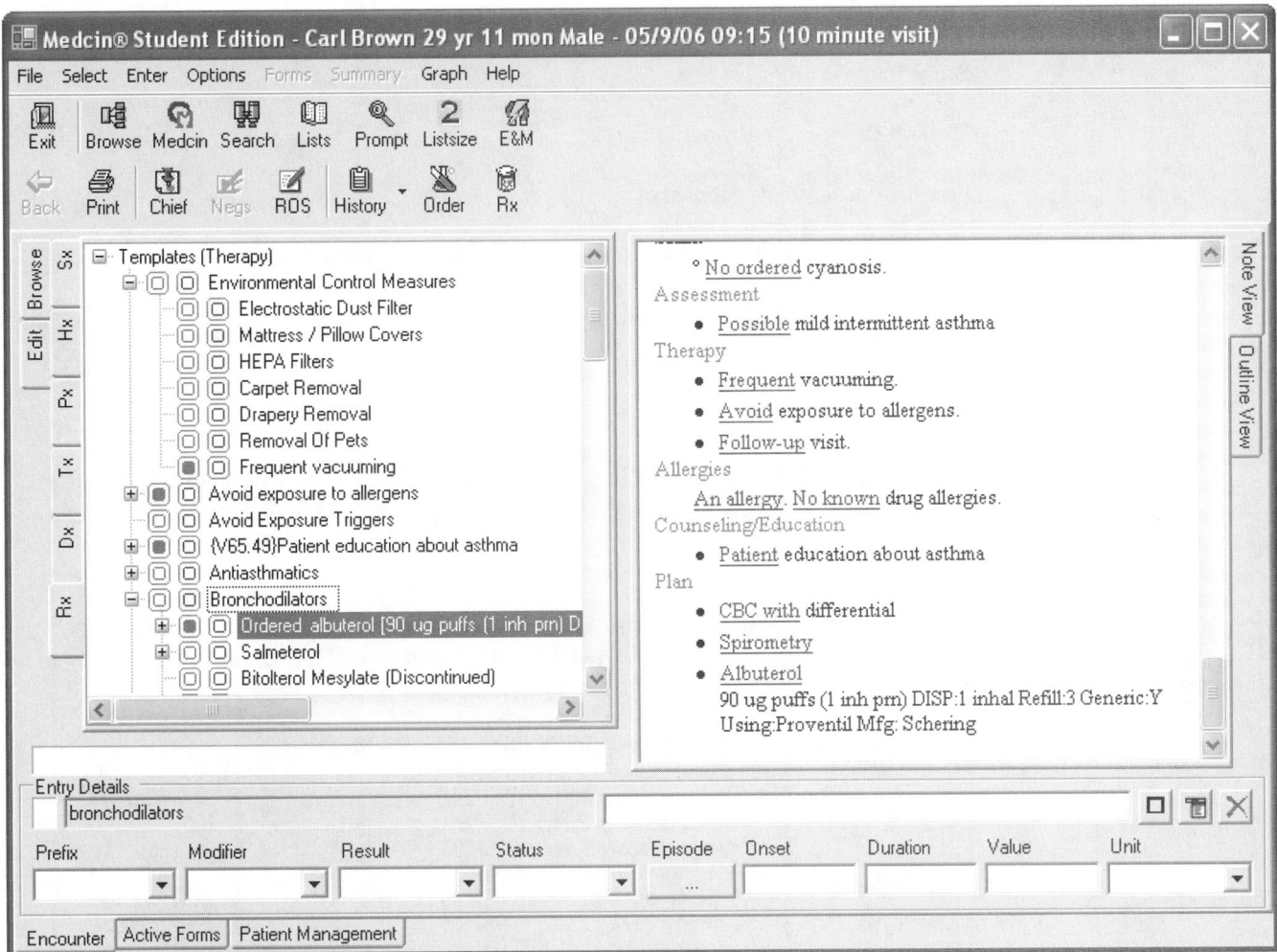

▲ **Figure 5-70 Environmental Orders for Carl Brown**

Step 16

Enter a prescription.

Expand the tree for Bronchodilators.

Locate and highlight **Albuterol.**

Click on the Rx button in the toolbar. The Prescription Writer window will be invoked.

Step 17 In the Rx Dosage Inquiry window, locate and click on the following Sig:

90 microgram puffs 1 inh prn DSP1

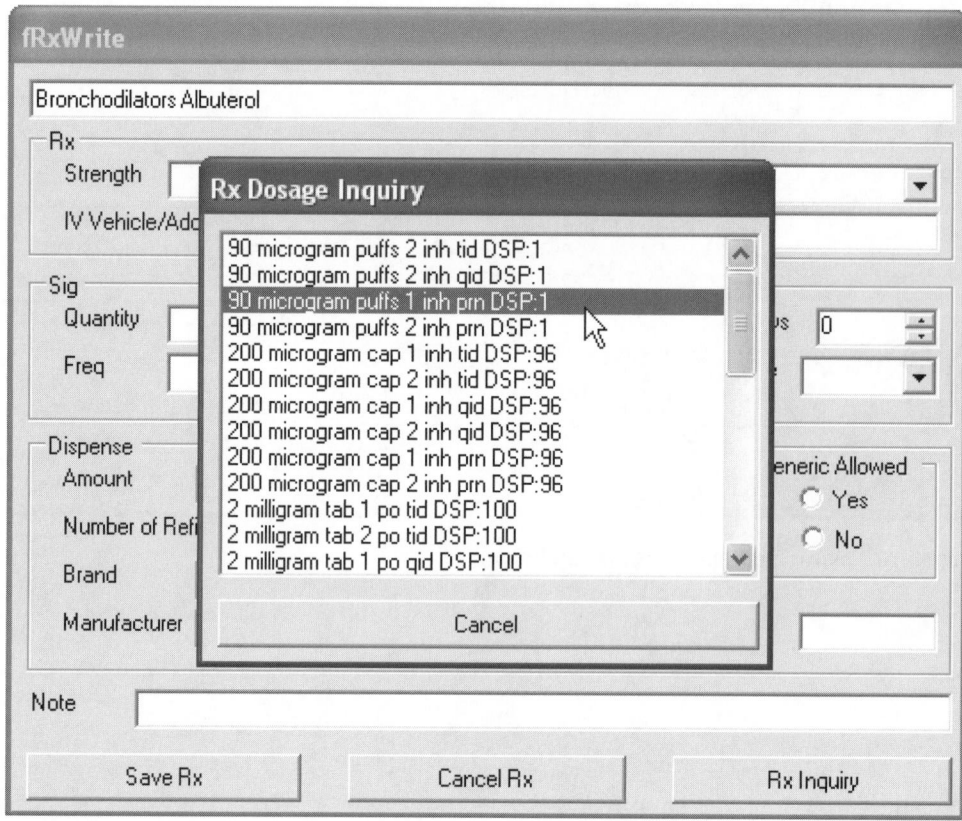

▲ **Figure 5-71 Prescription Rx Dosage Inquiry**

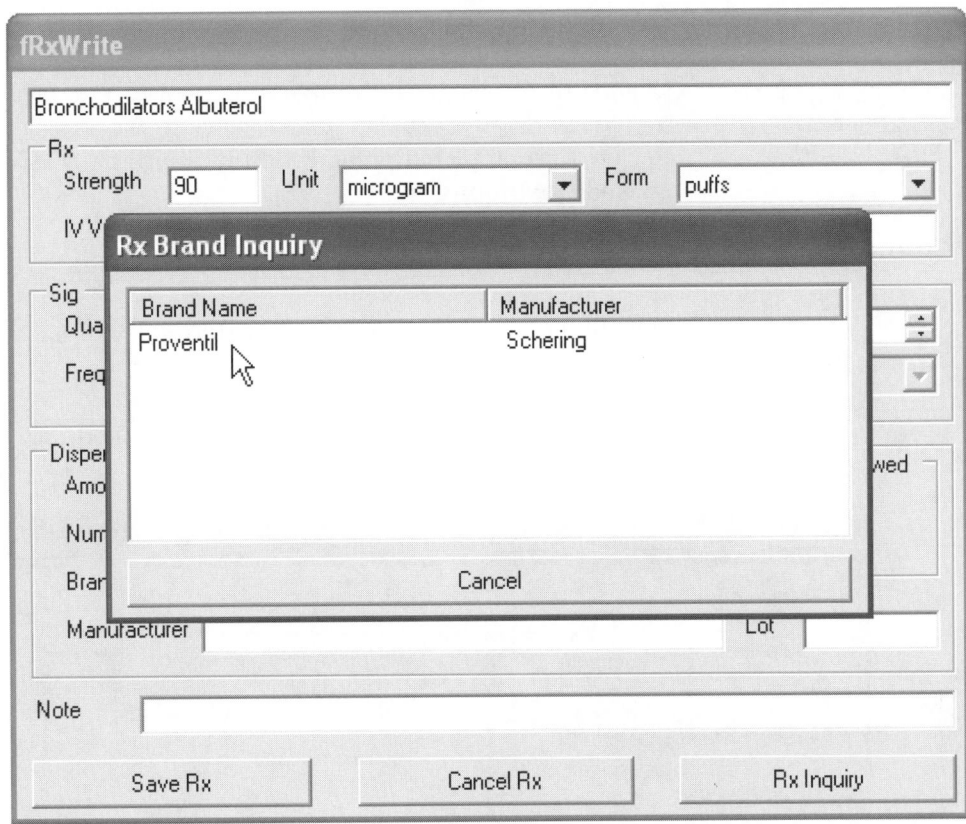

When the Rx Brand Inquiry window is displayed, position your mouse over the brand Proventil and click your mouse button.

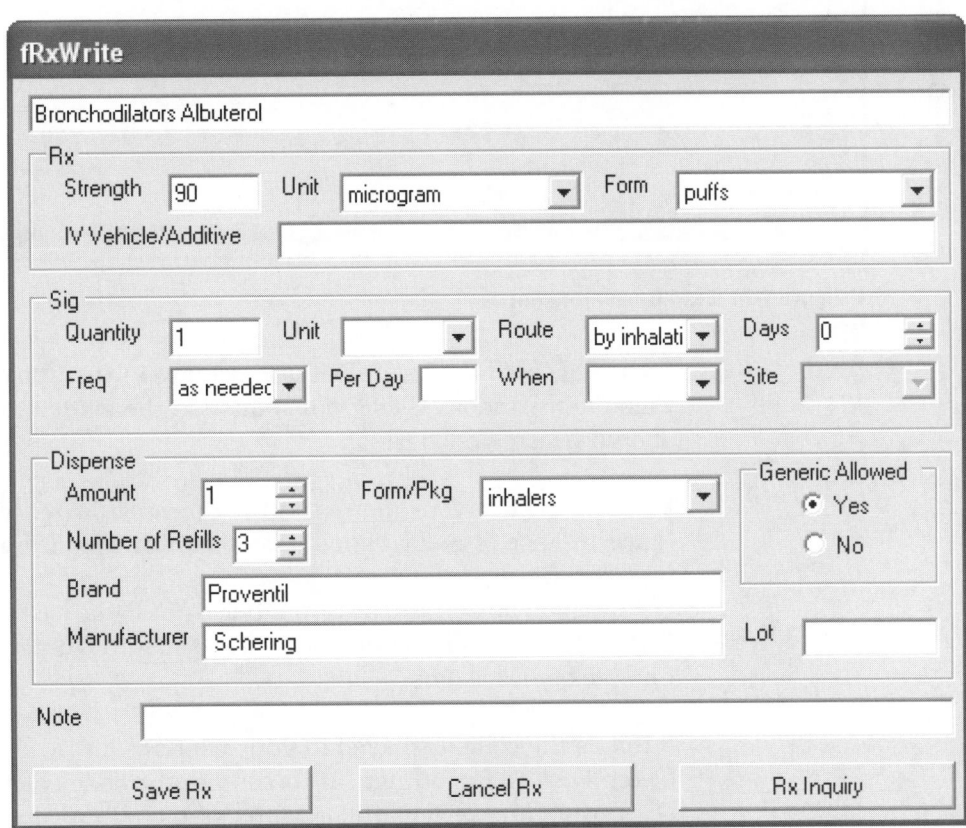

Locate the field labeled "Generic Allowed."

Click your mouse in the white circle next to Yes. It should become filled in.

Review the completed prescription. If anything is incorrect, click on the button labeled "Rx Inquiry" to correct it.

Locate and click on the button labeled "Save Rx."

Step 18 Locate and click on the button labeled "E&M" in the toolbar at the top of your screen.

The E&M Calculator window should be invoked.

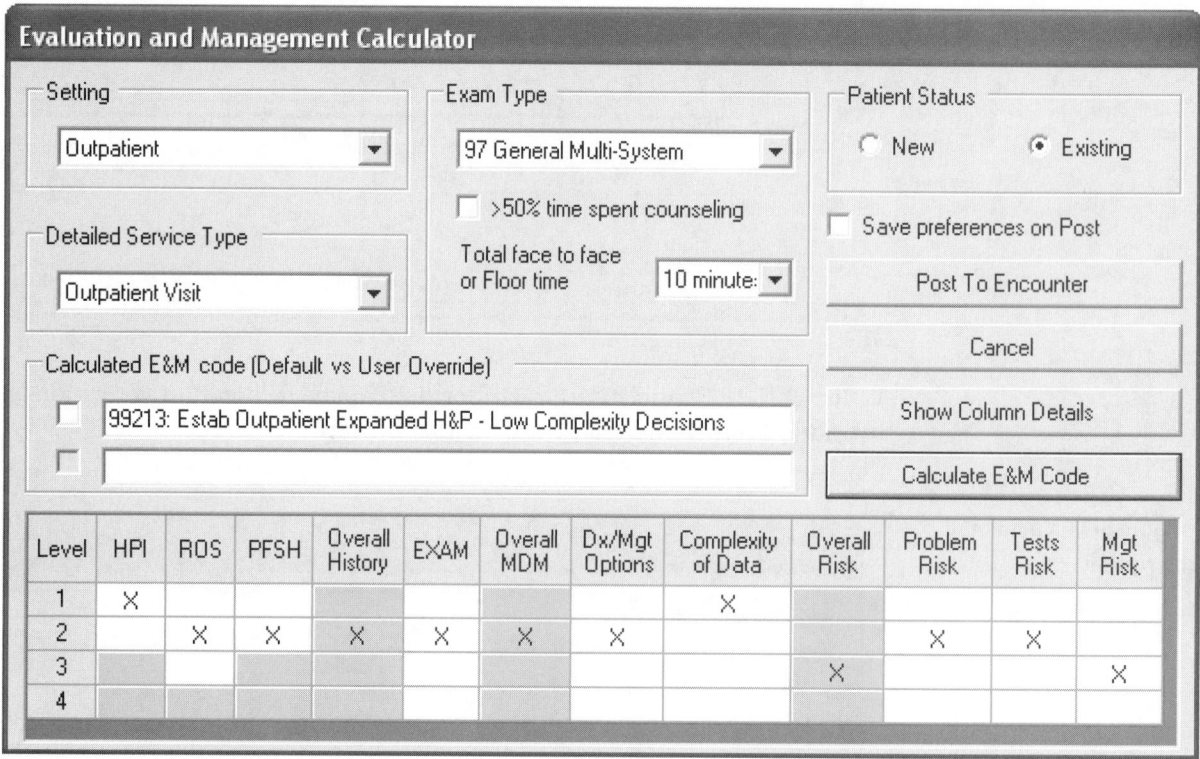

▲ **Figure 5-74 E&M Calculator Window**

Step 19 Locate the Patient Status section in the upper right corner of the E&M Calculator window. Click your mouse in the white circle next to **Existing**. It should become filled in.

Locate and click your mouse on the down arrow button in the field labeled "Face-to-Face or Floor Time." Select **10 minutes** from the drop-down list.

Locate and click on the button labeled "Calculate E&M Code." The Calculated E&M Code field should display "99213: Estab Outpatient Expanded H&P—Low Complexity Decisions."

If this is the code displayed in your window, locate and click on the button labeled "Post To Encounter." If this is not the code calculated, click on the "Cancel" button and review the previous steps to find your error.

Step 20 Click File on the menu bar, and then click Print Encounter or Print To HTML (as directed by your instructor).

If you are printing your work, you may alternatively click the "Print" button on the toolbar at the top of your screen.

Hand in the completed printout or HTML file to your instructor.

Remember: **Do not close or exit the encounter until you have a printed copy in your hand.** You will lose your work if you exit before printing.

6

Advanced Techniques Speed Data Entry

Chapter 6 enlarges upon concepts introduced in Chapters 1–4. Hands-on exercises allow students to experiment with other methods of documenting the exam and introduce the concepts of patient management, problem lists, and graphing lab trends. Standards for electronic interchange of data discussed in Chapter 1 are given further meaning by explanations of medical devices and electronic lab interfaces in this chapter. The workflow of electronic lab order and result systems is also discussed.

Data entry by the patient is first introduced in this chapter by Dr. Allen Wenner. The concept is tied to making better use of the clinician's time and to improving accuracy of the record because, as Dr. Wenner points out, the only person who actually knows the symptoms and history of present illness is the patient. However, the idea of patient involvement in the EHR introduced here is further developed in Chapter 9 where we will explore different styles of practice and the use of different technologies for EHR input.

Important Information About the Student Edition Patient History Program

One important technical item for instructors in this chapter is the use of the Student History program. In this and subsequent chapters the students will work with patients' complete medical history using information from years of previous encounters for some patients. This presents a challenge for the computer program because the exercises require multiple students to simultaneously retrieve patient charts and enter findings for the same patient without disturbing the sample data for the next class.

To accommodate this, a special software program loads previous patient history into the computer's memory just for these exercises. If your classroom is part of a school network, only one copy of the History program on the network server needs to be running. Information in the installation instructions encourages the network administrator to set this program to run automatically so you will not have to think about it. However, if it has not been set up to run automatically, you will need to make sure it is started and running during the periods your students are working in this and subsequent chapters.

If your students work on independent workstations or are in a distance learning program, you will have to remind them to start the program before each of the remaining exercises. In a nonnetwork environment, each workstation must start the History program before starting the Student Edition software.

The program must be running during the time students are performing the exercises in Chapter 6, Chapter 7, and the comprehensive exam at the end of Chapter 9. Warnings at key steps in the exercises will explain how to detect if the History program is not running and needs to be restarted. These are also described in the textbook in Appendix B.

Instructions for Starting History Program Software

If your classroom is on the school network, go to the network server that is running the Medcin Server and perform the following steps once for the entire network. If students are running on individual workstations, perform the following steps for each student workstation.

Step 1 Exit the Student Edition software on all participating workstations.

Step 2 (On the server, if networked) Click on the Windows "Start" button. Locate and click on Programs or All Programs.

From the list of programs displayed, locate and click on the program labeled "Medcin History Pool Loader." This is the Student Edition History program.

Step 3 The Medcin History Pool Loader window will be invoked; patient names will be displayed as their charts are loaded into memory.

Step 4 When the program has loaded all the patients, the message "All Patients Are Now Loaded" will be displayed at the end of the list.

Step 5 Locate and click on the button labeled "Minimize the Dialog to the Task Bar" in the History program window.

Step 6 Have students restart the Student Edition software.

Notes:

1. An illustrated version of these instructions is provided in Appendix B of the textbook.

2. There is no need to stop the History Pool program between classes. It can run continuously.

Learning Outcomes

After completing this chapter, students should be able to:

♦ Understand and use Patient Management

♦ Understand and use problem lists

♦ Cite information from previous visits in a new encounter

♦ Explain how vital signs and diagnostic tests can be recorded in the EHR

♦ Describe the workflow of electronic lab orders and results

♦ View pending orders and lab results

♦ Create a graph of lab results

♦ Describe triage by a nurse

♦ Discuss patient entry of symptoms and previous history

Teaching Recommendations

■ Some of the advantages of an EHR begin to reveal themselves in this chapter. The ability to sort, organize, and assemble like items of health data from numerous patient encounters helps the clinician better manage the patient's health. This feature is often called Patient Management or Patient Health Management.

Nearly every commercial EHR system available will have some version of the features covered in this chapter. However, commercial EHR vendors differentiate their products by using unique visual styles to present patient charts. Students should be made aware that the software they will use in a medical office will have concepts and features for Patient Management similar to the Student Edition, but the presentation of the information will likely have a different appearance.

■ The first exercise (37) explores Patient Management tabs of the software and introduces the concept of the problem list. The problem list provides an up-to-date list of the diagnoses and conditions that affect a particular patient's care.

Problem lists are used to track both acute and chronic conditions related to the care of the patient. In some systems problem lists can include findings that are not disease related but rather are *wellness conditions*. Wellness conditions are based on the age and sex of the patient and used in health maintenance and preventative screening programs to keep healthy patients healthy.

The purpose of the first exercise is to experience firsthand how findings from multiple encounters can be organized and displayed with similar findings, such as vital signs, patient history, immunizations, and so on. Since most clinical information recorded in the chart will be related to one or more problems, the Problem List tab and Care Plan tabs show how data can be displayed related to the problem under consideration.

At the beginning of Exercise 37 students create a new encounter but students do not print and turn in their work from this exercise. You do not have to get through this entire section in one class period. Students may quit and resume Exercise 37 at any point by repeating Steps 1–3.

■ Exercise 38 begins with the same patient and date and, therefore, can be continued directly after Exercise 37 if time permits. In this exercise, students will enter new data, print out their exam note, and turn in their work.

Where the previous exercise showed the value of the EHR for reviewing previous encounter data, Exercise 38 further explores the problem list and shows students how these data can be cited (i.e., brought forward into the current encounter).

The value of learning how to do this is that a large number of patient visits are concerned with following up on conditions for which the patient was previously seen and for following up on chronic conditions that require evaluation at every visit. Using an EHR, the clinician can follow up on and document each previous problem or chronic condition more thoroughly and more quickly.

Students will need time to complete Exercise 38 and print out the exam notes in a single class period. Therefore, do not begin the exercise if there is not sufficient class time remaining after Exercise 37.

■ The next section concerns obtaining data from external sources, which is a concept we have followed from Chapter 1. There are large portions of the patient chart that can be populated without using the clinician's time.

Since you will not likely have access to the type of equipment discussed here, this section is illustrated with photographs and descriptive examples. However, you may be able to find a guest speaker who can discuss the real-world application of this technology for the class. Suggested resources:

♦ A representative of a local reference lab that offers electronic connectivity to its clients

♦ A nurse or instructor from a nursing program who has worked in a hospital intensive care unit that captured data continuously (as many ICU systems do)

♦ A respiratory therapist or an instructor from such a program who has experience using electronic or digital spirometry equipment

♦ A sample of a paper ECG strip to show students what an ECG looks like followed by a discussion of how you might store the type of information on the paper strip in an electronic health record

This section also mentions "Wi-Fi" wireless communications between the devices and the EHR system. Chapter 9 contains a breakout section that explains how Wi-Fi works; curious students may want to read ahead.

■ As discussed earlier, the Student Edition does not contain a true electronic order and result system as it would be inappropriate for students to be transmitting actual orders. However, the chapter does discuss the workflow of electronic orders and a PowerPoint presentation of the workflow figure is provided on the Instructor's Resource CD that can be used for class discussion.

Exercise 39 uses several features of the Student Edition software to simulate some of the benefits of using an electronic order and result system. It would be useful to make sure that the students are aware that this is only simulating pieces of the process and that in an actual medical office the electronic order and result system will be more unified and even more efficient.

Students need to complete and print out the exam note from Exercise 39 in one class period.

■ Since Chapter 1, the text has emphasized the value of a codified EHR record and the benefits to be realized including trending. Students should realize that it is the use of a standardized nomenclature and a codified medical record that makes possible the Patient Management and Cite features discussed thus far. Exercise 40 should make that even more apparent as students create a graph of a patient's cholesterol over a period of time.

Students should print out and turn in their graph with their other work. Note the graphs do not print the students' names, so you will have to ask them to write their name on their work.

If your students have been using the Print to HTML feature to turn their work in on files instead of printouts, be aware that graphs cannot print to HTML. You must provide students directions on how to turn in their work for the five exercises that involve graphics. You may choose to have students print and send you just their graph exercises or you may wish to have them capture the screens and send them electronically. A suggested method for screen capture is provided in the chapter of this manual concerning installation of the software in a section titled "Distance Learning—Print to HTML."

■ The remainder of the chapter describes patient-entered data and introduces concepts that will be expanded in Chapter 9. However, in this section Dr. Wenner also introduces many other new concepts, such as that of triage. These concepts may be points for interesting class discussions.

■ The real-life story for this chapter not only discusses patient-entered data but also introduces the concept of preventative screening, which will be explained in Chapter 7. As you teach Chapter 7, you may want to remind students of the story in this chapter.

■ Have students review the Chapter Summary and answer the 15 questions at the end of the chapter. The answer key for the questions is provided after the chapter outline. Students should also turn in a printout or file of their exam notes for two exercises and their printout of the graph created in Exercise 40. Answer keys showing the steps used to create the patient note are provided for each.

A bank of test questions to create your own chapter exam is also available on the Prentice Hall Health Instructor's Resource CD.

Chapter 6 Outline

I. About the Student Edition Patient History Program

II. Improved Data Entry

Answer Key 6-1

Testing Your Knowledge of Chapter 6

1. What is a problem list?

ANSWER: An up-to-date list of the diagnoses and conditions that affect a particular patient's care.

2. What is the idea of a problem list?

ANSWER: The idea of a problem list is to make sure everyone who touches the patient knows what conditions are present.

3. Name at least two reasons why clinicians use a problem list.

ANSWER: Any two of the following:

Easy to see the active problems for a patient and also view the history of problems.

Most clinical information recorded in the chart will be related to one or more problems.

Everyone who touches the patient knows what conditions are present.

Problem lists are used to track both acute and chronic conditions.

Helps the clinician remember to follow up on conditions from previous visits.

Maintaining a problem list is a requirement for accreditation by JCAHO.

4. What is a reason why a "wellness" condition would appear on a problem list?

ANSWER: Any portion of the following concepts:
Items on the problem list are used to determine the type and frequency of tests and preventative measures. Wellness conditions on the problem lists are used to generate preventative care recommendations for healthy patients. Wellness conditions are based on the age and sex of the patient and used in health maintenance and preventative screening programs to keep healthy patients healthy.

5. Where do the data that appear in the Patient Management tab come from?

ANSWER: Previous encounters or patient visits.

6. What does it mean to cite a finding?

ANSWER: Citing from a previous exam note means to bring a finding into the current encounter, usually as a follow-up to a previous visit.

7. Name at least three external sources of data for populating the EHR.

ANSWER: Any three of the following:

Electronic lab orders and results

Vital signs

ECG

Digital spirometers

Ultrasound equipment

Holter monitors

In-house LIS systems

8. Define trending of lab values.

ANSWER: Comparing the change of certain test components over a period of time.

9. What type of lab results can be graphed?

ANSWER: Those with numerical values.

10. Describe the workflow of an office using an electronic lab interface.

ANSWER:

1. The clinician orders the test.
2. The lab order initiates a "task" for someone in the office to act on. The task involves at least two actions: completing the requisition and obtaining a specimen.

A. Complete the electronic requisition to be transmitted to the laboratory.

B. The specimen to be tested is collected either at the practice or at an outside lab.

3. If a blood or urine specimen is taken at the practice, a phlebotomist or nurse will obtain it. The clinician usually only takes the specimen when it is part of the exam or procedure, for example, taking a swab for a throat culture or removing a mole that is to be sent to pathology.

4. Specimens taken at the medical office for tests performed at an outside lab are picked up by a courier and transported to the lab one or more times a day.

5. If the patient is sent to an outside lab for a blood test, a phlebotomist or lab technician will draw the blood.

6. The lab performs the requested tests. As soon as any results are ready they are made available to the medical office EHR.

7. The clinician reviews the lab results and "signs" them.

8. A nurse or other staff member calls the patient with the results.

9. Alternatively, some practices allow the patient to view the test results online via a medical office Web site.

11. What is a pending order?

ANSWER: An order that has been sent to the lab for which no results have been received.

12. Name at least two benefits of having patients enter their own symptoms and history.

ANSWER: Any two of the following:

Only the patient has the information about the symptoms that were present at the outset of the illness.

Only the patient has the information about the outcome of medical treatment of those symptoms.

The patient is also the source of past medical, family, and social history.

Patient-entered data are a more accurate reflection of a patient's complaints.

Patients who can review their histories are better prepared for the visit.

13. What is triage (as used in this chapter)?

ANSWER: The screening of patients for allocation of treatment based on the urgency of their need for care; often a simplified, organ-specific review of systems conducted by the triage nurse based on the presenting complaint.

14. What percentage of a clinician's time is spent entering patient symptoms and history into the chart?

ANSWER: Up to 67%.

15. List the steps you would take to graph a lab value.

ANSWER: Highlight the lab finding you want to graph.

Click Graph on the menu bar, and then click "Current Finding."

(Note in Exercise 40 students searched for their finding so some may also add Search to their answer. This is acceptable.)

Answer Key 6-2

Evaluation of Printed Exam Note for Exercise 38: Following Up on a Problem

The following corresponds to Figure 6-24 in the textbook. A "Print to HTML" file named "fig6-24_ juan_garcia.htm" is available on the Instructor's Resource CD.

Juan Garcia Student: *(name or ID)*	Page 1 of 1	
Patient: Juan Garcia: M: 7/31/1978: 5/10/2006 03:00PM		*Steps 1 and 2*
CHIEF COMPLAINT The Chief Complaint is: Knee injury follow-up.		*Step 3*
HISTORY OF PRESENT ILLNESS Juan Garcia is a 27-year-old male. • No knee joint pain • No knee joint swelling **PAST MEDICAL/SURGICAL HISTORY** **Reported History:** Reported medications: Not taking antibiotics.		*Step 6*
Medical: A recent URI.		
Physical trauma: Trauma to the knee due to twisting.		*Step 6*
PHYSICAL FINDINGS **Vital signs:**		*Step 4*

Vital Signs/Measurements Range	Value	Normal
Oral temperature	97 F	97.6–99.6
RR	27 breaths/min	18–26
PR	67 bpm	50–100
Blood pressure	120/87 mmHg	100–120/60–80
DBP	80 mmHg	60–80
Weight	149 lbs	125–225
Height	68 in	65.4–74

Ears: General/bilateral: • Ears: normal. **Nose:** • Tenderness of the sinus. **Pharynx:** • Normal. **Lymph Nodes:** • Normal. **Lungs:** • Normal. **Musculoskeletal system:** Knee: Right knee. • No localized swelling. • No warmth. • Motion was normal. • No pain was elicited by motion. • No instability. **Neurological:** Motor (Motor Strength): • No weakness of the right knee was observed	*Steps 6 and 7*

ASSESSMENT	
• Acute sinusitis, which is resolved	*Step 11*
• Sprained anterior cruciate ligament of the knee, which is resolved	*Step 8*
THERAPY	
• Order canceled for cool mist vaporizer.	*Step 11*
• Order canceled for reduced physical activity. • Order canceled for acetaminophen. • Order canceled for ice. • Order canceled for Ace bandage.	*Step 9*
PRACTICE MANAGEMENT Estab outpatient focused h&p-straightforward decisions; Total face to face time 15 min	*Step 12*

Answer Key 6-3

Evaluation of Printed Exam Note for Exercise 39: Viewing Pending Orders and Lab Results

The following corresponds to Figure 6-44 in the textbook. A "Print to HTML" file named "fig6-44_ greg_natell.htm" is available on the Instructor's Resource CD.

Gregory Natell Page 1 of 1 Student: *(name or ID)*	
Patient: Gregory Natell: M: 3/18/1990: 5/11/2006 09:00AM	*Steps 1 and 2*
CHIEF COMPLAINT The Chief Complaint is: Rule out lead poisoning	*Step 3*
PERSONAL HISTORY Home environment: Housing has peeling lead-based paint.	*Step 8*
REVIEW OF SYSTEMS **Head symptoms:** No headache. **Gastrointestinal symptoms:** No nausea, no vomiting, and no abdominal pain. **Neurological symptoms:** No generalized convulsions. No decrease in concentrating ability, no confusion, and no disorientation. No memory lapses or loss. **Psychological symptoms:** No unexplained poor school performance. No change in personality.	*Step 7*
PHYSICAL FINDINGS **Vital signs:**	*Step 4*

Vital Signs/Measurements Range	Value	Normal
Oral temperature	98.6 F	97.6–99.6
RR	26 breaths/min	18–26
PR	76 bpm	50–100
Blood pressure	120/80 mmHg	100–120/56–80
Weight	155 lbs	94–188
Height	73 in	62.6–72.8

Oral cavity:	
Gums: • Showed no gingival line	*Step 9*
TESTS	*Step 10*
Hematology:	
Normal CBC with differential	
Blood Chemistry:	
Pending results for a basic metabolic panel	*Step 13*
Normal serum lead level	*Step 10*
Urine Tests:	
Normal urine lead, 24 hr	
ASSESSMENT	
• Poisoning by lead, which is ruled out	*Step 14*
PRACTICE MANAGEMENT	
Estab outpatient focused h&p–straightforward decisions; Total face to face time 15 min	*Step 15*

Answer Key 6-4

Evaluation of Printed Graph for Exercise 40: Graphing Lab Results

The student should print out and hand in a graph of Total Cholesterol for Sally Sutherland, which corresponds to Figure 6-49 in the textbook. The figure is not reprinted here. Since students did not enter data, the graph data should automatically match. Having successfully printed the graph is proof of successful completion of the exercise.

7 Using the EHR to Improve Patient Care

Chapter 7 focuses on benefits derived from an EHR that were named in the IOM report discussed in Chapter 1, Disease Management, Prevention, and Alerts. In this chapter students also learn about flow sheets, pediatric wellness visits, immunizations, growth charts, and preventative care screening. Students extend their ability to analyze trends in the patient's health by learning to graph additional types of data.

Flow sheets are commonly used in many types of practices and are ideal for chronic disease management such as diabetes or long-term conditions such as pregnancy. Flow sheets present data from multiple encounters in column form. This format allows for a side-by-side comparison of findings over a period of time. Students use their experience "citing" findings from the previous chapter as they learn to cite from flow sheets in this chapter.

Chapter 7 discusses medical alerts generated from EHR data and shows drug interaction checking using illustrations from actual electronic prescription writing software; however, students do not actually use the electronic prescription software.

The real-life story in this chapter ties together many of the concepts in this and previous chapters. The story is by a physician assistant who uses a commercial EHR based on Medcin, which is very similar to the Student Edition. She shares her experiences creating and using forms as well as a preventative screening component and health maintenance. She also discusses pediatrics and immunizations.

Learning Outcomes

After completing this chapter, students should be able to:

♦ Describe flow sheets

♦ Work with a flow sheet

♦ Create a graph of vital signs in the chart

♦ Document a well-baby check-up using a wellness form

♦ Explain the relationship between vitals signs and growth charts

♦ Create a pediatric growth chart

♦ Understand immunization schedules

♦ Order immunizations for a child

♦ Describe preventative care screening

Teaching Recommendations

■ Most exercises in this chapter use the Student Edition History program to share past encounter data. Remember to have the History program running during exercises in this chapter.

Warnings at key steps in the exercises will explain how to detect if the History program is not running and needs to be restarted. These are also described in the textbook in Appendix B.

■ Exercise 41 introduces flow sheets. Here are some tips on flow sheets:

● If the dated columns on the right side of the flow sheet are empty, the History program is not running. Stop the exercise, exit the Student Edition, start the History program, and restart the Student Edition.

● Changing in and out of Flow Sheet view with the "Cite" button on can affect the appearance of the "Cite" button so that it is difficult to tell whether is depressed or not. The directions in the steps have been carefully arranged to avoid getting the student into this state. However, should this occur, use the following guide:

● While the "Cite" button is on, the mouse pointer will change to resemble a large question mark whenever the mouse pointer moves over the cells of the flow sheet. If it looks like the usual mouse pointer instead of the question mark, then "Cite" is not on; have the student click on the "Cite" button in the toolbar again.

Students must print out and hand in their work from Exercise 41. If sufficient class time remains, students may continue directly into Exercise 42 and proceed to Step 3. Otherwise this is a good stopping point for the day, and you can begin with Exercise 42 at the next class session.

■ Exercise 42 teaches students to view a flow sheet based on a problem instead of a form. Students learn by comparing the two styles of flow sheets, but they should not enter new data. A printout is not required. If remaining class time is sufficient, students can continue directly into Exercise 43.

■ In this chapter students will learn to graph different types of EHR data. In Exercise 43 the students create a graph of the patient's weight, which they print out and turn in. As discussed in the previous chapter, graphs do not include the students' names, so you will have to ask them to write their name or student ID on their work.

As also mentioned previously, if your students have been using the Print to HTML feature to turn their work in on files instead of printouts, you must provide directions to students on how to turn in their work for the exercises that involve graphics.

■ In the next few exercises students will learn about pediatric visits, create a different kind of graph called a growth chart, and learn about childhood immunizations. This is a lot of material to cover and for that reason the pediatric visit will span several exercises.

■ Exercise 44 teaches the students about pediatric visits and instructs them to create and print out a growth chart. Students should hand in their growth chart. It is left up to the instructor to decide if students should printout and turn in the patient exam note for grading. This grading is optional because the student data have a correct copy of the same encounter already stored for use in Exercise 46 and students are not provided with a figure for final comparison.

If students are not printing the exam note for this exercise they will get a warning while attempting to exit that the encounter has not been printed. Instruct the students to click the "OK" button.

■ Have students read the subsequent section about the relationship between vital signs and growth charts. A PowerPoint on the Instructor's Resource CD on growth charts may be used to explain the concept of percentile.

■ Exercise 45 and Exercise 47 require access to the Internet. Both exercises encourage students to use tools on the CDC Web site to monitor their own health. Since both exercises are concerned with the student's personal health data they are marked optional. Students should be encouraged to complete the exercises, but the results should not be used for grading.

■ Exercise 46 will focus on immunizations for children. In order to move quickly through the exam and into the immunization section students will retrieve an existing encounter for patient Tyrell Williams that contains essentially the same data students were entering in Exercise 44.

The first portion of this exercise is to compare the child's record of vaccines with the recommended CDC immunization schedule. This is something that is done in every pediatric office nationwide. You may find it helpful to display the immunization schedule overhead while the students work through the comparison portion. Note that the immunization schedule did not change in 2006. The 2005 schedule shown in the book was current at the time of printing.

Once the comparison is completed, the students then record the vaccines administered to the patient in this visit and print out their exam note. However, a significant portion of the findings in the note was not entered by the students. You should focus grading only on the vaccination and practice management items.

■ The remainder of the chapter covers preventative care screening and alerts. Both topics are illustrated with screen captures from commercial EHR systems as the Student Edition software does not contain those functions.

As discussed earlier, the Student Edition does not contain a true electronic prescription system as it would be inappropriate for student software. Therefore, the section on alerts uses screen captures from commercial prescription writing software to illustrate the process.

In addition to the real-life story in this chapter, which discusses preventative screening, the real-life story in Chapter 6 provided an example of the impact it had on one man's life. You may want to remind students of that story when discussing preventative screening in this chapter.

■ Have students review the Chapter Summary and answer the 15 questions at the end of the chapter. The answer key for the questions is provided after the chapter outline. Students should also turn in a printout or file of their exam notes for Exercises 41, 46, and optionally Exercise 44. They should also print out and turn in the graphs created in Exercises 43 and 44. Answer keys showing the steps used to create the patient note are provided for each note.

A bank of test questions to create your own chapter exam is also available on the Prentice Hall Health Instructor's Resource CD.

Chapter 7 Outline

I. Important Information About the Student History Program

II. Disease Management and Prevention

III. Flow Sheets

    A. Hands-On Exercise 41: Working with a Flow Sheet
    B. About the Flow Sheet view

        1. Flow sheet from a form
        2. Flow sheet of a problem
        3. Flow sheet from a list
        4. A brief review of the buttons "FS Flow" and "Cite"

    C. Hands-On Exercise 42: Creating a Problem-Oriented Flow Sheet

IV. Patient Involvement in Their Own Health Care

    A. Hands-On Exercise 43: Graphing Vital Signs in the Chart
    B. Patient-entered data graphs

V. Prevention and Early Detection

VI. Pediatric Wellness Visit

    A. Hands-On Exercise 44: A Well-Baby Check-Up

VII. The Relation Between Vitals and Growth Charts

    A. What is a percentile?
    B. Body Mass Index
    C. Optional Hands-On Exercise 45: Calculate Your Own BMI

VIII. The Importance of Childhood Immunizations

    A. Hands-On Exercise 46: Immunizations
    B. Immunization schedules from the CDC
    C. Optional Hands-On Exercise 47: Determine Your Adult Immunizations

IX. Preventative Care Screening

Answer Key 7-1

Testing Your Knowledge of Chapter 7

1. List at least three ways codified data in the EHR can be used to manage and prevent disease.

ANSWER: Any of the following:

    Disease management

    Graphic analysis

    Trending

    Preventative screening

    Interactive alerts

2. What is a flow sheet?

ANSWER: Flow sheets present data from multiple encounters in columns allowing a side-by-side comparison of findings over a period of time.

3. Describe how to create a flow sheet from a form.

ANSWER: On the tab labeled "Active Forms" load a form from the Forms Manager and click on the button labeled "FS Form" in the toolbar at the top of the screen.

4. Describe how to create a problem-oriented flow sheet.

ANSWER: From Patient Management, on the tab labeled Problem List click on the diagnosis of the problem. Then click on the button labeled "Flowsheet" in the toolbar at the top of the screen.

5. Describe how to cite a finding from a flow sheet.

ANSWER: There are two possible answers both with the "Cite" button on:

    Click on the date at the top of a column. This will invoke a window from which you may cite findings.

    Or instead of clicking the date at the top of the column, click on an individual cell of a column to cite a single finding.

6. Describe how to graph a patient's weight.

ANSWER: Click Graph on the menu bar, and then click "Weight."

7. Why are childhood immunizations important?

ANSWER: Immunization slows down or stops disease outbreaks. Vaccines prevent disease in the people who receive them and protect those who come into contact with unvaccinated individuals. Through childhood immunization we are now able to control many infectious diseases that were once common in this country and from which many children died.

8. **Describe how to change the order vaccines are displayed in Patient Management.**

   ANSWER: If you click the mouse on the column header labeled "Finding," the vaccines are sorted into groups, allowing you to easily see how many doses have been given of each vaccine. If you click the mouse on the column header for date, the list will be reordered so you can see exactly which vaccines were administered during each well-baby check-up.

Give the full name for the following acronyms:

9. **DTaP**

   ANSWER: Diphtheria, Tetanus, Pertussis

10. **HepB**

    ANSWER: Hepatitis B

11. **BMI**

    ANSWER: Body Mass Index

12. **DUR**

    ANSWER: Drug Utilization Review

13. **What are evidence-based guidelines?**

    ANSWER: Using "evidence-based guidelines" means analyzing scientific evidence from current research and studies to determine the effectiveness of preventive services.

14. **Name the organization that developed pediatric growth charts**

    ANSWER: Growth charts were developed by the National Center for Health Statistics. (NCHS is also acceptable.)

15. **What is a growth chart percentile?**

    ANSWER: Curved lines representing the percentage of the reference population the individual would equal or exceed at a given size for age.

Answer Key 7-2

Evaluation of Printed Exam Note for Exercise 41: Working with a Flow Sheet

The following corresponds to Figure 7-23 in the textbook. A "Print to HTML" file named "fig7-23_daniels.htm" is available on the Instructor's Resource CD for review and comparison.

Guy Daniels	Page 1 of 1	
Student: *(name or ID)*		
Patient: Guy Daniels: M: 3/25/1960: 10/15/2005 02:15PM	*Steps 1* and *2*
CHIEF COMPLAINT	
The Chief Complaint is: 3 month check up	*Step 3*
REVIEW OF SYSTEMS	*Step 19*
Systemic symptoms:	
Not feeling tired or poorly and no recent weight change	

Eye symptoms:

No worsening vision

Genitourinary symptoms:

No increase in urinary frequency

Endocrine symptoms:

No polydipsia

Neurological symptoms:

No tingling of the limbs and no numbness of the limbs

PHYSICAL FINDINGS			Step 5

Vital signs:

Vital Signs/Measurements Range	Value	Normal	
Oral temperature	98.2 F	97.6–99.6	
RR 25 breaths/min	18–26		
PR 73 bpm	50–100		
Blood pressure	125/85 mmHg	100–120/60–80	
Weight	229 lbs	125–225	

Eyes: — *Step 6*

General/bilateral:
Optic Disc: • Normal
Retina: • Normal

Cardiovascular system:

Heart Rate and Rhythm: • Normal
Heart Borders: • By percussion the heart size and position were normal
Heart Sounds: • S1 was normal • S2 was normal • No S3 was heard.
• No S4 was heard
Murmurs: • No murmurs were heard

TESTS			Step 13
Urinalysis Results: Range	Value	Normal	
Urinalysis results: protein	0 +	0–0	

Hematology:

Hematology: Range	Value	Normal	
Hematocrit level	51%	42–52	
Hemoglobin level	16.2 g/dl	14–18	

Blood Chemistry:

An electrolyte panel was performed and a lipid profile was performed.

Blood Chemistry: Range	Value	Normal	
Potassium level	4.8 mEq/l	3.5–5.5	
Total calcium level	9.8 mg/dl	8.5–10.5	
Random blood glucose level	110 mg/dl	75–110	Step 12
Serum creatinine level	1.4 mg/dl	0.7–1.5	Step 13
Total plasma cholesterol level	185 mg/dl	140–200	
Plasma HDL cholesterol level	65 mg/dl	30–70	
Normal plasma LDL cholesterol level			Step 14

ASSESSMENT			Step 5
• Hypertension			
• Type-II diabetes mellitus which is well-controlled			Step 18

COUNSELING/EDUCATION	Step 20
• Weight loss diet	

PLAN	Step 13
• Hematocrit level • Hemoglobin level • Random blood glucose level	

• Weight loss diet • Diabetic diet • Controlled carbohydrate diet	Step 22

• Metformin HCl 500 mg tab Generic:Y Using:Glucophage Mfg: Bristol	Step 21

PRACTICE MANAGEMENT	Step 23
Estab outpatient focused h&p - straightforward decisions; Total face to face time 15 min	

Answer Key 7-3

Evaluation of Printed Graph for Exercise 43: Graphing Weight

Students should print out and hand in a graph of Guy Daniels's weight, which corresponds to Figure 7-27 in the textbook. The figure is not reprinted here. Since students did not enter data, the graph data should automatically match. Having successfully printed the graph is proof of successful completion of the exercise.

Answer Key 7-4

Evaluation of Printed Exam Note for Exercise 44: A Well-Baby Check-Up

Following are the data entered by the students in Exercise 44. The instructor may optionally choose to have students turn in this printout. However, students are not given a comparison figure to check their work. No "Print to HTML" file is available from this exercise for the instructor; however, the file would be the same as the file for Exercise 46 without the vaccinations and practice management sections.

Tyrell Williams Student: *(name or ID)*	Page 1 of 3	
Patient: Tyrell Williams: M: 11/10/2005: 5/16/2006 11:00AM		*Steps 1* and *2*
CHIEF COMPLAINT		*Step 5*
The Chief Complaint is: 6-month check-up		
HISTORY OF PRESENT ILLNESS		*Step 6*
Tyrell Williams is a 6-month-old male. Source of patient information was mother. • Babbles • Rolls over from back to front • Passes objects from hand to hand • Sits independently • Pulls self to a standing position • Shy with strangers • No constipation • A normal number of wet diapers per day		

PAST MEDICAL/SURGICAL HISTORY

Reported History:

Past medical history - No significant past medical history

Exposure: No exposure to tuberculosis Environmental exposure: No exposure to lead	*Step 10*
Surgical/procedural: Prior surgery - No significant surgical history	*Step 8*
Dietary: Infant is breast-feeding Pediatric history: No difficulty breast-feeding, rice cereal introduced, with pureed fruit introduced, and with pureed vegetables introduced	*Step 6*

PERSONAL HISTORY — *Step 7*

Habits: An abnormal sleep pattern

Home environment: Lives with parents and the living — *Step 9*
environment has secondhand tobacco smoke

FAMILY HISTORY

Family medical history - No significant family history
Tobacco use
Alcohol
Not using drugs

REVIEW OF SYSTEMS — *Step 10*

Systemic symptoms:

No systemic symptoms

Head symptoms:

No head symptoms

Eye symptoms:

No eye symptoms

Otolaryngeal symptoms:

No ear symptoms, no nasal symptoms, and no throat symptoms

Cardiovascular symptoms:

No cardiovascular symptoms

Pulmonary symptoms:

No pulmonary symptoms

Skin symptoms:

No skin symptoms

Musculoskeletal symptoms:

No musculoskeletal symptoms

Psychological symptoms:

No psychological symptoms

PHYSICAL FINDINGS — *Step 11*

Vital signs:

Vital Signs/Measurements	Value	Normal Range
Tympanic membrane temperature	99 F	99–101
RR	25 breaths/min	36–44
PR	78 bpm	110–175
Weight	8.7 kg	6.1–10
Body length	27.5 in	25.6–29.1
Head circumference	43.9 cm	42–47

General appearance:

• Alert • Well hydrated • Active

Head:

• Showed no evidence of cephalohematoma • No skull molding was seen
• Fontanelle was normal

Eyes:

General/bilateral:
Extraocular Movements: • Normal
Pupils: • Normal

Ears:

General/bilateral:
Outer Ear: • Auricle was normal
External Auditory Canal: • External auditory meatus showed no abnormalities
Tympanic Membrane: • Normal

Nose:

• External nose showed no deformities • No nasal discharge was seen

Oral cavity:

• Normal

Pharynx:

• Normal

Neck:

• Not swollen • Demonstrated no decrease in suppleness

Lungs:

• Clear to auscultation

Cardiovascular system: *Step 12*

Heart Rate and Rhythm: • Normal
Heart Sounds: • Normal
Murmurs: • No murmurs were heard
Venous Filling Time: • Normal
Arterial Pulses: • Equal bilaterally and normal

Abdomen:

Auscultation: • Bowel sounds were normal
Palpation: • Abdomen was soft. • No mass was palpated in the abdomen
Hepatic Findings: • Liver was normal to palpation
Splenic Findings: • Spleen was normal to palpation
Hernia: • No umbilical hernia was discovered

Genitalia:

Penis: • Normal
Testes: • No cryptorchism was observed

Skin:

• General appearance was normal • Showed no erythema
• No cyanosis • Not dry • No exfoliation was seen

Musculoskeletal system:

General/bilateral: • Normal movement of all extremities
Hips:
General/bilateral: • Hips showed no abnormalities

Neurological:

• System: normal

Growth and development:

• Normal

ASSESSMENT

• Normal routine history and physical well-baby (birth–2 yr)   *Step 13*

COUNSELING/EDUCATION	
• Discussed safety practices • Discussed stranger safety • Discussed nutritional needs • Discussed concerns about teething • Discussed concerns about dental hygiene	*Step 14*
Student generates and prints growth chart	*Steps 15 and 16*

Answer Key 7-5

Evaluation of Printed Graph for Exercise 44: A Well-Baby Check-Up

The student should print out and hand in a graph of Tyrell Williams's growth chart, which corresponds to Figure 7-42 in the textbook. The figure is not reprinted here. Having successfully printed the graph is proof of successful completion of the exercise.

Answer Key 7-6

Evaluation of Printed Exam Note for Exercise 46: Immunizations

The following corresponds to Figure 7-49 in the textbook. A "Print to HTML" file named "fig7-49_t_williams.htm" is available on the Instructor's Resource CD. Grade only on the vaccinations and practice management sections.

Tyrell Williams	Page 1 of 3	
Student: *(name or ID)*		
Patient: Tyrell Williams: M: 11/10/2005: 5/16/2006 11:00AM		*Steps 1 and 2*

CHIEF COMPLAINT

The Chief Complaint is: 6-month check-up

HISTORY OF PRESENT ILLNESS

Tyrell Williams is a 6-month-old male. Source of patient information was mother.
• Babbles • Rolls over from back to front • Passes objects from hand to hand
• Sits independently • Pulls self to a standing position • Shy with strangers
• No constipation • A normal number of wet diapers per day

PAST MEDICAL/SURGICAL HISTORY

Reported History:

Past medical history - No significant past medical history
Exposure: No exposure to tuberculosis
Environmental exposure: No exposure to lead
Surgical/procedural: Prior surgery - No significant surgical history
Dietary: Infant is breast-feeding
Pediatric history: No difficulty breast-feeding, rice cereal introduced, with pureed fruit introduced, and with pureed vegetables introduced

PERSONAL HISTORY

Habits: An abnormal sleep pattern
Home environment: Lives with parents and the living environment has secondhand tobacco smoke

FAMILY HISTORY

Family medical history - No significant family history
Tobacco use
Alcohol
Not using drugs

REVIEW OF SYSTEMS

Systemic symptoms:

No systemic symptoms

Head symptoms:

No head symptoms

Eye symptoms:

No eye symptoms

Otolaryngeal symptoms:

No ear symptoms, no nasal symptoms, and no throat symptoms

Cardiovascular symptoms:

No cardiovascular symptoms

Pulmonary symptoms:

No pulmonary symptoms

Skin symptoms:

No skin symptoms

Musculoskeletal symptoms:

No musculoskeletal symptoms

Psychological symptoms:

No psychological symptoms

PHYSICAL FINDINGS

Vital signs:

Vital Signs/Measurements	Value	Normal Range
Tympanic membrane temperature	99 F	99–101
RR	25 breaths/min	36–44
PR	78 bpm	110–175
Weight	8.7 kg	6.1–10
Body length	27.5 in	25.6–29.1
Head circumference	43.9 cm	42–47

General appearance:

• Alert • Well hydrated • Active

Head:

• Showed no evidence of cephalohematoma • No skull molding was seen
• Fontanelle was normal

Eyes:

General/bilateral:
Extraocular Movements: • Normal
Pupils: • Normal

Ears:

General/bilateral:
Outer Ear: • Auricle was normal
External Auditory Canal: • External auditory meatus showed no abnormalities
Tympanic Membrane: • Normal

Nose:

• External nose showed no deformities • No nasal discharge was seen

Oral cavity:

• Normal

Pharynx:

• Normal

Neck:

• Not swollen • Demonstrated no decrease in suppleness

Lungs:

• Clear to auscultation

Cardiovascular system:

Heart Rate and Rhythm: • Normal
Heart Sounds: • Normal
Murmurs: • No murmurs were heard
Venous Filling Time: • Normal
Arterial Pulses: • Equal bilaterally and normal

Abdomen:

Auscultation: • Bowel sounds were normal
Palpation: • Abdomen was soft • No mass was palpated in the abdomen
Hepatic Findings: • Liver was normal to palpation
Splenic Findings: • Spleen was normal to palpation
Hernia: • No umbilical hernia was discovered

Genitalia:

Penis: • Normal
Testes: • No cryptorchism was observed

Skin:

• General appearance was normal • Showed no erythema • No cyanosis
• Not dry • No exfoliation was seen

Musculoskeletal system:

General/bilateral: • Normal movement of all extremities
Hips:
General/bilateral: • Hips showed no abnormalities

Neurological:

• System: normal

Growth and development:

• Normal

ASSESSMENT

• Normal routine history and physical well-baby (birth–2 yr)

VACCINATIONS • Received dose of polio virus vaccine, inactivated (Salk) • Received dose of DTaP vaccine • Received dose of haemophilus influenzae B vaccine, PRP-T conjugate (4 dose schedule), for intramuscular use • Received dose of pneumococcal conjugate vaccine, polyvalent, IM use	*Step 6*
COUNSELING/EDUCATION • Discussed safety practices • Discussed stranger safety • Discussed nutritional needs • Discussed concerns about teething • Discussed concerns about dental hygiene	*Step 2*
PRACTICE MANAGEMENT Estab outpatient detailed h&p - moderate complexity decision; Total face to face time 40 min	*Step 7*

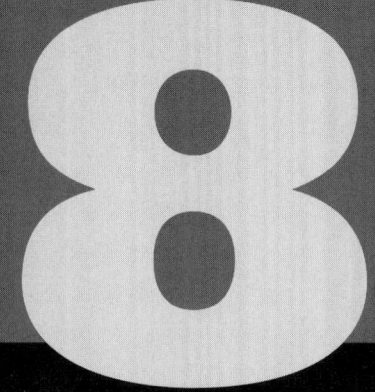

Privacy and Security of Health Records

The HIPAA law regulates many things, including portability and continuity of health care insurance, long-term care, elimination of fraud and abuse, and administrative simplification. In fact, the subsection known as Administrative Simplification is only a fraction of HIPAA, but it has had such a strong impact on medical providers that they often use the term *HIPAA* when they actually mean only the Administrative Simplification Subsection of HIPAA. This chapter mentions all of HIPAA but focuses on the Administrative Simplification Subsection and primarily on Privacy and Security.

Chapter 8 provides a thorough presentation of HIPAA privacy and security regulations that are of paramount concern in any medical setting. Since both rules apply to patient data stored and transmitted electronically, understanding the rules is a prerequisite to portions of Chapter 9 concerning the Internet. Chapter 8 also explains data encryption, electronic signatures, and how records are signed electronically.

Learning Outcomes

After completing this chapter, students should be able to:

- List HIPPA transactions and uniform identifiers
- Apply HIPAA privacy policy in a medical office
- Discuss HIPAA security requirements
- Follow security policy guidelines in a medical office
- Explain electronic signatures

Teaching Recommendations

This chapter is important because every employee in a medical facility is required to be trained and diligent in protecting PHI and EPHI. However, the chapter consists mostly of reading and learning the regulations. Class discussions are the best way to teach and personalize this material. Following are some discussion suggestions.

Privacy

■ Each of us has health records. Most of us feel strongly about the privacy of those records. Begin the privacy section with a class discussion eliciting how students feel about their own privacy.

1. How many are aware of HIPAA privacy?

2. Has any one received a copy of a privacy policy from a provider office?

3. Can anyone share a story of a good example of privacy in an office setting?

4. Does anyone have an example of a setting where the PHI was handled poorly?

Figure 8-3 is a brochure published by the Department of Health and Human Services to make patients aware of their rights. (The figure will also be used later in Exercise 48.) Have the students review the brochure.

1. How many class members were aware of their rights?

2. Were there any rights listed that students did not know they had?

Consent versus Authorization

■ In this area there can be confusion because there are two meanings of consent in a medical practice. First, there is a medical or "informed consent," which patients often sign prior to surgery or a procedure that explains a medical procedure and its risks. Second, there is HIPAA consent as discussed in this chapter, which gives the provider the right to share PHI with others for the purposes of treatment, obtaining payment, and operation of the health care facility.

HIPAA consent is granted by the patient acknowledging receipt of the medical practice's privacy policy. This consent does not give the practice the right to use PHI for marketing or research; that use requires authorization.

Authorization is a specific release granted by the patient to disclose PHI for a particular purpose. The patient must sign a new authorization for each different purpose or need for disclosure.

1. Ask students to name some examples that would require an Authorization for the disclosure. (Examples include school physicals, employment physicals, school athletic physicals, insurance records, immunization records, having a manufacturer send the patient information about a drug or medical device, and clinical drug studies.)

2. Can patients give their records to a school or employer or athletic group? Yes, there is no restriction on those with whom patients may share their PHI. A patient can obtain a copy of the information from the doctor and

give it to the school. The doctor would not require an authorization form in this case because the doctor did not disclose the information.

3. Can the government or law enforcement agency obtain PHI without a patient's authorization or consent? Yes, but law enforcement agencies will generally need a subpoena or court order, and the practice must record the disclosure. After a reasonable period of time, the disclosure will show up on a report of disclosures (which patients have a right to obtain annually at no charge). Public health reporting is another exception in which immunization records and the diagnosis of certain diseases are required by state law to be reported to health departments.

Personal Representatives and Minor Children

■ This topic can generate some interesting discussions. The rule concerning minors defers to state law, so you may want to assign someone to research the laws for your state.

The point to this discussion is to help the students look at the material in terms of how it affects them and their families.

1. Does a parent have a right to access a student's medical records if the student still lives at home? (This question assumes students are no longer minors.)

2. Should married persons have a right to their spouse's records?

Business Associates

■ This is often a new concept for students. A brief discussion will help clarify it:

Medical practices often use the services of a variety of other persons or businesses that do not work for the practice but need to access PHI to do work for the practice.

1. Can students think of some examples? (Examples include an outside transcription service, a billing service, a claims clearinghouse, and a computer company that installs or maintains the EHR computer system.)

Civil and Criminal Penalties

■ The real-life story in this chapter emphasizes the responsibility of maintaining privacy in a health care workplace. Though identity theft is serious, the consequences are much greater in a medical setting than if the same information had been stolen from a different type of business. Why? Because even the patient's name and date of birth are part of the PHI.

Additionally, the disclosure of PHI for financial gain could have a maximum sentence of 10 years for each violation. The ex-employee in this case applied for four credit cards. Therefore, what penalty could he have received? (The total penalty is 40 years.)

Discuss this story in comparison with other breaches, for example:

■ A chart was lost while transporting it from one multioffice location to another. (This would *not* be a violation of the rule, but the loss *would* have to be reported to the privacy official and logged as an incident.)

■ An unscrupulous employee sells a famous movie star's health information to a tabloid for a large sum of money. (It is likely that this employee would receive severe fines and prison time when convicted.)

Why Have a Security Rule?

■ After having read the four paragraphs under the section "Why Security?" students should be able to name several of the reason why the rule is necessary. These include the move to electronic health records, the use of the Internet, and that you cannot comply with the privacy rule if you cannot protect the electronic data.

Administrative Safeguards

■ Security may make students think of something very technical, but over half of the rule is administrative and essentially involves figuring out what the risks are, making a plan to mitigate them, selecting someone to be in charge, and training the staff. It also includes creating a contingency plan, keeping track of any security incidents, and periodically evaluating things to see if there need to be changes.

Suggested exercise: After reading the administrative safeguards, have students look at them in light of their own personal computers to create a risk analysis of their own system. Doing so will help them understand what the security officer must think about. Some suggested questions for the students:

1. Do students share their home computer with others or are they the only user?

2. Even though Windows offers passwords and individual identities, do students have their system set up for different users or does everyone share the same area (for example, My Documents, Outlook Express, etc.)?

3. Can anyone log on to their computer or does the person have to know a password?

4. Have students ever given anyone else their password?

5. How often do students change their password?

6. Do they have antivirus software? Is it kept up-to-date?

7. Have students ever had a virus or malicious software attack their computer? What did they do about it?

8. Do students have or know what firewall software is?

9. What is the risk of someone on the Internet gaining access to their computer? (Answers include dial-up connection, low; DSL or cable modem connection without firewall, higher.)

10. Do students make backup copies of their files on their home computer?

11. Have students ever had to restore a backup and discovered the files were not there or not readable? If this happened, what would they do to get their work back?

Physical Safeguards

■ As the name implies, the physical safeguards are about the building, the computer room, door locks, passwords, backups, and such.

After reading this section, have students apply these ideas to their own personal computers.

1. Do students have a desktop computer or a laptop?

2. How do they limit who can use it?

3. Have students ever needed access to their computer and the power was out (or the battery was dead)? What were the consequences?

4. If students have laptops, how do they protect them from being stolen?

5. If their computer was stolen, how could it be identified?

6. Have students given an old computer to someone else or been given a computer previously used by someone else? If so, did they erase any personal files before the computer changed hands?

Technical Safeguards

■ As the name implies, the technical safeguards are about making use of computer technology to protect EPHI. Since technology evolves so rapidly, no specific technologies are required by the rule.

After reading this section, have students discuss personal experiences of technical safeguards. Some examples:

1. Have any students ever worked at a job in which they had to enter an ID to log on to a cash register or other computer system? What were the risks of letting someone else use their ID?

2. Have students ever worked at a facility in which they had to use a key card or a code to open the employee entrance or other door?

3. Have students ever used a computer (or a cash register) that automatically logged them out if they left it idle for a period of time?

4. How many students have an ATM card? Do they have a secret PIN to use in conjunction with the card? This is a method of user authentication.

Exercise 48: Medical Office Privacy Policy

■ The purpose of this exercise is let the students apply this chapter to the real world. Students should obtain a copy of the privacy policy from a local health care facility. This could be their own doctor's office, the student infirmary, or even a Web site of a local medical practice (as many offices provide their privacy policy on their Web site.)

Students then write a brief paper comparing the contents of the privacy policy they obtained with the points in the CMS brochure shown in Figure 8-3. Note you may also wish to have students compare the policy with the required elements of a privacy policy listed in this chapter under the subheading "Privacy Policy." Students should turn in the privacy policy they obtained along with their essay.

■ Have students review the Chapter Summary and answer the 15 questions at the end of the chapter. The answer key for the questions is provided after the chapter outline.

A bank of test questions to create your own chapter exam is also available on the Prentice Hall Health Instructor's Resource CD.

Chapter 8 Outline

I. Understanding HIPAA

II. HIPAA Transactions and Code Sets
   A. Claims of equivalent encounters and coordination of benefits (COB)
   B. Remittance and payment advice
   C. Claims status
   D. Eligibility and benefit inquiry and response
   E. Referral certification and authorization
   F. Premium payments
   G. Enrollment and de-enrollment in a health plan
   H. Health claims attachments (not final)
   I. First report of injury (not final)
   J. Retail drug claims, coordination of drug benefits, and eligibility inquiry

III. HIPAA Uniform Identifiers
   A. National provider identifier
   B. Employer identifier
   C. National health plan identifier

IV. HIPAA Privacy Rule
   A. Privacy policy
   B. Consent
   C. Authorization
      1. Research
      2. Marketing
   D. Government agencies
   E. Minimum necessary
   F. A patient's right to know about disclosures
   G. Patient access to medical records
   H. Incidental disclosures
   I. Personal representatives
   J. Minor children
   K. Summary of patient privacy rights
   L. Business associates
   M. Civil and criminal penalties
      1. The First HIPAA Privacy Case—A Real-Life Story

V. HIPAA Security Rule
   A. Why security?
   B. Privacy rule and security rule compared

VI. Security Standards
   A. Implementation specifications

VII. Administrative Safeguards

    A. Security management process

        1. Risk analysis

        2. Risk management

        3. Sanction policy

        4. Information system activity review

    B. Assigned security responsibility

    C. Workforce security

        1. Authorization and or supervision

        2. Workforce clearance procedure

        3. Termination procedures

    D. Information access management

        1. Access authorization

        2. Access establishment and modification

        3. Isolating health care clearinghouse functions

    E. Security awareness and training

        1. Security reminders

        2. Protection from malicious software

        3. Log-in monitoring

        4. Password management

    F. Security incident procedures

        1. Response and reporting

    G. Contingency plan

        1. Data backup plan

        2. Disaster recovery plan

        3. Emergency mode operation plan

        4. Testing and revision procedures

        5. Application and data criticality analysis

    H. Evaluation

    I. Business associate contracts and other arrangements

        1. Written contract or other arrangement

VIII. Physical Safeguards

    A. Facility access controls

        1. Access control and validation procedures

        2. Contingency operations

        3. Facility security plan

        4. Maintenance records

    B. Workstation use

    C. Workstation security

    D. Device and media controls

        1. Disposal

        2. Media reuse

        3. Accountability

        4. Data backup and storage

IX. Technical safeguards

    A. Access control

        1. Unique user identification

2. Emergency access procedure
3. Automatic logoff
4. Encryption and decryption
- B. Audit controls
- C. Integrity
    1. Mechanism to authenticate electronic protected health information
- D. Person or entity authentication
- E. Transmission security
    1. Integrity controls
    2. Encryption

X. Organizational, policies and procedures, and documentation requirements

- A. Organizational requirements
    1. Business associate contracts
    2. Other arrangements
        a) Memorandum of understanding (MOU)
        b) Law or regulations
- B. Policies and procedures
- C. Documentation
    1. Time limit
    2. Availability
    3. Updates

XI. Electronic Signatures for Medical Records

- A. What is an electronic signature and what is not
    1. Valid electronic signatures must meet three criteria
        a) Message integrity
        b) Nonrepudiation
        c) User authentication
- B. How digital signatures work
- C. Some electronic signatures are not truly signatures
- D. The future of electronic signatures

XII. HIPAA Privacy, Security, and You
- A. Hands-On Exercise 48: Medical Office Privacy Policy

XIII. Chapter Summary

Answer Key 8-1

Testing Your Knowledge of Chapter 8

1. **What do the acronyms PHI and EPHI stand for?**

    ANSWER: PHI stands for protected health information.

    EPHI stands for protected health information in an electronic format.

2. **List the three criteria of an electronic signature.**

    ANSWER:

    message integrity

    Nonrepudiation

    User authentication

3. **Compare the difference between consent and authorization.**

   ANSWER: Authorization differs from consent in that authorization requires the patient's permission to disclose PHI.

   Signed consent is optional. The patient gives consent for the provider to disclose PHI for purposes of treatment, obtaining payment, or operation of the health care facility by acknowledging receipt of a copy of the office privacy policy.

4. **Does a provider need the patient's consent to share PHI with an authorized government agency?**

   ANSWER: No.

5. **List the four components of the HIPAA Administrative Simplification Subsection.**

   ANSWER:

   Transactions and Code Sets

   Uniform Identifiers

   Privacy

   Security

6. **Which part of the regulation went into effect first?**

   ANSWER: Transactions and Code Sets

7. **Which part of the regulation went into effect last?**

   ANSWER: Uniform Identifiers; however, Security is also an acceptable answer.

8. **Business associate agreements apply to which components of the Administrative Simplification Subsection?**

   ANSWER: Privacy and Security

9. **What department of the U.S. government enforces HIPAA?**

   ANSWER: Department of Health and Human Services or HHS. (Also acceptable are the specific subdivisions of CMS and OCR.)

10. **List the three categories of the security rule.**

    ANSWER:

    Administrative Safeguards

    Physical Safeguards

    Technical Safeguards

11. **Name the covered entities under HIPAA**

    ANSWER: Health care providers, health plans, clearinghouses

12. **Which components of the Administrative Simplification Subsection require employee training?**

    ANSWER: Privacy and Security

13. **List the requirements for the medical office privacy policy.**

    ANSWER:

    Notice must be in plain language.

How the covered entity may use and disclose protected health information about an individual.

The individual's rights with respect to the information.

How the individual may exercise these rights.

How the individual may complain to the covered entity.

The covered entity's legal duties with respect to the information, including a statement that the covered entity is required by law to maintain the privacy of protected health information.

Whom individuals can contact for further information about the covered entity's privacy policies.

14. Name three of the technical safeguards.

ANSWER: Any three of the following:

Access control

Unique user identification

Emergency access procedure

Automatic logoff

Encryption and decryption

Audit controls

Integrity

Mechanism to authenticate electronic protected health information

Person or entity authentication

Transmission security

Integrity controls

15. Who may sign an authorization to release PHI?

ANSWER: The patient or the patient's personal representative

Answer Key 8-2

Evaluation of Essay for Exercise 48: Medical Office Privacy Policy

Students should obtain a copy of the privacy policy of a local medical office and then write an essay comparing that policy with the information in Figure 8-3 in the textbook. The figure is not reprinted here. Students should hand in both their essay and the privacy policy they obtained for comparison.

Answer:

A privacy policy should meet the criteria required by the privacy rule (listed previously in the answer to question 13). Some of the key elements that students should be able to identify include the following (in any order):

The practice will take appropriate and reasonable steps to keep health information secure.

PHI will be used for treatment and care coordination, to obtain payment, and to help run the medical practice (operations).

The patient has a right to receive a notice that describes how health information may be used and shared.

Patients can decide if they want to give permission before their health information can be used or shared for certain purposes, such as for marketing. (Alternatively, some privacy policies may state that they never share PHI for marketing.)

Patients can get a report on when and why their health information was shared for certain purposes.

The practice may state that information will be shared with family members or other personal representatives whom the patients identify.

Patients have a right to see and get a copy of their health records and to have corrections made. (Usually a procedure or contact person for doing this will be listed.)

The practice will disclose PHI to government agencies for public health reporting and law enforcement.

The privacy policy will identify individuals to contact for further information about the covered entity's privacy policies or to file a complaint. (Usually the privacy policy will name a particular person or position, for example, office manager, as the Privacy Officer.)

EHR and Technology

Chapter 9 explores and compares an array of methods and devices used for EHR entry as well as alternative solutions that may improve the patient experience. How the style of a medical practice is reflected in the selection and placement of input devices and the recommended configurations are illustrated with numerous photos of medical personnel using the devices. An exercise teaches students how to electronically annotate medical illustrations for patient education or for documenting observations in the EHR.

Chapter 9 also includes a thorough discussion of medicine on the Internet, research tools, what is necessary for secure patient–provider communications, and the newest innovation, E-visits.

The real-life story for this final chapter is fitting because it ties together nearly every concept discussed in this book in one real-life practice. Hinsdale Hematology Oncology Associates uses a commercial EHR that is based on Medcin; therefore, its real-time patient encounters are very similar to the ones demonstrated in the software the students have been using. The practice scans incoming documents, merges transcription records, receives electronic lab results, and documents exams in real time (while the patient is present) into a codified EHR using Medcin; the practice uses workstations, laptops, Tablet PCs, and PDA devices in a wireless network and provides the clinicians with remote access to the EHR when they are away from the office. The practice also has a Web site providing educational information for patients (though not patient access to their records.)

This real-life example provides students with practical proof that there are medical offices today that incorporate in everyday practice most of what the students have learned in this course. As students take what they have learned into their local community, more offices will follow suit.

Learning Outcomes

After completing this chapter, students should be able to:

- ◆ Explain how technology impacts the implementation of EHR
- ◆ Compare the use of workstations, laptop computers, Tablet PCs, and PDA devices
- ◆ Understand how the clinician's style and mobility affect the choice of EHR devices
- ◆ Understand how wireless networks work
- ◆ Understand how speech recognition works
- ◆ Use an EHR drawing tool to annotate drawings in an exam note
- ◆ Discuss the effect of the Internet on the future of EHR
- ◆ Describe the differences between provider-to-patient e-mail, secure messaging, and E-visits
- ◆ Discuss patient access to electronic health records

Teaching Recommendations

■ A PowerPoint is available showing the various ways the choice of device and its location affect the doctor–patient relationship. These are the same photos printed in the textbook as Figures 9-11 through Figure 9-17, but the Power-Point may be useful for classroom discussion.

■ In Exercise 49 students create an annotated drawing of a dermatology patient. Here are some areas in which students may experience trouble.

■ *The patient's front, not back, is displayed.* The finding is for the skin; the student may need to select the center and right drop-down lists at the top of the drawing to select "Back" and "Trunk."

■ *Students have difficulty drawing small circles.* Movements of the mouse vary on different computer systems. The broader the movement of the mouse while holding down the button, the larger circle it will make. If circles are too large, have students delete them and start again. Have students make very small movements with the mouse while holding down the left button.

■ *The circle tool disappears after one or two circles.* (1) The padlock is not locked in the toolbar, or (2) students are just clicking in the drawing instead of simultaneously holding the button and moving the mouse. Have students reselect the circle and set the padlock, then try again.

■ *After entering text, students cannot display the right click menu to select the option "Complete Text Entry."* Students are right clicking while still in the textbox. They must move the cursor elsewhere on the canvas (not over the textbox) before right clicking the mouse.

- *Students get a printout of the exam note instead of the drawing.* Students are using the wrong print button at this step. To print the drawing students must use the print button in the drawing toolbar and then the print button in the Preview window, not the print button in the main program.

- *Students get a warning that they haven't printed the encounter when trying to close the drawing tool.* Students are using the wrong close button. After printing the drawing, the student must click the exit button in the drawing toolbar, not another exit button elsewhere in the program.

At the conclusion of this exercise, the students print out their annotated drawing to hand in. This graphic will automatically include the student's name. Students also enter text on a finding and print out the exam note. You should receive two documents from each student.

If your students have been using the Print to HTML feature to turn their work in on files instead of printouts, you are by now aware that graphics cannot print to HTML. You must provide students direction on how to turn in their graphic drawing as you did for graphs in previous exercises.

- Exercise 50 is optional. Its purpose is to allow those students who wish to participate in their own health record to use a secure site to do so. Students should not be graded on their participation in this exercise.

- Have students review the Chapter Summary and answer the 15 questions at the end of the chapter. The answer key for the questions is provided after the chapter outline. Students should also turn in a printout or file of their exam note for Exercise 49 and their annotated drawing also produced in Exercise 49. Answer keys showing the steps used to create the patient note and drawing are provided later.

A bank of test questions to create your own chapter exam is also available on the Prentice Hall Health Instructor's Resource CD.

Chapter 9 Outline

I. How Technology Impacts Implementation of EHR

    A. Style of practice

        1. The doctor is paternalistic telling the patient what to do

        2. The doctor gives the patient information; the patient decides

        3. Patients and doctors share information to determine the best plan

    B. Physical clinic and clinician mobility

II. EHR on Computer Workstations

III. EHR on Laptop Computers

IV. EHR on a Tablet PC

V. EHR on Handheld PDA Devices

VI. How Wireless Networks Work

VII. EHR Devices and the Patient

VIII. Remote EHR Access for the Provider

    A. Enhancing process efficiency through remote access

Answer Key 9-1

Testing Your Knowledge of Chapter 9

List the advantages of using each type of computer for an EHR:

1. **Workstations**

   ANSWER: Computer workstations are cheap, reliable, dependable, easier for the IT department to manage, and can be upgraded when necessary.

2. **Laptop computers**

   ANSWER: Laptop computers package everything in a unit about the size of a notebook. They provide mobility for clinicians who want to take their work from room to room. Laptops can use a wireless network to gain that mobility and can operate on a battery.

3. **Tablet PCs**

   ANSWER: Tablet PCs offer the size and portability of laptop computers and users can move and click the mouse by just touching the screen with a special stylus. They work well for EHR systems that involve primarily opening lists and clicking findings with a mouse. They can use a wireless network to gain that mobility and can operate on a battery.

4. **PDAs**

   ANSWER: PDAs or personal digital assistants are small, pocket-sized, and convenient for writing prescriptions or reading messages. PDAs that are to be used for an EHR access require a wireless network and require an EHR "client" software that has been specially written to communicate with their small screen size and limited memory.

5. **Explain how the physical layout of the office impacts the choice of devices.**

   ANSWER:

       1. How much space is available may determine the type of device you can use.

       2. What type of clinician–patient interaction the clinicians are striving for.

3. The mobility of the clinicians. (That is, do clinicians have a preassigned set of exam rooms used for their patients? Are the clinicians likely to complete the note and all orders while in the exam room? Where/when will the clinicians review lab results, radiology reports, e-mail—on the move throughout the day, at their office desk, from home after hours?)

6. **What is used in place of a mouse on a Tablet PC?**

   ANSWER: A stylus

7. **How does the clinician's mobility affect the choice of EHR devices?**

   ANSWER: Wireless devices such as laptop computers or Tablet PCs work better for a clinician who does not have assigned rooms or who reviews and finishes work between exams or from home.

   Clinicians who have their own exam rooms, always complete the exam in the exam room, and always review e-mail and results from their desk could use workstations if there is space in the exam room for these devices.

8. **List three styles of physician–patient relationship.**

   ANSWER:

   1. The doctor is paternalistic telling the patient what to do.
   2. The doctor gives the patient information and the patient decides what to do.
   3. Patients and doctors share information to determine the best plan for given conditions.

9. **Give an example of a specialty that might use speech recognition to create reports.**

   ANSWER: Radiology or pathology

10. **What types of specialties typically incorporate annotated drawings in an exam note?**

    ANSWER: Ophthalmology, dermatology (allow for other reasonable answers, such as cardiovascular, obstetrics, orthopedic, and general surgeons).

11. **Discuss the effect of the Internet on health care and give examples of changes.**

    ANSWER: People shop for doctors online; insurance companies provide on-line participating provider lists; physician specialty associations and state and local medical societies all offer Web sites that help patients locate a provider near them.

    Patients and clinicians are both using the Internet for research. Clinicians can obtain decision support and continuing education online. E-visits allow patients to be treated by their regular doctor for nonurgent matters online.

12. **Describe the differences between provider-to-patient e-mail and E-visits.**

    ANSWER: An E-visit is secure, but e-mail is not.

    The E-visit gathers symptom and HPI information creating a documented medical exam. E-mail is free text.

    When it is integrated with the EHR the E-visit becomes a part of the patient's chart, just like any other visit. It would be difficult for a provider to save an e-mail exchange into a patient's EHR record.

E-visits are reimburseable as a legitimate E&M visit, whereas e-mail exchanges are not.

E-mail is directed at a particular individual and, therefore, not likely to be accessible by another provider. E-visits can be directed to the "doctor on call" allowing practicing partners to share "being on call."

13. Discuss patient access to electronic health records.

ANSWER: A number of medical offices offer interactive Web sites that allow the patient to request an appointment time or a prescription renewal. Some even allow patients secure access to information from their medical record. This is usually not the full access the provider has to the chart but rather specific portions of the chart, for example, the results of recent lab tests.

Online services that are independent of any one medical group also offer patients the ability to maintain their own EHR online.

14. Briefly define and describe Wi-Fi.

ANSWER: *Wi-Fi* stands for wireless fidelity and is also called wireless networking. The network sends its information over radio waves instead of network cables.

Because Wi-Fi has a limited range, it requires multiple access points to be installed throughout the building in close enough proximity so that the laptop (or other wireless device) can always find the radio signal. The system switches access points seamlessly.

15. What CPT code is used to bill for an E-visit?

ANSWER: 0074T

(FYI to instructors: This question has a typo—the code is not actually a CPT-4 code; it is a procedure billing code.)

Answer Key 9-2

Evaluation of Printed Exam Note for Exercise 49: Annotated Dermatology Exam

The following corresponds to Figure 9-40 in the textbook. A "Print to HTML" file named "fig9-40_greensher.htm" is available on the Instructor's Resource CD for review and comparison. Students added only one item to this existing encounter shown in Step 18.

Arnie Greensher Student: *(name or ID)*	Page 1 of 1	
Patient: Arnie Greensher: M: 3/11/1940: 5/19/2006 01:00PM		*Steps 1 and 2*
CHIEF COMPLAINT The Chief Complaint is: Follow-up visit, routine lesion recheck		*Step 2*
HISTORY OF PRESENT ILLNESS Arnie Greensher is a 66-year-old male • No skin symptoms • No change in a mole and no other reported skin problems		

PHYSICAL FINDINGS

Skin:

	Value	Normal Range	
Skin Lesions [On exam]:			
Lesions on the back 15 Nevi	< 1 cm		*Step 18*

• No lesions on the back of the scalp • No lesions on the face • No lesions on the upper extremities in the front • No lesions on the upper extremities in the back • No lesions on the chest • No lesions on the lower extremities in the front • No lesions on the lower extremities in the back	*Step 2*

ASSESSMENT

• Dysplastic nevus

THERAPY

• Follow-up visit in 3 months

COUNSELING/EDUCATION

• Discussed avoiding sun exposure

PRACTICE MANAGEMENT

• Estab outpatient focused h&p - straightforward decisions; Total face to face time 15 min

Answer Key 9-3

Evaluation of Printed Drawing for Exercise 49: Annotated Dermatology Exam

The following corresponds to Figure 9-37 in the textbook. It is not reprinted here. The students were to draw 15 small circles on the patient's back, enter some text, and draw a blue line from the text to the circles. The student's name will automatically print on the drawing.

Depending on the various settings of the mouse, it is sometimes difficult to draw really small circles. Grade based on whether the student successfully got the correct number of elements on the drawing in approximate positions. Do not count off if the circles are a bit large or not exactly placed in the same location as the figure in the book. The following is a guide to the steps related to possible errors in the exercise.

Arnie Greensher Student: *(name or ID)*	(Drawing)	*Step 1*
Not patient's back or trunk		*Step 4*
Circles not solid		*Step 7*
Circles not orange		*Step 8*
Not enough circles		*Step 11*
Text in box does not read **"15 Nevi < 1 cm. unchanged"**		*Step 12*
Text is orange instead of blue		*Step 12*
Text missing entirely		*Step 13*
Blue line incorrect or missing		*Step 14*
Line that should be blue is orange		*Step 12*

Comprehensive Evaluation of Chapters 6–9

This comprehensive evaluation covers the last four chapters of the book to help you measure your students' mastery of the material. Students complete both a written test and hands-on exercise. Answer keys are provided later.

Detailed steps guide the student through the hands-on exercise in the same manner as previous exercises except there are no figures to compare against. Figures 9-44–9-88 only appear in the instructor's materials and do not appear in the student text. Students must be able to follow directions and document the patient visit without visual cues. An illustrated, step-by-step walkthrough of the exercise is provided later in this chapter. A PowerPoint show of Exercise 51 included on the Instructor's Resource CD can be used for class review after the exams have been graded.

> **(!) Important!**
>
> Part II of the Comprehensive Evaluation requires the Patient History program. Make sure the Medcin History Pool Loader is running before students begin the exercise.

Students should be permitted to run the Student Edition software during both the written and practical exams.

Part II—Hands-On Exercise 51 is more extensive than the previous comprehensive exam (Exercise 36) and, therefore, may take more time to complete. It is recommended that you administer the written exam in one class period and the hands-on exercise in another so that there will be time to complete the hands-on exercise.

Students may have difficulty in Step 8 locating and citing the test finding "bilateral angiography" in the problem-oriented flow sheet. The author ran this exercise several times and on at least one occasion the test (which had displayed on the Problem tab) did not appear on the problem flow sheet. The most likely cause was a misstep with the flow sheet and cite buttons earlier in the exercise. Warn students about this before they begin their hands-on exercise. Should students encounter this provide the following remedy.

Step 8 Solution:

Before citing anything in Step 8, locate and click on the button labeled "Cite" in the toolbar at the top of the screen to turn off the Cite feature.

Then locate and click on the button labeled "Flowsheet" in the toolbar at the top of the screen to close the flow sheet and return to the Patient Management Problem tab.

Locate and click on the Encounter tab to return to the Exam Note view.

Start Step 8 over again from the beginning. The test item should then appear in the flow sheet as indicated in the directions.

Upon completion of the exam students should hand in four printouts:

1. Graph of total cholesterol

2. Graph of Gloria Green's weight

3. Annotated drawing of femoral artery

4. Printed exam note for May 22, 2006, for Gloria Green

Remind students to write their names on their graphs.

Since three of these printouts are graphic, if students have been submitting "Print to HTML" files, provide them with directions on how you want to receive the graphic files.

Answer Key 9-4

Part I—Written Exam

1. **Where do the data that appear in the Patient Management tab come from?**

   ANSWER: Previous patient visits or previous patient encounters

2. **Why would clinicians use trending of lab results and what type of results can be graphed?**

   ANSWER: To compare the change of certain test components over a period of time. Results with numerical values can be graphed.

3. **Describe the benefits of having patients entering their own symptoms and history.**

   ANSWER: Any of the following:

   Only the patient has the information about the symptoms that were present at the outset of the illness.

   Only the patient has the information about the outcome of the medical treatment of those symptoms.

   The patient is also the source of past medical, family, and social history.

   Patient-entered data are a more accurate reflection of a patient's complaints.

   Patients who can review their histories are better prepared for the visit.

4. **What is triage (as used in this book)?**

   ANSWER: The screening of patients for allocation of treatment based on the urgency of their need for care; often a simplified, organ-specific review of systems conducted by the triage nurse based on the presenting complaint.

5. **List at least three ways codified data in the EHR can be used to manage and prevent disease.**

   ANSWER: Any of the following:

   Disease management

   Graphic analysis

   Trending

   Preventative screening

   Interactive alerts

6. **Describe a problem list and provide at least two reasons why clinicians use a problem list.**

   ANSWER: A problem list is an up-to-date list of the diagnoses and conditions that affect a particular patient's care.

   Clinicians might use a problem list for any two of the following reasons:

   Easy to see the active problems for a patient and also view the history of problems.

   Most clinical information recorded in the chart will be related to one or more problems.

   Everyone who touches the patient knows what conditions are present.

Problem lists are used to track both acute and chronic conditions.

Helps the clinician remember to follow up on conditions from previous visits.

Maintaining a problem list is a requirement for accreditation by JCAHO.

7. **Describe how to create a flow sheet from a form.**

   ANSWER: On the tab labeled "Active Forms," load a form from the Forms Manager. Click on the button labeled "FS Form" in the toolbar at the top of the screen.

8. **What does it mean to cite a finding and how would you do it from a flow sheet?**

   ANSWER: Citing from a previous exam note means to bring a finding into the current encounter, usually as a follow-up to a previous visit.

   Click the "Cite" button on, and then click on a single finding in one of the columns, or click the date at the top of the column.

9. **Why are childhood immunizations important?**

   ANSWER: Immunization slows down or stops disease outbreaks. Vaccines prevent disease in the people who receive them and protect those who come into contact with unvaccinated individuals. Through childhood immunizations we are now able to control many infectious diseases that were once common in this country and from which many children died.

10. **What are "evidence-based" guidelines?**

    ANSWER: Using "evidence-based guidelines" means analyzing scientific evidence from current research and studies to determine the effectiveness of preventive services.

11. **Name at least three external sources of data for populating the EHR.**

    ANSWER: Any three of the following:

    Electronic lab orders and results

    Vital signs

    ECG

    Digital spirometers

    Ultrasound equipment

    Holter monitors

    In-house LIS systems

12. **What is a growth chart percentile?**

    ANSWER: Curved lines representing what percentage of the reference population the individual would equal or exceed at a given size for age.

13. **List the four components of the HIPAA Administrative Simplification Subsection.**

    ANSWER:

    Transactions and Code Sets

    Uniform Identifiers

    Privacy

    Security

14. **Compare the difference between consent and authorization.**

    ANSWER: Authorization differs from consent in that authorization require the patient's permission to disclose PHI.

Signed consent is optional. The patient gives consent for the provider to disclose PHI for purposes of treatment, obtaining payment, and operation of the health care facility by acknowledging receipt of a copy of the office privacy policy.

15. Does a provider need the patient's consent to share PHI with an authorized government agency?

ANSWER: No.

16. Name the covered entities under HIPAA.

ANSWER: Health care providers, health insurance plans, and clearinghouses

17. Describe how the clinician's style of practice impacts the choice of EHR devices.

ANSWER: If the doctor is paternalistic and tells the patient what to do, the device will not be positioned where the patient can easily see it.

If the doctor gives the patient information and then the patient decides what to do, laptops or Tablet PC computers that can be shown to the patient may be used.

The doctors who share information with patients to determine the best plan for given conditions will configure exam rooms and devices so the doctor and patient can both view the screen during relevant portions of the encounter.

18. Give an example of a specialty that might use speech recognition to create reports.

ANSWER: Radiology or pathology were examples given in the textbook.

19. Give an example of a specialty that might use annotated drawings in an exam note.

ANSWER: Ophthalmology and dermatology were examples provided in the textbook. (Allow for other reasonable answers, such as cardiovascular, obstetrics, orthopedic, and general surgeons.)

20. How is the Internet changing health care? Give examples of changes.

ANSWER: People shop for doctors online, insurance companies provide online participating provider lists, and physician specialty associations, state, and local medical societies all offer Web sites that help patients locate a provider near them.

21. List the three criteria of an electronic signature.

ANSWER:

Message integrity

Nonrepudiation

User authentication

22. How does an E-visit differ from provider-to-patient e-mails?

ANSWER:

An E-visit is secure, but e-mail is not.

The E-visit gathers symptom and HPI information creating a documented medical exam. E-mail is free text.

When it is integrated with the EHR, the E-visit becomes a part of the patient's chart, just like any other visit. It would be difficult for a provider to save an e-mail exchange into a patient's EHR record.

E-visits are reimburseable as a legitimate E&M visit, whereas e-mail exchanges are not.

E-mail is directed at a particular individual and, therefore, not likely to be accessible by another provider. E-visits can be directed to the "doctor on call" allowing practicing partners to share "being on call."

For questions 23–30 select the acronym from the list that best matches the description and write it next to the number:

23. Information protected by the security rule
ANSWER: EPHI

24. Electronic signature standard
ANSWER: PKI

25. Calculation for height/weight ratio
ANSWER: BMI

26. Normal findings
ANSWER: WNL

27. Three vaccines
ANSWER: MMR

28. Enforces HIPAA privacy rule
ANSWER: OCR

29. Elements of a patient exam
ANSWER: H&P

30. Method of Internet security
ANSWER: VPN

Student: Terry Jones
Patient: Gloria Green: F: 12/02/1951: 5/22/2006 10:15AM
Chief complaint
The Chief Complaint is: Patient reports leg pain after exercise
History of present illness
    Gloria Green is a 54 year old female.
    • Intermittent leg claudication • Both feet are cold
    • Pain in the middle of the thigh • In the thigh near the knee
Past medical/surgical history
Reported History:
    Reported prior tests: A cholesterol test was high.
Physical findings
Vital signs:

Vital Signs/Measurements	Value	Normal Range
Oral temperature	98.6 F	97.6-99.6
RR	28 breaths/min	18-26
PR	78 bpm	50-100
Blood pressure	130/90 mmHg	100-120/60-80
Weight	210 lbs	125-225

Eyes:
General/bilateral:
Optic Disc: ° Normal
Retina: ° Normal
Cardiovascular system:
Heart Rate And Rhythm: ° Normal
Heart Borders: ° By percussion the heart size and position were normal
Heart Sounds: ° S1 was normal ° S2 was normal ° No S3 was heard ° No S4 was heard
Murmurs: ° No murmurs were heard
Musculoskeletal system:
Ankle:
Left ankle: • Swelling
Tests
Urinalysis

Urinalysis Results:	Value	Normal Range
Urinalysis results: protein	+0	0-0

Hematology:

Hematology:	Value	Normal Range
Hematocrit level	51%	37-47
Hemoglobin level	16.2 g/dl	12-16

Blood Chemistry:
An electrolyte panel was performed and a lipid profile was performed.

Blood Chemistry:	Value	Normal Range
Potassium level	4.8 mEq/l	3.5-5.5
Total calcium level	9.8 mg/dl	8.5-10.5
Random blood glucose level	120 mg/dl	75-110
Serum creatinine level	1.4 mg/dl	0.6-1.3
Total plasma cholesterol level	205 mg/dl	140-200
Plasma HDL cholesterol level	65 mg/dl	30-80
Plasma LDL cholesterol level	130 mg/dl	80-130

▲ **Figure 9-44 Printed Exam Note—Gloria Green Page 1 of 2**

Gloria Green

Pulmonary Function Tests:
Pulse oximetry with ankle/brachial index.

Imaging Studies:
Angiography:
Bilateral angiography of the extremity was performed.

Assessment

- Hypertension
- Atherosclerosis of the femoral artery

Counseling/Education

- Low fat diet
- Low fat cooking
- Changing eating habits

Plan

- Random blood glucose level

- Warfarin sodium (Coumadin)
  2 mg tab (1 qd 30) DISP:30 Generic:Y Using:Coumadin Mfg: Du Pont Pharma

Practice Management
Estab outpatient comprehensive h&p - high complex decisions; Total face to face time 50 min; Counseling and coordination of care was more than 50% of encounter time 30 minutes of visit spent on dietary and Coumadin counseling.

▲ **Figure 9-44 Printed Exam Note—Gloria Green Page 2 of 2**

Answer Key 9-5

Evaluation of Printed Exam Note for Exercise 51: Examination of a Patient with Arterial Disease

The following corresponds to Figure 9-44 in this Instructor's Manual. A "Print to HTML" file named "fig9-44_exam_(green).htm" is available on the Instructor's Resource CD.

A PowerPoint file is also available for class review after the exam has been graded. The steps in the answer key that follows may be used by the instructor to help students find where they made any error.

Gloria Green	Page 1 of 2	
Student: *(name or ID)*		
Patient: Gloria Green: F: 12/02/1951: 5/22/2006 10:15AM		*Steps 1 and 2*
CHIEF COMPLAINT		*Step 3*
The Chief Complaint is: Patient reports leg pain after exercise		

HISTORY OF PRESENT ILLNESS

Step 8

Gloria Green is a 54-year old female
• Intermittent leg claudication • Both feet are cold
• Pain in the middle of the thigh • In the thigh near the knee

PAST MEDICAL/SURGICAL HISTORY

Step 8

Reported History:

Reported prior tests: A cholesterol test was high

PHYSICAL FINDINGS

Step 4

Vital signs:

Vital Signs/Measurements Range	Value	Normal
Oral temperature	98.6 F	97.6–99.6
RR	28 breaths/min	18–26
PR	78 bpm	50–100
Blood pressure	130/90 mmHg	100–120/60–80
Weight	210 lbs	125–225

Eyes:

Step 5

General/bilateral:
Optic Disc: • Normal
Retina: • Normal

Cardiovascular system:

Heart Rate and Rhythm: • Normal
Heart Borders: • By percussion the heart size and position were normal
Heart Sounds: • S1 was normal • S2 was normal • No S3 was heard
• No S4 was heard
Murmurs: • No murmurs were heard

Musculoskeletal system:

Step 8

Ankle:
Left ankle: • Swelling

TESTS

Step 6

Urinalysis

Urinalysis Results: Range	Value	Normal
Urinalysis results: protein	+0	0–0

Hematology:

Hematology: Range	Value	Normal
Hematocrit level	51%	37–47
Hemoglobin level	16.2 g/dl	12–16

Blood Chemistry:

An electrolyte panel was performed and
a lipid profile was performed

Blood Chemistry: Range	Value	Normal
Potassium level	4.8 mEq/l	3.5–5.5
Total calcium level	9.8 mg/dl	8.5–10.5
Random blood glucose level	120 mg/dl	75–110
Serum creatinine level	1.4 mg/dl	0.6–1.3
Total plasma cholesterol level	205 mg/dl	140–200
Plasma HDL cholesterol level	65 mg/dl	30–80
Plasma LDL cholesterol level	130 mg/dl	80–130

Pulmonary Function Tests:

Step 8

Pulse oximetry with ankle/brachial index

Imaging Studies: Angiography: Bilateral angiography of the extremity was performed	*Step 8* *(cite)*
ASSESSMENT • Hypertension	*Step 5*
• Atherosclerosis of the femoral artery	*Step 8*
COUNSELING/EDUCATION • Low-fat diet • Low-fat cooking • Changing eating habits	*Step 12*
PLAN • Random blood glucose level	*Step 6*
• Warfarin sodium (Coumadin) 2 mg tab (1 qd 30) DISP:30 Generic:Y Using:Coumadin Mfg: Du Pont Pharm	*Steps 10–11*
PRACTICE MANAGEMENT Estab outpatient comprehensive H&P - high complex decisions; Total face to face time 50 min; Counseling and coordination of care was more than 50% of encounter time;	*Step 19*
30 minutes of visit spent on dietary and Coumadin counseling	*Step 20*

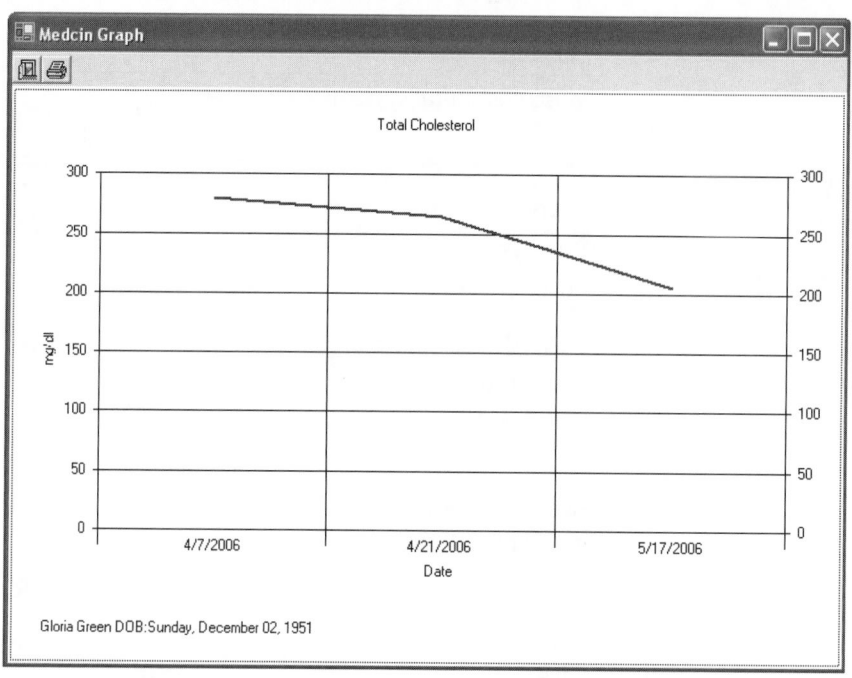

▲ **Figure 9-45 Printed Graph of Total Cholesterol for Gloria Green**

Answer Key 9-6

Evaluation of Printed Graph for Exercise 51: Graphing Lab Results

Students should print out and hand in a graph of total cholesterol for Gloria Green, which corresponds to Figure 9-45 in this manual. Because students did not enter data, the graph data should automatically match. Having successfully printed the graph is proof of successful completion of the exercise.

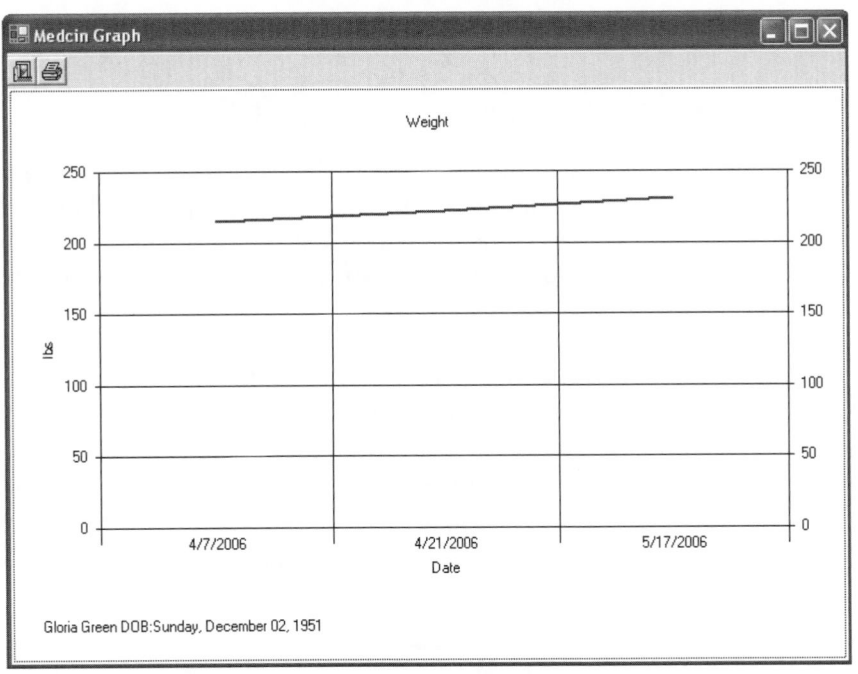

▲ **Figure 9-46 Printed Weight Graph for Gloria Green**

Answer Key 9-7

Evaluation of Printed Graph for Exercise 51: Graphing Weight

Students should print out and hand in a graph of Gloria Green's weight chart, which corresponds to Figure 9-46 in this manual. The figure is not reprinted here. Since students did not enter data, the graph data should automatically match. Having successfully printed the graph is proof of successful completion of the exercise.

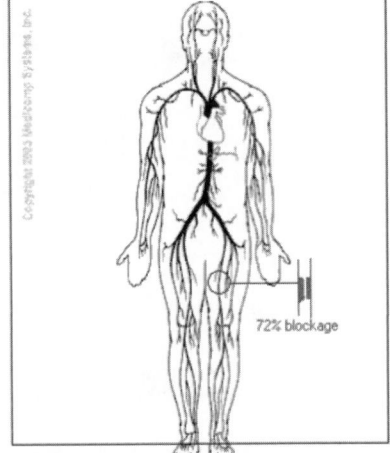

Medcin® Student Edition - Gloria Green 53 yr 11 mon Female - 05/22/06 10:15 (Office Visit)
Terry Jones, Printed: 05/22/2006 1:33 PM

▲ **Figure 9-47 Printed Annotated Drawing for Gloria Green**

Answer Key 9-8

Evaluation of Printed Drawing for Exercise 51: Examination of a Patient with Arterial Disease

Student drawings should closely resemble Figure 1 in the Comprehensive Exam 6–9 in the textbook. The figure is reprinted here as Figure 9-47. The students were to circle the femoral artery and illustrate freehand a blockage, then add text "72% blockage." The student's name will automatically print on the drawing.

Depending on the various settings of the mouse, it is sometimes difficult to draw well. Grade based on whether the student successfully got the correct number of elements on the drawing in approximate positions. Do not count off if the circle or lines are not exactly placed in the same location as the figure in the book. The following is a guide to the steps related to possible errors in the exercise.

Gloria Green	(Drawing)	*Step 1*
Student: *(name or ID)* *Not patient's back or trunk*		*Step 15*
Circle not blue		*Step 17*
Blue line incorrect or missing		*Step 17*
Freehand artery is blue, not red		*Step 17*
Freehand artery is missing		*Step 17*
Blockage is missing		*Step 17*
Text in box does not read **"72% blockage"**		*Step 17*
Text is blue instead of red		*Step 17*
Text missing entirely		*Step 17*

Instructor's Illustrated Steps for Hands-On Exercise 51

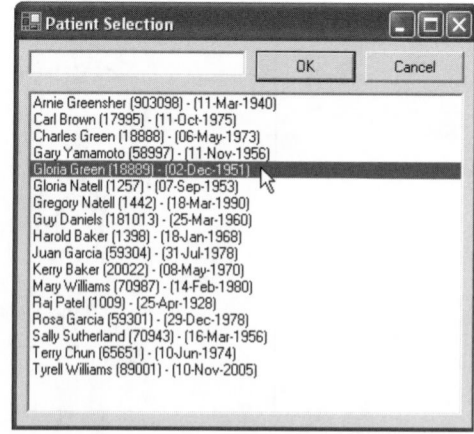

▲ **Figure 9-48 Select Patient Gloria Green**

Step 1 If you have not already done so, make sure the Student Edition History program is running; *then* start the Student Edition software.

Click Select on the menu bar, and then click Patient.

In the Patient Selection window, locate and click on **Gloria Green.**

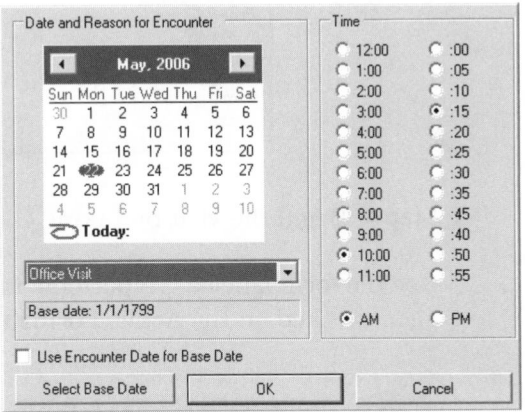

▲ **Figure 9-49 New Encounter for May 22, 2006, 10:15 AM Office Visit**

Step 2 Click Select on the menu bar, and then click New Encounter.

Select the date **May 22, 2006,** the time **10:15 AM,** and the reason **Office Visit.**

Make certain you set the date and reason correctly. Compare your screen to the date, time, and reason printed in bold type before clicking on the "OK" button.

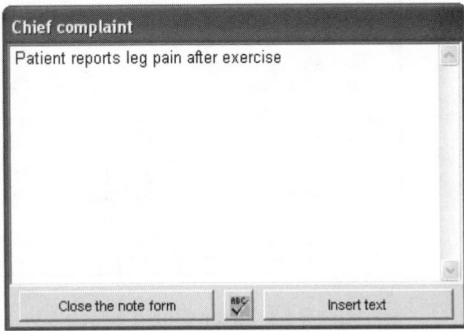

▲ **Figure 9-50 Chief Complaint "Patient Reports Leg Pain After Exercise"**

Step 3 Enter the chief complaint by locating the button in the toolbar labeled "Chief" and clicking on it.

In the dialog window that will open, type "**Patient reports leg pain after exercise.**"

When you have finished typing, click on the button labeled "Close the Note Dialog."

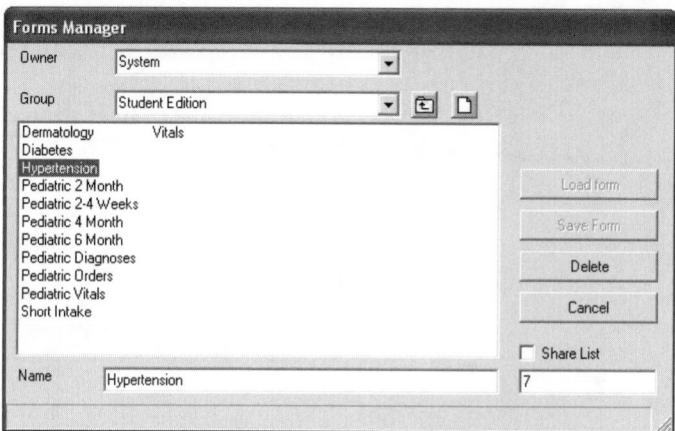

Step 4 Begin the visit by taking Gloria's vital signs and quick exam.

Use the form labeled "Hypertension," which you will select from the Forms Manager, invoked on the Active Forms tab (as you have done in previous exercises).

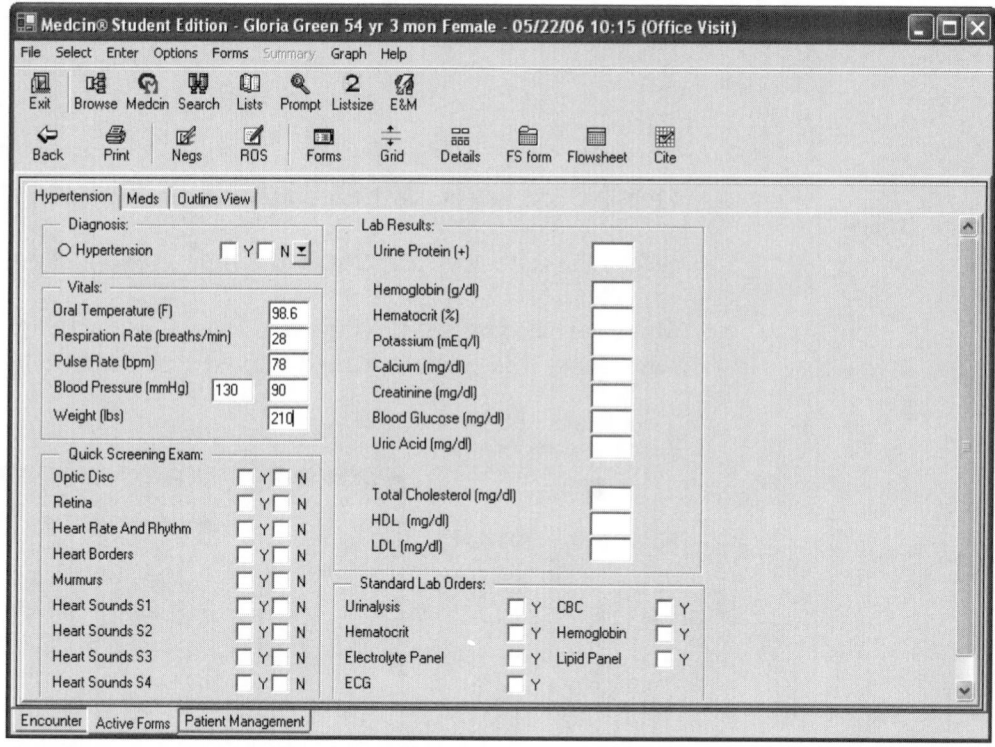

▲ **Figure 9-52 Enter Gloria Green's Vital Signs**

Enter Gloria's vital signs in the corresponding fields on the form as follows:

Temperature:	**98.6**
Respiration:	**28**
Pulse:	**78**
BP	**130/90**
Weight:	**210**

When you have finished, check your work; if it is correct, proceed to Step 5.

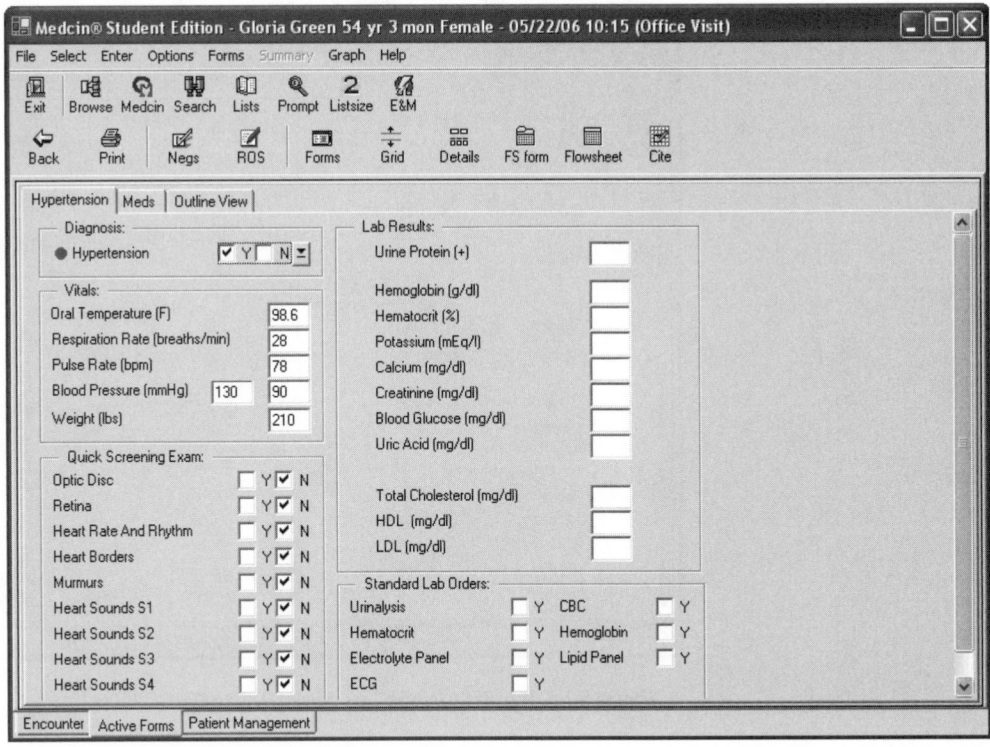

▲ Figure 9-53 Quick History and Physical

Step 5 Remain on the Active Forms tab.

Locate and click on check box for hypertension. The small circle will turn red.

● Hypertension   ✓ **Y**

Enter the Quick Exam portion by using the "Negs" button in the toolbar at the top of your screen. The Quick Exam items should be checked as follows:

Retina	✓ **N**
Optic Disc	✓ **N**
Heart Rate and Rhythm	✓ **N**
Heart Borders	✓ **N**
Murmurs	✓ **N**
Heart Sounds S1	✓ **N**
Heart Sounds S2	✓ **N**
Heart Sounds S3	✓ **N**
Heart Sounds S4	✓ **N**

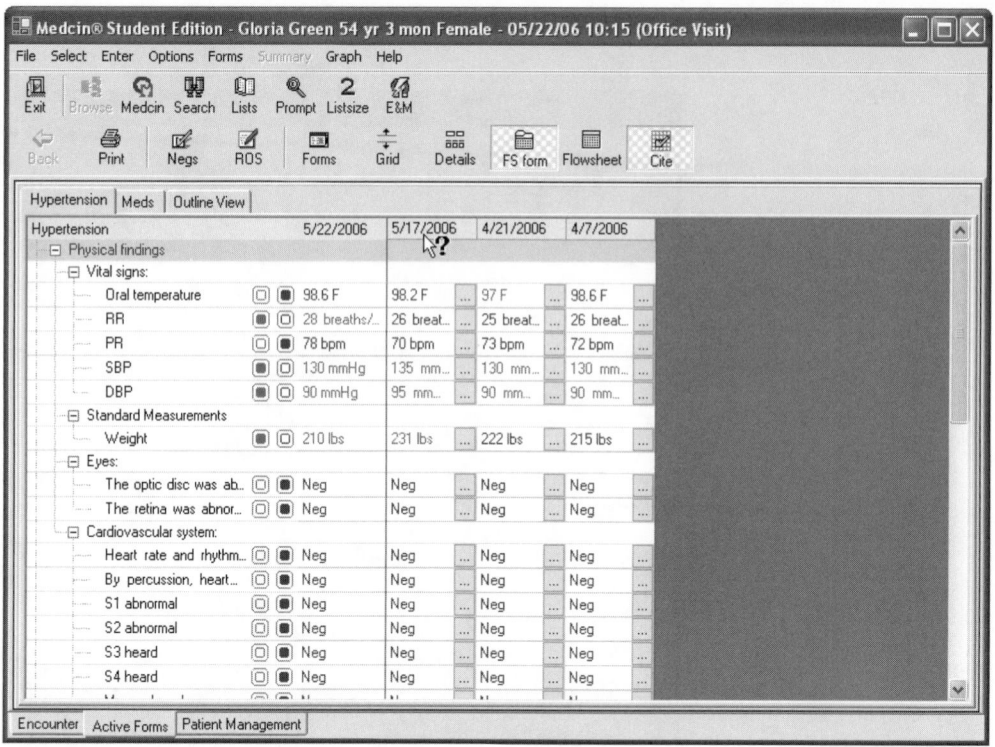

▲ **Figure 9-54 Hypertension Flow Sheet—Cite 05/17/2006**

Step 6 Locate and click on the button labeled "FS Form" in the toolbar at the top of your screen to invoke the Flow Sheet view.

Locate and click on the button labeled "Cite" in the toolbar at the top of your screen.

Move your mouse pointer over the column date "5/17/2006." The pointer should change to include a large question mark. Click on the column date. A window of findings from that encounter will be displayed.

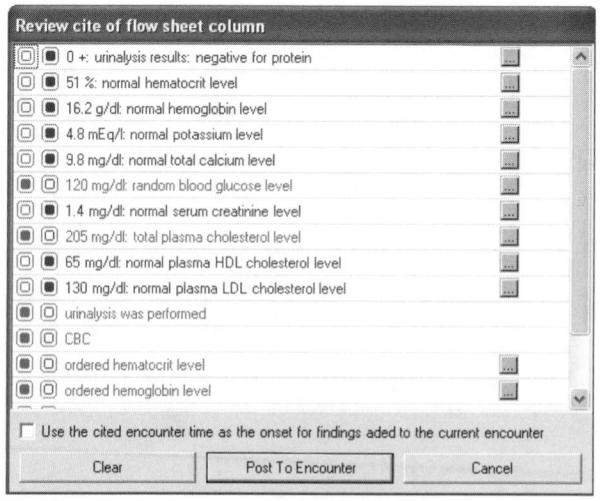

▲ **Figure 9-55 Review Cite of 05/17/2006**

Review the findings and then click the button labeled "Post To Encounter."

Locate and click on the button labeled "Cite" in the toolbar at the top of your screen to turn off the Cite feature. Then locate and click on the button labeled "FS Form" in the toolbar at the top of your screen to return to the Hypertension form.

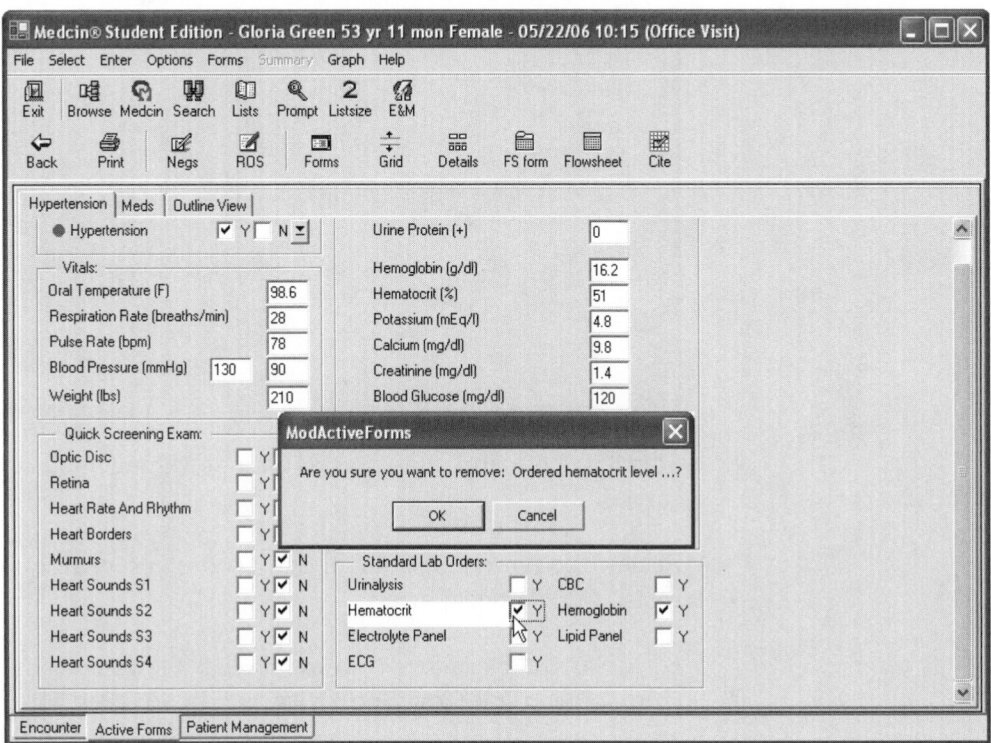

▲ **Figure 9-56 Delete Hematocrit and Hemoglobin Tests**

Step 7 Locate the section of the Hypertension form labeled "Standard Orders."

Click on the checked boxes to remove the orders for the tests:

☐ **Hematocrit**

☐ **Hemoglobin**

Confirm each deletion by clicking on the "OK" button in the confirmation dialog box that will appear.

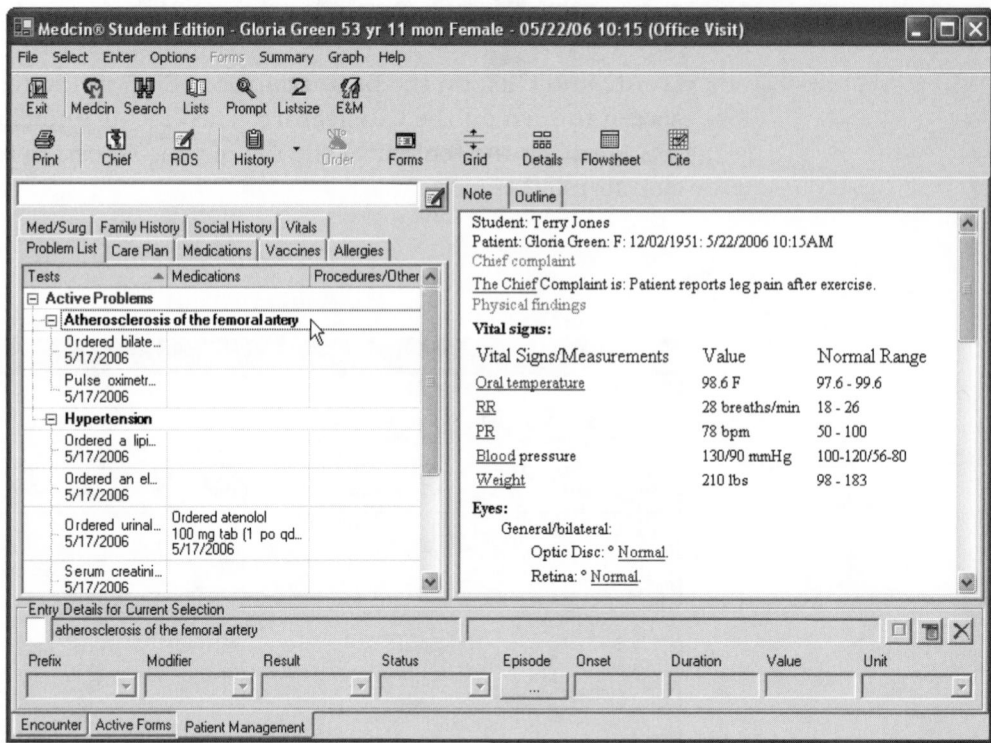

Step 8 Locate and click on the Patient Management tab at the bottom of the screen.

Review the patient's problem list. Locate and click on the problem "Atherosclerosis of the femoral artery."

Locate and click on the button labeled "Flowsheet" in the toolbar at the top of your screen. The Flow Sheet view will be invoked for the specific problem.

▶ Figure 9-58 Cite Test Finding Bilateral Angiography

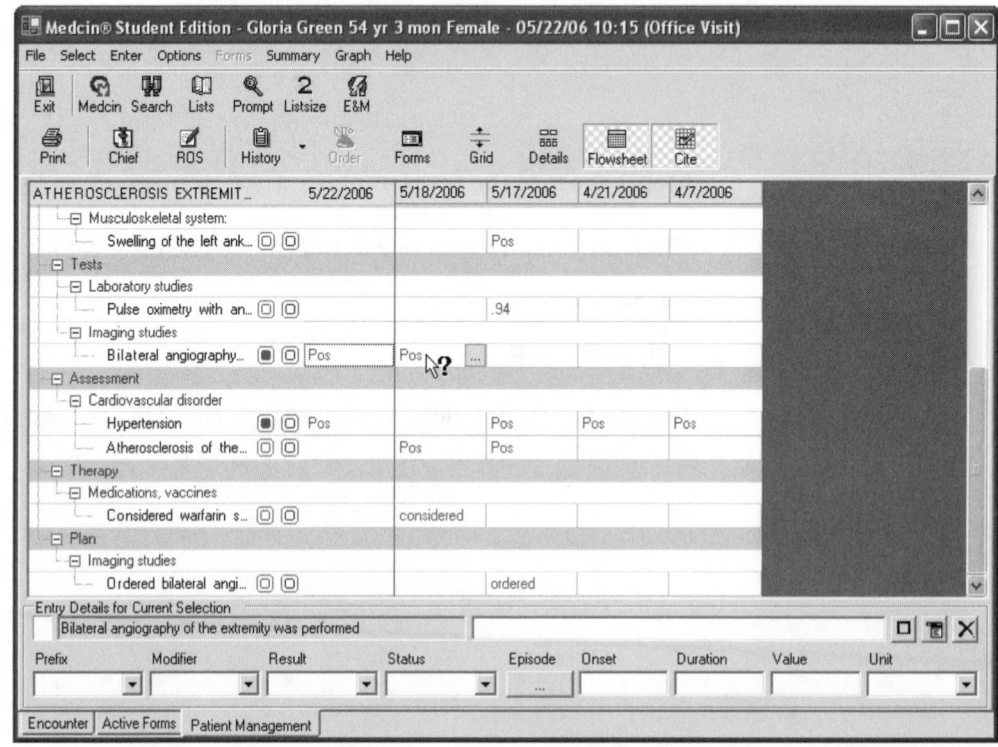

Locate and click on the button labeled "Cite" in the toolbar at the top of your screen.

Locate the section of the flow sheet with the label "Tests" (in a teal divider) by scrolling the window.

Cite an individual test result by moving your mouse pointer over the column "**5/18/2006**." The pointer should change to include a large question mark.

Locate the finding "Bilateral Angiography" and click on the column with the abbreviation "POS" (in red). The finding will be recorded in the current encounter.

► **Figure 9-59 Cite 05/17/2006 for Problem**

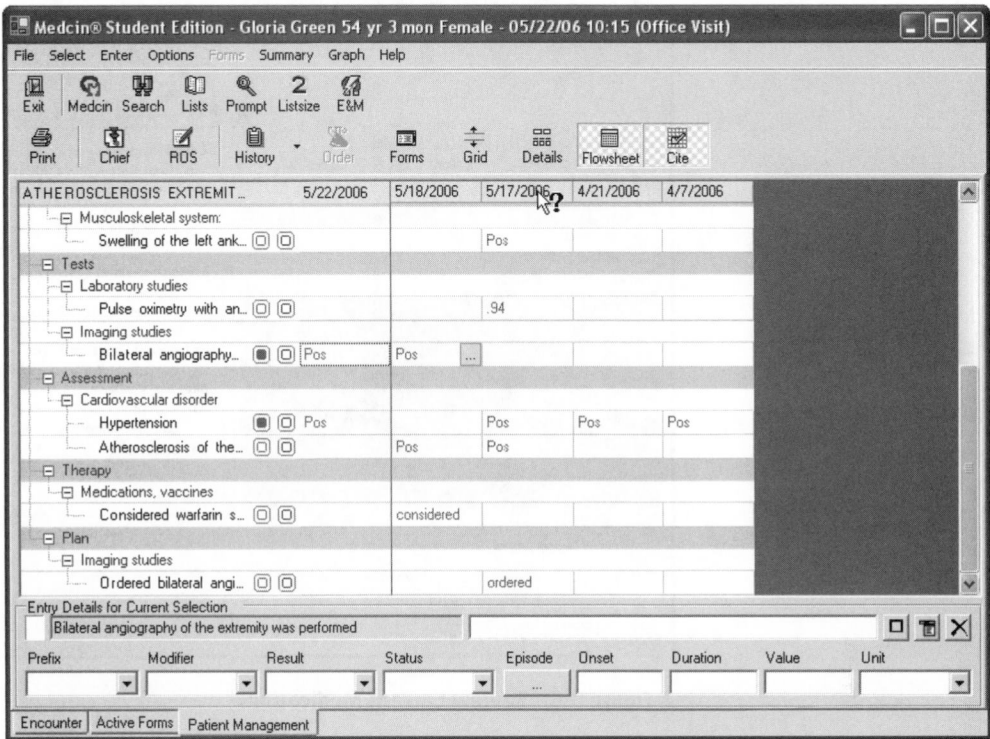

Cite the findings from the previous exam by moving your mouse pointer over the date "**5/17/2006**" at the top of the column and click on the date.

► **Figure 9-60 Review Cite for Problem**

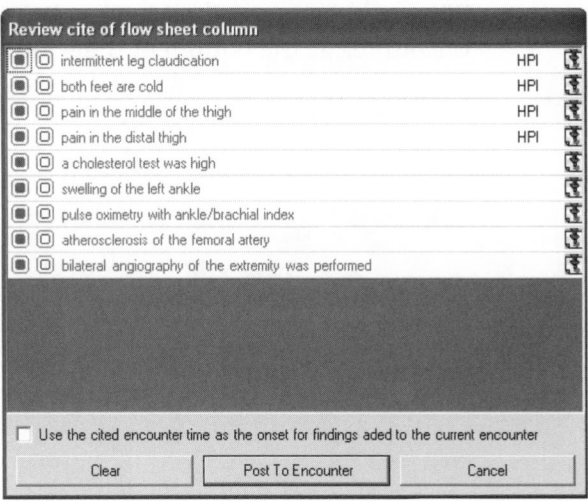

A window of findings from that encounter will be displayed.

Review the findings and then click the button labeled "Post To Encounter."

Step 9 Locate and click on the button labeled "Cite" in the toolbar at the top of your screen to turn off the Cite feature. Then locate and click on the button labeled "Flowsheet" in the toolbar at the top of your screen to return to the Patient Management tab.

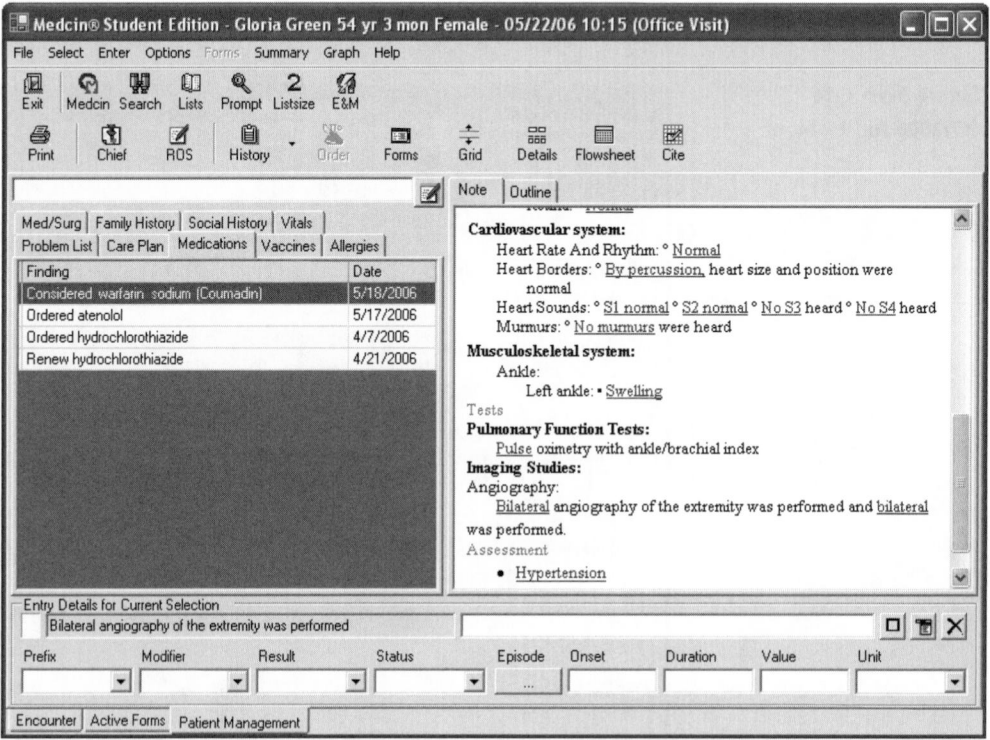

▲ **Figure 9-61 Review Current Medications**

Locate and click on the Patient Management tab labeled "Medications." Review the patient's current medications.

When you have reviewed her medications, locate and click on the tab labeled Encounter at the bottom of the window to return to the Exam Note view.

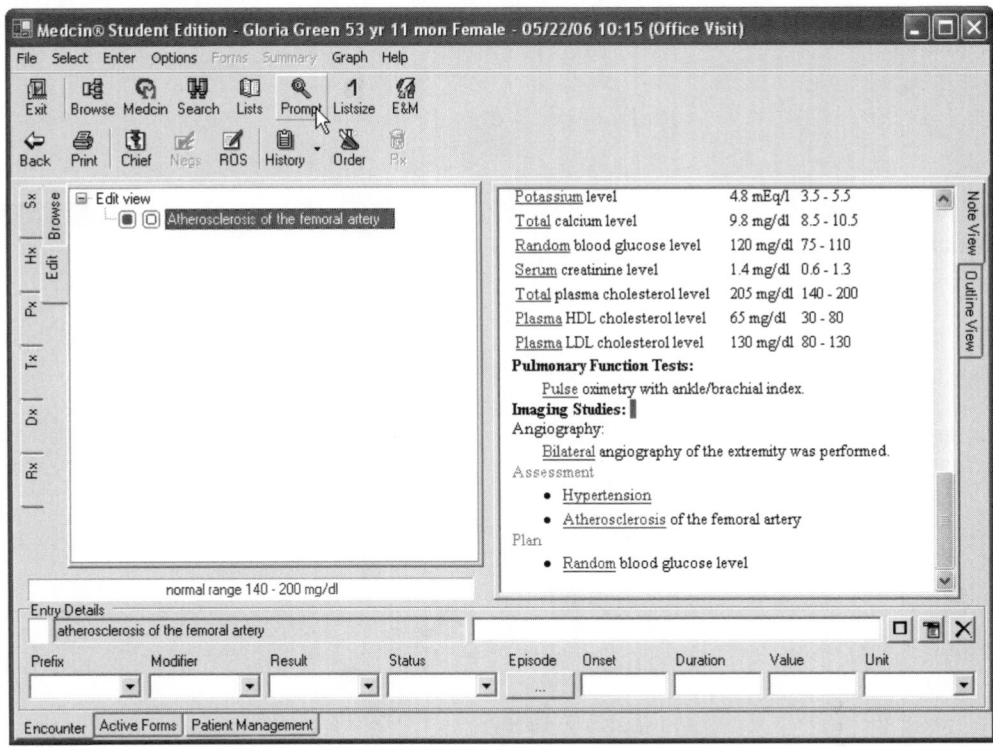

Step 10 Locate and click the assessment "Atherosclerosis of the femoral artery" in the exam note. The finding will then be displayed in the left pane on the Edit tab.

Highlight the diagnosis description. Then locate and click on the button labeled "Prompt" in the toolbar at the top of your screen.

Locate and click on the Rx tab in the left pane. Locate and click on the following medication:

● (red button) Anticoagulants Warfarin Sodium (Coumadin)

This will invoke the prescription writer.

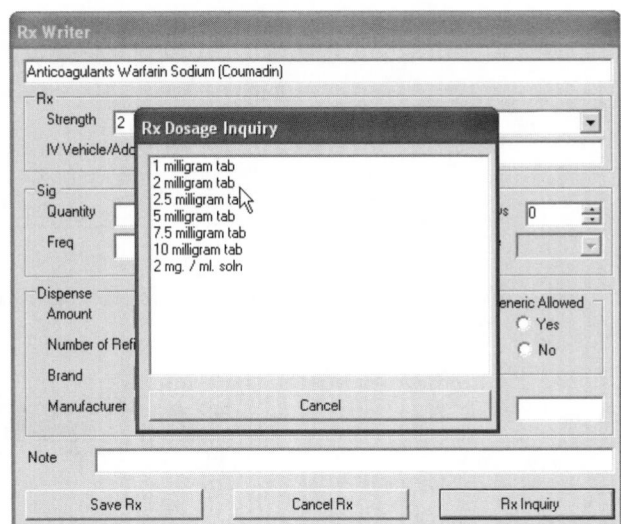

Step 11 Enter the following prescription by selecting the following options as they are presented:

Rx Dosage: **2 mg**

▶ **Figure 9-64 Select Coumadin Brand**

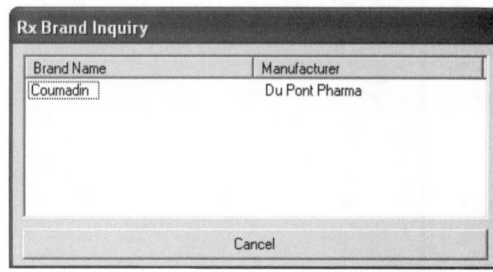

Rx Brand: **Coumadin**

Enter the following data in the prescription fields:

Quantity: **1**

Frequency: **daily**

Days: **30**

Dispense Amount: **30**

Generic: **Y**

▶ **Figure 9-65 Save Completed Prescription**

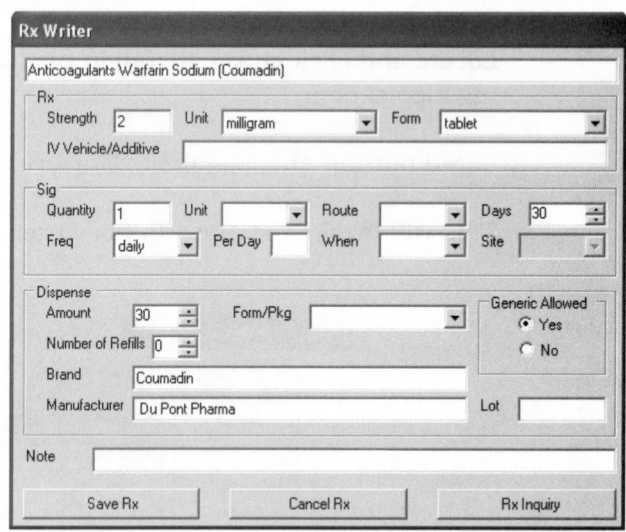

Verify you have entered the information correctly; then click the button labeled "Save Rx."

▶ **Figure 9-66 Search for Low-Fat Diet**

Step 12 Locate and click the button labeled "Search" in the toolbar at the top of your screen. The Search window will be invoked. Type: "Low fat diet" and click the "Search" button.

▶ **Figure 9-67 Counseling and Education**

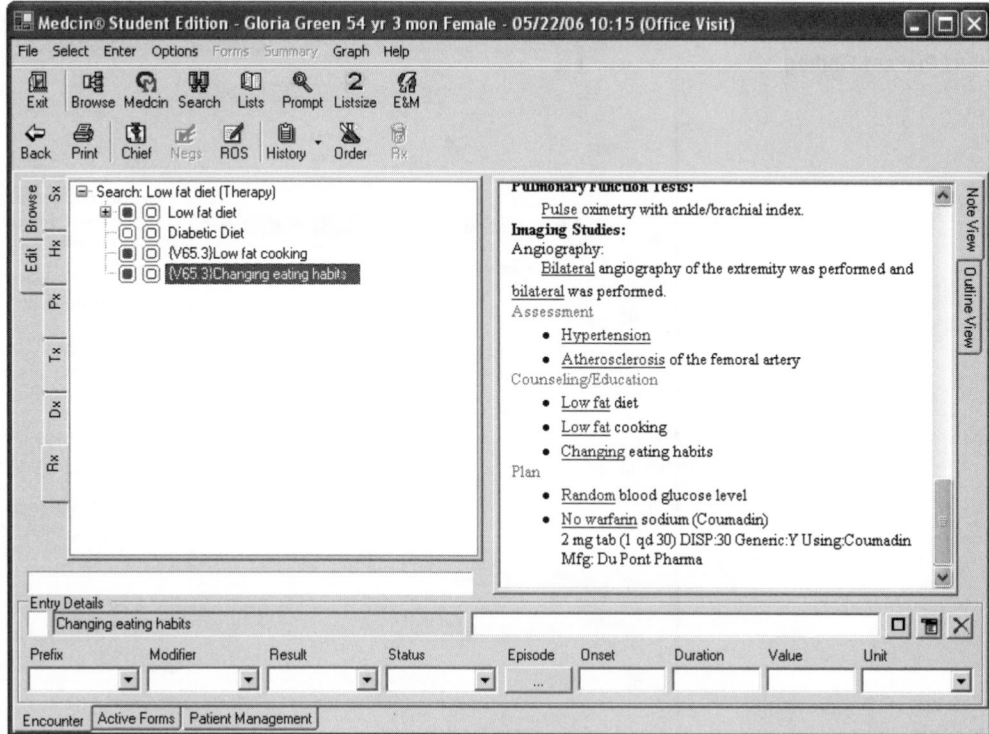

Locate and select the following findings from the list displayed in the Rx tab:

● (red button) Low Fat Diet

● (red button) Patient Education Dietary Low Fat Cooking

● (red button) Patient Education Dietary Changing Eating Habits

▶ **Figure 9-68 Search for Total Cholesterol**

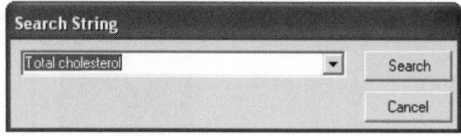

Step 13 In the next steps you will create some materials to be used for patient education.

Click on the button labeled "Search" on the toolbar near the top of the screen. The Search String window will be invoked.

Type the search string "Total cholesterol" and click on the "Search" button in the window.

The left pane should change to the Tx tab and display several findings with the words "Total Cholesterol" in them.

Locate and highlight the finding "Total plasma cholesterol" (the finding with the red button selected).

▶ **Figure 9-69 Graph Menu—Select Current Finding**

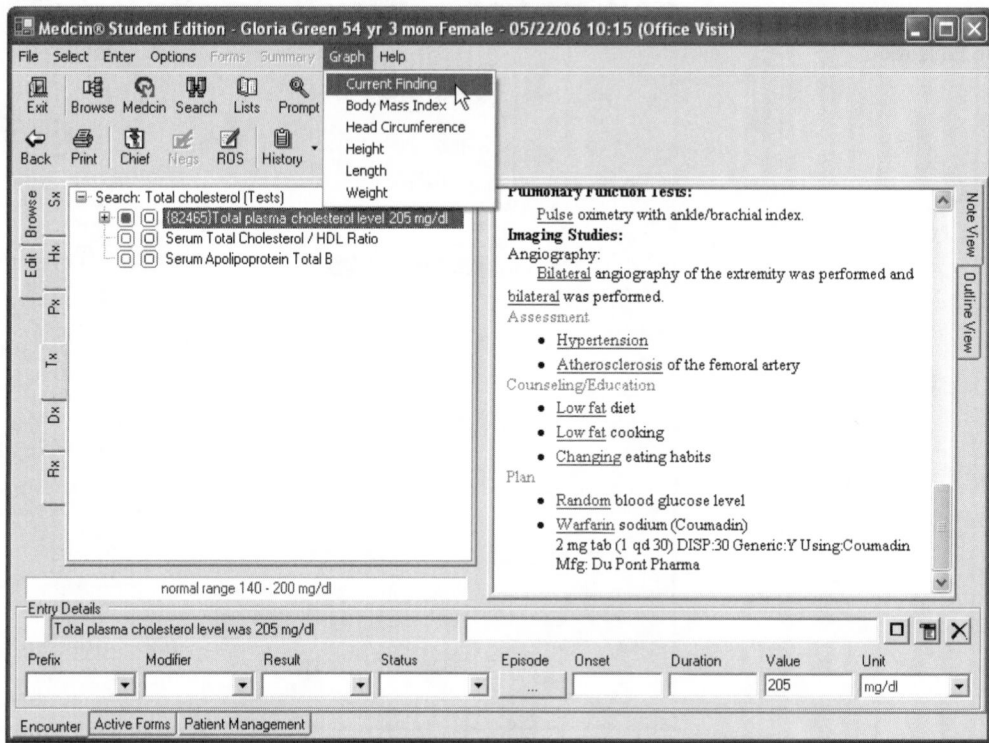

Click Graph on the menu bar, and then click "Current Finding" from the drop-down list. The Graph window will be invoked with a graph of Gloria's recent cholesterol results (shown in Figure 9-45).

Print a copy of the graph by locating and clicking the "Print" button in the upper left corner of the Graph window. A Print Preview window for graphs will be invoked.

▶ **Figure 9-70 Total Choles-terol Graph Preview**

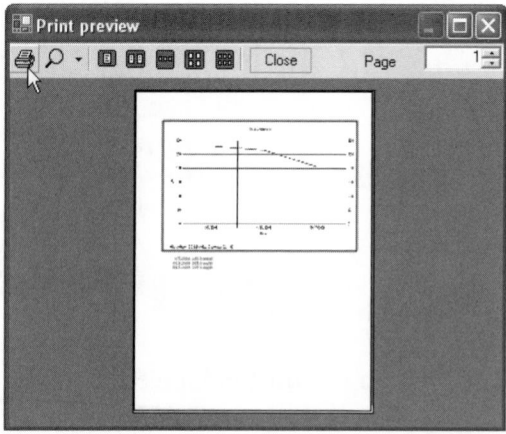

Locate the click on the "Print" button in the upper left corner *of the Preview window.*

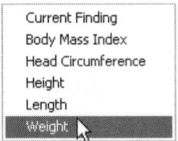

Current Finding
Body Mass Index
Head Circumference
Height
Length
Weight

▲ **Figure 9-71 Graph Menu—Select Weight**

When your graph has printed successfully, click on the button labeled "Close" to close the Print Preview window. Do not close or exit the Preview window until you have your printed copy in hand.

Write your name on your printout and save it to turn in to your instructor.

Step 14 Print a chart of Gloria's weight.

Click Graph on the menu bar, and then click "Weight" from the drop-down list. The Graph window will be invoked with a graph of Gloria's weight measurements (shown in Figure 9-46).

▶ **Figure 9-72 Gloria Green Weight Graph Preview**

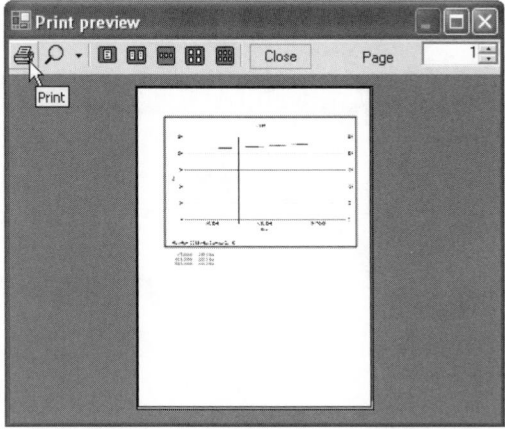

Print a copy of the graph by following the print procedures you used in Step 13.

When your graph has printed successfully, click on the button labeled "Close" to close the Print Preview window. Do not close or exit the Preview window until you have your printed copy in hand.

Write your name on your printout and save it to turn in to your instructor.

▶ **Figure 9-73 Select Add Object to Finding for Bilateral Angiography**

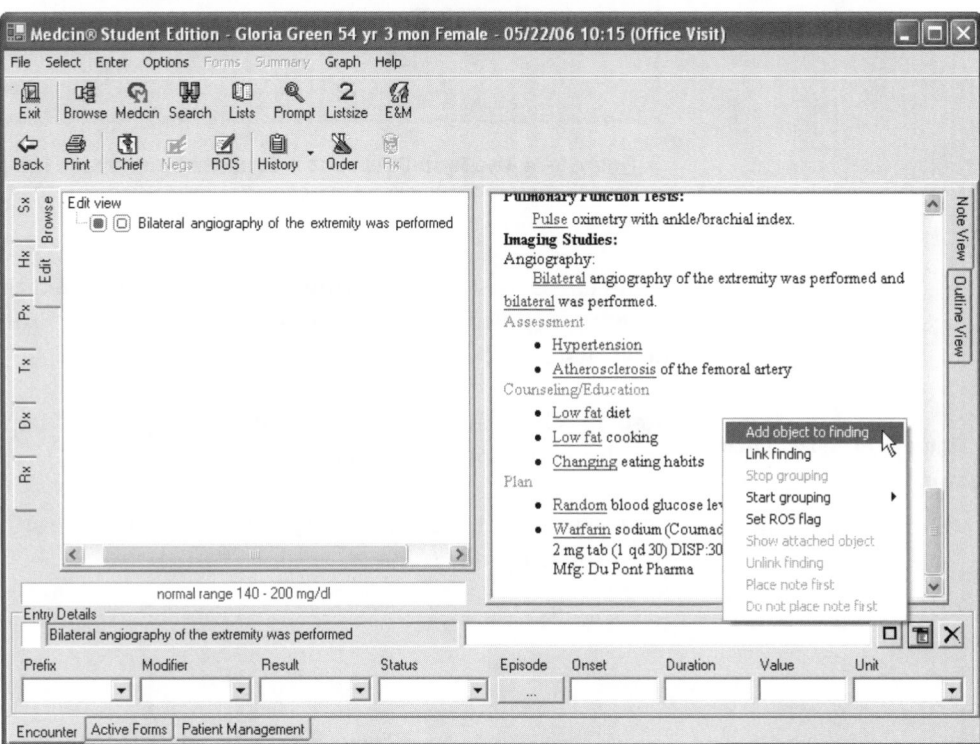

Step 15 Create an annotated drawing to explain the angiography to the patient.

Scroll the Exam Note in the right pane to locate the imaging study finding "Bilateral Angiography." Click on the word "Bilateral." The left pane should change to the Edit tab.

Locate the center button of the three buttons in the lower right-hand corner of your window and click on it. From the drop-down list displayed choose "Add Object to Finding."

The drawing window will be invoked in the right pane.

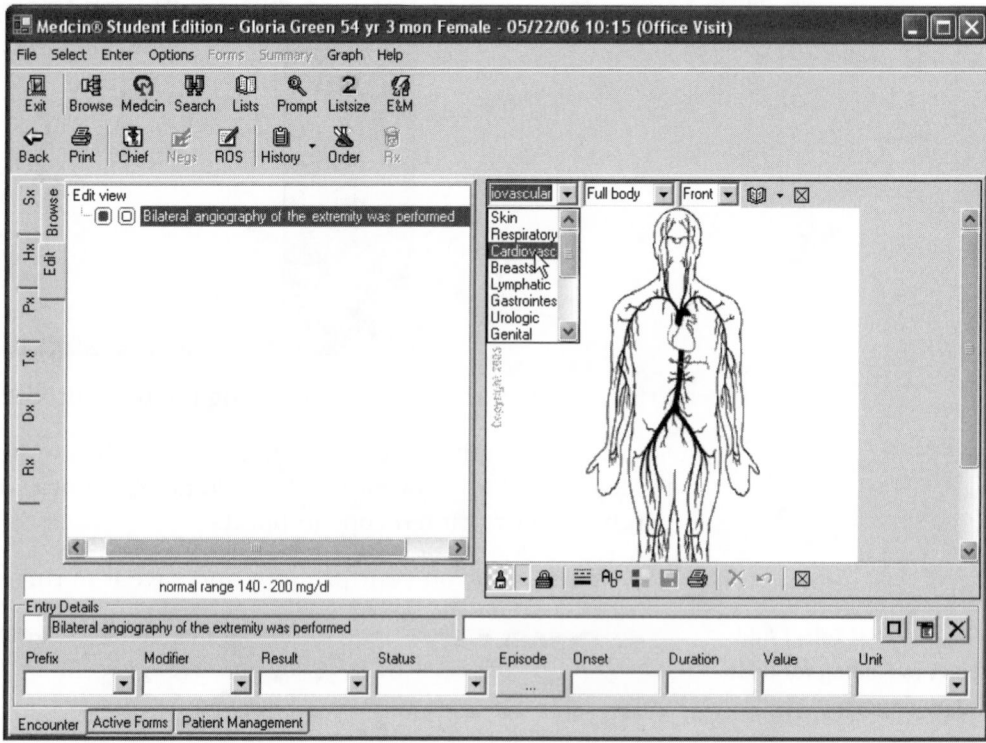

▲ **Figure 9-74 Use Drop-Down List If Cardiovascular Image Is Not Displayed**

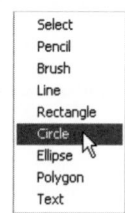

▲ **Figure 9-75 Select Circle Drawing Tool**

If the cardiovascular drawing is not displayed, use the fields at the top of the drawing to select the Cardiovascular, Full Body, Front view from the drop-down lists.

Step 16 Once the correct illustration template is displayed, use the toolbar in the drawing tool to set up the tool as follows:

Locate and click on the down arrow next to the first button; then select "Circle" from the drop-down list.

▲ **Figure 9-76 Set Padlock in Toolbar**

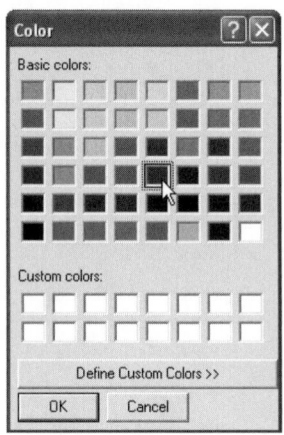

▲ **Figure 9-77 Select Blue from Color Pallet**

Locate and click on the "Lock" button (with the padlock). It should then appear depressed.

Locate and click on the "Color" pallet button. When the window is displayed, select Blue. Click OK to close the Color pallet window.

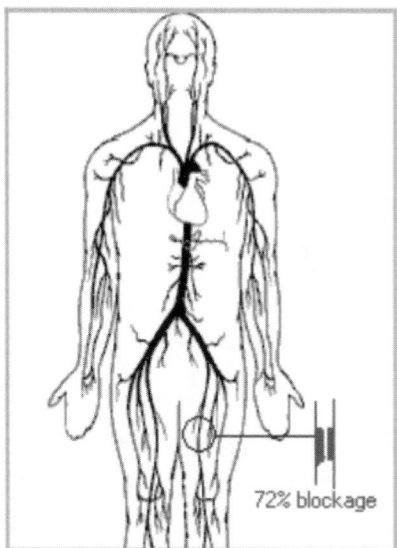

▲ **Figure 9-78 Anatomical Figure ©
Medicomp Systems, Inc.**

Step 17 As closely as possible replicate the drawing in Figure 1 as follows:

Draw a blue circle over the femoral artery midway between the groin and the knee (as shown in Figure 1).

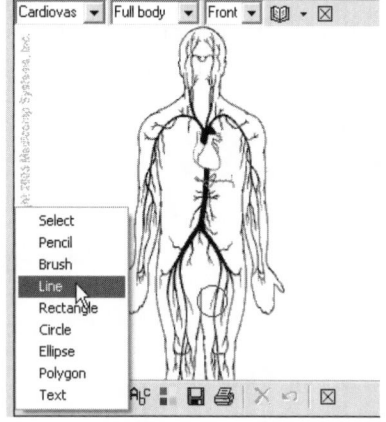

▲ **Figure 9-79 Select Line Drawing Tool**

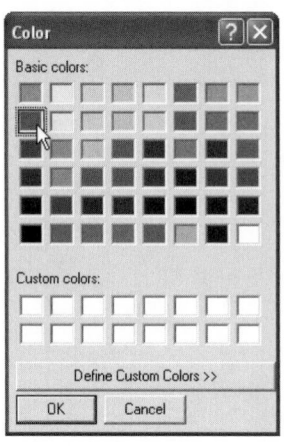

▲ **Figure 9-80 Select Red from Color Pallet**

Change the drawing tool.

Locate and click on the down arrow next to the first button; then select "Line" from the drop-down list.

Draw a horizontal line from the circle to the blank area of the drawing on the right.

Next, change the color to Red, by selecting the "Color" pallet button.

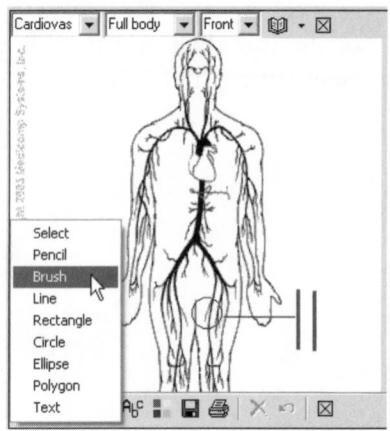

▲ **Figure 9-81 Select Brush Drawing Tool**

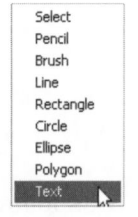

▲ **Figure 9-82 Select Text Tool**

In the blank area of the drawing, draw two vertical, parallel lines to represent an enlarged view of the artery.

Change the drawing tool.

Locate and click on the down arrow next to the first button; then select "Brush" from the drop-down list.

Using the brush, make a thick line on the interior of each of the parallel lines to represent the blockage in the artery (similar to Figure 1).

Annotate the drawing.

Locate and click on the down arrow next to the first button; then select "Text" from the drop-down list.

Click your mouse in the image to the right of the knee and a text field will open. Type: "72% blockage."

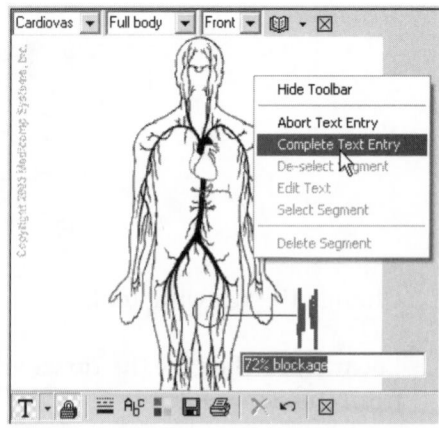

▲ **Figure 9-83 Right Click on Drawing, Select "Complete Text Entry"**

Right click anywhere on the drawing *except in the text box* to display a list of options; click on "Complete Text" from the list displayed.

Compare your drawing to Figure 9-78. If you need to correct the line or circle, change the tool button to "Select" and click on the object. Use the "Delete" button in the toolbar and then redraw the correct element.

Step 18

▲ **Figure 9-84 Click Print Icon on Drawing Toolbar**

When your drawing is satisfactory, select the "Print" button on the *drawing toolbar* (**not** the "Print" button on the main toolbar). A Print Preview window will be invoked.

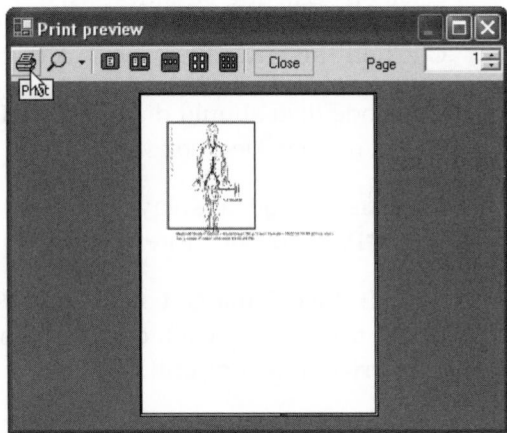

▲ **Figure 9-85 Print Preview of Annotated Drawing**

Locate and click on the "Print" button in the Preview window to print a copy you can turn in to your instructor at the end of this exercise.

When your drawing has printed successfully, click on the button labeled "Close" to close the Print Preview window. Do not close or exit the Preview window until you have your printed copy in hand.

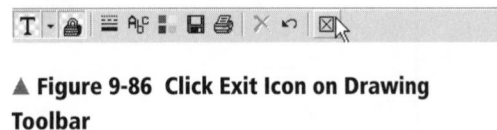

▲ **Figure 9-86 Click Exit Icon on Drawing Toolbar**

Step 19 Locate and click on the "Exit" button in the drawing toolbar to close the drawing tool and redisplay the exam note.

Locate and click on the button labeled "E&M" in the toolbar at the top of the screen to invoke the E&M Calculator.

► Figure 9-87 Evaluation and Management Calculator

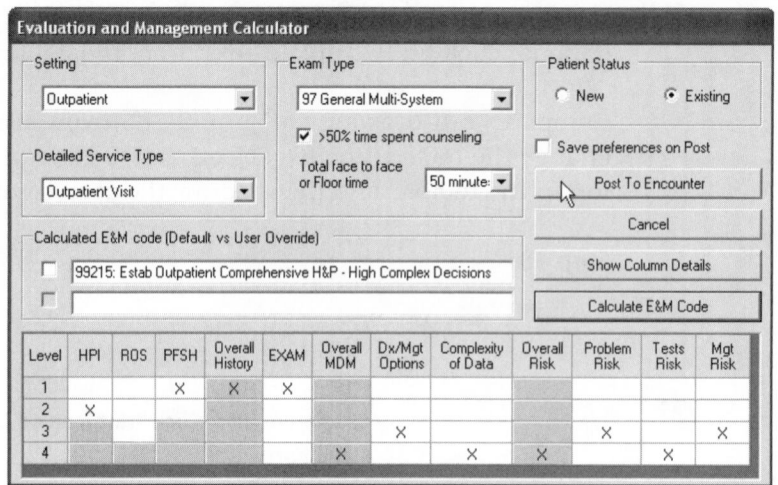

Click on the check box labeled "> 50% time spent counseling."

Set face to face/floor time to 50 minutes.

Click on "Existing Patient."

Click on the button labeled "Calculate E&M Code."

The Code field should display "99215: Estab Outpatient Comprehensive H&P – High Complex Decisions."

If this is the code displayed in your window, locate and click on the button labeled "Post To Encounter."

Note: If the calculated code is not 99215, verify you have followed Step 18. If it is still not correct, click on the "Cancel" button and review Steps 4–13 to find your error and correct it.

► Figure 9-88 Enter Free-Text Counseling Note

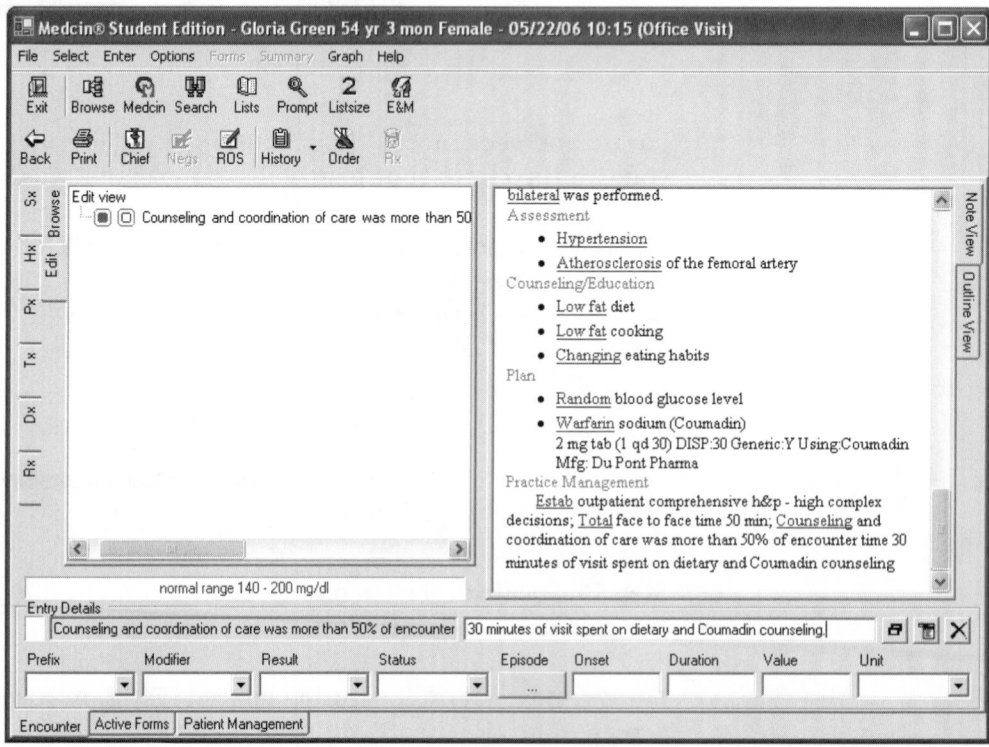

Step 20 Locate and click on the finding "Counseling" in the exam note. The finding should appear on the Edit tab in the left pane.

In the free-text field type: "30 minutes of visit spent on dietary and Coumadin counseling."

Press the Enter key.

Step 21 Click File on the menu bar, and then click "Print Encounter" or "Print To HTML" (as directed by your instructor).

If you are printing your work, you may alternatively click the "Print" button on the toolbar at the top of your screen.

Remember: **Do not close or exit the encounter until you have a printed copy in your hand.** You will lose your work if you exit before printing.

Hand in the following printouts to your instructor:

1. Graph of total cholesterol
2. Graph of Gloria Green's weight
3. Annotated drawing of femoral artery
4. Printed exam note for May 22, 2006, for Gloria Green